Abnormal Psychology

4th Edition

Susan Nolen-Hoeksema
Yale University

Boston   Burr Ridge, IL   Dubuque, IA   Madison, WI   New York   San Francisco   St. Louis
Bangkok   Bogotá   Caracas   Kuala Lumpur   Lisbon   London   Madrid   Mexico City
Milan   Montreal   New Delhi   Santiago   Seoul   Singapore   Sydney   Taipei   Toronto

Higher Education

ABNORMAL PSYCHOLOGY

Published by McGraw-Hill, a business unit of The McGraw-Hill Companies, Inc., 1221 Avenue of the Americas, New York, NY 10020.

This book is printed on acid-free paper.

1 2 3 4 5 6 7 8 9 0 DOW/DOW 0 9 8 7 6 5

ISBN-13: 978-0-07-110708-2
ISBN-10: 0-07-110708-8

www.mhhe.com

To Michael and Richard

CONTENTS IN BRIEF

CONTENTS

PREFACE

Abnormal Psychology, fourth edition, is about people—people who suffer and struggle and sometimes triumph over their mental-health problems. Beginning with the first edition of this book, my goal has been to bring readers face to face with people diagnosed with mental disorders, to increase their understanding and compassion. The voices of these people are heard loudly and clearly throughout this book, giving us glimpses of the personal experience of mental disorders. I have also dealt directly with the fact that many readers of this book will have experienced mental disorders in themselves or close family members or friends. These concerns with the personal experience of mental disorders continue in the fourth edition.

As our understanding and treatment of many types of abnormality progress, we are beginning to understand how biological and psychosocial factors interact to create psychological disorders. These interactions are a major focus of *Abnormal Psychology*. In this edition, I have highlighted theoretical models and new research that integrate biological and psychosocial approaches to mental disorders. I have also incorporated research on how biological treatments affect psychosocial functioning and how psychosocial treatments change biological processes. As a result, *Abnormal Psychology*, fourth edition, provides readers with the most advanced integrative perspectives in the field.

EMPHASIS ON EMPIRICAL RESEARCH

Empirical research is the gold standard for evaluating theories and treatments of mental disorders. In *Abnormal Psychology*, fourth edition, I have updated the reviews of research on theories and treatments for each disorder. Moreover, I have stated clearly when particular theories or treatments have not been supported empirically or have not been tested adequately. These reviews of recent research have benefited greatly from the many pre-prints and in-press manuscripts sent to me by some of the most respected researchers in the field. As a result, I have been able to provide readers with a sense of what the best and brightest researchers believe is the most important new work and where the field is going.

EMPHASIS ON INTEGRATION

Students often come to a course in abnormal psychology asking whether mental disorders are the result of biological factors *or* psychosocial factors. It is increasingly clear that this is the wrong question and that both biological and psychosocial factors are involved in most disorders. I highlighted integrative models of biological and psychosocial factors in previous editions of this book, but, in the fourth edition, these integrative models are central. In every chapter, a new section called *Chapter Integration* describes an integrative approach to the disorders discussed in that chapter and illustrates this approach with a new figure. In addition, specific disorders are often discussed in terms of integrative bio-psycho-social models. Thus, the fourth edition features an enhanced emphasis on how biology, psychology, and social contexts come together to create vulnerability to disorders.

EMPHASIS ON CLARITY

I have always attempted to write clearly, so that readers can comprehend the vast array of theories, research, and treatments available for various disorders. This emphasis on clarity continues in the fourth edition. Because students sometimes find biological theories and research especially difficult to understand, in this edition I have made a major effort to make this material clear and comprehensible. Toward this end, throughout the book I have added small diagrams of the brain, highlighting structures in which abnormalities have been associated with a particular disorder. These standardized illustrations will help students learn the parts of the brain and identify areas relevant to particular disorders.

EMPHASIS ON CULTURE AND GENDER

Beginning with the first edition of *Abnormal Psychology*, I have tried to help readers understand how culture and gender play a role in mental disorders, influencing people's vulnerability to a disorder, expression of a disorder, or response to treatment. I have relied as much as possible on empirical research in describing how culture and gender impact a disorder. In the fourth edition, I have updated the discussions of the research on culture and gender and have highlighted new debates, such as the debate on how culture influences the diagnosis of personality disorders. As always, my coverage of gender and cultural issues is not marginalized into "boxes" but is integrated as critical material readers should know about the disorders being discussed.

EMPHASIS ON UNDERSTANDING PERSONAL EXPERIENCE

Whenever I teach abnormal psychology, students approach me to talk about their own experience with mental disorders in their family, friends, or themselves. Often, these students begin by saying, "I've never told anyone else at school this, but . . ." They have many questions and concerns about these experiences—what can be done to help them, what it means for their future, how they can be supportive of family members or friends who suffer from a mental disorder.

I want students to come away from this book with the power of knowledge. I want them to be empowered not to suffer in silence, feeling victimized and helpless, but to understand better the sources of their distress and to make good choices that help them overcome this suffering. This knowledge comes, in part, from learning about research on explanations and treatments for disorders.

In addition, the feature titled *Taking Psychology Personally* directly addresses the personal questions and concerns students bring to a course on abnormal psychology, such as questions on how to find a therapist and how to support a loved one. In consultation with the major organizations that serve mental-health consumers (such as the American Psychological Association), I present ideas for how students can think about the meaning of the research they are reading for their own lives and how they can find appropriate help for their concerns.

EMPHASIS ON THE VOICES OF PEOPLE WITH DISORDERS

How can students understand what it is like to suffer from a mental disorder? They can read the criteria for diagnosing the disorder. But these criteria are often no more than lists of symptoms that are foreign and incomprehensible to students. In each chapter of this book, I let people who have experienced these symptoms describe them in their own words. Every chapter of the fourth edition begins with the feature *Extraordinary People*, which highlights the experiences of people who suffer from mental disorders and gives us a window into the hearts and minds of these people. Some of these extraordinary people, including Nobelist John Nash and psychology researcher and professor Kay Redfield Jamison, have achieved tremendous success despite their mental disorders. Others have led more ordinary lives, which in itself is a great accomplishment for people with serious mental disorders. These stories take students far beyond lists of diagnostic criteria and into the subjective experience of a disorder.

Also, within the text of each chapter are features called *Voices*, first-person accounts from people with mental disorders. These quotes give students a subjective sense of the symptoms of each disorder, allowing people who suffer these symptoms to describe their experiences. The quotes also illustrate key points about a disorder, such as how it affects the functioning of the individual or his or her family members or friends. This feature helps students get inside the experiences of people with mental disorders to gain a deeper understanding of the symptoms and the impact of the symptoms on people's lives.

MAJOR CHANGES ACROSS ALL CHAPTERS IN THE FOURTH EDITION

The fourth edition of *Abnormal Psychology* includes a number of major changes that were implemented in all chapters. These changes, some of which I have already mentioned, reflect a greater emphasis on integrated approaches to abnormal psychology and a concerted effort to make biological information clear to students.

1. *Integrative bio-psycho-social models* of mental disorders are featured in each chapter of the fourth edition. Where appropriate, these models are discussed and illustrated with regard to individual disorders. Then, at the end of each chapter, a new section called *Chapter Integration* describes an integrative approach to the group of disorders discussed in that chapter and illustrates this approach with a new figure. Color-coding helps students distinguish among the biological, psychological, and social factors in these figures and others.

2. *Extraordinary People*, a feature that usually highlights an individual diagnosed with a mental disorder, now opens and closes each chapter. The individual's own words and experiences introduce the characteristics of a mental disorder discussed in the chapter. Where appropriate, I refer to that individual in the chapter to illustrate important points about the disorder, its causes and treatments. At the end of the chapter, the *Extraordinary People* follow-up gives the reader a sense of how the individual is living with the mental disorder and its consequences. In some cases, the individual highlighted in *Extraordinary People* is a celebrity; in others, he or she is generally unknown but provides a compelling account of living with a mental disorder.

3. New *standardized brain diagrams* in most chapters help students understand which parts of the brain are implicated in a disorder. These small diagrams of the brain highlight areas where abnormalities have been associated with a particular disorder. These standardized illustrations will help students learn the parts of the brain and identify areas relevant to particular disorders.

4. The *biological theories* of mental disorders and evidence for these theories have been thoroughly updated. I have also rewritten much of the material on biological approaches to make it more accessible.

5. *Concept Overviews* in each chapter highlight, summarize, and illustrate the main "take-home" messages about theories of and treatments for disorders. Some of these *Concept Overviews* are tables; others are figures.

6. The *Chapter Summary* now includes references to relevant *Concept Overviews*, tables, and figures. These references point students to the summary material that will be most helpful in reviewing the material.

PROVEN FEATURES RETAINED IN THE FOURTH EDITION

Instructors and students liked a number of features in the third edition of *Abnormal Psychology*. I have kept—and strengthened—these popular features in the fourth edition:

1. *Taking Psychology Personally* addresses in each chapter the personal issues and questions students often bring to a course on abnormal psychology. Some examples include how to look for a therapist, how to cope with a family member who has a mental disorder, and what to do if a friend is suicidal.

2. *Voices* excerpts bring alive the characteristics of mental disorders in the words of people who live with them.

3. *Case Studies* illustrate the disorders, possible contributors to the disorders, and treatments for the disorders.

4. Several *learning tools* help students identify the most important information, organize it, understand it, and remember it:

   a. A *Chapter Overview* at the beginning of each chapter previews and frames the main sections of the chapter, including the *Chapter Integration* section.

   b. *Summing Up* provides a bulleted summary of key points at the end of each major section.

c. *DSM-IV-TR tables* list the symptoms and criteria for diagnosis of each major disorder.

d. *Concept Overviews* summarize key material in table form or as figures, which provide a more visual summary.

e. *Key Terms* are listed at the end of each chapter, with page references, for easy review.

CHAPTER-BY-CHAPTER CHANGES IN THE FOURTH EDITION

In addition to the major changes across all the chapters, I have made the following key changes in individual chapters:

Chapter 1: Looking at Abnormality

■ Added a discussion of how various criteria for abnormality can be summarized and remembered as the 3Ds: distress, dysfunction, and deviance

■ Expanded and updated the discussion of managed care

Chapter 2: Contemporary Theories of Abnormality

■ Revised the sections on biological theories for greater clarity and added new figures on the brain and other biological systems

■ Added more information on the empirical support for various theories

Chapter 3: The Research Endeavor

■ Clarified the meanings and roles of theory and hypothesis in the scientific method

■ Added a section on epidemiological research

■ Added discussions of prevalence and incidence

■ Added a section on single-case experimental designs

■ Added discussions of efficacy and effectiveness in therapy outcome research

■ Added a section on meta-analysis

Chapter 4: Assessing and Diagnosing Abnormality

■ Revised the *Extraordinary People* feature to focus on Michael J. Fox's autobiography and used examples from this autobiography throughout the chapter to illustrate how clinicians would assess his symptoms

■ Expanded and updated sections on neuroimaging technologies in assessment

■ Expanded and updated section on concerns about the DSM-IV-TR

■ Added a section in differential diagnosis

Chapter 5: Treatments for Abnormality

■ Added a section on the multiple caregivers often involved in the treatment of an individual diagnosed with a mental disorder

■ Updated the section on herbal medicines to reflect recent evidence questioning their safety and efficacy

■ Added a section on repetitive transcranial magnetic stimulation

■ Revised the section on evaluating therapies for greater clarity and to reflect recent critiques of the lack of data on the efficacy of therapies across ethnic groups

■ Added a discussion of recent concerns about the safety of antidepressant drugs for children and adolescents

Chapter 6: Stress Disorders and Health Psychology

■ Integrated material on the effects of stress on physical health (formerly in Chapter 18) with material on posttraumatic stress disorder (formerly in Chapter 7) to create one chapter on stress-related disorders

■ Expanded the discussion of acute stress disorder

■ Added a discussion of adjustment disorder

■ Added information on PTSD in the survivors of recent disasters and wars

- Updated the section on the biological factors in PTSD to reflect substantial new research in this field, including on the role of early childhood trauma on the development of the physiological stress response

Chapter 7: Anxiety Disorders

- Gathered material on all anxiety disorders except PTSD into this chapter
- Clarified the distinctions between adaptive fear and maladaptive anxiety
- Added a discussion of the role of interoceptive awareness in panic disorder
- Added a discussion of the role of negative reinforcement in phobias
- Reduced the number of *Voices* segments in the section on obsessive-compulsive disorder to improve the flow of that section

Chapter 8: Somatoform and Dissociative Disorders

- Reversed the order of discussion of somatoform and dissociative disorders, so that the more typical disorders are discussed first
- Clarified the distinctions among malingering, factitious disorders, and psychosomatic disorders
- Updated the section on the repressed or false memory debate

Chapter 9: Mood Disorders

- Updated epidemiology based on new data from the National Comorbidity Survey
- Added a section on the neurobiological changes accompanying early abuse that could contribute to risk for mood disorders
- Added a discussion of the role of excessive reassurance seeking in depression
- Added discussions of repetitive transcranial magnetic stimulation in the treatment of depression

- Added a section on vagus nerve stimulation in the treatment of depression

Chapter 10: Suicide

- Updated epidemiology of suicide with new data from the Centers for Disease Control and Prevention and the World Health Organization

Chapter 11: Schizophrenia

- Added a discussion of research on smooth pursuit eye movement in schizophrenia
- Added a discussion of deficits in working memory in schizophrenia
- Added a discussion of the integrative model of Barch on how neuropsychological deficits may contribute to schizophrenia
- Condensed the discussion on older and unsupported theories of schizophrenia

Chapter 12: Personality Disorders

- Emphasized empirically supported theories and treatments for personality disorders and deemphasized unsupported theories and treatments
- Clarified the distinction between antisocial personality disorder and psychopathy
- Expanded the discussions of problems with the DSM-IV-TR conceptualization of personality disorders, including possible gender and cultural bias
- Emphasized the trend toward dimensional models of personality disorders

Chapter 13: Childhood Disorders

- Added a section on college students coping with mental disorders
- Expanded the discussion of the subtypes of attention-deficit/hyperactivity disorder,

including information on the role of sluggish cognitive tempo

- Expanded the discussion of the distinctions between conduct disorder and oppositional defiant disorder
- Added a section on Asperger's disorder

Chapter 14: Cognitive Disorders and Life-Span Issues

- Added information on the causes of and treatments for Alzheimer's disorder

Chapter 15: Eating Disorders

- Expanded the section on binge-eating disorder
- Updated the research on social pressures toward eating disorders, including new experimental work
- Added a discussion of dieting subtype versus depressive subtype binge eating
- Reorganized and updated the section on the psychosocial factors in eating disorders

Chapter 16: Sexual Disorders

- Extensively revised the entire chapter to reflect new research and treatments
- Expanded the discussion of the role of Viagra and similar drugs in the treatment of sexual dysfunctions
- Clarified the role of sex therapy in the psychotherapy of sexual dysfunction
- Added a discussion of the history of thought on homosexuality
- Clarified the characteristics of the paraphilias
- Substantially updated the section on gender identity disorder

Chapter 17: Substance-Related Disorders

- Updated epidemiology and historical trends of drug use
- Added a section on club drugs

- Expanded the discussion of the role of GABA in drug effects
- Expanded and updated the section on the explanations for gender differences in alcohol use

Chapter 18: Mental Health and the Law

- Added a discussion of the "Zoloft defense" as a type of insanity defense
- Added new data on violence among people with mental illness

SUPPLEMENTS

The text has an outstanding ancillary package to support student learning and classroom teaching.

For the Student

Student Study Guide (prepared by Jennifer Boothby, Indiana State University)   This study tool provides students with a comprehensive review of the material in the textbook. Each chapter of the study guide includes learning objectives, a list of essential ideas from each chapter, a guided review through all of the major sections, a 20-item practice multiple-choice exam with answers, and a practice essay exam with answers.

MindMap Student CD-ROM   A rich resource for students, this CD-ROM includes short video excerpts from McGraw-Hill's *Faces of Abnormal Psychology* series and other sources with wrap-around pedagogy, interactive exercises, chapter quizzes, and other valuable tools to help students master the concepts of abnormal psychology.

Online Learning Center for Students (updated by Gail Edmunds)   The official Web site for the text contains PowerWeb articles, *New York Times* news feeds, chapter outlines, practice quizzes that can be e-mailed to the professor, key term flashcards, interactive exercises, Internet activities, Web links to relevant abnormal psychology sites, an Internet primer, a career appendix, and a statistics primer. www.mhhe.com/nolen4

PowerWeb This unique online tool provides students with current articles, curriculum-based materials, weekly updates with assessment, informative and timely world news, refereed Web links, research tools, study tools, and interactive exercises. A PowerWeb access password is bound into the front of each new copy of the text.

For the Instructor

Instructor's Manual (revised by Linda Raasch, Normandale Community College, and NiCole Buchanan, Michigan State University) This comprehensive guide includes an overview of each chapter, learning objectives, suggestions and resources for lecture topics, classroom activities, projects, suggestions for video and multimedia lecture enhancements, and a media integration guide to help link the electronic resources to the syllabus. For this edition, NiCole Buchanan has provided ideas for addressing in the classroom differences in gender and culture that affect the way individuals experience psychological disorders in a diverse society. The *Instructor's Manual* is available on the password-protected Instructor's Center of the text Web site and on the *Instructor's Resource CD-ROM*.

Test Item File (revised by Brenda Flippen, Durham Technical Community College) Available on the *Instructor's Resource CD-ROM*, the *Test Item File* provides a wide variety of book-specific test questions. Available as Word files, the questions in the *Test Item File* are also provided in EZ Test. McGraw-Hill's EZ Test is a flexible and easy-to-use electronic testing program that allows instructors to create tests from book-specific items. It accommodates a wide range of question types and allows instructors to add their own questions. Multiple versions of a test can be created and any test can be exported for use with course management systems such as WebCT, BlackBoard, or PageOut. EZ Test Online is a new service that gives instructors a place to easily administer EZ Test–created exams and quizzes online. The program is available for Windows and Macintosh environments.

PowerPoint Lectures (revised by Crystal Park, University of Connecticut, Storrs) Available on the text Web site as well as on the *Instructor's Resource CD-ROM,* these presentations cover the key points of the chapter and include graphics. Helpful lecture guidelines are provided in the "notes" section for each slide. They can be used as-is or modified to meet the instructor's needs.

Classroom Performance System (CPS) The Classroom Performance System (CPS) from **eInstruction** allows instructors to gauge immediately what students are learning during lectures. With CPS, instructors can ask questions, take polls, or host classroom demonstrations and get instant feedback. In addition, CPS makes it easy to take attendance, give and grade pop quizzes, or give formal, paper-based class tests with multiple versions of the test using CPS for immediate grading.

For instructors who want to use CPS in their classroom, McGraw-Hill is pleased to offer text-specific multiple-choice questions and polling questions created by Elisabeth Sherwin (University of Arkansas, Little Rock) for in-class use. The questions are available on the *Instructor's Resource CD-ROM* and can be downloaded from the Web site for *Abnormal Psychology,* fourth edition.

Instructor's Resource CD-ROM This comprehensive CD-ROM includes the *Instructor's Manual, Test Item Files,* PowerPoint slides, CPS questions, and an image gallery. An easy-to-use interface is provided for the design and delivery of multimedia classroom presentations.

Faces of Abnormal Psychology, **Volumes I and II** This series of 20 8- to 10-minute video short clips suitable for classroom viewing is available on DVD and VHS for instructors who adopt this text. Each video features an interview with an individual who has experienced a mental disorder. Schizophrenia, posttraumatic stress disorder, bulimia nervosa, obsessive-compulsive disorder, and Asperger's disorder are some of the conditions covered.

Taking Sides: Clashing Views on Controversial Issues in Abnormal Psychology This debate-style reader introduces students to controversial viewpoints on important issues in the field. Each topic is carefully framed for students, and the pro and con essays represent the arguments of leading scholars and commentators in their fields. An instructor's guide containing testing materials is also available.

Online Learning Center for Instructors The password-protected instructor side of the text Web site contains the *Instructor's Manual*, a sample chapter from the text, PowerPoint presentations, Web links, *New York Times News* feeds, and other teaching resources. www.mhhe.com/nolen4

PageOut™ With this tool from McGraw-Hill, instructors can build their own course Web sites in less than an hour. PageOut™ requires no prior knowledge of HTML, no long hours of coding, and no design skills. With PageOut™, even the most inexperienced computer user can quickly and easily create a professional-looking course Web site. Instructors simply fill in templates with their information and with content provided by McGraw-Hill, then choose a design, to create a Web site specifically designed for their course. Instructors can visit www.pageout.net to find out more about this free course management system.

Populated **WebCT and Blackboard** course cartridges are also available for use with this text. Instructors should contact their McGraw-Hill sales representative for details.

ACKNOWLEDGMENTS

I greatly appreciate the hard work and creativity of the McGraw-Hill staff who have contributed to this fourth edition. I especially wish to thank Anne Reid for her careful and patient editing of the manuscript, as well as for her creativity in helping me develop new features for this edition. I also wish to thank Judith Kromm, John Wannemacher, Melissa Caughlin, Laura Kuhn, Emily Hatteberg, Laurie Entringer, Emma Ghiselli, Nora Agbayani, Alex Rohrs, Stephanie George, Louis Swaim, and Carol Bielski at McGraw-Hill. Laura Lawrie coordinated the development of the supplements. I also thank Richard Liu and Thomas Flanagan for being diligent research assistants during this revision.

Many colleagues reviewed sections of the book and provided invaluable feedback for the fourth edition. My heartfelt thanks go to

Carol Shaw Austad
Central Connecticut State University

Jason Bowman
University of Florida, Gainesville

Seth Brown
University of Northern Iowa

Michael Connor
California State University, Long Beach

Miriam Ehrenberg
John Jay College, CUNY

Timothy R. Elliott
University of Alabama, Birmingham

Tom Ersfeld
Central Lakes College

Marc Feldman
University of Alabama, Birmingham (retired)

Karen Freiberg
University of Maryland, Baltimore County

Debra Hollister
Valencia Community College

Gloria Lawrence
Wayne State College

Dianne Leader
Georgia Institute of Technology

Karsten Look
Columbus State University

Terri Messman-Moore
Miami University of Ohio

Kurt Michael
Appalachian State University

Crystal Park
University of Connecticut, Storrs

Karen Pfost
Illinois State University

Brady Phelps
South Dakota State University

Mirjam Quinn
Purdue University

Linda Raasch
Normandale Community College

Kim Renk
University of Central Florida

Carolyn Roecker Phelps
University of Dayton

Esther Rothblum
University of Vermont

David Sbarra
University of Arizona

Glenn Shean
College of William
and Mary

Elisabeth Sherwin
University of Arkansas,
Little Rock

**Persephanie
Silverthorn**
University of New
Orleans

Ari Solmon
Williams College

Marian Underwood
University of Texas
at Dallas

As always, my family provided tremendous support as I worked on this edition, particularly given that we moved halfway across the country just before work on the revision began. I thank Richard Nolen-Hoeksema and Michael Hoeksema, John Nolen, and Renze and Marjorie Hoeksema.

Susan Nolen-Hoeksema
New Haven, Connecticut

Susan Nolen-Hoeksema, Ph.D., is professor of psychology at Yale University. She has also been a professor at Stanford University and the University of Michigan. She received her B.A. from Yale University and her Ph.D. from the University of Pennsylvania. Her research focuses on mood regulation and on gender differences in psychopathology. The recipient of two major teaching awards, Professor Nolen-Hoeksema has received research funding from the National Institutes of Health, the National Science Foundation, and the William T. Grant Foundation. She was awarded the Leadership Award from the Committee on Women, as well as the Early Career Award from the American Psychological Association. She lives near New Haven, Connecticut, with her husband, Richard, and her son, Michael.

Abnormal Psychology: The Intersection of Science and Humanity

Challenging Material with Pedagogy that Motivates Learning

Sometimes students find it difficult to appreciate the scientific side of abnormal psychology as well as the human side. Susan Nolen-Hoeksema took special care to make the content as clear and precise as possible and to provide engaging pedagogy that promotes understanding of abnormal psychology as a science.

CONCEPT REVIEW TABLES AND FIGURES summarize the major conceptual points, such as the leading theories of what causes a disorder and the principal treatment options. These visual displays organize the material in ways that make it easier to retain.

TABLE 12.3　Concept Overview

Dramatic-Emotional Personality Disorders

People with dramatic-emotional personality disorders tend to have unstable emotions and to engage in dramatic and impulsive behavior.

Label	Key Features	Similar Disorders on Axis I
Antisocial personality disorder	Pervasive pattern of criminal, impulsive, callous, or ruthless behavior; disregard for the rights of others; no respect for social norms	Conduct disorder (diagnosed in children)
Borderline personality disorder	Rapidly shifting and unstable mood, self-concept, and interpersonal relationships; impulsive behavior; transient dissociative states; self-effacement	Mood disorders
Histrionic personality disorder	Rapidly shifting moods, unstable relationships, and intense need for attention and approval; dramatic, seductive behavior	Somatoform disorders, mood disorders
Narcissistic personality disorder	Grandiose thoughts and feelings of one's own worth; obliviousness to others' needs; exploitative, arrogant demeanor	Manic symptoms

Source: Reprinted with permission from the *Diagnostic and Statistical Manual of Mental Disorders*, Fourth Edition, Text Revision. Copyright © 2000 American Psychiatric Association.

DSM-IV-TR TABLES list the symptoms and diagnostic criteria of each major disorder.

TABLE 12.1　DSM-IV-TR

Personality Disorders

The DSM-IV-TR groups personality disorders into three clusters.

Cluster A: Odd-Eccentric Personality Disorders

People with these disorders have symptoms similar to those of people with schizophrenia, including inappropriate or flat affect, odd thought and speech patterns, and paranoia. People with these disorders maintain their grasp on reality, however.

Cluster B: Dramatic-Emotional Personality Disorders

People with these disorders tend to be manipulative, volatile, and uncaring in social relationships. They are prone to impulsive, sometimes violent behaviors that show little regard for their own safety or the safety or needs of others.

Cluster C: Anxious-Fearful Personality Disorders

People with these disorders are extremely concerned about being criticized or abandoned by others and, thus, have dysfunctional relationships with others.

Source: Reprinted with permission from the *Diagnostic and Statistical Manual of Mental Disorders*, Fourth Edition, Text Revision. Copyright © 2000 American Psychiatric Association.

CASE STUDIES illustrate the disorders, possible contributing factors to the disorders, and treatments for the disorders.

CASE STUDY

Debbie was a 26-year-old woman who worked as a salesclerk in a trendy clothing store and who sought therapy for panic disorder with agoraphobia. She dressed flamboyantly, with an elaborate and dramatic hairdo. Her appearance was especially striking, since she was quite short (under 5 feet tall) and at least 75 pounds overweight. She wore sunglasses indoors throughout the evaluation and constantly fiddled with them, taking them on and off nervously and waving them to emphasize a point. She cried loudly and dramatically at various points in the interview, going through large numbers of tissue. She continually asked for reassurance. ("Will I be OK?" "Can I get over this?") She talked nonstop throughout the evaluation. When gently interrupted by the evaluator, she was very apologetic, laughing and saying, "I know I talk too much"; yet she continued to do so throughout the session.

SUMMING UP

- People diagnosed with the odd-eccentric personality disorders—paranoid, schizoid, and schizotypal personality disorders—have odd thought processes, emotional reactions, and behaviors similar to those of people with schizophrenia, but they retain their grasp on reality.
- People diagnosed with paranoid personality disorder are chronically suspicious of others but maintain their grasp on reality.
- People diagnosed with schizoid personality disorder are emotionally cold and distant from others and have great trouble forming interpersonal relationships.
- People diagnosed with schizotypal personality disorder have a variety of odd beliefs and perceptual experiences but maintain their grasp on reality.
- These personality disorders, especially schizotypal personality disorder, have been linked to familial histories of schizophrenia and some of the biological abnormalities of schizophrenia.

SUMMING UP SECTIONS provide a bulleted review of key points at the end of each major section in a chapter.

CHAPTER INTEGRATIONS at the end of each chapter emphasize how biology, psychology, and social context come together to create vulnerability to disorders and illustrate this approach with a figure.

CHAPTER INTEGRATION

Although the empirical research on the personality disorders is too lacking to allow a clear integration

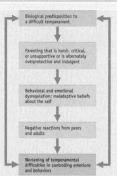

FIGURE 12.3 **An Integrated Model of the Personality Disorders.** A difficult temperament may combine with difficult parenting to lead to personality disorders.

- Biological predisposition to a difficult temperament
- Parenting that is harsh, critical, or unsupportive or is alternately overprotective and indulgent
- Behavioral and emotional dysregulation; maladaptive beliefs about the self
- Negative reactions from peers and adults
- Worsening of temperamental difficulties in controlling emotions and behaviors

of the biological, psychological, and social factors impinging on these disorders, some theoretical models have attempted this integration. They serve as the basis for current research (Millon et al., 2000; Siever & Davis, 1991; Trull & Durrett, 2005). According to these models, at the root of many of the personality disorders may be a biological predisposition to a certain kind of difficult temperament (see Figure 12.3).

For example, in the case of avoidant, dependent, and obsessive-compulsive personality disorders, an anxious and fearful temperament may be involved. In narcissistic and antisocial personality disorders, an impulsive and aggressive temperament may contribute. In borderline and histrionic personality disorders, a unstable, overly emotional temperament may be involved.

Children born with any of these temperaments are difficult to parent effectively. If parents can be supportive of these children yet set appropriate

limits on their behavior, the children may never develop severe enough behavior or emotional problems to be diagnosed with a personality disorder. If parents are unable to counteract children's temperamental vulnerabilities with harsh, critical, unsupportive parenting or overprotective, indulgent parenting, then the children's temperamental vulnerabilities may grow into severe behavior and emotional problems, as well as maladaptive beliefs about the self. These problems will influence how others—teachers, peers, and eventually employers and mates—interact with the individuals, perhaps in ways that further exacerbate their temperamental vulnerabilities.

In this way, a lifelong pattern of dysfunction, called a personality disorder, may emerge out of the interaction between a child's biologically based temperament and others' reactions to that temperament.

Extraordinary People

Susanna Kaysen: *Girl, Interrupted*

Susanna Kaysen was 18 and depressed, drifting through life and endlessly oppositional toward her parents and teachers. She tried to commit suicide. She began having strange perceptions:

> I was having a problem with patterns. Oriental rugs, tile floors, printed curtains, things like that. Supermarkets were especially bad, because of the long, hypnotic checkerboard aisles. When I looked at these things, I saw other things within them. That sounds as though I was hallucinating, and I wasn't. I knew I was looking at a floor or a curtain. But all patterns seemed to contain potential representations, which in a dizzying array would flicker briefly to life. That could be . . . a forest, a flock of birds, my second grade class picture. Well, it wasn't—it was a rug, or whatever it was, but my glimpses of the other things it might be were exhausting. Reality was getting too dense. (Kaysen, 1993, pp. 40–41)

Kaysen went to see a psychiatrist for a routine evaluation. At the end of one session, he put her in a taxi and sent her to McLean Hospital outside Boston. When she signed herself in, she was told that her stay would be about two weeks. Instead, Kaysen was not released for nearly two years.

Years after she was released from the hospital, Kaysen discovered that her diagnosis had been borderline personality disorder. In her autobiography, *Girl, Interrupted*, she raises many questions about this disorder:

> . . . I had to locate a copy of the *Diagnostic and Statistical Manual of Mental Disorders* and look up Borderline Personality to see what they really thought about me.
>
> It's a fairly accurate picture of me at eighteen, minus a few quirks like reckless driving and eating binges. . . . I'm tempted to try refuting it, but then I would be open to the further charges of "defensiveness" and "resistance."
>
> All I can do is give the particulars: an annotated diagnosis.
>
> . . . "Instability of self-image, interpersonal relationships, and mood . . . uncer-

tainty about . . . long-term goals or career choice. . . ." Isn't this a good description of adolescence? Moody, fickle, faddish, insecure: in short, impossible.

> "Self-mutilating behavior (e.g., wrist-scratching). . . ." I've skipped forward a bit. This is the one that caught me by surprise as I sat on the floor of the bookstore reading my diagnosis. Wrist-scratching! I thought I'd invented it. Wrist-banging, to be precise. . . .
>
> I had a butterfly chair. In the sixties, everyone in Cambridge had a butterfly chair. The metal edge of its upturned seat was perfectly placed for wrist-banging. I had tried breaking ashtrays and walking on the shards, but I didn't have the nerve to tread firmly. Wrist-banging—slow, steady, mindless—was a better solution. It was cumulative injury, so each bang was tolerable. . . .
>
> I spent hours in my butterfly chair banging my wrist. I did it in the evenings, like homework. I'd do some homework, then I'd spend half an hour wrist-banging, then finish my homework, then back in the chair for some more banging before brushing my teeth and going to bed.
>
> I was trying to explain my situation to myself. My situation was that I was in pain and nobody knew it. So I told myself, over and over, You are in pain. It was the only way I could get through to myself ("counteract feelings of 'numbness'"). I was demonstrating, externally and irrefutably, an inward condition. . . .

Understanding Brings Compassion and Choices

EXTRAORDINARY PEOPLE VIGNETTES

at the beginning of each chapter highlight the experiences of people who suffer from one of the disorders discussed in the chapter. Within the chapter, these vignettes are used to illustrate key points about the disorder. At the end of the chapter, a follow-up section places the chapter content in the personal context of these Extraordinary People.

VOICES quotations throughout each chapter allow individuals to speak from their own experience about their disorder and put a human face on the clinical aspects of abnormal psychology.

compulsions may often seem purposeful, they are not functional. In some cases, the family members of people with OCD become accomplices in the disorder, as did the husband of writer Emily Colas, who has written about her OCD (Colas, 1998, pp. 70–72).

VOICES

My husband and I generally kept a pile of about twenty garbage bags in one corner of our apartment. Which may seem out of character, for me to let them stay, but it was our trash and I knew nothing bad was in there. It was the communal trash that made me shake. So when it was time to take the bags out to the dumpster, my husband had to follow the whole hygienic procedure. To keep the neighbors' germs out of our place. First the water had to be turned on and left that way because if he touched the garbage and then the spigot, the spigot would get contaminated. Next he'd take one bag in his right hand and open the door with his left. Then he'd shut the door behind him and lock it so that no one could get into the house. I guess I could have monitored, but he wanted me upstairs so I couldn't critique him. He'd take the bag down, stand a few feet from the dumpster to be sure not to touch it, and throw the bag in. Then he'd unlock the door, open it, slip his shoes off, come inside, and wash his hands. He used a pump soap so

that he could use his clean wrist to pump some in the palm of his hand and not contaminate the dispenser. The water would stay on, and he'd move to the next bag. He went through this procedure twenty times, once for each bag, until they were gone.

Theories of OCD

The biological theories of OCD have dominated research in recent years, and they have provided some intriguing hypotheses about its sources. Psychodynamic and cognitive-behavioral theories of OCD have also been proposed. These theories are summarized in the Concept Overview in Table 7.10.

Biological Theories

Biological theories of obsessive-compulsive disorder view it as a neurobiological disorder. Much of this research has focused on a circuit in the brain that is involved in the execution of primitive patterns of behavior, such as aggression, sexuality, and bodily excretion (Baxter et al., 2001; Rapoport, 1990; Saxena & Rauch, 2000). This circuit begins in the orbital region of the frontal cortex (see Figure 7.11). These impulses are then carried to a part of the basal ganglia called the **caudate nucleus**, which allows only the strongest of these impulses to carry through to the thalamus. If these impulses reach the thalamus, the person is motivated to think further about and possibly act on these impulses. The action might involve a set of stereotyped behaviors appropriate to the impulse. Once these behaviors are executed, the impulse diminishes.

Seeing Yourself in the Personality Disorders

In Chapter 1, we discussed the tendency for students reading an abnormal psychology textbook to see signs of many mental disorders in themselves or in the people in their lives. Students may be especially prone to see personality disorders in themselves or in others. Indeed, people are considerably more likely to diagnose themselves on self-report questionnaires as having a personality disorder than are clinicians to diagnose them in the context of psychiatric interviews (Weissman, 1993).

Why might this be so? It may occur because people tend to attribute behaviors to personality traits and to ignore the influence of situations on those behaviors (see Ross & Nisbett, 1991). This tendency is often referred to as *fundamental attribution error*.

A classic study demonstrating how strongly people discount situational influences over personality influences was conducted by Jones and Harris (1967). They asked participants to read essays presumably written by other participants. The participants were told that the persons writing the essays had been assigned to present a particular viewpoint on the topic of the essay. For example, they were told that a political science student had been assigned to write an essay defending communism in Cuba or that a debate student had been assigned to attack the proposition that marijuana should be legalized. Despite the fact that the participants were told that the essay writers had been assigned to take a particular viewpoint (and had not chosen that viewpoint), they tended to believe that the essay writers actually held the viewpoint they presented in their essays.

If you think you see signs of one or more personality disorders in yourself or someone close to you, stop and ask yourself the following questions:

■ *What are the situational influences that might be driving my behavior or my friend's or relative's behavior?* For example, let's say that you are concerned that your brother has developed an obsessive-compulsive personality disorder (see pp. 451–452) since he has taken on two jobs to try to help your family with finances. He is preoccupied with schedules and always has lists of things to do; he has become a workaholic; he has become a perfectionist to the point of not being able to get things done; and he has become even more moralistic than he was in high school.

It is true that certain situations can exaggerate the already dysfunctional behaviors of people with obsessive-compulsive personality disorder. However, consider the possibility that your brother's behaviors, particularly the ones that he has developed since taking these two jobs, are largely driven by the demands of his life rather than by enduring personality traits. Your brother's preoccupation with lists and schedules and his working 20 hours a day are probably behaviors that he believes are necessary, given the demands of the situation. This kind of pressure can cause many people to try to be perfectionists but to become so anxious about the possibility of failing that they cannot do their work. When you find yourself wondering if you or someone you care about has developed a personality disorder, stop to consider the aspects of the situation that might really be responsible for the behaviors you observe.

■ *Am I selectively remembering behaviors that are signs of a personality disorder and selectively forgetting behaviors that contradict the diagnosis of a personality disorder?* One of the strongest reasons people overestimate the influence of personality traits on behaviors is that they selectively pay attention to and remember behaviors that are consistent with personality traits and ignore or forget behaviors that are inconsistent with the traits. For example, if you fear that you are an overly dependent person, you will probably find it quite easy to remember times in the past when you have had trouble making decisions without much advice from others, have felt uncomfortable and helpless when alone, or have been passive in voicing your opinions or needs to others. You will probably forget the many more times when you made decisions with no help from others, actually enjoyed being alone, or spoke up to express your opinions or needs.

It can be helpful to write down all the times in the recent or distant past when you behaved in ways that contradicted the troubling personality trait you think you have. Or you might want to ask a trusted friend to help you sort out whether your behaviors are always consistent with a negative personality trait.

■ *Are the behaviors I am observing part of a longtime pattern of behavior, or do they occur only occasionally?* Most of us occasionally act in dysfunctional or plainly stupid ways. Sometimes, these actions are driven by the situations in which we find ourselves, but sometimes we act in stupid ways even when there is no apparent situational excuse for doing so. A personality disorder is a pattern of behavior that has existed most of a person's life and that the person demonstrates across a range of situations.

(continued)

TAKING PSYCHOLOGY PERSONALLY boxes address personal questions and concerns that sometimes come up in the abnormal psychology course, such as concern about one's own mental health and questions about how to get help for oneself or others.

Electronic Resources to Enhance Teaching and Learning

ONLINE LEARNING CENTER www.mhhe.com/nolen4

STUDENT RESOURCES include chapter outlines and practice quizzes keyed to learning goals, flashcards, interactive review exercises, Abnormal Psychology Box Office guide to related movies, and access, via **PowerWeb**, to current news about psychology, research tools, and other valuable study tools.

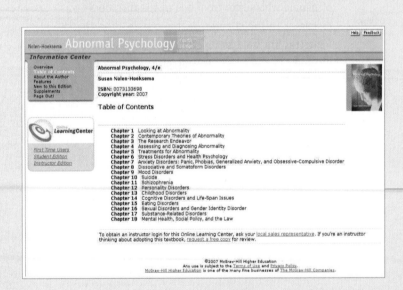

The **MINDMAP CD-ROM** for students comes with new copies of the text. This CD-ROM contains numerous video exercises featuring short excerpts from McGraw-Hill's *Faces of Abnormal Psychology* series and other sources, interactive exercises, chapter quizzes, and other valuable study tools.

MindMap CD-ROM

The following resources on the MindMap CD-ROM that came with this text will help you to master the content of this chapter and prepare for tests:

■ Video: Borderline Personality Disorder
■ Chapter Timeline
■ Chapter Quiz

> Chapter 1

People Flying
by Peter Sickles

Who, except the gods, can live time through forever
without any pain.

—Aeschylus

Looking at Abnormality <

CHAPTER OVERVIEW

Extraordinary People

■ **Clifford Beers:** *A Mind That Found Itself*

Defining Abnormality

The context for a behavior often determines whether it is considered abnormal. Criteria that have been used to determine the abnormality of behaviors are cultural norms for behaviors, how unusual the behaviors are, whether the behaviors cause the person discomfort, the presence of an identifiable illness, and whether the behaviors interfere with the person's functioning. Today, mental-health professionals tend to view behaviors as maladaptive or abnormal if they cause distress or dysfunction or if they are deviant.

Taking Psychology Personally

■ **When You Wonder If You Are Abnormal**

Historical Perspectives on Abnormality

Theories of abnormality across the ages have included biological theories, supernatural theories, and psychological theories. In prehistoric times, supernatural theories of abnormality may have dominated, and a primitive form of brain surgery designed to release demons may have been performed. Some of the most ancient writings about abnormality are in Chinese texts from around 2674 B.C. Other prominent writings include the papyri of Egypt and Mesopotamia, the Old Testament, and the works of Greek and Roman philosophers and physicians. In the Middle Ages, many people with mental disorders may have been accused of being witches and killed out of fear. Throughout history, people who acted abnormally have been imprisoned, tortured, or cast out. In the eighteenth and nineteenth centuries, however, several advocates of more gentle treatment of people with mental disorders helped establish facilities where they could be treated with kindness.

The Emergence of Modern Perspectives

Biological and psychosocial theories of abnormality dominate in mainstream science and practice in abnormal psychology. Some people still take their own lay and supernatural theories of abnormality into their interactions with therapists, however.

Modern Mental-Health Care

Major breakthroughs in drug therapies for serious mental disorders in the mid-twentieth century made it possible to move many people out of institutional care and into community-based care. Deinstitutionalization never lived up to its lofty goals, however, because the resources to support people in the community were never adequate. The late twentieth century saw the rise of managed care systems, some of which severely limit access to mental-health care.

Professions Within Abnormal Psychology

Mental-health professionals treat people with psychological problems and do research on these problems. Several professions are available in the field.

Chapter Integration

Modern approaches to abnormality emphasize the integration and interaction of biological, psychological, and social factors.

Extraordinary People

Clifford Beers: *A Mind That Found Itself*

Clifford Beers was always an energetic child, moody with little self-control. Still, he was intelligent and ambitious enough to do well in school and eventually to graduate from a university. Beers' moodiness increased with time, however, particularly after his brother Sam began to have severe convulsive seizures. These seizures were diagnosed as epilepsy (but were probably due to a massive brain tumor discovered after the brother's death). Clifford Beers developed a morbid fear that he would be overcome with epilepsy.

In March 1890, as his brother lay dying in the family home, Beers' moodiness grew to despair, accompanied by deep paranoia. By June, Beers' despair had become so great that he was unable to speak. He began contemplating suicide and eventually jumped out a fourth-floor window. He escaped with only broken bones. Beers' obsession with becoming epileptic passed with this incident but was replaced with other paranoid and grandiose beliefs. Beers was hospitalized, first in a private mental hospital and later in public mental hospitals when his family ran out of money. His mood alternated between depression and manic excitement.

In the early 1900s, there were no drugs that significantly affected symptoms such as those suffered by Clifford Beers. He endured some of the drugs of the day—strychnine and arsenic tonics. He also was beaten; choked; locked away for long periods in dark, cold cells with no clothes; and put in a straitjacket for up to 21 days. Beers wrote volumes about the hospital conditions, describing the need for better care for the "insane." Over those three years of hospitalization, Beers' mood swings became less severe, and in 1903 he was declared recovered enough to be released.

Clifford Beers survived the harsh treatment he received in early twentieth-century mental hospitals and recovered from his symptoms of fear, depression, and paranoia, perhaps despite these treatments. Later in this chapter, we will pick up the story of Clifford Beers and will see how he transformed his terrible experience into a social movement to improve the treatment of people with mental-health problems.

The study of abnormal psychology is the study of people, like Clifford Beers, who suffer mental, emotional, and often physical pain as a result of some form of psychological or mental disorder, often referred to as **psychopathology.** Sometimes the experiences of people with psychopathology are as unusual as the experiences of a young woman named Julia, whose voice we listen to in the following.

VOICES

My illness began slowly, gradually, when I was between the ages of 15 and 17. During that time reality became distant and I began to wander around in a sort of haze, foreshadowing the delusional world that was to come later. I also began to have visual hallucinations in which people changed into different characters, the change indicating to me their moral value. For example, the mother of a good friend always changed into a witch, and I believed this to be indicative of her evil nature. Another type of visual hallucination I had at this time is exemplified by an occurrence during a family trip through Utah: The cliffs along

(continued)

the side of the road took on a human appearance, and I perceived them as women, bedraggled and weeping. At the time I didn't know what to make of these changes in my perceptions. On the one hand, I thought they came as a gift from God, but on the other hand, I feared that something was dreadfully wrong. However, I didn't tell anyone what was happening; I was afraid of being called insane. I also feared, perhaps incredibly, that someone would take it lightly and tell me nothing was wrong, that I was just having a rough adolescence, which was what I was telling myself. (Anonymous, 1992, pp. 333–334)

Sometimes, however, people with psychopathology have experiences that are familiar to many of us but more extreme, as Jamison (1995, p. 110) describes:

VOICES

From the time I woke up in the morning until the time I went to bed at night, I was unbearably miserable and seemingly incapable of any kind of joy or enthusiasm. Everything—every thought, word, movement—was an effort. Everything that once was sparkling now was flat. I seemed to myself to be dull, boring, inadequate, thick brained, unlit, unresponsive, chill skinned, bloodless, and sparrow drab. I doubted, completely, my ability to do anything well. It seemed as though my mind had slowed down and burned out to the point of being virtually useless. The wretched, convoluted, and pathetically confused mass of gray worked only well enough to torment me with a dreary litany of my inadequacies and shortcomings in character and to taunt me with the total, the desperate hopelessness of it all.

In this book, we explore the lives of people with troubling psychological symptoms to understand how they think, what they feel, and how they behave. We investigate what is known about the causes of and treatments for various types of symptoms. The purpose of this book is not only to provide you with information, facts and figures, theories, and research. It is also to take you into the lives of people with psychological symptoms and to help you understand their experience. You may recognize yourself in some of these people, and you may attain the knowledge you need to seek effective treatment. The good news is that, thanks to an explosion of research in the last few decades, there *are* effective biological and psychological treatments for many of the mental-health problems we discuss in this book.

DEFINING ABNORMALITY

Let us start by defining what is meant by *psychopathology*, or, more generally, by *abnormality*. This key step is often more difficult than it might seem at first glance. Consider the following behaviors:

1. A man kissing another man
2. A woman slapping a child
3. A man driving a nail through his hand
4. A woman refusing to eat for several days
5. A man barking like a dog and crawling on the floor on his hands and knees
6. A woman building a shrine to her dead husband in a corner of her living room and leaving food and gifts for him at the altar

Do you think these behaviors are abnormal? You may reply, "It depends." In some circumstances, several of these behaviors may seem perfectly normal. In many European cultures, for example, men commonly greet other men with a kiss. In many religious traditions, refusing to eat for a period, or fasting, is a common ritual of cleansing and penitence. You might expect that some of the other listed behaviors, such as driving a nail through one's hand or barking like a dog, are abnormal in all circumstances, yet even these behaviors are accepted by some people and indeed are prescribed for specific situations. In Mexico, some Christians have themselves nailed to crosses at Easter to commemorate the crucifixion of Jesus. Among the Yoruba of Africa, traditional healers act as dogs, barking and crawling on the floor, during healing rituals (Murphy, 1976). In Shinto and Buddhist religions, it is customary to build altars to dead loved ones, to offer them food and gifts, and to speak with them as if they were in the room (Stroebe et al., 1992). Thus, the **context,** or circumstances surrounding a behavior, influences whether a behavior is viewed as abnormal.

Some theorists have gone so far as to argue that deviation from cultural or societal norms is the only criterion for labeling a behavior as abnormal (see Mezzich et al., 1999). A parallel perspective argues that behaviors become defined as abnormal if they

In Mexico, some Christians have themselves nailed to a cross to commemorate the crucifixion of Jesus.

violate a culture's **gender roles,** which are expectations for the behavior of an individual based on his or her gender. For example, a woman crying in public is not viewed as terribly abnormal in our culture, but a man crying in public is seen as abnormal, because this violates gender roles for men's display of emotions.

Other theorists have argued for what might appear, on the surface, to be more objective criteria, or standards, for defining abnormality. Such standards do not rely on cultural traditions or gender roles. Instead, they focus on the *unusualness* of the behavior, the *discomfort* of the person exhibiting the behavior, the presence of *mental illness,* and the *maladaptiveness* of the behavior. Each of these standards has its advantages and disadvantages, as we will see in the following sections.

Cultural Relativism

The **cultural relativism** perspective holds that there are no universal standards or rules for labeling a behavior as abnormal. Instead, behaviors can only be abnormal relative to cultural norms (Snowden & Yamada, 2005). Cultural relativists believe that there are different definitions of abnormality across different cultures.

Bereavement practices provide a good example of cultural relativism. In Western countries, bereaved people are expected to mourn their dead loved ones for a period of time, perhaps a few weeks or months, then to "let go" of the loved ones and move on in their lives (Stroebe et al., 1992). People who continue to think and talk about their dead loved ones a great deal after the specified period of mourning are thought to have "compli-

cated bereavement" and may be encouraged to seek counseling. More often, their family members and friends simply tell them to "get over it." The norm in these cultures is to break emotional bonds with dead loved ones, and people who seem not to have adequately broken those bonds may be labeled as abnormal.

In contrast, people in other cultures believe that we cannot and should not break psychological ties with dead loved ones. For example, in Japan, maintaining emotional bonds with deceased loved ones is not only normal but also prescribed for bereaved people (Yamamoto, 1970). In Egypt, the bereaved are encouraged to dwell profusely on their grief, and other people support them by recounting their own losses and openly expressing their sorrow in emotional outpourings (Wikan, 1991).

Even in Western countries, during the romantic age of the nineteenth century, expectations of the bereaved were radically different from current expectations (Rosenblatt, 2001; Stroebe et al., 1992). People's close relationships were at the center of their self-definitions, and the loss of a loved one was a critical defining moment in the survivor's life. "To grieve was to signal the significance of the relationship, and the depth of one's own spirit. Dissolving bonds with the deceased would not only define the relationship as superficial, but would deny as well one's own sense of profundity and self-worth" (Stroebe et al., 1992, p. 1208). People clung to the lost loved one and wrote about their grief in poetry, diaries, and fiction.

Opponents of cultural relativism argue that dangers arise when societal norms are allowed to dictate what is normal and abnormal. In particular, psychiatrist Thomas Szasz noted that, throughout history, societies have labeled individuals and groups abnormal in order to justify controlling or silencing them. Hitler branded Jews abnormal and used this as one justification for the Holocaust. The former Soviet Union branded political dissidents mentally ill and jailed them in mental hospitals.

When the slave trade was active in the United States, slaves who tried to escape their masters could be diagnosed as having *drapetomania*, a sickness that caused them to desire freedom. This provided a justification for capturing them and returning them to their masters (Szasz, 1971). In 1851, Dr. Samuel Cartwright, a prominent physician, published an essay in the prestigious *New Orleans Medical and Surgical Journal* titled "Report on the Diseases and Physical Peculiarities of the Negro Race," in which he argued that

the cause, in most cases, that induces the Negro to run away from service, is as

When the slave trade was active, slaves who tried to escape were sometimes labeled as having a mental illness and beaten to "cure" them.

much a disease of the mind as any other species of mental alienation, and much more curable, as a general rule. With the advantages of proper medical advice, strictly followed, this troublesome practice that many Negroes have of running away, can be almost entirely prevented.

Cartwright also described a disease called *dysaesthesia Aethiopis*, the refusal to work for one's master. To cure this "disease," Cartwright prescribed the following:

The liver, skin and kidneys should be stimulated to activity, and be made to assist in decarbonising the blood. The best means to stimulate the skin is, first, to have the patient well washed with warm water and soap; then to anoint it all over with oil, and to slap the oil with a broad leather strap; then to put the patient to some hard kind of work in the open air and sunshine, that will compel him to expand his lungs, as chopping wood, splitting rails, or sawing with the cross-cut or whip saw.

According to Cartwright, whipping slaves who refused to work and then forcing them to do hard labor would "revitalize" their lungs and bring them

back to their senses. We might like to believe that Cartwright's essay represented the extreme views of just one person, but he was writing on behalf of a prestigious medical association.

As noted earlier, in our modern society, gender-role expectations heavily influence the labeling of behaviors as normal or abnormal (Hartung & Widiger, 1998). Men who display sadness or anxiety, who choose to stay home to raise their children while their wives work, or who otherwise violate the male gender role are at risk for being labeled as abnormal. Women who are too aggressive, who don't want to have children, or who otherwise violate the female gender role are at risk for being labeled as abnormal. On the other hand, aggression in men and chronic anxiety or sadness in women are often dismissed as normal, because they do not violate gender roles—we expect these behaviors, so we label them as normal.

The cultural relativist perspective creates many difficulties in defining abnormality. Most psychologists these days do not take an extreme relativist view on abnormality, recognizing the dangers of completely accepting society's definitions of what is normal and abnormal. There is increasing sensitivity, however, to the reality that cultural norms and gender roles strongly influence people's feelings and actions.

Unusualness

A second standard that has been used for designating behaviors as abnormal is **unusualness.** Behaviors that are unusual, or rare, are considered abnormal, whereas behaviors that are typical, or usual, are considered normal. This criterion has some ties to the relativist criterion, because the unusualness of any behavior depends in part on a culture's norms for that behavior. For example, how unusual it is for a bereaved person to be wailing in public? The answer depends on whether that person is in Minneapolis or Cairo.

The unusualness criterion for abnormality has two other problems. First, although the criterion may seem objective, someone still has to decide how rare a behavior must be in order to call it abnormal. Are behaviors that only 10 percent of the population exhibits abnormal? Or do we want to set a more strict cutoff and say that only behaviors that 1 percent or less of the population exhibits are abnormal? Choosing a cutoff is as subjective as relying on personal opinions as to what is abnormal and normal.

The second problem with the unusualness criterion is that many rare behaviors are positive for the individual and for society, and most people would object to labeling such behaviors as abnormal. For example, we don't label the playing of a piano virtuoso abnormal; we label it gifted. Other people have hobbies or activities that are rare but

are a source of great joy for them and do no harm to others. These people are often referred to as *eccentrics*. For example, consider Gary Holloway, an environmental planner who works for the city of San Francisco and who is described in the following case study.

"Do people hate us because we dress this way or do we dress this way because people hate us?" © *Sidney Harris, courtesy ScienceCartoonsPlus.com*

CASE STUDY

He is fascinated by Martin Van Buren, the eighth president of the United States. Eighteen years ago, he discovered that Van Buren was the only president not to have a society dedicated to his memory, so he promptly founded the Martin Van Buren Fan Club. "This man did absolutely nothing to further the course of our national destiny," Holloway told us proudly, "yet hundreds of people now follow me in commemorating him." Holloway has served as the club's president for eighteen consecutive terms, and he has also been the winner for eighteen consecutive years of the Marty, its award for excellence in Van Burenism. Holloway is also a lifelong devotee of St. Francis of Assisi, and frequently dresses in the habit of a Franciscan monk. "It's comfortable, fun to wear, and I like the response I get when I wear it," he explained. "People always offer me a seat on the bus." Holloway has an obsession with the British Commonwealth and has an encyclopedic knowledge of places such as Tristan da Cunha and Fiji. During the Falklands war he passionately espoused the cause of the islanders, to the point of flying the Falklands flag on the flagpole on his front lawn. After the war he celebrated Britain's victory by renaming his home Falklands House, where he continues to fly its flag. His bedroom at Falklands House still has everything in it that it had when he was a boy. He calls it the Peanuts Room because of his huge collection of stuffed Snoopies and other memorabilia pertaining to the comic strip *Peanuts*. He has slept on the same twin bed there for forty years. He has dozens of toy airplanes, relics of his boyhood, and the walls are covered with pennants. "As a monk," he explained, "I'm always doing pennants"—thereby demonstrating the sly sense of humor that many eccentrics possess. (Weeks & James, 1995, pp. 36–37)

Gary Holloway's activities certainly are eccentric, but would we call them abnormal?

One of the few studies of eccentrics estimates that only about 1 in 10,000 people is a true eccentric. This study found that eccentrics certainly have unusual tastes but are generally very happy and function well in society (Weeks & James, 1995). Indeed, the rate of serious dysfunction among the eccentrics in this study was lower than the rate among noneccentrics.

Discomfort

Proponents of a **discomfort** criterion for abnormality suggest that behaviors should be considered abnormal only if the individual suffers discomfort and wishes to be rid of the behaviors. This criterion avoids, to some extent, the problems of using societal norms as the criterion for abnormality. If a person's behaviors violate societal norms but do not cause him or her any discomfort, then the behaviors should not be considered abnormal.

This viewpoint has contributed to a change in how psychologists and psychiatrists viewed one behavior pattern—homosexuality. Gay men and lesbians have argued that their sexual orientation is a natural part of themselves and a characteristic that causes them no discomfort and that they don't wish to alter or eliminate. Partly because of these arguments, in 1973 the American Psychiatric Association removed homosexuality from its list of recognized psychological disorders (Spitzer, 1981).

Some therapists object to the subjective discomfort criterion, however, because people are not always aware of problems their behaviors create for themselves or for others. For example, some

people who have lost touch with reality wander the streets aimlessly, not eating or taking care of themselves, in danger of starvation or exposure to the elements. These people may not be fully aware that they have severe problems and do not seek help. If we require that people acknowledge and seek help for their behaviors before we call those behaviors abnormal, some people who could benefit greatly from help might never get it.

In addition, the behaviors of some people cause great discomfort in others, if not in themselves. An example is people who engage in highly antisocial behavior, lying, cheating, and even being violent toward others. They may suffer no discomfort, and even may experience pleasure, at causing others great pain. Thus, we may want to call their behaviors abnormal.

Mental Illness

A fourth way of defining abnormality is as behaviors that result from mental disease or illness. This **mental illness** criterion implies that there is a clear, identifiable physical process that differs from "health" and that leads to specific behaviors or symptoms. For example, when many people say that an individual "has schizophrenia," they imply that he or she has a disease that should show up on some sort of biological test, just as hypertension shows up when a person's blood pressure is taken.

To date, however, there is no biological test available to diagnose any of the types of abnormality we will discuss in this book. This may be simply because we do not yet have the right biological tests. But many theorists believe that most mental-health problems are due to a number of complex biological and psychosocial factors, rather than to single abnormal genes or disease processes.

When we give a person's psychological symptoms a diagnosis, it is simply a label for that set of symptoms. For example, when we say someone "has" obsessive-compulsive disorder, we can mean only that he or she is exhibiting a set of symptoms, including obsessive thoughts and compulsive behaviors. The term *obsessive-compulsive disorder* does not refer to an identifiable physical process that is found in all people who exhibit these symptoms.

Maladaptiveness

How do the majority of researchers and clinicians in the mental-health field decide whether a set of behaviors is abnormal? The consensus is that behaviors and feelings that are **maladaptive**—that cause people to *suffer distress* and that *prevent them from functioning in daily life*—are abnormal and should be the focus of research and intervention (Spitzer, 1981). In addition, mental-health professionals tend

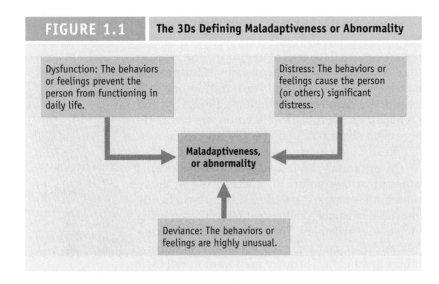

FIGURE 1.1   **The 3Ds Defining Maladaptiveness or Abnormality**

Dysfunction: The behaviors or feelings prevent the person from functioning in daily life.

Distress: The behaviors or feelings cause the person (or others) significant distress.

Maladaptiveness, or abnormality

Deviance: The behaviors or feelings are highly unusual.

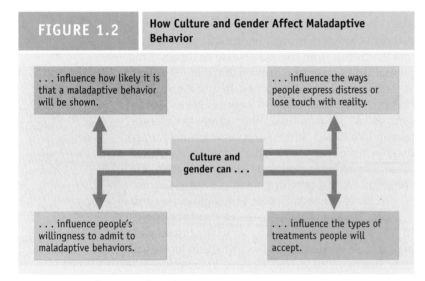

FIGURE 1.2   **How Culture and Gender Affect Maladaptive Behavior**

. . . influence how likely it is that a maladaptive behavior will be shown.

. . . influence the ways people express distress or lose touch with reality.

Culture and gender can . . .

. . . influence people's willingness to admit to maladaptive behaviors.

. . . influence the types of treatments people will accept.

How much should the behaviors be interfering with daily functioning? Who determines what is adequate functioning? And the criteria still depend on societal norms. Many behaviors are physically damaging but are accepted by society, such as smoking cigarettes. There are also many beliefs that some people think are "crazy," such as the belief in an afterlife, but that are accepted by society. Throughout this book, as we apply the maladaptiveness criteria to specific types of behavior, we will keep in mind the subjectivity of these criteria and the fuzziness of definitions of abnormality.

Even when the maladaptiveness criteria can be used confidently to identify a certain group of behaviors as abnormal, culture and gender can still influence the expression of those behaviors and the way those behaviors are treated (see Figure 1.2). First, culture and gender influence how likely it is that a given maladaptive behavior will be shown. For example, men are twice as likely as women to suffer problems related to alcohol use. This fact suggests that something about being male—male biology, male personality, or the social pressures put on men—contributes to the development of alcoholism.

Second, culture and gender can influence the ways people express distress or lose touch with reality. People who lose touch with reality often believe that they have divine powers, but whether an individual believes he or she is Jesus Christ or Buddha depends on his or her religious background.

Third, culture and gender can influence people's willingness to admit to certain types of maladaptive behaviors (Snowden & Yamada, 2005). People in Eskimo and Tahitian cultures may be reluctant to admit to angry feelings because of strong cultural norms against the expression of anger. However, the Kaluli of New Guinea and the Yanamamo of Brazil value the expression of anger and have elaborate and complex rituals for expressing anger (Jenkins, Kleinman, & Good, 1991).

Fourth, culture and gender can influence the types of treatments that are deemed acceptable or helpful for maladaptive behaviors (Snowden & Yamada, 2005). For example, women may be more willing than men to accept psychological treatments for problems. Throughout this book, we will explore these influences of culture and gender on maladaptive behaviors.

Many students take a course on abnormal psychology, wondering if they are abnormal, because they feel unusual, are uncomfortable with themselves, or fear they have inherited a mental illness. *Taking Psychology Personally: When You Wonder If You Are Abnormal* addresses this concern and what to do about it.

to reserve the label *maladaptive* for behaviors and feelings that are highly unusual or deviant.

Thus, the three components of maladaptiveness can be remembered with the heuristic of the *3Ds: dysfunction, distress,* and *deviance* (see Figure 1.1). Julia's experiences and the feelings described by Jamison, presented at the beginning of this chapter, would be labeled as abnormal by these criteria because they caused them suffering, they interfere with their ability to function in daily life, and they are highly unusual.

The maladaptiveness criteria have attracted widespread support among mental-health professionals, because they seem to capture what most of us mean when we call something abnormal, while avoiding some of the problems of using only the cultural relativism, unusualness, discomfort, and illness criteria. Still, the maladaptiveness criteria call for subjective judgments—how much emotional pain or harm must a person be suffering?

Taking Psychology Personally

When You Wonder If You Are Abnormal

As you read in this book about behaviors labeled as abnormal, you may find yourself thinking, "That's me!" or "That's someone I know!" You should be aware that many of the behaviors discussed in this book occur occasionally, in mild form, in many people. For example, many people between the ages of 18 and 25, even when not under the influence of a drug, have brief "out-of-body" experiences, in which they feel their "soul" or "self" is floating out of their body. It is even more common for people of all ages to have periods of sad or anxious moods or times when they feel that life is "out of control." For most people, these periods are relatively brief, and these behaviors or feelings do not severely interfere with their ability to function in life. If, however, you have been behaving in ways that interfere with daily functioning or that cause you or others much suffering, it is a good idea to talk with a professional about these experiences. Your instructor may be willing to speak with you or to provide you with referrals to professionals with whom you may speak. Many colleges offer confidential counseling for students at no cost or minimal cost. Some counties have mental-health associations that provide information on professionals or groups that serve people with specific types of problems. The phone number for your local mental-health association may be in the *Yellow Pages* or available through an operator.

SUMMING UP

- Cultural relativism is a perspective on abnormality that argues that the norms of a society must be used to determine the normality or abnormality of a behavior.
- The unusualness criterion for abnormality suggests that unusual, or rare, behaviors should be labeled abnormal.
- The discomfort criterion suggests that only behaviors or emotions that an individual finds distressing should be labeled abnormal.
- The mental illness criterion for abnormality suggests that only behaviors resulting from mental illness are abnormal.
- The consensus among professionals in the mental-health field is that behaviors that cause people to suffer distress, that prevent them from functioning in daily life, and that are unusual are abnormal. Often these behaviors are referred to as *maladaptive* and can be remembered as the 3Ds: distress, dysfunction, and deviance.

HISTORICAL PERSPECTIVES ON ABNORMALITY

References to madness, insanity, or other forms of abnormal behavior can be found throughout human history. Three types of theories of the causes of abnormal behaviors have competed for dominance across time. The **biological theories** saw abnormal behavior as similar to physical diseases, caused by the breakdown of systems in the body. The appropriate cure for mental disorders, according to the biological theories, was the restoration of the body to good health. The **supernatural theories** saw abnormal behavior as a result of divine intervention, curses, demonic possession, and personal sin. To rid the person of the disorder, religious rituals, exorcisms, confessions, and atonement were prescribed. The **psychological theories** saw abnormal behavior as a result of traumas, such as bereavement, or chronic stress. According to these theories, rest, relaxation, a change of environment, and certain herbal medicines were sometimes helpful to the afflicted person. These three types of theories influenced how people afflicted with disorders were regarded in the society. A person thought to be insane because he or she was a sinner would be regarded differently than would a person thought to be insane because of a medical disorder.

Ancient Theories

Our understanding of prehistoric people's conceptions of abnormality is based on inferences from archeological artifacts—fragments of bones, tools, artwork, and so on. Ever since humans developed written language, they have been writing about abnormal behavior. It seems that humans have always viewed abnormality as something needing special explanation.

Evil Spirits of the Stone Age

Historians speculate that even prehistoric people had a concept of insanity, probably one rooted in supernatural beliefs (Selling, 1940). Demons and ghosts were the cause of abnormal behavior. When a person acted oddly, he or she was suspected of being possessed by evil spirits.

The typical treatment for abnormality, according to supernatural beliefs, was exorcism—driving the evil spirits from the body of the suffering person. Shamans, or healers, would say prayers or incantations, try to talk the spirits out of the body, or make the body an uncomfortable place for the spirits to reside, often through extreme measures, such as starving or beating the person. At other times, the person thought to be possessed by evil spirits would simply be killed.

One treatment for abnormality in the Stone Age may have been to drill holes in the skulls of people displaying abnormal behavior to allow the spirits to depart. Archeologists have found skulls dating back to the Stone Age a half-million years ago, in which circular sections of the skull had been drilled away (Maher & Maher, 1985). The tool used for this drilling is called a trephine and the operation is called **trephination.** Some historians believe that people who were seeing or hearing things that were not real and people who were chronically sad were subjected to this prehistoric form of brain surgery (Selling, 1940). Presumably, if the person survived this surgery, the evil spirits would have been released and his or her abnormal behavior would have declined. However, we cannot know with certainty that trephination was used to drive away evil spirits. Some historians suggest that trephination was used primarily to remove blood clots caused by stone weapons during warfare and for other medical purposes (Maher & Maher, 1985). It is clear, however, that supernatural theories of abnormality have been around for a very long time.

Ancient China: Balancing Yin and Yang

Some of the earliest written sources on abnormality are ancient Chinese texts on medicine (Tseng, 1973). *Nei Ching* (*Classic of Internal Medicine*) was probably written around 2674 B.C. by Huang Ti, the third legendary emperor of China.

Ancient Chinese medicine was based on the concept of yin and yang. The human body was said to contain a positive force (yang) and a negative force (yin), which confronted and complemented each other. If the two forces were in balance, the individual was healthy. If not, illness, including insanity, could result. For example, *excited insanity* was considered the result of an excessive positive force:

> The person suffering from excited insanity initially feels sad, eating and sleeping

Some scholars believe that holes found in ancient skulls are from trephination, a crude form of brain surgery performed on people acting abnormally.

less; he then becomes grandiose, feeling that he is very smart and noble, talking and scolding day and night, singing, behaving strangely, seeing strange things, hearing strange voices, believing that he can see the devil or gods, etc. As treatment for such an excited condition withholding food was suggested, since food was considered to be the source of positive force and the patient was thought to be in need of a decrease in such force. (Tseng, 1973, p. 570)

Another theory in ancient Chinese medical philosophy was that human emotions were controlled by internal organs. When the "vital air" was flowing on one of these organs, an individual experienced a particular emotion. For example, when air flowed on the heart, a person felt joy; when on the lungs, sorrow; when on the liver, anger; when on the spleen, worry; and when on the kidney, fear. This theory encouraged people to live in an orderly and harmonious way, so as to maintain the proper movement of vital air.

Although the ancient Chinese perspective on psychological symptoms was largely a biological theory in ancient times, the rise of Taoism and Buddhism during the Chin and T'ang dynasties (A.D. 420 to 618) led to some religious interpretations of abnormal behavior. Evil winds and ghosts were blamed for bewitching people, and for people's erratic emotional displays and uncontrolled behavior. Religious theories of abnormality declined in China after this period.

Some of the earliest medical writings on mental disorders came from ancient Chinese texts. The illustration shows a healer at work.

Ancient Egypt, Greece, and Rome: Biological Theories Dominate

Other ancient writings on abnormal behavior are found in the papyri of Egypt and Mesopotamia (Veith, 1965). The oldest of these is a document known as the Kahun Papyrus, after the ancient Egyptian city in which it was found, and it dates from about 1900 B.C. This document lists a number of disorders, each followed by a physician's judgment of the cause of the disorder and the appropriate treatment.

Several of the disorders apparently left people with unexplainable aches and pains, sadness or distress, and apathy about life. Some examples are "a woman who loves bed; she does not rise and she does not shake it"; "a woman who is pained in her teeth and jaws; she knows not how to open her mouth"; and "a woman aching in all her limbs with pain in the sockets of her eyes" (Veith, 1965, p. 3). These disorders were said to occur only in women and were attributed to a "wandering uterus." Apparently, the Egyptians believed that the uterus could become dislodged and wander throughout a woman's body, interfering with her other organs and causing these symptoms. Later the Greeks, holding to the same theory of the anatomy of women, named this disorder hysteria (from the Greek word *hysteria*, which means "uterus"). These days, the term *hysteria* is used to refer to physiological symptoms that are probably the result of psychological processes. In the Egyptian papyri, the prescribed treatment for this disorder involved the use of strong-smelling substances to drive the uterus back to its proper place.

Another, more complete papyrus, the Papyrus Ebers, recommends a combination of physiological interventions and incantations to the gods to assist in the healing process (Veith, 1965). One astounding feature of the Papyrus Ebers is that it provides a detailed description of the brain and clearly ascribes mental functioning to the brain. The ancient Egyptians' perspective on abnormal behavior was clearly driven by biological theories of these disorders, but they also believed that supernatural powers could intervene in the cure (and perhaps cause) of disorders.

The Old Testament makes several references to madness. In Deuteronomy, which dates from the seventh century B.C., Moses warns his people that if they "will not obey the voice of the Lord your God or be careful to do all his commandments and his statutes . . . the Lord will smite you with madness and blindness and confusion of the mind . . ." (Deuteronomy 28:15, 28). Thus, the Hebrews saw madness as a punishment from God. People stricken with madness were to confess their sins and repent in order to achieve relief. There are several passages in the Old Testament in which people thought to be mad were also attended by physicians, however (e.g., Job 13:4), so the Hebrews believed that physicians could at least comfort people, if not cure them of madness.

Beginning with Homer, the Greeks wrote frequently of people thought to be mad (Veith, 1965). Flute music played an important role in religious rituals, and there are accounts of people hearing and seeing phantom flute players by day and night. Physician Hippocrates (460–377 B.C.) described a case of a common phobia. A man could not walk alongside a cliff, pass over a bridge, or jump over even a shallow ditch without feeling unable to control his limbs and having his vision impaired. Another physician, Aretaeus (A.D. 50–130), described an artisan who appears to have had symptoms of what we now call *agoraphobia* (people with this disorder become housebound because they experience episodes of panic when away from their safe abodes): "If at any time he went away to the market, the bath, or on any other engagement, having laid down his tools, he would first groan, then shrug his shoulders as he went out. But when he had got out of sight of the domestics, or of the work and the place where it was performed, he became completely mad; yet if he returned speedily he recovered his reason again" (cited in Veith, 1965, p. 96).

The traditional interpretation of madness throughout much of Greek and Roman history was

Hippocrates argued that mental disorders are caused by imbalances in the body's essential humors, or elements.

that it was an affliction from the gods. The afflicted retreated to temples honoring the god Aesculapius, where priests held healing ceremonies. Plato (429–347 B.C.) and Socrates (384–322 B.C.) argued that some forms of madness were divine and could be the source of great literary and prophetic gifts.

For the most part, however, Greek physicians rejected supernatural explanations of abnormal behavior. Hippocrates, often regarded as the father of medicine, argued that abnormal behavior was like other diseases of the body. According to Hippocrates, the body was composed of four basic humors: blood, phlegm, yellow bile, and black bile. All diseases, including abnormal behavior, were caused by imbalances in the body's essential humors, typically an excess of one of the humors. Based on careful observation of his many patients, including listening to their dreams, Hippocrates classified abnormal behavior into epilepsy, mania, melancholia, and brain fever. He also recognized hysteria, although he did not view it as a mental disease. Like others, he thought that this was a disorder confined to women and caused by a wandering uterus.

The treatments prescribed by the Greek physicians were intended to restore the balance of the humors. Sometimes these treatments were physiological and intrusive; for example, bleeding a patient was a common practice for disorders thought to result from an excess of blood. Other treatments were rest, relaxation, a change of climate or scenery, a change of diet, and a temperate life. Some of the nonmedical treatments prescribed by these physicians sound remarkably like prescriptions made by

modern psychotherapists. Hippocrates, for example, believed that removing a patient from a difficult family could help restore mental health. Plato took a decidedly psychological view of abnormal behavior. He argued that madness arose when the rational mind was overcome by impulse, passion, or appetite. Sanity could be restored by a restoration of the rational process through a discussion with the individual designed to induce emotional control (Maher & Maher, 1985).

Throughout ancient times, the relatives of people considered mad were encouraged to confine the afflicted people to the home. The state claimed no responsibility for insane people; there were no asylums or institutions, other than the religious temples, to house and care for them. The state could, however, take rights away from people declared mad. Relatives could bring suit against those they considered mad, and the state could award the property of insane people to their relatives. People declared mad could not marry or acquire or dispose of their own property. Poor people who were considered mad were simply left to roam the streets if they were not violent. If they were violent, they were locked away in stocks and chains. The general public greatly feared madness of any form, and people thought to be mad, even if divinely mad, were often shunned or even stoned.

Medieval Views

The Middle Ages (around A.D. 400–1400) are often described as a time of backward thinking, dominated by an obsession with witchcraft and supernatural forces, yet even within Europe supernatural theories of abnormal behavior did not dominate until late in the Middle Ages, between the eleventh and fifteenth centuries. Prior to the eleventh century, witches and witchcraft were accepted as real but considered merely nuisances that were overrated by superstitious people. Severe emotional shock and physical illness and injury were most often seen as the causes of bizarre behaviors. For example, English court records on persons thought to be mentally ill attributed their illnesses to factors such as a "blow received on the head," explained that symptoms were "induced by fear of his father," or noted that "he has lost his reason owing to a long and incurable infirmity" (Neugebauer, 1979, p. 481). Laypeople probably did believe in demons and curses as causes of abnormal behavior, but there is strong evidence that physicians and government officials attributed abnormal behavior to physical causes or traumas.

Witchcraft

Beginning in the eleventh century, the power of the Church was threatened by the breakdown of feudalism and rebellions caused by the economic and political inequalities of the times. The Church chose to interpret these threats in terms of heresy and satanism. The Inquisition was established originally to rid the earth of religious heretics, but eventually those practicing witchcraft or satanism were also the focus of hunts. The witch hunts continued long after the Reformation and were perhaps at their height during the fifteenth to seventeenth centuries, the period known as the Renaissance (Kroll, 1973).

Some psychiatric historians have argued that persons accused of witchcraft must have been mentally ill (Veith, 1965; Zilboorg & Henry, 1941). Accused witches sometimes confessed to speaking with the devil, flying on the backs of animals, and engaging in other unusual behaviors. Such people may have been experiencing delusions (false beliefs) or hallucinations (unreal perceptual experiences), which are signs of some psychological disorders.

Accused witches were also said to have a devil's mark on their bodies, which was often invisible but was insensitive to even the most severe pain. Professional "witch prickers" poked accused witches all over their bodies to find the devil's mark, and areas of insensitivity were found in some of the accused. Psychiatric historians have interpreted this insensitivity as a sign of hysteria or self-hypnosis.

The accused witches' supposed insensitivity to pain indeed could have been real but may have been due to poor nutrition and ill health, common in medieval times, as opposed to any influence of the devil. Professional witch prickers were also known to use techniques to make it falsely appear that a person was insensitive to pain. For example, some witch prickers used collapsible needles attached to hollow shafts, making it appear that the needle pierced deeply into the accused's flesh without inducing pain. However, many of the confessions of accused witches may have been extracted through brutal torture or under the promise of a stay of execution in exchange for a confession (Spanos, 1978).

Accusations of witchcraft were also used as a means of social punishment or control. For example, in 1581, Johann Klenke was accused of witchcraft by the mayor of his town. This accusation came after Klenke had lent the mayor money and then insisted on having it paid back (Rosen, 1968). In England, during the sixteenth and seventeenth centuries, persons accused of being witches were

Some people burned at the stake as witches may have been suffering from mental disorders that caused them to act abnormally.

typically older women, unmarried and poor, who often begged for food and money and were considered by their neighbors to be foul-mouthed and disgusting. These women sometimes cultivated the myth that they were witches to frighten their neighbors into giving them money. This ploy could backfire, however, if their neighbors attributed some misfortune to a spell cast by the self-acclaimed witch. The woman would be arrested and the neighbor could be rid of her.

Some people truly believed themselves to be witches. These people may have been suffering from abnormal behavior. Indeed, even during the witch hunts, some physicians risked condemnation by the Church and even death by arguing that accused witches were suffering from mental illnesses.

In 1563, Johann Weyer published *The Deception of Dreams*, in which he argued that the people accused of being witches were suffering from melancholy (depression) and senility. The Church banned Weyer's writings, however, and he was scorned by many of his peers. Twenty years later, Reginald Scot, in his *Discovery of Witchcraft* (1584), supported Weyer's beliefs: "These women are but diseased wretches suffering from melancholy, and their words, actions, reasoning, and gestures show that sickness has affected their brains and impaired their powers of judgment" (Castiglioni, 1946, p. 253). Again, the Church, and this time the state, refuted the arguments and banned Scot's writings.

As is often the case, change came from within. In the sixteenth century, Teresa of Avila, a Spanish nun who was later canonized, explained that the mass hysteria that had broken out among a group of nuns was not the work of the devil but the effect of infirmities or sickness. She argued that these nuns were *comas enfermas*, or "as if sick." She sought out natural causes for the nuns' strange behaviors and concluded that they were due to melancholy, a weak imagination, or drowsiness and sleepiness (Sarbin & Juhasz, 1967).

It is also possible that some people who truly believed they were witches were not suffering from abnormal behavior. The culture in which they lived so completely accepted the existence of witches and witchcraft that these people may simply have used these cultural beliefs to explain their own feelings and behaviors, even when these feelings and behaviors were not components of a mental disorder. In addition, most writings of medieval and Renaissance times, as well as writings from the witch hunt period in Salem, Massachusetts, clearly distinguish between people who were mad and people who were witches. This distinction between madness and witchcraft continues to this day in cultures that believe in witchcraft.

Psychic Epidemics

Psychic epidemics are defined today as a phenomenon in which large numbers of people begin to engage in unusual behaviors that appear to have a psychological origin. During the Middle Ages, reports of dance frenzies or manias were frequent. A monk, Peter of Herental, described a rash of dance frenzies that broke out over a four-month period in 1374 in Germany:

> Both men and women were abused by the devil to such a degree that they danced in their homes, in the churches and in the streets, holding each other's hands and leaping in the air. While they danced they called out the names of demons, such as Friskes and others, but they were unaware of this nor did they pay attention to modesty even though people watched them. At the end of the dance, they felt such pains in the chest, that if their friends did not tie linen clothes tightly around their waists, they cried out like madmen that they were dying. (cited in Rosen, 1968, pp. 196–197)

Other instances of dance frenzy were reported in 1428 during the feast of Saint Vitus, at Schaffhausen, at which a monk danced himself to death. Again, in 1518, a large epidemic of uncontrolled dance frenzy occurred at the chapel of Saint Vitus at Hohlenstein, near Zabern. According to one account, more than 400 people danced during the four-week period the frenzy lasted. Some writers of the time began to call the frenzied dancing *Saint Vitus' dance*.

A similar phenomenon was *tarantism*, which was seen in Italy as early as the fourteenth century but became prominent in the seventeenth century. People suddenly developed an acute pain, which they attributed to the bite of a tarantula. They jumped around and danced wildly in the streets, tearing at their clothes and beating each other with whips. Some people dug holes in the earth and rolled on the ground; others howled and made obscene gestures. At the time, many people interpreted dance frenzies and tarantism as the results of possession by the devil. The behaviors may have been the remnants of ancient rituals performed by people worshipping the Greek god Dionysus.

Although dance frenzies and similar psychic epidemics were observed frequently in the Middle Ages, this phenomenon is not confined to that period in history. Dance frenzies and similar behavior patterns were observed later, in the eighteenth century, in some religious sects. These sects included the Shakers; the mystical Russian sects, such as the Chlysti; certain Jewish sects; congregations of the early Methodist movement; and the Quakers. During religious services, members of these sects might become so emotionally charged that they would jerk around violently, running, singing, screaming, and dancing. This type of religious service tended to be more popular among people suffering great economic and social deprivation and alienation. The enthusiastic expression of religious fervor can act as a welcome release from the tensions and stresses of simply trying to survive in a hostile world.

Even today, we see episodes of psychic epidemics. On February 8, 1991, a number of students and teachers in a high school in Rhode Island thought they smelled noxious fumes coming from the ventilation system. The first person to detect these fumes, a 14-year-old girl, fell to the floor, crying and saying that her stomach hurt and her eyes stung. Other students and the teacher in that room then began to experience symptoms. They were moved into the hallway with a great deal of commotion. Soon, students and teachers from adjacent rooms, who could clearly see into the hallway, began to experience symptoms. Eventually, 21 people (17 students and 4 teachers) were admitted to the local hospital emergency room. All were hyperventilating, and most complained of dizziness, headache, and nausea. Although some of them initially showed symptoms of mild carbon monoxide intoxication in blood tests, no evidence of toxic gas in the school could be found. The physicians treating the children and teachers concluded that the outbreak was a case of mass hysteria prompted by the fear of chemical warfare during the Persian Gulf War (Rockney & Lemke, 1992).

Psychic epidemics are no longer viewed as the result of spirit possession or the bite of a tarantula. Rather, psychologists attempt to understand them using research from social psychology about the influence of others on individuals' self-perceptions. The social context can affect even our perceptions of our own bodies, as we will see when we discuss people's differing reactions to psychoactive substances, such as marijuana (see Chapter 17) and people's interpretations of physiological arousal in their bodies (see Chapters 6 and 7).

The Spread of Asylums During the Renaissance

As early as the twelfth century, many towns in Europe took some responsibility for housing and caring for people considered mentally ill (Kroll, 1973). Remarkable among these towns was Gheel, in Belgium, where townspeople regularly took into their homes the mentally ill who visited the shrine of Saint Dymphna for cures.

General hospitals began to include special rooms or facilities for people with abnormal behavior in about the eleventh or twelfth century. In 1326, a *Dollhaus* (madhouse) was constructed as part of the Georgehospital at Elbing. In 1375, a *Tollkiste* (mad cell) was mentioned in the municipal records of Hamburg (Kroll, 1973). Unlike the humane treatment people with abnormal behavior received in such places as Gheel, the treatment in these early hospitals was far from humane. The mentally ill were little more than inmates, housed against their will, often in extremely harsh conditions.

One of the most famous of these hospitals was the Hospital of Saint Mary of Bethlehem, in London, which officially became a mental hospital in 1547. This hospital, nicknamed *Bedlam*, was famous for its deplorable conditions, which were highlights in Shakespeare's *King Lear:*

> Bedlam beggers, who, with roaring voices
> . . . sometimes with lunatic bans, sometimes with prayers enforce their charity.
> (*King Lear*, Act II, Scene iii)

Shakespeare is referring to the practice of forcing patients at this hospital to beg in the streets for money. At Bedlam and other mental hospitals established in Europe in the sixteenth, seventeenth, and eighteenth centuries, patients were exhibited to the public for a fee. They lived in filth and confinement, often chained to walls or locked in small boxes. The following description of the treatment of patients in La Bicêtre Hospital, an asylum for male patients in Paris, provides an example of typical care:

> The patients were ordinarily shackled to the walls of their dark, unlighted cells by iron collars which held them flat against the wall and permitted little movement. Ofttimes there were also iron hoops around the waists of the patients and both their hands and feet were chained. Although these chains usually permitted enough movement that the patients could feed themselves out of bowls, they often kept them from being able to lie down at night. Since little was known about dietetics, and the patients were presumed to be animals anyway, little attention was paid to whether they were adequately fed or whether the food was good or bad. The cells were furnished only with straw and were never swept or cleaned; the patient remained in the midst of all the accumulated

Bedlam—the Hospital of St. Mary of Bethlehem—was famous for the chaotic and deplorable conditions in which people with mental disorders were kept.

ordure. No one visited the cells except at feeding time, no provision was made for warmth, and even the most elementary gestures of humanity were lacking. (adapted from Selling, 1940, pp. 54–55)

The laws regarding the confinement of the mentally ill in Europe and the United States were concerned with the protection of the public and the ill person's relatives (Busfield, 1986; Scull, 1993). For example, Dalton's 1618 edition of the *Common Law* states that "it is lawful for the parents, kinsmen or other friends of a man that is mad, or frantic . . . to take him and put him into a house, to bind or chain him, and to beat him with rods, and to do any other forcible act to reclaim him, or to keep him so he shall do no hurt" (Allderidge, 1979).

The first *Act for Regulating Madhouses* in England was not passed until 1774, with the intentions of cleaning up the deplorable conditions in hospitals and madhouses and protecting people from being unjustly jailed for insanity. This act provided for the licensing and inspection of madhouses and required that a physician, a surgeon, or an apothecary sign a certificate before a patient could be admitted. These provisions applied only to paying patients in private madhouses, however, and not to the poor people confined to workhouses for lunatics.

The conditions of asylums in America were not much better. In 1756, Benjamin Franklin helped establish the Pennsylvania Hospital in Philadelphia, which included some cells or wards for mental patients. In 1773, the Public Hospital in Williamsburg, Virginia, became the first hospital exclusively for the mentally ill. The treatment of patients, although designed to restore health and balance to the mind, included powerful electrical shocks, plunging of the person into ice water or hot water, starvation, and the heavy use of restraints (Bennett, 1947).

It is worth noting that these asylums typically were established and run by people who thought that abnormal behaviors were medical illnesses. For example, Benjamin Rush (1745–1813), one of the founders of American psychiatry, believed that abnormal behavior was caused by excessive blood in the brain and prescribed bleeding the patient— drawing huge amounts of blood from the body. Thus, although the demonology and witchcraft theories of the Middle Ages have often been decried as leading to brutal treatment of people with mental illnesses, the medical theories of those times and of the next couple of centuries did not always lead to much more gentle treatment. These treatments were based on beliefs and understandings about anatomy and physiology that we now know to be incorrect.

Moral Treatment in the Eighteenth Century

Fortunately, the eighteenth and nineteenth centuries saw the growth of a movement toward a more humane treatment of the mentally ill. This new form of treatment was based on the psychological view that people became mad because they were separated from nature and succumbed to the stresses imposed by the rapid social changes of the period (Rosen, 1968). This was a heavily psychological theory of abnormal behavior, which suggested that the appropriate treatment for madness was rest and relaxation in a serene and physically appealing place.

In 1796, Quaker William Tuke (1732–1819) opened an asylum in England called The Retreat, in direct response to the brutal treatment he saw being delivered to people with abnormal behavior at other facilities. Tuke's intent was to provide a "mild system of treatment," which he referred to as **moral treatment** (Busfield, 1986). This treatment was designed to restore patients' self-restraint by treating them with respect and dignity and encouraging them to exercise self-control.

One of the most militant crusaders for moral treatment of the insane was Dorothea Dix (1802–1877). A retired schoolteacher living in Boston in 1841, Dix visited a jail on a cold Sunday morning to teach a Sunday School class to women inmates. There she discovered the negligence and brutality that characterized the treatment of poor people with abnormal behavior, many of whom were simply warehoused in jails:

> Following the lesson, Miss Dix focused her attention on conditions in the jail. Prostitutes, drunks, criminals, retarded individuals, and the mentally ill were housed together in unheated, unfurnished, and foul-smelling quarters. Inmates without adequate clothing were huddled and shivering in the chill March New England climate. The conditions offended all the senses. When Dorothea Dix asked why heat was not provided, she was informed that the insane do not feel heat and cold. (Viney & Zorich, 1982, p. 212)

That encounter began Dix's tireless quest to improve the treatment of people with abnormal behavior. Dix was armed with dogged determinism and considerable political savvy, and she went from state to state, speaking to legislators and laypeople about the conditions in mental hospitals. Dix's lobbying efforts led to the passage of laws and appropriations to fund the clean-up of mental hospitals and the training of mental-health professionals dedicated to the moral treatment of patients. Be-

Dorothea Dix crusaded for the moral treatment of mental patients in the United States.

tween 1841 and 1881, Dix personally helped establish more than 30 mental institutions in the United States, Canada, Newfoundland, and Scotland. Hundreds more public hospitals for the insane were established during this period by others and were run according to humanitarian perspectives.

Another leader of the moral treatment of people with abnormality was Philippe Pinel (1745–1826), a French physician, who was put in charge of La Bicêtre in Paris in 1793. Pinel argued, "To detain maniacs in constant seclusion and to load them with chains; to leave them defenceless, to the brutality of underlings . . . in a word, to rule them with a rod of iron . . . is a system of superintendence, more distinguished for its convenience than for its humanity or success" (Grob, 1994, p. 27). Pinel rejected supernatural theories of abnormality and believed that many forms of abnormality could be cured by restoring the dignity and tranquility of patients.

Pinel ordered that patients be released from their chains and allowed to walk freely around the asylum. They were provided with clean and sunny rooms, comfortable sleeping quarters, and good food. Nurses and professional therapists were trained to work with the patients, to help them restore their sense of tranquility, and to help them engage in planned social activities. Although many other physicians thought Pinel himself was mad for releasing the patients, his approach was remarkably successful. Many people who had been locked away in darkness for decades became able to control their behavior and reengage in life. Some improved so much that they could be released. Pinel later reformed a mental hospital in Paris for female patients, La Salpetrière, and had remarkable success there as well.

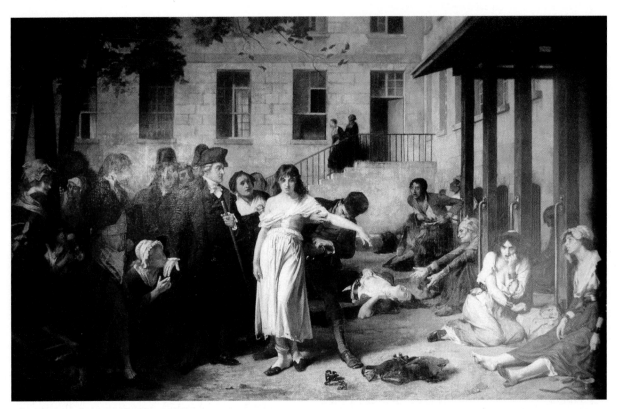

Philippe Pinel, a leader in the moral movement in France, helped free mental patients from the horrible conditions of the hospitals.

Unfortunately, the moral treatment movement grew too fast. As more asylums were built, and more people went into these asylums, the capacity of the asylums to recruit mental-health professionals and to maintain a humane, individual approach to each patient declined (Grob, 1994; Scull, 1993). The physicians, nurses, and other caretakers simply did not have enough time to give each patient the calm and dedicated attention he or she needed. The fantastic successes of the early moral treatment movement gave way to more modest successes, and many outright failures, as patients remained impaired or even got worse. Even some patients who received the best of moral treatment could not benefit from it, because their problems were not due to a loss of dignity or tranquility. Because so many patients were being given the moral treatment, the number of patients who failed to benefit from it increased, and questions about the effectiveness of moral treatment grew louder.

At the same time, the rapid pace of immigration into the United States in the late nineteenth century meant that an increasing percentage of its asylum patients were from different cultures and often were of lower socioeconomic classes. Prejudice against these "foreigners," combined with increasing attention to the failures of moral treatment

to cure many patients, led to declines in public support for funding these institutions. This reduced funding led to even greater declines in the quality of care given to patients. At the turn of the twentieth century, many public hospitals were no better than warehouses, where patients were kept in restraints for long periods of time simply to control their behavior (Grob, 1994; McGovern, 1985; Scull, 1993).

Effective biological treatments were not developed for most major psychological disorders until well into the twentieth century. Until these treatments were developed, mental patients who could not afford private care were basically warehoused in large state institutions and not given the psychological and social rehabilitation prescribed by the moral management theories. Many of these institutions were overcrowded and isolated far from cities or towns. The physical isolation of the mental hospitals contributed to the slow progress in the application of medical advances to the treatment of abnormal behavior (Deutsch, 1937). Clifford Beers, highlighted at the beginning and ending of this chapter, was one extraordinary man who suffered the conditions of mental hospitals at the turn of the twentieth century, survived them, and worked to change them.

SUMMING UP

- Three types of theories have influenced the definition and treatment of abnormality over the ages: the biological theories, the supernatural theories, and the psychological theories.

- Stone Age people probably viewed abnormal behavior as a result of supernatural forces. They may have drilled holes in the skulls of sufferers—a procedure known as trephination—to release the evil forces causing the abnormal behavior.

- Some of the earliest written references to abnormal behavior can be found in Chinese medical texts around 2674 B.C. and then in the papyri of Egypt and Mesopotamia, in the Old Testament, and in the writings of ancient Greek and Roman philosophers and physicians. Abnormal behaviors were often described as medical disorders in these ancient writings, although there is also evidence that they were viewed as due to supernatural forces.

- The witch hunts began in the late Middle Ages. Some accused witches may have suffered from abnormal behavior.

- Psychic epidemics have occurred throughout history. They were formerly explained as due to spirit possession but are now seen as a result of the effects of social conditions on people's self-perceptions.

- In the eighteenth and nineteenth centuries, advocates of more gentle treatment of people with abnormal behavior began to establish asylums for these people.

THE EMERGENCE OF MODERN PERSPECTIVES

Although the quality of the treatment of people with abnormal behavior had declined somewhat at the turn of the twentieth century, tremendous advances in the scientific study of disorders took place in the early twentieth century. These advances laid the groundwork for the biological, psychological, and social theories of abnormality that now dominate psychology and psychiatry.

The Beginnings of Modern Biological Perspectives

Basic knowledge of the anatomy, physiology, neurology, and chemistry of the body increased rapidly in the late nineteenth century. With the advancement of this basic knowledge came increasing focus on biological causes of abnormality. In 1845, Ger-

Emil Kraepelin (1856–1926) developed a classification system for mental disorders that remains very influential today.

man psychiatrist Wilhelm Griesinger (1817–1868) published *The Pathology and Therapy of Psychic Disorders*, the first systematic argument that all psychological disorders can be explained in terms of brain pathology. In 1883, one of Griesinger's followers, Emil Kraepelin (1856–1926), also published a textbook emphasizing the importance of brain pathology in psychological disorders. More important, Kraepelin developed a scheme of classifying symptoms into discrete disorders that has stood the test of time and is the basis for our modern classification systems, as we will discuss in Chapter 4. Having a good classification system gives investigators a common set of labels for disorders, as well as a set of criteria for distinguishing between disorders. This contributes immensely to the advancement of the scientific study of the disorders.

One of the most important discoveries underpinning modern biological theories of abnormality was the discovery of the cause of **general paresis,** a disease that leads to paralysis, insanity, and eventually death. In the mid-1800s, reports that patients with paresis also had a history of syphilis led to the suspicion that syphilis might be a cause of paresis. In 1897, Viennese psychiatrist Richard Krafft-Ebing conducted a daring experiment that would not pass scientific ethics boards today. He injected paretic patients with matter from syphilis sores. None of the patients developed syphilis, and Krafft-Ebing concluded that they must already have been infected with syphilis. The discovery that syphilis is the cause of one form of insanity lent great weight to the idea that biological factors can cause abnormal behaviors.

As we will discuss in more detail in Chapter 2, modern biological theories of the psychological disorders have focused on the role of genetics, structural abnormalities in the brain, and biochemical imbalances. The advances in our understanding of the biological aspects of psychological disorders have contributed to the development of a large number of medications that are useful in the treatment of these disorders, as we will discuss in Chapter 5.

The Psychoanalytic Perspective

The development of psychoanalytic theory begins with the odd story of Franz Anton Mesmer (1734–1815), an Austrian physician who believed that people had a magnetic fluid in the body that must be distributed in a particular pattern in order to maintain health. The distribution of magnetic fluid in one person could be influenced by the magnetic forces of other people, as well as by the alignments of the planets. In 1778, Mesmer opened a clinic in Paris to treat all sorts of diseases by "animal magnetism."

The psychological disorders that were the focus of much of Mesmer's treatment were the hysterical disorders, in which people lose functioning or feeling in some part of the body for no apparent physiological reason. The patients sat in darkness around a tub containing various chemicals, the affected areas of their bodies prodded by iron rods emerging from the tub. With music playing, Mesmer emerged in an elaborate robe, touching each patient as he passed by, supposedly realigning people's magnetic fluids through his own powerful magnetic force. This process, Mesmer said, cured illness, including psychological disorders.

Mesmer was eventually labeled a charlatan by a scientific review committee, which included Benjamin Franklin, yet his methods, known as **mesmerism,** continued to fuel debate long after he had faded into obscurity. The "cures" Mesmer caused in his psychiatric patients were attributed to the trancelike state that Mesmer seemed to induce in his patients. Later, this state was relabeled *hypnosis*. Under hypnosis, Mesmer's patients appeared very suggestible, and the suggestion that their ailments would disappear seemed enough to make them actually disappear.

The connection between hypnosis and hysteria fascinated several leading scientists of the time, although not all scientists accepted this connection. In particular, Jean Charcot (1825–1893), head of La Salpetrière Hospital in Paris and the leading neurologist of his time, argued that hysteria was caused by degeneration in the brain and had nothing to do with hypnosis. The work of two physicians practicing in the French town of Nancy, Hippolyte-Marie Bernheim (1840–1919) and Ambroise-Auguste Liebault (1823–1904), eventually won Charcot over, however. Bernheim and Liebault argued that hysteria was caused by self-hypnosis. They showed that they could induce the symptoms of hysteria, such as paralysis in an arm or the loss of feeling in a leg, by suggesting these symptoms to patients who were hypnotized. Fortunately, they could also remove these symptoms under hypnosis. Charcot was so impressed by the evidence that hysteria has psychological roots that he became a leading researcher of the psychological causes of abnormal behavior. The experiments of Bernheim and Liebault, and the leadership of Charcot, did a great deal to advance psychological perspectives on abnormality.

One of Charcot's students was Sigmund Freud (1856–1939), a Viennese neurologist. He went to study with Charcot in 1885 and, in this work, became convinced that much of the mental life of an individual remains hidden from consciousness. This view was further supported by Freud's interactions with Pierre Janet (1858–1947) in Paris, who was investigating multiple personality disorder, in which people appear to have multiple, distinct personalities, each of which operates independently of the others, often not knowing the others exist (Matarazzo, 1985).

When he returned to Vienna, Freud worked with another physician who was interested in

Anton Mesmer's (1734–1815) work on animal magnetism set the stage for the study of hypnosis.

hypnosis and the unconscious processes behind psychological problems, Josef Breuer (1842–1925). Breuer had discovered that encouraging patients to talk about their problems while under hypnosis led to a great upswelling and release of emotion, which was eventually called catharsis. The patient's discussion of his or her problems under hypnosis was less censored than conscious discussion, allowing the therapist to elicit important psychological material more easily.

Breuer and Freud collaborated on a paper published in 1893 as *On the Psychical Mechanisms of Hysterical Phemonena*, which laid out their discoveries about hypnosis, the unconscious, and the therapeutic value of catharsis. This paper proved to be a foundation stone in the development of **psychoanalysis,** the study of the unconscious. Freud introduced his ideas to America in a series of lectures in 1909 at Clark University in Worcester, Massachusetts, at the invitation of G. Stanley Hall, one of the founders of American psychology.

Freud went on to write dozens of papers and books describing his theory of psychoanalysis, and he became the best-known figure in psychiatry and psychology. The impact of Freud's theories on the development of psychology over the next century cannot be overestimated. Freudian ideas not only influenced the professional literature on psychopathology but also are used heavily in literary theory, anthropology, and other humanities. They pervade popular notions of psychological processes to this day.

The Roots of Behaviorism

In what seems now like a parallel universe, while psychoanalytic theory was being born, the roots of behaviorism were being planted in Europe and then the United States. Wilhelm Wundt (1832–1920) established the first experimental psychology laboratory in 1879 in Leipzig, Germany. His work focused on memory and sensation, but he and others developed many of the basic experimental techniques that are the mainstay of behavioral experimentation. In 1896, one of Wundt's students, Lightner Witmer (1867–1956), established the first psychological clinic at the University of Pennsylvania to study the causes and treatment of mental deficiency in children. Witmer thus brought the experimental techniques of the new behaviorism to bear on an important clinical issue—the functioning of children.

Ivan Pavlov (1849–1936), a Russian physiologist, was also developing methods and theories to understand behavior in terms of stimuli and responses, rather than in terms of the internal workings of the unconscious mind. He discovered that dogs could be conditioned to salivate to stimuli other than food if the food was paired with these other stimuli—a process later called *classical conditioning.* Pavlov's discoveries inspired American John Watson (1878–1958) to study important human behaviors, such as phobias, in terms of classical conditioning (see Chapter 7). Watson rejected psychoanalytic and biological theories of abnormal behaviors, such as phobias, and explained them entirely on the basis of the individual's history of conditioning. Watson went so far as to boast that he could train any healthy child to become any kind of adult one wished:

> Give me a dozen healthy infants, well-formed, and my own specified world to bring them up in, and I'll guarantee to take any one at random and train him to be any type of specialist I might select—doctor, lawyer, artist, merchant-chief, and yes, even beggar-man and thief, regardless of his talents, penchants, tendencies, abilities, vocations, and the race of his ancestors. (Watson, 1930, p. 104)

In the meantime, two other psychologists, E. L. Thorndike (1874–1949) and B. F. Skinner (1904–1990), were studying how the consequences of behaviors shape their likelihood of recurrence. They argued that behaviors that are followed by positive consequences are more likely to be repeated than behaviors followed by negative consequences. This process came to be known as *operant,* or *instrumental, conditioning.* This idea may seem simple to us now (which is one sign of how much it has influenced thinking over the past century), but at the time it was radical to argue that even complex behaviors, such as violence against others, can be explained by the reinforcement or punishment these behaviors have had in the past.

Behaviorism—the study of the impact of reinforcements and punishments on behavior—has had as profound an impact on psychology and on our common knowledge of psychology as has psychoanalytic theory. Behavioral theories have led to many of the effective psychological treatments for disorders that we will discuss in this book.

The Cognitive Revolution

In the 1950s, some experimental psychologists began to argue that behaviorism is limited in its explanatory power by its refusal to look at some of the internal thought processes that mediate the relationship between stimulus and response. It wasn't until the 1970s that psychology shifted its focus substantially to the study of **cognitions**—thought processes that influence behavior and emotion. An important player in this cognitive revolution was Albert Bandura, a clinical psychologist trained in behaviorism who had contributed a great deal to the application of behaviorism to psychopathology (see Chapters 2 and 7). Bandura argued that people's beliefs about their ability to execute the behaviors necessary to control important events—which he called **self-efficacy beliefs**—are crucial in determining their well-being. Again, this idea seems obvious to us now, but that is only because it took hold of both professional psychology and lay notions of psychology.

Another key figure in cognitive perspectives was Albert Ellis, who argued that people prone to psychological disorders are plagued by irrational negative assumptions about themselves and the world. Ellis developed a therapy for emotional problems based on his theory, called rational-emotive therapy. This therapy was controversial, because it required therapists to challenge, sometimes quite harshly, their patients' irrational belief systems. It became very popular, however, and moved psychology into the study of the thought processes behind serious emotional problems. Another therapy focused on the irrational thoughts of people with psychological problems was developed by Aaron Beck. Beck's cognitive therapy has become one of the widest used therapies for many disorders (see Chapters 2 and 5). Since the 1970s, theorists have continued to emphasize cognitive factors in psychopathology, although behavioral theories have remained strong, and interpersonal theories, which we will examine in the next chapter, have become more prominent.

SUMMING UP

- Modern biological theories and therapies began with the development of Kraepelin's classification scheme for psychological disorders and the discovery that syphilis causes general paresis, a disease with symptoms including loss of touch with reality.

- The roots of psychoanalytic theory can be found in the work of Mesmer and the suggestion that psychological symptoms can be relieved through hypnosis. Jean Charcot, Sigmund Freud, and Josef Breuer are among the founders of modern psychoanalytic theory, which focuses on the role of the unconscious in psychological symptoms.

- Behavioral approaches to psychopathology began with the development of basic experimental techniques to study the effects of reinforcement and punishment in producing normal, and abnormal, behavior.

- Cognitive approaches to abnormality emerged in the mid-twentieth century, when theorists began arguing that the way people think about events in their environment determines their emotional and behavioral responses to those events.

MODERN MENTAL-HEALTH CARE

Halfway through the twentieth century, major breakthroughs were made in drug treatments for some of the major forms of abnormality. In particular, the discovery of a class of drugs that can reduce the symptoms of schizophrenia, known as the phenothiazines (see Chapter 5), made it possible for many people who had been institutionalized for years to be released from asylums and hospitals. Since then, there has been an explosion of new drug therapies for psychopathology. In addition, as we will discuss in Chapter 5, several types of psychotherapy have been developed, and continue to be developed, that have proven effective in treating a wide range of psychological problems. Still, there are significant problems in the delivery of mental-health care, some of which began with the deinstitutionalization movement of the mid-twentieth century.

Deinstitutionalization

By 1960, a large and vocal movement, known as the **patients' rights movement,** had emerged. Patients' rights advocates argued that mental patients can recover more fully or live more satisfying lives if they are integrated into the community, with the support of community-based treatment facilities—a process known as **deinstitutionalization.** Many of these patients would continue to need around-the-clock care, but it could be given in treatment centers based in neighborhoods, rather than in large, impersonal institutions. The **community mental-health movement** was officially launched in 1963 by President John Kennedy as a "bold new approach" to mental-health care. This movement attempted to provide coordinated mental-health services to people in community-based centers.

The deinstitutionalization movement had massive effects on the lives of people with serious psychological problems. Between 1955 and 1998, the number of patients in state psychiatric hospitals went from a high of 559,000 to about 57,000—almost a 90 percent reduction (Lamb & Weinberger, 2001). Many former mental patients who had lived for years in cold, sterile facilities, receiving little useful care, experienced dramatic increases in the quality of life on their release. Moreover, they suddenly had the freedom to live where they wanted to, as they saw fit.

Unfortunately, the resources to care for all the mental patients released from institutions were never adequate. There were not enough halfway houses built or community mental-health centers funded to serve the thousands of men and women who were formerly institutionalized or who would have been if the movement had not happened. In the meantime, the state psychiatric hospitals to which they would have retreated were closed down by the hundreds. These men and women began living in nursing homes and other types of group homes, where they received little mental-health treatment, or with their families, many of whom were ill-equipped to handle serious mental illness (Lamb, 2001). Some of these people began living on the streets. Certainly not all homeless people are mentally ill, but some researchers estimate that one-third to one-half of all long-term homeless adults in the United States have a major mental disorder, and up to four-fifths have a mental disorder, a severe substance use disorder (such as alcoholism), or both (Baum & Burnes, 1993). In emergencies, these people end up in general or private hospitals that are not equipped to treat them appropriately (Kiesler & Sibulkin, 1983). Many end up in jail (Torrey, 1997). It is estimated that 10 to 15 percent of the prison population has a serious mental disorder (Lamb & Weinberger, 2001).

Thus, deinstitutionalization began with laudatory goals, but many of these goals were never fully reached, leaving many people who formerly would have been institutionalized in mental hospitals no better off. In recent years, the financial strains on local, state, and federal governments have led to the closing of many more community mental-health centers.

Managed Care

The entire system of private insurance for health care underwent a revolution in the second half of the twentieth century. Managed care emerged as the dominant means for organizing health care. The exact nature of managed care systems varies greatly from one company to another, but **managed care** is generally a loose collection of methods for organizing health care that ranges from simple monitoring all the way to total control over what care can be provided and paid for. The goals are to coordinate services for an existing medical problem and to prevent future medical problems before they arise. Often, health care providers are given a set amount of money per member (patient) per month and then must determine how best to serve their patients with that money.

Under managed care, some of the problems created by deinstitutionalization can be solved. For example, instead of leaving it up to people with a serious psychological problem, or their families, to find appropriate care, the primary provider might find this care and ensure that patients have access to it. Say an individual patient reported to his physician that he was hearing voices when there was no one around. The physician might refer the patient to a psychiatrist for an evaluation, to determine if the patient might be suffering from schizophrenia. In some cases, the primary care physician might coordinate care offered by other providers, such as drug treatments, psychotherapy, and rehabilitation services. And the primary provider might ensure continuity of care, so that patients did not "fall through the cracks." Thus, theoretically, managed care could have tremendous benefits for people with long-term, serious mental-health problems. For people with less severe psychological problems, the availability of mental-health care through managed care systems and other private insurance systems has led to a tremendous increase in the number of people seeking psychotherapy and other types of mental-health care.

Unfortunately, however, mental-health care is often not covered, or covered fully, by health insurance. For people who need hospitalization, insurance often pays for a very limited stay. For those who need outpatient care, insurance may pay for only a few sessions of psychotherapy and often pays only for drugs, not psychotherapy. Then, of course, many people do not have any kind of health insurance, because they are not employed or their employer does not offer it.

The Medicaid Program, which covers one-fifth of all mental-health care spending in the United States, has been a target for reductions in recent years. Many states have reduced or restricted eligibility and benefits for mental-health care, have increased copayments, have controlled drug costs, and have reduced or frozen payments to providers (Mechanic & Bilder, 2004). In the meantime, the number of people seeking mental-health care has risen. For example, the Veterans Administration provides health care for poor and disabled veterans, and the number of people seeking mental-health care has increased by 4 percent per year since 1990 (Rosenheck, 1999). At the same time, reductions in state and city welfare programs and other community services to the poor have made daily life more difficult for poor people in general, and in particular for people with serious mental disorders, who often have exhausted their financial resources. At the turn of the millennium, it was estimated that about 50 percent of the people in the United States with serious psychological problems were not receiving stable mental-health treatment (Kessler et al., 2001). This situation is particularly distressing, given that effective biological and psychosocial treatments now exist for the majority of mental-health problems, as we will discuss throughout this book.

PROFESSIONS WITHIN ABNORMAL PSYCHOLOGY

In our times, a number of professions are concerned with abnormal or maladaptive behavior. Psychiatry is a branch of medicine that focuses on psychological disorders. *Psychiatrists* have an M.D. degree and have specialized training in the treatment of psychological problems. Psychiatrists can prescribe medications for the treatment of these problems, and some also have been trained to conduct psychotherapies that involve talking with people about their problems.

Clinical psychologists typically have a Ph.D. in psychology, with a specialization in psychological problems. Clinical psychologists can conduct psychotherapy, but in most states they do not currently prescribe medications (although they do have limited prescription privileges in some programs and many psychologists are lobbying for prescription privileges in many states).

Marriage and family therapists specialize in helping families, couples, and children overcome problems that are interfering with their well-being. *Clinical social workers* have a master's degree in social work and often focus on helping people with psychological problems overcome the social conditions contributing to their problems, such as joblessness or homelessness. *Psychiatric nurses* have a degree in nursing, with a specialization in the treatment of people with severe psychological problems. They often work on inpatient psychiatric wards in hospitals, delivering medical care and certain forms of psychotherapy, such as group therapy to increase patients' contacts with one another. They have privileges to write prescriptions for psychotherapeutic drugs in some states.

Dramatic changes are currently taking place in the field of mental health, due to changes in the funding of mental-health care. There have been some increases in insurance funding for psychiatric medications, but many people in the United States either have no insurance to cover mental-health care or have only limited coverage. The practice of psychiatry has declined in status somewhat over the past two decades, and fewer and fewer students with new M.D.s are pursuing psychiatry

(Appelbaum, 2003). In contrast, there has been a substantial increase in the number of clinical psychologists, clinical social workers, and marriage and family therapists (Mechanic & Bilder, 2004). The increased competition for the mental-health dollar has led to political disagreements between the types of mental-health professionals over who has the right to treat which kinds of disorders.

Each of these professions has its rewards and its limitations. Students who are interested in one or more of these professions often find it helpful to volunteer to be a research assistant in studies of psychological problems or to volunteer to work in a psychiatric clinic or hospital, to learn more about these professions. This type of volunteering can help students determine what type of work within abnormal psychology is most comfortable for them. Some students find tremendous gratification working with people with psychological problems, whereas others find it more gratifying to conduct research that might answer important questions about psychological problems. Many mental-health professionals of all types combine clinical practice and research in their careers.

SUMMING UP

- The goal of the deinstitutionalization movement was to move mental patients from custodial mental-health facilities, where they were isolated and received little treatment, to community-based mental-health centers. Thousands of patients were released from mental institutions. Unfortunately, community-based mental-health centers have never been fully funded or supported, leaving many former mental patients with few resources in the community.

- Managed care systems are meant to provide coordinated, comprehensive medical care to patients. This can be a great asset to people with long-term, serious disorders. Coverage for mental-health problems tends to be limited, however, and many people have no insurance at all.

- A number of professions provide care to people with mental-health problems, including psychiatrists, psychologists, marriage and family therapists, clinical social workers, and psychiatric nurses.

CHAPTER INTEGRATION

Although the biological, psychological, and social theories of abnormality have traditionally been viewed as competing with each other to explain psychological disorders, many clinicians and researchers now believe that theories that integrate biological, psychological, and social perspectives on abnormality will prove most useful (see Figure 1.3). For example, in Chapter 7, we will discuss theories of anxiety disorders that take into account individuals' genetic and biochemical vulnerabilities, the impact of stressful events, and the role of cognitions in explaining why some people suffer debilitating anxiety. Throughout this book, we will first examine the biological, psychological, and social theories of a given disorder, but we will focus on how these factors interact and influence each other to produce and maintain mental-health problems. In other words, we will take an **integrationist approach** to psychological problems. Note that the color-coding scheme in Figue 1.3 reinforces this approach and will be used in other figures throughout the book, with green for biological factors, blue for social factors, and orange for psychological factors.

What about supernatural theories? Most cultures still have *spiritual healers*. Throughout this book, we will consider cross-cultural perspectives on psychological disorders, and we will note the supernatural theories some cultures hold about abnormality and the healing rituals that emerge from these theories. Even in cultures in which most healers do not subscribe to supernatural theories of abnormality, however, laypeople often still believe in the power of supernatural forces to cause or cure their psychological problems. These beliefs influence the type of healer a person with a psychologi-

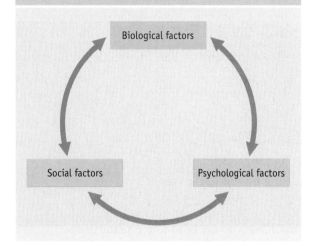

FIGURE 1.3

The Integrationist Approach to Understanding Mental Health. Many mental health theories today strive to integrate biological, psychological, and social factors in understanding mental-health issues, and this integrationist approach will be emphasized in this book.

Biological factors

Social factors

Psychological factors

cal problem might seek out and how he or she might present the psychological problem to a potential therapist. Thus, supernatural theories arise in the practice of treating people with psychological problems, because these clients take them into discussions with their therapists. In turn, therapists must work within a client's framework to help the client understand his or her mental-health problems.

Extraordinary People: Follow-Up

At the beginning of this chapter, we met Clifford Beers, a young man whose paranoia of becoming epileptic evolved into a three-year nightmare of depression, a break from reality, and horrific treatments in mental hospitals in the early 1900s. One of the extraordinary things about Beers is that this experience did not break him—instead, it inspired him to start a movement for the reform of mental-health treatment, which he called the **mental hygiene movement.** After his release from the mental hospital, Beers wrote a personal account of his time there, which was published in 1908 as *A Mind That Found Itself.* This book changed how physicians and the lay public viewed mental patients and hospitals. He argued that all psychological disorders are medical diseases and should be treated biologically. Beers outlined a plan for reforms in the treatment of the mentally ill and for the prevention of mental illness. He advocated public education about mental illness and early treatment for those who were afflicted. One of Beers' supporters was Dr. Adolph Meyer, who was himself revolutionizing the treatment of mental patients by advocating the treatment of the "whole individual," including assisting former mental patients in their reintegration into society. Beers eventually founded the National and International Committees on Mental Hygiene and became a fund-raiser and lobbyist for the rights of mental patients.

In *A Mind That Found Itself,* Beers explained his motivations and drive to use his experiences to change the lives of others who suffered from psychological disorders:

> When I set out upon a career of reform, I was impelled to do so by motives in part like those which seem to have possessed Don Quixote when he set forth, as Cervantes says, with the intention "of righting every kind of wrong, and exposing himself to peril and danger, from which in the issue he would obtain eternal renown and fame." In likening myself to Cervantes' mad hero my purpose is quite other than to push myself within the charmed circle of the chivalrous. What I wish to do is to make plain that a man abnormally elated may be swayed irresistibly by his best instincts, and that while under the spell of an exaltation, idealistic in degree, he may not only be willing, but eager to assume risks and endure hardships which under normal conditions he would assume reluctantly, if at all. In justice to myself, however, I may remark that my plans for reform have never assumed quixotic, and therefore impracticable, proportions. At no time have I

gone a-tilting at windmills. A pen rather than a lance has been my weapon of offense and defense; for with its point I have felt sure that I should one day prick the civic conscience into a compassionate activity, and thus bring into a neglected field earnest men and women who should act as champions for those afflicted thousands least able to fight for themselves.

Beers' biographer, Norman Dain, writes:

> [Beers] significantly contributed toward making public discussion of psychological disorders legitimate, informed, and matter-of-fact. The movement helped to introduce mental health considerations into many aspects of American life, such as the schools and the courts, not for sensational exploitation but to develop systematic means of dealing with children's emotional problems. On a personal plane, Clifford Beers was a living refutation of the view that mental disorder forever incapacitated a person for useful public activity. His life experience educated people to the complexities and surprising possibilities that lie within so many men and women whom society tends to discard. (Dain, 1980, p. 331)

Chapter Summary

- Cultural relativists argue that the norms of a society must be used to determine the normality of a behavior. Others have suggested that unusual behaviors, or behaviors that cause subjective discomfort in a person, should be labeled abnormal. Still others have suggested that only behaviors resulting from mental illness or disease are abnormal. All these criteria have serious limitations, however.

- Currently, the consensus among professionals is that behaviors that cause people to suffer distress, that prevent them from functioning in daily life, and that are unusual are abnormal. These behaviors are often referred to as maladaptive and can be remembered with the

heuristic of the 3Ds: distress, dysfunction, and deviance (review Figure 1.1).

- Historically, theories of abnormality have fallen into one of three categories. Biological theories saw psychological disorders as similar to physical diseases, caused by the breakdown of a system of the body. Supernatural theories saw abnormal behavior as a result of divine intervention, curses, demonic possession, and personal sin. Psychological theories saw abnormal behavior as a result of stress. These three types of theories led to very different types of treatment of people who acted abnormally.

- In prehistoric times, people probably had largely supernatural theories of abnormal behavior, attributing it to demons or ghosts. A treatment for abnormality in the Stone Age may have been to drill holes in the skull to allow demons to depart, a procedure known as trephination.

- Ancient Chinese, Egyptian, and Greek texts suggest that these cultures took a natural, or biological, view of abnormal behavior, although references to supernatural and psychological theories also can be found.

- During the Middle Ages, abnormal behavior may have been interpreted as due to witchcraft.

- History provides many examples of psychic epidemics and mass hysterias. Groups of people have shown similar psychological and behavioral symptoms, which usually have been attributed to common stresses or beliefs.

- Even well into the nineteenth and twentieth centuries, many people who acted abnormally were shut away in prisonlike conditions, tortured, starved, and ignored.

- As part of the mental hygiene movement, the moral management of mental hospitals became more widespread. Patients in these hospitals were treated with kindness and the best biological treatments available. Effective biological treatments for most psychological problems were not available until the mid-twentieth century, however.

- Modern biological perspectives on psychological disorders were advanced by Kraepelin's development of a classification system and the discovery that the syndrome known as general paresis is caused by a syphilis infection.

- The psychoanalytic perspective began with the odd work of Anton Mesmer, but then it grew as Jean Charcot, and eventually Sigmund Freud, became interested in the role of the unconscious in producing abnormality.

- Behaviorist views on abnormal behavior began with the basic research of John Watson and B. F. Skinner, who used principles of classical and operant conditioning to explain both normal and abnormal behavior.

- The cognitive revolution was spurred by theorists such as Albert Ellis, Albert Bandura, and Aaron Beck and focused on the role of thinking processes in abnormality.

- The deinstitutionalization movement attempted to move mental patients from mental-health facilities, where they were isolated and received little treatment, to community-based mental-health centers. Unfortunately, community-based mental-health centers have never been fully funded or supported, leaving many former mental patients with few resources in the community.

- Managed care systems are meant to provide coordinated, comprehensive medical care to patients. This can be a great asset to people with long-term, serious psychological disorders. Insurance coverage for mental-health problems tends to be limited, however, and many people have no insurance at all.

- The professions within abnormal psychology include psychiatrists, psychologists, marriage and family therapists, clinical social workers, and psychiatric nurses.

MindMap CD-ROM

The following resources on the MindMap CD-ROM that came with this text will help you to master the content of this chapter and prepare for tests:

- Video: History of Mental Illness
- Chapter Timeline
- Chapter Quiz

Key Terms

psychopathology 4
context 5
gender roles 6
cultural relativism 6
unusualness 8
discomfort 9

mental illness 9
maladaptive 9
biological theories 11
supernatural theories 11
psychological theories 11
trephination 12

Chapter 2

Heart of the Hunter
by Michelle Puleo

It can be no dishonor to learn from others when they speak good sense.

—Sophocles, *Antigone*
(442–441 B.C.; translated by Elizabeth Wyckoff)

Contemporary Theories of Abnormality <

CHAPTER OVERVIEW

Extraordinary People

■ **Albert Ellis:** *The Phobic Psychologist*

Biological Approaches

Biological theories suggest that psychological symptoms are due to structural abnormalities in the brain, poor functioning of brain neurotransmitter systems, or faulty genes. These three types of biological abnormalities may work independently to create psychological symptoms, or genetic abnormalities are often the cause of other abnormalities.

Taking Psychology Personally

■ **Do "Bad Genes" Doom You to a Disorder?**

Psychological Approaches

Psychodynamic theories of abnormality suggest that psychological symptoms are due to unconscious conflicts. Newer psychodynamic theories focus on concepts of the self that develop from early experiences. Behavioral theories say symptoms result from the reinforcements and punishments people have received for their behaviors. Cognitive theories say that people's ways of interpreting situations determine their emotional and behavioral symptoms. Humanist and existential theories suggest that symptoms arise when people are not allowed to pursue their potential and, instead, try to conform to others' wishes.

Social and Interpersonal Approaches

Interpersonal theorists focus on the role of interpersonal relationships in shaping normal and abnormal behavior. Family systems theories suggest that psychopathology within individual family members is the result of dysfunctional patterns of interaction within families that encourage and maintain the psychopathology within the individual members. Social structural theorists focus on the influence of the environment and culture on individuals' behavior.

Chapter Integration

Many scientists believe that only models that *integrate* biological, psychological, and social factors can provide comprehensive explanations of psychological disorders. Integrated models are often called vulnerability-stress models.

Extraordinary People

Albert Ellis: *The Phobic Psychologist*

Albert Ellis is best known as the psychologist who developed a cognitive theory of emotional problems called rational-emotive theory, as well as a form of therapy based on this theory. According to Ellis' theory, which we will discuss in more detail in this chapter, emotional problems are the result of irrational beliefs. In rational-emotive therapy, therapists confront clients with their irrational beliefs in an attempt to change those beliefs (see Chapter 5).

What most people don't know about Albert Ellis is that he suffered from a fear of public speaking that was so severe that it could have prevented his career. Fortunately, Ellis was a born psychologist. He devised methods for treating himself that hadn't been discovered by psychologists at the time but now are part of many therapists' tool kit:

> At 19, Ellis became active in a political group but was hampered by his terror of public speaking. Confronting his worst demons in the first of many "shame-attacking" exercises he would devise, Ellis repeatedly forced himself to speak up in any political context that would permit it. "Without calling it that, I was doing early desensitization on myself," he says. "Instead of just getting good at this, I found I was very good at it. And now you can't keep me away from a public platform." After mastering his fear of public speaking, Ellis decided to work on the terrors of more private communication. "I was always . . . interested in women," he says. "I would see them and flirt and exchange glances, but I always made excuses not to talk to them and was terrified of being rejected. Since I lived near The New York Botanical Garden in the Bronx, I decided to attack my fear and shame with an exercise in the park. I vowed that whenever I saw a reasonably attractive woman up to the age of 35, rather than sitting a bench away as I normally would, I would sit next to her with the specific goal of opening a conversation within one minute. I sat next to 130 consecutive women who fit my criteria. Thirty of the women got up and walked away, but about 100 spoke to me—about their knitting, the birds, a book, whatever. I made only one date out of all these contacts—and she stood me up. According to learning theory and strict behavior therapy, my lack of rewards should have extinguished my efforts to meet women. But I realized that throughout this exercise no one vomited, no one called a cop, and I didn't die. The process of trying new behaviors and understanding what happened in the real world instead of in my imagination led me to overcome my fear of speaking to women." (Warga, 1988, p. 56)

Thus, rational-emotive therapy was born.

Albert Ellis was able to integrate his personal perspective with contemporary theory and research on anxiety to develop a new theory of his own. A **theory** is a set of ideas that provides a framework for asking questions about a phenomenon, as well as gathering and interpreting information about that phenomenon.

Ellis believed that his fears were due to irrational beliefs, but other theories suggest alternative causes of his fears. If you took a **biological approach** to abnormality, you would suspect that Ellis' symptoms were caused by a biological factor, such as a genetic vulnerability to anxiety, inherited from his parents. Ellis' own rational-emotive theory is a **psychological approach** to abnormality, which suggests that symptoms are rooted in psychological factors, such as belief systems or early childhood experiences. If you took a **social approach** to understanding Ellis' symptoms, you would look to his interpersonal relationships and the social environment in which he lived.

Traditionally, biological, psychological, and social approaches have been seen as incompatible with one another. People frequently ask, "Is the cause of this disorder biological *or* psychological *or* social?" This question is often called the *nature-nurture question*—is the cause of the disorder something in the *nature*, or biology, of the person or in the person's *nurturing*, or history of events to which the person was exposed? This question implies that there has to be one cause of a disorder, rather than multiple causes. Indeed, most theories of psychological disorders over history have searched for the one factor—the one gene, the one traumatic experience, the one personality trait—that causes people to develop that disorder.

Many contemporary theorists recognize that there are often many pathways that all lead to the same end—namely, the development of a specific disorder. In some cases, it takes only one of these factors to cause a disorder. In most cases, however, it takes an accumulation of several factors before an individual develops the disorder. Just one or two of the factors working together may not be enough to create the disorder, but, when multiple factors are present in the life of an individual, a threshold is reached and the disorder develops.

Biological, psychological, and social approaches are being integrated to develop comprehensive models of the many factors that lead some people to develop a given mental disorder (e.g., Caspi, 1993; Cicchetti & Rogosch, 1996). These integrated models are sometimes referred to as **vulnerability-stress models** (see Figure 2.1). According to these models, a person must carry a vulnerability to the disorder

in order to develop it. This vulnerability can be a biological one, such as a genetic predisposition to the disorder. It can also be a psychological one, such as a personality trait that increases the person's risk of developing the disorder or a history of poor interpersonal relationships.

In order for the person to develop the disorder, however, he or she has to experience some type of stress, or trigger. Again, this trigger can be a biological one, such as illness that changes the person's balance of certain hormones. Or the trigger can be a psychological or social one, such as a traumatic event. Only when the vulnerability and the stress come together in the same individual does the full-blown disorder emerge. Although Ellis may indeed have had a genetic vulnerability to anxiety, he may have experienced stressers that triggered this vulnerability.

How do vulnerability and stress interact to cause a disorder? Another feature of contemporary theories of abnormality is that they recognize the *feedback effects* that biological and psychosocial factors have on each other. Feedback effects develop, so that changes in one factor result in changes in a second factor, but then those changes in the second factor feed back to change the first factor again (see Figure 2.2 on page 36). For example, a change in a person's biology, such as an increase in the levels of certain brain chemicals, might make the person angry and irritable. The person acts angrily and irritably around her friends, and in turn her friends react angrily toward her and begin to avoid her. The rejection of her friends only makes her more angry and irritable, which then causes even greater changes in her brain chemistry.

In this chapter, we examine the major biological, psychological, and social theories of

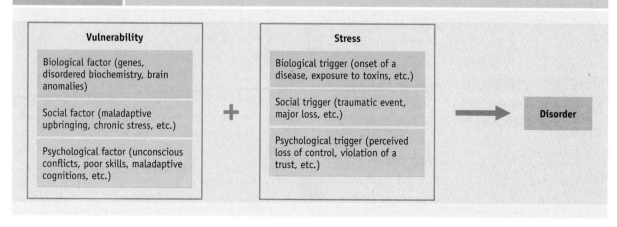

| **FIGURE 2.1** | **The Vulnerability-Stress Model of the Development of Disorders.** The vulnerability-stress model says that it takes both an existing vulnerability to a disorder and a trigger, or stress, to create the disorder. |

Vulnerability

Biological factor (genes, disordered biochemistry, brain anomalies)

Social factor (maladaptive upbringing, chronic stress, etc.)

Psychological factor (unconscious conflicts, poor skills, maladaptive cognitions, etc.)

+

Stress

Biological trigger (onset of a disease, exposure to toxins, etc.)

Social trigger (traumatic event, major loss, etc.)

Psychological trigger (perceived loss of control, violation of a trust, etc.)

⟶ **Disorder**

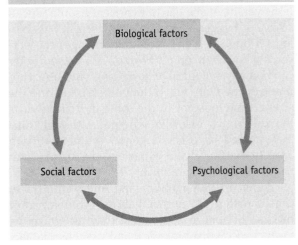

FIGURE 2.2   **Feedback Effects Among Biological, Social, and Psychological Factors.** Some integrative models of psychopathology suggest that biological, social, and psychological factors all affect each other in feedback loops that maintain and enhance psychopathological processes.

abnormality that have dominated the field in its modern history. They provide a background for understanding specific disorders and their treatments. Then in Chapter 5 we explore the treatments and therapies deriving from these theories. We look at the theories and treatments one at a time, so that they are easier to understand. Keep in mind, however, that most mental-health professionals now take an integrated approach to understanding mental disorders, viewing them as the result of a combination of biological, psychological, social vulnerabilities, and stresses that come together and feed off one another. We will return to this integrationist theme at the end of this chapter.

BIOLOGICAL APPROACHES

Let's start by considering the story of Phineas Gage, one of the most dramatic examples of the effect of biological factors on psychological functioning.

On 13 September 1848, Phineas P. Gage, a 25-year old construction foreman for the Rutland and Burlington Railroad in New England, became the victim of a bizarre accident. In order to lay new rail tracks across Vermont, it was necessary to level the uneven terrain by controlled blasting. Among other tasks, Gage was

CASE STUDY

in charge of the detonations, which involved drilling holes in the stone, partially filling the holes with explosive powder, covering the powder with sand, and using a fuse and a tamping iron to trigger an explosion into the rock. On the fateful day, a momentary distraction let Gage begin tamping directly over the powder before his assistant had had a chance to cover it with sand. The result was a powerful explosion away from the rock and toward Gage. The fine-pointed, 3-cm-thick, 109-cm-long tamping iron was hurled, rocket-like, through his face, skull, and brain, and then into the sky. Gage was momentarily stunned but regained full consciousness immediately thereafter. He was able to talk and even walk with the help of his men. The iron landed many yards away.

Phineas Gage not only survived the momentous injury, in itself enough to earn him a place in the annals of medicine, but he survived as a different man, and therein lies the greater significance of this case. Gage had been a responsible, intelligent, and socially well-adapted individual, a favorite with peers and elders. He had made progress and showed promise. The signs of a profound change in personality were already evident during the convalescence under the care of his physician, John Harlow. But as the months passed, it became apparent that the transformation was not only radical but difficult to comprehend. In some respects, Gage was fully recovered. He remained as able-bodied and appeared to be as intelligent as before the accident; he had no impairment of movement or speech; new learning was intact, and neither memory nor intelligence in the conventional sense had been affected. On the other hand, he had become irreverent and capricious. His respect for the social conventions by which he once abided had vanished. His abundant profanity offended those around him. Perhaps most troubling, he had taken leave of his sense of responsibility. He could not be trusted to honor his commitments. His employers had deemed him "the

(continued)

most efficient and capable" man in their "employ" but now they had to dismiss him. In the words of his physician, "the equilibrium or balance, so to speak, between his intellectual faculty and animal propensities" had been destroyed. In the words of his friends and acquaintances, "Gage was no longer Gage." (Damasio et al., 1994, p. 1102)

As a result of damage to his brain from the accident, Gage's basic personality seemed to change. He was transformed from a responsible, socially appropriate man to an impulsive, emotional, and socially inappropriate man. Almost 150 years later, researchers using modern neuroimaging techniques on Gage's preserved skull and a computer simulation of the tamping-iron accident determined the precise location of the damage to Gage's brain (see Figure 2.3). (We will discuss neuroimaging techniques, such as MRI, CT, and PET scanning, in Chapter 4.)

Studies of people today who suffer damage to the same area of the brain as Gage's injury reveal that they have trouble making rational decisions in personal and social matters and have trouble processing information about emotions. They do not have trouble, however, with the logic of an abstract problem, with arithmetic calculations, or with memory. Like Gage, their basic intellectual functioning remains intact, but their emotional control and judgment in personal and social matters are impaired (Damasio et al., 1994).

Gage's psychological changes were the result of damage to his brain. *Structural damage to the brain* is one of three causes of abnormality on

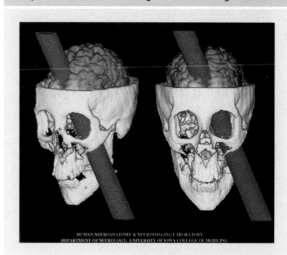

FIGURE 2.3   **Phineas Gage's Brain Injury.** Modern neuroimaging techniques have helped identify the precise location of damage to Phineas Gage's brain.

which biological approaches to abnormality often focus (see Figure 2.4). The other two are *biochemical imbalances* and *genetic abnormalities*. Structural abnormalities, biochemical imbalances, and genetic abnormalities can all influence each other. For example, structural abnormalities may be the result of genetic factors and may cause biochemical imbalances. We explore these three biological causes of abnormality in this section.

Structural Brain Abnormalities

It may seem obvious to us today that damage to the areas of the brain responsible for personality

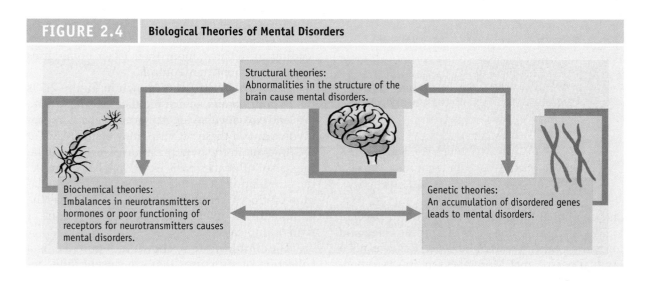

FIGURE 2.4   **Biological Theories of Mental Disorders**

Structural theories: Abnormalities in the structure of the brain cause mental disorders.

Biochemical theories: Imbalances in neurotransmitters or hormones or poor functioning of receptors for neurotransmitters causes mental disorders.

Genetic theories: An accumulation of disordered genes leads to mental disorders.

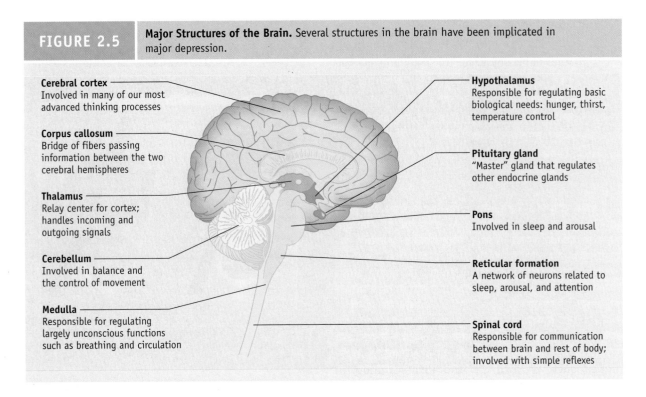

FIGURE 2.5 **Major Structures of the Brain.** Several structures in the brain have been implicated in major depression.

Cerebral cortex
Involved in many of our most advanced thinking processes

Corpus callosum
Bridge of fibers passing information between the two cerebral hemispheres

Thalamus
Relay center for cortex; handles incoming and outgoing signals

Cerebellum
Involved in balance and the control of movement

Medulla
Responsible for regulating largely unconscious functions such as breathing and circulation

Hypothalamus
Responsible for regulating basic biological needs: hunger, thirst, temperature control

Pituitary gland
"Master" gland that regulates other endocrine glands

Pons
Involved in sleep and arousal

Reticular formation
A network of neurons related to sleep, arousal, and attention

Spinal cord
Responsible for communication between brain and rest of body; involved with simple reflexes

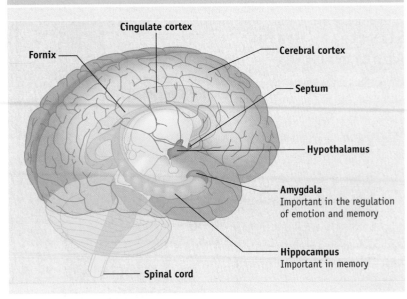

FIGURE 2.6 **Structures of the Limbic System.** The limbic system is a collection of structures that are closely interconnected with the hypothalamus. They appear to exert additional control over some of the instinctive behaviors regulated by the hypothalamus, such as eating, sexual behavior, and reactions to stressful situations.

Cingulate cortex

Fornix

Cerebral cortex

Septum

Hypothalamus

Amygdala
Important in the regulation of emotion and memory

Hippocampus
Important in memory

Spinal cord

and emotional functioning will result in psychological changes. In the days of Phineas Gage and for many years thereafter, however, this was not a popular perspective. More precisely, it was unpopular to believe that a person's character and control over his or her behavior rest, at least in part, in biology and are not completely the result of will and upbringing.

We now know that people who suffer damage to the brain (often referred to as *lesions*) or who have major abnormalities in the structure of the brain often show problems in psychological functioning. The location of the structural damage influences the specific psychological problems they have. Figure 2.5 shows some of the major structures in the brain. The damage that Phineas Gage suffered was primarily to the **cerebral cortex,** an area of the brain involved in many of our most advanced thinking processes. Some of the brain structures shown in Figure 2.5 are clearly separated. Others gradually merge into each other, leading to debates about their exact boundaries and the functions they control.

Another key structure shown in Figure 2.5 is the **hypothalamus,** which regulates eating, drinking, and sexual behavior. Abnormal behaviors that involve any of these activities may be the result of dysfunction in the hypothalamus. The hypothalamus also influences basic emotions. For example, the stimulation of certain areas of the hypothalamus produces sensations of pleasure, whereas the stimulation of other areas produces sensations of pain or unpleasantness.

The **limbic system,** shown in Figure 2.6, is a collection of structures that are closely interconnected with the hypothalamus and appear to exert additional control over some of the instinctive behaviors regulated by the hypothalamus, such as eating, sexual behavior, and reactions to stressful situations. Monkeys with damage to the limbic system sometimes become chronically aggressive, reacting with rage to the slightest provocation. At other times, they become excessively passive and do not react even to direct threats.

Structural damage to the brain can result from injury, such as from an automobile accident, and from diseases that cause deterioration. In schizophrenia, a severe disorder in which people lose touch with reality, the cerebral cortex does not function effectively or normally. In this book, we will encounter other examples of psychological disorders that appear to be associated with structural abnormalities in the brain.

Often, even modern neuroimaging techniques detect no structural abnormalities in the brains of people with psychological disorders, including some severe disorders. Instead, these disorders may be tied to biochemical processes in the brain.

Biochemical Causes of Abnormality

The brain requires a number of chemicals to work efficiently and effectively. Chief among these are **neurotransmitters,** biochemicals that act as messengers, carrying impulses from one *neuron*, or nerve cell, to another in the brain and in other parts of the nervous system (see Figure 2.7). Each neuron has a *cell body* and a number of short branches, called *dendrites*. The dendrites and cell body receive impulses from adjacent neurons. The impulse then travels down the length of a slender, tubelike extension, called an *axon*, to small swellings at the end of the axon, called *synaptic terminals*. Here the impulse stimulates the release of neurotransmitters.

The synaptic terminals do not actually touch the adjacent neurons. There is a slight gap between the synaptic terminals and the adjacent neurons. This gap is called the *synaptic gap*, or **synapse.** The neurotransmitter is released into the synapse. It then binds to **receptors,** which are molecules on the membranes of adjacent neurons. This binding works somewhat as a key fits into a lock. The binding stimulates the adjacent neurons to initiate the impulse, which then runs through the neuron's dendrites and cell body and down the axon to cause the release of more neurotransmitter between that neuron and other neurons.

Neurotransmitter Theories

Many of the biochemical theories of psychopathology suggest that too much or too little of certain neurotransmitters in the synapses causes specific types of psychopathology. The amount of a neurotransmitter available in the synapse can be affected by two processes. The process of **reuptake** occurs when the initial neuron releasing the neurotransmitter into the synapse reabsorbs the neurotransmitter, decreasing the amount left in the synapse. Another process, called **degradation,** occurs when the receiving neuron releases an enzyme into the synapse that breaks down the neurotransmitter into other biochemicals. The reuptake and degradation of neurotransmitters happens naturally. When one or both of these processes malfunction, abnormally high or low levels of neurotransmitter in the synapse result.

Psychological symptoms may also be linked to the number and functioning of the receptors for neurotransmitters on the dendrites. If there are too few receptors or the receptors are not sensitive

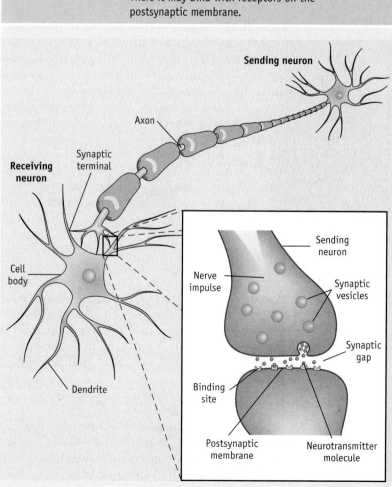

FIGURE 2.7 **Neurotransmitters and the Synapse.** The neurotransmitter is released into the synaptic gap. There it may bind with receptors on the postsynaptic membrane.

| FIGURE 2.8 | **Some Major Neurotransmitter Systems.** Serotonin and dopamine are two neurotransmitters important in many mental disorders. |

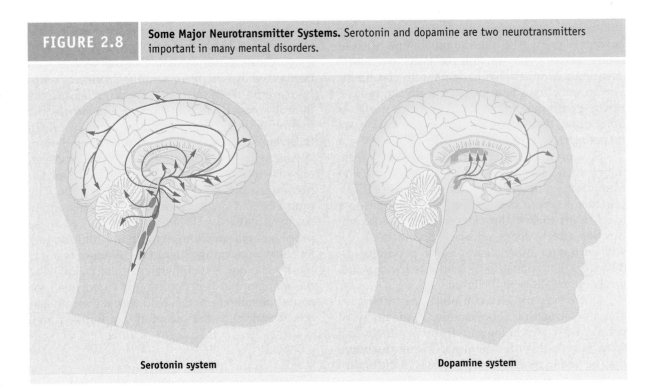

Serotonin system

Dopamine system

enough, the neuron will be unable to make adequate use of the neurotransmitter available in the synapse. If there are too many receptors or they are too sensitive, the neuron may be overexposed to the neurotransmitter that is in the synapse.

Scientists have identified more than 100 neurotransmitters. *Serotonin* plays a particularly important role in mental health, regulating emotions and impulses, such as aggression. Serotonin travels through many key areas of the brain, affecting the function of those areas (see Figure 2.8).

Dopamine is a neurotransmitter that is prominent in the areas of the brain that regulate our experience of reinforcements or rewards (see Figure 2.8), and it is affected by substances, such as alcohol, that we find rewarding. Dopamine also is important to the functioning of muscle systems, and it plays a role in disorders involving control over muscles, such as Parkinson's disease.

Norepinephrine (also known as noradrenaline) is a neurotransmitter that is produced mainly by neurons in the brain stem. Two well-known drugs, cocaine and amphetamines, prolong the action of norepinephrine by slowing its reuptake process. Because of the delay in the reuptake, the receiving neurons are activated for a longer period of time, causing the stimulating psychological effects of these drugs. On the other hand, when there is too little norepinephrine in the brain, the person's mood level is depressed.

Another prominent neurotransmitter is *gamma-aminobutyric acid*, or *GABA*, which inhibits the action of other neurotransmitters. Certain drugs have a tranquilizing effect because they increase the inhibitory activity of GABA. GABA is thought to play an important role in anxiety symptoms, so one contributor to Albert Ellis' anxiety could have been a dysfunction in his GABA system.

These are but a few of the neurotransmitters we discuss in this book. You will find that some neurotransmitters are implicated in a number of disorders. This is probably because each neurotransmitter plays crucial roles in the functioning of several basic systems in the brain. Several functions in the brain can go awry when the level of a particular neurotransmitter is too high or low, when receptors for that neurotransmitter are not working properly, or when there are too few receptors or too many.

The Endocrine System

Other biochemical theories of psychopathology focus on the body's **endocrine system** (see Figure 2.9). This system of glands produces many different chemicals called *hormones*, which are released directly into the blood. A **hormone** carries messages throughout the body, potentially affecting a person's moods, levels of energy, and reactions to stress.

| FIGURE 2.9 | **The Endocrine System.** The hypothalamus regulates the endocrine system, which produces most of the major hormones of the body. |

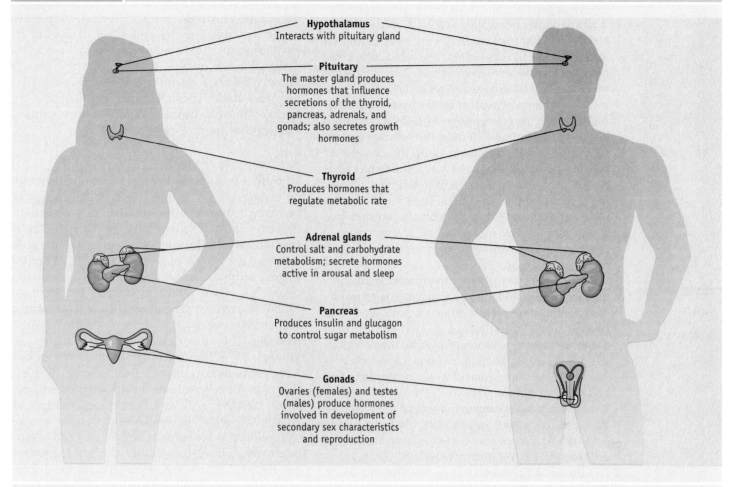

Hypothalamus
Interacts with pituitary gland

Pituitary
The master gland produces
hormones that influence
secretions of the thyroid,
pancreas, adrenals, and
gonads; also secretes growth
hormones

Thyroid
Produces hormones that
regulate metabolic rate

Adrenal glands
Control salt and carbohydrate
metabolism; secrete hormones
active in arousal and sleep

Pancreas
Produces insulin and glucagon
to control sugar metabolism

Gonads
Ovaries (females) and testes
(males) produce hormones
involved in development of
secondary sex characteristics
and reproduction

Source: From Goldstein and Noble, *Psychology*, 1st edition. Copyright © 1994. Reprinted with permission of Wadsworth, a division of Thomson Learning: www.thomsonrights.com. Fax 800-730-2215.

One of the major endocrine glands, the **pituitary,** has been called the "master gland" because it produces the largest number of different hormones and controls the secretion of other endocrine glands. It is partly an outgrowth of the brain and lies just below the hypothalamus (review Figure 2.5).

The relationship between the pituitary gland and the hypothalamus illustrates the complex interactions that take place between the endocrine system and the nervous system. For example, in response to stress (fear, anxiety, pain, and so forth), certain neurons on the hypothalamus secrete a substance called corticotropin-release factor (CRF). CRF is carried from the hypothalamus to the pituitary through a channel-like structure. The CRF stimulates the pituitary to release the body's major stress hormone, adrenocorticotrophic hormone (ACTH). In turn, ACTH is carried by the blood-stream to the adrenal glands and to various other organs of the body, causing the release of about 30 hormones, each of which plays a role in the body's adjustment to emergency situations.

As we discuss in Chapters 7, 8, and 9, some theories of anxiety and depression suggest that these disorders result from dysregulation of this relationship, called the *hypothalamic-pituitary-adrenal axis* (or *HPA axis*). People who have a dysregulated HPA axis may have abnormal physiological reactions to stress, which make it more difficult for them to cope psychologically with the stress resulting in symptoms of anxiety and depression.

The proper working of neurotransmitter and endocrine systems requires a delicate balance, and many forces can upset this balance. One of these is a genetic abnormality, which can affect biochemical systems as well as brain development. The end result can be a psychological disturbance.

Genetic Factors in Abnormality

Behavior genetics, the study of the genetics of personality and abnormality, is a relatively new and fast-growing area of research concerned with two questions: (1) To what extent are behaviors or behavioral tendencies inherited and (2) what are the processes by which genes affect behavior?

Let us begin by reviewing the basics of genetic transmission. At conception, the fertilized embryo has 46 chromosomes, 23 from the female egg and 23 from the male sperm, making up 23 pairs of chromosomes. One of these pairs is referred to as the *sex chromosomes* because it determines the sex of the embryo: The XX combination results in a female embryo, and the XY combination results in a male embryo. The mother of an embryo always contributes an X chromosome, and the father can contribute an X or a Y.

Alterations in the structure or number of chromosomes can cause major defects. For example, Down syndrome results when chromosome 21 is present in triplicate instead of as the usual pair. Down syndrome is characterized by mental retardation, heart malformations, and facial features such as a flat face, a small nose, protruding lips and tongue, and slanted eyes.

Chromosomes contain individual genes, which are segments of long molecules of deoxyribonucleic acid (DNA). Genes give coded instructions to the cells to perform certain functions, usually to manufacture certain proteins. Genes, like chromosomes, come in pairs. One half of the pair comes from the mother, the other from the father. Abnormalities in genes that make up chromosomes are much more common than are major abnormalities in the structure or number of chromosomes.

Although you may often hear of scientists having discovered "the gene" for a major disorder, most disorders are not the result of single faulty genes but of combinations of altered genes. Each of these altered genes makes only a small contribution to a vulnerability for the disorder. However, when a critical number of these altered genes come together, the individual may develop the disorder. This is known as a multigene, or **polygenic** process—it takes multiple genetic abnormalities coming together in one individual to create a disorder. Most of the genetic models of the major types of mental disorders are also polygenic. A number of physiological disorders, such as diabetes, coronary heart disease, epilepsy, and cleft lip and palate, result from such polygenic processes. As we discuss in *Taking Psychology Personally: Do "Bad Genes" Doom You to a Disorder?*, genetic factors increase vulnerablility to a disorder rather than determining whether it occurs.

As we discuss the specific psychological disorders in this textbook, we will consider the ways genetic predispositions and other biological or psychosocial factors may interact to increase an individual's risk for the disorder. But how do we know whether a disorder is heritable? Scientists use three basic types of studies to determine the heritability of a disorder: family history studies, twin studies, and adoption studies.

Family History Studies

Disorders that are genetically transmitted should, on average, show up more often in the families of people who have the disorder than they do in families of people who do not have the disorder. This is true whether the disorder is caused by a single gene or by a combination of genes. To conduct a **family history study,** scientists first identify people who clearly have the disorder in question. This group is called the *probands.* The researchers also identify a *control group* of people who clearly do not have the disorder. They then trace the *family pedigrees,* or family trees, of the individuals in these two groups and determine how many of their relatives have the disorder. Researchers are most interested in *first-degree* relatives, such as full siblings, parents, and children, because these relatives are most genetically similar to the subjects (unless they have identical twins, who are genetically identical to them).

Figure 2.10 (on page 44) illustrates the degree of genetic relationship between an individual and various categories of relatives. This figure gives you an idea of why the risk of inheriting the genes for a disorder quickly decreases as the relationship between an individual and the relative with the disorder becomes more distant: The percentage of genes the individual and relative with the disorder have in common decreases greatly with distance.

Although family history studies provide very useful information about the possible genetic transmission of a disorder, they have their problems. The most obvious one is that families share not only genes but also environment. Several members of a family might have a disorder because they share the same environmental stresses. Family history studies cannot tease apart genetic and environmental contributions to a disorder. Researchers often turn to twin studies to do that.

Twin Studies

Notice in Figure 2.10 that identical, or **monozygotic (MZ), twins** share 100 percent of their genes. This is

Taking Psychology Personally

Do "Bad Genes" Doom You to a Disorder?

The media are full of stories about scientists discovering the genes that contribute to serious mental disorders. These stories are fascinating, and the advances in our understanding of the genetics of mental disorders over the last decade or two are critical to the development of more effective biological treatments for these disorders.

In the general public, however, there is widespread misunderstanding of the meanings of genetic findings. First, people usually don't understand, and the media don't make clear, that mental disorders, like most physical disorders, are rarely the result of a single "bad gene." Instead, they are usually the result of polygenic processes, in which a number of irregular genes must come together in an individual to produce a disorder.

People who have disorders caused by polygenic processes often wonder why they have no family history of the disorder. It may be because none of their relatives accumulated all the different genes necessary for the disorder to develop fully. It just happened that, when the people with disorders were conceived, all the genes necessary for the disorders were present in the chromosomes contributed by their mothers and fathers. When their brothers or sisters were conceived, however, different sets of chromosomes were contributed by their mothers and fathers, and these may not have contained all the necessary genes for the disorders, so their siblings did not develop the disorders.

Conversely, many people who have relatives with disorders that are heritable worry that they will inevitably develop the disorders. In most cases, however, the odds of an individual's inheriting all the genes necessary for a disorder are fairly low, even if a relative who has the disorder is a parent or sibling. For example, the sibling of a person with schizophrenia,

which is probably the psychological disorder in which genes play the strongest role, has only about a 9 percent chance of developing schizophrenia at some point in his or her life (see Chapter 11).

Another widely misunderstood characteristic of polygenic disorders involves what is inherited. A person inherits the **predisposition** to the disorder—a tendency to develop it. The disorder is not inevitable. Often the predisposition must interact with other biological or environmental influences for the individual to fully develop the disorder. A good example from the medical field is coronary heart disease. A person can inherit a predisposition to coronary heart disease by inheriting the genes for hypertension, diabetes, or hyperlipidemia (too much fat in the blood). Whether he or she actually develops coronary heart disease depends, however, on a number of environmental and behavioral factors, such as obesity, smoking, exercise, alcohol abuse, a hard-driving personality, and life in an industrialized society.

The same characteristic may be true of many psychological disorders. What is inherited is a predisposition to the disorder. Whether an individual ever fully develops the disorder may depend on exposure to other biological risks (such as malnutrition or negative intrauterine experiences) and other psychosocial risks (such as growing up in a dysfunctional family).

If you have a family history of a particular psychological disorder, or worry that you may carry the genes for a disorder, you are not "doomed" to develop the disorder. You may have an increased risk for the disorder, but there may also be steps you can take to reduce that risk. You can learn about these steps by talking with a mental-health professional.

because they come from a single fertilized egg, which splits into two identical parts. In contrast, nonidentical, or **dizygotic (DZ), twins** share, on average, 50 percent of their genes, because they come from two separate eggs fertilized by separate sperm, just as regular siblings do.

Researchers have capitalized on this difference between MZ and DZ twins to investigate through **twin studies** the contribution of genetics to many disorders. If a disorder is determined *entirely* by ge-

netics, when one member of a monozygotic (MZ) twin pair has a disorder, the other member of the pair should always have the disorder. This probability that both twins have the disorder if one twin has the disorder is called the **concordance rate** for the disorder. Thus, if a disorder is entirely determined by genes, the concordance rate among MZ twins should be 100 percent. The concordance rate for the disorder among dizygotic (DZ) twins should be much lower than 100 percent. Even when a disorder

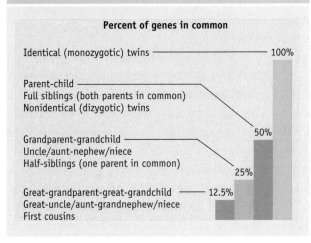

FIGURE 2.10 **Degrees of Genetic Relationship.** People with whom you share 50 percent of your genes are your first-degree relatives. People with whom you share 25 percent of your genes are your second-degree relatives. People with whom you share 12.5 percent of your genes are your third-degree relatives.

Percent of genes in common

Identical (monozygotic) twins ——————————— 100%

Parent-child
Full siblings (both parents in common)
Nonidentical (dizygotic) twins

50%

Grandparent-grandchild
Uncle/aunt-nephew/niece
Half-siblings (one parent in common)

25%

Great-grandparent-great-grandchild ——— 12.5%
Great-uncle/aunt-grandnephew/niece
First cousins

is transmitted only partially by genetics, the concordance rate for MZ twins should be considerably higher than the concordance rate for DZ twins, because MZ twins are genetically identical, but DZ twins share only about half the same genes.

For example, let us say that the concordance rate for Disorder X for MZ twins is 48 percent, whereas the concordance rate for DZ twins is 17 percent. These concordance rates tell us two things. First, because the concordance rate for MZ twins is considerably higher than the concordance rate for DZ twins, we have evidence that Disorder X is genetically transmitted. Second, because the concordance rate for MZ twins is well under 100 percent, we have evidence that it takes a combination of a genetic predisposition and other factors (biological or environmental) for an individual to develop Disorder X.

By now, you may be objecting that twin studies do not fully tease apart genetic factors from environmental factors, because MZ twins may have much more similar environments and experiences than do DZ twins. For example, MZ twins typically look alike, whereas DZ twins often do not look alike, and physical appearance can strongly affect other people's reactions to an individual. MZ twins may also be more likely than DZ twins to share talents that influence the opportunities they are given in life. For instance, MZ twins may both be athletic or very talented academically or musically, which then affects

their treatment by others and their opportunities in life. In contrast, DZ twins much less often share the same talents and thus are less likely to be treated similarly by others. Finally, parents may simply treat MZ twins more similarly than they do DZ twins, for a variety of reasons. To address these problems, researchers have turned to a third method for studying heritability, adoption studies.

Adoption Studies

An **adoption study** can be carried out in a number of ways. Most commonly, researchers first identify people who have the disorder of interest who were adopted shortly after birth. Then they determine the rates of the disorder in the biological relatives of these adoptees and the adoptive relatives of the adoptees. If a disorder is strongly influenced by genetics, researchers should see higher rates of the disorder among the biological relatives of the adoptee than among the adoptive relatives. If the disorder is strongly influenced by environment, they should see higher rates of the disorder among the adoptive relatives than among the biological relatives.

Some of the most interesting studies of the genetics of personality combine the strategies of adoption studies and the twin studies. Researchers at the University of Minnesota identified several dozen pairs of MZ and DZ twins who had been reared apart and brought them together to assess their personalities. Some of the twins reared apart had never met each other and had not even known that they had a twin. The personalities and behavioral patterns of the MZ twins reared apart were compared with the personalities of the DZ twins reared apart and with MZ and DZ twins reared in the same households.

The results of this study have provided evidence that some aspects of personality and everyday behavior are substantially affected by genetics. Some of the characteristics affected by genetics will not surprise you, nor have they surprised many other scientists. For example, it appears that traits such as shyness and the tendency to become easily upset are heavily influenced by genetics (Bouchard & Loehlin, 2001; Johnson et al., 2004).

What stunned the world of behavior genetics, however, was evidence that even the most mundane behaviors, which were thought to be shaped by circumstance and rearing, are heavily influenced by genetics, such as the amount of television we watch and what we snack on while we're watching TV (Bouchard, 1994; Hur, Bouchard, & Eckert, 1998). There are startling examples of iden-

Studies of identical twins reared apart have revealed amazing similarities. Jim Lewis and Jim Springer were reared apart but, when reunited, found that they were identical in more than appearance.

tical twins reared apart who are amazingly similar, even though they have never met. Consider, for example, the "Jim twins" (Holden, 1980). Jim Lewis and Jim Springer were identical twins reunited at the age of 39 after being separated since infancy. Both had married and later divorced women named Linda. Their second wives were both named Betty. Both had sons named James Allan and dogs named Toy. Both chain-smoked Salem cigarettes, worked as sheriffs' deputies, drove Chevrolets, chewed their fingernails, enjoyed stock car racing, had basement workshops, and had built circular white benches around trees in their yards.

Genetic researchers do not argue that there are genes for marrying women named Linda or Betty or genes for having basement workshops. Given similar circumstances, however, people with identical genes may choose the same activities and have the same likes and dislikes.

Not surprisingly, the work on behavior genetics has been controversial. Some scientists believe that behavior geneticists are underestimating the role of the environment as they overestimate the role of genetics. This work clearly has stimulated a lively and interesting discussion, however, about how deeply and broadly genes affect our behavior.

In sum, adoption studies, twin studies, and family history studies all help to determine whether a characteristic or disorder is influenced by genetics and the degree of this influence. Each type of study has its limitations. Family history and twin studies cannot fully tease apart the impacts of genetics and shared environment. Adoption studies suffer from the fact that it is difficult to find large numbers of adoptees with the disorder

of interest, so the sample sizes in these studies tend to be very small.

Assessing the Biological Theories

Modern biological theories have greatly advanced our understanding of the human mind and the biological influences on behavior. Research on these theories seems to be advancing at a rapid pace, with new discoveries about the role of biology in mental disorders in the news every day. These theories have led to new treatments, which have restored the lives of people who suffer with disorders.

The biological theories have their flaws, however. They often seem reductionistic, boiling down the complex human behavior called psychopathology into the firing of neurons and abnormal genes. Some of these theories ignore the influence of social factors and the environment in shaping the behavior of people who may carry a biological risk for psychopathology. More generally, the biological theories often have trouble explaining why not everyone who carries a biological risk for a disorder, such as an unusual level of a hormone or neurotransmitter, eventually develops the disorder.

Although we may think of biological research as "harder science" than the research done to test the psychosocial theories of abnormality, biological research is often at least as messy and nondefinitive as psychosocial research (Valenstein, 1998). Most of the processes thought to cause psychopathology, such as changes in neurotransmitter levels, can be measured only indirectly and quite imprecisely in the brains of live humans. As a result, much of the evidence for the biological theories comes from studies of animals rather than humans. Although animal studies can be informative, it is sometimes difficult to generalize from animals to humans.

Many of the biological theories of psychopathology were based on accidental discoveries that certain drugs change behavior in animals or humans. Reasoning backward from the effects of drugs on behavior to a theory of what causes that behavior is a tricky business, particularly because the drugs that are used to alleviate psychopathology have widespread effects on many areas and systems in the brain (Valenstein, 1998).

The biological theories of abnormality have many proponents, however, and seem to have captured the hearts of the general public. Many people find biological theories of psychopathology appealing, because they seem to take away any stigma or blame on the individual sufferer for having the disorder. Indeed, many organizations for people with psychological disorders explicitly advocate a biological view of these disorders, emphasizing that people with the disorders need to stop blaming themselves, accept the fact that they have a "disease," and obtain the appropriate medical treatment. In addition, many insurance companies will pay only for biological treatments, even though psychological treatments have longer-lasting positive effects for some disorders.

SUMMING UP

- The biological theories of psychopathology hold that psychological symptoms and disorders are caused by structural abnormalities in the brain, disordered biochemistry, or faulty genes.

- Structural abnormalities in the brain can be caused by injury or disease processes. The location of brain damage influences the type of psychological symptoms shown.

- Most biochemical theories focus on neurotransmitters, the biochemicals that facilitate the transmission of impulses in the brain. Some theories say that psychological symptoms are caused by too little or too much of a particular neurotransmitter in the synapses of the brain. Other theories focus on the number of receptors for neurotransmitters.

- Some people may be genetically predisposed to psychological disorders. Most of these disorders are probably linked not to a single faulty gene but to an accumulation of faulty genes.

- Three methods of determining the heritability of a disorder are family history studies, twin studies, and adoption studies.

PSYCHOLOGICAL APPROACHES

Psychological theories of abnormality vary greatly. Some theories focus on unconscious conflicts and anxiety, some focus on the effects of rewards and punishments in the environment, some focus on thought processes, and others focus on the difficulties humans have in striving to realize their full potential in a capricious world (see Figure 2.11). In this book, we will discuss the psychological theories that have had the largest and most enduring impacts on how psychologists view abnormality and on the types of psychological therapies that are currently used to treat people.

Psychodynamic Theories of Abnormality

The **psychodynamic theories** of abnormality suggest that all behavior, thoughts, and emotions, whether normal or abnormal, are influenced to a large extent by unconscious processes (McWilliams & Weinberger, 2003). The psychodynamic theories began with Sigmund Freud in the late nineteenth century and have expanded to include several newer theories. These theories accept many of Freud's basic assumptions about the working of the human mind but emphasize different processes from those that Freud emphasized.

Freud developed **psychoanalysis,** which is (1) a theory of personality and psychopathology, (2) a

| **FIGURE 2.11** | **Psychological Theories of Mental Disorders.** Psychological theories of mental disorders describe a variety of causes of symptoms. |

Psychodynamic theories: Unconscious conflicts between primitive desires and constraints on those desires cause symptoms of mental disorders.

Behavioral theories: Symptoms of mental disorders are due to reinforcements and punishments for specific behaviors.

Cognitive theories: People's ways of interpreting situations, their assumptions about the world, and their self-concepts cause negative feelings and behaviors.

Humanistic and existential theories: Mental disorders arise when people do not pursue their own values and potentials and, instead, feel they must conform to the demands of others.

Sigmund Freud believed that normal and abnormal behaviors are driven by needs and drives, most of which are unconscious.

method of investigating the mind, and (3) a form of treatment for psychopathology (McWilliams & Weinberger, 2003). As we noted in Chapter 1, Freud was a Viennese neurologist who became interested in unconscious processes while working with Jean Charcot in Paris in the late nineteenth century. He then returned to Vienna and worked with physician Josef Breuer, most notably on the case of "Anna O."

Anna O. had extensive symptoms of hysteria—physical ailments with no apparent physical cause—including paralysis of the legs and right arm, deafness, and disorganized speech. Breuer attempted to hypnotize Anna O., hoping he could cure her symptoms by suggestion. Anna O. began to talk about painful memories from her past, which were apparently tied to the development of her hysterical symptoms. She expressed a great deal of distress about these memories, but, following the recounting of the memories under hypnosis, many of her symptoms went away. Breuer labeled the release of emotions connected to these memories **catharsis,** and Anna O. labeled the entire process her "talking cure." (Later Anna O., whose real name was Bertha Pappenheim, rejected the psychoanalytic explanation for her symptoms and believed Breuer's treatment had had no positive effects.)

Breuer and Freud published papers on their cases together and suggested that hysteria is the result of traumatic memories that have been repressed from consciousness because they are too painful. **Repression** was defined as the motivated forgetting of a difficult experience, such as being abused as a child, or an unacceptable wish, such as

the desire to hurt someone. Repression does not dissolve the emotion associated with the memory or wish. Instead, this emotion is "dammed-up" and emerges as symptoms.

Freud went on to develop these ideas about dynamic processes within the unconscious into an elaborate and comprehensive theory of human thought and behavior. Freud was a passionate reader of history, archeology, philosophy, and many other fields, and he developed theories reaching far beyond psychology and psychiatry. In this book, we will review the central assumptions of Freudian theory that are most pertinent to abnormal behavior. Some of these ideas are summarized in the Concept Overview in Table 2.1 (on page 48).

The Id, Ego, and Superego

Freud believed that the two basic drives that motivate human behavior are the sexual drive, which he referred to as **libido,** and the aggressive drive. The energy from these drives continually seeks to be released but can be channeled or harnessed by various psychological systems. Most of Freud's writings focused primarily on libido (or libidinal drive), so our discussion will do so as well.

According to Freud, the three systems of the human psyche that help regulate the libido are the id, the ego, and the superego. The **id** is the system from which the libido emerges, and its drives and impulses seek immediate release. The id operates by the **pleasure principle**—the drive to maximize pleasure and to minimize pain, as quickly as possible. A number of reflex actions, such as an infant's turning to the mother's breast for milk, are direct expressions of the pleasure principle. When direct action cannot be taken, humans may use fantasies or memories to conjure up the desired object or

© Sidney Harris, courtesy ScienceCartoonsPlus.com

TABLE 2.1	Concept Overview

Key Concepts in Freudian Theory

Freudian theory includes a number of complex concepts.

Name	Description
Repression	The motivated forgetting of memories or desires that cause anxiety
Catharsis	The release of energy bound up in painful emotions
Libido	Psychical energy emerging from sexual drive
Id	The most primitive part of the unconscious, which consists of drives and impulses seeking immediate gratification
Ego	The part of the psyche that channels libido into activities that balance the demands of society and the superego
Superego	The part of the unconscious that consists of absolute moral standards internalized from one's parents and culture
Pleasure principle	The principle that desires and wishes should be immediately gratified, without concern for the constraints of society
Primary process thinking	Thinking oriented toward satisfying primitive urges, perhaps through fantasy
Reality principle	The realization that primitive urges cannot always be immediately gratified because of the constraints of society
Secondary process thinking	Rational deliberation about how to satisfy primitive urges within the constraints of society
Introjection	Incorporating or internalizing the standards or view of others into one's own ways of thinking
Unconscious	The vast area of the psyche holding desires, memories, and emotions of which we are not aware
Preconscious	The "way station" between the unconscious and conscious, holding material that is somewhat accessible to consciousness
Conscious	The aspect of the psyche holding material of which we are aware
Defense mechanisms	Strategies for transforming unacceptable desires, thoughts, and feelings into a more acceptable form
Neurotic paradox	When an individual's defense mechanisms become maladaptive and distressing
Oedipus complex	The stage of development in which a boy desires his mother and hates his father
Castration anxiety	Anxiety a little boy feels when he fears his father will castrate him in retaliation for his desire for his mother
Electra complex	The stage of development in which a girl becomes attached to her father in hopes he will provide her with a replacement for the penis she lacks
Penis envy	A female's desire to have a penis

action. This is known as **primary process thinking,** or *wish fulfillment*. A hungry infant, for example, may imagine the mother's breast when she is not readily available.

As children grow older, they become aware that they cannot always quickly satisfy their impulses without paying a price. They cannot immediately satisfy sexual urges and cannot carry out aggressive impulses without being punished by society. A part of the id splits off and becomes the **ego,** the force that seeks to gratify wishes and needs in ways that remain within the rules of society for their appropriate expression. The ego follows the **reality principle**—the drive to satisfy our needs within the realities of society's rules—rather than the pleasure principle. **Secondary process**

thinking, or *rational deliberation*, is the ego's primary mode of operation, rather than primary process thinking. A preschooler, who may wish to suckle at the mother's breast but is aware that this is no longer allowed, may satisfy himself with cuddling in his mother's lap.

The **superego** develops from the ego a little later in childhood. It is the storehouse of rules and regulations for the conduct of behavior that are learned from one's parents and from society. These rules and regulations are in the form of absolute moral standards. We **introject,** or *internalize*, these moral standards, because following them makes us feel good and reduces anxiety. The superego is made up of two components, the conscience and the ego ideal. The *conscience* constantly evaluates whether we are conforming our behavior to our internalized moral standards. The *ego ideal* is an image of the person we wish to become, formed from images of those people with whom we identified in our early years, usually our parents.

Most of the interactions among the id, ego, and superego occur in the **unconscious**—completely out of our awareness. The **preconscious** is a way station, or buffer, between the unconscious and the **conscious.** Wishes, needs, and memories from the unconscious can make their way into the preconscious, but they rarely reach the conscious level. The ego deflects this material back into the unconscious or changes the material in such a way as to protect the conscious from being fully aware of the unconscious material. This pushing material back into the unconscious is repression.

Why must the conscious be protected from unconscious material? In their raw form, unconscious wishes, needs, and memories represent our basic instincts and drives, seeking to be satisfied in the quickest and fullest way possible. Because these unconscious desires are often unacceptable to the individual or society, they cause anxiety if they seep into the conscious, prompting the ego to push the material back into the unconscious.

The psychoanalytic explanation for depression illustrates how repression can lead to symptoms. Freud argued that at the root of depression is a deep rage against important people in your life, such as your caregivers. Expressing, or even consciously acknowledging, this rage causes anxiety, however, so the rage is repressed and made unconscious. The ego turns this rage on itself, leading to the self-criticism and even suicidal behaviors of depression.

Freud—and later his daughter, Anna Freud described certain strategies, or **defense mechanisms,** that the ego uses to disguise or transform unconscious wishes. The particular defense mechanisms that a person regularly uses shape his or her behav-

Anna Freud, daughter of Sigmund Freud, was a major contributor to psychodynamic theory and described the basic defense mechanisms people use to control anxiety.

ior and personality. Table 2.2 (on page 50) provides a list and examples of the basic defense mechanisms. Everyone uses defense mechanisms to a degree, because everyone must protect against an awareness of unacceptable wishes and conform his or her behavior to societal norms.

When a person's behavior becomes ruled by defense mechanisms or when the mechanisms themselves are maladaptive, the defense mechanisms can result in abnormal, pathological behavior. Freud called this situation the **neurotic paradox.** For example, a man whose father physically abused him as a child may develop the tendency to displace his rage—to transfer his feelings to another target—because it is too dangerous to express his anger directly against his father. This displacement may take the form of beating his wife or getting into frequent fist fights with other men. The displacement behavior is maladaptive in itself, and the man is stuck in the neurotic paradox.

Psychosexual Stages

Psychoanalytic theory argues that the nurturance a child receives from his or her early caregivers strongly influences personality development. Freud proposed that, as children develop, they pass through a series of universal **psychosexual stages.** In each stage, sexual drives are focused on the stimulation of certain body areas, and particular psychological issues can arouse anxiety. The id, ego, and superego must negotiate and develop successfully through these stages for the child to become a psychologically healthy adult.

The responses of caregivers, usually parents, to the child's attempts to satisfy basic needs and wishes can greatly influence whether a given stage is negotiated successfully. If the parents are not

TABLE 2.2   Defense Mechanisms

These defense mechanisms were described by Sigmund and Anna Freud.

Defense Mechanism	Definition	Example
Regression	Retreating to a behavior of an earlier developmental period to prevent anxiety and satisfy current needs	A woman abandoned by her lover curls up in a chair, rocking and sucking her fingers.
Denial	Refusing to perceive or accept reality	A husband whose wife recently died denies she is gone and actively searches for her.
Displacement	Discharging unacceptable feelings against someone or something other than the true target of these feelings	A woman who is angry at her children kicks a dog.
Rationalization	Inventing an acceptable motive to explain unacceptably motivated behavior	A soldier who killed innocent civilians rationalizes that he was only following orders.
Intellectualization	Adopting a cold, distanced perspective on a matter that actually creates strong, unpleasant feelings	An emergency room physician who is troubled by seeing young people with severe gunshot wounds every night has discussions with colleagues that focus only on the technical aspects of treatment.
Projection	Attributing one's own unacceptable motives or desires to someone else	A husband who is sexually attracted to a colleague accuses his wife of cheating on him.
Reaction formation	Adopting a set of attitudes and behaviors that are the opposite of one's true dispositions	A man who cannot accept his own homosexuality becomes extremely homophobic.
Identification	Adopting the ideas, values, and tendencies of someone in a superior position in order to elevate self-worth	Prisoners adopt the attitudes of their captors toward other prisoners.
Sublimation	Translating wishes and needs into socially acceptable behavior	An adolescent with strong aggressive impulses trains to be a boxer.

appropriately responsive, helping the child learn acceptable ways of satisfying and controlling drives and impulses, the child can become *fixated* at a stage, trapped in the concerns and issues of that stage, never successfully moving beyond that stage and through the subsequent stages.

According to Freud, the earliest stage of life, the **oral stage,** lasts for the first 18 months following birth. In the oral stage, libidinal impulses are best satisfied through stimulation of the mouth area, usually through feeding or sucking. At this stage, the child is entirely dependent on caregivers for gratification, and the central issues of this stage are issues of one's dependence and the reliability of others. If the child's caregiver, typically the mother,

is not adequately available to the child, he or she can develop deep mistrust and fear of abandonment. Children fixated at the oral stage develop an "oral character"—a personality characterized by excessive dependence on others but mistrust of their love. A number of habits focused on the mouth area—for example, smoking or excessive drinking and eating—are said to reflect an oral character.

The **anal stage** lasts from about 18 months to 3 years of age. During this phase, the focus of gratification is the anus. The child becomes very interested in toilet activities, particularly the passing and retaining of feces. Parents can cause a child to become fixated at this stage by being too harsh or critical during toilet training. People with an "anal personality" are said to be stubborn, overcontrolling, stingy, and too focused on orderliness and tidiness.

During the **phallic stage,** lasting from about ages 3 to 6, the focus of pleasure is the genitals. During this stage, one of the most important conflicts of sexual development occurs, and it occurs differently for boys and girls. Freud believed that boys become sexually attracted to their mothers and hate their fathers as rivals. Freud labeled this the **Oedipus complex,** after the character in Greek mythology who unknowingly kills his father and marries his mother. Boys fear that their fathers will retaliate against them by castrating them, however. This fear arouses **castration anxiety,** which is then the motivation for putting aside their desire for their mothers and aspiring to become like their fathers. The successful resolution of the Oedipal complex helps instill a strong superego in boys, because it results in boys' identifying with their fathers and their fathers' value systems.

Freud believed that, during the phallic stage, girls recognize that they do not have a penis and are horrified at this discovery. They also recognize that their mothers do not have a penis and disdain their mothers and all other females for this deficit. Girls develop an attraction for their fathers, in hopes that their fathers will provide the penis they lack. He labeled this the **Electra complex,** after the character in Greek mythology who conspires to murder her mother to avenge her father's death. Girls cannot have castration anxiety, because, according to Freud, they feel they have already been castrated. As a result, girls do not have as strong a motivation as boys to develop a superego. Freud argued that females never do develop superegos as strong as males' and this leads to a greater reliance on emotion than on reason in the lives of women. Freud also thought that much of women's behavior is driven by **penis envy**—the wish to have the male sex organ.

The unsuccessful resolution of the phallic stage can lead to a number of psychological problems in children. If children do not fully identify with their same-sex parents, they may not develop "appropriate" gender roles or a heterosexual orientation. They also may not develop a healthy superego and may become either too self-aggrandizing or too self-deprecating. If children's sexual attraction to their parents is not met with gentle but firm discouragement, they may become overly seductive or sexualized and have a number of problems in romantic relationships.

After the turmoil of the phallic stage, children enter the **latency stage,** during which libidinal drives are quelled somewhat. Their attention turns to developing skills and interests and becoming fully socialized into the world in which they live. They play with friends of the same sex and avoid children of the opposite sex. This is the time when girls hate boys and boys hate girls.

At about the age of 12, children's sexual desires emerge again as they enter puberty, and they enter the **genital stage.** If they have successfully resolved the phallic stage, their sexual interests turn to heterosexual relationships. They begin to pursue romantic alliances and learn to negotiate the world of dating and early sexual encounters with members of the opposite sex.

Later Psychodynamic Theories

Freud's theories are some of the most intriguing and enduring in psychology, but they have had critics, even among Freud's followers. Freud viewed behavior and thought as the products of energies that were either contained or released. Where, many people asked, was the person, the self, in Freud's human being?

Several of Freud's followers developed new theories, which emphasized the role of the ego as an independent force striving for mastery and competence (e.g., Jacobson, 1964; Mahler, 1968). Others talked explicitly about the concept of a self and argued that the development of a positive sense of the self is an individual's primary aim (e.g., Kohut, 1984). Freud downplayed the roles of the environment and interpersonal relationships in the development of personality, and several of his contemporaries believed this was a mistake. In the section "Interpersonal Theories of Abnormality," we will review the interpersonal theories, which view social relationships as the driving force of psychological development within individuals. These interpersonal theories grew out of splits between Freud and his followers.

One new school of thought within psychodynamic theory retained significant aspects of Freud's drive theory but integrated them with the role of early relationships in the development of self-concept and personality. This theory is known as **object relations** theory. According to proponents of this school, such as Melanie Klein, Margaret Mahler, Otto Kernberg, and Heinz Kohut, our early relationships create images, or representations, of ourselves and others. We carry these images throughout adulthood and they affect all our subsequent relationships.

According to this theory, there are four fundamental stages in the development of the self-concept. In the first stage, known as the *undifferentiated stage,* the newborn has only an image of the self and no sense that other people and

Melanie Klein questioned some of the principles of Freudian psychoanalytic theory and helped develop object relations theory.

Otto Kernberg is one of the leaders of the object relations school.

objects are separate from the self. The infant believes that the caregiver and itself are one and that everything the infant feels or wants the caregiver feels or wants.

In the second stage, known as *symbiosis*, the infant still does not distinguish between self and other but does distinguish between good and bad aspects of the self-plus-other image. That is, the child has an image of the good self-plus-other and an image of the bad self-plus-other. These images are either all good or all bad.

In the third stage, the *separation-individuation stage*, the child begins to differentiate between the self and the other. The child's images of the good self and the bad self are not integrated, however. The child focuses on either the good self or the bad self exclusively. Similarly, the child's images of the good other and the bad other are not integrated, and the child focuses on only the good other or the bad other. A child who is frustrated with a parent may say, "I hate you!" and mean it with all her heart, because she is focusing only on the bad image of the parent at the time.

In the fourth stage, the *integration stage*, the child is able to distinguish clearly between the self and the other and to integrate the good and bad images of the self and the other into complex representations. This new ability allows a frustrated child to say to a parent, "I am really mad at you, but I still love you."

According to the object relations theorists, many people with psychopathology never fully resolve Stage 2 or 3 and are prone to seeing the self and others as all good or all bad. This tendency is known as **splitting,** because the image of the self

and other is split into the good image and the bad image, with no appreciation for the mixed qualities of good and bad that are true of all people. Also, a person stuck in Stage 2 or 3 never fully differentiates between the self and other and expects others to know what he or she feels and wants.

As we will see, the notion of splitting provides an intriguing explanation for the syndrome known as *borderline personality disorder*. People with this disorder tend to view themselves and other people as either all good or all bad and vacillate between these two images. They either idealize themselves and others or hate themselves and others to the point of wanting to hurt themselves or others. People with borderline personality disorder also tend to have trouble accepting the boundaries between themselves and others. When even slightly rejected by another, they feel completely abandoned and empty.

Assessing Psychodynamic Theories

Freud and the psychodynamic theorists who came after him were the first to establish a systematic explanation of abnormal behavior in terms of psychological principles rather than purely biological or supernatural principles. They were truly the founders of a psychological approach to the study of psychopathology. Moreover, psychodynamic theories are probably the most comprehensive theories of human behavior established to date. For some people, they are also the most satisfying theories. They explain both normal and abnormal behavior with similar processes. And they have an "aha!" quality about them that leads us to believe they hold important insights.

Karen Horney was an early critic of Freud's assertions that personality is fixed in childhood and that women suffer from penis envy.

Psychodynamic theories also have many limitations and weaknesses. One of the earliest critics of Freud's conceptualization of female development was Karen Horney, who was trained in Berlin by Freud's colleagues, Abraham and Sachs, in the early 1900s. Using research from anthropology, sociology, and her own therapy practice, Horney (1934/1967) challenged several assumptions and methods in classical psychoanalysis. These included (1) the emphasis on sexual drives and anatomy in personality and the exclusion of environmental and cultural influences on personality development, (2) the view that the male is the prototypical human being, and (3) the claim that one can describe a universally applicable psychology based on a small sample.

Another major problem with most psychodynamic theories is that it is difficult or impossible to scientifically test their fundamental assumptions (Erdelyi, 1992; although see Westen, 1998). The processes described by these theories are abstract and difficult to measure. The theories themselves often provide ways of explaining away the results of studies that seem to dispute their fundamental assumptions. Perhaps as a result, there is little controlled research testing traditional psychodynamic theories or the newer theories.

Finally, Freud believed that personality is essentially fixed in childhood, with little opportunity for significant change later on, even with therapy. Many of his early critics believed that human personality continues to grow and change in response to changes in the environment and in personal relationships. They believed that therapy does offer significant hope for people who want to change fundamental aspects of their personalities.

In spite of their weaknesses, psychodynamic theories have played a major role in shaping psychology and psychiatry in the past century. The fundamental assumption of traditional psychodynamic theory that unconscious processes drive our behaviors has become a fundamental assumption of laypeople's views of human behaviors. When we find ourselves questioning the "real" motives behind our own or others' behaviors, when we "realize" we are attracted to a certain person because we know our mother would disapprove, or when we recall a traumatic event from the past that we believe we have been repressing, we are applying psychodynamic theories.

Behavioral Theories of Abnormality

Behavioral theories reject claims that unconscious conflicts drive human behavior. Instead, behaviorists focus on the influences of reinforcements and punishments in producing behavior. Like the psychodynamic theorists, behavioral theorists seek to explain both normal and abnormal behavior through the same principles. The principles of behaviorism, however, focus on how behaviors are learned through experiences in the environment. The two core principles or processes of learning according to behaviorism are *classical conditioning* and *operant conditioning*. In later developments of the theory behaviorists acknowledged that learning can occur through *modeling* and *observational learning*.

Classical Conditioning

Ivan Pavlov, a Russian physiologist, was conducting experiments on the salivary glands of dogs when he made discoveries that would revolutionize psychological theory. Not surprisingly, his dogs salivated when Pavlov or an assistant put food in their mouths. Pavlov noticed that, after a while, the dogs began to salivate when he or his assistant simply walked into the room. This process gained the name **classical conditioning.**

Pavlov had paired a previously neutral stimulus (himself) with a stimulus that naturally leads to a certain response (the dish of food, which leads to salivating), and eventually the neutral stimulus (Pavlov) was able to elicit that response (salivation). He named the stimulus that naturally produced the desired response the **unconditioned stimulus (US),** and he named the response created by the unconditioned stimulus the **unconditioned response (UR).** Thus, in Pavlov's experiments, the dish of food was the US and salivation in response

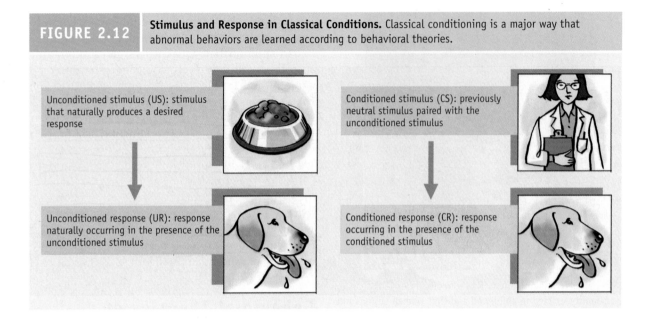

FIGURE 2.12   **Stimulus and Response in Classical Conditions.** Classical conditioning is a major way that abnormal behaviors are learned according to behavioral theories.

Unconditioned stimulus (US): stimulus that naturally produces a desired response

Unconditioned response (UR): response naturally occurring in the presence of the unconditioned stimulus

Conditioned stimulus (CS): previously neutral stimulus paired with the unconditioned stimulus

Conditioned response (CR): response occurring in the presence of the conditioned stimulus

to this food was the UR. He named the previously neutral stimulus the **conditioned stimulus (CS)** and the response that it elicited the **conditioned response (CR).** Thus, Pavlov was the CS, and, when the dogs salivated in response to seeing him, this salivation became the CR (see Figure 2.12).

Classical conditioning has been used to explain people's seemingly irrational responses to a host of neutral stimuli. For example, a college student who failed a test in a particular classroom may break out in a cold sweat when she enters that room again—this response is the result of classical conditioning. The room has become a conditioned stimulus, eliciting a response of anxiety, because it was paired with an unconditioned stimulus (failing an exam) that elicited anxiety.

Classical conditioning can also explain why heroin addicts, if they simply see a syringe, sometimes have physiological responses similar to those they have had when they have injected heroin in the past. They have developed a conditioned physiological response to syringes (which have become a conditioned stimulus), because of the frequent pairing of the syringes with the physiological action of the drugs.

Operant Conditioning

E. L. Thorndike observed that behaviors that are followed by a reward are strengthened, whereas behaviors that are followed by a punishment are weakened. This simple but important observation, which Thorndike labeled the *law of effect,* led to the development of the principles of **operant conditioning**—the shaping of behaviors by providing rewards for desired behaviors and punishments for undesired behaviors.

B. F. Skinner is the psychologist most strongly associated with operant conditioning. In the 1930s, he showed that a pigeon will learn to press on a bar if pressing it is associated with the delivery of food, and it will learn to avoid pressing another bar if pressing it is associated with an electric shock. Similarly, a child will learn to make his bed if he receives a hug and kiss from his mother each time he makes the bed, and he will learn to stop hitting his brother if, every time he hits his brother, he is not allowed to watch his favorite television show that week.

In operant conditioning, behaviors will be learned most quickly if they are paired with the reward or punishment every time the behavior is emitted. This consistent response is called a **continuous reinforcement schedule.** Behaviors can be learned and maintained, however, on a **partial reinforcement schedule,** in which the reward or punishment occurs only sometimes in response to the behavior. **Extinction**—the elimination of a learned behavior—is more difficult when the behavior has been learned through a partial reinforcement schedule than it is when the behavior has been learned through a continuous reinforcement schedule. This is because the behavior has been learned under conditions of occasional reward, so a constant reward is not needed to maintain the behavior. A good example is gambling behavior. People who frequently gamble are seldom rewarded, but they continue to gamble in anticipation of that occasional, unpredictable win.

Combinations of classical and operant conditioning can help explain responses people develop to avoid situations that arouse fear in them. For example, consider a woman who developed a fear of bridges through classical conditioning: She fell off a bridge into icy waters as a child, and now anytime she nears a bridge, she feels very anxious. This woman has developed elaborate means of getting around her hometown without having to cross any bridges. Avoiding the bridges reduces her anxiety, and thus her avoidant behavior is reinforced. This woman has developed a *conditioned avoidance response* through operant conditioning. As a result, however, she never exposes herself to a bridge and never has the opportunity to extinguish her initial fear of bridges. As we will see, many of the therapeutic techniques developed by behavioral theorists are designed to extinguish conditioned avoidance responses, which can interfere greatly with a person's ability to function in everyday life.

Modeling and Observational Learning

Skinner and other "pure" behaviorists have argued that humans and animals learn behaviors only by directly experiencing the rewards or punishments for these behaviors. In the 1950s, however, psychologist Albert Bandura argued that people can also learn behaviors by watching other people, a view that came to be known as **social learning theory.** First, in **modeling,** people learn new behaviors from imitating the behaviors modeled by important people in their lives, such as their parents. Learning through modeling is more likely to occur when the person modeling the behavior is seen as an authority figure or is perceived to be like oneself. For example, Bandura (1969) argued that children are most likely to imitate the behaviors modeled by their same-sex parent, because this parent is an authority figure and because the same-sex parent seems more similar to them than does the opposite-sex parent.

Second, **observational learning** takes place when a person observes the rewards and punishments that another person receives for his or her behavior and then behaves in accord with those rewards and punishments. For example, a child who views her sibling being punished for dropping food on the floor will learn, through observation, the consequences of dropping food on the floor and will be less likely to engage in this behavior herself. Some theorists argue that even extremely negative behaviors, such as teenagers going on a shooting rampage, are also due to observational learning. Teenagers see heroes in the media being rewarded for violent behavior and thus learn that behavior. They also are directly rewarded for violent behavior in certain video games.

The behavioral theory of anxiety would suggest that Albert Ellis' symptoms were the result of experiences of being punished in some way for his

Gambling is reinforced only occasionally by wins, but this makes it more difficult to extinguish the behavior.

public speaking—for example, being ridiculed by an audience member. He learned, through operant conditioning, that he could reduce his anxiety by avoiding speaking engagements.

Assessing Behavioral Theories

The behavioral theorists set the standard for scientifically testing hypotheses about how normal and abnormal behaviors develop. The hypotheses developed from these theories are precise, and the studies that have been done to test these hypotheses are rigorously controlled and exact. These studies have provided strong support for behavioral explanations of many types of abnormal behavior.

The behavioral theories have limitations, however. Certain types of abnormal behaviors can be created in the laboratory, but is this how they develop in the real world? Laboratory studies are artificial and cannot capture the complexity of environmental experiences that shape people's behavior. Like the psychodynamic theories, the behavioral theories have been criticized for not recognizing free will in people's behaviors—the active choices they make to defy the external forces upon them.

Cognitive Theories of Abnormality

The movement that followed the development of the behavioral theories is now known as the cognitive revolution in psychology. Cognitive psychologists made great strides in understanding the processes of memory, attention, and information processing and, by the late 1960s and early 1970s, much of the theorizing about the causes of abnormal behavior had focused on the role of cognitions. The cognitive theorists argued that it is not just rewards, punishments, or even drives that motivate human behavior. Instead, humans actively construct meaning out of their experiences and act in accord with their interpretations of the world.

Cognitive theories of abnormality argue that **cognitions**—thoughts and beliefs—shape our behaviors and the emotions we experience. Several theories of abnormal behavior have focused on three types of cognitions: causal attributions, control beliefs, and dysfunctional assumptions.

When something happens to us, we ask ourselves why that event happened (Abramson, Metalsky, & Alloy, 1989; Abramson, Seligman, & Teasdale, 1978). The answer to this "why" question is our **causal attribution** for the event. The attributions we make for events can influence our behavior, because they influence the meaning we give to events and our expectations for similar events in the future.

For example, if we attribute a friend's rude behavior to temporary or situational factors (he is under a lot of pressure), we do not evaluate that friend too harshly, and we do not expect the friend to act rudely again in the future. However, if we attribute the friend's behavior to personality factors (he is a mean guy), our evaluations of the friend will be more harsh, and we will expect the friend to act rudely again. A personality attribution for the friend's behavior might lead us to avoid the friend or even break up the relationship, whereas a situational attribution would not.

The attributions we make for our own behavior can have a strong effect on our emotions and self-concept. For example, if we act meanly toward another person and attribute this behavior to situational factors (the other person acted meanly first), we may feel slightly guilty but we may also feel justified. However, if we attribute this behavior to personality factors (we are mean), we may feel quite guilty and lose self-esteem. Our attributions for our performance in achievement settings can also affect our self-esteem, our emotions, and our willingness to continue striving. Attributing failure on an exam to situational factors (the exam was too hard) will result in less negative emotion than attributing failure on an exam to personality factors (a lack of intelligence).

A **control theory** focuses on people's expectations regarding their abilities to control important events (Bandura, 1977; Rotter, 1954; Seligman, 1975). When people believe they can control an important event, they behave in ways to control that event. When they believe they are unable to control an event, they do not attempt to control it or easily give up when they have difficulty controlling it. Martin Seligman (1975) argued that repeated experiences with uncontrollable events lead a person to develop *learned helplessness*, the general expectation that future events will be uncontrollable. He described a set of learned helplessness deficits that result from this expectation, including lowered self-esteem, lowered persistence and motivation, and the inability to see opportunities for control when they do arise.

In an update of his social learning theory, Albert Bandura (1977) argued that a major contributor to people's sense of well-being, motivation, and persistence is their sense of *self-efficacy*. Self-efficacy is a person's belief that he or she can successfully execute the behaviors necessary to control desired outcomes. A good example of high self-efficacy is "the little engine that could," which kept saying, "I think I can! I think I can! I think I can!" People with high self-efficacy in a given situation exert more control over that situation, try harder, are more per-

Garfield ®   **by Jim Davis**

Garfield © *Paws, Inc. Reprinted with permission of Universal Press Syndicate. All Rights Reserved.*

sistent, and are more successful in that situation than are people with low self-efficacy (Bandura, 1986). High self-efficacy also protects a person against negative emotional reactions to a situation. For example, consider a person whose home has been ruined in a flood. If she has high self-efficacy, she will maintain her motivation to rebuild her home, will make better decisions about how to rebuild, and will be less likely to become depressed over the loss of her home than if she has a low sense of self-efficacy.

A different set of cognitive theories of psychopathology suggests that we have broad beliefs about how things work, which can be either positive and helpful to us or negative and destructive. These broad beliefs are called **global assumptions.** Two of the prominent proponents of this view are Albert Ellis, whom we met in the Extraordinary People opening segment, and Aaron Beck. They argued that most negative emotions and maladaptive behaviors are the result of one or more of the dysfunctional global assumptions that guide a person's life. Some of the most common dysfunctional assumptions are:

1. I should be loved by everyone for everything I do.
2. Things should turn out the way I want them to turn out.
3. I should be terribly upset by dangerous situations.
4. It is better to avoid problems than to face them.
5. I need someone stronger and more powerful than me to rely on.
6. I should be completely competent, intelligent, and achieving in all I do.
7. Once something affects my life, it will affect it forever.
8. I must have perfect self-control.
9. I have no control over my emotions and cannot help feeling certain feelings.

People who hold such beliefs will often react to situations with irrational thoughts and behaviors and negative emotions. For example, someone who believes that she must be completely competent, intelligent, and achieving in all areas in her life will be extremely upset by even minor failures or bad events, such as tearing her blouse or forgetting to return a phone call. If she were to score poorly on an exam, she could have thoughts such as "I am a total failure. I will never amount to anything. I should have gotten a perfect score on that exam." Similarly, someone who believes that things should

always turn out the way he wants them to may be unable to respond flexibly to the obstacles and setbacks that inevitably stand in the way of achieving goals in daily life. Rather than finding a way around these obstacles, he may focus on the obstacles, distressed that things are not going his way.

In the 1960s and 1970s, effective therapies were developed for the mood and anxiety disorders, based on Beck's and Ellis' theories, and we will discuss these therapies in Chapter 5. These cognitive therapies help clients identify and challenge these negative thoughts and dysfunctional belief systems.

Assessing the Cognitive Theories

The cognitive theories may seem the most comfortable or familiar to you of all the theories we have discussed thus far. If so, that is probably because they are a product of our times and dominate much of current clinical, personality, and social psychology. The cognitive theories are also attractive because they focus on that distinctly human process of abstract thinking. Cognitive theorists have worked hard to provide scientific evidence for their explanations of specific disorders and have been successful in many domains. Particularly in studies of mood disorders and anxiety disorders, and increasingly in studies of sexual disorders and substance use disorders, the cognitive theories have helped explain how unwanted emotions, thoughts, and behaviors develop and are maintained.

The greatest limitation of the cognitive theories has been the difficulty of proving that maladaptive cognitions precede and cause disorders, rather than being the symptoms or consequences

Aaron Beck is one of the founders of cognitive theories of psychopathology.

of the disorders. For example, it is clear that depressed people think depressing thoughts. But is this a cause of their depression or a symptom of it? It turns out to be harder than you might think to answer this question definitively (Coyne & Gotlib, 1983). Even if cognitions can cause changes in mood and behavior, it is clear that changes in mood and behavior can also cause cognitions (Bower, 1981). In other words, there are reciprocal effects, or feedback loops, among cognitions, behaviors, and moods, making it difficult to distinguish cause from effect.

The cognitive theories have also been criticized for assuming that negative beliefs are always irrational and for ignoring the negative lives that some people truly lead. People who believe they have little control over their environments, that they are not good at most things, or that no one loves them may be correct in their beliefs and not distorting reality. Many cognitive theorists would argue, however, that reality is always in the eye of the beholder to some extent and that there are more and less adaptive ways of viewing even the most difficult circumstances.

Humanistic and Existential Theories of Abnormality

More than any of the other theories of abnormality, **humanistic theories** and **existential theories** focus on what we might call "the person" behind the cognitions, the behaviors, and the unconscious conflicts. These theories are based on the assumption that humans have an innate capacity for goodness and for living a full life. Pressure from society to conform to certain norms, rather than to seek one's most developed self, interferes with the fulfillment of this capacity.

The humanistic theories emerged in the 1950s and 1960s, partly in reaction to the pessimistic and deterministic view of human behavior provided by traditional psychodynamic theory and to the claims of traditional behavioral theory that humans are only products of their environment. The humanistic theorists recognized that we are often not aware of the forces shaping our behavior and that the environment can play a strong role in our happiness or unhappiness. But they were optimistic that, once people were made aware of these forces and freed to make choices about the direction of their lives, they would naturally make good choices and be happier.

Carl Rogers (1951) developed the most widely known version of humanistic theory. Rogers believed that, without undue pressure from others, individuals naturally move toward personal growth, self-acceptance, and **self-actualization,** which is the

Carl Rogers (1902–1987) was one of the founders of humanistic theory.

fulfillment of one's potential for love, creativity, and meaning. We can develop a set of values that is all our own, as well as an identity that is free from the expectations of others. Under the stress of pressure from society and family, however, people can develop rigid and distorted perspectives of the self and can lose touch with their own values and needs. This can lead to emotional distress, unhealthy behaviors, and even loss of touch with reality. Rogers developed a form of therapy, called **client-centered therapy,** that is designed to help people realize their genuine selves, accept themselves entirely, and begin growing toward self-actualization (see Chapter 5).

Abraham Maslow, another key figure in the development of the humanistic perspective, argued that humans have a hierarchy of needs, and self-actualization can occur only after lower-order needs are satisfied (see Figure 2.13). The most basic needs are physiological needs, such as hunger. At the highest level of the hierarchy is the need to fulfill one's own personal values and to reach self-actualization. Maslow said that people who are at this highest level of the hierarchy "no longer strive in the ordinary sense, but rather develop. They attempt to grow to perfection and to develop more and more fully in their own style" (Maslow, 1954, p. 211). Maladaptive behavior and general distress can result from a person's inability to fulfill lower-order needs and reach a point of growth instead of striving.

The existential theories of Fritz Perls, Martin Heidegger, and Soren Kierkegaard were based on many of the same beliefs as the humanistic theories. Humans are in control—they have the capacity and the responsibility to direct their lives in meaningful and constructive ways. They also believed that the

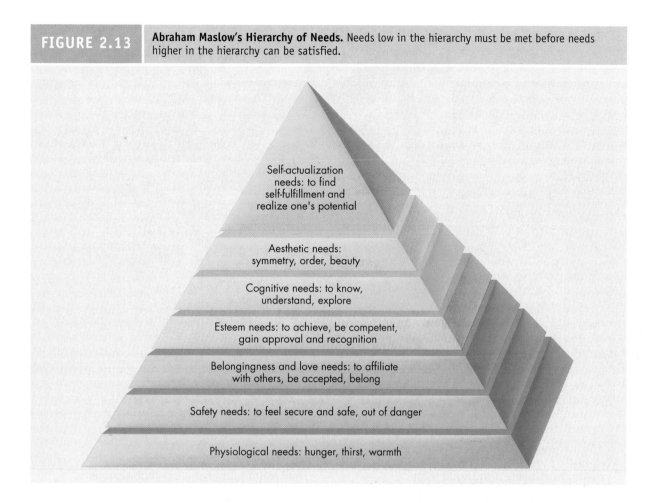

Self-actualization
needs: to find
self-fulfillment and
realize one's potential

Aesthetic needs:
symmetry, order, beauty

Cognitive needs: to know,
understand, explore

Esteem needs: to achieve, be competent,
gain approval and recognition

Belongingness and love needs: to affiliate
with others, be accepted, belong

Safety needs: to feel secure and safe, out of danger

Physiological needs: hunger, thirst, warmth

ultimate goals in human growth are the discovery of one's own values and meaning and the living of one's life by these values.

The existentialists, however, put more emphasis on the difficulties inherent in self-actualization, recognizing that society puts many obstacles in the way of living according to one's own values. *Existential anxiety,* created by the realization of our ultimate death, leads many people to abandon their personal growth and search for meaning. We must overcome this anxiety by choosing to live full and meaningful lives, or our lives will be wasted and corrupted and likely will be filled with misery and maladaptive behaviors.

Assessing Humanistic and Existential Theories

The humanistic theories struck a positive chord in the 1960s and still have many proponents, especially among self-help groups and peer counseling programs. The optimism and attribution of free will of these theories is a refreshing change from the emphasis on pathology and external forces in other theories. These theories change the focus from what is wrong with people to questions about how people can be helped to achieve their greatest potential.

The humanistic and existential theories have been criticized, however, for being vague and impossible to test scientifically. And, as we discuss in Chapter 5, the humanistic therapies may be helpful and interesting to people who are generally healthy and functioning in society, but it is not clear they can help people with serious psychopathology.

SUMMING UP

- Psychodynamic theories of psychopathology focus on unconscious conflicts that cause anxiety and result in maladaptive behavior.

- The ways people handle their conflicts are defined by the types of defense mechanisms they use. Children can become fixated on certain needs or concerns if their transitions through psychosexual stages are not managed well.

- More recent psychodynamic theories focus less on the role of unconscious impulses and more on the development of the individual's self-concept in the context of interpersonal relationships. They describe a greater role for the environment in the shaping of personality

Calvin and Hobbes © *Watterson. Dist. By Universal Press Syndicate. Reprinted with permission. All Rights Reserved.*

and provide more hope for change in personality during adulthood than Freud did.

- The behavioral theories of abnormality focus only on the rewards and punishments in the environment that shape and maintain behavior. Classical conditioning takes place when a previously neutral stimulus is paired with a stimulus that naturally creates a certain response. Eventually the neutral stimulus will also elicit the response.

- Operant conditioning involves rewarding desired behaviors and punishing undesired behaviors.

- People also learn by imitating the behaviors modeled by others and by observing the rewards and punishments others receive for their behaviors.

- Cognitive theories suggest that people's attributions for events, their perceptions of control and self-efficacy, and their global assumptions about themselves and the world influence their behaviors and emotions in reaction to situations.

- Humanistic and existential theories suggest that all humans strive to fulfill their potential for good and to self-actualize. The inability to fulfill one's potential arises from the pressures

of society to conform to others' expectations and values and from existential anxiety.

SOCIAL AND INTERPERSONAL APPROACHES

The psychological theories we have discussed so far focus primarily on the individual. They attribute problematic psychological symptoms to unconscious conflicts, negative cognitions, existential anxiety, and other factors within the individual. Although these theories may suggest that the environment plays a role in creating these problems, they still consider the individual to be the primary focus of analysis. The social approaches to abnormality focus more on the larger social structures within which an individual lives (see Figure 2.14). These structures can include the individual's marriage or family and his or her neighborhood, social class, or culture.

Interpersonal Theories of Abnormality

Humans are social beings. The **interpersonal theories** put this fact at the center of their explanations of the development of normal and abnormal behavior more than any of the theories we have discussed so far. Contemporary interpersonal theories grew out of a split between Freud and one of his students,

FIGURE 2.14

FIGURE 2.14 **Social Approaches to Mental Disorders.** Social approaches to mental disorders look to an individual's relationships to others and place in society for the source of mental disorders.

Interpersonal theories: Mental disorders are the result of long-standing patterns of negative relationships, which have their roots in early experiences with caregivers.

Social structural theories: Societies create mental disorders in individuals by putting them under unbearable stress and by sanctioning abnormal behavior.

Family systems theories: Families create and maintain mental disorders in individual family members to maintain the status quo.

Contrast to Freudian Theory

Alfred Adler. Adler disagreed with Freud's singular focus on unconscious processes within the individual as the force behind human behavior, as well as on Freud's concern with instinctual drives. Adler argued that the primary motivation of humans is to belong to and participate in social groups. Later, other psychodynamic theorists also split with Freud and emphasized social motives and social forces more than sexual drives in shaping humans' behaviors. These theorists included Erich Fromm, Karen Horney, and Erik Erikson.

Erik Erikson proposed a series of stages of psychosocial development that are not concerned with gratifying sexual needs, as in Freud's stages, but with resolving crises in our understanding of the world, ourselves, and our relationships (see Figure 2.15 on page 62). We never fully resolve all of these issues, but some people make better resolutions than others, and these people tend to be happier and better adjusted.

Harry Stack Sullivan (1953) developed ideas similar to those of the object relations school about the roles of important others in the development of self-concept, but he used very different language. He noted that children constantly receive feedback from others for their behaviors—criticism for some behaviors and praise for others. The behaviors and aspects of self that are continually criticized become part of the child's self-concept as the *bad-me*, and the aspects of self that are praised become part of the self-concept as the *good-me*. The bad-me arouses anxiety, so the child develops ways of averting attention from those aspects of the self. If enough anxiety is aroused by those aspects of the self, the child may develop it as the *not-me*, blocking it from consciousness.

All of us have aspects of ourselves we wish to deny—perhaps our anger, our sexual urges, or our competitiveness. Even when these not-me aspects are repressed, they still exert influence on our behavior. We may deny we are angry, but everyone else knows we are angry, for instance. People with severe psychopathology have images of the self and others that are so painful that they engage in self-destructive behavior to avoid these images. For example, a woman whose father secretly abused her as a child may be completely unable to confront these truths about herself and her father and may drink heavily to numb her feelings.

The child's self-concept is part of a broader system of **prototypes**—images of the self and others in relation to the self—that are formed from experiences with family members during childhood. Throughout life, our reactions to others reflect these prototypes. The influence of these prototypes can lead to irrational and exaggerated reactions. For example, an innocent remark by our boss can lead to extreme anxiety or anger because it activates our prototype of our father, who was constantly critical.

More recently, interpersonal theorists have focused on the "scripts" people develop for their relationships—the sets of expectations for how each person in a relationship should behave toward the other. Wives and husbands each have implicit scripts for how the other should behave in the marriage, parents and children have implicit scripts for each other's behaviors, and so on. When these expectations are violated, people can become confused, angry, and frightened, and relationships can dissolve. Other relationships are filled with conflict because patterns of communication break down and the methods partners use to negotiate common goals do not work (Leary, 1957; Wiggins, 1982).

Finally, several theorists have formulated theories of normal and abnormal behavior based on the

FIGURE 2.15	**Erikson's Stages of Psychosocial Development.** Erickson proposed eight stages of psychosocial crises, which can lead to positive or negative development across the life span.

Stage of life	Psychosocial crisis	Favorable outcome
I. Infancy	Trust vs. mistrust	Trust and hope
II. Early childhood	Autonomy vs. shame, doubt	Self-control, sense of adequacy
III. Years 3 to 5	Initiative vs. guilt	Purpose and direction, initiative
IV. Years 6 to puberty	Industry vs. inferiority	Competence
V. Adolescence	Identity vs. confusion	Integrated view of self as unique
VI. Early adulthood	Intimacy vs. isolation	Ability to form close relationships
VII. Middle adulthood	Generativity vs. stagnation	Concern for family, society
VIII. Old age	Integrity vs. despair	Fulfillment and satisfaction, willingness to face death

work of John Bowlby (1969), whose ideas were influenced by psychodynamic thought but also by *ethology*—the study of animal behavior. Bowlby argued that early in life we form strong attachments to our caregivers, and the quality of these attachments then determines our expectations for ourselves and our relationships. On one hand, children who form *secure attachments* are confident that their caregivers will be there when they need them. This confidence gives them the courage to explore their environment, returning to their caregivers for comfort and assistance when necessary. As they mature, children expect other relationships to be secure and seek out and form positive, strong relationships with others.

On the other hand, children who have *insecure attachments* do not have confidence in their caregivers, because their caregivers have not been consistently trustworthy. They may be anxious and clinging to their caregivers, refusing to leave their side. Or they may be hostile and avoidant of caregivers. In either case, these children then have negative expectations for future relationships, which essentially become self-fulfilling prophecies. Children with anxious, insecure attachments become adults who are prone to anxiety, depression, and excessive dependence on others. Children with avoidant, insecure attachments may become adults who are hostile, isolated, and even violent. When we discuss childhood disorders in Chapter 13, we will see that the field of developmental psychopathology, which focuses on how normal development goes awry to produce psychopathology in children, has incorporated attachment theory into several of its theories of the development of specific disorders.

A number of empirical studies have tested the interpersonal theories in recent years. Some of the hypotheses about the importance of prototypes, or "mental models," of early relationships in shaping adult relationships have been supported (Banse, 2004; Fraley & Bonanno, 2004; Roisman, Tsai, & Chiang, 2004). In addition, new therapies based on the interpersonal theories are proving helpful in several disorders, as we discuss in Chapter 5.

Family Systems Theories of Abnormality

Most of the theories we have discussed thus far have implicated the family in the development of both normal and abnormal behavior. The **family systems theories** and therapies focus on the family in quite a different manner from the other theories, however (Minuchin, 1981; Mirsalimi et al., 2003; Satir, 1967). These theories see the family as a complex system, which works to maintain the status quo or *homeostasis*. Each family has its own hierarchy and set of rules, which govern the behavior of the members and help maintain homeostasis. The family system can function well and be healthy for its individual members, supporting their growth and accepting their change. Or the family system can be dysfunctional, in essence requiring psychopathology in one or more members in order to maintain the status quo.

When a member of the family has a psychological disorder, family systems theorists see it not as a problem within the individual but as an indication of a dysfunctional family system. Psychopathology in an individual reflects pathology or dysfunction in the family, according to family systems theory. The particular form that any individual's psychopathology takes depends on the complex interactions among the family's cohesiveness, adaptability to change, and communication style.

For example, an *inflexible family* is resistant to and isolated from all forces outside the family and does not adapt well to changes within the family, such as a child moving into adolescence. In an *enmeshed family*, each member is too greatly involved in the lives of the other members, to the point that individuals do not have personal autonomy and can feel controlled. In contrast, a *disengaged family* is one in which the members pay no attention to each other and operate as independent units isolated from other family members. And in *pathological triangular relationships*, parents avoid dealing with conflicts with each other by always keeping their children involved in their conversations and activities (Mirsalimi et al., 2003). Thus, a family theorist trying to understand Albert Ellis' anxiety would examine how his family functioned as he grew up and how that continued to influence him an adult.

Some of the research on family systems theories of psychopathology has focused on disorders in the children in the family, particularly eating disorders (e.g., Minuchin, Rosman, & Baker, 1978). This research suggests that many young girls who develop eating disorders are members of enmeshed families. The parents of these girls are overcontrolling and overinvested in their children's success, and in turn the children feel smothered and dependent on their parents. Anorexia nervosa, a disorder in which an individual refuses to eat and becomes emaciated, may be a girl's way of claiming some control over her life. The family system of these girls maintains and supports the anorexia, rather than working to help her overcome her anorexia. The anorexia becomes a focal point and excuse for the family's enmeshment.

As we discuss in Chapter 5, the family systems theories have led to therapeutic approaches that have proven useful for some types of disorders. Family systems therapies may be particularly appropriate in the treatment of children, because children are so much more entwined in their families than adults. Although the details of many family systems theories have not been thoroughly tested in research, it is clear that families can contribute to or help diminish psychological symptoms in their members (e.g., Mirsalimi et al., 2003).

Social Structural Theories of Abnormality

Social structural theories suggest that we need to look beyond the family to the larger society to find

Family therapists believe that individuals' problems are rooted in patterns of interaction among family members.

the causes of psychopathology in individuals. First, society can create stresses on individuals that increase their risk for psychopathology. These stresses may come in the form of a massive reorganization of the society, such as the industrialization of America in the early twentieth century or the great increases in the presence of people of Hispanic origins in the American West in the past decade. Such societal reorganization changes people's roles and relationships to the society—from factory worker to unemployed person or from member of the majority culture to member of a multicultural society. Societies undergoing significant social change often experience increases in the rates of mental disorders. This is especially true if the change is generally seen as a negative one, as during an economic depression.

Second, some people live in more chronically stressful circumstances than others, and these people appear to be at greater risk for psychopathology. For example, people living in poverty-stricken urban neighborhoods experience more problems, especially substance abuse, juvenile delinquency, depression, and anxiety (Belle & Doucet, 2003). Just what makes some neighborhoods toxic is a matter of debate among researchers.

One model for the effects of neighborhoods on mental health is given in Figure 2.16 (on page 64). Certain characteristics of neighborhoods seem important, such as high rates of poverty, the frequent experience of prejudice and discrimination due to ethnic minority status, families moving in and out of neighborhoods frequently, a lack of cultural or

FIGURE 2.16   **A Social Structural Model of Mental Health.** Social structural theories focus on the effects of the larger society on individuals' mental health.

Neighborhood characteristics
Widespread poverty
Prejudice and discrimination
Lack of cultural or ethnic ties
High residential turnover
High child-to-adult ratio

+

Social organization
Lack of common values
Lack of social control
Open conflict

Psychological stress
Insufficient resources
Chronic agitation and fear

Subcultural influences
Development of gangs
and drug use

→

Mental-health outcomes
Child maltreatment
Juvenile delinquency
Behavioral disorders
Depression
Anxiety
Schizophrenia
Substance abuse

Source: Based on Wandersman & Nation, 1998.

ethnic ties among neighbors, and high numbers of children relative to the numbers of adults (Earls, 2001; Leventhal & Brooks-Gunn, 2003). These characteristics contribute to a scarcity of financial resources for individual families, a lack of cohesion and common values in the neighborhood, an unwillingness of neighbors to monitor and constrain the behavior of each other's children, and often open conflict between neighbors. In such neighborhoods, subcultures often emerge that offer members a means of coping with the stresses they face, but in maladaptive ways, such as through drugs and crime. Other people are chronically agitated and afraid, seeing no way out. All these forces then result in high rates of a number of mental-health problems, from behavioral disorders to depression (Wandersman & Nation, 1998).

Finally, societies may influence the types of psychopathology their members show by having implicit or explicit rules about what types of abnormal behavior are acceptable and in what circumstances. Throughout this book, we will see that the rates of disorders vary from one culture or ethnic group to another and between males and females. For example, people from "traditional" cultures, such as the Old Order Amish in the United States, appear to have less depression than people in modern cultures (Egeland & Hostetter, 1983). In addition, the particular manifestations of disorders seem to vary from one culture to another. For example, the symptoms of anorexia nervosa, the disorder in which people refuse to eat, appear to be different in Asian cultures than in American culture. Finally, there may be many disorders that are specific to certain cultures.

Assessing Social Approaches

The social approaches to abnormality argue that we should analyze the larger social and cultural forces that may be influencing people's behavior. It is not enough to look only at what is going on within individuals or their immediate surroundings. Social approaches are often credited for not "blaming the victim," as other theories seem to do, by placing responsibility for psychopathology within the individual. The social approaches also raise our consciousness about our responsibility within families and as a society to change the social conditions that put some individual members at risk for psychopathology.

The social structural theories can be criticized, however, for being somewhat vague about the exact ways in which social and cultural forces lead to psychological disturbance in individuals. Just how is it that social change or stress leads to depression, schizophrenia, and so on? Why does it lead to depression in some people but to drug abuse in others? Why do most people exposed to social stress and change develop no psychological disturbance at all? These theories and the studies testing them are becoming more complex as they attempt to answer such questions.

SUMMING UP

- The interpersonal theories assert that our self-concepts and expectations of others are based on our early attachments and relationships to caregivers.

- Family systems theories suggest that families form cohesive systems, which regulate the behavior of each member in the system. Sometimes these systems support and enhance the well-being of their members but sometimes they do not.

- Social structural theories suggest that society contributes to psychopathology in some people by creating severe stresses for them, then allowing or encouraging them to cope with these stresses with psychological symptoms. People living in chronically stressful environments have higher rates of psychopathology.

CHAPTER INTEGRATION

Surely, you might be saying to yourself, after decades of research and with the modern scientific techniques available, we must know which of the many theories covered in this chapter is right or correct. Or at least we should know which of these theories best explains specific disorders. As we go through each disorder, we will discuss which theories have been supported best by modern scientific methods.

As we noted at the beginning of this chapter, however, many scientists believe that only models that *integrate* biological, psychological, and social factors can provide comprehensive explanations of psychological disorders. Only integrated models can explain why many people with disordered genes or deficiencies in neurotransmitters do *not* develop painful emotional symptoms or bizarre thoughts. Similarly, only integrated models can suggest how traumatic experiences and toxic interpersonal relationships can cause changes in the basic biochemistry of the brain, which then cause changes in a person's emotions, thoughts, and behaviors.

Figure 2.17 illustrates how some of the biological, psychological, and social factors discussed in this chapter might come together to contribute, for example, to symptoms of depression. First, some people are born with certain genetic characteristics that lead to poor functioning of the hypothalamic-pituitary-adrenal axis. Chronic arousal of this axis may lead individuals to be overly responsive to stress. If they tend to interpret their reactions to stress in terms of "I can't cope!" this can lead them

FIGURE 2.17 How Some Biological, Psychological, and Social Factors Might Interact to Cause Depression

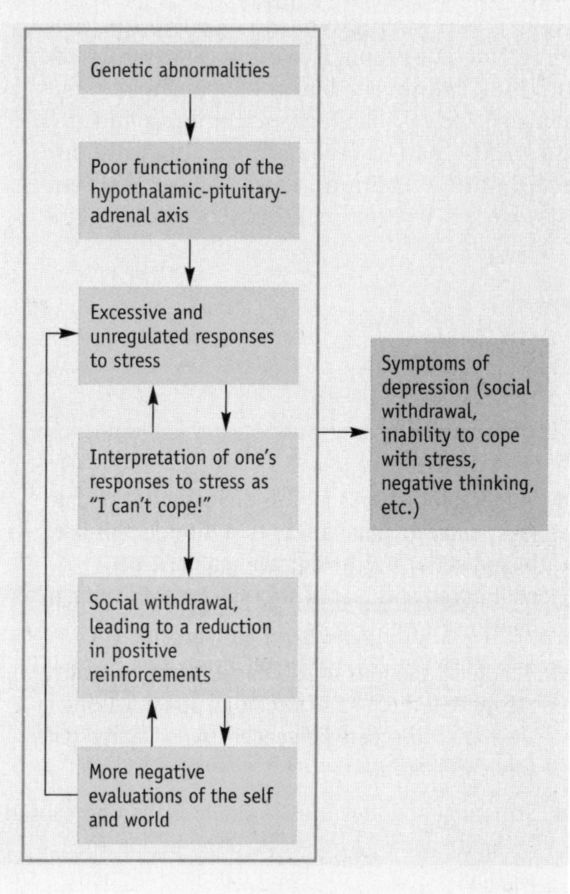

to develop a negative thinking style. This negative thinking style then can cause them to withdraw socially, leading to a reduction in positive reinforcements. This could feed negative evaluations of themselves and the world, further contributing to depression. Then, when they are confronted with new stressors, they might not have good strategies for coping with them and might overreact psychologically as well as physiologically. All these processes come together to produce the key symptoms of depression—social withdrawal, an inability to cope with stress, negative thinking, and so on.

Extraordinary People: Follow-Up

After Ellis had his personal insights into the sources of his own anxiety symptoms, he received his doctorate in psychology from Columbia Teacher's College and took training to become a psychoanalyst. He soon rejected psychoanalytic thinking and, by the late 1950s, had established the Institute for Rational-Emotive Therapy. Over the subsequent 50 years, he has written many books on this type of therapy, as well as on sexuality, has treated thousands of clients, and has given thousands of public lectures. He says, "I love my work . . . I like helping people." (Warga, 1988, p. 58)

Chapter Summary

- Vulnerability-stress models suggest that people must carry a vulnerability to a disorder (usually biological or psychological) and must be confronted with social stresses for a disorder to develop (review Figure 2.1).

- Biological theories of psychopathology typically attribute symptoms to structural abnormalities in the brain, disordered biochemistry, or faulty genes (review Figure 2.4).

- Structural abnormalities in the brain can be caused by faulty genes, by disease, or by injury. The particular area of the brain damaged influences the symptoms individuals show.

- Many biological theories attribute psychopathology to imbalances in neurotransmitters or to the functioning of receptors for neurotransmitters.

- Genetic theories of abnormality usually suggest that it takes an accumulation of faulty genes to cause a psychopathology. Genetic theories are tested with family history studies, twin studies, and adoption studies.

- Psychodynamic theories of psychopathology focus on unconscious conflicts that cause anxiety in the individual and result in maladaptive behavior (review Concept Overview in Table 2.1). Freud argued that these conflicts arise when the libidinal impulses of the id clash with the constraints on behavior imposed by the ego and superego.

- Psychodynamic theories say that the ways people handle their conflicts are defined by the types of defense mechanisms they use (review Table 2.2). How caregivers handle children's transitions through the psychosexual stages determines the concerns or issues the children may become fixated upon.

- More recent psychodynamic theorists focus less on the role of unconscious impulses and more on the development of the individual's self-concept in the context of interpersonal relationships. They see a greater role for the environment in shaping personality and have more hope for change during adulthood than Freud did.

- The behaviorist theories of abnormality reject notions of unconscious conflicts and focus only on the rewards and punishments in the environment that shape and maintain behavior.

- Classical conditioning takes place when a previously neutral stimulus is paired with a stimulus that naturally creates a certain response; eventually, the neutral stimulus will also elicit the response (review Figure 2.12).

- Operant conditioning involves rewarding desired behaviors and punishing undesired behaviors.

- People also learn by imitating the behaviors modeled by others and by observing the rewards and punishments others receive for their behaviors.

- Cognitive theories suggest that people's attributions for events, their perceptions of control and self-efficacy, and their global beliefs and assumptions influence the behaviors and emotions they have in reaction to situations.

- Humanist and existential theories suggest that all humans strive to fulfill their potential for good and to self-actualize. The inability to fulfill one's potential arises from the pressures of society to conform to others' expectations and values and from existential anxiety.

- Interpersonal theories suggest that children develop internal models of the self and others through their attachments and relationships with early caregivers. These models then affect their behaviors and later relationships, sometimes in unhealthy ways.

- Family systems theories suggest that psychopathology in individual family members is due to dysfunctional patterns of interaction within families, which create and maintain the abnormal behaviors.

- Social structural theories suggest that societies create severe stresses for some people, and then subcultures can sanction maladaptive ways of coping with these stresses. Cultures also have implicit and explicit rules for the types of abnormal behavior that are permissible in the society.

MindMap CD-ROM

The following resources on the MindMap CD-ROM that came with this text will help you to master the content of this chapter and prepare for tests:

- Interactive segment: Parts of the Brain
- Video: Functions of Neurotransmitters
- Interactive segment: Identifying Psychological Perspectives
- Chapter Timeline
- Chapter Quiz

Key Terms

theory 34
biological approach 34
psychological approach 34
social approach 34
vulnerability-stress models 35
cerebral cortex 38
hypothalamus 38
limbic system 38
neurotransmitters 39
synapse 39
receptors 39
reuptake 39
degradation 39
endocrine system 40
hormone 40
pituitary 41
behavior genetics 42
polygenic 42
family history study 42
monozygotic (MZ) twins 42
predisposition 43
dizygotic (DZ) twins 43
twin studies 43
concordance rate 43

adoption study 44
psychodynamic theories 46
psychoanalysis 46
catharsis 47
repression 47
libido 47
id 47
pleasure principle 47
primary process thinking 48
ego 48
reality principle 48
secondary process thinking 48
superego 49
introject 49
unconscious 49
preconscious 49
conscious 49
defense mechanisms 49
neurotic paradox 49
psychosexual stages 49
oral stage 50
anal stage 50
phallic stage 51
Oedipus complex 51

> Chapter 3

The Global Seat
by Christian Pierre

There's no limit to how complicated things can get, on account of one thing always leading to another.

—E. B. White

The Research Endeavor <

Extraordinary People

The Old Order Amish of Pennsylvania

Imagine that you live in a quiet, close-knit rural community, surrounded by family and friends. You purposely live a simple life and shun notoriety and attention.

Then imagine having a team of investigators come into your community, asking detailed questions about the most distressing, embarrassing, and intimate experiences of your life and the lives of your family members and closest friends. The team also asks community leaders to report on unusual behaviors by members of the community.

Most of us would not agree to such an experience. We value our privacy and don't want anyone making public the problems that we or our loved ones have faced, yet one extraordinary community agreed to open itself to researchers, and from that research has come some of the most interesting and important work on the mood disorders—depression and mania (see Chapter 9)—that has been published in the scientific literature. That community is the Old Order Amish of southeastern Pennsylvania.

The Amish are a religious sect who avoid contact with the "modern" world and live a simple, agrarian life, much as people lived in the eighteenth century. The Amish use horse and buggy as transportation, most of their homes do not have electricity or telephones, and there is little movement of people into or out of this culture. It is a theocratic society, with the community divided according to church districts and led by church elders. The Amish are pacifists, and they avoid involvement with local and national politics and practices. The rules of social behavior among the Amish are very strict, and roles within the community are clearly set. Members who do not comply with community norms are isolated or shunned.

Despite their self-enforced isolation from mainstream American society, the Amish of southeastern Pennsylvania welcomed researcher Janice Egeland and several of her colleagues to conduct some of the most intensive studies of depression and mania ever done (Egeland, 1986, 1994; Egeland & Hostetter, 1983; Pauls, Morton, & Egeland, 1992). These researchers first attempted to ascertain how common depression and mania were among the Amish. They searched the records of local hospitals for Amish people who had been hospitalized for psychological problems. They also interviewed thousands of members of this community (which, in total, numbered about 12,000) to discover people with mood disorders who had not yet been hospitalized.

Thanks to this closed community, which opened itself to research on psychological disorders, and to the tireless work by researcher Janice Egeland and colleagues, researchers have come a long way in understanding the major mood disorders.

Research in abnormal psychology is similar in many ways to research in many other fields. There are some special challenges in studying psychopathology, however. One of the greatest is that the populations of interest—such as the Old Order Amish in the *Extraordinary People* feature, or people who are paranoid and hearing voices—can be difficult to convince to participate in research.

Another challenge is that abnormal behaviors and feelings are extremely difficult to measure accurately. We cannot see, hear, or feel other people's emotions and thoughts. Researchers must often rely on people's own accounts, or *self-reports*, of their internal states and experiences. Self-reports can be distorted in a number of ways, intentionally or unintentionally. Similarly, relying on an observer's assessments of a person also has pitfalls. The observer's assessments can be biased by stereotypes involving gender and culture, idiosyncratic biases, and lack of information.

A third challenge is that most forms of abnormality probably have multiple causes. Unless a single study can capture the biological, psychological, and social causes of the abnormality of interest, it cannot fully explain the causes of that abnormality. Rarely can a single study accomplish so much. Instead, we are usually left with partial answers to the question of what causes a certain abnormality, and we must piece together the partial answers from several studies to get a full picture of that abnormality.

Despite these challenges, tremendous strides have been made in our understanding of many forms of abnormality in the past 50 years or so, thanks to the cleverness and persistence of researchers. Researchers overcome many of the challenges of researching abnormality by using a *multimethod approach*, which means they use a variety of methodologies. Each method may have some limitations, but taken together, the various methods can provide convincing evidence concerning an abnormality.

In this chapter, we discuss the most common methods of doing research on abnormality. We consider one very common psychological problem, depression, and talk about how to test a simple idea about this problem—the idea that stress is a cause of depression—using various research methods. Of course, the research methods we discuss can be used to test many different ideas, but, by applying all the methods to one idea, we can see how many tools researchers have at their disposal to test a given idea.

THE SCIENTIFIC METHOD

Any research project involves a basic series of steps. These steps are designed to obtain and evaluate information relevant to a problem in a systematic way—a process often called the **scientific method.**

The first step is to select and define a problem. In our case, the problem is to determine the relationship between stress and depression. Then, a testable statement of what is predicted to happen in the study must be formulated. Next, the method for testing the prediction must be chosen and implemented. Once the data have been collected and analyzed, the researcher draws the appropriate conclusions. Finally, the results are written in a research report.

Defining the Problem and Stating a Hypothesis

Throughout this chapter, we examine the idea that stress causes depression. Even this simple idea is too broad and abstract to test directly. Thus, we must state a hypothesis based on this idea. A **hypothesis** is a testable statement of what we predict will happen in the study.

To generate a hypothesis, we might ask, "What kind of evidence would support the idea that stress causes depression?" If we find that people who had recently experienced stress are more likely to be depressed than people who had not recently experienced stress, this evidence would support our idea. One hypothesis, then, is that people who have recently experienced stress are more likely to be depressed than people who have not. This hypothesis can be tested by a number of research methods.

If we find support for this hypothesis, we will have support for our idea. Our idea will not be proven correct, however. No one study can do that. However, a series of studies supporting our idea will bolster our confidence in the idea, particularly if these studies have different methodologies.

The alternative version of our hypothesis is that people who experience stress are *not* more likely to develop depression than are people who do not experience stress. This expectation, that there is *no relationship* between the phenomena being studied—in this case, stress and depression, is called the **null hypothesis.** Results often support the null hypothesis instead of the researcher's primary hypothesis.

Does support for the null hypothesis mean that the underlying idea has been disproved? No. The null hypothesis can be supported for many reasons. Most important, the study may not be designed well enough to provide support for the primary hypothesis. Researchers will often continue to test their primary hypothesis, using a variety of methodologies. If the null hypothesis continues to get much more support than the primary hypothesis, they eventually either modify or drop the primary hypothesis.

Choosing and Implementing a Research Method

Once we have stated a hypothesis, the next step in testing our idea that stress leads to depression is to choose how we are going to define the phenomena we are studying.

A **variable** is a factor or characteristic that can vary within an individual or between individuals. Weight, mood, neurotransmitter levels, and attitudes toward one's mother are all factors that can vary over time, so they are considered variables. Similarly, height, sex, and ethnicity are factors that do not vary for an individual over time, but they can vary from one individual to another, so they, too, can be considered variables.

A **dependent variable** is the factor being predicted in a study. In our studies of stress and depression, we will be trying to predict depressive symptoms, so depression is our dependent variable.

An **independent variable** is the factor that is believed to affect the dependent variable. In our studies, stress is our independent variable.

In order to research depression and stress, we must define what we mean by these terms. As we will discuss in Chapter 9, *depression* is a syndrome or collection of the following symptoms: sadness, loss of interest in one's usual activities, weight loss or gain, changes in sleep, agitation or slowing down, fatigue and loss of energy, feelings of worthlessness or excessive guilt, problems in concentration or indecisiveness, and suicidal thoughts (American Psychiatric Association, 2000). Some researchers define depressed people as those who can be diagnosed with a depressive disorder. Anyone who had some of these symptoms of depression but has not been diagnosed with a depressive disorder would be considered not depressed. Other researchers focus on the full range of depressive symptoms, from no symptoms to moderate symptoms to the most severe symptoms. They divide people into those who show depressive symptoms, those who show moderately severe depressive symptoms, and those who show severe depressive symptoms.

Stress is more difficult to define, because the term has been used in so many ways in research and the popular press. *Stressor* refers to an *event* that is uncontrollable, is unpredictable, and challenges the limits of people's abilities to cope. *Stress* has been used to refer to people's *emotions and behaviors* in response to such stressful events.

Operationalization is the way a researcher measures or manipulates the variables in a study. Our definitions of depression and stress will influence how we operationalize these variables. For example, if we define depression as symptoms meeting criteria for a depressive disorder, then we will operationalize depression as diagnoses. If we define depression as symptoms along the entire range of severity, then we might operationalize depression as scores on a depression questionnaire.

In operationalizing stress, we must first decide whether to focus on stressful events or on people's stress reactions to these events. Then we must devise a measure of what we define as stress or a way of manipulating or creating stress, so that we can then examine people's reactions to this stress. As

we discuss different research methods in this chapter, we examine several operationalizations of stress. In the remaining sections of the book, we discuss various methods of testing hypotheses, as well as the conclusions one can and cannot draw from these methods.

SUMMING UP

- The scientific method is a set of steps designed to obtain and evaluate information relevant to a problem in a systematic way.
- A hypothesis is a testable statement of what a researcher expects to happen in a study.
- A null hypothesis is the statement that the outcome of the study will contradict the primary hypothesis of the study. Usually, the null hypothesis says that the variables (such as stress and depression) are unrelated to one another.
- A variable is a factor that can vary within an individual or between individuals.
- A dependent variable is the factor that is being predicted in a study.
- An independent variable is the factor being used to predict the dependent variable.
- Operationalization is the way the variables of interest are measured or manipulated.

CASE STUDIES

Throughout this book, you will see **case studies**— detailed histories of individuals who have suffered a form of psychological disorder. Case studies have been used for centuries as a way of trying to understand the experiences of individuals and to make more general inferences about the sources of psychopathology.

If we wanted to use a case study to test our idea that stress causes depression, we would focus on an individual, interviewing him or her at length to discover the links between periods of depression and stressful events in his or her life. We might also interview close friends and family to obtain additional information. Based on the information we gathered, we would create a detailed description of the causes of his or her depressive episodes, with an emphasis on the role of stressful events in these episodes. For example, the following brief case study describes singer Kurt Cobain of the hit 1990s rock band Nirvana. It was written by a reporter a week after Cobain committed suicide.

Cobain always had a fragile constitution (he was subject to bronchitis, as well as the recurrent stomach pains he claimed drove him to a heroin addiction). The image one gets is that of a frail kid batted between warring parents. "[The divorce] just destroyed his life," Wendy O'Connor tells Michael Averred in the Nirvana biography *Come As You Are*. "He changed completely. I think he was ashamed. And he became very inward—he just held everything [in]. . . . I think he's *still* suffering." As a teen, Cobain dabbled in drugs and punk rock and dropped out of school. His father persuaded him to pawn his guitar and take an entrance exam for the navy. But Cobain soon returned for the guitar. "To them, I was wasting my life," he told the *Los Angeles Times*. "To me, I was fighting for it." Cobain didn't speak to his father for 8 years. When Nirvana went to the top of the charts, Don Cobain began keeping a scrapbook. "Everything I know about Kurt," he told Azerrad, "I've read in newspapers and magazines."

The more famous Nirvana became, the more Cobain wanted none of it. . . . Nirvana—with their stringy hair, plaid work shirts, and torn jeans—appealed to a mass of young fans who were tired of false idols like Madonna and Michael Jackson and who'd never had a dangerous rock-and-roll hero to call their own. Unfortunately, the band also appealed to the sort of people Cobain had always hated: poseurs and band wagoneers, not to mention record company execs and fashion designers who fell over themselves cashing in on the new sights and sounds. Cobain, who'd grown up as an angry outsider, tried to shake his celebrity. . . .

By 1992, it became clear that Cobain's personal life was as tangled and troubling as his music. The singer married [Courtney] Love in Waikiki—the bride wore a moth-eaten dress once owned by actress Frances Farmer—and the couple embarked on a self destructive pas de deux widely referred to as a 90s version of *Sid and Nancy*. As Cobain put it, "I was going off with Courtney and we were scoring drugs and we were f—king up against a wall and stuff . . . and causing scenes just to do it. It was fun to be with someone who would stand up all of a sudden and smash a glass on the table." In September 1992, *VanityFair* reported that Love had used heroin while she was pregnant with [their daughter] Frances Bean. She and Cobain denied the story (the baby is healthy). But authorities were reportedly concerned enough to force them to surrender custody of Frances to Love's sister, Jamie, for a month, during which time the couple was, in Cobain's words, "totally suicidal.". . .

[T]hose who knew the singer say there was a real fragility buried beneath the noise of his music and his life. . . . If only someone had heard the alarms ringing at that rambling, gray-shingled home near the lake. Long before there was a void in our hearts, there was a void in Kurt Cobain's. (Giles, 1994, pp. 46–47)

In-depth histories of troubled people, such as, Kurt Cobain, may be rich in detail but not generalizable.

Case studies are a time-honored method of research for several reasons. No other method captures the uniqueness of the individual as much as a case study. The nuances of an individual's life and experiences can be detailed, and the individual's own words can be used to describe his or her experiences. Exploring the unique experiences of individuals and honoring their own perspectives on these experiences are important goals for many researchers, and in-depth case studies of individual lives have become more popular in recent years.

Case studies are sometimes the only way to study rare problems, because there simply are not enough people with that problem to study through any other method. For example, much of the research on people with multiple personalities has come from case studies, because this form of psychopathology has historically been quite rare.

Case studies can be invaluable in helping generate new ideas and provide tentative support for those ideas. Most of Freud's theories came from his case studies of people he treated. Freud would listen for hours to his patients' descriptions of their lives, their dreams, and their memories and would notice themes in these reports, which he speculated were related to the psychological symptoms they were suffering. Freud was often quite hesitant in stating his ideas in his reports of his work, encouraging further research to test his ideas.

Today one of the most common uses of case studies is in drug treatment research to report unusual reactions patients have had to certain drugs. These reports can alert other clinicians to watch for similar reactions in their patients. If enough case reports of these unusual reactions emerge in the literature, larger-scale research to study the sources of these reactions may be warranted.

Evaluating Case Studies

Case studies have their drawbacks, however. The first involves **generalizability**—the ability to apply what has been learned to other individuals or groups. The conclusions drawn from the study of an individual may not apply to many other individuals. This limitation is especially true when case studies focus on people whose experiences have been dramatic but unusual. For example, the circumstances leading to Kurt Cobain's death may be very interesting, but they may not tell us anything about why other people commit suicide. As we noted in Chapter 2, even some of Freud's contemporaries criticized him for attempting to generate universal theories of human psychological functioning based on the experiences of his patients who were suffering from psychopathology.

Case studies also suffer from a lack of *objectivity* on the part of both the people telling their stories and the therapists or researchers listening to the stories. The people telling their stories might have biased recollections of their pasts and may selectively report events that happen to them in the present. The therapists or researchers listening to the stories filter them through their own beliefs and assumptions about the causes of human behavior and might selectively remember the parts of the stories that support their beliefs and assumptions and selectively forget the parts that do not. Thus, two case studies of the same person, if conducted by two researchers, may come to very different conclusions about the motivations and key events in that person's life.

Researchers bring their own perspectives to a case study; as a result, one case study may not *replicate*—repeat the conclusions of—another. **Replication** is a key feature of the scientific method. Difficulties in replication are one of the major drawbacks of case studies.

SUMMING UP

- Case studies are in-depth histories of the experiences of individuals.

- The advantages of case studies are their richness in detail, their attention to the unique experiences of individuals, their ability to focus on rare problems, and their ability to generate new ideas.

- The disadvantages of case studies are their lack of generalizability, their lack of objectivity, and difficulties in replication.

CORRELATIONAL STUDIES

Correlational studies examine the relationship between an independent variable and a dependent variable without manipulating either variable. Correlational studies are the most common type of study in psychology and medicine. For example, you will often read about studies of the relationship between television watching and violence, smoking and heart disease, or Internet use and depression, in which researchers have not manipulated any variables but have examined the naturally occurring relationships between the variables.

There are many kinds of correlational studies. The most common type in abnormal psychology is a study of two or more continuous variables. A **continuous variable** is measured along a continuum. For example, on a scale measuring the severity of depression, scores might fall along a continuum from 0 (no depression) to 100 (extreme

Calvin and Hobbes

by Bill Watterson

depression). On a scale measuring the number of recent stressors, scores might fall along a continuum from 0 (no stressors) to 20 (20 or more recent stressors). If we measured severity of depression and number of recent stressors in the same group of people and then looked at the relationship between these two continuous variables, we would be doing a continuous variable correlational study.

Another type of correlational study is a **group comparison study.** In this type of study, researchers are interested in the relationship between people's membership in a particular group and their scores on some other variable. For example, we might be interested in the relationship between depression and whether or not people have experienced a specific type of stress, such as the loss of a loved one. In this case, the groups of interest are bereaved and nonbereaved people. We would find people who represented these two groups, then measure depression in both groups. This is still a correlational study because we are only observing the relationship between two variables—bereavement and depression—not manipulating any variable. In this type of study, however, at least one of the variables—group membership—is not a continuous variable.

Both continuous variable studies and group comparison studies can be either **cross-sectional**—they observe people at only one point in time—or **longitudinal**—they observe people on two more occasions over time. Longitudinal studies have a major advantage over cross-sectional studies, because they can show that the independent variable precedes and predicts changes in the dependent variable over time. For example, a longitudinal study of stress and depression can show that people who are not depressed at the beginning of the study are much more likely to be depressed later in the study if they have experienced a stressful event in the interim than if they have not.

| **FIGURE 3.1** | **A Positive Correlation.** A positive correlation indicates that, as values of the independent variable increase, values of the dependent variable increase. This graph illustrates a correlation of +1.00. |

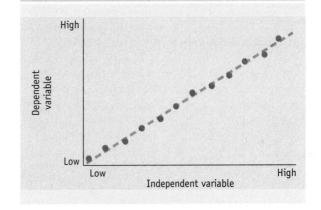

Measuring the Relationship Between Variables

In most correlational studies, the relationship between the variables is indicated by a correlation coefficient. Let us review what this statistic is and how to interpret it.

Correlation Coefficient

A **correlation coefficient** is a statistic used to represent the relationship between variables, and it is usually denoted with the symbol r. A correlation coefficient can fall between -1.00 and $+1.00$. A positively valued correlation coefficient indicates that, as values of the independent variable increase, values of the dependent variable increase (see Figure 3.1). For example, a *positive correlation* between stress and depression would mean that people who reported more stressors had higher levels of depression.

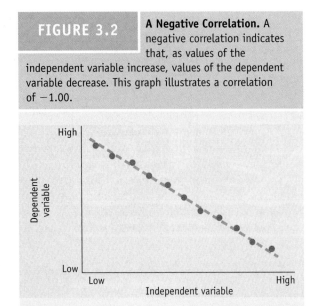

FIGURE 3.2 | **A Negative Correlation.** A negative correlation indicates that, as values of the independent variable increase, values of the dependent variable decrease. This graph illustrates a correlation of −1.00.

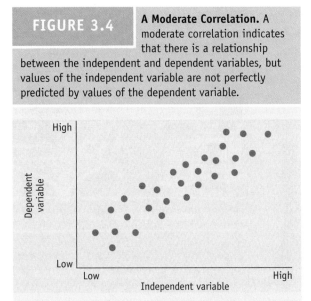

FIGURE 3.4 | **A Moderate Correlation.** A moderate correlation indicates that there is a relationship between the independent and dependent variables, but values of the independent variable are not perfectly predicted by values of the dependent variable.

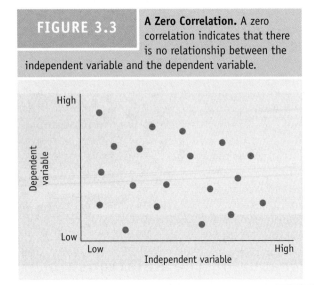

FIGURE 3.3 | **A Zero Correlation.** A zero correlation indicates that there is no relationship between the independent variable and the dependent variable.

A negatively valued correlation coefficient indicates that, as values of the independent variable increase, values of the dependent variable decrease (see Figure 3.2). If we were still measuring stressors and depression, a *negative correlation* would mean that people who reported more stressors actually had lower levels of depression. This is an unlikely scenario, but there are many instances of negative correlations between variables. For example, people who have more positive social support from others typically have lower levels of depression.

The magnitude (size) of a correlation is the degree to which the variables move in tandem with each other. It is indicated by how close the correla-

tion coefficient is to either −1.00 or +1.00. A correlation (*r*) of 0, a zero correlation, indicates no relationship between the variables (see Figure 3.3). An *r* of −1.00 or +1.00 indicates a perfect relationship between the two variables (as illustrated in Figures 3.1 and 3.2). The value of one variable is perfectly predictable by the value of the other variable—for example, every time people experience stress, they become depressed.

Seldom do we see perfect correlations in psychological research. Instead, correlations are often in the low to moderate range, indicating some relationship between the two variables, but far from a perfect relationship (see Figure 3.4). Many relationships between variables happen by chance and are not meaningful. Scientists evaluate the importance of correlation coefficient by examining its statistical significance.

Statistical Significance

The **statistical significance** of a result such as a correlation coefficient is an index of how likely that result occurred simply by chance. You will often see statements in research studies such as "The result was statistically significant at $p < .05$." This means that the probability (*p*) is less than 5 in 100 that the result occurred only by chance. Researchers typically accept results at this level of significance as support of their hypotheses, although the choice of an acceptable significance level is somewhat arbitrary.

Whether a correlation coefficient will be statistically significant at the $p < .05$ level is determined by its magnitude and the size of the sample on which it is based. Both larger correlations and larger sample sizes increase the likelihood of achieving statistical significance. A correlation of .30 will be significant if it is based on a large sample, say 200 or more, but will not be significant if it is based on a small sample, such as 10 or fewer participants. On the other hand, a correlation of .90 will be statistically significant even if the sample is as small as 30 people.

Correlation versus Causation

One of the most important things to understand about correlations is that they do not tell us anything about causation. That is, even though we may find that an independent and a dependent variable are highly correlated, this correlation does not tell us that the independent variable caused the dependent variable. In other words, even if we found a strong positive correlation between stress and depression, we could not conclude that stress causes depression.

All that a positive correlation could tell us is that there is a relationship between stress and depression. It could be that depression causes stress. Or some other variable might cause both stress and depression. This latter situation is called the **third variable problem**—the possibility that variables not measured in a study are the real cause of the relationship between the variables measured in the study. For example, perhaps some people with difficult temperaments both generate stressful experiences in their lives by being difficult to live with and are prone to depression. If we measure only stress and depression, we might observe a relationship between them because they co-occur within the same individuals. But this relationship is actually due to their common relationship to temperament.

Selecting a Sample

One of the critical choices in a correlational study is the choice of the sample. A **sample** is a group of people taken from the population that we want to study.

Representativeness

A *representative sample* is a sample that is highly similar to the population of interest in terms of sex, ethnicity, age, and other important variables. If a sample is not representative—for example, if there are more women or people of color in the sample than in the general population of interest—then the sample is said to have *bias*. The representativeness of a sample is important to the generalization we want to make from the study. If the sample represents only a small or an unusual group of people, then we cannot generalize the results of the

study to the larger population. For example, if all of the people in our study are white, middle-class females, we cannot know whether our results generalize to males, people of color, or people in other socioeconomic classes.

Some methods of recruiting participants into a study create more representative samples than do others. For example, in our study of stress and depression, we could put an advertisement in the local newspaper, asking people who had recently experienced stressful experiences to volunteer for our study. This would bias our sample in favor of people who have experienced stress, however, and leave out people who have not. Perhaps many people who have not experienced stress are depressed. This is important information we need in order to evaluate our hypothesis that stress causes depression.

An effective way of obtaining a representative sample of a population is to generate a random sample of that population. For example, some studies have obtained random samples of the entire U.S. population by randomly dialing phone numbers throughout the country and then recruiting the people who answered the phone into the study. Often, researchers can settle for random samples of smaller populations, such as random samples of particular cities. When a sample is truly random, the chances are high that it will be similar to the population of interest in ethnicity, sex, age, and all the other important variables in the study.

Selection of a Comparison Group

In a group comparison study, we are interested in comparing the experiences of one group with those of another. For example, we may be interested in the depression levels of bereaved and nonbereaved people. We might begin by recruiting our sample of bereaved people, attempting to make this sample as representative as possible of bereaved people in our community.

In selecting the comparison group of nonbereaved people, it is a good idea to match our bereaved group with this comparison group on any variable (other than stress) we think might influence levels of depression, so that the two groups are alike on these variables. If we did not do this matching process, any differences we found between the two groups on levels of depression could be attributable to variables for which we did not match—the third variable problem again.

For example, women are generally more likely to be depressed than men. If we happen to have more women in our bereaved group than in our comparison group, higher levels of depression in the bereaved group might be attributable to a third

Some studies of depression have focused on people who have experienced the stressor of bereavement.

variable—the fact that there are more women in that group—not to the fact that the group has recently been bereaved. For this reason, we need to match our bereaved and comparison groups on all third variables that might influence our dependent variable of depression.

If we decide to match our two groups on sex, age, ethnicity, and socioeconomic status, we can then generate the comparison group by consulting the local census records. For every person in our bereaved group, we can recruit a person of the same sex, age, ethnicity, and socioeconomic status from the local area into our comparison group. Although not a simple task, this is good way to generate a matched comparison group.

Evaluating Correlational Studies

Correlational studies have provided much important information for abnormal psychology. One of the major advantages of correlational studies is that they focus on situations occurring in the real world, rather than those manipulated in a laboratory. This gives them relatively good **external validity,** the extent to which a study's results can be generalized to the phenomena in real life. In other words, the results of these studies are generalizable to wider populations and to people's actual experiences in life.

Longitudinal correlational studies have several advantages over cross-sectional correlational studies. In longitudinal correlational studies, researchers can determine whether there are differences between the groups before the crucial event occurs. If there are no differences before the event but significant differences after the event, researchers can have more confidence that it was the event that actually led to the differences between the groups. Longitu-

dinal designs also allow researchers to follow groups long enough to assess both short-term and long-term reactions to the event.

The most significant disadvantage of all correlational studies is that they cannot tease apart what is a cause and what is a consequence. For example, many stressful events that depressed people report may be the consequences of their depression, rather than the causes. In addition, the symptoms of depression can cause stress by impairing interpersonal skills, interfering with concentration on the job, and causing insomnia. The same problem exists for many types of psychopathology. The symptoms of schizophrenia can disrupt social relationships, alcoholism can lead to unemployment, and so on. Some psychological symptoms may even cause physiological changes in people. For example, people who have recently experienced psychological trauma often develop medical diseases, because the traumas reduce the effectiveness of their immune systems, which help fight disease (Schneiderman, Ironson, & Siegel, 2005).

Another disadvantage of correlational studies is their potential for bad timing. Stress may indeed cause depression, but if we do not assess these two variables at the right point in time, we may not observe this relationship. For example, in our study of bereavement, we could miss many of the depressed people in our bereaved group if we measured depression either before they developed it or after they had recovered from it.

Longitudinal studies can be time-consuming and expensive to run. Chapter 11 reports studies in which children at high risk for schizophrenia were studied from their preschool years to their early adult years to determine what characteristics could predict who would develop schizophrenia and who would not (Erlenmeyer-Kimling et al., 1991). Some longitudinal studies have been going on for more than 25 years and have cost millions of dollars. They are producing extremely valuable data but at a high cost in researchers' time and research dollars.

Finally, all correlational studies suffer from the third variable problem. Researchers seldom can measure all the possible influences on their participants' levels of depression or other psychopathologies.

SUMMING UP

- A correlational study examines the relationship between two variables without manipulating either variable.

- A correlation coefficient is an index of the relationship between two variables. It ranges from -1.00 to $+1.00$. The magnitude of the correlation indicates how strong the relationship between the variables is.

- A positive correlation indicates that, as values of one variable increase, values of the other variable increase. A negative correlation indicates that, as values of one variable increase, values of the other variable decrease.

- A result is said to be statistically significant if it is unlikely to have happened by chance. The convention in psychological research is to accept results that have a probability of less than 5 in 100 of happening by chance.

- A correlational study can show that two variables are related, but it cannot show that one variable caused the other.

- All correlational studies suffer from the third variable problem—the possibility that variables not measured in the study actually account for the relationship between the variables measured in the study.

- Continuous variable studies evaluate the relationship between two variables that vary along a continuum.

- A sample is a subset of a population of interest. A representative sample is similar to the population on all important variables. One way to generate a representative sample is to obtain a random sample.

- Cross-sectional studies assess a sample at one point in time, and longitudinal studies assess a sample at multiple points in time.

- Group comparison studies evaluate differences between key groups, such as a group that has experienced a specific type of stressor and a comparison group that has not experienced the stressor but is matched on all important variables.

- Potential problems in correlational studies include the potential for bad timing and the expense of longitudinal studies.

EPIDEMIOLOGICAL STUDIES

Epidemiology is the study of the frequency and distribution of a disorder, or a group of disorders, in a population. An epidemiological study asks how many people in a population have the disorder and how this number varies across important groups within the population, such as men and women or people with high and low incomes.

Epidemiological research focuses on three types of data: the prevalence of a disorder, the incidence of a disorder, and the risk factors for a disorder. The

TABLE 3.1 Lifetime and 12-Month Prevalence of Major Depressive Disorder		
	Lifetime Prevalence (%)	**12-Month Prevalence (%)**
Males	12.7	7.7
Females	21.3	12.9
Total	17.1	10.3

Source: Kessler et al., 1994.

prevalence of a disorder is the proportion of the population that has the disorder at a given point or period in time. For example, a study might report the *lifetime prevalence* of a disorder, or the number of people who will have the disorder at sometime in their lives. The *12-month prevalence* of a disorder is the proportion of the population who will be diagnosed with the disorder in any 12-month period.

Table 3.1 shows the lifetime prevalence and 12-month prevalence of one of the more severe forms of depression, major depressive disorder, from a nationwide epidemiological study conducted in the United States (Kessler et al., 1994). Not surprisingly, the proportion of the population who will be diagnosed with major depressive disorder at sometime in their lives is larger than the proportion who will be diagnosed with the disorder in any 12-month period. Another interesting thing seen in Table 3.1 is that the prevalence of major depression is greater for women than for men. As we will discuss in Chapter 9, this fact, revealed by many epidemiological studies, has been an important focus of research in depression.

Epidemiological research also seeks to determine the **incidence** of a disorder, the number of new cases of the disorder that develop during a specific period of time. The one-year incidence of a disorder is the number of people who develop the disorder during a one-year period.

Finally, epidemiological research is concerned with the **risk factors** for a disorder—conditions or variables that are associated with a higher risk of having the disorder. Thus, if women are more likely than men to have a disorder, being a woman is a risk factor for the disorder. In terms of our interest in the relationship between stress and depression, an epidemiological study might show that people who live in high-stress areas of a city are more likely to have depression than are people who live in low-stress areas of a city.

How do researchers determine the prevalence of, incidence of, and risk factors for a disorder? Epidemiological researchers first identify the population of interest, then identify a random sample of that population—for example, by randomly phoning residential telephone numbers. They then use *structured clinical interviews,* in which interviewers use a specific set of questions with every participant to assess whether he or she has the symptoms that make up the disorders and risk factors, such as gender or socioeconomic status, being studied. We will discuss structured clinical interviews more in Chapter 4. From these data, epidemiologists are able to estimate how many people in different categories of risk factors have the disorder.

Evaluating Epidemiological Research

Epidemiological studies have provided valuable information on the prevalence of, incidence of, and risk factors for disorders, and we will discuss evidence from some of the major nationwide studies throughout this book. This research can give us important clues as to who is at highest risk for a disorder, and this information can then be used to test hypotheses about why those people are at higher risk.

Epidemiological studies suffer many of the same limitations as correlational studies. First and foremost, they cannot establish that any risk factor causes a disorder. That is, even though a study may show that people living in higher-stress neighborhoods are more likely to have a disorder, this finding does not mean that the high stress of the neighborhoods caused the disorder. Similarly, as in correlational studies, third variables may explain the relationship between any risk factor and the rates of a disorder.

SUMMING UP

- Epidemiology is the study of the frequency and distribution of a disorder in a population.
- The prevalence of a disorder is the proportion of the population that has the disorder at a give point or period in time.
- The incidence of a disorder is the number of new cases of the disorder that develop during a specific period of time.
- Risk factors for a disorder are conditions or variables that are associated with a higher risk of having the disorder.

EXPERIMENTAL STUDIES

The hallmark of **experimental studies** is control. Researchers attempt to control the independent variable and any potentially problematic third variables, rather than simply observing them as they naturally occur.

We turn now to the various types of experimental studies we could do to test our idea that stress leads to depression. We will examine three types in particular. The first, the *human laboratory study,* has the goal of inducing the conditions that we predict will lead to our outcome of interest (e.g., increasing stress to cause depression) in people. The second, the *therapy outcome study,* also is conducted with humans but has the opposite focus of the first type of study. In a therapy outcome study, the researcher wants to reduce the conditions leading to the outcome of interest so as to reduce that outcome (e.g., decreasing stress to decrease depression). The third, the *animal study,* attempts to model what happens in humans by manipulating animals in a laboratory.

Human Laboratory Studies

One experimental method for testing our hypothesis that people exposed to stress will become depressed, whereas those not exposed will not become depressed, is to expose participants to a stressor in a laboratory and then determine whether it causes an increase in depressed mood—a method known as a **human laboratory study.**

Several experimental studies on stress and depression have been done (see Peterson & Seligman, 1984). The stressor that is often used in these studies is an unsolvable task or puzzle, such as an unsolvable anagram. If we chose this as the type of stress we would induce, our operationalization would be participants' exposure to unsolvable anagrams. We would be manipulating stress, not just measuring it. This would give us the advantage of knowing precisely what type of stress participants were exposed to and when.

A human laboratory study is also called an **analogue study,** because researchers are attempting to create conditions in the laboratory that resemble certain conditions in the real world but that are not exactly like those real conditions. We cannot create in the laboratory many of the types of stress that may cause depression in the real world, such as the destruction of a person's home in a hurricane or continual assaults. Instead, we can create analogues—situations that capture some of the key characteristics of these real-world events, such as their uncontrollability and unpredictability.

Internal Validity

Researchers want to ensure that the experiment has **internal validity,** meaning that changes in the dependent variable can be confidently attributed to the manipulation of the independent variable, not

Researchers cannot reproduce some kinds of stress, such as losing a home in a hurricane, in the laboratory, so they must settle for creating analogues of these stressors.

to other factors. For example, people who participate in our experiment using anagrams might become more depressed over the course of the experiment simply because participating in an experiment is a negative experience, not because of the unsolvable anagrams. This threat to internal validity is basically the same type of third variable problem we encountered in correlational studies.

To control third variables, researchers create a **control group,** or a *control condition*, in which participants have all the same experiences as the group of main interest in the study, except that they do not receive the key manipulation—in our case, the experience of the unsolvable puzzles. The control group for our study could be made to do puzzles very similar to the unsolvable anagrams the other group works on, but the control group's anagrams could be solvable. Thus, the control group's experience would be identical to that of the other group—the **experimental group,** or *experimental condition*—except that the control group would not receive the stressor of unsolvable anagrams.

Another threat to internal validity can arise if the participants for our experimental group (the one that does the unsolvable anagrams) and for our control group (the one that does the solvable anagrams) differ in important ways before they begin the experiment. Because of such differences, we could not be sure that our manipulation was

the cause of any changes in our dependent variable. To safeguard internal validity, random assignment to the experimental and control groups is a critical step. **Random assignment** occurs when each participant has an equal chance of being assigned to the experimental or the control group. Often, a researcher will use a table of random numbers to assign participants to groups.

Yet another threat to internal validity is the presence of **demand characteristics**—situations that cause participants to guess the hypothesis of the study and change their behavior as a result. For example, if our measure of depression were too obvious, participants could guess what hypothesis we were testing. To avoid demand characteristics, we could use more subtle measures of depression, such as those illustrated in Figure 3.5 on page 84, embedded in other measures, so as to obscure the real purpose of our study. These other measures are often called *filler measures*. Researchers also often use *cover stories:* Participants are told false stories to prevent them from guessing the true purpose of the experiment and changing their behavior accordingly.

In order to reduce demand characteristics further, the experimenters who actually interact with the participants should be *unaware* of which condition the participants are in, the experimental condition or control condition, so that the experimenters do not give off subtle cues as to what they expect

| FIGURE 3.5 | **Scales to Measure Depression, Embedded in Other Scales.** The researcher may be interested only |

in participants' answers on the scales measuring happiness and depression but may embed these scales in other scales to obscure the purpose of the study.

Instructions: On each scale, mark off how you feel right now.

Happy |--|--|--|--|--|--| Unhappy

Curious |--|--|--|--|--|--| Not curious

Thoughtful |--|--|--|--|--|--| Not thoughtful

Depressed |--|--|--|--|--|--| Not depressed

Smart |--|--|--|--|--|--| Not smart

the participants to do in the experiment. For example, if experimenters know that a participant is in the experimental condition, they might suggest to the participant in subtle ways that the anagrams are unsolvable. This creates demands for the participant to behave in ways he or she otherwise might not.

Assume that we have instituted a number of safeguards for internal validity on our study: The participants have been randomly selected and assigned, and the experimenters they interact with are unaware of the hypothesis of our study and of the condition that participants are in. Now the study can be conducted. When our data have been collected and analyzed, we find that, as we predicted, the participants given the unsolvable anagrams showed greater increases in depressed mood than did participants given the solvable anagrams.

What can we conclude about our idea of depression, based on this study? Our experimental controls have helped us rule out third variable explanations, so we can be relatively confident that it was the experience of the uncontrollable stressor that led to the increases in depression in the experimental group. Thus, we can say that we have supported our hypothesis that people exposed to uncontrollable stress will show more depressed mood than will people not exposed to uncontrollable stress.

Evaluating Human Laboratory Studies

The primary advantage of human laboratory studies is control. Researchers have more control over

third variables, the independent variable, and the dependent variable in these studies than they do in any other type of study they can do with humans. However, human laboratory studies have their own limitations.

Generalizability The primary limitation of human laboratory studies is that we cannot know if our results generalize to what happens outside the laboratory. For this reason, their external validity can be low. Is being exposed to unsolvable anagrams anything like being exposed to major, real-world, uncontrollable stressors, such as the death of a loved one? Clearly, there is a difference in the severity of the two types of experiences, but is this the only important difference? Similarly, do the increases in depressed mood in the participants in our study, which were probably small increases, tell us anything about why some people develop extremely severe, debilitating episodes of depression? Experimental analogue studies such as ours have been criticized for the lack of generalizability of their results to the major psychopathology that occurs in everyday life.

Ethical Issues Apart from posing the problems of generalizability, human laboratory studies sometimes pose serious ethical issues. Is it ethical to induce distress, even mild distress, in people? Participants in an experiment can be warned of possible discomfort or distress and told that they can end their participation at any time. Even so, participants rarely stop experiments, even if they are uncomfortable, because of the subtle pressures of the social situation. (See *Taking Psychology Personally: Your Rights as a Research Participant* for further discussion.)

What if participants, even after being told that the stressful experience they had (e.g., being given an unsolvable anagram) was completely out of their control, believe that they should have been able to control the situation or solve the tasks? It turns out that many participants, especially college students, continue to believe that they should have been able to solve unsolvable tasks or that negative feedback they received in an experiment was a true indication of their abilities, even after being told that they were deceived by the experimenter. The researchers who discovered this phenomenon recommended conducting a *process debriefing* with participants following any potentially upsetting experiments (Ross, Lepper, & Hubbard, 1975). In such debriefings, experimenters slowly draw out the participants' assumptions about the experiments

Taking Psychology Personally

Your Rights as a Research Participant

You may participate in a research study at sometime. You have certain basic rights, which you should expect to be honored, regardless of the type of research being conducted:

■ *Understanding of the study*. You have the right to understand the nature of the research you are participating in, particularly any factors that might influence your willingness to participate. For example, if you are likely to experience discomfort (psychological or physical) as a result of participating in the study or if there are any risks to your well-being as a result of participation, the researcher should spell these out in plain language to you.

■ *Confidentiality*. You should expect your identity and any information gathered from you in the study to be held in strict confidence. This usually means that the researcher will report data from the study aggregated across participants, rather than reporting data from individual participants. If the researcher intends to report data from individual participants, he or she should explain this to you and obtain your explicit permission.

■ *Right to refuse participation*. You should be allowed to refuse to participate in the study, or to withdraw from participation once the study has begun, without suffering adverse consequences. If you are participating as a course requirement or as an opportunity for extra credit for a class, you should be given the choice of equitable alternative activities if you choose not to participate in the study. If you are offered payment or other inducements for participating in the study, they should not be so great that you basically cannot afford to refuse to participate.

■ *Informed consent*. Usually, your consent to participate in the study should be documented in writing. In some cases, a written informed consent document is not used, as when you are filling out an anonymous survey (in this case, your willingness to complete the survey is taken as your consent to participate).

■ *Deception*. Researchers should use deception in studies only when such techniques are absolutely essential and justified by the study's potential contributions. Participants should not be deceived about the aspects of the research that might affect their willingness to participate, such as physical risks, discomfort, or unpleasant emotional experiences. Researchers should explain the deception to the participants once the research is complete.

■ *Debriefing*. At the end of the study, researchers should explain the purpose of the research and answer any questions you have about the research.

Colleges and universities have institutional review boards (IRBs), which review proposed research studies to ensure that they honor the rights of participants; IRBs also handle complaints from participants about research. If you have any concerns about a study you have participated in, you can contact the IRB at your school to discuss these concerns. Some IRBs also have student members who assist in reviewing proposed research studies. This is a good way of learning about the variety of research going on at your college or university.

---

and their performances. They conduct extended conversations with the participants about the purposes and procedures of the experiments, explaining how their behavior was beyond their control and certainly not a reflection of their abilities.

Experimenters must always be aware of the ethical concerns raised by experiments of this sort and take all possible means to limit dangers to participants. All colleges and universities have a human participants committee, which reviews the procedures of studies done with humans to ensure that the benefits of the study substantially outweigh any risks to the participants and that the risks to the participants have been minimized.

Therapy Outcome Studies

The ethical concerns surrounding human laboratory studies have led some researchers to advocate studies that attempt to *reduce* psychopathology by reducing the factors believed to cause it. Applying this type of study to our idea would mean intervening with depressed participants to reduce stress, which should, in turn, decrease depression, according to our idea. This type of study is called a **therapy outcome study.**

Therapy outcome studies are appealing because they involve helping people while obtaining information. The goal of therapy outcome studies is to determine the effectiveness of an experimental therapy over no therapy or as compared with other, often established therapies. We discuss many therapy outcome studies in this book, including some that have compared psychological therapies with drug therapies in the treatment of specific disorders.

Control Groups

Sometimes, people get better simply because of the passage of time. Thus, researchers need to compare the experiences of people who receive an experimental therapy with those of a control group of people who do not receive the therapy to see if the experimental group's improvement has anything to do with the therapy. Sometimes, researchers use a *simple control group* consisting of participants who do not receive the experimental therapy but are tracked for the same period of time as the participants who do receive the therapy.

A variation on this simple control group is the **wait list control group.** The participants in this type of group do not receive the therapy when the experimental group does, but they go onto a wait list to receive the intervention at a later date when the study is complete. Both groups of participants are assessed at the beginning and end of the study, but only the experimental group receives the therapy as part of the study.

Another type of control group is the **placebo control group.** This type of group is used most often in studies of the effectiveness of drugs. The participants in this group have the same interactions with experimenters as do the participants in the experimental group, but they take pills that are *placebos* (inactive substances) rather than the real drug. Usually, to prevent demand effects, both the participants and the experimenters in these studies are unaware of what condition the participants are in. In this case, the experiment is known as a **double-blind experiment.**

A placebo control group can also be used to control for the possibility that the simple interaction with the therapist affected the outcome of the participants. This placebo group interacts with a therapist for the same amount of time but receives no therapy. However, some theorists have objected to the idea that interacting with a warm and caring therapist without experiencing any other experimental conditions is a placebo. They suggest that the active ingredient in therapy is receiving unconditional support and encouragement from a warm and caring therapist, not the actual program of therapy (Rogers, 1951). Indeed, psychological placebo interventions have been found to be quite effective with some types of problems (Elkin et al., 1989). It seems that a little bit of human caring goes a long way in helping people overcome their distress. It also seems nearly impossible to construct a true psychological placebo.

Evaluating Therapy Outcome Studies

Although therapy outcome studies might seem the most ethical way of conducting research on people in distress, they carry their own methodological challenges and ethical issues. Most psychological therapies involve a package of techniques for responding to people's problems. For example, depressed people in an experimental therapy group might be taught assertiveness skills, social problem-solving skills, and skills in changing self-defeating thinking. Which of these skills was most responsible for alleviating their depression? Even when a therapy works, researchers often cannot know exactly what it is about the therapy that works.

This uncertainty has practical implications, because we need to know what the effective elements of a therapy are in order to bolster those elements and to reduce other elements that may be useless or even harmful. The uncertainty also has important theoretical and scientific implications. If we conduct a therapy outcome study to test a particular idea about the cause of a psychopathology, we need to know whether the therapy works for the reasons we have theorized. For example, if we are testing our idea that stress causes depression, we need to know that our intervention reduced depression because it reduced stress, not because it provided the participants with an opportunity to ventilate their feelings, because it provided social support in the form of a therapist, or because of some other factor unrelated to our idea.

Ethical Issues Ethical problems arise in using simple control groups, wait list control groups, and placebo control groups in therapy outcome research. Some researchers believe it is unethical to withhold treatment or to provide a treatment they believe is ineffective for people in distress. For example, many depressed participants assigned to a control group may be in severe distress or in danger of harming themselves or someone else and, therefore, require immediate treatment.

In response to this concern, many therapy outcome studies now compare the effectiveness of two or more therapies that are expected to have positive effects. These studies basically are a competition between rival therapies and the theories behind these therapies. There is reason to believe that all the participants in such a study will benefit from participation in the study but that the study

Real-world settings where therapy is delivered, such as busy mental-health clinics, may differ substantially from the controlled conditions of a therapy outcome study.

will yield useful information about the most effective type of therapy for the participants.

Another ethical issue concerns the therapist's obligation to respond to the patients' needs. How much can a therapy be modified to respond to a specific participant's needs without compromising the scientific element of the study? Therapists may feel the need to vary the dosage of a drug or to deviate from a study's procedure for psychological intervention. If they depart too far from the standard therapy, however, there will be great variation in the therapy that participants in the intervention group receive, which could compromise the results of the study.

Generalizability A related methodological issue has to do with generalizing results from therapy outcome studies to the real world. In these studies, the therapeutic intervention is usually delivered to patients in a controlled, high-quality atmosphere by the most competent therapists. The patients are usually screened, so that they fit a narrow set of criteria for inclusion in the study, and often only the patients who stick with the therapy to its end are included in the final analyses.

In the real world, mental-health services are not always delivered in controlled, high-quality atmospheres by the most competent therapists. Patients are who they are, with their complicated symptom pictures and lives that may not fit neatly

into the criteria for an "optimal patient." Patients often leave and return to therapy and may not receive "full trials" of the therapy before they drop out for financial or personal reasons.

Therapy outcome research that tests how well a therapy works in highly controlled settings with a narrowly defined group of people is said to test the **efficacy** of a therapy. In contrast, therapy outcome research that tests how well a therapy works in real-world settings with all the complications we've just discussed is said to test the **effectiveness** of a therapy.

Single-Case Experimental Designs

Another type of experimental study is the **single-case experimental design,** in which one individual or a small group of people is studied intensively. This design may sound like the case studies we discussed earlier. The major difference is that, in a single-case experimental design, the individual is put through a manipulation or an intervention, and his or her behavior is examined before and after this to determine the effects. (In a case study, usually no manipulation or intervention is attempted.) In addition, in a single-case experimental design, the participants' behaviors are measured through a standard method, repeatedly over time, whereas a case study is often based on the researcher's

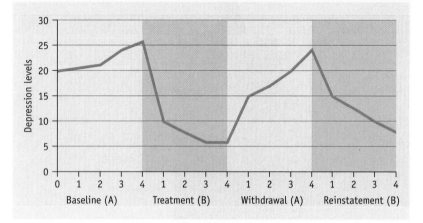

FIGURE 3.6 **Effects over Time of Drug Treatment for Depression in an Individual.** This graph shows an individual's level of depression during a 4-week baseline assessment (A), during 4 weeks of drug treatment (B), when the drug treatment is withdrawn for 4 weeks (A), and when the drug treatment is reinstated for 4 weeks (B).

impressions of the participant and the factors that are affecting him or her.

A specific type of single-case experimental design is the **ABAB,** or **reversal design,** in which an intervention is introduced, withdrawn, and then reinstated, and the behavior of the participant is examined on and off the treatment. For example, in a study on the effect of a drug for depression, a depressed person might be assessed for her level of depression each day for 4 weeks. This is the baseline assessment (A) (see Figure 3.6). Then the participant is given the drug for 4 weeks (B), and her level of depression assessed each day during that period. Then the drug is withdrawn for 4 weeks (A), and her level of depression assessed each day during that time. Finally, the drug is reinstated for 4 weeks (B), and her level of depression reassessed each day during that period. If the participant's levels of depression follows the pattern seen in Figure 3.6, this result suggests that her depression level was much lower during the periods when she was taking the drug (B) than when she was not taking the drug (A).

Evaluating Single-Case Experimental Designs

A major advantage of single-case experimental designs is that they allow for much more intensive assessment of participants than might be possible if there were many more participants. For example, an individual child could be observed for hours each day as he was put on, then taken off, a treatment. This intensity of assessment can allow researchers to pinpoint the types of behaviors that are and are not affected by their interventions.

The major disadvantage of single-case experimental designs is that their results may not generalize to the wider population. One individual's experience on or off a treatment may not be the same as others experiences. In addition, not all hypotheses can be tested with single-case experimental designs. Some treatments have lingering effects after they end. For example, if a person is taught new skills at coping with stress during the treatment, these skills might continue to be present after the treatment has been withdrawn.

Animal Studies

Researchers sometimes try to avoid the ethical issues involved in experimental studies with humans by conducting such studies with animals. Animal research has its own set of ethical issues, but many researchers feel it is acceptable to subject animals to situations in the laboratory that would not be ethical to impose on humans. **Animal studies** thus provide researchers with even more control over laboratory conditions and third variables than is possible in human laboratory studies.

In a well-known series of animal studies designed to investigate depression (discussed in Chapter 9), Martin Seligman, Bruce Overmier, Steven Maier, and their colleagues subjected dogs to an uncontrollable stressor in the laboratory (Overmier & Seligman, 1967; Seligman & Maier, 1967). They did not ask the dogs to do unsolvable anagrams. Instead, they used a stressor over which the researchers could have complete control: a painful electric shock. The experimental group of dogs received a series of uncontrollable shocks. Let us call this *Group E* for *experimental.*

In addition, there were two control groups. One control group of dogs received shocks of the same magnitude as the dogs in the experimental group, but they could control the shocks by jumping over a short barrier in their cage (see Figure 3.7). Let us call this *Group J* for *jump.* The dogs in this control group and the dogs in Group E received exactly the same number and duration of shocks. The only difference between the groups was that the dogs in Group E could not control their shocks, whereas the dogs in control Group J could. The second control group of dogs received no shock. Let us call this *Group N* for *none.*

The dogs in Group E initially responded to the shocks by jumping around their cages and protesting loudly. Soon, however, the majority became passive and simply hovered in one part of their cages, whimpering. Later, when the researchers provided the dogs with the opportunity to escape the shock by jumping over a barrier, these dogs did not learn to do this. It seemed that they had an expectation that they could not control the shock, so they were unable to recognize the opportunities for control that arose. They seemed to have given up. The researchers labeled this set of behaviors *learned helplessness deficits* and argued that the dogs had learned they were helpless to control their situation.

The dogs in controllable shock Group J, however, quickly learned how to control the shock and did not develop the learned helplessness deficits shown by the dogs in the uncontrollable shock group. The fact that the two groups of dogs experienced the same amount of shock suggests that lack of control, not the shock alone, led to the learned helplessness deficits in the experimental group. The dogs in control Group N, which received no shock, also did not develop learned helplessness deficits.

Seligman and his colleagues likened the learned helplessness deficits shown by the dogs to the symptoms of depression in humans: apathy, low initiation of behavior, and the inability to see opportunities to improve one's environment (see Seligman, 1975). They argued that many human depressions result from people learning they have no control over important outcomes in their lives. This learned helplessness theory of depression seems useful in explaining the depression and passivity seen in chronically oppressed groups, such as battered spouses and some people who grow up in poverty.

A second type of animal study is similar to therapy outcome studies. In studies of the effectiveness of drugs, animals are often given the drugs to determine the effects of the drugs on different bodily systems and behaviors. Sometimes, the animals are sacrificed after receiving the drugs, so that detailed physiological analyses of the effects of the drugs can be determined. Obviously, such studies could not be done with humans. Animal studies of drugs are particularly useful in the early stages of research, when the possible side effects of the drugs are unknown.

Evaluating Animal Studies

There clearly are problems with animal studies. First, some people believe it is no more ethical to conduct painful, dangerous, or fatal experiments with animals than it is to do so with humans. Second, from a scientific vantage point, we must ask whether we can generalize the results of experiments with animals to humans. Are learned helplessness deficits in dogs really analogous to human depression? The debate over the ethical and scientific issues of animal research continues, sometimes leading to violent clashes between proponents and opponents of animal research. Particularly in the case of research on drug effectiveness, however,

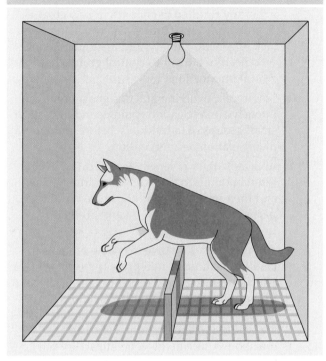

FIGURE 3.7   **Shuttle Box for Learned Helplessness Experiments.** Researchers used an apparatus like this to deliver controllable or uncontrollable shocks to dogs in order to investigate the phenomenon of learned helplessness.

animal research is crucial to the advancement of our knowledge of how to help people overcome psychopathology.

SUMMING UP

■ Experimental studies attempt to control all the variables affecting the dependent variable.

■ In human laboratory studies, the independent variable is manipulated and the effects on people participating in the study are examined. To control for the effects of being in the experimental situation and the passage of time, researchers use control groups, in which participants have all the same experiences as the group of main interest in the study, except that they do not receive the key manipulation.

■ Demand characteristics are aspects of the experimental situation that cause participants to guess the purpose of the study and change their behavior as a result.

■ The disadvantages of human laboratory studies are their lack of generalizability and the ethical issues involved in manipulating people.

■ Therapy outcome studies assess the impact of an intervention designed to relieve symptoms.

Simple control groups, wait list control groups, and placebo control groups are used to compare the effects of the intervention with other alternatives.

- It can be difficult to determine what aspects of a therapy resulted in changes in participants. Therapy outcome studies also can suffer from lack of generalizability, and assigning people who need treatment to control groups holds ethical implications.

- Single-case experimental designs involve the intensive investigation of single individuals or small groups of individuals, before and after a manipulation or intervention.

- In an ABAB, or reversal, design, an intervention is introduced, withdrawn, and then reinstated, and the behavior of the participant is examined on and off the treatment.

- Animal studies involve exposing animals to conditions thought to represent the causes of a psychopathology and then measuring changes in the animals' behavior or physiology. The ethics of exposing animals to conditions that we would not expose humans to can be questioned, as can the generalizability of animal studies.

CROSS-CULTURAL RESEARCH

Not long ago, most psychological research was conducted with college students, many of whom were White and middleclass, and researchers believed that any results they obtained from these samples could be generalized to any other relevant sample. Only anthropologists and a handful of psychologists and psychiatrists argued that what is true of one ethnic group, culture, or gender is not necessarily true of others.

In the past two decades, however, there has been an explosion of cross-cultural research in abnormal psychology. Researchers are investigating the similarities and differences across culture in the nature, causes, and treatment of psychopathology. Cross-cultural researchers face their own special challenges in addition to the ones common to all research.

First, gaining access to the people one wants to study can be difficult. People who have never participated in research may be wary of cooperating with researchers. In addition, some cultures explicitly shun contact with outsiders. An example was described in *Extraordinary People: The Old Order Amish of Pennsylvania* at the beginning of this chapter. Researcher Janice Egeland spent 20 years gaining the trust of the Amish, and eventually they allowed her to bring in a research team to study major psychopathology in the culture (Egeland & Hostetter, 1983). The result was some of the most exciting research ever published on cross-cultural similarities and differences in bipolar disorder.

Most of us do not have 20 years to gain the trust of the people we want to study and thus will not choose to study populations that are that difficult to access. Nevertheless, most groups of people need some time to warm up to research. Researchers can usually do some things to facilitate this warming up. For example, they can enlist the support of important leaders in the group, provide things that the group needs or wants in exchange for its participation, and learn the group's customs and adhere to these customs in all interactions with the group.

The second challenge is that researchers must be careful in applying theories or concepts developed in one culture to another culture (Rogler, 1999). Because the manifestations of disorders can differ across cultures, researchers who insist on narrow definitions of disorders may fail to identify many people suffering from disorders in culturally defined ways. Similarly, theoretical variables can have different meanings or manifestations across cultures.

A good example is the variable known as *expressed emotion*. Families high in expressed emotion are highly critical and hostile toward other family members and emotionally overinvolved with each other. Several studies of the majority cultures in America and Europe have shown that people with schizophrenia whose families are high in expressed emotion have higher rates of relapse than do those whose families are low in expressed emotion (Brown, Birley, & Wing, 1972; Vaughn & Leff, 1976). The meaning and manifestation of expressed emotion can differ greatly across cultures, however:

Criticism within Anglo-American family settings, for example, may focus on allegations of faulty personality traits (e.g., laziness) or psychotic symptom behaviors (e.g., strange ideas). However, in other societies, such as those of Latin America, the same behaviors may not be met with criticism. Among Mexican-descent families, for example, criticism tends to focus on disrespectful or disruptive behaviors that affect the family but not on psychotic symptom behavior and individual personality characteristics. Thus, culture plays a role in creating the content or targets of criticism. Perhaps most importantly, culture is influential in determining *whether* criticism is a prominent part of the familial emotional atmosphere. (Jenkins & Karno, 1992, p. 10)

For this reason, today's researchers are more careful to search for culturally specific manifestations of the characteristics of interest in their studies and for the possibility that the characteristics or variables that predict psychopathology in one culture are irrelevant in other cultures.

Third, even if researchers believe they can apply their theories across cultures, they may have difficulty translating their questionnaires or other assessment tools into different languages (Rogler, 1999). A key concept in English may not be precisely translated into another language. Subtle problems can arise because many languages contain variations on pronouns and verbs whose usage is determined by the social relationship between the speaker and the person being addressed. For example, in Spanish, the second-person pronoun *usted* (you) connotes respect, establishes an appropriate distance in a social relationship, and is the correct way for a young interviewer to address an older respondent (Rogler, 1989). By contrast, when a young interviewer addresses a young respondent, the relationship is more informal, and the appropriate form of address is *tú* (also *you*). If an interviewer violates the social norms implicit in a language, he or she can alienate a respondent and impair the quality of the research.

Fourth, there may be cultural or gender differences in people's responses to the social demands of interacting with researchers. For example, people of Mexican origin, older people, and people of lower socioeconomic class are more likely to answer yes to researchers' questions, regardless of the content, and to attempt to answer questions in socially desirable ways than are Anglo Americans, younger people, and people of higher socioeconomic class. These differences appear to result from differences among groups in deference to authority figures and concern over presenting a proper appearance (Ross & Mirowsky, 1984). Similarly, it is often said that men are less likely than women to admit to "weaknesses," such as symptoms of distress or problems in coping. If researchers do not take biases into account when designing assessment tools and analyzing data, erroneous conclusions can result.

Fifth, researchers may face pressure to designate one culture as the healthy, or normative, one and another culture as the unhealthy, or aberrant, one. Researchers must constantly guard against such assumptions and must be willing to interpret differences simply as differences, acknowledging that each culture and gender has its healthy and unhealthy characteristics. Despite the difficulties

in conducting cross-cultural research, the need for such research is clear as our understanding of the diversity of human experience of psychopathology becomes greater.

SUMMING UP

- Cross-cultural research has expanded greatly in recent decades.
- Some special challenges of cross-cultural research include difficulty in accessing populations, in applying theories appropriate in one culture to other cultures, in translating concepts and measures across cultures, in predicting the responses of people in different cultures to being studied, and avoiding defining "healthy" and "unhealthy" cultures.

META-ANALYSIS

Often there are a large number of studies in the research literature that have investigated a particular idea (for example, that stress leads to depression) by testing various hypotheses that are based on it. Some of these studies have supported their hypothesis; some have not. An investigator may want to find out the overall trend of the results across all the studies, as well as what factors might account for some studies' supporting their hypothesis and others' failing to do so. One way to determine the overall trend is simply to read all the studies and draw conclusions about whether most of them support or do not support their hypothesis. These conclusions can be biased, however, in the reader's assumptions about the hypotheses and impressions of the studies.

A more objective way to draw conclusions about a body of research is to conduct a **meta-analysis,** a statistical technique for summarizing the results across several studies. The first step in a meta-analysis is to do a thorough literature search, usually with the help of computer search engines that identify all studies with certain key words. Studies often use different methods and measures for testing a hypothesis, so the second step of a meta-analysis is to transform the results of each study into a statistic that is common across all the studies. This statistic is called the *effect size,* and it gives an indication of how big the differences are between two groups (such as a group that received a specific form of therapy and one that did not), or how large the relationship between two continuous variables is (such as the correlation between levels of stress and levels of depression). Researchers can then examine the average effect size across studies and relate the effect size to characteristics of the study, such as the year it was published, the type of measures used, or the age or gender of the participants.

Evaluating Meta-Analysis

As we noted, a major advantage of meta-analysis is that it removes much of the bias that can be introduced when individual investigators read various studies and try to draw conclusions. It also allows researchers to examine the characteristics of studies that can account for differences in effect sizes. For example, in a meta-analysis of studies of children's depression levels, Twenge and Nolen-Hoeksema (2002) found that studies done in more recent years tend to find lower depression scores than studies done several years ago. This finding suggests that levels of depression may be going down in more recent groups of children.

In addition, meta-analysis can overcome some of the problems of small numbers of participants in an individual study by pooling the data from thousands of participants, providing more power to find significant effects. The studies examined by Twenge and Nolen-Hoeksema (2002) generally have small numbers of ethnic minority children, making it difficult to compare their depression scores with those of other children. By pooling studies, however, the overall sample size of Hispanic and African American children was large enough to do comparisons by race/ethnicity. The meta-analysis found that the Hispanic children generally had higher depression scores than the African American or White children.

Meta-analyses have their problems, however. First, some studies have methodological flaws but still are published. These flawed studies may be included in a meta-analysis, along with methodologically stronger studies, influencing the overall results.

Second, is the *file drawer effect*—studies that do not support the hypothesis they are designed to test are less likely to get published than studies that do. For example, a study that finds that a psychotherapy is not any more effective than a wait list control is less likely to get published than a study that finds that the same psychotherapy is more effective than the wait list control. Note that some studies do not support the investigator's hypothesis because they are methodologically flawed, so you wouldn't want them to be published. But the bias toward publishing studies with positive results means that many perfectly good studies that fail to find the expected effects do not get published and therefore do not end up in meta-analyses. This file drawer effect biases the results of meta-analyses toward finding an overall posi-

tive effect of a treatment, or another type of difference between groups.

SUMMING UP

- Meta-analysis is a statistical technique for summarizing results across several studies.

- In a meta-analysis, the results of individual studies are standardized into a statistic called the effect size. Then the magnitude of the effect size and its relationship to characteristics of the study are examined.

- Meta-analyses reduce the bias that can occur when investigators draw conclusions across studies in a more subjective manner; however, they can include studies that have poor methods and can exclude good studies that were not published because they did not find significant effects.

CHAPTER INTEGRATION

We noted in Chapter 2 that theories and models of psychopathology are increasingly based on the integration of concepts from biological, psychological, and social approaches. These concepts are often viewed from a vulnerability-stress perspective. The characteristics that make a person more vulnerable to abnormality might include biological characteristics, such as genetic predisposition, or psychological characteristics, such as maladaptive styles of thinking about the world. These personal characteristics must interact with characteristics of the situation or environment to create the abnormality. For example, a woman with a genetic predisposition to depression may never develop the disorder in its full form if she has a supportive family and never faces major stressors.

Conducting research that reflects this integrationist perspective on abnormality is not easy. Researchers must gather information about people's biological, psychological, and social vulnerabilities and strengths. This work may require specialized equipment or expertise. It may also require following participants longitudinally to observe what happens when people with vulnerabilities face stressors that may trigger episodes of their disorders.

Increasingly, researchers are working together in teams to share their expertise in specialized research methods and to share resources that make multidisciplinary longitudinal research possible (see Figure 3.8). Researchers are also receiving training in disciplines and methods that are not their primary disciplines. For example, psychologists are learning to use magnetic resonance imaging (MRI), positron-emission tomography (PET)

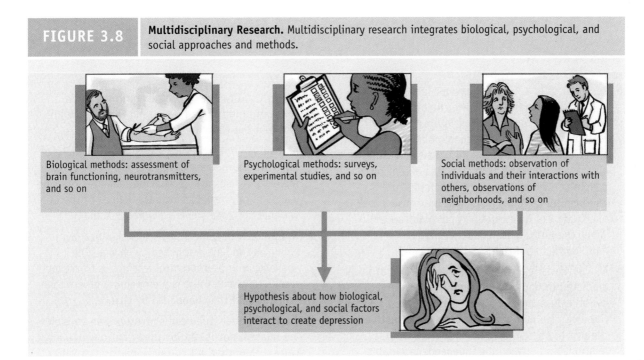

FIGURE 3.8 **Multidisciplinary Research.** Multidisciplinary research integrates biological, psychological, and social approaches and methods.

Biological methods: assessment of brain functioning, neurotransmitters, and so on

Psychological methods: surveys, experimental studies, and so on

Social methods: observation of individuals and their interactions with others, observations of neighborhoods, and so on

Hypothesis about how biological, psychological, and social factors interact to create depression

scans, and other advanced biological methods to investigate abnormality.

If you pursue a career researching abnormality, you may find yourself integrating methods from psychology (which have been the focus of this chapter), sociology, and biology to create the most comprehensive picture of the disorder you are investigating. This task may seem daunting right now, but the interactionist approach holds the possibility of producing breakthroughs that greatly improve the lives of people vulnerable to psychopathology.

Extraordinary People: Follow-Up

The researchers who studied the Old Order Amish quickly realized that they would have to adjust their definitions of depression and mania to take into account the cultural context of the Amish. As we discuss in more depth in Chapter 9, the manifestations of mood problems, particularly mania, among the Amish were quite different from the manifestations in mainstream culture, due to the strong social norms for behavior among the Amish. This realization alone brought the study of cross-cultural differences in psychiatric disorders into the mainstream psychiatric literature and gave cross-cultural research a legitimacy in that literature it had not had before (Egeland, Hostetter, & Eshleman, 1983).

Egeland and colleagues did not simply describe and count cases of mood disorders among the Amish, however. They took advantage of the fact that the Amish are a closed society, with little movement of individuals in or out, and that the Amish keep extensive genealogical records on their members. In addition, the Amish have essentially only one social class—everyone has the same level of education and similar occupational pursuits, and there is little variation in income. This setting was perfect for genetic studies of mood disorders. Egeland and colleagues conducted groundbreaking work that shaped how researchers think about the role of heritability in depression and mania (e.g., Ginns et al., 1996, 1998).

This study of the Old Order Amish set important precedents for how cross-cultural work is done in psychology and psychiatry. The researchers entered this study with respect and understanding for this culture's norms for behavior and relationships to the outside world, and they worked within these expectations as much as possible. As a result, they accomplished extraordinary research that has had important effects on the field of mood disorders and on cross-cultural research in general.

Chapter Summary

- Researchers of abnormal behavior face certain special challenges. First is the challenge of convincing the population of interest to participate in research. Second, abnormal behaviors and feelings are difficult to measure objectively and must rely to a large extent on people's self-reports. Third, most forms of abnormality probably have multiple causes, and no one study can investigate all possible causes simultaneously. These challenges require a multimethod approach.

- A hypothesis is a testable statement of what is predicted to happen in a study. The primary hypothesis is the one believed to be true based on the idea. The null hypothesis is the alternative to the primary hypothesis, stating there is no relationship between the independent variable and the dependent variable.

- The dependent variable is the factor being predicted in a study. The independent variable is the factor being used to predict the dependent variable.

- In any study, the variables of interest must be operationalized: The researcher must decide how to measure or manipulate the variables.

- A sample is a group of people taken from the population of interest to participate in the study. The samples for the study must be representative of the population of interest, and the research must be generalizable to the population of interest.

- A control group consists of people who are similar in most ways to the primary group of interest but who do not experience the variable the theory says causes changes in the dependent variable. Matching the control group to the group of primary interest can help control third variables, which are variables unrelated to the theory that may still have some effect on the dependent variable.

- Case studies of individuals provide rich and detailed information about their subjects. They are helpful in the generation of new ideas and the study of rare problems. Case studies suffer from problems in generalizability and in the subjectivity of both the person being studied and the person conducting the study.

- Correlational studies examine the relationship between two variables without manipulating the variables. A correlation coefficient is an index of the relationship between two variables. It ranges

from -1.00 to $+1.00$. The magnitude of the correlation indicates how strong the relationship between the variables is.

- A positive correlation indicates that, as values of one variable increase, values of the other variable increase. A negative correlation indicates that, as values of one variable increase, values of the other variable decrease (review Figures 3.1 and 3.2).

- A result is said to be statistically significant if it is unlikely to have happened by chance. The convention in psychological research is to accept results for which there is a probability of less than 5 in 100 that they happened by chance.

- A correlational study can show that two variables are related, but it cannot show that one variable caused the other. All correlational studies suffer from the third variable problem—the possibility that variables not measured in the study actually account for the relationship between the variables measured in the study.

- Continuous variable studies evaluate the relationship between two variables that vary along a continuum.

- A representative sample is similar to the population of interest on all important variables. One way to generate a representative sample is to obtain a random sample.

- Whereas cross-sectional studies assess a sample at one point in time, longitudinal studies assess a sample at multiple points in time. Group comparison studies evaluate differences between key groups, such as a group that has experienced a certain stressor and a matched comparison group that has not.

- Epidemiology is the study of the frequency and distribution of a disorder in a population. The prevalence of a disorder is the proportion of the population that has the disorder at a give point or period in time. The incidence of a disorder is the number of new cases of the disorder that develop during a specific period of time. Risk factors for a disorder are conditions or variables that are associated with a higher risk of having the disorder.

- Experimental studies can provide evidence that a given variable causes psychopathology. The goal of a human laboratory study is to induce the conditions that are hypothesized to lead to the outcome of interest (for example, increasing stress to cause depression) in people in a controlled setting. Participants are randomly assigned to either the experimental group, which receives a manipulation, or a control group, which does not.

■ Generalizing experimental studies to real-world phenomena is sometimes not possible. In addition, manipulating people who are in distress in an experimental study can create ethical problems.

■ A special type of experimental study is the therapy outcome study. It allows researchers to test a hypothesis about the causes of a psychopathology while providing a service to participants.

■ Difficult issues associated with therapy outcome studies include problems in knowing what elements of therapy were effective, questions about the appropriate control groups to use, questions about whether to allow modifications of the therapy to fit individual participants' needs, and the lack of generalizability of the results of these studies to the real world.

■ In therapy outcome studies, researchers sometimes use wait list control groups, in which control participants wait to receive the interventions after the studies are complete. Alternatively, researchers may try to construct psychological placebo control groups, in which participants receive the general support of therapists but none of the elements of the therapy thought to be active. Both of these types of control groups have practical and ethical limitations.

■ Single-case experimental designs involve the intensive investigation of single individuals or small groups of individuals, before and after a manipulation or an intervention. In an ABAB, or reversal, design, an intervention is introduced, withdrawn, and then reinstated, and the behavior of a participant is examined on and off the treatment (review Figure 3.6).

■ Animal studies allow researchers to manipulate their subjects in ways that are not ethically permissible with human participants, although many people feel that such animal studies are equally unethical. Animal studies suffer from problems in generalizability to humans.

■ In doing cross-cultural research, researchers face special challenges. Access to the populations of interest can be difficult. Theories and concepts that make sense in one culture may not be applicable to other cultures. Questionnaires and other assessment tools must be translated accurately. Culture can affect how people respond to the social demands of research. Finally, researchers must be careful not to build into their research assumptions that one culture is healthy and another culture is deviant.

■ Meta-analysis is a statistical technique for summarizing the results across several studies. In a meta-analysis, the results of individual studies are standardized into a statistic called the effect size. Then the magnitude of the effect size and its relationship to characteristics of the study are examined.

■ Meta-analyses reduce bias that can occur when investigators draw conclusions across studies in a more subjective manner but can include studies that have poor methods and exclude good studies that were not published because they did not find significant effects.

MindMap CD-ROM

The following resources on the MindMap CD-ROM that came with this text will help you to master the content of this chapter and prepare for tests:

■ Interactive Segments: Self-Report Bias in Surveys; Correlational Research; Samples and Populations; Independent and Dependent Variables; Reliability, Validity, and Variability

■ Chapter Timeline

■ Chapter Quiz

Key Terms

scientific method 73

hypothesis 73

null hypothesis 73

variable 73

dependent variable 74

independent variable 74

operationalization 74

case studies 74

generalizability 76

replication 76

correlational studies 76

continuous variable 76

group comparison study 77

cross-sectional 77

longitudinal 77

correlation coefficient 77

statistical significance 78

third variable problem 79

sample 79

external validity 80

epidemiology 81

prevalence 81

incidence 81

risk factors 81

experimental studies 82

human laboratory study 82

analogue study 82

internal validity 82

control group 83

experimental group 83

random assignment 83

demand characteristics 83

therapy outcome study 85

wait list control group 86

placebo control group 86

double-blind experiment 86

efficacy 87

effectiveness 87

single-case experimental design 87

ABAB (reversal) design 88

animal studies 88

meta-analysis 91

Chapter 4

Essor
by André Rouillard

Beauty cannot disguise nor music melt
A pain undiagnosable but felt.

—Anne Morrow Lindbergh, *The Unicorn and Other*
Poems, 1935–1955 (1956)

Assessing and Diagnosing Abnormality <

CHAPTER OVERVIEW

Extraordinary People

■ Michael J. Fox: *Lucky Man*

Gathering Information

Assessment is the process of gathering information about the symptoms people are suffering and the possible causes of these symptoms. Many types of information are gathered during an assessment, including information about current symptoms and ways of coping with stress, recent events and physical condition, drug and alcohol use, personal and family history of psychological disorders, cognitive functioning, and sociocultural background. This information helps in planning treatment.

Assessment Tools

Clinicians use many types of assessment tools. An assessment tool should provide valid and reliable information. Neuropsychological tests can help detect neurological problems that may be causing symptoms. Intellectual tests indicate cognitive functioning. Structured clinical interviews and symptom questionnaires provide direct information about symptoms. Personality inventories, behavioral observations, self-monitoring, and projective tests can indicate personality styles and behavioral deficits. At some point in the future, brain-imaging techniques may prove useful in assessing psychopathology, but the technology does not allow this today.

Taking Psychology Personally

■ Is Self-Assessment a Good Idea?

Problems in Assessment

Clients may be resistant to providing information. Some clients may be unable to provide information because of cognitive impairment or youth. Children's manifestation of distress can change significantly with age. Cultural biases can impair the accuracy of clinicians' assessments of clients from other cultures.

Diagnosis

The *Diagnostic and Statistical Manual of Mental Disorders* (DSM) provides the primary set of rules used for diagnosing psychological disorders in the United States. The first two editions of the DSM had diagnostic criteria that were vague and based on theory. In the third edition of the DSM in 1980, the diagnostic criteria were revised to be as observable and atheoretical as possible. The current edition, DSM-IV-TR, specifies five axes to be used in making diagnoses. Critics of the DSM have charged that it reflects Western, masculine ideals for a "healthy" person and thus pathologizes the normal behaviors of women and people from other cultures. In addition, the subjectivity inherent in psychiatric diagnoses and the stigma attached to these diagnoses raise concerns about the application of these diagnoses, yet having clear criteria for diagnosis is necessary for the progress of research on psychological disorders and for communication among clinicians.

Chapter Integration

Understanding the context and possible sources of a person's psychological symptoms requires a comprehensive, integrated assessment of biological, psychological, and social factors.

Extraordinary People

Michael J. Fox: *Lucky Man*

Michael J. Fox was one of the most successful movie and television actors of the late twentieth century. He starred in the long-running sitcom *Family Ties* and in the blockbuster movies *Back to the Future, The Secret of My Success,* and *Doc Hollywood.* When he was just 30 years old and at the height of his career, however, Fox began to have strange symptoms, which he could not control. It started with a twitching in his pinkie finger. Over the next few months, the twitching progressed to his ring and middle fingers, and he began to have weakness in his left hand, stiffness in his shoulder, and aches in the muscles on one side of his chest.

Fox attributed these symptoms to having accidentally been hanged for a few moments in a botched scene in *Back to the Future* and tried his best to ignore them. Over the next few years, Fox's symptoms progressed, so that at their worst he was experiencing rigidity, shuffling, a lack of balance, difficulty in expressing his feelings and ideas, and a weakening of his voice. He felt terrific frustration over his difficulties of expression, finding that he could form his thoughts and ideas into words and sentences but had trouble getting them out of his mouth. He spoke in a halting monotone and his face became expressionless.

Fox attempted to drown his symptoms, and his fear of them, in alcohol. He describes one of the binges he and his film crew went on after finishing the taping of his movie *For Love or Money.* They had already consumed three pitchers of Margaritas on the set, but the party continued at a local restaurant and bar as the group switched from tequila to beer and finally to vodka. After each shot, they threw their glasses into the fireplace. Well after closing time and yet more beer, Fox was driven home, where he grabbed another beer from the refrigerator and passed out on the couch.

Fox eventually went to see a neurologist for an evaluation of his tremors and difficulties in moving and speaking. At first, the neurologist dismissed the symptoms as insignificant, but, the more testing he did, the more grave his expression became. At the end of the appointment, he dropped a bombshell— Fox had a rare, early-onset form of Parkinson's disease, a progressive, degenerative, and incurable neurological disease. He probably had 10 years left of being able to function normally.

Suppose that Michael J. Fox showed up at your clinic, asking you to determine what was wrong with him before he had the diagnosis of Parkinson's disease. How would you do this? The assessment and diagnosis of symptoms is the focus of this chapter.

Assessment is the process of gathering information about people's symptoms and the possible causes of those symptoms. The information gathered in an assessment is used to determine the appropriate diagnosis for a person's problems. A **diagnosis** is a label attached to a set of symptoms that tend to occur with one another. Michael J. Fox

was diagnosed with Parkinson's disease. If his alcohol use had come under the scrutiny of a clinician, he might also have been diagnosed with alcohol abuse or dependence (which is discussed in Chapter 17).

In this chapter, we discuss the modern tools of assessment and how they are used to determine the proper diagnosis of psychological symptoms and to understand the nature and causes of psychological problems. Some of these tools are very new, but others have been around for many years. These tools provide information on personality characteristics, cognitive deficits (such as learning disabilities or problems in maintaining attention), emotional well-being, and biological functioning. Increasingly, comprehensive assessments that take into account a person's biological, psychological, and social functioning are being done so that the contribution of each of these factors to symptoms can be understood.

We also consider modern systems of diagnosing psychological problems. There are a number of dangers and problems in applying a psychiatric diagnosis to a person, such as the stigmatizing effects of having a psychiatric diagnosis. We will discuss these dangers. Still, having a standardized system of diagnosis is crucial to communication among mental-health professionals and to good research on psychological problems. Clinicians must agree on what diagnostic labels mean, and a standardized diagnostic system provides agreed-upon definitions of disorders.

First, however, we explore the types of information to be gathered during an assessment. Then we review several methods that can be used to gather this information. Throughout the process of gathering information, the clinician must watch for many pitfalls in the assessment process, and we examine several of these in the following sections.

GATHERING INFORMATION

Let's look at three types of information—symptoms and history, physiological and neurophysiological factors, and sociocultural factors—that guide the formation of a diagnosis and treatment plan.

Symptoms and History

If you were Michael J. Fox's clinician, you would want to ask about his *current symptoms*, including their severity and chronicity. You would try to ascertain how much the symptoms are interfering with Fox's *ability to function* in the various domains of his life (e.g., in his work, his relationships with others, and his role as a parent). Is Fox experiencing the symptoms across a wide variety of situations or only in specific types of situations? The criteria for diagnosing most of the major psychological disorders require that the symptoms be severe and pervasive enough that they are interfering with the person's ability to function in daily life. If the symptoms are not that severe and are specific to one situation, then a diagnosis may not be warranted. Information about the pervasiveness and duration of Fox's symptoms will also help you formulate a plan for treatment that addresses all the areas in which he is having problems.

"I was beginning to think of myself as a visionary. Turned out they were hallucinations." © *Sidney Harris, courtesy ScienceCartoonsPlus.com*

In Fox's case, it would also be very helpful to know how he is *coping* with the stress of his life and his symptoms. Rather than seeking out people with whom he trusted to talk about his stresses, Fox initially turned to alcohol to drown his awareness of them. As is frequently the case, his way of coping with his symptoms and stressors created significant problems over and above his initial symptoms. Indeed, it turned out that his symptoms were the result of a neurological disorder, but he developed psychological symptoms of alcohol abuse in response to his neurological symptoms.

You would want to know about any *recent events* in Fox's life and whether the onset of the symptoms is tied to these life events. Fox thought his symptoms were due to his accidental hanging on a movie set. Symptoms that arise in response to a specific event are often given a different diagnosis (or, in some cases, no diagnosis) from the same symptoms when they arise with no apparent trigger.

For example, a child who becomes depressed after his or her parents separate might be given a diagnosis of adjustment disorder with depressed mood, whereas a child who gradually becomes more and more depressed for no apparent reason might be given a diagnosis of major depressive disorder. This distinction is made because symptoms that are triggered by a specific event often have a different prognosis and require different treatment than do symptoms that arise "out of the blue." A child whose symptoms of depression are triggered by a specific event is more likely to recover from these symptoms after a few talks with a supportive counselor than is a child who gradually becomes more and more depressed for no apparent reason.

An individual's *history of psychological problems* is also important in the assessment. For example, if Fox had a history of heavy drinking, his bout of

It is important for clients to receive a physical examination to determine whether medical problems are affecting their mental health.

drinking in response to his neurological symptoms might not just be a reaction to a stressor but rather, a longer-standing problem with alcohol abuse. It is also helpful to know an individual's *family history of disorders*. As we will discuss repeatedly in this book, many disorders appear to have genetic roots, so knowing that an individual has a family history of a particular disorder can assist in diagnosing that disorder.

Physiological and Neurophysiological Factors

Michael J. Fox's story is an interesting one from the perspective of assessment, because he was experiencing both severe neurological symptoms (tremors and weakness) and significant psychological symptoms (heavy drinking). It would be easy for a clinician to focus on one set of symptoms and to ignore the other.

When clients seek an assessment of what appear to be primarily psychological symptoms, it is still a good idea for the clinician to have them obtain a complete *physical examination* to determine if they are suffering from any medical conditions that can create psychological symptoms. For example, some brain tumors can create disorientation and agitation that are similar to symptoms of the psychological disorder schizophrenia.

Unfortunately, there are no definitive biological tests for any of the psychological disorders. What biological tests can sometimes tell, however, is whether there is a medical disease that is causing psychological symptoms as side effects. For example, thyroid disorders can cause people to experience the classic symptoms of depression, but most people who get depressed do not have a thyroid disorder. However, if an individual's depression is caused by a thyroid disorder, clinicians can often simply treat the thyroid disorder and the symptoms of depression will also disappear without any additional antidepressant treatment. For this reason, it is important to determine whether a medical disease, such as a thyroid disorder, might be causing a person's psychological symptoms.

Clinicians also need to know about any *drugs*—legal or illegal—their clients are taking. Many drugs can induce distressing psychological symptoms as side effects during drug use or withdrawal from the drug. In such cases, a different diagnosis is given from that given when the symptoms are not the consequence of a drug. Clinicians also need to know about any drugs a client is taking to protect against interactions between those drugs and medications the clinician might prescribe.

Clinicians often assess their clients' *cognitive functioning* and *intellectual abilities*. This information can be relevant to making a **differential diagnosis**—a determination of which of several possible disorders an individual may be suffering. For example, symptoms of paranoia can be the result of several psychological disorders, such as paranoid personality disorder or schizophrenia. They can also be the result of difficulties in short-term memory. People who cannot remember conversations they have had or where they have left items sometimes begin to believe that other people are doing things behind their backs. Determining whether or not symptoms of paranoia are due to cognitive deficits, such as memory loss, can have a major impact on the diagnosis and type of treatment the person receives.

Sociocultural Factors

Clients' social environment and cultural background can influence their symptoms and thus need to be assessed. Clinicians often ask about the *social resources* their clients have available—the number of friends and family members they have contact with and the quality of their relationships with these people. Michael J. Fox was fortunate to have tremendous support from his wife, Tracy. Social isolation can make it much more difficult for people to overcome psychological problems. On the other hand, friends and family members can also be burdens when these relationships are marked by conflict or create unreasonable demands.

An important step for clinicians working with a culturally diverse clientele is to obtain information on clients' *sociocultural background.* For immigrant clients, this background includes the specific culture in which they were raised, the number of years they have been in this country, the circumstances that brought them to this country (e.g., to escape war or oppression or to seek work), their continuing connections to their homeland, and whether they are currently living with people from their homeland (Dana, 2001; Westermeyer, 1993). As we will see, immigrants who left their homeland under difficult circumstances and who do not have a strong support system of people from their culture in their new homes are at especially high risk for disorders such as posttraumatic stress disorder (see Chapter 7). It is also useful to know as much as possible about the clients' socioeconomic status and occupation in their homeland—perhaps they were physicians in their homeland but now are street cleaners—because the contrast between their lives in the homeland and their current lives can be a source of difficulty.

Immigrants and other members of ethnic minority groups differ in their levels of acculturation. **Acculturation** is the extent to which a person identifies with his or her group of origin and its culture or with the dominant, mainstream culture (Dana, 2000). Some members of ethnic minority groups retain as much of their culture of origin as possible and reject the dominant, mainstream culture. They may continue to speak their language of origin and refuse to learn the dominant language. Other members fully identify with the dominant culture and reject their culture of origin. Still others are bicultural—they continue to identify with their culture of origin and celebrate it but also assimilate as necessary into the dominant culture.

Clinicians need to understand their clients' level of acculturation, because it can affect how clients talk about and present their problems, the kinds of stresses clients will be exposed to, and clients' responses to interventions (Lopez & Guarnaccia, 2000). We discuss these issues in more depth in Chapter 5, but let's briefly examine three examples. First, members of some cultures experience psychological distress in somatic symptoms, such as headaches and stomachaches (Kirmayer, 2001).

Parents and children can have different levels of acculturation, leading to conflicts.

Knowing that a client remains fully identified with a culture that tends to present psychological symptoms in somatic terms can help a clinician interpret a client's complaints. Second, when members of a family differ in their levels of acculturation, this difference can cause significant stress for family members. For example, an adolescent who is fully acculturated to the dominant culture may have many conflicts with a parent who remains identified with his or her culture of origin and does not want the adolescent to adopt the mainstream culture. Third, a client who is acculturated to the mainstream American culture will respond differently to certain suggestions a clinician makes, such as to confront an abusive boss, than will a client who remains identified with a culture in which authority figures are never questioned.

SUMMING UP

- Information concerning clients' symptoms and history is obtained in an assessment. This information includes the details of their current symptoms, their ability to function, their coping strategies, recent events, their history of psychological problems, and their family history of psychological problems.

- Clients' physiological and neurophysiological functioning is assessed as well. Clients may be asked to undergo a physical examination to detect medical conditions, questioned about their drug use, and tested for their cognitive functioning and intellectual abilities.

- Clients' sociocultural background—including their social resources and cultural heritage—is important to ascertain in an assessment.

ASSESSMENT TOOLS

A number of assessment tools have been developed to ensure that clinicians gather all the information needed for an accurate assessment.

Clinical Interviews

Much of the information for an assessment is gathered in an initial interview, often called an *intake interview,* or a *mental status exam,* when the clinician first meets the client. The interview may be an **unstructured interview,** with only a few questions that are open-ended, such as "Tell me about yourself." The clinician will listen to the client's answers to the questions and observe how the client answers—whether the client hesitates when talking about her marriage, whether she avoids questions about her drinking habits, whether she looks sad when talking about her career—to obtain nonverbal indicators of what is bothering her.

The clinician may also interview the client's family members for information about the family's history of psychological problems, the client's history, and the client's current symptoms. Information from family members is especially important if the client is a child, because children cannot always state what they are feeling or thinking. In addition, some adults are so impaired that they cannot provide adequate information to the assessor. They may be so depressed, anxious, or confused that they cannot properly answer questions. In such cases, an assessor often must rely entirely on family members and friends for information about a client's functioning.

Unstructured interviews have an important place in an assessment. The specific questions asked in an unstructured interview may vary from one assessor to the next, however, making comparisons of the information gathered by different assessors difficult. Increasingly, clinicians and researchers are using what is known as a **structured interview** to gather information about clients. In a structured interview, the clinician asks the respondent a series of questions about symptoms he or she is experiencing or has experienced in the past. The format of the questions and the entire interview is highly structured and standardized, and the clinician uses concrete criteria to score the person's answers to each question (see Table 4.1). At the end of the interview, the clinician should have enough information from the respondent to determine whether he or she has symptoms that qualify for a diagnosis of any of the major types of psychological problems.

Several such structured interviews have been developed in recent decades, including the Diagnostic Interview Schedule, or DIS (Robins et al., 1981), and the Structured Clinical Interview for the DSM (First et al., 1997). Structured interviews have also been adapted for diagnosing children's problems. Much of the information about a child's symptoms must often come from parents and other sources.

Structured and unstructured interviews can be valuable tools in assessment, but they have limitations. One of the greatest can be **resistance** on the part of the client who is being interviewed. Sometimes, the individual being assessed does not want to be assessed or treated. For example, the parents of a teenager may have forced him to see a psychologist because they are worried about recent changes in his behavior. This teenager may be resistant to providing any information to the assessor. Because much of the information a clinician needs must come directly from the person being assessed, resistance can be a formidable problem.

Even when the client is not completely resistant to being assessed, he or she may have a strong interest in the outcome of that assessment and thus may be highly selective in the information provided, may bias his or her presentation of the information, or may even lie to the assessor. Such problems often arise when assessments are being done as part of a legal case, such as when parents are fighting for custody of their children in divorce. Each parent will want to present him- or herself in the best light but may negatively bias his or her reports on the other parent when speaking to psychologists who have been appointed to assess each parent's fitness for custody of the children.

Cognitive, Symptom, and Personality Tests

Clinicians have a number of tests they use to aid in gathering information from clients. Before we discuss several of these tests, let's define two criteria that are used to evaluate the quality of any test: validity and reliability.

Validity

If you administer a test to determine what is wrong with a client, you want to be sure that the test is an accurate measure. The *accuracy* of a test in assessing what it is supposed to measure is called its **validity.** The best way to determine the validity of a test is to see if the results of the test yield the same information as an objective and accurate indicator of what the test is supposed to measure. For example, if there was a blood test that definitively proved

TABLE 4.1 Sample Structured Interview

Anxiety Disorders

Panic Disorder Questions

Have you ever had a panic attack, when you *suddenly* felt frightened, anxious, or extremely uncomfortable?

If Yes: Tell me about it. When does that happen? (Have you ever had one that just seemed to come out of the blue?) IF PANIC ATTACKS IN EXPECTED SITUATIONS: Did you ever have one of these attacks when you weren't in (EXPECTED SITUATION)?

Have you ever had four attacks like that in a four-week period?

If No: Did you worry a lot about having another one? (How long did you worry?)

When was the last bad one (EXPECTED OR UNEXPECTED)?

Now I am going to ask you about that attack. What was the first thing you noticed? Then what?

During the attack . . .

. . . were you short of breath? (have trouble catching your breath?)

. . . did you feel dizzy, unsteady, or as if you might faint?

. . . did your heart race, pound, or skip?

. . . did you tremble or shake?

. . . did you sweat?

. . . did you feel as if you were choking?

. . . did you have nausea, upset stomach, or the feeling that you were going to have diarrhea?

. . . did things around you seem unreal or did you feel detached from things around you or detached from part of your body?

Panic Disorder Criteria

A. At some time during the disturbance, one or more panic attacks (discrete periods of intense fear or discomfort) have occurred that were (1) unexpected, i.e., did not occur immediately before or on exposure to a situation that almost always causes anxiety, and (2) not triggered by situations in which the person was the focus of others' attention.

B. Either four attacks, as defined in criterion A, have occurred within a four-week period, or one or more attacks have been followed by a period of at least a month of persistent fear of having another attack.

C. At least four of the following symptoms developed during at least one of the attacks:

1. Shortness of breath (dyspnea) or smothering sensations
2. Dizziness, unsteady feelings, or faintness
3. Palpitations or accelerated heart rate (tachycardia)
4. Trembling or shaking
5. Sweating
6. Choking
7. Nausea or abdominal distress
8. Depersonalization or derealization

Source: Data from First et al., 1997.

whether a person had a particular psychological disorder, you would want any other test for that disorder (such as a questionnaire) to yield the same results when administered to the person. (You may remember that we talked about internal and external validity in Chapter 3 in reference to experimental studies. The types of validity we discuss here refer specifically to the validity of questionnaires or tests.)

So far, there are no definitive blood tests, brain scans, or other objective tests for any of the psychological disorders we discuss in this book. Fortunately, the validity of a test can be estimated in a number of other ways (see Figure 4.1 on page 106). A test is said to have **face validity** when, on face value, the items seem to be measuring what the test is intended to measure. For example, a questionnaire for anxiety that includes questions such

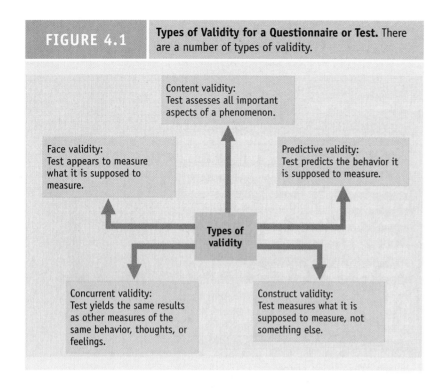

FIGURE 4.1   **Types of Validity for a Questionnaire or Test.** There are a number of types of validity.

Content validity:
Test assesses all important aspects of a phenomenon.

Face validity:
Test appears to measure what it is supposed to measure.

Predictive validity:
Test predicts the behavior it is supposed to measure.

Types of validity

Concurrent validity:
Test yields the same results as other measures of the same behavior, thoughts, or feelings.

Construct validity:
Test measures what it is supposed to measure, not something else.

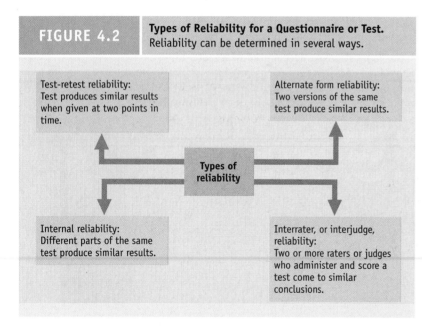

FIGURE 4.2   **Types of Reliability for a Questionnaire or Test.** Reliability can be determined in several ways.

Test-retest reliability:
Test produces similar results when given at two points in time.

Alternate form reliability:
Two versions of the same test produce similar results.

Types of reliability

Internal reliability:
Different parts of the same test produce similar results.

Interrater, or interjudge, reliability:
Two or more raters or judges who administer and score a test come to similar conclusions.

as "Do you feel jittery much of the time?" "Do you feel as if you can't sit still?" and "Do you worry about many things?" has face validity, because it seems to assess the symptoms of anxiety.

Content validity is the extent to which a test assesses all the important aspects of a phenomenon that it purports to measure. For example, if our measure of anxiety included only questions about the physical symptoms of anxiety (nervousness, restlessness, stomach distress, rapid heartbeat) and none of the cognitive symptoms of anxiety (appre-

hensions about the future, anticipation of negative events), then we might question whether it is a good measure of anxiety.

Concurrent validity is the extent to which a test yields the same results as other measures of the same behavior, thoughts, or feelings. A person's scores on our anxiety questionnaire should bear some relation to information gathered from the client's family members and friends about his or her typical level of anxiety. Information from family members and friends may not be completely accurate or valid, so it is not a definitive standard against which to judge our anxiety questionnaire. However, the notion behind concurrent validity is that any new measure of a variable should yield results similar to established measures of that variable.

A test that has **predictive validity** is good at predicting how a person will think, act, or feel in the future. Our anxiety measure has good predictive validity if it correctly predicts which people will behave in anxious ways when confronted with stressors in the future and which people will not be anxious.

Construct validity is the extent to which the test measures what it is supposed to measure, not something else altogether (Cronbach & Meehl, 1955). Consider the construct validity of multiple-choice exams given in courses. These exams are supposed to measure a student's knowledge and understanding of what has been taught in a course. What they may often measure, however, is the student's ability to take multiple-choice examinations—to determine what the instructor is trying to get at with the questions and to recognize any tricks or distractors in the questions.

Reliability

It is important that a test provide consistent information about a client. The **reliability** of a test is an indicator of the *consistency* of a test in measuring what it is supposed to measure. As with validity, there are several types of reliability (see Figure 4.2). **Test-retest reliability** is an index of how consistent the results of a test are over time. If a test supposedly measures an enduring characteristic of a person, then the person's scores on that test should be similar when he or she takes the test at two different points in time. For example, if our anxiety questionnaire is supposed to measure people's general tendencies to be anxious, then their scores on this questionnaire should be similar if they complete the questionnaire once this week and then again next week. On the other hand, if our anxiety questionnaire is a measure of people's current symptoms of anxiety (with questions such as "Do you feel jittery right now?"), then we might expect low test-retest reliability on this measure. Typically, measures of general and enduring characteristics should have higher test-retest reliability than measures of momentary, or transient, characteristics.

When people take the same test a second time, they may remember their answers from the first time and try to repeat these answers to seem consistent. For this reason, researchers often develop two or more forms of a test. When people's answers to these different forms of a test are similar, the tests are said to have **alternate form reliability.** Similarly, a researcher may simply split a test into two or more parts to determine if people's answers to one part of a test are similar to their answers to another part of the test. When there is similarity in people's answers among different parts of the same test, the test is said to have high **internal reliability.**

Finally, many of the tests we examine in this chapter are not self-report questionnaires but interviews or observational measures that require a clinician or researcher to make judgments about the people being assessed. These tests should have high **interrater,** or *interjudge,* **reliability.** That is, different raters or judges who administer and score the interview or test should come to similar conclusions when they are evaluating the same people.

Neuropsychological Tests

If the clinician suspects neurological impairment in a client, paper-and-pencil **neuropsychological tests** may be useful in detecting specific cognitive and fine-motor deficits, such as an attentional problem or a tendency to ignore items in one part of the visual field (Golden & Freshwater, 2001). One frequently used neuropsychological test is the Bender-Gestalt Test (Bender, 1938). This test assesses clients' sensorimotor skills by having them reproduce a set of nine drawings (see Figure 4.3). Clients with brain damage may rotate or change parts of the drawings or be unable to reproduce the drawings. When asked to remember the drawings after a delay, they may show significant memory deficits. The Bender-Gestalt Test appears to be good at differentiating people with brain damage from those without brain damage, but it does not reliably identify the specific type of brain damage a person has (Goldstein & Hersen, 1990).

More extensive batteries of tests have been developed to pinpoint types of brain damage. Two of the most popular batteries are the Halstead-Reitan Test (Reitan & Davidson, 1974) and the Luria-Nebraska Test (Luria, 1973). These batteries contain several tests that provide specific information about an individual's functioning in several skill

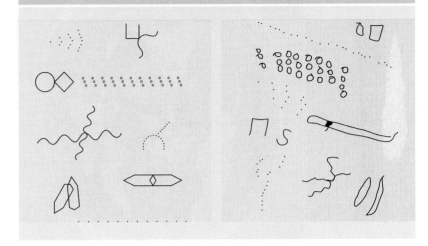

FIGURE 4.3   **The Bender-Gestalt Test.** On the left are the figures presented to clients. On the right are the figures as copied by a child with a brain tumor that is creating perceptual-motor difficulties.

areas, such as concentration, dexterity, and speed of comprehension.

Brain-Imaging Techniques

Increasingly, neuropsychological tests are being used in conjunction with brain-imaging techniques to identify specific deficits and possible brain abnormalities. Clinicians use brain scans to determine if a patient has a brain injury or tumor. Blood tests can detect medical problems (such as low blood sugar) that might be contributing to certain psychological symptoms. Researchers use brain scans and blood tests to search for differences in biochemicals or in brain activity or structure between people with a psychological disorder and people with no disorder. Ideally, this research will reveal enough about the biology of psychological disorders that researchers can develop valid and reliable biological tests for these disorders in the future.

Indeed, both technology and clinicians' understanding of the biology of disorders are advancing so rapidly that there will probably be major breakthroughs in biological techniques for assessing and diagnosing psychological disorders in the near future. Let's review existing brain-imaging technologies and what they can tell us now. This technology is providing some of the most exciting new findings in the search for biological underpinnings of psychological disorders. Michael J. Fox underwent several of these procedures when his physicians were trying to determine the sources of his symptoms.

Computerized tomography (CT) is an enhancement of X-ray procedures. In CT, narrow

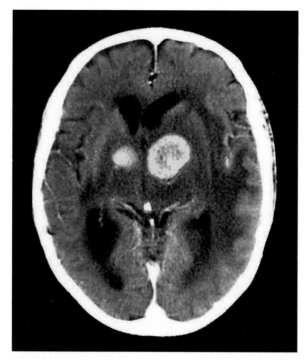

CT scan of a patient with a tumor in the tissues near the basal ganglia (tumor appears orange).

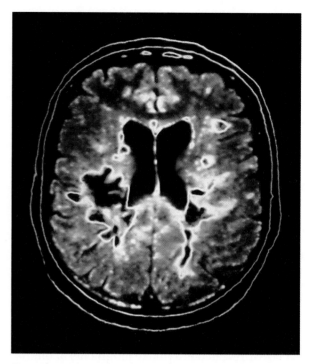

Magnetic resonance imaging (MRI) scan of a patient with multiple sclerosis. The orange/black areas are lesions of the myelin sheaths around axon nerve fibers.

X-ray beams are passed through the person's head in a single plane from a variety of angles. The amount of radiation absorbed by each beam is measured, and from these measurements a computer program constructs an image that looks like a slice of the brain. By taking many slices of the brain, the computer can reconstruct a three-dimensional image, showing the major structures of the brain. A CT scan can reveal brain injury, tumors, and structural abnormalities. The two major limitations of CT technology are that it exposes patients to X rays, which can be harmful, and it provides only an image of the *structure* of the brain, rather than an image of the *activity* in the brain.

Positron-emission tomography (PET) can provide a picture of activity in the brain. PET requires injecting the patient with a harmless radioactive isotope, such as fluorodeoxyglucose (FDG). This substance travels through the blood to the brain. The parts of the brain that are active need the glucose in FDG for nutrition, so FDG accumulates in the active parts of the brain. Subatomic particles in FDG, called *positrons*, are emitted as the isotope decays. These positrons collide with electrons, and both are annihilated and converted to two photons, traveling away from each other in opposite directions. The PET scanner detects these photons and the point at which they are annihilated and constructs an image of the brain, showing the areas that are most active.

PET scans can be used to show differences in the activity level of specific areas of the brain between people with a psychological disorder and people without a disorder.

Magnetic resonance imaging (MRI) holds several advantages over both CT and PET technology. It does not require exposing the patient to any form of radiation or injection of radioisotopes. It is safe to use repeatedly in the same patient. It provides much more finely detailed pictures of the anatomy of the brain than do other technologies, and it can image the brain at any angle. It can also provide pictures of the activity and functioning in the brain.

MRI involves creating a magnetic field around the brain that is so powerful that it causes a realignment of hydrogen atoms in the brain. When the magnetic field is turned off and on, the hydrogen atoms change position, causing them to emit magnetic signals. These signals are read by a computer, which reconstructs a three-dimensional image of the brain. Researchers are using MRI to study functional and structural brain abnormalities in almost every psychological disorder.

Intelligence Tests

In clinical practice, **intelligence tests** are used to get a sense of a client's intellectual strengths and weaknesses, particularly when mental retardation or brain damage is suspected (Ryan & Lopez, 2001).

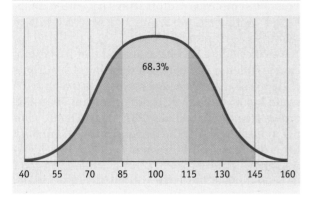

FIGURE 4.4 **IQ Distribution.** If the entire population took an IQ test, the scores would fall into a bell-shaped curve around the most frequent score of 100. More than two-thirds of all people score between 85 and 115 on IQ tests.

Intelligence tests are also used in schools to identify children with intellectual difficulties and to place children in "gifted" classrooms. They are used in occupational settings and the military to evaluate adults' capabilities for certain jobs or types of service. Some examples of these tests are the *Wechsler Adult Intelligence Scale*, the *Stanford-Binet Intelligence Test*, and the *Wechsler Intelligence Scale for Children*.

These tests were designed to measure basic intellectual abilities, such as the ability for abstract reasoning, verbal fluency, and spatial memory. The term *IQ* is used to describe a method of comparing an individual's score on an intelligence test with the performance of individuals of the same age group. An IQ score of 100 means that the person performed similarly to the average performance of other people his or her age (see Figure 4.4).

Intelligence tests are controversial in part because there is little consensus as to what is meant by intelligence (Sternberg, 2004). The most widely used *intelligence* tests assess verbal and analytical abilities but do not assess other talents or skills, such as artistic and musical ability. Some psychologists argue that success in life is as strongly influenced by social skills and other talents not measured by intelligence tests as by verbal and analytical skills (Gardner, 2003; Sternberg, 2004).

Another important criticism of intelligence tests is that they are biased in favor of middle- and upper-class, educated European Americans because these people have more familiarity with the kinds of reasoning that are assessed on the intelligence tests (Sternberg, 2004). In addition, educated European Americans may be more comfortable in taking intelligence tests, because testers are often also European Americans, and the testing situation resembles testing situations in their educational experience. In contrast, different cultures within the United States and in other countries may emphasize other forms of reasoning over those assessed on intelligence tests and may not be comfortable with the testing situations of intelligence tests.

A "culture-fair" test would have to include items that are equally applicable to all groups or items that are different for each culture but are psychologically equivalent for the groups being tested. Attempts have been made to develop culture-fair tests, but the results have been disappointing. Even if a universal test were created, it would be difficult to make statements about intelligence in different cultures, because different nations and cultures vary in the emphasis they place on "intellectual achievement."

So far, we have focused on tests to assess brain abnormalities and cognitive and intellectual functioning. Much of the information that must be gathered in an assessment, however, has to do with the client's emotional, social, and behavioral

Garfield ® by Jim Davis

TABLE 4.2 Sample Items from the Beck Depression Inventory®—Second Edition (BDI®—II)

Unhappiness

0   I do not feel unhappy.

1   I feel unhappy.

2   I am unhappy.

3   I am so unhappy that I can't stand it.

Changes in Activity Level

0   I have not experienced any change in activity level.

1a I am somewhat more active than usual.

1b I am somewhat less active than usual.

2a I am a lot more active than usual.

2b I am a lot less active than usual.

3a I am not active most of the day.

3b I am active all of the day.

Source: Beck Depression Inventory®—Second Edition. Copyright © 1996 by Aaron T. Beck. Reproduced with permission of Publisher, Harcourt Assessment, Inc. All rights reserved. Beck Depression Inventory and BDI are trademarks of Harcourt Assessment, Inc. registered in the United States and/or other jurisdictions.

Information concerning the BDI®—II is available from: Harcourt Assessment, Inc.
Attn: Customer Service
19500 Bulverde Road
San Antonio, TX 78259
Phone: (800) 211-8378
Fax: (800) 232-1223
Web site: www.harcourtassessment.com
Email: Customer_Service@harcourt.com

functioning. Now let's turn to tools that help the clinician assess these characteristics.

Symptom Questionnaires

Often, when a clinician or researcher wants a quick way to assess what symptoms a person is experiencing, he or she will ask the person to complete a **symptom questionnaire.** Some questionnaires cover a wide variety of symptoms, representing several different disorders. Others focus on the symptoms of specific disorders.

One of the most common questionnaires used to assess the symptoms of depression is the *Beck Depression Inventory*, or *BDI* (Beck & Beck, 1972).

The most recent form of the BDI has 21 items, each of which describes four levels of a given symptom of depression (see Table 4.2). The respondent is asked to indicate which of the descriptions best fits how he or she has been feeling in the past week. The items are scored to indicate the level of the depressive symptoms. Cutoff scores have been established to indicate moderate and severe levels of depressive symptoms.

Critics of the BDI have argued that it does not clearly differentiate between the clinical syndrome of depression and the general distress that may be related to an anxiety disorder or several other disorders (see Kendall et al., 1987). The BDI also cannot indicate whether the respondent would qualify for a diagnosis of depression. But the BDI is extremely quick and easy to administer and has good test-retest reliability. Hence, it is widely used, especially in research on depression.

Clinicians treating depressed people also use the BDI to keep track of their clients' symptom levels from week to week. They use it as a monitoring tool rather than as a diagnostic tool. A client may be asked to complete the BDI at the beginning of each therapy session, and both the client and the clinician then have a concrete indicator of the progress of the client's symptoms.

Personality Inventories

Personality inventories are usually questionnaires that are meant to assess people's typical ways of thinking, feeling, and behaving. These inventories are used as part of an assessment procedure to obtain information on people's well-being, self-concept, attitudes and beliefs, ways of coping, perceptions of their environment and social resources, and vulnerabilities. You have probably seen versions of personality inventories in popular magazines, although often these versions have not undergone much scientific scrutiny, as we discuss in *Taking Psychology Personally: Is Self-Assessment a Good Idea?*

The most widely used personality inventory in professional clinical assessments is the *Minnesota Multiphasic Personality Inventory (MMPI),* which has been translated into more than 150 languages and used in more than 50 countries (Dana, 1998). The original MMPI was first published in 1945 and contained 550 items. In 1990, an updated version, published under the name MMPI-2, contained 567 items (Butcher, 1990). Both versions of the MMPI present respondents with sentences describing moral and social attitudes, behaviors, psychological states, and physical conditions and ask them to respond "true," "false," or "can't say" to each sentence.

Taking Psychology Personally

Is Self-Assessment a Good Idea?

Self-help books and magazine articles often feature questionnaires that allow readers to assess their own personal characteristics or weaknesses or the characteristics of their relationships with others. These self-assessment tools typically involve a set of questions that help readers "diagnose" problems and some guidelines on how to interpret the scores on the questionnaires. Are these self-assessment tools a good idea?

In this chapter, we have discussed the problems with the reliability and validity of many assessment tools. The tools described in this chapter are the "best of the bunch"—those most widely used and accepted by professional psychologists and psychiatrists—yet even these tools have many critics. The self-assessment questionnaires in books and magazines are often not as well tested or well conceived as those we discuss in this chapter. In addition, the writers of these questionnaires often make claims about the diagnoses they produce that are overly conclusive and extreme, such as "If you scored between 10 and 20 on the Relationship Diagnostic Inventory, then your relationship is definitely going to fail. You might as well dump him and find someone else now!"

This does not mean that all self-assessment tools are a bad idea. People often want to deny their problems or are not aware that their symptoms are part of syndromes that can be treated successfully, and self-assessment tools can help people recognize their troubles and seek help. For example, questionnaires that lead people to recognize that they consume much more alcohol than the average person and that withdrawal from the effects of alcohol often interferes with their daily functioning can help these people moderate their alcohol consumption or seek treatment for alcohol addiction if necessary. Similarly, questionnaires or guidelines that make people aware that the symptoms they have been experiencing add up to the syndrome of an anxiety disorder can lead these people into therapy.

One of the most important points to remember about any self-assessment tool is that the information it provides is only suggestive, not conclusive. If you are concerned about the outcome of any self-assessment tool—your score on a questionnaire or how you have answered individual questions—it is a good idea to consult with a professional counselor about your concerns. Doing so would enable you to obtain a more thorough and expert assessment of how you are doing.

The MMPI was developed *empirically*, meaning that a large group of possible items were given to psychologically "healthy" people and to people suffering from various psychological problems. Then the items that reliably differentiated among the groups of people were included in the inventory.

The items on the original MMPI cluster into 10 scales, which measure different types of psychological characteristics or problems, such as paranoia, anxiety, and social introversion. An additional 4 scales were added to the MMPI-2 to assess vulnerability to eating disorders, substance abuse, and poor functioning at work. A respondent's scores on each of the scales are compared with scores from the normal population, and a profile of the respondent's personality and psychological problems is derived. There are also 4 validity scales that determine whether the person tends to respond to the items on the scale in an honest and straightforward manner or tends to distort his or her answers in a way that might invalidate the test (see Table 4.3 on page 112). For example, the Lie scale measures the respondent's tendency to respond to items in a socially desirable way that makes him or her look unusually positive or good.

Because the items on the MMPI were chosen for their ability to differentiate people with specific types of psychological problems from people without psychological problems, the concurrent validity of the MMPI scales was built in during their development. The MMPI may be especially useful as a general screening device for detecting people who are functioning very poorly psychologically. The test-retest reliability of the MMPI has also proven to be quite high (Dorfman & Leonard, 2001).

Many criticisms have been raised about the use of the MMPI in culturally diverse samples (Dana, 1998; Tsai et al., 2001). The norms for the original MMPI—the scores considered "healthy" scores—were based on samples of people in the United States that were not representative of people from a wide range of ethnic backgrounds, age groups, and social classes. In response to this problem, the publishers of the MMPI established new norms based

TABLE 4.3 Clinical and Validity Scales of the Original MMPI

The MMPI is one of the most widely used questionnaires to assess people's symptoms and personalities. It also includes scales to assess whether respondents are lying or trying to obfuscate their answers.

CLINICAL SCALES

SCALE NUMBER	SCALE NAME	WHAT IT MEASURES
Scale 1	Hypochondriasis	Excessive somatic concern and physical complaints
Scale 2	Depression	Symptomatic depression
Scale 3	Hysteria	Hysterical personality features and tendency to develop physical symptoms under stress
Scale 4	Psychopathic deviate	Antisocial tendencies
Scale 5	Masculinity-femininity	Sex role conflict
Scale 6	Paranoia	Suspicious, paranoid thinking
Scale 7	Psychasthenia	Anxiety and obsessive behavior
Scale 8	Schizophrenia	Bizarre thoughts and disordered affect
Scale 9	Hypomania	Behavior found in mania
Scale 0	Social introversion	Social anxiety, withdrawal, overcontrol

VALIDITY SCALES

	SCALE NAME	WHAT IT MEASURES
	Cannot say scale	Total number of unanswered items
	Lie scale	Tendency to present favorable image
	Infrequency scale	Tendency to falsely claim psychological problems
	Defensiveness scale	Tendency to see oneself in unrealistically positive manner

Source: Clinical and Validity Scales of the Original MMPI Minnesota Multiphasic Personality Inventory (MMPI). Copyright © 1942, 1943, 1951, 1967 (renewed 1970), 1983. Reprinted by permission of the University of Minnesota. "MMPI" and "Minnesota Multiphasic Personality Inventory" are trademarks owned by the University of Minnesota.

on more representative samples of eight communities across the United States. Still, there are concerns that the MMPI norms do not reflect variations across cultures in what is considered normal or abnormal. In addition, the linguistic accuracy of the translated versions of the MMPI and the comparability of these versions to the English version have been questioned (Dana, 1998).

Projective Tests

A **projective test** is based on the assumption that, when people are presented with an ambiguous stimulus, such as an oddly shaped inkblot or a captionless picture, they will interpret the stimulus in line with their current concerns and feelings, their relationships with others, and their conflicts or desires. The people are said to project these issues as they describe the content of the stimulus,

hence the name *projective tests*. Proponents of these tests argue that they are useful in uncovering the unconscious issues or motives of a person or in assessing a person who is resistant or heavily biasing the information he or she presents to the assessor. Four of the most frequently used projective tests are the Rorschach Inkblot Test, the Thematic Apperception Test (TAT), the Sentence Completion Test, and the Draw-a-Person Test.

The *Rorschach Inkblot Test*, commonly referred to simply as the *Rorschach*, was developed in 1921 by Swiss psychiatrist Hermann Rorschach. The test consists of 10 cards, each containing a symmetrical inkblot in black, gray, and white or in color (see Figure 4.5). The examiner tells the respondent something like "People may see many different things in these inkblot pictures; now tell me what you see, what it makes you think of, what it means

"Rorschach! What's to become of you?" © *Sidney Harris, courtesy ScienceCartoonsPlus.com*

the inkblot as a whole or the clients' hesitations in responding to certain inkblots (Exner, 1993).

The *Thematic Apperception Test (TAT)* consists of a series of pictures. The client is asked to make up a story about what is happening in the pictures (Murray, 1943). Proponents of the TAT argue that clients' stories reflect their concerns and wishes and their personality traits and motives. As with the Rorschach, clinicians are interested in both the content and the style of clients' responses to the TAT cards. Some cards may stimulate more emotional responses than others or no responses at all. These cards are considered to tap the clients' most important issues. The following is a story that a person made up about a picture of a man and young woman (Allison, Blatt, & Zimet, 1968).

to you" (Exner, 1993). Clinicians are interested in both the content of the clients' responses to the inkblots and the style of their responses. In the content of responses, they look for particular themes or concerns, such as the frequent mention of aggression or fear of abandonment. Important stylistic features may include the clients' tendency to focus on small details of the inkblot rather than

> This looks like a nice man and—a sweet girl—They look like this is a happy moment—Looks like he's telling her that he loves her—or something that's tender and sweet. She looks very confident and happy! It looks nice; I like it. Hm! Wait now! Maybe—well—that's right—he looks kind of older—but she looks efficient—
> *(continued)*

| **FIGURE 4.5** | **Projective Tests.** Clinicians analyze people's answers to projective tests for particular themes or concerns. |

VOICES

and sweet. [Efficient?] Yes [laughs]. Doesn't look particularly efficient at the moment, but I imagine—[puts card away]. [What led up to this?] Well—I think maybe he taught school nearby, and she was a girl in the village—It strikes me as a sort of sweet, old fashioned romance. Maybe she's seen him a long time, and now it has just come to the state where he tells her that he loves her. [What will the outcome be?] I think they will get married, get some children and be happy—not that they will live happily ever after, not like a fairy tale. They look like ordinary people.

In interpreting the client's story, the clinician might note that it exhibits a romanticized, naive, and childlike quality. The client presents a very conventional scenario but with moral themes and much emotional expression. The clinician might interpret these tendencies as part of the client's basic personality style (Allison et al., 1968).

A third test that is based on the idea that people project their concerns and wishes onto ambiguous stimuli is the *Sentence Completion Test*. Sentence Completion Tests have been designed for children, adolescents, and adults. The tests provide a "stem," which is the beginning of a sentence, such as "My mother is . . ." or "I wish. . . ." The individual is asked to complete the sentence. Although more structured than the Rorschach and TAT, Sentence Completion Tests are also interpreted subjectively by the examiner. Clinicians might look for indications of the person's concerns in both what he or she says in response to the sentence stem and what he or she avoids saying in response to the stem. For example, a clinician might find it interesting that the person seems unable to come up with any response to the stem "Sex is. . . ."

A fourth test is the *Draw-a-Person Test* (Machover, 1949). The client is asked to draw a picture of him- or herself and then to draw a picture of another person of the opposite sex. The clinician examines how the client depicts him- or herself: Does he draw himself as a small figure, huddled in the corner of the page, or as a large figure, filling the page? The drawings of self are thought to reflect the client's self-concept as a strong person or weak person, a smart person or unintelligent person, and so on. The drawing of the other person is thought to reflect the client's attitudes toward the opposite sex and his or her relationships with important members of the opposite sex.

Clinicians from psychodynamic perspectives see projective tests as valuable tools for assessing the underlying conflicts and concerns that clients cannot or will not report directly. Clinicians from other perspectives question the usefulness of these tests. The validity and reliability of all of the projective tests have not proven strong in research (Garb, Florio, & Grove, 1998; Kline, 1993). In addition, because these tests rely so greatly on subjective interpretations by clinicians, they are open to a number of biases. Finally, criteria for interpreting the tests do not take into account the cultural context from which an individual comes (Dana, 2001).

Behavioral Observation and Self-Monitoring

Clinicians often use **behavioral observation** of clients to assess deficits in their skills or ways of handling situations. For example, a clinician might watch a child interact with other children to determine what situations seem to provoke the child to act aggressively. The clinician can then use information from behavioral observation to help the client learn new skills, stop negative habits, and understand and change the way he or she reacts to certain situations. A couple seeking marital therapy might be asked to discuss with each other a topic on which they disagree. The clinician observes this interaction, noting the specific ways that the couple handles conflict. For example, one member of the couple may lapse into statements that blame the other for problems in their marriage, escalating conflict to a boiling point.

Behavioral observation is a good way to gather data, but these observations should be reliable.

The advantages of direct behavioral observation are that it does not rely on the clients' reporting and interpretation of their behaviors. Instead, the clinician sees just how skilled a client is or is not in handling important situations. One disadvantage is that different observers may draw different conclusions about an individual's skills. That is, direct behavioral observations may have low interrater reliability, especially when no standard means of making the observations are established. In addition, any individual rater may have difficulty catching everything that is happening in a situation, particularly when he or she is observing two or more people interacting.

It can be time-consuming and sometimes impossible for a clinician to observe a client's behaviors in key situations. If direct observation is not possible, the clinician may require client **self-monitoring**—that is, may ask the client to keep track of the number of times per day he or she engages in a specific behavior (e.g., smoking a cigarette) and the conditions under which this behavior happens. The following is an example (adapted from Thorpe & Olson, 1997, p. 149):

> Steve, a binge drinker, was asked to self-monitor his drinking behavior for two weeks, noting the situational context of urges to drink and his associated thoughts and feelings. These data revealed that Steve's drinking was completely confined to bar situations, where he drank in the company of friends. Gaining relief from stress was a recurring theme.

Self-monitoring is open to biases in what the client notices about his or her behavior and is willing to report. However, the client can gain valuable insight into the triggers of unwanted behaviors through self-monitoring, which can lead to changing these behaviors.

SUMMING UP

- Paper-and-pencil neuropsychological tests can help identify specific cognitive deficits that may be tied to brain damage.
- CT, PET, and MRI technologies are used to investigate the structural and functional differences between the brains of people with psychological disorders and those of people without disorders. We cannot yet use these technologies to diagnose specific psychological disorders in individual patients.
- Intelligence tests can indicate a client's general level of intellectual functioning in verbal and analytic tasks.

- Structured interviews provide a standardized way to assess, in an interview format, people's symptoms.
- Symptom questionnaires allow for the mass screening of large numbers of people to determine self-reported symptoms.
- Personality inventories assess stable personality characteristics.
- Projective tests are used to uncover unconscious conflicts and concerns but are open to interpretive biases.
- Behavioral observation and self-monitoring can help detect behavioral deficits and the environmental triggers for symptoms.

PROBLEMS IN ASSESSMENT

Some of the problems that arise in assessing clients' problems include the client's inability to provide information or resistance to providing information and the weaknesses of the tests used to gain information. In this section, we examine the challenges that arise in assessing certain groups of clients—children and people from cultures different from the assessor's culture.

Evaluating Children

Consider the following conversation between a mother and her 5-year-old son, Jonathon, who has been sent home from preschool for fighting with another child.

Mom: Jonathon, why did you hit that boy?

Jonathon: I dunno. I just did.

Mom: But I want to understand what happened. Did he do something that made you mad?

Jonathon: Yeah, I guess.

Mom: What did he do? Did he hit you?

Jonathon: Yeah.

Mom: Why did he hit you?

Jonathon: I dunno. He just did. Can I go now?

Mom: I need to know more about what happened.

Jonathon: [Silence]

Mom: Can you tell me more about what happened?

Jonathon: No. He just hit me and I just hit him. Can I go now?

Anyone who has tried to have a conversation with a distressed child about why he or she misbehaved has a sense of how difficult it can be to engage a child in a discussion about emotions or behaviors. Even when a child talks readily, his or

It can be difficult to talk with a distressed child or teenager who doesn't want to talk about his or her feelings.

her understanding of the causes of his or her behaviors or emotions may not be very well developed. Children, particularly preschool-age children, cannot describe their feelings, or the events associated with these feelings, as easily as adults can. Young children do not differentiate among different types of emotions, often just saying that they feel "bad," for example (Harter, 1983). When distressed, children may talk about physical aches and pains rather than the emotional pain they are feeling. Or a child might not verbalize that he or she is distressed and show this distress only in nonverbal behavior, such as making a sad face, withdrawing, or behaving aggressively. Children who have behavior problems, such as excessive distractibility or lack of control over their anger, may not believe that they have problems and thus may deny that anything is wrong (Kazdin, 1991).

These problems with children's self-reporting of emotional and behavior problems have led clinicians and researchers to rely on other people, usually adults in children's lives, to provide information about children's functioning. Parents are often the first source of information about a child's functioning. A clinician may interview a child's parents when the child is taken for treatment, asking the parents about changes in the child's behavior and corresponding events in the child's life. A researcher studying children's functioning may ask parents to complete questionnaires assessing the children's behavior in a variety of settings.

Because parents typically spend more time with their child than any other person does, they potentially have the most complete information about the child's functioning and a sense of how the child's behavior has or has not changed over time. Unfortunately, however, parents are not always accurate in their assessments of their children's functioning. One study found that the parents and children disagreed as to what prob-

lems had brought the child to a psychiatric clinic in 63 percent of the cases (Yeh & Weisz, 2001). Parents' perceptions of their children's well-being can be influenced by their own symptoms of psychopathology and their expectations for their children's behavior (Nock & Kazdin, 2001). Indeed, sometimes parents take children for assessment and treatment of psychological problems as a way of seeking treatment for themselves.

Parents may also be the source of a child's psychological problems and, as a result, unwilling to acknowledge or seek help for the child's problems. The most extreme example is parents who are physically or sexually abusing a child. These parents are unlikely to acknowledge the psychological or physical harm they are causing the child or to seek treatment for that harm. A less extreme example is parents who do not want to believe that an action they have taken, such as filing for a divorce or moving the family across the country, is the cause of the child's emotional or behavior problems. Again, such parents may be slow in taking a child who is distressed to a mental-health professional or in admitting to the child's problems when asked by a researcher.

Cultural norms for children's behaviors differ, and parents' expectations for their children and their tolerance of "deviant" behavior in children are affected by these norms. For example, Jamaican parents appear more tolerant than American parents of unusual behaviors in children, including both aggressive behavior and behavior indicating that a child is shy and inhibited. In turn, Jamaican parents have a higher threshold than American parents in terms of the appropriate time to take a child to a clinician (Lambert et al., 1992).

Teachers are another source of information about children's functioning. Teachers and other school personnel (such as guidance counselors and coaches) are often the first to recognize that a child has a problem and to initiate an intervention for the problem. Teachers' assessments of children, however, are often different from the assessments by other adults, including parents and trained clinicians (Weisz et al., 1995). Such discrepancies may arise because these other adults are providing invalid assessments of the children, whereas the teachers are providing valid assessments. The discrepancies may also arise because children function at different levels in different settings. At home a child may be well behaved, quiet, and withdrawn, but at school the same child may be impulsive, easily angered, and distractible. These differences in a child's behavior in different settings might make it seem that either a parent's report of the child's behavior or the teacher's report is invalid, when the truth is that the child simply acts differently, depending on the situation.

Evaluating Clients from Other Cultures

A number of challenges to assessment arise when there are significant cultural differences between the assessor and the person being assessed (Dana, 2000; Tsai et al., 2001; Tseng, 2001). Imagine having to obtain all the information needed to assess what is wrong with someone from a culture very different from your own. The first problem you may run into is that the client does not speak the same language you do or speaks your language only partially (and you do not speak his or hers at all). There is evidence that symptoms can go both underdiagnosed and overdiagnosed when the client and assessor do not speak the same language (Okazaki & Sue, 2003). Overdiagnosis often occurs because a client tries to describe his or her symptoms in the assessor's language, but the assessor interprets a client's slow and somewhat confused description of symptoms as indicating more pathology than is really present. Underdiagnosis can occur when the client cannot articulate complex emotions or strange perceptual experiences in the assessor's language and thus does not even try.

One solution is to find an interpreter to translate between the clinician and the client. Interpreters can be invaluable to good communication. However, interpreters who are not trained assessors themselves can misunderstand and mistranslate a clinician's questions and the client's answers, as in the following example (Marcos, 1979, p. 173):

> **Clinician to Spanish-speaking patient:** "Do you feel sad or blue, do you feel that life is not worthwhile sometimes?"
>
> **Interpreter to patient:** "The doctor wants to know if you feel sad and if you like your life."
>
> **Patient's response:** "No, yes, I know that my children need me, I cannot give up, I prefer not to think about it."
>
> **Interpreter to clinician:** "She says that no, she says that she loves her children and that her children need her."

In this case, the interpreter did not accurately reflect the client's answer to the clinician's question, giving the clinician a sense that the client was doing much better than the client reported she was. In addition, different people from the same country can speak different dialects of a language or can have different means of expressing feelings and attitudes. Mistranslation can occur when the interpreter does not speak the client's dialect or comes from a different subculture than the client.

Cultural differences between clients and clinicians can lead to misinterpretations of clients' problems.

Even when mistranslation is not a problem, some of the questions that the assessor asks or that appear on a test or questionnaire may be so culture-bound that they do not make sense to the client, or they can be interpreted by the client in ways the assessor did not anticipate. This can happen on even the most objective of tests. For example, several assessment tests ask whether a client ever believes that forces or powers other than herself control her behavior or if she ever hears voices talking in her head. According to Western conceptualizations, these are signs of psychosis, yet many cultures, such as the Xhosa of South Africa, believe that ancestors live in the same psychic world as living relatives and that ancestors speak to the living and advise them on their behavior (Gillis et al., 1982). Thus, members of this culture might answer yes to questions intended to assess psychotic thinking, when they are really reporting on the beliefs of their culture.

Cultural biases can arise when everyone is supposedly speaking the same language but each person comes from a unique cultural background. There is evidence that African Americans in the United States are overdiagnosed as suffering from schizophrenia (Neighbors et al., 2003). For example, African Americans are more likely than European Americans to be misdiagnosed as schizophrenic when their symptoms actually fit the diagnosis of bipolar disorder (Mukherjee et al., 1983). Some investigators believe that cultural differences in the presentation of symptoms play a role (Neighbors, 1984). African Americans may present more intense symptoms than European Americans, and these symptoms are then misunderstood by European American assessors as representing more severe psychopathology. Another possibility is that some European American assessors are too quick to diagnose severe psychopathology in African Americans because of negative stereotypes of them.

Finally, even when clinicians avoid all these biases, they are still left with the fact that people from other cultures often think about and talk about their psychological symptoms quite differently than do members of their own culture. We discuss several examples of cultural differences in the presentation of symptoms throughout this book. One of the most pervasive differences is in whether cultures experience and report psychological distress in emotional symptoms or in somatic (physical) symptoms. European Americans tend to view the body and mind separately, whereas many other cultures do not make sharp distinctions between the experiences of the body and the experiences of the mind (Okazaki & Sue, 2003). Following a psychologically distressing event, European Americans tend to report that they feel anxious or sad, but members of many other cultures report having physical aches and maladies. To conduct an accurate assessment, clinicians must know about cultural differences in the manifestation of disorders and in the presentation of symptoms, and they must use this information correctly in interpreting the symptoms that their clients report. Cultural differences are further complicated by the fact that not every member of a culture conforms to what is known about that culture. That is, within every culture, people differ in their acceptance of cultural norms for behavior.

SUMMING UP

- It is often difficult to obtain accurate information on children's problems because children are unable to report their thoughts and feelings. Parents and teachers may provide information about children, but they can be biased in their own assessments of children's symptoms and needs.

- When the clinician and client are from different cultures, language difficulties and cultural expectations can make assessment difficult. Interpreters can help in the assessment process but must be well trained in psychological assessment.

DIAGNOSIS

Recall that a *diagnosis* is a label attached to a set of symptoms that tend to occur together. This set of symptoms is referred to as a **syndrome.** In medical models of psychological disorders, a syndrome is thought to be the observable manifestation of an underlying biological disorder. Thus, if you have the symptoms that make up the syndrome *schizophrenia*, you are thought also to have a biological disorder called *schizophrenia*. As we have noted, however, there are no definitive biological tests for psychological disorders. For this reason, it is impossible to verify whether a given person *has* schizophrenia by giving him or her a biological test for schizophrenia.

We are left to observe humans and identify what symptoms typically occur together in them, and then we call those co-occurring symptoms a *syndrome*. Identifying naturally occurring syndromes is no easy task. Typically, several symptoms make up a syndrome, but people differ in which of these symptoms they experience most strongly. Think about the last time you were in a sad or depressed mood. Did you also feel tired and have trouble sleeping? Do you always feel tired and have trouble sleeping every time you are in a sad or depressed mood or just sometimes? Does everyone you know also experience fatigue and sleeplessness when in a sad mood? Or do some of them simply lose their appetite and their ability to concentrate?

Thus, syndromes are not lists of symptoms that all people have all of the time, if they have any of the symptoms at all. Rather, they are lists of symptoms that tend to co-occur within individuals. There may be overlap between the symptoms of one syndrome and the symptoms of another. Figure 4.6 shows the overlap in the symptoms that make up two common psychological disorders, major depressive disorder (see Chapter 9) and generalized anxiety disorder (see Chapter 7). Both disorders include the symptoms fatigue, sleep disturbances, and concentration problems. Each disorder has symptoms that are more specific to it, however.

For centuries, people have tried to organize the confusing array of psychological symptoms into a limited set of syndromes. This set of syndromes and the rules for determining whether an individual's symptoms are part of one of these syndromes constitute a **classification system.**

One of the first classification systems for psychological symptoms was proposed by Hippocrates in the fourth century B.C. Hippocrates divided all mental disorders into mania (states of abnormal excitement), melancholia (states of abnormal depression), paranoia, and epilepsy. Modern classification systems divide the world of psychological symptoms into a many more syndromes than did Hippocrates. Let's focus on the classification system most widely used in the United States. Then we will examine the dangers of *diagnosis*.

Diagnostic and Statistical Manual of Mental Disorders (DSM)

For more than 50 years, the official manual for diagnosing psychological disorders in the United States has been the ***Diagnostic and Statistical Manual of Mental Disorders*** **(DSM)** of the American Psychiatric Association. The first edition of the DSM was published in 1952. It outlined the diagnostic criteria for all the mental disorders recognized by the psychiatric community at the time. These criteria were somewhat vague descriptions heavily influenced by psychoanalytic theory. For example, the diagnosis of *anxiety neurosis* could have been manifested in a great variety of specific behavioral and emotional symptoms. The key to the diagnosis was whether the clinician inferred that unconscious conflicts were causing the client to experience anxiety. The second edition of the DSM (DSM-II), published in 1968, included some new disorders that had been recognized since the publication of the first edition but was not much different.

Because the descriptions of disorders were so abstract and theory based in the first and second editions of the DSM, the reliability of the diagnoses was low. For example, one study found that 4 experienced clinicians using the first edition of the DSM to diagnose 153 patients agreed on their diagnoses only 54 percent of the time (Beck et al., 1962). This low reliability eventually led psychiatrists and psychologists to call for a radically new system of diagnosing mental disorders.

DSM-III, DSM-IIIR, DSM-IV, and DSM-IV-TR

In response to the reliability problems of the first and second editions of the DSM, in 1980 the American Psychiatric Association published the third edition of the DSM, known as DSM-III. The third edition was followed by a revised third edition, known as DSM-IIIR, published in 1987, and a fourth edition, known as DSM-IV, originally published in 1994 and revised as DSM-IV-TR in 2000.

In the newer editions of the DSM, the developers replaced the vague descriptions of disorders with specific and concrete criteria for each disorder. These criteria are in the form of behaviors people must show and experiences or feelings they must report in order to be given a diagnosis. The developers tried to be as atheoretical and descriptive as possible in listing the criteria for each disorder. Good examples are the diagnostic criteria for panic disorder in the DSM-IV-TR, which are given

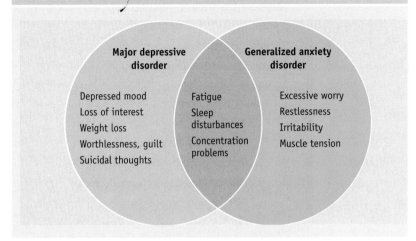

FIGURE 4.6 **Syndromes as Clusters of Symptoms.** Syndromes are clusters of symptoms that frequently co-occur. The symptoms of one syndrome, such as major depressive disorder, can overlap with the symptoms of another syndrome, such as generalized anxiety disorder.

in Table 4.4. As you can see, a person must have 4 of 13 possible symptoms in order to be given the diagnosis of panic disorder. These criteria reflect the fact that not all the symptoms of panic disorder will be present in every assessed individual.

Two other elements distinguish the DSM-III, DSM-IIIR, DSM-IV, and DSM-IV-TR from their predecessors. First, the later editions specify how long a person must show symptoms of the disorder to be given the diagnosis (see Table 4.4 on page 120, item B). Second, the criteria for most disorders require that the symptoms interfere with occupational or social functioning for the person to be diagnosed. This emphasis on symptoms that are long-lasting and severe reflects the consensus among psychiatrists and psychologists that abnormality should be defined in terms of the impact of behaviors on the individual's ability to function and on his or her sense of well-being (see Chapter 1).

Reliability of the DSM

Despite the use of explicit criteria for disorders, the reliability of many of the diagnoses listed in the DSM-III and DSM-IIIR was disappointing. On average, experienced clinicians agreed on their diagnoses using these manuals only about 70 percent of the time (Kirk & Kutchins, 1992). The reliability of some of the diagnoses, particularly the personality disorder diagnoses, was much lower.

Low reliability of diagnoses can be caused by many factors. Although the developers of the DSM-III and DSM-IIIR attempted to make the criteria for each disorder explicit, many of the criteria were still vague and required the clinician to make

TABLE 4.4   DSM-IV-TR

Diagnostic Criteria for Panic Disorder

These are the DSM-IV-TR criteria for a diagnosis of panic disorder. They specify core symptoms that must be present and several other symptoms, a certain number of which must be present, for the diagnosis.

A. At some time during the disturbance, one or more panic attacks have occurred that were (1) unexpected, and (2) not triggered by situations in which the person was the focus of another's attention.

B. Either four attacks, as defined in criterion A, have occurred within a four-week period, or one or more attacks have been followed by a period of at least a month of persistent fear of having another attack.

C. At least four of the following symptoms developed during at least one of the attacks:

1. Shortness of breath or smothering sensations
2. Dizziness, unsteady feelings, or faintness
3. Palpitations or accelerated heart rate
4. Trembling or shaking
5. Sweating
6. Choking
7. Nausea or abdominal distress
8. Depersonalization or derealization
9. Numbness or tingling sensations
0. Flushes or chills
11. Chest pain or discomfort
12. Fear of dying
13. Fear of going crazy or doing something uncontrolled

D. During at least some of the attacks, at least four of the C symptoms developed suddenly and increased in intensity within 10 minutes of the beginning of the first C symptom.

E. It cannot be established that an organic factor initiated the disturbance, such as caffeine intoxication.

Source: Reprinted with permission from the *Diagnostic and Statistical Manual of Mental Disorders,* Fourth Edition, Text Revision. Copyright © 2000 American Psychiatric Association.

inferences about the client's symptoms or to rely on the client's willingness to report symptoms. For example, most of the symptoms of the mood disorders and anxiety disorders (e.g., sadness, apprehensiveness, hopelessness) are subjective experiences, and only clients can report whether they have these symptoms and how severe they are. To diagnose any of the personality disorders, the clinician must establish that the client has a lifelong history of specific dysfunctional behaviors or ways of relating to the world. Unless the clinician has known the client all his or her life, the clinician must rely on the client and the client's family to provide information about the client's history, and different sources of information can provide very different pictures of the client's functioning.

In an effort to increase the reliability of diagnoses in the DSM-IV, the task force that developed the DSM-IV conducted numerous field trials, in which the criteria for most of the diagnoses to be included in the DSM-IV were tested in clinical and research settings. In a field trial, testing determines if diagnostic criteria can be applied reliably and if they fit clients' experiences. As a result, the reliability of the DSM-IV diagnoses are higher than the reliability of the predecessors, although clearly they are not perfectly reliable (Widiger, 2002).

Multiaxial System

In a system introduced in the third edition of the DSM, the manual specifies five *axes*, or dimensions, along which a clinician evaluates a client's behavior (see Table 4.5). Only the first two axes list actual disorders and the criteria required for their diagnoses. The other three axes are meant to provide information on physical conditions that might

TABLE 4.5	DSM-IV-TR

The DSM-IV-TR has five axes, along which each client should be evaluated.

Axis I	Clinical disorders
Axis II	Personality disorders
	Mental retardation
Axis III	General medical conditions
Axis IV	Psychosocial and environmental problems
Axis V	Global assessment of functioning

Source: Reprinted with permission from the *Diagnostic and Statistical Manual of Mental Disorders,* Fourth Edition, Text Revision. Copyright © 2000 American Psychiatric Association.

TABLE 4.6	Disorders Listed on Axis I

These disorders, most of which we discuss in this book, represent conditions that typically cause people significant distress or impairment.

Disorders usually first diagnosed in infancy, childhood, or adolescence

- Attention-deficit disorder
- Hyperactivity
- Conduct and oppositional disorder
- Separation anxiety disorder
- Pervasive developmental disorder
- Learning disorders
- Feeding, tic, and elimination disorders

Delirium, dementia, and amnesic or other cognitive disorders

Substance-related disorders

Schizophrenia and other psychotic disorders

Mood disorders

Anxiety disorders

Somatoform disorders

Factitious disorders

Dissociative disorders

Sexual and gender identity disorders

Eating disorders

Sleep disorders

Adjustment disorders

Other conditions that may be a focus of clinical attention

Source: Reprinted with permission from the *Diagnostic and Statistical Manual of Mental Disorders,* Fourth Edition, Text Revision. Copyright © 2000 American Psychiatric Association.

be affecting the person's mental health (Axis III), psychosocial and environmental stressors in the person's life (Axis IV), and the degree of impairment in the person's mental health and functioning (Axis V). Let's take a look at these five axes, one by one, and then apply them to a case study.

On Axis I, a clinician lists any major disorders for which the person qualifies, with the exclusion of mental retardation and personality disorders (see Table 4.6). The clinician also notes whether these disorders are chronic or acute. *Chronic* disorders last for long periods of time. *Acute* disorders have a more recent and abrupt onset of severe symptoms.

On Axis II, the clinician lists mental retardation or any personality disorders for which the person qualifies (see Table 4.7 on page 122). Mental retardation is listed on Axis II instead of Axis I because it is a lifelong condition, whereas most of the disorders on Axis I tend to wax and wane across the life span. Similarly, a personality disorder is characterized by a chronic and pervasive pattern of dysfunctional behavior that the person has shown since at least adolescence. For example, a person with an antisocial personality disorder has a lifelong pattern of being abusive toward others and violating basic norms of social relationships.

On Axis III, the clinician notes any medical or physical diseases from which the person is suffering. These diseases may or may not be directly related to the psychological disorders from which the person is also suffering. For example, a person may have lung cancer, which has nothing to do with the fact that he or she also has schizophrenia. However, it is important for the clinician to know about any physical diseases for two reasons. First, these diseases could be related to the person's mental health.

For example, Michael J. Fox was abusing alcohol in part because he was distressed over his neurological symptoms. Also, a clinician must guard against any interactions between the drugs the patient is taking for the physical disease and the drugs the clinician will prescribe for the mental disorder.

On Axis IV, the clinician rates the severity of the psychosocial stressors the client is facing, such as those listed in Table 4.8 on page 122. Again, these psychosocial stressors may be related to the client's mental disorder, as causes or consequences. Or they may merely be coincidental with the disorder. However, it is important for the clinician to know what

TABLE 4.7 Disorders Listed on Axis II

These disorders typically represent lifelong disorders that pervade every area of the person's life.

Mental retardation
Personality disorders
- Paranoid personality disorder
- Schizoid personality disorder
- Schizotypal personality disorder
- Antisocial personality disorder
- Borderline personality disorder
- Histrionic personality disorder
- Narcissistic personalty disorder
- Avoidant personality disorder
- Dependent personality disorder
- Obsessive-compulsive personality disorder

Source: Reprinted with permission from the *Diagnostic and Statistical Manual of Mental Disorders,* Fourth Edition, Text Revision. Copyright © 2000 American Psychiatric Association.

TABLE 4.8 Axis IV Psychosocial and Environmental Problems to Note

These are some of the important problems people might face that should be noted on Axis IV.

Problems with primary support group
Problems related to the social environment
Education problems
Occupational problems
Housing problems
Economic problems
Problems with access to health care services
Problems related to interaction with the legal system and to crime

Source: Reprinted with permission from the *Diagnostic and Statistical Manual of Mental Disorders,* Fourth Edition, Text Revision. Copyright © 2000 American Psychiatric Association.

types of stressors the client is facing in order to provide a successful treatment plan.

On Axis V, the clinician rates the level at which the client is able to function in daily life on the scale given in Table 4.9. This helps the clinician quantify and communicate the degree to which the disorder is impairing the client's functioning.

Consider the following case study of a woman who is seeking help for some distressing symptoms. Think about how the clinician would incorporate all five of the DSM-IV-TR axes in making a diagnosis.

CASE STUDY

Jonelle is a 35-year-old African American woman who works as a manager of a large bank. She reports at least a dozen incidents from the past six weeks in which she suddenly felt her heart pounding, her pulse racing, and her breathing become rapid and shallow; she felt faint and dizzy; and she was sure that she was about to die. These attacks lasted for several minutes. Jonelle consulted with her physician, who conducted a complete physical checkup and concluded that there was no evidence of cardiac problems or other physical problems that could be causing her symptoms. Jonelle is becoming so afraid of having one of these attacks that it is interfering with her ability to do her job. She is constantly vigilant for signs of an impending attack, and this vigilance is interfering with her concentration and her ability to converse with customers and employees. When she feels an attack may be coming on, she rushes to the rest room or out to her car and remains there, often for over an hour, until she is convinced she will not have an attack. Jonelle reports that the attacks began shortly after her mother died of a heart attack. She and her mother were extremely close, and Jonelle still feels devastated by her loss.

In consulting the five axes, Jonelle's clinician would likely come up with the following list:

Axis I: Panic disorder

Axis II: None

Axis III: None

Axis IV: Psychosocial and environmental stressors: recent bereavement

Axis V: Global functioning: 60 (moderate difficulty)

TABLE 4.9 Axis V Global Assessment of Functioning Scale

This is the scale for indicating how well the person is functioning across the domains of his or her life.

Code

100	Superior functioning in a wide range of areas
90	Absent or minimal symptoms; good functioning in all areas
80	If symptoms present, they are transient and expectable reactions to psychosocial stressors; only slight impairment in functioning
70	Some mild symptoms or difficulty in functioning
60	Moderate symptoms and difficulty in functioning
50	Serious symptoms and difficulty in functioning
40	Some impairment in reality testing or communication or major impairment in several domains
30	Considerable delusions and hallucinations or serious impairment in communication and judgment
20	Some danger of hurting self or others or gross impairment in communication
10	Persistent danger of severely hurting self or others

Source: Reprinted with permission from the *Diagnostic and Statistical Manual of Mental Disorders*, Fourth Edition, Text Revision. Copyright © 2000 American Psychiatric Association.

What is particularly interesting is that this case study provides a good example of the importance of Axes III (physical conditions) and IV (psychosocial and environmental stressors). The clinician would certainly want to know if Jonelle had a physical condition that was creating her panic attacks before diagnosing them as a psychological disorder. Similarly, knowing that the panic attacks began to occur shortly after the death of Jonelle's mother from a heart attack gives the clinician a good clue about their possible psychological origins. It is fairly common for people suffering from panic attacks to have lost a close relative or friend to a heart attack or stroke and then to experience symptoms mimicking a heart attack or stroke.

Continuing Concerns About the DSM-IV-TR
Although the past two decades have seen substantial improvement in the scheme for diagnosing mental disorders now represented by the DSM-IV-TR, many researchers believe there is much more room for improvement (Widiger, 2002).

Where to Draw the Line One of the greatest controversies concerns the assumption in the DSM-IV-TR that it is possible to define where normality ends and psychopathology begins. This is an old controversy, which we highlighted at the beginning of Chapter 1. It has gained momentum, however, based on recent research supporting the claim that there is no clear demarcation between "normal" responses and "pathological" responses in many domains.

For example, the predictors of mild depression are highly similar to the predictors of severe depression (e.g., Judd et al., 1996; Klein, Lewinsohn, & Seeley, 1996). Another example, which we discuss in Chapter 12, concerns the personality disorders. According to the DSM-IV-TR, these disorders represent pathologies that are qualitatively different from normal human personality. Several researchers have argued, however, that it is more useful and valid to conceptualize personality disorders as extreme variants of normal personality traits (Widiger & Coker, 2003).

In sum, many believe that it would be better to have a diagnostic system that recognizes many disorders as the extremes of continuums, rather than implying that they are categories of thought, behavior, and mood that are qualitatively different from normal functioning.

Differentiating Mental Disorders from Each Other Another ongoing problem with the DSM-IV-TR is the difficulty in differentiating the mental disorders from each other (Widiger & Clark, 2000). Most people who are diagnosed with one DSM-IV-TR disorder also meet the criteria for a diagnosis of at least one other disorder (Kessler et al., 1994). This overlap occurs, in part, because certain symptoms show up in the criteria for several disorders. For

TABLE 4.10 Culture-Bound Syndromes

Certain syndromes appear to occur only in some cultures.

Syndrome	Cultures Where Found	Symptoms
Amok	Malaysia, Laos, Philippines, Polynesia, Papua New Guinea, Puerto Rico	Brooding followed by an outburst of violent, aggressive, or homicidal behavior
Ataque de nervios	Latin American and Latin Mediterranean cultures	Uncontrollable shouting, attacks of crying, trembling, heat in the chest rising into the head, verbal or physical aggression, a sense of being out of control
Dhat	India, Sri Lanka, China	Severe anxiety about the discharge of semen, whitish discoloration of the urine, feelings of weakness and exhaustion
Ghost sickness	Native American cultures	Preoccupation with death and the deceased; manifested in dreams and in severe anxiety
Koro	Malaysia, China, Thailand	Episode of sudden and intense anxiety that the penis (or, in women, the vulva and nipples) will recede into the body and possibly cause death
Mal de ojo	Mediterranean cultures	Fitful sleep, crying without apparent cause, diarrhea, vomiting, fever
Shinjing shuairuo	China	Physical and mental fatigue, dizziness, headaches, other pains, concentration difficulties, sleep disturbance, memory loss
Susto	U.S. Latinos, Mexico, Central America, South America	Appetite disturbances, sleep problems, sadness, lack of motivation, low self-worth, aches and pains; follows a frightening experience
Taijin kyofusho	Japan	Intense fear that one's body displeases, embarrasses, or is offensive to other people

example, irritability or agitation can be part of depression, mania, anxiety, and schizophrenia; some of the personality disorders; and some of the childhood disorders.

We might want to "clean up" the diagnostic criteria for disorders to make them more distinct from each other, but recent research suggests that much of the overlap (or *comorbidity,*) among disorders represents how problems in mood, behavior, and thought co-occur in nature (Krueger, 2002). This finding suggests that there are some fundamental dimensions of functioning and that people vary in where they fall along these dimensions, with the extremes being "maladaptive" or "dysfunctional." Diagnostic systems of the future might specify how these dimensions come together to create different types of psychopathology, as well as how and why these psychopathologies are related to each other. This dimensional approach to diagnosis is very different from the DSM-IV-TR, which designates discrete categories of disorders, which supposedly represent distinct types of pathology.

Cultural Issues A third concern many researchers and clinicians have with the DSM-IV-TR is with its treatment of culture. We noted in Chapter 1 that different cultures have different ways of conceptualizing mental disorders. There are some disorders defined in one culture that do not seem to occur in other cultures. The developers of the DSM-IV-TR included an appendix that lists many of these culture-specific disorders and brief guidelines for gathering information during the assessment process regarding a client's culture. Table 4.10 describes some of these culture-bound syndromes.

The DSM-IV-TR also includes short descriptions of cultural variation in the presentation of the each of the major mental disorders recognized in the manual. For example, it notes differences among cultures in the content of delusions (beliefs out of touch with reality) in schizophrenia. Some critics do not believe it goes nearly far enough in recognizing cultural variation in what is healthy or unhealthy (see Kirmayer, 2001; Tsai, et al., 2001). Throughout the remainder of this book, we comment on cultural variations in the experience and prevalence of each of the disorders recognized by the DSM.

How the DSM Was Developed A final issue has to do with the process by which recent editions of the DSM were developed. The diagnostic criteria for the DSM-III, DSM-IIIR, DSM-IV, and DSM-IV-TR were derived by committees of experts on each of the disorders. These committees conducted reviews of the published literature to determine the evidence for and against the existence of the syndromes being considered for inclusion in the DSM. The developers of the DSM-IV and DSM-IV-TR also conducted field trials to determine the reliability and usefulness of criteria sets in clinical and research settings. Despite the efforts of the developers of the DSM to be objective and accurate in their definitions of disorders, these definitions represent a process of consensus building and compromise among experts with different opinions. The opportunity for political, cultural, and ideological influences on the establishment of the diagnostic criteria for disorders in such a process is considerable (Widiger, 2005).

One good example of the politicization of the DSM process was the debate over the addition of two personality disorders in an earlier version of the DSM, the DSM-IIIR. Some members of the committee revising the DSM-IIIR argued for the inclusion of a disorder that they felt was very common and was distinct from all the disorders that were already recognized in the DSM-IIIR. People with this proposed disorder had a lifelong practice of getting themselves into and remaining in situations in which other people used and abused them. The proponents of this disorder suggested that it be labeled *masochistic personality disorder.*

When news of this proposed disorder became public, some psychologists and psychiatrists strongly objected to it (Caplan & Gans, 1991). They argued that it would be used to pathologize women who, because of their lack of power and their social upbringing, found themselves trapped in abusive relationships, such as wife-battering relationships. They demanded a hearing before the committee to discuss the scientific merits of the masochistic personality disorder diagnosis and the social implications of including it as a disorder in the DSM. To address the concerns of the opponents of the masochistic personality disorder diagnosis, some of the committee members suggested adding yet another disorder, called sadistic personality disorder, which then would pathologize the behavior of the abusers in wife-battering relationships. Soon, however, several people pointed out that one of the political implications of this

"solution" was that some wife batterers could plead "not guilty" by reason of a mental disorder when charged with beating their wives.

In the end, the committee could not reach consensus and simply voted on what to do. The masochistic personality disorder was relabeled *self-defeating personality disorder,* and both it and sadistic personality disorder were included in an appendix of the DSM-IIIR as "Proposed Diagnostic Categories Needing Further Study." The further study of these diagnoses after the publication of the DSM-IIIR did not strongly support the reliability or validity of the diagnoses. For this reason, they were dropped altogether from the DSM-IV.

The Dangers of Diagnosis

One influential critic of psychiatry, Thomas Szasz, has argued that there are so many biases inherent in who is labeled as having a mental disorder that the entire system of diagnosis is corrupt and should be abandoned. Szasz (1961) believes that people in power use psychiatric diagnoses to label and dispose of people who do not "fit in." He suggests that mental disorders do not really exist and that people who seem to be suffering from mental disorders are suffering only from the oppression of a society that does not accept their alternative ways of behaving and looking at the world.

Even psychiatrists and psychologists who do not fully agree with Szasz's perspective on labeling recognize the great dangers of labeling behaviors or people as abnormal. A person labeled abnormal is treated differently by society, and this treatment can continue long after the person stops exhibiting behaviors labeled abnormal. This point was made in a classic study of the effects of labeling by psychologist David Rosenhan (1973). He and a group of seven colleagues had themselves admitted to 12 different mental hospitals by reporting to hospital staff that they had been hearing voices saying the words *empty, hollow,* and *thud.* When they were questioned by hospital personnel, they told the truth about every other aspect of their lives, including the fact that they had never experienced mental-health problems before. All eight were admitted to the hospital, all but one with a diagnosis of schizophrenia (see Chapter 11).

Once they were admitted to the hospital, the pseudopatients stopped reporting they were hearing voices and behaved as "normally" as they usually did. When asked how they were doing by hospital staff, the pseudopatients said they felt fine and they no longer heard voices. They cooperated in activities. The only thing they did differently than other patients was to write down their observations on notepads occasionally during the day.

Not one of the pseudopatients was ever detected as normal by the hospital staff, although they remained in the hospital for an average of 19 days each. Several of the other patients in the mental hospital detected the pseudopatients' normality, however, making comments such as "You're not crazy, you're a journalist, or a professor [referring to the continual note taking]. You're checking up on the hospital" (Rosenhan, 1973). When the pseudopatients were discharged, they were given the diagnosis of schizophrenia in remission, meaning that the physicians still believed they had schizophrenia but the symptoms had subsided for the time being.

Rosenhan concluded, "It is clear that we cannot distinguish the sane from the insane in psychiatric hospitals. The hospital itself imposes a special environment in which the meanings of behavior can be easily misunderstood" (Rosenhan, 1973, p. 257). He also noted that, if mental-health professionals cannot distinguish sanity from insanity, the dangers of diagnostic labels are even greater in the hands of nonprofessionals: "Such labels, conferred by mental health professionals, are as influential on the patient as they are on his relatives and friends, and it should not surprise anyone that the diagnosis acts on all of them as a self-fulfilling prophecy. Eventually, the patient himself accepts the diagnosis, with all of its surplus meanings and expectations, and behaves accordingly" (Rosenhan, 1973, pp. 253–254).

Not surprisingly, Rosenhan's study created a furor in the mental-health community. How could seasoned professionals have made such mistakes—admitting mentally healthy people to a psychiatric hospital on the basis of one symptom (hearing voices), not recognizing the pseudopatients' behavior as normal, and allowing them to be discharged carrying a diagnosis that suggests they still had schizophrenia? Even today, Rosenhan's study is held up as an example of the abuses of power—the power to label people as sane or insane, normal or abnormal, good or bad.

The label *abnormal* may be even more dangerous when it is applied to children, as is illustrated by one study of boys in grades 3 through 6 (Harris et al., 1992). Researchers paired boys who were the same age but who were previously unacquainted. In half of the pairs, one of the boys was told that his partner had a behavior problem that made him disruptive. In reality, only some of the boys labeled as having a behavior problem actually had a behavior problem. In the other half of the pairs, the boys were not told anything about each other, although some of the boys actually did have behavior problems. All the pairs worked together on a task while researchers videotaped their interaction. After the interaction, the boys were asked several questions about each other and about their enjoyment of the interaction.

The boys who had been told that their partners had a behavior problem were less friendly toward their partners during the task, talked with them less often, and were less involved in the interaction than were the boys who had been told nothing about their partners. In turn, the boys who had been labeled as having a behavior problem enjoyed the interaction less, took less credit for their performance on the task, and said their partners were less friendly toward them than did the boys who had not been labeled as having a behavior

Children who are labeled as "different" can be ostracized by other children.

problem. Most important, labeling a boy as having a behavior problem influenced his partner's behaviors toward him and his enjoyment of the task, regardless of whether he actually had a behavior problem. These results show that labeling a child as abnormal strongly affects other children's behaviors toward him or her, even when there is no reason for the child to be labeled as abnormal.

Should we avoid psychiatric diagnoses altogether? Probably not—despite the potential dangers of diagnostic systems, they serve vital functions. The primary role of diagnostic systems is to organize the confusing array of psychological systems in an agreed-upon manner. This facilitates communication from one clinician to another and across time.

For example, if Dr. Jones reads in a patient's history that he was diagnosed with schizophrenia according to the DSM-IV-TR, she knows what criteria were used to make that diagnosis and can compare the patient's diagnosis then with his symptoms now. Such information can assist Dr. Jones in making an accurate assessment of the patient's current symptoms and in determining the proper treatment for his symptoms. For example, if the patient's current symptoms also suggest schizophrenia and the patient responded to Drug X when he had schizophrenia a few years ago, this suggests that the patient might respond well to Drug X now.

Having a standard diagnostic system also greatly facilitates research on psychological disorders. For example, if a researcher at State University is using the DSM-IV-TR criteria to identify people with obsessive-compulsive disorder, and a researcher at Private University is using the same criteria for the same purpose, the two researchers will be better able to compare the results of their research than if they were using different criteria to diagnose obsessive-compulsive disorder. This can lead to faster advances in our understanding of the causes of and effective treatment for disorders.

SUMMING UP

- The *Diagnostic and Statistical Manual of Mental Disorders* (DSM) provides criteria for diagnosing all psychological disorders currently recognized in the United States.

- The first two editions of the DSM provided vague descriptions of disorders based on psychoanalytic theory; thus, the reliability of the diagnoses made according to these manuals was low. More recent editions of the DSM contain more specific, observable criteria that are not as strongly based on theory for the diagnosis of disorders.

- Five axes, or dimensions, of information are specified in determining a DSM diagnosis:

  - On Axis I, clinicians list all significant clinical syndromes.
  - On Axis II, clinicians indicate if the client is suffering from a personality disorder or mental retardation.
  - On Axis III, clinicians list the client's general medical condition.
  - On Axis IV, clinicians list the psychosocial and environmental problems the client is facing.
  - On Axis V, clinicians indicate the client's global level of functioning.

- Many critics of the DSM argue that it reflects Western, male perspectives on abnormality and pathologizes the behavior of women and other cultures. The DSM-IV-TR includes descriptions of culture-bound syndromes—groups of symptoms that seem to occur only in specific cultures.

- Diagnoses can be misapplied for political or social reasons. The negative social implications of having a psychiatric diagnosis can be great, but having a standard diagnostic system helps in treatment and research.

CHAPTER INTEGRATION

Assessment is inherently a process of biopsychosocial integration of pieces of information about an individual. After clinicians administer a battery of assessment tests to a client, they must then integrate the information from these tests to form a coherent picture of the client's strengths and weaknesses. This picture weaves together information on the client's biological functioning (major illnesses, possible genetic vulnerability to psychopathology), psychological functioning (personality, coping skills, intellectual strengths), and social functioning (support networks, work relationships, social skills), as depicted in Figure 4.7 on page 128. The clinician comments on ways in which strengths or deficits in one area are influencing functioning in another area.

For example, Michael J. Fox had increasing difficulties performing his job as his neurological symptoms got worse; as a result, he became anxious and depressed. To cope with that anxiety and depression, he began drinking heavily. This drinking caused conflict in his marriage, which then made him even more anxious and depressed.

The latest editions of the DSM were revised to reflect a more integrated and dynamic view of how biology, psychology, and social factors influence each other. The manual now includes information on cultural differences and similarities for each disorder and biological symptoms associated with

FIGURE 4.7	Integration of Biological, Psychological, and Social Factors in Assessment and Diagnosis

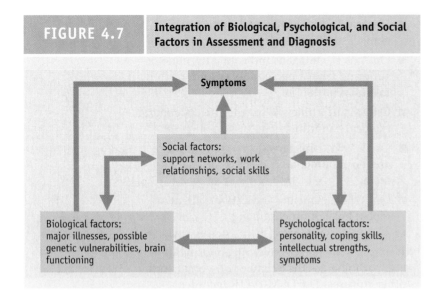

each disorder. In addition, the DSM-IV changed the label for an entire set of disorders to enhance an integrated biopsychosocial view of disorders. The editions prior to the DSM-IV included a category called *organic disorders*, which included delirium, dementia, and amnesia. These disorders were included in the DSM-IV, but not under the label *organic disorders*. The DSM-IV developers dropped the label *organic disorders* because labeling one category of disorders as organic implied that these disorders were caused by biological factors but that other disorders listed under other labels were not. This philosophy continued in the DSM-IV-TR.

Thus, both the assessment process and the DSM-IV-TR itself reflect a biopsychosocial approach to psychopathology. As we will see as we discuss each of the major disorders recognized by the DSM-IV-TR, this type of approach appears warranted.

Extraordinary People: Follow-Up

What happened to Michael J. Fox after receiving his diagnosis of early-onset Parkinson's disease? Over the 10 years following his diagnosis, Fox attempted to hide his Parkinson's symptoms from all but his family and closest friends and to drown out his own consciousness of it in alcohol abuse. His autobiography, *Lucky Man*, takes us through that decade as he hit bottom with alcohol, recovered with a great deal of help from his wife and a psychotherapist, and finally was forced to admit his Parkinson's publicly.

He fought against the Parkinson's even while sitting with his therapist. During their sessions, he sometimes punched his own tremoring left arm until he raised bruises on it. But they worked on his denial and, with time, Fox gained the courage to acknowledge his Parkinson's, at least to his wife, Tracy, and his young son, Sam. His family's loving acceptance of his disorder gave him the courage to accept it himself.

Fox's left-side tremors eventually became so severe that his arm flapped uncontrollably, shaking his entire body. It couldn't be controlled by drugs any longer, so in 1998 he underwent brain surgery to lesion a small part of his thalamus, which was responsible for the tremor. This was at the end of the second season of his hit sitcom, *Spin City*. The surgery was successful in eliminating the tremor in his left side, but that only made the emerging tremor in his right side more evident.

Fox revealed his Parkinson's disease publicly in November 1998 and was overwhelmed by the outpouring of support he received from the public. He continued on *Spin City* until May 2000, when he retired from acting to take care of himself and to advocate for Parkinson's patients and research. Fox's book, *Lucky Man*, is a story of personal triumph, not so much over the disease he has but over his former approach to life. He writes that, if he could trade the years since his diagnosis for "more years as the person [he] was before," he would not do so.

Chapter Summary

- Assessment is the process of gathering information about people's symptoms and the causes of the symptoms. A diagnosis is a label attached to symptoms that tend to co-occur with one another.

- During an assessment, a clinician gathers information about an individual's symptoms and history. This includes information about the nature, duration, and severity of the symptoms, as well as the person's ability to function, coping strategies, recent life events, history of psychological problems, and family history of psychological problems.

- An assessment also obtains information about physiological and neurophysiological functioning. This includes any medical conditions from which the client is suffering, any drugs the client is taking, and the client's cognitive and intellectual abilities.

- An assessment should also examine the client's social resources and cultural background.

- The validity and reliability of assessment tools are indices of their quality. Validity is the accuracy of a test in assessing what it is supposed to assess. Five types of validity are face validity, content validity, concurrent validity, predictive validity, and construct validity (review Figure 4.1). Reliability is the consistency of a test. The types of reliability are test-retest reliability, alternate form reliability, internal reliability, and interrater reliability (review Figure 4.2).

- Paper-and-pencil neuropsychological tests can assess specific cognitive deficits that may be related to brain damage in patients. Intelligence tests provide a more general measure of verbal and analytical skills.

- Brain-imaging techniques, such as CT, MRI, and PET scans, are being used primarily for research purposes but in the future may contribute to the assessment of psychological disorders.

- To assess emotional and behavioral functioning, clinicians use structured clinical interviews, symptom questionnaires, personality inventories, behavioral observation and self-monitoring, and projective tests. Each test has its advantages and disadvantages.

- During the assessment procedure, many problems and biases can be introduced. Clients may be resistant to being assessed and thus distort the information they provide. Clients may be too impaired by cognitive deficits, distress, or a lack of development of verbal skills to provide information.

Finally, many biases can arise when the clinician and client are from different cultures.

- A classification system is a set of definitions for syndromes and rules for determining when a person's symptoms are part of each syndrome. The predominant classification system for psychological problems in the United States is the *Diagnostic and Statistical Manual of Mental Disorders* (DSM) of the American Psychiatric Association. Its most recent editions provide specific criteria for diagnosing each of the recognized psychological disorders, as well as information on the course and prevalence of disorders.

- The explicit criteria in the DSM have increased the reliability of diagnoses, but there is still room for improvement.

- The DSM provides five axes, along which clinicians should assess client (review Table 4.5). On Axis I, major clinical syndromes are noted. Axis II contains diagnoses of mental retardation and personality disorders. On Axis III, the clinician notes any medical conditions that clients have. On Axis IV, psychosocial and environmental stressors are noted. On Axis V, clients' general levels of functioning are assessed.

- Critics have charged that the DSM reflects cultural and gender biases in its views of what is psychologically healthy and unhealthy. They also point to many dangers in labeling people with psychiatric disorders, including the danger of stigmatization. Diagnosis is important, however, to communication between clinicians and researchers. Only when a system of definitions of disorders is agreed upon can communication about disorders be improved.

MindMap CD-ROM

The following resources on your MindMap CD-ROM that came with this text will help you to master the content of this chapter and prepare for tests:

- Interactive Segment: DSM-IV-TR
- Chaper Timeline
- Chapter Quiz

Key Terms

assessment 100

diagnosis 100

differential diagnosis 102

acculturation 103

unstructured interview 104

structured interview 104

resistance 104

validity 104

face validity 105

content validity 106

concurrent validity 106

predictive validity 106

construct validity 106

reliability 106

test-retest reliability 106

alternate form reliability 107

internal reliability 107

interrater reliability 107

neuropsychological tests 107

computerized tomography (CT) 107

positron-emission tomography (PET) 108

magnetic resonance imaging (MRI) 108

intelligence tests 108

symptom questionnaire 110

personality inventories 110

projective test 112

behavioral observation 114

self-monitoring 115

syndrome 118

classification system 118

Diagnostic and Statistical Manual of Mental Disorders (DSM) 119

Chapter 5

Window of Opportunity
by Christian Pierre

The wish for healing has ever been the half of health.

—Seneca

Treatments for Abnormality <

Extraordinary People

■ **The Inside Story on Coping with Schizophrenia**

Taking Psychology Personally

■ **How to Look for a Therapist**

Biological Treatments

Biological therapies most often involve the prescription of drugs. Antipsychotic medications help reduce unreal perceptual experiences, unreal beliefs, and other symptoms of psychosis. Antidepressant drugs help reduce symptoms of depression. Lithium, anticonvulsants, and calcium channel blockers help reduce mania. Barbiturates and benzodiazepines help reduce anxiety. Herbal medicines have been popular for psychological symptoms, but their effectiveness has not been proven in many cases and they can be dangerous. Electroconvulsive therapy is used to treat severe depression. Psychosurgery is used in rare circumstances. A new therapy is repetitive transcranial magnetic stimulation (rTMS), in which magnets are used to stimulate specific areas of the brain.

Psychological Therapies

Psychodynamic therapies focus on uncovering and resolving unconscious conflicts. Humanistic therapy seeks to help people discover their greatest potentials and self-heal. Behavior therapies try to reshape people's maladaptive behaviors. Cognitive therapies attempt to change people's maladaptive ways of thinking.

Interpersonal and Social Approaches

Interpersonal therapy is a short-term version of psychodynamic therapies focused more on current relationships. Family systems therapists attempt to change maladaptive systems of behavior within families. Prevention programs attempt to stop or retard the development of disorders or to help people reduce the impact of disorders on their daily lives. Culturally specific therapies use the beliefs and rituals of a culture in treating clients of that culture.

Evaluating Treatments

It is very difficult to conduct good, ethical research on the effectiveness of treatments. Many studies have compared the various treatments for mental disorders. Some have found that they are equally effective; others have found that certain therapies are more effective than others for specific disorders. All successful psychotherapies share certain components, although their specific techniques may differ greatly. These common components include the development of a positive relationship with a therapist and the client's belief that the therapy will help.

Special Issues in Treating Children

A number of special issues arise in the treatment of children with psychological problems. First, therapies must be adapted so that they are appropriate to children's developmental levels. Second, there are concerns about the long-term effects of drug therapies on children's physical development. Third, it is often necessary to treat a child's family as well as the child. Fourth, children typically do not seek treatment for themselves but are taken to treatment by others.

Chapter Integration

A comprehensive, integrated approach to treatment for people with psychological problems involves teams of mental-health professionals with different specializations, including psychologists, psychiatrists, and social workers. In addition, some theorists are arguing for the integration of the elements of various therapies.

Extraordinary People

The Inside Story on Coping with Schizophrenia

"In lectures on antipsychotic drugs I want to tell the faculty and fellow students what it feels like to take these medicines and have to depend on them to function 'outside' and what it is like to be titrated as an individual to the proper medication and dosage and the problems involved. . . .

"During my first semester of pharmacy school I was on 2 mg of Haldol (haloperidol) and 2 mg of Cogentin (benztropine, an anticholinergic drug used to reduce such side effects of antipsychotic drugs, such as speech slurring, rigid neck muscles, and fixed gaze) h.s. (at bedtime) as prescribed for me after hospitalization the summer before entry to school. My condition improved psychologically and I seemed to be in remission until I entered school. I found I could neither read the board nor my notes; everything was blurred no matter where I sat. I called the psychiatrist who had prescribed the drugs and remembered his suggesting that I should take 2 more mg of Cogentin. . . . I complied and the next few days I not only had blurry vision, but I could not even see the lines on my notebook paper nor my writing—it was all one blur. In fact, the paper looked colorless. After 2 to 3 days of this, I called the physician back and told him I just could not take this medicine anymore, because I could not read or see with it. I could not even tell if I was taking notes on the lines. This side effect, he said, was as he expected; his recommendation now was to drop down to only 2 mg of Cogentin and switch from Haldol to Stelazine (trifluoperazine) 6 mg every day h.s. This was a compromise solution because, although I could now read and write, my schizophrenia was not so well-controlled. I wanted to drop out of school 3 weeks into the semester; I was afraid to go outside and felt as though I did not belong in pharmacy school or would not be able to overcome the stresses to be faced there. Fellow students were remarking to me that I seemed to be more impatient, hyperactive, and depressed. I also had problems with what a friend of mine called the 'Stelazine stroll'—akathesia (restlessness). I continued to go out of the city once a week to see my psychologist, who helped me with aspects of the pressures I could not face alone or with only the drugs. . . .

"In my first semester of my second year . . . I had just restarted Stelazine (after going off it by myself) at 8 mg h.s., an increased dose, and began having what I thought were seizures. In my classes I experienced an aura and then a wave hit me. I felt overstimulated and could hear a lecture but not process the information and take notes. My hand tremor was so bad during these episodes that I could not write. My psychologist suggested a consultation with the psychiatrist who had supervised my previous hospitalizations and prescribed the medications.

"Although the psychiatrist was hesitant to give me the label for what was happening, I insisted, and he said it was 'transient psychotic episodes.' The problem with this development was that it began after I had already been taking an increased amount of the medication. Where could we go from here? The psychiatrist recommended titration, increasing the dose of Stelazine. However, it didn't work. He then suggested taking Stelazine along with another antipsychotic drug with more milligram potency (Navane [thiothixene] 5 mg h.s.), but I was still having acute psychotic episodes in my classes. I had taken to sitting in the back of the classroom, although I could not see the board, because I needed to be able to leave the room when this occurred. When I got up in the morning, I could predict that the episodes would occur and where—I had a prodrome (a premonitory symptom). There were many frantic long distance calls to my psychologist after these episodes. I had to tell someone who could help me with what was happening to me. I, at this point, felt scared enough that never again would I have a compliance problem. I didn't want to lose all I had worked for in pharmacy school. I noticed the episodes were worse when emotionally volatile material was discussed in classes, such as antipsychotic agents, characteristics of schizophrenia, depression—all problems I had to cope with daily and that remained unresolved for me. . . .

"As a consequence of the psychotic episodes and occasionally having to leave the classroom, I missed a lot of notes in my classes. All this work had to be made up. This increased the pressure I was under, which in turn worsened the schizophrenic symptoms and almost forced me into hospitalization. I did not

(continued)

want to drop out of school or receive too many incomplete grades, which would have been the result of 4 to 8 weeks of hospitalization to get properly titrated on the medication and to decrease disease symptoms. However, most of my instructors had rigid rules about missing exams and taking makeup exams. To reduce the pressure, I told the professor with whom I was doing independent study that for medical reasons I would not be able to finish the paper due in that course. I decided to tell him why and he allowed me the Incomplete grade without requiring a medical letter on file, saving me the possible consequences of having this information on written record. And, most importantly, he did not treat me differently as a result of knowing. This reduced my stress and gave me time to make up work and take my final examinations. It also allowed me to work on my independent study paper during vacation and to do a good job on it while I was finally beginning to get a positive response to the medication.

"When classes started, I still felt overstimulated and again had prodromes of psychotic episodes. I could not process information when people were talking; everything just seemed like noise. I was now on 5 mg of Navane b.i.d. (twice daily) and 2 mg of Cogentin h.s. I got enough courage to sit in front of the class again, but I was very fearful. My psychologist explained that I had begun to associate that classroom with these episodes and that extreme anxiety was causing dissociation reactions in me: I felt I was outside my body; I was watching everything. I wanted an antianxiety agent to get rid of these feelings and that constant impending feeling that a psychotic episode would begin. The psychiatrist prescribed 5 mg of Valium (diazepam) in the morning and at bedtime when necessary. I took it only in the morning when I could not restructure my environment and situation to reduce the anxiety. For the first several weeks I was falling asleep in my first class and had double vision because I could not keep my eyes open. Finally, I became tolerant to the sedative effect. So this is the answer right now for me: a neuroleptic, an antianxiety agent, an anti-Parkinsonian agent, and intense long-term psychotherapy with my psychologist. And I still look around at my fellow students and say to myself, 'They do it without medicine, or doctors, or going to a psychiatric ward,' but I needed all these things to cope with the pressure and stress of pharmacy school and life." (Anonymous, 1983, pp. 152–155)

When we read about the treatments for mental disorders, particularly the biological treatments, they can seem very straightforward. You determine what is wrong with a person, prescribe a medication and/or a psychotherapy, administer it competently, and the person gets better. As this young pharmacy student's story illustrates, however, it often isn't that straightforward.

As was the case with this pharmacy student, multiple caregivers are often involved in the treatment of any one individual. The system of mental-health services has four major sectors. The *specialty mental-health* sector includes psychiatrists, psychologists, psychiatric nurses, and psychiatric social workers who are trained specifically to treat people with mental disorders. The *general medical* or *primary care* sector includes health care professionals, such as internists, pediatricians, and nurse practitioners, who may not be specifically trained in mental-health treatment, but are often the initial point of contact, or the only source of mental-health

services, for people with mental-health problems. The *human services* sector includes social services, school-based counseling services, residential rehabilitation services, criminal justice services, and religious professional counselors. Finally, the *voluntary support network* sector, which consists of self-help groups such as Alcoholics Anonymous, is a growing component of the mental-health treatment system. In all, about 15 percent of adults in the United States use one or more of these services in any given year (U.S. Department of Health and Human Services, 1999).

Unfortunately, however, most people who might benefit from treatment are getting no treatment at all (see Figure 5.1 on page 136). About 28 percent of the U.S. population has a diagnosable mental-health problem, but only 8 percent of the population receives professional treatment in a given year (U.S. Department of Health and Human Services, 1999). Although they may eventually seek out treatment, they typically delay telling a health

FIGURE 5.1   **Mental-Health Care.** The majority of people with diagnosable mental disorders do not seek treatment in a given year, whereas about half of people who do seek treatment do not have a diagnosis of a mental disorder.

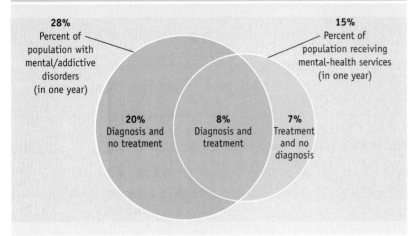

28%
Percent of
population with
mental/addictive
disorders
(in one year)

15%
Percent of
population receiving
mental-health services
(in one year)

20%
Diagnosis and
no treatment

8%
Diagnosis and
treatment

7%
Treatment
and no
diagnosis

care professional about their psychological symptoms for several years after these symptoms first appear (Kessler, Olfson, & Berglund, 1998). Almost half of the people who receive treatment in any given year don't have symptoms that would qualify for a diagnosis.

What does mental-health treatment consist of? That depends greatly on the theoretical approach of the person providing the treatment. Proponents of biological theories of mental disorders most often prescribe *medication,* although several other types of biological treatments are discussed in this chapter and throughout this book. Proponents of psychological and some social approaches to abnormality most often prescribe **psychotherapy.** There are many forms of psychotherapy, but most involve a therapist (psychiatrist, psychologist, clinical social worker, or marriage or family counselor) talking with the person suffering from the disorder (typically called a patient or client) about his or her symptoms and what is contributing to these symptoms. The specific topic of these conversations depends on the therapist's theoretical approach. Many of the psychotherapies have been adapted for work with couples or families, or with groups of people who have something in common, usually the experience of specific symptoms or disorders.

Both drug therapies and psychotherapy have proven effective in the treatment of many disorders. Drugs and psychotherapy may work on different aspects of a disorder, and they are increasingly being used together in an integrated approach to disorders, as we discuss in the Chapter Integration at the end of this chapter.

BIOLOGICAL TREATMENTS

Most of the biological treatments for abnormality are drug therapies (see Table 5.1). These drugs are thought to relieve psychological symptoms by correcting imbalances of neurotransmitters in the brain. They may also compensate for structural deficits in the brain or the effects of genetic abnormalities. Other biologically based therapies include electroconvulsive therapy, psychosurgery, and transcranial magnetic stimulation. Some people turn to herbal remedies for psychological problems, and we will discuss these here.

Drug Therapies

You might imagine that most drugs used to treat psychopathology were discovered through a perfectly rational and systematic application of basic science. A clever scientist did the basic research to discover which systems of the body and brain are responsible for a particular form of psychopathology and then, using his or her understanding of basic biology, developed a drug that would reverse the bodily processes known to cause the disorder. In truth, most of the drugs now used to treat mental disorders were discovered in roundabout ways, typically by accident.

Antipsychotic Drugs

The beginning of modern drug treatment is generally thought to have occurred with the discovery of **chlorpromazine,** a drug now used to treat the symptoms of psychosis (Valenstein, 1998). *Psychosis* involves the loss of touch with reality, hallucinations (unreal perceptual experiences), and delusions (fantastic, unrealistic beliefs). The pharmacy student at the beginning of this chapter was suffering from psychotic symptoms.

Chlorpromazine belongs to a group of chemical compounds called **phenothiazines.** While working to produce synthetic dyes in 1883, August Bernthsen, a research chemist in Heidelberg, synthesized a phenothiazine, which has a chemical structure very similar to that of synthetic violet and blue dye products. Later, it was discovered that phenothiazine compounds have a number of biological effects on humans. They can act as antihistamines and thus were initially thought useful in the treatment of allergies.

In the 1940s, researchers in a pharmaceutical company in Paris learned that phenothiazines also result in a decrease in muscle tone, the reduction of nausea, and in some cases either sedation or euphoria. At first, these effects were considered unwanted side effects. Some physicians began to use phenoth-

TABLE 5.1   Drug Therapies for Mental Disorders

These are the major types of drugs used to treat several kinds of mental disorders.

Type of Drug	Purpose	Examples
Antipsychotic drugs	Reduce symptoms of psychosis (loss of reality testing, hallucinations, delusions)	Thorazine (a phenothiazine) Haldol (a butyrophenone) Clozaril (an atypical antipsychotic)
Antidepressant drugs	Reduce symptoms of depression (sadness, loss of appetite, sleep disturbances)	Parnate (an MAO inhibitor) Elavil (a tricyclic) Prozac (a selective serotonin reuptake inhibitor)
Lithium	Reduce symptoms of mania (agitation, excitement, grandiosity)	Lithobid Cibalith-S
Antianxiety drugs	Reduce symptoms of anxiety (fearfulness, worry, tension)	Nembutal (a barbiturate) Valium (a benzodiazepine)

iazines to calm agitated patients, however, and to reduce tremors in patients with Parkinson's disease.

Shortly after World War II, French surgeon Henri Laborit became interested in using phenothiazines as a presurgery drug to reduce postsurgical shock, a neuroendocrine response to stress that can be fatal. Laborit found that the administration of a phenothiazine called promethazine creates a "euphoric quietude. . . . Patients are calm and somnolent, with a relaxed and detached expression" (Swazey, 1974, p. 79). Pain was reduced so greatly in some patients that they did not require morphine. Laborit went back to the pharmaceutical company that had produced promethazine to ask for a phenothiazine with even greater central nervous system effects. The company suggested he try a compound it had recently synthesized, which was eventually called chlorpromazine.

In the early 1950s, Laborit and a number of other researchers were investigating the effects of chlorpromazine on psychological symptoms. Reports were published that chlorpromazine reduces the hallucinations and delusions of some psychiatric patients. Particularly influential were reports in 1952 by French psychiatrists Jean Delay and Pierre Deniker that chlorpromazine reduces agitation, excitation, confusion, and paranoia in psychotic patients (Delay, Deniker, & Harl, 1952; Valenstein, 1998). Delay labeled chlorpromazine a **neuroleptic,** implying that this drug depresses the activity of the nervous system. In 1953, Delay and Deniker in France, and other physicians in Switzerland and Great Britain, were reporting that chlorpromazine was having such remarkable effects on

psychotic patients that it was transforming psychiatric hospitals.

Soon, chlorpromazine was introduced to North American psychiatrists. American drug company Smith Kline & French began marketing the drug for use in psychiatry in 1954 under the name Thorazine. At that time, there was little regulation of the prescription drug market, compared with today's standards, so Thorazine was introduced before much research had been done on its effectiveness or side effects.

Word spread quickly about the remarkable effects of Thorazine on patients with psychotic disorders, however. Within a year of the introduction of Thorazine on the market, more than 2 million prescriptions for the drug were written in the United States. By 1965, chlorpromazine had been the subject of about 10,000 publications worldwide (Valenstein, 1998). By 1970, Smith Kline & French's Thorazine sales had totaled over $116 million.

The success of chlorpromazine led other drug companies to develop and patent similar drugs. Some of the more successful phenothiazines that were developed were thioridazine (Mellaril) and trifluoperazine (Stelazine). During the 1950s, researcher Paul Janssen discovered another class of drugs that can reduce psychotic symptoms, **butyrophenone.** The first drug in this class to be marketed was haloperidol (Haldol), in 1957, and it proved at least as effective as chlorpromazine.

Unfortunately, both the phenothiazines and butyrophenone also produce a number of dangerous side effects. These side effects are detailed in Chapter 11 and include severe sedation, visual disturbances, and tardive dyskinesia, a neurological disorder characterized by involuntary movements of the tongue, face, mouth, or jaw. The pharmacy student we met at the beginning of this chapter was suffering several of these side effects. Fortunately, new drugs, such as clozapine and risperidone, which are part of a class referred to as the *atypical antipsychotics*, seem to be effective in treating psychosis without inducing some of the serious side effects of the phenothiazines and butyrophenone (see Chapter 11).

How do these drugs work to reduce psychotic symptoms? The answer to this question is less clear than you might think. Indeed, their use became widespread before researchers had any evidence of how they work (Valenstein, 1998). The leading theories today, however, suggest that these drugs reduce levels of the neurotransmitter dopamine or influence receptors for dopamine in the brain.

Antipsychotic drugs—drugs that relieve the symptoms of psychosis—led to a revolution in the treatment and lives of people with psychosis, who had been locked away in mental hospitals and state institutions, perhaps for life, often completely out of touch. These are the major types of drugs used to treat several kinds of mental disorders.

Antidepressant Drugs

The discovery of drugs to treat the symptoms of depression—sadness, low motivation, and sleep and appetite disturbances—was just as fortuitous as the discovery of the antipsychotic drugs (Valenstein, 1998). One of the fuels used by the Germans for the V-2 rocket during World War II was hydrazine. When the war ended, drug companies acquired much of the leftover hydrazine, believing that modifications of the chemical could make it useful for medical purposes. In 1951, researchers in the Hoffman-LaRoche pharmaceutical company in New Jersey found that two hydrazine compounds, isoniazid and iproniazid, were effective in treating tuberculosis. One of the side effects of these drugs, however, seemed to be euphoria—the tuberculosis patients were dancing with joy in the hospital corridors after treatment with these drugs.

French psychiatrist Jean Delay, who also played a role in the discovery of chlorpromazine for psychiatric uses, suspected that isoniazid and iproniazid could be useful as **antidepressants**—drugs to treat the symptoms of depression. The initial tests done by him and other physicians, however, proved unsuccessful, probably because they did not allow enough time for the drugs to have any effect. Several years passed before enough research was done to establish that isoniazid and iproniazid truly do have antidepressant effects. These drugs are part of

a class of drugs now called the **monoamine oxidase inhibitors,** or **MAOIs.**

Some trade names of the MAOIs are Nardil and Parnate. These drugs inhibit the enzyme monoamine oxidase in the brain, which results in higher levels of a number of neurotransmitters, such as norepinephrine. Unfortunately, the MAOIs have potentially dangerous side effects, including throbbing headaches, jaundice, and a precipitous rise in blood pressure, especially when mixed with certain foods (see Chapter 9). Because of these side effects, other drugs are used more often.

Until the 1980s, the antidepressants most often used were **tricyclic antidepressants.** In the 1950s, Swiss psychiatrist Roland Kuhn was trying different drugs in an attempt to improve sleep in mental patients. One drug he tried was imipramine, which has a chemical structure similar to that of a phenothiazine. Imipramine did not induce sleep but, rather, energized patients and elevated their moods. Kuhn treated more than 500 psychiatric patients with imipramine over the next three years and reported that imipramine is not simply a stimulant but a true antidepressant:

> The patients get up in the morning of their own accord, they speak louder and more rapidly, their facial expression becomes more vivacious. They commence some activity on their own, again seeking contact with other people, they begin to entertain themselves, take part in games, become more cheerful and are once again able to laugh. . . . The patients express themselves as feeling much better, fatigue disappears, the feeling of heaviness in the limbs vanishes, and the sense of oppression in the chest gives way to a feeling of relief. The general inhibition, which led to retardation, subsides. They declare that they are now able to follow other persons' train of thought, and that once more new thoughts occur to them, whereas previously they were continually tortured by the same fixed idea. . . . Instead of being concerned about imagined or real guilt in their past, they become occupied with plans concerning their own future. Actual delusions of guilt, or loss, or hypochondriacal delusions become less evident. The patients declare "I don't think of it anymore" or "the thought doesn't enter my head now." Suicidal tendencies also diminish, become more controllable or disappear altogether. . . . Not infrequently the cure is complete, sufferers and their relatives confirming the fact that

they had not been so well for a long time. (Kuhn, 1958, pp. 459–460)

The Geigy pharmaceutical company started marketing imipramine (Tofranil) in 1958. Other tricyclic antidepressants, such as Elavil and Anafranil, were soon introduced by other pharmaceutical companies. By 1980, approximately 10 million prescriptions for antidepressant drugs were being written annually in the United States, and most of these were for tricyclic antidepressants (Valenstein, 1998). Tricyclic antidepressants quickly became favored over MAOIs because they seemed more effective and had fewer dangerous side effects. Tricyclics do have their side effects, however, including sedation, dry mouth, and blurred vision.

The tricyclic antidepressants were thought to work by inhibiting the reuptake of the neurotransmitters norepinephrine, serotonin, and perhaps dopamine in the brain. Because they have effects on so many neurotransmitter systems, the tricyclic antidepressants are sometimes referred to as "dirty drugs." Researchers thought that, if they could synthesize drugs that had more specific effects on individual neurotransmitter systems, these drugs could be more effective in treating depression. By the 1980s, the technology for synthesizing drugs that bind to specific neurotransmitter subtypes had advanced enough to make it possible to test many new drugs.

In 1986, pharmaceutical company Eli Lilly introduced the drug fluoxetine, under the trade name Prozac, as an antidepressant. Prozac is one of the **selective serotonin reuptake inhibitors (SSRIs),** which means that it is thought to act more selectively on serotonin receptors than do the tricyclic antidepressants. Some psychiatrists have touted Prozac as the "SCUD missile of psychopharmacology," able to zero in on its target with amazing precision (Slater, 1998, p. 10). Other SSRIs, including Zoloft and Paxil, were soon introduced by other drug companies. In the 12 months between August 1996 and August 1997, more than 3.5 million prescriptions were written for SSRIs. Lilly's sales of Prozac alone were over $1.8 billion, and Pfizer's sales of Zoloft were almost $1.2 billion. Today, more than 40 million people worldwide have taken Prozac, and many more millions have taken one of the other SSRIs.

Why did the SSRIs become so popular so fast? It is not because they are more effective than the tricyclic antidepressants. Most studies comparing the two classes of drugs find they are equally effective in treating depression (Thase, Jindal, & Howland, 2002). One reason the SSRIs became so popular is that many people can tolerate the side effects of the

Media stories about so-called "wonder drugs," including Prozac, touted their ability to alleviate a wide range of problems beyond the treatment of serious psychological disorders.

SSRIs better than the side effects of the tricyclics. Some of the common side effects of the SSRIs are nausea, diarrhea, headache, tremor, daytime sedation, failure to achieve orgasm, nervousness, and insomnia. Another reason for the rapid proliferation of the SSRIs is that they seem useful in the treatment of a number of other psychological problems in addition to depression, including anxiety, poor impulse control, and eating disorders.

Finally, the impact of stories in the media on the SSRIs cannot be underestimated. These drugs enjoyed unprecedented coverage as "wonder drugs" in their early days, and several popular books have promoted these drugs as the cures not only for depression but also for lack of self-confidence, shyness, impulsiveness, and a host of other problems.

Some of the newest antidepressant drugs are designed to target both serotonin and norepinephrine; they include venlafaxine (Effexor) and mirtazapine (Remeron). In addition, people with depression are often given combinations of antidepressant drugs and lithium or an antianxiety drug.

Lithium and Other Mood Stabilizers

Lithium is a metallic element that is present in the sea, in natural springs, and in animal and plant tissue. It has been used to treat a number of medical disorders, with weak results. In the middle of the nineteenth century, it was widely used to treat rheumatism and gout, and several physicians thought there was a relationship between these disorders and mania—a condition in which people experience agitated, excited, and grandiose ideas. Indeed, mania was often referred to as "brain gout." In 1871, William Hammand, a neurologist at Bellevue Hospital in New York and a former surgeon general of the United States, recommended lithium as a treatment for mania. His recommendation got little attention, however.

The introduction of lithium as a treatment followed a rather unusual path. During World War II, Australian physician John Cade was captured by the Japanese and spent three and a half years in a military prison. He observed the onset of mania in some of his fellow prisoners and wondered if it was caused by an excessive accumulation of a metabolite that had a toxic effect on the brain (Valenstein, 1998). Cade did not know what the metabolite was, but he pursued this idea vigorously when he was released after the war. His research subjects were guinea pigs. A series of unusual experiments led Cade to discover, quite accidentally, that lithium had a powerful calming effect on the guinea pigs: The animals remained fully awake, but after about two hours they became so calm that they lost their "startle-reaction" and frantic righting-reflex when placed on their backs. It was this observation that prompted the trial of lithium salts in that overexcitable state of mania (Cade, 1949, pp. 70–71).

Cade proceeded to experiment on himself to determine the safety of lithium. After being convinced of its safety, he tried a lithium regimen on 19 patients, 10 of whom had frequent bouts of mania. He published his report of the successful treatment of these patients with lithium in 1949. Unfortunately, however, this was published in an Australian medical journal not widely read outside of Australia, and Cade was an unknown psychiatrist with no research training working in a small hospital. Thus, Cade's work went unnoticed for the most part.

It wasn't until a Danish psychiatrist, Mogens Schou, published a series of studies on the effectiveness of lithium in 1970 that lithium was legitimized as a treatment for mania. Schou had come across Cade's report in the early 1950s and had begun experimenting with lithium in a more carefully controlled research procedure. His initial findings had shown lithium to be effective in treating mania. But lithium is a dangerous substance and can have many severe side effects, even death. American and European psychiatrists had been reluctant to accept lithium because of its toxicity. Schou's 1970 paper had such convincing evidence of the effectiveness of lithium, however, that psychiatrists were forced to consider using it, especially because there were no effective alternatives in the treatment of mania.

Lithium continues to be widely used in the treatment of mania today. Other drugs, known as the **anticonvulsants,** and **calcium channel blockers** are also being used in the treatment of mania (see Chapter 9). Fortunately, these newer drugs appear to have fewer side effects than lithium.

Antianxiety Drugs

Anxiety and insomnia are the symptoms for which drugs are most often prescribed. The first group of **antianxiety drugs** were the **barbiturates,** introduced at the beginning of the twentieth century. Barbiturates suppress the central nervous system, decreasing the activity of a variety of types of neurons. Although these drugs are effective for inducing relaxation and sleep, they are quite addictive, and withdrawal from them can cause life-threatening symptoms, such as increased heart rate, delirium, and convulsions.

The other major class of anxiety-reducing drugs, the **benzodiazepines,** was discovered in the 1940s, but these drugs were not widely available until the 1960s, when drug companies began selling them under names such as Librium, Valium, and Serax. These drugs appear to reduce the symptoms of anxiety without interfering substantially with an individual's ability to function in daily life. The most frequent use of benzodiazepines, accurately referred to as minor tranquilizers, is as sleeping pills. As many as 70 million prescriptions are written each year in the United States for benzodiazepines. The pharmacy student featured in *Extraordinary People* was using benzodiazepines to quell her symptoms of anxiety.

Unfortunately, benzodiazepines are also highly addictive, and up to 80 percent of the people who take them for six weeks or more show withdrawal symptoms, including heart rate acceleration, irritability, and profuse sweating. The active metabolites of benzodiazepines remain in the body for days and can create toxic interaction effects with alcohol and other drugs.

Herbal Medicines

You have probably heard of St. John's wort (technically known as *Hypericum perforatum*). This little roadside weed became big news in the mid-1990s, when the media became aware of studies in Europe suggesting that St. John's wort is an effective treatment for depression. Psychiatrist Harold Bloomfield published the book *Hypericum & Depression,* which reviewed the European studies and concluded that St. John's wort is a reasonable alternative to medications in the treatment of mild or moderate depression. Since then, sales of St. John's wort, which can be bought without prescription in

St. John's Wort became a popular treatment for depression in the 1990s, but studies have raised questions about its safety and efficacy.

most pharmacies, have soared, hitting $48 million in the United States in 1997.

American researchers jumped to action to test whether St. John's wort is effective for depression on this side of the ocean. They actually had serious questions about how depression was defined in many of the European studies and differences between the people studied in Europe and those who might seek out St. John's wort in the United States. The National Institutes of Health initiated a large study in America comparing St. John's wort with a placebo in treating serious depression (Hypericum Depression Trial Study Group, 2002). St. John's wort did not fare well in this study—it proved no more effective than placebo on several measures of depression (but, then, neither did the selective serotonin reuptake inhibitor it was compared with).

One reason people had hoped that St. John's wort would prove helpful for depression is that its side effects tend to be less severe than the side effects of antidepressant drugs. One study found that less than 3 percent of the people taking St. John's wort experienced any side effects (Woelk, Burkard, & Grunwald, 1994). The most common side effects are gastrointestinal irritation, allergic reactions, dry mouth, sedation, headache, and increased sensitivity to light.

In the past few years, however, the safety of St. John's wort has been seriously questioned by evidence that it can interact with a number of medications people take for medical ailments (Zhou et al., 2004). For example, there are several reports that St. John's wort interferes with the efficacy of drugs used to treat patients who have recently received organ transplants, resulting in the rejection of the new organs. It may also interfere with drugs used to treat heart disease, seizures, and certain cancers. Thus, there are increasing concerns about the widespread use of St. John's wort, because people may be exposing themselves to potential drug-drug interactions with little reason for hope that they will gain relief from depressive symptoms.

What about other "natural" remedies for psychological problems? These have been referred to as phytomedicines, and their use dates back to the beginning of civilization. For example, *Rauwolfia serpentina* was used at least 3,000 years ago by Hindu Ayurvedic healers as a treatment for insanity. In the twentieth century, it was "rediscovered," and chemical analysis of the root extracts of *R. serpentina* led to the discovery of dopamine and its role in Parkinson's disease and schizophrenia.

Phytomedicines are a regular part of modern mainstream medicine in Asia and parts of Western Europe, particularly Germany (Beaubrun & Gray, 2000). Herbal products account for over $4 billion in sales in the United States annually, with as many as 40 percent of Americans reporting they use herbal products at least occasionally (Astin, 1998; Brevoort, 1998). These products are typically sold as foods. They can range from simple and mild products, such as chamomile and peppermint, to products with potent pharmacological activity, such as foxglove, from which digitalis is derived. Two of the most common ailments for which people take herbal products are anxiety and depression (Astin, 1998). People also use herbals to treat chronic pain, chronic fatigue syndrome, addictions, and memory problems.

What is the effectiveness of these products? Only a few of them have been tested in rigorous research. We have already discussed the research on St. John's wort for depression. Two products used to treat anxiety, valerian and kava, have also undergone close scientific scrutiny. Valerian is made from the root of *Valeriana officinalis,* a common herb native to both Europe and Asia (Cott, 1995). Valerian appears to be a safe, mild sedative that produces no morning hangover (Fugh-Berman & Cott, 1999). Kava is the psychoactive member of the pepper family, widely used in Polynesia, Micronesia, and Melanesia as a ceremonial, tranquilizing beverage, as well as in Europe and the United

States for anxiety and insomnia. Several placebo-controlled studies have shown that kava is a safe herb for short-term relief from stress and anxiety (Fugh-Berman & Cott, 1999; Volz & Kieser, 1997). Although most people who take kava report no side effects, some report mild gastrointestinal complaints or allergic skin reactions. Kava may also interact with benzodiazepines.

Ginkgo biloba is the most widely prescribed phytomedicine in Germany. It is an antioxidant, and some reports suggest it enhances cognitive functioning in people with Alzheimer's disease and other memory impairments (Le Bars et al., 1997). One review of studies of the cognitive effects of ginkgo biloba concluded that it enhances cognitive functions, but weakly and inconsistently across studies (Gold, Cahill, & Wenk, 2002). Although it is rare for humans to experience significant side effects from gingko, it does have anticoagulant effects and in rare cases has been associated with serious bleeding problems, usually in people who are already taking anticoagulant drugs.

Concerns have been raised that many people are using the more potent substances without any supervision from a physician, putting themselves at risk for side effects or interactions with drugs or other substances, when sufficient research on their efficacy and safety has not been done. In addition, even for the products that do seem to be effective, little is known about how they work. Unfortunately, it is unlikely that herbal products will ever be researched to the degree that drugs produced by pharmaceutical companies are researched.

Doing sufficient research to have herbal products approved as drugs is extremely expensive in the United States. Meanwhile, botanicals are not patentable and are chemically very complex. The U.S. Congress passed the Dietary Supplement Health and Education Act in 1994 to encourage more research on nutrition and dietary supplements, as well as increased regulation of this industry.

Thus, although herbal treatments for psychological disorders have been used for centuries, they were largely considered a thing of the past by the mainstream medical community until very recently. Now, in part because the public is asking for more "natural" approaches in medicine, these products are becoming one of the newest tools in the treatment of mental disorders.

Electroconvulsive Therapy

An alternative to drug therapies in the treatment of some disorders is **electroconvulsive therapy,** or **ECT.** ECT was introduced in the early twentieth century, originally as a treatment for schizophrenia. Italian physicians Ugo Cerletti and Lucio Bini decided to experiment with the use of ECT to treat schizophrenia, reasoning that ECT can calm people with schizophrenia, much as experiencing an epileptic seizure can calm and sedate people with epilepsy. Eventually, clinicians found that ECT is not effective for schizophrenia, but it is effective for depression.

ECT consists of a series of treatments in which a brain seizure is induced by passing electrical current through the patient's brain. Patients are first anesthetized and given muscle relaxants, so that they are not conscious when they have the seizure and so that their muscles do not jerk violently during the seizure. Metal electrodes are taped to the head and a current of 70 to 150 volts is passed through one side of the brain for about one-half of a second. Patients typically have a convulsion, which lasts about one minute. The full series of treatments consists of 6 to 12 sessions.

In Chapter 9, we discuss the use of ECT in the treatment of depression. Although many mental-health professionals believe that ECT can be useful, it remains a controversial treatment. The idea of passing electrical current through the brain of a person to relieve psychiatric symptoms seems somewhat bizarre. And some critics argue that ECT results in significant and permanent cognitive damage, even when done according to modern guidelines (Breggin, 1997). For some seriously depressed people who do not respond to medications, however, ECT may be the only effective alternative.

Psychosurgery

In Chapter 1, we examined theories that prehistoric people performed crude brain surgery, called

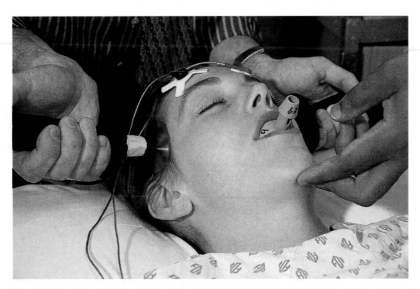

Electroconvulsive therapy has been controversial for much of its history but can be effective for certain disorders in its present form.

trephining, on people with mental disorders in order to release evil spirits thought to be causing the mental disorders. In modern times, brain surgery did not become a mode of treatment for mental disorders until the early twentieth century. A Portuguese neurologist named Antonio de Egas Moniz introduced a procedure in 1935 in which the frontal lobes of the brain were severed from the lower centers of the brain in people suffering from psychosis. This procedure eventually developed into the procedure known as **prefrontal lobotomy.** Although Moniz won the Nobel Prize for his work, prefrontal lobotomies were eventually criticized as a cruel and ineffective means of treating psychosis (Valenstein, 1986). Many patients suffered severe and permanent side effects, including either an inability to control impulses or a loss of the ability to initiate activity, extreme listlessness and loss of emotions, seizures, and sometimes even death.

By the 1950s, the use of **psychosurgery** had declined dramatically, especially in countries outside the United States. These days, psychosurgery is used rarely, and only with people who have severe disorders that do not respond to other forms of treatment. Modern neurological assessment and surgical techniques make psychosurgery more precise and safer than it was, although it remains highly controversial, even among professionals. Neurosurgeons attempt to lesion, or destroy, minute areas of the brain thought to be involved in a patient's symptoms. One of the greatest remaining problems in psychosurgery, however, is that it is not yet known what areas of the brain are involved in the production of most psychiatric symptoms, and it is likely that many areas of the brain are involved in any given disorder (Valenstein, 1986).

Repetitive Transcranial Magnetic Stimulation

One of the newest biologically based therapies uses powerful magnets, such as those used in magnetic resonance imaging (see Chapter 4), to stimulate targeted areas of the brain. The procedure, known as **repetitive transcranial magnetic stimulation (rTMS),** exposes patients to repeated, high-intensity magnetic pulses, which are focused on particular brain structures. When treating depressed people, researchers have targeted the left prefrontal cortex, which tends to show abnormally low metabolic activity in some depressed people.

Several studies have suggested that depressed patients given rTMS daily for at least a week tend to experience relief from their symptoms (Chae et al., 2001; George et al., 2003; Jorge et al., 2004; Martin et al., 2003). In addition, rTMS relieved auditory hallucinations (hearing voices that aren't there) in patients in some studies (Hoffman et al., 2000, 2003).

How does rTMS work? Electrical stimulation of neurons can result in long-term changes in neurotransmission across synapses (George et al., 2003). Neurotransmission can be enhanced or blunted, depending on the frequency of the stimulation. Patients who receive rTMS report few side effects, usually only minor headaches treatable by aspirin. Patients can remain awake, rather than having to be anesthetized, as in electroconvulsive therapy (ECT), thereby avoiding possible complications of anesthesia. Thus, there is a great deal of hope that rTMS will be an effective and safe alternative therapy, particularly for people who do not respond to drug therapies and cannot tolerate ECT.

The Social Impact of the Biological Approach to Treatment

The biological therapies have revolutionized the treatment of people with psychological disorders. At the beginning of the twentieth century clinicians were able only to warehouse and comfort people with severe psychological disturbances. We entered the twenty-first century able to treat many of these people so successfully that they can lead

Peanuts: © United Features Syndicate.

normal lives, thanks to many of the biological therapies that have been developed in recent decades.

Many people find the biological theories appealing, because they seem to erase any blame or responsibility that might be put on the sufferer of a disorder. Indeed, many organizations that advocate for people with mental disorders argue vehemently that mental disorders should be seen as medical diseases, just like diabetes or high blood pressure. They argue that people who suffer these disorders simply must accept they have a disease and obtain the appropriate medical treatment.

Despite their current popularity, the biological therapies are not a panacea. They do not work for everyone. Indeed, significant percentages of people with psychological disorders do not respond to any of the drugs or other biological treatments currently available. With time, new and more effective treatments may be developed that help these people, too.

Most of the biological therapies have significant side effects. Often, these side effects are tolerable, and people endure them because they are getting relief from their psychological disorder. For some people, however, the side effects are worse than the disorder itself. For others, the side effects can be dangerous and even deadly.

Some critics of biological theories and drug therapies worry that people will turn to the drugs rather than dealing with the difficult issues in their lives that are causing their psychological problems. If people can rid themselves of troubling symptoms by popping a pill, they may never make changes in their lives that could have permanent positive effects on their own psychological health and their relationships with others. As we will discuss later, there are several highly effective psychological therapies, and the combination of drug treatment and psychotherapy can be especially effective for some disorders.

Finally, the widespread use of some drugs, such as the SSRIs and the benzodiazepines, by people who are not suffering from severe depression or anxiety, but who just want a little help getting through the day, has raised many questions about the appropriateness of "changing your personality with a pill." We are grappling with the ethical and philosophical issues raised by the availability of drugs that offer us the opportunity to be smarter, more confident, less shy, and more energetic. Is this how we want these drugs to be used? Writer Lauren Slater, whose own symptoms of obsessions and compulsions (see Chapter 7) were relieved by Prozac, writes the following.

VOICES

Much has been said about the meanings we make of illness, but what about the meanings we make out of cure? Cure is complex, disorienting, a revisioning of the self, either subtle or stark. Cure is the new, strange planet, pressing in. (Slater, 1998, p. 9)

No doubt these issues will continue to be debated for many years to come. Biological science is advancing at a rapid pace, presenting us with more alternatives in the treatment of mental disorders and more questions about how we view the relationship between the body and the mind.

SUMMING UP

- Antipsychotic drugs, such as phenothiazines and butyrophenone, help reduce the symptoms of psychosis.
- Antidepressant drugs, including the monoamine oxidase inhibitors, the tricyclic antidepressants, and the selective serotonin reuptake inhibitors, help reduce the symptoms of depression.
- Lithium is used to treat the symptoms of mania.
- Anticonvulsant drugs and calcium channel blockers also help treat mania.
- Antianxiety drugs include the barbiturates and the benzodiazepines.
- Herbal medicines are popular, but the efficacy and safety of some of these drugs has not been definitively shown.
- Electroconvulsive therapy (ECT) is useful in treating severe depression.
- Psychosurgery is used on rare occasions to help people with severe psychopathology that is not affected by drugs or other treatments.
- Repetitive transcranial magnetic stimulation (rTMS) is a new technique that involves exposing the brain to magnets. It may be helpful in the treatment of depression.

PSYCHOLOGICAL THERAPIES

Drug treatments can go a long way toward helping people with psychological problems. For many disorders, however, psychotherapy is an effective alternative to drugs; in addition, psychotherapy and drug therapy in combination can be particularly helpful for some disorders. There are many types of psychotherapy, which we dis-

TABLE 5.2	Psychological Therapies for Mental Disorders

These are some of the most commonly used psychologically based therapies used to treat mental disorders.

Type of Therapy	Description
Psychodynamic therapies	Help clients gain insight into unconscious motives and conflicts, through analysis of free associations, resistances, dreams, and transferences
Humanistic therapy	Helps clients explore their own values and potentials and fulfill their potential more fully by providing a warm and supportive relationship
Behavior therapies	Help clients extinguish unwanted behaviors or teach clients new, desired behaviors, with techniques such as systematic desensitization and response shaping
Cognitive therapies	Help clients change maladaptive thought patterns by challenging irrational thoughts and learning new skills

cuss in this section (see Table 5.2). In the remaining chapters of this book, you will see how these therapies are applied to treat specific disorders. In *Taking Psychology Personally: How to Look for a Therapist,* we discuss how people go about finding a clinician who will provide them with the kind of treatment they believe they need.

Psychodynamic Therapies

Psychodynamic therapies focus on uncovering and resolving unconscious conflicts that are thought to drive psychological symptoms. The goal is to help clients recognize the maladaptive ways in which they have been trying to cope and the sources of their unconscious conflicts. These insights are thought to free clients from the grip of the past and give them a sense of agency in making changes in the present (Vakoch & Strupp, 2000). Another goal is to help clients integrate aspects of their personality that have been split off or denied into a unified sense of self. As Freud stated in 1923,

> It may be laid down that the aim of the treatment is to remove the patient's resistances and to pass his repressions in review and thus to bring about the most far-reaching unification and strengthening of his ego, to enable him to save the mental energy which he is expending on internal conflicts, to make the best of him that his inherited capacities will allow and so to make him as efficient and as capable of enjoyment as possible. The removal of the symptoms of the illness is not specifically aimed at, but is achieved, as it were, as a by-product if the analysis is properly carried through. (Freud, 1923, p. 251)

It is not easy to uncover unconscious conflicts. Freud and others developed the method of **free association,** in which a client is taught to talk about whatever comes to mind, trying not to censor any thoughts. By "turning off" the censor, a client might find herself talking about subjects or memories that she did not even realize were on her mind. The therapist notices what themes seem to recur in a client's free associations, just how one thought seems to lead to another thought, and the specific memories that a client recalls.

The material that the client is reluctant to talk about during psychotherapy—that is, the client's **resistance** to certain material—is an especially important clue to the client's most central unconscious conflicts, because the most threatening conflicts are the ones the ego tries hardest to repress. The therapist eventually puts together these pieces of the puzzle into a suggestion or an interpretation of a conflict the client might be facing and voices this interpretation to the client. Sometimes, the client accepts this interpretation as a revelation. Other times, the client is resistant to this interpretation. The therapist might interpret this resistance as a good indication that the interpretation has identified an important issue in the client's unconscious.

The client's **transference** to the therapist is also a clue to unconscious conflicts and needs. A transference occurs when the client reacts to the therapist as if the therapist were an important person in the client's early development, such as his father or mother. For example, a client may find himself reacting with rage or extreme fear when a therapist is just a few minutes late for an appointment, and this might stem from his feelings of having been emotionally abandoned by a parent during childhood. The therapist might point out the ways the client

Taking Psychology Personally

How to Look for a Therapist

How do you know when you or someone you care about needs a therapist? How do you find a therapist once you decide to seek one? The American Psychological Association has published the following guidelines for evaluating whether you should seek a therapist and for finding a therapist (from *Choosing a Therapist Who Is Right for You,* distributed by the Practice Directorate of the American Psychological Association).

Consider Therapy If . . .

- You feel helpless and problems do not seem to get better despite your efforts.
- You feel sad or blue, nervous, or tense for a prolonged period of time.
- You or others notice changes in your mood or behavior or a decrease in your ability to carry out everyday activities.
- You are concerned about the emotional health of a family member or partner.
- You want to look at life and make decisions in a different way.
- You want to find ways of changing your life to feel more satisfied.

How Do You Find a Therapist?

- Talk to friends and family.
- Call your local or state psychological association.
- Contact your community mental-health center.
- Inquire at your church, synagogue, or mosque.
- Ask your physician or other health professional.
- Consult counseling centers at local colleges and universities.
- Consult your local *Yellow Pages.*

What Should You Consider When Making a Choice?

A therapist and client work together. The right match is important. Also, as you will see in later chapters of this book, some therapies have been shown to be more effective than others in treating certain disorders. The following are sample interview questions that may be useful when considering a particular psychologist:

- Are you a licensed psychologist?
- How many years have you been practicing psychology?
- I've been feeling (anxious, tense, depressed, etc.). I'm having problems (with my job, my marriage, eating, sleeping, etc.). What kind of experience do you have in helping people with these types of problems?
- What are your specialty areas (children, marriage, etc.)?
- What might I expect during our sessions?
- What are your fees? (Fees are usually based on a 45-minute to 50-minute session.)
- Do you use a sliding-fee scale? Please explain how this works.
- What types of insurance do you accept?
- Do you accept Medicare/Medicaid patients?
- How do you bill for services? Will you bill my insurance company directly, or do I bill for reimbursement?

Interview several therapists—by telephone or in person—before making a choice. Following the initial contact, you may want to meet two or three times before you decide to work together. These sessions, called *consultation sessions,* will help you determine if the therapist is right for you. It may also be recommended that you work with therapists with different specializations to create a comprehensive treatment plan.

For further information on choosing a therapist, you can contact the American Psychological Association, Practice Directorate, 1200 17th Street NW, Washington, DC 20036, or visit www.apa.org.

---

behaves that represent a transference and might help the client explore the roots of his behavior in his relationships with significant others.

Following is a simulation of how a psychodynamic therapist might use transference to help the pharmacy student at the beginning of this chapter understand the sources of her ambivalence about her studies.

Therapist: Each time I notice that you are doing well in school, you get tearful and cry.

Pharmacy student [crying]: I worry that your praise is not sincere. Father said I would never amount to anything because of my illness.

Therapist: I see, so you feel you have some well-established old reasons for feeling that way with me.

Some psychodynamic therapists also have their clients recount their dreams, and they use this material in the analysis of their conflicts. Freud believed that, during sleep, the ego loosens its control over the unconscious, and some unconscious material slips out in the form of dreams. These dreams are seldom direct representations of unconscious material, however, because this would be too threatening. Instead, dreams symbolize unconscious material in fascinating and creative ways.

By **working through,** or going over and over, painful memories and difficult issues, clients are able to understanding them and weave them into their self-definition in ways that are acceptable. This allows them to move forward in their lives. Many therapists believe that **catharsis,** or the expression of emotions connected to memories and conflicts, is also central to the healing processes in psychodynamic therapies. Catharsis unleashes the energy bound in unconscious memories and conflicts, allowing this material to be incorporated into more adaptive self-views.

An important issue in psychodynamic therapies is the **therapeutic alliance.** By being empathic and supportive, and by listening nonjudgmentally, the therapist creates a relationship of trust with the client, which gives the client the freedom and

"Have a couple of dreams, and call me in the morning."
© *Sidney Harris, courtesy ScienceCartoonsPlus.com*

courage to explore difficult issues. This does not mean that the therapist never confronts the client about issues he or she may be avoiding. But the therapist carefully times confrontations and interpretations, so that the client can receive and respond to these without undue anxiety. Several studies have shown that the strength of the therapeutic alliance between a therapist and a client, even in the early sessions of therapy, is a strong predictor of whether or not the client will benefit from therapy (Luborsky & Crits-Christoph, 1990). Indeed, clients who do not experience their therapists as supportive are prone to quit therapy altogether.

What is the difference between **psychoanalysis** and psychodynamic therapies? Psychoanalysis typically involves three or four sessions per week over a period of many years. The focus of psychoanalysis is primarily on the interpretation of transferences and resistances, as well as on experiences in the client's past (Wolitzky, 1995). Psychodynamic therapies may also go on for years, but they can be as short-term as 12 weeks (Crits-Christoph & Barber, 2000). Transferences, resistances, and the client's relationship with early caregivers are also the focus of psychodynamic therapies, but the psychodynamic therapist, compared with the psychoanalyst, may focus more on current situations in the client's life.

Many people report that the self-exploration of psychodynamic therapies has been valuable to them. The long-term, intensive nature of psychodynamic therapies makes them unaffordable for many people, however. In addition, people suffering from acute problems, such as severe depression or anxiety, often cannot tolerate the lack of structure in traditional psychodynamic therapies and need more immediate relief from their symptoms (Bachrach et al., 1991). Finally, it is unclear whether traditional psychodynamic therapies are effective in the treatment of many mental disorders, largely because the therapies last so long that studies have not been conducted to test their effectiveness empirically (Wolitzky, 1995).

For these reasons, modern psychodynamic therapists have developed some shorter-term, more structured versions of psychodynamic therapies (Luborsky, 1984). In these short-term therapies, the therapist and patient contract with each other for a limited number of sessions, usually fewer than 30, and focus on a limited set of problems the client identifies as causing him or her the most trouble. The few studies conducted on the effectiveness of these short-term therapies suggest they can result in significant improvement in symptoms for many clients (Crits-Christoph, 1992).

Some of these new therapies have incorporated the revisions in psychodynamic thought offered by object relations theorists and other theorists who argued that interpersonal relationships throughout the life span can shape people's behaviors and self-concepts (Anderson & Lambert, 1995). Interpersonal therapies explicitly focus on people's roles and relationships within their network of relationships with friends, family, and the larger community.

Humanistic Therapy

The stated goal of **humanistic therapy,** often referred to as **person-centered therapy**, is to help clients discover their greatest potential through self-exploration. Person-centered therapy is unique in the extent to which it emphasizes the self-healing capacities of the person (Bohart, 1995). The job of the therapist in person-centered therapy is not to act as an authority or expert who provides healing to the client. Rather, the therapist's job is to provide the optimal conditions for the client to heal him- or herself.

This therapy rests on the assumption that the natural tendency for humans is toward growth. When obstacles toward growth are removed, then the client will let go of symptoms and move forward in his or her life. Person-centered therapists do not push clients to uncover repressed painful memories or unconscious conflicts. Instead, they believe that, when clients are supported and empowered to grow, they will eventually face their past when it is necessary for their further development (Bohart, 1995).

The best known of this type of therapy is Carl Rogers' **client-centered therapy (CCT).** Rogers (1951) said there are three essential ingredients of CCT. First, the therapist communicates a genuineness in his or her role as helper to the client, acting as an authentic, real, living, behaving person rather than as an authority figure. Second, the therapist shows **unconditional positive regard** for the client. Third, the therapist communicates an empathic understanding of the client by making it clear that he or she understands and accepts the client's underlying feelings and search for self.

Through these conditions, the therapist helps the client know that he or she understands what the client is experiencing and feeling and what the client is trying to bring forth and understand. Rogers believed that this experience of being understood helps clients bring forth their own self-healing powers and have the courage to recognize and pursue their potential.

The main strategy for accomplishing these goals is the use of reflection. **Reflection** is a method of responding in which the therapist expresses an attempt to understand what the client is experiencing and trying to communicate (Bohart, 1995). The therapist does not attempt to interpret the unconscious aspects of the client's experience. Rather, the therapist tries to communicate an understanding of the client and explicitly asks for feedback from the client about this understanding.

Following is an example of the difference between how a humanistic therapist would use reflection and how a psychodynamic therapist would use interpretation to respond to the pharmacy student's feelings about her schoolwork and career (adapted from Bohart, 1995, p. 101).

VOICES

Pharmacy student: I'm feeling so lost in my career. Every time I seem to be getting close to doing something really good, like acing a class, I somehow manage to screw it up. I never feel like I am really using my potential. There is a block there.

Reflection: It's really frustrating to screw up and kill your chances; and it feels like it's something in you that's making that happen again and again.

A psychodynamic interpretation: It sounds like every time you get close to success you unconsciously sabotage yourself. Perhaps success means something to you that is troubling or uncomfortable, and you are not aware of what that is.

GARFIELD © *Paws, Inc. Reprinted with permission of Universal Press Syndicate. All Rights Reserved.*

The psychodynamic interpretation may be true, but the client-centered therapist would view it as inappropriate, because it brings to the client's attention something that is not currently in the client's awareness.

Client-centered therapy has been used to treat people with a wide range of problems, including depression, alcoholism, schizophrenia, anxiety disorders, and personality disorders (Bohart, 1990). An analysis of more than 20 studies comparing client-centered and other humanistic therapies with more structured therapies found that the humanistic therapies were generally as effective as the more structured therapies for a variety of disorders (Greenberg, Elliot, & Lietaer, 1994). For example, Borkovec and Mathews (1988) found client-centered therapy to be as effective as behavior and cognitive therapies in the treatment of anxiety disorders.

Not all studies find client-centered therapy to be an effective treatment, however (Bohart, 1990). Some therapists believe that CCT may be appropriate and sufficient for people who are moderately distressed, but not sufficient for people who are seriously distressed.

Behavior Therapies

Just as behavior *theories* of psychopathology are radically different from psychodynamic and humanistic *theories*, **behavior therapies** seem to be the polar opposite of these other therapies. Whereas psychodynamic therapies focus on uncovering unconscious conflicts and relational issues that develop during childhood and humanistic therapy focuses on helping the client discover the inner self, behavior therapies focus on identifying the reinforcements and punishments contributing to a person's maladaptive behaviors and on changing specific behaviors.

The foundation for behavior therapy is the **behavioral assessment** of the client's problem. The therapist works with the client to identify the specific circumstances that seem to elicit the client's unwanted behavior or emotional responses: What situations seem to trigger anxiety symptoms? When is the client most likely to begin heavy drinking? What types of interactions with other people make the client feel most distressed? The therapist may ask the client to use some of the techniques of self-monitoring described in Chapter 4 to identify triggers for symptoms. For example, the pharmacy student in *Extraordinary People* may be asked to keep a journal in which she notes each time she feels anxious and specifically what is happening in those situations.

The therapist may also **role-play** situations with the client, with the therapist taking the role of a person to whom the client feels she reacts badly. The therapist would observe the client's behavior in the role-play to assess what aspects of that behavior need to change for the client to be effective in interpersonal interactions.

Although there are many specific techniques for behavior change (see Table 5.3 on page 150), they can be grouped into two main categories: techniques that extinguish unwanted behaviors and techniques for teaching a person new, desired behaviors. We discuss some examples of each category in this chapter. The application of the other techniques, listed in Table 5.3, to specific disorders is discussed in the later chapters on those disorders.

Techniques for Extinguishing Unwanted Behaviors

Systematic desensitization therapy is based on Mowrer's (1939) two-factor model, which suggests that people develop fear and anxiety responses to previously neutral stimuli through classical conditioning. Then, through operant conditioning, they develop behaviors designed to avoid triggers for that anxiety. It is a gradual method for extinguishing anxiety responses to stimuli and the maladaptive behavior that often accompanies this anxiety.

In systematic desensitization, the client first creates a hierarchy of feared stimuli, ranging from stimuli that would cause him or her only mild anxiety to stimuli that would cause severe anxiety or panic. A person with a snake phobia might generate the hierarchy in Table 5.4 on page 150. Then the therapist would help the person proceed through this hierarchy, starting with the least feared stimulus. The person would be instructed to vividly imagine the feared stimulus or would even be exposed to the feared stimulus for a short period, while implementing relaxation exercises to control the anxiety. When the person gets to the point where he or she can imagine or experience the first and least feared stimulus without feeling anxious, the person moves on to the next most feared stimulus, imagining or experiencing it while implementing relaxation exercises. This proceeds until he or she reaches the most feared stimulus on the list and is able to experience this stimulus without feeling extremely anxious. Thus, by the end of systematic desensitization therapy, a person with a snake phobia should be able to pick up and handle a large snake without becoming very anxious.

Often, systematic desensitization therapy is combined with **modeling**—the client might watch a therapist pick up a snake, pet it, and play with it, observing that the therapist is not afraid, is not bitten or choked, and seems to enjoy playing with the snake. Eventually, the client is encouraged to imitate the therapist's behaviors with and reactions to

TABLE 5.3 Behavior Change Techniques

These are some of the methods used in behavior therapy.

Label	Description
Removal of reinforcements	Removes the individual from the reinforcing situation or environment
Aversion therapy	Makes the situation or stimulus that was once reinforcing no longer reinforcing
Relaxation exercises	Helps the individual voluntarily control physiological manifestations of anxiety
Distraction techniques	Helps the individual temporarily distract from anxiety-producing situations; diverts attention from physiological manifestations of anxiety
Flooding, or implosive, therapy	Exposes the individual to the dreaded or feared stimulus while preventing avoidant behavior
Systematic desensitization	Pairs the implementation of relaxation techniques with hierarchical exposure to the aversive stimulus
Response shaping through operant conditioning	Pairs rewards with desired behaviors
Behavioral contracting	Provides rewards for reaching proximal goals
Modeling and observational learning	Models desired behaviors, so that the client can learn through observation

TABLE 5.4 Hierarchy of Fears for Snake Phobia

This is a hierarchy of feared stimuli for a person with a snake phobia, ranging from the least feared stimulus to the most feared stimulus.

1. Hearing the word *snake*
2. Imagining a snake in a closed container at a distance
3. Imagining a snake uncontained at a distance
4. Imagining a snake nearby in a closed container
5. Looking at a picture of a snake
6. Viewing a movie or video of a snake
7. Seeing a snake in a container in the same room
8. Seeing a snake uncontained in the same room
9. Watching someone handle a snake
10. Touching a snake
11. Handling a snake
12. Playing with a snake

the snake. In some cases, people undergoing systematic desensitization are asked only to imagine experiencing the feared stimuli. In other cases, they are asked to experience these stimuli directly, actually touching and holding the snake, for example. The latter method is known as **in vivo expo-** sure, and it generally has stronger results than exposure only in the client's imagination (Follette & Hayes, 2000).

Another technique for extinguishing unwanted behaviors is **flooding,** or **implosive therapy,** which involves exposing clients to feared stimuli or situations to an excessive degree while preventing them from avoiding that situation. One example is having a person with a deep fear of germs soil her hands with dirt and then not wash her hands for several hours. This may sound relatively benign to you, but, for person with a germ obsession, that would arouse a great deal of anxiety. Over time, however, the anxiety tends to extinguish.

Techniques for Learning Desirable Behaviors

The techniques we have just discussed are designed to extinguish maladaptive responses or behaviors. Often, however, a person wishes to learn a new set of behaviors. A student of B. F. Skinner's, named Ogden Lindsley, first conceived of using the methods of operant conditioning to create new, positive behaviors in people with serious mental disorders. He began working with severely impaired mental patients in the Metropolitan State Hospital just outside Boston, setting up a system whereby they were given rewards for positive, nonpsychotic behavior, whereas rewards were withheld when they exhibited psychotic behavior. This method of shaping the responses of severely impaired people proved extremely successful.

Soon, during the 1950s and 1960s, whole wards of state hospitals were being turned over to behavior therapists. In these wards, a **token economy** was often set up, in which a patient would receive a small chip or token each time he or she exhibited a desired behavior (e.g., spoke to another person, made his or her bed). These tokens could be exchanged for privileges, such as a walk on the hospital grounds, or desired objects, such as special food. This technique is credited, along with the introduction of antipsychotic drugs, with helping cut the population of inpatient mental hospitals by 67 percent between 1955 and 1980 (Bellack, Morrison, & Mueser, 1992). This type of operant conditioning is frequently used to treat children with severe disorders, such as autism.

Response shaping through operant conditioning is also an effective tool in working with children who have behavior problems in the normal range for children. For example, suppose that a child tends to have tantrums in his school class. A behavior therapist might observe that the child initiates these tantrums when it appears he wants, but is not receiving, the teacher's attention. The therapist might prescribe that the teacher put the child in a small, empty room for three or four minutes each time he begins to tantrum—in other words, to give the child a time-out. At the same time, the therapist might train the child to ask the teacher in an appropriate manner to come and look at his drawing or another accomplishment, rather than to tantrum. At first, the child may use these new communication skills poorly, but even a minor attempt at using them instead of tantruming would be rewarded by the teacher's attention. Over time, only completely appropriate communications with the teacher would be rewarded. This is a form of **social skills training,** which has been adapted to help people with a variety of problems in interacting and communicating with others.

Behavior therapies have proven effective for a wide range of psychological problems, including several of the anxiety disorders, and behavior problems, particularly in children (Thorpe & Olson, 1997). Many therapists combine behavioral strategies with cognitive strategies.

Cognitive Therapies

Cognitive therapies focus on challenging people's maladaptive interpretations of events or ways of thinking and replacing them with more adaptive ways of thinking. Cognitive therapists also help clients learn more effective problem-solving techniques to deal with the concrete problems in their lives.

One of the most widely used cognitive therapies was developed by Aaron Beck (1976). There are many specific techniques in cognitive therapies (see Table 5.5 on page 152). They reflect three main goals.

The first goal is to assist clients in identifying their irrational and maladaptive thoughts. People often do not recognize the negative thoughts that are swirling in their minds and affecting their emotions and behaviors. Cognitive therapists encourage clients to pay attention to the thoughts that are associated with their moods or with unwanted behaviors, to write down these thoughts, and to bring the thoughts into the therapy session. If the pharmacy student we have been discussing did this, she would discover that every time she begins to feel somewhat anxious in class, thoughts such as "I'll never succeed! I can't do this! My illness is too debilitating!" rush through her mind.

The second goal is to teach clients to challenge their irrational or maladaptive thoughts and to consider alternative ways of thinking. Many of the specific techniques listed in Table 5.5 are designed to challenge clients' irrational thoughts.

These techniques tend to be implemented through a Socratic method of asking questions that help clients come to insights about their thoughts on their own. For example, a therapist might ask the pharmacy student, "What's the evidence for your belief that you'll never finish pharmacy school?" Sometimes, a client will have no evidence for his or her belief about a situation. For example, the pharmacy student may be pulling straight As and have little evidence that she is about to flunk out of school. Other times, a client will have identified pieces of evidence for his or her perspective.

The therapist might ask a second question: "Are there other ways of looking at this evidence or this situation?" The therapist is encouraging the client to think of alternative perspectives to his or her own. The pharmacy student might answer, "Well, I have been bouncing back each time I have a setback, I guess, so it's not a sure thing that I will flunk out of school."

The third goal of the cognitive therapist is to get the client to face his or her worst fears about a situation and recognize ways the client could cope with them. The therapist might ask the pharmacy student, "What's the worst that could happen?" and "What could you do if the worst did happen?" The point of these questions is to get clients to generate ways they can cope with their worst fears, diminishing the fears and developing a set of coping strategies they can use if these fears come to pass. The pharmacy student may say that her worst fear is that she will have a psychotic episode in class, which everyone will see, and she will be forced to

TABLE 5.5   Techniques in Cognitive Therapies

Cognitive therapists use many different techniques to challenge clients' thinking.

Label	Description	Example
Challenge idiosyncratic meanings	Explore personal meaning attached to the client's words and ask the client to consider alternatives	When a client says he will be "devastated" by his spouse leaving, ask just how he would be devastated and ways he could avoid being devastated.
Question the evidence	Systematically examine the evidence for the client's beliefs or assertions	When a client says she can't live without her spouse, explore how she lived without the spouse before she was married.
Reattribution	Help the client distribute responsibility for events appropriately	When a client says that her son's failure in school must be her fault, explore other possibilities, such as the quality of the school.
Examine options and alternatives	Help the client generate alternative actions to maladaptive ones	If a client considers leaving school, explore whether tutoring or going part-time to school are good alternatives.
Decatastrophize	Help the client evaluate whether he or she is overestimating the nature of a situation	If a client states that failure in a course means he must give up the dream of medical school, question whether this is a necessary conclusion.
Fantasize consequences	Explore fantasies of a feared situation; if unrealistic, the client may recognize this; if realistic, work on effective coping strategies	Help a client who fantasizes "falling apart" when asking the boss for a raise to role-play the situation and develop effective skills for making the request.
Examine advantages and disadvantages	Examine advantages and disadvantages of an issue, to instill a broader perspective	If a client says she "was just born depressed and will always be that way," explore the advantages and disadvantages of holding that perspective versus other perspectives.
Turn adversity to advantage	Explore ways that difficult situations can be transformed into opportunities	If a client has just been laid off, explore whether this is an opportunity for him to return to school.
Guided association	Help the client see connections between different thoughts or ideas	Draw the connections between a client's anger at his wife for going on a business trip and his fear of being alone.
Scaling	Ask the client to rate his or her emotions or thoughts on scales to help gain perspective	If a client says she was overwhelmed by an emotion, ask her to rate it on a scale from 0 (not at all present) to 100 (fell down in a faint).
Thought stopping	Provide the client with ways of stopping a cascade of negative thoughts	Teach an anxious client to picture a stop sign or hear a bell when anxious thoughts begin to snowball.
Distraction	Help the client find benign or positive distractions to take attention away temporarily from negative thoughts or emotions	Have a client count to 200 by 13s when he feels himself becoming anxious.
Labeling of distortions	Provide labels for specific types of distorted thinking to help the client gain more distance and perspective	Have a client keep a record of the number of times per day she engages in all-or-nothing thinking—seeing things as all bad or all good.

Source: Freeman & Reinecke, 1995.

drop out of pharmacy school. The therapist would then help her explore ways of coping with this if it were true. For example, the therapist might work with the pharmacy student to identify the early signs of her anxiety attacks and psychotic symptoms and to develop a specific plan for leaving class and contacting the therapist at this time.

Behavioral Assignments

An important component of cognitive therapies is the use of **behavioral assignments** to help the client gather evidence concerning his or her beliefs, to test alternative viewpoints about a situation, and to try new methods of coping with different situations. These assignments are presented to the client as ways of testing hypotheses and gathering information that will be useful in therapy, regardless of the outcome. The assignments can also involve trying out new skills, such as skills at communicating more effectively, between therapy sessions.

The following simulation illustrates how a therapist might use behavioral assignments to provide the *Extraordinary People* pharmacy student with opportunities to practice new skills and to gather information about thoughts that contribute to negative emotions:

A socially anxious client may be given the behavioral assignment to talk to a clerk in a checkout line.

CASE STUDY

The pharmacy student was unable to complete her degree because she feared meeting with a professor to discuss an incomplete grade she had received in a course. She was quite convinced that the professor would "scream at her" and had been unable to complete a homework assignment to call the professor's secretary to arrange a meeting. An in vivo task was agreed on, in which she called the professor from her therapist's office. Her thoughts and feelings before, during, and after the call were carefully examined. As might be expected, the professor was quite glad to hear from his former student and was pleased to accept her final paper. The origins of her beliefs about how others feel toward her were then reviewed and she was able to see that these beliefs were both maladaptive and erroneous. (Adapted from Freeman & Reinecke, 1995, pp. 203–204)

Therapists also often use role-plays during therapy sessions to elicit the client's reactions to feared situations and to help the client rehearse positive responses to such situations. For example, a therapist might engage the pharmacy student in a role-play in which the therapist plays the part of the student's professor and the client rehearses how she might talk with him about her concerns about her homework assignment.

Taking Control

Cognitive therapists attempt to teach clients skills, so that clients can become their own therapists (Beck et al., 1979). Therapists try to get clients to take responsibility for and control over their own thoughts and actions, rather than looking to the therapist to tell them what to do, or only reacting to external forces. By learning these strategies and gaining a sense of control over their thinking and emotions, clients not only can overcome current problems but also can handle new problems that arise more effectively.

Do cognitive therapists ever get around to exploring the "deeper" meanings of clients' emotions and irrational thoughts? Most cognitive therapists are not against exploring the origins of clients' negative ways of thinking in their earlier experiences in life. Most believe, however, that clients must first learn how to manage and control these thoughts and emotions. Once clients have become effective at challenging their irrational thoughts and coping with negative emotions and difficult situations, cognitive therapists may then help them investigate the roots of these patterns.

Cognitive therapies are designed to be short-term, 12 to 20 weeks in duration, with one or two sessions per week (Beck et al., 1979). They have been compared with drug therapies and interpersonal therapy in the treatment of depression, anxiety, substance use problems, and eating disorders and have been shown to be highly effective (Hollon, Haman, & Brown, 2002).

SUMMING UP

- Psychodynamic therapies focus on uncovering the unconscious motives and concerns behind psychopathology through free association and the analysis of transferences and dreams.

- Humanistic, or client-centered, therapy attempts to help clients find their own answers to problems by supporting them and reflecting back these concerns, so they can self-reflect and self-actualize.

- Behavior therapies focus on altering the reinforcements and punishments people receive for maladaptive behavior. Behavior therapists also help clients learn new behavioral skills.

- Cognitive therapies focus on changing the maladaptive cognitions behind distressing feelings and behaviors.

INTERPERSONAL AND SOCIAL APPROACHES

The psychological therapies focus primarily on changing the ways people think and behave. The interpersonal and social approaches to treatment view the individual as part of a larger system of relationships, influenced by social forces and culture, and hold that this larger system must be addressed in therapy.

The treatments discussed in this section vary greatly in how broadly they reach beyond the individual into the social system in attempting to alleviate the individual's symptoms. *Interpersonal therapists* work primarily with individuals to help them understand their place in their social system and change their behaviors and roles in that social system. *Family systems therapists* insist that the whole family needs to be part of therapy, because the dynamics that cause and maintain psychopathology rise from the family unit, not from the individual. *Group therapies* capitalize on the presence of other group members to help individuals learn to cope with their problems more effectively. The *community mental-health movement* was designed to be a wholistic approach to the treatment of mental disorders that involves the entire community in an individual's treatment. *Cultural perspectives* on treatment acknowledge the impact of cultural values and norms on people's experiences of mental disorders.

Interpersonal Therapy

As we noted in Chapter 2, **interpersonal therapy,** or **IPT,** emerged out of modern psychodynamic theories of psychopathology, which shifted their focus from the unconscious conflicts of the individual to the client's pattern of relationships with important people in his or her life (Klerman et al., 1984; Weissman & Markowitz, 2002). IPT differs from psychodynamic therapies in that the therapist is much more structuring and directive in the therapy, offering interpretations much earlier and focusing on how to change current relationships. In addition, IPT is designed to be a short-term therapy, often lasting only about 12 weeks. An example of the application of IPT and some of the differences between an IPT approach and a traditional psychodynamic approach comes in the following case study (adapted from Klerman et al., 1984, pp. 155–182).

CASE STUDY

Mrs. C. was an older woman whose husband died a year earlier after a long and painful illness. Mrs. C. had been extremely dependent on her husband prior to his illness, relying on him to lead their social life and manage all their finances. Over the course of his illness, Mrs. C. became resentful both that her husband was "abandoning her" by becoming incapacitated by his illness at a time they were supposed to be enjoying their retirement and that he was becoming a severe burden on her. Following his death, she still felt a great deal of anger toward him, but also a great deal of guilt for her anger. She came into therapy suffering from unshakable sadness, preoccupation with memories of her husband's death and her guilty feelings, problems in sleeping, and complete social withdrawal. The IPT therapist began by reassuring Mrs. C. that her feelings were not unusual and telling her that the goal of therapy would be to help her confront all that she has lost and learn to manage her new life better. Much of the therapy then focused on eliciting Mrs. C.'s feelings about her husband and her loss, helping her clarify the reasons for these feelings and accept these feelings. At the end of the first session, the therapist said:

> One of the reasons why people sometimes have difficulty starting up again after losing a loved one is be-

(continued)

cause it's been hard to really look the loss straight in the face, and to really think about what it means, and allow yourself to feel the painful feelings. I think one of the things we can do in therapy is to try to look at what's happened with you and your husband, to look at what he meant to you. . . . The other side of trying to look at what's happened with the loss of your husband is for us to look into the ways you can start enjoying life again. And it seems that in fact you've made a start as far as that kind of thing is concerned. However, it also seems that you have a number of long-term attitudes that to some extent you realize aren't realistic, such as the difference between the way things turn out and the way you anticipate them. Also, you have a lot of fears, that somehow people won't like you, that they're avoiding you or perhaps going to exploit you. We will spend some time trying to look at just what makes these things seem so powerful and likely to happen. Also we'll look at ways you can overcome these hesitations.

Like a psychodynamic therapist, the IPT therapist believed that Mrs. C.'s inability to accept the anger she felt against her husband caused her depression. The therapy focused on helping Mrs. C. express her guilt and anger. Unlike a psychodynamic therapist, who would have focused on the roots of Mrs. C.'s relationship with her husband and feelings about that relationship in her early childhood, the IPT therapist was concerned primarily with Mrs. C.'s recent and current relationships. In addition, the IPT therapist was directive in gently but consistently urging Mrs. C. to increase her social contacts and her activities. The following interchange between the therapist and Mrs. C. illustrates how the therapist focused on helping Mrs. C. express and clarify her feelings but stayed in the present:

Mrs. C.: I like Christmas. I like decorating the house. So . . . I-I just, when my husband isn't there, I still will . . . decorate.

Therapist: It's still hard to think about doing things for yourself.

Mrs. C.: Well, I think that's where the guilt comes in, that he isn't here, you know. I get

CASE STUDY

this pang of guilt, thinking, well, gee, you shouldn't be, you shouldn't be so happy about things.

Therapist: Because if you're enjoying things, that means you can't be thinking about him?

Mrs. C.: I think about him less and less, but I don't . . . suddenly, all of a sudden, when I'm doing something that I'm enjoying, the thought intrudes that, you know, you shouldn't be so happy [chuckles]. I'm sure he wouldn't want me to be—sad. . . .

Therapist: But in a way, hanging on to those sad thoughts . . . is a little like hanging on to him?

Mrs. C.: Probably.

Because IPT is short-term, it has been relatively easy for its proponents to test its effectiveness and to compare its effectiveness with that of a number of other treatments. IPT has been shown effective in the treatment of depression, anxiety, drug addiction, and eating disorders (Weissman & Markowitz, 2002). In addition, it appears as effective as drug treatments for most of these disorders.

Family Systems Therapy

Family systems therapy is based on the belief that an individual's problems are always rooted in interpersonal systems, particularly in the systems called *families*. According to this viewpoint, a therapist cannot help an individual without treating the entire family system that created and is maintaining the individual's problems. In fact, family systems theorists argue that the individual may not actually have a problem but has become the "identified patient" in the family, carrying the responsibility or blame for the dysfunction of the family system.

Two of the most frequently used types of family systems therapy are Virginia Satir's Conjoint Family Therapy (Satir, 1967) and Salvador Minuchin's Structural Family Therapy (Minuchin, 1981). Satir's therapy focuses on the patterns and processes of communication among family members. The therapist identifies and points out dysfunctional communication patterns and teaches family members to communicate better by modeling for them effective communication and by teaching members to be clear and to refrain from inferring meaning.

Minuchin's Structural Family Therapy focuses more on the role each member of the family has

Family therapists work with the entire family rather than only the "identified patient."

come to play in the family system and on changing the structure and dynamics of the relationships among family members. The therapist attempts to "join" with the family, becoming a part of the family so as to exert influence over the processes by which family members interact. By questioning family members about their feelings about one another's behaviors and commenting on the behaviors and feelings of the members, the therapist attempts to bring the family dynamics into the open. What follows is an example of an interchange between Minuchin and a husband and wife with whom he was working (1981, adapted from pp. 35–36).

V O I C E S

Husband: I think when something irritates me, it builds up and I hold it in until some little thing will trigger it, and then I'll be very, very critical and get angry. Then I'll tell her that I just don't understand why it has to be this way. But then I try to be very careful not to be unreasonable or too harsh because, when I'm harsh, I feel guilty about it.

Minuchin: So, sometimes the family feels like a trap.

Husband: It's not the family so much; it's just—[indicates wife].

Minuchin [completing husband's gesture]: Your wife?

Husband [looking at wife]: No, not her either. It's just the things she doesn't do versus the things she does in terms of how she spends her time. Sometimes I think her priorities should be changed.

Minuchin: I think you are soft-pedaling.

Wife: About being trapped?

Minuchin: Yes, about being trapped. I think people sometimes get depressed when they are, like your husband, unable to be direct. He's not a straight talker. There's a tremendous amount of indirection in your family, because you are essentially very good people who are very concerned not to hurt one another. And you need to tell white lies a lot. . . .

Wife [to husband]: Am I indirect?

Husband: I don't really know. Sometimes you seem very direct, but I find myself wondering if you are telling me everything about what's bothering you. You know, if you seem upset, I'm not always sure that I know what's bugging you.

Wife: That I can be upset for something like that because it wouldn't upset you?

Husband: Maybe that's part of it.

Wife [smiling, but at the same time her eyes are watering]: Because you always seem to know better than I do what is really upsetting me, what my problem is at the moment.

Minuchin [to husband]: You see what's happening now? She's talking straight, but she's afraid that, if she talks straight, you will be hurt, so she begins to cry and she begins to smile, so she's saying, "Don't take my straight talk seriously, because it is just the product of a person who is under stress." And that is the kind of thing you do to each other, so you cannot change too much. Because you don't tell each other in what direction to change.

The goal of the family systems therapist is to challenge and disrupt the current dysfunctional dynamics of the family, so that the family is forced to change these dynamics, ideally toward more adaptive dynamics. The following are the three primary strategies of family systems therapy:

1. To challenge the family's assumption that "the problem" lies in one member of the family, rather than in the family dynamics

2. To challenge dysfunctional family structures, such as those in which the family members are overinvolved with each other and do not allow each other sufficient autonomy

3. To challenge the family's defensive conception of reality, such as in challenging the parents' belief that there is nothing wrong with their daughter, when she is suffering from a serious eating disorder

If the pharmacy student we have been discussing had family systems therapy to deal with her anxiety symptoms, the therapist might explore how these symptoms are part of a larger system of the family's seeing her as weak and damaged, possibly communicating their low expectations to her. The therapist might work with her and her family, so that the family provides her with the support she needs without undermining her attempts at autonomy.

Group therapies bring together people experiencing a common problem to learn from and support each other.

Group Therapy

Most of the psychotherapies we have discussed in this chapter have been applied in **group therapy** as well as in one-on-one interactions between a therapist and a client. Often, the members of the group share an experience, such as a history of sexual abuse, severe problems in social interactions, or the diagnosis of a life-threatening disease. The pharmacy student we have been discussing might join a group of people with serious mental-health problems who are attempting to finish their education, to obtain support and understanding from people having some of the same life experiences she is.

Group therapy offers many potential benefits over individual therapy. Groups provide individuals with unique opportunities to view their problems from a broader perspective than their own, as well as to practice new attitudes and skills in a safe environment. Group therapy also is an efficient, cost-effective way for therapists to provide their services to larger numbers of clients. Many studies of group therapies for specific disorders have found them to be effective (Forsyth & Corazzini, 2000), as we will discuss in their application to the specific disorders.

Many group therapy sessions are not led by professional therapists, however. Many **self-help groups**—people who come together to deal with a common experience or need—organize themselves without the help of mental-health professionals. Many of these groups subscribe to the perspective of Rogers' client-centered therapy that it does not necessarily require a professional to help people in self-exploration—what it really takes is a listening, caring person. In colleges, client-centered approaches are taught in many courses on *peer coun-*

seling, in which students learn to counsel other college students. Client-centered therapy is considered appropriate for such situations, because it does not require years of training for the counselor and is based on the premise that the counselor and client are equals.

Self-help groups are extremely popular, with as many as 15 million people in the United States alone attending these groups. One popular type of self-help group is the *bereavement support group* for people who have recently experienced a loss. The loss of a loved one can be an overwhelming experience, and grief can involve frightening symptoms, such as severe problems in concentration or the sense that the deceased loved one is present. Bereavement support groups provide a safe place for the expression of grief, education on grief, and validation of members' experiences of grief. Support groups can also help decrease the isolation that many bereaved people feel. Group members may learn new coping strategies as they hear about how others have approached the tasks of mourning. Many people find bereavement support groups helpful, as the following 65-year-old man who lost his wife describes (Nolen-Hoeksema & Larson, 1999, p. 171).

VOICES

I've been going to the support group they have once a week, for all the people who lost their loved ones—over a year now. With some other people, we sit around, you know, and everybody tells their problems. You feel then you're not the only one, that some other people are hurting, too.

Evaluating the effectiveness of bereavement groups and other self-help groups has not been easy. These groups tend to be fluid, with members coming and going, getting different "dosages" of the group. The effectiveness of one of the most widespread and popular self-help groups, Alcoholics Anonymous, has been evaluated, and it appears that this form of self-help group therapy can be quite effective in the treatment of alcoholism (see Chapter 17).

Community Treatment

As we noted in Chapter 1, *the community mental-health movement* was officially launched in 1963 by President John Kennedy to provide coordinated mental-health services to people in community-based centers. Let's take a look at some of these community treatment centers.

Community Treatment Centers

Community mental-health centers are intended to provide mental-health care based in the community, often from teams of social workers, therapists, and physicians who coordinate care. **Halfway houses** offer people with long-term mental-health problems the opportunity to live in a structured, supportive environment while they are trying to reestablish a job and ties to family and friends. **Day treatment centers** allow people to obtain treatment all day, as well as occupational and rehabilitative therapies, but to live at home at night.

People who have acute problems that require hospitalization may go to inpatient wards of general hospitals or specialized psychiatric hospitals. Sometimes, their first contact with a mental-health professional is in the emergency room of a hospital. Once their acute problems have subsided, however, they often are released back to their community treatment center, rather than remaining for the long term in a psychiatric hospital.

Deinstitutionalization was successful in getting patients out of psychiatric hospitals. The number of patients in large state psychiatric hospitals decreased by 75 percent in the 1960s and 1970s after the movement was launched (Lamb & Weinberger, 2001). Unfortunately, the resources to care for all the mental patients released from institutions were never adequate. Not enough halfway houses were built or community mental-health centers funded to serve the thousands of men and women who had been institutionalized or who would have been if the movement had not happened.

The mental-health care system in the United States has hit another turning point in the early twenty-first century (Torrey, 1997). Mental-health services are expensive, because mental-health problems are sometimes chronic and mental-health treatment can take a long time. Many people are not insured, and those who have insurance often find that their mental-health coverage is limited (Rosenheck, 1999). People with long-term, severe mental disorders, such as schizophrenia, often exhaust all sources of funding for their mental-health care, and many end up homeless or incarcerated for crimes they commit while not being treated.

Although 50 to 60 percent of people with a severe mental illness receive some sort of care, that leaves about half who receive none (Kessler et al., 2001; Narrow et al., 1993; Torrey, 1997). Sometimes, people refuse care that might help them; other times, they fall through holes in the medical safety net because of bureaucratic rules designed to shift the burden of the cost of mental-health care from one agency to another, as in the case of Rebecca J. (Torrey, 1997, pp. 105–106):

CASE STUDY

Because of severe schizoaffective disorder, Rebecca J., age 56, had spent 25 years in a New York State psychiatric hospital. She lived in a group home in the community but required rehospitalization for several weeks approximately once a year when she relapsed despite taking medications. As a result of the reduction in state hospital beds (for people with mental disorders) and attempts by the state to shift readmissions for fiscal reasons, these rehospitalizations increasingly took place on the psychiatric wards of general hospitals that varied widely in quality. In 1994, she was admitted to a new hospital because the general hospital where she usually went was full. The new hospital was inadequately staffed to provide care for patients as sick as Rebecca J. In addition, the psychiatrist was poorly trained and had access to only a small fraction of Rebecca J.'s complex and voluminous past history. During her 6-week hospitalization, Rebecca J. lost 10 pounds because the nursing staff did not help her eat, had virtually all her clothing and personal effects lost or stolen, became toxic from her lithium medication, which was not noticed until she was semicomatose, and was prematurely discharged while she was still so psychotic that she had to be rehospitalized in another hospital less than 24

(continued)

hours later. Meanwhile, less than a mile away in the state psychiatric hospital where she had spent many years, a bed sat empty on a ward with nursing staff and a psychiatrist who knew her case well and with her case records readily available in a file cabinet.

As we discuss the research showing the effectiveness of various treatments for specific disorders throughout the remainder of the book, it is important to keep in mind that those treatments can work only if people have access to them. A critical question for society is whether we will ensure that the people who can benefit from the treatments researches have worked so hard to develop will get access to them.

Community Prevention Programs

It would be better to prevent people from developing psychopathology in the first place than to treat it once it had developed. This approach is known as **primary prevention**—stopping the development of disorders before they start. Some primary prevention strategies for reducing drug abuse and delinquency might include changing some of the neighborhood characteristics that seem to contribute to delinquency and drug use. Education is a big part of primary prevention. For example, researchers in the Stanford Heart Disease Program educated townspeople through the local media about how they could reduce their risk for cardiovascular disease (for example, by stopping smoking and reducing fat in their diets). This effort led to measurable decreases in blood pressure and cholesterol in the townspeople (Maccoby & Altman, 1988).

Secondary prevention is focused on catching disorders in their earliest stages and providing treatment designed to reduce their development. Secondary prevention usually focuses on people at high risk for the disorder. For example, one highly successful study targeted people in low-income minority groups who were suffering from physical ailments (Munoz, 1997; Munoz, Mrazek, & Haggerty, 1996). The people in these groups also were at high risk for serious depression. This program provided cognitive-behavioral therapy to the people in these groups, teaching them strategies for overcoming or preventing the symptoms of depression. It also helped them learn skills for coping more effectively with their physical illnesses and for dealing with medical professionals. The people who went through this program were less likely to develop serious depression over the year they were followed than was a control group of people who did not go through the program. The program participants were also physically healthier at the end of their follow-up year.

Cross-Cultural and Gender Issues in Treatment

A number of assumptions or values are inherent in the psychological therapies we have discussed. They can clash with the values and norms of cultures different from the Western cultures that created those psychotherapies (Sue & Lam, 2002, Snowden & Yamada, 2005). First, most psychotherapies are focused on the individual—the individual's unconscious conflicts, dysfunctional ways of thinking, maladaptive behavior patterns, and so on. In contrast, many cultures focus on the group, or collective, rather than the individual (Sue & Sue, 2003). The identity of the individual is not seen apart from the groups to which that individual belongs—his or her family, community, ethnic group, and religion. If therapists fail to recognize this when working with clients from collectivist cultures, they may make recommendations that are useless or perhaps even harmful, leading to conflicts between clients and important groups in the clients' lives that clients cannot handle.

Second, most psychotherapies value the expression of emotions and the disclosure of personal concerns, whereas the restraint of emotions and personal concerns is valued in many cultures, such as Japanese culture (Sue & Sue, 2003). Some counselors may see this restraint as a problem and try to encourage clients to become more expressive. Again, this effort can clash badly with the self-concepts of clients and with the norms of their culture.

Third, in many psychotherapies, clients are expected to take the initiative in communicating their concerns and desires to the therapist and in generating ideas about what is causing their symptoms and what changes they might want to make. These expectations can clash with cultural norms that require deference to people in authority (Sue & Sue, 2003). A client from a culture in which one speaks only when spoken to and never challenges an elder or authority figure may be extremely uncomfortable with a therapist who does not tell the client what is wrong and how to fix it in a very direct manner.

In addition, many clients who are in ethnic minority groups may also be in lower socioeconomic groups, whereas their therapists are likely to be in middle- or upper-class socioeconomic groups. This can create tensions due to class differences as well as cultural differences.

Some studies suggest that people from Latino, Asian, and Native American cultures are more comfortable with structured and action-oriented therapies, such as behavior and cognitive-behavioral therapies, than with the less structured therapies (see Miranda et al., 2005). The specific form of therapy may not matter as much as the cultural sensitivity the therapist shows the client. Sue and Zane (1987, pp. 42–43) give the following example of the importance of cultural sensitivity in the interaction between a client and a therapist. First, they describe the problems the client faced; second, they describe how the therapist (one of the authors of the study) responded to these problems.

CASE STUDY

At the advice of a close friend, Mae C. decided to seek services at a mental health center. She was extremely distraught and tearful as she related her dilemma. An immigrant from Hong Kong several years ago, Mae met and married her husband (also a recent immigrant from Hong Kong). Their marriage was apparently going fairly well until six months ago when her husband succeeded in bringing over his parents from Hong Kong. While not enthusiastic about having her parents-in-law live with her, Mae realized that her husband wanted them and that both she and her husband were obligated to help their parents (her own parents were still in Hong Kong).

After the parents arrived, Mae found that she was expected to serve them. For example, the mother-in-law would expect Mae to cook and serve dinner, to wash all the clothes, and to do other chores. At the same time, she would constantly complain that Mae did not cook the dinner right, that the house was always messy, and that Mae should wash certain clothes separately. The parents-in-law also displaced Mae and her husband from the master bedroom. The guest room was located in the basement, and the parents refused to sleep in the basement because it reminded them of a tomb.

Mae would occasionally complain to her husband about his parents. The husband would excuse his parents' demands by indicating "They are my parents and they're getting old." In general, he avoided any potential

conflict; if he took sides, he supported his parents. Although Mae realized that she had an obligation to his parents, the situation was becoming intolerable to her.

I (the therapist) indicated (to Mae) that conflicts with in-laws were very common, especially for Chinese, who are obligated to take care of their parents. I attempted to normalize the problems because she was suffering from a great deal of guilt over her perceived failure to be the perfect daughter-in-law. I also conveyed my belief that in therapy we could try to generate new ideas to resolve the problem—ideas that did not simply involve extreme courses of action such as divorce or total submission to the in-laws (which she believed were the only options).

I discussed Mae during a case conference with other mental health personnel. It is interesting that many suggestions were generated: Teach Mae how to confront her parents-in-law; have her invite the husband for marital counseling so that husband and wife could form a team in negotiation with his parents; conduct extended family therapy so that Mae, her husband, and her in-laws could agree on contractual give-and-take relationships. The staff agreed that working solely with Mae would not change the situation. . . . Confronting her in-laws was discrepant with her role of daughter-in-law, and she felt very uncomfortable in asserting herself in the situation. Trying to involve her husband or in-laws in treatment was ill advised. Her husband did not want to confront his parents. More important, Mae was extremely fearful that her family might find out that she had sought psychotherapy. Her husband as well as her in-laws would be appalled at her disclosure of family problems to a therapist who was an outsider. . . . How could Mae's case be handled? During the case conference, we discussed the ways that Chinese handle interpersonal family conflicts which are not unusual to see. Chinese often use third-party intermediaries to resolve conflicts. The intermediaries obviously have to be credible and influential with the conflicting parties. At the next ses-

(continued)

sion with Mae, I asked her to list the persons who might act as intermediaries, so that we could discuss the suitability of having someone else intervene. Almost immediately, Mae mentioned her uncle (the older brother of the mother-in-law) whom she described as being quite understanding and sensitive. We discussed what she should say to the uncle. After calling her uncle, who lived about 50 miles from Mae, she reported that he wanted to visit them. The uncle apparently realized the gravity of the situation and offered to help. He came for dinner, and Mae told me that she overheard a discussion between the uncle and Mae's mother-in-law. Essentially, he told her that Mae looked unhappy, that possibly she was working too hard, and that she needed a little more praise for the work that she was doing in taking care of everyone. The mother-in-law expressed surprise over Mae's unhappiness and agreed that Mae was doing a fine job. Without directly confronting each other, the uncle and his younger sister understood the subtle messages each conveyed. Older brother was saying that something was wrong and younger sister acknowledged it. After this interaction, Mae reported that her mother-in-law's criticisms did noticeably diminish and that she had even begun to help Mae with the chores.

If Mae's therapist had not been sensitive to Mae's cultural beliefs about her role as a daughter-in-law and had suggested some of the solutions put forward by his colleagues in the case conference, Mae might have dropped out of therapy. People from ethnic minority groups in the United States are much more likely than European Americans to drop out of psychosocial therapy (Snowden & Yamada, 2005). Ethnic minority clients often find therapists' suggestions strange, unhelpful, and even insulting. Because Mae's therapist was willing to work within the constraints of her cultural beliefs, he and Mae found a solution to her problem that was acceptable to her.

In treating children, cultural norms about child-rearing practices and the proper role of doctors can make it difficult to include the family in a child's treatment. For example, in a study of behavior therapy for children, Hong Kong Chinese parents were very reluctant to be trained to engage

Therapists working with children must be sensitive to parents' expectations concerning the role of the therapist.

in behavioral techniques, such as responding with praise or ignoring certain behaviors. Such techniques violated the parents' views of appropriate child-rearing practices and their expectations that the therapist should be the person "curing" the child. However, several clinicians argue that family-based therapies are more appropriate than individual therapy in cultures that are highly family-oriented, including Native American, Hispanic, African American, and Asian American cultures (Hall, 2001; Tharp, 1991).

Rosselló and Bernal (2004) adapted both cognitive-behavioral therapy and interpersonal therapy to be more culturally sensitive in the treatment of depressed Puerto Rican adolescents. The Puerto Rican value of *familism*, a strong attachment to family, was incorporated into the therapy. Issues of the balance between dependence and independence were explicitly discussed in family groups. The adapted therapies proved effective in treating the adolescents' depression.

Matching Therapist and Client

Must a therapist come from the same culture as the client to understand the client fully? A review of several studies suggests that ethnic matching is not an important predictor of how long clients remain in therapy or of the outcomes of therapy (Maramba & Nagayama Hall, 2002).

Cultural sensitivity can probably be acquired through training and experience to a large degree (D'Andrea & Daniels, 1995; Sue et al., 1998). In fact, just because a therapist is from the same ethnic group as the client does not mean that the therapist and client share a value system (Teyber & McClure, 2000). For example, a fourth-generation Japanese American who has fully adopted American competitive and individualistic values may clash with a recent immigrant from Japan who subscribes to the self-sacrificing, community-oriented values of

Japanese culture. These value differences among people of the same ethnic group may explain why studies show that matching the ethnicity or gender of the therapist and client does not necessarily lead to a better outcome for the client (Maramba & Nagayama Hall, 2002). On the other hand, the relationship between a client and a therapist and a client's beliefs about the likely effectiveness of a therapy contribute strongly to a client's full engagement in the therapy and the effectiveness of the therapy.

As for gender, there is little evidence that women or men do better in therapy with a therapist of the same gender (Garfield, 1994; Huppert et al., 2001; Teyber & McClure, 2000). In the largest study of the treatment of depression, for example, clients who were matched with a therapist of their gender did not recover more quickly or more fully than clients who were matched with a therapist of the other gender (Zlotnick, Elkin, & Shea, 1998). This was true whether the client received cognitive-behavioral therapy, interpersonal therapy, or drug therapy.

Women and men do tend to report that they prefer a therapist of the same gender, however (Garfield, 1994; Simons & Helms, 1976). Again, because the client's comfort with a therapist is an important contributor to a client's seeking therapy and remaining in therapy for an entire course, gender matching may still be important in therapy.

Culturally Specific Therapies

Our review of the relationships among culture and therapy has focused on the forms of therapy most often practiced in modern, industrialized cultures, such as psychodynamic, behavior, and cognitive therapies. Cultural groups, even within modern, industrialized countries, often have their own forms of therapy for distressed people, however (Hall, 2001). Let's examine two of these.

Native American healing processes simultaneously focus on the physiology, psychology, and religious practices of the individual (LaFromboise, Trimble, & Mohatt, 1998). "Clients" are encouraged to transcend the self and experience the self as embedded in the community and as an expression of the community. Family and friends are brought together with the individual in traditional ceremonies involving prayers, songs, and dances that emphasize the Native American cultural heritage and the reintegration of the individual into the cultural network. These ceremonies may be supplemented by a variety of herbal medicines, used for hundreds of years to treat people with physical and psychological symptoms.

Several cultures have healing rituals that have been part of their cultural traditions for generations.

Hispanics in the southwestern United States and in Mexico suffering from psychological problems may consult folk healers, known as *curanderos* or *curanderas* (Koss-Chioino, 1995; Rivera, 1988). One survey of urban Hispanic American women in Colorado found that 20 percent had consulted a curandero for treatment (Rivera, 1988). Curanderos use religion-based rituals to overcome the folk illnesses believed to cause psychological and physical problems. These illnesses may be the result of hexes placed on the individual, soul loss, or magical fright. The healing rituals include prayers, the use of holy palm, and incantations. Curanderos may also apply healing ointments or oils and prescribe herbal medicines.

Native Americans and Hispanics often seek both folk healers and psychiatric care from mental-health professionals practicing the therapies described in this chapter. Mental-health professionals need to be aware of the practices and beliefs of folk healing when treating clients from these cultural groups. They need to keep in mind the possibility that clients will combine these forms of therapy, following some of the recommendations of both types of healers.

SUMMING UP

- Interpersonal therapy is a short-term therapy that focuses on clients' current relationships and concerns but explores the roots of their problems in past relationships.

- Family systems therapists focus on changing maladaptive patterns of behavior within family systems to reduce psychopathology in individual members.

- In group therapy, people who share a problem come together to support each other, learn from each other, and practice new skills. Self-help groups are a form of group therapy that does not involve a mental-health professional.

- The community mental-health movement was aimed at deinstitutionalizing people with mental disorders and treating them through community mental-health centers, halfway houses, and day treatment centers. The resources for these community treatment centers have never been adequate, however, and many people do not have access to mental-health care.

- Primary prevention programs aim to stop the development of disorders before they start.

- Secondary prevention programs provide treatment to people in the early stages of their disorders, in the hope of reducing the development of the disorders.

- The values inherent in most psychotherapies that can clash with the values of certain cultures include the focus on the individual, the expression of emotions and disclosure of personal concerns, and the expectation that clients take initiative.

- People from minority groups may be more likely to remain in treatment if matched with a therapist from their own cultural group, but there are large individual differences in these preferences.

- There are a number of culturally specific therapies designed by cultural groups to address psychopathology within the traditions of those cultures.

EVALUATING TREATMENTS

In 1952, well-known British psychologist Hans Eysenck stunned the field when he reviewed studies evaluating the effectiveness of psychotherapy and concluded that psychotherapy does not work. People who had received psychotherapy apparently fared no better than people who were untreated or who were placed on a waiting list.

The number and quality of studies evaluating psychotherapies prior to 1952 were limited. Not surprisingly, Eysenck's review prompted a great deal of new research. Several reviews of this research over the past five decades have concluded that psychotherapy does, indeed, have positive effects and is better than no treatment at all or than various placebos (see Westen, Novotny, & Thompson-Brenner, 2004).

Are some psychotherapies clearly better than others? Some reviews have concluded the answer is no (see Wampold et al., 1997). Rosenweig (1936) called this the *Dodo bird verdict*—"Everybody has won and all must have prizes"—quoting from the Dodo bird in *Alice in Wonderland.* Other reviews suggest that some therapies are better than others, at least for some disorders (Crits-Christoph, 1997; Dobson, 1989; Engels, Garnefski, & Diekstra, 1993; Lambert & Bergen, 1994; Shadish et al., 1993; Smith, Glass, & Miller, 1980).

Some theorists argue that one therapy is unlikely to win over another in therapy outcome studies, because all therapies share certain components that make them successful. This may seem an outrageous idea—on the surface, the different types of therapy described in this chapter may seem radically different. Indeed, proponents of a given approach have often been loud in their opposition to other approaches, decrying these other approaches as useless or even harmful to clients. There is increasing evidence, however, that there are some common components to successful therapies, even when the specific techniques of the therapies differ greatly (see Table 5.6).

The first of these components is a *positive relationship* with the therapist (Norcross, 2002). Clients

TABLE 5.6   Common Components of Successful Therapies

All successful therapies may share certain components that contribute to their success.

Component	Result
Positive relationship with therapist	Affirmation and safety to explore difficult issues or to make difficult changes
Explanation for symptoms	Insight into symptoms and a plan for how to alleviate them
Confrontation of negative emotions	Habituation to emotions and/or catharsis

who trust their therapists and believe that the therapists understand them are more willing to reveal important information, to engage in homework assignments, and to try new skills or coping techniques that the therapists suggest. In addition, simply having a positive relationship with a caring, understanding human being goes a long way toward helping people overcome distress and change behaviors.

Second, all therapies provide clients with an *explanation or interpretation* of why they are suffering (Ingram, Hayes, & Scott, 2000). Simply having a label for painful symptoms and an explanation for those symptoms seems to help many people feel better, much as having a diagnosis for a physical ailment can bring relief. This may suggest that insight provides relief. In addition, however, the explanations that therapies provide for symptoms are usually accompanied by a set of recommendations for how to overcome those symptoms. Following these recommendations may provide the main relief from the symptoms.

In any case, it seems clear that a client has to believe the explanation given to him or her for the symptoms in order for the therapy to help (Frank, 1978). For example, studies of cognitive-behavioral therapy for depression have found that the extent to which clients believe and accept the rationale behind this therapy is a significant predictor of the effectiveness of the therapy (Fennell & Teasdale, 1987). Clients to whom the rationale behind cognitive therapy makes sense engage more actively in therapy and are less depressed after a course of therapy than are those who don't accept the rationale for the therapy from the outset. A major problem in drug therapies is the high dropout rate from these therapies. Often, people drop out either because they do not experience quick enough relief from the drugs and therefore believe the drugs will not work or because they feel they need to talk about problems to overcome them.

A number of other common components across psychotherapies have been suggested (Frank, 1978; Prochaska, 1995; Snyder et al., 2000). For example, most therapies encourage clients to *confront painful emotions* and have techniques for helping them become less sensitive to these emotions. In behavior therapy, systematic desensitization or flooding might be used. In psychodynamic therapies, interpretation of transference and catharsis might be used. Whatever technique is used, the goal is to help the client stop denying, avoiding, or repressing the painful emotions and become able to accept and experience the emotions without being debilitated by them.

Finally, the treatment outcome literature has essentially ignored the question of whether the efficacy of treatments varies by cultural group or ethnicity (Miranda et al., 2005). An analysis conducted for the report of the surgeon general entitled "Mental Health: Culture, Race and Ethnicity" (U.S. Department of Health and Human Services [USDHHS], 2001) found that, of 9,266 participants involved in efficacy studies forming the major treatment guidelines for bipolar disorder, schizophrenia, depression and attention deficit/hyper-activity disorder (ADHD), only 561 African Americans, 99 Latinos, 11 Asian American/Pacific Islanders, and 0 American Indian/Alaskan Natives were included. Few of these studies had the power necessary to examine the impact of care on specific minorities. The need for more studies specifically examining the cultural variation in the efficacy of therapy is obvious.

SUMMING UP

- Some reviews of studies of the effectiveness of psychological treatments find they are all equally effective, but others suggest that certain treatments are more effective than others in treating specific disorders.

- Methodological and ethical problems make doing good research on the effectiveness of therapy difficult.

- Most successful therapies establish a positive relationship between a therapist and client, provide an explanation or interpretation to the client, and encourage the client to confront painful emotions.

SPECIAL ISSUES IN TREATING CHILDREN

Every therapy described in this chapter has probably been used to treat children and adolescents with psychological disorders. Studies of the effectiveness of biological, psychological, and interpersonal, and social therapies generally show that children and adolescents receiving therapy have better outcomes than do those receiving no therapy (Kazdin, 2003a; Kazdin & Weisz, 2003). The effectiveness of any type of therapy may depend largely on the type of disorder the child or adolescent has.

Designing and applying effective therapies for children and adolescents involve problems similar to those that arise in assessing and diagnosing disorders in children and adolescents (refer to Chapter 4). These problems include the need to match the therapy to the child's developmental level; the possibility that a therapy, especially a drug therapy, will have long-term negative effects on the child's development; the fact that children are embedded in families that often need to be treated as well; and the fact that children and adolescents seldom refer themselves for treatment and thus often are not motivated to engage in treatment.

Psychotherapies Matched to Children's Developmental Levels

As we discussed in Chapter 4, children can have difficulty expressing their feelings and concerns in words, particularly when they are very distressed. Therapists use a variety of methods to elicit information from children about their feelings. For example, they may have children draw pictures or engage in play that symbolizes how they are feeling.

Psychodynamically oriented therapists believe that expressing feelings and concerns through play can help the child master these feelings and concerns and overcome negative behaviors. Their therapy with a child may consist primarily of helping the child engage in this indirect expression and exploration of feelings and concerns. Other therapists use play or other projective techniques only as tools to assess a child's feelings and concerns.

Can children participate in talking therapies, such as cognitive-behavioral therapy? It seems that the answer is yes, although the conversations between the therapist and child must be at a level that is appropriate for the child's age (Roberts, Vernberg, & Jackson, 2000). However, many therapists believe that, for children, behavior-oriented therapies are more appropriate than are talking therapies, because behavior therapies are not as dependent on children's verbal abilities. Moreover, children may have trouble changing their behaviors only by changing their thinking—it may take repeated practicing of new behaviors and reinforcement of these behaviors for children to learn them. Comparisons of behavior and nonbehavior therapies for children have suggested that behavior therapies produce a larger and more reliable effect, although nonbehavior therapies do have positive effects on children (Weisz & Hawley, 2002).

The Effects of Drugs on Children and Adolescents

Drug therapies are becoming increasingly popular in treating children and adolescents with psychological problems (Martin, et al., 2002). Drugs were initially used to treat only the most severe disorders in children, such as autism, but they are now being used to treat disorders such as depression and phobias. The use of drugs in children has been extremely controversial, largely because of fears that drugs will have toxic effects both in the short term and in the long term. Finding a safe dosage of drugs for children is initially tricky, because body size, age, and hormones all affect the metabolism of drugs, and there is more variability in the proper dosage of a drug among children than there is among adults.

Most of the drugs used to treat psychological problems in children and adolescents are not approved for use in these populations. Fears of possible negative effects of these drugs were heightened by reports that the serotonin reuptake inhibitors (SSRIs), which are widely prescribed for depression, anxiety, and other conditions in children and adolescents, increase the risk of children committing suicide (see Couzin, 2004; Ramchandani, 2004; Wessely & Kerwin, 2004). Close monitoring is clearly needed when children or adolescents must use psychotherapeutic drugs.

The Need to Treat the Child's Family

Most children live in some sort of family, whether in the traditional two-parent family, with a single parent or perhaps a grandparent, in a foster-care family, or in some other configuration. Many clinicians believe that children's disorders cannot be treated effectively outside the context of the family (Mirsalimi et al., 2003). The family may be the direct cause of a child's disorder, such as when one parent is physically abusive to the child and perhaps to other members of the family. In such cases, treating the child without correcting the cause of

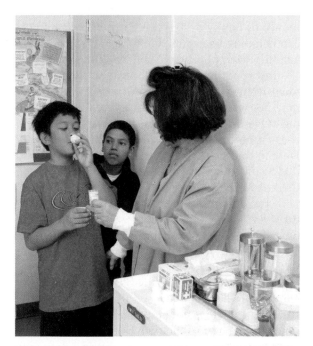

The use of medications to treat children with mental-health problems is controversial.

"Don't you realize, Jason, that when you throw furniture out the window and tie your sister to a tree, you make mommy and daddy very sad?" © *Sidney Harris, courtesy ScienceCartoonsPlus.com*

the child's problem (i.e., the parental abuse) is ineffective. Indeed, sometimes the parent needs therapy even more than the child.

In other cases, the family may not have directly caused the child's problem but may be reinforcing or supporting it in some way. For example, a child may have trouble controlling aggressive behavior, perhaps because of a biological dysfunction, but the family reinforces the child's aggressivity by allowing her to have what she wants when she threatens to lose control. In such cases, teaching family members how to extinguish the child's aggressive behavior can help the child gain control over that behavior, even if the initial cause of the behavior is biological (Estrada & Pinsof, 1995). Children and their families are sometimes treated with the techniques of family systems therapy, but all the psychotherapies we explored in this chapter have been adapted for application to children and families.

Incorporating the family into a child's treatment creates many difficulties, however. A child may not want his or her family involved in treatment. For example, an adolescent who is depressed because his mother is emotionally abusive may not want to confront his mother in therapy and instead may want an exclusive relationship with the caring therapist. The therapist may still choose to meet with the parent, apart from the adolescent, if the therapist believes the parent must be dealt with in order for the adolescent's problems to be overcome. The adolescent must know the therapist is meeting with the parent, however, and must be helped to trust that his relationship with the therapist is not compromised by these meetings with the parent. Family members may not want to join therapy, particularly if they feel they are being blamed for the child's problems. If they do join therapy, they may not cooperate with the therapist in overcoming the child's and family's problems.

Therapists are sometimes faced with extremely difficult decisions about whether to remove children from their families, such as when a therapist believes a family poses a danger to a child. They also must decide when to allow a child to return to a family from which he or she has been removed because of a perceived danger. A therapist's perceptions of the danger a family poses to a child can be influenced by the therapist's biases against the ethnicity or culture of the family or by misunderstandings of the parenting practices of that ethnic or cultural group. For example, Gray and Cosgrove (1985) note that spanking is an accepted form of discipline in some ethnic and socioeconomic groups in the United States but can be taken as evidence of child abuse by social workers and therapists who do not believe spanking is appropriate. Certain cultures may accept some parenting practices that therapists never want to endorse, but therapists must be careful to take into account the cultural context of a parent's behaviors before passing judgment.

Children's Unwillingness to Seek Therapy

Most children and adolescents who enter therapy do not seek it for themselves (Yeh & Weisz, 2001). They may be taken by their parents, who are overwhelmed by their children's behavior or emotional difficulties. Often, troubled children are first identified by school officials, by their pediatricians, by social service agents (e.g., welfare workers), or by the criminal justice system (Snowden & Yamada, 2005). Children who enter psychotherapy through any of these avenues may enter it reluctantly and thus may not participate wholeheartedly in therapy. Little research has been done on the effects of the relationship between a child and a therapist on the outcome of child psychotherapy, but it is likely that a warm, positive relationship with a therapist is as important in therapy with children as it is in therapy with adults. Therapists usually must work against a child's initial reluctance to enter therapy in order to establish a good therapeutic relationship.

Unfortunately, most children who could benefit from therapy do not receive it. Treatment facilities specializing in children's problems are unavailable in many parts of the United States and other industrialized countries and are nonexistent in other parts of the world. The child welfare system sees many troubled children, often the victims of abuse and neglect. Such children are increasingly placed in long-term foster care, rather than given specialized psychological treatment. Many children in the juvenile justice system suffer from psychological disorders, including conduct disorders, depression, and drug addiction, but few receive long-term, intensive treatment (Cauce et al., 2002). There is much room for expanding services to children with psychological problems.

SUMMING UP

- Treatments for children must take into account their cognitive skills and developmental levels and must adapt to their ability to comprehend and participate in therapy.

- There are reasons to be concerned about the possible toxic effects of drugs on children.

- Often, a child's family must be brought into therapy, but the child or the family may object.

- Most children who enter therapy do not seek it out themselves but are taken by others, raising issues about children's willingness to participate in therapy.

CHAPTER INTEGRATION

Many theorists have argued for integration of the different psychotherapies (e.g., Norcross, Beutler, & Caldwell, 2002). Although it may be difficult to integrate the theories behind the therapies because these theories disagree too profoundly on the causes of psychopathology, it may be possible to integrate the techniques of the therapies into a group of strategies used as the therapist sees fit (see Figure 5.2). Indeed, therapists commonly see themselves as eclectics—using the techniques of various therapies depending on the specific issues needing to be addressed. For example, a psychologist might use behavioral techniques for treating phobias but more psychodynamic techniques for treating people who have chronic moderate anxiety.

In addition, team approaches to treatment are becoming increasingly common. A psychologist may provide psychotherapy to clients, with a psychiatrist available to prescribe medications if warranted. A team approach to treatment is especially important for people with chronic mental disorders that can be debilitating, such as schizophrenia. As we discuss in Chapter 11, people with schizophrenia often need drug therapies, psychotherapy that helps them cope with their illnesses, and community-oriented interventions that help them find jobs and housing and reintegrate into society. The pharmacy student in *Extraordinary People* is working with a team such as this. Those people who are able to receive comprehensive care often can live full, productive lives.

FIGURE 5.2 Integrated treatments capitalize on the most effective elements of different therapies.

"I utilize the best from Freud, the best from Jung and the best from my uncle Marty, a very smart fellow." © *Sidney Harris, courtesy ScienceCartoonsPlus.com*

Extraordinary People: Follow-Up

"What I have been trying to express here is the actual reality of what being 'individually titrated to an antipsychotic medicine' and having schizophrenia means to someone personally going through it as opposed to how objectively and easily it is expressed in pharmacy classes. My instructors have stated that 'antipsychotics alleviate symptoms but do not cure psychoses,' but this matter-of-fact statement has very personal meaning for me. It involves internal conflicts and many complicated adjustments—getting to a psychologist outside the city, or if the necessity of hospitalization occurs, getting hospitalized outside the city so fellow students and the pharmacy

school will not have access to that information about me. It means never being able to see well because of the side effects of the medication. It also means enormous medical bills and debts. . . .

"Finally, I heard a teacher in one class talk about long-term chronic illness such as schizophrenia in a way that suggested the teacher knew something about the disease and had looked beyond the myths. Through this class, I began to understand a little better my own noncompliance with the psychotropic drugs; how unacceptable my illness was not only to me, but would have been to others if they had known my diagnosis. I didn't take the medicine at times because I didn't want the disease, its problems, and its stigma. I wanted to be normal. And even now in a professional pharmacy school it would probably shock many people to know a schizophrenic was in their class, would be a pharmacist, and could do a good job. And knowledge of it could cause loss of many friends and acquaintances. So even now I must write this article anonymously. But I want people to know I have schizophrenia, that I need medicine and psychotherapy, and at some times I have required hospitalization. But, I also want them to

know that I have been on the dean's list, and have friends, and expect to receive my pharmacy degree from a major university.

"When you think about schizophrenia next time, try to remember me; there are more people like me out there trying to overcome a poorly understood disease and doing the best they can with what medicine and psychotherapy have to offer them. And some of them are making it." (Anonymous, 1983, pp. 152–155).

Chapter Summary

- A wide variety of biological and psychological approaches to the treatment of psychological disorders have been developed in line with different theories of the causes of these disorders. Biological therapies most often involve drugs intended to regulate the functioning of the brain neurotransmitters associated with a psychological disorder or to compensate for structural brain abnormalities or the effects of genetics (review Table 5.1).

- Antipsychotic medications help reduce unreal perceptual experiences, unreal beliefs, and other symptoms of psychosis. Antidepressant drugs help reduce the symptoms of depression. Lithium, anticonvulsants, and calcium channel blockers help reduce mania. Barbiturates and benzodiazepines help reduce anxiety.

- Herbal medicines have been used for centuries to treat psychological symptoms and have increased in popularity in recent years. Most herbal medicines have not been sufficiently tested, however, and some have been shown not to be very effective.

- Electroconvulsive therapy is used to treat severe depression. Psychosurgery is used in rare circumstances.

- Repetitive transcranial magnetic stimulation (rTMS) is a technique in which powerful magnets are used to stimulate the brain. It has proven useful for some psychological disorders.

- Psychological therapies can be delivered to individual clients or used in a group setting. They include

  1. Psychodynamic therapies, which focus on unconscious conflicts and interpersonal conflicts that lead to maladaptive behaviors and emotions

  2. Behavior therapies, which focus on changing specific maladaptive behaviors and emotions by changing the reinforcements for them

  3. Cognitive therapies, which focus on changing the way clients think about important situations

  4. Humanistic therapy, which intends to help clients realize their potential for self-actualization (review Table 5.2)

- Two types of treatment focus on the individual's relationships and roles in social systems. Interpersonal therapies are based on psychodynamic theories but focus more on current relationships and concerns. Family systems therapies attempt to break maladaptive patterns of relating among family members.

- The community mental-health movement intended to coordinate community services for people with mental disorders. Patients were deinstitutionalized and treated in community mental-health centers, day treatment centers, and halfway houses. Because adequate resources were never put into this movement, its goals were never fully realized.

- Prevention programs focus on preventing disorders before they develop, retarding the development of disorders in their early stages, and reducing the impact of disorders on people's functioning.

- Some clients may wish to work with therapists of the same culture or gender, but it is unclear whether matching a therapist and client in terms of culture and gender is necessary for therapy to be effective. It is important for therapists to be sensitive to the influences of culture and gender on a client's attitudes toward therapy and various solutions to problems.

- Some studies comparing different therapies suggest they are equally effective, whereas others suggest that certain therapies are more effective than others in the treatment of specific disorders. Common components of effective therapy seem to be a good therapist-client relationship, an explanation for symptoms, and the confrontation of negative emotions.

- Therapy with children has its own set of challenges. First, a therapy must be matched to a child's developmental level for the child to be able to participate fully. Second, therapists must be concerned about the short-term and long-term effects of drugs on children's development. Third, children's families may need to be brought into therapy. Fourth, children do not tend to seek therapy for themselves and thus are sometimes reluctant to participate.

MindMap CD-ROM

The following resources on the MindMap CD-ROM that came with this text will help you to master the content of this chapter and prepare for tests:

- Interactive Segment: Systematic Desensitization
- Chapter Timeline
- Chapter Quiz

Key Terms

psychotherapy 136

chlorpromazine 136

phenothiazines 136

neuroleptic 137

butyrophenone 137

antipsychotic drugs 138

antidepressants 138

monoamine oxidase inhibitors (MAOIs) 138

tricyclic antidepressants 138

selective serotonin reuptake inhibitors (SSRIs) 139

lithium 139

anticonvulsants 140

calcium channel blockers 140

antianxiety drugs 140

barbiturates 140

benzodiazepines 140

electroconvulsive therapy (ECT) 142

prefrontal lobotomy 143

psychosurgery 143

repetitive transcranial magnetic stimulation (rTMS) 143

psychodynamic therapies 145

free association 145

resistance 145

transference 145

working through 147

catharsis 147

therapeutic alliance 147

psychoanalysis 147

humanistic therapy (person-centered therapy) 148

client-centered therapy (CCT) 148

unconditional positive regard 148

reflection 148

behavior therapies 149

behavioral assessment 149

role-play 149

systematic desensitization therapy 149

modeling 149

in vivo exposure 150

flooding (implosive therapy) 150

token economy 151

response shaping 151

social skills training 151

cognitive therapies 151

behavioral assignments 153

interpersonal therapy (IPT) 154

family systems therapy 155

group therapy 157

self-help groups 157

community mental-health centers 158

halfway houses 158

day treatment centers 158

primary prevention 159

secondary prevention 159

Chapter 6

The Dream Tree
by Daniel Nevins

*If the mind, which rules the body, ever forgets itself so
far as to trample upon its slave, the slave is never
generous enough to forgive the injury; but will rise
and smite its oppressor.*

—Longfellow, *Hyperion* (1839)

Stress Disorders and
Health Psychology <

CHAPTER OVERVIEW

Extraordinary People

■ **Norman Cousins: *Healing with Laughter***

Physiological Responses to Stress

Our bodies have a natural physiological response to stress, known as the fight-or-flight response. In the short term, this physiological response is adaptive, because it helps the body fight or flee from a threat. When this physiological response is prolonged, however, it causes wear and tear on the body, potentially contributing to ulcers, asthma, headaches, coronary heart disease, high blood pressure, and impairment of the immune system. Events that people perceive as stressful are often uncontrollable or unpredictable.

Sleep and Health

Stress can affect health indirectly by leading people to engage in less healthy behaviors, such as not sleeping enough. Some people develop sleep disorders, which the DSM-IV-TR divides into four categories: sleep disorders due to another mental disorder, sleep disorders due to a general medical condition, substance-induced sleep disorders, and primary sleep disorders. The most well-known primary sleep disorder is insomnia.

Personality and Health

Some personality styles that have been linked to poor physical health include dispositional pessimism and the Type A behavior pattern. Each of these may contribute to poor health by causing a chronic hyperarousal of the fight-or-flight response or by causing people to engage in unhealthy behaviors. One coping style associated with better health is seeking positive social support.

Interventions to Improve Health

Health psychologists have designed a variety of cognitive and behavioral interventions to improve people's physical health, including guided mastery techniques that help people learn healthy behaviors and biofeedback. Social interventions for health focus on helping people use or change their social environment to improve their health.

Posttraumatic Stress Disorder, Acute Stress Disorder, and Adjustment Disorder

Posttraumatic stress disorder (PTSD) is a set of symptoms—including hypervigilance, reexperiencing of trauma, and emotional numbing—experienced by trauma survivors. Acute stress disorder has the same symptoms as PTSD but is experienced for a short time after the trauma. Adjustment disorder is diagnosed when people experience depressive or anxiety symptoms or antisocial behavior in the 3 months following a stressor. Some predictors of people's vulnerability to PTSD are the proximity, duration, and severity of the stressor; the availability of social support; pretrauma distress; and coping strategies. Treatment generally involves exposing people to their fears, challenging their cognitions, and helping them manage ongoing problems. Eye movement desensitization and reprocessing therapy is a controversial intervention for PTSD. Drug therapies may be used to quell distress.

Taking Psychology Personally

■ **What to Do If You've Been Sexually Assaulted**

Chapter Integration

Social factors, such as the experience of trauma; psychological factors, such as personality and health-related behaviors; and biological factors, such as the physiological stress response, have reciprocal effects on each other that contribute to an individual's vulnerability to a stress-related disorder.

Extraordinary People

Norman Cousins: *Healing with Laughter*

In 1964, Norman Cousins, a successful writer at the *Saturday Review,* was diagnosed with ankylosing spondylitis, a painful collagen disease. After many medical tests and days in the hospital, doctors gave him a 1 in 500 chance of living.

Cousins refused to believe that he would succumb to the disease and set out to find a course of action that might reverse its progression. His 1979 book *Anatomy of an Illness* describes his use of comedy and movies to raise his levels of positive emotions and thereby affect the functioning of his adrenal and endocrine systems. Cousins eventually recovered from his illness and became known for his view that laughter cured his fatal disease.

Although many scientists criticized Cousins' conclusions about the role of laughter in his recovery, Cousins objected that these criticisms tended to oversimplify his theorizing about the role of positive emotions in recovery and the scientific evidence that positive emotions have healing powers. After returning to his career as a writer for several years, Cousins spent the last 12 years of his life at the UCLA Medical School, working with researchers to find scientific proof for his beliefs. It is clear that Cousins played a pivotal role in the movement toward more holistic approaches to patient care by physicians and hospitals. Following is an excerpt of an essay Cousins wrote, based on his experience:

> A good place to begin, I thought, was with amusing movies. Allen Funt, producer of the spoofing television program "Candid Camera," sent films of some of his "CC" classics, along with a motion-picture projector. The nurse was instructed in its use.
>
> It worked. I made the joyous discovery that ten minutes of genuine belly laughter had an anesthetic effect and would give me at least two hours of pain-free sleep. When the painkilling effect of the laughter wore off, we would switch on the motion-picture projector again, and not infrequently, it would lead to another pain-free sleep interval. Sometimes the nurse read to me out of a trove of humor books.
>
> How scientific was it to believe that laughter—as well as the positive emotions in general—was affecting my body chemistry for the better? If laughter did in fact have a salutary effect on the body's chemistry, it seemed at least theoretically likely that it would enhance the system's ability to fight the inflammation. So we took sedimentation-rate readings just before as well as several hours after the laughter episodes. Each time, there was a drop of at least five points. The drop by itself was not substantial, but it held and was cumulative.
>
> I was greatly elated by the discovery that there is a physiological basis for the ancient theory that laughter is good medicine. . . . (Cousins, 1976, pp. 1458–63)

Many years have passed since Cousins' discovery that laughter was good medicine for him. Since then, there has been considerable new evidence that positive emotions speed physiological and psychological recovery from stress (Fredrickson & Joiner, 2002; Fredrickson et al., 2003). These findings evoke the ancient mind-body question: Does the mind affect the body, or does the body affect the mind?

In this chapter, we will review research on how stress affects us psychologically and physiologically. We will examine the psychological and social factors that make it harder or easier to cope with stress, as well as interventions to help people who have been exposed to considerable stress. Finally, we will consider two diagnosable psychological disorders, acute stress disorder and posttraumatic stress disorder (PTSD), as well as possible treatments.

First, what is stress? In general terms, experiencing **stress** means experiencing events that we perceive as endangering our physical or psychological well-being. These events are usually referred to as *stressors,* and people's reactions to them are labeled *stress responses* (Schneiderman, Ironson, & Siegel, 2005).

What makes some events especially stressful? Uncontrollable negative events, such as the loss of a job, the sudden death of a loved one, or the loss of one's home to a natural disaster, are perceived by most people as stressful. Indeed, any negative event is perceived as more stressful if it is *uncontrollable.* For example, in a classic experimental study, participants were shown vivid photographs of victims of violent deaths. One group of participants, the experimental group, could terminate their viewing by pressing a button. The other group, the control group, could not terminate their viewing by pressing a button. Both groups of participants saw the same photographs for the same duration of time. The level of anxiety in both groups was measured by their *galvanic skin response (GSR),* a drop in the electrical resistance of the skin, which is an index of physiological arousal. The experimental group showed much less anxiety while viewing the photographs than did the control group, even though the only difference between the groups was their control over their viewing (Geer & Maisel, 1972).

Similarly, a person who has a traffic accident because he or she is not wearing glasses while driving may experience the accident as less stressful than if he or she had not perceived a reason for the accident. An accident that happens because a person has forgotten to wear glasses can presumably be prevented from happening again by wearing glasses. An accident that appears to have no explanation cannot be prevented from happening again.

Unpredictability also makes some events especially stressful. Experimental studies have confirmed that unpredictable events are more stressful than predictable events. These studies show that both rats and human participants prefer mild but painful electric shocks or loud bursts of noise that are preceded by a warning tone (and therefore are predictable) to electric shocks or noise that is preceded by no warning tone (Abbott, Schoen, & Badia, 1984; Glass & Singer, 1972; Katz & Wykes, 1985).

Having sufficient warning of upcoming aversive events may allow people to prepare themselves in ways that reduce the impact of those events. Predictable aversive events may also be less stressful because people know they can relax until they get the warning that the events are about to occur. With unpredictable events, people feel they can never relax, because the events may occur at any time, so they remain anxious all the time. This explanation has been called the *safety signal hypothesis* (Seligman & Binik, 1977).

For example, perhaps a woman's boss occasionally flies into a rage, criticizing her in front of others. If these outbursts are completely unpredictable, then the employee is always on guard and may chronically feel stressed. If, however, she knows these outbursts happen only around the end of each fiscal quarter, when her boss is upset because he has to prepare a fiscal account for the firm, then she can relax to some extent during the remainder of the fiscal year.

Finally, any *change* in life that requires numerous readjustments—even a positive change—can be perceived as stressful. A positive change can challenge our self-concept or the limits of our capabilities (Holmes & Rahe, 1967). For example, most people think of marriage as a positive event, but it requires many readjustments in daily life and self-concept as two people go from living as single individuals to living as lifetime partners.

Nevertheless, negative events are more likely than positive events to be perceived as stressful and to have impacts on physical and psychological health (e.g., Sarason, Johnson, & Siegel, 1978). This may be because of the different consequences of positive and negative events. Although some positive events require people to make adjustments and to change their self-concepts, these changes tend to be for the better. The person affected usually gains

Unpredictable and uncontrollable negative events are often perceived as stressful.

something from the events and from the new roles that he or she takes. In contrast, negative events often involve loss and can threaten a person's self-esteem or sense of mastery of the world (Monroe & Hadjiyannakis, 2002).

PHYSIOLOGICAL RESPONSES TO STRESS

How do we respond to stress? When we face any type of stressor—a saber-toothed tiger, a burglar with a weapon, a first bungee jump—the body mobilizes to handle the stressor. The liver releases extra sugar (glucose) to fuel our muscles, and hormones are released to stimulate the conversion of fats and proteins to sugar. The body's metabolism increases in preparation for expending energy on physical action. Heart rate, blood pressure, and breathing rate increase and the muscles tense. At the same time, less essential activities, such as digestion, are curtailed. Saliva and mucus dry up, increasing the size of the air passages to the lungs.

FIGURE 6.1   **The Fight-or-Flight Response.** The body's fight-or-flight response is initiated by the part of the brain known as the hypothalamus. The hypothalamus stimulates the sympathetic division of the autonomic nervous system, which acts on smooth muscles and internal organs to produce the bodily changes shown in the figure. The hypothalamus also releases corticotropin-release factor (CRF), which triggers the pituitary gland to release adrenocorticotropic hormone (ACTH). In turn, ACTH then stimulates the adrenal glands to release about 30 other hormones. These hormones act on organs and muscles to prepare the body to fight or flee.

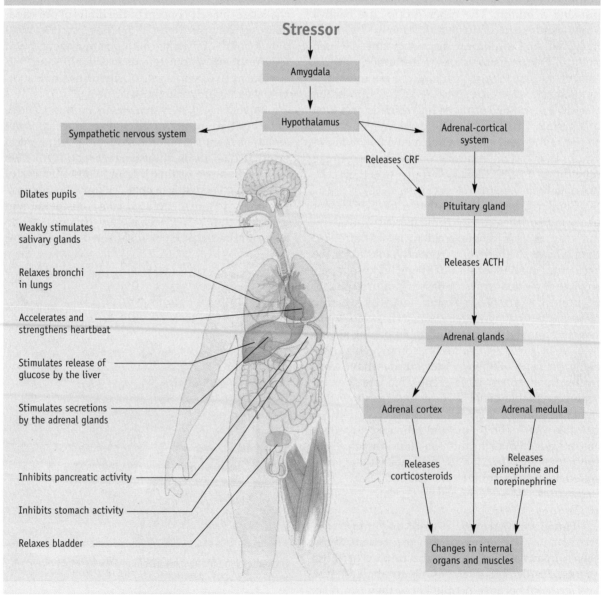

The body's natural painkillers, endorphins, are secreted, and the surface blood vessels constrict to reduce bleeding in case of injury. The spleen releases more red blood cells to help carry oxygen.

Most of these physiological changes result from the activation of two systems controlled by the hypothalamus, as shown in Figure 6.1: the *autonomic nervous system* (in particular, the sympathetic division of this system) and the *adrenal-cortical system* (a hormone-releasing system). These physiological responses have developed through evolution to prepare the body to fight a threat or to flee from it—to attack a saber-toothed tiger or to run away from it—and have been labeled **fight-or-flight response.** The hypothalamus first activates the sympathetic division of the autonomic nervous system. The sympathetic system acts directly on the smooth muscles and internal organs to produce some of the bodily changes—for example, increased heart rate and elevated blood pressure. The sympathetic system also stimulates the release of a number of hormones, including epinephrine (adrenaline) and norepinephrine, which perpetuate a state of physiological arousal.

The hypothalamus activates the adrenal-cortical system by releasing corticotrophin-release factor (CRF), which signals the pituitary gland to secrete adrenocorticotrophic hormone (ACTH), the body's major stress hormone. ACTH stimulates the outer layer of the adrenal glands (the adrenal cortex), resulting in the release of a group of hormones, the major one being **cortisol.** The amount of cortisol in blood or urine samples is often used as a measure of stress. ACTH also signals the adrenal glands to release about 30 other hormones, each of which plays a role in the body's adjustment to emergency situations. Eventually, the hormones signal the hippocampus, a part of the brain that helps regulate emotions, to turn off this physiological cascade when the threatening stimulus has passed. The fight-or-flight system thus has its own feedback loop, which normally regulates the level of physiological arousal experienced in response to a stressor.

This response is very adaptive when the stressor or threat is immediate and fight or flight is possible and useful. However, when a stressor is chronic and a person or an animal cannot fight it or flee from it, the chronic physiological arousal that results can be severely damaging to the body (Schneiderman et al., 2005).

In groundbreaking work that continues to be influential today, researcher Hans Selye (1979) described such physiological changes as part of the **general adaptation syndrome** that all organisms show in response to stress. The general adaptation syndrome consists of three phases (see Figure 6.2).

In the first phase, *alarm,* the body mobilizes to confront a threat by triggering sympathetic nervous system activity. In the second phase, *resistance,* the organism makes efforts to cope with the threat, by fighting it or fleeing from it. The third phase, *exhaustion,* occurs if the organism is unable to fight or flee from the threat and depletes physiological resources while trying to do so.

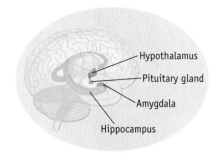

These structures of the brain are involved in activating or turning off the fight-or-flight response.

Selye argued that a wide variety of physical and psychological stressors trigger this response pattern. He also argued that the repeated or prolonged exhaustion of physiological resources, due to exposure to prolonged stressors that one cannot fight or flee from, is responsible for a wide array of physiological diseases. He conducted laboratory studies in which he exposed animals to several types of prolonged stressors—such as extreme cold and fatigue—and found that, regardless of the stress, certain bodily changes inevitably occurred: enlarged adrenal glands, shrunken lymph nodes, and stomach ulcers (Selye, 1979). Although some of Selye's specific hypotheses have not been supported in subsequent work, his general assertion that stress is an important determinant of the degree of physiological damage in several diseases has been supported (Schneiderman et al., 2005).

Taylor, Iacono, and McGue (2000) have suggested that, due to evolutionary pressures, there are gender differences in responses to stressful circumstances. Instead of engaging in fight or flight when faced with a threat, females engage in a

FIGURE 6.2 — **The General Adaptation Syndrome.** According to Hans Selye, the body reacts in three phases to a stressor. In the first phase, alarm, the body mobilizes to confront the threat, which temporarily expends resources and lowers resistance. In the resistance phase, the body is actively confronting the threat and resistance is high. If the threat continues, the body moves into exhaustion.

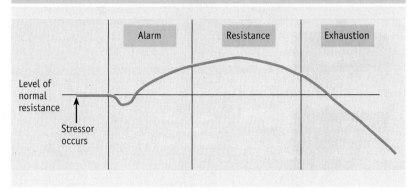

When confronted with an extremely stressful situation, some women focus on caring for others.

pattern they term "tend and befriend." Females are not as physically capable of fighting off many aggressors as men, and across evolutionary history they have had more responsibility than men for their offspring. As a result, rather than attempting to fight or flee from an aggressor, females join social groups to reduce their vulnerability and to gain resources, and they focus on caring for their offspring. This gender difference does not mean that stress has less impact on the physical health of women; in some cases, it may have more. It does suggest that the ways in which stress affects health in women may be different from those in men.

Health Psychology

Selye's work inspired the development of an entire field of psychology, known as **health psychology,** which investigates the effects of stress and other psychological factors on physical illness. This field has grown considerably over the past 30 years or so. Health psychologists are concerned with the roles of personality factors, coping styles, stressful events, and health-related behaviors, such as maintaining good sleep and diet habits, in the development and progress of physical disease. They also study whether changing a person's psychology—for example, by teaching stress-reduction techniques or inducing positive emotions—can influence the course of a physical disease and whether diseases can be prevented by helping people adopt healthy lifestyles and attitudes about the world.

Three models of the ways in which psychological factors affect physical disease drive most of the work in health psychology. The *direct effects model* suggests that psychological factors, such as stressful experiences or certain personality characteristics, directly cause changes in the physiology of the body, which in turn cause or exacerbate disease (see Figure 6.3a).

The *interactive model* suggests that psychological factors must interact with a preexisting biological vulnerability to a disease in order for an individual to develop the disease. According to this model, prolonged stress contributes to disease only in people who already have a biological vulnerability to the disease or perhaps have already developed mild forms of the disease (see Figure 6.3b).

The *indirect effects model* suggests that psychological factors affect disease largely by influencing whether people engage in health-promoting behaviors (see Figure 6.3c). Our diets, the amount of exercise we get, and whether we smoke can all influence our vulnerability to certain diseases, such as heart disease or lung cancer, and can influence the progression of many diseases once we have developed

FIGURE 6.3 **Three Models for the Effects of Psychological Factors on Disease.** These three models posit quite different pathways by which psychological factors, such as stress or personality style, might affect physical disease.

a. The direct effects model

Psychological factors (stress, personality styles) → Physiological changes → Disease

b. The interactive model

Psychological factors X Vulnerability to disease → Physiological changes → Disease

c. The indirect effects model

Psychological factors → Health-related behaviors (smoking, sleep) → Disease

them. People under stress or with certain personality characteristics may be less prone to engage in healthy behaviors and more prone to engage in unhealthy behaviors. According to this model, psychological factors do not directly affect health but, rather, affect health indirectly by influencing health-related behaviors. Similarly, Norman Cousins' use of laughter to reduce his symptoms is an example of how health-promoting behaviors may help reduce physical disease.

Now let's examine some of the research into stress and disorders that modern health psychology has been particularly concerned with, such as coronary heart disease, hypertension, colds, and cancer.

Stress, Coronary Heart Disease, and Hypertension

Coronary heart disease occurs when blood vessels supplying the heart are blocked by plaque; complete blockage causes a myocardial infarction—a heart attack.

CASE STUDY

Orrin was so mad he could scream. He had been told at 3:00 that afternoon to prepare a report on the financial status of his division of the company in time for a meeting of the board of directors the next morning. On the way home from work, someone rear-ended him at a stoplight and caused several hundred dollars in damage to his new car. When he got home from work, there was a message from his wife, saying she had been delayed at work and would not be home in time to cook dinner for the children, so Orrin would have to do it. Then, at dinner, Orrin's 12-year-old son revealed that he had flunked his math exam that afternoon.

After finishing the dishes, Orrin went to his study to work on the report. The kids had the TV on so loud he couldn't concentrate. Orrin yelled to the kids to turn off the TV, but they couldn't hear him. Furious, he stalked into the family room and began yelling at the children about the television and anything else that came to his mind.

Then, suddenly, Orrin began to feel a tremendous pressure on his chest, as if a truck were driving across it. Pain shot through his chest and down his left arm. Orrin felt dizzy and terrified. He collapsed onto the floor. His 7-year-old began screaming. Luckily, his 12-year-old called 911 for an ambulance.

Orrin was having a *myocardial infarction*—a heart attack. A myocardial infarction is one endpoint of **coronary heart disease,** or **CHD.** CHD occurs when the blood vessels that supply the heart muscles are narrowed or closed by the gradual buildup of a hard, fatty substance called *plaque*, blocking the flow of oxygen and nutrients to the heart. This can lead to pain, called *angina pectoris*, which radiates across the chest and arm. When the oxygen to the heart is completely blocked, it can cause a myocardial infarction.

Coronary heart disease is the leading cause of death and chronic illness in the United States today, accounting for 20 percent of all deaths, most before the age of 65 (American Heart Association, 2002). CHD is also a chronic disease, and more than 12 million Americans live daily with its symptoms. Men are more prone to CHD than are women, but CHD is still the leading cause of death of women. African Americans and Hispanic Americans have higher rates of CHD than European Americans. People with family histories of CHD are more susceptible to CHD. CHD has been linked to high serum cholesterol, diabetes, smoking, and obesity.

People who live in chronically stressful environments over which they have little control appear to be at increased risk for CHD. For example, one study followed about 900 middle-aged men and women for over 10 years, tracking the emergence of coronary heart disease (Karasek, Russell, & Theorell, 1982). These people worked in a variety of jobs, and the researchers categorized these jobs in terms of how demanding they were and how much control they allowed a worker. Over the 10 years of this study, workers in jobs that were highly demanding but low in control had a risk for coronary heart disease that was one and one-half times greater than that of those in other occupations.

Hypertension, or high blood pressure, is a condition in which the supply of blood through the vessels is excessive, putting pressure on the vessel walls. Chronic high blood pressure can cause hardening of the arterial walls and deterioration of the cell tissue, leading eventually to coronary heart disease, kidney failure, and stroke. Approximately 50 million people in the United States have hypertension, and about 16,000 die each year due to hypertensive disease. Genetics appears to play a role in the predisposition to hypertension, but only about 10 percent of all cases of hypertension can be traced to genetics or to specific organic causes, such as kidney dysfunction. The other 90 percent of cases are known as *essential hypertension*, meaning the causes are unknown.

Because part of the body's response to stress—the fight-or-flight response—is to increase blood pressure, it is not surprising that people who live in chronically stressful circumstances are more likely to develop hypertension (Schneiderman et al., 2005). As an example, persons who move from quiet rural settings to crowded, noisy urban settings show increases in rates of hypertension.

One group that lives in chronically stressful settings and has particularly high rates of hypertension is low-income African Americans (American Heart Association, 2002). Many do not have adequate financial resources for daily living, are poorly educated and have trouble finding good employment, live in neighborhoods racked with violence, and are frequently exposed to racism. All these conditions have been linked to higher blood pressure. In addition, African Americans may be genetically prone to a particular pattern of cardiovascular response to stress that contributes to the development of hypertension (Anderson et al., 1989; Light & Sherwood, 1989).

Persons with hypertension and the children of parents with hypertension tend to show a stronger blood pressure response to a wide variety of stressors. In experimental situations, solving arithmetic problems and immersing their hands in ice water, people with no personal or family histories of hypertension showed much less response than those with a history of hypertension (Harrell, 1980). In addition, it takes longer for the blood pressure of persons with hypertension to return to normal following stressors than it does the blood pressure of those without hypertension.

This information suggests that people with hypertension and people with family/genetic histories of hypertension may have a heightened physiological reactivity to stress. If they are exposed to chronic stress, their chronically elevated blood pressure can lead to hardening and narrowing of the arteries, which creates a physiologically based hypertension (Harrell, 1980). Low-income African Americans may have both this physiological predisposition to heightened reactivity to stress *and* chronic exposure to stressful environments, making them doubly vulnerable to hypertension.

Stress and the Immune System

The **immune system** protects the body from disease-causing microorganisms. This system affects our susceptibility to infections, diseases, allergies, cancer, and autoimmune disorders, such as rheumatoid arthritis, in which the immune cells attack normal tissues of the body. Many components of the immune system fight disease. One of the fastest-growing areas of health psychology is *psychoneuroimmunology*, the study of the effects of psychological factors on the functioning of the immune system. Stress can affect the immune system in several ways. In particular, some of the biochemicals released as part of the fight-or-flight response, such as the corticosteroids, may suppress the immune system.

The most controlled research linking stress and immune system functioning has been conducted with animals. They are experimentally exposed to stressors and then the functioning of their immune system is measured directly. Studies have shown that **lymphocytes,** the cells of the immune system that attack viruses, are suppressed in animals that have been exposed to loud noise, electric shock, separation from their mothers as infants, separation from peers, and a variety of other stressors (Segerstrom & Miller, 2004).

Animals are most likely to show impairment of their immune system if exposed to stressors that are uncontrollable. In one experiment, one group of rats was subjected to electric shock that they could turn off by pressing a lever (Laudenslager et al., 1983). Another group received an identical sequence of shocks but could not control the shocks by pressing the lever. A third group received no shock. The investigators examined how well the rats' *T-cells,* lymphocytes that secrete chemicals that kill harmful

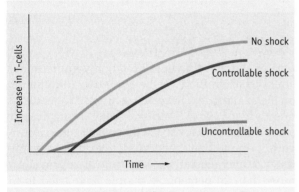

FIGURE 6.4 **The Effects of Controllable and Uncontrollable Shock on Rats' Immune Systems.** In one study, rats given uncontrollable shocks showed less increase in T-cells, which kill harmful cells, than did rats given controllable shocks or no shock.

Source: Laudenslager et al., 1983.

Studies suggest that immune-related diseases, such as colds, are more common among those who are under stress.

cells, multiplied when challenged by invaders. They found that the T-cells in the rats that could control the shock multiplied, as did those in the rats that were not shocked at all (see Figure 6.4). The T-cells in the rats exposed to uncontrollable shock multiplied only weakly, however. In another study following the same experimental design, investigators implanted tumor cells into rats, gave them controllable or uncontrollable shocks, and examined whether the rats' natural defenses rejected the tumors. Only 27 percent of the rats given uncontrollable shock rejected the tumors, whereas 63 percent of the rats given controllable shock rejected the tumors (Visintainer, Volpicelli, & Seligman, 1982).

Uncontrollable stress also is related to impaired immune system functioning in humans (Schneiderman et al., 2005). In one study, investigators exposed about 400 healthy volunteers either to a nasal wash containing one of five cold viruses or to an innocuous salt solution (Cohen, Tyrrell, & Smith, 1991). Each participant was assigned a stress score ranging from 3 (lowest stress) to 12 (highest stress), based on the number of stressful events they had experienced in the past year, the degree to which they felt able to cope with daily demands, and their frequency of negative emotions, such as anger and depression. The participants were examined daily for cold symptoms and for the presence of cold viruses or virus-specific antibodies in their upper respiratory secretions. About 35 percent of the volunteers who reported the highest stress in their lives developed colds, compared with about 18 percent of those with the lowest stress scores.

Most other studies of humans simply have compared the functioning of the immune system in persons undergoing particular stressors with that of persons not undergoing these stressors (see Cohen, 1996). For example, a study of people who survived Hurricane Andrew in 1992 found that those who had experienced more damage to their homes or whose lives had been more threatened by the storm showed poorer immune system functioning than people whose homes and lives had been safer (Ironson et al., 1997). Similarly, following the 1994 Northridge earthquake in the Los Angeles area, people whose lives had been more severely disrupted showed more decline in immune system functioning than those who had not experienced as much stress as a result of the earthquake (Solomon et al., 1997). People who worried more about the impact of the earthquake on their lives were especially likely to show detriments in *natural killer cells,* a type of T-cell that seeks out and destroys cells that have been infected with a virus (Segerstrom et al., 1998).

More common events have also been linked to deficits in immune system functioning. For example, students often complain that they become ill during exam times. Studies have verified the idea that college students and medical students are more prone to infectious illness during exam periods than at other times of the academic year (Glaser et al., 1986).

Negative interpersonal events seem particularly likely to affect immune system functioning. Married couples who have more conflictual interactions with each other show poorer immunological functioning than married couples with fewer conflictual interactions (Kiecolt-Glaser & Newton, 2001). Men and women who have recently been separated or divorced show poorer immune functioning than matched control subjects who are still married (Robles & Kiecolt-Glaser, 2003). However, the partner who has more control over the divorce or separation—that is, the partner who initiated the divorce or separation—shows better immune system functioning and better health than does the partner who has less control over the divorce or separation. This is one example of how perceptions of the controllability of a stressor can influence the impact of that stressor on health.

Several studies have examined whether stress can contribute to the development or progression of cancer in humans (see Segerstrom & Miller, 2004). The results of these studies have been mixed, some showing that people who are more stressed are more vulnerable to developing cancer or have faster progressions of their cancer than people who are less stressed. Again, it may be that people's perceptions or appraisals of stressors, not the presence of the stressors alone, determine the impact of the stressors on immune system functioning. For example, one study of women with breast cancer found that those who felt they had little control over their cancer and over other aspects of their lives were more likely to develop new tumors over a five-year period were women who felt more in control, even though the two groups of women did not differ in the type or initial seriousness of their cancers (Levy & Heiden, 1991; Watson et al., 1999). Similarly, although studies have not shown conclusively that stress contributes to the progression of acquired immune deficiency syndrome (AIDS), perceptions of control may be related to the progression of this disease (Baum & Posluszny, 2001).

SUMMING UP

- The body has a natural response to stress that prepares it for fight or flight. In the short term, this response is highly adaptive but, if it is chronically aroused, it can cause physical damage.

- There is substantial evidence that stress, particularly uncontrollable stress, increases the risks for coronary heart disease and hypertension, probably through chronic hyperarousal of the body's fight-or-flight response.

- There is mounting evidence from animal and human studies that stress impairs the functioning of the immune system, possibly leading to higher rates of infectious diseases.

SLEEP AND HEALTH

One of the first things to go when you are under stress is sleep. In 1993, the National Commission on Sleep Disorders Research estimated that at least one-third of all U.S. adults suffer from chronic sleep disturbances, especially chronic sleep deprivation due to busy schedules. Over the past century, the average night's sleep time has declined by more than 20 percent, as people have tried to fit more and more into the 24-hour day.

The costs to society of sleep disorders and sleepiness include lost lives, lost income, disabilities, accidents, and family dysfunction (Drake, Roehrs, & Roth, 2003; Léger, et al., 2002; McConnell, Bretz, & Dwyer, 2003). For example, each year in the United States, there are 200,000 sleep-related automobile accidents, and 5,000 of these are fatal. Twenty percent of automobile drivers admit to having fallen asleep at the wheel at least once. Some of the most serious disasters in modern history have been caused by mistakes made by sleepy people (Mitler & Miller, 1995). In 1979, the worst nuclear plant accident in the United States resulted from fatigued workers at Three Mile Island failing to respond to a mechanical problem at the plant. In 1986, the world's worst nuclear disaster happened in Chernobyl in the former Soviet Union while a test was being conducted by an exhausted team of engineers.

Young adults will sleep, on average, 9.2 hours per day when they have no environmental influences to interfere with sleep patterns, yet most young adults sleep 7.5 or fewer hours per day (Wolfson & Carskadon, 1998). Similarly, most middle-aged adults seem to need at least 7 or 8 hours of sleep per day but, on average, get less than 7 hours. People who work rotating shifts or in jobs demanding long periods of activity, such as nurses, doctors, firefighters, police, and rescue personnel, are often chronically sleep deprived. Even when they have time to sleep, they have trouble doing so, because their bodies' natural rhythms that promote sleep are disrupted by their irregular schedules. The effects of sleep deprivation are cumulative: A person builds up an increasing sleep debt for every 24-hour period in which he or she does not get adequate sleep.

Sleep Deprivation

Lack of sleep can impair health. In addition to the increased risk for accidents due to sleepiness, lack of sleep also appears to impair the immune system (Cruess et al., 2003). People who sleep fewer than six hours per night have a 70 percent higher mortality rate than do those sleeping at least seven or eight hours per night (Kryger, Roth, & Dement, 1994). This is true for both men and women, for people of many ethnicities, and for people with many different health backgrounds. People who work rotating shifts have higher rates of illness, including cardiovascular and gastrointestinal disease, than do people who do not work such shifts. Traumatic events can also cause loss of sleep, and the sleep deprivation then can affect the immune system. One study of people who survived Hurricane Andrew found that those with the most sleep problems also had the greatest decreases in immune system functioning (Ironson et al., 1997).

Sleep deprivation also has a number of psychological effects. Cognitive impairments caused by sleep deprivation include impairments in memory, learning, logical reasoning, arithmetic skills, complex verbal processing, and decision making. For example, reducing the amount of sleep to five hours per night for just two nights significantly reduces performance on math problems and creative thinking tasks. Thus, staying up to study for exams for just a couple of nights can significantly impair your ability to do as well as possible on those exams. A study of more than 3,000 high school students found that those who were getting Cs, Ds, and Fs in school were getting significantly less sleep than those getting As and Bs (Wolfson, 2002). Sleep deprivation also causes irritability, emotional ups and downs, and perceptual distortions, such as mild hallucinations.

How can people reduce sleepiness and the effects of sleep deprivation? First of all, they can get enough sleep. Although the social lives of college students often begin at 10 P.M. or later, it is important to keep in mind that the sleep lost on the weekend can affect performance and health for the rest of the week. Students who have families and/or jobs are especially prone to skipping sleep in order to get everything done. Good time-management skills can help people find more time in their days to accomplish all their tasks without having to give up much sleep. Avoiding alcohol, nicotine, and caffeine in the evening can also help people fall asleep and sleep well.

In addition to its direct positive effects on health, adequate sleep helps us feel more in control of the stressful events that befall us during the day. When we are alert and rested, challenging events may not seem so overwhelming, because we can marshal our best coping responses. Indeed, when we are rested, we may be better able to prevent stressful events from happening, because we are alert enough to anticipate them and to take action before they occur. Thus, sleep has both direct and indirect effects on our health by enhancing our ability to prevent or cope with stressful events.

Sleep Disorders

Some people experience so much difficulty in sleeping that they may be diagnosed with a sleep disorder. The DSM-IV-TR recognizes four general types of sleep disorders. *Sleep disorders related to another mental disorder* are sleep disturbances that are directly attributable to psychological disorders, such as depression or anxiety. *Sleep disorders due to a general medical condition* are sleep disturbances that result from the physiological effects of a medical condition. Many medical conditions can disturb sleep, including degenerative neurological illnesses (such as Parkinson's disease), cerebrovascular disease (such as vascular lesions to the upper brain stem), endocrine conditions (such as hypo- or hyperthyroidism), viral and bacterial infections (such as viral encephalitis), pulmonary diseases (such as chronic bronchitis), and pain from musculoskeletal diseases (such as rheumatoid arthritis or fibromyalgia). Norman Cousins mentioned that pain kept him awake many nights and that his laughter treatments helped him get a few hours of pain-free sleep.

Substance-induced sleep disorders are sleep disturbances due to the use of substances, including

Busy students are often sleep deprived.

TABLE 6.1	Concept Overview

Dyssomnias

These are the primary sleep disorders known as dyssomnias. Each condition must not be due to a general medical condition or substance use and must cause significant impairment in functioning to be diagnosed.

Type	Definition
Primary insomnia	Difficulty initiating or maintaining sleep, or nonrestorative sleep, for at least a month
Primary hypersomnia	Excessive sleepiness for at least one month, as evidenced by either prolonged sleep episodes or daytime sleep episodes that occur almost daily
Narcolepsy	Irresistible attacks of refreshing sleep that occur daily over at least three months plus either sudden loss of muscle tone or recurrent intrusions of elements of rapid eye movement (REM) sleep
Breathing-related sleep disorder	Sleep disruption leading to excessive sleepiness or insomnia that is due to a sleep-related breathing condition, such as apnea
Circadian rhythm sleep disorder	Sleep disruption leading to excessive sleepiness or insomnia that is due to a mismatch between the sleep-wake schedule required by a person's environment and his or her circadian sleep-wake pattern

Source: Reprinted with permission from the *Diagnostic and Statistical Manual of Mental Disorders*, Fourth Edition, Text Revision. Copyright © 2000. American Psychiatric Association.

prescription medications (such as medications that control hypertension or cardiac arrhythmias) and nonprescription substances (such as alcohol and caffeine).

The fourth category of sleep disorders is *primary sleep disorders*. These are further subdivided into **dyssomnias** (see the Concept Overview in Table 6.1), which involve abnormalities in the amount, quality, or timing of sleep, and **parasomnias** (see the Concept Overview in Table 6.2), which involve abnormal behavioral and physiological events occurring during sleep.

Insomnia

Probably the most familiar dyssomnia is **insomnia,** difficulty in initiating or maintaining sleep or sleep that chronically does not restore energy and alertness. People with insomnia usually report a combination of difficulty falling asleep and intermittent wakefulness during the night. A vicious cycle often develops in people with insomnia. The longer they lie in bed, unable to go to sleep, the more distressed and aroused they become. This arousal makes it even more difficult for them to fall asleep. Their arousal then becomes conditioned to their environment—to their bed and bedroom—so that their arousal levels go up when they try to go to bed the

next night. In addition, they may consciously worry about having trouble falling asleep, which adds more to their arousal level. Many people with insomnia report that they sleep better when they are in unfamiliar settings, such as hotel rooms. In contrast, people without insomnia report they sleep worse in unfamiliar settings (Hauri & Fisher, 1986).

Occasional problems with insomnia are extremely common, with as many as 50 percent of adults reporting they have had insomnia sometime in their lives and one in three adults complaining they have had insomnia in the past year (Nowell et al., 1998). Complaints of insomnia increase with age but decrease with socioeconomic status.

To be diagnosed with primary insomnia, people must have the symptoms of insomnia for at least one month, and the sleep disturbance must cause significant distress or impairment in their functioning. In addition, the insomnia must not be due to another mental disorder, to a medical condition, or to substance use. It is unclear how prevalent diagnosable insomnia is in the general population, but in one long-term study of young adults, 9 percent reported chronic insomnia (Angst et al., 1989).

Various medications are used to treat insomnia, including antidepressants, antihistamines, tryptophan, delta-sleep-inducing peptide (DSIP), mela-

TABLE 6.2   Concept Overview

Parasomnias

These are the primary sleep disorders known as parasomnias. Each condition must not be due to a general medical condition or substance use and must cause significant impairment in functioning to be diagnosed.

Type	Definition
Nightmare disorder	Repeated awakenings with detailed recall of extended and extremely frightening dreams, usually involving threats to survival, security, or self-esteem; on awakening, the person is alert and oriented.
Sleep terror disorder	Repeated, abrupt awakenings beginning with a panicky scream; intense fear and signs of autonomic arousal; relative unresponsiveness to the efforts of others to comfort the person; no detailed dream is recalled and there is amnesia for the episode.
Sleepwalking disorder	Repeated episodes of rising from the bed during sleep and walking about; while sleepwalking, the person has a blank, staring face, is relatively unresponsive to others, and can be awakened only with great difficulty; on awakening, the person has amnesia for the episode; within several minutes after awakening, there is no impairment of mental activity or behavior, although there may initially be a short period of confusion and disorientation.

Source: Reprinted with permission from the *Diagnostic and Statistical Manual of Mental Disorders,* Fourth Edition, Text Revision. Copyright © 2000. American Psychiatric Association.

tonin, and benzodiazepines (Dündar et al., 2004). All of these have proven effective in at least some studies, although the number of studies done on most of these agents is small. The agents that have proven most reliably effective are the benzoidiazepines and zolpidem (trade name Ambien). Those that have the least clear benefit are antihistamines and tryptophan (Lee, 2004; Nowell et al., 1998).

Several studies have shown that cognitive-behavioral interventions for insomnia can be highly effective (e.g., Bastien et al., 2004). These interventions have a number of components. **Stimulus-control therapy** involves a set of instructions designed to curtail behaviors that might interfere with sleep and to regulate sleep-wake schedules (Bootzin & Perlis, 1992):

1. Go to bed only when sleepy.

2. Use the bed and bedroom only for sleep and sex, not for reading, television watching, eating, or working.

3. Get out of bed and go to another room if you are unable to sleep for 15 to 20 minutes, and do not return to bed until you are sleepy.

4. Get out of bed at the same time each morning.

5. Don't nap during the day.

Sleep restriction therapy involves initially restricting the amount of time insomniacs can try to sleep in the night (Smith, 2001). Once their sleep becomes more efficient, the amount of time they are allowed to spend in bed is gradually increased, until they reach the greatest total amount of sleep possible while maintaining efficient sleep. In addition, people are often taught relaxation exercises (see the *Taking Psychology Personally* feature in Chapter 7) and are educated about the effect of diet, exercise, and substance use on sleep. Cognitive-behavioral interventions may be used to help counteract people's maladaptive cognitions about sleep, such as "There's no way I can go to sleep quickly." Although these behavioral and cognitive interventions typically take longer than the drug therapies to begin working with insomniacs, they tend to have more long-lasting effects (Nowell et al., 1998).

Other Sleep Disorders

Primary **hypersomnia** is the opposite of insomnia. People with hypersomnia are chronically sleepy and sleep for long periods at a time. They may sleep 12 hours at a stretch and still wake up sleepy. A nap during the day may last for an hour or more, and people may wake up unrefreshed. If their environment is not stimulating (for example, they are sitting in a boring lecture), they are sure to fall asleep.

They may even fall asleep at the wheel while driving. To qualify for a diagnosis, the hypersomnia must be present for at least a month and must cause significant distress or impairment in functioning. Again, the prevalence of hypersomnia in the general population is not known, but about 5 to 16 percent of people who go to sleep disorders clinics are diagnosed with primary hypersomnia (APA, 2000).

Narcolepsy involves irresistible attacks of sleep. People must experience these attacks for at least three months to be diagnosed. These sleep attacks are most likely to come during low-stimulation, low-activity situations but may also occur while the person is carrying on a conversation or driving a car. Sleep episodes generally last 10 to 20 minutes but can last up to an hour, and people may dream during the episodes. They wake up from these sleep attacks refreshed but then become sleepy again after several hours and may have chronic sleepiness. Narcolepsy most often starts in adolescence and is quite rare, affecting less than .05 percent of the general population.

If untreated, people with narcolepsy typically have two to six episodes of sleep per day. In addition to sleepiness, people diagnosed with narcolepsy must experience (1) cataplexy or (2) recurrent intrusions of elements of rapid eye movement (REM) sleep into the transition between sleep and wakefulness. **Cataplexy** consists of episodes of sudden loss of muscle tone, lasting from a few seconds to minutes. It occurs in about 70 percent of people with narcolepsy. They may suddenly drop objects, buckle at the knees, or even fall to the ground. Cataplexy is usually triggered by a strong emotion, such as anger or surprise. The intrusions of REM sleep often involve the experience of intense, dreamlike imagery just before falling asleep or just after awakening. Sometimes, these hallucinations are accompanied by a sense of paralysis, so people report seeing or hearing unusual things but being unable to move.

The most common *breathing-related sleep disorder* is obstructive **sleep apnea,** which involves repeated episodes of upper-airway obstruction during sleep. People with sleep apnea typically snore loudly, go silent and do not breathe for several seconds at a time, then gasp for air. Apnea occurs in up to 10 percent of the population and can begin anytime throughout the life span. It is most common, however, in overweight, middle-aged men and prepubertal children with enlarged tonsils.

Other primary sleep disorders include circadian rhythm sleep disorder, nightmare disorder, sleep terror disorder, and sleepwalking disorder (review Tables 6.1 and 6.2). Occasional problems with the symptoms of these disorders are very common, but only a small percentage of the population ever develops one of these sleep disorders. For example, most children have occasional nightmares but do not develop a disorder.

SUMMING UP

- The sleep disorders are divided into sleep disorders related to another mental disorder, sleep disorders due to a general medical condition, substance-induced sleep disorders, and primary sleep disorders.

- The primary sleep disorders are further divided into dyssomnias and parasomnias.

- The most common dyssomnia is insomnia. Hypersomnia, narcolepsy, and breathing-related sleep disorders, such as sleep apnea, are also dyssomnias.

- Sleep disorders, particularly insomnia, can be treated with a variety of drugs or through behavioral and cognitive-behavioral therapies that change sleep-related behavior and thinking patterns.

PERSONALITY AND HEALTH

In recent years, psychologists have explored certain personality characteristics and coping strategies that seem to be associated with an increased risk for a variety of diseases. Individuals with these characteristics or strategies appraise a wider range of events as stressful or do not readily engage in behaviors that reduce the stressfulness of events. Thus, these people are more chronically stressed, and their bodies are more chronically in the fight-or-flight response.

Pessimism

Being pessimistic appears to be bad for your health. In one study of 412 patients with human immunodeficiency virus (HIV), those who were pessimistic at a baseline assessment had a greater load of the virus 18 months later than those who were less pessimistic (Milam et al., 2004). Similarly, a study of gay men who were HIV-positive found that those who blamed themselves for negative events and those with more negative expectations showed more decline in immune functioning and greater development of HIV symptoms over time than those who were more optimistic (Reed et al., 1999; Segerstrom et al., 1996).

Pessimists' vulnerability to illness seems to be lifelong. In a long-term study of men in the Harvard classes of 1939 and 1940, those who were pessimistic in college were more likely to develop physical illness over the subsequent 35 years than were the men who were more optimistic (Peterson, Seligman, & Vaillant, 1988; see also Peterson et al., 1998). Other studies have found that pessimists recover more slowly from coronary bypass surgery and have more severe angina than optimists (Fitzgerald et al., 1993; Scheier et al., 1989). Also, pessimistic cancer patients are more likely than optimistic patients to die during the first few years after their diagnosis (Schulz et al., 1996).

How does pessimism affect health? People who are pessimistic tend to feel they have less control over their lives than people who are more optimistic and, therefore, may appraise more events as stressful. Thus, pessimism may contribute to poor health by causing chronic arousal of the body's fight-or-flight response, resulting in physiological damage (see Figure 6.5).

Several studies have found evidence for this explanation. In one, the blood pressure of pessimists and optimists was monitored daily for three days. The pessimists had chronically higher blood pressure levels than the optimists across the three days (Raikkonen et al., 1999). Another study found that older adults who were pessimistic showed poorer immune system functioning on two biological indices than those were optimistic, even after the researchers statistically controlled for differences between the pessimists and optimists on current health, depression, medication, sleep, and alcohol use (Kamen-Siegel et al., 1991).

A pessimistic outlook may also impair health by leading people to engage in unhealthy behaviors. In the previously mentioned work with people who were HIV-positive, researchers found that those who were more pessimistic were less likely to be engaging in healthy behaviors, such as maintaining proper diets, getting enough sleep, and exercising (Milam et al., 2004; Taylor et al., 1992). These behaviors are particularly important for HIV-positive people, because these healthy behaviors can reduce the risk of developing AIDS.

In short, a pessimistic outlook may affect health directly by causing hyperarousal of the body's physiological response to stress or indirectly by reducing positive coping strategies and, more specifically, reducing healthy behaviors. In contrast, an optimistic outlook, such as Norman Cousins attempted to create in himself through laughter, may promote physical health by reducing physiological stress responses and promoting positive coping strategies.

The Type A Behavior Pattern

Like the word *stress*, the term **Type A behavior pattern** is often used loosely to describe friends, colleagues, and family members. Let's try to pin down the definition of this important personality style. The Type A pattern was initially identified by two physicians, Meyer Friedman and Ray Rosenman, who noticed that the chairs in the waiting room of their offices seemed to wear out very quickly (Friedman & Rosenman, 1974). Specifically, the edges of the seats became threadbare, as if their patients were sitting on the edges, anxiously waiting to spring up. These patients were most frequently cardiology patients who had histories of coronary artery disease. Friedman and Rosenman eventually described a personality pattern seen in many of their cardiology patients, which was given the label Type A behavior pattern.

The three components of the Type A pattern, according to these physicians, are a sense of time urgency, easily aroused hostility, and competitive achievement strivings. People who are Type A are always in a hurry, setting unnecessary deadlines for themselves and trying to do multiple things at once. They are competitive, even in situations in

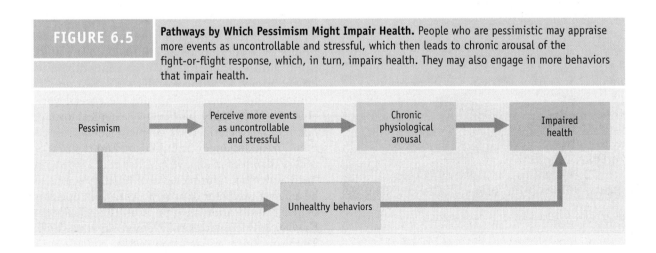

FIGURE 6.5 **Pathways by Which Pessimism Might Impair Health.** People who are pessimistic may appraise more events as uncontrollable and stressful, which then leads to chronic arousal of the fight-or-flight response, which, in turn, impairs health. They may also engage in more behaviors that impair health.

which it is ridiculous to be competitive. For example, they rush to be the first in line at a restaurant or at the movies, even when the wait would be only two or three minutes if they were last in line. They are also chronically hostile and fly into a rage with little provocation. Persons who are not Type A are referred to as *Type B*. They are able to relax without feeling guilty, are able to work without feeling pressured or becoming impatient, and are not easily aroused to hostility.

Although we tend to think of Type A people as angry and aggressive, always fighting to get their way and to accomplish a great deal, there is evidence that they are often anxious and depressed and that these negative emotions may contribute to their risk for disease (Kiecolt-Glaser et al., 2002). Type As may be anxious and depressed because they tend to be dissatisfied with their careers; they tend to spend little time with their families and, thus, jeopardize their home lives; and their social lives in general are not as satisfying as they might be. Regardless of the source of their negative emotions, it appears that these emotions are risk factors for both coronary heart disease and death as the result of a variety of other diseases (Kiecolt-Glaser et al., 2002).

Type A Personality and Coronary Heart Disease

One of the most compelling studies to demonstrate the relationship between Type A behavior and coronary heart disease followed more than

Hostility is the component of Type A behavior that is most strongly linked to heart disease.

3,000 healthy, middle-aged men for 8½ years (Rosenman et al., 1976). At the beginning of the study, the men were evaluated for the Type A pattern by means of an interview that was designed to be irritating. The interviewer kept the participants waiting without explanation and then asked a series of questions about being competitive, hostile, and pressed for time: Do you ever feel rushed or under pressure? Do you eat quickly? Would you describe yourself as ambitious and hard driving or relaxed and easygoing? Do you resent it if someone is late?

The interviewer interrupted participants, asked questions in a challenging manner, and threw in non sequiturs. A participant's level of Type A behavior was determined more on the way he behaved in answering the questions and responding to the interviewer's rudeness than on his answers to the questions themselves. For example, a man was labeled as extremely Type A if he spoke loudly in an explosive manner, talked over the interviewer so as not to be interrupted, appeared tense and tight-lipped, and described hostile incidents with great emotional intensity. The Type B men tended to sit in a relaxed manner, spoke slowly and softly, were easily interrupted, and smiled often.

Over the 8½ years of the study, the Type A men had twice as many heart attacks or other forms of coronary heart disease than did the Type B men. These results held up even after diet, age, smoking, and other variables associated with coronary heart disease were taken into account. Other studies have confirmed this twofold risk and have linked Type A behavior to heart disease in both men and women (Haynes, Feinlieb, & Kannel, 1980; Schneiderman et al., 2001). In addition, Type A behavior correlates with severity of coronary artery blockage as determined at autopsy or in X-ray studies (Friedman et al., 1968; Williams et al., 1988). Based on such evidence, in 1981 the American Heart Association classified Type A behavior as a risk factor for coronary heart disease.

More recent research suggests that the definition of Type A behavior, as originally formulated, is too diffuse. Time urgency and competitiveness do not appear to be the variables that best predict coronary heart disease. Instead, the crucial variable may be hostility, particularly a cynical form of hostility characterized by suspiciousness, resentment, frequent anger, antagonism, and distrust of others (Barefoot et al., 1989; Miller et al., 1996). Indeed, a person's chronic level of hostility seems to be a better predictor of heart disease than does his or her classification as Type A or Type B (Booth-Kewley & Friedman, 1987; Dembroski et al., 1985; Thoresen, Telch, & Eagleston, 1981).

For example, a 25-year study of 118 male lawyers found that those who scored high on hostility traits on a personality inventory taken in law school were five times more likely to die before the age of 50 than were classmates who were not hostile (Barefoot et al., 1989). Similarly, in a study of physicians, hostility scores obtained in medical school predicted the incidence of coronary heart disease as well as mortality from all causes (Barefoot, Dahlstrom, & Williams, 1983). In both studies, the relationship between hostility and illness was independent of the effects of smoking, age, and high blood pressure.

How does Type A behavior—or, more specifically, hostility and related negative emotions—lead to coronary heart disease? Again, overarousal of the sympathetic nervous system may play a role (see Figure 6.6). Hostile people show greater physiological arousal in the anticipation of stressors and in the early stages of dealing with stressors (Benotsch, Christensen, & McKelvey, 1997; Lepore, 1995): Their heart rates and blood pressures are higher and they have greater secretion of the stress-related biochemicals known as *catecholamines*. They also return more slowly to baseline levels of sympathetic nervous system activity following stressors than do nonhostile people. This hyperreactivity may cause wear and tear on the coronary arteries, leading to coronary heart disease. Alternately, the excessive secretion of catecholamines in response to stress in hostile people may exert a direct chemical effect on blood vessels. The frequent rise and fall of catecholamine levels may cause frequent changes in blood pressure, which reduce the resilience of the blood vessels. Finally, hostile people may also engage in behaviors that increase their propensity for heart disease, including smoking, heavy drinking, and high-cholesterol diets (Schneiderman et al., 2001).

Gender Differences

Some research has suggested that men are more likely than women to have the Type A personality pattern and to be chronically hostile (Barefoot et al., 1987; Haynes et al., 1980). Men also are more likely than women to carry three other risk factors for CHD: smoking, hypertension, and elevated cholesterol. In turn, among young and middle-aged people, far more men than women die of cardiovascular disease (Stoney, 2003).

Newer research, however, suggests that women may carry as much anger and hostility as men—they just don't express it as readily (Kring, 2000; Lavoie et al., 2001; Nolen-Hoeksema & Rusting, 2002). In addition, excessive hostility and anger—whether expressed or suppressed—are associated with risk factors for coronary heart disease in both women and men (Matthews et al., 1995). Depression and anxiety are also risk factors for coronary heart disease, and women are more likely than men to suffer these negative emotions (see Chapters 7 and 9).

Coronary heart disease is the number one killer of women, as well as men, and the rates of CHD in women go up dramatically after menopause (Stoney, 2003). Women are less likely than men to recognize the signs of a heart attack, possibly in part because the signs in women are different from those in men. They are also less likely than men to seek help for heart attack symptoms and, even after

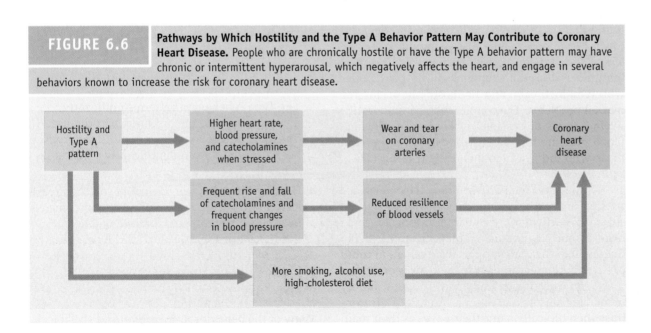

FIGURE 6.6   **Pathways by Which Hostility and the Type A Behavior Pattern May Contribute to Coronary Heart Disease.** People who are chronically hostile or have the Type A behavior pattern may have chronic or intermittent hyperarousal, which negatively affects the heart, and engage in several behaviors known to increase the risk for coronary heart disease.

they seek help, they are less likely to be given aggressive treatment. After a heart attack, women are more likely than men to die, to have chronic impairment, to have a lower quality of life, and to drop out of rehabilitative therapy. The sources of these gender differences are currently unknown, but cardiac disease in women is a fast-growing area of research.

Social Support

So far, we have discussed psychosocial factors that may contribute to poorer health. What about factors that contribute to better health? One such factor that appears to promote adjustment to stressors is social support. A wide variety of studies have found that people who seek and receive positive emotional support from others show more positive health outcomes, both on micro-level measures, such as natural killer cell activity, and on macrolevel outcomes, such as the progression of major diseases (Pennebaker, 1990). For example, studies of women with breast cancer found that those who actively sought social support from others had higher natural killer cell activity (Levy et al., 1990; Turner-Cobb et al., 2000). Similarly, Dixon and colleagues (2001) found that HIV-positive men who experienced declines in social support and increases in loneliness showed biological signs of poorer control over the virus.

One of the main sources of social support is a partner or spouse. Married people have less physical illness and are less likely to die from a variety of conditions, including cancer, heart disease, and surgery, compared with nonmarried people (see Kiecolt-Glaser & Newton, 2001). When a marriage is conflictual, however, it can be a major detriment to health. Experimental studies of married couples found that those who became hostile and negative toward each other while discussing marital problems showed more decrements in four indicators of immune system functioning than did the couples who remained calm and nonhostile in discussing marital problems. The couples who became hostile during these discussions also showed elevated blood pressure for longer periods of time than did those who did not become hostile (Kiecolt-Glaser et al., 1993).

Women and men differ in how they use social support and in the benefits they derive from social support, particularly from the support derived from a marital partner. Women are more likely than men to seek out support from others in times of stress and have larger social networks on whom they rely, including friends and extended family members (Kiecolt-Glaser & Newton, 2001). In contrast, men typically name their wives as their main source of support and the only person in whom

they confide. Marriage is greatly beneficial to men's health—unmarried men have a 250 percent higher mortality rate than married men, compared with a 50 percent difference in mortality rates between unmarried and married women (Ross, Mirowsky, & Goldsteen, 1990).

Why would women not benefit from marriage as much as men do? Women are more physiologically reactive to marital conflict than men (Kiecolt-Glaser & Newton, 2001). This may be because women's self-concepts, as well as their financial well-being, tend to be more closely tied to their marital partner than are men's (Cross & Madson, 1997). Women are more emotionally tuned to their partners and are more conscious of conflict in their relationships than are men. For these reasons, women may be more emotionally, cognitively, and physiologically sensitive to marital conflict, and this sensitivity may counteract any positive health effects they could derive from the support provided to them by their partners (Kiecolt-Glaser & Newton, 2001).

Psychologists can work with people facing stress and illness to help them identify their sources of positive social support and use these resources better. This might involve helping people organize their time, so that they have opportunities for quiet walks or evenings with a friend. Or a psychologist might help an individual whose relationships with important others are conflictual to deal more effectively with those relationships, so that they are a source of strength, rather than a burden.

SUMMING UP

- People who are chronically pessimistic may show poorer physical health because they appraise more events as uncontrollable or because they engage in poorer health-related behaviors.

- People with the Type A behavior pattern are highly competitive, time urgent, and hostile. The Type A behavior pattern significantly increases the risk for coronary heart disease. The most potent component of this pattern is hostility, which alone significantly predicts heart disease.

- People who receive high-quality social support have more positive physical health outcomes in stressful situations than those who have little social support or much social friction.

INTERVENTIONS TO IMPROVE HEALTH

Many of the behavioral, cognitive, and social techniques that are useful in the treatment of psychological disorders (see Chapter 5) can also improve physical health.

Guided Mastery Techniques

When told what they have to do to protect or improve their health, people often feel unable or unwilling to engage in these behaviors. **Guided mastery techniques** provide people with explicit information about how to engage in positive health-related behaviors and with opportunities to engage in these behaviors in increasingly challenging situations (Taylor, 1999). The goals are to increase people's skills at engaging in the behaviors and their beliefs that they can engage in the behaviors.

A guided mastery program for teaching women how to negotiate safe sexual practices in sexual encounters with men could begin with information on condom use. A counselor could then model how a woman can tell a man that she wants him to use a condom when they have sex. The women would watch the counselor and then practice insisting on condom use in role-plays with the counselor or other group participants. In these role-plays, the women would face increasingly difficult challenges to their insistence on condom use, receive feedback on effective means for meeting these challenges, and practice meeting these challenges. The women could also be taught techniques for determining when it is useless to argue with their partners any longer about condom use and skills for withdraw-ing from sexual encounters in which their partners want to practice unsafe sex.

Guided mastery techniques have been used successfully in AIDS prevention programs with African American female and male adolescents (Jemmott & Jemmott, 1992). In the programs with the young women, researchers gave participants information about the cause, transmission, and prevention of AIDS. The young women then participated in guided mastery exercises to increase their skills and self-confidence for negotiating condom use by their male partners. The young women were also given instruction on how to eroticize condom use—how to incorporate putting on condoms into foreplay and intercourse in ways that increase positive attitudes toward condoms. Compared with young women who received only information, not guided mastery exercises, these young women showed a greater sense of efficacy in negotiating condom use, more positive expectations for sexual enjoyment with condoms, and stronger intentions to use condoms. These effects were found in a similar program with sexually active African American female adolescents drawn from the inner city (Jemmott & Jemmott, 1992).

In a program with African American male adolescents, the young men were first given information about the cause, transmission, and prevention of AIDS. Then they participated in guided mastery exercises that taught them how to negotiate condom use with their partners and to eroticize

Programs to increase safe sexual behavior and promote the use of condoms may help prevent the spread of sexually transmitted diseases, especially if the programs are culturally sensitive.

condom use. Follow-up assessments showed that, compared with a control group, these adolescents were more knowledgeable about the risks for AIDS, were less accepting of risky practices, and engaged in lower-risk sexual behavior with fewer sexual partners (Jemmott et al., 1992).

Biofeedback

Biofeedback has been used to treat a wide variety of health problems—most frequently, migraine headaches, chronic pain, and hypertension. Biofeedback actually involves several techniques designed to help people change bodily processes by learning to identify signs that the processes are going awry and then learning ways of controlling the processes. For example, a person with hypertension might be hooked up to a machine that converts his heartbeats to tones. He sits quietly, listening to his heart rate and trying various means to change it, such as breathing slowly or concentrating on a pleasant image. The goal in biofeedback is for people to detect early signs of dysfunction in their bodies, such as signs that their blood pressure is rising, and to use the techniques they learned while hooked up to machines to control their bodies even when they are independent of the machines. Several controlled studies have found that biofeedback training can significantly reduce blood pressure among people with hypertension (Glasgow, Engel, & D'Lugoff, 1989; Glasgow, Gaader, & Engel, 1982; Nakao et al., 1997).

Biofeedback also seems to be successful in reducing tension-related headaches (Gannon et al., 1987). Headache sufferers learn to detect when they are tensing the muscles in their heads. They then use techniques for reducing this tension, thus relieving their headaches.

Biofeedback is used for migraine sufferers to increase the blood flow to the body's periphery, thereby decreasing the blood flow to the head and reducing pressure on the arteries. Migraine patients are hooked up to machines that give them temperature readings from their head and fingers. They are taught to relax fully and to notice the effects of relaxation on their temperatures. Then they may be encouraged to increase the temperature of their fingers, using the machine's feedback as an aid. It is not clear just how patients do this—it is a matter of using trial and error to find a way of changing their temperatures. Eventually, patients attempt to use these techniques to control headaches at home. When they feel headaches coming on, they concentrate on warming their fingers to divert blood flow from the arteries in their head to the periphery (see Turk, Meichenbaum, & Berman, 1979).

Although biofeedback can be successful in treating hypertension and pain conditions, such as headaches, it is not clear that it works the way its proponents believe it works. For example, although biofeedback can reduce migraine headaches, the evidence that it does so by temperature control is mixed. In addition, biofeedback appears to be no more successful than simple relaxation techniques in reducing headaches, pain, and hypertension (see Chapter 7 for a description of relaxation techniques). Indeed, biofeedback may work largely because individuals often learn relaxation techniques as a part of biofeedback training. Relaxation techniques have the advantage over biofeedback of being much less expensive and time-consuming to learn.

Sociocultural Interventions

Many people facing stressors, including physical illness, participate in support groups. A provocative study of breast cancer patients found evidence that support groups may not only help women cope emotionally with their cancer but also prolong their lives (Spiegel et al., 1989). Several years ago, researchers began a study in which they randomly assigned women with advanced breast cancer either to a series of weekly support groups or to no support groups. All the women received standard medical care for their cancer. The focus in the groups was on facing death and learning to live one's remaining days to the fullest. The researchers did not expect to alter the course of the cancer; they wanted only to improve the quality of life for the women with advanced cancer. They were quite surprised when, 48 months after the study began, all of the women who had not been

Biofeedback helps people learn to detect when bodily processes are going awry and to counteract these processes.

in the support groups were dead from their cancer but a third of the women in the support groups were still alive. From the time the study began, the average survival time for the women in the support groups was about 40 months, compared with about 19 months for the women who were not in the support groups. There were no differences between the groups other than their participation in the weekly support meetings that could explain the differences in the average survival times. It appears that the support groups actually increased the number of months that the women in the support groups lived. Some subsequent studies have found similar results (e.g., Fawzy et al., 1990; Richardson et al., 1990), whereas others have not (e.g., Goodwin et al., 2001).

If support groups can improve the physical health of cancer patients, how might this work? In the Spiegel et al. (1989) study, the women in the support groups had lower levels of emotional distress, and they learned how to control their physical pain better than the women who did not participate in the support groups. This lowering of distress may have improved the functioning of their immune systems. The ways in which the lowering of distress can affect immune functioning are not yet known, but one possibility is that reducing distress reduces levels of stress-related hormones, including the corticosteroids. Excessive levels of corticosteroids promote the growth of some cancers (Spiegel, 2001).

SUMMING UP

- Guided mastery techniques help people learn positive health-related behaviors by teaching them the most effective ways of engaging in these behaviors and by giving them an opportunity to practice the behaviors in increasingly challenging situations.

- Biofeedback is used to help people learn to control their own negative physiological responses.

- Support groups are one source of social support for some people. Some research suggests that they can improve both psychological and physical well-being.

POSTTRAUMATIC STRESS DISORDER, ACUTE STRESS DISORDER, AND ADJUSTMENT DISORDER

We've considered the effects of stressful experiences on physical health, but stress also takes a toll on emotional health. Three psychological disorders, **posttraumatic stress disorder (PTSD)**, **acute stress disorder**, and **adjustment disorder**, are by definition the consequences of more extreme stressors and are the focus of the remainder of this chapter.

Here one survivor of the terrorist attacks on the World Trade Center on September 11, 2001, describes many of the core symptoms of PTSD and acute stress disorder:

VOICES

I just can't let go of it. I was working at my desk on the 10th floor of the World Trade Center when the first plane hit. We heard it but couldn't imagine what it was. Pretty soon someone started yelling, "Get out—it's a bomb!" and we all ran for the stairs.

The dust and smoke were pouring down as we took step by step. It seemed to take an eternity to get down to the ground. When I got outside, I saw people running away but also people just standing, looking up, in pure horror. When I looked up and saw that the top of the tower was on fire, I just froze; I couldn't move. Then the second plane hit. Someone grabbed my arm and we started running. Concrete and glass began to fly everywhere. People were falling down, stumbling. Everyone was covered in dust. When I got far enough away, I just stood and stared as the towers fell. I couldn't believe what I was seeing. Other people were crying and screaming, but I just stared. I couldn't believe it.

Now, I don't sleep very well. I try, but just as I'm falling asleep, the images come flooding into my mind. I see the towers falling. I see people with cuts on their faces. I see the ones who didn't make it out, crushed and dead. I smell the dust and smoke. Sometimes, I cry to the point that my pillow is soaked. Sometimes, I just stare at the ceiling, as I stared at the towers as they fell. During the day, I go to work, but often it's as if my head is in another place. Someone will say something to me, and I won't hear them. I often feel as if I'm floating around, not touching or really seeing anything around me. But if I do hear a siren, which you do a lot in the city, I jump out of my skin.

Traumatic events such as the attacks on the World Trade Center can lead to posttraumatic stress.

Studies done immediately after the World Trade Center attacks found that about 20 percent of the people living very nearby had symptoms meeting the diagnosis of PTSD (Galea et al., 2002). Even people who were not present at the World Trade Center attack were traumatized by it. Nationwide studies showed that, just after September 11, 2001, 44 percent of adults reported symptoms of PTSD (Schuster et al., 2001). Two months later, in November 2001, 21 percent of adults nationwide still reported being "quite a bit" or "extremely" bothered by one of five distress symptoms (Stein et al., 2004). Those with persistent distress reported accomplishing less at work (65 percent); avoiding public gathering places (24 percent); and using alcohol or other drugs to quell worries about terrorism (38 percent).

A wide range of traumas can induce posttraumatic stress disorder or acute stress disorder, ranging from extraordinary events, such as a terrorist attack, to common events, such as a traffic accident. About 20 percent of women and 8 percent of men exposed to trauma will suffer from posttraumatic stress disorder at sometime in their lives (Kessler et al., 1995). The symptoms can be mild to moderate, and some people function adequately with these symptoms without seeking treatment. For other people, however, the symptoms can be immobilizing, causing deterioration in their work, family, and social lives (Putnam, 1996).

The diagnosis of PTSD requires that three types of symptoms be present (see Table 6.3). The first set of PTSD symptoms is repeated *reexperiencing of the traumatic event*. PTSD sufferers may experience intrusive images or thoughts, recurring nightmares, or flashbacks in which they relive the event. They react psychologically and physiologically to stimuli that remind them of the

event. One survivor of war atrocities in Bosnia in the 1990s said films of traumas constantly play in his head, and, although he tries to look away from them, they continue to intrude on his consciousness (Weine et al., 1995). The quoted World Trade Center survivor vividly remembers her traumatic event to the point of reliving it. Memories of the attack intrude into her consciousness against her will, particularly when she encounters something that reminds her of the event. She

TABLE 6.3   DSM-IV-TR

Symptoms of Posttraumatic Stress Disorder

Three categories of symptoms characterize PTSD.

Reexperiencing of the Traumatic Event

Distressing memories of the event

Distressing dreams about the event

Reliving of the event by acting or feeling as if the event were recurring

Intense psychological and physiological distress when exposed to situations reminiscent of the event

Emotional Numbing and Detachment

Avoidance of thoughts, feelings, or conversations about the event

Avoidance of activities, places, or people associated with the event

Trouble recalling important aspects of the event

Loss of interest in activities

Feelings of detachment from others

Inability to have loving feelings toward others and a general restriction of feelings

Sense that the future is bleak

Hypervigilance and Chronic Arousal

Difficulty falling or staying asleep

Irritability or outbursts of anger

Difficulty concentrating

Hypervigilance

Exaggerated startle response

Source: Reprinted with permission from the *Diagnostic and Statistical Manual of Mental Disorders*, Fourth Edition, Text Revision. Copyright © 2000. American Psychiatric Association.

also relives her emotional reaction to the event, and since the event she has chronically experienced negative emotions, which have not diminished with time.

The second set of symptoms in PTSD is *emotional numbing and detachment.* People become withdrawn, reporting that they feel numb and detached from others. Especially just after the trauma, they may also feel detached from themselves and their ongoing experiences, with a general sense of unreality, as does the quoted World Trade Center survivor.

The third set of symptoms involves *hypervigilance* and *chronic arousal.* PTSD sufferers are always on guard for the traumatic event to recur. Sounds or images that remind them of their trauma can instantly create panic and flight. A war veteran, on hearing a car backfire, may jump into a ditch and begin to have flashbacks of the war, reexperiencing the terror he felt on the front lines. PTSD sufferers may report "survivor guilt," painful guilt feelings over the fact that they survived the traumatic event or about things that they had to do to survive. Many Holocaust survivors report guilt for having survived when their families did not or for not having fought more strongly against the Nazis (Krystal, 1968).

Children can experience PTSD in much the same way that adults can, but they may have their own ways of manifesting it (Fremont, 2004; LaGreca et al., 1996; Pfefferbaum et al., 2000; Ruggiero, Morris, & Scotti, 2001). Children's memories and fears of a traumatic event may generalize to fears of a wide range of stimuli (Baker & Shalhoub-Kevorkian, 1999). One 12-year-old girl who had been kidnapped, along with several of her friends, spoke of her feelings several months later (Terr, 1981, p. 18):

VOICES I don't like to turn off the lights. I'm afraid someone would come in and shoot and rob us. When I wake up I turn on the light. . . . I've been in Bakersfield helping my brother. . . . At night in Bakersfield it feels like someone broke in. Nothing is there. I hear footsteps again. I keep going to check. . . . I check where the sound is coming from. . . . I'm very frightened of the kitchen because no one's there at all. I completely avoid it. At home I kept feeling someone was looking in and watching me. I kept the light on. I was afraid they'd come in and kill us all or take us away again.

Acute stress disorder occurs in response to traumas, as does PTSD, and it has symptoms simi-

lar to those of PTSD (see Table 6.4). The main difference is that acute stress disorder occurs within one month of exposure to the stressor and is short-lived, not lasting more than four weeks. Also, in acute stress disorder, **dissociative symptoms**—symptoms that indicate a detachment from the trauma and from ongoing events—are especially prominent. People may become emotionally unresponsive, finding it impossible to experience pleasure. They may have difficulty concentrating, feel detached from their bodies, experience the world as unreal or dreamlike, and have increasing difficulty recalling the details of the trauma. In addition, as in PTSD, the sufferer of acute stress disorder persistently reexperiences the trauma through flashbacks, nightmares, and intrusive thoughts; avoids reminders of the trauma; and is constantly aroused.

TABLE 6.4 DSM-IV-TR

Symptoms of Acute Stress Disorder

Acute stress disorder has symptoms similar to those of PTSD but occurs within one month of a stressor and is less than four weeks in duration.

A. While experiencing or after experiencing a traumatic event, the individual has three or more of the following dissociative symptoms:

1. sense of numbing, detachment, or emotional unresponsiveness

2. reduced awareness of one's surroundings ("being in a daze")

3. sense that things are not real

4. sense that one's body and mind are not connected

5. inability to recall an important aspect of the trauma

B. Reexperiencing the traumatic event through recurrent images, thoughts, dreams, illusions, flashbacks, or sense of reliving the experience; distress when exposed to reminders of the trauma

C. Avoidance of stimuli that arouse recollections of the trauma

D. Symptoms of anxiety or increased arousal (such as difficulty sleeping, irritability, poor concentration, hypervigilance, exaggerated startle response, motor restlessness)

Source: Reprinted with permission from the *Diagnostic and Statistical Manual of Mental Disorders,* Fourth Edition, Text Revision. Copyright © 2000. American Psychiatric Association.

Although acute stress disorder is defined as a short-term response to trauma, it appears that people who experience acute stress disorder are at high risk of continuing to experience posttraumatic stress symptoms for many months following the trauma (Classen et al., 1998).

Another stress-related diagnosis is adjustment disorder, which consists of emotional and behavioral symptoms (depressive symptoms, anxiety symptoms, and/or antisocial behaviors) that arise within three months of the onset of a stressor. Adjustment disorder differs from PTSD and acute stress disorder in that the stressors that lead to adjustment disorder can be of any severity, whereas the stressors that lead to PTSD and acute stress disorder are extreme. In addition, PTSD and acute stress disorder have some specific symptoms that do not occur in adjustment disorder, including re-experiencing of the traumatic event. Adjustment disorder is a residual category in DSM-IV-TR, used for people who are experiencing emotional and behavioral symptoms following a stressor but who do not meet the criteria for a diagnosis of PTSD, acute stress disorder, or another anxiety or mood disorder (which are described in Chapters 7 and 9) that is the result of the stressful experience.

The Role of Trauma in PTSD

A wide variety of traumatic events can induce posttraumatic stress disorder. We will focus on four types of events: natural disasters, abuse, combat- and war-related traumas, and common traumatic events, such as the loss of a loved one in a car accident. These are the traumatic events that have been researched most thoroughly.

Natural Disasters

Natural disasters, such as floods, tsunami, earthquakes, fires, hurricanes, and tornadoes, can trigger a wave of PTSD among the survivors. A study of Florida children who lived through Hurricane Andrew in 1992 found that nearly 20 percent were still suffering from PTSD a year after the disaster (LaGreca et al., 1996). Another study of children in South Carolina who survived Hurricane Hugo in 1993 found that, three years after the hurricane, one-third still experienced a sense of detachment and avoided thoughts or feelings associated with the hurricane, one-quarter were irritable and angry, and one-fifth experienced physiological arousal (Garrison et al., 1995).

Other studies have focused on survivors of major earthquakes. For example, a study of survivors of an earthquake in Turkey found that

Survivors of natural disasters, such as the tsunami in Asia in 2004 or Hurricane Katrina in 2005, often experience posttraumatic stress disorder.

23 percent of those who were at the epicenter had PTSD 14 months later, and 16 percent had PTSD plus depression (Basoglu et al., 2004). Similar rates of PTSD were found in survivors of a large earthquake in Taiwan (Lai et al., 2004).

Rescue workers are at high risk for PTSD and acute stress disorder. Another study of the Taiwan earthquake found that 20 percent of professional rescuers and 32 percent of nonprofessional rescuers had significant symptoms of PTSD one month following the disaster (Guo et al., 2004).

Culture and gender appear to interact in interesting ways to influence vulnerability to PTSD. One study compared random community samples of survivors of Hurricane Andrew, which hit Florida in 1992, with survivors of Hurricane Paulina, which hit Acapulco, Mexico, in 1997 (Norris et al., 2001). These two hurricanes were similar in many ways, rated as Category 4 hurricanes and causing widespread property damage, physical injury, and death. Rates of PTSD symptoms were high in both countries. Women had more symptoms than men in both countries (see Figure 6.7), yet the difference in PTSD symptoms between Mexican women and men was much greater than the difference between American women and men. In addition, within the American sample, the difference in PTSD symptoms between non-Hispanic White women and men was significantly greater than the difference between African American women and men.

The researchers suggest that the relative strength of traditional sex roles across these three cultures (Mexican, non-Hispanic White, and African American) influenced the magnitude of sex differences in PTSD symptoms. There is more social pressure in Mexican culture than in American culture for women to be passive, self-sacrificing, and compliant and for men to be dominant, fearless, and strong (Vazquez-Nuttall, Romero-Garcia, & DeLeon, 1987). This may lead Mexican women to feel more helpless following a trauma and to be less able to get the material support they need, compared with Mexican men. Within American culture, there is some evidence that sex roles are more egalitarian among African Americans than among non-Hispanic Whites (Davenport & Yurich, 1991). Thus, African American women did not suffer much more PTSD than African American men. It is noteworthy that African Americans in the Norris et al. (2001) study generally had higher rates of PTSD than non-Hispanic Whites, perhaps because they had fewer financial and material resources to cope with the disaster. Many of the victims of Hurricane Katrina in 2005 were poor African Americans, and future studies may reveal high rates of PTSD in this group.

Abuse

There are many kinds of abuse—physical abuse (such as in battering relationships), sexual abuse (as in rape and incest), and emotional abuse (as when parents continually ridicule their children). Each of these forms of abuse can contribute to long-term PTSD. Studies of rape survivors have found that about 95 percent experience posttraumatic stress symptoms severe enough to qualify for a diagnosis of the disorder in the first two weeks following the rape (see Figure 6.8 on page 196). About 50 percent still qualify for the diagnosis three months after the rape. As many as 25 percent still suffer from PTSD four to five years after the rape (Faravelli et al., 2004; Foa & Riggs, 1995; Resnick et al., 1993; Rothbaum et al., 1992).

In the United States alone, more than 200,000 cases of verified child sexual abuse and more than 380,000 cases of physical abuse are reported each year. Studies of children who have been sexually and/or physically assaulted show that they remain at increased risk for PTSD, as well as other anxiety disorders, depression, substance abuse, and sexual dysfunction, well into adulthood (Cicchetti & Toth, 2005; Kessler et al., 1997; Saunders et al., 1992). Indeed, over 60 percent of childhood rape survivors develop PTSD at sometime in their lives (Saunders et al., 1992).

The risk of long-term PTSD can be reduced when a child or an adult receives compassionate support from family members and friends and

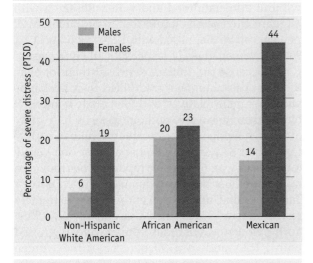

FIGURE 6.7   **Cultural and Sex Differences in PTSD.** Sex differences in rates of PTSD were greatest among Mexicans, followed by non-Hispanic White Americans, then least among African Americans in a study of reactions to a hurricane.

Source: Norris et al., 2001.

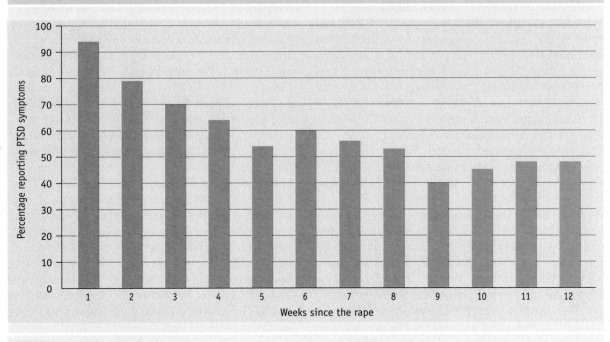

FIGURE 6.8   **Posttraumatic Symptoms in Rape.** Almost all women show symptoms of posttraumatic stress disorder severe enough to be diagnosed with it in the first or second week following a rape. Over the three months following a rape, the percentage of women continuing to show PTSD declines. However, almost 50 percent of women continue to be diagnosed with PTSD three months after a rape.

Source: Adapted from Foa & Riggs, 1995.

professional mental-health care as needed. PTSD and other psychological problems are more likely when abused people try to hide or deny their abuse. *Taking Psychology Personally: What to Do If You Have Been Sexually Assaulted* describes what people who have been sexually abused can do to get the help they need.

Combat- and War-Related Traumas

Much of what is known about PTSD comes from studies of men and women who fought in wars and were taken as prisoners of war. There are well-documented cases of "combat fatigue syndrome," "war zone stress," and "shell shock" among soldiers and former prisoners of the two world wars and the Korean War. Follow-up studies of some of these people show chronic posttraumatic stress symptoms for decades after the war (Elder & Clipp, 1989; Sutker, Allain, & Winstead, 1993; Sutker et al., 1991). PTSD came into the national limelight after the Vietnam War, when it was revealed that large numbers of Vietnam veterans suffered PTSD shortly after the war, and as many as half a million still suffered PTSD 15 years after their service had ended (Schlenger et al., 1992).

Recent and ongoing wars and conflicts have left thousands of sufferers of PTSD in their wake. A study of U.S. army soldiers and Marines deployed to Iraq found that approximately 13 percent could be diagnosed with PTSD (Hoge et al., 2004).

The citizens of countries besieged by war are at even higher risk for PTSD. The Afghan people have endured decades of war and occupation, the repressive regime of the Taliban, and then the bombing of their country by the United States after the attacks on the World Trade Center and the Pentagon. Thousands of Afghanis have been killed, injured, or displaced from their homes. Thousands still live in make-shift tents on a barren landscape without adequate food and water. Research with Afghani citizens has found that approximately 20 percent can be diagnosed with PTSD (Scholte et al., 2004). Women may be especially likely to suffer PTSD because the Taliban deprived them of even the most basic human rights, killed their husbands and other male relatives, and then made it impossible for them to survive without these men. A study of women living in Kabul under the Taliban regime found that 84 percent had lost at least one family member in war, 69 percent reported that they or a family member had been detained and abused by Taliban militia, and 68 percent reported extremely restricted social activities (Rasekh et al., 1998). Forty-two percent of these women were diagnosed with PTSD, and over 90 percent of the women reported some symptoms of PTSD (see also Scholte et al., 2004).

Taking Psychology Personally

What to Do If You've Been Sexually Assaulted

You probably don't want to think about how you would cope with being sexually assaulted. One study estimated that, across the globe, one woman in three has been beaten, coerced into sex, or otherwise abused in her lifetime (Heise, Ellsberg, & Gottemuller, 1999). Large studies in the United States suggest that about 13 to 15 percent of women are the victims of completed rape at sometime in their lives, and over half of these women experience their first sexual assault during childhood and adolescence (Kilpatrick, Edmunds, & Seymour, 1992; Kilpatrick & Saunders, 1996).

Sexual assault can be defined as unwanted sexual contact obtained without consent or obtained through the use of force, threat of force, intimidation, or coercion. It includes unwanted sexual contact that occurs after the administration of intoxicants to lower the victim's resistance. Following are some tips from the Sexual Assault Prevention and Awareness Center of the University of Michigan on what to do if you have been sexually assaulted.

- *Believe in yourself.* Don't blame yourself; take care of yourself.

- *Tell someone you can trust.* Sexual assaults can be terrifying and traumatic. It is an enormous burden to bear alone. Think about whom you might trust to tell—maybe

a friend, relative, or faculty member. You may also be able to call a 24-hour sexual assault crisis line in your community—it should be listed in your phone book.

- *Have a medical examination.* Even if you don't think you have been physically hurt, you may want to be checked for internal injuries; sexually transmitted diseases; and, if you are a woman, pregnancy as soon as possible. Also, a medical exam within 72 hours is the best time for collecting physical evidence of the rape. Even if you are not sure about pressing charges, it can be reassuring to have the evidence in case you decide to do so.

- *Report it to the police.* Choosing whether or not to report the assault is your right. Whether to press charges is a decision you do not have to make immediately, but making a criminal report sooner may help if the case is prosecuted. Your local sexual assault counseling center may be able to help you make a third-party report. If you are making an immediate criminal report, do not clean yourself up or touch anything in the area where the assault took place.

- *Seek additional supportive counseling.* Regardless of whether you get a medical exam or report the assault, you may need help to deal with the consequences of the assault. Recovering from a sexual assault may take time and professional counseling.

People from Southeast Asia (Vietnamese, Cambodians, Laotians, and Hmong) have undergone decades of civil war, invasions by other countries, and death at the hands of despots. In the few years that Pol Pot and the Khmer Rouge ruled Cambodia (1975–1979), perhaps one-third of Cambodia's 7 million people died. Many others were tortured, starved, and permanently separated from their families. Hundreds of thousands of Southeast Asians fled to Thailand, Europe, the United States, and Canada. Unfortunately, many of these refugees faced further trauma, being imprisoned in refugee camps for years, often separated from their families (Kinzie, 2001). Studies of refugees who have relocated to the United States suggest that as many as half suffer PTSD, and these symptoms may persist for years if untreated (Kinzie, 2001).

The wars in the former Yugoslavia in the 1990s were marked by "ethnic cleansing"—the torture and slaughter of thousands and displacement of millions of former Yugoslavians. This campaign

was one of the most brutal in history, with many atrocities, concentration camps, organized mass rapes, and neighbors murdering neighbors. A survey of a random sample of 1,358 Kosovar Albanians done in 1998–1999 found that one-quarter had experienced the murder of a family member or friend, two-thirds had been in a combat situation during the war, and over 80 percent had been displaced from their homes during the war (Cardozo et al., 2000). Seventeen percent of these people had symptoms that met the criteria for posttraumatic stress disorder in 1999, and a follow-up survey in 2000 found that 25 percent reported PTSD symptoms (Cardozo, et al., 2003).

People who have been forced to flee their country, never to return, may be even more likely to suffer PTSD: A study of Bosnian refugees just after they had resettled in the United States found that 65 percent suffered from posttraumatic stress disorder (Weine et al., 1995). The following woman's story is far too common.

The people of Afghanistan have lived in desperate conditions for many years and many suffer PTSD.

CASE STUDY

A woman in her 40s worked the family farm in a rural village until the day the siege began, when mortar shells turned most of their house to rubble. A few months before, she and her husband had sent their son away to be with relatives in Slovenia. The morning after the shelling, the Chetniks—Serbian nationalist forces—came and ordered everyone to leave their houses at once. Many neighbors and friends were shot dead before the woman's eyes. She and her husband were forced to sign over the title to their house, car, and bank deposits—and watched as the looting began. Looters included neighbors who were their friends. Over the next few days they traveled back from the Muslim ghetto to their land to feed the animals. One day, as she and her husband stood in the garden, the Chetniks cap-

tured them. Her husband was taken away with other men. For the next 6 months she did not know if he was dead or alive. She spent days on transport trains with no food or water, where many suffocated to death beside her. On forced marches she had to step over the dead bodies of friends and relatives. Once her group was forced across a bridge that was lined with Chetnik machine gunners randomly shooting to kill and ordering them to throw all valuables over the edge into nets. She spent weeks in severely deprived conditions in a big tent with many women and children, where constant sobbing could be heard. When she herself could not stop crying she thought that something had broken in her head and that she had gone "crazy." Now she says, "I will never be happy again." When alone, everything comes back to her. But when she is with others or busy doing chores, she can forget. "My soul hurts inside, but I'm able to pull it together." She is able to sleep without nightmares only by using a nightly ritual: "I lie down and go through every step of the house in Bosnia—the stable, everything they took, the rugs, the horses, the doors. I see it all again." (Weine et al., 1995, p. 540)

A follow-up of the Bosnian refugees one year later found that 44 percent still suffered from PTSD, with the older refugees more vulnerable to PTSD than the younger refugees (Weine et al., 1998). Many refugees from Bosnia and other war-torn countries were tortured before they escaped their homeland, and the experience of torture significantly increases the chance that an individual will develop PTSD (Basoglu et al., 1997; Shrestha et al., 1998). Torture survivors who have been political activists appear less prone to develop PTSD than those who have not been political activists (Basoglu et al., 1997). Political activists appear more psychologically prepared for torture than nonactivists, because they expect at sometime to be tortured, often have previous experience with torture, and have a belief system whereby torture is viewed merely as an instrument of repression.

Common Traumatic Events
PTSD can occur following more common events: being in an automobile accident or another serious accident; experiencing the sudden, unexpected death of a loved one; learning that one's child has a

life-threatening disease; or observing someone else being severely injured or killed. Studies of people who attended an emergency room shortly after a motor vehicle accident found that half of them reported intrusive reexperiencing of the accident, hyperarousal, or distress (Ehlers, Mayou, & Bryant, 1998; Mayou, Bryant, & Ehlers, 2001). Over 20 percent suffered symptoms severe enough to meet the diagnostic criteria for PTSD 3 months after the accident, and 17 percent were diagnosed with PTSD 1 year after the accident. Another study found that adults who had lost children or spouses in fatal car accidents were still experiencing high levels of anxiety and depression 4 to 7 years after their losses, and those who had lost children were more likely than people in a control group to have divorced (Lehman, Wortman, & Williams, 1987). As these studies illustrate, PTSD symptoms can last a long time after a trauma. About half the people experiencing a trauma appear to recover from PTSD within 3 months of the trauma, but many others continue to experience symptoms for at least 12 months or much longer (APA, 2000).

Explanations of PTSD Vulnerability

The cause of PTSD seems obvious: trauma. It seems perfectly understandable for PTSD to develop in assault or torture victims, people who have lost a loved one in a car accident, people who have lost their homes in a hurricane, and so on. But just what is it about traumatic events that can cause long-term, severe psychological impairment in some people? And why do some people develop PTSD in the wake of a trauma, whereas others do not? Researchers have identified a number of social, psychological, and biological factors that seem to contribute to PTSD (Scheiderman et al., 2005) (see the Concept Overview in Table 6.5).

TABLE 6.5	Concept Overview

Contributors to PTSD

A number of social, psychological, and biological factors may contribute to vulnerability to PTSD.

Contributor	Description	Example
Social factors		
1. Severity, duration, and proximity of trauma	1. More severe and longer traumas, and traumas directly affecting people, are more likely to lead to PTSD.	1. War veterans who were on the front lines for months at a time are more prone to PTSD.
2. Social support	2. Good social support protects against PTSD.	2. Women whose husbands commit suicide are less prone to PTSD if they can discuss it with friends.
Psychological factors		
1. Shattered assumptions	1. People whose basic assumptions are shattered are more prone to PTSD.	1. People who believe that bad things happen to others may be more traumatized when they experience a trauma.
2. Preexisting distress	2. People who are already distressed before a trauma are at greater risk for PTSD.	2. People distressed before a natural disaster are more at risk for PTSD after the disaster.
3. Coping styles	3. Use of avoidance, rumination, or dissociation or inability to make sense of trauma increases risk for PTSD.	3. People who cannot make sense of the loss of a loved one are more prone to PTSD.
Biological factors		
1. Physiological hyperreactivity	1. PTSD sufferers show greater arousal of neurotransmitters, hormones, and brain regions associated with stress response.	1. While imaging combat scenes, combat veterans with PTSD show greater blood flow in areas of the brain involved in emotion and memory.
2. Genetics	2. Vulnerability to PTSD may be influenced by genetic factors.	2. Identical twins show higher concordance for PTSD than fraternal twins.

Environmental and Social Factors

Not surprisingly, the nature of a traumatic event plays an important role in determining people's likelihood of developing PTSD in response to the event. In addition, the response of family members and friends to a trauma survivor is a critical influence on the survivor's vulnerability to PTSD.

Severity, Duration, and Proximity of Trauma The most potent predictors of people's reactions to trauma are the *severity* and *duration* of the trauma and the individual's *proximity* to the trauma (Cardozo et al., 2000; Ehlers, Mayou, et al., 1998; Hoge et al., 2004; Kessler et al., 1995). That is, people who experience more severe and longer-lasting traumas and are directly affected by a traumatic event are more prone to develop PTSD. For example, soldiers are more likely to experience PTSD if they were on the front lines of the war for an extended period of time or if they were taken prisoner of war than if they were not (Hoge et al., 2004; Schlenger et al., 1992; Wolfe et al., 1999). People who were at Ground Zero during the World Trade Center attacks were more likely to develop PTSD than those who were not (Galea et al., 2002). Rape survivors who are violently and repeatedly raped over an extended period are more likely to experience PTSD than are those whose experiences are shorter and less violent (Epstein, Saunders, & Kilpatrick, 1997; Merrill et al., 2001; Resick, 1993). Victims of natural disasters who lose their homes or loved ones or are themselves injured are more likely to experience PTSD than are those whose lives are less affected by the natural disaster (Basoglu et al., 2004; Nolen-Hoeksema & Morrow, 1991; Norris & Uhl, 1993).

Social Support Another predictor of people's vulnerability to PTSD following trauma is the *social support* available to them (Shalev, Tuval-Mashiach, & Hadar, 2004). People who have others who will support them emotionally through recovery from their traumas, allowing them to discuss their feelings and memories of the traumas, recover more quickly than do those who do not (Kendall-Tackett, Williams, & Finkelhor, 1993; King et al., 1999; La-Greca et al., 1996; Sutker et al., 1995). For example, women whose husbands have committed suicide show better physical and emotional health and fewer intrusive thoughts about the suicides if they are able to discuss the suicides with supportive friends than if they had not discussed the suicides with others (Pennebaker & O'Heeron, 1984).

Some events may be more difficult to discuss with others and less likely to engender social support from others because of social stigmas against people who experience such events. Examples are the suicides of family members, sexual assault, and the loss of loved ones to AIDS, particularly if the loved ones were homosexual. Some theorists have argued that veterans of the Vietnam War were more likely than veterans from previous wars to experience PTSD, because they received less social support from friends and family members on returning from combat, due to the social controversy over the war (Figley & Leventman, 1980). Similarly, one reason women are more likely than men to develop PTSD may be because the types of traumas women most frequently suffer (for example, sexual abuse) are stigmatized, whereas men are more likely to suffer traumas that don't carry as much stigma, such as exposure to war (Resick & Calhoun, 2001).

Differences among ethnic or cultural groups in vulnerability to PTSD may also be linked to differences in the social support available to members of these groups before and after traumas. Groups in which individuals have strong social support networks may be less prone to PTSD than those with weaker networks. For example, Southeast Asian refugees who are able to move into existing communities of people from their homeland when emigrating to a new country are less likely to show PTSD than are those who do not have existing communities in their new home (Beiser, 1988).

Psychological Factors

People facing the same circumstances around a trauma vary greatly in their risk for PTSD. At least three psychological factors have been identified to explain differences between people in response to trauma. First, for some people, a trauma shatters certain basic assumptions about life, and the shattering of these assumptions can contribute to long-term psychological distress. Second, some people are already distressed before a trauma occurs and they appear at greater risk for PTSD. Third, certain coping styles seem to increase people's chances of developing PTSD.

Shattered Assumptions We tend to go through life with a number of assumptions about ourselves and how the world works that help us feel good most of the time but can be shattered by a trauma (Janoff-Bulman, 1992). The first is the assumption of *personal invulnerability*. Most people believe that bad things happen to other people and that they are relatively invulnerable to traumas, such as being in a severe car accident, having their homes destroyed in natural disasters, or being kidnapped or raped. When such events do happen, people lose their illusion of invulnerability. Chronically feeling vulnerable, they are hypervigilant for signs of new traumas and may show signs of chronic anxiety (Janoff-Bulman, 1992).

The second basic assumption is that *the world is meaningful and just and that things happen for a good reason* (Lerner, 1980). This assumption can be shattered by events that seem senseless, unjust, or perhaps evil, such as the terrorist bombing of a children's day-care center or teenagers randomly shooting their classmates.

The third assumption is that *people who are good, who "play by the rules," do not experience bad things.* Trauma victims often will say that they have lived a good life, have been good people, and thus can't understand how the trauma happened to them (Janoff-Bulman & Frieze, 1983). A study of refugees from Bhutan, a region near Nepal, who had been forced from their homes and often tortured, found that many saw their misfortune as a result of past deeds, in line with cultural beliefs (Shrestha et al., 1998). A study of rape survivors found that those who engaged in self-blame involving their character—saying there was something bad about themselves that resulted in their being raped—showed greater distress than those who did not engage in such self-blame (Boeschen et al., 2001). Blaming themselves for causing a trauma can shatter people's views of themselves as good people (Janoff-Bulman & Frieze, 1983).

Preexisting Distress Another predictor of people's vulnerability to PTSD is the level of *distress* they were experiencing *before* the trauma hit (Shalev et al., 2004). People who are already experiencing increased symptoms of anxiety or depression are more likely to develop PTSD than are those who were not anxious or depressed (Blanchard et al., 1996; Cardozo et al., 2003; Hoge et al., 2004; Mayou et al., 2001). For example, a study of the victims of Hurricane Andrew found that the children who had already been anxious before the hurricane were more likely to develop posttraumatic stress reactions than were those who had not been anxious prior to the hurricane (LaGreca, Silverman, & Wasserstein, 1998). War veterans who have psychological problems or poor interpersonal relationships before they enter combat are more likely to develop symptoms of PTSD (Chemtob et al., 1990; King et al., 1999; Orsillo et al., 1996). African American, Hispanic American, and Native American combat veterans from the Vietnam and Persian Gulf wars appear to have been more vulnerable to PTSD than White veterans (Manson et al., 1996). This may be because they faced discrimination in the United States both before and after the war, increasing their base levels of distress and making it more likely they would respond to the traumas of combat with PTSD.

Coping Styles People's styles of *coping* with stressful events and with their own symptoms of

distress may also influence their vulnerability to PTSD. Several studies have shown that people who use self-destructive or avoidant coping strategies, such as drinking and self-isolation, are more likely to experience PTSD (Fairbank, Hansen, & Fitterling, 1991; Merrill et al., 2001; Sutker et al., 1995).

A similar form of coping that may increase the likelihood of PTSD is the use of dissociation (Foa & Hearst-Ikeda, 1996; Spiegel, 1991). Dissociation involves a range of psychological processes that indicate a detachment from the trauma and from ongoing events. People who dissociate following a trauma may feel they are in another place or in someone else's body, watching the trauma and its aftermath unfold. Studies have shown that people who dissociate shortly after a trauma are at increased risk to develop PTSD (Ehlers, Mayou et al., 1998; Fauerbach et al., 2000; Koopman, Classen, & Spiegel, 1994; Mayou et al., 2001; Shalev et al., 1996). Some studies suggest that Latinos are more prone to dissociate in response to severe stress, and this may increase their vulnerability to PTSD (Hough et al., 1996; Marshall & Orlando, 2002).

On the other hand, many studies have found that, following a trauma, most people try to *make sense* of the trauma somehow as a way of coping (Lehman et al., 1987; Silver, Boon, & Stones, 1983). They try to find a reason or purpose for the trauma or to understand what the trauma means in their lives. Psychodynamic and existential theorists have argued that searching for meaning in a trauma is a healthy process, which can lead people to gain a sense of mastery over their traumas and to integrate their traumas into their understanding of themselves (Frankl, 1963; Freud, 1920; Horowitz, 1976). They suggest that people who are able to make sense of their traumas are less likely to develop PTSD or other chronic emotional problems and may recover more quickly from their traumas than do people who cannot make sense of their traumas (Bulman & Wortman, 1977; Silver et al., 1983).

How do people make sense of traumas? Some people have religious or philosophical beliefs that assist them. For example, many recently bereaved people who are religious say that God needed their loved ones in heaven or had a special purpose for taking their loved ones, and this view seems to help them understand their losses (McIntosh, Silver, & Wortman, 1993; Nolen-Hoeksema & Larson, 1999). Other people say that the deaths of loved ones made them reevaluate their lives and their relationships with others and make positive changes, and this process helped them deal with the loss. For example, the following are some comments from a person who had lost a close loved one in recent months (Nolen-Hoeksema & Larson, 1999, p. 143).

VOICES

Thinking back on it, if I had not done this, look at all I would have missed—all this growth, all this understanding. I tend to look at it generally as if all the things that happen in my life are a gift, for whatever reason, or however they happen. It doesn't necessarily have to be only pleasant gifts, but everything that happens . . . there's a meaning. I've had a lot of suffering in my life . . . and through that I've learned a great deal. While I wouldn't want to go back and relive that, I'm grateful for that because it makes me who I am. There's a lot of joys and sorrows, but they all enrich life. I like who I am now because I find at 44 that I really like myself. If I didn't go through a lot of the hardships that I had, I wouldn't be who I am. So in a lot of ways, it's been an OK journey. And if I hadn't had people like that in my life, I wouldn't have a good sense of humor, which is one of the things that helps us get through, right? I feel extremely fortunate lately.

Some people are never able to make sense of their losses or other traumas, and these people are more likely to experience chronic and severe symptoms of PTSD and depression. For example, researchers questioned 77 women who were the survivors of incest an average of 20 years after the incest had ended. They found that 50 percent of the women were still actively searching for meaning in their incest. These women said things such as "I always ask myself why, over and over, but there is no answer" and "There is no sense to be made. This should not have happened to me or any child" (Silver et al., 1983). The more actively a woman was still searching for meaning in her incest, the more likely she was to be experiencing recurrent and intrusive thoughts about the incest experience, the more distress she was experiencing, and the lower her level of social functioning was. Because those who search for meaning are ruminating about the past, perhaps they are also less able to focus coping efforts on the present and the future. In trying to understand, they may, in effect, get stuck in the past. Finding meaning may be particularly difficult in traumas such as sexual assault or genocide, in which the nature of the event violates basic moral codes and destroys people's basic trust in others (Resick, 1993; Silver et al., 1983).

Biological Factors

In recent years, researchers have been searching for biological factors that determine whether an individual will develop PTSD following a trauma. That search has focused on differences between PTSD sufferers and nonsufferers in the functioning of the brain and biochemical systems involved in the stress response. Some research also suggests that genetics play a role in vulnerability to PTSD.

Physiological Hyperreactivity Studies using neuroimaging techniques, such as positron-emission tomography (PET) and functional magnetic resonance imaging (MRI) (see Chapter 3), have found differences between PTSD sufferers and nonsufferers. The differences occur in activity levels in the parts of the brain involved in the regulation of emotion and the fight-or-flight response and in memory, including the amygdala and hippocampus (Ballenger et al., 2004; Nutt & Malizia, 2004). The *amygdala* appears to be hyperreactive to trauma-related stimuli in PTSD sufferers. In one study, combat veterans with PTSD show increased blood flow in the amygdala while imagining combat-related scenes, compared with when they were imagining neutral scenes (Liberzon & Phan, 2003; Shin et al., 1997) (see Figure 6.9). Similar results have been found in studies comparing survivors of childhood sexual assault with and without PTSD (Shin et al., 1999).

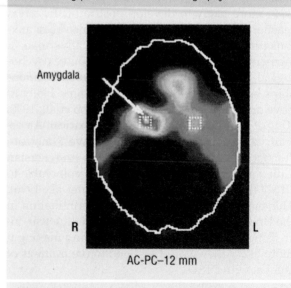

FIGURE 6.9 **Amygdala Activity in PTSD.** Combat veterans with PTSD showed increased blood flow in the amygdala when asked to imagine combat scenes in studies using positron-emission tomography.

Amygdala

R   L

AC-PC–12 mm

Source: Shin et al., 1997.

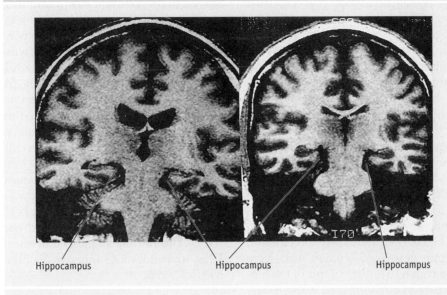

FIGURE 6.10 **Hippocampal Deterioration in PTSD.** Studies using magnetic resonance imaging show deterioration in the hippocampus of people with PTSD (right), compared to someone without PTSD (left).

Hippocampus   Hippocampus   Hippocampus

Source: Bremner, 1998.

Some studies also show shrinkage in the *hippocampus* among PTSD patients (Bremner et al., 2000; Villarreal et al., 2002) (see Figure 6.10). The hippocampus is involved in memory. Damage to it may result in some of the memory problems that PTSD sufferers report. In addition, the hippocampus plays a role in the extinction of fear responses, so damage could interfere with an individual's ability to overcome fearful responses to stimuli reminiscent of the trauma.

Recall that one of the major hormones released as part of the fight-or-flight response is *cortisol* and that high levels of cortisol usually indicate an elevated stress response. Interestingly, resting levels of cortisol among PTSD sufferers (when they are not being exposed to reminders of their trauma) tend to be *lower* than among people without PTSD (Ballenger et al., 2004; Yehuda, 2004). Cortisol shuts down sympathetic nervous system activity after stress, so the lower levels of cortisol among PTSD sufferers may result in prolonged activity of the sympathetic nervous system following stress. As a result, they may more easily develop a conditioned fear of stimuli associated with the trauma and subsequently develop PTSD.

One longitudinal study assessed cortisol levels in people who had been injured in a traffic accident one to two hours previously (Yehuda, McFarlane, & Shalev, 1998). Six months later, these people were evaluated for the presence of PTSD. Those who developed the disorder had had signif-

icantly lower cortisol levels immediately after the trauma than had the people who did not develop the disorder. Similar results were found in a study of rape survivors (Resnick et al., 1995). These data suggest that people who develop PTSD have lower baseline levels of cortisol before they experience their trauma and possibly that abnormally low cortisol levels contribute to the development of PTSD.

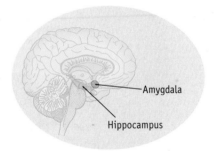

Amygdala

Hippocampus

These structures of the limbic system have been implicated in PTSD.

Although PTSD sufferers have low levels of cortisol, some of their other physiological responses to stress are exaggerated, including elevated heart rate and increased secretion of the neurotransmitters epinephrine and norepinephrine (Ballenger et al., 2004; Yehuda, 2004). One possibility is that people who are vulnerable to the development of PTSD in the wake of trauma show a decoupling, or dissociation, among the various regulators of the tress response, including the hypothalamic-pituitary-adrenal (HPA) axis and the sympathetic nervous system. The HPA axis may be unable to shut down the response of the sympathetic nervous system to a trauma by secreting the necessary levels of cortisol, resulting in the brain's overexposure to epinephrine, norepinephrine, and other neurochemicals. This overexposure then may lead to memories of the traumatic event being "over-consolidated," or inappropriately remembered (Pitman, 1989).

There is increasing evidence that exposure to trauma during childhood may permanently alter children's biological stress response, making them more vulnerable to PTSD and to other anxiety disorders and depression throughout their lives (Cicchetti & Toth; 2005; Nemeroff, 2004). Studies of children who have been maltreated (severely neglected or physically, emotionally, or sexually abused) show that they have abnormal cortisol responses to stressors (Cicchetti, Toth, & Rogosch, 2001) and a diminished startle response (Klorman et al., 2003). Studies of adults who were abused as children show that they continue to have abnormal cortisol responses to laboratory stressors, even if they do not continue to show symptoms of PTSD or depression (Heim, Meinlschmidt, & Nemeroff, 2003). In addition, depressed women who were abused as children show a lower volume of the hippocampus, compared with depressed women who were not abused as children (Vythilingam et al., 2002). Thus, early childhood trauma may leave permanent physical scars, as well as emotional scars, that predispose individuals to later psychological problems.

Genetics There is some evidence that a vulnerability to PTSD can be inherited (Segman & Shalev, 2003). One study of about 4,000 twins who had served in the Vietnam War found that, if one twin developed PTSD, the other twin was much more likely also to develop PTSD if he was an identical twin than if he was a fraternal twin (True et al., 1993). Fascinating studies of the adult children of Holocaust survivors find that they are three times more likely to develop PTSD than matched comparison groups, and the children of Holocaust survivors who developed PTSD are even more likely to develop the disorder than the children of survivors who did not develop PTSD (Yehuda et al., 1998). In turn, the adult children whose parents developed PTSD have abnormally low levels of cortisol, whether or not they had ever been exposed to traumatic events themselves and had developed PTSD. This finding suggests that one risk factor for PTSD that might be inherited is abnormally low cortisol levels.

Treatments for PTSD

Psychotherapies for PTSD generally have three goals: exposing clients to what they fear in order to extinguish that fear, challenging distorted cognitions that are contributing to symptoms, and

---

TABLE 6.6   Concept Overview

Treatments for PTSD

Treatments for PTSD focus on exposing clients to feared images, challenging distorted cognitions, managing stressful circumstances, and reducing painful anxiety symptoms.

Treatment	Description	Example
Cognitive-behavioral therapy	Systematic desensitization is used to extinguish fear reactions to memories; cognitive techniques are used to challenge irrational thoughts.	Rape survivor works through hierarchy of feared memories of rape using relaxation techniques; therapist helps her confront self-blaming thoughts.
Stress management	Therapist helps the client solve concrete problems to reduce stress; may use thought-stopping strategies to quell intrusive thoughts.	Disaster survivor is helped to find a new home and job.
Biological therapies	Antianxiety and antidepressant drugs are used to quell symptoms.	Person uses Valium (a benzodiazeine) to help induce sleep at night.
Sociocultural approaches	PTSD symptoms are understood and treated within the norms of people's culture.	Culture-specific rituals might be used to help a PTSD sufferer make peace with the trauma and reintegrate into the community.

helping clients manage their ongoing life problems to reduce the stress in their lives. These goals are addressed in cognitive-behavioral therapy for PTSD and in stress-management therapies. Some people with PTSD also benefit from the use of antianxiety and antidepressant medications (see the Concept Overview in Table 6.6). After we discuss psychotherapies and drug therapies for PTSD, we will address social perspectives on PTSD and its treatment.

Cognitive-Behavioral Therapy

Cognitive-behavioral therapy has proven effective in the treatment of PTSD in adults (Davidson, 2004; Resick & Calhoun, 2001; Van Etten & Taylor, 1998) and in children (Cohen et al., 2004). A major element of cognitive-behavioral treatment for PTSD is **systematic desensitization therapy.** The client identifies thoughts and situations that create anxiety, ranking them from most anxiety-provoking to least. The therapist then begins to take the client through this hierarchy, using relaxation techniques to quell anxiety. The focus of anxiety in PTSD is the memory of the traumatic event and stimuli that remind the person of the event. It is impossible to return to the actual event that triggered the PTSD in many cases, so imagining the event vividly must replace actual exposure to the event. A combat veteran being treated for PTSD imagines the bloody battles and scenes of killing and death that haunt him; a rape survivor imagines the minute details of the assault. The therapist also watches for distorted thinking patterns, such as survivor guilt, and helps the client challenge these thoughts, as in the following interchange between a therapist and a woman named Cindy, who developed PTSD after being raped (adapted from Resick & Calhoun, 2001, p. 81).

VOICES

Cindy: Why did this have to happen? Why? Why?

Therapist: Why did the rape have to happen?

Cindy: Yeah. Why did he do that to me? Why should I have to feel this? I'm a product of my environment. I really feel like that.

Therapist: We all are to a certain extent.

Cindy: Yeah. We are.

Therapist: What answer have you given yourself up to this point to that "why" question?

Cindy: Because, just, that's my life, that was my past. That is what happened.

Therapist: But you still keep asking why.

Cindy: I think my "why" question just stems from, you know, you stupid idiot, you don't take that from people. [Long pause] You know, it's not why did he take it from me. One thing I get mad at myself is [crying], why did I let him?

Therapist: You didn't let him.

Cindy: I know.

Therapist: Did you? He just did it.

Cindy: It happened. I was 15. I was so scared.

Therapist: And confused.

Cindy: Yeah, and alone. I think that's why I'm mad. Because I was so alone and I walked away from so many people. It kind of wiped away all the good memories.

Therapist: It's a scary decision for a 15-year-old to try to reach out to people when she's feeling bad about herself. At times a person in that position is going to pull away, because she's so afraid of compounding the trauma by other people rejecting her. It seems almost better to walk away yourself than let other people reject you. So you were rejecting them first.

Repeatedly and vividly imagining and describing the feared events in the safety of the therapist's office, the client has an opportunity to habituate to his or her anxiety and to distinguish the memory from present reality (Foa & Jaycox, 1999; Resick & Calhoun, 2001). Repeatedly imagining and discussing the traumatic events may also allow the client to work through them and integrate them into his or her concepts of the self and the world (Foa & Jaycox, 1999; Horowitz, 1976).

Studies of rape survivors, combat veterans, survivors of road traffic collisions, and refugees have found that this kind of repeated exposure therapy significantly decreases PTSD symptoms and helps prevent relapse (Foa et al., 1991, 1999; Keane et al., 1992; Paunovic & Öst, 2001; Resick & Schnicke, 1992; Tarrier et al., 1999; Taylor et al., 2001). In another type of imagery intervention, rape survivors who had repeated nightmares about their rape experience were taught to use positive imagery to change the content of their nightmares. Even after only a few sessions of imagery training, these women showed decreases in nightmares, improved sleep quality, and decreased PTSD symptoms (Krakow et al., 2000, 2001).

Stress Management

What about those people who are constantly ruminating about their traumas, even years after they are over? Will intensive exposure to thoughts about the traumas help them? Some theorists argue that, for PTSD sufferers who cannot find any meaning in their traumas or cannot "resolve" their traumas and who experience very frequent, intrusive thoughts, it may be more useful to help them find ways of blocking their intrusive thoughts (Ehlers, Clark, et al., 1998; Horowitz, 1976; Silver et al., 1983). **Thought-stopping techniques** include the client's yelling "No!" loudly when realizing he or she is thinking about the trauma, as well as learning to engage in positive activities that distract thoughts away from the trauma (Rachman, 1978). These thought-stopping techniques are often combined with **stress-management interventions** that teach clients skills for overcoming problems in their lives that are increasing their stress and that may be the result of PTSD, such as marital problems or social isolation (Keane et al., 1992; Wolfsdorf & Zlotnick, 2001). The following case study illustrates the use of several stress-management interventions with a combat veteran suffering from PTSD (Keane et al., 1992, p. 91):

CASE STUDY

D. P. was a male Vietnam veteran referred to the PTSD unit of his local DVA [Department of Veterans Affairs] Medical Center. D. P. reported feeling extremely stressed over the past six months because of problems on his job. He complained of sleep disturbance, angry outbursts, intrusive thoughts, nightmares, and avoidance of movies, books, and television shows associated with Vietnam. He also was experiencing marital difficulties, constriction of affect, and numbing of emotions. Since his discharge from the military, D. P. had avoided discussing Vietnam (his friends over the past 20 years were unaware that D. P. had even been in the military), and he stated that he did not want to discuss Vietnam in treatment. Respecting his wishes, treatment began by addressing sleep disturbance and interpersonal difficulties. D. P. learned progressive muscle relaxation and began using the technique to prepare for sleep, to get back to sleep after awakening, and at times throughout the day when he felt himself becoming stressed. Interpersonal difficulties were then addressed in couples sessions using communication and problem-solving skills. D. P. and his wife had developed a relatively noncommunicative style over a number of years. Mrs. P. complained about a lack of intimacy in their relationship and being overburdened with decisions that were better made by both of them. In therapy, the couple learned to listen to one another and to give constructive positive and negative feedback. As is common among combat veterans with PTSD, D. P. was afraid of his anger, even though he had not been violent in over 17 years. To address this concern, he was taught several strategies for anger control. For example, D. P. was given permission by the therapist to remove himself from a situation or discussion that created stress for him. He was taught to request a time and place to later continue working on that specific problem. This allowed D. P. to work on problem-solving skills while titrating his exposure to aversive, arousing circumstances. Initially, problem solving was conducted only during the session; however, after several weeks, the couple began problem solving at home and reviewed the contracts and solution processes in the following session. As D. P. learned a variety of new skills that enhanced his ability to manage his stress and his interpersonal problems, he became less defensive about Vietnam and began to address those issues more directly in therapy.

Wolfsdorf and Zlotnick (2001) recommend a variation on stress-management therapy for survivors of sexual abuse, which they call *affect-management therapy*. This therapy uses a variety of behavioral and cognitive methods to help clients manage their negative moods better, with the hope that eventually they will be able to confront the overwhelming memories of their abuse. An interchange between a therapist and client who is self-destructive in response to her negative feelings goes like this (adapted from Wolfsdorf & Zlotnick, 2001, pp. 178–179):

Client: Once I'm upset, that's it. There's nothing I can do. I just sit on the floor and chain smoke.

Therapist: Then what?

Client: I usually end up bingeing. If it's really bad, I burn myself with a cigarette.

Therapist: Does that work for you?

Client: Kind of. I mean, it does usually stop me from doing something more drastic. But I'm getting fat, and I'm sick of all these little scars. I end up feeling worse the next day because I did it again.

Therapist: Yes, that's hard. I think it's important for you to have other options for feeling better when you are in a crisis. Something that could help you feel better in the moment and also longer term. What do you think?

Client: Well, it *sounds* okay.

Therapist: One thing that can be very important at those times is to have a plan of healthy things you could do. If you have a crisis plan, then you don't have to come up with other options when you're upset; it's already done for you. Does that make sense?

Client: Yes.

Therapist: Okay, good. So what kinds of things could you do in a crisis instead of hurting yourself?

Client: I could get away. Take a trip. That would really help. To be able to just get on a plane and go visit a friend.

Therapist: Yes, visiting friends is a great idea. It can really help deal with stress. But I'm concerned that you might not always be able to do that in a crisis. And for a crisis plan to work, we need to focus on things you could do any time. Does that make sense?

Client: I guess.

Therapist: So what could you do that would help you feel better any time you were in crisis? What do you enjoy doing?

Client: I like to go for walks in the park near my house. There are some beautiful trees in that park. And I like to give my dog a bath. He loves the water, so it's fun.

Therapist: Those are great ideas. Do you think that would help if you were in crisis?

Client: Yes. They're both distracting, and they get me out of the house, which is good.

Therapist: Excellent. Now, if you needed to do something else, what else could you do?

Client: I could call a friend and let her know how I'm feeling.

Therapist: Okay, do you have someone specific in mind?

Studies find that these affect- and stress-management interventions are helpful both to combat veterans with PTSD and to persons suffering PTSD after rape (Foa et al., 1999; Kilpatrick, Veronen, & Resick, 1979; Meichenbaum & Jaremko, 1983; Veronen & Kilpatrick, 1983; Wolfsdorf & Zlotnick, 2001). There is still much work to do, however, before it is known just how to treat persons with PTSD.

Eye Movement Desensitization and Reprocessing

Eye movement desensitization and reprocessing, or **EMDR,** is a highly controversial therapy for trauma survivors that evolved from a personal observation. The originator of this therapy, Francine Shapiro (1995), noticed that her troubling thoughts were resolved when her eyes followed the waving of leaves during a walk in the park. She suggested that lateral eye movements facilitate the cognitive processing of trauma and developed EMDR from this hypothesis.

During a session of EMDR, a client attends to the image of the trauma, thoughts about the trauma, and the physical sensations of anxiety aroused by the trauma. At the same time, the therapist quickly moves a finger back and forth in front of the client's eyes to elicit a series of repeated, rapid, jerky, side-to-side eye movements ("saccades"). During the session, the client provides ratings of his or her anxiety level and how strongly he or she believes negative thoughts pertaining to the trauma.

In its early days, EMDR was described as a one-session cure for PTSD and related disorders. More recently, proponents have suggested that it requires multiple sessions. The fantastic claims made by early proponents of EMDR led to a flurry of studies of its effectiveness. A statistical summary, or meta-analysis (review Chapter 3), of 34 studies examining EMDR with a variety of populations and measures concluded that EMDR is significantly more effective at reducing PTSD symptoms than no treatment or nonspecific treatments that do not expose people to their traumatic memories (Davidson & Parker, 2001). EMDR had effects similar to those of behavior therapies focused on exposing people to their traumatic memories and cognitive-behavioral therapies.

Interestingly, this meta-analysis also compared EMDR with a form of the therapy that has all the components of EMDR except the eye movements (i.e., directing clients' attention to images and thoughts of the trauma), and it concluded that the eye movements are unnecessary for reducing PTSD symptoms. This analysis suggests that the active components of EMDR are the exposure and habituation of clients to their traumas and the cognitive restructuring of their thoughts about the traumas—not the eye movements (see also Resick & Calhoun, 2001).

Biological Therapies

Studies have shown the selective serotonin reuptake inhibitors (SSRIs) and, to a lesser extent, the benzodiazepines, to be useful in treating the symptoms of PTSD, particularly the sleep problems, nightmares, and irritability (Ballenger et al., 2004; Brady et al., 2000; Davidson, 2004; Marshall et al., 2001). One study showed that PTSD patients who had had a successful treatment with an SSRI were more likely to be symptom-free for five months, compared with patients who had not received an SSRI (Martenyi et al., 2002). Patients who continue to take an SSRI after their acute symptoms have subsided are even more likely to remain symptom-free (Davidson, Rothmaum, et al., 2001).

Sociocultural Approaches

Treatments for PTSD often must consider the cultural context for this disorder. Some cultural groups have suffered a tremendous number of traumas and, thus, are more likely to have high rates of PTSD. The appropriateness of any given treatment for PTSD, however, may depend on the norms and values of that culture. In addition, when whole communities have been the victims of traumas, treatment must often be at a community level as well as at an individual level.

Cross-Cultural Issues Southeast Asians may be especially vulnerable to PTSD because of the chronic and severe traumas to which many of them have been exposed. When they do seek treatment for psychological distress, Southeast Asians often have bodily symptoms, such as pain, poor sleeping, and stomachaches, rather than the psychological symptoms of posttraumatic stress disorder. They often do not believe that the primary symptoms of PTSD, such as startle reaction, nightmares, reexperiencing of the trauma, and irritability, are worth mentioning to a physician, and they steadfastly avoid thinking about or talking about the traumas they experienced (Kinzie & Leung, 1993). Dissociative experiences, such as transient hallucinations or loss of physical functioning for no medical reason, are also common. What follows is a case history of a Cambodian woman with PTSD (adapted from Kinzie & Leung, 1993, p. 292).

CASE STUDY

When originally seen, S. A. was 38 years old. She was a Cambodian refugee brought because she believed she was possessed by her dead mother. During the original evaluation, the patient was so distressed and agitated that no real history could be obtained. A subsequent evaluation showed that she had recently been angry and depressed much of the time and actually felt that her mother had entered her body. This intrusion caused her to become very irritable and angry, and during these episodes, she would lose control. . . . S. A.'s past history was very disturbing. She was born in a rural area in Cambodia, the third of five children. She worked as a secretary for 1½ years and married at the age of 17. During the Pol Pot regime, she was subjected to 4 years of forced labor. Her father died, and her husband was executed at the time she was in labor with her second child. S. A.'s child died of starvation, and her mother died of disease and starvation. She felt most distressed about the death of her mother, who was the person closest to her and who had helped her with the delivery of her child. In 1979, she left Cambodia and lived in refugee camps for 1½ years before coming to the United States. . . . At her original presentation, S. A. was extremely agitated and appeared to be in a dissociated state. However, in the second interview, after a week of benzodiazepine treatment, she demonstrated a good fund of knowledge and a good memory for past events. She appeared to be numb and saddened about what she had suffered. Her symptoms included frequent nightmares, intrusive

(continued)

thoughts about the past, startle reaction, irritability, and marked attempts to avoid all memories of the past or any events that would remind her of Cambodia. . . .

The treatment of PTSD in Southeast Asian refugees, such as S. A., can be especially delicate. They may never have told anyone about the traumas they experienced in their homeland because of strong cultural taboos against discussing these traumas in their families. Thus, therapists must be highly sensitive and supportive in encouraging the refugee to tell his or her own story (Kinzie, 2001). The therapist must be careful to avoid any suggestion of interrogating the client, as he or she might have been interrogated in the homeland.

These refugees may need to protect themselves against the agony that memories of their severe traumas arouse and focus more on solving current problems. For example, the therapist treating S. A. might want to ensure that she is getting all the financial support and education available to her to stabilize her income and living situation. Although refugees may be having significant problems in their marital and family relationships due to their PTSD symptoms and the amount of stress their families are facing, they may be reluctant to talk to the therapist about these, due to cultural taboos against doing so.

Some cultures have their own treatments for PTSD-like symptoms. For example, some Native American groups have cleansing rituals that absolve combat veterans from their actions during combat and reintegrate veterans into the community and with the values of his or her group. The Navajo have a healing ceremony called the *Enemy Way*, which is explicitly oriented toward returning combat veterans. The ceremony lasts for seven days and seven nights. The veteran, his or her family and community members, and a tribal healer actively participate in ritual song designed to return balance and harmony to the veteran and the entire community (Manson et al., 1996).

Community-Level Interventions Often, whole communities are ravaged by traumas—a tornado might wipe out most businesses in a community or a flood might make most of the homes in a community uninhabitable. Human-made disasters can also ravage whole communities, such as the atrocities committed under "ethnic cleansing" and apartheid. Hundreds of thousands of people in many communities around the world—Afghanistan, Kosovo, Bosnia, Rwanda, South Africa, Eritrea—have been forced from their homes, driven out of their countries, tortured, raped, and killed. Mental-health professionals have been on the front lines of these conflicts, attempting to help survivors cope with the traumas they have suffered.

A community-level intervention helped women refugees in Kwazulu-Natal, South Africa cope with the traumas they suffered.

Following is the story of one of these helpers, a psychologist in South Africa (Burnette, 1997, pp. 10–11).

When the civil strife started two years ago, the men of Bhambayi went off to fight and the women were forced to move from their middle-class homes into rundown shacks on barren land. The war, fought by two factions in conflict over apartheid, drastically altered the lives of the people in Bhambayi, a town in KwaZulu-Natal, South Africa. Hundreds of people were killed and the people's homes were destroyed.

Psychologist Craig Higson-Smith, a 27-year-old South African native, became aware of the region's problems while teaching at the University of Natal and founded the KwaZulu-Natal Program for Survivors of Violence. He first brought a team of South African community researchers to help the beleaguered people there in 1992 and their work continues today.

Before the war, most of the families owned their own homes, benefited from two incomes and had gardens where they grew their own vegetables. So, as one of the first priorities, the staff of the KwaZulu-Natal Program for the Survivors of Violence secured a 3,000-square-foot piece of land from the government. While the women toiled, they discussed how the violence had affected their lives and how it felt to lose their husbands and their children.

The garden fulfilled many needs. The 25 women turned the once-barren soil into a flourishing vegetable patch. The garden also became a therapeutic oasis as the women supported each other, and spoke with program staff about their experiences, and gained self-esteem from being productive.

"What happened was the same interaction that psychologists think of as group therapy," says Higson-Smith. "But it happened in a different context and was facilitated by a process that we wouldn't have necessarily thought of using."

The program is geared primarily toward communities, although staff conduct some work at the individual, small group, and societal levels. With individuals, they conduct traditional psychotherapy to help people cope psychologically in their war-torn environment. At the small group level, they work with families, schools, and churches to restore support systems and foster community empowerment.

And at the societal level, they advocate for government funding for their program, discuss the violence in the region with lawmakers, and advocate for conflict resolution programs in the school curricula.

"The interventions we conduct mean rethinking what we as psychologists understand as our role, particularly in underdeveloped countries," Higson-Smith says. "Our job often includes facilitating, promoting and networking so that the structures [that already exist in the community] can mobilize.

"Even the most fragmented communities contain structures," Higson-Smith said. Church groups, stokvels (savings clubs), social clubs and paramilitary units are examples of such networks. His group works with those structures to link people in the communities.

Higson-Smith's team worked with a paramilitary group whose members had become involved in criminal activities, such as stealing and selling drugs. The researchers facilitated discussion among the group members about their problems and helped them come up with concrete strategies they could use to improve their lives, such as getting job training.

At the same time, Higson-Smith and his group were working with nurses at a local clinic, training them in trauma management. The team connected the two groups and now some of the group members are volunteering at the clinic.

Higson-Smith and his staff also have programs designed specifically for the young people whose lives have been ravaged by the war. They recruit youth who have been involved in the conflict to help them resume normal lives and use group discussions to explore topics such as unemployment and coping with anger and grief. They also focus on other issues young people must face, including peer pres-

(continued)

sure and substance abuse, and explore how those issues relate to the violence they have experienced.

"Political violence is the most salient feature of their lives. Most of the teens there have killed someone, know someone who's been killed or have been forced to leave their homes," Higson-Smith says. "So in the groups we discuss how the violence relates to these other issues they must contend with as adolescents."

The youth groups play games and work on projects aimed at teaching life skills. Last year when the youth group organized a community sports day, they learned to communicate with each other as well as youth from other communities, and take responsibility by seeing the event through to completion.

Higson-Smith and his colleagues also conduct psychodrama, art and music groups that serve as a venue for the youth to express how it felt to live through the conflict. The youth write poems, for example, to express their feelings, some of which were published in a book, *On Common Ground* (KwaZulu-Natal Program for Survivors of Violence, 1996).

Higson-Smith says the team's work is difficult yet rewarding. He also emphasizes that he and his colleagues are not the sole cause of healing in these devastated communities. "Before we came, the people here survived, coped, and found joy in their lives," he said.

Therapists who work with refugees and other groups that have undergone tremendous, chronic stressors emphasize the need for flexibility—adapting therapeutic methods to the cultural norms of the groups—and for respect and recognition of the resilience of these people in the face of overwhelming conditions (Eisenbruch, de Jong, & van de Put, 2004; Lemaire & Despret, 2001).

SUMMING UP

- People with posttraumatic stress disorder repeatedly reexperience the traumatic event, avoid situations that might arouse memories of their trauma, and are hypervigilant and chronically aroused.
- PTSD may be most likely to occur following traumas that shatter people's assumptions that

they are invulnerable, that the world is a just place, and that bad things do not happen to good people.

- People who experience severe and long-lasting traumas, who have lower levels of social support, who experience socially stigmatizing traumas, who were already depressed or anxious before the trauma, or who have maladaptive coping styles may be at increased risk for PTSD.
- People who are unable to make sense of a trauma appear more likely to have chronic PTSD symptoms.
- PTSD sufferers show greater physiological reactivity to stressors, greater activity in the areas of the brain involved in emotion and memory, but lower resting cortisol levels.
- Effective psychotherapy for PTSD involves exposing the person to memories of the trauma and extinguishing his or her anxiety over these memories through systematic desensitization and flooding.
- Some people cannot tolerate such exposure, however, and may do better with supportive therapy focused on solving current interpersonal difficulties and life problems.
- Benzodiazepines and antidepressant drugs can quell some of the symptoms of PTSD.
- Clinicians must be sensitive both to the extraordinary circumstances that may have led to PTSD and to the cultural norms of the person or group being treated.

CHAPTER INTEGRATION

This chapter amply illustrates the reciprocal effects of the body, the mind, and the environment (see Figure 6.11 on page 212). Psychological and social factors can have direct effects on the physiology of the body and indirect effects on health by leading people to engage in behaviors that either promote or impair health. On the other hand, our physical health affects our emotional health and self-concept. People with life-threatening or debilitating physical illnesses are at a much increased risk for depression and other emotional problems. At a more subtle level, physiology may influence many characteristics we think of as personality, such as how quick we are to react with anger when someone confronts us or how adaptable we are to new situations. For these reasons, health psychologists begin with the assumption that biology, psychology, and the social environment have reciprocal influences on each other. Then they attempt to characterize these influences and determine their importance.

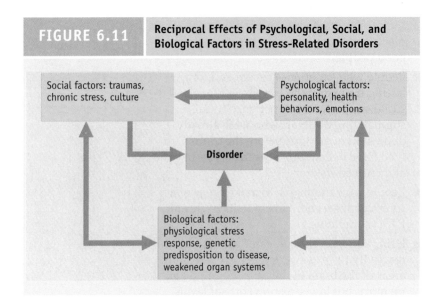

FIGURE 6.11 Reciprocal Effects of Psychological, Social, and Biological Factors in Stress-Related Disorders

By definition, posttraumatic stress disorder is the result of a psychological experience of trauma, yet new research is showing just how much traumatic experiences can permanently change an individual's biology. As we discussed in this chapter, people with PTSD show changes in how their brains function and how they respond to stimuli. Studies of young children who have suffered traumas, such as emotional or sexual abuse, show that their brains develop differently than do the brains of children who have not suffered traumas (Cicchetti & Toth, 2005). In turn, the risk of developing serious PTSD following a trauma may be influenced by genetics or by other types of predisposing vulnerability factors.

Does the mind affect the body, or does the body affect the mind? The work in health psychology and the research on PTSD show that this ancient mind-body question can only be answered with *"Both."*

Extraordinary People: Follow-Up

We end this chapter with powerful encouragement from Norman Cousins for anyone who has faced serious disease or the impact of traumatic events on the mind and body.

What we are talking about essentially, I suppose, is the chemistry of the will to live. If I had to guess, I would say that the principal contribution made by my doctor to the taming, and possibly the conquest, of my illness was that he encouraged me to believe I was a respected partner with him in the total undertaking. He fully engaged my subjective energies. He may not have been able to define or diagnose the process through which self-confidence (wild hunches securely believed) was somehow picked up by the body's immunologic mechanisms and translated into anti-morbid effects. But he was acting, I believe, in the best tradition of medicine in recognizing that he had to reach out in my case beyond the usual verifiable modalities. . . .

Something else I have learned. I have learned never to underestimate the capacity of the human mind and body to regenerate—even when the prospects seem most wretched. The life-force may be the least understood force on earth. William James (1948) said that human beings tend to live too far within self-imposed limits. It is possible that those limits will recede when we respect more fully the natural drive of the human mind and body toward perfectibility and regeneration. Protecting and cherishing that natural drive may well represent the finest exercise of human freedom. (Cousins, 1976, pp. 1458–63)

Chapter Summary

- Events that are uncontrollable or unpredictable are perceived as more stressful. Stress can have a direct effect on health by causing chronic arousal of the physiological responses that make up the fight-or-flight response. These physiological responses result from the activation of the sympathetic nervous system and the adrenal-cortical system. Although these physiological changes are useful in helping the body fight or flee from a threat, they can cause damage to the body if they are chronically aroused due to stress. (Review Figures 6.1 and 6.2.)

- Health psychologists are concerned with the roles of personality factors, coping styles, stressful events, and health-related behaviors in the development of physical disease and in the progress of disease. Health psychologists use three models for explaining how psychological factors affect health (review Figure 6.3):

  1. The direct effects model suggests that psychological factors, such as stressful experiences or certain personality characteristics, directly cause changes in the physiology of the body, which, in turn cause or exacerbate disease.

  2. The interactive model suggests that psychological factors must interact with a pre-existing biological vulnerability to disease in order for a disease to develop.

  3. The indirect effects model suggests that psychological factors affect disease largely by influencing whether people engage in health-promoting behaviors.

- Chronic physiological arousal in response to stress can contribute to coronary heart disease, hypertension, and possibly impairment of the immune system.

- Many of us give up sleep when we are under stress. The amount and quality of sleep we get on a daily basis have a significant impact on our physical health and psychological functioning.

- Some people develop sleep disorders. Dyssomnias, such as insomnia, involve abnormalities in the amount, quality, or timing of sleep. Parasomnias involve abnormal behavioral and psychological events during sleep. (Review Tables 6.1 and 6.2.)

- Pessimism is a personality characteristic that has been linked to poor health. (Review Figure 6.5.)

- The Type A behavior pattern is strongly related to a high risk for coronary heart disease and possibly other diseases. People who have the Type A pattern have a sense of time urgency, are easily made hostile, and are competitive in many situations. The component of this pattern that has been most consistently linked to coronary heart disease is a cynical form of hostility. (Review Figure 6.6.)

- People who seek and receive positive social support appear to fare better after stressful experiences.

- Guided mastery techniques have been effective in increasing self-efficacy for engaging in healthy behaviors and skill in conducting healthy behaviors. They include modeling and role-playing

to provide people with new skills and opportunities to practice them in increasingly challenging circumstances.

- Biofeedback is sometimes used to help people gain control over the bodily processes that contribute to disease. It is unclear how biofeedback works, but it has been shown to be useful in reducing hypertension and headaches.

- Sociocultural interventions focus on changing and using people's social networks to improve their health. Some research suggests that support groups may improve physical well-being.

- Posttraumatic stress disorder (PTSD) occurs after a person experiences a severe trauma. It involves three types of symptoms: (1) repeatedly reexperiencing of the traumatic event through intrusive images or thoughts, recurring nightmares, flashbacks, and psychological and physiological reactivity to stimuli that remind the person of the event; (2) withdrawal, emotional numbing, and avoidance of anything that might arouse memories of the event; and (3) hypervigilance and chronic arousal. In addition to having these symptoms, PTSD sufferers report survival guilt. (Review Table 6.3.)

- Acute stress disorder has symptoms similar to those of PTSD but occurs within one month of a stressor and lasts less than four weeks. (Review Table 6.4.)

- Adjustment disorder is diagnosed when depressive or anxiety symptoms or antisocial behavior occurs within three months after a stressor.

- Social factors appear involved in the risk for PTSD. The more severe and longer-lasting a trauma and the more involved a person is in the trauma, the more likely he or she is to show PTSD. People who have lower levels of social support and who experience socially stigmatizing traumas are at increased risk for PTSD.

- Psychological factors also play a role in PTSD. People who are already depressed or anxious before a trauma, cope through dissociation, or have difficulty making sense of the trauma may be at increased risk for PTSD.

- The biological factors involved in vulnerability to PTSD may include abnormally low cortisol levels and a genetic risk. In addition, people with PTSD show hyperarousal of the amygdala, atrophy in the hippocampus, and exaggerated heart rate responses to stressors. (Review Table 6.5.)

- An effective treatment for PTSD involves exposing a person to his or her memories of a trauma, through systematic desensitization and flooding, to extinguish his or her anxiety over these memories. Some people cannot tolerate such exposure, however, and may do better with supportive therapy focused on solving current interpersonal difficulties and life problems.

- Benzodiazepines and antidepressant drugs can quell some of the symptoms of PTSD. (Review Table 6.6.)

- Alternative approaches to the treatment of PTSD include eye movement desensitization and reprocessing as well as culturally specific practices.

MindMap CD-ROM

The following resources on the MindMap CD-ROM that came with this text will help you to master the content of this chapter and prepare for tests:

- Interactive Segments: Stress and Life Events; Type A Behavior
- Video: PTSD
- Chapter Timeline
- Chapter Quiz

Key Terms

stress 173

fight-or-flight response 175

cortisol 175

general adaptation syndrome 175

health psychology 176

coronary heart disease (CHD) 177

hypertension 178

immune system 178

lymphocytes 178

dyssomnias 182

parasomnias 182

insomnia 182

stimulus-control therapy 183

sleep restriction therapy 183

hypersomnia 183

narcolepsy 184

cataplexy 184

sleep apnea 184

Type A behavior pattern 185

guided mastery techniques 189

biofeedback 190

posttraumatic stress disorder (PTSD) 191

acute stress disorder 191

adjustment disorder 191

dissociative symptoms 193

systematic desensitization therapy 205

thought-stopping techniques 206

stress-management interventions 206

eye movement desensitization and reprocessing (EMDR) 207

> Chapter 7

Birddog
by Diana Ong

*All emotions are pure which gather you and lift you up;
that emotion is impure which seizes only one side of
your being and so distorts you.*

—Rainer Maria Rilke, *Letters to a Young Poet*
(1904, November 4; translated by M. D. Herter)

Anxiety Disorders <

Extraordinary People

■ **Marc Summers:** *Everything in Its Place*

Panic Disorder

People with panic disorder experience sudden bursts of anxiety symptoms, feel out of control, and think they are dying. They may have an overreactive autonomic nervous system, which easily turns on a fight-or-flight response. They also tend to catastrophize their symptoms and have an excessive sensitivity to anxiety. Antidepressant and antianxiety drugs can reduce symptoms of panic, and cognitive-behavioral treatments are effective for panic disorder.

Taking Psychology Personally

■ **Relaxation Exercises**

Phobias

People with agoraphobia fear being in places where they might be trapped or unable to get help in an emergency. The emergency they often fear is having a panic attack. The specific phobias focus on animals, elements of the environment (such as water), certain situations (such as flying), blood, injections, and injuries. Social phobia involves a pervasive fear of scrutiny by others.

Psychodynamic theories attribute phobias to the displacement of unconscious conflicts onto symbolic objects. Behavioral theories argue that phobias develop from classical and operant conditioning. Cognitive theories of social phobia suggest that this disorder develops in people who have excessively high standards for their social performance, assume that others are judging them harshly, and are hypervigilant to signs of rejection from others. Biological theories attribute phobias to genetics. The most effective treatments for phobias are behavioral treatments that expose people to their phobic objects and teach them skills for reducing their anxiety.

Generalized Anxiety Disorder

People with generalized anxiety disorder have chronic and pervasive anxiety about most aspects of their lives. Both consciously and unconsciously, they are hypervigilant for threat. They worry constantly about both important and unimportant things. Cognitive-behavioral therapies have proven effective for generalized anxiety disorder. Antianxiety drugs and antidepressants can also reduce anxiety symptoms.

Obsessive-Compulsive Disorder

Obsessive-compulsive disorder (OCD) is classified as an anxiety disorder but has many distinct characteristics. Obsessions are unwanted, intrusive thoughts that the individual feels are uncontrollable. Compulsions are ritualized behaviors that the individual feels forced to engage in. Biological theories attribute obsessive-compulsive disorder to genetics and to dysfunction in areas of the brain regulating impulses. Psychodynamic theories view obsessions and compulsions as symbols of unconscious conflicts. Cognitive-behavioral theories attribute obsessions to rigid thinking and compulsions to operant conditioning. Treatment for obsessive-compulsive disorder generally involves a combination of drug therapy and cognitive-behavioral therapy.

Social Approaches to the Anxiety Disorders

Sociocultural theorists focus on group differences in anxiety disorders and look to environmental demands and social and cultural norms to explain these differences. Sociocultural perspectives shed some light on the fact that women are more likely than men to have any of the anxiety disorders discussed in this chapter. They also help explain cross-cultural differences in the manifestation of anxiety.

Chapter Integration

Vulnerability-stress models of the anxiety disorders argue that individuals who develop these disorders have underlying biological or psychological vulnerabilities to anxiety, which may be due in part to past experiences with traumas, and these vulnerabilities interact with new stressors to produce anxiety symptoms.

Extraordinary People

Marc Summers: *Everything in Its Place*

Marc Summers has had a successful television career as the host of the game show Double Dare and the Food TV show Unwrapped. He is funny, self-confident, and good on his feet.

Marc Summers is also a man with a significant anxiety disorder called obsessive-compulsive disorder. In his autobiography, *Everything in Its Place* (Summers, 2000), Marc Summers describes how his obsession with orderliness and cleanliness has plagued him all his life. On Sunday afternoons, when the other children in the neighborhood were playing outside together, Marc Summers was in his room, cleaning it from top to bottom (pp. 33–34):

> This was no ordinary cleaning. First I'd strip my bunk bed, and dust the woodwork behind the bed and the bed itself. I'd walk around and around the bed as I made it, back and forth, until the bedding was perfectly smooth and symmetrical. The bedspread couldn't touch the floor. It had to be perfectly even along the bottom. I put the bed back into its indentations in our dark green carpet so I wouldn't make new ones. If by chance, the bed had left any slight indentations in its temporary position, I would get down on my hands and knees and rub them out.
>
> I then turned my attention to our bookshelf. I dusted each book with a rag—the cover, binding, spine, bottom, top, every surface. I dusted and Pledged the shelves, put each book back in its place, taking care that the edges were exactly flush with the lip of the bookshelf. The bookshelf alone could take an hour to clean. . . .
>
> Once a month, I'd binge, moving everything away from the walls and dusting behind the furniture. . . . There was nothing in my room that wasn't Pledged to death, wiped, Windexed, vacuumed. Nothing. Everything was shiny and perfect. I loved the way a clean room smelled. Cleaning gave me an incredible feeling of satisfaction. It fulfilled a very deep inner need.

So far, you may be saying that Marc Summers was just a quirky little boy who liked a clean room. That's what his parents thought. But he harbored a terrible sense of responsibility for the welfare of his family, which could be allayed only by compulsive rituals (p. 42):

> I thought my parents would die if I didn't do everything in exactly the right way. When I took my glasses off at night I'd have to place them on the dresser at a particular angle. Sometimes I'd turn on the light and get out of bed seven times until I felt comfortable with the angle. If the angle wasn't right, I felt that my parents would die. The feeling ate up my insides.
>
> If I didn't grab the molding on the wall just the right way as I entered or exited my room; if I didn't hang a shirt in the closet perfectly; if I didn't read a paragraph a certain way; if my hands and nails weren't perfectly clean, I thought my incorrect behavior would kill my parents.

Ever since he was a boy, Marc Summers had wanted to be on television, and he credits his perfectionism and drive with helping him become a success in the hypercompetitive world of TV. Ironically, his first big hit, *Double Dare,* was a show in which the goal was to get the guests and the host (Marc Summers) as dirty as possible with the slimiest, most disgusting substances the producers could imagine. On every show, he ended up covered in gooey globs of green slime, swimming in vats of baked beans, or otherwise covered with something revolting. After each show, Marc Summers took multiple showers at the studio and then went home and showered again until he finally felt clean.

His obsessions about others being hurt and his compulsions to try to prevent this harm continued into adulthood. Marc Summers lived in New York for a couple of years when he hosted a talk show called *Biggers and Summers,* and he developed a set of compulsions that involved street signs (pp. 133–134):

> I'd walk up and down Madison when I returned to Manhattan after a day in the Queens studio. I would read the signs in the shop windows over and over again.

If I didn't read the signs correctly, I was convinced that Meredith [his daughter] wouldn't get a part in the school play or Matthew [his son] wouldn't make the sports team. I was afraid that if I didn't read the sign just right, the plane I took every Thursday to California would crash.

I obsessed endlessly about those Thursday flights, following strict rituals to ensure that disaster didn't strike. I was especially drawn to the window of one particular watch store. I vividly remember standing in front of the store's window one blustery fall evening. A sale was on for Breitling watches. There was a sign in the window that explained the watches' special features: dual time zones, perpetual calendar, day-and-date display. I read the sales pitch from top to bottom at least 25 times, a sickening feeling gripping my stomach and chest, utterly convinced that if I didn't read the ad copy perfectly my plane would hurtle downward in a ball of flame somewhere over Missouri.

VOICES

We all have our fears, but they usually are mild, short-term, or reasonable, given the circumstances. People with anxiety disorders, like Marc Summers, live with fears that are not mild, short-term, or reasonable. The fears of people with anxiety disorders are severe and ultimately lower the quality of their lives. Their fears are chronic and frequent enough to interfere with their functioning. Finally, their fears are out of proportion to the dangers that they truly face. In the following segment, one man named Harry describes his debilitating fears:

> My wife keeps telling me to calm down. If only I could. There is something wrong with me, I just know it. I feel tense all the time, even when I try to relax. My heart skips beats, or I think it's going to jump out of my chest. I have a constant stomachache. I need to pee all the time. If only the doctor could find a diagnosis. I have a lot of reasons to be tense. My father had a heart attack last year, and, although his cardiologist says he's doing well, I worry that he will have another one. I go over to Dad's house every day to check on him, and I call him several times a day. He gets annoyed and tells me he's okay, but I have to check to make sure. And then there's my job. Supposedly, the company is in good shape, but I worry constantly about being laid off. If that happened, I don't know what I'd do. My wife probably wouldn't put up with my being unemployed. She'd probably leave me. I worry she'll leave me just because I'm tense. Lately, I just can't stand to go out with her. The noise and bustle of stores and

(continued)

restaurants make me feel worse. Sometimes, I get dizzy and think I'm going to faint right on the street. I feel better when I'm home. But she doesn't want to stay home all the time. I don't know what I'll do if she leaves me.

Harry is experiencing four types of symptoms that make up **anxiety** (see Table 7.1). First, he has *physiological*, or *somatic*, *symptoms*, including muscle tension, heart palpitations, stomach pain, and the need to urinate. Second, he has *emotional symptoms*—primarily a sense of fearfulness and watchfulness. Third, he has *cognitive symptoms*, including unrealistic worries that something bad is happening (that his father is ill) or is about to happen (that he will lose his job). Finally, he has *behavioral symptoms*—he avoids situations because of his fears.

The physiological and behavioral symptoms listed in Table 7.1 are similar to those those of the *fight-or-flight response*, which we discussed in Chapter 6. In addition, Harry is experiencing the emotion of fear. These physiological, behavioral, and emotional symptoms can occur whether we are facing a poisonous snake or a midterm exam.

We can draw several distinctions between an adaptive response to a threat, which we will refer to as *adaptive fear*, and a *maladaptive anxiety* response, although these distinctions are often not sharp:

- In adaptive fear, people's concerns are realistic, given the circumstances, but, in maladaptive anxiety, their concerns are *unrealistic*. What they are anxious about cannot hurt them or is very unlikely to come about. For example, people having a panic attack may fear they will suddenly keel over and die, although this is highly unlikely.

- In adaptive fear, the amount of fear people experience is in proportion to the reality of the threat, but, in maladaptive anxiety, the amount of fear experienced is *out of proportion* to the harm the threat could cause. For example, a person with a social phobia may become absolutely panicked over the thought that she could say something that would embarrass her if she were called on in class, so she therefore avoids going to class at all.

- In adaptive fear, people's fear response subsides when the threat ends, but, in maladaptive anxiety, people's concern is *persistent* when a threat passes, and they may have a great deal of *anticipatory anxiety* about the future. For example, the man previously quoted continues to worry about his father's health after his heart attack, even though his father now seems healthy.

Anxiety is a prominent feature in many psychological disorders. For example, the majority of people with serious depression also report bouts of anxiety (Kessler et al., 1994; Lewinsohn et al., 1997). People with schizophrenia often feel anxious when

TABLE 7.1 Symptoms of Anxiety

Somatic	Emotional	Cognitive	Behavioral
Goosebumps	Sense of dread	Anticipation of harm	Escape
Tense muscles	Terror	Exaggeration of danger	Avoidance
Increased heart rate	Restlessness	Problems in concentrating	Aggression
Accelerated respiration	Irritability	Hypervigilance	Freezing
Deepened respiration		Worried, ruminative thinking	Decreased appetitive responding
Spleen contraction		Fear of losing control	Increased aversive responding
Dilated peripheral blood vessels		Fear of dying	
Widened bronchioles		Sense of unreality	
Dilated pupils			
Increased perspiration			
Adrenaline secretion			
Inhibited stomach acid			
Decreased salivation			
Bladder relaxation			

they believe they are slipping into a new episode of psychosis. Many people who abuse alcohol and other drugs do so to dampen anxious symptoms. In addition, the anxiety disorders are highly comorbid with each other, meaning that they co-occur (Craske & Waters, 2005), so people who have one of the anxiety disorders appear to be at increased risk for another.

Freud and many other early theorists believed that anxiety was the underlying cause of most forms of psychopathology. He used the term **neurosis** to refer to disorders in which the anxiety aroused by unconscious conflicts could not be quelled or channeled by defense mechanisms. This anxiety could be experienced more or less directly as conscious symptoms of anxiety. It could also take a number of maladaptive forms, such as depression or hypocondriasis (unrealistic worry about one's health).

The DSM no longer uses the term *neurosis*. Instead, it classifies disorders in which the predominant symptoms are anxiety as anxiety disorders. Depression, hypocondriasis, and other disorders are classified separately, and it is no longer assumed that anxiety underlies these disorders.

Research suggests that some people do have a general tendency toward anxiety from a very early age (Biederman et al., 1993). This tendency is sometimes referred to as neuroticism (Eysenck, 1967), negative affectivity (Watson & Clark, 1984), or behavioral inhibition (Gray, 1987). Children and adults who have high levels of neuroticism, negative affectivity, or behavioral inhibition become anxious or depressed easily in response to stressors, and they may chronically carry a low level of anxiety. High levels of these characteristics in childhood have been shown to predict several of the anxiety disorders in adulthood (see Craske & Waters, 2005).

Children who are neurotic or behaviorally inhibited may not develop a full-blown anxiety disorder unless they also experience parenting that exacerbates their anxious tendencies rather than quells them (Craske & Waters, 2005; Neal & Edelmann, 2003). The parents of anxious children tend to be overprotective, controlling, and intrusive (Hudson & Rapee, 2001; Siqueland, Kendall, & Steinberg, 1996). Anxious children perceive their parents as being less accepting of them, compared with nonanxious children (Siqueland et al., 1996). Parents may be overinvolved and controlling with their anxious children in an attempt to prevent the children's distress, but this behavior promotes their children's perceptions that the world is a dangerous place over which they have no control (Craske & Waters, 2005).

In addition, the parents of anxious children tend to be anxious themselves. Anxious mothers

Fear is adaptive in truly dangerous situations.

interacting with their children tend to catastrophize and criticize more, are less likely to grant autonomy, and display less warmth than nonanxious mothers (e.g., Whaley, Pinto, & Sigman, 1999). In turn, these parenting behaviors foster anxiety in their children. Thus, the interactions between anxious parents and anxious children may be reciprocal, feeding the anxiety of both.

In this chapter, we focus on disorders classified in the DSM-IV-TR as anxiety disorders. We begin with a discussion of panic, which can be a part of many of the anxiety disorders or, when frequent, can be a disorder in itself. We then discuss agoraphobia, which usually develops in response to a history of panic attacks, and then simple phobias and social phobias. We discuss generalized anxiety disorder (GAD), which is characterized not by acute panic attacks but by chronic, diffuse anxiety. Finally, we discuss obsessive-compulsive disorder, which is categorized as an anxiety disorder but has some intriguing features that distinguish it from the other anxiety disorders. (Posttraumatic stress disorder, which we discussed in Chapter 6 in the context of responses to stress, is also classified as an anxiety disorder.)

PANIC DISORDER

The first time Celia had a panic attack, she was working at McDonald's. It was two days before her 20th birthday. As she was handing a customer a Big Mac, she had the worst experience

(continued)

CASE STUDY

of her life. The earth seemed to open up beneath her. Her heart began to pound, she felt she was smothering, she broke into a sweat, and she was sure she was going to have a heart attack and die. After about twenty minutes of terror, the panic subsided. Trembling, she got in her car, raced home, and barely left the house for the next three months.

Since that time, Celia has had about three attacks a month. She does not know when they are coming. During an attack she feels dread, searing chest pain, smothering and choking, dizziness, and shakiness. She sometimes thinks this is all not real and she is going crazy. She also thinks she is going to die. (Seligman, 1993, p. 61)

Celia is suffering from **panic attacks,** short but intense periods in which she experiences many symptoms of anxiety: heart palpitations, trembling, a feeling of choking, dizziness, intense dread, and so on (see Table 7.2). Celia's panic attacks appear to come out of the blue, in the absence of any environmental triggers. Simply handing a customer a hamburger should not cause such terror. This is one of the baffling characteristics of some panic attacks.

Some people have panic attacks that are triggered by specific situations or events. For example, people with a social phobia may have panic attacks when forced into a social situation. Most commonly, panic attacks are related to certain situations: The person is more likely to have them in certain situations but does not always have them when in those situations. In all cases, however, a panic attack is a terrifying experience, causing a person intense fear or discomfort, the physiological symptoms of anxiety, and the feeling of losing control, going crazy, or dying.

As many as 40 percent of all young adults have occasional panic attacks, especially during times of intense stress, such as exams week (King, Gullone, & Tonge, 1993). Similarly, many people facing a severely traumatic event will have a panic attack. For most of these people, the panic attacks are annoying but isolated events and do not change how they live their lives. When panic attacks become a common occurrence, when the panic attacks are usually not provoked by any particular situation, and when a person begins to worry about having attacks and changes behaviors as a result of this worry, a diagnosis of **panic**

TABLE 7.2 Symptoms of a Panic Attack

These are the common symptoms of a panic attack. Occasional experiences of these symptoms are common. When four or more symptoms occur frequently and interfere with daily living, the individual may be diagnosed with panic disorder.

Heart palpitations

Pounding heartbeat

Numbness or tingling sensations

Chills or hot flashes

Sweating

Trembling or shaking

Sensations of shortness of breath or smothering

Feeling of choking

Chest pain or discomfort

Nausea and upset stomach

Dizziness, unsteadiness, lightheadedness, or faintness

Feelings of unreality or being detached from oneself

Fear of losing control or going crazy

Fear of dying

disorder may be given (American Psychiatric Association [APA], 2000).

Some people with panic disorder have many attacks in a short period of time, such as every day for a week, and then go for weeks or months without having another attack, followed by another period in which the attacks come often. Other people have attacks less frequently but more regularly, such as once every week for months. Between full-blown panic attacks, they might have more minor bouts of panic.

People who have panic disorder often fear that they have life-threatening illnesses, and they are more likely to have a history of serious chronic illness in themselves or family members (Craske & Waters, 2005). However, even after such illnesses are ruled out, people with panic disorder may continue to believe that they are about to die of a heart attack, a seizure, or another physical crisis. They may seek medical care frequently, going from physician to physician to find out what is wrong with them. Another common but erroneous belief among people with panic disorder is that they are going crazy or losing control. Many people with panic disorder feel ashamed of their disorder and try to hide it from others. If the disorder is left untreated, they may become demoralized and depressed.

Each year, about 7 percent of people experience a panic attack, and 3 to 4 percent of people will develop panic disorder at sometime in their lives (Craske & Waters, 2005; Culpepper, 2004). Most people who develop panic disorder usually do so between late adolescence and their mid-thirties. The disorder tends to be chronic once it begins. One study found that 92 percent of patients with panic disorder continued to experience panic attacks for at least one year, and, among those whose symptoms subsided at sometime during the year, 41 percent relapsed into panic attacks within the year (Ehlers, 1995).

Panic disorder can be debilitating in its own right. Many people with panic disorder also suffer from chronic generalized anxiety, depression, and alcohol abuse (Wilson & Hayward, 2005). People with panic disorder who are also depressed or abuse alcohol may be at increased risk for suicide attempts (Hornig & McNally, 1995; McNally, 1994). And one-third to one-half of people diagnosed with panic disorder develop agoraphobia, as we discuss in the section "Phobias."

Theories of Panic Disorder

The biological and psychological theories of panic disorder have been integrated into a model (see Figure 7.1) to clarify how these factors work together to create the disorder (Bouton, Mineka, & Barlow, 2001; Craske & Waters, 2005; White & Barlow, 2002). We will review each of the components of this model.

The Role of Genetics

Panic disorder appears to run in families (Craske & Waters, 2005). A review of family history studies of panic disorder found that about 10 percent of the first-degree relatives of people with panic disorder also have panic disorder. In comparison, only about 2 percent of the first-degree relatives of people without panic disorder have the disorder (Hettema, Neale, & Kendler, 2001). In particular, the children of parents with panic disorder are at increased risk of developing panic disorder (Biederman et al., 2001). Twin studies of panic disorder report a broad range of concordance rates for monozygotic and dizygotic twins, but generally find that 30 to 40 percent of the variation in rates of panic disorder is due to genetics (e.g., Kendler, Neale, Kessler, & Heath, 1993; Scherrer et al., 2000; also see a review by Hettema et al., 2001). These studies suggest that a bio-

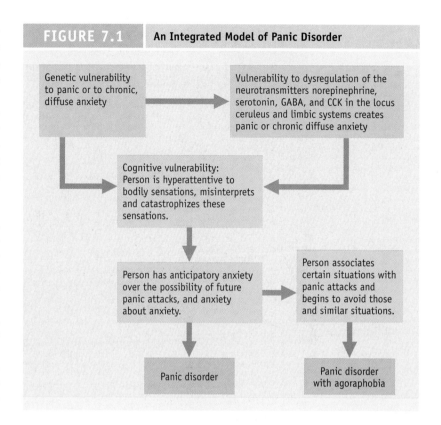

FIGURE 7.1   **An Integrated Model of Panic Disorder**

logical vulnerability to panic disorder, or to a chronic diffuse anxiety that predisposes one to panic disorder, may be transmitted at least in part through genes.

Neurotransmitters and the Brain

Most of the modern neurological theories of panic disorder are the result of the fortuitous discovery by psychiatrist Donald Klein in the 1960s that antidepressant medications reduce panic attacks (Klein, 1964). Because these medications affect the levels of the neurotransmitter **norepinephrine** in the brain, Klein and others reasoned that norepinephrine may be involved in panic disorder. Over the years, evidence has mounted that norepinephrine may be poorly regulated in people with panic disorder, especially in an area of the brain stem called the **locus ceruleus** (see Figure 7.2 on page 224). Electrical stimulation of this brain area in monkeys produces paniclike responses, and the destruction of this area in monkeys renders them unable to experience fear, even in the presence of real threats (Redmond, 1985).

.   Other research suggests that, when people are given drugs that alter the activity of norepinephrine, particularly in the locus ceruleus, this alteration can induce panic attacks (Bourin, Baker, & Bradwejn, 1998; Charney et al., 2000). For example, the drug yohimbine alters norepinephrine, but not other neurotransmitters, in the locus ceruleus.

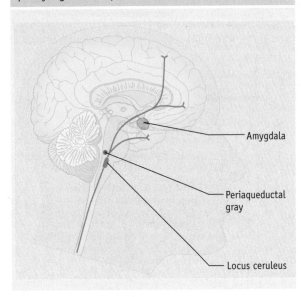

When people with panic disorder take this drug, they typically have a panic attack immediately. On the other hand, other drugs that alter norepinephrine activity have been shown to reduce panic attacks in people who suffer from the disorder (Charney et al., 2000). This, and other evidence, suggests that abnormal activity of norepinephrine, particularly in the locus ceruleus, is involved in human panic attacks.

Other neurotransmitters, particularly serotonin, gamma-aminobutyric acid (GABA), and cholecystokinin (CCK), have been implicated in panic disorders (Bell & Nutt, 1998; Bourin et al., 1998; Charney et al., 2000). Research also has focused on serotonin, following evidence that drugs that alter the functioning of serotonin systems are helpful in reducing panic attacks (Bell & Nutt, 1998). Some theories suggest that panic disorder is due to excessively high levels of serotonin in key areas of the brain, but other theories suggest it is due to deficiencies in serotonin levels (Bell & Nutt, 1998; Bourin et al., 1998). It may be that acute panic attacks have a different association with serotonin than does anticipatory anxiety. Animal studies suggest that increases in serotonin in certain areas of the brain stem (specifically the *periaqueductal gray*) reduce paniclike responses

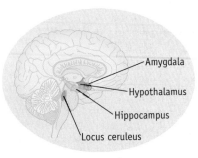

The locus ceruleus and these structures of the limbic system may be involved in panic attacks.

in animals, whereas increases in serotonin in the amygdala increase anxiety, particularly anticipatory anxiety (review Figure 7.2) (Graeff et al., 1996).

Some women with panic disorder report increases in anxiety symptoms during their premenstrual periods and the postpartum period (Brawman-Mintzer & Yonkers, 2001). It may be that the ovarian hormones, particularly progesterone, play a role in vulnerability to panic attacks. Progesterone can affect the activity of both the serotonin and the GABA neurotransmitter systems. Fluctuations in progesterone levels with the menstrual cycle or in the postpartum period thus might lead to imbalances in or dysfunctioning of the serotonin or GABA system, thereby influencing their susceptibility to panic. In addition, increases in progesterone can induce mild, chronic hyperventilation. In women prone to panic attacks, this may be enough to induce full panic attacks.

Gorman and colleagues (Gorman, Papp, & Coplan, 1995) have suggested a "kindling" model of panic disorder, which suggests that the anticipatory anxiety that many people with the disorder have chronically kindles, or sets the stage for, the experience of panic attacks (see Figure 7.3). This link has to do with two parts of the brain, the locus ceruleus and the **limbic system,** which have well-defined pathways between them. Gorman and colleagues argue that, whereas the locus ceruleus is involved in the production of panic attacks, the limbic system is involved in diffuse, anticipatory anxiety. Poor regulation in the locus ceruleus causes panic attacks, which then stimulate and kindle the limbic system, lowering the threshold for the activation of diffuse and chronic anxiety. This anticipatory anxiety, in turn, may increase the likelihood of dysregulation of the locus ceruleus and thereby a new panic attack.

One thing is clear—people with panic disorders can be easily induced into a panic attack through a number of procedures. For example, researchers may have them hyperventilate, inhale a small amount of carbon dioxide, ingest caffeine, breathe into a paper bag, or take infusions of sodium lactate, a substance that resembles the lactate produced by the body during exercise (Craske & Barlow, 2001; McNally, 1999b). In contrast, people without a history of panic attacks may experience some physical discomfort while doing these activities but rarely experience a full panic attack (see Figure 7.4).

What these panic-inducing procedures may have in common is that they initiate the physiological changes of the fight-or-flight response. People who develop panic disorder appear to have a poorly regulated fight-or-flight response, perhaps due to poor regulation of norepinephrine or serotonin in the brain circuits that regulate this response (Gorman et al., 1986; Margraf, 1993). The fight-or-flight response can be initiated without the provocation of a fear stimulus. Once the fight-or-flight response gets going, it operates out of control.

The Cognitive Model

Although many people who develop panic disorder may have a biological vulnerability to this disorder, psychological factors also appear to play a heavy role in determining who will develop the disorder. Cognitive theorists argue that people prone to panic attacks tend to (1) pay very close attention to their bodily sensations, (2) misinterpret bodily sensations in a negative way, and (3) engage in snowballing catastrophic thinking, exaggerating their symptoms and the consequences of the symptoms (Beck & Emery, 1985; Clark, 1988; Craske & Barlow, 2001). For example, when a person prone to panic disorder feels a bit dizzy because she has stood up too quickly, she might think, "I'm really dizzy. I think I'm going to faint. Maybe I'm having a seizure. Oh God, what's happening?" This kind of thinking increases the subjective sense of anxiety and sympathetic nervous system activity. These feelings then are interpreted catastrophically, and the person is on her way into a full panic attack. Between full panic attacks, the person is hypervigilant for any bodily sensations. She worries about her health generally and about having more panic attacks specifically. This constant arousal makes it more likely that she will have more panic attacks.

The belief that bodily symptoms have harmful consequences has been labeled **anxiety sensitivity** (McNally, 1999a). Several studies have shown that

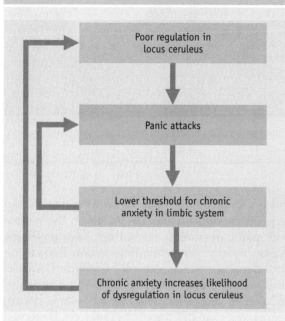

FIGURE 7.3 **The Kindling Model of Panic Disorder.** This model suggests that poor regulation in the locus ceruleus initiates panic attacks, lowering the threshold for chronic anxiety in the limbic system. This chronic anxiety then increases the likelihood of dysregulation in the locus ceruleus, inducing more frequent panic attacks.

FIGURE 7.4 **Panic Attacks of Patients and Controls.** People with panic disorder are much more likely than people without panic disorder to have a panic attack when made to hyperventilate or inhale small amounts of carbon dioxide in laboratory experiments.

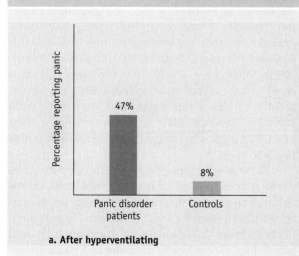

a. After hyperventilating

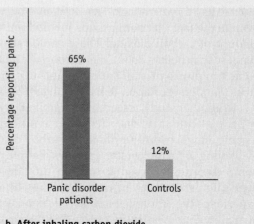

b. After inhaling carbon dioxide

Source: Rapee et al., 1992.

people high in anxiety sensitivity are more likely to have panic disorder already, to have more frequent panic attacks, or to develop panic attacks over time, compared with people low in anxiety sensitivity (Hayward et al., 2000; Pauli et al., 1997; Shipherd, Beck, & Ohtake, 2001; Zoellner, Craske, & Rapee, 1996).

People prone to panic attacks also appear to have increased **interoceptive awareness**—a heightened awareness of bodily cues that a panic attack may soon happen. Slight sensations of arousal or anxiety become conditioned stimuli for more severe symptoms of anxiety or panic (Bouton, et al., 2001). Thus, slight changes in relevant bodily functions that are not necessarily consciously recognized may elicit conditional fear due to previous pairings with panic, thereby accounting for the apparent spontaneity of panic attacks (Craske & Waters, 2005).

Evidence for the role of psychological factors in panic disorder comes from several studies (see Craske & Waters, 2005). In one study, researchers examined the influence of beliefs about the controllability of panic symptoms on the actual experience of panic in the laboratory. Two groups of people with panic disorder were asked to wear breathing masks, which delivered air that was slightly enriched with carbon dioxide. They were warned that inhaling carbon dioxide could induce a panic attack. One group was told that they could not control the amount of carbon dioxide that came through their masks. The other group was told they could control the amount of carbon dioxide that came through their masks by turning a knob. Actually, neither group had any control over the amount of carbon dioxide they inhaled. Eighty percent of the people who believed they had no control experienced a panic attack, but only 20 percent of the people who believed they could control the carbon dioxide had a panic attack. This difference occurred despite the fact that both groups inhaled the same amount of carbon dioxide. These results strongly suggest that beliefs about the uncontrollability of panic symptoms play an important role in panic attacks (Sanderson, Rapee, & Barlow, 1989).

In another study, researchers examined whether people with panic disorder could avoid having a panic attack, even after inhaling carbon dioxide, by having a "safe person" nearby. People with panic disorder exposed to carbon dioxide with their safe person present were much less likely to experience the emotional and physical symptoms of anxiety than were those exposed to carbon dioxide without their safe person present. Indeed, those who had their safe person with them did not experience significantly more anxiety than a con-

People prone to panic attacks may seek comfort and security in others.

trol group of people who were not prone to any type of anxiety disorder. In addition, the people with panic disorder who did not have their safe person nearby when inhaling carbon dioxide reported many more catastrophic cognitions, such as "I'm losing control" and "I'm having a heart attack," than did those who did have their person nearby and than did the control subjects. It seemed that having the safe person nearby reduced the tendency to interpret the bodily changes they were experiencing as dangerous (Carter et al., 1995).

The Integrated Model

As shown in Figure 7.5, the biological and cognitive theories of panic disorder have been integrated to create a vulnerability-stress model of this disorder (Craske & Barlow, 2001; Craske & Waters, 2005). Many people who develop panic disorder seem to have a biological vulnerability to a hypersensitive fight-or-flight response. With just a mild stimulus, these people's hearts begin to race, their breathing begins to become rapid, and their palms begin to sweat.

These people typically do not develop frequent panic attacks or a panic disorder, however, unless they also engage in catastrophizing cognitions about their physiological symptoms. These cognitions increase the intensity of their initially mild physiological systems to the point of a panic attack. They also cause them to become hypervigilant for signs of another panic attack, which puts them con-

FIGURE 7.5 | **The Vulnerability-Stress Model of Panic Disorder.** The vulnerability-stress model of panic disorder suggests that a biological vulnerability to a hypersensitive fight-or-flight response interacts with the tendency to engage in catastrophizing cognitions to create panic attacks and panic disorder.

Biological vulnerability to hypersensitive fight-or-flight response

X

Tendency to engage in catastrophizing cognitions about physiological symptoms

Panic attacks and hypervigilance for signs of panic

TABLE 7.3 | Concept Overview

Treatments for Panic Disorder

A number of biological treatments and one psychological treatment help people with panic disorder.

Treatment	How It Works
Tricyclic antidepressants	Increase levels of norepinephrine and a number of other neurotransmitters
Selective serotonin reuptake inhibitors	Increase levels of serotonin
Benzodiazepines	Suppress the central nervous system and influence functioning in the GABA, norepinephrine, and serotonin neurotransmitter systems
Cognitive-behavioral therapy	Teaches clients ways to reduce anxiety symptoms, to reinterpret these symptoms in a more positive way; systematic desensitization used to expose clients gradually to feared situations as they use new skills to quell anxiety symptoms

stantly at a mild to moderate level of anxiety. This anxiety level increases the probability that they will become panicked again, and the cycle continues. As we will discuss in more detail later, some people then begin to associate certain places or situations with symptoms of anxiety and panic. If they then avoid those situations, and generalize to a wide range of situations, they may also develop agoraphobia, which we will discuss shortly.

Treatments for Panic Disorder

Both biological and psychological treatments have been developed for panic disorder (see the Concept Overview in Table 7.3). Some of the most effective drugs for the treatment of panic disorder are classified as antidepressant drugs. These include the tricyclic antidepressants and selective serotonin reuptake inhibitors. In addition, the benzodiazepines, which are antianxiety drugs, help some people. Antidepressant drugs and benzodiazepines quell the immediate symptoms of panic disorder, but most people relapse if they discontinue the drugs. Relapse rates can be greatly diminished, however, if cognitive-behavioral therapies are combined with the benzodiazepines or antidepressants (Doyle & Pollack, 2004).

Tricyclic Antidepressants

The **tricyclic antidepressants,** such as imipramine, can reduce panic attacks in the majority of patients (Doyle & Pollack, 2004). Recall that one of the neurotransmitters that may be involved in panic disorder is norepinephrine. The tricyclic antidepressants are thought to improve the functioning of the norepinephrine system, and this may be why they are effective in treating panic. These drugs also may affect the levels of a number of other neurotransmitters, including serotonin, thereby affecting anxiety levels.

The disadvantages of the tricyclic antidepressants are their side effects and the relapse rate once patients discontinue the drugs. Possible side effects include blurred vision, dry mouth, difficulty urinating, constipation, weight gain, and sexual dysfunction.

Selective Serotonin Reuptake Inhibitors

Another type of drug used to treat people with panic disorder is the **selective serotonin reuptake inhibitors (SSRIs).** Some commonly used SSRIs include Paxil, Prozac, Zoloft, and Celexa. These drugs increase the functional levels of the neurotransmitter serotonin in the brain. The possible side effects of these drugs include gastrointestinal upset and irritability, initial feelings of agitation, insomnia, drowsiness, tremor, and sexual dysfunction. Studies suggest that the SSRIs are more effective than placebo and about as effective as the tricyclic antidepressants in reducing acute anxiety symptoms (Culpepper, 2004; Doyle & Pollack, 2004).

Benzodiazepines

The third type of drugs used to treat panic disorder is the **benzodiazepines,** which suppress the central nervous system and influence functioning in the GABA, norepinephrine, and serotonin neurotransmitter systems. The benzodiazepines approved to treat panic are alprazolam and clonazepam. These drugs work quickly to reduce panic attacks and general symptoms of anxiety in most people with panic disorder (Culpepper, 2004).

Unfortunately, the benzodiazepines have three major disadvantages (Chouinard, 2004). First, they are physically and psychologically addictive. People build up a tolerance to these drugs, so that they need increasing dosages of the drug to get a positive effect. In turn, when they stop using the drug, they experience difficult withdrawal symptoms, including irritability, tremors, insomnia, anxiety, tingling sensations, and, more rarely, seizures and paranoia. These withdrawal symptoms can occur even if people are tapered off the drug gradually.

The second major disadvantage of benzodiazepines is that they can interfere with cognitive and motor functioning. People's ability to drive or to avoid accidents is impaired, and their performance on the job, at school, and in the home suffers. These impairments can be especially severe if the benzodiazepines are combined with alcohol.

The third major disadvantage of the benzodiazepines is that about half of the patients begin having panic attacks again shortly after discontinuing treatment with these drugs, and 90 percent of the patients eventually relapse into panic disorder after being taken off these drugs (Fyer et al., 1987; Spiegel, 1998).

Cognitive-Behavioral Therapy

Cognitive-behavioral therapy (CBT) for all the anxiety disorders, including panic disorder, involves getting clients to confront the situations or thoughts that arouse anxiety in them. Confrontation seems to help in two ways: Irrational thoughts about these situations can be challenged and changed, and anxious behaviors can be extinguished.

Cognitive-behavioral therapy appears to be at least as effective in eliminating panic disorder as drug therapies, and it is more effective in preventing relapse following treatment (Barlow et al., 2000; Clark et al., 1999; Kenardy et al., 2003; Telch et al., 1993). There are a number of components to cognitive-behavioral interventions.

First, clients are taught relaxation and breathing exercises, such as those described in *Taking Psychology Personally: Relaxation Exercises.* These exercises are useful in therapy for anxiety disorders because they give clients some control over their symptoms, which then permits them to engage in the other components of the therapy.

Second, the clinician guides clients in identifying the catastrophizing cognitions they have about changes in bodily sensations. Clients may do this by keeping diaries of the thoughts they have about their bodies on days between therapy sessions, particularly when they begin to feel they are going to panic. Figure 7.6 shows the entries in one man's panic thoughts diary. He noted that he had had mild symptoms of panic while in his office at work but more severe symptoms while riding the subway home. In both situations, he had had thoughts about feeling trapped and suffocating and had thought he was going to faint.

Many clients need to experience panic symptoms in the presence of their therapist before they can begin to identify their catastrophizing cognitions. They are too overwhelmed by their symptoms when they are having them outside the therapy office to pay attention to their thoughts. For this reason, the therapist may try to induce panic symptoms in clients during therapy sessions by having them exercise to elevate their heart rates, spin to get dizzy, or put their heads between their knees and then stand up quickly to get lightheaded (due to sudden changes in blood pressure). None of these activities is dangerous, but all are likely to produce the kinds of symptoms that clients catastrophize. As clients are experiencing these symptoms and their catastrophizing cognitions, the therapist helps them collect these thoughts.

Third, clients practice using their relaxation and breathing exercises while experiencing panic symptoms in the therapy session. If the panic attacks occur during sessions, the therapist talks clients through them, coaching them in the use of relaxation and breathing skills, suggesting ways of improving their skills, and noting successes clients have in using these skills to stop the attacks.

Fourth, the therapist challenges clients' catastrophizing thoughts about their bodily sensations and teaches them to challenge their thoughts for themselves, using the cognitive techniques described in Chapter 5. The therapist might help clients reinterpret bodily sensations accurately. For example, the client whose thoughts are illustrated in Figure 7.6 frequently felt he was choking. His therapist could explore whether his choking sensation might be due to the stuffiness of a small office or a subway on a warm summer day. If he interprets the increase in his heart rate as a heart attack, the therapist might have him collect evidence from his physician that he is in perfect cardiac health.

FIGURE 7.6   **A Panic Thoughts Diary.** This man recorded the thoughts he had had during panic attacks and then worked on these thoughts in cognitive therapy.

SITUATION	SYMPTOMS AND SEVERITY	THOUGHTS
Office at work	Choking (mild)	Oh, I can't have an attack
	Dizziness (mild)	here. People will see me
	Heart racing (mild)	and I might get fired. I'm
		suffocating! I'm going to
		faint.
Riding subway home	Sweating (severe)	I can't stand this! I've got to
	Choking (severe)	get out of here. I'm going to
	Shaking (severe)	choke to death. I'm trapped.
	Heart racing (severe)	I'm going to faint!
	Dizziness (severe)	
At home	Sweating (mild)	I can't believe I made it
	Heart still racing	home.
	(moderate)	
	A little faintness	

The therapist and client might also explore the client's expectations that he is sure to die of a heart attack because a relative of his did. If the therapist induces panic symptoms in the client during a therapy session, and the client is able to reduce these symptoms with relaxation or breathing skills, the therapist will use this success to challenge the client's belief that there is nothing that can be done to control the panic symptoms once they begin.

Fifth, the therapist uses **systematic desensitization therapy** to expose the client gradually to the situations they most fear while helping them maintain control over their panic symptoms. The client and therapist compose a list of panic-inducing situations, from most threatening to least threatening. Then, after learning relaxation and breathing skills and perhaps gaining some control over panic symptoms induced during therapy sessions, the client begins to expose him- or herself to the panic-inducing situations, beginning with the least threatening. The therapist may accompany the client on trips to the panic-inducing situations, coaching the client in the use of relaxation and breathing skills and skills in challenging catastrophic cognitions that arise in these situations. The following is an example of an interchange between a therapist and a client as they ride together in the client's car.

VOICES

Client: I really don't think we should be doing this. I might have a panic attack while I'm driving. I wouldn't want to be responsible for an accident while you're in the car.

Therapist: Do you think I would have gotten in the car if I thought that it was likely you would have a panic attack and wreck the car?

Client: No, probably not, but I'm really scared.

Therapist: Yes, I understand. Have you ever had a car wreck?

Client: No, I just always worry about one.

Therapist: Remember, our worries are not reality. Tell me what else is going through your mind.

Client: I feel like my chest is about to cave in. I'm having trouble breathing. Oh no, here I go.

Therapist: Okay, let's begin using some of your exercises. Try counting backward from one hundred by sevens. Breathe in deeply the

(continued)

Taking Psychology Personally

Relaxation Exercises

Therapists often teach clients with anxiety disorders to use relaxation exercises to quell their anxiety. These exercises can also be used to combat the everyday anxiety and tension associated with anger. Following are a few exercises that you can use when you feel tense or anxious (Rimm & Masters, 1979; Schafer, 1992).

Six-Second Quieting Response

This is a simple breathing technique that you can use very quickly (it takes only six seconds) and in almost any situation to relax when you feel anxious or angry. (1) Draw a long, deep breath. (2) Hold it for two or three seconds. (3) Exhale slowly and completely. (4) As you exhale, let your jaw and shoulders drop. Feel relaxation flow into your arms and hands.

Quick Head, Neck, and Shoulder Relaxers

The remainder of the exercises described involve tensing or stretching certain muscles. (If you have had a significant injury, such as whiplash or an injured back, you should not try these exercises without first consulting your physician or physical therapist.)

Some of the muscles that most commonly tense up when we are anxious or angry are the neck and shoulder muscles. A quick way to release some of this tension is first to tighten the neck and shoulder muscles as much as possible and then hold this tension for 5 to 10 seconds. Then completely release the muscles. Repeat this exercise a number of times, focusing on the contrast between the tension and the relaxation.

You can also release some neck and shoulder tension by gently rotating your shoulders, first forward and then backward. You can also gently rotate your head from side to side and from front to back in a circular motion. Then repeat the movements in the opposite direction. Continue this exercise a number of times until you feel more relaxed. Perform this exercise very slowly and gently to avoid straining your neck muscles.

The muscles on the forehead are also tensed when you are anxious or angry, and your teeth may be clenched. To relax your forehead, lift your eyebrows gently and release lines of tension or fatigue. Then relax your forehead as you use the six-second quieting response.

Check to see if your teeth are clenched and, if so, relax your jaw while breathing deeply and slowly.

Progressive Muscle Relaxation

Progressive muscle relaxation is a set of techniques for successively tensing and then relaxing voluntary muscles in an orderly sequence until all the muscles are relaxed. Before beginning this exercise, you should get as comfortable as possible, sitting down, with any tight clothing loosened. You might also want to begin by using the six-second quieting response to start you down the path to relaxation.

Go through each of the following steps in the order given. Spend 10 seconds tensing each muscle group, then at least 10 to 15 seconds relaxing. Repeat the 10 seconds of tensing that muscle group, followed by another 10 to 15 seconds of relaxation. During the relaxation period, focus on the positive sensations of relaxation and try not to worry about anything else. If you feel that muscle group has relaxed sufficiently, move on to the next one. As you progress through the muscle groups, concentrate hard on tensing only the muscle group you are working on in that step. Try not to let any of the other muscle groups, particularly the ones you have already tensed and relaxed, become tense again (Rimm & Masters, 1979):

- *Hands*. Tense your fists and then relax them. Extend your fingers as far as possible and then relax them.
- *Biceps and triceps*. Tense your biceps and then relax. Tense your triceps and then relax.
- *Shoulders*. Pull your shoulders back and then relax. Push your shoulders forward and then relax.
- *Neck*. Slowly roll your head on your neck's axis three or four times in one direction, then in the opposite direction.
- *Mouth*. Open your mouth as widely as possible and then relax. Purse your lips in an exaggerated pout and then relax.
- *Tongue*. With your mouth open, extend your tongue as far as possible and then relax. Next bring your tongue back into your throat as far as possible and then relax. Next dig your tongue into the roof of your mouth as hard as possible and then relax. Finally, dig your tongue into the floor of your mouth as hard as possible and then relax.
- *Eyes and forehead*. Close your eyes and imagine you are looking at something pleasant far away. Focus your eyes so that you can see and enjoy the distant object. Continue this for about one minute.
- *Breathing*. Take as deep a breath as possible and then relax.
- *Back*. With your shoulders resting against a chair, push the trunk of your body forward so as to arch your entire back

Taking Psychology Personally (*continued*)

and then relax. Do this very slowly; if you experience any pain, relax immediately and do not repeat this exercise.

- *Midsection.* Raise your midsection slightly by tensing your buttocks and then relax. Lower your midsection slightly by digging your buttocks into the seat of your chair and then relax.

- *Thighs.* Extend and raise your legs about 6 inches off the floor, trying not to tense your stomach muscles, and then relax. Dig your heels or the backs of your feet into the floor and then relax.

- *Stomach.* Pull your stomach in as hard as possible and then relax. Extend your stomach out as much as possible and then relax.

- *Calves and feet.* Support your legs, bend your feet so that your toes are pointed toward your head, and then relax. Next bend your feet in the opposite direction and then relax. If your muscles cramp during this exercise, relax them and shake them loose.

- *Toes.* With your legs supported and your feet relaxed, dig your toes into the bottoms of your shoes and then relax. Then bend your toes in the opposite direction until they dig into the tops of your shoes and then relax.

- *Breathing.* Breathe slowly and deeply for two to three minutes. Each time you exhale, say the word *calm* to yourself.

---

first count, then out with the second count, and so on.

Client: Okay, I'll try. [Breathes in] One hundred. [Breathes out] Ninety-three. [Breathes in] Eighty-six. [Breathes out]

Therapist: How are you feeling now?

Client: Better. I'm not as panicked. Oh, my gosh, here comes a bridge. I hate bridges.

Therapist: What do you hate about bridges?

Client: If I ever had an accident on a bridge, I'd be more likely to die.

Therapist: What do you think is the likelihood that you are going to have an accident on a bridge?

Client: Well, sometimes it feels like it's 100 percent!

Therapist: But what do you think it really is?

Client: Probably very low. Hey, we're already over that bridge!

Therapist: Okay, there's another bridge coming up in a couple of miles. I want you to decide what strategies you're going to use to help yourself feel less panicked as we approach the bridge.

A large-scale, multisite study compared cognitive-behavioral therapy (CBT) with tricyclic antidepressants in the treatment of 312 people

with panic disorder and found the two treatments to be equally effective in eliminating panic symptoms (Barlow et al., 2000). Several other studies have found that 85 to 90 percent of panic disorder patients treated with CBT experience complete relief from their panic attacks within 12 weeks (Addis et al., 2004; Barlow et al., 1989; Clark et al., 1994; Klosko et al., 1990; Westen & Morrison, 2001). Follow-up studies of patients receiving CBT found that nearly 90 percent were classified as panic-free two years after the treatment (Craske, Brown, & Barlow, 1991; Fava et al., 2001; Margraf et al., 1993; Westen & Morrison, 2001). Cognitive-behavioral therapy appears to be considerably better than antidepressants at preventing relapse after treatment ends (Barlow et al., 2000), probably because this therapy teaches people strategies to prevent the recurrence of panic symptoms.

SUMMING UP

- Panic disorder is characterized by sudden bursts of anxiety symptoms, a sense of loss of control or unreality, and the sense that one is dying.

- Several neurotransmitters, including norepinephrine, serotonin, GABA, and CCK, have been implicated in panic disorder.

- Panic disorder runs in families, and twin studies suggest that genetics plays a role.

- The cognitive model suggests that people with panic disorder are hypersensitive to bodily symptoms and tend to catastrophize these symptoms.

- The vulnerability-stress model suggests that people who develop panic disorder are born with a biological predisposition to an overactive fight-or-flight response, but they don't develop the disorder unless they also tend to catastrophize their bodily symptoms.

- Tricyclic antidepressants, selective serotonin reuptake inhibitors, and benzodiazepines can be helpful in reducing symptoms, but these symptoms tend to recur once the drugs are discontinued.

- Cognitive-behavioral therapy has proven as useful as antidepressants in reducing panic symptoms and more useful in preventing relapse in panic disorder.

PHOBIAS

People can develop phobias of many things. In this section, we consider three groups of phobias: agoraphobia, specific phobias about objects or situations, and social phobia about social situations in particular (see Figure 7.7).

Agoraphobia

The term *agoraphobia* comes from the Greek for "fear of the marketplace." People with **agoraphobia** fear crowded, bustling places, such as the marketplace or, in our times, the shopping mall. They also fear enclosed spaces, such as buses, subways, and elevators. Also, they fear wide open spaces, such as open fields, particularly if they are alone. In general, people with agoraphobia fear any places where they might have trouble escaping or getting help in an emergency. The emergency that they often fear is a panic attack. Thus, the person with agoraphobia thinks, "If I have a panic attack while I'm in this mall [or on this airplane, or in this movie theater, or on this deserted beach], it will be hard for me to get away quickly or to find help." People with agoraphobia also often fear that they will embarrass themselves if others see their symptoms of panic or their frantic efforts to escape during a panic attack. Actually, other people can rarely tell when a person is having a panic attack.

Agoraphobia can occur in people who do not have panic attacks, but most people who seek treatment for agoraphobia do experience full-blown panic attacks, more moderate panic attacks, or severe social phobia, in which they experience panic-

FIGURE 7.7   **Phobic Disorders.** These are the phobic disorders recognized in the DSM-IV-TR.

Phobic Disorder	Description	Example
Agoraphobia	Fear of places where help might not be available in case of emergency	Person becomes housebound because anyplace other than the person's home arouses extreme anxiety symptoms.
Specific phobias	Fear of specific objects, places, or situations	
Animal type	Specific animals or insects	Person has extreme fear of dogs, cats, or spiders.
Natural environment type	Events or situations in the natural environment	Person has extreme fear of storms, heights, or water.
Situational type	Public transportation, tunnels, bridges, elevators, flying, driving	Person becomes extremely claustrophobic in elevators.
Blood-injection-injury type	Blood, injury, injections	Person panics when viewing a child's scraped knee.
Social phobia	Fear of being judged or embarrassed by others	Person avoids all social situations and becomes a recluse for fear of encountering others' judgment.

like symptoms in social situations (Craske & Barlow, 2001). In most cases, agoraphobia begins within one year after a person begins experiencing frequent anxiety symptoms.

The lives of people with agoraphobia can be terribly disrupted, even brought to a complete halt. Think how difficult it would be to carry on daily life if you could not ride in a car, a bus, a train, or an airplane; if you could not go into a store; or if you could not stand being in any kind of crowd. Lia's case illustrates how debilitating agoraphobia can be:

People with agoraphobia may become housebound.

CASE STUDY

Lia was a graduate student who was conducting research on children's styles of learning in the classroom. For her research, Lia needed to travel to local elementary schools and observe children in classrooms for a couple of hours each day. Lia had spent months developing good relationships with the schools, teachers, and children who were participating in her research. Everyone was excited about the potential for Lia's research to improve classroom teaching. It seemed that Lia was on her way toward a promising career as an educational researcher.

The problem was that Lia could not leave her apartment. Over the past year, she had become terrified at the idea of driving her car, convinced that she would have a fatal car accident. She had tried to ride the public bus instead, but, when she got onto the bus, she felt as if she was choking, and she was so dizzy she almost missed her stop, so she began walking everywhere she went. The elementary schools participating in her research were too far away for her to walk to them, however. Moreover, Lia was becoming afraid even when she stepped out of her apartment. When she walked onto her street, it seemed to open into a big chasm. The thought of being confined in a small elementary school classroom for two hours was just intolerable.

Lia was beginning to believe that she was going to have to abandon her research and her degree. She could not see any way to finish her work. Even if she did get her degree, how could she possibly hold a job if she could not even leave her apartment?

Like Lia, people with agoraphobia often get to the point at which they will not leave their own homes. Sometimes, they can venture out with a close family member who makes them feel safe. However, family members and friends often have trouble understanding their anxiety and may not be willing to chaperone them everywhere they go. People with agoraphobia may force themselves to enter situations that frighten them, as Lia had been forcing herself to travel for her research. The persistent and intense anxiety they experience in these situations can be miserable, however, and, like Lia, many people give up and remain confined to their homes. Some people with this disorder turn to alcohol and other substances to dampen these anxiety symptoms.

Agoraphobia strikes people in their youth. In one large study, more than 70 percent of the people who developed agoraphobia did so before the age of 25, and 50 percent developed the disorder before the age of 15 (Bourden et al., 1988).

Specific Phobias

Agoraphobia is different from many people's conception of a phobia, because people with agoraphobia fear such a wide variety of situations. In contrast, the **specific phobias** conform more to popular conceptions of phobia. Most specific phobias fall into one of four categories (APA, 2000): animal type, natural environment type, situational type, and blood-injection-injury type. When people with these phobias encounter their feared objects or situations, their anxiety is immediate and intense, and they may even have full panic attacks. They also become anxious if they believe there is any chance they will encounter their feared objects or situations, and they will go to great lengths to avoid the objects or situations.

Most phobias develop during childhood. Adults with phobias recognize that their anxieties are illogical and unreasonable. Children, however, may not have this insight and just have the anxiety. As many as 1 in 10 people will have a specific phobia at sometime, making it one of the most common disorders (Kessler et al., 1994). Almost 90 percent of people with a specific phobia never seek treatment (Regier et al., 1993).

Animal type phobias are focused on specific animals or insects, such as dogs, cats, snakes, or spiders. A snake phobia appears to be the most common type of animal phobia in the United States (Agras, Sylvester, & Oliveau, 1969). Other animals or insects, such as scorpions, may be more commonly feared in other countries. Many people who come across a feared animal or insect may startle and move away quickly. Most of these people would not be diagnosed with a phobia, however, because they can get through daily life without worrying constantly about encountering a feared animal or insect. People with phobias go to great lengths to avoid the objects of their fears. For example, one woman with a severe spider phobia sprayed powerful insecticide around the perimeter of her apartment (which was in a new, pristine apartment building) once a week to prevent spiders from coming in. The fumes from this insecticide made her physically ill, and her neighbors complained of the smell. However, this woman was so fearful of encountering a spider that she withstood the fumes and her neighbors' complaints, remaining vigilant for any signs of a spider web in her apartment. She refused to go into older buildings, because she believed they were more likely to hold spiders. Since she lived in a city with many old buildings, this meant that she could not enter the homes of many of her friends or establishments where she might want to do business.

Natural environment type phobias are focused on events or situations in the natural environment, such as storms, heights, or water. As with fears of animals or insects, mild to moderate fears of these natural events or situations are ex-

tremely common and, of course, adaptive in that they prevent people from getting into dangerous situations. Again, however, these fears do not usually cause people much inconvenience or concern in their daily lives and thus are not considered phobias. It is only when people begin reorganizing their lives to avoid their feared situations or having severe anxiety attacks when confronted with the situations that a diagnosis of phobia is warranted.

Situational type phobias usually involve a fear of public transportation, tunnels, bridges, elevators, flying, and driving. *Claustrophobia*, the fear of enclosed spaces, is a common situational type phobia. People with situational type phobias believe they might have panic attacks in their phobic situations. Indeed, they often have had panic attacks when forced into those situations. Unlike people with agoraphobia, people with situational type phobias tend to have panic attacks only in the specific situations they fear. Situational type phobias often arise in people between 2 and 7 years of age, but another common period of onset is the mid-twenties.

The final type, **blood-injection-injury type phobias,** was first recognized in the DSM-IV-TR. People with this type of phobia fear seeing blood or an injury:

CASE STUDY

When her son José was born, Irene decided to quit her job and become a full-time mother. She enjoyed José's infancy tremendously. He was a happy baby and had hardly been ill for the first two years of his life. Now that he was a toddler, however, José was beginning to get the usual skinned knees and bumps and bruises that small children do. Irene had always been squeamish about blood, but she thought she could overcome this when it came to caring for her son. The first time José scraped his knee seriously enough for it to bleed, however, Irene became dizzy on seeing it and fainted. José screamed and cried in terror at seeing his mother faint. Fortunately, a neighbor saw what happened and quickly went over to comfort José and to see that Irene was okay. Since then, Irene has fainted three more times on seeing José injured. She has begun to think that she will not be able to care for José by herself any longer.

Fear of heights is a common specific phobia.

Irene's reaction to seeing José's scraped knee illustrates the unusual physiological reaction of people with blood-injection-injury type phobias to their feared objects. Whereas people with one of the other specific phobias typically experience increases in heart rate, blood pressure, and other fight-or-flight physiological changes when confronted with their feared objects or situations, people with a blood-injection-injury type phobia experience significant *drops* in heart rate and blood pressure when confronted with their feared stimuli and are likely to faint. This type of phobia runs more strongly in families than do the other types (Öst, 1992).

Social Phobia

Social phobia is not categorized as a specific phobia because, rather than fearing a specific (often inanimate) object or situation, people with social phobia fear being judged or embarrassing themselves in front of other people. Social phobia also differs from the specific phobias in that it is more likely to severely disrupt a person's daily life (Kessler, 2003). It is easier in most cultures to avoid snakes or spiders than it is to avoid social situations in which one might embarrass oneself. Con-

sider the inner pain that this man with social phobia suffered and the way that he has organized his life to avoid social situations:

CASE STUDY

Malcolm was a computer expert who worked for a large software firm. One of the things he hated to do most was ride the elevator at the building where he worked when other people were on it. He felt that everyone was watching him, commenting silently on his ruffled clothes and noticing every time he moved his body. He held his breath for almost the entire elevator ride, afraid that he might say something or make a sound that would embarrass him. Often, he walked up the eight flights of stairs to his office, rather than take the risk that someone would get on the elevator with him.

Malcolm rarely went anywhere except to work and home. He hated even to go to the grocery store for fear he would run his cart into someone else or say something stupid to

(*continued*)

a grocery clerk. He found a grocery store and several restaurants that allowed customers to send orders for food over the computer to be delivered to their homes. He liked this service, because he could use it to avoid even talking to someone over the phone to place the order.

In the past, Malcolm's job had allowed him to remain quietly in his office all day, without interacting with other people. Recently, however, his company was reorganized, and it took on a number of new projects. Malcolm's supervisor said that everyone in Malcolm's group needed to begin to work together more closely to develop these new products. Malcolm was supposed to make a presentation to his group on some software he was developing, but he called in sick the day of the presentation, because he could not face it. Malcolm was thinking that he had to change jobs and that perhaps he would go into private consulting, so that he could work from his home, rather than having to work with anyone else.

Many people get a little nervous when speaking in front of a group of people or when they must join a group of people already engaged in conversation (see Table 7.4). In one study of college students, 48 percent could be classified as "shy" (Heiser, Turner, & Beidel, 2003). Only 18 percent of these shy students, however, had symptoms qualifying for a diagnosis of social phobia.

People with social phobia, like Malcolm, get more than a little nervous in social situations. They may begin trembling and perspiring, feel confused and dizzy, have heart palpitations, and eventually have a full panic attack. They are sure that others see their nervousness and judge them as inarticulate, weak, stupid, or "crazy." Malcolm avoided speaking in public and having conversations with others for fear of being judged. People with a social phobia may avoid eating or drinking in public, for fear they will make noises when they eat, drop food, or otherwise embarrass themselves. They may avoid writing in public, including signing their names, for fear that others will see their hands tremble. Many with social phobia avoid urinating in public bathrooms for fear of embarrassing themselves.

People with social phobia tend to fall into three groups (Eng et al., 2000). Some people with social phobia fear only public speaking. Others have moderate anxiety about a variety of social situations. Finally, people who have severe fear of many social situations, from speaking in public to having a conversation with another person, are said to have a generalized type of social phobia.

Social phobia is relatively common, with lifetime prevalence rates of about 7 percent across countries (Neal & Edelmann, 2003; Wittchen & Fehm, 2003). Women are somewhat more likely than men to develop this disorder (Lang & Stein, 2001). In addition, one study found that women with social phobia have more severe social fears than men, particularly with regard to performance situations, such as giving a presentation (Turk, Heimberg, & Hope, 2001).

There are two periods in life when social phobia tends to develop—in the early preschool years and in the adolescent years, when many people become excessively self-conscious and concerned about others' opinions of them (Lang & Stein, 2001; Turk et al., 2001). Some people report having had humiliating experiences that triggered their social phobia, but others report having felt extremely uncomfortable in social situations all their lives. Social phobia often co-occurs with mood disorders, other anxiety disorders, and antisocial personality disorder (Neal & Edelmann, 2003; Wittchen & Fehm, 2003). Once it develops, social phobia tends to be a chronic problem if untreated. Most people with a social phobia do not seek treatment for their symptoms (Kessler, 2003).

Theories of Phobias

The phobias have been the battleground for various psychological approaches to abnormality, as

TABLE 7.4	Lifetime Prevalence of Social Fears in a National Survey	
Social Fear	**Percentage of People Saying They Experienced the Fear in Their Lifetimes**
Public speaking	30.2%
Talking in front of a small group	15.2
Talking with others	13.7
Using a toilet away from home	6.6
Writing while someone watches	6.4
Eating or drinking in public	2.7
Any social fear	38.6

Source: Kessler, Stein, & Berglund, 1998, p. 614.

well as the focus of some of the most revolutionary psychological theories developed in the past century. Biological theories have also been proposed. The Concept Overview in Table 7.5 summarizes the theories reviewed in this section.

Psychodynamic Theories

Freud's theory of the development of phobias is one of his most well known. He argued that phobias result when unconscious anxiety is displaced onto a neutral or symbolic object (Freud, 1909). That is, people become phobic of objects not because they have any real fear of the objects but because they have displaced their anxiety over other issues onto the object.

This theory is detailed in a 150-page case history of a little boy named Hans, who had a phobia of horses after seeing a horse fall on the ground and writhe around violently. How did Hans' phobia develop? According to Freud, young boys have a sexual desire for their mothers and jealously hate their fathers, but they fear that their fathers will castrate them in retaliation for this desire. As we

discussed in Chapter 2, this phenomenon is known as the Oedipus complex. In Freud's interpretation, Hans found the anxiety created by this conflict so unbearable that he unconsciously displaced this anxiety onto horses, which somehow symbolized his father for him. Freud's evidence for this formulation came from Hans' answers to a series of leading questions asked by Freud and by Hans' father. After long conversations about horses and what Hans was "really" afraid of, Hans reportedly became less fearful of horses, because, according to Freud, he had gained insight into the true source of his anxiety.

There is little reason to accept Freud's theory of phobias, either in the case of Hans or in general. Hans never provided any spontaneous or direct evidence that his real concerns were Oedipal concerns instead of a fear of horses. In addition, Hans' phobia of horses decreased slowly over time, rather than suddenly in response to an insight. Many children have specific fears that simply fade with time with no intervention. In general, psychodynamic therapies for phobias are not highly effective, suggesting

---

TABLE 7.5   Concept Overview

Theories of Phobias

The psychodynamic, behavioral, biological, and cognitive theories of phobias take very different approaches to explaining these disorders.

Theory	Description	Example
Psychodynamic theories	Phobias result when unconscious anxiety is displaced onto a neutral object.	Little Hans developed a horse phobia, which represented his Oedipal fears of his father.
Behavioral theories	1. Classical conditioning leads to fear of the object when it is paired with a naturally frightening event.	1. A child who falls into a river and cannot swim develops a fear of water.
	2. Avoidance of the object reduces anxiety; thus, it is reinforced through operant conditioning.	2. A person with agoraphobia learns that, by staying in her apartment, panic attacks are less likely, and thus staying in her apartment is reinforced.
	3. Humans are prepared through evolutionary history to develop phobias to objects or situations that were dangerous to our ancient ancestors.	3. Humans develop phobias to spiders and heights more easily than to guns or powerlines.
Cognitive theories (of social phobia)	Social phobia develops in people with excessively high standards for their social performance, who assume others judge them harshly, and who are attentive to signs of social rejection.	A man who believes that he always stammers in conversations and that others think he is stupid as a result might develop a social phobia.
Biological theories	Genetics contribute to risk for phobias, either directly or by creating certain temperaments that are more prone to phobias.	Children with phobias often have relatives with the same phobia, or the children tend to be excessively timid or shy.

that insight into unconscious anxieties is not what is needed in treating phobias.

Behavioral Theories

In contrast to the psychodynamic theories, the behavioral theories have been very successful in explaining phobias. According to these theories, classical conditioning leads to the fear of the phobic object, and operant conditioning helps maintain that fear (Mowrer, 1939). Recall that, in classical conditioning, a previously neutral object (the conditioned stimulus) is paired with an object that naturally elicits a reaction (an unconditioned stimulus that elicits an unconditioned response) until the previously neutral object elicits the same reaction (which is now called the conditioned response). For example, when a tone is paired with an electric shock, the conditioned stimulus is the tone, the electric shock is the unconditioned stimulus, the unconditioned response is anxiety in response to the shock, and the conditioned response is anxiety in response to the tone.

The first application of these theories to phobias came in a series of studies done 80 years ago by a philosopher turned behaviorist, John Watson, and a graduate student named Rosalie Raynor (1920). Their subject in these studies was an 11-month-old boy named Little Albert. One day, Watson and Raynor placed a white rat in front of Little Albert. As Little Albert playfully reached for the white rat, they banged a metal bar loudly just above his head. Naturally, Little Albert was completely startled,

nearly jumped out of his diapers, quickly pulled his hand away from the rat, and then broke down, whimpering. This only encouraged Watson and Raynor to continue their study, however. After several more pairings of the white rat with the loud noise from the metal bar, Little Albert would have nothing to do with the creature—in effect, developing a fear of the white rat. When presented with it, he retreated and showed distress. Little Albert's fear also generalized to other white, furry animals—he would not approach white rabbits, either.

Although by today's standards this experiment with Little Albert would raise serious ethical questions, it laid the groundwork for the behavioral theories of phobias by showing powerfully that a phobia can easily be created through classical conditioning. In the case of Little Albert, the unconditioned stimulus (US) was the loud noise from the banged bar, and the unconditioned response (UR) was his startle response to the loud noise. The conditioned stimulus (CS) was the white rat, and the conditioned response (CR) was the startle and fear response to the white rat (see Figure 7.8). If Little Albert had been subsequently presented with the white rat several times without the bar being banged behind his head, his fear of white rats should have been extinguished, according to what we know about classical conditioning.

Most people who develop a phobia, however, try to avoid being exposed to their feared object. Thus, they avoid the exposure that could extinguish their phobia. In addition, if they are suddenly confronted with their feared object, they experience extreme anxiety and run away as quickly as possible. The running away, or avoidance, is reinforced by the subsequent reduction of their anxiety—a process known as **negative reinforcement.** In this way, behaviors that help maintain the phobia are negatively reinforced through operant conditioning.

For example, Malcolm, the person with social phobia described in the section "Social Phobia," had developed a wide array of avoidant behaviors to prevent him from exposing himself to what he feared most: the possibility of scrutiny by others. He walked up several flights of stairs rather than be trapped in an elevator for a few minutes with another person who might notice something odd about Malcolm's clothes or mannerisms. He paid a great deal of money to have his groceries delivered, rather than risk going to a crowded grocery store, where he might embarrass himself in front of other people. He was even prepared to quit his job to avoid having to make presentations or work closely with others on projects. These avoidant behaviors created much hardship for Malcolm, but

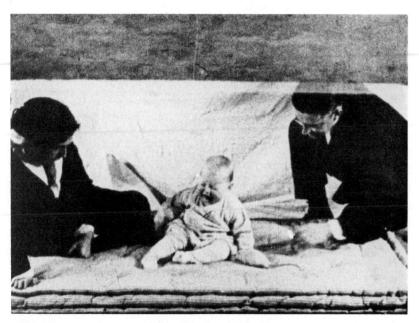

Little Albert, shown in this photo, developed a fear of white rats through classical conditioning.

they reduced his anxiety and therefore were greatly reinforced. Also, as a result of this avoidance, Malcolm never had the opportunity to extinguish his anxiety about social situations.

Behavioral theory also does a good job of explaining why agoraphobia so often develops in people with panic disorder (see Figure 7.9). The fear of panic attacks leads the individual to search for safe people and places that are associated with a low risk for panic attacks. These safe people and places have been referred to as *safety signals*, which we discussed briefly in Chapter 6. According to the *safety signal hypothesis* (Seligman & Binik, 1977), people remember vividly the places in which they have had panic attacks, even if the panic attacks have come on by surprise, with no obvious environmental triggers. They associate these places with their symptoms of panic and may begin to feel these symptoms again if they return to these places. By avoiding these places, they reduce their

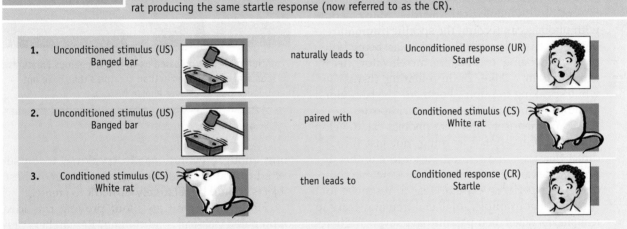

FIGURE 7.8 **The Behavioral Account of Little Albert's Phobia.** The pairing of the banged bar (the US), which naturally leads to a startle response (the UR), and the white rat (the CS) leads eventually to the white rat producing the same startle response (now referred to as the CR).

1. Unconditioned stimulus (US) Banged bar   naturally leads to   Unconditioned response (UR) Startle

2. Unconditioned stimulus (US) Banged bar   paired with   Conditioned stimulus (CS) White rat

3. Conditioned stimulus (CS) White rat   then leads to   Conditioned response (CR) Startle

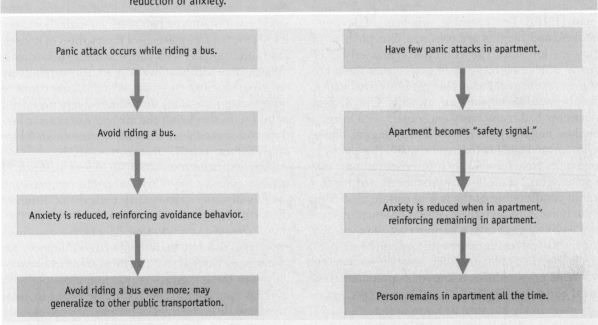

FIGURE 7.9 **How Agoraphobic Behaviors Develop in Panic Disorder.** Behavioral theories argue that agoraphobic behaviors develop when avoiding situations in which panic has often occurred and remaining in situations where panic has occurred less often are reinforced by the reduction of anxiety.

Panic attack occurs while riding a bus.

Avoid riding a bus.

Anxiety is reduced, reinforcing avoidance behavior.

Avoid riding a bus even more; may generalize to other public transportation.

Have few panic attacks in apartment.

Apartment becomes "safety signal."

Anxiety is reduced when in apartment, reinforcing remaining in apartment.

Person remains in apartment all the time.

symptoms; thus, their avoidance behavior is highly reinforced. If a man has a panic attack while sitting in a theater, he may later associate a theater with his panic symptoms and begin to feel anxious whenever he is near the theater. He can reduce his anxiety by avoiding the theater. In addition, other places, such as his own home or a specific room in his home, may become associated with lowered anxiety levels, and being in these places is thus reinforcing. Through classical and operant conditioning, the person's behavior becomes shaped in ways that lead to the development of agoraphobia.

The behavioral theories of phobias are one of the most elegant examples of the application of basic learning principles to the understanding of a mysterious psychological disorder. Many people with phobias can recount the specific traumatic experiences that triggered their phobias: being bitten by a dog, being trapped in an elevator, nearly drowning in a lake, or humiliating themselves while speaking in public. For them, the behavioral accounts of their phobias seem to ring true.

Some theorists argue that phobias can develop through observational learning, not just through direct classical conditioning. According to this theory, people can develop phobias by watching someone else experience extreme fear in response to a situation. For example, small children may learn to fear snakes when their parents have severe fright reactions on seeing snakes (Bandura, 1969; Mineka et al., 1984).

An extension of the behavioral theories of phobias seems to answer an interesting question about phobias: Why do humans develop phobias to some objects or situations but not to others (deSilva, Rachman, & Seligman, 1977; Mineka, 1985; Seligman, 1970)? For example, phobias of spiders, snakes, and heights are common, but phobias of flowers are not. The common characteristic of many phobic objects appears to be that these are things whose avoidance, over evolutionary history, has been advantageous for humans. Our distant ancestors had many nasty encounters with insects, snakes, heights, loud noises, and strangers. Those who learned quickly to fear and avoid these objects or events were more likely to survive and bear offspring. Thus, evolution may have selected for the rapid conditioning of the fear of certain objects or situations. Although these objects or situations are not as likely to cause us harm today, we carry the vestiges of our evolutionary history and are biologically prepared to learn certain associations quickly.

This preparedness is known as **prepared classical conditioning.** In contrast, many objects that are more likely to cause us harm in today's world (such as guns and knives) have not been around

Evolution may have prepared us to fear dangerous creatures, such as snakes, more easily than creatures that have not been dangerous to us over human history.

long enough, evolutionarily speaking, to be selected for rapid conditioning, so phobias of these objects should be relatively difficult to create.

How would you go about proving this idea of prepared classical conditioning? Researchers presented subjects with pictures of objects that theoretically should be evolutionarily selected for conditioning (snakes or spiders) and objects that should not be selected (houses, faces, and flowers) and paired the presentation of these pictures with short but painful electric shocks. The subjects developed anxiety reactions to the pictures of snakes and spiders within one or two pairings with shock, but it took four or five pairings of the pictures of houses, faces, and flowers with shock to create a fear reaction to these pictures. In addition, it was relatively easy to extinguish the subjects' anxiety reactions to houses and faces once the pictures were no longer paired with shock, but the anxiety reactions to spiders and snakes were difficult to extinguish (Hugdahl & Ohman, 1977; Ohman et al., 1976).

As we have seen, the behavioral theories of phobias seem to provide a compelling explanation for this disorder, particularly with the addition of the principles of observational learning and prepared classical conditioning. The behavioral theories have also led to very effective therapies for phobias, as we will see. The most significant problem with these theories is that many people with phobias can identify no traumatic event in their own lives or in the lives of people they are close to that triggered their phobias. Without conditioned stimuli, it is hard to argue that they developed their phobias through classical conditioning or observational learning. Craske and Waters (2005) argue that many individuals who develop phobias have a chronic low-level anxiety or reactivity, which makes them more susceptible to the development of phobias, given even mild aversive experiences.

Cognitive Theories

The cognitive theories of phobias have primarily focused on the development of social phobia (Clark & Wells, 1995; Rapee & Heimberg, 1997; Turk et al., 2001). According to these theories, people with social phobia have excessively high standards for their social performance—for example, believing that they should be liked by everyone they meet and never do anything embarrassing in front of others. Unfortunately, they also tend to focus on what is going wrong in social interactions instead of what is going right, and they evaluate their own behavior extremely harshly. They enter social situations assuming that others will find them boring, peculiar, or unattractive. People with social phobia also show biases in attention, picking up on socially threatening cues (such as a grimace on the face of the person they are speaking to) and then interpreting them in self-defeating ways (Heinrichs & Hofman, 2001). They are exquisitely attuned to their own self-presentation and their internal feelings, and they tend to assume that, if they feel anxious, it is because the social interaction is not going well (Clark & Wells, 1995).

Several studies have supported the claims of the cognitive theories that people with social phobia have biases in attention and in evaluating social situations (see Heinrichs & Hofman, 2001; McNally, 1996; Turk et al., 2001). Where do these biases come from? Adults with social phobia often describe their parents as having been overprotective and controlling but also critical and negative (see Craske & Waters, 2005; Neal & Edelmann, 2003). These are retrospective accounts, however, and could be incorrect. To date, there are no prospective studies of the family environments of people who develop social phobia. In addition, studies have not yet established whether the beliefs and cognitive biases described by the cognitive theories are the causes of social phobia or only the symptoms. Cognitive-behavioral therapies based on these theories, however, can help people with social phobia overcome their avoidant and anxious symptoms.

Biological Theories

The first-degree relatives of people with phobias are three to four times as likely to have a phobia as the first-degree relatives of people without pho-bias, and twin studies suggest that this is due, at least in part, to genetics (Hettema et al., 2001; Merikangas et al., 2003). For example, family history studies of agoraphobia find that 10 to 11 percent of the first-degree relatives of people with this disorder also have the disorder, compared with 3 to 4 percent of the relatives of people without the disorder (Fyer et al., 1995; Noyes et al., 1986).

There is an interesting gender difference in the heritability of agoraphobia. The female relatives of people with this disorder are even more likely than the male relatives to have the disorder (Crowe, 1990). In addition, twin studies of females find evidence for a genetic contribution to agoraphobia (Kendler, Myers, Prescott, & Neale, 2001), whereas twin studies of males do not (Kendler et al., 2001). This evidence suggests that the genetic vulnerability to agoraphobia is sex-linked.

Several researchers suggest that a particular phobia in itself is not strongly heritable but that the general tendency toward anxiety is heritable, leading to a temperament that makes it easier for phobias to be conditioned (Eysenck, 1967; Gray, 1987; Pavlov, 1927). Children who, as toddlers, are behaviorally inhibited—that is, excessively timid and shy—are at higher risk to develop specific phobias and social phobia than are those who are not inhibited (Biederman et al., 2001; Craske & Waters, 2005; Turner, Beidel, & Wolff, 1996). For example, one study found that children who were socially inhibited were four times more likely to develop social phobia in high school than those who were not socially inhibited (Hayward et al., 1998). Again, however, children with a genetic predisposition toward anxiety or who are behaviorally inhibited may not develop social phobia, or a specific phobia, unless the parenting they receive exacerbates their anxiety (Craske & Waters, 2005; Neal & Edelmann, 2003).

Treatments for Phobias

A number of behavioral techniques are used to treat phobias. In addition, some therapists add cognitive techniques and certain drug therapies to their treatment regime for people with phobias (see the Concept Overview in Table 7.6 on page 242).

Behavioral Treatments

The goal of behavior therapies for phobias is to extinguish the fear of the object or situation by exposing the person to the object or situation. The majority of phobias can be cured with these therapies (Christopherson & Mortweet, 2001; Emmelkamp, 1994; Wolpe, 1997). Some studies suggest that just one session of behavior therapy leads to major reductions in phobic behaviors and anxiety (Öst et al., 2001). There are three basic components of behavior

TABLE 7.6 Concept Overview

Treatments for Phobias

A number of treatments have proven useful for phobias.

Treatment	Description	Example
Behavioral treatments	Focus on extinguishing fear by exposing the person to the feared object or situation.	
1. Systematic desensitization therapy	1. It gradually exposes the person to a hierarchy of fears while the person practices techniques to reduce the fear response.	A person with agoraphobia ventures out to the least feared situation (such as the local grocery) first, practicing relaxation, and then gradually ventures to more and more fearful situations.
2. Modeling	2. Therapist models behaviors most feared by the client before asking the client to engage in behaviors.	Therapist handles a snake before asking the person with a snake phobia to do so.
3. Flooding	3. It intensively exposes the client to the feared object until anxiety extinguishes.	Person with a fear of heights may look out the window of the 100th floor of a building until her anxiety passes.
Cognitive-behavioral therapy	It helps clients identify and challenge negative, catastrophizing thoughts about feared situations.	Therapist accompanies a person with agoraphobia to the local grocery, helping him challenge thoughts that he is about to have a panic attack.
Biological treatments	They reduce symptoms of anxiety generally, so that they do not arise in the feared situation.	Benzodiazepines, monoamine oxidase inhibitors, and selective serotonin reuptake inhibitors are used.

therapy for phobias: *systematic desensitization therapy, modeling,* and *flooding.*

Systematic Desensitization In systematic desensitization therapy, clients formulate lists of situations or objects they fear, ranked from most feared to least feared. They learn relaxation techniques, which will reduce the symptoms of anxiety they will experience when they are exposed to their feared objects. They then begin to expose themselves to the items on their hierarchy of fears, beginning with the least feared item. For example, a person with a severe dog phobia might have as the first item on his list "seeing a picture of a dog in a magazine." This client might then first visualize a picture of a dog. As the client begins to feel anxious, the therapist coaches him to use his relaxation techniques to quell his anxious feelings. The point is to help the client replace his anxious reaction with the calm that comes with the relaxation techniques. When the client can visualize a picture of a dog without experiencing anxiety, he might move on to looking at a picture of a dog in a magazine, again using relaxation techniques to lower his anxiety reaction and replace it with a calm reac-

tion. Gradually, the client and therapist move through the entire list, until the client is able to pet a big dog without feeling overwhelming anxiety.

One of the specific phobias, blood-injection-injury type phobia, requires a different approach than the other phobias (Öst & Sterner, 1987). Recall that, unlike people with other specific phobias, whose blood pressure and heart rate increase when they confront their phobic objects, people with a blood-injection-injury type phobia experience severe decreases in heart rate and blood pressure when confronted with their phobic objects. Sometimes, because less blood is circulating to their head, they faint. Relaxation techniques would only worsen these people's natural response to their phobic object, because such techniques also decrease blood pressure and heart rate. Thus, therapists must take the opposite approach, teaching them to tense the muscles in their arms, legs, and chest until they feel the warmth of their blood rising in their face. This **applied tension technique** increases blood pressure and heart rate. When a person with a blood-injection-injury type phobia learns this technique, she can use it when confronted with her phobic object to counteract her typical biological

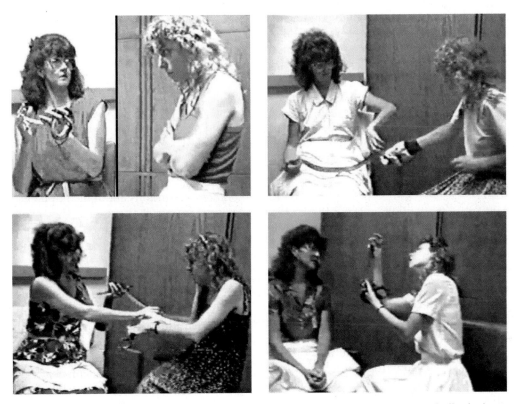

The therapist first models handling a snake for this woman with a snake phobia, then gradually she is able to handle it herself.

response and prevent fainting. Then systematic desensitization therapy can be implemented to extinguish her fear of blood, injury, or injections.

Modeling Techniques of **modeling** are often used in conjunction with systematic desensitization therapy in the treatment of phobias. The therapist models the behaviors most feared by clients before they attempt behaviors themselves. For example, if a therapist is treating a person with a snake phobia, the therapist may perform each of the behaviors on the client's hierarchy of fears before asking the client to perform them. The therapist stands in the room with the snake before asking the client to do so, touches the snake before asking the client to do so, and holds the snake before the client does. Eventually, the therapist allows the snake to crawl around on her before asking the client to attempt this. Through observational learning, the client begins to associate these behaviors with a calm, nonanxious response in the therapist, which reduces the client's own anxiety about engaging in the behaviors. Modeling is as effective as systematic desensitization therapy in reducing phobias (Bandura, 1969; Thorpe & Olson, 1997).

Flooding The idea behind **flooding** (also called implosive therapy) is to intensively expose a client to his or her feared object until anxiety extinguishes. In a flooding treatment, a person with claustrophobia might lock himself in a closet for several hours, a person with a dog phobia might spend the night in a dog kennel, and a person with social phobia might volunteer to teach a class that meets every day for a semester. The therapist typically prepares clients with relaxation techniques they can use to reduce their fear during the flooding procedure. Flooding is as effective as systematic desensitization therapy or modeling and often works more quickly. It is more difficult to get clients to agree to this type of therapy, though, because it is frightening to contemplate (Thorpe & Olson, 1997).

Cognitive-Behavioral Therapy

Many therapists combine behavioral techniques with cognitive techniques that help clients identify and challenge the negative, catastrophizing thoughts they are having when they are anxious (Beck & Emery, 1985; Turk et al., 2001). For example, when a person with a snake phobia is saying, "I just can't do this. I can't stand this anxiety. I'll never get over this," the therapist might point out the progress the client has already made on his hierarchy of fears and the client's previous statements that the relaxation techniques have been a great help to him. Creating the expectations in clients that they can master their problems, known as *self-efficacy expectations*, is a potent factor in curing phobias (Bandura, 1986).

In the treatment of social phobia, cognitive-behavioral therapy (CBT) is more effective than the SSRIs both in the short term and in 6-month and 1-year follow-ups (Clark et al., 2003; Hofmann, 2004). CBT can be implemented in a group setting, where all the members, except the therapist, suffer from a social phobia (Coles, Hart, & Heimberg, 2005; Heimberg, 2001; Turk et al., 2001). The group members are an audience for one another, providing exposure to the very situation each member fears. An individual group member can practice her feared behaviors in front of the other members while the therapist coaches her in the use of relaxation techniques to calm her anxiety. The group can also help the individual challenge her negative, catastrophizing thoughts about her behavior, as in the following excerpt from a group cognitive therapy session with Gina, a woman with social phobia (adapted from Turk et al., 2001, pp. 124–125):

VOICES

Therapist: So your automatic thought is "I don't know how to have a conversation," is that right?

Gina: Yeah, I always screw it up.

Therapist: All right, let's ask the rest of the group what they think about that. Who has had a conversation with Gina or noticed her talking with someone else?

Ed: We walked out to our cars together last week and talked in the parking lot for a while. [Several other group members list similar conversations.]

Therapist: So it sounds like you have had a number of conversations with the rest of the group.

Gina: I guess so.

Therapist: Group, how did she do? How did the conversations go?

Sally: It was fine. She was asking me about my car, because she has been looking for a new one, so we talked mostly about that.

[Other group members provide similar answers.]

Therapist: Well, Gina, the rest of the group doesn't seem to agree that you don't know how to have conversations.

Gina: I guess I have always been so nervous that I never stopped to think that sometimes the conversations go OK.

Through observational learning, the group members' cognitions about incompetence and embarrassment are challenged as they challenge one another. Group-administered cognitive-behavioral therapy has proven effective even for people with generalized social phobia (Heimberg, 2001; Turk et al., 2001). For example, in one study, 133 people with social phobia were randomly assigned to receive group cognitive-behavioral therapy (CBT), to take an antidepressant, to receive a pill placebo, or simply to meet in a group to receive support and education about social phobia (Heimberg et al., 1998). After 12 weeks of treatment, 75 percent of the group cognitive-behavioral therapy -patients were significantly improved in their symptoms, compared with 77 percent of the people who had received the antidepressant. These response rates were similar, but both the CBT group and the antidepressant group had significantly better recovery than the pill placebo group or the education/support group. A follow-up showed that cognitive-behavioral therapy was much better at preventing relapse into social phobia than the antidepressant treatment: Only 17 percent of the CBT group had relapsed one year later, compared with 50 percent of the antidepressant treatment group (Heimberg, 2001).

Biological Treatments

Some people use the benzodiazepines to reduce their anxiety when forced to confront their phobic objects. For example, when people with a phobia of flying are forced to take a flight, they might take a high dose of the benzodiazepine Valium or drink alcohol to relieve their anxiety. Many people who become very nervous in public presentations take a benzodiazepine to reduce their anxiety before giving a speech or a performance. These drugs produce temporary relief (Jefferson, 2001), but the phobia remains.

Antidepressants, particularly the monoamine oxidase inhibitors and the selective serotonin reuptake inhibitors, are more effective than placebos in the treatment of social phobia (Davidson, 2003; Schneier, 2001; Van Ameringen et al., 2001). However, follow-up studies suggest that people soon relapse into social phobia after discontinuing their use of the drug (Davidson, 2003). Of course, these drugs also have potential significant side effects, and the benzodiazepines are addictive.

In contrast, the vast majority of people can be cured of phobias with behavioral techniques after only a few hours of treatment (Öst et al., 2001), and cognitive-behavioral therapy is effective in the treatment of social phobia (Zaider & Heimberg, 2003). For now, it appears that the old advice to "confront your fears" through behavior therapy is the best advice for people with phobias.

SUMMING UP

- People with agoraphobia fear a wide variety of situations in which they might have an emergency but not be able to escape or get help. Many people with agoraphobia also suffer from panic disorder.

- The specific phobias include animal type phobias, natural environment type phobias, situational type phobias, and blood-injection-injury type phobias.

- People with social phobia fear social situations in which they might be embarrassed or judged by others.

- Psychodynamic theories of phobias suggest that they represent unconscious anxiety that has been displaced. These theories have not been supported, however.

- Behavioral theories of phobias suggest that they develop through classical conditioning and are maintained by operant conditioning. Humans may be evolutionarily prepared to develop some types of phobias more easily than others.

- Cognitive theories have focused on social phobia and suggest that this disorder develops in people who have excessively high standards for their social performance, assume that others are judging them harshly, and are hypervigilant to signs of rejection from others.

- Biological theories of phobias attribute their development to heredity.

- Behavioral treatments for phobias include systematic desensitization therapy, modeling, and flooding.

- Cognitive techniques are used to help clients identify and challenge the negative, catastrophizing thoughts they have when anxious. Group cognitive therapy has proven

highly effective in the treatment of social phobia and in preventing relapse.

- The benzodiazepines and antidepressant drugs can help quell anxiety symptoms, but people soon relapse into phobias after the drugs are discontinued.

GENERALIZED ANXIETY DISORDER

The phobias, panic, and agoraphobia involve periods of anxiety that are acute, usually short-lived, and more or less specific to certain situations. Some people are anxious all the time, however, in almost all situations. These people may be diagnosed with a **generalized anxiety disorder (GAD)** (see Table 7.7 on page 246). People with GAD worry about many things in their lives, as Claire describes in the following excerpt (adapted from Brown, O'Leary, & Barlow, 2001, p. 187):

VOICES

I just feel anxious and tense all the time. It all started in high school. I was a straight-A student, and I worried constantly about my grades, whether the other kids and the teachers liked me, being prompt for classes—things like that. . . . My husband thinks I'm neurotic. For example, I vacuum four times a week and clean the bathrooms every day. There have even been times when I've backed out of going out to dinner with my husband because the house needed to be cleaned. Generally, my husband is supportive, but it has caused a strain on our marriage.

I get so upset and irritated over minor things, and it'll blow up into an argument. . . . I still worry about being on time to church and to appointments. Now I find I worry a lot about my husband. He's been doing a tremendous amount of traveling for his job, some of it by car, but most of it by plane. Because he works on the northeastern seaboard, and because he frequently has to travel in the winter, I worry that he'll be stuck in bad weather and get into an accident or, God forbid, a plane crash. It's just so scary.

Oh, and I worry about my son. He just started playing on the varsity football team, so he's bound to get an injury sometime. It's

(continued)

so nerve-wracking to watch him play that I've stopped going to his games with my husband. I'm sure my son must be disappointed that I'm not watching him play, but it's simply too much for me to take.

People with GAD may worry about their performance on the job, about how their relationships are going, and about their own health. Like Claire, they also may worry about minor issues, such as whether they will be late for an appointment, whether the hair stylist will cut their hair the right way, or whether they will have time to mop the kitchen floor before dinner guests arrive. The focus of their worries may shift frequently, and they tend to worry about many different things, instead of just focusing on one issue of concern.

Their worry is accompanied by many of the physiological symptoms of anxiety, including muscle tension, sleep disturbances, and a chronic sense of restlessness. Claire's worries give her a chronically upset stomach and sense of nausea. People with GAD report feeling tired much of the time, probably due to their chronic muscle tension and sleep loss.

GAD is a relatively common type of anxiety disorder, with cross-national studies showing lifetime prevalences of about 5 percent of women and 3 percent of men (Kessler et al., 2002). Many people with this disorder report they have been anxious all their lives, and the disorder most commonly first appears in childhood or adolescence. Over half of people with GAD also develop another anxiety disorder, such as phobias or panic disorder. Over 70 percent experience a mood disorder, and a third have a substance use disorder as well (Craske & Waters, 2005; Kessler et al., 2002). Many recent psychological theories, and the biological theories, have come to view generalized anxiety disorder as a distinct disorder that has many differences even from other anxiety disorders (see the Concept Overview in Table 7.8).

Theories of Generalized Anxiety Disorder

Many of the earliest psychological theories saw chronic, generalized anxiety not only as a problem in itself but also as the core issue behind many other disorders.

Psychodynamic Theories

Freud (1917) developed the first psychodynamic theory of generalized anxiety. He distinguished among three kinds of anxiety: realistic, neurotic,

and moral. **Realistic anxiety** occurs when we face a real danger or threat, such as an oncoming tornado. **Neurotic anxiety** occurs when we are repeatedly prevented from expressing our id impulses. The energy of those impulses is not allowed release, and it causes anxiety. For example, a person who feels she can never act on her sexual urges may experience neurotic anxiety. **Moral anxiety** occurs when we have been punished for expressing our id impulses, and we come to associate those impulses with punishment, causing anxiety. For example, a child who is harshly punished for fondling his genitals may, as an adult, have moral anxiety over any sexual impulses.

Generalized anxiety occurs when our defense mechanisms can no longer contain either the id impulses or the neurotic or moral anxiety that arises from these impulses. We are anxious all the time because we cannot find healthy ways to express our id impulses and greatly fear the expression of those impulses.

Because more recent psychodynamic theories focus more on the development of self-concept through early close relationships, it is not surprising that these theories have attributed generalized anxiety to poor upbringing, which results in fragile and conflicted images of the self and others (Zerbe, 1990). Children whose parents are not sufficiently

---

TABLE 7.7 DSM-IV-TR

Symptoms of Generalized Anxiety Disorder

People diagnosed with GAD must show excessive anxiety and worry, difficulty in controlling the worry, and at least three of the other symptoms on this list chronically for at least six months.

Excessive anxiety and worry

Difficulty in controlling the worry

Restlessness or feeling keyed-up or on edge

Easily fatigued

Difficulty concentrating, mind goes blank

Irritability

Muscle tension

Sleep disturbance

Source: Reprinted with permission from the *Diagnostic and Statistical Manual of Mental Disorders,* Fourth Edition, Text Revision. Copyright © 2000. American Psychiatric Association.

TABLE 7.8 Concept Overview

Theories of Generalized Anxiety Disorder

These are the major theories of generalized anxiety disorder.

Theory	Description
Psychodynamic theories	
Freud's theory	GAD results when impulses are feared and cannot be expressed.
Newer psychodynamic theories	Children whose parents are not warm and nurturing develop images of the self as vulnerable and images of others as hostile, which results in chronic anxiety.
Humanistic theory	GAD occurs in children who develop a harsh set of self-standards they feel they must achieve in order to be acceptable.
Existential theory	GAD is due to existential anxiety, a universal fear of the limits and responsibilities of one's existence.
Cognitive theories	Both the conscious and unconscious thoughts of people with GAD are focused on threat, leading to chronic anxiety.
Biological theories	
GABA theory	People with GAD have a deficiency in GABA receptors, resulting in excessive firing in the limbic system.
Genetic theory	A biological vulnerability to GAD is inherited.

warm and nurturing, and may have been overly strict or critical, may develop images of the self as vulnerable and images of others as hostile. As adults, their lives are filled with frantic attempts to overcome or hide their vulnerability, but stressors often overwhelm their coping capacities, causing frequent bouts of anxiety.

These psychodynamic formulations have been studied in some empirical research (Eisenberg, 1958; Jenkins, 1968; Luborsky, 1973). Most of these studies are open to multiple interpretations and do not really get at the heart of the causal factors implicated in psychodynamic theories of generalized anxiety disorder.

Humanistic and Existential Theories

Carl Rogers' humanistic explanation of generalized anxiety suggests that children who do not receive unconditional positive regard from significant others become overly critical of themselves and develop **conditions of worth,** harsh self-standards they feel they must meet in order to be acceptable. Throughout their lives, these people then strive to meet these conditions of worth by denying their true selves and remaining constantly vigilant for the approval of others. They typically fail to meet their self-standards, causing them to feel chronically anxious or depressed.

Existential theorists attribute generalized anxiety disorder to **existential anxiety,** a universal hu-

man fear of the limits and responsibilities of one's existence (Bugental, 1997; May & Yalom, 1995; Tillich, 1952). Existential anxiety arises when we face the finality of death, the fact that we may unintentionally hurt someone, or the prospect that our lives have no meaning. We can avoid existential anxiety by accepting our limits and striving to make our lives meaningful, or we can try to silence that anxiety by avoiding responsibility or by conforming to others' rules. Failing to confront life's existential issues only leaves the anxiety in place, however, and leads us to "inauthentic lives."

Neither the humanistic nor the existential theory of generalized anxiety disorder has been extensively researched. Instead, most research attention these days is focused on the cognitive theories of GAD.

Cognitive Theories

The cognitive theories of GAD suggest that the cognitions of people with GAD are focused on threat, at both the conscious and nonconscious levels (Beck, 1997; Beck & Emery, 1985; Borkovec, 1994; Ellis, 1997; Mathews & MacLeod, 2005). At the conscious level, people with GAD have a number of maladaptive assumptions that set them up for anxiety, such as "I must be loved or approved of by everyone," "It's always best to expect the worst," and "I must anticipate and prepare myself at all times for any possible danger" (Beck & Emery, 1985; Ellis, 1997).

Munch's painting *The Scream* seems to capture the experiences of generalized anxiety.

Many of these assumptions reflect issues of being in control and losing control.

People with GAD believe that worrying can prevent bad events from happening. Many of these beliefs are superstitious, but people with GAD also believe that worrying motivates them and facilitates their problem solving, yet people with GAD seldom get around to problem solving. Although they are always anticipating a negative event, they do not tend to think through this anticipated event and vividly imagine it happening to them (Borkovec, 2002). Indeed, they actively avoid visual images of what they worry about, perhaps as a way of avoiding the negative emotion associated with those images. By avoiding fully processing those images, while anticipating that something bad is going to happen, people with GAD do not allow themselves to consider the ways they might cope with an event if it were to happen. Neither do they allow themselves to habituate to the negative emotions associated with the image of an event.

Their maladaptive assumptions lead people with GAD to respond to situations with **automatic thoughts,** which directly stir up anxiety, cause them to be hypervigilant, and lead them to overreact to situations. For example, when facing an exam, a person with GAD might reactively think, "I don't think I can do this," "I'll fall apart if I fail

this test," and "My parents will be furious if I don't get good grades."

The unconscious cognitions of people with GAD also appear to be focused on detecting possible threats in the environment (Mathews & MacLeod, 2005). One paradigm in which this has been shown is the Stroop color naming task. In this task, a participant is presented with words printed in color on a computer screen (see Figure 7.10). The participant's task is to say what color the word is printed in. Some of the words have special significance for a person with chronic anxiety, such as *disease* or *failure,* whereas other words have no special significance. In general, participants are slower in naming the color of words that have special significance to them than in naming nonsignificant words. The reason is that they are paying more attention to the content of the significant words than to the colors in which the words are printed.

One study presented threatening and nonthreatening words to GAD patients and nonpatient controls on the computer screen for only 20 milliseconds, too short a period for the subjects to consciously process the content of the word. The GAD patients were slower in naming the colors of the threatening words than were the nonpatients, but the two groups of subjects did not differ in the time it took them to name the colors of the nonthreatening words. This suggests that people suffering from GAD are always vigilant for signs of impending threat, even at an unconscious level (Mathews & MacLeod, 2005).

Why do some people become vigilant to signs of threat? One theory is that they have had experiences in which they have been confronted with stressors or traumas that were uncontrollable and came on without warning (Mineka & Kelly, 1989; Mineka & Zinbarg, 1998). Animal studies show that animals given unpredictable and uncontrollable shock often show symptoms of chronic fear or anxiety (Mineka, 1985). People who have had unpredictable and uncontrollable life experiences—such as an unpredictably abusive parent—may also develop chronic anxiety. Although these ideas are difficult to test in humans, studies of monkeys have shown that the level of control and predictability in an infant monkey's life is related to the monkey's symptoms of anxiety as an adolescent or adult (Mineka, Gunnar, & Champoux, 1986).

Biological Theories

Recall that the discovery that antidepressant medications reduce panic attacks led to the hypothesis that norepinephrine is involved in panic disorder. Similarly, the discovery in the 1950s that the benzodiazepines provide relief from generalized anxiety has led to theories about the neurotransmitters involved in generalized anxiety. The benzodiazepines increase the activity of **gamma-aminobutyric acid (GABA),** a neurotransmitter that carries inhibitory messages from one neuron to another. When GABA binds to a neuronal receptor, the neuron is inhibited from firing. One theory is that people with generalized anxiety disorder may have a deficiency of GABA or GABA receptors, which results in the excessive firing of neurons through many areas of the brain, but particularly in the limbic system, which is involved in emotional, physiological, and behavioral responses to threat (Charney, 2004; LeDoux, 1995). As a result of excessive and chronic neuronal activity, the person experiences chronic, diffuse symptoms of anxiety.

Genetic studies suggest that GAD, as a specific disorder, has a modest heritability (Kendler et al., 1992; Rapee & Barlow, 1993). The more general trait of anxiety is much more clearly heritable, and it puts individuals at risk for the diagnosis of GAD (Craske & Waters, 2005).

Treatments for Generalized Anxiety Disorder

The effective treatments for GAD are cognitive-behavioral or biological.

Cognitive-Behavioral Treatments

Cognitive-behavioral treatments focus on helping people with GAD confront the issues they worry most about; challenge their negative, catastrophizing thoughts; and develop coping strategies. We see in the following excerpt how a cognitive-behavioral therapist helps Claire challenge her tendency to overestimate the probability that her son will have an injury playing football (Brown, O'Leary, & Barlow, 2001, pp. 193–194):

VOICES

Therapist: Claire, you wrote that you were afraid about your son playing in his football game. What specifically were you worried about?

Claire: That he'd get seriously hurt. His team was playing last year's state champions, so you know that those boys are big and strong. My son is good, but he hasn't been playing for years and years.

Therapist: How specifically do you imagine your son getting hurt?

FIGURE 7.10 **The Stroop Color Naming Task.** In this task, words are flashed on a computer screen for a brief period of time, and the person is asked to name the color the word is printed in. People with generalized anxiety disorder are slower to name the color of words with threatening content than of neutral words, presumably because they are attending to the content of the threatening words.

Claire: Getting a broken back or neck. Something that will result in paralysis or death. It happened to two NFL players this past year, remember?

Therapist: What happened to your son when he played in the game?

Claire: Nothing, really. He came home that afternoon with a sore thumb, but that went away after a while. He said he scored a touchdown and had an interception. I guess he played really well.

Therapist: So what you're saying is that you had predicted that he would be injured during the game, but that didn't happen. When we're anxious, we tend to commit a common cognitive error, called "probability overestimation." In other words, we overestimate the likelihood of an unlikely event. While you were feeling anxious and worried, what was the probability in your mind that your son would be hurt, from 0 to 100%?

Claire: About 75%.

Therapist: And now what would you rate the probability of your son getting hurt in a future game?

Claire: Well, if you put it that way, I suppose around a 50% chance of him getting injured.

Therapist: So that means for every two times that your son plays football, he gets hurt once. Is that correct?

(continued)

Claire: Umm, no. I don't think it's that high. Maybe about 30%.

Therapist: That would be one out of every three times that your son gets hurt. To counter the tendency to overestimate the probability of negative future events, it's helpful to ask yourself what evidence from the past supports your anxious belief. What evidence can you provide from your son's playing history to account for your belief that he'll get hurt one out of every three games?

Claire: Well, none. He had a sprained ankle during summer training, but that's it.

Therapist: So what you're saying is that you don't have very much evidence at all to prove that your son has a 30% chance of getting hurt in a game.

Claire: Gee, I never thought of it that way.

Therapist: What are some alternatives to your son getting seriously hurt in a football game? . . .

Claire: He could get a minor injury, like a sprained ankle or something of that nature.

Therapist: Right. And what would be the probability of your son getting a minor versus a major injury?

Claire: Probably higher, like 60% or 70%.

Therapist: To go back to your original worry, what would you rate the probability of your son getting seriously injured during a football game?

Claire: Low, about 10%.

Therapist: So 1 out of every 10 times your son will get seriously hurt playing football. How many times has your son played football?

Claire: He just started varsity this year and he's a junior. But he's been playing since he got to high school, about 3 years. All in all, about 25 games.

Therapist: And how many times in those 3 years has he been seriously injured?

Claire: Not once. I see what you're doing.

Cognitive-behavioral therapy has been shown to be more effective than benzodiazepine therapy, placebos, or humanistic therapy in the treatment of GAD (Borkovec, Newman, & Castonguay, 2003;

Borkovec & Ruscio, 2001; Borkovec & Whisman, 1996; Butler et al., 1991; Harvey & Rapee, 1995). In one study, the positive effects of cognitive-behavioral therapy remained in a two-year follow-up of GAD clients (Borkovec et al., 2002).

Biological Treatments

The benzodiazepine drugs (such as Xanax, Librium, Valium, and Serax) provide short-term relief from the symptoms of anxiety (Gorman, 2003). The side effects and addictiveness of the benzodiazepines preclude their long-term use. Once people discontinue using these drugs, their anxiety symptoms return (Davidson, 2001).

A drug named **buspirone** (trade name BuSpar) appears to alleviate the symptoms of generalized anxiety for some people; it has few side effects and is unlikely to lead to physical dependence (Gorman, 2003). Buspirone is not a benzodiazepine but one of a class of drugs called azaspirones. It appears to reduce anxiety by blocking serotonin receptors.

Both the tricyclic antidepressant imipramine (trade name Tofranil) and the selective serotonin reuptake inhibitor paroxetine (trade name Paxil) have been shown to be better than placebo in reducing anxiety symptoms in GAD, and paroxetine improves anxiety more than a benzodiazepine does (Rocca et al., 1997). Venlafaxine (trade name Effexor), which is a serotonin-norepinephrine reuptake inhibitor, has also been shown to reduce the symptoms of anxiety in GAD better than placebo and in some studies better than busiprone (Davidson et al., 1999; Gelenberg et al., 2000; Rickels et al., 2000; Stocchi et al., 2001).

SUMMING UP

- Generalized anxiety disorder is characterized by chronic symptoms of anxiety across most situations.

- Freud suggested that GAD develops when people cannot find ways to express their impulses and fear the expression of these impulses. Newer psychodynamic theories suggest that children whose parents are not sufficiently warm and nurturing develop images of the self as vulnerable and images of others as hostile, which results in chronic anxiety. Neither of these theories has been supported empirically.

- Humanistic theory suggests that generalized anxiety results in children who develop a harsh set of self-standards they feel they must achieve in order to be acceptable.

- Existential theory attributes generalized anxiety to existential anxiety, a universal fear of the limits and responsibilities of one's existence.

■ Cognitive theories suggest that both the conscious and unconscious thoughts of people with GAD are focused on threat.

■ Biological theories suggest that people with GAD have a deficiency in GABA or GABA receptors. They may also have a genetic predisposition to generalized anxiety.

■ Cognitive-behavioral treatments for people with GAD focus on helping them confront their negative thinking.

■ Drug therapies have included the use of benzodiazepines and a newer drug called buspirone, as well as the tricyclic antidepressants and the selective serotonin reuptake inhibitors.

OBSESSIVE-COMPULSIVE DISORDER

Recall the obsessions and compulsions of Marc Summers, whom we met at the beginning of the chapter. **Obsessions** are thoughts, images, ideas, or impulses that are persistent, that the individual feels intrude upon his or her consciousness without control, and that cause significant anxiety or distress. **Compulsions** are repetitive behaviors or mental acts that an individual feels he or she must perform.

Obsessive-compulsive disorder (OCD) is classified as an anxiety disorder because people with OCD experience anxiety as a result of their obsessional thoughts and when they cannot carry out their compulsive behaviors (see Table 7.9 on page 252). This disorder has quite a different character than the other anxiety disorders we have discussed and may eventually be declassified as an anxiety disorder. Children can suffer OCD, just as adults can, and the little boy's personal account of OCD in the following excerpt illustrates how overwhelming this disorder can be (Rapoport, 1990, pp. 43–44). His name is Zach.

VOICES

When I was 6 I started doing all these strange things when I swallowed saliva. When I swallowed saliva I had to crouch down and touch the ground. I didn't want to lose any saliva—for a bit I had to sweep the ground with my hand—and later I had to blink my eyes if I swallowed. I was frustrated because I couldn't stop the compulsions. Each time I swallowed I had to do something. For a while I had to touch my shoulders to my chin. I don't know why. I had no reason. I was afraid. It was just so unpleasant if I didn't. If I tried not to do these things, all I got was failure. I had to do it, and no matter how hard I tried, I just *still* had to.

I tried to tell my ma. I told her I had to do it. She ways, "You're doing some strange things, why do you do it?" I said, "Cause I don't want to lose any saliva," and she says, "Maybe you'll want to talk about it later." I don't want to lose any saliva and there's no good reason. I just don't want to. I was afraid to tell anybody. People would think I was crazy or something. I don't want to tell Dr. Kaufman. I was nervous when I first came to him and then I just didn't want to talk about it. It just bothered me to talk about it. I felt ashamed. I didn't want anyone to know. I wanted it to be just for me to know, no one else.

It wrecked my life. It took away all the time. I couldn't do anything. If you put it all together I did it maybe an hour and a half or sometimes three hours a day.

I had bathroom problems too. I had to take some toilet paper and rip them up a lot of times into teeny pieces that had to be just the right size—only about a millimeter. They had to be torn perfect and then I'd flush them away.

I had to do all kinds of things with my fingers and my mouth. I had to touch all my fingers to my lips a few times if I swallowed saliva. Swallowing was one of the first things.

You may be thinking that the thoughts and behaviors that Zach describes, as well as those of Marc Summers, are "crazy"—that they are out of touch with reality. The thoughts and behaviors of people with OCD are not considered psychotic, however, because these people are very aware of how irrational their thoughts and behaviors are, yet they cannot seem to control them.

OCD often begins at a young age, as it did for Marc Summers. The peak age of onset for males is between 6 and 15 years, and for females it is between 20 and 29 years (Angst et al., 2004; Foa & Franklin, 2001). Children often hide their symptoms, even from their parents; as a result, their symptoms can go undetected for years (Rapoport

TABLE 7.9 DSM-IV-TR

Symptoms of Obsessive-Compulsive Disorder

Obsessive-compulsive disorder is classified as an anxiety disorder but differs from other anxiety disorders in many ways.

The person must show either obsessions or compulsions, which he or she recognizes are excessive or unreasonable.

Obsessions are defined as

1. recurrent and persistent thoughts, impulses, or images that are experienced as intrusive and inappropriate and that cause anxiety or distress

2. thoughts, impulses, or images that are not simply excessive worries about real-life problems

3. thoughts, impulses, or images that the person attempts to ignore or suppress or to neutralize with some other thought or action

4. obsessional thoughts, impulses, or images that the person recognizes are a product of his or her own mind

Compulsions are defined as

1. repetitive behaviors (such as handwashing, ordering, checking) or mental acts (such as praying, counting, repeating words silently) that the person feels driven to perform in response to an obsession or according to rules that must be applied rigidly

2. behaviors or mental acts that are aimed at preventing or reducing distress or preventing some dreaded event or situation; however, these behaviors or mental acts either are not connected in a realistic way with what they are designed to neutralize or prevent or are clearly excessive

Source: Reprinted with permission from the *Diagnostic and Statistical Manual of Mental Disorders*, Fourth Edition, Text Revision. Copyright © 2000. American Psychiatric Association.

States, Canada, Mexico, England, Norway, Hong Kong, India, Egypt, Japan, and Korea (Escobar, 1993; Insel, 1984; Kim, 1993). Although some studies have found slightly higher rates of OCD in women than in men (Angst et al., 2004), other studies have not (Edelmann, 1992; Karno & Golding, 1991).

OCD Symptoms

Zach's and Marc Summers' obsessions involve dirt. The focus of obsessive thoughts seems to be similar across cultures, with the most common type of obsession focusing on dirt and contamination (Akhtar et al., 1975; Hewlett, 2000; Rachman & Hodgson, 1980). Other common obsessions include aggressive impulses (such as to hurt one's child), sexual thoughts (such as recurrent pornographic images), impulses to do something against one's moral code (such as to shout obscenities in church), and repeated doubts (such as worrying that one has not turned off the stove). Although thoughts of this kind occur to most people occasionally, most of us can turn them off by dismissing or ignoring them. People with OCD cannot turn off these thoughts.

People with OCD do not carry out the impulses they have (e.g., hurting a baby or shouting obscenities in church), but they are so bothered by the fact that they even have these thoughts that they feel extremely guilty and anxious. Most people who have severe and persistent obsessions engage in compulsions to try to erase their thoughts and the anxiety they create. Sometimes, an individual's compulsion is tied to his or her specific obsession by obvious logic. The compulsive behavior becomes so extreme and repetitive, however, that it is irrational. For example, Zach washes his hands 35 times a day, until they crack and bleed, to rid himself of contamination obsessions. "Checking" compulsions, which are extremely common, are tied to obsessional doubts, as is illustrated in the following story (Rapoport, 1990, pp. 21–22).

et al., 2000). Marc Summers' parents thought he just liked a clean room.

OCD tends to be a chronic disorder if left untreated. Obsessional thoughts are very distressing to people with OCD, and engaging in compulsive behaviors can take a great deal of time and can even be dangerous (e.g., washing your hands so often that they bleed). As many as 66 percent of people with OCD are also significantly depressed (Foa & Franklin, 2001). Panic attacks, phobias, and substance abuse are also common in OCD.

Between 1 and 3 percent of people will develop OCD at sometime in their lives (Angst et al., 2004; Hewlett, 2000; Robins et al., 1984). In the United States, European Americans show a higher prevalence of OCD than do African Americans or Hispanic Americans (Hewlett, 2000). The prevalence of OCD does not seem to differ greatly across countries that have been studied, including the United

VOICES

I'm driving down the highway doing 55 MPH. I'm on my way to take a final exam. My seat belt is buckled and I'm vigilantly following all the rules of the road. No one is on the highway—not a living soul.

Out of nowhere an obsessive-compulsive disorder (OCD) attack strikes. It's almost magical the way it distorts my perception of reality. While in reality no one is on the road, I'm intruded with the heinous thought that I *might* have hit someone . . . a human being! God knows where such a fantasy comes from.

(continued)

I think about this for a second and then say to myself, "That's ridiculous. I didn't hit anybody." Nonetheless, a gnawing anxiety is born. An anxiety I will ultimately not be able to put away until an enormous emotional price has been paid.

I try to make reality chase away this fantasy. I reason, "Well, if I hit someone while driving, I would have *felt* it." This brief trip into reality helps the pain dissipate . . . but only for a second. Why? Because the gnawing anxiety that I really did commit the illusionary accident is growing larger—so is the pain.

The pain is a terrible guilt that I have committed an unthinkable, negligent act. At one level, I know this is ridiculous, but there's a terrible pain in my stomach telling me something quite different.

Again, I try putting to rest this insane thought and that ugly feeling of guilt. "Come on," I think to myself, "this is *really* insane!"

But the awful feeling persists. The anxious pain says to me, "You Really Did Hit Someone." The attack is now in full control. Reality no longer has meaning. My sensory system is distorted. I have to get rid of the pain. Checking out this fantasy is the only way I know how.

I start ruminating, "Maybe I did hit someone and didn't realize it. . . . Oh, my God! I might have killed somebody! I have to go back and check." Checking is the only way to calm the anxiety. It brings me closer to truth somehow. I can't live with the thought that I actually may have killed someone—I have to check it out.

Now I'm sweating . . . literally. I pray this outrageous act of negligence never happened. My fantasies run wild. I desperately hope the jury will be merciful. I'm particularly concerned about whether my parents will be understanding. After all, I'm now a criminal. I must control the anxiety by checking it out. Did it really happen? There's always an infinitesimally small kernel of truth (or potential truth) in all my OC fantasies.

I think to myself, "Rush to check it out. Get rid of the hurt by checking it out."

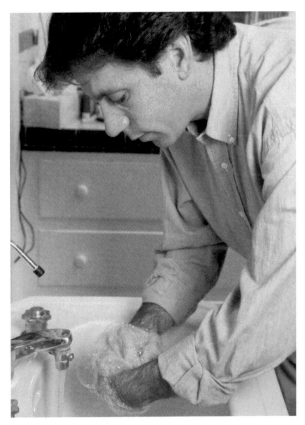

Handwashing is one of the most common compulsions in OCD.

This man's compulsive checking makes some sense, given what he is thinking. However, what he is thinking—that he hit someone on the road without knowing it—is highly improbable. The compulsive checking quells obsessional thoughts briefly, but the obsessional thoughts come back with even more force.

Often, the link between the obsession and the compulsion is the result of "magical thinking." For example, many people with OCD believe that repeating a ritual a certain number of times will ward off danger to themselves or others. Their rituals often become stereotyped and rigid, and they develop obsessions and compulsions about not performing the rituals correctly. For example, Marc Summers felt compelled to read the advertisement for a watch 25 times perfectly, and he feared something would happen to his family if he didn't.

At times, there is no discernible link between the specific obsession a person has and the specific compulsion that helps dispel the obsession. Recall that Zach engages in several behaviors, such as touching the floor and touching his shoulders to his chin, when he has an obsession about losing his saliva. He cannot even say how these behaviors are related to his obsession; he just knows he has to engage in them. Thus, although compulsions may often seem purposeful, they are not functional. In some cases, the family members of people with OCD become accomplices in the disorder, as did the husband of writer Emily Colas, who has written about her OCD (Colas, 1998, pp. 70–72).

My husband and I generally kept a pile of about twenty garbage bags in one corner of our apartment. Which may seem out of character, for me to let them stay, but it was our trash and I knew nothing bad was in there. It was the communal trash that made me shake. So when it was time to take the bags out to the dumpster, my husband had to follow the whole hygienic procedure. To keep the neighbors' germs out of our place. First the water had to be turned on and left that way because if he touched the garbage and then the spigot, the spigot would get contaminated. Next he'd take one bag in his right hand and open the door with his left. Then he'd shut the door behind him and lock it so that no one could get into the house. I guess I could have monitored, but he wanted me upstairs so I couldn't critique him. He'd take the bag down, stand a few feet from the dumpster to be sure not to touch it, and throw the bag in. Then he'd unlock the door, open it, slip his shoes off, come inside, and wash his hands. He used a pump soap so that he could use his clean wrist to pump some in the palm of his hand and not contaminate the dispenser. The water would stay on, and he'd move to the next bag. He went through this procedure twenty times, once for each bag, until they were gone.

Theories of OCD

The biological theories of OCD have dominated research in recent years, and they have provided some intriguing hypotheses about its sources. Psychodynamic and cognitive-behavioral theories of OCD have also been proposed. These theories are summarized in the Concept Overview in Table 7.10.

Biological Theories

Biological theories of obsessive-compulsive disorder view it as a neurobiological disorder. Much of this research has focused on a circuit in the brain that is involved in the execution of primitive patterns of behavior, such as aggression, sexuality, and bodily excretion (Baxter et al., 2001; Rapoport, 1990; Saxena & Rauch, 2000). This circuit begins in the orbital region of the frontal cortex (see Figure 7.11). These impulses are then carried to a part of the basal ganglia called the **caudate nucleus,** which allows only the strongest of these impulses to carry through to the thalamus. If these impulses reach the thalamus, the person is motivated to think further about and possibly act on these impulses. The action might involve a set of stereotyped behaviors appropriate to the impulse. Once these behaviors are executed, the impulse diminishes.

TABLE 7.10 Concept Overview

Theories of OCD

The biological theories of OCD have been dominant in recent years, but psychodynamic and cognitive-behavioral theories have also been proposed.

Theory	Description
Biological theories	People with OCD suffer from a dysfunction in the circuits in the brain regulating primitive impulses, possibly due to deficiencies in serotonin, which cause OCD.
Psychodynamic theories	The obsessions and compulsions of people with OCD represent unconscious wishes or conflicts.
Cognitive-behavioral theories	People with OCD have difficulty turning off intrusive thoughts because of chronic distress, a tendency toward rigid thinking, and the belief they should be able to control their thoughts.

FIGURE 7.11 **OCD in the Brain.** A three-dimensional view of the human brain (with parts shown as they would look if the overlying cerebral cortex were transparent) clarifies the locations of the orbital frontal cortex and the basal ganglia—areas implicated in obsessive-compulsive disorder. Among the basal ganglia's structures are the caudate nucleus, which filters powerful impulses that arise in the orbital frontal cortex, so that only the most powerful ones reach the thalamus. Perhaps the orbital frontal cortex, the caudate nucleus, or both are so active in people with obsessive-compulsive disorder that numerous impulses reach the thalamus, generating obsessive thoughts or compulsive actions.

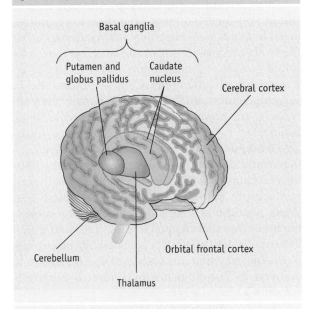

Source: Adapted from Rapoport, 1989, p. 85.

FIGURE 7.12 **PET Scans of OCD.** PET scans of people with OCD show more activity in the frontal cortex, basal ganglia, and thalamus than do PET scans of people without OCD.

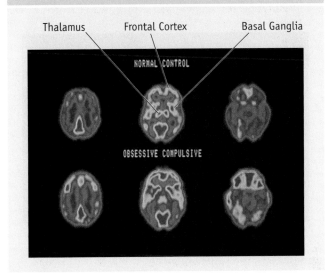

For people with OCD, dysfunction in this circuit may result in the system's inability to turn off these primitive impulses or to turn off the execution of the stereotyped behaviors once they are engaged. For example, when most of us have the thought that we are dirty, we engage in a fairly stereotyped form of cleansing: We wash our hands. People with OCD, however, continue to have the impulse to wash their hands, because their brains do not shut off their thoughts about dirt or their behavior when the behavior is no longer necessary. Proponents of this theory have pointed out that many of the obsessions and compulsions of people with OCD have to do with contamination, sex, aggression, and the repetition of behavior patterns—all issues with which this primitive brain circuit deals.

PET scans of people with OCD show more activity in the areas of the brain involved in this primitive circuit than do PET scans of people without

OCD (Micallef & Blin, 2001; Saxena et al., 1998) (see Figure 7.12). In addition, people with OCD often get some relief from their symptoms when they take drugs that better regulate the neurotransmitter serotonin, which plays an important role in the proper functioning of this primitive circuit in the brain (Micallef & Blin, 2001; Saxena et al., 1998). OCD patients who do respond to serotonin-enhancing drugs tend to show more reductions in the rate of activity in these brain areas than do OCD patients who do not respond well to these drugs (Baxter et al., 1992; Saxena et al., 1999, 2003). Interestingly, OCD patients who respond to behavior therapy also tend to show decreases in rate of activity in the caudate nucleus and thalamus (Schwartz et al., 1996) (see Figure 7.13 on page 256).

Piecing together these studies, researchers have argued that people with OCD have a fundamental dysfunction in the areas of the brain regulating primitive impulses, perhaps due to a depletion of serotonin in these systems. As a result, primitive impulses about sex, aggression, and cleanliness break through to their consciousness and motivate the execution of stereotyped behaviors much more often than in people without OCD (Baxter et al., 2001; Rapoport, 1989, 1991). Whether these differences in brain functioning are a cause or a consequence of OCD is not clear.

Finally, there is evidence that genes may play a role determining who is vulnerable to OCD (Hettema et al., 2001; Jonnal, Gardner, & Prescott, 2000; Nestadt et al., 2000). Family history studies clearly show that OCD runs in families, and twin studies

FIGURE 7.13 **The Effects of Behavior Therapy.** PET scans show decreases in metabolic activity in the caudate nucleus (rCd) and thalamus (Thal) in OCD patients after they have received behavior therapy.

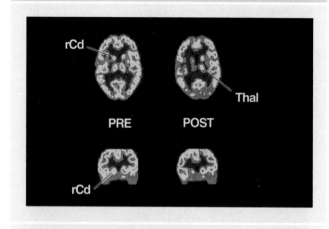

Source: Schwartz et al., 1996.

provide evidence for a substantial genetic effect on obsessive and compulsive behaviors (Eley et al., 2003; Hudziak et al., 2004).

Psychodynamic Theories

Psychodynamic theorists suggest that the particular obsessions and compulsions of people with OCD are symbolic of unconscious conflicts that they are guarding against (Freud, 1909). These conflicts create such anxiety for people that they can confront them only indirectly, by displacing the anxiety created by the conflict onto a more acceptable thought or behavior.

According to these theories, the reason that so many obsessions and compulsions involve contamination, sex, and aggression is that unconscious conflicts have to do with sexual and aggressive impulses. Psychodynamic theories suggest that the way to cure people of their OCD is to help them gain insight into the conflicts their obsessions and compulsions symbolize and to help them better resolve these conflicts. Psychodynamic therapy generally is not considered effective for the most OCD patients, however (Salzman, 1980).

Cognitive-Behavioral Theories

Most people, including people who do *not* have OCD, occasionally have negative, intrusive thoughts (Angst et al., 2004; Rachman & deSilva, 1978). People are more prone to have negative, intrusive thoughts and to engage in rigid, ritualistic behaviors when they are distressed (Clark & Purdon, 1993; Rachman, 1997). For example, many new mothers, exhausted from sleep deprivation

and the stresses of caring for a newborn, have thoughts about harming their newborn, even though they are horrified by such thoughts and would never carry them out.

According to the cognitive-behavioral theories of OCD, what differentiates people with OCD from people without the disorder is the ability to turn off these negative, intrusive thoughts (Clark, 1988; Rachman & Hodgson, 1980; Salkovskis, 1998). People who do not develop OCD are able to turn them off by ignoring or dismissing them, attributing them to their distress, and simply letting them subside with the passage of time.

Why do people who develop OCD have trouble turning off their thoughts, according to cognitive-behavioral theories? First, they may be depressed or generally anxious much of the time, so that even minor negative events are more likely to invoke intrusive, negative thoughts (Clark & Purdon, 1993). Second, people with OCD may have a tendency toward rigid, moralistic thinking (Rachman, 1993; Salkovskis, 1998). They judge their negative, intrusive thoughts as more unacceptable than most people would and become more anxious and guilty over having them. This anxiety then makes it even harder for them to dismiss the thoughts (Salkovskis, 1998). In addition, people who feel more responsible for events that happen in their lives and in the lives of others than other people do have more trouble dismissing thoughts such as "Did I hit someone on the road?" and thus might be more likely to develop OCD.

Third, people with OCD appear to believe that they *should* be able to control all thoughts, and they have trouble accepting that everyone has horrific thoughts from time to time (Clark & Purdon, 1993; Freeston et al., 1992). They tend to believe that having these thoughts means they are going crazy, or they equate having the thoughts with actually engaging in the behaviors (e.g., "If I'm thinking about hurting my child, I'm as guilty as if I actually did hurt my child"). Of course, this just makes them that much more anxious when they have the thoughts, which makes it harder for them to dismiss the thoughts.

How do compulsions develop, according to these theories? They develop largely through operant conditioning. People with anxiety-provoking obsessions discover that, if they engage in certain behaviors, their anxiety is reduced. The reduction in anxiety negatively reinforces the behaviors. Each time the obsessions return and they use the behaviors to reduce the obsessions, the behaviors are reinforced. Compulsions are born.

As with the biological theories of OCD, research has supported pieces of the cognitive-

TABLE 7.11 Concept Overview

Treatments for OCD

Often, drug therapies and cognitive-behavioral therapies are combined in the treatment of OCD.

Treatment	Description	Example
Biological treatments	Use serotonin-enhancing drugs.	Paxil, Prozac
Cognitive-behavioral treatments	Expose the client to obsessions until anxiety about obsessions decreases; prevent compulsive behaviors and help the client manage anxiety that is aroused.	Systematic desensitization therapy to help a person with a germ obsession gradually tolerate exposure to "dirty" materials

behavioral view of OCD, but much more research needs to be done. In particular, it is not clear whether the dysfunctions that the biological and cognitive-behavioral theories point to are the causes or the consequences of OCD. The reason is that almost all studies investigating these theories have compared people who already have OCD with those who do not.

Treatments for OCD

Just as biological theories dominate research on OCD, biological therapies have come to dominate the treatment of OCD. Cognitive-behavioral therapies also appear very helpful in treating OCD (see the Concept Overview in Table 7.11).

Biological Treatments

Until the 1980s, there were few effective biological treatments for OCD. The antianxiety drugs, the benzodiazepines, were not useful in most cases of OCD. This is one clue that OCD is not like the other anxiety disorders.

Then, it was discovered that antidepressant drugs that affect levels of the neurotransmitter serotonin helped relieve symptoms of OCD in many patients (Abramowitz, 1997; Rapoport, 1989, 1991). These drugs include clomipramine (trade name Anafranil), fluoxetine (trade name Prozac), paroxetine (trade name Paxil), sertraline (trade name Zoloft), and fluvoxamine (trade name Luvox). Controlled studies suggest that 50 to 80 percent of OCD patients experience decreases in their obsessions and compulsions when on these drugs, compared with only 5 percent of patients on placebos (March et al., 1998; Riddle et al., 2001).

These drugs may work by inhibiting the reuptake of the neurotransmitter serotonin, increasing the functional levels of serotonin in the brain. Recall that the latest biological theories of OCD suggest that this disorder involves dysfunctioning of the areas of the brain rich in serotonin.

These drugs are not the complete answer for people with OCD, however. A substantial number of patients do not respond to SSRIs, and, even among people who respond to the drug, obsessions and compulsions are reduced by only 40 or 50 percent, and people tend to relapse if the drugs are discontinued (Hewlett, 2000). Also, the drugs have significant side effects, including drowsiness, constipation, and loss of sexual interest, which prevent many people from taking them. Recent studies suggest that adding an atypical antipsychotic (a new form of antipsychotic drug described in Chapter 11) to an SSRI can further help people who do not respond fully to the SSRI (Bystritsky et al., 2004).

As writer Emily Colas observes, after living a lifetime with OCD, she needed to learn how to live a normal life once the drugs removed her symptoms (Colas, 1998, p. 138):

VOICES

You can try really hard not to get better. Use all your strength and will. But when you're on the pill, you get better and there's not a whole lot you can do about it. It takes a little while to kick in, so there are about four or five weeks when you're basically taking medication for the sheer benefit of the side effects. Tired, spacey, constipated. But then it happens. Not dramatically. It comes on slowly, but you can tell. The thoughts and worries become less gripping. I guess I figured that once that began to happen I'd instantly become happy. But the startling realization I made as I was coming to my senses was that life's kind of a

(continued)

drag. There didn't seem to be much to it. And my rituals had been a nice diversion. Without them, I wasn't quite sure what to do with myself. This thought made my head ache. I got anxious, nervous, wondering if I was destined to live this dull and uninteresting life. But because of those damn pills, I wasn't even able to obsess about *that*.

Cognitive-Behavioral Treatments

Many clinicians believe that drugs must be combined with cognitive-behavioral therapies in order to help people recover completely from OCD. The cognitive-behavioral therapies for OCD focus on repeatedly exposing the client to the focus of the obsession and preventing compulsive responses to the anxiety aroused by the obsession (Foa & Franklin, 2001; Marks & Swinson, 1992; Rachman & Hodgson, 1980). The repeated exposure to the content of the obsession is thought to habituate the client to obsession, so that it does not arouse as much anxiety as it formerly did. Preventing the person from engaging in compulsive behavior allows this habituation to take place. In addition, the person comes to learn that not engaging in the compulsive behavior does not lead to a terrible result. To implement this repeated exposure and response prevention, the therapist might first model the behavior he or she wants the client to practice.

For example, if the client has an obsession about contamination and a washing compulsion, the therapist might model rubbing dirt on his hands and then not wash his hands during the therapy session. At the next session, the therapist might again rub dirt on his hands but this time encourage the client to get her hands dirty as well. As the client's compulsion to wash her hands grows, the therapist encourages her not to do so but sits with her and uses relaxation techniques to control her anxiety. After several such sessions, the client may be able to sit with dirty hands without feeling anxious and to control her washing compulsion herself.

The client may also be given homework assignments that help her confront her obsession. For example, early in therapy, she might be assigned simply to refrain from cleaning the house every day of the week, as she normally does, and clean it only every three days. Later in therapy, she might be assigned to drop a cookie on a dirty kitchen floor and then pick it up and eat it or drop the kitchen knives on the floor and then use them to prepare food.

These behavior therapies have been shown to lead to significant improvement in obsessions and compulsive behavior in 60 to 90 percent of OCD clients (Abramowitz, 1997; Fals-Stewart, Marks, & Schafer, 1993; Foa & Franklin, 2001; Marks & Swinson, 1992; McLean et al., 2001; Steketee & Frost, 2003). Moreover, these improvements are maintained in most clients over periods of up to six years (Foa & Franklin, 2001; Foa & Kozak, 1993). Unfortunately, however, this therapy does not eliminate all obsessions and compulsions in OCD patients, and a substantial minority are not helped at all. Much work remains to be done to find a universally and completely effective therapy for OCD. The treatments available now, however, are great improvements over what was available only a few years ago.

SUMMING UP

- Obsessions are thoughts, images, ideas, or impulses that are persistent, are intrusive, and cause distress, and they commonly focus on contamination, sex, violence, and repeated doubts.

- Compulsions are repetitive behaviors or mental acts that the individual feels he or she must perform to erase his or her obsessions.

- Biological theories of OCD speculate that the areas of the brain involved in the execution of primitive patterns of behavior, such as washing rituals, may be impaired in people with OCD. These areas of the brain are rich in the neurotransmitter serotonin, and drugs that regulate serotonin have proven helpful in the treatment of OCD.

- Psychodynamic theories of OCD suggest that the obsessions and compulsions symbolize unconscious conflict or impulses and that the proper therapy for OCD involves uncovering these unconscious thoughts. These theories have not been supported.

- Cognitive-behavioral theories suggest that people with OCD are chronically distressed, think in rigid and moralistic ways, judge negative thoughts as more acceptable than other people do, and feel more responsible for their thoughts and behaviors. This makes them unable to turn off the negative, intrusive thoughts that most people have occasionally.

- Compulsive behaviors develop through operant conditioning. People are reinforced for compulsive behaviors by the fact that they reduce anxiety.

- Effective therapies for OCD involve a combination of selective serotonin reuptake inhibitors and cognitive-behavioral therapy.

SOCIAL APPROACHES TO THE ANXIETY DISORDERS

Social theorists have drawn attention to the fact that some groups and cultures are more prone than others to panic disorders, phobias, and generalized anxiety disorder (although there are not large cultural differences in OCD). They have tried to understand these differences in light of the environmental demands faced by these groups and their cultural norms for behavior.

Studies across the world show that people living in countries undergoing rapid societal change, political oppression, and war are much more likely to show anxiety symptoms than are those in more stable countries (Compton et al., 1991). In the United States, anxiety disorders are more common among people in disadvantaged minority groups and those in lower educational and socioeconomic groups than among Whites and people in higher educational and socioeconomic groups (Manson et al., 1996; Schlenger et al., 1992; Sheikh, 1992).

The stressful environment in which disadvantaged people live may create a chronic and pervasive anxiousness, which increases their risk for the development of anxiety disorders (Barlow, 1988; Manson et al., 1996). For example, consider a woman living in poverty who is anxious about the unsafe neighborhood in which she lives. Her chronic apprehensiveness could make it easier for even minor events, such as being trapped briefly in the elevator of her apartment building, to create paniclike symptoms. She would then be likely to associate her panic symptoms with elevators or, perhaps more generally, with enclosed spaces. Claustrophobia might develop.

Gender Differences

Women are more prone than men to develop most of the anxiety disorders we have discussed in this chapter. Compared with men, women have two or three times the rate of panic with agoraphobia, three or four times more specific phobias, one and one-half times more social phobias, and two times more generalized anxiety disorder (Kessler et al., 1995; Yonkers & Gurguis, 1995). Why would women be more likely than men to develop these disorders?

Some social theories suggest that women have a greater risk for anxiety disorders because of their place in society and the nature of their relationships with others (Chodorow, 1978; Horney, 1934/1967; Miller, 1976). Women generally have less power in society than do men, and their status is typically tied to the men they are related to. This causes women to cling to others, to play passive and subservient roles in relationships, to have a sense of being vulnerable and defenseless, and to be hypervigilant to any signs of problems in their relationships. This suppression of their own desires and fearfulness of loss, however, leave women chronically anxious, as in generalized anxiety disorder. Panic attacks and phobias are simply extreme expressions of these women's ongoing anxiety. Agoraphobia may be another way to express vulnerability and to conform to the passive role. This intriguing and popular theory has not been extensively studied in empirical research.

A different but related perspective is that sex-role socialization and pressures influence how men and women cope with symptoms of distress and thus whether they develop anxiety disorders. First, men may feel it is socially unacceptable to express anxiety and thus may be more prone to confront their feared situations and thereby extinguish their anxiety (Bruch & Cheek, 1995). Second, men appear more likely than women to seek medical help for anxiety symptoms, especially panic attacks (Yonkers & Gurguis, 1995). Men may view these symptoms as annoying medical problems, rather than as signs that there is something wrong in their lives or in their personalities. As a result, men may be more likely than women to receive effective treatment in the early stages of possible anxiety disorders.

Not all men who have anxiety symptoms seek appropriate help for them, however. Many men who have panic attacks appear to self-medicate by consuming large amounts of alcohol to decrease their panic symptoms, a coping behavior that is more acceptable for men than for women (Chambless et al., 1987; Johannessen et al., 1989). In contrast, because it is more acceptable for women to remain home and to avoid the kinds of situations that people with agoraphobia avoid, women may be more likely than men to develop agoraphobia as a way of coping with their panic attacks.

Women in many cultures face threats in daily life that quite reasonably would lead them to be chronically anxious and more prone to all of the anxiety disorders. In particular, women are more likely than men to be the targets of physical and sexual abuse. Girls and women who have been physically or sexually abused are at increased risk for most anxiety disorders (Burnam et al., 1988).

Victimization has a tragic, cyclical nature. Women are more at risk for abuse when they have very low incomes and are newly divorced. In turn, women who have been abused are more likely to become unemployed, to have reduced income, and to become divorced. Thus, these women suffer a host of circumstances that are difficult to control, may be unpredictable, and may contribute to anxiety. Even women who have not yet been victimized may be chronically anxious due to the pervasive threat of violence.

Cross-Cultural Differences

Culture appears to strongly influence the manifestation of anxiety. People in Latino cultures report a syndrome known as *ataque de nervios* (attack of the nerves). A typical *ataque de nervios* might include trembling, heart palpitations, a sense of heat in the chest rising into the head, difficulty moving limbs, loss of consciousness or mind going blank, memory loss, a sensation of needles in parts of the body (paresthesia), chest tightness, difficulty breathing (dyspnea), dizziness, and faintness. Behaviorally, the person begins to shout, swear, and strike out at others. The person then falls to the ground and either experiences convulsive body movements or lies "as if dead" (Guarnaccia et al., 1996).

When *ataque de nervios* comes out of the blue, it is often attributed to the stresses of daily living or to spiritual causes. Like panic attacks, *ataque de nervios* is more common among recent trauma victims. A study of Puerto Ricans after the 1985 floods and mudslides in Puerto Rico found that 16 percent of the victims reported experiencing *ataque de nervios* (Guarnaccia et al., 1993).

More chronic anxiety-like symptoms, known as *nervios*, are quite common in Latino communities, particularly among the poor and uneducated. The term *nervios* encompasses a broad array of symptoms, including physical ailments (e.g., headaches, stomach problems, dizziness) and emotional symptoms (sadness, irritability, anger, absent-mindedness), as well as the presence of intrusive worries or negative thoughts. One study of 942 adults in rural Mexico found that 21 percent of the women and 10 percent of the men had chronic *nervios* (de Snyder, Diaz-Perez, & Ojeda, 2000). The authors suggest that, among the underprivileged, particularly women, *nervios* is a way of expressing the anger and frustration of "being at the bottom" and provides temporary release from grinding, everyday burdens of life (see also Lopez & Guarnaccia, 2000).

In Japan, the term *taijin kyofu-sho* has been used to describe an intense fear of interpersonal relations. *Taijin kyofu-sho* is characterized by shame about and persistent fears of causing others offense, embarrassment, or even harm through one's own inadequacies. It is most frequently encountered, at least in treatment settings, among young males. People with this disorder may fear blushing, emitting body odor, displaying unsightly body parts, speaking one's thoughts aloud, or irritating others (Chapman, Manuzza, & Fyer, 1995). Although *taijin kyofu-sho* may share some features with social phobia, it

In Latino cultures, *ataque de nervios* is a common anxiety syndrome.

reflects concerns about offending others, rather than embarrassing oneself. This is in line with the emphasis in Japan on deference to others (Kirmayer, 2001).

Are these just different manifestations of disorders that we call panic attacks or social phobias? Or are they truly culture-bound disorders that don't exactly match any disorders in the DSM? The study of people with *ataque de nervios* following the Puerto Rican mudslides found that most of these people could also be diagnosed with anxiety or depressive disorders, according to DSM criteria (Guarnaccia et al., 1993). The authors of this study noted, however, that these people conceptualized their symptoms as *ataque de nervios*, and accepting their conceptualization may be more useful and respectful than imposing a DSM diagnosis on them.

Clinicians are only beginning to understand such differences in the anxiety disorders. The sociocultural perspective draws attention to these differences, as well as differences between other groups, and suggests that we look to factors within the environment, and within interpersonal relationships and culture, for their causes.

SUMMING UP

■ Social perspectives on anxiety disorders suggest that group differences are tied to environmental pressures and to social and cultural norms.

- Women are more prone than men to panic disorder, phobias, and generalized anxiety disorder. This tendency may be tied to women's roles in society and to gender roles.

- The manifestation of anxiety may differ across cultures. As examples, Latino cultures have *ataque de nervios* and more chronic *nervios,* and the Japanese culture has *taijin kyofu-sho.* These difficulties may represent culturally acceptable forms of panic attacks, generalized anxiety disorder, and social phobia, respectively, or they may be true culture-bound syndromes.

CHAPTER INTEGRATION

Biology is clearly involved in the experience of anxiety. Evolution has prepared our bodies to respond to threatening situations with physiological changes that make it easier for us to flee from or fight an attacker. For some people, this natural physiological response may be impaired, leading to chronic arousal, to overreactivity, or to poorly regulated arousal. These people may be more prone to severe anxiety reactions to threatening stimuli and to the anxiety disorders.

Psychological and social factors also clearly play a role in anxiety and the anxiety disorders. People differ in what they perceive as threatening, and these differences in perception lead to differences in the level of anxiety people fear when faced with potentially threatening situations. These differences in perception may be due to upbringing. For example, a child may develop a phobia of dogs because her mother modeled a fearful response to dogs. Another child may be chronically anxious and may believe he must be perfect because his parents punish him severely if he makes any type of mistake. Differences in perceptions of what is threaten-

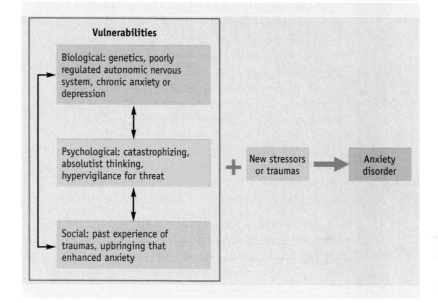

FIGURE 7.14   **Vulnerability-Stress Models.** Vulnerability-stress models of anxiety disorders describe how biological, psychological, and social factors work together to create these disorders.

ing may also be due to specific traumatic experiences that some people have suffered.

Some of the most successful models of the anxiety disorders are vulnerability-stress models (see Figure 7.14). These models stipulate that a person who develops an anxiety disorder has preexisting biological or psychological vulnerabilities, which are due in part to a history of trauma or severe stress. These vulnerabilities interact with new stressors to create the symptoms of anxiety disorders. These models go far in explaining why some people, but not others, experience anxiety that is so severe and chronic that it develops into a disorder.

Extraordinary People: Follow-Up

Marc Summers never knew he had OCD, had never heard of the disorder, until a psychiatrist went on his talk show one day to discuss the disorder, along with Mariette Hartley, an actress who was a spokesperson for the Obsessive Compulsive Foundation. As Marc Summers was reading about the disorder in preparation for interviewing the psychiatrist, he suddenly realized that he had it. He was both extremely relieved to find that what he had experienced all his life was a treatable disorder and extremely distressed at the thought of going on national television to discuss the disorder he now realized he had. He did go on the air with the psychiatrist, and in the middle of the program he admitted that he thought he had OCD. The psychiatrist and everyone else in the studio were supportive of him and congratulated him on his courage.

It was six more months before Marc Summers sought any help. He felt that just having a label for his troubles somehow made them manageable. When his talk show was abruptly canceled, however,

Marc Summers went into a tailspin of OCD symptoms and developed a serious episode of depression. His symptoms caused a great deal of agitation and distress in his family as well: His teenage daughter would be in her room with a friend, and Marc Summers would come in and insist on cleaning around them. After several overwhelming weeks, he finally called the psychiatrist he had interviewed on his TV show to talk about treatment. Eventually, he began taking a selective serotonin reuptake inhibitor and participating in behavior therapy. This treatment has helped him gain substantial control over his symptoms, but vestiges still linger. He thinks of OCD as a chronic disorder that he has not overcome but is in the process of overcoming (Summers, 2000 p. 209):

> My wife and kids have seen the change in me—that I'm better. But there are still things I'm working on. I want people to walk into our house and feel comfortable, but I'm still uptight, and it gnaws at me. I still get antsy when there are little children in the house; I think they're going to put their hands on the walls, or toddle around with a mouth full of cookies, dribbling crumbs on the floor. And I'm still waiting for the day when I'll be able to say to [my daughter] Meredith, "Why don't you invite fifty of your friends over for a party?" That's my goal: to feel comfortable with fifty teenagers partying hard late into the night in our house, leaning against the walls, dancing on the carpets, their jackets tossed hither and yon, bowls of chips knocked over on the living room floor, glasses spilled, glasses broken, chaos and mayhem, everything out of place.

Chapter Summary

- Anxiety has physiological and somatic, emotional, cognitive, and behavioral symptoms. (Review Table 7.1.)

- A panic attack is a short, intense experience of several of the physiological symptoms of anxiety, plus cognitions that one is going crazy, losing control, or dying. (Review Table 7.2.) The diagnosis of panic disorder is given when a person has spontaneous panic attacks frequently, begins to worry about having attacks, and changes his or her ways of living as a result of this worry. About one-third to one-half of people diagnosed with panic disorder also develop agoraphobia.

- One biological theory of panic disorder is that these people have overreactive autonomic nervous systems, which put them into a full fight-or-flight response with little provocation. This may be the result of imbalances in norepinephrine or serotonin or in hypersensitivity to feelings of suffocation. There also is some evidence that panic disorder may be transmitted genetically.

- Psychological theories of panic suggest that people who suffer from panic disorder pay very close attention to their bodily sensations, misinterpret bodily sensations in a negative way, and engage in snowballing, catastrophic thinking. This thinking then increases physiological activation, and a full panic attack ensues.

- Antidepressants and benzodiazepines are effective in reducing panic attacks and agoraphobic behavior, but people tend to relapse into these disorders when they discontinue these drugs. (Review Table 7.3.)

- An effective cognitive-behavioral therapy has been developed for panic and agoraphobia. (Review Table 7.3.) Clients are taught relaxation exercises and then learn to identify and challenge their catastrophic styles of thinking, often while having panic attacks induced in the therapy sessions. Systematic desensitization techniques are used to reduce agoraphobic behavior.

- People with agoraphobia fear places from which they might have trouble escaping or where they might have trouble getting help if they should have a panic attack.

- The specific phobias involve fears of specific objects or situations. Most fall into one of four categories: animal type, natural environment type, situational type, and blood-injection-injury type.

Social phobia involves fears of being judged or embarrassed. (Review Figure 7.8.)

■ There is little support for Freud's theory that phobias symbolize unconscious conflicts and fears that have been displaced onto neutral objects or for psychoanalytic treatment of phobias.

■ Behavioral theories suggest that phobias develop through classical and operant conditioning. (Review Table 7.5.) This fear is maintained because, through operant conditioning, the person has learned that avoiding the phobic object reduces the fear, so the avoidance is negatively reinforced. Phobias can also develop through observational learning. Finally, it appears that, through classical conditioning, humans develop phobias more readily to objects that our distant ancestors had reason to fear, such as snakes and spiders.

■ Cognitive theories have focused on social phobia and suggest that this disorder develops in people who have excessively high standards for their performance in social situations, assume that others will judge them harshly, and have biased attention to signs of social rejection. (Review Table 7.5.)

■ Behavioral treatments focus on extinguishing fear responses to phobic objects and have proven quite effective. (Review Table 7.6.) People with blood-injection-injury type phobias must also learn to tense up when they confront their phobic objects to prevent the decreases in blood pressure and heart rate they experience. Drug therapies have not proven useful for phobias.

■ Group cognitive-behavioral therapy has proven highly effective in the treatment of social phobia.

■ Benzodiazepines and antidepressant drugs can reduce acute symptoms of anxiety in people with phobias, but these symptoms return when the drugs are discontinued. (Review Table 7.6.)

■ People with generalized anxiety disorder (GAD) are chronically anxious and worried in most situations. (Review Table 7.7.) Psychodynamic theories attribute GAD to the inability to quell neurotic and moral anxiety. Humanistic theory attributes GAD to being compelled to meet conditions of worth in order to feel good about oneself. Existential theory attributes GAD to existential or death anxiety. Cognitive theories argue that people with GAD appear more vigilant for threatening information, even on an unconscious level. (Review Table 7.8.)

■ Benzodiazepines can produce short-term relief for some people with GAD but are not suitable in the long-term treatment of GAD. A new drug called buspirone and the antidepressants appear helpful in treating GAD.

■ Cognitive-behavioral therapies focus on changing the catastrophic thinking styles of people with GAD and have been shown to reduce acute symptoms and to prevent relapse in the majority of people.

■ Obsessions are thoughts, images, ideas, or impulses that are persistent, are intrusive, and cause distress, and they commonly focus on contamination, sex, violence, and repeated doubts. (Review Table 7.9.) Compulsions are repetitive behaviors or mental acts that the individual feels he or she must perform to erase his or her obsessions.

■ One biological theory of obsessive-compulsive disorder (OCD) speculates that the areas of the brain involved in the execution of primitive patterns of behavior, such as washing rituals, may be impaired in people with OCD. These areas of the brain are rich in the neurotransmitter serotonin, and drugs that regulate serotonin have proven helpful in the treatment of OCD. (Review Table 7.10 and Figure 7.12.)

■ Psychodynamic theories of OCD suggest that obsessions and compulsions symbolize unconscious conflicts or impulses. Psychodynamic therapies, which focus on helping clients gain insight into these unconscious conflicts or impulses, are not effective with OCD, however.

■ Cognitive-behavioral theories suggest that people with OCD think in ways that make them unable to turn off the negative, intrusive thoughts that most people have occasionally. Compulsive behaviors develop through operant conditioning when people are reinforced for behaviors that reduce anxiety. (Review Table 7.10.)

■ The most effective drug therapies for OCD are the antidepressants known as selective serotonin reuptake inhibitors.

■ Cognitive-behavioral therapies have also proven helpful for OCD. These therapies expose OCD clients to the content of their obsessions while preventing compulsive behavior, so that the anxiety over the obsessions and the compulsions to do the behaviors are extinguished.

■ Social perspectives on the anxiety disorders focus on differences between groups in the rates and expression of anxiety disorders. Women have higher rates of almost all the anxiety disorders than do men.

- Social theorists suggest that women are chronically anxious because they fear separation from others or because they truly are in greater danger of sexual or physical abuse than are men. Another theory is that men are punished for exhibiting signs of anxiety, whereas women are not, so men cope with their anxiety through adaptive or maladaptive activities, whereas women go on to develop anxiety disorders.

- Cultures may differ in their expression of anxiety disorders, or they may have distinct types of anxiety disorders not found in other cultures.

MindMap CD-ROM

The following resources on the MindMap CD-ROM that came with this text will help you to master the content of this chapter and prepare for tests:

- Interactive Segment: Measuring Anxiety
- Videos: Agoraphobia; OCD
- Chapter Timeline
- Chapter Quiz

Key Terms

anxiety 220

neurosis 221

panic attacks 222

panic disorder 222

norepinephrine 223

locus ceruleus 223

limbic system 224

anxiety sensitivity 225

interoceptive awareness 226

tricyclic antidepressants 227

selective serotonin reuptake inhibitors (SSRIs) 227

benzodiazepines 228

systematic desensitization therapy 229

agoraphobia 232

specific phobias 234

animal type phobias 234

natural environment type phobias 234

situational type phobias 234

blood-injection-injury type phobias 234

social phobia 235

negative reinforcement 238

prepared classical conditioning 240

applied tension technique 242

modeling 243

flooding 243

generalized anxiety disorder (GAD) 245

realistic anxiety 246

neurotic anxiety 246

moral anxiety 246

conditions of worth 247

existential anxiety 247

automatic thoughts 248

gamma-aminobutyric acid (GABA) 249

buspirone 250

obsessions 251

compulsions 251

obsessive-compulsive disorder (OCD) 251

caudate nucleus 254

Chapter 8

Day Dream
by Daniel Nevis

The image of myself which I try to create in my own mind in order that I may love myself is very different from the image which I try to create in the minds of others in order that they may love me.

—W. H. Auden, "Hic et Ille," *The Dyer's Hand* (1963)

Somatoform and Dissociative Disorders <

Extraordinary People

- **Anna O.**

Somatoform Disorders

People with conversion disorder completely lose functioning in a part of their bodies, apparently for psychological reasons. These disorders arise most commonly in response to extreme stress. Psychodynamic treatments involve helping people make the links between their symptoms and traumatic memories. Behavioral treatments focus on relieving people's anxiety about the initiating traumas through desensitization and exposure treatments.

People with somatization disorder have histories of multiple physical complaints for which there are no organic causes but for which they have sought a great deal of medical help. People with pain disorder focus their complaints on pain symptoms. These disorders may represent acceptable ways of expressing distress, especially for people in certain cultures. Cognitive theories of these disorders suggest that they are due to the catastrophization of physical symptoms. Treatment for these disorders involves helping people cope more adaptively with the stresses they face.

People with hypochondriasis worry chronically that they may be ill, even when they have no physical symptoms and have been thoroughly checked by medical professionals. The causes and treatments for hypochondriasis are similar to those for somatization disorder.

People with body dysmorphic disorder are excessively preoccupied with a part of their bodies and go to elaborate means to change that part of their bodies. This disorder may be a form of obsessive-compulsive disorder.

Dissociative Disorders

People with dissociative identity disorder (DID) develop multiple separate personalities. Dissociative identity disorder may develop in people who experience severe traumas, especially during childhood, and who use self-hypnosis to create "alters" to help them cope with these traumas. Treatment for dissociative identity disorder involves discovering the functions of all the personalities and helping the individual integrate these personalities and find more adaptive ways of coping with stress.

People with dissociative fugue move away from home and assume a new identity, with complete amnesia for their previous lives. Fugue states may arise following major traumas.

People with dissociative amnesia lose their memory for important facts about their lives and personal identities, apparently for psychological reasons. Psychologically based amnesias most frequently occur following traumatic events, such as sexual assaults. Depersonalization experiences involve a sense that one is detached from one's own mental processes or body.

Taking Psychology Personally

- **Dissociation in Everyday Life**

Chapter Integration

The somatoform and dissociative disorders provide several examples of how psychological factors can influence apparent physical functioning.

Extraordinary People

Anna O.

One of the most famous single cases in the annals of psychology and psychiatry was that of Anna O., a young Viennese woman whose real name was Bertha Pappenheim. She was born in Vienna on February 27, 1859, in a wealthy Orthodox Jewish family. Pappenheim became ill in 1880 at the age of 21, around the time of her father's serious illness and eventual death. Josef Breuer, a colleague of Freud's who had treated Pappenheim, wrote about her:

> Up to the onset of the disease, the patient showed no sign of nervousness, not even during pubescence. She had a keen, intuitive intellect, and a craving for psychic fodder, which she did not, however, receive after she left school. She was endowed with a sensitiveness for poetry and fantasy, which was, however, controlled by a very strong and critical mind. . . . Her will was energetic, impenetrable, and persevering, sometimes mounting to selfishness; it relinquished its aim only out of kindness and for the sake of others. . . . Her moods always showed a slight tendency to an excess of merriment or sadness, which made her more or less temperamental. . . . With her puritanically-minded family, this girl of overflowing mental vitality led a most monotonous existence. . . .
>
> Upon her father's illness, in rapid succession there seemingly developed a series of new and severe disturbances.
>
> Left-sided occipital pain; convergent strabismus (diplopia), which was markedly aggravated through excitement. She complained that the wall was falling over (obliquus affection). Profound analyzable visual disturbances, paresis of the anterior muscles of the throat, to the extent that the head could finally be moved only if the patient pressed it backward between her raised shoulders and then moved her whole back. Contractures and anesthesia of the right upper extremity, and somewhat later of the right lower extremity. . . . (Quoted in Edinger, 1963)

Bertha Pappenheim, a patient of Breuer's and Freud's, had several conversion symptoms. Breuer treated Pappenheim by asking her to talk about her symptoms under hypnosis, and after 18 months she seemed to be losing her symptoms. Pappenheim dubbed this the "talking cure." After Breuer told Pappenheim he thought she was well and he would not be seeing her again, later that evening he was called back to her house, where he found Pappenheim thrashing around in her bed, going through imaginary childbirth. Pappenheim claimed that the baby was Breuer's. He calmed her down by hypnotizing her but soon fled the house and never saw her again. Pappenheim remained ill intermittently for six years but, by age 30, had recovered. Breuer collaborated with Sigmund Freud in writing about Anna O., and their descriptions of the talking cure launched psychoanalysis as a form of psychotherapy.

Bertha Pappenheim, or Anna O., appeared to suffer from what is now called a *somatoform disorder*—she experienced physiological symptoms that Breuer argued were the result of painful memories or emotions she was not able to confront. In this chapter, we discuss the somatoform disorders, as well as the *dissociative disorders*, in which people develop multiple separate personalities or completely lose their memory for significant portions of their lives.

Some theorists consider both of these sets of disorders to be the result of an extreme form of escape used by some people facing traumatic experiences or intolerable distress. This form of escape is known as dissociation, a process in which different parts of an individual's identity, memories, or consciousness become split off from one another.

The somatoform and dissociative disorders have a long history in psychology. As the story of Bertha Pappenheim illustrates, these phenomena were the material for much of the early theorizing by Breuer, Freud, and other psychoanalysts. In recent years, these disorders, and the idea that people can completely lose conscious access to painful memories and emotions through dissociation, have become very controversial, and we will discuss that controversy at the end of this chapter. First, however, let's explore the nature of somatoform disorders.

SOMATOFORM DISORDERS

The **somatoform disorders** are a group of disorders in which people experience significant physical symptoms for which there is no apparent organic cause. Often, these symptoms are inconsistent with possible physiological processes, and there is strong reason to believe that psychological factors are involved. People with somatoform disorders usually do not consciously produce or control the symptoms. Instead, they truly experience the symptoms, and the symptoms pass only when the psychological factors that led to the symptoms are resolved.

One of the great difficulties in diagnosing somatoform disorders is the possibility that an individual has a real physical disorder that is simply difficult to detect or diagnose. Many of us have friends or relatives who complained to their physicians for years about specific physical symptoms, which the physicians attributed to "nervousness" or "attention seeking" but which later were determined to be early symptoms of serious disease. The diagnosis of somatoform disorder is easier when the psychological factors leading to the development of the symptoms can clearly be identi-fied or when physical examination can prove that the symptoms cannot be physiologically possible. For example, when a child is perfectly healthy on weekends but has terrible stomachaches in the morning on school days, the stomachaches may be due to distress over going to school. A more extreme example of a somatoform disorder is *pseudocyesis*, or false pregnancy, in which a woman believes she is pregnant but physical examination and laboratory tests confirm that she is not.

Distinction Between Somatoform and Related Disorders

The somatoform disorders are not the same as the **psychosomatic disorders**, which are medical disorders in which people have an actual physical illness or defect, such as high blood pressure, that can be documented with medical tests and that is being worsened by psychological factors. Instead, a person with a somatoform disorder does not have any illness or defect that can be documented with tests (see the Concept Overview in Table 8.1).

Somatoform disorders are also different from **malingering,** in which people fake a symptom or disorder in order to avoid an unwanted situation, such as military service, or in order to gain something, such as insurance payments. Again, an individual with a somatoform disorder subjectively experiences the symptoms, but there is no organic basis for the symptoms.

Finally, somatoform disorders are different from **factitious disorders,** in which a person deliberately fakes an illness to gain medical attention. Factitious disorders are also referred to as *Munchhausen's syndrome*. Note that the major difference between malingering and factitious disorders is the motivation for faking symptoms—in malingering the symptoms help an individual avoid an unwanted situation, whereas in factitious disorders

---

TABLE 8.1 Concept Overview

Distinctions Between Somatoform and Related Syndromes

Somatoform Disorders	Psychosomatic Disorders	Malingering	Factitious Disorders
Subjective experience of many physical symptoms, with no organic cause	Actual physical illness present and psychological factors seem to be contributing to the illness	Deliberate faking of physical symptoms to avoid an unpleasant situation, such as military duty	Deliberate faking of physical illness to gain medical attention

the symptoms are intentionally created to gain medical attention.

In recent years, several cases of **factitious disorder by proxy** have come to light. In these tragic cases, parents have faked or even created illnesses in their children in order to gain attention for themselves. They act as devoted and long-suffering protectors of their children, drawing praise for their dedicated nursing. Their children are subjected to unnecessary and often dangerous medical procedures and may actually die from their parents' attempts to make them ill. Seven-year-old Jennifer Bush appeared to be one victim of factitious disorder by proxy:

Sitting beside Hillary Clinton at a meeting on Capitol Hill, Jennifer Bush cut a heart-breaking figure. The 7-year-old Coral Springs, Florida, girl with big eyes and a perky red bow atop her little Dutch-boy coif seemed the perfect poster child for the Administration's health-care reform plan. Chronically ill almost from birth, Jennifer had already endured nearly 200 hospitalizations and 40 operations, and her $2 million–plus medical bill had exhausted the family's health-insurance benefits. Not surprisingly, Jennifer became a media darling, appearing on the *Today* show and on the front page of many newspapers.

Now it appears that Jennifer's suffering may have been much worse than was ever reported. Florida officials arrested Jennifer's seemingly devoted mother Kathleen Bush and charged her with aggravated child abuse and fraud. According to authorities, Bush, 38, deliberately caused her daughter's ailments by dosing her with unprescribed drugs, tampering with her medications, and even contaminating her feeding tube with fecal bacteria. As a result, say officials, Jennifer was subjected to dozens of needless operations and invasive procedures. Bush has denied all charges.

Almost as shocking as the charges against Jennifer's mother, however, is the fact that it took more than 4 years of warnings before state authorities placed the child under protective custody. Nurses at Coral Springs Medical Center began noticing as early as 1991—when Jennifer was just 4—that her condition seemed to worsen whenever her mother visited. . . .

State officials reopened the investigation last April, after receiving an anonymous complaint. According to the arrest affidavit, once her mother was informed of the inquiry, Jennifer's condition improved dramatically. In the preceding 9 months she had been hospitalized seven times for a total of 83 days. In the 9 months afterward she was admitted just once for 4 days. (Toufexis, 1996, p. 70)

Why would it take so long for authorities to intervene in a case such as this? Parents with factitious disorder by proxy may be very adept at hiding what they are doing to their children, especially if they have a medical background. Also, authorities must be extremely cautious about accusing a parent of causing harm to his or her children because of the great repercussions of falsely accusing parents, including the destruction of reputations, careers, and family relationships.

There are five types of somatoform disorders: conversion disorder, somatization disorder, pain disorder, hypochondriasis, and body dysmorphic disorder (see the Concept Overview in Table 8.2). Except for body dysmorphic disorder, each of these is characterized by the experience of one or

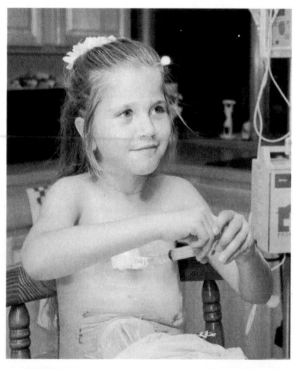

Jennifer Bush has endured hundreds of medical treatments and surgeries in her young life. Her mother was accused of causing Jennifer's illness to gain attention of physicians and the media.

TABLE 8.2 Concept Overview

Somatoform Disorders

The somatoform disorders are characterized by physical symptoms or complaints that appear to have psychological causes.

Disorders	Key Features
Conversion disorder	Loss of functioning in a part of the body for psychological rather than the physical reasons
Somatization disorder	History of complaints about physical symptoms, affecting many different areas of the body, for which medical attention has been sought but that appear to have no physical cause
Pain disorder	History of complaints about pain for which medical attention has been sought but that appears to have no physical cause
Hypochondriasis	Chronic worry that one has a physical disease in the absence of evidence that one does; frequent seeking of medical attention
Body dysmorphic disorder	Excessive preoccupation with a part of the body the person believes is defective

more physical symptoms. Body dysmorphic disorder involves a preoccupation with an imagined defect in one's appearance that is so severe that it interferes with one's functioning in life.

One study of 294 patients admitted to a hospital for medical symptoms examined the prevalence of somatoform disorders (excluding body dysmorphic disorder) and found them quite common. About 20 percent of patients were diagnosed with one or more somatoform disorders (Fink, Hansen, & Oxhøj, 2004). About one-third of these patients also had another psychiatric diagnosis, most often depression or anxiety. These patients were four times more likely than patients without somatoform disorders to have frequently been admitted to the hospital in the past and six times more likely to be heavy users of outpatient primary care facilities.

Conversion Disorder

The most dramatic type of somatoform disorder is **conversion disorder.** People with this disorder lose functioning in a part of their bodies, apparently due to neurological or other medical causes. Some of the most common conversion symptoms are paralysis, blindness, mutism, seizures, hearing loss, severe loss of coordination, and anesthesia in a limb. Conversion disorder typically involves one specific symptom, such as blindness or paralysis, but a person can have repeated episodes of conversion involving different parts of the body. Usually, the symptom develops suddenly following an extreme psychological stressor. A fascinating but

TABLE 8.3 DSM-IV-TR

Diagnostic Criteria for Conversion Disorder

Conversion disorder is diagnosed when individuals lose functioning in a part of their bodies apparently due to neurological or other medical conditions.

A. One or more symptoms or deficits affecting voluntary motor or sensory function that appear due to a neurological or medical condition.

B. Pyschological factors appear to be associated with the onset worsening of the symptoms or deficit.

C. The symptom or deficit is not intentionally produced or faked.

D. The symptom of deficit cannot be fully explained by a condition, the effects of drugs.

Source: Reprinted with permission from the *Diagnostic and Statistical Manual of Mental Disorders,* Fourth Edition, Text Revision. Copyright © 2000 American Psychiatric Association.

controversial feature of conversion disorders is *la belle indifference,* "the beautiful indifference"— people appear completely unconcerned about the loss of functioning they are experiencing (see the DSM-IV-TR criteria in Table 8.3).

Conversion disorder is relatively rare. One study of nearly 300 hospital patients estimated that 2.7 percent of the men and none of the women were suffering from a conversion disorder (Fink et al., 2004).

Theories of Conversion Disorder

Conversion disorder was formerly referred to as *conversion hysteria*, after the Greek word *hystera*, for "womb." Centuries ago, physicians believed that only women develop conversion symptoms and that these symptoms arose when a woman's desires for sexual gratification and children were not fulfilled, causing her womb to dislodge and wander (Veith, 1965). The theory was that the womb wandered into various parts of the body, such as the throat or the leg, causing related symptoms, such as a sensation of choking or paralysis. It is known now that conversion symptoms have nothing to do with wandering wombs and that, although they are more common in women than in men, men as well as women can develop these symptoms (Phillips, 2001).

Sigmund Freud became fascinated with conversion symptoms early in his career. One particularly dramatic conversion symptom is **glove anesthesia,** in which people lose all feeling in one hand, as if they were wearing a glove that wiped out physical sensation. This pattern of feeling loss cannot be caused physiologically, however, because the nerves in the hand do not provide feeling in a glovelike pattern. Freud found that these people tended to regain feeling in their hands when, usually under hypnosis, they recalled painful memories or emotions that had been blocked from consciousness.

The study of patients with severe dissociative experiences contributed much to Freud's theory of the structure of the mind and the role of repression in serious psychopathology. Freud and his contemporaries viewed conversion symptoms as results of the transfer of the psychic energy attached to repressed emotions or memories into physical symptoms. The symptoms often symbolized the specific concerns or memories that were being repressed.

It is difficult to prove the psychoanalytic theory, but some studies have provided evidence that could be interpreted as supporting it. Conversion symptoms were apparently quite common during the two world wars, when soldiers inexplicably became paralyzed or blind and therefore were unable to return to the front (Ironside & Batchelor, 1945). Many of the soldiers seemed unconcerned about their paralysis or blindness, showing *la belle indifference.* Sometimes, the physical symptoms represented traumas the soldiers had witnessed. For example, a soldier who has stabbed a civilian in the throat might lose the ability to talk.

Children can have conversion symptoms as well. Most often, their symptoms mimic those of someone they are close to who has a real illness (Grattan-Smith, Fairly, & Procopis, 1988; Spierings et al., 1990). For example, a child whose cherished grandfather has had a stroke and has lost functioning on his right side may become unable to use his right arm.

Conversion symptoms may be more common among sexual abuse survivors (Anderson, Yasenik, & Ross, 1993). Consider the following case of a woman who was raped and later developed both posttraumatic stress disorder (see Chapter 6) and conversion mutism.

At the time she sought treatment, Jane was a 32-year-old woman living with her 15-year-old son and employed as a lower-level executive. When she was 24, two men entered her home after midnight, held a knife to her throat, and threatened to kill her if she made a sound or struggled. They raped her orally and vaginally in front of her son, who was 7 at the time, and then locked them in the basement before leaving. Several weeks after the rape, Jane's mother, to whom she was very close, died of cancer. Jane felt she had to be "the strong one" in the family and prided herself because she "never broke down."

At the age of 31, during an abusive relationship with a live-in boyfriend, Jane developed conversion mutism. In the midst of attempting to ask her boyfriend to leave her house, she was unable to produce any sound. After several months of treatment with a speech therapist, Jane became able to whisper quietly but did not regain her normal speech. The speech therapist referred Jane to a clinic for the treatment of rape-related PTSD.

The pretreatment interview confirmed that Jane suffered from chronic PTSD as a result of the rape. She presented with fears, panicky reactions, nightmares, flashbacks, and intrusive thoughts about the assault. She reported attempts to avoid thinking about the assault and situations that reminded her of it and feelings of detachment from others. She also complained of sleep problems, exaggerated startle, and hyperalertness. Jane was moderately depressed and quite anxious. During the intake interview, Jane indicated that

(continued)

she had never verbally expressed her feelings about the assault and believed that this constriction underlied her inability to speak. (Rothbaum & Foa, 1991, pp. 453–454)

Recent research suggests that people with conversion symptoms are highly hypnotizable (Roelofs et al., 2002). This supports the idea that conversion symptoms result from spontaneous self-hypnosis, in which sensory or motor functions are dissociated, or split off, from consciousness in reaction to extreme stress.

A behavioral theory of conversion disorder was proposed by Ullman and Krasner (1975), who argued that people with this disorder attempt to behave in accord with their conception of how a person with a neurological disease would act in order to secure some end. Thus, this theory views conversion disorder as being created by an individual to gain attention or support, or to avoid an aversive situation, such as being returned to combat duty.

Distinguishing Conversion Disorder from Physical Disorders

For a conversion disorder to be diagnosed, it must be shown that there is no physiological cause for the individual's symptoms. Sometimes, a physiological cause of symptoms can be definitively ruled out, as in false pregnancy. Often, however, physiological tests cannot give definitive proof that a person's symptoms do not have physical causes.

Over the years, a number of studies have suggested that many people diagnosed with conversion disorder were actually suffering from a physical disorder that the diagnostic tests of the times could not identify. For example, one study found that 62.5 percent of people diagnosed with conversion symptoms later were found to have a medical disease, compared with only 5.3 percent of people not diagnosed with conversion symptoms (Watson & Buranen, 1979). The most common medical problem found in the conversion group was head injury, which usually occurred about six months before the conversion symptoms began. Other common problems were stroke, encephalitis, and brain tumors (see also Fishbain & Goldberg, 1991; Watson & Buranen, 1979).

If diagnostic tests cannot establish a physical cause for puzzling symptoms, then clinicians will try to determine whether the conversion symptoms are consistent with the way the body works. For example, recall that glove anesthesia violates what is known about the innervation of the hand, because the anesthesia usually begins abruptly at the wrist and extends throughout the hand. As Figure 8.1 shows, however, the nerves in the hand are distributed in a way that makes this pattern of anesthesia highly unlikely. Similarly, a person with a conversion paralysis from the waist down may not show the deterioration of the muscles in the legs that a person with a physical paralysis typically shows over time. Still, distinguishing conversion disorder from a physical disorder that is simply difficult to diagnose can be tricky.

With increases in the sophistication of tests to diagnose physical disorders, such as the use of neuroimaging techniques to identify pathologies that are not detectable by other methods, physicians have become better able to differentiate physical disorders from conversion symptoms. Interestingly, a few investigators are using neuroimaging techniques to try to understand how conversion symptoms occur (Ron, 2001).

For example, Vuilleumier and colleagues (2001) used single photon emission computerized tomography (SPECT) to examine seven patients for whom no organic cause could be found for their loss of functioning. They applied a vibration to both hands, a stimulus that typically causes widespread activity in the sensory and motor areas of the brain. The SPECT recorded activity in sensory and motor areas on both sides of the brain but recorded reduced activity in the thalamus and basal ganglia on the sides of the brain opposite the side of the body in which the patient had loss of

FIGURE 8.1 **Glove Anesthesia.** In the conversion symptom called glove anesthesia, the entire hand from finger tips to wrist become numb. Actual physical damage to the ulnar nerve, in contrast, causes anesthesia in the ring finger and little finger and beyond the wrist partway up the arm; damage to the radial nerve causes insensitivity only in parts of the ring, middle, and index fingers and the thumb and partway up the arm.

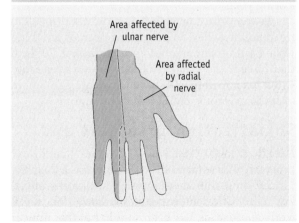

functioning. The authors suggested that emotional stressors can inhibit the circuits between sensorimotor areas of the brain and areas more involved in emotions (such as the thalamus and basal ganglia), resulting in loss of sensation or motor control.

Treating Conversion Disorder

Psychoanalytic treatment for conversion disorder focuses on the expression of painful emotions and memories and insight into the relationship between these and the conversion symptoms (Temple, 2001). Chronic conversion disorder is more difficult to treat. When symptoms are present for more than a month, the person's history often resembles somatization disorder (discussed in the section "Somatization Disorders and Pain Disorders") and is treated as such.

Behavioral treatments focus on relieving the person's anxiety around the initial trauma that caused the conversion symptoms and on reducing any benefits the person is receiving from the conversion symptoms. For example, the treatment of Jane, the woman in the case study, involved both systematic desensitization therapy and exposure therapy (refer to Chapter 6). A hierarchy of situations that Jane avoided, mostly situations that reminded her of her rape, was constructed. For the exposure, Jane was aided in approaching the situations that made her feel anxious and in progressing up her hierarchy to increasingly more feared situations, while practicing relaxation techniques. During the imagery sessions, Jane recounted the details of the assault first in general terms and later in great detail, including the details of the situation and the details of her physiological and cognitive reactions to the assault. At first, Jane was able to describe the assault in only a whisper, but she cried in full volume. After crying, Jane's speech became increasingly louder, with occasional words uttered in full volume. Eventually, she regained a full-volume voice. Following treatment, Jane's PTSD symptoms also decreased and diminished further over the following year.

People with conversion disorder are difficult to treat, because they do not believe there is anything wrong with them psychologically (Brown, 2004). If they have *la belle indifference,* they are not even motivated to cooperate with psychological treatment in order to overcome their physical symptoms.

Somatization Disorders and Pain Disorders

A person with **somatization disorder** has a long history of complaints about physical symptoms, affecting many different areas of the body, for which medical attention has been sought but that appear to have no physical cause (see the DSM-IV-TR crite-

---

TABLE 8.4 DSM-IV-TR

Diagnostic Criteria for Somatization Disorder

Somatization is diagnosed when individuals have a history of numerous physical complains for which no medical causes can be found.

A. A history of many physical complaints over a period of several years, for which the person seeks treatment

B. Symptoms in each of the following areas must occur at some time during the course of the disorder:

   a. Pain symptoms in at least four areas of the body (e.g., head, back, rectum, legs)

   b. At least two gastrointestinal symptoms other that pain (e.g., nausea, diarrhea)

   c. At least one sexual symptom

   d. At least one apparently neurological symptom (e.g., paralysis, double vision, deafness)

C. The symptom or deficit cannot be fully explained by a medical condition, the effects of drugs.

Source: Reprinted with permission from the *Diagnostic and Statistical Manual of Mental Disorders,* Fourth Edition, Text Revision. Copyright © 2000 American Psychiatric Association.

---

ria in Table 8.4). To receive a diagnosis of somatization disorder, a person has to complain of pain symptoms in at least four areas of the body, including two gastrointestinal symptoms (such as nausea and diarrhea), a sexual symptom (such as menstrual difficulties or painful intercourse), and an apparent neurological symptom (such as double vision or paralysis) (APA, 2000). A person with somatization disorder often goes from physician to physician, looking for attention and sympathy and for that one test that will prove that he or she really is sick.

People with somatization disorder may also report loss of functioning in a part of the body, as do people with conversion disorder. In somatization disorder, this loss of functioning is just one of a multitude of physical complaints, but, in conversion disorder, the loss of functioning may be the person's only complaint.

People who complain only of chronic pain may be given the diagnosis of **pain disorder.** In contrast, people with somatization disorder must report symptoms in each of four areas in order to be diagnosed with this disorder. Because most of what is known about pain disorder is encompassed in what is known about somatization disorder, we will discuss these two disorders together in this section.

It is extremely important for physicians not to assume that an individual has a psychological problem just because he or she cannot identify the cause of the physical complaints. Somatization disorder should be diagnosed only when the person has a clear history of multiple physical complaints for which no organic causes can be found. These complaints are usually presented in vague, dramatic, or exaggerated ways, and the individual may have insisted on medical procedures, even surgeries, that clearly were not necessary. One study of 191 persons in a general medicine outpatient clinic found that about 40 percent who had physical symptoms for which no organic causes could be found met the diagnostic criteria for a somatization disorder, meaning they had long histories of vague and multiple physical complaints with no apparent organic causes (Van Hemert et al., 1993).

As with conversion disorder, people with somatization or pain disorder may be prone to periods of anxiety and depression that they cannot express or cope with adaptively. They either somatize their distress or mask the distress in alcohol abuse or antisocial behavior. One large study of people with somatization disorder found that 76 percent had lifetime histories of episodes of major depression (Rief, Hiller, & Margraf, 1998; see also Feder et al., 2001; Katon, Sullivan, & Walker, 2001). In addition, people with the disorder frequently have histories of anxiety disorders, drug abuse, and personality disorders (Noyes et al., 2001).

Moderate degrees of somatization are apparently quite common. Very few people tend to meet the diagnostic criteria for somatization disorder (Katon et al., 2001). For example, one study found that 4.40 percent of a randomly selected sample of adults had a history of significant somatization, but only 0.03 percent met the criteria for somatization disorder (Escobar et al., 1987). A more recent study of hospital patients found that 3.3 percent of the women but none of the men qualified for a diagnosis of somatization disorder (Fink et al., 2004). Somatization tends to be more common in women than in men (Feder et al., 2001). Women have more periods of depression and anxiety than do men but are not always comfortable in expressing their distress directly, instead experiencing it in physical symptoms.

There also appear to be cultural variations in the prevalence of somatization disorder. Studies in China, Latin America, and Rwanda and studies of Asian and Hispanic/Latino groups in the United States have found that persons from these cultures are more likely to have somatization disorder than

are European Americans (Canino, Rubio-Stipec, & Bravo, 1988; Escobar et al., 1987; Hagengimana et al., 2003; Jun-mian, 1987; Shrout et al., 1992; Westermeyer et al., 1989). People from these cultures may have higher rates of somatization disorder because of norms of expressing distress in physical complaints rather than admitting to negative emotions. Traumatic events contributing to somatization and pain disorders may also be more common in people from these ethnic groups.

In the United States, somatization disorder also appears more common in older adults than in middle-aged adults (Feder et al., 2001). The cultural norms with which older adults were raised often prohibited admitting to depression or anxiety. For this reason, older adults who are depressed or anxious may be more likely to express their negative emotions in somatic complaints, which are acceptable and expected in old age. Young children also often express their distress in somatic complaints (Garber, Walker, & Zeman, 1991). They may not have the language to express difficult emotions but can say that they feel "bad" or that they have stomachaches or headaches. Ten to 30 percent of children and adolescents report having headaches or abdominal pain on a weekly basis (Fritz, Fritsch, & Hagino, 1997).

Somatization disorder tends to be a long-term problem. In a two-year study of people with somatization disorder and people with similar physical complaints for which an organic cause could be found, Craig and colleagues (1993) found that the symptoms of the people with somatization disorder lasted longer than the symptoms of those with medical illnesses. Moreover, changes in the symptoms of

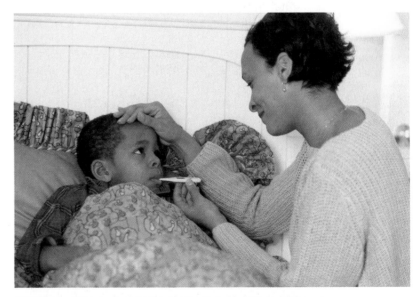

Children sometimes express distress through somatic symptoms.

the people with somatization disorder mirrored their emotional well-being: When they were anxious or depressed, they reported more physical complaints than when they were not anxious or depressed.

It can be extremely difficult to differentiate between somatization disorder and organic disorders for which there are no definitive tests. For example, one disorder that is often confused with, or overlaps with, somatization disorder is chronic fatigue syndrome. Chronic fatigue syndrome involves a persistent, debilitating fatigue accompanied by symptoms resembling those of common viral infections (Manu, Lane, & Matthews, 1992). Chronic fatigue syndrome is a real medical syndrome, probably caused by infections and a poorly

functioning immune system. It is difficult to diagnose, and it involves many of the symptoms identified by people diagnosed with somatization disorder. In one study of 100 adults complaining of chronic fatigue syndrome, 15 met the diagnostic criteria of somatization disorder, meaning they had long histories of vague physical complaints involving many parts of their bodies (Manu, Lane, & Matthews, 1989). However, 85 percent had no history of somatic complaints.

Theories of Somatization Disorders and Pain Disorders

Family history studies of somatization and pain disorders find that the disorders run in families, primarily among female relatives (Phillips, 2001). Anxiety and depression are also common in the female relatives of people with somatization disorder (Garber et al., 1991). The male relatives of persons with somatization disorder also have higher than usual rates of alcoholism and personality disorder. Similarly, patients with pain disorder tend to have family histories of psychological problems, most often pain disorder in the female relatives and alcoholism in the male relatives (Phillips, 2001).

It is not clear that the transmission of somatization or pain disorder in families has to do with genetics. A large study of over 3,400 twins could not determine whether genetics or shared environments were responsible for the aggregation within families of somatization (Gillespie et al., 2000). The children of parents with somatization or pain disorder may model their parents' tendencies to somatize distress (Craig et al., 1993). Parents who are somatizers also are more likely to neglect their children, and the children may learn that the only way to receive care and attention is to be ill. This finding is in accord with a behavioral account of somatization and pain disorders, which views them as the result of reinforcements for "sickness behavior" that the individual has received over much of his or her lifetime (Ullman & Krasner, 1975).

A cognitive theory of somatization and pain disorders suggests that persons with these disorders tend to experience bodily sensations more intensely than other people, to pay more attention than others to physical symptoms, and to catastrophize these symptoms (Kirmayer & Taillefer, 1997) (see Figure 8.2). For example, such a person might have a slight case of indigestion but experience it as severe chest pain and interpret the pain as a sure sign of a heart attack. The person's interpretation of his experience may have a direct influence on his physiological processes, by increasing his heart rate or blood pressure, thereby maintaining and exacerbating his pain. Further, his cognitions will influence the way he presents symptoms to

FIGURE 8.2   **A Model of Somatization Disorder.** Biological and psychosocial factors may combine to lead to somatization disorder.

Source: Reprinted from p. 353 of "Somatoform Disorders,"by L. J. Kirmayer and S. Taillefer. In S. M. Turner and M. Hersen (Eds.), *Adult Psychopatholgy and Diagnosis*, 3rd ed., 1997, pp. 333–383. Copyright © 1997 John Wiley & Sons, Inc. Reprinted with permission of John Wiley & Sons, Inc.

his physician and family. As a result, physicians may prescribe more potent medication or order more diagnostic tests, and family members may express more sympathy, excuse the person from responsibilities, and otherwise encourage passive behavior (Turk & Ruby, 1992). In this way, the person's misinterpreting and catastrophizing of his symptoms are reinforced by his physician and family, increasing the likelihood that he will interpret future symptoms in similar ways.

As with conversion disorder, somatization disorder may be part of posttraumatic stress disorder experienced by a person who has experienced a severe stressor. Many people with somatization disorder have histories of physical or sexual abuse or other severe childhood adversity (Katon et al., 2001; Pribor et al., 1993).

Refugees and recent immigrants also have an increased risk for somatization disorder. For example, a study of Bhutanese refugees found that over half of those who had been tortured, and over one-fourth of those who had not been tortured, had a persistent pain disorder (van Ommeren et al., 2001). Another study found that immigrants to the United States from Central America and Mexico had higher rates of posttraumatic stress disorder and somatization disorder than either U.S.–born Mexican Americans or European Americans. Fifty-two percent of the Central Americans who had fled to the United States to escape war or political unrest had posttraumatic stress disorder and somatization disorder (Cervantes, Salgado de Snyder, & Padilla, 1989). Similarly, a study of Hmong immigrants to the United States, who had fled Cambodia during the Khmer Rouge regime, found 17 percent to have posttraumatic stress disorder characterized by moderate to severe somatizing symptoms (Westermeyer et al., 1989).

Treatments for Somatization and Pain Disorders

Convincing people with somatization or pain disorder that they need psychological treatment is not easy. These people have held tightly to the belief that they are physically ill despite dozens of physicians' telling them they are not and hundreds of medical tests' failing to establish a physical illness. If they do agree to psychological treatment, people with these disorders appear to respond well to intervention that teaches them to express negative feelings or memories and to understand the relationship between their emotions and their physical symptoms (Beutler et al., 1988).

Psychodynamic therapies focus on providing this insight into the connections between emotions and physical symptoms by helping people recall events and memories that may have triggered the symptoms. Behavior therapies attempt to determine the reinforcements the individual receives for his or her symptoms and to eliminate these reinforcements while increasing positive rewards for healthy behavior. Cognitive therapies for these disorders help people learn to interpret their physical symptoms appropriately and to avoid catastrophizing physical symptoms, much as in the cognitive treatment of panic symptoms (see Chapter 6 and Campo & Fritz, 2001). One study found that antidepressant medications (selective serotonin reuptake inhibitors) led to significant improvement in somatization symptoms in a sample of 15 people with somatization disorder (Menza et al., 2001).

Some clinicians use the belief systems and cultural traditions of the clients they are treating to motivate the clients to engage in therapy and to help them overcome their physical complaints. Following is an example of the use of cultural beliefs to treat a Hispanic woman with somatization disorder.

> **CASE STUDY**
>
> Ellen was a 45-year-old woman who consulted many doctors for "high fever, vomiting, diarrhea, inability to eat, and rapid weight loss." After numerous negative lab tests, her doctor told her, "I can't go on with you; go to one of the *espiritistas* or a *curandera* (traditional healers)." A cousin then took her to a Spiritist center "for medicine." She was given herbal remedies: some baths and a tea of *molinillo* to take in the morning before eating. But the treatment focused mainly on the appearance of the spirit of a close friend who had died a month earlier from cancer. The spirit was looking for help from Ellen who had not gone to help during her friend's illness because of her own family problems. The main thrust of the healers' treatment plan was to help Ellen understand how she had to deal with the feelings of distress related to the stress of a paralyzed husband and caring for two small daughters alone. The spirit's influence on Ellen's body was an object lesson that was aimed at increasing her awareness of how her lifestyle was causing her to neglect the care of her own body and feelings much as she had neglected her dying friend. (Adapted from Koss, 1990, p. 82)

The spiritual healer in this case recognized the cause of Ellen's somatic complaints as stress, anger, and guilt; helped her link her physical symptoms with these emotions; and helped her find ways to cope more adaptively with the emotions. The context for this intervention was not cognitive therapy or another type of psychotherapy used by the dominant, non-Hispanic culture. Instead, the context was the cultural belief system concerning the role of spirits in producing physical symptoms.

Hypochondriasis

Somatization disorder and **hypochondriasis** are quite similar and may be variations of the same disorder. The primary distinction in the DSM-IV-TR between the two disorders is that people with somatization disorder actually experience physical symptoms and seek help for them, whereas people with hypochondriasis worry that they have a serious disease but do not always experience severe physical symptoms. However, when they do have any physical complaints, people with hypochondriasis are more likely to believe they should seek out medical attention immediately, whereas people with somatization disorder are more likely to wait and see how the bodily sensations develop (Rief et al., 1998). People with hypochondriasis may go through many medical procedures and float from physician to physician, sure that they have a dreaded disease. Often, their fears focus on a particular organ system. For example, a woman may be totally convinced that she has heart disease, even though the most sophisticated medical diagnostic tests have shown no evidence of heart disease. Carlos, in the following case study, was convinced something was wrong with his bowels.

CASE STUDY

Carlos, a married man of 39, came to the clinic, complaining, "I have trouble in my bowels and then it gets me in my head. My bowels just spasm on me, I get constipated." The patient's complaints dated back 12 years to an attack of "acute indigestion," in which he seemed to bloat up and pains developed in his abdomen and spread in several directions. He traced some of these pathways with his finger as he spoke. Carlos spent a month in bed at this time and then, based on an interpretation of something the doctor said, rested for another 2 months before working again. Words of reassurance from his doctor failed to take effect. He felt "sick, worried, and scared," feeling that he really would never get well again.

Carlos became very dependent upon the woman he married when he was 22 years old. He left most of the decisions to her and

showed little interest in sexual relations. His wife was several years older than he and did not seem to mind his totally passive approach to life. His attack of "acute indigestion" followed her death, 5 years after marriage, by 3 months during which he felt lost and hopeless. In time, he moved to a rural area and remarried. His second wife proved less willing to assume major responsibilities for him than the first, and she made sexual demands upon him that he felt unable to meet. He became more and more preoccupied with his gastrointestinal welfare. In the complete absence of community facilities for psychological assistance where he lived, prognosis for recovery from chronic partially disabling hypochondria was deemed poor. (Adapted from Cameron & Rychlak, 1985)

Diagnosable hypochondriasis is not very common. A study of 1,456 patients in a general medical practice found that only 3 percent met the diagnostic criteria for hypochondriasis (Escobar et al., 1998). Another study of hospital patients found that 2.1 percent of the men and 7.8 percent of the women were diagnosed with hypochondriasis (Fink et al., 2004).

Most studies of hypochondriasis have grouped people who have this disorder with people who have somatization disorder, in part because many people qualify for the diagnosis of both disorders. Thus, most of what is known about the causes of somatization disorder also applies to the causes of hypochondriasis. In particular, people with hypochondriasis appear very prone to chronic depression and anxiety and have family histories of these disorders (Barsky, Wyshak, & Klerman, 1992; Escobar et al., 1998). Their fears about their health often stem from general distress and an inability to cope with that distress in adaptive ways. People with hypochondriasis also tend to have dysfunctional beliefs about illness, assuming that serious illnesses are common, and they tend to misinterpret any physical change in themselves as a sign for concern (Marcus & Church, 2003).

As is the case with people who have somatization disorder, people who have hypochondriasis do not appreciate suggestions that their problems are caused by psychological factors and thus tend not to seek psychological treatment. When they do receive psychological treatment, it focuses on helping them understand the association between their symptoms and emotional distress and on helping

Dial 123-SICK and reach out to your fellow hypochondriacs.
© *The New Yorker Collection 1989 J.B. Handelsman from cartoonbank.com. All rights reserved.*

them find more adaptive ways of coping with their distress.

Body Dysmorphic Disorder

People with **body dysmorphic disorder** are excessively preoccupied with a part of their bodies that they believe is defective. Although it is not clear whether there are gender differences in the prevalence of this disorder, men and women with body dysmorphic disorder tend to obsess about different parts of their bodies (Perugi et al., 1997; Phillips & Diaz, 1997). Women seem to be more concerned with their breasts, legs, hips, and weight, whereas men tend to be preoccupied with a small body build, their genitals, excessive body hair, and hair thinning. People with this disorder spend hours looking at their "deformed" body parts, perhaps in a mirror, and perform elaborate rituals to try to improve the parts or hide them. For example, they may spend hours styling their hair to hide the defects in their ears or wear heavy makeup to hide their defects. Many people with this disorder also seek out plastic surgery to change the offensive body parts (Phillips, 2001).

Case studies of some people with this disorder indicate that their perceptions of deformation can be so severe and bizarre as to be considered out of touch with reality (Phillips, 1991). Even if they do not lose touch with reality, some people with body dysmorphic disorder have severe impairment in their functioning due to the disorder. For example, a study of 188 people with this disorder found that 98 percent avoided social activities because of their "deformity," 30 percent had become housebound, and about 20 percent had attempted suicide (Phillips & Diaz, 1997). Approximately 25 percent attempt suicide (Phillips, Kim, & Hudson, 1995).

Body dysmorphic disorder tends to begin in the teenage years and to become chronic if untreated. The average age of onset of this disorder is 16 years; on average, these people have four or more bodily preoccupations. Those who seek treatment wait an average of 6 years from the onset of their concerns before seeking treatment (Cororve & Gleaves, 2001).

CASE STUDY

Sydney was a popular 17-year-old who attended a suburban high school near Washington, DC. During the spring of her senior year, Sydney became preoccupied with her appearance and began to look constantly for her own image in windows and mirrors. In particular, Sydney began to notice that her nose was abnormally shaped. Her friends all told her that she was crazy when she expressed her concern, so she stopped talking about it to them. She began to apply makeup in an attempt to offset what she believed to be the contemptible contour of her nose. She started wearing her hair loosely, holding her head down much of the time, so that her face was partially obscured, and brushing her hair excessively to encourage it to fall forward around her face. Her distress grew, and she repeatedly begged her parents to let her have surgery to correct the shape of her nose, which she regarded as hideous. Her pleas turned to volatile arguments when her parents told her that her nose was fine and that they would not agree to surgery. Sydney started finding excuses not to go out with her friends and refused to date, because she could not stand the thought of anyone looking at her up close. She stayed home in her room, staring for hours in the mirror. She refused to attend her senior prom or graduation ceremony.

After high school, Sydney got a job as a night security guard, so that she could isolate herself as much as possible and not be seen by others. During the next seven years, she had

(continued)

five surgeries to change the shape of her nose. Each time, she became even more dissatisfied and obsessed with her appearance. Although everyone who knew Sydney thought she looked fine, she remained obsessed and tormented by her "defect," which dominated her life.

Although clinicians in Europe have frequently written about body dysmorphic disorder, it has been relatively ignored in the United States (Corove & Gleaves, 2001). The diagnosis was introduced in the DSM in the 1987 edition. Body dysmorphic disorder is highly comorbid with several disorders, including anxiety and depressive disorders, personality disorders, and substance use disorders (Corove & Gleaves, 2001).

One anxiety disorder that is relatively common among people with body dysmorphic disorder is obsessive-compulsive disorder (Phillips & Diaz, 1997). Some theorists believe that body dysmorphic disorder may be a form of obsessive-compulsive disorder, in which the person obsesses about a part of the body and engages in compulsive behaviors to change that part (see Corove & Gleaves, 2001; Phillips, 2001). An MRI study of the brains of eight women with body dysmorphic disorder found that they showed some of the same abnormalities in the caudate nucleus as are seen in obsessive-compulsive disorder (Rauch et al., 2003).

Other theorists point out the commonalities between body dysmorphic disorder and eating disorders, particularly the extreme overvaluing of

appearance, and suggest they are both variants of a body image disorder (Rosen & Ramirez, 1998). For now, body dysmorphic disorder remains classified as a somatoform disorder because it involves a preoccupation with bodily complaints.

Psychoanalytically oriented therapy for body dysmorphic disorder focuses on helping clients gain insight into the real concerns behind their obsession with a body part. Cognitive-behavioral therapies focus on challenging clients' maladaptive cognitions about the body, exposing them to feared situations concerning their bodies, extinguishing anxiety about their body parts, and preventing compulsive responses to those body parts (Corove & Gleaves, 2001). For example, a client may identify her ears as her deformed body part. The client could develop her hierarchy of things she would fear doing related to her ears, ranging from looking at herself in the mirror with her hair fully covering her ears to going out in public with her hair pulled back and her ears fully exposed. After the client has learned relaxation techniques, she would begin to work through the hierarchy, engaging in the feared behaviors, beginning with the least feared and using the relaxation techniques to quell anxiety. Eventually, the client would work up to the greatly feared situation of exposing her ears in public. At first, the therapist might contract with the client that she cannot engage in behaviors intended to hide the body part (such as putting her hair over her ears) for at least five minutes after going out in public. The eventual goal in therapy would be for the client's concerns about the body part to diminish totally and not affect her behavior or functioning. Empirical studies have supported the efficacy of cognitive-behavioral therapies in treating body dysmorphic disorder (Corove & Gleaves, 2001).

Finally, studies suggest that selective serotonin reuptake inhibitors (SSRIs) can be effective in some cases in reducing obsessional thought and compulsive behavior in persons with this disorder (Phillips & Najjar, 2003; Saxena, Winegrad, Duncan et al., 2001). This finding fuels theories that body dysmorphic disorder is a form of obsessive-compulsive disorder, because SSRIs are effective in treating obsessive-compulsive disorder as well (see Chapter 7).

SUMMING UP

- Somatoform disorders are a group of disorders in which people experience significant physical symptoms for which there is no apparent organic cause.

- Conversion disorder involves loss of functioning in a body part for no organic

People with body dysmorphic disorder spend a great deal of time examining the parts of their body they feel are defective.

reason. Conversion symptoms often occur after trauma or stress, perhaps because the person cannot face memories or emotions associated with the trauma. Treatment for conversion disorder focuses on the expression of emotions or memories associated with the symptoms.

■ Somatization disorder involves a long history of multiple physical complaints for which people have sought treatment but for which there is no apparent organic cause. Pain disorder involves only the experience of chronic, unexplainable pain. These disorders appear to be common, particularly among women, young children, the elderly, and people of Asian or Hispanic heritage.

■ Hypochondriasis is a condition in which people worry chronically about having a dreaded disease, despite evidence that they do not. This disorder appears to be rare.

■ In somatization disorder, pain disorder, and hypochondriasis, individuals often have a history of anxiety and depression. These disorders may represent acceptable ways of expressing emotional pain.

■ Cognitive theories of the disorders say that they are due to excessive focus on physical symptoms and the tendency to catastrophize symptoms. Treatment for these disorders involves helping people identify the feelings and thoughts behind the symptoms and find more adaptive ways of coping.

■ People with body dysmorphic disorder have an obsessional preoccupation with some parts of their bodies and make elaborate attempts to change these body parts. Treatments for body dysmorphic disorder include psychodynamic therapies to reveal underlying concerns, systematic desensitization therapy to reduce obsessions and compulsions about the body, and the use of selective serotonin reuptake inhibitors.

DISSOCIATIVE DISORDERS

Most of us occasionally have mild dissociative experiences (Aderibigbe, Bloch, & Walker, 2001; Seedat, Stein, & Forde, 2003). Daydreaming is a dissociative experience. When we daydream, we can lose consciousness of where we are and of what is going on around us. Becoming absorbed in a movie is also a dissociative experience.

Dissociative experiences are especially common when we are sleep-deprived and under stress. For example, a study of mentally healthy soldiers undergoing survival training in the U.S. Army found that over 90 percent reported dissociative symptoms, such as feeling as if they were separated from what was happening, as if they were watching themselves in a movie, in response to the stress of the training (Morgan et al., 2001). We discuss common dissociative symptoms in *Taking Psychology Personally: Dissociation in Everyday Life*.

Scientific interest in dissociative experiences has waxed and waned for more than a century (Kihlstrom, 2005). There was a great deal of interest in dissociation in nineteenth-century France and in the United States among neurologists and psychologists. French neurologist Pierre Janet viewed dissociation as a process in which systems of ideas are

Taking Psychology Personally

Dissociation in Everyday Life

You are driving down a familiar road, thinking about a recent conversation with a friend. Suddenly, you realize that you've driven several miles and don't remember traveling that section of the road. How did you get where you currently are? Obviously, you must have driven there, but you have no memory of passing the usual landmarks.

This kind of dissociative experience is quite common (Aderibigbe et al., 2001; Seedat et al., 2003). Researcher Colin Ross (1997) asked more than 1,000 adults, randomly selected from the community of Winnipeg in Canada, about a number of different dissociative experiences. The accompanying table on page 282 presents some of Ross' findings. Miss-

ing part of a conversation appears to be the most common dissociative experience, followed by being unsure whether you have actually carried through with something (such as brushing your teeth) or have only thought about it. These experiences seem quite benign. Farther down the list are somewhat more bizarre experiences, such as hearing voices in your head, feeling as though your body is not your own, and not recognizing objects or other people as real. As the table shows, even these rather bizarre experiences are reported as happening at least occasionally by a substantial percentage of "normal" people.

(continued)

Taking Psychology Personally (*continued*)

Dissociative Experiences in the General Population

These are the percentages of people in a random sample of 1,055 adults in Winnipeg, Canada who acknowledged ever having experienced each item and who fell into the pathological range for frequency of experiences of the item.

Experience	Percentage Acknowledging	Percentage in Pathological Range
Missing part of a conversation	83	29
Not sure whether one has done something or only thought about it	73	25
Remembering the past so vividly one seems to be reliving it	60	19
Talking out loud to oneself when alone	56	18
Not sure if remembered event happened or was a dream	55	13
Feeling as though one were two different people	47	12
So involved in fantasy that it seems real	45	11
Driving a car and realizing that one doesn't remember part of the trip	48	8
Finding notes or drawings that one must have done but doesn't remember doing	34	6
Seeing oneself as if looking at another person	29	4
Hearing voices inside one's head	26	7
Other people and objects do not seem real	26	4
Finding unfamiliar things among one's belongings	22	4
Feeling as though one's body is not one's own	23	4
Finding oneself in a place but unaware of how one got there	19	2
Finding oneself dressed in clothes one doesn't remember putting on	15	1
Not recognizing one's reflection in a mirror	14	1

Source: From C. A. Ross, *Dissociative Identity Disorder*. Copyright © 1997 John Wiley & Sons, Inc. Reprinted with permission of John Wiley & Sons, Inc.

How can we explain everyday dissociative experiences? They can be caused by many factors. Fatigue and stress are probably the most common causes. Binge drinking alcohol or taking other psychoactive drugs can cause many of the memory lapses shown in the table. Older adults whose short-term memories are fading often forget having done things, and, as we discuss in Chapter 14, several cognitive disorders can lead to memory lapses, even the inability to recognize faces. Most of the time, however, dissociative experiences are transient and do not signal any long-term problems.

Some people have dissociative experiences frequently enough that they interfere with their functioning. Ross (1997) categorized these people as in the "pathological range" of dissociative experiences. The percentage of people in his sample falling in this range for each of the experiences he studied is given in the righthand column of the table. You can see that occasional dissociative experiences are extremely common, but most of the more bizarre dissociative experiences occur infrequently enough that only a small percentage of people are categorized in the pathological range.

The next time you find yourself wondering how you got to where you are standing, or not remembering dressing in the clothes you are wearing, don't panic. Chances are that it is one of those everyday dissociative experiences we all have.

split off from consciousness but accessible through dreams and hypnosis. One case he investigated was that of a woman named Irene, who had no memory of the fact that her mother had died. However, during her sleep, Irene physically dramatized the events surrounding her mother's death.

After about 1910, interest in dissociative phenomena waned, partly because of the rise of behaviorism and biological approaches within psychology, which rejected the concept of repression and the use of techniques such as hypnosis in therapy. Ernest Hilgard (1977/1986) revitalized interest in dissociation in his experiments on the "hidden observer" phenomenon. He argued that there is an *active mode* to consciousness, which includes our conscious plans and desires and voluntary actions. In its passive *receptive mode,* the conscious registers and stores information in memory without being aware that the information has been processed, as if hidden observers were watching and recording events in people's lives without their awareness.

Hilgard and his associates (Hilgard, 1977/1986) conducted experimental studies in which participants were hypnotized and given a suggestion that they would feel no pain during a painful procedure but that they would remember the pain when the hypnotist gave them a specific cue. These participants, indeed, showed no awareness of pain during the procedure. When cued, they reported memories of the pain in a matter-of-fact fashion, as if a lucid, rational observer of the event had registered the event for the participant.

Other research has shown that some anesthetized surgical patients can later recall, under hypnosis, specific pieces of music played during the surgery. Again, it is as if a "hidden observer" is registering the events of the operations even while the patients are completely unconscious under anesthesia (see Kihlstrom, 2001; Kihlstrom & Couture, 1992; Kirsch & Lynn, 1998).

For most of us, the active and receptive modes of consciousness weave our experiences together so seamlessly that we do not notice any division between them. People who develop dissociative disorders may have chronic problems integrating their active and their receptive consciousness (Hilgard, 1992; Kihlstrom, 2001). That is, different aspects of consciousness in these people do not communicate with each other in normal ways but, rather remain split and operate independently of each other.

We begin our discussion of specific dissociative disorders with dissociative identity disorder (DID), formerly known as *multiple personality disorder.* We then move to dissociative fugue, dissociative amnesia, and depersonalization disorder (see

the Concept Overview in Table 8.5). All these disorders involve frequent experiences in which various aspects of a person's "self" are split off from each other and felt as separate.

TABLE 8.5	Concept Overview

Key Features of the Dissociative Disorders in DSM-IV-TR

The dissociative disorders represent extreme experiences in which aspects of people identities split apart.

Disorder	Key Features
Dissociative identity disorder	There are separate, multiple personalities in the same individual. The personalitites may be aware of each other or may have amnesia for each other.
Dissociative fugue	The person moves away and assumes a new identity, with amnesia for the previous identity. There is no switching among personalities, as there is in dissociative identity disorder.
Dissociative amnesia	The person loses memory for important personal facts, including personal identity, with no apparent organic cause.
Depersonalization disorder	There are frequent episodes in which the individual feels detached from his or her mental state of body. The person does not develop new identities or have amnesia for these episodes.

Dissociative Identity Disorder

CASE STUDY

Eve White was a quiet, proper, unassuming woman, a full-time homemaker and devoted mother of a young daughter. She sought help from a psychiatrist for painful headaches that were occurring with increasing frequency. The psychiatrist decided that her headaches were related to arguments she was having with her husband over whether to raise their young daughter in the husband's church (Catholic) or in her church (Baptist). After undergoing some marital therapy, Mrs. White's marriage improved and her headaches subsided for a year or so.

Then, her husband recontacted her therapist, alarmed over changes in his wife's behavior. She had gone to visit a favorite cousin in a town 50 miles away and during the visit

(continued)

had behaved in a much more carefree and reckless manner than she usually did. Mrs. White told her husband over the phone that she was not going to return home, and the two had a terrible fight, which ended in an agreement to divorce. When Mrs. White did return home a few days later, however, she said she had no memory of the fight with her husband or, for that matter, of the visit with her cousin.

Shortly thereafter, Mrs. White apparently went shopping and bought hundreds of dollars worth of elaborate clothing, which the couple could not afford. When confronted by her husband about her expenditures, Mrs. White claimed to have no memory of buying the clothing.

At the urging of her husband, Mrs. White made an appointment with the therapist whom she had originally consulted about her headaches. In the session, she admitted that her headaches had returned and were much more severe now than before. Eventually, she also tearfully admitted that she had begun to hear a voice other than her own speaking inside her head and that she feared she was going insane. The therapist asked her more questions about the clothes-buying spree, and Mrs. White became more tense and had difficulty getting words out to discuss the incident. Then, as her therapist reported,

> The brooding look in her eyes became almost a stare. Eve seemed momentarily dazed. Suddenly her posture began to change. Her body slowly stiffened until she sat rigidly erect. An alien, inexplicable expression then came over her face. This was suddenly erased into utter blankness. The lines of her countenance seemed to shift in a barely visible, slow, rippling transformation. For a moment there was the impression of something arcane. Closing her eyes, she winced as she put her hands to her temples, pressed hard, and twisted them as if to combat sudden pain. A slight shudder passed over her entire body.
>
> Then the hands lightly dropped. She relaxed easily into an attitude of comfort the physician had never before seen in this patient. A pair of blue eyes popped open. There was a quick reckless smile. In a bright, unfamiliar voice that sparked, the woman said, "Hi, there, Doc!"
>
> Still busy with his own unassimilated surprise, the doctor heard himself say, "How do you feel now?"
>
> "Why just fine—never better! How you doing yourself, Doc?"
>
> Eve looked for a moment straight into his eyes. Her expression was that of one who is just barely able to restrain laughter. Her eyes rolled up and to one side for an instant, then the lids flicked softly before opening wide again. She tossed her head lightly with a little gesture that threw the fine dark hair forward onto her shoulder. A five-year-old might have so reacted to some sudden, unforeseen amusement. In the patient's gesture there was something of pert sauciness, something in which the artless play of a child and a scarcely conscious flirtatiousness mingled. . . .
>
> "She's been having a real rough time. There's no doubt about that," the girl said carelessly. "I feel right sorry for her sometimes. She's such a damn dope though. . . . What she puts up with from that sorry Ralph White— and all her mooning over that little brat . . . ! To hell with it, I say!"
>
> The doctor asked, "Who is 'she'?"
>
> "Why, Eve White, of course. Your longsuffering, saintly, little patient."
>
> "But aren't you Eve White?" he asked.
>
> "That's for laughs," she exclaimed, a ripple of mirth in her tone. . . . "Why, I'm Eve Black," she said. . . . "I'm me and she's herself," the girl added. "I like to live and she don't. . . . Those dresses—well, I can tell you about them. I got out the other day, and I needed some dresses. I like good clothes. So I just went into town and bought what I wanted. I charged 'em to her husband, too!" She began to laugh softly. "You ought've seen the look on her silly face when he showed her what was in the cupboard!"

In later sessions, Eve Black told the psychiatrist of escapades in which she had stayed out all night, drinking, and then had gone "back in" in the morning to let Eve White deal with the hangover. At the beginning of therapy, Eve White had no consciousness of Eve Black or of more than 20 personalities eventually identified during therapy.

This story of *The Three Faces of Eve* is one of the most detailed and gripping accounts of someone diagnosed with dissociative identity disorder. Eve White eventually recovered from her disorder, integrating the aspects of her personality represented by Eve Black and her other personalities into one entity and living a healthy, normal life.

Dissociative identity disorder (DID) is one of the most controversial and fascinating disorders recognized in clinical psychology and psychiatry. People with this disorder have more than one distinct identity or personality, and many people have more than a dozen personalities. Each personality appears to have different ways of perceiving and relating to the world. Some theorists claim the alternate personalities, or *alters,* can have distinct facial expressions, speech characteristics, physiological responses, gestures, interpersonal styles, and attitudes (Miller, 1989; Putnam, 1991). They often are different ages and different genders and perform specific functions.

The movie *The Three Faces of Eve* depicted the story of a woman with dissociative identity disorder, who discovered extravagant articles of clothing in her closet that she didn't remember buying.

Reliable estimates of the prevalence of dissociative identity disorder are hard to come by. One study of psychiatric inpatients found that 1 percent could be diagnosed with DID (Rifkin et al., 1998). The vast majority of persons diagnosed with this disorder are adult women. It may be that the conditions leading to dissociative identity disorder are more commonly experienced by women than by men (Peterson, 1991). Among children diagnosed with dissociative identity disorder, however, the numbers of females and males appear to be more equal (Dell & Eisenhower, 1990). It may be that boys with dissociative identity disorder are more likely to be taken for treatment than are girls, so, as adults, males are less likely to continue to have the disorder than are females (Dell & Eisenhower, 1990). Or girls may be more likely than boys to experience traumas in adolescence that lead to dissociative identity disorder, which continues into adulthood.

There are some differences between the characteristics of the personalities of males and females with dissociative identity disorder. Males with dissociative identity disorder appear to be more aggressive than females with the disorder. In one study, 29 percent of male dissociative identity disorder patients had been convicted of crimes, compared with 10 percent of female dissociative identity disorder patients (Ross & Norton, 1989). Case reports suggest that females with dissociative identity disorder tend to have more somatic complaints than do males and may engage in more suicidal behavior (Kluft, 1985).

Symptoms of Dissociative Identity Disorder

The cardinal symptom in dissociative identity disorder is the presence of multiple alters with distinct qualities. These alters can take many forms and perform many functions. *Child alters—* alters who are young children, who do not age as the individual ages—appear to be the most common type (Ross, Norton, & Wozney, 1989). Childhood trauma is often associated with the development of dissociative identity disorder. A child alter may be created during a traumatic experience to become the victim of the trauma, while the "host" personality escapes into the protection of psychological oblivion. Alternately, an alter may be created as a type of big brother or sister to protect the host personality from traumas. When a child alter is "out," or in control of the individual's behavior, the adult may speak and act in a childlike way.

A second type of alter is the *persecutor personality.* These alters inflict pain or punishment on the

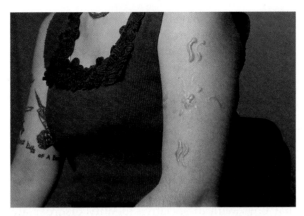

People with dissociative identity disorder may engage in self-mutilative behavior

other personalities by engaging in self-mutilative behaviors, such as self-cutting or -burning and suicide attempts (Coons & Milstein, 1990; Ross, Norton & Wozney, 1989). A persecutor personality may engage in a dangerous behavior, such as taking an overdose of pills or jumping in front of a truck, and then "go back inside," leaving the host personality to experience the pain. Persecutors may have the belief that they can harm other personalities without harming themselves.

A third type of alter is the protector, or *helper, personality.* The function of this personality is to offer advice to other personalities or to perform functions the host personality is unable to perform, such as engaging in sexual relations or hiding from abusive parents. Helpers sometimes control the switching from one personality to another or act as passive observers who can report on the thoughts and intentions of all the other personalities (Ross, 1989).

People with dissociative identity disorder typically claim to have significant periods of amnesia, or blank spells. They describe being completely amnesic for the periods when other personalities are in control or having one-way amnesia between certain personalities. In these instances, one personality is aware of what the other is doing, but the second personality is completely amnesic for periods when the first personality is in control. As with Eve White, people with dissociative identity disorder may suddenly discover unknown objects in their homes, or they may lose objects. People they do not recognize might approach them on the street, claiming to know them. They may consistently receive phone calls or mail addressed to someone with a different first or last name. Verifying claims of amnesia is difficult, but some studies by cognitive psy-

chologists suggest that information and memories tend to transfer between identities, even in individuals who believe certain personalities experience amnesia (Allen & Iacono, 2001). Other studies support claims of amnesic barriers between personalities (Dorahy, 2001).

Self-destructive behavior is very common among people with dissociative identity disorder and is often the reason they seek or are taken for treatment (Ross, 1999). This behavior includes self-inflicted burns or other injuries, wrist slashing, and overdoses. About three-quarters of patients with dissociative identity disorder have a history of suicide attempts, and over 90 percent report recurrent suicidal thoughts (Ross, 1997).

Like adults, children with dissociative identity disorder exhibit a host of behavior and emotional problems (Putnam, 1991). Their performance in school may be erratic, sometimes very good and sometimes very poor. They are prone to antisocial behavior, such as stealing, fire-setting, and aggression. They may engage in sexual relations and abuse alcohol or illicit drugs at an early age. They tend to show many symptoms of posttraumatic stress disorder (see Chapter 6), including hypervigilance, flashbacks to traumas they have endured, traumatic nightmares, and an exaggerated startle response. Their emotions are unstable, alternating among explosive outbursts of anger, deep depression, and severe anxiety.

Most children and many adults with dissociative identity disorder report hearing voices inside their heads. Some report being aware that their actions or words are being controlled by other personalities. For example, Joe, an 8-year-old boy with dissociative identity disorder, described how "a guy inside of me," called B. J. (for Bad Joey), would make him do "bad things" (Hornstein & Putnam, 1992, p. 1081):

VOICES

Well, say B. J. hears someone call me names, then he would strike me to do something, like I'd be running at the other kid, but it wouldn't be my legs, I'd be saying to my legs, "no . . . , stop . . . ," but they'd keep going on their own because that's B. J. doing that. Then my arm would be going at the other kid, hitting him, and I could see my arm doing that, but I couldn't stop it, and it wouldn't hurt when my hand hit him, not until later when B. J. goes back in and then my arm is my own arm. Then it starts hurting.

Issues in Diagnosis

Dissociative identity disorder was rarely diagnosed before about 1980, but there was a great increase in the number of reported cases after 1980 (APA, 2000; Braun, 1986; Coons, 1986). This is due in part to the fact that dissociative identity disorder was first included as a diagnostic category in the DSM in its third edition, published in 1980. The availability of specific diagnostic criteria for this disorder made it more likely that it would be used as a diagnosis. At the same time, the diagnostic criteria for schizophrenia were made more specific in the 1980 version of the DSM, possibly leading to some cases that would have been diagnosed as schizophrenia being diagnosed as dissociative identity disorder. One final, and important, influence on trends in diagnosis was the publication of a series of influential papers by psychiatrists describing persons with dissociative identity disorder whom they had treated (Bliss, 1980; Coons, 1980; Greaves, 1980; Rosenbaum, 1980). These cases aroused interest in the disorder in the psychiatric community.

Still, most mental-health professionals are reluctant to give this diagnosis. Most people diagnosed with dissociative identity disorder have already been diagnosed with at least three other disorders (Kluft, 1987). Some of the other disorders diagnosed may be secondary to or the result of the dissociative identity disorder. For example, one study of 135 patients with dissociative identity disorder found that 97 percent could also be diagnosed with major depression; 90 percent had an anxiety disorder, most often posttraumatic stress disorder; 65 percent were abusing substances; and 38 percent had an eating disorder (Ellason, Ross, & Fuchs, 1996). In addition, most people with dissociative identity disorder also are diagnosed with a personality disorder (Dell, 1998).

Many of the earler diagnoses may be misdiagnoses of the dissociative symptoms, however. For example, when people with dissociative identity disorder report hearing voices talking inside their heads, they are often misdiagnosed as having schizophrenia (Kluft, 1987). The voices that people with schizophrenia hear, however, often are experienced as coming from outside their heads. Conversely, people with dissociative identity disorder do not show schizophrenic symptoms, such as flat or inappropriate affect or loose or illogical associations (Ellason et al., 1996).

There are substantial cross-national differences in rates of diagnosed dissociative identity disorder. This disorder is diagnosed much more frequently in the United States than in Great Britain, Europe, India, or Japan (Ross, 1989; Saxena & Prasad, 1989;

Takahashi, 1990). Some studies suggest that Latinos, both within and outside the United States, may be more likely than other ethnic groups to experience dissociative symptoms in response to traumas. For example, a study of Vietnam veterans found that Latino veterans were more likely than non-Latino veterans to have dissociative symptoms (Koopman et al., 2001). Another study, conducted with Latino survivors of community violence in the United States, found that those who were less acculturated to mainstream U.S. culture were more likely to have dissociative symptoms than those who were more acculturated (Marshall & Orlando, 2002). This finding suggests that something about the Latino culture may increase vulnerability to dissociation. Dissociative symptoms may be part of the syndrome of *ataque de nervios,* a culturally accepted reaction to stress among Latinos that involves transient periods of loss of consciousness, convulsive movements of a psychological origin, hyperactivity, assaultive behaviors, and impulsive suicidal or homicidal acts (see the discussion of *ataque de nervios* in Chapter 7). The following case study describes a Hispanic woman believed to experience *ataque de nervios* but later diagnosed with dissociative identity disorder by a non-Hispanic psychiatrist (adapted from Steinberg, 1990, pp. 31–32).

CASE STUDY

Mrs. C., a 40-year-old divorced Hispanic woman, contacted a Hispanic clinic in Connecticut on the suggestion of her previous psychiatrist in Puerto Rico. Over an 18-year period Mrs. C. had made numerous emergency room and follow-up visits to a Puerto Rican psychiatric hospital. Her previous diagnoses included psychotic depression, schizophrenia, posttraumatic stress disorder, schizoaffective disorder, and hysterical personality. A variety of neuroleptics and antidepressants in therapeutic dosages had been prescribed but had provided no relief.

Mrs. C. was the youngest of three daughters born to indigent parents in Puerto Rico and was raised among numerous relatives in an overcrowded setting. Mrs. C. suffered extreme physical and emotional abuse from her mother, including administration of enemas and emetics every other day as punishment "if she was bad." Mrs. C. also recalled being sexually abused by her father and suffered recurrent dreams of this abuse.

(continued)

Married at age 17, she had three children by her first husband, who was physically abusive. After 4 years, Mrs. C. left him and shortly thereafter married another man, whom she described as physically and emotionally abusive. They separated 4 months later. Recently, she moved to Connecticut to be near her grown daughter.

Mrs. C.'s first presentation in Connecticut was with a classic episode of *ataque*. She described an acute onset of distressing auditory and visual hallucinations, stating that the voices were commanding her to harm herself. The initial diagnostic impression at the clinic was of a psychotic depression and she was given a prescription for an antipsychotic drug. Four days later, in a follow-up visit, she had not used the medication, denied having had auditory or visual hallucinations, and was free of any psychotic symptoms. She described rapid mood swings, "out of body experiences," and amnesic episodes, which she had experienced since childhood.

At this time, Mrs. C. was scheduled for biweekly supportive therapy with a mental-health worker. She attended sessions irregularly. Her demeanor, level of functioning, and symptoms fluctuated radically. Several times she spontaneously began acting as though she were a child. Frequently she came to therapy referring to herself by another name and did not remember previous sessions.

During this period, Mrs. C. was brought to the Hispanic clinic by her boyfriend for an emergency consultation due to the acute onset of bizarre behavior. She was childlike and disoriented, suffered auditory and visual hallucinations of a suicidal and homicidal nature, and rapidly became restless and agitated. She stated her name was *Rosa*. At that time the emergency room psychiatrist noted the similarity of her symptoms to the *ataque* and described her behavior: "When she came into the screening area, she took one of the balloons and began to play with it and asked me if I had a doll for her; she also said she was hungry and wanted some cookies and milk."

His diagnostic impression was "atypical psychosis." Re-evaluation several hours later revealed a "dramatic change in state." She said she was not Rosa, was not 6 years old, had no interest in playing with a doll, and she did not feel like someone was following her or was telling her to hurt herself.

At this time Mrs. C. began a new course of weekly psychotherapy sessions, which she attended fairly regularly. Mrs. C.'s sense of identity, her demeanor, and the content of each session varied significantly. During this treatment, five distinct personalities emerged with different names, ages, memories, and characteristic behaviors. Frequently she would state that she was "unable to remember" what she had discussed in a previous session. Recurrent themes included identity confusion and severe abuse by both parents. Throughout this year she remained off medication.

Some researchers have argued that psychiatrists in the United States are too quick to diagnose dissociative identity disorder, and others have argued that psychiatrists in other countries misdiagnose it as another disorder (Coons et al., 1990; Fahy, 1988).

Explanations of Dissociative Identity Disorder

Many theorists who study dissociative identity disorder view it as the result of coping strategies used by persons faced with intolerable trauma, most often childhood sexual and/or physical abuse, which they are powerless to escape (Bliss, 1986; Kluft, 1987). As Ross (1997, p. 64) describes,

The little girl being sexually abused by her father at night imagines that the abuse is happening to someone else, as a way to distance herself from the overwhelming emotions she is experiencing. She may float up to the ceiling and watch the abuse in a detached fashion. Now not only is the abuse not happening to her, but she blocks it out of her mind—that other little girl remembers it, not the original self. In this model, DID is an internal divide-and-conquer strategy in which intolerable knowledge and feeling is split up into manageable compartments. These compartments are personified and take on a life of their own.

In most studies, the majority of people diagnosed with dissociative identity disorder self-report having been the victims of sexual or physical abuse

Children who are abused may dissociate and even develop alter personalities as a way of dealing with their abuse.

during childhood (Coons, 1994; Dell & Eisenhower, 1990; Hornstein & Putnam, 1992), and dissociative experiences are commonly reported by survivors of child sexual abuse (Butzel et al., 2000; Kisiel & Lyons, 2001). For example, in a study of 135 persons with dissociative identity disorder, 92 percent reported having been sexually abused and 90 percent reported having been repeatedly physically abused (Ellason et al., 1996; see also Putnam et al., 1986). Similar results have been found in studies in which patients' reports of abuse were corroborated by at least one family member or by emergency room reports (Coons, 1994; Coons & Milstein, 1986). This abuse was most often carried out by parents or other family members and was chronic over an extended period of childhood. Other types of trauma that have been associated with the development of dissociative identity disorder include kidnapping, natural disasters, war, famine, and religious persecution (Ross, 1999).

People who develop dissociative identity disorder tend to be highly suggestible and hypnotizable and may use self-hypnosis to dissociate and escape their traumas (Kihlstrom, Glisky, & Angiulo, 1994). They may create the alter personalities to help then cope with their traumas, much as a child might create imaginary playmates to ease pangs of loneliness. These alter personalities can provide the safety, security, and nurturing that they are not receiving from their real caregivers. People with dissociative identity disorder may become trapped in their own defense mechanisms. Retreating into their alter personalities or using these personalities

to perform frightening functions may become a chronic way of coping with life.

There is evidence from a few family history studies that dissociative identity disorder runs in some families (Coons, 1984; Dell & Eisenhower, 1990). In addition, studies of twins and of adopted children have found evidence that the tendency to dissociate is substantially affected by genetics (Becker-Blease et al., 2004). Perhaps the ability and tendency to dissociate as a defense mechanism is, to some extent, biologically determined.

Treatment of Dissociative Identity Disorder

Treating dissociative identity disorder can be extremely challenging (Ross & Ellason, 1999). The goal of treatment is the integration of all the alter personalities into one, coherent personality. This integration is done by identifying the functions or roles of each personality, helping each personality confront and work through the traumas that led to the disorder and the concerns each one has or represents, and negotiating with the personalities for fusion into one personality who has learned adaptive styles of coping with stress. Hypnosis is used heavily in the treatment of dissociative identity disorder to contact alters (Putnam & Lowenstein, 1993).

Patients who have been treated successfully report a sense of unity in their personality, no longer report hearing voices, and are consistent in their expression of one personality. In treating children with dissociative identity disorder, it is often necessary to work with their parents to improve the children's family life, and it is sometimes necessary to remove the children from abusive homes (Dell & Eisenhower, 1990). Antidepressants and antianxiety drugs are sometimes used as adjuncts to supportive psychotherapy.

Experts in the treatment of dissociative identity disorder argue that treatment is successful in most cases (Coons & Bowman, 2001; Kluft, 1987; Ross, 1999), particularly if the treatment is begun in childhood shortly after a child first develops alter personalities (Peterson, 1991). One of the few studies that has empirically evaluated the treatment of DID found that patients who were able to integrate their personalities through treatment remained relatively free of symptoms over the subsequent two years (Ellason & Ross, 1997). These patients also reported few symptoms of substance abuse and depression, and they were able to reduce their use of antidepressant and antipsychotic medications. In contrast, patients who had not achieved integration during treatment continued to show DID symptoms and a number of other disorders. This study did not compare the outcome of the patients who received therapy with that of those who did not, and it did not compare different types of therapy.

Dissociative Fugue

A person in the midst of a **dissociative fugue** will suddenly pick up and move to a new place, assume a new identity, and have no memory for his previous identity. He will behave quite normally in his new environment, and it will not seem odd to him that he cannot remember anything from his past. Just as suddenly, he may return to his previous identity and home, resuming his life as if nothing had happened, with no memory for what he did during the fugue. A fugue may last for days or years, and a person may experience repeated fugue states or a single episode. An extreme and classic case of fugue was that of Reverend Ansel Bourne, reported by American philosopher and psychologist William James (1890, pp. 391–393).

CASE STUDY

The Rev. Ansel Bourne, of Greene, R.I., was brought up to the trade of a carpenter; but, in consequence of a sudden temporary loss of sight and hearing under very peculiar circumstances, he became converted from Atheism to Christianity just before his thirtieth year, and has since that time for the most part lived the life of an itinerant preacher. He has been subject to headaches and temporary fits of depression of spirits during most of his life, and has had a few fits of unconsciousness lasting an hour or less. He also has a region of somewhat diminished cutaneous sensibility on the left thigh. Otherwise his health is good, and his muscular strength and endurance excellent. He is of a firm and self-reliant disposition, a man whose yea is yea and his nay, nay; and his character for uprightness is such in the community that no person who knows him will for a moment admit the possibility of his case not being perfectly genuine.

On January 17, 1887, he drew 551 dollars from a bank in Providence with which to pay for a certain lot of land in Greene, paid certain bills, and got into a Pawtucket horse-car. This is the last incident which he remembers. He did not return home that day, and nothing was heard of him for two months. He was published in the papers as missing, and foul play being suspected, the police sought in vain his whereabouts. On the morning of March 14th, however, at Norristown, Pennsylvania, a man calling himself A. J. Brown, who had rented a

small shop six weeks previously, stocked it with stationery, confectionery, fruit, and small articles, and carried on his quiet trade without seeming to anyone unnatural or eccentric, woke up in a fright and called the people of the house to tell him where he was. He said that his name was Ansel Bourne, that he was entirely ignorant of Norristown, and that he knew nothing of shop-keeping, and that the last thing he remembered—it seemed only yesterday—was drawing the money from the bank, etc. in Providence. He would not believe that two months had elapsed. The people of the house thought him insane; and so, at first, did Dr. Louis H. Read, whom they called in to see him. But on telegraphing to Providence, confirmatory messages came, and presently his nephew, Mr. Andrew Harris, arrived upon the scene, made everything straight, and took him home. He was very weak, having lost apparently over twenty pounds of flesh during his escapade, and had such a horror of the idea of the candy-store that he refused to set foot in it again.

The first two weeks of the period remained unaccounted for, as he had no memory, after he had once resumed his normal personality, of any part of the time, and no one who knew him seems to have seen him after he left home. The remarkable part of the change is, of course, the peculiar occupation which the so-called Brown indulged in. Mr. Bourne has never in his life had the slightest contact with trade. "Brown" was described by the neighbors as taciturn, orderly in his habits, and in no way queer. He went to Philadelphia several times, replenished his stock; cooked for himself in the back shop, where he also slept; went regularly to church; and once at prayer-meeting made what was considered by the hearers as a good address, in the course of which he related an incident which he had witnessed in his natural state of Bourne.

This was all that was known of the case up to June 1890, when I induced Mr. Bourne to submit to hypnotism, so as to see whether, in the hypnotic trance, his "Brown" memory would not come back. It did so with surprising

(continued)

readiness; so much so indeed that it proved quite impossible to make him whilst in the hypnosis remember any of the facts of his normal life. He had heard of Ansel Bourne, but "didn't know as he had ever met the man." When confronted with Mrs. Bourne he said that he had "never seen the woman before," etc. On the other hand, he told of his peregrinations during the lost fortnight, and gave all sorts of details about the Norristown episode. The whole thing was prosaic enough; and the Brown-personality seems to be nothing but a rather shrunken, dejected, and amnesic extract of Mr. Bourne himself. He gives no motive for the wandering except that there was "trouble back there" and "he wanted rest." During the trance he looks old, the corners of his mouth are drawn down, his voice is slow and weak, and he sits screening his eyes and trying vainly to remember what lay before and after the two months of the Brown experience. "I'm all hedged in," he says: "I can't get out at the other end. I don't know what set me down in the Pawtucket horse-car, and I don't know how I ever left that store, or what became of it." His eyes are practically normal, and all his sensibilities (save for tardier response) about the same in hypnosis as in waking. I had hoped by suggestion, etc., to run the two personalities into one, and make the memories continuous, but no artifice would avail to accomplish this, and Mr. Bourne's skill to-day still covers two distinct personal selves.

Some, but not all, persons who experience fugue episodes do so after traumatic events. Many others, such as the Reverend Bourne, seem to escape into a fugue state in response to chronic stress in their lives that is within the realm of most people's experience. People are typically depressed before the onset of fugues (Kopelman, 1987). As in dissociative identity disorder, fugue states may be more common in people who are highly hypnotizable. Unlike a person with dissociative identity disorder, however, a person in a fugue state actually leaves the scene of the trauma or stress and leaves his or her former identity behind.

Fugue states appear to be more common among people who have histories of amnesia, including amnesias due to head injuries (Kopelman, 1987). There is no accurate estimate of the preva-

lence of fugue states, although they appear to be quite rare, and not much is known about the causes of fugue states, in part because of their rarity. Clinicians who treat people with this disorder tend to use many of the same techniques used to treat dissociative identity disorder, but, again, because the disorder is rare, little is known about the outcomes of treatment.

Dissociative Amnesia

In both dissociative identity disorder and dissociative fugue states, individuals may have amnesia for the periods of time when their alter personalities are in control or when they have been in fugue states, yet some people have significant periods of amnesia but do not assume new personalities or identities. They cannot remember important facts about their lives and their personal identities and are typically aware that there are large gaps in their memory or knowledge of themselves. These people are said to have **dissociative amnesia.**

Amnesia is considered either organic or psychogenic (see the Concept Overview in Table 8.6 on page 292). **Organic amnesia** is caused by a brain injury resulting from disease, drugs, accidents (such as blows to the head), or surgery. Organic amnesia often involves the inability to remember new information, known as **anterograde amnesia.**

Psychogenic amnesia arises in the absence of any brain injury or disease and is thought to have psychological causes. Psychogenic amnesia rarely involves anterograde amnesia. The inability to remember information from the past, known as **retrograde amnesia,** can have both organic and psychogenic causes. For example, people who have been in serious car accidents can have retrograde amnesia for the few minutes just before the accident. This retrograde amnesia can be due to a brain injury resulting from blows to the head during accidents, or it can be a motivated forgetting of the events leading up to traumatic accidents. Retrograde amnesia can also occur for longer periods of time than just a few minutes.

When such amnesias are due to organic causes, people usually forget everything about the past, including both personal information, such as where they lived and who they knew, and general information, such as who was president and major historical events of the period. They typically retain memory of their personal identities, however. They may not remember their children, but they know their own names. When long-term retrograde amnesias are due to psychological causes, people typically lose their identities and forget personal information but retain memories for general information.

TABLE 8.6	Concept Overview

Differences Between Psychogenic and Organic Amnesia

There are several important differences between psychogenic amnesia and organic amnesia.

Psychogenic Amnesia	Organic Amnesia
Caused by psychological factors	Caused by biological factors (such as disease, drugs, and blows to the head)
Seldom involves anterograde amnesia (inability to learn new information acquired since onset of amnesia)	Often involves anterograde amnesia
Can involve retrograde amnesia (inability to remember events from the past)	Can involve retrograde amnesia
Retrograde amnesia often only for personal information, not for general information	Retrograde amnesia usually for both personal and general information

The following is a case study of a man with a psychogenic retrograde amnesia (Hilgard, 1977/1986, p. 68).

CASE STUDY

Some years ago a man was found wandering the streets of Eugene, Oregon, not knowing his name or where he had come from. The police, who were baffled by his inability to identify himself, called in Lester Beck . . . , a psychologist they knew to be familiar with hypnosis, to see if he could be of assistance. He found the man eager to cooperate and by means of hypnosis and other methods was able to reconstruct the man's history. . . .

Following domestic difficulties, the man had gone on a drunken spree completely out of keeping with his earlier social behavior, and he had subsequently suffered deep remorse. His amnesia was motivated in the first place by the desire to exclude from memory the mortifying experiences that had gone on during the guilt-producing episode. He succeeded in forgetting all the events before and after this behavior that reminded him of it. Hence the amnesia spread from the critical incident to events before and after it, and he completely lost his sense of personal identity.

Loss of memory due to alcohol intoxication is common, but usually the person forgets only the events occurring during the period of intoxication.

Severe alcoholics can develop a more global retrograde amnesia, known as *Korsakoff's syndrome* (see Chapter 17), in which they cannot remember much personal or general information for a period of several years or decades. However, the type of retrograde amnesia in the previous case study, which apparently involved only one episode of heavy drinking and the loss of only personal information, typically has psychological causes.

Some theorists argue that psychogenic amnesias may be the result of using dissociation as a defense against intolerable memories or stressors (Freyd, 1996; Gleaves et al., 2004). Psychogenic amnesias most frequently occur following traumatic events, such as wars or sexual assaults. Alternately, amnesia for specific events may occur because individuals were in such a high state of arousal during the events that they did not encode and store information during the period of the event and thus were unable to retrieve the information later.

A third explanation for amnesia for specific events is that information about events is stored at the time of the events but is associated with a high state of arousal of painful emotions. Later on, people avoid these emotions and therefore do not gain access to the information associated with them (Bower, 1981).

Amnesias for specific periods of time around traumas appear to be fairly common, but generalized retrograde amnesias for people's entire pasts and identities appear to be very rare. Studies of people in countries that have been the site of attempted genocides, "ethnic cleansings," and wars have suggested that the rate of dissociative amnesias in these country may be elevated. For example, a study of 810 Bhutanese refugees in Nepal found that almost 20 percent of those who had been tortured during

Lorena Bobbit cut off her husband's penis, after years of experiencing his abuse. She claimed to have amnesia for the act of cutting it off.

conflicts in their country could be diagnosed with a dissociative disorder (van Ommeren et al., 2001).

One complication that arises in diagnosing amnesias is the possibility that amnesias are being faked by people trying to escape punishment for crimes committed during the periods for which they claim to be amnesic. True amnesias can occur in conjunction with the commission of crimes. Many crimes are committed by persons under the influence of alcohol or other drugs, and the drugs can cause blackouts for the periods of intoxication (Kopelman, 1987). Similarly, people who incur head injuries during the commission of crimes—for example, by falling while trying to escape the scene of a crime—can have amnesia for the commission of the crimes. Psychogenic amnesias can also occur for the commission of crimes, particularly if the criminals feel extremely guilty about the crimes. For example, a man who beat his wife may feel so guilty for doing so that he develops amnesia for the beating.

Amnesia is most often seen in homicide cases, with between 25 and 45 percent of persons arrested for homicide claiming to have amnesia for the killings (Kopelman, 1987). In most of these cases, the victims are closely related to the killers (as lovers, spouses, close friends, or family members), the offenses appear to be unpremeditated, and the killers are in states of extreme emotional arousal at the time of the killings. More rarely, the killers appear to have been in psychotic states at the time of the killings.

There is no clear-cut way to differentiate true amnesias from feigned ones. Head injuries leading to amnesia may be detectable through neuroimag-

ing of the brain. Some clinicians advocate the use of hypnosis to assist people in remembering events around crimes, if it is suspected that the amnesia is due to psychological causes. However, the possibility that hypnosis will "create" memories through the power of suggestion leads many courts to deny the use of hypnosis in such cases (Kopelman, 1987). In most cases, it is impossible to determine whether the amnesia is true.

Depersonalization Disorder

People with **depersonalization disorder** have frequent episodes in which they feel detached from their own mental processes or bodies, as if they are outside observers of themselves. Occasional experiences of depersonalization are common, particularly when people are sleep-deprived or under the influence of drugs (Baker et al., 2003). Approximately half of all adults report having at least one brief episode of depersonalization, usually following a severe stressor (APA, 2000).

Depersonalization disorder is diagnosed when episodes of depersonalization are so frequent and distressing that they interfere with individuals' ability to function. One study of people diagnosed with depersonalization disorder found that the average age of onset was about 23 years, and two-thirds reported they had chronic experiences of depersonalization since the onset (Baker et al., 2003). Seventy-nine percent reported impaired social or work functioning, and the majority also had another psychiatric diagnosis, most often depression. People diagnosed with depersonalization disorder often report a history of childhood emotional, physical, or sexual abuse (Simeon et al., 2001).

Controversies Around the Dissociative Disorders

Surveys of psychiatrists in the United States and Canada find that fewer than one-quarter of them believe that there is strong empirical evidence that the dissociative disorders represent valid diagnoses (Lalonde et al., 2001; Pope et al., 1999a). Skeptics argue that the disorders are artificially created in suggestible clients by clinicians who reinforce clients for "admitting" to symptoms of dissociative identity disorder and who induce the symptoms of the disorder through hypnotic suggestion (see Kihlstrom, 2005; Lilienfeld et al., 1999; Weekes, Spanos, & Bertrand, 1985). Even clinicians who believe dissociative identity disorder exists and is more common than was originally believed acknowledge that some clinicians are too quick to diagnose DID and can badger clients into believing that they have it (Ross, 1997).

Controversy over the diagnosis of dissociative amnesia has become particularly heated in recent years because of increased attention to claims that some survivors of childhood sexual abuse repressed their memories of the abuse for years and then eventually recalled these memories, often in the context of psychotherapy. These *repressed memories* represent a form of dissociative amnesia. Believers in repressed memories argue that the clinical evidence for dissociative or psychogenic amnesia is ample and the empirical evidence is increasing (Brown, Scheflin, & Whitfield, 1999). Nonbelievers argue that the empirical evidence against the validity of dissociative amnesia is ample and the clinical evidence is biased (Kihlstrom, 2005).

Most of the evidence for repressed memories comes from studies of people who are known to have been abused or who self-report abuse. Researchers then typically look for evidence that these people have forgotten or repressed their abuse. For example, Williams (1995) surveyed 129 women who had documented histories of having been sexually abused sometime between 1973 and 1975. These women, who were between 10 months and 12 years old at the time of their abuse, were interviewed about 17 years after their abuse. Williams found that 49 of these 129 women had no memory of the abuse events that were documented.

Briere and Conte (1993) located 450 therapy patients who identified themselves as abuse victims. They asked the patients if there had ever been a time before their eighteenth birthdays when they "could not remember" their abuse. Fifty-nine percent answered yes. As a final example, Herman and Harvey (1997) examined interviews of 77 women who had reported memories of childhood trauma and found that 17 percent had spontaneously reported they had had some delayed recall of the trauma, and 16 percent had said there had been a period of complete amnesia following the trauma.

Critics of repressed memories have raised questions about the methods and conclusions of these studies (Kihlstrom, 2005; Loftus, 2003; McNally, 2003). For example, regarding the Williams (1995) study, it turns out that 33 of the 49 women who said they could not remember the specific abuse incidents they were asked about could remember other abuse incidents during their childhoods. Thus, they had not completely forgotten or repressed all memories of abuse. Instead, they simply could not remember the specific incident about which they were being asked. Williams did not give any additional information about the 16 women who could remember no incidents of molestation in their childhoods. They may have been too young to remember these incidents, because memory for anything that happens before the age of about 3 tends to be very bad.

Critics of repressed memories also cite numerous studies from the literature on eyewitness identification and testimony indicating that people can be made to believe that events occurred, when, in fact, they never did (Ceci & Bruck, 1995; Loftus, 1993; Read & Lindsay, 1997). For example, Elizabeth Loftus and her colleagues developed a method for instilling a specific childhood memory of being lost on a specific occasion at the age of 5 (Loftus, 1993, 2003). This method involved a trusted family member engaging the subject in a conversation about the time he or she was lost (Loftus, 1993, p. 532):

> Chris (14 years old) was convinced by his older brother Jim that he had been lost in a shopping mall when he was 5 years old. Jim told Chris this story as if it were the truth: "It was 1981 or 1982. I remember that Chris was 5. We had gone shopping in the University City shopping mall in Spokane. After some panic, we found Chris being led down the mall by a tall, oldish man (I think he was wearing a flannel shirt). Chris was crying and holding the man's hand. The man explained that he had found Chris walking around crying his eyes out just a few moments before and was trying to help him find his parents." Just two days later, Chris recalled his feelings about being lost: "That day I was so scared that I would never see my family again. I knew that I was in trouble." On the third day, he recalled a conversation with his mother: "I remember Mom telling me never to do that again." On the fourth day: "I also remember that old man's flannel shirt." On the fifth day, he started remembering the mall itself: "I sort of remember the stores." In his last recollection, he could even remember a conversation with the man who found him: "I remember the man asking me if I was lost." . . . A couple of weeks later, Chris described his false memory and he greatly expanded on it. "I was with you guys for a second and I think I went over to look at the toy store, the Kay-bee Toy and uh, we got lost and I was looking around and I thought, 'Uh-oh, I'm in trouble now.' You know. And then I . . . I thought I was never going to see my family again. I was really scared you know. And then this old man, I think he was wearing a blue flannel, came up to me. . . . He was kind of old. He was kind

of bald on top. . . . He had like a ring of gray hair . . . and he had glasses."

Other studies have found that repeatedly asking adults about childhood events that never actually happened leads some (perhaps 20 to 40 percent) eventually to "remember" these events and even explain them in detail (Hyman & Billings, 1998; Schacter, 1999). In addition, Mazzoni and Loftus (1998) found that, if a psychologist suggests that an individual's dreams reflect repressed memories of childhood events, a majority of subjects subsequently report that the events depicted in their dreams actually happened.

Believers in repressed memories question the application of these studies to claims of repressed memories of sexual abuse (Gleaves & Freyd, 1997; Gleaves, Hernandez, & Warner, 2003). They argue that people might be willing to go along with experimenters or therapists who try to convince them that they were lost in a shopping mall as a child, but it is unlikely that people would be willing to go along with therapists or experimenters trying to convince them they were sexually abused if this abuse did not happen.

Freyd (1996) further argues that childhood abuse and incest are exactly the kinds of events that might be blocked, repressed, or forgotten for a period of time, because they so greatly violate a child's expectations that caregiving adults can be trusted. To survive, the child may dissociate from the ongoing experience of abuse and thus form no explicit memory of the abuse, although an implicit memory lies blocked from consciousness.

Recently, researchers have been using paradigms from cognitive psychology to test hypotheses about the reality of repressed memories. In a series of studies, Richard McNally and colleagues (McNally, 2003; McNally, Clancy, & Schacter, 2001; McNally et al., 2000a, 2000b) have found that individuals reporting recovered memories of either childhood sexual abuse or abduction by space aliens are characterized by a heightened proneness to form false memories in certain laboratory tasks. For example, one task required participants to say whether they recognized words that are similar to words they previously learned but are not exactly the same. Women with recovered memories of abuse, and people who had recovered memories of alien abductions, were more prone than control groups to falsely recognize words that had not appeared on the first list (Clancy et al., 2000, 2002). The researchers argue that these people are characterized by an information-processing style that may render them prone to believing they experienced specific events (such as childhood abuse)

when, in fact, they experienced other, broadly similar events (such as physical abuse or emotional neglect).

Freyd and colleagues have argued that the kinds of cognitive tasks McNally and colleagues have used in their studies do not tap the specific cognitive phenomena that are associated with repressed memories. Specifically, they suggest that women who dissociate from, and forget, their abusive experiences are most likely to perform differently than other women on cognitive tasks that require divided attention—attending to more than one thing at a time—because dividing one's attention is critical to dissociation (DePrince & Freyd, 1999, 2001; Freyd et al., 1998). One divided attention task requires participants to press a key on a keyboard in response to a secondary task while attending to words on a computer screen and committing them to memory. Researchers have shown that, under these divided attention conditions, women who score high on measures of dissociation recall fewer trauma-related words but more neutral words that they had previously been instructed to remember, compared with low-dissociation participants, who show the opposite pattern (DePrince & Freyd, 1999, 2001; Freyd et al., 1998). They suggest that women high in dissociation are better able to keep threatening information from explicit awareness, particularly if they can turn that attention to other things they are doing or that are going on in their environment at the time.

The repressed memory debate will not go away or be resolved soon. Not only are basic researchers in the middle of this debate but psychotherapists are often called upon to testify in court cases involving claims of recovered memories of abuse. People trying to understand their distressing symptoms are at the center of this scientific maelstrom.

SUMMING UP

- The dissociative disorders include dissociative identity disorder (DID), dissociative fugue, dissociative amnesia, and depersonalization disorder.

- In all the dissociative disorders, people's conscious experiences of themselves become fragmented, they may lack awareness of core aspects of themselves, and they may experience amnesia for important events.

- The distinctive feature of dissociative identity disorder is the development of multiple separate personalities within the same person. The personalities take turns being in control.

- People with dissociative fugue move away from home and assume entirely new identities, with complete amnesia for their previous identities. They do not switch back and forth between personalities.

- People with dissociative amnesia lose important memories due to psychological causes.

- People with depersonalization disorder have frequent experiences of feeling detached from their mental processes or their bodies.

- These disorders are often, although not always, associated with traumatic experiences.

- Therapists often treat these disorders by helping people explore past experiences and feelings that they have blocked from consciousness and by supporting them as they develop more integrated experiences of self and more adaptive ways of coping with stress.

- Significant controversy exists over the validity of the diagnoses of dissociative disorders and the notion of repressed memories.

CHAPTER INTEGRATION

As we noted in Chapter 6, philosophers and scientists have long debated the *mind-body problem*—does the mind influence bodily processes? Do changes in the body affect a person's sense of "self"? Exactly how do the body and the mind influence each other?

The somatoform and dissociative disorders are excellent evidence that the mind and body are complexly interwoven (see Figure 8.3). In a person with dissociative identity disorder, different personalities may actually have different physiological characteristics, such as different heart rates or blood pressure, even though they reside in the same body. In conversion disorder, psychological stress causes the person to lose eyesight, hearing, or functioning in another important physiological system. In somatization and pain disorders, a person under psychological stress experiences physiological symptoms, such as severe headaches. An underlying theme of these disorders is that it is easier or more acceptable for some people to experience psychological distress through changes in their bodies than to express it more directly as sadness, fear, or anger, perhaps because of cultural or social norms.

We all somatize our distress to some degree—we feel more aches and pains when we are upset about something than when we are happy. People who develop somatoform and perhaps dissociative disorders may somatize their distress to an extreme degree. Their tendency to differentiate between what is going on in their minds and what is going on in their bodies may be low, and they may favor an extreme bodily expression of what is going on in their minds.

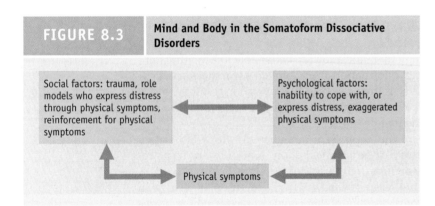

| FIGURE 8.3 | Mind and Body in the Somatoform Dissociative Disorders |

Social factors: trauma, role models who express distress through physical symptoms, reinforcement for physical symptoms ⟷ Psychological factors: inability to cope with, or express distress, exaggerated physical symptoms → Physical symptoms ←

Extraordinary People: Follow-Up

Although Bertha Pappenheim eventually lost her painful and mysterious physical symptoms, she did not credit psychoanalysis with her cure. She stated, "Psychoanalysis in the hands of the physician is what confession is in the hands of the Catholic priest. It depends on its user and its use, whether it becomes a beneficial tool or a two-edged sword" (Edinger, 1963, p. 12). Apparently, Pappenheim did not think much of Breuer's use of psychoanalysis in her case.

The remainder of Pappenheim's life after psychoanalysis, however, was not spent bashing Breuer or Freud but serving the poor and afflicted of Vienna.

Pappenheim became a social worker and a tireless advocate for the poor and for the Jewish minority in Europe. She was director of the Jewish Orphanage for Girls and founded other welfare organizations to help the poor, homeless, and outcast and to lift prostitutes out of their hopeless lives. Pappenheim was a strong proponent of emancipation and education for women. She wrote plays on women's rights and translated Mary Wollstonecraft's book *A Vindication of the Rights of Women* (1792).

Many theorists—psychoanalytic ones and feminist ones—have reinterpreted Breuer's and Freud's case history of Anna O., and many have analyzed Pappenheim's life after psychoanalysis. Was her fight for women's rights a fight against Breuer and Freud? Was her advocacy of the poor and outcasts—which was seen as unusual and inexplicable behavior for a wealthy Viennese socialite—a repudiation of her parents, who were strict and deprived her of opportunities to exercise her own capabilities as a youngster?

Bertha Pappenheim described her own motivations in a prayer she wrote, which was published after her death (Pappenheim, 1936):

> I am grateful that I can dam up
> As in a cool mill-pond
> Whatever power grows in my mind
> Unintentionally and unforced,
> Solely for my own pleasure.
> I thank also for the hour
> In which I found the words
> For what moves me, so that I could
> Move others by them.
> To feel strength is to live—to live is to wish
> to serve. Allow me to . . .

Chapter Summary

- The somatoform disorders are a group of disorders in which the individual experiences or fears physical symptoms for which no organic cause can be found. (Review Table 8.2.) These disorders may result from the dissociation of painful emotions or memories and the reemergence of these emotions or memories as cries for help or for the secondary gain people receive for these symptoms.

- One of the most dramatic somatoform disorders is conversion disorder, in which the individual loses all functioning in a part of the body, such as the eyes or legs. (Review Table 8.3.) Conversion symptoms often occur after trauma or stress. People with conversion disorder tend to have high rates of depression, anxiety, alcohol abuse, and personality disorder. Treatment for the disorder focuses on the expression of emotions or memories associated with the symptoms.

- Somatization disorder involves a long history of multiple physical complaints for which people have sought treatment but for which there is no apparent organic cause. (Review Table 8.4.) Pain disorder involves only the experience of chronic, unexplainable pain. People with these disorders show high rates of anxiety and depression. The disorders are apparently common and are more common in women, in Asians and Hispanics, and among the elderly and children.

- Somatization and pain disorders run in families. The cognitive theory of these disorders is that affected people focus excessively on physical symptoms and catastrophize these symptoms. People with these disorders often have experienced recent traumas. Treatment involves understanding the traumas and helping the person find adaptive ways of coping with distress.

- Hypochondriasis is a disorder in which the individual fears he or she has a disease, despite medical proof to the contrary. Hypochondriasis shares many of the features and causes of somatization disorder and is typically comorbid with somatization disorder.

- In body dysmorphic disorder individuals have an obsessional preoccupation with parts of their bodies and engage in elaborate behaviors to mask or get rid of these body parts. They are frequently depressed, anxious, and suicidal. This disorder may be a feature of an underlying depression or anxiety disorder or may be a form of obsessive-compulsive disorder. Treatment includes psychodynamic therapies to uncover the emotions driving the obsession about the body, systematic desensitization therapy to decrease obsessions and compulsive behaviors focused on the body part, and the use of selective serotonin reuptake inhibitors to reduce obsessional thought.

■ In the dissociative disorders, the individual's identity, memories, and consciousness become separated, or dissociated, from one another. (Review Table 8.5.) In dissociative identity disorder (DID), the individual develops two or more distinct personalities, which alternate in their control over the individual's behavior. Persons with dissociative identity disorder often engage in self-destructive and mutilative behaviors.

■ The vast majority of diagnosed cases of dissociative identity disorder are women, and recent cases tend to have histories of childhood sexual and/or physical abuse. The alter personalities may have been formed during the traumatic experiences as a way of defending against these experiences, particularly among people who are highly hypnotizable. The treatment of dissociative identity disorder has typically involved helping the various personalities integrate into one functional personality.

■ Fugue is a disorder in which the person suddenly moves away from home and assumes an entirely new identity, with complete amnesia for the previous identity. Fugue states usually occur in response to a stressor and can disappear suddenly, with the person returning to his or her previous identity. Little is known about the prevalence or causes of fugue states.

■ Dissociative, or psychogenic, amnesia involves the loss of memory due to psychological causes. It is different from organic amnesia, which is caused by brain injury and in which a person may have difficulty remembering new information (anterograde amnesia), which is rare in psychogenic amnesia. (Review Table 8.6.) In addition, with organic amnesia, loss of memory for the past (retrograde amnesia) is usually complete, whereas, with psychogenic amnesia, it is limited to personal information.

■ Psychogenic amnesia typically occurs following traumatic events. It may be due to motivated forgetting of events, to poor storage of information during events due to hyperarousal, or to avoidance of the emotions experienced during events and of the associated memories of events.

■ Depersonalization disorder involves frequent episodes in which the individual feels detached from his or her mental processes or body. Transient depersonalization experiences are common, especially under the influence of drugs or sleep deprivation. The causes of depersonalization disorder are unknown.

MindMap CD-ROM

The following resources on the MindMap CD-ROM that came with this text will help you to master the content of this chapter and prepare for tests:

■ Video: Dissociative Features
■ Chapter Timeline
■ Chapter Quiz

Key Terms

somatoform disorders 269
psychosomatic disorders 269
malingering 269
factitious disorders 269
factitious disorder by proxy 270
conversion disorder 271
la belle indifference 271
glove anesthesia 272
somatization disorder 274
pain disorder 274

hypochondriasis 278
body dysmorphic disorder 279
dissociative identity disorder (DID) 285
dissociative fugue 290
dissociative amnesia 291
organic amnesia 291
anterograde amnesia 291
psychogenic amnesia 291
retrograde amnesia 291
depersonalization disorder 293

Chapter 9

Watching from the Steps
by Hyacinth Manning-Carner

How much pain have cost us the evils which have never happened.

—Thomas Jefferson, letter to Thomas Jefferson Smith
(February 21, 1825)

Mood Disorders <

CHAPTER OVERVIEW

Extraordinary People

■ **Kay Redfield Jamison: *An Unquiet Mind***

Unipolar Depression

People with unipolar depression experience sadness, loss of interest in their usual activities, changes in sleep and activity levels, and thoughts of worthlessness, hopelessness, and suicide.

Bipolar Mood Disorders

People with bipolar disorder experience both periods of depression and periods of mania, during which their mood is elevated or irritable, and they have great energy and self-esteem. Bipolar disorder is much less common than is unipolar depression.

Biological Theories of Mood Disorders

There clearly is a heritable component to bipolar disorder and for some forms of unipolar depression. Biochemical theories suggest that imbalances in certain neurotransmitters or the malfunctioning of receptors for these neurotransmitters contributes to mood disorders. People with depression show disturbances on neuroimaging scans. They also show chronic hyperactivity of the bodily system that regulates stress responses.

Psychological Theories of Mood Disorders

Behavioral theories suggest that a lack of positive reinforcements and the presence of many aversive circumstances lead to depression. Cognitive theories suggest that people with depression interpret stressful experiences in negative and distorted ways, contributing to their depression. Psychodynamic theories describe depression as anger turned inward on the self. Interpersonal theories of depression attribute it to maladaptive social roles and patterns of relationships.

Social Perspectives on Mood Disorders

Sociologists have examined the large age, gender, and cross-cultural differences in depression for clues to its origins.

Mood Disorders Treatments

Several drugs are effective in the treatment of depression. Electroconvulsive therapy is also used to treat serious depression. The newest treatments include repetitive transcranial magnetic stimulation (rTMS) and vagus nerve stimulation. Lithium, anticonvulsants, antipsychotics, and calcium channel blockers are used to treat mania. The psychological therapies aim to reverse the processes that specific theories say lead to depression. Prevention programs intervene with high-risk groups to prevent first onsets of depression.

Taking Psychology Personally

■ **Primary Care Physicians Treating Depression**

Chapter Integration

New models of mood disorders describe how genetics may affect both the individual's biological sensitivity to stress and personality characteristics that heighten reactivity to stress, contributing to depression.

Extraordinary People

Kay Redfield Jamison: *An Unquiet Mind*

I was a senior in high school when I had my first attack. At first, everything seemed so easy. I raced about like a crazed weasel, bubbling with plans and enthusiasms, immersed in sports, and staying up all night, night after night, out with friends, reading everything that wasn't nailed down, filling manuscript books with poems and fragments of plays, and making expansive, completely unrealistic plans for my future. The world was filled with pleasure and promise; I felt great. Not just great, I felt *really* great. I felt I could do anything, that no task was too difficult. My mind seemed clear, fabulously focused, and able to make intuitive mathematical leaps that had up to that point entirely eluded me. Indeed, they elude me still. At the time, however, not only did everything make perfect sense, but it all began to fit into a marvelous kind of cosmic relatedness. My sense of enchantment with the laws of the natural world caused me to fizz over, and I found myself buttonholing my friends to tell them how beautiful it all was. They were less than transfixed by my insights into the webbings and beauties of the universe although considerably impressed at how exhausting it was to be around my enthusiastic ramblings: You're talking too fast, Kay. Slow down, Kay. You're wearing me out, Kay. Slow down, Kay. And those times when they didn't actually come out and say it, I still could see it in their eyes: For God's sake, Kay, slow down.

I did, finally, slow down. In fact, I came to a grinding halt. The bottom began to fall out of my life and my mind. My thinking, far from being clearer than a crystal, was tortuous. I would read the same passage over and over again only to realize that I had no memory at all for what I had just read. My mind had turned on me: It mocked me for my vapid enthusiasms; it laughed at all my foolish plans; it no longer found anything interesting or enjoyable or worthwhile. It was incapable of concentrated thought and turned time and again to the subject of death: I was going to die, what difference did anything make? Life's run was only a short and meaningless one; why live? I was totally exhausted and could scarcely pull myself out of bed in the mornings. It took me twice as long to walk anywhere as it ordinarily did, and I wore the same clothes over and over again, as it was otherwise too much of an effort to make a decision about what to put on. I dreaded having to talk with people, avoided my friends whenever possible, and sat in the school library in the early mornings and late afternoons, virtually inert, with a dead heart and a brain as cold as clay. (Jamison, 1995, pp. 35–38)

So writes author Kay Redfield Jamison in her autobiography, *An Unquiet Mind: A Memoir of Moods and Madness*. In *An Unquiet Mind*, Jamison describes her moods, her psychotic episodes, her suicide attempts, some outrageous things she did while manic, and her resistance to taking medication. It is an intimate look inside the life of a person with severe bipolar disorder, in all its mystery and tragedy.

When Jamison published this book in 1995, it garnered a great deal of attention in both the professional psychology and psychiatry literatures as well as in the general public media. This was because it was one of the most eloquent accounts of the experience of bipolar disorder published in years. It was also because Dr. Jamison is one of the most prolific and respected researchers of mood disorders in the field. Seldom does a person in Jamison's position—a

(*continued*)

professor of psychiatry at Johns Hopkins Medical School, a leading researcher and author in the field of mood disorders, an active clinician who specializes in treating people with mood disorders, and a winner of a MacArthur Foundation "genius" award— reveal that she suffers from the very disorder she researches and treats. Throughout this chapter, we will hear more of Jamison's powerful descriptions of what it is like to have a serious mood disorder.

The emotional roller-coaster ride Kay Jamison describes is known as **bipolar disorder,** or *manic-depression*. First, Jamison had **mania,** with great energy and enthusiasm for everything, fizzing over with ideas, talking and thinking so fast that her friends could not keep up with her. Eventually, though, she crashed into a **depression.** Her energy and enthusiasm were gone, and she was slow to think, to talk, and to move. The joy was drained from her life. Bipolar disorder is one of the two major types of mood disorders. The other type is **unipolar depression.** People with unipolar depression experience only depression, no mania.

The symptoms of unipolar depression and bipolar disorder may, at first glance, seem very familiar. We often talk of feeling depressed when something bad happens. And some people get a "fizzing over" feeling of exuberance and invincibility when things are going really well in their world. People who develop mood disorders, however, experience highs and lows that most of us can only imagine.

UNIPOLAR DEPRESSION

VOICES

From the time I woke up in the morning until the time I went to bed at night, I was unbearably miserable and seemingly incapable of any kind of joy or enthusiasm. Everything—every thought, word, movement—was an effort. Everything that once was sparkling now was flat. I seemed to myself to be dull, boring, inadequate, thick brained, unlit, unresponsive, chill skinned, bloodless, and sparrow drab. I doubted, completely, my ability to do anything well. It seemed as though my mind had slowed down and burned out to the point of being virtually useless. The wretched, convoluted, and pathetically confused mass of gray worked only well enough to torment me with a dreary litany of my inadequacies and shortcomings in character and to taunt me with the total, the desperate hopelessness of it all. (Jamison, 1995, p. 110)

Symptoms of Depression

Depression takes over the whole person—emotions, bodily functions, behaviors, and thoughts (see DSM-IV-TR criteria in Table 9.1 on page 304).

Emotional Symptoms

The most common emotion in depression is *sadness*. This sadness is not the garden variety type, which we all feel sometimes, but is a deep, unrelenting pain. As Kay Jamison wrote, she was "unbearably miserable and seemingly incapable of any kind of joy or enthusiasm." In addition, many people diagnosed with depression report that they have lost interest in everything in life—a symptom referred to as *anhedonia*. Even when they try to do something enjoyable, they may feel no emotional reaction.

Physiological and Behavioral Symptoms

In depression, many bodily functions are disrupted. These *changes in appetite, sleep, and activity levels* can take many forms. Some people with depression lose their appetite, but others find themselves eating more, perhaps even binge eating. Some people with depression want to sleep all day. Others find it difficult to sleep and may experience a form of insomnia known as *early morning wakening,* in which they awaken at 3 or 4 A.M. every day and cannot go back to sleep.

Behaviorally, many people with depression are slowed down, a condition known as *psychomotor retardation*. They walk more slowly, gesture more slowly, and talk more slowly and quietly. They

TABLE 9.1 DSM-IV-TR

Symptoms of Depression

Depression includes a variety of emotional, physiological, behavioral, and cognitive symptoms.

Emotional Symptoms

Sadness

Depressed mood

Anhedonia (loss of interest or pleasure in usual activities)

Irritability (particularly in children and adolescents)

Physiological and Behavioral Symptoms

Sleep disturbances (hypersomnia or insomnia)

Appetite disturbances

Pyschomotor retardation or agitation

Catatonia (unusual behaviors ranging from complete lack of movement to excited agitation)

Fatigue and loss of energy

Cognitive Symptoms

Poor concentration and attention

Indecisiveness

Sense of worthlessness or guilt

Poor self-esteem

Hopelessness

Suicidal thoughts

Delusions and hallucinations with depressing themes

Source: Reprinted with permission from the *Diagnostic and Statistical Manual of Mental Disorders,* Fourth Edition, Text Revision. Copyright © 2000 American Psychiatric Association.

have more accidents, because they cannot react to crises as quickly as necessary to avoid them. Many people with depression *lack energy* and report feeling chronically *fatigued*. A subset of people with depression have *psychomotor agitation* instead of retardation. They feel physically agitated, cannot sit still, and may move around or fidget aimlessly.

Cognitive Symptoms

The thoughts of people with depression may be filled with themes of *worthlessness, guilt, hopelessness,* and even *suicide.* They often have trouble concentrating and making decisions. Again, as Kay

Jamison described, "It seemed as though my mind had slowed down and burned out to the point of being virtually useless."

In some severe cases, the cognitions of people with depression lose complete touch with reality, and they experience delusions and hallucinations. **Delusions** are beliefs with no basis in reality, and **hallucinations** involve seeing, hearing, or feeling things that are not real. The delusions and hallucinations that people with depression experience usually are depressing and negative in content. For example, people have delusions that they have committed a terrible sin, that they are being punished, or that they have killed or hurt someone. They may have auditory hallucinations in which voices accuse them of having committed an atrocity or instruct them to kill themselves.

The Diagnosis of Unipolar Depressive Disorders

Depression takes several forms. The DSM-IV-TR recognizes two categories of unipolar depression: **major depression** and **dysthymic disorder.** The diagnosis of major depression requires that a person experience either depressed mood or loss of interest in usual activities, plus at least four other symptoms of depression chronically for at least two weeks. In addition, these symptoms have to be severe enough to interfere with the person's ability to function in everyday life.

Dysthymic disorder is a less severe form of depressive disorder than is major depression, but it is more chronic. To be diagnosed with dysthymic disorder, a person must be experiencing depressed mood plus two other symptoms of depression for at least *two years.* During these two years, the person must never have been without the symptoms of depression for more than a two-month period. Said one woman with dysthymic disorder, "It just goes on and on. I never feel really good; I always feel kind of bad, and it seems it's never going to end."

Some unfortunate people experience both major depression and dysthymic disorder. This has been referred to as **double depression.** People with double depression are chronically dysthymic, then occasionally sink into episodes of major depression. As the major depression passes, however, they return to dysthymia rather than recover to a normal mood. As one might imagine, people with double depression are even more debilitated than are people with major depression or dysthymia. One study that followed people with double depression over about nine years found that they remained free of the symptoms of minor or severe depression only about one-third of that time (Judd

TABLE 9.2 DSM-IV-TR

Subtypes of Major Depression (and the Depressive Phase of Bipolar Disorder)

The DSM-IV-TR specifies a number of subtypes of major depression and the depressive phase of bipolar disorder.

Subtype	Characteristic Symptoms
With melancholic features	Inability to experience pleasure, distinct depressed mood, depression regularly worse in morning, early morning awakening, marked psychomotor retardation or agitation, significant anorexia or weight loss, excessive guilt
With psychotic features	Presence of depressing delusions or hallucinations
With catatonic features	Catatonic behaviors: catalepsy, excessive motor activity, severe disturbances in speech
With atypical features	Positive mood reactions to some events, significant weight gain or increase in appetite, hypersomnia, heavy or laden feelings in arms or legs, long-standing pattern of sensitivity to interpersonal rejection
With postpartum onset	Onset of major depressive episode within four weeks of delivery of child
With seasonal pattern	History of at least two years in which major depressive episodes occur during one season of the year (usually the winter) and remit when the season is over

Source: Reprinted with permission from the *Diagnostic and Statistical Manual of Mental Disorders,* Fourth Edition, Text Revision. Copyright © 2000 American Psychiatric Association.

et al., 1998). People with double depression also are less likely to respond to treatments.

Over half of the people diagnosed with major depression or dysthymia also have another psychological disorder. The most common disorders to co-occur with depression are substance abuse, such as alcohol abuse; anxiety disorders, such as panic disorder; and eating disorders (Blazer et al., 1994). Sometimes, the depression precedes and perhaps causes the other disorder. In other cases, depression follows and may be the consequence of the other disorder.

The DSM-IV-TR also recognizes several subtypes of depression—different forms the disorder can take (see DSM-IV-TR criteria in Table 9.2). These subtypes apply both to major depression and to the depressive phase of a bipolar disorder.

The first subtype of depression is *depression with melancholic features,* in which the physiological symptoms of depression are particularly prominent. Second is *depression with psychotic features,* in which people experience delusions and hallucinations during a major depressive episode. Third, people with *depression with catatonic features* show the strange behaviors collectively known as *catatonia,* which can range from a complete lack of movement to excited agitation. Fourth, there is *depression with atypical features.* The criteria for this subtype are an odd assortment of symptoms (review Table 9.2).

The fifth subtype is *depression with postpartum onset.* This diagnosis is given to women when the

onset of a major depressive episode occurs within four weeks of the delivery of a child. More rarely, women develop mania postpartum and are given the diagnosis of *bipolar disorder with postpartum onset.* As many as 30 percent of women experience the *postpartum blues*—emotional lability (unstable and quickly shifting moods), frequent crying, irritability, and fatigue—in the first few weeks after giving birth. For most women, these symptoms are only annoying and pass completely within two weeks of the birth. Only about 1 in 10 women experience postpartum depressions serious enough to warrant a diagnosis of a depressive disorder (Steiner, Dunn & Born, 2003).

The final subtype of major depressive disorder is *depression with seasonal pattern,* sometimes referred to as **seasonal affective disorder,** or **SAD.** People with SAD have a history of at least two years of experiencing major depressive episodes and fully recovering from them. The symptoms seem to be tied to the number of daylight hours in a day. People become depressed when the daylight hours are short and recover when the daylight hours are long. In the northern hemisphere, this means people are depressed November through February and not depressed the remainder of the year. Some people with this disorder actually develop mild forms of mania or have full manic episodes during the summer months and are diagnosed with *bipolar disorder with seasonal pattern.* In order to be diagnosed with seasonal affective disorder, a person's mood

People in northern latitudes have higher rates of seasonal affective disorder.

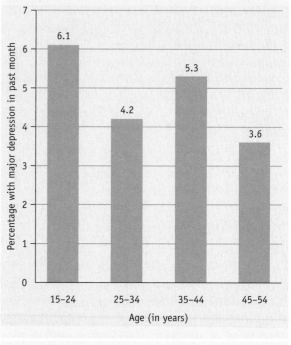

FIGURE 9.1   **Age Differences in Depression.** Shown are the percentages, in one study, of people in each age group who were diagnosed with major depression in a one-month period. Those 15 to 24 years old have the highest rates of depression, and those 45 to 54 years old have the lowest rates.

Source: Blazer et al., 1994.

changes cannot be the result of psychosocial events, such as regularly being unemployed during the winter. Rather, the mood changes must seem to come on without reason or cause.

Although many of us may feel our mood changes with the seasons, only about 1 percent of the U.S. population experiences a diagnosable seasonal affective disorder (Blazer, Kessler, & Swartz, 1998). This disorder is more common in latitudes where there are fewer hours of daylight in the winter months (Rosen et al., 1990). For example, people in Norway and Sweden are more prone to SAD than are people in Mexico and southern Italy.

Prevalence and Course of Depression

Depression is one of the most common psychological problems. At sometime in their lives, 16 percent of Americans experience an episode of major depression (Kessler et al., 2003). Among adults, 15- to 24-year-olds are most likely to have had a major depressive episode in the past month (Blazer et al., 1994; Kessler et al., 2003) (see Figure 9.1). There are lower rates among 45- to 54-year-olds, and other studies have found even lower rates in people 55 to 70 years of age, with only about 2 percent diagnosable with a major depression (Kessler et al., 2003; Newmann, 1989; Zisook & Downs, 1998). The rates of depression go up, however, among the "old-old," those over 85 years of age. When they do occur, depressions in older people tend to be quite severe, chronic, and debilitating (Lyness, 2004).

Perhaps it is surprising that the rate of depression is so low among older adults. The diagnosis of depression in older adults is complicated (Lyness, 2004). First, older adults may be less willing than younger adults to report the symptoms of depression, because they grew up in a society less accepting of the disorder.

Second, depressive symptoms in the elderly often occur in the context of a serious medical illness, which can interfere with making an appropriate diagnosis. Third, older people are more likely than younger people to have mild to severe cognitive impairment, and it is often difficult to distinguish between a depressive disorder and the early stages of a cognitive disorder.

Although these factors are important, some researchers suggest that the low rate is valid and have offered explanations. The first is quite grim: Depression appears to interfere with physical health; as a result, people with a history of depression may be more likely to die before they reach old age (Lyness, 2004). The second explanation is more hopeful: As people age, they may develop more adaptive coping skills and a psychologically healthier outlook on life, and this may lead them to experience fewer episodes of depression (Elder, Liker, & Jaworski, 1984).

Most studies show that women are about twice as likely as men to experience both mild depressive symptoms and severe depressive disorders (Nolen-Hoeksema, 2002). This gender difference in depression has been found in many countries, in most ethnic groups, and in all adult age groups. Could it be that females are more willing to admit to depression than males? The gender difference in depression is found even in studies that use relatively objective measures of depression that do not rely much on self-reports, such as clinicians' ratings of depression, or the reports of family members or friends. As we discuss the various theories of depression in this chapter, we will explore how these theories explain this gender difference in depression.

Depression appears to be a long-lasting, recurrent problem for some people (Boland & Keller, 2002). One nationwide study found that people with major depression spent an average of 16 weeks during the previous year with significant symptoms of depression (Kessler et al., 2003). The picture one gets is of a depressed person spending much of his or her time at least moderately depressed (Judd & Akiskal, 2000). Then, even after the depressed person recovers from one episode of depression, he or she remains at high risk for relapses into new episodes. People with a history of multiple episodes of depression are even more likely to remain depressed for long periods of time.

Depression is a costly disorder to the individual and to society. A study of over 1,100 employed people found that those who had significant symptoms of depression lost an average of 5.6 hours per week in productive work time, compared with 1.5 hours per week in those not depressed. The authors suggest that depression in workers costs employers an estimated $44 billion per year in lost productivity alone (not including the costs of treatment) (Stewart et al., 2003).

The good news is that, once people undergo treatment for their depression, they tend to recover much more quickly and their risk for relapse is reduced. The bad news is that many people with depression never seek care, or they wait years after their symptoms have begun to seek care (Kessler et al., 2003). Why don't people suffering the terrible symptoms of depression seek treatment? It may be because they do not have the money or insurance to pay for care. But often it is because they feel they should be able to get over their symptoms on their own. They believe that the symptoms are just a phase they are going through, that they will pass with time and won't affect their lives in the long term.

Depression does sometimes pass without treatment, and without long-term consequences. Some people seem to be left with scars from their bouts of depression, however. Their ways of thinking, their views of themselves, their social relationships, and their academic and work histories may be changed for the worse by the depression and may remain impaired long after the symptoms of depression have passed. Even if they do not relapse into additional major depressive episodes, people with previous episodes of major depression tend to have enduring problems in many areas of their lives (Boland & Keller, 2002). Their functioning on the job tends to remain impaired even after their depression has subsided. They report that they are not interested in sex or do not enjoy sex as much as they used to, and there is chronic conflict and dissatisfaction in their intimate relationships (Joiner, 2002).

Depression in Childhood and Adolescence

Depression is less common among children than among adults. At any point in time, as many as 2.5 percent of children and 8.3 percent of adolescents can be diagnosed with major depression, and as many as 1.7 percent of children and 8.0 percent of adolescents can be diagnosed with dysthymic disorder (for reviews, see Garber & Horowitz, 2002; Lewinsohn & Essau, 2002). Between 15 and 20 percent of youth will experience an episode of major depression before the age of 20 (Lewinsohn & Essau, 2002).

Depressive symptoms that don't quite meet the diagnostic criteria for major depression are even more common in adolescents. A study of 9,863 students in grades 6, 8, and 10 in the United States found that 25 percent of the girls versus 10 percent of the boys reported elevated depressive symptoms. The highest rates were among American Indians (29 percent), followed by 22 percent of Hispanics, 18 percent of Whites, 17 percent of Asian Americans, and 15 percent of African Americans. Youth who were using substances were more likely to be depressed (Saluja et al., 2004).

The Scars of Childhood Depression

Depression may be most likely to leave psychological and social scars if it occurs initially during childhood, rather than during adulthood (Cole et al., 1998). Self-concept is still being developed in childhood and adolescence, much more so than in adulthood. A period of significant depressive symptoms while one's self-concept is undergoing substantial change can have long-lasting effects on the content or structure of one's self-concept. Similarly, the development of skills and abilities in school is cumulative during childhood and adolescence. For this reason, a bout of depression that interferes with learning can have long-term effects on children's achievement. Finally, children and adolescents are dependent on and connected with other people to a greater extent than are adults, so a bout of depression that impairs social skills can have long-term effects on social relationships.

Depression may also increase negative thinking, because it brings with it a host of new negative events. Stress-generation models suggest that the symptoms of depression—such as low motivation, fatigue, problems in concentration, low self-esteem, and decreases in social interactions and skills—can interfere with youngsters' functioning in all domains of their lives (Hammen, 1991, 1992). Because depression affects so many domains of functioning in a youngster's life, it may lead to increases in many kinds of stressors. For example, having a depressed child in the family can cause strains on parents, which may affect their relationships, perhaps putting a fragile marriage or partnership over the edge and contributing to separation. Or the cost of treatment for a depressed child may cause significant financial strain in a family.

Depression in less common in children than in adults, but can be debilitating and have long-term consequences.

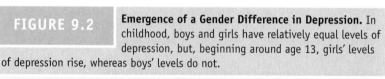

FIGURE 9.2   **Emergence of a Gender Difference in Depression.** In childhood, boys and girls have relatively equal levels of depression, but, beginning around age 13, girls' levels of depression rise, whereas boys' levels do not.

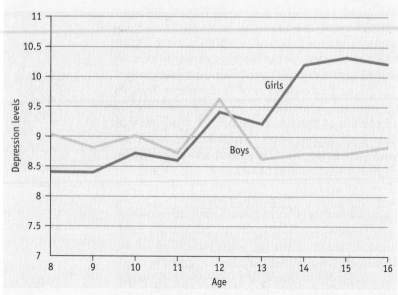

Source: Twenge & Nolen-Hoeksema, 2002.

The Effects of Puberty

Girls' rates of depression escalate dramatically over the course of puberty, but boys' rates do not (Twenge & Nolen- Hoeksema, 2002) (see Figure 9.2). Although there is some evidence that girls' increase in depressive symptoms is correlated with the hormonal changes of puberty (Angold, Costello, & Worthman, 1998), the observable physical changes of adolescence may have more to do with the emotional development of girls and boys than with hormonal development, because these characteristics affect boys' and girls' self-esteem differently. Girls appear to value the physical changes that accompany puberty much less than do boys. In particular, girls dislike the weight they gain in fat and their loss of the long, lithe look that is idealized in modern fashions. In contrast, boys like the increase in muscle mass and other pubertal changes their bodies undergo (Dornbusch et al., 1984). Body dissatisfaction appears to be more closely related to low self-esteem and depression in girls than in boys (Allgood-Merten, Lewinsohn, & Hops, 1990).

The pubertal increase in depression for girls may occur only among European American girls, however, not among African American and Latino girls (Hayward et al., 1999). It may be that African American and Latino girls do not accept the pressures to be thin as much as European American girls do, and this protects them against declines in their self-image and well-being with the onset of puberty. The social environment of African American and Latino girls may also protect them against depression in other ways, although currently there is too little research to determine what factors are important.

SUMMING UP

- Depression includes disturbances in emotion (sadness, loss of interest), bodily function (loss of sleep, appetite, and sexual drive), behavior (retardation or agitation), and thought (worthlessness, guilt, suicidality).

- The two primary categories of unipolar depression are major depression and dysthymic disorder. There are several subtypes of major depression.

- Young adults have the highest rates of depression.

- Many people who become depressed remain so for several months or more and have multiple relapses over their lifetimes.

BIPOLAR MOOD DISORDERS

VOICES

There is a particular kind of pain, elation, loneliness, and terror involved in this kind of madness. When you're high it's tremendous. The ideas and feelings are fast and frequent like shooting stars and you follow them until you find better and brighter ones. Shyness goes, the right words and gestures are suddenly there, the power to seduce and captivate others a felt certainty. There are interests found in uninteresting people. Sensuality is pervasive and the desire to seduce and be seduced irresistible. Feelings of ease, intensity, power, well-being, financial omnipotence, and euphoria now pervade one's marrow.

But, somewhere, this changes. The fast ideas are far too fast and there are far too many; overwhelming confusion replaces clarity. Memory goes. Humor and absorption on friends' faces are replaced by fear and concern. Everything previously moving with the grain is now against—you are irritable, angry, frightened,

TABLE 9.3	DSM-IV-TR

Symptoms of Mania

A diagnosis of mania requires that a person show an elevated, expansive, or irritable mood for at least one week, plus at least three of the other symptoms listed here.

Elevated, expansive, or irritable mood

Inflated self-esteem or grandiosity

Decreased need for sleep

More talkative than usual, a pressure to keep talking

Flight of ideas or sense that your thoughts are racing

Distractibility

Increase in activity directed at achieving goals

Excessive involvement in potentially dangerous activities

Source: Reprinted with permission from the *Diagnostic and Statistical Manual of Mental Disorders,* Fourth Edition, Text Revision. Copyright © 2000 American Psychiatric Association.

uncontrollable, and enmeshed totally in the blackest caves of the mind. You never knew those caves were there. It will never end. (Goodwin & Jamison, 1990, pp. 17–18)

This person is describing an episode of bipolar disorder. When she is manic, she has tremendous energy and vibrancy, her self-esteem is soaring, and she is filled with ideas and confidence. Then, when she becomes depressed, she is despairing and fearful, she doubts herself and everyone around her, and she wishes to die. This alternation between periods of mania and periods of depression is the classic manifestation of bipolar disorder.

Symptoms of Mania

We have already discussed the symptoms of depression in detail, so let's focus on the symptoms of mania (see the DSM-IV-TR criteria in Table 9.3). The moods of people who are manic can be *elated,* but that elation is often mixed with *irritation* and *agitation.*

First and foremost comes a general sense of intense well-being. I know of course that this sense is illusory and transient—

(*continued*)

V O I C E S

Although, however, the restrictions of confinement are apt at times to produce extreme irritation and even paroxysms of anger, the general sense of wellbeing, the pleasurable and sometimes ecstatic feeling-tone, remains as a sort of permanent background of all experience during a manic period. (Goodwin & Jamison, 1990, pp. 25–26)

The manic person is filled with a *grandiose self-esteem,* meaning that his view of himself is unrealistically positive and inflated. *Thoughts* and *impulses* race through his mind. At times, these grandiose thoughts are delusional and may be accompanied by grandiose hallucinations. A manic person may *speak rapidly* and *forcefully,* trying to convey the rapid stream of fantastic thoughts he is having. He may become agitated and irritable, particularly with people he perceives as "getting in his way." He may engage in a variety of *impulsive behaviors,* such as ill-advised sexual liaisons or spending sprees. He may have *grand plans* and *goals,* which he pursues frenetically.

The Diagnosis of Mania

In order to be diagnosed with mania, an individual must show an elevated, expansive, or irritable mood for at least one week, plus at least three of the other symptoms listed in Table 9.3. These symptoms must impair the individual's ability to function in order to qualify for the diagnosis.

People who experience manic episodes meeting these criteria are said to have **bipolar I disorder.** Most of these people eventually fall into a depressive episode. For some people with bipolar I disorder, the depressions are as severe as major depressive episodes, whereas others have episodes of depression that are relatively mild and infrequent. People with **bipolar II disorder** experience severe episodes of depression that meet the criteria for major depression, but their episodes of mania are milder and are known as **hypomania** (see the DSM-IV-TR criteria in Table 9.4). Hypomania has the same symptoms as mania. The major difference is that, in hypomania, these symptoms are not severe enough to interfere with daily functioning and do not involve hallucinations or delusions.

Just as dysthymic disorder is the less severe but more chronic form of unipolar depression, there is a less severe but more chronic form of bipolar disorder, known as **cyclothymic disorder.** A person with cyclothymic disorder alternates between episodes of hypomania and moderate depression chronically over at least a two-year period. During the periods of hypomania, the person may be able to function reasonably well in daily life. Often, however, the periods of depression significantly interfere with daily functioning, although these periods are not as severe as those qualifying as major depressive episodes.

About 90 percent of people with bipolar disorder have multiple episodes or cycles during their lifetime (APA, 2000). The length of an individual episode of bipolar disorder varies greatly from one person to the next. Some people are in a manic state for several weeks or months before moving into a depressed state. More rarely, people switch from mania to depression and back within a matter of days. The number of lifetime episodes also varies tremendously from one person to the next,

---

TABLE 9.4 DSM-IV-TR

Criteria for Bipolar I and Bipolar II Disorders

Bipolar I and II disorders differ in the presence of major depressive episodes, episodes meeting the full criteria for mania, and hypomanic episodes.

Criteria	Bipolar I	Bipolar II
Major depressive episodes	Can occur but are not necessary for diagnosis	Are necessary for diagnosis
Episodes meeting full criteria for mania	Are necessary for diagnosis	Cannot be present for diagnosis
Hypomanic episodes	Can occur between episodes of severe mania or major depression but are not necessary for diagnosis	Are necessary for diagnosis

Source: Reprinted with permission from the *Diagnostic and Statistical Manual of Mental Disorders,* Fourth Edition, Text Revision. Copyright © 2000 American Psychiatric Association.

but a relatively common pattern is for episodes to become more frequent and closer together over time. If a person has four or more cycles of mania and depression within a year, this is known as **rapid cycling bipolar disorder.**

Prevalence and Course of Bipolar Disorder

Bipolar disorder is less common than unipolar depression. About 1 or 2 in 100 people experience at least one episode of bipolar disorder at sometime in their lives (Judd & Akiskal, 2003; Kessler et al., 1994; Lewinsohn, Klein, & Seeley, 2000). Men and women seem equally likely to develop the disorder, and there are no consistent differences among ethnic groups in the prevalence of the disorder (Weissman et al., 1996). Most people who develop bipolar disorder do so in late adolescence or early adulthood (Lewinsohn, Seeley, Klein, 2003). About half of the people who eventually develop a bipolar disorder have experienced their first episode by early adulthood (Judd & Akiskal, 2003).

Like people with unipolar depression, people with bipolar disorder often face chronic problems on the job and in their relationships between their episodes (Keck et al., 1998). One study, which followed people who had been hospitalized for an episode of bipolar disorder, found that, over the year following their hospitalization, only about one in four recovered fully from their symptoms and were able to lead a relatively normal life (Keck et al., 1998). The best predictors of recovery were full compliance with medication taking and higher social class, which may have afforded people better health care and social support. Judd and colleagues (2002) followed 146 patients with bipolar I disorder for almost 13 years and found that they experienced significant symptoms during 47 percent of the weeks. Depressive symptoms were more common, occurring 32 percent of the weeks, than manic symptoms, which occurred about 9 percent of the weeks, or cycling/mixed symptoms of depression and mania, which occurred 6 percent of the weeks. The presence of symptoms, even if they do not meet the criteria for an episode of mania or depression, is associated with deficits in both social and occupational functioning, and the symptoms appear to increase the risk for relapse (Marangell, 2004). In addition, people with bipolar disorder often abuse substances (such as alcohol and hard drugs), which also impairs their control over their disorder, their willingness to take medications, and their functioning in life (Goodwin & Ghaemi, 1998; Keck et al., 1998; van Gorp et al., 1998).

A controversial issue in research on bipolar disorder is the extent to which it exists and can be diagnosed reliably in children and young adolescents. One longitudinal study followed 86 prepubertal children who had been diagnosed with bipolar disorder using strict criteria (Geller et al., 2004). They found that, over a two-year period, these children continued to show the symptoms of mania or hypomania for an average of 57 weeks and the symptoms of depression for an average of 47 weeks. These data supported the initial diagnosis of bipolar disorder and suggest that pediatric bipolar disorder tends to be chronic.

Creativity and Bipolar Disorder

Could there possibly be anything good about suffering from a bipolar disorder? Some theorists have argued that the symptoms of mania—increased self-esteem, a rush of ideas, the courage to pursue these ideas, high energy, little need for sleep, hypervigilance, and decisiveness—can actually benefit certain people, especially highly intelligent or talented people. In turn, the melancholy of depression is often seen as inspirational for artists. Indeed, some of the most influential people in history have suffered, and perhaps to some extent benefited, from a mood disorder.

Some political leaders, including Abraham Lincoln, Alexander Hamilton, Winston Churchill, Napoleon Bonaparte, and Benito Mussolini, and some religious leaders, including Martin Luther and George Fox (founder of the Society of Friends, or Quakers), have been posthumously diagnosed by psychiatric biographers as having periods of mania, hypomania, or depression (Jamison, 1993). Although during periods of depression these leaders were often incapacitated, during periods of mania and hypomania they accomplished extraordinary feats. While manic, they devised brilliant and daring strategies for winning wars and solving domestic problems and had the energy, self-esteem, and persistence to carry out these strategies. The Duke of Marlborough, a great English military commander, was able to put his chronic hypomania to great use:

> No one can read the whole mass of the letters which Marlborough either wrote, dictated, or signed personally without being astounded at the mental and physical energy which it attests. . . . After 12 or 14 hours in the saddle on the long reconnaissances often under cannon-fire; after endless inspections of troops in camp and garrison; after ceaseless calculations about food and supplies, and all the anxieties of direct command in war, Marlborough

would reach his tent and conduct the foreign policy of England, decided the main issues of its Cabinet, and of party politics at home. (Rowse, 1969, pp. 249–250)

Marlborough was an ancestor of Winston Churchill, who was also able to put his cyclothymic temperament to use in his career. However, Churchill's biographer also documented how the grandiosity, scheming, and impulsiveness that are part of mania can be a liability in a leader:

> All those who worked with Churchill paid tribute to the enormous fertility of his new ideas, the inexhaustible stream of invention which poured from him, both when he was Home Secretary, and later when he was Prime Minister and director of the war effort. All who worked with him also agreed that he needed the most severe restraint put upon him, and that many of his ideas, if they had been put into practice, would have been utterly disastrous. (Storr, 1988, pp. 14–15)

Writers, artists, and composers of music have a higher than normal prevalence of mania and depression. For example, a study of 1,005 famous twentieth-century artists, writers, and other professionals found that the artists and writers experienced two to three times the rate of mood disorders, psychosis, and suicide attempts than did comparably successful people in business, science, and public life. The poets in this group were most likely to have been manic (Ludwig, 1992).

Does mania simply enhance (and depression inhibit) productivity in naturally creative people? Or is there a deeper link between creativity and bipolar disorder? This is a difficult question to answer by simply examining how many creative people are also manic. However, one group of researchers found an ingenious way to address this question (Richards et al., 1988). They hypothesized that the genetic abnormalities that cause bipolar disorder are in close proximity to the genetic abnormalities that cause great creativity. According to this hypothesis, the close relatives of patients with bipolar disorder should be more creative, even if they do not have bipolar disorder, than the close relatives of people without bipolar disorder. The participants in this study were patients with bipolar disorder or cyclothymia, their first-degree relatives (siblings, parents, and children), a control group of people with no psychiatric disorders, and their first-degree relatives. The relatives in both

Winston Churchill had periods of manic symptoms that may have been both an asset and a liability.

Abraham Lincoln suffered periods of severe depression.

these groups had no history themselves of mood disorders, so any creativity they showed was in the absence of mania or depression.

To measure creativity, the researchers examined the lives of these participants for evidence that they had used their special talents in original, and creative ways. For example, one participant who was rated as extremely creative was an entrepreneur who had advanced from a chemist's apprentice to an independent researcher of new products. He then had started a major paint manufacturing company, and, during the Danish Resistance of World War II, he had surreptitiously manufactured and smuggled explosives for the Resistance. A participant who was rated as low in creativity had been a bricklayer for 20 years and then inherited a large trust fund and retired to a passive life on a country estate. An advantage of this measure of creativity is that it did not require that a person receive social recognition to be considered creative.

The results of this study suggested that the relatives of the people with bipolar disorder or cyclothymia were more creative than the participants with no history of bipolar disorder or cyclothymia or their relatives. The people with cyclothymia and the healthy relatives of those with bipolar disorder had somewhat higher creativity scores than did the patients who had bipolar disorder. This suggests that creativity that is associated with a predisposition toward bipolar disorder is more easily expressed in people who do not suffer from full episodes of mania and depression but may suffer from milder mood swings (Richards et al., 1988).

We should not overemphasize the benefits of bipolar disorder. Although many creative people with bipolar disorder may have been able to learn from their periods of depression and to exploit their periods of mania, many also have found the highs and lows of the disorder unbearable and have attempted or completed suicide. As Wurtzel (1995, p. 295) notes,

> While it may be true that a great deal of art finds its inspirational wellspring in sorrow, let's not kid ourselves in how much time each of those people wasted and lost by being mired in misery. So many productive hours slipped by as paralyzing despair took over. This is not to say that we should deny sadness its rightful place among the muses of poetry and of all art forms, but let's stop calling it madness, let's stop pretending that the feeling itself is interesting. Let's call it depression and admit that it is very bleak.

SUMMING UP

- The symptoms of mania include elation, irritation and agitation, grandiosity, impulsivity, and racing thoughts and speech. People with bipolar disorder experience periods of both mania and depression.
- The two major diagnostic categories of bipolar mood disorders are bipolar disorder and cyclothymic disorder.
- Bipolar mood disorders are less common than unipolar depression, but they are equally common in men and women.
- The onset of bipolar disorder is most often in late adolescence or early adulthood. Most people with bipolar disorder have multiple episodes.
- There is some evidence that people with bipolar disorder are more creative.

BIOLOGICAL THEORIES OF MOOD DISORDERS

Most of the modern biological theories of the causes of mood disorders focus on genetic abnormalities or dysfunctions in certain neurobiological systems. These two types of theories complement each other: Genetic abnormalities may cause mood disorders by altering a person's neurobiology. In this section, we first review the evidence for a genetic contribution to depression and mania. Second, we review the evidence that neurotransmitters play a role in depression and mania. Third, we examine a variety of abnormalities that have been found in the brains of people with mood disorders. Fourth, we explore hypotheses that the neuroendocrine system, which regulates hormones throughout the body, becomes dysregulated in the mood disorders (see the Concept Overview in Table 9.5 on page 314).

The Role of Genetics

Family history and twin studies suggest that the mood disorders can be transmitted genetically (Southwick, Vythilingam, & Charney, 2005; Wallace, Schneider, & McGuffin, 2002).

Family History Studies

Family history studies of people with bipolar disorder find that their first-degree relatives (i.e., parents, children, and siblings) have rates of both bipolar disorder and unipolar depression at least two to three times higher than the rates of relatives of people without bipolar disorder (MacKinnon, Jamison, & DePaulo, 1997; Wallace et al., 2002) (Figure 9.3 on page 314).

TABLE 9.5 Concept Overview

Biological Theories of Mood Disorders

A number of biological factors have been implicated in the mood disorders.

Theory	Description
Genetic theory	Disordered genes predispose people to depression or bipolar disorder.
Neurotransmitter theories	Dysregulation of neurotransmitters and their receptors causes depression and mania. The monoamine neurotransmitters—norepinephrine, serotonin, and dopamine—have been most researched.
Neurophysiological abnormalities	Abnormalities in the structure and functioning of the prefrontal cortex, hippocampus, anterior cingulate cortex, and amygdala.
Neuroendocrine abnormalities	Depressed people show chronic hyperactivity in the hypothalamic-pituitary-adrenal axis and slow return to baseline after a stressor, which affects the functioning of neurotransmitters.

FIGURE 9.3

Risk for Bipolar Disorder in Relatives of People with Bipolar Disorder and in the General Population. The risk of developing bipolar disorder decreases as the genetic similarity between an individual and a relative with bipolar disorder decreases.

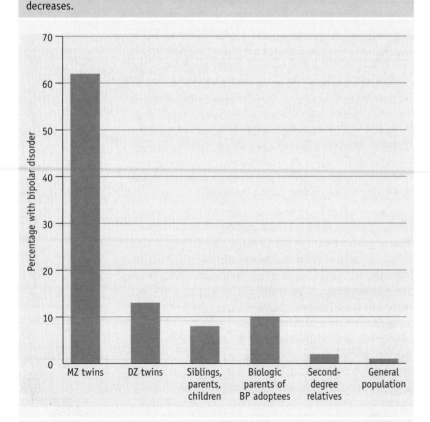

Source: With permission, from *Annual Review of Neuroscience*, Volume 20, copyright © 1997, by Annual Reviews, www.AnnualReviews.org

Does this mean that, if you have a close relative with bipolar disorder, you are destined to develop the disorder? No—most studies find that fewer than 10 percent (and often less than 5 percent) of the first-degree relatives of people with bipolar disorder develop the disorder themselves (MacKinnon et al., 1997) (review Figure 9.3). In other words, the risk is higher for people with a bipolar relative, but only a minority of them develop the disorder.

Unipolar depression also clearly runs in families. Family history studies find that the first-degree relatives of people with unipolar depression are two to three times more likely also to have depression, compared with the first-degree relatives of people without the disorder (Klein et al., 2001). Interestingly, the relatives of people with depression do *not* tend to have any greater risk for bipolar disorder than do the relatives of people with no mood disorder. This suggests that bipolar disorder has a genetic basis different from that of unipolar depression.

Twin Studies

Twin studies of bipolar disorder have shown that the probability that both twins will develop the disorder, or its *concordance rate*, is about 60 percent among monozygotic (identical) twins, compared with about 13 percent among dizygotic (nonidentical) twins (MacKinnon et al., 1997; McGuffin & Katz, 1989; Wallace et al., 2002). This finding suggests that genetics plays a substantial role in vulnerability to bipolar disorder.

Twin studies of major depression also find higher concordance rates for monozygotic twins than for dizygotic twins (e.g., Kendler et al., 2001). Some twin studies of major depression suggest that genetics plays a heavier role in this disorder for women than for men (Kendler et al., 2001). Other twin studies, however, have found no gender difference in the heritability of depression (Eaves et al., 1997; Kendler & Prescott, 1999; Rutter et al., 1999). Still other studies suggest that the types of genes responsible for depression may differ between women and men (Zubenko et al., 2002).

Specific Genetic Abnormalities

What kinds of genetic abnormalities might play a role in these disorders? One specific genetic abnormality that some studies suggest may be involved in the vulnerability to depression is on the serotonin transporter gene (Southwick et al., 2005). As we will discuss shortly, serotonin is one of the neurotransmitters implicated in depression. Abnormalities on the serotonin transporter gene could lead to dysfunction in the regulation of serotonin, which in turn could affect the stability of individuals' moods. In a longitudinal study, Caspi and colleagues (2003) found that people with abnormalities on the serotonin transporter gene were at increased risk for depression when they faced negative life events.

It is likely that there is no single location on a gene that leads to mood disorders. Many researchers believe that the genetic predisposition to mood disorders is *multifactorial*—it involves many factors. That is, a particular configuration of several disordered genes may be necessary to create a mood disorder.

Neurotransmitter Dysregulation

Most of the biochemical theories of mood disorders have focused on neurotransmitters, the biochemicals that facilitate the transmission of impulses across the synapses between neurons. Many different neurotransmitters may play a role in the mood disorders, but the neurotransmitters that have been implicated most often in the mood disorders are the **monoamines.**

The specific monoamines that have been implicated are **norepinephrine, serotonin,** and, to a lesser extent, **dopamine.** These neurotransmitters are found in large concentrations in the *limbic system*, a part of the brain associated with the regulation of sleep, appetite, and emotional processes. These neurotransmitters are thought to cause both depression and mania—imbalances in one direction may cause depression and imbalances in the other direction may cause mania.

The early theory of the roles of these neurotransmitters in mood disorders was that depression was caused by a reduction in the amount of norepinephrine or serotonin in the synapses between neurons (Glassman, 1969; Schildkraut, 1965). This depletion could occur for numerous reasons: decreased synthesis of the neurotransmitter from its precursors, increased degradation of the neurotransmitter by enzymes, or impaired release or reuptake of the neurotransmitter (see Chapter 2 to review these processes). Mania was thought to be caused by an excess of the monoamines or perhaps dysregulation of the levels of these amines, especially dopamine. Taken together, these theories are known as the **monoamine theories** of mood disorders (Bunney & Davis, 1965; Schildkraut, 1965).

More recent studies of the monoamine theories have focused on the number and functioning of receptors for the monoamines on neurons in people suffering from mood disorders (Southwick et al., 2005). Recall from Chapter 2 that neurotransmitters and their receptors interact, somewhat as locks and keys do. Each neurotransmitter fits a particular type of receptor on the nerve cell membrane. If there is the wrong number of receptors for a given type of neurotransmitter or if the receptors for that neurotransmitter are too sensitive or not sensitive enough, then the neurons do not efficiently use the neurotransmitter that is available in the synapse.

Several studies suggest that people with major depression or bipolar disorder may have abnormalities in the number and sensitivity of receptors for the monoamine neurotransmitters (Hasler et al., 2004; Southwick et al., 2005). In major depression, receptors for serotonin and norepinephrine appear to be too few or insensitive. In bipolar disorder, the picture is less clear, but it is likely that receptors for the monoamines undergo poorly timed changes in sensitivity, which are correlated with mood changes (Kujawa & Nemeroff, 2000).

Most of the neurotransmitter abnormalities found in people with mood disorders are state-dependent. That is, these differences are present when the mood disorder is present but tend to disappear when the mood disorder subsides. Certain neurotransmitter abnormalities may be correlated with, but may not necessarily cause, the mood disorders. As the technology for determining the functioning of neurotransmitter systems develops, our understanding of the relationship between neurotransmitters and mood disorders will no doubt increase.

Brain Abnormalities

Neuroimaging studies using computerized tomography (CT) scans, positron-emission tomography

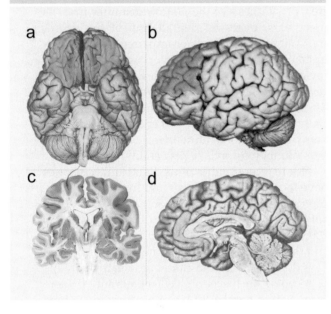

FIGURE 9.4 **Brain Areas That May Be Involved in Mood Disorders.** *(a)* Orbital prefrontal cortex *(green)* and ventromedial prefrontal cortex *(red)*. *(b)* Dorsolateral prefrontal cortex *(purple)*. *(c)* Hippocampus *(pink)* and amygdala *(orange)*. *(d)* Anterior cingulated cortex *(yellow)*.

(PET), and magnetic resonance imaging (MRI) have found consistent abnormalities in at least four areas of the brain in people with mood disorders. These areas are the prefrontal cortex, the hippocampus, the anterior cingulate cortex, and the amygdala (Davidson et al., 2002; Southwick et al., 2005) (see Figure 9.4).

Both reductions in metabolic activity and a reduction in the volume of gray matter in the *prefrontal cortex*, particularly on the left side, have been found in people with serious depression or bipolar disorder (review Figure 9.4a, green and red areas, and b, purple areas) (Buchsbaum et al., 1997; Drevets, 2001; Drevets et al., 1997). Davidson, Pizzagalli, Nitschke, and Putnam (2002) have suggested that the left prefrontal cortex is more involved in approach-related goals and that inactivity in this region is associated with the lack of motivation and goal orientation in depression. The successful treatment of depression with antidepressant medications is associated with increases in metabolic activity in the left prefrontal cortex (Kennedy et al., 2001).

The *anterior cingulate* plays an important role in the body's response to stress, in emotional expression, and in social behavior, as well as in the processing of difficult information (Davidson et al., 2002) (review Figure 9.4d, yellow area). Peo-

ple with depression show decreased activity in the anterior cingulate relative to controls (Buchsbaum et al., 1997; Drevets et al., 1997). This lack of activity may be associated with problems in attention, in the planning of appropriate responses, and in coping, as well as with anhedonia found in depression. Again, activity increases in this region of the brain when people are successfully treated for their depression (Mayberg et al., 1997; Pizzagalli et al., 2001).

The *hippocampus* is critical in memory and in fear-related learning (review Figure 9.4c, purple area). MRI studies show a smaller volume in the hippocampus of people with major depression or bipolar disorder (Bremner et al., 2000; Noga, Vladar, & Torrey, 2001). Similarly, PET studies show lower metabolic activity in the hippocampus in people with major depression (Saxena, Brody, et al., 2001). Damage to the hippocampus could be the result of chronic arousal of the body's stress response. People with depression show chronically high levels of the hormone cortisol, particularly in response to stress, indicating that their bodies overreact to stress and do not return to normal levels of cortisol as quickly as the bodies of healthy people do. The hippocampus contains many receptors for cortisol, and chronically elevated levels of cortisol may inhibit the development of new neurons in the hippocampus (see Pariante & Miller, 2001; Sapolsky, Krey, & McEwen, 1986).

Abnormalities in the structure and functioning of the amygdala are found in several disorders involving mood (Davidson et al., 2002) (review Figure 9.4c, orange area). The amygdala helps direct attention to stimuli that are emotionally salient and have major significance for the individual. Studies of people with mood disorders show an enlargement of the amygdala (Altshuler et al., 1998; Mervaala et al., 2000) and increased activity in this part of the brain (Drevets, 2001). Activity in the amygdala has been observed to decrease to normal values in people successfully treated for depression (Drevets, 2001). The effects of overactivity in the amygdala are not yet entirely clear, but Drevets (2001) and Davidson and colleagues (2002) suggest that it may bias people toward aversive or emotionally arousing information and lead to rumination over negative memories and negative aspects of the environment.

It is not known whether any of these abnormalities in the structure or functioning of the brain are causes of the mood disorders or the consequences of these disorders (Davidson, Pizzagalli, & Nitschke, 2002; Thase et al., 2002). Animal studies suggest that many of these brain abnormalities can be caused by conditions in the environment, including chronic stress and chronic lack of control (Leverenz et al., 1999). Thus, for some people with mood disorders, the initial cause of their disorder may have been environmental, but the disorder may cause changes in the brain that increase their vulnerability to future episodes. For other people with mood disorders, brain dysfunction may be caused by abnormal genes.

Neuroendocrine Factors

Hormones have long been thought to play a role in mood disorders, especially depression. The *neuroendocrine system* regulates a number of important hormones, which in turn affect basic functions, such as sleep, appetite, sexual drive, and the ability to experience pleasure (to review the neuroendocrine system, see Chapter 2). These hormones also help the body respond to environmental stressors.

FIGURE 9.5	**The Hypothalamic-Pituitary-Adrenal Axis.** The

hypothalamus synthesizes corticotropin-releasing hormone (CRH). CRH is transported to the pituitary gland, where it stimulates the synthesis and release of adrenocorticotropic hormone (ACTH), which then circulates to the adrenal glands, producing cortisol. Cortisol then inhibits the production of further ACTH and CRH. Normally, this process prevents too much or too prolonged physiological arousal following a stressor. In major depression, however, people often show abnormal cortisol functioning, suggesting that there is dysregulation in the hypothalamic-pituitary-adrenal (HPA) axis.

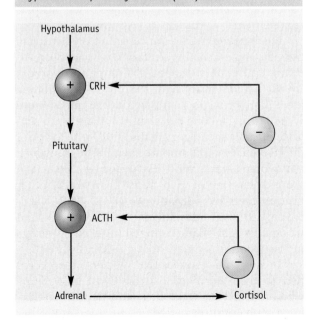

Three key components of the neuroendocrine system—the hypothalamus, pituitary, and adrenal cortex—work together in a biological feedback system that is richly interconnected with the limbic system and the cerebral cortex. This system is often referred to as the **hypothalamic-pituitary-adrenal axis, or HPA axis**, and is involved in the fight-or-flight response, as discussed in Chapter 6.

Normally, when we are confronted with a stressor, the HPA axis becomes more active (see Figure 9.5). It increases the body's levels of major stress hormones, such as **cortisol**, which help the body respond to the stressor by making it possible to fight the stressor or flee from it. Once the stressor is gone, the HPA axis activity returns to its baseline levels. Thus, this biological feedback loop both helps activate the HPA system during stress and calms the system when the stress is over.

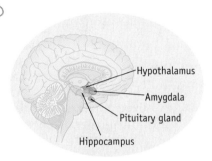

The hypothalamic-pituitary-adrenal (HPA) axis and structures of the limbic system may be involved in the development of depression.

People with depression tend to show chronic hyperactivity in the HPA axis and an inability for the HPA axis to return to normal functioning following a stressor (Southwick et al., 2005; Young & Korzun, 1998). In turn, the excess hormones produced by heightened HPA activity seem to have an inhibiting effect on receptors for the monoamines. One model for the development of depression is that people exposed to chronic stress may develop poorly regulated neuroendocrine systems. Then, when they are exposed even to minor stressors later in life, the HPA axis overreacts and does not easily return to baseline. This overreaction creates change in the functioning of the monoamine neurotransmitters in the brain, and an episode of depression is likely to ensue (Southwick et al., 2005).

Women's Hormonal Cycles as a Factor

Many people have argued over the years that women's greater vulnerability to depression is tied to hormones—specifically, the so-called ovarian hormones, estrogen and progesterone. The main fuel for this idea comes from evidence that women are more prone to depression during the premenstrual period of the menstrual cycle, the postpartum period, and menopause. These are times when estrogen and progesterone levels change dramatically.

Research over the past several decades has shown that most women do not experience significant changes in their moods during times of hormonal change (Nolen-Hoeksema, 2002; Young &

Korszun, 1998). However, there is a small group of women, about 3 percent of the population, who frequently experience increases in depressive symptoms during the premenstrual phase. Many of these women also have a history of frequent major depressive episodes or anxiety disorders with no connection to the menstrual cycle or of other psychiatric disorders (Steiner et al., 2003). This history suggests that these women have a general vulnerability to depression or anxiety, rather than a specific vulnerability to premenstrual depression.

This information has led many researchers to argue that depressions during the premenstrual period should not be given a separate diagnosis, such as **premenstrual dysphoric disorder,** but, rather, should be considered only exacerbations of major depression or dysthymia. Others argue that premenstrual depression should be recognized separately, with its own diagnosis, because it is different from depression that has no link with the menstrual cycle and therefore should be studied separately. The authors of the DSM-IV-TR dealt with this controversy by putting diagnostic criteria for premenstrual dysphoric disorder in an appendix, rather than in the main body of its text with other officially recognized diagnoses.

Even among women who clearly do have premenstrual symptoms (PMS), there is little evidence that their symptoms are due to changes in estrogen or progesterone levels across the menstrual cycle (Steiner et al., 2003; Young & Korzun, 1998). Many studies have found no differences in estrogen or progesterone levels between women with PMS and those without PMS. There clearly is something about the menstrual cycle that is worsening mood in women with PMS, but it appears that estrogen or progesterone does not have consistent direct effects on mood.

About 1 in 10 women experience a severe postpartum depression in the first few months after giving birth. This might seem like strong evidence that hormonal changes play a role in women's depressions, because this is a period of great hormonal change in women's bodies. However, studies comparing rates of depression in women who are and are not postpartum have tended not to find differences in rates of depression (O'Hara & Swain, 1996). Even among women who do become seriously depressed during the postpartum period, depressions do not seem to be linked to any specific imbalances in hormones (Hendrick, Altshuler, & Suri, 1998).

Postpartum depressions are often linked to severe stress in women's lives, such as financial strain, marital difficulties, lack of social support, and fussy babies (Brugha et al., 1998; Hendrick et al., 1998; O'Hara & Swain, 1996). In addition, women who

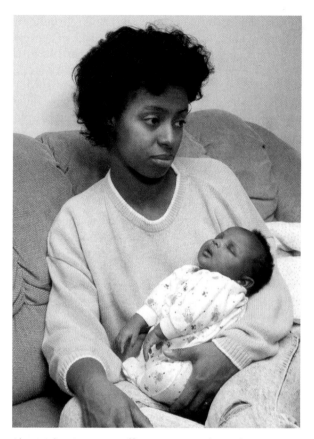

About 1 in 10 women suffer postpartum depression.

have a history of depression clearly are at increased risk for postpartum depression (Steiner et al., 2003). These women may carry a general vulnerability to depression, which is triggered by either the physiological or the environmental changes of the postpartum period.

Menopause marks the cessation of menstrual periods, and circulating ovarian hormones decrease dramatically at menopause (Young & Korzun, 1998). Twenty years ago, the belief that women were more prone to depression during menopause was so strong among clinicians that there was a separate diagnostic category in the DSM for this type of depression. Several studies have found, however, that women are no more likely to show depression around the time of menopause than at any other time in their lives (Matthews et al., 1990; Nicol-Smith, 1996). In addition, there are no consistent mood effects of taking estrogen replacement drugs for menopausal women (Young & Korzun, 1998).

In sum, the evidence that women's moods are tied to their hormones is mixed, at best. Some women clearly do experience more depression during the postpartum period, menopause, and other times when their hormone levels change rapidly.

The extent to which these experiences of depression account for the generally higher rates of depression among women compared with men is less clear.

Early Stress as a Cause of Neurobiological Vulnerability to Depression

There is increasing evidence that early traumatic stress, such as being the victim of incest, severe neglect, or other serious, chronic stress, can lead to some of the neurobiological abnormalities that may predispose people to depression (Southwick et al., 2005). Studies of children who have been abused or neglected show that their biological responses to stress, particularly the response of their HPA axis, often are either exaggerated or blunted (Cicchetti & Toth, 2005). Heim and colleagues (Heim & Nemeroff, 2002; Heim, Plotsky, & Nemeroff, 2004) have found that women who were sexually abused as children show altered HPA responses to stress as adults, even when they are not depressed. Similarly, animal studies show that early stress (such as separation from their mothers) promotes exaggerated neurobiological stress reactivity and vulnerability to depression-like responses to future stressors (see Southwick et al., 2005). These neurobiological vulnerabilities can be reduced in animals by providing them with subsequent supportive maternal care and/or pharmacological interventions.

SUMMING UP

- Genetic factors clearly play a role in bipolar disorder, although it is somewhat less clear what role genetics plays in many forms of unipolar depression.

- The neurotransmitter theories suggest that imbalances in levels of norepinephrine or serotonin or the dysregulation of receptors for these neurotransmitters contribute to depression, and dysregulation of norepinephrine, serotonin, or dopamine is involved in bipolar disorder.

- Neuroimaging studies have shown abnormalities in the structure and functioning of the prefrontal cortex, hippocampus, anterior cingulate cortex, and amygdala in people with mood disorders.

- People with depression have chronic hyperactivity of the hypothalamic-pituitary-adrenal (HPA) axis, which helps regulate the body's response to stress.

- Abnormalities in the biological stress response may result from early stressors in some people and contribute to depression.

PSYCHOLOGICAL THEORIES OF MOOD DISORDERS

Psychological theories have focused almost exclusively on depression, because the evidence that bipolar disorder is caused by biological factors is strong. However, new episodes of bipolar disorder may be triggered by experiencing stressful events or living in an unsupportive family (Frank, Schwartz, & Kupfer, 2000; Hlastsala et al., 2000). This pattern suggests a diathesis-stress model of bipolar disorder, in which the *diathesis*, or vulnerability, is a biological one, such as a genetic predisposition to the disorder, and stressors, such as the loss of a job, can trigger new episodes. In this section, however, we focus on depression and the psychological theories that have tried to explain it (see the Concept Overview in Table 9.6 on page 320).

Behavioral Theories

Depression often arises as a reaction to stressful negative events, such as the breakup of a relationship, the death of a loved one, a job loss, or a serious medical illness (Hammen, 2005). Sixty-five percent of people with depression in one study reported a negative life event in the six months prior to the onset of their depression (Frank et al., 1994). People with depression are more likely than nondepressed people to have chronic life stressors, such as financial strain or a bad marriage. People who suffer depression also tend to have a history of traumatic life events, particularly events involving loss (Hammen, 2005).

The Reduction of Positive Reinforcers

Peter Lewinsohn's **behavioral theory of depression** suggests that life stress leads to depression because it reduces the positive reinforcers in a person's life (Lewinsohn & Gotlib, 1995). The person begins to withdraw, which only results in a further reduction in reinforcers, which leads to more withdrawal, and a self-perpetuating chain is created.

For example, imagine that a man is having difficulty in his relationship with his wife. Interactions with her are no longer as positively reinforcing as they formerly were, so he stops initiating these interactions as often. This only worsens the communication between him and his wife, so the relationship becomes even worse. He withdraws further and becomes depressed about this area of his life. Lewinsohn suggests that such a pattern is especially likely in people with poor social skills, because they are more likely to experience rejection by others and to withdraw in response to this rejection, rather than to find ways to overcome the rejection (Lewinsohn, 1974). In addition, once a person begins engaging in

TABLE 9.6	Concept Overview

Psychological Theories of Mood Disorders

The psychological theories of depression have focused on aspects of the environment, of thinking, and of a person's past.

Theory	Description
Behavioral theories	
Lewinsohn's theory	Depressed people experience a reduction in positive reinforcers and an increase in aversive events, which leads to their depression.
Learned helplessness theory	Depressed people lack control, which leads to the belief that they are helpless, which leads to depressive symptoms.
Cognitive theories	
Aaron Beck's theory	Depressed people have a negative cognitive triad of beliefs about the self, the world, and the future, which is maintained by distorted thinking.
Reformulated learned helplessness theory	Depressed people have the tendency to attribute events to internal, stable, and global factors, which contributes to depression.
Ruminative response styles theory	Depressed people tend to ruminate about their symptoms and problems.
Psychodynamic theory	Depressed people are unconsciously punishing themselves because they feel abandoned by another person but cannot punish that person; dependency and perfectionism are risk factors for depression.
Interpersonal theories	Depressed people have poor relationships with others.

depressive behaviors, these behaviors are reinforced by the sympathy and attention they engender in others.

Learned Helplessness Theory

Another behavioral theory—the **learned helplessness theory**—suggests that the type of stressful event most likely to lead to depression is uncontrollable negative events (Seligman, 1975). Such events, especially if frequent or chronic, can lead people to believe that they are helpless to control important outcomes in their environment. In turn, this belief in helplessness leads people to lose their motivation, to reduce actions that might control the environment, and to be unable to learn how to control situations that are controllable. These deficits, known as **learned helplessness deficits**, are similar to the symptoms of depression: low motivation, passivity, and indecisiveness (Seligman, 1975).

The initial evidence for the learned helplessness theory came from studies with animals, as described in Chapter 2. A group of researchers conducted a series of studies in which dogs were given controllable shock, uncontrollable shock, or no

shock (Overmier & Seligman, 1967; Seligman & Maier, 1967). The dogs in the controllable shock group could turn off the shock by jumping a short barrier, and they quickly learned how to do so (as did the dogs that had previously received no shock). The dogs in the uncontrollable shock group could not turn off or otherwise escape the shock. The dogs in the controllable and uncontrollable shock conditions received the same total amount of shock. However, when the dogs in the uncontrollable shock group were put into a situation in which they could control the shock, they seemed unable to learn how to do so. They just sat in the box, passive and whimpering, until the shock went off. Even when the experimenter dragged these dogs across the barrier in an attempt to teach them how to turn off the shock, the dogs did not learn the response. The researchers argued that the dogs in the uncontrollable shock group had learned they were helpless to control the shock, and their passivity and inability to learn to control the shock were the result of this learned helplessness.

In turn, the researchers argued that many human depressions are *helplessness depressions*, result-

Children who lose a parent may come to believe that important areas of their lives are not under their control and, thus, develop a helplessness depression.

ing when people come to believe they are helpless to control important outcomes in their environment. For example, children who lose their mothers may come to believe that important areas of their lives are not under their control. The loss of a mother may mean not only the loss of the person to whom the child is most closely attached but also years of disruption and instability as the child is moved from one set of relatives to another, if the father is not able to care for the child. Such chronic instability might persuade the child that life truly is uncontrollable, and this may be why childhood bereavement is a predisposing factor for depression. Similarly, women who are frequently battered by their husbands may develop the belief that there is nothing they can do to control their beatings or other parts of their lives, and this may explain the high rates of depression among battered women (Koss & Kilpatrick, 2001).

Cognitive Theories

> "Good morning, Eeyore," shouted Piglet.
> "Good morning, Little Piglet," said
>   Eeyore.

"If it *is* a good morning," he said.
"Which I doubt," said he.
"Not that it matters," he said.
(Milne, 1961, p. 54)

Like poor Eeyore, some people have a chronically gloomy way of interpreting the things that happen to them. According to the cognitive theories of depression, these gloomy ways of thinking are a cause of depression.

Aaron Beck's Theory

One of the first cognitive theories of depression was developed by psychiatrist Aaron Beck. Beck (1967) argued that people with depression look at the world through a **negative cognitive triad:** They have negative views of themselves, of the world, and of the future. People with depression then commit many types of errors in thinking—such as jumping to negative conclusions on the basis of little evidence, ignoring good events, focusing only on negative events, and exaggerating negative events—that support their negative cognitive triad (see Table 9.7 on page 322).

People with depression may not be aware that they hold these negative views or that they make these errors in thinking. Often, these negative thoughts are so automatic that people with depression do not realize how they are interpreting situations. A wide range of studies have supported the hypothesis that people with depression show these negative ways of thinking, and some longitudinal studies have shown that these thinking styles predict depression over time (Abramson et al., 2002). Beck's theory led to one of the most widely used and successful therapies for depression, cognitive-behavioral therapy.

Reformulated Learned Helplessness Theory

Another influential cognitive theory of depression, the **reformulated learned helplessness theory,** was proposed to explain how cognitive factors might influence whether a person becomes helpless and depressed following a negative event (Abramson, et al., 1978; Peterson & Seligman, 1984). This theory focuses on people's causal attributions for events. A **causal attribution** is an explanation of why an event happened. According to this theory, people who habitually explain negative events by causes that are internal, stable, and global blame themselves for these negative events, expect negative events to recur in the future, and expect to experience negative events in many areas of their lives. In turn, these expectations lead them to experience long-term learned helplessness deficits plus self-esteem loss in many areas of their lives.

TABLE 9.7 Errors or Distortions in Thinking in Depression

Error	Description
All-or-nothing thinking	You see things in black-and-white categories. If your performance falls short of perfect, you see yourself as a total failure.
Overgeneralization	You see a single negative event as a never-ending pattern of defeat.
Mental filter	You pick out a single negative detail and dwell on it exclusively, so that your vision of all reality becomes darkened, like a drop of ink that discolors an entire beaker of water.
Disqualifying the positive	You reject positive experiences by insisting they "don't count" for some reason. In this way, you can maintain a negative belief that is contradicted by your everyday experiences.
Jumping to conclusions	You make a negative interpretation, even though there are no definite facts that convincingly support your conclusion: (a) *Mind Reading*. You arbitrarily conclude that someone is reacting negatively to you, and you don't bother to check this out. (b) *The Fortune Teller Error*. You anticipate that things will turn out badly, and you feel convinced that your prediction is an already established fact.
Magnification (catastrophizing) or minimization	You exaggerate the importance of things (such as your goof-up or someone else's achievement), or you inappropriately shrink things until they appear tiny (your own desirable qualities or another's imperfections). This is also called the "binocular trick."
Emotional reasoning	You assume that your negative emotions necessarily reflect the way things really are: "I feel it; therefore, it must be true."
"Should" statements	You try to motivate yourself with "shoulds" and "shouldn'ts", as if you had to be whipped and punished before you could be expected to do anything. "Must" and "oughts" are also offenders. The emotional consequence is guilt. When you direct "should" statements toward others, you feel anger, frustration, and resentment.
Labeling and mislabeling	This is an extreme form of overgeneralization. Instead of describing your error, you attach a negative label to yourself: "I'm a *loser*." When someone else's behavior rubs you the wrong way, you attach a negative label to that person. Mislabeling involves describing an event with language that is highly colored and emotionally loaded.
Personalization	You see yourself as the cause of a negative external event, which, in fact, you were not primarily responsible for.

Source: Burns, 1980.

For example, consider a student who becomes depressed after failing a psychology exam. The reformulated learned helplessness theory would suggest that she has blamed her failure on internal causes—she didn't study hard enough—rather than external causes—the exam was too hard. Further, she has assumed that the failure was due to stable causes, such as a lack of aptitude in psychology, rather than unstable causes, such as the instructor's not allowing enough time, and she can expect to fail again. Finally, she has attributed her failure to a global cause, such as her difficulty in learning the material for this particular test. This global attribution would lead to failure in other academic areas.

Again, researchers equate learned helplessness deficits with depression and argue that an internal-stable-global attributional style for negative events puts people at risk for depression. Abramson et al. (1989) argued that hopelessness depression develops when people make pessimistic attributions for the most important events in their lives and perceive that they have no way of coping with the consequences of these events. The reformulated learned helplessness theory and the hopelessness theory have motivated a great deal of research (Abramson et al., 2002).

One of the most definitive studies of this theory of depression was a long-term study of college students (Alloy, Abramson, & Francis, 1999). Researchers interviewed first-year students at two universities and identified those with hopeless attributional styles and those with optimistic attributional styles. They then tracked these students for the next 2½ years, interviewing them every 6 weeks. Among the students with no history of depression, those with a hopeless cognitive style were much more likely to develop a first onset of major depression than were those with an optimistic attributional style (17 percent versus 1 percent). In addition, among those who had a history of depression, students with a hopeless style were more likely to have a relapse of depression than those with an optimistic style (27 percent versus 6 percent). Thus, a pessimistic attributional style predicted both first onsets of depression and relapses of depression.

Is it possible that people with depression are not distorted in their negative views of the world but actually are seeing the world realistically for the terrible place that it is? Researchers began investigating this possibility when they stumbled on a phenomenon now referred to as **depressive realism:** When asked to make judgments about how much control they have over situations that are actually uncontrollable, people with depression are quite accurate. In contrast, nondepressed people greatly overestimate the amount of control they have, especially over positive events. For example, in one study (Alloy & Abramson, 1979), depressed and nondepressed people were asked to judge to what degree they could control the onset of a green light by pushing a button on a display panel. In truth, none of the subjects had control over the onset of the light. In conditions in which the subjects were rewarded whenever the green light came on, the nondepressed people grossly overestimated their control over the onset

of the light. In contrast, the depressed subjects accurately judged that they had no control over the onset of the light.

Subsequently, a long line of research has shown that nondepressed people have a robust illusion that they can control all sorts of situations that truly are out of their control and that they have superior skills, compared with most people (Taylor & Brown, 1988). For example, nondepressed people believe they can control games of chance, such as the lottery; that they are more likely than the average person to succeed in life; that they are more immune to car accidents than other people; and that their social skills are better than most people's. In contrast, people with depression do not seem to hold these illusions of control and superiority. Indeed, people with depression seem amazingly accurate in judging the amount of control they have over situations and their skills at various tasks. This research on illusion of control calls into question the notion that depression results from unrealistic beliefs that one cannot control one's environment or from negative errors in thinking about oneself and the world. Perhaps it is not accurate, realistic thinking that prevents people from becoming depressed but, rather, hope and optimism.

Ruminative Response Styles Theory

Another cognitive theory, the **ruminative response styles theory,** focuses more on the process of thinking, rather than the content of thinking, as a contributor to depression (Nolen-Hoeksema, 2003). Some people, when sad and upset, focus intently on how they feel—their symptoms of fatigue and poor concentration and their sadness and hopelessness—and can identify many possible causes of these symptoms. They do not attempt to do anything about these causes, however, and continue to engage in **rumination** about their depression.

Several studies have shown that people with this more ruminative coping style are more likely to develop major depression and may remain depressed longer than people with a more action-oriented coping style (Nolen-Hoeksema, 2000; Nolen-Hoeksema, Larson, & Grayson, 1999; Nolen-Hoeksema & Morrow, 1991; Nolen-Hoeksema, Parker, & Larson, 1994). Rumination is not just another symptom of depression, although people who are more depressed have more to ruminate about. People with depression differ in the extent to which they ruminate, and those who ruminate more become more severely depressed over time and remain depressed longer than those who do not.

Women are more likely than men to ruminate when they are depressed (Nolen-Hoeksema, 2002; Nolen-Hoeksema et al., 1999). This may be because women are exposed to more circumstances that make them ruminate—more negative events and circumstances over which they feel they have no control. Regardless of the reasons for this gender difference in rumination, women's tendency to ruminate appears to contribute to their higher rates of depression, compared with men (Nolen-Hoeksema et al., 1999).

Psychodynamic Theories

Some people seem to find themselves in unhealthy, destructive relationships over and over again. Each time these relationships end, they vow never to get into similar relationships again. However, they do and then find themselves depressed over the problems in the new relationships or when the relationships inevitably end.

Psychodynamic theorists suggest that such patterns of unhealthy relationships stem from people's childhood experiences that prevented them from developing a strong and positive sense of self reasonably independent of others' evaluations (Arieti & Bemporad, 1980; Bibring, 1953; Blatt & Zuroff, 1992; Freud, 1917). As adults, these people are constantly searching for approval and security in their relationships with others. They are anxious about separation and abandonment and may allow others to take advantage and even abuse them, rather than risk losing the relationship by complaining. They are constantly striving to be "perfect," so that they will be loved. Even when they accomplish great things, they do not feel secure or positive about themselves. Eventually, a problem in a close relationship or a failure to achieve perfection occurs, and they plunge into depression.

Many modern psychodynamic theorists still rely on the groundbreaking work Freud published in his paper *Mourning and Melancholia* to describe just how depression develops when a person per-

ceives he or she has been abandoned or has failed. Freud pointed out that people who are depressed have many of the symptoms of people who are grieving the death of a loved one: They feel sad, alone, unmotivated, and lethargic. Unlike grieving people, people with depression display severe self-hate and self-blame. Indeed, said Freud, people with depression appear to want to punish themselves, even to the point of killing themselves.

Freud argued that people with depression are not actually blaming or punishing themselves. Instead, they are blaming or punishing those who they perceive have abandoned them. People with depression are so dependent on the approval and love of others that much of their ego or sense of self is made up of their images of these others— what Freud called the "love objects." When they believe others have rejected them, people with depression are too frightened to express their rage outwardly. Instead, they turn their anger inward on the parts of their own egos that have incorporated the love objects. Their self-blame and punishment is actually blame and punishment of the others who have abandoned them. This is Freud's **introjected hostility theory** of depression. The case of Giselle illustrates the processes described by the psychodynamic theories of depression.

CASE STUDY

Giselle was raised by two well-meaning but emotionally inhibited parents. The parents had emigrated to the United States from Eastern Europe in the 1970s, fleeing persecution for their anticommunist beliefs. Even after settling in the United States, Giselle's parents remained paranoid about the family's security and constantly told Giselle she had to be "good" or the family would be in danger. Thus, from an early age, Giselle suppressed any childhood willfulness or exuberance. She was not allowed to play with other children; she spent most of her time with the family maid, who had followed them to the United States. Her parents were preoccupied with their uncertain circumstances and unnecessarily belittled Giselle's childhood concerns. For example, when there was an epidemic of flu at Giselle's school, her mother told her not to worry, because only the smart and pretty girls were getting sick. The mother doted on the father when he was in the house, ignoring Giselle.

(continued)

The father paid attention to Giselle only when she was deferential or complimentary.

As an adult, Giselle chose to become a nurse, because she felt it would gain her acceptance and love by patients. Giselle married a man who was somewhat solitary and hypercritical. He was prone to periods of depression and always preoccupied with his own concerns. Giselle became the major source of financial support during her marriage, often taking on extra shifts to earn more money. She had done remarkably well in her career because of her hard work and her repeated efforts to please others. She was also the emotional mainstay in her family, being responsible for taking care of the children and for fulfilling the usual responsibilities of running a household. Giselle rarely complained, however. She needed to be certain that everyone liked her and thought well of her, and she went to extremes of self-sacrifice to ensure the high regard of others.

After several years, her husband left her, telling her that he did not love her any longer and that she no longer gave him any pleasure in his life. In the first few days after her husband announced he was going to leave, Giselle desperately tried to win back his love by indulging his every whim. Eventually, however, they had a violent confrontation, during which he walked out. Later that evening, Giselle emptied her medicine cabinet of all drugs, drove to a secluded area, and ingested the drugs in an effort to kill herself. (Adapted from Bemporad, 1995)

Some research has supported elements of the psychodynamic perspective on depression. For example, people with depression tend to display many of Giselle's personality traits: They are dependent on others, believe that they must be perfect, have poor self-esteem, and are unable to express anger openly (Klein et al., 2002). In addition, many people with depression describe their parents as having characteristics similar to those of Giselle's parents: They are cold and neglectful, excessively moralistic and demanding of perfection, or requiring of complete devotion and dependency from their children in exchange for their love (Blatt & Zuroff, 1992). Most of these studies are cross-

sectional, however, so it is not known whether these characteristics and views are symptoms of the depression or actual causes of it. A few longitudinal studies support elements of psychodynamic theories. For example, one study of middle-aged women found that those who tended to inhibit any expression of anger and who were unassertive in interpersonal interactions were more likely to become depressed over a three-year period (Bromberger & Matthews, 1996).

Traditional psychodynamic perspectives on depression have been adapted by modern theorists to develop the interpersonal theories of depression and therapies based on these theories. We turn now to the interpersonal theories.

Interpersonal Theories

Like psychodynamic theories, **interpersonal theories of depression** are concerned with people's close relationships and their roles in those relationships (Klerman et al., 1984). Disturbances in these roles are thought to be the main source of depression. These disturbances may be recent, as when a woman who believes that her marriage has been successful for years suddenly finds that her husband is having an affair. Often, the disturbances are rooted in long-standing patterns of interactions the people with depression typically have with important others. Drawing from attachment theory (Bowlby, 1982), interpersonal theorists argue that children who do not experience their caregivers as reliable, responsive, and warm develop an insecure attachment to their caregivers, which sets the stage for all future relationships (see Chapter 2). These problematic relationships become represented mentally as negative working models of others and of the self in relation to others. These models are essentially operating rules and expectations about the availability of support from others and the implications of others' lack of support for one's self-worth.

Children with insecure attachments develop expectations that they must be or do certain things in order to win the approval of others, which have been called **contingencies of self-worth** (Kuiper & Olinger, 1986; Kuiper, Olinger, & MacDonald, 1988). These are "if-then" rules concerning self-worth, such as "I'm nothing if a person I care about doesn't love me." If these contingencies of self-worth sound like the dysfunctional beliefs that Beck and other cognitive theories describe, they are—the interpersonal theorists argue that dysfunctional beliefs are the result of insecure attachments in childhood. As long as an individual meets the contingencies of self-worth set up in his or her working model, then he or she will maintain positive self-esteem and remain nondepressed. Failures to meet these contingencies are inevitable, however, and plunge the person into depression.

According to the interpersonal theories, people who are so insecure in their relationships with others engage in **excessive reassurance seeking**— constantly looking for assurances from others that they are accepted and loved (Joiner, 2002). They never quite believe the affirmations other people give, however, and anxiously keep going back for more. After a while, their family members and friends can become weary of this behavior and become frustrated or hostile. The insecure person picks up on these cues of annoyance and becomes panicked over them, leading him or her to feel even more insecure and to engage in even more excessive reassurance seeking. Eventually, the person's social support may withdraw altogether, leading him or her to develop even more depression, as is illustrated in the following case study (from Nolen-Hoeksema, 2006).

CASE STUDY

Rachel was a 48-year-old homemaker from the Bronx, married to her husband, Phil, for 15 years. Phil never really gave Rachel good cause to doubt that he loved her. He was attentive and loving. He was at her side when she had medical problems a few years ago and when her mother died last year. He supported her decision to stay home to raise their two children and was sincerely interested in what she and the kids did during the day while he was working at his law firm.

But still Rachel doubted, and these doubts had grown stronger in the last few months as another one of her depressive periods had set in. How could he love her, when she was so boring? Surely he was just being nice when he asked about her day—he couldn't really be interested, given how exciting his own work was. She had gained weight over the years and felt she was no longer attractive to him. She wondered what he would do if one of the young women lawyers in his firm expressed interest in him.

Rachel tried to keep these concerns to herself, but they leaked out, in little comments to Phil. When he came home in the evening and said, "How was your day?" she sometimes responded, "Oh, boring as usual; you wouldn't be interested." Then, she waited to see what his response was. Phil would usu-

ally say something like, "Sure, I'm interested; tell me what you did." Then Rachel would tell him a few incidents from the day but label each one as "nothing" and "silly" as she went along. She listened intently for his response, wanting him to deny that her activities were nothing or silly and becoming anxious and disappointed if he didn't explicitly do so.

When Rachel mentioned that she felt fat or unattractive, Phil would usually respond that she was still his beautiful bride. She responded, "Oh, you have to say that; you're stuck with me." Phil felt frustrated and put off by this but tried to stay calm. "I don't have to say that; I mean it. I love you and I love how you look." But Rachel would not be satisfied: "You love me now, but will you always love me no matter what happens?"

Rachel set up all sorts of other tests of Phil's love for her and ploys to gain assurance of his devotion. If they disagreed with each other about something in the morning, Rachel would ruminate about it after Phil left for work. In her mind, she implicitly believed that, if he hadn't called to talk with her about the disagreement by 10 A.M. this meant he was really angry and their relationship was in trouble. Sometimes, if he hadn't called or e-mailed her by 11 A.M. she'd call or e-mail him with a neutral message, just to see whether he'd mention the morning's disagreement. If he didn't respond almost immediately, Rachel took this as further evidence that he was angry with her, even though she knew he was probably just very busy. If he did respond to her message, but didn't mention the disagreement and how sorry he was for it, Rachel would ruminate about this for the rest of the afternoon. By the time Phil got home in the evening, she was ripe with fear and anger, when he hadn't thought about the disagreement all day because it had been so minor.

A number of influential theories have suggested that women are socialized to base most of their self-concept and self-worth on their relationships with others, and this is what makes them more prone than men to depression. Jack (1991) and Helgeson (1994) both argue that females are

Difficulties in close relationships are often tied to depression.

more likely than males to silence their own wants and needs in a relationship in favor of maintaining a positive emotional tone in the relationship and to feel too responsible for the quality of the relationship. This leads females to have less power and to obtain less benefit from relationships. Some support has been found for this perspective on the gender difference in depression (Baron & Peixoto, 1991; Nolen-Hoeksema & Jackson, 2001).

The interpersonal theories of depression have been supported in several studies (Joiner, 2002). For example, one longitudinal study of college students found that those with an anxious, insecure attachment style had more dysfunctional negative beliefs and subsequently developed lower self-esteem and more depressive symptoms (Roberts, Gotlib, & Kassel, 1996). Most of the research on the interpersonal models of depression has focused on evaluating the therapy that was developed based on this model.

SUMMING UP

- The behavioral theories of depression suggest that stress can induce depression by reducing the number of reinforcers available to people.

- The learned helplessness theory of depression says that uncontrollable events can lead people to believe that important outcomes are outside of their control and thus can lead them to develop depression.

- The cognitive theories of depression argue that people with depression think in distorted and negative ways, and this leads them to become depressed, particularly in the face of negative events. In addition, people who ruminate about their depressive symptoms and the causes and consequences of those symptoms appear more prone to develop severe levels of depression.

- Psychodynamic theories posit that people with depression are overly dependent on the evaluations and approval of others for their self-esteem, as a result of poor nurturing by parents.

- The interpersonal theories of depression suggest that poor attachment relationships early in life can lead children to develop expectations that they must be or do certain things in order to win the approval of others, which puts them at risk for depression. They may also engage in excessive reassurance seeking, which drives away their social support.

SOCIAL PERSPECTIVES ON MOOD DISORDERS

Sociologists have focused on the large age, gender, and cross-cultural differences in rates of depression, and they have tried to understand these disorders in light of those differences.

The Cohort Effect in Depression

Recall that the rates of depression appear to be lower in people over the age of 65 than in younger people and that there are several explanations for this age difference. One further explanation highlights sociocultural changes over history that may have resulted in more recent generations' being at higher risk for depression than people who were born a few generations ago (Klerman & Weissman, 1989). This type of explanation is called a **cohort effect:** People born in one historical period are at different risk for a disorder than are people born in another historical period. For example, fewer than 15 percent of people born before 1940 have experienced episodes of major depression at some time in their lives, whereas over 25 percent of people born after 1970 have already experienced major depression by the age of 30 (see Figure 9.6 on page 328). Proponents of the cohort explanation suggest that more recent generations are more at risk for depression because of the rapid changes in social values that began in the 1960s and the disintegration of the family unit (Klerman & Weissman, 1989).

This decrease in social support and in identification with common social values may have put younger generations at higher risk for depression than older generations were. Another possible explanation is that younger generations have higher expectations for themselves than did older generations, but these expectations are too high to be met.

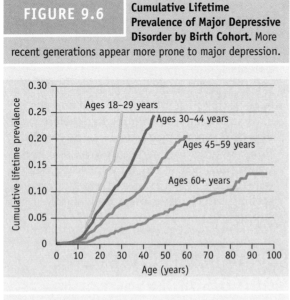

FIGURE 9.6 **Cumulative Lifetime Prevalence of Major Depressive Disorder by Birth Cohort.** More recent generations appear more prone to major depression.

Source: Kessler et al., 2003.

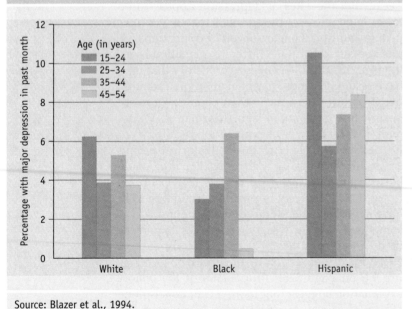

FIGURE 9.7 **Ethnic Differences in Major Depression.** These are the percentages of people in each age group and by ethnicity diagnosed with major depression in the previous month in one study. Hispanic Americans showed the highest rates across all age groups.

Source: Blazer et al., 1994.

Social Status

People who have lower status in society generally tend to show more depression. For example, in one large study done in the United States, people of Hispanic origin had a higher prevalence of major depression in the previous year than European Americans (Blazer et al., 1994) (see Figure 9.7).

This may reflect the higher rate of poverty, unemployment, and discrimination that Hispanics suffer, compared with European Americans.

Figure 9.7 also suggests, however, that African Americans of most ages have even lower rates of major depression than European Americans. This may seem puzzling, given the disadvantaged status of African Americans in U.S. society. However, African Americans have high rates of anxiety disorders, suggesting that the stress of their social status may make them especially prone to anxiety disorders rather than depression. Other studies have found extremely high rates of depression among Native Americans, especially the young (Saluja et al., 2004). Depression among these Native American youth is tied to poverty, hopelessness, and alcoholism.

One of the most compelling social explanations for women's higher rates of depression is that women's lower social status puts them at high risk for physical and sexual abuse, and these experiences often lead to depression. Women are much more likely than men to be the victims of rape, incest, battering, and sexual harassment (Koss & Kilpatrick, 2001). The rates of these types of violence against women are staggering. Most studies of rape estimate that between 14 and 25 percent of women are raped in their lives, most often before the age of 30 (Koss, 1993). One in eight women reports that she has been physically assaulted by her husband in the past year, and 1.8 million women report having been severely assaulted (punched, kicked, choked, or threatened with a gun or knife) (Straus & Gelles, 1990). Survivors of physical and sexual assault show high rates of major depression, anxiety disorders, and substance abuse. Thus, it seems likely that at least some of the difference between women's and men's rates of depression may be tied to the higher rates of abuse of women than of men and the resulting depression in female abuse survivors (Nolen-Hoeksema, 2002).

Cross-Cultural Differences

One cultural group within the United States that has an especially low prevalence of unipolar depression is the Old Order Amish of central Pennsylvania. As noted in Chapter 3, the Amish are a religious community of people who maintain a very simple lifestyle oriented around farming and the church and who reject modern conveniences, such as automobiles, electricity, and telephones. Essentially, the Amish live as people did in nineteenth-century rural America. Extensive research on the mood disorders among the Amish has suggested that their prevalence of major depression is only one-tenth of that of mainstream groups in the

United States (Egeland et al., 1987). Perhaps the simple, agrarian lifestyle of the Amish, with its emphasis on family and community, helps protect its members against depression.

Similarly, cross-national studies have suggested that the prevalence of major depression is lower among less industrialized and less modern countries than among more industrialized and more modern countries (Cross-National Collaborative Group, 1992; Lepine, 2001). Again, it may be that the fast-paced lifestyles of people in modern, industrialized societies, with their lack of stable social support and community values, are toxic to mental health. In contrast, the community- and family-oriented lifestyles of less modern societies may be beneficial to mental health, despite the physical hardships that many people in these societies face because of their lack of modern conveniences.

Alternately, some researchers have suggested that people in less modern cultures may tend to manifest depression with physical complaints, rather than psychological symptoms of depression, such as sadness, loss of motivation, and hopelessness about the future (Tsai & Chentsova-Dutton, 2002). For example, a study of refugees in Somalia found that they had a concept similar to the concept of sadness, which they called *murug* (Carroll, 2004). *Murug* arises when an individual has lost a loved one or another major negative life event has occurred. The symptoms of *murug*, however, are headaches and social withdrawal.

Similarly, in China, people facing severe stress often complain of *neurasthenia*, a collection of physical symptoms such as chronic headaches, pain in the joints, nausea, lack of energy, and palpitations, as illustrated in the following case study (adapted from Kleinman & Kleinman, 1985, pp. 454–455).

CASE STUDY

Lin Hung is a 24-year-old worker in a machine factory in China who complains of headaches, dizziness, weakness, lack of energy, insomnia, bad dreams, poor memory, and a stiff neck. Pain, weakness, and dizziness, along with bouts of palpitations are his chief symptoms. His symptoms began 6 months ago, and they are gradually worsening. His factory doctors believe he has a heart problem, but repeated electrocardiograms have been normal. He believes he has a serious bodily disorder that is worsened by his work and that interferes with his ability to carry out his job responsibilities. Until his father retired from the job Lin now occupies, he was a soldier living not far from home. He didn't want to leave the army, but his father was anxious to retire so he could move to a new apartment owned by his factory in another city. Fearing that his son would not be able to stay in the army and thereafter would not find work, Lin's father pressured him to take over his job, a job the younger Lin never liked or wanted for himself. Lin Hung reluctantly agreed but now finds he cannot adjust to the work. He did not want to be a machinist and cries when he recounts that this is what he must be for the rest of his life. Moreover, he is despondent and lonely living so far away from his parents. He has no friends at work and feels lonely living in the dormitory. He has a girlfriend, but he cannot see her regularly anymore, owing to the change in work sites. They wish to marry, but his parents, who have a serious financial problem because of a very low pension, cannot provide the expected furniture, room, or any financial help. The leaders of his work unit are against the marriage because he is too young. They also criticize him for his poor work performance and frequent days missed from work owing to sickness.

On questioning Lin Hung, psychiatrists trained in Western medicine diagnosed major depression. Like many Chinese, Lin rejected the psychological diagnosis, believing firmly that he was suffering solely from a physical disorder. A psychological diagnosis would not have garnered any sympathy from Lin's coworkers or family, but a physical diagnosis could provide him with an acceptable reason to leave his job and return to his family.

Indeed, the very concept of depression may be unique to Western cultures (Tsai & Chentsova-Dutton, 2002). Symptoms such as decreases in self-esteem and lack of interest in pleasurable activities are only abnormal in cultures that expect people to have high self-esteem and to seek out positive emotions. These are expectations in Western culture, but not in many other cultures of the world.

SUMMING UP

■ More recent generations appear to be at higher risk for depression than earlier generations, perhaps because of historical changes in values and social structures related to depression.

- People of lower social status tend to have higher rates of depression. Women's greater vulnerability to depression may be tied to their lower social status and the risks of abuse that accompany this social status.

- Less industrialized cultures may have lower rates of depression than more industrialized cultures. Some studies suggest that the manifestation of depression and mania may be different across cultures.

MOOD DISORDERS TREATMENTS

The mood disorders have a tremendous impact on individuals and on society. In the United States alone, between $3 billion and $6 billion per year is spent on the treatment of depression, and over $40 billion per year goes to cover losses in productivity plus the health care costs of people with mood disorders (Rost et al., 1998). By the year 2020, depression is expected to be the fourth leading cause of disability in the world (Murray & Lopez, 1996).

In any given year, about 60 percent of people suffering from bipolar disorder and about half of people suffering from major depression will seek out treatment for their disorder (Regier et al., 1993; Rost et al., 1998). The rest will suffer through their symptoms without any care. People who do seek treatment tend to be more severely impaired by their symptoms than those who do not seek treatment (Angst, 1998). Most often, the people who eventually seek treatment wait a number of years after their symptoms begin to obtain any help (Kessler et al., 1998).

Fortunately, many forms of treatment are now available for mood disorders, particularly depression. Most of these types of treatment have been shown to work for the majority of people. Thus, although there are many pathways into a mood disorder, there now are many pathways by which people can overcome or control mood disorders as well.

Biological Treatments for Mood Disorders

Most of the biological treatments for depression and mania are drug treatments (see the Concept Overview in Table 9.8). Several classes of antidepressant drugs are used to treat depression. In addition to being treated with drugs, some people with depression are treated with electroconvulsive therapy (ECT). Two new treatments for mood disorders, repetitive transcranial magnetic stimulation (rTMS) and vagus nerve stimulation, hold hope for many people. People with seasonal affective disorder (SAD) seem to benefit from a unique type of therapy: exposure to bright lights. Lithium is the treatment of choice for bipolar disorder, but anti-

---

TABLE 9.8 Concept Overview

Biological Treatments for Mood Disorders

Type of Treatment	Description and Mode of Action
Medication: antidepressants (tricyclics, monoamine oxidase inhibitors, selective serotonin reuptake inhibitors), lithium, anticonvulsants, calcium channel blockers, antipsychotics	Alter the levels of neurotransmitters or sensitivity of receptors for them
Electroconvulsive therapy	Apply electrical current to the brain; may increase permeability of the blood-brain barrier, cause release of neurotransmitters, stimulate the hypothalamus, increase sensitivity of receptors
Repetitive transcranial magnetic stimulation	Expose patients to repeated, high-intensity magnetic pulses focused on particular brain structures; may change the functioning of neurotransmitters
Vagus nerve stimulation	Stimulate by a small electronic device much like a cardiac pacemaker, which is surgically implanted under a patient's skin in the left chest wall; may increase activity in the hypothalamus and amygdala
Light therapy	Expose the individual to bright light; may "reset" circadian rhythms

convulsants, antipsychotics, and calcium channel blockers are also used.

Drug Treatments for Depression

Effective drug treatments for depression have been around since the 1960s. The late twentieth century, however, saw a rapid growth in the number of drugs available for depression and in the use of these drugs by large numbers of people.

Tricyclic Antidepressants The **tricyclic antidepressants** help reduce the symptoms of depression apparently by preventing the reuptake of norepinephrine and serotonin in the synapses or by changing the responsiveness of the receptors for these neurotransmitters. These drugs are reasonably effective, leading to the relief of acute symptoms of depression in about 60 percent of people with depression (Gijsman et al., 2004; Nemeroff, 2000). Some of the most commonly prescribed tricyclic antidepressants are imipramine, amitriptylene, and desipramine.

Unfortunately, however, the tricyclic antidepressants have a number of side effects. The most common ones are dry mouth, excessive perspiration, blurring of vision, constipation, urinary retention, and sexual dysfunction. Another problem with the tricyclic antidepressants is that they can take four to eight weeks to show an effect (Fava & Rosenbaum, 1995). This is an excruciatingly long time to wait for relief from depression. Finally, the tricyclics can be fatal in overdose, which is only three to four times the average daily prescription for the drug. For this reason, physicians are wary of prescribing these drugs, particularly for people with depression who might be suicidal.

Monoamine Oxidase Inhibitors A second class of drugs used to treat depression is the **monoamine oxidase inhibitors (MAOIs).** MAO is an enzyme that causes the breakdown of the monoamine neurotransmitters in the synapse (Stahl, 1998). MAO inhibitors decrease the action of MAO and thus bring about increases in the levels of the neurotransmitters in the synapses.

The MAOIs are as effective as the tricyclic antidepressants, but physicians are more cautious in prescribing MAOIs, because their side effects are potentially more dangerous (Gitlin, 2002). When people taking MAOIs ingest food rich in an amino acid called *tyramine,* they can experience a rise in blood pressure that can be fatal. The foods that can interact with MAOIs include aged or ripened cheeses, red wine, beer, and chocolate. The MAOIs can also interact with several drugs, including antihypertension medications and over-the-counter drugs such as antihistamines. Finally, MAOIs can cause liver damage, weight gain, severe lowering of blood pressure, several of the same side effects of the tricyclic antidepressants.

Selective Serotonin Reuptake Inhibitors and Related Drugs A newer class of antidepressant drugs consists of the **selective serotonin reuptake inhibitors,** or **SSRIs.** These drugs are similar in structure to the tricyclic antidepressants, but they work more directly to affect serotonin than do the tricyclics. These drugs have become extremely popular in the treatment of depression. The SSRIs are not more effective in the treatment of depression than the antidepressants we have already discussed—about the same percentage of people respond to an SSRI as respond to a tricyclic or an MAOI (Gitlin, 2002; Montgomery et al., 2004).

These drugs have several advantages over the other antidepressants, however, which have made them extremely popular. First, many people begin experiencing relief from their depression after a couple of weeks of using these drugs, whereas it often takes four weeks or more for the other drugs to show significant effects. Second, the side effects of the SSRIs tend to be less severe than the side effects of the other antidepressants. Third, these drugs do not tend to be fatal in overdose and thus are safer than the other antidepressants (Nemeroff & Schatzberg, 1998). Fourth, the SSRIs appear to be helpful in a wide range of symptoms in addition to depression, or those often associated with depression, such as anxiety symptoms, binge eating, and premenstrual symptoms. The SSRIs may be useful in the treatment of the most chronic and persistent types of depression (Frank, Grochocinski, et al., 2000; Keller et al., 1998).

The SSRIs do have side effects, however (Gitlin, 2002). One of the most common is increased agitation or nervousness. People on SSRIs often report

The selective serotonin reuptake inhibitors have become the widest selling antidepressant drugs.

feeling "jittery" or "hyper" and that they cannot sit still. They may have mild tremors and increased perspiration and feel weak. Some find themselves becoming angry or hostile more often. Nausea and stomach cramps or gas are common side effects, as is a decrease in appetite. Sexual dysfunction and decreased sexual drive are reported by some. Finally, there appears to be an increase in risk for suicide among people on SSRIs.

A number of other drugs that have been introduced for the treatment of depression in the past decade share some similarities with the SSRIs or the older antidepressants but cannot be classified in the same categories. Some of these antidepressants were designed to affect the levels of norepinephrine as well as serotonin and thus are referred to as selective serotonin and norepinephrine reuptake inhibitors (SSNRIs). Some examples are mirtazapine (Remeron), nefazodone (Serzone), venlafaxine (Effexor), and duloxetine (Cymbalata).

Bupropion (which goes by the trade names Wellbutrin and Zyban) affects the norepinephrine and dopamine systems. It may be especially useful in people suffering from psychomotor retardation, anhedonia, hypersomnia, cognitive slowing, inattention, and craving; for example, bupropion can help people stop craving cigarettes. In addition, bupropion appears to overcome the sexual side effects of the SSRIs and thus is sometimes used in conjunction with them. The side effects of bupropion include agitation, insomnia, nausea, and seizures.

Although a large selection of drug therapies is now available for the treatment of depression, there are no consistent rules for determining which of the antidepressant drugs to try first with a person with depression. Many clinicians begin with the selective serotonin reuptake inhibitors because their side effects tend to be less significant. As we discuss in *Taking Psychology Personally: Primary Care Physicians Treating Depression,* most people with depression in treatment are being treated by their primary care physicians. People with depression often must try several drugs before finding one that works well for them and has tolerable side effects. When they find the drug that works for them, it is often as if they have regained their lives (Wurtzel, 1995, p. 329):

> And then something just kind of changed in me. Over the next few days, I became all right, safe in my own skin. It happened just like that. One morning I woke up, and I really did want to live, really looked forward to greeting

VOICES

the day, imagined errands to run, phone calls to return, and it was not with a feeling of great dread, not with the sense that the first person who stepped on my toe as I walked through the square may well have driven me to suicide. It was as if the miasma of depression had lifted off me, gone smoothly about its business, in the same way that the fog in San Francisco rises as the day wears on.

Electroconvulsive Therapy for Depression

Perhaps the most controversial of the biological treatments for depression is **electroconvulsive therapy (ECT).** ECT was introduced in the early twentieth century, originally as a treatment for schizophrenia. Italian physicians Ugo Cerlettii and Lucio Bini decided to experiment with the use of ECT to treat people with schizophrenia, reasoning that ECT could calm them much as experiencing an epileptic seizure would calm and sedate epileptics. Eventually, clinicians found that ECT is not effective for schizophrenia, but it is effective for depression.

ECT consists of a series of treatments in which a brain seizure is induced by passing electrical current through the brain. Patients are first anesthetized and given muscle relaxants, so that they are not conscious when they have the seizure and so that their muscles do not jerk violently during the seizure. Metal electrodes are taped to the head, and a current of 70 to 130 volts is passed through one side of the brain for about one-half of a second. Patients typically go into a convulsion, which lasts about one minute. The full ECT treatment consists of 6 to 12 sessions. ECT is most often given to people with depression who have not responded to drug therapies, and it relieves depression in 50 to 60 percent of these people (Fink, 2001).

Neuroimaging studies show that ECT results in decreases in metabolic activity in several regions of the brain, including the frontal cortex, and the anterior cingulate (Henry et al., 2001; Oquendo et al., 2001) It is not entirely clear, however, how ECT lifts depression.

ECT is controversial for several reasons. First, there were reports in the past of ECT being used as a punishment for patients who were unruly, as was depicted in the movie *One Flew over the Cuckoo's Nest.* Second, ECT can lead to memory loss and difficulties in learning new information. When ECT was first developed, it was administered to both sides of the brain, and the effects on memory and learning were sometimes severe and permanent.

Taking Psychology Personally

Primary Care Physicians Treating Depression

In most of the research on the efficacy of treatments for depression that we've discussed in this chapter, the treatment was administered by a trained clinical psychologist or psychiatrist. The majority of people treated for depression, however, never see a psychologist or psychiatrist (Rost et al., 1998). Instead, most consult their primary care physician (e.g., their "family doctor," internist, or gynecologist).

Actually, patients rarely state that they are depressed. They are more likely to report physical symptoms, such as fatigue, loss of appetite, problems sleeping, or general aches and pains. This is one reason that depression is never detected by primary care physicians in 40 to 50 percent of patients who would qualify for a diagnosis of major depression (Katon et al., 2001). Other reasons include the rushed nature of interactions between physicians and patients in today's world of managed care and the competing demands for that time—if the patient has other, more pressing or obvious medical problems, the physician is likely to attend to those instead of to complaints of malaise (Rost et al., 2000). Many physicians also report that they feel uncomfortable asking patients about depressive symptoms or other mental-health problems, and they worry about offending a patient with such questions.

When a physician does detect depression in a patient, about three-quarters of the time he or she prescribes an antidepressant medication (Williams et al., 1999). At best, only about one-third of patients are given a referral to a mental-health specialist. This may be because many patients do not have insurance benefits that cover mental-health care, and many patients refuse to see a mental-health specialist because of stigmas.

Unfortunately, the care that many primary care physicians provide for patients with depression is inadequate (Simon et al., 2001). The dosages of antidepressants prescribed often are less than what research suggests is necessary for an effective response. Side effects are not monitored systematically. Over 20 percent of patients never fill their prescriptions for antidepressant medications, and as many as 50 percent stop taking the medication without consulting their doctor (Greden, 2001).

Fortunately, studies in primary care settings have shown that the quality of care given to patients with depression can be increased significantly by collaborative care programs, in which primary care physicians work with psychiatrists and psychologists (Katon et al., 2001; Simon et al., 2001). In these programs, the primary care physician continues to be responsible for the care of the patient, but the patient is given educational materials about depression, referrals to psychotherapy or community social services if necessary, and a relatively small number of visits (two to four) with a psychiatrist specializing in depression care. Patients receiving this collaborative care are more likely to take prescribed antidepressant medications, show greater reductions in depression in the short term, and are less likely to relapse over the long term.

If you or someone you know seeks care from a primary care physician for depression, what can you do to ensure that you receive adequate care? First, be honest with your doctor. Talk about your symptoms, even if it makes you uncomfortable. In particular, if you have been having suicidal thoughts, tell your doctor explicitly. If your doctor seems to ignore your reports of depressive symptoms, find another doctor.

Second, ask for a referral to a mental-health specialist if your health insurance covers this. If you don't have insurance for mental-health care, ask your doctor for recommendations for community services that are low-cost or free.

Third, if your doctor prescribes antidepressant medications for you, make sure he or she knows about any medications you are taking, including herbal remedies, such as St. John's wort, to prevent possible interactions between medications. (See Chapter 5 for a discussion of the dangers of mixing herbal remedies with prescription medications.)

Fourth, if you have no intention of taking the antidepressants prescribed for you, tell your doctor—don't just accept the prescription, then ignore it. Ask your doctor about alternative treatments.

Finally, if you begin taking an antidepressant and it doesn't give you serious side effects, continue taking it for a few weeks before you judge whether it's effective. Many antidepressants take awhile to begin to work. If after a few weeks you still are not experiencing any benefits from the antidepressant, or if your symptoms of depression get worse, tell your doctor, so that he or she can change or adjust the prescription or suggest an alternative treatment.

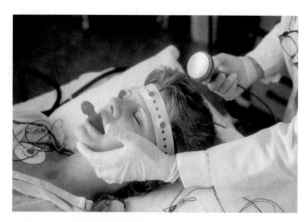

Electroconvulsive therapy is a controversial but effective treatment for depression.

These days, ECT is usually delivered to only one side of the brain, usually the right side, because it is less involved in learning and memory. As a result, patients undergoing modern ECT do not tend to experience significant or long-term memory or learning difficulties (Glass, 2001). Because this unilateral administration is sometimes not as effective as bilateral administration, some people are still given bilateral ECT. Third, although ECT can be extremely effective in eliminating the symptoms of depression, the relapse rate among people who have undergone ECT is as high as 85 percent (Fink, 2001). Fourth, perhaps the strongest reason ECT is controversial is that the idea of having electrical current passed through a person's brain is very frightening and seems like a primitive form of treatment.

Still, ECT is sometimes the only form of treatment that works for people with severe depression. One survey found that about 10 percent of people admitted to the psychiatric wards of general hospitals in the United States with diagnoses of recurrent major depression received ECT (Olfson et al., 1998). The people most likely to receive ECT were older, White, privately insured, and more affluent. It may be that people of color and poor people do not have access to ECT in the hospitals in their neighborhoods. In addition, ECT is used more frequently in eastern and midwestern states than in western states. This may be because ECT is regulated more closely, and frowned upon more, in western states, such as California. Those people who did receive ECT early in their hospital stays had shorter stays than those who did not, suggesting they recovered more quickly from their depression.

Repetitive Transcranial Magnetic Stimulation

In recent years, researchers have been investigating new methods for stimulating the brain without the application of electric current (Sackheim &

Lisanby, 2001). Scientists are using powerful magnets, such as those used in magnetic resonance imaging, to stimulate targeted areas of the brain. The procedure known as **repetitive transcranial magnetic stimulation (rTMS)** exposes patients to repeated, high-intensity magnetic pulses focused on particular brain structures, such as the left prefrontal cortex, which tends to show abnormally low metabolic activity in some people with depression. Studies have suggested that patients with depression given rTMS daily for at least a week tend to experience relief from their symptoms (Chae et al., 2001; George et al., 2003).

How does rTMS work? The electrical stimulation of neurons can result in long-term changes in neurotransmission across synapses (George et al., 2003). Neurotransmission can be enhanced or blunted, depending on the frequency of the stimulation. By stimulating the left prefrontal cortex of people with depression at particular frequencies, researchers have been able to increase neuronal activity, which in turn has had an antidepressant effect. Patients who receive rTMS report few side effects, usually only minor headaches treatable by aspirin. Patients can remain awake, rather than having to be anesthetized, as in electroconvulsive therapy (ECT), thereby avoiding the possible complications of anesthesia. There is a great deal of hope that rTMS will be an effective and safe alternative therapy, particularly for people who do not respond to drug therapies and cannot tolerate ECT.

Vagus Nerve Stimulation (not yet available)

Another new method that holds considerable promise in the treatment of serious depression is **vagus nerve stimulation (VNS)** (Marangell, Martinez, & Niazi, 2004). The vagus nerve is part of the autonomic nervous system; it carries information from the head, neck, thorax, and abdomen to several areas of the brain, including the hypothalamus and amygdala, which are involved in depression. In VNS, the vagus nerve is stimulated by a small electronic device much like a cardiac pacemaker, which is surgically implanted under a patient's skin in the left chest wall. Vagus nerve stimulation was originally used to control seizures in epileptic patients, and some investigators noticed that the therapy also improved mood in these patients (George et al., 2000). The mood effects of VNS occurred even in epileptic patients who were still having seizures, so researchers began studying the mood effects of VNS in patients with depression.

In one study of 38 patients with depressions that had not responded to other forms of treatment, 40 percent got substantial relief from their depression with VNS (George et al., 2000). Another 30 percent of the patients got minimal relief through

VNS. Four patients had negative side effects, including agitation, and 3 patients' surgical wounds did not heal promptly. In another study, of 59 depressed patients, 31 percent obtained significant relief from their depression with VNS; among those who had previously responded to antidepressant medications, 40 percent responded to VNS (Sackheim et al., 2001). About half of all the patients reported mild voice alteration or hoarseness as a side effect of VNS.

How does VNS work when it relieves depression? That is unknown currently, but positron-emission studies show that VNS increases activity in the hypothalamus and amygdala, which may have antidepressant effects (George et al., 2000). Additional research is currently being done on VNS in hopes that it will provide a relatively safe alternative treatment for some people with depression.

Light Therapy To treat SAD

Recall that seasonal affective disorder (SAD) is a form of mood disorder in which people become depressed during the winter months, when there are the fewest hours of daylight. Their moods then brighten in the summer months, when there is more daylight each day. It turns out that many people with SAD who are exposed to bright lights for a few hours each day during the winter months experience complete relief from their depression within a couple of days (Koorengevel et al., 2001; Wileman et al., 2001).

Light therapy may help reduce seasonal affective disorder by resetting *circadian rhythms,* natural cycles of biological activities that occur every 24 hours. The production of several hormones and neurotransmitters varies over the course of the day,

according to circadian rhythms. These rhythms are regulated by internal clocks but can be affected by environmental stimuli, including light. People with depression sometimes show dysregulation of their circadian rhythms. Light therapy may work by resetting circadian rhythms and thereby normalizing the production of hormones and neurotransmitters (Koorengevel et al., 2001).

Another theory is that light therapy works by decreasing levels of the hormone melatonin, secreted by the pineal gland (Wehr et al., 2001). Decreasing melatonin levels can increase levels of norepinephrine and serotonin, thereby reducing the symptoms of depression. Finally, studies suggest that exposure to bright lights may directly increase serotonin levels, thereby decreasing depression (Rosenthal, 1995).

Drug Treatments for Bipolar Disorder

Many fewer drugs are available to treat bipolar disorder than to treat unipolar depression, because this disorder is understood less well than depression and because it is more rare. Fortunately, however, recent years have seen an increase in the number of drugs designed to treat bipolar disorder.

Lithium   Lithium is the most common treatment for bipolar disorder. A number of controlled trials show that lithium is effective in preventing relapses of bipolar disorder (Geddes et al., 2004; Ghaemi, Pardo, & Hsu, 2004).

Lithium seems to stabilize a number of neurotransmitter systems, including serotonin, dopamine, and glutamate (Dixon & Hokin, 1998; Lenox & Manji, 1995). It appears to be more effective in reducing the symptoms of mania than the symptoms of depression. People with bipolar disorder are often prescribed lithium to help curb their mania and an antidepressant drug to curb their depression (Nemeroff, 2000).

Most people with bipolar disorder take lithium even when they have no symptoms of mania or depression, in order to prevent relapses. People maintained on adequate doses of lithium have significantly fewer relapses than those not maintained on lithium (Maj et al., 1998; Tondo, Jamison, & Baldessarini, 1997). Up to 55 percent of patients develop a resistance to lithium within three years, however, and only about one-third remain symptom-free on lithium (Nemeroff, 2000).

Although lithium has been a lifesaver for many people with bipolar disorder, it poses some problems. First, there are enormous differences among people in their rates of lithium absorption, so the proper dosage varies greatly from one person to the next. Second, the difference between an effective dose of lithium and a toxic dose is small, leaving a

Light therapy can be helpful to people with seasonal affective disorder.

very narrow window of therapeutic effectiveness. People who take lithium must be monitored carefully by physicians, who can determine whether the dosage of lithium is adequate to relieve the symptoms of bipolar disorder but not too large to induce toxic side effects. The side effects of lithium range from annoying to life-threatening. Many patients experience abdominal pain, nausea, vomiting, diarrhea, tremors, and twitches (Jamison, 1995, p. 93):

VOICES

I found myself beholden to a medication that also caused severe nausea and vomiting many times a month—I often slept on my bathroom floor with a pillow under my head and my warm, woolen St. Andrews gown tucked over me. I have been violently ill more places than I choose to remember, and quite embarrassingly so in public places.

People on lithium complain of blurred vision and problems in concentration and attention that interfere with their ability to work. Lithium can cause diabetes, hypothyroidism, and kidney dysfunction. It can also contribute to birth defects if taken during the first trimester of a woman's pregnancy.

It is not surprising that many people with bipolar disorder will not take lithium or will go on and off of it, against their physicians' advice. In addition to experiencing side effects, many patients complain that they miss the positive symptoms of their mania—the elated moods, flowing ideas, and heightened self-esteem—and feel washed-out on lithium. Especially during periods of calm, they feel they can manage their illness without lithium and that they can detect when a new episode is coming and go back on the medication then. Usually, however, as a new episode of mania becomes more and more severe, their judgment becomes more impaired, and they do not go back on the lithium.

Anticonvulsants, Antipsychotics, and Calcium Channel Blockers Sometimes, lithium does not overcome mania and, even if it is effective, some people cannot tolerate its side effects. Three other classes of drugs, **anticonvulsants, antipsychotic drugs,** and **calcium channel blockers,** are alternatives to lithium for the treatment of mania.

The most commonly prescribed anticonvulsants are carbamazepine (trade name Tegretol), valproic acid (trade names Depakene and Valproate), and divalproex sodium (trade name Depakote). These drugs can be effective in reducing the symptoms of severe and acute mania, although it is not clear if they are as effective as lithium in

the long-term treatment of bipolar disorder. For this reason, lithium is still usually used first, before trying the anticonvulsants (Ghaemi et al., 2004; Grunze & Walden, 2002). The side effects of carbamazepine include blurred vision, fatigue, vertigo, dizziness, rash, nausea, drowsiness, and liver disease (Nemeroff, 2000). Valproic acid and divalproex sodium seem to induce many fewer side effects and are now used more often than carbamazepine (Frances et al., 1998). But the anticonvulsants can cause birth defects if women take them while pregnant. The anticonvulsants have effects on a multitude of neurotransmitters, but the way in which the anticonvulsants reduce mania is not yet clear (Nemeroff, 2000).

The antipsychotic drugs, which are described in more detail in Chapter 11, are also used to quell the symptoms of severe mania (Nemeroff, 2000). These drugs reduce functional levels of dopamine and seem especially useful in the treatment of psychotic manic symptoms. They have many neurological side effects, however, the most severe of which is an irreversible condition known as *tardive dyskinesia*. People with tardive dyskinesia have uncontrollable tics and movements of their face and limbs. Newer drugs, such as clozapine, olanzapine, and risperidone, do not induce these neurological side effects and are being investigated for use in bipolar disorder (Post, Frye, et al., 2000).

Most recently, drugs known as calcium channel blockers, such as verapamil and nimodipine, have been shown to be effective in treating mania in some, but not all, studies (Keck et al., 2000). The calcium channel blockers are safe for women to take during pregnancy. They seem to induce fewer side effects than lithium and perhaps the anticonvulsants, but they can create dizziness, headache, nausea, and changes in heart rate. It is not currently known how these drugs work to lower mania.

Psychological Treatments for Depression

Each of the psychological theories of depression has led to a treatment designed to overcome the factors that the theory asserts causes depression. Behavior therapy focuses on changing the depressed person's schedule of reinforcements and punishments. Cognitive-behavioral therapy focuses on changing both negative cognitions and maladaptive behaviors. Interpersonal therapy works on dysfunctional relationship patterns, and psychodynamic therapy focus on uncovering the unconscious hostility toward others that is the source of the person's self-punishment (see the Concept Overview in Table 9.9).

TABLE 9.9 Concept Overview

Psychological Treatments for Depression

Each of the psychological treatments for depression aims to reverse the processes contributing to depression.

Type of Treatment	Proposed Mechanism of Action
Behavior therapies	Increase positive reinforcers and decrease aversive events by teaching the person new skills for managing interpersonal situations and the environment and engaging in pleasant activities
Cognitive-behavioral therapy	Challenges distorted thinking and helps the person learn more adaptive ways of thinking and new behavioral skills
Interpersonal therapy	Helps the person change dysfunctional relationship patterns
Psychodynamic therapies	Help the person gain insight into unconscious hostility and fears of abandonment to facilitate change in self-concept and behaviors

Behavior Therapies

Behavior therapies for depression focus on increasing the number of positive reinforcers and decreasing the number of aversive experiences in an individual's life by helping the depressed person change his or her ways of interacting with the environment and other people (Hollon, Haman, & Brown, 2002). Behavior therapies are designed to be short-term, about 12 weeks long.

The first phase of behavior therapies requires a *functional analysis* of the connections between specific circumstances and the depressed person's symptoms. When does the depressed person feel the worst? Are there any situations in which he or she feels better? The therapist may visit the depressed client's home to observe his or her interactions with family members. The client may fill out questionnaires to assess what events he or she finds pleasant or unpleasant. This analysis helps the therapist pinpoint the behaviors and interaction patterns that need to be the focus of therapy. It also helps the client understand the intimate connections between his or her symptoms and daily activities or interactions. This understanding challenges the client's belief that he or she is the helpless victim of uncontrollable forces and sets the stage for the therapist's suggestions for changes in behavior.

Once the therapist and client identify the circumstances that precipitate the client's depressive symptoms, a variety of strategies can be used to make the necessary changes in the client's life. These generally fall into three categories (Thorpe & Olson, 1997):

1. *Change the aspects of the environment that are related to the depressive symptoms.* The depressed person may be encouraged to engage in specific rewarding activities and to avoid depressing activities. For example, a depressed man who typically spends all evening in front of the television, being bored and depressed, might be encouraged to take a half-hour walk around his neighborhood every evening and to limit his television watching to one hour.

2. *Teach the depressed person skills to change his or her negative circumstances, particularly negative social interactions.* For example, a depressed woman who feels her relationship with her child is out of control might be taught parenting skills, so that she is able to interact more effectively and pleasantly with her child.

3. *Teach the client mood-management skills that can be used in unpleasant situations.* It is inevitable that people with depression will find themselves in unpleasant situations some of the time. The therapist may teach the person to use strategies, such as relaxation techniques (see Chapter 7), to reduce negative symptoms even while an unpleasant event is happening. These strategies must be woven together to meet the specific needs of an individual client. For example, consider the following case (adapted from Yapko, 1997).

Mark worked constantly. When he was not actually at work, he was working at home. He had a position of considerable responsibility and was convinced that, if he didn't stay focused on his job, he'd miss something that

(continued)

would result in his being fired or kicked off the career ladder. Mark had not taken a vacation in several years. Although he wanted to continue to get pay raises and promotions, as he has each year, he was also painfully aware that life was passing him by. He felt stressed, depressed, and hopeless about ever having a "normal" life.

Mark clearly felt rewarded for his one-dimensional life with praise, pay raises, promotions, and the absence of mistakes for which he might get punished. Mark's behavior was governed by his work focus. He engaged in no social activities, lived alone, and did not organize his time to include anything but his work. The behavior therapist suggested that, if he wanted to improve his quality of life, and his outlook on life, he must learn some very specific new behaviors. Mark was encouraged to organize his schedule so that he'd have time for social and recreational opportunities. He learned he needed to actively and deliberately do things that are fun and pleasurable. The therapist practiced with him new ways to meet people and form social relationships (friendships, dating). The therapist also taught him relaxation skills to reduce his stress. Eventually, Mark felt a new sense of control over his life and his depression lifted.

CBT way forward.

*Cognitive-Behavioral Therapy

Cognitive-behavioral therapy represents a blending of cognitive and behavioral theories of depression (Beck et al., 1974; Ellis & Harper, 1961; Lewinsohn et al., 1986; Rehm, 1977). There are two general goals in this therapy. First, it aims to change the negative, hopeless patterns of thinking described by the cognitive models of depression. Second, it aims to help people with depression solve concrete problems in their lives and develop skills for being more effective in their worlds, so that they no longer have the deficits in reinforcers described by behavioral theories of depression.

Like behavior therapy, cognitive-behavioral therapy is designed to be brief. The therapist and client usually agree on a set of goals they wish to accomplish in 6 to 12 weeks. These goals focus on specific problems that clients believe are connected to their depression, such as problems in their marriage or dissatisfaction with their job. From the very beginning of therapy, the therapist urges clients to take charge of the therapy as much as possible, setting goals and making decisions themselves, rather than relying on the therapist to give them all the answers.

Cognitive Techniques The first step in cognitive-behavioral therapy is to help clients discover the negative, automatic thoughts they habitually have and to understand the link between those thoughts and their depression. Often, the therapist will assign clients the homework of keeping track of times when they feel sad or depressed and writing down on sheets, such as the one in Figure 9.8, what is going through their minds at such times. Clients often report that they did not realize the types of thoughts that went through their heads when certain types of events happened. For example, the client whose automatic thought record is shown in Figure 9.8 did not realize that she had catastrophic thoughts about losing her job every time her boss was a little cross with her.

The second step in cognitive-behavioral therapy is to help clients challenge their negative thoughts. People with depression often believe that there is only one way to interpret a situation—their negative way. Therapists will use a series of questions to help clients consider alternative ways of thinking about a situation and the pros and cons of these alternatives, such as "What is the evidence that you are right in the way you are interpreting this situation?" "Are there other ways of looking at this situation?" and "What can you do if the worst-case scenario comes true?" Of course, these questions don't always move the client toward more positive ways of thinking about the situation. It is important for the therapist to be flexible in pursuing a line of questions or comments, dropping approaches that are not helpful and trying new approaches to which the client might respond better.

The third step in cognitive-behavioral therapy is to help clients recognize the deeper, basic beliefs or assumptions they hold that are feeding their depression. These basic beliefs might be ones such as "If I'm not loved by everyone, I'm a failure" or "If I'm not a complete success at everything, my life is worthless." The therapist will help clients question these beliefs and decide if they truly want to live their lives according to these beliefs. The case of Susan illustrates some of the cognitive components of cognitive-behavioral therapy (adapted from Thorpe & Olson, 1997, pp. 225–227):

| | FIGURE 9.8 | **An Automatic Thoughts Record Used in Cognitive-Behavioral Therapy.** In cognitive-behavioral therapy, patients keep records of the negative thoughts that arise when they feel negative emotions. These records are then used in therapy to challenge the patients' depressive thinking. |

Date	Event	Emotion	Automatic thoughts
April 4	Boss seemed annoyed.	Sad, anxious, worried	Oh, what have I done now? If I keep making him mad, I'm going to get fired.
April 5	Husband didn't want to make love.	Sad	I'm so fat and ugly.
April 7	Boss yelled at another employee.	Anxious	I'm next.
April 9	Husband said he's taking a long business trip next month.	Sad, defeated	He's probably got a mistress somewhere. My marriage is falling apart.
April 10	Neighbor brought over some cookies.	A little happy, mostly sad	She probably thinks I can't cook. I look like such a mess all the time. And my house was a disaster when she came in!

CASE STUDY

Susan was seen for 14 sessions of psychotherapy. She was a young, single, 24-year-old woman. Her goals for therapy were to learn how to overcome chronic feelings of depression and to learn how to deal with temptations to overeat. Susan was unemployed and living with her aunt and uncle in a rural area. She had no means of personal transportation. Hypersensitivity to the reactions of significant others and the belief that they could control her feelings seemed to be central to her low self-concept and feelings of helplessness. Susan described her mother as knowing which "buttons to push." This metaphor was examined and challenged. She was questioned as to how her mother controlled her emotions: Where were these buttons? Did they have a physical reality? Once again, the principle was asserted that it is not the actions of others

that cause emotions, but one's cognitions about them.

Then the cognitions she had concerning certain looks or critical statements were examined. When her aunt was looking "sickly and silent," Susan believed that it was because she was displeased with her for not helping enough. The evidence for this belief was examined, and there was none. Alternative explanations were explored, such as the aunt might be truly ill, having a bad day, or upset with her spouse. Susan admitted that all explanations were equally plausible. Furthermore, it was noted that, in ambiguous social situations, she tended to draw the most negative and personalized conclusions.

Her consistent tendency to evaluate her self-worth in terms of her family's approval

(continued)

was examined. Susan still had fantasies of her family becoming like the "Walton" family (e.g., a "normal" family that was loving and accepting of one another; instead, her own family was distant and argumentative with one another). Susan began to let go of this fantasy and grieved over this loss. Once this had been done, she began to gain a better understanding of how her current cognitive distortions could be related to overconcern with familial approval. As she began to let go of her desire to live up to imagined expectations, she stopped seeing herself as a failure.

During the last stage of therapy, Susan's mother visited. This provided a real test of the gains she had made, as it was her mother's criticism that Susan feared the most. At first, she reported feeling easily wounded by her mother's criticism. These examples were used as opportunities to identify and challenge self-defeating thoughts. Soon, Susan was able to see her mother's critical statements as her mother's problem, not her own. She also discovered that, as she became better at ignoring her mother's critical remarks and not taking them to heart, her mother began to be more relaxed and open around her and criticized her less.

Behavioral Techniques Cognitive-behavioral therapists also use behavioral techniques to train clients in new skills they might need to cope better in their life. Often, people with depression are unassertive in making requests of other people or in standing up for their rights and needs. This unassertiveness can be the result of their negative automatic thoughts. For example, a person who often thinks, "I can't ask for what I need, because the other person might get mad and that would be horrible," is not likely to make even reasonable requests of other people. The therapist will first help clients recognize the thoughts behind their actions (or lack of action). Then, the therapist may work with clients to devise exercises or homework assignments in which they practice new skills, such as assertiveness, between therapy sessions.

The Effectiveness of Cognitive-Behavioral Therapy Cognitive-behavioral therapy has proven quite effective in treating depression, including major depression. About 60 to 70 percent of people with depression experience full relief from their symp-

toms with 12 weeks of cognitive therapy (Hollon et al., 2002; Lewinsohn & Clarke, 1999). Cognitive-behavioral therapy has been successfully adapted for the treatment of depressed children, adolescents, and older persons (Futterman et al., 1995; Garber & Horowitz, 2002; Lewinsohn & Clarke, 1999; Treatment for Adolescents with Depression Study [TADS] Team, 2004).

Interpersonal Therapy

In **interpersonal therapy (IPT),** therapists look for four types of problems in depressed patients (see the Concept Overview in Table 9.10). First, many depressed patients truly are grieving the loss of loved ones, perhaps not from death but from the breakup of important relationships. Interpersonal therapists help clients face such losses and explore their feelings about the losses. Often, clients idealize the people they have lost, feeling as if they will never have relationships as good. Therapists help clients reconstruct their relationships with the lost loved ones, recognizing both the good and bad aspects of the relationships and developing more balanced views of the relationships. Therapists also help clients let go of the past relationships and begin to invest in new relationships.

The second type of problem interpersonal therapy focuses on is interpersonal role disputes. Such disputes arise when people do not agree on their roles in a relationship. For example, a husband and wife may disagree on the proper roles each should play in relation to their children. Or a college student and a parent may disagree on the extent to which the student should follow the parent's wishes in choosing a career. Interpersonal therapists first help the clients recognize the disputes and then guide clients in making choices about concessions they are or are not willing to make to the other people in the relationships.

Therapists may also need to help clients modify and improve their patterns of communicating with others in relationships. For example, a student who resents his parents' intrusions into his private life may tend to withdraw and sulk rather than directly confront his parents about their intrusions. He would be helped in developing more effective ways of communicating his distress over his parents' intrusions.

The third type of problem addressed in interpersonal therapy is role transitions, such as the transition from college to work or from work to full-time motherhood. Sometimes, people become depressed out of grief over the roles they must leave behind. Therapists help clients develop more realistic perspectives toward roles that are lost and help clients regard new roles in a more positive manner. If clients feel unsure about their capabili-

TABLE 9.10	Concept Overview

Interpersonal Therapy

Interpersonal therapists focus on four types of interpersonal problems as sources of depression.

Type of Problem	Therapeutic Approach
Grief, loss	Help the client accept feelings and evaluate a relationship with a lost person; help the client invest in new relationships
Interpersonal role disputes	Help the client make decisions about concessions willing to be made and learn better ways of communicating
Role transitions	Help the client develop more realistic perspectives toward roles that are lost and regard new roles in a more positive manner
Interpersonal skills deficits	Review the client's past relationships, helping the client understand these relationships and how they might be affecting current relationships; directly teach the client social skills, such as assertiveness

ties in new roles, therapists help them develop a sense of mastery in the new roles. Sometimes, clients need help in developing new networks of social support within their new roles, to replace the support systems they left behind in old roles.

The fourth type of problem people with depression take to interpersonal therapy involves deficits in interpersonal skills. Such skill deficits can be the reason that people with depression have inadequate social support networks. Therapists review with clients past relationships, especially important childhood relationships, helping clients understand these relationships and how they might be affecting current relationships. Therapists might also directly teach clients social skills, such as assertiveness.

Interpersonal therapy has been shown to be highly effective in the treatment of depression, with 60 to 80 percent of people with depression recovering during this form of therapy (Weissman & Markowitz, 2002). Like cognitive-behavioral therapy, interpersonal therapy has been successfully adapted for the treatment of children and older adults with depression. It can be used both in individual therapy and in group therapy settings.

An interesting application of interpersonal therapy in a group setting occurred in a study conducted in rural Uganda (Bolton et al., 2003). The people of Uganda have suffered terrible trauma over the decades, and the rate of depression in this country is high. A group of researchers conducted a randomized clinical trial to test the effectiveness of group interpersonal psychotherapy in treating villagers in rural Uganda who were depressed. Their intervention resulted in significant decreases in depression in the villagers who received it, compared with villagers in the control group.

Interpersonal therapy for depression focuses on problems in interpersonal relationships that lead to depression.

Psychodynamic Therapies

In **psychodynamic therapies,** the therapist will closely observe a depressed client's behavior to analyze the sources of his or her depression, just as a behavior or cognitive therapist will. The types of behavior the psychodynamic therapist examines, and the therapist's assumptions about the potential causes of that behavior, are very different from those that concern the behavior or cognitive therapist.

The psychodynamic therapist will closely observe the client's *transference* to the therapist—the ways in which the client treats the therapist as though the therapist were someone else, such as a parent—with the assumption that the client's transference represents unconscious conflicts and concerns with important people in his or her life. The therapist will also observe the client's recollections of both recent events and distant events, searching for themes of abandonment, hostility, and disappointment. The therapist may listen to the client's recounting of dreams for further clues as to the unconscious concerns behind the depression. The therapist will acknowledge and interpret the themes he or she observes in the client's behaviors and recollections, to help the client gain insight, accept these unconscious concerns, and move beyond them.

Although it may seem necessary to have insight to fully gain control over one's depression, long-term psychodynamic therapies have not proven very effective in the treatment of depression (Robinson, Berman, & Neimeyer, 1990). The nature of depression may make it particularly unsuitable for long-term psychodynamic therapies. Many people with depression are too overcome by symptoms of lethargy, poor attention and concentration, and a sense of hopelessness to participate in these therapies. They may not have the energy or motivation to engage in the long process of uncovering and exploring old psychological wounds. They may be so acutely depressed that they need more immediate relief, particularly if they are suicidal.

Comparisons of Cognitive-Behavioral, Interpersonal, and Drug Therapies

Which of the many treatments for mood disorders is the best? In the past few decades, several studies have compared cognitive-behavioral therapy, interpersonal therapy, and drug therapies with each other. Perhaps surprisingly, these three therapies, despite their vast differences, appear equally effective for the treatment of most people with depression (see DeRubeis et al., 1999; Hollon et al., 2002; Weissman & Markowitz, 2002). A growing number of studies suggest that the combination of psychotherapy and drug therapy is more effective in treating people with chronic depression than is either type of therapy alone (e.g., Hollon et al., 1992; Frank, Grochocinski, 2000; Thase et al., 1997; TADS Team, 2004).

For example, in one study, 681 patients with chronic major depression were randomly assigned to receive nefazodone (trade name Serzone), cognitive-behavioral therapy, or both for 12 weeks (Keller et al., 2000). About half of the people receiving nefazodone or cognitive-behavioral therapy alone experienced relief from their depression (see Figure 9.9). Eighty-five percent of the patients receiving both nefazodone and cognitive-behavioral therapy experienced relief from their depression.

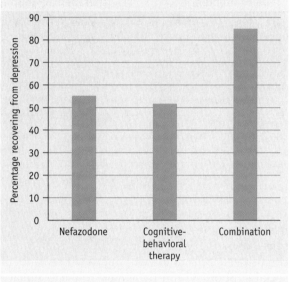

FIGURE 9.9   **Comparison of Drug Therapy and Psychotherapy.** In one study, people with chronic major depression responded equally well to a drug therapy (nefazodone) and cognitive-behavioral therapy but responded best to the combination of the two therapies.

Source: Keller et al., 2000.

The relapse rates in depression are quite high, even among people whose depression completely disappears in treatment. For this reason, many psychiatrists and psychologists argue that people with a history of recurrent depression should be kept on a maintenance dose of therapy even after their depression has been relieved (Hirschfeld, 1994). Usually, the maintenance therapy is a drug therapy, and many people remain on antidepressant drugs for years after their initial episodes of depression have passed. Studies of interpersonal therapy and cognitive-behavioral therapy show that maintenance doses of these therapies, usually consisting of once-a-month meetings with therapists, can also reduce relapse just as well as drugs (Hollon et al., 2002; Jarrett et al., 1998; Weissman & Markowitz, 2002).

Studies suggest that similar changes in the brain occur whether people with depression undergo psychotherapy or drug therapy. For example, Brody and colleagues (2001) put people with major depression through a PET scan to assess their brain functioning. Compared with control participants, the depressed participants showed abnormal activity in the prefrontal cortex and the temporal lobe. The depressed participants were then given either interpersonal therapy or a selective serotonin reuptake inhibitor for 12 weeks, and their brain functioning was reevaluated at the end of the therapies. The interpersonal therapy group and drug therapy group both showed normalization of their brain functioning over the course of therapy, to similar levels.

In bipolar disorder, combining drug treatment with the psychological therapies may reduce the rate at which patients stop taking their medications and may lead more patients to achieve full remission of their symptoms, compared with lithium treatment alone (Miklowitz et al., 2000; Swarz & Frank, 2001). Psychotherapy can help people with bipolar disorder understand and accept their need for lithium treatment. It also can help them cope with the impact of the disorder on their lives (Jamison, 1995, pp. 88–89):

VOICES

At this point in my existence, I cannot imagine leading a normal life without both taking lithium and having had the benefits of psychotherapy. Lithium prevents my seductive but disastrous highs, diminishes my depressions, clears out the wool and webbing from my disordered thinking, slows me down, gentles me out, keeps me from ruining my career and relationships, keeps me out of a hospital, alive, and makes psychotherapy possible. But, ineffably, psychotherapy *heals*. It makes some sense of the confusion, reins in the terrifying thoughts and feelings, returns some control and hope and possibility of learning from it all. Pills cannot, do not, ease one back into reality; they only bring one back headlong, careening, and faster than can be endured at times. Psychotherapy is a sanctuary; it is a battleground; it is a place I have been psychotic, neurotic, elated, confused, and despairing beyond belief. But, always, it is where I have believed—or have learned to believe—that I might someday be able to contend with all of this.

Depression Prevention

Given the devastating effects depression can have on people's lives, an important goal for the future is to prevent depression in vulnerable people before it ever begins. Several studies using cognitive-behavioral and interpersonal therapy techniques have shown that community-based interventions can prevent first onsets of depression in people at high risk (Munoz et al., 2002). For example, cognitive-behavioral techniques can be used to prevent depression in low-income, minority people who are faced with chronic and overwhelming stressors (Munoz, 1997; Munoz et al., 1995).

Evidence that depression first arises in adolescence has led several researchers to focus on preventing depression in high-risk adolescents. In one study, adolescents at high risk to develop major depression because they already had mild to moderate symptoms of depression were randomly assigned to a cognitive-behavioral intervention or to a no-intervention control group. The students receiving the cognitive-behavioral intervention met for 15 sessions in small groups after school. They received therapy designed to help them overcome negative ways of thinking and to learn more effective coping strategies. Following the therapy, both the intervention group and the no-treatment control group were followed for up to 18 months. The children in the prevention group got some immediate benefit from this intervention; their levels of depressive symptoms declined over the course of the 15 sessions. The remarkable finding of this study was that the intervention seemed to reduce the risk for future depression in these children (Clarke et al., 1995) (see Figure 9.10). Over the year after the intervention ended, a relatively low percentage of the children who received it developed

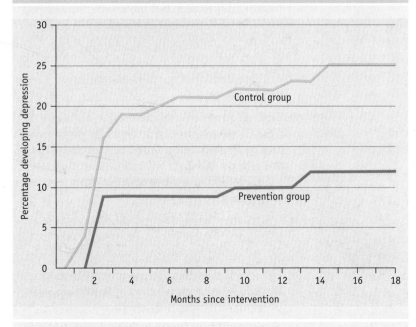

FIGURE 9.10   **Effects of a Preventive Intervention.** In one study, adolescents undergoing 15 sessions of cognitive-behavioral therapy were less likely to develop major depression over the next 18 months than a control group who received no therapy.

Source: Clarke et al., 1995.

Studies have shown that group therapy for teenagers can prevent or reduce depression.

depression. In contrast, many of the children in the control group developed depression (for similar results, see Gillham et al., 1995; Jaycox et al., 1994). This study gives us hope that many vulnerable children can be spared from the debilitating effects of depressive episodes.

SUMMING UP

- Tricyclic antidepressants are effective in treating depression but have some side effects and can be dangerous in overdose.

- The monoamine oxidase inhibitors (MAOIs) also are effective treatments for depression but can interact with certain medications and foods.

- The selective serotonin reuptake inhibitors (SSRIs) are effective treatments for depression and have become popular because they are less dangerous and their side effects are more tolerable than are those of other drug treatments.

- Electroconvulsive therapy (ECT) involves inducing seizures in people with depression. It can be quite effective but is controversial.

- Lithium is useful in the treatment of mood disorders but requires careful monitoring to prevent dangerous side effects.

- Anticonvulsants, antipsychotics, and calcium channel blockers can help relieve mania.

- Behavioral treatment focuses on increasing positive reinforcers and decreasing aversive events by helping clients change their environments, learn social skills, and learn mood-management skills.

- Cognitive-behavioral treatment combines the techniques of behavior therapies with techniques to identify and challenge depressive thinking patterns.

- Psychodynamic therapies focus on uncovering unconscious hostility and fears of abandonment through the interpretation of transference, memories, and dreams.

- Interpersonal therapy seeks to identify and overcome problems with grief, role transitions, interpersonal role disputes, and deficits in interpersonal skills that contribute to depression.

- Cognitive-behavioral therapy, interpersonal therapy, and drug treatments seem to work equally well with most people with depression, and the combination of drug therapy and one of the psychotherapies may be the most effective.

- Some research suggests that interventions targeting high-risk groups can help prevent or delay first onsets of depression.

CHAPTER INTEGRATION

The mood disorders affect the whole person. Depression and mania involve changes in every aspect of functioning, including biology, cognitions, personality, social skills, and relationships. Some of these changes may be causes of the depression or mania, and some of them may be consequences of the depression or mania.

The fact that the mood disorders are phenomena of the whole person illustrates the intricate connections among the various aspects of functioning: biology, cognitions, personality, and social interactions. These areas of functioning are so intertwined that major changes in any one area will almost necessarily provoke changes in other areas. Many recent models of the mood disorders, particularly depression, suggest that most people who become depressed carry a vulnerability to depression for much of their lives. This may be a biological vulnerability, such as dysfunctions in neurotransmitter systems, or a psychological vulnerability, such as overdependence on others. It is not until these vulnerabilities interact with certain stressors that a full-blown depression is triggered, however.

Kendler and colleagues (Kendler, 1998; Kendler & Karkowski-Shuman, 1997) have suggested that, in major depression, genetic factors may influence vulnerability to depression by altering the individual's relationship to the environment, in addition to inducing biological abnormalities that directly cause depression (see Figure 9.11). First, genetic factors may increase the individual's biological sensitivity to stressors in the environment, by altering the neurotransmitter and neuroendocrine systems involved in the stress response. This makes it more likely that these individuals will react to a stressor with depression. In their large study of twins, they found statistical evidence that being at genetic risk for depression made twins more prone to depression in the face of negative life events. In twins with a low genetic risk for depression (e.g., a monozygotic twin whose cotwin had no history of depression), the probability of a depression, given exposure to a severe life event, was 6.2 percent. In twins with a high genetic risk for depression (a monozygotic twin whose cotwin had a history of depression), the probability of depression, given exposure to a severe life event, was 14.6 percent (Kendler & Karkowski-Shuman, 1997).

Second, genetic factors may influence the probability that individuals will select high- versus low-risk environments for the production of depression. People actively help create their environments by choosing which people they spend time with, where they live, the type of occupation they pursue, and so on. In their twin studies, Kendler

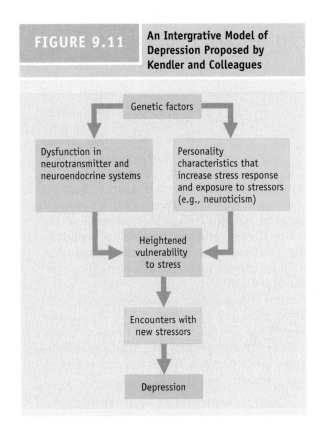

FIGURE 9.11   **An Intergrative Model of Depression Proposed by Kendler and Colleagues**

Genetic factors

Dysfunction in neurotransmitter and neuroendocrine systems

Personality characteristics that increase stress response and exposure to stressors (e.g., neuroticism)

Heightened vulnerability to stress

Encounters with new stressors

Depression

and colleagues (1993) found, not surprisingly, that cotwins often shared the same life events, such as the death of a family member. This seems mostly likely due to environmental factors—specifically, having the same family members. But certain other stressors, including being robbed or assaulted or experiencing a major financial stressor, appeared to be influenced primarily by genetic factors. That is, similarities in the twins' environments could not account for their common risk of experiencing these events. In addition, these events did not seem to be solely the result of both twins' being depressed. Kendler and Karkowski-Shuman (1997) suggest that genetic factors may contribute to broad personality characteristics, such as neuroticism or impulsivity, which then lead to greater risk both for negative life events and for depression.

Fortunately, the interconnections among these areas of functioning may mean that improving functioning in one area can improve functioning in other areas. Improving people's biological functioning can improve their cognitive and social functioning and their personalities. Improving people's cognitive and social functioning can improve their biological functioning, and so on. Thus, although there may be many pathways into mood disorders (biological, psychological, and social), there may also be many pathways out of the mood disorders, particularly depression.

346 **Chapter 9** Mood Disorders

Extraordinary People: Follow-Up

We began this chapter noting the courage of one prominent theorist and researcher of abnormality, Kay Redfield Jamison, in publishing her autobiography describing her experiences with a serious mental disorder. Although many psychiatrists and psychologists have personal histories of mental disorder, they are often reluctant to let it be known, because they fear that it will bias others' attitudes toward their ideas or will affect their professional licenses or their privileges to admit patients to hospitals. They are also concerned, as was Jamison, that their revelation of mental illness would have repercussions for their families.

Why did Jamison feel the need to go public with her illness? Jamison's explanation of her decision to reveal her disorder indicates her personal triumph over fears of others' opinions and her dedication to changing cultural attitudes toward mental disorders (Jamison, 1995, pp. 7–8):

> I have no idea what the long-term effects of discussing such issues so openly will be on my personal and professional life, but whatever the consequences, they are bound to be better than continuing to be silent. I am tired of hiding, tired of misspent and knotted energies, tired of the hypocrisy, and tired of acting as though I have something to hide. One is what one is, and the dishon-

esty of hiding behind a degree, or a title, or any manner and collection of words, is still exactly that: dishonest. Necessary, perhaps, but dishonest. I continue to have concerns about my decision to be public about my illness, but one of the advantages of having had manic-depressive illness for more than thirty years is that very little seems insurmountably difficult. Much like crossing the Bay Bridge when there is a storm over the Chesapeake, one may be terrified to go forward, but there is no question of going back. I find myself somewhat inevitably taking a certain solace in Robert Lowell's essential question, *Yet why not say what happened?*

We can only hope that, as the public understands more about the causes of mental disorders, fewer people with these disorders will have to fear the consequences of letting it be known that they suffer. Kay Redfield Jamison, through her courageous decision to talk about her disorder and her eloquent and thoughtful writing and speaking on mental disorders, has moved us a bit closer to the fulfillment of that hope.

Chapter Summary

- There are two general categories of mood disorder: unipolar depression and bipolar disorder. People with unipolar depression experience only the symptoms of depression (sad mood, loss of interest, disruption in sleep and appetite, motor retardation or agitation, loss of energy, worthlessness and guilt, suicidality). (Review Table 9.1.) People with bipolar disorder experience both depression and mania (elated or agitated mood, grandiosity, little need for sleep, racing thoughts and speech, increase in goals and dangerous behavior). (Review Table 9.3.)

- Within unipolar depression, the two major diagnostic categories are major depression and dysthymic disorder. In addition, there are several subtypes of major depression: with melancholic

features, with psychotic features, with catatonic features, with atypical features, with postpartum onset, and with seasonal pattern. (Review Table 9.2.)

- Depression is one of the most common disorders, but there are substantial age, gender, and cross-cultural differences in depression. Bipolar disorder is much less common than the depressive disorders. It tends to be a lifelong problem. The length of individual episodes of bipolar disorder varies dramatically from one person to the next and over the life course, as in depression. The expression of mania may depend on cultural norms.

- Genetic factors probably play a role in determining vulnerability to the mood disorders, especially bipolar disorder. (Review Table 9.5.) Disordered genes may lead to dysfunction in the monoamine neurotransmitter systems. The neurotransmitters norepinephrine, serotonin, and dopamine have been implicated in the mood disorders. In addition, neuroimaging studies show abnormal structure or activity in several areas of the brain, including the prefrontal cortex, hippocampus, anterior cingulate cortex, and amygdala. There is evidence that people with depression have chronic hyperactivity in the hypothalamic-pituitary-adrenal axis, which may make them more susceptible to stress.

- Behavioral theories of depression suggest that people with much stress in their lives may have too low a rate of reinforcement and too high a rate of punishment, which then leads to depression. (Review Table 9.6.) Stressful events can also lead to learned helplessness—the belief that nothing one does can control one's environment—which is linked to depression. Most people who are faced with stressful events do not become depressed, however.

- The cognitive theories of depression argue that the ways people interpret the events in their lives determine whether they become depressed. (Review Table 9.7.) Some evidence suggests that people with depression are actually quite realistic in their negative views of life and that nondepressed people are unrealistically optimistic about life. People who ruminate in response to distress are more prone to depression.

- Interpersonal theories of depression suggest that poor attachment relationships early in life can lead children to develop expectations that they must be or do certain things in order to win the approval of others, which puts them at risk for depression. (Review Table 9.6.)

- Psychodynamic theories of depression suggest that people with depression have chronic patterns of negative relationships and tend to internalize their hostility against others.

- Social theories attribute depression to the effects of low social status, as well as changes in the social conditions that different generations face. In addition, there appear to be differences across cultures in how depression is manifested.

- Most of the biological therapies for the mood disorders are drug therapies. (Review Table 9.8.) Three classes of drugs are commonly used to treat depression: tricyclic antidepressants, monoamine oxidase inhibitors, and selective serotonin reuptake inhibitors. Each of these is highly effective in treating depression, but each has significant side effects. Electroconvulsive therapy is used to treat severe depressions, particularly those that do not respond to drugs.

- Lithium is the most effective drug for the treatment of bipolar disorder. It has a number of side effects, including nausea, vomiting, diarrhea, tremors, twitches, kidney dysfunction, and birth defects. Alternatives to lithium include anticonvulsant drugs, antipsychotic drugs, and calcium channel blockers.

- Behavior therapies focus on increasing positive reinforcers and decreasing negative events by building social skills and teaching clients how to engage in pleasant activities and cope with their moods. Cognitive-behavioral therapies focus on helping people with depression develop more adaptive ways of thinking and are very effective in treating depression. Interpersonal therapy helps people with depression identify and change their patterns in relationships and is highly effective in treating depression. Psychodynamic therapy helps people with depression uncover unconscious hostility and fears of abandonment. (Review Table 9.9.)

- Direct comparisons of drug therapies with cognitive-behavioral and interpersonal therapies show that they tend to be equally effective in the treatment of depression. The combination of drug therapy and psychotherapy may be more effective than either treatment alone for people with chronic depression.

- Effective prevention programs have been designed to reduce the risk for onset of major depression in high-risk groups.

MindMap CD-ROM

The following resources on the MindMap CD-ROM that came with this text will help you to master the content of this chapter and prepare for tests:

- Videos: Major Depression; Dysthymia; Bipolar Disorder
- Chapter Timeline
- Chapter Quiz

Key Terms

bipolar disorder 303

mania 303

depression 303

unipolar depression 303

delusions 304

hallucinations 304

major depression 304

dysthymic disorder 304

double depression 304

seasonal affective disorder (SAD) 305

bipolar I disorder 310

bipolar II disorder 310

hypomania 310

cyclothymic disorder 310

rapid cycling bipolar disorder 311

monoamines 315

norepinephrine 315

serotonin 315

dopamine 315

monoamine theories 315

hypothalamic-pituitary-adrenal axis (HPA axis) 317

cortisol 317

premenstrual dysphoric disorder 318

behavioral theory of depression 319

learned helplessness theory 320

learned helplessness deficits 320

negative cognitive triad 321

reformulated learned helplessness theory 321

causal attribution 321

depressive realism 323

ruminative response styles theory 323

rumination 323

introjected hostility theory 324

interpersonal theories of depression 325

contingencies of self-worth 325

excessive reasurrance seeking 326

cohort effect 327

tricyclic antidepressants 331

monoamine oxidase inhibitors (MAOIs) 331

selective serotonin reuptake inhibitors (SSRIs) 331

electroconvulsive therapy (ECT) 332

repetitive transcranial magnetic stimulation (rTMS) 334

vagus nerve stimulation (VNS) 334

light therapy 335

lithium 335

anticonvulsants 336

antipsychotic drugs 336

calcium channel blockers 336

behavior therapies 337

cognitive-behavioral therapy 338

interpersonal therapy (IPT) 340

psychodynamic therapies 341

Chapter 10

Florista
by Bernadita Zegers

Razors pain you;
Rivers are damp;
Acids stain you;
And drugs cause cramp.
Guns aren't lawful;
Nooses give;
Gas smells awful;   —Dorothy Parker, "Resume,"
You might as well live.   *Dorothy Parker: Complete Poems* (1999)

Suicide <

Extraordinary People

- **William Styron: *Darkness Visible***

Defining and Measuring Suicide

Suicide is the intentional taking of one's own life. Suicidal thoughts and behaviors are on a continuum from those representing a clear intention to die to those representing ambivalence about dying. Suicide is the eighth leading cause of death in the United States, and internationally an estimated 1 million people die by suicide and 2 million other people make suicide attempts each year. Women are more likely than men to attempt suicide, but men are more likely than women to complete suicide. There are substantial cross-cultural and age differences in suicide.

Understanding Suicide

Generally, suicide notes are brief and concrete and leave few clues. Social approaches to suicide have identified several negative life events or circumstances that increase the risk for suicide. Influential theorist Emil Durkheim described several types of suicide that result from individuals' relationships to society. Sometimes, suicides occur in groups of people, a phenomenon known as suicide clusters or suicide contagion. Psychodynamic theorists attribute suicide to repressed rage, which leads to self-destruction. Several mental disorders increase the risk for suicide, including depression, bipolar disorder, substance abuse, schizophrenia, and anxiety disorders. Cognitive-behavioral theorists argue that hopelessness and dichotomous thinking contribute to suicide. Impulsivity is a behavioral characteristic common to people who commit suicide. Finally, biological theories attribute suicidality to genetic vulnerabilities and to low serotonin levels.

Treating and Preventing Suicidal Tendencies

Drug treatments for suicidality most often consist of lithium or antidepressant medications to reduce impulsive and violent behavior, depression, and mania. Antipsychotic medications and other medications that treat the symptoms of an existing mental disorder may also be used. The psychotherapies for suicide are similar to those used for depression. Dialectical behavior therapy has been designed specifically to address skills deficits and thinking patterns in people who are suicidal. Suicide hot lines and crisis intervention programs provide immediate help to people who are suicidal. Community prevention programs aim to educate the public about suicide and encourage suicidal people to enter treatment. Guns are involved in the majority of suicides, and some research suggests that restricting access to guns can reduce the number of suicide attempts. Society is debating whether people have a right to choose to commit suicide.

Taking Psychology Personally

- **What to Do If a Friend Is Suicidal**

Chapter Integration

Suicide seems to fit a vulnerability-stress model. Several factors determine an individual's vulnerability to suicide, and various events or circumstances can serve as a trigger. Psychological treatments for suicidality help people recognize suicidal feelings and their personal triggers and develop more effective ways of coping.

Extraordinary People

William Styron: *Darkness Visible*

You may have read some of William Styron's books in your courses on great American literature. This Pulitzer Prize–winning author of such classics as *Sophie's Choice* and *The Confessions of Nat Turner* was at the top of his profession in late October 1985. Styron was in Paris to receive the Prix Mondial Cino del Duca, given yearly to an artist or a scientist whose work reflects certain principles of humanism. This prize was a high honor, and Styron knew he should be feeling full of joy and pride. Instead, as Styron writes, "I was feeling in my mind a sensation close to, but indescribably different from, actual pain. . . . For myself, the pain is most closely connected to drowning or suffocation" (1990, pp. 16–17).

In June 1985, Styron had begun drifting into a deep, severe depression, which overtook his life. He could not sleep at night or during the day. As each day wore on, his mood became worse and his thinking more clouded. He began to loathe his work and himself. On the day he received the Prix Mondial Cino del Duca, he found himself sitting at a dinner in his honor, unable to speak, to eat, or to respond in any way to his hosts. He reached into his coat pocket and realized he had lost the check for $25,000 that was the cash prize for the del Duca award. He thought it was fitting that this had happened, because he did not believe he deserved the award. Later that night, on the way back to his hotel, Styron thought of his many friends and heroes who had committed suicide and realized he would be facing the same decision very soon.

Styron was 60 when depression first cast a shadow over his mind in June 1985. He had been addicted to alcohol for 20 years, but, suddenly that June, his body began to reject alcohol. Even a mouthful of wine made him woozy and dizzy, and he quickly became unable to drink at all. As his alcohol intake stopped, his depression began. At first, it was mild:

> It was not really alarming at first, since the change was subtle, but I did notice that my surroundings took on a different tone at certain times: the shadows of nightfall seemed more somber, my mornings were less buoyant, walks in the woods became less zestful, and there was a moment during my working hours in the late afternoon when a kind of panic and anxiety overtook me, just for a few minutes, accompanied by a visceral queasiness. (Styron, 1990, p. 42)

By December, though, Styron had become so deeply mired in his depression that he began taking steps to commit suicide. He consulted his lawyer to ensure that his will and estate were in good order. He destroyed his diary in which he had written about his despair. He wrote a few words of parting but tore up all his efforts in disgust. Late one night, after his wife had gone to bed, Styron sat watching the tape of a movie in his living room. A passage from the Brahms *Alto Rhapsody* was played in the movie. Styron writes:

> This sound, which like all music—indeed, like all pleasure—I had been numbly unresponsive to for months, pierced my heart like a dagger, and in a flood of swift recollection I thought of all the joys the house had known: the children who had rushed through its rooms, the festivals, the love and work, the honestly earned slumber, the voices and the nimble commotion, the perennial tribe of cats and dogs and birds, "laughter and ability and Sighing, / And Frocks and Curls." All this I realized was more than I could ever abandon, even as what I had set out so deliberately to do was more than I could inflict on those memories, and upon those, so close to me, with whom the memories were bound. And just as powerfully I realized I could not commit this desecration on myself. I drew upon some last gleam of sanity to perceive the terrifying dimensions of the mortal predicament I had fallen into. I woke up my wife and soon telephone calls were made. The next day I was admitted to the hospital. (1990, pp. 66–67)

Suicide is both an unusual act and a surprisingly familiar one. We can all name movie stars, political leaders, and other people of prominence who killed themselves. Most of us also have come into personal contact with suicide. Nearly half of all teenagers in the United States say that they know someone who has tried to commit suicide (*New York Times/CBS News Poll*, 1999) (see Figure 10.1). One in four teenagers admits to attempting or seriously contemplating suicide (van Heeringen, 2001). Suicide is among the three leading causes of death worldwide among people 15 to 44 years of age (World Health Organization [WHO], 2005). Across the world, more people die from suicide than from homicide.

The impact of suicide on surviving family members and friends can be huge. There is guilt—over not having prevented the suicide, over things that were said to the person who committed suicide, over things that may have contributed to the suicide. There is the shame and stigma of suicide. And there is anger at the person who committed suicide.

In this chapter, we try to understand suicide. With the help of biographies and autobiographies, we peer into the minds of people who have attempted or completed suicide to get a glimpse of what they were feeling and thinking. We examine statistics that reveal substantial differences among age groups, between the genders, and among cultural groups in the rates of suicide. We review explanations of why some people commit suicide. Finally, we discuss programs designed to prevent suicide in high-risk groups and those designed to help survivors of suicide.

Although many people who commit suicide are depressed, as was William Styron, suicidal thoughts and behaviors occur in the context of several disorders in this book. This is why we are discussing suicide in a separate chapter. You'll see that there are several explanations for why some people become suicidal. Most researchers and clinicians view suicide as the result of an intersection of several biological, psychological, and social factors.

DEFINING AND MEASURING SUICIDE

We need to define **suicide**. This may seem simple—it is the purposeful taking of one's own life. This definition is close to that used by the Centers for Disease Control and Prevention (CDC), one of the federal agencies in the United States that track suicide rates. The CDC says that suicide is death from injury, poisoning, or suffocation where there is evidence that the damage was self-inflicted and

FIGURE 10.1 **Teenagers' Experience with Suicide.** These are the percentages of teenagers in a national poll who answered yes or no to the question "Do you know anyone your age who has ever tried to commit suicide?"

Do you know anyone your age who has ever tried to commit suicide?

	YES	NO
All teens	46%	53%
Girls	56%	44%
Boys	37%	62%
White	50%	50%
Black	28%	72%
Hispanic	39%	61%

Note: Hispanic may be of any race. There were too few Asian respondents to give separate percentages.

Based on surveys of 13- to 17-year-olds nationwide. The latest poll was conducted Oct. 11 to 14 with 1,038 teenagers. Those with no answer are not shown.

Source: *New York Times/CBS News Poll* 1999, p. 1.

that the individual intended to kill himself or herself.

As crisp and clear as this definition seems, there is great variability in the form that suicide takes, and there can be debate over whether to call particular types of death suicide. We may easily agree that a young man who is despondent and shoots himself in the head has committed suicide. It is harder to agree whether a despondent young man who goes on a drinking binge and then crashes his car into a tree has committed suicide. Is an Indian woman who throws herself on her husband's funeral fire committing suicide? Is an elderly person who refuses life support when dying from a painful disease committing suicide? Is a middle-aged person with severe heart disease who continues to smoke cigarettes, eat fatty foods, and drink excessive amounts of alcohol committing suicide? Clearly, suicide-like behaviors fall on a continuum.

Types of Suicide

Influential suicide theorist Edwin Shneidman (1963, 1981, 1993) described four types of people who commit suicide: death seekers, death initiators, death ignorers, and death darers. **Death seekers** clearly and explicitly seek to end their lives. Their intentions to commit suicide may be present for a long period of time, during which they prepare for their death by giving away possessions, writing a will, buying a gun, and so on, as did William Styron. Most often, their intentions are fleeting, and, if they are prevented from committing suicide, they may become ambivalent about their desire to die.

Death initiators also have a clear intention to die but believe that they are simply hastening an inevitable death. Many people with serious illnesses who commit suicide fall into this category. For example, particularly before effective drug treatments for human immunodeficiency virus (HIV) were available, some people infected with HIV committed suicide rather than face the severe illnesses, mental decline, and wasting away that can accompany advanced stages of acquired immune deficiency syndrome (AIDS).

Death ignorers intend to end their lives but do not believe that this means the end of their existence. They see their death as the beginning of a new and better life. Mass suicides by members of religious groups, such as the 1997 suicides of 39 members of the Heaven's Gate religious cult, fall into this category. Similarly, suicide bombers who believe they will receive tremendous rewards from God for their acts are considered death ignorers.

Death darers are ambivalent about dying, and they take actions that greatly increase their chances of death but that do not guarantee they will die. A person who swallows a handful of pills from the medicine cabinet without knowing how lethal they are, then calls a friend, is a death

Suicide bombers have wreaked havoc in many areas of the world, including the Middle East. Those who believe they will receive tremendous rewards from God for their acts are considered death ignorers.

darer. A youngster who randomly loads a gun with one bullet, then points the barrel at his head and pulls the trigger, is a death darer. Death darers may want attention or may want to make someone else feel guilty, more than they want to die (Brent et al., 1988).

What about the people who chronically make lifestyle choices that increase their risk for early death, such as a heart patient who continues to smoke cigarettes? Shneidman (1981, 1993, 2001) describes acts in which people indirectly contribute to their own death, perhaps unconsciously, as **subintentional deaths.** Most researchers and theorists, however, reserve the label *suicide* for deaths that are intentionally caused by the individual.

Suicide Rates

Not surprisingly, it is difficult to obtain accurate suicide rates. The stigma against suicide is a great incentive for labeling a death as anything but a suicide. Sometimes, it is absolutely clear that a death was a suicide—a note is left, the person had been threatening suicide, or a revolver is still in the victim's hand, with powder stains that could mean only a self-inflicted wound. Many deaths are more ambiguous, however, particularly when there are no notes left behind and no clues as to the victim's mental state before the death. Local officials, such as police and coroners, may conspire with family members to label ambiguous deaths as accidents, rather than have the family face the questions that come with suicide (Madge & Harvey, 1999). Accurate data on nonlethal suicide attempts are even more difficult to obtain, particularly since over half of all people who attempt, but do not complete, suicide never seek professional help and thus may not be diagnosed (Crosby, Cheltenham, & Sacks, 1999).

As a result, the statistics on the rates of suicide in various groups are probably gross underestimates. Even so, the statistics indicate that suicide is more common than we would like to believe. It is the eighth leading cause of death in the United States. About 31,000 people kill themselves each year in the United States, which averages to nearly 85 people per day (Centers for Disease Control and Prevention [CDC], 2004). In addition, as many as 3 percent of the population contemplate suicide at sometime in their lives, and between 5 and 16 percent report having had suicidal thoughts at sometime (Crosby et al., 1999; Statham et al., 1998). Suicide is not just an American phenomenon, however. Internationally, an estimated 1 million people die by suicide each year, or one person every 40 seconds (WHO, 2005).

There are large differences in suicide rates between men and women, among age groups, and among cultural groups. We now turn to a description of some of these differences.

Gender Differences

We might expect that, since women are more prone to depression than men and depression is often associated with suicide, rates of suicide in women are much higher than in men. Indeed, three times more women than men *attempt* suicide (Brockington, 2001; Canetto & Sakinofsky, 1998; Welch, 2001). And a study of high school students found that the girls were much more likely than the boys to have considered or planned a suicide attempt (Lewinsohn, Rohde, & Seeley, 1996a). However, men and boys are four times more likely than women and girls to complete suicide (CDC, 2004). This gender difference in suicide completion rate is true in many nations of the world, and across all age ranges, as can be seen in Figure 10.2 (WHO, 2004).

The gender difference in rates of completed suicides may be due in part to gender differences in the means of attempting suicide. Men tend to choose more lethal means of suicide than do women (Canetto & Sakinofsky, 1998; Crosby et al., 1999; Denning et al., 2000). In the United States, men are more likely than women to shoot, stab, or hang themselves. Although guns are still the most common way women commit suicide, women are more likely than men to choose less lethal means, such as drug overdoses. Even if men are often ambivalent about dying, the means they choose to attempt suicide are more likely to be lethal than the means women tend to choose. Some theorists argue, however, that men tend to be more sure in their intent to die when they attempt suicide than women and this is why they choose more lethal means (Jack, 1992; Linehan, 1973). Men may feel that it is not masculine to be ambivalent about their intent to die or to communicate this intent to others in hopes that they will be prevented from succeeding (Canetto & Sakinofsky, 1998). Women, on the other hand, may be more comfortable in using suicide attempts as cries for help.

Finally, guns and alcohol play a role in many suicides. Alcohol lowers inhibitions and increases impulsive behavior, and guns provide a means for carrying out suicidal thoughts. Men are more likely than women to drink alcohol when they are highly distressed and may have more ready access to guns. This may contribute to men's higher rates of completed suicides.

In some countries, women are at least as likely as men to commit suicide. For example, in China, women account for 55 percent of all suicide deaths

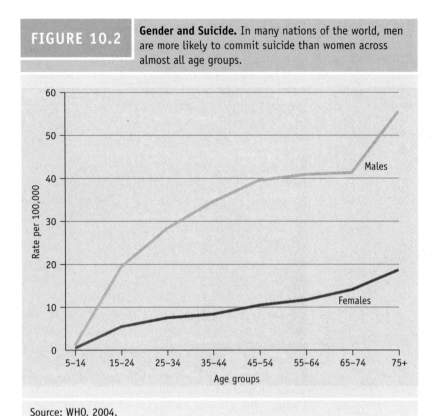

FIGURE 10.2 **Gender and Suicide.** In many nations of the world, men are more likely to commit suicide than women across almost all age groups.

Source: WHO, 2004.

(Ji, Kleinman, & Becker, 2001). The reasons are unclear, but gender roles probably interact with cultural beliefs about suicide to influence rates in both women and men.

Ethnic and Cross-Cultural Differences

Within the United States, there are substantial differences among ethnic groups in rates of suicide (CDC, 2004; Oquendo et al., 2001). European Americans have higher suicide rates than all other groups, at approximately 12 people per 100,000 in the population, and Native Americans are close behind at approximately 11 per 100,000 people. Suicide among Native Americans is tied to poverty, lack of education and hope, discrimination, substance abuse, and the easy availability of firearms (Berman & Jobes, 1995).

Several studies have compared the suicide rates of African Americans and European Americans (Burr, Hartman, & Matteson, 1999; Joe & Kaplan, 2001; O'Donnell et al., 2004). European Americans have higher rates of completed suicide than African Americans, but the rates among African American males have increased greatly in recent decades (Joe & Kaplan, 2001). Other studies show that Hispanic youth in the United States are more likely to contemplate and attempt suicide than African American youth or European American

TABLE 10.1   Reports of Suicidal Thoughts and Attempts over the Past Year Among Urban Ethnic Minority Youth

Item	Black (%)	Hispanic (%)	Black-Hispanic (%)	Other (%)
Seriously considered suicide	14.8	20.2	11.7	9.9
Told someone they have thought about killing themselves	14.8	20.7	15.0	9.9
Thought killing themselves a solution	15.1	17.2	15.0	11.3
Made a suicide plan	12.3	15.2	11.7	11.3
Attempted suicide at least once	8.1	17.9	10.0	16.9
Made multiple suicide attempts	3.8	4.1	8.3	5.6

Source: O'Donnell et al., 2004.

youth, as illustrated by a study of urban youth shown in Table 10.1 (O'Donnell et al., 2004). The rate of completed suicide is not higher for Hispanic youth than for youth in other ethnic groups in the United States, however, and studies of adults tend to find lower completed suicide rates in Hispanic groups than in other groups (Oquendo et al., 2001).

There are cross-national differences in suicide rates, with higher rates in much of Europe, the former Soviet Union, and Australia, and lower rates in Latin America and South America (WHO, 2004) (see Figure 10.3). The suicide rates in the United States, Canada, and England fall between these two extremes. These differences may have to do with cultural and religious norms against suicide. People who belong to religions that expressly forbid suicide are less likely to attempt it (O'Donnell et al., 2004; Statham et al., 1998).

Suicide in Children and Adolescents

Unfortunately, most adults often do not believe children when they voice their suicidal thoughts. Even clinicians formerly thought that young children could not have a concept of suicide and thus were not vulnerable. Now it is understood that, although suicide is relatively rare in young children, it is not impossible. One 10-year-old girl had no history of suicide attempts or mental disorder yet spoke explicitly of her suicidal thoughts (Pfeffer, 1985, p. 80):

VOICES

I often think of killing myself. It started when I was almost hit by a car. Now I want to kill myself. I think of stabbing myself with a knife. When Mom yells at me, I think she does not love me. I worry a lot about my family. Mom is always depressed and sometimes she says she will die soon. My brother becomes very angry, often for no reason. He tried to kill himself last year and had to go to the hospital. Mom was in the hospital once also. I worry a lot about my family. I worry that if something happens to them, no one will take care of me. I feel sad about this.

Another child, a 10-year-old boy, described how anger so often drives suicidal thoughts and actions (Pfeffer, 1985, p. 80):

VOICES

I want to hurt myself when I get upset and angry. I bang my head against the wall or punch the wall with my fist. I wish I were dead. I often think about how to kill myself. I think I will go to France to have myself guillotined. It would be quick and painless. Guns are too painful, so is stabbing myself. Once, I put my head into a sink of water and I got scared. My grandmother found me. I told her I was washing my face. Mom was shocked when she heard about this. She began to cry. She worries a lot and always seems sad.

Girls are much more likely to attempt suicide, but boys are more likely to complete suicide. The gender ratio for completed suicide is even greater

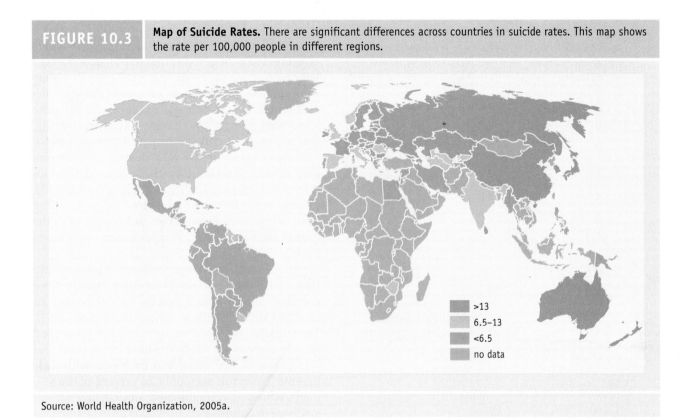

FIGURE 10.3 **Map of Suicide Rates.** There are significant differences across countries in suicide rates. This map shows the rate per 100,000 people in different regions.

>13
6.5–13
<6.5
no data

Source: World Health Organization, 2005a.

among adolescents and young adults than among older adults: Males are six times more likely than females in this age range to commit suicide (CDC, 2004).

The rate of suicide increases substantially in early adolescence. Each year, one in five teenagers in the United States seriously considers suicide; 15 percent make a specific plan to attempt suicide; nearly 9 percent of adolescents attempt suicide; and about 3 percent make a serious suicide attempt that requires medical attention (Gould, Greenberg, Velting & Shaffer, 2003). Suicide may be more common in adolescence than in childhood because the rate of several types of psychopathology tied to suicide, including depression, anxiety disorders, and substance abuse, increase in adolescence. Suicide rates may also rise at this age because adolescents are more sophisticated in their thinking than are children and can contemplate suicide more clearly. Finally, adolescents may simply have the means to commit suicide (such as access to drugs and guns) more than do children.

There are interesting historical trends in suicide rates among adolescents, particularly among males. Between 1964 and 1988, there was nearly a threefold increase in adolescent male suicides (Gould, Greenberg et al., 2003; Spirito & Esposito-

Smythers, 2006) (see Figure 10.4 on page 358). This increase continued among white males until the mid 1990s, then started to decline. Rates among African American males, although still lower than among European Americans, showed no sign of decline until 1995. The increase in earlier decades has been attributed to increases in adolescents' access to alcohol and other drugs, whereas the relatively recent decrease in suicide rates may be due to the tremendous increase in the prescription of antidepressants for adolescents (Gould, Greensberg et al., 2003). African American youth typically have greater difficulty accessing treatments for mental-health problems, and this may account for the fact that their decline in suicide rates came a bit later than that of European American youth.

The risk factors for suicide in adolescents include current depression, interpersonal problems, insecure relationships with parents, negative thinking and hopelessness, appetite problems, increased substance abuse, aggression, and a suicide attempt by a friend (King et al., 2001; Lewinsohn et al., 1996a, Lewinsohn et al., 2001; Spirito & Esposito-Smythers, 2006; Wagner et al., 2003). In addition, several studies suggest that gay and bisexual youth are at significantly greater risk for suicidal behavior, although the vast majority report no suicidal

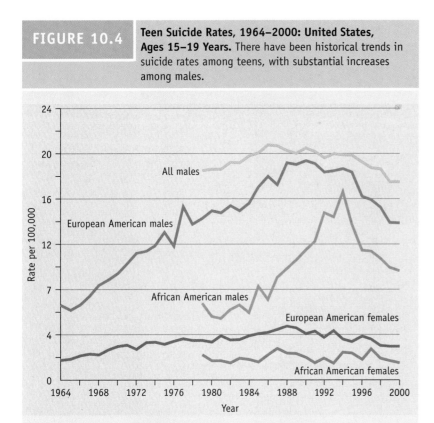

Source: Gould, Greenberg, et al., 2003.

posed in high school. Academic material is much more difficult and standards are higher. Students who entered college expecting to pursue a particular career, such as medicine, may find that they cannot make the grades in necessary classes, such as chemistry and biology. Student athletes who were stars in high school may play second-string, if at all, on their college team. Student musicians, performers, and artists may despair of pursuing their dreams. And there are the social and developmental challenges of college—making new friends, dealing with the drug and alcohol culture, coping with being away from home, and coping with the changes in values that come with exposure to new ideas.

In a survey of college students, 9 percent said they had thought about committing suicide since entering college, and 1 percent said they had attempted suicide while at college (Furr et al., 2001). The students who had contemplated or attempted suicide were more likely to suffer depression and hopelessness, loneliness, and problems with their parents. Unfortunately, only 20 percent of the students who had contemplated suicide had sought any type of counseling.

Suicide in Older Adults

Although there has been a 50 percent decline in suicide rates among older adults over the past few decades, older adults, particularly older men, still remain at relatively high risk for suicide. The highest risk is among European American men over the age of 85 (CDC, 2004). When they attempt suicide, older people are much more likely than younger people to be successful. It seems that most older people who attempt suicide fully intend to die (McIntosh, 1995). In contrast, most young people who attempt suicide are highly ambivalent about it.

Some older people who commit suicide do so because they cannot tolerate the loss of their spouse or other loved ones. For example, an elderly woman who had recently lost her husband to prostate cancer said the following (Nolen-Hoeksema & Larson, 1999, p. 43):

thoughts or behaviors at all (see Gould, Greenberg, et al., 2003; Russell, 2003; Spirito & Esposito-Smythers, 2006). Many adolescents contemplating suicide write letters to friends to say good-bye and give away their possessions. Almost all have thought about committing suicide for sometime before actually attempting it.

Many more adolescents attempt suicide than die by suicide. Adolescents may be especially prone to use suicide attempts as a way of getting attention and help for problems. This does not mean that adolescent suicide attempts are unimportant, however. A history of a suicide attempt is the single best predictor of future suicide attempts and completions (King et al., 2001; Lewinsohn et al., 1996a; Spirito & Esposito-Smythers, 2006). As Kay Redfield Jamison says, referring to suicide in her book *Night Falls Fast: Understanding Suicide,* "If it has ever been taken up as an option, however, the black knight has a tendency to remain in play." (1999, p. 4). Thus, adolescents who attempt suicide once are at high risk for future attempts, which might be successful.

College Students

The college years are full of pressures and changes. Students may face challenges far beyond those

VOICES

I think when you live with someone for a long time, that when they go, you should be able to go, too. I think people should be able to go together. I think it's useless for one person of a pair to stick around. I just think that it should be a natural order of things that if you're together with somebody a long
(continued)

time, you should just go with them when they go. It doesn't make any sense. . . . We grew up together, really. All those years and all the things we did. I don't want to do anything by myself. I don't want to be alone. It was great with him. It's sure a big zero without him.

Suicide rates are highest in the first year after a loss but remain relatively high for several years after the loss (McIntosh, 1995).

Some older persons who commit suicide suffer from debilitating illnesses and wish to escape their pain and suffering. Escape from illness and disabilities may be a particularly strong motive for suicide among men (Canetto & Hollenshead, 2000). An older man may have been strong and healthy his entire life; then, when stricken with a serious disease in old age, he may become confined to a wheelchair or his bed or be forced to enter a nursing home. One study of older people who had committed suicide found that 44 percent had said they could not bear being placed in a nursing home and would rather be dead (Loebel et al., 1991).

Some researchers argue that intentional life-threatening behavior, such as refusing food or medication, is a common form of suicidal behavior in older people (see Harwood et al., 2000). These behaviors range from clearly self-destructive behaviors, such as refusing food with the intent of starving to death, to behaviors with less obvious intent, such as failing to follow a prescribed treatment for an illness or continuing to smoke with emphysema.

Most older persons who lose a spouse or become ill do not commit suicide. Again, those who enter older age with a history of depression or other psychological problems are at greatest risk of responding to the challenges of old age with suicide (Harwood et al., 2000).

SUMMING UP

- Suicide is defined as death from injury, poisoning, or suffocation when there is evidence (either explicit or implicit) that the injury was self-inflicted and that the decedent intended to kill him- or herself.

- Death seekers clearly and explicitly seek to end their lives. Death initiators also have a clear intention to die but believe that they are simply hastening an inevitable death. Death ignorers intend to end their lives but do not believe this

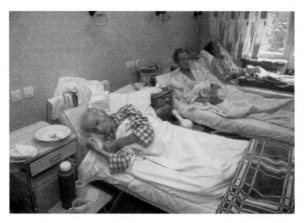

Illness is often a precursor to suicide among older adults.

means the end of their existence. Death darers are ambivalent about dying and take actions that greatly increase their chances of death but that do not guarantee they will die.

- Suicide is the eighth leading cause of death in the United States, and internationally at least 160,000 people die by suicide and 2 million other people make suicide attempts each year.

- Women are more likely than men to attempt suicide, but men are more likely than women to complete suicide.

- Cross-cultural differences in suicide rates may have to do with religious doctrines, stressors, and cultural norms about suicide.

- Young people are less likely than adults to commit suicide, but suicide rates have been rising dramatically for young people in recent decades. The elderly, particularly elderly men, are at high risk for suicide.

UNDERSTANDING SUICIDE

Our ability to understand the causes of suicide is hampered by many factors. First, although it is more common than we would hope, it is still rare enough that it is difficult to study scientifically. Second, in the wake of a suicide, family members and friends may selectively remember certain information about the victim (such as evidence that he or she was depressed) and forget other information. Third, the majority of people who contemplate suicide never actually commit suicide, so it is difficult to determine what causes some people to go through with the act.

Suicide Notes

It would be very helpful if we could get some clues as to the reasons for suicide from the notes left behind by those who commit suicide. Only about one in four people leave a suicide note, however, and often these notes provide only a glimpse into their motives (Jamison, 1999). These notes are often brief and vague and may simply say, "I could not bear it any longer," or "I am tired of living." On the other hand, some suicide notes are very concrete, with explicit instructions or requests, such as how to handle the body, what to tell others about the suicide, and how to distribute assets. Occasionally, the mental anguish that leads to suicide is expressed more fully in the suicide note (Leenaars, 1988, pp. 247–248):

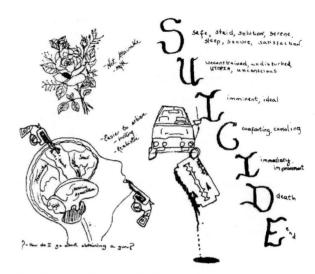

Drawings by a 19-year-old college sophomore.

VOICES

I wish I could explain it so someone could understand it. I'm afraid it's something I can't put into words. There's just this heavy, overwhelming despair—dreading everything. Dreading life. Empty inside, to the point of numbness. It's like there's something already dead inside. My whole being has been pulling back into that void for months. . . . But there's some core-level spark of life that just isn't there. Despite what's been said about my having "gotten better" lately—the voice in my head that's driving me crazy is louder than ever. It's way beyond being reached by anyone or anything, it seems. I can't bear it anymore. I think there's something psychologically twisted—reversed—that has taken over; that I can't fight anymore. I wish that I could disappear without hurting anyone. I'm sorry.

This writer mentions that family members and friends believe she is "getting better." Suicides often happen when people are not in the deepest depths of depression and despair but, rather, when they seem to be getting better, having more energy and engagement in life. This energy, however, can simply give them the energy and freedom to commit suicide, as Elizabeth Wurtzel explains in her autobiography, *Prozac Nation* (1995, p. 315):

The suicide attempt startled even me. It seemed to happen out of context, like something that should have taken place months and months ago. It should never have happened

VOICES

within a few days of returning to Cambridge, at a point when, even I had to admit, the fluoxetine (Prozac) was starting to kick in. After all, I was able to get out of bed in the morning, which may not seem like much, but in my life it was up there with Moses parting the Red Sea. Anybody would have thought that these were signs that my mood was on the upswing, and I guess it was. But just as a little bit of knowledge is a dangerous thing, a little bit of energy, in the hands of someone hell-bent on suicide, is a very dangerous thing.

My improved affect did not in any way sway me from the philosophical conviction that life, at its height and depth, basically sucks.

For people with long-term mental disorders, the prospect of sinking once again into despair leads them to take "preventive action"—to kill themselves before it happens again. Virginia Woolf suffered psychotic depressions and manias and committed suicide when she sensed a new episode coming (1975–1980a, pp. 486–487):

Dearest,
I want to tell you that you have given me complete happiness. No one could have done more than you have done. Please believe that.

(continued)

But I know that I shall never get over this: and I am wasting your life. It is this madness. Nothing anyone says can persuade me. You can work, and you will be much better without me. You see I can't write this even, which shows I am right. All I want to say is that until this disease came on we were perfectly happy. It was all due to you. No one could have been so good as you have been, from the very first day till now. Everyone knows that.

Most suicide notes are positive in their remarks about remaining family members, expressing love and thanks. Sometimes, the note is meant to relieve family members of guilt (Leenaars, 1988, p. 249):

Everyone has been so good to me—has tried so hard. I truly wish that I could be different, for the sake of my family. Hurting my family is the worst of it, and that guilt has been wrestling with the part of me that wanted only to disappear.

Thus, suicide notes often reveal only the obvious—that suicide tends to be driven by mental anguish and a sense of futility about going on.

Social Perspectives on Suicide

Social theorists have been at the forefront of research and theorizing about suicide. They have identified a number of events, and characteristics of societies, that may contribute to a vulnerability to suicide (see the Concept Overview in Table 10.2 on page 362).

Economic Hardship

A variety of stressful life events appear to contribute to an increased risk for suicide (Statham et al., 1998). One type of stressful event consistently linked to increased suicide vulnerability is economic hardship (Fanous, Prescott, & Kendler, 2004; Welch, 2001). For example, the loss of a job can precipitate suicidal thoughts and attempts (Crosby et al., 1999; Platt & Hawton, 2000); as the farm economy has collapsed in the United States in recent decades, the rate of suicide among farmers has increased considerably (Ragland & Berman, 1990–1991). Men and women who have spent their entire lives trying to make a living from land that may have been in their families for generations can find their dreams shattered and their farms lost forever.

Chronic economic hardship also contributes to suicidality. One nationwide study found that 8.5 percent of people living below the poverty level had thought about committing suicide in the previous year, compared with 5.4 percent of people living above the poverty level (Crosby et al., 1999). The high suicide rate among African American males in recent years may also be tied to perceptions that their economic futures are uncertain at best, as well as comparisons of their economic status with the status of the majority culture. One study found that suicide rates among African American males in the United States were highest in communities where the occupational and income inequalities between African Americans and European Americans were the greatest (Burr et al., 1999).

Serious Illness

Some people who commit suicide, especially older people, suffer from serious illnesses that bring them constant pain and debilitation (Canetto & Hollenshead, 2000). Some illnesses especially likely to increase the risk for suicide are HIV/AIDS, cancers of the brain, and some neurological conditions, including multiple sclerosis (Hughes & Kleespies, 2001). Although people who are seriously ill may always have been at increased risk for suicide, increases in the ability of medical practices to keep people alive long after they have been diagnosed with a serious illness have contributed to the number of seriously ill people wishing they could die. Interestingly, physical illness is a risk factor for suicidal thoughts and attempts in adolescents as well as in older adults (Lewinsohn et al., 1996a). The pain and burden of chronic physical illness are clearly not being well managed by the medical professions, leaving some people feeling incapable of bearing them on their own.

Loss and Abuse

Loss of a loved one through death, divorce, or separation often immediately precedes suicide attempts or completions (Spirito & Esposito-Smythers, 2006). People feel they cannot go on without the lost relationship and wish to end their pain. In addition, people who have experienced certain traumas in childhood, especially sexual abuse or the loss of a parent also appear at increased risk for suicide (Fanous et al., 2004; Spirito & Esposito-Smythers, 2006). For example, a nationwide study

TABLE 10.2   Concept Overview

Social Perspectives on Suicide

Social theorists have attributed suicide to larger events happening in a culture or to major traumas in an individual's life.

Theory	Description
Economic hardship	People who are chronically impoverished or who recently have lost a job are at increased risk for suicide.
Serious illness	People with serious illnesses are at increased risk for suicide.
Loss and abuse	People who have experienced loss or abuse in the distant or recent past are at increased risk for suicide.
Durkheim's theory	Egoistic suicide is committed by people who feel alienated from others, empty of social contacts, and alone in an unsupportive world. Anomic suicide is committed by people who experience severe disorientation because of a major change in their relationships to society. Altruistic suicide is committed by people who believe that taking their own lives will benefit society in some way.
Suicide contagion	When one member of group commits suicide, other members are at increased risk for suicide, perhaps because of "contagion" effects, modeling, increased acceptability of suicide, or the impact of the traumatic event on already vulnerable people.

in the United States found that a history of child-hood sexual abuse increases the odds of a suicide attempt by 2 to 4 times for women and 4 to 11 times for men (Molnar, Berkman, & Buka, 2001; see also Brent et al., 2002). Studies focusing on women have found that physical abuse by a partner is a potent predictor of suicide attempts (Kaslow et al., 2000; Ragin et al., 2002). The loss of a parent during child-hood may create a lifetime of instability and feelings of abandonment, which can contribute to suicidal intentions. Sexual abuse during childhood may shatter people's trust in others and prevent the development of a strong self-concept, which can protect against suicide.

Durkheim's Theory

In his classic work on suicide, sociologist Emil Durkheim (1897) focused not on specific events that precipitate suicide but, rather, on the mindsets that certain societal conditions can create that increase the risk for suicide. He proposed that there are three types of suicide, based on his analysis of records of suicide for various countries and across historical periods.

Egoistic suicide is committed by people who feel alienated from others, empty of social contacts, and alone in an unsupportive world. A person with schizophrenia who kills herself because she is completely isolated from society may be committing egoistic suicide. **Anomic suicide** is committed by people who experience severe disorientation because of a major change in their relationships to society. A man who loses his job after 20 years of service may feel *anomie*, a complete confusion of his role and worth in society, and may commit anomic suicide. Finally, **altruistic suicide** is committed by people who believe that taking their own lives will benefit society in some way. For instance, during the Vietnam War, Buddhist monks burned themselves to death in public suicides to protest the war.

Durkheim's theory suggests that social ties and integration into a society help prevent suicide if the society discourages suicide and supports individuals in overcoming negative situations in ways other than suicide. However, if a society supports suicide as an act that benefits the society in some situations, then ties with such a society may actually promote suicide. For example, some terrorist groups promote suicide as an honorable, even glorious, act in the service of striking at enemies. William Styron saw suicide as an acceptable act in part because so many of his friends and heroes had committed suicide.

Suicide Contagion

When a well-known member of a society commits suicide, people who closely identify with that person may see suicide as more acceptable (Gould,

Jamieson, & Romer, 2003). When two or more suicides or attempted suicides are nonrandomly bunched in space or time, such as a series of suicide attempts in the same high school or a series of completed suicides in response to the suicide of a celebrity, scientists refer to this as a **suicide cluster** (Joiner, 1999).

Suicide clusters appear most likely to occur among people who knew the person who committed suicide. One well-documented example occurred in a high school of about 1,500 students. Two students committed suicide within 4 days. Then, over an 18-day span, 7 other students attempted suicide, and an additional 23 reported having suicidal thoughts (Brent et al., 1989). Many of those who attempted suicide or had active suicidal thoughts were friends of each other and of the two students who had completed suicide.

Other suicide clusters occur not among close friends but among people who are linked only by media exposure to the suicide of a stranger, often a celebrity. Some studies have suggested that suicide rates, at least among adolescents, increase after a publicized suicide (for a review, see Gould, Jamieson, & Romer, 2003). For example, in the week after Marilyn Monroe committed suicide in 1963, the national suicide rate rose 12 percent. More recently, after the suicide of the popular lead singer of the band Nirvana, Kurt Cobain, there were concerns that young people who identified with Cobain and the message in his music would view suicide as an appropriate way of dealing with the social anomie expressed in that music. At least one fan, a 28-year-old man, went home after a candlelight vigil honoring Cobain and killed himself with a shotgun, just as Cobain had.

What is the reason for suicide clustering? Some theorists have argued these clusters are due to **suicide contagion,** meaning that people somehow "catch" suicidal intentions and behaviors from those who commit suicide (Stack, 1991). Survivors who become suicidal may be modeling the behavior of the friend or admired celebrity who committed suicide. The suicide may also make the idea of suicide more acceptable and thus lower inhibitions for suicidal behavior in survivors. In addition, the local and media attention given to a suicide can be attractive to some people who are feeling alienated and abandoned. After the murder/suicide rampage of two teenagers at Columbine High School in Littleton, Colorado, in 1999, some teenagers said that having the media attention given to the shooters would be an attractive way to "go out."

Thomas Joiner (1999) argues that suicide clusters are best understood as the result of several sets of factors coming together in the same time and place. First, people form relationships with others who possess similar qualities or problems—known as *assortative relationships.* People who are at risk for suicide, because of psychopathology, life problems, or lack of social support from families, may be more likely to gravitate together. For example, teenagers who are outcasts from the popular groups at their high school may hang out together, with social alienation as the primary bond between them.

Second, severe negative events can be triggers for suicide, and these negative events often happen to groups of people as well as to individuals. The suicide of a close friend qualifies as a severe negative event and, thus, may increase the risk for suicide among others, as would any other severe negative event. But when the close friends of the person who committed suicide also carry other risk factors for suicide, then the suicide may be especially likely to trigger suicidality in the survivors.

Psychological Theories of Suicide

Psychological theorists have focused on what goes through the mind of a person who commits suicide. Psychodynamic theorists attribute suicide to repressed rage. Cognitive theorists have identified patterns of thinking that appear to increase the risk for suicide, and a great deal of evidence shows that certain mental disorders increase the risk for suicide (see the Concept Overview in Table 10.3).

TABLE 10.3 Concept Overview

Psychological Theories of Suicide

Psychological theories of suicide focus on the thoughts and motivations of people who attempt suicide.

Theory	Description
Psychodynamic theories	Suicide is the extreme expression of anger at the love object who has abandoned the person.
Mental disorders	Several mental disorders increase the risk for suicide, including depression, bipolar disorder, schizophrenia, substance abuse, and anxiety disorders.
Impulsivity	People who commit suicide have a general tendency toward impulsive acts.
Cognitive theories	Hopelessness and dichotomous thinking increase the risk for suicide.

Psychodynamic Theories

Recall that Freud (1917) argued that depression is anger turned inward on the self. Instead of expressing anger at people they feel have betrayed or abandoned them, depressed people express that anger at themselves, specifically at the part of their ego that represents the lost person. Sometimes, that anger is so great that the depressed person wishes to annihilate that image of the lost person. This means annihilating the self—suicide.

This line of reasoning suggests that suicidal people tend to be filled with rage against others. For example, teenagers who are enraged at their parents but cannot express it may attempt suicide as a means of punishing their parents. As noted in the section "Suicide Notes," however, anger and rage are not the most common emotions that suicidal people express (Shneidman, 1979). Instead, guilt and emotional despair are more common. A psychodynamic theorist might argue that suicidal people don't express anger in suicide notes or in other ways precisely because they cannot express these emotions and are turning the feelings in on themselves. Unfortunately, this argument makes the theory difficult to test.

Near the end of his career, Freud was dissatisfied with his own theory of suicide and believed it a more complex phenomenon than anger turned inward. Although newer psychodynamic theories of suicide have emerged, most still focus on self-directed anger as the core problem in suicidality (Maltsberger, 1999).

Mental Disorders

Over 90 percent of people who commit suicide have probably been suffering from a diagnosable mental disorder (Joiner, Brown, & Wingate, 2005; Spirito & Esposito-Smythers, 2006). The most common disorder among people who commit suicide is a mood disorder—for example, William Styron's suicidal thoughts were part of a debilitating depression. Suicide is associated with several other disorders as well, including borderline personality disorder, disruptive behavior disorders (such as conduct disorder), alcohol and other drug use disorders, anxiety disorders, anorexia nervosa, and schizophrenia (Joiner, Brown, & Wingate, 2005; Spirito & Esposito-Smythers, 2006). Often, psychiatric diagnoses have not been made before an individual commits suicide. Instead, researchers conduct a *psychological autopsy*—an analysis of the person's moods, thoughts, and behaviors based on the reports of family and friends and the individual's writings—after the suicide has occurred.

One group of researchers was able to conduct a prospective study of people who attempted suicide during a year-long study of 13,673 adults randomly chosen from a community sample. All these adults were interviewed twice, one year apart. A structured clinical interview was used to determine whether each adult qualified for the diagnosis of a psychological disorder. Over the year between the two interviews, 40 people in the sample attempted suicide. The researchers randomly chose 40 other people from the rest of the sample who had not attempted suicide to make comparisons with the 40 suicide attempters. When the researchers examined the data from the first interview, they found that 53 percent of those who had attempted suicide had been diagnosed with major depression, compared with 6 percent of those who had not made an attempt (Petronis et al., 1990). Similarly, a prospective study of suicide attempts in adolescents found that major depression greatly increases the risk for suicide (Lewinsohn et al., 1996a).

In the longitudinal study by Petronis and colleagues (1990), 8 percent of the people who attempted suicide had been diagnosed with mania at the first interview, compared with 0.6 percent of the nonattempters. As many as half of people with bipolar disorder attempt suicide, and perhaps one in five will complete suicide (Dunner, 2004; Goodwin & Jamison, 1990). It might seem strange that a manic person would attempt suicide, because the symptoms of mania include elation and heightened self-esteem. However, often the predominant feelings of mania are agitation and irritation mixed with despair over having the illness or in contemplating falling into a debilitating depression. Kay Redfield Jamison, who was featured in the *Extraordinary People* segment of Chapter 9, described one of her suicide attempts, which occurred when she was in a mixed manic and depressive state and was highly agitated (Jamison, 1995, pp. 113–114):

VOICES

In a rage I pulled the bathroom lamp off the wall and felt the violence go through me but not yet out of me. "For Christ's sake," he said, rushing in—and then stopping very quietly. Jesus, I must be crazy, I can see it in his eyes a dreadful mix of concern, terror, irritation, resignation, and why me, Lord? "Are you hurt?" he asks. Turning my head with its fast-scanning eyes I see in the mirror blood running down my arms. I bang my head over and over against the door. God, make it stop, I can't stand it, I know I'm insane again. He really cares, I think, but within ten minutes he too is screaming, and his eyes have a wild

(continued)

look from contagious madness, from the lightning adrenaline between the two of us. "I can't leave you like this," but I say a few truly awful things and then go for his throat in a more literal way, and he does leave me, provoked beyond endurance and unable to see the devastation and despair inside. I can't convey it and he can't see it; there's nothing to be done. I can't think, I can't calm this murderous cauldron, my grand ideas of an hour ago seem absurd and pathetic, my life is in ruins, and worse still—ruinous; my body is uninhabitable. It is raging and weeping and full of destruction and wild energy gone amok. In the mirror I see a creature I don't know but must live and share my mind with.

I understand why Jekyll killed himself before Hyde had taken over completely. I took a massive overdose of lithium with no regrets.

Another psychological disorder that greatly increases the risk for suicide attempts is substance abuse (Fanous et al., 2004; Welch, 2001; Yen et al., 2003). Recall that William Styron had been abusing alcohol for years before he became suicidal. In the prospective study of suicide attempts we have been discussing (Petronis et al., 1990), 33.0 percent of the individuals who attempted suicide were identified as heavy drinkers, compared with 2.5 percent of those who did not make an attempt. The lifetime risk for suicide among people who are dependent on alcohol is seven times greater than the lifetime risk among people who are not alcohol dependent (Joiner et al., 2005). When alcoholism co-occurs with depression, as in Styron's case, the risk for suicide is especially high (Waller, Lyons, & Costantini-Ferrando, 1999). Alcohol lowers people's inhibitions to engage in impulsive acts, even self-destructive ones, such as suicide attempts. Also, people with chronic alcohol problems may have a general tendency toward self-destructive acts and may wreck many of their relationships and their careers, making them feel they do not have much reason to live.

Between 10 and 15 percent of people with schizophrenia commit suicide, a rate 20 times higher than in the general population (Joiner et al., 2005; Tsuang, Fleming, & Simpson, 1999). They may kill themselves to end the torment of accusatory hallucinations telling them they are evil or to end the excruciating social isolation they feel. Most suicide attempts among people with schizophrenia happen not when the people are psychotic but when they are lucid but depressed. Those who are most likely

Alcohol is involved in many suicides.

to commit suicide are young males who have frequent relapses into psychosis but who had a good education and high expectations for themselves before they developed schizophrenia. It seems that these young men cannot face a future that is likely to be so much less than what they had envisioned for themselves (Joiner et al., 2005).

Whatever mental disorder a suicidal individual is suffering from, the most common reason expressed for attempting suicide is to escape intolerable distress (Brown, Comtois, & Linehan, 2002). In addition, people say they want to relieve their loved ones of the burdens of their existence and of caring for them.

Impulsivity

The behavioral characteristic that seems to predict suicide best is **impulsivity,** the general tendency to act on one's impulses rather than to inhibit them when it is appropriate to do so (Joiner et al., 2005). For example, a study of incarcerated men found that those with a history of suicide attempts were more likely to score high on scales measuring impulsivity and sensation seeking (Verona, Patrick, & Joiner, 2001). When impulsivity is overlaid on other psychological problems—such as depression, substance abuse, or life in a chronically stressful environment—it can be a potent contributor to suicide. One family history study showed that the children of parents with a mood disorder who also scored high on measures of impulsivity were at a much greater risk of attempting suicide (Brent et al., 2002). As we discuss in the section "Biological Theories of Suicides," there also is increasing evidence that impulsivity has biological roots (Oquendo & Mann, 2000).

Cognitive Theories

Cognitive theorists have examined the beliefs and attitudes that may contribute to suicide. The cognitive variable that has most consistently predicted

TABLE 10.4	Concept Overview

Biological Theories of Suicide

Biological theories of suicide focus on genetic and biochemical factors that may increase the risk for suicide.

Theory	Description
Genetic theory	Disordered genes increase the risk for suicide.
Neurotransmitter theory	Deficiencies in serotonin lead to impulsive, violent, and suicidal behavior.

suicide is **hopelessness**—the sense that the future is bleak and there is no way of making it more positive (Beck et al., 1985). One group of researchers examined 207 patients who had been hospitalized while contemplating suicide and found that 89 of them expressed utter hopelessness about their futures. Over the next five years, 13 of these 89 hopeless patients committed suicide, compared with only 1 patient who had not expressed hopelessness (Beck et al., 1985). Joiner and colleagues (2005) suggest that hopeless feelings about being a burden on others and about never belonging with others are especially linked to suicidality. Hopelessness may also be one reason people who are suicidal often do not seek treatment.

In addition, some research suggests that people who attempt or commit suicide tend to be rigid in their thinking (Linehan et al., 1987). They engage in **dichotomous thinking**, seeing everything in either/or terms. This inflexibility makes it more difficult for them to consider alternative solutions to their situations or simply to hold out until the suicidal feelings pass.

Biological Theories of Suicide

Genetics and neurotransmitters have been the focus of biological theories of suicide risk (see the Concept Overview in Table 10.4).

Genetic Theory

Suicide runs in families. For example, one study found that the children of parents who had attempted suicide were six times more likely to attempt suicide than were the children of parents who had a mood disorder but had not attempted suicide (Brent et al., 2002, 2003). The study of the Old Order Amish mentioned in Chapters 3 and 9 found that almost three-quarters of the suicides occurring in this culture come from just four large families, all of which have high rates of mood disorders (Egeland & Sussex, 1985).

One extraordinary family that has been plagued by suicide is the Hemingways. Five members of this family, spread across four generations, have committed suicide. Acclaimed novelist Ernest Hemingway killed himself with a shotgun after two treatments with electroconvulsive therapy failed to heal his severe depression. His granddaughter Margaux killed herself with an overdose of barbiturates on the thirty-fifth anniversary of her grandfather's suicide. Margaux had suffered from bulimia and alcoholism. She had had a successful modeling career but, after a series of failed movie appearances, her career had begun to decline. Just before her death, Margaux was reduced to taking parts in low-budget pictures and making guest appearances at European conventions. She allowed the BBC to tape a therapy session in which she said, "There's so much inside, and . . . sometimes I'm afraid that it's so full that it might kill me" (Masters, 1996, p. 148).

Although some of this clustering of suicide within families may be due to environmental factors, such as family members' modeling each other or having common stressors, twin and adoption studies suggest that genetics are involved as well (Joiner et al., 2005). Twin studies estimate that the risk for suicide attempts increase by 5.6 times if one's monozygotic twin has attempted suicide, 4.0 times if one's dizygotic twin has attempted suicide (Glowinski et al., 2001; Joiner et al., 2005). Strong evidence of a genetic component of suicidality remains when researchers control for histories of psychiatric problems in the twins and their families, recent and past negative life events, the twins' closeness to each other socially, and personality factors.

Neurotransmitter Theory

Many studies have found a link between suicide and low levels of the neurotransmitter serotonin in the brain (Asberg & Forslund, 2000; Mann, Brent, & Arango, 2001). For example, postmortem studies of the brains of people who committed suicide find lower than average levels of serotonin (Gross-Isseroff et al., 1998). People with a family history of suicide or who have attempted suicide are more likely to have abnormalities on genes that regulate serotonin (Courtet et al., 2004; Joiner et al., 2005; Joiner, Johnson, & Soderstrom, 2002). People who attempt suicide who have low serotonin levels are 10 times more likely to make another suicide attempt than those with higher serotonin levels (Roy,

1992). Low serotonin levels are linked with suicidality even among people who are not depressed, suggesting that the connection between serotonin and suicidality is not due entirely to a common connection to depression.

Serotonin may generally be linked to impulsive and aggressive behavior (Courtet et al., 2004; Mann et al., 2001). Low serotonin levels are most strongly associated with impulsive and violent suicides. Although these pieces of evidence do not prove that low serotonin levels cause suicidal behavior, they suggest that people with low serotonin levels may be at high risk for impulsive and violent behavior that sometimes results in suicide.

SUMMING UP

- Suicide notes suggest that mental anguish and escape from pain are behind many suicides.

- Several negative life events or circumstances increase the risk for suicide, including economic hardship, serious illness, loss, and abuse.

- Durkheim distinguished among egoistic suicide, which is committed by people who feel alienated from others, empty of social contacts, and alone in an unsupportive world; anomic suicide, which is committed by people who experience severe disorientation because of a major change in their relationships to society; and altruistic suicide, which is committed by people who believe that taking their own lives will benefit society in some way.

- Suicide clusters occur when two or more suicides or attempted suicides are nonrandomly bunched in space or time. This phenomenon is also sometimes called suicide contagion.

- Psychodynamic theorists attribute suicide to repressed rage, which leads to self-destruction.

- Several mental disorders increase the risk for suicide, including depression, bipolar disorder, substance abuse, schizophrenia, and anxiety disorders.

- Cognitive theorists argue that hopelessness and dichotomous thinking contribute to suicide.

- Impulsivity is a behavioral characteristic common to many people who commit suicide.

- Family history, twin, and adoption studies all suggest there is a genetic vulnerability to suicide.

- Many studies have found a link between low serotonin levels and suicide.

The Hemingway family has experienced the suicides of five of its members, including Ernest and Margaux.

TREATING AND PREVENTING SUICIDAL TENDENCIES

A person who is gravely suicidal needs immediate care. In *Taking Psychology Personally: What to Do If a Friend Is Suicidal* on pae 368, we discuss useful tips. Sometimes, people require hospitalization to prevent an imminent suicide attempt. They may voluntarily agree to be hospitalized, but, if they do not agree, they can be hospitalized involuntarily for a short period of time (usually about three days). We discuss the pros and cons of involuntary hospitalization in Chapter 18.

Community-based **crisis intervention** programs are available to help people who are highly suicidal deal in the short term with their feelings and then refer them for longer care to mental-health specialists. Some crisis intervention is done over the phone, on **suicide hot lines.** Some communities have suicide prevention centers, which may be part of a larger mental-health system, or stand-alone clinics, where suicidal people can walk in and receive immediate care.

Crisis intervention aims to reduce the risk for an imminent suicide attempt by providing suicidal persons someone to talk with, someone who understands their feelings and problems. The counselor can help them mobilize support from family members and friends and can make a plan to deal with specific problem situations in the short term. The crisis intervention counselor may make a contract with the suicidal person that he or she will not attempt suicide, or at least will recontact the counselor as soon as the suicidal feelings return. The counselor will help the person identify other people he or she can turn to when panicked or overwhelmed. And the counselor will make follow-up appointments with the suicidal person or refer the person to another counselor for long-term treatment.

Taking Psychology Personally

What to Do If a Friend Is Suicidal

What should you do if you suspect that a friend or family member is suicidal? The National Depressive and Manic-Depressive Association (1996), a patient-run advocacy group, makes the following suggestions in *Suicide and Depressive Illness*:

- *Take the person seriously*. Although most people who express suicidal thoughts do not go on to attempt suicide, most people who do commit suicide communicate their suicidal intentions to friends or family members beforehand. Stay calm, but don't ignore the situation.

- *Get help*. Call the person's therapist, a suicide hot line, 911, or any other source of professional mental-health care.

- *Express concern*. Tell the person concretely why you think he or she is suicidal.

- *Pay attention*. Listen closely, maintain eye contact, and use body language to indicate that you are attending to everything the person says.

- *Ask direct questions about whether the person has a plan for suicide and, if so, what that plan is*. Many people fear that asking a person if he or she is thinking about suicide will give him or her the idea, but this is not the case.

- *Acknowledge the person's feelings in a nonjudgmental way*. For example, you might say something like "I know you're feeling really horrible right now, but I want to help you get through this" or "I can't begin to understand completely how you feel, but I want to help you."

- *Reassure the person that things can be better*. Emphasize that suicide is a permanent solution to a temporary problem.

- *Don't promise confidentiality*. You need the freedom to contact mental-health professionals and tell them precisely what is going on.

- *If possible, don't leave the person alone until he or she is in the hands of professionals*. Go with him or her to the emergency room, if need be. Then, once he or she has been hospitalized or has received other treatment, follow up to show you care.

- *Take care of yourself*. Interacting with a person who is suicidal can be an extremely stressful and disturbing experience. Talk with someone you trust about it—perhaps a friend, family member, or counselor—particularly if you worry about how you handled the situation or about finding yourself in that situation again.

People who receive longer-term treatment for suicidality typically receive psychotherapies and medications similar to those used to treat mood disorders. Preventive measures are taken with high-risk people who have not yet attempted suicide to try to reduce the risk for future attempts.

What is most clear from the literature on the treatment of suicidal people is that they are woefully undertreated. Most people who are suicidal never seek treatment (Crosby et al., 1999). Even when their families know they are suicidal, they may not be taken for treatment because of denial and a fear of the stigma of suicide. The people who do receive treatment typically receive inadequate care. One study of depressed people on an inpatient psychiatric ward found that less than a third of those with a history of suicide attempts were being adequately treated (Oquendo et al., 1999).

Drug Treatments

The medication most consistently shown to reduce the risk for suicide is *lithium*. Baldessarini, Tondo,

and Hennen (2001) reviewed 33 published treatment studies of people with major depression or bipolar disorder and found that those *not* treated with lithium were 13 times more likely to commit or attempt suicide than those who had been treated with lithium.

As noted in Chapter 9, however, many people have difficulty taking lithium, because of its side effects and toxicity. Most recently, studies have focused on the *selective serotonin reuptake inhibitors (SSRIs)*, such as Celexa, Prozac, Luvox, Zoloft, and Paxil, in the treatment of suicide risk. Some studies suggest that these drugs can reduce impulsive and violent behaviors in general, and suicidal behaviors specifically (see Gould, Greensberg, et al., 2003). Paradoxically, however, some studies suggest that the SSRIs can increase the risk for suicide in some people. It is not clear who is at most risk for this "side effect" of the SSRIs or when it is most likely to happen. This risk is just one of many reasons it is crucial for people taking psychotherapeutic drugs to be closely monitored by physicians with expertise in these drugs.

Antipsychotic medications can be used to treat psychotic symptoms in people with psychotic mood disorders or schizophrenia. Reducing psychotic symptoms may also reduce the risk for suicidality.

Psychological Treatments

The psychological therapies designed for depression, and described in Chapter 9, are most frequently used in the treatment of suicidality. Psychodynamic therapists focus more on exploring unexpressed anger at others, whereas cognitive therapists focus more on the client's hopelessness and dichotomous thinking, as well as on the environmental triggers for suicidal behavior (Henriques, Beck, & Brown, 2003).

Psychologist Marcia Linehan (1999) has developed a cognitive-behavioral intervention designed specifically to address suicidal behaviors and thoughts, which she calls **dialectical behavior therapy.** This therapy was originally developed to treat people with borderline personality disorder, whose moods and self-images have a tendency to swing between extremes (see Chapter 12). (The term *dialectical* in *dialectical behavior therapy* refers to this constant tension between conflicting images or emotions in people with borderline personality disorder.) Dialectical behavior therapy is somewhat like cognitive-behavioral therapy, but it focuses on difficulties in managing negative emotions and in controlling impulsive behaviors. The therapy involves a number of techniques aimed at increasing problem-solving skills, interpersonal skills, and skills in managing negative emotions. Studies comparing this therapy with control conditions suggest that it can reduce suicidal thoughts and behaviors, as well as improve interpersonal skills (Linehan, 1999; Linehan et al., 1991; Shearin & Linehan, 1989).

Therapists often include spouses, partners, and family members in the treatment of people who are suicidal. Some of the problems behind a suicide attempt may reside in troubled relationships and family environments. Even if this is not the case, family members can play a role in preventing future attempts by helping suicidal members recognize when they are vulnerable and actively seek professional help. Finally, suicidality in one member can devastate a family, and often the entire family is in need of psychological help.

Social Approaches and Prevention

Suicide hot lines and crisis intervention centers are forms of suicide prevention programs. They provide help to suicidal people in times of greatest

Psychotherapies for people at high risk for suicide help them identify times when they are vulnerable and develop more adaptive coping skills during these times.

need, hoping to prevent a suicidal act until suicidal feelings have passed.

In addition, many prevention programs aim to educate entire communities about suicide. Many of these programs are based in schools and colleges. Students are given information about the suicide rates in their age group, the risk factors for suicide, and what to do if they or a friend is suicidal.

Unfortunately, studies of the effects of broadly based prevention/education programs have suggested that they are not very helpful and, indeed, might cause harm (Gould, Greenberg, et al., 2003). One major problem with these programs is that they often simultaneously target both the general population of students and students who are at high risk for suicide. The programs may attempt to destigmatize suicide by making it appear quite common and by not mentioning that most suicidal people are suffering from a psychological disorder, in hopes that suicidal students will feel more free to seek help. But such messages can backfire among students who are not suicidal, making suicide seem to be an understandable response to stress. In addition, studies of school-based suicide prevention programs have found that adolescents who had made prior suicide attempts generally reacted negatively to the programs, saying they were less inclined to seek help after seeing the program than before they had seen the program (Gould, Greenberg, et al., 2003).

Recently, researchers have begun tailoring suicide prevention messages to specific populations, particularly high-risk populations, in hopes that the right kind of help will get to the most needy people. David Shaffer and colleagues at Columbia University have designed a program that involves screening adolescents for suicidality, doing a diagnostic interview with the adolescents with the help of a laptop computer, and then interviewing the adolescents to determine the most appropriate referral to a mental-health specialist (Shaffer & Gould, 2000). This program has shown success in identifying high-risk youth and getting them into effective treatment. A similar program for college students has been implemented at Emory University (Haas, Hendin, & Mann, 2003).

Guns and Suicide

In the United States, the majority of suicides, particularly those by men, involve guns (National Institute of Mental Health [NIMH], 2002). Most people who commit suicide by gun do not buy guns expressly to commit suicide. Instead, they use guns that have been in their households for sometime. Often, suicide with guns is an impulsive act committed by people under the influence of alcohol: They may be depressed, get drunk, and retrieve family handguns and shoot themselves. The risk for a suicide attempt with a gun is increased if there is a loaded, unlocked gun in the household (Conwell et al., 2002). Unfortunately, a gunshot to the head is highly likely to end in death, whether or not the person truly intended to commit suicide.

Can we reduce the number of such suicides by restricting people's access to guns? The answer may be yes. Several studies have found that suicide rates decrease when cities and states enact strict antigun legislation that limits people's access to guns (Lambert & Silva, 1998). For example, one study compared two similar metropolitan areas with different degrees of firearms restrictions and found that the urban area with less strict handgun laws had almost six times more suicides involving firearms than the urban area with stricter handgun laws (Sloan et al., 1990). Although people who are intent on committing suicide can find other means to do so if guns are not available, restricting ready access to guns appears to reduce impulsive suicides with guns, particularly among males. In addition, several studies suggest that there is no increase in suicides by means other than guns (e.g., by jumping off buildings or inhaling carbon monoxide) when access to guns is restricted, suggesting that people do not simply substitute different means of committing suicide when guns are not available (Lambert & Silva, 1998). Instead, the lack of availability of guns gives them a cooling off period, during which suicidal impulses can wane.

Opponents of gun control argue that restricting access to guns only makes people more vulnerable to intruders in their homes or to others wishing to do them harm. One study strongly suggests that

this is not the case, however. Researchers examined 398 consecutive deaths by gun in the homes of families who owned guns (usually handguns). Of these deaths, only 0.5 percent were intruders shot by families protecting themselves. In contrast, 83 percent of these deaths were suicides of adolescent or adult family members. Another 12 percent were homicides of one adult in the home by another family member, usually in the midst of quarrels. The final 3 percent of deaths were due to accidental gunshots of one of the family members (Kellermann et al., 1992). The mere presence of a firearm in the home appears to be a risk factor for suicide when other risk factors are taken into account, especially when handguns are improperly secured or are kept loaded (Brent et al., 1991). These data strongly suggest that removing guns from the home is an important preventive measure against suicide.

The "Right" to Commit Suicide

Many societies, including the United States, are currently debating whether people have a right to commit suicide. Some people, such as psychiatrist Thomas Szasz and physician Jack Kevorkian, argue that the right to die as one chooses and when one

Restricting access to guns appears to lower suicide rates.

chooses is a fundamental human right that cannot be regulated by the state. Others note that most people who attempt suicide but do not complete it do not later commit suicide, suggesting that they do not truly wish to die (Harwood et al., 2000). More generally, most people who contemplate suicide, particularly if they are depressed and not suffering from terminal medical illness, are ambivalent about it, and their suicidal wishes pass after relatively short periods of time. This information suggests that preventing suicide is appropriate, at least for people who have serious mental disorders, because many people who attempt suicide are not making rational or permanent choices.

Gender and Assisted Suicide

In most cases of suicide by the seriously ill, ill people kill themselves, but, in a substantial number of cases, they are killed by a medical professional or a family member or friend, an act sometimes referred to as "mercy killing." Although mercy killing, or **euthanasia,** is not legal in the United States, it is not uncommon. Surveys of medical professionals in the United States show that perhaps 20 percent or more have assisted in a patient's suicide or have hastened the death of a seriously ill patient, even without that patient's consent (Canetto & Hollenshead, 2000).

Studies conducted in the United States and Australia show that most mercy killings involve older married couples, with the husband killing his ill wife (Canetto & Hollenshead, 2000). This gender balance stands in stark contrast to the data showing that many more men than women commit suicide, especially among older people. Men may be more willing than women to kill, whether it be themselves or an ill family member. Men may also find it more intolerable to be caught in the caregiver role to an ill spouse than do women (Canetto & Hollenshead, 2000). Ill women are not only killed by their husbands but are also more likely than ill men to be the recipients of physician-assisted death (Canetto & Hollenshead, 1999).

It is not known why women are more likely than men to be assisted in suicide. Some researchers suggest that women's lives are less valued than men's, particularly once they are seriously, chronically ill. For this reason, family members and physicians may agree to assist women in killing themselves (Canetto & Hollenshead, 1999, 2000).

SUMMING UP

- Drug treatments for suicidality most often include lithium or antidepressant medications to reduce impulsive and violent behavior, depression, and mania. Antipsychotic medications and other medications that treat the symptoms of an existing mental disorder may also be used.

- The psychotherapies for suicide are similar to those used for depression. Dialectical behavior therapy has been specifically designed to address skill deficits and thinking patterns in people who are suicidal.

- Suicide hot lines and crisis intervention programs provide immediate help to people who are highly suicidal.

- Community prevention programs aim to educate the public about suicide and encourage suicidal people to enter treatment.

- Guns are involved in the majority of suicides, and some research suggests that restricting access to guns can reduce the number of suicide attempts.

- Society is debating whether people have a right to choose to commit suicide.

- Women are more likely than men to be assisted in suicide by a spouse or a physician.

CHAPTER INTEGRATION

Suicide seems to fit a diathesis-stress model (see Figure 10.5). Several factors seem to determine an individual's vulnerability to suicide, including a genetic vulnerability to suicide and possibly deficient serotonin levels. Other factors are early life experiences with loss and abuse and later life experiences with traumatic events. Hopeless and dichotomous thinking styles and impulsivity also can lower the threshold for suicidal behavior. And several psychological disorders clearly increase the

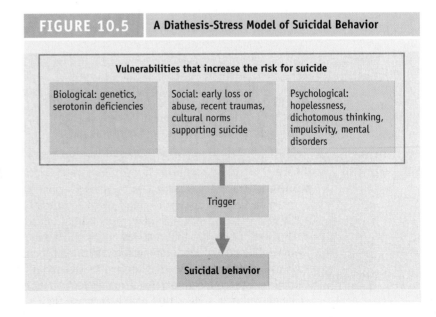

FIGURE 10.5   **A Diathesis-Stress Model of Suicidal Behavior**

risk for suicide. Many people carry these risk factors, however, and never become suicidal.

Something must trigger active suicidal behavior. These triggers also appear to be legion—the suicide of a close friend or relative, a recent traumatic event, and alcohol or other drug abuse. The difficulty in predicting suicidal behavior is that the specific trigger for one individual may be very different from the trigger for another. This is one reason that psychological treatments for suicidality have focused a great deal on helping people recognize when suicidal feelings are rising, learn what their personal triggers are, and develop more effective ways of coping with mood swings and transient suicidality, so that the trigger never gets fully pulled.

Extraordinary People: Follow-Up

What happened to William Styron, the author we met at the beginning of this chapter, who was seriously depressed and suicidal? Styron was hospitalized and, after seven weeks of antidepressant drugs and psychotherapy, overcame his depression.

What was the cause of Styron's depression? Styron speculates that he has always had a propensity for depression and anxiety. His father apparently suffered from depression, although it was never called depression back then. Styron's mother died when he was 13, and he believes this loss created a psychological vulnerability in him that compounded the genetic vulnerability to depression he may have inherited from his father. Forty years of alcohol abuse may have altered the workings of his neurotransmitter systems, but Styron also believes that he used alcohol to dampen his feelings of anxiety and depression all those years.

A few years after he emerged from his depression, Styron wrote *Darkness Visible*, a memoir of his descent into depression and suicide and his triumph over it. This book became a national best-seller, but not only because Styron was able to describe with great skill and poetry the deepest horrors of depression and suicidality. *Darkness Visible* also gives hope to those who suffer:

> For those who have dwelt on depression's dark wood, and known its inexplicable agony, their return from the abyss is not unlike the ascent of the poet, trudging upward and upward out of hell's black depths and at last emerging into what he saw as "the shining world." There, whoever has been restored to health has almost always been restored to the capacity for serenity and joy, and this may be indemnity enough for having endured the despair beyond despair. (Styron, 1990, p. 84)

Chapter Summary

- Suicide is defined as death from injury, poisoning, or suffocation when there is evidence (either explicit or implicit) that the injury was self-inflicted and that the decedent intended to kill him- or herself.

- Theorist Edwin Shneidman has described four types of suicide: Death seekers clearly seek to end their lives; death initiators also have a clear intention to die but believe that they are simply hastening an inevitable death; death ignorers intend to end their lives but do not believe that this means the end of their existence; death darers are ambivalent about dying and take actions that greatly increase their

chances of death but that do not guarantee they will die.

- Suicide is the eighth leading cause of death in the United States. There are substantial differences across ethnic groups within the United States, and across countries worldwide, in rates of suicide.

- Women are more likely than men to attempt suicide, but men are more likely than women to complete suicide. Cross-cultural differences in suicide rates may have to do with religious doctrines, stressors, and cultural norms about suicide. Young people are less likely than adults to commit suicide, but suicide rates have been rising dramatically for young people in recent decades. The elderly, particularly elderly men, are at high risk for suicide.

- Suicide notes suggest that mental anguish and escape from pain are behind many suicides. Generally, suicide notes are brief and concrete, however, and leave few clues.

- Several negative life events or circumstances increase the risk for suicide, including economic hardship, serious illness, loss, and abuse. (Review Table 10.2.)

- Durkheim distinguished among egoistic suicide, which is committed by people who feel alienated from others, empty of social contacts, and alone in an unsupportive world; anomic suicide, which is committed by people who experience severe disorientation because of a major change in their relationships to society; and altruistic suicide, which is committed by people who believe that taking their own lives will benefit society in some way.

- Suicide clusters (thought to be due to suicide contagion) occur when two or more suicides or attempted suicides are nonrandomly bunched in space or time.

- Psychodynamic theorists attribute suicide to repressed rage, which leads to self-destruction. Several mental disorders increase the risk for suicide, including depression, bipolar disorder, substance abuse, schizophrenia, and anxiety disorders. Cognitive theorists argue that hopelessness and dichotomous thinking contribute to suicide. Impulsivity is a behavioral characteristic common to people who commit suicide. (Review Table 10.3.)

- Family history, twin, and adoption studies all suggest there is a genetic vulnerability to suicide. Many studies have found a link between low serotonin levels and suicide. (Review Table 10.4.)

- Drug treatments for suicidality most often include lithium or antidepressant medications to reduce impulsive and violent behavior, depression, and mania. Antipsychotic medications and other medications that treat the symptoms of an existing mental disorder may also be used.

- The psychotherapies for suicide are similar to those used for depression. Dialectical behavior therapy has been specifically designed to address skill deficits and thinking patterns in people who are suicidal.

- Suicide hot lines and crisis intervention programs provide immediate help to people who are highly suicidal. Community prevention programs aim to educate the public about suicide and encourage suicidal people to enter treatment.

- Guns are involved in the majority of suicides, and some research suggests that restricting access to guns can reduce the number of suicide attempts. Society is debating whether people have a right to choose to commit suicide. Women are more likely than men to be assisted in suicide by a spouse or a physician.

- Suicide seems to fit a diathesis-stress model. Various biological, psychological, and social factors can contribute to a person's vulnerability to suicide, and events or circumstances can trigger suicidal behavior. (Review Figure 10.5.)

MindMap CD-ROM

The following resources on the MindMap CD-ROM that came with this text will help you to master the content of this chapter and prepare for tests:

- Chapter Quiz

Key Terms

suicide 353

death seekers 353

death initiators 354

death ignorers 354

death darers 354

subintentional deaths 354

egoistic suicide 362

anomic suicide 362

altruistic suicide 362

suicide cluster 363

suicide contagion 363

impulsivity 365

hopelessness 366

dichotomous thinking 366

crisis intervention 367

suicide hot lines 367

dialectical behavior therapy 369

euthanasia 371

Chapter 11

My Dog and I Are One
by Patricia Schwimmer

Whom Fortune wishes to destroy she first makes mad.

—Publilius Syrus, *Moral Sayings*
(first century B.C.; translated by Darius Lyman)

Schizophrenia <

Extraordinary People

■ John Nash: *A Beautiful Mind*

Taking Psychology Personally

■ Helping Families Cope with Schizophrenia

Symptoms, Diagnosis, and Prognosis of Schizophrenia

People with schizophrenia have delusions (beliefs with little grounding in reality), hallucinations (unreal perceptual experiences, such as hearing voices), and disorganized thought, speech, and behavior. Their motivation, affective responses, and quality of communication can also be unusual. Four types of schizophrenia have been identified: paranoid, disorganized, catatonic, and undifferentiated.

Biological Theories of Schizophrenia

There is strong evidence that schizophrenia is transmitted genetically. People with schizophrenia show abnormalities in several areas of the brain, including the prefrontal cortex, ventricles, and hippocampus. A number of prenatal difficulties and obstetrical problems at birth are implicated in the development of schizophrenia, including prenatal hypoxia and exposure to the influenza virus during the second trimester of gestation. Imbalances in the neurotransmitters dopamine, serotonin, glutamate, and GABA are also implicated in schizophrenia.

Psychosocial Perspectives on Schizophrenia

A variety of stressors may worsen the course of schizophrenia. Early psychodynamic theorists suggested that schizophrenia resulted from overwhelmingly negative experiences in early childhood with primary caregivers. More recent theories have focused on the aspects of family life that may increase stress and relapse in schizophrenia. Behavioral theories suggest that the symptoms of schizophrenia can develop through operant conditioning. Cognitive theories accept that there is a biological vulnerability to schizophrenia but see many symptoms as attempts to understand and cope with basic perceptual and attentional problems.

Treatments for Schizophrenia

Drugs called neuroleptics have proven useful in the treatment of schizophrenia; however, they have significant neurological side effects. Newer drugs, known as atypical antipsychotics, appear to be effective without inducing as many side effects as previous drugs. Psychosocial therapies focus on teaching communication and living skills and reducing isolation in people with schizophrenia.

Chapter Integration

There is compelling evidence that the fundamental vulnerability to schizophrenia is a biological one, yet there is also a growing consensus that psychosocial factors contribute to the risk for schizophrenia among people with the biological vulnerability. Theorists are increasingly developing models that integrate the biological and psychosocial factors. The most effective therapies for schizophrenia address both the biological and the psychosocial contributors to the disorder.

Extraordinary People

John Nash: *A Beautiful Mind*

In 1959, at the age of 30, John Nash was widely regarded as one of the premier mathematical minds of his generation. As a young professor at the Massachusetts Institute of Technology, he was tackling mathematical problems others thought were impossible to solve, and solving them with unconventional but highly successful approaches. While still a graduate student at Princeton, he had introduced the notion of equilibrium to game theory, which would eventually revolutionize the field of economics and win him the Nobel Prize.

As writer Sylvia Nasar details in her biography of John Nash, called *A Beautiful Mind*, Nash had always been flamboyant and eccentric, with few social skills and little emotional connection to other people. In 1959, however, Nash's wife noticed a change in his behavior. He became increasingly distant and cold to her, and his behavior grew more and more bizarre:

> Several times, Nash had cornered her with odd questions when they were alone, either at home or driving in the car. "Why don't you tell me about it?" he asked in an angry, agitated tone, apropos of nothing. "Tell me what you know," he demanded. (Nasar, 1998, p. 248)

Nash began writing letters to the United Nations, the FBI, and other government agencies, complaining of conspiracies to take over the world. He also began talking openly about his beliefs that powers from outer space, or perhaps from foreign governments, were communicating with him through the front page of the *New York Times*. Nash gave a series of lectures at Columbia and Yale Universities that were totally incoherent. Nash states,

> I got the impression that other people at MIT were wearing red neckties so I would notice them. As I became more and more delusional, not only persons at MIT but people in Boston wearing red neckties [would seem significant to me]. . . . [There was some relation to] a crypto-communist part. (Nasar, 1998, p. 242)

Nash's wife, Alicia, had him committed to McLean Hospital in April 1959 after his threats to harm her became more severe and as his behavior became increasingly unpredictable. There, Nash was diagnosed as having paranoid schizophrenia and was given medication and daily psychoanalytic therapy.

His behavior calmed. Nash spent much of his time with poet Robert Lowell, who suffered from manic-depression and was hospitalized for the fifth time in 10 years with severe mania. Nash learned to hide his delusions and hallucinations and to behave completely rationally, although his inner world remained much the same as it had been before the hospitalization. After 50 days of confinement, a week after the birth of his first son, Nash was released. On his release, Nash resigned from MIT, furious that the institution had "conspired" in his commitment to McLean Hospital. He withdrew his pension fund and sailed to Europe, vowing never to return.

In Geneva, Nash tried to renounce his American citizenship and eventually destroyed his passport. After being deported from Geneva and Paris, Nash ended up in Princeton two years later, still suffering from the acute symptoms of his schizophrenia. He walked up and down the streets of Princeton with a fixed expression and dead gaze, wearing Russian peasant garments and going into restaurants with bare feet. He talked in lofty terms of world peace and made it clear that he was intimately involved in the development of a world government. He wrote endless letters and made many phone calls to friends and eminaries around the world, talking of numerology and world affairs.

Various people—university officials, psychiatrists, friends—began to urge Alicia to have him committed again. This time, Alicia could not afford a private hospital, and Nash ended up in Trenton State Hospital. Nash was assigned a serial number, as if he were a prison inmate, and shared a room with 30 or 40 other patients. The nearly 600 patients in Nash's section of Trenton State were cared for by just 6 psychiatrists. At Trenton State, Nash was given insulin shock therapy, which was a popular treatment for schizophrenia in the early 1960s but is now discredited. Nonetheless, after six weeks, Nash was considered much improved and was moved to another ward of the hospital. There, he began to work on a paper on fluid dynamics. After six months of hospitalization, a month after his thirty-third birthday, he was discharged. Nash appeared to be well for sometime, but then his thinking, speech, and behavior began to slip again. Eventually, he ended up living with his mother in Roanoke, Virginia.

His daily rounds extended no farther than the library or the shops at the end of Grandin Road in Roanoke, but, in his own mind, he traveled to the remotest reaches of the globe: Cairo, Zebak, Kabul, Bangui, Thebes, Guyana, Mongolia. In these faraway places, he lived in refugee camps, foreign embassies, prisons, and bomb shelters. At other times, he felt that he was inhabiting an Inferno, a purgatory, or a polluted heaven ("a decayed rotting house infested by rats and termites and other vermin"). His identities were like the skins of an onion. Underneath each one lurked another: He was C.O.R.P.S.E. (a Palestinian refugee), a great Japanese shogun, C1423, Esau, L'homme d'Or, Chin Hsiang, Job, Jorap Castro, Janos Norses, and even at times a mouse (Nasar, 1998).

After his mother died, Nash returned to Princeton and lived with Alicia, who had long since divorced him. Nonetheless, she felt some responsibility for him and provided him with as much support as she could muster. There, Nash finally came to know his son. Nash also slowly reintegrated into the world of mathematics at Princeton.

Most of us walk around so secure in our perceptions of the world that we would never think to ask whether those perceptions were real or not. We look at a chair, recognize it as an object for sitting in, and use it accordingly. We hear a friend call our name and look for that friend, confident that he or she is somewhere nearby. We have an idea, realize that if others are going to appreciate that idea we have to communicate it to them, and articulate the idea clearly enough for them to understand it.

What must it be like to walk around not knowing whether your perceptions map onto reality, as did John Nash during the acute phases of his illness? You might question whether the things you see before you really exist. You might wonder if the voices you are hearing come from other people or are only in your head. You might believe that the ideas you are having are being broadcast over the television, so that others already know what you are thinking. If you are unable to tell the difference between what is real and what is unreal, you are suffering from **psychosis.**

Psychosis can take many forms and has many causes. In Chapter 9, we noted that people who suffer mood disorders can become psychotic and have hallucinations and delusions that are horribly depressing or wildly grandiose in content. In addition, the DSM-IV-TR recognizes a number of disorders in which psychosis is the primary feature (see the DSM-IV-TR information in Table 11.1 on page 378).

One of the most common psychotic disorders is **schizophrenia,** a truly puzzling disorder. At times, people with schizophrenia think and communicate clearly, have an accurate view of reality, and function well in daily life. At other times, their thinking and speech are garbled, they lose touch with reality, and they are not able to care for themselves in even the most basic ways.

Schizophrenia exacts heavy costs. There are medical costs: Over 90 percent of people with schizophrenia seek treatment in a mental-health facility or general medicine facility in any given year (Narrow et al., 1993). Studies have estimated that direct medical care alone for people with schizophrenia costs almost $20 billion per year in the United States (Torrey, 1995). Tens of billions of dollars more are lost in productivity. Most people who develop schizophrenia do so in the late teenage or early adult years. By then, they have been educated and are ready to assume their place in society, contributing their unique talents. Then the disorder strikes, often preventing them from making their contributions. Instead, people with schizophrenia may need continual services, including placement in halfway houses and other residential care facilities, rehabilitative therapy, subsidized income, and the help of social workers to obtain needed resources. And they need these

TABLE 11.1   DSM-IV-TR

Psychotic Disorders in the DSM-IV-TR

The DSM-IV-TR recognizes a number of psychotic disorders as well as schizophrenia. In addition, depression and bipolar disorder can include psychotic symptoms, as discussed in Chapter 9.

Disorder	Description
Schizophrenia	At least one month of acute symptoms of delusions, hallucinations, disorganized thought and speech, disorganized behavior, and negative symptoms and at least six months of some symptoms of disorder
Schizophreniform disorder	Same symptoms as schizophrenia, lasting more than one month but less than six months
Schizoaffective disorder	Symptoms of schizophrenia coinciding with symptoms of depression or mania, but at least a two-week period when only symptoms of schizophrenia present
Delusional disorder	Evidence only of nonbizarre delusions (e.g., that one is being followed or deceived) of at least one month's duration; functioning at relatively high level
Brief psychotic disorder	Presence of delusions, hallucinations, disorganized speech or behavior for at least one day but less than one month
Shared psychotic disorder	The individual in a close relationship with someone who is delusional with similar delusions (also known as *folie à deux*)
Substance-induced psychotic disorder	Hallucinations or delusions caused by the direct physiological effects of a substance (such as cocaine)

Source: Reprinted with permission from the *Diagnostic and Statistical Manual of Mental Disorders,* Fourth Edition, Text Revision. Copyright © 2000 American Psychiatric Association.

services for the rest of their lives, because schizophrenia tends to be a lifelong disorder. Author Greg Bottoms (2000, pp. 63–64) describes his brother Michael's descent into schizophrenia:

VOICES

Michael's decline, both mentally and physically, was astonishingly fast. He had gone from being a decent student and an amazing athlete to failing everything in the space of four years; he had gone from being a black belt in karate—lithe, aggressive, handsome—to being a disheveled, Bible-toting one-man show in less than one year. The rapidity of his decline once he hit twenty—particularly the physical decline—caught us all off guard. His poor marks in school had nothing to do with aptitude, but rather with his shifting of focus. He had a mission in life and little time to pursue other things, even if people insisted these things—school, a job, friends—were important.

His body softened dramatically, his hygiene could produce a gag reflex. Where he had once been inordinately handsome, he now had smears of blackheads across his nose, a double chin, greasy hair. . . . He started smoking three packs of Camels a day, sometimes rocked back and forth uncontrollably in the school smoking section during lunch, looking up through his long bangs at the other dopers to tell them that Jesus loved them. . . . He never slept—or if he did, it was maybe an hour or two at a time. . . . Sometimes he'd scream in the middle of the night.

In the United States, 1 to 2 percent of the population will develop schizophrenia at sometime in their lives (Walker et al., 2004). Similarly, studies across the globe find that between 0.5 and 2 percent of the general population suffers with schizophrenia (Gottesman, 1991; Jablensky, 2000). Unfortunately, schizophrenia is one of the most stigmatized psychological disorders, and people have become experts at hiding away loved ones with this disorder. As E. Fuller Torrey, a schizophrenia expert, has said, "People with schizophrenia are the lepers of the twentieth century" (Torrey, 1995, p. 8).

Torrey compiled data from several sources to estimate where people with schizophrenia are being kept, and his estimates are given in Figure 11.1. Note that the majority of people with schizophrenia are living independently or in their family's home. *Taking Psychology Personally: Helping Families Cope with Schizophrenia* highlights the challenges that families of people with schizophrenia face in coping with their loved one's disorder, particularly when that loved one lives at home. Note also in Figure 11.1 that almost as many people with schizophrenia are in jails, prisons, and homeless shelters and on the street as are in hospitals and nursing homes. The criminal system and the shelters are often the repositories for people with schizophrenia who do not have families to support them or the resources to get psychiatric help.

There are differences across groups within the United States in rates of schizophrenia. One large epidemiological study found the highest rates of schizophrenia in African Americans, somewhat lower rates in European Americans, and the lowest rates in Hispanic Americans, although these ethnic differences diminished when socioeconomic status was taken into account (Escobar, 1993). Studies of persons hospitalized for serious mental disorders have found that African Americans are more likely than other groups to be misdiagnosed with schizophrenia, when they are actually suffering from a severe mood disorder (Arnold et al., 2004; Neighbors et al., 2003).

Schizophrenia may be more common in men than in women, although the gender difference in rates of schizophrenia varies among studies and with the criteria used to diagnose schizophrenia (Cannon et al., 1998; Goldstein et al., 2002). Women with schizophrenia tend to have better premorbid (predisorder) histories than men (Goldstein & Lewine, 2000; Jablensky, 2000). They are more likely to have graduated from high school or college, to have married and had children, and to have developed good social skills. This may be, in part, because the onset of schizophrenia in women tends to be later in life, often in the late twenties or early thirties, than for men, who more often develop schizophrenia in their late teens or early twenties (Goldstein & Lewine, 2000). Women also show fewer cognitive deficits than men, particularly in verbal processing (Goldstein et al., 2002).

The reasons for these gender differences in the age of onset, course, and cognitive deficits in

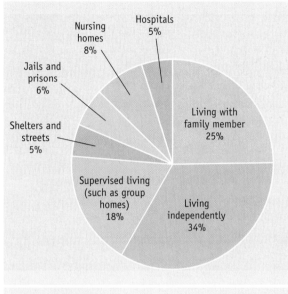

FIGURE 11.1 **Distribution of People with Schizophrenia.** Most people with schizophrenia live with family members or independently, but a number are in hospitals, in nursing homes, in group homes, in jail, or on the street.

Source: Torrey, 2001.

schizophrenia are not well understood yet. Estrogen may affect the regulation of dopamine, a neurotransmitter implicated in schizophrenia, in ways that are protective for women. Some of the sex differences, particularly in cognitive deficits, may also be due to normal sexual differences in the brain (Goldstein et al., 2002). The pace of prenatal brain development, which is hormonally regulated, is slower in males than in females and may place males at higher risk than females for brain insults. Exposure to a wide variety of toxins and illnesses in utero increases the risk for abnormal brain development and the development of schizophrenia. Several studies suggest that males with schizophrenia show greater abnormalities in brain structure and functioning than females with schizophrenia (Goldstein & Lewine, 2000).

In this chapter, we first consider the symptoms of schizophrenia and the various forms that schizophrenia can take. After reviewing the prognosis of schizophrenia, we examine its causes. Most theorists view schizophrenia primarily as a biological disorder, but psychological and social factors can influence how severe this disorder becomes and how often an individual has relapses. Effective biological treatments for schizophrenia have been developed in the past 50 years, as we will learn. These biological treatments are often supplemented

Taking Psychology Personally

Helping Families Cope with Schizophrenia

The anguish and confusion of family members who learn that a loved one has been diagnosed with schizophrenia can be huge. Before their eyes, a son, daughter, or sibling who once was full of hope and plans for the future has disintegrated into a being whom they may hardly recognize. The opportunities for blame are many—blaming each other for causing the disorder, blaming the afflicted family member for his or her symptoms, blaming mental-health professionals for not being able to cure the disorder, and blaming themselves. On top of this, families are now being asked to bear the brunt of the care for their members with schizophrenia, acting as psychotherapist, medication specialist, caretaker, rehabilitator, intermediary with the mental-health system, and unconditional emotional support system. It is no wonder that burnout and despair are common among these families.

One advocate on behalf of these families is E. Fuller Torrey. A very personal and painful experience led Torrey to psychiatry and the study of schizophrenia. While Torrey was an undergraduate, his sister, then 17, was diagnosed with schizophrenia. Torrey accompanied his mother and sister to a treatment facility and was appalled at the explanations and treatments offered for her illness. As he pursued a career in medicine, Torrey dedicated himself to finding better explanations and treatments for schizophrenia than those that had been offered to his sister, as well as to improving the treatment of people with serious mental disorders.

One of Torrey's books, *Surviving Schizophrenia* (1995), helps the families of people with schizophrenia understand the disorder and find appropriate treatment for their afflicted family members. This book educates family members on what schizophrenia is and is not, and it includes many specific tips on how to live with the schizophrenic family member and cope with the disorder. The key to surviving schizophrenia, according to Torrey, is having a "SAFE" attitude: a Sense of humor, an Acceptance of the illness, Family balance, and Expectations that are realistic.

Sense of Humor

It may seem strange to think that family members can approach schizophrenia with a sense of humor, but Torrey argues that the families most successful at managing schizophrenia maintain a sense of humor and an appreciation for the absurd. Family members cannot laugh *at* the person with schizophrenia, but they can laugh *with* him or her. For example, one family in which the son typically relapsed in the autumn and required hospitalization had a standing family joke that the son always carved his pumpkins in the hospital.

Acceptance of the Illness

Acceptance of the illness does not mean giving up but, rather, accepting the reality that the disorder will not go away, is likely to place limitations on the family member, and will need active management by the family. Unfortunately, it is more

---

by psychological and social therapies that help people with schizophrenia cope with the impact of the disorder on their lives, and we discuss those as well. We end this chapter considering theoretical perspectives and treatments that integrate knowledge of the biological and psychosocial contributors to schizophrenia.

SYMPTOMS, DIAGNOSIS, AND PROGNOSIS OF SCHIZOPHRENIA

Schizophrenia is a complex disorder that can take many forms. Indeed, many researchers and clinicians talk about "the schizophrenias," reflecting their belief that several types of schizophrenia are currently captured by the diagnostic criteria for schizophrenia.

Symptoms

There are two categories of symptoms. **Positive symptoms,** also called *Type I symptoms,* are characterized by the presence of unusual perceptions, thoughts, or behaviors. *Positive* refers to the fact that these symptoms represent very salient experiences. In contrast, **negative symptoms,** or *Type II symptoms,* represent losses or deficits in certain domains. They involve the absence of behaviors, rather than the presence of behaviors. People with schizophrenia may also suffer with depression, anxiety, substance abuse, inappropriate affect, anhedonia, and impaired social skills.

Positive Symptoms

The positive, or Type I, symptoms of schizophrenia include delusions, hallucinations, disorganized thought and speech, and disorganized or catatonic

Taking Psychology Personally (*continued*)

common for families to be angry at themselves, at the afflicted family member, at God, and so on. Their anger can be overtly expressed, or it can seethe quietly until a trigger causes a family member to explode. Educating family members about the illness and what they can reasonably expect is one of the most important jobs of mental-health professionals, because it can be the foundation of acceptance.

Family Balance

Caring for a family member with schizophrenia can be overwhelming. Some families put the needs of their member with schizophrenia before those of all the rest. Such families are prone to burnout, and neglected family members can become resentful and hostile. Families must achieve a balance of concern for the afflicted member and appreciation for the needs of the other family members. Caregivers may need to get away occasionally and to find resources, so that they are not providing round-the-clock care and ignoring their own needs.

Expectations That Are Realistic

It can be especially difficult for families to have realistic expectations of their family member with schizophrenia if that person had a particularly promising future before the illness struck. Pressure put on that family member may help trigger new episodes of acute symptoms. Lowering expectations can help family members appreciate the member with schizophre-

nia for who he or she is now, rather than focusing on what they wish were true:

> Several relatives mentioned that giving up hope had paradoxically been the turning point for them in coming to terms with their unhappiness. "Once you give up hope," one mother said, "you start to perk up." "Once you realise he'll never be cured you start to relax." These relatives had lowered their expectations and aspirations for the patient, and had found that doing this had been the first step in cutting the problem down to manageable size. (Creer & Wing, 1974, p. 33)

Clearly, family members should not abandon all expectations of the person with schizophrenia. What is important is having realistic expectations. Again, educating the family about the disease is critical to creating such expectations.

Some family members find that becoming politically active on behalf of people with schizophrenia helps them cope. The National Alliance for the Mentally Ill (NAMI) is the largest national organization focusing on serious mental disorders, including schizophrenia. NAMI was created and is run by consumers (people with disorders) and their families to advocate for more research, better health care and access to health care, and public education. It also runs support groups and educational courses for people with schizophrenia and their families. Many communities have local chapters of NAMI, which can usually be found in the phone book and at **www.nami.org.**

behavior (see the Concept Overview in Table 11.2 on page 382). These symptoms can occur in other disorders, particularly in depression and bipolar disorder (see Chapter 9). On the other hand, many people with schizophrenia are also depressed or show tremendous mood swings. This can make the differentiation between schizophrenia and a mood disorder with psychotic features very tricky. If psychotic symptoms occur only during periods of clear depression or mania, then the most appropriate diagnosis is mood disorder with psychotic features. If psychotic symptoms occur substantially in the absence of depression or mania, or if the depression or mania does not meet the criteria for a diagnosis of a mood disorder, then the appropriate diagnosis is schizophrenia or schizoaffective disorder (review Table 11.1).

Delusions **Delusions** are ideas that an individual believes are true but are highly unlikely and often simply impossible. Of course, most people occasionally hold beliefs that are likely to be wrong, such as the belief that they will win the lottery. These kinds of *self-deceptions* differ from delusions in at least three ways (Strauss, 1969). First, self-deceptions are not completely implausible, whereas delusions often are. It is possible, if highly unlikely, to win the lottery, but it is not possible that one's body is dissolving and floating into space. Second, people harboring self-deceptions may think about these beliefs occasionally, but people harboring delusions tend to be preoccupied with them. Delusional people look for evidence in support of their beliefs, attempt to convince others of these beliefs, and take actions based on them, such as filing

TABLE 11.2	Concept Overview

Positive Symptoms of Schizophrenia

The positive symptoms of schizophrenia represent the presence of unusual perceptions, thoughts, or behaviors.

Symptom	Definition and Example
Delusions	Beliefs with little grounding in reality (e.g., beliefs that one is being persecuted or that one is the Messiah)
Hallucinations	Unreal perceptual or sensory experiences (e.g., hearing, seeing, and feeling things that are not there)
Disorganized thought and speech	Grossly disorganized patterns of speech (e.g., complete incoherence, linking together of words based on sounds instead of meaning)
Disorganized or catatonic behavior	Behavior that is highly unpredictable, is bizarre, and/or shows a complete lack of responsiveness to the outside world (e.g., complete motionlessness for long periods; sudden, untriggered outbursts)

Source: Reprinted with permission from the *Diagnostic and Statistical Manual of Mental Disorders*, Fourth Edition, Text Revision. Copyright © 2000 American Psychiatric Association.

lawsuits against the people they believe are trying to control their minds. Third, people holding self-deceptions typically acknowledge that their beliefs may be wrong, but people holding delusions are often highly resistant to arguments or compelling facts contradicting their delusions. They may view others' arguments against their beliefs as a conspiracy to silence them and as evidence for the truth of their beliefs.

Table 11.3 lists some of the most common types of delusions. A **persecutory delusion** is the type of delusion we hear about most often in media depictions of people with schizophrenia and, indeed, is the most common form. People with persecutory delusions may believe they are being watched or tormented by people they know, such as their professors, or by agencies or persons in authority with whom they have never had direct contact, such as the FBI or a particular congressperson.

Another common type of delusion, the **delusion of reference,** in which people believe that random events or comments by others are directed at them, is related to persecutory delusion. People with delusions of reference may believe that the newscaster on the local television news is reporting on their movements or that the comments of a local politician at a rally are directed at them. John Nash believed that people in Boston were wearing red neckties so he would notice them as part of a crypto-communist plot. Sometimes, delusions of reference are part of a grandiose belief system in which all events are meaningful to the believer. For example, one person with schizophre-

nia was lying in bed, feeling cold and shivering, when a small earthquake occurred near his house. He believed that he had caused the earthquake with his shivering.

Grandiose delusions are beliefs that one is a special person or being or possesses special powers. A person may believe that she is a deity incarnated. She may believe she is the most intelligent, insightful, and creative person on earth or that she has discovered the cure for a disease.

Another common type of delusion is a **delusion of thought insertion,** the belief that one's thoughts are being controlled by outside forces, as the following person with schizophrenia describes:

VOICES

"Suggestions" or "commands" are being transmitted (by a parapsychologist) straight into an unknowing victim's hearing-center, becoming strong impressions on his mind. Those "voices" (which are sometimes accompanied by melodious tones and sounds that either please or irritate the mind) will subliminally change his personality by controlling what kinds of suggestions go into his "subconscious memory" to govern how he feels, or mind-boggle him (trick his mind into believing that they are its own thoughts) during these brainwash and thought-control techniques. Psy-

(continued)

TABLE 11.3   Types of Delusions

These are some types of delusions that are often woven together in a complex and frightening system of beliefs.

Delusion	Definition	Example
Persecutory delusion	False belief that oneself or one's loved ones are being persecuted, watched, or conspired against by others	Belief that the CIA, FBI, and local police are conspiring to catch you in a "sting" operation
Delusion of reference	Belief that random events are directed at oneself	Belief that a newscaster is reporting on your movements
Grandiose delusion	False belief that one has great power, knowledge, or talent or that one is a famous and powerful person	Belief that you are Martin Luther King, Jr., reincarnated
Delusions of being controlled	Beliefs that one's thoughts, feelings, or behaviors are being imposed or controlled by an external force	Belief that an alien has taken over your body and is controlling your behavior
Thought broadcasting	Belief that one's thoughts are being broadcast from one's mind for others to hear	Belief that your thoughts are being transmitted via the Internet against your will
Thought insertion	Belief that another person or object is inserting thoughts into one's head	Belief that your spouse is inserting blasphemous thoughts into your mind through the microwave
Thought withdrawal	Belief that thoughts are being removed from one's head by another person or an object	Belief that your roommate is stealing all your thoughts while you sleep
Delusion of guilt or sin	False belief that one has committed a terrible act or is responsible for a terrible event	Belief that you have killed someone
Somatic delusion	False belief that one's appearance or part of one's body is diseased or altered	Belief that your intestines have been replaced by snakes

chotropic medications are given to the victims who can "discern the voices" over other sounds in order to keep them ignorant to the real truth about their dilemma, and to enhance the chemical-reaction in the brain to the stimulation as their souls: (minds): are enslaved by computers programmed to "think" for them here in George Orwell's America.

Delusional beliefs can be simple and transient, such as when a person with schizophrenia believes the pain he just experienced in his stomach is the result of someone across the room shooting a laser beam at him. Delusional beliefs are often complex and elaborate, however, and the person clings to these beliefs for long periods. The following account illustrates how several types of delusions— grandiose delusions, persecutory delusions, delusions of reference, and delusions of thought control—can co-occur and work together in one person's belief system. Note that, although the following passage is written by a person with schizo-

phrenia about his own experience, he speaks of himself in the third person (Zelt, 1981, pp. 527–531).

VOICES

A drama that profoundly transformed David Zelt began at a conference on human psychology. David respected the speakers as scholars and wanted their approval of a paper he had written about telepathy. A week before the conference, David had sent his paper "On the Origins of Telepathy" to one speaker, and the other speakers had all read it. He proposed the novel scientific idea that telepathy could only be optimally studied during the process of birth. . . .

David's paper was viewed as a monumental contribution to the conference and potentially to psychology in general. If scientifically verified, his concept of telepathy, universally present at birth and measurable, might have

(continued)

as much influence as the basic ideas of Darwin and Freud. Each speaker focused on David. By using allusions and nonverbal communications that included pointing and glancing, each illuminated different aspects of David's contribution. Although his name was never mentioned, the speakers enticed David into feeling that he had accomplished something supernatural in writing the paper. . . . David was described as having a halo around his head, and the Second Coming was announced as forthcoming. Messianic feelings took hold of him. His mission would be to aid the poor and needy, especially in underdeveloped countries. . . .

David's sensitivity to nonverbal communication was extreme; he was adept at reading people's minds. His perceptual powers were so developed that he could not discriminate between telepathic reception and spoken language by others. He was distracted by others in a way that he had never been before. It was as if the nonverbal behavior of people interacting with him was a kind of code. Facial expressions, gestures, and postures of others often determined what he felt and thought.

Several hundred people at the conference were talking about David. He was the subject of enormous mystery, profound in his silence. Criticism, though, was often expressed by skeptics of the anticipated Second Coming. David felt the intense communication about him as torturous. He wished the talking, nonverbal behavior, and pervasive train of thoughts about him would stop.

content of delusions may differ across cultures (Suhail & Cochrane, 2002; Tateyama et al., 1998). For example, persecutory delusions often focus on intelligence agencies or persons of authority in the person's culture. Urban European Americans might fear that the Central Intelligence Agency is after them; Afro Caribbeans may believe that people are killing them with curses (Westermeyer, 1993; for similar results comparing British and Pakistani patients, see Suhail & Cochrane, 2002). Studies comparing Japanese people who have schizophrenia with people in Western Europe who have schizophrenia have found that, among the Japanese, delusions of being slandered by others and delusions that others know something terrible about them are relatively common, perhaps due to the emphasis in Japanese culture on how one is thought of by others. In contrast, among German and Austrian people with schizophrenia, religious delusions of having committed a sin (e.g., "Satan orders me to pray to him; I will be punished") are relatively common, perhaps due to the influence of Christianity in Western Europe (Tateyama et al., 1993).

Some theorists argue that odd or impossible beliefs that are part of a culture's shared belief system cannot be considered delusions when these beliefs are held by individuals in that culture (Fabrega, 1993). For example, if the people of a culture believe that the spirits of dead relatives watch over the living, then individuals in that culture who hold that belief are not considered delusional, although people in other cultures might consider such a belief untrue and impossible. However, even theorists who hold cultural relativist positions on delusions tend to view people who hold extreme manifestations of their culture's shared belief systems as delusional. For example, a person who believed that her dead relatives were tor-

David's *grandiose delusions* were that he had discovered the source of telepathy, that all the scientists thought highly of him, and that he might be the Messiah. As is often the case, these grandiose delusions were accompanied by *persecutory delusions*—that the scientists were criticizing him because they were jealous. David's delusions of reference were that all the scientists were talking about him, directly and indirectly. David believed that he could read others' minds. Finally, he had *delusions of being controlled,* that the scientists were determining what he felt with their facial expressions, gestures, and postures.

Although the types of delusions we have discussed probably occur in all cultures, the specific

The specific content of hallucinations and delusions may be influenced by culture.

menting her by causing her heart and lungs to rot would be considered delusional, even if she were part of a culture that holds the belief that dead relatives watch over the living.

Hallucinations Have you ever had a strange perceptual experience, such as thinking you saw someone when no one was near, thinking you heard a voice talking to you, or feeling as though your body were floating through the air? If so, you are not alone. One study found that 15 percent of mentally healthy college students report sometimes hearing voices, such as the voice of God telling them to do something, their "conscience" giving them advice, or two voices (usually both their own) debating a topic (Chapman, Edell, & Chapman, 1980). Six percent of students believe they have transmitted thoughts into other people's heads. Most of these students probably would not be diagnosed with schizophrenia because their "hallucinations" were occasional and brief; often occurred when they were tired, stressed, or under the influence of alcohol or other drugs; and did not impair their daily functioning in any way.

The **hallucinations**—unreal perceptual experiences—of people with schizophrenia tend to be much more bizarre and troubling than college students' hallucinations and are precipitated not only by sleep deprivation, stress, or drugs, as this person describes (Long, 1996):

> **VOICES**
> At one point, I would look at my coworkers and their faces would become distorted. Their teeth looked like fangs ready to devour me. Most of the time I couldn't trust myself to look at anyone for fear of being swallowed. I had no respite from the illness. Even when I tried to sleep, the demons would keep me awake, and at times I would roam the house searching for them. I was being consumed on all sides whether I was awake or asleep. I felt I was being consumed by demons.

An **auditory hallucination** (hearing voices, music, and so on) is the most common type of hallucination, and it is even more common in women than in men. Often, people hear voices accusing them of evil deeds or threatening them. The voices may also tell them to harm themselves. People with schizophrenia may talk back to the voices, even as they are trying to talk to people who are actually in the room with them. The second most common hallucination is the **visual hallucination,** often accompanied by auditory hallucinations. For

example, a person may see Satan standing at her bedside, telling her she is damned and must die.

Hallucinations can involve any sensory modality. **Tactile hallucinations** involve the perception that something is happening to the outside of one's body—for example, that bugs are crawling up one's back. **Somatic hallucinations** involve the perception that something is happening inside one's body—for example, that worms are eating one's intestines. These hallucinations are often frightening, even terrifying.

As with delusions, the types of hallucinations people have in different cultures appear similar, but the specific content of hallucinations may be culturally specific. For example, a person from Asia may see the ghosts of ancestors haunting him or her, but this is not a common experience for Europeans (Browne, 2001; Westermeyer, 1993). As with delusions, clinicians must interpret hallucinations in a cultural context. For example, a Puerto Rican woman might be diagnosed with schizophrenia by a European American interviewer because she believes she has special powers to anticipate events and because she describes what sound like hallucinations, such as "I see images of saints and virgins in the house. I also see the image of Jesus Christ, with the crown of thorns and bleeding." Interviewers who know Puerto Rican culture, however, might recognize this woman's beliefs and experiences as consistent with a spiritual group common in Latin America, which believes in clairvoyance and religious visions (Guarnaccia et al., 1992).

Disorganized Thought and Speech The disorganized thinking of people with schizophrenia is often referred to as a **formal thought disorder.** One of the most common forms of disorganization in schizophrenia is a tendency to slip from one topic to a seemingly unrelated topic with little coherent transition, often referred to as the *loosening of associations,* or *derailment.* For example, one person with schizophrenia posted the following "announcement":

> **VOICES**
> Things that relate, the town of Antelope, Oregon, Jonestown, Charlie Manson, the Hillside Strangler, the Zodiac Killer, Watergate, King's trial in L.A., and many more. In the last 7 years alone, over 23 Starwars scientists committed suicide for no apparent reason. The AIDS coverup, the conference in South America in 87 had over 1,000 doctors claim that insects can transmit it. To be able to read
> *(continued)*

> one's thoughts and place thoughts in one's mind without the person knowing it's being done. Realization is a reality of bioelectromagnetic control, which is thought transfer and emotional control, recording individual brain-wave frequencies of thought, sensation, and emotions.

The person who wrote this announcement saw clear connections among the events he listed in the first half of the paragraph and between these events and his concerns about mind reading and bioelectromagnetic control. However, it is hard for us to see these connections.

A person with schizophrenia may answer questions with comments that are barely related to the questions or are completely unrelated to the questions. For example, when asked why he is in the hospital, a man with schizophrenia might answer, "Spaghetti looks like worms. I really think it's worms. Gophers dig tunnels but rats build nests." At times, the person's speech is so disorganized as to be totally *incoherent* to the listener, when it is often referred to as **word salad.** The person may make up words that mean something only to him or her, which are known as *neologisms.* The person with schizophrenia may make associations between words that are based on the sounds of the words, rather than on the content, and these are known as *clangs.* For example, in response to the question "Is that your dog?" a person with schizophrenia might say, "Dog. Dog is Spog. Frog. Leap. Heap, steep, creep, deep, gotta go beep." Or the person may *perseverate* on the same word or statement, saying it over and over again.

The disorganized thought and speech in schizophrenia may be tied to fundamental deficits in cognition and attention (Barch, 2005). People with schizophrenia have difficulty on a wide range of cognitive tasks. For example, they show deficits in **smooth pursuit eye movement** (sometimes referred to as eye tracking). When they are asked to keep their head still and track a moving object, people with schizophrenia have greater difficulty doing this than people without schizophrenia. This suggests they have deficiencies in fundamental attention processes.

In addition, people with schizophrenia show deficits in **working memory,** that is, deficits in the capacity to hold information in memory and manipulate it (Barch, 2005). In turn, these deficits in working memory make it difficult for people with schizophrenia to suppress unwanted or irrelevant information or to pay attention to relevant information. In other words, they find it difficult to identify their thoughts that are relevant to an ongoing conversation or to the situation at hand and to ignore the environmental stimuli that are not relevant to what they are doing or thinking. Working memory deficits also impair their ability to learn and retrieve new information. These deficits together may contribute to the difficulties in reasoning, communication, and problem solving in people with schizophrenia.

Men with schizophrenia tend to show more severe deficits in language, compared with women who have schizophrenia (Goldstein et al., 2002). Some researchers have speculated that this is because language is controlled more bilaterally—by both sides of the brain—in women than in men. Thus, the brain abnormalities associated with schizophrenia may not impact women's language and thought as much as men's because women can use both sides of their brains to compensate for problems. In contrast, language is more localized in men, so that, when these areas of the brain are affected by schizophrenia, men may not be as able to compensate for these deficits.

Disorganized or Catatonic Behavior The disorganized behavior of people with schizophrenia is often what leads others to be afraid of them. People with schizophrenia may display unpredictable and apparently untriggered agitation, suddenly shouting, swearing, or pacing rapidly up and down the street. They may engage in socially unacceptable behavior, such as public masturbation. Many are disheveled and dirty, sometimes wearing few clothes on a cold day or heavy clothes on a very hot day. Short of these more bizarre behaviors, persons with schizophrenia often have trouble organizing their daily routines to ensure that they bathe, dress properly, and eat regularly. It is as if all their concentration must be used to accomplish even one simple task, such as brushing their teeth, and other tasks just do not get done.

In Chapter 9, we discussed **catatonia,** a group of disorganized behaviors that reflect an extreme lack of responsiveness to the outside world. One form of catatonia in schizophrenia is **catatonic excitement,** in which the person becomes wildly agitated for no apparent reason and is difficult to subdue. During a period of catatonic excitement, the individual may articulate a number of delusions or hallucinations or may be largely incoherent. In 1905, German psychiatrist Emil Kraepelin gave the following account of a patient showing signs of catatonic excitement (Laing, 1971, pp. 29–30).

The patient I will show you today has almost to be carried into the rooms, as he walks in a straddling fashion on the outside of his feet. On coming in, he throws off his slippers, sings a hymn loudly, and then cries twice (in English), "My father, my real father!" He is eighteen years old, and a pupil . . . , tall and rather strongly built, but with a pale complexion, on which there is very often a transient flush. The patient sits with his eyes shut, and pays no attention to his surroundings. He does not look up even when he is spoken to, but answers beginning in a low voice, and gradually screaming louder and louder. When asked where he is, he says, "You want to know that too. I tell you who is being measured and is measured and shall be measured. I know all that, and could tell you, but I do not want to." When asked his name, he screams, "What is your name? What does he shut? He shuts his eyes. What does he hear? He does not understand; he understands not. How? Who? Where? When? What does he mean? When I tell him to look he does not look properly. You there, just look. What is it? What is the matter? Attend; he attends not. I say, what is it, then? Why do you give me no answer? Are you getting impudent again? How can you be so impudent? I'm coming! I'll show you! You don't whore for me. You mustn't be smart either; you're an impudent, lousy fellow, such an impudent, lousy fellow I've never met with. Is he beginning again? You understand nothing at all, nothing at all; nothing at all does he understand. If you follow now, he won't follow, will not follow. Are you getting still more impudent? Are you getting impudent still more? How they attend, they do attend," and so on. At the end, he scolds in quite inarticulate sounds.

This patient's catatonic excitement is infused with angry and agitated outbursts, which also have the characteristic disorganization of schizophrenic thought.

Negative Symptoms

The negative, or Type II, symptoms of schizophrenia involve losses, or deficits, in certain domains.

Three types of negative symptoms are recognized by the DSM-IV-TR as core symptoms of schizophrenia: affective flattening, alogia, and avolition (see the Concept Overview in Table 11.4) on page 388.

Affective Flattening Affective flattening is a severe reduction in, or even the complete absence of, affective (emotional) responses to the environment. Often, this symptom is also referred to as *blunted affect*. The person's face may remain immobile most of the time, no matter what happens, and his or her body language may be unresponsive to what is going on in the environment. One man set fire to his house, then sat down to watch TV. When it was called to his attention that his house was on fire, he calmly got up and walked outside (Torrey, 1995). People with blunted affect may speak in a monotone voice, without any emotional expression, and may not make eye contact with others.

Affective flattening is a person's lack of overt expression of emotion. We must be cautious, however, in assuming that people demonstrating affective flattening are actually experiencing no emotion. In one study, people with schizophrenia and people without the disorder were shown emotionally charged films while their facial expressions were observed and their physiological arousal was recorded (Kring & Neale, 1996). The

People with catatonia strike strange poses and maintain them for long periods of time without moving.

TABLE 11.4	Concept Overview

Negative Symptoms of Schizophrenia

The negative symptoms of schizophrenia represent the absence of usual emotional and behavioral responses.

Symptom	Description	Examples
Affective flattening (blunted affect)	Severe reduction or complete absence of affective (emotional) responses to the environment	No facial expressions in response to emotionally charged stimuli; no emotional expression in voice
Alogia	Severe reduction or complete absence of speech	Complete mutism for weeks
Avolition	Inability to persist at common, goal-oriented tasks	Inability to get dressed, brush teeth, eat breakfast in morning

Source: Reprinted with permission from the *Diagnostic and Statistical Manual of Mental Disorders,* Fourth Edition, Text Revision. Copyright © 2000 American Psychiatric Association.

people with schizophrenia showed less facial responsiveness to the films than the normal group but reported experiencing just as much emotion and showed even more physiological arousal. Thus, people with schizophrenia who are showing no emotion may be experiencing intense emotion, which they cannot express.

Alogia Alogia, or poverty of speech, is a reduction in speaking. The person may not initiate speech with others and, when asked direct questions, may give brief, empty replies. The person's lack of speech presumably reflects a lack of thinking, although it may be caused in part by a lack of motivation to speak.

People with schizophrenia may have trouble caring for their own daily needs and may end up on the streets.

Avolition Avolition is an inability to persist at common, goal-directed activities, including those at work, school, and home. The person has great trouble completing tasks and is disorganized and careless, apparently completely unmotivated. She may sit around all day, doing almost nothing. She may withdraw and become socially isolated.

The negative symptoms of schizophrenia can be difficult to diagnose reliably. First, they involve the absence of behaviors, rather than the presence of behaviors, making them more difficult to detect. Second, they lie on a continuum between normal and abnormal, rather than being clearly bizarre behaviors, as are the positive symptoms. Third, they can be caused by a host of factors other than schizophrenia, such as depression or social isolation, or they may be side effects of medications.

Other Symptoms of Schizophrenia

People with schizophrenia often also suffer significant symptoms of depression and anxiety, and many abuse alcohol and other drugs. A number of other symptoms, or features, of schizophrenia are not part of the formal diagnostic criteria for the disorder but occur frequently. Among these are inappropriate affect, anhedonia, and impaired social skills.

Inappropriate Affect Instead of showing flattened, or blunted, affect, a person with schizophrenia may show *inappropriate affect*, such as laughing at sad things and crying at happy things. This may happen because he or she is thinking about and responding to something other than what is going on in the environment (McGhie & Chapman, 1961, p. 104):

It must look queer to people when I laugh about something that has got nothing to do with what I am talking about, but they don't know what's going on inside and how much of it is running round in my head. You see I might be talking about something quite serious to you and other things come into my head at the same time that are funny and this makes me laugh. If only I could concentrate on the one thing at the one time and I wouldn't look half so silly.

Inappropriate displays of affect may also occur because the brain processes that match stimuli with the proper emotions and emotional responses to those stimuli are not working properly. Unhappy stimuli somehow trigger laughter and happy stimuli trigger sadness. Whatever the cause, inappropriate affect is one of the most striking symptoms of schizophrenia. Often, the person switches from one extreme emotional expression to another for no apparent reason.

Anhedonia Recall that many people who display flattened, or blunted, affect are actually experiencing emotions, although they are not showing them. Some people with schizophrenia, however, experience severe *anhedonia* (a loss of interest in everything in life), similar to the anhedonia that characterizes depression (see Chapter 9). They lose the ability to experience emotion and, no matter what happens, do not feel happy or sad. This emotional void itself can be miserable.

Impaired Social Skills Not surprisingly, the symptoms of schizophrenia make it difficult to have normal interactions with other people. People with schizophrenia show a wide range of *impaired social skills*, including difficulty in holding conversations, in maintaining relationships, and in holding a job. You may be surprised to learn, however, that the difficulties in social skills in schizophrenia may be due more to the negative symptoms than to the positive symptoms of the disorder.

Although the negative symptoms of schizophrenia are less bizarre than the positive symptoms, they are major causes of the problems people with schizophrenia have in functioning in society. People with schizophrenia with many negative symptoms have lower educational attainments and less success in holding jobs, poorer performance on cognitive tasks, and a poorer prognosis than do those with few negative symptoms and predominantly positive symptoms (Andreasen et al., 1990;

Eaton et al., 1998). In addition, the negative symptoms are less responsive to medication than are the positive symptoms: A person with schizophrenia may be able to overcome the hallucinations, delusions, and thought disturbances with medication but may not be able to overcome the affective flattening, alogia, and avolition. Thus, the person may remain chronically unresponsive, unmotivated, and socially isolated, even when he or she is not acutely psychotic (Fenton & McGlashan, 1994).

Diagnosis

Schizophrenia has been recognized as a psychological disorder since the early 1800s (Gottesman, 1991). German psychiatrist Emil Kraepelin is credited with the most comprehensive and accurate description of schizophrenia. In 1883, Kraepelin labeled the disorder **dementia praecox** (precocious dementia), because he believed that the disorder resulted from premature deterioration of the brain. He viewed the disorder as progressive, irreversible, and chronic. Kraepelin's definition of this disorder was a narrow one, which resulted in only a small percentage of people receiving this diagnosis.

The other major figure in the early history of schizophrenia research was Eugen Bleuler. Bleuler disagreed with Kraepelin's view that this disorder always developed at an early age and always led to severe deterioration of the brain. Bleuler introduced the label *schizophrenia* for the disorder, from the Greek words *schizein*, meaning "to split," and *phren*, meaning "mind." Bleuler believed that this disorder involved the splitting of usually integrated psychic functions of mental associations, thoughts, and emotions. (Bleuler did not view schizophrenia as the splitting of distinct personalities, as in dissociative identity disorder, nor do modern psychiatrists and psychologists.)

Bleuler argued that the primary problem underlying the many different symptoms of schizophrenia was the "breaking of associative threads," referring to a breaking of associations among thought, language, memory, and problem solving. He argued that the attentional problems seen in schizophrenia were due to a lack of the necessary links between aspects of the mind. In turn, the behavioral symptoms of schizophrenia (such as alogia) were similarly due to an inability to maintain a train of thought.

Bleuler's view of schizophrenia was much broader than Kraepelin's and led to a broader range of people being given this diagnosis. Bleuler's definition of schizophrenia was adopted by clinicians in the United States in the early twentieth century, whereas the Europeans stuck with Kraepelin's narrower definition. Over the first few decades of the

TABLE 11.5   DSM-IV-TR

Diagnostic Criteria for Schizophrenia

The DSM-IV-TR criteria for schizophrenia require the presence of severe symptoms for at least one month and the presence of some symptoms for at least six months.

A. Core symptoms: two or more of the following present for at least a one-month period:

   1. Delusions

   2. Hallucinations

   3. Disorganized speech

   4. Grossly disorganized or catatonic behavior

   5. Negative symptoms

B. Social/occupational functioning: significant impairment in work, academic performance, interpersonal relationships, and/or self-care

C. Duration: continuous signs of the disturbance for at least six months; at least one month of this period must include symptoms that meet Criterion A above

Source: Reprinted with permission from the *Diagnostic and Statistical Manual of Mental Disorders*, Fourth Edition, Text Revision. Copyright © 2000 American Psychiatric Association.

twentieth century, U.S. clinicians further broadened their definition of schizophrenia, so that eventually anyone experiencing delusions and hallucinations was given the diagnosis (even though delusions and hallucinations can also occur in mood disorders).

Beginning in 1980 with the third edition of the DSM, the pendulum began to swing back toward a narrower definition of schizophrenia in the United States. Now, the DSM-IV-TR states that, in order to be diagnosed with schizophrenia, an individual must show some symptoms of the disorder for at least six months. During this six months, there must be at least one month of acute symptoms, during which two or more of the broad groups of symptoms (e.g., delusions, hallucinations, disorganized speech, disorganized or catatonic behavior, negative symptoms) are present and severe enough to impair the individual's social or occupational functioning (see the DSM-IV-TR diagnostic criteria in Table 11.5). Some people seek treatment shortly after the onset of their symptoms, but most do not and have experienced significant symptoms for many months, even years, before being treated.

Prodromal symptoms are present before people go into the acute phase of schizophrenia, and **residual symptoms** are present after they come out of the acute phase. During the prodromal and residual phases, people with schizophrenia may express beliefs that are not delusional but are unusual. They may have strange perceptual experiences, such as sensing another person in the room, without reporting full-blown hallucinations. They may speak in a somewhat disorganized and tangential way but remain coherent. Their behavior may be peculiar—for example, collecting scraps of paper—but not grossly disorganized. The negative symptoms are especially prominent in the prodromal and residual phases of the disorder. The person may be withdrawn and uninterested in others or in work or school. During the prodromal phase, family members and friends may experience the person with schizophrenia as "gradually slipping away."

Recall from Chapter 9 some of the difficulties in distinguishing schizophrenia from *mood disorders with psychotic features*. Another differential diagnosis that is difficult to make is between schizophrenia and schizoaffective disorder (see the DSM-IV-TR criteria in Table 11.6). *Schizoaffective disorder* is a mix of schizophrenia and mood disorders, with evidence that the schizophrenic symptoms are present even when the mood symptoms are absent. People with schizoaffective disorder simultaneously experience symptoms that meet Criterion A for the diagnosis of schizophrenia (review Table 11.5) and mood symptoms meeting the criteria for a major depressive episode, a manic episode, or an episode of mixed mania/depression. Their mood symptoms must be present for a substantial duration of the time that their schizophrenic symptoms are present. But the main difference between schizoaffective disorder and mood disorders with psychotic features is that, in schizoaffective disorder, people experience schizophrenic symptoms, specifically delusions and hallucinations, in the absence of mood symptoms for at least two weeks.

This all may sound a bit confusing to you, and it is confusing to mental-health professionals as well. The diagnosis of schizoaffective disorder is a controversial one, because many clinicians believe that it is used as a default when clinicians can't decide whether an individual has schizophrenia or a mood disorder. The reliability of the diagnosis of schizoaffective disorder is low, meaning that clinicians don't often agree that an individual warrants this diagnosis.

Within the diagnosis of schizophrenia, many subtypes have been described. In *Type I schizophrenia,* the positive symptoms are much more promi-

TABLE 11.6 DSM-IV-TR

Diagnostic Criteria for Schizoaffective Disorder

The major distinction between schizoaffective disorder and schizophrenia is the presence of severe mood symptoms in schizoaffective disorder.

A. An uninterrupted period of illness during which, at some time, there is either a major depressive episode, a manic episode, or a mixed episode concurrent with symptoms that meet Criterion A for schizophrenia.

B. During the same period of illness, there have been delusions or hallucinations for at least two weeks in the absence of prominent mood symptoms.

C. Symptoms that meet criteria for a mood episode are present for a substantial portion of the total duration of the active and residual periods of the illness.

Source: Reprinted with permission from the *Diagnostic and Statistical Manual of Mental Disorders*, Fourth Edition, Text Revision. Copyright © 2000 American Psychiatric Association.

TABLE 11.7 DSM-IV-TR

Types of Schizophrenia

The DSM-IV-TR recognizes five subtypes of schizophrenia.

Type	Major Features
Paranoid schizophrenia	Delusions and hallucinations with themes of persecution and grandiosity
Disorganized schizophrenia	Incoherence in cognition, speech, and behavior and flat or inappropriate affect
Catatonic schizophrenia	Nearly total unresponsiveness to the environment, as well as motor and verbal abnormalities
Undifferentiated schizophrenia	Diagnosed when a person experiences schizophrenic symptoms but does not meet the criteria for paranoid, disorganized, or catatonic schizophrenia
Residual schizophrenia	History of at least one episode of acute positive symptoms but currently no prominent positive symptoms

Source: Reprinted with permission from the *Diagnostic and Statistical Manual of Mental Disorders*, Fourth Edition, Text Revision. Copyright © 2000 American Psychiatric Association.

nent than the negative symptoms. In *Type II schizophrenia*, the negative symptoms are more prominent than the positive symptoms. This distinction between Type I and Type II schizophrenia is not part of the official DSM-IV-TR diagnostic framework, but it has turned out to be a useful distinction in research on schizophrenia.

The DSM-IV-TR officially divides schizophrenia into five subtypes (see the DSM-IV-TR information in Table 11.7). Three of these types, the *paranoid*, *disorganized*, and *catatonic* types, have specific symptoms that differentiate them from each other. The other two types, *undifferentiated* and *residual schizophrenia*, are not characterized by specific differentiating symptoms but, rather, by a mix of symptoms that are either acute (in the undifferentiated type) or attenuated (in the residual type).

Paranoid Schizophrenia

The best-known, and most researched, type of schizophrenia is the paranoid type. This is the type that John Nash appeared to suffer from. People with **paranoid schizophrenia** have prominent delusions and hallucinations that involve themes of persecution and grandiosity. Many do not show the grossly disorganized speech or behavior that people with other types of schizophrenia show. They may be lu-

cid and articulate, with elaborate stories of how someone is plotting against them. They may also be able to articulate the deep pain and anguish of believing that they are being persecuted (Torrey, 1995, pp. 53–54):

> Anxiety:
> like metal on metal in my brain
> Paranoia: it is
> making me run away, away, away
> and back again quickly
> to see if I've been caught
> Or lied to
> Or laughed at
> Ha ha ha. The ferris wheel
> in Looney Land is not so funny.

People with paranoid schizophrenia are highly resistant to any arguments against their delusions and may become very irritated with anyone who argues with them. They may act arrogantly and as if they were superior to others or may remain aloof and suspicious. The combination of persecutory and grandiose delusions can lead people with this type of schizophrenia to be suicidal or violent toward others.

The prognosis for people with paranoid schizophrenia is actually better than the prognosis for people with other types of schizophrenia (Hwu et al., 2002). They are more likely to be able to live independently and hold down a job and, thus, show better cognitive and social functioning (Kendler et al., 1994). The onset of paranoid schizophrenia tends to occur later in life than does the onset of other forms of schizophrenia, and episodes of psychosis are often triggered by stress. In general, paranoid schizophrenia is considered a milder, less insidious form of schizophrenia.

Disorganized Schizophrenia

Unlike people with the paranoid type of schizophrenia, people with **disorganized schizophrenia** do not have well-formed delusions or hallucinations. Instead, their thoughts and behaviors are severely disorganized. People with this type of schizophrenia may speak in word salads, completely incoherent to others. They are prone to odd, stereotyped behaviors, such as frequent grimacing or mannerisms such as flapping their hands. They may be so disorganized that they do not bathe, dress, or eat if left on their own.

The emotional experiences and expressions of people with disorganized schizophrenia are also quite disturbed. They may not show any emotional reactions to anything, or they may have unusual and inappropriate emotional reactions to events, such as laughing uncontrollably at a funeral. When they talk, they may display emotions that are apparently unrelated to what they are saying or to what is going on in the environment. For example, a young woman with disorganized schizophrenia responded in the following manner when asked about her mother, who had been recently hospitalized for a serious illness: "Mama's sick. [Giggle.] Sicky, sicky, sicky. [Giggle.] I flipped off a doctor once, did you know that? Flip. I wanta wear my blue dress tomorrow. Dress mess. [Giggle.]"

This type of schizophrenia tends to have an early onset and a continuous course, which is often unresponsive to treatment. People with this type of schizophrenia are among the most disabled by the disorder.

Catatonic Schizophrenia

Catatonic schizophrenia has some of the most distinct features of all the types of schizophrenia. It is very rare, however, and thus has not been well researched. People with catatonic schizophrenia show a variety of motor behaviors and ways of speaking that suggest almost complete unresponsiveness to their environment. The diagnostic criteria for catatonic schizophrenia require two of the following symptoms: (1) catatonic stupor (remaining motionless for long periods of time); (2) catatonic excitement (excessive and purposeless motor activity); (3) the maintenance of rigid postures or complete mutism for long periods of time; (4) odd mannerisms, such as grimacing or hand flapping; and (5) **echolalia** (the senseless repetition of words just spoken by others) or **echopraxia** (repetitive imitation of the movements of another person).

Undifferentiated Schizophrenia and Residual Schizophrenia

People with **undifferentiated schizophrenia** have symptoms that meet the criteria for schizophrenia (delusions, hallucinations, disorganized speech, disorganized behavior, negative symptoms) but do not meet the criteria for paranoid, disorganized, or catatonic schizophrenia. This type of schizophrenia tends to have an onset relatively early in life and to be chronic and difficult to treat.

People with **residual schizophrenia** have had at least one acute episode of acute positive symptoms of schizophrenia but do not currently have any prominent positive symptoms of schizophrenia. They continue to have signs of the disorder, however, including the negative symptoms and mild versions of the positive symptoms. People may have these residual symptoms chronically for several years.

Prognosis

Schizophrenia is more chronic and debilitating than most other mental disorders. Between 50 and 80 percent of people who are hospitalized for one schizophrenic episode will be rehospitalized for another episode at sometime in their lives (Eaton et al., 1992). The life expectancy of people with schizophrenia is as much as 10 years shorter than that of people without schizophrenia (McGlashan, 1988; Mortensen, 2003). People with schizophrenia suffer from infectious and circulatory diseases at a higher rate than do people without the disorder, for reasons that are unclear. As many as 10 to 15 percent of people with schizophrenia commit suicide (Joiner et al., 2005). The following account of a woman about her suicidal thoughts gives a sense of the pain that many people with schizophrenia live with and wish to end through suicide (Anonymous, 1992, p. 334).

I had major fantasies of suicide by decapitation and was reading up on the construction of guillotines. I had written several essays on the problem of the complete destruction of myself; I thought my inner being to be a deeply poisonous substance. The problem, as I saw it, was to kill myself, but then to get rid of my essence in such a way that it did not harm creation.

Despite the pain that many people with schizophrenia suffer for years, most people with schizophrenia do not show a progressive deterioration in functioning across the life span. Instead, most stabilize within 5 to 10 years of their first episode, and the duration of episodes and number of rehospitalizations decline as the person grows older (Eaton et al., 1992, 1998). Studies suggest that between 20 and 30 percent of treated people with schizophrenia recover substantially or completely from their illness within 10 to 20 years of its onset (Breier et al., 1991; Jablensky, 2000). One very long-term study that followed people with schizophrenia for an average of 32 years found that 62 percent had completely recovered or showed only minor impairment in functioning at follow-up (Harding, Zubin, & Strauss, 1987).

Age and Gender Factors

Women who develop schizophrenia have a more favorable course of the disorder than do men who develop it (Goldstein & Lewine, 2000). Women are hospitalized less often and for briefer periods of time than are men, show milder negative symptoms between periods of acute positive symptoms, and have better social adjustment when they are not psychotic. This more favorable course may occur in part because women tend to develop schizophrenia at a later age than do men, and, the later the age of onset of schizophrenia, the more favorable the course of the disorder tends to be.

Why does the functioning of people with schizophrenia often improve with age? Perhaps it is because they find treatments that help them stabilize, or they and their families learn to recognize the early symptoms of a relapse and seek aggressive treatment before their symptoms become acute. Alternatively, the aging of the brain might somehow reduce the likelihood of new episodes of schizophrenia. It has been speculated that the improvement of people with schizophrenia with age might be related to a reduction of dopamine in the brain with age; excess levels of dopamine

have been implicated in schizophrenia (Breier et al., 1991).

Sociocultural Factors

Culture appears to play a strong role in the course of schizophrenia. Schizophrenia tends to have a more benign course in developing countries than in developed countries (Anders, 2003; Jablensky, 2000). Cross-national studies conducted in 10 countries by the World Health Organization and other studies conducted by individual investigators have found that persons who develop schizophrenia in countries such as India, Nigeria, and Colombia are less likely to remain incapacitated by the disorder in the long term than are persons who develop schizophrenia in countries such as Great Britain, Denmark, and the United States (Jablensky, 2000) (see Figure 11.2).

The social environments of people with schizophrenia in developing countries may facilitate adaptation and recovery better than do the social environments of people with schizophrenia in developed countries (Anders, 2003; Karno & Jenkins, 1993). In developing countries, there are broader and closer family networks around the person

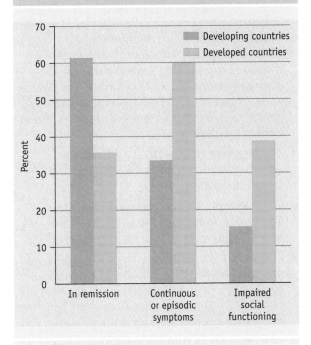

FIGURE 11.2 **Cultural Differences in the Course of Schizophrenia.** People with schizophrenia in developing countries show a more positive course of the disorder than people in developed countries.

Source: Jablensky, 2000.

with schizophrenia, providing more people to care for the person with schizophrenia. This ensures that no one person is solely responsible for the care of someone with schizophrenia, which is risky for both the person with schizophrenia and the caregiver. Families in some developing countries also score lower on measures of hostility, criticism, and overinvolvement than do families in some developed countries. This may help lower relapse rates for their family members with schizophrenia.

Social factors likely contribute to the gender differences in the course of schizophrenia (Mueser et al., 1990). Deviant behavior may be more socially acceptable in women than in men, so women who develop schizophrenia may experience less loss of social support than do men, which helps them cope better with their disorder. Also, women with schizophrenia may have better social skills than do men with schizophrenia. These social skills may help women maintain and make use of their social support networks and reduce stress in their lives, thereby reducing their risk for a relapse of symptoms.

Whatever the reasons for variations among cultures and between men and women in the course of schizophrenia, the conventional wisdom that schizophrenia is inevitably a progressive disorder, marked by more deterioration with time, has been replaced by new evidence that many people with schizophrenia achieve a level of good functioning over time.

SUMMING UP

- The positive, or Type I, symptoms of schizophrenia are delusions, hallucinations, disorganized thinking and speech, and disorganized or catatonic behavior. The forms of delusions and hallucinations are relatively similar across cultures, but the specific content varies by culture.

- The negative, or Type II, symptoms are affective flattening, poverty of speech, and loss of motivation.

- Other symptoms of schizophrenia include anhedonia, inappropriate affect, and impaired social skills.

- Prodromal symptoms are more moderate positive and negative symptoms that are present before an individual goes into an acute phase of the illness, and residual symptoms are symptoms present after an acute phase.

- The DSM-IV-TR differentiates between schizophrenia and two other disorders that include severe mood symptoms. In mood

disorders with psychotic features, the mood symptoms occur in the absence of the schizophrenic symptoms at least some of the time. In schizoaffective disorder, the schizophrenic symptoms occur in the absence of the mood symptoms.

- The DSM-IV-TR further differentiates among paranoid, disorganized, catatonic, undifferentiated, and residual schizophrenia.

BIOLOGICAL THEORIES OF SCHIZOPHRENIA

Given the similarity in the symptoms and prevalence of schizophrenia across cultures and across time, it is not surprising that biological factors have long been thought to play a strong role in the development of schizophrenia. There are several biological theories of schizophrenia (see Concept Overview in Table 11.8). First, there is good evidence for a genetic transmission of schizophrenia, although genetics do not fully explain who gets this disorder. Second, some people with schizophrenia show structural and functional abnormalities in specific areas of the brain, which may contribute to the disorder. Third, many people with schizophrenia have a history of birth complications or prenatal exposure to viruses, which may have affected the development of their brains. Fourth, the neurotransmitter theories of schizophrenia hold that excess levels of the neurotransmitter dopamine play a causal role in schizophrenia. New research is also focusing on the neurotransmitters serotonin, GABA, and glutamate.

Genetic Contributors to Schizophrenia

Family, twin, and adoption studies have all provided evidence that genes are involved in the transmission of schizophrenia (Gottesman & Reilly, 2003; Lichtermann, Karbe, & Maier, 2000). So far, however, the gene for schizophrenia has not been found, and many scientists believe that no single genetic abnormality accounts for this complex disorder (or set of disorders). Some researchers have argued for a polygenic, additive model, in which it takes a certain number and configuration of abnormal genes to create schizophrenia (Gottesman, 1991; Gottesman & Erlenmeyer-Kimling, 2001). Having more disordered genes increases both the likelihood of developing schizophrenia and the severity of the disorder. Individuals born with some of these genes but not enough to reach the threshold for creating full-blown schizophrenia may still show mild symp-

TABLE 11.8   Concept Overview

Biological Theories of Schizophrenia

Biological theories of schizophrenia have attributed the disorder to genetics, structural brain abnormalities, birth complications, prenatal exposure to viruses, and deficits in dopamine and other neurotransmitters.

Theory	Description
Genetic theories	Disordered genes cause schizophrenia, or at least a vulnerability to schizophrenia.
Structural brain abnormalities	Enlarged ventricles may indicate deterioration of a number of brain areas, leading to cognitive and emotional deficits. Reduced volume and neuron density in the frontal cortex and the temporal and limbic areas cause widespread cognitive and emotional deficits.
Birth complications	Delivery complications, particularly those causing loss of oxygen, might damage the brain.
Prenatal viral exposure	Exposure to viruses during the prenatal period might damage the brain.
Neurotransmitter theories	Imbalances in levels of or receptors for dopamine cause symptoms; serotonin, GABA, and glutamate may also play roles.
Integrated theory	Abnormal dopamine levels in prefrontal cortex lead to deficits in working memory, which make it difficult to attend to relevant information, leading to difficulties in reasoning, communication, and problem-solving.

toms of schizophrenia, such as oddities in their speech patterns or thought processes and strange beliefs.

Family Studies

Psychologist Irving Gottesman (1991) compiled more than 40 studies to determine the lifetime risk of developing schizophrenia for people with various familial relationships to a person with schizophrenia. His conclusions are summarized in Figure 11.3 on page 396. Children of two parents with schizophrenia and monozygotic (identical) twins of people with schizophrenia share the greatest number of genes with people with schizophrenia. As the top bars of the graph in Figure 11.3 show, these individuals have the greatest risk of developing schizophrenia sometime in their lives.

As the genetic similarity to a person with schizophrenia decreases, an individual's risk of developing schizophrenia also decreases. Thus, a first-degree relative of a person with schizophrenia, such as a nontwin sibling, who shares about 50 percent of genes with the person with schizophrenia, has about a 10 percent chance of developing schizophrenia. In contrast, a niece or nephew of a person with schizophrenia, who shares about 25 percent of genes with the person with schizophrenia, has only a 3 percent chance of developing schizophrenia.

This is not much different from the general population, in which the risk is about 1 to 2 percent. This relationship between an individual's degree of genetic similarity to a relative with schizophrenia and the individual's own risk of developing schizophrenia strongly suggests that genes play a role in the development of the disorder.

It's important to understand that having a biological relative with schizophrenia increases an individual's risk for schizophrenia but does not mean that an individual will develop schizophrenia. For example, of all children who have one parent with schizophrenia, 87 percent will *not* develop the disorder. On the other hand, 63 percent of people with schizophrenia have *no* first- or second-degree relatives with the disorder (Gottesman & Erlenmeyer-Kimling, 2001).

Even when the child of a person with schizophrenia develops the disorder, this doesn't necessarily mean it is transmitted genetically. Growing up with a parent with schizophrenia, and particularly with two parents with the disorder, is likely to mean growing up in a stressful atmosphere. When a parent is psychotic, the child may be exposed to illogical thought, mood swings, and chaotic behavior. Even when the parent is not acutely psychotic, the residual negative symptoms of schizophrenia—the flattening of affect, lack of

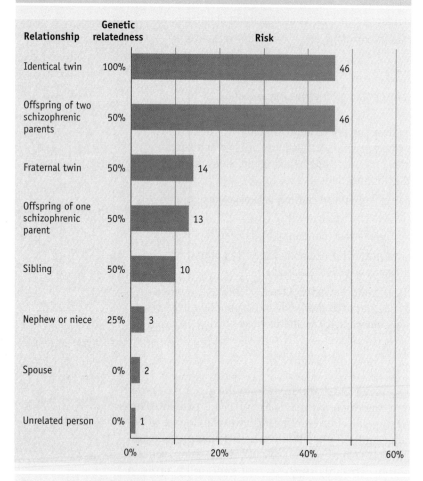

FIGURE 11.3   **Risk for Schizophrenia and Genetic Relatedness.** One's risk of developing schizophrenia decreases substantially as one's genetic relationship to a person with schizophrenia becomes more distant.

Relationship	Genetic relatedness	Risk
Identical twin	100%	46
Offspring of two schizophrenic parents	50%	46
Fraternal twin	50%	14
Offspring of one schizophrenic parent	50%	13
Sibling	50%	10
Nephew or niece	25%	3
Spouse	0%	2
Unrelated person	0%	1

Source: Gottesman, 1991.

motivation, and disorganization—may impair the parent's child-care skills.

Is it possible that the high risk of developing schizophrenia seen in the children of people with schizophrenia is due, at least in part, to the stress of living with parents who have schizophrenia? This question has been addressed to some extent in adoption studies.

Adoption Studies

Several adoption studies have found evidence that genetics play an important role in schizophrenia. An early and classic adoption study was conducted by Leonard Heston (1966) in the United States and Canada. He interviewed the adult children of 47 women who had been diagnosed with schizophrenia in the Oregon state mental hospitals in the 1930s. All of these children had been placed in orphanages or with nonmaternal relatives within three days of their birth. He also interviewed a group of 50 adults who had been adopted shortly after birth but whose mothers had no record of mental illness. If living with a parent with schizophrenia contributes significantly to a child's vulnerability to schizophrenia, then the children of people with schizophrenia who were adopted away from their mothers should have had a lower rate of developing schizophrenia than the 13 percent rate for children who grow up with one parent with schizophrenia (review Figure 11.3).

Heston found, however, that about 17 percent of the adopted-away children of the people with schizophrenia developed schizophrenia as adults, a rate even higher than the average rate of 13 percent for children of one parent with schizophrenia, providing strong evidence that these adoptees carry a genetic risk for schizophrenia. The rate may have been higher for the adopted-away children in the Heston study because the mothers of these children were probably experiencing particularly severe forms of schizophrenia. They had all been hospitalized and had been deemed unfit to be mothers. In contrast, none of the 50 control-group children in the Heston study whose mothers had no mental illness developed schizophrenia as adults.

Other adoption studies have examined the rates of schizophrenia in the biological versus the adoptive relatives of adoptees with schizophrenia, and these studies also support a role for genetics in schizophrenia. For example, Kety and colleagues (1994) found that the biological relatives of adoptees with schizophrenia were 10 times more likely to have a diagnosis of schizophrenia than the biological relatives of adoptees who did not have schizophrenia. In contrast, the adoptive relatives of adoptees with schizophrenia showed no increased risk for schizophrenia.

In one of the largest adoption studies, Tienari (1991) has tracked 155 offspring of mothers with schizophrenia and 185 children of mothers without schizophrenia; all of the children were given up for adoption early in life. To date, approximately 10 percent of the children whose biological mothers had schizophrenia have developed schizophrenia or another psychotic disorder, compared with about 1 percent of the children whose biological mothers did not have schizophrenia.

Twin Studies

In Figure 11.3 are the compiled results of several twin studies of schizophrenia that suggest that the concordance rate for monozygotic (identical) twins is 46 percent, whereas the concordance rate for dizygotic (fraternal) twins is 14 percent. A study that assessed all twins born in Finland between

The Genain quadruplets all have schizophrenia, but the specific forms of schizophrenia differ among the sisters.

1940 and 1957 used statistical modeling to estimate that 83 percent of the variation in schizophrenia is due to genetic factors (Cannon et al., 1998).

Genetic factors may play an even greater role in the more severe forms of schizophrenia than in the mild forms. Gottesman and Shields (1982) found concordance rates for monozygotic (MZ) twins of between 75 and 91 percent when they restricted their sample to persons with only the most severe forms of schizophrenia. In comparison, the concordance rates for MZ twins with mild forms of schizophrenia ranged from 17 to 33 percent.

Even when a person carries a genetic risk for schizophrenia, many other biological and environmental factors may influence whether and how he or she manifests the disorder. The classic illustration of this point is found in the Genain quadruplets, who are now in their sixties. These four women, who shared exactly the same genes and grew up in the same family environment, all developed schizophrenia, but the specific symptoms, onset, course, and outcomes of the disorder varied substantially among them (Mirsky et al., 2000). It's likely that other factors, such as birth complications, contributed to the variation in their risk for schizophrenia, although the specific causes of each twin's disorder have not been pinpointed. Their experiences are evidence that, even if the genes for schizophrenia could be cloned, there would still be a great deal to learn about how this disorder, or group of disorders, emerges out of a genetic predisposition.

Structural Brain Abnormalities

Clinicians and researchers have long believed that there is something fundamentally different about the brains of people with schizophrenia, compared with the brains of people without schizophrenia. Only in the past 20 years, with the development of technologies such as positron-emission tomography (PET scans), computerized axial tomography (CAT scans), and magnetic resonance imaging (MRI), have scientists been able to examine in detail the structure and functioning of the brain. The picture emerging from the use of these technologies is not entirely clear, again probably because there are many different types of schizophrenia, which are often grouped together in studies.

There is increasing evidence, however, for major structural and functional deficits in the brains of some people with schizophrenia (Andreasen, 2001; Barch, 2005). Most theorists of schizophrenia think of it as a *neurodevelopmental disorder*, in which a variety of factors lead to abnormal development of the brain in utero and early in life.

Enlarged Ventricles

The major structural brain abnormality found most consistently in schizophrenia is **enlarged ventricles** (Andreasen et al., 1990; Lieberman et al., 2001) (see Figure 11.4 on page 398). *Ventricles* are fluid-filled spaces in the brain. Enlarged ventricles suggest atrophy, or deterioration, in other brain tissue. People with schizophrenia with ventricular enlargement also show reductions in the prefrontal areas of the brain and an abnormal connection between the prefrontal cortex and the amygdala and hippocampus. Ventricular enlargement might indicate structural deficits in many other areas of the brain, however. Indeed, the different areas of the brain that can deteriorate to create ventricular enlargement might lead to different manifestations of schizophrenia.

People with schizophrenia with ventricular enlargement tend to show social, emotional, and behavioral deficits long before they develop the core symptoms of schizophrenia. They also tend to have more severe symptoms than others with schizophrenia and are less responsive to medication. These characteristics suggest gross alterations in the functioning of the brain, which are difficult to alleviate with treatment.

The gender differences in schizophrenia may be tied, in part, to gender differences in ventricular size. Some studies find that men with schizophrenia have more severely enlarged ventricles than women with schizophrenia (Nopoulos, Flaum, & Andreasen, 1997). This difference may be because men generally show greater loss of tissue volume and increase in ventricle size with age than do women. The normal effects of aging on men's brains may exacerbate the neuroanatomical abnormalities of schizophrenia, causing more severe symptoms and, thus, a worse course.

| FIGURE 11.4 | **Enlarged Ventricles in People with Schizophrenia.** The left panel shows the enlarged, fluid-filled ventricles (in gray) of a person with schizophrenia, compared with those of a normal person (right panel). This image was taken by Nancy Andreasen. |

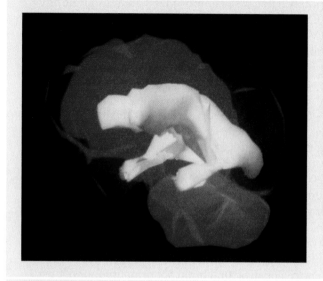 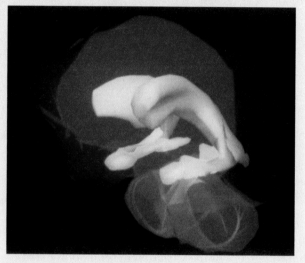

Source: Gershon & Rieder, 1992, p. 128.

Prefrontal Cortex and Other Key Areas

Studies have shown abnormalities in volume, neuron density, and metabolic rate in a number of areas of the brain in people with schizophrenia. These areas include the frontal cortex, temporal lobe, basal ganglia, and limbic area, including the hippocampus, thalamus, and amygdala (Andreasen, 2001; Barch, 2005; Suhara et al., 2002). Some of the most consistent findings are in the **prefrontal cortex.** The prefrontal cortex of the brain is smaller and shows less activity in some areas in people with schizophrenia than in people without schizophrenia (Barch, 2005) (see Figure 11.5). In addition, people at risk for schizophrenia because of a family history, but who have not yet developed the disorder, have been shown to have abnormalities of prefrontal activity (Lawrie et al., 2001).

The prefrontal cortex has connections to all other cortical regions, as well as to the *limbic system*, which is involved in emotion and cognition, and the *basal ganglia*, which are involved in motor movement. The prefrontal cortex is important in language, emotional expression, the planning and producing of new ideas, and the mediation of social interactions. Thus, it seems logical that a person with a pre-

frontal cortex that is unusually small or inactive would show a wide range of deficits in cognition, emotion, and social interactions, as people with schizophrenia do.

Evidence of this lower level of activity is not found in all people with schizophrenia, however. It is more common in people who predominantly exhibit negative symptoms of schizophrenia (e.g., low motivation, poor social interactions, blunted affect) than in those who predominantly exhibit positive symptoms (e.g., hallucinations and delusions) or mixed symptoms (Fitzgerald et al., 2004).

The *hippocampus* is another area of the brain where differences are being found between people with schizophrenia and people without the disorder (Barch, 2005). The hippocampus plays a critical role in the formation of long-term memories. People with schizophrenia show abnormal hippocampal activation when they are doing tasks that require them to encode information for storage in memory or to retrieve information from memory (Barch et al., 2002; Schacter et al., 2003). Other studies show that people with schizophrenia have abnormalities in the volume and shape of their hippocampus at the cellular level (Knable et al., 2004; Shenton et al., 2001). Similar abnormalities in the hippocampus are found in first-degree relatives of people with schizophrenia (Seidman et al., 2002). These abnormalities in the structure and functioning of the hippocampus might make it difficult for people with schizophrenia to recall information and to use it in

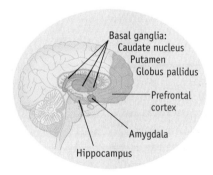

Basal ganglia:
Caudate nucleus
Putamen
Globus pallidus

Prefrontal cortex

Amygdala

Hippocampus

The prefrontal cortex has connections to the basal ganglia and the limbic area, including the hippocampus, thalamus, and amygdala.

ongoing conversations or in understanding current situations. These problems, in turn, may contribute to difficulties in maintaining coherent conversations and accurately interpreting ongoing situations.

Causes of Abnormalities

What causes the neuroanatomical abnormalities in schizophrenia? There might be a number of causes, including specific genetic abnormalities, brain injury due to birth injury, head injury, viral infections, deficiencies in nutrition, and deficiencies in cognitive stimulation (Barch, 2005; Conklin & Iacono, 2002). Recall that some studies have shown that family members of people with schizophrenia also exhibit several of these neuroanatomical abnormalities (Barch, 2005). Similarities between family members might be due either to genetic causes or to other biological or environmental factors shared by family members. In some studies of MZ twins in which one twin has schizophrenia but the other does not, the twin with schizophrenia tends to show neuroanatomical abnormalities, but the other twin does not, even though both twins have identical genetic makeups (Suddath et al., 1990; Thermenos et al., 2004). These studies argue against a solely genetic contribution to family similarities in neuroanatomical abnormalities.

Birth Complications

Serious prenatal and birth difficulties are more frequent in the histories of people with schizophrenia than in those of people without schizophrenia and may play a role in the development of neurological difficulties (Cannon, in press). Delivery complications have been found to combine with a familial risk for schizophrenia to predict the degree of enlargement of the ventricles and abnormalities in the hippocampus in people with schizophrenia.

One type of birth complication that may be especially important in neurological development is oxygen deprivation during labor and delivery, known as **perinatal hypoxia** (Goldstein et al., 2000). As many as 30 percent of people with schizophrenia have a history of perinatal hypoxia. A prospective study of 9,236 people born in Philadelphia between 1959 and 1966 found that the odds of an adult diagnosis of schizophrenia increased in direct proportion to the degree of perinatal hypoxia (Cannon et al., 1999). The authors of this study suggest that the effects of oxygen deprivation interact with a genetic vulnerability for schizophrenia to result in a person's developing this disorder, because the majority of people suffering oxygen deprivation prenatally or at birth do not develop schizophrenia.

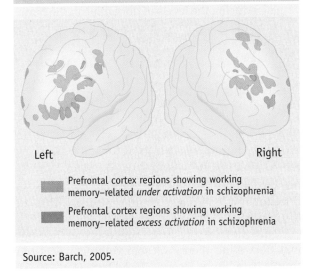

FIGURE 11.5 Areas of the Prefrontal Cortex Showing Abnormal Activity in People with Schizophrenia.

Several areas of the prefrontal cortex show abnormally high or low levels of activity when people with schizophrenia do tasks requiring working memory.

Left   Right

Prefrontal cortex regions showing working memory-related *under activation* in schizophrenia

Prefrontal cortex regions showing working memory-related *excess activation* in schizophrenia

Source: Barch, 2005.

Prenatal Viral Exposure

Epidemiological studies have shown high rates of schizophrenia among persons whose mothers were exposed to the influenza virus while pregnant (Cannon, in press). For example, persons whose mothers were exposed to the influenza epidemic that swept Helsinki, Finland, in 1957 were significantly more likely to develop schizophrenia than people in control groups, particularly if their mothers were exposed during the second trimester of pregnancy (Mednick et al., 1988, 1998). The second trimester is a crucial period for the development of the central nervous system of the fetus. Disruption in this phase of brain development could cause the major structural deficits found in the brains of some people with schizophrenia.

Neurotransmitters

The neurotransmitter **dopamine** has been thought to play a role in schizophrenia for many years (Burt, Creese, & Snyder, 1977). The original dopamine theory was that the symptoms of schizophrenia were caused by excess levels of dopamine in the brain, particularly in the frontal lobe and limbic system. This theory was supported by several lines of evidence.

On one hand, drugs that tend to reduce the symptoms of schizophrenia—the **phenothiazines**—reduce the functional level of dopamine in the brain. Some people who take phenothiazines to reduce their psychotic symptoms develop motor movement disorders similar to those of Parkinson's disease. It is well established that Parkinson's disease is caused by a deficiency of dopamine in the brain. Thus, the movement disorders that people with schizophrenia develop as a result of taking phenothiazines are likely to be caused by these drugs' reducing the levels of dopamine in the brain.

On the other hand, drugs that increase the functional level of dopamine in the brain, such as amphetamines, tend to increase the psychotic symptoms of schizophrenia. Finally, neuroimaging studies suggest that there are more receptors for dopamine and sometimes higher levels of dopamine in some areas of the brain in people with schizophrenia than in people without the disorder. The opposite effects of the phenothiazines and amphetamines on dopamine levels, and subsequently on symptoms of schizophrenia, suggested that excess dopamine led to schizophrenia, according to the original theory.

Now, however, research suggests that the original dopamine theory of schizophrenia was too simple (Conklin & Iacono, 2002; Davis et al., 1991). Many people with schizophrenia do not respond to the phenothiazines, indicating that neurotransmitter systems other than the dopamine system may be involved in the disorder. Even people with schizophrenia who do respond to phenothiazines tend to experience relief only from their positive symptoms (e.g., hallucinations and delusions), not from their negative symptoms. This pattern of relief suggests that simple dopamine depletion does not explain these negative symptoms.

Although the original version of the dopamine theory of schizophrenia (that there are generally higher levels of dopamine in the brains of people with schizophrenia) is not holding up, it is clear that dopamine is involved in schizophrenia. Let's consider a more complex version of the dopamine theory, which can explain both the positive and the negative symptoms of schizophrenia (Conklin & Iacono, 2002; Davis et al., 1991).

First, there may be *excess* dopamine activity in the **mesolimbic pathway,** a subcortical part of the brain involved in cognition and emotion (see Figure 11.6). The mesolimbic pathway is rich with certain types of receptors for dopamine. High dopamine activity in the mesolimbic system may lead to the positive symptoms of schizophrenia: hallucinations, delusions, and thought disorder. In turn, new drugs in the treatment of schizophrenia, known as the **atypical antipsychotics,** may work to reduce the symptoms of schizophrenia by binding to D4 receptors in the mesolimbic pathway, blocking the action of dopamine in this system.

Second, there may be *unusually low* dopamine activity in the prefrontal area of the brain, which is

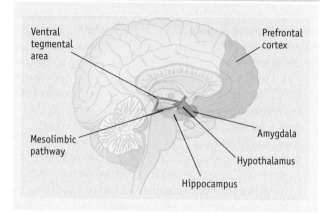

FIGURE 11.6   **Areas of Abnormal Dopamine Activity in the Brain in Schizophrenia.** There may be excess dopamine activity in the mesolimbic pathway, which begins in the ventral tegmental area and projects to the hypothalamus, amygdala, and hippocampus. But there may be unusually low dopamine activity in the prefrontal cortex.

involved in attention, motivation, and the organization of behavior. Low dopamine activity here may lead to the negative symptoms of schizophrenia: lack of motivation, an inability to care for oneself in daily activities, and the blunting of affect. This idea fits well with the evidence that structural and functional abnormalities in this part of the brain are associated with the negative symptoms. This idea also helps explain why the phenothiazines, which reduce dopamine activity, do not alleviate the negative symptoms of schizophrenia.

This more complex dopamine theory of schizophrenia seems to integrate research and clinical findings that, at first glance, seem to contradict one another. Another theory posits that, whereas the positive symptoms of schizophrenia are caused by excess dopamine activity in the brain, the negative symptoms are not the result of dopamine imbalances. Instead, the negative symptoms result from structural abnormalities in the frontal lobes of the brain (see Barch, 2005).

Finally, other research suggests that dopamine is not the only neurotransmitter to play an important role in schizophrenia. Serotonin neurons regulate dopamine neurons in the mesolimbic pathway, and some of the newest drugs that treat schizophrenia bind to serotonin receptors (Bondolfi et al., 1998). It may be that the interaction between serotonin and dopamine is critical in schizophrenia (Breier, 1995).

Other research has found abnormal levels of the neurotransmitters glutamate and gamma-aminobutyric acid (GABA) in people with schizophrenia (Goff & Coyle, 2001; Tsai & Coyle, 2002).

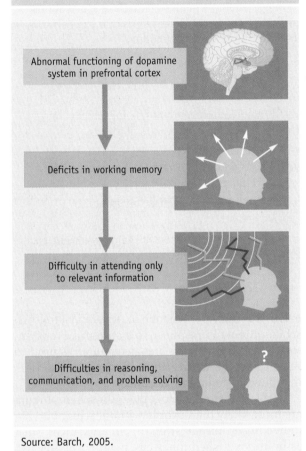

FIGURE 11.7 An Integrated Model of the Links Between Cognitive Deficits and the Symptoms of Schizophrenia. Theorists have argued that abnormalities in the function of the dopamine system, particularly in the prefrontal cortex, lead to deficits in the working memory, which then make it difficult for people with schizophrenia to attend only to relevant information. This difficulty impairs their ability to reason, communicate, and solve problems.

Abnormal functioning of dopamine system in prefrontal cortex

Deficits in working memory

Difficulty in attending only to relevant information

Difficulties in reasoning, communication, and problem solving

Source: Barch, 2005.

Glutamate and GABA are widespread in the human brain, and deficiencies in these neurotransmitters might contribute to a host of cognitive and emotional symptoms. Glutamate neurons are the major excitatory pathways linking the cortex, limbic system, and thalamus, regions of the brain shown to behave abnormally in people with schizophrenia.

An Integrative Model

Barch (2003, 2005) and others (Docherty et al., 1996; Fitzgerald et al., 2004) have argued that many of the core symptoms of schizophrenia are due to fundamental problems in basic cognitive processes resulting from functional and structural abnormalities in the brain (see Figure 11.7). These core symptoms include disorganized speech and difficulties in communication, logical reasoning, and the tasks of daily life (such as getting oneself out of bed, dressed, fed, and to work).

Specifically, abnormalities in the dopamine system, particularly in the prefrontal cortex, lead to deficits in working memory. These deficits make it difficult to inhibit irrelevant information from intruding into one's attention and interfere with communication with others, as the following woman with schizophrenia describes (McGhie & Chapman, 1961, p. 104).

VOICES

Everything seems to grip my attention although I am not particularly interested in anything. I am speaking to you just now, but I can hear noises going on next door and in the corridor. I find it difficult to shut these out, and it makes it more difficult for me to concentrate on what I am saying to you.

Working memory deficits also impair the ability to learn new information and to retrieve it when needed. Together, these deficits contribute to the difficulties in reasoning, communication, and problem solving experienced by people with schizophrenia.

This model has been supported by a wide range of studies showing deficits in working memory and related cognitive functions in people with schizophrenia, as well as in the first-degree relatives of people with schizophrenia (Barch, 2005). In addition, these cognitive deficits are linked to abnormalities in the functioning of the prefrontal cortex and in the dopamine system. This model does not explain all the symptoms of schizophrenia (such as the delusions and hallucinations), but it does explain how basic cognitive deficits, tied to brain functioning, can lead to problems in communication, reasoning, and functioning in daily life, which are some of the most damaging symptoms of schizophrenia.

SUMMING UP

■ There is strong evidence for a genetic contribution to schizophrenia, although genetics do not fully explain who has the disorder.

■ Many people with schizophrenia show significant structural and functional abnormalities in the brain, including low frontal activity and enlarged ventricles.

■ A number of prenatal and birth difficulties are implicated in the development of

TABLE 11.9	Concept Overview

Psychosocial Perspectives on Schizophrenia

A number of psychosocial factors may increase the risk of relapse in schizophrenia, even if they do not directly cause the onset of schizophrenia.

Perspective	Description
Social drift and urban birth	Schizophrenia impairs functioning, leading an individual to lose social status; also, people born in poor urban settings are at increased risk for the perinatal diseases and injuries that may contribute to schizophrenia.
Stress and relapse	A variety of stressful events increase risk for relapse.
Psychodynamic theories	Overwhelming rejection by an infant's mother causes the child to lose the ability to distinguish reality from unreality.
Communication patterns	Oddities in communication by a caregiver to a child at risk for schizophrenia increase stress and impair the development of the child's ability to communicate with others.
Expressed emotion	Families that are overinvolved with and hostile toward their member with schizophrenia increase stress, which leads to relapse.
Cognitive theories	The symptoms of schizophrenia arise from an individual's attempts to understand and manage cognitive deficits.
Behavioral theories	People with schizophrenia attend to irrelevant stimuli in the environment and don't know socially acceptable responses to others.

schizophrenia, including prenatal hypoxia and exposure to the influenza virus during the second trimester of gestation.

■ Difficulties in deploying attention may be at the core of many symptoms of schizophrenia.

■ Excess dopamine activity in the mesolimbic pathway and unusually low dopamine activity in the prefrontal area of the brain may work together to create the symptoms of schizophrenia.

■ New research suggests that serotonin, glutamate, and GABA may also play a role in schizophrenia.

PSYCHOSOCIAL PERSPECTIVES ON SCHIZOPHRENIA

Although schizophrenia is strongly linked to biological factors, there is a history of psychological theories of schizophrenia, and contemporary research shows that social factors can clearly influence the course of schizophrenia (see the Concept Overview in Table 11.9).

Social Drift and Urban Birth

Although you may have heard of someone having a "nervous breakdown" following a traumatic

event, it is rare for someone to develop full-blown schizophrenia in response to a stressful event. Instead, the term *nervous breakdown* often is used to refer to severe depressions or anxiety disorders that develop following trauma.

Still, it is true that people with schizophrenia are more likely than people without schizophrenia to live in chronically stressful circumstances, such as in impoverished inner-city neighborhoods and in low-status occupations or unemployment (Dohrenwend, 2000). Most research supports a **social selection** explanation of this link. According to this explanation, the symptoms of schizophrenia interfere with a person's ability to complete an education and hold a job. For these reasons, people with schizophrenia tend to drift downward in social class, compared with their families of origin.

One of the classic studies showing the process of social selection in schizophrenia tracked the socioeconomic status of men with schizophrenia and compared it with the status of their brothers and fathers (Goldberg & Morrison, 1963). The men with schizophrenia tended to end up in socioeconomic classes that were well below those of their fathers. For example, if their fathers were in the middle class, the men with schizophrenia were likely to be in the lower classes. In contrast, the healthy brothers of the people with schizophrenia tended to end up in socioeconomic classes that were equal to or higher than those of their fathers. More recent data also support the social selection theory (Dohrenwend, 2000).

Several studies have shown that people with schizophrenia and other forms of psychosis (such as bipolar disorder with psychotic features) are more likely to have been born in a large city than in a small town (Kendler et al., 1996; Lewis et al., 1992; Takei et al., 1992, 1995; Torrey, Bowler, & Clark, 1997; van Os et al., 2001). For example, studies in the United States find that people with psychotic disorders are as many as five times more likely to have been born and raised in a large metropolitan area than a rural area. Is it the stress of the city that leads to psychosis? Torrey and Yolken (1998) argue that the link between urban living and psychosis is due not to stress but to overcrowding, which increases the risk that a pregnant woman or newborn will be exposed to infectious agents. Many studies have shown that the rates of many infectious diseases, including influenza, tuberculosis, respiratory infections, herpes, and measles, are higher in crowded urban areas than in less crowded areas. As noted earlier, there is a link between prenatal or perinatal exposure to infectious disease and schizophrenia.

Stress and Relapse

Stressful circumstances may not cause someone to develop schizophrenia, but they may trigger new episodes in people who are vulnerable to schizophrenia. When researchers looked at the timing of stressful events relative to the onset of new episodes of psychosis, they found higher levels of stress occurring shortly before the onset of a new episode of psychosis, as compared with other times in the lives of people with schizophrenia (Norman & Malla, 1993).

For example, in one study, researchers followed 30 people with schizophrenia for one year, interviewing them every two weeks to determine if they had experienced any stressful events and/or any increase in their symptoms. They found that the people who had experienced relapses of symptoms were more likely to have experienced negative life events in the month before their relapse (Ventura et al., 1989). It is important not to overstate the link between stressful life events and new episodes of schizophrenia. Over half the people in this study who had had a relapse of their schizophrenia in the year they were followed had *not* experienced negative life events just before their relapse (Ventura et al., 1989). In addition, other studies suggest that many of the life events that people with schizophrenia experience in the weeks before they relapse may actually be caused by the prodromal symptoms that occur just

Poverty is often related to schizophrenia, perhaps as both a contributor and a consequence.

before a relapse into psychosis (Dohrenwend et al., 1987). For example, one of the prodromal symptoms of a schizophrenic relapse is social withdrawal. In turn, the negative life events most often preceding a relapse, such as the breakup of a relationship or the loss of a job, might be caused partially by the person's social withdrawal.

Psychodynamic Theories

Early psychodynamic theorists suggested that schizophrenia resulted from overwhelmingly negative experiences in early childhood with primary caregivers (usually the mother). Freud (1924) argued that, when mothers are extremely harsh and withhold their love from a child, the child regresses to infantile levels of functioning, and the ego loses its ability to distinguish reality from unreality. Later, psychoanalysts Freida Fromm-Reichmann (1948) and Silvano Arieti (1955) elaborated on Freud's theory and more fully described parenting styles in mothers that might cause their children to become schizophrenic. These *schizophrenogenic (schizophrenia-causing) mothers* are at the same time overprotective and rejecting of their children. They dominate their children, not letting them develop an autonomous sense of self and simultaneously making the children feel worthless and unlovable.

These theories did not hold up to scientific scrutiny. Research comparing the parenting styles of mothers of people with schizophrenia and the styles of mothers of people without the disorder did not confirm this theory. Later psychodynamic theorists generally see schizophrenia as the result of biological forces that prevent these individuals from developing an integrated sense of self (Kohut & Wolf, 1978).

Communication Patterns

Another early family theory of schizophrenia, proposed by Gregory Bateson and colleagues (Bateson et al., 1956), was that parents (particularly mothers) of children who become schizophrenic put their children in *double binds* by constantly communicating conflicting messages to the children. Such a mother might physically comfort her child when he falls down and is hurt but, at the same time, be verbally hostile to and critical of the child. Children chronically exposed to such mixed messages supposedly cannot trust their own feelings or their perceptions of the world and, thus, develop distorted views of themselves, of others, and of the environment, which contribute to schizophrenia. Again, however, empirical research has not supported the specific predictions of this double-bind theory of schizophrenia.

Although the double-bind theory of schizophrenia has not been supported, investigations of the *communication patterns* in families of people with schizophrenia have revealed oddities. Most investigators do not believe that these oddities alone cause schizophrenia in children. Rather, the oddities create a stressful environment, which makes it more likely that a child with a biological vulnerability to schizophrenia will develop the full syndrome of schizophrenia or that a person with schizophrenia will have more frequent relapses of psychosis.

Margaret Singer and Lyman Wynne (1965) described *communication deviance* within schizophrenic families as involving vague communications; misperceptions and misinterpretations; odd or inappropriate word usage; and fragmented, disrupted, and poorly integrated communication. Controlled comparisons of interactions in families with a person with schizophrenia and in families without a person with schizophrenia have found significantly higher levels of communication deviance in the families of people with schizophrenia. Some examples of this are statements such as "But the thing is as I said, there's got . . . you can't drive in the alley" and "It's gonna be up and downwards along the process all the while to go through something like this" (Miklowitz et al., 1991).

Such deviant patterns of communication do not appear to have serious, long-lasting effects on children who do not have family histories of schizophrenia (Gottesman, 1991). However, among children at risk for schizophrenia because they have family histories of the disorder, those whose families show high levels of communication deviance are more likely to develop schizophrenia than are those whose families have low levels of communication deviance (Goldstein, 1987).

Expressed Emotion

The family interaction style that has received the most attention by researchers of schizophrenia is **expressed emotion.** Families high in expressed emotion are overinvolved with each other, are overprotective of the disturbed family member, and voice self-sacrificing attitudes toward the disturbed family member, while being critical, hostile, and resentful of the disturbed family member (Brown, Birley, & Wing, 1972; Vaughn & Leff, 1976). Although high expressed-emotion family members do not doubt the legitimacy of their schizophrenic family member's illness, they talk as if the ill family member can exert quite a bit of control over the symptoms (Hooley & Campbell, 2002). They often have many ideas about what the family member can do to improve his or her symptoms, as is illustrated in the following comments from two high expressed-emotion mothers of people with schizophrenia (Hooley, 1998, p. 636):

> I tell him, "Sit down, you're driving me crazy!" Back and forth, back and forth [pacing]. I say, "Why don't you take some good deep breaths and just relax!"

> She was reading in the hospital. I don't know why she stopped. I've been trying to get her to start again. I said, "Read—even if it's only for 15 minutes, Lori. Try!"

Expressed emotion has been assessed through lengthy interviews with people with schizophrenia and their families, through projective tests, and through direct observation of family interactions. A number of studies have shown that people with schizophrenia whose families are high in expressed emotion are much more likely to suffer relapses of psychosis than are those whose families are low in expressed emotion (e.g., Butzlaff & Hooley, 1998; Hooley & Hiller, 1998). An analysis of 27 studies of expressed emotion and schizophrenia showed that 70 percent of patients in high expressed-emotion families relapsed within a follow-up year, compared with 31 percent of patients in low expressed-emotion families (Butzlaff & Hooley, 1998). Being in a high expressed-emotion family may create stresses for a person with schizophrenia, which overwhelm his or her ability to cope and trigger new episodes of psychosis.

The link between high levels of family expressed emotion and higher relapse rates has been found in several cultures, including European countries, the United States, Mexico, and India. In

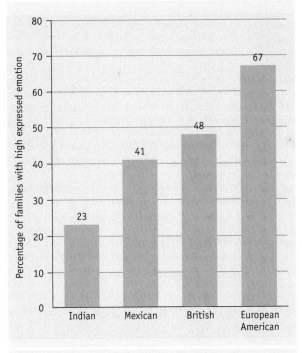

FIGURE 11.8 **Cultural Differences in the Prevalence of Expressed Emotion in Families of People with Schizophrenia.** Families of people with schizophrenia from developing countries tend to show lower levels of expressed emotion than do families of people with schizophrenia from developed countries. This may be one reason that people with schizophrenia from developing countries have fewer relapses than do those from developed countries.

Source: Karno & Jenkins, 1993.

Mexico and India, however, the families of people with schizophrenia tend to score lower on measures of expressed emotion than do their counterparts in Europe and the United States (Karno & Jenkins, 1993; Karno et al., 1987) (see Figure 11.8).

Critics of the literature on expressed emotion argue that the hostility and intrusiveness observed in some families of people with schizophrenia might be the result of the symptoms exhibited by the person with schizophrenia, rather than contributors to relapse (Parker, Johnston, & Hayward, 1988). Although families are often forgiving of the positive symptoms of schizophrenia (e.g., hallucinations, delusions, thought disturbances) because they view them as uncontrollable, they can be unforgiving of the negative symptoms (e.g., lack of motivation, blunted affect), viewing them as under the control of the person with schizophrenia (Hooley & Campbell, 2002). People with schizophrenia who have more of these symptoms may elicit more negative expressed emotion from their

families. They may also be especially prone to relapse, but for reasons other than their exposure to expressed emotion.

Another alternative explanation for the link between family expressed emotion and relapse in people with schizophrenia comes from evidence that family members who are particularly high on expressed emotion are themselves more likely to have some form of psychopathology (Goldstein et al., 1992). Thus, it may be that people with schizophrenia in these families have high rates of relapse because they have a greater genetic loading for psychopathology, as evidenced by the presence of psychopathology in their family members, rather than because their family members are high in expressed emotion. Perhaps the best evidence that family expressed emotion actually influences relapse in schizophrenic patients is that interventions that reduce family expressed emotion tend to reduce the relapse rate in schizophrenic family members.

Cognitive and Behavioral Perspectives

Aaron Beck, a founder of cognitive therapy, and Neil Rector have recently formulated a cognitive model of schizophrenia (Beck & Rector, 2005). They suggest that the neurological abnormalities of schizophrenia create fundamental difficulties in attention, inhibition, and the adherence to rules of communication, which lead people with schizophrenia to try to conserve their limited cognitive resources. One way they do so is to use, to an excessive degree, certain biases or schemas for understanding the overwhelming information streaming through their brains. Delusions arise as a person with schizophrenia tries to explain strange perceptual experiences. Hallucinations result from a hypersensitivity to perceptual input, coupled with a tendency to attribute experiences to external sources. For example, rather than thinking, "I'm hearing things," a person with schizophrenia tends to think, "Someone is trying to talk to me." The negative symptoms of schizophrenia arise from exaggerations of personality characteristics, expectations that social interactions will be aversive, and the need to withdraw and conserve scarce cognitive resources.

This cognitive conceptualization has led to cognitive strategies for treating people with schizophrenia. These strategies help patients identify stressful circumstances associated with the development and worsening of symptoms and learn better ways of coping with that stress. They also teach patients ways of disputing their delusional beliefs and hallucinatory experiences. Negative symptoms are treated by helping patients develop expectations that being more active and interacting more with other people will have positive benefits. Studies testing this cognitive intervention have shown it to be more effective in reducing symptoms than simply providing support to patients (Beck & Rector, 2005).

Some behaviorists have tried to explain schizophrenic symptoms as having developed through operant conditioning (see Belcher, 1988). They suggest that most people learn what stimuli to attend to in the social environment—such as another person's face or what that person is saying—through experiences in which they attend to these stimuli and are rewarded for doing so. People with schizophrenia do not receive this basic training in what social stimuli to attend to, and how to respond, because of inadequate parenting or extremely unusual circumstances. As a result, they attend to irrelevant stimuli in the environment and do not know the socially acceptable responses to other people.

This behavioral theory of how schizophrenia develops has not been well tested or accepted. But it is clear that behavioral techniques can help people with schizophrenia learn more socially acceptable ways of interacting with others (Belcher, 1988; Braginsky, Braginsky, & Ring, 1969). For example, if family members begin to ignore bizarre comments or behaviors by the person with schizophrenia, and provide reinforcement for socially acceptable behavior, the person with schizophrenia gradually reduces the bizarre behaviors and increases the socially acceptable behaviors.

Cross-Cultural Perspectives

Cultures vary greatly in their explanations for schizophrenia (Anders, 2003; Karno & Jenkins, 1993). Most cultures have a biological explanation for the disorder, including the general idea that it runs in families. Intermingled with biological explanations are theories that attribute the disorder to stress, lack of spiritual piety, and family dynamics. Browne (2001) offers a case study of a woman from Java, whose understanding of her own schizophrenic symptoms included all these factors:

Anik is a 29 year old Javanese woman who was born in a rural area but has lived in the city of Yogyakarta for the last four years. She has been married 1½ years, but is very unhappy in her marriage, feeling her husband was lacking in openness and compassion. Anik has an 8 month-old daughter, but has been unable to care for her for the last several

CASE STUDY

months, so the daughter was living with Anik's aunt in Jakarta. When her illness began, Anik first became withdrawn and didn't sleep or eat. She developed hallucinations of accusatory voices criticizing her husband, his family, and their landlady. Anik also suffered from jealous delusions that her husband was having an affair. She was taken to the hospital by her brother, where her symptoms included *mondarmandir* ("wandering without purpose"), *ngamuk*, being easily offended and suspicious, talking to herself, crying, insomnia, *malmun* ("daydreaming"), and quickly changing emotions. Her sister-in-law reported that she had been chronically fearful and irritable for some time and would frequently slam doors and yell. In Javanese culture, the control of emotions in social situations is of great importance, so Anik's outbursts were seen as clear signs of some sort of pathology.

Anik had several explanations for her behavior. First and foremost, she believed that she was in a bad marriage, and this stress was a contributing factor. Shortly before her symptoms began, her landlady said something harsh to her, and Anik believed that her startle reaction to this (*goncangan*) led to *sajit hati*, literally "liver sickness." In addition, Anik's mother had a brief period during Anik's childhood when she "went crazy," becoming loud and violent, and Anik believes she may have inherited this tendency from her mother. Anik initially sought to overcome her symptoms by increasing the frequency with which she repeated Muslim prayers and asking to be taken to a Muslim boarding house. Once she was taken to the hospital, she agreed to take antipsychotic medications, which helped her symptoms somewhat. She was discharged from the hospital after a short time, but was rehospitalized multiple times over the next year.

Anik's experience illustrates the interweaving of traditional beliefs and practices concerning people with schizophrenic symptoms and modern biological treatments. Although she agreed to take antipsychotic medicines, the understanding she and her family had of her symptoms was not primarily a biological one but, rather, one rooted in concerns about stress and, to some extent, religion.

SUMMING UP

- People with schizophrenia tend to live in highly stressful circumstances. Most theorists see this as a consequence, rather than as a cause, of schizophrenia.

- Early psychodynamic theories viewed schizophrenia as the result of harsh and inconsistent parenting, which causes an individual to regress to infantile forms of coping. According to other theories, families put schizophrenic members in double binds or have deviant patterns of communication. These theories have not been supported.

- Families high in expressed emotion are overinvolved and overprotective while being critical and resentful. People with schizophrenia who live in families high in expressed emotion may be at increased risk for relapse.

- Cognitive theorists see some schizophrenic symptoms as attempts to understand perceptual and attentional disturbances.

- Behavioral theorists view schizophrenic behaviors as the result of operant conditioning.

- Different cultures have different native theories of schizophrenia.

TREATMENTS FOR SCHIZOPHRENIA

NB

Comprehensive treatment for people with schizophrenia means providing them with medications to help quell symptoms, therapy to help them cope with the consequences of the disorder, and social services to aid in their reintegration into society and to ensure that they have access to all the resources they need for daily life.

Biological Treatments: Drug Therapy

Over the centuries, many treatments for schizophrenia have been developed, based on the scientific theories of the time. Physicians have performed brain surgery on people with schizophrenia in an attempt to "fix" or eliminate the part of the brain causing hallucinations or delusions. These patients were sometimes calmer after their surgeries but often also experienced significant cognitive and emotional deficits as a result of the surgery. *Insulin coma therapy* was used in the 1930s to treat schizophrenia. People with schizophrenia were given massive doses of insulin—the drug used to treat diabetes—until they went into a coma. When they emerged from this coma, however, patients were rarely much better, and the procedure was a highly dangerous one. *Electroconvulsive therapy,* or *ECT,* was also used to treat schizophrenia for a time, until it was clear that it had little effect on the symptoms of schizophrenia (although it is effective in treating serious depression, as we discussed in Chapters 5 and 9).

Mostly, however, people with schizophrenia were simply warehoused. In 1955, one out of every two people in psychiatric hospitals had been diagnosed with schizophrenia, although, by today's standards of diagnosis, they may have suffered from disorders other than schizophrenia (Rosenstein, Milazzo-Sayre, & Manderscheid, 1989). These patients received custodial care—they were bathed, fed, and prevented from hurting themselves physically, often with the use of physical restraints—but few received any treatment that actually reduced their symptoms of schizophrenia. It wasn't until the 1950s that an effective drug treatment for schizophrenia was introduced. Since then, several other antipsychotic drugs have been added to the arsenal of treatments for schizophrenia. Most recently, new types of antipsychotics, the atypical antipsychotics, hold the promise of relieving psychotic symptoms without inducing as many side effects as the traditional antipsychotics.

As we discussed in Chapter 5, in the early 1950s, French researchers Jean Delay and Pierre Deniker found that **chlorpromazine** (Thorazine), one of a class of drugs called the *phenothiazines,* calms agitation and reduces hallucinations and delusions in patients with schizophrenia. Other phenothiazines that became widely used include trifluoperazine (Stelazine), thioridazine (Mellaril), and fluphenazine (Prolixin). They appear to work by blocking receptors for dopamine, thereby reducing dopamine's action in the brain. Many people with schizophrenia can control the positive symptoms of schizophrenia (hallucinations, delusions, thought disturbances) by taking this drug prophylactically—that is, even when they are not experiencing acute symptoms.

The need for the long-term custodial hospitalization of people with schizophrenia was greatly reduced over the next 20 years, so that, by 1971, the number of people with schizophrenia who were hospitalized had decreased to half of what would have been expected if these drugs had not been available. Other classes of antipsychotic drugs were introduced after the phenothiazines, including the *butyrophenones* (such as Haldol) and the *thioxanthenes* (such as Navane). Collectively, these drugs are known as the *neuroleptics.*

[handwritten margin notes:] Prior other Methods of Biological treatments failed.

[handwritten margin note:] - resulted in less hospitalisation

Effectiveness and Side Effects of Neuroleptics

Although the neuroleptic drugs revolutionized the treatment of schizophrenia, they do not work for everyone with the disorder. About 25 percent of people with schizophrenia do not respond to the neuroleptics (Spaulding, Johnson, & Coursey, 2001). Even among people who do respond, the neuroleptics are more effective in treating the positive symptoms of schizophrenia than the negative symptoms (e.g., lack of motivation and interpersonal deficits). Many people with schizophrenia who take neuroleptics are not actively psychotic but are still unable to lead normal lives, holding a job and building positive social relationships. People with schizophrenia typically must take neuroleptic drugs prophylactically—that is, all the time to prevent new episodes of acute symptoms. If the drug is discontinued, about 78 percent of people with schizophrenia relapse within one year, and 98 percent within two years, compared with about a third of people who continue on their medications (Gitlin et al., 2001; Sampath et al., 1992).

Unfortunately, however, the neuroleptics have significant side effects, which cause many people to want to discontinue their use. The side effects include grogginess, dry mouth, blurred vision, drooling, sexual dysfunction, visual disturbances, weight gain or loss, constipation, menstrual disturbances in women, and depression. Another common side effect, **akinesia,** is characterized by slowed motor activity, monotonous speech, and an expressionless face (Blanchard & Neale, 1992). Patients taking the phenothiazines often show symptoms similar to those seen in Parkinson's disease, including muscle stiffness, freezing of the facial muscles, tremors and spasms in the extremities, and **akathesis,** an agitation that causes people to pace and be unable to sit still. The fact that Parkinson's disease is caused by a lack of dopamine in the brain suggests that these side effects occur because the drugs reduce the functional levels of dopamine in the brain.

One of the most serious side effects of the neuroleptics is a neurological disorder known as **tardive dyskinesia,** which involves involuntary movements of the tongue, face, mouth, or jaw. People with this disorder may involuntarily smack their lips, make sucking sounds, stick out their tongues, puff their cheeks, or make other bizarre movements over and over again. Tardive dyskinesia is often irreversible and may occur in over 20 percent of persons with long-term use of the phenothiazines (Spaulding et al., 2001).

The side effects of the neuroleptics can be reduced by reducing dosages. For this reason, many clinicians maintain people with schizophrenia on the lowest possible dosage that still keeps acute symptoms at bay, known as a *maintenance dose.* Unfortunately, maintenance doses are often not enough to restore an individual to full functioning. The negative symptoms of schizophrenia may still be present in strong form, and the individual may experience mild versions of the positive symptoms. This clearly makes it hard to function in daily life. Some people with schizophrenia live a revolving-door life of frequent hospitalizations and a marginal life outside the hospital.

Physicians prescribing neuroleptics also have to take cultural differences into consideration. There is some evidence that persons of Asian descent need less neuroleptic medication than do persons of European descent to reach desired blood levels of the drug and to show symptom relief (Lin & Shen, 1991). Asians may also experience the side effects of neuroleptics at lower dosages. It is currently unclear whether these differences in response are due to biological differences or to differences in diet or another environmental variable.

Atypical Antipsychotics

Fortunately, newer drugs, referred to as the *atypical antipsychotics,* seem to be even more effective in treating schizophrenia than the neuroleptics, without inducing the neurological side effects of the neuroleptics (Dossenbach et al., 2004). One of the most common of these drugs, *clozapine,* binds to the D4 dopamine receptor, but it also influences several other neurotransmitters, including serotonin. Clozapine has been effective with many people with schizophrenia who have never responded to the phenothiazines, and it appears to reduce the negative as well as the positive symptoms in many patients (Dossenbach et al., 2004; Spaulding et al., 2001).

Clozapine does not induce tardive dyskinesia, but it does have some side effects. These include dizziness, nausea, sedation, seizures, hypersalivation, weight gain, and irregular heartbeat. In addition, in 1 to 2 percent of the people who take clozapine, a disease called **agranulocytosis** develops. This is a deficiency of granulocytes, which are substances produced by bone marrow to fight infection. This condition can be fatal, so patients taking clozapine must be carefully monitored for the development of this disease.

Physicians often begin treatment with atypical antipsychotics developed in more recent years, such as risperidone. This drug affects serotonin receptors and is a weak blocker of dopamine receptors (Ananth et al., 2001). Risperidone is as effective as clozapine and may work more quickly than clozapine (Bondolfi et al., 1998). It has also been shown to be more effective at preventing relapse than the typical antipsychotic medications, such as haloperidol (Csernansky, Mahmoud, & Brenner, 2002). Risperidone also does not induce tardive dyskinesia, but it can cause sexual dysfunction, sedation, low blood pressure, weight gain, seizures, and problems with concentration.

Other atypical antipsychotic drugs are designed to stabilize dopamine levels across the brain, increasing dopamine where it is deficient and decreasing it where it is excessive (Stahl, 2001). Some of these drugs, including olanzapine, have been shown to decrease the symptoms of schizophrenia while inducing significantly fewer neurological side effects than either the typical antipsychotics or clozapine (Dossenbach et al., 2004; Lieberman et al., 2003).

Despite the potentially serious side effects of the drugs used to treat schizophrenia, many people with schizophrenia and their families regard these drugs as true lifesavers. These drugs have released many people with schizophrenia from lives of psychosis and isolation and have made it possible for them to pursue the everyday activities and goals that most of us take for granted.

Psychological and Social Treatments

With the availability of drugs that control the symptoms of schizophrenia, why would anyone need psychological or social interventions? As the following essay illustrates, drugs cannot completely restore the life of a person with schizophrenia (Anonymous, 1992, p. 335).

VOICES

A note about becoming "sane": Medicine did not cause sanity; it only made it possible. Sanity came through a minute-by-minute choice of outer reality, which was often without meaning, over inside reality, which was full of meaning. Sanity meant choosing reality that was not real and having faith that someday the choice would be worth the fear involved and that it would someday hold meaning.

Many individuals who are able to control the acute psychotic symptoms of schizophrenia with drugs still experience many of the negative symptoms, particularly problems in motivation and in social interactions. Psychological interventions can help them increase their social skills and reduce their isolation and immobility (Bustillo et al., 2001). These interventions can help people with schizophrenia and their families learn to reduce the stress and conflict in their lives, thereby reducing the risk for relapse into psychosis. Psychological interventions can help people with schizophrenia understand their disorder, appreciate the need to remain on their medications, and cope more effectively with the side effects of the medications. Finally, because of the severity of their disorder, many people with schizophrenia have trouble finding or holding jobs, finding enough money to feed and shelter themselves, and obtaining necessary medical or psychiatric care. Psychologists, social workers, and other mental-health professionals can assist people with schizophrenia in meeting these basic needs.

Behavioral, Cognitive, and Social Interventions

Most experts in the treatment of schizophrenia argue for a comprehensive approach that addresses the wide array of behavioral, cognitive, and social deficits in schizophrenia and is tailored to the specific deficits of each individual with schizophrenia (Liberman et al., 2002) (see Table 11.10 on page 410). These treatments are given in addition to medication and can increase everyday functioning and can significantly reduce the risk for relapse (Gumley et al., 2003; Spaulding et al., 2001).

Cognitive interventions include helping people with schizophrenia recognize demoralizing attitudes they may have toward their illness and then change those attitudes, so that they will seek help when they need it and will participate in society to the extent that they can. Behavioral interventions, based on social learning theory (see Chapter 5), include the use of operant conditioning and modeling to teach persons with schizophrenia skills such as initiating and maintaining conversations with others, asking for help or information from physicians, and persisting in an activity, such as cooking or cleaning. These interventions may be administered by the family. A therapist might teach a client's family members to ignore schizophrenic symptoms, such as bizarre comments, but to reinforce socially appropriate behavior by giving attention and positive emotional responses. In psychiatric hospitals and residential treatment centers, *token economies* are sometimes established, based on the principles of operant conditioning. Patients earn tokens, which they can exchange for privileges, such as time watching television or walks on the hospital grounds, by completing assigned duties (such as making their beds) or even just by engaging in appropriate conversations with others.

Social interventions include increasing contact between people with schizophrenia and supportive others, often through self-help support groups. These groups meet to discuss the impact of the

TABLE 11.10 Skill Areas Targeted in Comprehensive Community Treatments

These skill areas are the focus of comprehensive community interventions.

Medication Management

Obtaining information about antipsychotic medication

Knowing the correct self-administration and evaluation of medications

Identifying side effects of medication

Negotiating medication issues with health care providers

Taking long-acting medication by injection

Symptom Management

Identifying and managing warning signs of relapse

Coping with persistent symptoms

Avoiding alcohol and street drugs

Conversation Skills

Starting and maintaining a friendly conversation

Ending a conversation pleasantly

Interpersonal Problem-Solving Skills

Paying attention

Describing problems

Thinking of ideas for solutions

Evaluating solutions

Putting solutions into action

Recreation for Leisure

Identifying the benefits of recreation

Getting information about recreational activities

Evaluating and maintaining a recreational activity

Community Re-entry

Planning community re-entry

Connecting with the community

Coping with stress in the community

Planning a daily schedule

Making and keeping appointments

Solving medication problems

Identifying warning signs of relapse

Developing an emergency relapse prevention program

Source: Liberman et al., 2002.

disorder on their lives, the frustrations of trying to make people understand their disorder, their fears of relapse, their experiences with various medications, and other concerns they must live with day to day. Group members can also help each other learn social skills and problem-solving skills, such as those described in Table 11.10, by giving each other feedback on problem areas and by providing a forum in which individual members can role-play new skills. People with schizophrenia are also often directly taught problem-solving skills for common social situations (Liberman, Eckman, & Marder, 2001). For example, they may practice generating and role-playing solutions when a receptionist tells them there is no one available at a company to interview them for a potential job.

Family Therapy

Recall that communication deviance and high levels of expressed emotion within the family of a person with schizophrenia can substantially increase the risk for and frequency of relapse. This increased risk has led many researchers to examine the effectiveness of family-oriented therapies for people with schizophrenia. The successful therapies tend to combine basic education on schizophrenia with the training of family members in coping with their loved one's inappropriate behaviors and with the disorder's impact on their lives (Bustillo et al., 2001; Falloon, Brooker, & Graham-Hole, 1992; Halford & Hayes, 1991; Hogarty et al., 1991; McFarlane et al., 1995).

In the educational portion of these therapies, families are given information about the biological causes of the disorder, the symptoms of the disorder, and the medications and their side effects. The hope is that this information will reduce self-blame in the family members, increase their tolerance for the uncontrollable symptoms of the disorder, and allow them to monitor their loved one's use of medication and possible side effects. Family members are also taught good communication skills, so as to reduce harsh, conflictual interactions with their member with schizophrenia. Family members learn problem-solving skills to manage problems in the family, such as lack of money, so as to reduce the overall level of stress. They also learn specific behavioral techniques for encouraging appropriate behavior and discouraging inappropriate behavior.

These family-oriented interventions, when combined with drug therapy, appear to be more effective at reducing relapse rates than drug therapy alone. On average, approximately 24 percent of people who receive family-oriented therapy in addition to drug therapy relapse into schizophrenia, compared with 64 percent of people who re-

ceive routine drug therapy alone (Bustillo et al., 2001; Pitschel-Walz et al., 2001).

For example, Hogarty and colleagues (1986, 1991) compared the effectiveness of four types of intervention for persons with schizophrenia. The first group received medication only. The other three groups received medication plus one of the following types of psychosocial intervention: social skills training for the person with schizophrenia only, family-oriented treatment, or a combination of social skills training for the person with schizophrenia and family-oriented treatment for his or her family members. In the first year following these treatments, 40 percent of the people in the medication-only group relapsed, compared with only 20 percent in the two psychosocial intervention groups and no one in the group that received both individual social skills training and family-oriented therapy (see Figure 11.9). In the second year of follow-up, the groups that received family-oriented therapy continued to fare better than did those who received medication alone. In this study and others, however, the effects of psychosocial interventions diminished with time if the interventions were not continued. Thus, as with the medications for schizophrenia, psychosocial interventions must be ongoing to continue to reduce the chances of relapse in people with schizophrenia.

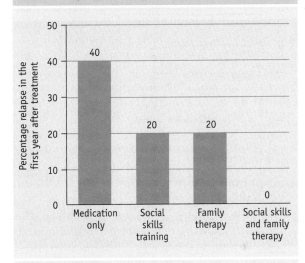

FIGURE 11.9 **Effects of Psychosocial Intervention (with Medication) on Relapse Rates.** In one study, patients with schizophrenia who received social skills training, family therapy, or both in addition to medication had much lower relapse rates in the first year after treatment than did patients who received only medication.

Source: Hogarty et al., 1986.

Some modern treatment facilities provide people with schizophrenia with comprehensive services in a positive, pleasant setting.

In some cultures, people with schizophrenia are more likely to be cared for and deeply embedded in their families than in other cultures. Lopez, Kopelowicz, and Canive (2002) argue that this makes family-oriented interventions even more critical for people from these cultures, but these interventions must be culturally sensitive. One study found that behavior therapies to increase communication actually backfired in some Hispanic families, perhaps because these families already had low levels of expressed emotion and found that the techniques suggested by therapists violated their cultural norms for how family members should interact (Telles et al., 1995). For example, some of the most traditional family members in this study expressed great discomfort during exercises that encouraged them to establish eye contact or express negative feelings to authority figures. These actions were considered disrespectful. This is just another example of how therapists must take into account the culture of clients in designing appropriate interventions for them.

Assertive Community Treatment Programs

Many people with schizophrenia do not have families who can care for them. Even those who do have families have such a wide array of needs—for the monitoring and adjustment of their medications, occupational training, assistance in getting financial resources (such as social security and Medicaid), social skills training, emotional support, and sometimes basic housing—that comprehensive community-based treatment programs are

necessary. **Assertive community treatment programs** provide comprehensive services to people with schizophrenia, using the expertise of medical professionals, social workers, and psychologists to meet the variety of patients' needs 24 hours a day.

In Chapter 5, we discussed the community mental-health movement, which was initiated by President Kennedy in the 1960s to transfer the care of people with serious mental disorders from primarily psychiatric hospitals to comprehensive community-based programs. The idea was that people with schizophrenia and other serious disorders would spend time in the hospital when their symptoms were so severe that hospitalization was necessary; however, when discharged from the hospital, they would go to community-based programs, which would help them reintegrate into society, maintain their medications, gain needed skills, and function at their highest possible levels. Hundreds of halfway houses, group homes, and therapeutic communities were established for people with serious mental disorders who needed a supportive place to live.

One classic example of this was The Lodge, a residential treatment center for people with schizophrenia established by George Fairweather and colleagues (1969). At the Lodge, mental-health professionals were available for support and assistance, but the residents were responsible for running the household and working with other residents to establish healthy behaviors and discourage inappropriate behaviors. The residents also established their own employment agency to find jobs. Follow-up studies showed that Lodge residents fared much better than people with schizophrenia who were simply discharged from the hospital into the care of their families or less intensive treatment programs (Fairweather et al., 1969). For example, Lodge residents were less likely to be rehospitalized and much more likely to hold jobs than were those in a comparison group, even after The Lodge closed.

Other comprehensive treatment programs provide skills training, vocational rehabilitation, and social support to people with schizophrenia who are living at home. Studies of these programs find that they reduce the amount of time spent in the hospital and, as a result, can be cost-effective (Bustillo et al., 2001).

In a model program established in Madison, Wisconsin, by founders of the assertive community treatment program movement (Test & Stein, 1980), mental-health professionals worked with people with schizophrenia who were also chronically disabled. These interventions were provided in the homes or communities of patients for 14 months, and then the patients were followed for another 28 months. Their progress was compared with that of another group of patients, who received standard hospital treatment for their psychotic symptoms. Both groups were treated with antipsychotic medications. The patients who received the home-based intensive skills interventions were less likely than the control-group patients to be hospitalized and more likely to be employed both during the treatment and in the 28 months of follow-up (see Figure 11.10). The home-based intervention group also showed lower levels of emotional distress and psychotic symptoms during the intervention than did the control group.

The differences in symptoms between the two groups diminished after the intervention period ended. In general, the gains that people in skills-based interventions make tend to decline once the interventions end, suggesting that these interventions need to be ongoing (Liberman, 1994). However, the benefits of these interventions can be great.

Despite the proven effectiveness of intensive treatment programs such as these, they have been few and far between. About 800 community mental-health centers are now operating in the United States, but this is only one-third of the number needed. Those that do exist tend to be understaffed, underfunded, and thus unable to provide adequate care to the people they serve.

From its beginning, the community mental-health movement was never funded to a level that could support its lofty goals. With the changes in medical insurance in recent years, funding for mental-health care for the seriously mentally ill has been even tighter. Although billions of dollars are spent on mental-health care per year in the United States, much of that money goes not to direct services to people with schizophrenia but, rather, to subsistence programs, such as social security disability income, and to community services for people with less serious mental disorders (Torrey, 1997). Much of the financial burden of caring for people with schizophrenia falls to state and local governments, which do not have the necessary financial resources, or to families, who are too often bankrupted by the cost of care.

As a result, nearly half of all people with schizophrenia receive little or no care in a given year (Regier et al., 1993; Torrey, 1997; Von Korff et al., 1985). Those who do receive care often are hospitalized only when their symptoms are acute, and then they remain in the hospital for inadequate periods of time for their symptoms to stabilize. They may be discharged with little or no follow-up. Some return to their families, but many end up in nursing homes, where they receive only custodial care, or in single-room-occupancy hotels or rooming houses, often in run-down inner-city neighbor-

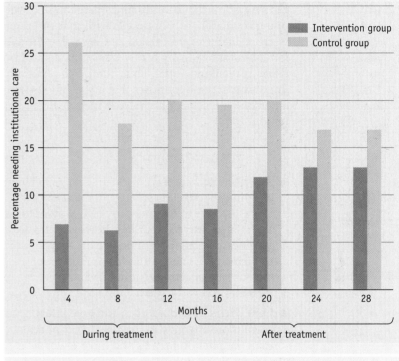

FIGURE 11.10   **Effects of Home-Based Treatment on Need for Institutional Care.** In one study, patients with schizophrenia who received intensive home-based skills training and care were much less likely to be hospitalized for psychotic symptoms or to need other types of institutional care.

Source: Test & Stein, 1980.

hoods. Many are homeless or end up in prison (Torrey, 1995).

Cross-Cultural Treatments: Traditional Healers

In developing countries and in parts of industrialized countries, the symptoms of schizophrenia are sometimes treated by folk or religious healers, according to the cultural beliefs about the meaning and causes of these symptoms. Anthropologists and cultural psychiatrists have described four models that traditional healers tend to follow in treating schizophrenic symptoms (Karno & Jenkins, 1993). According to the *structural model,* there are interrelated levels of experience, such as the body, emotion, and cognition, or the person, society, and culture, and symptoms arise when the integration of these levels is lost. Healing, thus, involves reintegrating these levels, through a change of diet or environment, the prescription of herbal medicines, or rituals.

The *social support model* holds that symptoms arise from conflictual social relationships and that healing involves mobilizing a patient's kin to support him or her through this crisis and reintegrating the patient into a positive social support network. The *persuasive model* suggests that rituals can transform the meaning of symptoms for the patient, diminishing the pain of the symptoms. Finally, in the *clinical model*, it is simply the faith that the patient puts in the traditional healer to provide a cure for the symptoms that leads to improvement. In developing countries, care for people with schizophrenia is more likely to be carried out by the extended family, rather than by a mental-health institution (Karno & Jenkins, 1993). Thus, it may be especially important in these countries that interventions with a person with schizophrenia also include his or her family.

SUMMING UP

- The phenothiazines were the first drugs to have a significant effect on schizophrenia. They are more effective in treating the positive symptoms than the negative symptoms, however, and a significant percentage of people do not respond to them at all. They can induce a number of serious side effects, including tardive dyskinesia.

- New drugs, called atypical antipsychotics, seem more effective in treating schizophrenia than the phenothiazines and have fewer side effects.

- Psychosocial therapies focus on helping people with schizophrenia and their families understand and cope with the consequences of the disorder. They also help the person with schizophrenia gain resources and integrate into the community as much as possible.

- Studies show that providing psychosocial therapy along with medication can significantly reduce the rate of relapse in schizophrenia.

- Community-based comprehensive treatment programs for people with schizophrenia have been underfunded. As a result, many people with this disorder receive little or no useful treatment.

- Traditional healers treat people with schizophrenia within the context of their cultural beliefs.

CHAPTER INTEGRATION

There is probably more consensus among mental-health professionals about the biological roots of schizophrenia than of any other psychopathology we discuss in this book. The evidence that the fundamental vulnerability to schizophrenia is a biological one is compelling, yet there is a growing consensus that psychosocial factors contribute to the risk for schizophrenia among people with the biological vulnerability. Theorists are increasingly developing models that integrate the biological and psychosocial contributors to schizophrenia to provide comprehensive explanations of the development of this disorder (see Figure 11.11).

| FIGURE 11.11 | The Interaction of Biological and Psychosocial Factors in Schizophrenia |

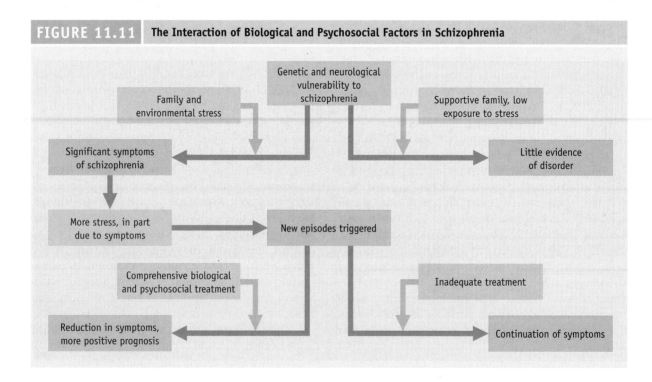

A person with a biological vulnerability to schizophrenia who is raised in a supportive, low-conflict family and who escapes exposure to major stressors may never develop the full syndrome of schizophrenia. He or she may still have mild symptoms, however, because the biological underpinnings of this disorder play such a strong role. On the other hand, a person who has a biological vulnerability and grows up in a stressful atmosphere is more likely to develop the full syndrome of the disorder. Psychosocial stress also clearly contributes to new episodes of psychosis in people with schizophrenia.

Finally, there is a widespread consensus among mental-health professionals that the most effective therapies for schizophrenia are those that address both the biological contributors and the psychosocial contributors to the disorder.

Extraordinary People: Follow-Up

When we left the story of John Nash at the beginning of this chapter, he was slowly reintegrating into the mathematics community at Princeton University. During the 1970s and 1980s, John Nash's illness gradually seemed to subside, although he was not taking any medications or receiving any other treatment. One of his colleagues, Hale Trotter, said,

> My impression was of a very gradual sort of improvement. In the early stages he was making up numbers out of names and being worried by what he found. Gradually, that went away. Then it was more mathematical numerology. Playing with formulas and factoring. It wasn't coherent math research, but it had lost its bizarre quality. Later it was real research. (Nasar, 1998, p. 350)

What accounted for the remission of his illness? Some, including the movie based on the book *A Beautiful Mind*, attribute it to the calm support of Alicia, Nash's wife. Some attribute it to the continued support of his mathematics colleagues. Nash believes he willed himself well, to some extent.

Whatever the reason, Nash was one of those lucky people with schizophrenia whose illness seems to diminish, or even subside altogether, with age. In 1994 John Nash was awarded the Nobel Prize in economics for his contributions to game theory. He and Alicia have remarried and now live in Princeton, where Nash works on his mathematical theories. Nash also helps care for their son, Johnny, who obtained his Ph.D. in mathematics several years ago and has developed paranoid schizophrenia. Although Johnny is receiving the newest treatments for schizophrenia, they help only a little, and he is frequently hospitalized.

As biographer Sylvia Nasar concludes,

The extraordinary journey of this American genius, this man who surprises people, continues. The self-deprecating humor suggests greater self-awareness. The straight-from-the-heart talk with friends about sadness, pleasure, and attachment suggests a wider range of emotional experiences. The daily effort to give others their due, and to recognize their right to ask this of him, bespeaks a very different man from the often cold and arrogant youth. And the disjunction of thought and emotion that characterized Nash's personality, not just when he was ill, but even before are much less evident today. In deed, if not always in word, Nash has come to a life in which thought and emotion are more closely entwined, where getting and giving are central, and relationships are more symmetrical. He may be less than he was intellectually, he may never achieve another breakthrough, but he has become a great deal more than he ever was—"a very fine person," as Alicia put it once. (Nasar, 1998, p. 388)

Even if you have seen the movie *A Beautiful Mind*, it's worth reading the book. Nasar's research into Nash's life is exemplary, and her account is more comprehensive than that in the movie.

- The positive (Type I) symptoms of schizophrenia include delusions (ideas the individual believes are true but are certainly false), hallucinations (unreal perceptual experiences), thought disturbances (incoherence of thought and speech), and grossly disorganized or catatonic behavior. (Review Table 11.2.)

- The negative (Type II) symptoms include affective flattening, alogia (poverty of speech), and avolition (the inability to initiate and persist in goal-directed activities). (Review Table 11.4.) Prodromal and residual symptoms are mild versions of the positive and negative symptoms that occur before and after episodes of acute symptoms.

- There are five subtypes of schizophrenia. (Review Table 11.7.) People with the paranoid subtype of schizophrenia have delusions and hallucinations with themes of persecution and grandiosity. This type of schizophrenia tends to begin later in life, and its episodes are often triggered by stress. People with this type of schizophrenia have a better prognosis than do people with other types of schizophrenia.

- The disorganized subtype of schizophrenia shows especially marked disorganization in thought and behavior and either a flattening of affect or frequent inappropriate affect. People with this subtype of schizophrenia are prone to odd, stereotyped behaviors, and their speech is often incoherent. This type of schizophrenia tends to have an early onset and a continuous course, which is often unresponsive to treatment.

- The catatonic subtype of schizophrenia is characterized by motor behaviors and ways of speaking that suggest that the person is completely unresponsive to the environment. The symptoms include motoric immobility, excessive and purposeless motor activity, extreme negativism, peculiar movements, and echolalia or echopraxia.

- People with the undifferentiated subtype of schizophrenia have symptoms that meet the criteria for schizophrenia but do not meet the criteria for paranoid, disorganized, or catatonic schizophrenia.

- People with the residual subtype of schizophrenia have had at least one episode of active symptoms but do not currently have prominent positive symptoms of schizophrenia. They continue to have mild positive symptoms and significant negative symptoms.

- Estimates of the prevalence of schizophrenia in various countries range from about 0.1 percent to 2.0 percent, but most estimates are between 0.5 and 1.0 percent. There are some slight ethnic differences in the rates of schizophrenia, but these may be due to differences in socioeconomic status.

- The content of delusions and hallucinations changes somewhat across cultures, but the form of these symptoms remains similar across cultures, and many clinicians and researchers believe that schizophrenia can be diagnosed reliably across cultures.

- Men may be more prone to schizophrenia than are women, and there are some differences in symptoms between the genders.

- Biological theories of schizophrenia have focused on genetics, structural abnormalities in the brain, and neurotransmitters. (Review Table 11.8.) There is clear evidence for a genetic transmission of schizophrenia, although genetics do not fully account for the disorder. People with schizophrenia show abnormal functioning in the prefrontal areas of the brain and the hippocampus and enlarged ventricles, suggesting atrophy in parts of the brain. Many people with schizophrenia have a history of prenatal difficulties, such as exposure to the influenza virus during the second trimester of gestation, or birth complications, including prenatal hypoxia. Dysfunction in the dopamine systems of the brain may contribute to schizophrenia.

- Stressful events probably cannot cause schizophrenia in people who do not have a vulnerability to the disorder, but they may trigger new episodes of psychosis in people with the disorder.

- Early psychodynamic theories argued that caregivers who are demanding and excessively harsh toward their children, so-called schizophrenogenic mothers, might cause the children to regress to infantile stages, resulting in schizophrenia. These theories have not been supported.

- Several theories have suggested that family communication patterns play a role in schizophrenia. The double-bind theory says that parents put their schizophrenic children in double binds by communicating mutually contradictory demands. The communication deviance theory says that parents create thought disorders in their children by communicating with them in deviant ways. Expressed-emotion theorists argue that some families of people with schizophrenia are simultaneously overprotective and hostile and that this increases the risk for relapse. Only the expressed-emotion theories have received strong empirical support.

■ Cognitive theories suggest that some schizophrenic symptoms are attempts by the individual to understand and manage cognitive deficits. Behavioral theories suggest that schizophrenic behaviors are operantly conditioned. (Review Table 11.9.)

■ Drugs known as the phenothiazines, introduced in the 1950s, bring relief to many people with schizophrenia. The phenothiazines reduce the positive symptoms of schizophrenia but often are not effective with the negative symptoms. Major side effects include tardive dyskinesia, an irreversible neurological disorder characterized by involuntary movements of the tongue, face, mouth, or jaw.

■ Newer drugs, called atypical antipsychotics, seem to induce fewer side effects and are effective in treating both the positive and the negative symptoms of schizophrenia for many people.

■ Psychological and social therapies focus on helping people with schizophrenia reduce stress, improve family interactions, learn social skills, and cope with the impact of the disorder on their lives. Comprehensive treatment programs combining drug therapy with an array of psychological and social therapies have been shown to reduce relapse significantly. These programs tend to be few and underfunded, however. (Review Table 11.10.)

■ People in developing countries tend to show a more positive course of schizophrenia than do people in developed countries. Women tend to have a more positive course than do men.

MindMap CD-ROM

The following resources on the MindMap CD-ROM that came with this text will help you to master the content of this chapter and prepare for tests:

■ Videos: Beautiful Mind: Interview with John Nash and Son; Paranoid Schizophrenia; Schizophrenia—Disorganized Type

■ Chapter Timeline

■ Chapter Quiz

Key Terms

psychosis 377

schizophrenia 377

positive symptoms 380

negative symptoms 380

delusions 381

persecutory delusion 382

delusion of reference 382

grandiose delusions 382

delusion of thought insertion 382

hallucinations 385

auditory hallucination 385

visual hallucination 385

tactile hallucinations 385

somatic hallucinations 385

formal thought disorder 385

word salad 386

smooth pursuit eye movement 386

working memory 386

catatonia 386

catatonic excitement 386

affective flattening 387

alogia 388

avolition 388

dementia praecox 389

prodromal symptoms 390

residual symptoms 390

paranoid schizophrenia 391

disorganized schizophrenia 392

catatonic schizophrenia 392

echolalia 392

echopraxia 392

undifferentiated schizophrenia 392

> Chapter 12

The Armour
by Gayle Ray

No man can climb out beyond the limitations of his own character.

—John Morley, "Robespierre," *Critical Miscellanies* (1871–1908)

Personality Disorders <

CHAPTER OVERVIEW

Extraordinary People

■ Susanna Kaysen, *Girl, Interrupted*

Defining and Diagnosing Personality Disorders

Personality disorders are long-standing patterns of maladaptive thought, behavior, and emotions. The DSM-IV-TR organizes personality disorders into three groups based on similarities in symptoms. A number of criticisms of the DSM-IV-TR categories have been raised.

Taking Psychology Personally

■ **Seeing Yourself in the Personality Disorders**

Odd-Eccentric Personality Disorders

People diagnosed with the odd-eccentric personality disorders—paranoid, schizoid, and schizotypal personality disorders—have odd or eccentric patterns of behavior and thought, including paranoia, extreme social withdrawal or inappropriate social interactions, and magical or illusory thinking. This group of disorders, particularly schizotypal personality disorder, may be linked genetically to schizophrenia and may represent mild variations of schizophrenia.

Dramatic-Emotional Personality Disorders

The dramatic-emotional personality disorders include four disorders characterized by dramatic, erratic, and emotional behavior and interpersonal relationships: antisocial personality disorder, histrionic personality disorder, borderline personality disorder, and narcissistic personality disorder.

Anxious-Fearful Personality Disorders

People diagnosed with anxious-fearful personality disorders—avoidant, dependent, and obsessive-compulsive personality disorders—become extremely concerned about being criticized or abandoned by others and thus have dysfunctional relationships with others.

Alternative Conceptualizations of Personality Disorders

Several alternative conceptualizations of personality disorders have been suggested, based on theories of normal personality. One alternative views personality disorders as extreme versions of five basic personality traits.

Chapter Integration

Although empirical research is lacking for many of the personality disorders, some theorists view them as the result of the interaction between a biologically determined temperament and parenting that enhances a child's biological vulnerabilities.

Extraordinary People

Susanna Kaysen: *Girl, Interrupted*

Susanna Kaysen was 18 and depressed, drifting through life and endlessly oppositional toward her parents and teachers. She tried to commit suicide. She began having strange perceptions:

> I was having a problem with patterns. Oriental rugs, tile floors, printed curtains, things like that. Supermarkets were especially bad, because of the long, hypnotic checkerboard aisles. When I looked at these things, I saw other things within them. That sounds as though I was hallucinating, and I wasn't. I knew I was looking at a floor or a curtain. But all patterns seemed to contain potential representations, which in a dizzying array would flicker briefly to life. That could be . . . a forest, a flock of birds, my second grade class picture. Well, it wasn't—it was a rug, or whatever it was, but my glimpses of the other things it might be were exhausting. Reality was getting too dense. (Kaysen, 1993, pp. 40–41)

Kaysen went to see a psychiatrist for a routine evaluation. At the end of one session, he put her in a taxi and sent her to McLean Hospital outside Boston. When she signed herself in, she was told that her stay would be about two weeks. Instead, Kaysen was not released for nearly two years.

Years after she was released from the hospital, Kaysen discovered that her diagnosis had been borderline personality disorder. In her autobiography, *Girl, Interrupted*, she raises many questions about this disorder:

> . . . I had to locate a copy of the *Diagnostic and Statistical Manual of Mental Disorders* and look up Borderline Personality to see what they really thought about me.
>
> It's a fairly accurate picture of me at eighteen, minus a few quirks like reckless driving and eating binges. . . . I'm tempted to try refuting it, but then I would be open to the further charges of "defensiveness" and "resistance."
>
> All I can do is give the particulars: an annotated diagnosis.
>
> . . . "Instability of self-image, interpersonal relationships, and mood . . . uncertainty about . . . long-term goals or career choice. . . ." Isn't this a good description of adolescence? Moody, fickle, faddish, insecure: in short, impossible.
>
> "Self-mutilating behavior (e.g., wrist-scratching). . . ." I've skipped forward a bit. This is the one that caught me by surprise as I sat on the floor of the bookstore reading my diagnosis. Wrist-scratching! I thought I'd invented it. Wrist-banging, to be precise. . . .
>
> I had a butterfly chair. In the sixties, everyone in Cambridge had a butterfly chair. The metal edge of its upturned seat was perfectly placed for wrist-banging. I had tried breaking ashtrays and walking on the shards, but I didn't have the nerve to tread firmly. Wrist-banging—slow, steady, mindless—was a better solution. It was cumulative injury, so each bang was tolerable. . . .
>
> I spent hours in my butterfly chair banging my wrist. I did it in the evenings, like homework. I'd do some homework, then I'd spend half an hour wrist-banging, then finish my homework, then back in the chair for some more banging before brushing my teeth and going to bed.
>
> I was trying to explain my situation to myself. My situation was that I was in pain and nobody knew it; even I had trouble knowing it. So I told myself, over and over, You are in pain. It was the only way I could get through to myself ("counteract feelings of 'numbness'"). I was demonstrating, externally and irrefutably, an inward condition. . . .

"The person often experiences this instability of self-image as chronic feelings of emptiness or boredom." My chronic feelings of emptiness and boredom came from the fact that I was living a life based on my incapacities, which were numerous. A partial list follows. I could not and did not want to: ski, play tennis, or go to gym class; attend to any subject in school other than English and biology; write papers on any assigned topics (I wrote poems instead of papers for English; I got Fs); plan to go or apply to college; give any reasonable explanation for these refusals.

My self-image was not unstable. I saw myself, quite correctly, as unfit for the educational and social systems. But my parents and teachers did not share my self-image. Their image of me was unstable, since it was out of kilter with reality and based on their needs and wishes. They did not put much value on my capacities, which were admittedly few, but genuine. I read everything, I wrote constantly, and I had boyfriends by the barrelful. . . .

I often ask myself if I'm crazy. I ask other people too. "Is this a crazy thing to say?" I'll ask before saying something that probably isn't crazy.

I start a lot of sentences with "Maybe I'm totally nuts," or "Maybe I've gone 'round the bend." If I do something out of the ordinary—take two baths in one day, for example—I say to myself: "Are you crazy?" (Kaysen, 1993, pp. 150–159)

Was Susanna Kaysen just a mixed-up adolescent, with parents who expected too much of her and locked her away when she didn't comply? Or was she a deeply troubled young woman, whose stay in the hospital prevented her complete psychological deterioration? Is the diagnosis of borderline personality disorder a valid psychological disorder, or is it a label we give to people who don't conform? Kaysen's *Girl, Interrupted* (which was made into a motion picture starring Winona Ryder) brings life to the enduring debates about the validity and ethics of the diagnosis of borderline personality disorder.

Personality is all the ways we have of acting, thinking, believing, and feeling that make each of us unique. A *personality trait* is a complex pattern of behavior, thought, and feeling that is stable across time and across many situations.

DEFINING AND DIAGNOSING PERSONALITY DISORDERS

A **personality disorder** is a long-standing pattern of maladaptive behaviors, thoughts, and feelings. To be diagnosed with a personality disorder, an adult must have shown these symptoms since adolescence or early adulthood. The personality disorders are highly controversial in modern clinical psychology because of problems theorists see in the current conceptualization of these disorders and their assessment.

The DSM-IV-TR calls special attention to personality disorders and treats them as different from the acute disorders, such as major depression and schizophrenia, by placing the personality disorders on Axis II of the diagnostic system, instead of on Axis I with the acute disorders (see Chapter 4). People diagnosed with a personality disorder often experience one of the acute disorders, such as major depression or substance abuse, at sometime in their lives (Grant et al., 2004). Indeed, these acute disorders are often what bring them to the attention of clinicians. People diagnosed with personality disorders tend not to seek therapy until they experience a bout of major depression or until their substance abuse lands them in jail or the hospital, because they often do not see the behaviors that constitute their personality disorder as maladaptive. In addition, they often have serious problems relating to other people, and these relationship problems may bring them into therapy.

The DSM-IV-TR groups personality disorders into three clusters (see the DSM-IV-TR information in Table 12.1 on page 424). *Cluster A* includes three

TABLE 12.1   DSM-IV-TR
Personality Disorders
The DSM-IV-TR groups personality disorders into three clusters.
Cluster A: Odd-Eccentric Personality Disorders
People with these disorders have symptoms similar to those of people with schizophrenia, including inappropriate or flat affect, odd thought and speech patterns, and paranoia. People with these disorders maintain their grasp on reality, however.
Cluster B: Dramatic-Emotional Personality Disorders
People with these disorders tend to be manipulative, volatile, and uncaring in social relationships. They are prone to impulsive, sometimes violent behaviors that show little regard for their own safety or the safety or needs of others.
Cluster C: Anxious-Fearful Personality Disorders
People with these disorders are extremely concerned about being criticized or abandoned by others and, thus, have dysfunctional relationships with others.

Source: Reprinted with permission from the *Diagnostic and Statistical Manual of Mental Disorders,* Fourth Edition, Text Revision. Copyright © 2000 American Psychiatric Association.

disorders characterized by *odd or eccentric behaviors and thinking:* paranoid personality disorder, schizoid personality disorder, and schizotypal personality disorder. Each of these disorders has some of the features of schizophrenia, but people diagnosed with these personality disorders are not psychotic. Their behaviors are simply odd and often inappropriate. For example, they may be chronically suspicious of others or speak in odd ways that are difficult to understand.

Cluster B includes four disorders characterized by *dramatic, erratic, and emotional behavior and interpersonal relationships:* antisocial personality disorder, histrionic personality disorder, borderline personality disorder, and narcissistic personality disorder. People diagnosed with these disorders tend to be manipulative, volatile, and uncaring in social relationships and prone to impulsive behaviors. They may behave in wild and exaggerated ways or even engage in suicidal attempts to try to gain attention.

Cluster C includes three disorders characterized by *anxious and fearful emotions and chronic self-doubt:* dependent personality disorder, avoidant personality disorder, and obsessive-compulsive personality disorder. People diagnosed with these disorders have little self-confidence and difficult relationships with others.

Some of the symptoms just described may sound very familiar. Indeed, the personality disorders are some of the easiest to see in yourself and your family members. The criteria for diagnosing personality disorders are more vague than the criteria for many of the other, more acute disorders and thus leave more room for misapplication (Costa & Widiger, 2002). For example, one of the symptoms of dependent personality disorder is "difficulty expressing disagreement with others because of fear of loss of support or approval." Most of us can probably see signs of this tendency in ourselves or in someone close to us. In *Taking Psychology Personally: Seeing Yourself in the Personality Disorders,* we discuss the problems with diagnosing oneself with the personality disorders.

Problems with the DSM Categories

Many theorists have raised objections to the DSM-IV-TR conceptualization and organization of the personality disorders (see Trull & Durrett, 2005). First, the DSM-IV-TR treats these disorders as categories. That is, each disorder is described as if it represents something qualitatively different from a "normal" personality, yet there is substantial evidence that several of the disorders recognized by the DSM-IV-TR represent the extreme versions of normal personality traits (Widiger, Costa, & McCrae, 2002). Later, we will

Taking Psychology Personally

Seeing Yourself in the Personality Disorders

In Chapter 1, we discussed the tendency for students reading an abnormal psychology textbook to see signs of many mental disorders in themselves or in the people in their lives. Students may be especially prone to see personality disorders in themselves or in others. Indeed, people are considerably more likely to diagnose themselves on self-report questionnaires as having a personality disorder than are clinicians to diagnose them in the context of psychiatric interviews (Weissman, 1993).

Why might this be so? It may occur because people tend to attribute behaviors to personality traits and to ignore the influence of situations on those behaviors (see Ross & Nisbett, 1991). This tendency is often referred to as *fundamental attribution error.*

A classic study demonstrating how strongly people discount situational influences over personality influences was conducted by Jones and Harris (1967). They asked participants to read essays presumably written by other participants. The participants were told that the persons writing the essays had been assigned to present a particular viewpoint on the topic of the essay. For example, they were told that a political science student had been assigned to write an essay defending communism in Cuba or that a debate student had been assigned to attack the proposition that marijuana should be legalized. Despite the fact that the participants were told that the essay writers had been assigned to take a particular viewpoint (and had not chosen that viewpoint), they tended to believe that the essay writers actually held the viewpoint they presented in their essays.

If you think you see signs of one or more personality disorders in yourself or someone close to you, stop and ask yourself the following questions:

- *What are the situational influences that might be driving my behavior or my friend's or relative's behavior?* For example, let's say that you are concerned that your brother has developed an obsessive-compulsive personality disorder (see pp. 451–452) since he has taken on two jobs to try to help your family with finances. He is preoccupied with schedules and always has lists of things to do; he has become a workaholic; he has become a perfectionist to the point of not being able to get things done; and he has become even more moralistic than he was in high school.

It is true that certain situations can exaggerate the already dysfunctional behaviors of people with obsessive-compulsive personality disorder. However, consider the possibility that your brother's behaviors, particularly the ones that he has developed since taking these two jobs, are largely driven by the demands of his life rather than by enduring personality traits. Your brother's preoccupation with lists and schedules and his working 20 hours a day are probably behaviors that he believes are necessary, given the demands of the situation. This kind of pressure can cause many people to try to be perfectionists but to become so anxious about the possibility of failing that they cannot do their work. When you find yourself wondering if you or someone you care about has developed a personality disorder, stop to consider the aspects of the situation that might really be responsible for the behaviors you observe.

- *Am I selectively remembering behaviors that are signs of a personality disorder and selectively forgetting behaviors that contradict the diagnosis of a personality disorder?* One of the strongest reasons people overestimate the influence of personality traits on behaviors is that they selectively pay attention to and remember behaviors that are consistent with personality traits and ignore or forget behaviors that are inconsistent with the traits. For example, if you fear that you are an overly dependent person, you will probably find it quite easy to remember times in the past when you have had trouble making decisions without much advice from others, have felt uncomfortable and helpless when alone, or have been passive in voicing your opinions or needs to others. You will probably forget the many more times when you made decisions with no help from others, actually enjoyed being alone, or spoke up to express your opinions or needs.

It can be helpful to write down all the times in the recent or distant past when you behaved in ways that contradicted the troubling personality trait you think you have. Or you might want to ask a trusted friend to help you sort out whether your behaviors are always consistent with a negative personality trait.

- *Are the behaviors I am observing part of a longtime pattern of behavior, or do they occur only occasionally?* Most of us occasionally act in dysfunctional or plainly stupid ways. Sometimes, these actions are driven by the situations in which we find ourselves, but sometimes we act in stupid ways even when there is no apparent situational excuse for doing so. A personality disorder is a pattern of behavior that has existed most of a person's life and that the person demonstrates across a range of situations.

(continued)

Taking Psychology Personally (*continued*)

Occasional lapses into dysfunctional behavior do not constitute a personality disorder.

■ *Are the behaviors I am observing significantly impairing or causing distress in my life or the lives of other people?* In order to qualify as a personality disorder, a set of behaviors has to cause significant distress or impairment in a person's life. We all have our quirks, our tendencies to act in ways we wish we would not. It can be helpful to examine these behaviors and make attempts to change them if they are not in line with our values or if they

occasionally get us into trouble. However, most quirks are relatively benign.

As always, if you are quite concerned about whether you or someone you care about has a significant psychological problem, it can be helpful to talk it out with a professional mental-health specialist who is trained to differentiate between psychological disorders and variations in people's behaviors that are not dangerous or unhealthy.

---

discuss proposals to replace the categorical organization of the personality disorders with one that characterizes them as extreme versions of normal personality traits.

Second, there is a great deal of overlap in the diagnostic criteria for the various personality disorders in the DSM-IV-TR. The majority of people who are diagnosed with one disorder tend to meet the diagnostic criteria for at least one more personality disorder. This overlap suggests that there actually may be fewer personality disorders that adequately account for the variation in personality disorder symptoms. The overlap also makes it very difficult to obtain reliable diagnoses of the personality disorders.

Third, diagnosing a personality disorder often requires information that is hard for a clinician to obtain. For example, the clinician may need accurate information about how an individual treats other people, information about how an individual behaves in a wide variety of situations, or information about how stable an individual's behaviors have been since childhood or adolescence. Again, this difficulty makes it hard to obtain reliable diagnoses of the personality disorders.

Fourth, the personality disorders are conceptualized as stable characteristics of an individual. Longitudinal studies have found, however, that people diagnosed with these disorders vary over time in how many symptoms they exhibit and the severity of these symptoms, so that they go in and out of the diagnosis over time (Shea et al., 2002). In particular, people often look as if they have a personality disorder when they are suffering from an acute Axis I disorder, such as major depression, but then their personality disorder symptoms seem to diminish when their Axis I disorder symptoms subside.

These problems make it difficult for clinicians to be confident of diagnoses of personality disorders. Indeed, the diagnostic reliability of the personality disorders is only fair (Trull & Durrett, 2005; Zanarini et al., 2000). The problems also make it difficult to do research on personality disorders. There is much less research on the epidemiology, causes, and treatment of the personality disorders than there is on most of the other disorders described in this book.

Gender and Ethnic Biases in Construction and Application

We will see throughout this chapter that there are differences in the frequency with which men and women are diagnosed with certain personality disorders, as well as some differences in the frequency with which different ethnic groups are diagnosed. One of the greatest controversies in the literature on personality disorders concerns claims that these apparent differences actually result from biases in the construction of these disorders in the DSM-IV-TR or in clinicians' applications of the diagnostic criteria (Cale & Lilienfeld, 2002; Hartung & Widiger, 1998; Widiger, 1998).

First, some theorists have argued that the diagnoses of histrionic, dependent, and borderline personality disorders, which are characterized by flamboyant behavior, emotionality, and dependence on others, are simply extreme versions of negative stereotypes of women's personalities (Kaplan, 1983; Sprock, 2000; Walker, 1994). For this reason, clinicians may sometimes be too quick to see these characteristics in women clients and to apply these diagnoses. It has also been argued that the diagnostic criteria for antisocial, paranoid, and obsessive-compulsive personality disorders, which are characterized by violent, hostile, and controlling behaviors, represent extremes of negative stereotypes of men. Clinicians may be biased to overapply these diagnoses to men but not to women (Sprock, Blashfield, & Smith, 1990). Similarly, clinicians may be biased to overapply diagnoses of antisocial and paranoid personality disorder to African Americans because they selectively perceive violence and hostility in African American clients (Iwamasa, Larrabee, & Merritt, 2000).

Another way that the DSM-IV-TR constructions of personality disorders may be biased is in not recognizing that the expressions of the symptoms of a disorder may naturally vary between groups. For example, the diagnostic criteria for antisocial personality disorder emphasize overt signs of callous and cruel antisocial behavior, including committing crimes against property and people. Women with antisocial personality disorder may be less likely than men with the disorder to engage in such overt antisocial behaviors, because of greater social sanc-

tions against women for doing so. Instead, women with antisocial personality disorder may find more subtle or covert ways of being antisocial, such as acting cruelly toward their children or covertly sabotaging people at work (Cale & Lilienfeld, 2002). As we will see when we discuss childhood disorders in Chapter 13, the same argument has been made about possible gender differences in the expression of a childhood precursor to antisocial personality disorder, conduct disorder. It may also be that certain ethnic groups, such as European Americans, are better able to hide their symptoms of callous and cruel behavior, because they hold more social power and can exercise these tendencies in ways that are deemed acceptable in the majority culture (e.g., being ruthless in business deals).

Similarly, some theorists have argued that the DSM-IV-TR ignores or downplays possible masculine ways of expressing dependent, histrionic, and borderline personality disorders, and this bias contributes to an underdiagnosis of these disorders in men (see Widiger et al., 1995). For example, one of the criteria for histrionic personality disorder is

Women and men may exhibit flamboyant and self-aggrandizing behavior in different ways.

"consistently uses physical appearance to draw attention to the self" (APA, 2000). Although the DSM-IV-TR notes that men may express this characteristic by acting "macho" and bragging about their athletic skills, the wording of the criterion brings to mind everyday behaviors more common among women, such as wearing makeup.

Even if the DSM-IV-TR criteria for personality disorders are not biased in their construction, they may be biased in their application. Clinicians may be too quick to see histrionic, dependent, and borderline personality disorders in women or antisocial personality disorder in men. Several studies have shown that, when clinicians are presented with the description of a person who exhibits many of the symptoms of one of these disorders—say, a histrionic personality disorder—they are more likely to make that diagnosis if the person is described as a female than if the person is described as a male (Widiger, 1998). It is important to note that these studies did not suggest that the DSM-IV-TR criteria are themselves gender-biased—only that clinicians seem to be misapplying the DSM-IV-TR according to gender stereotypes.

In response to these concerns about the biased application of the criteria for personality disorders, Widiger (1998) argues that structured interviews, rather than unstructured interviews, should be used in assessing personality disorders. The idea is that the use of structured interviews would increase the chances that the DSM-IV-TR criteria would be applied systematically and fairly to men and women and to people of different ethnic groups. Studies that have used structured interviews tend to show less gender bias in clinicians' applications of the DSM-IV-TR personality disorder criteria than do studies that have used unstructured interviews. However, the structured interviews still yield greater numbers of women than men being diagnosed with histrionic, dependent, and borderline personality disorder and more men than women being diagnosed with antisocial personality disorder (e.g., Kessler et al., 1994). Studies that have compared the impact of structured clinical interviews with that of self-report instruments on the distribution of personality disorder diagnoses among ethnic groups have found that the two methods of assessment produce similar results (Chavira et al., 2003). These results suggest that it is not just clinicians' bias in applying the DSM-IV-TR criteria that leads to gender and ethnic differences in the apparent prevalence of the disorder.

Other theorists have argued that the DSM-IV-TR criteria should be balanced to include equal numbers of symptoms and diagnoses that are pathological variants of masculine and feminine personality traits (Frances, First, & Pincus, 1995; Kaplan, 1983; Walker, 1994). Indeed, the authors of the DSM-IV-TR attempted to include more masculine variations of symptoms thought to be more common in women (e.g., masculine forms of dependency) and more feminine versions of stereotypical masculine symptoms (e.g., feminine forms of antisocial behavior). Some theorists argue the DSM-IV-TR did not go far enough and that the next edition of the DSM should strive for even greater balance in pathologizing men and women. However, others argue that, just because it would be possible to construct a set of diagnostic criteria that yields equal numbers of men and women with each personality disorder, or equal numbers of people in different ethnic groups with each disorder, it does not mean that these criteria reflect the true structure and distribution of personality disorders in people.

ODD-ECCENTRIC PERSONALITY DISORDERS

People diagnosed with the **odd-eccentric personality disorders** (see the Concept Overview in Table 12.2) behave in ways that are similar to the behaviors of people with schizophrenia or paranoid psychotic disorder, but they retain their grasp on reality to a greater degree than do people who are psychotic. That is, they may be paranoid, speak in odd and eccentric ways that make them difficult to understand, have difficulty relating to other people, and have unusual beliefs or perceptual experiences that fall short of delusions and hallucinations. Some researchers consider this group of personality disorders to be part of the "schizophrenia spectrum" (see Nigg & Goldsmith, 1994). That is, these disorders may be precursors to schizophrenia in some people or may be milder versions of schizophrenia. These disorders often occur in people who have first-degree relatives with schizophrenia.

Paranoid Personality Disorder

The defining feature of **paranoid personality disorder** is a pervasive and unwarranted mistrust of others. People diagnosed with this disorder deeply believe that other people are chronically trying to deceive them or to exploit them and are preoccupied with concerns about the loyalty and trustworthiness of others. They are hypervigilant for confirming evidence of their suspicions. They are often penetrating observers of situations, noting details that most other people miss. For example, they notice a slight grimace on the face of their boss or an apparently trivial slip of the tongue by

TABLE 12.2   Concept Overview

Odd-Eccentric Personality Disorders

People with an odd-eccentric personality disorder may exhibit mild signs of schizophrenia.

Label	Key Features	Relationship to Schizophrenia
Paranoid personality disorder	Chronic and pervasive mistrust and suspicion of other people that is unwarranted and maladaptive	Weak relationship
Schizoid personality disorder	Chronic lack of interest in and avoidance of interpersonal relationships, emotional coldness toward others	Unclear relationship
Schizotypal personality disorder	Chronic pattern of inhibited or inappropriate emotion and social behavior, aberrant cognitions, disorganized speech	Strong relationship—considered a mild version of schizophrenia

Source: Reprinted with permission from the *Diagnostic and Statistical Manual of Mental Disorders,* Fourth Edition, Text Revision. Copyright © 2000 American Psychiatric Association.

their spouse, when these would have gone unnoticed by everyone else. Moreover, people diagnosed with paranoid personality disorder consider these events highly meaningful and spend a great deal of time trying to decipher these clues about other people's true intentions. They are also overly sensitive to criticism or potential criticism.

People with paranoid personality disorder tend to misinterpret or overinterpret situations in line with their suspicions. For example, a husband might interpret his wife's cheerfulness one evening as evidence that she is having an affair with a man at work. They are resistant to rational arguments against their suspicions and may take the fact that another person is arguing with them as evidence that this person is part of the conspiracy against them. Some become withdrawn from others in an attempt to protect themselves, but others are aggressive and arrogant, sure that their way of looking at the world is right and superior and that the best defense against the conspiring of others is a good offense. In the following case study, Felix is diagnosed with paranoid personality disorder.

CASE STUDY

Felix is a 59-year-old construction worker who worries that his coworkers might hurt him. Last week, while he was using a table saw, Felix's hand slipped and his fingers came very close to being cut badly. Felix wonders if someone sabotaged the saw, so that somehow the piece of wood he was working with slipped and drew his hand into the saw blade. Since this incident, Felix has observed his coworkers looking at him and whispering to each other. He mentioned his suspicion that the saw had been tampered with to his boss, but the boss told him that was a crazy idea and that Felix obviously had just been careless.

Felix does not have any close friends. Even his brothers and sisters avoid him, because he frequently misinterprets things they say to be criticisms of him. Felix was married for a few years, but his wife left him when he began to demand that she not see any of her friends or go out without him, because he suspected she was having affairs with other men. Felix lives in a middle-class neighborhood in a small town that has very little crime. Still, he owns three handguns and a shotgun, which are always loaded, in expectation of someone breaking into his house.

Prevalence and Prognosis of Paranoid Personality Disorder

Epidemiological studies suggest that between 0.5 and 5.6 percent of people in the general population can be diagnosed with paranoid personality disorder (Bernstein, Useda, & Siever, 1995; Ekselius et al., 2001). Among people treated for the disorder, males outnumber females three to one (Fabrega et al.,

Garfield ® by Jim Davis

1991). People diagnosed with paranoid personality disorder appear to be at increased risk for a number of acute psychological problems, including major depression, anxiety disorders, substance abuse, and psychotic episodes (Bernstein et al., 1995; Grant et al., 2004). Not surprisingly, their interpersonal relationships, including intimate ones, tend to be unstable. Retrospective studies suggest that their prognosis is generally poor, with their symptoms intensifying under stress.

Theories and Treatment of Paranoid Personality Disorder

Some family history studies have shown that paranoid personality disorder is somewhat more common in the families of people with schizophrenia than in the families of healthy control subjects. This finding suggests that paranoid personality disorder may be part of the schizophrenic spectrum of disorders (Chang et al., 2002; Kendler et al., 1994; Nigg & Goldsmith, 1994). Twin and adoption studies have not been done to tease apart genetic influences and environmental influences on the development of this disorder.

Cognitive theorists see paranoid personality disorder as the result of an underlying belief that other people are malevolent and deceptive, combined with a lack of self-confidence about being able to defend oneself against others (Beck & Freeman, 1990; Colby, 1981). Thus, the person must always be vigilant for signs of others' deceit or criticism and must be quick to act against others. A study of 17 patients diagnosed with paranoid personality disorder found that they endorsed beliefs as predicted by this cognitive theory more than did patients diagnosed with other personality disorders (Beck et al., 2001).

People diagnosed with paranoid personality disorder usually come into contact with clinicians only when they are in crisis. They may seek treatment for severe symptoms of depression or anxiety but often do not feel a need for treatment of their paranoia. In addition, therapists' attempts to challenge their paranoid thinking are likely to be misinterpreted in line with their paranoid belief systems. For example, a man with paranoid personality disorder may believe his wife paid his therapist to convince him that the wife is not having an affair. For this reason, it can be quite difficult to treat paranoid personality disorder (Millon et al., 2000).

In order to gain the trust of a person diagnosed with a paranoid personality disorder, the therapist must be calm, respectful, and extremely straightforward (Siever & Kendler, 1985). The therapist must behave in a highly professional manner at all times, not attempting to engender a warm, personal relationship with the client that might be misinterpreted. The therapist cannot directly confront the client's paranoid thinking but must rely on more indirect means of raising questions in the client's mind about his or her typical way of interpreting situations. Although many therapists do not expect paranoid clients to achieve full insight into their problems, they hope that, by developing at least some degree of trust in the therapist, the client can learn to trust others a bit more and thereby develop somewhat improved interpersonal relationships.

Cognitive therapy for people diagnosed with this disorder focuses on increasing their sense of self-efficacy for dealing with difficult situations, thus decreasing their fear and hostility toward others. As an example, consider the following interchange between a cognitive therapist and a woman named Ann, who believed that her coworkers were intentionally trying to annoy her and to turn her supervisor against her (Beck & Freeman, 1990, pp. 111–112):

VOICES

Therapist: You're reacting as though this is a very dangerous situation. What are the risks you see?

Ann: They'll keep dropping things and making noise to annoy me.

Therapist: Are you sure nothing worse is at risk?

Ann: Yeah.

Therapist: So you don't think there's much chance of them attacking you or anything?

Ann: Nah, they wouldn't do that.

Therapist: If they do keep dropping things and making noises, how bad will that be?

Ann: Like I told you, it's real aggravating. It really bugs me.

Therapist: So it would continue pretty much as it's been going for years now.

Ann: Yeah. It bugs me, but I can take it.

Therapist: And you know that if it keeps happening, at the very least you can keep handling it the way you have been—holding the aggravation in, then taking it out on your husband when you get home. Suppose we could come up with some ways to handle the aggravation even better or to have them get to you less. Is that something you'd be interested in?

Ann: Yeah, that sounds good.

Therapist: Another risk you mentioned earlier is that they might talk to your supervisor and turn her against you. As you see it, how long have they been trying to do this?

Ann: Ever since I've been there.

Therapist: How much luck have they had so far in doing that?

Ann: Not much.

Therapist: Do you see any indications that they're going to have any more success now than they have so far?

Ann: No, I don't guess so.

Therapist: So your gut reaction is as though the situation at work is really dangerous. But when you stop and think it through, you conclude that the worst they're going to do is to be really aggravating, and that even if we don't come up with anything new, you can handle it well enough to get by. Does that sound right?

Ann: [Smiling] Yeah, I guess so.

Therapist: And if we can come up with some ways to handle the stress better or handle them better, there will be even less they can do to you.

In this interchange, the therapist did not directly challenge Ann's beliefs about her coworkers' intentions but did try to reduce the sense of danger Ann felt about her workplace by helping her redefine the situation as aggravating rather than threatening. The therapist also enlisted Ann in an effort to develop new coping skills that might further reduce her aggravation.

Schizoid Personality Disorder

People diagnosed with **schizoid personality disorder** lack the desire to form interpersonal relationships and are emotionally cold in interactions with others. Other people describe them as aloof, reclusive, and detached or as dull, uninteresting, and humorless. People diagnosed with this disorder show little emotion in interpersonal interactions. They view relationships with others as unrewarding, messy, and intrusive. The man described next shows several of these symptoms (adapted from Spitzer et al., 1981, p. 209):

CASE STUDY

The patient is a 50-year-old retired police officer who is seeking treatment a few weeks after his dog was run over and died. Since that time he has felt sad, tired, and has had trouble sleeping and concentrating. The patient lives alone and has for many years had virtually no conversational contacts with other human beings beyond a "Hello" or "How are you?" He prefers to be by himself, finds talk a waste of time, and feels awkward when other people try to initiate a relationship. He occasionally spends some time in a bar but always off by himself and not really following the general

(continued)

conversation. He reads newspapers avidly and is well informed in many areas but takes no particular interest in the people around him. He is employed as a security guard but is known by his fellow workers as a "cold fish" and a "loner." They no longer even notice or tease him, especially since he never seems to notice or care about their teasing anyway.

The patient floats through life without relationships. His only companion was his dog, whom he dearly loved. At Christmas he bought the dog elaborate gifts and gave himself a wrapped bottle of scotch as if it were a gift from the dog. He believes that dogs are more sensitive and loving than people, and he can express toward them a tenderness and emotion not possible in his relationships with people. The loss of his pets are the only events in his life that have caused him sadness. He experienced the death of his parents without emotion and feels no regret at being completely out of contact with the rest of his family. He considers himself different from other people and regards emotionality in others with bewilderment.

This man would be diagnosed with schizoid personality disorder because of his long-standing avoidance of relationships with other people and his lack of emotions or emotional understanding. As is often the case with people diagnosed with

Group therapy can help people with schizoid personality disorder increase their social skills.

personality disorders, he seeks the help of a clinician only when a crisis occurs.

Prevalence of Schizoid Personality Disorder

Schizoid personality disorder is quite rare, with about 0.4 to 1.7 percent of adults manifesting the disorder at sometime in their lives (Ekselius et al., 2001; Weissman, 1993). Among people seeking treatment for this disorder, males outnumber females about three to one (Fabrega et al., 1991). They can function in society, particularly in occupations that do not require interpersonal interactions.

Theories and Treatment of Schizoid Personality Disorder

There is a slightly increased rate of schizoid personality disorder in the relatives of persons with schizophrenia, but the link between the two disorders is not clear (Kendler, Neale, Kessler, Heath, & Eaves, 1993; Nigg & Goldsmith, 1994). Twin studies of the personality traits associated with schizoid personality disorder, such as low sociability and low warmth, strongly suggest that these personality traits may be partially inherited (Costa & Widiger, 2002). This evidence for the heritability of schizoid personality disorder is only indirect, however.

Psychosocial treatments for schizoid personality disorder focus on increasing the person's social skills, social contacts, and awareness of his or her own feelings (Beck & Freeman, 1990; Quality Assurance Project, 1990). The therapist may model the expression of feelings for the client and help the client identify and express his or her own feelings. Social skills training, done through role-plays with the therapist and through homework assignments in which the client tries out new social skills with other people, is an important component of cognitive therapies. Some therapists recommend group therapy for people with schizoid personality disorder. In the context of group sessions, the group members can model interpersonal relationships and the person with schizoid personality disorder can practice new social skills directly with others.

Schizotypal Personality Disorder

Like people diagnosed with schizoid personality disorder, people diagnosed with **schizotypal personality disorder** tend to be socially isolated, to have a restricted range of emotions, and to be uncomfortable in interpersonal interactions. As children, people who develop schizotypal personality disorder are passive, socially unengaged, and hypersensitive to criticism (Olin et al., 1999).

The distinguishing characteristics of schizotypal personality disorder are its oddities in cognition, which generally fall into four categories (Beck & Freeman, 1990). The first is *paranoia or suspiciousness*. People diagnosed with schizotypal personality disorder perceive other people as deceitful and hostile, and much of their social anxiety emerges from this paranoia. The second category is *ideas of reference*. People diagnosed with schizotypal personality disorder tend to believe that random events or circumstances are related to them. For example, they may think it is highly significant that a fire has occurred in a store in which they shopped only yesterday. The third type of odd cognition is *odd beliefs* and *magical thinking*. For example, they may believe that others know what they are thinking. The fourth category of odd thought consists of *illusions* that are just short of hallucinations. For example, they may think they see people in the patterns of wallpaper.

In addition to having these oddities of thought, people diagnosed with schizotypal personality disorder tend to have speech that is tangential, circumstantial, vague, or overelaborate. In interactions with others, they may have inappropriate or no emotional responses to what other people say or do. Their behaviors are also odd, sometimes reflecting their odd thoughts. They may be easily distracted or fixate on an object for long periods of time, lost in thought or fantasy. On neuropsychological tests (see Chapter 4), people with schizotypal personality disorder show deficits in working memory, learning, and recall that are similar to those shown by people with schizophrenia (Barch, 2005).

Although the quality of these oddities of thought, speech, and behavior is similar to that in schizophrenia, it is not as severe as in schizophrenia, and people diagnosed with schizotypal personality disorder maintain basic contact with reality. The woman in the following case study shows many of the oddities of schizotypal personality disorder (adapted from Spitzer et al., 1981, pp. 95–96).

CASE STUDY

The patient is a 32-year-old unmarried, unemployed woman on welfare who complains that she feels "spacey." Her feelings of detachment have gradually become stronger and more uncomfortable. For many hours each day she feels as if she were watching herself move through life, and the world around her seems unreal. She feels especially strange when she looks into a mirror. For many years she has felt able to read people's minds by a "kind of clairvoyance I don't understand." According to her, several people in her family apparently also have this ability. She is preoccupied by the thought that she has some special mission in life but is not sure what it is; she is not particularly religious. She is very self-conscious in public, often feels that people are paying special attention to her, and sometimes thinks that strangers cross the street to avoid her. She is lonely and isolated and spends much of each day lost in fantasies or watching TV soap operas. She speaks in a vague, abstract, digressive manner, generally just missing the point, but she is never incoherent. She seems shy, suspicious, and afraid she will be criticized. She has no gross loss of contact with reality, such as hallucinations or delusions, and she has never been treated for emotional problems. She has had occasional jobs but drifts away from them because of lack of interest.

Prevalence of Schizotypal Personality Disorder

Between 0.6 and 5.2 percent of people will be diagnosed with schizotypal personality disorder at sometime in their lives (Ekselius et al., 2001; Weissman, 1993). Among people seeking treatment, it is over twice as commonly diagnosed in males as in females (Fabrega et al., 1991). As with the other odd-eccentric personality disorders, people diagnosed with schizotypal personality disorder are at an increased risk for depression and for schizophrenia or isolated psychotic episodes (Siever, Bernstein, & Silverman, 1995).

For a person to be given a diagnosis of schizotypal personality disorder, his or her odd or eccentric thoughts cannot be part of cultural beliefs, such as a cultural belief in magic or specific superstitions. Still, some psychologists have argued that people of color are more often diagnosed with schizophrenic-like disorders, such as schizotypal personality disorder, than are Whites, because White clinicians often misinterpret culturally bound beliefs as evidence of schizotypal thinking (Snowden & Cheung, 1990).

One large study of people in treatment found that the African American patients were more likely than the Caucasian or Hispanic patients to be diagnosed with schizotypal personality disorder on both self-report and standardized diagnostic interviews (Chavira et al., 2003). This finding suggests that African Americans may be diagnosed with this disorder relatively frequently, even when steps are taken to avoid clinician bias. It is possible that African Americans are more likely to be exposed to conditions that enhance a biological vulnerability to schizophrenia-like disorders. Such conditions include perinatal brain damage, urban living, and low socioeconomic status (see Chapter 11 for a discussion of these conditions in schizophrenia).

Theories and Treatment of Schizotypal Personality Disorder

Many more studies of the genetics of schizotypal personality disorder have been conducted than studies of the other odd-eccentric personality disorders. Family history, adoption, and twin studies all suggest that schizotypal personality disorder is transmitted genetically, at least to some degree (see Nigg & Goldsmith, 1994; Siever et al., 1998). In addition, schizotypal personality disorder is much more common in the first-degree relatives of people with schizophrenia than in the relatives of either psychiatric patients or healthy control groups (Gilvarry et al., 2001; Kendler, Neale, Kessler, Heath, & Eaves, 1993). This finding supports the view that schizotypal personality disorder is a mild form of schizophrenia, which is transmitted through genes in ways similar to those of schizophrenia.

Similarly, some of the nongenetic biological factors implicated in schizophrenia are also present in people with schizotypal personality disorder (Barch, 2005). In particular, people diagnosed with this disorder show problems in the ability to sustain attention on cognitive tasks, as well as deficits in memory similar to those seen in people with schizophrenia (e.g., Mitropoulou et al., 2003). People with schizotypal personality disorder also tend to show a dysregulation of the neurotransmitter dopamine in the brain, as do people with schizophrenia (Abi-Dargham et al., 2004). Thus, like people with schizophrenia, people with schizotypal personality disorder may have abnormally high levels of dopamine in some areas of their brains. Finally, people with schizotypal personality disorder show abnormalities in the structure of their brains that are similar to those seen in people with schizophrenia (Barch, 2005).

Schizotypal personality disorder is most often treated with the same drugs that are used to treat schizophrenia, including traditional neuroleptics, such as haloperidol and thiothixene, and the atypical antipsychotics, such as olanzapine (Keshavan et al., 2004; Siever et al., 1998). As in schizophrenia, these drugs appear to relieve psychotic-like symptoms, including ideas of reference, magical thinking, and illusions. Antidepressants are sometimes used to help people with schizotypal personality disorder who are experiencing significant distress.

Although there are few psychological theories of schizotypal personality disorder, psycho-

logical therapies have been developed to help these people overcome some of their symptoms. In psychotherapy, it is especially important for therapists to establish good relationships with clients, because these clients typically have few close relationships and tend to be paranoid (Beck & Freeman, 1990). The next step in therapy is to help clients increase social contacts and learn socially appropriate behaviors through social skills training. Group therapy may be especially helpful in increasing clients' social skills. The crucial component of cognitive therapy with clients diagnosed with schizotypal personality disorder is teaching them to look for objective evidence in the environment for their thoughts and to disregard bizarre thoughts. For example, a client who often thinks that he or she is not real can be taught to identify that thought as bizarre and to discount the thought when it occurs, rather than taking it seriously and acting on it.

SUMMING UP

- People diagnosed with the odd-eccentric personality disorders—paranoid, schizoid, and schizotypal personality disorders—have odd thought processes, emotional reactions, and behaviors similar to those of people with schizophrenia, but they retain their grasp on reality.

- People diagnosed with paranoid personality disorder are chronically suspicious of others but maintain their grasp on reality.

- People diagnosed with schizoid personality disorder are emotionally cold and distant from others and have great trouble forming interpersonal relationships.

- People diagnosed with schizotypal personality disorder have a variety of odd beliefs and perceptual experiences but maintain their grasp on reality.

- These personality disorders, especially schizotypal personality disorder, have been linked to familial histories of schizophrenia and some of the biological abnormalities of schizophrenia.

- People diagnosed with these disorders tend not to seek treatment, but, when they do, therapists pay close attention to the therapeutic relationship and help the clients learn to reality-test their unusual thinking.

- Antipsychotics may help people with schizotypal personality disorder reduce their odd thinking.

TABLE 12.3 Concept Overview

Dramatic-Emotional Personality Disorders

People with dramatic-emotional personality disorders tend to have unstable emotions and to engage in dramatic and impulsive behavior.

Label	Key Features	Similar Disorders on Axis I
Antisocial personality disorder	Pervasive pattern of criminal, impulsive, callous, or ruthless behavior; disregard for the rights of others; no respect for social norms	Conduct disorder (diagnosed in children)
Borderline personality disorder	Rapidly shifting and unstable mood, self-concept, and interpersonal relationships; impulsive behavior; transient dissociative states; self-effacement	Mood disorders
Histrionic personality disorder	Rapidly shifting moods, unstable relationships, and intense need for attention and approval; dramatic, seductive behavior	Somatoform disorders, mood disorders
Narcissistic personality disorder	Grandiose thoughts and feelings of one's own worth; obliviousness to others' needs; exploitative, arrogant demeanor	Manic symptoms

Source: Reprinted with permission from the *Diagnostic and Statistical Manual of Mental Disorders*, Fourth Edition, Text Revision. Copyright © 2000 American Psychiatric Association.

DRAMATIC-EMOTIONAL PERSONALITY DISORDERS

People diagnosed with the **dramatic-emotional personality disorders** engage in behaviors that are dramatic and impulsive, and they often show little regard for their own safety or the safety of others (see the Concept Overview in Table 12.3). For example, they may engage in suicidal behaviors or self-damaging acts, such as self-cutting. They may also act in hostile, even violent ways against others. One of the core features of this group of disorders is a lack of concern for others. Two of the disorders in this cluster, antisocial personality disorder and borderline personality disorder, have been the focus of a great deal of research, whereas the other two, narcissistic personality disorder and histrionic personality disorder, have not.

Antisocial Personality Disorder

Severe antisocial tendencies have been recognized under various names as a serious disorder for over two centuries (Sher & Trull, 1994). Pritchard (1837) used the term *moral insanity* to describe people with little self-control and no concern for the rights of others. Later, in 1891, Koch applied the term *psychopathic* to the same individuals. Subsequent writers in the late nineteenth and early twentieth centuries often applied the term *psychopath* to anyone who had a severely maladaptive personality. Today, the label *psychopath* is not part of the official DSM-IV-TR nomenclature. Instead, the DSM-IV-TR diagnoses people with chronic antisocial behaviors as having **antisocial personality disorder (ASPD).**

The key features of antisocial personality disorder, as defined by the DSM-IV-TR, are an impairment in the ability to form positive relationships with others and a tendency to engage in behaviors that violate basic social norms and values. People with this disorder are deceitful, as indicated by the repeated lying to or conning of others for personal profit or pleasure. They commit violent criminal offenses against others, including assault, murder, and rape, much more frequently than do people without the disorder (Hart & Hare, 1997). When caught, they tend to have little remorse, seeming indifferent to the pain and suffering they have caused others.

A prominent characteristic of antisocial personality disorder is poor control of one's impulses.

People with this disorder have a low tolerance for frustration and often act impetuously, with no apparent concern for the consequences of their behavior. They often take chances and seek thrills with no concern for danger. They are easily bored and restless, unable to endure the tedium of routine or to persist at the day-to-day responsibilities of marriage or a job (Millon et al., 2000). As a result, they tend to drift from one relationship to another and often are in lower-status jobs. They may engage in criminal activity impulsively, and 50 to 80 percent of men in jail may be diagnosable with antisocial personality disorder (Cale & Lilienfeld, 2002).

Antisocial personality disorder (ASPD), as defined by the DSM-IV-TR, differs in some important ways from the characterization of **psychopathy**. Whereas the DSM-IV-TR emphasizes observable antisocial behaviors in the diagnosis of ASPD, a pioneer in the study of psychopathy, Hervey Cleckley (1941), emphasized certain broad personality traits in psychopathy. More recently, Robert Hare (1991) has built on Cleckley's work to develop criteria for the diagnosis of psychopathy, which have been supported in research. These criteria include a superficial charm, a grandiose sense of self-worth, a tendency toward boredom and need for stimulation, pathological lying, an ability to be conning and manipulative, and a lack of remorse. People with psychopathy are cold and callous, gaining pleasure by competing with and humiliating others. They can be cruel and malicious, and they often insist on being seen as faultless. They are dogmatic in their opinions. However, when they need to be, people with psychopathy can be gracious and cheerful, until they get what they want. They then may revert to being brash and arrogant. Cleckley (1941) noted that, although psychopaths often end up in prisons or dead, many of them become successful businesspeople and professionals (see Cleckley, 1941). He suggested that the difference between psychopaths who become successful people and psychopaths who end up in jail is that the successful ones are better able to maintain an outward appearance of being normal. They may be able to do so because they have superior intelligence and can put on a "mask of sanity" and superficial social charm in order to achieve their goals.

Research on people with antisocial tendencies is mixed as to whether people are defined in terms of the Cleckley/Hare criteria for psychopathy, the DSM-IV-TR criteria for antisocial personality disorder, or simply in terms of having a record of severe criminal conduct. For example, several of the genetic studies we will review used prison inmates as their "antisocial" group. Although most inmates may be diagnosable with antisocial personality disorder, formal assessments of this diagnosis are often not done. These ambiguities in the research literature are important to keep in mind as we discuss the possible causes of and treatments for this disorder.

Prevalence of Antisocial Personality Disorder

Epidemiological studies doing formal assessments of antisocial personality disorder, as defined by the DSM-IV-TR, suggest it is one of the most common personality disorders, with approximately 3 percent of the general population being diagnosed with the disorder at sometime in their lives (Cale & Lilienfeld, 2002; Ekselius et al., 2001). Men are substantially more likely than women to be diagnosed with this disorder. Although some theorists have argued that clinicians are more likely to see antisociality in African Americans than in Caucasians (Iwamasa et al., 2000), epidemiological studies have not found ethnic differences in rates of diagnosis (Cale & Lilienfeld, 2002; Chavira et al., 2003; Cloninger, Bayon, & Przybeck, 1997). People diag-

Over half of men in jail may be diagnosable with antisocial personality disorder.

nosed with this personality disorder are somewhat more likely than people diagnosed with the other personality disorders to have low levels of education (Fabrega et al., 1991).

As many as 80 percent of people with antisocial personality disorder abuse substances, such as alcohol and illicit drugs (Kraus & Reynolds, 2001; Trull, Waudby, & Sher, 2004). Substance abuse, such as binge drinking, may be just one form of the impulsive behavior that is part of antisocial personality disorder. Substance abuse probably feeds impulsive and antisocial behavior among people with this personality disorder. Alcohol and other substances may reduce any inhibitions they do have, making it more likely they will lash out violently at others. People with this disorder are also at a somewhat increased risk for suicide attempts (particularly females) and for violent death (Cale & Lilienfeld, 2002).

The tendency to engage in antisocial behaviors is one of the most stable personality characteristics in this disorder (Loeber & Farrington, 1997; Moffitt, 1993; Perry, 1993). Many adults with antisocial personality disorder show a disregard for societal norms and a tendency for antisocial behavior beginning in childhood, and most would have been diagnosed with conduct disorder as children. For some people with this disorder, however, the antisocial behavior diminishes as they age. This is particularly true of people who were not antisocial as children but became antisocial as adolescents or young adults (Moffitt, 1993). This tendency may be due to a psychological or biological maturation process, or many people with this disorder may simply be jailed or otherwise constrained by society from acting out their antisocial tendencies.

Theories of Antisocial Personality Disorder

A variety of biological and psychosocial theories of antisocial personality disorder have received some empirical support. These theories are summarized in the Concept Overview in Table 12.4 on page 438.

There is substantial support for a genetic influence on antisocial behaviors, particularly criminal behaviors (Eley, Lichenstein, & Stevenson, 1999; Taylor, Iacono, et al., 2000). Twin studies find that the concordance rate for such behaviors is near 50 percent in MZ twins, compared with 20 percent or lower in DZ twins (Carey & Goldman, 1997; Rutter, MacDonald, et al., 1990). Adoption studies find that the criminal records of adopted sons are more similar to the records of their biological fathers than to those of their adoptive fathers (Cloninger & Gottesman, 1987; Mednick et al., 1987). Family history studies show that the family members of people with antisocial personality disorder have

increased rates of this disorder, as well as increased rates of alcoholism and criminal activity (Perry, 1993).

Most theorists suggest that antisocial behavior is not the result of one gene or even a small number of genes. Instead, some people appear to be born with a number of genetically influenced deficits that make them ill-equipped to manage ordinary life, putting them at risk for antisocial behavior (Dodge & Pettit, 2003).

One long-standing theory is that aggressiveness, such as that shown by people with antisocial personality disorder, is linked to the hormone testosterone. Although some studies have found that highly aggressive males have higher levels of testosterone than nonaggressive males, the evidence for a role for testosterone in most forms of aggression is weak (Brain & Susman, 1997). Hormones such as testosterone may play a more important role during prenatal development in organizing the fetal brain in ways that promote or inhibit aggressiveness, rather than having a direct influence on behavior in adolescence or adulthood.

Anthony Hopkins played a terrifying antisocial personality in the film *Silence of the Lambs*.

TABLE 12.4   Concept Overview

Contributors to Antisocial Personality Disorder

There may be many contributors to antisocial personality disorder.

Contributor	Description
Genetic predisposition	Genetic factors contribute to antisocial behavior.
Testosterone	Aggressiveness is associated with high levels of testosterone; alternatively, high levels of testosterone present in utero affect the development of the fetal brain in ways that promote aggressiveness.
Serotonin	Low levels of serotonin contribute to impulsive and aggressive behaviors.
Attention-deficit/hyperactivity disorder	Children with attention-deficit/hyperactivity disorder develop antisocial behavior in response to social rejection and punishment.
Executive functions	People with antisocial personality disorder have deficits in the parts of the brain that are involved in executive functions (planful behavior and self-monitoring).
Arousability	Low levels of arousability lead to fearlessness in dangerous situations and/or stimulation-seeking behavior, which contributes to antisocial personality disorder.
Social cognitive factors	Children with antisocial tendencies have parents who are harsh and neglectful, and the children interpret interpersonal situations in ways that promote aggression.

Recall that a prominent characteristic of antisocial personality disorder is a difficulty in inhibiting impulsive behaviors (Morey, 1993; Rutter, 1997; Sher & Trull, 1994). Some researchers argue that poor impulse control is at the heart of antisocial personality disorder (Rutter, 1997). What might be the biological causes of poor impulse control? Many animal studies have shown that impulsive and aggressive behaviors are linked to low levels of the neurotransmitter **serotonin,** leading to the suggestion that people with antisocial personality disorder may also have low levels of serotonin (Krakowski, 2003). Several studies of humans also suggest that impulsiveness and aggressiveness are correlated with low levels of serotonin (Mann et al., 2001).

Research with children who show antisocial tendencies indicates that a significant percentage, perhaps the majority, have *attention-deficit/hyperactivity disorder (ADHD),* which involves significant problems with inhibiting impulsive behaviors and maintaining attention (see Chapter 13). The disruptive behavior of these children leads to frequent punishment and to rejection by peers, teachers, and other adults. These children then become even more disruptive, and some become overtly aggressive and antisocial in their behaviors and attitudes. Thus, at least some adults with antisocial personality disorder may have lifelong problems with attentional deficits and hyperactivity, which then contribute to lifelong problems with controlling their behaviors.

People with antisocial personalities also show deficits in verbal skills and in the **executive functions** of the brain. These functions include the ability to sustain concentration, abstract reasoning, concept and goal formation, the ability to anticipate and plan, the capacity to program and initiate purposive sequences of behavior, self-monitoring and self-awareness, and the ability to shift from maladaptive patterns of behavior to more adaptive ones (see Henry & Moffitt, 1997). In turn, some, but not all, studies have found differences between antisocial adults (usually prison inmates) and the general population in the structure or functioning of the temporal and frontal lobes of the brain (Morgan & Lilienfeld, 2000). These deficits in brain func-

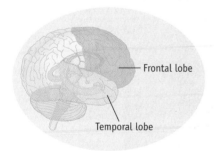

Frontal lobe

Temporal lobe

The temporal and frontal lobes of the brain may be implicated in deficits in executive functions in antisocial personality disorder.

tioning and structure might be tied to medical illnesses and exposure to toxins during infancy and childhood, both of which are more common among people who develop criminal records than among those who do not (see Chapter 13). On the other hand, these deficits might be tied to genetic abnormalities. Whatever their causes, low verbal intelligence and deficits in executive functions might contribute to poor impulse control and difficulty in anticipating the consequences of one's actions.

Many studies have suggested that persons with antisocial personality disorder show low levels of arousability, measured by relatively low resting heart rates, low skin conductance activity, and excessive slow-wave electroencephalogram readings (Herpertz et al., 2001; Raine, 1997). One interpretation of these data is that low levels of arousal indicate low levels of fear in response to threatening situations (Raine, 1997). Fearlessness can be put to good use—for instance, bomb disposal experts and British paratroopers also show low levels of arousal (McMillan & Rachman, 1987; O'Connor, Hallam, & Rachman, 1985). However, fearlessness may also predispose some people to antisocial and violent behaviors, such as fighting and robbery, which require fearlessness to execute. In addition, low-arousal children may not fear punishment and may not be deterred from antisocial behavior by the threat of punishment.

A second theory of how low arousability contributes to antisocial personality is that chronically low arousal is an uncomfortable state and leads to stimulation seeking (Eysenck, 1994). Again, if an individual seeks stimulation through prosocial or neutral acts, such as skydiving, stimulation seeking may not lead to antisocial behavior. But some individuals may seek stimulation through antisocial acts that are dangerous or impulsive, such as robbery or fights. The direction that stimulation seeking takes—toward antisocial activities or toward more neutral activities— may depend on the reinforcement that individuals receive for their behaviors. Those who are rewarded for antisocial behavior by family and peers may develop antisocial personalities, whereas those who are consistently punished for such behaviors and given alternative, more neutral behaviors may not (Dishion & Patterson, 1997).

Intelligence may also influence the direction that stimulation seeking takes (Henry & Moffitt, 1997). Children who are intelligent experience more rewards from school and, thus, may be more influenced by the norms of adults and positive peer groups in the choices they make for seeking stimulation. In contrast, children who are less intelligent may find school punishing and may turn to deviant peer groups for gratification and stimulating activities.

Much of the empirical research on the social and cognitive factors that contribute to antisocial behavior has been conducted with children. Many children with antisocial tendencies come from homes in which they have experienced harsh and inconsistent parenting and physical abuse (Dishion & Patterson, 1997; Dodge & Pettit, 2003). The parents of these children alternate between being neglectful and being hostile and violent toward their children. These children learn ways of thinking about the world that promote antisocial behavior (Crick & Dodge, 1994). They enter social interactions with the assumption that other children will be aggressive toward them, and they interpret the actions of their peers in line with this assumption. As a result, they are quick to engage in aggressive behaviors toward others. These social and cognitive factors alone may be enough to lead to antisocial personalities in some children and adults.

Dodge and Pettit (2003) integrated the myriad biological, social, and cognitive factors associated with antisociality into a comprehensive model (see Figure 12.1 on page 440). According to this model, some people are born with neural, endocrine, and psychophysiological dispositions, or are born into sociocultural contexts, that put them at risk for antisocial behavior throughout their lifetimes. Early symptoms of aggression and oppositional behavior in a child lead to, and interact with, harsh discipline and a lack of warmth from parents, as well as conflicts with aggressive peers. These children are at risk for academic and social problems in school, which can motivate them to turn to deviant peer groups, where they are encouraged in antisocial behavior. All along, such children learn that the world is hostile and that they must defend themselves rapidly and often aggressively, and they are prone to impulsive behaviors or reactions to others. These children enter adulthood with a long history of negative interactions with others, violent and impulsive outbursts, and alienation from mainstream society. All these factors feed back on each other, perpetuating the cycle of antisocial behavior into adulthood.

Treatments for Antisocial Personality Disorder

People with antisocial personality disorder tend to believe they do not need treatment. They may submit to therapy when forced to because of marital discord, work conflicts, or incarceration, but they are prone to blaming others for their current situations, rather than accepting responsibility for their actions. As a result, many clinicians do not hold much hope for effectively treating persons with

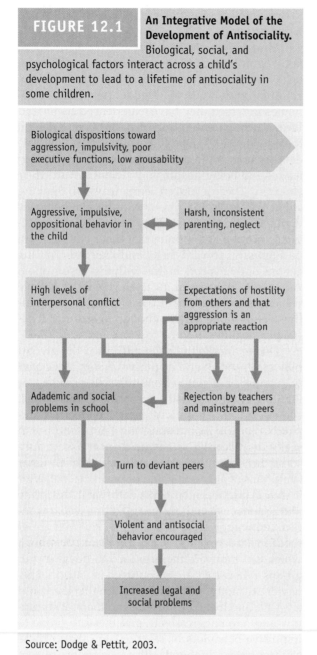

FIGURE 12.1   **An Integrative Model of the Development of Antisociality.** Biological, social, and psychological factors interact across a child's development to lead to a lifetime of antisociality in some children.

Source: Dodge & Pettit, 2003.

this disorder through psychotherapy (Kraus & Reynolds, 2001; Millon et al., 2000).

When clinicians attempt psychotherapy, they tend to focus on helping the person with antisocial personality disorder gain control over his or her anger and impulsive behaviors by recognizing triggers and developing alternative coping strategies (Kraus & Reynolds, 2001). Some clinicians also try to increase the individual's empathy for the effects of his or her behaviors on others (Hare & Hart, 1993).

Lithium and the atypical antipsychotics have been used successfully to control impulsive/aggres-

sive behaviors in people with antisocial personality disorder (Karper & Krystal, 1997; Markovitz, 2004). More recently, based on the evidence for low levels of serotonin in some animals prone to impulsive and aggressive behavior, researchers have been suggesting the use of drugs that inhibit the reuptake of serotonin into the synapses, such as the selective serotonin reuptake inhibitors (Karper & Krystal, 1997; Kraus & Reynolds, 2001). The efficacy of these drugs in treating antisocial personality disorder is not clear yet.

Borderline Personality Disorder

Recall that Susanna Kaysen, whom we met in the opener to this chapter, suffered a variety of disturbing symptoms and was given a diagnosis of **borderline personality disorder,** which she strongly questioned later in her life. In the following passage, a clinician describes another woman who was later diagnosed with borderline personality disorder (adapted from Linehan, Cochran, & Kehrer, 2001, pp. 502–504).

CASE STUDY

At the initial meeting, Cindy was a 30-year-old, white, married woman with no children who was living in a middle-class suburban area with her husband. She had a college education and had successfully completed almost 2 years of medical school. Cindy was referred by her psychiatrist of 1½ years, who was no longer willing to provide more than pharmacotherapy following a recent hospitalization for a near-lethal suicide attempt. In the 2 years prior to referral, Cindy had been hospitalized at least 10 times (one lasting 6 months) for psychiatric treatment of suicidal ideation; had engaged in numerous instances of parasuicidal behavior, including at least 10 instances of drinking Clorox bleach, multiple deep cuts, and burns; and had had three medically severe or nearly lethal suicide attempts, including cutting an artery in her neck.

Until age 27 Cindy was able to function well in work and school settings, and her marriage was reasonably satisfactory to both partners, although the husband complained of Cindy's excessive anger. When Cindy was in the second year of medical school, a classmate she

(continued)

knew only slightly committed suicide. Cindy stated that when she heard about the suicide, she immediately decided to kill herself also, but had very little insight into what about the situation actually elicited the inclination to kill herself. Within weeks she left medical school and became severely depressed and actively suicidal. Although Cindy presented herself as a person with few psychological problems before the classmate's suicide, further questioning revealed a history of severe anorexia nervosa, bulimia nervosa, and alcohol and prescription medication abuse, originating at the age of 14 years.

Over the course of therapy, a consistent pattern associated with self-harm became apparent. The chain of events would often begin with an interpersonal encounter (almost always with her husband), which culminated in her feeling threatened, criticized, or unloved. These feelings would often be followed by urges either to self-mutilate or to kill herself, depending somewhat on her levels of hopelessness, anger, and sadness. Decisions to self-mutilate and/or to attempt suicide were often accompanied by the thought "I'll show you." At other times, hopelessness and a desire to end the pain permanently seemed predominant. Following the conscious decision to self-mutilate or attempt suicide, Cindy would then immediately dissociate and at some later point cut or burn herself, usually while in a state of "automatic pilot." Consequently, Cindy often had difficulty remembering specifics of the actual acts. At one point, Cindy burned her leg so badly (and then injected it with dirt to convince the doctor that he should give her more attention) that reconstructive surgery was required.

Glenn Close portrayed a woman with borderline personality disorder in *Fatal Attraction*.

Cindy's symptoms represent some of the benchmarks of borderline personality disorder: out-of-control emotions that cannot be smoothed, a hypersensitivity to abandonment, a tendency to cling too tightly to other people, and a history of hurting oneself.

Instability is a key feature of borderline personality disorder. The *mood* of people with borderline personality disorder is unstable, with bouts of severe depression, anxiety, or anger seeming to arise frequently and often without good reason. Their *self-concept* is unstable, with periods of extreme self-doubt and periods of grandiose self-importance. Their *interpersonal relationships* are extremely unstable, and they can switch from idealizing others to despising them without provocation. People with borderline personality disorder often describe a desperate emptiness, which leads them to cling to new acquaintances or therapists in hopes that they will fill the tremendous void they experience in themselves. They are greatly concerned about abandonment and misinterpret other people's innocent actions as abandonment or rejection. For example, if a therapist has to cancel an appointment because she is ill, a client with borderline personality disorder might interpret this as a rejection by the therapist and become extremely depressed or angry.

Along with the instability of mood, self-concept, and interpersonal relationships comes a tendency toward impulsive, self-damaging behaviors, including self-mutilating behaviors and suicidal behavior. Cindy's self-mutilating behavior was to cut and burn herself. Finally, like Cindy, people with borderline personality disorder are prone to transient dissociative states, in which they feel unreal, lose track of time, and may even forget who they are. Glenn Close's depiction of a woman with borderline personality disorder in the movie *Fatal Attraction* aptly captured this diagnosis.

The variety of symptoms that make up the criteria for a diagnosis of borderline personality disorder reflects, to some extent, the complexity of this disorder. The manifestation of this disorder can be quite different from one person to the next and from one day to the next within any one person. Indeed, Trull and Durrett (2005) note that there are 126 ways an individual can meet the criteria for borderline personality disorder. The varied list of symptoms also reflects the difficulty that clinicians have had in agreeing on a conceptualization of this disorder (Gunderson, Zanarini, & Kisiel, 1995).

The term *borderline* has been used loosely for many years to refer to people who could not be fit easily into existing diagnoses of emotional disorders or psychotic disorders and who were extremely difficult to treat (Millon et al., 2000). One result of the variety of symptoms listed in the diagnostic criteria for the disorder is that there is a great deal of overlap between the borderline diagnosis and several of the other personality disorders, including paranoid, antisocial, narcissistic, histrionic, and schizotypal personality disorders (Grilo, Sanislow, & McGlashan, 2002). Indeed, most people diagnosed with borderline personality disorder also meet the diagnostic criteria for at least one other personality disorder.

People with borderline personality disorder also tend to receive diagnoses of one of the acute disorders, including substance abuse, depression, and generalized anxiety disorder; simple phobias; agoraphobia; posttraumatic stress disorder; panic disorder; or somatization disorder (Fabrega et al., 1991; Kraus & Reynolds, 2001; Weissman, 1993). About 75 percent of people with this disorder attempt suicide and about 10 percent die by suicide (Kraus & Reynolds, 2001; Linehan et al., 2001). The greatest risk for suicide appears to be in the first year or two after people diagnosis. This may be because people are often not diagnosed with this disorder until a crisis brings them to the attention of the mental-health system.

The symptoms of borderline personality disorder create a number of severe and debilitating problems for people with this disorder and for people in their environment. A longitudinal study that followed 351 young adults diagnosed with the disorder found that their impulsivity and emotional instability led to difficulties in relating with other people, in meeting their social role obligations (for example, as a parent), and in achieving their academic and work goals (Bagge et al., 2004).

Prevalence of Borderline Personality Disorder

Epidemiological studies suggest that between 1 and 2 percent of the population will develop borderline personality disorder in their lives (Kraus & Reynolds, 2001; Weissman, 1993). In clinical settings, borderline personality disorder is much more often diagnosed in women than in men. It is somewhat more commonly diagnosed in people of color than in Whites and in people in lower socioeconomic classes (Chavira et al., 2003; Grilo et al., 2002). A large study of people in treatment for personality disorders found that Hispanics were more likely than Caucasians or African Americans to be diagnosed with borderline personality disorder (Chavira et al., 2003). This difference might occur because factors that contribute to this disorder, such as extreme stress, are more common among Hispanics. On the other hand, clinicians may overdiagnose this disorder in Hispanic people because they do not take into account the Hispanic cultural norms that permit a greater expression of strong emotions, such as anger, aggressiveness, and sexual attraction (Chavira et al., 2003).

People with this disorder are high users of outpatient mental-health services (Bender et al., 2001). One community study found that 50 percent had used some form of mental-health service in the past six months (Swartz et al., 1990). Follow-up studies of people treated as inpatients for borderline personality disorder suggest that about 50 percent continue to meet the diagnostic criteria for the disorder seven years later (Links, Heslegrave, & van Reekum, 1998). The more severe the symptoms at the time of treatment, the more likely the disorder is to be chronic.

Theories of Borderline Personality Disorder

Several family history studies of borderline personality disorder have been conducted, and the evidence that this disorder is transmitted genetically is mixed (Dahl, 1993; Nigg & Goldsmith, 1994). There are high rates of mood disorders in the families of persons diagnosed with borderline personality disorder, however (Kendler, Meale, Kessler, Heath, & Eaves, 1993). Functional magnetic resonance imaging (fMRI) studies show that people with borderline personality disorder have greater activation of the amygdala in response to pictures of emotional faces, as do people with mood and anxiety disorders, which may contribute to their difficulties in regulating their moods (Donegan et al., 2003) (see Figure 12.2). Recall that the amygdala is a part of the brain that is important in the processing of emotion. Similarly, positron-emission tomography studies have found decreased metabolism in the prefrontal cortex of patients with borderline personality disorder, as is also found in patients with mood disorders (Soloff et al., 2000). Most researchers do not suggest that borderline personality disorder is simply a type of affective disorder, but there clearly are links between the two disorders.

Impulsive behaviors in people with borderline personality disorder are correlated with low levels of serotonin (see Weston & Siever, 1993). Recall

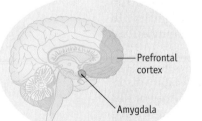

Prefrontal cortex

Amygdala

The amygdala and the prefrontal cortex have been implicated in borderline personality disorder.

Map Showing Activated Regions in the Amygdala for Normal Control and Borderline Personality Disorder Groups for Four Facial Expressions. People with borderline personality disorder showed more activity in the amygdala in response to all emotional faces.

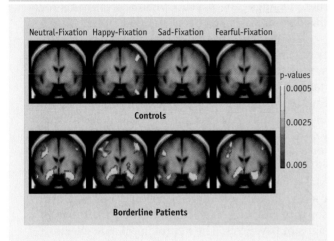

that impulsive behaviors in people with antisocial personality disorder have also been linked to low serotonin levels. This link suggests that low serotonin levels are not associated with one diagnostic category but, rather, with impulsive behaviors in general.

Psychoanalytic theorists, particularly those in the object relations school (see Chapter 2), have been extremely interested in borderline personality disorder (see Kernberg, 1979; Klein, 1952). They suggest that people with this disorder have very poorly developed views of themselves and others, stemming from poor early relationships with caregivers. These early caregivers may have encouraged the children's dependence on them. They may have punished the children's attempts at individuation and separation, so the children never learned to fully differentiate their views of themselves from their views of others. This makes them extremely reactive to others' opinions of them and to the possibility of being abandoned by others. When they perceive others as rejecting them, they reject themselves and may engage in self-punishment or self-mutilation.

They also have never been able to integrate the positive and negative qualities of either their self-concept or their concept of others, because their early caregivers were comforting and rewarding when they remained dependent and compliant toward them but hostile and rejecting when they tried to individuate from them. They tend to see themselves and other people as either all good or all bad and vacillate between these two views, a process known as **splitting.** The instability in emo-

tions and interpersonal relationships is due to splitting: Their emotions and their perspectives on their interpersonal relationships reflect their vacillation between the all-good and the all-bad self and the all-good and all-bad other.

Empirical studies have found that people with borderline personality disorder are more likely than people without the disorder to report childhoods marked by instability, abuse, neglect, and parental psychopathology (Helgeland & Torgersen, 2004). Of course, this is true of the childhoods of people with many different types of psychopathology and does not directly address the object relations theory of the development of this disorder.

One influential theorist, Marcia Linehan (Linehan et al., 2001), focuses on deficits in the ability to regulate emotions, which are probably physiologically based. Extreme emotional reactions to situations lead to impulsive actions. In addition, Linehan argues that people with borderline personality disorder have histories of significant others' discounting and criticizing their emotional experiences. Such histories make it even harder for them to learn appropriate emotion-regulation skills and to understand and accept their emotional reactions to events. People with this disorder come to rely on others to help them cope with difficult situations but do not have enough self-confidence to ask for help from others in mature ways. They become manipulative and indirect in trying to gain support from others.

Finally, research suggests that a number of people with borderline personality disorder have histories of physical and sexual abuse during childhood (Zanarini, 1997). Some theorists believe that the severe problems in self-concept seen in people with borderline personality disorder frequently are the result of childhood abuse (Kraus & Reynolds, 2001). Recently, researchers have found a variety of abnormalities in the structure and functioning of brain regions in people with both a history of sexual abuse and borderline personality disorder, including reductions in the volume of the hippocampus and amygdala and an abnormal change in blood flow in the prefrontal cortex with exposure to trauma-related memories (Schmahl et al., 2004; Tebartz van Elst et al., 2003). Although the implications of these findings are not yet known, they may suggest that early trauma alters the functioning of the brain in ways that contribute to the symptoms of borderline personality disorder.

Treatments for Borderline Personality Disorder

Over the past two decades, Linehan and colleagues have developed a therapy blending cognitive-behavioral techniques with interpersonal and psychodynamic techniques for the treatment of people with borderline personality disorder, which they call **dialectical behavior therapy** (Linehan et al., 2001). This therapy focuses on helping clients gain a more realistic and positive sense of self, learn adaptive skills for solving problems and regulating emotions, and correct their dichotomous thinking. Therapists teach clients to monitor their self-disparaging thoughts and black-or-white evaluations of people and situations and to challenge these thoughts and evaluations. Therapists also help clients learn appropriate assertiveness skills for close relationships, so that they can express their needs and feelings in a mature manner. Clients may learn how to control impulsive behavior by monitoring the situations most likely to lead to such behaviors and learn alternative ways to handle such situations. Controlled clinical trials testing dialectical behavior therapy have found that the therapy reduces depression, anxiety, and self-mutilating behavior while increasing interpersonal functioning (Bohus et al., 2004; Linehan, Heard, & Armstrong, 1993).

Psychodynamic treatments for people with borderline personality disorder involve helping clients clarify feelings, confronting them with their tendency to split images of the self and other, and interpreting clients' transference relationships with therapists (Kernberg, 1989). Many people with borderline personality disorder at times become extremely angry toward their therapists, as they move from idealizing to devaluing them. Therapists can use such times to help clients understand their splitting defenses and to set clear limits on the clients'

behaviors. Clients may also be taught more adaptive means of solving everyday problems, so that the world does not appear so overwhelming. Self-destructive tendencies are addressed, with therapists helping clients identify the feelings leading to these acts and develop healthy ways of coping with these feelings. The psychodynamic treatments for this disorder have not been studied empirically.

The drug treatments for people with borderline personality disorder have focused on reducing the symptoms of anxiety and depression through antianxiety drugs and antidepressants and on controlling impulsive behaviors with selective serotonin reuptake inhibitors. The antidepressants have been found to have some positive effects on the symptoms of this disorder and may help reduce aggressiveness and impulsivity (Hollander et al., 2001; Markovitz, 2004). Antipsychotics are sometimes used with people who have severe borderline personality disorder, particularly when they exhibit signs of psychosis. The neurological side effects of the phenothiazines (see Chapter 11) lead many people to discontinue taking these drugs (Soloff et al., 1993). Studies of the atypical antipsychotics clozapine and olanzapine have suggested that these drugs may relieve psychotic-like symptoms and other symptoms of borderline personality disorder in many people (Benedetti et al., 1998; Hough, 2001; Markovitz, 2004). Overall, however, the results of drug treatment studies have been mixed, and adding a drug treatment to an effective psychotherapy, such as dialectical behavior therapy, does not appear to improve recovery rates (Linehan et al., 2001; Simpson et al., 2004).

Histrionic Personality Disorder

Histrionic personality disorder shares features with borderline personality disorder, including rapidly shifting emotions and intense, unstable relationships. Whereas people with borderline personality disorder are often self-effacing in an attempt to win favor from others, people with histrionic personality disorder usually want to be the center of attention. People with borderline personality disorder may desperately cling to others in self-doubt and need, but people with histrionic personality disorder simply want the attention of others. These individuals pursue others' attention by being highly dramatic, being overtly seductive, and emphasizing the positive qualities of their physical appearance. They tend to speak in global terms. Others see them as self-centered and shallow, unable to delay gratification, demanding, and overly dependent. In the following case study, Debbie was diagnosed with

Suicidal behavior is common among people with borderline personality disorder.

histrionic personality disorder (Beck & Freeman, 1990, pp. 211–212).

> **CASE STUDY**
>
> Debbie was a 26-year-old woman who worked as a salesclerk in a trendy clothing store and who sought therapy for panic disorder with agoraphobia. She dressed flamboyantly, with an elaborate and dramatic hairdo. Her appearance was especially striking, since she was quite short (under 5 feet tall) and at least 75 pounds overweight. She wore sunglasses indoors throughout the evaluation and constantly fiddled with them, taking them on and off nervously and waving them to emphasize a point. She cried loudly and dramatically at various points in the interview, going through large numbers of tissue. She continually asked for reassurance. ("Will I be OK?" "Can I get over this?") She talked nonstop throughout the evaluation. When gently interrupted by the evaluator, she was very apologetic, laughing and saying, "I know I talk too much"; yet she continued to do so throughout the session.

Prevalence of Histrionic Personality Disorder

Between 1.3 and 2.2 percent of the population will develop this disorder at sometime in their lives, and the vast majority of persons diagnosed with this disorder are women (Ekselius et al., 2001; Weissman, 1993). People with this disorder are more likely to be separated or divorced than married. They tend to exaggerate medical problems and make more medical visits than the average person, as do people with somatoform disorders, and there is an increased rate of suicidal behavior and threats in this group (Kraus & Reynolds, 2001; Nestadt et al., 1990). People with this disorder most often seek treatment for depression or anxiety (Fabrega et al., 1991).

Theories and Treatment of Histrionic Personality Disorder

Although discussions of histrionic personalities date back to the ancient Greek philosophers, little is known about its causes or effective treatments. Family history studies indicate that histrionic personality disorder clusters in families, along with borderline personality disorder, antisocial personality disorder, and somatization disorder (Dahl,

1993). It is unclear whether this disorder is genetically related or results from processes within the family or environment.

Psychodynamic treatments focus on uncovering repressed emotions and needs and helping people with histrionic personality disorder express these emotions and needs in more socially appropriate ways. Cognitive therapy focuses on identifying these patients' assumptions that they cannot function on their own and helping them formulate goals and plans for their lives that do not rely on the approval of others (Beck & Freeman, 1990). Therapists attempt to help clients tone down their dramatic evaluations of situations by challenging these evaluations and suggesting more reasonable evaluations. None of the therapies for this disorder have been tested empirically.

Narcissistic Personality Disorder

The characteristics of **narcissistic personality disorder** are similar to those of histrionic personality disorder. In both disorders, individuals act in a dramatic and grandiose manner, seek admiration from others, and are shallow in their emotional expressions and relationships with others. Whereas people with histrionic personality disorder look to others for approval, however, people with narcissistic personality disorder rely on their own self-evaluations and see dependency on others as weak and dangerous. They are preoccupied with thoughts of their self-importance and with fantasies of power and success and view themselves as superior to most others. In interpersonal relationships, they make unreasonable demands for others to follow their wishes, ignore the needs and wants of others, exploit others to gain power, and are arrogant and demeaning. David, in the

Flamboyance is one symptom of histrionic personality disorder.

following case study, has been diagnosed with narcissistic personality disorder (adapted from Beck & Freeman, 1990, pp. 245–247).

David was an attorney in his early 40s when he sought treatment for depressed mood. He cited business and marital problems as the source of his distress and wondered if he was having a midlife crisis. David had grown up in a comfortable suburb of a large city, the oldest of three children and the only son of a successful businessman and a former secretary. Always known to have a bit of a temper, David usually provoked his parents and his sisters into giving in to his wishes. Even if they didn't give in to his demands, he reported that he usually went ahead and did what he wanted, anyway. David spoke of being an "ace" student and a "super" athlete but could not provide any details that would validate a superior performance in these areas. He also recollected that he had his pick of girlfriends, as most women were "thrilled" to have a date with him.

David went to college, fantasizing about being famous in a high-profile career. He majored in communications, planning to go on to law school and eventually into politics. He met his first wife during college, the year she was the university homecoming queen. They married shortly after their joint graduation. He then went on to law school, and she went to work to support the couple.

During law school, David became a workaholic, fueled by fantasies of brilliant work and international recognition. He spent minimal time with his wife and, after their son was born, even less time with either of them. At the same time, he continued a string of extramarital affairs, mostly brief sexual encounters. He spoke of his wife in an annoyed, devaluing way, complaining about how she just did not live up to his expectations. He waited until he felt reasonably secure in his first job so that he could let go of her financial support and then he sought a divorce. He continued to see his son occasionally, but he rarely paid his child support.

After his divorce, David decided that he was totally free to just please himself. He loved spending all his money on himself, and he lavishly decorated his condominium and bought an attention-getting wardrobe. He constantly sought the companionship of attractive women. He was very successful at making initial contacts and getting dates, but he rarely found anyone good enough to date more than once or twice. Sometimes he played sexual games to amuse himself, such as seeing how fast he could make sexual contact or how many women would agree to have sex with him. He eventually married Susan, the daughter of a well-known politician, and was presently unhappy with her and what she expected of him. He thought that she was lucky to have him and therefore did not really have the right to make demands. He knew that there would be plenty of other, prettier women who would be glad to cater to his needs.

At work, David believed that, because he was "different" from other people, they had no right to criticize him. But he had every right to criticize others. He also believed that other people were weak and needed contact with someone like him in order to bring direction or pleasure into their lives. He saw no problem in taking advantage of other people if they were "stupid" enough to allow him to do so.

David felt better when someone flattered him; when he was in a group social situation where he could easily grab the center of attention; and when he could fantasize about obtaining a high-level position, being honored for his great talent, or just being fabulously wealthy.

People with narcissistic personality disorder can be extremely successful in societies that reward self-confidence and assertiveness, such as the United States (Millon et al., 2000). When they grossly overestimate their abilities, however, they can make poor choices in their careers and may experience many failures. In addition, they annoy other people and can alienate the important people in their lives. People with this disorder seek treatment most often for depression and for trouble adjusting to life stressors (Fabrega et al., 1991).

Prevalence of Narcissistic Personality Disorder

Most epidemiological studies suggest that narcissistic personality disorder is rare, with a lifetime prevalence of less than 1 percent (Gunderson, Ronningstam, & Smith, 1995; Weissman, 1993), although one community study found a prevalence of 2.9 percent (Ekselius et al., 2001). It is more frequently diagnosed in men.

Theories and Treatment of Narcissistic Personality Disorder

Sigmund Freud (1914) viewed narcissism as a phase that all children pass through before transferring their love for themselves to significant others. Children can become fixated in this narcissistic phase, however, if they experience caregivers as untrustworthy and decide that they can rely only on themselves or if they have parents who indulge them and instill in them a grandiose sense of their abilities and worth (see also Horney, 1939). Later psychodynamic writers (Kernberg, 1998; Kohut, 1971) argued that narcissistic people actually suffer from low self-esteem and feelings of emptiness and pain as a result of rejection from parents and that narcissistic behaviors are reaction formations against these problems with self-worth.

Cognitive theorists Beck and Freeman (1990) argued that some narcissistic people develop assumptions about their self-worth that are unrealistically positive as the result of indulgence and overvaluation by significant others during childhood. Other narcissists develop the belief that they are unique or exceptional in reaction to being singled out as different from others due to ethnic or economic status or as a defense against rejection by important people in their lives. One study found that people diagnosed with narcissistic personality disorder were significantly more likely to endorse beliefs such as "I don't have to be bound by rules that apply to other people" than were people diagnosed with other disorders (Beck et al., 2001).

People with narcissistic personality disorder do not tend to seek treatment, except when they develop depression or are confronted with severe interpersonal problems (Beck & Freeman, 1990). They generally see any problems they encounter as due to the weaknesses of others, rather than their own weaknesses. Cognitive techniques can help these clients develop more sensitivity to the needs of others and more realistic expectations of their own abilities by learning to challenge their initially self-aggrandizing ways of interpreting situations (Millon et al., 2000). Such self-challenging doesn't come easily for these people, however, and they often do not remain in therapy once their acute symptoms or interpersonal problems decrease.

SUMMING UP

- People with dramatic-emotional personality disorders—antisocial, borderline, histrionic, and narcissistic personality disorders—have histories of unstable relationships and emotional experiences and of dramatic, erratic behavior.
- People with antisocial personality disorder regularly violate the basic rights of others and many engage in criminal acts.
- Antisocial personality disorder may have strong biological roots but is also associated with harsh and nonsupportive parenting.
- People with borderline personality disorder vacillate between all-good and all-bad evaluations of themselves and others.
- People with histrionic and narcissistic personality disorder act in flamboyant manners. People with histrionic personality disorder are overly dependent and solicitous of others, whereas people with narcissistic personality disorder are dismissive of others.
- None of these personality disorders responds consistently well to current treatments.

ANXIOUS-FEARFUL PERSONALITY DISORDERS

The **anxious-fearful personality disorders**—avoidant personality disorder, dependent personality disorder, and obsessive-compulsive personality disorder—are all characterized by a chronic sense of anxiety or fearfulness and behaviors intended to ward off feared situations (see the Concept Overview in Table 12.5 on page 448). In each of the three disorders, people fear something different, but they are all nervous and not very happy.

Avoidant Personality Disorder

Avoidant personality disorder has been studied more than the other two anxious-fearful personality disorders. People with avoidant personality disorder are extremely anxious about being criticized by others, so they avoid interactions with others in which there is any possibility of being criticized. They might choose occupations that are socially isolated, such as park rangers in the wilderness. When they must interact with others, people with avoidant personality disorder are restrained, nervous, and hypersensitive to signs of

TABLE 12.5   Concept Overview

Anxious-Fearful Personality Disorders

People with the anxious-fearful personality disorders are chronically anxious.

Label	Key Features	Similar Disorders on Axis I
Avoidant personality disorder	Pervasive anxiety, a sense of inadequacy, and a fear of being criticized, which lead to the avoidance of social interactions and nervousness	Social phobia
Dependent personality disorder	Pervasive selflessness, a need to be cared for, and a fear of rejection, leading to total dependence on and submission to others	Separation anxiety disorder, dysthymic disorder
Obsessive-compulsive personality disorder	Pervasive rigidity in one's activities and interpersonal relationships, including emotional constriction, extreme perfectionism, and anxiety about even minor disruptions in one's routine	Obsessive-compulsive disorder

Source: Reprinted with permission from the *Diagnostic and Statistical Manual of Mental Disorders,* Fourth Edition, Text Revision. Copyright © 2000 American Psychiatric Association.

being evaluated or criticized. They are terrified of saying something silly or doing something that will embarrass themselves. They tend to be depressed and lonely. They may crave relationships with others, but they feel unworthy of these relationships and isolate themselves, as the following case study illustrates (Spitzer et al., 1981, p. 59).

<div class="case-study">

CASE STUDY

A 27-year-old, single, male bookkeeper was referred to a consulting psychologist because of a recent upsurge in anxiety that seemed to begin when a group of new employees was assigned to his office section. He feared that he was going to be fired, though his work was always highly commended. A clique had recently formed in the office, and, though very much wanting to be accepted into this "in group," the patient hesitated to join the clique unless explicitly asked to do so. Moreover, he "knew he had nothing to offer them" and thought that he would ultimately be rejected anyway.

The patient spoke of himself as having always been a shy, fearful, quiet boy. Although he had two "good friends" whom he continued to see occasionally, he was characterized by fellow workers as a loner, a nice young man

</div>

who usually did his work efficiently but on his own. They noted that he always ate by himself in the company cafeteria and never joined in the "horsing around."

Prevalence of Avoidant Personality Disorder

Studies suggest that from 1 to 7 percent of people can be diagnosed with avoidant personality disorder. There are no strong gender differences in its prevalence (Ekselius et al., 2001; Fabrega et al., 1991; Weissman, 1993). People with this disorder are prone to chronic dysthymic disorder and to bouts of major depression and severe anxiety (Grant et al., 2004).

There is overlap between the characteristics of avoidant personality disorder and those of social phobia (van Velzen, Emmelkamp, & Scholing, 2000) (see Chapter 7). People with avoidant personality disorder have a general sense of inadequacy and a pervasive, general fear of being criticized, which leads them to avoid most types of social interaction. People with social phobia tend to fear specific social situations in which they will be expected to perform (such as giving a talk in class) and tend not to have a general sense of inadequacy. People with social phobia tend to want to connect with others, whereas people with avoidant personality disorder do not. People with schizoid personality disorder also withdraw from social situations; however, unlike people with avoidant personality disorder, they do not view themselves as inadequate and incompetent.

Theories and Treatment of Avoidant Personality Disorder

Family history studies show that avoidant personality disorder is more common in the first-degree relatives of people with the disorder than in the relatives of normal control groups (Dahl, 1993). Studies have not been done to determine whether this is due to a genetic transmission of the disorder or to certain family environments. What may be transmitted is a particular type of *temperament,* or level of emotional arousal and reactivity. Studies of temperamental differences among very young children suggest that some children may be born with a shy, fearful temperament, which causes them to avoid most people (Pilkonis, 1995).

Cognitive theorists suggest that people with avoidant personality disorder develop dysfunctional beliefs about being worthless as a result of rejection by important others early in life (Beck & Freeman, 1990). Cognitive theorists contend that the children whose parents reject them conclude, "I must be a bad person for my mother to treat me so badly," "I must be different or defective," and "If my parents don't like me, how could anyone?" (Beck & Freeman, 1990, p. 261). They assume that they will be rejected by others, as they were rejected by their parents, and thus avoid interactions with others. Their thoughts are of this sort: "Once people get to know me, they see I'm really inferior." When they must interact with others, they are unassertive and nervous, because they think, "I must please this person in every way or she will criticize me." They also tend to discount any positive feedback they receive from others, believing that others are just being nice or do not see how incompetent they really are. A study of 130 patients with avoidant personality disorder found that they endorsed beliefs such as this more often than patients with other personality disorders (Beck et al., 2001).

Cognitive and behavior therapies have proven helpful for people with avoidant personality disorder (Shea, 1993). These therapies have included graduated exposure to social settings, social skills training, and challenges to negative automatic thoughts about social situations. People receiving these therapies show increases in the frequency and range of social contacts, decreases in avoidance behaviors, and increases in comfort and satisfaction in social activities (Pretzer, 2004).

People with avoidant personality disorder may choose professions that allow them to avoid other people.

Dependent Personality Disorder

People with **dependent personality disorder** are anxious about interpersonal interactions, but their anxiety stems from a deep need to be cared for by others, rather than a concern that they will be criticized. Their desire to be loved and taken care of by others leads persons with dependent personality disorder to deny any of their own thoughts and feelings that might displease others, to submit to even the most unreasonable demands, and to cling frantically to others. People with this personality disorder cannot make decisions for themselves and do not initiate new activities, except in an effort to please others. In contrast to people with avoidant personality disorder, who avoid relationships, people with dependent personality disorder can function only within a relationship. They deeply fear rejection and abandonment and may allow themselves to be exploited and abused rather than lose relationships, as in the case of Francesca:

> Francesca was in a panic, because her husband seemed to be getting increasingly annoyed with her. Last night, he became very angry when Francesca asked him to cancel an upcoming business trip, because she was terrified of being left at home alone. In a rage, her husband shouted, "You can't ever be alone! You can't do anything by yourself! You can't even decide what to have for dinner by yourself! I'm sick of it. Grow up and act like an adult!"

(continued)

It was true that Francesca had a very difficult time making decisions for herself. While she was in high school, she couldn't decide which courses to take and talked with her parents and friends for hours about what she should do, finally doing whatever her best friend or her mother told her to do. When she graduated from high school, she didn't feel smart enough to go to college, even though she had gotten good grades in high school. She drifted into a job because her best friend had a job with the same company, and she wanted to remain close to that friend. The friend eventually dumped Francesca, however, because she was tired of Francesca's incessant demands for reassurance. Francesca frequently bought gifts for the friend and offered to do the friend's laundry or cooking, in obvious attempts to win the friend's favor. But Francesca also talked to the friend for hours in the evening, asking her whether she thought Francesca had made the right decision about some trivial issue, such as what to buy her mother for Christmas and how she thought Francesca was performing on the job.

Soon after her friend dumped her, Francesca met her future husband, and, when he showed some interest in her, she quickly tried to form a close relationship with him. She liked the fact that he seemed strong and confident, and, when he asked her to marry him, Francesca thought that perhaps finally she would feel safe and secure. However, especially since he has begun to get angry with her frequently, Francesca has been worrying constantly that he is going to leave her.

Prevalence of Dependent Personality Disorder

Between 1.6 percent and 6.7 percent of people will develop dependent personality disorder at sometime in their lives (Ekselius et al., 2001; Weissman, 1993). Higher rates of the disorder are found when self-report research methods are used than when structured clinical interviews are used, suggesting that many people feel they have this disorder, when clinicians would not diagnose it in them. More women than men are diagnosed with this disorder in clinical settings (Fabrega et al., 1991). Periods of dysthymia, major depression, and chronic anxiety over being separated from important others are common in people with the disorder (Grant et al., 2004).

Theories and Treatment of Dependent Personality Disorder

Dependent personality disorder runs in families, but it is unclear whether this is due to genetics or to family environments (Dahl, 1993). Children with histories of anxiety about separation from their parents or of chronic physical illness appear more prone to develop dependent personality disorder.

Cognitive theories argue that people with dependent personality disorder have beliefs such as "I am needy and weak," which drive their dependent behaviors. A study of 38 patients with dependent personality disorder found that they endorsed such beliefs more often than patients with other personality disorders (Beck et al., 2001).

Unlike people with many of the other personality disorders, persons with dependent personality disorder frequently seek treatment (Millon et al., 2000). Although many psychosocial therapies are used in the treatment of this disorder, none have been systematically tested for their effectiveness. Psychodynamic treatment focuses on helping clients gain insight into the early experiences with caregivers that led to their dependent behaviors through the use of free association, dream interpretation, and interpretation of the transference process. Nondirective and humanistic therapies may be helpful in fostering autonomy and self-confidence in persons with dependent personality disorder (Millon et al., 2000).

Cognitive-behavioral therapy for dependent personality disorder includes behavioral techniques designed to increase assertive behaviors and to decrease anxiety, as well as cognitive techniques designed to challenge assumptions about the need to rely on others (Beck & Freeman, 1990). Clients might be given graded exposure to anxiety-provoking situations, such as requesting help from a salesperson. Clients might also be taught relaxation skills, so that they can overcome anxiety enough to engage in homework assignments. They and their therapists might develop a hierarchy of increasingly difficult independent actions that the clients gradually attempt on their own—for example, beginning with deciding what to have for lunch and ending with deciding what job to take. After making each decision, clients are encouraged to recognize their competence and challenge the negative thoughts they had about making the decision.

"RONALD IS EXTREMELY COMPULSIVE."

© *Sidney Harris, courtesy ScienceCartoonsPlus.com*

Obsessive-Compulsive Personality Disorder

The characteristics of self-control, attention to detail, perseverance, and reliability are highly valued in many societies, including U.S. society. Some people, however, carry these traits to an extreme and become rigid, perfectionistic, dogmatic, ruminative, and emotionally blocked. These people are said to have **obsessive-compulsive personality disorder.** The obsessive-compulsive personality disorder shares features with obsessive-compulsive disorder (see Chapter 7), but obsessive-compulsive personality disorder represents a more generalized way of interacting with the world than does obsessive-compulsive disorder, which often involves only specific and constrained obsessional thoughts and compulsive behaviors.

People with obsessive-compulsive personality disorder seem grim and austere, tensely in control of their emotions, and lacking in spontaneity (Millon et al., 2000). They are workaholics and see little need for leisure activities or friendships. Other people experience them as stubborn, stingy, possessive, moralistic, and officious. They tend to relate to others in terms of rank or status and are ingratiating and deferential to "superiors" but dis-

missive, demeaning, or authoritarian toward "inferiors." Although they are extremely concerned with efficiency, their perfectionism and obsessions about following rules often interfere with their completion of tasks, as in the following case study (Spitzer et al., 1983, pp. 63–64).

CASE STUDY

Ronald Lewis is a 32-year-old accountant who is "having trouble holding on to a woman." He does not understand why, but the reasons become very clear as he tells his story. Mr. Lewis is a remarkably neat and well-organized man who tends to regard others as an interference to the otherwise mechanically perfect progression of his life. For many years he has maintained an almost inviolate schedule. On weekdays he arises at 6:47, has two eggs soft-boiled for 2 minutes, 45 seconds, and is at his desk at 8:15. Lunch is at 12:00, dinner at 6:00, bedtime at 11:00. He has separate Saturday and Sunday schedules, the latter characterized by a methodical and thorough trip through *The New York Times*. Any change in schedule causes him to feel varying degrees of anxiety, annoyance, and a sense that he is doing something wrong and wasting time.

Orderliness pervades Mr. Lewis's life. His apartment is immaculately clean and meticulously arranged. His extensive collections of books, records, and stamps are all carefully catalogued, and each item is reassuringly always in the right and familiar place. Mr. Lewis is highly valued at his work because his attention to detail has, at times, saved the company considerable embarrassment. . . . His perfectionism also presents something of a problem, however. He is the slowest worker in the office and probably the least productive. He gets the details right but may fail to put them in perspective. His relationships to coworkers are cordial but formal. He is on a "Mr. and Ms." basis with people he has known for years in an office that generally favors first names. Mr. Lewis's major problems are with women and follow the same repetitive pattern. At first, things go well.

(continued)

Soon, however, he begins to resent the intrusion upon his schedule a woman inevitably causes. This is most strongly illustrated in the bedtime arrangements. Mr. Lewis is a light and nervous sleeper with a rather elaborate routine preceding his going to bed. He must spray his sinuses, take two aspirin, straighten up the apartment, do 35 sit-ups and read two pages of the dictionary. The sheets must be of just the right crispness and temperature and the room must be noiseless. Obviously, a woman sleeping over interferes with his inner sanctum and, after sex, Mr. Lewis tries either to have the woman go home or sleep in the living room. No woman has put up with this for very long.

Prevalence of Obsessive-Compulsive Personality Disorder

Between 1.7 and 7.7 percent of the population can be diagnosed with obsessive-compulsive personality disorder, and it is more common in men than women (Ekselius et al., 2001; Fabrega et al., 1991; Weissman, 1993). People with this disorder are prone to depression and anxiety, but not to the same extent as people with avoidant or dependent personality disorder (Grant et al., 2004).

Theories and Treatment of Obsessive-Compulsive Personality Disorder

There are no family history, twin, or adoption studies specifically focusing on obsessive-compulsive personality disorder.

Early psychodynamic theorists attributed this personality disorder to fixation at the anal stage of development because the patient's parents were overly strict and punitive during toilet training (Freud, 1923). Harry Stack Sullivan (1953) argued that obsessive-compulsive personalities arise when children grow up in homes where there is much anger and hate that is hidden behind superficial love and niceness. The children do not develop interpersonal skills and, instead, avoid intimacy and follow rigid rules to gain a sense of self-esteem and self-control. These theories have not been empirically tested.

Cognitive theories suggest that people with this disorder harbor beliefs such as "Flaws, defects or mistakes are intolerable." One study found that people diagnosed with obsessive-compulsive personality disorder endorsed such beliefs significantly more often than people diagnosed with other personality disorders (Beck et al., 2001).

Supportive therapies may assist people with this disorder in overcoming the crises that send them for treatment, and behavior therapies can be used to decrease their compulsive behaviors (Beck & Freeman, 1990; Millon et al., 2000). For example, a client may be given the assignment to alter her usual rigid schedule for the day, first by simply getting up 15 minutes later than she usually does and then gradually changing additional elements of her schedule. The client may be taught to use relaxation techniques to overcome the anxiety created by alterations in the schedule. She might also write down the automatic negative thoughts she has about changes in the schedule ("Getting up 15 minutes later is going to put my entire day off"). In the next therapy session, she and the therapist might discuss the evidence for and against these automatic thoughts.

SUMMING UP

- People with the anxious-fearful personality disorders—avoidant, dependent, and obsessive-compulsive personality disorders—are chronically fearful or concerned.

- People with avoidant personality disorder worry about being criticized.

- People with dependent personality disorder worry about being abandoned.

- People with obsessive-compulsive personality disorder are locked into rigid routines of behavior and become anxious when their routines are violated.

- Some children may be born with temperamental predispositions toward shy and avoidant behaviors, or childhood anxiety may contribute to dependent personalities.

- These disorders may arise from a lack of nurturing parenting and basic fears about one's ability to function competently.

ALTERNATIVE CONCEPTUALIZATIONS OF PERSONALITY DISORDERS

The DSM-IV-TR scheme for conceptualizing and categorizing personality disorders is intentionally atheoretical. In other words, the authors of the DSM-IV-TR sought to describe the personality disorders that had been observed in clinical practice and research, independent of any theoretical conceptualization of personality that suggests which personality disorders should exist in humans. Many theorists have criticized this lack of theory, however, saying that it impedes the progress of research on personality disorders, because a good theory of personality disorders suggests which specific hypotheses about these disorders researchers should be tested.

Several theoretical schemes for the personality disorders have been suggested (see Trull & Durrett, 2005). Many of these schemes view the personality disorders as extreme variants of normal personality traits.

Five-Factor Model

One of the leading theories of "normal" personality is the **five-factor model,** which posits that any individual's personality is organized along five broad dimensions, or factors, of personality. These factors are often referred to as the Big 5: *neuroticism, extraversion, openness to experience, agreeableness, and conscientiousness* (McCrae & Costa, 1999) (see the Concept Overview in Table 12.6). Considerable research suggests that these five dimensions capture a great deal of the variation in people's personalities, and that the personality traits these dimensions describe are strongly influenced by genetics (Jang, McCrae, et al., 1998). These traits have

also been replicated in cultures very different from that of the United States, where they have been studied most (Benet-Martinez & John, 1998; Yang et al., 2002).

In turn, the DSM-IV-TR personality disorders can be conceptualized along these five dimensions (Costa & Widiger, 2002; Lynam & Widiger, 2001). For example, people with antisocial personality disorder can be characterized as high in antagonism and low in conscientiousness. People with dependent personality disorder can be characterized as high in agreeableness and high in neuroticism.

Several studies have found that people diagnosed with a personality disorder score higher on the traits that the five-factor model suggests they should score higher on (see Trull & Durrett, 2005). In addition, a longitudinal study of people in treatment for borderline, avoidant, or schizotypal personality disorder found that the degree to which they changed over time in the manifestation of their personality disorder was predicted by the degree to which they had previously changed in their scores on relevant Big 5 dimensions (Warner et al., 2004).

One advantage of translating the personality disorders into the Big 5 personality traits is that

---

TABLE 12.6 Concept Overview

Big 5 Personality Factors

The five-factor model of personality posits that all personalities can be characterized by combinations of the five personality factors described in this table.

Factor	Key Characteristics
Neuroticism	Individuals high on neuroticism scales are chronically anxious, hostile, depressed, self-conscious, and impulsive and have poor coping skills; people low on neuroticism scales lack these problems.
Extraversion	Individuals high on extraversion scales are sociable, active, talkative, interpersonally oriented, optimistic, fun-loving, and affectionate; people low on extraversion scales (referred to as introverts) are reserved, sober, aloof, independent, and quiet.
Openness to experience	Individuals high in this factor actively seek and appreciate experiences for their own sake and are curious, imaginative, and willing to entertain new and unconventional ideas; people low in this factor are conventional in their beliefs and attitudes, conservative in their tastes, dogmatic, rigid in their beliefs, set in their ways, and emotionally unresponsive.
Agreeableness	Individuals high in this factor are softhearted, good-natured, trusting, helpful, forgiving, and altruistic; people low in this factor are cynical, rude, suspicious, uncooperative, and irritable and can be manipulative, vengeful, and ruthless.
Conscientiousness	Individuals high in this factor are organized, reliable, hardworking, self-directed, punctual, scrupulous, ambitious, and persevering; people low in this factor are aimless, unreliable, lazy, careless, lax, negligent, and hedonistic.

Source: Costa & McCrae, 1992.

research on gender differences in the Big 5 can be used to make hypotheses about what kinds of gender differences are likely to occur in the personality disorders (Corbitt & Widiger, 1995). For example, women tend to score higher than men on both neuroticism and agreeableness. If dependent personality disorder is an extreme version of this personality constellation, then we would expect women to be diagnosed with this personality disorder more than men, as they are (Widiger et al., 1994). On the other hand, the five-factor model suggests that there should be a personality disorder characterized by antagonistic closed-mindedness, and, because men tend to score higher on both antagonism and closed-mindedness, this personality disorder should be more frequently diagnosed in men than in women (Widiger, 1998). There is, however, no personality disorder in the DSM-IV-TR for antagonistic closed-mindedness. Thus, the five-factor model suggests a new personality disorder, which could be the focus of new research, and it suggests some hypotheses about the distribution of this disorder in males versus females. It is this guiding of research, provided by a theory such as the five-factor model, that leads many researchers to argue that the DSM-IV-TR should not be so atheoretical.

Evaluations of Dimensional Models

Critics of dimensional models note that redefining personality disorders in light of theories of normal personality does not avoid the difficult questions of where cutoffs should be drawn between what is normal and what is pathological. In addition, just because dimensional models, such as the five-factor model, describe normal personality well, this does not mean that they describe personality disorders well (Davis & Millon, 1993). Dimensional models are usually based on extensive empirical research on people in the general population, and they may be unlikely to capture the personality characteristics of the small portion of the population that has extreme personality disturbances. However, studies have replicated the five-factor model in psychiatric samples (Bagby et al., 1999). In addition, the empirical evidence that dimensional models capture the DSM-IV-TR personality disorders well is growing rapidly (Trull & Durrett, 2005).

These debates about the appropriate conceptualization and categorization of personality disorders are likely to continue for many years. They are difficult to resolve in part because it is inherently difficult to determine where normality ends and abnormality begins and to derive accurate ways of describing personality and its variants.

These debates are also difficult to resolve because the personality disorders do not represent discrete and acute sets of symptoms, as do many of the Axis I disorders. Instead, they appear to be naturally chronic, pervasive, and amorphous.

SUMMING UP

- Some critics of the definitions of personality disorders in the DSM-IV-TR have suggested that the personality disorders represent extremes of normal personality traits. These critics argue for dimensional models of these disorders.

- One scheme suggests organizing the personality disorders along dimensions of the Big 5 personality traits: neuroticism, extraversion, openness to experience, agreeableness, and conscientiousness.

CHAPTER INTEGRATION

Although the empirical research on the personality disorders is too lacking to allow a clear integration

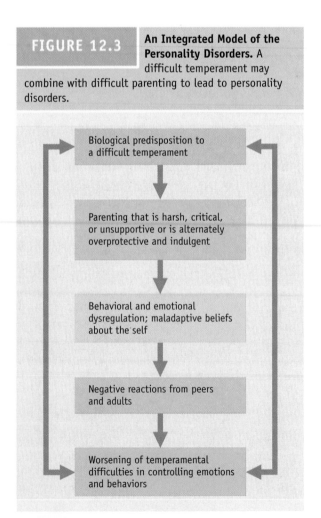

FIGURE 12.3 **An Integrated Model of the Personality Disorders.** A difficult temperament may combine with difficult parenting to lead to personality disorders.

Biological predisposition to a difficult temperament

Parenting that is harsh, critical, or unsupportive or is alternately overprotective and indulgent

Behavioral and emotional dysregulation; maladaptive beliefs about the self

Negative reactions from peers and adults

Worsening of temperamental difficulties in controlling emotions and behaviors of the biological, psychological, and social factors impinging on these disorders, some theoretical models have attempted this integration. They serve as the basis for current research (Millon et al., 2000; Siever & Davis, 1991; Trull & Durrett, 2005). According to these models, at the root of many of the personality disorders may be a biological predisposition to a certain kind of difficult temperament (see Figure 12.3).

For example, in the case of avoidant, dependent, and obsessive-compulsive personality disorders, an anxious and fearful temperament may be involved. In narcissistic and antisocial personality disorders, an impulsive and aggressive temperament may contribute. In borderline and histrionic personality disorders, a unstable, overly emotional temperament may be involved.

Children born with any of these temperaments are difficult to parent effectively. If parents can be supportive of these children yet set appropriate limits on their behavior, the children may never develop severe enough behavior or emotional problems to be diagnosed with a personality disorder. If parents are unable to counteract children's temperamental vulnerabilities or if they exacerbate these vulnerabilities with harsh, critical, unsupportive parenting or overprotective, indulgent parenting, then the children's temperamental vulnerabilities may grow into severe behavior and emotional problems, as well as maladaptive beliefs about the self. These problems will influence how others—teachers, peers, and eventually employers and mates—interact with the individuals, perhaps in ways that further exacerbate their temperamental vulnerabilities.

In this way, a lifelong pattern of dysfunction, called a personality disorder, may emerge out of the interaction between a child's biologically based temperament and others' reactions to that temperament.

Extraordinary People: Follow-Up

One of the fascinating aspects of Susanna Kaysen's autobiography, *Girl, Interrupted,* is that it provides a rare look inside an inpatient psychiatric ward from the perspective of a patient. The snippets of daily life on the ward are simultaneously touching and disturbing—friends who hurt themselves and attempt suicide, patients given powerful drugs and electroconvulsive therapy, young women wandering through life.

Kaysen's evaluation of the hospital is as complex as her own symptoms of distress:

> For many of us, the hospital was as much a refuge as it was a prison. Though we were cut off from the world and all the trouble we enjoyed stirring up out there, we were also cut off from the demands and expectations that had driven us crazy. What could be expected of us now that we were stowed away in a loony bin?
>
> The hospital shielded us from all sorts of things. We'd tell the staff to refuse phone calls or visits from anyone we didn't want to talk to, including our parents.
>
> "I'm too upset!" we'd wail, and we wouldn't have to talk to whoever it was.
>
> As long as we were willing to be upset, we didn't have to get jobs or go to school. We could weasel out of anything except eating and taking our medication.
>
> In a strange way we were free. We'd reached the end of the line. We had nothing more to lose. Our privacy, our liberty, our dignity: All of this was gone and we were stripped down to the bare bones of our selves.
>
> Naked, we needed protection, and the hospital protected us. Of course, the hospital had stripped us naked in the first place—but that just underscored its obligation to shelter us. (Kaysen, 1993, p. 94)

If you read *Girl, Interrupted,* or see the movie by the same name, you will get a flavor of the controversies surrounding the personality disorders, particularly borderline personality disorder. Are they just extreme versions of normal personalities? Are they vehicles for pathologizing people who don't "fit in"? Or are they legitimate diagnoses for people suffering from significant mental-health problems?

Chapter Summary

- The DSM-IV-TR divides the personality disorders into three clusters: the odd-eccentric disorders, the dramatic-emotional disorders, and the anxious-fearful disorders (Table 12.1). This organization is based on symptom clusters. It assumes that there is a dividing line between normal personality and pathological personality.

- The odd-eccentric disorders are characterized by odd or eccentric patterns of behavior and thought, including paranoia, extreme social withdrawal or inappropriate social interactions, and magical or illusory thinking. (Review Table 12.2.) This group of disorders, particularly schizotypal personality disorder, may be genetically linked to schizophrenia and may represent mild variations of schizophrenia. People with these disorders tend to have poor social relationships and are at increased risk for some acute psychiatric disorders, especially depression and schizophrenia.

- Psychoanalytic and cognitive therapies have been devised for these disorders, but they have not been empirically tested for their efficacy. Neuroleptic and atypical antipsychotic drugs appear to reduce the odd thinking of people with schizotypal personality disorder.

- The dramatic-emotional personality disorders include four disorders characterized by dramatic, erratic, and emotional behavior and interpersonal relationships: antisocial personality disorder, borderline personality disorder, histrionic personality disorder, and narcissistic personality disorder. (Review Table 12.3.) Persons with these disorders tend to be manipulative, volatile, uncaring in social relationships, and prone to impulsive behaviors.

- Antisocial personality disorder (ASPD) is one of the most common personality disorders and is more common in men than in women. There are several possible contributors to antisocial personality disorder. (Review Table 12.4.) These contributors include a genetic predisposition; the effects of testosterone on fetal brain development; low levels of serotonin; low arousability; attention-deficit-hyperactivity disorder; harsh, inconsistent parenting; and assumptions about the world that promote aggressive responses. (Review Figure 12.1.)

- Psychotherapy is not considered extremely effective for people with antisocial personality disorder.

Lithium, the selective serotonin reuptake inhibitors, and antipsychotics may help control impulsive behaviors.

- People with borderline personality disorder show instability in their moods, self-concept, and interpersonal relationships. This disorder is more common in women than in men. People with the disorder may suffer from low levels of serotonin, which lead to impulsive behaviors. There is little evidence that borderline personality disorder is transmitted genetically, but the family members of people with this disorder show high rates of mood disorders.

- Psychoanalytic theorists argue that borderline personality disorder is the result of poorly developed and integrated views of the self, which are due to poor early relationships with caregivers. Cognitive theorists see this disorder as stemming from deficits in self-concept. Many people with this disorder were the victims of physical and sexual abuse in childhood.

- Drug treatments have not proven very effective for borderline personality disorder. Psychoanalytic and cognitive therapies focus on establishing a stronger self-identity in people with this disorder.

- Histrionic and narcissistic personality disorders are both characterized by dramatic self-presentations and unstable personal relationships. A person with histrionic personality disorder looks to others for approval, whereas a person with narcissistic personality disorder relies on self-evaluations.

- The anxious-fearful personality disorders include three disorders characterized by anxious and fearful emotions and chronic self-doubt, leading to maladaptive behaviors: dependent personality disorder, avoidant personality disorder, and obsessive-compulsive personality disorder. (Review Table 12.5.)

- Dependent personality disorder is more common in women, obsessive-compulsive personality disorder is more common in men, and avoidant personality disorder is equally common in men and women. Dependent and avoidant personality disorders tend to run in families, but it is not clear whether this is due to genetics or to family environments.

- Several alternative models of the personality disorders have been developed. One prominent model is based on theories of normal personality. The five-factor model of personality suggests that five basic factors describe most of personality: neuroticism, extraversion, openness to experience, agreeableness, and conscientiousness. (Review Table 12.6.) Personality disorders may be extreme variants of these factors.

MindMap CD-ROM

The following resources on the MindMap CD-ROM that came with this text will help you to master the content of this chapter and prepare for tests:

- Video: Borderline Personality Disorder
- Chapter Timeline
- Chapter Quiz

Key Terms

personality 423

personality disorder 423

odd-eccentric personality disorders 428

paranoid personality disorder 428

schizoid personality disorder 431

schizotypal personality disorder 432

dramatic-emotional personality disorders 435

antisocial personality disorder (ASPD) 435

psychopathy 436

serotonin 438

executive functions 438

borderline personality disorder 440

splitting 443

dialectical behavior therapy 444

histrionic personality disorder 444

narcissistic personality disorder 445

anxious-fearful personality disorders 447

avoidant personality disorder 447

dependent personality disorder 449

obsessive-compulsive personality disorder 451

five-factor model 453

Chapter 13

In the Fields
by Daniel Nevins

Youth, even in its sorrows, always has a brilliancy of its own.

—Victor Hugo, "Saint Denis," *Les Miserables*
(1962; translated by Charles E. Wilbour)

Childhood Disorders <

CHAPTER OVERVIEW

Extraordinary People

■ **Temple Grandin:** *Thinking in Pictures*

Behavior Disorders

The behavior disorders include attention-deficit/hyperactivity disorder (ADHD), conduct disorder, and oppositional defiant disorder. Children with attention-deficit/hyperactivity disorder have trouble maintaining attention and controlling impulsive behavior and are hyperactive. Children with conduct or oppositional defiant disorder engage in frequent antisocial or defiant behavior.

Separation Anxiety Disorder

One of the most common emotional disorders of childhood is separation anxiety disorder, in which children are extremely anxious about any separation from their primary caregivers. Behavioral and cognitive therapies are often used to treat this disorder.

Elimination Disorders

The two elimination disorders are enuresis—uncontrolled wetting—and encopresis—uncontrolled bowel movements. The most effective treatment is a behavioral technique that teaches children to awaken at night when they need to go to the bathroom.

Disorders of Cognitive, Motor, and Communication Skills

Disorders of cognitive, motor, and communication skills involve deficits and delays in the development of fundamental skills. These include learning disorders, a motor skills disorder, and the communication disorders.

Taking Psychology Personally

■ **College Students with Mental Disorders**

Mental Retardation

Children diagnosed with mental retardation have deficits in cognitive skills that range from mild to severe. A number of genetic factors and biological traumas in the early years of life can contribute to mental retardation. Social factors, such as poverty or lack of a good education, can also contribute to mental retardation.

Pervasive Developmental Disorders

The pervasive developmental disorders include autism, Asperger's disorder, Rett's disorder, and childhood disintegrative disorder. These disorders are characterized by severe and lasting impairment in several areas of development, including social interaction, communication with others, everyday behaviors, interests, and activities. Autism, the most researched of these disorders, has biological roots but often responds well to behavioral interventions.

Chapter Integration

The study of psychological disorders in children is often referred to as developmental psychopathology. Researchers in this field are concerned with the interdependence of biological, psychological, and social development in children, recognizing that disruptions in any one of these three systems are likely to affect the other systems.

Extraordinary People

Temple Grandin: *Thinking in Pictures*

Dr. Temple Grandin, professor of animal sciences at Colorado State University, has designed one-third of all the livestock-handling facilities in the United States. She has published dozens of scientific papers and gives lectures throughout the world. Sometimes, those lectures describe the new equipment and procedures she has designed for safer and more humane handling of animals. Sometimes, however, those lectures describe her life with autism.

As a young child, Grandin had all the classic symptoms of autism. When she was a baby, she had no desire to be held by her mother and struggled to get away, but she was calm if left alone in a baby carriage. She seldom made eye contact with others, seemed to have no interest in people, and was constantly staring off into space. She frequently threw wild tantrums and smeared her feces around. If left alone, she rocked back and forth or spun around indefinitely. She could sit for hours on the beach, watching sand dribbling through her fingers, in a trancelike state. She still had not begun talking at age 2½. She was labeled as "brain-damaged," because 40 years ago doctors did not know about autism.

Fortunately, Grandin's mother was dogged about finding good teachers, learning ways to calm her daughter, and encouraging her daughter to speak and engage in the social world. Grandin had learned to speak by the time she entered elementary school, although most of her deficits in social interactions remained. When she was 12 years old, Grandin scored 137 on an IQ test but still was thrown out of a regular school because she didn't fit in. She persisted, however, and eventually went to college, earning a degree in psychology, and then to graduate school, where she earned a Ph.D. in animal sciences.

Grandin's autobiography *Thinking in Pictures* (1995), and her most recent book, *Animals in Translation* (Grandin & Johnson, 2005), provide remarkable insights into the motivations and experiences behind some of the strange symptoms of autism. She describes how she, like many people with autism, thinks visually instead of verbally:

> Today, everyone is excited about the new virtual reality computer systems in which the user wears special goggles and is fully immersed in video game action. To me, these systems are like crude cartoons. My imagination works like the computer graphics programs that created the lifelike dinosaurs in Jurassic Park. When I do an equipment simulation in my imagination or work on an engineering problem, it is like seeing it on a videotape in my mind. I can view it from any angle, placing myself above or below the equipment and rotating it at the same time. I don't need any fancy graphics program that can produce three-dimensional design simulations. I can do it better and faster in my head. (Grandin, 1995, p. 21)

This ability to visualize has been of tremendous value in Grandin's career as a facilities designer. She can literally take a "cow's-eye view" of holding facilities and equipment, seeing what a cow sees as it is shuttled down a shoot, even before the equipment is built. This has led her to develop revolutionary new designs for this equipment that prevent animals from panicking and, thus, either hurting themselves, possibly fatally, or being exposed to cruel tactics, such as electric cattle prods.

Thinking in pictures instead of words is part of what made it difficult for her to learn language, however. She was able to learn nouns relatively easily, because she could visualize the objects to which these words refer. Other components of language were more difficult, until she developed a means for visualizing them, too:

> I also visualize verbs. The word "jumping" triggers a memory of jumping hurdles at the mock Olympics held at my elementary school. Adverbs often trigger inappropriate images—"quickly" reminds me of Nestle's

Quick—unless they are paired with a verb, which modifies my visual image. For example, "he ran quickly" triggers an animated image of Dick from the first grade reading book running fast, and "he walked slowly" slows the image down. As a child, I left out words such as "is," "the," and "it," because they had no meaning by themselves. Similarly, words like "of" and "an" made no sense. Eventually, I learned how to use them properly, because my parents always spoke correct English and I mimicked their speech patterns. To this day certain verb conjugations, such as "to be," are absolutely meaningless to me. (Grandin, 1995, pp. 30–31)

Still, Grandin has been able to thrive in her career and her personal life, channeling some of her symptoms of autism into good use and overcoming other symptoms with intellect and good humor. Not all people with autism are able to do this, but Grandin's autobiography is a testimony to the importance of early detection and intervention for children with serious mental-health problems.

We like to think of childhood as a time relatively free from stress, when boys and girls can enjoy the simple pleasures of everyday life and are immune from major psychological problems. Yet this was not the case for Temple Grandin, nor is it the case for many children. Large-scale epidemiological studies suggest that more than a third of all children suffer from a significant emotional or behavior disorder by the time they are 16 (Costello et al., 2003). As you can see in Table 13.1 on page 462, boys are more vulnerable to mental-health problems than are girls prior to age 16. Overall, a substantial minority of children and adolescents do not live a carefree existence. Instead, they experience distressing symptoms severe enough to warrant attention from mental-health professionals.

For some children, psychological symptoms and disorders are linked to major stressors in their environment. A large and growing number of children in the United States and other countries are faced with severe circumstances that would overwhelm the coping capacities of many adults. In the United States, about 18 percent of children live below the poverty line (*Washington Post,* 2004). Children living in the inner cities—particularly in housing projects, where many poor families reside—are often exposed to violence. For example, in one study of 9- to 12-year-old children in an urban area in the United States, 97 percent reported witnessing or being the victim of some sort of violence in the past year; 37 percent of the children had been beaten up; 19 percent had been chased or threatened (Purugganan et al., 2003). Those who had been exposed to violence had significantly more negative mental-health symptoms than those who had not been exposed.

Most children who face one such stressor are beset by multiple stressors. For example, children in poverty are more likely than other children to witness or be the victims of violence, to use illicit drugs, to engage in unprotected sexual intercourse, and to face racial and ethnic discrimination and harassment. These stressors appear to have a cumulative effect on children's risk for psychological problems. The more stressors a child encounters, the more likely he or she is to experience severe psychological symptoms (Cicchetti & Toth, 2005).

What is remarkable is that many, perhaps most, children who face major stressors do *not* develop severe psychological symptoms or disorders. These children have been referred to as *resilient* children (Garmezy, 1991; Luthar, 2003). It is not known exactly what makes these children so resilient in the face of stress, but having at least one healthy, competent adult to rely on seems to help. Temple Grandin's mother, for example, played a key role in her daughter's early life. In addition, studies of homeless children suggest that those who have high-quality interactions with a parent are no more likely to develop psychological problems than are children who are not homeless (Masten & Powell, 2003).

Conversely, many children who develop psychological disorders do not have any major stressors in their lives to which the development of the

TABLE 13.1 Prevalence of Mental Disorders in Children.

Estimated percentages of children who suffer psychological disorders by age 16 years (note that children can be diagnosed with more than one disorder).

Diagnosis	Total	Girls	Boys
Any disorder	36.7	31.0	42.3
Any anxiety disorder	9.9	12.1	7.7
Any depressive disorder	9.5	11.7	7.3
Any behavior disorder	23.0	16.1	29.9
Conduct disorder	9.0	3.8	14.1
Oppositional defiant disorder	11.3	9.1	13.4
ADHD*	4.1	1.1	7.0
Substance use disorder (e.g., alcohol abuse)	12.2	10.1	14.3

Source: Costello, Mustillo, et al., 2003.
*ADHD = attention-deficit/hyperactivity disorder.

disorders can be linked. These children may come from privileged backgrounds, in which they have not been exposed to any traumas or chronic problems. However, they still develop psychological disorders or symptoms.

It seems that among children, as among adults, most psychological disorders are the result of multiple factors, such as biological predispositions plus environmental stressors. One biological factor that has been implicated in the development of many psychological disorders in children is temperament. As noted in Chapter 12, *temperament* is a child's arousability and general mood. Children with "difficult" temperaments are highly sensitive to stimulation, become upset easily, and have trouble calming themselves when upset. They also tend to have generally negative moods and trouble adapting to new situations, particularly social situations (Thomas & Chess, 1984). Children with difficult temperaments are more likely than other children to have both minor and major psychological problems during childhood and later in life (Caspi et al., 2003).

Temperament probably has strong biological roots, including genetic roots (Rothbart & Bates, 1998). The link between temperament and the development of psychological problems is not exclusively biological, however. Children with difficult temperaments elicit more negative interactions from others, including their parents. Adults act less affectionately toward children with difficult temperaments, and other children are more likely

Children with difficult temperaments can make parenting stressful.

to be hostile toward these children. The negative environments that children with difficult temperaments create for themselves may contribute to their psychological problems, rather than the actual difficult temperaments. Conversely, children with difficult temperaments who receive high-quality parenting are not at high risk for psychological problems, whereas children with difficult

TABLE 13.2 Concept Overview

Disorders of Childhood

These disorders have their first onset in childhood.

Category	Specific Disorders
Behavior disorders	Attention-deficit/hyperactivity disorder
	Conduct disorder
	Oppositional defiant disorder
Separation/anxiety disorder	
Elimination disorders	Enuresis
	Encopresis
Disorders in cognitive, motor, and communication skills	Learning disorders
	Reading disorder (dyslexia)
	Mathematics disorder
	Disorder of written expression
	Motor skills disorder
	Developmental coordination disorder
	Communication disorders
	Expressive language disorder
	Mixed receptive-expressive language disorder
	Phonological disorder
	Stuttering
Mental retardation	Mild, moderate, severe, and profound mental retardation
Pervasive developmental disorders	Autism
	Rett's disorder
	Childhood disintegrative disorder
	Asperger's disorder
Tic disorders	Tourette's disorder
	Chronic motor or focal tic disorder
	Transient tic disorder
Feeding and eating disorders	Pica
	Rumination disorder
	Feeding disorder of infancy or early childhood
Other disorders	Selective mutism
	Reactive attachment disorder
	Stereotypic movement disorder

temperaments who are part of dysfunctional families are at high risk (Plomin, 1994).

In this chapter, we examine the roles that biology and psychosocial factors play in the development of specific psychological disorders in children. A large number of disorders can be diagnosed in children. The Concept Overview in Table 13.2 lists several disorders that are usually first diagnosed in childhood or infancy. In addition, several disorders we have already discussed can also occur for the first time during childhood or adolescence. We reviewed information on childhood depression in Chapter 9 and on the anxiety disorders in childhood in Chapters 6 and 7.

We focus on some of the most common and severe of the disorders that usually begin in infancy or childhood. First, we discuss the behavior disorders, specifically attention-deficit/hyperactivity disorder, conduct disorder, and oppositional defiant disorder. Children with these disorders have trouble paying attention and controlling socially inappropriate behaviors. Then we turn to an anxiety disorder that is prevalent in children, separation anxiety disorder.

The third group of disorders we discuss is the elimination disorders, enuresis and encopresis. Children with these disorders have trouble controlling bladder and bowel movements far beyond the age at which most children learn to control them. The fourth group is disorders of cognitive, motor, and communication skills, and the fifth is mental retardation. Finally, the sixth group is pervasive developmental disorders. Within this sixth group, we focus on autism, the disorder that Temple Grandin has had since infancy, because it has been the focus of more research.

The study of childhood disorders has expanded greatly in the past two decades and has grown into a field known as *developmental psychopathology.* Developmental psychopathologists try to understand when children's behaviors cross the line from the normal difficulties of childhood into unusual or abnormal problems that warrant concern (Cicchetti & Toth, 2005). Most children have transient emotional or behavior problems sometime during childhood. That is, most children go through periods in which they are unusually fearful or easily distressed or engage in behaviors such as lying or stealing, but these periods pass relatively quickly and are often specific to certain situations. Differentiating these normal periods of distress from signs of a developing psychological disorder is not easy. Developmental psychologists also try to understand the impact of normal development on the form that abnormal behaviors take. That is, children's levels of cognitive, social, and emotional development can affect the types of symptoms they show. These developmental considerations make the assessment, diagnosis, and treatment of childhood disorders quite challenging, but helping children overcome their problems and get back on the path to healthy development can be highly rewarding.

BEHAVIOR DISORDERS

The *behavior disorders* have been the focus of a great deal of research, probably because children with these disorders can be quite difficult to deal with, and their behaviors can exact a heavy toll on society. The three behavior disorders we discuss are *attention-deficit/hyperactivity disorder, conduct disorder,* and *oppositional defiant disorder.* These are distinct disorders, but they often co-occur in the same child (see the Concept Overview in Table 13.3).

Attention-Deficit/ Hyperactivity Disorder

"Pay attention! Slow down! You're so hyper today!" These are phrases that most children hear their parents saying to them at least occasionally. A major focus of socialization is helping children learn to pay attention, control their impulses, and organize their behaviors, so that they can accomplish long-term goals. Some children have tremendous trouble learning these skills, however, and may be diagnosed with **attention-deficit/ hyperactivity disorder,** or **ADHD.** Eddie is a young boy with ADHD (adapted from Spitzer et al., 1994, pp. 351–352):

CASE STUDY

Eddie, age 9, was referred to a child psychiatrist at the request of his school because of the difficulties he creates in class. His teacher complains that he is so restless that his classmates are unable to concentrate. He is hardly ever in his seat and mostly roams around the class, talking to other children while they are working. When the teacher is able to get him to stay in his seat, he fidgets with his hands and feet and drops things on the floor. He never seems to know what he is going to do next and may suddenly do something quite outrageous. His most recent suspension from school was for swinging from the fluorescent light fixture over the blackboard. Because he was unable to climb down again, the class was in an uproar.

His mother says that Eddie's behavior has been difficult since he was a toddler and that, as a 3-year-old, he was unbearably restless and demanding. He has always required little sleep and been awake before anyone else.

(continued)

TABLE 13.3 Concept Overview

Behavior Disorders

The behavior disorders involve extreme inattention, hyperactivity, and socially inappropriate behavior.

Disorder	Symptoms	Proposed Etiologies	Treatments
Attention-deficit/hyperactivity disorder (ADHD)	Inattention, hyperactivity, impulsivity	1. Immaturity of the brain, particularly frontal lobes, caudate nucleus, and corpus callosum 2. Genetic predisposition 3. Prenatal and birth complications 4. Disrupted families	1. Stimulant drugs (e.g., Ritalin) 2. Behavior therapy focused on reinforcing attentive, goal-directed behaviors and extinguishing impulsive, hyperactive behaviors
Conduct disorder	Behaviors that violate the basic rights of others and the norms for social behavior	1. Genetic predisposition 2. Deficits in brain regions involved in planning and controlling behavior 3. Difficult temperament 4. Lower physiological arousal to punishment 5. Serotonin imbalances 6. Higher testosterone level 7. Poor parental supervision, parental uninvolvement, parental violence 8. Delinquent peer groups 9. Cognitions that promote aggression	1. Antidepressants, neuroleptics, stimulants, lithium 2. Cognitive-behavioral therapy focused on changing hostile cognitions, teaching children to take others' perspectives, and teaching problem-solving skills
Oppositional defiant disorder	Argumentativeness, negativity, irritability, defiance, but behaviors not as severe as in conduct disorder	Same as conduct disorder	Same as conduct disorder

When he was small, "he got into everything," particularly in the early morning, when he would awaken at 4:30 A.M. or 5:00 A.M. and go downstairs by himself. His parents would awaken to find the living room or kitchen "demolished." When he was 4 years old, he managed to unlock the door of the apartment and wander off into a busy main street but, fortunately, was rescued from oncoming traffic by a passerby.

Eddie has no interest in TV and dislikes games or toys that require any concentration or patience. He is not popular with other children and at home prefers to be outdoors, playing with his dog or riding his bike. If he does play with toys, his games are messy and destructive, and his mother cannot get him to keep his things in any order.

Eddie's difficulties in paying attention and his impulsivity go far beyond what is normal for a child his age. Most elementary school age children can sit still for a period of time and like to engage in at least some games that require patience and concentration. They can inhibit their impulses to jump up in class and talk to other children or to walk out into busy traffic. Eddie cannot do any of these things. His behavior has a character of being driven and disorganized, following one whim and then the next, as is common in children with ADHD (see Table 13.4 for DSM-IV-TR symptoms).

There are three subtypes of ADHD. Most children and adolescents with ADHD have the *Combined Type*, which is defined by the presence of six or more of the symptoms of inattention and six or more of the symptoms of hyperactivity-impulsivity listed in Table 13.4. The *Predominantly Inattentive Type* is diagnosed if six or more symptoms of inattention but fewer than six symptoms of hyperactivity-impulsivity are present. Some researchers argue that certain symptoms indicating a *sluggish cognitive tempo* are also important parts of the Predominantly Inattentive Type. These symptoms include the slow retrieval of information from memory and slow processing of infor-

---

TABLE 13.4 DSM-IV-TR

Symptoms of Attention-Deficit/Hyperactivity Disorder (ADHD)

The symptoms of attention-deficit/hyperactivity disorder fall into three clusters: inattention, hyperactivity, and impulsivity.

Inattention

Does not pay attention to details and makes careless mistakes

Has difficulty sustaining attention

Does not seem to be listening when others are talking

Does not follow through on instructions or finish tasks

Has difficulty organizing behaviors

Avoids activities that require sustained effort and attention

Loses things frequently

Is easily distracted

Is forgetful

Hyperactivity

Fidgets with hands or feet and squirms in seat

Leaves his or her seat when it is inappropriate

Runs around or climbs excessively

Has difficulty engaging in quiet activities

Often acts as if "driven by a motor"

Often talks excessively

Impulsivity

Blurts out responses while others are talking

Has difficulty waiting his or her turn

Often interrupts or intrudes on others

Source: Reprinted with permission from the *Diagnostic and Statistical Manual of Mental Disorders*, Fourth Edition, Text Revision. Copyright © 2000 American Psychiatric Association.

mation, low levels of alertness, drowsiness, and daydreaming (McBurnett, Pfiffner, & Frick, 2001). The *Predominantly Hyperactive-Impulsive Type* is diagnosed if six or more symptoms of hyperactivity-impulsivity but fewer than six symptoms of inattention are present. Eddie appears to have this type. Jason, however, in the following case study, appears to have the Predominantly Inattentive Type:

CASE STUDY

Jason, a second-grade student, was known by his classmates as "The Space Cadet." He often spent classtime drawing pictures of space ships and aliens instead of paying attention to what was going on. When the teacher tried to get his attention, she often had to nearly shout at him, and then he would raise his head slowly, as if he'd been in another world.

On the playground, Jason was not popular. He was seldom chosen for baseball teams because he tended to ignore what was happening in the field and, instead, gazed at the vehicles passing by on the road or the children playing in an adjacent playground. Jason also had a temper, and he sometimes exploded at another child if he felt he was being insulted. Most days on the playground, Jason just flitted from one group of children to another, intrusively inserting himself into ongoing games, getting angry when something didn't go his way, and stalking off to the next group of children.

At home, Jason's parents had to watch over him closely. He was constantly losing things, particularly books and materials related to school, so every morning was a panic as he and his parents searched far and wide for books and homework sheets, which Jason usually had forgotten to complete the night before.

Many children like Eddie and Jason do poorly in school. Because they cannot pay attention or quell their hyperactivity, they do not learn the material they are being taught and perform below their intellectual capabilities (Whalen & Henker, 1998). In addition, 20 to 25 percent of children with ADHD have serious learning disabilities that make it doubly hard for them to concentrate in school and to learn (Wilens, Biederman, & Spencer, 2002).

Some children with ADHD have extremely poor relationships with other children and, like Eddie and Jason, are rejected outright by other children (Hinshaw & Melnick, 1995). When interacting with their peers, children with ADHD are disorganized and never finish anything. They are intrusive, irritable, and demanding. They want to play by their own rules and have explosive tempers, so that, when things do not go their way, they may become physically violent (Whalen & Henker, 1998).

The behavior problems of some children with ADHD are so severe that they may also be diagnosed with a *conduct disorder.* Children with conduct disorders grossly violate the norms for appropriate behavior toward others by acting in uncaring and even violent ways. Between 45 and 60 percent of children with ADHD develop conduct disorders, abuse drugs, or become juvenile delinquents (Waschbusch, 2002; Wilens et al., 2002). The conduct problems that some children with ADHD have persist into adulthood (Abramowitz, Kosson, & Seidenberg, 2004).

ADHD has become a popular diagnosis to give to children who are disruptive in school or at home, and the media attention on ADHD over the past decade has made it seem that there is an epidemic of this disorder. However, various epidemiological studies indicate that only 1 to 7 percent of children develop ADHD (Angold et al., 2002; Wilens et al., 2002). Boys are about three times more likely than girls to develop ADHD in childhood and early adolescence (Angold et al., 2002). Boys with ADHD tend to have more disruptive behavior than girls with ADHD, and this may lead to an underidentification of ADHD in girls (Biederman et al., 2002). ADHD is found across most cultures and ethnic groups.

The long-term outcomes for children with ADHD vary considerably. The symptoms of ADHD persist from childhood into young adulthood for about three-quarters of these children (Wilens et al., 2002). Adults who were diagnosed with ADHD as children are at increased risk for antisocial personality disorder, substance abuse, mood and anxiety disorders, marital problems, traffic accidents, legal infractions, and frequent job changes (Barkley et al., 2004; Wilens et al., 2002). Adults who have ADHD are at high risk for depression, anxiety disorders, substance abuse, and antisocial personality disorder (Biederman et al., 2004). However, many children grow out of ADHD. By early adulthood, their ADHD

Children normally have high energy levels but only a minority of children can be labeled hyperactive.

symptoms have passed, and they go on to lead normal, healthy lives (Mannuza et al., 1998).

Biological Contributors to ADHD

ADHD was formerly referred to as *minimal brain damage,* under the assumption that the attentional deficits and hyperactivity were due to mild brain damage. Most children who develop ADHD, however, have no history of brain injury, and most children with some brain injury do not develop ADHD.

Modern studies have shown that children with ADHD differ from children with no psychological disorders on a variety of measures of neurological functioning and cerebral blood flow (Barkley, 1996; Wilens et al., 2002). The areas of the brain most likely involved in ADHD include the frontal lobes; the caudate nucleus within the basal ganglia; the corpus callosum, which connects the two lobes of the brain; and the pathways between these structures (Bradley & Golden, 2001). Each of these brain areas and pathways plays an important role in the deployment of attention, the regulation of impulses, and the planning of complex behavior. One hypothesis is that children with ADHD are neurologically immature— their brains are slower in developing than are other children's—and this is why they

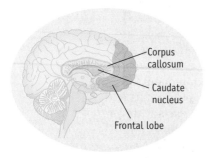

Corpus callosum

Caudate nucleus

Frontal lobe

These areas of the brain are most likely involved in ADHD.

are unable to maintain attention and control their behavior at a level that is appropriate for their age. This *immaturity hypothesis* helps explain why the symptoms of ADHD decline with age in many children.

The neurotransmitter that is most consistently implicated in ADHD is dopamine (Dougherty et al., 1999; Krause et al., 2000). Although serotonin seems to play a role in aggressive behavior, it does not appear to be central to ADHD (Wilens et al., 2002).

ADHD runs in families. Between 10 and 35 percent of the immediate family members of children with ADHD are also likely to have the disorder (Barkley, 1996; Biederman et al., 1986, 1990). Several other disorders also tend to run in the families of children with ADHD, including antisocial personality disorder, alcoholism, and depression (Barkley, 1991; Faraone et al., 1991). Twin studies and adoption studies also suggest that genetic factors play a role in vulnerability to ADHD (Eaves et al., 1997; Gilger, Pennington, & DeFries, 1992; Nadder et al., 1998; Rhee et al., 1999). It is not clear exactly what aspects of the ADHD syndrome are inherited, whether they are problems with attention, hyperactivity, impulsivity, or aggressivity. Molecular genetics studies suggest that the dopamine transporter genes may be abnormal in ADHD (Wilens et al., 2002).

Many children with ADHD have histories of prenatal and birth complications, including maternal ingestion of large amounts of nicotine or barbiturates during pregnancy, low birthweight, premature delivery, and difficult delivery, leading to oxygen deprivation (Bradley & Golden, 2001). Some investigators suspect that moderate to severe drinking by mothers during pregnancy can lead to the kinds of problems in inhibiting behaviors seen in children with ADHD. As preschoolers, some of these children were exposed to high concentrations of lead, when they ingested lead-based paint (Fergusson, Horwood, & Lynskey, 1993).

The popular notion that hyperactivity in children is caused by dietary factors, such as consuming large amounts of sugar, has not been supported in controlled studies (Whalen & Henker, 1998). A few studies do suggest, however, that a subset of children with ADHD have severe allergies to food additives and that removing these additives from these children's diets can reduce hyperactivity (Bradley & Golden, 2001).

Psychological and Social Contributors to ADHD

Children with ADHD are more likely than children without psychological disturbances to belong to families in which there are frequent disruptions, such as changes in residence or parental divorce (Barkley et al., 1990). Their fathers are more prone to antisocial and criminal behavior, and the children's interactions with their mothers are often marked with hostility and conflict (Barkley et al., 1990). Some investigators argue that there is a nongenetic form of ADHD that is caused by environmental adversity (Bauermeister et al., 1992). Others argue, however, that both ADHD and difficult family environments are the result of genetic predispositions to problems with lack of control (see Barkley, 1996).

Certainly, having a child with ADHD can impose significant stress on parents and a family. The explosive temper; the impulsive, dangerous activities; the school difficulties; and the rejection by peers can lead to constant conflict between children and the parents and siblings. Family members may not understand that a child with ADHD cannot voluntarily control his or her behavior simply when told to and, thus, may blame the child. Much of the treatment of ADHD in a child involves the parents, and sometimes siblings, in reshaping the family's interactions to reduce the symptoms of ADHD in the target child and to improve overall family functioning.

Treatments for ADHD

The most common treatment for ADHD in children is the use of stimulant drugs, such as Ritalin, Dexedrine, and Adderall. It may seem odd to give a stimulant drug to a hyperactive child, but between 70 and 85 percent of ADHD children respond to these drugs with *decreases* in demanding, disruptive, and noncompliant behavior (Joshi, 2004). They also show increases in positive mood, in the ability to be goal-directed, and in the quality of their interactions with others. The stimulants may work because they increase dopamine levels in the synapses of the brain by enhancing the release and inhibiting the reuptake of this neurotransmitter (Joshi, 2004).

The side effects of stimulants include reduced appetite, insomnia, edginess, and gastrointestinal upset. They can also increase the frequency of tics in children with ADHD. Some youth abuse stimulants, and recent reports have focused on college students who "fake" ADHD in order to get a prescription for stimulants, which they use to help them stay awake and work long hours in college (Joshi, 2004; Wilens et al., 2002).

Nationwide, the number of children prescribed stimulant medications increased by 200 to 300 percent in the past two decades (Joshi, 2004). Some researchers have argued that this greater use

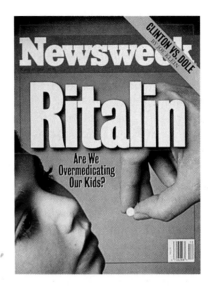

Some people think that attention-deficit/hyperactivity disorder is being overdiagnosed and that too many children are being prescribed Ritalin and other stimulant drugs.

is due to an increase in recognition of the disorder and treatment-seeking for children with ADHD. Others argue that it represents an inappropriate overuse of drugs, particularly for children who are difficult to control (see Angold et al., 2000). However, there is scant empirical evidence on which to judge these competing claims.

In one cross-sectional study of four U.S. communities, only 12 percent of the children meeting the diagnostic criteria for ADHD had received stimulants in the preceding year, suggesting that most children with the disorder are going untreated (Jensen et al., 1999). On the other hand, in a longitudinal study of children in a predominantly rural area, 72 percent of those with ADHD received stimulants at some point during the four years they were followed, suggesting that most children with ADHD are being treated (Angold et al., 2000). In this study, most of the children who were taking stimulants, however, did *not* have symptoms meeting the diagnostic criteria for ADHD. The boys and younger children in this study were especially likely to be prescribed stimulants in the absence of symptoms meeting the criteria for ADHD. More research is needed to determine how appropriately stimulants are being used.

Other drugs that are used to treat ADHD include clonidine and guanfacine, which affect levels of norepinephrine. These drugs can help reduce tics, which are common in children with ADHD, and increase cognitive performance (Joshi, 2004). The side effects of these drugs include dry mouth, fatigue, dizziness, constipation, and sedation. More recently, atomoxetine, which inhibits the reuptake of norepinephrine, has been approved for use in the treatment of ADHD.

Antidepressant medications are sometimes prescribed to children and adolescents with ADHD, particularly if they also have depression. These drugs have some positive effects on cognitive performance but are not as effective against ADHD as the stimulants (Wilens et al., 2002). Bupropion is an antidepressant with particularly strong effects on dopamine levels, and it appears to be more effective against ADHD than some of the other antidepressants.

Unfortunately, the gains made by children with ADHD when treated with medications alone are short-term (Joshi, 2004). Longer-term gains can be had by combining stimulant therapy with behavior therapy that focuses on reinforcing attentive, goal-directed, and prosocial behaviors and extinguishing impulsive and hyperactive behaviors (DuPaul & Barkley, 1993). Parents can be taught behavioral methods for promoting positive behaviors and extinguishing maladaptive behaviors in their children (Anastopoulos & Farley, 2003). In addition, parents' own psychological problems and the impairments in parenting skills that these problems create may be the focus of psychosocial interventions for children with ADHD.

Behavioral training programs for children with ADHD and their parents have been shown to improve functioning significantly in the children and their families (Anastopoulos & Farley, 2003; Chronis et al., 2004). For example, the child and his parents might design a contract that says that, every time the child complies with a request from his parents to wash his hands, to set the dinner table, and to put away his toys, he earns a chip. At the end of each week, he can exchange his chips for toys or fun activities. Each time the child refuses to comply, however, he loses a chip. If the child throws a tantrum or becomes aggressive, he must go to his room for a time-out. Such techniques can help parents break the cycle of arguments with their children that leads to escalations in the children's behaviors, which in turn lead to more arguments and perhaps physical violence. These techniques also help children learn to anticipate the consequences of their behaviors and to make less impulsive choices about their behaviors.

Several studies suggest that the combination of stimulant therapy and psychosocial therapy is more likely to lead to both short-term and long-term improvements than either type of therapy alone. For example, in one multisite study, 579 children with ADHD, average age about 8 years, were randomly assigned to receive the combination of Ritalin and behavior therapy, one of these therapies alone, or routine community care (Jensen et al., 2001). After 14 months of treatment, 68 percent of the children in the combined treatment group showed a reduction in or complete discontinuation of their ADHD behaviors, such as aggression and lack of concentration. In the medication-alone group, 56 percent showed a reduction in or discontinuation of symptoms. Behavior therapy alone led to a reduction of symptoms in only 34 percent of the group members, and only 25 percent of the children given routine community care showed reductions in symptoms over that time period.

Conduct Disorder and Oppositional Defiant Disorder

Have you ever lied? Have you ever stolen something? Have you ever hit someone? Most of us would have to answer yes to some and probably all of these questions. Fewer of us would answer yes to the following questions:

- Have you ever pulled a knife or a gun on another person?
- Have you ever forced someone into sexual activity?
- Have you ever deliberately set a fire, with the hope of doing serious damage to someone else's property?
- Have you ever broken into someone else's car or house with the intention of stealing?

Many children who have **conduct disorder** answer yes to these questions and engage in other serious transgressions of societal norms for behavior (see the DSM-IV-TR symptoms in Table 13.5). These children have chronic patterns of unconcern for the basic rights of others. Consider the following case of a boy named Phillip (Jenkins, 1973, pp. 60–64):

> Phillip, age 12, was suspended from a small-town Iowa school and referred for psychiatric treatment by his principal, who sent along the following note with Phillip:
>
>> This child has been a continual problem since coming to our school. He does not get along on the playground because he is mean to other children.

(continued)

He disobeys school rules, teases the patrol children, steals from the other children, and defies all authority. Phillip keeps getting into fights with other children on the bus.

He has been suspended from cafeteria privileges several times for fighting, pushing, and shoving. After he misbehaved one day at the cafeteria, the teacher told him to come up to my office to see me. He flatly refused, lay on the floor, and threw a temper tantrum, kicking and screaming.

The truth is not in Phillip. When caught in actual misdeeds, he denies everything and takes upon himself an air of injured innocence. He believes we are picking on him. His attitude is sullen when he is refused anything. He pouts, and when asked why he does these things, he points to his head and says, "Because I'm not right up here." This boy needs help badly. He does not seem to have any friends. His aggressive behavior prevents the children from liking him. Our school psychologist tested Phillip, and the results indicated average intelligence, but his school achievement is only at the third- and low fourth-grade level.

TABLE 13.5   DSM-IV-TR

Symptoms of Conduct Disorder

The symptoms of conduct disorder include behaviors that violate the basic rights of others and the norms for appropriate social behavior.

Bullies, threatens, or intimidates others

Initiates physical fights

Uses weapons in fights

Engages in theft and burglary

Is physically abusive to people and animals

Forces others into sexual activity

Lies and breaks promises often

Violates parents' rules about staying out at night

Runs away from home

Sets fires deliberately

Vandalizes and destroys others' property deliberately

Often skips school

Source: Reprinted with permission from the *Diagnostic and Statistical Manual of Mental Disorders,* Fourth Edition, Text Revision. Copyright © 2000 American Psychiatric Association.

We all have known bullies and children who often get into trouble. Only 3 to 7 percent of children exhibit behaviors serious enough to qualify for a diagnosis of conduct disorder, however (Costello, Compton, et al., 2003; Maughan et al., 2004). Still, the behaviors of children with conduct disorder exact a high cost to society. For example, the cost of vandalism to schools by juveniles in the United States is estimated to be over $600 million per year. Juveniles account for almost 20 percent of all violent-crime arrests (*Newsweek,* 1993). About half of all adolescent boys and 25 percent of adolescent girls report being attacked by someone at school (Offord, 1997).

Unfortunately, many children with conduct disorder continue to have serious difficulty conforming to societal norms in adolescence and adulthood (Maughan et al., 2000; Offord et al., 1992). As adolescents, about half engage in criminal behavior and drug abuse. As adults, about 75 to 85 percent are chronically unemployed, have histories of unstable personal relationships, frequently engage in impulsive physical aggression, or abuse their spouses (Lahey & Loeber, 1997). Between 35 and 40 percent will be diagnosed with antisocial personality disorder as adults. Youth who develop conduct disorder as children are more likely than those whose conduct problems begin in adolescence to show a wide range of psychological problems and violent behavior as adults (Loeber & Farrington, 2000; Moffitt, Caspi, Rutter, et al., 2001). For example, one study that followed children in three countries found that boys who exhibited physical aggression early in life were especially likely to show chronic conduct problems into adulthood (Broidy et al., 2003).

The DSM-IV-TR also recognizes a less severe pattern of chronic misbehavior than is seen in conduct disorder, known as **oppositional defiant disorder.** Children with oppositional defiant disorder frequently lose their temper or have temper tantrums, argue with adults, actively defy requests or rules, deliberately do things to annoy other people, blame others for their own mistakes, are easily annoyed by others, are angry and resentful, and are spiteful or vindictive (see the DSM-IV-TR symptoms in Table 13.6). Unlike children with conduct disorder, however, children with oppositional defiant disorder are not aggressive toward people or animals, do not destroy property, and do not show a pattern of theft and deceit. Several of the symptoms of oppositional defiant disorder can be seen in the case of 9-year-old Jeremy (adapted from Spitzer et al., 1994, p. 343):

CASE STUDY

Jeremy has been difficult to manage since nursery school. The problems have slowly escalated. Whenever he is without close supervision, he gets into trouble. At school, he teases and kicks other children, trips them, and calls them names. He is described as bad-tempered and irritable, even though at times he seems to enjoy school. Often he appears to be deliberately trying to annoy other children, though he always claims that others have started the arguments. He does not become involved in serious fights but does occasionally exchange a few blows with another child.

Jeremy sometimes refuses to do what his two teachers tell him to do, and this year has been particularly difficult with one who takes him in the afternoon for arithmetic, art, and science lessons. He gives many reasons why he should not have to do his work and argues when told to do it. At home, Jeremy's behavior is quite variable. On some days he is defiant and rude to his mother, needing to be told to do everything several times before he will do it, though eventually he usually complies. On other days he is charming and volunteers to help, but his unhelpful days predominate. His mother says, "The least little thing upsets him, and then he shouts and screams." Jeremy is described as spiteful and mean with his younger brother, Rickie. His mother also comments that he tells many minor lies, though, when pressed, is truthful about important things.

The symptoms of oppositional defiant disorder often begin very early in life, during the toddler and preschool years. Some children with oppositional defiant disorder, however, seem to outgrow their behaviors by late childhood or early

---

TABLE 13.6   DSM-IV-TR

Symptoms of Oppositional Defiant Disorder

The symptoms of oppositional defiant disorder are not as severe as the symptoms of conduct disorder but have their onset at an earlier age, and oppositional defiant disorder often develops into conduct disorder.

Often loses temper

Often argues with adults

Often refuses to comply with requests or rules

Deliberately tries to annoy others

Blames others for his or her mistakes or misbehaviors

Is touchy or easily annoyed

Is angry and resentful

Is spiteful or vindictive

Source: Reprinted with permission from the *Diagnostic and Statistical Manual of Mental Disorders,* Fourth Edition, Text Revision. Copyright © 2000 American Psychiatric Association.

---

adolescence. A subset of children with oppositional defiant disorder, particularly those who tend to be aggressive, go on to develop conduct disorder in childhood and adolescence. Indeed, it seems that almost all children who develop conduct disorder during elementary school had symptoms of oppositional defiant disorder in the earlier years of their lives.

Boys are about three times more likely than girls to be diagnosed with conduct disorder or oppositional defiant disorder (Angold et al., 2002; Maughan et al., 2004). This pattern may exist because the causes of these disorders are more frequently present in boys than in girls. Also, boys with conduct disorder tend to be more physically aggressive than girls with conduct disorder and, thus, may be more likely to draw attention to themselves (Maughan et al., 2000; Tiet et al., 2001).

Some researchers have suggested that antisocial aggressive behavior is not rarer in girls than in boys—it just looks different (Crick & Grotpeter, 1995; Zoccolillo, 1993). Girls' aggression is more likely to be indirect and verbal, rather than physical, and to involve the alienation, ostracism, and character defamation of others. Girls exclude their peers, gossip about them, and collude with others to damage the social status of their targets.

It is clear, however, that girls with conduct and oppositional defiant disorders, like boys with these disorders, are at risk for severe problems throughout their lives. Girls with conduct disorder are just as likely as boys with conduct disorders to engage in stealing, lying, and substance abuse (Tiet et al., 2001). Long-term studies of girls diagnosed with conduct disorder find that, as adolescents and adults, they show high rates of depression and anxiety disorders, severe marital problems, criminal activity, and early, unplanned pregnancies (Moffitt et al., 2001).

Biological Contributors to Conduct Disorder and Oppositional Defiant Disorder

Antisocial behavior clearly runs in families. Children with conduct disorder are much more likely than children without this disorder to have parents with antisocial personalities (Smith & Farrington, 2004). Their fathers are also highly likely to have histories of criminal arrest and alcohol abuse, and their mothers tend to have histories of depression.

Twin and adoption studies indicate that both conduct disorder and oppositional defiant disorder are heritable. For example, one study examined 1,116 pairs of 5-year-old twins and found that 82 percent of the variability in conduct disorder was due to genetic factors (Arseneault et al., 2003).

Some researchers have suggested that children with conduct disorder have fundamental neurological deficits in the frontal lobes, brain systems involved in planning and controlling behavior (Seguin et al., 1995). One piece of evidence that neurological deficits play a role in the development of conduct disorder is the fact that many children with conduct disorder also have attention-deficit/hyperactivity disorder (Moffitt & Silva, 1988). Recall that children with ADHD have trouble maintaining attention and tend to be irritable and impulsive in their actions. These problems can lead to the development of conduct disorder when they bring about failure in school and, thus, to a rejection of school, to poor peer relationships, and to rejection by their peers.

One source of the neurological deficits these children suffer may be exposure to neurotoxins and drugs while in the womb or during the preschool years (Loeber, 1990). These neurological deficits then lead to oppositional behavior in early childhood, followed by increasingly more aggressive and severe antisocial behavior as the child ages.

Another clue that biological factors are involved in conduct disorder is that there are often signs of trouble in diagnosed children, even in infancy. Children who develop conduct disorder tend to have been difficult babies and toddlers, at least by their parents' reports (Henry et al., 1996; Shaw, Keenan, & Vondra, 1994; Shaw & Winslow, 1997). They were irritable and demanding and did not comply with their parents' requests. They were impulsive, seemed to have little control over their behaviors, and responded to frustration with aggression. This correlation suggests that diagnosed children are born with a particular kind of difficult temperament that portends the antisocial behaviors they will engage in as older children (Frick & Morris, 2004).

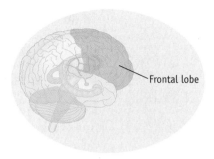

The frontal lobes, which are involved in planning and controlling behavior, may be implicated in conduct disorder.

One way that children learn to control their behavior is by associating punishment with misbehavior and rewards with good behavior. Children with conduct disorder may have more difficulty learning from punishments and rewards, because they tend to become less physiologically aroused than other children by the reinforcements and punishments they receive (Quay, 1993; Raine, Venables, & Williams, 1996). Some studies have found that boys with aggressive conduct disorder have unusually low levels of cortisol. This hormone is secreted by the hypothalamus-pituitary-adrenal axis of the neuroendocrine system and is an indicator of the body's responsiveness to stress (McBurnett et al., 2000).

The role of serotonin in violent behavior has been the focus of many studies (Berman, Kavoussi, & Coccaro, 1997). One study of a large, community-based sample found that young men whose blood serotonin levels were high relative to other men their age were much more likely to have committed a violent crime (Moffitt et al., 1998). Serotonin levels were not correlated with propensity to violence in women, however.

Finally, a popular theory of aggressive behavior is that it is linked to the hormone testosterone. A meta-analysis (see Chapter 3) of studies of testosterone and aggression in humans found a small but statistically significant correlation of .14 (Book, Starzyk, & Quinsey, 2001). Rowe and colleagues (2004) found that the association between testosterone and aggression depends on the social context of the individuals being tested. In a study of 9- to 15-year-old boys, they found that higher levels of testosterone were associated with more conduct disorder symptoms in boys whose peers were prone to engage in socially deviant behaviors. In boys whose peers were not deviant, testosterone was associated with leadership rather than conduct disorder symptoms.

Social Contributors to Conduct and Oppositional Defiant Disorders

Conduct disorder and oppositional defiant disorder are found more frequently in children in lower socioeconomic classes and in urban areas than in children in higher socioeconomic classes and rural areas (Costello, Keeler, & Angold, 2001). This may be because a tendency toward antisocial behavior runs in families, and families with members who engage in antisocial behavior may experience "downward social drift": The adults in these families cannot maintain good jobs, and the families tend to decline in socioeconomic status. Alternatively, this tendency may be due to differences between socioeconomic groups in some of the environmental causes of antisocial behavior, such as poverty and poor parenting.

A recent "experiment of nature" provided more evidence for a causal role of poverty on antisocial behavior than for a "downward drift" hypothesis. Costello, Compton, et al. (2003) had been following 1,420 children in rural North Carolina for several years. About one-quarter of these children were Native American. During their study, a casino operated by Native Americans opened, providing a sudden and substantial increase in income for some of the Native American children. The rates of conduct and oppositional defiant disorders went down among Native American children whose families benefited from the casino money, but not among the Native American children whose families did not benefit from the money.

The quality of parenting children receive, particularly children with a vulnerability to hyperactivity and conduct disturbances, is strongly related to whether they develop the full syndrome of conduct disorder (Bird et al., 2001; Smith & Farrington, 2004). Children who are physically maltreated by their parents or severely neglected are more likely to develop disruptive and delinquent behavior (Stouthamer-Loeber et al., 2001). A related variable is parental uninvolvement: Children whose parents are not involved in their everyday lives—for example, children whose parents do not know who their friends are or what they are doing in school—are more likely to develop conduct disturbances. When the parents of children with conduct disturbances do interact with their children, these

Children who are physically maltreated by their parents are more likely to develop symptoms of conduct disorders.

interactions often are characterized by hostility, physical violence, and ridicule (Dishion & Patterson, 1997). The picture of these families is one in which parents frequently ignore the children or are absent from home but when the children transgress in some way, the parents lash out violently at them (Lochman, White, & Wayland, 1991; Smith & Farrington, 2004). Also, these parents are more likely to give severe physical punishments to boys than to girls, which may partially account for the higher rate of conduct disturbances in boys (Lytton & Romney, 1991).

Children living in such families may turn to their peers to receive validation and to escape their parents. Unfortunately, these peer groups may consist of other children with conduct disturbances. Deviant peer groups tend to encourage delinquent acts, even providing opportunities for such acts (Dishion & Patterson, 1997). For example, the members of a peer group of adolescents may dare a new member to commit a robbery to "show he is a man" and provide him with a weapon and a getaway car. Children who become part of deviant peer groups are especially likely to begin abusing alcohol and illicit drugs, which in turn leads to increases in deviant acts (McBride, Joe, & Simpson, 1991).

Individuals with antisocial tendencies tend to choose mates with similar tendencies (Smith & Farrington, 2004). Conversely, adolescents and young adults with conduct disturbances who form close relationships with others who do not have such problems are much more likely to grow out of their conduct disturbances. For example, delinquent young men who marry young women with no histories of conduct problems tend to cease their delinquent acts and never engage in such acts again (Sampson & Laub, 1992).

The biological factors and family factors that contribute to conduct disorder may coincide, sending a child on a trajectory toward antisocial behaviors that is difficult to stop (Loeber, 1990; Reid & Eddy, 1997) (see Figure 13.1 on page 476). The neuropsychological problems associated with antisocial behaviors are linked to maternal drug use, poor prenatal nutrition, pre- and postnatal exposure to toxic agents, child abuse, birth complications, and low birthweight (Moffitt, 1993; Silberg et al., 2003). Infants and toddlers with these neuropsychological problems are more irritable, impulsive, awkward, overreactive, and inattentive than their peers and are slower learners. This makes them difficult for parents to care for, and they are at increased risk for maltreatment and neglect. Added to this, the parents of these children are likely to be teenagers and to have psychological problems of their own that contribute to ineffective, harsh, or inconsistent parenting. Thus, children may carry a biological predisposition to disruptive, antisocial behaviors and may experience parenting that contributes to these behaviors.

In a longitudinal study following children from age 3 into adulthood, Moffitt, Caspi, and colleagues (Moffitt & Caspi, 2001; Moffitt et al., 2001) gathered information on a particularly pernicious form of conduct disorder that begins early in childhood and persists into a violent adulthood. They found that this disorder is the outcome of an interaction between a biological disposition to a difficult temperament and cognitive deficits and a risky environment characterized by inadequate parenting and disrupted family bonds. In contrast, youth who are antisocial only in adolescence are much less likely to carry this combination of biological and environmental risk factors. Similarly, another study found that impulsivity in boys is linked to a greater risk for delinquency in late adolescence only among those who grow up in violent, poor neighborhoods (Lynam et al., 2000).

Cognitive Contributors to Conduct Disorder

Children with conduct disorder tend to process information about social interactions in ways that promote aggressive reactions to these interactions (Crick & Dodge, 1994). They enter social interactions with assumptions that other children will be aggressive toward them, and they use these assumptions, rather than cues from specific situations, to interpret the actions of their peers (Dodge & Schwartz, 1997). For example, when another child accidentally bumps into him or her, a child with a conduct disorder assumes that the bumping was intentional and meant to provoke a fight. In addition, children with conduct disorder tend to believe that any negative actions that peers take against them, such as taking their favorite pencils, are intentional rather than accidental. When deciding on what action to take in response to a perceived provocation by a peer, children with conduct disorder tend to think of a narrow range of responses, usually including aggression (Pettit, Dodge, & Brown, 1988; Rubin, Daniels-Bierness, & Hayvren, 1982; Spivack & Shure, 1974). When pressed to consider responses other than aggression, these children generate ineffective or vague responses. They often consider responses other than aggression to be useless or unattractive (Crick & Ladd, 1990).

Children who think about their social interactions in these ways are likely to act aggressively toward others. Then others may retaliate: Other children will hit them, parents and teachers will punish them, and others will perceive them negatively. In turn, these actions by others may feed the children's assumptions that the world is against them, causing them to misinterpret future actions by others. A cycle of interactions can be built that maintains and encourages aggressive, antisocial behaviors.

Again, the best evidence that thinking patterns are causes, rather than just correlates, of antisocial behavior in children comes from studies showing that changing aggressive children's thinking patterns can change their tendencies to act aggressively. Let's turn to these interventions and others for children with conduct disorder.

Drug Therapies for Conduct Disorder

Children with severely aggressive behavior have been prescribed a variety of drugs, although medications have not proven consistently helpful for them (Chang, 2004). Antidepressant drugs, particularly the selective serotonin reuptake inhibitors, may help reduce irritable and agitated behavior in children (Emslie et al., 2004). Children with conduct disorder are sometimes prescribed neuroleptic drugs, and controlled studies suggest that these drugs suppress aggressive behavior in these children (Gadow, 1992). It is unclear whether the drugs have any effect on the other symptoms of conduct

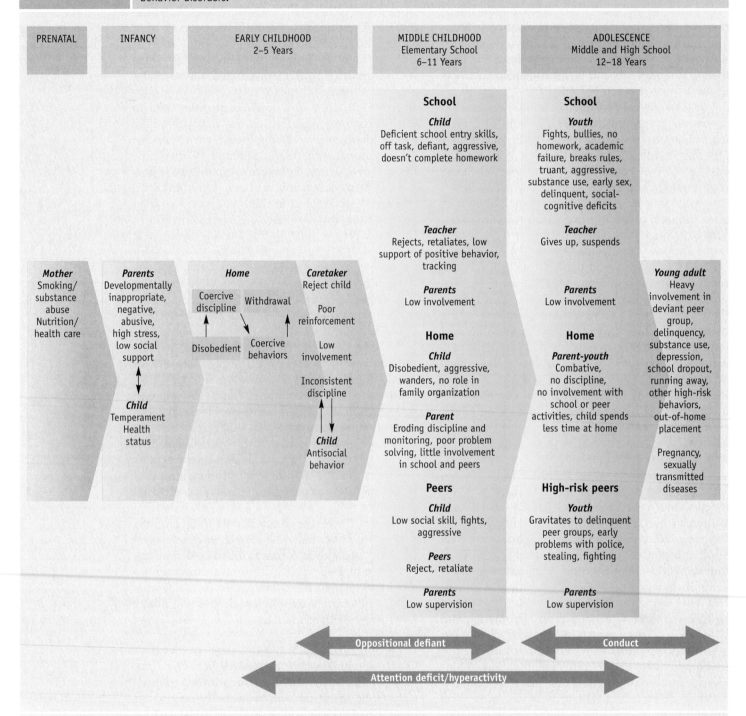

FIGURE 13.1 | **Developmental Model of Behavior Disorders.** Several biological and environmental factors come together to create behavior disorders.

Source: From J. B. Reid and J. M. Eddy, "The Prevention of Antisocial Behavior: Some Considerations in the Search for Effective Interventions" in D. M. Stoff et al. (Eds.), *Handbook of Antisocial Personality Disorder.* Copyright © 1997 John Wiley & Sons, Inc.

disorder, such as lying and stealing. Children with conduct disorder are frequently prescribed stimulant drugs, and these drugs also suppress aggressive behaviors (Joshi, 2004). Finally, controlled studies suggest that mood stabilizers, including lithium and anticonvulsant drugs, may be an effective treatment for children with aggressive conduct disorder (Chang & Simeonova, 2004).

Psychological and Social Therapies for Conduct and Oppositional Defiant Disorders

Most psychotherapies for conduct disorder are derived from social learning theory (see Chapter 2). They focus on changing the children's ways of interpreting interpersonal interactions, teaching them to take the perspectives of others and to care about those perspectives, to use self-talk as a way of controlling impulsive behaviors, and to use more adaptive ways of solving conflicts than aggression (Kazdin, 2003a; Lochman, Barry, & Pardini, 2003). Many therapies try to involve parents as well as children and to change the interaction patterns in the family that help maintain children's antisocial behavior (Webster-Stratton & Reid, 2003).

Cognitive-Behavioral Therapy The first step in cognitive-behavioral therapy is to teach children to recognize situations that trigger anger or aggressive behaviors or in which they tend to be impulsive. This is done through observing children in their natural settings and then pointing out to them situations in which they misbehave or seem angry, discussing hypothetical situations and how the children would react to them and having children keep diaries of their feelings and behaviors. The children also are taught to analyze their thoughts in these situations and to consider alternative ways of interpreting situations. Their assumptions that other children or adults act meanly toward them intentionally are challenged, and they are helped to take other people's perspectives on situations.

Next, the children may be taught to use self-talk to help them avoid negative reactions to situations: They learn to talk to themselves in difficult situations, repeating phrases that help them calm themselves, and to consider adaptive ways of coping with situations. For example, a child who tends to respond to provocation by others by immediately beginning to hit and kick might learn to think,

> Slow down, slow down, slow down. Breathe deeply. Count to five. Slow down, slow down, slow down—think about what to do. Don't want to get mad. Slow down, slow down.

Therapists teach adaptive problem-solving skills by discussing real and hypothetical problem situations with children and by helping them generate a variety of positive solutions to the problems. These solutions might be modeled by the therapists and then practiced by the children in role-plays. For example, if a therapist and child are discussing how to respond to another child who has cut in line in the school lunchroom, the therapist might initially model an assertive (rather than aggressive) response, such as saying, "I would like you to move to the back of the line," to the cutting child. Then, the child in therapy might practice the assertive response and pretend to be the child cutting in line in order to gain some perspective on why the child is doing this.

Some psychosocial therapies for children with conduct disorder also include parents, particularly if the family dynamics are supporting the children's conduct disorder (Kazdin, 2003b; Reid & Eddy, 1997; Webster-Stratton & Reid, 2003). Parents are taught to reinforce positive behaviors in their children and to discourage aggressive or antisocial behaviors. Parents are also taught strategies similar to the ones already described for controlling their own angry outbursts and discipline techniques that are not violent.

Unfortunately, it can be difficult to get the parents who need the most improvement in parenting skills to participate in therapy (Kazdin, 2003a). In addition, to be effective, therapists need to be sensitive to cultural differences in the norms for the behavior of children and parents. For example, in families of color, it is often useful to engage the extended family (grandparents, aunts, uncles) in family therapy, as well as the parents of a child with conduct disorder (Dudley-Grant, 2001).

Studies of the therapies based on social learning theory suggest that they can be very effective in reducing aggressive and impulsive behavior in children, particularly interventions made in the home, in the classroom, and in peer groups (August et al., 2001; Kazdin, 2003a; Webster-Stratton & Reid, 2003). Unfortunately, many children relapse into conduct disorder after a while, particularly if their parents have poor parenting skills, alcoholism or other drug abuse, or other psychopathology. Interventions are most likely to have long-term, positive effects if they begin early in a disturbed child's life (Estrada & Pinsof, 1995). Booster sessions of additional therapy after a course of initial therapy also help a child avoid relapsing into conduct disorder (Lochman et al., 1991).

Ethnic Differences in Interventions for Antisocial Behavior A recent study of youth growing up in a largely rural area of North Carolina found no differences between African American and European American youth in rates of conduct disorder, but the European American youth had higher rates of oppositional defiant disorder (Angold et al.,

2002). The European American youth were more likely to obtain treatment from mental-health specialists than the African American youth, who tended to receive what treatment they got in the context of the school system.

The criminal justice system may deal differently with African American and European American adolescents who behave in antisocial ways (Tolan & Gorman-Smith, 1997). Researchers examined the case records of all adolescents who were sent to correctional schools or to state psychiatric hospitals in one area of Connecticut over a year (Lewis, Balla, & Shanok, 1979). The adolescents sent to psychiatric hospitals and those sent to jail were just as likely to have histories of violence and had equal levels of emotional problems. However, the adolescents sent to jail were much more likely to be African American than European American, whereas those sent to psychiatric hospitals were much more likely to be European American than African American. It appears that disturbed African American adolescents are incarcerated, whereas disturbed European Americans are hospitalized.

SUMMING UP

- The behavior disorders include attention-deficit/hyperactivity disorder, conduct disorder, and oppositional defiant disorder.

- Children with attention-deficit/hyperactivity disorder are inattentive, impulsive, and overactive. Many do not do well in school, and their relationships with their peers are extremely impaired.

- Some children with attention-deficit/hyperactivity disorder grow out of this disorder, but some continue to show the symptoms into adulthood, and they are at high risk for conduct problems and emotional problems throughout their lives.

- The two therapies that are effective in treating ADHD are stimulant drugs and behavior therapies that teach children how to control their behaviors. The combination of medications and behavior therapies appears to lead to the most long-lasting improvement.

- Children with conduct disorder engage in behaviors that severely violate societal norms, including chronic lying, stealing, and violence toward others.

- Children with oppositional defiant disorder engage in antisocial behaviors that are less severe than those of conduct disorder but that indicate a negative, irritable approach to others.

- Some children outgrow oppositional defiant disorder, but a subset develop full conduct disorder.

- Children who develop conduct disorder often continue to engage in antisocial behaviors into adulthood and have high rates of criminal activity and drug abuse.

- Neurological deficits may be involved in conduct disorder. These deficits may make it more difficult for children with this disorder to learn from reinforcements and punishments and to control their behaviors.

- Children with conduct disorder tend to have parents who are neglectful much of the time and violent when annoyed with them.

- Children with conduct disorder tend to think about interactions with others in ways that contribute to their aggressive reactions.

- Drug therapies are sometimes used to help children with conduct disorder control their behavior, and cognitive-behavioral therapies help them learn to interpret and respond to situations differently.

SEPARATION ANXIETY DISORDER

Children can suffer from depression, panic attacks, obsessive-compulsive disorder, generalized anxiety disorder, posttraumatic stress disorder, and phobias. The childhood versions of most of these disorders are discussed in the chapters on the individual disorders. One emotional disorder that is specific to childhood is **separation anxiety disorder** (see the DSM-IV-TR symptoms in Table 13.7).

Many infants become anxious and upset if separated from their primary caregivers. They cry loudly and cannot be consoled by anyone but their primary caregivers. This is a normal consequence of an infant's development of the understanding that objects (including mothers and fathers) continue to exist even when they are not in direct sight, as well as a consequence of the infant's attachment to caregivers. With development, however, most infants come to understand that their caregivers will return, and they find ways to comfort themselves while their caregivers are away, so that they are not excessively anxious.

Some children continue to be extremely anxious when separated from their caregivers, even into childhood and adolescence. They may refuse to go to school, because they fear the separation from their caregivers. They cannot sleep at night unless they are with their caregivers. They have nightmares with themes of separation. They follow their caregivers around the house. If they are sepa-

TABLE 13.7 DSM-IV-TR

Symptoms of Separation Anxiety Disorder

Children who show much more than the usual anxiety when separated from caregivers may be diagnosed with separation anxiety disorder.

Excessive distress when separated from home or caregivers or when anticipating separation

Persistent and excessive worry about losing, or harm coming to, caregivers

Persistent reluctance or refusal to go to school or elsewhere because of fear of separation

Excessive fear about being alone

Reluctance to go to sleep without caregivers nearby

Repeated nightmares involving themes of separation

Repeated complaints of physical symptoms when separation from caregivers occurs or is anticipated

Source: Reprinted with permission from the *Diagnostic and Statistical Manual of Mental Disorders,* Fourth Edition, Text Revision. Copyright © 2000 American Psychiatric Association.

Children with separation anxiety disorder often cling desperately to their parents.

rated from their caregivers, they worry tremendously that something bad will happen to the caregivers. They have exaggerated fears of natural disasters (e.g., tornadoes, earthquakes) and of robbers, kidnappers, and accidents. They may have stomachaches and headaches and become nauseated if forced to separate from their caregivers. Younger children may cry unconsolably. Older children may avoid activities, such as being on a baseball team, that might take them away from their caregivers, preferring to spend all the time possible with their caregivers.

Many children go through short episodes of a few days of these symptoms after traumatic events, such as getting lost in a shopping mall. Separation anxiety disorder is not diagnosed unless a child shows symptoms for at least four weeks and the symptoms significantly impair the child's ability to function in everyday life. Children with this disorder may be very shy, sensitive, and demanding of adults.

About 3 percent of children under 11 years of age experience separation anxiety disorder (Angold et al., 2002; Bowen, Offord, & Boyle, 1990). It

is more common in girls than in boys. Left untreated, this disorder can recur frequently throughout childhood and adolescence, significantly interfering with the child's academic progress and peer relationships. One study examined the adult outcomes of children with separation anxiety who had refused to go to school because of their anxiety, comparing them with people who had had no psychiatric disorders as children. The investigators found that those who had had separation anxiety disorder had more psychiatric problems as adults than the comparison group, were more likely to continue to live with their parents even though they were adults, and were less likely to have married and had children (Flakierska-Praquin, Lindstrom, & Gilberg, 1997).

Biological Contributors to Separation Anxiety Disorder

Biological factors may be involved in the development of separation anxiety disorder (see the Concept Overview in Table 13.8 on page 480). Children with this disorder tend to have family histories of anxiety and depressive disorders (Biederman et al., 2001; Manicavasagar et al., 2001). Twin studies suggest that separation anxiety disorder is heritable, but more so in girls than in boys (Eaves et al., 1997; Feigon et al., 2001).

Earlier, we discussed the role of difficult temperament in the development of conduct disorder. A different kind of temperament is implicated in the development of anxiety disorders in children. Kagan, Reznick, and Snidman (1987) suggest that some children are born high in **behavioral inhibition**—they are shy, fearful, and irritable as toddlers and cautious, quiet, and introverted as

TABLE 13.8 Concept Overview

Proposed Causes of and Treatments for Separation Anxiety Disorder

Biological and environmental factors may contribute to separation anxiety disorder, which is often treated with cognitive-behavioral therapy.

Proposed Causes	Description
Biological predisposition	There may be a genetic predisposition to anxiety disorders, including separation anxiety and panic attacks.
Behavioral inhibition	Children are born with an inhibited, fearful temperament.
Traumatic and uncontrollable events	Some children develop separation anxiety after a traumatic event; studies of nonhuman primates show that chronic uncontrollability can contribute to anxiety.
Parenting experiences	Parents may encourage fearful behavior and not encourage appropriate independence.

Treatment	Description
Cognitive-behavioral therapy	Children are taught self-talk to challenge negative thoughts and relaxation to quell anxiety; periods of separation from parents are increased gradually; parents are taught to model and reinforce nonanxious behavior.

school-age children. These children tend to avoid or withdraw from novel situations, are clingy with parents, and become excessively aroused when exposed to unfamiliar situations.

Some studies suggest that children high in behavioral inhibition as infants are at increased risk to develop anxiety disorders in childhood (Biederman et al., 1990, 1993; Caspi et al., 2003). These children's parents also are prone to anxiety disorders, particularly panic disorder, and many have a history of anxiety disorders that dates back to their own childhood. One study found that children who were behaviorally inhibited had abnormalities on the gene that regulates corticotropin-releasing hormone (CRH), which plays an important role in stress responses (Smoller et al., 2003). This association between the abnormal gene and behavioral inhibition was particularly strong in children whose parents also had an anxiety disorder.

Psychological and Sociocultural Contributors to Separation Anxiety Disorder

Children may learn to be anxious from their parents or as an understandable response to their environments. In some cases, separation anxiety disorder develops following traumatic events:

CASE STUDY

In the early morning hours, 7-year-old Maria was abruptly awakened by a loud rumbling and violent shaking. She sat upright in bed and called out to her 10-year-old sister, Rosemary, who was leaping out of her own bed 3 feet away. The two girls ran for their mother's bedroom as their toys and books plummeted from shelves and dresser tops. The china hutch in the hallway teetered in front of them and then fell forward with a crash, blocking their path to their mother's room. Mrs. Marshall called out to them to go back and stay in their doorway. They knew the doorway was a place you were supposed to go during an earthquake, so they huddled there together until the shaking finally stopped. Mrs. Marshall climbed over the hutch and broken china to her daughters. Although they were all very shaken and scared, they were unhurt.

Two weeks later, Maria began to complain every morning of stomachaches, headaches, and dizziness, asking to stay home from

(continued)

school with her mother. After four days, when a medical examination revealed no physical problems, Maria was told she must return to school. She protested tearfully, but her mother insisted, and Rosemary promised to hold her hand all the way to school. In the classroom, Maria could not concentrate on her schoolwork and was often out of her seat, looking out the window in the direction of home. She told her teacher she needed to go home to see if her mother was okay. When she was told she couldn't go home, she began to cry and shake so violently that the school nurse called Mrs. Marshall, who picked up Maria and took her home. The next morning, Maria's protests grew stronger and she refused to go to school until her mother promised to go with her and sit in her classroom for the first hour. When Mrs. Marshall began to leave, Maria clung to her, crying, pleading for her not to leave, and following her into the hallway. The next day, Maria refused to leave the house for her Brownie meeting and her dancing lessons or even to play in the front yard. She followed her mother around the house and insisted on sleeping with her at night. "I need to be with you, Mommy, in case something happens," she declared.

Parents may contribute to the development of a separation anxiety disorder in their children by being overprotective and by modeling anxious reactions to separations from their children (Kendall, 1992). The families of children with separation anxiety disorder tend to be especially close-knit, not encouraging developmentally appropriate levels of independence in the children.

Some of the best evidence that environmental and parenting factors can influence the development of anxiety disorders in youngsters comes from studies of nonhuman primates. Mineka and colleagues (1986) found that rhesus monkeys who were given adequate food and water from ages 2 to 6 months, but could not control their access to food and water, developed a fearfulness and became generally inhibited in their behavior. Other monkeys given the same amount of food and water, but under conditions that they could exert some control over, did not become fearful. This re-

sult suggests that some human children who are raised in conditions over which they have little control may develop anxiety symptoms.

Moreover, Suomi (1999) found that, although some rhesus monkeys seem to be born behaviorally inhibited, the extent to which they develop serious signs of fearfulness and anxiety later in life depends on the parenting they receive. Those who are raised by anxious mothers, which also are inhibited and inappropriately responsive to the infants, are prone to develop monkey versions of anxiety disorders. Those that are raised by calm, responsive mothers that model appropriate reactions to stressful situations typically are not any more likely to develop anxiety problems as adolescents or adults than are those that are not born behaviorally inhibited.

Treatments for Separation Anxiety Disorder

Cognitive-behavioral therapies are most often used to treat separation anxiety disorder (Kendall, Aschenbrand, & Hudson, 2003). Children are taught to manage their anxiety better by developing new skills at coping and at challenging cognitions that feed their anxiety. They might be taught relaxation exercises to practice during periods of separation from their parents. Their fears about separation are challenged, and they are taught to use self-talk to calm themselves when they become anxious.

As therapy progresses, periods of separation from their parents are increased in number and duration. Parents must be willing to participate in the therapy and to cope with their children's (and their own) reactions to attempts to increase periods of separation. Parents may need to be taught to model nonanxious reactions to separations from their children and to reinforce nonanxious behavior in their children.

Controlled clinical trials of this type of therapy show that it can be effective in the short term and maintain its effects in the long term (Shortt, Barrett, & Fox, 2001; Velting, Setzer, & Albano, 2004). For example, Mark Dadds and colleagues (1999) provided a 10-week school-based intervention for anxiety-ridden children and their parents. They found that these children were much less likely than a control group who received no intervention to be diagnosed with separation anxiety or another anxiety disorder over the 2 years following the intervention (see Figure 13.2 on page 482).

Here is how Maria was treated for her separation anxiety:

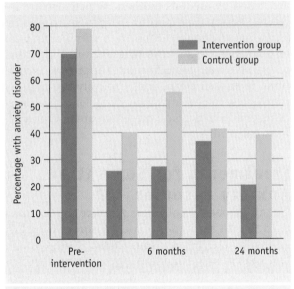

FIGURE 13.2 **Effects of Cognitive-Behavioral Therapy for Separation Anxiety Disorder.**
Schoolchildren with separation anxiety and other anxiety disorders and their parents were given a 10-week cognitive-behavioral intervention. These children were less likely than a control group of children over the next 2 years to be diagnosed with an anxiety disorder.

Source: Dadds et al., 1999.

and praise each morning for sleeping in her own bed.

The first few times Mrs. Marshall left the classroom, Maria followed her out. Soon, however, she began to stay in her chair and received stickers. At home, she remained in her own bed the first night, even though she was told she had to stay only two hours to earn her sticker. At her own request, she returned to Brownie meetings and attended summer camp.

Many kinds of drugs are used in the treatment of childhood anxiety disorders, including antidepressants; antianxiety drugs, such as the benzodiazepines; stimulants; and antihistamines. The selective serotonin reuptake inhibitors, such as fluoxetine, are most frequently used and have been most consistently shown to be effective in reducing anxiety symptoms in children (Birmaher et al., 2003; Thienemann, 2004). There is greater support for the efficacy of cognitive-behavioral therapy than for drug therapies in the treatment of separation anxiety disorder, however.

SUMMING UP

- Children can suffer from all the emotional disorders, including depression and all the anxiety disorders. Separation anxiety disorder is one disorder specific to children.
- Children with separation anxiety disorder are excessively fearful about separation from primary caregivers. They may become extremely agitated or ill when they anticipate separation, and they may curtail usual activities to avoid separation.
- Separation anxiety disorder appears to be associated with a family history of anxiety disorders.
- Children who are behaviorally inhibited as infants appear at risk for separation anxiety disorder as adults.
- Parents may enhance a vulnerability to separation anxiety disorder by their reactions to children's distress.
- Cognitive-behavioral therapies can help children with separation anxiety disorder quiet their anxieties and resume everyday activities.

CASE STUDY

Mrs. Marshall was instructed to take Maria to school and leave four times during the period she was there. Initially, Mrs. Marshall left for 30 seconds each time. Over time, she gradually increased the amount of time and distance she was away while Maria remained in the classroom. Maria was given a sticker at the end of the school day for each time she remained in her seat while her mother was out of the room. In addition, she was praised by her teacher and her mother, and positive self-statements (e.g., "My mommy will be okay; I'm a big girl and I can stay at school") were encouraged. No response was made when Maria failed to stay in her chair. Maria could exchange her stickers for prizes at the end of each week.

At home, Mrs. Marshall gave minimal attention to Maria's inquiries about her well-being and ignored excessive, inappropriate crying. Eventually, Maria was given a sticker

ELIMINATION DISORDERS

CASE STUDY

On the morning of her third birthday, Gretchen walked into the kitchen and announced to her mother, "I'm a big girl now, and I'm going to wear big girl underpants. No more diapers." She, indeed, did wear "big girl underpants" that day, and, although she had a couple of accidents during the day, at bedtime Gretchen was extremely proud of herself for being such a big girl. Within a few weeks, she was able to wear big girl underpants all day without any accidents.

Most children gain sufficient control over their bladder and bowel movements by about age 4 that they no longer need to wear diapers during the day or night. Like Gretchen, many children view the ability to control their bladder and bowel movements as a marker of their passage into being "big boys or girls." It is understandable, then, that children who lose this control, particularly when they are far past the preschool years and into middle childhood, can experience shame and distress. These children might be diagnosed with one of the two **elimination disorders,** enuresis or encopresis (see the Concept Overview in Table 13.9 on page 484).

Enuresis

Occasional wetting of the bed at night is common among elementary school children, particularly during times of stress. Children over age 5 are diagnosed with **enuresis** when they have wet the bed or their clothes at least twice a week for three months (APA, 2000). Most children with enuresis wet only at night. A subset of children with enuresis wet during the daytime only, most often at school. These children may be socially anxious about using the public toilets at school or prone to becoming preoccupied with other things they are doing. They do not use the toilet as they need to and tend to have wetting accidents.

Bed-wetting is relatively common, as disorders go, among young children, but the prevalence decreases with age. About 15 to 20 percent of 5-year-olds wet the bed at least once per month. By adolescence, the prevalence of bed-wetting decreases to 1 to 2 percent (Angold et al., 2002; Houts, 2003).

Enuresis runs in families, and approximately 75 percent of children with enuresis have biological relatives who had the disorder. Some of these children may have inherited a biological vulnerability to the disorder in the form of unusually small bladders or lower bladder threshold for involuntary voiding. About 5 to 10 percent of children with enuresis have urinary tract infections (Mellon & McGrath, 2000). A variety of other biological causes for enuresis have been suggested, but none have received consistent empirical support (Ondersma & Walker, 1998).

Psychodynamic and family systems theorists suggest that enuresis is due to conflicts and anxiety caused by disruptions or dysfunction in the family (Olmos de Paz, 1990). For example, some children develop enuresis when new babies are born into the family, perhaps because they feel threatened by the attention their parents are giving to the new baby and resentful toward the new baby but cannot express their feelings freely. Behaviorists suggest that enuresis may be due to lax or inappropriate toilet training, that enuretic children never learned appropriate bladder control and, thus, have recurrent problems during childhood (Erickson, 1992).

Children with enuresis are usually taken to their pediatricians rather than mental-health specialists, and physicians often prescribe antidepressants to treat enuresis (Ondersma & Walker, 1998). Tricyclic antidepressants, particularly imipramine, are commonly used. It is not clear how these drugs affect wetting, but increases in norepinephrine may help in bladder control. About half the children treated with imipramine show reductions in wetting, but up to 95 percent relapse once the medication is discontinued (Ondersma & Walker, 1998). In addition, the tricyclic antidepressants have dangerous side effects in children, including sleep disturbances, tiredness, gastrointestinal distress, and cardiac irregularities. Overdoses can be fatal.

Synthetic antidiuretic hormone (ADH) has emerged as the drug of choice for nighttime enuresis (Houts, 2003; Ondersma & Walker, 1998). This drug concentrates urine, thereby reducing urine output from the kidney to the bladder. It reliably reduces nighttime wetting; however, children typically relapse into wetting once the medication is discontinued.

A behavioral method referred to as the **bell and pad method** is a reliable, long-term solution to enuresis (Houts, 2003). A pad is placed under the

---

TABLE 13.9 Concept Overview

Elimination Disorders

The elimination disorders involve uncontrolled wetting and defecation far beyond the age at which children usually gain control over these functions.

Disorder	Symptoms	Proposed Causes	Treatments
Enuresis	Unintended urination at least two times per week for 3 months; child over 5 years of age	1. Genetic vulnerability 2. Conflicts or anxiety 3. Lax or inappropriate toilet training	1. Antidepressant drugs, synthetic antidiuretic hormone 2. Bell and pad behavioral method
Encopresis	Unintended defecation at least one time per month for 3 months; child over 4 years of age	Usually begins after episodes of severe constipation; changes in colon reduce ability to know when to use toilet, leading to accidents	1. Medication to clear out colon, laxatives or mineral oil to soften stools, increase in dietary fiber 2. Behavioral contracting to increase appropriate toilet use and diet change, relaxation methods

child while she sleeps. This pad has a sensory device to detect even small amounts of urine. If the child wets during her sleep, a bell connected to the pad rings and awakens the child. Through classical conditioning, the child learns to wake up when she has a full bladder and needs to urinate. Reviews of dozens of studies of the bell and pad method and related methods conclude that they are highly effective, with over 70 percent of chil-

dren completely cured of bed-wetting, often within four weeks (Houts, 2003; Mellon & McGrath, 2000).

Encopresis

Encopresis is repeated defecation into clothing or onto the floor and is rarer than enuresis. To be diagnosed with encopresis, children must have at least one such event a month for at least 3 months and must be at least 4 years of age. Fewer than 1 percent of children can be diagnosed with encopresis, and it is more common in boys than in girls (Angold et al., 2002).

Encopresis usually begins after one or more episodes of severe constipation, which may result from environmental factors, such as the withholding of bowel movements during toilet training or a refusal to use the toilet during school; a genetic predisposition toward decreased bowl motility; food intolerance; or certain medications (Stark et al., 1997). Constipation can cause distention of the colon, decreasing the child's ability to detect the urge to have a bowel movement, fecal hardening and buildup in the colon, and subsequent leakage of fecal material. The child may then increase the problem by avoiding using the toilet because of large or painful bowel movements, which in turn makes him or her more insensitive to fecal matter in the colon and, thus, less able to know when it is time to use the toilet.

Encopresis is typically treated by a combination of medications to clear out the colon, laxatives

Children are very proud of themselves when they learn to control their bowel and bladder movements; thus, loss of control can be very distressing.

or mineral oil to soften stools, recommendations to increase dietary fiber, and encouragement to the child to sit on the toilet a certain amount of time each day. This medical management strategy works for 60 to 80 percent of children with encopresis.

Stark and colleagues (1997) used a behavioral treatment program for a group of children with encopresis who did not respond to medical management. This behavioral program included contracting around toileting behaviors and diet, the use of rewards for appropriate toilet usage, and relaxation techniques. In addition, all the children received standard medical management. Eighty-six percent of the children had stopped soiling by the end of the treatment and did not require further treatment.

SUMMING UP

- Enuresis—persistent, uncontrolled wetting by children who have attained bladder control—runs in families and has been attributed to a variety of biological causes. Psychodynamic theories attribute it to emotional distress. Behavioral theories attribute it to poor toilet training.

- Antidepressants help reduce enuresis in the short term, but not in the long term, and carry significant side effects.

- Behavioral methods that help children learn to awaken and go to the bathroom can help reduce nighttime enuresis.

- Encopresis—persistent, uncontrolled soiling by children who have attained control of defecation—typically begins after one or more episodes of constipation, which creates distention in the colon and decreases a child's ability to detect needed bowel movements.

- Medical management and behavioral techniques can help reduce encopresis.

DISORDERS OF COGNITIVE, MOTOR, AND COMMUNICATION SKILLS

Beginning from the first day home from the hospital with a new baby, parents eagerly track their child's development, watching for the emergence of cognitive skills, motor skills, and communication skills. The first responsive smile from a child, the first tentative steps, and the first babbling words are occasions for major celebrations. Although most parents become anxious when it seems their children are not developing a skill "on time" (or perhaps even ahead of other children), their fears usually are allayed as their children's skills eventually emerge.

Sometimes, though, important skills do not emerge or develop fully in a child. A child might not learn to crawl or walk until many months after most children do. A child might have severe trouble with reading or arithmetic, despite having good teachers. Approximately 20 percent of children have significant impairment in important cognitive, motor, or communication skills (APA, 2000). These problems are more common in boys than in girls. They can greatly affect a child's achievement in school and can lower self-esteem and well-being. When deficits in fundamental skills are severe enough to interfere with a child's progress, the child may be diagnosed with a learning disorder, a motor skills disorder, or a communication disorder (see the Concept Overview in Table 13.10).

Learning Disorders

The DSM-IV-TR describes three *learning disorders*. These disorders are diagnosed only when a child's performance on standardized tests is significantly below that expected for his or her age, schooling, and overall level of intelligence. **Reading disorder,** also known as *dyslexia*, involves deficits in the ability to read. This disorder is usually apparent by the fourth grade. About 4 percent of children have a reading disorder, and they are more common in boys than girls (Rutter et al., 2004).

Mathematics disorder involves deficits in the ability to learn math. It includes problems in understanding mathematical terms, in recognizing numerical symbols, in clustering objects into groups, in counting, and in following mathematical principles. Although many of us feel that we are not great at math, deficits in math skills severe enough to warrant this diagnosis occur in only about 1 percent of children (APA, 2000). The disorder is usually apparent at about second or third grade.

A **disorder of written expression** involves deficits in the ability to write. Children with this disorder have severe trouble spelling, constructing a sentence or paragraph, or writing legibly. This disorder is rare.

Children with learning disorders can become demoralized and disruptive in class. If their learning disorder is never treated, they are at high risk of dropping out of school, with as many as 40 percent never finishing high school (APA, 2000). As adults, they may have problems getting and keeping good jobs. The emotional side effects of

TABLE 13.10   Concept Overview

Disorders of Cognitive, Motor, and Communication Skills

These disorders involve deficits in specific skills.

Disorder	Description
Learning Disorders	
Reading disorder (dyslexia)	Deficits in ability to read
Mathematics disorder	Deficits in mathematics skills
Disorder of written expression	Deficits in the ability to write
Motor Skills Disorder	
Developmental coordination disorder	Deficits in the ability to walk, run, hold on to objects
Communication Disorders	
Expressive language disorder	Deficits in the ability to express oneself through language
Mixed receptive-expressive language disorder	Deficits in the ability both to express oneself through language and to understand the language of others
Phonological disorder	Use of speech sounds inappropriate for age or dialect
Stuttering	Severe problems in word fluency

Actor Tom Cruise has struggled with dyslexia

learning disorders may also affect their social relationships.

On the other hand, many children overcome learning disorders. For example, actor Tom Cruise suffers from dyslexia.

Motor Skills Disorder

The one *motor skills disorder*, called **developmental coordination disorder**, involves deficits in fundamental motor skills, such as walking, running, or holding on to objects. This disorder is not diagnosed if a child's motor skills deficits are due to a medical condition, such as cerebral palsy or muscular dystrophy, or to a serious mental disorder, such as autism. A young child with developmental coordination disorder may be clumsy and very slow in achieving major milestones, such as walking, crawling, sitting, tying shoelaces, or zipping pants. Older children may be unable to assemble puzzles, build models, play ball, or write their names. This disorder is relatively common, with as many as 6 percent of children between 5 and 11 years of age suffering from it (APA, 2000).

Communication Disorders

The *communication disorders* involve deficits in the ability to communicate verbally, because of a severely limited vocabulary, severe stuttering, or an inability to articulate words correctly. Children with **expressive language disorder** have a limited vocabulary, difficulty in learning new words, difficulty in retrieving words or the right word, and poor grammar. They may use a limited variety of sentence types (such as only questions or declarations), omit critical parts of sentences, or use words in an unusual order. Some children with this disorder show signs of it from a very early age, whereas others develop language normally for a while but then begin to show signs of the disorder. Between 3 and 7 percent of children may be affected by this disorder (APA, 2000). Some children also have problems in understanding the language produced by others, as well as in expressing their own thoughts. These children are said to have a **mixed receptive-expressive language disorder.**

Children with **phonological disorder** do not use speech sounds that are appropriate for their age or dialect. They may substitute one sound for another (e.g., use a *t* for a *k* sound) or omit certain sounds (such as final consonants on words). Their words come out sounding like baby talk. They may say *wabbit* for *rabbit*, or *bu* for *blue*. Approximately 2 to 3 percent of 6- to 7-year-olds have moderate to severe phonological disorder. The prevalence falls to 0.5 percent by age 17 (APA, 2000).

Finally, children who suffer from **stuttering** have significant problems in speech fluency, often including frequent repetitions of sounds or syllables (such as "I-I-I-I see him"). The severity of their speech problems varies from situation to situation but is usually worse when they are under pressure to speak well, as when giving a verbal report. Stuttering often begins gradually and almost always before the age of 10 (APA, 2000). As many as 80 percent of children who stutter recover on their own by age 16. Others, however, go on to stutter as adults. Stuttering can reduce a child's self-esteem and cause him or her to limit goals and activities. The more aware the child is of stuttering, the more nervous he or she may become, which just increases the stuttering.

Causes and Treatment of Disorders of Cognitive, Motor, and Communication Skills

The causes of the disorders of cognitive, motor, and communication skills are not well understood. Genetic factors are implicated in several of the disorders, especially reading disorder and stuttering.

Learning disorders can lead to frustration and low self-esteem.

These disorders may also be linked to lead poisoning, birth defects, sensory dysfunction, or impoverished environments. The treatment of these disorders usually involves therapies designed to build and correct missing skills, such as reading therapy for dyslexia, physical therapy for developmental coordination disorder, and speech therapy for the communication disorders. The use of computerized exercises has proven helpful to children with learning and communication disorders (Merzenich et al., 1996). Studies suggest that the atypical antipsychotic medication risperidone can reduce stuttering (Maguire et al., 2000).

SUMMING UP

- Learning disorders include reading disorder (an inability to read, also known as dyslexia), mathematics disorder (an inability to learn math), and disorder of written expression (an inability to write).

- Developmental coordination disorder involves deficits in fundamental motor skills.

- Communication disorders include expressive language disorder (an inability to express

Taking Psychology Personally

College Students with Mental Disorders

We've noted throughout this chapter that many of the disorders that first arise in childhood persist at least into the young adult years. In addition, as you've read other chapters in this book, you've probably noticed that many other disorders have their first onset during the young adult years, including depression, bipolar disorder, anxiety disorders, and schizophrenia. That means that a significant proportion of young adults are suffering from significant emotional problems, or disorders of cognitive, motor, or communication skills, that they either have had since childhood or are just beginning to experience.

Several years ago, young adults with mental disorders or learning problems often did not attend college or dropped out before completing their degree, because the stresses of college so exacerbated their symptoms that they could not control their symptoms. These days, however, the treatments for many mental disorders and learning disabilities are effective enough that many more young people with mental disorders are attending college (Megivern, 2002). This group includes students with severe mental disorders, such as schizophrenia.

For many of these students, attending and completing college is a critical and positive experience, building their self-esteem and launching them into a productive and happy adult life.

For some students, however, the stress of college is very difficult to cope with. They may feel cut off from their usual sources of support in their family, their friends, and the psychologist or psychiatrist they have developed a relationship with. They may find it difficult to obtain high-quality, consistent care at their college. Many students report experiences of stigmatization and discrimination against them when professors or other students find out about their diagnoses (Megivern, 2002).

If you or someone you know is coping with the combined stress of college life and a significant mental disorder, what can you, or someone you know, do? Here are a few ideas:

■ *Develop a relationship with a mental-health professional.* Some students prefer to maintain a relationship with a therapist or physician with whom they were working before they came to college, because they feel that this person knows their history and what treatments have

oneself through language), mixed receptive-expressive language disorder (an inability to express oneself through language or to understand the language of others), phonological disorder (the use of speech sounds inappropriate for the age and dialect), and stuttering (deficits in word fluency).

■ Some of these disorders, particularly reading disorder and stuttering, may have genetic roots. Many other factors have been implicated in these disorders, but they are not well understood.

■ Treatment usually focuses on building skills in problem areas through specialized training and computerized exercises.

MENTAL RETARDATION

Mental retardation involves deficits in a wide range of skills. It is defined as significantly subaverage intellectual functioning. A child's level of intellectual functioning can be assessed by standardized tests, usually referred to as *IQ tests* (see Chapter 4

for a discussion of these tests). Low scores on an IQ test do not, by themselves, warrant a diagnosis of mental retardation. This diagnosis requires that a child also show significant problems in performing the tasks of daily life. Specifically, in order to be diagnosed with mental retardation, a child must show deficits, relative to other children that age, in at least two of the following skill areas: communication, self-care, home living, social or interpersonal skills, use of community resources (such as riding a bus), self-direction, academic skills, work, leisure, health, and personal safety (see the DSM-IV-TR criteria in Table 13.11 on page 486).

The severity of mental retardation varies greatly. Children with *mild mental retardation* can feed and dress themselves with minimal help, may or may not have average motor skills, and can learn to talk and write in simple terms. They can get around their own neighborhoods well, although they may not be able to venture beyond their neighborhoods without help. If they are put in special education classes that address their specific deficits, they can achieve a high school education and become self-sufficient. As adults, they can

Taking Psychology Personally (*continued*)

worked or not worked in the past. Other students feel the need to have a mental-health provider near their college, so that they can interact with this person face to face on a regular basis. In addition, a mental-health specialist who practices near the college may be able to intervene for a student with college administrators or professionals if the need arises. What is important is to establish a relationship with a specialist whom you trust and who is available as your symptoms wax and wane. You can consult *Taking Psychology Personally* in Chapter 5 for tips on how to find a mental-health professional in your area.

■ *Investigate support services for students with mental disorders at your college.* Services are often available for students with mental-health problems through the student disabilities office in a college. For example, if you sometimes require longer periods to take tests or complete assignments because of your disorder, your student disabilities office may be able to help you negotiate this issue with your professor.

■ *Investigate peer support groups for students with mental disorders.* Many colleges have support groups or outreach groups for students with mental disorders. These groups

may be run by students, and they may have a mental-health specialist as a consultant or an advisor. Such groups can provide peers who understand what it is like to have a mental disorder and who can help other students obtain treatment and other resources. Some groups have community education or action programs to inform students about mental disorders and increase resources for students with mental disorders.

■ *Take college at your own pace.* Just as students with chronic and severe medical disorders, such as diabetes or cystic fibrosis, sometimes need to take extra time to complete their college courses and degrees, students with serious mental disorders sometimes need some extra time. Pressuring yourself to take a full load of classes and press on at a high speed when your symptoms are quite severe can be risky. Work with your mental-health provider and your college to design a course of study that fits your needs and maximizes your chances of completing your goals.

---

shop for specific items and cook simple meals for themselves. They may be employed in unskilled or semiskilled jobs. Their scores on IQ tests tend to be between about 50 and 70.

Children with *moderate mental retardation* typically have significant delays in language development, such as using only 4 to 10 words by the age of 3. They may be physically clumsy and, thus, have some trouble dressing and feeding themselves. They typically do not achieve beyond the second-grade level in academic skills but, with special education, can acquire simple vocational skills. As adults, they may not be able to travel alone or shop or cook for themselves. Their scores on IQ tests tend to be between about 35 and 50.

Children with *severe mental retardation* have very limited vocabularies and speak in two- or three-word sentences. They may have significant deficits in motor development and may play with toys inappropriately (e.g., banging two dolls together, rather than having them interact symbolically). As adults, they can feed themselves with spoons and dress themselves if the clothing is not complicated with many buttons or zippers. They

cannot travel alone for any distance and cannot shop or cook for themselves. They may be able to learn some unskilled manual labor, but many do not. Their IQ scores tend to run between 20 and 35.

Children and adults with *profound mental retardation* are severely impaired and require full-time custodial care. They cannot dress themselves completely. They may be able to use spoons, but not knives and forks. They tend not to interact with others socially, although they may respond to simple commands. They may achieve vocabularies of 300 to 400 words as adults. Many persons with profound mental retardation suffer from frequent illnesses, and their life expectancy is shorter than normal. Their IQ scores tend to be under 20.

Experts on mental retardation divide this disorder into two types: *organic retardation* and *cultural-familial retardation* (Hodapp, Burack, & Zigler, 1998). In cases of organic retardation, there is clear evidence of a biological cause for the disorder, and the level of retardation tends to be more severe. In cases of cultural-familial retardation, there is less evidence for the role of biology and more evidence for the role of environment in the development of the

TABLE 13.11 DSM-IV-TR

Criteria for Diagnosing Mental Retardation

The diagnosis of mental retardation requires that a child show both poor intellectual functioning and significant defects in everyday skills.

A. Significantly subaverage intellectual functioning, indicated by an IQ of approximately 70 or below

B. Significant deficits in at least two of the following areas:

1. communication
2. self-care
3. home living
4. social or interpersonal skills
5. use of community resources
6. self-direction
7. academic skills
8. work
9. leisure
10. health
11. personal safety

C. Onset before age 18

Source: Reprinted with permission from the *Diagnostic and Statistical Manual of Mental Disorders,* Fourth Edition, Text Revision. Copyright © 2000 American Psychiatric Association.

disorder. The retardation tends to be less severe, and there is a good chance that, with the right intervention, the child will eventually develop normal abilities.

Biological Causes of Mental Retardation

A large number of biological factors can cause mental retardation, including chromosomal and gestational disorders, exposure to toxins prenatally and in early childhood, infections, physical trauma, metabolism and nutrition problems, and gross brain disease (see the Concept Overview in Table 13.12). We examine these factors first and then turn to the sociocultural factors implicated in mental retardation.

Genetic Contributors to Mental Retardation

Intellectual skills are at least partially inherited. The IQs of adopted children correlate much more strongly with those of their biological parents than with those of their adoptive parents. Similarly, the IQs of monozygotic twins are much more strongly correlated than are the IQs of dizygotic twins, even when the twins are reared apart (Scarr, Weinberg, & Waldman, 1993; Simonoff, Bolton, & Rutter, 1998). Families of children with mental retardation tend to have high incidences of a variety of intellectual problems, including the different levels of mental retardation and autism (Camp et al., 1998).

Two metabolic disorders that are genetically transmitted and that cause mental retardation are *phenylketonuria (PKU)* and *Tay-Sachs disease.* PKU is carried by a recessive gene and occurs in about 1 in 20,000 births. Children with PKU are unable to metabolize phenylalanine, an amino acid. As a result, phenylalanine and its derivative, phenyl pyruvic acid, build up in the body and cause permanent brain damage. Fortunately, an effective treatment is available, and children who receive this treatment from an early age can develop an average level of intelligence. Most states mandate testing for PKU in newborns. If untreated, children with PKU typically have IQs below 50.

Tay-Sachs disease also is carried by a recessive gene and occurs primarily in Jewish populations. It usually does not appear until a child is between 3 and 6 months old. At this point, a progressive degeneration of the nervous system begins, leading to mental and physical deterioration. These children usually die before the age of 6 years, and there is no effective treatment.

Several types of chromosomal disorders can lead to mental retardation. Recall from Chapter 2 that children are born with 23 pairs of chromosomes. Twenty-two of these pairs are known as *autosomes,* and the 23rd pair contains the *sex chromosomes.* One of the best-known causes of mental retardation is *Down syndrome,* which occurs when chromosome 21 is present in triplicate rather than in duplicate. (For this reason, Down syndrome is also referred to as *Trisomy 21*). Down syndrome occurs in about 1 in every 800 children born in the United States.

From childhood, almost all people with Down syndrome have mental retardation, although the level of their retardation varies from mild to profound. Children with Down syndrome have round, flat faces and almond-shaped eyes; small noses; slightly protruding lips and tongues; and short, square hands. They tend to be short in stature and somewhat obese. Many of these chil-

TABLE 13.12	Concept Overview

Factors Associated with Mental Retardation

A large number of factors contribute to mental retardation.

Predisposing Factor	Examples of Specific Disorders or Conditions
Genetic disorders	Down syndrome, Tay-Sachs disease, Fragile X syndrome, phenylketonuria, Trisomy 13 and 18
Early alterations of embryonic development	Down syndrome, prenatal exposure to toxins (e.g., maternal alcohol consumption or other substance abuse)
Later pregnancy and perinatal problems	Fetal malnutrition, placental insufficiency, prematurity, hypoxia, low birthweight, intracranial hemorrhage
Acquired childhood diseases/accidents	Infections (e.g., meningitis, encephalitis), malnutrition, head trauma (e.g., car or household accident, child abuse), poisoning (e.g., lead, mercury), environmental deprivation (psychosocial disadvantage, neglect)
Environmental influences and other mental disorders	Deprivation, child abuse, severe mental disorders
Unknown	

dren have congenital heart defects and gastrointestinal difficulties. As adults, they seem to age more rapidly than normal, and their life expectancy is shorter than average. People with Down syndrome have abnormalities in the neurons in their brains that resemble those found in Alzheimer's disease. About 25 to 40 percent of them lose their memories and the ability to care for themselves in adulthood.

Fragile X syndrome, which is the second most common cause of mental retardation in males after Down syndrome, is caused when a tip of the X chromosome breaks off. This syndrome is characterized by severe to profound mental retardation, speech defects, and severe deficits in interpersonal interaction. Males with Fragile X syndrome have large ears, long faces, and enlarged testes. Two other chromosomal abnormalities that cause mental retardation are *Trisomy 13* (chromosome 13 is present in triplicate) and *Trisomy 18* (chromosome 18 is present in triplicate). Both of these disorders lead to severe retardation and shortened life expectancy.

The risk of having a child with Down syndrome or any other chromosomal abnormalities increases the older the mother or father is when they conceive the child. This may be because, the older a parent is, the more likely his or her chro-

mosomes are to have degenerated or to have been damaged by toxins.

The Prenatal Environment: Alcohol and Other Drugs

The intellectual development of a fetus can be profoundly affected by the quality of its prenatal environment. When a pregnant woman contracts the rubella (German measles) virus, the herpes virus, or syphilis, there is a risk of physical damage to the fetus that can cause mental retardation. Chronic maternal disorders, such as high blood pressure and diabetes, can interfere with fetal nutrition and brain development and, therefore, can affect the intellectual capacities of the fetus. If these disorders are treated effectively throughout the pregnancy, the risk of damage to the fetus is low.

Most drugs that a pregnant woman takes can pass through the placenta to the fetus. It is estimated that 325,000 babies born in the United States each year are exposed prenatally to illicit drugs (Gonzalez & Campbell, 1994). Much media attention has been focused on "crack babies," infants born to women who smoked crack cocaine while pregnant. Any form of cocaine constricts the mother's blood vessels, reducing oxygen and blood flow to the fetus and possibly resulting in brain damage and retardation. Crack babies tend to be less alert than other babies and not as responsive, either emotionally or cognitively. They are more excitable and less able to regulate their sleep-wake patterns. They tend to be irritable and distractible (Napiorkowski et al., 1996; Tronick et al., 1996). Studies suggest that mothers who take cocaine during pregnancy differ in many ways from mothers who do not: They are older, more socially disadvantaged, and more likely to use tobacco, alcohol, marijuana, and other illicit drugs (Tronick et al., 1996). These other risk factors, in addition to exposure to cocaine, may severely impair the intellectual growth of their children.

Fetuses whose mothers abuse alcohol during pregnancy are at increased risk for mental retardation and a collection of physical defects known as **fetal alcohol syndrome (FAS)** (Fried & Watkinson, 1990). Children with fetal alcohol syndrome have an average IQ of only 68, along with poor judgment, distractibility, difficulty in perceiving social cues, and the inability to learn from experience. As adolescents, their academic functioning is only at the second- to fourth-grade level, and they have great trouble following directions. It is estimated that about 1 in 700 children in the United States is born with fetal alcohol syndrome (Streissguth, Randels, & Smith, 1991). Abel Dorris was one such child (adapted from Dorris, 1989; Lyman, 1997):

CASE STUDY

Abel Dorris was adopted when he was 3 years old by Michael Dorris. Abel's mother had been a heavy drinker throughout the pregnancy and after Abel was born, and she later died at age 35 of alcohol poisoning. Abel had been born almost seven weeks premature, with low birthweight. He had been abused and malnourished before being removed to a foster home. At age 3, Abel was small for his age, was not yet toilet-trained, and could speak only about 20 words. He had been diagnosed as mildly retarded. His adoptive father hoped that, in a positive environment, Abel could catch up.

At age 4, Abel was still in diapers and weighed only 27 pounds. He had trouble remembering the names of other children and his activity level was unusually high. When alone, he would rock back and forth rhythmically. At age 4, he suffered the first of several severe seizures, which caused him to lose consciousness for days. No drug treatments seemed to help.

When he entered school, Abel had trouble learning to count, to identify colors, and to tie his shoes. He had a short attention span and difficulty following simple instructions. Despite devoted teachers, when he finished elementary school, Abel still could not add, subtract, or identify his place of residence. His IQ was measured in the mid-60s.

Eventually, at age 20, Abel entered a vocational training program and moved into a supervised home. His main preoccupations were his collections of stuffed animals, paper dolls, newspaper cartoons, family photographs, and old birthday cards. At age 23, he was hit by a car and killed.

Is it safe for a woman to drink alcohol at all during pregnancy? The answer may be no. Studies of the effects of moderate maternal drinking on reproductive outcomes such as birthweight, gestational age, rate of miscarriage or stillbirth, congenital abnormalities, and social and cognitive development suggest that even low to moderate levels of drinking during pregnancy are associated with subtle alcohol-related birth defects (Jacobson & Jacobson, 2000; Kelly, Day, & Streissguth, 2000; Olson et al., 1998). For example, longitudinal studies of children exposed prenatally to alcohol show negative effects on growth at 6 years of age and on learning and memory skills at 10 years of age, even if they do not evidence the full syndrome of FAS (Cornelius et al., 2002).

The First Years of Life

Severe head traumas that damage children's brains can lead to mental retardation. *Shaken baby syndrome* is caused when a baby is shaken violently, leading to intracranial injury and retinal hemorrhage (Caffey, 1972). Babies' heads are relatively large and heavy, compared with the rest of their bodies, and their neck muscles are too weak to control their heads when they are shaken back and forth in whiplash fashion. The rapid movement of their heads when shaken can lead to their brains' being bruised from being banged against the skull wall. Bleeding can also occur in and around the brain and behind the eyes. This bleeding can lead to seizures, partial or total blindness, paralysis, mental retardation, or death. Although the violent shaking of a baby sometimes is part of a pattern of physical abuse by a parent, it often happens innocently. A frustrated parent may not know that shaking a baby can lead to permanent brain damage, as in the following case of a father of a young infant.

> **CASE STUDY**
>
> Jill's mother was very ill, so she left me with the baby for the day while she went to her mother's house to help her. About 2 o'clock, the baby started crying for some reason. I changed him, I fed him, I rocked him, I sang to him. Nothing would quiet him down. He kept crying and crying, for hours. Finally, around 6 P.M., I got so overwhelmed with his crying that I just shook him, hard, but only for a few seconds. He immediately quieted down, so I thought I had done the right thing. I put him to bed and he seemed to sleep peacefully. But then we had trouble waking him for his feeding. The next day, he was listless, just like a rag doll. Jill rushed him to the doctor. They did a series of tests and said that he might have brain damage! That was four years ago. Since then, he has been delayed in many areas of his development. The doctors say he will never be normal. I just wish I had known that you aren't supposed to shake a baby.

Young children face a number of other hazards in addition to shaken baby syndrome. Exposure to toxic substances, such as lead, arsenic, and mercury, during early childhood can lead to mental retardation by damaging specific areas of the brain. The importance of protecting children from accidental ingestion of these substances cannot be overemphasized. Children can also incur brain damage, leading to mental retardation, through accidents, including traffic accidents in cars in which they are not properly buckled.

Social Contributors to Mental Retardation

Children who have either organic or cultural-familial mental retardation are more likely to come from low socioeconomic groups (Brooks-Gunn, Klebanov, & Duncan, 1996; Camp et al., 1998). This may be because their parents also have mental retardation and have not been able to acquire well-paying jobs. The social disadvantages of being poor may also contribute to lower than average intellectual development. Poor mothers are less likely to receive good prenatal care, increasing the risk of their children being born prematurely. Chil-

dren living in lower socioeconomic areas are at increased risk for exposure to lead, because many old, run-down buildings have lead paint, which chips off and is ingested by the children. Poor children are concentrated in the inner cities in poorly funded schools, and this is especially true for poor minority children. Poor children who have lower IQs receive less favorable attention from teachers and fewer learning opportunities, especially if they are also members of minorities (Alexander, Entwisle, & Thompson, 1987). Poor children are less likely to have parents who read to them, who encourage academic success, and who are involved in their schooling. These factors may directly affect a child's intellectual development and may exacerbate the biological conditions that interfere with a child's cognitive development (Camp et al., 1998).

Treatments for Mental Retardation

Interventions for mentally retarded children must be comprehensive, intensive, and probably long-term to show benefits (Singh, Oswald, & Ellis, 1998). The Concept Overview in Table 13.13 on page 494 summarizes these treatments.

Behavioral Strategies

Typically, a child's parents or caregivers are enlisted in treatment and are taught new skills for enhancing the child's positive behaviors and reducing negative behaviors. Behavioral strategies are often used to help children and adults learn new skills, from identifying colors correctly to using vocational skills. The desired behavior may be modeled in incremental steps and rewards given to the child or adult as he or she comes closer and closer to mastering the skill. Behavioral strategies can also help to reduce self-injurious and other maladaptive behaviors. Behavioral methods do not simply focus on isolated skills but, rather, are typically integrated into a comprehensive program designed to maximize the individual's ability to integrate into the community.

Drug Therapies

Medications are used to reduce seizures, which are common among people with mental retardation; to help control aggressive or self-injurious behavior; and to help improve mood (Singh et al., 1998). Neuroleptic medications (see Chapter 11) can reduce aggressive, destructive, and antisocial behavior. The potential for neurological side effects has made these medications controversial, however. The atypical antipsychotics, such as risperidone, have been shown to reduce aggression and self-injurious behavior in adults with mental retardation without

TABLE 13.13   Concept Overview

Treatments for Mental Retardation

Comprehensive treatment programs for mental retardation involve behavioral, biological, and sociocultural interventions.

Behavioral Strategies

Caregivers are taught skills for enhancing the child's positive behaviors and reducing negative behaviors.

Desired behaviors are modeled in incremental steps; rewards are given to the child as he or she masters the skill.

Self-injurious behavior is extinguished.

Drug Therapies

Neuroleptic medications reduce aggressive and antisocial behavior.

Atypical antipsychotics reduce aggression and self-injury.

Antidepressant medications reduce depression, improve sleep, and reduce self-injury.

Social Programs

Early intervention programs are provided, including comprehensive services addressing physical, developmental, and educational needs and the training of parents.

Children are mainstreamed into regular classrooms.

Group homes provide comprehensive services to adults.

Children or adults with severe physical disabilities or behavior problems are institutionalized.

inducing serious neurological side effects (Cohen et al., 1998). Antidepressant medications can reduce depressive symptoms, improve sleep patterns, and help control self-injurious behavior in mentally retarded individuals (Singh et al., 1998).

Social Programs

Social programs have focused on early intervention—integration of the child into the mainstream of other children where possible, group homes that provide comprehensive care, and institutionalization when necessary.

Early Intervention Programs Many experts recommend beginning comprehensive interventions with children at risk for mental retardation from the first days of life. These measures include intensive one-on-one interventions with children to enhance their development of basic skills; efforts to reduce the social conditions that might interfere with the children's development, such as child abuse, malnutrition, or exposure to toxins; and adequate medical care.

One such program was the Infant Health and Development Program (Gross, Brooks-Gunn, & Spiker, 1992). This program focused on children with a birthweight of 2,500 grams or less and a gestational age of 37 completed weeks or less. The program enrolled a total of 985 infants across eight sites in the United States. Two-thirds of these infants were randomly assigned to receive high-quality pediatric care for high-risk infants. The other third received the same pediatric care plus an early educational intervention program.

The intervention had three components. First, specially trained counselors visited each child's home during the first three years of the child's life, providing support to the mothers and fostering parent-child activities that would enhance the children's development. The mothers were given training in good parenting practices and in ways of facilitating their children's cognitive development. For example, the mothers were taught ways to calm their babies (who tended to be irritable), ways to provide appropriate levels of stimulation and opportunities for self-motivated actions and explorations, and ways to reduce stress in their environments. Second, the children in the intervention program went daily to a child development center with specially trained teachers, who worked to overcome the children's intellectual and physical deficits. Third, parent support groups were started to help the parents cope with the stresses of parenting.

At 36 months of age, the children in the intervention group were significantly less likely to have IQ scores in the low range than were those in the control group, who received only medical care (Infant Health and Development Program, 1990). Among the infants with birthweights between 2,001 and 2,500 grams, the effects of the program were especially strong: At age 36 months, they had IQ scores an average of 13 points higher than the infants in the control group with similar birthweights. The infants with birthweights under 2,000 grams also benefited from the program, but to a lesser degree: Their 36-month IQ scores were an average of 6.6 points higher than the control-group infants with similar birthweights. Both the "heavier" and "lighter" birthweight groups who received the intervention condition also showed fewer behavior and emotional problems at 36 months than did the children in the control groups.

The "heavier" birthweight children continued to show benefits in cognitive development from the intervention at 60 months and 96 months of age, compared with the control groups (Brooks-Gunn, Klebanov, & Liaw, 1995). Differences between the intervention groups and the control groups in behavior and emotional problems had disappeared by this age, however. Thus, as has been the case with many early intervention programs, benefits were seen in the short term; however, without continuation of the intervention, such benefits often diminish with time.

What accounted for the positive effects of the intervention? The home environments of the children in the intervention improved significantly (Berlin et al., 1998; McCormick et al., 1998). There were more learning materials available, and their mothers more actively stimulated the children's learning. The mothers of the children in the intervention program were better at assisting their children in problem solving, remaining more responsive and persistent with their children. In turn, these children showed more enthusiasm and involvement in learning tasks. In addition, the mothers in the intervention program reported better mental health than the mothers in the control group. The mothers in the intervention group were also less likely to use harsh disciplinary strategies with their children than the mothers in the control group. All of these factors were associated with the better outcomes of the children in the intervention groups.

When interventions with children with learning difficulties involve parents, they tend to be more effective.

Adults with Down syndrome are often mainstreamed into jobs in the public sector.

Mainstreaming Controversy exists over whether children with mental retardation should be placed in special education classes or *mainstreamed*—that is, put into regular classrooms. On one hand, special education classes can concentrate on the children's needs, providing them with extra training in skills they lack. On the other hand, some critics argue that these classes stigmatize children and provide them with an education that asks less of them than they are capable of achieving. Critics also have charged that minority children often are placed inappropriately in special education classes because they score lower on culturally biased achievement tests and IQ tests.

Placing children with mental retardation in a classroom with children of average intelligence, however, can put them at certain disadvantages.

One study found that children with mental retardation were viewed negatively by the other children in their classrooms. Zigler and Hodapp (1991) argue that children with mental retardation who are mainstreamed may often not receive the special training they need. Studies of the academic progress of children with mental retardation in special education programs and in regular classrooms, however, tend to find little difference in the performance of these two groups. Many children today spend some time in special education and some time in regular classrooms over the course of the week.

Group Homes Many adults with mental retardation live in group homes, where they receive assistance in the tasks of daily living (e.g., cooking, cleaning) and training in vocational and social skills. They may work in sheltered workshops during the day, doing unskilled or semiskilled labor. Increasingly, they are being mainstreamed into the general workforce, often in service-related jobs (e.g., in fast-food restaurants or as baggers in grocery stores). Community-based programs for adults with mental retardartion have been shown to be effective in enhancing their social and vocational skills in some studies of specific programs.

Institutionalization In the past, most children with mental retardation were institutionalized for life. Institutionalization is less common these days, but children with severe physical disabilities or with significant behavior problems, such as problems controlling aggression, may still be institutionalized (Blacher, Hanneman, & Rousey, 1992). African American and Latino families are less likely to institutionalize their children with mental retardation than are European American families (Blacher et al., 1992). This may be because African American and Latino families are less likely than European American families to have the financial resources to place their children in high-quality institutions. It may also be because African American and Latino cultures place a stronger emphasis on caring for ill or disabled family members within the family.

SUMMING UP

- Mental retardation is defined as subaverage intellectual functioning, indexed by an IQ score of under 70 and deficits in adaptive behavioral functioning. There are four levels of mental retardation, ranging from mild to profound.
- A number of biological factors are implicated in mental retardation, including metabolic disorders (PKU, Tay-Sachs disease); chromosomal disorders (Down syndrome, Fragile X, Trisomy 13, and Trisomy 18); prenatal exposure to rubella, herpes, syphilis, or drugs (especially alcohol); premature delivery; and head traumas (such as those arising from being violently shaken).
- There is some evidence that intensive and comprehensive educational interventions, administered very early in life, can help decrease the level of mental retardation.
- Controversy exists over whether children with mental retardation should be put in special education classes or mainstreamed into normal classrooms.

PERVASIVE DEVELOPMENTAL DISORDERS

The **pervasive developmental disorders** are characterized by severe and lasting impairment in several areas of development, including social interactions, communication with others, everyday behaviors, interests, and activities. The pervasive developmental disorder that is probably most familiar is **autism**—a disorder in which children show deficits in social interaction, communication, activities, and interests. Many children with autism also show at least mild levels of mental retardation, although this was not true of Temple Grandin, whose life with autism is described in the chapter opener.

Autism affects many aspects of a child's development: communication skills, social interactions, cognitive skills, and motor development (see the DSM-IV-TR symptoms in Table 13.14). The most salient features of autism, however, are the impairments in social interaction (Kanner, 1943). Some autistic children seem to live in worlds of their own, uninterested in other children or in their own caregivers. Richard is a child with autism (adapted from Spitzer et al., 1994, pp. 336–337):

CASE STUDY

Richard, age 3½, appeared to be self-sufficient and aloof from others. He did not greet his mother in the mornings or his father when he returned from work, though, if left with a baby-sitter, he tended to scream much of the time. He had no interest in other children and ignored his younger brother. His babbling had no conversational intonation. At age 3 he could understand simple practical instructions. His speech consisted of echoing some words and phrases he had heard in the past, with the original speaker's accent and intonation; he could use one or two such phrases to indicate his simple needs. For example, if he said, "Do you want a drink?" he meant he was thirsty. He did not communicate by facial expression or use gesture or mime, except for pulling someone along with him and placing his or her hand on an object he wanted. He was fascinated by bright lights and spinning objects and would stare at them while laughing, flapping his hands, and dancing on tiptoe. He also

(continued)

TABLE 13.14 DSM-IV-TR

Symptoms of Autism

The symptoms of autism include a range of deficits in social interaction, communication, and activities and interests. To be diagnosed with autism, children must show these deficits before the age of 3.

Deficits in Social Interaction

Little use of nonverbal behaviors that indicate a social "connection," such as eye-to-eye gazes, facial reactions to others (smiling or frowning at others' remarks as appropriate), body postures that indicate interest in others (leaning toward a person who is speaking), or gestures (waving good-bye to a parent)

Failure to develop peer relationships as other children do

Little expression of pleasure when others are happy

Little reciprocity in social interactions

Deficits in Communication

Delay in, or total absence of, spoken language

In children who do speak, significant trouble in initiating and maintaining conversations

Unusual language, including repetition of certain phrases and pronoun reversal

Lack of make-believe play or imitation of others at a level appropriate for the child's age

Deficits in Activities and Interests

Preoccupation with certain activities or toys and compulsive adherence to routines and rituals

Stereotyped and repetitive movements, such as hand flapping and head banging

Preoccupation with parts of objects (such as the arm of a doll instead of the whole doll) and unusual uses of objects (lining up toys in rows instead of playing "pretend" with them)

Source: Reprinted with permission from the *Diagnostic and Statistical Manual of Mental Disorders*, Fourth Edition, Text Revision. Copyright © 2000 American Psychiatric Association.

---

displayed the same movements while listening to music, which he liked from infancy. He was intensely attached to a miniature car, which he held in his hand, day and night, but he never played imaginatively with this or any other toy. He could assemble jigsaw puzzles rapidly (with one hand because of the car held in the other), whether the picture side was exposed or hidden. From age 2 he had collected kitchen utensils and arranged them in repetitive patterns all over the floors of the house. These pursuits, together with occasional periods of aimless running around, constituted his whole repertoire of spontaneous activities.

The major management problem was Richard's intense resistance to any attempt to change or extend his interests. Removing his toy car, disturbing his puzzles or patterns, even retrieving, for example, an egg whisk or a spoon for its legitimate use in cooking, or trying to make him look at a picture book precipitated temper tantrums that could last an hour or more, with screaming, kicking, and the biting of himself or others. These tantrums could be cut short by restoring the status quo. Otherwise, playing his favorite music or going for a long car ride were sometimes effective.

(continued)

His parents had wondered if Richard might be deaf, but his love of music, his accurate echoing, and his sensitivity to some very soft sounds, such as those made by unwrapping chocolate in the next room, convinced them that this was not the cause of his abnormal behavior. Psychological testing gave Richard a mental age of 3 years in non-language-dependent skills (such as assembling objects) but only 18 months in language comprehension.

The Diagnosis of Autism

Autism involves three types of deficits. The first type includes deficits in *social interaction,* such as a lack of interaction with family members. Even as infants, children with autism seem not to connect with other people, including their parents, as Temple Grandin did not. They may not smile and coo in response to their caregivers or initiate play with their caregivers, the way most young infants do. They may not want to cuddle with their parents, even when they are frightened. Whereas most infants love to gaze on their caregivers as the caregivers gaze adoringly at them, autistic infants may hardly ever make eye-to-eye contact. When they are a bit older, children with autism may not be interested in playing with other children, preferring to remain in solitary play. They also do not seem to react to other people's emotions. In the chapter opener, Temple Grandin described how she had to work hard to overcome her lack of understanding of social interactions.

It was formerly thought that children with autism were preoccupied with internal thoughts and fantasies, much as people with schizophrenia might be preoccupied with hallucinations and delusions. Indeed, autism in children formerly was considered a precursor to adult schizophrenia. Studies have shown, however, that these children do not develop the classic symptoms of schizophrenia as adults (for example, they show no evidence of hallucinations and delusions) and that adults with schizophrenia do not have histories of full autistic disorder as young children (Gillberg, 1991). In addition, autism and schizophrenia do not co-occur in families at a high rate, suggesting that they have different genetic causes.

The second type of deficit in autism has to do with *communication.* Approximately 50 percent of children with autism do not develop useful speech (Gillberg, 1991). Those who do develop language may not use it as other children do. In the previous case study, Richard showed several of the communication problems of children with autism. Rather than generating his own words, he simply echoed what he had just heard, in a phenomenon called *echolalia.* He reversed pronouns, using *you* when he meant *I.* When he did try to generate his own words or sentences, he did not modulate his voice for expressiveness, sounding almost like a voice-generating machine.

The third type of deficit concerns the *activities and interests* of children with autism. Rather than engaging in symbolic play with toys, they are preoccupied with one part of a toy or an object, as Richard was preoccupied with his miniature car, or as Temple Grandin was interested only in watching sand drip through her fingers. Children with autism may engage in bizarre, repetitive behaviors with toys. For example, rather than using two dolls to play "dollies have tea," a child with autism might take the arm off one doll and simply pass it back and forth between her two hands. Routines and rituals are often extremely important to children with autism: When any aspect of their daily routine is changed—for example, if a child's mother stops at the bank on the way to school—they may fly into a rage. Some children perform stereotyped and repetitive behaviors using parts of their own bodies, such as incessantly flapping their hands or banging their heads against walls. These behaviors are sometimes referred to as *self-stimulatory behaviors,* under the assumption that these children engage in these behaviors for self-stimulation. It is not clear, however, that this is their true purpose.

Children with autism often do poorly on measures of intellectual ability, such as IQ tests, with 29 percent having mild to moderate intellectual impairments and 42 percent having severe intellectual impairments (Fombonne, 1999). The deficits of some children with autism, however, are confined to skills that require language and perspective-taking skills, and they may score in the average range on subtests that do not require language skills. Temple Grandin is one person with autism who is clearly of above-average intelligence. Much has been made in the popular press about the special talents that some children with autism have, such as the ability to play music without having been taught or to draw extremely well, or exceptional memory and mathematical calculation abilities, as was depicted in the movie *Rain Man.* These persons are sometimes referred to as *savants.* These cases are quite rare, however (Poutska & Bolte, 2004).

Dustin Hoffman played a man with autism who had some extraordinary abilities.

By definition, the symptoms of autism have their onset before the age of 3. However, children with autism are not simply delayed in their development of important skills. When they do develop language or social interaction patterns, there is a deviancy in the nature of these that is striking. It is important to note, though, that there is a wide variation in the severity and outcome of this disorder. Howlin and colleagues (2004) followed 68 individuals who had been diagnosed with autism as children and who had a performance IQ of at least 50. As adults, one-fifth of them had been able to obtain some sort of academic degree, five had gone on to college, and two had obtained postgraduate degrees. Almost a third were employed and about a quarter had close friendships. The majority, however, remained very dependent on their parents or required some form of residential care. Fifty-eight percent had overall outcomes that were rated as "poor" or "very

poor." They were unable to live alone or hold a job and had persistent problems in communication and social interactions.

By far, the best predictor of the outcome of autism is a child's IQ and amount of language development before the age of 6 (Howlin et al., 2004; Nordin & Gillberg, 1998). Children who have IQs above 50 and communicative speech before age 6 have a much better prognosis than do those with IQs below 50 and no communicative speech before age 6. In the study by Howlin and colleagues (2004), people with an IQ of 70 or above were especially likely to achieve a "good" or "very good" outcome.

The prevalence of autism has been rising in recent years, probably because of the increased attention to and recognition of the disorder (Tager-Flusberg, Joseph, & Folstein, 2001). A review of epidemiological studies estimated that the prevalence of autism is about 5 per 10,000 children, and the prevalence of all forms of pervasive developmental disorder is 14 per 10,000 children (Fombonne, 1999). Boys outnumber girls about three to one. The prevalence of autism does not appear to vary by national origin, ethnicity, socioeconomic status, or parental education.

Pervasive Developmental Disorders Other Than Autism

Other pervasive developmental disorders include *Rett's disorder, childhood disintegrative disorder,* and *Asperger's disorder* (see the Concept Overview in Table 13.15 on page 500). In both **Rett's disorder** and **childhood disintegrative disorder**, children appear to develop normally for a while and then show apparently permanent loss of basic skills in social interaction, language, and/or movement.

Asperger's disorder is characterized by deficits in social interaction and in activities and interests that are similar to those of autism (review these deficits in Table 13.14). Asperger's disorder differs from autism in that there are no significant delays or deviance in language, and, in the first three years of life, children show normal levels of curiosity about the environment and acquire most normal cognitive skills. Children with Asperger's syndrome tend to have IQ scores within the average range.

Children with Asperger's disorder tend to have difficulty in relationships with others and to engage in unusual behaviors (such as memorizing ZIP codes) to the point of being obsessed with arcane facts and issues. They can be rather formal in their speech, and the disorder has sometimes been referred to as the "little professor syndrome."

TABLE 13.15 Concept Overview

Pervasive Developmental Disorders

The pervasive developmental disorders are characterized by severe and lasting deficits in several areas of development.

Disorder	Description
Autism	Deficits in social interaction; in communication, including significant language deficits; and in activities and interests
Rett's disorder	Apparently normal development through the first 5 months of life and normal head circumference at birth but then deceleration of head growth between 5 and 48 months, loss of motor and social skills already learned, and poor development of motor skills and language
Childhood disintegrative disorder	Apparently normal development for the first 2 years, followed by significant loss of previously acquired skills between ages 2 and 10 and abnormalities of functioning in social interaction, communication, and activities
Asperger's disorder	Deficits in social interaction and in activities and interests, but not in language or basic cognitive skills

The prevalence of Asperger's disorder is not clear, and many individuals are able to function well enough in life that they go undiagnosed. Current estimates suggest that the prevalence is between 1 and 36 people per 10,000 (Volkmar et al., 2004). It is an increasingly popular diagnosis, so its apparent prevalence may increase in future years.

Controversy currently exists over whether Asperger's disorder is simply a mild variant of autism or a disorder distinct from autism (Macintosh & Dissanayake, 2004). The amount of research on Asperger's disorder is increasing, however, and it should be better understood in the years to come. For now, most of what is known about pervasive developmental disorders comes from studies of autism.

Contributors to Autism

Over the years, a wide variety of theories of autism have been proposed (see the Concept Overview in Table 13.16). The psychiatrist who first described autism, Leo Kanner (1943), thought that it was caused partly by biological factors and partly by poor parenting. He and later psychoanalytic theorists (Bettelheim, 1967) described the parents of children with autism as cold, distant, and uncaring (hence the description "refrigerator mothers"). The child's symptoms were seen as a retreat inward to a secret world of fantasies in response to unavailable parents. Research over the decades has clearly shown, though, that parenting practices play little or no role in the development of autism.

Deficits in Theory of Mind

One of the leading theories of autism is that these children have deficits in *theory of mind*, which is the ability both to understand that people—including oneself—have mental states and to use this understanding to interact and communicate with others (Baron-Cohen & Swettenham, 1997). Having a theory of mind is essential to comprehending, explaining, predicting, and manipulating the behavior of others.

Most young children show signs of developing a theory of mind by 18 months, by engaging in symbolic play, using objects to represent something other than what they really are (Lillard, 1993, 1996). By about age 3, children are able to understand the difference between their own mental states and those of others. They seem to understand what others can perceive, and they know that people may differ in what they see, know, expect, like, and want (Yirmiya et al., 1998). By age 4 to 5, children understand false beliefs (for example, that Mommy thinks they are hiding in the closet when they are really hiding in the bedroom), realize the distinction between appearance and reality, understand the concepts of desire and intention, and understand that people's actions are guided by their thoughts, beliefs, and desires (Wellman, 1994).

TABLE 13.16 Concept Overview

Contributors to Autism

The modern theories of autism view it as the result of biological factors.

Contributor	Description
Deficits in theory of mind	Deficits in the ability to understand that people have mental states and to use this understanding to interact and communicate with others
Genetic predisposition	Predisposition to a broad range of cognitive impairments
Chromosomal abnormalities	Possible aberrations on the long arm of chromosome 15 or in the number and structure of the sex chromosomes
Neurological deficits	Broad array of neurological problems, including seizure disorders
Prenatal and birth complications	Neurological deficits that could be caused by a number of complications
Neurotransmitter imbalances	Possible imbalances in serotonin and norepinephrine levels

Children with autism often fail tasks assessing theory of mind, even when they perform appropriately on other cognitive tasks for their age group (Yirmiya et al., 1998). Temple Grandin describes how the interests and perspectives of other people often strike her as odd and incomprehensible. The absence of a theory of mind may make it impossible for these children to understand and operate in the social world and to communicate appropriately with others. Their strange play behavior—specifically, the absence of symbolic play—may also represent an inability to understand anything but the concrete realities before them.

Biological Factors

Biological factors have been implicated in the development of autism. Family and twin studies strongly suggest that genetics play a role in the development of the disorder. The siblings of children with autism are 50 times more likely to have the disorder than are the siblings of children without autism (Szatmari et al., 1998; Tager-Flusberg et al., 2001). Twin studies show concordance rates for autism to be about 60 to 80 percent for monozygotic twins and 0 to 10 percent for dizygotic twins (Bailey et al., 1995). In addition, about 90 percent of the MZ twins of children with autism have a significant cognitive impairment, compared with 10 percent of DZ twins. Finally, children with autism have a higher than average rate of other genetic disorders associated with cognitive impairment, including Fragile X syndrome and PKU (Szatmari et al., 1998). These data

suggest that a general vulnerability to several types of cognitive impairment, only one of which is manifested as autism, runs in families.

Aberrations in almost all of the chromosomes have been found in studies comparing individuals with and without autism (Gillberg, 1998). The most frequently and consistently reported chromosomal abnormalities found in autism are aberrations on the long arm of chromosome 15 and in the sex chromosomes.

It seems likely that neurological factors are involved in autism. The broad array of deficits seen in autism suggests disruption in the normal development and organization of the brain (Minshew, Sweeney, & Bauman, 1997). In addition, approximately 30 percent of children with autism develop seizure disorders by adolescence, suggesting a severe neurological dysfunction (Fombonne, 1999).

Neuroimaging studies have suggested a variety of structural and functional deficits in the brains of individuals with autism. A consistent finding is a greater head and brain size in children with the disorder than in those without the disorder (Lotspeich et al., 2004). Functional MRI studies suggest that, when doing tasks tapping theory of mind, people with autism show less activity in the medial frontal cortex and medial temporal cortex than

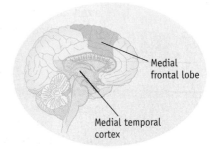

These areas of the brain have been implicated in autism.

people without autism (Frith & Frith, 2000). At a more fundamental level, people with autism do not show the same pattern of brain activation as people without autism when doing face perception and recognition tasks (Schultz et al., 2000).

Neuorological dysfunctions could be the result of genetic factors. Alternately, there is a higher than average rate of prenatal and birth complications among children with autism. These complications might have created neurological damage (Dykens & Volkmar, 1997). Finally, studies have found differences between children with and without the disorder in levels of the neurotransmitters serotonin and dopamine, although the meaning of these differences is not entirely clear (Anderson & Hoshino, 1997).

The variety of biological factors implicated in autism may indicate that there are several subtypes of autism, each with its own biological cause. With a disorder as rare as autism, it is difficult to study enough children to discover subtypes. Ideally, recent advances in the technology of biomedical research, such as the use of magnetic resonance imagery and genetic mapping, will provide more detailed data on the biology of autism.

Treatments for Autism

A number of drugs have been shown to improve some of the symptoms of autism, such as overactivity, stereotyped behaviors (e.g., head-banging, hand-flapping), sleep disturbances, and tension (Kerbeshian, Burd, & Avery, 2001; Volkmar, 2001). The selective serotonin reuptake inhibitors appear to reduce repetitive behavior and aggression, and they improve social interactions in some people

Intensive behavior therapy can help children with autism learn communication and social skills.

with autism. The antipsychotic medications are used to reduce obsessive and repetitive behavior and to improve self-control. Naltrexone, a drug that blocks receptors for opiates, has been shown to be useful in reducing hyperactivity in some children with autism. Finally, stimulants are used to improve attention. These drugs do not alter the basic autistic disorder, but they may make it easier for people with the disorder to participate in school and in interventions.

Psychosocial therapies for autism combine behavioral techniques and structured educational services (Koegel, Koegel, & Brookman, 2003; Lovaas & Smith, 2003). Operant conditioning strategies are used to reduce excessive behaviors, such as repetitive or ritualistic behaviors, tantrums, and aggression, and to alleviate deficits or delays, such as deficits in communication, and deficits in interactions with caregivers and peers. These techniques may be implemented in highly structured schools designed especially for children with autism or in regular classrooms if the child is mainstreamed. The specific deficits a child has in cognitive, motor, or communication skills are targeted, and materials that reduce possible distractions (such as reading books that do not have words printed in bright colors) are used. Parents may be taught to implement the techniques continually when the children are at home.

One pioneering study showed that 47 percent of children with autism given this intensive behavioral treatment for at least 40 hours per week for at least 2 years achieved normal intellectual and educational functioning by age 7, compared with 2 percent of children who received only institutional care (Lovaas, 1987). Several other studies have shown remarkable improvements in cognitive skills and behavioral control in children with autism when they were treated with a comprehensive behavior therapy administered both by their parents and in their school setting (Bregman & Gerdtz, 1997; Koegel et al., 2003; Lovaas & Smith, 2003; Ozonoff & Cathcart, 1998; Schreibman & Charlop-Christy, 1998).

SUMMING UP

- The pervasive developmental disorders are characterized by severe and lasting impairment in several areas of development, including social interaction, communication, everyday behaviors, interests, and activities. They include Asperger's disorder, Rett's disorder, childhood disintegrative disorder, and autism.

- Autism is characterized by significant interpersonal, communication, and behavioral deficits. Two-thirds of children with autism score in the mentally retarded range on IQ tests.

- There is wide variation in the outcome of autism, although the majority of autistic children must have continual care as adults. The best predictors of a good outcome in autism are an IQ above 50 and language development before the age of 6.

- The biological causes of autism may include a genetic predisposition to cognitive impairment, central nervous system damage, prenatal complications, and neurotransmitter imbalances.

- Drugs reduce some behaviors in autism but do not eliminate the core of the disorder.

- Behavior therapy is used to reduce inappropriate and self-injurious behaviors and to encourage prosocial behaviors in children with autism.

CHAPTER INTEGRATION

As noted earlier, the study of psychological disorders in children is often referred to as developmental psychopathology. This label explicitly recognizes that, in order to understand psychopathology in children, researchers must understand normal biological, psychological, and social development. Moreover, developmental psychopathologists are concerned with the interdependence of biological, psychological, and social development in children, recognizing that disruptions in any one of these three systems send perturbations through the other systems. The interdependence of these systems is probably even greater in children than in adults, because children are not mature enough to compartmentalize their troubles and are highly dependent on their caregivers and environment for even their most basic needs.

One example of the interplay among biology, psychology, and the social environment comes from a study of adopted children (Ge et al., 1996) (see Figure 13.3). Some of the adopted children in this study had biological parents who had antisocial personalities or histories of substance abuse. The other adopted children had biological parents with no histories of psychological problems. The children whose biological parents had histories of psychopathology were more likely than the other children to be hostile and antisocial themselves. Most researchers who do not take a biopsychosocial approach to childhood disorders would stop with these results and declare them clear evidence

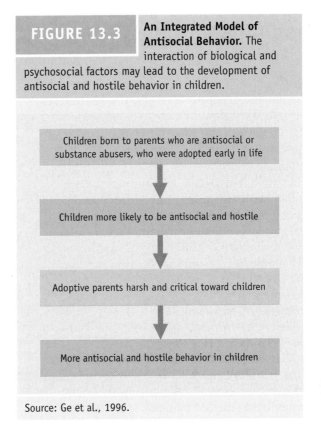

FIGURE 13.3 **An Integrated Model of Antisocial Behavior.** The interaction of biological and psychosocial factors may lead to the development of antisocial and hostile behavior in children.

Children born to parents who are antisocial or substance abusers, who were adopted early in life

↓

Children more likely to be antisocial and hostile

↓

Adoptive parents harsh and critical toward children

↓

More antisocial and hostile behavior in children

Source: Ge et al., 1996.

for the genetic inheritance of antisocial and hostile tendencies.

The researchers in this study, however, went further and looked at the parenting behaviors of the children's adoptive parents. They found that the adoptive parents of the antisocial/hostile children were more harsh and critical in their parenting than were the adoptive parents of the children who were not antisocial and hostile. It appeared that the antisocial/hostile children drew out harsh and critical behaviors from their adoptive parents. The harsh and critical parenting these children received only exacerbated the children's antisocial behaviors. Thus, the children with biological parents who were antisocial or were substance abusers appeared to have a genetic predisposition to being antisocial and hostile. Then, in effect, their genes also created an environment of parenting practices by their adoptive parents that contributed to more antisocial behavior by the children.

These children were on a developmental trajectory in which their biology and social environment were acting in synergy to lead them toward serious conduct disturbances. This kind of synergy among biology, psychology, and the social environment is the rule, rather than the exception, in the development of psychopathology, particularly in children.

Extraordinary People: Follow-Up

Temple Grandin, whom we met at the beginning of this chapter, has generally been able to overcome, or even use, the symptoms of autism to succeed in her profession, but she still finds it very difficult to understand emotions and social relationships. She explains,

> I get great satisfaction out of doing clever things with my mind, but I don't know what it is like to feel rapturous joy. I know I am missing something when other people swoon over a beautiful sunset. Intellectually I know it is beautiful, but I don't feel it. The closest thing I have to joy is the excited pleasure I feel when I have solved a design problem. When I get this feeling, I just want to kick up my heels. I'm like a calf gamboling about on a spring day.
>
> My emotions are simpler than those of most people. I don't know what complex emotion in a human relationship is. I only understand simple emotions, such as fear, anger, happiness, and sadness. I cry during sad movies, and sometimes I cry when I see something that really moves me. But complex emotional relationships are beyond my comprehension. (Grandin, 1995, p. 89)

Grandin often finds it difficult to operate in the social world. She does not "read" other people well, and she often finds herself offending people or being stared at for her social awkwardness:

> Social interactions that come naturally to most people can be daunting for people

with autism. As a child, I was like an animal that had no instincts to guide me; I just had to learn by trial and error. I was always observing, trying to work out the best way to behave, but I never fit in. I had to think about every social interaction. When other students swooned over the Beatles, I called their reaction an ISP—interesting sociological phenomenon. I was a scientist trying to figure out the ways of the natives. I wanted to participate, but did not know how. . . .
>
> All my life I have been an observer, and I have always felt like someone who watches from the outside. I could not participate in the social interactions of high school life. . . . My peers spent hours standing around talking about jewelry or some other topic with no real substance. What did they get out of this? I just did not fit in. I never fit in with the crowd, but I had a few friends who were interested in the same things, such as skiing and riding horses. Friendship always revolved around what I did rather than who I was. (p. 132)

Still, Grandin does not regret that she has autism. She says,

> If I could snap my fingers and be a nonautistic person, I would not. Autism is part of what I am. (p. 60)

Chapter Summary

- More than a third of children suffer from a significant emotional or behavior disorder by the time they are 16. (Review Table 13.1.)

- The behavior disorders include attention-deficit/hyperactivity disorder (ADHD), conduct disorder, and oppositional defiant disorder. (Review Table 13.3.)

- ADHD is characterized by inattentiveness, impulsivity, and hyperactivity. (Review Table 13.4.) Children with ADHD do poorly in school and in peer relationships and are at increased risk of

developing conduct disorder. ADHD is more common in boys than in girls.

- Biological factors that have been implicated in the development of ADHD include genetics, exposure to toxins prenatally and early in childhood, and abnormalities in neurological functioning. In addition, many children with ADHD come from families in which there are many disruptions, although it is not clear if this is a cause or just a correlate of ADHD.

- Treatments for ADHD usually involve stimulant drugs and behavior therapy designed to decrease children's impulsivity and hyperactivity and to help them control aggression.

- Conduct disorder is characterized by extreme antisocial behavior and the violation of other people's rights and of social norms. (Review Table 13.5.) Conduct disorder is more common in boys than in girls and is highly stable across childhood and adolescence. Adults who had conduct disorder as children are at increased risk for criminal behavior and a host of problems in fitting into society.

- Children with oppositional defiant disorder are easily angered and tend to violate rules and requests. (Review Table 13.6.) Unlike children with conduct disorder, they do not tend to be aggressive toward other people or animals, to steal, or to destroy property.

- Genetics and neurological problems leading to attention deficits are implicated in the development of conduct disorder. In addition, children with conduct disorder tend to have parents who are harsh and inconsistent in their discipline practices and who model aggressive, antisocial behavior. Psychologically, children with conduct disorder tend to process information in ways that are likely to lead to aggressive reactions to others' behaviors.

- The treatment for conduct disorder is most often cognitive-behavioral, focusing on changing children's ways of interpreting interpersonal situations and helping them control their angry impulses. Neuroleptic drugs and stimulant drugs are also sometimes used to treat conduct disorder.

- Children can develop all the major emotional disorders (such as mood disorders and anxiety disorders), but separation anxiety disorder, by definition, begins in childhood. Its symptoms include chronic worry about separation from parents or about parents' well-being, dreams and fantasies about separation from parents, refusal to go to school, and somatic complaints. (Review Table 13.7.) This disorder is more common in girls.

- Separation anxiety disorder runs in families, which may suggest either that genetics plays a role in its development or that parents model anxious behavior for their children. Separation anxiety often arises following major traumas, particularly if parents are anxious and overprotective of their children. (Review Table 13.8.)

- The therapy for separation anxiety follows behaviorist principles and involves relaxation training and increasing periods of separation from parents.

- The elimination disorders are enuresis, the repeated wetting of clothes or bed linens in children over the age of 5, and encopresis, repeated defecation in the clothes or on the floor in children over the age of 4. (Review Table 13.9.) Enuresis is more common and has been studied more extensively than encopresis and has been linked to psychological stress, inappropriate or lax toilet training, and genetics.

- Enuresis is often treated with the bell and pad method, which helps children learn to awaken when their bladders are full, so that they can go to the bathroom. Antidepressants are also used to treat enuresis, but their effects disappear when the children stop taking them.

- Encopresis most often begins after episodes of constipation. It is treated by medical management and regular toilet sitting.

- The disorders of cognitive, motor, and communication skills involve deficits and delays in the development of fundamental skills. (Review Table 13.10.)

- The learning disorders include reading disorder (an inability to read, also known as dyslexia), mathematics disorder (an inability to learn math), and disorder of written expression (an inability to write).

- Developmental coordination disorder involves deficits in fundamental motor skills.

- The communication disorders include expressive language disorder (an inability to express oneself through language), mixed receptive-expressive language disorder (an inability to express oneself through language or to understand the language of others), phonological disorder (the use of speech sounds inappropriate for one's age and dialect), and stuttering (deficits in word fluency).

- Some of these disorders, particularly reading disorder and stuttering, may have genetic roots. Many other factors have been implicated in these disorders, but they are not well understood.

- Treatment usually focuses on building skills in problem areas through specialized training, as well as the use of computerized exercises.

- Mental retardation is defined as subaverage intellectual functioning, indexed by an IQ score below 70 and deficits in adaptive behavioral functioning. (Review Table 13.11.) There are four levels of mental retardation, ranging from mild to profound.

- A number of biological factors are implicated in mental retardation, including metabolic disorders (PKU, Tay-Sachs disease); chromosomal disorders

(Down syndrome, Fragile X syndrome, Trisomy 13, and Trisomy 18); prenatal exposure to rubella, herpes, syphilis, or drugs (especially alcohol, as in fetal alcohol syndrome); premature delivery; and head traumas (such as those arising from being violently shaken as an infant). (Review Table 13.12.)

■ There is some evidence that intensive and comprehensive educational interventions, administered very early in an affected child's life, can help decrease the level of mental retardation.

■ Controversy exists over whether children with mental retardation should be put in special education classes or mainstreamed into normal classrooms.

■ The pervasive developmental disorders are characterized by severe and lasting impairment in several areas of development, including social interaction, communication with others, everyday behaviors, interests, and activities. They include Asperger's disorder, Rett's disorder, childhood disintegrative disorder, and autism. (Review Table 13.15.)

■ Autism is characterized by significant interpersonal, communication, and behavioral deficits. (Review Table 13.14.) Many children with autism score in the range for mental retardation on IQ tests. The outcomes of autism vary widely, although the majority of people with autism must have continual care, even as adults. The best predictors of a good outcome in autism are an IQ above 50 and language development before the age of 6.

■ The possible biological causes of autism include a genetic predisposition to cognitive impairment, chromosomal abnormalities, central nervous system damage, prenatal and birth complications, and neurotransmitter imbalances. (Review Table 13.16.)

■ Drugs reduce some behaviors in autism but do not eliminate the core of the disorder. Behavior therapy is used to reduce inappropriate and self-injurious behaviors and to encourage prosocial behaviors.

MindMap CD-ROM

The following resources on the MindMap CD-ROM that came with this text will help you to master the content of this chapter and prepare for tests:

■ Videos: ADHD; Asperger's Disorder
■ Chapter Timeline
■ Chapter Quiz

Key Terms

attention-deficit/hyperactivity disorder (ADHD) 464
conduct disorder 470
oppositional defiant disorder 471
separation anxiety disorder 478
behavioral inhibition 479
elimination disorders 483
enuresis 483
bell and pad method 483
encopresis 484
reading disorder 485
mathematics disorder 485
disorder of written expression 485

developmental coordination disorder 486
expressive language disorder 487
mixed receptive-expressive language disorder 487
phonological disorder 487
stuttering 487
mental retardation 488
fetal alcohol syndrome (FAS) 492
pervasive developmental disorders 496
autism 496
Rett's disorder 499
childhood disintegrative disorder 499
Asperger's disorder 499

Chapter 14

Untitled #4
by Deborah Schneider

Men are not prisoners of fate, but only prisoners of their own minds.

—Franklin D. Roosevelt,
Pan American Day address (1939)

Cognitive Disorders and Life-Span Issues <

Extraordinary People

Iris Murdoch: *Elegy for Iris*

When she was a young woman teaching philosophy at Oxford University, Iris Murdoch met John Bayley, a recent graduate in English. They fell in love, married two years later, and settled in Oxford, where John eventually taught and became an eminent literary critic. Iris went on to write a total of 26 novels and several textbooks on philosophy and to be considered one of the greatest writers of the twentieth century. She received honorary doctorates from many major universities and was named a Dame of the British Empire. These two intellectual giants shared a life and love that was extraordinary for its passion, its intimacy, and its fun.

John Bayley writes,

> The more I got to know Iris during the early days of our relationship, the less I understood her. Indeed, I soon began not to want to understand her. I was far too preoccupied at the time to think of such parallels, but it was like living in a fairy story—the kind with sinister overtones and not always a happy ending— in which a young man loves a beautiful maiden who returns his love but is always disappearing into some unknown and mysterious world, about which she will reveal nothing. (Bayley, 1999, pp. 45–46)

Tragedy eventually did befall the couple, although not until John and Iris had been married nearly 40 years. In 1994, Iris developed Alzheimer's disease. This brilliant novelist and philosopher was reduced to grunts, squeaks, and murmurs, asking the same questions over and over and not being able to care for her own basic needs.

John's account of his life with Iris after she developed Alzheimer's disease, published in *Elegy for Iris* (1999), is a story of the triumph of love over the great stresses of caring for a person with severe dementia. Following are some passages from this wonderful love story:

> Alzheimer's is, in fact, like an insidious fog, barely noticeable until everything around has disappeared. After that, it is no longer possible to believe that a world outside the fog exists. (p. 281)

The sense of someone's mind. Only now an awareness of it; other minds are usually taken for granted. I wonder sometimes if Iris is secretly thinking: How can I escape? What am I to do? Has nothing replaced the play of her mind when she was writing, cogitating, living in her mind? I find myself devoutly hoping not. (p. 228)

Our mode of communication seems like underwater sonar, each bouncing pulsations off the other, then listening for an echo. The baffling moments at which I cannot understand what Iris is saying, or about whom or what—moments which can produce tears and anxieties, though never, thank goodness, the raging frustration typical of many Alzheimer's sufferers—can sometimes be dispelled by embarking on a jokey parody of helplessness, and trying to make it mutual, both of us at a loss of words. (pp. 51–52)

The face of an Alzheimer's patient has been clinically described as the "lion face." An apparently odd comparison, but in fact a very apt one. The features settle into a leonine impassivity which does remind one of the king of beasts, and the way his broad expressionless mask is represented in painting and sculpture. . . .

The face of the Alzheimer's sufferer indicates only an absence: It is a mask in the most literal sense. That is why the sudden appearance of a smile is so extraordinary. The lion face becomes the face of the Virgin Mary, tranquil in sculpture and painting, with a gravity that gives such a smile its deepest meaning. (pp. 53–54)

This terror of being alone, of being cut off for even a few seconds from the familiar object, is a feature of Alzheimer's. If Iris could climb inside my skin now, or enter me as if I had a pouch like a kangaroo, she would do so. She has no awareness of what I am doing, only an awareness of what I am. The worlds and gestures of love still come naturally, but they cannot be accompanied by that wordless communication which depends on the ability to use words. (p. 127)

I make a savage comment today about the grimness of our outlook. Iris looks relieved and intelligent. She says, "But I love you." (p. 233)

"When are we going?"

"I'll tell you when we go."

Iris always responds to a jokey tone. But it is sometimes hard to maintain. Violent irritation possesses me and I shout out before I can stop myself, "Don't keep asking me when we are going!" . . .

Her face just crumples into tears. I hasten to comfort her, and she always responds to comfort. We kiss and embrace now much more than we used to. (p. 235)

[A lady] told me in her own deliberately jolly way that living with an Alzheimer's victim was like being chained to a corpse [and] went on to an even greater access of desperate facetiousness, saying, "And, as you and I know, it's a corpse that complains all the time."

I don't know it. In spite of her anxious and perpetual queries, Iris seems not to know how to complain. She never has. Alzheimer's, which can accentuate personality traits to the point of demonic parody, has only been able to exaggerate a natural goodness in her.

On a good day, her need for a loving presence, mutual pattings and murmurs, has something angelic about it; she seems herself in the presence found in an ikon. It is more important for her still on days of silent tears, a grief seemingly unaware of that mysterious world of creation she has lost, and yet aware that something is missing. (pp. 76–77)

Our modern culture tends to equate aging with disease and decline. Stories such as that of Iris Murdoch paint a picture of deterioration and emotional turmoil, which many young people think are inevitable in old age. Some diseases are more likely to occur late in life, and normal aging involves some decline in cognitive and physical abilities. Most older people, however, are physically and mentally healthy, living happy and productive lives. Indeed, the rate of most psychological disorders is lower among older people than among younger people (Whitbourne, 2000).

However, between 10 and 20 percent of people over the age of 65 have psychological problems severe enough to qualify for a diagnosis and to warrant treatment (Gatz, Kasl-Godley, & Karel, 1996). The rate of psychological problems is even higher among the "old-old," those over 85 years of age. The subfield of psychology concerned with psychological disorders in late life is known as *geropsychology.* Just as developmental psychopathologists try to understand children's psychological problems in the context of normal development during childhood and adolescence, geropsychologists try to understand psychological problems in older people in the context of the many biological, psychological, and social changes people undergo in later life.

All of the disorders we have discussed so far in this book can occur among older people. Near the end of this chapter, we will discuss the prevalence, characteristics, and treatment of depression, anxiety, and substance use disorders in older people. First, however, we focus on disorders that most often arise for the first time in old age—the **cognitive disorders**—dementia, delirium, and amnesia. These disorders are characterized by impairments in cognition caused by a medical condition

Most older people are physically and mentally healthy, leading productive lives.

(such as Alzheimer's disease, which Iris Murdoch suffered) or by substance intoxication or withdrawal. The impairments in cognition include memory deficits, language disturbances, perceptual disturbances, impairment in the capacity to plan and organize, and the failure to recognize or identify objects. These disorders were formerly called *organic brain disorders*. This label was discontinued in the DSM-IV-TR, however, because it implies that other disorders are *not* caused by biological factors, when it is clear that many disorders recognized by the DSM-IV-TR have biological causes.

The cognitive impairments seen in dementia, delirium, and amnesia can also occur in other psychological disorders. For example, people with schizophrenia have language impairments and perceptual disturbances. People with depression may have problems with concentration and memory. Dementia, delirium, and amnesia are diagnosed when cognitive impairments appear to be the result of nonpsychiatric medical diseases, sub-

stance intoxication, or substance withdrawal, but not when the cognitive impairments appear only to be symptoms of other psychiatric disorders, such as schizophrenia or depression.

DEMENTIA

CASE STUDY

Aside from sustaining a head injury of uncertain significance while a young man in the service, Mr. Abbot B. Carrington had no medical or psychiatric problems until the age of 56. At that time, employed as an officer of a bank, he began to be forgetful. For example, he would forget to bring his briefcase to work or he would misplace his eyeglasses. His efficiency at work declined. He failed to follow through with assignments. Reports that he prepared were incomplete. Although still friendly and sociable, Mr. Carrington began to lose interest in many of his usual activities. He ignored his coin collection. He no longer thoroughly perused *The Wall Street Journal* each day. When he discussed economics, it was without his previous grasp of the subject. After about a year of these difficulties, he was gradually eased out of his responsible position at the bank and eventually retired permanently. At home, he tended to withdraw into himself. He would arise early each morning and go for a long walk, occasionally losing his way if he reached an unfamiliar neighborhood. He needed to be reminded constantly of the time of day, of upcoming events, and of his son's progress in college. He tried to use electric appliances without first plugging them into the socket. He shaved with the wrong side of the razor. Mostly, he remained a quiet, pleasant, and tractable person, but sometimes, particularly at night, he became exceptionally confused, and at these times he might be somewhat irritable, loud, and difficult to control.

Approximately 2 years following the onset of these symptoms, he was seen by a neurologist, who conducted a detailed examination of his mental status. The examiner noted that Mr. Carrington was neatly dressed, polite, and cooperative. He sat passively in the office as his

(continued)

wife described his problems to the doctor. He himself offered very little information. In fact, at one point, apparently bored by the proceedings, he unceremoniously got up from his chair and left the room to wander in the corridor. He did not know the correct date or the name and location of the hospital in which he was being examined. Mr. Carrington was then told the date and place, but 10 minutes later he had forgotten this information. Although a presidential election campaign was then in progress, he did not know the names of the candidates. Despite his background in banking and economics, he could not give any relevant information concerning inflation, unemployment, or the prime lending rate. When questioned about the events of his own life, Mr. Carrington was also frequently in error. He confused recent and remote events. For example, he thought his father had recently died, but in fact this had occurred many years earlier. He could not provide a good description of his occupation.

Mr. Carrington's speech was fluent and well articulated, but vague and imprecise. He used long, roundabout, cliché-filled phrases to express rather simple ideas. Sometimes he would use the wrong word, as when he substituted *prescribe* for *subscribe*. Despite his past facility with figures, he was unable to do simple calculations. With a pencil and paper, he could not copy two-dimensional figures or a cube. When instructed to draw a house, he drew a succession of attached squares. Asked to give a single word that would define the similarity between an apple and an orange, he replied, "Round." He interpreted the proverb "People who live in glass houses shouldn't throw stones" to mean that "People don't want their windows broken." He seemed to have little insight into his problem. He appeared apathetic rather than anxious or depressed. (Adapted from Spitzer et al., 1981, pp. 243–244)

Mr. Carrington was slowly losing his ability to remember the most fundamental facts of his life, to express himself through language, and to carry out the basic activities of everyday life. This is the picture of **dementia**, the most common cognitive disorder.

Dementia most commonly occurs in later life. The estimated prevalence of the most common type of dementia—that due to Alzheimer's disease—is 5 to 10 percent in people over 65 years of age (Aguero-Torres, Fratiglioni, & Winblad, 1998; Epple, 2002). The prevalence of most types of dementia increases with age, with an estimated prevalence of 20 to 50 percent in people over 85 years of age.

News coverage on dementia has increased substantially in recent years, and at times it seems that there is an epidemic of this disorder. Three factors have probably contributed to the increased public attention to dementia. First, there have been substantial advances in the understanding of some types of dementia in the past decade, which have made the news. Second, in previous generations, people died of heart disease, cancer, and infectious diseases at younger ages and, therefore, did not reach the age at which dementia often has its onset. These days, however, people are living long enough for dementia to develop and affect their functioning. Third, as the baby-boom generation ages, the number of people who reach the age at which dementia typically emerges is increasing. Indeed, the number of people with dementia is expected to double in the next 50 years, due to the aging of the general population (Max, 1993). The cost to society in health care and to individuals in time spent caring for family members with dementia is likely to be staggering.

Symptoms of Dementia

There are five types of cognitive deficits in dementia (see the DSM-IV-TR symptoms in Table 14.1 on page 514). The most prominent is a *memory deficit*, which is required for the diagnosis of dementia. In the early stages of dementia, the memory lapses may be similar to those that we all experience from time to time—forgetting the name of someone we know casually, our own phone number, or what we went into the next room to get. Most of us eventually remember what we temporarily forget, either spontaneously or by tricks that jog our memories. The difference with dementia is that memory does not return spontaneously and may not respond to reminders or other memory cues.

People in the early stages of dementia may repeat questions because they do not remember asking them moments ago, or they do not remember getting answers. They frequently misplace items, such as keys or wallets. They may try to compensate for the memory loss. For example, they may

TABLE 14.1   DSM-IV-TR

Major Symptoms of Dementia

Dementia is characterized by the permanent loss of basic cognitive functions.

Memory impairment, including impaired ability to learn new information or to recall previously learned information

Aphasia (language disturbance)

Apraxia (inability to carry out motor activities despite intact motor function)

Agnosia (failure to recognize or identify objects despite intact sensory functioning)

Disturbance in executive functioning (such as planning, organizing, sequencing, and abstracting information)

Source: Reprinted with permission from the *Diagnostic and Statistical Manual of Mental Disorders,* Fourth Edition, Text Revision. Copyright © 2000 American Psychiatric Association.

carefully write down their appointments or things they need to do. Eventually, however, they forget to look at their calendars or lists. As the memory problems become more apparent, they may become angry when asked questions or make up answers in an attempt to hide memory loss. Later, as dementia progresses, they may become lost in familiar surroundings and be unable to find their way unaccompanied.

Eventually, long-term memory also becomes impaired. People with dementia forget the order of major events in their lives, such as graduation from college, marriage, and the birth of their children. After a time, they unable to recall the events at all and may not even know their own names.

The second type of cognitive impairment is a *deterioration of language*, known as **aphasia.** People with dementia have tremendous difficulty producing the names of objects or people and may often use terms such as *thing* or vague references to *them* to hide their inability to produce names. If asked to identify a cup, for example, they may say that it is a *thing for drinking* but be unable to name it as a cup. They may be unable to understand what another person is saying and to follow simple requests, such as "Turn on the lights and shut the door." In advanced stages of dementia, people may exhibit **echolalia**—the repetition of what they hear—or **palialia**—the repetition of sounds or words.

The third cognitive deficit is **apraxia,** impairment in the ability to execute common actions, such as waving good-bye or putting on a shirt. This deficit is not caused by problems in motor functioning (such as moving the arm), in sensory functioning, or in the comprehension of what action is required. People with dementia simply are unable to carry out actions that are requested of them or that they wish to carry out.

The fourth cognitive deficit is **agnosia,** the failure to recognize objects or people. People with dementia may not be able to identify common objects, such as chairs or tables. At first, they fail to recognize casual friends or distant family members. With time, they may not recognize their spouses or children or even their own reflections in a mirror.

The fifth cognitive deficit is a loss of **executive functions.** Executive functions are the functions of the brain that involve the ability to plan, initiate, monitor, and stop complex behaviors. Cooking Thanksgiving dinner requires executive functioning. Each menu item (e.g., the turkey, the stuffing, the pumpkin pie) requires different ingredients and preparation. The cooking of various menu items must be coordinated, so that all the items are ready at the same time. People in the early stages of dementia may attempt to cook Thanksgiving dinner but forget important components (such as the turkey) or fail to coordinate the dinner, burning certain items while undercooking others. People in later stages of dementia are unable even to plan or initiate a complex task such as this.

Deficits in executive functions also involve problems in the kind of abstract thinking required to evaluate new situations and respond appropriately to these situations. For example, in the previous case study, when Mr. Carrington was presented with the proverb "People who live in glass houses shouldn't throw stones," he was unable to interpret the abstract meaning of the proverb. Instead, he interpreted it concretely to mean "People don't want their windows broken."

In addition to having these cognitive deficits, people with dementia often show changes in emotional and personality functioning. Shoplifting and exhibitionism are common occurrences caused by declines in judgment and the ability to control impulses. People with dementia may become depressed when they recognize their cognitive deterioration. Often, however, they do not recognize or admit to their cognitive deficits. This can lead them to take unrealistic or dangerous actions, such as driving a car when they are too impaired to do so safely. People with dementia may become paranoid and angry with family members and friends, whom they see as thwarting their desires and freedoms. They may accuse others of stealing the belongings they have misplaced. They may believe that others are conspiring against them—the only conclusion left for them when they simply do not remember conversations in which they agreed to some action, such as starting a new medication or moving into a treatment facility for people with dementia. Violent outbursts are not unusual.

Types of Dementia

Dementia has several causes (see Figure 14.1). The most common is Alzheimer's disease, and great strides are being made in the understanding of Alzheimer's dementia. Dementia can also be caused by vascular disease (a blockage of blood to the brain, commonly referred to as a stroke); by head injury; by progressive diseases, such as Parkinson's disease and HIV disease; and by chronic drug abuse (see the Concept Overview in Table 14.2).

Dementia of the Alzheimer's Type

In 1995, the family of former President Ronald Reagan announced that he had been diagnosed with Alzheimer's disease. Although the family decided to maintain their privacy concerning the specific manifestations of the disease, their announcement of Reagan's diagnosis helped bring attention to this disease, which affects nearly 4 million Americans (Max, 1993).

Dementia due to **Alzheimer's disease** is the most common type of dementia and accounts for over 50 percent of all dementias (Torti et al., 2004). Alzheimer's dementias typically begin with mild memory loss, but as the disease progresses, the memory loss and disorientation quickly become profound, as did Iris Murdoch's. About two-thirds of Alzheimer's patients show psychiatric symptoms, including agitation, irritability, apathy, and dysphoria. John Bayley writes in *Elegy for Iris* that these emotional symptoms were as difficult as the cognitive symptoms for him to deal with. As the disease worsens, people may become violent and experience hallucinations and delusions. The disease usually begins after the age

Former President Ronald Reagan, who died in 2004 at the age of 93, was diagnosed with Alzheimer's disease.

FIGURE 14.1	**Leading Causes of Dementia.** Alzheimer's disease causes over half of all cases of dementia.

"Other causes" of dementia are chronic alcoholism, nutritional deficiencies, and metabolic imbalances.

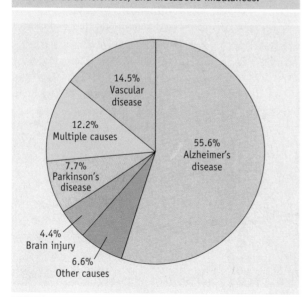

14.5% Vascular disease

12.2% Multiple causes

7.7% Parkinson's disease

4.4% Brain injury

6.6% Other causes

55.6% Alzheimer's disease

Source: Max, 1993.

TABLE 14.2	Concept Overview

Types of Dementia

Dementia can be caused by a number of progressive diseases, as well as by repeated head injury.

Alzheimer's type

Vascular dementia

Dementia due to head injury

Dementia associated with other medical conditions

  Parkinson's disease

  HIV disease

  Huntington's disease

  Pick's disease

  Creutzfeldt-Jakob disease

  Chronic heavy use of alcohol, inhalants, and sedative drugs

of 65, but there is an early-onset type of Alzheimer's disease that tends to progress more quickly than the late-onset type. On average, people with this disease die within 8 to 10 years of its diagnosis, usually as a result of physical decline or independent diseases common in old age, such as heart disease. Iris Murdoch was diagnosed with Alzheimer's disease in 1994 and died in 1999.

Brain Abnormalities in Alzheimer's Disease

This type of dementia was first described in 1906 by Alois Alzheimer. He observed severe memory loss and disorientation in a 51-year-old female patient. Following her death at age 55, an autopsy revealed that filaments within nerve cells in her brain were twisted and tangled. These **neurofibrillary tangles** are common in the brains of Alzheimer's patients but rare in people without cognitive disorders (Beatty, 1995). They appear to interfere with the basic functioning of neurons in many areas of the brain. Another brain abnormality seen in Alzheimer's disease is **plaques.** These plaques are deposits of a class of protein, called **amyloid,** that accumulate in the spaces between the cells of the cerebral cortex, hippocampus, amyg-

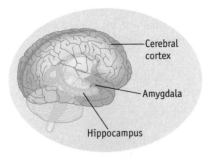

Plaques that accumulate between cells in these and other areas of the brain are seen in Alzheimer's disease.

dala, and other areas of the brain structures critical to memory and cognitive functioning (Atiya et al., 2003; Du et al., 2001).

There is extensive cell death in the cortex of Alzheimer's patients, resulting in the shrinkage, or atrophy, of the cortex and enlargement of the ventricles of the brain (see Figure 14.2). The remaining cells lose much of their dendrites—the branches that link one cell to other cells (see Figure 14.3). The results of all these brain abnormalities are profound memory loss and an inability to coordinate one's activities.

Causes of Alzheimer's Disease What causes the brain deterioration of Alzheimer's disease? This is an area of tremendous research activity, and new answers to this question emerge each day. Alzheimer's disease has been attributed to viral infections, immune system dysfunction, exposure to toxic levels of aluminum, deficiencies of the vitamin folate, and head traumas.

Much of the current research, however, has focused on genes that might transmit a vulnerability to this disorder and on the amyloid proteins that form the plaques found in the brains of almost all Alzheimer's patients. Family history studies suggest that 25 to 50 percent of relatives of patients with Alzheimer's disease eventually develop the disease, compared with only about 10 percent of family members of elderly people without Alzheimer's disease (Plassman & Breitner, 1996).

FIGURE 14.2 **Cortical Atrophy in Alzheimer's Disease.** Alzheimer's patients show widespread atrophy, or shrinkage, in the cortex and enlargement in the ventricular areas of the brain (butterfly-shaped spaces in the center).

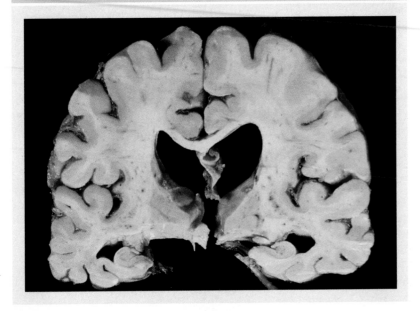

FIGURE 14.3 **Loss of Neuronal Dendrites in Alzheimer's Disease.**

(a) Dendrites in the brain of a healthy person. *(b)* Shrunken and deteriorated dendrites in the brain of an Alzheimer's patient.

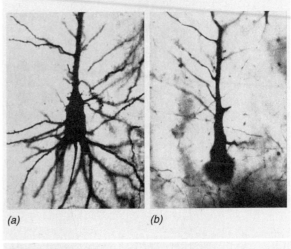

(a) (b)

Source: Beatty, 1995.

Several genes have been linked to Alzheimer's disease. A defective gene on chromosome 19 is associated with an increased risk for the late-onset form of Alzheimer's disease, which is the most common form. This gene appears to be responsible for a rare protein, known as ApoE4. ApoE4 is one of a group of proteins that transport cholesterol through the blood. ApoE4 binds to the amyloid protein and may play a role in the regulation of amyloid protein. The ApoE4 gene has been estimated to account for 45 to 60 percent of all cases of Alzheimer's disease (Atiya et al., 2003; Petegnief et al., 2001). One study found that people with two copies of the ApoE4 gene (one on both of their chromosome 19s) were eight times more likely to have Alzheimer's disease than were people with no copies of the ApoE4 gene on either of their chromosome 19s (Corder, Saunders, & Strittmatter, 1993).

One of the most fascinating studies to show a link between ApoE4 and Alzheimer's disease is the Nun Study, a longitudinal study of several hundred elderly nuns in the School Sisters of Notre Dame. Research David Snowdon and colleagues confirmed that the nuns without the ApoE4 gene were much more likely to maintain high levels of intellectual functioning into advanced age (Riley et al., 2000). Even more remarkable was evidence that the nuns who entered old age with greater intellectual strengths were less likely to develop severe dementia, even when their brains showed evidence of significant neurofibrillary tangles and senile plaques (Snowdon, 1997). For example, the level of linguistic skills that the nuns showed in journal writings when they were in their twenties significantly predicted their risk of developing dementia in later life (Snowdon et al., 1996). The best example was Sister Mary, who had high cognitive test scores right up until her death at 101 years of age. An evaluation of Sister Mary's brain revealed that Alzheimer's disease had spread widely through her brain, but her cognitive test scores had slipped only from the "superior" range to the "very good" range as she aged. Other results from this study showed that tiny strokes may lead a mildly deteriorating brain to develop full-fledged dementia (Snowdon et al., 1997).

Other genes are implicated in the development of less common forms of Alzheimer's disease, which begin in middle age and are more strongly familial. The first of these genes is on chromosome 21 (Bird et al., 1998). The first clue that a defective gene on chromosome 21 may be linked with Alzheimer's disease came from the fact that people with Down syndrome are more

The Sisters of Notre Dame have participated in a fascinating study of the effects of early experiences on mental and physical health in old age.

likely than people in the general population to develop Alzheimer's disease in later life. Down syndrome is caused by an extra chromosome 21. Researchers hypothesized that the gene responsible for some forms of Alzheimer's disease may be on chromosome 21 and that people with Down syndrome are more prone to Alzheimer's disease because they have an extra chromosome 21 (Mayeux, 1996).

This hypothesis has been supported by linkage studies of families with high rates of Alzheimer's disease. These studies have found links between the presence of the disease and the presence of an abnormal gene on chromosome 21 (see Goate et al., 1991; St. George-Hyslop et al., 1987). In turn, this abnormal gene on chromosome 21 is near the gene responsible for producing a precursor of the amyloid protein known as the amyloid precursor protein gene, or APP gene. It may be that defects along this section of chromosome 21 cause an abnormal production and buildup of amyloid proteins in the brain, resulting in Alzheimer's disease.

A defective gene on chromosome 14 has been linked to early-onset Alzheimer's disease (Sherrington, Rogaev, & Liang, 1995). This discovery is especially exciting because this defective chromosome 14 gene may be implicated in almost 80 percent of early-onset Alzheimer's disease. This gene appears to be responsible for a protein, on the membranes of cells, known as S182. The link between S182 and the amyloid protein or other processes responsible for Alzheimer's disease is not yet known. Finally, another gene, E5-1, on chromosome 1, has been linked to Alzheimer's disease (Lendon, Ashall, & Goate, 1997).

People with Alzheimer's disease also show deficits in a number of neurotransmitters, including acetylcholine, norepinephrine, serotonin, somatostatin (a corticotropin-releasing factor), and peptide Y (Small, 1998). The deficits in acetylcholine are particularly noteworthy, because this neurotransmitter is thought to be critical in memory function. The degree of cognitive decline seen in patients with Alzheimer's disease is significantly correlated with the degree of deficits in acetylcholine (Knopman, 2003). In turn, drugs that enhance acetylcholine levels can slow the rate of cognitive decline in some Alzheimer's sufferers.

It is likely that much more about the causes of Alzheimer's disease will be learned in the next few years, because the technologies to study the genetic and neurological processes of the disease are advancing rapidly and because many researchers are investigating this disorder. Four and a half million people in the United States and 18 million people worldwide have been diagnosed with Alzheimer's disease, and this number is expected to increase by at least 300 percent by the year 2050 (Tariot, 2003). We can hope that, by then, this disorder will be understood well enough to be treated effectively.

Vascular Dementia

The second most common type of dementia, after Alzheimer's dementia, is **vascular dementia** (formerly called *multi-infarct dementia*). To be diagnosed with vascular dementia, a person must have symptoms or laboratory evidence of **cerebrovascular disease.** Cerebrovascular disease occurs when the blood supply to areas of the brain is blocked, causing tissue damage in the brain. Neuroimaging techniques, such as PET and MRI, can detect areas of tissue damage and reduced blood flow in the brain, confirming cerebrovascular disease (see Figure 14.4).

Sudden damage to an area of the brain due to the blockage of blood flow or to hemorrhaging (bleeding) is called a **stroke.** Vascular dementia

| **FIGURE 14.4** | **MRI Showing Tissue Damage Following a Stroke (Dark Blue Areas)** |

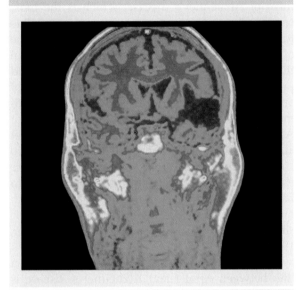

Source: Beatty, 1995.

can occur after one large stroke or an accumulation of small strokes. Cerebrovascular disease can be caused by high blood pressure and the accumulation of fatty deposits in the arteries, which block blood flow to the brain. It can also be a complication of head injuries and diseases that inflame the brain. The specific cognitive deficits and emotional changes a person experiences depend on the extent and location of the brain tissue damage (Desmond & Tatemichi, 1998).

About 25 percent of stroke patients develop cognitive deficits severe enough to qualify for a diagnosis of dementia (Stephens et al., 2004). A greater risk of developing dementia is seen in stroke patients who are older (over 80 years of age), who have less education, who have a history of strokes, and who have diabetes. The finding that greater education protects against the development of vascular dementia corresponds the with findings of studies of Alzheimer's disease.

Even stroke patients who do not immediately develop dementia are at increased risk of developing dementia, compared with people the same age who do not suffer a stroke. Follow-ups of stroke victims who remained free of dementia in the 3 months after their stroke found that about one-third of them developed dementia within the next 52 months, compared with 10 percent of a control group (Desmond & Tatemichi, 1998). The patients most likely to develop dementia eventually tended to have additional strokes over this time, some of which were obvious and others of which were "silent" and only detected later. In addition, patients who had medical events or conditions that caused widespread oxygen or blood deficiency, such as seizures, cardiac arrhythmias, congestive heart failure, and pneumonia, were more likely to develop dementia.

Dementia Due to Head Injury

A 41-year-old factory worker named Leland was returning home along a rural road one night after work. A drunk driver ran a stop sign and collided at a high rate of speed with the driver's side of Leland's car. Leland was not wearing a seat belt. The collision sent Leland through the windshield and onto the pavement. He lived but sustained substantial head injuries, as well as many broken bones and cuts. Leland was unconscious for over two weeks and then spent another two months in the hospital, recovering from his injuries.

When he returned home to his family, Leland was not himself. Before the accident, he was a quiet man who doted on his family and frequently displayed a wry sense of humor. After the accident, Leland was sullen and chronically irritable. He screamed at his wife or children for the slightest annoyance. He even slapped his wife once when she confronted him about his verbal abuse of the children.

Leland did not fare much better at work. He found he now had great trouble concentrating on his job, and he could not follow his boss's instructions. When his boss approached Leland about his inability to perform his job, Leland could not express much about the trouble he was having. He became angry at his boss and accused him of wanting to fire him. Leland had always been much liked by his coworkers, and they welcomed him back after the accident with sincere joy, but soon he began to lash out at them, as he was at his wife and children. He accused a close friend of stealing from him.

These symptoms continued acutely for about 3 months. Gradually, they declined. Finally, about 18 months after the accident, Leland's emotional and personality functioning appear to be back to normal. His cognitive functioning has also improved greatly, but he still finds it more difficult to pay attention and to complete tasks than he did before the accident.

Leland's symptoms were characteristic of people with traumatic brain injury (see the symptoms in Table 14.3). He showed changes in both his cognitive abilities and his usual emotional and personality functioning. Fortunately, Leland's symptoms subsided after several months. Many victims of brain injury never fully recover (Beatty, 1995).

Brain damage can be caused by penetrating injuries, such as those caused by gunshots, or closed head injuries, typically caused by blows to the head. The most common causes of closed head injuries are motor vehicle accidents, followed by falls, blows to the head during violent assault, and sports injuries. Dementia that follows a single closed head injury is more likely to dissipate with time than is dementia that follows repeated closed head injuries, such as experienced by boxers. Young men are most likely to suffer dementia due to head injury, because they take more risks associated with head injuries than do other groups.

Dementia pugilistica is a type of dementia due to repetitive head injuries (Jordan, 1998). It was first described in boxers but has been seen frequently in professional football, soccer, and ice hockey players. Dementia pugilistica is characterized by the cognitive symptoms of dementia described thus far;

People engaged in sports such as boxing are at risk for brain injuries that can lead to severe cognitive deficits.

TABLE 14.3 Symptoms of Frontal Lobe Injuries

Social and Behavioral Changes

Disorderliness, suspiciousness, argumentativeness, disruptiveness, anxiousness

Apathy, lack of concern for others

Uncharacteristic lewdness, inattention to personal appearance or hygiene

Intrusiveness, boisterousness, pervasive profanity, loud talking

Risk taking, poor impulse control, increased alcohol use

Affective Changes

Apathy, indifference, shallowness

Lability of affect, irritability, mania

Inability to control rage and violent behavior

Intellectual Changes

Reduced capacity to use language, symbols, logic

Reduced ability to use mathematics, to calculate, to process abstract information, to reason

Diminished ability to focus, to concentrate, to be oriented in time and place

Source: Beatty, 1995.

---

various personality changes, such as excessive jealousy and rage; and shaking and loss of motor functioning, such as in Parkinson's disease. In one study of exprofessional boxers, 17 percent had clinical evidence of central nervous system damage attributable to boxing (Roberts, 1969). About half of these men showed some signs of impairment in intellectual functioning, and about 30 percent showed severe cognitive impairment.

Dementia Associated with Other Medical Conditions

A variety of serious medical conditions can produce dementia. The most common ones are Parkinson's disease, HIV disease, and Huntington's disease, and these will be discussed here. Other types of dementia we won't be discussing include those caused by two rare diseases, Pick's disease and Creutzfeldt-Jakob disease; brain tumors; endocrine conditions (such as hypothyroidism); nutritional conditions (such as deficiencies of thiamine, niacin, and vitamin B-12), infectious conditions (such as syphilis), and other neurological diseases (such as multiple sclerosis). In addition, the chronic, heavy use of alcohol, inhalants, and the sedative drugs, especially in combination with nu-

tritional deficiencies, can cause brain damage and dementia. As many as 10 percent of chronic alcohol abusers may develop dementia (Winger, Hofmann, & Woods, 1992). Alcohol-related dementia usually has a slow, insidious onset. It can be slowed with nutritional supplements but is often irreversible.

Parkinson's Disease *Parkinson's disease* is a degenerative brain disorder that affects about 1 of every 100,000 people (Mayeux et al., 1992). The primary symptoms of Parkinson's disease are tremors, muscle rigidity, and the inability to initiate movement. In a longitudinal community-based study of patients with Parkinson's disease, 78 percent developed dementia over the eight years they were followed (Aarsland et al., 2003). Parkinson's disease results from the death of the brain cells that produce the neurotransmitter dopamine. The death of these cells can be caused by certain drugs or by inflammation of the brain, but the cause of Parkinson's disease is often unclear. Muhammed Ali and Michael J. Fox (see Chapter 4) are just two well-known people with Parkinson's disease.

HIV Disease The *human immunodeficiency virus (HIV)*, the virus that causes AIDS, can cause dementia, as Mariel's story illustrates.

Mariel is a 29-year-old single Puerto Rican woman. She has no children and currently lives with her mother and aunt in the Bronx. Since June 1993, she has been unemployed and supported by her family. Mariel was found to be HIV-positive eight years ago, when she was donating blood. She had contracted the virus when raped at age 17 by a family friend. The offender later died of AIDS. For two years, Mariel lived and worked as a store clerk in Puerto Rico. When she developed *Pneumocystis carinii* pneumonia, her mother insisted that she return to New York City to obtain better medical care.

In the hospital, Mariel was referred for a psychiatric consultation, because she was found wandering in a corridor distant from her room. When the psychiatrist arrived in her room, he found her lying on her bed, with half her body outside the covers, rocking back and forth while clutching a pink teddy bear, appearing to stare at the television expressionlessly. When asked a series of questions about where she was, what day it was, and so on, she answered correctly, indicating she was oriented to the time and place, but her responses were greatly delayed, and it was almost impossible to engage her in conversation. She said she wanted to leave the hospital to find a place to think. Her mother reported that Mariel had told her she wanted to die.

Over the next few days in the hospital, Mariel became increasingly withdrawn. She sat motionless for hours, not eating voluntarily, and did not recognize her mother when she visited. At times, Mariel became agitated and appeared to be responding to visual hallucinations. When asked to state where she was and her own birthdate, Mariel did not answer and either turned away or became angry and agitated.

As the pneumonia subsided, these acute psychological symptoms dissipated, but Mariel continued to be inattentive, apathetic, and withdrawn and to take a long time to answer simple questions. Suspecting depression, the psychiatrist prescribed an antidepressant medication, but it had little effect on Mariel's symptoms. After being discharged from the hospital, Mariel showed increasing trouble in expressing herself to her mother and in remembering things her mother had told her. She spent all day in her room, staring out the window, with little interest in the activities her mother suggested to her.

HIV probably enters the brain in the early stages of infection (Price, 1998). Memory and concentration become impaired. Infected persons' mental processes slow—they may have difficulty following conversations or plots in movies or may take much longer to organize their thoughts and to complete simple, familiar tasks. Their behaviors may change—they may withdraw socially, become indifferent to familiar people and responsibilities, and lose their spontaneity. They may complain of fatigue, depression, irritability, agitation, emotional instability, and reduced sex drive. Sometimes, although rarely, they experience hallucinations or delusions. Weakness in the legs or hands, clumsiness, loss of balance, and lack of coordination are common complaints. People may trip more frequently, drop things, or have difficulty writing or eating. If the dementia progresses, the deficits become more global and more severe. Speech becomes increasingly impaired, as does the understanding of language. The ability to walk is lost, and people are confined to bed, often with indifference to their surroundings and their illness.

HIV-associated dementia is diagnosed when the deficits and symptoms become severe and global, with a significant disruption of daily activities and functioning. Epidemiological studies estimate that from 20 to 50 percent of HIV-infected persons will develop dementia, although the incidence and severity of HIV-associated dementia have decreased as antiretroviral drugs have become widely used in treating people with HIV (Sperber & Shao, 2003). These drugs have had greater success in treating the opportunistic infections of HIV than in treating HIV's effects on the brain, however.

Huntington's Disease Huntington's disease is a rare genetic disorder that afflicts people early in life, usually between the ages of 25 and 55. People with this disease develop severe dementia and chorea—irregular jerks, grimaces, and twitches. Huntington's disease is transmitted by a single dominant gene on chromosome 4 (Gusella et al., 1993). If one parent has the gene, his or her children have a 50 percent chance of inheriting the gene and developing the disease. There are many neurotransmitter changes in the brains of people with Huntington's disease. It is not yet clear which of these changes is responsible for the dementia and chorea.

Treatments for Dementia

There are two classes of drugs approved to treat the cognitive symptoms of dementia. The first includes the cholinesterase inhibitors, such as donepezil (Aricept), rivastigmine (Exelon), and galantamine (Reminyl). These drugs help prevent the breakdown of the neurotransmitter acetylcholine, and randomized trials show they have a modest positive effect on the symptoms of dementia (Knopman, 2003; Trinh et al., 2003). The side effects of these drugs include nausea, diarrhea, and anorexia.

A drug called memantine (Namenda) was approved in 2003 for the treatment of moderate to severe Alzheimer's disease. It appears to work by regulating the activity of the neurotransmitter glutamate, which plays an essential role in learning and memory. Because Parkinson's disease is also associated with too little of the neurotransmitter dopamine in the brain, some Parkinson's patients are given other drugs that increase dopamine levels and, thus, provide some relief from their symptoms.

A great deal of media attention has been given to the role of antioxidants in slowing cognitive decline in Alzheimer's disease. Antioxidants include natural products, such as vitamin E, and manufactured products, such as a selective monoamine oxidase-B inhibitor known as selegiline. A few controlled trials have shown that Alzheimer's patients given antioxidants show slower rates of decline than those given placebo treatment, although they do not show improvement in cognitive functioning (Knopman, 2003; Sano et al., 1997). Ginkgo biloba, a plant extract sold without prescription, has been shown to stabilize and improve cognitive functioning in some Alzheimer's patients (see Le Bars et al., 1997). Antioxidants may work by reducing levels of monoamine oxidase-B in the brain, which normally increase with aging but increase at excessive rates among people with Alzheimer's disease—particularly in the hippocampus, which plays an important role in memory—causing cell damage (Thal, 1998).

Many of the other drugs used to treat people with dementia are meant to treat the secondary symptoms of the disorder, rather than the primary cognitive symptoms. Antidepressant and antianxiety drugs are used to help control the emotional symptoms of people with dementia. Antipsychotic drugs help control hallucinations, delusions, and agitation (Trinh et al., 2003).

Behavior therapies can be helpful in controlling patients' angry outbursts and emotional insta-

bility (Rovner et al., 1996). Often, family members are given training in behavioral techniques to help them manage patients at home. These techniques not only reduce stress and emotional distress among caregiving family members but also may result in fewer behavior problems in the family member with dementia (Teri et al., 2003). For more information about the effects of a patient's dementia on caregiving family members, see *Taking Psychology Personally: How Does Dementia Affect Caregivers?* on pages 524–525.

The Impact of Gender and Culture on Dementia

There are more elderly women than men with dementia, particularly Alzheimer's dementia (Gao et al., 1998). This simply may be because women tend to live longer than men and, thus, live long enough to develop age-related dementias. Among people with dementia, women tend to show greater decline in language skills than do men—even though, among people without dementia, women tend to score better on tests of language skills than do men (Buckwalter et al., 1993). The reason for the greater impact of dementia on language in women compared with men is unknown. Some researchers have speculated that language skills are distributed across both sides of the brain in women but are more localized in the left side of the brain in men, and this somehow makes women's language skills more vulnerable to the effects of dementia.

In general, African Americans are more frequently diagnosed with dementia than are European Americans. The types of dementias that African Americans and European Americans develop differ, however (Chun et al., 1998). African Americans are more likely than European Americans to be diagnosed with vascular dementia. The reason may be that African Americans have higher rates of hypertension and cardiovascular disease, which contribute to vascular dementia. In contrast, European Americans may be more likely than African Americans to have dementias due to Alzheimer's disease and Parkinson's disease. The genetic factors leading to these diseases may be more prevalent in European Americans than in African Americans.

The likelihood that a person with dementia will be institutionalized instead of being cared for in the family is greater for European Americans than for Asians and Latinos (Mausbach et al., 2004; Torti et al., 2004). The reason may be that Asian and Latino cultures have a more positive view of caring for sick and elderly family members than does the European American culture. There is also greater societal pressure in Asian and Latino cultures to care for ill family members in the home.

Perhaps the greatest cross-cultural issue in dementia is the impact of culture and education on the validity of the instruments used to assess cognitive impairment. One of the most common paper-and-pencil assessment tools is the *Mini-Mental State Examination* (Folstein, Folstein, & McHugh, 1975). Selected items from this questionnaire are presented in Figure 14.5. People with low levels of education tend to perform more poorly on this questionnaire than do people with more education, whether or not they have dementia (Murden et al., 1991). This performance may lead to some poorly educated elderly people being misdiagnosed as having dementia.

Indeed, studies in the United States, Europe, Israel, and China show that people with low levels of education are more likely to be diagnosed with dementia than are people with more education (Katzman, 1993; Stern et al., 1994). The relationship between lower education and dementia is not just a factor of the measures used to assess dementia, however. Neuroimaging studies of people with dementia find that those with less education show more of the brain deterioration associated with dementia than do those with more education. It may be that people with more education have a higher socioeconomic status, which in turn provides them with better nutrition and health care, which protect them against the conditions contributing to Alzheimer's disease. Education and, more generally, cognitive activity throughout one's life may actually increase brain resources in ways that forestall the development of dementia in people prone to the disorder (Snowdon et al., 1996).

SUMMING UP

- Dementia is typically a permanent deterioration in cognitive functioning, often accompanied by emotional changes.

- The five types of cognitive impairments in dementia are memory impairment, aphasia, apraxia, agnosia, and loss of executive functions.

- The most common type of dementia is due to Alzheimer's disease.

- The brains of Alzheimer's patients show neurofibrillary tangles, plaques made up of amyloid protein, and cortical atrophy.

- Recent theories of Alzheimer's disease focus on three genes that might contribute to the buildup of amyloid in the brains of Alzheimer's disease patients.

| FIGURE 14.5 | **Mini-Mental State Examination.** The Mini-Mental State Examination is one of the most commonly used tests to assess patients' cognitive functioning and orientation. |

Mini-Mental State Examination
(Add points for each correct response.)

Orientation			Score	Points
1. What is the	Year?		___	1
	Season?		___	1
	Date?		___	1
	Day?		___	1
	Month?		___	1
2. Where are we?	State?		___	1
	County?		___	1
	Town or city?		___	1
	Hospital?		___	1
	Floor?		___	1

Registration
3. Name three objects, taking one second to say each. Then ask the patient all three after you have said them. Give one point for each correct answer. Repeat the answers until patient learns all three. ___ 3

Attention and calculation
4. Serial sevens. Give one point for each correct answer. Stop after five answers. Alternate: Spell WORLD backwards. ___ 5

Recall
5. Ask for names of three objects learned in Q.3. Give one point for each correct answer. ___ 3

Language
6. Point to a pencil and a watch. Have the patient name them as you point. ___ 2
7. Have the patient repeat 'No ifs, ands, or buts.' ___ 1
8. Have the patient follow a three-stage command: 'Take a paper in your right hand. Fold the paper in half. Put the paper on the floor.' ___ 3
9. Have the patient read and obey the following: 'CLOSE YOUR EYES.' (Write it in large letters.) ___ 1
10. Have the patient write a sentence of his or her choice. (The sentence should contain a subject and an object, and should make sense. Ignore spelling errors when scoring.) ___ 1
11. Enlarge the design printed below to 1.5 cm per side, and have the patient copy it. (Give one point if all sides and angles are preserved and if the intersecting sides form a quadrangle.) ___ 1

_____ = Total 30

- Dementia can also be caused by cerebrovascular disorder, head injury, and progressive disorders, such as Parkinson's disease, HIV disease, Huntington's disease, and, more rarely, Pick's disease, Creutzfeldt-Jakob disease, and a number of other medical conditions. Finally, chronic drug abuse and the

Taking Psychology Personally

How Does Dementia Affect Caregivers?

Dementia exacts a heavy toll on the family members of patients, as well as on the patients themselves, as is depicted in the book *Elegy for Iris*. From the first onset of symptoms, patients with dementia live an average of 8 years, and as many as 20 years, with the lifetime cost for treatment averaging $175,000 per patient in the United States (Tariot, 2003). In the United States, the societal cost of Alzheimer's disease alone is estimated at $100 billion per year in medical care, loss of productivity, and personal caregiving expenses (DeKosky & Orgogozo, 2001).

If a person with dementia is cared for in the home, the caregivers must deal with a wide range of troubling symptoms. The patient's confusion and memory loss may cause him or her to lose important items, to wander away from home into dangerous situations, or to engage in dangerous behaviors, such as putting clothes in the oven and turning it on. The emotional and behavioral symptoms of dementia—paranoia, agitation, anxiety, and depression—can be very stressful for family members to deal with, as John Bayley describes in *Elegy for Iris*.

The primary caregiver to a person with dementia is most often a woman—the daughter, daughter-in-law, or wife of the patient (Dunkin & Anderson-Hanley, 1998; Torti et al., 2004). Often, this primary caregiver is also raising her own children and trying to hold down a job. This is the *sandwich generation* of women, caught in the middle of caring for young children and for elderly parents or parents-in-law. These primary caregivers show higher rates of depression, anxiety, and physical illness than do noncaregivers, particularly when they do not have the financial resources to pay for assistance (Dunkin & Anderson-Hanley, 1998; Torti et al., 2004). Some caregivers become so frustrated with their family members with dementia that they resort to violence and abuse (adapted from Gallagher-Thompson, Lovett, & Rose, 1991, pp. 68–69):

> Mr. E was a 60-year-old caregiver of a rather frail younger brother (Robert) who had been diagnosed with dementia. Robert had been an alcoholic earlier in life and was the type of person who settled disagreements with verbal and/or physical abuse. Mr. E and his brother had begun sharing a household following the

CASE STUDY

deaths of both their wives about 5 years before. Shortly thereafter, Robert was diagnosed with Alzheimer's disease and eventually developed substantial cognitive and physical deficits. Mr. E felt guilty about doing anything other than keeping his brother in the home with him, although Robert's disabilities were very distressing to him and Robert's increasing hostility and angry verbal outbursts were hard to handle. At the same time, Mr. E was developing a romantic interest and resented not being able to follow through with that as he pleased; instead, he felt quite inhibited by his brother's presence in his home. The situation gradually worsened to the point where the two brothers were given to frequent angry outbursts, leading, at times, to Mr. E hitting Robert. Afterwards, he would feel extremely guilty about this and concerned that he might lose control during one of these episodes and actually hurt his brother.

A number of communities provide support groups for caregivers and therapy focused on developing problem-solving skills for managing the person with dementia at home. For example, the man in the case study, Mr. E, joined an anger-management class and learned new ways of interpreting and reacting to his brother's behaviors. He read about Alzheimer's disease and learned to challenge his beliefs that his brother was intentionally acting in ways to annoy him. He learned to walk away from his brother's angry outbursts. He found other resources in the community to help him care for his brother, so that he could pursue his own interests more fully. These programs have proven effective in reducing caregivers' emotional problems and feelings of burden in some studies, although not in all studies (Miller, Newcomer, & Fox, 1999).

Medications can help control some of the patients' behaviors. Antipsychotic medications may decrease agitation and psychosis. The cholinesterase inhibitors help reduce the symptoms of dementia. The changes brought about by these medications appear to reduce the burden on caregivers as well (Torti et al., 2004).

Taking Psychology Personally (*continued*)

If you become a caregiver to someone with dementia, how can you manage the stress? The following are some tips from the Alzheimer's Association (www.alz.org).

■ *Investigate the resources in your community.* There may be support groups for you, financial resources for medical and custodial care for your family member, or groups that will provide respite care (for example, sitting with your family member when you need to be away from the house). You can find out about these resources through your family physician, your religious institution, or local chapters of the Alzheimer's Association or other groups focused on people with dementia.

■ *Become educated about dementia and caregiving techniques.* It can be helpful to know what to expect from your family member, as well as how to interpret and cope with his or her symptoms.

■ *Engage in legal and financial planning.* You may need to consult a financial advisor or an attorney to plan for the day when you may need to place your family member in a care facility or to ensure that his or her finances are appropriately managed. The Alzheimer's Association Web site has lots of good information about the legal and financial issues you may need to deal with.

■ *Take care of yourself by watching your diet, exercising, and getting plenty of rest.* Caregivers often neglect their own well-being, but this doesn't help their ill family member any more than it helps them. Consult your physician if you develop health problems, and consider getting help from a support group or a counselor to deal with the emotional issues you are facing.

■ *Be realistic about what you can do.* There may come a time when you cannot manage your family member physically because of his or her symptoms, or the stress of caregiving becomes too much for you or your family. Give yourself credit for what you have done, and don't blame yourself if you can't do it all on your own. Ask for help from other family members, friends, and anyone else who may be able to relieve your stress.

nutritional deficiencies that often accompany it can lead to dementia.

■ Some drugs help reduce the cognitive symptoms and accompanying depression, anxiety, and psychotic symptoms in some patients with dementia.

■ Gender, culture, and education all play roles in vulnerability to dementia.

DELIRIUM

Delirium is characterized by disorientation, recent memory loss, and a clouding of consciousness (see the DSM-IV-TR criteria in Table 14.4 on page 526). A delirious person has difficulty focusing, sustaining, or shifting attention. These signs arise suddenly, within several hours or days. They fluctuate over the course of a day and often become worse at night, a condition known as *sundowning*. The duration of these signs is short—rarely more than a month. Delirious patients are often agitated or frightened. They may also experience disrupted sleep-wake cycles, incoherent speech, illusions, and hallucinations.

The signs of delirium usually follow a common progression (Cole, 2004). In the early phase, patients report mild symptoms, such as fatigue, decreased concentration, irritability, restlessness, or depression. They may experience mild cognitive impairments or perceptual disturbances. As the delirium worsens, the person's orientation becomes disrupted. For example, the patient may think she is in her childhood home, when she is actually in the hospital. If undetected, the delirium progresses, and the person's orientation to familiar people becomes distorted. For example, a delirious patient misidentifies his wife or fails to recognize his child. Immediate memory is the first to be affected, followed by intermediate memory (memories of events occurring in the past 10 minutes), and finally remote, or distant, memory. When intervals of these symptoms alternate with intervals of lucid functioning and the symptoms become worse at night, a diagnosis of delirium is likely. If the person is not disoriented (to time, place, or person) or recent memory loss is absent, a diagnosis of delirium is unlikely.

The onset of delirium may be very dramatic, as when a normally quiet person suddenly becomes loud, verbally abusive, and combative or when a compliant hospital patient tries to pull out his IVs and will not be calmed by family or medical staff. Sometimes, though, the onset of delirium is subtle and manifests as an exaggerated form of an individual's normal personality

TABLE 14.4 DSM-IV-TR
Diagnostic Criteria for Delirium
Delirium is characterized by disorientation, recent memory loss, and a clouding of consciousness.
Disturbance of consciousness, such as reduced clarity of awareness of the environment, with reduced ability to focus, sustain, or shift attention
Change in cognition (such as memory deficit, disorientation, language disturbance) or development of a perceptual disturbance that is not accounted for by a dementia
Disturbance that develops over a short period of time, usually hours to days, and tends to fluctutate during the course of the day
Evidence that the disturbance is caused by the direct physiological consequences of a medical condition

Source: Reprinted with permission from the *Diagnostic and Statistical Manual of Mental Disorders*, Fourth Edition, Text Revision. Copyright © 2000 American Psychiatric Association.

traits. For example, a perfectionistic nurse recovering from surgery may complain loudly and harshly about the "inadequate" care she is receiving from the attending nurses. It would be easy for attending staff to regard her irritability as consistent with her personality style and her recovery: "She must be feeling better; she's beginning to complain." In this type of case, the delirium may go unrecognized until severe symptoms of delirium emerge.

Sometimes, delirious patients just appear confused. People who know them well say, "He just doesn't seem like himself." These delirious patients may call acquaintances by the wrong names or forget how to get to familiar locations. For example, they may not remember where their rooms are. In such cases, often the first indication of delirium comes from the observations of family or medical staff. They notice that the person seems calm during the day but agitated at night. It is important to monitor such a patient around the clock. Detecting delirium may require the frequent testing of the person's orientation. Close monitoring is also important because, with delirium, accidents, such as falling out of bed or stepping into traffic, are common.

Delirium typically is a signal of a serious medical condition. When it is detected and the underlying medical condition treated, delirium is temporary and reversible. The longer delirium continues, however, the more likely it is that the person will suffer permanent brain damage, because the causes of delirium, if left untreated, can induce permanent changes in the functioning of the brain.

Causes of Delirium

The specific causes of delirium are not known (Cole, 2004). Patients with delirium often show abnormal EEG activity. There is evidence that delirium may be mediated by abnormal activity in the neurotransmitter acetylcholine, and drugs affecting acetylcholine activity can reduce the symptoms of delirium (Cole, 2004).

Dementia is the strongest predictor of delirium, increasing the risk fivefold. A wide range of medical disorders, including stroke, congestive heart failure, HIV infection and other infectious diseases, and high fever, are associated with a risk for delirium. Intoxication with illicit drugs and withdrawal from these drugs or prescription medications can lead to delirium. Other possible causes include fluid and electrolyte imbalances, and toxic substances (see Table 14.5).

Delirium is probably the most common psychiatric syndrome found in the general hospital, particularly in older people. About 15 to 20 percent of older people are delirious on admission to the hospital for a serious illness, and another 10 to 15 percent develop delirium while in the hospital. Older people often experience delirium following surgery (Brown & Boyle, 2002; Cole, 2004). The delirium may be the result of the patient's medical disorder or the effects of medications. It may also result from sensory isolation. A syndrome known as *ICU/CCU psychosis* occurs in intensive care and cardiac care units (Maxmen & Ward, 1995): When patients are kept in unfamiliar surroundings that are monotonous, they may hear noises from machines as human voices, see the walls quiver, or hallucinate that someone is tapping them on the shoulder.

TABLE 14.5 Substances That Can Induce Delirium

A wide range of substances can cause delirium.

Alcohol	Antimicrobials	Inhalants
Amphetamines	Antiparkinsonian drugs	Muscle relaxants
Anesthetics	Cannabis	Opioids
Analgesics	Carbon dioxide	Organophosphate insecticides
Antiasthmatic agents	Carbon monoxide	Phencyclidine
Anticholinesterase	Cocaine	Psychotropic medications with anticholinergic side effects
Anticonvulsants	Corticosteroids	
Antihistamines	Gastrointestinal medications	Sedatives, hypnotics, and anxiolytics
Antihypertensive and cardiovascular medications	Hallucinogens	Volatile substances, such as fuel or paint

Source: Reprinted with permission from the *Diagnostic and Statistical Manual of Mental Disorders,* Fourth Edition, Text Revision. Copyright © 2000 American Psychiatric Association.

Among the elderly, a high mortality rate is associated with delirium (Byrne, 1994; Cole, 2004). Typically, the reason is that the underlying condition or the cause of the delirium is very serious. Between 15 and 40 percent of delirious hospital patients die within one month, as compared with half that rate in nondelirious patients.

Some people are at increased risk for delirium. The risk factors include age (the older the person, the higher the risk), gender (males are more at risk than females), and preexisting brain damage or dementia (Brown & Boyle, 2002). African Americans have higher rates of delirium than European Americans. This higher rate may occur because African Americans are less likely to have health insurance, so many do not receive early medical care for serious illnesses. As a result, their illnesses may be more likely to become severe enough to cause delirium.

Treatments for Delirium

It is extremely important that delirium be recognized and treated quickly. If a delirious person is not already hospitalized, an immediate referral to a physician should be made. If another medical condition is associated with the delirium (such as stroke or congestive heart failure), the first priority is to treat that condition (Cole, 2004). Drugs that may be contributing to the delirium must be discontinued. Antipsychotic medications are sometimes used to treat the patient's confusion. It may also be necessary to prevent people with delirium from harming themselves (Maxmen & Ward, 1995). Often, nursing care is required to monitor people's states and to prevent them from wandering off, tripping, or ripping out intravenous tubes and to manage their behavior if they should become noncompliant or violent. In some instances, restraints are necessary.

SUMMING UP

- Delirium is characterized by disorientation, recent memory loss, and a clouding of consciousness.

- The onset of delirium can be either sudden or slow.

- The many causes of delirium include medical diseases, the trauma of surgery, illicit drugs, medications, high fever, and infections.

- Delirium must be treated immediately by treating its underlying causes, to prevent brain damage and to prevent people from hurting themselves.

AMNESIA

A 46-year-old divorced housepainter is admitted to the hospital with a history of 30 years of heavy drinking. He has had two previous admissions for detoxification, but his family states that he has not had a drink in several weeks, and he shows no signs of alcohol withdrawal. He looks malnourished, however, and

(continued)

appears confused and mistakes one of his physicians for a dead uncle.

Within a week, the patient seems less confused and can find his way to the bathroom without direction. He remembers the names and birthdays of his siblings but has difficulty naming the past five presidents. More strikingly, he has great difficulty in retaining information for longer than a few minutes. He can repeat a list of numbers immediately after he has heard them but a few minutes later does not recall being asked to perform the task. Shown three objects (keys, comb, ring), he cannot recall them 3 minutes later. He does not seem worried about this. Asked if he can recall the name of his doctor, he replies, "Certainly," and proceeds to call the doctor "Dr. Masters" (not his name), and he claims to have met him in the Korean War. He tells a long, untrue story about how he and Dr. Masters served as fellow soldiers. (Adapted from Spitzer et al., 1981, pp. 41–42)

In dementia and delirium, people show multiple cognitive deficits, including memory deficits, language deficits, disorientation, an inability to recognize objects or people, and an inability to think abstractly or plan and carry through with an activity. In **amnesia,** only memory is affected. A person with amnesia is impaired in the ability to learn new information (**anterograde amnesia**) or to recall previously learned information or past events (**retrograde amnesia**). Amnesic disorders often follow periods of confusion and disorientation and delirium.

The patterns of amnesia represented in soap operas and other television shows—with people suddenly losing their memories for everything they previously knew—are unrealistic. Commonly, people with amnesia can remember events from the distant past but not from the recent past. For example, a 60-year-old patient may be able to tell where he went to high school and college but be unable to remember that he was admitted to the hospital yesterday. He will also forget meeting his doctor from one day to the next. In profound amnesia, a person may be completely disoriented about place or time, but rarely does a person with amnesia forget his or her own identity.

Often, people with amnesia do not realize they have profound memory deficits and deny evidence of these deficits. They may seem unconcerned with obvious lapses in memory or may make up stories to cover their lapses in memory. They may become agitated with others who point out their memory lapses. They may even accuse others of conspiring against them.

Amnesia can be caused by brain damage due to strokes, head injuries, chronic nutritional deficiencies, exposure to toxins (such as through carbon monoxide poisoning), or chronic substance abuse. *Korsakoff's syndrome* is a form of amnesia caused by damage to the thalamus, a part of the brain that acts as a relay station to other parts of the brain. Chronic, heavy alcohol use is associated with Korsakoff's syndrome, probably because the alcoholic neglects nutrition and thus develops thiamine deficiencies (see Chapter 17).

The course of amnesia depends on the cause. If, for example, a stroke occurs in the hippocampus, the memory loss that results will include events after the date of the stroke. Memories prior to the stroke will remain intact. If the memory loss is caused by alcohol or other toxins, it is often broader and the onset can be insidious. For some people, remote memory may also become impaired.

The first step in the treatment of amnesia is to remove, if possible, any conditions contributing to the amnesia, such as alcohol use or exposure to toxins. In addition, attention to nutrition and the treatment of any accompanying health condition (such as hypertension) can help prevent further deterioration. Finally, because new surroundings and routines may prove too difficult or impossible for the person with amnesia to learn, the environment should be kept as familiar as possible. Often, as with dementia, it can be helpful to have clocks, calendars, photographs, labels, and other kinds of reminders prominent.

SUMMING UP

- Amnesia is characterized only by memory loss.
- Retrograde amnesia is a loss of memory for past events. Anterograde amnesia is an inability to remember new information.
- Amnesia can be caused by brain damage due to strokes, head injuries, chronic nutritional deficiencies, exposure to toxins (such as through carbon monoxide poisoning), or chronic substance abuse.

— Thalamus

— Hippocampus

Damage to the thalamus causes Korsakoff's syndrome, and stroke damage to the hippocampus causes memory loss for events after the stroke.

- The treatment of amnesia can involve removing the agents contributing to the amnesia and helping the person develop memory aids.

MENTAL DISORDERS IN LATER LIFE

All of the disorders we have considered in previous chapters of this book also can occur in later life, and in several chapters we have discussed the characteristics of disorders as people move into old age. For the remainder of this chapter, we focus on three of the most common mental disorders among older adults—the anxiety disorders, depression, and the substance use disorders.

Assessing psychopathology in older people can be difficult, in part because psychological problems very often co-occur with medical problems (Zarit & Haynie, 2000). Sometimes, the symptoms of depression, anxiety, or confusion, for example, can be the consequences of medical problems. Other times, they are independent of medical problems but contribute to them, as when a depressed person is not motivated to take the medications needed to overcome a medical problem. Still other times, emotional symptoms arise in response to the disability, pain, or loss that occurs because of a medical problem. Finally, some psychological symptoms are side effects of the many medications an ill older person is taking. Teasing apart psychological symptoms from medical problems is critical to an accurate assessment, but it can be very difficult.

Assessment is also complicated by the fact that older people may not present the same symptoms of a disorder as do younger people. In the mood and anxiety disorders, older people often complain of physical problems, rather than the psychological concerns associated with these disorders. This can lead to misdiagnosis, or to people ignoring the elderly person's somatic complaints as "normal for old age." Older people may be more reluctant to admit to psychological problems as well, because they grew up in a period in which these problems were heavily stigmatized.

Anxiety Disorders

Anxiety is one of the most common problems among older adults, with up to 15 percent of people over the age of 65 experiencing an anxiety disorder (Scogin, Floyd, & Forde, 2000). Some anxiety disorders among older people are continuations of persistent disorders they have had all their lives. Other times, anxiety first arises in old age. It often takes the form of worry about loved ones or about the older person's own health or safety, and it frequently exists along with medical illnesses and depression, as with Mrs. Johnson (adapted from Scogin et al., 2000, pp. 117–118):

CASE STUDY

Mrs. Johnson is a 71-year-old female who was referred by a family practice physician who works in a nearby town. Mrs. Johnson had become extremely anxious and moderately depressed following a major orthopedic surgery, a total hip replacement. She was a retired office worker.

I was immediately struck by her general level of anxiety. For example, she expressed fears about her ability to get her husband to take her to an appointment and was concerned that she might not be the right type of person for psychological treatment. Her anxiety seemed to interfere with her ability to adequately attend to and process information. For example, she seemed to have difficulty getting down the directions to my office. She stated that she was concerned about being able to find the building and that she would leave her house early in case she got lost. Mrs. Johnson was early to her appointment. She looked distraught throughout the session. She wrung her hands, cried on a couple of occasions, and repeatedly stated, "I don't want to be a burden." Her main concern was that, due to her recent surgery, she might not be able to continue living in the home she and her husband had lived in most of her adult life. She was extremely afraid of having a fall and not being found for hours.

Mrs. Johnson stated that, when she was raising her children, she worried about their education and about money. Her children were living various distances away from her, so that their involvement, at least physically, was not an option. Mrs. Johnson indicated that she loved all her children but that she worried about two of them. Both had been divorced and she was concerned about their well-being and that of her three grandchildren. She reported not having the desire to eat because her stomach was "fluttery." I asked, "Do you

(continued)

find yourself worrying about things?" to which she responded, "Yes, a lot. I worry that I've begun to be a burden for my husband. I worry about my hip and I worry about not being able to get around. I guess I'm crazy because I worry about being worried so much." I assured her that she was not crazy, just anxious, which can oftentimes make you feel like you are crazy.

Mrs. Johnson was diagnosed with generalized anxiety disorder, or GAD (see Chapter 7). One study estimated that 1.9 percent of older adults suffer from GAD in any given six-month period (Blazer, George, & Hughes, 1991). This rate is lower than the rate among young adults, but, as in young adults, older women are about twice as likely as older men to suffer from the disorder. Older adults may worry more about health and family issues than do younger adults (Scogin et al., 2000). Too often, their worries about health are dismissed as understandable, when they are part of the larger picture of GAD.

Panic disorder is relatively rare in older age. One epidemiological study estimated that only 0.1 percent of people over 65 can be diagnosed with this disorder (Regier et al., 1988). Obsessive-compulsive disorder is also quite rare. It was diagnosed in only 0.8 percent of the older people in this study.

The symptoms of posttraumatic stress disorder (PTSD) and acute stress disorder are relatively common among older people, often occurring in response to the loss of a loved one (Bonanno & Kaltman, 1999). PTSD is also common among combat veterans. Some of these veterans have experienced the flashbacks and other symptoms of PTSD their entire lives, but late-onset PTSD can occur in older veterans (Schnurr, Spiro, & Paris, 2000). Vietnam veterans are just beginning to reach the period known as old age. Given the high rates of PTSD in these veterans (see Chapter 6), the rates of PTSD among the elderly may increase in the next couple of decades.

Very few older adults seek treatment for anxiety disorders, and those who do tend to consult their family physicians, rather than mental-health professionals (Scogin et al., 2000). For the older people who do seek help, cognitive-behavioral therapy and supportive therapy based on a more humanistic model have both been shown to be effective in the treatment of anxiety symptoms (Stanley & Novy, 2000). Simple relaxation training is

also effective in reducing tension and anxiety (Scogin et al., 1992).

Physicians frequently prescribe an antianxiety drug, such as a benzodiazepine, when an older patient complains of anxiety. With age, there are changes in drug absorption, distribution, metabolism, and sensitivity to side effects. Side effects, such as unsteadiness, can lead to falls and bone fractures in frail elderly people. With the benzodiazepines, tolerance can develop with prolonged use, leading to severe withdrawal effects, as well as the rebound of anxiety symptoms, once the person discontinues use. Antidepressant drugs, including buspirone and the selective serotonin reuptake inhibitors, are increasingly being used to treat anxiety symptoms, with fewer side effects and withdrawal effects than occur with the benzodiazepines. Older adults often are taking several prescription and over-the-counter medications that can interact with psychotropic drugs. All of these factors make the management of drug therapy in older adults more complex than in younger adults (Scogin et al., 2000).

Depression

CASE STUDY

Mrs. Scott was a 76-year-old widowed mother of three children who came to the Clinic for Older Adults, an ambulatory psychiatric clinic for seniors, at the behest of her oldest son, Roger. When first greeted in the waiting room, Mrs. Scott was sitting on the edge of her seat, wringing her hands, looking anxiously from one corner of the room to another. Roger was sitting next to his mother, slumped in his chair and visibly irritated. Once she was alone with the interviewer, Mrs. Scott explained that she was terribly upset because her bowel was no longer working. She had been constipated for five days and took this as evidence that her bowel had "died" and that she would likely be dead within a matter of days. She further stated that she had been to see her primary care physician repeatedly for the problem and got only false reassurances that she was basically healthy but needed to adjust her diet and take a daily fiber supplement. She then tearfully related how "fed up" her children were with her and her bowel problems and fervently asked the interviewer not to tell

(continued)

Roger that she had been talking about her problems again. She hinted that her children would be better off without her because "they just don't understand what I'm going through and are too busy with their own lives to worry about me." When asked if she had other difficulties, Mrs. Scott stated only that she was quite lonely and wished her children would visit her more often. In response to specific questions about depressive symptoms, Mrs. Scott stated that her sleep had been quite interrupted for the past several months and that she woke typically around 5 A.M. with abdominal cramping and fears about dying. She estimated that in the past six months she had lost about 20 pounds, in part because she had lost her appetite and in part because she was afraid to eat and "clog up" her body. Although she had been an avid reader in the past, she now found it difficult to focus or concentrate on anything other than her bowel. When asked if her problems had gotten so bad that she thought about dying or hurting herself, her eyes welled with tears and she admitted that she asked the Lord each night to take her and put her out of her misery.

Later when asked about her sister, who had died unexpectedly from a stroke 6 months previously, Mrs. Scott initially turned away and then wept bitterly. She began to describe how her sister had been her close companion throughout life and especially since Mrs. Scott's husband died 10 years earlier. After this brief release of sorrow, she then abruptly asked that the interview be terminated because she could not imagine how any of this could help her with her "real" problem. (Adapted from King & Markus, 2000, pp. 141–142)

Among older people living in the community, only about 1 to 3 percent can be diagnosed with major depression (Gatz et al., 1996). Depression is much more common among those in acute care or chronic care settings, where the prevalence reaches 12 to 20 percent. Symptoms not quite meeting the criteria for major depression occur in approximately 15 percent of the community-dwelling elderly and up to 30 percent of the institutionalized

Depression can be a life threatening disorder in elderly people.

elderly (King & Marcus, 2000). As we discussed in Chapter 9, women outnumber men among depressed people, but this age gap narrows, and in some studies disappears, among people over 65 (Gatz et al., 1996). Bipolar disorder is quite rare among the elderly and is even more rarely diagnosed for the first time in old age (King & Markus, 2000). Thus, we will focus our discussion on unipolar depression.

Depression greatly reduces the quality of life for older people. One study estimated that depression ranks with arthritis and heart disease as the diseases inflicting the greatest burden on quality of life in the elderly (Unützer et al., 2000). In fact, depression can be lethal for older people. The suicide rate among older White males is the highest of any group in the United States, and 60 to 75 percent of older suicide victims are depressed (Conwell, 1996) (see the discussion of suicide among the elderly in Chapter 10). In addition, depression may hasten the progression of several medical diseases. Among people who have had a heart attack, depression increases the risk of dying from the heart attack by five times (Frasure-Smith, Lesperance, & Talajic, 1995). In nursing home patients, major depression hastens mortality, regardless of what physical ailment the person suffers from (Rovner, 1993).

About half of older people who are depressed were depressed as younger adults, and about half have symptoms that initially arose in older age (King & Marcus, 2000). Older people are less likely than younger people to report the psychological symptoms of depression, such as depressed mood, guilt, low self-esteem, and suicidal ideation. They are more likely to complain of somatic problems (such as the case study's Mrs. Scott's abdominal cramps), psychomotor abnormalities (such as agitation or extreme slowing), and cognitive impairments (King & Markus, 2000). Many depressed elders show a **depletion syndrome**, consisting of loss of interest, loss of energy, hopelessness, helplessness, and psychomotor retardation (Newmann, Engel, & Jensen, 1991). Depression is less likely to lead to impairment in functioning in older people, perhaps because they are less likely to be in the workforce or in the process of raising children. As a result, depression is often misdiagnosed, or missed altogether, by family members and physicians.

Differentiating a primary depression from one caused by medical illness or medications can be quite difficult. Several medical illnesses can cause depression-like symptoms, including multiple sclerosis, Cushing's disease, Parkinson's disease, Huntington's disease, Addison's disease, cerebrovascular disease, hypothyroidism, chronic obstructive pulmonary disease, and vitamin deficiency (King & Markus, 2000). It is important for an older adult who appears to be depressed to have a thorough medical examination in an attempt to rule out any medical disorders that may be causing his or her symptoms.

One of the most difficult differential diagnoses to make is between depression and dementia, particularly because the two disorders often occur together. Dementia can cause depression, and depression can cause changes in brain functioning that increase the risk for future irreversible dementia (King & Markus, 2000). Some rules of thumb can help differentiate depression from dementia, although they are not foolproof.

First, although depressed people often complain about memory problems, their cognitive deficits tend to be less severe than those found in people with dementia, and they tend to be more aware of their cognitive problems than are people with dementia. Second, the noncognitive symptoms of depression tend to be more severe in people with primary depression than in people with dementia. Third, depressed people often have trouble doing "free recall" memory tasks but can recognize things they know if shown them, whereas people with dementia have difficulty in both free recall and recognition memory tasks. Finally, depressed people are more likely to have a rapid onset of symptoms, whereas the onset of dementia is much more gradual.

Depression that occurs first in old age is very often associated with the disability and pain due to medical illness (King & Marcus, 2000). In addition, older people are often caring for spouses or other loved ones who are seriously ill, and caregiving is a risk factor for depression. The loss of a spouse or another loved one to death leads to depressive symptoms in most people. These grief-related symptoms are normal and are not diagnosed as depression unless they persist for several months beyond the loss. "Complicated grief," or grief that eventually is diagnosed as major depression, also tends to be characterized by profound guilt, thoughts that one would be better off dead, profound inactivity, persistent impairment in functioning, and hallucinations that go beyond the common experience of hearing or seeing a dead loved one (APA, 2000).

There is a substantial amount of research on the treatment of depression in the elderly, and it is clear that several treatments can be successful (see Lyness, 2004). Antidepressant medications are frequently used, and they are effective in 50 to 70 percent of older depressed people (King & Markus, 2000). The tricyclic antidepressants and monoamine oxidase inhibitors can have cardiac side effects that are dangerous for older people, however, so the selective serotonin reuptake inhibitors are used more often. Physicians must still monitor older patients to ensure that dosage levels are not too high and serious side effects do not emerge. Electroconvulsive therapy is disproportionately used with older depressed people than with younger ones, particularly among those who have not responded to medication therapy or whose medical conditions (e.g., cardiac problems) preclude the use of antidepressant medications.

Gallagher-Thompson, Thompson, and colleagues have conducted a number of studies comparing cognitive, behavior, and interpersonal therapies for depressed elders and have found all of these treatments to be effective (Powers et al., 2002). Thompson and colleagues (2001) compared cognitive-behavioral therapy (CBT) alone, a tricyclic antidepressant alone, and combined CBT and a tricyclic and found that the CBT alone and the combined treatment were both superior to the drug treatment alone. There was no difference between the combined treatment and CBT alone. Reynolds and colleagues (2000) have used the combination of interpersonal therapy with drug therapy (a tricyclic or a selective sertonin reuptake inhibitor) to treat older people with recurrent or chronic depression with consistent success.

Substance Use Disorders

We tend to think of substance use disorders as problems of the young. Indeed, the use of "hard" drugs, such as cocaine or heroin, is quite rare

Some elderly people abuse prescription drugs.

among the elderly. Many chronic users of illicit substances die before they reach old age, and others grow out of their use. Adults currently above the age of 65 probably never did use illicit substances as frequently as people in younger generations, because the use of these drugs was less acceptable and the drugs were less available when they were adolescents and young adults. Certain types of substance abuse and dependence are a frequent problem among older people, however, including alcohol-related problems and the misuse of prescription drugs (Lisansky-Gomberg, 2000).

Approximately 2 percent of people over 65 can be diagnosed with alcohol abuse or dependence, and about 8 percent can be considered heavy drinkers (Helzer, Burnam, & McEvoy, 1991; Molgaard et al., 1990). You might assume that most older people with alcohol problems have been alcoholics most of their lives, but one-third to one-half first develop problems after the age of 65 (Liberto, Oslin, & Ruskin, 1996). Tolerance for alcohol decreases with age, so it takes fewer drinks for an older person to have a high blood-alcohol concentration. Older people also metabolize alcohol

(and other drugs and medications) more slowly, so it can more readily cause toxic effects in the body, including changes in brain chemistry and cognitive deficits. In addition, women tend to metabolize alcohol and some other drugs less efficiently than men, so the same doses can lead to greater toxic effects, especially if usage occurs over many years.

The abuse of and dependence on prescription drugs is a much greater problem among the elderly. Although only 13 percent of the U.S. population is over the age of 65, they account for a third of all prescription drug expenditures (Lisansky-Gomberg, 2000). The most commonly prescribed drugs are diuretics, cardiovascular drugs, and sedatives. Older people are also more likely than younger people to purchase over-the-counter drugs, including analgesics, vitamins, and laxatives.

The abuse of drugs, such as benzodiazepines, may begin innocently. Physicians tend to be liberal in their prescription of these drugs to older patients, and as many as a third of older people take these drugs at least occasionally—for insomnia or after a loss, for example (Wetherell et al., 2005). As tolerance for the drug develops, and an older person learns of the withdrawal effects of discontinuing the drug, he or she may seek out ways to get more of it, by copying prescriptions or seeing multiple physicians. The slurred speech and memory problems that can be caused by drugs may be overlooked in the elderly as normal symptoms of old age. They can often hide their drug abuse for long periods of time. Eventually, the side effects of the drugs, the withdrawal symptoms they experience when they try to go "cold turkey" off the drugs, or interaction effects with other medications may land them in a hospital emergency room, as with Eleanor (Lisansky-Gomberg, 2000, p. 277):

CASE STUDY

Eleanor is a widow of 72; she keeps reasonably busy by volunteering in a few community organizations. Since her husband died 10 years ago, she has had difficulty sleeping. Her physician, who perceives the sleep difficulties as based on depression and grieving, prescribed antidepressants. Because her insomnia continued, he also prescribed sedatives. She is now a regular user of sedatives and has appeared in the emergency department of the local hospital recently complaining of logginess and fatigue.

The treatment for older substance abusers is similar to that for younger abusers (see Chapter 17), although withdrawal symptoms may be more dangerous for older abusers and, thus, must be monitored more carefully (Lisansky-Gomberg, 2000). Psychotherapies that have been shown to be useful tend to have the following characteristics (Schonfeld & Dupree, 1997):

■ Elders are treated along with people their age in a supportive, nonconfrontational approach.

■ Negative emotional states (such as depression and loneliness) and their relationship to the substance abuse are a focus of the intervention.

■ Social skills and social networks are rebuilt.

■ Staff members are respectful and interested in working with older adults.

■ Linkages are made with medical facilities and community resources (such as housing services).

Due to increasing longevity and the size of the baby-boom generation, the proportion of the population that is above the age of 65 will increase dramatically over the next few decades (King & Marcus, 2000). In addition, the older adult population will become much more ethnically diverse: Although 85 percent of Americans over 65 in 1995 were non-Hispanic White, this proportion is expected to decrease to 66 percent by 2030 (Whitbourne, 2000). In turn, the proportion of older people who are of Hispanic and Asian descent will increase. Much more research is needed on the psychological health needs of older people, particularly older people of color.

SUMMING UP

■ Mental disorders are less common among older adults than younger adults, but 10 to 20 percent of older people suffer significant psychopathology.

■ Psychological problems can be difficult to differentiate from medical problems. In addition, older people may complain of different symptoms than younger people do or may be less likely to seek help.

■ Anxiety disorders are fairly common among older people, particularly generalized anxiety disorder and posttraumatic stress disorder.

■ Anxiety disorders can be treated with antianxiety drugs, antidepressants, or psychotherapy.

■ Depression is a common problem among the elderly, and suicide rates are extremely high among elderly White males.

■ Some older people show a depletion syndrome, consisting of loss of interest, loss of energy, hopelessness, helplessness, and psychomotor retardation.

■ Differentiating depression from dementia can be particularly difficult, but certain patterns of memory loss can help in the differentiation.

■ Antidepressant medications and ECT are commonly used to treat severe depression in older people. Cognitive-behavioral and interpersonal therapies have been shown to work very well.

■ Alcohol use problems can begin in older age, particularly since the metabolism of and tolerance for alcohol change with age.

■ The abuse of and dependence on prescription drugs are significant problems among older people.

■ The treatment of substance use disorders for older people is similar to that for younger people.

CHAPTER INTEGRATION

Geropsychologists have emphasized the importance of understanding the cognitive disorders and psychological problems experienced by older people in the context of normal aging. Aging is not just a biological process—it is the interaction of biological, psychological, and social processes, as depicted in Figure 14.6.

Certain changes take place in the brain and the rest of the body with aging, and these are influenced by our genetic and other biological vulnerabilities. The impact of these changes on the everyday behavior of older people varies tremendously, however, in part due to differences in personality and the social environment. Some people become sedentary when their bodies lose some of the strength and endurance they had as younger adults, whereas others institute exercise programs that help them maintain much of their youthful fitness. Similarly, the likelihood of developing many diseases in old age is substantially influenced by a person's behaviors as a younger adult. For example, people who keep mentally active into middle and old age may be less likely to develop Alzheimer's disease.

Much of what we attribute to biological aging—for example, memory loss—is not the result of aging per se but, rather, of diseases such as those discussed in this chapter. But even the pro-

| FIGURE 14.6 | **Integrating Biological and Psychosocial Factors in Aging** |

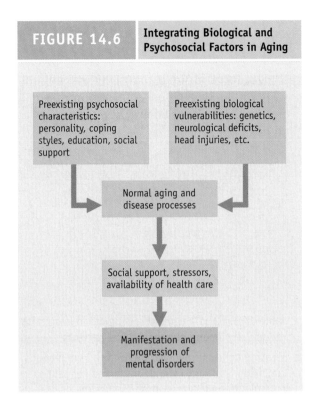

Preexisting psychosocial characteristics: personality, coping styles, education, social support

Preexisting biological vulnerabilities: genetics, neurological deficits, head injuries, etc.

Normal aging and disease processes

Social support, stressors, availability of health care

Manifestation and progression of mental disorders

gression of these biological diseases is substantially affected by psychological and social variables. For example, many people in the early stages of dementia become paranoid, irritable, and impulsive. These symptoms may be especially pronounced in people who were somewhat paranoid, irritable, or impulsive even before they developed dementia.

The social environment can greatly affect the severity of cognitive deficits. If a person who is easily confused or forgetful is further stressed by family members who frequently become annoyed with the person or expect too much of him or her, the cognitive deficits can become even more severe. Thus, even though the cognitive disorders are rooted in medical disease or in chronic intoxication with substances such as alcohol, there are several ways in which psychosocial factors can influence the severity and manifestation of these disorders.

Extraordinary People: Follow-Up

John Bayley's depiction of his life with Iris Murdoch after she developed Alzheimer's disease is remarkable for his elegant and engaging description of her symptoms and the impact of those symptoms on their life together. It is even more remarkable, however, for the fact that it is first and foremost a love story.

> There are so many doubts and illusions and concealments in any close relationship. Even in our present situation, they can come as an unexpected shock. Iris's tears sometimes seem to signify a whole inner world which she is determined to keep from me and shield me from. There is something ghastly in the feeling of relief that this can't be so; and yet the illusion of such an inner world still there—if it is an illusion—can't help haunting me from time to time. There are moments when I almost welcome it. Iris has always had—must have had—so vast and rich and complex an inner world, which it used to give me immense pleasure not to know anything about. Like looking at a map of South Africa as a child and wondering about the sources of the Amazon, and what unknown cities might be hidden there in the jungle. Have any of those hidden places survived in her? (Bayley, 1999, pp. 258–259)

> Life is no longer bringing the pair of us "closer and closer apart," in the poet's tenderly ambiguous words. Every day we move closer and closer together. We could not do otherwise. There is a certain comic irony—happily, not darkly comic—that after more than forty years of taking marriage for granted, marriage has decided it is tired of this, and is taking a hand in the game. Purposefully, persistently, involuntarily, our marriage is now getting somewhere. It is giving us no choice—and I am glad of that.

> Every day, we are physically closer; and Iris's little "mouse cry," as I think of it,

(continued)

Extraordinary People: Follow-Up (*continued*)

signifying loneliness in the next room, the wish to be back beside me, seems less and less forlorn, more simple, more natural. She is not sailing into the dark: The voyage is over, and under the dark escort of Alzheimer's she has arrived somewhere. So have I. (pp. 265–266)

Iris Murdoch died in February 1999, just a few months after *Elegy for Iris* was published. A movie based on this extraordinary book and couple was released in 2001.

Chapter Summary

- Aging is not simpy a biological process. Rather, it involves the interaction of biological, psychological, and social processes. (Review Figure 14.6.) Most older people are physically and mentally healthy.

- Dementia is typically a permanent deterioration in cognitive functioning, often accompanied by emotional changes. The five types of cognitive impairment in dementia are memory impairment, aphasia, apraxia, agnosia, and loss of executive functions. (Review Table 14.1.)

- The most common type of dementia is due to Alzheimer's disease. The brains of Alzheimer's patients show neurofibrillary tangles, plaques made up of amyloid protein, and cortical atrophy. (Review Figures 14.2 and 14.3.) Recent theories of Alzheimer's disease focus on three genes that might contribute to the buildup of amyloid protein in the brains of Alzheimer's patients.

- Dementia can also be caused by cerebrovascular disorder, head injury, and progressive disorders, such as Parkinson's disease, HIV disease, Huntington's disease, Pick's disease, and Creutzfeldt-Jakob disease. Chronic drug abuse and the nutritional deficiencies that often accompany it can lead to dementia.

- Drugs help reduce the cognitive symptoms of dementia and the accompanying depression, anxiety, and psychotic symptoms in some patients.

- Delirium is characterized by disorientation, recent memory loss, and a clouding of consciousness. (Review Table 14.4.) Delirium typically is a signal of a serious medical condition, such as a stroke, congestive heart failure, an infectious disease, high fever, or drug intoxication or withdrawal. (Review

Table 14.5.) It is a common syndrome in hospitals, particularly among elderly surgical patients.

- Treating delirium involves treating the underlying condition leading to the delirium and keeping the patient safe until the symptoms subside.

- In amnesia, only patients' memories are affected. Anterograde amnesia is the most common form of amnesia and is characterized by the inability to learn or retain new information. Retrograde amnesia is the inability to recall previously learned information or past events.

- Amnesic disorders can be caused by strokes, head injuries, chronic nutritional deficiencies, exposure to toxins, and chronic substance abuse. The course and treatment of amnesia depend on the cause.

- Mental disorders are less common among older adults than younger adults, but 10 to 20 percent of older people suffer significant psychopathology.

- Anxiety disorders are fairly common among older people, particularly generalized anxiety disorder and posttraumatic stress disorder. Anxiety disorders can be treated with antianxiety drugs, antidepressants, or psychotherapy.

- Depression is a common problem among the elderly, and suicide rates are extremely high among elderly White males. Some older people show a depletion syndrome, consisting of loss of interest, loss of energy, hopelessness, helplessness, and psychomotor retardation. Differentiating depression from dementia can be particularly difficult, but certain patterns of memory loss can help in the differentiation.

- Antidepressant medications and ECT are commonly used to treat severe depression in older people. Cognitive-behavioral and interpersonal therapies have been shown to work very well.

■ Alcohol use problems can begin in older age, particularly since the metabolism of and tolerance for alcohol change with age. The abuse of and dependence on prescription drugs are significant problems among older people. The treatment of substance use disorders for older people is similar to that for younger people.

MindMap CD-ROM

The following resources on the MindMap CD-ROM that came with this text will help you to master the content of this chapter and prepare for tests:

■ Video: Alzheimer's Disease
■ Chapter Timeline
■ Chapter Quiz

Key Terms

cognitive disorders 511

dementia 513

aphasia 514

echolalia 514

palialia 514

apraxia 514

agnosia 514

executive functions 514

Alzheimer's disease 515

neurofibrillary tangles 516

plaques 516

amyloid 516

vascular dementia 518

cerebrovascular disease 518

stroke 518

delirium 525

amnesia 528

anterograde amnesia 528

retrograde amnesia 528

depletion syndrome 532

Chapter 15

Wednesday's Child
by John S. Bunker

We love good looks rather than what is practical,
Though good looks may prove destructive.

—La Fontaine, "The Stag and His Reflection," *Fables*
(1668–1694; translated by Marianne Moore)

Eating Disorders <

Taking Psychology Personally

■ **Is There Such a Thing as a Healthy Diet?**

Chapter Integration

Interacting social, psychological, and biological factors may lead a person to develop an eating disorder.

There may be more than one pathway into an eating disorder. Once disordered behaviors begin, they tend to be maintained.

Extraordinary People

Diana, Princess of Wales

Perhaps the most famous person to suffer from bulimia nervosa, Diana, Princess of Wales, shocked the world when she made her suffering public. Never before had a member of the British royal family been so open, particularly about symptoms that could be diagnosed as a psychological disorder. After the birth of her first son, William, Diana suffered a postpartum depression (see Chapter 9). She attributed this depression to an accumulation of great changes in her life—her marriage at 19 to the Prince of Wales; her difficult pregnancy, which came early in that marriage; the tremendous media attention given her; and the early signs that her marriage was falling apart. Diana felt she had little support from her husband or family, however, in fighting this depression and, thus, began to cope with her pain in maladaptive ways. The following is her story of how her bulimia developed, as told to a British Broadcasting Corporation (BBC) interviewer in November 1995.

Diana: When no one listens to you, or you feel no one's listening to you, all sorts of things start to happen. For instance, you have so much pain inside yourself that you try and hurt yourself on the outside because you want help, but it's the wrong help you're asking for. People see it as crying wolf or attention-seeking, and they think because you're in the media all the time you've got enough attention. But I was actually crying out because I wanted to get better in order to go forward and continue my duty and my role as wife, mother, Princess of Wales. So yes, I did inflict it upon myself. I didn't like myself, I was ashamed because I couldn't cope with the pressures.

Question: Were you able to admit that you were in fact unwell, or did you feel compelled simply to carry on performing as the Princess of Wales?

Diana: I felt compelled to perform. Well, when I say perform, I was compelled to go out and do my engagements and not let people down and support them and love them. And in a way by being out in public they supported me, although they weren't aware just how much healing they were giving me, and it carried me through.

Question: But did you feel that you had to maintain the public image of a successful Princess of Wales?

Diana: Yes I did, yes I did.

Question: The depression was resolved, as you say, but it was subsequently reported that you suffered bulimia. Is that true?

Diana: Yes, I did. I had bulimia for a number of years. And that's like a secret disease. You inflict it upon yourself because your self-esteem is at a low ebb, and you don't think you're worthy or valuable. You fill your stomach up four or five times a day—some do it more—and it gives you a feeling of comfort. It's like having a pair of arms around you, but it's temporarily, temporary. Then you're disgusted at the bloatedness of your stomach, and then you bring it all up again. And it's a repetitive pattern which is very destructive to yourself.

Question: How often would you do that on a daily basis?

Diana: Depends on the pressures going on. If I'd been on what I call an awayday, or I'd been up part of the country all day, I'd come home feeling pretty empty, because my engagements at that time would be to do with people dying, people very sick, people's marriage problems, and I'd come home and it would be very difficult to know how to comfort myself having been comforting lots of other people, so it would be a regular pattern to jump into the fridge. It was a symptom of what was going on in my marriage. I was crying out for help, but giving the wrong signals, and people were using my bulimia as a coat on a hanger: they decided that was the problem—Diana was unstable.

Princess Diana certainly led an unusual life, and some of the pressures that may have contributed to her eating disorder were ones very few of us can expect to encounter. Still, the kind of love-hate relationship she had with food is familiar to many of us, as this excerpt from a college student's diary shows:

VOICES

Dear Diary: This morning I had a half of a grapefruit for breakfast, and some coffee—no sugar or cream. For lunch, I had an apple and a diet soda. For dinner, I had some plain white rice and a salad with just some lemon squeezed over it. So I was feeling really good about myself, really virtuous. That is, until Jackie came over, and completely messed up my day. She brought over a movie to watch, which was fine. But then she insisted on ordering a pizza. I told her I didn't want any, that I wasn't hungry (which was a lie, because I was starving). But she ordered it anyway. The pizza arrived, and I thought I could be good and not have any. But it was just sitting there on the table, and I couldn't think of anything except having some. I couldn't concentrate on the movie. I kept smelling the pizza and feeling the emptiness in my stomach. Like a weakling, I reached out and got one piece, a small piece. It was ice cold by then, and kind of greasy, but I didn't care. I ate that piece in about 5 seconds flat. Then I had another piece. And another. I stopped after four pieces. But I still couldn't pay attention to the movie. All I could think about was what a pig I was for eating that pizza, and how I'll never lose the 10 pounds I need to lose to fit into a smaller size dress. Jackie's gone now, and I still keep thinking about how ugly and fat I am, and how I have no willpower. I didn't deserve to have that pizza tonight, because I haven't lost enough weight this month. I'm going to have to skip breakfast and lunch tomorrow, and exercise for a couple of hours, to make up for being a complete pig tonight.

Our culture is obsessed with weight and with how much food we eat. A nationwide study in the United States found that 38 percent of normal-weight women thought they were overweight (Chang & Christakis, 2003). Weight concerns are even greater among college women; a study of 2,200 college students in six universities across the United States found that two-thirds of the women were unhappy with their weight (Rozin, Bauer, & Catanese, 2003). Dissatisfaction with the shape and size of the body is greater among women than men (Lewinsohn et al., 2002; Rozin et al., 2003) (see Figure 15.1 on page 542).

Dieting is the most common way people try to overcome their body dissatisfaction. Only one-third

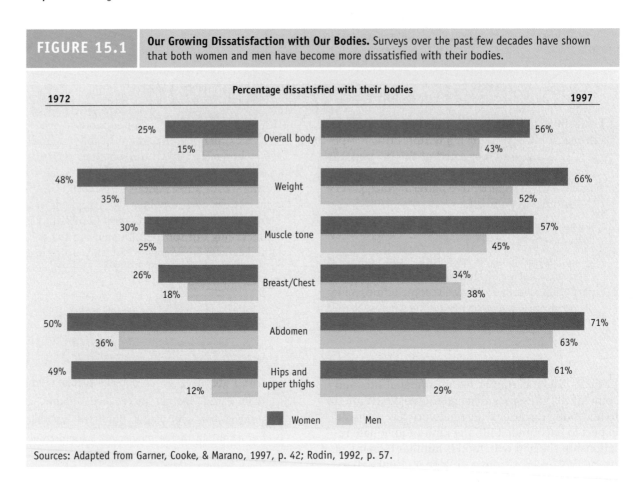

FIGURE 15.1   **Our Growing Dissatisfaction with Our Bodies.** Surveys over the past few decades have shown that both women and men have become more dissatisfied with their bodies.

Percentage dissatisfied with their bodies

1972

1997

	Women	Men
Overall body	25% → 56%	15% → 43%
Weight	48% → 66%	35% → 52%
Muscle tone	30% → 57%	25% → 45%
Breast/Chest	26% → 34%	18% → 38%
Abdomen	50% → 71%	36% → 63%
Hips and upper thighs	49% → 61%	12% → 29%

Sources: Adapted from Garner, Cooke, & Marano, 1997, p. 42; Rodin, 1992, p. 57.

of college women say they "never" diet, compared with 58 percent of college men (Rozin et al., 2003). Dieting is hard, however, and almost everyone who loses weight through dieting gains it all back and often more (Byrne, Cooper, & Fairburn, 2003). Many people spend their lives losing and gaining back tens of pounds in a cycle of "yo-yo" dieting.

Some people turn to more extreme means to make themselves look "better." The popularity of cosmetic surgery to improve appearance has exploded in recent years, with procedures such as liposuction and breast augmentation doubling in popularity in four years (Sarwer, Magee, & Crerand, 2004). The most popular procedure these days is injections of *Botulinum* toxin (e.g., Botox) to reduce wrinkles, with 1.6 million people receiving this procedure per year. In all, Americans spend over $30 billion per year on weight-loss products, including $8 billion per year on spas and exercise clubs, $382 million on diet books, $10 billion on diet soft drinks, and billions of dollars on low-calorie foods and artificial sweeteners. To put this into perspective, consider that the federal government spends about $30 billion per year on all education, training, employment, and social services programs.

Why do people care so much about their weight? There are health concerns that drive the attempt to lose weight. Being overweight can contribute to serious diseases, such as high blood pressure, heart disease, and diabetes. Overweight people have shorter life spans than do people who are not overweight.

The driving force behind most people's attempts to eat less and lose weight, however, is the desire to be more attractive and increase self-esteem (Gruber et al., 2001). Food has become more than something we eat to maintain healthy bodies or because it tastes good, and exercise is not just something we do to improve our health. What we eat and how much we exercise have become linked to feelings of worth, merit, guilt, sin, rebelliousness, and defiance. Weight and how attractive we feel are integral parts of our self-esteem.

For some people, concerns about eating and weight become so overwhelming and behaviors oriented toward eating or avoiding eating get so out of control that they are said to have eating disorders. There are three specific types of eating disorders: anorexia nervosa, bulimia nervosa, and binge-eating disorder. **Anorexia nervosa** is characterized by a pursuit of thinness that leads peo-

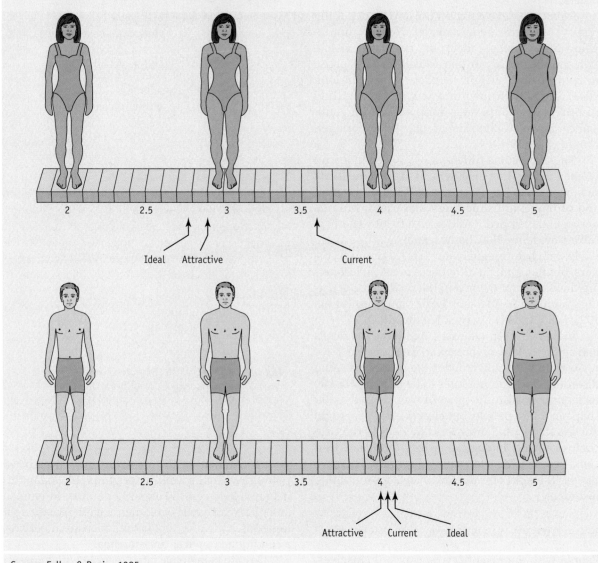

FIGURE 15.2   **Women's and Men's Body Images.** Female and male undergraduates were shown figures of their own sex and asked to indicate figures that looked most like their current shape, their ideal figure, and the figure they felt would be most attractive to the opposite sex. Men selected very similar figures for all three choices, but women selected very different figures for their current figure and either their ideal figure or the figure they thought would be most attractive.

Source: Fallon & Rozin, 1985.

ple to starve themselves. As Princess Diana described, **bulimia nervosa** is characterized by a cycle of bingeing followed by extreme behaviors to prevent weight gain, such as self-induced vomiting. People with **binge-eating disorder** regularly binge but do not engage in behaviors to purge what they eat. The eating disorders are the focus of this chapter.

Traditionally, women have felt more pressure than men to be very thin (see Figure 15.2), and we will see that the eating disorders are much more common among women than men. In recent years,

however, there has been an increased emphasis on men attaining a superfit look, having lean lower bodies and strong, toned upper bodies. A study of boys' action toys found that they have grown more muscular over time, with many contemporary action figures far exceeding the muscularity of even the largest human bodybuilders (Pope et al., 1999b). The number of articles in men's magazines on achieving such a look has risen dramatically, and television stars reach stardom in part because they have this look (Nemeroff et al., 1994). The male centerfolds in *Playgirl* magazine have become increasingly muscular over the past two decades (Leit, Pope, & Gray, 2001). One study found that, on average, men want to be much more muscular than they actually are (Pope et al., 2000). This look is more difficult for some men to attain than for others.

Men who develop eating disorders generally display the same symptoms as women who develop the disorders, including body dissatisfaction and the use of purging and excessive exercise to control their weight (McCabe & Ricciardelli, 2004). Also, both men and women with eating disorders have high rates of depression and substance abuse (Olivardia et al., 1995; Striegel-Moore et al., 1998).

There are some differences between men and women with eating disorders. Men are more likely than women to have histories of being overweight and of bingeing before their anorexia or bulimia nervosa developed (Andersen, 1990). There is mixed evidence that homosexual men are more likely than heterosexual men to have eating disorders, but there are no differences between lesbians and heterosexual women in the prevalence of eating disorders (Andersen, 1990; Mangweth et al., 1997; Schneider, O'Leary, & Jenkins, 1995).

In this chapter, we first explore the diagnosis and epidemiology of the eating disorders. Next, we review what is known about the causes of eating disorders. Societal pressures to be thin may create maladaptive attitudes toward weight and body shape in many people, but clearly most people do not develop eating disorders. We discuss the psychological and biological factors that may lead some people to develop eating disorders. Then, we discuss the most effective treatments for the eating disorders.

ANOREXIA NERVOSA

People with anorexia nervosa starve themselves, subsisting on little or no food for very long periods of time, yet they remain sure that they still need to lose more weight.

Diagnosis, Prevalence, and Prognosis of Anorexia Nervosa

The diagnosis of anorexia nervosa requires that a person refuse to maintain a body weight that is healthy and normal for his or her age and height (see the DSM-IV-TR criteria in Table 15.1). The DSM-IV-TR criteria for anorexia nervosa require that a person's weight be at least 15 percent below the minimum healthy weight for his or her age and height (APA, 2000). Often, the person's weight is much below this. For example, a 5-foot 6-inch

| TABLE 15.1 | DSM-IV-TR |

Diagnostic Criteria for Anorexia Nervosa

The DSM-IV-TR specifies that both intentional extreme weight loss and distorted thoughts about one's body are key features of anorexia nervosa.

A. Refusal to maintain body weight at or above a minimally normal weight for age and height (e.g., weight loss leading to a weight at least 15 percent below minimum healthy body weight, or failure to make expected weight gain during a period of growth, resulting in a weight at least 15 percent below minimum healthy body weight)

B. Intense fear of gaining weight or becoming fat, despite being underweight

C. Distortions in the perception of one's body weight or shape, undue influence of body weight or shape on self-evaluation, or denial of the seriousness of the current low body weight

D. In females who have reached menarche, amenorrhea (absence of at least three consecutive menstrual cycles)

Source: Reprinted with permission from the *Diagnostic and Statistical Manual of Mental Disorders*, Fourth Edition, Text Revision. Copyright © 2000 American Psychiatric Association.

young woman with anorexia may weigh 95 pounds, when the healthy weight for a woman this height is between 120 and 159 pounds. In women and girls who have begun menstruating, the weight loss causes them to stop having menstrual periods, a condition known as **amenorrhea.**

Despite being emaciated, people with anorexia nervosa have intense fears of becoming fat. They have very distorted images of their bodies, often believing they are fat and needing to lose more weight. The self-evaluations of anorexics hinge entirely on their weight and their control over their eating. They believe they are good and worthwhile only when they have complete control over their eating and when they are losing weight. The weight loss causes people with anorexia to be chronically fatigued, yet they drive themselves to exercise excessively and to keep up a grueling schedule at work or school.

People with anorexia often develop elaborate rituals around food, as writer Marya Hornbacher describes in her autobiography, *Wasted* (Hornbacher, 1998, pp. 254–255):

I would spread my paper out in front of me, set the yogurt aside, check my watch. I'd read the same sentence over and over, to prove that I could sit in front of food without snarfing it up, to prove it was no big deal. When five minutes had passed, I would start to skim my yogurt. . . . You take the edge of your spoon and run it over the top of the yogurt, being careful to get only the melted part. Then let the yogurt drip off until there's only a sheen of it on the spoon. Lick it—wait, be careful, you have to only lick a teeny bit at a time, the sheen should last at least four or five licks, and you have to lick the back of the spoon first, then turn the spoon over and lick the front, with the tip of your tongue. Then set the yogurt aside again. Read a full page, but don't look at the yogurt to check the melt progression. Repeat. Repeat. Do not take a mouthful, do not eat any of the yogurt unless it's melted. Do not fantasize about toppings, crumbled Oreos, or chocolate sauce. Do not fantasize about a sandwich. A sandwich would be so *complicated*.

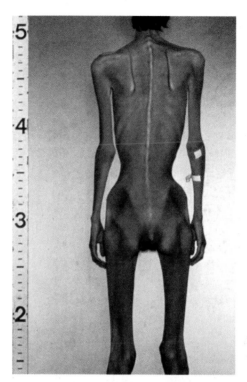

People with anorexia nervosa weigh significantly less than what they should for their height and weight.

About 1 percent of people will develop anorexia nervosa at sometime in their lives, and between 90 and 95 percent of people diagnosed with anorexia nervosa are female (Hoek & van Hoeken, 2003; Striegel-Moore, Dohm, et al., 2003). White women are somewhat more likely than Black women to develop the disorder. Anorexia nervosa usually begins in adolescence, between the ages of 15 and 19 (Striegel-Moore, 1995). The course of the disorder varies greatly from person to person. Long-term studies done in Europe suggest that as many as half of the women who develop anorexia nervosa are fully recovered 10 years after treatment, but the remainder continue to suffer from eating-related problems or other psychopathology, particularly depression (Herpertz-Dahlmann, Muller, et al., 2001; Lowe et al., 2001; Wentz et al., 2001).

Anorexia nervosa is a very dangerous disorder physiologically. The death rate among people with anorexia is 5 to 8 percent (Polivy & Herman, 2002). Some of the most serious consequences of anorexia are the cardiovascular complications, including bradycardia (extreme slowing of heart rate), arrhythmia (irregular heart beat), and heart failure. Another potentially serious complication of anorexia is acute expansion of the stomach, to the point of rupturing. Bone strength is an issue for women with anorexia who have amenorrhea, presumably because low es-

trogen levels affect bone strength. Kidney damage has been seen in some patients with anorexia, and impaired immune system functioning may make people with anorexia more vulnerable to severe illnesses.

Types of Anorexia Nervosa

In the previous Voices excerpt, Hornbacher describes one of the two types of anorexia, the restricting type (see the Concept Overview in Table 15.2 on page 546). People with the **restricting type of anorexia nervosa** simply refuse to eat as a way of preventing weight gain. Some people with anorexia who are restrictors attempt to go for days without eating anything. Most eat very small amounts of food each day, in part simply to stay alive and in part because of pressures from others to eat. Hornbacher survived for months on one cup of yogurt and one fat-free muffin per day. Daphne, in the following case study, also has the restricting type of anorexia nervosa.

Daphne is 5 feet 11 inches tall and weighs 102 pounds. She has felt "large" since her height soared above her schoolmates in the fifth grade. She has been on a diet ever since. During her junior year in high school, Daphne

(continued)

TABLE 15.2 Concept Overview

Comparisons of Eating Disorders

The eating disorders vary on these characteristics.

Symptom	AN*— Restricting Type	AN*— Binge/Purge Type	BN*— Purging Type	BN*— Nonpurging Type	Binge-Eating Disorder
Body weight	Must be underweight by more than 15 percent	Must be underweight by more than 15 percent	Often normal or somewhat overweight	Often normal or somewhat overweight	Often significantly overweight
Body image	Severely disturbed	Severely disturbed	Overconcerned with weight	Overconcerned with weight	Often disgusted with overweight
Binges	No	Yes	Yes	Yes	Yes
Purges or other compensatory behaviors	No	Yes	Yes	No	No
Sense of lack of control over eating	No	During binges	Yes	Yes	Yes
Amenorrhea in females	Yes	Yes	Not usually	Not usually	No

*AN refers to anorexia nervosa, BN to bulimia nervosa.

decided that she had to take drastic measures to lose more weight. She began by cutting her calorie intake to about 1,000 calories per day. She lost several pounds, but not fast enough for her liking, so she cut her intake to 500 calories per day. She also began a vigorous exercise program of cross-country running. Each day, Daphne would not let herself eat until she had run at least 10 miles. Then she would have just a few vegetables and a handful of cereal. Later in the day, she might have some more vegetables and some fruit, but she would wait until she was so hungry that she was faint. Daphne dropped to 110 pounds and she stopped menstruating. Her mother expressed some concern about how little Daphne was eating, but since her mother tended to be overweight, she did not discourage Daphne from dieting.

When it came time to go to college, Daphne was excited but also frightened, because she had always been a star student in high school and wasn't sure she could maintain her straight *As* in college. In the first examination period in college, Daphne got mostly *As*

but one *B*. She felt very vulnerable, like a failure, and as if she was losing control. She also was unhappy with her social life, which, by the middle of the first semester, was going nowhere. Daphne decided that things might be better if she lost more weight, so she cut her food intake to two apples and a handful of cereal each day. She also ran at least 15 miles each day. By the end of fall semester, she was down to 102 pounds. She was also chronically tired, had trouble concentrating, and occasionally fainted. Still, when Daphne looked in the mirror, she saw a fat, homely young woman who needed to lose more weight.

The other type is the **binge/purge type of anorexia nervosa,** in which people periodically engage in bingeing or purging behaviors (e.g., self-induced vomiting or the misuse of laxatives or diuretics). This disorder is different from bulimia nervosa in at least two ways. First, people with the binge/purge type of anorexia continue to be at least 15 percent below a healthy body weight, whereas people with bulimia nervosa are typically at normal weight or somewhat overweight. Second, women with binge/purge anorexia often develop amenorrhea, whereas women with bulimia nervosa usually do not. Often, a person with the binge/purge type of anorexia nervosa does not engage in binges in which she eats large amounts of food; however, if she eats even a small amount of food, she feels as if she has binged and will purge this food.

People with the restricting type of anorexia are more likely than those with the binge/purge type to have deep feelings of mistrust of others and a tendency to deny they have a problem. People with binge/purge anorexia are more likely to have problems with unstable moods and impulse control, with alcohol and other drug abuse, and with self-mutilation (Garner, Garfinkel, & O'Shaughnessy, 1985). They also tend to have more chronic courses of the disorder.

SUMMING UP

- Anorexia nervosa is characterized by self-starvation, a distorted body image, intense fears of becoming fat, and amenorrhea.

- The lifetime prevalence of anorexia is about 1 percent, with 90 to 95 percent of cases being female.

- Anorexia usually begins in adolescence, and the course is variable from one person to another.

- People with the restricting type refuse to eat in order to prevent weight gain.

- People with the binge/purge type periodically engage in bingeing and then purge to prevent weight gain.

BULIMIA NERVOSA

The core characteristics of bulimia nervosa, from which Princess Diana suffered, are uncontrolled eating, or **bingeing**, followed by behaviors designed to prevent weight gain from the binges (see the DSM-IV-TR criteria in Table 15.3). The DSM-IV-TR defines a binge as occurring in a discrete period of time, such as an hour or two, and involving eating an amount of food that is definitely larger than most people would eat during a similar period of time and in similar circumstances. There are tremendous variations among people with eating disorders in the sizes of their binges, however. The average binge is about 1,500 calories. Less than a third of binge episodes contain more than 2,000 calories. One-third of the binge episodes contain only 600 calories, and many people will say that they consider eating just one piece of cake a binge. What makes that a binge for people with an eating disorder is the sense that they have no control over their

TABLE 15.3 DSM-IV-TR
Diagnostic Criteria for Bulimia Nervosa
People with bulimia nervosa regularly binge eat and then attempt to avoid gaining weight from their binge.

A. Recurrent episodes of binge eating, characterized by both of the following:
  1. eating, in a discrete period of time (such as within a two-hour period), an amount of food that is definitely larger than most people would eat during a similar period of time and under similar circumstances
  2. a sense of lack of control over eating during the episode
B. Recurrent inappropriate behaviors to prevent weight gain, such as self-induced vomiting; misuse of laxatives, diuretics, enemas, or other medications; fasting; or excessive exercise
C. The binge eating and inappropriate purging behaviors both occur, on average, at least twice a week for three months.
D. Self-evaluation is unduly influenced by body shape and weight.

Source: Reprinted with permission from the *Diagnostic and Statisical Manual of Mental Disorders,* Fourth Edition, Text Revision. Copyright © 2000 American Psychiatric Association.

eating, that they feel compelled to eat, even though they are not hungry. The DSM-IV-TR recognizes this aspect of binges, and the criteria for a binge include a sense of lack of control over eating.

The behaviors people with bulimia use to control their weight include self-induced vomiting; the abuse of laxatives, diuretics, or other purging medications; fasting; and excessive exercise. As with people with anorexia nervosa, the self-evaluations of people with bulimia nervosa are heavily influenced by their body shapes and weights. When they are thin, they feel like a "good person." People with bulimia nervosa do not tend to show gross distortions in their body images, as people with anorexia nervosa do. Whereas a woman with anorexia nervosa who is emaciated and sees herself as obese, a woman with bulimia nervosa has more realistic perceptions of her actual body shape. Still, people with bulimia are constantly dissatisfied with their shapes and weights and concerned about losing weight.

People with bulimia nervosa are distinguished from people with the binge/purge type of anorexia nervosa primarily by their body weight: The criteria for binge/purge anorexia require that a person be at least 15 percent below normal body weight, whereas there are no weight criteria for bulimia nervosa. People with the restricting type of anorexia nervosa also differ from people with bulimia nervosa in that they do not engage in binges—restrictors severely limit their food intake all of the time (review Table 15.2).

Self-induced vomiting is the behavior people associate most often with bulimia. Bulimia is often discovered by family members, roommates, and friends when people with the disorder are caught vomiting or when they leave messes after they vomit. In one sorority, the frequent purging behavior of the members was discovered in a particularly odd way (Hubbard et al., 1999, p. 52):

> At first it seemed like a minor, if mystifying, problem: In the spring of 1996, plastic sandwich bags began disappearing by the hundreds from the kitchen of a sorority house at a large northeastern university. When the sorority's president investigated, she found a disturbing explanation: The bags, filled with vomit, were hidden in a basement bathroom. "I was shocked," says the president (who later learned that the building's pipes, eroded by gallons of stomach acid, would have to be replaced). "Yet in a way it made sense." Most of her 45 housemates, she recalls, worried about

weight. "It was like a competition to see who could eat the least. At dinner they would say, 'All I had today was an apple,' or 'I haven't had anything.' It was surreal."

Dentists recognize people with bulimia, because frequent vomiting can rot teeth from exposure to stomach acid. People who use self-induced vomiting or purging medications are said to have the **purging type of bulimia nervosa.** The cycle of bingeing and then purging or other compensatory behaviors to control weight becomes a way of life, as in the case of Alice (Spitzer et al., 1981, p. 146):

CASE STUDY

Alice is a single 17-year-old who lives with her parents, who insisted that she be seen because of binge eating and vomiting. She achieved her greatest weight of 180 pounds at 16 years of age. Her lowest weight since she reached her present height of 5 feet 9 inches has been 150 pounds, and her present weight is about 160 pounds. Alice states she has been dieting since age ten and says she has always been . . . slightly chubby. At age 12 she started binge eating and vomiting. She was a serious competitive swimmer at that time, and it was necessary for her to keep her weight down. She would deprive herself of all food for a few days and then get an urge to eat. She could not control this urge, and would raid the refrigerator and cupboards for ice cream, pastries, and other desserts. She would often do this at night, when nobody was looking, and would eat, for example, a quart of ice cream, an entire pie, and any other desserts she could find. She would eat until she felt physical discomfort and then she would become depressed and fearful of gaining weight, following which she would self-induce vomiting. When she was 15 she was having eating binges and vomiting four days a week. Since age 13 she has gone through only one period of six weeks without gaining weight or eating binges and vomiting.

Some social settings, such as being part of a cheerleading team, may increase the risk for eating disorders.

People who use excessive exercise or fasting to control their weight but do not engage in purging are said to have the **nonpurging type of bulimia nervosa.** People who use excessive exercise to control their weight can easily hide their bulimia if they are part of a group that values exercise, such as students on a college campus. The following passage was written by a male psychologist who developed the nonpurging type of bulimia nervosa over a period of years. This man grew up viewing food as a source of comfort and bingeing as a way of escaping from overbearing and disapproving parents. He fasted for a day or more after a binge to control his weight. As the pressures of his job and a failed marriage increased, his bulimic pattern of bingeing and then fasting grew more serious (Wilps, 1990, pp. 19–21).

VOICES

I would sigh with relief when Sunday evening came, since I had no work responsibilities until the next morning, and I would have just returned my son to his mother's custody. I would then carefully shop at convenience stores for "just right" combinations of cheese, lunch meats, snack chips, and sweets such as chocolate bars. I would also make a stop at a neighborhood newsstand to buy escapist paperback novels (an essential part of the binge) and then settle down for a three-hour session of reading and slow eating until I could barely keep my eyes open. My binges took the place of Sunday dinner, averaging approximately 6,000 kilocalories in size. Following the binge, my stomach aching with distension, I would carefully clean my teeth, wash all the dishes, and fall into a drugged slumber. I would typically schedule the following day as a heavy working day with evening meetings in order to distract myself from increasing hunger as I fasted. I began running. . . . I would typically run for one hour, four to five days per week, and walked to work as a further weight control measure. . . . As time went on, I increased the frequency of these binges, probably because of the decreasing structured demands for my time. They went from weekly to twice per week, then I was either bingeing or fasting with no normal days in my week at all. My sleep patterns were either near-comatose or restless, with either sweating after a binge or shivering after a fast. I became increasingly irritable and withdrawn . . . prompting increased guilt on my part that I resented the intrusion of my friends, my patients, and even my son into my cycle. . . . The nadir of my life as a bulimic occurred when I found myself calling patients whom I had scheduled for evening appointments, explaining to them that I was ill, then using the freed evening for bingeing. . . . I was physically exhausted most of the time, and my hands, feet, and abdomen were frequently puffy and edematous, which I, of course, interpreted as gain in body fat and which contributed to my obsession with weight and food. I weighed myself several times per day in various locations, attending to half pound variations as though my life depended on them.

The prevalence of bulimia nervosa is estimated to be between 0.5 and 3 percent in the general population (Wilson, 2005; Striegel-Moore & Franko, 2003). It is much more common in women than in men, and in European Americans than in African Americans (Striegel-Moore, Dohm, et al., 2003).

Symptoms of bulimia nervosa are quite common, particularly among adolescent and young adult women, and Figure 15.3 on page 550 lists questions from one of the surveys commonly used to measure maladaptive eating attitudes. One study of 2,200 students in six colleges around the United States found that 15 percent of the women admitted to having engaged in some purging behavior, and 28 percent classified themselves as obsessed with their weight (rates for men on the two questions were 4 percent and 11 percent, respectively) (Rozin et al., 2003).

Researchers in Oregon followed a large group of adolescents for several years, examining the ebb and flow of what they called *partial-syndrome eating disorders*—behaviors that smack of anorexia or bulimia nervosa but don't meet the full criteria for the disorders (Lewinsohn, Striegel-Moore, & Seeley, 2000; Striegel-Moore, Seeley, & Lewinsohn, 2003). Adolescents with partial-syndrome eating disorders may binge at least once a week, but not multiple times per week. They may be underweight, but not a full 15 percent underweight. They tend to be highly concerned with their weight and judge themselves on the basis of their weight. However, their symptoms don't add up to a full-blown eating disorder.

The researchers found that the adolescents with partial-syndrome eating disorders, the vast majority of whom were girls, were just as likely as those with full-blown eating disorders to have several psychological problems, both as adolescents and later in their twenties. These problems included anxiety disorders, substance abuse, depression,

FIGURE 15.3

Check Your Own Attitudes Toward Eating. Psychologist David Garner and colleagues (Garner, Olmstead, & Polivy, 1984) developed the Eating Disorder Inventory to assess people's attitudes and behaviors toward eating and their bodies. People who score higher on this questionnaire are more prone to eating disorders. As you read through these items, think about whether you would say each one is true of you always, usually, often, sometimes, rarely, or never. If you find you have answered "usually" or "always" to many of these items, you might want to reconsider your attitudes toward food and your body and perhaps talk to someone you trust about them.

Eating Disorder Inventory

I think my stomach is too big.

I eat when I am upset.

I stuff myself with food.

I think about dieting.

I think that my thighs are too large.

I feel ineffective as a person.

I feel extremely guilty after overeating.

I am terrified of gaining weight.

I get confused as to whether or not I am hungry.

If I gain a pound, I worry that I will keep gaining.

I have the thought of trying to vomit in order to lose weight.

I eat or drink in secrecy.

Source: From D. Garner, A. K. Cooke, and H. E. Marano, "The 1997 Body Image Survey" in *Psychology Today,* 30–44, 1997. Reprinted with permission from *Psychology Today Magazine,* Copyright © 1997 Sussex Publishers, Inc.

and attempted suicide. Almost 90 percent had a full-blown psychiatric disorder when they were in their early twenties. Those with partial-syndrome eating disorders also had lower self-esteem, poorer social relationships, poorer physical health, and lower life satisfaction than those with no signs of an eating disorder. They were less likely to have earned a bachelor's degree and more likely to be unemployed.

The onset of bulimia nervosa most often occurs between the ages of 15 and 29 (Striegel-Moore,

1995). Many people with bulimia nervosa are of normal weight or are slightly overweight. You might conclude, then, that bulimia is not as physically dangerous as anorexia. Although the death rate among people with bulimia is not as high as among people with anorexia, bulimia also has serious medical complications. One of the most serious is an imbalance in the body's electrolytes, which results from fluid loss following excessive and chronic vomiting, laxative abuse, and diuretic abuse. Electrolytes are biochemicals that help regulate the heart, and imbalances in electrolytes can lead to heart failure.

Bulimia nervosa tends to be a chronic condition. People seeking treatment for this disorder typically report years of unremitting symptoms. A study of the natural course of bulimia nervosa in 102 women, most of whom did not receive treatment, found that, over a five-year period, half to two-thirds had some form of eating disorder of clinical severity at each of several assessment points over that period (Fairburn et al., 2000, 2003). One-third still had a diagnosable eating disorder at the end of five years. The factors associated with a more persistent course include obesity as a child, an excessive valuation of shape and low weight, increasing dietary restraint, and a high level of social maladjustment.

Cultural and Historical Trends

Several theorists have argued that the eating disorders are culture-bound syndromes, occurring primarily in wealthy, developed countries in which food is abundant and thinness is highly valued (Garner & Garfinkel, 1980; McCarthy, 1990; Sobal & Stunkard, 1989). In addition, the prevalence of eating disorders may have increased over recent decades, as the availability of food has increased but cultural norms (at least in the United States and Europe) have increasingly prized thinness for women (Striegel-Moore, 1995; Stunkard, 1997).

Keel and Klump (2003) did a meta-analysis of existing studies to test these ideas. As we discussed in Chapter 3, in a meta-analysis, all studies relevant to a hypothesis—in this case, that the prevalence of the eating disorders varies across cultures and over time—are analyzed together and the trends across the studies are summarized statistically. Keel and Klump found that the evidence for cultural and historical differences in the prevalence of eating disorders was different for anorexia and bulimia nervosa.

There was only modest evidence of cultural or historical differences in the prevalence of anorexia nervosa. Cases of self-starvation have been described since the medieval times and in most re-

Standards of beauty vary greatly across cultures.

gions of the world. The motivations given for self-starvation do seem to vary across culture and time. In "non-Westernized" countries and in centuries past, the stated motivations for excessive fasting have had less to do with weight concerns and more to do with stomach discomfort, or with religious reasons (Keel & Klump, 2003). Patients with anorexia in Asian countries also do not have the distorted body images that are characteristic of anorexia in the United States and Europe and readily admit that they are very thin. Nonetheless, they stubbornly refuse to eat, as is illustrated by the case of one Chinese woman (adapted from Sing, 1995, pp. 27–29):

CASE STUDY

Miss Y, aged 31, was 5 foot 3 inches. She had formerly weighed 110 pounds but now weighed 48 pounds. Her anorexia began four years previously, when she was suddenly deserted by her boyfriend, who came from a neighboring village. Greatly saddened by his departure for England, Miss Y started to complain of abdominal discomfort and reduced her food intake. She became socially withdrawn and unemployed. At her psychiatric examination, she wore long hair and was shockingly emaciated—virtually a skeleton. She had sunken eyes, hollow cheeks, and pale, cold skin. She recognized her striking wasting readily but claimed a complete lack of hunger and blamed the weight loss on an unidentifiable abdominal problem. Her concern over the seriousness of her physical condition was perfunctory. When asked whether she consciously tried to restrict the amount she ate, she said, "No." When questioned why she had gone for periods of eight or more waking hours without eating anything, she said it was because she had no hunger and felt distended, pointing to the lower left side of her abdomen. All physical examinations revealed no biological source for her feelings of distension, however. Miss Y was often in a low mood and became

(continued)

transiently tearful when her grief over the broken relationship was acknowledged. However, she resisted all attempts to discuss this loss in detail and all other psychological and medical treatments. Miss Y later died of cardiac arrest. Postmortem examination revealed no specific pathology other than multiple organ atrophy due to starvation.

One question that can be raised is whether self-starvation in the absence of weight concerns can be called anorexia nervosa, since weight concerns are a defining feature of the disorder in the DSM-IV-TR. On the other hand, the DSM-IV-TR itself is a culture-bound document, representing Western views of mental disorders.

In contrast to the prevalence data for anorexia nervosa, the prevalence of bulimia nervosa does seem to vary substantially across cultures and across historical time. It is considerably more common in the past 50 years than previously, and in Westernized cultures than in non-Westernized cultures. Keel and Klump (2003) suggest that bulimia nervosa may vary more by culture and historical period because the bingeing that is part of this disorder requires the availability of abundant food, whereas people can starve themselves, as in anorexia nervosa, whether or not food is abundant.

SUMMING UP

- Bulimia nervosa is characterized by uncontrolled bingeing, followed by behaviors designed to prevent weight gain from the binges.

- People with the purging type use self-induced vomiting, diuretics, or laxatives to prevent weight gain.

- People with the nonpurging type use fasting and exercise to prevent weight gain.

- The definition of a binge has been controversial, but the DSM-IV-TR specifies that it must involve the consumption of an unusually large amount of food in a short time, as well as a sense of lack of control.

- The prevalence of the full syndrome of bulimia nervosa is estimated to be between 0.5 and 3 percent. It is much more common in women than in men.

- The onset of bulimia nervosa is most often in adolescence, and its course, if left untreated, is unclear.

- Although people with bulimia nervosa do not tend to be severely underweight, there are a

variety of possible medical complications of the disorder.

BINGE-EATING DISORDER

The DSM-IV-TR mentions one further eating disorder, called binge-eating disorder. This disorder resembles bulimia nervosa in many ways, except that a person with binge-eating disorder does not regularly engage in purging, fasting, or excessive exercise to compensate for binges. Binge-eating disorder is not one of the officially recognized forms of eating disorders in the DSM-IV-TR largely because its authors felt that there has been too little research on this disorder to sanction the diagnosis. Rather, the diagnostic criteria for binge-eating disorder were placed in the appendix of the DSM-IV-TR for further study.

People with binge-eating disorder may eat continuously throughout the day, with no planned mealtimes. Others engage in discrete binges on large amounts of food, often in response to stress and feelings of anxiety or depression. They may eat very rapidly and be almost in a daze as they eat, as the man in the following case study describes.

CASE STUDY

"The day after New Year's Day I got my check cashed. I usually eat to celebrate the occasion, so I knew it might happen. On the way to the bank I steeled myself against it. I kept reminding myself of the treatment and about my New Year's resolution about dieting. . . .

"Then I got the check cashed. And I kept out a hundred. And everything just seemed to go blank. I don't know what it was. All of my good intentions just seemed to fade away. They just didn't seem to mean anything anymore. I just said, 'What the hell,' and started eating, and what I did then was an absolute sin."

He described starting in a grocery store where he bought a cake, several pieces of pie, and boxes of cookies. Then he drove through heavy midtown traffic with one hand, pulling food out of the bag with the other hand and eating as fast as he could. After consuming all of his groceries, he set out on a furtive round of restaurants, staying only a short time in each and eating only small amounts. Although in constant dread of discovery, he had no idea what "sin" he felt he was committing. He knew only that it was not pleasurable. "I didn't en-

(continued)

joy it at all. It just happened. It's like a part of me just blacked out. And when that happened there was nothing there except the food and me, all alone." Finally he went into a delicatessen, bought another $20 worth of food and drove home, eating all the way, "until my gut ached." (Stunkard, 1993, pp. 20–21)

People with binge-eating disorder are often significantly overweight and say they are disgusted with their bodies and ashamed of their bingeing. They typically have histories of frequent dieting, memberships in weight-control programs, and family obesity (Fairburn et al., 1997). As many as 30 percent of people currently in weight-loss programs may have binge-eating disorder. In contrast, approximately 1 to 3 percent of the general population has the disorder (Striegel-Moore et al., 2003; Striegel-Moore & Franko, 2003).

As with anorexia and bulimia nervosa, binge-eating disorder is more common in women than in men, in both the general community and among people in weight-loss programs. The symptom of binge-eating is more common in African American women than European American women, but at least one study found that European American women are more likely than African American women to be diagnosed with the full syndrome of binge-eating disorder (Striegel-Moore, Dohm, et al., 2003; Striegel-Moore & Franko, 2003). People with binge-eating disorder have high rates of depression and anxiety and possibly more alcohol abuse and personality disorders than those without binge-eating disorder (Castonguay, Eldredge, & Agras, 1995; Telch & Stice, 1998). One study found that 18 percent of a group of 48 women with binge-eating disorder, most of whom had sought no treatment, still had an eating disorder five years later, usually binge-eating disorder (Fairburn et al., 2000). This suggests that the course of this disorder is more favorable than that of anorexia nervosa or bulimia nervosa, but a subset of people with this disorder do have it chronically.

SUMMING UP

- Binge-eating disorder is a provisional diagnosis in the DSM-IV-TR. It is characterized by binge eating in the absence of behaviors designed to prevent weight gain.
- Binge eating is common, perhaps more so among African Americans than among European Americans, but binge-eating disorder affects only about 2 percent of the population.

- Women are more likely than men to develop binge-eating disorder.

UNDERSTANDING EATING DISORDERS

A number of biological, sociocultural, and psychological factors have been implicated in the development of the eating disorders (see the Concept Overview in Table 15.4). It is likely that it takes an accumulation of several of these factors for any individual to develop an eating disorder. In this section, we consider each of these factors, as well as the evidence regarding each factor.

Biological Theories

As is the case with most psychological disorders, anorexia and bulimia nervosa tend to run in families (Bulik, 2004). There are a few large, population-based twin studies of anorexia nervosa, and they have found that 48 to 74 percent of the variability in the disorder is due to genetic factors (Klump et al., 2001; Kortegaard et al., 2001; Wade et al., 2000). Twin studies of bulimia nervosa put the heritability

TABLE 15.4 Concept Overview
Contributors to the Eating Disorders
A number of biological, sociocultural, and psychological factors have been said to contribute to the eating disorders.
Biological Factors
Genetic predisposition to eating disorders
Predisposition to depression
Dysregulation of hypothalamus
Serotonin imbalances
Sociocultural and Psychological Factors
Pressures to be thin
Cultural norms of attractiveness
Food used as a way of coping with negative emotions
Overconcern with others' opinions
Rigid, dichotomous thinking style, perfectionism
Family dynamics characterized by overcontrolling parents who do not allow the expression of emotion
History of sexual abuse

[handwritten margin notes: "Bio." ; "Psycho Social" ; "ie Biopsychosocial Method."]

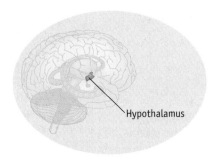

The hypothalamus plays a central role in regulating eating and is implicated in disordered eating behavior in bulimia and anorexia.

of this disorder at 59 to 83 percent (Bulik, Sullivan, & Kendler, 1998; Wade et al., 1999).

Much of the current research on the biological causes of bulimia and anorexia focuses on the bodily systems that regulate appetite, hunger, satiety, the initiation of eating, and the cessation of eating. The *hypothalamus* plays a central role in regulating eating. It receives messages about the body's recent food consumption and nutrient level and sends messages to cease eating when the body's nutritional needs have been met. These messages are carried by a variety of neurotransmitters, including norepinephrine, serotonin, and dopamine, and a number of hormones, such as cortisol and insulin. Disordered eating behavior might be caused by imbalances in or the dysregulation of any of the neurochemicals involved in this system or by structural or functional problems in the hypothalamus. For example, if this system were disrupted, it could cause the individual to have trouble detecting hunger accurately or to stop eating when full, which are both characteristics of people with eating disorders.

There is evidence that people with eating disorders have disruptions in the hypothalamus (Study Group on Anorexia Nervosa, 1995). People with anorexia nervosa show lowered functioning of the hypothalamus and abnormalities in the levels or regulation of several hormones important to the functioning of the hypothalamus, including serotonin and dopamine (Brambilla et al., 2001; Frank et al., 2001). It is unclear whether these disruptions are causes or consequences of the self-starvation of anorexia. Some studies find that people with anorexia continue to show abnormalities in hypothalamic and hormonal functioning and in neurotransmitter levels after they gain some weight, whereas other studies show that these abnormalities disappear with weight gain (Polivy & Herman, 2002).

Many people with bulimia show abnormalities in the neurotransmitter serotonin (Franko et al., 2004; Wurtman, 1987; Wurtman & Wurtman, 1984). Deficiencies in serotonin might lead the body to crave carbohydrates, and people with bulimia often binge on high-carbohydrate foods. They may then take up self-induced vomiting or other types of purges in order to avoid gaining weight from eating carbohydrates.

Thus, a number of biological abnormalities are associated with anorexia nervosa and bulimia ner-

vosa. These abnormalities could contribute to disordered eating behavior by causing the body to crave certain foods or by making it difficult for a person to read the body's signals of hunger and fullness. Just why people with eating disorders also develop the distorted body images and other cognitive and emotional problems seen in the eating disorders is not clear. In addition, many of the biological abnormalities seen in the eating disorders might be the consequences, rather than the causes, of the disorders.

Sociocultural and Psychological Factors

Societal pressures to be thin and attractive probably play a role in the eating disorders, although many people who are exposed to these pressures do not develop eating disorders. Certain psychological factors may also need to come into play for an eating disorder to develop.

Societal Pressures and Cultural Norms

Psychologists have linked the historical and cross-cultural differences in the prevalence of eating disorders to differences in the standards of beauty for women at different historical times and in different cultures (Garner & Garfinkel, 1980; McCarthy, 1990; Sobal & Stunkard, 1989). In addition, certain groups within a culture, such as athletes, may have standards for appearance that put them at greater risk for eating disorders.

Standards of Beauty The ideal shape for women in the United States and Europe has become thinner over the past 45 years. Models in fashion magazines, winners of the Miss America and Miss Universe pageants, and Barbie dolls—all icons of beauty for women—have been getting thinner (Garner & Garfinkel, 1980; Keel & Klump, 2003; Wiseman et al., 1992) (see Figure 15.4). Indeed, the average model in a fashion magazine these days is pencil thin, with a figure that is physically unattainable by most adult women.

Both anorexia nervosa and bulimia nervosa are much more common in females than in males. This gender difference has largely been attributed to the fact that thinness is more valued and encouraged in females than in males. For example, studies of popular women's and men's magazines find 10 times more diet articles in women's magazines than in men's magazines (Andersen & DiDomenico, 1992; Nemeroff et al., 1994). Half of all women report frequent dissatisfaction with their appearance, whereas fewer than one-third of men report the same (Thompson & Stice, 2001). In recent years, women's magazines have moved somewhat away

FIGURE 15.4 | **Our Changing Beauty Standards.** In the period from 1959 to 1978, the average weight of women who were *Playboy* centerfolds or who won the Miss America contest became lower and lower, relative to what would be expected for women of their height.

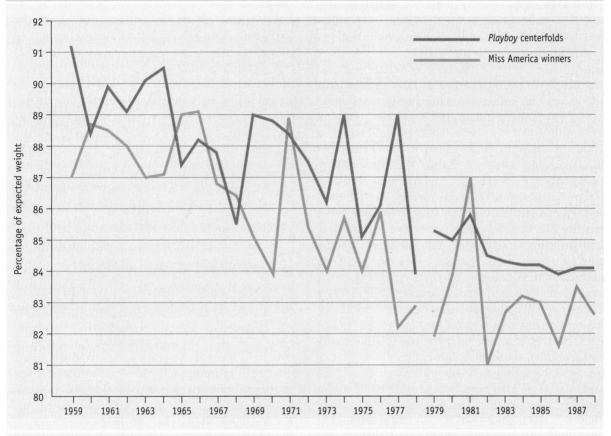

Source: From C. V. Wiseman, et al., "Cultural Expectations of Thinness in Women: An Update" in *International Journal of Eating Disorders,* 11. Copyright © 1992 John Wiley & Sons, Inc.

from articles solely on dieting toward articles on fitness and exercise (Nemeroff et al., 1994). Unfortunately, however, women's motivations for exercise are still more likely to be for weight control than are men's motivations, and exercising for weight control is more likely to contribute to eating-disordered behavior than is exercising for health (McDonald & Thompson, 1992).

The thin-ideal promoted in women's magazines seems to have an effect on women's attitudes toward themselves. Stice and Shaw (1994) showed young women images from fashion magazines of ultra-thin models, or images from magazines that didn't portray thin models, for a three-minute period (Stice & Shaw, 1994). These women who saw the fashion magazine images experienced increases in depression, shame, guilt, stress, insecurity, and body dissatisfaction, compared with the women exposed to the other images. In turn, those women who had the most increases in negative mood and body dissatisfaction, and who most strongly sub-

scribed to the thin-ideal for women, showed increases in the symptoms of bulimia. If just three minutes of exposure to these fashion models can have such effects, think what the constant exposure that young women experience does to their self-image and well-being.

Stice and colleagues looked at what chronic exposure to the thin-ideal in fashion magazines actually does to adolescent girls' mental health (Stice, Spangler, & Agras, 2001). They randomly gave 219 girls, ages 13 to 17, a 15-month subscription to a leading fashion magazine or no subscription, then followed them over time. They found that the girls who already felt pressured to be thin and dissatisfied with their bodies became more depressed over time if they had been given the subscription to the fashion magazine than if they had not. In addition, the girls who started the study with little social support from family members and friends became more dissatisfied with their bodies, dieted more, and showed more bulimic symptoms if they were given the fashion magazine subscription than if they were not.

Adolescent girls and women can avoid pressures to be thin to some extent by avoiding fashion magazines and other media depictions of the thin-ideal. We can't completely avoid our friends, however, and they are sometimes the worst carriers of the thin-ideal message. In another study, Stice, Maxfield, and Wells (2003) had women college students talk to another college woman whom they thought was just another student, but who was really an accomplice in their study. This accomplice was a thin, attractive 19-year-old woman who was 5 foot 10 inches tall and weighed only 127 pounds (they also had a second accomplice who was 20 years old, 5 foot 9 inches, and 126 pounds). First, both the target woman student and the accomplice watched a neutral film about a seascape, supposedly so they could rate how they felt about the film. But, after the film, the accomplice launched into a prescripted conversation with the target woman student. In the *pressure condition*, the accomplice complained about how dissatisfied she was with her weight and discussed the extreme exercise routine and restrictive diet she was using to reduce her weight. In the *neutral condition*, the accomplice talked about classes she was currently taking and her plans for the weekend. Then, the experimenter entered the room and both women filled out questionnaires on how they felt about their bodies. The target women in the pressure condition became significantly more dissatisfied with their own bodies after talking with the thin accomplice about her own weight concerns. In contrast, the women in the neutral condition did not become more dissatisfied with their bodies after talking with the same woman about matters unrelated to weight or dieting.

Of course, not all women accept the thin-ideal for themselves. Table 15.5 lists some items from questionnaires designed to assess the internalization of the thin-ideal. Longitudinal studies have shown that women who internalize the thin-ideal are more likely to develop bulimic symptoms, as well as to show increases in dieting and body dissatisfaction over time (Stice, 2003; Thompson & Stice, 2001). Experimental studies have shown that interventions designed to get women to argue against the thin-ideal and recognize pressures from the media to subscribe to this ideal result in reductions in women's acceptance of this ideal and decreases in body dissatisfaction, dieting, and bulimic pathology (Stice et al., 2000; Stice, Chase, Stormer, et al., 2001; Stormer & Thompson, 1998).

Athletes and Eating Disorders One group that appears to be at increased risk for unhealthy eating habits and full-blown eating disorders is athletes,

---

TABLE 15.5 Items from Questionnaires Measuring Internalization of the Thin-Ideal

These are some items assessing women's internalization of the thin-ideal promoted in today's media.

I would like my body to look like the women that appear in TV shows and movies.

I wish I looked like the women pictured in magazines that model underwear.

Music videos that show women who are in good physical shape make me wish that I were in better physical shape.

Slender women are more attractive.

Women with toned bodies are more attractive.

Women with long legs are more attractive.

Sources: Stice & Agras, 1998; Thompson et al., 1999.

---

especially those in sports in which weight is considered an important factor in competitiveness, such as gymnastics, ice skating, dancing, horse racing, wrestling, and bodybuilding (Smolak, Murnen, & Ruble, 2000). Researchers in Norway assessed all the 522 elite female athletes between the ages of 12 and 35 in that country for the presence of eating disorders. They found that those in sports classified as "aesthetic" or "weight-dependent," including diving, figure skating, gymnastics, dance, judo, karate, and wrestling, were most likely to have anorexia or bulimia nervosa (Sundgot-Borgen, 1994) (see Table 15.6). When the women athletes with eating disorders were asked about the triggers for their eating disorders, many said they felt that the physical changes of puberty came too early for them and decreased their competitive edge. They had started dieting severely to try to maintain their prepubescent figures. The case of Heidi, described by her therapist, illustrates several of these triggers (adapted from Pipher, 1994, pp. 165–168):

> Heidi arrived in my office after gymnastics practice. Blond and pretty, she was dressed in a shiny red and white warm-up suit. We talked about gymnastics, which Heidi had been involved in since she was six. At that time, she was selected to train with the university coaches. Now she trained four hours a day, six
> *(continued)*

TABLE 15.6 Rates of Eating Disorders in Elite Women Athletes

Sports that emphasize weight are especially likely to encourage eating disorders.

Sport	Percentage with an Eating Disorder
Aesthetic sports (e.g., figure skating, gymnastics)	35
Weight-dependent sports (e.g., judo, wrestling)	29
Endurance sports (e.g., cycling, running, swimming)	20
Technical sports (e.g., golf, high jumping)	14
Ball game sports (e.g., volleyball, soccer)	12

Source: Data from Sundgot-Borgen, 1994.

CASE STUDY

days a week. She didn't expect to make an Olympic team, but she anticipated a scholarship to a Big-8 school.

Heidi glowed when she talked about gymnastics, but I noticed her eyes were red and she had a small scar on the index finger of her right hand. (When a hand is repeatedly stuck down the throat, it can be scarred by the acids in the mouth.) I wasn't surprised when she said she was coming in for help with bulimia.

Heidi said, "I've had this problem for two years, but lately it's affecting my gymnastics. I am too weak, particularly on the vault, which requires strength. It's hard to concentrate.

"I blame my training for my eating disorder," Heidi continued. "Our coach has weekly weigh-ins where we count each others' ribs. If they are hard to count we're in trouble."

I clucked in disapproval. Heidi explained that since puberty she had had trouble keeping her weight down. After meals, she was nervous that she'd eaten too much. She counted calories; she was hungry but afraid to eat. In class she pinched the fat on her side and freaked out. The first time she vomited after a gymnastics meet. Coach took her and the other gymnasts to a steak house. Heidi ordered a double cheeseburger and onion rings. After she ate, she obsessed about the weigh-in the next day, so she decided, just this once, to get rid of her meal. She slipped into the restaurant bathroom and threw up.

She blushed. "It was harder than you would think. My body resisted, but I was able to do it. It was so gross that I thought, 'I'll never do that again,' but a week later I did. At first it was weekly, then twice a week. Now it's almost every day. My dentist said that acid is eating away the enamel of my teeth."

Bodybuilding is an increasingly popular sport, but bodybuilders routinely have substantial weight fluctuations as they try to shape their bodies for competition and then binge in the off-seasons. For example, one study compared male bodybuilders with men with diagnosed eating disorders. This study found that the bodybuilders had a pattern of eating and exercising as obsessive as that of the men with eating disorders, but with a focus on gaining muscle, rather than losing fat (Mangweth et al., 2001). In another study of male bodybuilders, 46 percent reported bingeing after most competitions, and 85 percent reported gaining significant weight (an average of 15 pounds) in the off-season. Then, they dieted to prepare for competition, losing an average of 14 pounds (Anderson et al., 1995). In a parallel study of female bodybuilders and weight lifters, 42 percent

Sports that require certain body shapes or weights, such as bodybuilding, seem to breed eating disorders.

reported having been anorexic at sometime in their lives, 67 percent were terrified of being fat, and 58 percent were obsessed with food (Anderson et al., 1995). A study of female weightlifters found that they often abused ephedrine, a stimulant that helps reduce body fat, particularly if they had symptoms of an eating disorder (Gruber & Pope, 1998).

Amateur athletics may actually protect some young women against eating disorders. Smolak et al. (2000) reviewed studies of the relationship between athletics and eating problems in women. They concluded that, although elite athletes do show increased rates of eating disorders, nonelite athletes, particularly those participating in high school sports in which thinness is not emphasized, show lower rates of eating problems than nonathletes.

Socioeconomics and Ethnicity In the United States and Europe, there may be differences among socioeconomic and ethnic groups in the prevalence of eating disorders. Some studies find that anorexia and bulimia nervosa are more prevalent among the upper and middle classes than among lower socioeconomic classes. This association between socioeconomic status and these eating disorders is found among Caucasians, African Americans, and Hispanics. Perhaps because African Americans and Hispanics are more likely than Caucasians to be in lower socioeconomic groups, the overall rates of anorexia and bulimia are lower in African Americans and Hispanics than in Caucasians (Mulholland & Mintz, 2001; Pate et al., 1992). Other researchers have argued that the rate of these eating disorders is lower in African Americans and Hispanics because they are less likely to accept the thin-ideal promoted in Caucasian culture (Osvold & Sodowsky, 1993).

Bingeing and Emotion Regulation

The bingeing of eating disorders sometimes serves as a maladaptive strategy for dealing with painful emotions, as Princess Diana described her own binge eating (Fairburn et al., 1995; McCarthy, 1990). Depressive symptoms and negative affect have been found to predict the future onset or exacerbation of bulimic symptoms (Cooley & Toray, 2001; Field et al., 1999; Killen et al., 1996; Stice, Burton, & Shaw, 2004; Stice, Presnell, & Spangler, 2002), as well as relapse into binge eating among obese people (Byrne et al., 2003). For example, Stice and colleagues (2002) followed a group of adolescent girls over two years. They found that the girls who engaged in emotional eating—eating when they felt distressed in an attempt to feel bet-

ter—were significantly more likely to develop chronic binge eating over the two years.

In addition, Stice and colleagues (2002) have identified two subtypes of disordered eating patterns involving binge eating. One subtype is connected to excessive attempts at losing weight. Women with this *dieting subtype* are greatly concerned about their body shapes and sizes, and they try their best to maintain a strict, low-calorie diet but frequently fall off the wagon and engage in binge eating. They then use vomiting or exercise to try to purge themselves of the food or the weight it puts on their bodies. The other subtype is the *depressive subtype.* These women are also concerned about weight and body size but are plagued by feelings of depression and low self-esteem; they often eat to quell these feelings.

Women with the depressive subtype of disordered eating patterns suffer even greater social and psychological consequences over time than women with the dieting subtype of disordered eating (Stice et al., 2002). They have more difficulties in their relationships with family and friends; are more likely to suffer significant psychiatric disorders, such as anxiety disorders; and are less likely to respond well to treatment. One long-term study found that, over a period of five years, women with the depressive subtype were more likely to be diagnosed with major depression or an anxiety disorder and were more likely to continue to engage in severe binge eating, compared with women who had the dieting subtype (Stice & Fairburn, 2003). Indeed, 80 percent of the women with the depressive subtype developed a full-blown major depression over that five years.

Cognitive Models of Eating Disorders

Several types of negative cognitions are associated with an increased risk for eating disorders, particularly bulimia nervosa in women. Fairburn (1997) proposed a cognitive model of bulimia nervosa that suggests that the overvaluation of appearance is of primary importance in the development of the disorder. According to Fairburn (1997), people who consider their body shape one of the most important aspects of their self-evaluation, and who believe that achieving thinness will bring social and psychological benefits, will engage in excessive dieting and purging behaviors to reduce their weight. In line with Fairburn's model, a meta-analysis of relevant studies found that women who internalize the thin-ideal for women and are dissatisfied with their own bodies show greater eating pathology (Stice, 2002).

Vohs and colleagues (1999, 2001) have suggested that disordered eating is especially likely to result when body dissatisfaction is combined with perfectionism and low self-esteem. Women who are dissatisfied with their bodies and have a deep need to be perfect, including to have a perfect body, but who have low self-esteem will engage in maladaptive strategies to control their weight, including excessive dieting and purging. Vohs and colleagues found that young women with all three of these cognitive characteristics were more likely to develop bulimic symptoms than women with just one or two of these characteristics.

Other research confirms that people with eating disorders are more concerned with the opinions of others, are more conforming to others' wishes, and are more rigid in their evaluations of themselves and others than are other people (Polivy & Herman, 2002; Striegel-Moore, Silberstein, & Rodin, 1993). Studies of the cognitions of people with eating disorders show that they have a dichotomous thinking style, in which everything is either all good or all bad. For example, if they eat one cookie, they may think that they have blown their diets and might as well eat the whole box of cookies. They will say they cannot break their rigid eating routines or they will completely lose control over their eating. They obsess over their eating routines and plan their days down to the smallest detail around these routines.

The cognitions of women with eating disorders may be organized around issues of body size and control even at a nonconscious level. Women with and without significant symptoms of bulimia were shown a variety of pictures of other women. The women in these pictures varied in terms of both their body size and the emotions shown on their faces, although the participants were not told that these were the critical dimensions along which the photos varied. Women with bulimic

symptoms were more likely than women without bulimic symptoms to attend to information about body size than information about facial emotion, as well as to classify the photos on the basis of body size rather than facial emotion (Viken et al., 2002). These results suggest that women who have bulimic symptoms organize their perceptions of the world around body size, even at an implicit level, more than women who do not have significant bulimic symptoms.

Family Dynamics

Hilde Bruch (1973, 1982) is a pioneer in the psychoanalytic study of eating disorders. Her theory is most concerned with girls who develop anorexia nervosa, although it has also been used to understand the development of bulimia nervosa and binge-eating disorder. Bruch noted that anorexia nervosa often occurs in girls who have been unusually "good girls," high achievers, dutiful and compliant daughters who are always trying to please their parents and others by being "perfect." These girls tend to have parents who are overinvested in their daughters' compliance and achievements, who are overcontrolling, and who will not allow the expression of feelings, especially negative feelings.

Another pioneer in theorizing about anorexia, Salvador Minuchin, describes the families of people with anorexia as **enmeshed families** (Minuchin et al., 1978). There is extreme interdependence and intensity in the family interactions, so that the boundaries between the identities of individual family members are weak and easily crossed. This might describe the family life of Princess Diana when she was part of the Royal Family.

Bruch argues that, throughout their daughters' lives, these parents are ineffective and inappropriate in their parenting, responding primarily to the parents' own schedules and needs, rather than to their daughters' needs for food or comfort (Bruch, 1973). As a result, the daughters do not learn to identify and accept their own feelings and desires. Instead, they learn to monitor closely the needs and desires of others and to comply with others' demands, as we can see in the case of Rachel and her family:

CASE STUDY

Rachel is a 16-year-old with anorexia nervosa. Her parents are highly educated and very successful, having spent most of their careers in the diplomatic corps. Rachel, her two brothers, and her parents are "very close, as are many families in the diplomatic corps, because we move so much," although the daily care of the children has always been left to nannies. The children had to follow strict rules for appropriate conduct, both in the home and outside. These rules were partly driven by the requirements of the families of diplomats to "be on their best behavior" in their host country and partly driven by Rachel's parents' very conservative religious beliefs. Rachel, as the only daughter in the family, always had to behave as "a proper lady" to counteract the stereotype of American girls as brash and sexually promiscuous. All the children were required to act mature beyond their years, controlling any emotional outbursts, taking defeats and disappointments without complaint, and happily picking up and moving every couple of years when their parents were reassigned to another country.

Rachel's anorexic behaviors began when her parents announced they were leaving the diplomatic corps to return to the United States. Rachel had grown very fond of their last post in Europe, because she had finally found a group of friends that she liked *and* whom her parents approved of, and she liked her school. She had always done well in school but often had hated the harshly strict schoolteachers. In her present school, she felt accepted by her teachers as well as challenged by the work. When Rachel told her parents she would like to finish her last year of high school in this school rather than go to the United States with them, they flatly refused to even consider it. Rachel tried to talk with her parents, suggesting she stay with the family of one of her friends, who was willing to have her, but her parents cut her off and told her they would not discuss the idea further. Rachel became sullen and withdrawn and stopped eating shortly after the family arrived in the United States.

As a result of such family dynamics, girls with anorexia have fundamental deficits in their senses of self and identities. They experience themselves as always acting in response to others, rather than in response to their own wishes and needs. They do not accurately identify their own feelings or desires and, thus, do not cope appropriately with distress. They do not even accurately identify bodily sensations, such as hunger, and this may contribute greatly to their ability to starve themselves for long periods of time.

Why do eating disorders often develop in adolescence? One of the important tasks of adolescence is separation and individuation from one's family. Girls from these families deeply fear separation, because they have not developed the ability to act and think independently of their families. They also fear involvement with peers, especially sexual involvement, because they do not understand their feelings or trust their judgment, yet they recognize at some level their need to separate from their families and take their place among their peers. They harbor rage against their parents for their overcontrol. They become angry, negativistic, defiant, and distrustful. They also discover that controlling their food intake both gives them a sense of control over their lives and elicits concern from their parents. The rigid control of their bodies provides a sense of power over the self and the family that the girls have never had before. It also provides a way of avoiding peer relationships—the girl dons the persona of someone with anorexia—sickly, distant, untouchable, and superior in her self-control. Other psychoanalytic theorists have taken this argument further to suggest that a girl with anorexia is primarily avoiding sexual maturity and relationships by stopping pubertal maturation by self-starvation (Lerner, 1986).

Why would girls, but not boys, in such families develop eating disorders? It may be because, in general, parents tend to appreciate the need for boys to separate from the family in adolescence and give them the freedom to separate. Especially in these enmeshed families, parents are terrified of their girls' independence. The mothers of these girls may need their daughters to remain dependent because their own identities are tied too closely to their daughters (Bruch, 1973; Palazzoli, 1974). Thus, there are tremendous pressures on girls to remain enmeshed with their families, but boys have more opportunity to break free and build their own identities.

Research has confirmed that the families of girls with eating disorders have high levels of conflict, that the expression of negative emotions is discouraged in the families, and that control and perfectionism are key family themes (Polivy & Herman, 2002). These negative characteristics are not specific to the families of girls with eating disorders, however. They are also prevalent in the families of children with depression, anxiety disorders, and several other forms of psychopathology. What may distinguish families in which eating disorders develop is that the mothers in these families believe their daughters should lose more weight, are critical of overweight in their daughters, and are themselves more likely to have disordered eating patterns (Hill & Franklin, 1998). In addition, a lack of awareness of their own bodily sensations may allow some girls in these families to ignore even the most severe hunger pangs (Leon et al., 1995). Girls who come from these troubled families but are not able to ignore their hunger completely may fall into a binge/purge form of anorexia nervosa or into bulimia nervosa.

Unfortunately, the majority of studies of the families and personality characteristics of people with anorexia or bulimia have compared people who already have eating disorders with those who do not (Polivy & Herman, 2002). As a result, it is not known to what extent these family and personality characteristics are causes of anorexia or bulimia. The controlling nature of parents' behaviors toward their children may be a consequence as well as a cause of the disorder—parents are exerting control to try to save their children's lives.

Similarly, many of the personality characteristics of people with eating disorders may be consequences as well as causes of the disorder. Studies of healthy people who engage in self-starvation as part of an experiment show that depression, anxiety, rigidity, obsessiveness, irritability, concrete thinking, and social withdrawal appear after a few weeks of self-starvation (Keys et al., 1950). The success of psychological therapies for eating disorders provides more evidence that psychological factors are implicated in the development or at least the maintenance of these disorders.

A controversial theory that has gained much attention is that the eating disorders often result from experiences of sexual abuse. One reason that this theory has been controversial is that it stems from clinical reports of high rates of sexual abuse among persons seeking therapy for eating disorders rather than from controlled studies. Another reason is that it has led some therapists to urge their clients with eating disorders to search through their pasts for memories of childhood sexual abuse and then take action against their abusers as part of their therapy. Proponents of this theory argue that survivors of sexual abuse develop eating disorders as a symbol of self-loathing and a way of making themselves unattractive in an attempt to prevent further sexual abuse.

Several careful studies have been done to examine the rates of sexual abuse among women and men with eating disorders and to compare these rates with those of people with other psychological disorders and people with no disorders (see the review by Polivy & Herman, 2002; also Bulik et al., 1997; Kinzl et al., 1994; Pope & Hudson, 1992; Rorty, Yager, & Rossotto, 1994; Welch & Fairburn, 1994). These studies have found that, although people with eating disorders tend to have higher rates of sexual abuse than people with no psychological disorders, they do not tend to have higher rates of sexual abuse than do people with other psychological disorders, such as depression or anxiety. In other words, sexual abuse seems to be a general risk factor for psychological problems, including eating disorders, depression, and anxiety, rather than a specific risk factor for eating disorders.

SUMMING UP

- There is evidence that tendencies toward both anorexia nervosa and bulimia nervosa are heritable.

- Eating disorders may be tied to dysfunction in the hypothalamus, a part of the brain that helps regulate eating behavior.

- Some studies show abnormalities in levels of the neurotransmitters serotonin and norepinephrine in people with eating disorders.

- Cultural and societal norms regarding beauty may play a role in the eating disorders. Eating disorders are more common in groups that consider extreme thinness attractive than in groups that consider a heavier weight attractive.

- Eating disorders develop as a means of gaining some control over or of coping with negative emotions. In addition, people with eating disorders tend to show rigid, dichotomous thinking.

- People who develop eating disorders tend to come from families that are overcontrolling and perfectionistic but that discourage the expression of negative emotions.
- People who are so unaware of their own bodily sensations that they can starve themselves may develop anorexia nervosa. People who remain aware of their bodily sensations and cannot starve themselves but who are prone to anxiety and impulsivity may develop binge-eating disorder or bulimia nervosa.
- Girls may be more likely than boys to develop eating disorders in adolescence because girls are not given as much freedom as boys to develop independence and their own identities.
- People with eating disorders are more likely than people without eating disorders to have a history of sexual abuse, but a history of sexual abuse is also common among people with several other disorders.

TREATMENTS FOR EATING DISORDERS

In this section, we discuss several psychotherapies and biological treatments that have proven successful in the treatment of anorexia, of bulimia, or both (see the Concept Overview in Table 15.7). There are several empirical studies of the effectiveness of treatments for bulimia nervosa and an increasing number for binge-eating disorder. The number of studies for anorexia nervosa is low, and many of these studies are plagued by small sample sizes and other methodological problems (Wilson, 2005).

Psychotherapy for Anorexia Nervosa

It can be very difficult to engage people who have anorexia nervosa in psychotherapy. Because they often feel that others try to control them and that they must maintain absolute control over their own behaviors, they can be extremely resistant to

---

TABLE 15.7   Concept Overview

Treatments for Eating Disorders

A number of treatments for the eating disorders have been developed.

Treatment	Description
Anorexia Nervosa	
1. Hospitalization and refeeding	1. Hospitalize the patient and force him or her to ingest food to prevent death from starvation.
2. Behavior therapy	2. Make rewards contingent upon eating. Teach relaxation techniques.
3. Techniques to help the patient accept and value his or her emotions	3. Use cognitive or supportive-expressive techniques to help the patient explore the emotions and issues underlying behavior.
4. Family therapy	4. Raise the family's concern about anorexic behavior. Confront the family's tendency to be overcontrolling and to have excessive expectations.
Bulimia Nervosa	
1. Cognitive-behavioral therapy	1. Teach the client to recognize the cognitions around eating and to confront the maladaptive cognitions. Introduce "forbidden foods" and regular diet and help the client confront irrational cognitions about these.
2. Interpersonal therapy	2. Help the client identify interpersonal problems associated with bulimic behaviors, such as problems in a marriage, and deal with these problems more effectively.
3. Supportive-expressive psychodynamic therapy	3. Provide support and encouragement for the client's expression of feelings about problems associated with bulimia in a nondirective manner.
4. Tricyclic antidepressants and selective serotonin reuptake inhibitors.	4. Help reduce impulsive eating and negative emotions that drive bulimic behaviors.

therapists' attempts to change their behaviors and attitudes. Regardless of the type of psychotherapy a therapist uses with client with anorexia, much work must be done to win the client's trust and participation in the therapy and to maintain this trust and participation as the client begins to regain that dreaded weight.

Winning the trust of someone with anorexia can be especially difficult if the therapist is forced to hospitalize her because she has lost so much weight that her life is in danger, yet hospitalization and forced refeeding are often necessary to save her life. Because people with anorexia nervosa typically do not seek treatment themselves, they often do not come to the attention of therapists until they are so emaciated and malnourished that they have a medical crisis, such as cardiac problems, or their families fear for their lives. The first job of the therapist is to help save the individual's life. Because a person with anorexia will not eat voluntarily, this may mean hospitalizing her and feeding her intravenously. During the hospitalization, the therapist begins the work of engaging the client in facing and solving the psychological issues causing her to starve herself.

Individual Therapy

Individual therapy with people with anorexia often focuses on their inability to recognize and trust their own feelings, with the goal of building their self-awareness and independence from others (Bruch, 1973). This can be very difficult, because many clients with anorexia are resistant to therapy and suspicious of therapists, whom they think are just other people trying to control their lives. Others may be engaged in therapy but look to therapists to define their feelings for them, just as their parents have done for years. Therapists must convey to clients that their feelings are their own, valuable and legitimate, and the proper focus of attention in therapy. Only when clients can learn to read their feelings accurately will they also read their sensations of hunger and fullness accurately and be able to respond to them.

Behavior therapies are often used in the treatment of anorexia. Rewards are made contingent upon the person's gaining weight. If the client is hospitalized, certain privileges in the hospital are used as rewards, such as watching television, going outside the hospital, or receiving visitors. The client may also be taught relaxation techniques, which she can use as she becomes extremely anxious about ingesting food. Some studies suggest that the majority of patients benefit from behavior therapies, gaining weight to within 15 percent of normal body weight (Agras, 1987; Fairburn, 2005).

However

The relapse rate with behavior therapies alone is very high, however. Most patients return to their anorexic eating patterns soon after therapy ends or they are released from the hospital, unless they are engaged in other therapies that confront some of the emotional issues accompanying their anorexia.

Family Therapy

In *family systems therapy,* the person with anorexia and her family are treated as a unit (Minuchin et al., 1978). With some families, therapists must first raise the parents' level of anxiety about their children's eating disorders, because the parents have been implicitly or explicitly supporting the children's avoidance of food. Therapists will identify the patterns in the families' interactions that are contributing to their children's sense of being controlled, such as being overprotective while not allowing their children the right to express their own needs and feelings. Parents' unreasonable expectations for their children are confronted, and families are helped to develop healthy ways of expressing and resolving conflict between the members.

One study of 50 girls with anorexia and their families found that family therapy was successful with 86 percent of the cases (Minuchin et al., 1978). These successful girls had normal eating patterns and good relations at home and at school even 2½ years after treatment. This study focused on young girls (an average age of 14 years) who had shown anorexic symptoms for only a short time. Other studies suggest that girls with anorexia who have shown symptoms for much longer and who are older when they enter treatment are not as likely to benefit from family therapy (Dare et al., 1990).

Psychotherapy can help many people with anorexia, but it typically is a long process, often taking years for full recovery. Along the way, many people with anorexia who have an initial period of *in the short term* recovery, with a restoration of their weight to normal levels and their eating to healthy patterns, relapse into bulimic or anorexic behaviors. They often continue to have self-esteem deficits, family problems, and periods of depression and anxiety (Eckert et al., 1995). Most therapists combine techniques from different modes of therapy to meet the individual needs of people with anorexia. Even multimethod inpatient treatment programs do not consistently overcome anorexia, however, and graduates of these programs often continue to show severely restrained eating, perfectionism, and low body weight (Sullivan et al., 1998). The difficulty in helping people with anorexia recover fully may indicate the depth of the psychological issues driving self-starvation.

Taking Psychology Personally

Is There Such a Thing as a Healthy Diet?

There are negative health effects of being overweight, as well as some radical public health policies to reduce the amount of high-calorie food people consume. But why not simply propose that overweight people go on a diet?

One big problem with diets is that many people who develop eating disorders begin their dysfunctional patterns simply by going on diets (Abbott et al., 1998; Fairburn et al., 1997). Their diets may be innocuous at first, the type of diets most people think are safe and healthy, such as diets that are low in fats and high in fruits and vegetables. The diets may then become more and more extreme, perhaps because the simple and healthy diets do not achieve the desired weight loss.

Even moderate dieting can create a set of psychological and physiological conditions that make it difficult for an individual to maintain healthy eating patterns. Dieting creates chronic frustration, irritability, and emotional reactivity, which can make people more impulsive in their eating patterns (Federoff, Polivy, & Herman, 1997; Polivy & Herman, 2002). Dieting also changes people's ability to read their bodies' cues about hunger and satiety and people's attitudes toward food.

In a classic study, researchers compared the eating patterns of chronic dieters with the patterns of people not dieting. These people were taken into a laboratory and first asked to drink two milkshakes, one milkshake, or no milkshake. Then they were asked to try three flavors of ice cream and to rate the ice cream. The people who were not dieting decreased the amount of ice cream they ate as a function of how many milkshakes they had consumed before the rating task: The more milkshakes they had consumed during the "preload," the less ice cream they ate during the rating task. The chronic dieters, however, ate more ice cream during the rating task if they had consumed milkshakes during the preload. Those who had consumed two milkshakes during the preload ate even more ice cream during the rating task than did those who had consumed only one milkshake (Herman & Mack, 1975). Dieters develop beliefs that, if they violate their diets in any way, they might as well violate them totally and binge. In addition, dieting may enhance the physiological appeal of forbidden foods, making it difficult to resist them, especially after a taste or smell of them. People actually prefer sweet-tasting foods more when they are on diets than when they are not (Rodin, Slochower, & Fleming, 1977).

Another physiological explanation is that each person has a "natural" weight, which the body will fight to maintain, even if the person attempts to lose weight (Keesey, 1986). This natural weight is often referred to as a **set point**. The set point is determined in part by a person's metabolic rate, which is known to be heavily influenced by genetics (Wadden, Brownell, & Foster, 2002). When a person diets, his metabolic rate actually slows down, reducing his body's need for food. Unfortunately, the slowing of the metabolic rate also means that the body is not using up the food he consumes as quickly, making it more likely that this food will turn to fat, even though he may be eating much less food than usual. The implication of this *set*

In *Taking Psychology Personally: Is There Such a Thing as a Healthy Diet?*, we explore whether people who do need to diet can do so healthily.

Psychotherapy for Bulimia Nervosa

Treatment for bulimia nervosa is different from treatment for anorexia nervosa in many ways. First, by the time a person with anorexia nervosa obtains treatment, she may be near death, so extreme measures may need to be taken to save her life, such as hospitalization and forced refeeding. This is less likely to be the case for a person with bulimia nervosa. Second, the psychological issues of anorexia and bulimia can be different. For people with anorexia, these issues often have to do with family dynamics, concerns about losing control, and a greatly distorted body image. For people with bulimia, psychological issues may involve learning to cope more effectively with emotions, learning to control binge and purge behaviors, and learning more adaptive ways to think about food and one's body.

Cognitive-behavioral therapy (CBT) has received the most empirical support for the effective treatment of bulimia nervosa (Whittal, Agras, & Gould, 1999; Wilson 2005). This therapy is based on the view that the extreme concerns about shape and weight are the central features of the disorder (Fairburn, 1997). The therapist teaches the client to monitor the cognitions that accompany her eating, particularly her binge episodes and her purging episodes (Wilson, Fairburn, & Agras, 1997). Then,

Taking Psychology Personally (*continued*)

point theory is that permanently changing weight may require some people to be on highly restrictive diets permanently.

People rarely stay on restrictive diets or keep their weight off after diets, however. In 1992, *Consumer Reports* did a survey of 95,000 of its readers who had tried to lose weight in the previous three years (*Consumer Reports*, 1993). One in five of these readers had joined commercial weight-loss programs, such as Weight Watchers. Interestingly, 25 percent of these people who had joined commercial weight-loss programs were not even moderately overweight at the start. On average, the people who had joined commercial weight-loss programs lost 10 to 20 percent of their starting weight, but they gained back half that weight in six months and two-thirds of the weight in two years. Only 25 percent of them kept the weight off for more than two years.

What's an overweight person to do, then? Exercise is one thing. Exercise may be the one way people can overcome the effects of dieting on metabolic rates and keep their weight off (Jeffery et al., 1998). People who exercise regularly increase their basal metabolic rate, so the body burns more calories, even when at rest. Thus, people who exercise may be able to maintain lower weights, even without continuing to restrict the amount of food they eat. In addition, several studies show that moderate exercise (the equivalent of 30 to 60 minutes per day of brisk walking, either in small spurts or all at once) is associated with substantial decreases in health risks and mortality, even among people with genetic predispositions to

major diseases, people who smoke, and people who are overweight (Blair, Lewis, & Booth, 1989; Paffenberger et al., 1986). Thus, even if people do not lose weight through exercise, they may be improving their health and increasing their longevity.

Obesity experts also agree that decreasing the intake of fats and salt and increasing the intake of complex carbohydrates have positive health effects, even if they do not lead to weight loss. Most of us can reduce fats in our diet by switching from whole milk to skim milk and from high-fat meats to lower-fat meats and fish and by using low-fat dressings and spreads. We can increase complex carbohydrates by snacking on fruits, vegetables, and whole grains, rather than on fatty foods, such as potato chips and cookies.

Overweight people who want to lose weight might consider trying to achieve "reasonable" weight loss, rather than "ideal" weights (Wadden et al., 2002). The effects of biological factors, such as genetics, on weight may be strong enough that overweight people can never achieve the ideal weights they wish to chieve, at least not without chronic self-starvation. Many overweight people find themselves bingeing out of hunger or frustration or yo-yo dieting, both of which harm their self-esteem and possibly their health. If overweight people can adopt healthier diets, exercise regularly, and stabilize at weights that are reasonable, given their family backgrounds and their histories of weight loss and gain, both their physical and psychological health may improve.

---

the therapist helps the client confront these cognitions and develop more adaptive attitudes toward her weight and body shape. An interchange between a therapist and client might go like this:

VOICES

Therapist: What were you thinking just before you began to binge?

Client: I was thinking that I felt really upset and sad about having no social life. I wanted to eat just to feel better.

Therapist: And, as you were eating, what were you thinking?

Client: I was thinking that the ice cream tasted really good, that it was making me feel

good. But I was also thinking that I shouldn't be eating this, that I'm bingeing again. But then I thought that my life is such a wreck that I deserve to eat what I want to make me feel better.

Therapist: And what were you thinking after you finished the binge?

Client: That I was a failure, a blimp, that I have no control, that this therapy isn't working.

Therapist: Okay, let's go back to the beginning. You said you wanted to eat because you thought it would make you feel better. Did it?

(continued)

Client: Well, as I said, the ice cream tasted good and it felt good to indulge myself.

Therapist: But, in the long run, did bingeing make you feel better?

Client: Of course not. I felt terrible afterward.

Therapist: Can you think of anything you might say to yourself the next time you get into such a state, when you want to eat in order to make yourself feel better?

Client: I could remind myself that I'll feel better only for a little while, but then I'll feel terrible.

Therapist: How likely do you think it is that you'll remember to say this to yourself?

Client: Not very likely.

Therapist: Is there any way to increase the likelihood?

Client: Well, I guess I could write it on a card or something and put the card near my refrigerator.

Therapist: That's a pretty good idea. What else could you do to prevent yourself from eating when you feel upset? What other things could you do to relieve your upset, other than eat?

Client: I could call my friend Keisha and talk about how I feel. Or I could go for a walk—someplace away from food—like up in the hills, where it's so pretty. Walking up there always makes me feel better.

Therapist: Those are really good ideas. It's important to have a variety of things you can do, other than eat, to relieve bad moods.

 The behavioral components of this therapy involve introducing forbidden foods (such as bread) back into the client's diet and helping her confront her irrational thoughts about these foods, such as "If I have just one doughnut, I'm inevitably going to binge." Similarly, the client is taught to eat three healthy meals a day and to challenge the thoughts she has about these meals and the possibility of gaining weight. Cognitive-behavioral therapy for bulimia usually lasts about three to six months and involves 10 to 20 sessions.

Controlled studies of the efficacy of cognitive-behavioral therapy for bulimia find that about one-half of clients completely stop the binge/purge cycle (Wilson, 2005; Wilson et al., 2002). Clients undergoing this therapy also show a decrease in depression and anxiety, an increase in social functioning, and a lessening of concern about dieting and weight. Comparisons with drug therapies show that cognitive-behavioral therapy is more effective than drug therapies in producing the complete cessation of binge eating and purging and in preventing relapse in the long term (Wilson, 2005).

Other studies of the treatment of bulimia have compared cognitive-behavioral therapy (CBT) with three other types of therapy—*interpersonal therapy (IPT), supportive-expressive psychodynamic therapy,* and behavior therapy without a focus on cognitions (Agras et al., 2000; Fairburn, Jones, et al., 1991; Fairburn et al., 1995; Garner et al., 1993; Wilson et al., 1999, 2002). In interpersonal therapy, client and therapist discuss interpersonal problems that are related to the client's eating disorder, and the therapist works actively with the client to develop strategies to solve these interpersonal problems. In supportive-expressive therapy, the therapist encourages the client to talk about problems related to the eating disorder, especially interpersonal problems, but in a highly nondirective manner. In behavior therapy, the client is taught how to monitor her food intake, is reinforced for introducing avoided foods into her diet, and is taught coping techniques for avoiding bingeing. In the studies, all the therapies resulted in significant improvement in the clients' eating behaviors and emotional well-being, but the cognitive-behavioral and interpersonal therapy clients showed the greatest and most enduring improvements. Comparisons of CBT and IPT suggest that CBT is significantly more effective than IPT and works more quickly, with substantial improvement being shown in CBT by three to six weeks into treatment (Agras et al., 2000; Fairburn, Jones, et al., 2001; Wilson et al., 1999, 2002).

For binge-eating disorder, cognitive-behavioral therapy has been shown to be more effective than no treatment and than antidepressant medications (Grilo et al., 2002; Ricca et al., 2001). Interpersonal therapy has proven equally effective as CBT for binge-eating disorder (Wilfley et al., 1993, 2002). In addition, *dialectical behavior therapy (DBT),* which was originally developed to treat borderline personality disorder (Linehan, Kanter, & Comtois, 1999), has proven effective in the treatment of binge-eating disorder. Dialectical behavior therapy has many of the components of cognitive-behavioral therapy, but it focuses on deficits of emotion regulation as key to disordered eating behavior. In one study, 44 women with binge-eating disorder were randomly assigned to group DBT or to no treatment (Telch, Agras, & Linehan, 2001). After 20 weeks of treatment, 89 percent of the women in the DBT group had stopped binge eating, compared with 12.5 percent of the women in the no treatment group. Six months following treatment, 56 percent of the women were still abstaining from binge eating. (The women in the control group received treatment during this time, so follow-up data were not available for them.)

In general, psychotherapies have had more success in reducing binge eating than in reducing weight in obese people with binge-eating disorder (Wonderlich et al., 2003).

Biological Therapies

Recall that many people with eating disorders are also depressed or have histories of depression in their families. This connection to depression has led many psychiatrists to use antidepressant drugs to treat the eating disorders, particularly bulimia nervosa (de Zwann, Roerig, & Mitchell, 2004). *Tricyclic antidepressants* are superior to placebos in reducing bingeing and vomiting and in enhancing a sense of control in people with bulimia (e.g., McCann & Agras, 1990). Patients with bulimia often continue to engage in severe dieting, however, and relapse into the binge/purge cycle shortly after stopping the drugs. The *monoamine oxidase (MAO) inhibitors* also have proven more effective than placebos in the treatment of bulimia but are not typically prescribed, because they require severe dietary restrictions to prevent dangerous side effects.

The *selective serotonin reuptake inhibitors (SSRIs)*, such as fluoxetine (trade name Prozac), have been the focus of much research on biological treatments for bulimia nervosa. These drugs appear to reduce binge-eating and purging behaviors, but they often do not restore the individual to normal eating habits (deZwann et al., 2004). Adding cognitive-behavioral therapy to antidepressant treatment increases the rate of recovery from the disorder (Wilson, 2005).

Tricyclic antidepressants and MAO inhibitors have not been proven effective in the treatment of anorexia in controlled clinical trials (deZwann et al., 2004). Fluoxetine may be helpful in treating anorexia, once patients have been restored to a normal weight (Kaye et al., 2001).

For people with binge-eating disorder, antidepressants do not appear to be as consistently effective in reducing binge eating as do cognitive-behavioral treatments (Wonderlich et al., 2003).

SUMMING UP

- People with anorexia nervosa often must be hospitalized, because they are so emaciated and malnourished that they are in a medical crisis.
- Behavior therapy for anorexia nervosa involves making rewards contingent upon the client's eating. Clients may be taught relaxation techniques to handle their anxiety about eating.
- Family therapy focuses on understanding the role of anorexic behaviors in the family unit. Therapists challenge parents' attitudes toward their children's behaviors and try to help the family find more adaptive ways of interacting with each other.
- Individual therapy for anorexia may focus on helping clients identify and accept their feelings and confront their distorted cognitions about their bodies.
- Psychotherapy can be helpful for anorexia but is usually a long process, and the risk for relapse is high.
- Several studies show that cognitive-behavioral therapy, which focuses on distorted cognitions about eating, is effective in the treatment of bulimia.
- Interpersonal therapy, which focuses on the quality of a client's relationships, and supportive-expressive therapy, can be effective in the treatment of bulimia.
- Tricyclic antidepressants and selective serotonin reuptake inhibitors have been shown to be helpful in the treatment of bulimia. The MAO inhibitors can also be helpful but are not usually prescribed, because they require dietary restrictions to avoid side effects.
- Antidepressants have not proven as useful in the treatment of anorexia nervosa, but some studies suggest that the selective serotonin reuptake inhibitors may be helpful.

CHAPTER INTEGRATION

Several experts have suggested that a group of biological, psychological, and social factors interact to create the eating disorders (Agras & Kirkley, 1986; Polivy & Herman, 2002; Striegel-Moore, 1993). Any one of these factors alone may not be enough to push someone to develop anorexia or bulimia nervosa but may do so when combined (see Figure 15.5 on page 568).

First, societal pressures for thinness clearly provide a potent impetus for the development of unhealthy attitudes toward eating, especially for women. If these pressures were simply toward

FIGURE 15.5   **Multiple Pathways into the Eating Disorders**

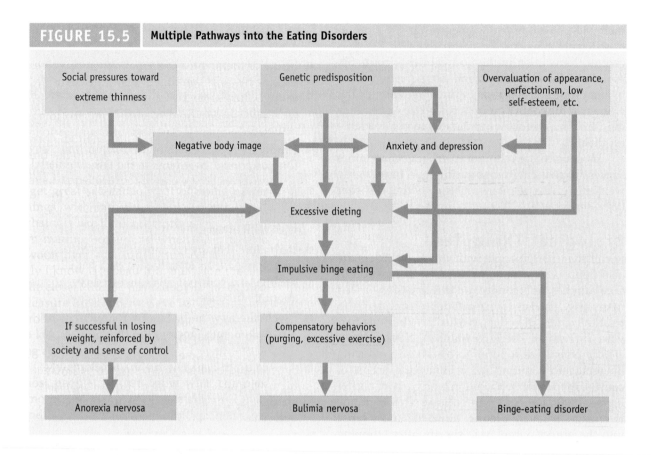

achieving a healthy weight and the maintenance of fitness, they would not be so dangerous. However, the ideal weight for women promoted by beauty symbols in developed countries is much lower than that considered healthy and normal for the average woman; thus, she develops a negative body image. This leads her to engage in excessive dieting. Unfortunately, excessive dieting sets up the conditions for impulsive binge eating, which then makes her have negative emotions and even lower self-esteem.

Second, biological factors may interact with these societal pressures to make some people more likely than others to develop eating disorders. People who develop eating disorders may have genetic predispositions to these disorders or to the dysregulation of their hormones or neurotransmitters. It is unclear just how their genetic vulnerabilities lead to the symptoms of eating disorders, but they may contribute to an ability to diet excessively. Another biological factor that may predispose some people to acquiesce to the pressures to diet and be thin is a tendency toward anxiety or mild depression. Many people with eating disorders, especially people with bulimia, are easily distressed and emotionally labile and tend to eat impulsively in response to their moods. Although problems in mood in people with eating disorders

may be the result of environmental circumstances or of the stresses of having eating disorders, they may also be biologically caused in at least some people who develop eating disorders.

Personality factors may also interact with societal pressures to be thin and/or with the biological predispositions described to lead some people to develop eating disorders. Perfectionism, all-or-nothing thinking, and low self-esteem may make people more likely to engage in extreme measures to control their weight in response to unwelcome weight gains or in an attempt to achieve an ideal of attractiveness and therefore increase their self-esteem. These personality characteristics are more likely to develop in children whose parents are lacking in affection and nurturance and, at the same time, are controlling and demanding of perfection.

Whatever pathway an individual takes into the eating disorders, these behaviors tend to be maintained once they begin. The excessive concern over weight among people with anorexia or bulimia nervosa is constantly reinforced by societal images, and any weight loss they achieve is reinforced by peers and family. People with anorexia may also be reinforced by the sense of control they gain over their lives by dieting. People with bulimia nervosa and binge-eating disorder may greatly desire control but are unable to maintain it and, so, fall into binge eating as an escape from negative emotions and thoughts about the self. The compensatory behaviors of bulimia nervosa help the individual regain some sense of control, however fragile, and thus are reinforced.

Thus, it may take a mixture of these factors, rather than any single one, to lead someone to de-velop a full eating disorder. Once the disorder sets in, however, it tends to be reinforced and perpetu-ated. Note also that many of the same factors con-tribute to each of the eating disorders.

Extraordinary People: Follow-Up

Although Diana, Princess of Wales led an extra-ordinary life, the triggers for her eating disorders were very common, as she explained in her BBC interview:

Question: What was the cause?

Diana: The cause was the situation where my husband and I had to keep everything together because we didn't want to disappoint the pub-lic, and yet obviously there was a lot of anxiety going on within our four walls.

Question: Do you mean between the two of you?

Diana: Uh, uh.

Question: And so you subjected yourself to this phase of bingeing and vomiting?

Diana: You could say the word subjected, but it was my escape mechanism, and it worked, for me, at that time.

Question: Did you seek help from any other members of the Royal Family?

Diana: No. You, you have to know that when you have bulimia you're very ashamed of your-self and you hate yourself, so—and people think you're wasting food—so you don't dis-cuss it with people. And the thing about bulimia is your weight always stays the same, whereas with anorexia you visibly shrink. So you can pre-tend the whole way through. There's no proof. . . .

Question: How long did this bulimia go on for?

Diana: A long time, a long time. But I'm free of it now.

Question: Two years, three years?

Diana: Mmm. A little bit more than that.

Diana suffered symptoms of depression, but she felt she had to be "perfect" at all times and show no weakness, even to her immediate family. The bu-limia became a release valve for her negative emo-tions, but it further damaged her self-esteem and sense of control. Diana perceived her family as un-supportive and overcontrolling and felt unable to reach out to them directly, so she used the bulimic behaviors as cries for help. As most of the world knows, Diana and her husband, Charles, divorced in 1996. She continued to live a glamorous life with the elite of Europe—and to be a devoted mother to her sons, William and Harry—until her death in a car crash in 1997.

Chapter Summary

- The eating disorders include anorexia nervosa, bulimia nervosa, and binge-eating disorder. (Review Table 15.2.)

- Anorexia nervosa is characterized by self-starvation, a distorted body image, intense fears of becoming fat, and amenorrhea. (Review Table 15.1.) People with the restricting type of anorexia nervosa refuse to eat in order to prevent weight gain. People with the binge/purge type periodically engage in bingeing and then purge to prevent weight gain.

- The lifetime prevalence of anorexia is about 1 percent, with 90 to 95 percent of cases being female. Anorexia nervosa usually begins in adolescence, and the course is variable from one person to another. It is a very dangerous disorder, and the death rate among people with anorexia is between 5 and 8 percent.

■ Bulimia nervosa is characterized by uncontrolled bingeing, followed by behaviors designed to prevent weight gain from the binges. (Review Table 15.3.) People with the purging type use self-induced vomiting, diuretics, or laxatives to prevent weight gain. People with the nonpurging type use fasting and exercise to prevent weight gain.

■ The prevalence of bulimia nervosa is between 0.5 and 3 percent. The onset of bulimia nervosa is most often in adolescence. Although people with bulimia do not tend to be underweight, there are several dangerous medical complications in bulimia nervosa.

■ People with binge-eating disorder engage in bingeing, but not in purging or behaviors designed to compensate for the binges. It is more common in women than in men, and people with the disorder tend to be significantly overweight. Binge-eating disorder is not officially recognized by the DSM-IV-TR, but the diagnostic criteria were placed in an appendix for further study.

■ The biological factors implicated in the development of the eating disorders include genetics, the dysregulation of hormonal and neurotransmitter systems, and generally lower functioning in the hypothalamus. (Review Table 15.4.)

■ Sociocultural theorists have attributed the eating disorders to pressures toward thinness in Western cultures and in the media. (Review Table 15.4.)

■ Eating disorders may develop in some people as maladaptive strategies for coping with negative emotions. Also, certain cognitive factors, including the overvaluation of appearance, perfectionism, low self-esteem, excessive concern about others' opinions, and a rigid, dichotomous thinking style may contribute to the development of the eating disorders. (Review Table 15.4.)

■ The families of girls with eating disorders may be overcontrolling, overprotective, and hostile and may not allow the expression of feelings. In adolescence, these girls may develop eating disorders as a way of exerting control. (Review Table 15.4.)

■ Sexual abuse is a risk factor for eating disorders, as well as for several other psychological problems. (Review Table 15.4.)

■ There are few treatments for anorexia shown to be successful in empirical studies. Cognitive-behavioral therapy has proven the most effective therapy for reducing the symptoms of bulimia and preventing relapse. Interpersonal therapy, supportive-expressive therapy, and behavior therapy also appear to be effective for bulimia nervosa. Antidepressants are effective in treating bulimia, but the relapse rate is high. (Review Table 15.7.)

■ Biological, psychological, and social factors may interact to create eating disorders. Any one factor alone may not be enough to push someone to develop an eating disorder, but combinations of these factors may do so. (Review Figure 15.5.) Whatever pathway an individual takes into the eating disorders, these behaviors tend to be maintained once they begin.

MindMap CD-ROM

The following resources on the MindMap CD-ROM that came with this text will help you to master the content of this chapter and prepare for tests:

■ Videos: Anorexia Nervosa; Bulimia Nervosa
■ Interactive Segment: Perception of Body Shape
■ Chapter Timeline
■ Chapter Quiz

Key Terms

anorexia nervosa 542
bulimia nervosa 543
binge-eating disorder 543
amenorrhea 544
restricting type of anorexia nervosa 545
binge/purge type of anorexia nervosa 546

bingeing 547
purging type of bulimia nervosa 548
nonpurging type of bulimia nervosa 548
enmeshed families 559
set point 564

> Chapter 16

Shadow of Her Former Self
by Diana Ong

I don't know whether it's normal or not, but sex has always been something that I take seriously. I would put it higher than tennis on my list of constructive things to do.

—Art Buchwald, *Leaving Home: A Memoir* (1993)

Sexual Disorders <

Extraordinary People

David Reimer: *The Boy Who Was Raised as a Girl*

In April 1966, 8-month-old Bruce Reimer was to undergo a routine circumcision to alleviate a painful medical condition on his penis. The operation went terribly wrong, however, and Bruce's penis was accidentally severed. None of the doctors whom Bruce's anguished parents consulted could offer any hope of restoring the penis and suggested that Bruce would never be able to function as a normal male. Dr. John Money of Johns Hopkins University offered them a solution, however—raise Bruce as a girl and have him undergo sex reassignment therapy. Money firmly believed that one's gender identity depends on the environment in which one is raised, not on the genes or genitals with which one is born. He had published several papers on his work with hermaphrodites—children born with a variety of anomalies of the internal and external sex organs that made them neither obviously male nor female. His research showed that the sex the children were assigned by their parents was the sex they later identified themselves as, regardless of their chromosomal makeup.

Money's theories were at the center of raging controversies in psychology and psychiatry in the 1950s and 1960s about the origins of gender identity. As writer John Colapinto (2001) chronicles in *As Nature Made Him: The Boy Who Was Raised as a Girl*, Money was the leader of a group of sex researchers who argued that gender identity is entirely determined by environment, not biology. On the opposite side were researchers such as Milton Diamond, who argued that the research clearly shows that chromosomal sex and exposure to hormones in utero heavily determine gender identity.

When Bruce's parents contacted Money, they presented him with the perfect opportunity to prove his points. Not only had Bruce been born a normal male, but he had an identical twin brother as well. If reassigning Bruce's sex to a girl with surgery, and raising him as a girl resulted in Bruce's fully accepting himself as a girl, when his identical twin brother identified himself as a boy, Money's theories of gender identity would be soundly supported.

Bruce's parents renamed him Brenda Lee and began dressing him in feminine clothes. They took the child to Johns Hopkins to undergo a bilateral orchidectomy—the removal of both testicles—at the age of 22 months. When Brenda's parents returned

home with the child, they furnished her with dolls and tried to reinforce in every way her identity as a girl. Brenda, however, resisted. She ripped at the frilly dresses her mother gave her to wear. As her brother, Brian, recalled, "When I say there was nothing feminine about Brenda . . . I mean there was *nothing* feminine. She walked like a guy. Sat with her legs apart. She talked about guy things, didn't give a crap about cleaning house, getting married, wearing makeup. We both wanted to play with guys, build forts and have snowball fights and play army. She'd get a skipping rope for a gift, and the only thing we'd use that for was to tie people up, whip people with it" (Colapinto, 2001, p. 57).

As Brenda grew up, she became more convinced that she was not a girl. Her parents kept reinforcing her femininity, but Brenda would have nothing of it. She was defiant and difficult in school. Other children teased her and rejected her for her "tomboyishness." She flatly refused further surgery to create a vagina for her and insisted on urinating standing up. Still, her parents persisted at treating Brenda as a girl, at Money's insistence. At the age of 12, Brenda began to take estrogen; as a result, she began to develop breasts. Her voice also began to crack, however, just like her brother Brian's. John Money and a host of psychiatrists kept trying to convince Brenda to submit to the vaginal surgery, but she steadfastly refused. Finally, when Brenda was 14, her father told her the entire truth about the botched circumcision and the surgery she underwent at age 22 months, as well as her parents' decision to raise her as a girl. She was amazed, but another emotion was even stronger: "I was *relieved*. . . . Suddenly it all made sense why I felt the way I did. I wasn't some sort of weirdo. I wasn't crazy" (Colapinto, 2001, p. 180).

Brenda immediately decided to revert to her biological sex. She renamed herself David, after the biblical king and giant-slayer. David began to take injections of testosterone and in 1980 underwent a double mastectomy to remove the breasts he had grown. Then, a month before his sixteenth birthday, he underwent surgery to create a rudimentary penis. David's reentry into life as a boy was rough, however. He was sexually attracted to girls but terrified at the thought of initiating sex with a girl because she would find out the truth about him. The artificial genitals that had been fashioned for him frequently became blocked, and he underwent several additional surgeries and treatments. Over the next few years, David attempted suicide and secluded himself in a mountain cabin for months at a time.

Finally, shortly after his 22nd birthday, David underwent a new kind of surgery to create a more acceptable and functional penis. In 1990, David married a young woman named Jane, who knew everything about his past and loved him completely.

Although any individual case study is limited in its generalizability, David Reimer's story raises many questions about the biological and social contributors to our self-concept as male and female, our sexual preferences, and the role of sexuality and gender in psychological well-being. In this chapter, we consider how biology interacts with social norms and psychological factors in producing both sexual health and sexual disorders.

Sexual disorders fall into three distinct categories. First, *sexual dysfunctions* involve problems in experiencing sexual arousal or in carrying through with a sexual act to the point of sexual satisfaction. Second, *paraphilias* involve sexual activities that are focused on nonhuman objects, children or nonconsenting adults, or suffering or humiliation. There are several types of paraphilias, and they vary in the severity of their impact on other people. Third, *gender identity disorder* involves the belief that one has been born with the body of the wrong gender. People with this disorder feel trapped in the wrong body, wish to be rid of their genitals, and want to live as a member of the other gender.

In this chapter, we discuss specific sexual disorders within each of these three categories. We begin with some of the most common disorders that both men and women suffer: sexual dysfunctions. Then we move to the paraphilias, which are less common and primarily experienced by men. Finally, we discuss the most uncommon sexual disorder, gender identity disorder.

SEXUAL DYSFUNCTIONS

The **sexual dysfunctions** are a set of disorders in which people have trouble engaging in and enjoying sexual relationships with other people. Occasional problems with sexual functioning are extremely common. In a representative sample of more than 3,000 adults in the United States, Laumann, Paik, and Rosen (1999) found that 43 percent of the women and 31 percent of the men reported occasional dysfunctions.

In order to understand the sexual dysfunctions, it is important to understand something about the human sexual response—what happens in our bodies when we feel sexually aroused, when we engage in sexual intercourse or other forms of sexual stimulation, and when we reach orgasm.

The Sexual Response Cycle

Before the work of William Masters and Virginia Johnson in the 1950s and 1960s, little was known about what happened in the human body during sexual arousal and activity. Masters and Johnson (1970) observed people engaging in a variety of sexual practices in a laboratory setting and recorded the physiological changes that occurred during sexual activity.

Masters and Johnson and later researchers argued that the sexual response cycle can be divided into five phases: desire, excitement or arousal, plateau, orgasm, and resolution (see Figures 16.1 and 16.2). **Sexual desire** is the urge to engage in any type of sexual activity. The **arousal phase**, or *excitement phase*, consists of a psychological experience of arousal and pleasure and the physiological changes known as *vasocongestion* and *myotonia*. **Vasocongestion** is the filling of blood vessels and tissues with blood, also known as *engorgement*. In males, erection of the penis is caused by an increased flow of blood into the arteries of the penis, accompanied by a decrease in the outflow of blood from the penis through the veins. In females, vasocongestion causes the clitoris to enlarge, the labia to swell, and the vagina to moisten. **Myotonia** is muscular tension. Dur-

---

FIGURE 16.1 | **Male Sexual Response Cycle.** Males experience characteristic changes in physiology during each phase of their sexual response cycle.

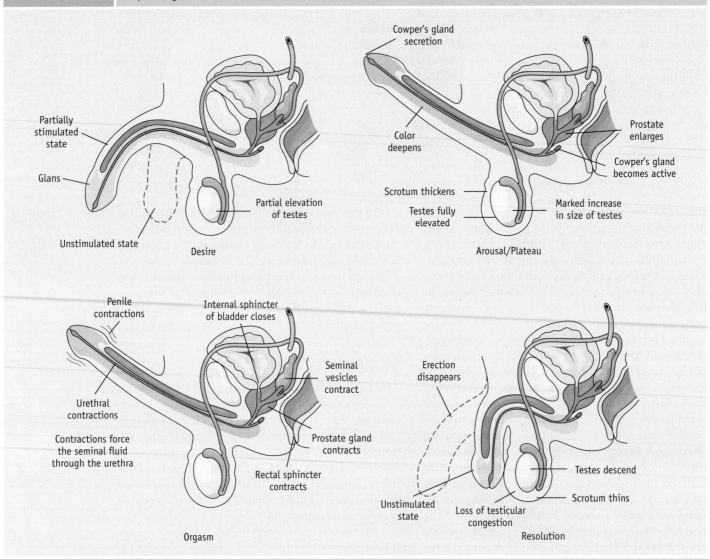

Source: Adapted from Hyde, 1990, p. 199.

ing the arousal phase, many muscles in the body may become more tense, culminating in the muscular contractions known as **orgasm.**

Following the arousal phase is the **plateau phase.** During this period, excitement remains at a high but stable level. This period is pleasurable in itself, and some people try to extend this period as long as possible before reaching orgasm. During both the arousal and the plateau phases, the person may feel tense all over, the skin is flushed, salivation increases, the nostrils flare, the heart pounds, breathing is heavy, and the person may be oblivious to external stimuli or events.

The arousal and plateau phases are followed by orgasm. Physiologically, orgasm is the discharge of the neuromuscular tension built up during the excitement and plateau phases. Both males and fe-

males experience a sense of the inevitability of orgasm just before it happens.

In males, orgasm involves rhythmic contractions of the prostate, the seminal vesicles, the vas deferens, and the entire length of the penis and urethra, accompanied by the ejaculation of semen (see Figure 16.1). In males, a *refractory period* follows ejaculation. During this period, the male cannot achieve full erection and another orgasm, regardless of the type or intensity of sexual stimulation. The refractory period lasts from a few minutes to several hours.

In females, orgasm generally involves rhythmic contractions of the orgasmic platform (see Figure 16.2) and more irregular contractions of the uterus, which are not always felt. Because females do not have a refractory period, they are capable of

| **FIGURE 16.2** | **Female Sexual Response Cycle.** At each phase of the sexual response cycle in females, there are characteristic changes in physiology. |

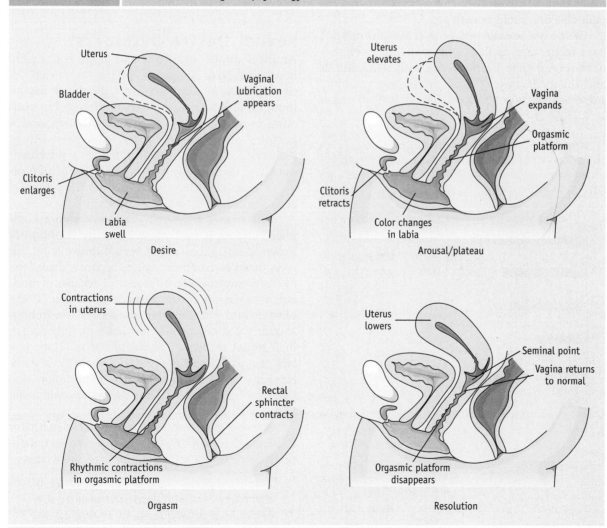

Source: Adapted from Hyde, 1990, p. 200.

experiencing additional orgasms immediately following one. However, not all women want to have multiple orgasms or find it easy to be aroused to multiple orgasms.

Following orgasm, the entire musculature of the body relaxes, and men and women tend to experience a state of deep relaxation, the stage known as **resolution.** A man loses his erection, and a woman's orgasmic platform subsides.

Both males and females experience the same five phases. There are some differences between the male and female sexual responses, however (Masters, Johnson, & Kolodny, 1993). First, there is greater variability in the female response pattern than in the male response pattern. Sometimes, the excitement and plateau phases are short for a female and she reaches a discernible orgasm quickly. At other times, the excitement and plateau phases are longer, and she may or may not experience a full orgasm. Second, as we have noted, there typically is a refractory period following orgasm for males but not for females. This refractory period in males becomes longer with age.

If you are sexually active, you may or may not have recognized all these phases in your own sexual response cycle. People vary greatly in the length and distinctiveness of each phase. For example, some people do not notice a distinct plateau phase and feel they go straight from arousal to orgasm. Being aware of how your body reacts to sexual stimulation can help you recognize what helps you get the most pleasure from sexual activity and what interferes with that pleasure.

Occasional, transient problems in sexual functioning are extremely common (see Figure 16.3). To qualify for a diagnosis of a sexual dysfunction, the difficulty must be more than occasional, and it must cause significant distress or interpersonal difficulty. The DSM-IV-TR divides sexual dysfunctions into four categories: sexual desire disorders, sexual arousal disorders, orgasmic disorders, and sexual pain disorders (see the Concept Overview in Table 16.1). (There are two other diagnoses in addition to those listed in Table 16.1: sexual dysfunction due to a medical condition and substance-induced sexual dysfunction, which we discuss in the section "Causes of Sexual Dysfunctions.") In reality, these dysfunctions overlap greatly, and many people who seek treatment for a sexual problem have more than one of these dysfunctions.

Sexual Desire Disorders

An individual's level of sexual desire is basically how much he or she wants to have sex. Sexual desire can be manifested in a person's sexual thoughts and fantasies, a person's interest in initiating or participating in sexual activities, and a person's awareness of sexual cues from others (Schiavi & Segraves, 1995). People vary tremendously in their levels of sexual desire, and an individual's level of sexual desire can vary greatly across time (see Tables 16.2 and 16.3).

Lack of sexual desire is the most common complaint of people seeking sex therapy (Leiblum & Rosen, 2000). Problems of sexual desire were not recognized as common, nor as separate disorders, by sex therapists in the first several decades of modern research on sexual disorders (Kaplan, 1995). Masters and Johnson, the pioneers of research on sexuality, did not include sexual desire disorders in their initial studies of sexual problems. They saw lack of sexual desire as a consequence of other problems in sexual functioning. The expectation was that treating these sexual dysfunctions would bring back sexual desire.

Another pioneer in sex research, Helen Singer Kaplan, was one of the first to recognize sexual desire disorders as a separate problem. She writes,

> I first became aware of the existence of disorders of sexual desire in the early seventies as a consequence of analyzing our treatment failures. As I reviewed the charts, it became clear that we had failed

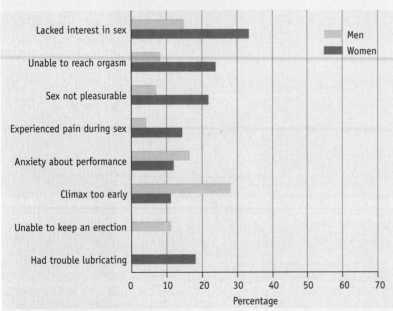

FIGURE 16.3 **Percentage of People Who Have Had a Sexual Difficulty in the Past Year.** A national survey found that many people report having had one or more sexual difficulties in the past year.

Source: Michael et al., 1994, p. 126.

TABLE 16.1 Concept Overview

Sexual Dysfunction Disorders

The DSM-IV-TR defines a number of sexual dysfunction disorders.

Sexual Desire Disorders	Description
Hypoactive sexual desire disorder	Persistent lack of sexual fantasies and desire for sexual activity
Sexual aversion disorder	Persistent and extreme aversion to genital sexual contact with a sexual partner

Sexual Arousal Disorders	Description
Female sexual arousal disorder	In women, recurrent inability to attain or maintain the swelling-lubrication response of sexual excitement
Male erectile disorder	In men, recurrent inability to attain or maintain an erection until the completion of sexual activity

Orgasmic Disorders	Description
Female orgasmic disorder	In women, recurrent delay in or absence of orgasm following sexual excitement
Premature ejaculation	In men, inability to delay ejaculation as desired
Male orgasmic disorder	In men, recurrent delay in or absence of orgasm following sexual excitement

Sexual Pain Disorders	Description
Dyspareunia	Genital pain associated with intercourse
Vaginismus	In women, involuntary contractions of the muscles surrounding the vagina, which interferes with sexual functioning

Source: Reprinted with permission from the *Diagnostic and Statistical Manual of Mental Disorders,* Fourth Edition, Text Revision. Copyright © 2000 American Psychiatric Association.

TABLE 16.2 Responses to the Question "How Often Do You Think About Sex?"

A national survey found a large variation in how often people think about sex and great differences between men and women.

	"Every Day" or "Several Times a Day"	"A Few Times a Month" or "A Few Times a Week"	"Less Than Once a Month" or "Never"
Men	54%	43%	4%
Women	19	67	14

Source: From R. T. Michael et al., *Sex in America.* Copyright © 1994 by CSG Enterprises, Inc. By permission of Little, Brown and Company.

TABLE 16.3 How Often Do People Have Sex?

A national survey of adults in the United States found a great deal of variation in how frequently people had sex.

Frequency	Percentage Reporting	
	Men	Women
Two to three times per week	30	26
A few times per month	36	37
A few times per year or not at all	27	30

Source: From E. O. Laumann et al., *The Social Organization of Sexuality: Sexual Practices in the United States.* Copyright © 1994 University of Chicago Press, Chicago, IL.

to recognize a considerable subgroup of patients who had little or no desire for sex or for sex with their partners. These patients had developed impotence or orgasmic disorders mainly because they had tried to make love without feeling lust or desire, and we had been trying to treat these secondary genital dysfunctions without being aware of the underlying desire disorders. This meant that some of our so-called "resistant" patients were not resistant to sex therapy at all. We had simply been treating them for the wrong thing! (Kaplan, 1995, p. 2)

Kaplan and other influential theorists (Kaplan, 1977; Masters, Johnson, & Kolodny, 1979) published their research on problems of sexual desire in the late 1970s. By the publication of the third edition of the DSM in 1980, these disorders had earned their own diagnostic category in the official nomenclature.

The percentage of people seeking therapy who report problems of sexual desire has increased sharply in the past 20 to 30 years (Bach, Wincze, & Barlow, 2001; Kaplan, 1995). Although the reasons for this increase are not clear, media attention to sexual desire disorders leads people to recognize that they have a problem that therapists can treat and, thus, to seek treatment. People who lack sexual desire can be diagnosed with one of two sexual desire disorders: hypoactive sexual desire disorder and sexual aversion disorder.

Hypoactive Sexual Desire Disorder

People with **hypoactive sexual desire disorder** have little desire for sex—they do not fantasize about sex or initiate sexual activity—and this lack of sexual desire causes them marked distress or interpersonal difficulty. In some rare cases, people report never having had much interest in sex, either with other people or privately, as in the viewing of erotic films, masturbation, or fantasy. In most cases of hypoactive sexual desire, the individual used to enjoy sex but has lost interest in it, despite the presence of a willing and desirable partner. A diagnosis of hypoactive sexual desire is not given if the individual's lack of desire is the result of transient circumstances in his or her life, such as being too busy or fatigued from overwork to care about sex. Also, a diagnosis of sexual desire disorder is not given if the lack of desire is actually caused by one of the other problems in sexual functioning, such as pain during intercourse or an inability to achieve orgasm. In such cases, the diagnosis a person receives focuses on the primary dysfunction, rather than on the lack of desire that is the result of the primary dysfunction.

Inhibited desire can be either generalized to all partners or situations or specific to certain partners or types of stimulation. A person who has had little desire for sexual activity most of his or her life has a *generalized sexual desire disorder.* A person who lacks the desire to have sex with his or her partner, but has sexual fantasies about other people, may be diagnosed with a *situational sexual desire disorder.* Obviously, the judgment about when a person's sexual desire has been too low for too long is a subjective one. Often, people seek treatment for a lack of sexual desire primarily because their partner's sexual desire appears to be considerably greater than their own and the difference is causing conflict in the relationship (Masters et al., 1993). Low sexual desire is one of the most common problems for which people seek treatment (Bach et al., 2001).

In the study of more than 3,000 adults done by Laumann and colleagues, 22 percent of the women and 5 percent of the men reported low sexual desire (Laumann et al., 1999). Men with this disorder tend to be older (average age 50) than women with the disorder (average age 33). Women with hypoactive sexual desire are more likely than men to report anxiety, depression, and life stress. Hypoactive sexual desire is more often connected to problems in relationships for women than for men.

Sexual Aversion Disorder

The other type of sexual desire disorder is **sexual aversion disorder.** People with this disorder do not simply have a passive lack of interest in sex; they actively avoid sexual activities. When they do engage in sex, they may feel sickened by it or experience acute anxiety. Some people experience a generalized aversion to all sexual activities, including kissing and touching.

Sexual aversion disorder in women is frequently tied to sexual assault experiences, as in the case of Norma (adapted from Spitzer et al., 1994, p. 213):

> Norma and Gary were having sex approximately once every 1 to 2 months, and only at Gary's insistence. Their sexual activity consisted primarily of Gary stimulating Norma to orgasm by manually caressing her genitals while he masturbated himself to orgasm.
>
> Norma had always had a strong aversion to looking at or touching her husband's penis. During an interview she explained that she had had no idea of the origin of this aversion until her uncle's recent funeral. At the funeral she was surprised to find herself becoming angry as the eulogy was read. Her uncle had been a world-famous concert musician and was widely respected and admired. She believes she suddenly recalled having been sexually molested by him when she was a child. From the ages of 9 to 12, her uncle had been her music teacher. The lessons included "teaching [her] rhythm" by having her caress his penis in time with the beating of the metronome. This repelled her, but she was frightened to tell her parents about it. She finally refused to continue lessons at age 12 without ever telling her parents why. At some point during her adolescence, she said, she "forgot what he did to me."

Sexual Arousal Disorders

People with *sexual arousal disorders* do not experience the physiological changes that make up the excitement or arousal phase of the sexual response cycle. **Female sexual arousal disorder** involves a recurrent inability to attain or maintain the swelling-lubrication response of sexual excitement. **Male erectile disorder** involves the recurrent inability to attain or maintain an erection until the completion of sexual activity. Much less is known about female sexual arousal disorder than about male erectile disorder (which is commonly referred to as *impo-*

tence). Female sexual arousal disorder is common, however. About 20 percent of women report difficulties with lubrication or arousal during sexual activity (Laumann et al., 1999; Michael et al., 1994). Men with the *lifelong* form of male erectile disorder have never been able to sustain erections for a desired period of time. Men with the *acquired* form of the disorder were able to sustain erections in the past but no longer can. Occasional problems in gaining or sustaining erections are very common, with as many as 30 million men in the United States having erectile problems at sometime in their lives. Such problems do not constitute a disorder until they become persistent and significantly interfere with a man's interpersonal relationships or cause him distress. Only 4 to 9 percent of men have problems sufficient to warrant a diagnosis of male erectile disorder (Laumann et al., 1999; Spector & Carey, 1990). Paul Petersen is one of these men (adapted from Spitzer et al., 1994, pp. 198–199):

> Paul and Geraldine Petersen have been living together for the last 6 months and are contemplating marriage. Geraldine describes the problem that has brought them to the sex therapy clinic.
>
> "For the last 2 months he hasn't been able to keep his erection after he enters me."
>
> The psychiatrist learns that Paul, age 26, is a recently graduated lawyer, and that Geraldine, age 24, is a successful buyer for a large department store. They both grew up in educated, middle-class, suburban families. They met through mutual friends and started to have sexual intercourse a few months after they met and had no problems at that time.
>
> Two months later, Paul moved from his family home into Geraldine's apartment. This was her idea, and Paul was unsure that he was ready for such an important step. Within a few weeks, Paul noticed that, although he continued to be sexually aroused and wanted intercourse, as soon as he entered his partner, he began to lose his erection and could not stay inside. They would try again, but by then his desire had waned and he was unable to achieve another erection. Geraldine would become extremely angry with Paul, but he would just walk away from her.

(continued)

The psychiatrist learned that sex was not the only area of contention in the relationship. Geraldine complained that Paul did not spend enough time with her and preferred to go to baseball games with his male friends. Even when he was home, he would watch all the sports events that were available on TV and was not interested in going to foreign movies, museums, or the theater with her. Despite these differences, Geraldine was eager to marry Paul and was pressuring him to set a date.

Male erectile disorder is sometimes, although not always, part of a constellation of problems in a couples relationship, as we will discuss later.

Orgasmic Disorders

Women with **female orgasmic disorder,** or *anorgasmia,* experience a recurrent delay in or the complete absence of orgasm after having reached the excitement phase of the sexual response cycle. The DSM-IV-TR specifies that this diagnosis should be made only when a woman is unable to achieve orgasm despite receiving adequate stimulation. About one in four women report difficulties reaching orgasm (Laumann et al., 1999). The problem is greater among postmenopausal women, with about one in three reporting some problems reaching orgasm during sexual stimulation (Rosen & Leiblum, 1995; Spector & Carey, 1990).

The most common form of orgasmic disorder in males is **premature ejaculation.** Men who have this disorder persistently ejaculate with minimal sexual stimulation before they wish to ejaculate. Laumann and colleagues (1999) found that 21 percent of men reported problems with premature ejaculation. Spector and Carey (1990) estimate that between 30 and 40 percent of men have significant trouble delaying ejaculation at will. Again, it is a judgment call about when premature ejaculation becomes a sexual dysfunction. Premature ejaculation must cause significant distress or interpersonal problems before it is considered a disorder. Some men seeking treatment for this problem simply cannot prevent ejaculation before their partner reaches orgasm. Others ejaculate after very little stimulation, long before their partner is fully aroused. One problem with the definition of premature ejaculation is that whether the ejaculation is premature depends in part on how quickly the man's partner becomes aroused to orgasm. Because of the inherent difficulty in defining "premature," this disorder is often referred to as *rapid* ejaculation.

Men with premature ejaculation resort to applying desensitizing creams to their penises before sex, wearing multiple condoms, distracting themselves by doing complex mathematical problems while making love, not allowing their partners to touch them, and masturbating multiple times shortly before having sex in an attempt to delay their ejaculations (Althof, 1995). These tactics are generally unsuccessful and can make their partner feel shut out of the sexual encounter, as in the following account (McCarthy, 1989, pp. 151–152).

CASE STUDY

Bill and Margaret were a couple in their late 20s who had been married for 2 years. Margaret was 27 and the owner of a hair-styling studio. Bill was 29 and a legislative lobbyist for a financial institution. This was a first marriage for both. They had had a rather tumultuous dating relationship before marriage. Margaret had been in individual and group therapy for 1½ years at a university counseling center before dropping out of school to enroll in a hair-styling program. During their dating period, Margaret reentered individual therapy, and Bill, who had never participated in therapy, attended five conjoint sessions. That therapist helped Bill and Margaret deal with issues in their relationship and increased their commitment to marrying. However, the therapist made an incorrect assumption in stating that with increased intimacy and the commitment of marriage, the ejaculatory control problem would disappear. . . .

Margaret saw the early ejaculation as a symbol of lack of love and caring on Bill's part. As the problem continued over the next 2 years, Margaret became increasingly frustrated and withdrawn. She demonstrated her displeasure by resisting his sexual advances, and their intercourse frequency decreased from three or four times per week to once every 10 days. A sexual and marital crisis was precipitated by Margaret's belief that Bill was acting more isolated and distant when they did have intercourse. When they talked about their sexual relationship, it was usually in bed after intercourse, and the communication quickly broke down into tears, anger, and ac-

(continued)

cusations. Bill was on the defensive and handled the sexual issue by avoiding talking to Margaret, which frustrated her even more.

Unbeknownst to Margaret, Bill had attempted a do-it-yourself technique to gain better control. He had bought a desensitizing cream he'd read about in a men's magazine and applied it to the glans of his penis (the caplike structure at the end of the penis) 20 minutes before initiating sex. He also masturbated the day before couple sex. During intercourse he tried to keep his leg muscles tense and think about sports as a way of keeping his arousal in check. Bill was unaware that Margaret felt emotionally shut out during sex. Bill was becoming more sensitized to his arousal cycle and was worrying about erection. He was not achieving better ejaculatory control, and he was enjoying sex less. The sexual relationship was heading downhill, and miscommunication and frustration were growing.

Men with **male orgasmic disorder** experience a recurrent delay in or the absence of orgasm following the excitement phase of the sexual response cycle. In most cases of this disorder, a man cannot ejaculate during intercourse but can ejaculate with manual or oral stimulation. Eight percent of men report problems in reaching orgasm (Laumann et al., 1999).

Sexual Pain Disorders

The final two sexual dysfunctions are sexual pain disorders, *dyspareunia* and *vaginismus*. **Dyspareunia** is genital pain associated with intercourse. It is rare in men but, in community surveys, 10 to 15 percent of women report frequent pain during intercourse (Laumann et al., 1994). In women, the pain may be shallow during intromission (insertion of the penis into the vagina) or deep during penile thrusting. Dyspareunia in women can be the result of dryness of the vagina, caused by antihistamines or other drugs; infection of the clitoris or vulval area; injury or irritation to the vagina; or tumors of the internal reproductive organs. In men, dyspareunia involves painful erections or pain during thrusting.

Vaginismus occurs only in women and involves the involuntary contraction of the muscles surrounding the outer third of the vagina when vaginal penetration with a penis, finger, tampon, or speculum is attempted. Women with vaginismus may experience sexual arousal and have orgasms

when their clitoris is stimulated. However, when a penis or another object is inserted into the vagina, the muscles surrounding its opening contract involuntarily. In other women with this disorder, even the anticipation of vaginal insertion may result in this muscle spasm. It is estimated that 5 to 17 percent of women experience vaginismus (Reissing, Binik, & Khalife, 1999).

Causes of Sexual Dysfunctions

How do sexual dysfunctions arise? Most sexual dysfunctions probably have multiple causes, including biological causes and psychosocial causes (see the Concept Overview in Table 16.4 on page 584). Perhaps the most common cause of one sexual dysfunction is another sexual dysfunction. For example, one study found that about 40 percent of people with hypoactive sexual desire disorder also had a diagnosis of an arousal or orgasmic disorder (Segraves & Segraves, 1991). That is, even when they do engage in sex, these people have difficulty becoming aroused or reaching orgasm. This, in turn, greatly reduces their desire to engage in sexual activity. Similarly, many people who experience pain during sexual activity lose all desire for sex.

When people seek help for sexual dysfunctions, clinicians conduct thorough assessments of their medical conditions, the drugs they are taking, the characteristics of their relationships, their attitudes toward their sexuality, and their sexual practices. Even when one of these factors can be identified as the primary cause of a sexual dysfunction, usually several areas of a person's life have been affected by the dysfunction, including his or her self-concept and relationships. All these areas need to be addressed in treatment.

Biological Causes

The DSM-IV-TR sets apart sexual dysfunctions that are caused by medical conditions by giving them a separate diagnosis. Many medical illnesses can cause problems in sexual functioning in both men and women. One of the most common contributors to sexual dysfunction is diabetes, which can result in reduced circulation, leading to reduced erectile tissue, and thus to reduced arousal (Bach et al., 2001; Schiavi et al., 1995). Diabetes often goes undiagnosed, so people may believe that psychological factors are causing their sexual dysfunction, when the cause is really undiagnosed diabetes. Other diseases that are common causes of sexual dysfunction, particularly in men, are cardiovascular disease, multiple sclerosis, renal failure, vascular disease, spinal cord injury, and injury of the autonomic nervous system by surgery or radiation (APA, 2000; Bach et al., 2001; Kelly, 1998).

TABLE 16.4 Concept Overview

Causes of Sexual Dysfunctions

A host of biological, psychological, and sociocultural factors can contribute to sexual dysfunctions.

Biological Causes	Psychological Causes	Sociocultural Causes
Medical conditions	Psychological disorders	Relationship problems
Diabetes	Depression	Lack of communication
Cardiovascular disease	Anxiety disorders	Differences in sexual expectations
Multiple sclerosis	Schizophrenia	Conflicts unrelated to sex
Renal failure	Attitudes and cognitions	Trauma
Vascular disease	Belief that sex is "dirty" or "disgusting"	Cultural taboos against sex
Spinal cord injury	Performance anxiety	
Autonomic nervous system injury		
Prescription drugs		
Antihypertensive medications		
Antipsychotic medications		
Antidepressant medications		
Lithium		
Tranquilizers		
Recreational drugs		
Marijuana		
Cocaine		
Amphetamines		
Nicotine		
Alcohol		
In men		
Low levels of androgen hormones or high levels of estrogen and prolactin		
Genital or urinary tract infections		
In women		
Low levels of estrogen		
Vaginal dryness or irritation		
Injuries during childbirth		

As many as 40 percent of cases of male erectile disorder are caused by one of these medical conditions. In men with cardiovascular disease, sexual dysfunction can be caused directly by the disease, which can, for example, reduce the functioning of the vascular system. Sexual dysfunction may be a psychological response to the presence of the disease. For example, a man who recently had a heart attack may fear he will have another if he has sex and, thus, loses his desire for sex.

In men, abnormally low levels of the androgen hormones, especially testosterone, or high levels of the hormones estrogen and prolactin can cause sexual dysfunction (Bach et al., 2001). In women, hormones do not seem to have a consistent, direct effect on sexual desire. For example, levels of most reproductive hormones change in women over the menstrual cycle, but there is no consistent effect of these hormones on sexual desire—simply, there is variance among women in what parts of their menstrual cycles they feel the most sexual desire (Beck, 1995; Schiavi & Segraves, 1995). Hormones may have an indirect effect on sexual desire by affecting sexual arousal, however. Low levels of estrogen can cause decreases in vasocongestion and vaginal lubrication, leading to diminished sexual arousal, pain during sexual activity, and therefore lowered sexual desire (Sherwin, 1991). Levels of estrogen drop greatly at menopause. Thus, postmenopausal women often complain of lowered sexual desire and arousal. Similarly, women who have had radical hysterectomies, which remove the main source of estrogen, the ovaries, can experience reductions in both sexual desire and arousal.

Vaginal dryness or irritation, which causes pain during sex and therefore lowers sexual desire and arousal, can be caused by radiation therapy, endometriosis, antihistamines, douches, tampons, vaginal contraceptives, and infections, such as vaginitis or pelvic inflammatory disease. Injuries during childbirth that have healed poorly, such as a poorly repaired episiotomy, can cause coital pain in women (Masters et al., 1993). The biological causes of pain during sex in men include genital or urinary tract infections, especially prostatitis, and a rare condition called *Peyronie's disease*, which causes deposits of fibrous tissue in the penis. Women who have had gynecological cancers sometimes report pain, changes in the vaginal anatomy, and problems with their body image or sexual self-concept (Lagana et al., 2001).

Several prescription drugs can diminish sexual drive and arousal and interfere with orgasm. These include antihypertensive drugs taken by people with high blood pressure, antipsychotic drugs, antidepressants, lithium, and tranquilizers. Indeed, one of the most common side effects of the widely used selective serotonin reuptake inhibitors is sexual dysfunction (Bach et al., 2001).

Many recreational drugs, including marijuana, cocaine, amphetamines, and nicotine, can impair sexual functioning (Schiavi & Segraves, 1995). Even though people often drink alcohol to make them feel more sexy and uninhibited, even small amounts of alcohol can significantly impair sexual functioning. Chronic alcoholics often have diagnosable sexual dysfunctions (Bach et al., 2001; Schiavi, 1990). When a sexual dysfunction is caused by substance use, it is given the diagnosis of **substance-induced sexual dysfunction.**

For a man with erectile disorder, one of the best ways to know if the dysfunction has biological causes is to determine whether he has erections during sleep, as healthy men do. If he is having nocturnal erections, then chances are that his erectile problems have psychological origins, at least in part. If he is not having nocturnal erections, then

Although many people drink alcohol to decrease their sexual inhibitions, alcohol can also decrease sexual performance.

chances are the erectile problems have biological causes (Ackerman & Carey, 1995). A thorough assessment of nocturnal erections can be done with devices that directly measure men's erections. In a sleep laboratory, strain gauges are attached to the base and glans (end structure) of the penis to record the magnitude, duration, and pattern of erections, while electroencephalographs record the sleep pattern.

Women also experience cyclic episodes of vasocongestion during sleep, which can be monitored to determine if a woman experiencing arousal problems has a biological disorder. Vasocongestion in women can be measured with a vaginal photoplethysmograph, a tampon-shaped device inserted into a woman's vagina, which records the changes that accompany vasocongestion.

In sum, a number of medical conditions and drugs can affect sexual desire, arousal, and orgasm. It is critical at the outset of any treatment program to determine if any of these factors are contributing to a sexual dysfunction.

Psychological Causes

Our emotional well-being and our beliefs and attitudes about sex greatly influence our sexuality.

Psychological Disorders A number of psychological disorders can cause sexual dysfunction (Bach et al., 2001). Loss of sexual functioning is a common symptom in depression. A person with depression may have no desire for sex or may experience any of the problems in sexual arousal and functioning we have discussed. Unfortunately, the medications used to treat depression often induce problems in sexual functioning. Similarly, people with an anxiety disorder, such as generalized anxiety disorder, panic disorder, or obsessive-compulsive disorder, may find their sexual desire and functioning waning. Loss of sexual desire and functioning is very common among people with schizophrenia.

Attitudes and Cognitions   People who have been taught that sex is dirty, disgusting, or sinful or is a "necessary evil" may understandably lack the desire to have sex. They may also know so little about their own bodies and sexual responses that they do not know how to make sex pleasurable. Such is the case with Mrs. Booth (adapted from Spitzer et al., 1994, pp. 251–252):

> **CASE STUDY**
>
> Mr. and Mrs. Booth have been married for 14 years and have three children, ages 8 through 12. They are both bright and well-educated. Both are from Scotland, from which they moved 10 years ago because of Mr. Booth's work as an industrial consultant. They present with the complaint that Mrs. Booth has been able to participate passively in sex "as a duty" but has never enjoyed it since they have been married.
>
> Before their marriage, although they had had intercourse only twice, Mrs. Booth had been highly aroused by kissing and petting and felt she used her attractiveness to "seduce" her husband into marriage. She did, however, feel intense guilt about their two episodes of premarital intercourse; during their honeymoon, she began to think of sex as a chore that could not be pleasing. Although she periodically passively complied with intercourse, she had almost no spontaneous desire for sex. She never masturbated, had never reached orgasm, thought of all variations such as oral sex as completely repulsive, and was preoccupied with a fantasy of how disapproving her family would be if she ever engaged in any of these activities.
>
> Mrs. Booth is almost totally certain that no woman she respects in any older generation has enjoyed sex and that despite the "new vogue" of sexuality, only sleazy, crude women let themselves act like "animals." These beliefs have led to a pattern of regular but infrequent sex that at best is accommodating and gives little or no pleasure to her or her husband.
>
> Whenever Mrs. Booth comes close to having a feeling of sexual arousal, numerous negative thoughts come into her mind such as, "What am I, a tramp?"; "If I like this, he'll just want it more often"; and "How could I look at myself in the mirror after something like this?" These thoughts almost inevitably are accompanied by a cold feeling and an insensitivity to sensual pleasure. As a result, sex is invariably an unhappy experience. Almost any excuse, such as fatigue or being busy, is sufficient for her to rationalize avoiding intercourse.

Women with severely negative attitudes toward sex, like Mrs. Booth's, also tend to experience dyspareunia and vaginismus, because they have been taught that sex is painful and frightening (Rosen & Leiblum, 1995). Although such attitudes toward sex may be declining among younger people, many younger and older women still report a fear of "letting go," which interferes with orgasm (Heiman & Grafton-Becker, 1989; Tugrul & Kabakci, 1997). They say they fear losing control or acting in a way that will embarrass them. This fear of loss of control may result from a distrust of one's partner, a sense of shame about sex, a poor body image, or a host of other factors.

Another set of attitudes that interfere with sexual functioning appear to be rampant among middle-aged and younger adults. These attitudes are often referred to as *performance concerns* or **performance anxiety** (LoPiccolo, 1992; Masters & Johnson, 1970). People worry so much about whether they are going to be aroused and have orgasms that this worry interferes with sexual functioning: "What if I can't get an erection? I'll die of embarrassment!" "I've got to have an orgasm, or he'll think I'm frigid!" "Oh, my God, I just can't get aroused tonight!" These worried thoughts are so distracting that people cannot focus on the pleasure that sexual stimulation is giving them and, thus, do not become as aroused as they want to or need to in order to reach orgasm (Barlow, Sakheim, & Beck, 1983; Cranston-Cuebas & Barlow, 1990) (see Figure 16.4).

In addition, many people engage in spectatoring: They anxiously attend to reactions and performance during sex as if they were spectators (Masters & Johnson, 1970). Spectatoring distracts from sexual pleasure and interferes with sexual functioning. Unfortunately, people who have had some problems in sexual functioning only develop more performance concerns, which then further interfere with their functioning. By the time they

FIGURE 16.4	A Model Showing How Anxiety and Cognitive Interference Can Produce Erectile Dysfunction and Other Sexual Disorders

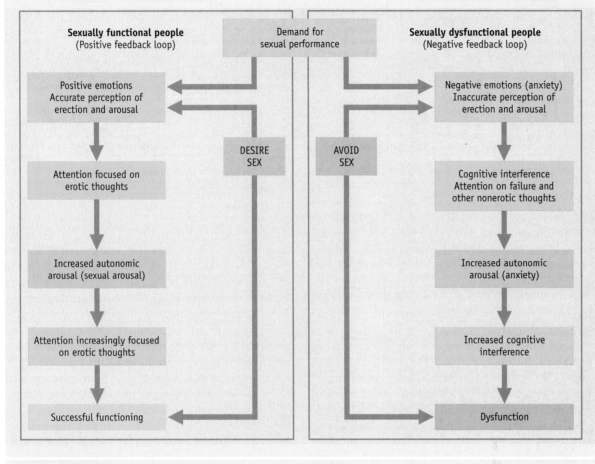

Source: Barlow, 1986.

seek treatment for sexual dysfunction, they may be so anxious about performing sexually that they avoid all sexual activity.

More chronic problems can develop from the way young men learn about their own sexual responses during adolescence. Most males, perhaps 90 percent, have their first orgasmic experience during masturbation as adolescents (McCarthy, 1989). Masturbation is usually practiced in an intense, rapid manner, where the only focus is on ejaculation. Many young men do not view masturbation as a positive, healthy exercise in which they are learning about their bodies. Rather, they feel guilty or embarrassed and anxious about being caught masturbating, so they hurry through it, not paying attention to their bodies' levels of arousal and not learning anything about ejaculatory control. In partner sex, they can become aroused without much stimulation from their partners and may fear ejaculating before their partners become aroused. Thus, they avoid allowing partners to stimulate them and focus, instead, on stimulating

their partners as quickly as possible, so that they can have intercourse. As a result, they come to associate high levels of arousal with anxiety over premature ejaculation, and this anxiety only increases the chance of premature ejaculation.

With experience and maturity, most males gain ejaculatory control through a number of processes, as described by Barry McCarthy (1989, p. 146): "(1) a regular rhythm of being sexual; (2) increased comfort with practice; (3) a more give-and-take 'pleasuring process' rather than goal-oriented foreplay; (4) allowance of more time for the variety of sensations in the sexual experience; (5) greater intimacy and security resulting in increased sexual comfort; (6) partner encouragement for a slower, more tender, rhythmic sexual interchange; and (7) shift of intercourse positions and/or thrusting movements."

Interpersonal and Sociocultural Factors

Although our internal psychological states and beliefs play important roles in our sexuality, sex is largely an interpersonal activity—one that societies

Garfield ®   by Jim Davis

attempt to control. For this reason, interpersonal and sociocultural factors also play important roles in people's sexual interests and activities.

Relationship Problems Problems in intimate relationships are extremely common among people with sexual dysfunctions. Sometimes, these problems are the consequences of sexual dysfunctions, as when a couple cannot communicate about the sexual dysfunction of one of the partners and grow distant from each other. Relationship problems can be direct causes of sexual dysfunctions as well (Bach et al., 2001; Beck, 1995).

Conflicts between partners may be about their sexual activities. One partner may want to engage in a type of sexual activity that the other partner is not comfortable with, or one partner may want to engage in sexual activity much more often than the other partner. People with inhibited desire, arousal, or orgasm often have sexual partners who do not know how to arouse them or are not concerned with their arousal and focus on only themselves. Partners often do not communicate with each other about what is arousing, so that, even if each partner intends to please the other, neither knows what the other wants him or her to do (Ackerman & Carey, 1995; Speckens et al., 1995).

Anorgasmia (lack of orgasm) in women may be tied to lack of communication between a woman and a male partner about what the woman needs to reach orgasm (Hurlbert, 1991). In sexual encounters between men and women, men are still more likely to be the ones who decide when to initiate sex, how long to engage in foreplay, when to penetrate, and what position to use during intercourse. A man's pattern of arousal is often not the same as a woman's pattern of arousal, and he may be making these decisions on the basis of his level of arousal and needs for stimulation, not understanding that hers may be different.

Most women have difficulty reaching orgasm by coitus alone and need oral or manual stimulation of the clitoris to become aroused enough to reach orgasm (Hite, 1976; Kaplan, 1974). Many men and women do not know this, however, or they believe that men should be able to bring women to orgasm by penile insertion and thrusting alone. Many women, thus, never receive the stimulation they need to be sufficiently aroused to orgasm. They may feel inhibited from telling their partners that they would like them to stimulate their clitoris more, because they are afraid of hurting their partners' feelings or angering them, or because they believe they do not have the right to ask for the kind of stimulation they want. Some women fake orgasms to protect their partners' egos. Often, their partners know that they are not fully satisfied, however. Communication between partners may break down further, and sex may become a forum for hostility rather than pleasure.

Conflicts between partners that are not directly about their sexual activity can affect their sexual relationship as well, as we saw in the case of Paul and Geraldine Peterson (Beck, 1995; Rosen & Leiblum, 1995). Anger, distrust, and lack of respect for one's partner can greatly interfere with sexual desire and functioning. When one partner suspects that the other partner has been unfaithful or is losing interest in the relationship, all sexual interest may disappear. Often, there is an imbalance of power in relationships, and people feel exploited, subjugated, and underappreciated by their partners, leading to problems in their sexual relationships (Rosen & Leiblum, 1995).

One study of men and women seeking treatment for hypoactive sexual desire disorder found that women are more likely than men to report problems in their marital relationships, other stressful events in their lives, and higher levels of psychological distress (Donahey & Carroll, 1993). Men seeking treatment are more likely than women to be experiencing other types of sexual dysfunction in addition to low sexual desire, such as erectile dysfunction. Thus, for men, it appears that issues of sexual functioning precipitate their entry into treatment, whereas, for women, lack of sexual desire is linked to a broader array of psychosocial problems.

Trauma Reductions in sexual desire and functioning often follow personal traumas, such as the loss of a loved one, the loss of a job, or the diagnosis of severe illness in one's child. Unemployment in men may contribute to declines in sexual desire and functioning (Morokoff & Gillilland, 1993). Traumas such as unemployment can challenge a person's self-esteem and self-concept, interfering with his or her sexual self-concept. Traumas can also cause a person to experience a depression that includes a loss of interest in most pleasurable activities, including sex. In such cases, clinicians typically focus on treating the depression, with the expectation that sexual desire will resume once the depression has lifted.

One type of personal trauma that is often associated with sexual desire disorders in women is sexual assault (DiLillo, 2001). A woman who has been raped may lose all interest in sex and be disgusted or extremely anxious when anyone, particularly a man, touches her. Her sexual aversion may be tied to a sense of vulnerability and loss of control or to a conditioned aversion to all forms of sexual contact (Leiblum & Rosen, 1988). In addition, male partners of women who have been raped sometimes cannot cope with the rapes and withdraw from sexual encounters with them. This withdrawal may be more common among men who accept rape myths, such as "Women who get raped were asking for it" and "Women enjoy being raped." Women rape survivors may then feel victimized yet again, and their interest in sex may decline even further.

Cross-Cultural Differences Other cultures recognize types of sexual dysfunction not described in the DSM-IV-TR. For example, both the traditional Chinese medical system and the Ayurvedic medical system, which is native to India, teach that loss of semen is detrimental to a man's health (Dewaraja & Sasaki, 1991). Masturbation is strongly discouraged, because it results in semen loss without the possibility of conception. A study of 1,000 consecutive patients seeking treatment in a sexual clinic in India found that 77 percent of the male patients reported difficulties with premature ejaculation and 71 percent were concerned about nocturnal emissions associated with erotic dreams (Verma, Khaitan, & Singh, 1998).

A depersonalization syndrome, known as *Koro*, thought to result from semen loss, has been reported among Malaysians, Southeast Asians, and southern Chinese. This syndrome involves an acute anxiety state, with a feeling of panic and impending death, and a delusion that the penis is shrinking into the body and disappearing. The patient or his relatives may grab and hold the penis until the attack of Koro is ended to stop the penis from disappearing into the body.

In Polynesian culture, there is no word for erection problems in men (Mannino, 1999). If a man does not have an erection, it is assumed that he does not want sex. In some African cultures, the preference is for women's vaginas to be dry and tight for sexual intercourse (Brown, Ayowa, & Brown, 1993). Several herbal treatments are used to achieve this dryness.

In surveys in the United States, less educated and poorer men and women tend to experience more sexual dysfunctions. These problems include having pain during sex, not finding sex pleasurable, being unable to reach orgasm, lacking interest in sex, climaxing too early, and, for men, having trouble maintaining erections (Laumann et al., 1994). People in lower educational and income groups may have more sexual dysfunctions because they are under more psychological stress, their physical health is worse, or they have not had the benefit of educational programs that teach people about their bodies and healthy social relationships.

Trends Across the Life Span

Our stereotypes tell us that young adults, particularly men, can't get enough sex but that sexual activity declines steadily with age, and older adults (i.e., over about 65 years old) hardly ever have sex.

Many older adults remain sexually active and experience little decline in sexual functioning.

It is true that sexual activity is greater among younger adults than older adults, but many older adults remain sexually active well into old age (Bartlik & Goldstein, 2001a, 2001b).

Age-related biological changes can affect sexual functioning. Adequate levels of testosterone are necessary for sexual desire in both men and women. Testosterone levels begin to decline in one's fifties for men and continue to decline steadily through life (Meston, 1997). It becomes more difficult for many men to achieve and maintain erections as they grow old, and the incidence of erectile dysfunction increases with age (Rosen, 1996). Diminished estrogen in postmenopausal women can lead to vaginal dryness and lack of lubrication and, thus, to a reduction in sexual responsivity (Bartlik & Goldstein, 2001a). In many cases of sexual dysfunction in men and women, the cause is not age per se but medical conditions, which are more common in older men and women than in younger people.

For both older men and women, the loss of a lifelong spouse, losses of other family members and friends, health concerns, and discomfort with one's own aging can contribute to sexual problems (Bartlik & Goldberg, 2000, Bartlik & Goldstein, 2001a, 2001b). Conflicts and dissatisfactions in a couple's relationship can become worse as they spend more time together because one or both retire and their children move out of the house. Older couples may need to learn to be more flexible and patient with each other as their bodies change and to try new techniques for stimulating each other. There are a number of biological and psychosocial treatments for sexual dysfunctions in both older and younger people.

Treatments for Sexual Dysfunctions

Because most sexual dysfunctions have multiple causes, treatments often involve a combination of approaches, often including biological interventions, psychosocial therapy focusing on problems in a relationship or the concerns of an individual client, and behavior therapies to help clients learn new skills for increasing sexual arousal and pleasure.

Biological Therapies

If a sexual dysfunction is the direct result of another medical condition, such as diabetes, treating the medical condition often reduces the sexual dysfunction. Similarly, if medications are contributing to a sexual dysfunction, adjusting the dosage or switching to a different type of medication that does not have the sexual side effects can relieve sexual difficulties. Also, getting a person to stop using recreational drugs, such as marijuana, that are causing a sexual dysfunction can often cure the dysfunction (Rosen & Ashton, 1993).

A number of biological treatments are available for men with male erectile disorder (see Table 16.5). A number of drugs have proven useful for the treatment of this disorder (Segraves, 2003). The one that has received the most media attention in recent years is sildenafil (trade name Viagra). Sildenafil is a selective inhibitor of cyclic guanosine monophosphate-specific phosphodiesterase type 5, which plays a critical role in erections. This drug has proven effective both in men whose erectile dysfunction has no known organic cause and in men whose erectile dysfunction is caused by medical conditions, such as hypertension, diabetes, or spinal cord injury (Segraves, 2003; Seidman et al., 2001). Sildenafil does have side effects, though, including headaches, flushing, and stomach irritation, and it does not work in up to 44 percent of men (Bach et al., 2001).

Yohimbine comes from the bark of the yohimbe tree, which Africans have chewed for centuries to increase their sexual desire and functioning. Yohimbine has been shown in some studies to improve erectile functioning in men (Segraves, 2003). Some people can have a severe allergic reaction to yohimbine, including difficulty swallowing and swelling in lips, tongue, and face. Other side effects can include fast or irregular heartbeat, dizziness, and tremors. The antidepressant trazadone, and apomorphine, which affects dopamine levels, can also help men with erectile dysfunction increase their ability to have erections (Segraves, 2003).

Some antidepressants, particularly the selective serotonin reuptake inhibitors (SSRIs), can cause sexual dysfunction. Other drugs can be used, in conjunction with these antidepressants, to reduce the sexual side effects of the antidepressants. One drug that has proven helpful in this regard is bupropion, which goes by the trade names Wellbutrin and Zyban (Ashton & Rosen, 1998). Bupropion appears to reduce the sexual side effects of the SSRIs and can be effective as an antidepressant on its own (Coleman et al., 2001). Sildenafil may also help men whose erectile dysfunction is caused by taking antidepressants, thereby allowing them to continue taking the antidepressants without losing sexual functioning (Balon, 1998).

For men suffering from premature ejaculation, antidepressants can be helpful, including fluoxetine (Prozac), clomipramine (Anafranil), and sertraline (Zoloft). Several studies suggest these drugs significantly reduce the frequency of premature ejaculation (Segraves, 2003).

Several studies have examined the effects of hormone therapy—specifically, the use of testos-

TABLE 16.5 Medical and Surgical Treatments for Male Erectile Disorder

A number of interventions can overcome male erectile disorder.

Treatments	How They Work	Effectiveness
Medications		
Oral medications		
Such as Viagra, Vasomax	Relax muscles that surround small blood vessels in the penis, allowing dilation, so that blood can flow more freely	Effective
Yohimbine, trazadone, apomorphine	Possible involvement of neurotransmitters	Modest improvement in some men
Injections	Injections of smooth muscle relaxants into penis	Moderately effective in most cases but high attrition rate
Topical creams	Topical cream or ointment with vasoactive properties	Uncertain efficacy
Surgery		
Vascular surgery	Unblocks blood vessels that supply the penis	May have limited, short-term benefit
Semirigid surgical prosthesis	Surgical implantation of silicone rods into the penis	Moderately effective, low partner satisfaction ratings
Inflatable prosthesis	Surgical implantation of an inflatable device	Highly effective, high patient and partner satisfaction ratings
Other		
Vacuum pump	Vacuum constriction device that creates a vacuum when held over the penis	Effective in producing erections but not sexual arousal

Sources: Kelly, 1998; Rosen, 1996.

terone—to increase sexual desire in men and women with hypoactive sexual desire disorder. Hormone replacement therapy can be very effective for men whose low levels of sexual desire or arousal are linked to low levels of testosterone, although not for men whose low sexual desire or arousal are not linked to low levels of testosterone (Segraves, 2003). For women, the effects of testosterone therapy are mixed. Some studies find that high levels of testosterone increase sexual desire and arousal in women but also run the risk of significant side effects, including masculinizing effects (e.g., chest hair and voice changes) (Shifren et al., 2000). More moderate levels of testosterone do not have consistent effects on libido for women. The antidepressant bupropion has proven helpful in treating some women with hypoactive sexual desire (Segraves et al., 2004).

A large multinational, double-blind, placebo-controlled study investigated the effects of sildenafil for women with sexual arousal disorder (Basson et al., 2001, 2002). In both premenopausal and postmenopausal women, sildenafil had no demonstrable effect in reversing sexual problems. Other studies have also failed to find that this drug helps women with arousal disorders (Segraves, 2003). Interestingly, the drug does increase vasocongestion and lubrication in women; however, these physiological changes do not consistently lead to greater subjective arousal in women. It seems that, particularly for women, sexual arousal and pleasure take more than physiological arousal.

Women with vaginal dryness may find that using vaginal lubricants significantly increases their ability to become sexually aroused. Hormone replacement therapy can be effective for men whose low levels of sexual desire or arousal are linked to low levels of testosterone or for women whose low sexual desire or arousal, or dyspareunia, are linked to low levels of estrogen (Schiavi & Segraves, 1995; Schiavi et al., 1997).

Psychotherapy

The introduction of drugs, such as sildenfil, that can overcome sexual dysfunctions, at least in men, has dramatically changed the nature of the treatments for these disorders. With the financial and time constraints imposed by managed care, many people seeking treatment for a sexual dysfunction are only offered a medication, not psychotherapy (Leiblum & Rosen, 2000). Many people want only a medication and do not want to engage in psychotherapy to address the possible psychological and interpersonal contributors to their sexual problems.

A variety of psychotherapeutic techniques have been developed, however, and have been shown to help people with sexual dysfunctions (Leiblum & Rosen, 2000). These techniques include individual psychotherapy, in which the person explores the thoughts and previous experiences that impede them from enjoying a positive sexual life. Couples therapy is often used to help couples develop more satisfying sexual relationships. And, as part of both individual and couples therapy, behavioral techniques are used to teach people skills to enhance their sexual experiences and to improve their communication and interactions with their sexual partners.

One psychosocial source of difficulties in sexual functioning can be a fear of contracting a sexually transmitted disease or of becoming pregnant. In *Taking Psychology Personally: Practicing Safe Sex*, we discuss strategies to enhance your safety in sexual encounters.

Individual and Couples Therapy A therapist begins treatment by assessing the attitudes, beliefs, and personal history of an individual client or both members of a couple, to discover the experiences, thoughts, and feelings that are contributing to sexual problems. Cognitive-behavioral interventions are often used to address the attitudes and beliefs that interfere with sexual functioning (McCarthy, 2001; Pridal & LoPiccolo, 2000; Rosen & Leiblum, 1995). For example, a man who fears that he will embarrass himself by not sustaining an erection in a sexual encounter may be challenged to examine the evidence for this having happened to him in the past. If this were a common occurrence for this man, his therapist would explore the cognitions surrounding the experience and help the man challenge these cognitions and practice more positive cognitions. Similarly, a woman who has low sexual desire or difficulties reaching orgasm because she was taught by her parents that sex is dirty would learn to challenge this belief and to adopt a more accepting attitude toward sex.

When one member of a couple has a sexual dysfunction, it may be the result of problems in the couple's relationship, and it may contribute to problems in the relationship. Many therapists prefer to treat sexual dysfunctions in the context of the couple's relationship, if possible, rather than focusing only on the individual suffering the sexual dysfunction. The therapist may use role plays during therapy sessions to observe how the couple talk about sex with each other and perceive each other's role in sexual encounters (e.g., Pridal & LoPiccolo, 2000).

Some couples in long-standing relationships have abandoned the *seduction rituals*—the activities that arouse sexual interest in both partners—they followed when they were first together (McCarthy, 2001; Verhulst & Heiman, 1988). Couples in which both partners work may be particularly prone to try to squeeze in sexual encounters late at night, when both partners are very tired and not very interested in sex. These encounters may be rushed or not fully satisfying and lead to a gradual decline in interest for any sexual intimacy. A therapist may encourage a couple to set aside enough time so that they can engage in seduction rituals and satisfying sexual encounters (McCarthy, 1997). For example, partners may decide to hire a baby-sitter for their children, have a romantic dinner out, and then go to a hotel, where they can have sex without rushing or being interrupted by their children.

Partners often differ in their *scripts* for sexual encounters—their expectations about what will take place during a sexual encounter and about what each partner's responsibilities are (Pridal & LoPiccolo, 2000). Resolving these differences in scripts may be a useful goal in therapy. For example, if a woman lacks desire for sex because she feels her partner is too rough during sex, a therapist may encourage the partner to slow down and show the woman the kind of gentle intimacy she needs to enjoy sex. In general, therapists help partners understand what each other wants and needs from sexual interactions and negotiate mutually acceptable and satisfying repertoires of sexual exchange.

When the conflicts between partners involve matters other than their sexual practices, the therapist focuses on these conflicts primarily and the sexual dysfunction only secondarily. Such conflicts may involve an imbalance of power in the relationship, distrust or hostility, or disagreements over important values or decisions. Cognitive-behavioral therapies are most commonly used, although some therapists use psychodynamic interventions, and some use interventions based on family systems therapy. Cognitive-behavioral therapies have been researched more than other types of therapy and have been shown to be effective for several types of sexual dysfunctions (see Leiblum & Rosen, 2000).

Whether a therapist uses a cognitive-behavioral or another therapeutic approach to addressing the psychological issues involved in a sexual dysfunc-

Taking Psychology Personally

Practicing Safe Sex

One of the most common causes of low sexual desire or problems in sexual functioning is fear—fear of being hurt, of getting pregnant or causing someone else to become pregnant, or of getting a sexually transmitted disease (STD). Practicing safe sex cannot protect you from violence by a partner or from a sexual dysfunction, but it can decrease your risk for pregnancy and sexually transmitted diseases, which can improve your sexual satisfaction and protect your health.

Sexually transmitted diseases, such as acquired immune deficiency syndrome (AIDS), chlamydia, herpes, genital warts, gonorrhea, and syphilis, often have no obvious signs or symptoms. You cannot know if a potential sexual partner has an STD by just looking at him or her. Thus, it is essential to practice safe sex if you are going to be sexually active.

What does practicing safe sex mean? The following are some general tips:

■ *Have monogamous sexual relationships.* Have sex with only one person, who in turn is having sex only with you. If you or your partner change sexual partners frequently, your risk of contracting a sexually transmitted disease is increased.

■ *Know your partner's sexual history before you engage in sexual activity.* It can be very difficult to talk about your partner's history or your own. Volunteer information about your own history and then ask your partner about his or hers. Persist if your partner tries to brush aside your concerns and be prepared to postpone or refuse sexual contact if your partner will not answer your questions. Consider having both of you tested for HIV.

■ *Avoid sexual activity if you or your partner might have been exposed to any sexually transmitted disease.* Most of the sexually transmitted diseases can be treated medically, and sex can be resumed when the disease is cured or under control.

■ *Wash your genitals after sexual contact.* Washing helps reduce the risk but does not eliminate it.

■ *Urinate immediately after intercourse.* Doing so helps flush out some germs.

■ *Do not have sex under the influence of alcohol or other drugs.* Alcohol and other drugs can lead you to practice unsafe sex, can lead to misunderstandings between partners about what sexual activities are acceptable, and can impair your ability to resist unwanted sexual activities.

■ *Use condoms for vaginal and anal intercourse.*

Use a condom *every* time you have sex.

Put condoms on during foreplay, before there is any pre-ejaculatory fluid.

After ejaculation and before the penis relaxes, remove the condom by holding it around the base and withdrawing it from the penis.

Use another condom if sex is repeated.

Store condoms in a cool, dry place (not a wallet or the glove compartment of a car).

Never test condoms by inflating them or stretching them.

Never use oil-based lubricants, such as petroleum jelly (Vaseline), on condoms.

Never reuse condoms.

■ *Know that oral sex can also spread STDs.* Males should wear condoms during oral sex. Partners performing oral sex on women should use dental dams or other latex barriers to protect their mouths from direct exposure to vaginal fluids.*

Many people do not practice safe sex because they feel it reduces spontaneity and excitement in sexual encounters. However, condom use can be eroticized so that it becomes a part of foreplay. Also, knowing that you are practicing safe sex can reduce fear and, therefore, increase your ability to enjoy sexual encounters. Most important, protecting yourself from sexually transmitted diseases, particularly AIDS, should always be a higher priority than having a little more spontaneity in any sexual encounter.

*Adapted from "Breaking the STD Chain," distributed by Cowell Student Health Center and the Office of Residential Education, Stanford University.

tion, direct sex therapy using behavioral techniques often is also a part of therapy. When a sexual dysfunction seems to be due, at least in part, to inadequate sexual skills of the client and his or her partner, sex therapy focusing on these practices can be useful. Some people have never learned what practices give them or their partners pleasure or have fallen out of the habit of engaging in these practices. Sex therapy teaches these practices and helps partners develop a regular pattern of satisfying sexual encounters (see the Concept Overview in Table 16.6 on page 594).

TABLE 16.6 Concept Overview

Sex Therapy

Sex therapy is designed to help individuals learn what their bodies need for sexual satisfaction.

Sensate Focus Therapy

Phase one: gentle nongenital touching, focusing on pleasurable sensations and communication

Phase two: stimulation of partner's breasts and genitals without intercourse

Phase three: intercourse with a focus on enhancing and sustaining pleasure, not orgasm and performance

Stop-Start Technique (for Premature Ejaculation)

Phase one: stimulation of the man's penis stops just before he ejaculates; he relaxes and concentrates on bodily sensations until arousal passes

Phase two (if female partner involved): the woman inserts the man's penis into her vagina but remains quiet

Phase three: the female partner creates some thrusting motion with slow, long strokes

Squeeze Technique (for Premature Ejaculation)

The man's partner stimulates him to erection but then applies a firm squeeze to his penis to reduce erection. Exercise continues until the man learns to control ejaculation.

Relaxation Technique (for Vaginismus)

The woman is taught to relax the muscles at the opening of her vagina; gradually, she inserts larger dilators while practicing relaxation exercises and becoming accustomed to the feel of the object in her vagina.

Sex therapy often includes teaching or encouraging clients to masturbate (Heiman, 2000). The goals of masturbation are for the people to explore their own bodies to discover what is arousing and to become less inhibited about their own sexuality. Then, individuals are taught to communicate what they have learned to their partners. This technique can be especially helpful for anorgasmic women, many of whom have never masturbated and have little knowledge of what they need to become aroused. Studies show that more than 80 percent of anorgasmic women are able to have an orgasm when they learn to masturbate, and 20 to 60 percent are able to have an orgasm with their partner after learning to masturbate (Heiman, 2000). Women also report increased enjoyment and satisfaction from sex, a more relaxed attitude toward sex and life, and increased acceptance of their bodies.

The client's cognitions while engaging in new sexual exercises can be evaluated and used as a focus of therapy sessions (McCarthy, 1997). For example, a woman who is learning how to masturbate for the first time may realize that she has thoughts such as "I'm going to get caught and I'll be so embarrassed," "I shouldn't be doing this—this is sinful," and "Only pathetic people do this" while masturbating. A cognitive-behavioral therapist can then help the woman address the accuracy of these thoughts and decide whether she wants to maintain this attitude toward masturbation. If the woman is in psychodynamic therapy, the therapist might explore the origins of the woman's attitudes about masturbation in her early relationships. Thus, the behavioral techniques of sex therapy not only directly teach the client new sexual skills but also provide material for discussion in therapy sessions.

Sensate Focus Therapy One of the mainstays of sex therapy is **sensate focus therapy** (Althof, 2000; Masters & Johnson, 1970). In this therapy, one partner is active, carrying out a set of exercises to stimulate the other partner, while the other partner is the passive recipient, focusing on the pleasure that the exercises bring. Then, the partners switch roles, so that each spends time being both the giver and the recipient of the stimulation. The exercises should be carried out at quiet, unhurried times, which the partners plan.

In the early phases of this therapy, partners are instructed *not* to be concerned about or even to attempt intercourse. Rather, they are told to focus intently on the pleasure created by the exercises.

These instructions are meant to reduce performance anxiety and concern about achieving orgasm.

In the first phase of sensate focus therapy, partners spend time gently touching each other, but not around the genitals. They are instructed to focus on the sensations and to communicate with each other about what does and does not feel good. The goal is to have the partners spend intimate time together, communicating, without pressure for intercourse. This first phase may continue for several weeks, until the partners feel comfortable with the exercise and have learned what gives each of them pleasure.

In the second phase of sensate focus therapy, the partners spend time directly stimulating each other's breasts and genitals but still without attempting to have intercourse and instead focusing on intimacy and communication. If the problem is a female arousal disorder, the woman guides her partner to stimulate her in arousing ways. It is acceptable for a woman to be aroused to orgasm during these exercises, but the partners are instructed not to attempt intercourse until she regularly becomes fully aroused by her partner during sensate focus exercises. If the problem is a male erectile disorder, the man guides his partner in touching him in ways that feel arousing. If he has an erection, he is to let it come and go naturally. Intercourse is forbidden until he is able to have erections easily and frequently during the sensate focus exercises.

Throughout these exercises, the partner with the problem is instructed to be selfish and to focus only on the arousing sensations and on communicating with his or her partner about what feels good. The touching should proceed in a relaxed and nondemanding atmosphere. Once the partner with the problem regularly experiences arousal with genital stimulation, the partners may begin having intercourse, but the focus remains on enhancing and sustaining pleasure, rather than on orgasm or performance.

The following case study indicates how the behavioral techniques of sensate focus therapy can help a couple recognize and confront the complex personal and interpersonal issues that may be interfering with their enjoyment of sex (Althof, 2000, p. 270).

In sensate focus therapy, people are encouraged to spend time exploring what sexually arouses each other without feeling pressured to reach orgasm.

CASE STUDY

Murray, a 53-year-old successful insurance agent, and his wife, a 50-year-old nutritional counselor, had been married for 28 years. With the exception of time spent on vacation, Murray had a 7-year history of erectile dysfunction. The frequency of their love making had gradually declined to its current level of once every 4 months. Murray reported considerable performance anxiety, enhanced by his competitive personality style. He summed up his dilemma: "When you have a life full of successes, you don't get much practice at how to deal with inadequacy."

During the first hour [of therapy], sensate focus exercises were suggested, and instructions given to engage in sensual nongenital touching. They returned in a week, noting how difficult it had been to find time to pleasure one another. Their mutual avoidance was discussed and understood as a means of warding off feelings of inadequacy. Working through the resistance allowed the couple to engage in the exercises three times over the course of

(continued)

the next week. With the pleasuring, Murray began to achieve good, long-lasting erections.

Therapy then progressed to include genital touching. After the first week, they talked about their problem of "silliness." They realized that humor had been used to cope with the dysfunction. Now, however, joking in bed seemed to inhibit sexual closeness. Murray's good erections were maintained, although he was having trouble concentrating on his sensations. Further exploration revealed that he was focusing his attention in a driven, intense manner. To counter this, [the therapist] redirected him to maintain a relaxed awareness akin to meditation. Murray found this analogy helpful, and the couple felt ready to proceed with vaginal containment. During the following week, they "disobeyed" and moved on to have mutually satisfying intercourse. They feared the recurrence of the old problem, but it did not return, and the remaining two sessions were spent talking about their sexual life. Despite otherwise good communication, they had never been able before to broach this topic with one another.

Techniques for Treating Premature Ejaculation
Two techniques are useful in helping a man with premature ejaculation gain control over his ejaculations: the stop-start technique (Semans, 1956) and the squeeze technique (Masters & Johnson, 1970). The **stop-start technique** can be carried out either through masturbation or with a partner. In the first phase, the man is told to stop stimulating himself or to tell his partner to stop stimulation just before he is about to ejaculate. He then relaxes and concentrates on the sensations in his body until his level of arousal declines. At that point, he or his partner can resume stimulation, again stopping before the point of ejaculatory inevitability. If stimulation stops too late and the man ejaculates, he is encouraged not to feel angry or disappointed but to enjoy the ejaculation and reflect on what he has learned about his body and then resume the exercise. If a man is engaging in this exercise with a female partner, they are instructed not to engage in intercourse until he has sufficient control over his ejaculations during her manual stimulation of him.

In the second phase of this process, when a female partner is involved, the man lies on his back, with his female partner on top of him, and she inserts his penis into her vagina but then remains quiet. Most men with premature ejaculation have intercourse only in the man-on-top position, with quick and short thrusting during intercourse, which makes it very difficult for them to exert control over their ejaculations. The goal is for the man to enjoy the sensation of being in the woman's vagina without ejaculating. During the exercise, he is encouraged to touch or massage his partner and to communicate with her about what each is experiencing. If he feels he is reaching ejaculatory inevitability, he can request that she dismount and lie next to him until his arousal subsides. The partners are encouraged to engage in this exercise for at least 10 to 15 minutes, even if they must interrupt it several times to prevent him from ejaculating.

In the third phase of the stop-start technique, she creates some thrusting motion while still on top of him, but using slow, long strokes. The partners typically reach orgasm and experience the entire encounter as highly intimate and pleasurable. Female partners of men with premature ejaculation often have trouble reaching orgasm themselves, because the men lose their erections after ejaculating long before the women are highly aroused, and tension is high between the partners during sex. The stop-start technique can create encounters in which female partners receive the stimulation they need to reach orgasm as well.

The **squeeze technique** is used somewhat less often, because it is harder to teach to partners (McCarthy, 2001). The man's partner stimulates him to an erection; then, when he signals that ejaculation is imminent, the partner applies a firm but gentle squeeze to his penis, either at the glans or at the base, for three or four seconds. This results in a partial loss of erection. The partner can then stimulate him again to the point of ejaculation and use the squeeze technique to stop the ejaculation. The goal of this technique, as with the stop-start technique, is for the man with a premature ejaculation disorder to learn to identify the point of ejaculatory inevitability and to control his arousal level at that point.

Techniques for Treating Vaginismus Vaginismus is often treated by deconditioning the woman's automatic tightening of the muscles of her vagina (Leiblum, 2000). She is taught about the muscular tension at the opening of her vagina and the need to learn to relax those muscles. In a safe setting, she is instructed to insert her own fingers into her vagina. She examines her vagina in a mirror and practices relaxation exercises. She may also use silicon or metal vaginal dilators made for this exercise. Gradually, she inserts larger and larger dilators, as she practices relaxation exercises and becomes accustomed to the feel of the dilator in her vagina. If she has a partner, his or her fingers may be used instead of the dilator. If the woman has a male partner, eventually she guides his penis into her vagina, while remaining in control.

Gay, Lesbian, and Bisexual People

Most of the treatments for sexual dysfunctions assume that the client is in a heterosexual relationship, but sexual dysfunctions can arise in gay, lesbian, and bisexual relationships as well. Often, the causes of their sexual dysfunctions are the same as the causes of sexual dysfunctions in heterosexual people, such as medical disorders or medications, biological aging, or conflicts with partners. Many of the problems in sexual functioning experienced by gay, lesbian, and bisexual people, however, may have to do with society's attitudes toward them and the particular stressors they face (Gilman et al., 2001). They may have lost partners and friends to AIDS, and grief and depression can impair sexual functioning. The fear of contracting the human immunodeficiency virus (HIV) can also heighten sexual anxiety and dampen sexual desire.

Gay, lesbian, and bisexual people must constantly deal with homophobia. They may face frequent discrimination and harassment. They have strong fear of homophobic violence against them. Gay, lesbian, and bisexual parents face chronic challenges to their legitimacy as parents. All of these pressures can interfere with normal sexual functioning.

Therapists treating gay, lesbian, or bisexual clients must be sensitive to the psychological conflicts and stresses these clients face as a result of society's rejection of their lifestyle, as well as to the contributions of these stresses to their sexual functioning (APA, 2000). Most of the sex therapy treatments can readily be adapted for gay, lesbian, or bisexual couples. It can be important to take into account the special social context in which any psychological problem reported by a gay, lesbian, or bisexual client occurs, however.

We should note that the attitude of clinical psychology as a profession toward homosexuality has changed over the past several decades. Early versions of the DSM listed homosexuality, particularly "ego-dystonic homosexuality" (which meant that the person did not want to be homosexual), as a mental disorder. Gay men, lesbians, and bisexual people argued that their sexual orientation is a natural part of themselves and a characteristic that causes them no discomfort and that they don't wish to alter or eliminate. In addition, there was little evidence that psychotherapy could lead a ho-

Sexual dysfunctions can also arise in the context of gay, lesbian, and bisexual relationships.

mosexual person to become heterosexual. In 1973, the American Psychiatric Association removed homosexuality from its list of recognized psychological disorders (Spitzer, 1981).

Large, epidemiological studies find that gay and bisexual men show a higher prevalence of depression and panic attacks than heterosexual men, however, and lesbian and bisexual women show a greater prevalence of generalized anxiety disorder than heterosexual women (Cochran, Sullivan, & Mays, 2003). These higher rates of mental-health problems seem to be due to the greater levels of stress in the lives of gay, lesbian, and bisexual individuals because of homophobia and discrimination.

Cultural Issues

The treatments for the sexual dysfunctions must also take into account the religious, moral, and cultural values that clients have concerning sex. The treatments described so far in this chapter tend to be based on the assumption that men and women should have sex when they wish and should enjoy it each time they have it. This assumption is not shared by persons of all backgrounds. Inhibitions about sex based on religious or cultural teachings are often seen as the causes of sexual dysfunctions by sex therapists. At the very least, cultural inhibitions against talking about sex can get in the way of therapy. The experienced therapist works within the values framework of the sexual partners, first finding out what is in their current repertoire of sexual activity and then building on that, according to their comfort.

Finally, many cultures have their own folk remedies for sexual dysfunctions (Kelly, 1998; Mannino, 1999). In Africa, impotent men drink potions and engage in ritual ceremonies to overcome their dysfunction. Hashish is the cure for sexual dysfunction in males in Morocco, whereas women who are anorgasmic are encouraged to take a younger lover or have a lesbian relationship. In Thailand, men drink a tonic made of the bile of a cobra, the blood of a monkey, and local liquor. In India, they apply an herb to the penis that is a potent irritant. In other parts of the world, the testes and penises of seals and tigers are consumed to overcome erectile problems in men. Traditional Chinese healers use a number of herbal preparations and acupuncture to treat sexual dysfunctions.

SUMMING UP

- The sexual response cycle includes five phases: desire, excitement or arousal, plateau, orgasm, and resolution.

- People with disorders of sexual desire have little or no desire to engage in sex. These disorders include hypoactive sexual desire disorder and sexual aversion disorder.

- People with sexual arousal disorders do not experience the physiological changes that make up the excitement or arousal phase of the sexual response cycle. These disorders include female sexual arousal disorder and male erectile disorder.

- Women with female orgasmic disorder do not experience orgasm or have greatly delayed orgasm after reaching the excitement phase. Men with premature ejaculation reach ejaculation before they wish. Men with male orgasmic disorder have a recurrent delay in or an absence of orgasm following sexual excitement.

- The two sexual pain disorders are dyspareunia, genital pain associated with intercourse, and vaginismus, involuntary contraction of the vaginal muscles in women.

- The biological causes of sexual dysfunctions include undiagnosed diabetes or other medical conditions, prescription or recreational drug use (including alcohol), and hormonal or vascular abnormalities.

- The psychological causes include psychological disorders and maladaptive attitudes and cognitions (especially performance concerns).

- The sociocultural and interpersonal causes include problems in intimate relationships, traumatic experiences, and an upbringing or a cultural environment that devalues or degrades sex.

- When the cause of a sexual dysfunction is biological, treatments that eradicate the cause can cure the sexual dysfunction. Alternately, drug therapies or prostheses can be used.

- Sex therapy corrects the inadequate sexual practices of a client and his or her partner. The techniques of sex therapy include sensate focus therapy, instruction in masturbation, the stop-start and squeeze techniques, and the deconditioning of vaginal contractions.

- Couples therapy focuses on decreasing conflicts between couples over their sexual practices or over other areas of their relationship.

- Individual psychotherapy helps people recognize conflicts or the negative attitudes behind their sexual dysfunctions and resolve these.

PARAPHILIAS

People find all sorts of creative ways to fulfill their sexual needs and desires while remaining within the limits set on sexual behavior by their society. Some examples in Western culture include the use of erotic fantasies, pictures or stories, or sex toys to enhance arousal while engaging in masturbation or sexual encounters with others. People vary greatly in what they do and do not find arousing (see Table 16.7). One person may find oral sex the most stimulating form of activity, whereas another person may be repulsed by oral sex. One man may become extremely aroused while watching a wet T-shirt contest, but another man may experience such a contest as silly. One woman may find men with beards extremely sexy, whereas another woman may dislike facial hair on men. Most of the time, these variations in preferences about sexually arousing stimuli simply provide spice to life.

Societies have always drawn lines between the types of sexual activities they allow and the types they do not allow. Judgments about what are acceptable sexual activities vary by culture and across historical periods. In Western cultures prior to the twentieth century and in some Islamic nations today, men are prohibited from seeing most of women's bodies, except their faces and hands, for fear that viewing women's legs and perhaps even their arms or their hair could sexually arouse men.

TABLE 16.7 What Kinds of Sexual Practices Do People Find Appealing?

A national survey of 18- to 44-year-olds found that many different sexual practices appeal to people, with men finding more activities appealing than women do.

Practice	Percentage Saying "Very Appealing"	
	Men	Women
Vaginal intercourse	83	78
Watching partner undress	50	30
Receiving oral sex	50	33
Giving oral sex	37	19
Group sex	14	1
Anus stimulated by partner's fingers	6	4
Using dildos/vibrators	5	3
Watching others do sexual things	6	2
Having a same-gender sex partner	4	3
Having sex with a stranger	5	1

Source: Michael et al., 1994.

Although we may like to think that, in our modern culture, we disallow only the sexual behaviors that are truly "abnormal," our judgments about what are normal and abnormal sexual behaviors are still subjective and culturally specific. Consider the following series of behaviors exhibited by three men. The first man goes to a public beach to watch women in skimpy bikinis. The second man pays to see a female topless dancer in a nightclub. The third man stands outside a woman's bedroom window at night, secretly watching her undress. The behavior of the first man is not only allowed but also is promoted in many movies, television shows, and commercials. The behavior of the second man is a form of allowed sexual commerce. Only the behavior of the third man is prohibited both by modern cultural norms and by laws. All three men, however, intend to view women's partially or fully nude bodies because they find such activity sexually arousing.

Atypical sexual behaviors that the DSM-IV-TR considers to be disorders are the **paraphilias** (Greek for "besides" and "love"). When people with paraphilias violate laws, they are referred to as *sex offenders*. The paraphilias are sexual activities that involve (1) nonhuman objects, (2) nonconsenting adults, (3) suffering or the humiliation of the person or the person's partner, or (4) children (see the Concept Overview in Table 16.8 on page 600). Paraphilias are sometimes divided into those that involve the consent of others (such as some sadomasochistic practices) and those that involve nonconsenting others (as in pedophilia). They can also be divided into those that involve contact with others (such as frotteurism) and those that do not necessarily involve contact with others (such as some fetishes).

Many people have occasional paraphilic fantasies. For example, one study of men's sexual fantasies found that 62 percent fantasized having sex with a young girl, 33 percent fantasized raping a woman, 12 percent fantasized being humiliated during sex, 5 percent fantasized having sexual activity with an animal, and 3 percent fantasized having sexual activity with a young boy (Crepault & Couture, 1980). In a study of male college undergraduates, 21 percent reported being sexually attracted to children, 9 percent fantasized having sex with children, 5 percent masturbated to fantasies of having sex with children, and 7 percent indicated they would become sexually involved with children if they could be assured they would never be discovered (Briere & Runtz, 1989). Most of these men would not be diagnosed with paraphilias because their fantasies were not the primary focus of their sexual arousal and they reported making no attempts to act out these fantasies.

For persons diagnosed with paraphilias, atypical sexual acts are their primary forms of sexual arousal. They often feel compelled to engage in their paraphilias, even though they know they could be punished by law or when they are distressed about feeling so compelled. Some people with paraphilia pay prostitutes to help them act out their fantasies, because it is difficult to find willing partners. Others with paraphilias force their fantasies on unwilling victims.

The paraphilias differ greatly in how severely they affect people other than the person with the paraphilia. We begin our discussion of the paraphilias with the one that is most benign: fetishism. People with *fetishism* do not typically impose their atypical sexual practices on other people. Indeed, the focus of their sexual activities are nonhuman objects. The second set of paraphilias we discuss,

TABLE 16.8 Concept Overview

The Paraphilias

The paraphilias are sexual activities that involve nonhuman objects, nonconsenting adults, suffering or the humiliation of oneself or one's partner, or children.

Diagnosis	Description
Fetishism	A person uses inanimate objects as the preferred or exclusive source of sexual arousal.
Transvestism	In this fetish, a heterosexual man dresses in women's clothing as his primary means of becoming sexually aroused.
Sexual sadism	Sexual gratification is obtained through inflicting pain and humiliation on one's partner.
Sexual masochism	Sexual gratification is obtained through experiencing pain and humiliation at the hands of one's partner.
Voyeurism	Sexual arousal is obtained by compulsively and secretly watching another person undressing, bathing, engaging in sex, or being naked.
Exhibitionism	Sexual gratification is obtained by exposing one's genitals to involuntary observers.
Frotteurism	Sexual gratification is obtained by rubbing one's genitals against or fondling the body parts of a nonconsenting person.
Pedophilia	Adults obtain sexual gratification by engaging in sexual activities with young children.

Source: Reprinted with permission from Diagnostic and Statistical Manual of Mental Disorders, Fourth Edition, Text Revision. Copyright © 2000 American Psychiatric Association.

sadism and *masochism,* are less benign, because they hold the potential for physical harm, even if both partners are engaging in the sexual activity willingly. The third set of paraphilias—*voyeurism, exhibitionism,* and *frotteurism*—are not benign, because, by definition, they require victims. Finally, the most severe paraphilia is *pedophilia,* because the victims of pedophiles are the most powerless victims: children.

Fetishism

Fetishism involves the use of inanimate objects (fetishes) as the preferred or exclusive source of sexual arousal or gratification. Soft fetishes are objects that are soft, furry, or lacy, such as frilly women's panties, stockings, and garters. Hard fetishes are objects that are smooth, harsh, or black, such as spike-heeled shoes, black gloves, and garments made of leather or rubber. These soft and hard objects are somewhat arousing to many people and, indeed, are promoted as arousing by their manufacturers. For most people, however, the objects simply add to the sexiness of the people wearing them, and their desire is for sex with those people. For the person with fetishism, the desire is linked to the object itself (adapted from Spitzer et al., 1994, p. 247):

CASE STUDY

A 32-year-old, single, male, freelance photographer presented with the chief complaint of "abnormal sex drive." The patient related that although he was somewhat sexually attracted by women, he was far more attracted by "their panties."

To the best of the patient's memory, sexual excitement began at about age 7, when he came upon a pornographic magazine and felt stimulated by pictures of partially nude women wearing panties. His first ejaculation occurred at 13 via masturbation to fantasies of women wearing panties. He masturbated into his older sister's panties, which he had stolen without her knowledge. Subsequently, he stole panties from her friends and from other women he met socially. He found pretexts to "wander" into the bedrooms of women during social occasions and would quickly rummage through their possessions until he found a pair of panties to his satis-

(continued)

faction. He later used these to masturbate into and then "saved them" in a "private cache." The pattern of masturbating into women's underwear had been his method of achieving sexual excitement and orgasm from adolescence until the present consultation.

The patient first had sexual intercourse at 18. Since then he had had intercourse on many occasions, and his preferred partner was a prostitute paid to wear panties, with the crotch area cut away, during the act. On less common occasions when sexual activity was attempted with a partner who did not wear panties, his sexual excitement was sometimes weak.

The patient felt uncomfortable dating "nice women" as he felt that friendliness might lead to sexual intimacy and that they would not understand his sexual needs. He avoided socializing with friends who might introduce him to such women. He recognized that his appearance, social style, and profession all resulted in his being perceived as a highly desirable bachelor. He felt anxious and depressed because his social life was limited by his sexual preference.

One elaborate form of fetishism is **transvestism,** also referred to as *cross-dressing,* in which heterosexual men dress in women's clothing as their primary means of becoming sexually aroused. They may surreptitiously wear only one women's garment, such as a pair of women's panties, under their business suits. The complete cross-dresser fully clothes himself in women's garments and applies makeup and a wig. Some men engage in cross-dressing alone. Others participate in transvestite subcultures, in which groups of men gather for drinks, meals, and dancing while elaborately dressed as women (adapted from Spitzer et al., 1994, pp. 257–258):

CASE STUDY

Mr. A., a 65-year-old security guard, is distressed about his wife's objections to his wearing a nightgown at home in the evening, now that his youngest child has left home. His appearance and demeanor, except when he is dressing in women's clothes, are always masculine, and he is exclusively heterosexual. Occasionally, over the past 5 years, he has worn an inconspicuous item of female clothing even when dressed as a man, sometimes a pair of panties, sometimes an ambiguous pinkie ring. He always carries a photograph of himself dressed as a woman.

His first recollection of an interest in female clothing was putting on his sister's underpants at age 12, an act accompanied by sexual excitement. He continued periodically to put on women's underpants—an activity that invariably resulted in an erection, sometimes a spontaneous emission, and sometimes masturbation but never accompanied by fantasy. Although he occasionally wished to be a girl, he never fantasized himself as one. During his single years he was always attracted to women but was shy about sex. Following his marriage at age 22, he had his first heterosexual intercourse.

His involvement with female clothes was of the same intensity even after his marriage. Beginning at age 45, after a chance exposure to a magazine called *Transvestia,* he began to increase his cross-dressing activity. He learned there were other men like himself, and he became more and more preoccupied with

(continued)

People with transvestism gain sexual pleasure by dressing in the clothes of the opposite sex.

female clothing in fantasy and progressed to periodically dressing completely as a woman. More recently he has become involved in a transvestite network, writing to other transvestites contacted through the magazine and occasionally attending transvestite parties. These parties have been the only times that he has cross-dressed outside his home.

Although still committed to his marriage, sex with his wife has dwindled over the past 20 years as his waking thoughts and activities have become increasingly centered on cross-dressing. Over time this activity has become less eroticized and more an end in itself, but it still is a source of some sexual excitement. He always has an increased urge to dress as a woman when under stress; it has a tranquilizing effect. If particular circumstances prevent him from cross-dressing, he feels extremely frustrated.

Some clinicians question whether fetishism should qualify as a psychiatric diagnosis or should be considered a variation in human sexual activity. Many, perhaps most, people with fetishism do not seek therapy or feel particularly disturbed about their behavior. In most cases, the behavior is socially harmless because it is done in private and does not involve the infliction of harm on others. Fetishism is one of the most common secondary diagnoses of persons with other types of paraphilias, however (Abel & Osborn, 1992). That is, many people who have fetishes also engage in other atypical sexual practices, including pedophilia, exhibitionism, and voyeurism. Thus, for some people, fetishes are part of a larger pattern of atypical sexual behaviors, including behaviors that have victims.

Sexual Sadism and Sexual Masochism

Sexual sadism and **sexual masochism** are two separate diagnoses, although sadistic and masochistic sexual practices often are considered together as a pattern referred to as **sadomasochism.** In sexual sadism, a person gains sexual gratification by inflicting pain and humiliation on his or her sex partner. In sexual masochism, a person gains sexual gratification by suffering pain or humiliation during sex. Some people occasionally engage in moderately sadistic or masochistic behaviors during sex or simulate such behaviors without actually carrying through with the infliction of pain or suffering. Persons who are diagnosed with sexual sadism or masochism engage in these behaviors as their primary form of sexual gratification.

The sexual rituals in sadism and masochism fall into four types: physical restriction, which involves the use of bondage, chains, or handcuffs as part of sex; the administration of pain, in which one partner inflicts pain or harm on the other with beatings, whippings, electrical shock, burning, cutting, stabbing, strangulation, torture, mutilation, and even death; hypermasculinity practices, including the aggressive use of enemas, fists, and dildos in the sexual act; and humiliation, in which one partner verbally and physically humiliates the other during sex (Sandnabba et al., 2002). The partner who is the victim in such encounters may be a willing victim or may be a nonconsenting victim on whom the person with sadism carries out his or her wishes. A variety of props may be used in such encounters, including black leather garments, chains, shackles, whips, harnesses, and ropes. Men are much more likely than women to enjoy sadomasochistic sex, in the roles of both sadist and masochist (Sandnabba et al., 2002). Some women find such activities exciting, but others consent to them only to please their partners or because they are paid to do so, and some are unconsenting victims.

Voyeurism, Exhibitionism, and Frotteurism

Voyeurism involves secretly watching another person undressing, bathing, doing things in the nude, or engaging in sex as a primary form of sexual arousal. For a diagnosis to be made, the voyeuristic behavior must be repetitive over six months and be compulsive. The person being observed must be unaware of it and would be upset if he or she knew about it. Almost all people who engage in voyeurism are men who watch women. They typically masturbate while watching or shortly after watching women.

Exhibitionism is, in some ways, the mirror image of voyeurism. The person who engages in exhibitionism obtains sexual gratification by exposing his or her genitals to involuntary observers, who are usually complete strangers. In the vast majority of cases, the person who engages in exhibitionism is a man who bares all to surprised women. He typically confronts women in a public place, such as a park, bus, or subway, either with his genitals already exposed or by flashing open his coat to expose his bare genitals. His arousal comes from observing the victim's surprise, fear, or disgust or from a fantasy that his victim is becoming sexually aroused. His behavior is often compulsive and impulsive: He feels a sense of excitement, fear, restlessness, and sexual arousal and then feels compelled to find relief by exhibiting himself. Some people with exhibitionism masturbate while exhibiting themselves. Others experience little or no arousal during the act, however, and instead they store these exhibitionist episodes in memory and use them during later masturbatory session (Becker, 2000), as in the following case study (adapted from Spitzer et al., 1994, pp. 117–118):

CASE STUDY

A 27-year-old engineer requested consultation at a psychiatric clinic because of irresistible urges to exhibit his penis to female strangers. At age 18, for reasons unknown to himself, he first experienced an overwhelming desire to engage in exhibitionism. He sought situations in which he was alone with a woman he did not know. As he approached her, he would become sexually excited. He would then walk up to her and display his erect penis. He found that her shock and fear further stimulated him, and usually he would then ejaculate. He also fantasized past encounters while masturbating. He feels guilty and ashamed after exhibiting himself and vows never to repeat it. Nevertheless, the desire often overwhelms him, and the behavior recurs frequently, usually at periods of tension.

People who engage in exhibitionism are more likely than most sex offenders to get caught, in part because of the public nature of their behavior but also because some of them seem to invite arrest by doing things such as repeatedly returning to places where they have already exhibited themselves. People who engage in exhibitionism are also likely to continue their behavior after having been caught.

Frotteurism is another paraphilia that often co-occurs with voyeurism and exhibitionism. The person who engages in frotteurism gains sexual gratification by rubbing against and fondling parts of the body of a nonconsenting person. Often, the person engages in this behavior in crowded places where his target may not realize that the contact has anything to do with sexuality, such as a crowded elevator. Most people with frotteurism are young men between 15 and 25 years of age, but little else is known about this disorder.

Pedophilia

The most troubling and most common paraphilia is **pedophilia.** People with pedophilia are sexually attracted to children and prefer to engage in sex with children rather than with other adults. The diagnosis of pedophilia generally requires that the sexual encounters be with children under the age of 13 and initiated by persons 16 years old or older and at least 5 years older than the children. Laws in most of the United States, however, define *child molesting* or *statutory rape* to include adults having sex with persons under the age of 18 (Green, 1993).

Sexual encounters between people with pedophilia and their child victims are often brief, although they may recur frequently. The contact most often consists of the person with pedophilia exposing and touching the child's genitals (Abel & Osborn, 1992). Other people with pedophilia perform fellatio (oral stimulation of the penis) or cunnilingus (oral stimulation of the female genitals) on children or penetrate children's vaginas, mouths, or anuses with their fingers, foreign objects, or their penises. People with pedophilia may threaten children with harm, physically restrain them, or tell them that they will punish them or their loved ones if the children do not comply with the pedophiles' wishes. Other people with pedophilia are loving, caring, and gentle to the child, using emotional closeness to gain sexual access to the child. This is especially true in incestuous relationships, in which people with pedophilia see themselves as simply being good, loving parents and believe that what they do to the child is not sexual but loving.

Defrocked priest Paul Shanley was convicted of pedophilia.

Most people with pedophilia are heterosexual men abusing young girls (Fagan et al., 2002). Homosexual men with pedophilia typically abuse young boys. Women can have pedophilia, but this is more rare.

CASE STUDY

Dr. Crone, a 35-year-old, single child psychiatrist, has been arrested and convicted of fondling several neighborhood girls, ages 6 to 12. Friends and colleagues were shocked and dismayed, as he had been considered by all to be particularly caring and supportive of children.

Dr. Crone's first sexual experience was at age 6, when a 15-year-old female camp counselor performed fellatio on him several times over the course of the summer—an experience that he had always kept to himself. As he grew older, he was surprised to notice that the age range of girls who attracted him sexually did not change, and he continued to have recurrent erotic urges and fantasies about girls between the ages of 6 and 12. Whenever he masturbated, he would fantasize about a girl in that age range, and on a couple of occasions over the years, he had felt himself to be in love with such a youngster.

Intellectually, Dr. Crone knew that others would disapprove of his many sexual involvements with young girls. He never believed, however, that he had caused any of these youngsters harm, feeling instead that they were simply sharing pleasurable feelings together. He frequently prayed for help and that his actions would go undetected. He kept promising himself that he would stop, but the temptations were such that he could not. (Adapted from Spitzer et al., 1994, pp. 187–188)

Mental-health experts are divided over whether people with pedophilia should be viewed primarily as persons with a psychiatric disorder that needs treating or as criminals who should be incarcerated (McConaghy, 1998). Even those who view pedophilia primarily as a disorder to be treated tend to agree that people with pedophilia should be prevented from engaging in their behaviors, often through incarceration.

Causes of Paraphilias

Many of the paraphilias may have similar causes, which may account for the fact that many people with paraphilia engage in a number of different paraphilic behaviors. Over 90 percent of people with paraphilias are men (McConaghy, 1998).

Attempts to link paraphilic behavior, particularly sexually aggressive paraphilias, to testosterone abnormalities have met with limited success (Langevin, 1992). Similarly, although some studies have found links between other hormones or endocrine abnormalities and paraphilias, no consistent biological cause of the paraphilias has been found (Maletzky, 1998).

Behavioral theories of the paraphilias explain them as due to an initial classical pairing of intense early sexual arousal with a particular stimulus (see Figure 16.5). For example, a youngster may become aroused when spying on the baby-sitter's lovemaking or when being held down and tickled erotically. This is followed by intensive operant conditioning in which the stimulus is present during masturbation. For example, the individual may repeatedly fantasize a particular scenario, such as watching the baby-sitter's lovemaking, while masturbating. This reinforces the association between the stimulus and sexual arousal. The individual may attempt to inhibit the undesired arousal or his behaviors, but, paradoxically, these attempts at inhibition increase the frequency and intensity of these fantasies. Eventually, the sexual arousal may generalize to other stimuli similar to the initial fantasy, such as actually watching other people's lovemaking or being naked, leading to paraphilic behavior (e.g., voyeurism). Often, the person with paraphilia also lacks adequate alternative sexual reinforcement opportunities and skills for relating appropriate to other adults.

These classic behavioral theories have been supplemented with principles of social learning theory (see Chapter 2), which suggest that the larger environment of a child's home and culture influence his or her tendency to develop deviant sexual behavior. Children whose parents frequently use physical punishment on them and who engage in aggressive, often sexual, contact with each other are more likely to engage in impulsive, aggressive, perhaps sexualized acts toward others as they grow older. Many people with pedophilia have poor interpersonal skills and feel intimidated when interacting sexually with adults.

A study of 64 convicted sex offenders with various types of paraphilias found that, compared with offenders who had committed property crimes and did not have paraphilias, the sex offenders had higher rates of childhood emotional abuse and family dysfunction and childhood sex-

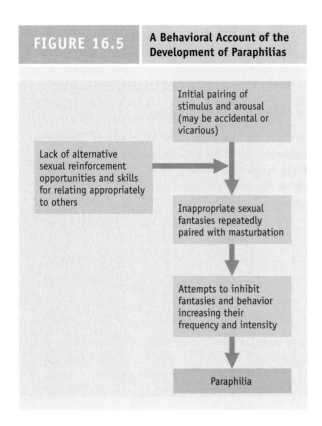

FIGURE 16.5   **A Behavioral Account of the Development of Paraphilias**

Lack of alternative sexual reinforcement opportunities and skills for relating appropriately to others

Initial pairing of stimulus and arousal (may be accidental or vicarious)

Inappropriate sexual fantasies repeatedly paired with masturbation

Attempts to inhibit fantasies and behavior increasing their frequency and intensity

Paraphilia

ual abuse (Lee et al., 2002). Childhood sexual abuse was a particularly strong predictor of pedophilia. Similarly, studies of juvenile sex offenders, most of whom had assaulted a younger child, find that many are likely to have suffered sexual abuse earlier in childhood (Gerardin & Thibaut, 2004).

Cognitive theorists have also identified a number of distortions and assumptions that people with paraphilias have about their behaviors and the behaviors of their victims, as shown in Table 16.9 on page 606 (Gerardin & Thibaut, 2004; Maletzky, 1998). These distortions may have been learned from their parents' deviant messages about sexual behavior. They justify the person's victimization of others.

Treatments for Paraphilias

Most people with paraphilia do not seek treatment for their behaviors. Treatment is often forced on those who engage in illegal acts (voyeurism, exhibitionism, frotteurism, pedophilia) after they are arrested for breaking the law by engaging in their behaviors. Simple incarceration does little to change these behaviors, and the recidivism rate among convicted sex offenders is very high.

Biological interventions have been tried, primarily with people with pedophilia and men who commit rape. These interventions formerly included surgery on the centers of the brain thought to control sexual behavior and surgery to stop the production of the hormones influencing sexual arousal. Ceasing the production of these hormones lowers recidivism rates among people with paraphilia who have committed sexual crimes (Maletsky & Field, 2003). Ethical concerns over the irreversibility of this treatment and the ability of offenders to freely consent to it have led to it being rarely used.

These days, sex offenders might be offered antiandrogen drugs that suppress the functioning of the testes, such as depo-Provera, thereby reducing the production of testosterone and possibly reducing the sex drive. These drugs are typically used in conjunction with psychotherapy and can be useful for hypersexual men who are motivated to change their behavior (Maletzky & Field, 2003). Follow-up studies have shown that people with paraphilia treated with antiandrogen drugs do show great reductions in their paraphilic behavior (Bradford, 1995; Gerardin & Thibaut, 2004; Maletzky & Field, 2003). These drugs can have significant side effects, however, and reduce overall sexual drive for the individual. Difficult ethical questions arise when the use of these drugs is part of a deal struck with a sex offender for a lighter sentence or parole.

Most recently, the selective serotonin reuptake inhibitors (SSRIs) have been used to reduce sexual drive and paraphilic behavior. Some studies find positive effects of these drugs on sexual drive and impulse control (e.g., Greenberg et al., 1996), although the effects are not totally consistent across studies (see Maletzky & Field, 2003).

Insight-oriented therapies alone have not proven extremely successful in changing behavior in people with paraphilia. Behavior modification therapies are commonly used to treat paraphilia and can be successful if people with paraphilia are willing to change their behavior. **Aversion therapy** is used to extinguish sexual responses to objects or situations that a person with paraphilia finds arousing. During such therapy, a person with paraphilia might receive painful but harmless electric shocks or loud bursts of noise while viewing photographs of what arouse him or her (such as children) or while actually touching objects that arouse him or her (such as women's panties). **Desensitization** procedures may be used to reduce the person's anxiety about engaging in normal sexual encounters with other adults. For example, people with paraphilia might be taught relaxation exercises, which they then use to control their anxiety as they gradually build up fantasies of interacting sexually with other adults in ways that are fulfilling to them and their partners (Maletzky, 1998).

Cognitive therapy is sometimes used to help people with a predatory paraphilia (i.e., pedophilia, exhibitionism, voyeurism) identify and challenge thoughts and situations that trigger their behaviors

TABLE 16.9 Distortions, Assumptions, and Justifications

People with paraphilia or who engage in rape may engage in cognitions that provide a rationale for their behaviors.

Category	Pedophilia	Exhibitionism	Rape
Misattributing blame	"She started it by being too cuddly." "She would always run around half dressed."	"She kept looking at me like she was expecting it." "The way she was dressed, she was asking for it."	"She was saying 'no' but her body said 'yes.'"
Minimizing or denying sexual intent	"I was teaching her about sex . . . better from her father than someone else."	"I was just looking for a place to pee." "My pants just slipped down."	"I was trying to teach her a lesson. . . . She deserved it."
Debasing the victim	"She'd had sex before with her boyfriend." "She always lies."	"She was just a slut anyway."	"The way she came on to me at the party, she deserved it." "She never fought back. . . . She must have liked it."
Minimizing consequences	"She's always been real friendly to me, even afterward." "She was messed up even before it happened."	"I never touched her so I couldn't have hurt her." "She smiled so she must have liked it."	"She'd had sex with hundreds of guys before. It was no big deal."
Deflecting censure	"This happened years ago. . . . Why can't everyone forget about it?"	"It's not like I raped anyone."	"I only did it once."
Justifying the cause	"If I wasn't molested as a kid, I'd never have done this."	"If I knew how to get dates, I wouldn't have to expose."	"If my girlfriend gave me what I want, I wouldn't be forced to rape."

Source: From "The Paraphilias: Research and Treatment" by Barry M. Maletsky, from *A Guide to Treatments That Work*, edited by Peter Nathan and Jack Gorman, copyright © 1998 by Peter E. Nathan and Jack M. Gorman. Used by permission of Oxford University Press, Inc.

and serve as justifications of their behaviors, such as those in Table 16.9 (Maletzky, 1998; McConaghy, 1998). Part of the work with people with a predatory paraphilia involves empathy training—getting the offender to understand the impact of his behavior on his victims and to care about it. Five components of empathy training include (1) encouraging identification with the victim, (2) getting the client to take responsibility for his acts, (3) encouraging his acceptance of the harm created by the acts, (4) encouraging the client to reverse roles with the victim, and (5) encouraging the client to empathize with the victim (Maletzky, 1998).

With nonpredatory paraphilias (e.g., fetishism), cognitive interventions may be combined with behavioral interventions designed to help people learn more appropriate ways of approaching and interacting with people they find attractive, in socially acceptable ways (Cole, 1992). Role-plays might be used to give the person with a paraphilia practice in initiating contact and eventually negotiating a positive sexual encounter with another person. Finally, group therapy in which people with paraphilias come together to support each other through changes in their behavior can be helpful.

Outcome studies comparing these treatments with control groups that receive no treatment have not been done for most types of therapy because of ethical concerns. Several studies, however, that have followed people with paraphilias after they have received treatment, usually consisting of a comprehensive program of various psychosocial interventions, suggest that these treatments are useful (Alexander, 1999). Table 16.10 summarizes the outcomes of more than 7,000 sex offenders with paraphilia treated in a clinic that emphasized cognitive and behavioral interventions (Maletzky, 1998). Successful treatment was defined as the completion of all treatment sessions, the reporting of no deviant sexual behavior at any follow-up ses-

TABLE 16.10	Treatment Outcomes for Sex Offenders with Paraphilias ($n = 7,156$)

These data suggest that cognitive-behavioral treatment may help reduce paraphilic behavior.

Category	n	Percentage Meeting Criteria For Success*
Situational pedophilia, heterosexual	3,012	96.6
Predatory pedophilia, heterosexual	864	88.3
Situational pedophilia, homosexual	717	91.8
Predatory pedophilia, homosexual	596	80.1
Exhibitionism	1,130	95.4
Voyeurism	83	93.9
Public masturbation	77	94.8
Frotteurism	65	89.3
Fetishism	33	94.0
Transvestic fetishism	14	78.6

Source: From "The Paraphilias: Research and Treatment" by Barry M. Maletsky, from *A Guide to Treatments That Work*, edited by Peter Nathan and Jack Gorman, copyright © 1998 by Peter E. Nathan and Jack M. Gorman. Used by permission of Oxford University Press, Inc.

*Treatment success was defined as (1) completing all treatment sessions, (2) reporting no deviant sexual behavior at any follow-up sessions, (3) demonstrating no deviant sexual arousal at any follow-up session, (4) having no repeat legal charges for a sexual crime at any follow-up session. Follow-up sessions occurred at 6, 12, 24, 36, 48, and 60 months after the end of active treatment.

sions up to five years after treatment, and no legal charges for sexual offenses during the follow-up period. A follow-up of these patients 25 years after treatment found that approximately 90 percent still met these criteria for successful treatment. The child molesters and exhibitionists achieved better overall success than the pedophiles and rapists (Maletzky & Steinhauser, 2002).

SUMMING UP

- The paraphilias are a group of disorders in which people's sexual activity is focused on (1) nonhuman objects, (2) nonconsenting adults, (3) suffering or the humiliation of oneself or one's partner, or (4) children.

- Fetishism involves the use of inanimate objects (such as panties or shoes) as the preferred or exclusive source of sexual arousal or gratification. Transvestism is when a man dresses in the clothes of a woman to sexually arouse himself.

- Voyeurism involves observing another person nude or engaging in sexual acts, without that person's knowledge or consent, in order to become sexually aroused.

- Exhibitionism involves exposing oneself to another without that person's consent, in order to become sexually aroused.

- Frotteurism involves rubbing up against another without his or her consent, in order to become sexually aroused.

- Sadism and masochism involve physically harming another or allowing oneself to be harmed for sexual arousal.

- Pedophilia involves engaging in sexual acts with a child.

- Behavioral theories suggest that the sexual behaviors of people with paraphilia result from classical and operant conditioning.

- Treatments for the paraphilias include biological interventions to reduce sexual drive, behavioral interventions to decondition arousal to paraphilic objects, and training in interpersonal and social skills.

GENDER IDENTITY DISORDER

For most people, their perception of themselves as male or female, referred to as **gender identity,** is a fundamental component of their self-concept, as is illustrated in the story of David Reimer that began this chapter. Gender identity differs from **gender role,** which is a person's belief about how he or she should behave as a male or female in society. Many females choose to engage in behaviors considered part of the masculine gender role, such as playing aggressive sports or pursuing competitive careers, but still have a fundamental sense of themselves as female. Similarly, many males choose to engage in behaviors considered part of the feminine gender role, such as caring for children, cooking, or sewing, but still have a fundamental sense of themselves as male. David Reimer was forced to behave as a girl in his early childhood, but he still had a fundamental sense of himself as male.

Gender identity and gender roles differ from **sexual orientation,** which is a person's preference for sexual partners either of the opposite sex or of the same sex. Most gay men have a fundamental sense of themselves as male and, therefore, have male gender identities. Most lesbians have a fundamental sense of themselves as female and, therefore, have female gender identities. Although gay men and lesbians are often portrayed as violating stereotypic gender roles, many adhere to traditional roles for their genders, except in their choices of sexual partners.

Gender identity disorder (GID) is diagnosed when individuals believe that they were born with the wrong sex's genitals and are fundamentally persons of the opposite sex (see the DSM-IV-TR criteria in Table 16.11). Stephanie, in the following case study, would be diagnosed with this disorder (adapted from Dickey & Stephens, 1995, pp. 442–443):

CASE STUDY

Stephanie was 30 when she first attended our clinic. She gave a history of conviction that she was, in fact, male and wished to rid herself of identifiably female attributes and acquire male traits and features. She said she had been cross-living and employed as a male for about 1 year, following the breakdown of a 10-year marriage. She was taking testosterone prescribed by her family physician. She presented at our clinic with a request for removal of her uterus and ovaries.

She did not give a childhood history of tomboy attitudes, thoughts, or behavior. She said social interaction with other children, boys or girls, was minimal. Desperate for a friend, she fantasized "an articulate and strong" boy,

exactly her own age, named Ronan. They were always together and they talked over everything: thoughts and feelings and the events of her life. Cross-dressing in her father's clothing also began during childhood. There was no history of sexual arousal associated with or erotic fantasy involving cross-dressing.

Puberty at age 12 and the accompanying bodily changes apparently did not overly distress Stephanie. Sexual and romantic feelings focused on "slender, feminine-appearing men." At 16, Stephanie met such a man and they were together for 2 years. Her next romantic involvement was with a "male bisexual transvestite." Sexual interaction according to Stephanie, included experimentation with drugs and "role reversals." She and her partner cross-dressed, and Stephanie took the dominant and active role. During vaginal sex, she imagined herself as a male with another male.

At 19, she met a slender, good-looking man. They were compatible and married soon after. The marriage was a success. Stephanie's preferred position for intercourse was with both kneeling, she behind her husband, rubbing her pubic area against him while masturbating him. She would imagine she had a penis and was penetrating him. Stephanie's marriage broke down after the couple's business failed. She decided to live full-time in the male role as Jacob. While on the West Coast, she started treatment with male hormones. She moved back east and presented at our clinic for assessment. She saw herself as a male, primarily attracted to gay or gay-appearing males. She was uninterested in relationships with women, except perhaps as purely sexual encounters of short duration.

Gender identity disorder of childhood is a rare condition in which a child persistently rejects his or her anatomic sex and desires to be or insists he or she is a member of the opposite sex. Girls with this disorder seek masculine-type activities and male peer groups to a degree far beyond that of a "tomboy." Sometimes, these girls express the belief that they will eventually grow penises. Boys with the disorder seek feminine-type activities and female peer groups and tend to begin cross-dressing

TABLE 16.11 DSM-IV-TR

Criteria for a Diagnosis of Gender Identity Disorder

People with gender identity disorder believe they were born with the wrong sex's body and are truly members of the other sex.

A. Strong and persistent identification with the other sex. In children, this is manifested by four or more of the following:

1. repeatedly stated desire to be, or insistence that he or she is, the other sex.

2. in boys, preference for cross-dressing or simulating female attire; in girls, insistence on wearing only stereotypic masculine clothing.

3. strong and persistent preferences for cross-sex roles in play and in fantasies.

4. intense desire to participate in the stereotypic games and pastimes of the other sex.

5. strong preference for playmates of the other sex.

In adolescents or adults, identification with the other sex may be manifested with symptoms such as the stated desire to be the other sex, frequently passing as the other sex, desire to live or be treated as the other sex, or the conviction that he or she has the typical feelings or reactions of the other sex.

B. Persistent discomfort with his or her sex and sense of inappropriateness in the gender role of that sex.

C. Disturbance is not concurrent with a physical intersex condition and causes significant distress or problems in functioning.

Source: Reprinted with permission from the *Diagnostic and Statistical Manual of Mental Disorders*, Fourth Edition, Text Revision. Copyright © 2000 American Psychiatric Association.

in girls' clothes at a very early age (Zucker, 2005). They express disgust with their penises and wish they would disappear. Boys with gender identity disturbances are more likely to be taken by their parents for counseling than are girls with the disturbance, probably because parents are more concerned about violations of gender roles in boys than in girls.

Adults who might be diagnosed with gender identity disorder are also referred to as **transsexuals.** Transsexual people may dress in the clothes of the opposite sex but, unlike transvestites, do not do this to gain sexual arousal. They simply believe they are putting on the clothes of the gender they really belong to. Some transsexual people who can afford it seek sex-change operations. The sexual preferences of transsexual people vary. Some are asexual, having little interest in either sex; some are heterosexual; and some are homosexual. Transsexualism is rare, with an estimated prevalence of 1 per 30,000 males and 1 per 100,000 females (Bradley & Zucker, 1997; Katchadourian, 1989).

Some transsexual people are so disturbed by their misassignment of gender that they develop alcohol and other drug abuse problems and other psychological disorders, but these problems seem to be consequences rather than causes of their transsexualism (Lombardi, 2001). Low self-esteem and psychological distress also result from their rejection by others. High rates of HIV infection among transsexual people have been reported in some studies (Lombardi, 2001). HIV may be contracted through risky sexual behaviors or through the sharing of needles during drug use or the injection of hormones. Many avoid seeking medical care because of negative interactions with physicians. Indeed, some physicians refuse to treat transsexual people. Leslie Feinberg, an activist and author, described her harrowing experiences in trying to receive medical care (Feinberg, 2001, pp. 897–898):

VOICES

Five years ago, while battling an undiagnosed case of bacterial endocarditis, I was refused care at a Jersey City emergency room. After the physician who examined me discovered that I am female-bodied, he ordered me out of the emergency room despite the fact that my temperature was above 104 degrees. He said I had a fever "because you are a very troubled person." Weeks later I was hospitalized with the same illness in New York City in a Catholic hospital where management insists patients be put in wards on the basis of birth sex. They place transsexual women who have completed sex-reassignment surgery in male wards. Putting me in a female ward created a furor. I awoke in

(continued)

the night to find staff standing around my bed ridiculing my body and referring to me as a "Martian." The next day the staff refused to work unless "it" was removed from the floor. These and other expressions of hatred forced me to leave.

In recent years, critics of the diagnosis of gender identity disorder have argued that it pathologizes a normal variant on human sexuality and gender roles (see Zucker, 2005). If you examine the criteria for "strong and persistent identification with the other sex," point A in the DSM-IV-TR criteria (review Table 16.11), you will notice that a child might be diagnosable with GID for having persistent cross-sex behavior without the stated desire that he or she is actually of the opposite sex. Thus, a child might be diagnosed with GID only for consistently refusing to conform with his or her stereotypic gender role. In addition, the dysphoria some children and adults who engage in cross-gender behavior experience might be due to social reactions to them, rather than to an inherent dysphoria about their own identity.

Zucker (2005) argues that the desire of people diagnosed with GID to undergo sex reassignment through surgery and hormonal treatment is evidence that people with this disorder are not just choosing an alternative lifestyle but truly have a psychological impairment. The debate over the legitimacy of GID as a diagnosis will continue for some time to come.

Contributors to Gender Identity Disorder

The genetic sex of an individual is determined at conception by the chromosomes received from the mother and father, but sexual development from that point on is influenced by many factors. For the first few weeks of gestation, the gonads and internal and external genital structures are neither male nor female. If the Y chromosome is present, the gonads of the embryo differentiate into testes. Then they secrete testosterone, and male genitalia develop in the fetus. If the Y chromosome is not present, the gonads develop into ovaries, which do not secrete androgen, and female genitalia develop.

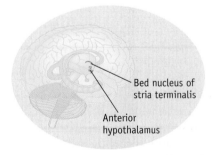

Parts of the hypothalamus, such as the anterior hypothalamus and the bed nucleus of stria terminalis, may be involved in gender identity disorder.

Biological theories of gender identity disorder have focused on the effects of prenatal hormones on brain development (Bradley, 1995; Bradley & Zucker, 1997). Although several specific mechanisms have been implicated, in general these theories suggest that people who develop gender identity disorder have been exposed to unusual levels of hormones, which influence later gender identity and sexual orientation by influencing the development of the hypothalamus and other brain structures involved in sexuality. These brain/hormone theories were bolstered when reports were published in the early 1990s of differences between homosexual and heterosexual men in the anterior hypothalamus (LeVay, 1993). To date, these reports have not been well replicated by other investigators, however. The relevance of studies of biological factors in homosexuality to gender identity disorder is not always clear, as well.

One of the few studies directly focusing on transsexual people found significant differences between male transsexuals and a group of nontranssexual men in a cluster of cells in the hypothalamus called the bed nucleus of stria terminalis (Zhou, Hofman, & Swaab, 1995). This cluster of cells was half as large in the transsexuals as in the nontranssexual men. Typically, this cluster of cells is smaller

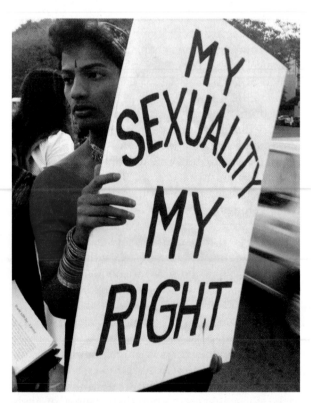

Some transsexual people argue they do not have a disorder but do have a right to live their life as they wish.

in women's brains than in men's, and the male transsexuals' cluster of cells was close to the size usually found in women's brains. This cluster of cells is known to play a role in sexual behavior, at least in male rats. Thus, it may be that the size of this cell cluster in the hypothalamus plays a role in gender identity disorder, at least in men.

Another group of studies that suggested that prenatal hormones play a role in gender identity disorder focused on girls who were exposed to elevated levels of testosterone in utero due to an illness in the mother or medications the mother took while pregnant (see Hines, 2004). Most of these girls were born with some degree of masculinization of their genitalia, which is treated early in infancy through surgical correction and hormone replacement; then they are raised as girls. Studies have suggested that these girls tend to have more masculine behavior than other girls (Berenbaum & Hines, 1992; Slijper et al., 1998). In addition, more of these girls have a homosexual or bisexual sexual orientation than girls not exposed to testosterone in utero (Dittman, Kappes, & Kappes, 1992; Money & Schwartz, 1976). Most of these girls do identify themselves as female, but they are at increased risk for gender identity disorder (Slijper et al., 1998). These findings lend some support to a prenatal hormone theory of gender identity disorder, although in general the evidence has been somewhat weak (Zucker, 2005).

Most of the psychosocial theories of gender identity disorder focus on the role parents play in shaping their children's gender identity. Parents encourage children to identify with one sex or the other, by reinforcing "gender-appropriate" behavior and punishing "gender-inappropriate" behavior. From early infancy, they buy male or female clothes for their children and sex-stereotyped toys (dolls or trucks). They encourage or discourage playing rough-and-tumble games or playing with dolls. In a long-term study of a large sample of boys with gender identity disorder, Green (1986) found that their parents were less likely than the parents of boys without gender identity disorder to discourage cross-gender behaviors. That is, these boys were not punished, subtly or overtly, for engaging in feminine behavior, such as playing with dolls or wearing dresses, as much as boys who did not have gender identity disorder. Further, boys who were highly feminine (although did not necessarily have gender identity disorder) tended to have mothers who had wanted a girl rather than a boy, saw their baby sons as girls, and dressed their baby sons as girls. When the boys were older, their mothers tended to prohibit rough-and-tumble play, and the boys had few opportunities to have male playmates. About one-third of these boys had no father in the home, and those who did have a father in the home tended to be very close to their mothers.

Other studies suggest that another factor in gender identity disorder, in addition to the reinforcements parents give for gender identification in their children, is parental psychopathology (Bradley, 1995; Marantz & Coates, 1991). Significant percentages of the parents of children with gender identity disorder suffer from depression, severe anxiety, or personality disorders. It may be that these parents create a difficult emotional atmosphere in the home, which makes the child anxious and unsure of him- or herself. Then, if the parent reinforces the child for cross-gendered behavior, the child may be especially likely to adopt a cross-gendered identity as a way of pleasing the parent and reducing his or her own anxiety.

In general, however, the evidence for various theories of gender identity disorder is weak. Most theorists believe that gender identity is the result of a number of biological and social factors, including chromosomes, hormones, and socialization. Gender identity disorder might result from variations in the development of any of these factors.

Treatments for Gender Identity Disorder

Therapists who work with people with gender identity disorder tend not to try to "cure" them by convincing them to accept the body with which they were born and the gender associated with that body (Bradley, 1995). This tactic simply does not work with most people with gender identity disorder. Instead, therapists help these individuals clarify their gender identity and sexual orientation. Some people with gender identity disorder choose to undergo gender reassignment treatment, which provides them with the genitalia and secondary sex characteristics (e.g., breasts) of the gender with which they identify. Sex reassignment cannot change their chromosomes, nor can it enable people born male to bear children or people born female to impregnate a woman.

Sex reassignment requires a series of surgeries and hormone treatments, often taking two or more years. Before undertaking any of these medical procedures, patients are usually asked to dress and live in their new gender for a year or two, to ensure that they are confident about their decisions before proceeding. Then, a lifetime of hormone treatments is begun. Male-to-female transsexuals take estrogen, which fosters the development of female secondary sex characteristics. This drug causes fatty deposits to develop in the breasts and hips, softens the skin, and inhibits the growth of a beard. Female-to-male transsexuals take androgens, which promote male secondary sex characteristics. This drug causes the voice to deepen, hair to become distributed in a male pattern, fatty tissue in the breast to recede, and muscles to enlarge. The clitoris may grow larger.

Sex reassignment surgery is primarily cosmetic. In male-to-female surgery, the penis and testicles are removed, and tissue from the penis is used to create an artificial vagina. The construction of male genitals for a female-to-male reassignment is technically more difficult. First, the internal sex organs (ovaries, fallopian tubes, uterus) and any fatty tissue remaining in the breasts are removed. The urethra is rerouted through the enlarged clitoris, or an artificial penis and scrotum are constructed from tissue taken from other parts of the body. This penis allows for urination while standing but cannot achieve a natural erection. Other procedures, such as artificial implants, may be used to create an erection

Sex reassignment surgery has always been controversial. Some follow-up studies suggest that the outcome tends to be positive when patients are carefully selected for such sex reassignment procedures based on their motivation for change and their overall psychological health and are given

psychological counseling to assist them through the change (Bradley & Zucker, 1997; Lindemalm, Korlin, & Uddenberg, 1986; Smith, van Goozen, & Cohen-Kettenis, 2001). Although many of these patients are unable to experience orgasm during sex, most are satisfied with their sex lives and are psychologically well adjusted to their new genders.

SUMMING UP

- Gender identity disorder (GID) is diagnosed when individuals believe they were born with the wrong sex's genitals and are fundamentally persons of the opposite sex. This disorder in adults is also called transsexualism.

- Biological theories suggest that unusual exposure to prenatal hormones affects the development of the hypothalamus and other brain structures involved in sexuality, leading to gender identity disorder.

- Socialization theories suggest that the parents of children (primarily boys) with gender identity disorder do not socialize gender-appropriate behaviors. Other theories suggest that the parents of children who develop this disorder have high rates of psychopathology.

- Some people with this disorder undergo sex reassignment treatment to change their genitalia and live as a member of the sex they believe they are.

CHAPTER INTEGRATION

Nowhere is the interplay of biological, psychological, and social forces more apparent than in matters of sexuality (see Figure 16.6). Biological factors influence gender identity, sexual orientation, and sexual functioning. These biological factors can be greatly moderated, however, by psychological and social factors. The meaning to people of a sexual dysfunction, an unusual sexual practice, or an atypical gender identity is heavily influenced by their attitudes toward their sexuality and by the reactions they get from people around them. In addition, as we saw with sexual dysfunctions, purely psychological and social conditions can cause a person's body to stop functioning as it normally would.

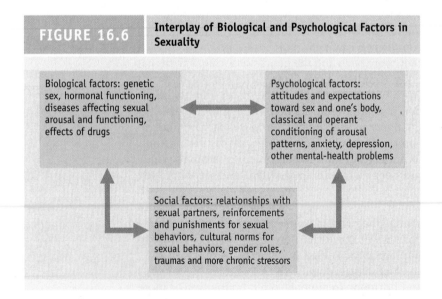

FIGURE 16.6 **Interplay of Biological and Psychological Factors in Sexuality**

Biological factors: genetic sex, hormonal functioning, diseases affecting sexual arousal and functioning, effects of drugs

Psychological factors: attitudes and expectations toward sex and one's body, classical and operant conditioning of arousal patterns, anxiety, depression, other mental-health problems

Social factors: relationships with sexual partners, reinforcements and punishments for sexual behaviors, cultural norms for sexual behaviors, gender roles, traumas and more chronic stressors

Extraordinary People: Follow-Up

What became of David Reimer, the boy who was raised as a girl, and the research that suggested this was an appropriate treatment for him? In 1997, researcher Milton Diamond and psychiatrist Keith Sigmundson, who had treated David when he was the child Brenda and had become convinced that the "experiment" to turn the child into a girl was a failure, published a paper revealing the outcome of this experiment. The paper hit the medical and psychological communities like a bombshell. Until that point, the academic community had assumed that the little boy raised as a girl had grown successfully into a woman. Diamond and Sigmundson's paper presented clear evidence from David's case and the cases of other children who had undergone sex reassignment that simply deciding which sex a child would be does not determine the child's gender identity. The cases of children who had been born with both male and female gonads or with ambiguous genitals also made it clear that gender identity is complex and often not binary—male or female.

Years later, David reflected on the assumptions that drove the decision to turn him into a girl after his penis was severed:

> You know, if I had lost my arms and my legs and wound up in a wheelchair where you're moving everything with a little rod in your mouth—would that make me less of a person? It just seems that they implied that you're nothing if your penis is gone. The second you lose that, you're nothing and they've got to do surgery and hormones to turn you into something. Like you're a zero. It's like your whole personality, everything about you is all directed—all pinpointed—toward what's between the legs. And to me, that's ignorant. (Colapinto, 2001, p. 262)

David's story, and Colapinto's book, *As Nature Made Him*, appear to argue that gender identity is completely determined by biological sex. The stories of many other children who eventually reject their biological sex or who live somewhere in between male and female argue against a purely biological origin of gender identity. Colapinto (2001, p. 280) writes,

> Despite [its] medical-scientific context, I've always believed that [David's] story transcends the incessant quibbling over the nature/nurture debate. David's is a story about identity in its largest sense—not simply *sexual* identity. His story, for all its uniqueness, is a universal one, and reminds us how it is every person's individual responsibility to define for himself who he is, and to assert that against a world that often opposes, ridicules, oppresses, or undermines him.

David Reimer committed suicide in 2004. He had lost his job, had financial difficulties, and been separated from his wife. His mother said he was still grieving the death of his brother two years before. In a newspaper story after David's death, however, John Colapinto, his biographer, noted, "David's blighted childhood was never far from his mind. Just before he died, he talked to his wife about his sexual 'inadequacy,' his inability to be a true husband. Jane tried to reassure him. But David was already heading for the door" (*Slate Magazine*, 2004).

Chapter Summary

- The interplay of biological, psychological, and social forces is nowhere more apparent than in matters of sexuality. (Review Figure 16.6.)

- The sexual response cycle can be divided into the desire, arousal, plateau, orgasm, and resolution phases. (Review Figures 16.1 and 16.2.)

- Sexual desire is manifested in sexual thoughts and fantasies, an awareness of sexual cues from others, and the initiation of or participation in sexual activities.

- The arousal phase consists of a psychological experience of arousal and pleasure and the

- physiological changes known as vasocongestion (the filling of blood vessels and tissues with blood) and myotonia (muscle tension).

- During the plateau phase, excitement remains at a high but stable level.

- Orgasm involves the discharge of built-up neuromuscular tension. In males, orgasm involves rhythmic contractions of the prostate, the seminal vesicles, the vas deferens, and the entire length of the penis and urethra, accompanied by the ejaculation of semen. In females, orgasm involves rhythmic contractions of the orgasmic platform and more irregular contractions of the uterus.

- Following orgasm, the entire musculature of the body relaxes, and men and women tend to experience a state of deep relaxation, the stage known as resolution. Males experience a refractory period following orgasm, during which they cannot be aroused to another orgasm. Females do not have a refractory period.

- Occasional problems with sexual functioning are extremely common. To qualify for a diagnosis of a sexual dysfunction, a person must be experiencing a problem that causes significant distress or interpersonal difficulty, that is not the result of another Axis I disorder, and that is not due exclusively to the direct effects of substance use or medical illness. (Review Table 16.1.)

- The psychological factors leading to sexual dysfunction most commonly involve negative attitudes toward sex, traumatic or stressful experiences, and conflicts with sexual partners. A variety of biological factors, including medical illnesses, the side effects of drugs, nervous system injury, and hormonal deficiencies, can cause sexual dysfunctions. (Review Table 16.4.)

- Sexual desire disorders (hypoactive sexual desire disorder and sexual aversion disorder) are among the most common sexual dysfunctions. Persons with these disorders experience a chronically lowered or absent desire for sex.

- The sexual arousal disorders include female sexual arousal disorder and male erectile disorder (formerly called impotence).

- Women with female orgasmic disorder experience a persistent or recurrent delay in or the complete absence of orgasm, after having reached the excitement phase of the sexual response cycle. Men with premature ejaculation persistently experience ejaculation (after minimal sexual stimulation) before, on, or shortly after penetration and before they wish it.

- Men with male orgasmic disorder experience a persistent or recurrent delay in or the absence of orgasm following the excitement phase of the sexual response cycle.

- The sexual pain disorders include dyspareunia, which is genital pain associated with intercourse, and vaginismus, in which a woman experiences involuntary contraction of the muscles surrounding the outer third of the vagina when the vagina is penetrated.

- Fortunately, most of the sexual dysfunctions can be treated successfully. Biological treatments include drugs that increase sexual functioning, such as Viagra, and the alleviation of medical conditions that might be contributing to sexual dysfunction. (Review Table 16.5.)

- The psychological treatments combine (1) psychotherapy focused on the personal concerns of the individual with the dysfunction and on the conflicts between the individual and his or her partner and (2) sex therapy designed to decrease inhibitions about sex and to teach new techniques for optimal sexual enjoyment. (Review Table 16.6.)

- One important set of techniques in sex therapy is sensate focus exercises. The exercises lead partners through three stages, from gentle nongenital touching, to direct genital stimulation, and finally to intercourse focused on enhancing and sustaining pleasure, rather than on orgasm and performance.

- Men with premature ejaculation can be helped with the stop-start technique or the squeeze technique.

- The paraphilias are a group of disorders in which the focus of the individual's sexual urges and activities are (1) nonhuman objects, (2) nonconsenting adults, (3) suffering or humiliation of oneself or one's partner, or (4) children. (Review Table 16.8.)

- People with pedophilia seek sexual gratification with young children. Most are heterosexual men seeking sex with young girls. Many people with pedophilia have poor interpersonal skills, feel intimidated when interacting sexually with adults, and are victims of childhood sexual abuse.

- Voyeurism involves secretly watching another person undressing, bathing, doing things in the nude, or engaging in sex as a preferred or exclusive form of sexual arousal. Almost all people who engage in voyeurism are men who watch women.

- Exhibitionism involves sexual gratification by exposing the genitals to involuntary observers, who are usually complete strangers. In the vast majority of cases, a person who engages in exhibitionism is a man who bares all to surprised women, typically in public places.

■ Frotteurism is another paraphilia, which often co-occurs with voyeurism and exhibitionism. A person who engages in frotteurism gains sexual gratification by rubbing against and fondling parts of the body of a nonconsenting person.

■ A person who engages in sexual sadism gains sexual gratification by inflicting pain and humiliation on his or her sex partner. A person who engages in sexual masochism gains sexual gratification by suffering pain or humiliation during sex. Some people occasionally engage in moderately sadistic or masochistic behaviors during sex or simulate such behaviors without actually inflicting pain or suffering. Persons who are diagnosed with sexual sadism or masochism engage in these behaviors as their preferred or exclusive forms of sexual gratification.

■ Fetishism is a paraphilia that involves the use of isolated body parts or inanimate objects as the preferred or exclusive sources of sexual arousal or gratification. A particular form of fetish is transvestism, in which an individual dresses in clothes of the opposite sex in order to become sexually aroused. Usually, transvestism involves a man dressing in women's clothes.

■ Gender identity disorder (GID) is diagnosed when an individual believes that he or she was born with the wrong genitals and is fundamentally a person of the opposite sex. Gender identity disorder of childhood is a rare condition in which a child persistently rejects his or her anatomic sex and desires to be or insists he or she is a member of the opposite sex. (Review Table 16.11.)

■ Gender identity disorder in adulthood is often referred to as transsexualism. Transsexual persons experience a chronic discomfort and sense of inappropriateness with their gender and genitals, wish to be rid of them, and want to live as members of the opposite sex. Transsexual individuals often dress in the clothes of the opposite sex but, unlike transvestites, do not do so to gain sexual arousal.

MindMap CD-ROM

The following resources on the MindMap CD-ROM that came with this text will help you to master the content of this chapter and prepare for tests:

■ Videos: Taking a Sexual History; Changing Genders
■ Interactive Segment: Androgeny
■ Chapter Timeline
■ Chapter Quiz

Key Terms

sexual dysfunctions 575

sexual desire 576

arousal phase 576

vasocongestion 576

myotonia 576

orgasm 577

plateau phase 577

resolution 578

hypoactive sexual desire disorder 580

sexual aversion disorder 580

female sexual arousal disorder 581

male erectile disorder 581

female orgasmic disorder 582

premature ejaculation 582

male orgasmic disorder 583

dyspareunia 583

vaginismus 583

substance-induced sexual dysfunction 585

performance anxiety 586

sensate focus therapy 594

stop-start technique 596

squeeze technique 596

paraphilias 599

fetishism 600

> Chapter 17

The Ferryman's
by George E. Dunne

Refrain to-night, And that shall lend a kind of easiness
To the next abstinence; the next more easy; For use
almost can change the stamp of nature.

—William Shakespeare, *Hamlet* (3:4:165; 1600)

Substance-Related Disorders <

Extraordinary People

■ **Celebrity Drug Users**

Society and Substance Use

Societies around the world and across time have had very different attitudes about substance use, leading to different responses to substance users.

Definitions of Substance-Related Disorders

Substance intoxication and withdrawal are characteristic behavioral and physical symptoms resulting from substance use. Substance abuse and dependence are diagnosed when substance use significantly interferes with an individual's functioning. Dependence also may involve the development of tolerance to substances.

Depressants

The depressants include alcohol, benzodiazepines, barbiturates, and inhalants. They produce the symptoms of depression and cognitive impairment.

Stimulants

The stimulants—cocaine, amphetamines, nicotine, and caffeine—activate the central nervous system and the parts of the brain that register pleasure.

Opioids

The opioids cause euphoria, lethargy, unconsciousness, and seizures and can be highly addictive.

Hallucinogens and PCP

The hallucinogens and PCP produce perceptual illusions and distortions and symptoms ranging from a sense of peace and tranquillity to feelings of unreality and violence.

Cannabis

Cannabis creates a high feeling, cognitive and motor impairments, and in some people, hallucinogenic effects.

Club Drugs

Some common club drugs, in addition to LSD, are ecstasy, GHB, ketamine, and rohypnol. They have a variety of euphoric and sedative effects and can be extremely dangerous.

Theories of Substance Use, Abuse, and Dependence

Biological theories attribute vulnerability to substance disorders largely to genetic predispositions. Psychosocial theories focus on environmental reinforcements and beliefs that support substance use.

Treatments for Substance-Related Disorders

Detoxification is the first step in treatment. Drugs may aid in withdrawal and abstinence. Alcoholics Anonymous is a widely used treatment. Behavioral and cognitive treatments extinguish substance use behaviors and change thoughts that motivate substance use.

Taking Psychology Personally

■ **Tips for Responsible Drinking**

Chapter Integration

The substances involved in substance use disorders are powerful biological agents that directly affect the brain. Some people may have biological predispositions that make substance use either more or less rewarding, but environmental influences can also affect the choices that they make. Both biological and psychosocial factors play a role in the familial transmission of substance use and dependence.

Extraordinary People

Celebrity Drug Users

Comedian Chris Farley was at the height of his career. This veteran of Chicago's famed Second City was catapulted to stardom when he landed a slot on *Saturday Night Live*. There, his slapstick and baudy routines made him an instant favorite and drew comparisons to one of his heroes, John Belushi. Like Belushi, Farley was overweight (weighing nearly 300 pounds) and had an "in your face" style of comedy. Also like Belushi, Farley lived hard and fast, abusing alcohol, cocaine, heroin, and other drugs. After *Saturday Night Live*, Farley moved on to star in movies such as *Tommy Boy*, *Black Sheep*, and *Beverly Hills Ninja*.

On December 18, 1997, Chris Farley was found dead at the age of 33 in his condominium on the sixtieth floor of the John Hancock Building in Chicago. He had spent the night drinking, drugging, and debauching with friends. An autopsy later showed

that he had overdosed on morphine and cocaine. There were also traces of marijuana in his urine. The coroner noted that heart disease, possibly due to Farley's excessive weight, also contributed to his death and that his liver showed clear evidence of damage from chronic heavy alcohol use.

Chris Farley is just one of many celebrities who have suffered, and even died, from substance abuse. For our purposes, a **substance** is any natural or synthesized product that has psychoactive effects—it changes perceptions, thoughts, emotions, and behaviors. Some of the substances we discuss in this chapter are cocaine, heroin, and amphetamines. These are popularly referred to as *drugs*, and people who have problems as a result of taking these drugs are often referred to as **drug addicts.** We use the more neutral term *substance*, however, because some of the disorders we discuss in this chapter involve substances that you might not normally think of as drugs, such as nicotine and alcohol. Also, as we see, a person need not be physically dependent on a substance, as is implied by the term *addict*, in order to have problems resulting from taking the substance.

Nearly half of the U.S. population admits to having tried an illegal substance at sometime in their lives, and approximately 15 percent have used one in the past year (Substance Abuse and Mental Health Services Administration [SAMHSA], 2005). Illicit drug use is highest among young adults (SAMHSA, 2005) (see Figure 17.1). Men are much more likely than women to

have used an illicit substance in their lives. Once women begin to use a substance, however, they are at least as likely to become dependent on it and may suffer greater physiological damage from some substances than men (Van Etten & Anthony, 2001). Substance use also varies quite substantially by ethnic group in the United States, as you can see in Figure 17.1.

The occasional use of illegal drugs peaked in the 1970s and has declined since then (Johnston et al., 2004). Most illegal drugs are now used by a minority of college students, although there is a recent increase in the use of ecstasy, and alcohol use has remained stable over time (see Figure 17.2 on page 622). One study surveyed seniors at a college in the eastern United States each decade since the 1960s and compared users and nonusers of illegal drugs on grades and extracurricular activities (Pope, Ionescu-Pioggia, & Pope, 2001). In the earlier decades, the users and nonusers did not differ, but, in 1999, the drug users had significantly lower grades and spent less time in extracurricular activities than the nonusers. Thus, college drug users appear to have become a more distinct group, whose lifestyle has diverged more from the rest of the student body in recent years.

SOCIETY AND SUBSTANCE USE

Societies differ in their attitudes about substances with psychoactive effects, some seeing their use as a matter of individual choice and others seeing it as a grave public health and security concern. These attitudes are reflected in different laws and approaches to treatment (Goldstein, 1994; Mac-Coun, 1998). Many Muslim countries following Islamic law strictly prohibit alcohol and enforce penalties against people caught using this or any other substance. When the Communists took over China in the late 1940s, they made it a major goal to eradicate the widespread use of opium. Traffickers were executed, and users were sent to the countryside for rehabilitation and reeducation. Today, antidrug laws are still strictly enforced, and punishments for the use or sale of illicit substances remain severe.

In Great Britain, substance addiction is considered a medical disease, and people who abuse or are dependent on substances are treated by physicians. Although traffickers in illegal substances are aggressively prosecuted by the British government, the users of illegal substances are more often referred for treatment than arrested for possession of substances. Heroin use is as prevalent as it is in the United States, but physicians in Great Britain are more comfortable with long-term methadone maintenance than are physicians in the United States. The Dutch make a distinction in their law enforcement between "soft" drugs (such as cannabis) and "hard" drugs (such as cocaine and heroin). Although both types of substances are illegal, the possession, use, and sale of cannabis are rarely prosecuted, whereas the importing, manufacture, and sale of the hard substances are subject to heavy penalties, which are enforced.

The Dutch system is based on the belief that enforcing a strict prohibition of softer drugs would drive users underground, where they would come into contact with persons trafficking in harder drugs and would be more likely to begin using these drugs.

In the mid-twentieth century, Zurich, Switzerland, became famous for its "needle park," where the sale and use of substances, including heroin and cocaine, were carried out in the open and allowed by authorities, while a doctor employed by the government stood by in a small kiosk to handle any emergencies and to distribute clean needles for the injection of substances. Opponents of the park argued that it made it extremely easy for troubled young people to become part of the drug scene and generally legitimized illicit drug use. In 1992, the park was closed because of evidence that

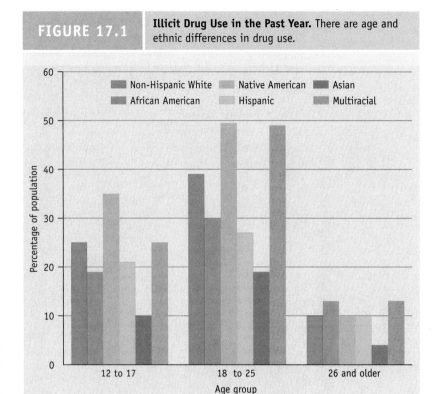

FIGURE 17.1 | **Illicit Drug Use in the Past Year.** There are age and ethnic differences in drug use.

addicts from around Europe had poured into the city and crime had soared.

Within the United States, attitudes toward substance use have varied greatly over time and across subgroups. The American ambivalence toward alcohol use is nicely illustrated in a letter written in the mid-twentieth century by a U.S. Congressman in response to a question from one of his constituents: "Dear Congressman, how do you stand on whiskey?" Because the congressman did not know how the constituent stood on alcohol, he fashioned the following safe response:

My dear friend, I had not intended to discuss this controversial subject at this particular time. However, I want you to know that I do not shun a controversy. On the contrary, I will take a stand on any issue at any time, regardless of how fraught with controversy it may be. You have asked me how I feel about whiskey. Here is how I stand on the issue.

If when you say whiskey, you mean the Devil's brew; the poison scourge; the bloody monster that defiles innocence, dethrones reason, destroys the home, creates misery, poverty, fear; literally takes the bread from the mouths of little children; if you mean the evil drink that topples the

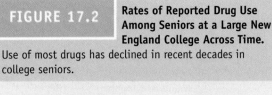

FIGURE 17.2   **Rates of Reported Drug Use Among Seniors at a Large New England College Across Time.**

Use of most drugs has declined in recent decades in college seniors.

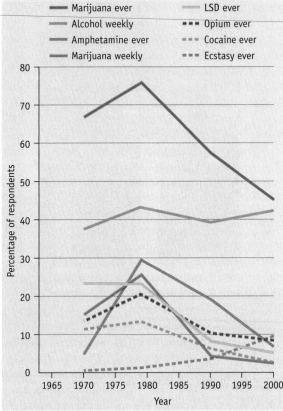

Source: From Pope, H. G., Jr., Ionescu-Pioggia, M. & Pope, K. W., 2001, "Drug Use and Lifestyle Among College Undergraduates: A 30-Year Longitudinal Study." Reprinted with permission from American Journal of Psychiatry, 158. Copyright © 2001 American Psychiatric Association.

forget, if only for a little while, life's great tragedies and heartbreaks and sorrows; if you mean that drink, the sale of which pours into our Treasury untold millions of dollars which are used to provide tender care for little crippled children, our blind, our deaf, our pitiful aged and infirm; to build highways, hospitals, and schools; then certainly, I am in favor of it. This is my stand, and I will not compromise. Your congressman. (Quoted in Marlatt et al., 1993, p. 462)

Many substances come from plants and have been used for medicinal purposes for centuries. As long ago as 1500 B.C., natives in the Andes highlands chewed coca leaves to increase their endurance (Cocores, Pottash, & Gold, 1991). Coca leaves can be manufactured into cocaine. Cocaine was used legally throughout Europe and then America into the twentieth century to relieve fatigue and was an ingredient in the original Coca-Cola drink and more than 50 other widely available drinks and elixirs.

Opium, a milky juice produced from the poppy plant, has been used for hundreds of years to relieve pain, particularly in Asian and European countries. The leaves of a plant called *khat* have been chewed in parts of eastern Africa, the Middle East, and South America for hundreds of years to produce a sense of well-being and relief from fatigue. Today, modern derivatives of khat are used

Christian man and woman from the pinnacles of righteous, gracious living into the bottomless pit of degradation and despair, shame and helplessness and hopelessness; then certainly, I am against it with all of my power.

But, if when you say whiskey, you mean the oil of conversation, the philosophic wine, the ale that is assumed when great fellows get together, that puts a song in their hearts and laughter on their lips, and the warm glow of contentment in their eyes; if you mean Christmas cheer; if you mean that stimulating drink that puts the spring in the old gentlemen's step on a frosty morning; if you mean the drink that enables the man to magnify his joy and his happiness and to

Coca-Cola originally contained cocaine.

to make amphetamines, a class of drugs used to treat attention-deficit/hyperactivity disorder, narcolepsy, and obesity and included in over-the-counter cold remedies and appetite suppressants for weight control.

Substances have also been used for religious ceremonies to produce psychological changes important for the ceremonies. For example, the peyote cactus contains a substance that, when chewed, causes people to experience visual hallucinations, in the form of brightly colored lights, or vivid, kaleidoscopic visions of geometric forms, animals, and people. The Aztecs and other native groups in Mexico and the Kiowa, Comanche, and other native groups in the United States and Canada have used peyote as part of religious rituals for hundreds of years.

When substances are used not as part of medical treatments or religious or ceremonial rituals but, rather, by individuals to change their moods, thoughts, and perceptions, other members of society begin to get nervous. This is because some individuals have great difficulty in using substances in moderation and begin to build their lives around using the substances. Their use of substances may lead to significant problems in their abilities to function in their daily lives—they may shirk their job and family responsibilities, they may act impulsively or bizarrely, and they may endanger their own lives and the lives of others. Such a person is said to have a **substance-related disorder.**

Societies have strong motivations for regulating the use of psychoactive substances. In the United States alone, the use of psychoactive substances for nonmedicinal and nonreligious purposes costs society over $240 billion a year in accidents, crime, health care costs, and lost productivity. Illnesses and accidents associated with alcohol alone result in about $6 billion in inpatient hospital costs and nearly $2 billion in outpatient medical costs. Alcohol is associated with over half of the deaths due to traffic accidents and homicides and with 30 percent of all suicides (Hunt, 1998).

DEFINITIONS OF SUBSTANCE-RELATED DISORDERS

There are four substance-related conditions recognized by the DSM-IV-TR: *substance intoxication, substance withdrawal, substance abuse,* and *substance dependence* (see the Concept Overview in Table 17.1). In the first part of this chapter, we discuss the criteria for each of these conditions. In the remainder of this chapter, we discuss how these conditions are manifested in the context of the substances most commonly linked to them.

These substances can be grouped into five categories: (1) central nervous system depressants, including alcohol, barbiturates, benzodiazepines, and inhalants; (2) central nervous system stimulants, including cocaine, amphetamines, nicotine, and caffeine; (3) opioids, including heroin and morphine; (4) hallucinogens and phencyclidine (PCP); and (5) cannabis. Intoxication, withdrawal, abuse, and dependence can occur with most, although not all, of these substances (see the DSM-IV-TR information in Table 17.2 on page 624). In addition, we will consider a mixed group of drugs referred to as club drugs, including ecstasy, GHB, ketamine, and rohypnol, which have become very popular among youth in recent years.

TABLE 17.1   Concept Overview

Definitions of Substance Intoxication, Withdrawal, Abuse, and Dependence

These definitions of substance intoxication, withdrawal, abuse, and dependence apply across a variety of substances, but the specific symptoms depend on the substance used.

Substance intoxication	Experience of significant maladaptive behavioral and psychological symptoms due to the effect of a substance on the central nervous system
Substance withdrawal	Experience of clinically significant distress in social, occupational, or other areas of functioning due to the cessation or reduction of substance use
Substance abuse	Diagnosis given when recurrent substance use leads to significant harmful consequences
Substance dependence	Diagnosis given when substance use leads to physiological dependence or significant impairment or distress

Source: Reprinted with permission from the *Diagnostic and Statistical Manual of Mental Disorders,* Fourth Edition, Text Revision. Copyright © 2000 American Psychiatric Association.

TABLE 17.2 DSM-IV-TR

Diagnosis for Each Class of Substances

The "X's" indicate which diagnoses are recognized for each substance in the DSM-IV-TR.

	Intoxication	Withdrawal	Abuse	Dependence
Alcohol	X	X	X	X
Barbiturates	X	X	X	X
Benzodiazepines	X	X	X	X
Inhalants	X		X	X
Cocaine	X	X	X	X
Amphetamines	X	X	X	X
Caffeine	X			
Opioids	X	X	X	X
Hallucinogens	X		X	X
Phencyclidine	X		X	X
Cannabis	X		X	X
Nicotine		X		X

Source: Reprinted with permission from the *Diagnostic and Statistical Manual of Mental Disorders,* Fourth Edition, Text Revision. Copyright © 2000 American Psychiatric Association.

TABLE 17.3 DSM-IV-TR

Other Substances That Can Lead to Substance Use Disorders

Anesthetics and analgesics	Muscle relaxants
Anticholinergic agents	Nonsteroidal anti-inflammatory medications
Anticonvulsants	Antidepressant medications
Antihistamines	Lead
Blood pressure medications	Rat poisons with strychnine
Antimicrobial medications	Pesticides
Antiparkinsonian medications	Nerve gas
Corticosteroids	Antifreeze
Gastrointestinal medications	Carbon monoxide or dioxide

Source: Reprinted with permission from the *Diagnostic and Statistical Manual of Mental Disorders,* Fourth Edition, Text Revision. Copyright © 2000 American Psychiatric Association.

There are many other substances used for intoxicating effects that more rarely lead to substance-related disorders (see the DSM-IV-TR information in Table 17.3). Although most people exposed to the substances listed in Table 17.3 experience either no psychoactive effects or only mild and transient effects, some people experience significant problems in cognition and mood, anxiety, hallucinations, delusions, and seizures when exposed. These people may be given the diagnosis of *other substance-related disorder.*

After we discuss specific substances and the disorders associated with them, we discuss the theories of why some people are more prone than others to develop substance-related disorders, examining gender and cultural differences. Then, we discuss the treatments available for people with substance-related disorders. Most of these theories and treatments focus on people with alcohol-related disorders but have been adapted for people with other disorders.

Intoxication

Substance intoxication is a set of behavioral and psychological changes that occur as a direct result of the physiological effects of a substance on the central nervous system. When people are intoxicated, their perceptions change and they may see or hear strange things. Their attention is often diminished or they are easily distracted. Their good judgment is gone and they may be unable to "think straight." They cannot control their bodies as well as they normally can, and they may stumble or be too slow or awkward in their reactions. They often want to sleep either a lot or not at all. Their interpersonal interactions change—they may become more gregarious than usual, more withdrawn, or more aggressive and impulsive. People begin to be intoxicated soon after they begin ingesting a substance, and, the more they ingest, the more intoxicated they become. Intoxication begins to decline as the amount of a substance in people's blood or tissue declines, but the symptoms of intoxication may last for hours or days after the substance is no longer detectable in the body.

The specific symptoms of intoxication depend on what substance is taken, how much is taken, how long the substance has been ingested, and the user's tolerance for the substance. Short-term, or acute, intoxication can produce different symptoms than chronic intoxication. For example, the first time people take a moderate dose of cocaine, they may be outgoing, friendly, and very upbeat. With chronic use over days or weeks, they may begin to withdraw socially and become less gregarious. People's expectations about a substance's effects can also influence the types of symptoms shown. People who expect marijuana to make them relaxed may experience relaxation, whereas people who are frightened of the disinhibition that marijuana creates may experience anxiety, as happened with the woman in the following case study (adapted from Spitzer et al., 1994, pp. 204–205):

> In the middle of a rainy October night, a family doctor in a Chicago suburb was awakened by an old friend who begged him to get out of bed and come quickly to a neighbor's house, where he and his wife had been visiting. The caller, Lou Wolff, was very upset because his

wife, Sybil, had smoked some marijuana and was "freaking out."

The doctor arrived at the neighbor's house to find Sybil lying on the couch looking quite frantic, unable to get up. She said she was too weak to stand, that she was dizzy, was having palpitations, and could feel her blood "rushing through [her] veins." She kept asking for water because her mouth was so dry she could not swallow. She was sure there was some poison in the marijuana.

Sybil, age 42, was the mother of three teenage boys. She worked as a librarian at a university. She was a very controlled, well-organized woman who prided herself on her rationality. It was she who had asked the neighbors to share some of their high-quality homegrown marijuana with her, because marijuana was a big thing with the students and she "wanted to see what all the fuss was about."

Her husband said that she took four or five puffs on a joint and then wailed, "There's something wrong with me. I can't stand up." Lou and the neighbors tried to calm her, telling her she should just lie down and she would soon feel better; but the more they reassured her, the more convinced she became that something was really wrong with her.

The doctor examined her. The only positive findings were that her heart rate was increased and her pupils dilated. He said to her, "For heaven's sake, Sybil, you're just a little stoned. Go home to bed." Sybil did go home to bed, where she stayed for 2 days, feeling "spacey" and weak but no longer terribly anxious. She recovered completely and vowed never to smoke marijuana again.

The setting in which a substance is taken can influence the types of symptoms people develop. For example, when people consume a few alcoholic drinks at a party, they may become uninhibited and loud, but, when they consume the same amount at home alone, they may simply become tired and depressed. The environment in which people become intoxicated can also influence how maladaptive the intoxication is: People who drink alcohol only at home may be at less risk of causing harm to themselves or others than are people who typically drink at bars and drive home under the influence of alcohol.

Most people have been intoxicated, usually with alcohol, at sometime in their lives. The diagnosis of substance intoxication is given only when the behavioral and psychological changes the person experiences are significantly maladaptive in that they substantially disrupt the person's social and family relationships, cause occupational or financial problems, or place the individual at significant risk for adverse effects, such as traffic accidents, severe medical complications, or legal problems.

Withdrawal

Substance withdrawal involves a set of physiological and behavioral symptoms that result when people who have been using substances heavily for prolonged periods of time stop using the substances or greatly reduce their use. The symptoms of withdrawal from a given substance are typically the opposite of the symptoms of intoxication with the same substance. The diagnosis of substance withdrawal is not made unless the withdrawal symptoms cause significant distress or impairment in a person's everyday functioning. For example, although the symptoms of caffeine withdrawal (nervousness, headaches) are annoying to many people, they do not typically cause significant impairment in people's functioning or great distress. For this reason, caffeine withdrawal is not included as a diagnostic category in the DSM-IV-TR.

The symptoms of withdrawal can begin a few hours after a person stops ingesting substances that break down quickly in the body, such as alcohol or heroin. The more intense symptoms of withdrawal usually end within a few days to a few weeks. However, withdrawal symptoms, including seizures, may develop several weeks after a person stops taking high doses of substances that take a long time to leave the body completely, such as some antianxiety substances. In addition, subtle physiological signs of withdrawal, such as problems in attention, perception, or motor skills, may be present for many weeks or months after a person stops using a substance.

Abuse

The diagnosis of **substance abuse** is given when a person's recurrent use of a substance results in significant harmful consequences. Thus, people may use substances, including illegal substances, without having a psychiatric diagnosis, but, when their use causes chronic harmful consequences, they are considered to have a substance use disorder. There are four categories of harmful consequences that suggest substance abuse (APA, 2000) (see the DSM-IV-TR criteria in Table 17.4) First, the individual *fails*

TABLE 17.4   DSM-IV-TR
Criteria for Diagnosing Substance Abuse
The criteria for diagnosing substance abuse require repeated problems as a result of the use of a substance.
One or more of the following occurs during a 12-month period, leading to significant impairment or distress:
1. failure to fulfill important obligations at work, home, or school as a result of substance use
2. repeated use of the substance in situations in which it is physically hazardous to do so
3. repeated legal problems as a result of substance use
4. continued use of the substance despite repeated social or legal problems as a result of use
Source: Reprinted with permission from the *Diagnostic and Statistical Manual of Mental Disorders*, Fourth Edition, Text Revision. Copyright © 2000 American Psychiatric Association.

to fulfill important obligations at work, school, or home. He or she may fail to show up at work or for classes, be unable to concentrate and therefore perform poorly, and perhaps even take the substance at work or at school. Second, the individual *repeatedly uses the substance in situations in which it is physically hazardous to do so*, such as while driving a car or a boat. Third, the individual *repeatedly has legal problems as a result of substance use*, such as arrests for the possession of illegal substances or for drunk driving. Fourth, the individual *continues to use the substance, even though he or she has repeatedly had social or legal problems as a result of the use*. A person has to show repeated problems in at least one of these categories within a 12-month period to qualify for a diagnosis of substance abuse.

For some people, the abuse of a particular group of substances evolves into dependence on those substances. In such cases, the diagnosis of substance dependence preempts the diagnosis of substance abuse, since dependence is considered a more advanced condition than abuse. Some individuals abuse substances for years without ever becoming dependent on them, however.

Dependence

The diagnosis of **substance dependence** is closest to what people often refer to as *drug addiction* (see the DSM-IV-TR criteria in Table 17.5). A person is

TABLE 17.5 DSM-IV-TR

Criteria for Diagnosing Substance Dependence

Substance dependence often involves evidence of physiological dependence plus repeated problems due to the use of the substance.

Maladaptive pattern of substance use, leading to three or more of the following:

1. tolerance, as defined by either
   a. the need for markedly increased amounts of the substance to achieve intoxication or desired effect
   b. markedly diminished effect with continued use of the same amount of the substance

2. withdrawal, as manifested by either
   a. the characteristic withdrawal syndrome for the substance
   b. the same or a closely related substance is taken to relieve or avoid withdrawal symptoms

3. the substance is often taken in larger amounts or over a longer period than was intended

4. there is a persistent desire or unsuccessful effort to cut down or control substance use

5. a great deal of time is spent in activities necessary to obtain the substance, use the substance, or recover from its effects

6. important social, occupational, or recreational activities are given up or reduced because of substance use

7. the substance use is continued despite knowledge of having a persistent or recurrent physical or psychological problem caused by or exacerbated by the substance.

Source: Reprinted with permission from the *Diagnostic and Statistical Manual of Mental Disorders*, Fourth Edition, Text Revision. Copyright © 2000 American Psychiatric Association.

physiologically dependent on a substance when he or she shows either tolerance or withdrawal from the substance. **Tolerance** is present when a person experiences less and less effect from the same dose of a substance and needs greater and greater doses of a substance in order to achieve intoxication. People who have smoked cigarettes for years often smoke more than 20 cigarettes a day, when the same amount would have made them violently ill when they first began smoking. A person who is highly tolerant to a substance may have a very high blood level of the substance without being aware of any effects of the substance. For example, people who are highly tolerant to alcohol may have blood-alcohol levels far above those used in the legal definition of intoxication but show few signs of alcohol intoxication. The risk for tolerance varies greatly from one substance to the next. Alcohol, opioids, stimulants, and nicotine have high risks for tolerance, whereas cannabis and PCP appear to have lower risks for tolerance.

People who are physiologically dependent on substances often show severe withdrawal symptoms when they stop using the substances. The symptoms may be so severe that the substances must be withdrawn gradually in order to prevent the symptoms from becoming overwhelming or dangerous. These people may take the substances to relieve or avoid withdrawal symptoms. For example, a person dependent on alcohol may have a drink first thing in the morning to relieve withdrawal symptoms.

Physiological dependence (i.e., evidence of tolerance or withdrawal) is not required for a diagnosis of substance dependence, however. The diagnosis can be given when a person compulsively uses a substance, despite experiencing significant social, occupational, psychological, or medical problems as a result of that use.

Most people who are dependent on a substance crave the substance and will do almost anything to get it (e.g., steal, lie, prostitute themselves) when the craving is strong. Their entire lives may revolve around obtaining and ingesting the substance. They may have attempted repeatedly to cut back on or quit using the substance, only to find themselves compulsively taking the substance again. In the following case study, Lucy is physically and psychologically dependent on both heroin and crack cocaine (adapted from Inciardi, Lockwood, & Pottieger, 1993, pp. 160–161):

By the time Lucy was 18, she was heavily addicted to heroin. Her mother took her to a detoxification program. After the 21-day regimen, Lucy was released but immediately relapsed to heroin use. By age 24, Lucy was mainlining heroin and turning tricks regularly to support both her and a boyfriend's drug habits. Lucy's boyfriend admitted himself to a drug rehabilitation program. When he completed his treatment stay, they both stopped their heroin use. However, they began snorting cocaine. Lucy left this boyfriend not too long afterwards. She went to work in a massage parlor, and the other women there introduced her to crack. This was 1984 and Lucy was 30 years old, a veteran drug addict and prostitute.

Lucy left the massage parlor and began working on the streets. Her crack use increased continually until 1986, when she tried to stop. In her opinion, crack was worse than heroin, so she started injecting narcotics again. But she never stopped using crack.

Because of her crack use, Lucy began doing things she had never even contemplated before, even while on heroin. For instance, she had anal sex and she sold herself for less money than ever before. She even began trading sex for drugs rather than money. Lucy also regularly worked in crack houses. She described them as "disgusting" and crowded. People would smoke and have sex in the same room in front of other people. Lucy insisted that her crack-house tricks rent rooms for sex, refusing to have sex in front of others. After having sex, Lucy would return to the stroll. Lucy would have five to seven customers a night, and most of the sex was oral. During this time, Lucy either stayed with her sister or slept in cars.

The way a substance is administered can be an important factor in determining how rapidly a person will become intoxicated and the likelihood that it will produce withdrawal symptoms or lead to abuse or dependence. The routes of administration that produce rapid and efficient absorption of the substance into the bloodstream lead to more intense intoxication and a greater likelihood of dependence. These routes include injecting, smoking,

Smoking, snorting, or injecting a substance can lead to more intense intoxication and a greater chance of dependence than eating or drinking it.

and snorting the substance. These routes of administration are also more likely to lead to overdose.

Some substances act more rapidly on the central nervous system and, thus, lead to faster intoxication. They are more likely to lead to dependence or abuse. Finally, substances whose effects wear off quickly are more likely to lead to dependence or abuse than are substances with longer-lasting effects.

Let's turn now to discussing what intoxication, withdrawal, abuse, and dependence look like for the substances associated with substance disorders in the DSM-IV-TR. We begin with the depressants, which include alcohol, benzodiazepines, barbiturates, and the inhalants.

DEPRESSANTS

The depressants slow the activity of the central nervous system. In moderate doses, they make people relaxed and somewhat sleepy, reduce concentration, and impair thinking and motor skills. In heavy doses, they can induce stupor (see the Concept Overview in Table 17.6).

Alcohol

Alcohol is a classic central nervous system depressant, but its effects on the brain occur in two distinct phases. In low doses, alcohol causes many people to feel more self-confident, more relaxed, and perhaps slightly euphoric. They may be less inhibited, and it may be this disinhibitory effect that many people find attractive. At increasing doses, however, alcohol induces many of the symptoms of depression, including fatigue and lethargy, decreased motivation, sleep disturbances, depressed mood, and confusion. Also, although many people take alcohol to feel more sexy (mainly by reducing

TABLE 17.6   Concept Overview

Intoxication with and Withdrawal from Depressants

The depressants are among the most widely used substances.

Drug	Intoxication Symptoms	Withdrawal Symptoms
Alcohol, benzodiazepines, and barbiturates	Behavioral changes (e.g., inappropriate sexual or aggressive behavior, mood lability, impaired judgment) Slurred speech Incoordination Unsteady gait Rapid eye movement Attention and memory problems Stupor or coma	Autonomic hyperactivity (e.g., sweating or a pulse rate greater than 100) Hand tremor Insomnia Nausea or vomiting Transient hallucinations or illusions Psychomotor agitation Anxiety Grand mal seizures
Inhalants	Behavioral changes (e.g., belligerence, assaultiveness, apathy, impaired judgment) Dizziness Involuntary rapid eyeball movements Incoordination Slurred speech Unsteady gait Lethargy Depressed reflexes Psychomotor retardation Tremor Muscle weakness Blurred vision Stupor or coma Euphoria	Not a diagnosis in DSM-IV-TR

Source: Reprinted with permission from the *Diagnostic and Statistical Manual of Mental Disorders,* Fourth Edition, Text Revision. Copyright © 2000 American Psychiatric Association.

their sexual inhibitions), even low doses of alcohol can severely impair sexual functioning.

People who are intoxicated with alcohol slur their words, walk with unsteady gaits, have trouble paying attention or remembering things, and are slow and awkward in their physical reactions. They may act inappropriately, becoming aggressive or saying rude things. Their moods may swing from exuberance to despair. With extreme intoxication, they may fall into a stupor or coma. Often, they do not recognize they are intoxicated or may flatly deny it, even though it is obvious. Once sober, they may have amnesia, known as a **blackout,** for the events that occurred while they were intoxicated.

One critical determinant of how quickly people become intoxicated with alcohol is whether their stomachs are full or empty. When the stomach is empty, alcohol is more quickly delivered from the stomach to the small intestine, where it is rapidly absorbed into the body. The person with a full stomach may drink significantly more drinks before reaching a dangerous blood-alcohol level or showing clear signs of intoxication. People in countries where alcohol is almost always consumed with

Drinking alcohol with food leads to slower absorption of the alcohol.

meals, such as in France, show lower rates of alcohol-related substance disorders than do people in countries where alcohol is often consumed on an empty stomach.

The *legal definition* of alcohol intoxication is much narrower than the criteria for a diagnosis of alcohol intoxication. Most states in the United States consider a person to be under the influence of alcohol if his or her blood-alcohol level is above 0.05, 0.08, or 0.10. As Table 17.7 indicates, it does not take very many drinks for most people to reach this blood-alcohol level. Deficits in attention, reaction time, and coordination arise even with the first drink and can interfere with the ability to operate a car or machinery safely and to perform other tasks requiring a steady hand, coordination, clear thinking, and clear vision. These deficits are not always readily observable, even to trained observers (Winger et al., 1992). People often leave parties or bars with blood-alcohol levels well above the legal limit and dangerous deficits in their ability to drive, without appearing drunk.

Drinking large quantities of alcohol can result in death, even in people who are not chronic abusers of alcohol. About one-third of these deaths occur as a result of respiratory paralysis, usually as a result of a final, large dose of alcohol in people who are already intoxicated. Alcohol can also interact fatally with a number of substances—for example, antidepressant drugs (Winger et al., 1992).

Most deaths due to alcohol, however, come from automobile accidents, private plane and boat accidents, and drownings. Nearly half of all fatal automobile accidents and deaths due to falls or fires and over a third of all drownings are alcohol-related (Flemming & Manwell, 2000; Hunt, 1998). More than half of all murderers and their victims are believed to be intoxicated with alcohol at the time of the murders, and people who commit suicide often do so under the influence of alcohol.

Alcohol Abuse and Dependence

People given the diagnosis of **alcohol abuse** use alcohol in dangerous situations (such as when driving), fail to meet important obligations at work or at home as a result of their alcohol use, and have recurrent legal or social problems as a result of their alcohol use. People given the diagnosis of **alcohol dependence** typically have all the problems of an alcohol abuser; plus they may show physiological tolerance to alcohol, they spend a great deal of time intoxicated or withdrawing from alcohol, they often organize their lives around drinking, or they continue to drink despite having significant social, occupational, medical, or legal problems that result from drinking. The characteristics of alcohol dependence match what most people associate with the label *alcoholism*. Table 17.8 on page 632 lists a variety of problems experienced by people who abuse or are dependent on alcohol.

There are at least three distinct patterns of alcohol use by alcohol abusers and dependents. Some people drink large amounts of alcohol every day and plan their days around their drinking. Others abstain from drinking for long periods of time and then go on binges, which last days or weeks. They may stop drinking when faced with crises they must deal with, such as their children's illnesses, or with threats of sanctions for drinking, such as threats of being fired. When they begin drinking again, they may be able to control their drinking for a while, but it may soon escalate until severe problems develop. Still others are sober during the weekdays but drink heavily during the evenings or perhaps only on weekends. Nick and his buddies fit into the third group:

Nick began drinking in high school, but his drinking escalated when he moved away from his parents' home to go to college. After just a couple of weeks at college, Nick became friends with a group of guys who liked to party really hard on the weekends. On Thursday nights, they would begin to drink beer, often getting quite drunk. They would get a little loud and obnoxious, and sometimes their neighbors in the dormitory would complain to the resident

(continued)

TABLE 17.7 Relationships Among Sex, Weight, Oral Alcohol Consumption, and Blood-Alcohol Level

It doesn't take very many drinks for most people to reach the blood-alcohol level of 0.05 or 0.10, which are the legal definitions of intoxication in most states.

Total Alcohol Content (Ounces)	Beverage Intake*	Blood-Alcohol Level (Percent)					
		Female (100 lb)	Male (100 lb)	Female (150 lb)	Male (150 lb)	Female (200 lb)	Male (200 lb)
1/2	1 oz spirits† 1 glass wine 1 can beer	0.045	0.037	0.03	0.025	0.022	0.019
1	2 oz spirits 2 glasses wine 2 cans beer	0.090	0.075	0.06	0.050	0.045	0.037
2	4 oz spirits 4 glasses wine 4 cans beer	0.180	0.150	0.12	0.100	0.090	0.070
3	6 oz spirits 6 glasses wine 6 cans beer	0.270	0.220	0.18	0.150	0.130	0.110
4	8 oz spirits 8 glasses wine 8 cans beer	0.360	0.300	0.24	0.200	0.180	0.150
5	10 oz spirits 10 glasses wine 10 cans beer	0.450	0.370	0.30	0.250	0.220	0.180

Source: Data from Ray & Ksir, 1993, p. 194.

*In one hour.

†100-proof spirits (50 percent alcohol).

CASE STUDY

assistant of the dorm about them. They would typically sleep off their hangovers on Friday, missing classes, and then begin drinking again Friday afternoon. They would continue to drink through Saturday, finally stopping on Sunday to sleep and recover. Nick was able to keep a decent grade average through his first year in college, despite missing many classes. In his sophomore year, however, the classes in his major were getting harder. Nick's drinking was also getting more out of hand. He still would abstain from drinking from about Sunday afternoon until noon on Thursday. But, when he would go get the keg of beer for his group of buddies on Thursday afternoon, he'd also pick up a few fifths of vodka or whatever hard liquor was the cheapest. His buddies would stick to the beer, but Nick would mix the beer with shots of hard liquor and was usually extremely drunk by dinner on Thursday. He started getting really mean and stupid when he was drunk. He punched a hole in the wall of his dorm room one night; when the resident assistant came up to investigate what was going on, he threatened her, saying he would "smack her across the room" if she didn't shut up and leave. That got him kicked out of his dormitory and off campus. Nick didn't mind being away from the "geeks" who studied all the time and liked (*continued*) having his own apartment, where his buddies could come to drink. Nick remained intoxicated from Thursday afternoon until Sunday morning, drinking all day and evening, except when he was passed out. He usually slept through most of his classes on Monday; when he did go, he was so hungover that he couldn't pay attention. His grades were falling, and even his drinking buddies were getting disgusted with Nick's behavior.

Binge drinking is defined as consuming five or more drinks within a couple of hours of each other (although some researchers define a binge for women as consuming four or more drinks within a

TABLE 17.8 Problems Experienced by People Who Are Diagnosed with Alcohol Abuse or Dependence

People with alcohol abuse or dependence typically have many problems due to their alcohol use.

Symptom	Percentage Saying Yes
Family objected to respondent's drinking	62
Thought him- or herself an excessive drinker	59
Consumed a fifth of liquor in one day	70
Engaged in daily or weekly heavy drinking	80
Told physician about drinking	22
Friends or professionals said drinking too much	39
Wanted to stop drinking but couldn't	21
Made efforts to control drinking	19
Engaged in morning drinking	21
Had job troubles due to drinking	15
Lost job	7
Had trouble driving	35
Was arrested while drinking	31
Had physical fights while drinking	50
Had two or more binges	29
Had blackouts while drinking	57
Had any withdrawal symptom	28
Had any medical complication	22
Continued to drink with serious illness	14
Couldn't do ordinary work without drinking	12

Source: Data from Helzer, Bucholz, & Robins, 1992.

short time). In a nationwide survey, 23 percent of Americans reported binge drinking in the previous month (SAMHSA, 2005). Binge drinking on college campuses is common. Nationwide, 44 percent of college students report binge drinking in the past month, compared with 39 percent of 18- to 22-year-olds not in college (SAMHSA, 2005). Binge drinking is especially common among members of fraternities and sororities, with 76 percent of members saying they binge drink and 15 percent having engaged in binge drinking at least six times in the previous two weeks (Wahlberg, 1999).

Family members, friends, and business associates often recognize when an individual is abusing or is dependent on alcohol, and they confront the individual. Sometimes, this leads the individual to seek help, but denial is strong. One confrontation or even a series of confrontations often does not motivate someone who is abusing alcohol to change his or her behavior or to seek help.

There is increasing evidence that alcohol dependence is a heterogeneous disorder and that different subtypes of alcohol dependence have different causes and prognoses. One reliable distinction is between alcoholics who also have antisocial personalities and alcoholics who do not have antisocial personalities (Zucker et al., 1996). Antisocial alcoholics have more severe symptoms of alcoholism, tend to remain alcoholic for longer, have poorer social functioning, have more marital failures, and have heavier drug involvement, compared with nonantisocial alcoholics (Zucker et al., 1996). Antisocial alcoholics are more likely to come from families with alcoholism and to have begun drinking earlier than nonantisocial alcoholics. In turn, the children of antisocial alco-

Heavy drinking can be part of the culture of a peer group, but it still can lead to alcohol abuse and dependence in some members.

holics are more likely to have behavior problems than are the children of nonantisocial alcoholics (Puttler et al., 1998).

Another distinction that has been made is between negative affect alcoholism and other alcoholisms (Sher, Grekin, & Williams, 2005). People with negative affect alcoholism tend to have had depressive and anxiety symptoms in childhood and adolescence and to have only begun severe alcohol use and abuse in adulthood. This pattern appears to be more common in women than in men (Nolen-Hoeksema, 2004).

Alcohol Withdrawal

People who are dependent on alcohol can experience severe alcohol withdrawal symptoms, which can be divided into three stages (Winger et al., 1992). The first stage, which usually begins within a few hours after drinking has been stopped or sharply curtailed, includes tremulousness (the "shakes"), weakness, and profuse perspiration. A person may complain of anxiety (the "jitters"), headache, nausea, and abdominal cramps. He or she may begin to retch and vomit. The person's face is flushed, and he or she is restless and easily startled but alert. The person's EEG pattern may be mildly abnormal. He or she may begin to see or hear things, at first only with eyes shut but with time also with eyes open. People whose dependence on alcohol is relatively moderate may experience only this first stage of withdrawal, and the symptoms may disappear within a few days.

The second stage of withdrawal involves convulsive seizures, which may begin as early as 12 hours after stopping drinking but more often appear during the second or third day. The third stage of withdrawal is characterized by **delirium tremens,** or **DTs.** Auditory, visual, and tactile hallucinations occur. The person may also develop bizarre, terrifying delusions, such as a belief that monsters are attacking. He or she may sleep little and become severely agitated, continuously active, and completely disoriented. Fever, profuse perspiration, and an irregular heartbeat may develop. Delirium tremens is a fatal condition in approximately 10 percent of cases. Death may occur from hyperthermia (greatly increased body temperature) or the collapse of the peripheral vascular system. Fortunately, only about 11 percent of individuals with alcohol dependence ever experience seizures or DTs (Schuckit et al., 1995). Seizures and DTs are more common among people who drink large amounts in single sittings and who have additional medical illnesses.

People who make it through the entire withdrawal syndrome can show complete recovery from withdrawal symptoms. The following is a case study presented by groundbreaking psychiatrist Emil Kraepelin to medical students in the nineteenth century. It is about a man going through delirium tremens after prolonged alcohol dependence (Spitzer et al., 1981, pp. 304–305).

CASE STUDY

The innkeeper, aged thirty-four, whom I am bringing before you to-day was admitted to the hospital only an hour ago. He understands the questions put to him, but cannot quite hear some of them, and gives a rather absent-minded impression. He states his name and age correctly. . . . Yet he does not know the doctors, calls them by the names of his acquaintances, and thinks he has been here for two or three days. It must be the Crown Hotel, or, rather, the "mad hospital." He does not know the date exactly. . . .

He moves about in his chair, looks round him a great deal, starts slightly several times, and keeps on playing with his hands. Suddenly he gets up, and begs to be allowed to play on the piano for a little at once. He sits down again immediately, on persuasion, but then wants to go away "to tell them something else that he has forgotten." He gradually gets more and more excited, saying that his fate is sealed; he must leave the world now; they might telegraph to his wife that her husband is lying at the point of death. We learn, by questioning him, that he is going to be executed by electricity, and also that he will be shot. "The picture is not clearly painted," he says; "every moment someone stands now here, now there, waiting for me with a revolver. When I open my eyes, they vanish." He says that a stinking fluid has been injected into his head and both his toes, which causes the pictures one takes for reality; that is the work of an international society, which makes away with those "who fell into misfortune innocently through false steps." With this he looks eagerly at the window, where he sees houses and trees vanishing and reappearing. With slight pressure on his eyes, he sees first sparks, then a hare, a picture, a head, a washstand-set, a half-moon, and a human head, first dully and then in colours. If you show him a speck on the floor,

(continued)

he tries to pick it up, saying that it is a piece of money. If you shut his hand and ask him what you have given him, he keeps his fingers carefully closed, and guesses that it is a leadpencil or a piece of indiarubber. The patient's mood is half apprehensive and half amused. His head is much flushed, and his pulse is small, weak, and rather hurried. His face is bloated and his eyes are watery. His breath smells strongly of alcohol and acetone. His tongue is thickly furred, and trembles when he puts it out, and his outspread fingers show strong, jerky tremors.

Long-Term Effects of Alcohol Abuse

Heavy, prolonged use of alcohol can have toxic effects on several systems of the body, including the stomach, esophagus, pancreas, and liver (for a review, see Nolen-Hoeksema, 2004). Comedian Chris Farley showed evidence of liver damage from chronic alcohol abuse. One of the most common medical conditions associated with alcohol abuse and dependence is low-grade hypertension. This factor, combined with increases in triglycerides and low-density lipoprotein (or "bad") cholesterol, puts alcohol abusers at increased risk for heart disease. Alcohol abusers and dependents are often malnourished, in part because chronic alcohol ingestion decreases the absorption of critical nutrients from the gastrointestinal system and in part because they tend to "drink their meals." Some alcohol abusers show chronic thiamine deficiencies, which can lead to several disorders of the central nervous system, including numbness and pain in the extremities, deterioration in the muscles, and the loss of visual acuity for both near and far objects (Martin & Bates, 1998).

Alcohol-induced persisting amnesic disorder, a permanent cognitive disorder caused by damage to the central nervous system, consists of two syndromes. **Wernicke's encephalopathy** involves mental confusion and disorientation and, in severe states, coma. **Korsakoff's psychosis** involves a loss of memory for recent events and problems in recalling distant events. The person may confabulate, telling implausible stories in an attempt to hide his or her inability to remember. **Alcohol-induced dementia** is the loss of intellectual abilities, including memory, abstract thinking, judgment, or problem solving, often accompanied by personality changes, such as increases in paranoia. This syndrome is found in approximately 9 percent of people who chronically abuse alcohol or are dependent and is a common cause of adult dementia (Winger et al.,

1992). More subtle deficits due to central nervous system damage are observed in many chronic abusers of alcohol, even after they have stopped using alcohol (Martin & Bates, 1998).

Children of mothers who chronically ingest large amounts of alcohol while pregnant may be born with **fetal alcohol syndrome (FAS)** (Streissguth et al., 1999). This syndrome is characterized by retarded growth, facial abnormalities, central nervous system damage, mental retardation, motor abnormalities, tremors, hyperactivity, heart defects, and skeletal anomalies (see also Chapter 13). The risk for fetal alcohol syndrome is highest among women who are chronic, heavy alcohol users while pregnant, particularly those who drink heavily early in pregnancy.

However, even low to moderate levels of drinking during pregnancy are associated with subtle alcohol-related birth defects (Jacobson & Jacobson, 2000; Kelly et al., 2000; Olson et al., 1998). For example, children exposed to alcohol in the womb are slower to grow physically by 6 years of age, and have deficits in learning and memory skills at 10 years of age (Cornelius et al., 2002). These results hold even after controlling for correlates of prenatal alcohol use, including income, and tobacco and marijuana use. Thus, experts believe that there is no level of drinking during pregnancy that is safe for the fetus.

Cultural Differences in Alcohol Disorders

There are marked differences across cultures in the use of alcohol and in rates of alcohol-related problems (see Figure 17.3). Low rates of alcohol consumption in Eastern Mediterranean and some African countries are tied to the influence of Islam and its prohibitions against alcohol. Low rates of alcohol consumption in Southeast Asia may be due in part to the absence, in 50 percent of people of Asian descent, of an enzyme that eliminates the first breakdown product of alcohol, acetaldehyde. When these individuals consume alcohol, they experience a flushed face and heart palpitations, and the discomfort of this effect often leads them to avoid alcohol altogether. Figure 17.3 shows moderate rates in the Western Pacific countries, which include Japan and China, where consumption is relatively low, but also include Australia, where consumption is relatively high.

Alcohol dependence and abuse are the most common disorders in the United States, with 8 to 24 percent of the population reporting symptoms that qualify them for a diagnosis of dependence or abuse at sometime in their lives, depending on which nationwide survey you look at (Sher, Grekin, & Williams, 2005). Within the United States, there are substantial differences among ethnic groups in alcohol use (see Figure 17.4 on page 636). One group in the United States that appears at high risk for alcohol abuse and dependence is Native Americans. For example, a study of adult members of a Pacific Northwest reservation community found that 27 percent qualified for a diagnosis of alcohol dependence. Deaths related to alcohol are as much as five times more common among Native Americans than in the general U.S. population (Manson et al., 1992). Hospital records indicate that alcohol-related illnesses are three times higher among Native Americans than among all people in the United States and twice the rates for other ethnic minority groups in the United States. The higher rates of alcohol-related problems among Native Americans have been tied to their excessive rates of poverty and unemployment, lower education, and greater sense of helplessness and hopelessness.

Gender and Alcohol Use

In a community survey done in the United States, about 62 percent of men over age 12 said they had consumed at least one alcoholic beverage in the past month, compared with 46 percent of women (SAMHSA, 2005) (see Figure 17.5 on page 636). Men are also more likely than women to binge drink, to drink heavily, and to have alcohol use disorders. About 13 percent of American men and 6 percent of American women will meet the criteria for alcohol abuse at sometime in their lives, and about 20 percent of men and 8 percent of women will meet the criteria for alcohol dependence at sometime in their lives (Kessler et al., 1994). The gender gap in alcohol use is much greater among men and women who subscribe to traditional gender roles, which condone drinking for men but not for women (Huselid & Cooper, 1992). Similarly, in ethnic minority groups of the United States in which traditional gender roles are more widely accepted, such as Hispanics and recent Asian immigrants, the gender gap in drinking is greater than it is among Whites, due largely to high percentages of women in the minority groups who completely abstain from alcohol.

Trends Across the Life Span

Studies of adolescents and young adults find a widespread abuse of alcohol (Lewinsohn et al., 1996b; Nelson & Wittchen, 1998), particularly among males. One nationwide sample found that the proportions of eighth-, tenth-, and twelfth-graders who reported drinking an alcoholic beverage in the 30-day period prior to the survey were 20 percent, 35 percent, and 48 percent, respectively (Johnston et al., 2004). One study of more than 3,000 14- to 24-year-olds found that 15 percent of

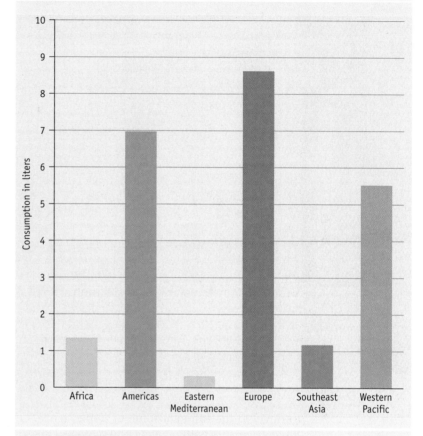

FIGURE 17.3 **Consumption of Pure Alcohol in Various Regions of the World.** Cultures vary greatly in their consumption of alcohol. (Southeast Asia includes India and neighboring countries. Western Pacific includes Australia, China, Japan, and the Pacific Rim Countries.)

Source: World Health Organization, 2005b.

the males and about 5 percent of the females could be diagnosed with alcohol abuse, according to the DSM-IV (Nelson & Wittchen, 1998). Alcohol dependence was lower, with about 10 percent of the males and 3 percent of the females qualifying for the diagnosis. Over time, about half of the adolescents and young adults who abused alcohol stopped abusing alcohol, but the alcohol abusers were much more likely than the nonabusers to become dependent on alcohol eventually.

Young and middle-aged adults who are diagnosed with alcohol dependence tend to show a chronic course, at least over a five-year period. One study, which followed 1,346 people, found that two-thirds of those diagnosed with alcohol dependence still had the diagnosis five years later (Schuckit, Smith, Danko, et al., 2001). Of those initially diagnosed with alcohol abuse, 55 percent continued to show some signs of abuse or dependence five years later, but only 3.5 percent went on

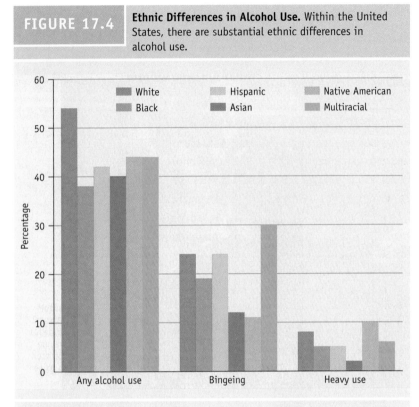

FIGURE 17.4   **Ethnic Differences in Alcohol Use.** Within the United States, there are substantial ethnic differences in alcohol use.

Source: SAMHSA, 2005.
Note: Bingeing is defined as five or more drinks on the same occasion at least once in the past 30 days. Heavy use is defined as five or more drinks on the same occasion on at least 5 different days in the past 30 days.

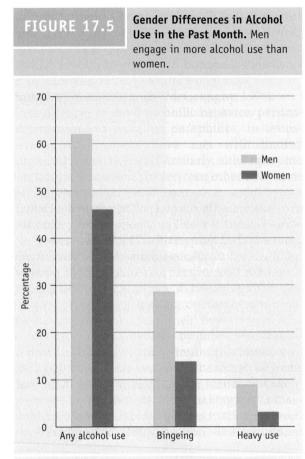

FIGURE 17.5   **Gender Differences in Alcohol Use in the Past Month.** Men engage in more alcohol use than women.

Source: SAMHSA, 2005.
Note: Bingeing is defined as five or more drinks on the same occasion at least once in the past 30 days. Heavy use is defined as five or more drinks on the same occasion on at least 5 different days in the past 30 days.

to develop the full syndrome of dependence. Of the participants with no alcohol diagnosis at baseline, only 2.5 percent met the criteria for alcohol dependence five years later, but 12.8 percent met the criteria for alcohol abuse at follow-up. Those who were more likely to have a diagnosis at follow-up included men, people with marital instability, and those who had also used illegal drugs.

As we saw in Figure 17.1, the use of illegal substances in general declines as adults get older, and this is true for alcohol as well (Sher, Grekin, & Williams, 2005). Elderly people are less likely than younger adults to abuse or be dependent on alcohol, probably for several reasons. First, with age, the liver metabolizes alcohol at a slower rate, and the lower percentage of body water increases the absorption of alcohol. As a result, older people can become intoxicated faster and experience the negative effects of alcohol more severely and quickly. Second, as people grow older, they may become more mature in their choices, including the choice about drinking alcohol to excess. Third, older people have grown up under stronger prohibitions against alcohol use and abuse and in a society in which there was more stigma associated with alcoholism, leading them to curtail their use of alcohol

more than younger people do. Finally, people who have used alcohol excessively for many years may die from alcohol-related diseases before they reach old age.

Benzodiazepines, Barbiturates, and Inhalants

Three other groups of substances that, like alcohol, depress the central nervous system are benzodiazepines, barbiturates, and inhalants. Intoxication with and withdrawal from these substances are quite similar to alcohol intoxication and withdrawal. Users initially may feel euphoric and become disinhibited but then experience depressed moods, lethargy, perceptual distortions, loss of coordination, and other signs of central nervous system depression.

Benzodiazepines (such as Xanax, Valium, Halcion, Librium, and Klonopin) and **barbiturates** (such as Quaalude) are legally manufactured and sold by prescription, usually for the treatment of anxiety and insomnia. In the United States, approximately 90 percent of people hospitalized for medical care or surgery are prescribed sedatives. Large quantities of these substances end up on the illegal black market, however. These substances are especially likely to be taken in combination with other psychoactive substances to produce greater feelings of euphoria or to relieve the agitation created by other substances (Schuckit, 1995).

There are two common patterns in the development of benzodiazapine or barbiturate abuse and dependence (Schuckit, 1995; Sowers, 1998). The most common pattern is followed by a teenager or young adult who begins using these substances recreationally, often at "bring your own drug" parties, to produce a sense of well-being or euphoria. Their use then escalates to chronic use and physiological dependence. This pattern is especially likely among persons who already have other substance abuse problems with alcohol, opioids, cocaine, amphetamines, or other substances.

A second pattern is seen in people, particularly women and older people, who initially use sedatives under physicians' care for anxiety or insomnia but then gradually increase their use as tolerance develops, without the knowledge of their physicians. They obtain prescriptions from several physicians or even photocopy their prescriptions. When confronted about their sedative use and dependency, they may deny that they use the drugs to produce euphoria or that they are dependent on the sedatives. Barbiturates and benzodiazepines cause decreases in blood pressure, respiratory rate, and heart rate. In overdose, they can be extremely dangerous and even fatal. Death can occur from respiratory arrest or cardiovascular collapse. Overdose is especially likely to occur when people take these substances (particularly the benzodiazepines) in combination with alcohol. Nationwide surveys find that, from 1995 to 2002, emergency room visits involving benzodiazepines increased 41 percent (SAMHSA, 2005).

Inhalants are volatile substances that produce chemical vapors, which can be inhaled and which depress the central nervous system. A recent user of an inhalant may appear drunk or disoriented, have slurred speech, be nauseated and lack appetite, and be inattentive, irritable, or depressed. One group of inhalants is solvents, such as gasoline, glue, paint thinners, and spray paints. Users may inhale vapors directly from the cans or bottles containing the substances, soak rags with the substances and then hold the rags to their mouths and noses, or place the substances in paper or plastic bags and then inhale the gases from the bags. The chemicals reach the lungs, bloodstream, and brain very rapidly. Others are

Older people may become addicted to sedatives after using them under a doctor's care.

medical anesthetic gases, such as nitrous oxide ("laughing gas"), which can also be found in whipped cream dispensers and products that boost octane levels. Nitrites are a special class of inhalants that dilate blood vessels and relax muscles and are used as sexual enhancers. Illegally packaged nitrites are called "poppers" or "snappers" on the street.

The greatest users of inhalants are young people. National surveys find that about 6 percent of U.S. children have tried inhalants by the time they have reached fourth grade, and inhalant abuse peaks between the seventh and ninth grades (National Institute on Drug Abuse [NIDA], 2002d). Seventeen percent of eighth-graders report having used inhalants at sometime in their lives (NIDA, 2002a). One group that appears especially prone to using inhalants is Native American teenagers. Some studies have found that nearly all the children on some Native American reservations have experimented with gasoline inhaling. Hispanic American teenagers also appear to have higher rates of inhalant use than other groups of teenagers in the United States, and it is estimated that 500,000

FIGURE 17.6   **Brain Damage in an Inhalant Abuser.** The right panel shows extensive shrinkage in the brain of an inhalant abuser, compared with the brain of a nonabuser (left panel).

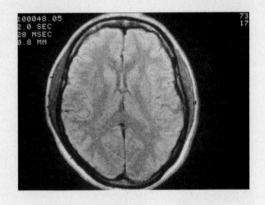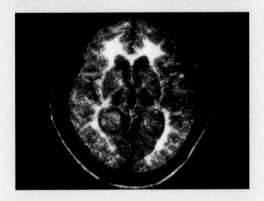

Source: http://www.drugabuse.gov/ResearchReports/

children in Mexico City are addicted to inhalants (Hartman, 1998). Males are more likely than females to use inhalants.

Chronic users of inhalants may have a variety of respiratory irritations and rashes due to the inhalants. Inhalants can cause permanent damage to the central nervous system, including degeneration and lesions of the brain, leading to cognitive deficits, including severe dementia (NIDA, 2002d) (see Figure 17.6). Recurrent use can also cause hepatitis and liver and kidney disease.

Death can occur from depression of the respiratory or cardiovascular systems. *Sudden sniffing death* is due to acute irregularities in the heartbeat or loss of oxygen. Sometimes, users suffocate themselves when they go unconscious with plastic bags filled with inhalants firmly placed over their noses and mouths. Users can also die or become seriously injured when the inhalants cause them to have delusions that they can do fantastic things, such as fly, and they jump off cliffs or tall buildings to try it.

SUMMING UP

- At low doses, alcohol produces relaxation and a mild euphoria. At higher doses, it produces the classic signs of depression and cognitive and motor impairment.

- A large proportion of deaths due to accidents, murders, and suicides are alcohol-related.

- Alcohol withdrawal symptoms can be mild or so severe as to be life threatening.

- People who abuse or are dependent on alcohol experience a wide range of social and interpersonal problems and are at risk for many serious health problems.

- Women drink less alcohol than do men in most cultures and are less likely to have alcohol-related disorders than are men.

- Benzodiazepines and barbiturates are sold legally by prescription for the treatment of anxiety and insomnia.

- Benzodiazepines and barbiturates can cause an initial rush plus a loss of inhibitions. These pleasurable sensations are then followed by depressed mood, lethargy, and physical signs of central nervous system depression.

- Benzodiazepines and barbiturates are dangerous in overdose and when mixed with other substances.

- Inhalants are substances that produce chemical vapors, such as gasoline or paint thinner. Inhalants can cause permanent organ and brain damage and accidental deaths due to suffocation or dangerous delusional behavior.

STIMULANTS

The stimulants are drugs that activate the central nervous system, causing feelings of energy, happiness, and power, a decreased desire for sleep, and a diminished appetite (see the Concept Overview in Table 17.9). Cocaine and amphetamines are the two types of stimulants associated with severe substance-related disorders. Both substances are used by people to get a psychological lift, or rush. Both substances cause dangerous increases in blood pressure and heart rate, changes in the rhythm and electrical activity of the heart, and constriction of the blood vessels, which can lead to heart attacks, respiratory arrest, and seizures. In the United States, toxic reactions to cocaine and amphetamines

TABLE 17.9 Concept Overview

Intoxication with and Withdrawal from Stimulants

The stimulants activate the central nervous system.

Drug	Intoxication Symptoms	Withdrawal Symptoms
Cocaine and amphetamines	Behavioral changes (e.g., euphoria or affective blunting; changes in sociability; hypervigilance; interpersonal sensitivity; anxiety, tension, or anger; impaired judgment) Rapid heartbeat Dilation of pupils Elevated or lowered blood pressure Perspiration or chills Nausea or vomiting Weight loss Psychomotor agitation or retardation Muscular weakness Slowed breathing Chest pain Confusion, seizures, coma	Dysphoric mood Fatigue Vivid, unpleasant dreams Insomnia or hypersomnia Increased appetite Psychomotor retardation or agitation
Nicotine	Not a diagnosis in DSM-IV-TR	Dysphoria or depressed mood Insomnia Irritability, frustration, or anger Anxiety Difficulty concentrating Restlessness Decreased heart rate Increased appetite or weight gain
Caffeine	Restlessness Nervousness Excitement Insomnia Flushed face Frequent urination Stomach upset Muscle twitching Rambling flow of thought or speech Rapid heartbeat Periods of inexhaustibility Psychomotor agitation	Marked fatigue or drowsiness Marked anxiety or depression Nausea or vomiting

Source: Reprinted with permission from the *Diagnostic and Statistical Manual of Mental Disorders*, Fourth Edition, Text Revision. Copyright © 2000 American Psychiatric Association.

account for 40 percent of all substance-related cases seen in hospital emergency rooms and for 50 percent of sudden deaths in which substances are involved (Goldstein, 1994). These substances are costly, both to users and to society.

Caffeine and nicotine are also stimulants and can result in diagnosable substance-related disorders. Although the psychological effects of caffeine and nicotine are not as severe as those of cocaine and amphetamines, these drugs, particularly nicotine, can have long-term negative effects, so we discuss them as well.

Prescription stimulants, including Dexedrine and Ritalin, are used to treat asthma and other respiratory problems, obesity, neurological disorders, and a variety of other diseases. Since 1990, the abuse

FIGURE 17.7 **Effects of Cocaine on Dopamine Systems.** Cocaine blocks transporters for the reuptake of dopamine, resulting in excess dopamine in the synapses.

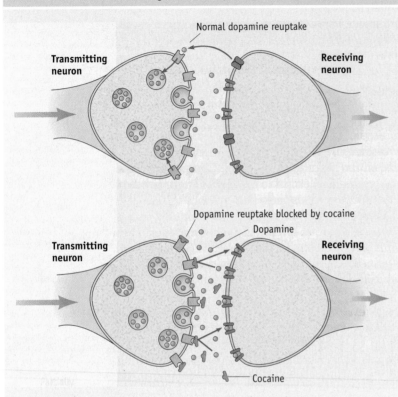

of these drugs has increased 165 percent (NIDA, 2002f), and about a million people in the United States use stimulants for nonmedical reasons.

Cocaine

Cocaine is a white powder extracted from the coca plant and one of the most highly addictive substances known. People can snort the powder, which causes its effects on the brain to be felt quickly, or dissolve the powder in water and inject it intravenously. In the 1970s, freebase cocaine appeared when users developed a method for separating the most potent chemicals in cocaine by heating it with ether. This process produced a cocaine base, or freebase, that is even more powerful. It is usually smoked in a water pipe or mixed in a tobacco or marijuana cigarette. Crack is a form of freebase cocaine that is boiled down into tiny chunks, or rocks, which are usually smoked.

Cocaine activates the ventral tegmental area and the nucleus accumbens, the areas of the brain that register reward and

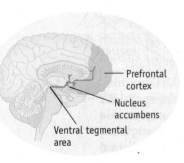

Cocaine activates the ventral tegmental area and the nucleus accumbens, the areas of the brain that register reward and pleasure.

pleasure (Gatley et al., 1998). Normally, when a pleasurable event occurs, dopamine is released into the synapses in these areas of the brain and then binds to receptors on neighboring synapses (see Figure 17.7). Cocaine blocks the reuptake of dopamine into the transmitting neuron, causing dopamine to accumulate in the synapse, maintaining the pleasurable feeling.

Initially, cocaine produces a sudden rush of intense euphoria, followed by great self-esteem, alertness, energy, and a general feeling of competence, creativity, and social acceptability. Users often do not feel drugged. Instead, they feel they have become the people they always wanted to be. When taken at high doses or chronically, however, cocaine leads to grandiosity, impulsiveness, hypersexuality, compulsive behavior, agitation, and anxiety, reaching the point of panic and paranoia. After stopping use of the substance, users may feel exhausted and depressed and sleep a great deal. Users also feel an intense craving for more of the substance, for both its physiological and its psychological effects.

Many current cocaine abusers and dependents started with heavy alcohol or marijuana use and then graduated to harder substances, including cocaine (Denison et al., 1998; Miller, 1991). The extraordinarily rapid and strong effects of cocaine on the brain's reward centers, however, seem to make this substance more likely than most illicit substances to result in patterns of abuse and dependence, even among people who have never been heavy users of any other substances, such as the dentist in the following case study.

CASE STUDY

Dr. Arnie Rosenthal is a 31-year-old white male dentist, married for 10 years with two children. His wife insisted he see a psychiatrist because of uncontrolled use of cocaine, which over the past year had made it increasingly difficult for him to function as a dentist. During the previous 5 years he used cocaine virtually every day, with only occasional periods of abstinence of 1 or 2 weeks. For the past 4 years he wanted to stop cocaine use, but his desire was overridden by a "compulsion" to take the drug. He estimates having spent $12,000 to $15,000 on cocaine during the past year.

The patient's wife, who accompanied him to the interview, complained primarily about her husband's lack of energy and motivation, which started with his drug use 5 years ago.

(continued)

She complained that "he isn't working; he has no interests outside of me and the kids—not even his music—and he spends all of his time alone watching TV." She is also bothered by his occasional temper outbursts, but that is less troubling to her. . . . During his second year in dental school he got married, while being supported comfortably by his inlaws. After having been married 1 year he began using marijuana, smoking a joint each day upon coming home from school, and spent the evenings "staring" at TV. When he graduated from dental school his wife was pregnant, and he was "scared to death" at the prospect of being a father. His deepening depression was characterized by social isolation, increased loss of interests, and frequent temper outbursts. He needed to be intoxicated with marijuana, or occasionally sedatives, for sex, relaxation, and socialization. Following the birth of the child he "never felt so crazy," and his marijuana and sedative use escalated. Two years later, a second child was born. Dr. Rosenthal was financially successful, had moved to an expensive suburban home with a swimming pool, and had two cars and "everything my parents wanted for me." He was 27 years old, felt he had nothing to look forward to, felt painfully isolated, and the drugs were no longer providing relief.

He tried cocaine for the first time and immediately felt good. "I was no longer depressed. I used cocaine as often as possible because all my problems seemed to vanish, but I had to keep doing it. The effects were brief and it was very expensive, but I didn't care. When the immediate effects wore off, I'd feel even more miserable and depressed so that I did as much cocaine as I was able to obtain." He is now continuously nervous and irritable. Practicing dentistry has become increasingly difficult. (Adapted from Spitzer et al., 1983, pp. 81–83)

Because cocaine has a short half-life (the time needed for half of the drug to disappear from the body), its effects wear off quickly. As a result, the person dependent on cocaine must take frequent doses of the substance to maintain a high. In addition, a tolerance to cocaine can develop, so that the individual must obtain larger and larger amounts of cocaine to experience any high. Cocaine dependents spend huge amounts of money on the substance and may become involved in theft, prostitution, or drug dealing to obtain enough money to purchase cocaine. The desperation to obtain cocaine seen in many frequent users also can lead them to engage in extremely dangerous behaviors. Many cocaine users contract HIV, the virus that causes AIDS, by sharing needles with infected users or by having unprotected sex in exchange for money or more cocaine.

Some other frequent medical complications of cocaine use are disturbances in heart rhythm and heart attacks; chest pain and respiratory failure; neurological effects, including strokes, seizure, and headaches; and gastrointestinal complications, including abdominal pain and nausea. The physical symptoms include chest pain, blurred vision, fever, muscle spasms, convulsions, and coma. Recall that, when comedian Chris Farley died, he had cocaine in his bloodstream, as well as morphine and heroin.

Although cocaine began as a wealthy person's substance because of its high cost, a sharp reduction in the cost of cocaine in the 1970s led to its widespread use at all socioeconomic levels. Fourteen percent of people in the United States have tried cocaine at least once in their lives (SAMHSA, 2005). Fortunately, the use of cocaine has fallen since the mid-1980s. In 1986, 13 percent of adolescents said they had used cocaine in the past year, but, in 2003, a survey of twelfth-graders in U.S. high schools found that 5 percent had used it in the past year (Johnston et al., 2004). This decline may have to do, in part, with antidrug campaigns in schools and in the media and with the highly publicized deaths of rock stars and athletes due to cocaine overdose. The decline has occurred primarily among casual users of cocaine. Chronic abusers and dependents have continued to use cocaine. There is also some evidence that the use of crack has not fallen off in recent years.

Amphetamines

The U.S. pharmaceutical industry annually manufactures 8 to 10 billion doses of the stimulants known as **amphetamines,** under names such as Dexedrine and Benzedrine (Miller, 1991). The drugs are most often swallowed as pills but can be injected intravenously, and methamphetamine can be snorted or smoked. These drugs were initially introduced as antihistamines, but people soon recognized their stimulant effects. These days, many people use them to combat depression or chronic fatigue from overwork or simply to boost their self-confidence and energy (Miller, 1991). They are also a component of diet drugs. Many of these drugs are used appropriately under the supervision of physicians, but a great many doses are diverted from prescription use to illegal use and abuse. On the street, amphetamines are known as "speed," "meth," and "chalk."

Amphetamines have their effects by causing the release of the neurotransmitters dopamine and norepinephrine and by blocking the reuptake of these neurotransmitters. The symptoms of intoxication with amphetamines are similar to the symptoms of cocaine intoxication: euphoria, self-confidence, alertness, agitation, and paranoia (Wyatt & Ziedonis, 1998).

Like cocaine, amphetamines can produce perceptual illusions that are frightening. The movement of other people and objects may seem distorted or exaggerated. Users may hear frightening voices making derogatory statements about them, see sores all over their bodies, or feel snakes crawling on their arms. They may have delusions that they are being stalked. They may act out violently against others as a result of their paranoid delusions. Some amphetamine users are aware that these experiences are not real, but some lose their reality testing and develop *amphetamine-induced psychotic disorders* (adapted from Spitzer et al., 1994, pp. 139–140):

People in fast-paced, highly demanding jobs, such as these commodities traders, sometimes use amphetamines to keep going.

CASE STUDY

An agitated 42-year-old businessman was admitted to the psychiatric service after a period of 2½ months in which he found himself becoming increasingly distrustful of others and suspicious of his business associates. He was taking their statements out of context, "twisting" their words, and making inappropriately hostile and accusatory comments; he had, in fact, lost several business deals that had been "virtually sealed." Finally, he fired a shotgun into the backyard late one night when he heard noises that convinced him that intruders were about to break into his house and kill him.

One and one-half years previously, he had been diagnosed as having narcolepsy because of daily irresistible sleep attacks and episodes of sudden loss of muscle tone, and he had been placed on an amphetaminelike stimulant, methylphenidate. His narcolepsy declined and he was able to work quite effectively as the sales manager of a small office-machine company and to participate in an active social life with his family and a small circle of friends.

In the 4 months before this admission, he had been using increasingly large doses of methylphenidate to maintain alertness late at night because of an increasing amount of work that could not be handled during the day. He reported that during this time he could often feel his heart race and he had trouble sitting still.

Legal problems for amphetamine abusers typically arise because of aggressive or inappropriate behavior while intoxicated or as a result of buying the drug illegally. Tolerance to amphetamines develops quickly, so frequent users can become physically dependent on the drug in a short period. They may switch from swallowing pills to injecting amphetamines intravenously. Some go on a speed run, in which they inject amphetamines frequently over several days, without eating or sleeping. When a speed run ends, they crash into a physical and emotional depression, which can be so severe that they may become suicidal. Acute withdrawal symptoms typically subside within a few days, but chronic users may experience mood instability, memory loss, confusion, paranoid thinking, and perceptual abnormalities for weeks, months, and perhaps even years. Most often, they battle the withdrawal symptoms with another speed run.

Abuse of amphetamines can cause a number of medical problems, particularly cardiovascular problems. These include rapid or irregular heartbeat, increased blood pressure, and irreversible, stroke-producing damage to the small blood vessels in the brain. Elevated body temperature and convulsions can occur during overdoses, leading to death. Sharing needles to inject amphetamines can lead to the contraction of HIV or hepatitis.

Nationwide surveys find that about 4 percent of the population has tried amphetamines in their lifetimes (SAMHSA, 2002b). Amphetamines are increasingly used in the workplace by people trying to keep up with the rapid pace of today's work world. Employers may even provide amphetamines to employees to keep them working and increase their productivity. When the employees finally go home, they may use depressants, such as alcohol, to come down off the speed. Although amphetamines may have the desired effects on employee morale and productivity in the short run, over time people become irritable and hostile and need more and more amphetamines to avoid withdrawal effects. Their health declines, as well as their personal relationships. Between 1995 and 2002, emergency room visits involving amphetamines increased 54 percent in the nation (SAMHSA, 2005).

Nicotine

All of the substances we have discussed thus far, except alcohol and the inhalants, are illegal for nonprescription use, and there are many laws regulating the use of alcohol. One of the most addictive substances, however, is fully legal for use by adults and readily available for use by adolescents.

Nicotine is an alkaloid found in tobacco. Cigarettes are the most popular nicotine delivery device. Cigarettes deliver nicotine to the brain within a few seconds after a person begins smoking. In the United States, 70 percent of people over age 12 have smoked cigarettes at sometime in their lives, and 30 percent currently smoke (SAMHSA, 2005). Smoking usually begins in the early teens. A survey of twelfth-graders done in 2001 found that 61 percent had smoked a cigarette at sometime in their lives, 30 percent had smoked in the past month, and 10 percent were smoking at least a half a pack a day (Monitoring the Future, 2002). Among people who continue to smoke through age 20, 95 percent become regular, daily smokers. In general, the use of tobacco has declined in the United States and other industrialized countries over the past few decades. In contrast, its use is increasing in developing countries (Giovini et al., 1994).

In the United States, the decrease in smoking rates over time has been greater for men than for women, so that today men are only slightly more likely than women to smoke (NIDA, 2002e; SAMHSA, 2005). In addition, female adolescents have been initiating smoking more frequently than male adolescents, and, once they are addicted to tobacco, women are less likely than men to quit. The ad campaigns by cigarette companies aimed specifically at women are also credited with increasing smoking among women.

Nicotine operates on both the central and peripheral nervous systems. It results in the release of several biochemicals that may have direct reinforcing effects on the brain, including dopamine, norepinephrine, serotonin, and the endogenous opioids. Although people often say they smoke to reduce stress, the physiological effects of nicotine actually resemble the fight-or-flight response—several systems in the body are aroused in preparation to fight or flee a stressor, including the cardiovascular and respiratory systems (see Chapter 6 for a discussion of the fight-or-flight response). The subjective sense that smoking reduces stress may actually reflect the

Cigarette companies often target women in their ad campaigns.

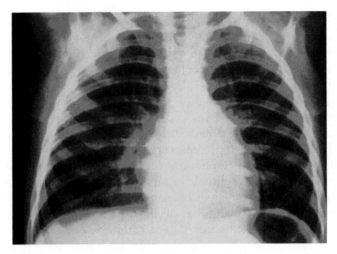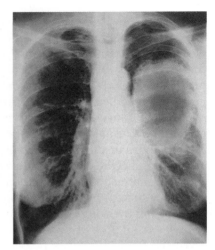

Smoking is the leading cause of lung cancer. The lungs on the left are healthy. The lungs on the right are from a smoker and show cancer in the red area.

reversal of tension and irritability that build in smokers between cigarettes because they are addicted to the nicotine (Parrott, 1998). In other words, nicotine addicts need nicotine to remain feeling normal because of nicotine's effects on the body and brain.

In 1964, on the basis of a review of 6,000 empirical studies, the surgeon general of the United States concluded that smoking, particularly cigarette smoking, causes lung cancer, bronchitis, and probably coronary heart disease. An estimated $80 billion of annual U.S. health care costs is attributable to smoking (NIDA, 2002e). Mortality rates for smokers are 70 percent greater than for nonsmokers. This means that a person between 30 and 35 years of age who smokes two packs of cigarettes a day will die eight to nine years earlier than will a nonsmoker. The chief causes of increased mortality rates among smokers are coronary heart disease, lung cancer, emphysema, and chronic bronchitis. Tobacco use accounts for 19 percent of all deaths in the United States (Goldstein, 1998). The babies of women who smoke while pregnant are smaller at birth. The longer a person smokes and the more he or she smokes per day, the greater the health risks.

Increasing attention is being paid to the effects of passive smoking—unintentionally inhaling the smoke from nearby smokers' cigarettes. This smoke contains more toxins than does the smoke that the smoker actively inhales, although the passive smoker does not inhale the smoke in concentrations as high as the smoker does. Children of parents who smoke have 30 to 80 percent more chronic respiratory problems than do nonsmokers and nearly 30 percent more hospitalizations for bronchitis and pneumonia (Winger et al., 1992).

Tobacco manufacturers have tried to claim that nicotine is not an addictive drug, but it causes most of the core symptoms of physiological and psychological dependence. The best evidence of nicotine dependence is the presence of tolerance to the substance and withdrawal symptoms after quitting. Chronic, heavy smokers become so tolerant to nicotine that they show no adverse physiological reactions to a dosage of nicotine that would have made them violently nauseated when they first began smoking. When they try to stop smoking or are prohibited from smoking for an extended period (such as at work or on an airplane), they show severe withdrawal symptoms: They are depressed, irritable, angry, anxious, frustrated, restless, and hungry; they have trouble concentrating; and they desperately crave another cigarette. These symptoms are immediately relieved by smoking another cigarette, another sign of physiological dependence.

Because nicotine is relatively cheap and available, people who are nicotine dependent do not tend to spend large amounts of time trying to obtain nicotine. They may, however, become panicked if they run out of cigarettes and replacements are not available. They may also spend large amounts of their day engaged in smoking or chewing tobacco and continue to use nicotine even though it is damaging their health, such as after they have been diagnosed with emphysema. They may skip social or recreational activities as a result of their habit. For example, people may turn down dinner invitations at the homes of friends who do not allow smoking. Or they may stop playing tennis because they have trouble breathing. With the increasing restrictions on smoking in the workplace, nicotine

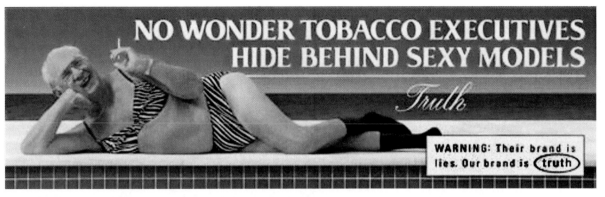

Programs to prevent and reduce smoking have become quite creative.

dependents may even begin to turn down or switch jobs to avoid these restrictions.

Over 70 percent of people who smoke say they wish they could quit (Goldstein, 1998). Quitting is difficult, however, in part because the withdrawal syndrome is so difficult to withstand. Only about 7 percent of smokers who attempt to quit smoking are still abstinent after one year, and most relapse within a few days of quitting (NIDA, 2002e). The craving for cigarettes can remain long after smokers have stopped smoking: 50 percent of people who quit smoking report they have desired cigarettes in the past 24 hours (Goldstein, 1994). Fortunately, the antidepressant bupropion (trade names Wellbutrin and Zyban) can significantly reduce the craving for nicotine and help smokers stop smoking permanently (Goldstein, 1998).

There are increasing calls for the U.S. government to declare nicotine a drug, much like marijuana and other substances that produce psychological changes and physiological dependence and are detrimental to health. Such a declaration would then lead to strict governmental regulation of the sale and use of tobacco. Antismoking advocates argue that nicotine dependence is a negative psychological and physiological condition just as bad as other substance dependencies. Moreover, between the effects of secondary smoke and the health care dollars spent treating diseases due to smoking, nicotine dependence exacts a much bigger toll on people who are not nicotine dependent than do most other substance dependencies.

Opponents of the antismoking movement argue that nicotine is not truly a psychoactive substance—nicotine does not cause great changes in mood, thought, or perceptions, as do cannabis, cocaine, heroin, and alcohol. They argue that the negative health effects of smoking are the smoker's business only and that people do many things that are not good for their health—they eat high-cholesterol foods, they sit in the sun without sunscreen—but these activities are not regulated by the government. This debate is likely to rage for some time to come, particularly given the issues of personal freedom and the massive amounts of money involved.

Caffeine

Caffeine is by far the most heavily used stimulant drug. Seventy-five percent of caffeine is ingested through coffee (Chou, 1992). The average American drinks about two cups of coffee per day, and a cup of brewed coffee has about 100 milligrams of caffeine. Other sources of caffeine include tea (about 40 milligrams of caffeine per 6 ounces), caffeinated soda (45 milligrams per 12 ounces), over-the-counter analgesics and cold remedies (25 to 50 milligrams per tablet), weight-loss drugs (75 to 200 milligrams per tablet), and chocolate and cocoa (5 milligrams per chocolate bar).

Caffeine stimulates the central nervous system, increasing levels of dopamine, norepinephrine, and serotonin. It causes metabolism, body temperature, and blood pressure to increase. Our appetite wanes and we feel more alert; however, in doses equivalent to just two to three cups of coffee, caffeine can cause a number of unpleasant symptoms, including restlessness, nervousness, and hand tremors. We may experience an upset stomach and feel our heart beating rapidly or irregularly. We may have trouble going to sleep later on and need to urinate frequently. These are the symptoms of *caffeine intoxication.* Extremely large doses of caffeine can cause extreme agitation, seizures, respiratory failure, and cardiac problems.

The DSM-IV-TR specifies that a diagnosis of caffeine intoxication should be given only if an individual experiences significant distress or impairment in functioning as a result of the symptoms. For example, someone drinking too much coffee

Garfield ®   by Jim Davis

GARFIELD © *Paws, Inc. Reprinted with permission of Universal Press Syndicate. All Rights Reserved.*

for several days in a row during exam week might be so agitated that she cannot sit through exams and so shaky she cannot drive a car.

Some heavy coffee drinkers joke that they are "caffeine addicts." Actually, they cannot be diagnosed with caffeine dependence disorder, according to the DSM-IV-TR, because to date there is little evidence that dependence on the drug causes significant social and occupational problems. Still, caffeine users can develop tolerance to caffeine and undergo withdrawal symptoms if they stop ingesting caffeine. They may find that they have to have several cups of coffee in the morning to feel "normal," and, if they do not get their coffee, they experience significant headaches, fatigue, and anxiety.

SUMMING UP

- Cocaine and amphetamines produce a rush of euphoria, followed by increases in self-esteem, alertness, and energy. With chronic use, however, they can lead to grandiosity, impulsiveness, hypersexuality, agitation, and paranoia.
- Withdrawal from cocaine and amphetamines causes the symptoms of depression, exhaustion, and an intense craving for more of the substance.
- Cocaine seems particularly prone to lead to dependence, because it has extraordinarily rapid, strong effects on the brain and its effects wear off quickly.
- The intense activation of the central nervous system caused by cocaine and amphetamines can lead to a number of cardiac, respiratory, and neurological problems, and these substances are responsible for a large percentage of substance-related medical emergencies and deaths.

- Nicotine is an alkaloid found in tobacco. It affects the release of several neurochemicals in the body. Nicotine subjectively reduces stress but causes physiological arousal similar to that seen in the fight-or-flight response.
- Smoking is associated with a higher rate of heart disease, lung cancer, emphysema, and chronic bronchitis, and it substantially increases mortality rates.
- The majority of people who smoke wish they could quit but have trouble doing so, in part because tolerance develops to nicotine and withdrawal symptoms are difficult to tolerate.
- Caffeine is the most commonly used stimulant drug. Caffeine intoxication can cause agitation, tremors, heart irregularities, and insomnia. People can develop a tolerance for and withdrawal from caffeine.

OPIOIDS

Morphine, heroin, codeine, and methadone are all known as **opioids.** They derive from the sap of the opium poppy, which has been used for thousands of years to relieve pain. Our bodies actually produce natural opioids, some of which are called *endorphins* and *enkaphalins*, to cope with pain. For example, a sports injury induces the body to produce endorphins to reduce the pain of the injury to avoid shock. Doctors may also prescribe synthetic opioids, such as hydrocodone (trade names Lorcet, Lortab, Vicodin) or oxycodone (Percodan, Percocet, Oxycontin) to help with pain.

Morphine was widely used as a pain reliever in the nineteenth century, until it was discovered that it is highly addictive. Heroin was developed from morphine in the late nineteenth century and used for a time for medicinal purposes. By 1917, however, it was clear that heroin and all opioids

TABLE 17.10 Intoxication with and Withdrawal from Opioids

The opioids include morphine, heroin, codeine, and methadone.

Drug	Intoxication Symptoms	Withdrawal Symptoms
Opioids	Behavioral changes (e.g., initial euphoria followed by apathy, dysphoria, psychomotor agitation or retardation, impaired judgment)	Dysphoric mood
	Constriction of pupils	Nausea or vomiting
	Drowsiness or coma	Muscle aches
	Slurred speech	Tearing or nasal mucus discharge
	Attention and memory problems	Dilation of pupils
	Hallucinations or illusions	Goose bumps
		Sweating
		Diarrhea
		Yawning
		Fever
		Insomnia

Source: Reprinted with permission from the *Diagnostic and Statistical Manual of Mental Disorders,* Fourth Edition, Text Revision. Copyright © 2000 American Psychiatric Association.

have dangerous addictive properties, and the U.S. Congress passed a law to make heroin illegal and to ban the other opioids except for specific medical needs. Heroin remained widely available on the street, however.

There was an explosion of heroin use during the Vietnam War, when young soldiers facing horrific circumstances found heroin cheap and easy to obtain in Vietnam. Fortunately, most of these soldiers stopped using heroin once they returned to the United States. But those who had experience with IV drugs or opioids before going to Vietnam tended to come back physically dependent on the drugs, which they continued to use when they returned to the United States. Current use of heroin expands and contracts with the drug's price and availability on the street. When the drug is cheap and highly available, "epidemics" of use occur.

When used illegally, opioids are often injected directly into the veins (*mainlining*), snorted, or smoked. The initial symptom of opioid intoxication is often euphoria (see Table 17.10). People describe a sensation in the abdomen like a sexual orgasm, referring to it as a *thrill, kick,* or *flash* (Winger et al., 1992). They may have a tingling sensation and a pervasive sense of warmth. Their pupils dilate, and they pass into a state of drowsiness, during which they are lethargic, their speech is slurred, and their mind may be clouded. They may experience periods of light sleep, with vivid dreams. Pain is reduced. A person in this state is referred to as being *on the nod.*

Severe intoxication with opioids can lead to unconsciousness, coma, and seizures. These substances can suppress the part of the brain stem controlling the respiratory and cardiovascular systems to the point of death. Basically, people stop breathing and their hearts stop pumping. The drugs are especially dangerous when used in combination with depressants, such as alcohol and sedatives. Withdrawal symptoms include dysphoria, anxiety, and agitation; an achy feeling in the back and legs; increased sensitivity to pain; and craving for more opioids. The person may be nauseated, vomit, and have profuse sweating and goose bumps, diarrhea, and fever. These symptoms usually come on within 8 to 16 hours of the last use of morphine or heroin and peak within 36 to 72 hours. In chronic or heavy users, the symptoms may continue strongly for 5 to 8 days and in a milder form for weeks to months.

Many people who develop opioid abuse or dependence begin using these drugs after having used alcohol, marijuana, and related drugs and perhaps some of the depressants and stimulants. The first use of heroin is typically in the late teen years, after people have experimented with several of these other drugs (Schuckit, 1995). About 1 percent of teenagers admit to having used heroin at sometime in the past year (Johnston et al., 2004). They may become psychologically dependent on the effects of the drugs first, then later become physiologically dependent. Once they are physiologically dependent, IV heroin users need to shoot up every four to six hours to avoid physical withdrawal. This is enormously expensive but makes it almost impossible to hold a regular job. As a result, many people dependent on opioids turn to stealing, prostitution, and other crimes to get money for the drug. Heavy users often have a police record by their early twenties.

Most street heroin is cut with other drugs or substances, so that users do not know the actual strength of the drug or its true contents. As a result, they are at high risk for overdose or death. One of the greatest dangers to opioid abusers and dependents is the risk of contracting HIV through contaminated needles or unprotected sex, in which many opioid abusers engage in exchange for more of the substance. In some areas of the United States, up to 60 percent of chronic heroin users are infected with HIV. Intravenous users also can contract hepatitis, tuberculosis, serious skin abscesses, and deep infections. Women who use heroin during pregnancy are at risk for miscarriage and premature delivery, and children born to addicted mothers are at increased risk for sudden infant death syndrome.

The abuse of, and dependence on, opioid pain relievers has increased significantly in recent years (SAMHSA, 2005). Emergency room visits involving pain relievers increased 153 percent from 1995 to 2002. The most frequently abused drug is *oxycodone*, and emergency room visits involving this drug increased 512 percent between 1995 and 2002. An estimated 11 million Americans age 12 and older have used oxycodone nonmedically at least once in their lifetime. In 2003, conservative commentator Rush Limbaugh admitted to being addicted to the prescription painkillers, creating a media sensation, given his previous arguments that drug abusers should be convicted and "sent up the river" (*Newsweek*, 2003).

SUMMING UP

- The opioids include heroin, morphine, codeine, and methadone, and the synthetic opioids include hydrocodone (Lorcet, Lortab, Vicodin) and oxycodone (Percodan, Percocet, Oxycontin).

- The opioids cause an initial rush, or euphoria, followed by a drowsy, dreamlike state. Severe intoxication can cause respiratory and cardiovascular failure.

- Withdrawal symptoms include dysphoria, anxiety, and agitation; an achy feeling in the back and legs; increased sensitivity to pain; and craving for more opioids.

- Opioid users who inject drugs can contract HIV and a number of other disorders by sharing needles.

HALLUCINOGENS AND PCP

Most of the substances we have discussed so far can produce perceptual illusions and distortions when taken in large doses. The hallucinogens and phenylcyclidine (PCP) produce perceptual changes even in small doses (see the Concept Overview in Table 17.11). A clear withdrawal syndrome from the hallucinogens and PCP has not been documented, so the DSM-IV-TR does not currently recognize withdrawal from these drugs as a diagnosis.

The **hallucinogens** are a mixed group of substances, including lysergic acid diethylamide (LSD) and peyote. Perhaps the best-known hallucinogen is LSD, which was first synthesized in 1938 by Swiss chemists. It was not until 1943 that the substance's psychoactive effects were discovered, when Dr. Albert Hoffman accidentally swallowed a minute amount of LSD and experienced visual hallucinations similar to those in schizophrenia. He later purposefully swallowed a small amount of LSD and reported the effects (Hoffman, 1968, pp. 185–186).

VOICES

As far as I remember, the following were the most outstanding symptoms: vertigo, visual disturbances; the faces of those around me appeared as grotesque, colored masks; marked motor unrest, alternating with paresis; an intermittent heavy feeling in the head, limbs, and the entire body, as if they were filled with metal; cramps in the legs, coldness, and loss of feeling in the hands; a metallic taste on the tongue; dry constricted sensation in the throat; feeling of choking; confusion alternating between clear recognition of my condition, in which state I sometimes observed, in the manner of an independent, neutral observer, that I shouted half insanely or babbled incoherent words. Occasionally, I felt as if I were out of my body. The doctor found a rather weak pulse but an otherwise normal circulation. Six hours after ingestion of the LSD my condition had already improved considerably. Only the visual disturbances were still pronounced. Everything seemed to sway and the proportions were distorted like the reflections in the surface of moving water. Moreover, all objects appeared in unpleasant, constantly changing colors, the predominant shades being sickly green and blue. When I

(continued)

closed my eyes, an unending series of colorful, very realistic and fantastic images surged in upon me. A remarkable feature was the manner in which all acoustic perceptions (e.g., the noise of a passing car) were transformed into optical effects, every sound causing a corresponding colored hallucination constantly changing in shape and color like pictures in a kaleidoscope.

As Hoffman describes, one of the symptoms of intoxication from LSD and other hallucinogens is synesthesia, the overflow from one sensory modality to another. People say they hear colors and see sounds. Time seems to pass very slowly. The boundaries between oneself and the environment seem gone. Moods may shift from depression to elation to fear. Some people become anxious, even panicked. Others feel a sense of detachment and a great sensitivity for art, music, and feelings. These experiences led to these drugs' being labeled psychedelic, from the Greek words for "soul" and "to make manifest." LSD was used in the 1960s as part of the consciousness-expanding movement. More recently, the hallucinogen known as ecstasy is used by people who believe that it enhances insight, relationships, and mood.

The hallucinogens are dangerous drugs, however. Although LSD was legal for use in the early 1960s, by 1967, reports of "bad acid trips," or "bummers," had become common, particularly in the Haight-Ashbury district of San Francisco, where many LSD enthusiasts from around the United States congregated (Smith & Seymour, 1994). The symptoms included severe anxiety, paranoia, and loss of control. Some people on bad trips would walk off roofs or jump out windows, believing they could fly, or walk into the sea, believing they were "one with the universe." For some people, the anxiety and hallucinations caused by hallucinogens are so severe that they become psychotic and require hospitalization and long-term treatment. Some people experience flashbacks to their psychedelic experiences long after the drug has worn off. These flashbacks can be extremely distressing. The most recent pattern of use for hallucinogens has been as part of the club scene and "raves" (Morrison, 1998).

Phenylcyclidine (PCP), also known as *angel dust, PeaCePill, Hog,* and *Tranq,* is manufactured as a powder to be snorted or smoked. Although PCP is not classified as a hallucinogen, it has many of the same effects. At lower doses, it produces a sense of intoxication, euphoria or affective dulling, talkativeness, lack of concern, slowed reaction time, vertigo, eye twitching, mild hypertension, abnormal invol-

TABLE 17.11	**Concept Overview**

Intoxication with Hallucinogens and PCP

The hallucinogens and PCP cause a variety of perceptual and behavioral changes.

Drug	Intoxication Symptoms
Hallucinogens	Behavioral changes (e.g., marked anxiety or depression, the feeling that others are talking about you, fear of losing your mind, paranoia, impaired judgment)
	Perceptual changes while awake (e.g., intensification of senses, depersonalization, illusions, hallucinations)
	Dilation of pupils
	Rapid heartbeat
	Sweating
	Palpitations
	Blurring of vision
	Tremors
	Incoordination
PCP	Behavioral changes (e.g., belligerence, assaultiveness, impulsiveness, unpredictability, psychomotor agitation, impaired judgment)
	Involuntary rapid eyeball movement
	Hypertension
	Numbness
	Loss of muscle coordination
	Problems speaking due to poor muscle control
	Muscle rigidity
	Seizures or coma
	Exceptionally acute hearing
	Perceptual disturbances

Source: Reprinted with permission from the *Diagnostic and Statistical Manual of Mental Disorders,* Fourth Edition, Text Revision. Copyright © 2000 American Psychiatric Association.

untary movements, and weakness. At intermediate doses, it leads to disorganized thinking, distortions of body image (such as feeling that one's arms do not belong to the rest of one's body), depersonalization, and feelings of unreality. A user may become hostile, belligerent, and even violent (Morrison, 1998). At higher doses, it produces amnesia and coma, analgesia sufficient to allow surgery, seizures, severe respiratory problems, hypothermia, and hyperthermia. The effects of PCP begin immediately after injecting, snorting, or smoking it, reaching a peak within minutes. The symptoms of severe intoxication can persist for several days. As a result, people with PCP intoxication are often misdiagnosed as having psychotic disorders not related to substance use.

As with the substances we have discussed so far, hallucinogen or PCP abuse is diagnosed when individuals repeatedly fail to fulfill major role obligations at school, work, or home due to intoxication with these drugs. They may use the drugs in dangerous situations, such as while driving a car, and may have legal troubles due to their possession of the drugs. Particularly because these drugs can cause paranoia or aggressive behavior, people who use them frequently may find their work and social relationships being affected. About 11 percent of the U.S. population reports ever having tried a hallucinogen or PCP, but only 0.4 percent report using it in the past month (SAMHSA, 2002a). Use is higher among teenagers, however, with 2 to 3 percent reporting using LSD, ecstasy, or a hallucinogen in the past month (Monitoring the Future, 2002).

SUMMING UP

- The hallucinogens create perceptual illusions and distortions—sometimes fantastic, sometimes frightening. Some people feel more sensitive to art, music, and other people. The hallucinogens also create mood swings and paranoia. Some people experience frightening flashbacks to experiences under the hallucinogens.

- PCP causes euphoria or affective dulling, abnormal involuntary movements, and weakness at low doses. At intermediate doses, it leads to disorganized thinking, depersonalization, feelings of unreality, and aggression. At higher doses, it produces amnesia and coma, analgesia sufficient to allow surgery, seizures, severe respiratory problems, hypothermia, and hyperthermia.

CANNABIS

The leaves of the **cannabis** (or hemp) plant can be cut, dried, and rolled into cigarettes or inserted into food and beverages. In North America, the product is known as *marijuana, weed, pot, grass, reefer,* and *Mary Jane.* It is called *ganja* in Jamaica, *kif* in North Africa, *dagga* in South Africa, *bhang* in In-

dia and the Middle East, and *macohna* in South America (Winger et al., 1992). It is the most widely used illicit substance in the world. Hashish is a dried resin extract from the cannabis plant, sold in cubes in America.

Cannabis is the most commonly used illegal drug in the United States, with about one-third of the population reporting they have used this drug at sometime in their lives, and 5 percent use it monthly (SAMHSA, 2002a). Teenagers are especially heavy users of marijuana, with about 50 percent of twelfth-graders saying they have used it at sometime in their lives and about 22 percent reporting using it in the past month (Johnston et al., 2004). The use of cannabis has increased in the past decade or so, and the potency of cannabis has become greater as well. About 7 percent of the population would qualify for a diagnosis of cannabis abuse, and 2 to 3 percent of the population would qualify for a diagnosis of cannabis dependence (Kendler & Prescott, 1998a).

The symptoms of cannabis intoxication may develop within minutes if the cannabis is smoked but may take a few hours to develop if taken orally (see the Concept Overview in Table 17.12). The acute symptoms last 3 to 4 hours, but some symptoms may linger or recur for 12 to 24 hours. Intoxication with cannabis usually begins with a "high" feeling of well-being, relaxation, and tranquillity. Users may feel dizzy, sleepy, or "dreamy." They may become more aware of their environments, and everything may seem funny. They may be-

---

TABLE 17.12 Concept Overview

Intoxication with Cannabis

Cannabis is the most commonly used illegal drug in the United States.

Drug	Intoxication Symptoms
Cannabis	Behavioral changes (e.g., impaired motor coordination, euphoria, anxiety, sensation of slowed time, impaired judgment)
	Red eyes
	Increased appetite
	Dry mouth
	Rapid heartbeat

Source: Reprinted with permission from the *Diagnostic and Statistical Manual of Mental Disorders,* Fourth Edition, Text Revision. Copyright © 2000 American Psychiatric Association.

come grandiose or lethargic. People who are very anxious, depressed, or angry may become more so under the influence of cannabis.

The cognitive symptoms of cannabis intoxication are negative. People may believe they are thinking profound thoughts, but their short-term memories are impaired to the point that they cannot remember thoughts long enough to express them in sentences (de Wit, Kirk, & Justice, 1998). Thus, they perform poorly on a wide range of tests and may not be able to hold a conversation. Motor performance is also impaired. People's reaction times are slower, and their concentration and judgment are deficient; as a result, they are at risk for accidents. The cognitive impairments caused by cannabis can last for up to a week after a person stops heavy use (Pope, Gruber, et al., 2001). These effects appear to be even greater for women than for men (Pope et al., 1997).

Cannabis has hallucinogenic effects at moderate to large doses. Users experience perceptual distortions, feelings of depersonalization, and paranoid thinking. The changes in perceptions may be experienced as pleasant by some but as very frightening by others. Some users may have severe anxiety episodes resembling panic attacks (Phariss, Millman, & Beeder, 1998).

The physiological symptoms of cannabis intoxication include increases in heart rate, an irregular heartbeat, increases in appetite, and dry mouth. Cannabis smoke is irritating and, thus, increases the risk for chronic cough, sinusitis, bronchitis, and emphysema. It contains even larger amounts of known carcinogens than does tobacco, so it creates a high risk for cancer. The chronic use of cannabis lowers sperm count in men and may cause irregular ovulation in women.

In part because of the increased potency of cannabis, many people who formerly might have been casual users of cannabis, including high school students, have developed problems with abuse and dependence. They may smoke marijuana often enough that their school performance suffers, their lives revolve around smoking, and they have frequent accidents as a result of intoxication. Physical tolerance to cannabis can develop, so users need greater amounts to avoid withdrawal symptoms. The symptoms of withdrawal include a loss of appetite, hot flashes, a runny nose, sweating, diarrhea, and hiccups (Kouri & Pope, 2000).

In recent years, several groups have advocated the legalization of marijuana cigarettes for medical uses (Grinspoon & Bakalar, 1995). THC, the active compound in cannabis, can help relieve nausea in cancer patients undergoing chemotherapy and increase appetite in AIDS patients. It also helps in the treatment of asthma and glaucoma. THC can be given in pill form, but some people argue that the level of THC that enters the body is more controllable when it is taken in a marijuana cigarette. People who ingest THC in pill form do not risk the respiratory damage caused by the smoke from marijuana cigarettes, however.

SUMMING UP

- Cannabis creates a high feeling, cognitive and motor impairments, and in some people hallucinogenic effects.

- Cannabis use is high. Significant numbers of people, especially teenagers, have impaired performance at school, on the job, and in relationships as a result of chronic use. Marijuana use can also lead to a number of physical problems, especially respiratory problems.

CLUB DRUGS

One of the most alarming developments in the world of illicit drug use in recent years is the increase in the use of drugs as part of the club scene among young adults, including at raves. Raves began in Europe in the 1980s. These events, which are often sponsored by club owners or businesspeople, are held in warehouses, basements, tenements, and other large spaces. Participants often ingest drugs with stimulant and hallucinogenic properties, then spend the night listening and dancing to "techno music." After the drug effects disappear, people are usually exhausted and may spend several hours sleeping. One of the greatest health concerns during

There has been an increase in recent years in the use of drugs as part of the club scene.

raves is dehydration, so some rave organizers encourage participants to drink fluids and take breaks from the dancing. Agitation and paranoia can set into the crowd, creating the possibility of a chaotic scene, which can result in injury.

Emergency room visits involving club drugs doubled from 1994 to 1999, although they have decreased somewhat in more recent years (SAMHSA, 2005). Some common club drugs, in addition to LSD, are *ecstasy* (3-4 methylenedioxymethamphetamine, or MDMA), *GHB* (gamma-hydroxybutyrate), *ketamine*, and *rohypnol* (flunitrazepam).

Ecstasy has the stimulant effects of an amphetamine along with occasional hallucinogenic properties. Users experience heightened energy and restlessness, and they claim that their social inhibitions decrease and their affection for others increases. These disinihibiting and "social" effects of ecstasy led a small number of unscrupulous therapists to use the drug as part of therapy for a short time.

Even the short-term use of ecstasy can have long-term negative effects on cognition and health, however. Studies of monkeys given ecstasy for just four days found that they had brain damage lasting six to seven years (SAMHSA, 2002b). Humans who use ecstasy score lower on tests related to attention, memory, learning, and general intelligence than people who do not use the drug. The euphoric effects of ecstasy, and some of the brain damage, may be due to alterations in the functioning of serotonin in the brain—serotonin levels in ecstasy users are half that of people who do not use ecstasy. One of the more bizarre effects of ecstasy is teeth-grinding; some users suck a baby pacifier at raves to relieve the grinding. One study showed that 60 percent of ecstasy users had worn their teeth through the enamel (Peroutka, Newman, & Harris, 1988). Long-term users of ecstasy are at risk for several cardiac problems and liver failure, and they show increased rates of anxiety, depression, psychotic symptoms, and paranoia (Gold, Tabrah, & Frost-Pineda, 2001).

GHB is an anabolic steroid (a synthetic derivative of the hormone testosterone) and a central nervous system depressant. At low doses, it can relieve anxiety and promote relaxation. At higher doses, it can result in sleep, coma, or death. In the 1980s, GHB was widely used by bodybuilders and athletes to lose fat and build muscle, and it was widely available over the counter in health food stores. In 1990, GHB was banned except under the supervision of a physician because of reports of severe side effects, including high blood pressure, wide mood swings, liver tumors, and violent behavior. Other side effects include sweating,

headache, decreased heart rate, nausea, vomiting, impaired breathing, loss of reflexes, and tremors. GHB is considered one of the date rape drugs, because it has been associated with several sexual assaults. It goes by the street names Grievous Bodily Harm, G., Liquid Ecstasy, and Georgia Home Boy.

Ketamine (which goes by the street names Vitamin K, Kit Kat, Keller, Super Acid, and Super C) is a rapid-acting anesthetic that produces hallucinogenic effects in users ranging from rapture to paranoia to boredom. Ketamine can elicit an out-of-body or near-death experience. It can also render the user comatose. It has effects similar to those of PCP, including numbness, loss of coordination, a sense of invulnerability, muscle rigidity, aggressive or violent behavior, slurred or blocked speech, an exaggerated sense of strength, and a blank stare. Because ketamine is an anesthetic, users feel no pain, which can lead them to injure themselves.

A ketamine "high" usually lasts an hour, but it can last 4 to 6 hours, and it takes 24 to 48 hours for users to feel completely normal again. Large doses can produce vomiting and convulsions and may lead to oxygen starvation of the brain and muscles. One gram can cause death. Ketamine is also a date rape drug, because it is used by sexual assault perpetrators to anesthetize victims.

A final club drug, and another date rape drug, is rohypnol, which goes by the slang names Roofies, Rophiees, Roche, and the Forget-Me-Not Pill. It is a member of the benzodiazepine family and has sedative and hypnotic effects. Users may experience a high, as well as muscle relaxation, drowsiness, impaired judgment, blackouts, hallucinations, dizziness, and confusion. Rohypnol is manufactured in tablet form, which can easily be crushed and slipped into someone's drink. It is odorless, colorless, and tasteless, so victims often don't notice that their drink has been altered. Some people take it willingly. The side effects of the drug include headaches, muscle pain, and seizures. When used in combination with alcohol or other depressants, rohypnol can be fatal.

SUMMING UP

- Some common club drugs, in addition to LSD, are ecstasy (3-4 methylenedioxymethamphetamine, or MDMA), GHB (gamma-hydroxybutyrate), ketamine, and rohypnol (flunitrazepam).

- Ecstasy has the stimulant effects of an amphetamine along with occasional hallucinogenic properties. Even the short-term use of ecstasy can have long-term negative effects on cognition and health. Long-term users of ecstasy are at risk for several cardiac problems and liver failure, and they show increased rates of anxiety, depression, psychotic symptoms, and paranoia.

- GHB is an anabolic steroid and a central nervous system depressant. At low doses, it can relieve anxiety and promote relaxation. At higher doses, it can result in sleep, coma, or death.

- Ketamine is an anesthetic that produces hallucinogenic effects. Large doses can produce vomiting and convulsions, even death.

- Rohypnol has sedative and hypnotic effects. It is one of the date rape drugs, along with GHB and ketamine. When used in combination with alcohol or other depressants, it can be fatal.

THEORIES OF SUBSTANCE USE, ABUSE, AND DEPENDENCE

All the substances we have discussed in this chapter affect several biochemicals in the brain, and these chemicals can have direct reinforcing effects on the brain. The brain appears to have its own "pleasure pathway" which affects our experience of reward. This pathway begins in the midbrain ventral tegmental area, then goes forward through the nucleus accumbens and on to the frontal cortex (Korenman & Barchas, 1993). This pathway is rich in neurons sensitive to the neurotransmitter dopamine.

Some drugs, such as amphetamines and cocaine, act directly to increase the availability of dopamine in this pathway, leading to the strong sense of reward or "high" that these drugs produce. Other drugs increase the availability of dopamine in more indirect ways. For example, the neurons in the ventral tegmental area are kept from continuous firing by GABA neurons, so the firing of GABA neurons reduces the "high" caused by activity in the dopamine neurons. The opiate drugs inhibit GABA, which in turn stops the GABA neurons from inhibiting dopamine, which makes dopamine available in the reward center.

The chronic use of psychoactive substances may produce permanent changes in the reward centers, causing a craving for these substances even after withdrawal symptoms pass. The repeated use of substances such as cocaine, heroin, and amphetamines causes dopamine neurons to become hyperactive, or sensitized. This sensitization can be permanent, so that these neurons will be activated more highly by subsequent exposure to the psychoactive substance or by stimuli that are associated with the substance (such as the pipe that a cocaine user formerly used to smoke crack). Subjectively, this sensitization creates a chronic, strong craving for the substance, which is made worse every time a former user comes into contact with stimuli that remind him or her of the substance. This craving can create a powerful physiological motivation for relapsing back into substance abuse and dependence (Robinson & Berridge, 1993). Susan, who was dependent on cocaine and alcohol but has been abstinent for three months, described this phenomenon (Engel, 1989, p. 40):

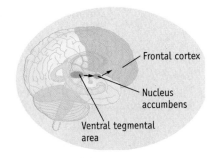

The brain's "pleasure pathway" begins in the ventral tegmental area, then goes through the nucleus accumbens and on to the frontal cortex. It is rich in neurons sensitive to dopamine.

VOICES

Right now, I mean, I wanna go out and—I mean I want a line so bad, you know, I can taste it. Right now. I know I'm not supposed to. I just want it, though. Coke.

The substances we have discussed in this chapter have powerful effects on the brain, in both the short term and the long term, which can make these substances hard for people to resist once they have used them. Substances such as cocaine that have especially rapid and powerful effects on the brain but that also wear off very quickly create great risk for dependency. Even people trying a substance casually can find the rapid, intense, but short-lived high so compelling that they crave more and soon increase their use.

Psychoactive drugs affect a number of other biochemical and brain systems. For example, alcohol has its sedative and anti-anxiety effects largely by enhancing the activity of the neurotransmitter GABA in the septal/hippocampal system. Alcohol also affects serotonin systems, which in turn are associated with changes in mood.

Most people never even try most of the substances discussed in this chapter, and, of those who do try them, most do not abuse them or become dependent on them. Why not? We turn now to other theories of substance abuse and dependence that have tried to explain the differences between people in terms of their vulnerability to substance-related

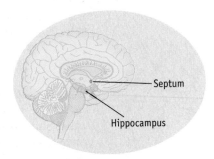

Alcohol has it sedative and anti-anxiety effects largely by enhancing the activity of the neurotransmitter GABA in the septal/hippocampal system. It also affects serotonin systems, which influence mood.

disorders. Most theories of substance-related disorders have focused on alcohol abuse and dependence, probably because alcohol-related disorders are more widespread than the other disorders. For this reason, much of our discussion of theories concerns the development of alcohol abuse and dependence. Several of these theories have been applied to explain the development of abuse and dependence on disorders other than alcohol, however, and we note these as we go along.

For years, alcoholism and other drug addictions were considered the result of a moral deficiency. Alcoholics and other drug addicts were simply perceived as weak, bad people who would not exert control over their impulses. Since the 1960s, that view has largely been replaced by the **disease model** of alcoholism and other drug addictions, which views these disorders as incurable physical diseases, like epilepsy or diabetes (Jellinek, 1960). This model has been supported somewhat by research on the genetics and biology of alcoholism and other drug addiction, but there clearly are social and psychological forces that make some people more prone to these disorders than are others. In the following sections, we discuss the biological, social, and psychological factors that increase people's vulnerability to substance abuse and dependence.

Biological Theories

As is the case with most disorders we have discussed in this book, many of the biological theories of substance use disorders focus on the role of genetics and neurotransmitters. In addition, research suggests that people who become substance dependent or abusive may react differently physiologically to substances than do those who do not become dependent or abusive. Third, some theorists have argued that alcoholism, and perhaps other forms of substance dependence, really represents an underlying biological depression.

Genetic Factors

Family history, adoption, and twin studies all suggest that genetics may play a substantial role in determining who is at risk for substance use disorders (Bierut et al., 1998; Crabbe, 2002; Kendler, Davis, & Kessler, 1997; McGue, 1999; Merikangas, Dierker, & Szatmari, 1998). For example, family studies show that the relatives of people with substance-related disorders are eight times more likely to also have a substance disorder than are the relatives of people with no substance-related disorder (Merikangas et al., 1998). There seems to be a common underlying genetic vulnerability to substance abuse and dependence in general (Tsuang et al., 1998), perhaps accounting for the fact that individuals who use one substance are likely to use multiple substances.

Similarly, twin studies have clearly shown that a substantial portion of the family transmission of substance abuse and dependence is due to genetics (Crabbe, 2002; Kendler & Prescott, 1998b; Lerman et al., 1999; Pomerleau & Kardia, 1999; Prescott & Kendler, 1999). For example, in a study of more than 3,000 male twins, Prescott and Kendler (1999) found concordance rates for alcohol dependence among monozygotic twins of .48, compared with .32 among dizygotic twins. The evidence for heritability was strong only for early-onset alcoholism (first symptoms before age 20), but not for late-onset alcoholism.

Until recently, studies often used all-male samples, or, if they had a female subsample, it tended to be small, and gender differences were not analyzed. In the past few years, however, data from mixed-sex samples have been reanalyzed and large-scale genetic studies have been reported. Some studies suggest that genetics play a stronger role in alcohol use disorders among men than women (Bierut et al., 1998; Jang, Livesley, & Vernon, 1997). For example, some twin studies find no evidence for a genetic contribution to alcohol dependence in women, or they find that the genetic contribution for women is less than that for men (Caldwell & Gottesman, 1991; McGue, 1999; McGue, Pickens, & Svikis, 1992). In contrast, one large twin study found similar heritability for alcohol dependence in women and men (Heath, Bucholz, Madden et al., 1997), whereas another study found modestly higher heritability for women than for men (Prescott & Kendler, 1999). Environmental circumstances, such as sexual abuse, are stronger predictors of alcoholism in women than in men, however (McGue, 1999). Researchers are currently debating whether the contributors to alcoholism and other drug dependencies are different, at least in magnitude, for women and men.

The first reports suggesting that genes play a role in smoking were published over 40 years ago by Fisher (1958), who found that the concordance rate for smoking is significantly higher in monozygotic twins than in dizygotic twins. Several subsequent publications confirmed this finding (Carmelli et al., 1992; Hannah, Hopper, & Mathews, 1983; Heath & Martin, 1993; Hughes, 1986). Hughes (1986) summarized the data from 18 twin studies of smoking and concluded that 53 percent of the variation in smoking behavior was attributable to genetic causes.

Genes affect vulnerability to substance use disorders in part by influencing the functioning of neurotransmitter systems involved in the metabolism and biosynthesis of substances. Research on alcoholism has shown that a variation in two genes (called ADH2 and ADH3) that control the enzymes that break down alcohol into its metabolite, acetaldehyde, is related to low alcohol risk in Asian populations (Reich et al., 1998). In addition, a variation in one of the genes for aldehyde dehydrogenase, the enzyme that breaks down acetaldehyde, the toxic metabolite of alcohol, into acetic acid, is associated with a very low risk for alcoholism in Asians. Persons with this genetic variant experience a buildup of acetaldehyde when they drink alcohol, leading to an aversive flushing response, which discourages alcohol use.

Other genes involved in drug abuse are related to central nervous system functioning, including genes associated with the GABA/benzodiazepine receptor complex, the NMDA receptor (a glutamate receptor that is sensitive to alcohol), calcium channels, cyclic AMP, and G proteins (see Sher, Grekin, & Williams, 2005). There also has been interest in the genes associated with the transport and metabolism of serotonin, because some substances, particularly alcohol, affect the functioning of serotonin systems in animals.

Much research has focused on the genes controlling the dopamine system, given its importance in the reinforcing properties of substances. Genetic variation in the dopamine receptor gene (labeled DRD2) and the dopamine transporter gene (labeled SLC6A3) may influence dopamine concentrations at the synapses and responses to dopamine, thereby influencing how reinforcing a person finds substances such as nicotine (Pomerleau & Kardia, 1999). People who have certain abnormalities in these genes that result in more dopamine at the synapses appear less likely to become smokers than people without these abnormalities (Lerman et al., 1999). In addition, smokers with the SLC6A3 abnormality are more likely to quit smoking than those without it (Sabol et al., 1999).

Alcohol Reactivity

When given moderate doses of alcohol, the sons of alcoholics, who are presumably at increased risk for alcoholism, experience less impairment, subjectively, in their cognitive and motor performance and on some physiological indicators than do the sons of nonalcoholics (Schuckit & Smith, 1996, 1997). At high doses of alcohol, however, the sons of alcoholics are just as intoxicated, by both subjective and objective measures, as are the sons of nonalcoholics. This lower reactivity to moderate doses of alcohol among the sons of alcoholics may lead them to drink substantially more before they begin to feel drunk. As a result, they may not learn to recognize subtle, early signs of intoxication and

may not learn to quit drinking before they become highly intoxicated. They may also develop a high physiological tolerance for alcohol, which leads them to ingest more and more alcohol to achieve any level of subjective intoxication.

Long-term studies of men with low reactivity to moderate doses of alcohol show that they are significantly more likely to become alcoholics over time than are men with greater reactivity to moderate doses of alcohol (Schuckit, 1998; Schuckit & Smith, 1997). The low-reactivity men are especially likely to develop alcohol problems if they encounter significant stress or if they have a tendency toward poor behavioral control. There is some evidence that low reactivity is genetically transmitted (Schuckit, Edenberg, et al., 2001).

Women may be less prone than men to alcoholism because they are much *more* sensitive than men to the intoxicating effects of alcohol (Lex, 1995). At a given dose of alcohol, about 30 percent more of the alcohol enters a woman's bloodstream than enters a man's, because women have less of an enzyme that neutralizes and breaks down alcohol. For these reasons, a woman experiences the subjective and overt symptoms of alcohol intoxication at lower doses than a man and may experience more severe withdrawal symptoms if she drinks too much. These factors may lead many women to drink less than men do. Women who do abuse alcohol, however, may be at more risk for the negative health effects of alcohol than are men, because their blood concentrations of alcohol are higher than those of men who abuse (see Nolen-Hoeksema, 2004).

Alcoholism as a Form of Depression

As many as 70 percent of people with alcohol dependency have depressive symptoms severe enough to interfere with daily living (Schuckit, 1991). In addition, early family history studies suggested that alcohol-related disorders and unipolar depression run together in families, with alcoholism more prevalent in male relatives and unipolar depression more prevalent in female relatives (Winokur & Clayton, 1967). These trends led some researchers to argue that alcoholism and depression are genetically related, or perhaps one disorder, and that many male alcoholics are actually depressed and denying their depression or self-medicating with alcohol (see Williams & Spitzer, 1983).

Although many people with alcohol-related problems appear to use alcohol to cope with daily stresses and emotional distress, it is probably not wise to consider alcoholism simply another form of depression for several reasons. First, although the children of alcoholics do have higher rates of depression than do the children of nonalcoholics, these depressions might result more from the stresses of having alcoholic parents than from genetics (Schuckit, 1995). Second, several family history studies have failed to find higher rates of alcoholism among the offspring of depressed people than among the offspring of nondepressed people, as one would suspect if depression and alcoholism were genetically related (Merikangas, Weissman, & Pauls, 1985).

Third, because alcohol is a central nervous system depressant, it can cause the classic symptoms of depression. In addition, the social consequences of alcohol abuse and dependency (e.g., loss of relationships, loss of job) can cause depression. Thus, when depression and alcohol dependency co-occur in individuals, the depression is just as likely to be a consequence as a cause of the alcohol dependency. Indeed, large epidemiological studies find that the odds of depression preceding alcoholism are equal to the odds that alcoholism will precede depression (Swendsen et al., 1998).

Fourth, studies show that adolescents who are depressed are not more likely to become alcoholics than are adolescents who are not depressed, as we might expect if alcoholism is often a response to depression (Schuckit, 1995). Fifth, simply prescribing antidepressant medications to a person with alcohol abuse or dependency is not enough to help him or her overcome the alcohol-related problems in the long run (Volpicelli, 2001). The risk of relapse is high unless he or she also undergoes treatment directly targeted at the drinking.

Sixth, depression among alcoholics usually disappears once they become abstinent, even without any antidepressant treatment, again suggesting that the depression is secondary to the alcoholism, rather than its cause (Brown et al., 1995). Finally, alcoholism and other drug addictions co-occur with a wide range of other psychological disorders in addition to depression—including bipolar disorder, the personality disorders, the anxiety disorders, and schizophrenia—as well as with histories of physical or sexual abuse (Schuckit et al., 1998).

Psychological Theories

Behavioral theories suggest that children and adolescents may learn substance use behaviors from the modeling of their parents and important others in their culture. Studies of the children of alcoholics find that, even as preschoolers, they are more likely than other children to be able to identify alcoholic drinks and to view alcohol use as a normal part of daily life (Zucker et al., 1995). The children of parents who abuse alcohol by frequently getting drunk or driving while intoxicated learn that these are acceptable behaviors and, thus, are more likely to engage in them as well (Chassin et al., 1999).

Because alcohol-related problems are more common among males than females, most of the adults modeling the inappropriate use of alcohol are male. In turn, because children are more likely to learn from adults who are similar to themselves, male children and male adolescents may be more likely to learn these behaviors from the adults in their world than are female children and female adolescents. Thus, maladaptive patterns of alcohol use may be passed down through the males in a family through modeling.

The cognitive theories of alcohol abuse have focused on people's expectations of the effects of alcohol and their beliefs about the appropriateness of using alcohol to cope with stress (Marlatt et al., 1988). People who expect alcohol to reduce their distress and who do not have other, more adaptive means of coping available to them (such as problem solving or supportive friends or family) are more likely than others to drink alcohol when they are upset and to have social problems related to drinking. For example, one study found that both men and women who believed that alcohol helped them relax and handle stress better and who tended to cope with stressful situations with avoidance rather than problem solving drank more often and had more drinking-related problems (Cooper et al., 1992). In long-term studies of the sons of alcoholics, men who used alcohol to cope and who expected alcohol to relax them were more likely to develop alcohol abuse or dependence, whether or not they had low reactivity to low doses of alcohol

Children may learn substance-related behaviors from their parents.

(Schuckit, 1998). In the section "Treatments for Substance-Related Disorders," we review therapies that try to change people's beliefs about alcohol as a coping tool and to give people more appropriate strategies for coping with their problems.

One personality characteristic that is consistently related to an increased risk for substance abuse and dependence is known as *behavioral undercontrol*, the tendency to be impulsive, sensation-seeking, and prone to antisocial behavior. People with high levels of behavioral undercontrol take psychoactive drugs at an earlier age, ingest more psychoactive drugs, and are more likely to be diagnosed with substance abuse or dependence (e.g., Mason & Windle, 2002; McGue et al., 2001; White, Xie, & Thompson, 2001). In turn, behavioral undercontrol runs strongly in families, and twin studies suggest that this may be due in part to genes (Rutter et al., 1999). Thus, it may be that genetics influence the presence of behavioral undercontrol, which in turn influences the risk of individuals to substance use disorders.

Sociocultural Approaches

VOICES

It was great being stoned. It was, you know, it was great. I just could evade all the bull—and just be stoned, do anything stoned. I just wanted to block everything out, is basically what it was. (Engel, 1989, p. 27)

The reinforcing effects of substances—the highs that stimulants produce, the calming and "zoning out" effects of the depressants and opioids—may be more attractive to people under great psychological stress, particularly those under chronic stress. Thus, there are higher rates of substance abuse and dependence among people facing chronic, severe stress—people living in poverty and with few hopes, women in abusive relationships, and adolescents whose parents fight frequently and violently (Stewart, 1996; Zucker, Chermack, & Curran, 1999). For these people, the effects of substances may be especially reinforcing. Plus, they may see few costs to becoming dependent on substances, because they feel they have little to lose.

Chronic stress combined with an environment that supports and even promotes the use of substances as an escape is a recipe for widespread substance abuse and dependence. Such was the situation for soldiers fighting in the Vietnam War.

The conditions under which they fought and lived created chronic stress. Illegal drugs, especially heroin and marijuana, were readily available, and the culture of the 1960s supported drug experimentation.

Only 1 percent of the soldiers who served in Vietnam had been dependent on heroin or other hard substances before the war. During the war, half the soldiers used these substances at least occasionally, and 20 percent were dependent on them. Fortunately, once these soldiers left that environment and returned home, their substance use dropped to the same level it was before they went to Vietnam (Robins, Helzer, & Davis, 1975).

Some people cannot leave their stress behind, because the stress is present where they live. Indeed, many people dependent on substances were introduced to these substances by their family members and grew up in horrible conditions, from which everyone around them was using substances to escape (Zucker et al., 1995), as is the case with LaTisha:

CASE STUDY

LaTisha, 35 years old when interviewed, was born and raised in Miami. Her mother was a barmaid and she never knew her father. She grew up with two brothers and four sisters, all of whom have different fathers. Her mother used pills during LaTisha's childhood, particularly Valium.

LaTisha took her first alcoholic drink when she was 12, introduced to her by her mother. However, she didn't drink regularly until she was 17, although she started sniffing glue at age 13. LaTisha's mother often brought men home from the bar to have sex with them for money. At 14, LaTisha's mother "turned her out" (introduced her to prostitution) by setting her up with "dates" from the bar. LaTisha was not aware until years later that the men had been paying her mother. LaTisha also recalls having been sexually abused by one of her mother's male friends when she was about 8.

When LaTisha was 16, her older brother returned home from the army. He and his friends would smoke marijuana. In an attempt to "be with the crowd," LaTisha also began smoking marijuana. At a party, her brother introduced her to "downers"—prescription sedatives and

(continued)

tranquilizers. LaTisha began taking pills regularly, eventually taking as many as 15 a day for about a year and a half. She was most often using both Valium and Quaalude.

By 17, LaTisha's brother had introduced her to heroin. Almost immediately, she began speedballing—injecting as well as snorting heroin, cocaine, and various amphetamines. During all the phases of LaTisha's injection-substance use, sharing needles was common. By age 24, LaTisha was mainlining heroin and turning tricks every day. (Adapted from Inciardi et al., 1993, pp. 160–161)

It does not take conditions as extreme as LaTisha's to create an atmosphere that promotes substance use and abuse. More subtle environmental reinforcements and punishments for substance use and abuse clearly influence people's substance use habits. Some societies discourage any use of alcohol, often as part of religious beliefs, and alcohol abuse and dependence in these societies are rare. Other societies, including many European cultures, allow the drinking of alcohol but strongly discourage excessive drinking and irresponsible behavior while intoxicated. Alcohol-related disorders are less common in these societies than in those with few restrictions, either legal or cultural, on alcohol use (Winger et al., 1992).

Most of the theories about the gender differences in substance use disorders have focused on alcohol use disorders, as well as on differences in the reinforcements and punishments for substance use between men and women and their resulting attitudes toward their own use (Nolen-Hoeksema, 2004). Substance use, particularly alcohol use, is much more acceptable for men than for women in many societies. Heavy drinking is part of what "masculine" men do, and it is modeled by heroes and cultural icons. In contrast, until quite recently, heavy drinking was a sign that a woman was "not a lady." Societal acceptance of heavy drinking by women has increased in recent generations, and so has the rate of alcohol use by young women.

Women tend to be less likely than men to carry several other risk factors for drug and alcohol abuse and dependence (see Nolen-Hoeksema, 2004). Women appear less likely than men to have undesirable personality traits associated with substance use disorder (aggressiveness, behavioral undercontrol, sensation-seeking). They also appear to be less motivated to drink to reduce distress (at least among social drinkers) and less likely to expect

drug consumption to have positive outcomes. On the other hand, women may carry certain protective factors against the development of substance-related problems, such as being more nurturant toward others.

The evidence regarding gender differences in the consequences of alcohol consumption suggests that women suffer alcohol-related physical illnesses at lower levels of exposure to alcohol than men. In addition, heavy alcohol use is associated with several reproductive problems in women. Women may be more likely than men to suffer more cognitive and motor impairment due to alcohol. Women may also be more likely than men to suffer physical harm and sexual assault when they are using alcohol.

Taken together, this pattern of results suggests that women's lower rates of alcohol-related disorders may be due both to the absence of risk factors for alcohol use and abuse in women and to women's sensitivity to the negative consequences of alcohol consumption. Women appear less likely to carry many of the risk factors for the initiation of heavy alcohol use. When they do use alcohol, women may notice they feel intoxicated at a much earlier stage of intoxication than men, and they may be more likely to find these effects aversive or frightening, leading them to inhibit their alcohol consumption. This lower consumption, in turn, protects women from developing a tolerance to high doses of alcohol, as well as alcohol-related social and occupational problems.

When women do become substance abusers, their patterns of use and reasons for use tend to differ from men's. Whereas men tend to begin using substances in the context of socializing with male friends, women are most often initiated into substance use by family members, partners, or lovers (Boyd & Guthrie, 1996; Gomberg, 1994; Inciardi et al., 1993; Sterk, 1999). One study found that 70 percent of female crack users were living with men who were also substance users, and many were living with multiple abusers (Inciardi et al., 1993).

SUMMING UP

- Psychoactive substances have powerful effects on the parts of the brain that register reward and pleasure. The repeated use of a substance may sensitize this system, causing a craving for more of the substance.

- Substance use disorders appear to be influenced by genetics. The genes involved in these disorders influence the neurotransmitters that regulate the metabolism and biosynthesis of substances.

- Some theorists view alcoholism as a form of depression, although the prevailing evidence suggests that alcoholism and depression are distinct disorders.

- Behavioral theories of alcoholism note that people are reinforced or punished by other people for their alcohol-related behaviors and model alcohol-related behaviors from parents and important others.

- Cognitive theories argue that people who develop alcohol-related problems have strong expectations that alcohol will help them feel better and cope better when they face stressful times.

- One personality trait associated with increased risk for substance use disorders is behavioral undercontrol, which in turn appears to be influenced by genetics.

- Sociocultural theorists note that alcohol and other drug use increases among people under severe stress.

- The gender differences in substance-related disorders may be due to men having more risk factors for substance use and women being more sensitive to the negative consequences of substance use.

TREATMENTS FOR SUBSTANCE-RELATED DISORDERS

Historically, the treatments for substance-related disorders have been based on the disease model, which views these disorders as medical diseases (MacCoun, 1998). The disease model suggests that biological treatments are most appropriate. It also suggests that people with these disorders have no control over their use of substances because of their disease and, thus, must avoid all use of the substances. Alcoholics Anonymous, a self-help group that focuses on helping alcoholics accept that they have a disease and abstain completely from drinking, is based on a disease model. It is the most widely prescribed intervention by the proponents of biological perspectives on alcoholism.

Psychological interventions have been based on a **harm-reduction model** of treatment (Marlatt, 1998). Proponents of this approach focus on the psychological and sociocultural factors that lead people to use substances inappropriately and on helping people gain control over their use of substances through behavioral and cognitive interventions. The harm-reduction model does not presume that people must avoid all use of substances—for example, that alcoholics must never take another

Men tend to begin using substances in the context of socializing with friends, whereas women are often introduced to substance use by their male partners.

drink—although it is strongly recommended that people with substance use disorders restrict their exposure to substances.

Whether a clinician follows the disease model or the harm-reduction model of intervention, he or she will most often recommend **detoxification** as the first step in any treatment program. Basically, individuals are assisted in stopping their use of the substance, and then the substance is allowed to be eliminated from the body. Many detoxification programs are in hospitals and clinics, so that physicians can monitor individuals through their withdrawal from the drug, making them more comfortable and intervening if their life is in danger. Detoxification is especially important when the substance being used can cause permanent organ or brain damage or is frequently lethal, such as cocaine, amphetamines, and inhalants.

Once people stop using the substance and are through the withdrawal process, a variety of biological and psychosocial therapies are used to help them prevent relapse. These therapies are often combined in comprehensive substance treatment programs. People check themselves into these programs, where they remain for a few weeks or months until they feel they have gained control over their substance use and dependence.

Biological Treatments

Medications can be used to help wean individuals off a substance, to reduce their desire for a substance, and to maintain their use of substances at a controlled level.

Antianxiety Drugs, Antidepressants, and Antagonists

Although many substance-dependent people can withstand withdrawal symptoms with emotional support, for other people the symptoms are so severe that medications may be prescribed to reduce these symptoms (Carroll, 2001; O'Brien & McKay, 1998). For people who are alcohol dependent, a benzodiazepine, which has depressant effects similar to those of alcohol, can be prescribed to reduce the symptoms of tremor and anxiety, to decrease pulse and respiration rates, and to stabilize blood pressure. The dosage of the drug is decreased each day, so that a patient withdraws from the alcohol slowly but does not become dependent on the benzodiazepine. Antidepressants are also used to help people weather the withdrawal syndrome so as to continue abstaining from substance use (O'Brien & McKay, 1998; Schuckit, 1996). The selective serotonin reuptake inhibitors can help reduce the impulsive consumption of and craving for alcohol.

Antidepressant drugs are sometimes used to treat alcoholics or other drug addicts who are depressed, but the efficacy of these drugs in treating either the alcohol or other drug problems or the depression in the absence of psychotherapy has not been consistently supported (Nunes & Levin, 2004). There are wide differences between people with substance use disorders in response to the SSRIs, which are not currently well understood (Naranjo & Knoke, 2001).

Antagonist drugs block or change the effects of the addictive drug, reducing the desire of the addict for the drug. **Naltrexone** and **naloxone** are opioid antagonists—they block the effects of opioids, such as heroin. Heroin dependents are also given other drugs that reduce the reinforcing effects of heroin and thus reduce their desire for it. If a person takes heroin while on naltrexone or naloxone, he or she will not experience the positive effects of the heroin. This, theoretically, can reduce the desire for the drug and, therefore, use of the drug. The opioid antagonists must be administered very carefully, however, because they can cause severe withdrawal reactions in people addicted to opioids.

Naltrexone has also proven useful in blocking the high that can be caused by alcohol. (Naltrexone may block the effects of alcohol as well as opioids, because it blocks the effects of the release of endorphins during drinking.) Alcoholics on naltrexone report that their craving for alcohol is diminished and they drink less (Anton, 2001). In one study, researchers administered naltrexone or a placebo to male and female alcoholics for 12 weeks (Volpicelli et al., 1997). The participants were also given individual therapy once per week to address their ad-

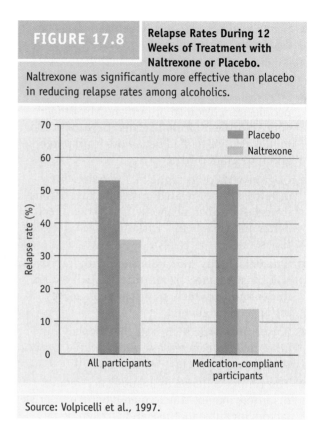

FIGURE 17.8   **Relapse Rates During 12 Weeks of Treatment with Naltrexone or Placebo.**

Naltrexone was significantly more effective than placebo in reducing relapse rates among alcoholics.

Source: Volpicelli et al., 1997.

diction. As Figure 17.8 shows, participants who took naltrexone were significantly less likely than those who took placebo to relapse during the 12 weeks of treatment. Moreover, participants who were more medication-compliant—who took 80 percent or more of their prescribed naltrexone—had a relapse rate of only 14 percent, compared with a relapse rate of 52 percent for the placebo group.

The drug acamprosate affects glutamate and GABA receptors in the brain, which in turn are involved in the craving for alcohol. Preliminary studies have suggested that alcoholics who are prescribed acamprosate stay abstinent longer and may crave alcohol less than alcoholics given placebo (Anton, 2001).

One drug that can make alcohol actually punishing is **disulfiram,** commonly referred to as *Antabuse* (Carroll, 2001). Just having one drink can make a person taking disulfiram feel sick and dizzy and can make him or her vomit, blush, and even faint. People must be very motivated to agree to remain on disulfiram, and it works to reduce alcohol consumption only as long as they take it.

In the pharmacological treatment of nicotine dependence, there are two general approaches (Mooney & Hatsukami, 2001). The first and most common is nicotine replacement therapy—the use of nicotine gum, the nicotine patch, nicotine nasal spray, or the nicotine inhaler to prevent withdrawal effects for a user who wishes to stop smoking. It is hoped that the individual will gradually reduce his or her use of the nicotine replacements, weaning off of the physiological effects of nicotine slowly.

The other approach is to prescribe a medication that reduces the craving for nicotine. The only medication currently approved for this use is bupropion (marketed for smoking cessation as Zyban), which is an antidepressant. The ways in which bupropion helps people stop smoking are not currently clear but may involve changes in the neurotransmitter dopamine (Mooney & Hatsukami, 2001).

Methadone Maintenance Programs

Gradual withdrawal from heroin can be achieved with the help of the synthetic drug **methadone.** This drug itself is an opioid, but it has less potent and longer-lasting effects than heroin when taken orally. The person dependent on heroin takes methadone while discontinuing the use of heroin. The methadone helps reduce the extreme, negative symptoms of withdrawal from heroin. Individuals who take heroin while on methadone do not experience the intense psychological effects of heroin, because methadone blocks receptors for heroin.

Although the goal of treatment is eventually to withdraw individuals from methadone, some patients continue to use methadone for years, under physicians' care, rather than taper off their use. These **methadone maintenance programs** are controversial. Some people believe that they allow the heroin dependent simply to transfer dependency to another substance that is legal and provided by a physician. Other people believe that methadone maintenance is the only way to keep some heroin dependents from going back on the street and becoming readdicted. Studies following patients in methadone maintenance programs do find that they are much more likely than patients who try to withdraw from heroin without methadone to remain in psychological treatment, and they are less likely to relapse into heroin use or to become reinvolved in criminal activity (Carroll, 2001; O'Brien & McKay, 1998).

Behavioral and Cognitive Treatments

Several behavioral and cognitive techniques are used in the treatment of substance use disorders, and several studies have shown these treatments to be quite effective (Volpicelli, 2001). These techniques have certain goals in common. The first is to motivate the individual to stop using the drug. People who enter treatment are often ambivalent about stopping use, and they may have been forced into treatment against their desires. The sec-

ond goal is to teach new coping skills to replace the use of substances to cope with stress and negative feelings. The third is to change the reinforcements a person has for using substances—for example, an individual may need to disengage from social circles in which drug use is "part of the scene." The fourth is to enhance the individual's supports from nonusing friends and family. The final goal is often to foster adherence to pharmacotherapies the person is using in conjunction with psychotherapy.

Behavioral Treatments

Behavioral treatments based on **aversive classical conditioning** are sometimes used to treat alcohol dependency and abuse, either alone or in combination with biological or other psychosocial therapies (Finney & Moos, 1998; Schuckit, 1995). Drugs, such as disulfiram (Antabuse), that make the ingestion of alcohol unpleasant or toxic, are given to people who are alcohol dependent. If they take drinks of alcohol, the drug interacts with the alcohol to cause nausea and vomiting. Eventually, through classical conditioning, they develop conditioned responses to the alcohol—namely, nausea and vomiting. They then learn to avoid the alcohol, through operant conditioning, in order to avoid the aversive response to it. Studies have shown such aversive conditioning to be effective in reducing alcohol consumption, at least in the short term (Schuckit, 1995). "Booster" sessions are often needed to reinforce the aversive conditioning, however, because it tends to weaken with time.

An alternative is **covert sensitization therapy,** in which people who are alcohol dependent use imagery to create associations between thoughts of alcohol use and thoughts of highly unpleasant consequences of alcohol use. An example of a sensitization scene that a therapist might take a client through begins as follows (Rimmele, Miller, & Dougher, 1989, p. 135):

VOICES | You finish the first sip of beer, and you . . . notice a funny feeling in your stomach. . . . Maybe another drink will help. . . . As you tip back . . . that funny feeling in your stomach is stronger, and you feel like you have to burp. . . . You swallow again, trying to force it down, but it doesn't work. You can feel the gas coming up. . . . You swallow more, but suddenly your mouth is filled with a sour liquid that burns the back of your throat and goes up your nose. . . . [You] spew the liquid all over the counter and sink. . . .

The imagery gets even more graphic from there. Covert sensitization techniques seem effective in creating conditioned aversive responses to the sight and smell of alcohol and in reducing alcohol consumption.

Finally, some people who are alcohol dependent develop classically conditioned responses to the environmental cues often present when they drink. For example, when they see or smell their favorite alcoholic beverages, they begin to salivate and report cravings to drink. These conditioned responses increase the risk for relapse among people who are abstinent or trying to quit drinking. A behavior therapy known as **cue exposure and response prevention** is used to extinguish this conditioned response to cues associated with alcohol intake (Rankin, Hodgson, & Stockwell, 1983). Clients are exposed to their favorite types of alcohol, are encouraged to hold glasses to their lips, and are urged to smell the alcohol, but they are prohibited from or strongly encouraged not to drink any of the alcohol. Eventually, this procedure reduces the desire to drink and increases the ability to avoid drinking when the opportunity arises (Rankin et al., 1983). The procedure probably should be coupled with strategies for coping with and removing oneself from tempting situations.

Cognitive Treatments

Interventions based on the cognitive models of alcohol abuse and dependency help clients identify the situations in which they are most likely to drink and to lose control over their drinking and their expectations that alcohol will help them cope better with those situations (Marlatt et al., 1998). Therapists then work with clients to challenge these expectations by reviewing the negative effects of alcohol on their behavior. For example, a therapist may focus on a recent party at which a client was feeling anxious and, thus, began to drink heavily. The therapist might have the client recount the embarrassing and socially inappropriate behaviors he engaged in while intoxicated, to challenge the notion that the alcohol helped him cope effectively with his party anxiety. Therapists also help clients learn to anticipate and reduce stress in their lives and to develop more adaptive ways of coping with stressful situations, such as seeking the help of others or engaging in active problem solving. Finally, therapists help clients learn to say, "No, thanks," when offered drinks and to deal effectively with social pressure to drink by using assertiveness skills.

The following is an excerpt from a discussion between a therapist and a client with alcohol-related problems in which the therapist is helping the client generate strategies for coping with the stress of a possible job promotion. The therapist encourages the client to brainstorm coping strategies, without evaluating them for the moment, so that the client feels free to generate as many possible strategies as he can (adapted from Sobell & Sobell, 1978, pp. 97–98).

VOICES

Client: I really want this job, and it'll mean a lot more money for me, not only now but also at retirement. Besides, if I refused the promotion, what would I tell my wife or my boss?

Therapist: Rather than worrying about that for the moment, why don't we explore what kinds of possible behavioral options you have regarding this job promotion? Remember, don't evaluate the options now. Alternatives, at this point, can include anything even remotely possible; what we want you to do is come up with a range of possible alternatives. You don't have to carry out an alternative just because you consider it.

Client: You know, I could do what I usually do in these kinds of situations. In fact, being as nervous as I've been these past couple of months, I've done that quite often.

Therapist: You mean drinking?

Client: Yeah, I've been drinking quite heavily some nights when I get home, and my wife is really complaining.

Therapist: Well, OK, drinking is one option. What other ways could you deal with this problem?

Client: Well, I could take the job, and on the side I could take some night courses in business at a local college. That way I could learn how to be a supervisor. But, gee, that would be a lot of work. I don't even know if I have the time. Besides, I don't know if they offer the kind of training I need.

Therapist: At this point, it's really not necessary to worry about how to carry out the options but simply to identify them. You're doing fine. What are some other ways you might handle the situation?

(continued)

Client: Well, another thing I could do is to simply tell the boss that I'm not sure I'm qualified and either tell him that I don't want the job or ask him if he could give me some time to learn my new role.

Therapist: OK. Go on, you're doing fine.

Client: But what if the boss tells me that I have to take the job, I don't have any choice?

Therapist: Well, what general kinds of things might happen in that case?

Client: Oh, I could take the job and fail. That's one option. I could take the job and learn how to be a supervisor. I could refuse the job, risk being fired, and maybe end up having to look for another job. You know, I could just go and talk to my supervisor right now and explain the problem to him and see what comes of that.

Therapist: Well, you've delineated a lot of options. Let's take some time to evaluate them before you reach any decision.

The therapist then helps the client evaluate the potential effectiveness of each option and anticipate any potential negative consequences of each action. The client decides to accept the promotion but to take some courses at the local college to increase his business background. The therapist discusses with the client the stresses of managing a new job and classes, and they generate ways the client can manage these stresses other than by drinking.

In most cases, therapists using these cognitive-behavioral approaches encourage clients to abstain from alcohol, especially when clients have histories of frequent relapses into alcohol abuse. When clients' goals are to learn to drink socially and therapists believe that clients have the capability to achieve these goals, therapists may focus on teaching clients to engage in social, or controlled, drinking.

A wide range of studies have shown that cognitive-behavioral approaches are effective in the treatment of abuse and dependence on alcohol, cannabis, nicotine, heroin, amphetamines, and cocaine (Dennis et al., 2000; McCrady, 2001; Mooney & Hatsukami, 2001; NIDA, 2002b, 2002c, 2002d; Waldron et al., 2001)

The Controlled Drinking Controversy

The notion that some alcoholics can learn to engage in controlled, social drinking directly clashes with the idea that alcoholism is a biological disease and that, if an alcoholic takes even one sip of alcohol, he or she will lose all control and plunge back into full alcoholism. In 1973, researchers Mark and Linda Sobell published one of the first studies showing that a cognitive-behaviorally oriented controlled drinking program can work for alcoholics, perhaps even better than a traditional abstinence program. They found that the alcoholics who had had their controlled drinking intervention were significantly less likely than alcoholics in the abstinence program to relapse into severe drinking, and they were significantly more likely to be functioning well over the two years following treatment.

These findings were assailed by proponents of the alcohol-as-a-disease model. For example, Pendery, Maltzman, and West (1982) published a 10-year follow-up of the alcoholics in the Sobells' controlled drinking group in the journal *Science*, based on interviews with these alcoholics, and their family members, as well as investigations of public records. Pendery and colleagues reported that, 10 years after the Sobells' study, 40 percent of the men in the controlled drinking treatment group were drinking excessively, 20 percent were dead from alcohol-related causes, 30 percent had given up attempts at controlled drinking in favor of becoming abstinent, and only 5 percent were engaging in controlled drinking. Subsequently, the TV program *60 Minutes* did a segment on the evils of controlled drinking treatments, which was introduced with Harry Reasoner standing at the graveside of one of the people from the Sobells' study. The Sobells were publicly charged with fraud, and multiple investigations of the Sobells' work followed, including one by the U.S. Congress, interrupting their research for years. They were eventually cleared of any wrongdoing.

Behavioral interventions help alcoholics learn new ways to cope with depression and anxiety.

In a response to the Pendery and colleagues article titled "Aftermath of a Heresy," Mark and Linda Sobell (Sobell & Sobell, 1984) detailed the many flaws in the Pendery article, the greatest of which was the lack of any information on the outcomes of the alcoholics who had been in the abstinence program in the Sobells' original study. They noted that claims that 30 percent of the men in their controlled drinking group were abstinent and 5 percent were engaging in controlled drinking suggest a much better long-term outcome for these men than other studies have suggested is true of alcoholics who are treated by abstinence programs. The Sobells were able to track down the mortality rates of the men in the abstinence treatment group in their study. Whereas Pendery and colleagues had reported that 20 percent of the men in the controlled drinking treatment group had died over the 10 years after the study, the Sobells found that 30 percent of the men in the abstinence treatment groups had died in the same 10 years, with all but one of these deaths directly attributable to alcohol.

Subsequent research by the Sobells and many others has shown that controlled drinking programs can work, at least for people with mild to moderate alcohol problems or dependence (see Marlatt, 1998, and Sobell & Sobell, 1995, for reviews). People who have had many alcohol-related problems generally have trouble with controlled drinking and must remain abstinent in order to avoid relapse into alcohol dependency.

Relapse Prevention

Unfortunately, the relapse rate for people undergoing any kind of treatment for alcohol abuse and dependency is high. The **abstinence violation effect** is a powerful contributor to relapse. There are two components to the abstinence violation effect. The first is a sense of conflict and guilt when an alcoholic who has been abstinent violates the abstinence and has a drink. He or she may then continue to drink to try to suppress the conflict and guilt. The second is a tendency to attribute the violation of abstinence to a lack of willpower and self-control, rather than to situational factors. Thus, the person may think, "I'm an alcoholic and there's no way I can control my drinking. The fact I had a drink proves this." This type of thinking may pave the way to continued, uncontrolled drinking.

Relapse prevention programs teach alcoholics to view slips as temporary and situationally caused. Therapists work with clients to identify high-risk situations for relapse and to avoid those situations or to exercise effective coping strategies for the situations. For example, a client may identify parties as high-risk situations for relapse. If she decides to go to a party, she may first practice with her therapist some assertiveness skills for resisting pressure from friends to drink and write down other coping strategies she can use if she feels tempted to drink, such as starting a conversation with a supportive friend or practicing deep breathing exercises. She may also decide that, if the temptation to drink becomes too great, she will ask a supportive friend to leave the party with her and go somewhere for coffee, until the temptation to drink passes.

Only about 10 percent of people who are alcohol dependents or abusers ever seek treatment. Another 40 percent may recover on their own, often as the result of maturation or positive changes in their environment (such as getting a good job or getting married to a supportive person) that help them and motivate them to get control of their drinking (Sobell & Sobell, 1995). The remainder of people with significant alcohol problems continue to have these problems throughout their lives. Some of these people become physically ill or completely unable to hold jobs or maintain their relationships. Others are able to hide or control their alcohol abuse and dependency enough to keep their jobs and may be in relationships with people who facilitate their alcohol dependency. Often, they have periods, sometimes long periods, of abstinence, but then, perhaps when facing stressful events, they begin drinking again. This is why preventing the development of alcohol abuse and dependency and other substance-related problems is so important.

Alcoholics Anonymous

Alcoholics Anonymous (AA) is an organization created by and for people with alcohol-related problems. Its philosophy is based on the disease model of alcoholism, which views alcoholism as a disease that causes alcoholics to lose all control over their drinking once they have the first drink. The implication of this model is that the only way to control alcoholism is to abstain completely from any alcohol. AA prescribes 12 steps that people dependent on alcohol must take toward recovery. The first step is to admit they are alcoholics and powerless to control the effects of alcohol. AA encourages members to seek help from a higher power, to admit to their weaknesses, and to ask for forgiveness. The goal for all members is complete abstinence.

Group members provide moral and social support for each other and make themselves available to each other in times of crisis. Once they are able, group members are expected to devote themselves to helping other alcoholics. AA members believe that people are never completely cured of alcoholism—they are always "recovering alcoholics," with the potential of falling back into alcohol dependency with one drink. AA meetings include testimonials from recovering alcoholics about their paths into alcoholism, such as the one that follows, which are meant to motivate others to abstain from alcohol (Spitzer et al., 1983, pp. 87–89).

VOICES

I am Duncan. I am an alcoholic. . . . I know that I will always be an alcoholic, that I can never again touch alcohol in any form. It'll kill me if I don't keep away from it. In fact, it almost did. . . . I must have been just past my 15th birthday when I had that first drink that everybody talks about. And like so many of them—and you—it was like a miracle. With a little beer in my gut, the world was transformed. I wasn't a weakling anymore, I could lick almost anybody on the block. And girls? Well, you can imagine how a couple of beers made me feel, like I could have any girl I wanted. So, like so many of you, my friends in the Fellowship, alcohol became the royal road to love, respect, and self-esteem. If I couldn't feel good about myself when I wasn't drinking, if I felt stupid or lazy or ugly or misunderstood, all I had to do was belt down a few and everything got better. Of course, I was fooling myself, wasn't I, because I was as ugly and dumb and lazy when I was drunk as when I was sober. But I didn't know it. . . .

Though it's obvious to me now that my drinking even then, in high school, and after I got to college, was a problem, I didn't think so at the time. After all, everybody was drinking and getting drunk and acting stupid, and I didn't really think I was different. A couple of minor auto accidents, one conviction for drunken driving, a few fights—nothing out of the ordinary, it seemed to me at the time. True, I was drinking quite a lot, even then, but my friends seemed to be able to down as much beer as I did. I guess the fact that I hadn't really had any blackouts and that I could go for days without having to drink reassured me that things hadn't gotten out of control. And that's the way it went, until I found myself drinking even more—and more often—and suffering more from my drinking, along about my third year of college. . . . [Eventually] I did cut down on my drinking by half or more. I only drank on weekends—and then only at night. And I set more-or-less arbitrary limits on how much I would drink, as well as where and when I would drink. And that got me through the rest of college and, actually, through law school as well. I'd drink enough to get very drunk once or twice a week, but only on weekends, and then I'd tough it out through the rest of the week.

[Later] on, the drinking began to affect both my marriage and my career. With enough booze in me and under the pressures of guilt over my failure to carry out my responsibilities to my wife and children, I sometimes got kind of rough physically with them. I would break furniture, throw things around, then rush out and drive off in the car. I had a couple of wrecks, lost my license for two years because of one of them. Worst of all was when I tried to stop. By then I was totally hooked, so every time I tried to stop drinking, I'd experience withdrawal in all its horrors. I never had DTs, but I came awfully close many times, with the vomiting and the "shakes" and being unable to sit still or to lie down. And that would go on for days at a time. . . . Then, about four years ago, with my life in ruins, my wife given up on me and the kids with her, out of a job, and way down on my luck, the Fellowship and I found each other. Jim, over there, bless his heart, decided to sponsor me—we'd been friends for a long time, and I knew he'd found sobriety through this group. I've been dry now for a little over two years, and with luck and support, I may stay sober. I've begun to make amends for my transgressions, I've faced my faults squarely again instead of hiding them with booze, and I think I may make it.

The practices and philosophies of AA do not appeal to everyone. The emphases on one's powerlessness, need for a higher power, and complete abstinence turn many people away. In addition, many people who subscribe to AA's philosophy still find it difficult to maintain complete abstinence and "fall off the wagon" at various times throughout their lives. However, many people have found AA

Many abstinence programs for substance abuse are based on Alcoholics Anonymous.

very helpful in their recovery from alcohol abuse and dependency, and AA remains the most common source of treatment for people with alcohol-related problems. There are about 23,000 chapters of AA across 90 countries, and it is estimated that 800,000 people attend meetings (Goodwin, 1988). Evaluations of 12-step programs, such as AA, have found that they are as effective as the behavioral and cognitive programs in the treatment of alcoholism (Finney & Moos, 1998; Project MATCH Research Group, 1998). Self-help groups modeled on Alcoholics Anonymous have also been formed to assist people with dependencies on other drugs, including Narcotics Anonymous, Cocaine Anonymous, and Potsmokers Anonymous.

Other self-help organizations have been developed that do not have the spiritual focus of AA and, instead, often apply cognitive-behavioral principles in a self-help format. These include Self-Management and Recovery Training (SMART), Secular Organizations for Sobriety/Save Ourselves (SOS), and Moderation Management (MM).

Prevention Programs for College Students

In the United States, young adults between 18 and 24 years of age have the highest rates of alcohol consumption and make up the largest proportion of problem drinkers of any age group. College students are even more likely to drink than are their peers who are not in college. Among college students, 73 to 98 percent drink alcohol, in response to

easy access to alcohol, social activities that focus on drinking, and peer pressure to drink. As much as 20 to 25 percent of college students report having experienced alcohol-related problems, such as an inability to complete schoolwork or an alcohol-related accident. Alcohol-related accidents are the leading cause of death in college students (Marlatt et al., 1993). Heavy drinking is also associated with acute alcohol toxicity (which can be lethal), date rape, unsafe sexual activity, vandalism, and impaired academic performance.

The pattern of drinking among college students has shifted over time. A greater percentage of students abstain completely from alcohol, but those who do drink are more likely to be heavy drinkers (Marlatt et al., 1993). These heavy drinkers are most likely to be binge drinkers, who drink large quantities of alcohol on weekends, typically at social events, often with the intention of getting drunk.

Many colleges are developing programs to reduce drinking and drinking-related problems among students. Most of these programs emphasize the health-related consequences of drinking, but such long-term concerns do not tend to impress young people, who are more likely to be focused on the short-term gains of alcohol use. Simply providing information about the dangers of alcohol abuse and trying to invoke a fear of these dangers have little effect. Some college counselors refer students with drinking problems to abstinence programs, such as Alcoholics Anonymous, but college students often find the focus on admitting one's powerlessness and the principle of lifelong abstinence so unattractive that they will not attend these programs. Finally, many colleges try to provide alternative recreational activities that do not focus on alcohol. In general, however, such prevention programs designed to stop drinking altogether have had limited success.

Psychologist Alan Marlatt and colleagues at the University of Washington (Marlatt, Blume, & Parks, 2001; Parks, Anderson, & Marlatt, 2001) have argued that a more credible approach to college drinking is to recognize alcohol use as normative behavior among young adults and to focus education on the immediate risks of the excessive use of alcohol (such as alcohol-related accidents) and on the payoffs of moderation (such as the avoidance of hangovers). They view young drinkers as relatively inexperienced in regulating their use of alcohol and as in need of skills training to prevent their abuse of alcohol. Learning to drink safely is compared to learning to drive safely, and people must learn to anticipate hazards and avoid "unnecessary accidents."

Based on this harm-reduction model, the Alcohol Skills Training Program (ASTP) targets heavy-drinking college students for intervention. In eight weekly sessions of 90 minutes, participants are first taught to be aware of their drinking habits, including when, where, and with whom they are most likely to overdrink, by keeping daily records of their alcohol consumption and the situations in which they drink. They are also taught to calculate their own blood-alcohol levels. It often comes as a surprise to people how few drinks it takes to be legally intoxicated.

Next, participants' beliefs about the "magical" effects of drinking on social skills and sexual prowess are challenged. They discuss the negative effects of alcohol on social behaviors, on the ability to drive, and on weight gain, and they discuss hangovers. Participants are encouraged to set personal goals for limiting alcohol consumption, based on their maximum blood-alcohol levels and their desires to avoid the negative effects of alcohol. They learn skills for limiting consumption, such as alternating alcoholic and nonalcoholic beverages and selecting drinks based on quality rather than quantity, such as buying two good beers rather than a six-pack of generic beer. In later sessions, members are taught to consider alternatives to drinking alcohol to reduce negative emotional states, such as using relaxation exercises or reducing sources of stress in their lives. Finally, in role-plays, participants are taught skills for avoiding high-risk situations in which they are likely to overdrink and skills for resisting peer pressure to drink. Some ideas from the ASTP program are described in *Taking Psychology Personally: Tips for Responsible Drinking*.

Evaluations of ASTP have shown that participants do decrease their alcohol consumption and problems and increase their social skills in resisting alcohol abuse (Fromme et al., 1994; Marlatt, Baer, & Larimer, 1995). ASTP was designed for a group format, and the use of group pressure to encourage change in individuals and as a forum for role playing has many advantages. Adaptations of this program delivered to individuals either in person or in written form as a self-help manual also have shown positive effects on drinking habits (Baer et al., 1992, 2001).

In one study, Marlatt and colleagues (Marlatt et al., 1998) attempted to intervene with high-risk drinkers when they might be most open to intervention, in their first year of college. They identified a group of high school students who were about to matriculate into the University of Washington and who were already drinking at least

monthly and consuming at least five to six drinks in one sitting or who reported frequent alcohol-related problems. These high-risk students were then randomly assigned to receive either a one-session intervention based on the Alcohol Skills Training Program or no intervention, sometime in January through March of their first year of college. Both groups of students were followed for the next two years. Over that two years, the intervention group showed less drinking overall and fewer harmful consequences of drinking (such as getting into alcohol-related accidents) over the subsequent two years than did the comparison group. In addition, approximately 90 percent of those receiving the intervention said it was helpful and that they would recommend it to friends. The work of Marlatt and colleagues suggests that problem drinkers of college age can learn to reduce their intake of alcohol and to avoid the harmful consequences of alcohol consumption if they receive nonconfrontational training on the skills necessary for harm reduction.

Gender-Sensitive Treatment Programs

The differences in the contexts for men's and women's substance abuse suggest the need for different approaches to treating men and women (Beckman, 1994). For men, treatment may need to focus on challenging the societal supports for their substance use and their view that substance use is an appropriate way to cope. It may also need to focus on men's tendency to act in aggressive and impulsive ways, particularly when intoxicated. For women, treatment may need to focus more on issues of self-esteem and powerlessness and on helping them remove themselves from abusive environments.

Women who violate social norms so greatly as to become substance abusers may have more severe underlying emotional problems than do men who become substance abusers (Beckman, 1994). In addition, because women substance abusers typically are living with partners and other family members who are also substance abusers, they may not have the necessary support from their environment to stop their substance use (Riehman, Hser, & Zeller, 2000). Rarely do husbands or boyfriends participate in the treatment of women substance users, and they may even oppose the woman's seeking treatment. In contrast, women partners often participate in male substance abusers' treatment (Higgins et al., 1994). One recent study found that, when male partners can be brought into treatment for women substance abusers, the women show greater remission of their substance abuse problems than if they receive only individual therapy (Winters et al., 2002). As substance use among women increases, however, treatment programs will need to become more sensitive to the differences in the patterns and motives of substance use in women and men and must design their programs to meet the needs of both genders.

SUMMING UP

- Detoxification is the first step in treating substance-related disorders.

- Antianxiety and antidepressant drugs can help ease withdrawal symptoms. Antagonist drugs can block the effects of substances, reduce desire for the drug, or make the ingestion of the drug aversive.

- Methadone maintenance programs substitute methadone for heroin in the treatment of heroin addicts. These programs are controversial but may be the only way some heroin addicts will get off the streets.

- Behavior therapies based on aversive classical conditioning are sometimes used to treat substance use disorders.

- Treatments based on social learning and cognitive theories focus on training people with substance use disorders in more adaptive coping skills and challenging their positive expectations about the effects of substances.

- The most common treatment for alcoholism is Alcoholics Anonymous, a self-help group that encourages alcoholics to admit their weaknesses and to call on a higher power and other group members to help them remain completely abstinent from alcohol. Related groups are available for people dependent on other substances.

- Prevention programs for college students aim to teach them the responsible use of alcohol.

- Different treatments may be needed for men and women that take into account the different contexts for their substance use.

CHAPTER INTEGRATION

The substances we have discussed in this chapter are powerful biological agents. They affect the brain directly, producing changes in mood, thoughts, and perceptions. Some people may find these changes more positive or rewarding than other people do, because they are genetically or biochemically predisposed to do so (see Figure 17.9). The rewards and punishments in the environment can clearly affect an individual's choice to pursue the effects of substances, however. Even many long-term, chronic substance abusers can abstain from use if they receive strong environmental support for abstention.

People who find substances more rewarding, for biological or environmental reasons, will develop expectations that substances will be rewarding, which in turn will enhance how rewarding they actually are. In turn, heavy substance users choose friends and environments that support their substance use. They also tend to find partners who are also heavy substance users, creating a biological and psychosocial environment for their children that promotes substance abuse and dependence. Thus, the cycle of familial transmission of substance abuse and dependence has intersecting biological and psychosocial components.

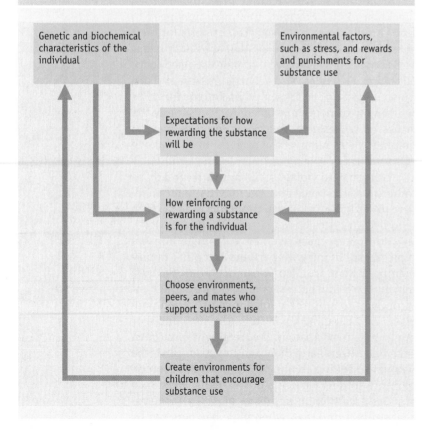

FIGURE 17.9   **Intergration of Biological and Psychological Pressures Toward the Development of Substance-Related Use Disorders**

Taking Psychology Personally

Tips for Responsible Drinking

The following are some tips for reducing your own drinking and for preventing problems due to drinking at social events, from the work of Alan Marlatt and colleagues (1998):

■ *Set a limit on how much you will drink* before you go to a party or another social function. You might want to use Table 17.7 to set your drink limit, so that you do not exceed a low to moderate blood-alcohol level. Tell a friend what your limit is and get a commitment from that friend to help you stick to that limit.

■ *Alternate between alcoholic and nonalcoholic beverages* at the party.

■ *Eat foods high in protein and carbohydrates* before and at the party.

■ *Designate someone in your group to drive*. That person should drink *no* alcoholic beverages at the party.

■ *If you are throwing the party, serve plenty of nonalcoholic beverages and attractive food and try to focus the party on something other than alcohol consumption*, such as music.

■ *If someone at the party appears to be very intoxicated, encourage him or her to stop drinking. Do not let him or her drive* away from the party. Instead, call a taxi or have someone who has not been drinking drive him or her home.

■ *If a person passes out after drinking heavily, lay the person on his or her side,* rather than on his or her back, in case of vomiting. Call medical personnel.

■ *If you get drunk at a party, after you have recovered, review the reasons for your overdrinking.* Were you trying to get rid of a bad mood? Were you nervous and trying to relax? Did certain people push you to drink? Did you tell yourself that you were not drinking that much? Try to develop concrete, realistic plans for avoiding, in future situations, the reasons you overdrank.

Extraordinary People: Follow-Up

Without much trouble, many of us could name a number of other celebrities besides Chris Farley who abuse or abused illicit drugs or have died from drug overdoses: rapper Ol' Dirty Bastard, Dee Dee Ramone of the punk band The Ramones, River Phoenix, Jimmy Hendrix, Charlie Parker, Janis Joplin, Jim Morrison, and, years ago, Marilyn Monroe and Elvis Presley. Comedian Richard Prior was permanently disfigured in an explosion while he was free-basing cocaine. As guitarist Keith Richards of the Rolling Stones said, "I used to know a few guys that did drugs all the time, but they're not alive anymore. . . . And you get the message after you've been to a few funerals."

But what message do fans, especially young fans, get from celebrities who use, and die from, drugs? It's easy to dismiss the celebrity drug deaths as the result of out-of-control excess by spoiled rich people who can't manage their drug use. The drug-related antics of people such as Chris Farley seem so outrageous that we can easily believe we'd never fall into such behavior.

At the same time, celebrity drug users—the ones who are alive—also can serve as models for cool and hip behavior. Many openly admit their drug use on talk shows and say little about the harm drugs are doing to their minds, bodies, and careers. They make snide jokes about their attempts to "get on the wagon." Alcohol and even illicit drug use is a staple of popular movies, where the star characters use these substances to cope with stress, to increase their sex appeal, and to live their lives each day.

Certainly, there are celebrities who have quit using drugs and who use their fame to campaign against drug use, especially by youth. But the overwhelming message that comes from the popular media is one that promotes alcohol and other drug use. What is extraordinary about celebrity drug users is their power to shape popular opinion about drug use and abuse.

■ A substance is any natural or synthesized product that has psychoactive effects. The five groups of substances most often leading to substance disorders are (1) central nervous system depressants, including alcohol, barbiturates and benzodiazepines, and inhalants; (2) central nervous system stimulants, including cocaine, amphetamines, nicotine, and caffeine; (3) opioids; (4) hallucinogens and PCP; and (5) cannabis.

■ Substance intoxication is indicated by a set of behavioral and psychological changes that occur as a direct result of the physiological effects of a substance on the central nervous system. Substance withdrawal involves a set of physiological and behavioral symptoms that result from the cessation of or reduction in heavy and prolonged use of a substance. The specific symptoms of intoxication and withdrawal depend on the substance being used, the amount of the substance ingested, and the method of ingestion. (Review Table 17.1.)

■ Substance abuse is indicated when an individual shows persistent problems in one of four categories: (1) failure to fulfill major role obligations at work, school, or home; (2) substance use in situations in which such use is physically hazardous; (3) substance-related legal problems; and (4) continued substance use despite social or interpersonal problems. (Review Table 17.4.)

■ Substance dependence is characterized by a maladaptive pattern of substance use, leading to significant problems in a person's life and usually leading to tolerance to the substance, withdrawal symptoms if the substance is discontinued, and compulsive substance-taking behavior. (Review Table 17.5.)

■ The routes of administration that produce rapid and efficient absorption of a substance into the bloodstream (intravenous injection, smoking, snorting) lead to a more intense intoxication, a greater likelihood of dependence, and a greater risk for overdose. Substances that act more rapidly on the central nervous system and whose effects wear off more quickly (such as cocaine) and that lead to faster intoxication are more likely to lead to dependence or abuse.

■ At low doses, alcohol produces relaxation and a mild euphoria. At higher doses, it produces the classic signs of depression and cognitive and motor impairment. A large proportion of deaths due to accidents, murders, and suicides are alcohol-related. Alcohol withdrawal symptoms can be mild or so severe as to be life threatening. Alcohol abusers

and dependents experience a wide range of social and interpersonal problems and are at risk for many serious health problems. (Review Table 17.8.)

■ Women drink less alcohol than men do in most cultures and are less likely to have alcohol-related problems. Persons of Asian descent typically drink less and thus are less prone to alcohol-related problems. (Review Figures 17.4, 17.5.)

■ Benzodiazepines and barbiturates are sold by prescription for the treatment of anxiety and insomnia. One pattern of the development of abuse of or dependence on these substances is reflected by the teenager or young adult who begins using the substances recreationally to produce a sense of well-being or euphoria but then escalates to chronic use and physiological dependence. A second pattern is shown by individuals who begin to use substances under physicians' care for insomnia or anxiety but then escalate their usage without the knowledge of their physicians.

■ The inhalants are volatile agents that people sniff to produce a sense of euphoria, disinhibition, and increased aggressiveness or sexual performance. The biggest users and abusers of inhalants are young boys, particularly Native American teenagers and Hispanic teenagers. Inhalants are extremely dangerous, because they can cause permanent brain damage even with casual use, several major diseases, and suffocation when the user goes unconscious with the plastic bag used for inhaling still over his or her head. (Review Table 17.6.)

■ Cocaine activates the parts of the brain that register reward and pleasure and produces a sudden rush of euphoria, followed by increased self-esteem, alertness, and energy and a greater sense of competence, creativity, and social acceptability. The user may also experience frightening perceptual changes. The withdrawal symptoms of cocaine include exhaustion, a need for sleep, and depression. The extraordinarily rapid, strong effects of cocaine on the brain's reward centers seem to make this substance more likely than most illicit substances to result in patterns of abuse and dependence. (Review Table 17.9.)

■ The amphetamines are readily available by prescription for the treatment of certain disorders but often end up in the black market and used by people to help them keep going through the day or to counteract the effects of depressants or heroin. They can make people feel euphoric, invigorated, self-confident, and gregarious, but they also can make people restless, hypervigilant, anxious, and aggressive and can result in several dangerous physiological symptoms and changes.

- The opioids are a group of substances developed from the juice of the poppy plant. The most commonly used illegal opioid is heroin. The initial symptom of opioid intoxication is euphoria. It is followed by a sense of drowsiness, lethargy, and periods of light sleep. Severe intoxication can lead to respiratory difficulties, unconsciousness, coma, and seizures. The withdrawal symptoms include dysphoria, anxiety, agitation, sensitivity to pain, and craving for more substance. (Review Table 17.10.)

- The hallucinogens, PCP, and cannabis all produce perceptual changes, which include sensory distortions and hallucinations. For some people, these are pleasant experiences, but, for others, they are extremely frightening. Similarly, some people experience a sense of euphoria or relaxation while on these substances, and others become anxious and agitated. (Review Tables 17.11, 17.12.)

- Some common club drugs, in addition to LSD, are ecstasy (3-4 methylenedioxymethamphetamine, or MDMA), GHB (gamma-hydroxybutyrate), ketamine, and rohypnol (flunitrazepam). They have several euphoric and sedative effects and are used by perpetrators of date rape.

- Nicotine is another widely available substance. Smoking tobacco is legal but causes cancer, bronchitis, and coronary heart disease in users and a range of birth defects in the children of women who smoke when pregnant. People can become physiologically dependent on nicotine and undergo difficult withdrawal symptoms when they stop smoking.

- The disease model of alcoholism views alcoholism as a biological disorder in which the individual has no control over his or her drinking and, therefore, must remain abstinent. Other theorists see alcoholism along a continuum of drinking habits, as modifiable through therapy.

- There is evidence that genes play a role in vulnerability to substance-related disorders, through their effects on the synthesis and metabolism of substances. Men genetically predisposed to alcoholism are less sensitive to the effects of low doses of alcohol.

- Some theorists view alcoholism as a form of depression, but the prevailing evidence suggests that alcoholism and depression are distinct disorders.

- Behavioral theories of alcoholism note that people are also reinforced or punished by other people for their alcohol-related behaviors and model the alcohol-related behaviors of important others.

Cognitive theories argue that people who develop alcohol-related problems have strong expectations that alcohol will help them feel better and cope better when they face stressful times. One personality characteristic aassociated with substance use disorders is behavioral undercontrol.

- Gender differences in substance-related disorders may be due to men having more risk factors for substance use and women being more sensitive to the negative consequences of substance use.

- Medications can be used to ease the symptoms of withdrawal from many substances and to reduce cravings for substances. The symptoms of withdrawal from opioids can be so severe that dependents are given the drug methadone to curtail the symptoms as they try to discontinue their heroin use. Methadone also blocks the effects of subsequent doses of heroin, reducing people's desire to obtain heroin. Methadone maintenance programs, which continue to administer methadone to former heroin dependents, are controversial.

- The most common treatment for alcoholism is Alcoholics Anonymous, a self-help group that encourages alcoholics to admit their weaknesses and to call on a higher power and other group members to help them remain completely abstinent from alcohol.

- Behavior therapies based on aversive classical conditioning are sometimes used to treat alcoholism. Alcoholics in these therapies use a drug that makes them ill if they ingest alcohol or use imagery to develop a conditioned aversive response to the sight and smell of alcohol.

- Treatments based on social learning and cognitive theories focus on training alcoholics in more adaptive coping skills and challenging their positive expectations about the effects of alcohol. Many therapists in the cognitive-behavioral tradition reject the disease model of alcoholism and suggest that some alcoholics may learn to engage in controlled social drinking.

MindMap CD-ROM

The following resources on the MindMap CD-ROM that came with this text will help you to master the content of this chapter and prepare for tests:

- Videos: Substance Abuse; Alcohol Addiction; Chemical Basis of Addiction
- Chapter Timelime
- Chapter Quiz

Key Terms

substance 620

drug addicts 620

substance-related disorder 623

substance intoxication 625

substance withdrawal 626

substance abuse 626

substance dependence 626

tolerance 627

blackout 629

alcohol abuse 630

alcohol dependence 630

delirium tremens (DTs) 633

alcohol-induced persisting amnesic disorder 634

Wernicke's encephalopathy 634

Korsakoff's psychosis 634

alcohol-induced dementia 634

fetal alcohol syndrome (FAS) 634

benzodiazepines 636

barbiturates 636

inhalants 637

cocaine 640

amphetamines 641

nicotine 643

caffeine 645

opioids 646

hallucinogens 648

phenylcyclidine (PCP) 649

cannabis 650

disease model 654

harm-reduction model 659

detoxification 659

antagonist drugs 660

naltrexone 660

naloxone 660

disulfiram 660

methadone 661

methadone maintenance programs 661

aversive classical conditioning 661

covert sensitization therapy 661

cue exposure and response prevention 662

abstinence violation effect 664

relapse prevention programs 664

Chapter 18

Sun and Moon (Subtitled *Starker Traum*) by Paul Klee

All, too, will bear in mind this sacred principle, that though the will of the majority is in all cases to prevail, that will to be rightful must be reasonable; that the minority possess their equal rights, which equal law must protect, and to violate would be oppression.

—Thomas Jefferson, first inaugural address (1801)

Mental Health and the Law <

CHAPTER OVERVIEW

Extraordinary People

■ **One Family's Struggle with Schizophrenia and the "System"**

Judgments About People Accused of Crimes

Mental-health professionals are called upon to help determine if accused people are competent to stand trial and if accused people were "sane" at the time the crimes were committed. The insanity defense has undergone many changes in recent history, often in response to its use in high-profile crimes. It is based on the notion that a person who was mentally incapacitated at the time of a crime should not be held responsible for the crime.

Involuntary Commitment and Civil Rights

People can be committed involuntarily to psychiatric facilities if they are gravely disabled by psychological disorders or are imminent dangers to themselves or others. These criteria are difficult to apply accurately and consistently.

Clinicians' Duties to Clients and Society

Some specific duties clinicians have are the duties to provide competent and appropriate treatment; to avoid multiple relationships, especially sexual relationships, with clients; and to protect clients' confidentiality. Client confidentiality can be broken, however, when clients are threatening others or abusing children or elderly people. Clinicians also have a duty to provide ethical service to diverse populations.

Taking Psychology Personally

■ **Guidelines for Ethical Service to Culturally Diverse Populations**

Chapter Integration

The law takes a largely biological view of psychological disorders, seeing them as similar to medical diseases. Mental-health professionals, on the other hand, tend to view psychological disorders in a more integrated way, considering the biological, psychological, and social vulnerabilities and circumstances that interact to influence an individual's behavior or mental health.

Extraordinary People

One Family's Struggle with Schizophrenia and the "System"

Greg Bottoms (shown at right), in his disturbing book *Angelhead* (2000), recalls his older brother Michael's descent into severe paranoid schizophrenia and the range of responses he and his family had to Michael's symptoms. This is a story of a family that had no idea what was happening to its eldest son, tried to cope with it on its own, finally got a diagnosis for Michael's symptoms, and then found the mental-health and judicial systems tragically inadequate in helping them cope.

The Bottoms family was newly moved to the suburbs, and the parents worked hard to afford their middle-class existence. The increasingly bizarre and violent behavior of their eldest son was met with restrictions on his freedoms (which he blatantly violated), screaming criticism, and beatings. Nothing would stop his disease, however, and his younger brother, Greg, watched him deteriorate with a mix of horror and fascination (Bottoms, 2000):

> Michael's world started breaking into tiny pieces. He laughed for no reason, nowhere near a punch-line. He said off-color things about death and dying and torture, about corpses and axes and Satan. He would look at a clock to tell the time, but then he'd see the round frame, the glass, the hands red and black, one sweeping, one still, and the actual calculation of time suddenly escaped him, moved just out of reach of his thoughts. (p. 22)

> He felt confused these days, once he knew he was outside of his dreams. People—teachers, my mother, his last few remaining friends—would talk to him but then their words would get lost before they reached his mind; it was as if the words would sometimes get caught up in the air, as if the air were heavy, almost solid, and the words, like hard objects, fell to the ground before they reached him. Other times, when the words did reach him, each word was wearing a disguise, each word actually contained the meanings of many words and

> how was he to know, how the ———— was he to know, if he could trust the legitimacy, the honesty of this word . . . ? Whenever I encountered him, he would stare at me until I walked out of a room, my heart pounding, a permanent frown on his face. Michael kept to himself—hunched, lonely, looking over his shoulder always. I thought of him as dangerous, someone to lock the door against. (pp. 38–40)

Michael's parents clearly felt completely overwhelmed with him. His father eventually gave up responding to him with violence, in part because he feared violent retribution from Michael, and took to throwing him out of the house on a regular basis. His mother tried to comfort and shield him, which Michael sometimes received with gratitude, but sometimes with derision and psychotic threats on her life:

> My mother, years later when I was badgering her with questions about Michael, told me that he used to hold a lighter up to her face while she drove him to the mall, saying that he would burn her if she didn't give him money, asking her if she knew what God did to stingy cunts. (p. 119)

Michael regularly beat up his younger brothers, Greg and Ron, and threatened the lives of everyone in the family. As much as he feared his brother's violence, however, Greg also suffered from the embarrassment of having a "crazy" brother. Avoidance and denial became a way of life:

Ours was a small Southern town—white colonial homes, churches. Community mattered. Everyone was friendly, even if only for appearances' sake. My mother and father knew the principal, the guidance counselor. These people began to feel sorry for them, concerned, in that administrative way, about Michael's tenuous—and dwindling—ability to function in the world. They would call my parents for conferences. My parents would often cancel, make up some excuse, their shame over their son having become nearly crippling. My own embarrassment over my brother's odd religion was at first debilitating, then simply numbing. . . .

He became the talk of the town, the bad boy who'd lost his mind, because of the Bible toting and random quoting of scripture. He would stop kids on the street, in the school parking lot, in hallways to remind them of their sins and quote scripture. He was a kind of village idiot, our small, all-white, suburban school's one truly great spectacle. (pp. 62–63)

Michael was not diagnosed with schizophrenia until he was in his early twenties. Instead of feeling some sort of relief that they finally had a label and a way of understanding Michael's behavior, his family felt tremendous guilt:

I have an image of my mother staring at the dark world of our kitchen table, saying, I don't know what we're going to do, saying this with no inflection, like the undead talking in a late-night movie. It was February. There was cold, sharp light in the room. A pitiful midday sun made geometric shapes in the color of stained teeth on the kitchen floor. My mother, after hearing the news, barely spoke for days. My father sat in his favorite chair, the TV droning on in front of him, but he wasn't even looking at the screen; he seemed to be looking at the blank wall behind it. It seemed so obvious once I knew—not that he was schizophrenic but that he was definitely severely mentally ill. I had known many "burnouts" or "heads" at school of one degree or another—I was, in a way, one myself—but no one came close to my brother's strangeness. . . .

I knew he was sick. And, most important, I realized for the first time it wasn't his fault. I had blamed Michael, hated Michael, for his behavior. So finding out suddenly, nearly a decade after his first psychotic break, that none of the behavior was entirely his fault, was nearly unbearable, making us all—particularly my father and I—feel immoral and ruthless to such a degree that shame is not a strong enough word. (pp. 92–93)

Unfortunately, Michael's diagnosis did not bring effective treatment. His parents spent all the money they had on doctors and occasional stints in institutions. Michael's symptoms did not respond to the antipsychotic drugs very well, at least when he actually took the medications. He came to believe they were part of a conspiracy to control his mind and usually refused them. He was increasingly violent toward his family members, so, when he lived at home, which was most of the time, his parents and brothers spent much of their time avoiding him. They locked their bedroom doors at night to protect themselves. One day, Michael went after his father and youngest brother with a bat, believing they had been talking about him and deserved to die. They tried everything they could to have him institutionalized but were constantly told that this was not possible unless they could prove he was a danger to himself or others. The stories of Michael's violent behaviors toward the family apparently weren't convincing enough.

Mental-health professionals are regularly asked to help families, such as the Bottoms family, battle the laws guiding the treatment of people with psychological disorders. Following are two other scenarios that raise legal and ethical issues for mental-health practitioners:

A 60-year-old man wanders the streets as the temperature plummets below freezing, talking to imaginary creatures and stripping off his warm clothes. When asked if he wants shelter or food, he curses and turns away. The police apprehend the man and take him to court. A psychologist is asked to determine whether the man is such a danger to himself that he should be held against his will.

A middle-aged man kills three people in a shooting rampage. When arrested, he says that he was obeying voices telling him to shoot "sinners." A psychiatrist is asked to evaluate whether this man is telling the truth.

Situations such as these raise fundamental questions about society's values: Do people have the right to conduct their lives as they wish, even if their behaviors pose a risk to their own health and well-being? Under what conditions should people be absolved of responsibility for behaviors that harm others? Should the diagnosis of a psychological disorder entitle a person to special services and protection against discrimination? Questions such as these are concerned with the values of personal freedom, society's obligation to protect its vulnerable members, and society's right to protect itself against the actions of individuals.

Mental-health professionals are increasingly being brought into such situations to help individuals and society make judgments about the appropriate actions to take. It would be nice if mental-health professionals could simply turn to the research literature for objective information that indicates which judgment is best in each situation. Frequently, however, there is no research literature relevant to a situation, or the research holds conflicting messages. Moreover, at its best, research can tell us only what is *likely* to be right or true in a given situation but not what is *definitely* right or true. That is, the predictions we can make from the research literature are *probabilistic*—they tell us how likely people are to do something but not that they definitely will do something. Also, we are limited in our ability to generalize from the research literature to individual cases. Finally, because most of such judgments involve conflicts between different values, ethical principles, or moral principles, research and clinical judgment can tell us only so much about the right resolution.

This chapter is about the interface between psychology and the law. Because the law has tended to regard at least some psychological disorders as medical illnesses or diseases, the phrase **mentally ill** is used throughout this chapter. Most previous chapters did not use this term because it connotes a medical view of psychological problems, which is only one of several ways to view psychological problems. We will see, however, that the law is inconsistent in its view of psychological disorders, and this view has changed quite frequently.

We first examine how the law regards people charged with crimes who might have psychological disorders. Mental-health professionals help legal authorities decide when people's psychological disorders make them incompetent to stand trial and when they should be considered not guilty by reason of insanity. Then, we discuss when a person can be held in a mental-health facility against his or her will. Over the past 50 years, the criteria for commitment and the rights of committed patients have changed greatly. Finally, we discuss certain duties that courts and professional organizations have argued clinicians have toward clients and society: the duty to provide competent treatment, the duty to avoid multiple relationships with clients, the duty to maintain clients' confidentiality, the duty to protect persons their clients are threatening to harm, the duty to report suspected child or elder abuse, and the duty to provide ethical service to diverse populations.

JUDGMENTS ABOUT PEOPLE ACCUSED OF CRIMES

Two critical judgments that mental-health professionals are asked to make about people accused of crimes are *whether they are competent to stand trial* and *whether they were sane at the time the crimes were committed*. Mental-health professionals actually do not make the final judgments about the dispensation of people accused of crimes. Instead, they only make recommendations to the court. Their recommendations can be influential in judges' or juries' decisions, however.

Competence to Stand Trial

One of the fundamental principles of law is that, in order to stand trial, accused individuals must have a rational understanding of the charges against them and the proceedings of the trial and must be able to participate in their defense. People who do not have an understanding of what is happening to them in a courtroom and who cannot participate in their own defense are said to be **incompetent to stand trial.** Incompetence may involve impairment in several capacities, including the capacity to understand information, to think rationally about alternative courses of action, to make good choices, and to appreciate one's situation as a criminal defendant (Hoge, Bonnie, et al., 1997).

Impaired competence may be a common problem: Defense attorneys suspect impaired competence in their clients in up to 10 percent of cases. Although only a handful of these clients are referred for formal evaluation, between 24,000 and 60,000 evaluations of criminal defendants for competence to stand trial are performed every year in the United States (MacArthur Research Network on Mental Health and the Law, 1998). Competence judgments are, thus, some of the most frequent types of judgments that mental-health professionals are asked to make for courts. Judges appear to value the testimony of mental-health experts concerning defendants' competence and rarely rule against the experts' recommendations.

As a result, the consequences of competence judgments for defendants are great. If they are judged incompetent, trials are postponed as long as there is reason to believe that they will become competent in the foreseeable future, and defendants

Competence to stand trial is one of the most common judgments psychologists are asked to help courts make.

may be forced to receive treatment. Incompetent defendants who are wrongly judged competent may not contribute adequately to their defense and may be wrongly convicted and incarcerated. Defendants who are suspected to be incompetent are described by their attorneys as much less helpful in establishing the facts of their case and much less actively involved in making decisions about their defense (MacArthur Research Network on Mental Health and the Law, 1998).

Not surprisingly, defendants with long histories of psychiatric problems, particularly schizophrenia or psychotic symptoms, are more likely to be referred for competence evaluations (Nicholson & Kugler, 1991). Defendants referred for competence evaluations also tend to have lower levels of education and to be poor, unemployed, and unmarried. Over half have been accused of violent offenses. Women are more likely than men, and members of ethnic minority groups are more likely than European Americans, to be judged incompetent (Nicholson & Kugler, 1991). This may be because women and ethnic minority persons who commit crimes are more likely to have severe psychological problems that make them incompetent to stand trial. On the other hand, evaluators may have lower thresholds for judging women and ethnic minorities incompetent. In addition, when evaluators do not speak the same languages as ethnic minority defendants, the defendants may not understand the evaluators' questions, and evaluators may not understand the defendants' answers. In these instances, evaluators may tend to interpret this lack of communication as an indication of defendants' incompetence to stand trial.

Psychologists have developed tests of cognitive abilities important to following legal proceedings, and people who perform poorly on these tests are more likely to be judged incompetent to stand trial. These tests have not been widely used, however. Instead, judgments of incompetence are usually given to people who have existing diagnoses of psychotic disorders or who have symptoms indicating severe psychopathology, such as gross disorientation, delusions, hallucinations, and thought disorder (Cochrane, et al., 2001).

Insanity Defense

Insanity is a legal term, rather than a psychological or medical term, and it has been defined in various ways. All of these definitions reflect the fundamental doctrine that people cannot be held fully responsible for their acts if they were so mentally incapacitated at the time of the acts that they could not conform to the rules of society. Note that people do not have to be chronically insane for the insanity defense to apply. They only have to be judged to have been insane at the time they committed the acts. This judgment can be difficult to make.

The **insanity defense** has been one of the most controversial applications of psychology to the law. The lay public often thinks of the insanity defense as a means by which guilty people "get off." When the insanity defense has been used successfully in celebrated cases, as when John Hinckley successfully used this defense after shooting for-

John Hinckley was judged not guilty by reason of insanity for shooting President Ronald Reagan. This judgment inspired a reappraisal of the insanity defense.

mer President Ronald Reagan and the president's press secretary, Jim Brady, in 1981, there have been calls to eliminate the insanity defense altogether (Steadman et al., 1993). Indeed, these celebrated cases have often led to reappraisals of the insanity defense and redefinitions of the legal meaning of insanity.

The insanity defense is used much less often than the public tends to think. As is shown in Table 18.1, fewer than 1 in 100 defendants in felony cases file an insanity plea, and of these, only 26 percent result in acquittal (Silver, Cirincione, & Steadman, 1994). Thus, only about 1 in 400 people charged with a felony are judged not guilty by reason of insanity. About two-thirds of these people have diagnoses of schizophrenia, and most have histories of psychiatric hospitalizations and previous crimes (McGreevy, Steadman, & Callahan, 1991).

Almost 90 percent of the people who are acquitted after pleading the insanity defense are male, and two-thirds of them are White (McGreevy et al., 1991; Warren et al., 2004). The reasons men and Whites are more likely to plead the insanity defense successfully are unclear but may have to do with their greater access to competent attorneys who can effectively argue the insanity defense. In the past decade or two, as society has become more aware of the plight of abused and battered women, increasing numbers of women are pleading the insanity defense after injuring or killing partners who had been abusing them for years.

TABLE 18.1   Comparison of Public Perceptions of the Insanity Defense with Actual Use and Results

The public perceives that many more accused persons use the insanity defense successfully than is actually the case.

	Public Perception	Reality
Percentage of felony indictments for which an insanity plea is made	37%	1%
Percentage of insanity pleas resulting in "not guilty by reason of insanity"	44%	26%
Percentage of persons "not guilty by reason of insanity" sent to mental hospitals	51%	85%
Percentage of persons "not guilty by reason of insanity" set free	26%	15%
Conditional release		12%
Outpatient treatment		3%
Unconditional release		1%
Length of confinement of persons "not guilty by reason of insanity" (in months)		
All crimes	21.8	32.5
Murder		76.4

Source: Data from Silver et al., 1994.

Andrea Yates argued that severe psychosis and postpartum depression led her to drown her five young children in 2001. Her argument was denied and she was convicted of murder.

Christopher Pittman argued that Zoloft led him to kill his grandparents, but a jury rejected this defense.

One case is that of Lorena and John Bobbitt. According to Lorena Bobbitt, her husband, John, had sexually and emotionally abused her for years. One night in 1994, John returned home drunk and raped Lorena. In what her attorneys described as a brief psychotic episode, Lorena cut off her husband's penis and threw it away. She was acquitted of charges of malicious injury by reason of temporary insanity. She was referred to a mental institution for further evaluation and released a few months later.

Another controversial application of the insanity defense by women has been its use by women who have committed infanticide, supposedly as the result of psychotic postpartum depression (Williamson, 1993). Severe postpartum depression with psychotic symptoms is very rare, and violence by these women against their newborns is even more rare (Nolen-Hoeksema, 1990). When such violence does occur, some courts have accepted that the mothers' behaviors were the result of the postpartum psychosis and have judged these women not guilty by reason of insanity. Often, however, the public cannot accept any excuse for a woman killing her own children and rejects the insanity defense in cases of postpartum depression.

Most recently, a version of the insanity defense referred to as the "Zoloft defense" has been used to argue that the antidepressant Zoloft can cause people to suddenly commit violent acts that are out of their control. In one case, 12-year-old Christopher Pittman shot both his grandparents, then burned their house down. His defense was that Zoloft had caused him to become violent and lose control. In February 2005, however, jurors rejected this defense and convicted Pittman of the crime.

Even when a defendant is judged not guilty by reason of insanity, it usually is not the case that he or she "gets off." Of those people acquitted because of insanity, about 85 percent are sent to mental hospitals, and all but 1 percent are put under some type of supervision and care. Of those who are sent to mental hospitals, the average length of stay (or incarceration) in the hospital is almost three years when all types of crimes are considered, and over six years for those who had been accused (and acquitted by reason of insanity) of murder. John Hinckley, who shot former President Reagan in 1981, has been incarcerated in St. Elizabeth's Hospital ever since he was found not guilty by reason of insanity. Some states require that people judged not guilty by reason of insanity cannot be incarcerated in mental institutions for longer than they would have served prison sentences if they had been judged guilty of their crimes, but not all states have this rule. In short, there is little evidence that the insanity defense is widely used to help people avoid incarceration for their crimes.

TABLE 18.2	Concept Overview

Insanity Defense Rules

Five rules have been used for determining whether an individual was insane at the time he or she committed the crime and therefore whether he or she should not be held responsible for the crime.

Rule	The Individual Is Not Held Responsible for a Crime If . . .
M'Naghten rule	At the time of the crime, the individual was so affected by a disease of the mind that he or she did not know the nature of the act he or she was committing or did not know it was wrong.
Irresistible impulse rule	At the time of the crime, the individual was driven by an irresistible impulse to perform the act or had a diminished capacity to resist performing the act.
Durham rule	The crime was a product of a mental disease or defect.
ALI rule	At the time of the crime, as a result of a mental disease or defect, the person lacked substantial capacity either to appreciate the criminality (wrongfulness) of the act or to conform his or her conduct to the law.
American Psychiatric Association definition of insanity	At the time of the crime, as a result of mental disease or mental retardation, the person was unable to appreciate the wrongfulness of his or her conduct.

Insanity Defense Rules

Five rules have been used in modern history to evaluate defendants' pleas that they should be judged not guilty by reason of insanity (see the Concept Overview in Table 18.2).

M'Naghten Rule The first insanity defense rule is the **M'Naghten rule.** Daniel M'Naghten lived in England in the mid-1800s and had the delusion that the English Tory party was persecuting him. He set out to kill the Tory prime minister but mistakenly shot the prime minister's secretary. At his trial, the jury judged M'Naghten not guilty by reason of insanity. There was a public outcry at this verdict, leading the House of Lords to formalize a rule for when a person could be absolved from responsibility for his or her acts because of a mental disorder. This rule became known as the M'Naghten rule, and it still is used in many jurisdictions today:

> To establish a defense on the ground of insanity, it must be clearly proved that at the time of committing the act, the party accused was labouring under such a defect of reason, from disease of the mind, as not to know the nature and quality of the act he was doing, or if he did know it, that he did not know he was doing what was wrong.

The M'Naghten rule reflects the doctrine that a person must have a "guilty mind"—in Latin, *mens rea*—or the intention to commit the illegal act in order to be held responsible for the act.

It might seem that applying the M'Naghten rule is a straightforward matter—one simply determines whether a person suffers from a disease of the mind and whether during the crime he or she understood that his or her actions were wrong. Unfortunately, it is not that simple. A major problem in applying the M'Naghten rule emerges in determining what is meant by a "disease of the mind." The law has been unclear and inconsistent in what disorders it recognizes as diseases of the mind. The most consistently recognized diseases are psychoses. It has been relatively easy for the courts and the public to accept that someone experiencing severe delusions and hallucinations is suffering from a disease and, at times, may not know right from wrong. However, defendants have argued that several other disorders, such as alcoholism, severe depression, and posttraumatic stress disorder, are diseases of the mind that impair judgments of right and wrong. It is much more difficult for courts, the lay public, and mental-health professionals to agree on these claims.

A second major problem is that the M'Naghten rule requires that a person did not know right from wrong at the time of the crime in order to be judged not guilty by reason of insanity. This is a difficult judgment to make, because it is a retrospective judgment. Even when everyone agrees that a defendant suffers from a severe psychological disorder, this does not necessarily mean that, at the time of the crime, he or she was incapable of knowing "right from wrong" as the M'Naghten rule requires. For example, serial killer Jeffrey Dahmer, who tortured, killed, dismembered, and ate his victims, clearly seemed to have a psychological disorder. Nevertheless, the jury denied his insanity defense in part because he took great care to hide his crimes from the local police, suggesting that he knew what he was doing was wrong or against the law.

Irresistible Impulse Rule The second rule used to judge the acceptability of the insanity defense is the **irresistible impulse rule.** First applied in Ohio in 1934, the irresistible impulse rule broadened the conditions under which a criminal act could be considered the product of insanity to include "acts of passion." Even if a person knew the act he or she was committing was wrong, if the person was driven by an irresistible impulse to perform the act or had a diminished capacity to resist performing the act, then he or she might be absolved of responsibility for performing the act.

One of the most celebrated applications of the notion of diminished capacity was the "Twinkie Defense" of Dan White. In 1979, Dan White assassinated San Francisco mayor George Moscone and a city council member named Harvey Milk. White argued that he had had diminished capacity to resist the impulse to shoot Moscone and Milk due to the psychological effects of extreme stress and the consumption of large amounts of junk food. Using a particularly broad definition of diminished capacity in force in California law at the time, the jury convicted White of manslaughter instead of first-degree murder. Variations of the Twinkie Defense have rarely been attempted since White's trial.

Durham Rule In 1954, Judge David Bazelon further broadened the criteria for the legal definition of insanity in his ruling on the case *Durham v. United States*, which produced the third rule for defining insanity, the **Durham rule.** According to the Durham rule, the insanity defense could be accepted for any crimes that were the "product of mental disease or mental defect." This rule allowed defendants to claim that the presence of any disorder recognized by mental-health professionals could be the "cause" of their crimes. The Durham rule did not require that defendants show they were incapacitated by their disorders or that they

did not understand that their acts were illegal. The Durham rule had been dropped by almost all jurisdictions by the early 1970s.

ALI Rule The fourth rule for deciding the acceptability of the insanity defense comes from the American Law Institute's Model Penal Code. Motivated by dissatisfaction with the existing legal definitions of insanity, a group of lawyers, judges, and scholars associated with the American Law Institute (ALI) worked to formulate a better definition, which eventually resulted in what is known as the **ALI rule:**

> A person is not responsible for criminal conduct if at the time of such conduct as the result of mental disease or defect he lacks substantial capacity either to appreciate the criminality (wrongfulness) of his conduct or to conform his conduct to the requirements of the law.

This rule is broader than the M'Naghten rule, because it requires only that the defendant have a lack of appreciation of the criminality of his or her act, not an absence of understanding of the criminality of the act. The defendant's inability to conform his or her conduct to the requirements of the law can come from the emotional symptoms of a psychological disorder, as well as from the cognitive deficits caused by the disorder. This expanded understanding incorporates some of the crimes recognized by the irresistible impulse rule. The ALI rule is clearly more restrictive than the Durham rule, however, because it requires some lack of appreciation of the criminality of one's act, rather than merely the presence of a mental disorder. The ALI rule further restricts the types of mental disorders that can contribute to a successful insanity defense:

> As used in this Article, the term "mental disease or defect" does not include an abnormality manifested only by repeated criminal or otherwise antisocial conduct.

This further restriction prohibits defense attorneys from arguing that a defendant's long history of antisocial acts is itself evidence of the presence of a mental disease or defect. Further, in 1977, in the case *Barrett v. United States*, it was ruled that "temporary insanity created by voluntary use of alcohol or drugs" also does not qualify a defendant for acquittal by reason of insanity.

The ALI rule was widely adopted in the United States, including in the jurisdiction in which John Hinckley was tried for shooting Ronald Reagan. Hinckley had a long-standing diagnosis of schizophrenia and an obsession with actress Jodi Foster. Letters he wrote to Foster before shooting Reagan indicated that he committed the act under the delusion that this would impress Foster and cause her to return his love. Hinckley's defense attorneys successfully argued that he had had a diminished capacity to understand the wrongfulness of shooting Reagan or to conform his behaviors to the requirements of the law. The public outcry over the judgment that Hinckley was "not guilty by reason of insanity" initiated another reappraisal of the legal definition of insanity and the use of the insanity defense (Steadman et al., 1993).

American Pyschiatric Association Definition The reappraisal led to the fifth legal redefinition of insanity in the **Insanity Defense Reform Act,** put into law by Congress in 1984. The Insanity Defense Reform Act adopted the **American Psychiatric Association definition of insanity** in 1983. This definition dropped the provision in the ALI rule that absolved people of responsibility for criminal acts if they were unable to conform their behavior to the law and retained the wrongfulness criterion initially proposed in the M'Naghten rule. This definition reads as follows:

> A person charged with a criminal offense should be found not guilty by reason of insanity if it is shown that, as a result of mental disease or mental retardation, he was unable to appreciate the wrongfulness of his conduct at the time of his offense.

This definition now applies in all cases tried in federal courts and in about half the states. Also, as a result of the Hinckley verdict, most states now require that a defendant pleading not guilty by reason of insanity prove he or she was insane at the time of the crime. Previously, the burden of proof had been on the prosecution to prove that the defendant was sane at the time the crime was committed (Steadman et al., 1993).

Problems with the Insanity Defense

Mental-health professionals tend to be strong proponents of the notion that psychological disorders can impair people's ability to follow the law. They believe that this should be taken into consideration when judging an individual's responsibility for his or her actions. Cases that are built on the insanity defense often use mental-health professionals to provide expert opinions in such cases. Despite their expertise, mental-health professionals often disagree about the nature and causes of psychological disorders, the presence or absence of psycho-

logical disorders, and the evaluation of defendants' states of mind at the time crimes were committed (Warren et al., 2004). Usually, lawyers on both sides of the case find mental-health professionals who support their point of view, and the two professionals are inevitably in disagreement with each other. This disagreement leads to confusion for judges, juries, and the public.

Mental-health professionals have also raised concerns about the rules used to determine the acceptability of the insanity defense. Behind these rules is the assumption that most people, including most people with psychological disorders, have free will and can usually choose how they will act in any given situation. Many current models of both normal and abnormal behavior suggest that people are not that much in control of their behaviors. Because of biological predispositions, early life experiences, or disordered patterns of thinking, people often act in irrational and perhaps uncontrolled ways. This view makes it more difficult to say when a person should or should not be held responsible for his or her behaviors.

Guilty but Mentally Ill

In a sixth, and most recent, reform of the insanity defense, some states have adopted as an alternative to the verdict "not guilty by reason of insanity" the verdict **guilty but mentally ill (GBMI).** Defendants convicted as guilty but mentally ill are incarcerated for the normal terms designated for their crimes, with the expectation that they will also receive treatment for their mental illness. Proponents of the GBMI verdict argue that it recognizes the mental illness of defendants while still holding them responsible for their actions. Critics argue that the GBMI verdict is essentially a guilty verdict and a means of eliminating the insanity defense (Tanay, 1992). In addition, juries may believe they are ensuring that a person gets treatment by judging him or her guilty but mentally ill, but there are no guarantees that a person convicted under GBMI will receive treatment. In most states, it is left up to legal authorities to decide whether to incarcerate these people in mental institutions or prisons and, if they are sent to prisons, whether to provide them with treatment for their mental illness.

SUMMING UP

- One judgment mental-health professionals are asked to make is about an accused person's competence to stand trial.

- Another judgment is whether the accused person was "sane" at the time he or she committed a crime.

- The insanity defense has undergone many changes over recent history, often in response to its use in high-profile crimes.

- Five rules have been used to evaluate the acceptability of a plea of not guilty by reason of insanity: the M'Naghten rule, the irresistible impulse rule, the Durham rule, the ALI rule, and the American Psychiatric Association definition of insanity.

- All of these rules require that a defendant be diagnosed with a "mental disease" but do not clearly define the term *mental disease.*

- Most of these rules also require that the defendant is unable to understand the criminality of his or her actions or conform his or her actions to the law in order to be judged not guilty by reason of insanity.

- Many states have introduced the alternative verdict of guilty but mentally ill.

INVOLUNTARY COMMITMENT AND CIVIL RIGHTS

In the best circumstances, people who need treatment for psychological disorders seek it themselves. They work with mental-health professionals to find the medication and/or psychotherapy that helps reduce their symptoms and keeps their disorder under control; however, many people who have serious psychological problems do not recognize their need for treatment or may refuse treatment for a variety of reasons. For example, a woman with persecutory delusions and hallucinations may fear treatment, believing that doctors are part of the conspiracy against her. A man in a manic episode may like many of the symptoms he is experiencing—the high energy, inflated self-esteem, and grandiose thoughts—and not want to take medication that would reduce these symptoms. A teenager who is abusing illegal drugs may believe that it is her right to do so and that there is nothing wrong with her. Can these people be forced into mental institutions and to undergo treatment against their will? These are the questions we address in this section.

Civil Commitment

Prior to 1969, in the United States the **need for treatment** was sufficient cause to hospitalize people against their will and force them to undergo treatment. Such involuntary hospitalization is called **civil commitment.** All that was needed for civil commitment was a certificate signed by two physicians, stating that a person needed treatment and was not agreeing to it voluntarily. The person could then be confined, often indefinitely, without the advice of an attorney, a hearing, or an appeal. In Great Britain and several other countries around the world, need for treatment still is one criterion for civil commitment.

Since 1969, however, the need for treatment alone is no longer sufficient legal cause for civil commitment in most states in the United States. This change came about as part of the patients' rights movement of the 1960s, in which concerns were raised about the personal freedom and civil liberties of mental patients (see Chapter 5). Opponents of the civil commitment process argued that it allowed people to be incarcerated simply for having "alternative lifestyles" or different political or moral values (Szasz, 1963a, 1977). Certainly, there were many cases in the former Soviet Union and other countries of political dissidents being labeled mentally ill and in need of treatment and then being incarcerated in prisons for years. In the United States, there also were disturbing cases of the misuse of civil commitment proceedings. For example, Mrs. E. P. W. Packard was one of several women involuntarily hospitalized by their husbands for holding "unacceptable" and "sick" political or moral views (Weiner & Wettstein, 1993). Mrs. Packard remained hospitalized for three years until she won her release and then began crusading against civil commitment.

Criteria for Involuntary Commitment

The three criteria currently used in the United States and in many other countries to commit someone to a psychiatric facility against his or her will are (1) grave disability, (2) dangerousness to self, and (3) dangerousness to others (see the Concept Overview in Table 18.3 on page 686). In addition, most states require that the danger people pose to themselves or to others be *imminent*—if they are not immediately incarcerated, they or someone else will likely be harmed in the very near future. Finally, all persons committed to psychiatric facilities must be diagnosed with mental disorders.

Grave Disability The **grave disability** criterion requires that people be so incapacitated by mental disorders that they cannot care for their basic needs for food, clothing, and shelter. This criterion is, in theory, much more severe than the need for treatment criterion, because it requires that the person's survival be in immediate danger due to illness. At least 30 states in the United States use the grave disability criterion in civil commitment hearings, and, in those states, about 80 percent of persons involuntarily committed are committed on the basis of grave disability (Turkheimer & Parry, 1992).

TABLE 18.3	Concept Overview

Criteria for Involuntary Commitment

Three criteria are currently used to determine if an individual can be involuntarily committed to a mental-health facility.

Criteria	Description
Grave disability	The individual is so incapacitated by a mental disorder that he or she cannot care for the basic needs for food, clothing, and shelter.
Dangerousness to self	The individual is an imminent danger to him- or herself.
Dangerousness to others	The individual presents an imminent danger to others.

One might think that the grave disability criterion could be used to hospitalize homeless people on the streets who appear to be psychotic and do not seem able to take care of their basic needs. This is what former New York mayor Ed Koch thought in the bitter winter of 1988, when he invoked the legal principle of *parens patriae* (sovereign as parent) to have mentally ill homeless people picked up from the streets of New York and taken to mental-health facilities. Mayor Koch argued that it was the city's duty to protect these mentally ill homeless people from the ravages of the winter weather, because they were unable to do it for themselves. One of the homeless people who was involuntarily taken to a psychiatric facility was 40-year-old Joyce Brown, who was subsequently given a diagnosis of paranoid schizophrenia. Brown had been living on the streets on and off for years, despite efforts by her family to get her into psychiatric treatment. She refused treatment of any kind. When Brown was involuntarily hospitalized in the winter of 1988 as part of Koch's campaign, she and the American Civil Liberties Union contested her commitment and won her release on the grounds that the city had no right to incarcerate Brown if she had no intention of being treated.

One of the legal precedents of Joyce Brown's release was *Donaldson v. O'Connor* (1975). Kenneth Donaldson had been committed to a Florida state hospital for 14 years. Donaldson's father had originally had him committed, believing that Donaldson was delusional and therefore a danger to himself. At the time, Florida law allowed people to be committed if their mental disorders might impair their ability to manage their finances or to protect themselves against being cheated by others. Throughout his hospitalization, Donaldson refused medication, because it violated his Christian Science beliefs. The superintendent, O'Connor, considered this refusal

to be a symptom of Donaldson's mental disorder. Even though Donaldson had been caring for himself adequately before his hospitalization and had friends who offered to help care for him if he was released from the hospital, O'Connor and the hospital continually refused Donaldson's requests for release. Donaldson sued, on the grounds that he had received only custodial care during his hospitalization and that he was not a danger to himself. He requested to be released to the care of his friends and family. The Supreme Court agreed and ruled that "a State cannot constitutionally confine . . . a nondangerous individual, who is capable of surviving safely in freedom by himself or with the help of willing and responsible family and friends."

In practice, however, most persons involuntarily committed because of grave disability do not have the American Civil Liberties Union championing their rights or the personal wherewithal to file suit. Often, these are people with few financial resources, friends, or families who have long histories of serious mental illness. The elderly mentally ill are especially likely to be committed because of grave disability (Turkheimer & Parry, 1992). Often, these people are committed to psychiatric facilities because there are not enough less restrictive treatment facilities available in their communities, and their families do not have the ability to care for them.

Dangerousness to Self The criterion of **dangerousness to self** is most often invoked when it is believed that a person is imminently suicidal. In such cases, the person is often held in an inpatient psychiatric facility for a few days while undergoing further evaluation and possibly treatment. Most states allow short-term commitments without a court hearing in emergency situations such as this. All that is needed is a certification by the attending mental-health professionals that the individual is in imminent danger to him- or herself. If the mental-health professionals judge that the person needs further treatment but the person does not voluntarily agree to treatment, they can go to court to ask that the person be committed for a longer period of time.

Dangerousness to Others The third criterion under which people can be committed involuntarily is **dangerousness to others**. If a mentally ill person is going to hurt another if set free, society has claimed the right to protect itself against this person by holding the person against his or her will. This action may seem completely justified, yet the appropriateness of this criterion rests on predictions of who will be dangerous and who will not. Some research has suggested that predictions of dangerousness tend to be wrong more often than they are correct (McNiel & Binder, 1991; Monahan & Walker, 1990). As a tragic example, serial killer Jeffrey Dahmer was arrested and jailed in 1988 for sexually molesting a 13-year-old boy. He was released in 1990 with only a limited follow-up by mental-health professionals, despite concerns raised by his family about his mental health. Dahmer proceeded to drug, molest, kill, and dismember at least 17 additional victims over the next few years before being apprehended.

Several states have adopted special laws concerning sex offenders, such as Dahmer (Winick, 2003). Under these laws, repeat offenders can be labeled "sexually violent predators" and can be kept in confinement even after their prison terms have been served. In 1997, the U.S. Supreme Court upheld the Kansas version of the sexual predator law, finding that the defendant in this case, who had committed sexual crimes against children, had a sufficient mental condition to authorize involuntary psychiatric hospitalization. All 50 states have some form of registration and community notification laws, in which sex offenders must register with the police and the communities where they live must be notified of their existence. Thus, our laws and society see sex offenders as especially dangerous and impose more constraints on their freedoms.

Violence Among People with Mental Disorders

Are people with psychological disorders more likely to be violent than people without disorders? Research suggests that there is some increased risk, particularly among people with substance abuse disorders, personality disorders, or schizophrenic disorders (Arseneault et al., 2000; Banks et al., 2004; Monahan & Steadman, 2001).

One ethical question facing society is whether it has an obligation to provide mental-health services to people who cannot take care of themselves.

Serial killer Jeffrey Dahmer clearly had psychological problems, but mental-health professionals did not foresee the terrible crimes he would commit.

In one major study, researchers followed 1,136 men and women with mental disorders for one year after being discharged from a psychiatric hospital, monitoring their own self-reports of violent behaviors, reports in police and hospital records, and reports by other informants, such as family members (Steadman et al., 1998). Their records of violent activity were compared with those of 519 people living in the same neighborhoods in which the former patients resided after their hospital discharge. The community group was interviewed only once, at the end of the year-long study, and asked about violent behavior in the past 10 weeks. Serious violent acts were defined as battery that resulted in physical injury, sexual assaults, assaultive acts that involved the use of a weapon, and threats made with a weapon in hand.

The likelihood that the former patients would commit a violent act was strongly related to their diagnosis and whether they had a substance abuse problem. About 18 percent of the former patients who had a diagnosis of a major mental disorder (e.g., schizophrenia, major depression, other psychotic disorder) *without* a history of substance abuse committed a serious violent act in the year following discharge, compared with 31 percent of those with a major mental disorder *and* a history of substance abuse, and 43 percent of those with a diagnosis of an "other" mental disorder (i.e., a personality or adjustment disorder) *and* a co-occurring substance abuse problem. The researchers were somewhat surprised to find that the former patients were most likely to commit a violent act in the first couple of months following their discharge and were less likely to do so as the year wore on (see Figure 18.1). They suggested that patients may still be in crisis shortly after their hospitalization, and it takes some months for social support systems and treatment to begin to affect their behavior.

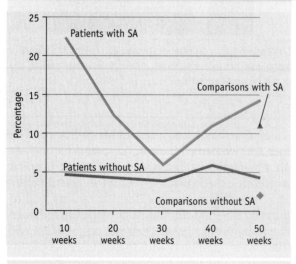

FIGURE 18.1   **Likelihood of Violence.** The lines represent the percentage of patients with or without a substance abuse problem, and the points represent community comparisons with or without a substance abuse problem, who committed a violent act in the previous 10 weeks, in this study.

Source: Steadman et al., 1998.

The rate of violence in the community sample was also strongly related to whether individuals had a history of substance abuse: 11 percent of those with a substance abuse problem committed a violent act during the year of the study, compared with 3 percent of those with no substance abuse problem. Although the overall rate of violence in the community sample was lower than in the patient sample, this difference was statistically significant only when the researchers considered violence by the former patients shortly after their discharge. At the end of that year, the former patients were no more likely to commit a violent act than the community comparison group.

The targets of violence by both the former patients and the community comparisons were most often family members, followed by friends and acquaintances. The former patients were actually somewhat less likely than the comparison group to commit a violent act against a stranger (13.8 percent of the acts committed by former patients versus 22.2 percent of acts committed by the comparison group).

The rates of violence committed in this study may seem high, for both the patient group and the comparison group. The patient group probably represented people with more serious psychological disorders, who were facing acute crises in their lives. The comparison group was largely from low socioeconomic backgrounds and in impoverished neighborhoods. These contextual factors may account for the relatively high rate of violence.

The researchers who conducted this study emphasized that their data show how inappropriate it is to consider "former mental patients" a homogeneous group of people who are all prone to violence. The presence of substance abuse problems was a strong predictor of violent behavior both in this group and in a group of people who had not been mental patients. Moreover, the majority of people with serious mental disorders did not commit any violent acts in the year after their discharge, particularly against random strangers, as media depictions of "former mental patients" often suggest.

Other research has suggested that violence by mentally ill women tends to be *underestimated* by clinicians (Coontz, Lidz, & Mulvey, 1994; Robbins, Monahan, & Silver, 2003). Clinicians do not expect mentally ill women to be violent to the same degree that they expect mentally ill men to be violent. As a result, they do not probe mentally ill women for evidence regarding violence as much as they probe mentally ill men. In reality, however, mentally ill women are as likely to commit violent acts toward others as are mentally ill men (Robbins et al., 2003).

The victims of mentally ill women's violent acts are most likely to be family members; mentally ill men also are most often violent toward family members, but they commit violent acts against strangers more often than do mentally ill women (Newhill, Mulvey, & Lidz, 1995). Mentally ill men who commit violence are more likely to have been drinking before the violence, and to be arrested, compared with mentally ill women who commit violence (Robbins et al., 2003).

Racial stereotypes lead people to expect that mentally ill persons from ethnic minority groups are more likely to commit acts of violence than are White mentally ill people. There are, however, no differences among the ethnic groups in rates of violence among mentally ill people (Mulvey, 1995). Thus, new research is clarifying the true rates of violence among the mentally ill and some predictors of violence in this group.

Prevalence of Involuntary Commitment

How often are people involuntarily committed to a psychiatric facility? There are sparse data to answer this question, but the available studies suggest that about one in four admissions to inpatient psychiatric facilities in the United States are involuntary, and about 15 to 20 percent of inpatient admissions in European countries are involuntary (Monahan et al., 1999). Admissions to state and county mental hospitals are much more likely to be involuntary than admissions to other types of hospitals (see Table 18.4).

These numbers probably underestimate the number of people coerced into mental-health care, because parents and legal guardians often "volunteer" a protesting child or an incompetent adult for admission (Monahan et al., 1999). One study found that nearly half of the adults admitted voluntarily to inpatient psychiatric facilities said that someone other than they had initiated their going to the hospital, and 14 percent of the patients were under the custody of someone else at the time they were admitted (Hoge, Poythress et al., 1997; see also Segal, Laurie, & Fanskoviak, 2004). Nearly 40 percent of the legally voluntary patients believed they would have been involuntarily committed if they had not "volunteered" to be hospitalized. Some of the patients felt they had been coerced by their own therapists, who did not include them in the admissions process (Monahan et al., 1999):

> I talked to him this morning. I said, "You . . . didn't even listen to me. You . . . call yourself a counselor. . . . Why did you decide to do this instead of . . . try to listen to me and under-

stand . . . what I was going through." And he said, "Well, it doesn't matter, you know, you're going anyway." . . . He didn't listen to what I had to say. . . . He didn't listen to the situation. . . . He had decided before he ever got to the house . . . that I was coming up here. Either I come freely or the officers would have to subdue me and bring me in.

Patients involuntarily committed often may need treatment that they cannot acknowledge they need. About half of patients who feel coerced into treatment eventually acknowledge that they needed treatment, but about half continue to believe they did not need treatment (Gardner et al., 1999).

Procedurally, most states mandate that persons being considered for involuntary commitment have the right to a public hearing, the right to counsel, the right to call and confront witnesses, the right to appeal decisions, and the right to be placed in the least restrictive treatment setting. In practice, however, attorneys and judges typically defer to the judgment of mental-health professionals about a person's mental illness and meeting of the criteria for commitment (Turkheimer & Parry, 1992). Thus, even the attorneys who are supposed to be upholding an individual's rights tend to acquiesce to the judgment of mental-health professionals, particularly if the attorney is court-appointed, as is often the case. Again, it appears that many attorneys who

---

TABLE 18.4 Frequency of Involuntary Admissions to Psychiatric Facilities

These data reveal the percentage of all admissions to various types of psychiatric facilities that involve involuntary commitments. Data are from the United States in 1986.

Type of Facility	Percentage of All Admissions That Are Involuntary
State and county hospitals	61.6
Multiservice mental-health organizations (e.g., community mental-health centers)	46.1
Private psychiatric hospitals	15.6
Nonfederal general hospitals	14.8
Veterans Administration hospitals	5.6

Source: Monahan et al., 2001.

are going along with the commitment of their clients are doing so because they believe the clients need treatment and that there are not enough facilities in the community to provide this treatment (Turkheimer & Parry, 1992).

Civil Rights

People who have been committed to a mental institution often feel that they have given up all their civil rights. But numerous court cases over the years have established that these people retain most of their civil rights and have certain additional rights, due to their committed status.

Right to Treatment

One fundamental right of people who have been committed is the **right to treatment.** In the past, mental patients, including those involuntarily committed and those who sought treatment voluntarily, were often warehoused. The conditions in which they lived were appalling, with little stimulation or pleasantries, let alone treatment for their disorders. In *Wyatt v. Stickney* (1972), patient Ricky Wyatt and others filed a class action suit against a custodial facility in Alabama, charging that they received no useful treatment and lived in minimally acceptable living conditions. They won their case. A federal court ruled that the state could not simply shelter patients who had been civilly committed but had to provide them with active treatment.

Many prison inmates have severe mental disorders (Lamb, Weinberger, & Gross, 2004). For example, one study of all 805 women felons entering prison in North Carolina in 1991 and 1992 found that 64 percent had a lifetime history of a major psychiatric disorder, including major depression, an anxiety disorder, a substance use disorder, or a personality disorder, and 46 percent had suffered

such a disorder in the previous six months (Jordan et al., 1996). In addition, nearly 80 percent of these women had been exposed to an extreme trauma, such as sexual abuse, at sometime in their lives. Another study of 1,272 women jail detainees awaiting trial in Chicago found that over 80 percent had a lifetime history of a psychiatric disorder, and 70 percent were symptomatic within the previous six months (Teplin, Abram, & McClelland, 1996). In both studies, the most common diagnosis the women received was substance abuse or dependence, but substantial percentages of the women also had major depression and/or borderline or antisocial personality disorder. Studies of male prison inmates also find that over 50 percent can be diagnosed with a mental disorder, most often a substance-related disorder or antisocial personality disorder (Collins & Schlenger, 1983; Hodgins & Cote, 1990; Neighbors et al., 1987).

Numerous court decisions have mandated that prison inmates receive necessary mental-health services, just as they should receive necessary medical services. Most inmates with mental disorders do not receive services, however. A study of male inmates found that only 37 percent of those with schizophrenia or a major mood disorder received services while in jail (Teplin, 1990), and a study of female inmates found that only 23.5 percent suffering schizophrenia or a major mood disorder received services in jail (Teplin, Abram, & McClelland, 1997). Depression in inmates is particularly likely to go unnoticed and untreated, yet suicide is the second most frequent cause of death among jail detainees, accounting for 39 percent of all inmate deaths (Patterson, 1994).

The services inmates do receive are often minimal. Drug treatments may involve only the provision of information about drugs and perhaps Alcoholics Anonymous or Narcotics Anonymous meetings in the prison. Treatment for schizophrenia or depression may involve only occasional visits with a prison physician, who prescribes a standard drug treatment but does not have the time or expertise to follow individuals closely.

Comprehensive treatment programs focusing on the special needs of prison inmates with mental disorders have been proven successful at reducing their symptoms of mental disorder, substance abuse, and recidivism. Many of these treatment programs are focused on male inmates, because they outnumber female inmates greatly. The female inmate population has grown more rapidly than the male inmate population in the past decade, however, more than tripling in that time frame (Teplin et al., 1997).

Female inmates may have different needs for services, compared with male inmates, for several

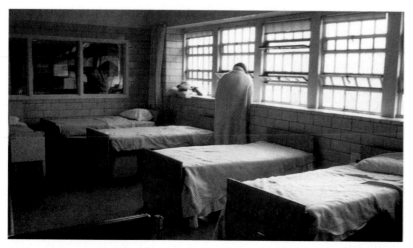

One fundamental right of people committed to a mental-health facility is the right to be treated rather than just warehoused.

reasons. Female inmates may be more likely than male inmates to have a history of sexual and physical abuse, which needs to be addressed in treatment. Female inmates are more likely than male inmates to be suffering from depression or anxiety. And female inmates are more likely than male inmates to have children for whom they will become caregivers once they are released from prison (Teplin et al., 1997).

Right to Refuse Treatment

Another basic right is the **right to refuse treatment.** One of the greatest fears of people committed against their will is that they will be given drugs or other treatments that rob them of their consciousness, personality, and free will. Many states do not allow mental institutions and prisons to administer treatments without the informed consent of patients. **Informed consent** means that a patient accepts treatment after receiving a full and understandable explanation of the treatment being offered and making a decision based on his or her own judgment of the risks and benefits of the treatment. The right to refuse treatment is not recognized in some states, however, and in most states this right can be overruled in many circumstances (Monahan et al., 2001). Particularly if a patient is psychotic or manic, it may be judged that he or she cannot make a reasonable decision about treatment; thus, the decision must be made by others. The simple fact that patients have a psychiatric diagnosis, particularly if it is a diagnosis of schizophrenia, is enough to declare them incompetent to make decisions about their treatment in some jurisdictions (Grisso & Appelbaum, 1998). However, studies using reliable measures of patients' abilities to make rational decisions suggest that as much as 75 percent of those with schizophrenia and 90 percent of those with depression have adequate decision-making capacity (Grisso & Appelbaum, 1995).

Patients' psychiatrists and perhaps families may seek court rulings allowing them to administer treatment even if patients refuse treatment. Judges most often agree with the psychiatrists' or families' requests to force treatment on patients. Most cases in which patients refuse treatment never get to court, however. Clinicians and family members pressure and persuade patients to accept treatment, and eventually most patients agree to treatment after initially refusing it (Griffin, Steadman, & Petrila, 2002; Monahan et al., 2001).

SUMMING UP

- People can be held in mental-health facilities involuntarily if they are judged to have grave disabilities that make it difficult for them to meet their own basic needs or that pose imminent danger to themselves or to others. Each of the criteria used to make such judgments has its flaws, however, creating concerns about the appropriateness of civil commitment.

- Short-term commitments can occur without court hearings on the certification of mental-health professionals that individuals are in emergency situations. Such commitments are most likely to happen for individuals who are actively suicidal.

- Longer-term commitments require court hearings. Patients have the rights to have attorneys and to appeal rulings.

- Other basic rights of patients are the right to be treated while being hospitalized and the right to refuse treatment (at least in some states).

- Research shows higher rates of violence by people with mental disorders, particularly those who also have a history of substance abuse, but the rates are not as high as some stereotypes would suggest.

CLINICIANS' DUTIES TO CLIENTS AND SOCIETY

A clinician's primary responsibility to the client is a *duty to provide competent and appropriate treatment* for the client's problems. A number of other duties also deserve mention.

First, according to the ethical guidelines that clinicians are expected to follow, there is a *duty to not become involved in multiple relationships* with clients. Thus, therapists should avoid becoming involved in business or social relationships with clients, and therapists should not treat members of their own families. Such multiple relationships can cloud therapists' judgments about the best treatment for their clients. Of great concern is the potential sexual involvement of therapists with clients. No matter how egalitarian a therapist is, the relationship between a therapist and client is always a relationship of power. The client goes to the therapist, vulnerable and seeking answers. The therapist is in a position to exploit the client's vulnerability. Current professional guidelines for psychologists and psychiatrists assert that it is not acceptable for a therapist to become sexually involved with a client, even if the client seems to be consenting voluntarily to such a liaison. Further, a therapist must not become intimately involved with a client for at least two years after the therapeutic relationship has ended. Sexual contact between a therapist and client is not just unethical—it is a felony in some states.

The vast majority of cases of sexual liaisons between therapists and clients involve male therapists and female clients. Older studies asking therapists (anonymously) if they had ever had sexual contact with their clients suggested that as much as 12 percent of male therapists and 3 percent of female therapists had, at sometime in their careers, had such relationships with clients (Holroyd & Brodsky, 1977). Fortunately, the rates of such abuse have decreased dramatically in more recent surveys, which suggest that about 1 to 4 percent of male therapists and less than 1 percent of female therapists have had sexual liaisons with clients (Borys & Pope, 1989; Pope, Tabachnick, & Keith-Spiegel, 1987). The decrease in rates of such liaisons is probably due to a number of factors, including the criminalization of the act, malpractice suits brought against therapists who have become sexually involved with clients, and increased sensitivity to the wrongness of such relationships among professionals and the organizations that govern them. On the other hand, therapists may be simply less willing to admit to having sexual relationships with their clients now than they were in previous years due to the increased sanctions against such relationships.

Second, therapists have a *duty to protect client confidentiality*. Therapists must not reveal information about their clients, including clients' identities, to anyone except with the clients' permission or under special circumstances. One of those special circumstances occurs when a therapist believes a client needs to be committed involuntarily and must convince a court of this.

Another condition under which therapists can violate their clients' confidentiality happens when they believe clients may harm other people. Based on the decision in *Tarasoff v. Regents of the University of California* (1974), in many jurisdictions clinicians now have a *duty to protect persons who might be in danger because of their clients*. Tatiana Tarasoff was a student at the University of California at Berkeley in the late 1960s. A graduate student named Prosenjit Poddar was infatuated with Tarasoff, who had rejected him. Poddar told his therapist in the student counseling service that he planned to kill Tarasoff when she returned from vacation. The therapist informed the campus police, who picked up Poddar for questioning. Poddar agreed to leave Tarasoff alone, and the campus police released him. Two months later, Poddar killed Tarasoff. Tarasoff's parents sued the university, arguing that the therapist should have protected Tarasoff from Poddar. The California courts agreed and established that therapists have a duty to warn persons who are threatened by their clients during therapy sessions and to take actions to protect these persons.

In addition, in most states, therapists have a *duty to report suspected child abuse* to the proper authorities, even when such reports violate their clients' confidentiality. These authorities then are required to investigate these reports and determine whether to file charges and to remove children from potentially abusive situations. In some states, therapists also have a *duty to report suspected abuse of elderly persons*. Therapists consider confidentiality to be one of the most fundamental rights of clients, but, in these cases, the courts have ruled that confidentiality must be broken to protect innocent people whom clients might harm or are harming.

Finally, in recent years, a new duty has been added to the clinicians' obligations: *to provide ethical service to culturally diverse populations*. We examine this duty in the *Taking Psychology Personally: Guidelines for Ethical Service to Culturally Diverse Populations*.

SUMMING UP

- First and foremost, clinicians have a duty to provide competent care to their clients.
- Clinicians must also avoid multiple relationships with their clients, particularly sexual relationships.
- They must protect their clients' confidentiality, except under special circumstances. One of these special circumstances occurs when therapists believe clients need to be committed involuntarily.
- Two other duties therapists have to society require them to break clients' confidentiality: the duty to protect people whom clients are threatening to harm and the duty to report suspected child or elder abuse.
- Recently, clinicians have been charged to provide ethical service to diverse populations.

CHAPTER INTEGRATION

There has been perhaps less integration of biological, social, and psychological viewpoints in the law's approach to issues of mental health than in the mental-health field itself. The rules governing the insanity defense suggest that the law takes a biological perspective on psychological disorders, conforming to the belief that a mental disease is like a medical disease (see Figure 18.2 on page 694). Similarly, civil commitment rules require certification that a person has a mental disorder or disease before he or she can be committed, further legitimizing psychiatric diagnostic systems that are based on medical models.

Taking Psychology Personally

Guidelines for Ethical Service to Culturally Diverse Populations

What can psychologists do to provide the best possible service and treatment to people who are of ethnicities or cultures different from their own? The following are some guidelines from the American Psychological Association for ethical conduct by psychologists treating culturally diverse populations (Office of Ethnic Minority Affairs, 1993). If you are hoping to become a psychologist, these guidelines provide a sense of the competencies you will be expected to gain in your training. If you are being treated by a psychologist, the guidelines provide some expectations you may have of your therapist, particularly if he or she is from a culture different from your own.

- *Psychologists educate their clients to the processes of psychological intervention,* such as goals and expectations; the scope and, where appropriate, legal limits of confidentiality; and the psychologists' orientations.

- *Psychologists are cognizant of relevant research and practice issues as related to the population being served.*

  Psychologists acknowledge that ethnicity and culture impact behavior and take those factors into account when working with various ethnic groups.

  Psychologists seek out educational and training experiences to enhance their understanding and thereby address the needs of these populations more appropriately and effectively. These experiences include cultural, social, psychological, political, economic, and historical material specific to the ethnic group being served.

  Psychologists recognize the limits of their competencies and expertise. Psychologists who do not possess knowledge and training about an ethnic group seek consultation with, and/or make referrals to, appropriate experts as necessary.

  Psychologists consider the validity of a given instrument or procedure and interpret resulting data, keeping in mind the cultural and linguistic characteristics of the person being assessed.

- *Psychologists recognize ethnicity and culture as significant parameters in understanding psychological processes.*

  Psychologists, regardless of ethnic background, are aware of how their own cultural background/experiences, attitudes, values, and biases influence psychological processes. They make efforts to correct any prejudices and biases.

  A psychologist's practice incorporates an understanding of the client's ethnic and cultural background. This includes the client's familiarity and comfort with the majority culture as well as ways in which the client's culture may add to or improve various aspects of the majority culture and/or of society at large.

  Psychologists help clients increase their awareness of their own cultural values and norms, and they facilitate the discovery of ways clients can apply this awareness to their own lives and to society at large. For example, psychologists may be able to help parents distinguish between generational conflict and culture gaps when problems arise between them and their children. In the process, psychologists can help both parents and children appreciate their own distinguishing cultural values.

  Psychologists seek to help a client determine whether a "problem" stems from racism or bias in others, so that the client does not inappropriately personalize problems. For example, the concept of "healthy paranoia," whereby ethnic minorities develop defensive behaviors in response to discrimination, illustrates this principle.

- *Psychologists respect the roles of family members and community structures, hierarchies, values, and beliefs within the client's culture.*

  Psychologists identify resources in the family and the larger community.

  Clarification of the psychologist's role and the client's expectations precedes intervention. For example, it is not uncommon for an entire Native American family to enter a clinic to provide support to the family member in distress. Many of the healing practices found in Native American communities are centered in the family and the whole community.

- *Psychologists respect clients' religious and/or spiritual beliefs and values,* including attributions and taboos, since they affect clients' worldview, psychosocial functioning, and expressions of distress.

- *Psychologists interact in the language requested by the client* and, if this is not feasible, make an appropriate referral.

- *Psychologists consider the impact of adverse social, environmental, and political factors* in assessing problems and designing interventions.

- *Psychologists attend to, as well as work to eliminate, biases, prejudices, and discriminatory practices.*

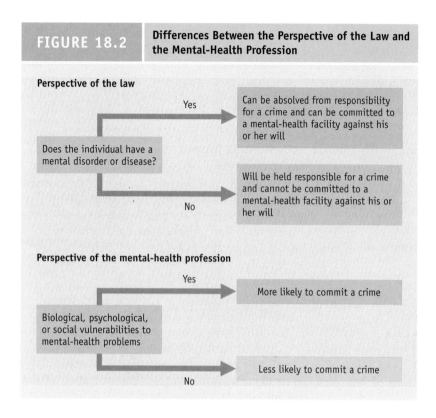

FIGURE 18.2 **Differences Between the Perspective of the Law and the Mental-Health Profession**

Perspective of the law

Does the individual have a mental disorder or disease?

Yes → Can be absolved from responsibility for a crime and can be committed to a mental-health facility against his or her will

No → Will be held responsible for a crime and cannot be committed to a mental-health facility against his or her will

Perspective of the mental-health profession

Biological, psychological, or social vulnerabilities to mental-health problems

Yes → More likely to commit a crime

No → Less likely to commit a crime

In each of the areas discussed in this chapter, however, there are mental-health professionals advocating a more integrated and complex view of mental disorders than that traditionally held by the law. These professionals are trying to educate judges, juries, and laypeople that some people have biological, psychological, or social predispositions to disorders and that other biological, psychological, or social factors can interact with predispositions to trigger the onset of disorders or certain manifestations of disorders. What is most difficult to explain is the probabilistic nature of the predictions that can be made about mental disorders and the behavior of people with these disorders. That is, a predisposition or certain recent life experiences may make it more likely that a person will develop a disorder or engage in a specific behavior (such as a violent behavior), but they do not determine the disorder or the specific behavior.

We all prefer to have predictions about the future that are definite, especially when we are making decisions that will determine a person's freedom or confinement. That kind of definitiveness is not possible, however, given the present knowledge of the ways biological, psychological, and social forces interact to influence people's behavior.

Extraordinary People: Follow-Up

Unfortunately, the story of Michael Bottoms' descent into schizophrenia, and his family's struggle with the mental-health system to get him treatment, doesn't have a happy ending. Eventually, the family found an institution that would take their insurance and placed Michael there. He hated the place, though, refused his medications, and attempted suicide. This landed him in a state psychiatric hospital for a while. Later, he "confessed" to a murder he had not committed, having been convinced by the voices in his head that this was the sin that he was paying such a high price for. He was jailed, but DNA evidence proved Michael couldn't have committed the murder.

After he was exonerated for this murder, Michael was back home again, on high doses of antipsychotic medications but totally delusional, believing that God spoke directly to him and that his family was evil. Indeed, he decided that his father was the antichrist and that, to save his family's souls, he had to kill them. One night, as his father lay dying of cancer and his family slept behind locked doors, Michael set the house on fire. He rode to the end of the street on his bicycle, then sat watching, expecting his family's souls to float past him on the way to Heaven. The family escaped. As they stood, watching the firefighters try to extinguish the fire, Mr. Bottoms told the other family members this was the best thing that could happen, because now Michael could really be put away. In the next instant, however, he feared that Michael had been in the house and was dying in the fire. He tried to run into the house to look for Michael but was held back by the firefighters. In the meantime, Michael rode up on his bicycle, completely nonchalant. A police officer asked Michael if he could ask him some questions, and Michael held out his hands for the handcuffs. Then, he turned to his mother and asked her casually what she was going to make for breakfast. Michael confessed to setting the fire with the purpose of killing his family. He was convicted for attempted murder and arson and was sent to prison for 30 years. Michael's father died shortly thereafter, in part from pneumonia contracted the night of the fire. Says Michael's brother, Greg,

> For a long time after Michael went to prison, I never spoke his name. When asked, I said I had only one brother, younger. I couldn't say the name "Michael" without feeling sick and anxious and embarrassed and sad. Acknowledging his existence was admitting his link to me and to all my weaknesses, failures, and humiliations. And it was, it is. Because no matter how I might define success, I am equally formed, if not more so, of human failure, mortal inadequacy, of loss as well as gain, and I am part of my brother just as he—whether he knows it or not, whether either of us want it or not—is part of me. . . .
>
> [In his letters from prison] he said he was sorry and asked for forgiveness, said that he loved our mother and he loved me and he loved my younger brother Ron. He said that he loved us all, always had and always would, and I believed him, because I don't think any of this happened for lack of love; I think, in fact, that the story of my brother, of my family, could be construed as a story of how wrong love might go, when mental illness—when spirits and angels and demons—invade your life. . . .
>
> Last year Michael came up for parole. I slept fitfully during the week before his hear-ing. I couldn't eat, I was petrified. It all seemed as if it were going to happen again. I called my mother every day that week, to see if she had heard anything, to see how she was doing, which was always better than I was, because she is, deep down, a stronger person. Finally, on a Saturday morning, she called to tell me that he had not been given parole, that the person from the parole board whom she had spoken with had said that he was "not doing well, not at all," that he was violent and uncooperative, and that he would most likely have to serve the full length of his sentence.
>
> My mother and I felt a sad sort of relief, yet being confronted with all this again rendered us both speechless. So we just stayed on the line, listening to each other breathe. (Bottoms 2000, pp. 201–203)

The story of the Bottoms family's inability to afford long-term care for Michael or to have him institutionalized due to his violence is all too familiar to families of people with serious mental disorders. Insurance coverage for mental-health care is lacking for many people and completely unavailable for others. In many cases, it takes an act as serious as Michael's attempt to kill his family to institutionalize an individual for more than a few weeks. A balance between protecting the rights of people with mental disorders and protecting their families from the consequences of their mental disorders is often difficult to find.

Chapter Summary

- One of the fundamental principles of law is that, in order to stand trial, an accused individual must have a reasonable degree of rational understanding of the charges against him or her and the proceedings of the trial and must be able to participate in his or her defense. People who do not have an understanding of what is happening to them in a courtroom and who cannot participate in their own defense are said to be incompetent to stand trial. Defendants who have histories of psychotic disorders, who have current symptoms of

psychosis, or who perform poorly on tests of important cognitive skills may be judged incompetent to stand trial.

- Five rules for judging the acceptability of the insanity defense have been used in recent history: the M'Naghten rule, the irresistible impulse rule, the Durham rule, the ALI rule, and the American Psychiatric Association definition of insanity. Each of these rules requires that the defendant be diagnosed with a mental disorder, and most of the rules require it be shown that the defendant did not appreciate the criminality of his or her act or could not control his or her behaviors at the time of the crime. (Review Table 18.2.)

■ The verdict of guilty but mentally ill was introduced following public uproar over recent uses of the insanity defense in high-profile cases. Persons judged guilty but mentally ill are confined for the duration of a regular prison term but with the presumption that they will be given psychiatric treatment.

■ Mental-health professionals have raised a number of concerns about the insanity defense. It requires after-the-fact judgments of a defendant's state of mind at the time of the crime. In addition, the rules governing the insanity defense presume that people have free will and usually can control their actions. These presumptions contradict some models of normal and abnormal behavior that suggest that behavior is strongly influenced by biological, psychological, and social forces.

■ Civil commitment is the procedure through which a person may be committed for treatment in a mental institution against his or her will. In most jurisdictions, three criteria are used to determine whether individuals may be committed: if they suffer from grave disability that impairs their ability to care for their own basic needs, if they are imminent dangers to themselves, and if they are imminent dangers to others. Each of these criteria requires a subjective judgment on the part of clinicians and often predictions about the future clinicians may not be good at making. In particular, the prediction of who will pose a danger to others in the future is a difficult one to make, and it is often incorrect. (Review Table 18.3.)

■ Once committed, patients have the right to be treated and the right to refuse treatment.

■ People with mental disorders, particularly those who also have a history of substance abuse, are somewhat more likely to commit violent acts, especially against family members and friends, than people without mental disorders.

■ Mental-health professionals have a number of duties to their clients and to society. They have a duty to provide competent care, to avoid multiple relationships with clients, and to uphold clients' confidentiality, except in unusual circumstances. They have a duty to warn people whom their client is threatening and to report suspected child or elder abuse. They also have a duty to provide ethical service to diverse populations.

■ In the areas of law discussed in this chapter, there are mental-health professionals advocating a more integrated and complex view of mental disorders than that traditionally held by the law, which takes a primarily biological view. (Review Figure 18.2.)

MindMap CD-ROM

The following resources on the MindMap CD-ROM that came with this text will help you to master the content of this chapter and prepare for tests:

■ Chapter Timeline
■ Chapter Quiz

Key Terms

mentally ill 678
incompetent to stand trial 679
insanity 679
insanity defense 680
M'Naghten rule 682
irresistible impulse rule 683
Durham rule 683
ALI rule 683
Insanity Defense Reform Act 684
American Psychiatric Association definition of insanity 684

guilty but mentally ill (GBMI) 684
need for treatment 685
civil commitment 685
grave disability 685
dangerousness to self 686
dangerousness to others 687
right to treatment 690
right to refuse treatment 691
informed consent 691

GLOSSARY

A

ABAB (reversal) design type of experimental design in which an intervention is introduced, withdrawn, and then reinstated, and the behavior of a participant is examined on and off the treatment

abstinence violation effect what happens when a person attempting to abstain from alcohol use ingests alcohol and then endures conflict and guilt by making an internal attribution to explain why he or she drank, thereby making him or her more likely to continue drinking in order to cope with the self-blame and guilt

acculturation extent to which a person identifies with his or her group of origin and its culture or with the mainstream dominant culture

acute stress disorder disorder similar to posttraumatic stress disorder but occurs within one month of exposure to the stressor and does not last more than four weeks; often involves dissociative symptoms

adjustment disorder stress-related disorder that involves emotional and behavioral symptoms (depressive symptoms, anxiety symptoms, and/or antisocial behaviors) that arise within three months of the onset of a stressor

adoption study study of the heritability of a disorder by finding adopted people with a disorder and then determining the prevalence of the disorder among their biological and adoptive relatives, in order to separate out contributing genetic and environmental factors

affective flattening negative symptom of schizophrenia that consists of a severe reduction or the complete absence of affective responses to the environment

agnosia impaired ability to recognize objects or people

agoraphobia anxiety disorder characterized by fear of places and situations in which it would be difficult to escape, such as enclosed places, open spaces, and crowds

agranulocytosis condition characterized by a deficiency of granulocytes, which are substances produced by the bone marrow and fight infection; 1 to 2 percent of people who take clozapine develop this condition

akathesis agitation caused by neuroleptic drugs

akinesia condition marked by slowed motor activity, a monotonous voice, and an expressionless face, resulting from taking neuroleptic drugs

alcohol abuse diagnosis given to someone who uses alcohol in dangerous situations, fails to meet obligations at work or at home due to alcohol use, and has recurrent legal or social problems as a result of alcohol use

alcohol dependence diagnosis given to someone who has a physiological tolerance to alcohol, spends a lot of time intoxicated or in withdrawal, or continues to drink despite significant legal, social, medical, or occupational problems that result from alcohol (often referred to as alcoholism)

alcohol-induced dementia loss of intellectual abilities due to prolonged alcohol abuse, including memory, abstract thinking, judgment, and problem solving, often accompanied by changes in personality, such as increases in paranoia

alcohol-induced persisting amnesic disorder permanent cognitive disorder caused by damage to the central nervous system due to prolonged alcohol abuse, consisting of Wernicke's encephalopathy and Korsakoff's psychosis

ALI rule legal principle stating that a person is not responsible for criminal conduct if he or she lacks the capacity to appreciate the criminality (wrongfulness) of the act or to conform his or her conduct to the requirements of the law as a result of mental disease

alogia deficit in both the quantity of speech and the quality of its expression

alternate form reliability extent to which a measure yields consistent results when presented in different forms

altruistic suicide suicide committed by people who believe that taking their own lives will benefit society

Alzheimer's disease progressive neurological disease that is the most common cause of dementia

amenorrhea cessation of the menses

American Psychiatric Association definition of insanity definition of insanity stating that people cannot be held responsible for their conduct if, at the time they commit crimes, as the result of mental disease or mental retardation they are unable to appreciate the wrongfulness of their conduct

amnesia impairment in the ability to learn new information or to recall previously learned information or past events

amphetamines stimulant drugs that can produce symptoms of euphoria, self-confidence, alertness, agitation, paranoia, perceptual illusions, and depression

amyloid class of proteins that can accumulate between cells in areas of the brain critical to memory and cognitive functioning

anal stage according to Freud, psycho-sexual stage that occurs between the ages of 18 months and 3 years; the focus of gratification is the anus, and children are interested in toilet activities; parents can cause children to be fixated in this stage by being too harsh and critical during toilet training

analogue study study that creates conditions in the laboratory meant to represent conditions in the real world

animal studies studies that attempt to test theories of psychopathology using animals

animal type phobias extreme fears of specific animals that may induce immediate and intense panic attacks and cause the individual to go to great lengths to avoid the animals

anomic suicide suicide committed by people who experience a severe disorientation and role confusion because of a large change in their relationship to society

anorexia nervosa eating disorder in which people fail to maintain body weights that are normal for their ages and heights and suffer from fears of becoming fat, distorted body images, and amenorrhea

antagonist drugs drugs that block or change the effects of an addictive drug, reducing desire for the drug

anterograde amnesia deficit in the ability to learn new information

antianxiety drugs drugs used to treat anxiety, insomnia, and other psychological symptoms

anticonvulsants drugs used to treat mania and depression

antidepressants drugs used to treat the symptoms of depression, such as sad mood, negative thinking, and disturbances of sleep and appetite; three common types are monoamine oxidase inhibitors, tricyclics, and selective serotonin reuptake inhibitors

antipsychotic drugs drugs used to treat psychotic symptoms, such as delusions, hallucinations, and disorganized thinking

antisocial personality disorder (ASPD) pervasive pattern of criminal, impulsive, callous, and/or ruthless behavior, predicated upon disregard for the rights of others and an absence of respect for social norms

anxiety state of apprehension, tension, and worry

anxiety sensitivity belief that bodily symptoms have harmful consequences

anxious-fearful personality disorders category including avoidant, dependent, and obsessive-compulsive personality disorders, which are characterized by a chronic sense of anxiety or fearfulness and behaviors intended to ward off feared situations

aphasia impaired ability to produce and comprehend language

applied tension technique technique used to treat blood-injection-injury type phobias in which the therapist teaches the client to increase his or her blood pressure and heart rate, thus preventing the client from fainting

apraxia impaired ability to initiate common voluntary behaviors

arousal phase in the sexual response cycle, psychological experience of arousal and pleasure as well as physiological changes, such as the tensing of muscles and enlargement of blood vessels and tissues (also called the excitement phase)

Asperger's disorder pervasive developmental disorder characterized by deficits in social skills and activities; similar to autism but does not include deficits in language or cognitive skills

assertive community treatment programs system of treatment that provides comprehensive services to people with schizophrenia, employing the expertise of medical professionals, social workers, and psychologists to meet the variety of patients' needs 24 hours per day

assessment process of gathering information about a person's symptoms and their possible causes

attention-deficit/hyperactivity disorder (ADHD) syndrome marked by deficits in controlling attention, inhibiting impulses, and organizing behavior to accomplish long-term goals

atypical antipsychotics drugs that seem to be even more effective in treating schizophrenia than phenothiazines without the same neurological side effects; they bind to a different type of dopamine receptor than other neuroleptic drugs

auditory hallucination auditory perception of a phenomenon that is not real, such as hearing a voice when one is alone

autism childhood disorder marked by deficits in social interaction (such as a lack of interest in one's family or other children), communication (such as failing to modulate one's voice to signify emotional expression), and activities and interests (such as engaging in bizarre, repetitive behaviors)

automatic thoughts thoughts that come to mind quickly and without intention, causing emotions such as fear or sadness

aversion therapy treatment that involves the pairing of unpleasant stimuli with deviant or maladaptive sources of pleasure in order to induce an aversive reaction to the formerly pleasurable stimulus

aversive classical conditioning pairing of alcohol with a substance (such as disulfiram) that will interact with it to cause nausea or vomiting in order to make alcohol itself a conditioned stimulus to be avoided

avoidant personality disorder pervasive anxiety, sense of inadequacy, and fear of being criticized that lead to the avoidance of most social interactions with others and to restraint and nervousness in social interactions

avolition inability to persist at common goal-directed activities

B

barbiturates drugs used to treat anxiety and insomnia that work by suppressing the central nervous system and decreasing the activity level of certain neurons

behavior genetics study of the processes by which genes affect behavior and the extent to which personality and abnormality are genetically inherited

behavior therapies therapies that focus on changing a person's specific behaviors by replacing unwanted behaviors with desired behaviors

behavioral assessment in behavior therapies, the therapist's assessment of the clients' adaptive and maladaptive behaviors and the triggers for these behaviors

behavioral assignments "homework" given to clients to practice new behaviors or gather new information between therapy sessions

behavioral inhibition set of behavioral traits including shyness, fearfulness, irritability, cautiousness, and introversion; behaviorally inhibited children tend to avoid or withdraw from novel situations, are clingy with parents, and become excessively aroused when exposed to unfamiliar situations

behavioral observation method for assessing the frequency of a client's behaviors and the specific situations in which they occur

behavioral theories theories that focus on an individual's history of reinforcements and punishments as causes for abnormal behavior

behavioral theory of depression view that depression results from negative life events that represent a reduction in positive reinforcement; sympathetic responses to depressive behavior then serve as positive reinforcement for the depression itself

behaviorism study of the impact of reinforcements and punishments on behavior

bell and pad method treatment for enuresis in which a pad placed under a sleeping child to detect traces of urine sets off a bell when urine is detected, awakening the child to condition him or her to wake up and use the bathroom before urinating

benzodiazepines drugs that reduce anxiety and insomnia

binge-eating disorder eating disorder in which people compulsively overeat either continuously or on discrete binges but do not behave in ways to compensate for the overeating

bingeing eating a large amount of food in one sitting

binge/purge type of anorexia nervosa type of anorexia nervosa in which periodic bingeing or purging behaviors occur along with behaviors that meet the criteria for anorexia nervosa

biofeedback group of techniques designed to help people change bodily processes by learning to identify signs that the processes are going awry and then learning ways of controlling the processes

biological approach view that biological factors cause and should be used to treat abnormality

biological theories theories of abnormality that focus on biological causes of abnormal behaviors

bipolar disorder disorder marked by cycles between manic episodes and depressive episodes; also called manic-depression

bipolar I disorder form of bipolar disorder in which the full symptoms of mania are experienced; depressive aspects may be more infrequent or mild

bipolar II disorder form of bipolar disorder in which only hypomanic episodes are experienced, and the depressive component is more pronounced

blackout amnesia for events that occurred during intoxication

blood-injection-injury type phobias extreme fears of seeing blood or an injury or of receiving an injection or another invasive medical procedure, which cause a drop in heart rate and blood pressure and fainting

body dysmorphic disorder syndrome involving obsessive concern over a part of the body the individual believes is defective

borderline personality disorder syndrome characterized by rapidly shifting and unstable mood, self-concept, and interpersonal relationships, as well as impulsive behavior and transient dissociative states

bulimia nervosa eating disorder in which people engage in bingeing and behave in ways to prevent weight gain from the binges, such as self-induced vomiting, excessive exercise, and abuse of purging drugs (such as laxatives)

buspirone drug that appears to alleviate the symptoms of general anxiety for some, has very few side effects, and is unlikely to lead to physical dependence

butyrophenone class of drug that can reduce psychotic symptoms; includes haloperidol (Haldol)

C

caffeine chemical compound with stimulant effects

calcium channel blockers drugs used to treat mania and depression

cannabis substance that causes feelings of well-being, perceptual distortions, and paranoid thinking

case studies in-depth analyses of individuals

castration anxiety according to Freud, boys' fear that their fathers will retaliate against them by castrating them; this fear serves as motivation for them to put aside their desires for their mothers and to aspire to become like their fathers

cataplexy episodes of sudden loss of muscle tone lasting from a few seconds to minutes

catatonia group of disorganized behaviors that reflect an extreme lack of responsiveness to the outside world

catatonic excitement state of constant agitation and excitability

catatonic schizophrenia type of schizophrenia in which people show a variety of motor behaviors and ways of speaking that suggest almost complete unresponsiveness to their environment

catharsis expression of emotions connected to memories and conflicts, which, according to Freud, leads to the release of energy used to keep these memories in the unconscious

caudate nucleus part of the basal ganglia that is involved in carrying the impulses to the thalamus that direct primitive patterns of primitive behavior, such as aggression, sexuality, and bodily excretion

causal attribution explanation for why an event occurred

cerebral cortex part of the brain that regulates complex activities, such as speech and analytical thinking

cerebrovascular disease disease that occurs when the blood supply to the brain is blocked, causing tissue damage to the brain

childhood disintegrative disorder pervasive developmental disorder in which children develop normally at first but later show permanent loss of basic skills in social interactions, language, and/or movement

chlorpromazine antipsychotic drug

civil commitment forcing of a person into a mental-health facility against his or her will

classical conditioning form of learning in which a neutral stimulus becomes associated with a stimulus that naturally elicits a response, thereby making the neutral stimulus itself sufficient to elicit the same response

classification system set of syndromes and the rules for determining whether an individual's symptoms are part of one of these syndromes

client-centered therapy (CCT) Carl Rogers' form of psychotherapy, which consists of an equal relationship between therapist and client as the client searches for his or her inner self, receiving unconditional positive regard and an empathic understanding from the therapist

cocaine central nervous system stimulant that causes a rush of positive feelings initially but that can lead to impulsiveness, agitation, and anxiety and can cause withdrawal symptoms of exhaustion and depression

cognitions thoughts or beliefs

cognitive-behavioral therapy treatment focused on changing negative patterns of thinking and solving concrete problems through brief sessions in which a therapist helps a client challenge negative thoughts, consider alternative perspectives, and take effective actions

cognitive disorders dementia, delirium, or amnesia characterized by impairments in cognition (such as deficits in memory, language, or planning) and caused by a medical condition or by substance intoxication or withdrawal

cognitive theories theories that focus on belief systems and ways of thinking as the causes of abnormal behavior

cognitive therapies therapeutic approaches that focus on changing people's maladaptive thought patterns

cohort effect effect that occurs when people born in one historical period are at different risk for a disorder than are people born in another historical period

community mental-health centers clinics that provide mental-health care based in the community through teams of social workers, therapists, and physicians who coordinate care

community mental-health movement movement launched in 1963 that attempted to provide coordinated mental-health services to people in community-based treatment centers.

compulsions repetitive behaviors or mental acts that an individual feels he or she must perform

computerized tomography (CT) method of analyzing brain structure by passing narrow X-ray beams through a person's head from several angles to produce measurements from which a computer can construct an image of the brain

concordance rate probability that both twins will develop a disorder if one twin has the disorder

concurrent validity extent to which a test yields the same results as other measures of the same phenomenon

conditioned response (CR) in classical conditioning, response that first followed a natural stimulus but that now follows a conditioned stimulus

conditioned stimulus (CS) in classical conditioning, previously neutral stimulus that, when paired with a natural stimulus, becomes sufficient to elicit a response

conditions of worth external standards some people feel they must meet in order to be acceptable

conduct disorder syndrome marked by chronic disregard for the rights of others, including specific behaviors, such as stealing, lying, and engaging in acts of violence

conscious mental contents and processes of which we are actively aware

construct validity extent to which a test measures only what it is intended to measure

content validity extent to which a measure assesses all the important aspects of a phenomenon that it purports to measure

context environment and circumstances in which a behavior occurs

contingencies of self-worth "if-then" rules concerning self-worth, such as "I'm nothing if a person I care about doesn't love me"

continuous reinforcement schedule system of behavior modification in which certain behaviors are always rewarded or punished, leading to rapid learning of desired responses

continuous variable factor that is measured along a continuum (such as 0–100) rather than falling into a discrete category (such as "diagnosed with depression")

control group in an experimental study, group of subjects whose experience resembles that of the experimental group in all ways, except that they do not receive the key manipulation

control theory cognitive theory that explains people's variance in behavior in certain domains in terms of their beliefs that they can or cannot effectively control situations in that domain

conversion disorder syndrome marked by a sudden loss of functioning in a part of the body, usually following an extreme psychological stressor

coronary heart disease (CHD) chronic illness that is a leading cause of death in the United States, occurring when the blood vessels that supply the heart with oxygen and nutrients are narrowed or closed by plaque, resulting in a myocardial infarction (heart attack) when closed completely

correlation coefficient statistic used to indicate the degree of relationship between two variables

correlational studies method in which researchers assess only the relationship between two variables and do not manipulate one variable to determine its effects on another variable

cortisol hormone that helps the body respond to stressors, inducing the fight-or-flight response

covert sensitization therapy pairing of mental images of alcohol with other images of highly unpleasant consequences resulting from its use in order to create an aversive reaction to the sight and smell of alcohol and reduce drinking

crisis intervention program that helps people who are highly suicidal and refers them to mental-health professionals

cross-sectional type of research examining people at one point in time but not following them over time

cue exposure and response prevention therapy to reduce relapse among alcoholics by tempting them with stimuli that induce cravings to drink while preventing them from actually drinking, allowing them to habituate to the cravings and reduce temptation

cultural relativism view that norms among cultures set the standard for what counts as normal behavior, which implies that abnormal behavior can only be defined relative to these norms; no universal definition of abnormality is therefore possible; only definitions of abnormality relative to a specific culture are possible

cyclothymic disorder milder but more chronic form of bipolar disorder that consists of alternation between hypomanic episodes and mild depressive episodes over a period of at least two years

D

dangerousness to others legal criterion for involuntary commitment that is met when a person would pose a threat or danger to other people if not incarcerated

dangerousness to self legal criterion for involuntary commitment that is met when a person is imminently suicidal or a danger to him- or herself as judged by a mental-health professional

day treatment centers centers where people with mental-health problems can obtain treatment all day, including occupational and rehabilitative therapies, but live at home at night

death darers individuals who are ambivalent about dying and take actions that increase their chances of death but that do not guarantee they will die

death ignorers individuals who intend to end their lives but do not believe this means the end of their existence

death initiators individuals who intend to die but believe that they are simply speeding up an inevitable death

death seekers individuals who clearly and explicitly seek to end their lives

defense mechanisms strategies the ego uses to disguise or transform unconscious wishes

degradation process in which a receiving neuron releases an enzyme into the synapse, breaking down neurotransmitters into other biochemicals

deinstitutionalization movement in which thousands of mental patients were released from mental institutions; a result of the patients' rights movement, which was aimed at stopping the dehumanizing of mental patients and at restoring their basic legal rights

delirium cognitive disorder that is acute and usually transient, including disorientation and memory loss

delirium tremens (DTs) symptoms that result during severe alcohol withdrawal, including hallucinations, delusions, agitation, and disorientation

delusion of reference false belief that external events, such as people's actions or natural disasters, relate somehow to oneself

delusions fixed beliefs with no basis in reality

delusions of thought insertion beliefs that one's thoughts are being controlled by outside forces

demand characteristics factors in an experiment that suggest to participants how the experimenter would like them to behave

dementia cognitive disorder in which a gradual and usually permanent decline of intellectual functioning occurs; can be caused by a medical condition, substance intoxication, or withdrawal

dementia praecox historical name for schizophrenia

dependent personality disorder pervasive selflessness, a need to be cared for, and fear of rejection, which lead to total dependence on and submission to others

dependent variable factor that an experimenter seeks to predict

depersonalization disorder syndrome marked by frequent episodes of feeling detached from one's own body and mental processes, as if one were an outside observer of oneself; symptoms must cause significant distress or interference with one's ability to function

depletion syndrome set of symptoms shown by depressed older people, consisting of loss of interest, loss of

energy, hopelessness, helplessness, and psychomotor retardation

depression state marked by either a sad mood or a loss of interest in one's usual activities, as well as feelings of hopelessness, suicidal ideation, psychomotor agitation or retardation, and trouble concentrating

depressive realism phenomenon whereby depressed people make more realistic judgments as to whether they can control actually uncontrollable events than do nondepressed people, who exhibit an illusion of control over the same events

desensitization treatment used to reduce anxiety by rendering a previously threatening stimulus innocuous by repeated and guided exposure to the stimulus under nonthreatening circumstances

detoxification first step in treatment for substance-related disorders, in which a person stops using the substance and allows it to exit the body fully

developmental coordination disorder disorder involving deficits in the ability to walk, run, or hold on to objects

diagnosis label given to a set of symptoms that tend to occur together

Diagnostic and Statistical Manual of Mental Disorders **(DSM)** official manual for diagnosing mental disorders in the United States, containing a list of specific criteria for each disorder, how long a person's symptoms must be present to qualify for a diagnosis, and requirements that the symptoms interfere with daily functioning in order to be called disorders

dialectical behavior therapy cognitive-behavioral intervention aimed at teaching problem-solving skills, interpersonal skills, and skills at managing negative emotions

dichotomous thinking inflexible way of thinking in which everything is viewed in either/or terms

differential diagnosis determination of which of two or more possible diagnoses is most appropriate for a client

discomfort criterion for abnormality that suggests that only behaviors that cause a person great distress should be labeled as abnormal

disease model view that alcoholism (or another drug addiction) is an incurable physical disease, like epilepsy or

diabetes, and that only total abstinence can control it

disorder of written expression developmental disorder involving deficits in the ability to write

disorganized schizophrenia syndrome marked by incoherence in cognition, speech, and behavior as well as flat or inappropriate affect (also called hebephrenic schizophrenia)

dissociation process whereby different facets of an individual's sense of self, memories, or consciousness become split off from one another

dissociative amnesia loss of memory for important facts about a person's own life and personal identity, usually including the awareness of this memory loss

dissociative fugue disorder in which a person moves away and assumes a new identity, with amnesia for the previous identity

dissociative identity disorder (DID) syndrome in which a person develops more than one distinct identity or personality, each of which can have distinct facial and verbal expressions, gestures, interpersonal styles, attitudes, and even physiological responses

dissociative symptoms symptoms suggesting that facets of the individual's sense of self, memories, or consciousness have become split off from one another

disulfiram drug that produces an aversive physical reaction to alcohol and is used to encourage abstinence; commonly referred to as Antabuse

dizygotic (DZ) twins twins who average only 50 percent of their genes in common because they developed from two separate fertilized eggs

dopamine neurotransmitter in the brain, excess amounts of which have been thought to cause schizophrenia

double depression disorder involving a cycle between major depression and dysthymic disorder

double-blind experiment study in which both the researchers and the participants are unaware of which experimental condition the participants are in, in order to prevent demand effects

dramatic-emotional personality disorders category including antisocial, borderline, narcissistic, and histrionic personality disorders, which are characterized by dramatic and impulsive behaviors that are maladaptive and dangerous

drug addicts people who are physically dependent on substances and who suffer from withdrawal when not taking the substances

Durham rule legal principle stating that the presence of a mental disorder is sufficient to absolve a criminal of responsibility for a crime

dyspareunia genital pain associated with sexual intercourse

dyssomnias primary sleep disorders that involve abnormalities in the amount, quality, or timing of sleep

dysthymic disorder type of depression that is less severe than major depression but more chronic; diagnosis requires the presence of a sad mood or anhedonia, plus two other symptoms of depression, for at least two years, during which symptoms do not remit for two months or longer

E

echolalia communication abnormality in which an individual simply repeats back what he or she hears rather than generating his or her own speech

echopraxia repetitive imitation of another person's movements

effectiveness in therapy outcome research, how well a therapy works in real-world settings

efficacy in therapy outcome research, how well a therapy works in highly controlled settings with a narrowly defined group of people

ego part of the psyche that channels libido acceptable to the superego and within the constraints of reality

egoistic suicide suicide committed by people who feel alienated from others and lack social support

Electra complex Freud's theory that girls realize during the phallic stage that they don't have a penis and are horrified at the discovery; they realize that their mothers also don't have penises and disdain females for this deficit; an attraction for the father ensues, following the belief that he can provide a penis

electroconvulsive therapy (ECT) treatment for depression that involves the induction of a brain seizure by passing electrical current through the patient's brain while he or she is anesthetized

elimination disorders disorders in which a child shows frequent, uncontrolled urination or defecation far beyond the age at which children usually develop control over these functions

encopresis diagnosis given to children who are at least 4 years old and who defecate inappropriately at least once a month for 3 months

endocrine system system of glands that produces many different hormones

enlarged ventricles fluid-filled spaces in the brain that are larger than normal and suggest atrophy or deterioration in other brain tissue

enmeshed families families in which there is extreme interdependence in family interactions, so that the boundaries between the identities of individual members are weak and easily crossed

enuresis diagnosis given to children over 5 years of age who wet the bed or their clothes at least twice a week for 3 months

epidemiology study of the frequency and distribution of a disorder, or a group of disorders, in a population

euthanasia killing of another person as an act of mercy

excessive reassurance seeking constantly looking for assurances from others that one is accepted and loved

executive functions functions of the brain that involve the ability to sustain concentration; use abstract reasoning and concept formation; anticipate, plan, program; initiate purposeful behavior; self-monitor; and shift from maladaptive patterns of behavior to more adaptive ones

exhibitionism obtainment of sexual gratification by exposing one's genitals to involuntary observers

existential anxiety universal human fear of the limits and responsibilities of one's existence

existential theories views that uphold personal responsibility for discovering one's personal values and meanings in life and then living in accordance with them; people face existential anxiety due to awareness of their life's finitude and must overcome both this anxiety and obstacles to a life governed by the meanings they give to it, in order to achieve mental health and avoid maladaptive behavior

experimental group in an experimental study, group of participants that receives the key manipulation

experimental studies studies in which the independent variables are directly manipulated and the effects on the dependent variable are examined

expressed emotion family interaction style in which families are overinvolved with each other, are overprotective of the disturbed family member, voice self-sacrificing attitudes to the disturbed family member, and simultaneously are critical, hostile, and resentful of this member

expressive language disorder disorder involving deficits in the ability to express oneself through language

external validity extent to which a study's results can be generalized to phenomena in real life

extinction abolition of a learned behavior

eye movement desensitization and reprocessing (EMDR) highly controversial therapy for trauma survivors in which a client attends to the image of the trauma, thoughts about the trauma, and the physical sensations of anxiety aroused by the trauma while the therapist quickly moves a finger back and forth in front of the client's eyes to elicit a series of repeated, rapid, jerky, side-to-side eye movements ("saccades")

F

face validity extent to which a test seems to measure a phenomenon on face value, or intuition

factitious disorder by proxy disorder in which the individual creates an illness in another individual in order to gain attention

factitious disorders disorders marked by deliberately faking physical or mental illness to gain medical attention

family history study study of the heritability of a disorder involving identifying people with the disorder and people without the disorder and then determining the disorder's frequency within each person's family

family systems theories theories that see the family as a complex system that works to maintain the status quo

family systems therapy psychotherapy that focuses on the family, rather than the individual, as the source of problems; family therapists challenge communication styles, disrupt pathological family dynamics, and challenge defensive conceptions in order to harmonize relationships among all members and within each member

female orgasmic disorder in women, recurrent delay in or absence of orgasm after having reached the excitement phase of the sexual response cycle (also called anorgasmia)

female sexual arousal disorder in women, recurrent inability to attain or maintain the swelling-lubrication response of sexual excitement

fetal alcohol syndrome (FAS) syndrome that occurs when a mother abuses alcohol during pregnancy, causing the baby to have lowered IQ, increased risk for mental retardation, distractibility, and difficulties with learning from experience

fetishism paraphilia in which a person uses inanimate objects as the preferred or exclusive source of sexual arousal

fight-or-flight response physiological changes in the human body that occur in response to a perceived threat, including the secretion of glucose, endorphins, and hormones as well as the elevation of heart rate, metabolism, blood pressure, breathing, and muscle tension

five-factor model personality theory that posits that any individual's personality is organized along five broad dimensions of personality: neuroticism, extraversion, openness to experience, agreeableness, and conscientiousness

flooding (implosive therapy) behavioral technique in which a client is intensively exposed to a feared object until the anxiety diminishes

formal thought disorder state of highly disorganized thinking (also known as loosening of associations)

free association method of uncovering unconscious conflicts in which the client is taught to talk about whatever comes to mind, without censoring any thoughts

frotteurism obtainment of sexual gratification by rubbing one's genitals against or fondling the body parts of a nonconsenting person

G

gamma-aminobutyric acid (GABA) neurotransmitter that carries inhibiting messages from one neuron to another

gender identity one's perception of oneself as male or female

gender identity disorder (GID) condition in which a person believes that he or she was born with the wrong sex's genitals and is fundamentally a person of the opposite sex

gender roles according to Freud, what society considers to be the appropriate behaviors for males or females

general adaptation syndrome physiological changes that occur when an organism reacts to stress; includes the stages of alarm, resistance, and exhaustion

general paresis disease that leads to paralysis, insanity, and eventually death; discovery of this disease helped establish a connection between biological diseases and mental disorders

generalizability extent to which the results of a study generalize to, or inform us about, people other than those who were studied

generalized anxiety disorder (GAD) anxiety disorder characterized by chronic anxiety in daily life

genital stage psychosexual stage that occurs around the age of 12, when children's sex drives reemerge; if a child has successfully resolved the phallic stage, interest in sex turns toward heterosexual relationships

global assumptions fundamental beliefs that encompass all types of situations

glove anesthesia state in which people lose all feeling in one hand as if they were wearing a glove that wiped out all physical symptoms

grandiose delusions elevated thinking about the self, ideas of omnipotence, and the taking of credit for occurrences not personally facilitated

grave disability legal criterion for involuntary commitment that is met when a person is so incapacitated by a mental disorder that he or she cannot care for his or her own basic needs, such as for food, clothing, or shelter, and his or her survival is threatened as a result

group comparison study study that compares two or more distinct groups on a variable of interest

group therapy therapy conducted with groups of people rather than one on one between a therapist and client

guided mastery techniques interventions designed to increase health-promoting behaviors by providing explicit information about how to engage in these behaviors as well as opportunities to engage in these behaviors in increasingly challenging situations

guilty but mentally ill (GBMI) verdict that requires a convicted criminal to serve the full sentence designated for his or her crime, with the expectation that he or she will also receive treatment for mental illness

H

halfway houses organizations that offer people with long-term mental-health problems a structured, supportive environment in which to live while they reestablish a job and ties to their friends and family

hallucinations perceptual experiences that are not real

hallucinogens substances, including LSD and MDMA, that produce perceptual illusions and distortions even in small doses

harm-reduction model approach to treating substance use disorders that views alcohol use as normative behavior and focuses education on the immediate risks of the excessive use of alcohol (such as alcohol-related accidents) and on the payoffs of moderation (such as avoidance of hangovers)

health psychology study of the effects of psychological factors on health

histrionic personality disorder syndrome marked by rapidly shifting moods, unstable relationships, and an intense need for attention and approval, which is sought by means of overly dramatic behavior, seductiveness, and dependence

hopelessness sense that the future is bleak and there is no way of making it more positive

hormone chemical that carries messages throughout the body, potentially affecting a person's moods, levels of energy, and reactions to stress

human laboratory study experimental study involving human participants

humanistic theories views that people strive to develop their innate potential for goodness and self-actualization; abnormality arises as a result of societal pressures to conform to unchosen dictates that clash with a person's self-actualization needs and from an inability to satisfy more basic needs, such as hunger

humanistic therapy (person-centered therapy) type of therapy in which the goal is to help the client discover his or her place in the world and to accomplish self-actualization through self-exploration; based on the assumption that the natural tendency for humans is toward growth

hypersomnia type of dyssomnia that involves being chronically sleepy and sleeping for long periods at a time

hypertension condition in which the blood supply through the blood vessels is excessive and can lead to deterioration of the cell tissue and hardening of the arterial walls

hypoactive sexual desire disorder condition in which a person's desire for sex is diminished to the point that it causes him or her significant distress or interpersonal difficulties and is not due to transient life circumstances or another sexual dysfunction

hypochondriasis syndrome marked by chronic worry that one has a physical symptom or disease that one clearly does not have

hypomania state in which an individual shows mild symptoms of mania

hypothalamic-pituitary-adrenal axis (HPA axis) three key components of the neuroendocrine system that work together in a feedback system interconnected with the limbic system and the cerebral cortex

hypothalamus component of the brain that regulates eating, drinking, sex, and basic emotions; abnormal behaviors involving any of these activities may be the result of dysfunction in the hypothalamus

hypothesis testable statement about two or more variables and the relationship between them

I

id according to Freud, most primitive part of the unconscious; consists of drives and impulses seeking immediate gratification

immune system system that protects the body from disease-causing microorganisms and affects our susceptibility to diseases

impulsivity difficulty in controlling behaviors; acting without thinking first

in vivo exposure technique of behavior therapy in which clients are encouraged to experience directly the stimuli that they fear

incidence number of new cases of a specific disorder that develop during a specific period of time

incompetent to stand trial legal status of an individual who lacks a rational understanding of the charges against him or her, an understanding of the proceedings of his or her trial, or the ability to participate in his or her own defense

independent variable factor that is manipulated by an experimenter or used to predict the dependent variable

informed consent procedure (often legally required prior to treatment administration) in which a patient receives a full and understandable explanation of the treatment being offered and makes a decision about whether to accept or refuse the treatment

inhalants solvents, such as gasoline, glue, or paint thinner, that one inhales to produce a high and that can cause permanent central nervous system damage as well as liver and kidney disease

insanity legal term denoting a state of mental incapacitation during the time a crime was committed

insanity defense defense used by people accused of a crime in which they state that they cannot be held responsible for their illegal acts because they were mentally incapacitated at the time of the act

Insanity Defense Reform Act 1984 law, affecting all federal courts and about half of the state courts, that finds a person not guilty by reason of insanity if it is shown that, as a result of mental disease or mental retardation, the accused was unable to appreciate the wrongfulness of his or her conduct at the time of the offense

insomnia type of dyssomnia that involves difficulty in initiating or maintaining sleep; chronically nonrestorative sleep

integrationist approach approach to psychopathology that emphasizes how biological, psychological, and social factors interact and influence each other to produce and maintain mental-health problems

intelligence tests tests that assess a person's intellectual strengths and weaknesses

internal reliability extent to which a measure yields similar results among its different parts as it measures a single phenomenon

internal validity extent to which all factors that could extraneously affect a

study's results are controlled within a laboratory study

interoceptive awareness heightened awareness of bodily cues that a panic attack may soon happen

interpersonal theories theories that attribute abnormal behavior to problems in interpersonal realtionships

interpersonal theories of depression theories that view the causes of depression as rooted in interpersonal relationships

interpersonal therapy (IPT) more structured, short-term version of psychodynamic therapies

interrater reliability extent to which an observational measure yields similar results across different judges (also called interjudge reliability)

introject to internalize moral standards because following them makes one feel good and reduces anxiety

introjected hostility theory Freud's theory explaining how depressive people, being too frightened to express their rage for their rejection outwardly, turn their anger inward on parts of their own egos; their self-blame and punishment is actually blame and punishment intended for others who have abandoned them

irresistible impulse rule legal principle stating that even a person who knowingly performs a wrongful act can be absolved of responsibility if he or she was driven by an irresistible impulse to perform the act or had a diminished capacity to resist performing the act

K

Korsakoff's psychosis alcohol-induced permanent cognitive disorder involving deficiencies in one's ability to recall both recent and distant events

L

la belle indifference feature of conversion disorders involving an odd lack of concern about one's loss of functioning in an area of one's body

latency stage according to Freud, period of psychosexual development, following the phallic stage, in which libidinal drives are quelled and children's energy turns toward the development of skills and interests and toward becoming fully socialized to the world; the opposite sex is avoided

learned helplessness deficits symptoms such as low motivation, passivity, indecisiveness, and an inability to control outcomes that result from exposure to uncontrollable negative events

learned helplessness theory view that exposure to uncontrollable negative events leads to a belief in one's inability to control important outcomes and a subsequent loss of motivation, indecisiveness, and failure of action,

libido according to Freud, psychical energy derived from physiological drives

light therapy treatment for seasonal affective disorder that involves exposure to bright lights during the winter months

limbic system part of the brain that relays information from the primitive brain stem about changes in bodily functions to the cortex, where the information is interpreted

lithium drug used to treat manic and depressive symptoms

locus ceruleus area of the brain stem that plays a part in the emergency response and may be involved in panic attacks

longitudinal type of research evaluating the same group(s) of people for an extended period of time

lymphocytes immune system cells that attack viruses

M

magnetic resonance imaging (MRI) method of measuring both brain structure and brain function through the construction of a magnetic field that affects hydrogen atoms in the brain, emitting signals that a computer then records and uses to produce a three-dimensional image of the brain

major depression disorder involving a sad mood or anhedonia plus four or more of the following symptoms: weight loss or a decrease in appetite, insomnia or hypersomnia, psychomotor agitation or retardation, fatigue, feelings of worthlessness or severe guilt, trouble concentrating, and suicidal ideation; these symptoms must be present for at least two weeks and must produce marked impairments in normal functioning

maladaptive in reference to behaviors, causing people who have the behaviors physical or emotional harm, preventing them from functioning in daily life, and/or indicating that they have lost

touch with reality and/or cannot control their thoughts and behavior (also called dysfunctional)

male erectile disorder in men, recurrent inability to attain or maintain an erection until the completion of sexual activity

male orgasmic disorder in men, recurrent delay in or absence of orgasm following the excitement phase of the sexual response cycle

malingering feigning of a symptom or a disorder for the purpose of avoiding an unwanted situation, such as military service

managed care health care system in which all necessary services for an individual patient are supposed to be coordinated by a primary care provider; the goals are to coordinate services for an existing medical problem and to prevent future medical problems before they arise

mania state of persistently elevated mood, feelings of grandiosity, overenthusiasm, racing thoughts, rapid speech, and impulsive actions

mathematics disorder developmental disorder involving deficits in the ability to learn mathematics

mental hygiene movement movement to treat mental patients more humanely and to view mental disorders as medical diseases

mental illness phrase used to refer to a physical illness that causes severe abnormal thoughts, behaviors, and feelings

mental retardation developmental disorder marked by significantly subaverage intellectual functioning, as well as deficits (relative to other children) in life skill areas, such as communication, self-care, work, and interpersonal relationships

mentally ill legal description of an individual who purportedly suffers from a mental illness, which is analogous (in this view) to suffering from a medical disease

mesmerism treatment for hysterical patients based on the idea that magnetic fluids in the patients' bodies are affected by the magnetic forces of other people and objects; the patients' magnetic forces are thought to be realigned by the practitioner through his or her own magnetic force

mesolimbic pathway subcortical part of the brain involved in cognition and emotion

meta-analysis statistical technique for summarizing the results across several studies

methadone opioid that is less potent and longer-lasting than heroin; taken by heroin users to decrease their cravings and help them cope with negative withdrawal symptoms

methadone maintenance programs treatments for heroin abusers that provide doses of methadone to replace heroin use and that seek eventually to wean addicted people from the methadone itself

mixed receptive-expressive language disorder disorder involving deficits in the ability to express oneself through language and to understand the language of others

M'Naghten rule legal principle stating that, in order to claim a defense of insanity, accused persons must have been burdened by such a defect of reason, from disease of the mind, as not to know the nature and quality of the act they were doing or, if they did know it, that they did not know what they were doing what was wrong

modeling process of learning behaviors by imitating others, especially authority figures or those like oneself

monoamine oxidase inhibitors (MAOIs) class of antidepressant drugs

monoamine theories theories that low levels of monoamines, particularly norepinephrine and serotonin, cause depression, whereas excessive or imbalanced levels of monoamines, particularly dopamine, cause mania

monoamines neurotransmitters, including catecholamines (epinephrine, norepinephrine, and dopamine) and serotonin, that have been implicated in the mood disorders

monozygotic (MZ) twins twins who share 100 percent of their genes, because they developed from a single fertilized egg

moral anxiety anxiety that occurs when one is punished for expressing id impulses and come to associate those with punishment

moral treatment type of treatment delivered in mental hospitals in which patients were treated with respect and dignity and were encouraged to exercise self-control

myotonia in the sexual response cycle, muscular tension in the body, which culminates in contractions during orgasm

N

naloxone drug that blocks the positive effects of heroin and can lead to a decreased desire to use it

naltrexone drug that blocks the positive effects of alcohol and heroin and can lead to a decreased desire to drink or use substances

narcissistic personality disorder syndrome marked by grandiose thoughts and feelings of one's own worth as well as an obliviousness to others' needs and an exploitive, arrogant demeanor

narcolepsy type of dyssomnia that involves irresistible attacks of sleep

natural environment type phobias extreme fears of events or situations in the natural environment that cause impairment in one's ability to function normally

need for treatment legal criterion operationalized as a signed certificate by two physicians stating that a person requires treatment but will not agree to it voluntarily; formerly a sufficient cause to hospitalize the person involuntarily and force him or her to undergo treatment

negative cognitive triad perspective seen in depressed people in which they have negative views of themselves, of the world, and of the future

negative reinforcement process in which people avoid being exposed to feared objects, and this avoidance is reinforced by the subsequent reduction of their anxiety

negative symptoms in schizophrenia, deficits in functioning that indicate the absence of a capacity present in normal people, such as affective flattening (also called Type II symptoms)

neurofibrillary tangles twists or tangles of filaments within nerve cells, especially prominent in the cerebral cortex and hippocampus, common in the brains of Alzheimer's disease patients

neuroleptic drug used to treat psychotic symptoms

neuropsychological tests tests of cognitive, sensory, and/or motor skills that attempt to differentiate people with deficits in these areas from normal subjects

neurosis according to Freud, a set of maladaptive symptoms caused by unconscious anxiety

neurotic anxiety according to Freud, anxiety that occurs when one is repeatedly prevented from expressing one's id impulses

neurotic paradox psychoanalytic term for a condition in which an individual's way of coping with unconscious concerns creates even more problems in that individual's life

neurotransmitters biochemicals, released from a sending neuron, that transmit messages to a receiving neuron in the brain and nervous system

nicotine alkaloid found in tobacco; operates on both the central and peripheral nervous systems, resulting in the release of biochemicals, including dopamine, norepinephrine, serotonin, and the endogenous opioids

nonpurging type of bulimia nervosa type of bulimia nervosa in which bingeing is followed by excessive exercise or fasting to control weight gain

norepinephrine neurotransmitter that is involved in the regulation of mood

null hypothesis alternative to a primary hypothesis, stating that there is no relationship between the independent variable and the dependent variable

O

object relations view held by a group of modern psychodynamic theorists that one develops a self-concept and appraisals of others in a four-stage process during childhood and retains them throughout adulthood; psychopathology consists of an incomplete progression through these stages or an acquisition of poor self and other concepts

observational learning learning that occurs when a person observes the rewards and punishments of another's behavior and then behaves in accordance with the same rewards and punishments

obsessions uncontrollable, persistent thoughts, images, ideas, or impulses that an individual feels intrude upon his or her consciousness and that cause significant anxiety or distress

obsessive-compulsive disorder (OCD) anxiety disorder characterized by obsessions (persistent thoughts) and compulsions (rituals)

obsessive-compulsive personality disorder pervasive rigidity in one's activities and interpersonal relationships; includes qualities such as emotional constriction, extreme perfectionism, and anxiety resulting from even slight disruptions in one's routine ways

odd-eccentric personality disorders disorders, including paranoid, schizotypal, and schizoid personality disorders, marked by chronic odd and/or inappropriate behavior with mild features of psychosis and/or paranoia

Oedipus complex according to Freud, major conflict of male sexual development, during which boys are sexually attracted to their mothers and hate their fathers as rivals

operant conditioning form of learning in which behaviors lead to consequences that either reinforce or punish the organism, leading to an increased or a decreased probability of a future response

operationalization specific manner in which one measures or manipulates variables in a study

opioids substances, including morphine and heroin, that produce euphoria followed by a tranquil state; in severe intoxication, can lead to unconsciousness, coma, and seizures; can cause withdrawal symptoms of emotional distress, severe nausea, sweating, diarrhea, and fever

oppositional defiant disorder syndrome of chronic misbehavior in childhood marked by belligerence, irritability, and defiance, although not to the extent found in a diagnosis of conduct disorder

oral stage according to Freud, earliest psychosexual stage, lasting for the first 18 months of life; libidinal impulses are best satisfied through the stimulation of the mouth area, including actions such as feeding or sucking; major issues of concern are dependence and the reliability of others

organic amnesia loss of memory caused by brain injury resulting from disease, drugs, accidents (blows to head), or surgery

orgasm discharge of neuromuscular tension built up during sexual activity; in men, entails rhythmic contractions of the prostate, seminal vesicles, vas deferens, and penis and seminal discharge; in women, entails contractions of the orgasmic platform and uterus

P

pain disorder syndrome marked by the chronic experience of acute pain that appears to have no physical cause

palialia continuous repetition of sounds and words

panic attacks short, intense periods during which an individual experiences physiological and cognitive symptoms of anxiety, characterized by intense fear and discomfort

panic disorder disorder characterized by recurrent, unexpected panic attacks

paranoid personality disorder chronic and pervasive mistrust and suspicion of other people that are unwarranted and maladaptive

paranoid schizophrenia syndrome marked by delusions and hallucinations that involve themes of persecution and grandiosity

paraphilias atypical sexual activities that involve one of the following: (1) nonhuman objects, (2) nonconsenting adults, (3) the suffering or humiliation of oneself or one's partner, or (4) children

parasomnias primary sleep disorders that involve abnormal behavioral and physiological events occurring during sleep

partial reinforcement schedule form of behavior modification in which a behavior is rewarded or punished only some of the time

patients' rights movement movement to ensure that mental patients retain their basic rights and to remove them from institutions and care for them in the community

pedophilia adult obtainment of sexual gratification by engaging in sexual activities with young children

penis envy according to Freud, wish to have the male sex organ

performance anxiety anxiety over sexual performance that interferes with sexual functioning

perinatal hypoxia oxygen deprivation during labor and delivery; an obstetrical complication that may be especially important in neurological development

persecutory delusion false, persistent belief that one is being pursued by other people

personality habitual and enduring ways of thinking, feeling, and acting that make each person unique

personality disorder chronic pattern of maladaptive cognition, emotion, and behavior that begins in adolescence or early adulthood and continues into later adulthood

personality inventories questionnaires that assess people's typical ways of thinking, feeling, and behaving; used to obtain information about people's well-being, self-concept, attitudes, and beliefs

pervasive developmental disorders disorders characterized by severe and persisting impairment in several areas of development

phallic stage according to Freud, psycho-sexual stage that occurs between the ages of 3 and 6: the focus of pleasure is the genitals; important conflicts of sexual development emerge this time, differing for boys and girls

phenothiazines drugs that reduce the functional level of dopamine in the brain and tend to reduce the symptoms of schizophrenia

phenylcyclidine (PCP) substance that produces euphoria, slowed reaction times, and involuntary movements at low doses; disorganized thinking, feelings of unreality, and hostility at intermediate doses; and amnesia, analgesia, respiratory problems, and changes in body temperature at high doses

phonological disorder disorder involving the use of speech sounds inappropriate for one's age or dialect

pituitary major endocrine gland that lies partly on the outgrowth of the brain and just below the hypothalamus; produces the largest number of different hormones and controls the secretions of other endocrine glands

placebo control group in a therapy outcome study, group of people whose treatment is an inactive substance (to compare with the effects of a drug) or a nontheory-based therapy providing social support (to compare with the effects of psychotherapy)

plaques deposits of amyloid protein that accumulate in the extracellular spaces of the cerebral cortex, hippocampus, and other forebrain structures in people with Alzheimer's disease

plateau phase in the sexual response cycle, period between arousal and orgasm, during which excitement remains high but stable

pleasure principle drive to maximize pleasure and minimize pain as quickly as possible

polygenic combination of many genes, each of which makes a small contribution to an inherited trait

positive symptoms in schizophrenia, hallucinations, delusions, and disorganization in thought and behavior (also called Type I symptoms)

positron-emission tomography (PET) method of localizing and measuring brain activity by detecting photons that result from the metabolization of an injected isotope

posttraumatic stress disorder (PTSD) anxiety disorder characterized by (1) repeated mental images of experiencing a traumatic event, (2) emotional numbing and detachment, and (3) hypervigilance and chronic arousal

preconscious according to Freud, area of the psyche that contains material from the unconscious before it reaches the conscious mind

predictive validity extent to which a measure accurately forecasts how a person will think, act, and feel in the future

predisposition tendency to develop a disorder that must interact with other biological, psychological, or environmental factors for the disorder to develop

prefrontal cortex region at the front of the brain important in language, emotional expression, the planning and producing of new ideas, and the mediation of social interactions

prefrontal lobotomy type of psychosurgery in which the frontal lobes of the brain are severed from the lower centers of the brain in people suffering from psychosis

premature ejaculation man's inability to delay ejaculation after minimal sexual stimulation or until one wishes to ejaculate, causing significant distress or interpersonal problems

premenstrual dysphoric disorder syndrome in which a woman experiences an increase in depressive symptoms during the premenstrual period and relief from these symptoms with the onset of menstruation

prepared classical conditioning theory that evolution has prepared people to be easily conditioned to fear objects or situations that were dangerous in ancient times

prevalence proportion of the population that has a specific disorder at a given point or period in time

primary prevention cessation of the development of psychological disorders before they start

primary process thinking wish fulfillment, or fantasies, humans use to conjure up desired objects or actions; an example is a hungry infant's imagining its mother's breast when she is not present

prodromal symptoms in schizophrenia, milder symptoms prior to an acute phase of the disorder, during which behaviors are unusual and peculiar but not yet psychotic or completely disorganized

projective test presentation of an ambiguous stimulus, such as an inkblot, to a client, who then projects unconscious motives and issues onto the stimulus in his or her interpretation of its content

prototypes images of the self and others in relation to the self formed from experiences with family during childhood

psychic epidemics phenomena in which large numbers of people begin to engage in unusual behaviors that appear to have a psychological origin

psychoanalysis form of treatment for psychopathology involving alleviating unconscious conflicts driving psychological symptoms by helping people gain insight into their conflicts and finding ways of resolving these conflicts

psychodynamic theories theories developed by Freud's followers but usually differing somewhat from Freud's original theories

psychodynamic therapies therapies focused on uncovering and resolving unconscious conflicts that drive psychological symptoms

psychogenic amnesia loss of memory in the absence of any brain injury or disease and thought to have psychological causes

psychological approach approach to abnormality that focuses on personality, behavior, and ways of thinking as possible causes of abnormality

psychological theories theories that view mental disorders as caused by psychological processes, such as beliefs, thinking styles, and coping styles

psychopathology symptoms that cause mental, emotional, and/or physical pain

psychopathy set of broad personality traits including superficial charm, a grandiose sense of self-worth, a tendency toward boredom and need for stimulation, pathological lying, an ability to be conning and manipulative, and a lack of remorse

psychosexual stages according to Freud, tages in the developmental process children pass through; in each stage, sex drives are focused on the stimulation of certain areas of the body and particular psychological issues can arouse anxiety

psychosis state involving a loss of contact with reality as well as an inability to differentiate between reality and one's subjective state

psychosomatic disorders syndromes marked by identifiable physical illness or defect caused at least partly by psychological factors

psychosurgery rare treatment for mental disorders in which a neurosurgeon attempts to destroy small areas of the brain thought to be involved in a patient's symptoms

psychotherapy treatment for abnormality that consists of a therapist and client discussing the client's symptoms and their causes; the therapist's theoretical orientation determines the foci of conversations with the client

purging type of bulimia nervosa type of bulimia nervosa in which bingeing is followed by the use of self-induced vomiting or purging medications to control weight gain

R

random assignment assignment of participants in an experiment to groups based on a random process

rapid cycling bipolar disorder diagnosis given when a person has four or more cycles of mania and depression within a single year

reading disorder developmental disorder involving deficits in reading ability

realistic anxiety anxiety that occurs when one faces a real danger or threat, such as a tornado

reality principle idea that the ego seeks to satisfy one's needs within the realities of society's rules, rather than following the abandon of the pleasure principle

receptors molecules on the membranes of neurons to which neurotransmitters bind

reflection method of responding in which a therapist expresses his or her attempt to understand what the client is experiencing and trying to communicate

reformulated learned helplessness theory view that people who attribute negative events to internal, stable, and global causes are more likely than other people to experience learned helplessness deficits following such events and are thus predisposed to depression

relapse prevention programs treatments that seek to offset continued alcohol use by identifying high-risk situations for those attempting to stop or cut down on drinking and teaching them either to avoid those situations or to use assertiveness skills when in them, while viewing setbacks as temporary

reliability degree of consistency in a measurement—that is, the extent to which it yields accurate measurements of a phenomenon across several trials, across different populations, and in different forms

repetitive transcranial magnetic stimulation (rTMS) biological treatment that exposes patients to repeated, high-intensity magnetic pulses that are focused on particular brain structures in order to stimulate those structures

replication repetition of the same results from study to study

repression defense mechanism in which the ego pushes anxiety-provoking material back into the unconscious

residual schizophrenia diagnosis made when a person has already experienced a single acute phase of schizophrenia but currently has milder and less debilitating symptoms

residual symptoms in schizophrenia, milder symptoms following an acute phase of the disorder, during which behaviors are unusual and peculiar but not psychotic or completely disorganized

resistance in psychodynamic therapy, when a client finds it difficult or impossible to address certain material, the client's resistance signals an unconscious conflict, which the therapist then tries to interpret

resolution in the sexual response cycle, state of deep relaxation following orgasm in which a man loses his erection and a woman's orgasmic platform subsides

response shaping technique used in behavior therapy in which a person's behavior problems are changed to desirable behaviors through operant conditioning

restricting type of anorexia nervosa type of anorexia nervosa in which weight gain is prevented by refusing to eat

retrograde amnesia deficit in the ability to recall previously learned information or past events

Rett's disorder pervasive developmental disorder in which children develop normally at first but later show permanent loss of basic skills in social interactions, language, and/or movement

reuptake process in which a sending neuron reabsorbs some of the neurotransmitter in the synapse, decreasing the amount left in the synapse

right to refuse treatment right, although not recognized by all states, of involuntarily committed people to refuse drugs or other treatment

right to treatment fundamental right of involuntarily committed people to active treatment for their disorders rather than shelter alone

risk factors conditions or variables associated with a higher risk of having a disorder

role-play technique used in behavioral therapy in which the client and the therapist take on the roles of people involved with the client's maladaptive behaviors; the therapist observes the client's behavior in the role-play to assess what aspects of that behavior need to change

rumination focusing on one's personal concerns and feelings of distress repetitively and passively

ruminative response styles theory theory stating that tendencies to focus on one's symptoms of distress and the possible causes and consequences of these symptoms, in a passive and repetitive manner, leads to depression

S

sadomasochism pattern of sexual rituals between a sexually sadistic "giver" and a sexually masochistic "receiver"

sample group of people taken from a population of interest to participate in a study

schizoid personality disorder syndrome marked by a chronic lack of interest in and avoidance of interpersonal relationships as well as emotional coldness in interactions with others

schizophrenia disorder consisting of unreal or disorganized thoughts and perceptions as well as verbal, cognitive, and behavioral deficits

schizotypal personality disorder chronic pattern of inhibited or inappropriate emotion and social behavior as well as aberrant cognitions and disorganized speech

scientific method systematic method of obtaining and evaluating information relevant to a problem

seasonal affective disorder (SAD) disorder identified by a two-year period in which a person experiences major depression during winter months and then recovers fully during the summer; some people with this disorder also experience mild mania during summer months

secondary prevention detection of psychological disorders in their earliest stages and treatment designed to reduce their development

secondary process thinking rational deliberation, as opposed to the irrational thought of primary process thinking

selective serotonin reuptake inhibitors (SSRIs) class of antidepressant drugs

self-actualization fulfillment of one's potential for love, creativity, and meaning

self-efficacy beliefs beliefs that one can engage in the behaviors necessary to overcome a situation

self-help groups groups that form to help the members deal with a common problem

self-monitoring method of assessment in which a client records the number of times per day that he or she engages in a specific behavior and the conditions surrounding the behavior

sensate focus therapy treatment for sexual dysfunction in which partners alternate between giving and receiving stimulation in a relaxed, openly communicative atmosphere, in order to reduce performance anxiety and concern over achieving orgasm by learning each partner's sexual fulfillment needs

separation anxiety disorder syndrome of childhood and adolescence marked by the presence of abnormal fear or worry over becoming separated from one's caregiver(s) as well as clinging behaviors in the presence of the caregiver(s)

serotonin neurotransmitter that is involved in the regulation of mood and impulsive responses

set point natural body weight determined by a person's metabolic rate, diet, and genetics

sexual aversion disorder condition in which a person actively avoids sexual activities and experiences sex as unpleasant or anxiety-provoking

sexual desire in the sexual response cycle, an urge or inclination to engage in sexual activity

sexual dysfunctions problems in experiencing sexual arousal or carrying through with sexual acts to the point of sexual arousal

sexual masochism sexual gratification obtained through experiencing pain and humiliation at the hands of one's partner

sexual orientation one's preference for partners of the same or opposite sex with respect to attraction and sexual desire

sexual sadism sexual gratification obtained through inflicting pain and humiliation on one's partner

single-case experimental design experimental design in which an individual or a small number of individuals is studied intensively; the individual is put through some sort of manipulation or intervention, and his or her behavior is examined before and after this manipulation to determine the effects

situational type phobias extreme fears of situations such as public transportation, tunnels, bridges, elevators, flying, driving, or enclosed spaces

sleep apnea repeated episodes of upper-airway obstruction during sleep; people with sleep apnea typically snore loudly, go silent and do not breathe for several seconds at a time, then gasp for air

sleep restriction therapy treatment for insomnia that involves initially restricting the amount of time that people with insomnia can try to sleep at night

smooth pursuit eye movement task in which individuals are asked to keep their head still and track a moving object (sometimes referred to as eye tracking); some people with schizophrenia show deficits on this task

social approach approach to abnormality that focuses on interpersonal relationships, culture, society, and the environment as possible causes of abnormality

social learning theory theory that people learn behaviors by imitating and observing others and by learning about the rewards and punishments that follow behaviors

social phobia extreme fear of being judged or embarrassed in front of people, causing the individual to avoid social situations

social selection explanation of the effects of the symptoms of schizophrenia on a person's life and the resulting tendency to drift downward in social class, as compared with the person's family of origin

social skills training technique often used in behavior therapy to help people with problems in interacting and communicating with others

social structural theories theories that focus on environmental and societal demands as causes of abnormal behavior

somatic hallucinations perceptions that something is happening inside one's body—for example, that worms are eating one's intestines

somatization disorder syndrome marked by the chronic experience of unpleasant or painful physical symptoms for which no organic cause can be found

somatoform disorders disorders marked by unpleasant or painful physical symptoms that have no apparent organic cause and that are often not physiologically possible, suggesting that psychological factors are involved

specific phobias extreme fears of specific objects or situations that cause an individual to routinely avoid those objects or situations

splitting in object relations theory, phenomenon wherein a person splits conceptions of self and others into either all-good or all-bad categories, neglecting to recognize people's mixed qualities

squeeze technique sex therapy technique used for premature ejaculation; the man's partner stimulates him to an erection, and then when he signals that ejaculation is imminent, the partner applies a firm but gentle squeeze to his

penis, either at the glands or at the base, for three or four seconds, the goal of this technique is for the man to learn to identify the point of ejaculatory inevitability and to control his arousal level at the point

statistical significance likelihood that a study's results have occurred only by chance

stimulus-control therapy behavioral intervention for insomnia that involves a set of instructions designed to reduce behaviors that might interfere with sleep and to regulate sleep wake schedules

stop-start technique sex therapy technique used for premature ejaculation; the man or his partner stimulates his penis until he is about to ejaculate; the man then relaxes and concentrates on the sensations in his body until his level of arousal declines; the goal of this technique is for the man to learn to identify the point of ejaculatory inevitability and to control his arousal level at that point

stress experience of events that we perceive as endangering our physical or psychological well-being

stress-management interventions strategies that teach clients to overcome the problems in their lives that are increasing their stress

stroke sudden damage to the brain due to blockage of blood flow or hemorrhaging

structured interview meeting between a clinician and a client or a client's associate(s) in which the clinician asks questions that are standardized, written in advance, and asked of every client

stuttering significant problem in speech fluency, often including frequent repetitions of sounds or syllables

subintentional deaths acts in which individuals indirectly contribute to their own deaths

substance naturally occurring or synthetically produced product that alters perceptions, thoughts, emotions, and behaviors when ingested, smoked, or injected

substance abuse diagnosis given when a person's recurrent substance use leads to significant harmful consequences, as manifested by a failure to fulfill obligations at work, school, or home, the use of substances in physically hazardous situations, legal problems, and continued use despite social and legal problems

substance dependence diagnosis given when a person's substance use leads to physiological dependence or significant impairment or distress, as manifested by an inability to use the substance in moderation; a decline in social, occupational, or recreational activities; or the spending of large amounts of time obtaining substances or recovering from their effects

substance intoxication experience of significantly maladaptive behavioral and psychological symptoms due to the effect of a substance on the central nervous system that develops during or shortly after use of the substance

substance withdrawal experience of clinically significant distress in social, occupational, or other areas of functioning due to the cessation or reduction of substance use

substance-induced sexual dysfunction problems in sexual functioning caused by substance use

substance-related disorder inability to use a substance in moderation and/or the intentional use of a substance to change one's thoughts, feelings, and/or behaviors, leading to impairment in work, academic, personal, or social endeavors

suicide purposeful taking of one's own life

suicide cluster when two or more suicides or attempted suicides nonrandomly occur closely together in space or time

suicide contagion phenomenon in which the suicide of a well-known person is linked to the acceptance of suicide by people who closely identify with that individual

suicide hot lines organizations in which suicide crisis intervention is done over the phone

superego part of the unconscious that consists of absolute moral standards internalized from one's parents during childhood and from one's culture

supernatural theories theories that see mental disorders as the result of supernatural forces, such as divine intervention, curses, demonic possession, and/or personal sins; mental disorders can be cured through religious rituals, exorcisms, confessions, and/or death

symptom questionnaire questionnaire that assesses what symptoms a person is experiencing

synapse space between a sending neuron and a receiving neuron into which neurotransmitters are first released (also known as the synaptic gap)

syndrome set of symptoms that tend to occur together

systematic desensitization therapy type of behavior therapy that attempts to reduce client anxiety through relaxation techniques and progressive exposure to feared stimuli

T

tactile hallucinations perceptions that something is happening to the outside of one's body—for example, that bugs are crawling up one's back

tardive dyskinesia neurological disorder marked by involuntary movements of the tongue, face, mouth, or jaw, resulting from taking neuroleptic drugs

test-retest reliability index of how consistent the results of a test are over time

theory set of assumptions about the likely causes of abnormality and appropriate treatments

therapeutic alliance during therapy, the therapist is empathetic and supportive of the client in order to create a relationship of trust with the client and to encourage the exploration of difficult issues

therapy outcome study experimental study that assesses the effects of an intervention designed to reduce psychopathology in an experimental group, while performing no intervention or a different type of intervention on another group

third variable problem possibility that variables not measured in a study are the real cause of the relationship between the variables measured in the study

thought-stopping techniques strategies that involve finding ways to stop intrusive thoughts

token economy application of operant conditioning in which patients receive tokens for exhibiting desired behaviors that are exchangeable for privileges and rewards; these tokens are withheld when a patient exhibits unwanted behaviors

tolerance condition of experiencing less and less effect from the same dose of a substance

transference in psychodynamic therapies, the client's reaction to the therapist as if the therapist were an important person in his or her early development; the client's feelings and beliefs about this other person are transferred onto the therapist

transsexuals people who experience chronic discomfort with their gender and genitals as well as a desire to be rid of their genitals and to live as a member of the opposite sex

transvestism paraphilia in which a heterosexual man dresses in women's clothing as his primary means of becoming sexually aroused

trephination procedure in which holes were drilled in the skulls of people displaying abnormal behavior to allow evil spirits to depart their bodies; performed in the Stone Age

tricyclic antidepressants class of antidepressant drugs

twin studies studies of the heritability of a disorder by comparing concordance rates between monozygotic and dizygotic twins

Type A behavior pattern personality pattern characterized by time urgency, hostility, and competitiveness

U

unconditional positive regard essential part of humanistic therapy; the therapist expresses that he or she accepts the client, no matter how unattractive, disturbed, or difficult the client is

unconditioned response (UR) in classical conditioning, response that naturally follows when a certain stimulus appears, such as a dog salivating when it smells food

unconditioned stimulus (US) in classical conditioning, stimulus that naturally elicits a reaction, as food elicits salivation in dogs

unconscious area of the psyche where memories, wishes, and needs are stored and where conflicts among the id, ego, and superego are played out

undifferentiated schizophrenia diagnosis made when a person experiences schizophrenic symptoms, such as delusions and hallucinations, but does not meet criteria for paranoid, disorganized, or catatonic schizophrenia

unipolar depression type of depression consisting of depressive symptoms but without manic episodes

unstructured interview meeting between a clinician and a client or a client's associate(s) that consists of open-ended, general questions that are particular to each person interviewed

unusualness criterion for abnormality that suggests that abnormal behaviors are rare or unexpected

V

vaginismus in women, involuntary contractions of the muscles surrounding the outer third of the vagina that interfere with penetration and sexual functioning

vagus nerve stimulation (VNS) treatment in which the vagus nerve—the part of the autonomic nervous system that carries information from the head, neck, thorax, and abdomen to several areas of the brain, including the hypothalamus and amygdala—is stimulated by a small electronic device much like a cardiac pacemaker, which is surgically implanted under a patient's skin in the left chest wall

validity degree of correspondence between a measurement and the phenomenon under study

variable measurable factor or characteristic that can vary within an individual, between individuals, or both

vascular dementia second most common type of dementia, associated with symptoms of cerebrovascular disease (tissue damage in the brain due to a blockage of blood flow)

vasocongestion in the sexual response cycle, the filling of blood vessels and tissues with blood, leading to erection of the penis in males and enlargement of the clitoris, swelling of the labia, and vaginal moistening in women (also called engorgement)

visual hallucination visual perception of something that is not actually present

voyeurism obtainment of sexual arousal by compulsively and secretly watching another person undressing, bathing, engaging in sex, or being naked

vulnerability-stress models comprehensive models of the many factors that lead some people to develop a given mental disorder

W

wait list control group in a therapy outcome study, group of people that functions as a control group while an experimental group receives an intervention and then receives the intervention itself after a waiting period

Wernicke's encephalopathy alcohol-induced permanent cognitive disorder involving mental disorientation, confusion, and, in severe states, coma

word salad speech that is so disorganized that a listener cannot comprehend it

working memory ability to hold information in memory and manipulate it

working through method used in psychodynamic therapies in which the client repeatedly goes over and over painful memories and difficult issues as a way to understand and accept them

REFERENCES

A

Aarsland, D., Andersen, K., Larsen, J. P., Lolk, A., & Kragh-Sørensen, P. (2003). Prevalence and characteristics of dementia in Parkinson disease. *Archives of Neurology, 60,* 387–392.

Abbott, B. B., Schoen, L. S., & Badia, P. (1984). Predictable and unpredictable shock: Behavioral measures of aversion and physiological measures of stress. *Psychological Bulletin, 96,* 45–71.

Abbott, D. W., de Zwaan, M., Mussell, M. P., Raymond, N. C., Seim, H. C., Crow, S. J., Crosby, R. D., & Mitchell, J. E. (1998). Onset of binge eating and dieting in overweight women: Implications for etiology, associated features and treatment. *Journal of Psychosomatic Research, 44,* 367–374.

Abel, G. G., & Osborn, C. (1992). The paraphilias: The extent and nature of sexually deviant and criminal behavior. *Psychiatric Clinics of North America, 15,* 675–687.

Abi-Dargham, A., Kegeles, L. S., Zea-Ponce, Y., Mawlawi, O., Martinez, D., Mitropoulou, V., O'Flynn, K., Koenigsberg, H. W., van Heertum, R., Cooper, T., Laruelle, M., & Siever, L. J. (2004). Striatal amphetamine-induced dopamine release in patients with schizotypal personality disorder studied with single photon emission computed tomography and [123I]Iodobenzamide. *Biological Psychiatry, 55,* 1001–1006.

Abramowitz, C. S., Kosson, D. S., & Seidenberg, M. (2004). The relationship between childhood attention deficit hyperactivity disorder and conduct problems and adult psychopathy in male inmates. *Personality and Individual Differences, 36,* 1031–1047.

Abramowitz, J. S. (1997). Effectiveness of psychological and pharmacological treatments for obsessive-compulsive disorder: A quantitative review. *Journal of Consulting & Clinical Psychology, 65,* 44–52.

Abramson, L. Y., Alloy, L. B., Hankin, B. L., Haeffel, G. J., MacCoon, D. G., & Gibb, B. E. (2002). Cognitive vulnerability-stress models of depression in a self-regulatory and psychobiological context. In I. H. Gotlib & C. L. Hammen (Eds.), *Handbook of depression* (pp. 268–294). New York: Guilford Press.

Abramson, L. Y., Metalsky, G. I., & Alloy, L. B. (1989). Hopelessness depression: A theory-based subtype of depression. *Psychological Review, 96,* 358–372.

Abramson, L. Y., Seligman, M. E. P., & Teasdale, J. (1978). Learned helplessness in humans: Critique and reformulation. *Journal of Abnormal Psychology, 87,* 49–74.

Ackerman, M. D., & Carey, M. P. (1995). Psychology's role in the assessment of erectile dysfunction: Historical perspectives, current knowledge, and methods. *Journal of Consulting & Clinical Psychology, 63,* 862–876.

Addis, M. E., Hatgis, C., Krasnow, A. D., Jacob, K., Bourne, L., & Mansfield, A. (2004). Effectiveness of cognitive-behavioral treatment for panic disorder versus treatment as usual in a managed care setting. *Journal of Consulting & Clinical Psychology, 72,* 625–635.

Ader, R. (2001). Psychoneuroimmunology. *Current Directions in Psychological Science, 10,* 94–98.

Aderibigbe, Y. A., Bloch, R. M., & Walker, W. R. (2001). Prevalence of depersonalization and derealization experiences in a rural population. *Social Psychiatry & Psychiatric Epidemiology, 36,* 63–69.

Agras, S., Sylvester, D., & Oliveau, D. (1969). The epidemiology of common fears and phobia. *Comprehensive Psychiatry, 10,* 151–156.

Agras, W. S. (1987). *Eating disorders: Management of obesity, bulimia, and anorexia nervosa.* New York: Pergamon Press.

Agras, W. S., & Kirkley, B. G. (1986). Bulimia: Theories of etiology. In K. D. Brownell & J. P. Foreyt (Eds.), *Handbook of eating disorders: Physiology, psychology, and treatment of obesity, anorexia, and bulimia* (pp. 367–378). New York: Basic Books.

Agras, W. S., Walsh, B. T., Fairburn, C. C., Wilson, G. T., & Kraemer, H. C. (2000). A multicenter comparison of cognitive-behavioral therapy and interpersonal psychotherapy for bulimia nervosa. *Archives of General Psychiatry, 57,* 459–466.

Aguero-Torres, H., Fratiglioni, L., & Winblad, B. (1998). Natural history of Alzheimer's disease and other dementias: Review of the literature in the light of the findings from the Kungholmen Project. *International Journal of Geriatric Psychiatry, 13,* 755–766.

Akhtar, S., Wig, N. N., Varma, V. K., Pershad, D., & Verma, S. K. (1975). A phenomenological analysis of symptoms in obsessive-compulsive neurosis. *British Journal of Psychiatry, 127,* 342–348.

Alexander, K. L., Entwisle, D. R., & Thompson, M. S. (1987). School performance, status relations, and the structure of sentiment: Bringing the teacher back in. *American Sociological Review, 52,* 665–682.

Alexander, M. A. (1999). Sexual offender treatment efficacy revisited. *Sexual Abuse: Journal of Research & Treatment, 11,* 101–116.

Allderidge, P. (1979). Hospitals, madhouses and asylums: Cycles in the care of the insane. *British Journal of Psychiatry, 134,* 321–334.

Allen, J. B., & Iacono, W. G. (2001). Assessing the validity of amnesia in dissociative identity disorder: A dilemma for the DSM and the courts. *Psychology, Public Policy, & Law, 7,* 311–344.

Allison, J., Blatt, S. J., & Zimet, C. N. (1968). *The interpretation of psychological tests.* New York: Harper & Row.

Alloy, L. B., & Abramson, L. Y. (1979). Judgment of contingency in depressed and nondepressed students: Sadder but wiser? *Journal of Experimental Psychology: General, 108,* 441–485.

Alloy, L. B., Abramson, L. Y., & Francis, E. L. (1999). Do negative cognitive styles confer vulnerability to depression? *Current Directions in Psychological Science, 8,* 128–132.

Althof, S. E. (1995). Pharmacologic treatment of rapid ejaculation. *Psychiatric Clinics of North America, 18,* 85–94.

Althof, S. E. (2000). Erectile dysfunction: Psychotherapy with men and couples. In S. R. Leiblum & R. C. Rosen (Eds.), *Principles and practice of sex therapy* (3rd ed., pp. 242–275). New York: Guilford Press.

Altshuler, L. L., Bartzokis, G., Grieder, T., Curran, J., & Mintz, J. (1998). Amygdala enlargement in bipolar disorder and hippocampal reduction in schizophrenia: An MRI study demonstrating neuroanatomic specificity. *Archives of General Psychiatry, 55,* 663–664.

American Heart Association. (2002). Diseases and conditions. Available at www.americanheart.org

American Psychiatric Association (APA). (1994). *Diagnostic and statistical manual of mental disorders* (4th ed.). Washington, DC: American Psychiatric Association.

American Psychiatric Association (APA). (2000). *Diagnostic and statistical manual of mental disorders* (4th ed., Text Revision). Washington, DC: American Psychiatric Association.

American Psychological Association. (2000). Guidelines for psychotherapy with lesbian, gay, and bisexual clients. *American Psychologist, 55,* 1440–1451.

Ananth, J., Burgoyne, K. S., Gadasalli, R., & Aquino, S. (2001). How do the atypical antipsychotics work? *Journal of Psychiatry & Neuroscience, 26,* 385–394.

Anastopoulos, A. D., & Farley, S. E. (2003). A cognitive-behavioral training program for parents of children with attention-deficit/hyperactivity disorder. In A. E. Kazdin & J. R. Weisz (Eds.), *Evidence-based psychotherapies for children and adolescents* (pp. 187–203). New York: Guilford Press.

Anders, S. L. (2003). Improving community-based care for the treatment of schizophrenia: Lessons from native Africa. *Psychiatric Rehabilitation Journal, 27*, 51–58.

Andersen, A. E. (Ed.). (1990). *Males with eating disorders*. New York: Brunner/Mazel.

Andersen, A. E., & DiDomenico, L. (1992). Diet vs. shape content of popular male and female magazines: A dose-response relationship to the incidence of eating disorders? *International Journal of Eating Disorders, 11*, 283–287.

Anderson, E. M., & Lambert, M. J. (1995). Short-term dynamically oriented psychotherapy: A review and meta-analysis. *Clinical Psychology Review, 15*, 503–514.

Anderson, G., Yasenik, L., & Ross, C. A. (1993). Dissociative experiences and disorders among women who identify themselves as sexual abuse survivors. *Child Abuse & Neglect, 17*, 677–686.

Anderson, G. M., & Hoshino, Y. (1997). Neurochemical studies of autism. In D. J. Cohen & F. R. Volkmar (Eds.), *Handbook of autism and pervasive developmental disorders* (pp. 325–343). Toronto: Wiley.

Anderson, N. B., Lane, J. D., Taguchi, F., & Williams, R. B. (1989). Patterns of cardiovascular responses to stress as a function of race and parental hypertension in men. *Health Psychology, 8*, 525–540.

Anderson, R. E., Bartlett, S. J., Morgan, G. D., & Brownell, K. D. (1995). Weight loss, psychological, and nutritional patterns in competitive male body builders. *International Journal of Eating Disorders, 18*, 49–57.

Andreasen, N. (2001). Neuroimaging and neurobiology of schizophrenia. In K. Miyoshi, C. M. Shapiro, M. Gaviria, & Y. Morita (Eds.), *Contemporary neuropsychiatry* (pp. 265–271). Tokyo: Springer-Verlag.

Andreasen, N. C., Flaum, M., Swayze, V. W., Tyrrell, G., & Arndt, S. (1990). Positive and negative symptoms in schizophrenia: A critical reappraisal. *Archives of General Psychiatry, 47*, 615–621.

Angold, A., Costello, E. J., & Worthman, C. M. (1998). Puberty and depression: The roles of age, pubertal status, and pubertal timing. *Psychological Medicine, 28*, 51–61.

Angold, A., Erkanli, A., Egger, H. L., & Costello, J. (2000). Stimulant treatment for children: A community perspective. *Journal of the American Academy of Child & Adolescent Psychiatry, 39*, 975–994.

Angold, A., Erkanli, A., Farmer, E. M. Z., Fairbank, J. A., Burns, B. J., Keeler, G., & Costello, J. (2002). Psychiatric disorder, impairment, and service use in rural African American and white youth. *Archives of General Psychiatry, 59*, 893–901.

Angst, J. (1998). Treated versus untreated major depressive episodes. *Psychopathology, 31*, 37–44.

Angst, J., Gamma, A., Endrass, J., Goodwin, R., Ajdacic, V., Eich, D., & Rössler, W. (2004). Obsessive-compulsive severity spectrum in the community: Prevalence, comorbidity, and course. *European Archives of Psychiatry & Clinical Neuroscience, 254*, 156–164.

Angst, J., Vollrath, M., Koch, R., & Dobler-Mikola, A. (1989). The Zurich Study: VII. Insomnia: Symptoms, classification and prevalence. *European Archives of Psychiatry & Clinical Neuroscience, 238*, 285–293.

Anonymous. (1983). First-person account. *Schizophrenia Bulletin, 9*, 152–155.

Anonymous. (1992). First-person account: Portrait of a schizophrenic. *Schizophrenia Bulletin, 18*, 333–334.

Anton, R. F. (2001). Pharmacologic approaches to the management of alcoholism. *Journal of Clinical Psychiatry, 62*(Suppl. 20), 11–17.

Appelbaum, P. S. (2003). The "quiet" crisis in mental health services. *Health Affairs, 22*, 110–116.

Arieti, S. (1955). *Interpretation of schizophrenia*. New York: R. Brunner.

Arieti, S., & Bemporad, J. R. (1980). The psychological organization of depression. *American Journal of Psychiatry, 137*, 1360–1365.

Arnold, L. M., Keck, P. E., Jr., Collins, J., Wilson, R., Fleck, D. E., Corey, K. B., Amicone, J., Adebimpe, V. R., & Strakowski, S. M. (2004). Ethnicity and first-rank symptoms in patients with psychosis. *Schizophrenia Research, 67*, 207–212.

Arseneault, L., Moffitt, T. E., Caspi, A., Taylor, A., Rijsdijk, F. V., Jaffee, S. R., Ablow, J. C., & Measelle, J. R. (2003). Strong genetic effects on cross-situational antisocial behaviour among 5-year-old children according to mothers, teachers, examiner-observers, and twins' self-reports. *Journal of Child Psychology & Psychiatry, 44*, 832–848.

Arseneault, L., Moffitt, T. E., Caspi, A., Taylor, P. J., & Silva, P. A. (2000). Mental disorders and violence in a total birth cohort. *Archives of General Psychiatry, 57*, 979–986.

Asberg, M., & Forslund, K. (2000). Neurobiological aspects of suicidal behavior. *International Review of Psychiatry, 12*, 62–74.

Ashton, A. K., & Rosen, R. C. (1998). Bupropion as an antidote for serotonin reuptake inhibitor–induced sexual dysfunction. *Journal of Clinical Psychiatry, 59*, 112–115.

Astin, J. A. (1998). Why patients use alternative medicine: Results of a national study. *Journal of the American Medical Association, 279*, 1548–1553.

Atiya, M., Hyman, B. T., Albert, M. S., & Killiany, R. (2003). Structural magnetic resonance imaging in established and prodromal Alzheimer's disease: A review. *Alzheimer's Disease & Associated Disorders, 17*, 177–195.

August, G. L., Realmutto, G. M., Hektner, J. M., & Bloomquist, M. L. (2001). An integrated components preventive intervention for aggressive elementary school children: The early risers' program. *Journal of Consulting & Clinical Psychology, 69*, 614–626.

B

Bach, A. K., Wincze, J. P., & Barlow, D. H. (2001). Sexual dysfunction. In D. H. Barlow (Ed.), *Clinical handbook of psychological disorders: A step-by-step treatment manual* (3rd ed., pp. 562–608). New York: Guilford Press.

Bachrach, H. M., Galatzer-Levy, R., Skolnikoff, A., & Waldron, S. (1991). On the efficacy of psychoanalysis. *Journal of the American Psychoanalytic Association, 39*, 871–916.

Baer, J. S., Kivlahan, D. R., Blume, A. W., McKnight, P., & Marlatt, G. A. (2001). Brief intervention for heavy-drinking college students: 4-year follow-up and natural history. *American Journal of Public Health, 91*, 1310–1316.

Baer, J. S., Marlatt, G. A., Kivlahan, D. R., & Fromme, K. (1992). An experimental test of three methods of alcohol risk reduction with young adults. *Journal of Consulting & Clinical Psychology, 60*, 974–979.

Bagby, R. M., Costa, P. T., McCrae, Robert R., Livesley, W. J., Kennedy, S. H., Levitan, R. D., Levitt, A. J., Joffe, R. T., & Young, L. T. (1999). Replicating the five factor model of personality in a psychiatric sample. *Personality & Individual Differences, 27*, 1135–1139.

Bagge, C., Nickell, A., Stepp, S., Durrett, C., Jackson, K., & Trull, T. J. (2004). Borderline personality disorder features predict negative outcomes 2 years later. *Journal of Abnormal Psychology, 113*, 279–288.

Baker, A., & Shalhoub-Kevorkian, N. (1999). Effects of political and military traumas on children: The Palestinian case. *Clinical Psychology Review, 19*, 935–950.

Baker, D., Hunter, E., Lawrence, E., Medford, N., Patel, M., Senior, C., Sierra, M., Lambert, M. V., Phillips, M. L., & David, A. S. (2003). Depersonalisation disorder: Clinical features of 204 cases. *British Journal of Psychiatry, 182*, 428–433.

Baldessarini, R. J., Tondo, L., & Hennen, J. (2001). Treating the suicidal patient with bipolar disorder: Reducing suicide risk with lithium. *Annals of the New York Academy of Sciences, 932*, 24–38.

Ballenger, J. C., Davidson, J. R. T., Lecrubier, Y., Nutt, D. J., Marshall, R. D., Nemeroff, C. B., Shalev, A. Y., & Yehuda, R. (2004). Consensus statement update on posttraumatic stress disorder from the International Consensus Group on Depression and Anxiety. *Journal of Clinical Psychiatry, 65*(Suppl. 1), 55–62.

Balon, R. (1998). Fluoxamine-induced erectile dysfunction responding to sildenafil. *Journal of Sex & Marital Therapy, 24*, 313–317.

Bandura, A. (1969). *Principles of behavior modification*. New York: Holt, Rinehart & Winston.

Bandura, A. (1977). Self-efficacy: Toward a unifying theory of behavioral change. *Psychological Review, 84*, 191–215.

Bandura, A. (1986). *Social foundations of thought and action*. Englewood Cliffs, NJ: Prentice Hall.

Bandura, A. (1995). *Self-efficacy in changing societies*. New York: Cambridge University Press.

Banks, S., Robbins, P. C., Silver, E., Vesselinov, R., Steadman, H. J., Monahan, J., Mulvey, E. P., Appelbaum, P. S., Grisso, T., & Roth, L. H. (2004). A multiple-models approach to violence risk assessment among people with mental disorder. *Criminal Justice & Behavior, 31*, 324–340.

Banse, R. (2004). Adult attachment and marital satisfaction: Evidence for dyadic configuration effects. *Journal of Social & Personal Relationships, 21*, 273–282.

Barch, D. M. (2003). Cognition in schizophrenia: Does working memory work? *Current Directions in Psychological Science, 12,* 146–150.

Barch, D. M. (2005). The cognitive neuroscience of schizophrenia. *Annual Review of Clinical Psychology, 1,* 321–353.

Barch, D. M., Csernansky, J. G., Conturo, T., & Snyder, A. Z. (2002). Working and long-term memory deficits in schizophrenia: Is there a common prefrontal mechanism? *Journal of Abnormal Psychology, 111,* 478–494.

Barefoot, J. C., Dahlstrom, W. G., & Williams, R. B. (1983). Hostility, CHD incidence, and total mortality: A 25-yr follow-up study of 255 physicians. *Psychosomatic Medicine, 45,* 59–63.

Barefoot, J. C., Dodge, K. A., Peterson, B. L., Dahlstrom, W. G., & Williams, R. B., Jr. (1989). The Cook-Medley Hostility Scale: Item content and ability to predict survival. *Psychosomatic Medicine, 51,* 46–57.

Barefoot, J. C., Siegler, I. C., Nowlin, J. B., & Peterson, B. L. (1987). Suspiciousness, health, and mortality: A follow-up study of 500 older adults. *Psychosomatic Medicine, 49,* 450–457.

Barkley, R. A. (1991). Attention deficit hyperactivity disorder. *Psychiatric Annals, 21,* 725–733.

Barkley, R. A. (1996). Attention deficit/ hyperactivity disorder. In E. J. Mash & R. A. Barkley (Eds.), *Child psychopathology* (pp. 63–112). New York: Guilford Press.

Barkley, R. A., Fischer, M., Edelbrock, C. S., & Smallish, L. (1990). The adolescent outcome of hyperactive children diagnosed by research criteria: I. An 8-year prospective follow-up study. *Journal of the American Academy of Child & Adolescent Psychiatry, 29,* 546–557.

Barkley, R. A., Fischer, M., Smallish, L., & Fletcher, K. (2004). Young adult follow-up of hyperactive children: Antisocial activities and drug use. *Journal of Child Psychology & Psychiatry, 45,* 195–211.

Barlow, D. H. (1986). Causes of sexual dysfunction: The role of anxiety and cognitive interference. *Journal of Consulting & Clinical Psychology, 54,* 140–148.

Barlow, D. H. (1988). *Anxiety and its disorders: The nature and treatment of anxiety and panic.* New York: Guilford Press.

Barlow, D. H., & Craske, M. G. (1994). *Mastery of your anxiety and panic (MAP II).* Albany, NY: Graywind.

Barlow, D. H., Craske, M. G., Cerny, J. A., & Klosko, J. S. (1989). Behavioral treatment of panic disorder. *Behavior Therapy, 20,* 261–282.

Barlow, D. H., Gorman, J. M., Shear, M. K., & Woods, S. W. (2000). Cognitive-behavioral therapy, imipramine, or their combination for panic disorder: A randomized controlled trial. *Journal of the American Medical Association, 283,* 2529–2536.

Barlow, D. H., Sakheim, D. K., & Beck, J. G. (1983). Anxiety increases sexual arousal. *Journal of Abnormal Psychology, 92,* 49–54.

Baron, P., & Peixoto, N. (1991). Depressive symptoms in adolescents as a function of personality factors. *Journal of Youth & Adolescence, 20,* 493–500.

Baron-Cohen, S., & Swettenham, J. (1997). Theory of mind in autism: Its relationship to executive function and central coherence. In D. J. Cohen & F. R. Volkmar (Eds.), *Handbook of autism and pervasive developmental disorders* (pp. 880–893). Toronto: Wiley.

Barsky, A. J., Wyshak, G., & Klerman, G. L. (1992). Psychiatric comorbidity in DSM-III-R hypochondriasis. *Archives of General Psychiatry, 49,* 101–108.

Bartlik, B., & Goldberg, J. (2000). Female sexual arousal disorder. In S. R. Leiblum & R. C. Rosen (Eds.), *Principles and practice of sex therapy* (3rd ed., pp. 85–117). New York: Guilford Press.

Bartlik, B., & Goldstein, M. Z. (2001a). Practical geriatrics: Maintaining sexual health after menopause. *Psychiatric Services, 51,* 751–753.

Bartlik, B., & Goldstein, M. Z. (2001b). Practical geriatrics: Men's sexual health after midlife. *Psychiatric Services, 52,* 291–293.

Basoglu, M., Kiliç, C., Salcioglu, E., & Livanou, M. (2004). Prevalence of posttraumatic stress disorder and comorbid depression in earthquake survivors in Turkey: An epidemiological study. *Journal of Traumatic Stress, 17,* 133–141.

Basoglu, M., Mineka, S., Paker, M., Aker, T., Livanou, M., & Gok, S. (1997). Psychological preparedness for trauma as a protective factor in survivors of torture. *Psychological Medicine, 27,* 1421–1433.

Basson, R., Berman, J., Burnett, A., Derogatis, L., Ferguson, D., Fourcroy, J., Goldstein, I., Graziottin, A., Heiman, J., Laan, E., Leiblum, S., Padma-Nathan, H., Rosen, R., Segraves, K., Segraves, R. T., Shabsigh, R., Sipski, M., Wagner, G., & Whippie, B. (2001). Report of the international consensus development conference on female sexual dysfunction: Definitions and classifications. *Journal of Sex & Marital Therapy, 27,* 83–94.

Basson, R., McInnes, R., Smith, M. D., Hodgson, G., & Koppiker, N. (2002). Efficacy and safety of sildenafil citrate in women with sexual dysfunction associated with female sexual arousal disorder. *Journal of Women's Health & Gender-Based Medicine, 11,* 367–377.

Bastien, C. H., Morin, C. M., Ouellet, M.-C., Blais, F. C., & Bouchard, S. (2004). Cognitive-behavioral therapy for insomnia: Comparison of individual therapy, group therapy, and telephone consultations. *Journal of Consulting & Clinical Psychology, 72,* 653–659.

Bateson, G., Jackson, D. D., Haley, J., & Weakland, J. (1956). Toward a theory of schizophrenia. *Behavioral Science, 1,* 251–264.

Bauermeister, J. J., Alegria, M., Bird, H. R., Rubio-Stipec, M., et al. (1992). Are attentional-hyperactivity deficits unidimensional or multidimensional syndromes? Empirical findings from a community survey. *Journal of the American Academy of Child & Adolescent Psychiatry, 31,* 423–431.

Baum, A., & Posluszny, D. M. (2001). Traumatic stress as a target for intervention with cancer patients. In A. Baum (Ed.), *Psychosocial interventions for cancer* (pp. 143–173). Washington, DC: American Psychological Association.

Baum, A. S., & Burnes, D. W. (1993). *A nation in denial: The truth about homelessness.* Boulder, CO: Westview Press.

Baxter, L., Schwartz, J., Bergman, K., & Szuba, M. (1992). Caudate glucose metabolic rate changes with both drug and behavior therapy for obsessive-compulsive disorder. *Archives of General Psychiatry, 49,* 681–689.

Baxter, L. R., Jr., Clark, E. C., Iqbal, M., & Ackermann, R. F. (2001). Cortical-subcortical systems in the mediation of obsessive-compulsive disorder: Modeling the brain's mediation of a classic "neurosis." In D. G. Lichter & J. L. Cummings (Eds.), *Frontal-subcortical circuits in psychiatric and neurological disorders* (pp. 207–230). New York: Guilford Press.

Bayley, J. (1999). *Elegy for Iris.* New York: St. Martin's Press.

Beatty, J. (1995). *Principles of behavioral neuroscience.* Dubuque, IA: Wm. C. Brown.

Beaubrun, G., & Gray, G. E. (2000). A review of herbal medicines for psychiatric disorders. *Psychiatric Services, 51,* 1130–1134.

Beck, A. T. (1967). *Depression: Clinical, experimental, and theoretical aspects.* New York: Harper & Row.

Beck, A. T. (1976). *Cognitive therapy and the emotional disorders.* New York: International Universities Press.

Beck, A. T. (1997). Cognitive therapy: Reflections. In J. K. Zeig (Ed.), *The evolution of psychotherapy: The third conference* (pp. 55–69). New York: Brunner/Mazel.

Beck, A. T., & Beck, R. W. (1972). Screening depressed patients in family practice: A rapid technique. *Postgraduate Medicine, 52,* 81–85.

Beck, A. T., Butler, A. C., Brown, G. K., Dahlsgaard, K. K., Newman, C. F., & Beck, J. S. (2001). Dysfunctional beliefs discriminate personality disorders. *Behaviour Research & Therapy, 39,* 1213–1225.

Beck, A. T., & Emery, G. (1985). *Anxiety disorders and phobias: A cognitive perspective.* New York: Basic Books.

Beck, A. T., & Freeman, A. M. (1990). *Cognitive therapy of personality disorders.* New York: Guilford Press.

Beck, A. T., & Rector, N. A. (2005). Cognitive approaches to schizophrenia: Theory and therapy. *Annual Review of Clinical Psychology, 1,* 577–606.

Beck, A. T., Rush, A. J., Shaw, B. F., & Emery, G. (1979). *Cognitive therapy of depression.* New York: Guilford Press.

Beck, A. T., Steer, R. A., Kovacs, M., & Garrison, B. (1985). Hopelessness and eventual suicide: A 10-year prospective study of patients hospitalized with suicidal ideation. *American Journal of Psychiatry, 142,* 559–563.

Beck, A. T., Ward, C. H., Mendelson, M., Moch, J. E., & Erbaugh, J. (1962). Reliability of psychiatric diagnosis: II. A study of consistency of clinical judgments and ratings. *American Journal of Psychiatry, 119,* 351–357.

Beck, A. T., Weissman, A., Lester, D., & Trexler, L. (1974). The measurement of pessimism: The Hopelessness Scale. *Journal of Consulting & Clinical Psychology, 42,* 861–865.

Beck, J. G. (1995). Hypoactive sexual desire: An overview. *Journal of Consulting & Clinical Psychology, 63,* 919–927.

Becker, J. V. (2000). Exhibitionism. In A. E. Kazdin (Ed.), *Encyclopedia of Psychology, Vol. 3* (pp. 288–290). Washington, DC: American Psychological Association.

Becker, J. V., & Kavoussi, R. J. (1996). Sexual and gender identity disorders. In R. E. Hales & S. C. Yudofsky (Eds.), *The American*

Psychiatric Press synopsis of psychiatry (pp. 605–623). Washington, DC: American Psychiatric Press.

Becker-Blease, K. A., Deater-Deckard, K., Eley, T., Freyd, J. J., Stevenson, J., & Plomin, R. (2004). A genetic analysis of individual differences in dissociative behaviors in childhood and adolescence. *Journal of Child Psychology & Psychiatry, 45*, 522–532.

Beckman, L. J. (1994). Treatment needs of women with alcohol problems. *Alcohol Health & Research World, 18*, 206–211.

Beiser, M. (1988). Influences of time, ethnicity, and attachment on depression in Southeast Asian refugees. *American Journal of Psychiatry, 145*, 46–51.

Belcher, J. R. (1988). The future role of state hospitals. *Psychiatric Hospitals, 19*, 79–83.

Bell, C. J., & Nutt, D. J. (1998). Serotonin and panic. *British Journal of Psychiatry, 172*, 465–471.

Bellack, A. S., Morrison, R. L., & Mueser, K. T. (1992). Behavioral interventions in schizophrenia. In S. M. Turner, K. S. Calhoun, & H. E. Adams (Eds.), *Handbook of clinical behavior therapy* (pp. 135–154). New York: Wiley.

Belle, D., & Doucet, J. (2003). Poverty, inequality, and discrimination as sources of depression among U.S. women. *Psychology of Women Quarterly, 27*, 101–113.

Bemporad, J. (1995). Long-term analytic treatment of depression. In E. E. Beckham & W. R. Leber (Eds.), *Handbook of depression* (2nd ed., pp. 391–403). New York: Guilford Press.

Bender, D. S., Dolan, R. T., Skodol, A. E., Sanislow, C. A., Dyck, I. R., McGlasgan, T. H., Shea, M. T., Zanarini, M. C., Oldham, J. M., & Gunderson, J. G. (2001). Treatment utilization by patients with personality disorders. *American Journal of Psychiatry, 158*, 295–302.

Bender, L. (1938). *A visual motor gestalt test and its clinical use.* New York: The American Orthopsychiatric Association.

Benedetti, F., Sforzini, L., Colombo, C., Maffei, C., & Smeraldi, E. (1998). Low-dose clozapine in acute and continuation treatment of severe borderline personality disorder. *Journal of Clinical Psychology, 59*, 103–107.

Benet-Martinez, V., & John, O. P. (1998). Los Cinco Grandes across cultures and ethnic groups: Multitrait-multimethod analyses of the Big Five in Spanish and English. *Journal of Personality & Social Psychology, 75*, 729–750.

Bennett, A. E. (1947). Mad doctors. *Journal of Nervous & Mental Disorders, 29*, 11–18.

Benotsch, E. G., Christensen, A. J., & McKelvey, L. (1997). Hostility, social support, and ambulatory cardiovascular activity. *Journal of Behavioral Medicine, 20*, 163–176.

Berenbaum, S. A., & Hines, M. (1992). Early androgens are related to childhood sex-typed toy preferences. *Psychological Science, 3*, 203–206.

Bergman, A. J., Harvey, P. D., Roitman, S. L., Mohs, R. C., Marder, D., Silverman, J. M., & Siever, L. J. (1998). Verbal learning and memory in schizotypal disorder. *Schizophrenia Bulletin, 24*, 635–641.

Berlin, L. J., Brooks-Gunn, J., McCartoon, C., & McCormick, M. C. (1998). The effectiveness of early intervention: Examining risk factors and pathways to enhanced development. *Preventive Medicine, 27*, 238–245.

Berman, A. L., & Jobes, D. A. (1995). Suicide prevention in adolescents (age 12–18). *Suicide & Life-Threatening Behavior, 25*, 143–154.

Berman, M. E., Kavoussi, R. J., & Coccaro, E. F. (1997). Neurotransmitter correlates of human aggression. In D. M. Stoff, J. Breiling, & J. D. Maser (Eds.), *Handbook of antisocial personality disorder* (pp. 305–314). New York: Wiley.

Bernstein, D. P., Useda, D., & Siever, L. J. (1995). Paranoid personality disorder. In W. J. Livesley (Ed.), *The DSM-IV personality disorders* (pp. 45–57). New York: Guilford Press.

Bettelheim, B. (1967). *The empty fortress: Infantile autism and the birth of the self.* New York: Free Press.

Beutler, L. E., Daldrup, R., Engle, D., & Guest, P. D. (1988). Family dynamics and emotional expression among patients with chronic pain and depression. *Pain, 32*, 65–72.

Bibring, E. (1953). The mechanism of depression. In P. Greenacre (Ed.), *Affective disorders* (pp. 13–48). New York: International Universities Press.

Biederman, J., Faraone, S. V., Hirschfeld-Becker, D. R., Friedman, D., Robin, J. A., & Rosenbaum, J. F. (2001). Patterns of psychopathology and dysfunction in high-risk children of parents with panic disorder and major depression. *American Journal of Psychiatry, 158*, 49–57.

Biederman, J., Faraone, S. V., Monuteaux, M. C., Bober, M., & Cadogen, E. (2004). Gender effects on attention-deficit/hyperactivity disorder in adults, revisited. *Biological Psychiatry, 55*, 692–700.

Biederman, J., Mick, E., Faraone, S. V., Braaten, E., Doyle, A., Spencer, T., Wilens, T. E., Frazier, E., & Johnson, M. (2002). Influence of gender on attention deficit hyperactivity disorder in children referred to a psychiatric clinic. *American Journal of Psychiatry, 159*, 36–42.

Biederman, J., Munir, K., Knee, D., Habelow, W., et al. (1986). A family study of patients with attention deficit disorder and normal controls. *Journal of Psychiatric Research, 20*, 263–274

Biederman, J., Rosenbaum, J. F., Bolduc-Murphy, E. A., Faraone, S. V., Chaloff, J., Hirshfeld, D. R., & Kagan, J. (1993). Behavioral inhibition as a temperamental risk factor for anxiety disorders. *Child & Adolescent Psychiatric Clinics of North America, 2*, 667–684.

Biederman, J., Rosenbaum, J. F., Hirshfeld, D. R., Faraone, V., Bolduc, E., Gersten, M., Meminger, S., & Reznick, J. S. (1990). Psychiatric correlates of behavioral inhibition in young children of parents with and without psychiatric disorders. *Archives of General Psychiatry, 47*, 21–26.

Bierut, L. J., Dinwiddie, S. H., Begleiter, H., Crowe, R. R., Hesselbrock, V., Nurnberger, J. I., Porjesz, B., Schuckit, M. A., & Reich, T. (1998). Familial transmission of substance dependence: Alcohol, marijuana, cocaine, and habitual smoking. *Archives of General Psychiatry, 55*, 982–988.

Bird, H. R., Canino, G. J., Davies, M., Zhang, H., Ramirez, R., & Lahey, B. B. (2001). Prevalence and correlates of antisocial behaviors among three ethnic groups. *Journal of Abnormal Child Psychology, 29*, 465–478.

Bird, T. D., Lampe, T. H., Wijsman, E. M., & Schellenberg, G. D. (1998). Familial Alzheimer's: Genetic studies. In M. F. Folstein (Ed.), *Neurobiology of primary dementia* (pp. 27–42). Washington, DC: American Psychiatric Press.

Birmaher, B., Axelson, D. A., Monk, K., Kalas, C., Clark, D. B., Ehmann, M., Bridge, J., Heo, J., & Brent, D. A. (2003). Fluoxetine for the treatment of childhood anxiety disorders. *Journal of the American Academy of Child & Adolescent Psychiatry, 42*, 415–423.

Blacher, J. B., Hanneman, R. A., & Rousey, A. B. (1992). Out-of-home placement of children with severe handicaps: A comparison of approaches. *American Journal on Mental Retardation, 96*, 607–616.

Blair, A. J., Lewis, J., & Booth, D. A. (1989). Behavior therapy for obesity: The role of clinicians in the reduction of overweight. *Counseling Psychology Quarterly, 2*, 289–301.

Blanchard, E. B., Hickling, E. J., Taylor, A. E., Loos, W. R., et al. (1996). Who develops PTSD from motor vehicle accidents. *Behavior Research & Therapy, 34*, 1–10.

Blanchard, J. J., & Neale, J. M. (1992). Medication effects: Conceptual and methodological issues in schizophrenia research. *Clinical Psychology Review, 12*, 345–361.

Blatt, S. J., & Zuroff, D. C. (1992). Interpersonal relatedness and self-definition: Two prototypes for depression. *Clinical Psychology Review, 12*, 527–562.

Blazer, D. G., George, L., & Hughes, D. (1991). The epidemiology of anxiety disorders. In C. Salzman & B. Liebowitz (Eds.), *Anxiety disorders in the elderly* (pp. 17–30). New York: Springer-Verlag.

Blazer, D. G., Kessler, R. C., McGonagle, K. A., & Swartz, M. S. (1994). The prevalence and distribution of major depression in a national community sample: The National Comorbidity Study. *American Journal of Psychiatry, 151*, 979–986.

Blazer, D. G., Kessler, R. C., & Swartz, M. (1998). Epidemiology of recurrent major and minor depression with a seasonal pattern: The National Comorbidity Study. *British Journal of Psychiatry, 172*, 164–167.

Bliss, E. L. (1980). Multiple personalities: A report of 14 cases with implications for schizophrenia and hysteria. *Archives of General Psychiatry, 37*, 1388–1397.

Bliss, E. L. (1986). *Multiple personality, allied disorders, and hypnosis.* New York: Oxford University Press.

Boeschen, L. E., Koss, M. P., Figueredo, J., & Coan, J. A. (2001). Experiential avoidance and post-traumatic stress disorder: A cognitive mediational model of rape recovery. *Journal of Aggression, Maltreatment & Trauma, 4*, 211–245.

Bohart, A. C. (1990). Psychotherapy integration from a client-centered perspective. In G. Lietaer (Ed.), *Client-centered and experiential psychotherapy in the nineties* (pp. 481–500). Leuven, Belgium: Leuven University Press.

Bohart, A. C. (1995). The person-centered psychotherapies. In A. S. Gurman (Ed.), *Essential psychotherapies: Theory and practice* (pp. 55–84). New York: Guilford Press.

Bohus, M., Haaf, B., Simms, T., Limberger, M. F., Schmahl, C., Unckel, C., Lieb, K., & Linehan, M. M. (2004). Effectiveness of inpatient dialectical behavioral therapy for borderline personality disorder: A controlled trial. *Behaviour Research & Therapy, 42,* 487–499.

Boland, R. J., & Keller, M. B. (2002). Course and outcome of depression. In I. H. Gotlib & C. L. Hammen (Eds.), *Handbook of depression* (pp. 43–60). New York: Guilford Press.

Bölte, S., & Poustka, F. (2004). Comparing the intelligence profiles of savant and nonsavant individuals with autistic disorder. *Intelligence, 32,* 121–131.

Bolton, P., Bass, J., Neugebauer, R., Verdeli, H., Clougherty, K. F., Wickramaratne, P., Speelman, L., Ndogoni, L., & Weissman, M. (2003). Group interpersonal psychotherapy for depression in rural Uganda. *Journal of the American Medical Association, 289,* 3117–3124.

Bonanno, G. A., & Kaltman, S. (1999). Toward an integrative perspective on bereavement. *Psychological Bulletin, 125,* 760–776.

Bondolfi, G., Dufour, H., Patris, M., May, J. P., Billeter, U., Eap, C. B., & Bauman, P. (1998). Risperidone versus clozapine in treatment-resistant chronic schizophrenia: A randomized double-blind study. *American Journal of Psychiatry, 155,* 449–504.

Book, A. S., Starzyk, K. B., & Quinsey, V. L. (2001). The relationship between testosterone and aggression: A meta-analysis. *Aggression & Violent Behavior, 6,* 579–599.

Booth-Kewley, S., & Friedman, H. S. (1987). Psychological predictors of heart disease: A quantitative review. *Psychological Bulletin, 101,* 343–362.

Bootzin, R. R., & Perlis, M. L. (1992). Nonpharmacologic treatments of insomnia. *Journal of Clinical Psychiatry, 53,* 37–41.

Borkovec, T. (2002). Life in the future versus life in the present. *Clinical Psychology: Science & Practice, 9,* 76–80.

Borkovec, T. D. (1994). The nature, functions, and origins of worry. In G. C. L. Davey & F. Tallis (Eds.), *Worrying: Perspectives on theory, assessment, and treatment* (pp. 5–34). Sussex, UK: Wiley.

Borkovec, T. D., & Mathews, A. M. (1988). Treatment of nonphobic anxiety disorders: A comparison of nondirective, cognitive, and coping desensitization therapy. *Journal of Consulting & Clinical Psychology, 56,* 877–884.

Borkovec, T. D., Newman, M. G., & Castonguay, L. G. (2003). Cognitive-behavioral therapy for generalized anxiety disorder with integrations from interpersonal and experiential therapies. *CNS Spectrums, 8,* 382–389.

Borkovec, T. D., Newman, M. G., Pincus, A. L., & Lytle, R. (2002). A component analysis of cognitive-behavioral therapy for generalized anxiety disorder and the role of interpersonal problems. *Journal of Consulting & Clinical Psychology, 70,* 288–298.

Borkovec, T. D., & Ruscio, A. M. (2001). Psychotherapy for generalized anxiety disorder. *Journal of Clinical Psychiatry, 62*(Suppl. 11), 37–42.

Borkovec, T. D., & Whisman, M. A. (1996). Psychosocial treatment for generalized anxiety disorder. In M. R. Mavissakalian (Ed.), *Long-term treatments of anxiety disorders* (pp. 171–199). Washington, DC: American Psychiatric Press.

Borys, D. S., & Pope, K. S. (1989). Dual relationships between therapist and client: A national study of psychologists, psychiatrists, and social workers. *Professional Psychology: Research & Practice, 20,* 283–293.

Bottoms, G. (2000). *Angelhead.* New York: Three Rivers Press.

Bouchard, T. J., & Loehlin, J. C. (2001). Genes, evolution, and personality. *Behavior Genetics, 31,* 243–273.

Bourden, K., Boyd, J., Rae, D., & Burns, B. (1988). Gender differences in phobias: Results of the EAC community survey. *Journal of Anxiety Disorders, 2,* 227–241.

Bourin, M., Baker, G. B., & Bradwejn, J. (1998). Neurobiology of panic disorder. *Journal of Psychosomatic Research, 44,* 163–180.

Bouton, M. E., Mineka, S., & Barlow, D. H. (2001). A modern learning theory perspective on the etiology of panic disorder. *Psychological Review, 108,* 4–32.

Bowen, R. C., Offord, D. R., & Boyle, M. H. (1990). The prevalence of overanxious disorder and separation anxiety disorder: Results from the Ontario Child Health Study. *Journal of the American Academy of Child & Adolescent Psychiatry, 29,* 753–758.

Bower, G. H. (1981). Mood and memory. *American Psychologist, 36,* 129–148.

Bowlby, J. (1982). *Attachment and loss* (2nd ed.). New York: Basic Books.

Boyd, C. J., & Guthrie, B. (1996). Women, their significant others, and crack cocaine. *American Journal on Addictions, 5,* 156–166.

Bradley, J. D. D., & Golden, C. J. (2001). Biological contributions to the presentation and understanding of attention-deficit/hyperactivity disorder: A review. *Clinical Psychology Review, 21,* 907–929.

Bradley, S. J. (1995). Psychosexual disorders in adolescence. In J. M. Oldham & M. B. Riba (Eds.), *Review of psychiatry* (Vol. 14, pp. 735–754). Washington, DC: American Psychiatric Press.

Bradley, S. J., & Zucker, K. J. (1997). Gender identity disorder: A review of the past 10 years. *Journal of the American Academy of Child & Adolescent Psychiatry, 36,* 872–880.

Brady, K., Pearlstein, T., Asnis, G. M., Baker, D., Rothbaum, B., Sikes, C. R., & Farfel, G. M. (2000). Efficacy and safety of sertraline treatment of posttraumatic stress disorder: A randomized controlled trial. *Journal of the American Medical Association, 283,* 1837–1844.

Braginsky, B. M., Braginsky, D. D., & Ring, K. (1969). *Methods of madness: The mental hospital as last resort.* New York: Holt.

Brain, P. F., & Susman, E. J. (1997). Hormonal aspects of aggression and violence. In D. M. Stoff, J. Breiling, & J. D. Maser (Eds.), *Handbook of antisocial personality disorder* (pp. 314–323). New York: Wiley.

Brambilla, F., Bellodi, L., Arancio, C., Ronchi, P., & Limonta, D. (2001). Central dopaminergic function in anorexia and bulimia nervosa: A psychoneuroendocrine approach. *Psychoneuroendocrinology, 26,* 393–409.

Braun, B. G. (Ed.). (1986). *Treatment of multiple personality disorder.* Washington, DC: American Psychiatric Press.

Brawman-Mintzer, O., & Yonkers, K. A. (2001). Psychopharmacology in women. In N. L. Stotland (Ed.), *Psychological aspects of women's health care: The interface between psychiatry and obstetrics and gynecology* (2nd ed., pp. 401–420). Washington, DC: American Psychiatric Press.

Breggin, P. R. (1997). *Brain-disabling treatments in psychiatry: Drugs, electroshock, and the role of the FDA.* New York: Springer.

Bregman, J. D., & Gerdtz, J. (1997). Behavioral interventions. In D. J. Cohen & F. R. Volkmar (Eds.), *Handbook of autism and pervasive developmental disorders* (pp. 606–630). Toronto: Wiley.

Breier, A. (1995). Serotonin, schizophrenia and antipsychotic drug action. *Schizophrenia Research, 14,* 187–202.

Breier, A., Schreiber, J. L., Dyer, J., & Pickar, D. (1991). National Institute of Mental Health longitudinal study of chronic schizophrenia: Prognosis and predictors of outcome. *Archives of General Psychiatry, 48,* 239–246.

Bremner, J. D. (1998). Neuroimaging of posttraumatic stress disorder. *Psychiatric Annals, 28,* 445–450.

Bremner, J. D., Narayan, M., Anderson, E. R., Staib, L. H., Miller, H. L., & Charney, D. S. (2000). Hippocampal volume reduction in major depression. *American Journal of Psychiatry, 157,* 115–118.

Bremner, J. D., Vythilingam, M., Anderson, G., Vermetten, E., McGlashan, T., Heninger, G., Rasmusson, A., Southwick, S. M., & Charney, D. S. (2003). Assessment of the hypothalamic-pituitary-adrenal axis over a 24-hour diurnal period and in response to neuroendocrine challenges in women with and without childhood sexual abuse and posttraumatic stress disorder. *Biological Psychiatry, 54,* 710–718.

Brent, D. A., Kerr, M. M., Goldstein, C., Bozigar, J., Wartella, M., & Allan, M. J. (1989). An outbreak of suicide and suicidal behavior in a high school. *Journal of the American Academy of Child & Adolescent Psychiatry, 28,* 918–924.

Brent, D. A., Kupfer, D. J., Bromet, E. J., & Dew, M. A. (1988). The assessment and treatment of patients at risk for suicide. In A. J. Frances & R. E. Hales (Eds.), *American Psychiatric Press review of psychiatry* (Vol. 7). Washington, DC: American Psychiatric Press.

Brent, D. A., Oquendo, M., Birmaher, B., Greenhill, L., Kolko, D., Stanley, B., Zelazny, J., Brodsky, B., Bridge, J., Ellis, S., Salazer, J. O., & Mann, J. J. (2002). Familial pathways to early-onset suicide attempt. *Archives of General Psychiatry, 59,* 801–807.

Brent, D. A., Oquendo, M., Birmaher, B., Greenhill, L., Kolko, D., Stanley, B., Zelazny, J., Brodsky, B., Firinciogullari, S., Ellis, S. P., & Mann, J. J. (2003). Peripubertal suicide attempts in offspring of suicide attempters with siblings concordant for suicidal behavior. *American Journal of Psychiatry, 160,* 1486–1493.

Brent, D. A., Perper, J. A., Allman, C. J., Moritz, G. M., Wartella, M. E., & Zelenak, J. P. (1991). The presence and accessibility of firearms in the homes of adolescent suicide: A case-control study. *Journal of the American Medical Association, 266,* 2989–2995.

Brevoort, P. (1998). The booming U.S. botanical market: A new overview. *HerbalGram, 44,* 33–46.

Briere, J., & Conte, J. R. (1993). Self-reported amnesia for abuse in adults molested as children. *Journal of Traumatic Stress, 6,* 21–31.

Briere, J., & Runtz, M. (1989). University males' sexual interest in children: Predicting potential indices of "pedophilia" in a nonforensic sample. *Child Abuse & Neglect, 13,* 65–75.

Brockington, I. (2001). Suicide in women. *International Clinical Psychopharmacology, 16*(Suppl. 12), 7–19.

Brody, A. L., Saxena, S., Stoessel, P., Gillies, L. A., Fairbanks, L. A., Alborzian, S., Phelps, M. E., Huang, S., Wu, H., Ho, M. L., Ho, M. K., Au, S. C., Maidment, K., & Baxter, L. R. (2001). Regional brain metabolic changes in patients with major depression treated with either paroxetine or interpersonal therapy: Preliminary findings. *Archives of General Psychiatry, 58,* 631–640.

Broidy, L. M., Nagin, D. S., Tremblay, R. E., Bates, J. E., Brame, B., Dodge, K. A., Fergusson, D., Horwood, J. L., Loeber, R., Laird, R., Lynam, D. R., Moffitt, T. E., Pettit, G. S., & Vitaro, F. (2003). Developmental trajectories of childhood disruptive behaviors and adolescent delinquency: A six-site, cross-national study. *Developmental Psychology, 39,* 222–245.

Bromberger, J. T., & Matthews, K. A. (1996). A longitudinal study of the effects of pessimism, trait anxiety, and life stress on depressive symptoms in middle-aged women. *Psychology & Aging, 11,* 207–213.

Brooks-Gunn, J., Klebanov, P. K., & Duncan, G. J. (1996). Ethnic differences in children's intelligence test scores: Role of economic deprivation, home environment, and maternal characteristics. *Child Development, 67,* 396–408.

Brooks-Gunn, J., Klebanov, P. K., & Liaw, F. (1995). The learning, physical, and emotional environment of the home in the context of poverty: The Infant Health and Development Program. *Children & Youth Services Review, 17,* 251–276.

Brown, D., Scheflin, A. W., & Whitfield, C. L. (1999). Recovered memories: The current weight of the evidence in science and in the courts. *Journal of Psychiatry & Law, 27,* 5–156.

Brown, G. W., Birley, J. L., & Wing, J. K. (1972). Influence of family life on the course of schizophrenic disorders: A replication. *British Journal of Psychiatry, 121,* 241–258.

Brown, J. E., Ayowa, O. B., & Brown, R. C. (1993). Dry and tight: Sexual practices and potential risks in Zaire. *Social Science & Medicine, 37,* 989–994.

Brown, M. Z., Comtois, K. A., & Linehan, M. M. (2002). Reasons for suicide attempts and nonsuicidal self-injury in women with borderline personality disorder. *Journal of Abnormal Psychology, 111,* 198–202.

Brown, S. A., Inaba, R. K., Gillin, J. C., & Schuckit, M. A. (1995). Alcoholism and affective disorder: Clinical course of depressive symptoms. *American Journal of Psychiatry, 152,* 45–52.

Brown, T. A., Campbell, L. A., Lehman, C. L., Grisham, J. R., & Mancill, R. B. (2001). Current and lifetime comorbidity of the DSM-IV anxiety and mood disorders in a large clinical sample. *Journal of Abnormal Psychology, 110,* 585–599.

Brown, T. A., Di Nardo, P. A., Lehman, C. L., & Campbell, L. A. (2001). Reliability of DSM-IV anxiety and mood disorders: Implications for the classification of emotional disorders. *Journal of Abnormal Psychology, 110,* 49–58.

Brown, T. A., O'Leary, T. A., & Barlow, D. H. (2001). Generalized anxiety disorder. *Clinical handbook of psychological disorders: A step-by-step treatment manual* (3rd ed., pp. 154–208). New York: Guilford Press.

Brown, T. M., & Boyle, M. F. (2002). The ABC of psychological medicine: Delirium. *British Medical Journal, 325,* 644–647.

Browne, K. O. (2001). Cultural formulation of psychiatric diagnoses. *Culture, Medicine, & Psychiatry, 25,* 411–425.

Brownell, K. D. (2003). Diet, obesity, public policy, and defiance. In R. J. Sternberg (Ed.), *Psychologists defying the crowd: Stories of those who battled the establishment and won* (pp. 47–64). Washington, DC: American Psychological Association.

Brownell, K. D., & Horgen, K. B. (2004). *Food fight: The inside story of the food industry, America's obesity crisis, and what we can do about it.* Chicago: Contemporary Books.

Bruch, H. (1973). *Eating disorders: Obesity, anorexia nervosa, and the person within.* New York: Basic Books.

Bruch, H. (1982). Anorexia nervosa: Therapy and theory. *American Journal of Psychiatry, 139,* 1531–1538.

Bruch, M. A., & Cheek, J. M. (1995). Developmental factors in childhood and adolescent shyness. In R. G. Heimberg, M. R. Liebowitz, D. A. Hope, & F. R. Schneier (Eds.), *Social phobia: Diagnosis, assessment, and treatment.* New York: Guilford Press.

Brugha, T. S., Sharp, H. M., Cooper, S. A., Weisender, C., Britto, D., Shrikwin, R., Sherrif, T., & Kirwan, P. H. (1998). The Leicester 500 Project. Social support and the development of postnatal depressive symptoms, a prospective cohort survey. *Psychological Medicine, 28,* 63–79.

Buchsbaum, M. S., Someya, T., Wu, J. C., Tang, C. Y., & Bunney, W. E. (1997). Neuroimaging bipolar illness with positron emission tomography and magnetic resonance imaging. *Psychiatric Annals, 27,* 489–495.

Buckwalter, J., Sobel, E., Dunn, M. E., & Diz, M. M. (1993). Gender differences on a brief measure of cognitive functioning in Alzheimer's disease. *Archives of Neurology, 50,* 757–760.

Bugental, J. F. T. (1997). There is a fundamental division in how psychotherapy is conceived. In J. K. Zeig (Ed.), *The evolution of psychotherapy: The third conference* (pp. 185–193). New York: Brunner/Mazel.

Bulik, C. M. (2004). Genetic and biological risk factors. In J. K. Thompson (Ed.), *Handbook of eating disorders and obesity* (pp. 3–16). Hoboken, NJ: Wiley.

Bulik, C. M., Sullivan, P. F., Fear, J., & Pickering, A. (1997). Predictors of the development of bulimia nervosa in women with anorexia nervosa. *Journal of Nervous & Mental Disease, 185,* 704–707.

Bulik, C. M., Sullivan, P. F., & Kendler, K. S. (1998). Heritability of binge-eating and broadly defined bulimia nervosa. *Biological Psychiatry, 44,* 1210–1218.

Bulik, C. M., Sullivan, P. F., Wade, T. D., & Kendler, K. S. (1999). Twin studies of eating disorders: A review. *International Journal of Eating Disorders, 27,* 1–20.

Bulman, R. J., & Wortman, C. G. (1977). Attributions of blame and coping in the "real world": Severe accident victims react to their lot. *Journal of Personality & Social Psychology, 35,* 351–363.

Bunney, W. E., & Davis, J. M. (1965). Norepinephrine in depressive reactions: A review. *Archives of General Psychiatry, 13,* 483–493.

Burnam, M. A., Stein, J. A., Golding, J. M., & Siegel, J. M. (1988). Sexual assault and mental disorders in a community population. *Journal of Consulting & Clinical Psychology, 56,* 843–850.

Burnette, E. (1997). Community psychologists help South Africans mend. *APA Monitor, 28.* Retrieved from the World Wide Web: www.apa.org/monitor/sep97/safrica.html

Burns, D. (1980). *Feeling good: The new mood therapy.* New York: Morrow.

Burns, D., & Nolen-Hoeksema, S. (1991). Coping styles, homework assignments and the effectiveness of cognitive-behavioral therapy. *Journal of Consulting & Clinical Psychology, 59,* 305–311.

Burr, J. A., Hartman, J. T., & Matteson, D. W. (1999). Black suicide in U.S. metropolitan areas: An examination of the racial inequality and social integration-regulation hypotheses. *Social Forces, 77,* 1049–1081.

Busfield, J. (1986). *Managing madness: Changing ideas and practice.* London: Hutchinson.

Bustillo, J. R., Lauriello, J., Horan, W. P., & Keith, S. J. (2001). The psychosocial treatment of schizophrenia: An update. *American Journal of Psychiatry, 158,* 163–175.

Butcher, J. N. (1990). *The MMPI-2 in psychological treatment.* New York: Oxford University Press.

Butler, G., Fennell, M., Robson, P., & Gelder, M. (1991). Comparison of behavior therapy and cognitive behavior therapy in the treatment of generalized anxiety disorder. *Journal of Consulting & Clinical Psychology, 59,* 167–175.

Butzel, J. S., Talbot, N. L., Duberstein, P. R., Houghtalen, R. P., Cox, C., & Giles, D. E. (2000). The relationship between traumatic events and dissociation among women with histories of childhood sexual abuse. *Journal of Nervous & Mental Disease, 188,* 547–549.

Butzlaff, R. L., & Hooley, J. M. (1998). Expressed emotion and psychiatric relapse. *Archives of General Psychiatry, 55,* 547–552.

Byrne, E. J. (1994). *Confusional states in older people.* Boston: E. Arnold.

Byrne, S., Cooper, Z., & Fairburn, C. (2003). Weight maintenance and relapse in obesity: A qualitative study. *International Journal of Obesity, 27,* 955–962.

Bystritsky, A., Ackerman, D. L., Rosen, R. M., Vapnik, T., Gorvis, E., Maidment, K. M., & Saxena, S. (2004). Augmentation of serotonin reuptake inhibitors in refractory obsessive-compulsive disorder using adjunctive olanzapine: A placebo-controlled trial. *Journal of Clinical Psychiatry, 65,* 565–568.

C

Cade, J. (1949). Lithium salts in the treatment of psychotic excitement. *Medical Journal of Australia, 36,* 349–352.

Cadoret, R. J., & Cain, C. A. (1980). Sex differences in predictors of antisocial behavior in adoptees. *Archives of General Psychiatry, 37,* 1171–1175.

Caffey, J. (1972). On the theory and practice of shaking infants. *American Journal of Diseases of Children, 124,* 161–172.

Caldwell, C. B., & Gottesman, I. I. (1991). Sex-differences in the risk for alcoholism—A twin study. *Behavior Genetics, 21,* 563.

Cale, E. M., & Lilienfeld, S. O. (2002). Sex differences in psychopathy and antisocial personality disorder: A review and integration. *Clinical Psychology Review, 22,* 1179–1207.

Cameron, N., & Rychlak, J. F. (1985). *Personality development and psychopathology: A dynamic approach.* Boston: Houghton Mifflin.

Camp, B. W., Broman, S. H., Nichols, P. L., & Leff, M. (1998). Maternal and neonatal risk factors for mental retardation: Defining the "at-risk" child. *Early Human Development, 50,* 159–173.

Campbell, M., Adams, P. B., Small, A. M., Kafantaris, V., Silva, R. R., Shell, J., Perry, R., & Overall, J. E. (1995). Lithium in hospitalized aggressive children with conduct disorder: A double-blind and placebo-controlled study. *Journal of the American Academy of Child & Adolescent Psychiatry, 34,* 445–453.

Campo, J. V., & Fritz, G. (2001). A management model for pediatric somatization. *Psychosomatics, 42,* 467–476.

Canetto, S. S., & Hollenshead, J. D. (1999). Gender and physician-assisted suicide: An analysis of the Kevorkian cases. *Omega, 40,* 165–208.

Canetto, S. S., & Hollenshead, J. D. (2000). Older women and mercy killing. *Omega, 42,* 83–99.

Canetto, S. S., & Sakinofsky, I. (1998). The gender paradox in suicide. *Suicide & Life-Threatening Behavior, 28,* 1–23.

Canino, G. J., Rubio-Stipec, M., & Bravo, M. (1988). Psychiatric diagnostic nosology in transcultural epidemiology research. *Acta Psiquiatrica Psicologica de America Latina, 34,* 251–259.

Cannon, T. D., Kapiro, J., Lonnqvist, J., Huttunen, M., & Koskenvuo, M. (1998). The genetic epidemiology of schizophrenia in a Finnish twin cohort. *Archives of General Psychiatry, 55,* 67–74.

Cannon, T. D., Rosso, I. M., Bearden, C. E., Sanchez, L. E., & Hadley, T. (1999). A prospective cohort study of neurodevelopmental processes in the genesis and epigenesis of schizophrenia. *Development & Psychopathology, 11,* 467–485.

Caplan, P. J., & Gans, M. (1991). Is there empirical justification for the category of "self-defeating personality disorder"? *Feminism & Psychology, 1,* 263–278.

Cardozo, B. L., Kaiser, R., Gotway, C. A., & Agani, F. (2003). Mental health, social functioning, and feelings of hatred and revenge in Kosovar Albanians one year after the war in Kosovo. *Journal of Traumatic Stress, 16,* 351–360.

Cardozo, B. L., Vergara, A., Agani, F., & Gotway, C. A. (2000). Mental health, social functioning, and attitudes of Kosovar Albanians following the war in Kosovo. *Journal of the American Medical Association, 284,* 569–577.

Carey, G., & Goldman, D. (1997). The genetics of antisocial behavior. In D. M. Stoff, J. Breiling, & J. D. Maser (Eds.), *Handbook of antisocial personality disorder* (pp. 243–254). New York: Wiley.

Carmelli, D. S., Swan, G. E., Robinette, D., & Fabsitz, R. (1992). Genetic influence on smoking: A study of male twins. *New England Journal of Medicine, 327,* 829–833.

Carroll, J. K. (2004). *Murug, waali,* and *gini:* Expressions of distress in refugees from Somolia. *Primary Care Companion to the Journal of Clinical Psychiatry, 6,* 119–125.

Carroll, K. M. (2001). Combined treatments for substance dependence. In M. T. Sammons & N. B. Schmidt (Eds.), *Combined treatments for mental disorders.* Washington, DC: American Psychological Association.

Carter, J. C., & Fairburn, C. G. (1998). Cognitive-behavioral self-help for binge eating disorder: A controlled effectiveness study. *Journal of Consulting & Clinical Psychology, 66,* 616–623.

Carter, M. M., Hollon, S. D., Carson, R. S., & Shelton, R. C. (1995). Effects of a safe person on induced distress following a biological challenge in panic disorder with agoraphobia. *Journal of Abnormal Psychology, 104,* 156–163.

Caspi, A. (1993). Why maladaptive behaviors persist: Sources of continuity and change across the life course. In D. C. Funder (Ed.), *Studying lives through time: Personality and development* (pp. 343–376). Washington, DC: American Psychological Association.

Caspi, A., Harrington, H., Milne, B., Amell, J. W., Theodore, R. F., & Moffitt, T. E. (2003). Children's behavioral styles at age 3 are linked to their adult personality traits at age 26. *Journal of Personality, 71,* 495–513.

Castiglioni, A. (1946). *Adventures of the mind* (1st American ed.). New York: Knopf.

Castonguay, L. G., Eldredge, K. L., & Agras, W. S. (1995). Binge eating disorder: Current state and future directions. *Clinical Psychology Review, 15,* 865–890.

Cauce, A. M., Domenech-Rodriguez, M., Pardise, M., Cochran, B. N., Shea, J. M., Srebnik, D., & Baydar, N. (2002). Cultural and contextual influences in mental health help seeking: A focus on ethnic minority youth. *Journal of Consulting and Clinical Psychology, 70,* 44–55.

Ceci, S. J., & Bruck, M. (1995). *Jeopardy in the courtroom.* Washington, DC: American Psychological Association.

Centers for Disease Control and Prevention (CDC), National Center for Injury Prevention and Control. (2004). Web-based injury statistics query and reporting system. Retrieved from http://www.cdc.gov/ncipc/wisqars/default.htm

Cervantes, R. C., Salgado de Snyder, V. N., & Padilla, A. M. (1989). Posttraumatic stress in immigrants from Central America and Mexico. *Hospital & Community Psychiatry, 40,* 615–619.

Chae, J.-H., Nahas, Z., Li, X., & George, M. S. (2001). Transcranial magnetic stimulation in psychiatry: Research and therapeutic applications. *International Review of Psychiatry, 13,* 18–23.

Chambless, D. C., Cherney, J., Caputo, G. C., & Rheinstein, B. J. (1987). Anxiety disorders and alcoholism: A study with inpatient alcoholics. *Journal of Anxiety Disorders, 1,* 29–40.

Chang, C.-J., Chen, W. J., Liu, S. K., Cheng, J. J., Yang, W.-C. O., Chang, H.-J., Lane, H.-Y., Lin, S.-K., Yang, T.-W., & Hwu, H.-G. (2002). Morbidity risk of psychiatric disorders among the first degree relatives of schizophrenia patients in Taiwan. *Schizophrenia Bulletin, 28,* 379–392.

Chang, K. D. (2004). Pediatric psychopharmacology: An overview. In H. Steiner (Ed.), *Handbook of mental health intervention in children and adolescents: an integrated developmental approach* (pp. 245–257). San Francisco: Jossey-Bass.

Chang, K. D., & Simeonova, D. I. (2004). Mood stabilizers: Use in pediatric psychopharmacology. In H. Steiner (Ed.), *Handbook of mental health intervention in children and adolescents: An integrated developmental approach* (pp. 363–412). San Francisco: Jossey-Bass.

Chang, V. W., & Christakis, N. A. (2003). Self-perception of weight appropriateness in the United States. *American Journal of Preventative Medicine, 24,* 332–339.

Chapman, L. J., Edell, W. S., & Chapman, J. P. (1980). Physical anhedonia, perceptual aberration, and psychosis proneness. *Schizophrenia Bulletin, 6,* 639–653.

Chapman, T. F., Manuzza, S., & Fyer, A. J. (1995). Epidemiology and family studies of social phobia. In R. G. Heimberg, M. R. Liebowitz, D. A. Hope, & F. R. Schneier (Eds.), *Social phobia: Diagnosis, assessment, and treatment* (pp. 21–40). New York: Guilford Press.

Charney, D. S. (2004). Psychobiological mechanisms of resilience and vulnerability: Implications for successful adaptation to extreme stress. *American Journal of Psychiatry, 161,* 195–216.

Charney, D. S., Nagy, L. M., Bremner, J. D., Goddard, A. W., Yehuda, R., & Southwick, S. M. (2000). Neurobiologic mechanisms of human anxiety. In B. S. Fogel (Ed.), *Synopsis of neuropsychiatry* (pp. 273–288). Philadelphia: Lippincott Williams & Wilkins.

Chassin, L., Pitts, S. C., DeLucia, C., & Todd, M. (1999). A longitudinal study of children of alcoholics: Predicting young adult substance use disorders, anxiety, and depression. *Journal of Abnormal Psychology, 108,* 106–119.

Chavira, D. A., Grilo, C. M., Shea, M. T., Yen, S., Gunderson, J. G., Morey, L. C., Skodol, A. E., Stout, R. L., Zanarini, M. C., & Mcglashan, T. H. (2003). Ethnicity and four personality disorders. *Comprehensive Psychiatry, 44,* 483–491.

Chemtob, C. M., Bauer, G. B., Neller, G., Hamada, R., Glisson, C., & Stevens, V. (1990). Posttraumatic stress disorder among

Special Forces Vietnam veterans. *Military Medicine, 155,* 16–20.

Chodorow, N. (1978). *The reproduction of mothering.* Berkeley: University of California Press.

Chou, T. (1992). Wake up and smell the coffee: Caffeine, coffee, and the medical consequences. *Western Journal of Medicine, 157,* 544–553.

Chouinard, G. (2004). Issues in the clinical use of benzodiazepines: Potency, withdrawal, and rebound. *Journal of Clinical Psychiatry, 65*(Suppl. 5), 7–12.

Christophersen, E. R., & Mortweet, S. L. (2001). *Treatments that work with children: Empirically supported strategies for managing childhood problems.* Washington, DC: American Psychological Association.

Chronis, A. M., Chacko, A., Fabiano, G. A., Wymbs, B. T., & Pelham, W. E., Jr. (2004). Enhancements to the behavioral parent training paradigm for families of children with ADHD: Review and future directions. *Clinical Child & Family Psychology Review, 7,* 1–27.

Chun, M. R., Schofield, P., Stern, Y., Tatemichi, T. K., & Mayeux, R. (1998). The epidemiology of dementia among the elderly: Experience in a community-based registry. In M. F. Folstein (Ed.), *Neurobiology of primary dementia* (pp. 1–26). Washington, DC: American Psychiatric Press.

Cicchetti, D., & Rogosch, F. A. (1996). Equifinality and multifinality in developmental psychopathology. *Development & Psychopathology, 8,* 597–600.

Cicchetti, D., & Rogosch, F. A. (2001a). Diverse patterns of neuroendocrine activity in maltreated children. *Development & Psychopathology, 13,* 677–694.

Cicchetti, D., & Rogosch, F. A. (2001b). The impact of child maltreatment and psychopathology upon neuroendocrine functioning. *Development & Psychopathology, 13,* 783–804.

Cicchetti, D., & Toth, S. L. (2005). Child maltreatment. *Annual Review of Clinical Psychology, 1,* 439–466.

Clancy, S. A., McNally, R. J., Schacter, D. L., Lenzenweger, M. F., & Pitman, R. K. (2002). Memory distortion in people reporting abduction by aliens. *Journal of Abnormal Psychology, 111,* 455–461.

Clancy, S. A., Schacter, D. L., McNally, R. J., & Pitman, R. (2000). False recognition in women reporting recovered memories of sexual abuse. *Psychological Science, 11,* 26–31.

Clark, D. A., & Purdon, C. (1993). New perspectives for a cognitive theory of obsessions. *Australian Psychologist, 28,* 161–167.

Clark, D. M. (1988). A cognitive model of panic attacks. In S. Rachman & J. D. Maser (Eds.), *Panic: Psychological perspectives* (pp. 71–89). Hillsdale, NJ: Erlbaum.

Clark, D. M., Ehlers, A., McManus, F., Hackmann, A., Fennell, M., Campbell, H., Flower, T., Davenport, C., & Louis, B. (2003). Cognitive therapy versus fluoxetine in generalized social phobia: A randomized placebo-controlled trial. *Journal of Consulting & Clinical Psychology, 71,* 1058–1067.

Clark, D. M., Salkovskis, P. M., Hackmann, A., Middleton, H., Anastasiades, P., & Gelder, M. (1994). A comparison of cognitive therapy, applied relaxation, and imipramine in the treatment of panic disorder. *British Journal of Psychiatry, 164,* 759–769.

Clark, D. M., Salkovskis, P. M., Hackmann, A., Wells, A., Ludgate, J., & Gelder, M. (1999). Brief cognitive therapy for panic disorder: A randomized controlled trial. *Journal of Consulting & Clinical Psychology, 67,* 583–589.

Clark, D. M., & Wells, A. (1995). A cognitive model of social phobia. In R. G. Heimberg, M. R. Liebowitz, D. A. Hope, & F. R. Schneier (Eds.), *Social phobia: Diagnosis, assessment and treatment* (pp. 69–93). New York: Guilford Press.

Clarke, G. N., Hawkins, W., Murphy, M., Sheeber, L. B., Lewinsohn, P. M., & Seeley, J. R. (1995). Targeted prevention of unipolar depressive disorder in an at-risk sample of high school adolescents: A randomized trial of a group cognitive intervention. *Journal of the American Academy of Child & Adolescent Psychiatry, 34,* 312–321.

Classen, C., Koopman, C., Hales, R., & Spiegel, D. (1998). Acute stress disorder as a predictor of posttraumatic stress symptoms. *American Journal of Psychiatry, 155,* 620–624.

Cleckley, H. M. (1941). *The mask of sanity: An attempt to reinterpret the so-called psychopathic personality.* St. Louis, MO: C. V. Mosby.

Cloninger, C. R., & Gottesman, I. I. (1987). Genetic and environmental factors in antisocial behavior disorders. In S. A. Mednick, T. E. Moffitt, & S. A. Stack (Eds.), *The causes of crime: New biological approaches* (pp. 92–109). New York: Cambridge University Press.

Cloninger, R., Bayon, C., & Przybeck, T. (1997). Epidemiology and Axis I comorbidity of antisocial personality. In D. M. Stoff, J. Breiling, & J. D. Maser (Eds.), *Handbook of antisocial personality disorder* (pp. 12–21). New York: Wiley.

Cochran, S. D., Sullivan, J. G., & Mays, V. M. (2003). Prevalence of mental disorders, psychological distress, and mental services use among lesbian, gay, and bisexual adults in the United States. *Journal of Consulting & Clinical Psychology, 71,* 53–61.

Cochrane, R. E., Grisso, T., & Frederick, R. I. (2001). The relationship between criminal charges, diagnoses, and psycholegal opinions among federal pretrial defendants. *Behavioral Sciences & the Law, 19,* 565–582.

Cocores, J., Pottash, A. C., & Gold, M. S. (1991). Cocaine. In N. S. Miller (Ed.), *Comprehensive handbook of drug and alcohol addiction* (pp. 341–352). New York: Marcel Dekker.

Cohen, J. A., Deblinger, E., Mannarino, A. P., & Steer, R. A. (2004). A multisite, randomized controlled trial for children with sexual abuse–related PTSD symptoms. *Journal of the American Academy of Child & Adolescent Psychiatry, 43,* 393–402.

Cohen, S. (1996). Psychological stress, immunity, and upper respiratory infections. *Current Directions in Psychological Science, 5,* 86–90.

Cohen, S., Tyrrell, D. A., & Smith, A. P. (1991). Psychological stress and susceptibility to the common cold. *New England Journal of Medicine, 325,* 606–612.

Cohen, S. A., Ohrig, K., Lott, R. S., & Kerrick, J. M. (1998). Risperidone for aggression and self-injurious behavior in adults with mental retardation. *Journal of Autism & Developmental Disorders, 28,* 229–233.

Colapinto, J. (2001). *As nature made him: The boy who was raised as a girl.* New York: HarperCollins.

Colas, E. (1998). *Just checking: Scenes from the life of an obsessive-compulsive.* New York: Pocket Books.

Colby, D. M. (1981). Modeling a paranoid mind. *Behavioral & Brain Sciences, 4,* 515–560.

Colder, C. R., & Chassin, L. (1993). The stress and negative affect model of adolescent alcohol use and the moderating effects of behavioral undercontrol. *Journal of Studies on Alcohol, 54,* 326–333.

Cole, D. A., Martin, J. M., Peeke, L. G., Seroczynski, A. D., & Hoffman, K. (1998). Are cognitive errors of underestimation predictive or reflective of depressive symptoms in children: A longitudinal study. *Journal of Abnormal Psychology, 107,* 481–496.

Cole, M. G. (2004). Delirium in elderly patients. *American Journal of Geriatric Psychiatry, 12,* 7–21.

Cole, W. (1992). Incest perpetrators: Their assessment and treatment. *Psychiatric Clinics of North America, 15,* 689–701.

Coleman, C. C., King, B. R., Bolden-Watson, C., Book, M. J., Segraves, R. T., Richard, N., Ascher, J., Batey, S., Jamerson, B., & Metz, A. (2001). A placebo-controlled comparison of the effects on sexual functioning of bupropion sustained release and fluoxetine. *Clinical Therapeutics: The International Peer-Reviewed Journal of Therapy, 23,* 1040–1058.

Coles, M. E., Hart, T. A., & Heimberg, R. G. (2005). Cognitive-behavioral group treatment for social phobia. In R. Crozier & L. E. Alden (Eds.), *International handbook of social anxiety.* London: Wiley.

Collins, J. J., & Schlenger, W. E. (1983, November 9–13). *The prevalence of psychiatric disorder among admissions to prison.* Paper presented at the American Society of Criminology 35th Annual Meeting, Denver.

Compton, W. M., Helzer, J. E., Hwu, H., Yeh, E., McEvoy, L., Tipp, J. E., & Spitznagel, E. L. (1991). New methods in cross-cultural psychiatry: Psychiatric illness in Taiwan and the United States. *American Journal of Psychiatry, 148,* 1697–1704.

Conklin, H. M., & Iacono, W. G. (2002). Schizophrenia: A neurodevelopmental perspective. *Current Directions in Psychological Science, 11,* 33–37.

Consumer Reports. (1993, June). Diets: What works—What doesn't. *Consumer Reports,* pp. 347–357.

Conwell, Y. (1996). Outcomes of depression. *American Journal of Geriatric Psychiatry, 4*(Suppl. 1), 34–44.

Conwell, Y., Duberstein, P. R., Connor, K., Eberly, S., Cox, C., & Caine, E. D. (2002). Access to firearms and risk for suicide in middle-aged and older adults. *American Journal of Geriatric Psychiatry, 10,* 407–416.

Cooley, E., & Toray, T. (2001). Body image and personality predictors of eating disorder symptoms during the college years. *International Journal of Eating Disorders, 30,* 28–36.

Coons, P. M. (1980). Multiple personality: Diagnostic considerations. *Journal of Clinical Psychiatry, 41,* 330–336.

Coons, P. M. (1984). *Childhood antecedents of multiple personality.* Paper presented at the Meeting of the American Psychiatric Association, Los Angeles.

Coons, P. M. (1986). Treatment progress in 20 patients with multiple personality disorder. *Journal of Nervous & Mental Disease, 174,* 715–721.

Coons, P. M. (1994). Confirmation of childhood abuse in child and adolescent cases of multiple personality disorder and dissociative disorder not otherwise specified. *Journal of Nervous & Mental Disease, 182,* 461–464.

Coons, P. M., & Bowman, E. S. (2001). Ten-year follow-up study of patients with dissociative identity disorder. *Journal of Trauma & Dissociation, 2,* 73–89.

Coons, P. M., Cole, C., Pellow, T. A., & Milstein, V. (1990). Symptoms of posttraumatic stress disorder and dissociation in women victims of abuse. In R. P. Kluft (Ed.), *Incest-related syndromes of adult psychopathology* (pp. 205–226). Washington, DC: American Psychiatric Press.

Coons, P. M., & Milstein, V. (1986). Psychosexual disturbances in multiple personality: Characteristics, etiology, and treatment. *Journal of Clinical Psychiatry, 47,* 106–110.

Coons, P. M., & Milstein, V. (1990). Self-mutilation associated with dissociative disorders. *Dissociation: Progress in the Dissociative Disorders, 3,* 81–87.

Coontz, P. D., Lidz, C. W., & Mulvey, E. P. (1994). Gender and the assessment of dangerousness in the psychiatric emergency room. *International Journal of Law & Psychiatry, 17,* 369–376.

Cooper, M. L., Russell, M., Skinner, J. B., Frone, M. R., & Mudar, P. (1992). Stress and alcohol use: Moderating effects of gender, coping, and alcohol expectancies. *Journal of Abnormal Psychology, 101,* 139–152.

Corbitt, E. M., & Widiger, T. A. (1995). Sex differences among the personality disorders: An exploration of the data. *Clinical Psychology: Science & Practice, 2,* 225–238.

Corder, E. H., Saunders, A. M., & Strittmatter, W. J. (1993). Gene dose of apolipoprotein E type 4 allele and the risk of Alzheimer's disease in late onset families. *Science, 261,* 921–923.

Cornblatt, B., Obuchowski, M., Andreasen, A., & Smith, C. (1998). High-risk research in schizophrenia: New strategies, new designs. In M. F. Lenzenweger & R. H. Dworkin (Eds.), *Origins of the development of schizophrenia* (pp. 349–383). Washington, DC: American Psychological Association.

Cornelius, M. D., Goldschmidt, L., Day, N. L., & Larkby, C. (2002). Alcohol, tobacco and marijuana use among pregnant teenagers: 6-year follow-up of offspring growth effects. *Neurotoxicology & Teratology, 24,* 703–710.

Corove, M. B., & Gleaves, D. H. (2001). Body dysmorphic disorder: A review of conceptualizations, assessments, and treatment strategies. *Clinical Psychology Review, 21,* 949–970.

Costa, P. T., & Widiger, T. A. (Eds.). (2002). *Personality disorders and the five-factor model of personality* (2nd ed., pp. 215–221). Washington, DC: American Psychological Association.

Costello, E. J., Compton, S. N., Keeler, G., & Angold, A. (2003). Relationships between poverty and psychopathology: A natural experiment. *Journal of the American Medical Association, 290,* 2023–2029.

Costello, E. J., Keeler, G. P., & Angold, A. (2001). Poverty, race/ethnicity, and psychiatric disorder: A study of rural children. *American Journal of Public Health, 91,* 1494–1498.

Costello, E. J., Mustillo, S., Erkanli, A., Keeler, G., & Angold, A. (2003). Prevalence and development of psychiatric disorders in children and adolescence. *Archives of General Psychiatry, 60,* 837–844.

Cott, J. (1995). Natural product formulations available in Europe for psychotropic indications. *Psychopharmacology, 31,* 745–751.

Courtet, P., Picot, M.-C., Bellivier, F., Torres, S., Jollant, F., Michelon, C., Castelnau, D., Astruc, B., Buresi, C., & Malafosse, A. (2004). Serotonin transporter gene may be involved in short-term risk of subsequent suicide attempts. *Biological Psychiatry, 55,* 46–51.

Cousins, N. (1976). Anatomy of an illness as perceived by the patient. *New England Journal of Medicine, 295,* 1458–1463.

Cousins, N. (1985). Therapeutic value of laughter. *Integrative Psychiatry, 3,* 112.

Couzin, J. (2004). Volatile chemistry: Children and antidepressants. *Science, 305,* 468–470.

Coyne, J. C., & Gotlib, I. H. (1983). The role of cognition in depression: A critical appraisal. *Psychological Bulletin, 94,* 472–505.

Crabbe, J. C. (2002). Genetic contributions to addiction. *Annual Review of Psychology, 53,* 435–462.

Craig, T. K., Boardman, A. P., Mills, K., & Daly-Jones, O. (1993). The South London Somatisation Study: I. Longitudinal course and the influence of early life experiences. *British Journal of Psychiatry, 163,* 579–588.

Cranston-Cuebas, M. A., & Barlow, D. H. (1990). Cognitive and affective contributions to sexual functioning. *Annual Review of Sex Research, 1,* 119–161.

Craske, M. G., & Barlow, D. H. (2001). Panic disorder and agoraphobia. In D. H. Barlow (Ed.), *Clinical handbook of psychological disorders: A step-by-step treatment manual* (3rd ed., pp. 1–59). New York: Guilford Press.

Craske, M. G., Brown, T. A., & Barlow, D. H. (1991). Behavioral treatment of panic disorder: A two-year follow-up. *Behavior Therapy, 22,* 289–304.

Craske, M. G., & Waters, A. M. (2005). Panic disorder, phobias, and generalized anxiety disorder. *Annual Review of Clinical Psychology, 1,* 197–226.

Creer, C., & Wing, J. K. (1974). *Several relatives mentioned.* London: Institute of Psychiatry.

Crepault, C., & Couture, M. (1980). Men's erotic fantasies. *Archives of Sexual Behavior, 9,* 565–581.

Crick, N. R., & Dodge, K. A. (1994). A review and reformulation of social information-processing mechanisms in children's social adjustment. *Psychological Bulletin, 115,* 74–101.

Crick, N. R., & Grotpeter, J. K. (1995). Relational aggression, gender, and social-psychological adjustment. *Child Development, 66,* 710–722.

Crick, N. R., & Ladd, G. W. (1990). Children's perceptions of the outcomes of social strategies: Do the ends justify being mean? *Developmental Psychology, 26,* 612–620.

Crits-Christoph, P. (1992). The efficacy of brief dynamic psychotherapy: A meta-analysis. *American Journal of Psychiatry, 149,* 151–158.

Crits-Christoph, P. (1997). Limitations of the dodo bird verdict and the role of clinical trials in psychotherapy research: Comment on Wampold et al. (1997). *Psychological Bulletin, 122,* 216–220.

Crits-Christoph, P., & Barber, J. P. (2000). Long-term psychotherapy. In C. R. Snyder & R. E. Ingram (Eds.), *Handbook of psychological change: Psychotherapy processes and practices for the 21st century* (pp. 455–473). New York: Wiley.

Cronbach, L. J., & Meehl, P. E. (1955). Construct validity in psychological tests. *Psychological Bulletin, 52,* 281–302.

Crosby, A. E., Cheltenham, M. P., & Sacks, J. J. (1999). Incidence of suicidal ideation and behavior in the United States, 1994. *Suicide & Life-Threatening Behavior, 29,* 131–140.

Cross, S. E., & Madson, L. (1997). Models of the self: Self-construals and gender. *Psychological Bulletin, 122,* 5–37.

Cross-National Collaborative Group. (1992). The changing rate of major depression. *Journal of the American Medical Association, 268,* 3098–3105.

Crowe, R. R. (1990). Panic disorder: Genetic considerations. *Journal of Psychiatric Research, 24*(Suppl. 2), 129–134.

Cruess, D. G., Antoni, M. H., Gonzalez, J., Fletcher, M. A., Klimas, N., Duran, R., Ironson, G., & Schneiderman, N. (2003). Sleep disturbance mediates and association between psychological distress and immune status among HIV-positive men and women on combination antiretroviral therapy. *Journal of Psychosomatic Research, 54,* 185–189.

Csernansky, J. G., Mahmoud, R., & Brenner, R. (2002). A comparison of risperidone and haloperidol for the prevention of relapse in patients with schizophrenia. *New England Journal of Medicine, 346,* 16–22.

Culpepper, L. (2004). Identifying and treating panic disorder in primary care. *Journal of Clinical Psychiatry, 65*(Suppl. 5), 19–23.

Curtis, J. (1998). *"Do not grieve for me," James Whale: A new world of gods and monsters.* Boston: Faber & Faber.

D

Dadds, M. R., Holland, D. E., Barrett, P. M., & Spence, S. H. (1999). Early intervention and prevention of anxiety disorders in children: Results at 2-year follow-up. *Journal of Consulting & Clinical Psychology, 67,* 145–150.

Dahl, A. A. (1993). The personality disorders: A critical review of family, twin, and adoption studies. *Journal of Personality Disorders* (Spr. Suppl. 1), 86–99.

Dain, N. (1980). *Clifford W. Beers, advocate for the insane.* Pittsburgh, PA: University of Pittsburgh Press.

Damasio, H., Grabowski, T., Frank, R., Galaburda, A. M., & Damasio, A. R. (1994). The return of Phineas Gage: Clues about the brain from the skull of a famous patient. *Science, 264,* 1102–1105.

Dana, R. H. (1998). *Understanding cultural identity in intervention and assessment.* Thousand Oaks, CA: Sage.

Dana, R. H. (2000). *Handbook on cross-cultural and multicultural personality assessment.* Mahwah, NJ: Erlbaum.

Dana, R. H. (2001). Clinical diagnosis of multicultural populations in the United States. In L. A. Suzuki & J. G. Ponterotto (Eds.), *Handbook of multicultural assessment: Clinical, psychological, and educational applications* (2nd ed., pp. 101–131). San Francisco: Jossey-Bass.

D'Andrea, M., & Daniels, J. (1995). Helping students learn to get along: Assessing the effectiveness of a multicultural developmental guidance project. *Elementary School Guidance & Counseling, 30,* 143–154.

Dare, C., Eisler, I., Russell, G. F., & Szmukler, G. I. (1990). The clinical and theoretical impact of a controlled trial of family therapy in anorexia nervosa. *Journal of Marital & Familial Therapy, 16,* 39–57.

Davenport, D. S., & Yurich, J. M. (1991). Multicultural gender issues. *Journal of Counseling & Development, 70,* 64–71.

Davidson, J., Pearlstein, T., Londborg, P., Brady, K. T., Rothbaum, B., Bell, J., Maddock, R., Hegel, M. T., & Farfel, G. (2001). Efficacy of sertraline in preventing relapse of posttraumatic stress disorder: Results of a 28-week double-blind, placebo-controlled study. *American Journal of Psychiatry, 158,* 1974–1981.

Davidson, J. R. T. (2001). Pharmacotherapy of generalized anxiety disorder. *Journal of Clinical Psychiatry, 62*(Suppl. 11), 46–50.

Davidson, J. R. T. (2003). Pharmacotherapy of social phobia. *Acta Psychiatrica Scandinavica, 108*(Suppl. 417), 65–71.

Davidson, J. R. T. (2004). Long-term treatment and prevention of posttraumatic stress disorder. *Journal of Clinical Psychiatry, 65*(Suppl. 1), 44–48.

Davidson, J. R. T., DuPont, R. L., Hedges, D., & Haskins, J. T. (1999). Efficacy, safety, and tolerability of venlafaxine extended release and buspirone in outpatients with generalized anxiety disorder. *Journal of Clinical Psychiatry, 60,* 528–535.

Davidson, J. R. T., Rothmaum, B. O., van der Kolk, B. A., Sikes, C. R., & Farfel, G. M. (2001). Multicenter, double-blind comparison of sertraline and placebo in the treatment of posttraumatic stress disorder. *Archives of General Psychiatry, 58,* 485–492.

Davidson, P. R., & Parker, K. C. H. (2001). Eye movement desensitization and reprocessing (EMDR): A meta-analysis. *Journal of Consulting & Clinical Psychology, 69,* 305–316.

Davidson, R. J., Pizzagalli, D., & Nitschke, J. B. (2002). The representation and regulation of emotion in depression: Perspectives from affective neuroscience. In I. H. Gotlib & C. L. Hammen (Eds.), *Handbook of depression* (pp. 219–244). New York: Guilford Press.

Davidson, R. J., Pizzagalli, D., Nitschke, J. B., & Putnam, K. (2002). Depression: Perspectives from affective neuroscience. *Annual Review of Psychology, 53,* 545–574.

Davis, K. L., Kahn, R. S., Ko, G., & Davidson, M. (1991). Dopamine in schizophrenia: A review and conceptualization. *American Journal of Psychiatry, 148,* 1474–1486.

Davis, R. D., & Millon, T. (1993). The five-factor model for personality disorders: Apt or misguided? *Psychological Inquiry, 4,* 104–109.

DeKosky, S. T., & Orgogozo, J.-M. (2001). Alzheimer disease: Diagnosis, costs, and dimensions of treatment. *Alzheimer Disease & Associated Disorders, 15*(Suppl. 1), 3–7.

Delay, J., Deniker, P., & Harl, J. M. (1952). Traitement des etats d'excitation et d'agitation par une methode medicamenteuse derivee de l'hibernotherapie. *Annuls Medicine Psychologie, 110,* 262–267.

Delizonna, L. L., Wincze, J. P., Litz, B. T., Brown, T. A., & Barlow, D. H. (2001). A comparison of subjective and physiological measures of mechanically produced and erotically produced erections (or, is an erection an erection?). *Journal of Sex & Marital Therapy, 27,* 21–31.

Dell, P. F. (1998). Axis II pathology in outpatients with dissociative identity disorder. *Journal of Nervous & Mental Disease, 186,* 352–356.

Dell, P. F., & Eisenhower, J. W. (1990). Adolescent multiple personality disorder: A preliminary study of eleven cases. *Journal of the American Academy of Child & Adolescent Psychiatry, 29,* 359–366.

Dembroski, T. M., MacDougall, J. M., Williams, J. M., & Haney, T. L. (1985). Components of Type A hostility and anger: Relationship to angiographic findings. *Psychosomatic Medicine, 47,* 219–233.

Denison, M. E., Paredes, A., Bacal, S., & Gawin, F. H. (1998). Psychological and psychiatric consequences of cocaine. In R. E. Tartar (Ed.), *Handbook of substance abuse: Neurobehavioral pharmacology* (pp. 201–213). New York: Plenum Press.

Denning, D. G., Conwell, Y., King, D., & Cox, C. (2000). Method choice, intent, and gender in completed suicide. *Suicide & Life-Threatening Behavior, 30,* 282–288.

Dennis, M. L., Babor, T. F., Diamond, G., Donaldson, J., Godley, S. H., Tims, F., Titus, J. C., Webb, C., Herrell, J., & the CYT Steering Committee. (2000). *The cannabis youth treatment (CYT) experiment: Preliminary findings.* Rockville, MD: Substance Abuse and Mental Health Services Administration, Center for Substance Abuse Treatment. Retrieved from the World Wide Web: http://samhsa.gov/centers/csat/content/recoverymonth/000907rptcover.html

DePrince, A. P., & Freyd, J. J. (1999). Dissociation, attention, and memory. *Psychological Science, 10,* 449–452.

DePrince, A. P., & Freyd, J. J. (2001). Memory and dissociative tendencies: The roles of attentional context and word meaning in a directed forgetting task. *Journal of Trauma & Dissociation, 2,* 67–82.

DeRubeis, R. J., Gelfand, L. A., Tang, T. Z., & Simons, A. D. (1999). Medications versus cognitive behavior therapy for severely depressed outpatients: Mega-analysis of four randomized comparisons. *American Journal of Psychiatry, 156,* 1001–1013.

deSilva, P., Rachman, S., & Seligman, M. (1977). Prepared phobias and obsessions. *Behaviour Research & Therapy, 15,* 65–77.

Desmond, D. W., & Tatemichi, T. K. (1998). Vascular dementia. In M. F. Folstein (Ed.), *Neurobiology of primary dementia* (pp. 167–190). Washington, DC: American Psychiatric Press.

de Snyder, V. N. S., Diaz-Perez, M. D., & Ojeda, V. D. (2000). The prevalence of nervios and associated symptomatology among inhabitants of Mexican rural communities. *Culture, Medicine & Psychiatry, 24,* 453–470.

Deutsch, A. (1937). *The mentally ill in America: A history of their care and treatment from colonial times.* Garden City, NY: Doubleday, Doran & Company.

Dewaraja, R., & Sasaki, Y. (1991). Semen-loss syndrome: A comparison between Sri Lanka and Japan. *American Journal of Psychotherapy, 45,* 14–20.

de Wit, H., Kirk, J. M., & Justice, A. (1998). Behavioral pharmacology of cannabinoids. In R. E. Tarter (Ed.), *Handbook of substance abuse: Neurobehavioral pharmacology* (pp. 131–146). New York: Plenum Press.

de Zwaan, M., Roerig, J. L., & Mitchell, J. E. (2004). Pharmacological treatment of anorexia nervosa, bulimia nervosa, and binge eating disorder. In J. K. Thompson (Ed.), *Handbook of eating disorders and obesity* (pp. 186–217). Hoboken, NJ: Wiley.

de Zwaan, M., Roerig, J. L., & Mitchell, J. E. (2004). Pharmacological treatment of anorexia nervosa, bulimia nervosa and binge-eating disorder. In J. K. Thompson (Ed.), *Handbook of eating disorders and obesity* (pp. 234–266). Hoboken, NJ: Wiley.

Dickinson, E. (1890/1955). *Poems: Including variant readings critically compared with all known manuscripts.* Cambridge, MA: Belknap Press.

DiLillo, D. (2001). Interpersonal functioning among women reporting a history of childhood sexual abuse: Empirical findings and methodological issues. *Clinical Psychology Review, 21,* 553–576.

Dishion, T. J., & Patterson, G. R. (1997). The timing and severity of antisocial behavior: Three hypotheses within an ecological framework. In D. M. Stoff, J. Breiling, & J. D. Maser (Eds.), *Handbook of antisocial personality disorder* (pp. 205–217). New York: Wiley.

Dittman, R. W., Kappes, M. E., & Kappes, M. H. (1992). Sexual behavior in adolescent and adult females with congenital and adrenal hyperplasia. *Psychoneuroendocrinology, 17,* 153–170.

Dixon, D., Cruess, S., Kilbourn, K., Klimas, N., Fletcher, M. A., Ironson, G., Baum, A., Schneiderman, N., & Antoni, M. H. (2001). Social support mediates loneliness and human herpes virus Type 6 (HHV-6) antibody titers. *Journal of Applied Social Psychology, 31,* 1111–1132.

Dixon, J. F., & Hokin, L. E. (1998). Lithium acutely inhibits and chronically up-regulates and stabilizes glutamate uptake by presynaptic nerve endings in mouse cerebral cortex. *Neurobiology, 95,* 8363–8368.

Dobson, K. S. (1989). A meta-analysis of the efficacy of cognitive therapy for depression.

Journal of Consulting & Clinical Psychology, 57, 414–419.

Dobson, K. S., Backs-Dermott, B. J., & Dozois, D. J. A. (2000). Cognitive and cognitive-behavioral therapies. In C. R. Snyder & R. E. Ingram (Eds.), *Handbook of psychological change: Psychotherapy processes and practices for the 21st century* (pp. 409–428). New York: Wiley.

Docherty, N. M., Grosh, E. S., Wexler, B. E. (1996). Affective reactivity of cognitive functioning and family history in schizophrenia. *Psychiatry, 139,* 59–64.

Dodge, K., & Schwartz, D. (1997). Social information processing mechanisms in aggressive behavior. In D. M. Stoff, J. Breiling, & J. D. Maser (Eds.), *Handbook of antisocial personality disorder* (pp. 171–180). New York: Wiley.

Dodge, K. A., & Pettit, G. S. (2003). A biopsychosocial model of the development of chronic conduct problems in adolescence. *Developmental Psychology, 39,* 349–371.

Dohrenwend, B. P. (2000). The role of adversity and stress in psychopathology: Some evidence and its implications for theory and research. *Journal of Health and Social Behavior, 41,* 1–19.

Dohrenwend, B. P., Levav, I., Shrout, P. E., Link, B. G., Skodol, A. E., & Martin, J. L. (1987). Life stress and psychopathology: Progress on research begun with Barbara Snell Dohrenwend. *American Journal of Community Psychology, 15,* 677–715.

Donahey, K. M., & Carroll, R. A. (1993). Gender differences in factors associated with hypoactive sexual desire. *Journal of Sex & Marital Therapy, 19,* 25–40.

Donegan, N. H., Sanislow, C. A., Blumberg, H. P., Fulbright, R. K., Lacadie, C., Skudlarski, P., Gore, J. C., Olson, I. R., McGlashan, T. H., & Wexler, B. E. (2003). Amygdala hyperreactivity in borderline personality disorder: Implications for emotional dysregulation. *Biological Psychiatry, 54,* 1284–1293.

Dorahy, M. J. (2001). Dissociative identity disorder and memory dysfunction: The current state of experimental research and its future directions. *Clinical Psychology Review, 21,* 771–795.

Dorfman, W. I., & Leonard, S. (2001). The Minnesota Multiphasic Personality Inventory-2 (MMPI-2). In W. I. Dorfman & S. M. Freshwater (Eds.), *Understanding psychological assessment* (pp. 145–171). Dordrecht, Netherlands: Kluwer Academic Publishers.

Dornbusch, S. M., Carlsmith, J. M., Duncan, P. D., Gross, R. T., Martin, J. A., Ritter, P. L., & Siegel-Gorelick, B. (1984). Sexual maturation, social class, and the desire to be thin among adolescent females. *Developmental & Behavioral Pediatrics, 5,* 308–314.

Dorris, M. (1989). *The unbroken cord.* New York: Harper & Row.

Dossenbach, M., Erol, A., el Mahfoud Kessaci, M., Shaheen, M. O., Sunbol, M. M., Boland, J., Hodge, A., O'Halloran, R. A., & Bitter, I. (2004). Effectiveness of antipsychotic treatments for schizophrenia: Interim 6-month observational analysis study from a prospective observational study (IC-SOHO) comparing olanzapine, quetiapine, risperidone, and

haloperidol. *Journal of Clinical Psychiatry, 65,* 312–321.

Dougherty, D., Donab, A., Spencer, T., et al. (1999). Dopamine transporter density in patients with attention deficit hyperactivity disorder. *The Lancet, 354,* 2132–2133.

Doyle, A., & Pollack, M. H. (2004). Long-term management of panic disorder. *Journal of Clinical Psychiatry, 65*(Suppl. 5), 24–28.

Drake, C. L., Roehrs, T., & Roth, T. (2003). Insomnia causes, consequences, and therapeutics: An overview. *Depression & Anxiety, 18,* 163–176.

Drevets, W. C. (2001). Neuroimaging and neuropathological studies of depression: Implications for the cognitive-emotional features of mood disorders. *Current Opinions in Neurobiology, 11,* 240–249.

Drevets, W. C., Price, J. L., Simpson, J. R. J., Todd, R. D., Reich, T., et al. (1997). Subgenual prefrontal cortex abnormalities in mood disorders. *Nature, 386,* 824–827.

Du, Y., Dodel, R., Hampel, H., Buerger, K., Lin, S., Eastwood, B., Bales, K., Gao, F., Moeller, H. J., Oertel, W., Farlow, M., & Paul, S. (2001). Reduced levels of amyloid B-peptide antibody in Alzheimer disease. *Neurology, 57,* 801–805.

Dudley-Grant, G. R. (2001). Eastern Caribbean family psychology with conduct disordered adolescents from the Virgin Islands. *American Psychologist, 56,* 47–57.

Dündar, Y., Dodd, S., Strobl, J., Boland, A., Dickson, R., & Walley, T. (2004). Comparative efficacy of newer hypnotic drugs for the short-term management of insomnia: A systematic review and meta-analysis. *Human Psychopharmacology: Clinical & Experimental, 19,* 305–322.

Dunkin, J. J., & Anderson-Hanley, C. (1998). Dementia caregiver burden: A review of the literature and guidelines for assessment and intervention. *Neurology, 51,* S53–S60.

Dunner, D. L. (2004). Correlates of suicidal behavior and lithium treatment in bipolar disorder. *Journal of Clinical Psychiatry, 65*(Suppl. 10), 5–10.

DuPaul, G. J., & Barkley, R. A. (1993). Behavioral contributions to pharmacology: The utility of behavioral methodology in medication treatment of children with attention deficit hyperactivity disorder. *Behavior Therapy, 24,* 47–65.

Durkheim, E. (1897). *Le suicide: Etude de sociologie.* Paris: F. Alcan.

Dykens, E. M., & Volkmar, F. R. (1997). Medical condition associated with autism. In D. J. Cohen & F. R. Volkmar (Eds.), *Handbook of autism and pervasive developmental disorders* (pp. 388–410). Toronto: Wiley.

E

Earls, F. (2001). Community factors supporting child mental health. *Child & Adolescent Psychiatric Clinics of North America, 10,* 693–709.

Eaton, W. W., Moortensenk, P. B., Herrman, H., & Freeman, H. (1992). Long-term course of hospitalization for schizophrenia: I. Risk for rehospitalization. *Schizophrenia Bulletin, 18,* 217–228.

Eaton, W. W., Thara, R., Federman, E., & Tien, A. (1998). Remission and relapse in

schizophrenia: The Madras longitudinal study. *Journal of Nervous & Mental Disease, 186,* 357–363.

Eaves, L. J., Silberg, J. L., Meyer, J. M., Maes, H. H., Simonoff, E., Pickles, A., Rutter, M., Neale, M. C., Reynolds, C. A., Erikson, M. T., Heath, A. C., Loeber, R., Truett, K. R., & Hewitt, J. K. (1997). Genetics and developmental psychopathology: 2. The main effects of genes and environment on behavior problems in the Virginia Twin Study of Adolescent Behavioral Development. *Journal of Child Psychology & Psychiatry, 38,* 965–980.

Eckert, E. D., Halmi, K. A., Marchi, P., & Grove, W. (1995). Ten-year follow-up of anorexia nervosa: Clinical course and outcome. *Psychological Medicine, 25,* 143–156.

Edelmann, R. J. (1992). *Anxiety: Theory, research, and intervention in clinical and health psychology.* Chichester, NY: Wiley.

Edinger, D. (1963). *Bertha Pappenheim, Leben und Schriften.* Frankfurt, Germany: Ner-Tamid Verlag.

Egeland, J. A. (1986). Cultural factors and social stigma for manic-depression: The Amish Study. *American Journal of Social Psychiatry, 6,* 279–286.

Egeland, J. A. (1994). An epidemiologic and genetic study of affective disorders among the Old Order Amish. In D. F. Papolos & H. M. Lachman (Eds.), *Genetic studies in affective disorders: Overview of basic methods, current directions, and critical research issues* (pp. 70–90). Oxford, UK: Wiley.

Egeland, J. A., Gerhard, D. S., Pauls, D. L., Sussex, J. N., Kidd, K. K., Allen, C. R., Hostetter, A. M., & Housman, D. E. (1987). Bipolar affective disorders linked to DNA markers on Chromosome 11. *Nature, 325,* 783–787.

Egeland, J. A., & Hostetter, A. M. (1983). Amish study: I. Affective disorders among the Amish, 1976–1980. *American Journal of Psychiatry, 140,* 56–61.

Egeland, J. A., Hostetter, A. M., & Eshleman, S. K. (1983). Amish study III: The impact of cultural factors on bipolar diagnosis. *American Journal of Psychiatry, 140,* 67–71.

Egeland, J. A., & Sussex, J. N. (1985). Suicide and family loading for affective disorders. *Journal of the American Medical Association, 254,* 915–918.

Ehlers, A. (1995). A 1-year prospective study of panic attacks: Clinical course and factors associated with maintenance. *Journal of Abnormal Psychology, 104,* 164–172.

Ehlers, A., Clark, D. M., Dunmore, E., Jaycox, L., Meadows, E., & Foa, E. (1998). Predicating response to exposure treatment in PTSD: The role of mental defeat and alienation. *Journal of Traumatic Stress, 11,* 457–471.

Ehlers, A., Mayou, R., & Bryant, B. (1998). Psychological predictors of chronic posttraumatic stress disorder after motor vehicle accidents. *Journal of Abnormal Psychology, 107,* 508–519.

Ehrensaft, M. K., Wasserman, G. A., Verdelli, L., Greenwald, S., Miller, L. S., & Davies, M. (2003). Maternal antisocial behavior, parenting practices, and behavior problems in boys at risk for antisocial behavior. *Journal of Child & Family Studies, 12,* 27–40.

Eisenberg, L. (1958). School phobia: A study in the communication of anxiety. *American Journal of Psychiatry, 114,* 712–718.

Eisenbruch, M., de Jong, J. T. V. M., & van de Put, W. (2004). Bringing order out of chaos: A culturally competent approach to managing the problems of refugees and victims of organized violence. *Journal of Traumatic Stress, 17,* 123–131.

Ekselius, L., Tilfors, M., Furmark, T., & Fredrikson, M. (2001). Personality disorders in the general population: DSM-IV and ICD-10 defined prevalence as related to sociodemographic profile. *Personality & Individual Differences, 30,* 311–320.

Elder, G. H., & Clipp, E. C. (1989). Combat experience and emotional health: Impairment and resilience in later life. *Journal of Personality, 57,* 311–341.

Elder, G. H., Liker, J. K., & Jaworski, B. J. (1984). Hardship in lives: Depression influences. In K. A. McCluskey & H. W. Reese (Eds.), *Lifespan developmental psychology: Historical and generational effects.* Orlando, FL: Academic Press.

Eley, T. C., Bolton, D., O'Connor, T. G., Perrin, S., Smith, P., & Plomin, R. (2003). A twin study of anxiety-related behaviours in pre-school children. *Journal of Child Psychology & Psychiatry, 44,* 945–960.

Eley, T. C., Lichenstein, P., & Stevenson, J. (1999). Sex differences in the etiology of aggressive and nonaggressive antisocial behavior: Results from two twin studies. *Child Development, 70,* 155–168.

Elkin, I., Shea, T., Watkins, J. T., Imber, S. D., Sotsky, S. M., Collins, J. F., Glass, D. R., Pilkonis, P. A., Leber, W. R., Docherty, J. P., Fiester, S. J., & Parloff, M. B. (1989). National Institute of Mental Health treatment of depression collaborative research program: General effectiveness of treatments. *Archives of General Psychiatry, 46,* 971–982.

Ellason, J. W., & Ross, C. A. (1997). Two-year follow-up of inpatients with dissociative identity disorder. *American Journal of Psychiatry, 154,* 832–839.

Ellason, J. W., Ross, C. A., & Fuchs, D. L. (1996). Lifetime Axis I and II comorbidity and childhood trauma history in dissociative identity disorder. *Psychiatry, 59,* 255–266.

Ellis, A. (1997). The evolution of Albert Ellis and emotive behavior therapy. In J. K. Zeig (Ed.), *The rational evolution of psychotherapy: The third conference* (pp. 69–78). New York: Brunner/Mazel.

Ellis, A., & Harper, R. A. (1961). *A guide to rational living.* Englewood Cliffs, NJ: Prentice Hall.

Ellison, L. F., & Morrison, H. I. (2001). Low serum cholesterol concentration and risk of suicide. *Epidemiology, 12,* 168–172.

Emmelkamp, P. M. G. (1994). Behavior therapy with adults. In A. E. Bergin (Ed.), *Handbook of psychotherapy and behavior change* (4th ed., pp. 379–427). New York: Wiley.

Emslie, G. J., Portteus, A. M., Kumar, E. C., & Hume, J. H. (2004). Antidepressants: SSRIs and novel atypical antidepressants—An update on psychopharmacology. In H. Steiner (Ed.), *Handbook of mental health intervention in children and adolescents: An integrated developmental approach* (pp. 318–362). San Francisco: Jossey-Bass.

Eng, W., Heimberg, R. G., Coles, M. E., Schneier, F. R., & Liebowitz, M. R. (2000). An empirical approach to subtype identification in individuals with social phobia. *Psychological Medicine, 30,* 1345–1357.

Engel, J. (1989). *Addicted: Kids talking about drugs in their own words.* New York: T. Doherty.

Engels, G. I., Garnefski, N., & Diekstra, R. F. W. (1993). Efficacy of rational-emotive therapy: A quantitative analysis. *Journal of Consulting & Clinical Psychology, 61,* 1083–1090.

Ensminger, M. E. (1995). Welfare and psychological distress: A longitudinal study of African/American urban mothers. *Journal of Health & Social Behavior, 36,* 346–359.

Ensminger, M. E., & Hee-Soon, J. (2001). The influence of patterns of welfare receipt during the child-rearing years on later physical and psychological health. *Women & Health, 32,* 25–46.

Epple, D. M. (2002). Senile dementia of the Alzheimer type. *Clinical Social Work Journal, 30,* 95–110.

Epstein, J., Saunders, B. E., & Kilpatrick, D. G. (1997). Predicting PTSD in women with a history of childhood rape. *Journal of Traumatic Stress, 10,* 573–588.

Erdelyi, M. H. (1992). Psychodynamics and the unconscious. *American Psychologist, 47,* 784–787.

Erickson, M. T. (1992). *Behavior disorders of children and adolescents.* Englewood Cliffs, NJ: Prentice Hall.

Erlenmeyer-Kimling, L. (2001). Early neurobehavioral deficits as phenotypic indicators of the schizophrenia genotype and predictors of later psychosis. *American Journal of Medical Genetics, 105,* 23–24.

Erlenmeyer-Kimling, L., Rock, D., Squires-Wheeler, E., & Roberts, S. (1991). Early life precursors of psychiatric outcomes in adulthood in subjects at risk for schizophrenia or affective disorders. *Psychiatry Research, 39,* 239–256.

Escobar, J. I. (1993). Psychiatric epidemiology. In A. C. Gaw (Ed.), *Culture, ethnicity, and mental illness* (pp. 43–73). Washington, DC: American Psychiatric Press.

Escobar, J. I., Burnam, M. A., Karno, M., & Forsythe, A. (1987). Somatization in the community. *Archives of General Psychiatry, 44,* 713–718.

Escobar, J. I., Gara, M., Waitzkin, H., Cohen Silver, R., Holman, A., & Compton, W. (1998). DSM-IV hypochondriasis in primary care. *General Hospital Psychiatry, 20,* 155–159.

Estrada, A. U., & Pinsof, W. M. (1995). The effectiveness of family therapies for selected behavioral disorders of childhood. *Journal of Marital & Family Therapy, 21,* 403–440.

Exner, J. E. (1993). *The Rorschach: A comprehensive system: Vol. 1. Basic foundations* (3rd ed.). New York: Wiley.

Eysenck, H. J. (1994). The biology of morality. In B. Puka (Ed.), *Defining perspectives in moral development* (pp. 212–229). New York: Garland.

Eysenck, H. J. (Ed.). (1967). *The biological basis of personality.* Springfield, IL: Charles C Thomas.

F

Fabrega, H. (1993). Toward a social theory of psychiatric phenomena. *Behavioral Science, 38,* 75–100.

Fabrega, H., Ulrich, R., Pilkonis, P., & Mezzich, J. (1991). On the homogeneity of personality disorder clusters. *Comprehensive Psychiatry, 32,* 373–386.

Fagan, P. J., Wise, T. N., Schmidt, C. W., Jr., & Berlin, F. S. (2002). Pedophilia. *Journal of the American Medical Association, 288,* 2458–2465.

Fahy, T. A. (1988). The diagnosis of multiple personality disorder: A critical review. *British Journal of Psychiatry, 153,* 597–606.

Fairbank, J. A., Hansen, D. J., & Fitterling, J. M. (1991). Patterns of appraisal and coping across different stressor conditions among former prisoners of war with and without posttraumatic stress disorder. *Journal of Consulting & Clinical Psychology, 59,* 274–281.

Fairburn, C. G. (1997). Eating disorders. In D. M. Clark & C. G. Fairburn (Eds.), *Science and practice of cognitive behaviour therapy* (pp. 209–241). London: Oxford University Press.

Fairburn, C. G. (2005). Evidence-based treatment of anorexia nervosa. *International Journal of Eating Disorders, 37,* 26–30.

Fairburn, C. G., & Harrison, P. J. (2003). Eating disorders. *Lancet, 361,* 407–416.

Fairburn, C. G., Cooper, Z., Doll, H. A., Norman, P., & O'Connor, M. (2000). The natural course of bulimia nervosa and binge eating disorder in young women. *Archives of General Psychiatry, 57,* 659–665.

Fairburn, C. G., Jones, R., Peveler, R. C., & Carr, S. J. (1991). Three psychological treatments for bulimia nervosa: A comparative trial. *Archives of General Psychiatry, 48,* 463–469.

Fairburn, C. G., Norman, P. A., Welch, S. L., O'Connor, M. E., Doll, H. A., & Peveler, R. C. (1995). A prospective study of outcome in bulimia nervosa and the long-term effects of three psychological treatments. *Archives of General Psychiatry, 52,* 304–312.

Fairburn, C. G., Stice, E., Cooper, Z., Doll, H. A., Norman, P. A., & O'Connor, M. E. (2003). Understanding persistence in bulimia nervosa: A 5-year naturalistic study. *Journal of Consulting & Clinical Psychology, 71,* 103–109.

Fairburn, C. G., Welsh, S. L., Doll, H. A., Davies, B. A., & O'Connor, M. E. (1997). Risk factors for bulimia nervosa. *Archives of General Psychiatry, 54,* 509–517.

Fairweather, G. W., Sanders, D. H., Maynard, H., & Cressler, D. L. (1969). *Community life for the mentally ill: An alternative to institutional care.* Chicago: Aldine.

Fallon, A. E., & Rozin, P. (1985). Sex differences in perceptions of desirable body shape. *Journal of Abnormal Psychology, 94,* 102–105.

Falloon, I. R., Brooker, C., & Graham-Hole, V. (1992). Psychosocial interventions for schizophrenia. *Behavior Change, 9,* 238–245.

Fals-Stewart, W., Marks, A. P., & Schafer, J. (1993). A comparison of behavioral group therapy and individual behavior therapy in treating obsessive-compulsive disorder. *Journal of Nervous & Mental Disease, 181,* 189–193.

Fanous, A. H., Prescott, C. A., & Kendler, K. S. (2004). The prediction of thoughts of death or self-harm in a population-based sample of female twins. *Psychological Medicine, 34,* 301–312.

Faraone, S. V., Biederman, J., Keenan, K., & Tsuang, M. T. (1991). A family-genetic study of girls with DSM-III attention deficit disorder. *American Journal of Psychiatry, 148,* 112–117.

Faravelli, C., Giugni, A., Salvatori, S., & Ricca, V. (2004). Psychopathology after rape. *American Journal of Psychiatry, 161,* 1483–1485.

Fauerbach, J. A., Lawrence, J. W., Schmidt, C. W., Munster, A. M., & Costa, P. T. (2000). Personality predictors of injury-related posttraumatic stress disorder. *Journal of Nervous & Mental Disease, 188,* 510–517.

Fava, G. A., Rafanelli, C., Grandi, S., Conti, S., Ruini, C., Magelli, L., & Belluardo, P. (2001). Long-term outcome of panic disorder with agoraphobia treated by exposure. *Psychological Medicine, 31,* 891–898.

Fava, M., Copeland, P. M., Schweiger, U., & Herzog, D. B. (1989). Neurochemical abnormalities of anorexia nervosa and bulimia nervosa. *American Journal of Psychiatry, 146,* 963–971.

Fava, M., & Rosenbaum, J. F. (1995). Pharmacotherapy and somatic therapies. In E. E. Beckham & W. R. Leber (Eds.), *Handbook of depression* (2nd ed., pp. 280–301). New York: Guilford Press.

Fawzy, F. I., Kemeny, M. E., Fawzy, N. W., Elashoff, R., et al. (1990). A structured psychiatric intervention for cancer patients: II. Changes over time in immunological measures. *Archives of General Psychiatry, 47,* 729–735.

Feder, A., Olfson, M., Fuentes, M., Shea, S., Lantigua, R. A., & Weissman, M. M. (2001). Medically unexplained symptoms in an urban general medicine practice. *Psychosomatics, 42,* 261–268.

Federoff, I. C., Polivy, J., & Herman, C. P. (1997). The effect of preexposure to food cues on the eating behavior of restrained and unrestrained eaters. *Appetite, 28,* 33–47.

Feigon, S. A., Waldman, I. D., Levy, F., & Hay, D. A. (2001). Genetic and environmental influences on separation anxiety disorder symptoms and their moderation by age and sex. *Behavior Genetics, 31,* 403–411.

Feinberg, L. (2001). Trans health crisis: For us it's life or death. *American Journal of Public Health, 91,* 897–900.

Fennell, M. J. V., & Teasdale, J. D. (1987). Cognitive therapy for depression: Individual differences and the process of change. *Cognitive Therapy & Research, 11,* 253–271.

Fenton, W. S., & McGlashan, T. H. (1994). Antecedents, symptom progression, and long-term outcome of the deficit syndrome in schizophrenia. *American Journal of Psychiatry, 151,* 351–356.

Fergusson, D. M., Horwood, J. L., & Lynskey, M. T. (1993). Early dentine lead levels and subsequent cognitive and behavioural development. *Journal of Child Psychology & Psychiatry & Allied Disciplines, 34,* 215–227.

Ferris, C. F., & de Vries, G. J. (1997). Ethological models for examining the neurobiology of aggressive and affiliative behaviors. In D. M. Stoff, J. Breiling, & J. D. Maser (Eds.), *Handbook of antisocial personality disorder* (pp. 255–268). New York: Wiley.

Field, A. E., Camargo, C. A., Jr., Taylor, C. B., Berkey, C. S., Frazier, L., Gillman, M. W., & Colditz, G. A. (1999). Overweight, weight concerns, and bulimic behaviors among girls and boys. *Journal of the American Academy of Child & Adolescent Psychiatry, 38,* 754–760.

Figley, C. R., & Leventman, S. (Eds.). (1980). *Strangers at home: Vietnam veterans since the war.* New York: Brunner/Mazel.

Fink, M. (2001). Convulsive therapy: A review of the first 55 years. *Journal of Affective Disorders, 63,* 1–15.

Fink, P., Hansen, M. S., & Oxhøj, M.-L. (2004). The prevalence of somatoform disorders among internal medical inpatients. *Journal of Psychosomatic Research, 56,* 413–418.

Finkelhor, D. (1984). *Child sexual abuse: New theory and research.* New York: Free Press.

Finkelhor, D., & Dzuiba-Leatherman, J. (1994). Victimization of children. *American Psychologist, 49,* 173–183.

Finney, J. W., & Moos, R. H. (1998). Psychosocial treatments for alcohol use disorders. In P. E. Nathan (Ed.), *A guide to treatments that work* (pp. 156–166). New York: Oxford University Press.

First, M. B., Spitzer, R. L., Gibbon, M., & Williams, J. B. W. (1997). *Structured Clinical Interview for DSM-IV Axis I Disorders—Nonpatient edition (version 2.0).* New York: New York State Psychiatric Institute, Biometrics Research Department.

Fishbain, D. A., & Goldberg, M. (1991). The misdiagnosis of conversion disorder in a psychiatric emergency service. *General Hospital Psychiatry, 13,* 177–181.

Fisher, R. A. (1958). *The cancer controversy.* London: Oliver & Boyd.

Fitzgerald, P. B., Brown, T. L., Daskalakis, Z. J., de Castella, A., Kulkarni, J., Marston, N. A. U, & Oxley, T. (2004). Reduced plastic brain responses in schizophrenia: A transcranial magnetic stimulation study. *Schizophrenia Research, 71,* 17–26.

Fitzgerald, T. E., Tennen, H., Affleck, G., & Pransky, G. S. (1993). The relative importance of dispositional optimism and control appraisals in quality of life after coronary artery bypass surgery. *Journal of Behavioral Medicine, 16,* 25–43.

Flakierska-Praquin, N., Lindstrom, M., & Gilberg, C. (1997). School phobia with separation anxiety disorder: A comparative 20- to 29-year follow up study of 35 school refusers. *Comprehensive Psychology, 38,* 17–22.

Flemming, M., & Manwell, L. B. (2000). Epidemiology. In G. Zernig (Ed.), *Handbook of alcoholism* (pp. 271–286). Boca Raton, FL: CRC Press.

Foa, E., & Kozak, M. (1993). Obsessive-compulsive disorder: Long-term outcome of psychological treatment. In M. Mavissakalian & R. Prien (Eds.), *Long-term treatment of anxiety disorders.* Washington, DC: American Psychiatric Press.

Foa, E. B., Dancu, C. V., Hembree, E., Jaycox, L. H., Anonymous, & Street, G. P. (1999). A comparison of exposure therapy, stress inoculation training, and their combination for reducing posttraumatic stress disorder in female assault victims. *Journal of Consulting & Clinical Psychology, 67,* 194–200.

Foa, E. B., Feske, U., Murdock, T. B., & Kozak, M. J. (1991). Processing threat-related information in rape victims. *Journal of Abnormal Psychology, 100,* 156–162.

Foa, E. B., & Franklin, E. (2001). Obsessive-compulsive disorder. In D. H. Barlow (Ed.), *Clinical handbook of psychological disorders: A step-by-step treatment manual* (3rd ed., pp. 209–263). New York: Guilford Press.

Foa, E. B., & Hearst-Ikeda, D. (1996). Emotional dissociation in response to trauma: An information-processing approach. In L. K. Michelson (Ed.), *Handbook of dissociation: Theoretical, empirical, and clinical perspectives* (pp. 207–224). New York: Plenum Press.

Foa, E. B., & Jaycox, L. H. (1999). Cognitive-behavioral theory and treatment of posttraumatic stress disorder. In D. Spiegel (Ed.), *Efficacy and cost-effectiveness of psychotherapy* (pp. 23–61). Washington, DC: American Psychiatric Association.

Foa, E. D., & Riggs, D. S. (1995). Posttraumatic stress disorder following assault: Theoretical considerations and empirical findings. *Current Directions in Psychological Science, 4,* 61–65.

Follette, W. C., & Hayes, S. C. (2000). Contemporary behavior therapy. In C. R. Snyder & R. E. Ingram (Eds.), *Handbook of psychological change: Psychotherapy processes and practices for the 21st century* (pp. 381–408). New York: Wiley.

Folstein, M. F., Folstein, S. E., & McHugh, P. R. (1975). Mini-mental state: A practical method for grading the cognitive state of patients for the clinician. *Journal of Psychiatric Research, 12,* 189–198.

Fombonne, E. (1999). The epidemiology of autism: A review. *Psychological Medicine, 29,* 769–786.

Forsyth, D. R., & Corazzini, J. G. (2000). Groups as change agents. In C. R. Snyder & R. E. Ingram (Eds.), *Handbook of psychological change: Psychotherapy processes and practices for the 21st century* (pp. 309–336). New York: Wiley.

Fox, M. J. (2002). *Lucky man: A memoir.* New York: Hyperion Press.

Fraley, R. C., & Bonanno, G. A. (2004). Attachment and loss: A test of three competing models on the association between attachment-related avoidance and adaptation to bereavement. *Personality & Social Psychology Bulletin, 30,* 878–890.

Frances, A., Kahn, D., Carpenter, D., Docherty, J., & Donovan, S. (1998). The expert consensus guidelines for treating depression in bipolar disorder. *Journal of Clinical Psychiatry, 59*(Suppl. 4), 73–79.

Frances, A. J., First, M. B., & Pincus, H. A. (1995). *DSM-IV guidebook.* Washington, DC: American Psychiatric Press.

Frank, E., Anderson, B., Reynolds, C. F., & Ritenour, A. (1994). Life events and the research diagnostic criteria endogenous subtype: A confirmation of the distinction using the Bedford College methods. *Archives of General Psychiatry, 51,* 519–524.

Frank, E., Grochocinski, V. J., Spanier, C. A., Buysse, D. J., Cherry, C. R., Houck, P. R., Stapf, D. M., & Kupfer, D. J. (2000). Interpersonal psychotherapy and antidepressant medication: Evaluation of a sequential treatment strategy in women with recurrent major depression. *Journal of Clinical Psychiatry, 61,* 51–57.

Frank, E., Swartz, H. A., & Kupfer, D. J. (2000). Interpersonal and social rhythm therapy: Managing the chaos of bipolar disorder. *Biological Psychiatry, 48*, 593–604.

Frank, G. K., Kaye, W. H., Weltzin, T. E., Perel, J., Moss, H., McConaha, C., & Pollice, C. (2001). Altered response to meta-chlorophenylpiperazine in anorexia nervosa: Support for a persistent alteration of serotonin activity after short-term weight restoration. *International Journal of Eating Disorders, 30*, 57–68.

Frank, J. D. (1978). *Effective ingredients of successful psychotherapy*. New York: Brunner/Mazel.

Frankl, V. E. (1963). *Man's search for meaning: An introduction to logotherapy*. Boston: Beacon Press.

Franko, D. L., Wonderlich, S. A., Little, D., & Herzog, D. B. (2004). Diagnosis and classification of eating disorders. In J. K. Thompson (Ed.), *Handbook of eating disorders and obesity* (pp. 58–80). Hoboken, NJ: Wiley.

Frasure-Smith, N., Lesperance, F., & Talajic, M. (1995). Depression and 18-month prognosis after myocardial infarction. *Circulation, 91*, 999–1005.

Fredrickson, B. L., & Joiner, T. (2002). Positive emotions trigger upward spirals toward emotional well-being. *Psychological Science, 13*, 172–175.

Fredrickson, B. L., Tugade, M. M., Waugh, C. E., & Larkin, G. R. (2003). What good are positive emotions in crisis? A prospective study of resilience and emotions following the terrorist attacks on the United States on September 11th, 2001. *Journal of Personality & Social Psychology, 84*, 365–376.

Freeman, A., & Reinecke, M. A. (1995). Cognitive therapy. In A. S. Gurman (Ed.), *Essential psychotherapies: Theory and practice* (pp. 182–225). New York: Guilford Press.

Freeston, M. H., Ladouceur, R., Thibodeau, N., & Gagnon, F. (1992). Cognitive intrusions in a non-clinical population: II. Associations with depressive, anxious, and compulsive symptoms. *Behaviour Research & Therapy, 30*, 263–271.

Fremont, W. P. (2004). Childhood reactions to terrorism-induced trauma: A review of the past 10 years. *Journal of the Academy of Child & Adolescent Psychiatry, 43*, 381–392.

Freud, S. (1905). *Collected works*. London: Hogarth Press.

Freud, S. (1909). *Analysis of a phobia of a five-year-old boy* (Vol. III). New York: Basic Books.

Freud, S. (1914). *Psychopathology of everyday life* (Authorized English ed.). New York: Macmillan.

Freud, S. (1917). *Mourning and melancholia. Collected works*. London: Hogarth Press.

Freud, S. (1920). *A general introduction to psychoanalysis*. New York: Boni & Liveright.

Freud, S. (1923). *The ego and id*. London: Hogarth Press.

Freud, S. (1924). The loss of reality in neurosis and psychosis. In J. Strachey (Ed.), *Sigmund Freud's collected papers* (Vol. 2, pp. 272–282). London: Hogarth Press.

Freyd, J. J. (1996). *Betrayal trauma: The logic of forgetting childhood abuse*. Cambridge, MA: Harvard University Press.

Freyd, J. J., Martorella, S. R., Alvarado, J. S., Hayes, A. E., & Christman, J. C. (1998).

Cognitive environments and dissociative tendencies: Performance on the standard Stroop task for high versus low dissociators. *Applied Cognitive Psychology, 12*, S91–S103.

Frick, P. J., & Morris, A. S. (2004). Temperament and developmental pathways to conduct problems. *Journal of Clinical Child & Adolescent Psychology, 33*, 54–68.

Fried, P. A., & Watkinson, B. (1990). 36- and 48-month neurobehavioral follow-up of children prenatally exposed to marijuana, cigarettes, and alcohol. *Journal of Developmental & Behavioral Pediatrics, 11*, 49–58.

Friedman, M., & Rosenman, R. H. (1974). *Type A behavior and your heart*. New York: Knopf.

Friedman, M., Rosenman, R. H., Straus, R., Wurm, M., & Kositcheck, R. (1968). The relationship of behavior pattern A to the state of coronary vasculature. *American Journal of Medicine, 44*, 525–537.

Frith, C., & Frith, U. (2000). The physiological basis of theory of mind: Functional neuroimaging studies. In S. Baron-Cohen, H. Tager-Flusberg, & D. Cohen (Eds.), *Understanding other minds: Perspectives from autism and developmental cognitive neuroscience* (2nd ed., pp. 334–356). Oxford, UK: Oxford University Press.

Fritz, G. K., Fritsch, S., & Hagino, O. (1997). Somatoform disorders in children and adolescents: A review of the past 10 years. *Journal of the American Academy of Child & Adolescent Psychiatry, 36*, 1329–1338.

Fromme, K., Marlatt, G. A., Baer, J. S., & Kivlahan, D. R. (1994). The Alcohol Skills Training Program: A group intervention for young adult drinkers. *Journal of Substance Abuse Treatment, 11*, 143–154.

Fromm-Reichmann, F. (1948). Notes on the development of treatments of schizophrenia by psychoanalytic psychotherapy. *Psychiatry, 2*, 263–273.

Fugh-Berman, A., & Cott, J. M. (1999). Dietary supplements and natural products as psychotherapeutic agents. *Psychosomatic Medicine, 61*, 712–728.

Furr, S. R., Westefeld, J. S., McConnell, G. N., & Jenkins, J. M. (2001). Suicide and depression among college students: A decade later. *Professional Psychology: Research & Practice, 32*, 97–100.

Futterman, A., Thompson, L., Gallagher-Thompson, D., & Ferris, R. (1995). Depression in later life: Epidemiology, assessment, etiology, and treatment. In E. E. Beckham & W. R. Leber (Eds.), *Handbook of depression* (2nd ed., pp. 494–525). New York: Guilford Press.

Fyer, A. J., Liebowitz, M. R., Gorman, J. M., & Campeas, R. (1987). Discontinuation of alprazolam treatment in panic patients. *American Journal of Psychiatry, 144*, 303–308.

Fyer, A. J., Mannuzza, S., Chapman, T. F., Martin, L. Y., et al. (1995). Specificity in familial aggregation of phobic disorders. *Archives of General Psychiatry, 52*, 564–573.

G

Gadow, K. D. (1991). Clinical issues in child and adolescent psychopharmacology. *Journal of Consulting & Clinical Psychology, 59*, 842–852.

Gadow, K. D. (1992). Pediatric psychopharmacology: A review of recent

research. *Journal of Child Psychology & Psychiatry & Allied Disciplines, 33*, 153–195.

Galea, S., Ahern, J., Resnick, H., Kilpatrick, D., Bucuvalas, M., Gold, J., & Vlahov, D. (2002). Psychological sequelae of the September 11 terrorist attacks in New York City. *New England Journal of Medicine, 346*, 982–987.

Gannon, L. R., Haynes, S. N., Cuevas, J., & Chavez, R. (1987). Psychophysiological correlates of induced headaches. *Journal of Behavioral Medicine, 10*, 411–423.

Gao, S., Hendrie, H., Hall, K., & Hui, S. (1998). The relationship between age, sex, and the incidence of dementia and Alzheimer's disease: A meta-analysis. *Archives of General Psychiatry, 55*, 809–815.

Garb, H. N., Florio, C. M., & Grove, W. M. (1998). The validity of the Rorschach and the Minnesota Multiphasic Personality Inventory. *Psychological Science, 9*, 402–404.

Garber, J., & Horowitz, J. L. (2002). Depression in children. In I. H. Gotlib & C. L. Hammen (Eds.), *Handbook of depression* (pp. 510–540). New York: Guilford Press.

Garber, J., Walker, L. S., & Zeman, J. (1991). Somatization symptoms in a community sample of children and adolescents: Further validation of the Children's Somatization Inventory. *Psychological Assessment, 3*, 588–595.

Gardner, H. (2003). Three distinct meanings of intelligence. In R. J. Sternberg & J. Lautrey (Eds.), *Models of intelligence: International perspectives* (pp. 43–54). Washington, DC: American Psychological Association.

Gardner, W., Lidz, C. W., Hoge, S. K., Monahan, J., Eisenberg, M. M., Bennett, N. S., Mulvey, E. P., & Roth, L. H. (1999). Patients' revisions of their beliefs about the need for hospitalization. *American Journal of Psychiatry, 156*, 1385–1391.

Garfield, S. L. (1994). Research on client variables in psychotherapy. In A. E. Bergin (Ed.), *Handbook of psychotherapy and behavior change* (4th ed., pp. 190–228). New York: Wiley.

Garmezy, N. (1991). Resilience and vulnerability to adverse developmental outcomes associated with poverty. *American Behavioral Scientist, 34*, 416–430.

Garner, D., Cooke, A. K., & Marano, H. E. (1997, January/February). The 1997 body image survey results. *Psychology Today*, pp. 30–44.

Garner, D. M., & Garfinkel, P. E. (1980). Sociocultural factors in the development of anorexia nervosa. *Psychological Medicine, 10*, 647–656.

Garner, D. M., & Garfinkel, P. E. (Eds.). (1985). *Handbook of psychotherapy for anorexia nervosa and bulimia*. New York: Guilford Press.

Garner, D. M., & Garfinkel, P. E. (Eds.). (1997). *Handbook for treatment for eating disorders* (2nd ed.). New York: Guilford Press.

Garner, D. M., Garfinkel, P. E., & O'Shaughnessy, M. (1985). The validity of the distinction between bulimia with and without anorexia nervosa. *American Journal of Psychiatry, 142*, 581–587.

Garner, D. M., Olmstead, M. P., & Polivy, J. (1984). *The EDI*. Odessa, FL: Psychological Assessment Resources.

Garner, D. M., Rockert, W., Davis, R., & Garner, M. V. (1993). Comparison of cognitive-behavioral and supportive-expressive therapy for bulimia nervosa. *American Journal of Psychiatry, 150,* 37–46.

Garner, D. M., & Wooley, S. C. (1991). Confronting the failure of behavioral and dietary treatments for obesity. *Clinical Psychology Review, 11,* 729–780.

Garrison, C. Z., Bryant, E. S., Addy, C. L., Spurrier, P. G., Freedy, J. R., & Kilpatrick, D. G. (1995). Posttraumatic stress disorder in adolescents after Hurricane Andrew. *Journal of the American Academy of Child & Adolescent Psychiatry, 34,* 1193–1201.

Gatley, S. J., Gifford, A. N., Volkow, N. D., & Fowler, J. S. (1998). Pharmacology of cocaine. In R. E. Tarter (Ed.), *Handbook of substance abuse: Neurobehavioral pharmacology* (pp. 161–185). New York: Plenum Press.

Gatz, M., Kasl-Godley, J. E., & Karel, M. J. (1996). Aging and mental disorders. In J. E. Birren (Ed.), *Handbook of the psychology of aging* (4th ed., pp. 365–382). San Diego, CA: Academic Press.

Ge, X., Conger, R. D., Cadoret, R. J., & Neiderhiser, J. M. (1996). The developmental interface between nature and nurture: A mutual influence model of child antisocial behavior and parent behaviors. *Developmental Psychology, 32,* 574–589.

Geddes, J. R., Burgess, S., Hawton K., Jamison, K., & Goodwin, G. M. (2004). Long-term lithium therapy for bipolar disorder: Systematic review and meta-analysis of randomized controlled trials. *American Journal of Psychiatry, 161,* 217–222.

Geer, J. H., & Maisel, E. (1972). Evaluating the effects of the prediction-control confound. *Journal of Personality & Social Psychology, 23,* 314–319.

Gelenberg, A. J., Lydiard, R. B., Rudolph, R. L., Aguiar, L., Haskins, J. T., & Salinas, E. (2000). Efficacy of venlafaxine extended-release capsules in nondepressed outpatients with generalized anxiety disorder: A 6-month randomized controlled trial. *Journal of the American Medical Association, 283,* 3082–3088.

Geller, B., Tillman, R., Craney, J. L., & Bolhofner, K. (2004). Four-year prospective outcome and natural history of mania in children with a prepubertal and early adolescent bipolar disorder phenotype. *Archives of General Psychiatry, 61,* 459–467.

George, M., Sackeim, H. A., Marangell, L. B., Husain, M. M., Nahas, Z., Lisanby, S. H., Ballenger, J. C., & Rush, A. J. (2000). Vagus nerve stimulation: A potential therapy for resistant depression? *Psychiatric Clinics of North America, 23,* 757–783.

George, M. S., Nahas, Z., Kozel, F. A., Li, X., Yamanaka, K., Mishory, A., & Bohning, D. E. (2003). Mechanisms and current state of transcranial magnetic stimulation. *CNS Spectrums, 8,* 511–514.

Gerardin, P., & Thibaut, F. (2004). Epidemiology and treatment of juvenile sexual offending. *Pediatric Drugs, 6,* 79–91.

Gershon, E. S., & Rieder, R. O. (1992, September). Major disorders of mind and brain. *Scientific American, 267,* 126–133.

Ghaemi, S. N., Pardo, T. B., & Hsu, D. J. (2004). Strategies for preventing the recurrence of bipolar disorder. *Journal of Clinical Psychiatry, 65*(Suppl. 10), 16–23.

Gijsman, H. J., Geddes, J. R., Rendell, J. M., Nolen, W. A., & Goodwin, G. M. (2004). Antidepressants for bipolar depression: A systematic review of randomized, controlled trials. *American Journal of Psychiatry, 161,* 1537–1547.

Giles, J. (1994, April 18). The poet of alienation. *Newsweek,* pp. 46–47.

Gilger, J. W., Pennington, B. F., & DeFries, J. C. (1992). A twin study of the etiology of comorbidity: Attention-deficit hyperactivity disorder and dyslexia. *Journal of the American Academy of Child & Adolescent Psychiatry, 31,* 343–348.

Gillberg, C. (1991). Outcome in autism and autistic-like conditions. *Journal of the American Academy of Child & Adolescent Psychiatry, 30,* 375–382.

Gillberg, C. (1998). Chromosomal disorders and autism. *Journal of Autism & Developmental Disorders, 28,* 415–425.

Gillespie, N. A., Zhu, G., Heath, A. C., Hickie, I. B., & Martin, N. G. (2000). The genetic aetiology of somatic distress. *Psychological Medicine, 30,* 1051–1061.

Gillham, J. E., Reivich, K. J., Jaycox, L. H., & Seligman, M. E. P. (1995). Prevention of depressive symptoms in schoolchildren: Two-year followup. *Psychological Science, 6,* 343–351.

Gillis, L. S., Elk, R., Ben-Arie, O., & Teggin, A. (1982). The Present State Examination: Experiences with Xhosa-speaking psychiatric patients. *British Journal of Psychiatry, 141,* 143–147.

Gilman, S. E., Cochran, S. D., Mays, V. M., Hughes, M., Ostrow, D., & Kessler, R. C. (2001). Risk of psychiatric disorders among individuals reporting same-sex sexual partners in the National Comorbidity Survey. *American Journal of Public Health, 91,* 933–939.

Gilvarry, C. M., Russell, A., Hemsley, D., & Murray, R. M. (2001). Neuropsychological performance and spectrum personality traits in the relatives of patients with schizophrenia and affective psychosis. *Psychiatry Research, 101,* 89–100.

Ginns, E. I., Ott, J., Egeland, J. A., Allen, C. R., Fann, C. S. J., Pauls, D. L., Weissenbach, J., Carulli, J. P., Falls, K. M., Keith, T. P., & Paul, S. (1996). A genome-wide search for chromosomal loci linked to bipolar affective disorder in the Old Order Amish. *Nature Genetics, 12,* 431–435.

Ginns, E. I., St. Jean, P., Philibert, R. A., Galdzicka, M., Damschroder-Williams, P., et al. (1998). A genomewide search for chromosomal loci linked to mental health wellness in relatives at high risk for bipolar affective disorder among the Old Order Amish. *Proceedings of the National Academy of Sciences, USA, 95,* 15531–15536.

Giovini, G. A., Schooley, M. W., Zhu, B., Chrisman, J. H., Tomar, S. L., Peddicord, J. P., Merritt, R. K., Husten, C. G., & Eriksen, M. P. (1994). Surveillance for selected tobacco-use behaviors—United States, 1900–1994. *Morbidity & Mortality Weekly Report, 43,* 1–43.

Gitlin, M. (2002). Pharmacological treatment of depression. In I. H. Gotlib & C. L. Hammen (Eds.), *Handbook of depression* (pp. 360–382). New York: Guilford Press.

Gitlin, M., Nuechterlein, K., Subotnik, K. L., Ventura, J., Mintz, J., Fogelson, D. L., Bartzokis, G., & Aravagiri, M. (2001). Clinical outcome following neuroleptic discontinuation in patients with remitted recent-onset schizophrenia. *American Journal of Psychiatry, 158,* 1835–1842.

Glaser, R., Rice, J., Speicher, C. E., Stout, J. C., & Kiecolt-Glaser, J. C. (1986). Stress depresses interferon production by leukocytes concomitant with a decrease in natural killer cell activity. *Behavioral Neuroscience, 100,* 675–678.

Glasgow, M. S., Engel, B. T., & D'Lugoff, B. C. (1989). A controlled study of a standardized behavioral stepped treatment for hypertension. *Psychosomatic Medicine, 51,* 10–26.

Glasgow, M. S., Gaader, K. R., & Engel, B. T. (1982). Behavioral treatment of high blood pressure: I. Acute and sustained effects of relaxation and systolic blood pressure biofeedback. *Psychosomatic Medicine, 44,* 155–170.

Glass, G. V., & Singer, J. E. (1972). *Urban stress: Experiments on noise and social stressors.* New York: Academic Press.

Glass, R. M. (2001). Electroconvulsive therapy: Time to bring it out of the shadows. *Journal of the American Medical Association, 285,* 1346–1348.

Glassman, A. (1969). Indoleamines and affective disorders. *Psychosomatic Medicine, 31,* 107–114.

Gleaves, D. H., & Freyd, J. J. (1997, September). Questioning additional claims about the false memory syndrome epidemic. *American Psychologist,* pp. 993–994.

Gleaves, D. H., Hernandez, E., & Warner, M. S. (2003). The etiology of dissociative identity disorder: Reply to Gee, Allen, and Powell (2003). *Professional Psychology: Research & Practice, 34,* 116–118.

Gleaves, D. H., May, M. C., & Cardena, E. (2001). An examination of the diagnostic validity of dissociative identity disorder. *Clinical Psychology Review, 21,* 577–608.

Gleaves, D. H., Smith, S. M., Butler, L. D., & Spiegel, D. (2004). False and recovered memories in the laboratory and clinic: A review of experimental and clinical evidence. *Clinical Psychology: Science & Practice, 11,* 3–28.

Glowinski, A. L., Bucholz, K. K., Nelson, E. C., Fu, Q., Madden, P. A. F., Reich, W., & Heath, A. C. (2001). Suicide attempts in an adolescent female twin sample. *Journal of the American Academy of Child & Adolescent Psychiatry, 40,* 1300–1307.

Goate, A., Chartier-Harlin, M.-C., Mullan, M., Brown, J., Crawford, F., Fidani, L., Giuffra, L., Haynes, A., Irving, N., James, L., et al. (1991). Segregation of a missense mutation in the amyloid precursor protein gene with familial Alzheimer's disease. *Nature, 349,* 704–706.

Goff, D. C., & Coyle, J. T. (2001). The emerging role of glutamate in the pathophysiology and treatment of schizophrenia. *American Journal of Psychiatry, 158,* 1367–1377.

Gold, M. S., Tabrah, H., & Frost-Pineda, K. (2001). Psychopharmacology of MDMA (ecstasy). *Psychiatric Annals, 31,* 675–681.

Gold, P. E., Cahill, L., & Wenk, G. L. (2002). Ginko biloba: A cognitive enhancer?

Psychological Science in the Public Interest, 3, 2–11.

Goldberg, E. M., & Morrison, S. L. (1963). Schizophrenia and social class. *British Journal of Psychiatry, 109,* 785–802.

Golden, C. J., & Freshwater, S. M. (2001). Luria-Nebraska Neuropsychological Battery. In W. I. Dorfman & S. M. Freshwater (Eds.), *Understanding psychological assessment* (pp. 59–75). Dordrecht, Netherlands: Kluwer Academic Publishers.

Goldstein, A. (1994). *Addiction: From biology to drug policy.* New York: W. H. Freeman.

Goldstein, G., & Hersen, M. (Eds.). (1990). *Handbook of psychological assessment.* Elmsford, NY: Pergamon Press.

Goldstein, J. M., & Lewine, R. R. J. (2000). Overview of sex differences in schizophrenia: Where have we been and where do we go from here? In D. J. Castle, J. McGrath, & J. Kulkarni (Eds.), *Women and schizophrenia* (pp. 111–141). Cambridge, UK: Cambridge University Press.

Goldstein, J. M., Seidman, L. J., Buka, S. L., Horton, N. J., Donatelli, J. L., Rieder, R. O., & Tsuang, M. T. (2000). Impact of genetic vulnerability and hypoxia on overall intelligence by age 7 in offspring at high risk for schizophrenia compared with affective psychoses. *Schizophrenia Bulletin, 26,* 323–334.

Goldstein, J. M., Seidman, L. J., O'Brien, L. M., Horton, N. J., Kennedy, D. N., Makris, N., Caviness, V. S., Faraone, S. V., & Tsuang, M. T. (2002). Impact of normal sexual dimorphisms on sex differences in structural brain abnormalities in schizophrenia assessed by magnetic resonance imaging. *Archives of General Psychiatry, 59,* 154–164.

Goldstein, M. G. (1998). Bupropion sustained release and smoking cessation. *Journal of Clinical Psychology, 59*(Suppl. 4), 66–72.

Goldstein, M. J. (1987) The UCLA high-risk project. *Schizophrenia Bulletin, 13,* 505–514.

Goldstein, M. J., Talovic, S. A., Nuechterlein, K. H., & Fogelson, D. L. (1992). Family interaction versus individual psychopathology: Do they indicate the same processes in the families of schizophrenia? *British Journal of Psychiatry, 161,* 97–102.

Gomberg, E. S. (1994). Risk factors for drinking over a woman's life span. *Alcohol Health & Research World, 18,* 220–227.

Gonzalez, N. M., & Campbell, M. (1994). Cocaine babies: Does prenatal exposure to cocaine affect development? *Journal of the American Academy of Child & Adolescent Psychiatry, 33,* 16–19.

Goodwin, D. W. (1988). *Alcohol and the writer.* Kansas City, MO: Andrews and McMeel.

Goodwin, F., & Ghaemi, S. (1998). Understanding manic-depressive illness. *Archives of General Psychiatry, 55,* 23–25.

Goodwin, F. K., & Jamison, K. R. (1990). *Manic-depressive illness.* New York: Oxford University Press.

Goodwin, P. J., Leszcz, M., Ennis, M., et al. (2001). The effect of group psychosocial support on survival in metastatic breast cancer. *New England Journal of Medicine, 345,* 1719–1726.

Gorman, J. M. (2003). Treating generalized anxiety disorder. *Journal of Clinical Psychiatry, 64*(Suppl. 2), 24–29.

Gorman, J. M., Liebowitz, M. R., Fyer, A. J., Fyer, M. R., & Klein, D. F. (1986). Possible respiratory abnormalities in panic disorder. *Psychopharmacological Bulletin, 221,* 797–801.

Gorman, J. M., Papp, L. A., & Coplan, J. D. (1995). Neuroanatomy and neurotransmitter function in panic disorder. In S. P. Roose & R. A. Glick (Eds.), *Anxiety as symptom and signal* (pp. 39–56). Hillsdale, NJ: Analytic Press.

Gottesman, I. I. (1991). *Schizophrenia genesis: The origins of madness.* New York: W. H. Freeman.

Gottesman, I. I., & Erlenmeyer-Kimling, L. (2001). Family and twin strategies as a head start in defining prodromes and endophenotypes for hypothetical early-interventions in schizophrenia. *Schizophrenic Research, 51,* 93–102.

Gottesman, I. I., & Reilly, J. L. (2003). Strengthening the evidence for genetic factors in schizophrenia (without abetting genetic discrimination). In M. F. Lenzenweger & J. M. Hooley (Eds.), *Principles of experimental psychopathology: Essays in honor of Brendan A. Maher* (pp. 31–44). Washington, DC: American Psychological Association.

Gottesman, I. I., & Shields, J. (1982). *Schizophrenia, the epigenetic puzzle.* New York: Cambridge University Press.

Gould, M., Jamieson, P., & Romer, D. (2003). Media contagion and suicide among the young. *American Behavioral Scientist, 46,* 1269–1284.

Gould, M. S., Greenberg, T., Velting, D. M., & Shaffer, D. (2003). Youth suicide risk and preventive interventions: A review of the past 10 years. *Journal of the American Academy of Child & Adolescent Psychiatry, 42,* 386–405.

Graeff, F. G., Guimaraes, F. S., Francisco, S., De Andrade, T. G. C. S., & Deakin, J. F. W. (1996). Role of 5-HT in stress, anxiety, and depression. *Pharmacology, Biochemistry, & Behavior, 54,* 129–141.

Grandin, T. (1995). *Thinking in pictures and my other reports from my life with autism.* New York: Vintage Books.

Grandin, T., & Johnson, C. (2005) *Animals in translation: Using the mysteries of autism to decode animal behavior.* New York: Scribner.

Grant, B., Stinson, F., Dawson, D., Chou, P., Dufour, M., Compton, W., Pickering, R., & Kaplan, K. (2004). Prevalence and co-occurrence of substance use disorders and independent mood and anxiety disorders: results from the national epidemiologic survey on alcohol and related conditions. *Archives of General Psychiatry, 61,* 807–816.

Grant, B. F., Hasin, D. S., Stinson, F. S., Dawson, D. A., Chou, S. P., Ruan, W. J., & Huang, B. (2005). Co-occurrence of 12-month mood and anxiety disorders and personality disorders in the US: Results from the national epidemiologic survey on alcohol and related conditions. *Journal of Psychiatric Research, 39,* 1–9.

Grattan-Smith, P., Fairly, M., & Procopis, P. (1988). Clinical features of conversion disorder. *Archives of Disease in Childhood, 63,* 408–414.

Gray, E., & Cosgrove, J. (1985). Ethnocentric perception of childbearing practices in protective services. *Child Abuse & Neglect, 9,* 389–396.

Gray, J. A. (1987). *The psychology of fear and stress* (2nd ed.). Cambridge, UK: Cambridge University Press.

Greaves, G. B. (1980). Multiple personality: 165 years after Mary Reynolds. *Journal of Nervous & Mental Disease, 168,* 577–596.

Greden, J. F. (2001). *Treatment of recurrent depression.* Washington, DC: American Psychiatric Association.

Green, A. H. (1993). Child sexual abuse: Immediate and long-term effects and intervention. *Journal of the American Academy of Child & Adolescent Psychiatry, 32,* 890–902.

Green, R. (1986). Gender identity in childhood and later sexual orientation: Follow-up of 78 males. *Annual Progress in Child Psychiatry & Child Development,* 214–220.

Greenberg, D. M., Bradford, J. M., Curry, S., & O'Rouche, A. (1996, May). *A controlled study of the treatment of paraphilia disorders with selective serotonin inhibitors.* Paper presented at the annual meeting of the Canadian Academy of Psychiatry and the Law, Tremblay, Quebec.

Greenberg, L. S., Elliot, R., & Lietaer, G. (1994). Research on humanistic and experiential psychotherapies. In A. Bergin & S. Garfield (Eds.), *Handbook of psychotherapy and behavior change* (4th ed., pp. 509–542). New York: Wiley.

Griffin, P. A., Steadman, H. J., & Petrila, J. (2002). The use of criminal charges and sanctions in mental health courts. *Psychiatric Services, 53,* 1285–1289.

Grilo, C. M., Sanislow, C. A., & McGlashan, T. H. (2002). Co-occurrence of DSM-IV personality disorders with borderline personality disorder. *Journal of Nervous & Mental Disease, 190,* 552–554.

Grinspoon, L., & Bakalar, J. B. (1995). Marihuana as medicine: A plea for reconsideration. *Journal of the American Medical Association, 273,* 1875–1876.

Grisso, T., & Applebaum, P. S. (1995). The MacArthur Treatment Competence Study: III. Abilities of patients to consent to psychiatric and medical treatments. *Law & Human Behavior, 19,* 149–174.

Grisso, T., & Applebaum, P. S. (1998). *Assessing competence to consent to treatment: A guide for physicians and other health professionals.* New York: Oxford University Press.

Grob, G. N. (1994). *The mad among us: A history of the care of America's mentally ill.* Cambridge, MA: Harvard University Press.

Gross, R. T., Brooks-Gunn, J., & Spiker, D. (1992). Efficacy of educational interventions for low birth weight infants: The Infant Health and Development Program. In S. L. Friedman & M. D. Sigman (Eds.), *The psychological development of low birth weight children: Advances in applied developmental psychology.* Norwood, NJ: Ablex.

Gross-Isseroff, R., Biegon, A., Voet, H., & Weizman, A. (1998). The suicide brain: A review of postmortem receptor/transporter binding studies. *Neuroscience & Biobehavioral Reviews, 22,* 653–661.

Gruber, A. J., & Pope, H. G. (1998). Ephedrine abuse among 36 female weightlifters. *American Journal of Addiction, 7,* 256–261.

Gruber, A. J., Pope, H. G., Lalonde, J. K., & Hudson, J. I. (2001). Why do young women diet? The roles of body fat, body perception, and body ideal. *Journal of Clinical Psychiatry*, *62*, 609–611.

Grunze, H., & Walden, J. (2002). Relevance of new and newly rediscovered anticonvulsants for atypical forms of bipolar disorder. *Journal of Affective Disorders, 72*(Suppl. 1), 15–21.

Guarnaccia, P. J., Canino, G., Rubio-Stipec, M., & Bravo, M. (1993). The prevalence of *ataques de nervios* in the Puerto Rico Disaster Study: The role of culture in psychiatric epidemiology. *Journal of Nervous & Mental Disease, 181*, 157–165.

Guarnaccia, P. J., Guevara-Ramos, L. M., Gonzales, G., Canino, G. J., & Bird, H. (1992). Cross-cultural aspects of psychiatric symptoms in Puerto Rico. *Community & Mental Health, 7*, 99–110.

Guarnaccia, P. J., Rivera, M., Franco, F., Neighbors, C., & Allende-Ramos, C. (1996). The experiences of *ataques de nervios:* Toward an anthropology of emotions in Puerto Rico. *Culture, Medicine, & Psychiatry, 15*, 139–165.

Gumley, A., O'Grady, M., McNay, L., Reilly, J., Power, K., & Norrie, J. (2003). Early intervention for relapse in schizophrenia: Results of a 12-month randomized controlled trial of cognitive behavioural therapy. *Psychological Medicine, 33*, 419–431.

Gunderson, J. G., Ronningstam, E., & Smith, L. E. (1995). Narcissistic personality disorder. In W. J. Livesley (Ed.), *The DSM-IV personality disorders* (pp. 201–212). New York: Guilford Press.

Gunderson, J. G., Zanarini, M. C., & Kisiel, C. L. (1995). Borderline personality disorder. In W. J. Livesley (Ed.), *The DSM-IV personality disorders* (pp. 141–157). New York: Guilford Press.

Guo, Y. J., Chen, C.-H., Lu, M.-L., Tan, H. K.-L., Lee, H.-W., & Wang, T.-N. (2004). Posttraumatic stress disorder among professional and non-professional rescuers involved in an earthquake in Taiwan. *Psychiatry Research, 127*, 35–41.

Gusella, J. F., MacDonald, M. E., Ambrose, C. M., & Duyao, M. P. (1993). Molecular genetics of Huntington's disease. *Archives of Neurology, 50*, 1157–1163.

H

Haas, A. P., Hendin, H., & Mann, J. J. (2003). Suicide in college students. *American Behavioral Scientist, 46*, 1224–1240.

Hagengimana, A., Hinton, D., Bird, B., Pollack, M., & Pitman, R. K. (2003). Somatic panic-attack equivalents in a community sample of Rwandan widows who survived the 1994 genocide. *Psychiatry Research, 117*, 1–9.

Halford, W. K., & Hayes, R. (1991). Psychological rehabilitation of chronic schizophrenic patients: Recent findings on social skills training and family psychoeducation. *Clinical Psychology Review, 11*, 23–44.

Hall, G. C. N. (2001). Psychotherapy research with ethnic minorities: Empirical, ethical, and conceptual issues. *Journal of Consulting & Clinical Psychology, 69*, 502–510.

Hammen, C. (1991). Generation of stress in the course of unipolar depression. *Journal of Abnormal Psychology, 100*, 555–561.

Hammen, C. (1992). Cognitive, life stress, and interpersonal approaches to a developmental psychopathology model of depression. *Development & Psychopathology, 4*, 189–206.

Hammen, C. (2005). Stress and depression. *Annual Review of Clinical Psychology, 1*, 293–320.

Harding, C. M., Zubin, J., & Strauss, J. S. (1987). Chronicity in schizophrenia: Fact, partial fact, or artifact? *Hospital & Community Psychiatry, 38*, 477–486.

Hare, R. (1991) *The Hare Psychopathy Checklist—Revised Manual.* Multi-Health Systems, Inc.

Hare, R. D., & Hart, S. D. (1993). Psychopathy, mental disorder, and crime. In S. Hodgins (Ed.), *Mental disorder and crime* (pp. 104–115). Thousand Oaks, CA: Sage.

Harrell, J. P. (1980). Psychological factors and hypertension: A status report. *Psychological Bulletin, 87*, 482–501.

Harris, M. J., Milich, R., Corbitt, E. M., & Hoover, D. W. (1992). Self-fulfilling effects of stigmatizing information on children's social interactions. *Journal of Personality & Social Psychology, 63*, 41–50.

Hart, S. D., & Hare, R. D. (1997). Psychopathy: Assessment and association with criminal conduct. In D. M. Stoff, J. Breiling, & J. D. Maser (Eds.), *Handbook of antisocial personality disorder* (pp. 22–35). New York: Wiley.

Harter, S. (1983). Developmental perspectives on the self-system. In P. H. Mussen (Ed.), *Handbook of child development* (pp. 275–385). New York: Wiley.

Hartman, D. E. (1998). Behavioral pharmacology of inhalants. In R. E. Tarter (Ed.), *Handbook of substance abuse: Neurobehavioral pharmacology* (pp. 263–268). New York: Plenum Press.

Hartung, C. M., & Widiger, T. A. (1998). Gender differences in the diagnosis of mental disorders: Conclusions and controversies of the DSM-IV. *Psychological Bulletin, 123*, 260–278.

Harvey, A. G., & Rapee, R. M. (1995). Cognitive-behavior therapy for generalized anxiety disorder. *Psychiatric Clinics of North America, 4*, 859–870.

Harwood, D. M. J., Hawton, K., Hope, T., & Jacoby, R. (2000). Suicide in older people: Mode of death, demographic factors, and medical contact before death. *International Journal of Geriatric Psychiatry, 15*, 736–743.

Hasler, G., Drevets, W. C., Manji, H. K., & Charney, D. S. (2004). Discovering endophenotypes for major depression. *Neuropsychopharmacology, 29*, 1765–1781.

Hauri, P., & Fisher, J. (1986). Persistent psychophysiologic (learned) insomnia. *Sleep, 9*, 38–53.

Haynes, S. G., Feinleib, M., & Kannel, W. B. (1980). The relationship of psychosocial factors to coronary heart disease in the Framingham study: III. Eight-year incidence of coronary heart disease. *American Journal of Epidemiology, 111*, 37–58.

Hayward, C., Gotlib, I. H., Schraedley, P. K., & Litt, I. F. (1999). Ethnic differences in the association between pubertal status and symptoms of depression in adolescent girls. *Journal of Adolescent Health, 25*, 143–149.

Hayward, C., Killen, J. D., Kraemer, H. C., & Taylor, C. B. (1998). Linking self-reported childhood behavioral inhibition to adolescent social phobia. *Journal of the American Academy of Child & Adolescent Psychiatry, 37*, 1308–1316.

Hayward, C., Killen, J. D., Kraemer, H. C., & Taylor, C. B. (2000). Predictors of panic attacks in adolescents. *Journal of the American Academy of Child & Adolescent Psychiatry, 39*, 207–214.

Heath, A. C., Bucholz, K. K., Madden, P. A. F., Dinwiddie, S. H., Slutske, W. S., Bierut, L. J., Statham, D. J., Dunne, M. P., Whitfield, J. B., & Martin, N. G. (1997). Genetic and environmental contributions to alcohol dependence risk in a national twin sample: Consistency of findings in women and men. *Psychological Medicine, 27*, 1381–1396.

Heath, A. C., & Martin, N. G. (1993). Genetic models for the natural history of smoking: Evidence for a genetic influence on smoking. *Addictive Behaviors, 18*, 19–34.

Hebert, L. E., Scherr, P. A., Bienias, J. L., Bennet, D. A., & Evans, D. A. (2003). Alzheimer disease in the US population: Prevalence estimates using the 2000 census. *Archives of Neurology, 60*, 1119–1122.

Heim, C., Meinlschmidt, G., & Nemeroff, C. B. (2003). Neurobiology of early-life stress. *Psychiatric Annals, 33*, 18–26.

Heim, C., Plotsky, P. M., & Nemeroff, C. B. (2004). Importance of studying the contributions of early adverse experience to neurobiological findings in depression. *Neuropsychopharmacology, 29*, 641–648.

Heiman, J. R. (2000). Orgasmic disorders in women. In S. R. Leiblum & R. C. Rosen (Eds.), *Principles and practice of sex therapy* (3rd ed., pp. 118–153) New York: Guilford Press.

Heiman, J. R., & Grafton-Becker, V. (1989). Orgasmic disorders in women. In S. R. Leiblum & R. C. Rosen (Eds.), *Principles and practice of sex therapy: Update for the 1990s* (pp. 51–88). New York: Guilford Press.

Heimberg, R. G. (2001). Current status of psychotherapeutic interventions for social phobia. *Journal of Clinical Psychiatry, 62*(Suppl. 1), 36–42.

Heimberg, R. G., Liebowitz, M., Hope, D. A., Schneier, F. R., Holt, C. S., Welkowitz, L. A., Juster, H. R., Campeas, R., Bruck, M. A., Cloitre, M., Fallon, B., & Klein, D. F. (1998). Cognitive behavioral group therapy vs. phenelzine therapy for social phobia: 12-week outcome. *Archives of General Psychiatry, 55*, 1113–1141.

Heinrichs, N., & Hofman, S. G. (2001). Information processing in social phobia: A critical review. *Clinical Psychology Review, 21*, 751–770.

Heise, L., Ellsberg, M. & Gottenmuller, M. (1999). Ending violence against women. *Population Reports*, Series L, No. 11, December 1-43. Baltimore: Johns Hopkins University School of Public Health, Population Information Program.

Heiser, N. A., Turner, S. M., & Beidel, D. C. (2003). Shyness: Relationship to social phobia and other psychiatric disorders. *Behaviour Research & Therapy, 41*, 209–221.

Helgeland, M. I., & Torgersen, S. (2004). Developmental antecedents of borderline personality disorder. *Comprehensive Psychiatry, 45*, 138–147.

Helgeson, V. S. (1994). Relation of agency and communion to well-being: Evidence and potential explanations. *Psychological Bulletin, 116,* 412–428.

Helzer, J. E., Bucholz, K., & Robins, L. N. (1992). Five communities in the United States: Results of the Epidemiologic Catchment Area Survey. In J. E. Helzer & G. J. Canino (Eds.), *Alcoholism in North America, Europe, and Asia.* New York: Oxford University Press.

Helzer, J. E., Burnam, A., & McEvoy, L. T. (1991). Alcohol abuse and dependence. In L. Robins & D. Reiger (Eds.), *Psychiatric disorders in America: The Epidemiologic Catchment Area Study* (pp. 9–38). New York: Free Press.

Hendrick, V., Altshuler, L., & Suri, R. (1998). Hormonal changes in the postpartum and implications for postpartum depression. *Psychosomatics, 39,* 93–101.

Henriques, G., Beck, A. T., & Brown, G. K. (2003). Cognitive therapy for adolescent and young adult suicide attempters. *American Behavioral Scientist, 46,* 1258–1268.

Henry, B., Caspi, A., Moffitt, T. E., & Silva, P. A. (1996). Temperamental and familial predictors of violent and nonviolent criminal convictions: Age 3 to age 18. *Developmental Psychology, 32,* 614–623.

Henry, B., & Moffitt, T. E. (1997). Neuropsychological and neuroimaging studies of juvenile delinquency and adult criminal behavior. In D. M. Stoff, J. Breiling, & J. D. Maser (Eds.), *Handbook of antisocial personality disorder* (pp. 280–288). New York: Wiley.

Henry, M. E., Schmidt, M. E., Matochik, J. A., Stoddard, E. P., & Potter, W. Z. (2001). The effects of ECT on brain glucose: A pilot FDG PET study. *Journal of ECT, 17,* 33–40.

Herman, C. P., & Mack, D. (1975). Restrained and unrestrained eating. *Journal of Personality, 43,* 647–660.

Herman, J. L., & Harvey, M. R. (1997). Adult memories of childhood trauma: A naturalistic clinical study. *Journal of Traumatic Stress, 10,* 557–571.

Herpertz, S. C., Werth, U., Lucas, G., Qunaibi, M., Schuerkens, A., Kunert, H., Freese, R., Flesch, M., Mueller-Isberner, R., Osterheider, M., & Sass, H. (2001). Emotion in criminal offenders with psychopathy and borderline personality disorders. *Archives of General Psychiatry, 58,* 737–745.

Herpertz-Dahlmann, B., Muller, B., Herpertz, S., & Heussen, N. (2001). Prospective 10-year follow-up in adolescent anorexia nervosa—Course, outcome, psychiatric comorbidity, and psychosocial adaptation. *Journal of Child Psychology & Psychiatry, 42,* 603–612.

Heston, L. L. (1966). Psychiatric disorders in foster home reared children of schizophrenic mothers. *British Journal of Psychiatry, 112,* 819–825.

Hettema, J. M., Neale, M. C., & Kendler, K. S. (2001). A review and meta-analysis of the genetic epidemiology of anxiety disorders. *American Journal of Psychiatry, 158,* 1568–1578.

Hewlett, W. A. (2000). Benzodiazepines in the treatment of obsessive-compulsive disorder. In W. K. Goodman (Ed.), *Obsessive-compulsive disorder: Contemporary issues in treatment* (pp. 405–429). Mahwah, NJ: Erlbaum.

Higgins, S. T., Budney, A. J., Beckel, W. K., & Badger, G. J. (1994). Participation of significant others in outpatient behavioral treatment predicts greater cocaine abstinence.

American Journal of Drug & Alcohol Abuse, 20, 47–56.

Hilgard, E. R. (1977/1986). *Divided consciousness: Multiple controls in human thought and action.* New York: Wiley.

Hilgard, E. R. (1992). Divided consciousness and dissociation. *Consciousness & Cognition: An International Journal, 1,* 16–31.

Hill, A. J., & Franklin, J. A. (1998). Mothers, daughters, and dieting: Investigating the transmission of weight control. *British Journal of Clinical Psychology, 37,* 3–13.

Hines, M. (2004). Psychosexual development in individuals who have female pseudohermaphroditism. *Child & Adolescent Psychiatric Clinics of North America, 13,* 641–656.

Hinshaw, S. P., & Melnick, S. M. (1995). Peer relationships in boys with attention-deficit hyperactivity disorder with and without comorbid aggression. *Development & Psychopathology, 7,* 627–647.

Hirschfeld, R. (1994). Guidelines for the long-term treatment of depression. *Journal of Clinical Psychiatry, 55*(Suppl. 12), 59–67.

Hite, S. (1976). *The Hite report: A nationwide study on female sexuality.* New York: Macmillan.

Hlastala, S. A., Frank, E., Kowalski, J., Sherrill, J. T., & Tu, X. M. (2000). Stressful life events, bipolar disorder, and the "kindling model." *Journal of Abnormal Psychology, 109,* 777–787.

Hodapp, R. M., Burack, J. A., & Zigler, E. (1998). Developmental approaches to mental retardation: A short introduction. In J. A. Burack, R. M. Hodapp, & E. Zigler (Eds.), *Handbook of mental retardation and development* (pp. 3–19). New York: Cambridge University Press.

Hodgins, S., & Cote, G. (1990). Prevalence of mental disorders among penitentiary inmates in Quebec. *Canadian Journal of Mental Health, 39,* 1–4.

Hoek, H. W., & van Hoeken, D. (2003). Review of the prevalence and incidence of eating disorders. *International Journal of Eating Disorders, 34,* 383–396.

Hoffman, A. (1968). Psychotomimetic agents. In A. Burger (Ed.), *Drugs affecting the central nervous system* (Vol. 2). New York: Marcel Dekker.

Hoffman, R. E., Boutros, N. N., Hu, S., Berman, R. M., Krystal, J. H., & Charney, D. S. (2000). Transcranial magnetic stimulation and auditory hallucinations in schizophrenia. *The Lancet, 355,* 1073–1075.

Hoffman, R. E., Hawkins, K. A., Gueorguieva, R., Boutros, N. N., Rachid, F., Carroll, K., & Krystal, J. H. (2003). Transcranial magnetic stimulation of left temporoparietal cortex and medication-resistant auditory hallucinations. *Archives of General Psychiatry, 60,* 49–56.

Hofmann, S. G. (2004). Cognitive mediation of treatment change in social phobia. *Journal of Consulting & Clinical Psychology, 72,* 393–399.

Hogarty, G. E., Anderson, C. M., Reiss, D. J., Kornblith, S. J., Greenwald, D. P., Jaund, C. D., & Madonia, M. J. (1986). Family psychoeducation, social skills training, and maintenance chemotherapy in the aftercare treatment of schizophrenia: I. One-year effects of a controlled study on relapse and expressed emotion. *Archives of General Psychiatry, 43,* 633–642.

Hogarty, G. E., Anderson, C. M., Reiss, D. J., Kornblith, S. J., Greenwald, D. P., Ulrich, R. F., & Carter, M. (1991). Family psychoeducation, social skills training, and maintenance chemotherapy in the aftercare treatment of schizophrenia: II. Two-year effects of a controlled study on relapse and adjustment. *Archives of General Psychiatry, 48,* 340–347.

Hogarty, G. E., Greenwald, D., Ulrich, R. F., Kornblith, S. J., DiBarry, A. L., Cooley, S., Carter, M., & Flesher, S. (1997). Three-year trials of personal therapy among schizophrenic patients living with or independent of family: II. Effects of adjustment of patients. *American Journal of Psychiatry, 154,* 1514–1524.

Hogarty, G. E., Kornblith, S. J., Greenwald, D., DiBarry, A. L., Cooley, S., Ulrich, R. F., Carter, M., & Flesher, S. (1997). Three-year trials of personal therapy among schizophrenic patients living with or independent of family: I. Description of study and effects on relapse rates. *American Journal of Psychiatry, 154,* 1504–1513.

Hoge, C. W., Castro, C. A., Messer, S. C., McGurk, D., Cotting, D. I., & Koffman, R. L. (2004). Combat duty in Iraq and Afghanistan, mental health problems, and barriers to care. *New England Journal of Medicine, 351,* 13–22.

Hoge, S. K., Bonnie, R. J., Poythress, N., Monahan, J., Eisenberg, M., & Feucht-Haviar, T. (1997). The MacArthur Adjudicative Competence Study: Development and validation of a research instrument. *Law & Human Behavior, 21,* 141–179.

Hoge, S. K., Poythress, N., Bonnie, R. J., Monahan, J., Eisenberg, M., & Feucht-Haviar, T. (1997). The MacArthur Adjudicative Competence Study: Diagnosis, psychopathology, and competence-related abilities. *Behavioral Sciences & the Law, 15,* 329–345.

Holden, C. (1980). Identical twins reared apart. *Science, 207,* 1323–1328.

Hollander, E., Allen, A., Lopez, R. P., Bienstock, C. A., Grossman, R., Siever, L. J., Merkatz, L., & Stein, D. J. (2001). A preliminary double-blind, placebo-controlled trial of divalproex sodium in borderline personality disorder. *Journal of Clinical Psychiatry, 62,* 199–203.

Hollon, S. D., DeRubeis, R. J., Evans, M. D., Wiemer, M. J., Garvey, M. J., Grove, W. M., & Tuason, V. B. (1992). Cognitive therapy and pharmacotherapy for depression: Singly and in combination. *Archives of General Psychiatry, 49,* 774–781.

Hollon, S. D., Haman, K. L., & Brown, L. L. (2002). Cognitive-behavioral treatment of depression. In I. H. Gotlib & C. L. Hammen (Eds.), *Handbook of depression* (pp. 383–403). New York: Guilford Press.

Holmes, T. H., & Rahe, R. H. (1967). The social readjustment rating scale. *Journal of Psychosomatic Research, 11,* 213–218.

Holroyd, J. C., & Brodsky, A. M. (1977). Psychologists' attitudes and practices regarding erotic and nonerotic physical contact with patients. *American Psychologist, 32,* 843–849.

Holstein, J. A. (1993). *Court-ordered insanity: Interpretive practice and involuntary commitment*. New York: A. de Gruyter.

Hooley, J. M. (1998). Expressed emotion and psychiatric illness: From empirical data to clinical practice. *Behavior Therapy, 29*, 631–646.

Hooley, J. M., & Campbell, C. (2002). Control and controllability: Beliefs and behaviour in high and low expressed emotion relatives. *Psychological Medicine, 32*, 1091–1099.

Hooley, J. M., & Hiller, J. B. (1998). Expressed emotion and the pathogenesis of relapse in schizophrenia. In M. F. Lenzenweger & R. H. Dworkin (Eds.), *Origins of the development of schizophrenia* (pp. 447–468). Washington, DC: American Psychological Association.

Hornbacher, M. (1998). *Wasted*. New York: HarperPerennial.

Horney, K. (1934/1967). The overvaluation of love: A study of present-day feminine type. In H. Kelman (Ed.), *Feminine psychology* (pp. 182–213). New York: W. W. Norton.

Horney, K. (1939). *New ways in psychoanalysis*. New York: W. W. Norton.

Hornig, C. D., & McNally, R. J. (1995). Panic disorder and suicide attempt: A reanalysis of data from the Epidemiologic Catchment Area study. *British Journal of Psychiatry, 167*, 76–79.

Hornstein, N. L., & Putnam, F. W. (1992). Clinical phenomenology of child and adolescent dissociative disorders. *Journal of the American Academy of Child & Adolescent Psychiatry, 31*, 1077–1085.

Horowitz, M. J. (1976). *Stress response syndromes*. New York: Aronson.

Hough, D. W. (2001). Low-dose olanzapine for self-mutilation behavior in patients with borderline personality disorder. *Journal of Clinical Psychiatry, 62*, 296–297.

Hough, R. L., Canino, G. J., Abueg, F. R., & Gusman, F. D. (1996). PTSD and related stress disorders among Hispanics. In A. J. Marsella, M. J. Friedman, E. T. Gerrity, & R. M. Scurfield (Eds.), *Ethnocultural aspects of posttraumatic stress disorder* (pp. 483–504). Washington, DC: American Psychological Association.

Houts, A. C. (2003). Behavioral treatment for enuresis. In A. E. Kazdin & J. R. Weisz (Eds.), *Evidence-based psychotherapies for children and adolescents* (pp. 389–406). New York: Guilford Press.

Howlin, P., Goode, S., Hutton, J., & Rutter, M. (2004). Adult outcome for children with autism. *Journal of Child Psychology & Psychiatry, 45*, 212–229.

Hubbard, K., O'Neill, A.-M., Cheakalos, C., Baker, K., Berenstein, L., Breu, G., Duffy, T., Fowler, J., Greissinger, L. K., Matsumoto, N., Smith, P., Weinstein, F., & York, M. (1999, April 12). Out of control. *People Magazine*, pp. 52–69.

Hudson, J. L., & Rapee, R. M. (2001). Parent-child interactions and anxiety disorders: An observational study. *Behaviour Research & Therapy, 39*, 1411–1427.

Hudziak, J. J., van Beijsterveldt, C. E. M., Althoff, R. R., Stanger, C., Rettew, D. C., Nelson, E. C., Todd, R. D., Bartels, M., & Boomsma, D. I. (2004). Genetic and environmental contributions to the Child Behavior Checklist Obsessive-Compulsive Scale: A cross-cultural twin study. *Archives of General Psychiatry, 61*, 608–616.

Hugdahl, K., & Ohman, A. (1977). Effects of instruction on acquisition and extinction of electrodermal response to fear-relevant stimuli. *Journal of Experimental Psychiatry: Human Learning & Memory, 3*, 608–618.

Hughes, D., & Kleespies, P. (2001). Suicide in the medically ill. Suicidal behavior among Latino youth. *Suicide & Life-Threatening Behavior, 31*, 48–59.

Hughes, J. R. (1986). Genetics of smoking: A review. *Behavior Therapy, 17*, 335–345.

Hunt, W. A. (1998). Pharmacology of alcohol. In R. E. Tarter, R. T. Ammerman, & P. J. Ott (Eds.), *Handbook of substance abuse: Neurobehavioral pharmacology* (pp. 7–21). New York: Plenum Press.

Huppert, J. D., Bufka, L. F., Barlow, D. H., Gorman, J. M., Shea, K. M., & Woods, S. W. (2001). Therapists, therapist variables, and cognitive-behavioral therapy outcome in a multicenter trial for panic disorder. *Journal of Consulting & Clinical Psychology, 69*, 747–755.

Hur, Y., Bouchard, T. J., Jr., & Eckert, E. (1998). Genetic and environmental influences on self-reported diet: A reared-apart twin study. *Physiology & Behavior, 64*, 629–636.

Hurlbert, D. F. (1991). The role of assertiveness in female sexuality: A comparative study between sexually assertive and sexually nonassertive women. *Journal of Sex & Marital Therapy, 17*, 183–190.

Huselid, R. F., & Cooper, M. L. (1992). Gender roles as mediators of sex differences in adolescent alcohol use and abuse. *Journal of Health & Social Behavior, 33*, 348–362.

Hwu, H.-G., Chen, C.-H., Hwang, T.-J., Liu, C.-M., Cheng, J. L., Lin, S.-K., Liu, S.-K., Chen, C.-H., Chi, Y.-Y., Ou-Young, C.-W., Lin, H.-N., & Chen, W. J. (2002). Symptom patterns and subgrouping of schizophrenic patients: Significance of negative symptoms assessed on admission. *Schizophrenic Research, 56*, 105–119.

Hyde, J. S. (1990). *Understanding human sexuality*. New York: McGraw-Hill.

Hyman, I. E., & Billings, F. J. (1998). Individual differences and the creation of false childhood memories. *Memory, 6*, 1–20.

Hypericum Depression Trial Study Group. (2002). Effects of *Hypericum perforatum* (St. John's wort) in major depressive disorder. *Journal of the American Medical Association, 287*, 1807–1814.

I

Inciardi, J. A., Lockwood, D., & Pottieger, A. E. (1993). *Women and crack cocaine*. New York: Macmillan.

Infant Health and Development Program. (1990). Enhancing the outcome of low-birth-weight, premature infants: A multisite randomized trial. *Journal of the American Medical Association, 263*, 3035–3042.

Ingram, R. E., Hayes, A., & Scott, W. (2000). Empirically supported treatments: A critical analysis. In C. R. Snyder & R. E. Ingram (Eds.), *Handbook of psychological change: Psychotherapy processes and practices for the 21st century* (pp. 40–60). New York: Wiley.

Insel, T. R. (Ed.). (1984). *New findings in obsessive-compulsive disorder*. Washington, DC: American Psychiatric Press.

Insel, T. R., Hoover, C., & Murphy, D. L. (1983). Parents of patients with obsessive-compulsive disorder. *Psychological Medicine, 13*, 807–811.

Ironside, R. N., & Batchelor, I. R. C. (1945). *Aviation neuro-psychiatry*. Baltimore: Williams & Wilkins.

Ironson, G., Wynings, C., Schneiderman, N., Baum, A., Rodriguez, M., Greenwood, D., Benight, C., Antoni, M., LaPerriere, A., Huang, H.-S., Klimas, N., & Fletcher, M. A. (1997). Posttraumatic stress symptoms, intrusive thoughts, loss and immune function after Hurricane Andrew. *Psychosomatic Medicine, 59*, 128–141.

Iwamasa, G. Y., Larrabee, A. L., & Merritt, R. D. (2000). Are personality disorder criteria ethnically biased? A card-sort analysis. *Cultural Diversity and Ethnic Minority Psychology, 6*, 284–296.

J

Jablensky, A. (2000) Epidemiology of schizophrenia: The global burden of disease and disability. *European Archives of Psychiatry & Clinical Neuroscience, 250*, 274–285.

Jack, D. C. (1991). *Silencing the self: Women and depression*. New York: HarperPerennial.

Jack, R. (1992). *Women and attempted suicide*. Hillsdale, NJ: Erlbaum.

Jacobson, E. (1964). *The self and the object world*. New York: International Universities Press.

Jacobson, S. W., & Jacobson, J. L. (2000). Teratogenic insult and neurobehavioral function in infancy and childhood. In C. A. Nelson (Ed.), *The Minnesota symposia on child psychology, Vol. 31: The effects of early adversity on neurobehavioral development* (pp. 61–112). Mahwah, NJ: Erlbaum.

James, W. (1890). *The principles of psychology*. New York: Henry Holt.

James, W. (1948). *Psychology*. (*Briefer Course*). Cleveland, OH: World.

Jamison, K. R. (1993). *Touched with fire: Manic-depressive illness and the artistic temperament*. New York: Free Press.

Jamison, K. R. (1995). *An unquiet mind: A memoir of moods and madness*. New York: Knopf.

Jamison, K. R. (1999). *Night falls fast: Understanding suicide*. New York: Knopf.

Jang, K. L., Livesley, W. J., & Vernon, P. A. (1997). Gender-specific etiological differences in alcohol and drug problems: A behavioral genetic analysis. *Addiction, 92*, 1265–1276.

Jang, K. L., McCrae, R. R., Angleitner, A., Riemann, R., & Livesley, W. J. (1998). Heritability of facet-level traits in a cross-cultural twin sample: Support for a hierarchical model of personality. *Journal of Personality & Social Psychology, 74*, 1556–1565.

Jang, K. L., Paris, J., Zweig-Frank, H., & Livesley, W. J. (1998). Twin study of dissociative experience. *Journal of Nervous & Mental Disease, 186*, 345–351.

Janoff-Bulman, R. (1992). *Shattered assumptions: Toward a new psychology of trauma*. New York: Maxwell Macmillan International.

Janoff-Bulman, R., & Frieze, I. H. (1983). A theoretical perspective for understanding reactions to victimization. *Journal of Social Issues, 39*, 1–17.

Jarrett, R. B., Basco, M. R., Risser, R., Ramanan, J., Marwill, M., Kraft, D., & Rush, A. J. (1998). Is there a role for continuation phase cognitive therapy for depressed patients? *Journal of Consulting & Clinical Psychology, 66*, 1036–1040.

Jaycox, L. H., Reivich, K. J., Gillham, J., & Seligman, M. E. P. (1994). Preventing depressive symptoms in school children. *Behaviour Research & Therapy, 32*, 801–816.

Jefferson, J. W. (2001). Benzodiazepines and anticonvulsants for social phobia (social anxiety disorder). *Journal of Clinical Psychiatry, 62*(Suppl. 1), 50–53.

Jeffery, R. W., Wing, R. R., Thorson, C., & Burton, L. R. (1998). Use of personal trainers and financial incentives to increase exercise in a behavioral weight-loss program. *Journal of Consulting & Clinical Psychology, 66*, 777–783.

Jellinek, E. (1960). *The disease concept of alcoholism.* Highland Park, NJ: Hillhouse.

Jemmott, J. B., Jemmott, L. S., Spears, H., & Hewitt, N. (1992). Self-efficacy, hedonistic expectancies, and condom-use intentions among inner-city black adolescent women: A social cognitive approach to AIDS risk behavior. *Journal of Adolescent Health, 13*, 512–519.

Jemmott, L. S., & Jemmott, J. B. (1992). Increasing condom-use intentions among sexually active adolescent women. *Nursing Research, 41*, 273–279.

Jenkins, J. H., & Karno, M. (1992). The meaning of expressed emotion: Theoretical issues raised by cross-cultural research. *American Journal of Psychiatry, 149*, 9–21.

Jenkins, J. H., Kleinman, A., & Good, B. J. (1991). Cross-cultural studies of depression. In J. Becker (Ed.), *Psychosocial aspects of depression* (pp. 67–99). Hillsdale, NJ: Erlbaum.

Jenkins, R. L. (1968). The varieties of children's behavioral problems and family dynamics. *American Journal of Psychiatry, 124*, 1440–1445.

Jenkins, R. L. (1973). *Behavior disorders of childhood and adolescence.* Springfield, IL: Charles C Thomas.

Jensen, P. S., Hinshaw, S. P., Swanson, J. M., Greenhill, L. L., Conners, C. K., Arnold, L. E., Abikoff, H. B., Elliott, G., Hechtman, L., Hoza, B., March, J. S., Newcorn, J. H., Severe, J. B., Vitiello, B., Wells, K., & Wigal, T. (2001). Findings from the NIMH Multimodal Treatment Study of ADHD (MTA): Implications and applications for primary care providers. *Journal of Developmental & Behavioral Pediatrics, 22*, 60–73.

Jensen, P. S., Kettle, L., Roper, M. T., Sloan, M. T., Dulcan, M. K., Hoven, C., Bird, H. R., Bauermeister, J. J., & Payne, J. D. (1999). Are stimulants overprescribed? Treatment of ADHD in four U.S. communities. *Journal of the American Academy of Child & Adolescent Psychiatry, 38*, 797–804.

Ji, J., Kleinman, A., & Becker, A. E. (2001). Suicide in contemporary China: A review of China's distinctive suicide demographics in their sociocultural context. *Harvard Review of Psychiatry, 9*, 1–12.

Joe, S., & Kaplan, M. S. (2001). Suicide among African American men. *Suicide & Life-Threatening Behavior, 31*(Suppl.), 106–121.

Johannessen, D. J., Cowley, D. S., Walker, D. R., & Jensen, C. F. (1989). Prevalence, onset and clinical recognition of panic states in hospitalized male alcoholics. *American Journal of Psychiatry, 146*, 1201–1203.

Johnson, W., McGue, M., Krueger, R. F., & Bouchard, T. J. (2004). Marriage and personality: A genetic analysis. *Journal of Personality & Social Psychology, 86*, 285–294.

Johnston, L. D., O'Malley, P. M., Bachman, J. G., & Schulenberg, J. E. (2004). *Monitoring the future national results on adolescent drug use: Overview of key findings, 2003.* Bethesda, MD: National Institute on Drug Abuse.

Joiner, T. E. (1999). The clustering and contagion of suicide. *Current Directions in Psychological Science, 8*, 89–92.

Joiner, T. E., Jr., Brown, J. S., & Wingate, L. R. (2005). The psychology and neurobiology of suicidal behavior. *Annual Review of Psychology, 56*, 287–314.

Joiner, T. E., Jr. (2002). Depression in its interpersonal context. In I. H. Gotlib & C. L. Hammen (Eds.), *Handbook of depression* (pp. 295–313). New York: Guilford Press.

Joiner, T. E., Johnson, F., & Soderstrom, K. (2002). Association between serotonin transporter gene polymorphism and family history of completed and attempted suicide. *Suicide & Life-Threatening Behavior, 32*, 329–332.

Jones, E. E., & Harris, V. A. (1967). The attribution of attitudes. *Journal of Experimental Social Psychology, 3*, 1–24.

Jonnal, A. H., Gardner, C. O., & Prescott, C. A. (2000). Obsessive and compulsive symptoms in a general population sample of female twins. *American Journal of Medical Genetics, 96*, 791–796.

Jordan, B. D. (1998). Dementia pugilistia. In M. F. Folstein (Ed.), *Neurobiology of primary dementia* (pp. 191–204). Washington, DC: American Psychiatric Press.

Jordan, B. K., Schlenger, W. E., Fairbank, J. A., & Caddell, J. M. (1996). Prevalence of psychiatric disorders among incarcerated women: II. Convicted felons entering prison. *Archives of General Psychiatry, 53*, 513–519.

Jorge, R. E., Robinson, R. G., Tateno, A., Narushima, K., Acion, L., Moser, D., Arndt, S., & Chemerinski, E. (2004). Repetitive transcranial magnetic stimulation as treatment of poststroke depression: A preliminary study. *Biological Psychiatry, 55*, 398–405.

Joshi, S. V. (2004). Psychostimulants, atomoxetine, and alpha-agonists. In H. Steiner (Ed.), *Handbook of mental health intervention in children and adolescents: An integrated developmental approach* (pp. 258–287). San Francisco: Jossey-Bass.

Joyce, P. R., Rogers, G. R., Miller, A. L., Mulder, R. T., Luty, S. E., & Kennedy, M. A. (2003). Polymorphisms of DRD4 and DRD3 and risk of avoidant and obsessive personality traits and disorders. *Psychiatry Research, 119*, 1–10.

Judd, L. L., & Akiskal, H. S. (2000). Delineating the longitudinal structure of depressive illness: Beyond clinical subtypes and duration thresholds. *Pharmacopsychiatry, 33*, 3–7.

Judd, L. L., & Akiskal, H. S. (2003). The prevalence and disability of bipolar spectrum disorders in the US population: Re-analysis of the ECA database taking into account subthreshold cases. *Journal of Affective Disorders, 73*, 123–131.

Judd, L. L., Akiskal, H., Maser, J., Zeller, P. J., Endicott, J., Coryell, W., Paulus, M., Kunovac, J., Leon, A., Mueller, T., Rice, J., & Keller, M. (1998). A prospective 12-year study of subsyndromal and syndromal depressive symptoms in unipolar major depressive disorders. *Archives of General Psychiatry, 55*, 694–700.

Judd, L. L., Akiskal, H. S., Schetteler, P. J., Endicott, J., Maser, J., Solomon, D. A., Leon, A. C., Rice, J. A., & Keller, M. B. (2002). The long-term natural history of the weekly symptomatic status of bipolar I disorder. *Archives of General Psychiatry, 59*, 530–537.

Judd, L. L., Paulus, M. P., Wells, K. B., & Rapaport, M. H. (1996). Socioeconomic burden of subsyndromal depressive symptoms and major depression in a sample of the general population. *American Journal of Psychiatry, 153*, 1411–1417.

Jun-mian, X. (1987). Some issues in the diagnosis of depression in China. *Canadian Journal of Psychiatry, 32*, 368–370.

K

Kagan, J., Reznick, J. S., & Snidman, M. (1987). The physiology and psychology of behavioral inhibition in children. *Child Development, 58*, 1459–1473.

Kamen-Siegel, L., Rodin, J., Seligman, M. E., & Dwyer, J. (1991). Explanatory style and cell-mediated immunity in elderly men and women. *Health Psychology, 10*, 229–235.

Kanner, L. (1943). Autistic disturbances of affective contact. *Nervous Child, 21*, 217–250.

Kaplan, H. S. (1974). *The new sex therapy: Active treatment of sexual dysfunction.* New York: Brunner/Mazel.

Kaplan, H. S. (1977). Hypoactive sexual desire. *Journal of Sex & Marital Therapy, 3*, 3–9.

Kaplan, H. S. (1995). *The sexual desire disorders: Dysfunctional regulation of sexual motivation.* New York: Brunner/Mazel.

Kaplan, M. (1983). The issue of sex bias in DSM-III: Comments on the articles by Spitzer, Williams, and Kass. *American Psychologist, 38*, 802–803.

Karasek, R. A., Russell, R. S., & Theorell, T. (1982). Physiology of stress and regeneration in job related cardiovascular illness. *Journal of Human Stress, 8*, 29–42.

Karno, M., & Golding, J. M. (1991). Obsessive compulsive disorder. In L. R. Robins & D. A. Regier (Eds.), *Psychiatric disorders in America: The Epidemiologic Catchment Area study.* New York: Maxwell Macmillan International.

Karno, M., Hough, R., Burnam, A., Escobar, J. I., Timbers, D. M., Santana, F., & Boyd, J. H. (1987). Lifetime prevalence of specific psychiatric disorders among Mexican Americans and non-Hispanic whites in Los Angeles. *Archives of General Psychiatry, 44*, 695–701.

Karno, M., & Jenkins, J. H. (1993). Cross-cultural issues in the course and treatment of schizophrenia. *Psychiatric Clinics of North America, 16*, 339–350.

Karper, L. P., & Krystal, J. H. (1997). Pharmacotherapy of violent behavior. In D.

M. Stoff, J. Breiling, & J. D. Maser (Eds.), *Handbook of antisocial personality disorder* (pp. 436–444). New York: Wiley.

Kaslow, N., Thompson, M., Meadows, L., Chance, S., Puett, R., Hollins, L., Jessee, S., & Kellermann, A. (2000). Risk factors for suicide attempts among African American women. *Depression & Anxiety, 12,* 13–20.

Katchadourian, H. A. (1989). *Fundamentals of human sexuality* (5th ed.). New York: Holt, Rinehart & Winston.

Katon, W., Rutter, C., Ludman, E. J., Von Korff, M., Lin, E., Simon, G., Bush, T., Walker, E., & Unützer, J. (2001). A randomized trial of relapse prevention of depression in primary care. *Archives of General Psychiatry, 58,* 241–247.

Katon, W., Sullivan, M., & Walker, E. (2001). Medical symptoms without identified pathology: Relationship to psychiatric disorders, childhood and adult trauma, and personality traits. *Annals of International Medicine, 134,* 917–925.

Katon, W., Von Korff, M., Lin, E., Simon, G., Walker, E., Unützer, J., Bush, T., Russo, J., & Ludman, E. (1999). Stepped collaborative care for primary care patients with persistent symptoms of depression: A randomized trial. *Archives of General Psychiatry, 56,* 1109–1115.

Katz, R., & Wykes, T. (1985). The psychological difference between temporally predictable and unpredictable stressful events: Evidence for information control theories. *Journal of Personality & Social Psychology, 48,* 781–790.

Katzman, R. (1993). Education and the prevalence of dementia and Alzheimer's disease. *Neurology, 43,* 13–20.

Kavanagh, D. J. (1992). Recent developments in expressed emotion and schizophrenia. *British Journal of Psychiatry, 160,* 601–620.

Kaye, W. H., Nagata, T., Weltzin, T. E., Hsu, G., Sokol, M. S., McConaha, C., Plotnicov, K. H., Weise, J., & Deep, D. (2001). Double-blind placebo-controlled administration of fluoxetine in restricting- and restricting-purging-type anorexia nervosa. *Biological Psychiatry, 49,* 644–652.

Kaysen, S. (1993). *Girl, interrupted.* New York: Random House.

Kazdin, A. E. (1991). Effectiveness of psychotherapy with children and adolescents. *Journal of Consulting & Clinical Psychology, 59,* 785–798.

Kazdin, A. E. (2003a). Problem-solving skills training and parent management training for conduct disorder. In A. E. Kazdin & J. R. Weisz (Eds.), *Evidence-based psychotherapies for children and adolescents* (pp. 241–262). New York: Guilford Press.

Kazdin, A. E. (2003b). Psychotherapy for children and adolescents. *Annual Review of Psychology, 54,* 253–276.

Kazdin, A. E., & Weisz, J. R. (2003). *Evidence-based psychotherapies for children and adolescents.* New York: Guilford Press.

Keane, T. M., Gerardi, R. J., Quinn, S. J., & Litz, B. T. (1992). Behavioral treatment of post-traumatic stress disorder. In S. M. Turner, K. S. Calhoun, & H. E. Adams (Eds.), *Handbook of clinical behavior therapy* (pp. 87–97). New York: Wiley.

Keck, P. E., McElroy, S. L., Strakowski, S., West, S., Sax, K., Hawkins, J., Bourne, M. L., & Haggard, P. (1998). 12-month outcome of patients with bipolar disorder following hospitalization or a manic or mixed episode. *American Journal of Psychiatry, 155,* 646–652.

Keck, P. E., Jr., Mendlwicz, J., Calabrese, J. R., Fawcett, J., Suppes, T., Vestergaard, P. A., & Carbonell, C. (2000). A review of randomized, controlled clinical trials in acute mania. *Journal of Affective Disorders, 59*(Suppl. 1), 31–37.

Keel, P. K., & Klump, K. L. (2003). Are eating disorders culture-bound syndromes? Implications for conceptualizing their etiology. *Psychological Bulletin, 129,* 747–769.

Keesey, R. E. (1986). A set-point theory of obesity. In K. D. Brownell & J. P. Foreyt (Eds.), *Handbook of eating disorders* (pp. 45–62). New York: Basic Books.

Keller, M. B., Kocsis, J. H., Thase, M. E., Gelenberg, A. J., Rush, A. J., Koran, L., Schatzberg, A., Russell, J., Hirschfeld, R., Klein, D., McCullough, J. P., Fawcett, J. A., Kornstein, S., LaVange, L., & Harrison, W. (1998). Maintenance phase efficacy of sertraline for chronic depression: A randomized controlled trial. *Journal of the American Medical Association, 280,* 1665–1672.

Keller, M. B., McCullough, J. P., Klein, D. N., Arnow, B., Dunner, D. L., Gelenberg, A. J., Markowitz, J. C., Nemeroff, C. B., Russell, J. M., Thase, M. E., Trivedi, M. H., & Zajecka, J. (2000). A comparison of nefazodone, the cognitive behavioral analysis system of psychotherapy, and their combination for the treatment of chronic depression. *New England Journal of Medicine, 342,* 1462–1470.

Kellermann, A. L., Rivara, F. P., Somes, G., & Reay, D. T. (1992). Suicide in the home in relation to gun ownership. *New England Journal of Medicine, 327,* 467–472.

Kelly, G. F. (1998). *Sexuality today: The human perspective.* New York: McGraw-Hill.

Kelly, S. J., Day, N., & Streissguth, A. P. (2000). Effects of prenatal alcohol exposure on social behavior in humans and other species. *Neurotoxicology & Teratology, 22,* 143–149.

Kemeny, M. E. (2003). The psychobiology of stress. *Current Directions in Psychological Science, 12,* 124–129.

Kenardy, J. A., Dow, M. G. T., Johnston, D. W., Newman, M. G., Thomson, A., & Taylor, C. B. (2003). A comparison of delivery methods of cognitive-behavioral therapy for panic disorder: An international multicenter trial. *Journal of Consulting and Clinical Psychology, 71,* 1068–1075.

Kendall, P. C. (1992). *Anxiety disorders in youth: Cognitive-behavioral interventions.* Boston: Allyn & Bacon.

Kendall, P. C., Aschenbrand, S. G., & Hudson, J. L. (2003). Child-focused treatment of anxiety. In A. E. Kazdin & J. R. Weisz (Eds.), *Evidence-based psychotherapies for children and adolescents* (pp. 81–100). New York: Guilford Press.

Kendall, P. C., Hollon, S. D., Beck, A. T., Hammen, C. L., & Ingram, R. E. (1987). Issues and recommendations regarding use of the Beck Depression Inventory. *Cognitive Therapy & Research, 11,* 289–299.

Kendall-Tackett, K. A., Williams, L. M., & Finkelhor, D. (1993). Impact of sexual abuse on children: A review and synthesis of recent empirical studies. *Psychological Bulletin, 113,* 164–180.

Kendler, K. (1998). Major depression and the environment: A psychiatric genetic perspective. *Pharmacopsychiatry, 31,* 5–9.

Kendler, K., & Karkowski-Shuman, L. (1997). Stressful life events and genetic liability to major depression: Genetic control of exposure to the environment? *Psychological Medicine, 27,* 539–547.

Kendler, K. S., Davis, C. G., & Kessler, R. C. (1997). The familial aggregation of common psychiatric and substance use disorders in the National Comorbidity Survey: A family history study. *British Journal of Psychiatry, 170,* 541–548.

Kendler, K. S., Gallagher, T. J., Abelson, J. M., & Kessler, R. C. (1996). Lifetime prevalence, demographic risk factors, and diagnostic validity of nonaffective psychosis as assessed in a U.S. community sample. *Archives of General Psychiatry, 53,* 1022–1031.

Kendler, K. S., McGuire, M., Gruenberg, A. M., & Walsh, D. (1994). Outcome and family study of the subtypes of schizophrenia in the west of Ireland. *American Journal of Psychiatry, 151,* 849–856.

Kendler, K. S., Myers, J., Prescott, C. A., & Neale, M. C. (2001). The genetic epidemiology of irrational fears and phobias in men. *Archives of General Psychiatry, 58,* 257–265.

Kendler, K. S., Neale, M. C., Kessler, R. C., & Heath, A. C. (1992). Major depression and generalized anxiety disorder: Same genes, (partly) different environments? *Archives of General Psychiatry, 49,* 716–722.

Kendler, K. S., Neale, M. C., Kessler, R. C., & Heath, A. C. (1993). Panic disorder in women: A population-based twin study. *Psychological Medicine, 23,* 397–406.

Kendler, K. S., Neale, M. C., Kessler, R. C., Heath, A. C., & Eaves, L. J. (1992). A population-based twin study of major depression in women. *Archives of General Psychiatry, 49,* 257–266.

Kendler, K. S., Neale, M. C., Kessler, R. C., Heath, A. C., & Eaves, L. J. (1993). A test of the equal-environment assumption in twin studies of psychiatric illness. *Behavior Genetics, 23,* 21–28.

Kendler, K. S., & Prescott, C. A. (1998a). Cannabis use, abuse, and dependence in a population-based sample of female twins. *American Journal of Psychiatry, 155,* 1016–1022.

Kendler, K. S., & Prescott, C. A. (1998b). Cocaine use, abuse, and dependence in a population-based sample of female twins. *British Journal of Psychiatry, 173,* 345–350.

Kendler, K. S., & Prescott, C. A. (1999). A population based twin study of lifetime major depression in men and women. *Archives of General Psychiatry, 56,* 39–44.

Kennedy, S. H., Evans, K. R., Kruger, S., Mayberg, H. S., Meyer, J. H., et al. (2001). Changes in regional brain glucose metabolism measured with positron emission tomography after paroxetine treatment of major depression. *American Journal of Psychiatry, 158,* 899–905.

Kerbeshian, J., Burd, L., & Avery, K. (2001). Pharmacotherapy of autism: A review and clinical approach. *Journal of Developmental and Physical Disabilities, 13,* 199–228.

Kernberg, O. F. (1979). Psychoanalytic profile of the borderline adolescent. *Adolescent Psychiatry, 7,* 234–256.

Kernberg, O. F. (1989). *Psychodynamic psychotherapy of borderline patients.* New York: Basic Books.

Kernberg, O. F. (1998). Pathological narcissism and narcissistic personality disorder: Theoretical background and diagnostic classification. In E. F. Ronningstam (Ed.), *Disorders of narcissism* (pp. 29–58). Washington, DC: American Psychiatric Press.

Keshavan, M., Shad, M., Soloff, P., & Schooler, N. (2004). Efficacy and tolerability of olanzapine in the treatment of schizotypal personality disorder. *Schizophrenia Research, 71,* 97–101.

Kessler, R. C. (2003). The impairments caused by social phobia in the general population: Implications for intervention. *Acta Psychiatrica Scandinavica, 108*(Suppl. 417), 19–27.

Kessler, R. C., Andrade, L. H., Bijl, R. V., Offord, D. R., Demler, O. V., & Stein, D. J. (2002). The effects of co-morbidity on the onset and persistence of generalized anxiety disorder in the ICPE surveys. *Psychological Medicine, 32,* 1213–1225.

Kessler, R. C., Berglund, P., Demler, O., Jin, R., Koretz, D., Merikangas, K. R., Rush, A. J., Walters, E. E., & Wang, P. S. (2003). The epidemiology of major depressive disorder: Results from the national comorbidity survey replication (NCS-R). *Journal of the American Medical Association, 289,* 3095–3105.

Kessler, R. C., Berglund, P. A., Bruce, M. L., Koch, J. R., et al. (2001). The prevalence and correlates of untreated serious mental illness. *Health Services Research, 36,* 987–1007.

Kessler, R. C., Davis, C. G., & Kendler, K. S. (1997). Childhood adversity and adult psychiatric disorder in the U.S. National Comorbidity Survey. *Psychological Medicine, 27,* 1101–1119.

Kessler, R. C., Frank, R. G., Edlund, M., Katz, S. J., Lin, E., & Leaf, P. (1997). Differences in the use of psychiatric outpatient services between the United States and Ontario. *New England Journal of Medicine, 336,* 551–557.

Kessler, R. C., McGonagle, K. A., Zhao, S., Nelson, C. B., Hughes, M., Eshleman, S., Wittchen, H., & Kendler, K. S. (1994). Lifetime and 12-month prevalence of DSM-III-R psychiatric disorders in the United States: Results from the National Comorbidity Study. *Archives of General Psychiatry, 51,* 8–19.

Kessler, R. C., Olfson, M., & Berglund, P. A. (1998). Patterns and predictors of treatment contact after first onset of psychiatric disorders. *American Journal of Psychiatry, 155,* 62–69.

Kessler, R. C., Sonnega, A., Bromet, E., Hughes, M., & Nelson, C. B. (1995). Posttraumatic stress disorder in the National Comorbidity Survey. *Archives of General Psychiatry, 52,* 1048–1060.

Kessler, R. C., Stein, M. B., & Berglund, P. (1998). Social phobia subtypes in the National Comorbidity Survey. *American Journal of Psychiatry, 155,* 613–619.

Kety, S. S., Wender, P. H., Jacobsen, B., Ingraham, L. J., Jansson, L., Faber, B., & Kinney, D. K. (1994). Mental illness in the biological and adoptive relative of schizophrenic adoptees: Replication of the Copenhagen study in the rest of Denmark. *Archives of General Psychiatry, 51,* 442–455.

Keys, A., Brozek, J., Henschel, A., Mickelsen, O., & Taylor, H. L. (1950). *The biology of human starvation.* Minneapolis: University of Minnesota Press.

Kiecolt-Glaser, J. K., Malarkey, W. B., Chee, M., & Newton, T. (1993). Negative behavior during marital conflict is associated with immunological down-regulation. *Psychosomatic Medicine, 55,* 395–409.

Kiecolt-Glaser, J. K., McGuire, L., Robles, T. F., & Glaser, R. (2002). Emotions, morbidity, and mortality: New perspectives from psychoneuroimmunology. *Annual Review of Psychology, 53,* 83–107.

Kiecolt-Glaser, J. K., & Newton, T. L. (2001). Marriage and health: His and hers. *Psychological Bulletin, 127,* 472–503.

Kiesler, C. A., & Sibulkin, A. E. (1983). Proportion of inpatient days for mental disorders: 1969–1978. *Hospital & Community Psychiatry, 34,* 606–611.

Kihlstrom, J. F. (2001). Dissociative disorders. In P. B. Sutker (Ed.), *Comprehensive handbook of psychopathology* (3rd ed., pp. 259–276). New York: Kluwer Academic/Plenum Publishers.

Kihlstrom, J. F. (2005). Dissociative disorders. *Annual Review of Clinical Psychology, 1,* 227–254.

Kihlstrom, J. F., & Couture, L. J. (1992). Awareness and information processing in general anesthesia. *Journal of Psychopharmacology, 6,* 410–417.

Kihlstrom, J. F., Glisky, M. L., & Angiulo, M. J. (1994). Dissociative tendencies and dissociative disorders. *Journal of Abnormal Psychology, 103,* 117–124.

Killen, J. D., Taylor, C. B., Hayward, C., Haydel, K. F., Wilson, D. M., Hammer, L., Kraemer, H., Blair-Greiner, A., & Strachowski, D. (1996). Weight concerns influence the development of eating disorders: A 4-year prospective study. *Journal of Consulting & Clinical Psychology, 64,* 936–940.

Kilpatrick, D. G., Edmunds, C., & Seymour, A. (1992). *Rape in America: A report to the nation.* Charleston: National Victims Center & the Crime Victims Research and Treatment Center, Medical University of South Carolina.

Kilpatrick, D. G., & Saunders, B. E. (1996). *Prevalence and consequences of child victimization: Results from the national survey of adolescents.* U.S. Department of Justice, Office of Justice Programs, National Institute of Justice, Grant No. 93-IJ-CX-0023.

Kilpatrick, D. G., Veronen, L. J., & Resick, P. A. (1979). The aftermath of rape: Recent empirical findings. *American Journal of Orthopsychiatry, 49,* 658–669.

Kim, L. I. C. (1993). Psychiatric care of Korean Americans. In A. C. Gaw (Ed.), *Culture, ethnicity, and mental illness* (pp. 347–375). Washington, DC: American Psychiatric Press.

King, D. A., & Markus, H. E. (2000). Mood disorders in older adults. In S. K. Whitbourne (Ed.), *Psychopathology in later adulthood* (pp. 141–172). New York: Wiley.

King, D. W., King, L. A., Foy, D. W., Keane, T. M., & Fairbank, F. A. (1999). Posttraumatic stress disorder in a national sample of female and male Vietnam veterans: Risk factors, war-zone stressors, and resilience-recovery variables. *Journal of Abnormal Psychology, 108,* 164–170.

King, N. H., Gullone, E., & Tonge, B. J. (1993). Self-reports of panic attacks and manifest anxiety in adolescents. *Behaviour Research & Therapy, 31,* 111–116.

King, R. A., Schwab-Stone, M., Flisher, A. J., Greenwald, S., Kramer, R. A., Goodman, S. H., Lahey, B. B., Shaffer, D., & Gould, M. S. (2001). Psychosocial and risk behavior correlates of youth suicide attempts and suicidal ideation. *Journal of the American Academy of Child & Adolescent Psychiatry, 40,* 837–846.

Kinzie, J. D. (2001). The Southeast Asian refugee: The legacy of severe trauma. In W.-S. Tseng (Ed.), *Culture and psychotherapy: A guide to clinical practice* (pp. 173–191). Washington, DC: American Psychiatric Press.

Kinzie, J. D., & Leung, P. K. (1993). Psychiatric care of Indochinese Americans. In A. C. Gaw (Ed.), *Culture, ethnicity, and mental illness* (pp. 281–304). Washington, DC: American Psychiatric Press.

Kinzl, J. F., Traweger, C., Guenther, V., & Biebl, W. (1994). Family background and sexual abuse associated with eating disorders. *American Journal of Psychiatry, 151,* 1127–1131.

Kirk, S. A., & Kutchins, H. (1992). *The selling of DSM: The rhetoric of science in psychiatry.* New York: A. de Gruyter.

Kirmayer, L. J. (2001). Cultural variations in the clinical presentation of depression and anxiety: Implications for diagnosis and treatment. *Journal of Clinical Psychiatry, 62*(Suppl. 13), 22–28.

Kirmayer, L. J., & Taillefer, S. (1997). Somatoform disorders. In S. M. Turner & M. Herseen (Eds.), *Adult psychopathology and diagnosis* (3rd ed., pp. 333–383). New York: Wiley.

Kirsch, I., & Lynn, S. J. (1998). Dissociation theories of hypnosis. *Psychological Bulletin, 123,* 100–115.

Kisiel, C. L., & Lyons, J. S. (2001). Dissociation as a mediator of psychopathology among sexually abused children and adolescents. *American Journal of Psychiatry, 158,* 1034–1039.

Klein, D. F. (1964). Delineation of two drug-responsive anxiety syndromes. *Psychopharmacologia, 5,* 397–408.

Klein, D. N., Durbin, C. E., Shankman, S. A., & Santiago, N. J. (2002). Depression and personality. In I. H. Gotlib & C. L. Hammen (Eds.), *Handbook of depression* (pp. 115–140). New York: Guilford Press.

Klein, D. N., Lewinsohn, P. M., & Seeley, J. R. (1996). Hypomanic personality traits in a community sample of adolescents. *Journal of Affective Disorders, 38,* 135–143.

Klein, D. N., Lewinsohn, P. M., Seeley, J. R., & Rohde, P. (2001). A family study of major depressive disorder in a community sample of adolescents. *Archives of General Psychiatry, 58,* 13–20.

Klein, M. (1952). Notes on some schizoid mechanisms. In M. Klein, P. Heimann, S. Isaacs, & J. Riviere (Eds.), *Developments in psychoanalysis.* London: Hogarth Press.

Kleinman, A., & Kleinman, J. (1985). Somatization: The interconnections in Chinese society among culture, depressive experiences, and meanings of pain. In A. Kleinman & B. Good (Eds.), *Culture and depression* (pp. 429–490). Berkeley: University of California Press.

Klerman, G. L., & Weissman, M. M. (1989). Increasing rates of depression. *Journal of the American Medical Association, 261,* 2229–2235.

Klerman, G. L., Weissman, M. M., Rounsaville, B., & Chevron, E. (1984). *Interpersonal psychotherapy of depression.* New York: Basic Books.

Kline, P. (1993). *The handbook of psychological testing.* New York: Routledge.

Klorman, R., Cicchetti, D., Thatcher, J. E., & Ison, J. R. (2003). Acoustic startle in maltreated children. *Journal of Abnormal Child Psychology, 31,* 359–370.

Klosko, J. S., Barlow, D. H., Tassinari, R., & Cerny, J. A. (1990). A comparison of alprazolam and behavior therapy in treatment of panic disorder. *Journal of Consulting & Clinical Psychology, 58,* 77–84.

Kluft, R. P. (1985). The natural history of multiple personality disorder. In R. P. Kluft (Ed.), *Childhood antecedents of multiple personality* (pp. 197–238). Washington, DC: American Psychiatric Press.

Kluft, R. P. (1987). Unsuspected multiple personality disorder: An uncommon source of protracted resistance, interruption, and failure in psychoanalysis. *Hillside Journal of Clinical Psychiatry, 9,* 100–115.

Klump, K. L., Miller, K. B., Keel, P. K., McGue, M., & Iacono, W. G. (2001). Genetics and environmental influences on anorexia nervosa syndromes in a population-based twin sample. *Psychological Medicine, 31,* 737–740.

Knable, M. B., Barci, B. M., Webster, M. J., Meador-Woodruff, J., & Torrey, E. F. (2004). Molecular abnormalities of the hippocampus in severe psychiatric illness: Postmortem findings from the Stanley Neuropathology Consortium. *Molecular Psychiatry, 9,* 609–620.

Knopman, D. (2003). Pharmacotherapy for Alzheimer's disease: 2002. *Clinical Neuropharmacology, 26,* 93–101.

Koegel, R. L., Koegel, L. K., & Brookman, L. I. (2003). Empirically supported pivotal response interventions for children with autism. In A. E. Kazdin & J. R. Weisz (Eds.), *Evidence-based psychotherapies for children and adolescents* (pp. 341–357). New York: Guilford Press.

Kohut, H. (1971). *The analysis of the self: A systematic approach to the treatment of narcissistic personality disorders.* New York: New York International Universities Press.

Kohut, H. (1984). *How does analysis cure?* Chicago: University of Chicago Press.

Kohut, H., & Wolf, E. S. (1978). The disorders of the self and their treatment: An outline. *International Journal of Psychoanalysis, 59,* 413–425.

Koopman, C., Classen, C., & Spiegel, D. A. (1994). Predictors of posttraumatic stress symptoms among survivors of the Oakland/Berkeley, California, firestorm. *American Journal of Psychiatry, 151,* 888–894.

Koopman, C., Drescher, K., Bowles, S., Gusman, F., Blake, D., Dondershine, H., Chang, V., Butler, L. D., & Spiegel, D. (2001). Acute, dissociative reactions in veterans with

PTSD. *Journal of Trauma & Dissociation, 2,* 91–111.

Koorengevel, K. M., Gordijn, M. C. M., Beersma, D. G. M., Meesters, Y., den Boer, J. A., & van der Hoofdakker, R. H. (2001). Extraocular light therapy in winter depression: A double-blind placebo-controlled study. *Biological Psychiatry, 50,* 691–698.

Kopelman, M. D. (1987). Crime and amnesia: A review. *Behavioral Sciences & the Law, 5,* 323–342.

Korenman, S. G., & Barchas, J. D. (1993). *Biological basis of substance abuse.* New York: Oxford University Press.

Kortegaard, L. S., Hoerder, K., Joergensen, J., Gillberg, C., & Kyvik, K. O. (2001). A preliminary population-based twin study of self-reported eating disorder. *Psychological Medicine, 31,* 361–365.

Koss, J. D. (1990). Somatization and somatic complaint syndromes among Hispanics: Overview and ethnopsychological perspectives. *Transcultural Psychiatric Research Review, 27,* 5–29.

Koss, M. P. (1993). Rape: Scope, impact, interventions, and public policy responses. *American Psychologist, 48,* 1062–1069.

Koss, M. P., Figueredo, A. J., & Prince, R. J. (2002). Cognitive mediation of rape's mental, physical, and social health impact: Tests of four models in cross-sectional data. *Journal of Consulting & Clinical Psychology, 70,* 926–941

Koss, M. P., & Kilpatrick, D. G. (2001). Rape and sexual assault. In E. Gerrity (Ed.), *The mental health consequences of torture* (pp. 177–193). New York: Kluwer Academic/Plenum Publishers.

Koss-Chioino, J. D. (1995). Traditional and folk approaches among ethnic minorities. In J. F. Aponte (Ed.), *Psychological interventions and cultural diversity* (pp. 145–163). Boston: Allyn & Bacon.

Kouri, E. M., & Pope, H. G. (2000). Abstinence symptoms during withdrawal from chronic marijuana use. *Experimental & Clinical Psychopharmacology, 8,* 483–492.

Krakow, B., Hollifield, M., Johnston, L., Koss, M., Schrader, R., Warner, T. D., Tandberg, D., Lauriello, J., McBride, L., Cutchen, L., Cheng, D., Emmons, S., Germain, A., Melendrez, D., Sandoval, D., & Prince, H. (2001). Imagery rehearsal therapy for chronic nightmares in sexual assault survivors with posttraumatic stress disorder: A randomized controlled trial. *Journal of the American Medical Association, 286,* 537–545.

Krakow, B., Hollifield, M., Schrader, R., Koss, M., Tandberg, D., Lauriello, J., McBride, L., Warner, T. D., Cheng, D., Edmond, T., & Kellner, R. (2000). A controlled study of imagery rehearsal for chronic nightmares in sexual assault survivors with PTSD: A preliminary report. *Journal of Traumatic Stress, 13,* 589–609.

Krakowski, M. (2003). Violence and serotonin: Influence of impulse control, affect regulation, and social functioning. *Journal of Neuropsychiatry & Clinical Neurosciences, 15,* 294–305.

Kraus, G., & Reynolds, D. J. (2001). The "A-B-C's" of the Cluster B's: Identifying, understanding, and treating Cluster B

personality disorders. *Clinical Psychology Review, 21,* 345–373.

Krause, K., Dresel, S. H., Krause, J., et al. (2000). Increased striatal dopamine transporter in adult patients with attention deficit hyperactivity disorder: Effects of methylphenidate as measured by single photon emission computed tomography. *Neuroscience & Letters, 285,* 107–110.

Kring, A. M. (2000). Gender and anger. In A. H. Fischer (Ed.), *Gender and emotion: Social psychological perspectives* (pp. 211–231). New York: Cambridge University Press.

Kring, A. M., & Neale, J. M. (1996). Do schizophrenic patients show a disjunctive relationship among expressive, experiential, and psychophysiological components of emotion? *Journal of Abnormal Psychology, 105,* 249–257.

Kroll, J. (1973). A reappraisal of psychiatry in the Middle Ages. *Archives of General Psychiatry, 29,* 276–283.

Krueger, R. F. (2002). Psychometric perspectives on comorbidity. In J. E. Helzer & J. J. Hudziak (Eds.), *Defining psychopathology in the 21st century: DSM-V and beyond* (pp. 41–54). Washington, DC: American Psychiatric Publishing.

Kryger, M. H., Roth, T., & Dement, W. C. (Eds.). (1994). *Principles and practice of sleep medicine.* Philadelphia: Saunders.

Krystal, H. (Ed.). (1968). *Massive psychic trauma.* New York: International Universities Press.

Kubany, E. S., Hill, E. E., Owens, J. A., Iannce-Spencer, C., McCaig, M. A., Tremayne, K. J., & Williams, P. L. (2004). Cognitive trauma therapy for battered women with PTSD (CTT-BW). *Journal of Consulting & Clinical Psychology, 72,* 3–18.

Kuhn, R. (1958). The treatment of depressive states with G22355 (imipramine hydrochloride). *American Journal of Psychiatry, 115,* 459–464.

Kuiper, N. A., & Olinger, L. J. (1986). Dysfunctional attitudes and a self-worth contingency model of depression. *Advances in Cognitive-Behavioral Research & Therapy, 5,* 115–142.

Kuiper, N. A., Olinger, L. J., & MacDonald, M. R. (1988). Vulnerability and episodic cognitions in a self-worth contingency model of depression. In L. B. Alloy (Ed.), *Cognitive processes in depression* (pp. 289–309). New York: Guilford Press.

Kujawa, M. J., & Nemeroff, C. B. (2000). The biology of bipolar disorder. In A. Marneros & J. Angst (Eds.), *Bipolar disorders: 100 years after manic-depressive insanity* (pp. 281–314). London: Kluwer Academic Publishers.

L

LaFromboise, T. D., Trimble, J. E., & Mohatt, G. V. (1998). Counseling intervention and American Indian tradition: An integrative approach. In D. R. Atkinson (Ed.), *Counseling American minorities* (5th ed., pp. 159–182). New York: McGraw-Hill.

Lagana, L., McGarvey, E. L., Classen, C., & Koopman, C. (2001). Psychosexual dysfunction among gynecological cancer survivors. *Journal of Clinical Psychology in Medical Settings, 8,* 73–84.

LaGreca, A. M., Silverman, W. K., Vernberg, E. M., & Prinstein, M. J. (1996). Symptoms of posttraumatic stress in children after Hurricane Andrew: A prospective study. *Journal of Consulting & Clinical Psychology, 64,* 712–723.

LaGreca, A. M., Silverman, W. K., & Wasserstein, S. B. (1998). Children's predisaster functioning as a predictor of posttraumatic stress following Hurricane Andrew. *Journal of Consulting & Clinical Psychology, 66,* 883–892.

Lahey, B. B., & Loeber, R. (1997). Attention-deficit/hyperactivity disorder, oppositional defiant disorder, conduct disorder, and adult antisocial behavior: A life span perspective. In D. M. Stoff, J. Breiling, & J. D. Maser (Eds.), *Handbook of antisocial personality disorder* (pp. 51–59). New York: Wiley.

Lai, T.-J., Chang, C.-M., Connor, K. M., Lee, L.-C., & Davidson, J. R. T. (2004). Full and partial PTSD among earthquake survivors in rural Taiwan. *Journal of Psychiatric Research, 38,* 313–322.

Laing, R. D. (1971). *Self and others.* Oxford, UK: Penguin Books.

Lalonde, J. K., Hudson, J. I., Gigante, R. A., & Pope, H. G. (2001). Canadian and American psychiatrists' attitudes towards dissociative disorders diagnoses. *Canadian Journal of Psychiatry, 46,* 407–412.

Lamb, H. R. (2001). *Best of new directions for mental health services, 1979–2001.* San Francisco: Jossey-Bass.

Lamb, H. R., & Weinberger, L. E. (Eds.). (2001). *Deinstitutionalization: Promise and problems.* San Francisco: Jossey-Bass.

Lamb, H. R., Weinberger, L. E., & Gross, B. H. (2004). Mentally ill persons in the criminal justice system: Some perspectives. *Psychiatric Quarterly, 75,* 107–126.

Lambert, M. C., Knight, F., Overly, K., Weisz, J. R., Desrosiers, M., & Thesiger, C. (1992). Jamaican and American adult perspectives on child psychopathology: Further exploration of the threshold model. *Journal of Consulting & Clinical Psychology, 60,* 146–149.

Lambert, M. J., & Bergen, A. E. (1994). The effectiveness of psychotherapy. In A. E. Bergen & S. L. Garfield (Eds.), *Handbook of psychotherapy and behavior change* (Vol. 4, pp. 143–189). New York: Wiley.

Lambert, M. T., & Silva, P. S. (1998). An update on the impact of gun control legislation on suicide. *Psychiatric Quarterly, 69,* 127–134.

Lang, A. J., & Stein, M. B. (2001). Social phobia: Prevalence and diagnostic threshold. *Journal of Clinical Psychiatry, 62*(Suppl. 1), 5–10.

Langevin, R. (1992). Biological factors contributing to paraphilic behavior. *Psychiatric Annals, 22,* 309–314.

Laudenslager, M. L., Ryan, S. M., Drugan, R. C., Hyson, R. L., & Maier, S. F. (1983). Coping and immunosuppression: Inescapable but not escapable shock suppresses lymphocyte proliferation. *Science, 221,* 569–570.

Laumann, E. O., Gagnon, J. H., Michael, R. T., & Michaels, S. (1994). *The social organization of sexuality: Sexual practices in the United States.* Chicago: University of Chicago Press.

Laumann, E. O., Paik, A., & Rosen, R. C. (1999). Sexual dysfunction in the United States. *Journal of the American Medical Association, 281,* 537–544.

Lavoie, K. L., Miller, S. B., Conway, M., & Fleet, R. P. (2001). Anger, negative emotions, and cardiovascular reactivity during interpersonal conflict in women. *Journal of Psychosomatic Research, 51,* 503–512.

Lawrie, S. M., Whalley, H. C., Abukmeil, S. S., Kestelman, J. N., Donnelly, L., Miller, P., Best, J. J. K., Owens, D. G. C., & Johnstone, E. C. (2001). Brain structure, genetic liability, and psychotic symptoms in subjects at high risk of developing schizophrenia. *Biological Psychiatry, 49,* 811–823.

Leary, T. (1957). *Interpersonal diagnosis of personality.* New York: Ronald.

LeBars, P. L., Katz, M. M., Berman, N., Itil, T. M., Freedman, A. M., & Schatzberg, A. F. (1997). A placebo-controlled, double-blind, randomized trial of an extract of ginkgo biloba for dementia. *Journal of the American Medical Association, 278,* 1327–1332.

Lee, J. K. P., Jackson, H. J., Pattison, P., & Ward, T. (2002). Developmental risk factors for sexual offending. *Child Abuse & Neglect, 26,* 73–92.

Lee, S., Lee, A. M., Ngai, E., Lee, D. T. S., & Wing, Y. K. (2001). Rationales for food refusal in Chinese patients with anorexia nervosa. *International Journal of Eating Disorders, 29,* 224–229.

Lee, Y.-J. (2004). Overview of the therapeutic management of insomnia with zolpidem. *CNS Drugs, 18*(Suppl. 1), 17–23.

Leenaars, A. A. (1988). *"I wish I could explain it," Suicide notes: Predictive clues and patterns.* New York: Human Sciences Press.

Lèger, D., Guilleminault, C., Bader, G., Levy, E., & Paillard, M. (2002). Medical and socio-professional impact of insomnia. *Sleep, 25,* 625–629.

Lehman, D. R., Wortman, C. B., & Williams, A. F. (1987). Long-term effects of losing a spouse or child in a motor vehicle crash. *Journal of Personality & Social Psychology, 52,* 218–231.

Leiblum, S. R. (2000). Vaginismus: A most perplexing problem. In S. R. Leiblum & R. C. Rosen (Eds.), *Principles and practice of sex therapy* (3rd ed., pp. 181–202) New York: Guilford Press.

Leiblum, S. R., & Rosen, R. C. (1988). *Sexual desire disorders.* New York: Guilford Press.

Leiblum, S. R., & Rosen, R. C. (2000). *Principles and practice of sex therapy* (3rd ed.). New York: Guilford Press.

Leit, R. A., Pope, H. G., & Gray, J. J. (2001). Cultural expectations of muscularity in men: The evolution of Playgirl centerfolds. *International Journal of Eating Disorders, 29,* 90–93.

Lemaire, J., & Despret, V. (2001). Collective post-traumatic disorders, residual resources, and an extensive context of trust: Creating a network in a refugee camp in former Yugoslavia. *International Journal of Mental Health, 30,* 22–26.

Lendon, C. L., Ashall, F., & Goate, A. M. (1997). Exploring the etiology of Alzheimer disease using molecular genetics. *Journal of the American Medical Association, 277,* 825–831.

Lenox, R. H., & Manji, H. K. (1995). Lithium. In A. F. Schatzberg & C. B. Nemeroff (Eds.), *The American psychiatric press textbook of psychopharmacology* (pp. 303–350). Washington, DC: American Psychiatric Press.

Leon, G. R., Fulkerson, J. A., Perry, C. L., & Early-Zald, M. B. (1995). Prospective analysis of personality and behavioral vulnerabilities and gender influences in the later development of disordered eating. *Journal of Abnormal Psychology, 104,* 140–149.

Lepine, J.-P. (2001). Epidemiology, burden, and disability in depression and anxiety. *Journal of Clinical Psychiatry, 62*(Suppl. 13), 4–10.

Lepore, S. J. (1995). Cynicism, social support and cardiovascular reactivity. *Health Psychology, 14,* 210–216.

Lerman, C., Caporaso, N. E., Audrain, J., Main, D., Bowman, E. D., Lockshin, B., Boyd, N. R., & Shields, P. G. (1999). Evidence suggesting the role of specific genetic factors in cigarette smoking. *Health Psychology, 18,* 14–20.

Lerner, H. D. (1986). Current developments in the psychoanalytic psychotherapy of anorexia nervosa and bulimia nervosa. *Clinical Psychologist, 39,* 39–43.

Lerner, M. J. (1980). *The belief in a just world: A fundamental delusion.* New York: Plenum Press.

Lester, D. (2003). Adolescent suicide from an international perspective. *American Behavioral Scientist, 46,* 1157–1170.

LeVay, S. (1993). *The sexual brain.* Cambridge, MA: MIT Press.

Leventhal, T., & Brooks-Gunn, J. (2003). Moving to opportunity: An experimental study of neighborhood effects on mental health. *American Journal of Public Health, 93,* 1576–1582.

Leverenz, J. B., Wilkinson, C. W., Wamble, M., Corbin, S., Grabber, J. E., et al. (1999). Effect of chronic high-dose exogenous cortisol on hippocampal neuronal number in aged nonhuman primates. *Journal of Neuroscience, 19,* 2356–2361.

Levy, S. M., & Heiden, L. (1991). Depression, distress, and immunity: Risk factors for infectious disease. *Stress Medicine, 7,* 45–51.

Levy, S. M., Herberman, R. B., Whiteside, T., & Sanzo, K. (1990). Perceived social support and tumor estrogen/progesterone receptor status as predictors of natural killer cell activity in breast cancer patients. *Psychosomatic Medicine, 52,* 73–85.

Lewinsohn, P. M. (1974). A behavioral approach to depression. In R. J. Friedman & M. M. Katz (Eds.), *The psychology of depression: Contemporary theory and research.* Washington, DC: Winston-Wiley.

Lewinsohn, P. M., & Clarke, G. N. (1999). Psychosocial treatments for adolescent depression. *Clinical Psychology Review, 19,* 329–342.

Lewinsohn, P. M., & Essau, C. A. (2002). Depression in adolescents. In I. H. Gotlib & C. L. Hammen (Eds.), *Handbook of depression* (pp. 541–559). New York: Guilford Press.

Lewinsohn, P. M., & Gotlib, I. H. (1995). Behavioral therapy and treatment of depression. In E. E. Beckham & W. R. Leber (Eds.), *Handbook of depression* (2nd ed., pp. 352–375). New York: Guilford Press.

Lewinsohn, P. M., Klein, D. N., & Seeley, J. R. (2000). Bipolar disorder during adolescence and young adulthood in a community sample. *Bipolar Disorders, 2,* 281–293.

Lewinsohn, P. M., Muñoz, R. F., Youngren, M. A., & Zeiss, A. M. (1986). *Control your depression.* Englewood Cliffs, NJ: Prentice Hall.

Lewinsohn, P. M., Rohde, P., & Seeley, J. R. (1996a). Adolescent suicidal ideation and attempts: Prevalence, risk factors, and clinical implications. *Clinical Psychology and Scientific Practice, 3,* 25–46.

Lewinsohn, P. M., Rohde, P., & Seeley, J. R. (1996b). Alcohol consumption in high school adolescents: Frequency of use and dimensional structure of associated problems. *Addiction, 91,* 375–390.

Lewinsohn, P. M., Rohde, P., Seeley, J. R., & Baldwin, C. L. (2001). Gender differences in suicide attempts from adolescence to young adulthood. *Journal of the American Academy of Child & Adolescent Psychiatry, 40,* 427–434.

Lewinsohn, P. M., Seeley, J. R., & Klein, D. N. (2003). Bipolar disorders during adolescence. *Acta Psychiatrica Scandinavica, 108,* 47–50.

Lewinsohn, P. M., Seeley, J. R., Moerk, K. C., & Striegel-Moore, R. H. (2002). Gender difference in eating disorder symptoms in young adults. *International Journal of Eating Disorders, 32,* 426–440.

Lewinsohn, P. M., Steinmetz, J. L., Larson, D. W., & Franklin, J. (1981). Depression-related cognitions: Antecedent or consequence? *Journal of Abnormal Psychology, 90,* 213–219.

Lewinsohn, P. M., Striegel-Moore, R. H., & Seeley, J. R. (2000). Epidemiology and natural course of eating disorders in young women from adolescence to young adulthood. *Journal of the American Academy of Child & Adolescent Psychiatry, 39,* 1284–1292.

Lewinsohn, P. M., Zinbarg, R., Seeley, J. R., Lewinsohn, M., & Sack, W. H. (1997). Lifetime comorbidity among anxiety disorders and between anxiety disorders and other mental disorders in adolescents. *Journal of Anxiety Disorders, 11,* 377–394.

Lewis, D. O., Balla, D. A., & Shanok, S. S. (1979). Some evidence of race bias in the diagnosis and treatment of the juvenile offender. *American Journal of Orthopsychiatry, 49,* 53–61.

Lewis, G., David, A., Andreasson, S., & Allebeck, P. (1992). Schizophrenia and city life. *The Lancet, 340,* 137–140.

Lex, B. W. (1995). Alcohol and other psychoactive substance dependence in women and men. In M. V. Seeman (Ed.), *Gender and psychopathology* (pp. 311–358). Washington, DC: American Psychiatric Association.

Liberman, R. P. (1994). Psychosocial treatments for schizophrenia. *Psychiatry, 57,* 104–114.

Liberman, R. P., Eckman, T. A., & Marder, S. R. (2001). Rehab rounds: Training in social problem solving among persons with schizophrenia. *Psychiatric Services, 52,* 31–33.

Liberman, R. P., Glynn, S., Blair, K. E., Ross, D., & Marder, S. R. (2002). In vivo amplified skills training: Promoting generalization of independent living skills for clients with schizophrenia. *Psychiatry: Interpersonal & Biological Processes, 65,* 137–155.

Liberto, J. G., Oslin, D. W., & Ruskin, P. E. (1996). Alcoholism in the older population. In L. L. Carstensen, B. A. Edelstein, & L. Dornbrand (Eds.), *The practical handbook of clinical gerontology* (pp. 324–348). Thousand Oaks, CA: Sage.

Liberzon, I., & Phan, K. (2003). Brain-imaging studies of posttraumatic stress disorder. *CNS Spectrums, 8,* 641–650.

Liberzon, I., Taylor, S. F., Amdur, R., Jung, T. D., Chamberlain, K. R., Minoshima, S., Koeppe, R. A., & Fig, L. M. (1999). Brain activation in PTSD in response to trauma-related stimuli. *Biological Psychiatry, 45,* 817–826.

Lichtermann, D., Karbe, E., & Maier, W. (2000). The genetic epidemiology of schizophrenia and of schizophrenia spectrum disorders. *European Archives of Psychiatry & Clinical Neuroscience, 250,* 304–310.

Lieberman, J., Chakos, M., Wu, H., Alvir, J., Hoffman, E., Robinson, D., & Bilder, R. (2001). Longitudinal study of brain morphology in first episode schizophrenia. *Biological Psychiatry, 49,* 487–499.

Lieberman, J. A., Tollefson, G., Tohen, M., Green, A. I., Gur, R. E., Kahn, R., McEvoy, J., Perkins, D., Sharma, T., Zipursky, R., Wei, H., & Hamer, R. M. (2003). Comparative efficacy and safety of atypical and conventional antipsychotic drugs in first-episode psychosis: A randomized, double-blind trial of olanzapine versus haloperidol. *American Journal of Psychiatry, 160,* 1396–1404.

Light, K. C., & Sherwood, A. (1989). Race, borderline hypertension, and hemodynamic responses to behavioral stress before and after beta-adrenergic blockage. *Health Psychology, 8,* 577–595.

Lilienfeld, S. O., Lynn, S. J., Kirsch, I., Chaves, J. F., Sarvin, T. R., Ganaway, G. K., & Powell, R. A. (1999). Dissociative identity disorders and the sociocognitive model: Recalling the lessons of the past. *Psychological Bulletin, 125,* 507–523.

Lillard, A. S. (1993). Young children's conceptualization of pretend: Action or mental representational states? *Child Development, 64,* 372–386.

Lillard, A. S. (1996). Body or mind: Children's categorizing of pretense. *Child Development, 67,* 1717–1734.

Lin, K.-M., & Shen, W. W. (1991). Pharmacotherapy for Southeast Asian psychiatric patients. *Journal of Nervous & Mental Disease, 179,* 346–350.

Lindemalm, G., Korlin, D., & Uddenberg, N. (1986). Long-term follow-up of "sex change" in 13 male-to-female transsexuals. *Archives of Sexual Behavior, 15,* 187–210.

Linehan, M. M. (1973). Suicide and attempted suicide: Study of perceived sex differences. *Perceptual & Motor Skills, 37,* 31–34.

Linehan, M. M. (1999). Standard protocol for assessing and treating suicidal behaviors for patients in treatment. In D. G. Jacobs (Ed.), *The Harvard Medical School guide to suicide assessment and intervention* (pp. 146–187). San Francisco: Jossey-Bass.

Linehan, M. M., Armstrong, H. E., Suarez, A., & Allmon, D. (1991). Cognitive-behavioral treatment of chronically parasuicidal borderline patients. *Archives of General Psychiatry, 48,* 1060–1064.

Linehan, M. M., Camper, P., Chiles, J. A., Strosahl, K., & Shearin, E. N. (1987). Interpersonal problem-solving and parasuicide. *Cognitive Therapy & Research, 11,* 1–12.

Linehan, M. M., Cochran, B. N., & Kehrer, C. A. (2001). Dialectical behavior therapy for borderline personality disorder. In D. H. Barlow (Ed.), *Clinical handbook of psychological disorders: A step-by-step treatment manual* (pp. 470–522). New York: Guilford Press.

Linehan, M. M., Heard, H. L., & Armstrong, H. E. (1993). Naturalistic follow-up of a behavioral treatment for chronically parasuicidal borderline patients. *Archives of General Psychiatry, 50,* 971–974.

Linehan, M. M., Kanter, J. W., & Comtois, K. A. (1999). Dialectical behavior therapy for borderline personality disorder: Efficacy, specificity, and cost effectiveness. In D. S. Janowsky (Ed.), *Psychotherapy indications and outcomes* (pp. 93–118). Washington, DC: American Psychiatric Press.

Linehan, M. M., Schmidt, H., Dimeff, L. A., Craft, J. C., Kanter, J., & Comtois, K. A. (1999). Dialectical behavior therapy for patients with borderline personality disorder and drug-dependence. *American Journal on Addiction, 8,* 279–292.

Links, P. S., Heslegrave, R., & van Reekum, R. (1998). Prospective follow-up study of borderline personality disorder: Prognosis, prediction of outcome, and Axis II comorbidity. *Canadian Journal of Psychiatry, 43,* 265–270.

Lipowski, Z. J. (1990). *Delirium: Acute confusional states.* New York: Oxford University Press.

Lisansky-Gomberg, E. S. (2000). Substance abuse disorders, In S. K. Whitbourne (Ed.), *Psychopathology in later adulthood* (pp. 277–298). New York: Wiley.

Lochman, J. E., Barry, T. D., & Pardini, D. A. (2003). Anger control training for aggressive youth. In A. E. Kazdin & J. R. Weisz (Eds.), *Evidence-based psychotherapies for children and adolescents* (pp. 263–281). New York: Guilford Press.

Lochman, J. E., White, K. J., & Wayland, K. K. (1991). Cognitive-behavioral assessment and treatment with aggressive children. In P. Kendall (Ed.), *Therapy with children and adolescents: Cognitive behavioral procedures* (pp. 25–65). New York: Guilford Press.

Loebel, J. P., Loebel, J. S., Dager, S. R., Centerwall, B. S., & Reay, D. T. (1991). Anticipation of nursing home placement may be a precipitant of suicide among the elderly. *Journal of the American Geriatric Society, 39,* 407–408.

Loeber, R. (1990). Development and risk factors of juvenile antisocial behavior and delinquency. *Clinical Psychology Review, 10,* 1–41.

Loeber, R., & Farrington, D. P. (1997). Strategies and yields of longitudinal studies on anti-social behavior. In D. M. Stoff, J. Breiling, & J. D. Maser (Eds.), *Handbook of antisocial personality disorder* (pp. 125–139). New York: Wiley.

Loeber, R., & Farrington, D. P. (2000). Young children who commit crime: Epidemiology, developmental origins, risk factors, early interventions, and policy implications. *Development & Psychopathology, 12,* 737–762.

Loftus, E. F. (1993). The reality of repressed memories. *American Psychologist, 48,* 518–537.

Loftus, E. F. (2003). Make-believe memories. *American Psychologist, 58,* 867–873.

Loftus, E. F., & Ketchum, K. (1994). *The myth of repressed memory.* New York: St. Martin's Press.

Lombardi, E. (2001). Enhancing transgender health care. *American Journal of Public Health, 91,* 869–872.

Long, P. W. (1996). Internet mental health. Retrieved from the World Wide Web: http://www.mentalhealth.com/

Lopez, S. R., & Guarnaccia, P. J. J. (2000). Cultural psychopathology: Uncovering the social world of mental illness. *Annual Review of Psychology, 51,* 571–598.

Lopez, S. R., Kopelowics, A., & Canive, J. M. (2002). Strategies in developing culturally congruent family interventions for schizophrenia: The case of Hispanics. In H. P. Lefley & D. L. Johnson (Eds.), *Family interventions in mental illness: International perspectives* (pp. 61–90). Westport, CT: Praeger.

LoPiccolo, J. (1992). Paraphilias. *Nordisk Sexolgi, 10,* 1–14.

Lotspeich, L. J., Kwon, H., Schumann, C. M., Fryer, S. L., Goodlin-Jones, B. L., Buonocore, M. H., Lammers, C. R., Amaral, D. G., & Reiss, A. L. (2004). Investigation of neuroanatomical differences between autism and Asperger syndrome. *Archives of General Psychiatry, 61,* 291–298.

Lovaas, O. I. (1987). Behavioral treatment and normal educational and intellectual functioning in young autistic children. *Journal of Consulting & Clinical Psychology, 55,* 3–9.

Lovaas, O. I., & Smith, T. (2003). Early and intensive behavioral intervention in autism. In A. E. Kazdin & J. R. Weisz (Eds.), *Evidence-based psychotherapies for children and adolescents* (pp. 325–340). New York: Guilford Press.

Lowe, B., Zipfel, S., Buchholz, C., Dupont, Y., Reas, D. L., & Herzog, W. (2001). Long-term outcome of anorexia nervosa in a prospective 21-year follow-up study. *Psychological Medicine, 31,* 881–890.

Luborsky, L. (1973). Forgetting and remembering (momentary forgetting) during psychotherapy. In M. Mayman (Ed.), *Psychoanalytic research and psychological issues* (pp. 29–55). New York: International Universities Press.

Luborksy, L. (1984). *Principles of psychoanalytic psychotherapy: A manual for supportive-expressive treatment.* New York: Basic Books.

Luborksy, L., & Crits-Cristoph, P. (1990). *Understanding transference: The core conflictual relationship theme method.* New York: Basic Books.

Ludwig, A. M. (1992). Creative achievement and psychopathology: Comparison among professions. *American Journal of Psychotherapy, 46,* 330–356.

Luria, A. (1973). *The working brain.* New York: Basic Books.

Luthar, S. S. (2003). *Resilience and vulnerability: Adaptation in the context of childhood adversities.* Cambridge, UK: Cambridge University Press.

Lyman, R. (1997, April 15). Michael Dorris dies at 52: Wrote of his son's suffering. *The New York Times,* p. 24.

Lynam, D. R., Caspi, A., Moffitt, T. E., Wikstrom, P. H., Loeber, R., & Novak, S. (2000). The interaction between impulsivity and neighborhood context on offending: The effects of impulsivity are stronger in poorer neighborhoods. *Journal of Abnormal Psychology, 109,* 563–574.

Lynam, D. R., & Widiger, T. A. (2001). Using the five factor model to represent the DSM-IV personality disorders: An expert consensus approach. *Journal of Abnormal Psychology, 110,* 401–402.

Lyness, J. M. (2004). Treatment of depressive conditions in later life: Real-world light for dark (or dim) tunnels. *Journal of the American Medical Association, 291,* 1626–1628.

Lytton, H., & Romney, D. M. (1991). Parents' differential socialization of boys and girls: A meta-analysis. *Psychological Bulletin, 109,* 267–296.

M

MacArthur Research Network on Mental Health and the Law. (1998). Executive summary. Retrieved from the World Wide Web: http://ness.sys.Virginia.EDU/macarthur/violence.html

Maccoby, N., & Altman, D. G. (1988). Disease prevention in communities: The Stanford Heart Disease Prevention Program. In R. H. Price (Ed.), *Fourteen ounces of prevention: A casebook for practitioners* (pp. 165–174). Washington, DC: American Psychological Association.

MacCoun, R. J. (1998). Toward a psychology of harm reduction. *American Psychologist, 53,* 1199–1208.

Machover, K. A. (1949). *Personality projection in the drawing of the human figure: A method of personality investigation.* Springfield, IL: Charles C Thomas.

Macintosh, K. E., & Dissanayake, C. (2004). Annotation: The similarities and differences between autistic disorder and Asperger's disorder: A review of the empirical evidence. *Journal of Child Psychology & Psychiatry, 45,* 421–434.

MacKinnon, D., Jamison, K. R., & DePaulo, J. R. (1997). Genetics of manic depressive illness. *Annual Review of Neuroscience, 20,* 355–373.

Madge, N., & Harvey, J. G. (1999). Suicide among the young—The size of the problem. *Journal of Adolescence, 22,* 145–155.

Maguire, G. A., Riley, G. D., Franklin, D. L., & Gottschalk, L. A. (2000). Risperidone for the treatment of stuttering. *Journal of Clinical Psychopharmacology, 20,* 479–482.

Maher, B. A. (1974). Delusional thinking and perceptual disorder. *Journal of Individual Psychology, 30,* 98–113.

Maher, W. B., & Maher, B. A. (1985). Psychopathology: I. From ancient times to eighteenth century. In G. A. Kimble & K. Schlesinger (Eds.), *Topics in the history of psychology* (Vol. 2). Hillsdale, NJ: Erlbaum.

Mahler, M. (1968). *On human symbiosis and the vicissitudes of individuation: Vol. I. Infantile psychosis.* New York: International Universities Press.

Maj, M., Pirozzi, R., Magliano, L., & Bartoli, L. (1998). Long-term outcome of lithium prophylaxis in bipolar disorder: A 5-year prospective study of 402 patients at a lithium clinic. *American Journal of Psychiatry, 155,* 30–35.

Maletzky, B. (1998). The paraphilias: Research and treatment. In P. E. Nathan (Ed.), *A guide to treatments that work* (pp. 472–500). New York: Oxford University Press.

Maletzky, B. M., & Field, G. (2003). The biological treatment of dangerous sexual offenders, a review and preliminary report of the Oregon pilot *depo-Provera* program. *Aggression and Violent Behavior, 8,* 391–412.

Maletzky, B. M., & Steinhauser, C. (2002). A 25-year follow-up of cognitive/behavioral therapy with 7,275 sexual offenders. *Behavior Modification, 26,* 123–147.

Maltsberger, J. T. (1999). The psychodynamic understanding of suicide. In D. G. Jacobs (Ed.), *The Harvard Medical School guide to suicide assessment and intervention* (pp. 72–82). San Francisco: Jossey-Bass.

Mangweth, B., Pope, H. G., Kemmler, G., Ebenbichler, C., Hausmann, A., De Col, C., Kreutner, B., Kinzl, J., & Biebl, W. (2001). Body image and psychopathology in male bodybuilders. *Psychotherapy & Psychosomatics, 70,* 38–43.

Manicavasagar, V., Silove, D., Rapee, R., Waters, F., & Momartin, S. (2001). Parent-child concordance for separation anxiety: A clinical study. *Journal of Affective Disorders, 65,* 81–84.

Mann, J. J., Brent, D. A., & Arango, V. (2001). The neurobiology and genetics of suicide and attempted suicide: A focus on the serotonergic system. *Neuropsycho-pharmacology, 24,* 467–477.

Mannino, J. D. (1999). *Sexually speaking.* New York: McGraw-Hill.

Mannuza, S., Klein, R. G., Bessler, A., Malloy, P., & LaPadula, M. (1998). Adult psychiatric status of hyperactive boys grown up. *American Journal of Psychiatry, 155,* 493–498.

Manson, S., Beals, J., O'Nell, T., Piasecki, J., Bechtold, D., Keane, E., & Jones, M. (1996). Wounded spirits, ailing hearts: PTSD and related disorders among American Indians. In A. J. Marsella, M. J. Friedman, E. T. Gerrity, & R. M. Scurfield (Eds.), *Ethnocultural aspects of posttraumatic stress disorder* (pp. 255–283). Washington, DC: American Psychiatric Press.

Manson, S. M., Shore, J. H., Baron, A. E., Ackerson, L., & Neligh, G. (1992). Alcohol abuse and dependence among American Indians. In J. E. Helzer & G. J. Canino (Eds.), *Alcoholism in North America, Europe, and Asia* (pp. 113–127). New York: Oxford University Press.

Manu, P., Lane, T. J., & Matthews, D. A. (1989). Somatization disorder in patients with chronic fatigue. *Psychosomatics, 30,* 388–395.

Manu, P., Lane, T. J., & Matthews, D. A. (1992). Chronic fatigue syndromes in clinical practice. *Psychotherapy & Psychosomatics, 58,* 60–68.

Maramba, G. G., & Nagayama Hall, G. C. (2002). Meta-analyses of ethnic match as a predictor of dropout, utilization, and level of functioning. *Cultural Diversity & Ethnic Minority Psychology, 8,* 290–297.

Marangell, L. B. (2004). The importance of subsyndromal symptoms in bipolar disorder. *Journal of Clinical Psychiatry, 65*(Suppl. 10), 24–27.

Marangell, L. B., Martinez, J. M., & Niazi, S. K. (2004). Vagus nerve stimulation as a potential option for treatment-resistant depression. *Clinical Neuroscience Research, 4,* 89–94.

Marantz, S., & Coates, S. (1991). Mothers of boys with gender identity disorder: A comparison of matched controls. *Journal of the American Academy of Child & Adolescent Psychiatry, 30,* 310–315.

Marcantonio, E. R., Simon, S. E., Bergmann, M. A., Jones, R. N., Murphy, J. M., & Morris, J. N. (2003). Delirium symptoms in post-acute care: Prevalent, persistent, and associated with poor functional recovery. *Journal of the American Geriatrics Society, 51,* 4–9.

March, J. S., Biederman, J., Wolkow, R., Safferman, A., Mardekian, J., Cook, E. H., Cutler, N. R., Dominguez, R., Ferguson, J., Muller, B., Riesenberg, R., Rosenthal, M., Sallee, F. E., & Wagner, K. D. (1998). Sertraline in children and adolescents with obsessive-compulsive disorder. *Journal of the American Medical Association, 280,* 1752–1756.

Marcos, L. R. (1979). Effects of interpreters on the evaluation of psychopathology in non-English-speaking patients. *American Journal of Psychiatry, 136,* 171–174.

Marcus, D. K., & Church, S. E. (2003). Are dysfunctional beliefs about illness unique to hypochondriasis? *Journal of Psychosomatic Research, 54,* 543–547.

Margraf, J. (1993). Hyperventilation and panic disorder: A psychophysiological connection. *Advances in Behaviour Research & Therapy, 15,* 49–74.

Margraf, J., Barlow, D. H., Clark, D. M., & Telch, M. J. (1993). Psychological treatment of panic: Work in progress on outcome, active ingredients, and follow-up. *Behaviour Research & Therapy, 31,* 1–8.

Markovitz, P. J. (2004). Recent trends in the pharmacotherapy of personality disorders. *Journal of Personality Disorders, 18,* 99–101.

Marks, I. M., & Swinson, R. (1992). Behavioral and/or drug therapy. In G. D. Burrows, S. M. Roth, & R. Noyes, Jr. (Eds.), *Handbook of anxiety* (Vol. 5). Oxford, UK: Elsevier.

Marlatt, G. A. (Ed.). (1998). *Harm reduction: Pragmatic strategies for managing high-risk behaviors.* New York: Guilford Press.

Marlatt, G. A., Baer, J. S., Donovan, D. M., & Kivlahan, D. R. (1988). Addictive behaviors: Etiology and treatment. *Annual Review of Psychology, 39,* 223–252.

Marlatt, G. A., Baer, J. S., Kivlahan, D. R., Dimeff, L. A., Larimer, M. E., Quigley, L. A., Somers, J. M., & Williams, E. (1998). Screening and brief intervention for high-risk college student drinkers: Results from a 2-year follow-up assessment. *Journal of Consulting & Clinical Psychology, 66,* 604–615.

Marlatt, G. A., Baer, J. S., & Larimer, M. (1995). Preventing alcohol abuse in college students: A harm reduction approach. In G. M. Boyd, J. Howard, & R. A. Zucker (Eds.), *Alcohol problems among adolescents: Current directions in prevention research* (pp. 147–172). Hillsdale, NJ: Erlbaum.

Marlatt, G. A., Blume, A. W., & Parks, G. A. (2001). Integrating harm reduction therapy and traditional substance abuse treatment. *Journal of Psychoactive Drugs, 33,* 13–21.

Marlatt, G. A., Larimer, M. E., Baer, J. S., & Quigley, L. A. (1993). Harm reduction for alcohol problems: Moving beyond the controlled drinking economy. *Behavior Therapy, 24,* 461–503.

Marshall, G. N., & Orlando, M. (2002). Acculturation and peritraumatic dissociation in young adult Latino survivors of community violence. *Journal of Abnormal Psychology, 111,* 166–174.

Marshall, R. D., Beebee, K., Oldham, M., & Zaninelli, R. (2001). Efficacy and safety of paroxetine treatment for chronic PTSD: A fixed-dose, placebo-controlled study. *American Journal of Psychiatry, 158,* 1982–1988.

Marshall, R. D., & Galea, S. (2004). Science for the community: Assessing mental health after 9/11. *Journal of Clinical Psychiatry, 65*(Suppl. 1), 37–43.

Martenyi, F., Brown, E. B., Zhang, H., Koke, S. C., & Prakash, A. (2002). Fluoxetine v. placebo in prevention of relapse in post-traumatic stress disorder. *British Journal of Psychiatry, 181,* 315–320.

Martin, A., Scahill, L., Charney, D. S., & Leckman, J. F. (2002). *Pediatric psychopharmacology: Principles and practice.* New York: Oxford University Press.

Martin, C. S., & Bates, M. E. (1998). Psychological and psychiatric consequences of alcohol. In R. E. Tarter, R. T. Ammerman, & P. J. Ott (Eds.), *Handbook of substance abuse: Neurobehavioral pharmacology* (pp. 33–50). New York: Plenum Press.

Martin, J. L. R., Barbanoj, M. J., Schlaepfer, T. E., Thompson, E., Perez, V., & Kulisevsky, J. (2003). Repetitive transcranial magnetic stimulation for the treatment of depression: Systematic review and meta-analysis. *British Journal of Psychiatry, 182,* 480–491.

Maslow, A. H. (1954). *Motivation and personality.* New York: Harper & Row.

Masten, A. S., & Powell, J. L. (2003). A resilience framework for research, policy, and practice. In S. E. Luthar (Ed.), *Resilience and vulnerability: Adaptation in the context of childhood adversities* (pp. 1–25). New York: Cambridge University Press.

Masters, K. (1996, July 15). It hurts so much. *Time,* p. 148.

Masters, W. H., & Johnson, V. E. (1970). *Human sexual inadequacy.* Boston: Little, Brown.

Masters, W. H., Johnson, V. E., & Kolodny, R. C. (1993). *Biological foundations of human sexuality.* New York: HarperCollins.

Masters, W. H., Johnson, V. E., & Kolodny, R. C. (Eds.). (1979). *Ethical issues in sex therapy & research.* Boston: Little, Brown.

Matarazzo, J. D. (1985). Psychotherapy. In G. A. Kimble & K. Schlesinger (Eds.), *Topics in the history of psychology.* Hillsdale, NJ: Erlbaum.

Mathews, A., & MacLeod, C. (1994). Cognitive approaches to emotion and emotional disorders. *Annual Review of Psychology, 45,* 25–50.

Mathews, A., & MacLeod, C. (2005). *Annual Review of Clinical Psychology, 1,* 167–196.

Mathews, J. (1996, July 30). Pressures of supporting business, family leave widow little time to mourn. *Baltimore Sun,* p. 5B.

Matthews, A., Mogg, K., Kentish, J., & Eysenck, M. (1995). Effect of psychological treatment on cognitive bias in generalized anxiety disorder. *Behavior Research & Therapy, 33,* 293–303.

Matthews, K. A., Wing, R. R., Kuller, L. H., & Meilhan, E. N. (1990). Influences of natural menopause on psychological characteristics and symptoms of middle-aged healthy women. *Journal of Consulting & Clinical Psychology, 58,* 345–351.

Maughan, B., Pickles, A., Rowe, R., Costello, E. J., & Angold, A. (2000). Developmental trajectories of aggressive and non-aggressive conduct problems. *Journal of Quantitative Criminology, 16,* 199–221.

Maughan, B., Rowe, R., Messer, J., Goodman, R., & Meltzer, H. (2004). Conduct disorder and oppositional defiant disorder in a national sample: Developmental epidemiology. *Journal of Child Psychology & Psychiatry, 45,* 609–621.

Mausbach, B. T., Coon, D. W., Depp, C., Rabinowitz, Y. G., Wilson-Arias, E., Kraemer, H. C., Thompson, L. W., Lane, G., & Gallagher-Thompson, D. (2004). Ethnicity and time to institutionalization of dementia patients: A comparison of Latina and Caucasian female family caregivers. *Journal of the American Geriatrics Society, 52,* 1077–1084.

Max, W. (1993). The economic impact of Alzheimer's disease. *Neurology, 43,* S6–S10.

Maxmen, J. S., & Ward, N. G. (1995). *Essential psychopathology and its treatment.* New York: W. W. Norton.

May, R., & Yalom, I. (1995). Existential psychotherapy. In R. J. Corsini & D. Wedding (Eds.), *Current psychotherapies* (5th ed., pp. 363–402). Itasca, IL: Peacock.

Mayberg, H. S., Brannan, S. K., Mahurin, R. K., Jerabek, P. A., Brickman, J. S., et al. (1997). Cingulate function in depression: A potential predictor of treatment response. *NeuroReport, 8,* 1057–1061.

Mayeux, R. (1996). Understanding Alzheimer's disease: Expect more genes and other things. *Annals of Neurology, 39,* 689–690.

Mayeux, R., Denaro, J., Hemenegildo, N., & Marder, K. (1992). A population-based investigation of Parkinson's disease with and without dementia: Relationship to age and gender. *Archives of Neurology, 49,* 492–497.

Mayou, R., Bryant, B., & Ehlers, A. (2001). Prediction of psychological outcomes one year after a motor vehicle accident. *American Journal of Psychiatry, 158,* 1231–1238.

Mazzoni, G., & Loftus, E. F. (1998). Dream interpretations can change beliefs about the past. *Psychotherapy, 35,* 177–187.

McBride, A. A., Joe, G. W., & Simpson, D. D. (1991). Prediction of long-term alcohol use, drug use, and criminality among inhalant users. *Hispanic Journal of Behavioral Sciences, 13,* 315–323.

McBurnett, K., Lahey, B. B., Rathouz, P. L., & Loeber, R. (2000). Low salivary cortisol and persistent aggression in boys referred for disruptive behavior. *Archives of General Psychiatry, 57,* 38–43.

McBurnett, K., Pfiffner, L. J., & Frick, P. J. (2001). Symptom properties as a function of ADHD type: An argument for continued study of sluggish cognitive tempo. *Journal of Abnormal Child Psychology, 29,* 207–213.

McCabe, M. P., & Ricciardelli, L. A. (2004). Weight and shape concerns of boys and men. In J. K. Thompson (Ed.), *Handbook of eating disorders and obesity* (pp. 606–634). Hoboken, NJ: Wiley.

McCann, U. D., & Agras, W. S. (1990). Successful treatment of nonpurging bulimia nervosa with desipramine: A double-blind, placebo-controlled study. *American Journal of Psychiatry, 147*, 1509–1513.

McCarthy, B. W. (1989). Cognitive-behavioral strategies and techniques in the treatment of early ejaculation. In S. R. Leiblum & R. C. Rosen (Eds.), *Principles and practice of sex therapy: Update for the 1990s* (pp. 141–167). New York: Guilford Press.

McCarthy, B. W. (1997). Strategies and techniques for revitalizing a nonsexual marriage. *Journal of Sex & Marital Therapy, 23*, 231–240.

McCarthy, B. W. (2001). Relapse prevention strategies and techniques with erectile dysfunction. *Journal of Sex & Marital Therapy, 27*, 1–8.

McCarthy, M. (1990). The thin ideal, depression and eating disorders in women. *Behaviour Research & Therapy, 28*, 205–215.

McConaghy, N. (1998). Paedophilia: A review of the evidence. *Australian & New Zealand Journal of Psychiatry, 32*, 252–265.

McConnell, C. F., Bretz, K. M., & Dwyer, W. O. (2003). Falling asleep at the wheel: A close look at 1,269 fatal and serious injury-producing crashes. *Behavioral Sleep Medicine, 1*, 171–183.

McCormick, M. C., McCarton, C., Brooks-Gunn, J., Belt, P., & Gross, R. T. (1998). The infant health development program: Interim summary. *Developmental & Behavioral Pediatrics, 19*, 359–370.

McCrady, B. S. (2001). Alcohol use disorders. In D. H. Barlow (Ed.), *Clinical handbook of psychological disorders: A step-by-step treatment manual* (3rd ed., pp. 376–433). New York: Guilford Press.

McCrae, R. R., & Costa, P. T. (1999). A five-factor theory of personality. In L. A. Pervin (Ed.), *Handbook of personality: Theory and research* (2nd ed., pp. 139–153). New York: Guilford Press.

McDonald, K., & Thompson, J. K. (1992). Eating disturbance, body image dissatisfaction, and reasons for exercising: Gender differences and correlational findings. *International Journal of Eating Disorders, 11*, 289–292.

McFarlane, W. R., Lukens, E., Link, B., & Dushay, R. (1995). Multiple-family groups and psychoeducation in the treatment of schizophrenia. *Archives of General Psychiatry, 52*, 679–687.

McGhie, A., & Chapman, J. (1961). Disorders in attention and perception in early schizophrenia. *Schizophrenia Bulletin, 34*, 103–116.

McGlashan, T. H. (1988). A selective review of recent North American long-term followup studies of schizophrenia. *Schizophrenia Bulletin, 14*, 515–542.

McGovern, C. M. (1985). *Masters of madness.* Hanover, NH: University Press of New England.

McGreevy, M. A., Steadman, H. J., & Callahan, L. A. (1991). The negligible effects of California's 1982 reform of the insanity defense test. *American Journal of Psychiatry, 148*, 744–750.

McGue, M. (1999). The behavioral genetics of alcoholism. *Current Directions in Psychological Science, 8*, 109–115.

McGue, M., Iacono, W. G., Legrand, L. N., Malone, S., & Elkins, I. (2001). Origins and consequences of age at first drink: I. Associations with substance-use disorders, disinhibitory behavior and psychopathology, and P3 amplitude. *Alcoholism: Clinical & Experimental Research, 25*, 1156–1165.

McGue, M., Pickens, R. W., & Svikis, D. S. (1992). Sex and age effects on the inheritance of alcohol problems: A twin study. *Journal of Abnormal Psychology, 101*, 3–17.

McGuffin, P., & Katz, R. (1989). The genetics of depression and manic-depressive disorder. *British Journal of Psychiatry, 155*, 294–304.

McGuire, R. J., Carlisle, J. M., & Young, B. G. (1965). Sexual deviation as conditioned behavior. *Behavior Research & Therapy, 2*, 185–190.

McIntosh, D. N., Silver, R. C., & Wortman, C. B. (1993). Religion's role in adjustment to a negative life event: Coping with the loss of a child. *Journal of Personality & Social Psychology, 65*, 812–821.

McIntosh, J. L. (1995). Suicide prevention in the elderly (age 65–99). *Suicide & Life-Threatening Behaviors, 25*, 180–192.

McLean, P. D., Whittal, M. L., Thordarson, D. S., Taylor, S., Soechting, I., Koch, W. J., Paterson, R., & Anderson, K. W. (2001). Cognitive versus behavior therapy in the group treatment of obsessive-compulsive disorder. *Journal of Consulting & Clinical Psychology, 69*, 205–214.

McMillan, T. M., & Rachman, S. J. (1987). Fearlessness and courage: A laboratory study of paratrooper veterans of the Falklands War. *British Journal of Psychology, 78*, 375–383.

McNally, R. J. (1994). *Panic disorder: A critical analysis.* New York: Guilford Press.

McNally, R. J. (1996). Cognitive bias in the anxiety disorders. *Nebraska Symposium on Motivation, 43*, 211–250.

McNally, R. J. (1999a). Anxiety sensitivity and information-processing biases for threat. In S. Taylor (Ed.), *Anxiety sensitivity: Theory, research, and treatment of the fear of anxiety* (pp. 183–197). Mahwah, NJ: Erlbaum.

McNally, R. J. (1999b). On the experimental induction of panic. *Behavior therapy, 30*, 331–339.

McNally, R. J. (2003). Recovering memories of trauma: A view from the laboratory. *Current Directions in Psychological Science, 12*, 32–35.

McNally, R. J., Clancy, S. A., & Schacter, D. L. (2001). Directed forgetting of trauma cues in adults reporting repressed or recovered memories of childhood sexual abuse. *Journal of Abnormal Psychology, 110*, 151–156.

McNally, R. J., Clancy, S. A., Schacter, D. L., & Pitman, R. K. (2000a). Cognitive processing of trauma cues in adults reporting repressed, recovered, or continuous memories of childhood sexual abuse. *Journal of Abnormal Psychology, 109*, 355–359.

McNally, R. J., Clancy, S. A, Schacter, D. L., & Pitman, R. K. (2000b). Personality profiles, dissociation, and absorption in women reporting repressed, recovered, or continuous memories of childhood sexual abuse. *Journal of Consulting Clinical Psychology, 68*, 1033–1037.

McNiel, D. E., & Binder, R. L. (1991). Clinical assessment of the risk of violence among psychiatric inpatients. *American Journal of Psychiatry, 148*, 1317–1321.

McWilliams, N., & Weinberger, J. (2003). Psychodynamic psychotherapy. In G. Stricker & T. A. Widiger (Eds.), *Handbook of psychology: Clinical psychology* (Vol. 8, pp. 253–277). New York: Wiley.

Mechanic, D., & Bilder, S. (2004). Treatment of people with mental illness: A decade-long perspective. *Health Affairs, 23*, 84–95.

Mednick, B., Reznick, C., Hocevar, D., & Baker, R. (1987). Long-term effects of parental divorce on young adult male crime. *Journal of Youth & Adolescence, 16*, 31–45.

Mednick, S. A., Machon, R. A., Huttunen, M. O., & Bonett, D. (1988). Adult schizophrenia following prenatal exposure to an influenza epidemic. *Archives of General Psychiatry, 45*, 189–192.

Mednick, S. A., Watson, J. B., Huttunen, M., Cannon, T. D., Katila, H., Machon, R., Mednick, B., Hollister, M., Parnas, J., Schulsinger, F., Sajaniemi, N., Voldsgaard, P., Pyhala, R., Gutkind, D., & Wang, X. (1998). A two-hit working model of the etiology of schizophrenia. In M. F. Lenzenweger & R. H. Dworkin (Eds.), *Origins of the development of schizophrenia* (pp. 27–66). Washington, DC: American Psychological Association.

Megivern, D. (2002). Disability services and college students with psychiatric disabilities. *Journal of Social Work in Disability and Rehabilitation, 1*, 25–42.

Meichenbaum, D., & Jaremko, M. (Eds.). (1983). *Stress reduction and prevention.* New York: Plenum Press.

Mellon, M. W., & McGrath, M. L. (2000). Empirically supported treatments in pediatric psychology: Nocturnal enuresis. *Journal of Pediatric Psychology, 25*, 193–214.

Menza, M., Lauritano, M., Allen, L., Warman, M., Ostella, F., Hamer, R. M., & Escobar, J. (2001). Treatment of somatization with nefazodone: A prospective, open-label study. *Annals of Clinical Psychiatry, 13*, 153–158.

Merikangas, K. R., Dierker, L. C., & Szatmari, P. (1998). Psychopathology among offspring of parents with substance abuse and/or anxiety disorders: A high-risk study. *Journal of Child Psychology & Psychiatry, 5*, 711–720.

Merikangas, K. R., Lieb, R., Wittchen, H.-U., & Avenevoli, S. (2003). Family and high-risk studies of social anxiety disorder. *Acta Psychiatrica Scandinavica, 108*(Suppl. 417), 28–37.

Merikangas, K. R., Weissman, M. M., & Pauls, D. L. (1985). Genetic factors in the sex ratio of major depression. *Psychological Medicine, 15*, 63–69.

Merrill, L. L., Thomsen, C. J., Sinclair, B. B., Gold, S. R., & Milner, J. S. (2001). Predicting the impact of child sexual abuse on women: The role of abuse severity, parental support, and coping strategies. *Journal of Consulting & Clinical Psychology, 69*, 992–1006.

Mervaala, E., Fohr, J., Kononen, M., Valkonen-Korhonen, M., Vainino, P., et al. (2000). Quantitative MRI of the hippocampus and amygdala in severe depression. *Psychological Medicine, 30*, 117–125.

Merzenich, M. M., Jenkins, W. M., Johnston, P., Schreiner, C., Miller, S. L., & Tallal, P. (1996). Temporal processing deficits of language-learning impaired children ameliorated by training. *Science, 271,* 77–81.

Meston, C. M. (1997). Aging and sexuality: In successful aging. *Western Journal of Medicine, 167,* 285–290.

Mezzich, J. E., Kirmayer, L. J., Kleinman, A., Fabrega, H., Jr., Parron, D. L., Good, B. J., Lin, K.-M., & Manson, S. M. (1999). The place of culture in DSM-IV. *Journal of Nervous & Mental Disease, 187,* 457–464.

Micallef, J., & Blin, O. (2001). Neurobiology and clinical pharmacology of obsessive-compulsive disorder. *Clinical Neuropharmacology, 24,* 191–207.

Michael, R. T., Gagnon, J. H., Laumann, E., & Kolata, G. (1994). *Sex in America: A definitive survey.* Boston: Little, Brown.

Miklowitz, D. J., Simoneau, T. L., George, E. L., Richards, J. A., Kalbag, A., Sachs-Ericsson, N., & Suddath, R. (2000). Family-focused treatment of bipolar disorder: 1-year effects of a psychoeducational program in conjunction with pharmacotherapy. *Biological Psychiatry, 48,* 582–592.

Miklowitz, D. J., Velligan, D. I., Goldstein, M. J., & Nuechterlein, K. H. (1991). Communication deviance in families of schizophrenic and manic patients. *Journal of Abnormal Psychology, 100,* 163–173.

Milam, J. E., Richardson, J. L., Marks, G., Kemper, C. A., & McCutchan, A. J. (2004). The roles of dispositional optimism and pessimism in HIV disease progression. *Psychology & Health, 19,* 167–181.

Miller, J. B. (1976). *Toward a new psychology of women.* Boston: Beacon Press.

Miller, N. S. (Ed.). (1991). *Comprehensive handbook of drug and alcohol addiction.* New York: Dekker.

Miller, R., Newcomer, R., & Fox, P. (1999). Effects of the Medicare Alzheimer's disease demonstration on nursing home entry. *Health Services Research, 34,* 691–714.

Miller, S. D. (1989). Optical differences in cases of multiple personality disorder. *Journal of Nervous & Mental Disease, 177,* 480–486.

Miller, T. Q., Smith, T. W., Turner, C. W., & Guijarro, M. L. (1996). Meta-analytic review of research on hostility and physical health. *Psychological Bulletin, 119,* 322–348.

Millon, T. (1969). *Modern psychopathology: A biosocial approach to maladaptive learning and functioning.* Philadelphia: Saunders.

Millon, T., Davis, R., Millon, C., Escovar, L., & Meagher, S. (2000). *Personality disorders in modern life.* New York: Wiley.

Milne, A. A. (1961). *Winnie-the-Pooh.* New York: E. P. Dutton.

Mineka, S. (1985). Animal models of anxiety based disorders: Their usefulness and limitations. In A. H. Tuma & J. Maser (Eds.), *Anxiety and the anxiety disorders* (pp. 199–244). Hillsdale, NJ: Erlbaum.

Mineka, S., Davidson, M., Cook, M., & Keir, R. (1984). Observational conditioning of snake fear in rhesus monkeys. *Journal of Abnormal Psychology, 93,* 355–372.

Mineka, S., Gunnar, M., & Champoux, M. (1986). Control and early socioemotional development: Infant rhesus monkeys reared in controllable versus uncontrollable environments. *Child Development, 57,* 1241–1256.

Mineka, S., & Kelly, K. A. (1989). The relationship between anxiety, lack of control and loss of control. In A. Steptoe (Ed.), *Stress, personal control and health* (pp. 163–191). Chichester, UK: Wiley.

Mineka, S., & Zinbarg, R. (1998). Experimental approaches to the anxiety and mood disorders. In J. G. Adair (Ed.), *Advances in psychological science: Vol. 1. Social, personal, and cultural aspects* (pp. 429–454). Hove, UK: Psychology Press/Erlbaum Taylor & Francis.

Minshew, N. J., Sweeney, J. A., & Bauman, M. L. (1997). Neurological aspects of autism. In D. J. Cohen & F. R. Volkmar (Eds.), *Handbook of autism and pervasive developmental disorders* (pp. 344–369). Toronto: Wiley.

Minuchin, S. (1981). *Family therapy techniques.* Cambridge, MA: Harvard University Press.

Minuchin, S., Rosman, B. L., & Baker, L. (1978). *Psychosomatic families: Anorexia nervosa in context.* Cambridge, MA: Harvard University Press.

Miranda, J., Bernal, G., Lau, A., Kohn, L., Hwang, W. C., & La Fromboise, T. (2005). *Annual Review of Clinical Psychology, 1,* 113–142.

Mirsalimi, H., Perleberg, S. H., Stovall, E. L., & Kaslow, N. J. (2003). Family psychotherapy. In G. Stricker & T. A. Widiger (Eds.), *Handbook of psychology: Clinical psychology* (Vol. 8, pp. 367–387). New York: Wiley.

Mirsky, A. E., Bieliauskas, L. A., French, L. M., Van Kammen, D. P., Joensson, E., & Sedvall, S. (2000). A 39-year follow-up on the Genain quadruplets. *Schizophrenia Bulletin, 26,* 699–708.

Mitler, M. M., & Miller, J. C. (1995). Some practical considerations and policy implications of studies and sleep patterns. *Behavioral Medicine, 21,* 184–185.

Mitropoulou, V., Barch, D., Harvey, P., Maldari, L., New, B., Cornblatt, B., & Siever, L. (2003). Two studies of attentional processing in schizotypal personality disorder. *Schizophrenia Research, 60,* S148.

Mitropoulou, V., Harvey, P. D., Maldari, L. A., Moriarty, P. J., New, A. S., Silverman, J. M., & Siever, L. J (2002). Neuropsychological performance in schizotypal personality disorder: Evidence regarding diagnostic specificity. *Biological Psychiatry, 52,* 1175–1182.

Moffitt, T. E. (1990). Juvenile delinquency and attention deficit disorder: Boys' developmental trajectories from age 3 to age 15. *Child Development, 61,* 893–910.

Moffitt, T. E. (1993). The neuropsychology of conduct disorder. *Development & Psychopathology, 5,* 135–151.

Moffitt, T. E., Brammer, G. L., Caspi, A., Fawcet, J. P., Raleigh, M., Yuwiler, A., & Silva, P. A. (1998). Whole blood serotonin relates to violence in an epidemiological study. *Biological Psychiatry, 43,* 446–457.

Moffitt, T. E., & Caspi, A. (2001). Childhood predictors differentiate life-course persistent and adolescence-limited antisocial pathways among males and females. *Development & Psychopathology, 13,* 355–375.

Moffitt, T. E., Caspi, A., Harrington, H., & Milne, B. J. (2001). Males on the life-course persistent and adolescence-limited antisocial pathways: Follow-up at age 26. *Developmental Psychology, 14,* 179–206.

Moffitt, T. E., Caspi, A., Rutter, M., & Silva, P. A. (2001). *Sex differences in antisocial behaviour: Conduct disorder, delinquency, and violence in the Dunedin Longitudinal Study.* Cambridge, UK: Cambridge University Press.

Moffitt, T. E., & Silva, P. A. (1988). Self-reported delinquency, neuropsychological deficit, and history of attention deficit disorder. *Journal of Abnormal Child Psychology, 16,* 553–569.

Molgaard, C. A., Nakamura, C. M., Stanford, E. P., Peddecord, K. M., & Morton, D. J. (1990). Prevalence of alcohol consumption among older persons. *Journal of Community Health, 15,* 239–251.

Molnar, B. E., Berkman, L. F., & Buka, S. L. (2001). Psychopathology, childhood sexual abuse and other childhood adversities: Relative links to subsequent suicidal behavior in the U.S. *Psychological Medicine, 31,* 965–977.

Monahan, J. (2001). Major mental disorder and violence: Epidemiology and risk assessment. In G. Pinard (Ed.), *Clinical assessment of dangerousness: Empirical contributions* (pp. 89–102). New York: Cambridge University Press.

Monahan, J., Bonnie, R. J., Appelbaum, P. S., Hyde, P. S., Steadman, H. J., & Swartz, M. S. (2001). Mandated community treatment: Beyond outpatient commitment. *Psychiatric Services, 52,* 1198–1205.

Monahan, J., Lidz, C. W., Hoge, S. K., Mulvey, E. P., Eisenberg, M. M., Roth, L. H., Gardner, W. P., & Bennett, N. (1999). Coercion in the provision of mental health services: The MacArthur studies. In J. Morrissey & J. Monahan (Eds.), *Research in community and mental health* (Vol. 10, pp. 13–30). Stamford, CT: JAI Press.

Monahan, J., & Steadman, H. J. (2001). Violence risk assessment: A quarter century of research. In L. E. Frost (Ed.), *The evolution of mental health law* (pp. 195–211). Washington, DC: American Psychological Association.

Monahan, J., & Walker, L. (1990). *Social science in law: Cases and materials.* Westbury, NY: Foundation Press.

Money, J., & Schwartz, M. (1976). Fetal androgens in the early treated adrenogenital syndrome of 46 XX hermaphroditism: Influence on assertive and aggressive types of behavior. *Aggressive Behavior, 2,* 19–30.

Monitoring the Future. (2002). 2002 data from in-school surveys of 8th, 10th, and 12th grade students. Retrieved November 1, 2004, from: http://monitoringthefuture.org/data/02data.html

Monroe, S. M., & Hadjiyannakis, K. (2002). The social environment and depression: Focusing on severe life stress. In I. H. Gotlib & C. L. Hammen (Eds.), *Handbook of depression* (pp. 314–340). New York: Guilford Press.

Montgomery, S. A., Entsuah, R., Hackett, D., Kunz, N. R., & Rudolph, R. L. (2004). Venlafaxine versus placebo in the preventive treatment of recurrent major depression. *Journal of Clinical Psychiatry, 65,* 328–336.

Mooney, M. E., & Hatsukami, D. K. (2001). Combined treatments for smoking cessation. In M. T. Sammons & N. B. Schmidt (Eds.), *Combined treatments for mental disorders* (pp. 191–213). Washington, DC: American Psychological Association.

Morey, L. C. (1993). Psychological correlates of personality disorder. *Journal of Personality Disorders* (Suppl.), 149–166.

Morgan, A. B., & Lilienfeld, S. O. (2000). A meta-analytic review of the relation between antisocial behavior and neuropsychological measures of executive function. *Clinical Psychological Review, 20,* 113–136.

Morgan, C. A., Hazlett, G., Wang, S., Richardson, E. G., Jr., Schnurr, P., & Southwick, S. M. (2001). Symptoms of dissociation in humans experiencing acute, uncontrollable stress: A prospective investigation. *American Journal of Psychiatry, 158,* 1239–1247.

Mori, D., Chaiken, S., & Pliner, P. (1987). "Eating lightly" and the self-presentation of femininity. *Journal of Personality & Social Psychology, 53,* 693–702.

Morokoff, P. J., & Gillilland, R. (1993). Stress, sexual functioning, and marital satisfaction. *Journal of Sex Research, 30,* 43–53.

Morrison, N. K. (1998). Behavioral pharmacology of hallucinogens. In R. E. Tarter (Ed.), *Handbook of substance abuse: Neurobehavioral pharmacology* (pp. 229–240). New York: Plenum Press.

Mortensen, P. B. (2003). Mortality and physical illness in schizophrenia. In R. M. Murray & P. B. Jones (Eds.), *The epidemiology of schizophrenia* (pp. 275–287). New York: Cambridge University Press.

Moscicki, E. (1995). Epidemiology of suicidal behavior. *Suicide & Life-Threatening Behavior, 25,* 22–35.

Mowrer, O. H. (1939). A stimulus-response analysis of anxiety and its role as a reinforcing agent. *Psychological Review, 46,* 553–566.

Mueser, K. T., Bellack, A. S., Morrison, R. L., & Wade, J. H. (1990). Gender, social competence, and symptomatology in schizophrenia: A longitudinal analysis. *Journal of Abnormal Psychology, 99,* 138–147.

Mukherjee, S., Shukla, S., Woodle, J., Rosen, A. M., & Olarte, S. (1983). Misdiagnosis of schizophrenia in bipolar patients: A multiethnic comparison. *American Journal of Psychiatry, 140,* 1571–1574.

Mulholland, A. M., & Mintz, L. B. (2001). Prevalence of eating disorders among African American women. *Journal of Consulting & Clinical Psychology, 48,* 111–116.

Mulvey, E. P. (1995). Personal communication.

Mulvey, E. P., Geller, J. L., & Roth, L. H. (1987). The promise and peril of involuntary outpatient commitment. *American Psychologist, 42,* 571–584.

Munoz, R. F. (1997). The San Francisco Depression Prevention Research Project. In G. W. Albee (Ed.), *Primary prevention works* (pp. 380–400). Thousand Oaks, CA: Sage.

Munoz, R. F., Le, H. N., Clarke, G., & Jaycox, L. (2002). Preventing the onset of major depression. In I. H. Gotlib & C. L. Hammen (Eds.), *Handbook of depression* (pp. 343–359). New York: Guilford Press.

Munoz, R. F., Mrazek, P. J., & Haggerty, R. J. (1996). Institute of Medicine report on prevention of mental disorders: Summary and commentary. *American Psychologist, 51,* 1116–1122.

Munoz, R. F., Ying, Y. W., Bernal, G., Perez-Stable, E. J., Sorensen, J. L., Hargreaves, W. A., Miranda, J., & Miller, L. S. (1995). Prevention of depression with primary care patients: A randomized controlled trial. *American Journal of Community Psychology, 23,* 199–222.

Murden, R. A., McRae, T. D., Kaner, S., & Bucknam, M. E. (1991). Minimental state exam scores vary with education in blacks and whites. *Journal of the American Geriatrics Society, 39,* 149–155.

Murphy, J. M. (1976). Psychiatric labeling in cross-cultural perspective. *Science, 191,* 1019–1028.

Murray, C. J., & Lopez, A. D. (1996). *The global burden of disease: A comprehensive assessment of mortality and disabilities from diseases, injuries, and risk factors in 1990 and projected to 2020.* Cambridge, MA: Harvard University School of Public Health.

Murray, H. A. (1943). *Thematic apperception test manual.* Cambridge, MA: Harvard University Press.

N

Nadder, T. S., Silberg, J. L., Eaves, L. J., Maes, H. H., & Meyer, J. M. (1998). Genetic effects on ADHD symptomatology in 7- to 13-year-old twins: Results from a telephone survey. *Behavior Genetics, 28,* 83–99.

Nakao, M., Nomura, S., Shimosawa, T., Yoshiuchi, K., Kumano, H., Kuboki, T., Suematsu, H., & Fujita, T. (1997). Clinical effects of blood pressure biofeedback treatment on hypertension by auto-shaping. *Psychosomatic Medicine, 59,* 331–338.

Napiorkowski, B., Lester, B. M., Freier, C., Brunner, S., Dietz, L., Nadra, A., & Oh, W. (1996). Effects of in utero substance exposure on infant neurobehavior. *Pediatrics, 98,* 71–75.

Naranjo, C. A., & Knoke, D. M. (2001). The role of selective serotonin reuptake inhibitors in reducing alcohol consumption. *Journal of Clinical Psychiatry, 62*(Suppl. 20), 18–25.

Narrow, W. E., Regier, D. A., Rae, D., Manderscheid, R. W., & Locke, B. Z. (1993). Use of services by persons with mental and addictive disorders. *Archives of General Psychiatry, 50,* 95–107.

Nasar, S. (1998). *A beautiful mind.* New York: Simon & Schuster.

National Institute of Mental Health (NIMH). (2002). Suicide facts. Retrieved from the World Wide Web: http://www.nimh.nih.gov/research/suifact.htm

National Institute on Drug Abuse (NIDA). (2002a). Cocaine abuse and addiction. Retrieved from the World Wide Web: http://www.drugabuse.gov/ResearchReports/Cocaine/ cocaine2.html

National Institute on Drug Abuse (NIDA). (2002b). Heroin: Abuse and addiction. Retrieved from the World Wide Web: http://www.drugabuse.gov/ResearchReports/heroin/ heroin2.html

National Institute on Drug Abuse (NIDA). (2002c). Inhalant abuse. Retrieved from the World Wide Web: http://www.drugabuse.gov/ResearchReports/Inhalants/inhalants2.html

National Institute on Drug Abuse (NIDA). (2002d). Methamphetamine: Abuse and addiction. Retrieved from the World Wide Web: http://www.drugabuse.gov/ResearchReports/Methamph/methamph2.html

National Institute on Drug Abuse (NIDA). (2002e). Nicotine addiction. Retrieved from the World Wide Web: http://www.drugabuse.gov/ResearchReports/ Nicotine/nicotine2.html

National Institute on Drug Abuse (NIDA). (2002f). Prescription drugs: Abuse and addiction. Retrieved from the World Wide Web: http://www.drugabuse.gov/ResearchReports/Prescription/prescription2.html

Neal, J. A., & Edelmann, R. J. (2003). The etiology of social phobia: Toward a developmental profile. *Clinical Psychology Review, 23,* 761–786.

Neighbors, H. W. (1984). Professional help use among black Americans: Implications for unmet need. *American Journal of Community Psychology, 12,* 551–566.

Neighbors, H. W., Trierweiler, S. J., Ford, B. C., & Muroff, J. R. (2003). Racial differences in DSM diagnosis using a semi-structured instrument: The importance of clinical judgment in the diagnosis of African Americans. *Journal of Health & Social Behavior, 43,* 237–256.

Neighbors, H. W., Williams, D. H., Gunnings, T. S., Lipscomb, W. D., Broman, C., & Lepkowski, J. (1987). *The prevalence of mental disorder in Michigan prisons: Final report.* Ann Arbor: Michigan Department of Corrections, University of Michigan, School of Public Health, Department of Community Health Programs, Community Mental Health Program.

Nelson, C. B., & Wittchen, H. (1998). DSM-IV alcohol disorders in a general population sample of adolescents and young adults. *Addiction, 93,* 1065–1077.

Nelson, J. C., Mazure, C. M., Jatlow, P. I., Bowers, M. B., Jr., & Price, L. H. (2004). Combining norepinephrine and serotonin reuptake inhibition mechanisms for treatment of depression: A double-blind, randomized study. *Biological Psychiatry, 55,* 296–300.

Nemeroff, C. B. (2000). An ever-increasing pharmacopoeia for the management of patients with bipolar disorder. *Journal of Clinical Psychiatry, 61*(Suppl. 13), 19–25.

Nemeroff, C. B. (2004). Neurobiological consequences of childhood trauma. *Journal of Clinical Psychiatry, 65*(Suppl. 1), 18–28.

Nemeroff, C. B., & Schatzberg, A. F. (1998). Pharmacological treatment of unipolar depression. In P. E. Nathan (Ed.), *A guide to treatments that work* (pp. 212–225). New York: Oxford University Press.

Nemeroff, C. J., Stein, R. I., Diehl, N. S., & Smilack, K. M. (1994). From the Cleavers to the Clintons: Role choices and body orientation as reflected in magazine article content. *International Journal of Eating Disorders, 16,* 167–176.

Nestadt, G., Romanoski, A. J., Chahal, R., & Merchant, A. (1990). An epidemiological study of histrionic personality disorder. *Psychological Medicine, 20,* 413–422.

Nestadt, G., Samuels, J., Riddle, M., Bienvenu, J., Liang, K., LaBuda, M., Walkup, J., Grados, M., & Hoehn-Saric, R. (2000). A family study of obsessive-compulsive disorder. *Archives of General Psychiatry, 57,* 358–363.

Neugebauer, R. (1979). Medieval and early modern theories of mental illness. *Archives of General Psychiatry, 36,* 477–483.

Neuner, F., Schauer, M., Klaschik, C., Karunakara, U., & Elbert, T. (2004). A comparison of narrative exposure therapy, supportive counseling, and psychoeducation for treating posttraumatic stress disorder in an African refugee settlement. *Journal of Consulting & Clinical Psychology, 72,* 579–587.

Newhill, C. E., Mulvey, E. P., & Lidz, C. W. (1995). Characteristics of violence in the community by female patients seen in a psychiatric emergency service. *Psychiatric Services, 46,* 785–789.

Newmann, J. P. (1989). Aging and depression. *Psychology & Aging, 4,* 150–165.

Newmann, J. P., Engel, R. J., & Jensen, J. E. (1991). Age differences in depressive symptom experiences. *Journal of Gerontology, 46,* P224–P235.

Newsweek. (2003, October 20). I am addicted to prescription pain medication. [Electronic version]. *Newsweek.*

New York Times/CBS News Poll. (1999, October 20). Teenagers' concerns. *New York Times,* p. A1.

Nicholson, R. A., & Kugler, K. E. (1991). Competent and incompetent criminal defendants: A quantitative review of comparative research. *Psychological Bulletin, 109,* 355–370.

Nicol-Smith, L. (1996). Causality, menopause, and depression: A critical review of the literature. *British Medical Journal, 313,* 1229–1232.

Nigg, J. T., & Goldsmith, H. H. (1994). Genetics of personality disorders: Perspectives from personality and psychopathology research. *Psychological Bulletin, 115,* 346–380.

Nock, M. K., & Kazdin, A. E. (2001). Parent expectancies for child therapy: Assessment and relation to participant in treatment. *Journal of Child & Family Studies, 10,* 155–180.

Noga, J. T., Vladar, K., & Torrey, E. F. (2001). A volumetric magnetic resonance imaging study of monozygotic twins discordant for bipolar disorder. *Psychiatry Research: Neuroimaging, 106,* 25–34.

Nolen-Hoeksema, S. (1990). *Sex differences in depression.* Stanford, CA: Stanford University Press.

Nolen-Hoeksema, S. (2000). The role of rumination in depressive disorders and mixed anxiety/depressive symptoms. *Journal of Abnormal Psychology, 109,* 504–511.

Nolen-Hoeksema, S. (2002). Gender differences in depression. In I. H. Gotlib & C. L. Hammen (Eds.), *Handbook of depression* (pp. 492–509). New York: Guilford Press.

Nolen-Hoeksema, S. (2003). The response styles theory. In C. Papageorgiou & A. Wells (Eds.), *Depressive rumination: Nature, theory, and treatment* (pp. 107–124). New York: Wiley.

Nolen-Hoeksema, S. (2004). Gender differences in risk factors and consequences for alcohol use and problems. *Clinical Psychology Review, 24,* 981–1010.

Nolen-Hoeksema, S. (2006). *Eating, Drinking, Overthinking: The Toxic Triangle of Food, Alcohol, and Depression—And Women Can Break Free.* New York: Henry Holt.

Nolen-Hoeksema, S., & Jackson, B. (2001). Mediators of the gender difference in rumination. *Psychology of Women Quarterly, 25,* 37–47.

Nolen-Hoeksema, S., & Larson, J. (1999). *Coping with loss.* Mahwah, NJ: Erlbaum.

Nolen-Hoeksema, S., Larson, J., & Grayson, C. (1999). Explaining the gender difference in depressive symptoms. *Journal of Personality & Social Psychology, 77,* 1061–1072.

Nolen-Hoeksema, S., & Morrow, J. (1991). A prospective study of depression and distress following a natural disaster: The 1989 Loma Prieta earthquake. *Journal of Personality & Social Psychology, 61,* 105–121.

Nolen-Hoeksema, S., Parker, L. E., & Larson, J. (1994). Ruminative coping with depressed mood following loss. *Journal of Personality & Social Psychology, 67,* 92–104.

Nopoulos, P., Flaum, M., & Andreasen, N. C. (1997). Sex differences in brain morphology in schizophrenia. *American Journal of Psychiatry, 154,* 1648–1654.

Norcross, J. C. (2002). Empirically supported therapy relationships. In J. C. Norcross (Ed.), *Psychotherapy relationships that work: Therapist contributions and responsiveness to patients* (pp. 3–16). London: Oxford University Press.

Norcross, J. C., Beutler, L. E., & Caldwell, R. (2002). Integrative conceptualization and treatment of depression. In M. A. Reinecke & M. R. Davidson (Eds.), *Comparative treatments of depression* (pp. 397–426). New York: Springer.

Nordin, V., & Gillberg, C. (1998). The long-term course of autistic disorders: Update on follow-up studies. *Acta Psychiatrica Scandinavica, 97,* 99–108.

Norman, R. M., & Malla, A. K. (1993). Stressful life events and schizophrenia: II. Conceptual and methodological issues. *British Journal of Psychiatry, 162,* 166–174.

Norris, F. H., Perilla, J. L., Ibanez, G. E., & Murphy, A. D. (2001). Sex differences in symptoms of posttraumatic stress: Does culture play a role? *Journal of Traumatic Stress, 14,* 7–28.

Norris, F. H., & Uhl, G. A. (1993). Chronic stress as a mediator of acute stress: The case of Hurricane Hugo. *Journal of Applied Social Psychology, 23,* 1263–1284.

Northey, W. F., Jr., & Primer, V. (2004). Comprehensive handbook of psychotherapy. *Journal of Marital & Family Therapy, 30,* 108–109.

Nowell, P. D., Buysse, D. J., Morin, C. M., Reynolds, III, C. F., & Kuper, D. J. (1998). Effective treatments for selected sleep disorders. In P. E. Nathan (Ed.), *A guide to treatments that work* (pp. 531–543). New York: Oxford University Press.

Noyes, R., Crowe, R. R., Harris, E. L., Hamra, B. J., McChesney, C. M., & Chaudhry, D. R. (1986). Relationship between panic disorder and agoraphobia: A family study. *Archives of General Psychiatry, 43,* 227–232.

Noyes, R., Langbehn, D. R., Happel, R. L., Stout, L. R., Muller, B. A., & Longley, S. L. (2001). Personality dysfunction among somatizing patients. *Psychosomatics, 42,* 320–329.

Nunes, E. V., & Levin, F. R. (2004). Treatment of depression in patients with alcohol or other drug dependence: A meta-analysis. *Journal of the American Medical Association, 291,* 1887–1896.

Nutt, D. J., & Malizia, A. L. (2004). Structural and functional brain changes in posttraumatic stress disorder. *Journal of Clinical Psychiatry, 65*(Suppl. 1), 11–17.

O

O'Brien, C. P., & McKay, J. R. (1998). Psychopharmacological treatments of substance use disorders. In P. E. Nathan (Ed.), *A guide to treatments that work* (pp. 127–155). New York: Oxford University Press.

O'Connor, K., Hallam, R., & Rachman, S. (1985). Fearlessness and courage: A replication experiment. *British Journal of Psychology, 76,* 187–197.

O'Donnell, L., O'Donnell, C., Wardlaw, D. M., & Stueve, A. (2004). Risk and resiliency factors influencing suicidality among urban African American and Latino youth. *American Journal of Community Psychology, 33,* 37–49.

Office of Ethnic Minority Affairs, American Psychological Association. (1993). Guidelines for providers of psychological services to ethnic, linguistic, and culturally diverse populations. *American Psychologist, 48,* 45–48.

Offord, D. R. (1997). Bridging development, prevention, and policy. In D. M. Stoff, J. Breiling, & J. D. Maser (Eds.), *Handbook of antisocial personality disorder* (pp. 357–364). New York: Wiley.

Offord, D. R., Boyle, M. H., Racine, Y. A., & Fleming, J. E. (1992). Outcome, prognosis, and risk in a longitudinal follow-up study. *Journal of the American Academy of Child & Adolescent Psychiatry, 31,* 916–923.

O'Hara, M. W., & Swain, A. M. (1996). Rates and risk of postpartum depression—A meta-analysis. *International Review of Psychiatry, 8,* 37–54.

Ohman, A., Fredrikson, M., Hugdahl, K., & Rimmo, P. (1976). The premise of equipotentiality in human classical conditioning: Conditioned electrodermal responses to potentially phobic stimuli. *Journal of Experimental Psychology: General, 105,* 313–337.

Okazaki, S., & Sue, S. (2003). Methodological issues in assessment research with ethnic minorities. In A. E. Kazdin (Ed.), *Methodological issues & strategies in clinical research* (3rd ed., pp. 349–367). Washington, DC: American Psychological Association.

O'Leary, A. (1990). Stress, emotion, and human immune function. *Psychological Bulletin, 108,* 363–382.

Olfson, M., Marcus, S., Sackheim, H. A., Thompson, J., & Pincus, H. A. (1998). Use of ECT for the inpatient treatment of recurrent major depression. *American Journal of Psychiatry, 155,* 22–29.

Olin, S. S., Raine, A., Cannon, T. D., Parnas, J., Schulsinger, F., & Mednick, S. A. (1999). Childhood behavior precursors of schizotypal personality disorder. *Schizophrenia Bulletin, 23,* 93–103.

Olivardia, R., Pope, H. G., Mangweth, B., & Hudson, J. I. (1995). Eating disorders in college men. *American Journal of Psychiatry, 152,* 1279–1285.

Olmos de Paz, T. (1990). Working-through and insight in child psychoanalysis. *Melanie Klein & Object Relations, 8,* 99–112.

Olson, H. C., Feldman, J. J., Streissguth, A. P., Sampson, P. D., & Boostein, F. L. (1998). Neuropsychological deficits in adolescents with fetal alcohol syndrome: Clinical findings. *Alcoholism: Clinical & Experimental Research, 22,* 1998–2012.

Ondersma, S. J., & Walker, C. E. (1998). Elimination disorders. In T. H. Ollendick & M. Hersen (Eds.), *Handbook of child psychopathology* (pp. 355–380). New York: Plenum Press.

Oquendo, M. A., Ellis, S. P., Greenwald, S., Malone, K. M., Weissman, M. M., & Mann, J. J. (2001). Ethnic and sex differences in suicide rates relative to major depression in the United States. *American Journal of Psychiatry, 158,* 1652–1658.

Oquendo, M. A., Malone, K. M., Ellis, S. P., Sackeim, H. A., & Mann, J. J. (1999). Inadequacy of antidepressant treatment for patients with major depression who are at risk for suicidal behavior. *American Journal of Psychiatry, 156,* 190–194.

Oquendo, M. A., & Mann, J. J. (2000). The biology of impulsivity and suicidality. *Psychiatric Clinics of North America, 23,* 11–25.

Orsillo, S. M., Weathers, F. W., Litz, B. T., Steinberg, H. R., Huska, J. A., & Keane, T. M. (1996). Current and lifetime psychiatric disorders among veterans with war zone–Related posttraumatic stress disorder. *Journal of Nervous & Mental Disease, 184,* 307–313.

Öst, L. (1992). Blood and injection phobia: Background and cognitive, physiological, and behavioral variables. *Journal of Abnormal Psychology, 101,* 68–74.

Öst, L., Svensson, L., Hellström, K., & Lindwall, R. (2001). One-session treatment of phobias in youths: A randomized clinical trial. *Journal of Consulting & Clinical Psychology, 69,* 814–824.

Öst, L. S., & Sterner, U. (1987). Applied tension: A specific behavioral method for treatment of blood phobia. *Behaviour Research & Therapy, 25,* 25–29.

Osvold, L. L., & Sodowsky, G. R. (1993). Eating disorders of white American, racial and ethnic minority American, and international women. Special issue: Multicultural health issues. *Journal of Multicultural Counseling & Development, 21,* 143–154.

Overmier, J. B., & Seligman, M. E. (1967). Effects of inescapable shock upon subsequent escape and avoidance responding. *Journal of Comparative & Physiological Psychology, 63,* 28–33.

Ozonoff, S., & Cathcart, K. (1998). Effectiveness of a home program intervention for young children with autism. *Journal of Autism & Developmental Disorders, 28,* 25–32.

P

Paffenberger, R. S., Hyde, R. T., Wing, A. L., & Hsieh, C. (1986). Physical activity, all-cause mortality, and longevity of college alumni. *New England Journal of Medicine, 314,* 605–613.

Palazzoli, M. S. (1974). *Self-starvation: From the intrapsychic to the transpersonal approach to anorexia nervosa* (A. Pomerans, Trans.). London: Chaucer.

Pappenheim, B. (1936). *Gebete. Ausgewahlt und herausgegeben vom Judischen Frauenbund.* Berlin: Philo Verlag.

Pariante, C. M., & Miller, A. H. (2001). Glucocorticoid receptors in major depression: Relevance to pathophysiology and treatment. *Biological Psychiatry, 49,* 391–404.

Parker, G., Johnston, P., & Hayward, L. (1988). Parental "expressed emotion" as a predictor of schizophrenic relapse. *Archives of General Psychiatry, 45,* 806–813.

Parks, G. A., Anderson, B. K., & Marlatt, G. A. (2001). Relapse prevention therapy. In N. Heather, T. J. Peters, & T. Stockwell (Eds.), *International handbook of alcohol dependence and problems* (pp. 575–592). New York: Wiley.

Parrott, A. C. (1998). Nesbitt's Paradox resolved? Stress and arousal modulation during cigarette smoking. *Addiction, 93,* 27–39.

Pate, J. E., Pumariega, A. J., Hester, C., & Garner, D. M. (1992). Cross-cultural patterns in eating disorders: A review. *Journal of the American Academy of Child & Adolescent Psychiatry, 31,* 802–809.

Patterson, R. (1994). *Opening remarks.* Paper presented at the National Forum on Creating Jail Mental Health Services for Tomorrow's Health Care Systems, San Francisco.

Pauli, P., Dengler, W., Wiedemann, G., Montoya, P., Flor, H., Birbaumer, N., & Buchkremer, G. (1997). Behavioral and neurophysiological evidence for altered processing of anxiety-related words in panic disorder. *Journal of Abnormal Psychology, 106,* 213–220.

Pauls, D. A., Morton, L. A., & Egeland, J. A. (1992). Risks of affective illness among first-degree relatives of bipolar I old-order Amish probands. *Archives of General Psychiatry, 49,* 703–708.

Paunovic, N., & Öst, L. (2001). Cognitive-behavior therapy vs exposure therapy in the treatment of PTSD in refugees. *Behaviour Research & Therapy, 39,* 1183–1197.

Pavlov, I. P. (1927). *Conditioned reflexes: An investigation of the physiological activity of the cerebral cortex.* London: Oxford University Press.

Pendery, M. L., Maltzman, I. M., & West, L. J. (1982). Controlled drinking by alcoholics? New findings and a reevaluation of a major affirmative study. *Science, 217,* 169–175.

Pennebaker, J. W. (1990). *Opening up: The healing power of confiding in others.* New York: William Morrow.

Pennebaker, J. W., & O'Heeron, R. C. (1984). Confiding in others and illness rates among spouses of suicide and accidental-death victims. *Journal of Abnormal Psychology, 93,* 473–476.

Perourka, S. J., Newman, H., & Harris, H. (1988). Subjective effects of 3, 4-methylenedioxymethamphetamine in recreational users. *Neuropsychopharmacology, 1,* 273–277.

Perry, J. C. (1993). Longitudinal studies of personality disorders. *Journal of Personality Disorders* (Suppl. 1), 63–85.

Perugi, G., Akiskal, H. S., Giannotti, D., Frare, F., Di Vaio, S., & Cassano, G. B. (1997). Gender-related differences in body dysmorphic disorder (dysmorphophobia). *Journal of Nervous & Mental Disease, 185,* 578–582.

Petegnief, V., Saura, J., De Gregorio-Rocasolano, N., & Paul, S. M. (2001). Neuronal injury-induced expression and release of apolipoprotein E in mixed neuron/GLIA co-cultures: Nuclear factor KB inhibitors reduce basal and lesion-induced secretion of apolipoprotein E. *Neuroscience, 104,* 223–234.

Peterson, C., & Seligman, M. E. (1984). Causal explanations as a risk factor for depression: Theory and evidence. *Psychological Review, 91,* 347–374.

Peterson, C., Seligman, M. E., & Vaillant, G. E. (1988). Pessimistic explanatory style is a risk factor for physical illness: A thirty-five-year longitudinal study. *Journal of Personality & Social Psychology, 55,* 23–27.

Peterson, C., Seligman, M. E. P., Yurko, K. H., Martin, L. R., & Friedman, H. S. (1998). Catastrophizing and untimely death. *Psychological Science, 9,* 127–130.

Peterson, G. (1991). Children coping with trauma: Diagnosis of "dissociation identity disorder." *Dissociation: Progress in the Dissociation Disorders, 4,* 152–164.

Petronis, K. R., Samuels, J. F., Moscicki, E. K., & Anthony, J. C. (1990). An epidemiologic investigation of potential risk factors for suicide attempts. *Social Psychiatry & Psychiatric Epidemiology, 25,* 193–199.

Pettit, G. S., Dodge, K. A., & Brown, M. M. (1988). Early family experience, social problem solving patterns, and children's social competence. *Child Development, 59,* 107–120.

Pfeffer, C. R. (1985). Suicidal tendencies in normal children. *Journal of Nervous & Mental Disease, 173,* 78–84.

Pfefferbaum, B., Gurwitch, R. H., McDonald, N. B., Leftwich, M. J. T., Sconzo, G. M., Messenbaugh, A. K., & Schultz, R. (2000). Posttraumatic stress among young children after the death of a friend or acquaintance in a terrorist bombing. *Psychiatric Services, 51,* 386–388.

Phares, E. J. (1992). *Clinical psychology: Concepts, methods and profession.* Pacific Grove, CA: Brooks/Cole.

Phariss, B., Millman, R. B., & Beeder, A. B. (1998). Psychological and psychiatric consequences of cannabis. In R. E. Tarter (Ed.), *Handbook of substance abuse: Neurobehavioral pharmacology* (pp. 147–158). New York: Plenum Press.

Phillips, K. A. (1991). Body dysmorphic disorder: The distress of imagined ugliness. *American Journal of Psychiatry, 148,* 1138–1149.

Phillips, K. A. (2001). *Somatoform and factitious disorders.* Washington, DC: American Psychiatric Association.

Phillips, K. A., & Diaz, S. F. (1997). Gender differences in body dysmorphic disorder. *Journal of Nervous & Mental Disease, 185,* 570–577.

Phillips, K. A., Kim, J. M., & Hudson, J. I. (1995). Body image disturbance in body dysmorphic disorder and eating disorders: Obsessions or delusions? *Psychiatric Clinics of North America, 18,* 317–334.

Phillips, K. A., & Najjar, F. (2003). An open-label study of citalophram in body dysmorphic disorder. *Journal of Clinical Psychiatry, 64,* 715–720.

Pilkonis, P. A. (1995). Commentary on avoidant personality disorder: Temperament, shame, or both? In W. J. Livesley (Ed.), *The DSM-IV personality disorders* (pp. 234–238). New York: Guilford Press.

Pipher, M. (1994). *Reviving Ophelia: Saving the selves of adolescent girls.* New York: Putnam.

Pitman, R. K. (1989). Posttraumatic stress disorder, hormones, and memory. *Biological Psychiatry, 26,* 221–223.

Pitman, R. K., Shalev, A. Y., & Orr, S. P. (2000). Posttraumatic stress disorder: Emotion, conditioning, and memory. In M. S. Gazzaniga (Ed.), *The new cognitive neurosciences* (2nd ed., pp. 1133–1147). Cambridge, MA: MIT Press.

Pitschel-Walz, G., Leucht, S., Baumi, J., Kissling, W., & Engel, R. (2001). The effect of family interventions on relapse and rehospitalization in schizophrenia—A meta-analysis. *Schizophrenia Bulletin, 27,* 73–92.

Pizzagalli, D., Pascual-Marqui, R. D., Nitschke, J. B., Oakes, T. R., Larson, C. L., et al. (2001). Anterior cingulated activity as a predictor of degree of treatment response in major depression: Evidence from brain electrical tomography analysis. *American Journal of Psychiatry, 158,* 405–415.

Plantenga, B. (1991). *Like open bright windows.* New York: Poets in Public Service.

Plassman, B. L., & Breitner, J. C. S. (1996). Recent advances in the genetics of Alzheimer's disease and vascular dementia with an emphasis on gene-environment interactions. *Journal of the American Geriatric Society, 44,* 1242–1250.

Platt, S., & Hawton, K. (2000). Repetition of suicidal behavior. In K. Hawton (Ed.), *International book of suicide and attempted suicide.* New York: Wiley.

Pliner, P., & Chaiken, S. (1990). Eating, social motives, and self-presentation in women and men. *Journal of Experimental Social Psychology, 26,* 240–254.

Plomin, R. (1994). *Genetics and experience: The interplay between nature and nurture.* Thousand Oaks, CA: Sage.

Polivy, J., & Herman, C. P. (2002). Causes of eating disorders. *Annual Review of Psychology, 53,* 187–213.

Pomerleau, O., & Kardia, S. (1999). Introduction to the featured section: Research on smoking. *Health Psychology, 18,* 3–6.

Pope, H. G., Gruber, A. J, Hudson, J. I., Huestis, M. A., & Yurgelun-Todd, D. (2001). Neuropsychological performance in long-term cannabis users. *Archives of General Psychiatry, 58,* 909–915.

Pope, H. G., Gruber, A. J., Mangweth, B., Bureau, B., deCol, C., Jouvent, R., & Hudson, J. I. (2000). Body image perception among men in three countries. *American Journal of Psychiatry, 157,* 1297–1301.

Pope, H. G., & Hudson, J. I. (1992). Is childhood sexual abuse a risk factor for bulimia nervosa? *American Journal of Psychiatry, 149,* 455–463.

Pope, H. G., Ionescu-Pioggia, M., & Pope, K. W. (2001). Drug use and lifestyle among college undergraduates: A 30-year longitudinal study. *American Journal of Psychiatry, 158,* 1519–1521.

Pope, H. G., Jacobs, A., Mialet, J., Yurgelun-Todd, D., & Gruber, S. (1997). Evidence for a sex-specific residual effect of cannabis on visuospatial memory. *Psychotherapy & Psychosomatics, 66,* 179–184.

Pope, H. G., Oliva, P. S., Hudson, J. I., Bodkin, J. A., & Grueber, A. J. (1999a). Attitudes toward DSM-IV dissociative disorders diagnoses among board-certified American psychiatrists. *American Journal of Psychiatry, 156,* 321–323.

Pope, H. G., Olivardia, R., Gruber, A., & Borowiecki, J. (1999b). Evolving ideals of male body image as seen through action toys. *International Journal of Eating Disorders, 26,* 65–72.

Pope, K. S., Tabachnick, B. G., & Keith-Spiegel, P. (1987). Ethics of practice: The beliefs and behaviors of psychologists as therapists. *American Psychologist, 42,* 993–1006.

Post, R. M., Frye, M. A., Denicoff, K. D., Leverich, G. S., Dunn, R. T., Osuch, E. A., Speer, A. M., Obrocea, G., & Jajodia, K. (2000). Emerging trends in the treatment of rapid cycling bipolar disorder: A selected review. *Bipolar Disorders, 2,* 305–315.

Powers, D. V., Thompson, L., Futterman, A., & Gallagher-Thompson, D. (2002). Depression later in life: Epidemiology, assessment, impact, and treatment. In I. H. Gotlib & C. L. Hammen (Eds.), *Handbook of depression* (pp. 560–580). New York: Guilford Press.

Prescott, C. A., & Kendler, K. S. (1999). Genetic and environmental contributions to alcohol abuse and dependence in a population-based sample of male twins. *American Journal of Psychiatry, 156,* 34–40.

Pretzer, J. (2004). Cognitive therapy of personality disorders. In G. G. Magnavita (Ed.), *Handbook of personality disorders: Theory and practice* (pp. 169–193). New York: Wiley.

Pribor, E. F., Yutzy, S. H., Dean, J. T, & Wetzel, R. D. (1993). Briquet's syndrome, dissociation, and abuse. *American Journal of Psychiatry, 150,* 1507–1511.

Price, R. W. (1998). Implications of the AIDS dementia complex viewed as an acquired genetic neurodegenerative disease. In M. F. Folstein (Ed.), *Neurobiology of primary dementia* (pp. 213–234). Washington, DC: American Psychiatric Press.

Pridal, C. G., & LoPiccolo, J. (2000). Multielement treatment of desire disorders: Integration of cognitive, behavioral, and systemic therapy. In S. R. Leiblum & R. C. Rosen (Eds.), *Principles and practice of sex therapy* (3rd ed., pp. 57–81). New York: Guilford Press.

Pritchard, J. C. (1837). *A treatise on insanity and other diseases affecting the mind.* Philadelphia: Harwell, Barrington, & Harwell.

Prochaska, J. O. (1995). Common problems: Common solutions. *Clinical Psychology: Science & Practice, 2,* 101–105.

Project MATCH Research Group. (1998). Matching alcoholism treatments to client heterogeneity: Treatment main effects and matching effects on drinking during treatment. *Journal of Studies on Alcohol, 59,* 631–639.

Pumariega, A. J., & Winters, N. C. (2003). *Handbook of child and adolescent systems of care: The new community psychology.* San Francisco: Jossey-Bass.

Purugganan, O. H., Stein, R. E. K., Silver, E. J., & Benenson, B. S. (2003). Exposure to violence and psychosocial adjustment among urban school-aged children. *Journal of Developmental & Behavioral Pediatrics, 24,* 424–430.

Putnam, F. W. (1991). Recent research on multiple personality disorder. *Psychiatric Clinics of North America, 14,* 489–502.

Putnam, F. W. (1996). Posttraumatic stress disorder in children and adolescents. In L. J. Dickstein, M. B. Riba, & J. M. Oldham (Eds.), *Review of psychiatry* (Vol. 15, pp. 447–467). Washington, DC: American Psychiatric Press.

Putnam, F. W., Guroff, J. J., Silberman, E. K., & Barban, L. (1986). The clinical phenomenology of multiple personality disorder: Review of 100 recent cases. *Journal of Clinical Psychiatry, 47,* 285–293.

Putnam, F. W., & Lowenstein, R. J. (1993). Treatment of multiple personality disorder: A survey of current practices. *American Journal of Psychiatry, 150,* 1048–1052.

Puttler, L. I., Zucker, R. A., Fitzgerald, H. E., & Bingham, C. R. (1998). Behavioral outcomes among children of alcoholics during the early and middle childhood years: Familial subtype variations. *Alcoholism: Clinical & Experimental Research, 22,* 1962–1972.

Q

Quality Assurance Project. (1990). Treatment outlines for paranoid, schizotypal, and schizoid personality disorders. *Australian & New Zealand Journal of Psychiatry, 24,* 339–350.

Quay, H. C. (1993). The psychobiology of undersocialized aggressive conduct disorder: A theoretical perspective. *Development & Psychopathology, 5,* 165–180.

R

Rachman, S. (1978). *Fear and courage.* San Francisco: W. H. Freeman.

Rachman, S. (1993). Obsessions, responsibility and guilt. *Behaviour Research & Therapy, 31,* 149–154.

Rachman, S. (1997). A cognitive theory of obsessions. *Behaviour Research & Therapy, 35,* 667–682.

Rachman, S., & deSilva, P. (1978). Abnormal and normal obsessions. *Behaviour Research & Therapy, 16,* 233–248.

Rachman, S. J., & Hodgson, R. J. (1980). *Obsessions and compulsions.* Englewood Cliffs, NJ: Prentice-Hall.

Ragin, D. F., Pilotti, M., Madry, L., Sage, R. E., Bingham, L. E., & Primm, B. J. (2002). Intergenerational substance abuse and domestic violence as familial risk factors for lifetime attempted suicide among battered women. *Journal of Interpersonal Violence, 17,* 1027–1045.

Ragland, J. D., & Berman, A. L. (1990–1991). Farm crisis and suicide: Dying on the vine? *Omega Journal of Death & Dying, 22,* 173–185.

Raikkonen, K., Matthews, K. A., Flory, J. D., Owens, J. F., & Gump, B. B. (1999). Effects of optimism, pessimism, and trait anxiety on ambulatory blood pressure and mood during everyday life. *Journal of Personality & Social Psychology, 76,* 104–113.

Raine, A. (1997). Antisocial behavior and psychophysiology: A biological perspective. In D. M. Stoff, J. Breiling, & J. D. Maser (Eds.), *Handbook of antisocial personality disorder* (pp. 289–304). New York: Wiley.

Raine, A., Venables, P. H., & Williams, M. (1996). Better autonomic conditioning and faster electrodermal half-recovery time at age 15 years as possible protective factors against crime at age 29 years. *Developmental Psychology, 32,* 624–630.

Ramchandani, P. (2004). A question of balance: How safe are the medicines that are prescribed to children? *Nature, 430,* 401–402.

Rankin, H., Hodgson, R., & Stockwell, T. (1983). Cue exposure and response prevention with alcoholics: A controlled trial. *Behaviour Research & Therapy, 21,* 435–446.

Rapee, R. M. (1994). Detection of somatic sensations in panic disorder. *Behaviour Research & Therapy, 32,* 825–831.

Rapee, R. M., & Barlow, D. H. (1993). Generalized anxiety disorder, panic disorder, and the phobias. In P. B. Sutker (Ed.), *Comprehensive handbook of psychopathology* (pp. 109–127). New York: Plenum Press.

Rapee, R. M., Brown, T. A., Antony, M. M., & Barlow, D. H. (1992). Response to hyperventilation and inhalation of 5.5% carbon dioxide-enriched air across the DSM-III-R anxiety disorders. *Journal of Abnormal Psychology, 101,* 538–552.

Rapee, R. M., & Heimberg, R. G. (1997). A cognitive-behavioral model of anxiety in social phobia. *Behaviour Research & Therapy, 35,* 741–756.

Rapoport, J. L. (1989). The biology of obsessions and compulsions. *Scientific American,* 83–89.

Rapoport, J. L. (1990). *The boy who couldn't stop washing.* New York: Plume.

Rapoport, J. L. (1991). Recent advances in obsessive-compulsive disorder. *Neuropsychopharmacology, 5,* 1–10.

Rapoport, J. L., Jensen, P. S., Inoff-Germain, G., Weissman, M. M., Greenwald, S., Narrow, W. E., Lahey, B. B., & Canino, G. (2000). Childhood obsessive-compulsive disorder in the NIMH MECA study: Parent versus child identification of cases. *Journal of Anxiety Disorders, 14,* 535–548.

Rasekh, Z., Bauer, H. M., Manos, M. M., & Iacopino, V. (1998). Women's health and human rights in Afghanistan. *Journal of the American Medical Association, 280,* 449–455.

Rauch, S. L., Phillips, K. A., Segal, E., Makris, N., Shin, L. M., Whalen, P. J., Jenike, M. A., Caviness, V. S., Jr., & Kennedy, D. N. (2003). A preliminary morphometric magnetic resonance imaging study of regional brain volumes in body dysmorphic disorder. *Psychiatry Research: Neuroimaging, 122,* 13–19.

Ray, O., & Ksir, C. (1993). *Drugs, society, and human behavior.* St. Louis: C. V. Mosby.

Read, J. D., & Lindsay, D. S. (Eds.). (1997). *Recollections of trauma: Scientific research and clinical practice.* New York: Plenum Press.

Redmond, D. E. (1985). Neurochemical basis for anxiety and anxiety disorders: Evidence from drugs which decrease human fear or anxiety. In A. H. Tuma & J. Maser (Eds.), *Anxiety and the anxiety disorders* (pp. 533–555). Hillsdale, NJ: Erlbaum.

Reed, G. M., Kemeny, M. E., Taylor, S. E., & Visscher, B. R. (1999). Negative HIV-specific expectancies and AIDS-related bereavement as predictors of symptom onset in asymptomatic HIV-positive gay men. *Health Psychology, 18,* 354–363.

Regier, D. A., Boyd, J. H., Burke, J. D., Rae, D. S., Myers, J. K., Kramer, M., Robins, L. N., George, L. K., Karno, M., & Locke, B. Z. (1988). One-month prevalence of mental disorders in the United States: Based on five epidemiologic catchment area sites. *Archives of General Psychiatry, 45,* 977–986.

Regier, D. A., Narrow, W. E., Rae, D. S., Manderscheid, R. W., Locke, B. Z., & Goodwin, F. K. (1993). The de facto U.S. mental and addictive disorders service system. *Archives of General Psychiatry, 50,* 85–94.

Rehm, L. P. (1977). A self-control model of depression. *Behavior Therapy, 8,* 787–804.

Reich, T., Edenberg, H. J., Goate, A., Williams, J. T., Rice, J. P., Van Eerdeweghm, P., Foroud, T., Hesselbrock, V., Schuckit, M. A., Bucholz, K., Porjesz, B., Li, T. K., Conneally, P. M., Nurnberger, J. I. Jr., Tischfield, J. A., Crowe, R. R., Cloninger, C. R., Wu, W., Shears, S., Carr, K., Crose, C., Willig, C., & Begleiter, H. (1998). Genome wide-research for genes affecting the risk for alcohol dependence. *American Journal of Medical Genetics, 81,* 207–215.

Reid, J. B., & Eddy, J. M. (1997). The prevention of antisocial behavior: Some considerations in the search for effective interventions. In D. M. Stoff, J. Breiling, & J. D. Maser (Eds.), *Handbook of antisocial personality disorder* (pp. 343–356). New York: Wiley.

Reissing, E. D., Binik, Y. M., & Khalife, S. (1999). Does vaginismus exist? *Journal of Nervous & Mental Disease, 187,* 261–274.

Reitan, R. M., & Davidson, L. A. (1974). *Clinical neuropsychology: Current status and applications.* Washington, DC: V. H. Winston & Sons.

Resick, P. A. (1993). The psychological impact of rape. *Journal of Interpersonal Violence, 8,* 223–255.

Resick, P. A., & Calhoun, K. S. (2001). Posttraumatic stress disorder. In D. H. Barlow (Ed.), *Clinical handbook of psychological disorders: A step-by-step treatment manual* (3rd ed., pp. 60–113). New York: Guilford Press.

Resick, P. A., & Schnicke, M. K. (1992). Cognitive processing therapy for sexual assault victims. *Journal of Consulting & Clinical Psychology, 60,* 748–756.

Resnick, H. S., Kilpatrick, D. G., Dansky, B. S., & Saunders, B. E. (1993). Prevalence of civilian trauma and posttraumatic stress disorder in a representative national sample of women. *Journal of Consulting & Clinical Psychology, 61,* 984–991.

Resnick, H. S., Yehuda, R., Pitman, R. K., & Foy, D. W. (1995). Effect of previous trauma on acute plasma cortisol level following rape. *American Journal of Psychiatry, 152,* 1675–1677.

Reynolds, C. F., Miller, M. D., Mulsant, B. H., Dew, M. A., & Pollock, B. G. (2000). Pharmacotherapy of geriatric depression: Taking the long view. In G. M. Williamson, D. R. Shaffer, & P. A. Parmelee (Eds.), *Physical illness and depression in older adults: A handbook of theory, research, and practice* (pp. 277–294).

New York: Kluwer Academic/Plenum Publishers.

Rhee, S. H., Waldman, I. D., Hay, D. A., & Levy, F. (1999). Sex differences in genetic and environmental influences on DSM-III-R attention-deficit/hyperactivity disorder. *Journal of Abnormal Psychology, 108,* 24–41.

Ricca, V., Mannucci, E., Mezzani, B., Moretti, S., Di Bernardo, M., Bertelli, M., Rotella, C. M., & Faravelli, C. (2001). Fluoxetine and fluvoxamine combined with individual cognitive-behaviour therapy in binge eating disorder: A one-year follow-up study. *Psychotherapy & Psychosomatics, 70,* 298–306.

Richards, R., Kinney, D. K., Lunde, I., & Benet, M. (1988). Creativity in manic-depressives, cyclothymes, their normal relatives, and control subjects. *Journal of Abnormal Psychology, 97,* 281–288.

Richardson, J. L., Shelton, D. R., Krailo, M., & Levine, A. M. (1990). The effect of compliance with treatment in survival among patients with hematologic malignancies. *Journal of Clinical Oncology, 8,* 356.

Rickels, K., Pollack, M. H., Sheehan, D. V., & Haskins, J. T. (2000). Efficacy of extended-release venlafaxine in nondepressed outpatients with generalized anxiety disorder. *American Journal of Psychiatry, 157,* 968–974.

Riddle, M. A., Reeve, E. A., Yaryura-Tobias, J. A., Yang, H. M., Claghorn, J. L., Gaffney, G., Greist, J. H., Holland, D., McConville, B. J., Pigott, T., & Walkup, J. T. (2001). Fluvoxamine for children and adolescents with obsessive-compulsive disorder: A randomized, controlled, multicenter trial. *Journal of the American Academy of Child & Adolescent Psychiatry, 40,* 222–229.

Rief, W., Hiller, W., & Margraf, J. (1998). Cognitive aspects of hypochondriasis and the somatization syndrome. *Journal of Abnormal Psychology, 107,* 587–595.

Riehman, K. S., Hser, Y., & Zeller, M. (2000). Gender differences in how intimate partners influence drug treatment motivation. *Journal of Drug Issues, 30,* 823–838.

Rifkin, A., Ghisalbert, D., Dimatou, S., Jin, C., & Sethi, M. (1998). Dissociative identity disorder in psychiatric inpatients. *American Journal of Psychiatry, 155,* 844–845.

Riley, K. P., Snowdon, D. A., Saunders, A. M., Roses, A. D., Mortimer, J. A., & Nanayakkara, N. (2000). Cognitive function and apolipoprotein in very old adults: Findings from the Nun Study. *Journal of Gerontology, 55B,* S69–S75.

Rimm, D. C., & Masters, J. C. (1979). *Behavior therapy: Techniques and empirical findings* (2nd ed.). New York: Academic Press.

Rimmele, C. T., Miller, W. R., & Dougher, M. J. (1989). Aversion therapies. In R. K. Hester & W. R. Miller (Eds.), *Handbook of alcoholism treatment approaches: Effective alternatives* (pp. 128–140). New York: Pergamon Press.

Rivera, G. (1988). Hispanic folk medicine utilization in urban Colorado. *Sociology & Social Research, 72,* 237–241.

Robbins, P. C., Monahan, J., & Silver, E. (2003). Mental disorder, violence, and gender. *Law and Human Behavior, 27,* 561–571.

Roberts, A. H. (1969). *Brain damage in boxers.* London: Pitman.

Roberts, J. E., Gotlib, I. H., & Kassel, J. D. (1996). Adult attachment security and symptoms of depression: The mediating roles of dysfunctional attitudes and low self-esteem. *Journal of Personality & Social Psychology, 60*, 310–320.

Roberts, M. C., Vernberg, E. M., & Jackson, Y. (2000). Psychotherapy with children and families. In C. R. Snyder & R. E. Ingram (Eds.), *Handbook of psychological change: Psychotherapy processes and practices for the 21st century* (pp. 500–519). New York: Wiley.

Robin, A. L. (2003). Behavioral family systems therapy for adolescents with anorexia nervosa. In A. E. Kazdin & J. R. Weisz (Eds.), *Evidence-based psychotherapies for children and adolescents* (pp. 358–373). New York: Guilford Press.

Robins, L. N., Helzer, J. E., Croughan, A., & Ratcliff, K. S. (1981). National Institute of Mental Health Diagnostic Interview Schedule. *Archives of General Psychiatry, 38*, 381–389.

Robins, L. N., Helzer, J. E., & Davis, D. H. (1975). Narcotic use in Southeast Asia and afterward: An interview of 898 Vietnam returnees. *Archives of General Psychiatry, 32*, 955–961.

Robins, L. N., Helzer, J. E., Weissman, M. M., Orvaschel, H., Gruenberg, E., Burke, J. D., & Regier, D. A. (1984). Lifetime prevalence of specific psychiatric disorders in three sites. *Archives of General Psychiatry, 41*, 949–958.

Robinson, L. A., Berman, J. S., & Neimeyer, R. A. (1990). Psychotherapy for the treatment of depression: A comprehensive review of controlled outcome research. *Psychological Bulletin, 109*, 30–49.

Robinson, T. E., & Berridge, K. C. (1993). The neural basis of drug craving: An incentive-sensitization theory of addiction. *Brain Research Reviews, 18*, 247–291.

Robles, T. F., & Kiecolt-Glaser, J. K. (2003). The physiology of marriage: Pathways to health. *Physiology & Behavior, 79*, 409–416.

Rockney, R. M., & Lemke, T. (1992). Casualties from a junior-senior high school during the Persian Gulf War: Toxic poisoning or mass hysteria? *Journal of Developmental & Behavioral Pediatrics, 13*, 339–342.

Rodin, J. (1992, January). Sick of worrying about the way you look? Read this. *Psychology Today*, pp. 56–60.

Rodin, J., Slochower, J., & Fleming, B. (1977). Effects of degree of obesity, age of onset, and weight loss on responsiveness to sensory and external stimuli. *Journal of Comparative & Physiological Psychology, 91*, 586–597.

Roelofs, K., Hoogduin, K. A. L., Keijsers, G. P. J., Naring, G. W. B., Moene, F. C., & Sandijck, P. (2002). Hypnotic susceptibility in patients with conversion disorder. *Journal of Abnormal Psychology, 111*, 390–395.

Rogers, C. R. (1951). *Client-centered therapy, its current practice, implications, and theory.* Boston: Houghton Mifflin.

Rogler, L. H. (1989). The meaning of culturally sensitive research in mental health. *American Journal of Psychiatry, 146*, 296–303.

Rogler, L. H. (1999). Methodological sources of cultural insensitivity in mental health research. *American Psychologist, 54*, 424–433.

Roisman, G. I., Tsai, J. L, & Chiang, K.-H. S. (2004). The emotional integration of childhood experience: Physiological, facial expressive, and self-reported emotional response during the Adult Attachment Interview. *Developmental Psychology, 40*, 776–789.

Ron, M. (2001). Explaining the unexplained: Understanding hysteria. *Brain, 124*, 1065–1066.

Rook, K. (1984). The negative side of social interaction: Impact on psychological well-being. *Journal of Personality & Social Psychology, 46*, 1097–1108.

Rorty, M., Yager, J., & Rossotto, E. (1994). Childhood sexual, physical, and psychological abuse in bulimia nervosa. *American Journal of Psychiatry, 151*, 1122–1126.

Rosen, G. (1968). *Madness in society: Chapters in the historical sociology of mental illness.* Chicago: University of Chicago Press.

Rosen, J. C., & Ramirez, E. (1998). A comparison of eating disorders and body dysmorphic disorder on body image and psychological adjustment. *Journal of Psychosomatic Research, 44*, 441–449.

Rosen, L. N., Targum, S. D., Terman, M., Bryant, M. J., Hoffman, H., Kasper, S. F., Hamovit, J. R., Docherty, J. P., Welch, B., & Rosenthal, N. E. (1990). Prevalence of seasonal affective disorder at four latitudes. *Psychiatry Research, 31*, 131–144.

Rosen, R. C. (1996). Erectile dysfunction: The medicalization of male sexuality. *Clinical Psychology Review, 16*, 497–519.

Rosen, R. C., & Ashton, A. K. (1993). Prosexual drugs: Empirical status of the "new aphrodisiacs." *Archives of Sexual Behavior, 22*, 521–543.

Rosen, R. C., & Leiblum, S. R. (1995). Treatment of sexual disorders in the 1990s: An integrated approach. *Journal of Consulting & Clinical Psychology, 63*, 877–890.

Rosenbaum, M. (1980). The role of the term schizophrenia in the decline of the diagnoses of multiple personality. *Archives of General Psychiatry, 37*, 1383–1385.

Rosenblatt, P. C. (2001). A social constructionist perspective on cultural differences in grief. In M. S. Stroebe & R. O. Hansson (Eds.), *Handbook of bereavement research: Consequences, coping and care* (pp. 285–300). Washington, DC: American Psychological Association.

Rosenhan, D. L. (1973). On being sane in insane places. *Science, 179*, 250–258.

Rosenheck, R. A. (1999). Principles for priority setting in mental health services and their implications for the least well off. *Psychiatric Services, 50*, 653–658.

Rosenman, R. H., Brand, R. J., Jenkins, C. D., Friedman, M., Straus, R., & Wrum, M. (1976). Coronary heart disease in the Western Collaborative Group Study: Final follow-up experience of 8 years. *Journal of the American Medical Association, 233*, 877–878.

Rosenstein, M. J., Milazzo-Sayre, L. J., & Manderscheid, R. W. (1989). Care of persons with schizophrenia: A statistical profile. *Schizophrenia Bulletin, 15*, 45–58.

Rosenthal, N. E. (1995, October 9–11). *The mechanism of action of light in the treatment of seasonal affective disorder.* Paper presented at the Biologic Effects of Light 1995, Atlanta.

Rosenweig, S. (1936). Some implicit common factors in diverse methods in psychotherapy. *American Journal of Orthopsychiatry, 6*, 412–415.

Ross, C. A. (1989). *Multiple personality disorder: Diagnosis, clinical features, and treatment.* New York: Wiley.

Ross, C. A. (1991). Epidemiology of multiple personality disorder and dissociation. *Psychiatric Clinics of North America, 14*, 503–517.

Ross, C. A. (1997). *Dissociative identity disorder: Diagnosis, clinical features, and treatment of multiple personality.* Toronto: Wiley.

Ross, C. A. (1999). Dissociative disorders. In T. Millon (Ed.), *Oxford textbook of psychopathology* (pp. 466–481). New York: Oxford University Press.

Ross, C. A., & Ellason, J. (1999). Comment on the effectiveness of treatment for dissociative identity disorder. *Psychological Reports, 84*, 1109–1110.

Ross, C. A., & Norton, G. R. (1989). Differences between men and women with multiple personality disorder. *Hospital & Community Psychiatry, 40*, 186–188.

Ross, C. A., Norton, G. R., & Fraser, G. A. (1989). Evidence against the iatrogenesis of multiple personality disorder. *Dissociation: Progress in the Dissociative Disorders, 2*, 61–65.

Ross, C. A., Norton, G. R., & Wozney, K. (1989). Multiple personality disorder: An analysis of 236 cases. *Canadian Journal of Psychiatry, 34*, 413–418.

Ross, C. E., & Mirowsky, J. (1984). Socially-desirable response and acquiescence in a cross-cultural survey of mental health. *Journal of Health & Social Behavior, 25*, 189–197.

Ross, C. E., Mirowsky, J., & Goldsteen, K. (1990). The impact of the family on health: The decade in review. *Journal of Marriage & the Family, 52*, 1059–1078.

Ross, L., Lepper, M. R., & Hubbard, M. (1975). Perseverance in self-perception and social preparation: Biased attributional processes in the debriefing paradigm. *Journal of Personality & Social Psychology, 32*, 880–892.

Ross, L., & Nisbett, R. E. (1991). *The person and the situation: Perspectives of social psychology.* Philadelphia: Temple University Press.

Rosselló, J., & Bernal, G. (2004). *Randomized trial of CBT and IPT in individual and group format for depression in Puerto Rican adolescents.* Paper under review.

Rost, K., Nutting, P., Smith, J., Coyne, J., Cooper-Patrick, L., & Rubenstein, L. (2000). The role of competing demands in the treatment provided primary care patients with major depression. *Archives of Family Medicine, 9*, 150–154.

Rost, K., Zhang, M., Fortney, J., Smith, J., & Smith, R. (1998). Expenditures for the treatment of major depression. *American Journal of Psychiatry, 155*, 883–888.

Rothbart, M., & Bates, J. (1998). Temperament. In W. Damon (Series Ed.) & N. Eisenberg (Vol. Ed.), *Handbook of child psychology: Vol. 3. Social, emotional, and personality development* (5th ed., pp. 105–176). New York: Wiley.

Rothbaum, B. O., & Foa, E. B. (1991). Exposure treatment of PTSD concomitant with conversion mutism: A case study. *Behavior Therapy, 22*, 449–456.

Rothbaum, B. O., Foa, E. D., Riggs, D. S., & Murdock, T. (1992). A prospective examination of post-traumatic stress disorder in rape victims. *Journal of Traumatic Stress, 5,* 455–475.

Rotter, J. B. (1954). *Social learning and clinical psychology.* Englewood Cliffs, NJ: Prentice Hall.

Rovner, B., Steele, C., Shmuely, Y., & Folstein, M. F. (1996). A randomized trial of dementia care in nursing homes. *Journal of the American Geriatric Society, 44,* 7–13.

Rovner, B. W. (1993). Depression and increased risk of mortality in the nursing home patient. *American Journal of Medicine, 94*(Suppl. 5A), 19S–22S.

Rowe, R., Maughan, B., Worthman, C. M., Costello, E. J., & Angold, A. (2004). Testosterone, antisocial behavior, and social dominance in boys: Pubertal development and biosocial interaction. *Biological Psychiatry, 55,* 546–552.

Rowse, A. L. (1969). *The early Churchills.* Middlesex, UK: Penguin Books.

Roy, A. (1992). Genetics, biology, and suicide in the family. In R. W. Maris, A. L. Berman, J. T. Maltsberger, & R. I. Yufit (Eds.), *Assessment and prediction of suicide* (pp. 574–588). New York: Guilford Press.

Rozin, P., Bauer, R., & Catanese, D. (2003). Food and life, pleasure and worry, among American college students: Gender differences and regional similarities. *Journal of Personality & Social Psychology, 85,* 132–141.

Rubin, K. H., Daniels-Beirness, T., & Hayvren, M. (1982). Social and social-cognitive correlates of sociometric status in preschool and kindergarten children. *Canadian Journal of Behavioural Science, 14,* 338–349.

Ruggiero, K. J., Morris, T. L., & Scotti, J. R. (2001). Treatment for children with posttraumatic stress disorder: Current status and future directions. *Clinical Psychology: Science & Practice, 8,* 210–227.

Russell, S. T. (2003). Sexual minority youth and suicide risk. *American Behavioral Scientist, 46,* 1241–1257.

Rutter, M. (1997). Antisocial behavior: Developmental psychopathology perspectives. In D. M. Stoff, J. Breiling, & J. D. Maser (Eds.), *Handbook of antisocial personality disorder* (pp. 115–124). New York: Wiley.

Rutter, M., Caspi, A., Fergusson, D., Horwood, L. J., Goodman, R., Maughan, B., Moffitt, T. E., Meltzer, H., & Carroll, J. (2004). Sex differences in developmental reading disability: New findings from 4 epidemiological studies. *Journal of the American Medical Association, 291,* 2007–2012.

Rutter, M., MacDonald, H., Couteur, A. L., Harrington, R., Bolton, P., & Bailey, A. (1990). Genetic factors in child psychiatric disorders: II. Empirical findings. *Journal of Child Psychology & Psychiatry, 31,* 39–83.

Rutter, M., Silberg, J., O'Connor, T., & Simonoff, E. (1999). Genetics and child psychiatry: II. Empirical research findings. *Journal of Child Psychology & Psychiatry, 40,* 19–55.

Ryan, J. J., & Lopez, S. J. (2001). Wechsler Adult Intelligence Scale–III. In W. I. Dorfman & S. M. Freshwater (Eds.), *Understanding psychological assessment* (pp. 19–42). Dordrecht, Netherlands: Kluwer Academic Publishers.

S

Sabol, S. Z., Nelson, M. L., Fisher, C., Gunzerath, L., Brody, C. L., Hu, S., Sirota, L. A., Marcus, S. E., Greenberg, B. D., Lucas, F. R., Benjamin, J., Murphy, D. L., & Hamer, D. H. (1999). A genetic association for cigarette smoking behavior. *Health Psychology, 18,* 7–13.

Sackheim, H. A., & Lisanby, S. H. (2001). Physical treatments in psychiatry: Advances in electroconvulsive therapy, transcranial magnetic stimulation, and vagus nerve stimulation. In M. Weissman (Ed.), *Treatment of depression: Bridging the 21st century* (pp. 151–174). Washington, DC: American Psychiatric Press.

Sackheim, H. A., Rush, A. J., George, M. S., Marangell, L. B., Husain, M. M., Nahas, Z., Johnson, C. R., Seidman, S., Giller, C., Haines, S., Simpson, R. K., & Goodman, R. R. (2001). Vagus nerve stimulation (VNS-super(TM)) for treatment-resistant depression: Efficacy, side effects, and predictors of outcome. *Neuropsychopharmacology, 25,* 713–728.

Salkovskis, P. M. (1998). Psychological approaches to the understanding of obsessional problems. In R. Swinson (Ed.), *Obsessive-compulsive disorder: Theory, research, and treatment* (pp. 33–50). New York: Guilford Press.

Saluja, G., Iachan, R., Scheidt, P. C., Overpeck, M. D., Sun, W., & Giedd, J. N. (2004). Prevalence of and risk factors for depressive symptoms among young adolescents. *Archives of Pediatrics & Adolescent Medicine, 158,* 760–765.

Salzman, L. (1980). *Psychotherapy of the obsessive personality.* New York: Jason Aronson.

Sampath, G., Shah, A., Krska, J., & Soni, S. D. (1992). Neuroleptic discontinuation in the very stable schizophrenic patient: Relapse rates and serum neuroleptic levels. *Human Psychopharmacology: Clinical & Experimental, 7,* 255–264.

Sampson, R. J., & Laub, J. H. (1992). Crime and deviance in the life course. *Annual Review of Sociology, 18,* 63–84.

Sanderson, W. C., Rapee, R. M., & Barlow, D. H. (1989). The influence of illusion of control on panic attacks induced via inhalation of 5.5% carbon dioxide–enriched air. *Archives of General Psychology, 46,* 157–162.

Sandnabba, N. K., Santtila, P., Alison, L., & Nordling, N. (2002). Demographics, sexual behaviour, family background and abuse experiences of practitioners of sadomasochistic sex: A review of recent research. *Sexual & Relationship Therapy, 17,* 39–55.

Sano, M., Ernesto, C., Thomas, R. G., & Klauber, M. R. (1997). A controlled trial of selegiline, alpha-tocopherol, or both as treatment for Alzheimer's disease. *New England Journal of Medicine, 336,* 1216–1222.

Sapolsky, R. M., Krey, L. C., & McEwen, B. S. (1986). The neuroendocrinology of stress and aging: The glucocorticoid cascade hypothesis. *Endocrinology Review, 7,* 284–301.

Sarason, I. G., Johnson, J. H., & Siegel, J. M. (1978). Assessing the impact of life changes: Development of the Life Experiences Survey.

Journal of Consulting & Clinical Psychology, 46, 932–946.

Sarbin, T. R., & Juhasz, J. B. (1967). The historical background of the concept of hallucination. *Journal of the History of the Behavioral Sciences, 3,* 339–358.

Sarwer, D. B., Magee, L., & Crerand, C. E. (2004). Cosmetic surgery and cosmetic medical treatments. In J. K. Thompson (Ed.), *Handbook of eating disorders and obesity* (pp. 718–737). Hoboken, NJ: Wiley.

Satir, V. (1967). Family systems and approaches to family therapy. *Journal of the Fort Logan Mental Health Center, 4,* 81–93.

Saunders, B. E., Villeponteaux, L. A., Lipovsky, J. A., Kilpatrick, D. G., et al. (1992). Child sexual assault as a risk factor for mental disorders among women: A community survey. *Journal of Interpersonal Violence, 7,* 189–204.

Saxena, S., Brody, A. L., Ho, M. L., Alborzian, S., Ho, M. K., Maidment, K. M., Huang, S.-C., Wu, H.-M., Au, S. C., & Baxter, L. R., Jr. (2001). Cerebral metabolism in major depression and obsessive-compulsive disorder occurring separately and concurrently. *Biological Psychiatry, 50,* 159–170.

Saxena, S., Brody, A. L., Ho, M. L., Zohrabi, N., Maidment, K. M., & Baxter, L. R., Jr. (2003). Differential brain metabolic predictors of response to paroxetine in obsessive-compulsive disorder versus major depression. *American Journal of Psychiatry, 160,* 522–532.

Saxena, S., Brody, A. L., Maidment, K. M., Dunkin, J. J., Colgan, M., Alborzian, S., Phelps, M. E., & Baxter, L. R. (1999). Localized orbitofrontal and subcortical metabolic changes and predictors of response to paroxetine treatment in obsessive-compulsive disorder. *Neuropsychopharmacology, 21,* 683–693.

Saxena, S., & Prasad, K. V. (1989). DSMIII subclassification of dissociative disorders applied to psychiatric outpatients in India. *American Journal of Psychiatry, 146,* 261–262.

Saxena, S., & Rauch, S. L. (2000). Functional neuroimaging and the neuroanatomy of obsessive-compulsive disorder. *Psychiatric Clinics of North America, 23,* 563–586.

Saxena, S., Winograd, A., Dunkin, J. J., Maidment, K., Rosen, R., Vapnik, T., Tarlow, G., & Bystritsky, A. (2001). A retrospective review of clinical characteristics and treatment response in body dysmorphic disorder versus obsessive-compulsive disorder. *Journal of Clinical Psychiatry, 62,* 67–72.

Scarr, S., Weinberg, R. A., & Waldman, I. D. (1993). IQ correlations in transracial adoptive families. *Intelligence, 17,* 541–555.

Schacter, D. L. (1999). The seven sins of memory. *American Psychologist, 54,* 182–203.

Schacter, D. L., Chiao, J. Y., & Mitchell, J. P. (2003). The seven sins of memory: Implications for the self. In J. LeDoux, J. Debiece, & H. Moss (Eds.), The self: From soul to brain. *Annals of the New York Academy of Sciences, 1001,* 226–239.

Schafer, W. (1992). *Stress management for wellness.* Fort Worth: Holt, Rinehart & Winston.

Scheff, T. J. (1966). *Being mentally ill: Sociological theory.* Chicago: Aldine.

Scheier, M. F., Matthews, K. A., Owens, J. F., Magovern, G. J., Lefebvre, R. C., Abbott, R. A., & Carver, C. S. (1989). Dispositional optimism and recovery from coronary artery surgery: The beneficial effects on physical and psychological well-being. *Journal of Personality & Social Psychology, 57,* 1024–1040.

Scherrer, J. F., True, W. R., Xian, H., Lyons, M. J., Eisen, S. A., Goldberg, J., Lin, N., & Tsuang, M. T. (2000). Evidence for genetic influences common and specific to symptoms of generalized anxiety and panic. *Journal of Affective Disorders, 57,* 25–35.

Schiavi, R. C. (1990). Sexuality and aging in men. *Annual Review of Sex Research, 1,* 227–249.

Schiavi, R. C., & Segraves, R. T. (1995). The biology of sexual dysfunction. *Psychiatric Clinics of North America, 18,* 7–23.

Schiavi, R. C., Stimmel, B. B., Mandeli, J., & Schreiner-Engel, P. (1995). Diabetes, psychological functioning, and male sexuality. *Journal of Psychosomatic Research, 39,* 305–314.

Schiavi, R. C., White, D., Mandeli, J., & Levine, A. (1997). Effect of testosterone administration on sexual behavior and mood in men with erectile dysfunction. *Archives of Sexual Behavior, 26,* 231–241.

Schildkraut, J. J. (1965). The catecholamine hypothesis of affective disorder: A review of supporting evidence. *American Journal of Psychiatry, 122,* 509–522.

Schlenger, W. E., Kulka, R. A., Fairbank, J. A., & Hough, R. L. (1992). The prevalence of post-traumatic stress disorder in the Vietnam generation: A multimethod, multisource assessment of psychiatric disorder. *Journal of Traumatic Stress, 5,* 333–363.

Schmahl, C. G., Vermetten, E., Elzinga, B. M., & Bremner, J. D. (2004). A positron emission tomography study of memories of childhood abuse in borderline personality disorder. *Biological Psychiatry, 55,* 759–765.

Schneider, J. A., O'Leary, A., & Jenkins, S. R. (1995). Gender, sexual orientation, and disordered eating. *Psychology & Health, 10,* 113–128.

Schneiderman, N., Antoni, M. H., Saab, P. G., & Ironson, G. (2001). Health psychology: Psychosocial and biobehavioral aspects of chronic disease management. *Annual Review of Psychology, 52,* 555–580.

Schneiderman, N., Ironson, G., & Siegel, S. D. (2005). Stress and health: Psychological, behavioral, and biological determinants. *Annual Review of Clinical Psychology, 1,* 607–628.

Schneier, F. R. (2001). Treatment of social phobia with antidepressants. *Journal of Clinical Psychiatry, 62*(Suppl. 1), 43–49.

Schnurr, P. P., Spiro, A., III, & Paris, A. H. (2000). Physician-diagnosed medical disorders in relation to PTSD symptoms in older male military veterans. *Health Psychology, 19,* 91–97.

Scholte, W. F., Olff, M., Ventevogel, P., de Vries, G.-J., Jansveld, E., Cardozo, B. L., & Crawford, C. A. G. (2004). Mental health symptoms following war and repression in eastern Afghanistan. *Journal of the American Medical Association, 292,* 585–593.

Schonfeld, L., & Dupree, L. W. (1997). Treatment alternatives for older alcohol abusers. In A. M. Gurnack (Ed.), *Older adults' misuse of alcohol, medicines, and other drugs: Research and practice issues* (pp. 113–131). New York: Springer.

Schreibman, L., & Charlop-Christy, M. H. (1998). Autistic disorder. In T. H. Ollendick & M. Hersen (Eds.), *Handbook of child psychopathology* (pp. 157–180). New York: Plenum Press.

Schuckit, M. A. (1991). A longitudinal study of children of alcoholics. In M. Galanter (Ed.), *Recent developments in alcoholism* (Vol. 9, pp. 5–19). New York: Plenum Press.

Schuckit, M. A. (1995). *Drug and alcohol abuse: A clinical guide to diagnosis and treatment.* New York: Plenum Medical Book Company.

Schuckit, M. A. (1996). Recent developments in the pharmacotherapy of alcohol dependence. *Journal of Consulting & Clinical Psychology, 64,* 669–676.

Schuckit, M. A. (1998). Biological, psychological, and environmental predictors of the alcoholism risk: A longitudinal study. *Journal of Studies on Alcohol, 59,* 485–494.

Schuckit, M. A., Daeppen, J. B., Tipp, J. E., Hesselbrock, M., & Bucholz, K. K. (1998). The clinical course of alcohol-related problems in alcohol dependent and nonalcohol dependent drinking men and women. *Journal of Studies in Alcohol, 59,* 581–590.

Schuckit, M. A., Edenberg, H. J., Kalmijn, J., Flury, L., Smith, T. L., Reich, T., Bierut, L., Goate, A., & Foroud, T. (2001). A genome-wide search for genes that relate to a low level response to alcohol. *Alcoholism: Clinical & Experimental Research, 25,* 323–329.

Schuckit, M. A., & Smith, T. L. (1996). An 8-year follow-up of 450 sons of alcoholic and control subjects. *Archives of General Psychiatry, 53,* 202–211.

Schuckit, M. A., & Smith, T. L. (1997). Assessing the risk for alcoholism among sons of alcoholics. *Journal of Studies on Alcohol, 58,* 141–145.

Schuckit, M. A., Smith, T. L., Danko, G. P., Bucholz, K. K., Reich, T., & Bierut, L. (2001). Five-year clinical course associated with DSM-IV alcohol abuse or dependence in a large group of men and women. *American Journal of Psychiatry, 158,* 1084–1090.

Schuckit, M. A., Tip, J. E., Reich, T., & Hesselbrock, V. M. (1995). The histories of withdrawal convulsions and delirium tremens in 1648 alcohol dependent subjects. *Addiction, 90,* 1335–1347.

Schultz, R., Gauthier, I., Klin, A. et al. (2000). Abnormal ventral temporal cortical activity during face discrimination among individuals with autism and Asperger syndrome. *Archives of General Psychiatry, 57,* 332–343.

Schulz, R., Bookwala, J., Knapp, J. E., Scheier, M., & Williamson, G. M. (1996). Pessimism, age, and cancer mortality. *Psychology & Aging, 11,* 304–309.

Schuster, M. A., Stein, B. D., Jaycox, L. H., Collins, R. L., Marshall, G. N., Elliott, M. N., Zhou, A. J., Kanouse, D. E., Morrison, J. L., & Berry, S. H. (2001). A national survey of stress reactions after the September 11, 2001, terrorist attacks. *New England Journal of Medicine, 345,* 1507–1512.

Schwartz, J., Stoessel, P. W., Baxter, L. R., Martin, K. M., & Phelps, M. C. (1996). Systemic changes in cerebral glucose metabolic rate after successful behavior modification treatment of obsessive-compulsive disorder. *Archives of General Psychiatry, 53,* 109–113.

Scogin, F., Floyd, M., & Forde, J. (2000). Anxiety in older adults. In S. K. Whitbourne (Ed.), *Psychopathology in later adulthood* (pp. 117–140). New York: Wiley.

Scogin, F., Rickard, H. C., Keith, S., Wilson, J., et al. (1992). Progressive and imaginal relaxation training for elderly persons with subjective anxiety. *Psychology & Aging, 7,* 419–424.

Scull, A. (1993). *The most solitary of afflictions.* New Haven: Yale University Press.

Sechehaye, M. (1951). *Autobiography of a schizophrenic girl.* New York: Grune & Stratton.

Seedat, S., Stein, M. B., & Forde, D. R. (2003). Prevalence of dissociative experiences in a community sample. *Journal of Nervous & Mental Disorders, 191,* 115–120.

Segal, S. P., Laurie, T. A., & Franskoviak, P. (2004). Ambivalence of PES patients toward hospitalization and factors in their disposition. *International Journal of Law & Psychiatry, 27,* 87–99.

Segerstrom, S. C., & Miller, G. E. (2004). Psychological stress and the human immune system: A meta-analytic study of 30 years of inquiry. *Psychological Bulletin, 130,* 601–630.

Segerstrom, S. C., Solomon, G. F., Kemeny, M. E., & Fahey, J. L. (1998). Relationship of worry to immune sequelae of the Northridge earthquake. *Journal of Behavioral Medicine, 21,* 433–450.

Segerstrom, S. C., Taylor, S. E., Kemeny, M. E., Reed, G. M., & Visscher, B. R. (1996). Causal attributions predict rate of immune decline in HIV seropositive gay men. *Health Psychology, 15,* 485–493.

Segman, R. H., & Shalev, A. Y. (2003). Genetics of posttraumatic stress disorder. *CNS Spectrums, 8,* 693–698.

Segraves, K. B., & Segraves, R. T. (1991). Multiple-phase sexual dysfunction. *Journal of Sex Education & Therapy, 17,* 153–156.

Segraves, R. T. (2003). Pharmacologic management of sexual dysfunction: Benefits and limitations. *CNS Spectrums, 8,* 225–229.

Segraves, R. T., Clayton, A., Croft, H., Wolf, A., & Warnock, J. (2004). Bupropion sustained release for the treatment of hypoactive sexual desire disorder in premenopausal women. *Journal of Clinical Psychopharmacology, 24,* 339–342.

Segraves, R. T., & Segraves, K. B. (1998). Pharmacotherapy for sexual disorders: Advantages and pitfalls. *Sexual & Marital Therapy, 13,* 295–309.

Seguin, J. R., Pihl, R. O., Harden, P. W., & Tremblay, R. E. (1995). Cognitive and neuropsychological characteristics of physically aggressive boys. *Journal of Abnormal Psychology, 104,* 614–624.

Seidman, L. J., Faraone, S. V., Goldstein, J. M., Kremen, W. S., Horton, N. J., Makris, N., Toomey, R., Kennedy, D., Caviness, V. S., &

Tsuang, M. T. (2002). Left hippocampal volume as a vulnerability indicator for schizophrenia. *Archives of General Psychiatry, 59*, 839–849.

Seidman, S. N., Roose, S. P., Menza, M. A., Shabsigh, R., & Rosen, R. C. (2001). Treatment of erectile dysfunction in men with depressive symptoms: Results of a placebo-controlled trial with sildenafil citrate. *American Journal of Psychiatry, 158*, 1623–1630.

Seligman, M. (1970). On the generality of the laws of learning. *Psychological Review, 77*, 406–418.

Seligman, M. E. (1993). *What you can change and what you can't: The complete guide to self-improvement.* New York: Knopf.

Seligman, M. E., & Maier, S. F. (1967). Failure to escape traumatic shock. *Journal of Experimental Psychology, 74*, 1–9.

Seligman, M. E. P. (1975). *Helplessness: On depression, development, and death.* San Francisco: Freeman, Cooper.

Seligman, M. E. P., & Binik, Y. M. (1977). The safety signal hypothesis. In H. Davis & H. Hurwitz (Eds.), *Pavlovian operant interactions.* Hillsdale, NJ: Erlbaum.

Selling, L. H. (1940). *Men against madness.* New York: Greenberg.

Selye, H. (1979). *The stress of life.* New York: McGraw-Hill.

Semans, J. H. (1956). Premature Ejaculation: A New Approach. *Southern Medical Journal, 49*, 353–357.

Shadish, W. R., Montgomery, L. M., Wilson, P., Wilson, M. R., Bright, I., & Okwumabua, T. (1993). Effects of family and marital psychotherapies: A meta-analysis. *Journal of Consulting & Clinical Psychology, 61*, 992–1002.

Shaffer, D., & Gould, M. (2000). Suicide prevention in the schools. In K. Hawton (Ed.), *The international handbook of suicide and attempted suicide* (pp. 585–724). New York: Wiley.

Shalev, A. Y., Peri, T., Canetti, L., & Schreiber, S. (1996). Predictors of PTSD in injured trauma survivors: A prospective study. *American Journal of Psychiatry, 153*, 219–225.

Shalev, A. Y., Tuval-Mashiach, R., & Hadar, H. (2004). Posttraumatic stress disorder as a result of mass trauma. *Journal of Clinical Psychiatry, 65*(Suppl. 1), 4–10.

Shapiro, F. (1995). *Eye movement desensitization and reprocessing: Basic principles, protocols, and procedures.* New York: Guilford Press.

Shaw, D. S., Keenan, K., & Vondra, J. I. (1994). Developmental precursors of externalizing behavior: Ages 1 to 3. *Developmental Psychology, 30*, 355–364.

Shaw, D. S., & Winslow, E. B. (1997). Precursors and correlates of antisocial behavior from infancy to preschool. In D. M. Stoff, J. Breiling, & J. D. Maser (Eds.), *Handbook of antisocial personality disorder* (pp. 148–158). New York: Wiley.

Shea, M. T. (1993). Psychosocial treatment of personality disorders. *Journal of Personality Disorders* (Suppl. 1), 167–180.

Shea, M. T., Stout, R., Gunderson, J., Morey, L. C., Grilo, C. M., McGlashan, T., Skodol, A. E., Dolan-Sewell, R., Dyck, I., Zanarini, M. C., & Keller, M. B. (2002). Short-term diagnostic stability of schizotypal, borderline, avoidant, and obsessive-compulsive personality disorders. *American Journal of Psychiatry, 159*, 2036–2041.

Sheard, M. H., Marini, J. L., Bridges, C. I., & Wagner, E. (1976). The effect of lithium on impulsive aggressive behavior in man. *American Journal of Psychiatry, 133*, 1409–1413.

Shearin, E. N., & Linehan, M. M. (1989). Dialectics and behavior therapy: A metaparadoxical approach to the treatment of borderline personality disorder. In L. M. Ascher (Ed.), *Therapeutic paradox* (pp. 255–288). New York: Guilford Press.

Sheikh, J. I. (1992). Anxiety and its disorders in old age. In J. E. Birren, K. Sloan, & G. D. Cohen (Eds.), *Handbook of mental health and aging* (pp. 410–432). New York: Academic Press.

Shenton, M. E., Frumin, M., McCarley, R. W., Maier, S. E., Westin, C.-F., Fischer, I. A., Dickey, C., & Kikinis, R. (2001). Morphometric magnetic resonance imaging studies: Findings in schizophrenia. In D. D. Dougherty & S. L. Rauch (Eds.), *Psychiatric neuroimaging research: Contemporary strategies* (pp. 1–60). Washington, DC: American Psychiatric Association.

Sher, K. J., Grekin, E. R., & Williams, N. A. (2005). The development of alcohol use disorders. In S. Nolen-Hoeksema, T. D. Cannon, & T. A. Widiger (Eds.), *Annual Review of Clinical Psychology* (Vol. 1, pp. 493–523). Palo Alto, CA: Annual Reviews.

Sher, K. J., & Trull, T. J. (1994). Personality and disinhibitory psychopathology: Alcoholism and antisocial personality disorder. *Journal of Abnormal Psychology, 103*, 92–102.

Sherrington, R., Rogaev, E. I., & Liang, Y. (1995). Cloning of a gene bearing missense mutations in early-onset familial Alzheimer's disease. *Nature, 375*, 754–760.

Sherwin, B. B. (1991). The psychoendocrinology of aging and female sexuality. *Annual Review of Sex Research, 2*, 191–198.

Shifren, J., Braunstein, G., Simon, J., Casson, P., Buster, J., Redmond, G., Burki, R., Ginsburg, E., Rosen, R., Leibum, S., Caramell, K., Mazer, N., Jones, K., & Daughery, C. (2000). Transdermal Testosterone Treatment in Women with Impaired Sexual Function after Oophorectomy. *The New England Journal of Medicine, 343*, 682–688.

Shin, L. M., Kosslyn, S. M., McNally, R. J., Alpert, N. M., Thompson, W. L., Rauch, S. L., Macklin, M. L., & Pitman, R. K. (1997). Visual imagery and perception in posttraumatic stress disorder: A positron emission tomographic investigation. *Archives of General Psychiatry, 54*, 233–241.

Shin, L. M., McNally, R. J., Kosslyn, S. M., Thompson, W. L., Rauch, S. L., Alpert, N. M., Metzger, L. J., Lasko, N. B., Orr, S. P., & Pitman, R. K. (1999). Regional cerebral blood flow during script-driven imagery in childhood sexual abuse–related PTSD: A PET investigation. *American Journal of Psychiatry, 156*, 575–584.

Shipherd, J. C., Beck, J. G., & Ohtake, P. J. (2001). Relationships between the anxiety sensitivity index, the suffocation fear scale, and responses to COsub-2 inhalation. *Journal of Anxiety Disorders, 15*(3), 247–258.

Shneidman, E. S. (1963). Orientations toward death: Subintentioned death and indirect suicide. In R. W. White (Ed.), *The study of lives.* New York: Atherton.

Shneidman, E. S. (1979). A bibliography of suicide notes: 1856–1979. *Suicide & Life-Threatening Behavior, 9*, 57–59.

Shneidman, E. S. (1981). Suicide. *Suicide & Life-Threatening Behavior, 11*, 198–220.

Shneidman, E. S. (1993). *Suicide as psychache: A clinical approach to self-destructive behavior.* Northvale, NJ: Jason Aronson.

Shneidman, E. S. (2001). *Comprehending suicide: Landmarks in 20th-century suicidology.* Washington, DC: American Psychological Association.

Shortt, A. L., Barrett, P. M., & Fox, T. L. (2001). Evaluating the FRIENDS program: A cognitive-behavioral group treatment for anxious children and their parents. *Journal of Clinical Child Psychology, 30*, 525–535.

Shrestha, N. M., Sharma, B., Van Ommeren, M., Regmi, S., Makaju, R., Komproe, I., Shrestha, G. B., & de Jong, J. T. V. M. (1998). Impact of torture on refugees displaced within the developing world. *Journal of the American Medical Association, 280*, 443–448.

Shrout, P. E., Canino, G. J., Bird, H. R., & Rubio-Stipec, M. (1992). Mental health status among Puerto Ricans, Mexican Americans, and non-Hispanic whites. *American Journal of Community Psychology, 20*, 729–752.

Siever, L. J., Bernstein, D. P., & Silverman, J. M. (1995). Schizotypal personality disorder. In W. J. Livesley (Ed.), *The DSM-IV personality disorders* (pp. 71–90). New York: Guilford Press.

Siever, L. J., & Davis, K. L. (1991). A psychobiological perspective on the personality disorders. *American Journal of Psychiatry, 148*, 1647–1658.

Siever, L. J., & Kendler, K. S. (1985). Paranoid personality disorder. In R. Michels, J. Cavenar, & H. Bradley (Eds.), *Psychiatry* (Vol. 1, pp. 1–11). New York: Basic Books.

Siever, L. J., New, A. S., Kirrane, R., Novotny, S., Koenigsberg, H., & Grossman, R. (1998). New biological research strategies for personality disorders. In K. R. Silk (Ed.), *Biology of personality disorders* (pp. 27–61). Washington, DC: American Psychiatric Press.

Silberg, J. L., Parr, T., Neale, M. C., Rutter, M., Angold, A., & Eaves, L. J. (2003). Maternal smoking during pregnancy and risk to boys' conduct disturbance: An examination of the causal hypothesis. *Biological Psychiatry, 53*, 130–135.

Silver, R. L., Boon, C., & Stones, M. H. (1983). Searching for meaning in misfortune: Making sense of incest. *Journal of Social Issues, 39*, 81–101.

Simeon, D., Guralnik, O., Schmeidler, J., Sirof, B., & Knutelska, M. (2001). The role of childhood interpersonal trauma in depersonalization disorder. *American Journal of Psychiatry, 158*, 1027–1033.

Simon, G. E., Katon, W. J., Von Korff, M., Un tzer, J., Lin, E., Walker, E. A., Bush, T., Rutter, C., & Ludman, E. (2001). Cost-effectiveness of a collaborative care program for primary care patients with persistent depression. *American Journal of Psychiatry, 158*(10), 1638–1644.

Simonoff, E., Bolton, P., & Rutter, M. (1998). Genetic perspectives on mental retardation. In J. A. Burack, R. M. Hodapp, & E. Zigler (Eds.), *Handbook of mental retardation and development* (pp. 41–79). New York: Cambridge University Press.

Simons, J. A., & Helms, J. E. (1976). Influence of counselors' marital status, sex, and age on college and noncollege women's counselor preferences. *Journal of Counseling Psychology, 23*, 380–386.

Simpson, E. B., Yen, S., Costello, E., Rosen, K., Begin, A., Pistorello, J., & Pearlstein, T. (2004). Combined dialectical behavior therapy and fluoxetine in the treatment of borderline personality disorder. *Journal of Clinical Psychiatry, 65*, 379–385.

Sing, L. (1995). Self-starvation in context: Towards a culturally sensitive understanding of anorexia nervosa. *Social Science & Medicine, 41*, 25–36.

Singer, M. T., & Wynne, L. C. (1965). Thought disorder and family relations of schizophrenics: IV. Results and implications. *Archives of General Psychiatry, 12*, 201–212.

Singh, N. N., Oswald, D. P., & Ellis, C. R. (1998). Mental retardation. In T. H. Ollendick & M. Hersen (Eds.), *Handbook of child psychopathology* (pp. 91–116). New York: Plenum Press.

Sipahimalani, A., & Masand, P. S. (1998). Olanzapine in the treatment of delirium. *Psychosomatics, 39*, 422–430.

Siqueland, L., Kendall, P. C., & Steinberg, L. (1996). Anxiety in children: Perceived family environments and observed family interaction. *Journal of Clinical Child Psychology, 25*, 225–237.

Slate Magazine. (2004, June 3). Gender gap: What were the real reasons behind David Reimer's suicide? Retrieved February 11, 2005, from http://slate.msn.com/id/2101678/

Slater, L. (1998). *Prozac diary.* New York: Random House.

Slijper, F. M. E., Drop, S. L. S., Molenaar, J. C., & de Munick Keizer-Schrama, S. M. P. F. (1998). Long-term psychological evaluation of intersex children. *Archives of Sexual Behavior, 27*, 125–144.

Sloan, J. H., Rivara, F. P., Reay, D. T., Ferris, J. A., Path, M. R. C., & Kellerman, A. L. (1990). Firearm regulations and rates of suicide: A comparison of two metropolitan areas. *New England Journal of Medicine, 322*, 369–373.

Small, G. W. (1998). The pathogenesis of Alzheimer's disease. *Journal of Clinical Psychiatry, 59*, 7–14.

Smith, C. A., & Farrington, D. P. (2004). Continuities in antisocial behavior and parenting across three generations. *Journal of Child Psychology & Psychiatry, 45*, 230–247.

Smith, D. (2001). Sleep psychologists in demand. *Monitor on Psychology, 32*, 36–38.

Smith, D. E., & Seymour, R. B. (1994). LSD: History and toxicity. *Psychiatric Annals, 24*, 145–147.

Smith, M. L., Glass, G. V., & Miller, T. I. (1980). *The benefits of psychotherapy.* Baltimore: Johns Hopkins University Press.

Smith, T. W., Turner, C. W., Ford, M. H., & Hunt, S. C. (1987). Blood pressure reactivity in adult male twins. *Health Psychology, 6*, 209–220.

Smith, Y. L. S., van Goozen, S. H. M., & Cohen-Kettenis, P. T. (2001). Adolescents with gender identity disorder who were accepted or rejected for sex reassignment surgery: A prospective follow-up study. *Journal of the American Academy of Child & Adolescent Psychiatry, 40*, 472–481.

Smolak, L., Murnen, S. K., & Ruble, A. E. (2000). Female athletes and eating problems: A meta-analysis. *International Journal of Eating Disorders, 27*, 371–380.

Smoller, J. W., Rosenbaum, J. F., Biederman, J., Kennedy, J., Dai, D., Racette, S. R., Laird, N. M., Kagan, J., Snidman, N., Hirshfeld-Becker, D., Tsuang, M. T., Sklar, P. B., & Slaugenhaupt, S. A. (2003). Association of a genetic marker at the corticotrophin-releasing hormone locus with behavioral inhibition. *Biological Psychiatry, 54*, 1376–1381.

Snowden, J. S., Neary, D., & Mann, D. M. A. (1996). *Frontotemporal lobar degeneration: Frontotemporal dementia, progressive aphasia, semantic dementia.* New York: Churchill Livingstone.

Snowden, L. R. (2003). Challenges to consensus in preparing the supplement to the surgeon general's report on mental health. *Culture, Medicine & Psychiatry, 27*, 409–418.

Snowden, L. R., & Cheung, F. K. (1990). Use of inpatient mental health services by members of ethnic minority groups. *American Psychologist, 45*, 347–355.

Snowden, L. R., & Yamada, A. M. (2005). Cultural differences in access to care. *Annual Review of Clinical Psychology, 1*, 143–166.

Snowdon, D. A. (1997). Aging and Alzheimer's disease: Lessons from the Nun Study. *Gerontologist, 37*, 150–156.

Snowdon, D. A., Greiner, L. H., Mortimer, J. A., Riley, K. P., et al. (1997). Brain infarction and the clinical expression of Alzheimer's disease: The Nun Study. *Journal of the American Medical Association, 277*, 813–817.

Snowdon, D. A., Kemper, S. J., Mortimer, J. A., Greiner, L. H., Wekstein, D. R., & Markesbery, W. R. (1996). Linguistic ability in early life and cognitive function and Alzheimer's disease in late life: Findings from the Nun Study. *Journal of the American Medical Association, 275*, 528–532.

Snyder, C. R., Ilardi, S., Michael, S. T., & Cheavens, J. (2000). Hope theory: Updating a common process for psychological change. In C. R. Snyder & R. E. Ingram (Eds.), *Handbook of psychological change: Psychotherapy processes and practices for the 21st century* (pp. 128–153). New York: Wiley.

Sobal, J., & Stunkard, A. J. (1989). Socioeconomic status and obesity: A review of the literature. *Psychological Bulletin, 105*, 260–275.

Sobell, M. B., & Sobell, L. C. (1973). Individualized behavior therapy for alcoholics. *Behavior Therapy, 4*, 49–72.

Sobell, M. B., & Sobell, L. C. (1978). *Behavioral treatment of alcohol problems.* New York: Plenum Press.

Sobell, M. B., & Sobell, L. C. (1984). The aftermath of heresy: A response to Pendery et al.'s (1982) critique of "Individualized behavior therapy for alcoholics." *Behavior Research & Therapy, 22*, 413–440.

Sobell, M. B., & Sobell, L. C. (1995). Controlled drinking after 25 years: How important was the great debate? *Addiction, 90*, 1145–1153.

Soloff, P. H., Cornelius, J., George, A., Nathan, S., Perel, J. M., & Ulrich, R. F. (1993). Efficacy of phenelzine and haloperidol in borderline personality disorder. *Archives of General Psychiatry, 50*, 377–385.

Soloff, P. H., Meltzer, C. C., Greer, P. J., Constantine, D., & Kelly, T. M. (2000). A fenfluramine-activated FDG-PET study of borderline personality disorder. *Biological Psychiatry, 47*, 540–547.

Solomon, G. F., Segerstrom, S. C., Grohr, P., Kemeny, M., & Fahey, J. (1997). Shaking up immunity: Psychological and immunologic changes following a natural disaster. *Psychosomatic Medicine, 59*, 114–127.

Southwick, S. M., Vythilingam, M., & Charney, D. S. (2005). The psychobiology of depression and resilience to stress: Implications for prevention and treatment. *Annual Review of Clinical Psychology, 1*, 255–292.

Sowers, W. (1998). Psychological and psychiatric consequences of sedatives, hypnotics, and anxiolytics. In R. E. Tarter (Ed.), *Handbook of substance abuse: Neurobehavioral pharmacology* (pp. 471–483). New York: Plenum Press.

Spanos, N. P. (1978). Witchcraft in histories of psychiatry: A critical analysis and an alternative conceptualization. *Psychological Bulletin, 85*, 417–439.

Spanos, N. P., Weekes, J. R., & Bertrand, L. D. (1985). Multiple personality: A social psychological perspective. *Journal of Abnormal Psychology, 94*, 362–376.

Speckens, A. E., Hengeveld, M. W., Nijeholt, G. L., & Van Hemert, A. M. (1995). Psychosexual functioning of partners of men with presumed nonorganic erectile dysfunction: Causes or consequences of the disorder? *Archives of Sexual Behavior, 24*, 157–172.

Spector, I. P., & Carey, M. P. (1990). Incidence and prevalence of the sexual dysfunctions: A critical review of the empirical literature. *Archives of Sexual Behavior, 19*, 389–408.

Sperber, K., & Shao, L. (2003). Neurologic consequences of HIV infection in the era of HAART. *AIDS Patient Care & STDs, 17*, 509–518.

Spiegel, D. (1991). Dissociation and trauma. In A. Tasman (Ed.), *American Psychiatric Press review of psychiatry* (Vol. 10, pp. 261–275). Washington, DC: American Psychiatric Press.

Spiegel, D. (2001). Mind matters—Group therapy and survival in breast cancer. *New England Journal of Medicine, 345*, 1767–1768.

Spiegel, D., Bollm, J. R., Kraemer, H. C., & Gottheil, E. (1989). Psychological support for cancer patients. *Lancet, 2*, 1447.

Spiegel, D. A. (1998). Efficacy studies of alprazolam in panic disorder. *Psychopharmacology Bulletin, 43*, 191–195.

Spierings, C., Poels, P. J., Sijben, N., Gabreels, F. J., & Renier, W. O. (1990). Conversion disorders in childhood: A retrospective follow-up study of 84 inpatients. *Developmental Medicine & Child Neurology, 32*, 865–871.

Spirito, A. (2006). Attempted and completed suicide in adolescence. *Annual Review of Clinical Psychology, 2.*

Spitzer, R. L. (1981). The diagnostic status of homosexuality in DSM-III: A reformulation of the issues. *American Journal of Psychiatry, 138,* 210–215.

Spitzer, R. L., Gibbon, M., Skodol, A. E., Williams, J. B. W., & First, M. B. (Eds.). (1994). *DSM-IV case book: A learning companion to the* Diagnostic and Statistical Manual of Mental Disorders (4th ed.). Washington, DC: American Psychiatric Association Press.

Spitzer, R. L., Skodol, A. E., Gibbon, M., & Williams, J. B. W. (1981). *DSM-III case book: A learning companion to the* Diagnostic and Statistical Manual of Mental Disorders (3rd ed.). Washington, DC: American Psychiatric Association.

Spitzer, R. L., Skodol, A. E., Gibbon, M., & Williams, J. B. W. (1983). *Psychopathology, a case book.* New York: McGraw-Hill.

Spitzer, R. L., Williams, J. B. W., Gibbon, M., & First, M. (1992). The Structured Clinical Interview for DSM-III-R (SCID): I. History, rationale, and description. *Archives of General Psychiatry, 49,* 624–636.

Spivack, G., & Shure, M. B. (1974). *Social adjustment of young children: A cognitive approach to solving real-life problems.* San Francisco: Jossey-Bass.

Sprock, J. (2000). Gender-typed behavioral examples of histrionic personality disorder. *Journal of Psychopathology and Behavioral Assessment, 22,* 107–122.

Sprock, J., Blashfield, R. K., & Smith, B. (1990). Gender weighting of DSM-IIIR personality disorder criteria. *American Journal of Psychiatry, 147,* 586–590.

Stack, S. (1987). Celebrities and suicide: A taxonomy and analysis, 1948–1983. *American Sociological Review, 52,* 401–412.

Stack, S. (1991). Social correlates of suicide by age: Media impacts. In A. A. Leenaars (Ed.), *Life span perspectives of suicide* (pp. 187–213). New York: Plenum Press.

Stahl, S. M. (1998). Basic psychopharmacology of antidepressants: Part 1. Antidepressants have seven distinct mechanisms of action. *Journal of Clinical Psychiatry 59*(Suppl. 4), 5–14.

Stahl, S. M. (2001). Dopamine system stabilizers, aripiprazole, and the next generation of antipsychotics, Part II: Illustrating their mechanisms of action. *Journal of Clinical Psychiatry, 62,* 923–924.

Stanley, M. A., & Novy, D. M. (2000). Cognitive-behavior therapy for generalized anxiety late in life: An evaluation overview. *Journal of Anxiety Disorders, 14,* 191–207.

Stark, L. J., Opipari, L. C., Donaldson, D. L., Danovsky, M. B., Rasile, D. A., & DelSanto, A. F. (1997). Evaluation of a standard protocol for retentive encopresis: A replication. *Journal of Pediatric Psychology, 22,* 619–633.

Statham, D. J., Heath, A. C., Madden, P., Bucholz, K., Bierut, L., Dinwiddie, S. H., Slutske, W. S., Dunne, M. P., & Martin, N. G. (1998). Suicidal behavior: An epidemiological study. *Psychological Medicine, 28,* 839–855.

Steadman, H. J., McGreevy, M. A., Morrissey, J. P., Callahan, L. A., Robbins, P. C., & Cirincione, C. (1993). *Before and after Hinckley: Evaluating insanity defense reform.* New York: Guilford Press.

Steadman, H. J., Mulvey, E. P., Monahan, J., Robbins, P. C., Appelbaum, P. S., Grisso, T., Roth, L. H., & Silver, E. (1998). Violence by people discharged from acute psychiatric inpatient facilities and by others in the same neighborhoods. *Archives of General Psychiatry, 55,* 393–401.

Stein, B. D., Elliott, M. N., Jaycox, L. H., Collins, R. L., Berry, S. H., Klein, D. J., & Schuster, M. A. (2004). A national longitudinal study of the psychological consequences of the September 11, 2001 terrorist attacks: Reactions, impairments, and help-seeking. *Psychiatry, 67,* 105–117.

Steinberg, M. (1990). Transcultural issues in psychiatry: The ataque and multiple personality disorder. *Dissociation: Progress in the Dissociative Disorders, 3,* 31–33.

Steiner, M., Dunn, E., & Born, L. (2003). Hormones and mood: From menarche to menopause and beyond. *Journal of Affective Disorders, 74,* 67–83.

Steketee, G., & Frost, R. (2003). Compulsive hoarding: Current status of the research. *Clinical Psychology Review, 23,* 905–927.

Stephens, S., Kenny, R. A., Rowan, E., Allan, L., Kalaria, R. N., Bradbury, M., & Ballard, C. G. (2004). Neuropsychological characteristics of mild vascular cognitive impairment and dementia after stroke. *International Journal of Geriatric Psychiatry, 19,* 1053–1057.

Sterk, C. E. (1999). *Fast lives: Women who use crack cocaine.* Philadelphia: Temple University Press.

Stern, Y., Gurland, B., Tatemichi, T. K., & Tang, M. X. (1994). Influence of education and occupation on the incidence of Alzheimer's disease. *Journal of the American Medical Association, 271,* 1004–1010.

Sternberg, R. J. (2004). Culture and intelligence. *American Psychologist, 59,* 325–338.

Stewart, S. H. (1996). Alcohol abuse in individuals exposed to trauma: A critical review. *Psychological Bulletin, 120,* 83–112.

Stewart, W. F., Ricci, J. A., Chee, E., Hahn, S. R., & Morganstein, D. (2003). Cost of lost productive work time among US workers with depression. *Journal of the American Medical Association, 289,* 3135–3144.

St. George-Hyslop, P. H., Tanzi, R. E., Polinsky, R. J., Haines, J. L., Nee, L., Watkins, P. C., & Meyers, R. H. (1987). The genetic defect causing familial Alzheimer's disease maps on chromosome 21. *Science, 235,* 885–890.

Stice, E. (2001). A prospective test of the dual-pathway model of bulimic pathology: Mediating effects of dieting and negative affect. *Journal of Abnormal Psychology, 110,* 124–135.

Stice, E. (2002). Risk and maintenance factors for eating pathology: A meta-analytic review. *Psychological Bulletin, 128,* 825–848.

Stice, E. (2003). Puberty and body image. In C. Hayward (Ed.), *Gender differences at puberty* (pp. 61–76). New York: Cambridge University Press.

Stice, E., & Agras, W. S. (1998). Predicting the onset and remission of bulimic behaviors in adolescence: A longitudinal grouping analysis. *Behavior Therapy, 29,* 257–276.

Stice, E., Agras, W. S., Telch, C. F., Halmi, K. A., Mitchell, J. E., & Wilson, T. (2001). Subtyping binge eating–disordered women along dieting and negative affect dimensions. *International Journal of Eating Disorders, 30,* 11–27.

Stice, E., Burton, E. M., & Shaw, H. (2004). Prospective relations between bulimic pathology, depression, and substance abuse: Unpacking comorbidity in adolescent girls. *Journal of Consulting & Clinical Psychology, 72,* 62–71.

Stice, E., Chase, A., Stormer, S., & Appel, A. (2001). A randomized trial of a dissonance-based eating disorder prevention program. *International Journal of Eating Disorders, 29,* 247–262.

Stice, E., & Fairburn, C. G. (2003). Dietary and dietary-depressive subtypes of bulimia nervosa show differential symptom presentation, social impairment, comorbidity, and course of illness. *Journal of Consulting & Clinical Psychology, 71,* 1090–1094.

Stice, E., Maxfield, J., & Wells, T. (2003). Adverse effects of social pressure to be thin on young women: An experimental investigation of the effects of "fat talk." *International Journal of Eating Disorders, 34,* 108–117.

Stice, E., Mazotti, L., Weibel, D., & Agras, W. S. (2000). Dissonance prevention program decreases thin-ideal internalization, body dissatisfaction, dieting, negative affect, and bulimic symptoms: A preliminary experiment. *International Journal of Eating Disorders, 27,* 206–217.

Stice, E., Presnell, K., & Spangler, D. (2002). Risk factors for binge eating onset in adolescent girls: A 2-year prospective investigation. *Health Psychology, 21,* 131–138.

Stice, E., & Shaw, H. E. (1994). Adverse effects of the media-portrayed thin-ideal on women and linkages to bulimic symptomatology. *Journal of Social & Clinical Psychology, 13,* 288–308.

Stice, E., Spangler, D., & Agras, W. S. (2001). Exposure to media-portrayed thin-ideal images adversely affects vulnerable girls: A longitudinal experiment. *Journal of Social & Clinical Psychology, 20,* 270–288.

Stocchi, F., Nordera, G., Jokinen, R., et al. (2001, May). *Efficacy and tolerability of paroxetine for long-term treatment of GAD.* Paper presented at 154th annual APA meeting, New Orleans.

Stoller, R. F. (1975). *Perversion: The erotic form of hatred.* New York: Pantheon Books.

Stoney, C. M. (2003). Gender and cardiovascular disease: A psychobiological and integrative approach. *Current Directions in Psychological Science, 12,* 129–133.

Stormer, S. M., & Thompson, J. K. (1998, November). *Challenging media messages regarding appearance: A psychoeducational program for males and females.* Paper presented at the annual meeting of the Association for the Advancement of Behavior Therapy, Washington, DC.

Storr, A. (1988). *Churchill's black dog, Kafka's mice, and other phenomena of the human mind.* New York: Grove Press.

Stouthamer-Loeber, M., Loeber, R., Homish, D. L., & Wei, E. (2001). Maltreatment of boys and the development of disruptive and delinquent behavior. *Development & Psychopathology, 13,* 941–955.

Straus, M. A., & Gelles, R. J. (1990). *Physical violence in American families: Risk factors and adaptations to violence in 8,145 families.* New Brunswick, NJ: Transaction.

Strauss, J. S. (1969). Hallucinations and delusions as points on continua function: Rating scale evidence. *Archives of General Psychiatry, 21,* 581–586.

Stravynski, A., Marks, I., & Yule, W. (1982). Social skills problems in neurotic outpatients: Social skills training with and without cognitive modification. *Archives of General Psychiatry, 39,* 1378–1385.

Streissguth, A. P., Barr, H. M., Bookstein, F. L., Sampson, P. D., & Olson, H. C. (1999). The long-term neurocognitive consequences of prenatal alcohol exposure: A 14-year study. *Psychological Science, 10,* 186–190.

Striegel-Moore, R. (1995). Psychological factors in the etiology of binge eating. *Addictive Behaviors, 20,* 713–723.

Striegel-Moore, R., Wilson, G. T., Wilfley, D. E., Elder, K. A., & Brownell, K. D. (1998). Binge eating in an obese community sample. *International Journal of Eating Disorders, 23,* 27–37.

Striegel-Moore, R. H. (1993). Etiology of binge eating: A developmental perspective. In C. G. Fairburn & G. T. Wilson (Eds.), *Binge eating: Nature, assessment, and treatment* (pp. 144–172). New York: Guilford Press.

Striegel-Moore, R. H., Dohm, F. A., Kraemer, H. C., Taylor, C. B., Daniels, S., Crawford, P. B., & Schreiber, G. B. (2003). Eating disorders in white and black women. *American Journal of Psychiatry, 160,* 1326–1331.

Striegel-Moore, R. H., & Franko, D. L. (2003). Epidemiology of binge eating disorder. *International Journal of Eating Disorders, 34*(Suppl. 1), 19–29.

Striegel-Moore, R. H., Seeley, J. R., & Lewinsohn, P. M. (2003). Psychosocial adjustment in young adulthood of women who experienced an eating disorder during adolescence. *Journal of the American Academy of Child & Adolescent Psychiatry, 42,* 587–593.

Striegel-Moore, R. H., Silberstein, L. R., & Rodin, J. (1993). The social self in bulimia nervosa: Public self-consciousness, social anxiety, and perceived fraudulence. *Journal of Abnormal Psychology, 102,* 297–303.

Stroebe, M., Gergen, M., Gergen, K., & Stroebe, W. (1992). Broken hearts or broken bonds: Love and death in historical perspective. *American Psychologist, 47,* 1205–1212.

Study Group on Anorexia Nervosa. (1995). Anorexia nervosa: Directions for future research. *International Journal of Eating Disorders, 17,* 235–241.

Stunkard, A. (1997). Eating disorders: The last 25 years. *Appetite, 29,* 181–190.

Stunkard, A. J. (1993). A history of binge eating. In C. G. Fairburn & G. T. Wilson (Eds.), *Binge eating: Nature, assessment, and treatment* (pp. 15–34). New York: Guilford Press.

Styron, W. (1990). *Darkness visible: A memoir of madness.* New York: Vintage Books.

Substance Abuse and Mental Health Services Administration (SAMHSA). (2002a). National household survey on drug abuse.

Retrieved November 1, 2004, from http://dawninfo.samhsa.gov/

Substance Abuse and Mental Health Services Administration (SAMHSA). (2002b). National survey on drug use and health. Retrieved November 1, 2004, from http://www.oas.samhsa.gov/nhsda2k2.htm

Substance Abuse and Mental Health Services Administration (SAMHSA). (2005). Overview of findings from the 2003 national survey on drug use and health. Retrieved November 1, 2004, from http://www.oas.samhsa.gov/nhsda/2k3nsduh/2k3Overview.htm

Suddath, R. L., Christison, G. W., Torrey, E. F., & Casanova, M. F. (1990). Anatomical abnormalities in the brains of monozygotic twins discordant for schizophrenia. *New England Journal of Medicine, 322,* 789–794.

Sudhansu, C., Hening, W. A., & Walters, A. S. (2003). *Sleep and movement disorders.* Burlington, MA: Butterworth-Heinemann.

Sue, D. W., Carter, R. T., Casas, J. M., Fouad, N. A., Ivey, A. E., Jensen, M., LaFromboise, T., Manese, J. E., Ponterotto, J. G., & Vazquez-Nutall, E. (1998). *Multicultural counseling competencies: Individual and organizational development.* Thousand Oaks, CA: Sage.

Sue, D. W., & Sue, D. (2003). *Counseling the culturally diverse: Theory and practice* (4th ed.). New York: Wiley.

Sue, S., & Lam, A. G. (2002). Cultural and demographic diversity. In J. C. Norcross (Ed.), *Psychotherapy relationships that work: Therapist contributions and responsiveness to patients* (pp. 401–421). London: Oxford University Press.

Sue, S., & Zane, N. (1987). The role of culture and cultural techniques in psychotherapy: A critique and reformulation. *American Psychologist, 42,* 37–51.

Suhail, K., & Cochrane, R. (2002). Effect of culture and environment on the phenomenology of delusions and hallucinations. *International Journal of Social Psychiatry, 48,* 126–138.

Suhara, T., Okubo, Y., Yasuno, F., Sudo, Y., Inoue, M., Ichimiya, T., Nakashima, Y., Nakayama, K., Tanada, S., Suzuki, K., Halldin, C., & Farde, L. (2002). Decreased dopamine D2 receptor binding in the anterior cingulated cortex in schizophrenia. *Archives of General Psychiatry, 59,* 25–30.

Sullivan, H. S. (1953). *The interpersonal theory of psychiatry.* New York: W. W. Norton.

Sullivan, P. F., Bulik, C. M., Fear, J. L., & Pickering, A. (1998). Outcome of anorexia nervosa: A case-control study. *American Journal of Psychiatry, 155,* 939–946.

Summers, M. (2000). *Everything in its place.* New York: Putnam.

Sundgot-Borgen, J. (1994). Risk and trigger factors for the development of eating disorders in female elite athletes. *Medicine & Science in Sports & Exercise, 26,* 414–419.

Suomi, S. J. (1999). Developmental trajectories, early experiences, and community consequences: Lessons from studies with rhesus monkeys. In D. P. Keating (Ed.), *Developmental health and the wealth of nations: Social, biological, and educational dynamics* (pp. 185–200). New York: Guilford Press.

Sutker, P. B., Allain, A. N., & Winstead, D. K. (1993). Psychopathology and psychiatric diagnoses of World War II Pacific theater prisoners of war and combat veterans. *American Journal of Psychiatry, 150,* 240–245.

Sutker, P. B., Davis, J. M., Uddo, M., & Ditta, S. R. (1995). Assessment of psychological distress in Persian Gulf troops: Ethnicity and gender comparisons. *Journal of Personality Assessment, 64,* 415–427.

Sutker, P. B., Winstead, D. K., Galina, Z. H., & Allain, A. N. (1991). Cognitive deficits and psychopathology among former prisoners of war and combat veterans of the Korean conflict. *American Journal of Psychiatry, 148,* 67–72.

Swartz, H. A., & Frank, E. (2001). Psychotherapy for bipolar depression: A phase-specific treatment strategy? *Bipolar Disorders, 3,* 11–12.

Swartz, M., Blazer, D., George, L., & Winfield, I. (1990). Estimating the prevalence of borderline personality disorder in the community. *Journal of Personality Disorders, 4,* 257–272.

Swazey, J. P. (1974). *Chlorpromazine in psychiatry: A study of therapeutic innovation.* Cambridge, MA: MIT Press.

Swendsen, J. D., Merikangas, K. R., Canino, G. J., Kessler, R. C., Rubio-Stipec, M., & Angst, J. (1998). The comorbidity of alcoholism with anxiety and depressive disorders in four geographic communities. *Comprehensive Psychiatry, 39,* 176–184.

Szasz, T. (1961). *The myth of mental illness.* New York: Hoeber-Harper.

Szasz, T. S. (1963a). *Law, liberty, and psychiatry: An inquiry into the social uses of mental health practice.* New York: Collier Books.

Szasz, T. S. (1963b). *The manufacture of madness.* New York: Harper & Row.

Szasz, T. S. (1971). The sane slave: An historical note on the use of medical diagnosis as justificatory rhetoric. *American Journal of Psychotherapy, 25,* 228–239.

Szasz, T. S. (1977). *Psychiatric slavery.* New York: Free Press.

Szatmari, P., Bartolucci, G., Bremner, R., & Bond, S. (1989). A follow-up study of high-functioning autistic children. *Journal of Autism & Developmental Disorders, 19,* 213–225.

Szatmari, P., Jones, M. B., Zwaigenbaum, L., & MacLean, J. E. (1998). Genetics of autism: Overview and new directions. *Journal of Autism & Developmental Disorders, 28,* 351–368.

T

Tager-Flusberg, H., Joseph, R., & Folstein, S. (2001). Current directions in research on autism. *Mental Retardation & Developmental Disabilities Research Review, 7,* 21–19.

Takahashi, Y. (1990). Is multiple personality disorder really rare in Japan? *Dissociation: Progress in the Dissociative Disorders, 3,* 57–59.

Takei, N., Sham, P. C., O'Callaghan, E., & Murray, R. M. (1992). Cities, winter birth, and schizophrenia. *Lancet, 340,* 558–559.

Takei, N., Sham, P. C., O'Callaghan, R., Glover, G., et al. (1995). Early risk factors in schizophrenia: Place and season of birth. *European Psychiatry, 10,* 165–170.

Tanay, E. (1992). The verdict with two names. *Psychiatric Annals, 22*, 571–573.

Tariot, P. N. (2003). Alzheimer disease: Current challenges, emerging treatments. *Alzheimer Disease & Associated Disorders, 17*(Suppl. 4), 98.

Tarrier, N., Pilgrim, H., Sommerfield, C., Faragher, B., Reynolds, M., Graham, E., & Barrowclough, C. (1999). A randomized trial of cognitive therapy and imaginal exposure in the treatment of chronic posttraumatic stress disorder. *Journal of Consulting & Clinical Psychology, 67*, 13–18.

Tateyama, M., Asai, M., Hashimoto, M., Bartels, M., & Kasper, S. (1998). Transcultural study of schizophrenic delusions: Tokyo versus Vienna versus Tuebingen (Germany). *Psychopathology, 31*, 59–68.

Tateyama, M., Asai, M., Kamisada, M., Hashimoto, M., Bartels, M., & Heimann, H. (1993). Comparison of schizophrenia delusions between Japan and Germany. *Psychopathology, 26*, 151–158.

Taylor, J., Iacono, W. G., & McGue, M. (2000). Evidence for a genetic etiology of early-onset delinquency. *Journal of Abnormal Psychology, 109*, 634–643.

Taylor, R. (1982). *Robert Schumann: His life and work.* London: Granada.

Taylor, S., Fedoroff, I., Koch, W. J., Thordarson, D. S., Fecteau, G., & Nicki, R. M. (2001). Posttraumatic stress disorder arising after road traffic collisions: Patterns of response to cognitive-behavior therapy. *Journal of Consulting & Clinical Psychology, 69*, 541–551.

Taylor, S. E. (1999). *Health psychology.* New York: McGraw-Hill.

Taylor, S. E., & Brown, J. D. (1988). Illusion and well-being: A social psychological perspective on mental health. *Psychological Bulletin, 103*, 193–210.

Taylor, S. E., Kemeny, M. E., Aspinwall, L. G., & Schneider, S. G. (1992). Optimism, coping, psychological distress, and high-risk sexual behavior among men at risk for acquired immunodeficiency syndrome (AIDS). *Journal of Personality & Social Psychology, 63*, 460–473.

Taylor, S. E., Klein, L. C., Lewis, B. P., Gruenwald, T. L., Gurung, R. A. R., & Updegraff, J. A. (2000). Biobehavioral responses to stress in females: Tend-and-befriend, not fight-or-flight. *Psychological Review, 3*, 411–429.

Tebartz van Elst, L., Hesslinger, B., Thiel, T., Geiger, E., Haegele, K., Lemieux, L., Lieb, K., Bohus, M., Hennig, J., & Ebert, J. (2003). Frontolimbic brain abnormalities in patients with borderline personality disorder: A volumetric magnetic resonance imaging study. *Biological Psychiatry, 54*, 163–171.

Telch, C. F., Agras, W. S., & Linehan, M. M. (2001). Dialectical behavior therapy for binge eating disorder. *Journal of Consulting & Clinical Psychology, 69*, 1061–1065.

Telch, C. F., & Stice, E. (1998). Psychiatric comorbidity in women with binge eating disorder: Prevalence rates from a non-treatment-seeking sample. *Journal of Consulting & Clinical Psychology, 66*, 768–776.

Telch, M. J., Lucas, J. A., Schmidt, N. B., Hanna, H. H., LaNae, J. T., & Lucas, R. A. (1993). Group cognitive-behavioral treatment

of panic disorder. *Behaviour Research & Therapy, 31*, 279–287.

Telles, C., Karno, M., Mintz, J., Paz, G., Arias, M., Tucker, D., & Lopez, S. (1995). Immigrant families coping with schizophrenia. *British Journal of Psychiatry, 167*, 473–479.

Temple, N. (2001). Psychodynamic psychotherapy in the treatment of conversion hysteria. In P. W. Halligan, C. Bass, & J. Marshall (Eds.), *Contemporary approaches to the study of hysteria: Clinical and theoretical perspectives* (pp. 283–297). Oxford, UK: Oxford University Press.

Teplin, L. A. (1990). The prevalence of severe mental disorder among male urban jail detainers: Comparison with the Epidemiologic Catchment Area program. *American Journal of Public Health, 80*, 663–669.

Teplin, L. A., Abram, K. M., & McClelland, G. M. (1996). Prevalence of psychiatric disorders among incarcerated women. I. Pretrial jail detainees. *Archives of General Psychiatry, 53*, 505–512.

Teplin, L. A., Abram, K. M., & McClelland, G. M. (1997). Mentally disordered women in jail: Who receives services? *American Journal of Public Health, 87*, 604–609.

Teri, L., Gibbons, L. E., McCurry, S. M., Logsdon, R. G., Buchner, D. M., Barlow, W. E., Kukull, W. A., LaCroix, A. Z., McCormick, W., & Larson, E. B. (2003). Exercise plus behavioral management in patients with Alzheimer disease: A randomized controlled trial. *Journal of the American Medical Association, 290*, 2015–2022.

Terr, L. C. (1981). Psychic trauma in children: Observations following the Chowchilla school-bus kidnapping. *American Journal of Psychiatry, 138*, 14–19.

Test, M. A., & Stein, L. I. (1980). Alternative to mental hospital treatment: III. Social cost. *Archives of General Psychiatry, 37*, 409–412.

Teyber, E., & McClure, F. (2000). Therapist variables. In C. R. Snyder & R. E. Ingram (Eds.), *Handbook of psychological change: Psychotherapy processes and practices for the 21st century* (pp. 62–87). New York: Wiley.

Tharp, R. G. (1991). Cultural diversity and treatment of children. *Journal of Consulting & Clinical Psychology, 59*, 799–812.

Thase, M. E., Greenhouse, J. B., Frank, E., Reynolds, C. F., III, Pilkonis, P. A., Hurley, K., Grochocinski, V., & Kupfer, D. J. (1997). Treatment of major depression with psychotherapy or psychotherapy-pharmacotherapy combinations. *Archives of General Psychiatry, 54*, 1009–1015.

Thase, M. E., Jindal, R., & Howland, R. H. (2002). Biological aspects of depression. In I. H. Gotlib & C. L. Hammen (Eds.), *Handbook of depression* (pp. 192–218). New York: Guilford Press.

Thermenos, H. W., Seidman, L. J., Breiter, H., Goldstein, J. M., Goodman, J. M., Poldrack, R., Faraone, S. V., & Tsuang, M. T. (2004). Functional magnetic resonance imaging during auditory verbal working memory in nonpsychotic relatives of persons with schizophrenia: A pilot study. *Biological Psychiatry, 55*, 490–500.

Thienemann, M. (2004). Medications for pediatric anxiety. In H. Steiner (Ed.), *Handbook of mental health intervention in*

children and adolescents: An integrated developmental approach* (pp. 288–317). San Francisco: Jossey-Bass.

Thomas, A., & Chess, S. (1984). Genesis and evolution of behavioral disorders: From infancy to early adult life. *American Journal of Psychiatry, 141*, 1–9.

Thompson, J. K., Heinberg, L. J., Altabe, M. N., & Tantleff-Dunn, S. (1999). *Exacting beauty: Theory, assessment and treatment of body image disturbance.* Washington, DC: American Psychological Association.

Thompson, J. K., & Stice, E. (2001). Thin ideal internalization: Mounting evidence for a new risk factor for body image disturbance and eating pathology. *Current Directions in Psychological Science, 10*, 181–183.

Thompson, L. W., Coon, D. W., Gallagher-Thompson, D., Sommer, B., & Koin, D. (2001). Comparison of desipramine and cognitive/behavioral therapy in the treatment of late-life depression. *American Journal of Geriatric Psychiatry, 9*, 225–240.

Thoresen, C. E., Telch, M. J., & Eagleston, J. R. (1981). Altering Type A behavior. *Psychosomatics, 8*, 472–482.

Thorpe, G. L., & Olson, S. L. (1997). *Behavior therapy: Concepts, procedures, and applications* (2nd ed.). Boston: Allyn & Bacon.

Tienari, P. (1991). Interaction between genetic vulnerability and family environment: The Finnish adoptive family study of schizophrenia. *Acta Psychiatrica Scandinavica, 84*, 460–465

Tienari, P., Wynne, L. C., Laksy, K., Moring, J., Nieminen, P., Sorri, A., Lahti, I., & Wahlberg, K.-E. (2003). Genetic boundaries of the schizophrenia spectrum: Evidence from the Finnish Adoptive Family Study of Schizophrenia. *American Journal of Psychiatry, 160*, 1587–1594.

Tiet, Q. Q., Wasserman, G. A., Loeber, R., McReynolds, L. S., & Miller, L. S. (2001). Developmental and sex differences in types of conduct problems. *Journal of Child & Family Studies, 10*, 181–197.

Tillich, P. (1952). Anxiety, religion, and medicine. *Pastoral Psychology, 3*, 11–17.

Tolan, P. H., & Gorman-Smith, D. (1997). Treatment of juvenile delinquency: Between punishment and therapy. In D. M. Stoff, J. Breiling, & J. D. Maser (Eds.), *Handbook of antisocial personality disorder* (pp. 405–415). New York: Wiley.

Tondo, L., Baldessarini, R. J., Floris, G., & Rudas, N. (1997). Effectiveness of restarting lithium treatment after its discontinuation in bipolar I and bipolar II disorders. *American Journal of Psychiatry, 154*, 548–550.

Tondo, L., Jamison, K. R., & Baldessarini, R. J. (1997). Effect of lithium maintenance on suicidal behavior in major mood disorders. *Annals of the New York Academy of Sciences, 836*, 339–351.

Torrey, E. F. (1995). *Surviving schizophrenia: A manual for families, consumers, and providers* (3rd ed.). New York: HarperPerennial.

Torrey, E. F. (1997). *Out of the shadows: Confronting America's mental illness crisis.* New York: Wiley.

Torrey, E. F., Bowler, A. E., & Clark, K. (1997). Urban birth and residence as risk factors for psychosis: An analysis of 1880 data. *Schizophrenia Research, 25*, 169–176.

Torrey, E. F., & Yolken, R. H. (1998). At issue: Is household crowding a risk factor for schizophrenia and bipolar disorder? *Schizophrenia Bulletin, 24,* 321–324.

Torti, F. M., Jr., Gwyther, L. P., Reed, S. D., Friedman, J. Y., & Schulman, K. A. (2004). A multinational review of recent trends and reports in dementia caregiver burden. *Alzheimer Disease & Associated Disorders, 18,* 99–109.

Toufexis, A. (1996, April 29). Why Jennifer got sick. *Time,* p. 70.

Treatment for Adolescents with Depression Study (TADS) Team. (2004). Fluoxetine, cognitive-behavioral therapy, and their combination for adolescents with depression: Treatment for adolescents with depression study (TADS) randomized controlled trial. *Journal of the American Medical Association, 292,* 807–820.

Trierweiler, S. J., & Stricker, G. (1998). *The scientific practice of professional psychology.* New York: Plenum Press.

Trinh, N.-H., Hoblyn, J., Mohanty, S., & Yaffe, K. (2003). Efficacy of cholinesterase inhibitors in the treatment of neuropsychiatric symptoms and functional impairment in Alzheimer disease: A meta-analysis. *Journal of the American Medical Association, 289,* 210–216.

Tronick, E. Z., Frank, D. A., Cabral, H., Mirochnick, M., & Zuckerman, B. (1996). Late dose-response effects of prenatal cocaine exposure on newborn neurobehavioral performance. *Pediatrics, 98,* 76–83.

True, W. R., Rice, J., Eisen, S. A., Heath, A. C., Goldberg, J., Lyons, M. J., & Nowak, J. (1993). A twin study of genetic and environmental contributions to liability for posttraumatic stress symptoms. *Archives of General Psychiatry, 50,* 257–264.

Trull, T. J., & Durrett, C. A. (2005). Categorical and dimensional models of personality disorder. In S. Nolen-Hoeksema, T. D. Cannon, & T. A. Widiger (Eds.), *Annual review of clinical psychology* (Vol. 1, pp. 355–380). Palo Alto, CA: Annual Reviews.

Trull, T. J., Waudby, C. J., & Sher, K. J. (2004). Alcohol, tobacco, and drug use disorders and personality disorder symptoms. *Experimental & Clinical Psychopharmacology, 12,* 65–75.

Tsai, G., & Coyle, J. T. (2002). Glutamatergic mechanisms in schizophrenia. *Annual Review of Pharmacological Toxicology, 42,* 165–179.

Tsai, J. L., Butcher, J. N., Munoz, R. F., & Vitousek, K. (2001). Culture, ethnicity, and psychopathology. In P. B. Sutker (Ed.), *Comprehensive handbook of psychopathology* (3rd ed., pp. 105–127). New York: Kluwer Academic/Plenum Publishers.

Tsai, J. L., & Chentsova-Dutton, Y. (2002). Understanding depression across cultures. In I. H. Gotlib & C. L. Hammen (Eds.), *Handbook of depression* (pp. 467–491). New York: Guilford Press.

Tseng, W. (1973). The development of psychiatric concepts in traditional Chinese medicine. *Archives of General Psychiatry, 29,* 569–575.

Tseng, W.-S. (2001). *Culture and psychotherapy: A guide to clinical practice.* Washington, DC: American Psychiatric Press.

Tsuang, M. T., Fleming, J. A., & Simpson, J. C. (1999). Suicide and schizophrenia. In D. G. Jacobs (Ed.), *The Harvard Medical School guide to suicide assessment and intervention* (pp. 287–299). San Francisco: Jossey-Bass.

Tsuang, M. T., Lyons, M. J., Meyer, J. M., Doyle, T., Eisen, S. A., Goldberg, J., True, W., Lin, N., Toomey, R., & Eaves, L. (1998). Co-occurrence of abuse of different drugs in men: The role of drug-specific and shared vulnerabilities. *Archives of General Psychiatry, 55,* 967–972.

Tugrul, C., & Kabakci, E. (1997). Vaginismus and its correlates. *Sexual & Marital Therapy, 12,* 23–34.

Tuma, J. M. (1989). Mental health services for children: The state of the art. *American Psychologist, 44,* 188–199.

Turk, C. L., Heimberg, R. G., & Hope, D. A. (2001). Social anxiety disorder. *Clinical handbook of psychological disorders: A step-by-step treatment manual* (3rd ed., pp. 114–153). New York: Guilford Press.

Turk, D. C., Meichenbaum, D. H., & Berman, W. H. (1979). Application of biofeedback for the regulation of pain: A critical review. *Psychological Bulletin, 86,* 1322–1338.

Turk, D. C., & Ruby, T. E. (1992). Cognitive factors and persistent pain: A glimpse into Pandora's box. *Cognitive Therapy & Research, 16,* 99–122.

Turkat, I. D. (1985). *Behavioral case formulation.* New York: Plenum Press.

Turkheimer, E., & Parry, C. D. (1992). Why the gap? Practice and policy in civil commitment hearings. *American Psychologist, 47,* 646–655.

Turnbull, J. E., & Gomberg, E. S. (1990). The structure of depression in alcoholic women. *Journal of Studies on Alcohol, 51,* 148–155.

Turner, R. J., & Lloyd, D. A. (2004). Stress burden and the lifetime incidence of psychiatric disorder in young adults: Racial and ethnic contrasts. *Archives of General Psychiatry, 61,* 481–488.

Turner, S. M., Beidel, D. C., & Wolff, P. L. (1996). Is behavioral inhibition related to the anxiety disorders? *Clinical Psychology Review, 16*(2) 157–172.

Turner-Cobb, J. M., Sephton, S. E., Koopman, C., Blake-Mortimer, J., & Spiegel, D. (2000). Social support and salivary cortisol in women with metastatic breast cancer. *Psychosomatic Medicine, 62,* 337–345.

Twenge, J. M., & Nolen-Hoeksema, S. (2002) Age, gender, race, SES, and birth cohort differences on the Children's Depression Inventory: A meta-analysis. *Journal of Abnormal Psychology, 111,* 578–588.

U

Ullman, L. P., & Krasner, L. (1975). *A psychological approach to abnormal behavior* (2nd ed.). Oxford, UK: Prentice Hall.

Unützer, J., Patrick, D. L., Diehr, P., Simon, G., Grembowski, D., & Katon, W. (2000). Quality adjusted life years in older adults with depressive symptoms and chronic medical disorders. *International Psychogeriatrics, 12,* 15–33.

U.S. Department of Health and Human Services (USDHHS). (1999). *Mental health: A report of the surgeon general—Executive summary.* Rockville, MD: U.S. Department of Health and Human Services, Substance Abuse and Mental Health Services Administration, Center for Mental Health Services, National Institutes of Health, National Institute of Mental Health.

U.S. Department of Health and Human Services (USDHHS). (2001). *Mental health: Culture, race, and ethnicity. A supplement to mental health: A report of the surgeon general.* Rockville, MD: U.S. Department of Health and Human Services, Public Health Services, Office of the Surgeon General.

Uva, J. L. (1995). Review: Autoerotic asphyxiation in the United States. *Journal of Forensic Sciences, 40,* 574–581.

V

Vakoch, D. A., & Strupp, H. H. (2000). Psychodynamic approaches to psychotherapy: Philosophical and theoretical foundations of effective practice. In C. R. Snyder & R. E. Ingram (Eds.), *Handbook of psychological change: Psychotherapy processes and practices for the 21st century* (pp. 200–216). New York: Wiley.

Valenstein, E. S. (1986). *Great and desperate cures: The rise and decline of psychosurgery and other radical treatments for mental illness.* New York: Basic Books.

Valenstein, R. S. (1998). *Blaming the brain: The truth about drugs and mental health.* New York: Free Press.

Van Ameringen, M. A., Lane, R. M., Walker, J. R., Bowen, R. C., Chokka, P. R., Goldner, E. M., Johnston, D. G., Lavallee, Y., Nandy, S., Pecknold, J. C., Hadrava, V., & Swinson, R. P. (2001). Sertraline treatment of generalized social phobia: A 20-week, double-blind, placebo-controlled study. *American Journal of Psychiatry, 158*(2), 275–281.

Van Etten, M. L., & Anthony, J. C. (2001). Male-female differences in transitions from first drug opportunity to first use: Searching for subgroup variation by age, race, region, and urban status. *Journal of Women's Health & Gender-Based Medicine, 10,* 797–804.

van Gorp, W. G., Altshuler, L., Theberge, D. C., Wilkins, J., & Dixon, W. (1998). Cognitive impairment in euthymic bipolar patients with and without prior alcohol dependence: A preliminary study. *Archives of General Psychiatry, 55,* 41–46.

Van Heeringen, C. (2001). Suicide in adolescents. *International Clinical Psychopharmacology, 16*(Suppl. 2), S1–S6.

Van Hemert, A. M., Hengeveld, M. W., Bolk, J. H., & Rooijmans, H. G. (1993). Psychiatric disorders in relation to medical illness among patients of a general medical outpatient clinic. *Psychological Medicine, 23,* 167–173.

van Ommeren, M., De Jong, J. T. V. M., Bhogendra, S., Komproe, I., Thapa, S. B., & Cardena, E. (2001). Psychiatric disorders among tortured Bhutanese refugees in Nepal. *Archives of General Psychiatry, 58,* 475–482.

van Os, J., Hanssen, M., Bijl, R. V., & Vollebergh, W. (2001). Prevalence of psychotic disorder and community level of psychotic symptoms. *Archives of General Psychiatry, 58,* 663–668.

van Velzen, C. J. M., Emmelkamp, P. M. G., & Scholing, A. (2000). Generalized social phobia versus avoidant personality disorder: Differences in psychopathology, personality traits, and social and occupational functioning. *Journal of Anxiety Disorders, 14,* 395–411.

Vaughn, C. E., & Leff, J. P. (1976). The influence of family and social factors on the course of psychiatric illness: A comparison of schizophrenic and depressed neurotic patients. *British Journal of Psychiatry, 129,* 125–137.

Vazquez-Nuttall, E., Avila-Vivas, Z., & Morales-Barreto, G. (1984). Working with Latin American families. *Family Therapy Collections, 9,* 74–90.

Vazquez-Nuttall, E., Romero-Garcia, I., & DeLeon, R. (1987). Sex roles and perceptions of femininity and masculinity of Hispanic women: A review of the literature. *Psychology of Women Quarterly, 11,* 409–425.

Veith, I. (1965). *Hysteria: The history of a disease.* Chicago: University of Chicago Press.

Velting, O. N., Setzer, N. J., & Albano, A. M. (2004). Update on and advances in assessment and cognitive-behavioral treatment of anxiety disorders in children and adolescents. *Professional Psychology: Research & Practice, 35,* 42–54.

Ventura, J., Neuchterlein, K. H., Lukoff, D., & Hardesty, J. P. (1989). A prospective study of stressful life events and schizophrenic relapse. *Journal of Abnormal Psychology, 98,* 407–411.

Verhulst, J., & Heiman, J. (1988). A systems perspective on sexual desire. In S. R. Leiblum & R. C. Rosen (Eds.), *Sexual desire disorders* (pp. 243–270). New York: Guilford Press.

Verma, K. K., Khaitan, B. K., & Singh, O. P. (1998). The frequency of sexual dysfunctions in patients attending a sex therapy clinic in north India. *Archives of Sexual Behavior, 27,* 309–314.

Verona, E., Patrick, C. J., Joiner, T. E. (2001). Psychopathy, antisocial personality, and suicide risk. *Journal of Abnormal Psychology, 110,* 462–470.

Veronen, L. J., & Kilpatrick, D. G. (1983). Stress management for rape victims. In D. Meichenbaum & M. E. Jaremko (Eds.), *Stress reduction and prevention.* New York: Plenum Press.

Viken, R. J., Treat, T. A., Nosofsky, R. M., McFall, R. M., & Palmeri, T. J. (2002). Modeling individual differences in perceptual and attentional processes. *Journal of Abnormal Psychology, 111,* 598–609.

Villarreal, G., Hamilton, D. A., Petropoulos, H., Driscoll, I., Rowland, L. M., Griego, J. A., Kodituwakku, P. W., Hart, B. L., Escalona, R., & Brooks, W. M. (2002). Reduced hippocampal volume and total white matter volume in posttraumatic stress disorder. *Biological Psychiatry, 52,* 119–125.

Visintainer, M. A., Volpicelli, J. R., & Seligman, M. E. (1982). Tumor rejection in rats after inescapable or escapable shock. *Science, 216,* 437–439.

Vohs, K. D., Bardone, A. M., Joiner, T. E., Jr., & Abramson, L. Y. (1999). Perfectionism, perceived weight status, and self-esteem interact to predict bulimic symptoms: A model of bulimic symptom development. *Journal of Abnormal Psychology, 108,* 695–700.

Vohs, K. D., Voelz, Z. R., Pettit, J. W., Bardone, A. M., Katz, J., Abramson, L. Y., Heatherton, T. F., & Joiner, T. E. (2001). Perfectionism, body dissatisfaction, and self-esteem: An interactive model of bulimic symptom development. *Journal of Social & Clinical Psychology, 20,* 476–497.

Volkmar, F. G. (2001). Pharmacological intervention in autism: Theoretical and practical issues. *Journal of Clinical Child Psychology, 30,* 80–87.

Volkmar, F. R., Lord, C., Bailey, A., Schultz, R. T., & Klin, A. (2004). Autism and pervasive developmental disorders. *Journal of Child Psychology and Psychiatry, 45,* 135–170.

Volpicelli, J. R. (2001). Alcohol abuse and alcoholism: An overview. *Journal of Clinical Psychiatry, 62*(Suppl. 20), 4–10.

Volpicelli, J. R., Rhines, K. C., Rhines, J. S., Volpicelli, L. A., Alterman, A. I., & O'Brien, C. P. (1997). Naltrexone and alcohol dependence: Role of subject compliance. *Archives of General Psychiatry, 54,* 737–742.

Volz, H.-P., & Kieser, M. (1997). Kavakava extract WS 1490 versus placebo in anxiety disorders: A randomized placebo-controlled 25-week outpatient trial. *Pharmacopsychiatry, 30,* 1–5.

von Buhler, J. M. (1998). Vacuum and constriction devices for erectile disorder—An integrative view. *Sexual & Marital Therapy, 13,* 257–276.

Von Korff, M., Nestadt, G., Romanoski, A., Anthony, J., Eaton, W., Merchant, A., Chahal, R., Kramer, M., Folstein, M., & Gruenberg, E. (1985). Prevalence of treated and untreated DSMIII schizophrenia: Results of a two-stage community survey. *Journal of Nervous & Mental Disease, 173,* 577–581.

Vuilleumier, P., Chicherio, C., Assal, F., Schwartz, S., Slosmen, D., & Landis, T. (2001). Functional neuroanatomical correlates of hysterical sensorimotor loss. *Brain, 124,* 1077–1090.

Vythilingam, M., Heim, C., Newport, J., Miller, A. H., Anderson, E., Bronen, R., Brummer, M., Staib, L., Vermetten, E., Charney, D. S., Nemeroff, C. B., & Bremner, J. D. (2002). Childhood trauma associated with smaller hippocampal volume in women with major depression. *American Journal of Psychiatry, 159,* 2072–2080.

W

Wadden, T. A., Brownell, K. D., & Foster, G. D. (2002). Obesity: Responding to the global epidemic. *Journal of Consulting & Clinical Psychology, 70,* 510–525.

Wade, T., Neale, M. C., Lake, R. I. E., & Martin, N. G. (1999). A genetic analysis of the eating and attitudes associated with bulimia nervosa: Dealing with the problem of ascertainment in twin studies. *Behavior Genetics, 99,* 1–10.

Wade, T. D., Bulik, C. M., Neale, M., & Kendler, K. S. (2000). Anorexia nervosa and major depression: Shared genetic and environmental risk factors. *American Journal of Psychiatry, 157,* 469–471.

Wagner, B. M., Silverman, M. A. C., & Martin, C. E. (2003). Family factors in youth suicidal behaviors. *American Behavioral Scientist, 46,* 1171–1191.

Wahlberg, D. (1999, October 21). Binge drinking remains problem. *Ann Arbor News,* p. A1.

Waldron, H. B., Slesnick, N., Brody, J. L., Turner, C. W., & Peterson, T. R. (2001). Treatment outcomes for adolescent substance abuse at 4- and 7-month assessments. *Journal of Consulting & Clinical Psychology, 69,* 802–813.

Walker, E., Kestler, L., Bollini, A., & Hochman, K. M. (2004). Schizophrenia: Etiology and course. *Annual Review of Psychology, 55,* 401–430.

Walker, L. E. A. (1994). Are personality disorders gender biased? In S. A. Kirk & S. D. Einbinder (Eds.), *Controversial issues in mental health* (pp. 22–29). Boston: Allyn & Bacon.

Wallace, J., Schneider, T., & McGuffin, P. (2002). Genetics of depression. In I. H. Gotlib & C. L. Hammen (Eds.), *Handbook of depression* (pp. 169–191). New York: Guilford Press.

Waller, S. J., Lyons, J. S., & Costantini-Ferrando, M. F. (1999). Impact of comorbid affective and alcohol use disorders on suicide ideation and attempts. *Journal of Clinical Psychology, 55,* 585–595.

Walters, E., & Kendler, K. (1999). Anorexia nervosa and anorexic-like syndromes in a population based female twin sample. *The American Journal of Psychiatry, 152,* 64–75.

Wampold, B. E., Mondin, G. W., Moody, M., Stich, F., Benson, K., & Ahn, H. (1997). A meta-analysis of outcome studies comparing bona fide psychotherapies: Empirically, "all must have prizes." *Psychological Bulletin, 122,* 203–215.

Wandersman, A., & Nation, M. (1998). Urban neighborhoods and mental health: Psychological contributions to understanding toxicity, resilience, and interventions. *American Psychologist, 53,* 647–656.

Warga, C. (1988, September). You are what you think. *Psychology Today,* pp. 54–58.

Warner, M. B., Morey, L. C., Finch, J. F., Gunderson, J. G., Skodol, A. E., Sanislow, C. A., Shea, M. T., McGlashan, T. H., & Grilo, C. M. (2004). The longitudinal relationship of personality traits and disorders. *Journal of Abnormal Psychology, 113,* 217–227.

Warren, J. I., Murrie, D. C., Chauhan, P., Dietz, P. E., & Morris, J. (2004). Opinion formation in evaluating sanity at the time of the offense: An examination of 5175 pre-trial evaluations. *Behavioral Sciences and the Law, 22,* 171–186.

Waschbusch, D. A. (2002). A meta-analytic examination of comorbid hyperactive-impulsive-attention problems and conduct problems. *Psychological Bulletin, 128,* 118–150.

Washington Post. (2004, August 27). Poverty rate up 3rd year in a row [Electronic version]. *Washington Post,* p. A01.

Waters, A., Hill, A., & Waller, G. (2001). Bulimics' response to food cravings: Is binge-eating a product of hunger or emotional state? *Behaviour Research & Therapy, 39,* 877–886.

Watson, C. G., & Buranen, C. (1979). The frequencies of conversion reaction symptoms. *Journal of Abnormal Psychology, 88,* 209–211.

Watson, D., & Clark, L. A. (1984). Negative affectivity: The disposition to experience aversive emotional states. *Psychological Bulletin, 96,* 465–490.

Watson, J. B. (1930). *Behaviorism.* Chicago: University of Chicago Press.

Watson, J. B., & Raynor, R. (1920). Conditioned emotional reactions. *Journal of Experimental Psychology, 3,* 1–14.

Watson, K. A., & Hayward, C. (2005). A prospective evaluation of agoraphobia and depression symptoms following panic attacks in a community sample of adolescents. *Journal of Anxiety Disorders, 19,* 87–103.

Watson, M., Haviland, J. S., Greer, S., Davidson, J., & Bliss, J. M. (1999). Influence of psychological response on survival in breast cancer: A population-based cohort study. *Lancet, 354,* 1331–1336.

Webster-Stratton, C., & Reid, M. J. (2003). The incredible years parents, teachers, and children training series: A multifaceted treatment approach for young children with conduct problems. In A. E. Kazdin & J. R. Weisz (Eds.), *Evidence-based psychotherapies for children and adolescents* (pp. 224–240). New York: Guilford Press.

Weeks, D., & James, J. (1995). *Eccentrics.* New York: Villard.

Wehr, T. A., Duncan, W. C., Sher, L., Aeschbach, D., Schwartz, P. J., Turner, E. H., Postolache, T. T., & Rosenthal, N. E. (2001). A circadian signal of change of season in patients with seasonal affective disorder. *Archives of General Psychiatry, 58,* 1108–1114.

Weine, S. M., Becker, D. F., McGlashan, T. H., Laub, D., Lazrove, S., Vojvoda, D., & Hyman, L. (1995). Psychiatric consequences of "ethnic cleansing": Clinical assessments and trauma testimonies of newly resettled Bosnian refugees. *American Journal of Psychiatry, 152,* 536–542.

Weine, S. M., Vojvoda, D., Becker, D. F., McGlashan, T. H., Hodzic, E., Laub, D., Hyman, L., Sawyer, M., & Lazrove, S. (1998). PTSD symptoms in Bosnian refugees 1 year after resettlement in the United States. *American Journal of Psychiatry, 155,* 562–564.

Weiner, B. A., & Wettstein, R. M. (1993). *Legal issues in mental health care.* New York: Plenum Press.

Weissman, M. M. (1993). The epidemiology of personality disorders: A 1990 update. NIMH Conference: Personality disorders (1990, Williamsburg, Virginia). *Journal of Personality Disorders* (Suppl. 1), 44–62.

Weissman, M. M., Bland, R. C., Canino, G. J., et al. (1996). Cross-national epidemiology of major depression and bipolar disorder. *Journal of the American Medical Association, 276,* 293–299.

Weissman, M. M., & Markowitz, J. C. (2002). Interpersonal psychotherapy for depression. In I. H. Gotlib & C. L. Hammen (Eds.), *Handbook of depression* (pp. 404–421). New York: Guilford Press.

Weisz, J. R., Donenberg, G., Han, S., & Kauneckis, D. (1995). Child and adolescent psychotherapy outcomes in experiments versus clinics: Why the disparity? *Journal of Abnormal Child Psychology, 23,* 83–106.

Weisz, J. R., & Hawley, K. M. (2002). Developmental factors in the treatment of adolescents. *Journal of Consulting & Clinical Psychology, 70,* 21–43.

Welch, S. L., & Fairburn, C. G. (1994). Sexual abuse and bulimia nervosa: Three integrated case control comparisons. 11th National Conference on Eating Disorders (1992, Columbus, Ohio). *American Journal of Psychiatry, 151,* 402–407.

Welch, S. S. (2001). A review of the literature on the epidemiology of parasuicide in the general population. *Psychiatric Services, 52,* 368–375.

Wellman, H. M. (1994). Early understanding of mind: The normal case. In S. Baron-Cohen (Ed.), *Understanding other minds: Perspectives from autism.* New York: Oxford University Press.

Wender, P. H., Kety, S. S., Rosenthal, D., Schulsinger, F., Ortmann, J., & Lunde, I. (1986). Psychiatric disorders in the biological and adoptive families of adopted individuals with affective disorders. *Archives of General Psychiatry, 43,* 923–929.

Wentz, E., Gillberg, C., Gillberg, I. C., & Ratsam, M. (2001). Ten-year follow-up of adolescent-onset anorexia nervosa: Psychiatric disorders and overall functioning scales. *Journal of Child Psychology & Psychiatry, 42,* 613–622.

Wessely, S., & Kerwin, R. (2004). Suicide risk and the SSRIs. *Journal of the American Medical Association, 292,* 379–381.

Westen, D. (1998). The scientific legacy of Sigmund Freud: Toward a psychodynamically informed psychological science. *Psychological Bulletin, 124,* 333–371.

Westen, D., & Morrison, K. (2001). A multidimensional meta-analysis of treatments for depression, panic, and generalized anxiety disorder: An empirical examination of the status of empirically supported therapies. *Journal of Consulting & Clinical Psychology, 69,* 875–899.

Westen, D., Novotny, C. M., & Thompson-Brenner, H. (2004). The empirical status of empirically supported psychotherapies: Assumptions, findings, and reporting in controlled clinical trials. *Psychological Bulletin, 130,* 631–663.

Westermeyer, J. (1993). Cross-cultural psychiatric assessment. In A. C. Gaw (Ed.), *Culture, ethnicity, and mental illness* (pp. 125–144). Washington, DC: American Psychiatric Press.

Westermeyer, J., Bouafuely, M., Neider, J., & Callies, A. (1989). Somatization among refugees: An epidemiologic study. *Psychosomatics, 30,* 34–43.

Weston, S. C., & Siever, L. J. (1993). Biologic correlates of personality disorders. NIMH Conference: Personality disorders (1990, Williamsburg, Virginia). *Journal of Personality Disorders* (Suppl. 1), 129–148.

Wetherell, J. L., Sorrell, J. T., Thorp, S. R., & Patterson, T. L. (2005). Psychological Interventions for Late-Life Anxiety: A Review and Early Lessons From the CALM Study. *Journal of Geriatric Psychiatry & Neurology, 18,* 72–82.

Whalen, C. K., & Henker, B. (1998). Attention-deficit/hyperactivity disorder. In T. H. Ollendick & M. Hersen (Eds.), *Handbook of child psychopathology* (pp. 181–212). New York: Plenum Press.

Whaley, S. E., Pinto, A., & Sigman, M. (1999). Characterizing interactions between anxious mothers and their children. *Journal of Consulting & Clinical Psychology, 67,* 826–836.

Whitbourne, S. K. (2000). The normal aging process. In S. K. Whitbourne (Ed.), *Psychopathology in later adulthood* (pp. 27–59). New York: Wiley.

White, H. R., Xie, M., & Thompson, W. (2001). Psychopathology as a predictor of adolescent drug use trajectories. *Psychology of Addictive Behaviors, 15,* 210–218.

White, K., & Barlow, D. H. (2002). Panic disorder and agoraphobia. In D. H. Barlow (Ed.), *Anxiety and its disorders: The nature and treatment of anxiety and panic* (2nd ed., pp. 328–379). New York: Guilford Press.

Whittal, M. L., Agras, W. S., & Gould, R. A. (1999). Bulimia nervosa: A meta-analysis of psychosocial and pharmacological treatments. *Behavior Therapy, 30,* 117–135.

Widiger, T. A. (1998). Invited essay: Sex biases in the diagnosis of personality disorders. *Journal of Personality Disorders, 12,* 95–118.

Widiger, T. A. (2002). Values, politics, and science in the construction of the DSMs. In J. Z. Sadler (Ed.), *Descriptions and prescriptions: Values, mental disorders, and the DSMs* (pp. 25–41). Baltimore: Johns Hopkins University Press.

+ Widiger, T. A. (2005). Classification and diagnosis: Historical development and contemporary issues. In J. E. Maddux & B. A. Winstead (Eds.), *Psychopathology: Foundations for a contemporary understanding* (pp. 63–83). Mahwah, NJ: Erlbaum.

Widiger, T. A., & Clark, L. A. (2000). Toward DSM-V and the classification of psychopathology. *Psychological Bulletin, 126,* 946–963.

Widiger, T. A., & Coker, L. A. (2003). Mental disorders as discrete clinical conditions: Dimensional versus categorical classification. In M. Hersen & S. M. Turner (Eds.), *Adult psychopathology and diagnosis* (4th ed., pp. 3–35). New York: Wiley.

Widiger, T. A., & Costa, P. T., Jr. (1994). Personality and personality disorders. Special Issue: Personality and psychopathology. *Journal of Abnormal Psychology, 103,* 78–91.

Widiger, T. A., Costa, P. T., Jr., & McCrae, R. R. (2002). A proposal for Axis II: Diagnosing personality disorders using the five-factor model. In P. T. Costa, Jr., & T. A. Widiger (Eds.), *Personality disorders and the five factor model of personality* (2nd ed., pp. 431–456). Washington, DC: American Psychological Association.

Widiger, T. A., Mangine, S., Corbitt, E. M., Ellis, C. G., & Thomas, G. V. (1995). *Personality disorder interview-IV: A semistructured interview for the assessment of personality disorders.* Odessa, FL: Psychological Assessment Resources.

Widiger, T. A., & Spitzer, R. L. (1991). Sex biases in the diagnosis of personality disorder: Conceptual and methodological issues. *Clinical Psychological Review, 11,* 1–22.

Widiger, T. A., Trull, T. J., Clarkin, J. F., Sanderson, C., & Costa, P. T. (1994). A description of the DSM-III-R and DSM-IV personality disorders with the five-factor model of personality. In P. T. Costa & T. A. Widiger (Eds.), *Personality disorders and the five-factor model of personality* (pp. 41–58). Washington, DC: American Psychological Association.

Wiggins, J. S. (1982). Circumplex models of interpersonal behavior in clinical psychology. In P. Kendall & J. Butcher (Eds.), *Handbook of research methods in clinical psychology.* New York: Wiley.

Wikan, U. (1991). *Managing turbulent hearts.* Chicago: University of Chicago Press.

Wileman, S. M., Eagles, J. M., Andrew, J. E., Howie, F. L., Cameron, I. M., McCormack, K., & Naji, S. A. (2001). Light therapy for seasonal affective disorder in primary care: Randomized controlled trial. *British Journal of Psychiatry, 178,* 311–316.

Wilens, T. E., Biederman, J., & Spencer, T. J. (2002). Attention deficit/hyperactivity disorder across the lifespan. *Annual Review of Medicine, 53,* 113–131.

Wilfley, D. E., Agras, W. S., Telch, C. F., Rossiter, E. M., Schneider, J. A., Cole, A. G., Sifford, L., & Raeburn, S. D. (1993). Group cognitive-behavioral therapy and group interpersonal psychotherapy for the nonpurging bulimic individual: A controlled comparison. *Journal of Consulting & Clinical Psychology, 61,* 296–305.

Wilfley, D. E., Welch, R. R., Stein, R. I., Spurrell, E. B., Cohen, L., R., Saelens, B. E., Dounchis, J. Z., Frank, M. A., Wiseman, C. V., & Matt, G. E. (2002). A randomized comparison of group cognitive-behavioral therapy and group interpersonal psychotherapy for the treatment of overweight individuals with binge-eating disorder. *Archives of General Psychiatry, 59,* 713–721.

Williams, J. B., & Spitzer, R. L. (1983). The issue of sex bias in DSM-III. *American Psychologist, 38,* 793–798.

Williams, J. W., Rost, K., Dietrich, A. J., Ciotti, M. C., Zyzanski, S. J., & Cornell, J. (1999). Primary care physicians' approach to depressive disorders. *Archives of Family Medicine, 8,* 58–67.

Williams, L. M. (1995). Recovered memories of abuse in women with documented child sexual victimization histories. *Journal of Traumatic Stress, 8,* 649–673.

Williams, R. B., Barefoot, J. C., Haney, T. L., & Harrell, F. E. (1988). Type A behavior and angiographically documented coronary atherosclerosis in a sample of 2,289 patients. *Psychosomatic Medicine, 50,* 139–152.

Williamson, G. L. (1993). Postpartum depression syndrome as a defense to criminal behavior. *Journal of Family Violence, 8,* 151–165.

Wilps, R. F., Jr. (1990). Male bulimia nervosa: An autobiographical case study. In A. E. Andersen (Ed.), *Males with eating disorders* (pp. 9–29). New York: Brunner/Mazel.

Wilson, G. R., Loeb, K. L., Walsh, B. T., Labouvie, R., Petkova, E., Xinhua, L., & Waternaux, C. (1999). Psychological versus pharmacological treatments of bulimia nervosa: Predictors and processes of change. *Journal of Consulting & Clinical Psychology, 67,* 451–459.

Wilson, G. T. (2005). Psychological treatment of eating disorders. *Annual Review of Clinical Psychology, 1,* 439–465.

Wilson, G. T., & Fairburn, C. G. (1998). Cognitive treatments for eating disorders. *Journal of Consulting & Clinical Psychology, 61,* 261–269.

Wilson, G. T., Fairburn, C. G., & Agras, W. S. (1997). Cognitive-behavioral treatment for anorexia nervosa. In D. M. Garner & P. E. Garfinkel (Eds.), *Handbook of treatment for eating disorders* (pp. 67–93). New York: Guilford Press.

Wilson, G. T, Fairburn, C. C., Agras, W. S., Walsh, B. T., & Kraemer, H. (2002). Cognitive-behavioral therapy for bulimia nervosa: Time course and mechanisms of change. *Journal of Consulting & Clinical Psychology, 70,* 267–274.

Wilson, K. A., & Hayward, C. (2005). A prospective evaluation of agoraphobia and depression symptoms following panic attacks in a community sample of adolescents. *Journal of Anxiety Disorders, 19,* 87–103.

Windholz, M. J., Marmar, C. R., & Horowitz, M. J. (1985). A review of the research on conjugal bereavement: Impact on health and efficacy of intervention. *Comprehensive Psychiatry, 26,* 433–447.

Winger, G., Hofmann, F. G., & Woods, J. H. (1992). *Handbook on drug and alcohol abuse.* New York: Oxford University Press.

Winick, B. J. (2003). A therapeutic jurisprudence assessment of sexually violent predator laws. In B. J. Winick & J. Q. LaFond (Eds.), *Protecting society from sexually dangerous offenders: Law, justice, and therapy* (pp. 317–331). Washington, DC: American Psychological Association.

Winokur, G., & Clayton, P. (1967). Family history studies: II. Sex differences and alcoholism in primary affective illness. *British Journal of Psychiatry, 113,* 973–979.

Winters, J., Fals-Stewart, W., O'Farrell, T. J., Birchler, G. R., & Kelley, M. L. (2002). Behavioral couples therapy for female substance-abusing patients: Effects on substance use and relationship adjustment. *Journal of Consulting & Clinical Psychology, 70,* 344–355.

Wiseman, C. V., Gray, J. J., Mosimann, J. E., & Ahrens, A. H. (1992). Cultural expectations of thinness in women: An update. *International Journal of Eating Disorders, 11,* 85–89.

Wittchen, H.-U., & Fehm, L. (2003). Epidemiology and natural course of social fears and social phobia. *Acta Psychiatrica Scandinavica, 108*(Suppl. 417), 4–18.

Woelk, H., Burkard, G., & Grunwald, J. (1994). Benefits and risks of the hypericum extract LI 160: Drug monitoring study with 3,250 patients. *Journal of Geriatric Psychiatry and Neurology, 7* (Suppl. 1), 34–38.

Wolfe, J., Erickson, D. J., Sharkansky, R. J., King, D. W., & King, L. A. (1999). Course and predictors of posttraumatic stress disorder among Gulf War veterans: A prospective analysis. *Journal of Consulting & Clinical Psychology, 67,* 520–528.

Wolff, S., & Wolff, H. G. (1947). An experimental study of changes in gastric function in response to varying life experiences. *Review of Gastroenterology, 14,* 419–426.

Wolfner, G. D., & Gelles, R. J. (1993). A profile of violence toward children: A national study. *Child Abuse & Neglect, 17,* 197–212.

Wolitzky, D. L. (1995). The theory and practice of traditional psychoanalytic psychotherapy. In A. S. Gurman (Ed.), *Essential psychotherapies: Theory and practice* (pp. 12–54). New York: Guilford Press.

Wollstonecraft, M. (1792). *A vindication of the rights of women.* London: J. Johnson.

Wolpe, J. (1997). Thirty years of behavior therapy. *Behavior Therapy, 28,* 633–635.

Wolfsdorf, B. A., & Zlotnick, C. (2001). Affect management in group therapy for women with posttraumatic stress disorder and histories of childhood sexual abuse. *Journal of Clinical Psychology, 57,* 169–181.

Wolfson, A. R. (2002). Bridging the gap between research and practice: What will adolescents' sleep-wake patterns look like in the 21st century? In M. A. Carskadon (Ed.), *Adolescent sleep patterns: Biological, social, and psychological influences* (pp. 198–219). New York: Cambridge University Press.

Wolfson, A. R., & Carskadon, M. A. (1998). Sleep schedules and daytime functioning in adolescents. *Child Development, 69,* 875–887.

Wonderlich, S. A., de Zwaan, M., Mitchell, J. E., Peterson, C., & Crow, S. (2003). Psychological and dietary treatments of binge eating disorder: Conceptual implications. *International Journal of Eating Disorders, 34*(Suppl. 1), 58–73.

Woolf, V. (1975–1980). "Dearest I want to tell you," Virginia Woolf, March 28, 1941. In N. Nicolson & J. Trautman (Eds.), *The letters* (Vol. 6, pp. 486–487). London: Hogarth Press.

World Health Organization (WHO). (2002). Mental health: Suicide prevention. Retrieved from the World Wide Web: http://www.who.int/mental_health/suicide

World Health Organization (WHO). (2004). Distribution of suicide rates (per 100,000) by gender and age, 2000. Retrieved from: http://www.who.int/mental_health/prevention/suicide/suicidecharts/en/

World Health Organization (WHO). (2005a). WHO SUPRE suicide prevention: Live your life. Retrieved from: http://www.who.int/mental_health/management/en/SUPRE_flyer1.pdf

World Health Organization (WHO). (2005b). *Global alcohol database.* Retrieved from the World Wide Web: http://www3.who.int/whosis.

Wurtman, J. J. (1987). Disorders of food intake: Excessive carbohydrate snack intake among a class of obese people. *Annals of the New York Academy of Sciences, 499,* 197–202.

Wurtman, R. J., & Wurtman, J. J. (1984). Nutritional control of central neurotransmitters. In K. M. Pirke & D. Plogg (Eds.), *The psychobiology of anorexia nervosa.* Berlin: Springer-Verlag.

Wurtzel, E. (1995). *Prozac nation.* New York: Berkley.

Wyatt, S. A., & Ziedonis, D. (1998). Psychological and psychiatric consequences of amphetamines. In R. E. Tarter (Ed.), *Handbook of substance abuse: Neurobehavioral pharmacology* (pp. 529–544). New York: Plenum Press.

Y

Yalom, I. D. (1985). *The theory and practice of group psychotherapy* (3rd ed.). New York: Basic Books.

Yamamoto, J. (1970). Cultural factors in loneliness, death, and separation. *Medical Times, 98,* 177–183.

Yang, J., Dai, X., Yao, S., Cai, T., Gao, B., McCrae, R. R., & Costa, P. T. (2002). Personality disorders and the five-factor model of personality in Chinese psychiatric patients. In P. T. Costa & T. A. Widiger (Eds.), *Personality Disorders and the Five-factor Model of Personality* (2nd ed., pp. 215–221). Washington, DC: American Psychological Association.

Yapko, M. D. (1997). *Breaking the patterns of depression*. New York: Golden Books.

Yeh, M., & Weisz, J. R. (2001). Why are we here at the clinic? Parent-child (dis)agreement on referral problems at outpatient treatment entry. *Journal of Consulting & Clinical Psychology, 69*, 1019–1025.

Yehuda, R. (2000). Biology of posttraumatic stress disorder. *Journal of Clinical Psychiatry, 61* (Suppl. 7), 14–21.

Yehuda, R. (2004). Risk and resilience in posttraumatic stress disorder. *Journal of Clinical Psychiatry, 65*(Suppl. 1), 29–36.

Yehuda, R., McFarlane, A. C., & Shalev, A. Y. (1998). Predicting the development of posttraumatic stress disorder from the acute response to a traumatic event. *Biological Psychiatry, 44*, 1305–1313.

Yen, S., Shea, M. T., Pagano, M., Sanislow, C. A., Grilo, C. M., McGlashan, T. H., Skodol, A. E., Bender, D. S., Zanarini, M. C., Gunderson, J. G., & Morey, L. C. (2003). Axis I and axis II disorders as predictors of prospective suicide attempts: Findings from the Collaborative Longitudinal Personality Disorders Study. *Journal of Abnormal Psychology, 112*, 375–381.

Yirmiya, N., Erel, O., Shaked, M., & Solomonica-Levi, D. (1998). Meta-analysis comparing theory of mind abilities of individuals with autism, individuals with mental retardation, and normally developed individuals. *Psychological Bulletin, 124*, 283–307.

Yonkers, K. A., & Gurguis, G. (1995). Gender differences in the prevalence and expression of anxiety disorders. In M. V. Seeman (Ed.), *Gender and psychopathology* (pp. 113–130). Washington, DC: American Psychiatric Press.

Young, E., & Korzun, A. (1998). Psychoneuroendocrinology of depression: Hypothalamic-pituitary-gonadal axis. *Psychiatric Clinics of North America, 21*, 309–323.

Z

Zaider, T. I., & Heimberg, R. G. (2003). Non-pharmacologic treatments for social anxiety disorder. *Acta Psychiatrica Scandinavica, 108*(Suppl. 417), 72–84.

Zanarini, M. C. (Ed.). (1997). *Role of sexual abuse in the etiology of borderline personality disorder*. Washington, DC: American Psychiatric Press.

Zanarini, M. C., Skodol, A.-E., Bender, D., Dolan, R., Sanislow, C., Schaefer, E., Morey, L., Grilo, C. M., Shea, M. T., McGlashan, T. H., & Gunderson, G. (2000). The Collaborative Longitudinal Personality Disorders Study: Reliability of Axis I and II diagnoses. *Journal of Personality Disorder, 14*, 291–299.

Zarit, S. H., & Haynie, D. A. (2000). Introduction to clinical issues. In S. K. Whitbourne (Ed.), *Psychopathology in later adulthood* (pp. 1–25). New York: Wiley.

Zelt, D. (1981). First person account: The Messiah quest. *Schizophrenia Bulletin, 7*, 527–531.

Zerbe, K. J. (1990). Through the storm: Psychoanalytic theory in the psychotherapy of anxiety disorders. *Bulletin of the Menninger Clinic, 54*, 171–183.

Zhou, J.-N., Hofman, M. A., & Swaab, D. F. (1995). No changes in the number of vasoactive intestinal polypeptide (VIP)-expressing neurons in the suprachiasmatic nucleus of homosexual men; comparison with vasopressin-expressing neurons. *Brain Research, 672*, 285–288.

Zhou, S., Chan, E., Pan, S.-Q., Huang, M., & Lee, E. J. D. (2004). Pharmacokinetic interactions of drugs with St. John's wort. *Journal of Psychopharmacology, 18*, 262–276.

Zigler, E., & Hodapp, R. M. (1991). Behavioral functioning in individuals with mental retardation. *Annual Review of Psychology, 42*, 29–50.

Zilboorg, G., & Henry, G. W. (1941). *A history of medical psychology*. New York: W. W. Norton.

Zimbardo, P. G. (1977). *Shyness: What it is, what to do about it*. New York: Addison-Wesley.

Zimbardo, P. G., Andersen, S. M., & Kabat, L. G. (1981). Induced hearing deficit generates experimental paranoia. *Science, 212*, 1529–1531.

Zisook, S., & Downs, N. (1998). Diagnosis and treatment of depression in late life. *Journal of Clinical Psychiatry, 59*(Suppl. 4), 80–91.

Zlotnik, C., Elkin, I., & Shea, M. T. (1998). Does the gender of a patient or the gender of a therapist affect the treatment of patients with major depression? *Journal of Consulting & Clinical Psychology, 66*, 655–659.

Zoccolillo, M. (1993). Gender and the development of conduct disorder. *Development & Psychopathology, 5*, 65–78.

Zoellner, L. A., Craske, M. G., & Rapee, R. M. (1996). Stability of catastrophic cognitions in panic disorder. *Behaviour Research & Therapy, 34*, 399–402.

Zubenko, G. S., Hughes, H. B., III, Stiffler, J. S., Zubenko, W. N., & Kaplan, B. B. (2002). D2S2944 identifies a likely susceptibility locus for recurrent, early-onset, major depression in women. *Molecular Psychiatry, 7*, 460–467.

Zubieta, J. K., & Alessi, N. E. (1992). Acute and chronic administration of trazodone in the treatment of disruptive behavior disorders in children. *Journal of Clinical Psychopharmacology, 12*, 346–351.

Zucker, K. J. (2005). Gender identity disorder in children and adolescents. In S. Nolen-Hoeksema, T. D. Cannon, & T. A. Widiger (Eds.), *Annual Review of Clinical Psychology* (Vol. 1, pp. 467–492). Palo Alto, CA: Annual Reviews.

Zucker, R. A., Chermack, S. T., & Curran, G. M. (1999). Alcoholism: A lifespan perspective on etiology and course. In M. Lewis & A. J. Sameroff (Eds.), *Handbook of developmental psychopatholgy* (2nd ed.). New York: Plenum Press.

Zucker, R. A., Ellis, D. A., Fitzgerald, H. E., Bingham, C. R., & Sanford, K. (1996). Other evidence for at least two alcoholisms: II. Life course variation in antisociality and heterogeneity of alcoholic outcome. *Development & Psychopathology, 8*, 831–848.

Zucker, R. A., Kincaid, S. B., Fitzgerald, H. E., & Bingham, C. R. (1995). Alcohol schema acquisition in preschoolers: Differences between children of alcoholics and children of nonalcoholics. *Alcoholism: Clinical & Experimental Research, 19*, 1011–1017.

CREDITS

CHAPTER 1
Opener: *People Flying* by Peter Sickles. American. Superstock. **P. 4:** © Corbis Images. **Pp. 4, 5:** Anonymous, 1992. "First-person account: Portrait of a schizophrenic." *Schizophrenia Bulletin*, 18, 333–334. **P. 5:** From *An Unquiet Mind: A Memoir of Moods and Madness* by K.R. Jamison. Copyright © 1995. Used by permission of Alfred A. Knopf, a Division of Random House, Inc. **P. 6:** © A.P./Wide World Photos. **P. 7:** © Archivo Iconografico, S.A./Corbis Images. **P. 9:** © Courtesy of Gary Holloway. Photo by Josef Astor. **P. 12:** © Sandved B. Kjell/Visuals Unlimited. **P. 13:** © The Granger Collection. **P. 14:** © Archivo Iconografico, S.A./Corbis Images. **P. 15:** © Bettmann/Corbis Images. **P. 18:** © National Library of Medicine/Science Photo Library/Photo Researchers. **P. 19:** © National Library of Medicine/Photo Researchers. **P. 20:** © Robert Fleeury/Photo Researchers. **Pp. 21, 22:** © The Granger Collection. **P. 27:** © Corbis Images.

CHAPTER 2
Opener: *Heart of the Hunter* by Michelle Puleo, B. 1967. American. Private Collection/Superstock. **P. 34:** Courtesy, Albert Ellis, Albert Ellis Institute. **Pp. 36, 37:** Adapted with permission from Damasio H, Grabowski T, Frank R, Galaburda AM, Damasio AR: The return of Phineas Gage: Clues about the brain from a famous patient. *Science*, 264:1102–1105, 1994. Department of Neurology and Image Analysis Facility, University of Iowa. Copyright © 1994 AAAS. **Figure 2.3:** Damasio H., Grabowski, T., Frank R., Galaburda A. M., Damasio A. R. (1994). The return of Phineas Gage: Clues about the brain from the skull of a famous patient. *Science*, 264, 1102–1105. Department of Neurology and Image Analysis Facility, University of Iowa. **Figure 2.5:** Adapted from Feldman, *Understanding Psychology*, 7e, Fig. 3, p. 83. Copyright © 2005 The McGraw-Hill Companies. Reprinted with permission from The McGraw-Hill Companies. **Figure 2.6:** Adapted from Feldman, *Understanding Psychology*, 7e, Fig. 4, p. 85. Copyright © 2005 The McGraw-Hill Companies. Reprinted with permission from The McGraw-Hill Companies. **Figure 2.8a&b:** Adapted from Feldman, *Understanding Psychology*, 7e, Fig. 5, p. 67. Copyright © 2005 The McGraw-Hill Companies. Reprinted with permission from The McGraw-Hill Companies. **P. 45:** © Enrico Ferorelli. **P. 47:** © Bettman/Corbis Images. **P. 49:** © Barton Silverman/NYT Pictures. **P. 52 (left):** © Wellcome Library, London. **P. 52 (right):** © Otto Kernberg. **P. 53:** © Bettman/Corbis Images. **P. 55:** © Syracuse Newspapers/Dennis Nett /Image Works. **P. 57:** Courtesy Aaron Beck. **P. 58:** National Library of Medicine. **P. 63:** ©Bruce Ayres/Getty Images. **P. 66:** Courtesy, Albert Ellis, Albert Ellis Institute.

CHAPTER 3
Opener: *The Global Seat* by Christian Pierre. American. Private Collection/Superstock. **P. 72:** © Lee Snider/Image Works. **P. 75:** From J. Giles, "The Poet of Alienation," *Newsweek*, April 18, 1994. Copyright © 1994 Newsweek, Inc. All rights reserved. Reprinted by permission. **P. 75:** © Jay Blakesberg/Corbis Sygma. **P. 80:** © Keith Brofsky/Getty Images. **P. 83:** © A.P./Wide World Photos. **P. 87:** © Michael Newman/PhotoEdit. **P. 93:** © Lee Snider/Image Works.

CHAPTER 4
Opener: *Essor* by Andrè Rouillard, 1981/Superstock. **P. 98:** From *The Unicorn and Other Poems* by Anne Morrow Lindbergh. Copyright © 1956. Used by permission of Pantheon Books, a Division of Random House, Inc. **P. 102:** © Steven Peters/Getty Images. **P. 103:** © Rhoda Sidney/PhotoEdit. **Figure 4.3:** From J. M. Sattler, *Assessment of Children*, 3rd edition. Reprinted with permission. **108 (both):** © ZEPHYR/Photo Researchers. **P. 113:** © Grantpix/Index Stock Imagery. **P. 114:** © Michael Newman/PhotoEdit. **P. 116:** © Camilla Smith/Rainbow. **P. 117:** © Michael Newman/PhotoEdit. **P. 126:** © Corbis Images. **P. 128:** © Frank Trapper/Corbis Sygma/Corbis Images.

CHAPTER 5
Opener: *Window of Opportunity* by Christian Pierre. American. Private Collection/Superstock. **Pp. 134, 135, 167, 168:** Anonymous, 1983. "First-person account," *Schizophrenia Bulletin*, 9, 152–155. **P. 139:** © 1994 Newsweek, Inc. All rights reserved. Reprinted by permission. Photo by Myko Photography. **P. 141:** © Don Farrall/Getty Images. **P. 142:** © Najlah Feanny/Stock Boston. **P. 153:** © David Young-Wolff/PhotoEdit. **P. 156:** © Michael Newman/PhotoEdit. **P. 157:** © Bob Daemmrich/Image Works. **Pp. 160, 161:** From Sue, S. & Zane, N., 1987, "The Role of Culture and Cultural Techniques in Psychotherapy: A Critique and Reformulation," *American Psychologist*, 42, pp. 37–45. Reproduced with permission. **P. 161:** © Michael Grecco/Stock Boston. **P. 162:** © David R. Frazier/Photo Researchers. **P. 165:** © Michael Newman/PhotoEdit.

Kobal Collection/20th Century Fox. **P. 286:** © Cindy Charles/Photo Edit. **Pp. 287–288:** Adapted from Steinberg, M. (1990). Transcultural issues in psychiatry: The ataque and multiple personality disorder. *Dissociation: Progress in the Dissociative Disorders, 3,* 31–32. Reprinted with permission from the Ridgeview Institute. **P. 289:** © Bettmann/Corbis Images. **P. 292:** From Hilgard, E. R. (1986). *Divided consciousness: Multiple controls in human thought and action,* p. 68. New York: Wiley. Reprinted with permission of the estate of Ernest R. Hilgard. **P. 293:** © Jeffrey Markowitz/Corbis Sygma. **P. 294:** From Loftus, E. F., 1993, "The Reality of Repressed Memories, *American Psychologist, 48,* 518–537. Copyright © 1993 by the American Psychological Association. Reproduced with permission. **P. 296:** © The Granger Collection.**P. 297:** Prayer by Bertha Pappenheim. From Pappenheim, B., 1936, Gebete, *Ausgewahlt und herausgegeben von Judischen Frauenbund,* Berline: Philo Verlag. Reproduced with permission.

CHAPTER 9

Opener: *Watching from the Steps* by Hyacinth Manning-Carner. African- American. Private Collection/Superstock. **P. 302:** © Johns Hopkins Medicine. **Pp. 302, 303, 336, 343, 346:** From *An Unquiet Mind: A Memoir of Moods and Madness* by K.R. Jamison. Copyright © 1995. Used by permission of Alfred A. Knopf, a Division of Random House, Inc. **P. 306:** © Peter Dazeley/Corbis Images. **P. 308:** © Tom Prettyman/PhotoEdit. **P. 312 (left):** © Hulton-Deutsch Collection/Corbis Images. **P. 312 (right):** © Bettmann/Corbis Images. **Figure 9.4a-d:** From Davidson, R. J., Pizzagalli, D., Nitschke, J. B., and Putnam, K. (2002). Depression: Perspectives from affective neuroscience. *Annual Review of Psychology, 53,* 545–74. **P. 318:** © Robert Brenner/PhotoEdit. **P. 321:** © Diaphor Agency/Index Stock Imagery. **Table 9.7:** From David H. Burns, *Feeling Good: The New Mood Therapy,* 1980, William Morrow. Copyright © 1980 HarperCollins Publishes. Used with permission. **Pp. 324, 325:** Adapted from J. Bemporad, 1995, "Long-Term Analytic Treatment of Depression," in E. E. Beckham & W. R. Leber (Eds.), *Handbook of Depression, Second Edition.* Copyright © 1995 Guilford Publications. Reprinted with permission. **P. 326:** "Rachel" Case Study from *Eating, Drinking, Overthinking: The Toxic Triangle of Food, Alcohol, and Depression— and How Women Can Break Free* by Susan Nolen-Hoeksema. Copyright © 2005 by Susan Nolen-Hoeksema. Reprinted by permission of Henry Holt and Company, LLC., Piatkus Books Ltd., and Zachary Shuster Harmsworth Literary Agency. **Figure 9.2:** From Twenge, J. & Nolen-Hoeksema, Susan. Age, gender, race, socioeconomic status, and birth cohort difference on the children's depression inventory: A meta-analysis. *Journal of Abnormal Psychology.* Vol 111(4) Nov 2002, 578–588. Copyright © 2002 by the American Psychological Association. Reproduced with permission. **Figure 9.3:** "Risk of Bipolar Disorder in Relatives of People with Bipolar and in the General Population." Reprinted, with permission, from *Annual Review of Neuroscience,* Volume 20, © 1997 by Annual Reviews www.annualreviews.org. **Figure 9.4:** From R. J. Davidson, et al., "Perspectives from Affective Neuroscience." Reprinted, with permission, from *Annual Review of Psychology,* Volume 53, © 2002 by Annual Reviews www.annualreviews.org. **P. 327:** © Gary Conner/Index Stock Imagery. **Figure 9.6:** Kessler, R. C., Berglund, P., Demler, O., Jin, R., Koretz, D., Merikangas, K. R., Rush, A. J., Walters, E. E., & Wang, P. S. (2003). The epidemiology of major depressive disorder: Results from the national comorbidity survey replication (NCS-R). *JAMA,* 2003, v. 289, pp. 3095–3105. Copyright © 2003 American Medical Association. All rights reserved. Reproduced with permission. **P. 329:** Adapted from Kleinman, A. & Kleinman, J., "Somatization: The Interconnections in Chinese Society Among Culture, Depressive Experiences, and Meanings of Pain," in A. Kleinman & B. Goods (Eds.), *Culture and Depression,* 454–455, 1986, Berkeley: University of California Press. Copyright © 1986 The Regents of the University of California. Used with permission. **P. 331:** © Bernard Annebicque/Corbis Sygma. **P. 332:** Excerpts from *Prozac Nation* by Elizabeth Wurtzel. Copyright © 1994 by Elizabeth Wurtzel. Reprinted by permission of Houghton Mifflin Company and Collins McCormick Literary Agency. All rights reserved. **P. 334:** © Will McIntyre/Photo Researchers. **P. 335:** © Pascal Goetgheluck/Photo Researchers. **Pp. 337, 338:** From *Breaking the Patterns of Depression* by Michael D. Yapko. Copyright © 1997 by Michael D. Yapko. Used by permission of Doubleday, a division of Random House, Inc. **Pp. 339, 340:** From Thorpe, G. & Olson, S. *Behavior Therapy: Concepts, Procedures and Application,* 2/e. Published by Allyn and Bacon, Boston, MA. Copyright © 1997 by Pearson Education. Reprinted/adapted by permission of the publisher. **P. 341:** © David Young-Wolff/PhotoEdit. **Figure 9.10:** From Clarke, G., Hawkins, W., Murphy, M., Sheeber, L. B., et al., 1995, "Targeted Prevention of Unipolar Depressive Disorder in an At-Risk Sample of High School Adolescents: A Randomized Trial of Group Cognitive Intervention," *Journal of the American Academy of Child and Adolescent Psychiatry, 34,* 312, 321. Copyright © 1995 Lippincott Williams and Wilkins. Used with permission. **P. 344:** © Mary Kate Denny/PhotoEdit. **P. 346:** © Johns Hopkins Medicine.

CHAPTER 10

Opener: *Florista* by Bernadita Zegers. Kactus Foto, Santiago, Chile/Superstock. **P. 350:** "Resume" from *Dorothy Parker: Complete Poems* by Dorothy Parker. Copyright © 1999 by The National Association for the Advancement of Colored People. Used by permission of Penguin, a division of Penguin Group (USA) Inc. **P. 352:** © Douglas Kirkland/Corbis Images. **Pp. 352, 372:** From *A Darkness Visible: A Memoir of Madness* by William Styron. Copyright © 1990 by William Styron. Used by permission of Vintage Books, a Division of Random House, Inc. **Figure 10.1:** From New York Times/CBS News Poll: Teenagers' Experience with Suicide, *New York Times,* October 20, 1999, p. 1.

Figure 10.2: Adapted from World Health Organization (WHO). (2004). Distribution of suicide rates (per 100,000) by gender and age, 2000. Retrieved from: http://www.who.int/mental_health/prevention/suicide/suicidecharts/en/. Reprinted with permission from the World Health Organization. **Table 10.1:** *American Journal of Community Psychology*, v. 33, 2004, "Risk and resiliency factors influencing suicidality among urban African American and Latin Youth" by L. O'Donnell, C. O'Donnell, D. M. Wardlaw, & A. Stueve, copyright © 2004. Used with kind permission of Springer Science and Business Media. **P. 356:** From Pfeffer, C. R., 1985, "Suicidal Tendencies in Normal Children," *Journal of Nervous & Mental Disease*, 173, 78–84. Copyright © 1985 Lippincott Williams & Wilkins. Reprinted with permission. **Figure 10.3:** From World Health Organization (WHO). (2005). WHO SUPRE suicide prevention: Live your life. Rretrieved from: http://www.who.int/mental_health/management/en/SUPRE_flyer1.pdf. Reprinted with permission from the World Health Organization. **Figure 10.4:** Gould, M. S., Greenberg, T., Velting, D. M., & Shaffer, D. (2003). Youth suicide risk and preventive interventions: A review of the past 10 years. *Journal of the American Academy of Child & Adolescent Psychiatry*, 42, 386–405. Copyright © 2003 by Lippincott Williams & Wilkins. Used with permission. **Pp. 358–359:** From Nolen-Hoeksema S, Larson J (1999), *Coping with Loss*. Mahweh, N.J.: Lawrence Erlbaum. Reprinted with permission. **P. 359:** © Chris Niedenthal/Black Star/PictureQuest. **P. 360:** Drawing from *Night Falls Fast* by Kay Redfield Jamison. Copyright © 1999 by Kay Redfield Jamison. Used by permission of Alfred A. Knopf, a division of Random House, Inc. and Picador. **Pp. 360, 361:** *Suicide Notes: Predictive Clues and Patterns*, 1988, "I wish I could explain it" by A. A. Leenaars. Copyright © 1998. Used with kind permission of Springer Science and Business Media. **Pp. 360, 361:** Excerpts from *Prozac Nation* by Elizabeth Wurtzel. Copyright © 1994 by Elizabeth Wurtzel. Reprinted by permission of Houghton Mifflin Company and Collins McCormick Literary Agency. All rights reserved. **P. 361:** Excerpt from The Letters of Virginia Woolf, Volume VI: 1936–1941. Copyright © 1980 by Quentin Bell and Angelica Garnett, reproduced by permission of Harcourt, Inc. Published in the UK as The Letters of Virginia Woolf, edited by N. Nicolson and J. Trautman, published by Hogarth Press. Reprinted by permission of The Random House Group Ltd. **Pp. 364, 365:** From *An Unquiet Mind: A Memoir of Moods and Madness* by K.R. Jamison. Copyright © 1995. Used by permission of Alfred A. Knopf, a Division of Random House, Inc. **P. 365:** © Esbin-Anderson/Image Works. **P. 367 (left):** © Corbis/Bettmann. **P. 367 (right):** © Alain Benainous/Gamma Press. **P. 369:** © Michael Newman/Photo Edit. **P. 370:** © Gary D. Landsman/Corbis Images. **P. 372:** © Douglas Kirkland/Corbis Images.

CHAPTER 11

Opener: *My Dog and I Are One* by Patricia Schwimmer. Canadian/Superstock. **P. 376:** © Reuters/Corbis Images. **Pp. 376, 415:** Reprinted with permission of Simon & Schuster Adult Publishing Group and the author from *A Beautiful Mind* by Sylvia Nasar. Copyright © 1998 by Sylvia Nasar. **P. 378:** From *Angelhead* by Greg Bottoms, copyright © 2000 by Greg Bottoms. Used by permission of Crown Publishers, a division of Random House, Inc. **Figure 11.1:** From *Surviving Schizophrenia: A Family Manual* by E. Fuller Torrey. Copyright © 1983 by E. Fuller Torrey. Reprinted by permission of HarperCollins Publishers. **P. 384:** © A.P./Wide World Photos. **P. 387:** From R. D. Laing, *The Divided Self*, 1971, pp. 29–30. Harmondsworth: Routledge. Reprinted with permission from Taylor & Francis. **P. 387:** © Grunnitus/Photo Researchers. **P. 388:** © Bob Daemmrich/Stock Boston. **P. 389:** From McGhie, A. & Chapman, J., 1961, "Disorders in Attention and Perception in Early Schizophrenia," *British Journal of Medical Psychology*, 34, p. 104. Reproduced with permission from Psychology and Psychotherapy: Theory Research and Practice (formerly the British Journal of Medical Psychology) © The British Psychological Society. **P. 391:** Poem "Anxiety" from *Surviving Schizophrenia: A Family Manual* by E. Fuller Torrey. Copyright © 1983 by E. Fuller Torrey. Reprinted by permission of HarperCollins Publishers. **Figure 11.3:** From *Schizophrenia Genesis: The Origins of Madness* by Irving I. Gottesman. © 1991 by Irving I. Gottesman. Used with permission of Worth Publishers. **P. 397:** Courtesy, The Genain Quadruplets. **P. 398 (both):** Courtesy, Dr. Nancy Andreasen. **Figure 11.5:** Barch, D. M., "The cognitive neuroscience of schizophrenia." Reprinted, with permission, from *Annual Review of Clinical Psychology*, Volume 1, © 2005 by Annual Reviews www.annualreviews.org. **Figure 11.7:** Barch, D. M., "The cognitive neuroscience of schizophrenia." Reprinted, with permission, from *Annual Review of Clinical Psychology*, Volume 1. Copyright © 2005 by Annual Reviews www.annualreviews.org. **P. 401:** From McGhie, A. & Chapman, J., 1961, "Disorders in Attention and Perception in Early Schizophrenia," *British Journal of Medical Psychology*, 34, p. 104. Reproduced with permission from Psychology and Psychotherapy: Theory Research and Practice (formerly the British Journal of Medical Psychology) © The British Psychological Society. **P. 403:** © Joseph Nettis/Photo Researchers. **P. 406:** From Brown, T. A., O'Leary, T. A. & Barlow, D. H., 2001, in Barlow, D. H. (Ed.) "Generalized Anxiety Disorder," *Clinical Handbook of Psychological Disorders: A Step-by-Step Treatment Manual*, Third Edition, New York: The Guilford Press. Reprinted with permission. **Table 11.10:** From Liberman, R. P., Glynn, S., Blair, K. E., Ross, D., & Marder, S. R. (2002). In vivo amplified skills training: Promoting generalization of independent living skills for clients with schizophrenia. *Psychiatry: Interpersonal & Biological Processes*, 65, 137–155. Reprinted with permission from The Guilford Press. **Figure 11.9:** From G.E. Hogarty, et al., "Family Psychoeducation," in

Archives of General Psychiatry, 1986, Vol. 43, pp. 633–642. Copyright © 1986 American Medical Association. All rights reserved. Reproduced with permission. **P. 412:** Courtesy, Skyland Trail, Atlanta, GA. **P. 415:** © Reuters/Corbis Images.

CHAPTER 12

Opener: *The Armour* by Gayle Ray. American/Superstock. **P. 422:** © Ed Quinn/Corbis Images. **Pp. 422, 423, 455:** From *Girl, Interrupted* by Susanna Kaysen. Copyright © 1993 by Susanna Kaysen. Used by permission of Turtle Bay Books, a division of Random House, Inc. **P. 427 (left):** © Coneyl Jay/Getty Images. **P. 427 (right):** Corbis Images. **P. 431:** From Beck, A. T. & Freeman, A. M., 1990, *Cognitive Therapy of Personality Disorders*, pp. 111–112. New York: Guilford Press. Reprinted with permission. **P. 431:** Reprinted with permission from Spitzer, R. L., Skodol, A. E., Gibbon, M. & Williams, J. B. W., 1981, *DSM-III Case Book: A Learning Companion to the Diagnostic and Statistical Manual of Mental Disorders*, Third Edition. Copyright © 1981 American Psychiatric Association. **432:** © Richard T. Nowitz/Corbis Images. **P. 433:** Reprinted with permission from Spitzer, R. L., Skodol, A. E., Gibbon, M. & Williams, J. B. W., 1981, *DSM-III Case Book: A Learning Companion to the Diagnostic and Statistical Manual of Mental Disorders*, Third Edition. Copyright © 1981 American Psychiatric Association. **P. 436:** © Joel Gordon. **P. 437:** © The Kobal Collection/Ken Regan/Orion. **Pp. 440, 441:** From Linehan, M. M., Cochran, B. N. & Kehrer, K. C., "Dialectical Behavior Therapy for Borderline Personality Disorder," in D. H. Barlow (Ed.), *Clinical Handbook of Psychological Disorders: A step-by-Step Treatment Manual*, Third edition, pp. 502–504. NY: Guilford Press. Reprinted with permission. **P. 441:** © The Kobal Collection/Paramount. **Figure 12.2:** Donegan, N. H., Sanislow, C. A., Blumberg, H. P., Fulbright, R. K., Lacadie, C., Skudlarski, P., Gore, J. C., Olson, I. R., McGlashan, T. H., & Wexler, B. E. Amygdala hyperreactivity in borderline personality disorder: Implications for emotional dysregulation. *Biological Psychiatry*, 54, 1284–1293. **P. 444:** © Esbin-Anderson/Image Works. **P. 445:** © Tordai/The Image Works. **Pp. 445, 446:** From Beck, A. T. & Freeman, A. M., 1990, *Cognitive Therapy of Personality Disorders*, pp. 211–212, 245–247. New York: Guilford Press. Reprinted with permission. **P. 448:** Reprinted with permission from Spitzer, R. L., Skodol, A. E., Gibbon, M. & Williams, J. B. W., 1981, *DSM-III Case Book: A Learning Companion to the Diagnostic and Statistical Manual of Mental Disorders*, Third Edition. Copyright © 1981 American Psychiatric Association. **P. 449:** © Walter Hodges/Getty Images. **P. 451:** From Spitzer, R. L., Skodol, A. E., Gibbon, M. & Williams, J. B. W., 1983, *Psychopathology: A Case Book*, pp. 63–64. NY: McGraw-Hill. Reprinted with permission from The McGraw-Hill Companies. **Table 12.6:** From P. T. Costa & R. R. McCrae, 1992, "The Five-Factor Model of Personality and its Relevance to Personality Disorders," *Journal of Personality Disorders*, 6, 343–359. Copyright © 1992

Guilford Publications. **P. 455:** © Ed Quinn/Corbis Images.

CHAPTER 13

Opener: *In the Fields* by Daniel Nevins. American. Private Collection/Superstock. **P. 460:** Courtesy, Temple Grandin. **Pp. 460, 461, 504:** From *Thinking in Pictures and My Other Reports from My Life with Autism* by Temple Grandin. Copyright © 1995. Used by permission of Vintage Books, a Division of Random House, Inc. **P. 462:** © Michael Newman/PhotoEdit. **P. 464:** Reprinted with permission from Spitzer, R. L., Gibbon, M., Skodol, A. E., Williams, J. B. W., and First, M.B. (Eds.), 1994, *DSM-IV Case Book: A Learning Companion to the Diagnostic and Statistical Manual of Mental Disorders*. Copyright © 1994 American Psychiatric Association. **P. 468:** © Dan McCoy/Rainbow. **P. 469:** © 1996 Newsweek, Inc. All rights reserved. Reprinted by permission. Photo by Ken Schles. **Pp. 470, 471:** From Jenkins, R. L., *Behavior Disorders of Childhood and Adolescence*, 1973. Courtesy of Charles C. Thomas Publisher, Ltd., Springfield, Illinois. **P. 472:** Reprinted with permission from Spitzer, R. L., Gibbon, M., Skodol, A. E., Williams, J. B. W., and First, M. B. (Eds.), 1994, *DSM-IV Case Book: A Learning Companion to the Diagnostic and Statistical Manual of Mental Disorders*, Copyright 1994. American Psychiatric Association. **P. 474:** © Colin Edwards/Photofusion Picture Library/Alamy. **Figure 13.1:** From J. B. Reid and J. M. Eddy, "The Prevention of Antisocial Behavior: Some Considerations in the Search for Effective Interventions," in D. M. Stoff, et al. (Eds.), *Handbook of Antisocial Personality Disorder*. Copyright © 1997 John Wiley & Sons, Inc. Reprinted with permission of John Wiley & Sons, Inc. **P. 479:** © Geri Engberg/Image Works. **Figure 13.2:** From Dadds, et al., 1999, "Early Intervention and Prevention of Anxiety Disorders in Children: Results at Two-Year Follow-Up," in *Journal of Consulting and Clinical Psychology*, Vol. 67, pp. 145–150. Copyright © 1999 by the American Psychological Association. Reproduced with permission. **P. 484:** © Eric A. Wessman/Stock Boston. **P. 486:** © A.P./Wide World Photos. **P. 487:** © Geoff Franklin. **P. 495 (top):** © Tony Freeman/PhotoEdit. **P. 495 (bottom):** © Michael Greenlar/Image Works. **Pp. 496, 497:** Reprinted with permission from Spitzer, R. L., Gibbon, M., Skodol, A. E., Williams, J. B. W., and First, M.B. (Eds.), 1994, *DSM-IV Case Book: A Learning Companion to the Diagnostic and Statistical Manual of Mental Disorders*. Copyright © 1994 American Psychiatric Association. **P. 499:** United Artists/The Kobal Collection/Stephen Vaughan. **P. 502:** © Ellen Senisi/Image Works. **P. 504:** Courtesy, Temple Grandin.

CHAPTER 14

Opener: *Untitled #4* by Deborah Schneider. © Bonnie Spiegel/Images.com/Corbis Images. **P. 510:** © Sophie Bassouls/Sygma/Corbis Images. **Pp. 510, 511, 535, 536:** From *Elegy for Iris* by John Bayley. Copyright © 1998 by the author and reprinted by permission of St. Martin's Press, LLC. and Duckworth Press. **P. 512:** © Corbis

Images. **P. 513:** Reprinted with permission from Spitzer, R. L., Gibbon, M., Skodol, A. E., Williams, J. B. W., and First, M. B. (Eds.), 1994, *DSM-IV Case Book: A Learning Companion to the Diagnostic and Statistical Manual of Mental Disorders.* Copyright © 1994 American Psychiatric Association. **P. 515:** © Bettman/Corbis Images. **Figure 14.2:** © D. Miller/Peter Arnold. **Figure 14.3a-b:** Courtesy, Dr. Arnold B. Scheibel. **P. 517:** © Judy Griesedieck/Getty Images. **P. 518:** © Science Photo Library/Photo Researchers. **P. 519:** © J. M. Loubat/Vandystadt/Photo Researchers. **P. 524:** From Gallagher-Thompson, D., Lovett, S. & Rose, J., 1991, "Psychotherapeutic Interventions for Stressed Family Caregivers." Reprinted with permission from W. A. Myers (Ed.) *New Techniques in Psychotherapy of Older Patients.* Copyright © 1991 American Psychiatric Association. **P. 528:** Reprinted with permission from Spitzer, R. L., Gibbon, M., Skodol, A. E., Williams, J. B. W., and First, M. B. (Eds.), 1994, *DSM-IV Case Book: A Learning Companion to the Diagnostic and Statistical Manual of Mental Disorders,* Copyright © 1994. American Psychiatric Association. **Pp. 529, 530:** Adapted from Scogin, F., Floyd, M. & Forde, J., 2000, Anxiety in Older Adults, in S. K. Whitbourne (Ed.)., *Psychopathology in Later Adulthood.* Copyright © John Wiley & Sons, Inc. Reprinted with permission of John Wiley & Sons, Inc. **P. 530, 531:** Adapted from D. A. King and H. W. Markus (2000). Mood Disorders in Older Adults in S. K. Whitbourne (Ed.)., *Psychopathology in Later Adulthood.* Copyright © John Wiley & Sons, Inc. Reprinted with permission of John Wiley & Sons, Inc. **P. 531:** © Fritz Hoffmann/Image Works. **P. 533:** © Macduff Everton/Getty Images. **P. 533:** Lisansky-Gomberg, E. (2000). Substance Abuse Disorders, in S. K. Whitbourne (Ed.), *Psychopathology in Later Adulthood.* Copyright © John Wiley & Sons, Inc. Reprinted with permission of John Wiley & Sons, Inc. **P. 535:** © Sophie Bassouls/Sygma/Corbis Images.

CHAPTER 15

Opener: *Wednesday's Child* by John S. Bunker. American/Superstock. **P. 540:** © Tim Graham Picture Library/A.P./Wide World Photos. **Pp. 540, 541, 569:** Diana, Princess of Wales, BBC Panorama Interview, November 1995. BBC. Reproduced with permission. **P. 545:** © N.M.S.B./Custom Medical Stock Photo. **P. 545:** Excerpt from pp. 254–5 from *Wasted: A Memoir of Anorexia and Bulimia* by Marya Hornbacher. Copyright © 1998 by Marya Hornbacher-Beard. Reprinted by permission of HarperCollins Publishers. **P. 548:** © Bill Losh/Getty Images. **P. 548:** Reprinted with permission from Spitzer, R. L., Skodol, A. E., Gibbon, M. & Williams, J. B. W., 1981, *DSM-III Case Book: A Learning Companion to the Diagnostic and Statistical Manual of Mental Disorders,* Third Edition. Copyright © 1981 American Psychiatric Association. **P. 548:** Kim Hubbard, Anne-Marie O'Neill and Christina Cheakalos/*People Weekly* © 1999. Reprinted with permission. **P. 549:** From Wilps, R. F., Jr., 1990, "Male Bulimia Nervosa: An Autobiographical Case Study." Copyright © 1990 From *Males with Eating Disorders*

by A. E. Andersen (Ed). Reproduced by permission of Routledge/Taylor & Francis Group. **Figure 15.3:** From D. Garner, A. K. Cooke, H. W. Marano, "The 1997 Body Image Survey," in *Psychology Today,* pp. 30–44. Reprinted with permission from Psychology Today Magazine. Copyright © 1997 www.psychologytoday.com. **P. 551 (left):** © Petre Buzoianu/ZUMA/Corbis Images. **P. 551 (right):** © Charles O'Rear/Corbis Images. **Pp. 551, 552:** Adapted from *Social Science & Medicine,* v. 41, L. Sing, "Self-starvation in context: Towards a culturally sensitive understanding of anorexia nervosa," pp. 27–29. Copyright © 1995, with permission from Elsevier. **Pp. 552, 553:** From Stunkard, A. J., 1993, "A History of Binge Eating," in C. G. Fairburn and G. T. Wilson (Eds.), *Binge Eating: Nature, Assessment, and Treatment,* pp. 20–21. New York: Guilford Press. Reprinted with permission. **Figure 15.4:** From C. V. Wiseman, et al., "Cultural Expectations of Thinness in Women: An Update," in *International Journal of Eating Disorders,* Vol. 11. Copyright © 1992 John Wiley & Sons, Inc. Reprinted with permission of John Wiley & Sons, Inc. **Pp. 556, 557:** "Worshipping The Gods Of Thinness," from *Reviving Ophelia* by Mary Pipher, Ph.D. Copyright © 1994 by Mary Pipher, Ph.D. Used by permission of G.P. Putnam's Sons, a division of Penguin Group (USA) Inc. and by permission of the author. **P. 557:** © Bob Daemmrich/Stock Boston. **P. 569:** © Tim Graham Picture Library/A.P./Wide World Photos.

CHAPTER 16

Opener: *Shadow of Her Former Self* by Diana Ong. 1940. Chinese/USA/Superstock. **P. 574 (top):** © Corbis Images. **P. 574 (bottom):** Courtesy, HarperCollins Publishers. **Figure 16.1:** From J. S. Hyde, *Understanding Human Sexuality,* p. 199. McGraw-Hill Companies, Copyright © 1990. Reprinted with permission from The McGraw-Hill Companies. **Figure 16.2:** From J.S. Hyde, *Understanding Human Sexuality,* p. 200. McGraw-Hill Companies, Copyright © 1990. Reprinted with permission from The McGraw-Hill Companies. **Pp. 574, 613:** Excerpts from pp. 57, 262, 280 from *As Nature Made Him* by JOHN COLAPINTO. Copyright © 1999 by John Colapinto. Reprinted by permission of HarperCollins Publishers. **Pp. 581, 582, 586, 600, 601, 602, 603, 604:** Reprinted with permission from Spitzer, R. L., Gibbon, M., Skodol, A. E., Williams, J. B. W., and First, M. B. (Eds.), 1994, *DSM-IV Case Book: A Learning Companion to the Diagnostic and Statistical Manual of Mental Disorders.* Copyright © 1994 American Psychiatric Association. **Table 16.2:** From *Sex in America* by Robert T. Michael. Copyright © 1994 by CSG Enterprises, Inc., Edward O. Laumann, Robert T. Michael, and Gina Kolata. By permission of Little, Brown and Co., Inc. and Edward Laumann. **Table 16.3:** From E. O. Laumann, et al., *The Social Organization of Sexuality: Sexual Practices in the United States.* Copyright © 1994 University of Chicago Press. Reprinted with permission of the publisher, University of Chicago Press. **Pp. 582, 583:** From McCarthy, B. W., 1989, "Cognitive Behavioral Strategies and Techniques in the Treatment of Early Ejaculation," in S. R. Leiblum & R. C. Rosen (Eds.), *Principles and*

Practice of Sex Therapy: Update for the 1990s, pp. 151–152. New York: Guilford Press. Reprinted with permission. **585:** © A. Collins/Image Works. **Figure 16.4:** From Barlow, D. H., 1986, "Causes of Sexual Dysfunction: The Role of Anxiety and Cognitive Interference," *Journal of Consulting and Clinical Psychology,* 54, 140–148. Copyright © 1986 by the American Psychological Association. Reproduced with permission. **P. 589:** © Bill Bachmann/PhotoEdit. **P. 595:** © Grace/Zefa/Corbis Images. **Pp. 595, 596:** From Althof, S. E. (2000). Erectile dysfunction: Psychotherapy with men and couples. In S. R. Leiblum & R. C. Rosen (Eds.), *Principles and Practice of Sex Therapy* (3rd ed.), p. 270. New York, NY: Guilford Press. Reprinted with permission. **P. 597:** © Digital Vision. **P. 601:** © Bill Aron/Photo Researchers. **P. 603, 610:** © A.P./Wide World Photos. **Tables 16.9 and 16.10:** From "The Paraphilias: Research and Treatment" by Barry Maletsky from *A Guide to Treatments That Work,* Second Edition, edited by Peter Nathan and Jack Gorman. Copyright © 1998 2002 by Peter E. Nathan and Jack M. Gorman. Used by permission of Oxford University Press, Inc. **P. 608:** Adapted from *Archives of Sexual Behavior,* v. 24, 1995, "Female-to-Male Transsexualism Type: Two Cases" by R. Dicky and J. Stephens, copyright © 1995. Used with kind permission of Springer Science and Business Media. **Pp. 609, 610:** From Feinberg, L. 2001 "Trans health crisis: For us it's life or death." *American Journal of Public Health,* 91, pp. 897–898. Reprinted with permission from The American Public Health Association. **P. 613:** © Corbis Images.

CHAPTER 17

Opener: *The Ferryman's* by George E. Dunne. Irish. New Apollo Gallery, Dublin/Superstock. **P. 620:** © Pacha/Corbis Images. **Pp. 621, 622:** Quoted in Marlatt, 1993, from *Behavior Therapy,* 24(4), p. 462. Copyright © 1993 by the Association for Advancement of Behavior Therapy. Reprinted by permission of the publisher. **P. 622:** © Bettmann/Corbis Images. **Figure 17.2:** From Pope, H. G., Jr., Ionescu-Pioggia, M., & Pope, K. W., 2001, "Drug Use and Lifestyle Among College Undergraduates: A 30-Year Longitudinal Study." Reprinted with permission from *American Journal of Psychiatry,* 158. Copyright © 2001 American Psychiatric Association. **Pp. 625, 633, 642:** Reprinted with permission from Spitzer, R. L., Gibbon, M., Skodol, A. E., Williams, J. B. W., and First, M. B. (Eds.), 1994, *DSM-IV Case Book: A Learning Companion to the Diagnostic and Statistical Manual of Mental Disorders.* Copyright © 1994 American Psychiatric Association. **Pp. 627, 628, 657, 658:** From Inciardi, J. A., Lockwood, D. & Pottieger, A. E. *Women and Crack-Cocaine.* Published by Allyn and Bacon, Boston, MA. Copyright © 1993 by Pearson Education. Reprinted/adapted by permission of the publisher. **P. 630:** © Philip Lee Harvey/Getty Images. **P. 632:** © Christopher Brown/Stock Boston. **Figure 17.3:** From Global Status Report on Alcohol, World Health Organization, 2001,

www.who.int/substance_abuse. Reprinted with permission from the World Health Organization. **Figures 17.4 and 17.5:** From the National Household Survey on Drug Abuse, 2000. Substance Abuse & Mental Health Services Administration. **P. 637:** © Kindra Clineff/Index Stock Imagery. **Figure 17.6a-b:** © Courtesy, Dr. Neil Rosenberg, Department of Medicine, University of Colorado School of Medicine and the International Institute on Inhalant Abuse. **Pp. 640, 641, 665** From Spitzer, R. L., Skodol, A. E., Gibbon, M. & Williams, J. B. W., 1983, *Psychopathology: A Case Book,* pp. 63–64. NY: McGraw-Hill. Reprinted with permission from The McGraw-Hill Companies. **P. 642:** © Tannen Maury/Image Works. **P. 643:** © A. Ramey/Stock Boston/PictureQuest. **P. 644 (left):** © Scott Camazine/Photo Researchers. **P. 644 (right):** © Dept. of Clinical Radiology, Salisbury District Hospital/Science Photo Library/Photo Researchers. **P. 45:** © A.P./Wide World Photos. **Pp. 648, 649:** From Hoffman, A. 1968, Psychotomimetic Agents, in A. Burger (Ed.) *Drugs Affecting the Central Nervous System,* Vol. 2, pp. 185–186. New York: Marcel Dekker. Copyright © 1968. Reprinted with permission of Routledge/Taylor & Francis Group, LLC. **P. 651:** © G. Baden/zefa/Corbis Images. **Pp. 653, 657:** Engel, J., *Addicted: Kids talking about drugs in their own words,* 1989, New York: Tom Doherty and Associates. Reproduced with permission of Palgrave MacMillan. **P. 656:** © Jeff Dunn/Index Stock Imagery. **P. 659:** © Tom & Dee Ann McCarthy/Corbis Images. **P. 661:** Reprinted from Hester, RK and WR Miller (Eds). *Handbook of Alcoholism Treatment Approaches: Effective Alternatives,* CT Rimmele, WR Miller, MJ Dougher, "Aversion Therapies," p. 135. Copyright © 1989, with permission from Elsevier. **Pp. 662, 663:** Adapted from *Behavioral Treatment of Alcohol Problems,* 1978, by M. B. Sobell and L. C. Sobell. Copyright © 1978. Used with kind permission of Springer Science and Business Media. **P. 663:** © Jill Sabella/Getty Images. **P. 666:** © Mary Kate Denny/PhotoEdit. **P. 669:** © Pacha/Corbis Images.

CHAPTER 18

Opener: *Sun and Moon* (Subtitled *Starker Traum*) by Paul Klee. Swiss. Bridgeman Art Library, London/Superstock. **P. 676:** Photo by William DiLillo. **Pp. 676, 677, 695:** From *Angelhead* by Greg Bottoms. Copyright © 2000 by Greg Bottoms. Used by permission of Crown Publishers, a division of Random House, Inc. **P. 679:** © Bob Daemmrich/Stock Boston. **P. 680:** © A.P./Wide World Photos. **P. 681 (left):** © Mike Stewart/Corbis Sygma. **P. 681 (right):** © A.P./Wide World Photos. **P. 687 (both):** © A.P./Wide World Photos. **P. 689:** Reprinted from Morrissey, J. and J. Monahan (eds.), *Research in Community and Mental Health,* v. 10, J. Monahan, et al., "Coercion in the Provision of Mental Health Services: The MacArthur Studies." Copyright © 2001, with permission from Elsevier. **P. 690:** © Eric Roth/Index Stock Imagery. **P. 694:** Photo by William DiLillo.

Information Technology Law

4TH EDITION

The Law & Society

ANDREW MURRAY

Reader in Law, London School of Economics and Political Science

OXFORD

UNIVERSITY PRESS

OXFORD
UNIVERSITY PRESS

Great Clarendon Street, Oxford, OX2 6DP,
United Kingdom

Oxford University Press is a department of the University of Oxford.
It furthers the University's objective of excellence in research, scholarship,
and education by publishing worldwide. Oxford is a registered trade mark of
Oxford University Press in the UK and in certain other countries

Published in the United States of America by Oxford University Press
198 Madison Avenue, New York, NY 10016, United States of America

British Library Cataloguing in Publication Data
Data available
Library of Congress Control Number: 2019942358

ISBN 978–0–19–880472–7

Printed in Great Britain by
Bell & Bain Ltd, Glasgow

To Andrew and Sarah Murray
Mervyn and Rosemary Miles
And especially to my wife Rachel
You have been with me every step of the way

PREFACE

It is impossible for me to imagine that it is time for a fourth edition. Earlier editions of this text are now for me a mark of the passage of time with nine years having now elapsed since the first edition, an age in terms of Information Technology Law and Society. Again I find myself noting that this is a subject which demands substantial rewriting from edition to edition; not just updates to reflect a few new developments in case law or statue. The world this book deals with changes from edition to edition. Once more, many chapters have been substantially rewritten to reflect changes in the law, technology, society, and developments in case law. The major legal development since the third edition has been the introduction of the General Data Protection Regulation and the Data Protection Act 2018. This completely reset legal framework for data protection law is now reflected in major changes in Part VI where three chapters on data protection law replace a single chapter in the third edition. Also, the passage of the Investigatory Powers Act 2016, see chapter 25 on state surveillance, has seen the law on data interception and surveillance completely rewritten since the previous edition. Other key changes include a major rewrite of the copyright in the information society section. The old single chapter on copyright and the digital environment has become three chapters, with the addition of chapters on digital creatives and copyright law and copyright infringement in the digital environment. The electronic payments chapter is expanded to look at cryptocurrency, and a new consumer protection chapter is added. To make some space, the old digital ownership chapter becomes online-only content, as does the future of IT Law chapter.

All other chapters have been substantially reviewed and updated to reflect emerging issues in law and technology. The key changes are:

- The law is updated throughout to that in force on 1 December 2018, except for one tiny update to account for the Advocate General's opinion in *Google v CNIL* published on 10 January 2018 (just as the text was being handed over to the publisher).

- The whole text has been reviewed and updated. All hyperlinks were active on 18 March 2019.

- Elements of the old chapter 3 on digitization and society have been incorporated into chapter 1.

- A new chapter 3 on net neutrality is added.

- The previous chapter 11 on copyright in the digital environment is expanded now to be three chapters: chapter 10 on digital creatives and copyright law, chapter 11 on copyright in the digital environment, and chapter 12 on copyright infringement in the digital environment.

- A new chapter 18 on consumer protection is added

- The previous chapter 20 on data protection is replaced with three new chapters: chapter 22 on the legal framework for data protection, chapter 23 on rights and obligations of data protection law, and chapter 24 on the international trade in personal data.

- Part VI on privacy and data protection has been completely rewritten to reflect the adoption of the General Data Protection Regulation, the Data Protection Act 2018, the Investigatory Powers Act 2016, the *Tele2*, *Liberty v Home Office*, *Ittihadieh*, and NT1 and NT2 decisions.

- There has been significant rewriting of chapter 3 (to reflect developments in net neutrality); chapter 4 (to discuss platform regulation and behavioural regulation); chapter 5 (to include a discussion of fake news, deception, and harmful political speech as well as the *Google v Equustek* and *Google v CNIL* cases); chapter 7 (to account for the *Monroe v Hopkins* decision among others); chapter 12 (to examine the impact of the Supreme Court decision in *Cartier v British Sky Broadcasting*); chapter 15 (to examine developments in the *Argos Ltd v Argos Systems Inc* and *Victoria Plum v Victorian Plumbing* cases); chapter 16 (to include a section on smart contracting); chapter 17 (to discuss blockchain technology and cryptocurrency); and chapter 20 (to discuss the Digital Economy Act 2018 (Age-verification) and other updates).

- Test questions and readings have been reviewed and updated.

- There are four further 'online only' chapters; chapter 26 on digital ownership, chapter 27 on the digital public sphere, chapter 28 on virtual environments, and chapter 29 on the future challenges for IT law. These chapters can only be accessed via the Online Resources.

Again I must thank my students, both undergraduate and postgraduate, for the great discussions we have in class. Thanks to all students of LL.210: Information Technology Law; LL4S1: Cyberlaw; LL4S2: Ecommerce Law; LL4S4: Digital Rights, Privacy and Security; and LL4S5 Piracy, Content, and Ownership in the Information Society. Particular thanks must go my panel of trusted advisors, a mixture of colleagues and PhD students past and present. In no particular order, thanks go to Dr Orla Lynskey who has been instrumental in my understanding of Data Protection Law, Dr Tatiana Cutts who explains blockchain and distributed ledgers in an approachable and understandable way (which is extremely difficult as I have learned), Dr Mark Leiser who was instrumental in the fake news and behavioural regulation additions and in a number of other areas, and Dr Emily Laidlaw who saw the importance of platform regulation almost before anyone else. Thanks also to all these people who listen to me talk and tell me when I'm wrong. You all know who you are but I pick out Professor Chris Reed, Dr Paul Bernal, Professor Daithi Mac Sithigh, Professor Lilian Edwards, Ms MacKenzie Common, Dr Tijman Wiseman, and Professor Arno Lodder. During the course of revising this text I was also an advisor to the House of Lords Communications Committee and I wish to thank in particular the Clerk to the Committee Mr Theo Pembroke for ensuring I always had time to work on this manuscript. Of course, as ever, thanks to everyone at OUP who do all the heavy lifting that turns this from manuscript to book, in particular my editors Hannah Crane, Lucy Read, and Carlotta Fanton.

Finally, thank you to all my supporters at home. In particular my wife Rachel. She again has to be singled out once more for her patience, attention to detail, and encouragement throughout the writing process. Again, I hope she is pleased with the end product, as I hope are all readers of this edition.

Andrew Murray, London, 10 January 2019

CONTENTS

GUIDE TO THE BOOK

Information Technology Law: The Law and Society contains a range of useful features, which have been designed to enhance your understanding of the subject.

> **Highlight** Kahn's four ground rules for internet
>
> 1. Each distinct network would have to stand on its own and n
>   required to any such network to connect it to the internet.
> 2. Communications would be on a best-effort basis. If a packet di
>   tination, it would shortly be retransmitted from the source.
> 3. Black boxes would be used to connect the networks (these wo
>   and routers). There would be no information retained by the

Highlights

Featuring definitions of crucial concepts, ideas, and principles, the highlight boxes give you an insight into the debates that surround the relationship between law and the information society. They may be a quotation from a leading figure, an outline of a legal term or procedure, or an extract from a case. In every instance they will help you to focus on and understand the key elements of the topic under discussion.

> **Example** Exhaustion of the first sale right
>
> Ana buys a legitimate copy of a computer program in Portugal. Sh
> when she moves to London. She later decided to sell her copy of
> The principle of exhaustion means Ana may legally sell her copy
> without the permission of the copyright owner (assuming she rem
> software from her computer).
>   Bárbara bought her copy of the same software in Brazil. She also
> tries to sell her copy of the software on eBay.co.uk she would tech

Examples

How do the legal rules developed to meet the challenges of the information society operate in practice? The example boxes use short fictional examples to demonstrate the application of the law clearly and concisely.

> **Case study** *Amazon's Conditions of sale*
>
> Your order is an offer to Amazon to buy the product(s) in your order
> purchase a product from Amazon, we will send you an e-mail confirm
> containing the details of your order (the 'Order Confirmation E-m
> E-mail is acknowledgement that we have received your order, and do
> your offer to buy the product(s) ordered. We only accept your offer,
> sale for a product ordered by you, when we dispatch the product to y
> tion to you that we've dispatched the product to you (the 'Dispatch

Case studies

From Napster to the economics behind recent US Presidential elections, the case study boxes illustrate the real-life examples that have shaped the developments of information technology law.

> **FURTHER READING**
>
> **Books**
>
> M Collins, *Collins on Defamation* (OUP 2014)
> A Kenyon (ed.), *Comparative Defamation and Privacy Law* (CUP
> J Riordan, *The Liability of Internet Intermediaries* (OUP 2016)
>
> **Chapters and Articles**

Further reading

Select and seek out titles from the further reading sources at the end of each chapter in order to broaden your knowledge of the individual topics covered.

GUIDE TO THE ONLINE RESOURCES

This book is accompanied by **Online Resources**—a website providing free and easy-to-use resources which complement and support the textbook.

www.oup.com/uk/murray4e/

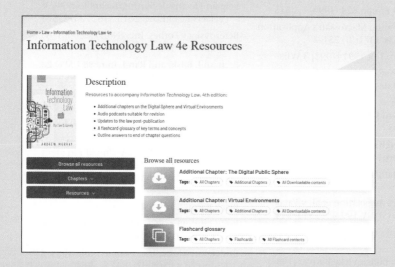

Audio updates

Audio updates from the author cover the latest developments in IT law.

Weblinks

A list of useful websites enables you to click straight through to reliable sources of online information, and efficiently direct your online study, including the author's blog which follows the latest developments in the subject.

Flashcard glossary of key terms

Test your knowledge and understanding of the specialized terminology used in information technology law, using this useful revision tool which can be downloaded to which can be downloaded to a range of portable devices.

Additional chapters

There are four additional chapters available to read and download, covering issues such as virtual environments, the digital public sphere, digital ownership and the future for IT law.

TABLE OF CASES

TABLE OF LEGISLATION

Statutory Instruments

Directives

Treaties and Conventions

PART I

The information society

How the world around us has changed as information has become the key to economic success and has become the foundation of much of our legal systems.

The world of bits

In reading this book you will be asked to think about the world around you slightly differently. While the question at the heart of most legal textbooks is: 'how does the rule of law affect individuals within the environment over which this law is effective?', the question at the heart of this book is: 'how does the environment over which the law seeks to be effective affect the rule of law?' The reason for this unique approach is the distinctive subject which this book examines; the relationship between established legal settlements and the rise of the information society.[1] While you may consider digital information, the internet, and applications such as YouTube or social networking tools like Instagram, Twitter, or Facebook to be simply part of the fabric of everyday life,[2] the British legal systems, which can trace their roots through at least 700 years of common law tradition,[3] find these developments to be extremely disruptive. These disruptive effects, once the preserve of the interested academic commentator,[4] have become of critical importance to politicians, economists, lawyers, and, in turn, to us all, as developed economies move from the traditional economic question of 'what can we produce?' to 'what can we control?'

This change in economic language reflects a wider change in modern developed economies. The traditional measure of an economic superpower was their output. Economies were measured by their ability to support communities. Agrarian economies

[1] While many books such as I Lloyd, *Information Technology Law* (8th edn, OUP 2017), D Bainbridge, *Information Technology and Intellectual Property Law* (7th edn, Bloomsbury 2018), and D Rowland, U Kohl, and A Charlesworth, *Information Technology Law* (5th edn, Routledge 2016) examine the effect of 'computerization' on the law, they take a technology-centred approach and focus on the narrow application of the law to computer systems, computer programmes, and technology-related legal issues such as data protection. This book will take a wider approach looking at the interaction of the law and the information society. A further analysis of this topic may be found in C Reed and A Murray, *Rethinking the Jurisprudence of Cyberspace* (Edward Elgar 2018).

[2] This may be determined by your age. If you are under 28, you were born after the release of the World Wide Web and have never known a world without it. You were probably active on social networking sites before you were a teenager and find a mobile telephone more useful as an instant messaging/social media device than as a telephone. Older readers though may remember the excitement of their first internet connection and signing their first mobile phone contract.

[3] For a discussion of the Common Law tradition of the English Legal System see SFC Milson, *Historical Foundations of the Common Law* (2nd edn, Lexis 1981). For a discussion of the different legal tradition of Scotland see A Kiralfy and H MacQueen (eds.), *New Perspectives in Scottish Legal History* (Routledge 1984).

[4] See L Lessig, *Code and Other Laws of Cyberspace* (Basic Books 1999); N Negroponte, *Being Digital* (Hodder & Stoughton 1995); M Castells, *The Internet Galaxy* (OUP 2001); F Webster, *Theories of the Information Society* (4th edn, Routledge 2014); R Mansell, *Inside the Communication Revolution: Evolving Patterns of Social and Technical Interaction* (OUP 2002).

measured how efficiently the land could be managed and farmed to support the surrounding community; freeing members of that community from the soil to allow
them to carry out more specialized roles such as fletcher, blacksmith, or cooper. Such
economies were though conspicuously inefficient, as demonstrated by Adam Smith in
The Wealth of Nations.[5] In this, Smith demonstrated how specialization could improve
individual output, a process which led eventually to the development of the factory,
the production line, and, with the introduction of steam power to the equation, the
Industrial Revolution.[6]

The industrial economic model became the dominant economic model of the nineteenth and early twentieth centuries. The industrial economy was driven by economies
of scale and by mechanization. No longer was economic success measured at a local level,
it was now measured by output at a national level.[7] It led industrialized nations such
as the UK to extend empires across the globe to secure the raw materials which could
be turned into textiles, iron, or later aluminium or steel. Industrial economies made
money by making things: ships, weapons, clothing, railway tracks, and later aircraft.
Industrialists grew wealthy but the workers did not: a few grew exceedingly wealthy
while exploiting the human capital of the many.[8] Following the economic downturn of
the 1920s, the effects of worker revolt such as the General Strike and the terrible impact
of two world wars on the industrial capital of European states, a new economic model
began to appear in post-war Europe. This new model of 'post-industrial economics' gives
us our first insight into the importance and value of this subject, and therefore this book.

Post-industrial economics emerged in the UK immediately after World War II. With
the cost of production of traditional industrial products such as shipbuilding and steel
production being cheaper offshore, the UK's industrial capital began to move to places
such as India, Malaysia, and Hong Kong. The UK economy started the painful transition
from industrial values of 'what can we produce?' to the newly developing service sector
and the question 'what can we provide?' With a massive growth in professional services
such as banking, insurance, legal services, education, and media, the UK became the
archetypal post-industrial, or service, economy. We no longer made money from making things, we made money from providing services. In the 1980s the last vestiges of our
old industrial economy were swept aside. We closed car plants, coal mines, shipyards,
and steelworks. The UK was going to be the world's leading service economy, but then
something happened and it is that something which is at the core of this book. The
post-industrial, or service, economy was itself overtaken only 40 years or so after it was
first developed. The new economic model is known as the 'information economy' while
its correspondent theory in social sciences is the 'information society'. While the UK
had invested in banking, insurance, and financial support services, the US, or at least
parts of it, had developed an economy built upon the systems that allowed information to be collected, stored, and processed. In so doing they created a new generation of
super-rich industrialists who far surpassed the wealth of the nineteenth-century industrialists. These were people like Steve Jobs, Larry Ellison, and most famously Bill Gates
who recognized that the value wasn't in the information itself; it was in what you could

---

[5] A Smith, *An Inquiry into the Nature and Causes of the Wealth of Nations* (1776; new edn, Capstone
2010).

[6] Ibid. Book 1, ch. 1.

[7] Gross Domestic Product became the touchstone of economic success.

[8] This of course had been explored by Karl Marx in his famous text *Das Kapital* (Verlag 1867).

enable people to do with it. They started to ask the question which is at the heart of this book: 'what can we control?'[9] This question is the thesis that underpins both the information society and the knowledge economy. It represents a shift from ownership or control of things to ownership of or control over information.[10] It represents the maturity of information technology and most importantly signals a change in economic value from owning things, or in physical terms *atoms*, to owning information which in the digital environment means *bits*. This transition from the world which saw economic value in atoms to a world which values information in bits will form the focus of the remainder of this chapter.

1.1 **An introduction to bits**

The move from economic value being sited within physical goods, to economic value being sited within information, is referred to by Nicholas Negroponte, formerly Director of the Media Laboratory at MIT, as the move from atoms to bits.[11] Negroponte, and others,[12] believe that in time this move from atomic value to value in bits may prove to be as important to social scientists and economists as the discovery of quantum physics was to physical scientists.[13] Before we embark on the deeper impact of the move from atoms to bits we need to answer the basic question, 'what is a "bit"'? We all know what atoms are, or at least I assume we do. If you do need to have a basic seminar on atoms and their role in the physical world, I suggest you read chapter 9 of Bill Bryson's excellent book *A Short History of Nearly Everything*.[14] On the assumption we know the role and position of atoms in the physical world, what then is a bit, and what is its role in the information society?

 Highlight What is a bit?

At its simplest 'bit' is a truncation of the term 'binary digit'. To expand, a binary digit is simply either a 0 or a 1.

The answer to what is a bit therefore doesn't get us any closer to the questions at the heart of this book, 'why are bits economically valuable?', 'how do bits effect social interaction?', and, most importantly for a legal textbook, 'why does the law have to take account of the effect of bits?' To answer these questions we must look, not narrowly at what a bit is, but more widely at what a bit does.

---

[9] To gain an insight into the thought process of Bill Gates during the early stages of what he calls the 'information age' read B Gates, *The Road Ahead* (Viking 1995), ch. 2.

[10] The post-industrial economic model may be seen as a step along this road being about ownership of or control over knowledge.

[11] Negroponte (n. 4).

[12] See Y Benkler, *The Wealth of Networks* (Yale UP 2007); M Castells, *The Rise of the Network Society: Information Age: Economy, Society, and Culture* (2nd edn, Wiley 2009); H Jenkins, *Convergence Culture: Where Old and New Media Collide* (NYU Press 2006).

[13] For more on this read A Murray, *The Regulation of Cyberspace: Control in the Online Environment* (Routledge 2007), ch. 9.

[14] B Bryson, *A Short History of Nearly Everything* (Broadway Books 2003).

At the most basic level therefore a bit is simply a 0 or a 1, but like atoms, which on their own are not very impressive either, it is how bits can be used to construct larger, more complex systems that give them their economic value and social importance. In the world of computer systems a bit represents a single instruction to the computer. This instruction is either to do (1) or not to do (0) a particular function. The brain of the computer, the microprocessor or central processing unit (CPU), reads the instruction.[15] The CPU may be thought of as a superfast calculator which works in binary. Bits of information are fed to the CPU from the computer memory, the CPU does a calculation and based upon the result the personal computer (or PC) carries out a predetermined function. The process that is followed is called von Neumann architecture after mathematician and computer pioneer Jon von Neumann.[16]

Von Neumann architecture is a four-step system that turns bits into computer operations or data. The first step is *fetch*, which involves the CPU retrieving an instruction (represented by bits) from program memory. These are instructions preloaded into the memory of the computer by a piece of software such as Microsoft Windows or Word. The second step is *decode*. In this step the single instruction is broken up by the CPU in separate instructions which require the CPU to do different operations. Thus a single instruction will usually contain an operational instruction telling the CPU what to do and a series of informational instructions giving the CPU the data it needs to fulfil the operational instruction. Step three is the *execute* step. In this step the CPU will carry out the operational instruction contained in the fetched data. This may be a purely internal process such as an autosave function managed completely by the software instructions fetched from the program memory or it may involve a user input where the actions of the user of the computer cause a particular event to happen (more will be said on this below). The execute step is a series of calculations using binary notation which gives a series of results managed by the CPU and carried out by a series of units on the microprocessor.[17] The final step is *writeback*. Here the CPU 'writes back' the result of its operational process to memory. This may be either the CPU memory (if it is about to carry out a further operation based on this result) or to the main memory if the operational process is complete for now. After writeback the whole process begins again with the cycle being repeated billions of times per second. At its most basic level therefore a computer CPU is simply a rather unimpressive calculator. It can add and subtract or multiply and divide but only in binary. It can do this billions of times per second and therefore is very powerful but as we are only dealing in 1s and 0s how does the manipulation of bits affect the established legal order? The answer is in the flexibility of the bit.

1.1.1 The process of digitization

Much as atoms can be used in the physical world to construct everything from the human liver to an Airbus A380, bits are the basic building blocks of the information society. In his book *The Road Ahead* Microsoft co-founder Bill Gates explains the

---

[15] This is the computer part that is advertised as 'Intel Core' or 'AMD Ryzen' or similar in promotional material.

[16] For more on von Neumann see N Macrae, *John Von Neumann: The Scientific Genius Who Pioneered the Modern Computer, Game Theory, Nuclear Deterrence, and Much More* (Pantheon 1992).

[17] For more on this see Gates (n. 9) ch. 2 which gives an exceedingly lucid description of this complex subject.

difference between the analogue world of atoms and the digital world of bits through a simple example.[18] He asks his readers to imagine a 250-watt light bulb attached to a dimmer switch. Using the dimmer the user may select graduated illumination from complete darkness (0) to full illumination (250). By turning the switch halfway you will get something around 125 watts of light and at one-quarter distance about 63 watts. But, as Gates points out, exact replication of the level of illumination achieved in such an analogue set-up is difficult. If I find one night that about one quarter turn is the perfect level of illumination to have a romantic dinner, I could make a mark on the dimmer switch and use this as a level for future reference, but if I want to tell my friend in Seattle this I need to try to communicate to him exactly where on the switch I made my mark (usually descriptively by telephone). If he then passes this information on to his friend in Calgary he repeats the process, but, as anyone who has played the childhood game of Chinese Whispers, or Telephone, knows, the message will over time change and deteriorate: this is known as analogue drop-off and affects all analogue transmissions as anyone who has made a copy of a copy of a friend's mix tape knows.[19] If, though, we replace the one 250-watt bulb with eight bulbs of differing output, each double the output of the previous, we create an analogy for a digital system. We now have eight switches, one for each bulb as seen below in Figure 1.1.

Figure 1.1 A 'digital lighting' system

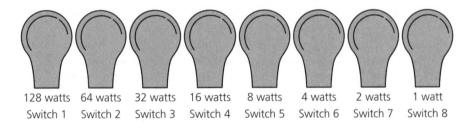

128 watts	64 watts	32 watts	16 watts	8 watts	4 watts	2 watts	1 watt
Switch 1	Switch 2	Switch 3	Switch 4	Switch 5	Switch 6	Switch 7	Switch 8

We can still control the level of lighting in the room from darkness (by switching all lights off) to full illumination (by switching them all on). But now instead of representing this as an analogue value between 0 and 250 we represent it using binary notation from 00000000 to 11111111 where 0 is 'off' and 1 is 'on'. Now, if I find that the perfect level of lighting for a romantic meal is in fact 93 watts, I can set my switches as 'off' 'on' 'off' 'on' 'on' 'on' 'off' 'on' or in binary notation 01011101. Now if I want my friend in Seattle to be able to replicate the *exact* level of lighting I had, I simply send him this code. He may then send this code to his friend in Calgary who can exactly replicate what I did without ever speaking to me. Thus digital transmissions are less likely to suffer drop-off as the message sent is short and precise, unlike analogue transmissions.

If we can represent levels of lighting in digital notation, what else can it be used to represent? The answer is almost anything. Gates gives the traditional example of ASCII or the American Standard Code for Information Interchange.[20] ASCII is the common

---

[18] What follows is based upon Gates' example contained at 26–8 of Gates (n. 9).

[19] If you are too young to know what a mix tape is ask your parents.

[20] For more on ASCII visit http://www.ascii-code.com/ where you can find the digital notation of all characters used on the keyboard.

system used by all computers to encode all the letters and punctuation of the English Language. ASCII gives each character a value between 0 and 255, 255 being the maximum number which can be created by an eight-character byte of bits.[21] Capitals A–Z are given values 65–90 while lower case a–z are given values 97–122, while a space is valued at 32. Thus in ASCII the message 'Long live the Queen' is given as:

01001100	01101111	01101110	01100111	00100000	01101100
01101001	01110110	01100101	00100000	01110100	01101000
01100101	00100000	01010001	01110101	01100101	01100101
01101110					

Of course it is not just text that may be represented in this way. As Negroponte points out we have been able over the years to represent more and more information in binary digits. Music has been distributed digitally since the early 1980s. It is digitally encoded by taking constant samples of the audio waveform (sound pressure measured as voltage): this is a numerical value which may then be encoded as bits. In digital photography each colour and shade is allocated a numerical value which allows for perfect replication and display of the encoded data on an output such as a computer monitor or smartphone screen. Digital video may be seen as a meshing of these two techniques. Here a constant stream of data replicating moving imagery is encoded on a carrier media. Indeed, the applications of bits are seemingly endless, with some physicists even believing that bits may eventually lead to the creation of a Star Trek-style matter transporter.[22] As Negroponte points out: 'the emergence of continuity in [individual bits] is analogous to a similar phenomenon in the familiar world of matter. Matter is made of atoms. If you could look at a smoothly polished metal surface at a subatomic scale, you would see mostly holes. It appears smooth and solid because the discrete pieces are so small. Likewise digital output.'[23]

In the information society we see a shift from encoding information in atoms (such as writing it on the page) to encoding it in bits (such as word processing it). But this move is not limited to the written word: it may be sounds, images, or electrical outputs. Almost anything which may be recorded may be digitized. As digital information is cheaper to store, cheaper to distribute, and cheaper to encode there has been a widely publicized migration from analogue technologies to digital technologies and with it a shift in economic values of information.

1.2 **Moving from atoms to bits**

The economic driver of the move from atoms to bits is clear from the final paragraph of the preceding section. During the 1980s the computer moved out of the research laboratory and the workplace into the home environment. The home computer of

---

[21] In case you wondered what the difference between a bit and a byte was, this is it. A bit is a single binary digit; a byte is a collection of eight bits used to create a single instruction to a CPU. Despite my earlier description of how a CPU works, information is always sent in bytes not bits to the CPU. I left this out of the description at the earlier stage to avoid confusion.

[22] See D Darling, *Teleportation: The Impossible Leap* (Wiley 2005).

[23] Negroponte (n. 4) 15.

the 1980s, devices such as the Sinclair Spectrum and the Commodore C64, were the trailblazers for the home PC or personal computer.[24] As the PC became a fixture of homes across North America, Europe, Australasia, and the Pacific Rim, computerization of media became the cutting-edge technology. The first entertainment media to be digitized were children's games (although they were often played by adults). The games console was the breakthrough technology of the 1970s. Although the first home games console, the Magnavox Odyssey released in 1972, was a failure, in 1977 games company Atari released the now legendary Atari 2600 games system which sold over 30 million units in its lifetime making it the iPhone/iPad of the home video games industry, an industry which remains at the cutting edge of home electronics through products such as the Nintendo Switch, the Xbox One, and the PS4.[25]

Most people though became aware of the digital revolution in the 1980s. Music was the first traditional mainstream media industry to go digital. With the advent of the Compact Disc, digital distribution became the norm. This was then followed by the film and TV industry with the advent of the DVD. These processes (the introduction of the CD and DVD) were evolutionary not revolutionary. The industry was in control of this evolution from the outset and the only discernible change to the consumer was a change in carrier media and in media player. Most importantly, both the CD and DVD retained the traditional distribution models of their predecessors the tape/vinyl disc and the videocassette. You still visited your local HMV, Virgin, or Woolworths to purchase them. They were still carried by road haulage and they were still 'pressed' and packaged in a far-off production line. This is why both CDs and DVDs are evolutionary: they are simply a better way to replicate what was already being done. But, as Negroponte points out, one of the key values of digitization is that it allows us to discard much of the baggage of the atomic world.[26]

This occurred with respect to the music industry in 1994 when the release of the MP3 sound compression technique allowed us to reduce the size of music files down to between 6 and 8 megabytes on average.[27] MP3, like all compression techniques, allows us to remove information not required for reproduction of the recorded data. With MP3 much of what is removed is information which refers to sounds recorded but outside normal levels of human hearing. There is a drop-off in quality compared with high bitrate recordings such as full CD quality, but for the purposes of most consumers the MP3 quality is 'good enough'. The smaller file size allowed by MP3 allowed for distribution of music in a completely revolutionary way. Instead of pressing discs and distributing them via traditional routes such as high street stores with all the accompanying overheads these carry, some enterprising individuals demonstrated that music could

---

[24] Now homes have several PC devices such as laptops, tablets, games systems, smart TVs, and desktops which share a wireless network creating a local area network or LAN which allows music, video, or other files to be streamed wirelessly between them.

[25] At this point I feel I should take a line or two of text to defend my decision to begin the story of digitization of the entertainment market with a short discussion of the early success of Atari. Too often academic commentators dismiss the home video games market as unimportant, yet gamers spent $137.9bn on home video games in 2018 globally. That is almost eight times the value of the global recorded-music sales in 2017, and almost half the combined film and TV revenue generated worldwide in 2017 which was $286.1bn. See Newzoo Games Market Research, *2018 Global Games Market Report.*

[26] See Negroponte (n. 4) 35–6.

[27] Allowing up to 100 tracks to be put on a single CD.

be shared directly from computer to computer cutting out all the middle men,[28] and uniquely music could now be passed on without the original owner of the music file losing possession of their copy.[29] Soon thereafter MPEG-4 and MP4 compression achieved the same effect with film expanding the impact of file sharing and similar technologies to the TV and movie industries.

1.2.1 Rivalrous and nonrivalrous goods

That development reflects one of the key differences between atomic and digital products. While atomic products are rivalrous, digital products are nonrivalrous. Rivalrous and nonrivalrous are terms of economic art. Rivalrous goods are goods whose consumption by one consumer prevents simultaneous consumption by other consumers. This is generally true of any 'atomic' good, for, notwithstanding some recent developments in quantum mechanics, it is generally accepted that no two atoms may occupy the same space simultaneously.

 Example Rivalrous and nonrivalrous goods

If one day it is raining and I decide to borrow my wife's umbrella, she cannot use it during the period it is in my possession: my possession is rivalrous to her possession. However, should I choose to watch the same TV broadcast as my neighbour, my consumption of that broadcast does not affect her ability to watch the same broadcast. My enjoyment of the TV broadcast is nonrivalrous to her enjoyment.

Atomic goods may be either durable or non-durable, but in general both are rivalrous goods. The umbrella example is an example of a durable rivalrous good. My use of the umbrella presents a barrier to others who desire to use that umbrella at the same time. However, my use of the umbrella does not 'use up' the umbrella, meaning that it, as with other durable rivalrous goods, can still be shared through time. By contrast nondurable rivalrous goods are destroyed by their use (consumption) and cannot be shared. A concert ticket is a non-durable rivalrous good: if I 'borrow' my wife's ticket to see a concert by her favourite band, the fact that I can return the ticket to her afterwards does not disguise the fact that I have 'consumed' the economic value of that ticket leaving her with a worthless piece of paper. Thus non-durable rivalrous goods cannot be shared through time. By contrast, nonrivalrous goods may be consumed by several consumers simultaneously. Nonrivalrous goods are usually intangible. The most famous example is probably that of an idea as presented by the eighteenth/nineteenth-century scientist, philosopher, and politician Thomas Jefferson.

[28] D Kusek and G Leonhard, *The Future of Music: Manifesto for the Digital Music Revolution* (Omnibus 2005); S Witt, *How Music Got Free: The Inventor, the Music Man, and the Thief* (Vintage 2016).
[29] S Bhattacharjee et al., 'Digital Music and Online Sharing: Software Piracy 2.0' (2003) 46(7) *Communication of the ACM* 107.

> **Highlight** Thomas Jefferson's letter to Isaac McPherson
>
> If nature has made any one thing less susceptible than all others of exclusive property, it is the action of the thinking power called an idea, which an individual may exclusively possess as long as he keeps it to himself; but the moment it is divulged, it forces itself into the possession of everyone, and the receiver cannot dispossess himself of it. Its peculiar character, too, is that no one possesses the less, because every other possesses the whole of it. He who receives an idea from me, receives instruction himself without lessening mine; as he who lights his taper at mine, receives light without darkening mine.

Here Jefferson captures the key elements of nonrivalrous goods. By taking from the original owner you do not deny them of their possession and enjoyment of the goods, nor do you deny anyone else the opportunity to consume, simultaneously, the same good. In the modern world, technology has enabled us to increase the number of nonrivalrous goods available to us. Television broadcasts are an example of a nonrivalrous good: if I turn on my TV set to watch a broadcast of 'The Good Place' this does not prevent my next-door neighbour, or anyone else, from watching the same show. Goods that are nonrivalrous are therefore goods that can be enjoyed simultaneously by an unlimited number of consumers.

If we list nonrivalrous goods we find an interesting commonality between them. Nonrivalrous goods include ideas, radio-communications broadcasts (TV and radio), visual light (think of a beautiful view or a sunset), digital media (you can 'give away' MP3 music while retaining the original), and sound (a speaker at Speaker's Corner may be heard by one person or one thousand without affecting the enjoyment of others). The commonality is that they are all 'informational goods'. All are about transmitting information from one source to another. To return to the earlier language of Negroponte, they are all susceptible to be encoded as binary digital information (bits) to be stored or shared: thus ideas may be written on a document file (as I am currently doing), radio-communications broadcasts are being replaced by digital broadcasts, digital photography and video is capturing that beautiful view, and, as we have seen, MP3s encode sound. Thus the move from the world of atoms to the world of bits, or the move from the industrial to informational society, can be similarly defined as a move from rivalrousness to nonrivalrousness.

1.2.2 Digital goods and society

The move from rivalrous to nonrivalrous supply in informational and entertainment products has been the fulcrum for massive social change. The concept of linear broadcasting or transmission, an album of music played in order, or a TV transmission broadcast at a certain time, is being replaced by the expectation of on-demand streaming of content.

Highlight Digital goods as utilities

The nonrivalrous nature of digital goods has seen digitally consumed content move from being goods (like groceries or clothes) which you pay for on demand, to utilities (like gas or water) which are streamed directly to your device and are normally paid for by monthly subscription rather than per item.

Today you are more likely (if at all) to consume mainstream television programmes such as 'The Handmaid's Tale' or 'Game of Thrones' via video sharing or streaming sites such as YouTube, Vimeo, Hulu, Netflix, or Amazon rather than through the traditional broadcast model. Music is not bought but rather is streamed by Spotify, YouTube, Apple, Amazon, and Google. Book publishers have recently discovered they are not exempt from such developments. The success of the Amazon Kindle family has seen Amazon launch Kindle Unlimited which gives access to, in Amazon's own words, 'over 1 million titles, thousands of audiobooks and a rotating selection of magazines on any device for just £7.99 a month' while Audible, another Amazon company, provides a subscription audiobook service.

These experiences to some extent answer the questions 'why are bits economically valuable?' and 'how do bits effect social interaction?' Although there is much more to explore in relation to both these questions, we can open by saying bits are economically valuable because they represent new and revolutionary models to market and deliver products or services, which are by nature informational products and which were traditionally embedded in or attached to a separate carrier media. The music industry has been through the full process of disintermediation; other industries are now going through the process including film and television production and broadcasting, telephone service providers, mail service providers, educational providers, publishing, advertising, print media, and even the legal profession.[30]

In addition, bits effect social interaction as they provide new avenues for communication, exchange of ideas, and for challenge to traditional orthodoxy. The reason the music industry was forced to embrace music streaming services was because of the ready availability and take up of early illegal file sharing services such as Napster and The Pirate Bay (the same is also true for film and television to a lesser extent). Although there is no doubt the vast majority of users of file sharing services were driven by economic desire to free-ride (for which read get free music, films, TV content, and video games), these services also demonstrated the convenience of being able to access content without going to the shops and for some the feeling of belonging to a wider community of viewers, listeners, and gamers. Although legal download sites such as iTunes replaced the convenience of file sharing sites, these corporate sites did not have the same community spirit. This led indirectly to the development of social networking sites, and in particular MySpace which was heavily influenced by popular culture and music culture. MySpace in return influenced popular music through the promotion of bands and singers such as the Arctic Monkeys and Lily Allen. Whereas in the 1970s and

---

[30] For a discussion of some of the challenges the legal profession may face see R Susskind, *Tomorrow's Lawyers: An Introduction to Your Future* (2nd edn, OUP 2017).

1980s groups of teenagers would meet in their local record shop to discuss music, now they do it on Tik Tok, Spotify, Instagram, Snapchat, SoundCloud, and YouTube. These sites succeeded mostly because the traditional iTunes model did not support social networking (a rare missed trick from Apple now corrected in Apple Music). What remains though is the most important question for a legal textbook, 'how does the law have to change to take account of the effect of bits?'

1.3 **The legal challenges of the information society**

What does this all mean to lawyers and to lawmakers? We have already identified three effects of the move from the industrial to the informational society:

> **Highlight** The three effects of the move from the industrial to the informational society
>
> 1. It represents a shift from ownership or control of things to ownership of or control over information.
> 2. It represents a new and revolutionary model to market and deliver products or services.
> 3. It represents a move from rivalrousness to nonrivalrousness.

All three of these pose serious challenges to traditional legal values and rules. All traditional legal systems, including the common law systems found in the UK and the civilian tradition found on Continental Europe, have a basic distinction between tangible and intangible goods. Tangible goods represent goods of economic value and are protected. Thus s. 1 of the Theft Act 1968 expects tangibility: 'A person is guilty of theft if they dishonestly appropriate property belonging to another with the intention to permanently deprive the other of it.' The key phrase is 'intention to permanently deprive' as this makes clear that to commit the offence of theft you must take something which is physical and rivalrous. Thus 'copying' an MP3 without the permission of the owner is not theft. Neither is intercepting a transmission without permission.[31] Both of these things are regulated elsewhere,[32] but neither is theft in the true sense of the word. This may not seem important: you may believe this is simply a matter of language, or you may believe it is simply a choice by lawmakers to distinguish between theft proper (the taking of a 'thing') and misappropriation of information. But this simple example reveals a greater tension between traditional legal values and the new economic values of the information society.

Traditional property theory examines how scarce resources ought to be put to use but in the world of bits scarcity loses its immediate impact. Although there are still

---

[31] Think here of erecting a satellite dish and installing an illegal decoder thus taking the economic benefit of the broadcast from the broadcaster without making payment.

[32] The copying without permission by the Copyright, Designs and Patents Act 1988, the broadcast example would be regulated by the Communications Act 2003 and/or the Investigatory Powers Act 2016.

limits which apply over storage space and bandwidth, the average user sees bits as almost limitless as they are infinitely scalable: want the new Ed Sheeran album but can't afford it? Someone will make it available for free, not by giving you access to their copy but by creating a brand-new copy for you. Bits never run out, and because bits never run out we can keep creating; the only limit is on how many bits we can transmit and store.

The traditional law of atomic property, and with it atomic values of wealth through owning and retaining things, is fundamentally altered by the scalability of bits, meaning those things which appear to be of economic value (information) seem perversely to be of no value because anyone can replicate it at any time at almost no outlay.[33]

 Highlight The informational paradox

Information is valuable. It is also (almost) infinitely scalable, nonrivalrous, and intangible.

Our traditional legal values are predicated on an environment where valuable goods are either physical, tangible, and rivalrous or where intangible goods (as protected by intellectual property laws) are fixed to some form of tangible carrier: books, vinyl or compact discs, compact music cassettes, videocassettes, patent specifications, or attached as 'badges' to products. But as John Perry Barlow demonstrated in his famous polemic: *The Economy of Ideas: Selling Wine Without Bottles on the Global Net*: 'with the advent of digitization, it is now possible to replace all previous information storage forms with complex and highly liquid patterns of ones and zeros'.[34] In Barlow's parlance the valuable content (the nonrivalrous good) is being separated from the traditional carrier (which was rivalrous). Not only is the move from atoms to bits affecting traditional property values; it also undermines our traditional models for enforcing intangible, intellectual property rights.

The move from atoms to bits is, as we have seen, a fundamental social, legal, and economic change. It is not however the only legal challenge posed by the process of digitalization. Two secondary effects of the process also fundamentally undermine our traditional legal settlement. The first is that digitalization also converges different types of content into a single category of digital, or binary, information. This is a process known as digital convergence and this brings unique challenges for law and lawyers. Additionally, the ease with which digital information and digital content can be transmitted around the globe adds an additional layer of complexity which challenges traditional concepts of the jurisdictional scope and reach of lawmakers, courts, and law enforcement bodies. We will now look briefly at both of these.

---

[33] This was recognized early on by Bill Gates (n. 9) who records, 'It seemed to me that too many people were accepting, at face value, uncritically the idea that information was becoming the most valuable commodity. Information was at the library. Anybody could check it out for nothing. Didn't that accessibility undermine its value?' at 22.

[34] 'The Economy of Ideas: Selling Wine without Bottles on the Global Net', *Wired 2.03*, March 1994.

1.3.1 **Digital convergence**

A smartphone is a truly remarkable device. On it you can (among other things): listen to music, phone people, text people, play games, watch videos, send and receive email, surf the web, manage your calendar, take pictures, store pictures, write text, check your stocks, and plan journeys (receiving turn-by-turn directions).[35] Think back 20 years (if you are old enough). To do all these things you would have needed to carry a Discman, a mobile phone, a Gameboy, a laptop computer, a journal or diary, a camera, and a road atlas. Now you have a hand-held device that weighs 168g.

 Highlight Digital convergence

Digital convergence[36] means inclination for various innovations, media sources, content that become similar with the time. It enables the convergence of access devices and content as well as the industry participant operations and strategy.

Convergence may be seen as another effect of the freeing of content from the carrier, or disintermediation. Whereas previously all content had a different carrier medium (photographs used photographic film or paper, music used magnetic tape, optical discs (CD), or vinyl disks, movies use magnetic tape or optical discs (DVD), while text used paper), now freed from these restrictions all content is carried equally, as 0s and 1s. The concept of convergence came to media and communications theory from the mathematical disciplines where it was used to refer to the coming together of physical things such as beams of light or non-parallel lines. Media and communications commentators began to apply the term to the coming together of media platforms in the late 1970s or early 1980s, it being extremely difficult to determine exactly when, and by whom, the term was first used in this context. What is clear though is that communications theorist Ithiel de Sola Pool adopted this contextual use of the term and popularized it among media and communications theorists. In his landmark 1983 book, *The Technologies of Freedom*,[37] Pool wrote of the 'convergence between historically separated modes of communication' and argued that 'electronic technology is bringing all modes of communications into one grand system'.[38]

Despite writing in 1983 it took close to 25 years for Pool's vision to become reality, why did it take so long? One obvious reason was the delay in developing a fully digital informational distribution chain. For complete digital convergence to become a reality we required technological innovations in every stage of the information infrastructure. Information

---

[35] Digital convergence or digital platform convergence or sometimes technological convergence should not be confused with the related but different phenomena of media convergence. Media convergence is an economic strategy in which communications companies seek financial benefit by making the various media properties they own work together. For a discussion of media convergence see G Meikle and S Young, *Media Convergence: Networked Digital Media in Everyday Life* (Palgrave Macmillan 2011).

[36] T Strader, *Digital Product Management, Technology and Practice: Interdisciplinary Perspectives* (IGI Global 2011), 113.

[37] I de Sola Pool, *The Technologies of Freedom* (Belknap 1983).

[38] Ibid. 28.

needed to be gathered digitally. This is now commonplace with reporters filing stories by email and the use of digital cameras to record news events and television broadcasts, with books being word-processed and with music being digitally recorded. Then information needed to be stored and delivered in digital form. All media outlets now store information in digital form and deliver it digitally, whether as digital television, digital radio, ebooks, digital music, or as online newspapers and magazines. Finally, it required a new generation of portable devices that would allow for delivery of a variety of text and audio-visual media. The arrival of smartphones and tablet devices finally signalled, 25 years after Pool predicted it, the opening of the golden age of media convergence.

What legal challenges does convergence bring? As information and content became cheaper to gather, cheaper to process, and cheaper to distribute, the intellectual connection between information or data and concepts such as personhood, privacy, autonomy, and respect for private property were initially swept aside in a rush to experiment with new technologies and to profit from content creation and sharing, data mining, date profiling, and data-gathering techniques. In comparison with digitization, digital platform convergence is still in its infancy and it is still too early to predict with certainty all of the issues that platform convergence will raise but some are already apparent.

These challenges include questions over ownership of both content and data. As we share ever more content online whether videos on YouTube, pictures or videos on Instagram, Snapchat, or Facebook, or micro content on Twitter, there is an inherent tension between the interests of the content creators, whether they are the user of the platform or a third party, and the platform itself. Two particular tensions are between the platform's right to use and monetize content produced by users and the user's rights and interests in their content and the right of third parties to prevent unlicensed use of their content. Both of these have been subject to extensive academic and policy discussion[39] and changes to the law have been both proposed and implemented.[40] Other questions surround the gathering, processing, and application of personal data gathered by these platforms, including location data, data on personal connections, device data, preferences (including data which can predict sexual preferences), and health data. A major scandal in 2018 surrounding the use of platform gathered data by the company Cambridge Analytica[41] has led to a number of legal developments in this regard and we will examine these developments in chapter 23.

Other challenges include a re-evaluation of the expectation one has to privacy in public spaces in a world where every movement is likely to be recorded via a smartphone and then uploaded to Twitter, Facebook, or YouTube[42] and the overwhelming

---

[39] P Samuelson, 'Does Copyright Law Need to Be Reformed?' (2007) 50 *Communications of the ACM* 19; N Elkin-Koren, 'Tailoring Copyright to Social Production' (2011) 12 *Theoretical Inquiries in Law* 309; Communia, *EU copyright should protect users' rights and prevent content filtering*: https://www.communia-association.org/2017/01/09/eu-copyright-protect-users-rights-prevent-content-filtering/. Discussed in ch. 10.

[40] Directive 2001/29/EC of the European Parliament and of the Council of 22 May 2001 on the harmonization of certain aspects of copyright and related rights in the information society (InfoSoc Directive); Proposal for a Directive of the European Parliament and of the Council on Copyright in the Digital Single Market (COM/2016/0593 final).

[41] P Greenfield, 'The Cambridge Analytica files: the story so far', *The Guardian*, 26 March 2018; Nathaniel Persily, 'The 2016 U.S. Election: Can Democracy Survive the Internet?' (2017) 28 *Journal of Democracy* 63.

[42] Discussed in chs. 22 and 23.

production of obscene and indecent material which digital convergence has allowed, including the alarming rise of obscenity and even child abuse images, through sexting and social networks.[43] The latter is aided by the final palpable effect digitization has had on society: the failure of laws to adequately cross borders.

1.3.2 The cross-border challenge of information law

Professors David Post and David Johnson first identified the cross-border effects of digital information transfers in their groundbreaking paper 'Law and Borders: The Rise of Law in Cyberspace'.[44] Here they laid for the first time a legal interpretation, known as classical cyberlibertarianism, which contends that regulation founded upon traditional state sovereignty, based as it is upon notions of physical borders, cannot function effectively in cyberspace as individuals may move seamlessly between zones governed by differing regulatory regimes in accordance with their personal preferences.[45] Simply put, they claimed the internet was unregulable as laws were confined to the jurisdiction in which they were promulgated while content hosted and carried on the internet, including obscene content, flowed seamlessly over these borders.

 Highlight Law and borders

Cyberspace radically undermines the relationship between legally significant (online) phenomena and physical location.[46] The rise of the global computer network is destroying the link between geographical location and: (1) the power of local governments to assert control over online behaviour; (2) the effects of online behaviour on individuals or things; (3) the legitimacy of the efforts of a local sovereign to enforce rules applicable to global phenomena; and (4) the ability of physical location to give notice of which sets of rules apply.

The overwhelming problem that lawmakers face in dealing with online pornography is which standard to apply. In the UK we use the Obscene Publication Act 1959 to determine whether an item is obscene (and therefore illegal) or merely indecent. This states: 'For the purposes of this Act an article shall be deemed to be obscene if its effect or (where the article comprises two or more distinct items) the effect of any one of its items is, if taken as a whole, such as to tend to deprave and corrupt persons who are likely, having regard to all relevant circumstances, to read, see or hear the matter contained or embodied in it.'[47] This standard is specifically designed to be flexible and to change over time as community standards change and over the 60 years it has been in force the UK standard of obscenity has changed quite dramatically.[48]

---

[43] Discussed in ch. 20.
[44] 48 *Stanford Law Review* 1367 (1996).
[45] The cyberlibertarian school will be discussed in depth in ch. 4.
[46] Johnson and Post (n. 44) 1370.
[47] Obscene Publications Act 1959, s. 1(1).
[48] For a discussion on the evolution of the obscenity standard see ch. 20. Also see Murray (n. 13) 205–9.

Internationally, individual states are continually altering their obscenity standard to meet contemporary community standards. What is considered sexually explicit but not obscene in the UK may well be considered to be obscene in the Republic of Ireland, and almost certainly material considered obscene in the Islamic Republic of Iran or in the Kingdom of Saudi Arabia would not be felt to be noteworthy in the UK. Similarly, material which would be considered to be obscene in the UK would probably not be censored in Germany, Spain, or Sweden where a more tolerant approach to erotica and pornographic material is taken. What we are seeing in these differences is a spectrum of community standards which range from extremely conservative to extremely liberal. In general, this system has functioned quite effectively in the real world due to the existence of physical borders and border controls. The easiest way for a state to apply its legal standard of obscenity within its borders is to prevent the importation of materials which offend the standard of that state, while simultaneously criminalizing the production of such materials within the state. In the UK, for example, it is an offence to import indecent or obscene prints, paintings, photographs, books, cards, lithographic or other engravings, or any other indecent or obscene articles under s. 42 of the Customs Consolidation Act 1876, while s. 2 of the Obscene Publications Act 1959 criminalizes the publication, or possession with intent to publish, of an obscene article.

The Customs Consolidation Act allows the UK to apply effective border controls. It allows HM Revenue and Customs to seize obscene items, and where necessary to prosecute those involved in their importation. This control provision continued to apply throughout the UK's membership of the European Union, with it being held on several occasions that this power subsists in relation to material deemed obscene under the Obscene Publications Act despite Art. 26 TFEU.[49] But these traditional measures are predicated upon the assumption that the items in question will be fixed in a physical medium, and that they will require physical carriage to enter the state. With the advent of the digital age both of these assumptions have been rendered null. The development of a global informational network has dismantled these traditional borders. The result of this is all too apparent, especially to parents trying to control what their children are exposed to. HM Revenue and Customs, along with the police, have given up all attempts to apply the provisions of the Customs Consolidation Act or the Obscene Publications Acts to content found on the internet.

Instead, until recently, the authorities have focused their attention on the storing and distribution of child abuse images,[50] non-photographic pornographic images of children under the Coroners and Justice Act 2009,[51] and extremely pornographic images under the Criminal Justice and Immigration Act 2008 (as amended by the Criminal Justice and Courts Act 2015),[52] and prosecuting those who run pornographic websites from overseas servers but who are resident in the UK and profit from this activity.[53] With

---

[49] *Conegate Ltd v HM Customs & Excise* [1987] QB 254 (ECJ); *R v Forbes* [2002] 2 AC 512 (HL).

[50] *R v Barry Philip Halloren* [2004] 2 Cr App R (S) 57; *R v Snelleman* [2001] EWCA Crim 1530 and *R v James* [2000] 2 Cr App R (S) 258.

[51] *R v Palmer* [2011] EWCA Crim 1286; *R v Milsom* [2011] EWCA Crim 2325.

[52] *R v Cheung* [2009] EWCA Crim 2965; *R v Burns* [2012] EWCA Crim 192; *R. v PW* [2012] EWCA Crim 1653.

[53] See *R v Ross Andrew McKinnon* [2004] 2 Cr App R (S) 46 and *R v Stephane Laurent Perrin* [2002] EWCA Crim 747.

the removal of the physical border between the UK and the rest of the world, internet users were afforded the opportunity to access and view pornography held overseas in the blink of an eye and with little opportunity for the authorities to intercept the content en route. This caused a huge upsurge in consumption and left the authorities with a difficult decision to make. They could either invest large sums to attempt to enforce the law in the digital environment,[54] or they could de facto deregulate adult obscenity and focus their attentions on more pressing problems such as child abuse images. The UK authorities, recognizing the limits of the law in relation to this subject, chose to focus their resources on only the most harmful content.

Recently, however, the UK government has adopted a new and to date unique approach which other governments are watching with interest to see if it succeeds. By s. 16 of the Digital Economy Act 2017 a new Age Verification Regulator was created. This role is being fulfilled by the British Board of Film Classification and under s. 14 of the same Act it will be illegal to allow access to pornographic content (wherever found) to persons from the UK who are under the age of 18. A complex age verification system has been implemented, which will be discussed in full at 20.2.5. Providers of pornographic materials who do not comply with the UK's age verification system may be blocked under s. 23 of the Act. This may be interpreted as an attempt to build a digital border where the physical border has failed. As noted, governments from around the globe are closely examining this idea of rebuilding borders digitally. If successful, it might be part of the solution to the problem first identified by Johnson and Post in 1996.

All of this does not deny that law can be effectively applied in the online environment. Throughout this book we will see the courts take effective jurisdiction over online defamation, pornography and child abuse images, computer hacking, computer fraud and data theft, copyright infringement, and a variety of other issues. The law is effective in cyberspace. The difficulty is in identifying which court has effective jurisdiction and in identifying who is the relevant person to pursue.

1.4 **Digitization and law**

This introductory chapter has outlined several of the challenges digitization brings to lawmakers. By replacing old-fashioned analogue data, which was expensive to gather, store, transfer, transmit, and search, and which was subject to decay in quality over time and would decay each time it was copied,[55] with digital data, which is cheap to gather, store, and search and which is perfectly replicated every time, we have created a number of challenges for the legal system and for lawyers.

The question of how we protect the value of information in an age where it is instantly replicable, transmissible, and is almost infinitely scalable is the challenge lawyers face today. It is also the core value of this book and it represents the thread that draws

---

[54] This could either be achieved by the investment of these funds into additional law enforcement personnel or by using the funds to design a technological solution to the problem such as a national firewall or filtering system which would in effect rebuild the natural border in cyberspace. See R Deibert et al., *Access Controlled* (MIT Press 2010).

[55] This is analogue drop-off discussed at 1.1.1.

together the chapters which follow on disparate subjects such as cyber-speech and defamation, databases, copyright in the information age, and computer crime. The common theme which will emerge is that attempts to broker a piecemeal settlement—here a Database Directive, there a Convention on Cybercrime—are wrong-headed and will eventually lead to a fragmented approach which will fracture not just along jurisdictional lines but also along lines of technology and types of information. This would be the informational age equivalent of fragmented responses to different types of physical things in traditional legal settlements: thus instead of a law of property and chattels we have a law of the steam engine, a law of the gramophone, and a law of the pocket watch. This is exactly what we are doing now in the world of bits by producing specific regulations to deal with copyright infringement, indecency, computer crime such as hacking, and informational products such as databases. This book will, in the traditional style, examine the extant and proposed legal-regulatory framework of each of these (and many others), but it will also encourage you, the reader, to question whether it is time to take a more comprehensive approach to the legal regulation of digital information rather than attempting to fit the square peg of the world of bits into the round hole of a legal system designed for a world of atoms.

TEST QUESTIONS

Question 1

John Perry Barlow argues that the valuable content that the law always protected is being separated from the traditional carrier, where the law gave protection. This move from atoms to bits is affecting traditional property values, and undermines our traditional legal enforcement models.

Write a reply to Barlow explaining why you think he is right or wrong.

Question 2

If bits have no economic value, should lawyers be part of the battle to give bits monetary value through the application of legal structures?

Question 3

Discuss the challenge posed by technological convergence. Is this a challenge of policy, technology, or law? What role should lawyers play in the convergence debate?

FURTHER READING

Books

B Gates, *The Road Ahead* (Viking 1995)

H Jenkins, *Convergence Culture: Where Old and New Media Collide* (NYU Press 2008)

N Negroponte, *Being Digital* (Hodder & Stoughton 1995)

J Palfrey and U Gasser, *Born Digital* (Basic Books 2010)

I de Sola Pool, *The Technologies of Freedom* (Belknap 1983)

Chapters and articles

D Johnson and D Post, 'Law and Borders: The Rise of Law in Cyberspace' 48 *Stanford Law Review* 1367 (1996)

M Lemley, 'Place and Cyberspace' 91 *California Law Review* 521 (2003)

D Svantesson, 'Jurisdictional issues and the internet—a brief overview 2.0' (2018) 34(4) *Computer Law and Security Review* 715

The network of networks

People use the term 'internet' every day without thinking what it actually means. It is in fact a compound word made up of 'inter' + 'net'. Inter is from the Latin root meaning between or among, while net is short for network.[1] In short, the internet is not a single computer network as you may have previously imagined; it is a system that connects together many individual computer networks allowing for the transfer of digital data, or bits, across networks. The internet is basically a telecommunications system for computer networks: this is why it is sometimes called the network of networks.

The idea for the first computer network was put forward by a group of computer visionaries in the 1960s. The original idea can probably be traced to the eminent experimental psychologist JCR Licklider. Licklider was a professor at the Massachusetts Institute of Technology (MIT). There he worked on the SAGE project as an expert on the interaction between humans and technology,[2] work which helped convince him of the great potential for human/computer interfaces. This led Licklider to write one of the most important papers in computer science, the 1960 paper, 'Man-Computer Symbiosis'[3] in which he stated:

> It seems reasonable to envision, for a time 10 or 15 years hence, a 'thinking center' that will incorporate the functions of present-day libraries together with anticipated advances in information storage and retrieval . . . *The picture readily enlarges itself into a network of such centers, connected to one another by wide-band communication lines and to individual users by leased-wire services.* In such a system, the speed of the computers would be balanced, and the cost of the gigantic memories and the sophisticated programs would be divided by the number of users.[4]

Licklider was particularly interested in the idea of using wires to tie expensive mainframe computers together. He went on to develop this idea with a colleague, Wes Clark, who at that time worked at MIT's Lincoln Lab and who had several years earlier taught Licklider how to program the TX-2 mainframe computer. Together they wrote another

---

[1] All definitions in this section are drawn from the *Oxford English Dictionary*.

[2] The Semi-Automatic Ground Environment (SAGE) system was the first major real-time, computer-based command-and-control system. It was designed as a new air defence system to protect the US from long-range bombers and other weapons. The SAGE system sent information from geographically dispersed radars over telephone lines and gathered it at a central location for processing by a newly designed, large-scale digital computer. For more information about SAGE see K Redmond and T Smith, *From Whirlwind to MITRE: The R&D Story of the SAGE Air Defense Computer* (MIT Press 2000).

[3] JCR Licklider, 'Man-Computer Symbiosis', *IRE Transactions on Human Factors in Electronics*, Vol. HFE-14 (March 1960). A digital reprint of the paper may be accessed at <http://memex.org/licklider.pdf>.

[4] Ibid. 11 (emphasis added).

groundbreaking paper, 'On-Line Man-Computer Communication', published in August 1962. In this they described a 'Galactic Network' which 'encompasses distributed social interactions through computer networks'.[5]

These papers and the visionary ideas contained therein may, like many other great ideas, have been destined to remain only an untested thought experiment, but fate was about to intervene. On 4 October 1957 the Soviet Union had launched the first man-made object into space, the satellite Sputnik I. Analysts in the West had not predicted this and it caused immense shock and surprise to the US military and scientific establishment. President Eisenhower determined that the US would never again be taken by surprise on a technological frontier. In response he created a new research agency tied directly to the Office of the President and funded from the Department of Defense budget. This new agency would oversee cutting-edge research of value to both the civilian and military establishments. It was to be called the Advanced Research Projects Agency or ARPA.[6]

As fortune would have it one of the first problems for ARPA was how to deal with the inefficient use of expensive scientific equipment. One particular problem was that computers were expensive pieces of equipment which were underutilized. They used batch processing techniques which meant that hours or days could be spent inputting data on punch cards before the program could be run, and then the slightest error in data entry would invalidate all this work. Between time, computers often lay idle. By the early 1960s every computer scientist wanted his own computer but the cost of providing this was prohibitive. The answer was clear: the users had to share the resources available more efficiently. This meant two things: first, the development of time-sharing mainframe resources, an idea first put forward by researchers at MIT's Lincoln Lab in the 1950s,[7] and, second, a network of machines which would allow researchers in different parts of the country to share results and resources easily. ARPA decided to appoint Licklider to deal with these problems and in October 1962, only two months after the publication of 'On-Line Man-Computer Communication', Licklider found himself appointed as the first Project Director of ARPA's Information Processing Techniques Office or IPTO. Once in post he surrounded himself with a group of like-minded men. This group included his co-author of 'On-Line Man-Computer Communication', Wes Clark, Bob Taylor of NASA and Larry Roberts and Leonard Kleinrock, both outstanding PhD students at the Lincoln Lab. Together they set out to build a communications system for computers: it would be called the Advanced Research Projects Agency Network or ARPANET.

2.1 **Introducing the internet (history)**

The number of histories of the internet which have been published, both online and offline are too great to list. I do not intend to examine the history of the internet in detail. Those who wish to learn in detail about the development of this fascinating

---

[5] The paper was originally published as an ARPA memo, one of a series by Licklider on this subject in 1962. Reprinted in *Proceedings of the IEEE*, Special Issue on Packet Communications Networks, 66(11) (November 1978).

[6] ARPA came into existence on 7 February 1958 <http://www.darpa.mil/about-us/darpa-history-and-timeline>.

[7] K Hafner and M Lyon, *Where Wizards Stay Up Late: The Origins of the Internet* (Simon & Schuster 1996) 25.

place should either read the excellent *Where Wizards Stay Up Late* by Katie Hafner and Matthew Lyon[8] or the Internet Society's *A Brief History of the Internet*[9] which is without doubt the best online history of cyberspace. Much of the following is drawn from these two sources.

2.1.1 Building the ARPANET

Immediately following his appointment, Licklider and his team set to work on developing a network technology which would give effect to his vision. Led by Bob Taylor, they started work on making a shared computer network a reality. One of the key players in this was Leonard Kleinrock, who in 1961 had published one of the first papers on packet-switching theory.[10] Packet switching was a radical new system being developed by Paul Baran of the RAND Corporation for military voice communications. In packet switching, a message or communication is broken into smaller packets which are then addressed and sent individually. Each packet can follow a different route to its destination, and can re-route itself if the connection is broken or damaged. Once all the packets forming a message arrive at the destination, they are recompiled to form the original message. Packet switching is generally seen as more efficient as there is no 'silent time' between sections of the message as there is with circuit switching and more robust as if part of the network is damaged the packets may be 'routed around' the damage.

Baran was working on packet switching as a method to ensure military voice communications could withstand a nuclear first strike,[11] Kleinrock was looking for a way to connect computers without tying up expensive leased lines. Kleinrock convinced Taylor that the best way to connect computers on a network was by using packet switching rather than conventional circuit switching.[12] The packet-switching model was adopted by ARPA and they began work on the network. One of the first problems faced by the fledgling ARPANET was how to make all computers on the network compatible with one another. In the 1960s there was no standard operating system such as Windows: each computer used a different programming language and operating system. Just to get the individual machines to interface, or 'talk', with each other was going to consume vast amounts of the ARPANET project's time and resources. At a meeting for Principal Investigators for the project at Ann Arbor, Michigan in April 1967, Wes Clark offered a solution. Instead of connecting each machine directly to the network they could install a minicomputer called an 'interface message processor' or IMP at each site. The IMP would handle the interface between the host computer and the ARPANET network. This meant each site would only have to write one interface: that between that host and the IMP and, as all the IMPs used the same programming language, the network of IMPs

[8] Ibid.

[9] <https://www.isoc.org/internet/history/brief.shtml>.

[10] L Kleinrock, 'Information Flow in Large Communication Nets', *RLE Quarterly Progress Report* (July 1961).

[11] For an explanation as to how this would work see P Baran, *On Distributed Communications* (1964) <http://rand.org/about/history/baran.list.html>.

[12] Circuit switching occurs when a dedicated channel (or circuit) is established for the duration of a transmission. All information is transmitted along this one dedicated link. The most ubiquitous circuit-switching network is the fixed-line telephone system, which links together wire segments to create a single unbroken line for each telephone call.

would handle the rest.[13] With all the principles of the ARPANET network now in place, it would be a 'layered' design with the IMPs supporting the host computers and it would use packet switching in place of traditional circuit switching. Larry Roberts and the project's engineering partners Bolt, Beranek & Newman, a small computer company in Cambridge, Massachusetts, started building the network. Finally, on 29 October 1969, the ARPANET vision became reality when Charley Kline, an undergraduate at UCLA, successfully logged in to the SDS 940 host at the Stanford Research Institute through the Sigma 7 host at UCLA.[14] Further hosts were added at the University of California at Santa Barbara and at the University of Utah, and by December 1969 the original four-node network was in place.

ARPANET may have been the first successful computer network, and it may also have been the forerunner of the modern internet, but it was quite dissimilar to the internet as we know it today. Modern definitions of the internet describe it as 'a computer network comprising or connecting a number of smaller networks, such as two or more local area networks connected by a shared communications protocol'.[15] ARPANET was a single network. Furthermore, ARPANET was what today would be described as a 'closed network': you could only gain access to the ARPANET network if you had a correctly configured IMP which had to be supplied by Bolt, Beranek & Newman. Thus the foundations of the modern internet architecture are not to be found in this part of the network's history. What happened next though was something quite special.

2.1.2 **Building the internet**

The ARPANET success was an exciting moment for network engineers. The design team had demonstrated that functioning computer networks could be constructed. As a result, the early 1970s were a time of intense experimentation with computer networking and other applications of packet switching. One of the first experiments was in the carrier medium. ARPANET used the existing AT&T telecoms system to carry its messages but this was less efficient in areas where there was a lack of good telecoms coverage: areas such as inter-island communications in Hawaii. In 1969 the IPTO awarded funding to Professor Norm Abramson at the University of Hawaii to develop a wireless network. Abramson used this money to construct a simple network of seven computers across the islands using radios similar to those used by taxis to transmit and receive data. This network, called ALOHANET, used a different transmission system to ARPANET. In ARPANET the IMPs would manage data transmission and reception, ensuring data was properly sent and received without interference. In ALOHANET the terminals were allowed to transmit whenever they wanted to; if the transmission was impeded by other traffic the recipient computer would ask for it to be resent, the sending computer would keep sending the message at random intervals until it got

---

[13] This is recorded by Hafner and Lyon (n. 7) 73.

[14] Commentators, including Leonard Kleinrock, recall that the first attempt by Kline to log in failed when the network crashed halfway through the procedure. A later attempt was successful. The record of that day including the log entries may be seen at L Kleinrock, *The Day the Infant Internet Uttered its First Words* <http://www.lk.cs.ucla.edu/internet_first_words.html>.

[15] This definition is taken from the *Oxford English Dictionary*, but it reflects the generally accepted view stated elsewhere.

an 'ok' message from the recipient. ALOHANET received a lot of attention, not least from the military who recognized the advantages of a wireless network. The problem was though that the range of the network was limited and to build larger transmitters would centralize the network leaving it open to attack. An alternative was to use satellites. Although slower than ARPANET due to transmission lag a satellite network would allow for international transmissions.[16] To this end the US, UK, and Norway collaborated on the development of a satellite network: SATNET. Concurrently, local fixed-line networks were being developed in the UK and in France.[17]

With the development of several independent networks interest in linking these resources grew. Bob Kahn, who had helped design the IMPs at Bolt, Beranek & Newman, was working on a packet-radio project at the time.[18] He wanted to connect his network to the ARPANET computer network but at the time this was impossible as they were radically different networks. Kahn and others sought to end their frustration. What they wanted was a network of networks: an inter-network. They formed a group called the International Network Working Group and appointed Vint Cerf to be its chair.[19] That same year, 1972, Kahn was invited by Larry Roberts to join the IPTO to work on a net project: the Internetting Project. Kahn accepted and immediately started developing designs to connect together all the independent networks which had sprung up since 1969. Kahn realized the solution to the problem was in open architecture networking. Open architecture allows for each individual network to retain its unique network architecture, while connections between networks take place at a higher 'Internetworking Architecture Layer' as seen in Figure 2.1.[20] In an open architecture network, the individual networks may be separately designed and developed and each may have its own unique interface which it may offer to users and/or other providers. Each network can be designed in accordance with the specific environment and user requirements of that network. There are generally no constraints on the types of network that can be included or on their geographic scope.

Figure 2.1 Simplified open architecture network

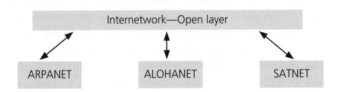

[16] At the time the fixed-line, or undersea, network, which was constructed of copper wire, lacked the necessary capacity between the US and Europe to allow for effective network transmission between the two. This was remedied soon after when the telecoms companies laid high-speed fibre-optic cable in its place.

[17] All this is discussed in Hafner and Lyon (n. 7) ch. 8.

[18] Kahn was a Professor of Electrical Engineering at MIT who joined Bolt, Beranek & Newman to help them overcome communications errors in data transmission.

[19] Vinton 'Vint' Cerf is the man most commonly called 'the father of the internet'. In 1972 he was an assistant professor at Stanford University.

[20] Set out more fully in *A Brief History of the Internet*, n. 9.

Designing this network was similar to designing the ARPANET. Like ARPANET the problem was that since each host (in this case host network) used its own language, what was needed was a version of the IMP which bridged this gap on the ARPANET. Unfortunately the IMPs were also one of Kahn's major obstacles. The language of ARPANET, the Network Control Protocol (NCP), did not have the ability to interface with networks or machines further downstream than a destination IMP on the ARPANET.[21] Thus Kahn would need to rewrite the NCP protocol.

Kahn set about designing a new, open architecture, protocol. In doing so he set out four ground rules for his new Internetwork Protocol:

 Highlight Kahn's four ground rules for internet protocols

1. Each distinct network would have to stand on its own and no internal changes could be required to any such network to connect it to the internet.

2. Communications would be on a best-effort basis. If a packet didn't make it to the final destination, it would shortly be retransmitted from the source.

3. Black boxes would be used to connect the networks (these would later be called gateways and routers). There would be no information retained by the black boxes about the individual flows of packets passing through them, thereby keeping them simple and avoiding complicated adaptation and recovery from various failure modes.

4. There would be no global control at the operations level.

Kahn began working on his new protocol with Vint Cerf who joined in his role as Chair of the International Network Working Group. According to Cerf, Kahn introduced the problem to him by saying: 'Look my problem is how I get a computer that's on a satellite net and a computer on a radio net and a computer on the ARPANET to communicate uniformly with each other without realizing what's going on in between.'[22] Cerf was fascinated by the problem and along with Kahn he worked on developing the new protocol which would allow transmission across networks. Each of these networks had its own set of rules though. They used different interfaces, different transmission rates, and each allowed for differently sized packets of information to be carried. How could they write a protocol which could be used uniformly across networks? Throughout 1973 Cerf and Kahn continued to work on these problems. Finally in September 1973 Cerf presented his and Kahn's ideas at the International Network Working Group meeting at the University of Sussex. Their idea, later refined and published as the seminal paper, *A Protocol for Packet Network Intercommunication*,[23] was deceptively simple. Cerf

---

[21] The reason for this short-sightedness was that in designing NCP, control over packets of data, and therefore network reliability, was given to the IMPs. This is because this was simpler and cheaper and at the time ARPANET was the only network envisaged by the designers.

[22] Hafner and Lyon (n. 7) 223.

[23] V Cerf and R Kahn, 'A Protocol for Packet Network Interconnection', *IEEE Trans on Comms*, Vol. Com-22, No. 5, 637 (May 1974).

realized that carriers of goods often carried packets without ever knowing what was in them. A transport container has a standard size and shape, yet it may be carrying anything from televisions to chocolate bars. Due to the common size of the container it can be carried by road, sea, or rail and neither the ship's captain nor the truck or train driver need know what he is carrying. The only people who need to know are the shipper and the recipient. Cerf applied this to digital data. He designed a new protocol: Transmission Control Protocol, or TCP, which would 'box up' the information and address it. Each message fragment, known as a datagram, would be the same size and could be handled by any of the networks. Once sent into the network, packets could take any route to their destination; they were not all destined to follow each other across busy networks. This design would work, and allowed for transmission of data across networks, but by removing the IMPs from the process, there remained the problem of missing or damaged datagrams.

In ARPANET the IMPs were responsible for sending and reassembling all message packets. They worked to ensure message integrity by checking the message at every stage of its journey, so-called hop-by-hop transmission. Cerf and Kahn changed all this in designing TCP. They returned to Norm Abramson's work on ALOHANET: to overcome the problem of interference or data corruption he placed the responsibility for data integrity on the sending and receiving computers, so-called end-to-end reliability. In Cerf and Kahn's TCP design when packets of information were sent they carried with them a request for acknowledgement. If safely received the recipient host would signal the transmission host of success. If the packet failed to arrive or was corrupted in transmission the recipient would not signal. If no acknowledgement was received the transmission host would retransmit the packet at random intervals until a successful acknowledgement was received. By placing all these responsibilities with the hosts, the network itself could be significantly simplified. Like the container transports of the real world, only the sender and recipient need know the details of the contents, all the network needed to know was where to send them.

TCP was not quite an instant success. Although it did lead to the development of the first internet, a network which between 1973 and 1975 grew at a rate of about one new network node per month, the protocol itself was redrafted and redeveloped continually over the next few years. The most important of these occurred in January 1978 when Vint Cerf and Jon Postel posted 'TCP Version 3 Specification', which suggested the splitting of TCP into a dual protocol Transmission Control Protocol/Internet Protocol or TCP/IP. TCP had always been a multifunctional protocol but by splitting it into the dual layer TCP/IP these functions could now be clearly seen. The release of the TCP/IP protocol is now seen by most network historians as the day the modern internet came into being and is therefore the logical place to end our short excurses into the history of the network.

2.2 **How the modern internet functions**

The modern internet still uses the TCP/IP protocol. The TCP element of the protocol breaks the data into packets ready for transmission and recombines them on the receiving end. The IP element handles the addressing and routing of the data and makes sure it gets sent to the proper destination. The easiest way to imagine this working is to think in terms of traditional postal communications.

Example Sending TCP/IP communications

Alistair wants to send a message to Barbara. In the real world he may write his message on a piece of paper and then place it inside an envelope before sealing the envelope and addressing it. He then places the envelope in the care of the Royal Mail who carries the envelope to Barbara. She then opens the envelope and reads the message.

TCP/IP works in a similar fashion, except in place of a single envelope the message is split into many 'packets' before being sent. If we were to use TCP/IP technology to send the simple message 'Meet me at 2pm' from Alistair to Barbara, the following operations would take place:

1. TCP would split the message into packets and numbers each packet $[Meet]_1$ $[me\ at]_2$ $[2pm]_3$.

2. Each packet is placed into a digital envelope before passing these envelopes on to the IP protocol.

3. IP would then address the envelopes with Barbara's IP address before sending them out across the network.

4. The network acts like the Royal Mail and carries these envelopes to their destination.

5. Upon arrival TCP opens the envelopes, checks all packets have been delivered safely and reassembles the message.

Let us take as an example the delivery of a file from one computer to another. This is a common internet operation and may occur where your operating system undertakes an automatic update, or it may be a requested download such as a video file from Netflix. We begin operations with two computers the Host (that is the computer on which the file is held) and the Recipient. The first thing to be aware of is that every digital device connected to the internet must have a unique identification or address. Like all communications networks, the internet relies upon the ability to deliver content to another party. The telephone network functions because each telephone connected to the network has a unique identifier, or telephone number. In internet terms a similar system is managed by the IP protocol, currently this may be a version known as IPv4 or IPv6. As internet communications are communications between computers the need for a linguistic addressing tool seemed minimal when the addressing protocol for the internet was developed. The primary addressing tool is therefore a numerical identifier called an IP address. As with a telephone number this number must be unique to allow for the smooth flow of information within the network. IP addresses are used when browsing the web to enable the transmission of communications between the user's web browser and server hosting the website. They are also used in the header of email messages and, in fact, are required for all programs that use the TCP/IP protocol.

Version 4 of the Internet Protocol (IPv4), which is still in use, uses an IP address consisting of 32 bits, usually shown as a 'dotted quad': four octets of binary numbers represented in decimal form in the range 0–255. For example, the IP address of the computer I am currently using is 151.224.85.103 but as computers do not work in decimal notation this will be converted by the network servers and routers into binary notation and be read by them as 10010111.11100000.01010101.01100111. As it is easier for humans to remember decimals than it is to remember binary numbers we use decimal notation to represent IP addresses when describing them. The address space of the IPv4 protocol (the number of available unique identifiers allowed) is 2^{32} or 4,294,967,296 unique host interface addresses. At the time it was adopted this seemed to be an almost limitless supply of addresses, but as the network has developed the strain on this resource has become quite heavy. For this reason a new version of the protocol, IPv6, has been adopted. In IPv6, addresses are 128 bits rather than 32 bits. This will allow 2^{128}, or about 3.403×10^{38}, unique host interface addresses: a mind-boggling availability of unique identifiers. An IPv6 address is written as eight four-digit hexadecimal numbers separated by colons. Thus to the human eye it looks something like: 21DA:00D3:0000:2F3B :02AA:00FF:FE28:9C5A. Computers, including hosts and routers, will continue to read this as binary notation, but space prevents me from reproducing the binary equivalent of a hexadecimal IPv6 address. Both IPv4 and IPv6 addresses are descending unique identifiers like telephone numbers. You read them from left to right with the first two sets of quads being used to identify the network location of your computer. For example, all computers on the London School of Economics network are allocated an IPv4 address which begins 158.143, while King's College, London operates from the 137.73 address space, while University of Oxford IP addresses begin 163.1, 129.67 or 192.76.[24] This information is of course double-edged. Not only is it essential for the functioning of the network it also allows data transmissions to be tracked to an end user. The privacy implications of this will be discussed in chapter 25.

With both computers in our transaction allocated an IP address the transaction between them can now take place. The host will have the file to be transferred and the IP address of the recipient. The TCP protocol now takes the file and breaks it up into smaller packets and prepares to send them. It places each packet into its electronic envelope and then attaches a header to that file. The header is basically all the information that is needed to deliver the packet and to reassemble the file. Thus it will contain the IP address of the recipient and basic information about the information contained in the packet to ensure that if it becomes damaged (corrupted) en route, the recipient is aware of this and can ask for the data to be resent if necessary.[25] These packets are all then sent into the physical infrastructure of the network which is made up of the wired network of telephone cables (both copper and fibre optic), wireless carriers such as Wireless Local Area Networks such as those provided in your local coffee shop or Wireless Wide Area Networks such as those operated by mobile telecommunications providers. How this physical layer carries this information from the host to the recipient is a result of all these early technology designs such as packet switching and network layering. If the host is a major website like YouTube it will have a permanent network connection through a leased data line; if it is a casual user, like your brother sending you a file by email, the connection will be created by their home broadband router to connect their computer to their Internet Service Provider (ISP). Whichever form the initial connection is made, the ISP will transfer the packets to the internet backbone. This is made up of several large telecommunications networks

---

[24] For more on the operation of IP addresses, including who regulates and assigns them, see A Murray, *The Regulation of Cyberspace: Control in the Online Environment* (Routledge 2007) ch. 4.

[25] For a more technically detailed description of the TCP Protocol see Information Sciences Institute, *Transmission Control Protocol: DARPA Internet Program Protocol Specification* (RFC 793, 1981): <http://www.netfor2.com/rfc793.txt>.

which interconnect with each other.[26] These backbone providers connect to each other to exchange packet traffic through a series of internet exchanges known as Network Access Points. These allow data packets to flow freely across the internet backbone. The management of the data flow across the backbone and thorough Network Access Points is controlled by a specialist piece of computer hardware known as a router. Routers are specially designed to manage the informational flow of the internet. When a data packet arrives at a router, the router examines the IP address put there by the IP protocol layer on the host. The router checks its records to see if it knows where the recipient is based. If the network containing the IP address is found, the packet is sent to that network. If the network containing the IP address is not found, then the router sends the packet on a default route, usually up the backbone hierarchy to the next router. Hopefully the next router will know where to send the packet. If it does not, again the packet is routed upwards until it reaches one of the routers actually on the backbone. These routers hold the largest records and here the packet will be routed to the correct backbone, where it will begin its journey downward through smaller and smaller networks until it finds its destination.[27]

There are some key operative parameters of the internet which may be gleaned from this short explanation of how TCP/IP works. Among these are that TCP works on a best-effort basis.[28] Routers do not usually attempt to repair damaged packets. If the IP address cannot be found, or if there is a network failure which makes it impossible for packets to be forwarded, they will be discarded. The recipient computer may request missing or damaged packets to be resent, the router will not. Second, the route taken by discrete packets may differ from that taken by other packets. Thus there is no reason to assume that if a file is transmitted from a computer in Glasgow to one in London that all will follow the same route, or even that they will take the most direct route. Routers will send packets by the most efficient route in terms of network capacity, not in terms of network geography. Thus if the network between Glasgow and London is extremely congested one packet may go via Stockholm, another via Amsterdam and another via Detroit. As the fibre optic cables which make up the backbone all carry data at the speed of light it should be completely unnoticeable to the end user that one packet of data has travelled 1,000 miles while another has travelled 12,000 miles.[29] Third, traditionally the network treated all data packets equally. Because the routers did not know what they were carrying they could not distinguish high-value data (perhaps a streaming video or a VoIP call) from low-value data (such as a spam email). This is the effect of two early network initiatives which are in many ways the opposite sides of the same coin: network neutrality and end-to-end architecture.

End-to-end architecture is a unique feature of distributed computing, as most famously employed in the current incarnation of the TCP protocol. The idea of end-to-end communications was first promulgated by Jerome Saltzer, David Reed, and David D Clark in

---

[26] The main carriers of internet backbone traffic are the so-called tier-1 providers. These are major telecoms companies such as AT&T, TeliaSonera, Sprint, Telstra, Verizon, BT, and Deutsche Telekom.

[27] For a technical discussion of how Internet Routers function see S Halabi, *Internet Routing Architectures* (2nd edn, Cisco Press 2000). For a more general discussion of internet architecture see B van Schewick, *Internet Architecture and Innovation* (MIT Press 2012).

[28] This is the second of Khan's four 'ground rules' for TCP.

[29] At the speed of light it takes approximately 0.06 seconds to travel 11,000 miles.

1984 in their *paper* 'End-to-end Arguments in System Design'.[30] The authors examined the developing internet, which at that time was beginning to play host to a variety of different end-user systems such as email, file transfers, online booking systems, and others, and concluded that: 'The function in question can completely and correctly be implemented only with the knowledge and help of the application standing at the end points of the communication system. Therefore, providing that questioned function as a feature of the communication system itself is not possible.'[31] In other words only the host who originated the file and the recipient of the file knew enough about the file to manage its transmission. The intelligence of the network was therefore in its applications held at each end of the communication rather than in the network architecture itself. This made the internet almost unique among communications media. Traditional media were centrally managed: think of the telephone exchange or the television broadcast facility, with dumb terminals at the ends. In fact the only other media of communication which used end-to-end principles was the mail delivery system. But as our discussion of the process of digitization in chapter 1 has demonstrated, the internet offered many more and exciting opportunities than traditional mail carriers. The network would be developed to carry a variety of digital products from simple text-based emails to MP3 files, to flash games, to streaming MP4 and MPEG videos, and on to VoIP telephone calls. The development of these new technologies, especially VoIP and streaming video, which are both bandwidth intense and which require for low latency, are challenging the continuing applicability of the end-to-end principle and its allied concept of network neutrality.[32]

2.3 **Higher-level protocols**

In Figure 2.1 I outlined how TCP/IP created an open layer built over or on top of the closed networks of the ARPANET, the ALOHANET, and the SATNET. In this section we turn to the third network layer, the applications layer where higher-level protocols such as Hypertext Transfer Protocol allow us to carry out operations such as web surfing. To explain how the modern internet lays higher-level functionality such as web surfing or video streaming on top of the basic networking functionality of TCP/IP, we start by looking at the environmental layering of the modern network.

Stratification or layering may be identified in any informational environment. Both network engineers and communications theorists recognize the vital function played by environmental layers in communications networks. In his book *Weaving the Web*,[33] the architect of the World Wide Web, Sir Tim Berners-Lee, identifies four layers within the architecture of the internet: the transmission layer, the computer layer, the software layer, and the content layer.[34] This may be seen as a simplified version of the seven-layer

---

[30] 2(4) *ACM Transactions on Computer Systems* 277 (1984).

[31] Ibid. 278.

[32] Latency is the time delay between the moment something is initiated, and the moment one of its effects begins or becomes detectable. In streaming video and voice communications high latency render the system ineffective due to lag. Network Neutrality will be discussed in chapter 3.

[33] T Berners-Lee, *Weaving the Web: The Original Design and Ultimate Destiny of the World Wide Web by Its Inventor* (Harper 1999).

[34] Ibid. 129–30.

Open Systems Interconnection Reference Model (OSI model) used by network engineers. This model divides the functions of a protocol into a series of layers. Each layer has the property that it only uses the functions of the layer below, and only exports functionality to the layer above. Typically, the lower layers are implemented in hardware, with the higher layers being implemented in software.[35] Although both the OSI model and the Berners-Lee model are network architecture models, designed to describe the purely functional aspects of the network, they can easily be adapted to illustrate the challenges faced by regulators. For lawyers and regulators this has been most successfully done by Yochai Benkler in his eloquent paper *From Consumers to Users*[36] and it is that model which will be employed here.

Benkler describes a three-layer network which is similar to Berners-Lee's four-layer environment. Benkler labels his layers (1) the physical infrastructure layer, (2) the logical infrastructure layer, and (3) the content layer. What Benkler does is to reduce the OSI/Berners-Lee model to the three key environmental layers found on the internet. The foundational layer is the physical infrastructure layer. This is the link between the physical world and cyberspace and is made up of wires, cables, spectrum, and hardware such as computers and routers. The second layer is the logical infrastructure layer. This encompasses the necessary software components to carry, store, and deliver content, software such as the TCP/IP protocol, operating systems, and browsers. Finally, the content layer encompasses all materials stored, transmitted, and accessed using the software tools of the logical infrastructure layer. Benkler's model was adapted by Lawrence Lessig in his book *The Future of Ideas*.[37] Lessig rebranded the layers the physical layer, the code layer, and the content layer. This allowed him to discuss the particular effectiveness in using the code layer to regulate the content layer; a subject he had previously raised in *Code and Other Laws of Cyberspace*,[38] and to which he would return in his third book, *Free Culture*.[39] Thus the role of TCP/IP is to act as the 'glue' which connects the physical infrastructure of the communications networks to the higher-level protocols which we use daily to read blogs, post Facebook updates, and send and receive emails. Among the everyday higher-level protocols you may use are SMTP—Simple Mail Transfer Protocol, used to send and receive emails; VoIP—Voice over IP, used for internet telephony such as Skype; and RTP—Real-time Transport Protocol, which streams audio and video content such as YouTube. One protocol suite stands out: it is HTTP—Hypertext Transfer Protocol and its allied programming language HTML—Hypertext Markup Language. Between them these protocols for the foundation of the World Wide Web, are by far the most important higher-level network to operate using TCP/IP.

The World Wide Web, or simply 'the web', is not synonymous with the internet. As we have seen, the internet is the network of computer networks which function using TCP/IP. The web is a higher-level network which uses the internet as its carrier medium. The invention of the web is usually credited to Sir Tim Berners-Lee. Berners-Lee is a

---

[35] The seven OSI layers are: (1) physical layer; (2) data link layer; (3) network layer; (4) transport layer; (5) session layer; (6) presentation layer; and (7) application layer. See D Comer, *Internetworking with TCP/IP: Principles, Protocols and Architecture* vol.1 (6th edn, Pearson 2013).

[36] Y Benkler 'From Consumers to Users: Shifting the Deeper Structures of Regulation toward Sustainable Commons and User Access', 52 *Federal Communications Law Journal* 561 (2000).

[37] L Lessig, *The Future of Ideas: The Fate of the Commons in a Connected World* (Random House 2001).

[38] L Lessig, *Code and Other Laws of Cyberspace* (Basic Books 1999).

[39] L Lessig, *Free Culture: The Nature and Future of Creativity* (Penguin 2005).

physicist who graduated from the University of Oxford in 1976. Upon leaving university he began working with Plessey Telecommunications as a software engineer, where he worked for two years on distributed systems, message relays, and bar-coding. He then joined DG Nash, a small software company, where he developed a multi-tasking operating system and typesetting software for intelligent printers. During this time he also developed a hypertexting system called Enquire.[40] Hypertext was not new, the term had been coined by filmmaker and computer programmer Ted Nelson in 1963 and the concept of hyper-linking was at the core of Project Xanadu, his hypertext project which ran from 1960 and which he discussed at length in his 1981 book, *Literary Machines*.[41] While Nelson was experimenting with hypertext, the first functioning hypertext system, Douglas Engelbart's NLS, or oN-Line System, was developed. Engelbart developed his system independently of Nelson's work and did not use the term hypertext to describe his system, but there is no doubt it was the first hypertext network. Engelbart had been hugely influenced by Vannevar Bush's 1945 paper *As We May Think*,[42] which described a mechanized library system, or memex, with embedded links between documents. In his attempts to build Bush's memex, Engelbart turned to the potential of digital computers. In 1962 he started work on Augment, a project to develop computer tools to augment human capabilities.[43] This was possibly the most important computer project of the time (arguably even more important than ARPANET) and it produced the first computer mouse, graphical user interface, and hypertext program. All these developments were demonstrated by Engelbart at the Fall Joint Computer Conference in San Francisco in December 1968. Engelbart received a standing ovation in tribute to his work on his NLS system; as a result, the SDS 940 computer he used for these applications was selected as the second ARPANET node. It took another 20 years though for Engelbart's invention to find a popular use, and that was in Tim Berners-Lee's web design.

After developing his Enquire system, Berners-Lee joined the European Particle Physics Laboratory (CERN)[44] as a consultant. During his time there he secured funding to develop a digital hypertext library of CERN research which could be accessed from any facility on the CERN network. By March 1989 Berners-Lee had completed his project design to allow researchers in the High Energy Physics Department to communicate information online. His design had two key features: (1) like TCP/IP his new protocol was to have an open architecture to allow researchers to connect any computer no matter what operating system it was using, and (2) information was to be distributed using the network itself. Berners-Lee was joined in his project by Robert Cailliau, a computer

---

[40] Hypertext is the now familiar user interface used on the web. It is designed to overcome some of the limitations of fixed written text. Rather than remaining static like traditional text, hypertext makes possible a dynamic organization of information through links and connections (called hyperlinks). Hypertext can be designed to perform various tasks; for instance, when a user clicks on the link it will usually cause his browser to load a related web page of information or if he allows his mouse to hover over it, a bubble with a description of the linked file may appear.

[41] T Nelson, *Literary Machines* (Mindful Press 1981).

[42] V Bush, 'As We May Think', *The Atlantic Monthly*, 101 (July 1945).

[43] The Augmentation Research Center at Stanford Research Institute in Menlo Park, CA was the precursor to the internationally famous Xerox PARC facility.

[44] CERN is the contraction of the Laboratory's French name: Conseil Européen pour la Recherché Nucléaire.

engineer from Belgium. Throughout 1990 Berners-Lee, assisted by Cailliau, developed the first web server, 'httpd', and the first client, 'WorldWideWeb' a hypertext browser/editor. This work was started in October 1990 and by Christmas Day 1990 Berners-Lee and Cailliau were conversing across the world's first web server at info.cern.ch. In August 1991, Berners-Lee posted a notice to the alt.hypertext newsgroup informing users where his web server and browser software could be downloaded. At this stage the web was still in its infancy, there was no certainty it would develop in the way we experienced in the 1990s, but on 30 April 1993 the future of the web was secured when CERN gave notification that they were not intending to take control of the technology developed by Berners-Lee and Cailliau. On that date CERN announced and certified that the WWW technology developed at CERN was to be put into the public domain 'to further compatibility, common practices, and standards in networking and computer supported collaboration'.[45] This allowed any interested party to use and improve the CERN software, assuring the future of the web.

With its freedom assured the web became the 'killer application' of the internet.[46] The number of internet users quickly increased[47] and today it is estimated that there are over 4.1 billion people online.[48] Thus, while it is important to bear in mind that the internet and the web are two different things, the importance of the web to the development and penetration of the internet cannot be underestimated. Throughout this book we will look at the challenges of both the internet and the web to governments, lawmakers, lawyers, and to regulators and users more generally. Much of the focus of this will be on the regulation of the web: issues such as the distribution of pornographic content across borders via the web, or the distribution of movies and music in breach of copyright via the web, but sometimes it is other aspects of the internet's unique communications media that are at the core of the problem, such as with BitTorrent a communications protocol which allows users to share large files between computers. BitTorrent is not a web protocol. Like HTTP it runs across TCP/IP and is therefore a question properly of internet governance. Thus this book will look at the regulation and governance of digital content wherever found. You need to be aware of the distinction between the internet and the web to allow you to distinguish whether we are talking about regulation of the logical infrastructure layer (internet regulation) or regulation at the content layer (usually regulation of web content). Where possible I will make this clear but on some occasions you will need to apply the distinction yourself.

---

[45] Original certificate at <http://cds.cern.ch/record/1164399>.

[46] The term killer application refers to any computer program or application that is so necessary or desirable that it affords the core value of some larger technology, such as an operating system, or a piece of computer hardware. Simply put, a killer application is so compelling that someone will buy the hardware or software components necessary to run it.

[47] Figures for 1993 are not reliable but estimates suggest there were about 1.3 million internet users in January 1993 mostly based in the US (Internet Society, *Global Internet Report 2014* <https://www.internetsociety.org/globalinternetreport/2014>). Accurate figures are available from 1995 when IDC Research began their user survey. From this we know there were 16 million internet users in December 1995, 36 million in December 1996, 76 million in November 1997, 147 million in September 1998, 195 million in August 1999, and 369 million in August 2000. See Gregory Gromov, *History of Internet and WWW: The Roads and Crossroads* <http://www.netvalley.com/intvalstat.html>.

[48] See *World Internet Users and Population Stats*: <https://ww.internetworldstats.com/stats.htm>.

TEST QUESTIONS

Question 1

The design of TCP means that internet carriers including telecommunications companies and ISPs have no way of knowing what they are carrying. They might be carrying terrorist content, child abuse images, or even simply content in breach of copyright. They therefore cannot ever be liable for content carried across the network using the TCP protocol.

Do you agree or disagree? Why?

Question 2

The existence of an IP address, as part of the TCP/IP protocol, means that every device connected to the internet can be identified and tracked at any time. This means one's correspondence can always be tracked and therefore the internet is incapable of complying with Art. 8 ECHR.

Discuss.

FURTHER READING

Books

T Berners-Lee, *Weaving the Web: The Original Design and Ultimate Destiny of the World Wide Web by Its Inventor* (Harper 1999)

K Hafner and M Lyon, *Where Wizards Stay Up Late: The Origins of the Internet* (Simon & Schuster 1996)

B van Schewick, *Internet Architecture and Innovation* (MIT Press 2012)

Chapters and articles

Y Benkler, 'From Consumers to Users: Shifting the Deeper Structures of Regulation Toward Sustainable Commons and User Access', 52 *Federal Communications Law Journal* 561 (2000)

V Cerf and R Kahn, 'A Protocol for Packet Network Interconnection', *IEEE Trans on Comms*, Vol. Com-22, No. 5, 637 (May 1974)

M Lemley and L Lessig, 'The End of End-to-End: Preserving the Architecture of the Internet in the Broadband Era', *Berkeley Law & Economics Working Papers* No. 8 (2000)

Net neutrality

Network neutrality, or more commonly net neutrality, is highly prized by many internet pioneers including Professor Sir Tim Berners-Lee creator of the World Wide Web.[1] This previously widely accepted concept has been subject to intense debate and review in recent years and remains at the heart of some of the most intense battles over internet regulation.[2]

 Highlight Net neutrality defined

Net neutrality is the principle that data packets on the internet should be moved impartially, without regard to content, destination, or source. It is sometimes referred to as 'The First Amendment of the Internet'.

Modern routers allow network carriers to prioritize certain traffic over others. Network providers argue this is a positive development as it allows them to prioritize traffic with a low latency threshold such as voice over internet protocol (VoIP) and streaming media over traffic with a higher latency threshold such as web browsing or a music download.[3] Network providers argue that in this way they can make a more efficient use of the limited resources available to them with everyone receiving the best service possible.[4] Critics argue that it also allows them to discriminate against certain applications

---

[1] T Berners-Lee, 'In defense of net neutrality', *Wall Street Journal* 22 June 2017; O Solon, 'Tim Berners-Lee on the future of the web: "The system is failing"', *The Guardian*, 16 November 2017.

[2] See e.g. Berners-Lee, ibid.; AA Gilroy, *Access to Broadband Networks: The Net Neutrality Debate*, Congressional Research Service, R40616, 16 April 2015: <https://www.fas.org/sgp/crs/misc/R40616.pdf>; Federal Communications Commission, *Restoring Internet Freedom* <https://www.fcc.gov/restoring-internet-freedom>.

[3] High Tech Broadband Coalition, *Appropriate Framework for Broadband Access to the Internet over Wireline Facilities* (CC Docket No. 96–45 (2002)); High Tech Broadband Coalition, *Appropriate Regulatory Treatment for Broadband Access to the Internet over Cable Facilities* (CC Docket No. 96–45 (2002)). For an excellent discussion of the issues see C Marsden, *Network Neutrality: From Policy to Law to Regulation* (Manchester University Press 2017).

[4] In 2016 Real Time Entertainment (audio/video streaming sites) accounted for 71 per cent of all fixed-line data (and 40 per cent of mobile data) downloaded at peak times to North American homes. Of that, two services Netflix (35.2 per cent) and YouTube (17.5 per cent) accounted for over 50 per cent of all fixed-line downloaded content—see Sandvine, *Global Internet Phenomena: Latin America & North America* 2016 <https://www.sandvine.com/hubfs/downloads/archive/2016-global-internet-phenomena-report-latin-america-and-north-america.pdf>.

or data types.[5] There are concerns that service providers may seek to deteriorate the quality of service of applications which compete with their products. Thus there are concerns that ISPs such as BT, Sky, or Virgin Media which provide integrated services (telephone, video on demand, and internet access) may degrade the quality of service of a competitor product such as Skype, YouTube, or Netflix.[6] In addition, they may place a restrictively low upload speed on your service making it difficult to use file or video sharing services such as YouTube or BitTorrent, or as was discovered by Professor Tim Wu when he surveyed ISPs' service contracts, you may simply be contractually barred from certain activities by your ISP.[7]

3.1 **Challenges to net neutrality**

As already noted there may be good reason for Internet service providers to carry out network traffic management. If, as is the case in North America, and increasingly the case in Europe, two service providers (Netflix and YouTube) are consuming over 50 per cent of the available network capacity, then it seems sensible that ISPs may want to manage that content to ensure that all users of their network get a reasonable experience online. It certainly doesn't seem fair that because my neighbour is streaming 'Stranger Things' in 4K on Netflix I should find that my browsing a price comparison site is affected. Returning to our discussion in chapter 1, although bits are nonrivalrous there is only so much capacity in the telecommunications network to carry them. So my neighbour's use of the network is rivalrous to my use.

As HD and later 4K video streaming has become commonplace the strain on the network has become pronounced. If we are to enjoy high latency services such as VoIP and streaming video we are faced with two choices: massive investment in improving network capacity, or network management. As the investment programme takes time to bear fruit, there is in the interim a strong argument in favour of some form of network management. Proponents of net neutrality accept this truth and are very clear that net neutrality does not mean a network that is not managed,[8] in fact as Tim Wu recognizes 'the goal of bandwidth management is, at a general level, aligned with network neutrality. Certain classes of applications will never function properly unless bandwidth and quality of service are guaranteed. Hence, the absence of bandwidth management can interfere with application development and competition.'[9]

Proponents of mandated net neutrality argue that there must be limits to acceptable network management for quality of service purposes, normally at the point where the actions of the ISP become discriminatory.[10] The main risk appears to be when network

---

[5] A Cooper and I Brown, 'Net Neutrality: Discrimination, Competition, and Innovation in the UK and US', 15 *ACM Transactions on Internet Technology* 2 (2015); T Wu, 'Network Neutrality, Broadband Discrimination' (2003) 2 *Journal of Telecommunications and High Technology Law* 141.

[6] See the discussion in L Lessig, *The Future of Ideas* (Random House 2001), ch. 10.

[7] Wu (n. 5) found that among the activities restricted were: Any commercial or business use of facilities; operating a server; overusing bandwidth; and in some cases even setting up a home network or wireless network (160–6).

[8] Wu (n. 5); RS Lee and T Wu, 'Subsidizing Creativity through Network Design: Zero-Pricing and Net Neutrality' (2009) 23 *Journal of Economic Perspectives* 61.

[9] Wu (n. 5) 155.

[10] Ibid. 142ff.

management techniques are applied without the knowledge of the customer. To be clear therefore, net neutrality is not about pricing: it is perfectly acceptable for an ISP to charge £6 per month for basic access at a download speed of 8Mbps, £20 per month for fibre at 38Mbps and £30 per month for superfast fibre at 63Mbps. Equally it is not about capping. If a provider offers a mobile internet package of 5Mb per month at £15 and another package at £30 for 30Mb per month that is acceptable. Net neutrality is simply the principle that you do not arbitrarily interfere in the transmission of data packets in an unclear and discriminatory fashion.

What sort of activities would normally be viewed as a breach of net neutrality principles? Most commonly these include blocking or filtering specific content or applications. For example, in 2007 it became apparent that one of the giant US cable companies, Comcast, was interfering with the ability of their cable modem customers to access BitTorrent services by resetting services that used BitTorrent packets. They were doing this as a traffic management tool to prevent BitTorrent from using up available bandwidth to the detriment of other customers. Two public advocacy groups, Free Press and Public Knowledge, referred them to the Federal Communications Commission (FCC). The complaint stated that Comcast's actions violated the FCC Internet Policy Statement, particularly violating the statement's principle that 'consumers are entitled to access the lawful Internet content of their choice . . . [and] to run applications and use services of their choice'. Comcast defended its interference as necessary to manage scarce network capacity. In August 2008 the FCC issued the results of its investigation. They found that Comcast's bandwidth management methods contravened federal policy by 'significantly impeding consumers' ability to access the content and use the applications of their choice'.[11] By the time the order was issued though Comcast had adopted new management methods and, as a result, the order effectively only required Comcast to disclose the details of those new methods and their implementation. Comcast agreed to comply with the order but also filed for review in the District of Columbia Circuit of the US Court of Appeals, claiming (among other things) that the FCC did not have jurisdiction over its network management methods. In April 2010 the Court vacated the FCC's order, holding that the FCC had no authority over Comcast's internet service because 'the Commission had failed to tie its assertion of ancillary authority over Comcast's internet service to any "statutorily mandated responsibility"'.[12] In essence the FCC had been found to have acted *ultra vires* as they had no mandate or authority to interfere in network management capability as such interference was not ancillary to their primary statutory role. This decision was to have a major impact on the ability of US regulators to police net neutrality, as we shall see at 3.3.

A second form of discrimination is access tiering, more commonly known as 'fast lanes'. This occurs when the broadband provider allows certain preferred partners access to a reserved area of the network taking their content away from the congested network. It is a little like paying for a toll road to avoid the congested public road. An example of such an agreement was revealed in 2014 when Netflix and Comcast signed a peering agreement. The agreement, it was reported, ensured 'faster and more reliable access to the Comcast's broadband customers' in return for an undisclosed payment

---

[11] *In re Formal Complaint of Free Press & Public Knowledge Against Comcast Corporation for Secretly Degrading Peer-to-Peer Applications*, 23 FCCR 13,028 at 13,054 (2008).
[12] *Comcast Corp. v FCC*, 600 F 3d 642, 661 (2010).

believed to be in the region of $15m–$20m per annum.[13] Netflix later challenged the agreement as unlawful under net neutrality rules introduced by the FCC, and discussed at 3.3. However, before the FCC could look at the deal, changes in the Federal Net Neutrality rules superseded events.

A third form of discrimination is the other side of the coin from 'fast lanes'. Throttling is the intentional slowing (or sometimes speeding) of specific content as a network management tool. Unlike access tiering this is a reactive measure employed to respond to network congestion. Like blocking and access tiering there is debate around the role of throttling with it being both a legitimate form of network management and also a threat to the principle of net neutrality that all packets may be moved equally. Throttling was reviewed by the FCC as part of their inquiry in the *Free Press & Public Knowledge* case. They found that it, like the resetting of connections, was an interference of the broadband service.[14]

Recently the practice of throttling has received some extremely bad publicity. The Mozilla Corporation and the Attorney Generals of twenty-two US States, as well as the District of Columbia, brought a legal challenge in February 2018 to the FCC's 2018 Restoring Internet Freedom Order,[15] in the United States Court of Appeals for the District of Columbia Circuit.[16] In a brief filed in August 2018[17] the petitioners outlined that while fighting the Mendocino Complex Fire, which started in July 2018 and which was described as the largest fire in California State history, the Santa Clara County Fire Department had their mobile data service throttled by Verizon. The briefing records that management and coordination of the firefighting operation was under the control of a specialist unit, OES Incident Support Unit 5262. As the brief explains 'OES 5262 relies heavily on the use of specialized software and Google Sheets to do near-real-time resource tracking through the use of cloud computing over the Internet. In doing so, the unit typically exchanges 5–10 gigabytes of data per day via the Internet using a mobile router and wireless connection.'[18] The brief goes on to state that 'in the midst of our response to the Fire, County Fire discovered the data connection for OES 5262 was being throttled by Verizon, and data rates had been reduced to 1/200, or less, than the previous speeds. Staff communicated directly with Verizon via email about the throttling, requesting it be immediately lifted for public safety purposes. Verizon representatives confirmed the throttling, but, rather than restoring us to an essential data transfer speed, they indicated that County Fire would have to switch to a new data plan at more than twice the cost, and they would only remove throttling after we contacted the Department that handles billing and switched to the new data plan.'[19] The brief then makes a strong accusation against Verizon: 'County Fire believes it is likely that Verizon will continue to use the exigent nature of public safety emergencies and catastrophic events to coerce public agencies into higher cost plans ultimately paying significantly more for mission critical service—even if that means risking harm to

---

[13] D Crow, 'Having signed the multiyear contract, Netflix wants to put Comcast genie back in "fast lane" bottle', *Financial Times* 9 November 2014.

[14] *Free Press & Public Knowledge* (n. 11).

[15] FCC-17-166 (14 December 2017). Discussed in depth at 3.3.

[16] *Mozilla Corporation v FCC*, et al. 0:18-rev-01051.

[17] Available from <https://ag.ny.gov/sites/default/files/nn_govt_petitioners_brief_and_addendum_final_filed.pdf>.

[18] Ibid. [6], [8].

[19] Ibid. [9].

public safety during negotiations.'[20] Verizon have not denied any of this but did issue a statement saying an error was made and that restrictions should have been immediately issued once the emergency notification was received from the Fire Department.[21] Despite this net neutrality, advocates have seized on the event as justification to repeal the Restoring Internet Freedom Order.[22]

A final form of discrimination is zero rating. Zero rating may be seen as a form of positive discrimination, but with negative consequences.

 Highlight What is zero rating?

Zero rating[23] is when an ISP applies a price of zero to the data traffic associated with a particular application or class of applications (and the data does not count towards any data cap in place on the internet access service). For example, if an internet access service does not charge a user for the data used to access a specific music streaming application or all music streaming applications, then the ISP is zero rating those applications.

You may have seen adverts for, or even benefited from, zero rating. Examples include the UK mobile network EE bundling Apple Music subscriptions (with zero-rated data) to its customers and Vodafone's pass scheme that allows unlimited video or music streaming or social media use for a fixed monthly payment. For the consumer, zero rating may seem like an unalloyed good. Who is going to object to receiving free data, or to the offer of unlimited data of a type for a single monthly payment (which is of course completely optional)?

Not everyone agrees though. In December 2017 the UK telecommunications regulator Ofcom opened an investigation into the activities of two UK mobile network operators, Three and Vodafone.[24] The Vodafone investigation included a specific investigation into the operation of the Vodafone passes scheme. They closed the investigation in August 2018 upon receiving written assurances from Vodafone that it had made changes to the scheme.[25] This investigation followed a similar action in Germany.

Why are regulators interested in these schemes if they are bringing only benefits to consumers? The answer is that zero rating has clear disbenefits as well as benefits. The most obvious is that zero rating schemes ring-fence certain content suppliers while shutting out others. The EE/Apple Music scheme while positive for Apple, locks out Spotify, Amazon Music, YouTube music, and other smaller providers. The Vodafone

[20] Ibid. [11].

[21] C Lecher, 'Verizon throttled California fire department during wildfire crisis', *The Verge* 21 August 2018.

[22] G Sohn, 'Verizon couldn't have restricted Santa Clara County's internet service during the fires under net neutrality', *NBC News* 24 August 2018; J Kruzel, 'Could net neutrality have shielded California firefighters from throttling?', *Politifact* 7 September 2018.

[23] Source: BEREC, *What is Zero Rating?*

[24] <https://www.ofcom.org.uk/about-ofcom/latest/bulletins/competition-bulletins/open-cases/cw_01210>.

[25] <https://www.ofcom.org.uk/about-ofcom/latest/bulletins/competition-bulletins/all-closed-cases/cw_01219>.

passes scheme favours established suppliers. The video pass for example covers video supplied only by Netflix, YouTube, Amazon Prime Video, DisneyLife, My5, TVPlayer, and UKTV Play. Other suppliers like Sky, BBC, and BT are excluded. This can have a distortive effect on competition in the supply side, entrenching some established providers while leaving competitors out in the cold. In addition, zero rating turns service providers into gatekeepers and transforms the internet from a permission-less environment in which anyone can develop a new app or protocol and deploy it, confident that the internet treats all traffic equally, into one in which developers effectively need to seek approval from ISPs if they want their new app or service to succeed.

3.2 **Regulating net neutrality**

Given the potential harms of net neutrality it is unsurprising to find that there are strong arguments around its regulation. However perhaps more surprisingly there is little agreement on whether there should be laws or regulations to enshrine the principle of net neutrality, and if so what form these should take.

There are some who believe that as internet access is a market it should be allowed to operate as a market without external interference from government or regulators. In other words net neutrality regulation is an unjustifiable intervention into the market. This is the position held by economists Robert Hahn and Scott Wallsten. In 2005 in their paper *The Economics of Net Neutrality*[26] they argued, 'net neutrality is actually a friendly-sounding name for price regulation'. They believe that net neutrality rules disincentivize investment by telecommunications companies in both network hardware and innovative software and services as they are unable to recover the full costs of their investments. In the words of Hahn and Wallsten 'A mandate erodes incentives to provide broadband Internet access and could prevent new applications or services from ever being developed.'

The position Hahn and Wallsten hold is prevalent in the economics literature. In his 2011 paper *Economics of net neutrality: A review*,[27] Gerald Faulhaber notes that 'given the level of interest in network neutrality, one could be forgiven that the Internet is being violated by rapacious broadband ISPs and there is not a moment to lose in protecting its openness. Since we have had broadband ISPs in the US for over a decade, one might think that the practices of blocking, discrimination, and disadvantaging competitors would be rife, and such practices well-documented. One might think, but one would be wrong.'[28] He goes on to note that in making the 2010 *Open Internet Report and Order* (discussed at 3.3) the FCC noted four examples of abusive behaviour in practice. This leads him to comment: 'in over a decade, there were only four examples of purported misconduct (one which was denied by the courts and another which didn't even rise to the level of a complaint) for the entire broadband ISP industry. By any standard, four complaints about an entire industry in over a decade would seem to be cause for a commendation, not for restrictive regulations.'[29] The argument made by Faulhaber is

---

[26] (2005) 3 *The Economist's Voice* <https://doi.org/10.2202/1553-3832.1194>.
[27] (2011) 3 *Communications & Convergence Review* 53.
[28] Ibid. 56.
[29] Ibid. 57.

the standard argument from economics. Allow markets to function and then regulate for market failures only where there is clear evidence of failure or harm. However for Faulhaber there is no evidence of such a failure or harm.[30]

This is the problem for economists. Economics is a (mostly) quantitative subject and however one looks at the data it seems to suggest the market works without the need for further regulatory intervention. In their 2010 paper *Net Neutrality and Consumer Welfare,*[31] Gary Becker, Dennis Carlton, and Hal Sider present a number of arguments to show that the broadband market is functioning and not in need of regulation. They state that broadband access speeds are increasing and price per MB is dropping; that customers are willing to switch providers for a better deal, and that there is no evidence to support the assertion that providers will charge for access in a manner that is discriminatory or harmful. They conclude 'the FCC's net neutrality rules are motivated by the concern that broadband access providers will harm competition by disadvantaging rival content providers. This concern does not justify the imposition of net neutrality rules today due, in part, to the existence of competition in the provision of broadband access service and new competition now emerging due to entry, expansion, and upgrades of existing broadband networks. Under these circumstances, broadband access providers have strong incentives to retain subscribers by providing services and pricing models that promote consumer welfare.'[32]

Of course one cannot be sure that markets will continue to function efficiently. The answer to this problem is to employ competition law to ensure that where market inefficiencies do lead to abuse these are corrected. This has been advocated by among others Federal Trade Commissioner Maureen Ohlhausen. In her 2016 paper *Antitrust over Net Neutrality: Why we should take competition in broadband seriously,*[33] she argues that 'market forces and antitrust policy can not only protect competition in ISP-related markets, but also safeguard nonmonetary goals like free speech and openness, at least to the extent that consumers share those values.'[34] This is achieved through vigorous application of competition law: 'Antitrust law is a formidable tool for promoting the public interest. If harmful exclusion, throttling, or paid prioritization by ISPs occurs, antitrust is well positioned to tackle those cases.'[35] These combined arguments lead to the common position of most economists and at least some competition lawyers, that internet access and carriage is no different to any other market. It is best regulated through competition in the market and when or if competition fails due to abuse of market inefficiencies, then competition law can step in.

These findings seem to suggest net neutrality is more of a philosophical concern than an actual concern. This brings us back to the concerns of net neutrality proponents such as Sir Tim Berners-Lee. Why should the creator of the World Wide Web hold such strong concerns if the market works? The answer is to be found in an early intervention to the debate on net neutrality. In 2006 he wrote a blog entry, unfortunately no longer available, called Net Neutrality: This is serious. He opened the entry with twelve words

---

[30] Ibid. 58.
[31] (2010) 6 *Journal of Competition Law & Economics* 497.
[32] Ibid. 519.
[33] 15(1) *Colorado Technology Law Journal* 119 (2016).
[34] Ibid. 133.
[35] Ibid. 141.

which explains the failure of the market approach—'When I invented the Web, I didn't have to ask anyone's permission.' Here Berners-Lee explains what is unique about the internet. The open architecture of the network, discussed at 2.1.2, allows anyone to build anything on the network. Net neutrality protects this. Markets may be generally effective regulators but at a specific level, where gatekeepers can make decisions about a single piece of technology, markets don't always work. This suggests that net neutrality is about more than just markets and market power.

This leads to the suggestion that net neutrality is about principles rather than economics. Lucie Audibert and Andrew Murray argue this in their 2016 paper *A Principled Approach to Network Neutrality*.[36] Audibert and Murray believe that 'mandating network neutrality through regulation is crucial to the protection of fundamental human rights [as well as] to ensure fair competition and innovation.'[37] According to Audibert and Murray the open internet has become part of our everyday lives and is now a vital sphere for democratic discourse and modern living.[38]

 Highlight The essential internet

Not only does the internet provide easy and free access to information sources, it also allows people to contribute to debates in a way not possible before: with the removal of spatial and temporal bounds, and the freedom to participate anonymously or pseudonymously, the internet facilitates town-hall-type gatherings and the creation of communities that might not otherwise have formed. Allowing everyone to vote is not enough for democracy to be realized—individuals must have the opportunity to voice their opinions, put them up to challenge by others, and exchange ideas. And the less costly it is to do so in terms of time and resources, the better it is. The internet provides for that, and in addition is an indispensable vector of participation in more routine, yet still crucial, activities. One need only to think of the amount of daily transactions and personal business or social activities we carry out through the internet. Almost all dealings with our banks, telephone companies, electricity and gas providers, gyms, universities, etc., are made online. Without an internet connection, we are automatically shut off from easy, streamlined access to these essential services.

The internet is, in the words of the authors, 'much more than a platform to post pictures of cute cats and silly videos. It has vital democratic and cultural functions and should be considered a public good to which open and free access is a fundamental right.'[39] The authors argue this space cannot be allowed to fall under the control of a small number of gatekeepers and in order to preserve the internet's openness and to expand its access, regulations should be enacted to prevent ISPs from carrying out illegitimate discrimination of certain types of data: net neutrality regulations.

This approach negates the need to explore market power, abuse, efficiency, or any of the economic arguments. According to this approach we regulate the internet to ensure

---

[36] (2016) 13 *Script*-Ed 118.
[37] Ibid. 120.
[38] Ibid. 134.
[39] Ibid. 119.

neutrality not because it is subject to market failure but because it should be managed according to the open network principles which applied when it was designed and built.

3.3 **The legal framework**

Against this backdrop the US Federal government and the European Union have both spent considerable time examining whether there is a need to enshrine the principle of net neutrality into Federal or European law. The debate in the US began around 2003 with the publication of Tim Wu's paper *Network Neutrality, Broadband Discrimination*[40] but it really came to the fore with the FCC's 2008 Comcast ruling, discussed at 3.1.[41] Buoyed by their initial success in regulating Comcast, the FCC decided to seek public input on a new set of draft rules that would codify and supplement existing principles to safeguard internet openness. After holding a series of reviews and public meetings the FCC adopted the *Open Internet Report and Order* in December 2010; this established three basic open internet rules designed to preserve the free and open internet. These took effect on 20 November 2011.

 Highlight FCC three basic open internet rules

1. Transparency—broadband providers must disclose information regarding their network management practices, performance, and the commercial terms of their broadband services.

2. No blocking—fixed broadband providers (such as DSL, cable modem, or fixed wireless providers) may not block lawful content, applications, services, or non-harmful devices. Mobile broadband providers may not block lawful websites, or applications that compete with their voice or video telephony services.

3. No unreasonable discrimination—fixed broadband providers may not unreasonably discriminate in transmitting lawful network traffic over a consumer's broadband internet access service. Unreasonable discrimination of network traffic could take the form of particular services or websites appearing slower or degraded in quality.

In the interim the appeal in *Comcast* had been heard. This decision suggested that any attempt to actually enforce the *Open Internet Report and Order* would be fruitless as applying Comcast, the FCC had no authority to intervene in network and traffic management. If this were true, the *Open Internet Report and Order* was merely a guideline not an order. As may therefore have been expected, the efficacy of the *Open Internet Report and Order* was immediately challenged by a number of telecommunications companies including Verizon and MetroPCS.[42] All these challenges were eventually consolidated

---

[40] Above (n. 5).
[41] *In re Formal Complaint of Free Press & Public Knowledge Against Comcast Corporation for Secretly Degrading Peer-to-Peer Applications*, above (n. 11).
[42] *Verizon v FCC*, Case No. 11–1014 (D.C. Cir. January 20, 2011); *MetroPCS Communications et al. v FCC*, Case No. 11–1016 (D.C. Cir. January 24, 2011).

into a single review before the US Court of Appeals for the Circuit of the District of Columbia.[43] In the consolidated action the telecommunications companies argued the *Comcast* decision rendered the FCC Open Internet Order *ultra vires* and in the alternative that it interfered with their First Amendment rights.

The Court issued its ruling in January 2014.[44] The Court began by framing its terms of reference: 'our task as a reviewing court is not to assess the wisdom of the Open Internet Order regulations, but rather to determine whether the Commission has demonstrated that the regulations fall within the scope of its statutory grant of authority.'[45] The Court then broke the Order up into its constituent parts and either vacated or upheld each part. Applying *Comcast* (among other authorities) the Court found that an earlier decision of the FCC to classify broadband providers as 'information services' and not 'telecommunication services' meant that broadband service providers were not subject to so-called common carrier regulation under Title II of the Communications Act 1934.[46] The effect of this was to render invalid the provisions of the Open Internet Order on anti-discrimination and anti-blocking as 'the Commission has failed to establish that the anti-discrimination and anti-blocking rules do not impose per se common carrier obligations.'[47] The decision to vacate the key anti-blocking and anti-discrimination provisions gutted the Open Internet Order of its capacity to enshrine and protect net neutrality, leaving only the provision on transparency, but brought about quite unexpected consequences and the next round of attempts to enshrine net neutrality through regulation in the United States.

While the telecommunications companies reacted positively to the outcome of the case by making announcements that they would not seek to interfere with the customer internet experience provided by an open internet,[48] pressure was quickly brought to bear on the US government by free internet advocates. A petition was launched on the White House petitions site. The petition called upon the Obama administration to 'Restore Net Neutrality By Directing the FCC to Classify Internet Providers as "Common Carriers"' and it quickly received over 105,000 signatures. In response the White House replied that 'preserving an open Internet is vital not just to the free flow of information, but also to promoting innovation and economic productivity', but cautioned that 'the FCC is an independent agency' and therefore the President was not able to mandate the FCC to take any action.

While the petition was open for signatures the new FCC Chairman Tom Wheeler issued a statement responding to the *Verizon* decision. In this he stated that the FCC would not appeal the decision, but instead would establish new rules for transparency, non-discrimination, and anti-blocking, based on the decision.[49] With the petition quickly gathering signatories the White House became fully engaged in November 2014. Despite the fact that the President had no power to mandate the FCC, he leveraged political pressure when he made a statement calling upon the FCC to 'implement

---

[43]   *Verizon Communications Inc. v FCC* 740 F.3d 623 (D.C. Cir. 2014).

[44]   Ibid. available from <https://www.cadc.uscourts.gov/internet/opinions.nsf/3AF8B4D938CD EEA685257C6000532062/$file/11-1355-1474943.pdf>.

[45]   At 17.

[46]   At 9.

[47]   Tatel CJ at 4.

[48]   J Lowensohn, 'Comcast, Verizon, and others promise net neutrality ruling won't hurt customers', *The Verge* 14 January 2014.

[49]   FCC, *Statement by FCC Chairman Tom Wheeler on the FCC's Open Internet Rules*, 19 February 2014 <https://www.fcc.gov/document/statement-fcc-chairman-tom-wheeler-fccs-open-internet-rules>.

the strongest possible rules to protect net neutrality' and setting out four bright line rules which he suggested 'reflect the Internet you and I use every day, and that some ISPs already observe': no blocking, no throttling, increased transparency, and no paid prioritization. Finally on 26 February 2015 the FCC issued a new 2015 Open Internet Rules and Order.[50] The order first dealt with the *Verizon* decision by reclassifying broadband internet access service as a telecommunications service under Title II of the Communications Act of 1934.[51] The Commission justified this, not only as a response to *Verizon* but because 'our reclassification of the broadband Internet access service means that we can regulate, consistent with the Communications Act, broadband providers to the extent they are "engaged" in providing the broadband Internet access service.'[52] In essence the argument made by the Commission is that in the modern world consumers see broadband providers as being similar to telecommunications providers of old: common carriers who are responsible for carrying and delivering our internet content from point to point. While this may not be technically true (the moment our email leaves our ISP servers anyone can be carrying it by any route), it is how broadband providers advertise themselves by promoting download (and to a lesser extent upload) speeds and network security. Thus, as far as the consumer is concerned, their broadband provider is the party responsible for delivering their email and making sure they can get access to Netflix. As the Commission noted: 'the representation to retail customers that they will be able to reach "all or substantially all Internet endpoints" necessarily includes the promise to make the interconnection arrangements necessary to allow that access.' As a telecommunications service, broadband internet access service implicitly includes an assertion that the broadband provider will make just and reasonable efforts to transmit and deliver its customers' traffic to and from 'all or substantially all Internet endpoints' under sections 201 and 202 of the Act . . . 'Thus, disputes involving a provider of broadband Internet access service regarding Internet traffic exchange arrangements that interfere with the delivery of a broadband Internet access service end user's traffic are subject to our authority under Title II of the Act.'[53]

Having secured a reason to regulate broadband providers under Title II the Order sets out a new 2015 series of bright line rules, based upon President Obama's statement.

 Highlight FCC four basic open internet rules (2015 version)

1. No blocking—A person engaged in the provision of broadband Internet access service, insofar as such person is so engaged, shall not block lawful content, applications, services, or non-harmful devices, subject to reasonable network management.

2. No throttling—A person engaged in the provision of broadband Internet access service, insofar as such person is so engaged, shall not impair or degrade lawful Internet traffic on

➡

---

[50] FCC15–24 <https://apps.fcc.gov/edocs_public/attachmatch/FCC-15-24A1.pdf>.
[51] Ibid. [59].
[52] Ibid. [339].
[53] Ibid. [204].

➡️

the basis of Internet content, application, or service, or use of a non-harmful device, subject to reasonable network management.

3. No paid prioritization—A person engaged in the provision of broadband Internet access service, insofar as such person is so engaged, shall not engage in paid prioritization.

4. No unreasonable interference or unreasonable disadvantage standard for Internet conduct—Any person engaged in the provision of broadband Internet access service, insofar as such person is so engaged, shall not unreasonably interfere with or unreasonably disadvantage (i) end users' ability to select, access, and use broadband Internet access service or the lawful Internet content, applications, services, or devices of their choice, or (ii) edge providers' ability to make lawful content, applications, services, or devices available to end users. Reasonable network management shall not be considered a violation of this rule.

In addition to the four basic open internet rules found in the 2015 Rules it should be remembered that the transparency provision of the 2010 rules remained in effect giving five basic open internet rules in total. The rules took effect on 12 June 2015 but, as may be expected, before they took effect they were challenged by broadband providers.

As soon as the new rules were promulgated the latest round of challenges began with a petition filed by the United States Telecom Association (USTA) claiming that: 'Broadband Internet access fits squarely within the 1996 [Telecommunications] Act's definition of "information service[s]," 47 USC §153(24), that may not be regulated as common carriage under Title II. And Congress explicitly stated that the term "information service" "includ[es] specifically a service . . . that provides access to the Internet." § 230(f)(2)' and that the FCC has tried 'to evade [the] Court's holding in Verizon'.[54] The claim went on to suggest that the whole action of the FCC was illegal as well as substantively invalid.[55] Although the Court declined to grant a motion preventing the 2015 Rules from coming into effect on 12 June,[56] they did grant a motion for an expedited hearing. The case was heard in December 2015 and in June 2016 US Court of Appeals for the District of Columbia issued its decision. Somewhat surprisingly, given predictions to the contrary,[57] the Court upheld the 2015 order and the reclassification of internet service providers as common carriers. The majority decision, given by Tatel and Srinivasan CJs, found that the Commission had not previously misclassified broadband service providers but had simply failed to classify them. By classifying providers as a telecommunications service provider the Commission had corrected that oversight and the Order was valid.[58] Chief Circuit Judge Williams dissented from this majority

---

[54] *United States Telecom Association v FCC & Ors.* CA D.C. Filed13/5/2015 <https://www.public-knowledge.org/assets/uploads/blog/15.05.13_Motion_for_Stay.pdf>, 2.

[55] Ibid. 3.

[56] J Kasperkevic, 'Net neutrality rules to go into effect after court rejects bid to block them', *The Guardian*, 11 June 2015.

[57] JP Tuthill, 'FCC throws in the towel, but public has right to know why' *SF Gate* 25 February 2014 <http://www.sfgate.com/opinion/openforum/article/FCC-throws-in-the-towel-but-public-has-right-to-5267613.php>; see also A Hurst, 'Neutering Net Neutrality: What *Verizon v FCC* Means for the Future of the Internet' (2015) 7 *Hastings Science and Technology Law Journal* 43.

[58] *United States Telecom Association v FCC* 825 F.3d 674, 728 (D.C. Cir. 2016).

position on the basis that 'the Commission's justification of its switch in classification of broadband from a Title I information service to a Title II telecommunications service fails for want of reasoned decision making' and 'to the extent that the Commission justified the switch on the basis of new policy perceptions, its explanation of the policy is watery thin and self-contradictory.'[59] By the narrowest of margins the DC Court of Appeals therefore found that the classification (in the views of the majority not a reclassification) of broadband service providers as telecommunications service providers was justified and therefore that the 2015 open internet rules were legal.

As might be expected the petitioners appealed and sought a fresh *en banc* hearing. This was denied in May 2017 with the Court finding that ISPs were more similar to telecommunications companies in that they did not exercise editorial controls than to entertainment and broadcast companies who did.[60] There were some very strong dissenting opinions issued as the Court seemed to fracture along political lines with some strong words from in particular Brown CJ who claimed that 'The President's intervention did not result from a "failure of Congress to legislate" on the issue of Internet access regulation, but because he desired "a different and inconsistent way of his own" respecting that regulation.'[61] Whatever the strong dissenting views the decision on whether to hold a new hearing was probably by this point moot, for as the majority recognized the FCC was about to replace the 2015 Order and Rules.

The pace of political change moves much faster than legal change. In November 2016 President Trump won election to the White House and one of his campaign pledges was to repeal the Open Internet Rules and Order. Upon taking over the reins of government in January 2017 he appointed Ajit Pai, a staunch supporter of less intervention, to be FCC Commissioner. Commissioner Pai immediately set about the task of repealing the Open Internet Rules and Order and in June 2018 the FCC implemented the Restoring Internet Freedom Order. This overrules the Open Internet Rules and Order. Vitally, the order also undoes the reclassification of internet broadband service providers carried out in 2015 rendering the *USTA* challenge moot. It also repealed all four open internet rules introduced in 2015, leaving only an enhanced transparency provision in place. In the words of Commissioner Pai 'It replaces unnecessary, heavy-handed regulations that were developed way back in 1934 with strong consumer protections, increased transparency, and common-sense rules that will promote investment and broadband deployment.'

 Highlight FCC Restoring Internet Freedom Order 2018

The FCC's new framework for protecting internet freedom has three key parts:

1. Consumer Protection—The Federal Trade Commission will police and take action against internet service providers for anticompetitive acts or unfair and deceptive practices.

2. Transparency—The FCC imposes enhanced transparency requirements. Internet service providers must publicly disclose information regarding their network management practices,

➡

---

[59] Ibid. 790.
[60] *United States Telecom Association v FCC* No. 15–1063 (D.C. Cir. 2017).
[61] Ibid. 45.

performance, and commercial terms of service. These disclosures must be made via a publicly available, easily accessible company website or through the FCC's website.

3. Removes Unnecessary Regulations to Promote Broadband Investment—The order removes the reclassification of broadband internet access service as a telecommunications service which occurred in 2015, reclassifying them once again as information service providers.

In passing the 2018 order the FCC has nailed its colours to the mast of market regulation. However, as everyone from Tim Berners-Lee to Vint Cerf has argued, the internet is not just a market like others in telecommunications and media.[62] As we saw at 3.1 the Mozilla Corporation and the Attorney Generals of twenty-two US States, as well as the District of Columbia, have brought a legal challenge to the Order in the United States Court of Appeals for the District of Columbia Circuit.[63] At the time of writing this is still pending.

Of course the issue of net neutrality is not only an American one. It is equally economically important, although historically was arguably less politicized, in Europe. One of the reasons the issue was less political was a more competitive European market for internet access. In the US, fixed-line broadband access was and is most commonly achieved via a cable provider. This means that for many subscribers they have a limited choice of perhaps only two or three (or even one) internet access providers. In the EU most people got, and still get, their fixed-line access over digital subscriber lines or DSL (more commonly known as telephone lines). This means that the average European consumer has a choice of several access providers. In the UK the comparison site ISP Review lists forty-two competing fixed-line service providers,[64] although admittedly most home users get their home broadband access from the 'big four' providers: BT, Sky, Virgin Media, and TalkTalk. The end user can change their ISP simply by requesting their new provider to change the service over to them.[65] Until recently the prevailing theory within Europe was that with greater competition in the internet access market, and with the regulatory authority ready to intervene should one of the behemoths of the internet access market decide to interfere with the quality of service of its customers, there was no need for proscriptive regulatory intervention.

More recently, however, Europe's reliance on market regulation has seemed less secure. As we moved from traditional DSL lines to fibre-optic access the market narrowed. As a result, European nations have taken steps to secure net neutrality. On 29 September 2010 a ministerial declaration from the Council of Europe stated that 'Users should have the greatest possible access to Internet-based content, applications and services of their choice, whether or not they are offered free of charge, using suitable devices of their choice. Such a general principle, commonly referred to as network neutrality,

---

[62] *In the Matter of Restoring Internet Freedom: Joint Comments of Internet Engineers, Pioneers, and Technologists on the Technical Flaws in the FCC's Notice of Proposed Rule-making and the Need for the Light-Touch, Bright-Line Rules from the Open Internet Order* (WC Docket No. 17–108).

[63] Above (n. 16).

[64] <https://www.ispreview.co.uk/review/top50.php>.

[65] <http://consumers.ofcom.org.uk/internet/broadband-switching/switching-broadband-provider/>.

should apply irrespective of the infrastructure or the network used for Internet connectivity.'[66] It then went on to acknowledge that although 'operators of electronic communication networks may have to manage Internet traffic [and] this management may relate to quality of service, the development of new services, network stability and resilience or combating cybercrime[67] . . . exceptions to this principle should be considered with great circumspection and need to be justified by overriding public interests'.[68] As well as the Council of Europe declaration there were developments at the EU level. Two communications from the Commission opened up debate and consultation on EU policy for net neutrality. In April 2011 a communication from the Commission to Parliament and the Council entitled *The Open Internet and Net Neutrality in Europe*,[69] noted that despite Art. 8(4)(g) of the Framework Directive[70] requiring national regulatory authorities to promote the interests of the citizens of the European Union by promoting the ability of end users to access and distribute information or run applications and services of their choice, concerns had been raised about throttling of peer-to-peer (P2P) file-sharing or video streaming by certain providers in France, Greece, Hungary, Lithuania, Poland, and the United Kingdom and blocking or charging extra for the provision of voice over internet protocol (VoIP) services in mobile networks by certain mobile operators in Austria, Germany, Italy, the Netherlands, Portugal, and Romania.[71] The Commission noted that the EU remained committed to 'preserving the open and neutral character of the internet, taking full account of the will of the co-legislators now to enshrine net neutrality as a policy objective and regulatory principle to be promoted by national regulatory authorities'.[72] The Commission also noted though that amendments made in the 2009 Telecoms Reform Package were still being implemented by member states and so recommended no immediate action be taken; rather they would monitor the situation.

The monitoring period ended in summer 2012. A study by the Body of European Regulators of European Communications (BEREC) found that 20 per cent of all internet users, and potentially up to half of EU mobile broadband users, had contracts that allowed their ISP to restrict services like VoIP or P2P. They further found that those fixed and mobile operators with contractual restrictions on P2P, 96 per cent of fixed-line providers, and 88 per cent of mobile providers, enforced them technically.[73] As a result the Commission launched a public consultation into transparency, switching, and internet traffic management with an aim to preserve net neutrality. The public consultation stage closed on 15 October 2012 after which the Commission put together a series of packages on net neutrality and mobile roaming which led on 11 September 2013 to the publication of the Connected Continent legislation package.[74] Key among this was the

---

[66] Council of Europe, Declaration of the Committee of Ministers on network neutrality (29 September 2010) para. 4 <http://archive1.diplomacy.edu/pool/fileInline.php?IDPool=1204>.

[67] Ibid. [5].

[68] Ibid. [6].

[69] COM(2011) 222 final.

[70] Dir. 2002/21/EC.

[71] See (n. 69) [4.1].

[72] EU telecoms reform package [2009] OJ L337.

[73] BEREC, *A View of Traffic Management and other Practices Resulting in Restrictions to the Open Internet in Europe* (29 May 2012) <https://ec.europa.eu/digital-single-market/en/news/view-traffic-management-and-other-practices-resulting-restrictions-open-internet-europe>.

[74] <http://ec.europa.eu/digital-agenda/en/node/67489/#open internet>.

proposal for a Regulation laying down measures concerning the European single market for electronic communications and to achieve a connected continent.[75]

The Regulation finally passed on 25 November 2015 as the Open Internet Access Regulation.[76] The key net neutrality provisions are found in Arts. 3–5 and allied regulations. Art. 3(1) ensures open standards, while Arts. 3(2) and (3) guard against discriminatory traffic management such as throttling or access tiering.

 Highlight Net neutrality in Europe (Art. 3)

1. End-users shall have the right to access and distribute information and content, use and provide applications and services, and use terminal equipment of their choice, irrespective of the end-user's or provider's location or the location, origin or destination of the information, content, application or service, via their internet access service.

2. Agreements between providers of internet access services and end-users on commercial and technical conditions and the characteristics of internet access services such as price, data volumes or speed, and any commercial practices conducted by providers of internet access services, shall not limit the exercise of the rights of end-users laid down in paragraph 1.

3. Providers of internet access services shall treat all traffic equally, when providing internet access services, without discrimination, restriction or interference, and irrespective of the sender and receiver, the content accessed or distributed, the applications or services used or provided, or the terminal equipment used.

The first subparagraph shall not prevent providers of internet access services from implementing reasonable traffic management measures. In order to be deemed to be reasonable, such measures shall be transparent, non-discriminatory, and proportionate, and shall not be based on commercial considerations but on objectively different technical quality of service requirements of specific categories of traffic. Such measures shall not monitor the specific content and shall not be maintained for longer than necessary.

Article 3 therefore prohibits blocking, filtering, access tiering, and throttling except in cases of 'reasonable traffic management'. To ensure compliance with Art. 3 transparency requirements are found in Art. 4. This provides that 'providers of internet access services shall ensure that any contract which includes internet access services specifies at least the following: (a) information on how traffic management measures applied by that provider could impact on the quality of the internet access services, on the privacy of end-users and on the protection of their personal data and (b) a clear and comprehensible explanation as to how any volume limitation, speed and other quality of service parameters may in practice have an impact on internet access services, and in particular on the use of content, applications and services.' Both Arts. 3 and 4 are backed up by the requirement that national regulatory authorities monitor service providers for compliance with the Regulation and the requirement of an annual report to BEREC.[77]

---

[75] COM(2013) 627 final <https://ec.europa.eu/digital-agenda/news-redirect/11950>.
[76] Reg. 2015/2120.
[77] Art. 5(1).

The more astute reader will have noticed that none of this appears to specifically prohibit zero rating. Even the regulator when asked the question 'is zero rating allowed under the Regulation?' answers: 'It depends'.[78] It appears from the BEREC guidelines that zero rating is allowed (subject to competition assessments) unless 'all applications are blocked (or slowed down) once the data cap is reached except for the zero-rated applications [as this] would infringe Article 3(3).'[79] Thus if your mobile network operator allows you to use unlimited Apple Music but then slows or blocks access to other services once you hit your data cap while allowing Apple Music to continue to stream unthrottled, that appears to be unlawful. However, the offering of zero-rated services is not in and of itself unlawful. This may be because the Commission sees zero rating as not necessarily harmful.[80] As was noted at 3.1 Ofcom recently closed an investigation into the Vodafone passes scheme thereby acknowledging that such schemes can be legal under the EU/UK framework.

3.4 **Conclusions**

Clearly the issue of net neutrality will remain to the fore of policy debate both in the United States and Europe, given the importance of the principle in both policy and economic terms. At the moment in the United States net neutrality is as much a political issue as it is a policy/legal issue. The current administration are strong advocates of market efficiency and minimum intervention (small government) which led directly to the Restoring Internet Freedom Order 2018. The Democrats have recently had some success in mid-term elections and remain strong advocates of mandated net neutrality. A key development in the United States will be the outcome of the challenge to the 2018 order in *Mozilla Corporation v FCC, et al.* It seems the debate between market regulation and legal intervention may not be settled for some time there.

Here in Europe the position is clearer: the Open Internet Access Regulation clearly mandates net neutrality in all areas other than zero rating, which as a result may remain a contentious issue in Europe. The UK has fully implemented the Regulation through the Open Internet Access (EU Regulation) Regulations 2016,[81] meaning that Brexit should have no implications for domestic enforcement of the net neutrality provisions of the Regulation. Clearly though the politicized nature of the net neutrality debate will ensure continued developments.

---

[78] BEREC, *What is Zero Rating?* <https://berec.europa.eu/eng/netneutrality/zero_rating/>.

[79] BEREC, *Guidelines on the Implementation by National Regulators of European Net Neutrality Rules*, BoR (16) 94, [38].

[80] European Commission, Directorate-General for Competition: *Zero-rating practices in broadband markets*, February 2017 <http://ec.europa.eu/competition/publications/reports/kd0217687enn.pdf>.

[81] SI 2016/607.

TEST QUESTIONS

Question 1

At present, it is argued, the existence of market failures requires government regulation to ensure net neutrality. Is this true? In particular, is it true in the United States? And is it true in the United Kingdom?

Question 2

Can it be said that there is, or should be, a fundamental right to a free and open internet?

Question 3

Does net neutrality necessarily entail a trade-off between competing values and interests?

FURTHER READING

Books

L Belli and P De Filippi (eds.), *Net Neutrality Compendium: Human Rights, Free Competition and the Future of the Internet* (Springer 2015)

C Marsden, *Network Neutrality: From Policy to Law to Regulation* (Manchester University Press 2017)

Chapters and articles

L Audibert and A Murray, 'A Principled Approach to Network Neutrality' (2016) 13 *Script-Ed* 118

A Cooper and I Brown, 'Net Neutrality: Discrimination, Competition, and Innovation in the UK and US', 15 *ACM Transactions on Internet Technology* 2 (2015)

T Wu, 'Network Neutrality, Broadband Discrimination' (2003) 2 *Journal of Telecommunications and High Technology Law* 141

Regulating the information society

As discussed in chapter 1, the process of digitization is proving to be a logistical challenge for lawmakers. In the real world we design laws to protect physical goods and to control the actions of corporeal individuals. The societal move from value in atoms to value in bits therefore offers a major challenge to lawmakers as it suggests traditional legal rules require to be re-evaluated when we consider extending them into the digital environment. For example, should the provisions of real world laws such as the Theft Act 1968 apply to online games where virtual property is acquired and sometimes stolen?[1] Similarly should the legal provision designed to prevent abuse of children in the production of child abuse images, found in s. 1 of the Protection of Children Act 1978, be extended to prevent the production and possession of pseudo-images: images which appear to portray the abuse of a child but which have been computer-generated?[2] These challenges of digitization, allied to the ability of internet communications to cross borders without being subjected to border controls, led some lawyers and academics to suggest that traditional legal rules, predicated on the dual foundations of physicality of goods and persons and jurisdictional boundaries, could not be extended to cyberspace. They believed that the incorporeal and borderless nature of the digital environment would render traditional lawmakers powerless, and would empower the community within cyberspace to elect its own lawmakers and to design its own laws tailored to that environment. Others disagreed, and for a period of time the argument was not about which laws should be applied in the digital environment: it was, more simply, could we regulate the actions of individuals in the digital environment at all?

4.1 **Cyberlibertarianism**

On 8 February 1996 John Perry Barlow published his declaration that cyberspace was a separate sovereign space where real-world laws and real-world governments were of little or no effect.[3] His *Declaration of Independence for Cyberspace* was a powerful challenge to lawmakers and law enforcement bodies.

---

[1] In January 2012 the Dutch Supreme Court (Hoge Raad) ruled that theft of a virtual amulet and mask in the online game Runescape could be regarded as 'goods' in Dutch law and are susceptible to theft. LJN: BQ9251, Hoge Raad, 10/00101 J.

[2] This question will be discussed in depth at 20.3.

[3] JP Barlow, *A Declaration of Independence for Cyberspace* <https://www.eff.org/cyberspace-independence>.

Highlight Barlow's Declaration of Independence for Cyberspace

Weary giants of flesh and steel you are not welcome among us and have no sovereignty where we gather . . . You have no moral right to rule us nor do you possess any methods of enforcement we have true reason to fear.

The final part of this sentence sets out one of the key supports utilized by the school of thought that was soon to become known as cyberlibertarianism or cyber-utopianism. They believed that as states may only enforce their laws within the confines of their jurisdiction, subject of course to a few specialized examples of extraterritorial effect,[4] when a citizen of a real-world jurisdiction, such as England and Wales, enters cyberspace they cross a virtual border to a new sovereign state where the laws of the old state they left are no longer legitimate or valid. Further, because this person is in a virtual (digital) environment, they have no corporeal body to imprison and any digital goods they own are in limitless supply, meaning that the sequestration of goods is an impractical method of punishment. This led to the belief, as expressed by Barlow, that traditional lawmakers could not enforce their laws against citizens of cyberspace.

There is an obvious weakness in this argument. When one visits cyberspace, one does not travel to that place. Unlike the imaginary worlds of childhood fantasy, such as Narnia or Alice's Wonderland, cyberspace is not somewhere to which we are physically transported. This means that if an individual were to engage in illegal or antisocial behaviour online their corporeal body (and all the assets owned by that individual) remains at all times subject to the direct regulation of the state in which they are resident at that time.[5] Thus a UK citizen who visits online paedophilic communities to engage in the trading and viewing of child abuse images remains at risk of apprehension and prosecution in the UK as their corporeal body is at all times subject to the actions of UK law enforcement authorities.[6] This belies Barlow's claim that traditional law-making and enforcement bodies 'do not possess any methods of enforcement we have true reason to fear' and led to a number of responses indicating that there is nothing about the nature of the digital environment which naturally protects individuals from the controls of real world lawmakers and law enforcement authorities. Professor Chris Reed calls this cyberlibertarian environmental argument 'the Cyberspace fallacy'[7] pointing out that:

> [this] states that the Internet is a new jurisdiction, in which none of the existing rules and regulations apply. This jurisdiction has no physical existence; it is a virtual space which expands and contracts as the different networks and computers, which collectively make up the Internet, connect to and disconnect from each other . . . A moment's thought reveals the fallacy. All the

---

[4] For example, s. 72 of the Criminal Justice and Immigration Act 2008 gives courts in the UK jurisdiction to prosecute UK nationals and residents who commit sex offences against children abroad. This law applies even where the person in question was not a UK national or resident at the time of the offence but has subsequently become one.

[5] Or the state in which the assets are to be found.

[6] As has been demonstrated on many occasions: see e.g. *R v Fellows and Arnold* [1997] 2 All ER 548; *R v Bowden* [2001] QB 88; *Atkins v Director of Public Prosecutions* [2000] 1 WLR 1427; or *R v Smith and Jayson* [2002] EWCA Crim 683.

[7] C Reed, *Internet Law: Text and Materials* (2nd edn, CUP 2004).

actors involved in an Internet transaction have a real-world existence, and are located in one or more legal jurisdictions . . . It is inconceivable that a real-world jurisdiction would deny that its laws potentially applied to the transaction.[8]

As Reed goes on to demonstrate, wherever traditional law enforcement bodies have faced the challenge of cross-border trade or harm, the ordinary rules of private international law, jurisdiction, and choice of law have proven effective in identifying the correct forum and legal rules to apply.

The lack of physicality found in the digital environment forms only part of the cyberlibertarian school of thought. The other key support, alluded to in Professor Reed's response, is that real-world law enforcement bodies lack legitimacy to interfere in the operations of 'Sovereign Cyberspace'. This is predicated upon the twin beliefs that there is a border between real space and cyberspace, a border not dissimilar to that which we find between jurisdictions in real space, and that. once one crosses this border into cyberspace, one may move freely about in 'Sovereign Cyberspace' without barrier or challenge. In other words, the cyberlibertarian school believed that cyberspace was a conceptually separate state.

This is most fully explored in the groundbreaking work of two US law professors, David Johnson and David Post, who in May 1996 published their highly influential paper 'Law and Borders: The Rise of Law in Cyberspace'.[9] In this paper they set out fully, and for the first time, a legal interpretation of the cyberlibertarian contention that regulation founded upon traditional state sovereignty cannot function effectively in cyberspace. They argued that, as individuals in cyberspace may move seamlessly between zones governed by differing regulatory regimes in accordance with their personal preferences, it was impossible to effectively regulate the activities of these individuals.

 Example Obscenity

Leo is a UK resident who wishes to access and download pornographic images which are in breach of the Obscene Publications Acts. Although illegal in the UK these images may be legal in the US. Leo therefore may access material hosted in the US and view it on his computer in the UK.

 Example Contempt of court

In 2007 two men attempted to blackmail a member of the UK Royal Family. A s.11 order was granted under the Contempt of Court Act 1981, meaning it was illegal to publish the name of the person involved (it still is). Despite this, it is extremely easy for a UK resident to find the name of the person involved with a quick Google search as the name has been published online by several overseas news organizations and gossip sites which are all accessible in the UK. It would even be possible for a UK resident to publish this person's name, in breach of the Contempt of Court Act, overseas but if identified they may face prosecution.

---

[8] Ibid. 174–5.
[9] 48 *Stanford Law Review* 1367 (1996).

This meant that citizens of cyberspace could engage in a practice known as regulatory arbitrage. This occurs when an individual or group may potentially be regulated by a number of alternate regulatory bodies and is offered the opportunity to choose which one to be regulated by. The individual then arbitrages (or plays off) these regulators against each other to seek the best regulatory settlement for the individual.[10] In our obscene publications example, our UK resident in the real world is directly regulated by the UK border and police forces. There is no opportunity to arbitrage their regulation (in enforcing the Obscene Publications Acts) against anyone else without leaving the jurisdiction of the UK courts. But in cyberspace he or she may seek the shelter of the US regulatory authorities by sourcing their pornographic content from US-based web servers. Technically the UK resident remains in breach of s. 42 of the Customs Consolidation Act 1876 which makes it an offence to import indecent or obscene prints, paintings, photographs, books, cards, lithographic or other engravings, or any other indecent or obscene articles. But with a 2014 survey reporting that 15 per cent of UK adults regularly visit pornographic websites, and 41 per cent occasionally do so,[11] it is clear the authorities simply do not have the resources to prosecute such a mass programme of disobedience. This is demonstrated by the fact that to date there have been no prosecutions in England and Wales under either the Customs Consolidation Act or the Obscene Publications Act 1959 for privately viewing obscene material using an internet connection. Thus the UK resident can safely arbitrage the UK regulatory framework of the Obscene Publications Acts and the Customs Consolidation Act for the US regulatory framework which has the protection of the US First Amendment.[12] This allows, at least in cyberlibertarian theory, the citizen of cyberspace to choose a different regulatory regime from that which regulates his or her activities in real space, undermining the effectiveness of traditional lawmaking processes and law enforcement institutions. Accordingly, the only effective 'Law of Cyberspace' would largely be determined by a free market in regulation in which network users would be able to choose those rule sets they found most congenial. Johnson and Post maintained that the various dimensions of inter-networking could be governed by 'decentralised, emergent law' wherein customary and privately produced laws, or rules, would be produced by decentralized collective action leading to the emergence of common standards for mutual coordination.[13] In other words, they believed that the decentralized and incorporeal nature of cyberspace meant that the only possible regulatory system was one which developed organically with the consent of the majority of the citizens of cyberspace.[14]

Cyberlibertarianism is clearly attractive for internet users. It suggests the development of new internet-only laws designed to reflect the values of the community of

[10] See AM Froomkin, 'The Internet as a Source of Regulatory Arbitrage', in B Kahin and C Nesson (eds.), *Borders in Cyberspace* (MIT Press 1997).

[11] J Mann, 'British sex survey 2014: "the nation has lost some of its sexual swagger"', *The Observer* 28 September 2014.

[12] *Reno v ACLU*, 521 US 844 (1997).

[13] This notion parallels the concept of polycentric or non-statist law. See T Bell, 'Polycentric Law' (1991/2) 7(1) *Humane Studies Review* 4; T Bell, 'Polycentric Law in the New Millennium', paper presented at the Mont Pelerin Society, 1998 Golden Anniversary Meeting, at Alexandria Virginia at <http://www.tomwbell.com/writings/FAH.html>.

[14] Johnson and Post (n. 9). See also D Johnson and D Post, 'The New "Civic Virtue" of the Internet: A Complex Systems Model for the Governance of Cyberspace', in CM Firestone (ed.), *The Emerging Internet* (1998 Annual Review of the Institute for Information Studies).

internet users and separate from the old-world values of state-based lawmakers. There are though clearly problems with such an approach. The first is who makes up the community of internet users, and who is authorized to speak for them?

The problem that the cyberlibertarians had to address was that there is no homogenous community of internet users; instead in cyberspace there are a series of heterogeneous communities with few shared values. This problem was highlighted by Professor Cass Sunstein in his book *Republic.com* where he suggested that the nature of the internet was to isolate individuals behind filters and screens rather than to provide for community building and democratic discourse.[15] Sunstein suggested that while a well-functioning system of deliberative democracy requires a certain degree of information so that citizens can engage in monitoring and deliberative tasks,[16] the ability to filter information offered by digital technologies interferes with the flow of this information in two ways. The first is that the user may simply choose not to receive some of this information by using filters to ensure they only receive information of interest to them. As such there is no homogeneity of information across the macro community of users of the internet making truly deliberative democratic discourse impossible. Further, Sunstein recognized that with the advent of internet communications it becomes easier to locate like-minded individuals whatever one's shared interests may be. This creates in Sunstein's words 'fringe communities that have a common ideology but are dispersed geographically'.[17] In turn this leads to community fragmentation. There are little in the way of common experiences and knowledge among the larger macro community of internet users. As Sunstein quickly demonstrated, there can be no cyberlibertarian ideal of a 'decentralised, emergent law' as decentralized collective action is highly unlikely to lead to the emergence of common standards for mutual coordination in the highly decentred and filtered environment of cyberspace.

If Sunstein was correct this meant that cyberspace lacked the necessary homogeneity to achieve the necessary levels of internal democratic discourse needed for the creation of cyberspace law and as a result the internet could not be effectively regulated from within. But, as Post and Johnson had demonstrated, attempts to impose external regulatory settlements in cyberspace would be equally ineffectual due to the effects of regulatory arbitrage and a lack of physical borders. This suggested an impasse. There had to be a legal framework which could be utilized in the online environment for it to flourish as a place to do business; further, there had to be a way to regulate and eliminate antisocial and anti-market activities such as the trade in pornography and copyright-infringing digital media files.[18] Fortunately Professor Sunstein was not the only theorist who had taken issue with the cyberlibertarian approach.

---

[15] C Sunstein, *Republic.com* 2.0 (Princeton University Press 2007). See also on this theme E Pariser, *The Filter Bubble: What the Internet Is Hiding from You* (Penguin 2011); S Turkle, *Alone Together* (Basic Books 2011).

[16] Sunstein ibid. 196.

[17] Ibid. 53.

[18] Note: I have not forgotten Professor Reed's point that the corpus of the individual user of online services remains subject to the direct control of the state where the individual is resident. Directly harmful activities such as the trade in child pornography will be directly regulated in this fashion. What is at issue here is more generally harmful or antisocial behaviour which is being engaged upon by a large number of users of online services and for whom direct legal regulation through the courts would be impracticable due to the large number of persons involved.

4.2 **Cyberpaternalism**

A new school of thought was developing; one which did not believe cyberspace was immune from regulatory intervention by real-world regulators. One of the strongest early critics of the cyberlibertarian position was Joel Reidenberg of Fordham Law School. Despite sympathizing with the cyberlibertarian view that the internet leads to the disintegration of territorial borders as the foundation for regulatory governance, Reidenberg argued that new models and sources of rules were being created in their place. He identified two new regulatory borders arising from new rule-making processes involving states, the private sector, technical interests, and citizens. He believed the first set of these were made up of the contractual agreements among various internet service providers. The second was to be found in the network architecture. The key to Reidenberg's analysis was this second border, the new geography of the internet which, unlike the geography of the natural world, was man-made and in our control.

Reidenberg claimed that technical standards could function like geographical borders as they establish default boundary rules that impose order in network environments. Using the network architecture as a proxy for regulatory architecture Reidenberg suggested a new way of looking at control and regulation in the online environment, a conceptualization he called '*Lex Informatica*'.[19] This draws upon the principle of *Lex Mercatoria* and refers to the 'laws' imposed on network users by technological capabilities and system design choices. Reidenberg asserted that, whereas political governance processes usually establish the substantive laws of nation states, in *Lex Informatica* the primary sources of default rule-making are the technology developer(s) and the social processes through which customary uses of the technology evolve.[20] To this end, he argued that, rather than being inherently unregulable due to its design or architecture, the internet is in fact closely regulated by its architecture.

Reidenberg contended that in the light of *Lex Informatica*'s dependence on design choices, the attributes of public oversight associated with regulatory regimes could be maintained by shifting the focus of government actions away from direct regulation of cyberspace, towards influencing changes to its architecture. Reidenberg's concept of regulatory control being implemented through the control mechanisms already in place in the network architecture led to development of the new cyberpaternalist school. This new school viewed legal controls as merely part of the network of effective regulatory controls in the online environment and suggested that lawmakers seeking to control the online activities of their citizens would seek to indirectly control these activities by mandating changes to the network architecture, or by supporting self-regulatory activities of network designers. This idea was most fully developed and explained by Professor Lawrence Lessig in his classic text *Code and Other Laws of Cyberspace*.[21]

Lessig contends that there are four 'Modalities of Regulation' which may be used individually or collectively, either directly or indirectly, by regulators to control the actions

---

[19] J Reidenberg, 'Governing Networks and Rule-Making in Cyberspace', 45 *Emory Law Journal* 911 (1996); J Reidenberg, 'Lex Informatica: The Formation of Information Policy Rules Through Technology', 76 *Texas Law Review* 553 (1998).

[20] On the role of software designers in default rule making see P Quintas, 'Software by Design', in R Mansell and R Silverstone (eds.), *Communication by Design: The Politics of Information and Communication Technologies* (OUP 1998).

[21] Basic Books (1999).

of individuals offline or online.[22] Further, Lessig suggests that Johnson and Post were wrong to suggest that regulatory arbitrage must undermine any attempt to regulate the activities of individuals online as regulators draw their legitimacy from the community they represent (and regulate) and as individuals we are therefore tied to the regulator in a way which Johnson and Post fail to recognize. As Lessig says:

> Even if we could construct cyberspace on the model of the market there are strong reasons not to. As life moves online, and more and more citizens from states X, Y and Z come to interact in cyberspaces A, B and C, these cyberspaces may well need to develop the kind of responsibility and attention that develops (ideally) within a democracy. Or, put differently, if cyberspace wants to be considered its own legitimate sovereign, and thus deserving of some measure of independence and respect, it must become more clearly a citizen sovereignty.[23]

Thus Johnson and Post's position that regulatory arbitrage, coupled with a physical border between real space and cyberspace, must lead to the development of a distinct and separate body of law for cyberspace is, in Lessig's view, tautologous. By attempting to reject real-world regulation, citizens within cyberspace undermine the possibility of competing real-world regulators recognizing the independence of cyberspace as a sovereign space, meaning that attempts to develop a separate set of principles for cyberspace will fail.

4.2.1 Lawrence Lessig's modalities of regulation

For Lessig the key to regulating all activity, whether it happens to be in the online or the offline environment is to be found in his four modalities of regulation: (1) laws, (2) markets, (3) architecture, and (4) norms. Lessig believes that regulators may, by using carefully selected hybrids of the four, achieve whatever regulatory outcome they desire. If Lessig is correct, there is no doubt that we can regulate the digital environment and the cyberlibertarians were mistaken in their claims to the contrary.

Lessig asked us to reconsider how one is regulated on a day-to-day basis. Although the law may say it is illegal to steal, it is not usually the legal imperative that prevents most of us from stealing; rather, the majority of people do not steal because they do not want to steal in the first place. We do not steal, not because we fear imprisonment but because we have been morally conditioned to accept that theft is a morally reprehensible act. Lessig concluded that four factors, or modalities, control the activities of individuals and each of these modalities functions by acting as a constraint on the choices of actions that individuals have. Thus law constrains through the threat of punishment; social norms constrain through the application of societal sanctions, such as criticism or ostracism; the market constrains through price and price-related signals; and architecture physically constrains (examples include the locked door and the concrete parking bollard). To demonstrate how these four modalities function collectively on the choice of actions for an individual, Lessig had us imagine a 'pathetic dot' which represents the individual and then graphically represented the four modalities as external forces which act upon that dot in control of its actions. This is seen in Figure 4.1.

---

[22] Ibid. 88ff.
[23] L Lessig, *Code Version 2.0*, (Basic Books 2006) 290.

Figure 4.1 Lessig's modalities in action

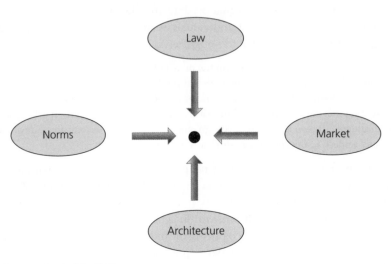

Source: Lawrence Lessig CC: BY: SA

Lessig demonstrated how these modalities function by using examples such as the regulation of smoking,[24] the supply of illegal drugs,[25] or the right of a woman to choose to have an abortion.[26] A relevant example from the online environment would be the regulation of pornographic and obscene content. The issue of online obscenity and pornography is a particularly vexed regulatory issue as the content flows over borders and different communities reflect different cultural and normative standards. Thus the first amendment culture of the United States allows far greater exploitation of pornographic content than the UK's culture which is more understanding of the need to balance the harm principle, while the UK's approach is again very different to that of the cultural values of the Kingdom of Saudi Arabia which is informed by Islamic religious teaching. Equally, community norms vary greatly so the community norms of online groups such as Christian Concern will vary wildly with those of pro-choice groups such as the Libertarian Alliance. The first modality a regulator will reach for is normally law. As we have already seen, much so-called hard-core pornography is regulated by a combination of the Customs Consolidation Act and the Obscene Publications Act 1959. However, the volume of disobedience to these laws render them impractical as a form of regulation. The government, cognizant of this, have to date focused the attention of law as a modality of regulation against only the most extreme and egregious forms of pornography, child abuse imagery,[27] and extreme forms of pornography, including bestiality, necrophilia, and rape imagery.[28] Markets generally fail to regulate

---

[24] Ibid. 122–3.
[25] Ibid. 131.
[26] Ibid. 132.
[27] Protection of Children Act 1978, s.1; Criminal Justice Act 1988, s. 160; Coroners and Justice Act 2009, s. 62.
[28] Criminal Justice and Immigration Act 2008, s. 63 (as amended).

online obscenity and pornography for, as Lessig acknowledged, as the cost of production approaches zero, the market demand increases meaning that 'free porn', especially amateur or home-produced porn, subverts normal market price controls.[29] This leaves norms and architecture (code) as possible modalities of regulation. Norms are an effective way to control porn production and consumption, as Lessig notes 'norms restrict the sale of porn generally—society for the most part sneers at consumers of porn, and this sneer undoubtedly inhibits its sale'[30] but this norm is undermined online by the remoteness of the consumer and supplier. No one sees you 'buy' online pornography and the seller is probably outside the regulator's jurisdiction. Thus normative values are undermined. This leaves architecture or code as a form of regulation and to date little use has been made of code in this regard.

The primary application of code controls to date has been the operation of the Internet Watch Foundation (IWF). The IWF operates the UK internet 'hotline' for the public to report potential child sexual-abuse imagery hosted in the UK or internationally. The IWF is a private industry body which is funded by industry partners and a European Union grant. It regulates content within its remit by reporting content to the police (and thereby ensuring its removal in the UK) and creating a blacklist of sites wherever found which contain illegal content. This blacklist is then distributed to all UK ISPs who are expected to block access to all sites contained on the list. The IWF have proven to be quite effective in reducing the availability of child abuse imagery in the UK and as a result the government has recently proposed a new form of code control for mainstream adult content. The age-verification requirement was introduced by the Digital Economy Act 2017, it requires 'any person [who] makes pornographic material available on the internet to persons in the United Kingdom on a commercial basis [to ensure] the material is not normally accessible by persons under the age of 18'.[31] The Act creates an Age-verification Regulator (currently the British Board of Film Classification) and requires them to ensure that providers of commercial online pornography have in place age-verification controls. The scheme will be discussed in more detail at 20.2.5 but the important thing to note here is that this is an attempt to use code to zone part of the internet as for adults only, ensuring children do not randomly encounter adult content.

Lessig shows that online activity is regulatable once one considers modalities of regulation which represent the regulatory framework beyond just law. The cyberlibertarians demonstrated the failure of traditional legal controls but the cyberpaternalists showed how traditional laws could be supplemented with other forms of control. This though left two challenges. First, who could legitimately make 'laws' for cyberspace, for example is it legitimate to Facebook or Google to regulate our online experience through code? And second, although governments could harness code and other modalities to regulation to regulate our online experience was it legitimate for them to do so, in other words, they could regulate in this fashion, but should they?[32]

---

[29] Lessig (n. 23) 247–8.
[30] Ibid. 247.
[31] Digital Economy Act 2017, s. 14.
[32] D Post, 'What Larry Doesn't Get: Code, Law, and Liberty in Cyberspace', (2000) 52 *Stanford Law Review* 1439.

4.3 **Network communitarianism**

That final question, should regulators use code to regulate, is at the heart of the debate between cyberlibertarians and cyberpaternalists. While cyberlibertarians believed the architecture of the network protected individuals from the attentions of real-world regulators and cyberpaternalists believed rather the opposite. Once the cyberpaternalists demonstrated the effectiveness of code as a form of regulation rather than as a tool for liberty the debate centred on the 'ought of it' question as David Post framed it. This is the question of who is best placed to make decisions about how it should be developed and deployed. Lessig and the cyberpaternalists believe this is a role for government (East Coast Codemakers as Lessig labels them) for if governments do not do this it will fall to private codemakers who are accountable to shareholders not users (West Coast Codemakers such as Google, Microsoft, and Facebook). David Post and the cyberlibertarians disagree. They believe that code, like language, is not in the control of a small number of designers: it develops organically by acquiescence of the community. As a result, governments should be kept out.

The problem with both theories is that they are techno-deterministic. Both assume that the code is deterministic of behaviour: either as permissive or restrictive of certain acts or actions.[33] Now while it is true that once implemented changes to code or architecture effect our actions: think of a locked door, a wall, or a set of bollards, we respond to the code individually and collectively. Locked doors may be kicked down, walls may be torn down, and bollards dug up. In other words, code is not a final determination of our actions; we must accept that code and not challenge it: code is not purely a design or architectural tool it also has a social or communicative function. This is the root of our third school of thought, the network communitarian school.

Unlike cyberlibertarianism and cyberpaternalism this developed in Europe with much of the early work taking place in the UK. I am the main proponent of network communitarianism and in my book *The Regulation of Cyberspace* I set out a model of network communitarian thought.[34] I believe that the cyberpaternalist model fails to account for the complexities of information flows found in a modern telecommunications/media system such as the internet. The main influences on network communitarianism are two European schools of thought which had yet to fully translate to the US, and which had therefore not influenced either cyberlibertarianism or cyberpaternalism. These are Actor Network Theory (ANT), developed in Paris in the 1980s by Michel Callon and Bruno Latour, and Social Systems Theory (SST), developed in Germany by Niklaus Luhmann and Gunther Teubner.

ANT is a theory of social transactions which accepts a role for non-human actors in any social situation. Thus, in a transaction between two individuals in a restaurant, their transaction is also affected by the restaurant itself: one would expect a different transaction in a luxury Michelin-starred restaurant than in a local café bar. The difference is not so much the surroundings themselves but the semiotic, or concepts, which the human actors have communicated to them through memory, experience

---

[33] V Mayer-Schönberger, 'Demystifying Lessig' (2008) *Wisconsin Law Review* 713.
[34] A Murray, *The Regulation of Cyberspace: Control in the Online Environment* (Routledge 2007).

and surroundings.[35] A key concept of ANT is that social communications are made up of parallel transactions between the material (things) and semiotic (concepts) which together form a single network. This has the potential to be particularly powerful when applied to the internet. The internet is the largest person-to-person communication network yet designed. It allows individuals to move social transactions in space and time and it allows transactions between people with shared experiences who are geographically remote and between people with no common history who are geographically close.[36] The potential for new networks to form, dissolve, and reform on the internet is massive, leading one to reconceptualize the internet not merely as a communications/media tool but as a cultural/social tool.[37]

SST shares some roots with ANT but is quite distinct. SST attempts to explain and study the flow of information within increasingly complex systems of social communication. Luhmann attempts to explain how communications affect social transactions by defining social systems as systems of communication, and society as the most encompassing social system. A system is defined by a boundary between itself and its surrounding environment, dividing it from the infinitely complex, or chaotic, exterior.[38] The interior of the system is thus a zone of reduced complexity: communication within a system operates by selecting only a limited amount of all information available outside. This process is also called reduction of complexity. The criterion according to which information is selected and processed is meaning.[39] Like ANT, SST is an attempt to map and study the complex process of social interactions in the increasingly complex and connected environment of modern society. Whereas ANT is about the evolution and formation of networks, SST is about the filtering of information flows in the decision-making process and the communication of ideas and concepts between systems.

Although these theories are quite distinct when taken together, they can illuminate much of our understanding of communications and social interaction in a networked environment such as the internet with a variety of actors, both human and non-human.[40] This is what is attempted in *The Regulation of Cyberspace*. I re-examined the classical cyberpaternalist model discussed earlier in which a pathetic dot is found to reside among four regulatory modalities which act as a constraint on the choice of actions of that 'dot'

---

[35] This is a woefully inadequate description of ANT which is extremely complex, rich, and valuable. Students interested in embarking on a study of ANT should start with B Latour, *Reassembling the Social: An Introduction to Actor-network-theory* (OUP 2005).

[36] And obviously between people geographically remote and also with no common history.

[37] This is actually well-worn ground in the field of communications and media studies although it seems quite alien to many lawyers and regulators. See e.g. M Castells, *The Internet Galaxy* (OUP 2001) or R Mansell, *Imagining the Internet: Communication, Innovation, and Governance* (OUP 2012).

[38] Thus a system may be the legal system where lawyers practice their trade and give advice against the background of the corpus of law. Lawyers may be asked 'is it legal to use offshore tax systems to process the profits of a particular transaction?' they will not be asked 'is it moral?' or is it 'socially harmful?' These are questions for, respectively, theologians (or philosophers) and politicians. Thus, in the internal language of the legal profession, the question is binary legal or illegal, rather than multifaceted in the wider system of society at large.

[39] As with ANT, this is a woefully inadequate description of SST which is extremely complex, rich, and valuable. Students interested in embarking on a study of SST should start with H-G Moeller, *Luhmann Explained* (Open Court 2006). Law students may then be interested in N Luhmann, *Law as a Social System* (OUP 2008).

[40] For a fascinating attempt to fuse the two together read G Teubner, 'Rights of Non-humans? Electronic Agents and Animals as New Actors in Politics and Law', 33 *Journal of Law and Society* 497 (2006).

and find that in applying the principles of ANT and SST we can consider the 'dot' rather differently. The dot is in ANT terms a material node in the network, while in SST terms is part of a system. In either term the dot is not isolated; it forms part of a matrix of dots or, to put it another way, the dot, which is designed to represent the individual, must always be considered to be part of the wider community and it is here that traditional cyberpaternalism runs into difficulty, for when one examines the modalities of regulation proposed by Lessig we find that of the four, three of them—laws, norms, and markets—are in fact a proxy for community-based control. Laws are passed by lawmakers elected by the community;[41] markets are merely a reflection of value, demand, supply, and scarcity as reflected by the community in monetary terms; and norms are merely the codification of community values. I recognized that these 'socially mediated modalities'[42] reflected an active role for the 'dot' in the regulatory process; far from being a 'pathetic dot' which was the subject of external regulatory forces, the dot was in fact an 'active dot' taking part in the regulatory process.[43] I believe there are two key distinctions between the classic cyberpaternalist model and the new network communitarian model. The first is to replace the isolated pathetic dot with a networked community (or matrix) of dots which share ideas, beliefs, ideals and opinions (see Figure 4.2). The second is to recognize that the regulatory modalities draw their legitimacy from, and are accountable to, the community (or matrix of dots), meaning the regulatory process is in nature a dialogue not an externally imposed set of constraints, as illustrated in Figure 4.3.

Figure 4.2 From the pathetic dot to the active dot matrix

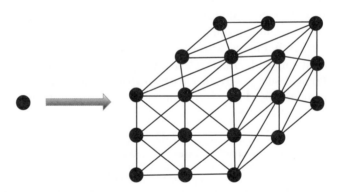

What does this mean for our understanding of internet regulation? First, it suggests that regulation in the online environment is little different to regulation in the real world. Regulation is a process of discourse and dialogue between the individual and society. Sometimes society, either directly through the application of norms, or indirectly by distilling its opinions, norms, or standards down to laws, wishes to force a change in

---

[41] At least in democratic representative politics as found in the UK. In the UK we may view the rights of MPs (our representatives) to make laws as being power drawn from the community at large as part of our social contract between the state and citizen. See J-J Rousseau, *The Social Contract* (1762, trans. M Cranston, 2004).

[42] Murray (n. 34) 37.

[43] Ibid. ch. 8.

behaviour of the individual.[44] But sometimes it is the regulatory settlement itself which is challenged by society when there is no longer any support for it. This is most clearly illustrated by the fact that the UK enforcement authorities have declined to prosecute individuals under either the Customs Consolidation Act or the Obscene Publications Act 1959 for privately viewing obscene material using an internet connection. We, the community of dots, have collectively decided that the viewing of pornography by internet connection is no longer to be viewed as morally objectionable and have communicated this decision both by driving the market for material of this type and by communicating to our lawmakers where a line is to be drawn. We wish to sanction and criminalize those who possess or trade in images of child abuse (including pseudo-images) and those who possess or trade in images of sexual violence, harm, bestiality, and necrophilia and to prevent the spread of so-called 'revenge porn'.[45] Thus the regulatory settlement is not imposed upon us—if it were, we would all avoid the viewing of obscene material for fear of prosecution under the Customs Consolidation and Obscene Publications Acts—but is rather part of a dialogue in which the regulatory settlement evolves to reflect changes in society. In network communitarian theory the power to determine the regulatory environment does not rest with the regulator alone.[46]

Figure 4.3 The regulatory discourse

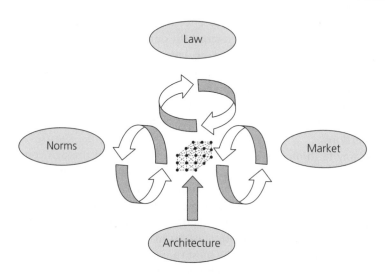

---

[44] A good example of such a change is s. 63 of the Criminal Justice and Immigration Act 2008 (as amended) which makes it an offence to possess 'extreme pornographic images'. These are images of sexual violence (including rape), bestiality, and necrophilia. This is society in the UK setting a limit on the free availability of pornographic images in the online environment. We cannot prevent pornography from entering the UK but we can criminalize the most offensive varieties of pornography to stifle demand, thus also allowing the market to make the production of such material less commercially attractive.

[45] Revenge porn is criminalized by s.33 of the Criminal Justice and Courts Act 2015.

[46] In this final analysis network communitarianism in the internet regulation context shares core values with decentred regulation in mainstream regulatory theory. See J Black, 'Decentring Regulation: Understanding the Role of Regulation and Self-Regulation in a "Post-Regulatory" World', 54 *Current Legal Problems* 103 (2001); C Scott, 'Regulation in the Age of Governance: The Rise of the Post Regulatory State', in J Jordana and D Levi-Faur (eds.), *The Politics of Regulation: Institutions and Regulatory Reforms for the Age of Governance* (Edward Elgar 2004).

4.3.1 **Symbiotic regulation**

The question of how to regulate online in the network communitarian model is somewhat complicated. It assumes the starting point of the other two models: that we may be regulated by code (as well as the other modalities) but then says the regulatory settlement is always open to challenge from the community. How can we effectively regulate in such a seemingly confused situation? I believe the answer is symbiotic regulation. The key difference between traditional models of command-and-control regulation and symbiotic regulation is that symbiotic regulation uses the communities' natural tendency towards order to bring about the regulatory settlement. The symbiotic regulation model begins with the regulator mapping the existing regulatory settlement and then defining the harm they wish to regulate. Then instead of bluntly applying one of Lessig's modalities in a command-and-control fashion they examine which form of regulation is most likely to capture the community, in other words what is the form of regulation that the community is likely to accept? This might be through market incentivization or price setting; changes to design, or variations of norms or laws.

The actual model of symbiotic regulation is complicated and I explained it fully in chapter 8 of my book *The Regulation of Cyberspace*[47] and in my paper 'Symbiotic Regulation',[48] but a clear and simple description is that the regulator uses computer modeling to model thousands of versions of their regulatory intervention across a series of repeated generations (or loops) to produce a model of which forms of regulation are likely to be accepted by, and thereby effective for, the majority of the community. Traditional enforcement models then target the outliers who will never accept the new regulatory settlement. I call this form of regulation symbiotic because it is a form of regulation which if applied correctly is mutually beneficial for both the regulator and the regulated community. The key to symbiotic regulation is that it recognizes the dynamic relationship between the regulated community, which I label as dynamic as opposed to Lessig's pathetic, and the regulator is a dialogue with information and values flowing in both directions.

The best way to think of symbiotic regulation is regulation through consensus and incentive rather than through coercion and threat. As Reed and Murray explain: 'The key distinction in practice between network communitarianism and cyberpaternalism is the compliance model. Cyberpaternalism proposes coercion whereas network communitarianism suggests incentivisation and persuasion. In cyberpaternalism the dot (or dots) acts in a certain way because of "constraint", whilst in network communitarianism it does so because of "encouragement". In the most simplistic terms they may be compared as regulation through the threat of the stick as against the incentive of the carrot.'[49]

It may be suggested that network communitarianism is close to anarchy or mob rule, that the community/mob decides what is or is not acceptable and then mobilizes their social and economic power to bring about the changes desired. Such a suggestion would though ignore the subtlety of the network communitarian school. The mob is not in charge, it is not regulation by group power; rather it is regulation by consent and democracy. As demonstrated by Cass Sunstein,[50] the nature of the internet is to

---

[47] Murray (n. 34).
[48] (2008) 26 *John Marshall Journal of Computer & Information Law* 207.
[49] C Reed and A Murray, *Rethinking the Jurisprudence of Cyberspace* (Edward Elgar 2018), 158–9.
[50] Sunstein (n. 15).

isolate individuals behind filters and screens rather than to provide for community building and democratic discourse. There is no such thing as an 'internet community' or even community of those who use the internet in a geographical location such as the UK. I am less likely to have something in common with my geographical next-door neighbour as with a professor of internet law in New Zealand. The key is that online we form micro communities, small or even large groups of like-minded people, rather than macro communities, large communities formed by geo-political connections. These micro communities are isolated from each other by barriers which impede the flow of communication between them. The true power online is not within the community; it is at the points where communities overlap, the gates through which information flows from one community to another, as illustrated in Figure 4.4.

Figure 4.4 Overlapping networks

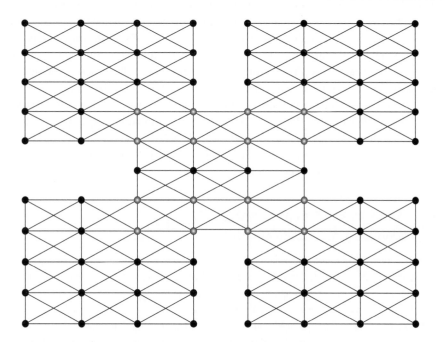

The points at which online networks meet or overlap are the key points where information flows from one micro community to another. These 'pinch points' in the communicative flows of the network are overseen by a small number of actors including search engines which index community information, social network sites such as Facebook or Twitter where people exchange information in an open environment, and telecommunications networks which carry the information. These key gatekeepers have greater influence on regulatory settlements than individuals, given their unique role.[51]

---

[51] A Murray, 'Nodes and Gravity in Virtual Space', 5 *Legisprudence* 195 (2011); EB Laidlaw, 'A Framework for Identifying Internet Information Gatekeepers', 24 *International Review of Law, Computers and Technology* 263 (2010).

It therefore becomes clear that mobs do not simply form or dissipate online; for the community to be activated it requires a considerable sense of injustice, over-regulation, or market advantage or disadvantage. For those who support network communitarianism, it reflects a more realistic dynamic of the way people come together and act in the online world.

These 'gatekeepers' are however the one key weakness in the symbiotic regulation model. For the community to communicate effectively with the regulator the communications between the nodes (or dots) must flow freely, but gatekeepers such as Google, Facebook, and ISPs can disrupt that information flow. This led to a refocusing of the regulatory model onto these key pinch points.

4.4 **Intermediary and platform regulation**

The problem of intermediaries interrupting the flow of information has been long recognized by lawyers and policymakers. It is the reason we have media plurality rules and the reason why freedom of expression and the prevention of state or private censorship is vital to democratic discourse. In the online environment the importance and role of intermediary gatekeepers is magnified, for as information flows across the network, intermediaries carry, filter, curate, and catalogue the data for us, they must as we could never make sense of such a volume of information ourselves. The key role intermediaries play in what information we receive has been studied extensively. Possibly the best-known discussion is Eli Pariser's *filter bubble*.[52] This is an extension of Nicholas Negroponte's *daily me*,[53] a personalized experience of the internet which divides us from other internet users in our experience.

 Highlight Filter bubbles

A filter bubble is the intellectual isolation that can occur when websites make use of algorithms to selectively assume the information a user would want to see, and then give information to the user according to this assumption. Websites make these assumptions based on the information related to the user, such as former click behaviour, browsing history, search history, and location. For that reason, the websites are more likely to present only information that will abide by the user's past activity. A filter bubble, therefore, can cause users to get significantly less contact with contradicting viewpoints, causing the user to become intellectually isolated.

The concept of the user being connected but isolated has major implications for network communitarianism and symbiotic regulation. If messages are not getting through between micro communities the discourse that symbiotic regulation requires is disrupted. I recognized this and tackled the issue in my paper *Nodes and Gravity in Virtual Space*.[54]

---

[52] Pariser (n. 15).
[53] N Negroponte, *Being Digital* (Hodder & Stoughton 1995) 153.
[54] Murray (n. 51).

Here I noted that 'the key control points in overlapping networks are the points of commonality. These are connections between communities: the pinch points of information flow. These macro-nodes may therefore function as gatekeepers of information flow from one area to another.'[55] I recognized that the nature of the network was changing: what had been a mostly decentred internet where users set up their own web pages and blogs, was being replaced by a new centralized internet where power was held in the hands of a smaller number of key intermediaries. I also recognized that regulators could leverage the power this small number of intermediaries wielded to bring effective regulation to the digital environment.[56]

4.4.1 Internet intermediaries

Perhaps in my original formulation of symbiotic regulation I discounted the special role of intermediaries because they had unique protection from the intervention of regulators. Articles 12–15 of the E-commerce Directive,[57] shields intermediaries from regulators by allowing them given specific liability exemptions. These are mirrored in the United States in §230 of the Communications Decency Act 1996. Intermediaries seemed therefore to be uniquely outside the ambit of regulators. However, the fact that regulators could not leverage intermediaries did not mean intermediaries were completely neutral, a fact demonstrated by Pariser. Further, the idea that intermediaries would always be shielded from intervention by regulators had already been shown to be false. In 2001 the Infosoc Directive[58] had allowed member states to implement domestic laws allowing for injunctions to be served in cases of copyright infringement.[59] This in UK terms became s.97A of the Copyright Designs & Patents Act 1988, a provision used extensively against internet service providers.[60] In the intervening years intermediaries have been pressed into service more and more to regulate among other things trademark infringements,[61] the so-called right to be forgotten at data protection law,[62] and even to regulate hate speech.[63]

The increasingly important role of intermediaries was picked up by, among others, Emily Laidlaw.[64] In her paper *A Framework for Identifying Internet Information Gatekeepers* she identified three different forms on internet gatekeepers. At the lowest level are micro gatekeepers. These are sites which have an impact on democratic discourse but which are normally closed or limited in impact. Examples would be news sites which allow

---

[55] Ibid. 212.

[56] Ibid. 213ff.

[57] Directive 2000/31/EC.

[58] Directive 2001/29/EC of the European Parliament and of the Council of 22 May 2001 on the harmonization of certain aspects of copyright and related rights in the information society.

[59] Art. 8(2).

[60] See e.g. *Twentieth Century Fox Film Corporation and Anor v Newzbin Ltd* [2010] EWHC 608 (Ch) and *Twentieth Century Fox and Others v Sky and Others* [2015] EWCA 1082 (Ch).

[61] *L'Oréal SA and Others v eBay International AG and Others* ECLI:EU:C:2011:474; *Cartier International AG v BSkyB* (CA). Reference [2016] EWCA Civ 658.

[62] *Google Spain SL and Google Inc. v AEPD and Mario Costeja González* ECLI:EU:C:2014:317.

[63] Act to Improve Enforcement of the Law in Social Networks (NetzDG), at: https://www.bmjv.de/SharedDocs/Gesetzgebungsverfahren/Dokumente/NetzDG_engl.pdf?__blob=publicationFile&v=2.

[64] EB Laidlaw, *Regulating Speech in Cyberspace: Gatekeepers, Human Rights and Corporate Responsibility* (CUP 2015); Laidlaw (n. 51).

comment such as the Huffington Post. Micro gatekeepers generally do not sit at the interface between communities and as such are less important. Next Laidlaw discusses authority gatekeepers; these are high-traffic sites which effect discourse. Laidlaw gives Wikipedia as an example and also, at the time Facebook, although it is clear Facebook has far outgrown this definition now. Sites which might still qualify include Twitter and Instagram, high-traffic sites but ones which tend not to act as an information broker between communities and groups. At the apex of Laidlaw's model sits macro gatekeepers. These control access across choke points and in Laidlaw's terms 'they are distinguished from the other levels because users must inevitably pass through them to use the Internet and thus engage all aspects of such rights as the right to freedom of expression.'[65] These are the same gatekeepers I identified in *Nodes and Gravity in Virtual Space*, the ones that have the capacity to interrupt the flow of information between communities. They include ISPs, search engine providers, designers of operating systems, and major platforms such as Facebook. These gatekeepers have the impact of recentring power in the network and re-establishing the ability to use code to coerce outcomes. Laidlaw's key contribution therefore is to identify a particular group of online actors that are uniquely positioned to implement code changes which disrupt the essential communication flows for network communitarianism to function effectively.

Laidlaw's gatekeeper analysis allows for a new wave of cyberpaternalist controls effected through the role of a few particularly powerful network actors, which can influence both code and communicative flows simultaneously. Gatekeepers, it seems, uniquely straddle the cyberpaternalist and network communitarian models and can be effective regulators in both. Laidlaw recognizes the implications of this model. She argues that the most powerful gatekeepers, which she labels Internet Information Gatekeepers (IIGs),[66] should have particular responsibilities reflecting their powerful role:

> An IIG is conceptually different than any other online gatekeeper, because it attracts human rights responsibilities. Whether human rights responsibilities should be incurred and the extent of the responsibilities depends on the extent to which the gatekeeper controls deliberation and participation in the forms of meaning-making in democratic society.[67]

Although Laidlaw here is identifying IIGs by their impact on democratic speech the same principles apply to the disruptive effects on internal discourse and network communitarianism. Thus we can more broadly identify IIGs by their disruptive effects on communicative discourse, whether democratic or otherwise. For Laidlaw the existence of democratic speech is important as it allows her to place human rights responsibilities onto IIGs, while for this analysis it is their disruptive effect that is the key.

The gatekeeper model has become the focus of much study following Laidlaw's breakthrough. Ben Wagner, in his 2016 book *Global Free Expression—Governing the Boundaries of Internet Content*,[68] makes three additions to Laidlaw's model. He first notes that traditional gatekeeper theory over-focuses upon the relationship between the gatekeeper and the gated and 'does not consider sufficiently situations in which there will be multiple

---

[65] Laidlaw (n. 51) 271.

[66] Internet gatekeepers are those gatekeepers that control the flow of information. IIGs, as a result of this control, impact participation and deliberation in democratic culture: ibid. 266.

[67] Ibid. 268.

[68] B Wagner, *Global Free Expression—Governing the Boundaries of Internet Content* (Springer 2016).

gateholders within the network'.[69] Second, he argues from a cyberpaternalist viewpoint that gatekeepers regulate through architecture,[70] and finally and perhaps most importantly, he argues that these gatekeepers are taking on a coercive enforcement role:

> Content Regulatory Agents (CRAs)—such as Facebook's Hate and Harassment team or the German Voluntary self-regulation of German media providers ('Freiwillige Selbstkontrolle Medienanbieter' or FSM)—serve as focal points for the control of online expression and create own expression governance regimes.[71]

In her work Natasha Tusikov highlights the focused power of a few essential gatekeepers which she labels 'chokepoints'.[72] She explains how gatekeepers that may not be traditionally labelled as such, for example, payment clearing systems, can influence communities and activities[73] and how 'macrointermediaries appear to be ideally suited to regulate a wide variety of activities, since they have specialized technical skills and a global enforcement reach'.[74]

The examination of intermediary regulation carried out by researchers such as Laidlaw, Wagner, and Tusikov, among others, has led to a second movement of cyberpaternalism. The current focus is not upon the diverse group of code developers, network engineers, and technical standards bodies discussed in the first movement, but rather upon a narrow group of IIGs, CRAs, or macrointermediaries. The essential lesson of the gatekeeper regulation movement is to reinvigorate the role of code-based regulation through its focus on the chokepoints in the network. It tells us that the network communitarian model can only work if the nodes in the network can communicate with each other, and although this may be possible within micro communities it is not necessarily true of the macro space that is the internet. The true model of regulation and governance in the online environment is probably somewhere between cyberpaternalism and network communitarianism, both of which recognize that much of the power to decide the future design of the space is in the hands of a few platforms. This leads us to look at the particular power of platforms.

4.4.2 **Platform power and platform regulation**

In recent years a particular form of intermediary has taken centre stage in the online environment. The groundbreaking work of Laidlaw and others looking at the gatekeeper function of certain intermediaries, such as IIGs, has given way to wider discussion of content regulation and curation of content by platform intermediaries. Platform intermediaries are difficult to define (as is common with intermediary regulation it seems) but one possible definition is to be found in the European Commission's public consultation on platform regulation which defines a platform as 'an undertaking operating in two (or multi)-sided markets, which uses the Internet to enable interactions between two or more distinct but interdependent groups of users so as to generate value

---

[69] Ibid. 14.

[70] Ibid. 20.

[71] Ibid. 18.

[72] N Tusikov, *Chokepoints: Global Private Regulation on the Internet* (University of California Press 2017).

[73] Ibid. 82–4.

[74] Ibid. 30.

for at least one of the groups.'[75] This focus on the two-sided nature of platforms has been critiqued by Dr Orla Lynskey who asks why Netflix, which is normally considered a platform, should be labelled as a platform or not based only on the form of market it supplies. As Lynskey points out: 'It is currently a single-sided service yet if it changed its revenue model and subsidized its content through advertising rather than through subscription fees it would become a two-sided platform. We must consider such a change in revenue model should be decisive in determining whether or not a digital actor is regulated.'[76] Lynskey suggests alternative definitional models for platforms including 'a broader definition was proposed in a study commissioned by the European Parliament according to which "a digital platform provides a (technological) basis for delivering or aggregating services/content from service/content providers to end-users"'.[77] Lynskey initially prefers this model as it 'incorporates two and multi-sided platforms but seemingly also includes services such as Spotify and Netflix that simply offer a service in exchange for remuneration' but even this model lacks the detail Lynskey is looking for 'yet, even this definition appears to provide a simplistic account of the relationship platforms facilitate between "providers" and "users". Moreover, it fails to shed light on why platforms might merit regulation.'[78] While this is no doubt true for our purposes it is suggested that that definition is acceptable. A platform is therefore at its heart an aggregating service which acts as an intermediary and which can act as a gatekeeper between content suppliers and consumers. To this we might add that platforms do more than just passively carry content. They curate it or manage it and present it to us in a manner which highlights some content and downplays other content. This gives them great power over information flows across platforms in a way arguably more finely grained than that discussed by Laidlaw, Wagner, and Tusikov.

Recently the power of platform intermediaries has been the focus of extensive political debate. With growing concern around the influence platforms hold in the democratic process, in particular news reports that Facebook may have influenced the US Presidential Elections in 2016,[79] the influence of both Facebook and Twitter in the UK Brexit referendum,[80] and failed attempts to use Facebook and Twitter to influence the French and German elections in 2017,[81] regulators have begun to focus on the particular power and influence of platforms.

This has led to developments in platform power and regulation. As Lynskey notes, the historical emphasis on platform power is on their market power.[82] This may be seen

---

[75] European Commission, *Public consultation on the regulatory environment for platforms, online intermediaries, data and cloud computing and the collaborative economy* (2015) 5 <https://ec.europa.eu/digital-single-market/en/news/public-consultation-regulatory-environmentplatforms-online-intermediaries-data-and-cloud>.

[76] O Lynskey, 'Regulating Platform Power' *LSE Law Society and Economy Working Paper Series*, 01/2017, 5.

[77] Ibid.

[78] Ibid. 5–6.

[79] A Madrigal, 'What Facebook Did to American Democracy and why it was so hard to see it coming', *The Atlantic* 12 October 2017.

[80] A Hern and D Pegg, 'Facebook fined for data breaches in Cambridge Analytica scandal', *The Guardian*, 11 July 2018; A Hern, 'Twitter's response to Brexit interference inquiry inadequate, MP says' *The Guardian*, 14 December 2017.

[81] C Farand, 'French social media awash with fake news stories from sources "exposed to Russian influence" ahead of presidential election', *The Independent*, 22 April 2017; I Lapowsky, 'Facebook's crackdown ahead of German election shows it's learning', *Wired*, 27 September 2017.

[82] Lynskey (n. 76) 7.

to be an effect of the focus on two-sided platforms with platforms gatekeeping access to customers or suppliers. This, Lynskey notes, is under inclusive since by equating power to market power a too narrow definition applies, instead developing Laidlaw; she argues that gatekeeping (by inclusion or exclusion) is a significant platform power distinct from market power. Regulators have quite recently acknowledged this as programmes of platform regulation begin to emerge. In addition to the Net DG law introduced in Germany[83] which requires online platforms to remove 'obviously illegal' hate speech and other postings within twenty-four hours of receiving a notification to face or potentially to face fines of up to €50m, a UK Commons select committee has recommended that media content platforms be reclassified not as platforms, which they describe as passive, but as something more like a publisher with greater legal responsibility for content which they curate and carry,[84] while the UK telecommunications regulator Ofcom has suggested that social media platforms should be regulated by an independent regulator in the same way that broadcasting and telecommunications are regulated.[85]

It seems the early work of Laidlaw and others into intermediaries and their gatekeeping function has now reached the ears of governments and regulators who see platforms as a unique and particularly potent form of intermediary with the ability not only to gatekeep content but also to curate and select content, increasing or decreasing visibility and influence. They are now clearly within the regulatory landscape and they will be the focus of a great deal of activity in the next few years.

4.5 **Behavioural regulation**

A recurring problem with all traditional models of internet regulation is that they expect the actors within the network to act in a predictable way. When you increase the price of a product or service you expect that to cause a reduction in demand for it. When you make something normatively unacceptable you expect fewer people want to take part in that activity. However, we know people are not always predictable. Veblen goods are a whole class of goods that become more desirable as the price goes up, pushing up demand. These are items like designer handbags and watches and luxury cars. Why do people demand them more as they cost more? Usually the demand for Veblen goods is explained by the snob effect: i.e. the desire to show your wealth and social standing through goods; other reasons may include the imitate-the-successful heuristic which sees the buyer seek to imitate the most successful person in their social group.[86] Whatever the reason, social psychologists and economists are now aware that people often act unpredictably, even irrationally and against their better interests on occasion. Knowing this is important for regulators as the assumption that a regulatory intervention will bring about a predictable, even rational, response cannot be assumed.

---

[83] (n. 63).

[84] House of Commons Digital, Culture, Media and Sport Committee, *Disinformation and 'fake news': Interim Report*, 24 July 2018 <https://publications.parliament.uk/pa/cm201719/cmselect/cmcumeds/363/363.pdf>.

[85] Ofcom, *Addressing harmful online content a perspective from broadcasting and on-demand standards regulation*, 18 September 2018 <https://www.ofcom.org.uk/__data/assets/pdf_file/0022/120991/Addressing-harmful-online-content.pdf>.

[86] R Boyd and P Richerson, *The Origin and Evolution of Cultures* (OUP 2005).

Traditionally when one maps a regulatory intervention you begin from the proposition that the regulatee will respond rationally in a way that maximizes his or her utility.[87] This rational actor is one who makes a 'cool and clear-headed ends-means calculation. He uses the best information available and chooses from the universe of possible responses that alternative most likely to maximize his goals.'[88] However more recently we have come to acknowledge that human actions are much more complex than this model assumes. Work by social psychologists such as Gerd Gigerenzer, Amos Tversky, and Daniel Kahneman, economists such as Herbert Simon and Richard Thaler, and regulatory theorist Cass Sunstein have shown the limitations of this approach. Simon demonstrated in the 1950s that the often-used economics model of Homo Economicus, an economic actor who is always rational, self-interested, and who pursues their subjectively defined ends optimally, was flawed as humans tend to work from incomplete information and have limited time to make decisions. As a result, Simon believed we made decisions partly out of rational choice but partly based on shortcuts or instinct. As Simon explained: 'the capacity of the human mind for formulating and solving complex problems is very small compared with the size of the problems whose solution is required for objectively rational behavior in the real world—or even for a reasonable approximation to such objective rationality.'[89]

Simon's work has influenced much that has been done in behavioural economics since. Knowing that we take mental shortcuts is important in understanding how we make decisions in the real world. This led to detailed discussion of heuristics, or mental shortcuts. Generally there are two schools of thought on heuristics: the errors and biases school, most closely connected with Kahneman and Tversky holds that reliance on heuristics leads to systemic errors in judgment;[90] the other main school, the fast and frugal school, most closely connected with Gerd Gigerenzer that using heuristics is an 'ecologically rational' strategy that makes best use of the limited information available to individuals.[91] Whichever school you subscribe to it is now widely accepted that bounded rationality involves the use of heuristics to deliver decision-making shortcuts. This is important information for regulators as it suggests they are always dealing with a limited form of bounded rationality in which errors or biases may influence the actions of the regulatee.[92]

[87] FA Hayek, *Individualism and Economic Order* (Routledge 1948); M Friedman, *Essays in Positive Economics* (University of Chicago Press 1953); HA Simon, *Models of Bounded Rationality* (MIT Press 1982).

[88] S Verba, 'Assumptions of Rationality and Non-rationality in Models of the International System,' (1961) 14 *World Politics* 93, 95.

[89] HA Simon, *Models of Man* (Wiley 1957).

[90] A Tversky and D Kahneman, 'Judgment Under Uncertainty: Heuristics and Biases' (1974) 185 *Science (NS)* 1124; D Kahneman and A Tversky, 'Prospect Theory: An Analysis of Decision Under Risk' (1979) 47 *Econometrica* 263; D Kahneman, *Thinking, Fast and Slow* (Allen Lane 2011).

[91] G Gigerenzer and DG Goldstein, 'Reasoning the Fast and Frugal Way: Models of Bounded Rationality' (1996) 103 *Psychological Review* 650; G Gigerenzer and PM Todd, *Simple Heuristics That Make Us Smart* (OUP 2000).

[92] Forms of social heuristics vary but include the availability heuristic, which leads us to assume an event is more likely to happen simply because we are able to recall a similar event faster, and the scarcity heuristic, a mental shortcut that places a value on an item based on how easily it might be lost, especially to competitors. This is often used by online booking sites which suggest there is 'only one room left', etc.

In 2016 Dr Mark Leiser in his paper *The problem with 'dots': questioning the role of rationality in the online environment* demonstrated the importance of this for internet regulators.[93] As Leiser observes:

> The online environment lacks the ability to provide users with the clues normally present during traditional methods of communication. Certain environments lack processing cues, leading users into making systematic errors and biases. Rationality is rooted in the concept that we make decisions when provided with the best information and make optimal decisions when based with clear information. On the contrary, users very rarely have access to complete information, nor do users seek complete information. Users do not calculate risks, nor compute all of the calculations before doing tasks normally associated with the online environment—entering into contracts, communicating in public forums and sharing personal data.[94]

Leiser argues that 'if we are to make better laws for the online environment, regulators should analyse the types of decisions whereby users are prone to act less than rationally and subsequently form policy where necessary to compensate for any irrational or quasi-rational behaviour.'[95] However the problem for a regulator is that predicting and mapping irrational behaviour is extremely difficult. Without the ability to assume rationality the regulator encounters Ludwig von Bertalanffy's concept of complex systems: that systems become too complex to model without anchoring assumptions.[96] A way which allows for us to adapt to the reality of bounded rationality and heuristics while providing a workable model for regulation is to return to code but in a slightly different form to that seen in Lessig's model.

4.5.1 Nudging and libertarian paternalism

Economist Richard Thaler and lawyer Cass Sunstein proposed an alternative regulatory model in 2003. Their model is labelled 'libertarian paternalism', which sounds like an impossible oxymoron. In fact, as they explain, it starts from the premise that people do not always make the best choices for themselves and that paternalistically it may be positive for law to intervene to ensure more positive outcomes. The second part of the premise is that it is false to assume that paternalism is always coercive. They argue instead that retaining the libertarian ideal that individuals should be free from coercion to make their own choices, while paternalistically intervening to bring about the best outcome, is achievable.[97]

How is this possible? The technique to be employed is what has universally become known as behavioural insights, or more commonly simply as 'nudge' after Thaler and Sunstein's famous book.[98] The central thesis of libertarian paternalism, or nudge, is that

---

[93] (2016) 30 *International Review of Law, Computers & Technology* 191.

[94] Ibid. 204.

[95] Ibid. 206.

[96] L von Bertalanffy, *General System Theory* (G Braziller 1969). Indeed, it is the existence of this problem which led Murray to suggest network communitarianism and symbiotic regulation in the first place: (Murray n. 34) ch. 2.

[97] R Thaler and C Sunstein, 'Libertarian Paternalism' (2003) 93 *The American Economic Review* 175, 175: 'If no coercion is involved, we think that some types of paternalism should be acceptable to even the most ardent libertarian. We call such actions libertarian paternalism.'

[98] R Thaler and C Sunstein, *Nudge: Improving Decisions About Health, Wealth, and Happiness* (Yale UP 2008).

humans are poor decision-makers. As we have seen, unlike the almost perfect superhu-
man decision-maker that is homo economicus, real humans are lazy decision-makers
and are subject to errors and biases. For Thaler and Sunstein the answer is to use laws, or
other regulatory techniques, to nudge the decision-maker towards the 'right' decision.
They illustrate this with a number of examples from the seemingly ridiculous:

 Example The 'Schiphol fly'

A wonderful example comes from, of all places, the men's rooms at Schiphol Airport in Amsterdam.[99] There the authorities have etched the image of a black housefly into each urinal. It seems
that men usually do not pay much attention to where they aim, which can create a bit of a mess,
but if they see a target, attention and therefore accuracy are much increased. According to the
man who came up with the idea, it works wonders. 'It improves the aim', says Aad Kieboom. 'If
a man sees a fly, he aims at it'. Kieboom, an economist, directs Schiphol's building expansion.
His staff conducted fly-in-urinal trials and found that etchings reduce spillage by 80 per cent.

to the potentially lifesaving:

 Example Organ donation

Many countries in Europe have adopted presumed consent laws [on organ donation].[100] Johnson
and Goldstein have analysed the effects of such laws by comparing countries with presumed consent to those with explicit consent. The effect on consent rates is enormous. To get a sense of the
power of the default rule, consider the difference in consent rates between two similar countries,
Austria and Germany. In Germany, which uses an opt-in system, only 12 per cent of the citizens gave
their consent, whereas in Austria (which has presumed consent), nearly everyone (99 per cent) did.

Essential to Thaler and Sunstein's model is an individual, group or government in a position of authority or influence who can engage in the process of nudging. This person is
labelled a choice architect and is described by Thaler and Sunstein as a person who 'has
the responsibility for organizing the context in which people make decisions'.[101] Choice
architects abound. As Thaler and Sunstein note, 'If you design the ballot voters use to
choose candidates, you are a choice architect. If you are a doctor and must describe the
alternative treatments available to a patient, you are a choice architect. If you design
the form that new employees fill out to enroll in the company health care plan, you are
a choice architect. If you are a parent, describing possible educational options to your
son or daughter, you are a choice architect. If you are a salesperson, you are a choice
architect (but you already knew that).'[102]

---

[99] Ibid. 3–4.
[100] Ibid. 178–9.
[101] Ibid. 3.
[102] Ibid.

Libertarian paternalism is essentially the rearrangement of default positions to encourage good decision-making and good behaviour. It might be something as simple as placing an etching of a fly in a urinal or changing the default position on organ donation. It may be slightly more complex such as changing the design of stores or cafés so that people see more clearly healthy choices such as fruit and vegetables and fewer clearly unhealthy choices such as fizzy drinks and chocolate, or it may be very complex such as designing pension plans in such a way as to encourage the best return for investors. They key, however, is identifying the behavioural outcome you hope to achieve, and a choice architect who can nudge actors towards the best outcome without ever coercing them to that end.[103]

Tantalizingly, libertarian paternalism and 'nudge' theory offer a model of regulation which mixes elements of cyberpaternalism and network communitarianism in a way which could be extremely effective in the online environment. From cyberpaternalism it draws on regulation through code or design: by changing defaults users are 'nudged' in a certain direction. From network communitarianism it draws upon the concept of discourse and choice—vitally in Thaler and Sunstein's model, unlike Lessig's, users are never coerced or constrained. It also accounts for the problem of heuristic shortcuts. If users are bound by time and informational overload the simplest decision, in most cases, is to accept the default. What is interesting about this model is that, just as Lessig warned in 1998, it returns power to the network and platform designers who acting as choice architects set the defaults. This suggests that the need for government oversight of platform power, as discussed at 4.4.2 is essential for the good health of the network, especially as platforms give over more control of their user environments to algorithms.

4.6 **Algorithmic regulation**

The current cutting edge of discourse in the field of online regulation sees humans mostly removed from the enforcement debate and replaced with intelligent computer algorithms. In what might be seen as a merging of several earlier theories: Lessig's 'code' thesis; network communitarianism; and Thaler and Sunstein's 'nudge', platforms, and intermediaries are looking to introduce smart technologies to regulate our online experience.

Drawing most clearly from the cyberpaternalist school's ethos that 'code is law', algorithmic regulation sees code deployed not as a fixed architecture or effector, as originally employed by the cyberpaternalists, but as a flexible detector of unacceptable or abhorrent behaviour. To explain the distinction: while cyberpaternalism saw code as a change to the architecture of cyberspace: a permissive or restrictive action which without discourse allowed or disallowed an action, think of the digital equivalent of a locked door, algorithmic regulation employs a discursive element, not dissimilar to network communitarian thought in which the algorithm learns and evaluates based on machine learning what is permissible and impermissible. In other words, instead of a locked door we have a digital custodian who can decide what to allow or disallow based upon a learning process.

---

[103] We should recognize that libertarian paternalism is not without critics. See R Baldwin, 'From Regulation to Behaviour Change: Giving Nudge the Third Degree' (2014) 77 *Modern Law Review* 831; M Lodge and K Wegrich, 'The Rationality Paradox of Nudge: Rational Tools of Government in a World of Bounded Rationality' (2016) 38 *Law & Policy* 250.

Algorithmic regulation is made up of three parts. First, the algorithmic process: algorithms are 'encoded procedures for transforming input data into a desired output, based on specified calculations';[104] they need not be software although the ones which we will discuss here will be software algorithms. Second, there is algorithmic decision-making, this 'refers to the use of algorithmically generated knowledge systems to execute or inform decisions, and which can vary widely in simplicity and sophistication.'[105] Finally, there is the regulation element: 'Algorithmic regulation refers to regulatory governance systems that utilise algorithmic decision making. Regulation (or regulatory governance) is intentional attempts to manage risk or alter behaviour in order to achieve some pre-specified goal.'[106] In essence, algorithmic regulation is the encoding of values (legal or community values) into software code with a process for making decisions based on input data leading to an output result.

At their most basic level, forms of algorithmic regulation are indistinguishable from cyberpaternalist code-based regulation. In her paper *Algorithmic regulation: A critical interrogation*, Yeung classifies forms of algorithmic regulation into eight classes: four of which are fixed, or code-based, and four of which are adaptive or truly algorithmic.[107] The fixed models include simple take-down procedures such as YouTube's content ID system which compares newly uploaded content against a database of copyright protected content allowing the copyright holder to take action against content which is recorded by the system as being in infringement,[108] or simple image-based or textual systems which look for triggers or keywords such as Twitter's sensitive content algorithm[109] or Facebook's Non-Consensual Intimate Image algorithm.[110] As noted, these fixed systems are simply modern incarnations of code-based control and suffer from the same weaknesses discussed earlier when we analysed cyberpaternalism.

However adaptive, or learning, algorithms are very different. They are not fixed points of architecture but are instead in a discursive relationship with their environment. Much like the active dots found in network communitarian thought these algorithms are always learning through feedback loops. Examples of smart or adaptive algorithms already in use include intelligent transportation systems that teach themselves to identify the most reliable predictor of traffic flow through machine learning processes that employ trial and error modelling applied to continuously updated real-time traffic data,[111] and credit card fraud detection systems that utilize machine learning techniques to profile the spending patterns of credit/debit card holders, aimed at detecting suspicious transactions when they occur, immediately alerting the credit

---

[104] T Gillespie, 'The Relevance of Algorithms' in Tarleton Gillespie, P Boczkowski, and K Foot (eds.) *Media Technologies* (MIT Press 2014) 167.

[105] K Yeung, 'Algorithmic regulation: A critical interrogation' (2018) 12 *Regulation and Governance* 505, 507.

[106] Ibid.

[107] Ibid. 508.

[108] YouTube, *How Content ID Works* <https://support.google.com/youtube/answer/2797370?hl=en-GB>.

[109] <http://thereputationalgorithm.com/2017/08/20/twitters-sensitive-content-algorithm/>.

[110] Facebook, *The Facts: Non-Consensual Intimate Image Pilot* 9 November 2017 <https://newsroom.fb.com/news/h/non-consensual-intimate-image-pilot-the-facts/>.

[111] Y Lv et al., 'Traffic Flow Prediction with Big Data: A Deep Learning Approach' (2015) 16 *IEEE Transactions on Intelligent Transportation Systems* 865.

provider and/or card holder to take action.[112] More ambitious programmes utilizing adaptive machine learning algorithms are planned. Facebook already uses algorithmic regulation to search for terrorist content, with apparently great success,[113] and they plan in future to use similar techniques to regulate hate speech over the coming years, although as CEO Mark Zuckerberg has admitted this is more complex than with terrorist content.

 Case Study Regulating hate speech

Some problems lend themselves more easily to AI solutions than others. So hate speech[114] is one of the hardest, because determining if something is hate speech is very linguistically nuanced, right? It's—you need to understand, you know, what is a slur and what—whether something is hateful not just in English, but the majority of people on Facebook use it in languages that are different across the world.

Contrast that, for example, with an area like finding terrorist propaganda, which we've actually been very successful at deploying AI tools on already. Today, as we sit here, 99 per cent of the ISIS and Al Qaida content that we take down on Facebook, our AI systems flag before any human sees it. So that's a success in terms of rolling out AI tools that can proactively police and enforce safety across the community.

Hate speech—I am optimistic that, over a 5 to 10-year period, we will have AI tools that can get into some of the nuances—the linguistic nuances of different types of content to be more accurate in flagging things for our systems.

What Zuckerberg is talking about is the final aim of most proponents of algorithmic regulatory systems. Smart, adaptive regulation utilizing machine learning to respond to risks and challenges by either taking steps to remove or screen content from view or to educate users through 'nudge' techniques to change their behaviour over time; all done automatically, without the need for human intervention. It appears to be the perfect merger of the code-based controls of cyberpaternalism, the discursive learning systems of network communitarianism, and the educational aims of libertarian paternalism. However, there are a number of risks associated with algorithmic regulation. It suffers many of the same problems of code-based regulation in that the designers, mostly platform regulators, set the parameters of acceptable behaviour. Further as a number of commentators have pointed out, the decision-making process takes place within a so-called 'black box' meaning that in many cases even the original designer does not know the complete decision-making process of a machine learning algorithm which continues to develop long after the original programming

---

[112] Al de Sá, A Pereira, and G Pappa, 'A customized classification algorithm for credit card fraud detection' (2018) 72 *Engineering Applications of Artificial Intelligence* 21.

[113] J Guynn, 'Facebook says artificial intelligence has sped up removal of terrorist content' (2017) *USA Today* 29 November 2017.

[114] Testimony of Mark Zuckerberg to Senate's Commerce and Judiciary Committees, 10 April 2018 <https://www.washingtonpost.com/news/the-switch/wp/2018/04/10/transcript-of-mark-zuckerbergs-senate-hearing/>.

is complete.[115] As a result, there is a developing legal framework surrounding algorithmic regulation. Like the process of algorithmic regulation itself, this is in the early stages of development. Currently primary protection is via net neutrality rules discussed in chapter 3 which prevent types of data from being treated differently and Art. 22 of the General Data Protection Regulation which allows individuals to opt out from automated decision-making processes. However, Art. 22 only applies to automated decision-making not to systems which make decisions based purely on non-personal data. Recently regulators have become more interested in the role of algorithmic regulation more widely in our lives, partly based on the fall-out from the Cambridge Analytica/Facebook scandal.[116] In early 2018 the Council of Europe published a report on algorithms and human rights.[117] This report highlighted the need for urgent public debate surrounding the issue and raised concerns about the role of private actors such as platform operators and designers of algorithms. It recommended a two-pronged approach. First, education and debate: 'all available means should be used to inform and engage the general public so that users are empowered to critically understand and deal with the logic and operation of algorithms';[118] second, oversight and transparency 'certification and auditing mechanisms for automated data processing techniques such as algorithms should be developed'.[119]

There is no doubt this is going to be at the cutting edge of debate and discourse on internet regulation in the next five to ten years. Algorithmic regulation, much like code-based regulation in the late 1990s and early 2000s seems to offer a tantalizing opportunity to take effective control over a variety of undesirable and harmful behaviour including trolling, extremism, copyright infringement, obscenity and indecency, hate speech, and fraud. However, much like the cyberpaternalist debate of twenty years ago there are concerns over lack of transparency, questions of accountability, private regulators and the risk of abuse of power, and the role of public discourse and democracy. Therefore, the debates of the early 2000s may attract new interest as we revisit the role of code in controlling online actions in a new form in the coming years.

4.7 **Conclusions**

What does all this mean for the study of cyber-regulation? Interestingly, many of the issues that were to the fore of the early debates between cyberlibertarians, cyberpaternalists ,and later network communitarians remain to the fore today. In discussions around platform power and algorithmic regulation, the same issues of code controls (and who designs the code) are still being discussed along with the role of the regulated

---

[115] F Pasquale, *The Black Box Society: The Secret Algorithms That Control Money and Information* (Harvard UP 2015); Cathy O'Neil, *Weapons of Math Destruction: How Big Data Increases Inequality and Threatens Democracy* (Penguin 2016).

[116] See <https://www.theguardian.com/news/series/cambridge-analytica-files>; <https://www.wired.com/story/wired-facebook-cambridge-analytica-coverage/>.

[117] Council of Europe, *Algorithms and Human Rights: Study on the human rights dimensions of automated data processing techniques and possible regulatory implications* (COE 2018).

[118] Ibid. 45.

[119] Ibid.

community and the wider role for public authorities (or in Lessig's terminology East Coast code). It seems we are caught in a long-term regulatory dialogue of the various roles of private vs public authorities, code vs discourse/community, choice vs architecture, and now also rationality vs irrationality. It is clear that the focus of the debates in the next five years or so will be on how to leverage the widespread power and influence of key platforms such as Facebook, Twitter, Google, and Apple. It is also clear that a new, more flexible code built upon learning algorithms which can mould to community values and standards will be developed. Code, like platforms, is no longer binary, applying simply a premissive/impermissive model. It now allows graduated responses and as such fits more fluidly into the network communitarian model. Thus it appears one may choose to see the regulation in the digital environment in a similar fashion as regulation in the physical environment. It may either be centred, command-and-control regulation or it may be decentred and part of the democratic process. What is clear is that there is nothing particularly special about designing effective regulation in the digital environment.

TEST QUESTIONS

Question 1

If code is law who are the regulators?

Question 2

Is network communitarianism a better regulatory model than cyberpaternalism? Explain why or why not?

Question 3

Can algorithms ever successfully substitute for human regulators? Can they ever account for human errors and biases? Should they?

FURTHER READING

Books

L Lessig, *Code Version 2.0* (Basic Books 2006)

A Murray, *The Regulation of Cyberspace: Control in the Online Environment* (Routledge 2007)

R Thaler and C Sunstein, *Nudge: Improving Decisions About Health, Wealth, and Happiness* (Yale UP 2008)

EB Laidlaw, *Regulating Speech in Cyberspace: Gatekeepers, Human Rights and Corporate Responsibility* (CUP 2015)

C O'Neil, *Weapons of Math Destruction: How Big Data Increases Inequality and Threatens Democracy* (Penguin 2016)

F Pasquale, *The Black Box Society: The Secret Algorithms That Control Money and Information* (Harvard UP 2015)

Chapters and articles

D Johnson and D Post, 'Law and Borders: The Rise of Law in Cyberspace' 48 *Stanford Law Review* 1367 (1996)

V Mayer-Schönberger, 'Demystifying Lessig', *Wisconsin Law Review* 714 (2008)

A Murray, 'Nodes and Gravity in Virtual Space' (2011) 5 *Legisprudence* 195

D Post, 'What Larry Doesn't Get: Code, Law and Liberty in Cyberspace' (2000) 52 *Stanford Law Review* 1439

J Reidenberg, 'Lex Informatica: The Formation of Information Policy Rules through Technology', 76 *Texas Law Review* 553 (1998)

K Yeung, 'Algorithmic regulation: A critical interrogation' (2018) 12 *Regulation and Governance* 505

PART II

Content and the information society

How internet content has become one of the most contentious legal issues of recent years. How do courts and judges deal with harmful, hateful, or violent expression and how can the law deal with the cross-jurisdictional nature of internet content?

Cyber-speech

5.1 **Introduction**

One of the most powerful developments of the digital society has been individual empowerment. By converging the functions of broadcast media and telecommunications systems the digital environment has subtly shifted the balance of power in modern society—empowering the individual, perhaps at a cost to society as a whole.

Historically power over information, and its mass distribution, rested with a few media organizations. When an event happened, be it mundane, such as the passing of planning permission for a new school, or world-shattering, such as the death of a major political or social figure, information about this occurrence could only be distributed via two discrete informational channels. First, individuals who had possession of the information could pass the information on to others who were within their circle of communications. They could do this by face-to-face meeting where they would directly pass on the information to other parties, or they could use one of the telecommunications (communication at a distance) methods developed more recently, such as a personal letter or a telephone call. These methods have become more efficient as technology has developed: the fax machine combines the two systems allowing for a letter to be sent instantaneously while mobile and satellite phones have made person-to-person voice calling more efficient and immediate. All these pre-digital personal communications systems, though, share the characteristic of narrowcasting: they may only be used to pass on information to one person or a small group of people at a time.[1]

To address a large group in the pre-digital era one had to have access to a form of broadcast or mass media. Broadcast and mass media are informational media that allow the transfer of information from one to many through a designated central broadcast point. Mass and broadcast media thus centralized the point of information control allowing for control of the information flow by an individual or a small group. Mass media tends to be the term applied to media with a mass reach with a centralized point of production but no centralized distribution point. This is newspapers and similar news media, including magazines, films, newsreels, books, and periodicals. Broadcast

---

[1] The largest group an ordinary individual would hope to address without some form of access to media would be a small public meeting in a town hall or at a designated venue such as Speaker's Corner in Hyde Park. A larger group would require considerable organization and the obtaining of permits from the authorities. With the help of technology systems such as Citizen Band, radio would allow a group to be addressed at a distance but only with the aid of costly and bulky equipment and specialist knowledge.

media describes mass media which is distributed via a broadcast centre; this is predominantly radio and television. The fact that mass media/broadcast media were in centralized control made these media forms easy to regulate[2] and led many to assume conspiracies of silence would be struck between media providers and states.[3] Digitization has interrupted the settled environment, both socially and legally with digital mass communications technology changing both the way people interact and the way regulators seek to control content. Nowhere is this more clearly demonstrated than in the development of Web 2.0, a term coined to describe this process of media/communications convergence which allows for enhanced creativity, communications, information sharing, collaboration, and functionality of the web.

This chapter will examine several aspects of this shift in power, and with it the responsibility to act with consideration to fellow citizens. It begins with a background discussion of the technologies involved: from web pages and internet forums to blogs, media-sharing syndication and ranking sites, and social networking platforms. In so doing it will look at the social implications of the shift in power from centralized media organizations to decentralized social media. We will explore what responsibilities citizens owe to each other in this new environment and ask how regulators may ensure social responsibility is met. We also ask and address the vital question: whose values predominate when regulating a global media tool which does not recognize traditional borders? From here we will examine two case studies political speech and hate speech.[4] By the end of the chapter the reader should be familiar with the key values, tensions, and current legal settlements in these areas.

5.2 **Platforms and content hosts**

Understanding how digital communications upset the established order of media and communications is essential to this chapter and our analysis of cyber-speech. As we saw in chapter 2, the internet has a longer history than most casual users are aware of. Dating from 1969 it is now 50 years old, but much of its life has been spent hidden away in universities and research labs. The internet only really came of age in the early 1990s when Berners-Lee and Cailliau's hypertext-based World Wide Web application was released to the general public through the Mosaic web browser. This development gave consumers their first experience of a converged media/communications tool. Now the average person could address large groups, as large as any media mogul could through their mass media outlet, and in addition they could address groups or individuals

---

[2] In the UK the BBC was regulated by the BBC Board of Governors and the Broadcasting Standards Commission (BSC); independent television was regulated by the Independent Television Commission (ITC); newspapers were regulated by the Press Complaints Commission; while commercial radio was regulated by the Radio Authority (RA). Three of these, the BSC, the ITC, and the RA became part of the merged super-regulator Ofcom on 1 January 2004, while the Press Complaints Commission was disbanded in 2014 following the Leveson Inquiry. The Independent Press Standards Organisation (IPSO) and IMPRESS, The Press Regulator, have taken up its duties.

[3] So-called conspiracy theories number in the thousands. Among the more famous are the Kennedy assassination; the death of Diana, Princess of Wales; and the Roswell cover-up.

[4] Further case studies in trolling, harassment, and other forms of criminal speech are discussed in ch. 6.

globally, not only locally. This is something that previously only a few media barons such as Rupert Murdoch could imagine.

5.2.1 Websites and internet forums

For most people their first experience of this newly liberated power came through their first experience of internet forums. An internet forum, or message board, is an online media exchange system that allows members to post messages which may be read at a later date by other forum users and to exchange information on a series of related (or even unrelated) issues. Well-known UK internet forums at the time included The Leaky Cauldron,[5] Outpost Gallifrey,[6] and The Student Room.[7]

Internet forums allowed an individual to address groups which could theoretically be numbered in the millions, although which more likely would be measured in the tens of thousands. Nevertheless, with nothing more specialist, or expensive, than a PC with an internet connection the individual for the first time could engage in a form of broadcasting. A posting on an internet forum could transcend space (and even time) and address audiences of a size previously only available to broadcasters. This empowered the individual internet user: it was a technology which magnified speech, since previously only commercial printworks and broadcast towers could.

Internet forums proved to be extremely powerful tools with Harry Potter fan forum The Leaky Cauldron credited with breaking the story in 2007 that Albus Dumbledore, a leading character in the Harry Potter book series, was gay.[8] Internet forums also allowed special interest groups to form; groups that due to physical remoteness or simply a lack of social acceptance may never have formed in the real world. Among the more unusual internet forums were The Marmite Forum, which brought together fans of a particular yeast extract; Worms Direct, a forum on worm farming; and Looner Fetish, a forum for individuals with a sexual fetish about balloons. The existence of these niche-interest forums, alongside the mass-audience sites such as The Student Room, were suggested to be evidence that predictions made by Nicholas Negroponte in the mid-1990s have come to pass.

Negroponte predicted individualization in delivery of informational content: that narrower common interests may support a community in the digital environment than in the physical environment.[9] If you have a very narrow or specialized interest, such as worm farming, you will find it extremely difficult to find others who share your interests in the physical world. This is because there are few people who share this interest and they are likely to be physically remote from you. The likelihood of finding people who share a socially marginalizing interest such as a sexual fetish about balloons is even less likely due to social pressures to conform. The introduction of internet forums changed all this. Negroponte cited two primary reasons for this: the first is that internet forums are 'places without space'—that is, they are places in which physical

---

[5] A Harry Potter-themed internet forum.
[6] A Dr Who-themed internet forum.
[7] A forum for students and young people.
[8] See   <http://www.the-leaky-cauldron.org/2007/10/20/j-k-rowling-at-carnegie-hall-reveals-dumbledore-is-gay-neville-marries-hannah-abbott-and-scores-more>.
[9] Discussed in N Negroponte, *Being Digital* (Hodder & Stoughton 1995) 164–71.

remoteness is unimportant. If an individual with a narrow interest, such as worm farming, is in a physically remote area, such as the Scottish Highlands, then through an internet forum he or she may form a community with worm farmers in Boise, Idaho, or Kendujhar in India. Thus digital communications shrink distances between people who share an interest. The second effect Negroponte cited was 'being asynchronous'. This allows people to share a two-way conversation across different time zones, with each able to leave a message for the other to collect at a later time. However, Negroponte also predicted that new media outlets such as internet forums would lead to a weakening of the social glue that holds society together. This was the negative effect of a multiplication of media and communication resources that he called the *Daily Me*, a personalized news service which only carries news of interest to the reader.[10] The danger of such a development is that internet users may become insular in their views even if they are seeking to normalize dangerous activities such as child abuse.

Around about the same time that internet forums began to flourish, individuals also began to offer personal websites. Personal websites were quite different from forums in that they were not designed to offer an interactive function. Instead, they functioned more like a traditional newspaper in that they allowed individuals to 'publish' their views on any subject and to address them to the world at large. Unlike traditional newspapers, of course, there were almost no start-up or production costs. Publication was instantaneous and, unlike newspapers, could stand as a (semi-)permanent record without the need to archive. Also, publication on the web was global. A personal web page, like an internet forum, could reach a potential audience that all but the most powerful media mogul could only dream of. They could even make the news as well as react to it. Probably the most famous example of a personal website reaching global acclaim was in January 1998 when Matt Drudge's *Drudge Report* published the story that President Bill Clinton was having an affair with Monica Lewinski, a White House intern.[11]

5.2.2 Social media platforms (SMPs)

The web has moved on from the pre-millennial explosion which led to, among other things, the dotcom bubble, and the creation of the first internet celebrities such as Matt Drudge. Today's internet user would not recognize the structure of the early web with static web pages and internet forums. These have been replaced by a dynamic, interactive and socially connected web experience. The kings of the new network are the SMPs: content aggregators and suppliers who connect people through social groupings. There are a number of these services such as Reddit, Tumblr, Spotify, Pinterest, Askfm, and Instagram—each designed to provide a personalized, Negroponte-style, service to news and business reports, ideas, photographs, music, video, or any other media. Unlike Negroponte's *Daily Me*, however, the content the users receive is selected by their social peers or friends rather than by the users themselves. Within this new space, some sites are more successful than others. The lords of this new space are Blogger, Tumblr, Wordpress, and Twitter for blogs and microblogs; Instagram and Pinterest for photo sharing; WhatsApp and Snapchat for instant communications; Reddit for

---

[10] Ibid. 152–4.

[11] The original Drudge Report is archived at <https://www.drudgereportarchives.com/data/2002/01/17/20020117_175502_ml.htm>.

aggregation; Vimeo and YouTube for video content; and, above all, Facebook for, well, just about everything.

 Highlight The Digital generation

Number of Facebook photo uploads per day (Sept., 2018): 350,000,000.
Number of Tweets per day (June, 2018): 500,000,000.
Number of Facebook daily active users (July, 2018): 1,470,000,000.
Number of Instagram photo uploads per day (July, 2018): 95,000,000.
Number of Facebook 'likes' per day (June, 2018): 4,750,000,000.

Interactivity is at the heart of SMPs. Whereas much of the early web was unidirective—content was held on central servers and directed to users—the modern network is built to encourage interactivity. The early web may be seen to be an extension of traditional broadcast media with content being radiated out from a central source. Sites such as BBC News, university websites like lse.ac.uk, and traditional first-generation e-commerce sites such as Amazon simply transported a traditional media/communications model to cyberspace. The modern networks, and in particular SMPs, are different. They have harnessed the network effects to create user interactivity on a previously unparalleled scale.

This brings both opportunities and challenges. While as a society the development of social networking sites such as Facebook may be seen to be a positive development, they carry risks. Some of these risks include social network stalking, as well as identity theft[12] and bullying.[13] Video networking site YouTube, while promoting the distribution of user-generated content, was the subject of a $1bn copyright infringement lawsuit[14] that went on for seven years before an undisclosed settlement was reached in 2014.[15] More recently, ongoing concerns about copyright infringement on video, audio, and image sharing platforms led the European Union to propose under Article 13 of the draft Copyright in the Digital Single Market Directive[16] that 'Information society service providers that store and provide to the public access to large amounts of works or other subject matter uploaded by their users shall use effective content recognition technologies, [which] shall be appropriate and proportionate.' The success of YouTube has also spawned a flurry of pornographic imitators. A particular problem with these services is that they are easily accessible to minors, a problem which led directly to the adoption of s. 14 of the Digital Economy Act 2017 and the creation of the Age Verification Regulator under s. 16.

---

[12] T Evans, 'Sharp rise in identity fraud as scammers use Facebook and other social media sites to hunt for information' *The Daily Telegraph* 5 July 2016.

[13] Cyberbullying is a major problem surrounding social media. This is discussed along with stalking in greater detail in ch. 6.

[14] *Viacom International, Inc. & Ors v YouTube, Inc. & Ors* 2010 WL 2532404 (SDNY 2010).

[15] S Rabil, 'Google, Viacom settle YouTube copyright suit, terms not disclosed' [2014] 28 WIPR 23; C Nemeth, '"Oh my God, they killed Kenny!"—copyright infringement on YouTube settled', *PA eBulletin*, May 2014, 6 <http://www.piperalderman.com.au/__files/f/6098/PB007%200514.pdf>.

[16] COM/2016/0593 final—2016/0280 (COD).

These issues collectively express the challenge SMPs pose from a regulatory perspective. New media has always empowered a challenge to the traditional regulatory settlement but the original network, with its traditional centralized distribution model, was subject to effective regulation (to an extent). The modern network functions quite differently with content being immediately sourced and distributed by individuals. Sites, if they are moderated, are usually moderated reactively not proactively. They give unprecedented media distribution ability to those least able to manage it: children and young people. The costs of the printing press and the broadcast tower, originally replaced in the 1990s by the cost of the PC and internet connection, have now been replaced by a free mobile phone with video capability: in other words, the cost of broadcasting is negligible.

5.3 Freedom of expression and social responsibility

5.3.1 Freedom of expression: the 'First Amendment' approach

The 'right' of free expression is jealously guarded in Western democratic culture. Many First Amendment scholars in the US argue that freedom of expression is vital for the functioning of a modern deliberative democracy: in a school of thought which mirrors the foundations of the adversarial system practiced at common law they argue that a 'free trade in ideas' advances the search for truth.[17]

 Highlight The First Amendment to the US Constitution

'Congress shall make no law respecting an establishment of religion, or prohibiting the free exercise thereof; or abridging the freedom of speech, or of the press; or the right of the people peaceably to assemble, and to petition the Government for a redress of grievances.'

As explained by Douglas Vick, this school of thought believes that 'when false ideas are expressed by some citizens, the best response is not sanction by the state but vigorous rebuttal by other citizens. Reliance on state regulation makes for an "inert people", the "greatest menace to freedom", but unimpeded public discussion allows the "power of reason" to triumph in the end.'[18] It is the belief of this 'marketplace of ideas' school that censorship or restriction of free speech is harmful as suppression of harmful speech may inadvertently boost its appeal. On the other hand, by allowing the unfettered expression of opinions despicable to the majority of citizens, the fundamental liberal value of tolerance should be promoted.[19]

---

[17] See F Schauer, *Free Speech: A Philosophical Enquiry* (CUP 1982), 15–34; WP Marshall, 'In Defense of the Search for Truth as a First Amendment Justification', 30 *Georgia Law Review* 1 (1995).

[18] D Vick, 'Regulating Hatred', in M Klang and A Murray (eds.), *Human Rights in the Digital Age* (Glasshouse 2005) 47.

[19] L Bollinger, *The Tolerant Society* (OUP 1986).

The other primary school of thought in the US emphasizes the need for free and unrestricted speech in the exercise of personal autonomy, arguing that free speech is a necessary precondition for individual autonomy, self-realization and self-fulfilment.[20] This school believes that individuals not only have the right to receive information uncensored by the state, 'they have the right to form their own beliefs and express them to others . . . state suppression of speech therefore violates the "sanctity of individual choice" and is an affront to the dignity of the individual'.[21]

5.3.2 Freedom of expression: the European approach

The European approach is slightly different. Although the philosophical foundations of free expression share certain common characteristics with the US, in particular John Stuart Mill's assertion that if we tolerate restrictions placed on speech this may restrict the ascertainment and publication of facts and valuable opinion,[22] we have different tolerances than those found in the US.

European values, perhaps shaped by our experiences of the first half of the twentieth century, particularly the powerful effect of the Nazi rhetoric which cost so many lives during the Reich and World War II, provides greater weighting to dignity when striking a balance between the interest of free expression and the (sometimes) conflicting value of respect for human dignity. Thus in Germany and France there are laws which restrict expression designed to deny the holocaust or offend the memory of the country.[23] Seeing how Hitler turned public opinion against disenfranchised groups such as communists, Jews, and homosexuals we in Europe have taken steps to protect groups within society who could otherwise feel stigmatized by their distinction from the mainstream, causing them to withdraw rather than to participate in public discourse. For instance, in the UK racial unrest in the 1960s led to the banning of 'threatening, abusive, or insulting' public statements made with the intent to incite racial hatred.[24] In addition, it is a criminal offence to possess with the intent to publish material or recordings which are likely to stir up racial hatred.[25]

It may be expected that laws such as those contained in the Public Order Act 1986 (as amended) which restrict speech on grounds of racial or religious hatred or found at the common law of blasphemy, which restricts speech harmful to Christianity,[26] would not survive the modern legal order where Art. 10 ECHR is given effect in the UK through the Human Rights Act 1998. But when one reads Art. 10 in full it becomes clear that such restrictions on speech are justified.

---

[20] See C Wells, 'Reinvigorating Autonomy: Freedom and Responsibility in the Supreme Court's First Amendment Jurisprudence', 32 *Harvard Civil Rights-Civil Liberties Law Review* 159 (1997).

[21] Vick (n. 18). See also Schauer (n. 17) 62, 68.

[22] Discussed in E Barendt, *Freedom of Speech* (2nd edn, OUP 2005) 7–13.

[23] For discussions of German law, see D Kommers and R Miller, *The Constitutional Jurisprudence of the Federal Republic of Germany* (3rd edn, Duke UP 2012). A discussion of the French position follows.

[24] Race Relations Act 1965, s. 6(1). The law, now found in the Public Order Act 1986, defines 'racial hatred' as hatred against a group based on their 'colour, race, nationality (including citizenship) or ethnic or national origins', s. 17.

[25] Public Order Act 1986, s. 23.

[26] A discussion of the common law of blasphemy may be found in Barendt (n. 22) 186–8.

Highlight European Convention on Human Rights, Art. 10

1. Everyone has the right to freedom of expression. This right shall include freedom to hold opinions and to receive and impart information and ideas without interference by public authority and regardless of frontiers. This Article shall not prevent States from requiring the licensing of broadcasting, television or cinema enterprises.

2. The exercise of these freedoms, since it carries with it duties and responsibilities, may be subject to such formalities, conditions, restrictions or penalties as are prescribed by law and *are necessary in a democratic society, in the interests of national security, territorial integrity or public safety, for the prevention of disorder or crime, for the protection of health or morals, for the protection of the reputation or rights of others, for preventing the disclosure of information received in confidence, or for maintaining the authority and impartiality of the judiciary* [emphasis added].

5.3.3 Freedom of expression: the approaches compared

The key distinction between the US First Amendment approach and the European approach is in the exceptions. The right given in Art. 10 is not absolute: in fact, the exceptions found in Art. 10(2) are extensive. This may be compared with the First Amendment to the US Constitution which states: 'Congress shall make no law respecting an establishment of religion, or prohibiting the free exercise thereof; or abridging the freedom of speech, or of the press; or the right of the people peaceably to assemble, and to petition the Government for a redress of grievances.' The First Amendment is noticeable for its lack of exceptions. This does not mean there are no exceptions to it: obscene speech is still illegal,[27] as are words designed to incite imminent violence (so-called 'fighting words').[28]

Despite these limitations the First Amendment is little restricted whereas European restrictions on Art. 10 are varied and extensive and include the aforementioned restrictions on racial and religious hatred and Nazi/Holocaust denial speech as well as restrictions on obscenity, libel, slander, and reporting of matters *sub judicae*, as well as allowing advertising restrictions on products such as tobacco, all of which are much more restrictive than their US counterparts.

This distinction in approaches between the US and the EU/UK has in the past been of little import. Media outlets tended to be focused on a particular state and would comply with the laws and practices of that state: individuals lacking the ability to be heard outside their home jurisdiction need only comply with the legal standard of that place. But as we have seen, the development of the web has both changed the focal point for media organizations who may now address an international audience as easily as a domestic one, and for individuals who are empowered to reach a global mass audience. It was only a matter of time until the inherent tensions between the European approach to free expression and the US approach came to light. It was eventually, and starkly,

---

[27] *Miller v California*, 413 US 15 (1973).
[28] *Chaplinsky v New Hampshire*, 315 US 568 (1941).

highlighted in a series of hearings in Paris and in San José and San Francisco, California. In total across six years a series of six judgments were required in the related cases of *et UEJF v Yahoo! Inc. and Yahoo! France*,[29] and *Yahoo! Inc. v LICRA*,[30] an action described by one US commentator as 'a backlash response to the cultural and technological hegemony of the United States in the on-line world'.[31]

5.3.4 *LICRA et UEJF v Yahoo! Inc. and Yahoo! France*

The cases began in Paris in May 2000 when the League Against Racism and Antisemitism (LICRA) and the Union of French Jewish Students (UEJF) raised an action against Yahoo! Inc. and Yahoo! France alleging that Yahoo! Inc. (the American parent company) hosted an auction site which offered for sale many items of Nazi memorabilia and paraphernalia, including copies of the book *Mein Kampf* by Adolph Hitler, and that Yahoo! France provided links and access to this material via the Yahoo.com website.

On 22 May 2000 the Tribunal de Grande Instance de Paris held that access by French internet users to the auction site was an offence under French law.[32] They ordered Yahoo! Inc. to 'take such measures as may be necessary to prevent the exhibition or sale on its Yahoo.com site of Nazi objects throughout the territory of France'. In addition, Yahoo! France was ordered to warn all internet users of the risk of viewing sites which contravene French law.

Yahoo! Inc. argued that the Grande Instance de Paris was not competent to make a ruling in this case as the services offered (the auction website and the Yahoo.com site) and Yahoo! Inc. itself were all offered in, or domiciled in, the US. The tribunal replied that as 'the harm is suffered in France; our jurisdiction is therefore competent over this matter pursuant to Article 46 of the New Code of Civil Procedure'. Yahoo! Inc. further argued that there were no technical means capable of allowing them to satisfy the order, and that even if such means were to exist their implementation would be at an undue cost to Yahoo! and would compromise the internet's character as a space of liberty and freedom. This they said was reflected in the application of the US Constitution which guaranteed freedom of opinion and expression to every US citizen, which had been recognized as applying to internet speech in *Reno v ACLU*,[33] and further that, as its services are directed primarily at internet users in the US and its servers are based in the

---

[29] Tribunal de Grande Instance de Paris (Superior Court of Paris). There are three separate orders in this case. To make sense of the case you should read all three. Of 22 May 2000: <http://www.lapres.net/yahen.html>; of 11 August 2000: <http://www.lapres.net/yahen8.html>; of 20 November 2000: <http://www.lapres.net/yahen11.html>.

[30] There were three hearings in California. A hearing before the District Court in which a decision was filed on 7 November 2001—*Yahoo! Inc. v LICRA*, 145 F Supp 2d 1168 (ND Cal 2001); an appeal to the 9th Circuit in which a ruling was filed on 23 August 2004—*Yahoo! Inc. v LICRA*, 379 F 3d 1120 (9th Cir. 2004); and an *en banc* rehearing before the 9th Circuit in which a ruling was filed on 12 January 2006—*Yahoo! Inc. v LICRA*, 433 F 3d 1199 (9th Cir. 2006).

[31] M Fagin, 'Regulating Speech Across Borders: Technology vs Values', (2003) 9 *Michigan Telecommunications and Technology Law Review* 395, 421.

[32] It is an offence under Art. R.645–1 of the Penal Code to display or offer for sale any material which offends the collective memory of the country. Such materials include any uniforms insignia or emblems resembling those worn by the Nazis. See the Order of 22 May 2000, <http://www.lapres.net/yahen.html>.

[33] 521 US 844 (1997).

US, the order of 22 May was 'a coercive measure [which] could have no application in the United States'.[34]

To answer the technical challenges that Yahoo! Inc. had raised, a panel of experts was convened and in August the court ordered that the panel be appointed to review Yahoo!'s technical claims. The panel was formed of one French expert (François Wallon),[35] one American expert (Vint Cerf),[36] and one independent European expert (Ben Laurie).[37] The experts reported to the tribunal on 6 November 2000. They estimated that 'almost 70 per cent of the IP addresses attributed to French internauts may be associated with certainty to a French domiciliation of the access provider and be filtered'.[38] In fact it was pointed out by the expert panel that 'Yahoo! carries out a posting of advertising banners targeting internauts which the company thinks are French and that it has available the technical means enabling it to identify them.'[39] Two of the consultants (Wallon and Laurie) suggested that in those cases where nationality was not clear from IP address identification, Yahoo! Inc. could ask visitors to Yahoo! sites to make a declaration of nationality. By a combination of these two techniques it was estimated by M. Wallon and Mr Laurie that Yahoo! would achieve a filtering success rate approaching 90 per cent. Vint Cerf disagreed with points of the technical report. He was concerned about privacy issues if this approach went ahead:

> Some users consider such questions to be an invasion of privacy. While I am not completely acquainted with privacy provisions in the Europe Union, it might be considered a violation of the rights of privacy of European users, including French users to request this information. Of course if this information is required solely because of the French Court Order, one might wonder on what grounds all other users all over the world are required to comply.[40]

Despite these concerns Cerf approved the report of the two other experts.

On the basis of this report the tribunal ordered that 'the combination of technical means available and of the initiatives which it can implement if only for the sake of elementary public morals therefore make it possible to satisfy the injunctions contained in the order of May 22, 2000: that is through filtering of access to the site auctioning Nazi [paraphernalia] and of any other site or service which contains an apology of Nazism' and that '[following] a period of three months which will be allowed for compliance with this order . . . it [Yahoo! Inc.] shall be liable to pay F100,000 per day of delay until execution shall have been fully accomplished'.[41]

5.3.5 Cross-border speech

Following the order of the court of 22 May Yahoo! France had made steps to ensure compliance with the part of the order directed at them. This was 'to warn all internet users

---

[34] For a discussion of this see D Vick, 'The Internet and the First Amendment' (1998) 61 MLR 414.
[35] A lawyer with considerable computer law experience.
[36] V (Vint) Cerf is known as the father of the internet and helped design the TCP/IP protocol. He is discussed in ch. 2.
[37] A software designer who among other things wrote Apache-SSL which is used for secure data transmission on the internet.
[38] Order of 20 November 2000—<http://ww.lapres.net/yahen11.html>.
[39] Ibid.
[40] Ibid.
[41] Ibid. At current values this is just over €15,244 per day.

of the risk of viewing sites which contravene French law'. To comply with this order, Yahoo! France modified its terms and conditions which could be accessed through the 'Find out about Yahoo!' link on the bottom of all Yahoo! web pages.[42] In addition Yahoo! France placed a warning when the user chose to search Yahoo.com from Yahoo.fr.[43] In the 20 November order the court noted that 'Yahoo! France has for the most part fulfilled the letter and the spirit of the decision of May 22, 2000 which contains an injunction applicable to Yahoo! France.' As a result of this Yahoo! France were exempted from further enforcement actions.[44] Yahoo! Inc. claimed the order was incompetent but the court reinforced it.

Rather than continue to pursue the action in France, Yahoo! Inc. retreated to the US. There Yahoo! raised a claim in the Federal District Court for the Northern District of California in San José. They sought a declaration that the French decisions were unenforceable in the US as they were in violation of the First Amendment.

Applying the precedents of earlier cases including *Telnikoff v Matusevitch*[45] and *Bachchan v India Abroad Publications Inc.*,[46] the District Court found that the French judgments had violated basic precepts of US law, noting: 'Although France has the sovereign right to regulate what speech is permissible in France, this court may not enforce a foreign order that . . . chills protected speech [occurring] simultaneously within our borders.'[47] In effect the District Court was stating publicly what had always been the issue in this series of hearings: the speech in question was, due to the borderless nature of internet communications, being broadcast simultaneously in both the US and in France (and in fact in every other state worldwide which had internet access). This is the pressure point where the freedom to express oneself and the duty to exercise that freedom responsibly meets: the very application of Shaw's principle.

 Highlight Shaw's principle

'Liberty means responsibility. That is why most men dread it.'[48]

---

[42] The new text read 'If in the context of a search conducted on https://www.yahoo.fr from a tree structure or keywords, the result of the search is to point to sites, pages or forums whose title and/or content contravenes French law, considering notably that Yahoo! France has no control over the content of those sites and external sources (including content referenced on other Yahoo! sites and services worldwide) you must desist from viewing the site concerned or you may be subject to the penalties provided in French law or legal action may be brought against you': ibid.

[43] This warning stated: 'If you continue this search on Yahoo! US, you could be invited to view revisionist sites of which the content contravenes French law and the viewing of which could lead to prosecution': ibid.

[44] Ibid.

[45] 702 A 2d 230 (Md 1997). In which case it was held that an attempt to enforce a libel judgment entered in England was contrary to the public policy of the State of Maryland as well as the First Amendment.

[46] 585 NYS 2d 661 (NY 1992). A similar case in which an attempt to enforce a libel judgment entered in England was contrary to the public policy of the State of New York as well as the First Amendment.

[47] *Yahoo! Inc. v LICRA*, 145 F Supp 2d 1168 (ND Cal. 2001), 1192.

[48] Source: *Oxford Dictionary of Quotations* (7th edn, OUP 2009).

With traditional broadcast and mass media we could entrust the publishers or broadcasters to act to protect wider social values. It did not matter if they agreed with those values or not; since they had made considerable financial investments in their distribution networks, they were susceptible to state-based regulation. Further, as the geographical reach of their media outlets was limited by the natural geography of the physical environment, it was often the case that a single state regulator could effectively police the speech of a single broadcast outlet. Television capable of reception in the UK was generally broadcast from the UK and was regulated by the Broadcasting Standards Council and the Independent Television Commission.[49] What the Yahoo! case demonstrated at a stroke was that the internet was different. There is no need of specialist equipment required to send or receive content: it was the first truly global media. Yahoo!'s sites were available both in the US and in France simultaneously. The pages were not simply published in the US, where the First Amendment applied, but were also published in France where Art. R.645-1 of the Penal Code applied. There were two competing regulators, each equally valid in their claim.

5.3.6 *Yahoo! Inc. v LICRA*

The Yahoo! case went on to have two appeals in California. In the first appeal,[50] LICRA and EUJF argued that the District Court erred in finding it had jurisdiction to hear the case. They argued that the District Court lacked personal jurisdiction, that the case was not ripe (because they have not yet sought to enforce the French judgment in the US), and that the abstention doctrine applied.[51] The majority (Judges Ferguson and Tashima) found that the District Court had erred in finding personal jurisdiction and reversed the decision.[52] Judge Brunetti wrote a strong dissenting judgment. He argued first that 'the case law in our circuit makes clear that, although wrongful conduct will satisfy the Supreme Court's constitutional standard for the exercise of in personam jurisdiction, it is not necessarily required in all cases; indeed, I believe that the Supreme Court's "express aiming" test may be met by a defendant's intentional targeting of his actions at the plaintiff in the forum state'.[53] Further, he argued that:

> the record provides ample indication that LICRA and UEJF targeted Yahoo! in California by successfully moving the French court to issue an order requiring Yahoo!'s American website to comply with French law, serving Yahoo! with such order in the US, and thereby subjecting Yahoo! to significant and daily accruing fines if Yahoo! refuses to so comply; it is immaterial to the analysis that LICRA and UEJF have yet to enforce the monetary implications of Yahoo!'s refusal to acquiesce in the French court order.[54]

With such a strong dissenting judgment it is no surprise that Yahoo! continued to press their case. They convinced the Court of Appeal to rehear the case and a rehearing *en*

---

[49] The one exception to this was that near to the border viewers in Northern Ireland could pick up television broadcasts from the Republic of Ireland.

[50] *Yahoo! Inc. v LICRA*, 379 F 3d 1120 (9th Cir. 2004).

[51] The abstention doctrine states that a court of law should (or in some cases must) refuse to hear a case, when hearing the case would potentially intrude upon the powers of another court (in this case the Tribunal de Grande Instance de Paris).

[52] They did not rule on the two other issues.

[53] *Yahoo!* (n. 50) 1127.

[54] Ibid.

banc by a panel of eleven judges was approved. The judgment of the court was given on 12 January 2006 with a narrow majority of 6:5 electing to refuse the appeal and dismiss the case, but this fact does not convey the complexity of this decision.[55] Of the eleven members of the panel eight found that the court did hold personal jurisdiction over the respondents and could hear the case. Thus on personal jurisdiction the majority verdict would have been 8:3 in favour of allowing the appeal. But, the question of ripeness (argued by UEJF and LICRA in the first appeal) remained. On this ground there were five votes for ripeness, three votes against ripeness, and three members of the court who did not reach the question (the three who had dismissed the appeal on the personal jurisdiction claim). This strange set of affairs led to a very unusual and complex result: the court held that because a three-judge plurality concluded that the suit was not ripe, '[w]hen the votes of the three judges who conclude that the suit is unripe are combined with the votes of the three dissenting judges who conclude that there is no personal jurisdiction over LICRA and UEJF, there are six votes to dismiss Yahoo!'s suit'.[56]

This is a highly unusual decision caused by a large *en banc* panel. Technically there never was a majority to dismiss the appeal on either of the grounds of appeal. Three judges rejected the first ground (personal jurisdiction) and three (different) judges rejected the second ground (ripeness) but because three of the panel never examined that ground we will never know what their decision may have been. It is possible that eight judges may have found in favour of each of Yahoo!'s grounds of appeal but they could still have lost on the narrow 6:5 decision. It is not surprising that following this decision that Yahoo! applied to the Supreme Court to hear the case. *Certiorari* was denied in May 2006, effectively ending the case. The Supreme Court was probably influenced in this decision by the fact that in January 2001 Yahoo! Inc. had announced that it would no longer allow Nazi or Ku Klux Klan memorabilia to be displayed on its websites and that a new proactive filtering and monitoring system would be installed.[57] This meant that since January 2001 Yahoo! Inc. had de facto been in compliance with the orders of 22 May and 20 November: the cases in California were in fact mostly moot.

5.3.7 **Post-*Yahoo!***

It is perhaps unsurprising that these issues have arisen occasionally since 2006. Perhaps the only surprise is that they occur occasionally rather than every day. In truth the conditions for further cases like the Yahoo! series do arise every day but it is quite uncommon that parties are willing to spend the vast sums required to litigate in two or more jurisdictions. As a result, Yahoo!-type cases remain rare, relative to the underlying conditions which cause them.

A case which reflected the *Yahoo! France* case emerged in 2012 as another case was brought by the Union of French Jewish Students. In October 2012 a rather unsavoury hashtag appeared on Twitter: #unbonjuif (a good Jew). The tweets tagged as such were antisemitic in nature. In November 2012, UEJF filed a summons requiring Twitter to reveal the identity of account holders who posted material in breach of Art. R.645-1 of

---

[55] *Yahoo! Inc. v LICRA* 433 F 3d 1199 (9th Cir. 2006).
[56] Ibid. 1248.
[57] M Ward, 'Yahoo! Looks for Hate', *BBC News* 3 January 2001 <http://news.bbc.co.uk/1/hi/sci/tech/1098761.stm>.

the French Penal Code using this hashtag. Taking a lead from Yahoo! Twitter had already voluntarily removed the offending tweets and had taken steps to prevent their republication. However, UEJF felt this did not go far enough. In January 2013 the Tribunal de Grande Instance agreed and issued an order requiring Twitter to identify a number of account holders or face a fine of €1,000 per day. Twitter responded by saying it was reviewing legal options, but earlier in the same month had asserted that it would need an order from a US court before it would, or could, disclose such personal details. The case was settled in July 2013 when Twitter handed over to the prosecutor of the Paris Tribunal de Grande Instance the data needed to enable him to identify users whom he believed had violated French law.[58] The settlement was prompted it seems by a decision of the Cour d'Appel to uphold the decision of the Tribunal de Grande Instance. This is in keeping with Twitter's policy that they may 'disclose your information if we believe that it is reasonably necessary to comply with a law, regulation, legal process, or governmental request.'[59] In fact there are many examples of such requests being met in Twitter's transparency reports. The 2017 report shows that Twitter received 12,716 requests for data (including 1366 from the UK) of which at least some data was produced in 57.5 per cent of cases (72 per cent in the UK) affecting 27,976 accounts (1993 in the UK).[60]

Recently there has been a small rush of cases where local orders are being made which are intended to have global impact. The first case in this recent tranche is *Google v Equustek*.[61] This played out very similarly to the Yahoo! case. On this occasion the case originated in Canada. Equustek Solutions, Inc., (Equustek) is a Canadian computer hardware seller and distributor. In 2011, Equustek filed a lawsuit in Canada against rival Datalink. Equustek alleged that Datalink had misappropriated Equustek's trade secrets with the help of a former Equustek engineer, as well as committing other illegal acts and unfair sales practices. The primary defendant fled Canada and refused to comply with several court orders. As a result, Equustek asked Google to remove links to Datalink websites from search results. Google removed links to more than 300 Datalink sites from its Canadian search results at https://www.google.ca, but only after Equustek requested and the court granted an order requiring it to do so. Google refused to remove Datalink's websites from its global and international search engine results (such as on google.com) beyond its Canada-specific results. Equustek requested a court order requiring that Google remove Datalink's websites from its global search results, which the Superior Court of British Columbia granted. Google appealed the global removal order to the Court of Appeal for British Columbia and then to the Supreme Court of Canada.

The Supreme Court of Canada rejected Google's appeal and upheld the order of the Court of Appeal. The Supreme Court built its argument on three pillars:

1. An injunction can be ordered against someone who is not a party to the underlying lawsuit when third parties are so involved in the wrongful acts of others that they facilitate the harm, even if they themselves are not guilty of wrongdoing. In this case it is established that Datalink was unable to carry on business in a commercially viable way without its websites appearing on Google.

---

[58] H Carnegy and T Bradshaw, 'Twitter hands over data to French prosecutors', *Financial Times*, 13 July 2013.

[59] Twitter Inc., *Privacy Policy* <https://twitter.com/privacy?lang=en>.

[60] For up-to-date data see <https://transparency.twitter.com/>.

[61] 2017 SCC 34.

The injunction in this case flows from the necessity of Google's assistance to prevent the facilitation of Datalink's ability to defy court orders and do irreparable harm to Equustek. Without the injunctive relief, it was clear that Google would continue to facilitate that ongoing harm.

2. Where it is necessary to ensure the injunction's effectiveness, a court can grant an injunction enjoining conduct anywhere in the world. The problem in this case is occurring online and globally. The Internet has no borders—its natural habitat is global. The only way to ensure that the interlocutory injunction attained its objective was to have it apply where Google operates—globally. If the injunction were restricted to Canada alone or to google.ca, the remedy would be deprived of its intended ability to prevent irreparable harm, since purchasers outside Canada could easily continue purchasing from Datalink's websites, and Canadian purchasers could find Datalink's websites even if those websites were de-indexed on google.ca.

3. Google's argument that a global injunction violates international comity because it is possible that the order could not have been obtained in a foreign jurisdiction, or that to comply with it would result in Google violating the laws of that jurisdiction, is theoretical. If Google has evidence that complying with such an injunction would require it to violate the laws of another jurisdiction, including interfering with freedom of expression, it is always free to apply to the British Columbia courts to vary the interlocutory order accordingly. As Google had not made such an application, in the absence of an evidentiary foundation, and given Google's right to seek a rectifying order, it is not equitable to deny Equustek the extraterritorial scope it needs to make the remedy effective, or even to put the onus on it to demonstrate, country by country, where such an order is legally permissible.

Google did as the Supreme Court of Canada suggested and sought evidence that the order would be illegal in the United States. They first took the case to the United States District Court for the Northern District of California seeking 'a declaratory judgment that the Canadian court's order cannot be enforced in the United States and an order enjoining that enforcement.'[62] Google argued that the Canadian court order was 'unenforceable in the United States because it directly conflicts with the First Amendment, disregards the Communication Decency Act's immunity for interactive service providers, and violates principles of international comity.'[63] Granting a preliminary injunction against enforcement District Judge Edward J Davila found that Google met all three limbs required of them to qualify for immunity under s. 230 of the Communications Decency Act 1996,[64] and as a result 'Google is harmed because the Canadian order restricts activity that Section 230 protects. In addition, the balance of equities favors Google because the injunction would deprive it of the benefits of U.S. federal law.' The preliminary injunction was made permanent in December 2017.[65]

---

[62] *Google LLC v Equustek Solutions Inc.*, Case No. 5:17-cv-04207-EJD (ND Cal. 2 Nov 2017).
[63] Ibid.
[64] These are: The claimant must show that (1) it is a 'provider or user of an interactive computer service', (2) the information in question was 'provided by another information content provider', and (3) it would be held liable as the 'publisher or speaker' of that information.
[65] *Google LLC v Equustek Solutions Inc.*, Case No. 5:17-cv-04207-EJD (ND Cal. Dec. 14, 2017).

Armed with their order from the District Court for the Northern District of California, Google, again as advised by the Canadian Supreme Court, returned to the Supreme Court of British Columbia seeking a variation of the original Canadian order.[66] Google argued that, as a result of the California judgment, the hypothetical situation that the Supreme Court of Canada had suggested had, in fact, arisen: another jurisdiction found the injunction to be 'offensive to its core values'.[67] However Smith J disagreed:

> The U.S. decision does not establish that the injunction requires Google to violate American law. That would be the case if, for example, the Datalink Defendants obtained an order from a U.S. court requiring Google to link to their websites. But there is no suggestion that any U.S. law prohibits Google from de-indexing those websites, either in compliance with the injunction or for any other reason. Absent the injunction, Google would be free to choose whether to list those websites and the injunction restricts that choice, but injunctions frequently restrain conduct that would otherwise be prima facie lawful. A party being restricted in its ability to exercise certain rights is not the same thing as that party being required to violate the law. I interpret the words of [the Supreme Court of Canada] as being primarily limited to the latter situation.[68]

On this basis Google's attempt to have the order varied was rejected. At the time of writing Google.ca continues to comply with the order while other global Google sites list Datalink pages. Google argued in *Equustek Solutions Inc. v Jack* that changes to their architecture meant they complied fully with the Canadian order in this architecture for 'it now delivers search results based by default on the user's location, regardless of the Google URL the user enters. That means website delisting would continue to be effective for all users identified as being in Canada [whichever Google site they visit], unless those users took specific steps to alter the settings on their computers.'[69] This however did not convince Smith J to vary the order. A further appeal may take place or Google may decide that with little risk of the order being enforced in the United States it might be best to leave the settled solution in place.

The Equustek case may be seen as the first shot in a developing battle around so-called geo-blocking and global effectiveness. While the original *Yahoo!* case resisted any attempt to leverage the French Penal Code beyond the borders of France and sought specifically to determine the effectiveness of geo-blocking content Equustek suggests more interventionist courts now see the internet as a global space to be policed if they are to effectively enforce their orders.

A related case to Equustek, which is instructive of the risks of such a development, is the *Deripaska* case. In February 2018 Russian opposition leader Aleksei Navalny posted a video to his own website as well as on YouTube and Instagram. The video showed an alleged meeting between billionaire Oleg Deripaska and Deputy Prime Minister Sergei Prikhodko, a long-time senior adviser to President Vladimir Putin. Navalny claimed that the video was part of a growing body of evidence of corruption in circles close to Putin. Mr Deripaska complained that the video was a breach of privacy and had been covertly filmed. He won an injunction from a court in his native Krasnodar region ordering the removal from websites of the videos and photographs and then followed this up with a complaint to Roskomnadzor (the Russian Federal Service for Supervision of

---

[66] *Equustek Solutions Inc. v Jack* 2018 BCSC 610.
[67] Ibid. [12].
[68] Ibid. [20].
[69] Ibid. [29].

Communications, Information Technology and Mass Media) when Mr Navalny failed to comply. The internal domestic elements are not important but the Russian order required YouTube and Instagram to delete the videos, meaning they would not be accessible globally. Like Equustek, the order of the Russian court would have a global effect: as Johnson and Post had predicted. Roskomnadzor warned that Russia would block all access to both YouTube and Instagram if they did not comply with the order. Instagram complied and took the video down[70] a decision that led to charges against Facebook/Instagram of bowing to censorship. YouTube however did not comply with the order and rather mysteriously Roskomnadzor announced it would not block YouTube, even though it did block Alexey Navalny's personal website for hosting the same video.[71] At the time of writing the video is still available on YouTube. The *Deripaska* case is instructive for it illustrates that when courts decide to make orders with global effect it is not only courts of states with strong rule of law traditions such as Canada, France, or the UK which will make such orders. We might expect more cases such as the *Deripaska* case originating in states like Russia, China, Turkey, or Myanmar. How global internet intermediaries respond to these cases is as instructive, arguably more so, than how they respond to cases such as *Equustek*.

A final case in our current run of such cases is *Google Inc. v Commission nationale de l'informatique et des libertés (CNIL)*.[72] This case arises from the right to be forgotten, which will be discussed in detail in at 23.2. The case began in 2013 when defamatory information about Dan Shefet, a lawyer in Paris, was placed online. Despite the claims being ludicrous they started to appear at the top of Google search returns for M. Shefet's name. Then in May 2014 in the case of *Google Spain v AEPD and Mario Costeja González*[73] the CJEU established the so-called right to be forgotten, more precisely the right to have personal data deleted or delinked by third parties under the rights of data rectification and objection to processing. Shefet argued in the Tribunal de Grande Instance de Paris that as the CJEU had found in the *Costeja González* case that Google Spain was a linked subsidiary to Google Inc. in Mountain View, California, that an order to delete or delink data could be served on Google Inc., with global effect as well as Google France. In September 2014, the Tribunal ordered Google to remove offending links from its entire global network, a much wider order than in the original *Costeja González* case which applied only in the EU. In November 2014, it threatened the company with daily €1,000 fines if it didn't comply. Then, in June 2015 CNIL, the French national data protection authority, stepped in and ordered Google to apply delisting on all versions of its search engine. They argued that removing links just from the French, or even European, versions of Google's websites does not sufficiently protect the right to be forgotten, since readers can still go to Google.com and find unexpurgated results. Google disputed this order and appealed all the way to the Conseil d'État, the French Supreme Court.

---

[70] A Kharpal, 'Facebook complies with Russia's request to take down an Instagram post linked to Putin's rival' *CNBC News* 16 February 2018 <https://www.cnbc.com/2018/02/16/instagram-removes-post-after-russia-watchdog-orders-navlany-deripaska-bribery-allegations.html>.

[71] <https://meduza.io/en/news/2018/02/20/russia-s-censor-says-it-won-t-block-youtube-despite-its-noncompliance-with-a-court-injunction>.

[72] Case C-507/17.

[73] ECLI:EU:C:2014:317.

In a blog post written by Google's Senior Vice President of Global Affairs the company explained its position.[74] In essence the company makes four arguments why it disagrees, both as a matter of policy and law, with the position taken by CNIL. The first is that Google already complies with the decision of *Costeja González* in all EU members states as the court required them to do, despite this coming with high compliance costs for Google. Second, he argues that the company have even gone beyond the *Costeja González* decision, as they have expanded their service to use geo-blocking which means that a French citizen (unless they take specific steps to spoof their location) will never be served a 'forgotten' link from any Google service wherever located. As the post explains 'if we detect you're in France, and you search for someone who had a link delisted under the right to be forgotten, you won't see that link anywhere on Google Search—regardless of which domain you use. Anyone outside the EU will continue see the link appear on non-European domains in response to the same search query.' Third, Google disputes CNIL's interpretation of the law. What CNIL is asking is that EU law be applied to global operations everywhere from Australia to Zambia and everywhere in between. This would see French law operating outside its jurisdiction. Finally, Google argue that 'if French law applies globally, how long will it be until other countries—perhaps less open and democratic—start demanding that their laws regulating information likewise have global reach? This order could lead to a global race to the bottom, harming access to information that is perfectly lawful to view in one's own country . . . This is not just a hypothetical concern. We have received demands from governments to remove content globally on various grounds—and we have resisted, even if that has sometimes led to the blocking of our services.'

The Conseil d'État referred three questions to the CJEU:

 Highlight Three questions

1. Must the 'right to de-referencing', as established by the CJEU in *Costeja González* be interpreted as meaning that a search engine operator is required, when granting a request for dereferencing, to deploy the dereferencing to all of the domain names used by its search engine so that the links at issue no longer appear, irrespective of the place from where the search initiated on the basis of the requester's name is conducted, and even if it is conducted from a place outside the territorial scope of EU law?

2. In the event that Question 1 is answered in the negative, must the 'right to de-referencing' be interpreted as meaning that a search engine operator is required, when granting a request for dereferencing, only to remove the links at issue from the results displayed, following a search conducted on the basis of the requester's name on the domain name corresponding to the State in which the request is deemed to have been made or, more generally, on the domain names distinguished by the national extensions used by that search engine for all of the Member States of the European Union?

→

---

[74] K Walker, A principle that should not be forgotten, 19 May 2016 <https://blog.google/around-the-globe/google-europe/a-principle-that-should-not-be-forgotten/>.

> →
>
> 3. In addition to the obligation mentioned in Question 2, must the 'right to de-referencing', be interpreted as meaning that a search engine operator is required, when granting a request for dereferencing, to remove the results at issue, by using the 'geo-blocking' technique, from searches conducted on the basis of the requester's name from an IP address deemed to be located in the State of residence of the person benefiting from the 'right to de-referencing', or even, more generally, from an IP address deemed to be located in one of the Member States, regardless of the domain name used by the internet user conducting the search?

The wider impact of the right to be forgotten will be discussed at 23.2; for our purposes here it is only the question of extraterritorial effect which is important.

Just as the text of this chapter was being prepared for publication the opinion of Advocate General Szpunar was published.[75] At the time of writing the opinion is only available in French, therefore the following is based on an unconfirmed translation from the original. In addressing the first question he first took aim at data protection maxmilists: 'the idea of a global dereference may seem appealing in its radicality, clarity, simplicity and efficiency. Nevertheless, this solution does not convince me, because it takes into account only one side of the coin, namely the protection of an individual's data.'[76] From this starting point he observed that neither Articles 7 nor 8 of the Charter, nor the result in *Google Spain* 'specify whether to treat a search request from Singapore differently than a request made from Paris or Katowice'[77] and went on to state that 'according to Article 52(1) TEU, the Treaties apply to the 28 Member States. The territory of a Member State is defined by national law and public international law. Article 52(2) TEU adds that the territorial scope of the Treaties is specified in Article 355 TFEU. Outside this territory, Union law cannot, in principle, apply or, consequently, create rights and obligations.'[78] This means that in AG Szpunar's opinion there can be no general application of EU law outside the borders of the EU Member States. He went on to analyse whether an 'exception case' can be made for data protection law. Noting that in some cases EU law can apply outside EU territory (such as in some cases in competition law and trademark law) he concluded there was no scope for data protection law to be so extended, finding that 'in both situations the effect [is] on the internal market (although other markets may also be affected). The internal market is a territory clearly defined by the Treaties. On the other hand, the internet is, by nature, global and, in some ways, everywhere. It is therefore difficult to make analogies and comparisons.'[79] This is a vital finding if supported by the Court when the full judgment is issued later in 2019. It suggests the CJEU may signal a retreat from attempts to impose extraterratorial provisions within the global sphere of the internet and a clear withdrawal from the line of cases developed in the *Yahoo!* and *Equustek*

---

[75] *Google Inc. v CNIL* ECLI:EU:C:2019:15.
[76] Ibid. [36].
[77] Ibid. [45].
[78] Ibid. [47].
[79] Ibid. [53].

cases. AG Szpunar goes further in also finding this approach satisfies the balancing principle in human rights law:

> It is established that data protection and privacy rights are rights deriving from Articles 7 and 8 of the Charter and must have a connection with Union law and its territoriality. The same goes for the legitimate interest of the public to access the information sought. As far as the Union is concerned, this right derives from Article 11 of the Charter. The target audience is not a global audience but is within the scope of the Charter, therefore European. Assuming a global misregistration, the Union authorities would not be able to define and determine a right to receive information, let alone weigh it against other fundamental rights of protection. data, and privacy. Especially since such public interest in accessing information will inevitably vary according to its geographical location, from one third state to another. Moreover, there is a danger that the Union will prevent people in third countries from accessing information. If an authority within the Union could order a global dereference, a fatal signal would be sent to third countries, which could also order a dereferencing under their own laws. Imagine that, for some reason, third countries interpret some of their rights in such a way as to prevent persons located in a Member State of the Union from accessing the information sought. There is a real risk of a leveling down, to the detriment of freedom of expression, at European and global level.[80]

On all of the above he had no difficulty in recommending that the first question be answered in the negative.

He then went on to answer the second and third questions together. He found that 'once a right to delisting is established, it is therefore the responsibility of the search engine operator to take any measure available to it in order to ensure efficient and complete dereferencing. This operator must take all the steps that are technically possible for him. This includes, in particular, the so-called "geo-blocking" technique, regardless of the domain name used by the user performing the search.'[81] Having established this he recommended that 'the answer to the second and third questions should be that the search engine operator is obliged to delete the disputed links from the results displayed following a search carried out on the basis of the name of the applicant made in a search engine in place in the European Union. In this context, this operator is required to take any measure at his disposal to ensure an efficient and complete dereferencing. This includes, in particular, the so-called "geo-blocking" technique, from a known IP address located in one of the Member States, regardless of the domain name used by the user who does the research.'[82]

It is of course not clear whether the Court will follow the opinion of the Advocate General in giving their judgment later in the year, however an immediate take on the opinion of the Advocate General is that following the earlier line of cases leading up to this it seems to be a sensible middle ground. It abandons the pretence that laws made at state (or supra-state as with the EU) level are of global effect in the online environment and instead seeks to settle a sensible middle ground that laws remain effective within their jurisdiction and operators of platforms and websites must try to assist lawmakers though technical tools such as geo-location and geo-blocking. In essence AG Szpunar is suggesting that just as Johnson and Post recorded that the internet took down the borders between states these borders can in a Lessigian sense be rebuilt by code and it is the duty of the code builders to do so.

---

[80] Ibid. [59]–[61].
[81] Ibid. [74].
[82] Ibid. [78].

The issues demonstrated in these cases, and in the Twitter transparency report, are likely to be substantially magnified in the future. The modern internet invites greater individual speech, facilitated by platforms. Whereas corporations have to fulfil standards of corporate social responsibility and must be sensitive to community values of all their customers wherever they are,[83] individuals have no such responsibility or sensitivities.[84] Furthermore individuals need not necessarily even be aware of different community or legal standards elsewhere. A real concern of the modern network is that it becomes a cacophony of speech rather than a marketplace for speech. Everyone feels they can say whatever they want, whenever they want and they feel it is their right not to be censored and to address the world in breach of Shaw's principle.

 Highlight Shaw's principle restated

'Liberty means Responsibility': to be allowed to speak in a public forum one must respect other members of that forum. The right to free expression should not be allowed to trump another individual's rights such as their privacy or their right to security or to a fair trial.

The problem with the information society in general and modern social network platforms in particular is that it will be very difficult to protect the rights of others as there seems to be an assumption that speech must be protected to protect the 'core values' of internet civil society and further, with the backbone of the modern network provided from the US, the primacy of free expression is again to the fore.

5.4 **Political speech**

When most commentators discuss the archetypal example of free expression they usually give political speech, or rather political debate and discourse, as the paradigm. The principle of free, that is unrestricted, speech in the political sphere is an extension of democracy itself. This is most clearly enunciated in the judgment of Justice Brandeis in the US Supreme Court case of *Whitney v California* in which he said:

> Those who won our independence believed that the final end of the State was to make men free to develop their faculties, and that, in its government, the deliberative forces should prevail over the arbitrary. They valued liberty both as an end, and as a means. They believed liberty to be the secret of happiness, and courage to be the secret of liberty. They believed that freedom to think as you will and to speak as you think are means indispensable to the discovery and spread of political truth; that, without free speech and assembly, discussion would be futile; that, with them, discussion affords ordinarily adequate protection against the dissemination of noxious doctrine; that the greatest menace to freedom is an inert people; that public discussion is a political duty, and that this should be a fundamental principle of the American government.[85]

---

[83] This may explain why Yahoo! voluntarily removed offensive material from its sites and why Twitter removed the offending tweets.

[84] The numbers of examples to demonstrate this are legion. There is the example of the Twitter users who defamed Conservative peer Lord McAlpine; the unmasking of privacy injunction holders like Ryan Giggs, again on Twitter; or the attempts made to organize violence and looting via Facebook in the 2011 English riots. These issues are discussed in chs. 6 and 7.

[85] *Whitney v California*, 274 US 357 (1927), 375–8.

In the latter half of the twentieth century the greatest proponent of this principle of 'democratic speech' was the American scholar Alexander Meiklejohn who suggested that the primary purpose of the First Amendment is to protect the right of all citizens to understand political issues and through this to participate in democracy.[86] Although Eric Barendt, writing from the UK point of view, is suspicious of the Meiklejohn position he recognizes that political speech is treated as a special case by courts.[87] He notes that two decisions in particular demonstrate that English courts are willing to give strong protection to political speech and perhaps even raise it above other forms of speech. In *Derbyshire County Council v Times Newspapers* the House of Lords held that it was contrary to public interest to allow any government authority to make a claim for libel as that would fetter free political discourse, with Lord Keith commenting that: 'it is vital that a democratically elected governmental body, or indeed any governmental body, should be open to uninhibited public criticism'.[88] Then in the later case of *R (on the application of ProLife Alliance) v BBC*,[89] the Court of Appeal gave explicit protection to 'freedom of political debate' in holding that the refusal of the BBC to transmit a party election broadcast of the ProLife Alliance on the grounds that it offended good taste and decency was unlawful. Although the House of Lords later upheld an appeal from the BBC, as Barendt notes, it did not in so doing question the value of political speech: its decision was solely based on the view that the BBC should not have to transmit any material which offended taste and decency.[90]

5.4.1 Political speech: economics and media

It is though another aspect of the democratic nature of free speech which draws the attention of lawyers in the information environment. If one accepts that political speech is a key component of democratic discourse one must face the challenge that potentially those individuals who have greatest access to media and other mass discourse tools have the potential to dominate political discourse, perhaps to the detriment of democracy.

This pattern is not uncommon in US politics where it is quite usual for the candidate who spends most on campaigning to win the presidency. In his paper *Campaign Spending and Presidential Election Results*, David Nice notes that:

> Of the thirty-one presidential elections held from 1860 through 1980, the winner outspent the loser 22 out of 31 times. If we focus just on open races, those with no incumbent running, the winner outspent the loser in 11 out of 12 races. By contrast, when an incumbent was running, a challenger who spent 41 percent or more of the two-party expenditure had a 50 per cent chance of victory. All challengers who spent less than 41 percent of the two-party expenditure lost.[91]

This suggests one is to be suspicious of unfettered free political speech at a time of election as the candidate financially best able to get across his or her campaign rhetoric to the electorate may subvert the democratic process.

To prevent the risk of subversion of the electorate in the UK we have strict campaign regulations. In the period immediately prior to a general election campaign a prospective

---

[86] See A Meiklejohn, *Political Freedom: The Constitutional Powers of the People* (Greenwood 1960); A Meiklejohn, 'The First Amendment is an Absolute', *Supreme Court Review* 245 (1961).

[87] Barendt (n. 22) 18–21, 154–5.

[88] [1993] AC 534, 547.

[89] [2002] 2 All ER 756.

[90] *R (on the application of ProLife Alliance) v BBC* [2004] 1 AC 185.

[91] 19 *Polity* 464 (1987), 468.

candidate may only spend £30,700 plus 6p for every registered voter (in a borough constituency) or 9p for every registered voter (in a county constituency).[92] Once selected for election, candidates may only spend £8,700 plus 6p for every registered voter (in a borough constituency) or 9p for every registered voter (in a county constituency).[93] The reason for the distinction between the two types of constituency is to reflect the fact that electioneering in a rural constituency costs more than in an urban one. As the average constituency size for parliamentary elections is approximately 66,250 registered voters this limits local spending by candidates during general elections to around £12,500. This does not, though, limit national spending by political parties which used to be unlimited. Yet this money could only be spent on newspaper or billboard advertising with the exception of party political and party election broadcasts, which are strictly regulated;[94] it is illegal to place political advertising on radio and television in the UK.[95]

Following the report of the Neill Committee into Standards in Public Life in 1999 even this provision was changed with new limits placed on national expenditure. By Schedule 9 of the Political Parties, Elections and Referendums Act 2000, in a general election a political party may only spend £30,000 multiplied by the number of constituencies contested by the party in that part of Great Britain or Northern Ireland; or if higher (a) in relation to England, £810,000; (b) in relation to Scotland, £120,000; and (c) in relation to Wales, £60,000. This means a party which campaigned in all 650 constituencies in the UK would have a maximum national campaign expenditure of £19,500,000.[96]

With political advertising strictly regulated, political parties often seek media coverage of speeches and events. To combat an imbalance of coverage between mainstream and minor parties the Representation of the People Act 1983 requires broadcasters to draw up codes of good practice, which are required to be reviewed by the Electoral Commission, to ensure fair and impartial coverage of political speech during elections.[97]

5.4.2 Online political speech

The question is how does online speech affect these provisions? These laws are predicated upon the idea that communication between political parties and candidates and the general public will be transmitted through traditional media routes. Whereas the Communications Act and the Broadcasting Act regulate electoral media transmissions through radio and television channels, they are silent as to new media channels such as social media sites, blogs, websites, and YouTube channels.[98] Any expenditure by political parties on new media messaging will, of course, have to be accounted for in their election returns and will count towards maximum expenditure limits discussed above.

---

[92] Representation of the People Act 1983, s. 76ZA.

[93] Representation of the People Act 1983, s. 76(2)(a).

[94] See Communications Act 2003, s. 333; Broadcasting Act 1990, ss. 36 and 107.

[95] Communications Act 2003, s. 319(2)(g).

[96] In the 2017 General Election the Labour Party spent £11,003,980; the Conservatives spent £18,592,590; and the Liberal Democrats £6,788,316 <https://www.electoralcommission.org.uk/find-information-by-subject/political-parties-campaigning-and-donations/political-party-spending-at-elections/details-of-party-spending-at-previous-elections>.

[97] Representation of the People Act 1983, s. 93.

[98] In the 2017 General Election Campaign the Conservative Party spent about £2.1m on Facebook advertising while the Labour Party spent slightly over £500,000 and the Liberal Democrats £244,000.

In this sense new media advertising may be seen to be akin to traditional billboard or newspaper advertising.

This was the view of the Electoral Commission in their 2003 report *Online Election Campaigns*.[99] Following an extensive review of the use of campaign websites, SMS messaging, and email campaigning (the report predates YouTube and most social networking sites such as Facebook) the Electoral Commission concluded that they: 'value the level playing field and platform for free speech which the internet and other online communication technologies can provide'. As a result they reported that 'while we do not accept that online campaign activities should be entirely free from regulatory restrictions, any regulatory action should be limited to the minimum necessary to protect a fair campaign environment'.[100] As a result they made no proposals to specifically regulate online activities of political parties, except to recommend that s. 146 of the Political Parties, Elections and Referendums Act 2000, which requires the name and address of the promoter of political communications to appear on the communication, be extended to digital communications.

It may be suggested though that the Electoral Commission underestimated the potential impact of digital communications in the field of political speech. At the time of the report it may have seemed that digital communications could be seen to be an incremental development of traditional mass media outlets such as newspapers or billboards. Even the use of SMS messaging suggested a 'broadcast' model with the information originating from a single source. It is therefore understandable that they focused on online campaigning rather than online political discourse more generally. However, with the advent of SMPs there were a number of new outlets for electioneering outside the control (and direct funding) of the political parties themselves. These outlets are therefore not subject to expenditure limits and, as they are not traditional media outlets, are not subject to the impartiality requirements of radio or television channels. These outlets include political YouTube channels and multimedia bloggers such as Guido Fawkes (Paul Staines), Iain Dale, and Mike Ferguson who operate blogs, Twitter feeds, and Facebook accounts. This issue came to a head ahead of the 2015 general election campaign when the Electoral Commission wrote to a number of high-profile political bloggers and commentators to inform them that they may need to register as a non-party campaigner and be made subject to Electoral Commission Regulation.[101]

 Case study *Guido Fawkes (Paul Staines)*

Letter from the Electoral Commission 8 January 2015

Dear Mr Staines,

I am writing to draw your attention to new rules on non-party campaigning in the Political Parties, Elections and Referendums Act 2000 ('PPERA') which were recently amended by the Transparency of Lobbying, Non-Party Campaigning and Trade Union Administration Act 2014.

➡

---

[99] Electoral Commission, *Online Election Campaigns: Report and Recommendations*, April 2003.
[100] Ibid. 4.
[101] The letter in full may be seen at <https://orderorder.files.wordpress.com/2015/01/guido-fawkes-non-party-campaigner-letter.pdf>.

➡

As it is possible the new rules could be relevant to your activities, particularly in relation to your website, I am writing to give a brief overview so that you can consider whether or not you may need to register with the Electoral Commission as a non-party campaigner ahead of the upcoming UK Parliamentary General Election.

Non-party campaigners are individuals or organisations that campaign in the run-up to elections, but are not standing as political parties or candidates. The rules cover spending on certain activities that can reasonably be seen as intended to influence voters to vote for or against political parties or categories of candidates, including political parties or candidates who support or do not support particular policies or issues (we call this the 'purpose test').

. . .

We are keen to ensure that we support everyone that we regulate, including those who are considering whether they need to register, by providing advice on the rules in relation to planned campaign activities. You may need to register with us now in which case we would be pleased to hear from you. Also, do let us know if you reach the view that you do not currently need to register with us. You may need to register in the future and we would advise you keep your activities under regular review.

The change in the law that the letter refers to is found in ss. 94A and 94B of the Political Parties, Elections and Referendums Act 2000. These require third parties to notify the Electoral Commission if the expenditure by that third party exceeds £20,000 in England, or £10,000 in Scotland, Wales, or Northern Ireland,[102] or within a single constituency 0.05 per cent of the total of the maximum campaign expenditure limits in England, Scotland, Wales, and Northern Ireland[103] which currently is £9,750, if that third party spends that money for reasons which can 'reasonably be regarded as intended to promote or procure electoral success at any relevant election' for:

(i) one or more particular registered parties,

(ii) one or more registered parties who advocate (or do not advocate) particular policies or who otherwise fall within a particular category of such parties, or

(iii)   candidates who hold (or do not hold) particular opinions or who advocate (or do not advocate) particular policies or who otherwise fall within a particular category of candidates.[104]

The reason for the amendments made by the Transparency of Lobbying, Non-party Campaigning and Trade Union Administration Act 2014 were not to do with blogging or other online activities. The change in the law was driven by a number of scandals in the 2010–2015 Parliament. Prime among this was a view, held by the coalition Conservative/Liberal Democrat government that trade unions exerted too much power and financial support in some Labour Party selection and election campaigns. There was a particular controversy in Falkirk in 2013 surrounding the influence of the UNITE

---

[102] Political Parties, Elections and Referendums Act 2000, s. 94(5).
[103] Political Parties, Elections and Referendums Act 2000, s. 94(5ZA).
[104] Political Parties, Elections and Referendums Act 2000, s. 85(2)(b).

union in candidate selection,[105] along with the more widespread view that lobbyists had too much influence. The Act was highly controversial and was seen as a party political act by Conservative-led government to use public outcry around lobbying scandals to regulate and control trade union funding of Labour Party candidates.[106] The Bill passed though and became law and one of the impacts of the Act, which was not entirely intended, was that bloggers such as Guido Fawkes who operates a clearly partisan right-wing blog and Labour List which operates a left-wing blog, were written to by the Electoral Commission. It seems that blogs, which were not clearly partisan such as the Spectator Blog, did not receive such guidance.

By registering, the blogs would have become regulated non-party campaigners, bringing a number of controls into financial management and reporting controls into play. The blogs in question felt that by being singled out they were being treated unfairly. *Conservative Home* editor Paul Goodman reported that he feels the site had no alternative, given the terms of the Lobbying Act, but to 'run some pieces by senior Labour MPs during the election campaign' to get around the issue of being a non-party campaign site.[107]

 Highlight Registered non-party campaign restrictions

Registered non-party campaigners[108] must

- have a system in place for authorizing spending on regulated campaign activity
- keep invoices and receipts for payments over £200 made as part of their spending on regulated campaign activity
- report to the Electoral Commission after the election their spending on regulated campaign activity if they have spent more than £20,000 in England or more than £10,000 in any of Scotland, Wales or Northern Ireland
- check that any donations received may be accepted, and record any donations over £500
- comply with the reporting requirements for donations received for spending on regulated campaign activity.

In addition, during a UK Parliamentary general election regulated period:

- they must report certain donations before and after the election
- they must provide the Electoral Commission with a list of constituencies in which their regulated campaign spending was more than £7,800
- they may need to provide the Electoral Commission with a statement of accounts after the election.

---

[105] J Cook, 'Labour's Falkirk row becomes national issue for Labour', *BBC News* 5 July 2013 <http://www.bbc.co.uk/news/uk-scotland-tayside-central-23193741>.

[106] N Morris, 'David Cameron is accused of using lobbying scandal to curb Labour's trade union support', *The Independent* 3 June 2013.

[107] <http://order-order.com/2015/01/09/electoral-commission-trying-to-regulate-blogsnotifies-guido-conservativehome-labourlist-libdemvoice/#_@/sYpgvAyueC9AFQ>.

[108] Electoral Commission, *Registering as a Non-party Campaigner* <http://www.electoralcommission.org.uk/__data/assets/pdf_file/0011/165962/sp-registering-npc.pdf>.

Mark Ferguson who operates the *Labour List* blog reported that 'It seems particularly bizarre (and that's being generous) that there's one law for "newspapers and periodicals" and another for "websites". Perhaps the government are finding this new-fangled internet thing very confusing. We're still working through what the most appropriate response is to this dreadful law—more worthy of a banana-Republic than a democracy—that clamps down on campaigning and free speech at a time when it's needed most, election time. Whatever response we decide on though, we will not be submitting ourselves to any form of regulation that stops us from writing, reporting and commenting on the election campaign as we see fit.'[109]

In the end none of the blogs registered with the Electoral Commission and no sanctions were forthcoming. In their report on the 2015 general election the Electoral Commission noted that 'it is sometimes harder to clearly differentiate between materials on the internet. This raises questions about internet content such as political material in blogs and whether it should fall under the exclusion for periodicals or be regarded as a piece of election campaign material.'[110] This led them to recommend that 'the way in which political blogs are treated in relation to the exemption on newspapers and periodicals should be clarified in legislation. In the meantime, we will continue to consider this exemption carefully at future elections and referendums.'[111] However events were about to overtake this rather simple recommendation.

5.4.3 **Astroturfing, #fakenews, and bots**

The following year an earthquake in the online conduct of political campaigns struck in two events: the UK referendum on continued membership of the European Union and the US presidential election. The UK referendum demonstrated a new kind of online political activism, one which had been developing for years through local and general elections and, in particular, the Scottish independence referendum of 2014 had come to maturity: the use of social media as a campaign tool, in particular Facebook and Twitter, both directly through official accounts and paid-for advertising, and indirectly by the employment of activists was well established. The 2016 referendum became famous for two particular reasons: (1) organized armies of social media accounts (including a large number of bot accounts) around specific hashtags and phrasings. and (2) detailed profiling and personalized political advertising.

The first may be seen as a modern version of AstroTurfing. AstroTurfing, as explained by Mark Leiser is 'a deceptive practice often deployed by marketers to create the false impression that a campaign has developed organically (the grass roots in AstroTurf are fake). "Classic" AstroTurfing involves the use of paid agents to falsely represent popular sentiment surrounding a product or service. As a result, consumers "follow the herd"'.[112] Classically AstroTurfing was a form of covert or guerrilla advertising. Leiser gives examples such as the formation of the National Smokers Alliance (NSA), a

---

[109] Ibid.
[110] Electoral Commission, *The May 2015 UK elections: Report on the administration of the 7 May 2015 elections, including the UK Parliamentary general election*, [3.161].
[111] Ibid. [3.162].
[112] M Leiser, 'AstroTurfing, "CyberTurfing" and other online persuasion campaigns' (2016) 7(1) *European Journal of Law and Technology* 1.

seemingly independent consumer group but actually created and funded by the tobacco industry and Americans for Technology Leadership (ATL) a Microsoft funded group which campaigned against an adverse anti-trust finding against the company in the 1990s. However, it did not take long for AstroTurfing to move into the political realm with politicians being targeted by what appeared to be grass-roots support for a number of programmes from legalization of fracking to both pro-choice and pro-life campaigns.

In the 2000s AstroTurfing moved online in a process Leiser calls CyberTurfing. Early forms of CyberTurfing included online campaigning via Twitter in a 2010 Massachusetts special election. In research carried out by Wellesley College it was identified that a concentrated spam attack originated from nine Twitter accounts, created within a thirteen-minute interval, which directed Twitter users to the website *coakleysaidit* created on the same day.[113] The Coakley mentioned in the site name was Democratic Candidate Martha Coakley and the website contained false claims that she was against Catholic medical professionals working in emergency medicine. The American Future Fund, a conservative organization based in Des Moines, which was supporting her Republican opponent, set up the accounts and the web page. The Wellesey research revealed that 'these 9 accounts sent 929 tweets addressed to 573 unique users in the course of 138 minutes . . . The attack was successful in terms of reaching the Twitter accounts of many users. We found 143 retweets in our corpus, the first after 5 minutes and the last after 24 hours of the attack. To estimate the audience of these messages, we calculated the set of all unique followers of the users that retweeted the original tweets. The audience size amounts to 61,732 Twitter users.'[114] Bots have since been deployed to manipulate political opinion in Venezuela[115] and to influence UK parliamentary elections,[116] however it was their use in the 2016 EU referendum debate that really brought their use to the fore of UK politics.

Immediately after the referendum, Philip Howard of Oxford University and Bence Kollanyi of Corvinus University ran an analysis on how both sides 'Stronger In' and 'Vote Leave/Brexit' used Twitter in campaigning.[117] They sampled 1.5 million tweets yielding 312,832 unique users. The hashtag #VoteLeave appeared 341,839 times in the data set, while #StrongerIn appeared 110,653 times. This suggests that pro-Brexit users generated a larger block of content and were better at deploying the Brexit hashtag 'so as to link messages to a larger argument and wider community of support.'[118] They found that 'the most active users—the accounts that tweeted 100 or more times with a related hashtag during the week—generated 32 percent of all Twitter traffic about Brexit. That volume is significant, considering that this number of posts was generated by fewer than 2,000 users in a collection of more than 300,000 users. In other words, less than 1 percent of the accounts generate almost a third of all the content.'[119] They conclude it is highly likely that a degree of automation was required to achieve this.

---

[113] E Mustafaraj and P Metaxas, 'From obscurity to prominence in minutes: Political speech and real-time search' (2010) *Proceedings of Web Science: Extending the Frontiers of Society On-Line* 317.

[114] Ibid. 323.

[115] M Forelle et al., *Political bots and the manipulation of public opinion in Venezuela* <https://arxiv.org/ftp/arxiv/papers/1507/1507.07109.pdf>.

[116] 'Jasper Admits to Using Twitter Bots to Drive Election Bid', *Inside Croydon*, 26 November 2012 <https://insidecroydon.com/2012/11/26/jasper-admits-to-using-twitter-bots-to-drive-election-bid/>.

[117] P Howard and B Kollanyi, 'Bots,# strongerin, and# brexit: Computational Propaganda during the UK-EU Referendum', *COMPROP Research Note* 2016.1 <https://arxiv.org/ftp/arxiv/papers/1606/1606.06356.pdf>.

[118] Ibid. 4.

[119] Ibid.

Worse they acknowledged the impact this could have had on the referendum result itself, noting that 'the measures of undecided voters suggest that 30 percent of UK voters will decide how to vote in the week before the election, and half of these will decide on polling day. The pervasive use of bots over social media heightens the risk of massive cascades of misinformation at a time when voters will be thinking about their options and canvasing their social networks for the sentiments of friends and family.'[120]

Since their report a number of allegations have surfaced about interference in the referendum campaign with Russia often being held out as a possible source of interference.[121] However later in 2016 President Trump was to introduce a new phrase into the political lexicon during his campaign: the phrase was fake news and this was about to take on a life all of its own.[122] President Trump used fake news as an attack against his democratic opponents, claiming any negative stories about his campaign, or positive stories about his opponent Hillary Clinton, were 'fake news'. However, at the heart of his bombastic rhetoric around the term a genuine social and legal problem around online deception was developing. Real fake news (if you pardon the term) was being fed into the political sphere. Much of this could be traced to Veles, a small town in Macedonia. In 2017 *Wired* ran a major story on this.[123] This revealed that this town of 55,000 people was the registered home of at least 100 pro-Trump websites 'filled with sensationalist, utterly fake news.' It seems the Veles operation was not a political one, it was instead simple economics. The young men of Veles could earn up to $4000 per month in advertising revenue by driving viewers to their sites, against an average Macedonian salary of $371. However, the Veles sites, which contained tales of imminent criminal indictment of Hillary Clinton and stories avowing the Pope's approval of Donald Trump, showed there was an appetite among people for stories which fitted their narrative. This is the logical end-point of Negroponte's *Daily Me*, a personalized experience of the internet which divides us from other internet users in our experience:[124] the end user no longer cares whether the story is true or false, only that it confirms their narrative.

Fake news brings particular political and democratic challenges.

 Highlight The democratic impact of 'fake news'

Following the 2016 election, a specific concern has been the effect of false stories—'fake news',[125] as it has been dubbed—circulated on social media. Recent evidence shows that: (1) 62 per cent of US adults get news on social media; (2) the most popular fake news stories were more widely shared on Facebook than the most popular mainstream news stories; (3) many people who see fake news stories report that they believe them; and (4) the most discussed fake news stories tended to favour Donald Trump over Hillary Clinton. Putting these facts together, a number of commentators have suggested that Donald Trump would not have been elected president were it not for the influence of fake news.

[120] Ibid. 5.
[121] A Mostrous, M Bridge, and K Gibbons, 'Russia used Twitter bots and trolls "to disrupt" Brexit vote', *The Times*, 15 November 2017.
[122] *Collins Dictionary* made fake news its word of the year for 2017.
[123] S Subramanian, 'Inside the Macedonian fake-news complex', *Wired*, 15 February 2017.
[124] Negroponte (n. 9) 153.
[125] H Allcott and M Gentzkow, 'Social Media and Fake News in the 2016 Election' 31 *Journal of Economic Perspectives* (2017) 211, 212.

Fake news also brings regulatory challenges. The first is how to define it. Allcot and Gentzkow define 'fake news' as 'news articles that are intentionally and verifiably false, and could mislead readers'.[126] However such a definition could cover satirical sources like *Private Eye* or *The Onion* while not covering news reports or stories delivered with a particular bias and which do not take steps to verify sources but which are not 'intentionally' false.[127] The problem of definition has been acknowledged by the House of Commons Digital, Culture, Media and Sport Committee, who in their report 'Disinformation and "fake news": Interim Report' note that 'the term "fake news" is bandied around with no clear idea of what it means, or agreed definition. The term has taken on a variety of meanings, including a description of any statement that is not liked or agreed with by the reader.'[128] The Committee instead suggest focusing on the intent of the communication by using terms such as 'misinformation' and 'disinformation'. This approach has also been suggested by the Independent High-level Group on Fake News and Online Disinformation, who in their report to the European Commission note that 'current debates about "fake news" encompass a spectrum of information types [from] relatively low-risk forms such as honest mistakes made by reporters, partisan political discourse, and the use of click bait headlines, to high-risk forms such as for instance foreign states or domestic groups that would try to undermine the political process in European Member States and the European Union.'[129] Like the House of Commons Digital, Culture, Media and Sport Committee, they seek to focus on 'disinformation' which they define as 'false, inaccurate, or misleading information designed, presented and promoted to intentionally cause public harm or for profit.'[130]

5.4.4 Regulating harmful online political speech

As is clear from the above discussion there is a concern growing that political speech online has strayed far from Meiklejohn's ideal as a system to understand political issues and through this to participate in democracy. With bots posing as people, fake news stories, and other forms of disinformation circulating online with increasing volume there are strongly held concerns, backed up by evidence, that key democratic votes such as the 2016 UK referendum on EU membership and the US presidential elections of the same year may have been undermined with results perhaps being altered as a consequence. As a result, regulators from around the globe, including the UK Parliament and the European Commission, have proposed new regulatory frameworks to alleviate the potential harms of mis- and disinformation in the online environment.

One of the first investigations launched was the House of Commons Digital, Culture, Media and Sport Committee inquiry. It issued a preliminary report in July 2018.[131] Here it proposed a two-pronged approach to regulate the problem of mis- and disinformation

---

[126] Ibid. 213.

[127] Allcot and Gentzkow state their definition does not cover satire, however this author is less sure.

[128] House of Commons Digital, Culture, Media and Sport Committee, *Disinformation and 'fake news': Interim Report* HC 363, 29 July 2018 [14].

[129] Independent High-level Group on Fake News and Online Disinformation, *A multi-dimensional approach to disinformation* (2018), 10.

[130] Ibid.

[131] House of Commons Digital, Culture, Media and Sport Committee (n. 128).

online. The first is a digital literacy programme. They note that 'most users do not understand how the content they read has got there, but accept it without question'. The solution is a programme of digital literacy enabling users to 'understand how social media works, and how the content that each user reads has appeared, as a result of specific algorithms.'[132] They propose a multilevel approach with children being taught digital literacy as part of the school curriculum and a public awareness initiative for adults. This will be paid for by an 'educational levy' paid by SMPs. The second prong, more directly relevant to us, is a new regulatory framework for social media companies. In June 2018 the Electoral Commission had returned to the issue of online campaigns in light of events since the 2015 general election. They called for the law to be strengthened around digital advertising and campaigning, including: a change in the law to require all digital political campaign material to state who paid for it; new legislation to make it clear that spending in UK elections and referendums by foreign organizations and individuals is not allowed; an increase in the maximum fine, currently £20,000 per offence, that the Electoral Commission can impose on organizations and individuals who break the rules; and a requirement for all campaigners to provide more details on how they spent money online.[133] Taking their lead from this report the DCMS Committee recommended that all political advertising should be identifiable and should show who paid for it. They also suggested increasing the ASA's fining powers, and vitally giving the ASA new authority to 'compel organisations that it does not specifically regulate, including tech companies and individuals, to provide information relevant to their inquiries, subject to due process.'[134]

Perhaps though the greatest change to the regulatory framework proposed by the report is to remove the safe harbour protection currently enjoyed by SMPs. Currently, as platforms rather than publishers, they enjoy the protections of Reg. 19 of The Electronic Commerce (EC Directive) Regulations 2002.[135] This provides that information society service providers who store content but who have 'no actual knowledge of unlawful activity or information' are shielded from both criminal and civil claims provided that they act expeditiously to remove or to disable access to the information upon obtaining knowledge or awareness of the nature of the content. This shield has been used extensively by SMPs to guard against claims of defamation and any criminal content distributed across their network. The DCMS Committee though believe the old platform/publishers divide is now out of date. They note that 'the definition of "platform" gives the impression that these companies do not create or control the content themselves, but are merely the channel through which content is made available. Yet Facebook is continually altering what we see, as is shown by its decision to prioritise content from friends and family, which then feeds into users' newsfeed algorithm.'[136] They therefore recommend that 'a new category of tech company is formulated, which tightens tech companies' liabilities, and which is not necessarily either a "platform"

---

[132] At [237].

[133] The Electoral Commission, *Digital campaigning: Increasing transparency for voters* (2018) <https://www.electoralcommission.org.uk/__data/assets/pdf_file/0010/244594/Digital-campaigning-improving-transparency-for-voters.pdf>.

[134] House of Commons Digital, Culture, Media and Sport Committee (n. 128) [49].

[135] SI 2002/2013.

[136] House of Commons Digital, Culture, Media and Sport Committee (n. 128) [51].

or a "publisher".'[137] Rather alarmingly for the SMPs they recommend that 'this process should establish clear legal liability for the tech companies to act against harmful and illegal content on their platforms. This should include both content that has been referred to them for takedown by their users, and other content that should have been easy for the tech companies to identify for themselves. In these cases, failure to act on behalf of the tech companies could leave them open to legal proceedings launched either by a public regulator, and/or by individuals or organisations who have suffered as a result of this content being freely disseminated on a social media platform.'[138]

This recommendation would leave platforms such as Twitter and Facebook liable for mis- and disinformation they host which they should have been able to identify as such or which has been reported to them as such. Unsurprisingly SMPs have not welcomed this proposal but it is based at least in part on a pre-existing legal framework elsewhere in Europe, the German Network Enforcement Act (or NetzDG).[139] This makes SMPs, and other intermediaries, liable for the policing of hate speech content. Failure to remove 'obviously illegal' content within 24 hours, or 'illegal' content within 7 days can lead to fines of up to €20 million. The law is highly contentious and it may be suggested is not the best model for the UK to follow.

Perhaps a better approach is the proposed EU approach. The Independent High-level Group recommended a five-point plan to fight mis- and disinformation: (a) enhanced transparency; (b) greater media and information literacy; (c) develop tools for empowering users and journalists (such as source verifiers); (d) safeguard the diversity and sustainability of the European news media ecosystem; and (e) calibrate the effectiveness of the responses through continuous research on the impact of disinformation in Europe.[140] In addition, the Commission has recently issued a draft code of practice on online disinformation.[141] This follows the structure of the report of the Independent High-level Group in focusing on transparency, robustness, and education. If adopted it will require signatories, including search and SMPs, to (1) implement policies and processes to disrupt advertising revenue from going to accounts and websites that repeatedly misrepresent material information about themselves; (2) ensure that advertisements are clearly distinguishable from editorial content; (3) enable public disclosure of political advertising; (4) have clear policies in place regarding identity and the use of automated bots on their services, and should have systems in place to enforce these; (5) invest in products, technologies, and programs to help people make informed decisions when they encounter online news that may be false, including by supporting efforts to develop and implement effective indicators of trustworthiness; and (6) partner with civil society, governments, educational institutions, and other stakeholders to support efforts aimed at improving critical thinking and digital media literacy.

The approach of the EU is clearly quite distinctive from the proposed approach of the DCMS Committee. It is rooted in principles-based co-regulation, giving the platforms responsibility, and requiring them to meet general principles. It avoids the

---

[137] Ibid. [58].

[138] Ibid. [60].

[139] Gesetz zur Verbesserung der Rechtsdurchsetzung in sozialen Netzwerken (Network Enforcement Act of 1 September 2017), *Federal Law Gazette* I, p. 3352.

[140] Independent High-level Group on Fake News and Online Disinformation (n. 129) 35.

[141] <https://ec.europa.eu/digital-single-market/en/news/draft-code-practice-online-disinformation>.

confrontational approach of both the NetzDG Law and the DCMS report. It might be suggested that this is a better approach in the longer term. While it might be fashionable to attack platforms such as Facebook and Twitter in the current environment, making them financially liable through fines or civil action for failure to adequately police mis- and disinformation by removing the current safe harbour may lead to over-regulation and indeed censorship by platforms. Unlike obscenity, violent threats, or hate speech verifying the veracity of a message is extremely difficult and time-consuming (except for the most obvious forms of fake news, which are not usually the issue). When complaints come in, rather than risk liability it will be the norm for the platform to take content down rather than risk liability. The answer may not be in making platforms liable for content they host, but as the EU have acknowledged through transparency, education, and the development of robust self-management systems.

5.5 **Hate speech**

While we seek to protect political speech, we seek to restrict hate speech. Sometimes there is a fine line between political speech and hate speech. For example, should the YouTube channel for the British National Party be protected as political speech or banned as hate speech? We have already touched upon these issues in our discussion of the distinctive approaches to be found in the US and Europe to potentially harmful speech, and in the analysis of the *LICRA et UEJF v Yahoo! Inc.* litigation in France and the US. The entire issue is one which is swathed in social responsibility. Every society suffers from bigotry and ignorance and in every society it is easy for the socially disenfranchised to blame another social, racial, or religious group. In a civilized society though these views are marginalized and mainstream public and media opinion is ranged against those who hold such socially harmful opinions. The internet, though, empowers those marginalized by mainstream society and it is not always to the benefit of society as a whole.

5.5.1 **Hate speech and society**

Digital media and, in particular, SMPs are allowing extremist viewpoints from all ends of the spectrum to proliferate. White supremacists find themselves online alongside Islamic fundamentalists, while transphobes find themselves alongside radical transgender groups. Those operating these sites and accounts do so without regard to their social responsibility: they view their right to represent their views and opinions as paramount. The problem is that in so doing they may cause harm to others. This is why the UK has taken steps to restrict such speech. Racially offensive speech is prohibited by the Public Order Act 1986,[142] as is the possession of, with intent to publish, material which is racially offensive.[143] Also prohibited by the Public Order Act is speech which is religiously offensive. The new Part 3A of the Act, introduced by the Racial and Religious Hatred Act 2006, extends the protections previously only available to racially abusive

---

[142] Public Order Act 1986, s. 17.
[143] Public Order Act 1986, s. 23.

material to prohibit the use of words or actions designed to stir up religious hatred[144] and the publication of material designed to stir up religious hatred.[145] In turn, these provisions were further extended by Sch. 16 of the Criminal Justice and Immigration Act 2008 to cover hatred on grounds of sexual orientation.[146]

The question of compatibility of such laws with Art. 10 of the ECHR is unsurprisingly common. In two key cases though the European Court of Human Rights has found provisions such as those found in the Public Order Act to be in compliance with the Convention. In *Jersild v Denmark*[147] the Court found that a Danish conviction of a journalist for aiding the distribution of race hate speech infringed Art. 10. However, this was on the narrow decision that in so doing they prevented a journalist from discharging his duty to aid discussion of matters in the public interest. As for the Danish law itself they found that the state was within the exceptions found in Art. 10(2) in passing a law which prohibited remarks which were insulting to members of targeted groups. In fact, the Court noted such a law was required by Denmark's obligations under the 1965 International Convention on the Elimination of all Forms of Racial Discrimination. More recently in the case of *Lehideux and Isorni v France*[148] the Court found that Art. R.645-1 of the French Penal Code (Restriction on Holocaust Denial Speech) is compatible with Art. 10.

5.5.2 Inter-state speech

With European lawmakers extending ever further the protections afforded to marginalized sections of society, in the UK the progression has been from racial hate speech to religious hate speech and most recently to sexual orientation hate speech; gender hate speech may be next[149] and, with the constitutional principles of the US protecting all but the most immediately harmful speech, a rise in conflicts between US-based content and European-based consumers becomes more likely.

We have already visited at length the best-known example of this ideological conflict, *LICRA et UEJF v Yahoo! Inc. and Yahoo! France*. This lengthy litigation produced a most unsatisfactory outcome which demonstrates that attempts to reach international consensus on this issue are unlikely to succeed. A further example closer to home highlights the difficulty of regulating the speech itself rather than the speaker. Some time prior to 2005 two individuals, Simon Sheppard and Stephen Whittle, began operating a website called heretical.com. The site is a standard white-supremacist, neo-Nazi site, common in the US but potentially illegal to operate in the UK under the Public Order Act. The site, and a number of others operated by Sheppard, is hosted in Torrance, California,

---

[144] Public Order Act 1986, s. 29B.

[145] Public Order Act 1986, s. 29C.

[146] Although it should be noted that a strong Christian lobby secured an exemption in Parliament. The new s. 29JA of the Public Order Act states: 'In this Part, for the avoidance of doubt, the discussion or criticism of sexual conduct or practices or the urging of persons to refrain from or modify such conduct or practices shall not be taken of itself to be threatening or intended to stir up hatred.'

[147] (1995) 19 EHRR 1.

[148] (2000) 30 EHRR 365.

[149] As part of the Parliamentary Debate on the Voyeurism (Offences) (No. 2) Bill, Parliament debated whether misogyny should be classified as a hate crime. This is now being reviewed by the Law Commission of England and Wales.

while Sheppard and Whittle live in the UK. On this site they placed a file called 'Tales of the Holohoax', a holocaust-denial comic strip. Sheppard and Whittle were questioned by police and charged under s. 19 of the Public Order Act 1986. While standing trial the two fled to the United States and claimed asylum which was refused. Eventually, after being convicted in their absence, they were returned to the UK and on 10 July 2009 Sheppard was sentenced to a total of four years and ten months' imprisonment and Whittle to a total of two years and four months' imprisonment.[150] Both later successfully appealed to have their sentences reduced but the interesting aspect of their story relates to jurisdiction and effective jurisdiction.

Sheppard and Whittle argued that the courts of England and Wales did not have jurisdiction to hear their case as the material was published in California and protected by the First Amendment. This was dismissed by the trial court where the judge applied *R v Smith (Wallace Duncan)*[151] to find that the court had jurisdiction to try them for their conduct because a substantial measure of the activities constituting the crime took place in England,[152] a position upheld on appeal.[153] Thus while the courts of England and Wales successfully established *de lege* jurisdiction, and de facto jurisdiction over Sheppard and Whittle, a problem remained, for while both Sheppard and Whittle could be remanded in prison for their breach of s. 19, there was nothing the English courts could do about the content itself which remained on the servers of the hosting company in Torrance, protected by the First Amendment. In essence the offence continued to be committed. Until early 2011 it was possible to visit heretical.com from the United Kingdom and download the material in question. The courts had successfully prosecuted the perpetrators of the crime, but the crime itself continued to be perpetrated. Eventually the will of the courts of England and Wales prevailed. With Sheppard seeking to obtain parole from prison in early 2011 he voluntarily removed the offending content as a condition of his release. There was a period though—between conviction and application for parole, from July 2009 to early 2011—where the will of the courts of England and Wales was defeated by the off-shoring of the content in question.

This is a problem for any content hosted in the United States. With the US Supreme Court ruling in *Reno v ACLU*[154] that the First Amendment applies to internet communications, the US government finds that it cannot enter into any international treaty or agreement which would conflict with its duty to uphold the US Constitution.[155] This was demonstrated in the negotiations of the Council of Europe Convention on Cybercrime.[156] The Convention which aims to provide a framework for the development of a common policy against all aspects of cybercrime including internet pornography, computer hacking, and distribution of malicious code was signed by the Council of Europe states and several invited non-member states including the US. It was the intent of the drafters that that Convention would have an article dealing with hate speech but the US delegation stated that due to the effect of *Reno v ACLU*, they would be unable

---

[150] All taken from *R v Sheppard & Anor* [2010] EWCA Crim 65, [1]–[8].
[151] (No. 4) [2004] EWCA Crim 631.
[152] *R v Sheppard & Anor* (n. 150) [20].
[153] Ibid. [20]–[33].
[154] 521 US 844 (1997).
[155] Vick (n. 34).
[156] CETS No. 185, Budapest, 23.XI.2001.

to sign a convention which restricted free expression. Because of this, and because the framers of the Convention wanted the US to sign, all references to hate and xenophobic speech were removed from the main Convention and were placed into a separate Additional Protocol to the Convention on Cybercrime Concerning the Criminalisation of Acts of a Racist and Xenophobic Nature Committed through Computer Systems.[157] This additional protocol was not signed by the US.[158]

We may never find common ground between the US and other leading democratic states including EU states on this issue, but as Douglas Vick points out 'it is far from certain that sexism, racism, homophobia or religious intolerance are greater problems in the US than in countries with well-developed anti-hate legislation'.[159] When the Programme in Comparative Media Law and Policy concluded its three-year research project into industry self-regulation and content,[160] it concluded that data havens were not unusual in digital communications, with Europe and in particular the UK, acting as a similar 'offshore centre' for online gambling for citizens of the US. Thus, short of blocking access to US-based websites which breach the Public Order Act, it appears UK regulators and UK citizens may have to accept that while as noted by District Judge Fogel in *Yahoo! Inc. v LICRA* 'the Internet in effect allows one to speak in more than one place at the same time'[161] individuals will in most cases be subject only to the effective jurisdiction of the place where they are domiciled or ordinarily resident.

5.6 Conclusions: cyber-speech and free expression

The internet is the best communications medium yet designed. For the first time an individual can address large groups and can do so without regard for traditional borders or nation states. Although we must view this as being on the whole positive, the breaking down of borders has affected the ability of nation states to protect their community values in the online environment. David Johnson and David Post first predicted this legal regulatory failure in 1996,[162] but it is only now we are seeing the effects of this. Speech in cyberspace is speech which crosses borders like the flow of a river, and, just as the government of France can do little to stop the waters of the River Rhone crossing the border from Switzerland into France, there is little they can do about content hosted on US-based servers being available to the citizens of France. The effect of this is that governments are being asked to reconsider if and how they wish to regulate expression. We have seen recent attempts to regulate speech acts outside the jurisdiction of the court have met with limited success despite an increase in attempts by regulators and courts to do so, and that such action carries risks. As Google have warned, attempts to apply domestic legal settlements globally may encourage other states, including less open and

---

[157] CETS No. 189, Strasbourg, 28.I.2003.

[158] It should be noted that the UK also have not signed the Protocol.

[159] Vick (n. 18) 51.

[160] Programme in Comparative Media Law and Policy, *Self-Regulation of Digital Media Converging on the Internet: Industry Codes of Conduct in Sectoral Analysis* (2004) <http://pcmlp.socleg.ox.ac.uk/wp-content/uploads/2014/12/IAPCODE final.pdf>.

[161] 145 F Supp 2d 1168 (ND Cal 2001), 1192.

[162] D Johnson and D Post, 'Law and Borders: The Rise of Law in Cyberspace' 48 *Stanford Law Review* 1367 (1996). Discussed in depth at 4.1.

democratic states, to seek to do the same, potentially leading to a global race to the bottom, harming access to information that is perfectly lawful to view in one's own country.

Major challenges remain though. One cannot simply allow the democratic process to be undermined through bias, disinformation, or simple fake news or for hatred to be allowed to flourish online. As this chapter has shown, the modern network and in particular SMPs are vulnerable to a number of attacks, including the use of bots to send and emphasize messages and the use of disinformation, or fake news, to try to bias an election or other form of democratic process. There is clear evidence that the UK Brexit referendum was influenced by Twitter bots and similar evidence that the US presidential election in 2016 was equally effected, perhaps to the point of changing the outcome of the election. While the internet empowers individual communication as never before, we cannot allow our democratic processes to be undermined by a few people harnessing the echo chamber effect seen in social media to magnify of their message. The current actions of both the European Commission and the DCMS Committee on this provide vital frameworks for the future regulation of political speech. It might be suggested the liability regime proposed by the DCMS Committee is unhelpful but at the same time it is clear that SMPs cannot simply continue to say they have no liability for content they carry which is so potentially harmful.

Whatever the future holds in all these areas, we should remember that the positive effects that digital communications have had on free expression and the free, full, and frank exchange of views and ideas between individuals far outweigh the negative; but it is to be hoped that those engaged in online expression remember their social responsibilities as well as their rights.

TEST QUESTIONS

Question 1

Critically analyse the complete *LICRA et UEJF v Yahoo! Inc*. litigation set. In particular, analyse whether the apparently divergent outcomes of the Tribunal de Grande Instance de Paris and the United States Court of Appeal for the 9th Circuit support Johnson and Post's thesis that in cyberspace traditional laws fail to be effective due to a lack of borders.

Question 2

Discuss critically the statement that 'the divergent approaches of the United States and European states in relation to the regulation of online expression, in particular the distinction between the "marketplace of speech" concept and the "human dignity" concept have left such international uncertainty in regulation of this area that the effect has been to effectively deregulate all forms of online speech'.

FURTHER READING

TG Ash, *Free Speech: Ten Principles for a Connected World* (Atlantic 2016)

E Barendt, *Freedom of Speech* (2nd edn, OUP 2005)

F Schauer, *Free Speech: A Philosophical Enquiry* (CUP 1982)

Chapters and articles

J Balkin, 'Free speech is a triangle' 118 *Columbia Law Review* 2011 (2018)

J Balkin, 'Digital Speech and Democratic Culture: A Theory of Freedom of Expression for the Information Society' (2004) 79 *NYU Law Review* 1

J Rowbottom, 'To Rant, Vent and Converse: Protecting Low Level Digital Speech' (2012) 71 *Cambridge Law Journal* 355

6

Social networking and antisocial conduct

6.1 **Introduction**

Speech, as we have seen in chapter 5 is not always harmless. The internet spreads anti-social comment as quickly and efficiently as it circulates news reports, political speech, and educational speech. In recent years the explosion in social networking has magnified this to the point where the internet now feels like a global hubbub of personalized views, expressions, and opinions. When Negroponte spoke of the *Daily Me*[1] in 1995 he did not address the other side of the *Daily Me* story: who produces content? Negroponte imagined a unidirectional experience where your local newspaper, wine shop, or national organization such as the National Trust would send you updates and news stories, tailored to your preferences.

> **Highlight** Negroponte's *Daily Me*
>
> Unique information about me determines news services that I might want to receive about a small obscure town, a not so famous person, and (for today) the anticipated weather conditions in Virginia . . . a machine could call your attention to a sale on a particular Chardonnay or beer that it knows the guests you have coming to dinner tomorrow night liked last time.[2]

Much more interesting today, for lawyers at least, is who is producing this content for us. It is not, as Negroponte imagined, corporations, local businesses, and public bodies; the explosion of social media platforms (SMPs) means that I get my daily news and updates via those I follow on Twitter, such as Graham Smith, who writes the Cyberleagle blog; Paul Bernal, a senior lecturer in law at UEA; and the enigmatic and slightly obsessive Ern Malley, whose (surprising) identity I know but I cannot share. On Facebook a similar selection process means I get news and updates from among others Mathias Klang, an Associate Professor at Fordham University; Daniel Paré, an Associate Professor in the Department of Communication at the University of Ottawa; and Emma Sadleir, South Africa's leading commentator on social media law and the author of the bestselling *Selfies, Sexts and Smartphones: A teenager's online survival guide*.[3]

---

[1] N Negroponte, *Being Digital* (Hodder & Stoughton 1995), 164–71.
[2] Ibid. 164–5.
[3] Penguin 2017.

It is not just the consumption of news and information that has been personalized; it is also its production. The internet, through SMPs, has become the world's most complex, most connected, most global, coffee shop. People treat SMPs like private conversations and do all the things they normally would in a private discussion with friends: they gossip,[4] they share (and break) confidences, they bully, and they act antisocially. The problem is that SMPs are not comparable to private conversations in pubs or coffee shops. Whereas conversations in pubs and cafés are ephemeral—there one second and gone the next, and localized: only available to those in very close proximity—conversations via SMPs are permanent, or at least semi-permanent and potentially global. In your café or pub conversation, you may address five or ten people who will quickly forget what you have said. Via Twitter a single tweet (before retweets) can reach over 107 million people, substantially more than the population of the UK;[5] retweets can send messages stratospheric in terms of readers. The most retweeted message (correct at October 2018) is Carter Wilkerson: 'HELP ME PLEASE. A MAN NEEDS HIS NUGGS' sent at 3:38 a.m. on 6 April 2017. It has been retweeted almost 3.6 million times.[6] These figures pale into insignificance when one considers the most popular videos on YouTube. The most watched YouTube video (again as of 30 November 2018) is Despacito by Luis Fonsi which has garnered 5.77 billion views, with the most popular viral video probably being Charlie bit my finger—again! with 865 million views.

The reach of individuals, powered by SMPs, is therefore quite staggering. Unfortunately, by treating SMPs like pub or café conversations without accounting for the reach of these messages can be extremely damaging. In the past Twitter trends have actively ignored court orders, defamed individuals, and promoted criminal messages. Below trending activity we find individuals being bullied and harassed on both Facebook and Twitter; hate speech; breaches of personal confidences; and, via YouTube, a video which caused riots throughout the Islamic world and which led to at least 54 deaths as a result.[7]

6.2 **Social networking, gossip, and privacy**

For several years SMPs like Facebook and Twitter have found themselves at the heart of a variety of antisocial activities, including a number of cases of defamation which will be discussed in the following chapter. For many in the mainstream, however, the first time they became aware of the legal implications of postings on SMPs was in relation to the Ryan Giggs privacy case in 2011.

Late 2009 to early 2011 brought a rash of applications to the English courts for privacy injunctions and super-injunctions.[8] For a period it seemed as if everyone, from the

---

[4] It is worth noting that it is reported by the Social Issues Research Centre at the University of Oxford that gossip accounts for 55 per cent of male conversation time and 67 per cent of female time. See K Fox, 'Evolution, Alienation and Gossip: The Role of Mobile Telecommunications in the 21st Century' *SIRC*: <http://www.sirc.org/publik/gossip.shtml>.

[5] The most followed individual on Twitter is Katy Perry with just over 107m followers (correct at 30 November 2018).

[6] The tweet may be found at <https://twitter.com/carterjwm/status/849813577770778624>.

[7] New York Times, 'The "Innocence of Muslims" Riots' (2012) *New York Times* 26 November 2012.

[8] Technically a super-injunction is an injunction with reporting restrictions which mean that the existence of the injunction, and the facts relating to it cannot be reported by anyone to whom it is known.

media itself to celebrities and businesses and politicians and individuals, was obsessed by who had injunctions and why they had them. A privacy injunction is usually applied for by an individual, or occasionally a business, under Art. 8 ECHR. The usual basis for such an injunction is that the reporting of the facts surrounding the application will unduly affect the children or spouse of the applicant, or that the information in the possession of the press was obtained illegally by invading the private sphere of the individual in question. Privacy injunctions are still quite a novel intervention of the English courts as, prior to the passing of the Human Rights Act 1998, it had been held that there was no common law right to privacy in English law. This was most clearly stated by Glidewell LJ in *Kaye v Robertson*.[9]

 Highlight Glidewell LJ in *Kaye v Robertson*

It is well known that in English law there is no right to privacy, and accordingly there is no right of action for breach of a person's privacy. The facts of the present case are a graphic illustration of the desirability of Parliament considering whether and in what circumstances statutory provision can be made to protect the privacy of individuals.[10]

The eventual passage of the Human Rights Act remedied this deficiency of English law. Section 1 ensured that Convention rights were woven into the fabric of English law, while s. 2 ensured English courts were required not only to take account of Convention rights but also the large body of jurisprudence which interpreted them. This meant a body of European privacy law now became part of English law. This included cases such as *Von Hannover v Germany*.[11] This case was brought by Caroline von Hannover, better known as Princess Caroline of Monaco. She was followed on a daily basis at home in France by paparazzi photographers who took pictures of her doing everyday things such as picking up her children from school, doing the shopping, or playing sport. These pictures were then published in German magazines. Under German law, Princess Caroline is deemed to be a 'public figure par excellence', and as such the public is deemed to have a legitimate interest in knowing how she generally behaves in public, even when not performing any kind of official function. Princess Caroline challenged this, first in the German courts, then at the European Court of Human Rights (ECtHR). The majority of the judges said that the question of the correct balance between Art. 8 and Art. 10 centred on 'the contribution that the published photos and articles make to a debate of general interest'.[12] In the case of Princess Caroline, the photographs made no such contribution as she exercised no official function and the photographs related solely to her private life.[13] The case was widely interpreted to create a positive obligation on states to ensure that the privacy of individuals can

---

[9] [1991] FSR 62.
[10] Ibid. 66.
[11] (2005) 40 EHRR 1.
[12] Ibid. [60].
[13] Ibid. [72].

be protected from interference by other private individuals, including the media. It should be noted though that before we move on to the domestic law in this area in the more recent case of *Von Hannover v Germany (No. 2)*,[14] the Court has retreated somewhat from this position. This action was brought by Caroline von Hannover because German courts had refused her injunctions preventing the publication of images which she claimed were obtained in breach of her Art. 8 rights. This time the ECtHR held that, in balancing Art. 8 and Art. 10 rights, 'An initial essential criterion is the contribution made by photos or articles in the press to a debate of general interest.'[15] In measuring this, courts are told that there are four relevant factors: (1) a distinction has to be made between private individuals and persons acting in a public context, as political figures or public figures; (2) the conduct of the person concerned prior to publication of the report or the fact; (3) the way in which the photo or report are published and the manner in which the person concerned is represented in the photo or report; and (4) the context and circumstances in which the published photos were taken.[16] In the *Von Hannover (No. 2)* case the Court found that 'the national courts [had] carefully balanced the right of the publishing companies to freedom of expression against the right of the applicants to respect for their private life' and that 'accordingly, there has not been a violation of [Art. 8]'.[17] This decision should be borne in mind as we consider the English law.

Around the same time that the *Von Hannover* case was being heard by the ECtHR, the House of Lords was considering privacy at English law. The case was *Campbell v MGN*.[18] Again this is a non-internet case but it forms the foundations of the privacy injunction cases that were to follow. The claimant in this case was the model Naomi Campbell. She was photographed leaving a Narcotics Anonymous meeting in London and then arriving for a further meeting at the same location. The photographs were then printed with a related story in the *Daily Mirror* newspaper. Ms Campbell admitted, perhaps predicting a *Von Hannover No. 2*-style decision, that there was a public interest justifying publication of the fact that she was a drug addict and was having therapy, but claimed damages for breach of confidentiality and compensation under s. 13 Data Protection Act 1998 for the publication of further details. Campbell won in the House of Lords. By a narrow 3:2 majority it was held that the additional information relayed in the photographs and story was confidential as its publication would have caused substantial offence to a person of ordinary sensibilities in her position,[19] and that her Art. 8 rights outweighed MGNs Art. 10 rights, so that publication of the additional information was an infringement of her Art. 8 rights.[20]

Thus by the end of the summer of 2004 a strong set of privacy rights had been established in English law thanks to the Human Rights Act, *Von Hannover*, and *Campbell*. This was later strongly confirmed by Eady J who responded to criticism in the media that

[14] (2012) 55 EHRR 15.
[15] Ibid. [109].
[16] Ibid. [109]–[113].
[17] Ibid. [124]–[126].
[18] [2004] UKHL 22.
[19] Ibid. [92].
[20] Ibid. [124].

judges had gone too far to protect privacy in his judgment in *Mosley v News Group*.[21] Here he stated that:

> the law now affords protection to information in respect of which there is a reasonable expecta-tion of privacy, even in circumstances where there is no pre-existing relationship giving rise of itself to an enforceable duty of confidence. That is because the law is concerned to prevent the violation of a citizen's autonomy, dignity and self-esteem. It is not simply a matter of 'unac-countable' judges running amok. Parliament enacted the 1998 statute which requires these values to be acknowledged and enforced by the courts. In any event, the courts had been increas-ingly taking them into account because of the need to interpret domestic law consistently with the United Kingdom's international obligations. It will be recalled that the United Kingdom government signed up to the Convention more than 50 years ago.[22]

Emboldened by the decisions of *Campbell* and *Mosley* a number of businesses and indi-viduals sought to use Art. 8 as a tool to obtain a prepublication privacy injunction. This often had the desired effect of preventing publication in the mainstream media of the content in question but the information, much like a dammed river, simply rerouted to find weaknesses elsewhere and overwhelmingly this was SMPs.

The wider public first became aware of the large number of privacy injunctions and super-injunctions the High Court was awarding in late 2009. The Dutch commodity trading company Trafigura has courted controversy for most of the 16 years it had traded at the time. It was named as being part of the Oil for Food scandal of the late 1990s and early 2000s,[23] and was forced to pay the Côte d'Ivoire government €152m in compensation in 2007 following an incident which saw illegal toxic waste dumped in Abidjan in 2006.[24] On 12 October 2009 Labour MP Paul Farrelly asked a parliamentary written question, it asked:

 Highlight Paul Farrelly's written question

To ask the Secretary of State for Justice, what assessment he has made of the effectiveness of legislation to protect: (a) whistleblowers and (b) press freedom following the injunctions obtained in the High Court by (i) Barclays and Freshfields solicitors on 19 March 2009 on the publication of internal Barclays reports documenting alleged tax avoidance schemes and (ii) Trafigura and Carter-Ruck solicitors on 11 September 2009 on the publication of the Minton report on the alleged dumping of toxic waste in the Ivory Coast, commissioned by Trafigura.

The second injunction he was referring to had been obtained by Trafigura on 11 September 2009. It barred *The Guardian* from reporting details from an expert report commissioned by Trafigura in the months following the Côte d'Ivoire scandal.[25] The

---

[21] [2008] EWHC 1777 (QB).

[22] Ibid. [7].

[23] For details on the scandal see 'The UN's Oil-for-Food Scandal: Rolling Up the Culprits', *The Economist*, 13 March 2008.

[24] BBC News, 'Two Jailed over Ivorian Pollution', *BBC News* 23 October 2008 <http://news.bbc.co.uk/1/hi/world/africa/7685561.stm>.

[25] *RJW & SJW v Guardian News and Media Ltd & Persons Unknown* [2009] EWHC 2540 (QB).

only thing *The Guardian* was allowed to state was that the injunction had been obtained by Carter-Ruck. On 12 October Mr Farrelly asked his question. In the ordinary course of things newspapers can report the proceedings of Parliament but this time it was confirmed the injunction remained in effect. *The Guardian* went on the offensive by saying as much as it could while remaining within the injunction. In a story on *The Guardian* website the paper's investigations executive editor, David Leigh, wrote:

> Today's published Commons order papers contain a question to be answered by a minister later this week. The Guardian is prevented from identifying the MP who has asked the question, what the question is, which minister might answer it, or where the question is to be found. The Guardian is also forbidden from telling its readers why the paper is prevented—for the first time in memory—from reporting Parliament. Legal obstacles, which cannot be identified, involve proceedings, which cannot be mentioned, on behalf of a client who must remain secret.[26]

This did enough to tip off the wider world as to what was going on. Very quickly a report on the Guido Fawkes blog suggested it was the Minton report and Paul Farrelly's question,[27] as did the Spectator blog.[28] Things really took off however once the story broke on Twitter. A number of leading Twitter users, including Stephen Fry, sent out tweets naming Trafigura. Following the lead of Guido Fawkes he tweeted: 'Outrageous gagging order. It's in reference to the Trafigura oil dumping scandal. Grotesque and squalid.' This made him, along with Guido Fawkes and *The Spectator*, potentially a high-profile target for any future legal action. Throughout the day of 13 October *The Guardian* editor Alan Rusbridger kept his followers updated on the moves to overturn the ban, while campaigners began to dig up and post links to all sorts of articles that the oil firm would surely have rather remained hidden. By midday on 13 October the trending topics on Twitter UK included 'Trafigura', 'Carter Ruck', 'Farrellys', 'dumping', 'gagging', 'toxic', and 'injunction'. This was all done in contempt of court. The order which Maddison J made on 11 September extended to 'persons unknown', meaning that this was a *contra mundum* order and could be enforced against anyone.[29] By 12.45 p.m. Trafigura had given up the fight. David Leigh tweeted 'It appears that carter-ruck have suddenly decided to abandon the fight. No court after all.'

Two lessons may be learned from the Trafigura tale. The first is that the internet, and particularly SMPs, view attempts to restrict freedom of expression as damage and route around it. This is the positive message that the internet in general, and SMPs in particular, will ensure that attempts to control or restrict free expression and comment will not succeed, even if draconian instruments such as super-injunctions are used. The second lesson is that individuals who use SMPs do not respect the rule of law. Whether it was right or not, there was a valid order of the court in place, an order that prohibited not only *The Guardian* but also persons unknown from reporting the question asked in Parliament, the details of the Minton report, or details of the company which had obtained the order. Following *The Guardian*'s hints on 12 October a number of individuals, some high-profile such as Paul Staines (Guido Fawkes), Allan Massie, and Stephen Fry, and many more just ordinary citizens, had willfully ignored and broken this order. In the instant case you may argue the end justifies the means, but when citizens ignore the rule of law so fundamentally it is only a matter of time until problems arise.

---

[26] D Leigh 'Guardian Gagged from Reporting Parliament', *The Guardian*, 12 October 2009.

[27] <http://order-order.com/2009/10/12/guardian-gagged-from-reporting-parliament/>.

[28] A Massie, 'British Press Banned from Reporting Parliament. Seriously' *The Spectator*, 13 October 2009.

[29] *RJW & SJW* (n. 25) [29].

6.2.1 **The spring of 2011 and the Ryan Giggs affair**

Matters finally came to a head in the spring of 2011. Throughout 2010 the existence of privacy injunctions had become widely acknowledged both in the mainstream media and online. A number of them involved famous celebrities and—the catnip of the tabloid media—the hint of a sex scandal or affair. In January 2010 Tugendhat J refused to grant a full injunction to England football captain John Terry, after granting initially an emergency injunction, to prevent publication of details of an affair he had had with Vanessa Perroncel, the girlfriend of then team mate Wayne Bridge.[30] In November 2010 the Court of Appeal lifted a super-injunction awarded by Eady J in April to Take That member Howard Donald. The injunction had prevented his ex-girlfriend Ms Ntuli from revealing details of their relationship, as well as preventing publication of details of his identity or the existence of the injunction;[31] the court lifted the anonymity order and the reporting restrictions but left the remainder of the injunction in place.

It seemed privacy and super-injunctions were suddenly everywhere. A number of orders were put in place in the spring of 2011. In January 2011 the Court of Appeal awarded a privacy and anonymity injunction, thereby overturning the earlier decision of Tugendhat J, to a well-known sportsman, who (in the words of the court):

> has, for some time, been in an apparently long-term and conventional relationship with another person, to whom I shall refer as 'XX'. Since his relationship with XX had started, but before August 2010, a story had been published, without JIH having received any prior notice, suggesting that he had had a sexual liaison with another person, whom I shall call 'YY'. The story whose publication JIH is seeking to prevent concerns an alleged sexual encounter he had with a different person, to whom I shall refer as 'ZZ', last year.[32]

In a separate case in April 2011 an order was made in favour of an individual who, in the words of Eady J, was being subjected to 'a straightforward and blatant blackmail case'.[33] The defendant had intimate photographs of the claimant which they initially were negotiating to sell to Associated Newspapers Ltd (the publishers of the *Daily Mail*) but which they then offered to pass on to the claimant for a sum of money. In a further case in April 2011 the Court of Appeal overturned an earlier decision of Collins J, and awarded an injunction to 'a married man, [who] works in the entertainment industry, [and who] had an affair with a colleague',[34] and the same month the High Court granted anonymity to both a 'leading actor' (originally reported as 'a world famous celebrity') and a prostitute, later named as Helen Wood, relating to sexual encounters that the actor, who is married with children, had with Ms Wood.[35]

Since there appeared to be a new privacy and anonymity injunction granted almost daily there was bound to be a point where the system would break under the pressure. The case which the media turned into a test case, and which SMPs broke, was *CTB v News Group Newspapers Ltd*[36] This was an application brought by a footballer

---

[30] *Terry v Persons Unknown (Rev 1)* [2010] EWHC 119 (QB).
[31] *Ntuli v Donald* [2010] EWCA Civ 1276.
[32] *JIH v News Group Newspapers Ltd (Rev 1)* [2011] EWCA Civ 42, [7]–[8].
[33] *OPQ v BJM & Anor* [2011] EWHC 1059 (QB), [1].
[34] *ETK v News Group Newspapers Ltd* [2011] EWCA Civ 439.
[35] *NEJ v Wood & Anor* [2011] EWHC 1972 (QB).
[36] [2011] EWHC 1232 (QB).

to prevent publication of an extra-marital affair he had entered into with former *Big Brother* contestant Imogen Thomas. An emergency injunction was awarded by Eady J on 14 April 2011 and then made permanent on 21 April. In this he granted the injunction partly on the basis that 'tawdry allegations about an individual's private life does not attract the robust protection under Article 10 afforded to more serious journalism'.[37] On 14 April *The Sun* newspaper ran a story revealing as much as they could while remaining within the confines of the injunction. They stated that a footballer had had an affair with Ms Thomas and that they had been made the subject of an injunction.[38] This began speculation as to who the footballer was, and in late April speculation became rife on Twitter as to the identity not only of CTB but also a number of others who had similar injunctions such as ETK, NEJ, JIH, and others. It was at this point that the worst excesses of SMPs became apparent. A mob mentality emerged with little regard for the rule of law, or indeed accuracy of reporting. Everyone began to speculate widely as to the identity of the people who had privacy and anonymity injunctions and why they had them. Few people were in possession of all the facts and indeed no one seemed to care that in each case a judge, or a panel of judges, had determined that, applying the balancing test, an injunction was in order. Fewer again concerned themselves that they may be committing an offence under the Contempt of Court Act 1981. A number of innocent parties (and some less innocent) found themselves dragged into the debate. Twitter users erroneously stated that TV presenter and journalist Jeremy Clarkson was having an affair with Jemima Khan and that she had intimate photographs of the two. This was not true: as has widely been reported since Jeremy Clarkson did have an injunction but it was to prevent publication of details of an affair he was having with his ex-wife, Alex Hall.[39] Jemima Khan was badly shaken by the vitriol shown towards her on Twitter. She originally tried to make light of the issue, tweeting 'Got a nice text from Francie Clarkson and also one from Jeremy. "it's odd I'm sure I would remember if any photos of us existed".' At the same time she sent tweets saying 'the proof that I haven't got a super-injunction is that the papers have printed my name (and no-one else's for fear of being sued)' and 'I've woken up trapped in a bloody nightmare'. As time went by and the messages she received became more vitriolic she tweeted 'I hope the people who made this story up realise that my sons will be bullied at school because of it.' This last comment was particularly ironic as one of the key reasons the privacy injunction in the *ETK* case had been awarded was 'to preserve the stability of the family while the appellant and his wife pursue a reconciliation and to save the children the ordeal of *playground ridicule* when that would inevitably follow publicity'.[40] Thus while the courts were awarding injunctions to prevent children from being ridiculed or bullied in the playground, the actions of Twitter users were causing innocent children to be so bullied and ridiculed. The absence of speech caused by the injunction had caused Twitter users to fill the vacuum with incorrect gossip and speculation.

Jemima Khan was not the only innocent victim of the mob mentality of Twitter users at this time. Speculation was rife as to the identity of the world-famous celebrity who

---

[37] Ibid. [33].
[38] The story may be seen at <https://www.thesun.co.uk/archives/news/488299/footie-stars-affair-with-big-brothers-imogen-thomas/>.
[39] *Jeremy Clarkson v Alexandra Hall (formerly known as AMM v HXW)* [2010] EWHC 2457.
[40] *ETK v News Group Newspapers Ltd* [2011] EWCA Civ 439, [17] (emphasis added).

was referred to in court as NEJ. Quickly Twitter users determined, quite erroneously, that it was Ewan McGregor. This led to the almost satirical outcome that an entirely innocent man was pilloried by Twitter and Facebook users for having an affair he did not have to protect another man who had an injunction. This of course affected not only Mr McGregor himself; like Jemima Khan it affected his wife and children also. What was becoming clear was that all privacy injunctions were doing was creating an information vacuum which users of SMPs would quickly fill without care for accuracy or the well-being of the people they were naming.

The focus on CTB became fiercer. A number of footballers' names were mentioned and journalist Giles Coren was threatened with a contempt of court action in relation to tweets he had made which (arguably) identified a different footballer (identified in court papers as TSE).[41] On 8 May a Twitter account, which still cannot be identified publicly in the UK as it also relates details of extant injunctions, posted the claim that CTB had been involved in a seven-month extra-marital relationship with model Imogen Thomas and naming CTB as Ryan Giggs. The same day a large number of Twitter users in breach of the order of 21 April started naming Giggs as CTB. On 16 May Eady J upheld the injunction. The dam finally broke on 20 May when lawyers for CTB indicated that they were likely to seek a Norwich Pharmical Order in California requiring Twitter Inc. to hand over customer data relating to a number of accounts which were naming Giggs as CTB. Within less than two hours the name of Ryan Giggs becomes the no. 1 trending item on Twitter worldwide (see Figure 6.1). By threatening Twitter users, Giggs's legal team had inadvertently triggered Twitter's autoimmune response known as #IamSpartacus. This occurs when members of the Twitter community feel that Twitter is under attack. The offending message or material is retweeted as often as possible often with the hashtag #IamSpartacus attached. The idea is, as in the classic movie *Spartacus*, to form a single group meaning that an attack on one is an attack on all. There is no way lawyers can sue all Twitter users so by banding together the group defends the users under threat.

Figure 6.1 Mentions of the name Ryan Giggs on Twitter on 20 May 2011

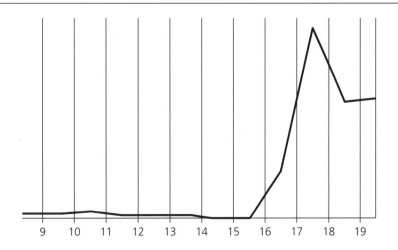

[41] *TSE & Anor v News Group Newspapers Ltd* [2011] EWHC 1308 (QB).

Faced with #IamSpartacus Giggs's lawyers dropped their plans to identify Twitter users. Immediately thereafter, on 22 May, the Scottish newspaper *The Sunday Herald*, which was not covered by the English court order, identified Giggs in Scotland and on 23 May John Hemming MP used parliamentary privilege to name Ryan Giggs as CTB. This meant that newspapers could now name Giggs using the defence of reporting parliamentary proceedings. Interestingly that wasn't quite the end of the CTB case. Attempts by News Group to have the order of 21 April varied failed,[42] but newspapers identified Giggs anyway. Eventually in March 2012 the case was finally disposed of with Tugendhat J finding that News Group had not breached the original injunction and that Giggs was not entitled to damages.[43] The most telling part of Tugendhat J's judgment is at paragraph 12 where he notes:

> NGN can hardly say that it has won this action. The fact that Mr Giggs was named as the subject of the Article was not something achieved by NGN in this action. *It was a consequence of the acts of third parties out of court.* There is no suggestion that NGN was behind the widespread publication of Mr Giggs's identity, so this is not a case where it could be said that his identity came into the public domain as a result of a breach by NGN of the injunction. And the effect of the undertaking given by Ms Thomas and NGN's own statement is that it is no more free to publish a story about Mr Giggs today than it was immediately after Eady J had granted the injunction on 14 April.

You can almost hear the disappointment in Tugendhat J's voice. Many claim the outcome of the CTB case to be victory for the power of SMPs and for free speech. For the judges involved in the maelstrom of spring 2011 it is quite the opposite. The will of the courts, the rule of law itself, was undermined by the actions of Twitter and Facebook users. Maybe if you are a free speech activist the end justifies the means. Attempts to gag the press in genuinely important cases such as Trafigura must be resisted but if one looks across the landscape of cases which became the focus of national attention in spring 2011 most of them are of the nature of sexual indiscretion. They are titillating stories—few are genuinely of national importance. We now know the identities of many involved but not always the full tale as injunctions remain in place. So we know that Ryan Giggs had an affair not only with Imogen Thomas but also with his sister-in-law Natasha Giggs. We know Jeremy Clarkson had an affair with his ex-wife, Alex Hall; and that journalist Andrew Marr had an affair and thought he had fathered a love child; that banker Fred Goodwin had an affair with a colleague;[44] and that Zac Goldsmith, his ex-wife Sheherazade Goldsmith, and his sister Jemima Khan (there was a reason she was falsely linked to Jeremy Clarkson) have an injunction covering hacked emails taken from the accounts of Mrs Khan and Mrs Goldsmith.[45] Interesting though this is I am not sure any of these pass the balancing test, and I am not sure we are any better informed for thousands of people having ignored the rule of law and the Contempt of Court Act. It is no surprise that the establishment felt something had to be done.

---

[42] *CTB v News Group Newspapers Ltd and anor* [2011] EWHC 1326 (QB).
[43] *Giggs (previously known as CTB) v News Group Newspapers Ltd & Anor* [2012] EWHC 431 (QB).
[44] *Goodwin v News Group Newspapers Ltd (Rev 1)* [2011] EWHC 1341 (QB).
[45] *Goldsmith & Anor v BCD* [2011] EWHC 674 (QB).

6.2.2 **The Neuberger report and the joint committee on privacy and injunctions**

There was already an ongoing enquiry in the light of growing public concerns about the use and effect of super-injunctions and the impact they were having on open justice. The Neuberger committee had been set up in April 2010 and by the time of the spring of discontent in 2011 they were near to reporting. As a result, the final Neuberger report said little about SMPs. Instead, as per its remit, it focused upon the effects of anonymity and super-injunctions on open justice and the operation of the courts. As a result, the final report, *Report of the Committee on Super-Injunctions: Super-Injunctions, Anonymised Injunctions and Open Justice*,[46] mentions the internet only twice. The first is in relation to the changing nature of the technological landscape: 'that anonymisation was a rare occurrence historically, and is less so now, may be due not only to the development of the law after the Human Rights Act but also, amongst other things, to changes in the nature of society and social attitudes, and to technological changes, such as the growth of the internet'.[47] The second relates to notification procedures for hearings:

> where a respondent, or non-party, is a media organisation only rarely will there be compelling reasons why advance notification is or was not possible on grounds of either urgency or secrecy. It will only be in truly exceptional circumstances that failure to give a media organisation advance notice will be justifiable on the ground that it would defeat the purpose of an interim non-disclosure order. Different considerations may however arise where a respondent or non-party is an internet-based organisation, tweeter or blogger, or where, for instance, there are allegations of blackmail.[48]

Thus it may be argued the report does little to solve the problems of *CTB*, *NEJ*, or *ETK*, the problem of speculation and gossip. But looking a little further into the report we find it does much indirectly to deal with the problem. The report makes a number of recommendations in relation to balancing the Art. 8 rights of individuals with the Art. 10 rights of media organizations, and in ensuring super-injunctions are not used to defeat the ends of open justice, as arguably appeared to be the case in *Trafigura*. It recorded that anonymity injunctions cannot be awarded at the agreement of the parties: 'interim non-disclosure orders which contain derogations from the principle of open justice cannot be granted by consent of the parties. Such orders affect the Article 10 Convention rights of the public at large. Parties cannot waive or give up the rights of the public.'[49] It also reiterated that 'derogations from open justice can only properly be made where, and to the extent that, they are strictly necessary in order to secure the proper administration of justice'.[50] The report went on to make a number of recommendations to ensure that the balancing principle was properly applied, that injunctions were only granted where strictly necessary and that injunctions be kept under review at regular intervals by the court.

It may be argued that, by tightening up the procedures for obtaining and retaining an anonymity or super-injunction, the need for the sort of speculation endured in spring 2011 in SMPs is removed. The actions of social network users in general and Twitter

---

[46] <https://www.judiciary.gov.uk/wp-content/uploads/JCO/Documents/Reports/super-injunction-report-20052011.pdf.
[47] Ibid. [1.14].
[48] Ibid. Annex A: Draft Practice Guidance for Interim Non-Disclosure Orders [22].
[49] Ibid. [16].
[50] Ibid. [1.36].

users in particular in spring 2011 were driven, arguably, by a sense of injustice: who were these people to decide what could and could not be reported about their private lives when it may be in the public interest? It was perhaps as much a sense of righteous indignation as much as idle speculation and gossip which drove on Twitter users: or rather, to be more accurate, there was a small core of indignant individuals who set up Twitter accounts with the specific aim of 'outing' the individuals who had obtained these injunctions and they fed or supported a much larger community of speculators and gossips. Another major factor in the spring 2011 events was that SMP users were driven by mainstream media. Throughout the CTB/Giggs affair mainstream media had been reporting the story almost every day, especially *The Sun* which often kept the story, which it had a pecuniary interest in, having paid Ms Thomas for her side of the story, on its front page. The mainstream media were at the centre of events in April/May 2011. They sensed that judges were giving weight to Art. 8 rights over Art. 10 and wanted to break that trend to ensure they could continue to report kiss'n'tell stories which are the staple of most UK tabloids. With the rebalancing exercise of the Neuberger report the drive of mainstream media to recruit and encourage SMP users was removed and since that eventful two months they have stopped stoking the fires. An extensive number of anonymity and super-injunctions remain in place—perhaps not quite as many as in the spring of 2011 but extensive all the less—so why is there no longer the same debate and gossip in SMPs? It is because the newspapers are no longer stoking the story.

A second enquiry was quickly set up. The Parliamentary Joint Committee on Privacy and Injunctions was, as it name suggests, a joint committee of the Commons and Lords. It was set up in summer 2011 and was to look specifically at the events of spring 2011 and to report to Parliament what, if any, changes to the law were required to prevent similar events from happening again. The Committee took evidence from expert witnesses throughout autumn/winter 2011 and then reported on 27 March 2012.[51] For most, the key recommendations of the Committee were in relation to whether the UK needed a new privacy statute designed to remove the problems seen in spring 2011: 'We conclude that a privacy statute would not clarify the law. The concepts of privacy and the public interest are not set in stone, and evolve over time. We conclude that the current approach, where judges balance the evidence and make a judgment on a case-by-case basis, provides the best mechanism for balancing Article 8 and Article 10 rights.'[52] For us, though, the most interesting outcomes are how they believed the law should deal with SMPs. The report concluded that:

> Where an individual has obtained a clear court order that certain material infringes their privacy and so should not be published we do not find it acceptable that he or she should have to return to court repeatedly in order to remove the same material from internet searches. Google acknowledged that it was possible to develop the technology proactively to monitor websites for such material in order that the material does not appear in the results of searches. We find their objections in principle to developing such technology totally unconvincing. Google and other search engines should take steps to ensure that their websites are not used as vehicles to breach the law and should actively develop and use such technology. We recommend that if legislation is necessary to require them to do so it should be introduced.[53]

---

[51] Joint Committee on Privacy and Injunctions, *Privacy and Injunctions*, 2010–12, HL 273, HC 1443 <http://www.publications.parliament.uk/pa/jt201012/jtselect/jtprivinj/273/273.pdf.
[52] Ibid.
[53] Ibid. [114]–[115].

This was a highly controversial move, but one which in a separate set of circumstances has come to pass, in some way.[54] In essence, the committee was attempting to force online information intermediaries to police content by actively filtering search results. It is arguable whether this is legal in EU law, following a series of CJEU decisions which say that the Art. 14 safe harbour provision of the Electronic Commerce Directive[55] is applicable to information gateways such as Google[56] and that those intermediaries cannot be compelled to design and implement filtering and blocking systems as to do so would be a breach of Art. 15(1) of the Electronic Commerce Directive.[57] Although active monitoring would not be compatible with EU law, passive removal of links and sites upon request is possible. Specifically with reference to defamation claims, s. 13 of the Defamation Act 2013 allows a court to make an order against 'any person who was not the author, editor or publisher of the defamatory statement to stop distributing, selling or exhibiting material containing the statement.' This is of course a reactive rather than proactive action and requires the court to make the order first. This is perfectly compliant with Arts. 14 and 15 but much narrower than suggested by the Joint Committee.

6.2.3 *PJS v News Group Newspapers*

In spring 2016 the SMPs were put under pressure once more to police their platforms. For the first time since the Ryan Giggs affair a celebrity cause célèbre became news. The case involved an individual, PJS, who is married to another well-known entertainer YMA. As is reported in the Supreme Court judgment: 'In 2007 or 2008, the claimant met AB and, starting in 2009, they had occasional sexual encounters. AB had a partner, CD. By text message on 15 December 2011, the claimant asked if CD was "up for a three-way", to which AB replied that CD was. The three then had a three-way sexual encounter, after which the sexual relationship between PJS and AB came to an end, though they remained friends for some time.'[58] In January 2016 AB and CD attempted to sell their story to *The Sun on Sunday* newspaper. The editor informed PJS of his intent to publish and PJS immediately sought an injunction against publication. Cranston J refused an interim injunction, but the Court of Appeal allowed an appeal and restrained publication of the relevant names and of details of their relationship.[59] The story took a twist on 6 April 2016 and at this point it became a challenge for SMPs and search intermediaries. On that date a US news magazine, apparently in a publication deal with AB, published details of the story including the names of PJS and YMA. In response to representations from PJSs lawyers the magazine agreed to restrict publication to hardcopy editions only, and geo-blocked the online publication so as to restrict this to the United States. However as the Supreme Court noted 'the evidence is that, apart from the one further state publication, the story was not taken up in America. Some other similar articles followed in Canada and in a Scottish newspaper. But, whatever the source, details started to appear on numerous websites, one of which contained equivalent detail to that which had appeared in the American magazine, as well as in social media hashtags.'[60]

[54] See discussion of the 'right to be forgotten' at 23.2.

[55] Dir. 2000/31/EC.

[56] *Google v Louis Vuitton Malletier* ECLI:EU:C:2010:159.

[57] *Scarlet Extended SA v Societe Belge des Auteurs, Compositeurs et Editeurs SCRL* (SABAM) ECLI:EU:C:2011:771.

[58] *PJS v News Group Newspapers Ltd* [2016] UKSC 26, [4].

[59] *PJS v News Group Newspapers Ltd* [2016] EWCA Civ 100.

[60] *PJS* (n. 58) [7].

These hashtags were of course to be found on Twitter and as a result for a period the names became known in England and Wales via that route. To attempt to combat this, lawyers for PJS informed Twitter of breaches of the injunction occurring on their platform. Acting on this information Twitter's legal team began sending letters to accounts identified, informing them that they were in breach of the injunction.

 Highlight Twitter's letter

Dear Twitter User,

We are writing to inform you that Twitter has received legal correspondence regarding specific content posted on your twitter account.

The complainant requests the following Tweet, allegedly in violation of local law in the UK, be removed immediately from your account [LINK].

Please confirm whether you will voluntarily comply with the request.

NOTE: The Twitter Rules state that users agree to comply with all local laws regarding their online conduct and acceptable content. Please be aware that abusive behaviour may lead to your account being suspended.

The action, although ultimately not as disastrous as the misjudged Ryan Giggs attempt to gag Twitter, did not fully succeed. A number of account holders who received the message noted they were not subject to the jurisdiction of the courts of England and Wales[61] including one US-based account that wrote an epic response.[62] In the interim the PJS case had made its way to the Supreme Court. Newspaper editors were arguing that as the names of PJS and YMA were identifiable through SMPs and internet search platforms the injunction should be lifted.

 Highlight The media campaign[63]

The Times on 8 April 2016 reported that the injunction was being 'flouted on social media' after the 'well-known' man was named in the US and that the Society of Editors had condemned such injunctions as 'bringing the whole system into disrepute'. *The Sun* on 10 April 2016 called 'on our loyal readers to help end the farce that means we can't tell you the full story of the celebrity father's threesome' by writing to their MPs 'to get them to voice the public outcry in Parliament and bring an end to this injustice'. It set out a suggested form of letter. It appears that an MP was by 11 April 2016 proposing to name the appellant in Parliament, something that intervention by the Speaker may have prevented. The *Mail Online* on 14 April 2016 reported that it had held a survey which 'found that 20 percent of the public already know who he is while others said they know how to find out'.

[61] S Hopkins, 'Celebrity Threesome Couple PJS, YMA Now Trying To Gag Twitter Users', *Huffington Post* 20 May 2016 <https://www.huffingtonpost.co.uk/entry/celebrity-threesome-couple-pjs-yma-now-trying-to-gag-twitter-users_uk_573f163fe4b00006e9ae9964>.

[62] <https://twitter.com/NeilRetail/status/733664060240076800>.

[63] *PJS* (n. 58) [8].

Based on the fact that a substantial proportion of the public already knew the identities of PJS and YMA the newspapers sought to have the injunction lifted. The Supreme Court though refused their application. Lord Mance who gave the majority verdict felt strongly that the internet and SMPs in particular should not be allowed to usurp the rule of law:

> Those interested in a prurient story can, if they try, probably read about the identities of those involved and in some cases about the detail of the conduct, according to where they may find it on the internet. The Court will be criticised for giving undue protection to a tawdry story by continuing the injunction to trial. There is undoubtedly also some risk of further internet, social media or other activity aimed at making the Court's injunction seem vain, whether or not encouraged in any way by any persons prevented from publishing themselves. On the other hand, the legal position, which the Court is obliged to respect, is clear. There is on present evidence no public interest in any legal sense in the story, however much the respondents may hope that one may emerge on further investigation and/or in evidence at trial, and it would involve significant additional intrusion into the privacy of the appellant, his partner and their children.[64]

In coming to this decision Lord Mance cites Tugendhat J in *CTB* that it is not merely the purpose of an injunction to preserve a secret also to prevent intrusion and harassment into the private life of the applicant, in fact as Tugendhat J observed at that time 'the fact that tens of thousands of people have named the claimant on the internet confirms that the claimant and his family need protection from intrusion into their private and family life.'[65] He also cited with approval Eady J in CTB: 'It is fairly obvious that wall-to-wall excoriation in national newspapers, whether tabloid or "broadsheet", is likely to be significantly more intrusive and distressing for those concerned than the availability of information on the Internet or in foreign journals to those, however many, who take the trouble to look it up.'[66] Agreeing with his brethren Lord Mance concludes that 'the media storm which discharge of the injunction would unleash would add a different and in some respects more enduring dimension to the existing invasions of privacy being perpetrated on the internet.'[67]

Lord Toulson issued a dissenting opinion. He took a distinctively different view to Lord Mance:

> As I read the words of the [Human Rights] Act, they require the court to take into account how generally available the information has become from whatever source, be it broadcast journalism, print journalism, the internet or social media. The evident underlying purpose of the subsection is to discourage the granting of an injunction to prevent publication of information which is already widely known. If the information is in wide, general circulation from whatever source or combination of sources, I do not see that it should make a significant difference whether the medium of the intended publication is the internet, print journalism or broadcast journalism. The world of public information is interactive and indivisible.[68]

This is an interesting argument from Lord Toulson. Essentially the justices were split (albeit by a 4:1 majority) as two whether the sphere of public information was uniform or layered. Lord Toulson saw the sphere as uniform and when the names of PJS and

[64] Ibid. [44].
[65] Ibid. [30].
[66] Ibid. [29].
[67] Ibid. [45].
[68] Ibid. [89].

YMA were published in the United States, Canada, and Scotland and then were circulated on SMPs and via search providers he believed the injunction was defeated and should be lifted. Lord Mance, for the majority, saw the sphere as layered where intrusion by mainstream media outlets would lead to in his words 'a different and in some respects more enduring dimension to the existing invasions of privacy'.

The PJS case gave the Supreme Court much to consider. It was acknowledged by Lord Neuberger that 'between 20 per cent and 25 per cent of the population know who PJS is' and indeed he acknowledged that if this had been a confidentiality injunction rather than a privacy one he would have been compelled to lift it on that basis.[69] However as he noted this meant that 75 per cent of the population did not know PJS's identity and presumably more than 75 per cent did not know much if anything about the details of the story. He acknowledged, as did Lord Mance, that the global nature of the internet was a challenge for injunctions such as this one admitting 'the internet and other electronic developments are likely to change our perceptions of privacy as well as other matters—and may already be doing so. The courts must of course be ready to consider changing their approach when it is clear that that approach has become unrealistic in practical terms or out of touch with the standards of contemporary society.' However he was strong in his opinion that the rule of law should not be undermined by actions taking place online and that the law should only be changed when required: 'we should not change our approach before it is reasonably clear that things have relevantly changed in a significant and long-term way'.[70]

When the third edition of this book was prepared I wrote 'it is far too soon to say another spring like 2011 is unlikely to be seen, and Twitter and Facebook remain awash with gossip. However stricter policing by Twitter and Facebook . . . will help those who possess privacy injunctions. *The real test of the new system though will be when a celebrity goes head to head with an established media outlet, as occurred between* The Sun *and Ryan Giggs in 2011*, for at the end of the day it seems unlikely Twitter users would have been discussing the identity of CTB were they not encouraged to do so by the tabloid press.'[71] PJS was precisely that case study. The facts closely mirror CTB/Giggs. A sex scandal involving a celebrity. An injunction preventing the English press from publishing details or their identity. Publication overseas and the persons involved named online and via SMPs. PJS ended differently to CTB following the Supreme Court decision. Throughout this section I have named Ryan Giggs but not PJS or YMA. It is clear a significant proportion of the UK population knows the identity of both PJS and YMA as the Supreme Court acknowledged. Indeed as Lord Mance acknowledged 'the online tool Google Trends shows a massive increase in the number of internet searches relating to the appellant and YMA by their true names.'[72] However, as time passed interest in the PJS story waned as newspapers realized they were not going to be able to publish their story. As I had suggested, the story was driven not by Twitter, Facebook, or Google but by mainstream media stoking interest. Once their financial interest was blunted by the Supreme Court judgment they stopped stoking the fires. Three years on there is no doubt that PJS and YMA suffered a major intrusion into their

---

[69] Ibid. [57].

[70] Ibid. [70].

[71] A Murray, *Information Technology Law: The Law and Society* (3rd edn, OUP 2016) 156 (emphasis added).

[72] *PJS* (n. 58) [8].

private lives but by the Supreme Court standing firm, despite newspapers depicting them as King Canute, the lives of PJS and YMA have not been torn apart in the way Ryan Giggs experienced. There will no doubt be future challenges to the authority of the courts and the rule of law in future celebrity privacy cases but for the moment PJS may be argued to have given the mainstream press pause for thought and it may help stem the argument of the press that because something is known online they should be allowed to publish it.

6.3 **Making criminal threats and organizing criminal activity**

6.3.1 **Criminal threats**

If gossip and speculation were the most antisocial form of activity occurring on SMPs we would have little to worry about. However SMPs are used for a variety of more antisocial activities including criminal activity. Probably the best-known case of this variety is *Chambers v DPP*.[73] Paul Chambers has become something of a cause célèbre of the Twitter community but some may not know the story of his prosecution. Paul Chambers, known on Twitter as @PaulJChambers, had begun a romantic exchange with another Twitter user, Sarah Tonner known as @Crazycolours. He had arranged to travel to Belfast to meet her on 15 January 2010. He and Sarah were exchanging messages via Twitter about his trip the week before on 6 January 2010 when they heard the news that the airport he was to fly from, Robin Hood Airport near Doncaster, might close due to snow conditions. They swapped tweets, joking about how he might get to Belfast the following week if the airport closed. Two messages sent by Chambers were: '@Crazycolours: I was thinking that if it does then I had decided to resort to terrorism' and '@Crazycolours: That's the plan! I am sure the pilots will be expecting me to demand a more exotic location than NI.'[74] Chambers then heard the news that Robin Hood Airport had closed. He tweeted his fateful message.

 Highlight Paul Chambers' tweet

Crap! Robin Hood Airport is closed. You've got a week and a bit to get your shit together otherwise I am blowing the airport sky high!!

It should be noted there is one essential difference between this final message and the ones before. Whereas the previous messages were in the form of replies to @Crazycolours this was a general tweet. This meant this tweet went to all his followers rather than just to @Crazycolours and into his timeline. There was no evidence that anyone found his tweet to be threatening or menacing and initially nothing more was said or thought of the tweet. Then, on 11 January 2010, five days after it was sent, the duty manager

---

[73] [2012] EWHC 2157.
[74] Ibid. [12].

responsible for security at Robin Hood Airport, while off duty at home, found the tweet. The court records:

> Mr Duffield did not see this 'tweet' on the appellant's time line, and it was never sent to him or to the airport. Rather he was at home searching generally for any 'tweets' which referred to Robin Hood Airport. In cross examination he said that he did not know whether the 'tweet' was a joke or not, but as even a joke could cause major disruption it had to be investigated. Accordingly he referred the 'tweet' to his manager, Mr Armson. Mr Armson was responsible for deciding whether any perceived threat to the airport should be graded as 'credible' or 'non-credible'. If 'credible', it was to be referred immediately to the Ministry of Defence, but if 'non-credible', as a matter of standard practice it was to be reported to the airport police. Mr Armson examined the appellant's 'tweet'. He regarded it as 'non-credible', not least because it featured the appellant's name and, as he noted, the appellant was due to fly from the airport in the near future. Nevertheless in accordance with airport procedure he passed this 'tweet' to the airport police. The airport police themselves took no action, presumably for exactly the same reason, but they decided to refer the matter on to the South Yorkshire police.[75]

On 13 January Chambers was arrested on suspicion of involvement in a bomb hoax and was eventually charged following advice from the Crown Prosecution Service (CPS) with sending by a public electronic communication network a message of a 'menacing character' contrary to s. 127(1)(a) of the Communications Act 2003.

Highlight Section 127(1) of the Communications Act 2003

A person is guilty of an offence if he or she:

(a) sends by means of a public electronic communications network a message or other matter that is grossly offensive or of an indecent, obscene or menacing character; or

(b) causes any such message or matter to be so sent.

On 10 May 2010 Chambers was found guilty by District Judge Jonathan Bennett at Doncaster Magistrates Court. Alarmingly for all users of SMPs, the CPS had argued that s. 127(1)(a) was a strict liability offence without the need to establish *mens rea*. Thankfully Judge Bennett rejected this assertion and relying on *DPP v Collins*,[76] found that 'the prosecution must show some *mens rea* to satisfy me, to the requisite standard of proof, for me to find this case is proved'. Judge Bennett was particularly convinced that Chambers had some form of *mens rea* because he posted the message to his timeline rather than in a reply to @Crazycolours as he had done previously. He recorded:

> I do not have to accept what the defendant tells me about his state of mind at face value. I also note the defendant is an experienced, and clearly very heavy user, of 'Twitter'. Furthermore he has travelled by air, although he had not used Robin Hood airport previously. I found strange his evidence in relation to airport threats not seeming to relate to him and appearing to be in another world. Of particular significance is the fact that this 'tweet' was posted to the public

---

[75] Ibid. [13].
[76] [2006] UKHL 40.

timeline, unlike most of his 'tweets' in the time frame around this particular posting. This message would have been of particular significance to the lady known as 'crazy colours' in Northern Ireland to whom the defendant was going to see on his air journey. He chose to post it in the public domain where in theory it was open for anyone to see, as indeed did Mr Duffield. I am therefore satisfied that the defendant sent the message via 'Twitter' and it was of a menacing nature in the context of the times in which we live. Furthermore I am satisfied the defendant was, at the very least, aware that this was of a menacing nature and I find him guilty of the offence.[77]

Chambers appealed and in November 2010 his appeal was lost. Her Honour Judge Davies, sitting with two magistrates, found that Chambers' tweet contained menace and that he must have known that it might be taken seriously. Judge Davies told the court that Chambers had been an unimpressive witness and said: 'Anyone in this country in the present climate of terrorist threats, especially at airports, could not be unaware of the possible consequences.'[78] An appeal by stated case was allowed and was stated on 3 March 2011. An initial hearing by the Divisional Court failed to produce a verdict after a highly unusual split between the two judges,[79] so a further hearing before three judges rather than the usual two was arranged. Finally, on 27 July 2012, Chambers saw his conviction quashed by a Divisional Court chaired by the Lord Chief Justice, Lord Judge.[80]

The court was quite scathing of the earlier decisions. After quickly disposing of a claim that a tweet was not a message sent by a public electronic communications network but was rather content created and published on a social media platform,[81] the court set about the key issue of Chambers' intent and actions. In considering the *actus reus* of the message Lord Judge made a strong policy statement. He noted that:

> The 2003 Act did not create some newly minted interference with the first of President Roosevelt's essential freedoms—freedom of speech and expression. Satirical, or iconoclastic, or rude comment, the expression of unpopular or unfashionable opinion about serious or trivial matters, banter or humour, even if distasteful to some or painful to those subjected to it should and no doubt will continue at their customary level, quite undiminished by this legislation. Given the submissions by Mr Cooper, we should perhaps add that for those who have the inclination to use 'Twitter' for the purpose, Shakespeare can be quoted unbowdlerised, and with Edgar, at the end of King Lear, they are free to speak not what they ought to say, but what they feel.[82]

Applying this policy, and taking account of the fact that none of Chambers' 600+ followers, nor the employees of the airport, nor the airport police had treated this as a credible threat, the message was not to be read as a 'menacing' message and as such could not make out the offence under s. 127(1).[83] Although this would have disposed

---

[77] Original source now deleted.

[78] M Wainwright, 'Twitter Joke Trial: Paul Chambers Loses Appeal against Conviction', *The Guardian*, 11 November 2010.

[79] DA Green, 'The High Court is Unable to Agree on Twitter Joke Trial Appeal', *New Statesman*, 28 May 2012.

[80] *Chambers* (n. 73).

[81] 'Whether one reads the "tweet" at a time when it was read as "content" rather than "message", at the time when it was posted it was indeed "a message" sent by an electronic communications service for the purposes of s. 127(1). Accordingly "Twitter" falls within its ambit': ibid. [25].

[82] Ibid. [28].

[83] Ibid. [31]–[34].

of the appeal the court continued to examine the *mens rea* element. Lord Judge usefully set out further guidance:

> The mental element of the offence is satisfied if the offender is proved to have intended that the message should be of a menacing character (the most serious form of the offence) or alternatively, if he is proved to have been aware of or to have recognised the risk at the time of sending the message that it may create fear or apprehension in any reasonable member of the public who reads or sees it. We would merely emphasise that even expressed in these terms, the mental element of the offence is directed exclusively to the state of the mind of the offender, and that if he may have intended the message as a joke, even if a poor joke in bad taste, it is unlikely that the *mens rea* required before conviction for the offence of sending a message of a menacing character will be established.[84]

This was a victory on every level, not only for Chambers and his legal team but also for all users of SMPs throughout England and Wales. It represented a significant rap on the knuckles for the CPS for bringing and continuing to press the case, and to the lower courts for not being sufficiently flexible in analysing both the *actus reus* and *mens rea* elements of the offence. Most important though, Lord Judge and the Divisional Court returned to SMP users everywhere the right to be offensive and rude without the fear of being criminalized. Though we may not agree with some of the more offensive content contained on Twitter and Facebook, such as jokes tweeted by comedian Frankie Boyle, which are often distasteful, it would be entirely incorrect to criminalize his actions because others found them to be 'grossly offensive' or to criminalize Paul Chambers because someone else deemed his message to be of a 'menacing character'.

There was great deal of fall-out from the *Chambers* decision—not least the publication of new guidance on social media prosecutions by the Director of Public Prosecutions.[85] The guidance divides offences into pre-existing offences against the person, public justice, sexual or public order offences, and communications offences. The guidance suggests that where social media is used to facilitate a substantive offence, prosecutors should proceed under the substantive offence in question. Thus communication offences, which tend to be more controversial, see *Chambers*, are not preferred. If a prosecution is to go forward for the communications offence, as in *Chambers*, prosecutors are reminded that Article 10 of the European Convention on Human Rights protects freedom of expression. The guidance given to prosecutors is that they 'must be satisfied that a prosecution is required in the public interest and, where Article 10 is engaged, this means on the facts and merits of the particular case that it has convincingly been established that a prosecution is necessary and proportionate.'[86] The guidelines list seven factors to be taken into account in determining the public interest:[87]

a. The likelihood of re-offending. The spectrum ranges from a suspect making a one–off remark to a suspect engaged in a sustained campaign against a victim;

---

[84] Ibid. [38].
[85] The revised guidance may be found at <https://www.cps.gov.uk/legal-guidance/social-media-guidelines-prosecuting-cases-involving-communications-sent-social-media>.
[86] Ibid. [30].
[87] Ibid. [31].

b. The suspect's age or maturity. This may be highly relevant where a young or immature person has not fully appreciated what they wrote;

c. The circumstances of and the harm caused to the victim, including whether they were serving the public, whether this was part of a coordinated attack (virtual mobbing), whether they were targeted because they reported a separate criminal offence, whether they were contacted by a person convicted of a crime against them, their friends or family;

d. Whether the suspect has expressed genuine remorse;

e. Whether swift and effective action has been taken by the suspect and/or others for example, service providers, to remove the communication in question or otherwise block access to it;

f. Whether the communication was or was not intended for a wide audience, or whether that was an obvious consequence of sending the communication; particularly where the intended audience did not include the victim or target of the communication in question; and

g. Whether the offence constitutes a hate crime.

The intention of these guidelines, implemented, as they were post-*Chambers*, was to reduce the volume of prosecutions, in particular prosecutions which to the media at least looked like an overreaction of the criminal law to this new sphere. However, a number of cases post-*Chambers* show an unhappy relationship between free expression and the application of the criminal law. Some cases seem quite straightforwardly to come to the right conclusion. Few would seek to defend Peter Nunn who sent rape threat messages to MP Stella Creasey and campaigner Caroline Criado-Perez,[88] however the abortive attempt to prosecute the controversial activist Bahar Mustafa for using the hashtag #killallwhitemen (without directing the message at any identifiable individual)[89] shows that even applying the new guidelines finding the line between acceptable free expression and unacceptable threats to cause harm can be difficult.

6.3.2 Organizing and inciting criminal activity

In the summer of 2011 civil unrest broke out in England. After a spring spent discussing the identity of CTB and NEJ, the summer was spent watching riots and looting break out in Tottenham, spreading quickly to several other London boroughs including Croydon and Enfield, and then over the next few nights to other parts of the country including the West Midlands and Manchester. The government initially found it difficult to control the spread of civil unrest with the riots beginning in Tottenham on Saturday 6 August and then spreading on successive nights to other London boroughs and other parts of England. The final night of unrest was Wednesday 10 August when a

---

[88] Press Association, 'Peter Nunn jailed for abusive tweets to MP Stella Creasy', *The Guardian*, 29 September 2014.

[89] J Elgot, 'London woman charged after alleged #killallwhitemen tweet', *The Guardian*, 6 October 2015. The charges were later dropped for lack of evidence not because of the public interest test—see <https://www.bbc.co.uk/news/uk-england-london-34711344>.

combination of bad weather and a full deployment of police following the cancellation of all leave saw an end to the unrest. One innovation of the unrest was the way it was organized. The overwhelming majority of those involved were under 30 and as a result they used SMPs and other media platforms to organize activities.

In the aftermath of the unrest, courts worked overtime to prosecute all the offenders. A large number of individuals were charged with public order offences as well as theft and burglary. A smaller number were charged with incitement offences relating to messages placed on Facebook in particular. Among these were Jordan Blackshaw and Perry Sutcliffe. Their cases became linked and formed part of the same appeal against sentence, *R v Blackshaw (Rev 1)*.[90] Jordan Blackshaw set up a Facebook page entitled 'Smash down in Northwich Town'. He set the page up at 10.30 a.m. on 8 August 2011, saying the action would start behind the McDonald's in Northwich at 1p.m. the next day. As the court notes:

> The riots were in full flow. The appellant knew perfectly well that they were. The purpose of his website was to wreak 'criminal damage and rioting in the centre of Northwich', and the event called for participants to meet in a restaurant in Northwich at lunchtime on 9th August. The website was aimed at his close associates, who he referred to as the 'Mob Hill Massive', and his friends, but he also opened it to public view and included in the website references to ongoing rioting in London, Birmingham and Liverpool. He posted a message of encouragement on the website that read 'we'll need to get on this, kicking off all over'.[91]

Instead of actually starting a riot in Northwich, all Blackshaw achieved was to draw attention to himself. Locals saw the event and reported him to the police. The police posted a warning to anyone thinking of taking part and nine people who said they would attend did not in fact turn up. There was no unrest in Northwich. The court records what happened next:

> Following his arrest at 11.00 on 9th August, the appellant admitted that he had watched media coverage of the riots on the television and that he set up the website. He agreed that the event would be carried out, and that he would have attended himself if he had had enough alcohol. He said that it was not something that he would have done sober, and claimed that he had set the site up for a 'laugh and to meet people to drink with', but in later discussions he agreed that what he had done was stupid and that the effect of his actions was to encourage rioting and looting. He accepted responsibility for his actions. As we have indicated, his later guilty plea made clear that he had not set up the website as a joke. He believed that the offences he was inciting would happen.[92]

Perry Sutcliffe's story is similar. In the early hours of 9 August he set up a Facebook page called 'The Warrington Riots'. The page contained a photograph of police officers in riot equipment in a stand-off with a group of rioters and a photograph of himself and others in a pose the police described as 'gangster like'. He then sent invitations to 400 Facebook friends inviting them to meet at a carvery in Warrington at 7.00 p.m. on 10 August. Like Blackshaw, he also made the page viewable to the general public. In Sutcliffe's case 47 people said they would attend but in the end, like Blackshaw, no one actually turned up and no unrest occurred after police closed the site down. Sutcliffe

---

[90]   [2011] EWCA Crim 2312.
[91]   Ibid. [55].
[92]   Ibid. [57].

was arrested on the morning of 9 August. Like Blackshaw, Sutcliffe pleaded guilty. The court records that:

> After he entered his plea it was said on his behalf that he went back to the Facebook site and cancelled the event. It was further said that he woke up at around 10.00 and received a telephone call from a friend who had seen the entry on Facebook and, asked him about it. This had prompted the appellant to go to the Facebook site and cancel the event, posting a remark to the effect that it was a joke . . . A forensic analysis of the appellant's computer equipment establishes that the posting on Facebook which cancelled the event and said it was 'only jokin f. . . hell' was created at 10.54am, literally a few minutes before the police arrived. Although we approach the decision in the appeal on the basis that the appellant decided to retract the Facebook entry, as his advocate suggested, the inference seems clear that this decision followed an intimation that the police were searching for him.[93]

The court therefore seems satisfied that Sutcliffe did cancel the event but believes this is only so because he had been tipped off that the police were searching for him.

As is clear already, neither contested the charges, both pleading guilty: Blackshaw to an offence contrary to s. 46 of the Serious Crime Act 2007 (encouraging or assisting offences believing one or more will be committed); Sutcliffe to an offence contrary to s. 44 of the same Act (intentionally encouraging or assisting an offence). Both were initially sentenced to four years' imprisonment, as in the judge's words 'a deterrent effect'. Both appealed their sentence and both were dismissed. The Court of Appeal noted that, although they were conscious of the fact that no unrest actually occurred as a consequence of their actions, 'the fact that no rioting occurred in the streets of Northwich or Warrington owed nothing to either appellant. The reality was that armed with information from members of the public who were disturbed at the prospect, the police were able to interfere and bring the possibility of riot to an end.'[94] The sentences though seem out of proportion with the harm caused despite this.

 Highlight Average prison sentences for the 2011 riots

As of 10 August 2012, there had been 2,138 persons found guilty and sentenced for their part in the disorder. Of those sentenced, 1,405 (66 per cent) were sentenced to immediate custody with an average custodial sentence length (ACSL) of 17.1 months.[95]

Thus the average sentence for taking part in the unrest including sentences for burglary, theft, and violent disorder, is 17.1 months while both Blackshaw and Sutcliffe were given four years, nearly three times the average, for something that did not happen. Why? The answer unfortunately appears to be a fear of technology on the part of the court, linked to a desire to send out a message to others who may consider using BBM or Facebook to organize disorder.

---

[93] Ibid. [61]–[63].
[94] Ibid. [72].
[95] Ministry of Justice, *Statistical Bulletin on the Public Disorder of 6th to 9th August 2011–September 2012 Update*: <www.gov.uk/government/uploads/system/uploads/attachment_data/file/219665/august-public-disorder-stats-bulletin-130912.pdf>.

> **Highlight** The court sends a message
>
> We are unimpressed with the suggestion that in each case the appellant did no more than make the appropriate entry in his Facebook. Neither went from door to door looking for friends or like minded people to join up with him in the riot. All that is true. But modern technology has done away with the need for such direct personal communication. It can all be done through Facebook or other social media. In other words, the abuse of modern technology for criminal purposes extends to and includes incitement of very many people by a single step. *Indeed it is a sinister feature of these cases that modern technology almost certainly assisted rioters in other places to organise the rapid movement and congregation of disorderly groups in new and unpoliced areas.*[96]

Clearly the message is being sent not just to Blackshaw and Sutcliffe, but to anyone else who may use SMPs to organize disorder: the courts will come down on you particularly hard. A group of individuals have found this out the hard way. They include Anthony Gristock who was sentenced to three years and eight months in prison after setting up a Facebook page entitled 'Bring the riots to Cardiff'. The online newspaper *Wales Online* records that 'Gristock posted messages on Facebook suggesting targets for rioting. He wrote: "Rolex, Post Office, Boss, the land of opportunity." In another message he told website users to target "the real banks" and named The Sony Centre and the Apple Store in Cardiff city centre as possible sites for disturbance.'[97] Also given long sentences were Shawn Divin and Jordan McGinley. They both set up a Facebook page called 'Riot in the toon', an attempt to incite members of the public to take part in a riot in Dundee. Again, no actual damage occurred and Divin was sentenced to three years and three months and McGinley to three years. On appeal their sentences were slightly reduced to two years five months and two years three months, less than their English and Welsh counterparts but in part this was due to their ages of 16 and 18.[98] In summing up Lord Mackay demonstrated the Scottish courts take this as seriously as their English counterparts: 'an appropriate starting point for sentencing the appellants on the offence to which they pled guilty is one of three years. A sentence of that length not only reinforces the view that the imposition of a custodial sentence is necessary. It reflects the gravity of the offence to which the appellants pled guilty. The appellants may have thought they were engaged in some form of prank. They were not. The agreed narrative and the transcript of the Facebook pages make that clear.'[99]

More recently we have seen the return of SMPs as a rallying point for criminal activity. Gangs, mostly in London, have used YouTube videos to incite violence. The rise of so-called 'drill rap' videos released by gangs of youths which contain violent lyrics and calls to violence has been credited with an increase in knife and gun crime and deaths. A number of youths involved in the drill scene have been victims, including

---

[96] *Blackshaw* (n. 90) [73] (emphasis added).

[97] S Morgan, 'London Riots: Jail for Facebook User who Wanted Riots in Cardiff', *Wales Online* 10 October 2012 <https://www.walesonline.co.uk/news/wales-news/london-riots-jail-facebook-user-2020720>.

[98] *Divin and McGinlay v Her Majesty's Advocate* [2012] HCJAC 81.

[99] Ibid. [30].

15-year-old Jordan Douherty known as Young Valenti who died when he was beaten and stabbed by more than five attackers near a community centre in Romford,[100] and 23-year-old Siddique Kamara known as Incognito who was stabbed in Camberwell. In an interview given before his death Kamara accepted that the drill music videos were inciting violence, saying 'the crime that's happening right music does influence it. You've got to put your hands up and say drill music does influence it.'[101]

In response to the apparent danger of drill music videos, some of which contain direct threats and incitement to violence, a combined effort of the Metropolitan Police and YouTube has seen a number of videos removed and at least one group banned from making videos. In May 2018 it was reported that following complaints from the Metropolitan Police, and a request to remove 50–60 videos YouTube had removed around 30 videos.[102] In addition, the Metropolitan Police obtained a Criminal Behaviour Order under s. 22 of the Anti-social Behaviour, Crime and Policing Act 2014 against members of the so-called 1011 gang banning them from mentioning death or injury, and from mentioning named postcodes in a gang context. They must also notify police within 24 hours of releasing new videos and give 48 hours' warning of the date and location of any performance or recording and permit officers to attend. The order will remain in place for three years.[103] At the time of writing there have been no prosecutions using communications offences for drill music but the police continue to treat the issue with seriousness and have indicated that they may seek further Criminal Behaviour Orders similar to the one issued against the 1011 gang.

6.4 **Cyberbullying, trolling, and harassment**

One of the most troubling forms of antisocial behaviour is bullying. The media abound with tragic tales of teenagers pushed beyond breaking point by the actions of others through a number of media, but in particular through SMPs, leading to their eventual suicide. Perhaps the most haunting tale is that of 15-year-old Amanda Todd. Todd committed suicide on 10 October 2012 at her home in Port Coquitlam, British Columbia, Canada. Prior to her death, she had posted a video on YouTube, entitled 'My Story: Struggling, bullying, suicide and self harm', which showed her using a series of flash cards to tell of her experiences being bullied. The video went viral after her death, resulting in international media attention. Todd had been bullied and stalked for years by a man who had obtained a topless picture of her via webcam while posing as a boy her age. According to Todd's mother 'The Internet stalker she flashed kept stalking her. Every time she moved schools he would go undercover and become a Facebook friend.'[104] Todd's story is unfortunately not at all unusual. Similar tales may be told by

[100] 'Teenager charged with murder over stabbing death of drill performer Jordan Douherty', *The Independent*, 28 June 2018.

[101] I Cobain, 'London drill rapper killed in knife attack admitted music's effect on crime', *The Guardian*, 2 August 2018.

[102] J Waterson, 'YouTube deletes 30 music videos after Met link with gang violence', *The Guardian*, 29 May 2018.

[103] I Cobain, 'London drill rap group banned from making music due to threat of violence', *The Guardian*, 15 June 2018.

[104] G Shaw, 'Amanda Todd's Mother Speaks Out about her Daughter, Bullying', *The Vancouver Sun*, 14 October 2012.

the families of 13-year-old Megan Meier of Dardenne Prairie, Missouri;[105] and closer to home 13-year-old Erin Gallagher from County Donegal[106] and 15-year-old Thomas Mullaney, from Bournville, in Birmingham.[107]

There is clearly a line between bullying and harassment. Bullying is an unfortunate fact of life for many youngsters and it is important that we do not create criminal records where one is not required. Equally, though, cyberbullying is a social problem that at times needs a legal response. Whereas in the past the bullied teenager could find space free from the actions of their tormentors such as the privacy of their own bedroom, the problem with WhatsApp, Snapchat, Facebook, Twitter, and Instagram is that it brings the bully into their private space: they find there is nowhere to escape to, often driving them to extreme actions. The law then needs to get involved when the bully goes beyond simple bullying and moves towards harassment. Harassment is behaviour intended to disturb or upset and which is usually found threatening or disturbing; it is regulated by the Protection from Harassment Act 1997. This provides that a person 'must not pursue a course of conduct (a) which amounts to harassment of another, and (b) which he knows or ought to know amounts to harassment of the other'.[108] This raises the question how one ought to know that their course of action amounts to harassment. However, this is covered by s. 1(2) which provides that 'the person whose course of conduct is in question ought to know that it amounts to harassment of another if a reasonable person in possession of the same information would think the course of conduct amounted to harassment of the other'. If found guilty of harassment the offender may both be charged under s. 2, which can lead to a maximum six months' imprisonment and may be issued with a restraining order under s. 5, which if breached may lead to up to five years' imprisonment.[109] If the harassment is of such a nature as to put the victim in fear of violence on at least two occasions then under s. 4 of the Act the offender may be charged with the aggravated offence of 'putting people in fear of violence'; this, like breaching a restraining order under s. 5, can lead to imprisonment of up to five years.

In addition to the provisions of the Protection from Harassment Act, cyberbullying may also lead to prosecutions under the Malicious Communications Act 1988, the Communications Act 2003, or the Crime and Disorder Act 1998. By s. 1 of the Malicious Communications Act 1988 it is an offence to send an indecent, offensive, or threatening letter, electronic communication, or other article to another person. This is a summary offence—and as such may only lead to a maximum sentence of imprisonment of six months—as is the already discussed offence of improper use of the public electronic communications system under s. 127 of the Communications Act 2003. As both these offences are summary in nature, the court cannot issue a restraining order. An alternative is to apply for an antisocial behaviour injunction under s.1 of the Anti-social Behaviour, Crime and Policing Act 2014 or alternatively for a Criminal Behaviour Order under s. 22 of the same Act.

---

[105] <https://meganmeierfoundation.org/megans-story/>.
[106] G Harkin, 'Family Devastated after Tragic Erin Takes Own Life after Vicious Online Bullying' *Irish Independent* 29 October 2012.
[107] BBC, 'Facebook Bullying Suicide Boy's Parents in Law Change Call' *BBC News* 12 July 2011 <https://www.bbc.co.uk/news/uk-england-birmingham-14121631>.
[108] Protection from Harassment Act 1997, s. 1(1).
[109] Protection from Harassment Act 1997, s. 5(6).

A mixture of all these strategies has been tried both in relation to cyberbullying, namely where an individual is bullied by someone they know or by someone who has formed an abusive relationship to them, and with the more widespread problem of trolling, namely where someone leaves abusive, insulting, or threatening messages to produce a response from the person being trolled. In 2009 Keeley Houghton, an 18-year-old from Malvern, Worcestershire, became probably the first person in the UK to be sentenced to a custodial sentence for Facebook harassment. She pleaded guilty to harassment and was sentenced to three months in a young offenders' institution after she posted a message on Facebook saying that she would kill another girl.[110] More recently, notorious troll Sean Duffy from Reading was sentenced to 18 weeks in prison having admitted two counts of sending offensive communications under s. 1 of the Malicious Communications Act 1988. He was also given a five-year Anti-social Behaviour Order which prevents him from signing up to, or uploading any content to, any social networking site or purchasing any device with internet access without notifying police. Duffy had posted a string of insulting comments on a Facebook page in memory of teenager Natasha MacBryde, who threw herself under a train in Bromsgrove after being bullied, as well as leaving similar comments on the memorial pages for Laura Drew, Hayley Bates, and Jordan Cooper.[111] Another troll, Colm Coss from Manchester, was also jailed for 18 weeks after admitting offences under s. 127 of the Communications Act 2003 in relation to Facebook comments,[112] while Liam Stacey was sentenced to 56 days in prison after admitting an offence under s. 4A of the Public Order Act 1986 for sending racially abusive tweets to footballer Fabrice Muamba.[113]

Some actions against bullies and trolls have been more controversial. During the 2012 Olympic Games, Twitter troll Reece Messer, a 17-year-old from Weymouth, was arrested at 2.45 a.m. by Dorset police and given a harassment warning under s. 1 of the Malicious Communications Act 1988. There is no doubt that Messer was an unapologetic troll but on this occasion the response seems like an overreaction. Why did they feel the need to formally arrest him at 2.45 a.m.? Could they not have waited until the morning? One of the tweets was probably in breach of the Act but in general the exchange between Messer and diver Tom Daley that began the police action was no different to many seen on Twitter. Messer began by tweeting after Daley had performed poorly in his first event, 'you let your dad down I hope you know that'. This was particularly upsetting to Daley who had recently lost his father after a battle with cancer. Daley retweeted the message to his followers with an addition stating 'After giving it my all . . . you get idiot's sending me this.' Two tweets followed from Messer 'hope your crying now you should be why can't you even produce for your country your just a diver anyway a over hyped [expletive deleted]' and 'haha Tom Daley just tweeted me now

---

[110] H Carter, 'Teenage Girl Is First to Be Jailed for Bullying on Facebook', *The Guardian*, 21 August 2009.

[111] S Morris, 'Internet Troll Jailed after Mocking Deaths of Teenagers', *The Guardian*, 13 September 2011.

[112] BBC, 'Jade Goody Website "Troll" from Manchester Jailed', *BBC News*, 29 October 2010 <https://www.bbc.co.uk/news/uk-england-manchester-11650593>.

[113] The details of his offence are found in the note of appeal against sentence. For some inexplicable reason the note suggests he pleaded guilty to an offence under s. 31(1)(b) of the Public Order Act 1986. This is impossible as this section was repealed in 2000. The author understands it was s. 4A under which he was charged and pleaded guilty <https://www.judiciary.uk/wp-content/uploads/JCO/Documents/Judgments/appeal-judgment-r-v-stacey.pdf>.

I know he's feeling bad'. Quickly Daley's followers began a campaign to have Messer banned from Twitter and set up a twitition for this purpose. Before he could grasp the situation, Messer realized he was trending, not only in the UK but worldwide: 'how am I trending worldwide?' Realizing the situation had got out of control he apologized to Daley: 'please I don't want to be hated I'm just sorry you didn't win I was rooting for you pal to do britain all proud just so upset'. He then realized he was on Sky News: 'what the hell I'm on sky news?' There is nothing in these tweets to suggest s. 1 of the Malicious Communications Act should be applied. Messer later stated he didn't know Daley had lost his father who famously was his coach for many years; this may or may not be true, but certainly none of these tweets merit a 2.45 a.m. arrest under the Act. It is the case that later on that day Messer did appear to send a tweet which clearly falls under the ambit of s. 1, 'i'm going to find you and i'm going to drown you in the pool you cocky [expletive deleted] you're a nobody people like you make me sick'. This is clearly a threat and qualifies under s. 1 of the Act; the question is why did Messer send this when he appeared to be repentant? The answer is that the Twitter mob had lit their torches and were battering at his door in a search for justice. A 17-year-old boy responded in the only way he knew how, by issuing threats. Although a record of threats issued to Messer has now been lost (unlike his tweets which were preserved) it seems at least one Twitter user expressed a desire that he burn to death while another recorded they would physically like to assault him. A hashtag was set up #ThingsBetterThanRiley69 in response to which the mob consensus appears to be 'being the middle person in The Human Centipede'. They wished him ill, harm, and trauma. Many of these tweets may also have been in breach of s. 1 or s. 127 of the Communications Act. In a real sense it can be argued that until he was incited to make such responses Messer did not break the law. The Twitter community led to his arrest.

Another controversial case with a whiff of mob justice is the Matthew Woods case. Woods, after a drunken night out, decided to post a number of sick and offensive jokes about April Jones, a 5-year-old from Wales who disappeared in October 2012, to his Facebook page. There is no doubt the jokes were offensive and in poor taste, but what happened next is an alarming example of mob justice. Police arrested Woods after a furious mob of 50 people turned up at his home the following night. Initially they said that this was for his own safety but then they charged him under s. 127(1) of the Communications Act. Woods pleaded guilty at a hearing the following day and was sentenced to 12 weeks in a young offenders' institute. It is unlikely that he would be prosecuted under the new CPS guidelines, which would be a step in the right direction as his 'jokes', although designed to be offensive, were not to the author's mind 'grossly offensive or of an indecent, obscene or menacing character'. Yet in a move which mirrored the statements of Judges Bennett and Davies in *Chambers*, magistrates said he (Woods) had committed a 'disgusting and despicable' crime.[114] But why was this? Well, as explained by the chairman of the Bench at Chorley Magistrates Court, Bill Hudson: 'The reason for the sentence is the seriousness of the offence, the public outrage that has been caused.'[115] In other words the statement of Woods was grossly offensive as the

---

[114] 'Fury over Chorley Man's Sick April Facebook Comments', *Lancashire Telegraph*, 9 October 2012.

[115] C Skelton, 'Matthew Woods Deserves Support as Much as Airport Tweeter Paul Chambers', *The Guardian*, 12 October 2012.

public were grossly offended. This would create a crazy situation where the perception of the audience would determine the criminality of SMP messages; the mob would rule. Thankfully the judgment of the court in *Chambers* overrules this: 'the mental element of the offence is satisfied if the *offender* is proved to have intended that the message should be of a menacing character'.[116] The same must surely be true of offensive content as well as of menacing content.

The *Chambers* position was tested in summer 2013 with the Twitter abuse of Caroline Criado-Perez and Stella Creasey. Ms Criado-Perez is a journalist and feminist campaigner. She has campaigned to increase the representation of women in the media and in 2013 was active in the campaign to feature a woman on the new £10 note when Winston Churchill was to replace Elizabeth Fry (then the only female to feature on the reverse of a Bank of England banknote) on the £5 note. This campaign was successful but immediately upon the announcement of the Bank's decision Criado-Perez began to receive harassment via Twitter. It was reported that the threats were of a number of 50 per hour and many were of the nature of rape and death threats. Also caught up in the Twitterstorm was MP Stella Creasy who also received threats. Following extensive investigations only three people were charged and subsequently found guilty, Isabella Sorley[117] who sent the graphic series of tweets 'Fuck off and die . . . you should have jumped in front of horses, go die; I will find you and you don't want to know what I will do when I do . . . kill yourself before I do; rape is the last of your worries; I've just got out of prison and would happily do more time to see you berried; seriously go kill yourself! I will get less time for that; rape?! I'd do a lot worse things than rape you'; John Nimmo who tweeted equally graphically 'Ya not that gd looking to rape u be fine; I will find you; come to geordieland bitch; just think it could be somebody that knows you personally; the police will do nothing; rape her nice ass; could I help with that lol; the things I cud do to u; dumb blond bitch'; and Peter Nunn who sent a series of messages to Stella Creasy including one too graphic to record here and another saying 'If you can't threaten to rape a celebrity, what is the point in having them?'[118]

Many people felt that the prosecution of only three people was an inappropriate response to the barrage of hateful messages sent. Had *Chambers* swung the pendulum too far the other way? This is the problem of SMPs such as Twitter, they are firehoses of speech which simply overwhelm common sense. Bullies and trolls appear on both sides: sometimes they are the mob demanding something be done about someone like Reece Messer or Matthew Woods, sometimes it is a mob objecting to a woman campaigning, quite reasonably, to have a woman represented on a banknote. The police are being caught in the middle of this. Free speech advocates argue they are far too involved with a public sphere. In their 2015 report 'Careless Whispers: How speech is policed by outdated communications legislation'[119] campaign group Big Brother Watch note that in the three years November 2010 to November 2013, 6,329 people were charged or cautioned under s. 127 of the Communications Act 2003 or under the Malicious

---

[116] *Chambers* (n. 73) [38].

[117] In an interview given after her release from prison Ms Sorley blames her actions on alcohol while Mr Nimmo says he was 'bored and leaped on a bandwagon'. See P Smith, 'This Is What It's Like To Go To Prison For Trolling' *Buzzfeed News* 2 March 2015 <https://www.buzzfeed.com/patricksmith/isabella-sorley-john-nimmo-interview>.

[118] Press Association (n. 88).

[119] <www.bigbrotherwatch.org.uk/wp-content/uploads/2015/02/Careless-Whisper.pdf>.

Communications Act 1988 (at least 4,259 people were charged and at least 2,070 people were cautioned). This led Big Brother Watch to find 'It is arguable that the outdated nature of the law is why we are seeing an increase in legal cases involving comments made on social media', and to recommend 'that there needs to be serious reform in this area, to ensure that the laws are brought up to date'. Following the Criado-Perez case and the subsequent #gamergate Twitter implemented a new 'report abusive' function[120] and a new filtering system which is supposed to prevent newly created accounts from sending abusive messages to recipients.[121]

The problem continues almost unabated though by either the criminal law or the operation of technological solutions. In September 2017 the *New Statesman* magazine published the results of an Amnesty investigation into tweets sent to female MPs in the preceding six months. This revealed that in the survey period Dianne Abbot, the Shadow Home Secretary, received 8,121 abusive tweets.[122] Alarmingly the data showed that this was 5.8 per cent of all tweets mentioning her twitter handle @HackneyAbbott. Of course she was not the only MP affected. The SNP MP Joanna Cherry received 1,025 abuse tweets, Labour MP Emily Thornberry 1,023 and another Labour MP Jess Phillips 1,002 abusive tweets.[123] More recently a debate over the borders between democratic speech and online harassment saw Infowars activist Alex Jones banned from Twitter, Facebook, Apple, YouTube, and Spotify.[124] It is clear therefore that there is an ongoing problem despite prosecutions being filed and steps taken by SMPs to control online harassment.

Voters who feel SMPs have not done enough to police hate and harassment on their platforms are calling politicians to step into this forum. In response the German government introduced the German Network Enforcement Act (or NetzDG).[125] This makes SMPs, and other intermediaries, liable for the policing of forms of speech content. Failure to remove 'obviously illegal' content within 24 hours, or 'illegal' content within 7 days can lead to fines of up to €20 million. Although wider in scope than just trolling and harassment, covering as it does insult, defamation, public incitement to crime, incitement to hatred, and dissemination of depictions of violence, it demonstrates a renewed vigour from lawmakers to intervene in the regulation of threatening and abusive content on SMPs. The NetzDG law is perhaps though not the best model to adopt. Even prior to the law coming into effect on 1 January 2018 it was the target of criticism. In a detailed report Art. 19 states that 'the likelihood of Social Networks being over-vigorous in deleting or blocking content is compounded by the legal uncertainty pervading the Act. [The law] does nothing to address over-blocking, and provides little protection or due process to Social Networks that in

---

[120] <https://support.twitter.com/articles/20169998-reporting-abusive-behavior>.

[121] A Hern, 'Twitter announces crackdown on abuse with new filter and tighter rules', *The Guardian*, 21 April 2015.

[122] This is 1,353 abusive tweets per month or over 44 abusive tweets per day.

[123] A Dhrodia, 'We tracked 25,688 abusive tweets sent to women MPs—half were directed at Diane Abbott', *New Statesman*, 5 September 2017.

[124] A Hern, 'Facebook, Apple, YouTube and Spotify ban Infowars' Alex Jones', *The Guardian*, 6 August 2018; JC Wong, 'Twitter permanently bans conspiracy theorist Alex Jones', *The Guardian*, 6 September 2018.

[125] Gesetz zur Verbesserung der Rechtsdurchsetzung in sozialen Netzwerken (Network Enforcement Act of 1 September 2017), *Federal Law Gazette* I p. 3352.

good faith refrain from blocking or removing content in the interests of respecting freedom of expression.'[126] Human Rights Watch meanwhile described the law as 'vague, overbroad, and turns private companies into overzealous censors to avoid steep fines, leaving users with no judicial oversight or right to appeal.'[127] However a contrary view is expressed by researcher Stefan Theil 'it is difficult to see why a social media platform operator, which ultimately requires continuous user engagement and content creation to be profitable would adopt an overly aggressive deletion policy. An exodus of users would be sure to follow the consistent and arbitrary deletion of legal content, and thus critically undermine the viability of the social media platform. It therefore appears more likely that the limited scope of the fines and the inherent economic interests of social networks encourage a more nuanced deletion policy: one that complies with existing laws but avoids removing more content than necessary.'[128]

Whatever the views of the critics or supporters of the law it appears the problems with it are more fundamental. On the day it came into effect two senior members of the far right AfD party sent messages via Twitter which were deemed to be in breach of the Act; both tweets were quickly flagged and deleted, as were a series of tweets from the satirical magazine *Titanic* parodying the remarks. However far from containing the problem the AfD have claimed political censorship and have produced adverts claiming they are being silenced. It has been commented that 'Germany's attempt to regulate speech online has seemingly amplified the voices it was trying to diminish.'[129] It was announced in March 2018 that, just a little over two months since the law came into effect, minsters were proposing to amend the law as there was evidence of over-blocking.[130]

UK ministers however continue to suggest that if SMPs do not take more active steps to police their networks they will introduce a legal framework to force them to do so. In September 2018 these appeared to come to a head with reports that the Department of Digital, Culture, Media and Sport, and the Home Office were jointly developing a White Paper on the regulation of SMPs which will 'introduce a mandatory code of practice for social media platforms and strict new rules such as "takedown times" forcing websites to remove illegal hate speech within a set timeframe or face penalties.'[131] At the same time Ofcom released a discussion document suggesting SMPs could be regulated in a manner similar to broadcasters.[132] At the time of writing this process was in its infancy. It may be expected that by the time you read this there will have been considerable development.

---

[126] Article 19, *Germany: The Act to Improve Enforcement of the Law in Social Networks* (2017).

[127] Human Rights Watch, *Germany: Flawed Social Media Law* (2018).

[128] S Theil, 'The new German social media law—a risk worth taking? An "extended look"', *UK Human Rights Blog* 19 February 2018 <https://ukhumanrightsblog.com/2018/02/19/the-new-german-social-media-law-a-risk-worth-taking-an-extended-look-by-stefan-theil/>.

[129] L Kinstler, 'Germany's Attempt to Fix Facebook Is Backfiring', *The Atlantic* 18 May 2018.

[130] E Thomasson, 'Germany looks to revise social media law as Europe watches' *Reuters* 8 March 2018.

[131] A Wickham, 'The UK Government Is Planning To Set Up A Regulator For The Internet', *Buzzfeed News* 20 September 2018 <https://www.buzzfeed.com/alexwickham/uk-government-regulator-internet>.

[132] Ofcom, *Addressing harmful online content* (September 2018) <https://www.ofcom.org.uk/__data/assets/pdf_file/0022/120991/Addressing-harmful-online-content.pdf>.

6.5 **YouTube and *Innocence of Muslims***

Of course the problem of determining what is offensive, or even grossly offensive, to individuals is magnified by the global audience for SMP content. This has already been seen in the related cases of *LICRA et UEJF v Yahoo! Inc. and Yahoo! France*,[133] and *Yahoo! Inc. v LICRA*[134] which were discussed extensively in chapter 5. There was a clear distinction between attitudes in France and in the United States in relation to the Nazi memorabilia which had been listed on Yahoo! auctions. This distinction was seen again in *R v Sheppard & Anor*,[135] also discussed in chapter 5, where the website host in California continued to host 'Tales of the Holohoax' despite Sheppard and Whittle being prosecuted and found guilty in the UK of an offence under the Public Order Act 1986.

That the internet fails to respect borders and with it distinctive national, cultural, and religious values was thrown into sharp relief in the autumn of 2012. A trailer and later a full 74-minute movie appeared on YouTube, entitled *Innocence of Muslims*. Both are designed to inflame controversy—they apparently show Christians being attacked and a medical clinic trashed by a Muslim mob in Egypt while the police stand idly by. Then it moves to a very poorly scripted and acted retelling of the life of the prophet Muhammad. There is little doubt that the film was designed to provoke outrage and so it proved. It was allegedly written and produced by a Coptic Christian, Nakoula Basseley Nakoula, who was born in Egypt but who lives in the United States. He claims he was driven to produce the movie because of the increasing persecution of Copts and poor human rights standards in Egypt, with a rise in church-burnings, growing religious intolerance, and sectarian violence that has been seen against the 10 per cent population of Egypt that are Copts, and complaints that authorities have failed to protect this population.[136] The movie provoked outcry in the Islamic world. Violent demonstrations took place in a number of countries including Egypt, Yemen, Pakistan, and Sudan. More peaceful demonstrations took place in over 20 other countries including the UK. A number of calls were made for YouTube to remove the videos but YouTube cited the First Amendment and refused to take them down. The White House itself requested YouTube to take down the video, a request that was turned down.[137] Instead YouTube and its parent company Google stated that they would block access to the movie locally where the content was illegal. On this basis they blocked local access from India and Indonesia, as well as in Libya, Singapore, Malaysia, Saudi

---

[133] Tribunal de Grande Instance de Paris (Superior Court of Paris). There are three separate orders in this case. To make sense of the case you should read all three. Order of 22 May 2000 <http://www.lapres.net/yahen.html>; Order of 11 August 2000 <http://www.lapres.net/yahen8.html>; Order of 20 November 2000 <http://www.lapres.net/yahen11.html>.

[134] There were three hearings in California. A hearing before the District Court in which a decision was filed on 7 November 2001: *Yahoo Inc. v LICRA*, 145 F Supp 2d 1168 (ND Cal 2001); an appeal to the 9th Circuit in which a ruling was filed on 23 August 2004: *Yahoo Inc. v LICRA*, 379 F 3d 1120 (9th Cir. 2004); and an *en banc* rehearing before the 9th Circuit in which a ruling was filed on 12 January 2006: *Yahoo Inc. v LICRA*, 433 F 3d 1199 (9th Cir. 2006).

[135] [2010] EWCA Crim 65.

[136] R Ibrahim, 'The Collective Punishment of Egypt's Christian Copts', *Middle East Forum*, 6 September 2012 <https://www.meforum.org/3338/egypt-christian-copts-collective-punishment>.

[137] Reuters, 'White House "Innocence Of Muslims" Request Denied: Google Will Not Remove Film From YouTube' *Huffington Post* 14 September 2012 <www.huffingtonpost.com/2012/09/14/white-house-innocence-of-_n_1885684.html>.

Arabia, and Egypt.[138] Google/YouTube were extremely bullish in their response. White House officials asked Google to reconsider whether the video had violated YouTube's terms of service. Google said that the video was within its guidelines, and added they would only 'further restrict the clip to comply with local law rather than as a response to political pressure'.[139]

In response to Google's bullish approach, courts around the world have dealt with the problems the movie has caused. A Brazilian court has ordered that YouTube remove the movies or face daily fines of $5,000.[140] In Egypt, Afghanistan, Pakistan, Bangladesh, and Sudan YouTube was blocked by local court orders or decrees of telecommunications regulators until in each case installed geo-blocks preventing the video from being locally accessed. Meanwhile back home (in YouTube terms) in California an action brought by one of the actresses seen in the movie, who claimed she was misled as to the nature of the movie, failed to see her gain the temporary restraining order she sought preventing YouTube from distributing the movie or trailer.[141] In rejecting her initial application Judge Fitzgerald of the District Court for the Central District of California noted that it was not clear the application had been properly served on all parties.[142] She then applied for a preliminary injunction on copyright infringement, an order also rejected by the court on the basis that 'Garcia [has not] established a likelihood of success on the merits. Even assuming both that Garcia's individual performance in the film is copyrightable and that she has not released this copyright interest, the nature of this copyright interest is not clear. Nor is it clear that Defendants would be liable for infringement.'[143] Upon appeal the Court of Appeals for the Ninth Circuit held that Garcia was entitled to a preliminary injunction because she was likely to succeed on the merits of her copyright claim. The court determined that Garcia likely owned an independent, copyrightable interest in her own performance in the film.[144] A later *en banc* decision of the Ninth Circuit though reversed that position.[145] The Court expressed its sympathy for Garcia but could not find in her favour 'at this stage of the proceedings, we have no reason to question Garcia's claims that she was duped by an unscrupulous filmmaker and has suffered greatly from her disastrous association with the *Innocence of Muslims* film. Nonetheless, the district court did not abuse its discretion when it denied Garcia's motion for a preliminary injunction under the copyright laws.'[146] Thus the route of using a copyright takedown notice to have the video removed from YouTube was closed. Currently the complete video cannot be found on YouTube. It was removed following the Ninth Circuit decision in favour of Garcia and has not been re-uploaded

---

[138] Ibid.

[139] Ibid.

[140] J Langlois, '"Innocence of Muslims" Ordered Removed from YouTube by Brazilian Court' *Global Post* 26 September 2012. This request has not been acceded to.

[141] *Garcia v Google Inc.* 743 F.3d 1258 (2014).

[142] *Garcia v Nakoula & Ors*, Case 2:12-cv-08315-MWF-VBK (CD Calif). Minute Order available at: <https://www.citmedialaw.org/sites/citmedialaw.org/files/2012-10-18-Minute%20Order%20on%20TRO.pdf>.

[143] *Garcia v Nakoula & Ors*, Case 2:12-cv-08315-MWF-VBK (CD Calif). Minute Order available at <http://pcmlp.socleg.ox.ac.uk/wp-content/uploads/2014/12/IAPCODEfinal.pdf>.

[144] *Garcia v Google Inc.* (n. 142).

[145] *Garcia v Google Inc.* D.C. No.2:12-cv-08315-MWF-VBK, 18 May 2015 <http://cdn.ca9.uscourts.gov/datastore/general/2015/05/18/12-57302%20EB%20opinion.pdf>.

[146] Ibid. 30.

by the copyright holder. However a 14-minute 'trailer' for the film may be found. It is preceded by a warning that 'the following content has been identified by the YouTube community as inappropriate or offensive to some audiences. Viewer discretion is advised.' The full 74-minute movie is however available from other sites.

Innocence of Muslims is a case very similar to the *Yahoo! France* cases: different cultural values and even legal values in different jurisdictions unable to agree a common approach. It is also very different to *Yahoo! France*. The ubiquitousness and open availability of SMPs turn everyone into a global publisher and SMPs themselves are going to have to ask themselves more clearly for which of their users' actions they ought to be responsible.

6.6 **Conclusions**

This chapter has covered a lot of ground: a number of unrelated legal concepts, privacy, the right to be offensive, blasphemy, and incitement to violence. In common they share a utility of social media platforms or SMPs. The modern internet experience has become focused on SMPs. A quick review of the most visited sites on the web shows that search engines and SMPs dominate. Google dominates as the most visited website but YouTube is no. 2, Facebook no. 3, Twitter no. 10, Instagram no. 13, VK no. 14,[147] Reddit no. 16, Weibo no. 20,[148] and LinkedIn no. 28. With the exception of Amazon, Taobao, TMall, eBay, and Wikipedia, all other sites in the top 25 are forms of search engines. With the exceptions of search and shopping, SMPs have come to define the modern user experience of the internet, yet strangely it is among the least regulated parts of the network. Most SMPs will allow anyone to post anything which does not offend against their decency and copyright policies. Thus you are much more likely to have a YouTube video removed because in the background a ten-second snippet of 'Empire State of Mind' can be heard playing on the radio than because your video offends a substantial number of people who belong to a faith with around 1.6 billion followers. This seems an odd way to promote freedom of speech: commercial speech seems to be given a higher order of protection than religious interests or other interests such as privacy and in *CTB*, *PJS*, and cases like them, a certified order of the court which is being willingly breached. I should state for the avoidance of doubt I am not in favour of censorship of SMPs and laws like the NetzDG law do not seem to be the answer, but perhaps the balance of interests and responsibilities of both users and SMPs themselves needs to be revisited. When a video or message is more likely to be removed because of incidental copyright inclusion rather than in accordance with a legal court order or because of potential offence to 1.6 billion people, the balance seems off. Maybe Facebook, Twitter, and YouTube/Google should reconsider Shaw's principle that 'Liberty means responsibility. That is why most men dread it.'[149]

---

[147] VK is a Russian language social networking site.
[148] Weibo is a Chinese language microblogging site.
[149] Source: *Oxford Dictionary of Quotations* (7th edn, OUP 2009).

TEST QUESTIONS

Question 1

People cannot say what they like on Twitter. It is a public space not a private one and all Twitter speech must be regulated accordingly. If you break the terms of an injunction you should expect to be prosecuted for contempt of court; trolls should expect prosecution under relevant criminal provisions while anyone who tweets 'You've got a week and a bit to get your shit together otherwise I'm blowing the airport sky high!' should expect to be treated as making a criminal threat or communication.

Discuss.

Question 2

Is there a right not to be offended in one's religious beliefs? Should YouTube take down copies of the movie *Innocence of Muslims*? Are they right to instead selectively block access to it on a country-by-country basis?

Question 3

According to Lord Toulson in *PJS* 'the court needs to be very cautious about granting an injunction preventing publication of what is widely known, if it is not to lose public respect for the law by giving the appearance of being out of touch with reality'.
Do you agree with him? Is Lord Toulson a cyber-libertarian?

FURTHER READING

Books

P Bernal, *The Internet, Warts and All: Free Speech, Privacy and Truth* (CUP 2018)

R Cohen-Almagor, *Speech, Media and Ethics: The Limits of Free Expression* (Palgrave 2008)

R Hayes and K Luther, *#Crime: Social Media, Crime, and the Criminal Legal System* (Palgrave 2018)

D Stewart (ed.), *Social Media and the Law* (2nd edn, 2017)

Chapters and articles

EB Laidlaw, 'What is a joke? Mapping the path of a speech complaint on social networks' in D Mangan and LE Gillies (eds.) *The Legal Challenges of Social Media* (Edward Elgar 2017)

G Letsas, 'Is S there a Right Not to Be Offended in one's Religious Beliefs?', in Lorenzo Zucca (ed.), *Law, State and Religion in the new Europe: Debates and Dilemmas* (CUP 2011)

J Bishop, 'The art of trolling law enforcement: A review and model for implementing "flame trolling" legislation enacted in Great Britain (1981–2012)' (2013) 27 *International Review of Law, Computers & Technology* 301

J Rowbottom, 'To Rant, Vent and Converse: Protecting Low Level Digital Speech' (2012) 71 *Cambridge Law Journal* 355

A Zuckerman, 'Common Law Repelling Super Injunctions, Limiting Anonymity and Banning Trial by Stealth', 30 *Civil Justice Quarterly* 223 (2011)

Defamation

Although the UK recognizes and seeks to protect the individual rights found in Article 10 of the European Convention on Human Rights and Article 19 of the Universal Declaration of Human Rights, one form of speech which has continually found itself subject to strict regulation in the UK is defamatory speech: that is speech harmful to the reputation of others. Defamation occurs when one publishes, or makes public, a statement which damages a person's reputation and tends to lower him in the estimation of right-thinking members of society. Defamatory statements are commonplace. Co-workers tend to defame other co-workers, students often defame lecturers, and individuals in pubs and bars defame a variety of public figures from footballers to actors to politicians. As an experiment think back to the last time you said something about someone that you either knew or suspected not to be true, or about which you were recklessly unaware of its veracity, and which was likely to lower the reputation of that person among those present.

It is a fact of life that we like to 'gossip' about other people,[1] and the best gossip as we all know is salacious and shocking gossip. This causes people to exaggerate, or even to make up stories about others to attain or secure social status. This was not an issue where the nature of discourse was just gossip. When gossip was passed over pints of beer or glasses of wine in the local pub or exchanged over coffees in Starbucks it was short-lived: in the air for a second and then gone again. Actionable defamation, that is the type of defamatory statement which causes a case to end up before a judge, was a world away from gossip. It tended to be statements published in the press or broadcast on television or radio. This is partly due to the extensive audience such statements could reach and partly due to the fact that a publisher or broadcaster indicated deep pockets which could be called upon to fulfil a damages award. As is the common theme of this book the nature of digital communication and the information society has changed all this. As was discussed at length in chapters 5 and 6 the nature of digital communications is that individuals now possess the broadcast abilities of the traditional mass media/broadcast sector. Further, as blogs, video and photo streams, IM platforms, and social network updates provide a semi-permanent record of statements, they lose the character of ephemera that gossip has. Finally, posts to blogs, social network sites, IM platforms, and video and photo sharing sites require the assistance of commercial internet service

---

[1] It is reported by the Social Issues Research Centre at the University of Oxford that gossip accounts for 55 per cent of male conversation time and 67 per cent of female time. See K Fox, *Evolution, Alienation and Gossip: The role of mobile telecommunications in the 21st century* SIRC <http://www.sirc.org/publik/gossip.shtml>.

providers and content hosts which assure the availability of deep pockets. It is therefore unsurprising that a number of defamation cases arising both from traditional media sites and from user-generated media entries have been brought in the UK and further afield.

7.1 **The tort of defamation**

The tort occurs when one individual makes a defamatory statement about another in which the defamed party may be identified.[2] The defamatory statement must be 'published' that is, it must be communicated to at least one other person. You may defame a natural person, either a living person[3] or a corporation;[4] although in English law it is against the public interest for local authorities, government-owned corporations, and political parties to bring defamation actions,[5] while trade unions lack personality to raise actions.[6] English law makes a distinction between libel: that is, a written or recorded defamatory statement including a statement made in a broadcast and slander: a spoken or otherwise transient defamatory statement. In general libel is treated more strictly by the courts than slander, at least in part on the basis that a recorded statement is more likely to be damaging than a transitory one.

Modern telecommunications and mass communication technologies have tended to blur this line somewhat. A statement made on a live television broadcast could reach a far greater audience than a statement written in a local newspaper or in an academic textbook and thus modern telecommunications caused an imbalance in the respective potential effects of libel and slander. Because of this s.166(1) of the Broadcasting Act 1990 states: 'For the purposes of the law of libel and slander (including the law of criminal libel so far as it relates to the publication of defamatory matter) the publication of words in the course of any programme included in a programme service shall be treated as publication in permanent form.' Digital communications have, of course, caused further imbalances in traditional defamation principles. As almost all content in the digital environment is recorded there can be little doubt that any defamatory statement contained therein would be subject to an action in libel rather than slander. Even in the unlikely event that the material was broadcast only as a live webcast which was not recorded, it would be treated as libel not slander for s. 201(1)(c) of the Broadcasting Act 1990 makes clear that a programme service includes 'any other service which consists in the sending, by means of a telecommunication system, of sounds or visual images or both'. Such a definition clearly includes all internet-based programme services from YouTube to Facebook Live.

---

[2] It is irrelevant whether or not you intended to identify the defamed party. If they *can* be identified they may then claim for defamation.

[3] Famously in *Rex v Ensor* (1887) 3 TLR 366 Stephen J stated: 'The dead have no rights and can suffer no wrongs. The living alone can be the subject of legal protection, and the law of libel is intended to protect them.' For a critique of this see FF Cameron, 'Defamation Survivability and the Demise of the Antiquated "Actio Personalis" Doctrine' (1985) 85 *Columbia Law Review* 1833.

[4] *Jameel v Wall Street Journal* [2007] 1 AC 359.

[5] *Derbyshire v Times Newspapers Ltd* [1993] AC 534; *Goldsmith v Boyrul* [1997] 4 All ER 268. However, it should be noted that individuals working within such organizations whose reputation is impaired could still commence proceedings. See *Reynolds v Times Newspapers Ltd* [1999] 4 All ER 609.

[6] *EETPU v Times Newspapers Ltd* [1980] 1 All ER 1097.

7.1.1 **Statements and publication**

When a defamatory statement is made, several issues arise. There are questions of who may be liable in damages, questions of when and where the statement was made, issues surrounding defences, and the role and potential liability for distributors of the defamatory statement. Although the law of defamation is well established and we have the assistance of the Defamation Acts 1996 and 2013 in interpreting the various roles and potential liabilities involved in an action for defamation, we find these issues have become extremely complex when dealing with a media that is capable of crossing borders, which keeps a constant record of all 'discussions', and which allows individuals access to a mass communication channel.

The first issue to address is who is responsible and potentially liable for an online defamatory statement? Primary liability for any defamatory statement rests with the author of the statement: that is the person who made the utterance or who wrote the defamatory text. Liability does not only rest with the author. Liability also arises for editors, publishers, and distributors of a defamatory statement. Distributors and publishers of defamatory statements have always proven to be popular defendants, or co-defendants, as they possess deep pockets, a character often not true of the author or even of the editor of the original libel. As distributors are in a particularly perilous position, distributors are rarely aware of all the content of the material they distribute, and even if they were they have little opportunity of knowing the veracity of statements made in material they distribute; they are offered a particular defence in s. 1 of the Defamation Act 1996, known somewhat unimaginatively as the distributor defence. This states that a distributor of a defamatory statement has a defence if he shows that he took reasonable care in relation to its publication, and he did not know, and had no reason to believe, that what he did caused or contributed to the publication of a defamatory statement. This defence, as we shall see, is important for ISPs and hosting services who cannot possibly be aware of all the content they host and/or supply. In fact the particular challenges faced by internet hosting services and ISPs, who deal with vastly more material than usual distributors of newspapers and magazines imagined in s. 1 of the 1996 Act, have led to the promulgation of a specific defence for operators of websites in s. 5 of the Defamation Act 2013, which will be discussed in more detail.

The next issue is where the harm occurs; although there are special considerations which arise with internet publication, which will be discussed further; the general rule on jurisdiction and harm is complex enough as was demonstrated in the case of *Berezovsky v Forbes, Inc. (No.1)*.[7]

 Case study *Berezovsky v Forbes, Inc. (No.1)*

Mr Berezovsky was a Russian businessman who at the time of the alleged defamation lived and worked in Russia. In 1996 *Forbes Magazine* published an article claiming that Mr Berezovsky was involved in criminal activity and labelling him as a Russian mafia godfather, insinuating that he was involved in the murder of television producer Vladislav Listiev.

---

[7] [2000] 1 WLR 1004.

Mr Berezovsky decided to litigate, claiming the article to be defamatory; surprisingly he chose to litigate in England. This seems a remarkable decision. Mr Berezovsky was living and working, at this time, in Russia; he was in fact a member of the Russian government holding the office of Deputy Secretary of the Security Council of the Russian Federation, while the magazine was published in the US. England therefore seemed an unusual forum for this dispute, but of course English libel laws are famously accommodating of plaintiffs, leading to complaints about so-called libel tourism.[8] Unsurprisingly, the defendant challenged the jurisdiction of the English courts. Evidence was laid before the court showing that of the 788,346 copies of the issue in question only 1,915 (0.25 per cent) were sold in England and Wales with over 98.9 per cent of the issues being sold in the US and Canada. Forbes claimed that as Mr Berezovsky was not resident in England and Wales and as the magazine was published in and marketed towards and overwhelmingly sold in the North American market the correct forum for this dispute was either Russia or the US. Mr Berezovsky countered that he had a considerable reputation to protect in England and Wales. He explained in an affidavit that 'Over the past several years I have had extensive contacts with England, in business, in government service and personally. During the years in which I pursued my career in international business and finance, I worked frequently in London and with persons and companies based in London. This is entirely understandable, given London's status as the international business and financial capital of Europe, where all of my business interests have been based, and of which Russia is an increasingly important part.'

The case eventually ended up before the House of Lords where Forbes's appeal was dismissed. In the leading judgment Lord Steyn found the necessary connection with the jurisdiction of the court was made out by the facts that Mr Berezovsky was a frequent visitor to England, owned an apartment in London, had an ex-wife and two children who lived in London, and had another two children who were students in England. There was also in Lord Steyn's words 'concrete evidence from three independent sources as to the effect of the Forbes article on Mr Berezovsky's business reputation' in England.[9]

Lord Steyn then dealt with three challenges to the assumption that the courts of England and Wales were the correct forum for the case, all of which are of key importance when dealing with issues of online jurisdiction as we shall see later when we discuss cases such as *Dow Jones v Gutnick*[10] and *Jameel v Dow Jones Inc.*[11] The first of these was whether Russia was a better forum for the case to be heard. Lord Steyn rejected this claim on the basis that 'only 19 copies [of the relevant issue of Forbes Magazine] were distributed in Russia . . . and most importantly . . . it is clear that a judgment in favour of the plaintiffs in Russia will not be seen to redress the damage to the reputations of the plaintiffs in England'.[12] Next, on the claim that the US was the better jurisdiction, Lord Steyn noted that: 'the connections of both plaintiffs with the United States are minimal. They cannot realistically claim to have reputations which need protection in the United States. It is therefore not an appropriate forum.'[13] Finally, and most importantly, Lord

---

[8] The Defamation Act 2013, s. 9 has taken steps to reduce the availability of libel tourism in England and Wales. It will be discussed in Section 7.1.2.

[9] *Berezovsky* (n. 7) 1010–11.

[10] [2002] HCA 56.

[11] [2005] EWCA Civ 75.

[12] *Berezovsky* (n. 7) 1014–15.

[13] Ibid. 1015.

Steyn addressed a claim raised by counsel for the appellant that 'the correct approach is to treat multi-jurisdiction cases like the present as giving rise to a single cause of action and then to ascertain where the global cause of action arose'.[14] Lord Steyn rejected this. He found that such an argument 'runs counter to well established principles of libel law . . . the present case is a multi-jurisdictional case. It is also a case in which all the constituent elements of the torts occurred in England . . . In such cases it is not unfair that the foreign publisher should be sued here.'[15] This last point is particularly important when dealing with online publication. Lord Steyn is directly rejecting a claim that when publication is of a global nature it is the role of the court to identify a single cause of action and raise a single claim where that cause arose; in the *Berezovsky* case this would probably be the US. Instead he reaffirms the principle of *lex loci delicti*: that is, wherever harm has occurred, those who are victims of that harm may raise an action. Thus a web page which is accessible worldwide may lead to an action in any jurisdiction in which the claimant's reputation has suffered. This is an application of the multiple publication rule (to which we will return). It states that whenever a new publication or republication of a defamatory statement takes place, a fresh cause of action arises wherever and whenever that occurs. This rule made sense in the real world when to republish a statement usually meant taking some form of affirmative action such as paying for redistribution or reprinting of the statement. In the digital environment though it has taken on a new dimension as material hosted on a single web server anywhere in the world may be continually republished in a variety of jurisdictions by the simple act of a new reader visiting the web page and downloading the defamatory statement to his computer screen. As we shall see, this has caused great difficulty for authors and publishers online.

7.1.2 Taking jurisdiction in claims against non-EU respondents

Such is the extent of the perceived injustice to publishers caused by the outcome of the *Berezovsky* case (and subsequent cases) that the law has been reformed in this area as part of the package of reforms brought forward in the Defamation Act 2013. The new law is found in s. 9 of the Act and sets out a series of standards for judges to apply in claims raised against respondents from outside the European Union, Iceland, Norway, and Switzerland.[16]

 Highlight Actions against a person not domiciled in the UK or EU

Defamation Act 2013: s. 9

(1) This section applies to an action for defamation against a person who is not domiciled—

  (a) in the United Kingdom;

  (b) in another Member State; or

➔

---

[14] Ibid. 1011.
[15] Ibid. 1012–13.
[16] Iceland, Norway, and Switzerland being the only non-EU Lugano Convention nations.

> ➡
>
>   (c) in a state which is for the time being a contracting party to the Lugano
>
>   (d) Convention.
>
> (2) A court does not have jurisdiction to hear and determine an action to which this section applies unless the court is satisfied that, of all the places in which the statement complained of has been published, England and Wales *is clearly the most appropriate place in which to bring an action in respect of the statement.*

The intent of this provision is to statutorily overrule the *Berezovsky* assumption that wherever harm has occurred those who are victims of that harm may raise an action. This is the specific response from Parliament to the challenge of the global digital network which sees communications replicated instantly and globally. As shall be discussed, the *Berezovsky* principle was to cause great difficulty with challenges founded upon minimal connections of the parties to the action with the jurisdiction of England and Wales but where the material could be accessed within the jurisdiction.[17] In essence the effect of s. 9 is to give statutory weight to the later decision of the Court of Appeal in *Jameel v Dow Jones, Inc.*[18] over the House of Lords decision in *Berezovsky*, a decision that would naturally be inferior in terms of judicial authority and precedence. The new standard does not, of course, prevent actions being brought against non-European respondents, it merely asks the judge in considering whether England and Wales is the most appropriate location for the hearing to balance the interests of justice in hearing the action in England and Wales with those of alternate jurisdictions.[19] The explanatory notes to the Act give guidance to Judges and Masters in deciding this: 'subsection (2) provides that a court does not have jurisdiction to hear and determine an action to which the section applies unless it is satisfied that, of all the places in which the statement complained of has been published, England and Wales is clearly the most appropriate place in which to bring an action in respect of the statement.' This means that in cases where a statement has been published in this jurisdiction and also abroad the court will be required to consider the overall global picture to determine where it would be most appropriate for a claim to be heard. It is intended that this will overcome the problem of courts readily accepting jurisdiction simply because a claimant frames their claim so as to focus on damage which has occurred in this jurisdiction only. This would mean that, for example, if a statement was published 100,000 times in Australia and only 5,000 times in England that would be a good basis on which to conclude that the most appropriate jurisdiction in which to bring an action in respect of the statement was Australia rather than England. There will however be a range of factors which the court may wish to take into account including, for example, the amount of damage to the claimant's reputation in this jurisdiction compared to elsewhere, the extent

---

[17] See *King v Lewis* [2004] EWCA Civ 1329 and *Jameel v Dow Jones* [2005] EWCA Civ 75 (discussed at 7.2.3).

[18] *Jameel*, ibid.

[19] As shall be seen in the discussion of *Sloutsker v Romanova* [2015] EWHC 2053 (QB), discussed at 7.2.3.

to which the publication was targeted at a readership in this jurisdiction compared to elsewhere, and whether there is reason to think that the claimant would not receive a fair hearing elsewhere.[20]

It must be said though that it is unlikely s. 9(2) would have changed the outcome in *Berezovsky* if it had been in effect at the time, given the strong wording of Lord Steyn's judgment. Further, the simple act of a new reader visiting the web page and download-ing the defamatory statement to his or her computer screen has caused great difficulty for authors and publishers online. The courts had already taken steps to close the win-dow of jurisdictional choice in cases such as *King v Lewis* and *Jameel v Dow Jones*.

7.1.3 **Defences**

The final general issue is to examine when defences may be raised to a claim in defa-mation. There are several defences; the most complete defence is truth.[21] This new statutory defence replaces the old common law justification defence that can be traced back to at least the case of *McPherson v Daniels* in 1829.[22] The new defence is arguably marginally wider than the old justification defence although it does follow the previ-ous formulation quite closely. It states that 'it is a defence to an action for defamation for the defendant to show that the imputation conveyed by the statement complained of is substantially true.' The interesting word there is substantially; there is no need for the defendant to be able to demonstrate that all aspects of the statement are true. This is the statutory version of the justification defence established in *Chase v News Group Newspapers Ltd*,[23] where the Court of Appeal indicated that in order for the defence of justification to be available 'the defendant does not have to prove that every word he or she published was true. He or she has to establish the "essential" or "substantial" truth of the sting of the libel.'[24] In short, were an individual to make a defamatory accusation about an individual; such as they are a paedophile who abused children at a hospital in Manchester, it would not matter to their defence if it turned out they could prove the truth of the charge of paedophilia but in fact following further investigation it was established that the abuse had taken place at a hospital in Oldham.

An alternative is 'honest opinion' which replaces the old 'fair comment' defence.[25] This defence may be available if the statement is expressed to be a personal opinion on a matter. To claim the defence, three factors need to be established: (1) the statement complained of must be a statement of opinion; (2) the statement should in general or specific terms give the basis of the opinion; and (3) it must be possible than an honest person could have held the opinion based upon the facts or available privileged state-ments at the time the opinion was given. It should be particularly noted though that the defence fails if it is established by the claimant that the respondent did not hold the opinion stated.[26] Thus, if I genuinely hold the opinion that the banking crisis and

---

[20] Explanatory note to s. 9 of the Defamation Act 2013. Available at: <www.legislation.gov.uk/ukpga/2013/26/notes/division/5/9>. See also *Sloutsker*, ibid.
[21] Defamation Act 2013 s. 2.
[22] (1829) 10B and C 263.
[23] [2002] EWCA Civ 1772.
[24] Ibid. [34].
[25] Defamation Act 2013 s 3.
[26] Defamation Act 2013 s. 3(5).

financial crash of 2008 was caused by the actions of one banker and I write a news story or blog entry stating this opinion and giving my reasons, I cannot be successfully sued by that banker in defamation because of the honest opinion defence, even if I am wrong in my assumptions. If though the banker could show that I only wrote the story because of a long-standing enmity between us, then any honest opinion defence would be swept aside.

The final generic defence open to the author of a defamatory statement is the public interest defence. In recent years the public interest defence has become known as 'the Reynolds defence' after the case that established the principles under which it may be raised. The case was *Reynolds v Times Newspapers Ltd and Others*,[27] and the principle established was that the public interest defence could be raised when a newspaper or other media organization published a defamatory statement if they could prove it was in the public interest to publish it and that it was the product of responsible journalism.[28] As with the other defences the Public Interest defence has been placed on a statutory footing by the Defamation Act 2013. The defence is found in s. 4 which states, 'It is a defence to an action for defamation for the defendant to show that (a) the statement complained of was, or formed part of, a statement on a matter of public interest; and (b) the defendant reasonably believed that publishing the statement complained of was in the public interest.' This defence seems simple to understand but is actually loaded with complexity. By replacing the old Reynolds defence with this new statutory defence, the old Reynold's test which contained clear guidance from Lord Nicholls as to the types of consideration which should be undertaken before deciding whether or not to publish a story is consigned to history. In the explanatory notes to the Act it is indicated it is the intent of the drafters to retain the Reynold's principles so it may be that the guidance given by Lord Nicholls remains applicable in the new framework but this also brings problems. As Jacob Rowbottom has pointed out, while the defence remains ostensibly the same the environment is different.[29] So while in *Reynolds*, and the later Privy Council case of *Seaga v Harper*,[30] the requirements of 'responsible journalism' formed the foundation of the privilege to publish, whether one were a professional journalist or an individual these requirements were 'devised in the late 1990s, before the full extent of the freedom to publish on the digital media had been realised. The standards

---

[27] [1999] UKHL 45.

[28] Lord Nicholls set out ten factors which should be taken account of in determining whether responsible journalism was practiced. They are: (1) The seriousness of the allegation. The more serious the charge, the more the public is misinformed and the individual harmed, if the allegation is not true. (2) The nature of the information, and the extent to which the subject matter is a matter of public concern. (3) The source of the information. Some informants have no direct knowledge of the events. Some have their own axes to grind, or are being paid for their stories. (4) The steps taken to verify the information. (5) The status of the information. The allegation may have already been the subject of an investigation which commands respect. (6) The urgency of the matter. News is often a perishable commodity. (7) Whether comment was sought from the claimant. He may have information others do not possess or have not disclosed. An approach to the plaintiff will not always be necessary. (8) Whether the article contained the gist of the claimant's side of the story. (9) The tone of the article. A newspaper can raise queries or call for an investigation. It need not adopt allegations as statements of fact. (10) The circumstances of the publication, including the timing.

[29] J Rowbottom, 'In the Shadow of Big Media: Freedom of Expression Participation and the Production of Knowledge Online' (2014) *Public Law* 491.

[30] [2008] UKPC 9.

of responsible journalism were therefore formulated with the practices associated with traditional investigative journalism in mind.' As Rowbottom notes these standards are difficult to meet even if you are a 'smaller title within the traditional mass media', they are almost impossible to meet if you are an individual blogger. The concern for digital media outputs is that they are overwhelmingly quick responses from individuals, they do not meet media standards of editorial control and thus it is unlikely that s. 4 will be very useful to individuals or even small to medium-sized digital media outlets. This is best captured by the response of Lord McNally, Minister of State for Justice, who when asked about the defence in Grand Committee responded:

> The noble Viscount, Lord Colville, and the noble Baroness, Lady Bakewell, explained to us what the responsible journalist does in these matters. The noble Lord, Lord Triesman, rightly reminded us of the question of what to do when the intention of the publisher or owner is to destroy a reputation. Do we give impunity to that? That is why, when our friends in the Libel Reform Campaign come close to asking for a blank cheque, I have to say that we cannot give it to them. We also have a responsibility, as well as a recognition that there is irresponsible publication. We are moving on to new media . . . I would say to Twitterers the Twittering equivalent of 'caveat emptor': 'Twitterer beware'. Twittering is not beyond the law. We somehow got the idea that new media is a law-free area. People are going to find that it is not.'[31]

It is clear therefore that the public interest defence is one to be approached with some degree of caution unless one is a professional journalist.

There are three further narrower and more specialized defences laid out in the 2013 Act. By s. 7 there is the defence of privilege. This allows the reporting of a number of official reports, documents, and records without fear of a subsequent action in defamation. There are absolute privileges for fair and accurate statements made in judicial proceedings[32] and contemporaneous reports of such proceedings,[33] and for statements made in either House of Parliament.[34] Qualified privilege is awarded for fair reports of judicial proceedings, Parliamentary proceedings (internationally not only the UK Parliament), public meetings and notices, press conferences at which matters of public interest are discussed, and reports of proceedings of a scientific or academic conferences held anywhere in the world.[35] The reason for these privileges is to allow journalists, including citizen journalists to report proceedings of judicial, legislative, and public meetings accurately without the risk of an action in defamation. By s. 6 there is a new extension of the privilege principle to peer-reviewed publications. This privileges publications in academic or scientific journals (whether paper published or electronic journals) as long as the publication is an academic or scientific publication and provided it has been peer-reviewed by the editor of the journal and at least one further peer-reviewer. The same privilege extends to the reviewer's report.[36] This privilege was brought forward after extended lobbying from the academic and scientific community following the case of *BCA v Singh*.[37]

---

31 HL Deb 19 December 2012, vol. 741, col. GC558.
32 *Watson v McEwan* [1905] AC 480.
33 Defamation Act 1996 s. 14.
34 Bill of Rights 1689. Although this may be waived under s. 13 of the Defamation Act 1996.
35 Defamation Act 1996 Sch.1 (as amended by s. 7 of the Defamation Act 2013).
36 Defamation Act 2013 s. 6(4).
37 [2009] EWHC 1101 (QB); [2010] EWCA Civ 350.

The final defence is one of particular importance to this text; it is the s. 5 defence available to operators of websites. This is a specialist defence open only to internet intermediaries. Although flagged up here it will be discussed in full at 7.3.3.

7.2 **Digital defamation: publication and republication**

It is clear that publication in any digital format qualifies as publication for the law of defamation. It is equally clear that in all cases the publication would be of the nature to raise an action in libel rather than slander. The first major issue raised by digital distribution of defamatory material is the method of distribution and what this means for publication and republication.

As we have already seen in *Berezovsky v Forbes*, the standard usually employed by a court in taking jurisdiction over a defamation action is that of *lex loci delicti*. This means that wherever a claimant suffers a loss or harm to his reputation an action may be raised. Traditional media outlets can take steps to limit their exposure to overseas actions. They have defined or specific markets where they broadcast or distribute their content. By targeting their publications or broadcasts to specific jurisdictions they can avoid extraterritorial claims as they are in a position to establish that, as publication took place only within a specific jurisdiction, harm could not have occurred outside that jurisdiction. This allows publishers and broadcasters to claim that publication did not take place in the jurisdiction in question even if a few copies of the defamatory material crossed borders in the bags or suitcases of travellers. Obviously, and as illustrated by *Berezovsky v Forbes*, once the publisher or broadcaster actively distributes their product in other states they run the risk of facing a libel action in any state in which they market their product. In *Berezovsky*, a key piece of evidence throughout was that *Forbes Magazine* had 566 subscribers in England and Wales and the issue in question sold a further 1,349 copies at newsstands. Thus traditional media publishers could balance the risks of being pursued in an overseas jurisdiction against the commercial benefits of trading in the jurisdiction.

The online distribution model is very different. A static or dynamic digital space (web page, SMP, or broadcast site) is stored and updated via a server. That server may then be accessed anywhere in the world, and at any time unless access to the server is geo blocked. At the risk of sounding repetitive it is the same central issue which has driven the discussion in chapters 4, 5, and 6: digital communications cross borders without challenge and may be stored and recovered at any time. The effect of this, when faced with the challenges raised by the law of defamation, is though potentially paralysing. Whereas previously publishers or broadcasters could choose to extend the audience for their publication or broadcast by entering a new market, or jurisdiction depending on whether you view this as a commercial or legal development, the suggested implication of digital publishing is that any publisher, no matter how small or localized their intended audience may be, could potentially be seen to publish simultaneously in every country worldwide where their content could be read, and even more potentially damaging: applying the principle in *Berezovsky*, every time their content was accessed by any user worldwide it would count for defamation law purposes as a republication of that content in the place where the user accessed it. Could defamation law really be that strict? If so would anyone publish anything which was remotely at risk of a defamation suit online given that they could potentially have to defend themselves in any court in any jurisdiction worldwide?

7.2.1 *Dow Jones v Gutnick*

The answer to some of these questions came in 2002 when the High Court of Australia handed down judgment in *Dow Jones & Co. Inc. v Gutnick*.[38] This case has many factual similarities to the *Berezovsky* case but was the first defamation case to answer the question 'does internet publication qualify as publication within a jurisdiction?'

 Case study *Dow Jones & Co. v Gutnick*

On 30 October 2000 *Barrons* magazine published an article entitled 'Unholy Gains' and placed a copy on the *Barrons Online* website.

The article raised a number of allegations about Mr Gutnick, a well-known Melbourne entrepreneur. It claimed that he was involved in the manipulation of stock prices, warning readers to avoid investment products with which the plaintiff was associated and calling for an investigation into the plaintiff's conduct by US securities regulators. It also questioned Mr Gutnick's connection with a convicted money launderer and tax evader called Nachum Goldberg and suggested that Mr Goldberg assisted Mr Gutnick in a tax evasion scheme by laundering money through religious charities.

Mr Gutnick raised a statement of claim in the Supreme Court of Victoria. In this he claimed he had been defamed within the State of Victoria both in print and online. Unlike *Berezovsky*, it seems a very small (though unspecified) number of physical copies of the magazine were distributed in Victoria.[39] Instead Mr Gutnick's claim focused upon the *Barrons Online* site. He produced evidence that there were 550,000 subscribers to the *Barrons Online* website worldwide at the relevant time: when questioned the defendant conceded that of that number 1,700 subscribers had paid by credit card from Australia, including several hundred subscribers in Victoria.

As with the *Berezovsky* case the defendant applied to have the proceedings stayed on the basis of the doctrine of *forum non conveniens*. The defendant claimed that the article was published in the US, specifically New Jersey, and that that was the correct forum for this claim. In particular the editor of *Barrons Online*, in an affidavit to the court, stated that: 'stories which were written and edited in New York are transmitted by a dedicated computer to [our] corporate campus in New Jersey. There the data is transferred from Barrons' two computers in New Jersey on to six further servers which hold the stories or articles. All six servers are physically located in New Jersey.'[40] At trial Hedigan J dismissed the defendant's claims citing with approval Lord Steyn's judgment in *Berezovsky*. Dow Jones sought leave to appeal to the Victoria Court of Appeal, but this was refused.

---

[38] [2002] HCA 56.
[39] *Gutnick v Dow Jones & Co. Inc.* [2001] VSC 305.
[40] Ibid. 309.

Almost three months later, Gleeson CJ and Hayne J granted special leave to appeal to the High Court of Australia.

The key issues in dispute in *Dow Jones* are exactly the same as in *Berezovsky*, but with the focus being on digital publishing rather than print publication. First, the court had to decide whether the article had been 'published' in Australia generally and Victoria in particular. The court examined both sides of the argument: the single publication argument put forward by Dow Jones which claimed that publication was a single event which took place in New Jersey and the multiple publication argument put forward by Mr Gutnick which argued that publication occurred wherever the consumer read the material and concluded that: '[b]ecause publication is an act or event to which there are at least two parties, the publisher and a person to whom material is published, publication to numerous persons may have as many territorial connections as there are those to whom particular words are published'.[41] Having established the multiple publication rule should apply equally to online publications as to other types of publications, they then turned their attention to the question of when an article was published in a given territory if it is made available via a web server in another jurisdiction.

 Highlight Gutnick before the High Court of Australia

Defamation is to be located at the place where the damage to reputation occurs. Ordinarily that will be where the material which is alleged to be defamatory is available in comprehensible form assuming, of course, that the person defamed has in that place a reputation which is thereby damaged. It is only when the material is in comprehensible form that the damage to reputation is done and it is damage to reputation which is the principal focus of defamation, not any quality of the defendant's conduct.

In the case of material on the World Wide Web, it is not available in comprehensible form until downloaded on to the computer of a person who has used a web browser to pull the material from the web server. It is where that person downloads the material that the damage to reputation may be done. Ordinarily then, that will be the place where the tort of defamation is committed.

The above is the key passage from the decision. It was the key passage both on a micro and a macro level. On the micro level it established that in *this* case the Supreme Court of Victoria was right to find jurisdiction, a finding that led eventually to Dow Jones settling the case for A$180,000 in damages and A$400,000 costs.[42] The effects on the macro level were much greater. The High Court of Australia had said explicitly what everyone had suspected following the *Berezovsky* decision: digital content hosted on a web server would be deemed to be 'published' at the point of access not at the point of storage. Thus a web server hosted in the US could publish material in any country which allowed access to that server. In other words an online publication could lead to litigation for defamation in potentially any jurisdiction worldwide.

---

[41] *Dow Jones* (n. 38) 63.
[42] ABC News, *Dow Jones settles Gutnick action*, 12 November 2004.

Some commentators suggested the potential chilling effects of *Dow Jones* on internet speech would be calamitous. The *New York Times* famously editorialized: 'To subject distant providers of on-line content to sanctions intent on curbing free speech— or even to 190 libel laws—is to undermine the internet's viability.'[43] Others though were more measured, pointing out that all the High Court of Australia had done was apply a well-established principle of libel laws that had been seen in a series of previous cases culminating in the *Berezovsky* case.[44] As these commentators pointed out, international communications and media had not proven to be hamstrung by the multiple publication rule in the past and there was no reason to suggest that things would be any different with online publications. Although the scale of international publication was undoubtedly magnified by online publishing, publishers had little to fear of being dragged before a succession of courts across the globe. As Professor Jonathan Zittrain pointed out, there still needs to be a reason for the court to take jurisdiction:

> The Australian court was unpersuaded by the 'pile on' argument that Gutnick could next sue the company in Zimbabwe, or Great Britain, or China. It pointed out that Gutnick himself lived in Australia, and Dow Jones quite explicitly sold subscriptions to the online Barron's to Australians. These facts helped Australia escape the dilemma of justifying almost any country's intervention if it was to justify its own. Without its special if not unique relationship to one party in the case, Australia may well have declined to intervene in the dispute.[45]

There is therefore little risk of a greater chilling effect with online speech as with any other form of speech. In fact it can be argued that as we saw in chapter 5, with the ease of access and widespread audience offered through digital publication, online publishing finds itself protected from the chilling effects of defamation law to a greater extent than other forms of publishing. Additionally, an order of an extraterritorial court can only be enforced against the author of a statement found to be defamatory if either: (a) the author is resident in or has assets domiciled within the jurisdiction in question, or (b) the local courts where the author is resident recognize the order of the foreign jurisdiction, something which a US court is unlikely to do when faced with libel orders from overseas.[46]

7.2.2 *Loutchansky v Times Newspapers*: republication and limitation

The fall-out from the *Gutnick* decision was predictable. Those states perceived to be plaintiff-friendly in defamation actions found cases were quickly raised following online publication of allegedly defamatory material. At the forefront of this were the courts of England and Wales.

---

[43] Editorial, 'A Blow to Online Freedom', *New York Times* 11 December 2002.

[44] D Rolph, 'The Message, Not the Medium: Defamation, Publication and the Internet in *Dow Jones & Co Inc v Gutnick*' (2002) 24 *Sydney Law Review* 263; M Richardson and R Garnett, 'Perils of Publishing on the Internet: Broader Implications of *Dow Jones v Gutnick*' (2004) 31 *Griffith Law Review* 4.

[45] J Zittrain, 'Be Careful What You Ask For: Reconciling a Global Internet and Local Law' in A Thierer (ed.) *Who Rules the Net?: Internet Governance and Jurisdiction* (Cato Institute 2003).

[46] *Telnikoff v Matusevitch* 702 A 2d 230 (Md 1997); *Bachchan v India Abroad Publications Inc*, 585 NYS 2d 661 (NY 1992).

The first of a series of cases which have helped establish the level of connection required for the English courts to take jurisdiction over an international defamation action was *Loutchansky v Times Newspapers Ltd*.[47] The *Loutchansky* case is very similar to the *Berezovsky* case.

 Case study *Loutchansky v Times Newspapers Ltd*

Dr Loutchansky, a Russian national, claimed that two news stories published in *The Times* newspaper on 8 September 1999 and 14 October 1999 were defamatory. The stories claimed that Dr Loutchansky was the boss of a major Russian criminal organization and that he was involved in, among other things, money laundering. The defendants accepted that the articles were defamatory of Dr Loutchansky, but argued qualified privilege, and also argued that Dr Loutchansky's action was time barred.

This claim was based on s. 4A of the Limitation Act 1980 which states that in actions of libel or slander 'no such action shall be brought after the expiration of one year from the date on which the cause of action accrued'. Dr Loutchansky had failed to raise the case in time, but he argued that, in relation to material *The Times* placed on its web servers, each time the material was accessed by a reader was a fresh publication of the stories, thus allowing him to comply with the Limitation Act. This is another application of the debate between a single publication rule and the multiple publication rule already discussed extensively in *Berezovsky* and *Gutnick*: in this case it is not the place of publication which is an issue; it is the time of the publication.

As we have already seen, common law courts would tend to apply the multiple publication rule when approaching this issue. In this case counsel for the newspaper argued that this approach had been rendered incompatible with the Limitation Act through the application of internet technology. Lord Lester of Herne Hill QC, acting for the respondents, argued that the Court of Appeal should adopt a single publication rule on the basis that the emergence of the internet and the extensive period for which material was archived and accessible through online services meant that, should the multiple publication rule be endorsed, there would be ongoing liability of an open-ended nature for material placed online. This he argued was incompatible with the intent of the Limitation Act which was to provide for a limited period following publication for an action to be brought.[48] Lord Lester went on to claim that the existence of internet-based libraries of newspaper stories provided an important public service and it was the law that was out of step with this service. If the law did not change he warned that: 'if a newspaper defendant which maintained a website of back numbers was to be indefinitely vulnerable to claims in defamation for years and even decades after the initial hard copy and internet publication, such a rule was bound to have an effect on the preparedness of the media to maintain such websites, and thus to limit freedom of expression'.[49]

[47] [2002] QB 783.
[48] Ibid. 814.
[49] Ibid. 817.

The court considered all Lord Lester's arguments, but ultimately dismissed them. They did not accept that the effect of the multiple publication rule in the information society was to undermine the intent of the Limitation Act. In the opinion of the court, given by Lord Phillips MR, it was pointed out that an action based on internet publication was subsidiary to the action based on print publication. In other words each publication was a separate action with separate twelve-month limitation periods, and essentially with separate quanta of damages attached thereto: as Lord Phillips says, 'the scale of such publication and any resulting damage is likely to be modest compared with that of the original publication'.[50] On this basis the court dismissed the claim that the multiple publication rule interfered with the working and intent of the Limitation Act.

This only left the claim that the multiple publication rule was out of step with the new order of internet publication and record keeping. The court quickly rejected this claim as well. Lord Phillips stated that although the court accepted:

> that the maintenance of archives, whether in hard copy or on the Internet, has a social utility ... [we] consider that the maintenance of archives is a comparatively insignificant aspect of freedom of expression. Archive material is stale news and its publication cannot rank in importance with the dissemination of contemporary material. Nor do we believe that the law of defamation need inhibit the responsible maintenance of archives. Where it is known that archive material is or may be defamatory, the attachment of an appropriate notice warning against treating it as the truth will normally remove any sting from the material.[51]

In other words once the publisher of the material becomes aware of the fact that it may be defamatory they may take simple steps to limit their exposure by simply adding an addendum to the archive material informing readers of this. This would work in much the same way as a retraction in print.

The passing of the Defamation Act has seen *Loutchansky* at least partially overruled. New provisions contained in s. 8 have introduced a specific single publication rule for the purposes of s. 4A of the Limitation Act. The rule though 'does not apply in relation to the subsequent publication if the manner of that publication is materially different from the manner of the first publication.'[52] The Act gives some definition to this in s. 8(5) noting that 'in determining whether the manner of a subsequent publication is materially different from the manner of the first publication, the matters to which the court may have regard include (amongst other matters): (a) the level of prominence that a statement is given; and (b) the extent of the subsequent publication'. This suggests that any attempt to use s. 8 to unreasonably avoid a defamation claim by first publishing the information in a hidden section of a website or blog before moving it to greater prominence once the limitation period has expired will fail. In relation to the *Loutchansky* case as the material was not moved or altered, just continually downloaded s. 8 would likely have been effective to bar Dr Loutchansky's claim. This is the key mischief s. 8 seeks to remedy. As every access is a republication, s. 4A of the Limitation Act had been in effect rendered pointless, absent the point made by Lord Phillips on quantum of damages; s. 8 ensures the effectiveness of s. 4A is reinvigorated.

---

[50] Ibid. 818.
[51] Ibid. 817–818.
[52] s. 8(4).

7.2.3 **Multiple publication and jurisdiction**

The next case to develop this principle was the case of *King v Lewis*.[53] This involved an action brought by Mr Don King, a famous boxing promoter and US resident, against three defendants: Mr Lennox Lewis, a UK citizen, but at the time a US resident; Mr Judd Burstein, a New York-based lawyer and US citizen; and Lion Promotions LLC, a Nevada-based promotion company. Mr Lewis and Lion Promotions were suing Mr King and a co-defendant, Mike Tyson, in New York claiming interference with an agreement between Mr Lewis and Mr Tyson in connection with a proposed rematch of their world heavyweight title contest. The proceedings in London followed the publication of two online articles surrounding the New York litigation. The first appeared on the site *fight-news.com* on 5 July 2003, was written by Mr Burstein and was entitled 'My Response to Don King.' In this Mr Burstein claimed that Mr King had made anti-Semitic remarks about him and accused him of bigotry.[54] The second appeared on *boxingtalk.com* on 8 July 2003 and was an interview with Mr Burstein. It repeated all the claims made by Mr Burstein in the earlier article.[55] Although it may seem that the Courts of New York were the most appropriate forum for a dispute between three US-based individuals and a US-based corporation involving claims made on US-based websites, Mr King chose to raise his action in England.

In dismissing an appeal from Mr Justice Eady's decision to allow Mr King to serve the claim form out of the jurisdiction, the Court of Appeal examined Mr King's claim to have the case heard in England and Wales. The court seemed to be convinced that Mr King had a reputation to protect in England,[56] and appeared to be particularly swayed by the fact that Mr King 'would wish to adduce evidence from a number of witnesses based in the UK, on such matters as his reputation and connection with this country and, in particular, his links with Jewish charity work in London'.[57] What is less satisfactory is that the court never sought, or was given, any actual evidence of publication occurring in England and Wales. Instead they were content to state that:

> The libels alleged consist in two texts stored on websites based in California. In the ordinary way they can be, and have been, downloaded here. It is common ground that by the law of England the tort of libel is committed where publication takes place, and each publication generates a separate cause of action. The parties also accept that a text on the Internet is published at the place where it is downloaded. Accordingly there is no contest but that subject to any defences on the merits the respondent has been libelled in this jurisdiction.[58]

The court never investigated the degree of publication in England and Wales. Were the stories downloaded on one occasion or one hundred? We may never know for this dispute was merely about the procedural issue of whether the courts of England and Wales could issue a claim against the defendants. The court was not interested in discussing the merits of the case at this time; this would be a matter for later trial.[59] It

---

[53] [2004] EWCA Civ 1329.
[54] Ibid. [8].
[55] Ibid. [9].
[56] Ibid. [13].
[57] Ibid. [38].
[58] Ibid. [2].
[59] There appears to have been no later trial on the merits of the claim. It may be suspected this was a negotiating lever designed to reach a settlement of the dispute in New York.

is unfortunate though that the court did not consider this issue as on the wording of the decision of the Court of Appeal in *King* a single download within the jurisdiction of England and Wales would be sufficient to enable a libel action to be raised within this jurisdiction if the plaintiff had a reputation to protect in the jurisdiction.

King v Lewis may be seen as the archetypal case of forum shopping and the reason why we need s. 9 of the Defamation Act 2013. Earlier I argued that s. 9 in fact makes little difference to the day-to-day operation of the courts in online defamation cases. This is because of the decision of the Court of Appeal in *Jameel v Dow Jones Inc.*[60] This is another in the long line of cases starting with *Berezovsky* and including *Gutnick* in which an international businessman has challenged stories in US-based business-oriented publications which accuse him of links to organized crime.

 Case study *Jameel v Dow Jones Inc.*

Saudi businessman Yousef Jameel and his brother Mohammed Jameel were accused in an article in the *Wall Street Journal* of providing financial support for al Qaeda. The story arose when the US obtained secret al Qaeda documents relating to the formation of the al Qaeda movement in 1988. Among these documents was one called 'the Golden Chain' which purported to list 20 Saudi financial backers of Osama Bin Laden: on this list was Mr Jameel. The *Wall Street Journal* published a news story based upon this discovery entitled 'War on Terror' by Glenn Simpson on 18 March 2003 and placed it on the *wsj.com* website. Via the website one could link to the list of names on the Golden Chain.[61]

On 15 April 2003 Mr Jameel's solicitors wrote to Dow Jones asking them to remove the Golden Chain document from their website and warning their client would take action to 'protect his reputation in England'.[62] When Dow Jones refused to do so a claim was raised in the High Court. Mr Justice Eady found in favour of the plaintiff but Dow Jones immediately appealed to the Court of Appeal and it was in the judgment of the court, handed down by Lord Phillips MR, that we see a new approach to internet defamation cases in England and Wales develop.

The question which was to become the focus of much of the court's time was whether Mr Jameel had suffered any actual harm in England and Wales. While Mr Jameel managed to force an admission from Dow Jones that there were approximately six thousand subscribers to *wsj.com* in England and Wales,[63] Dow Jones countered that only five subscribers had actually followed the hyperlink from the story to read the Golden Chain document, and that of these five one was Mr Jameel's solicitor, one was a consultant to the claimant's businesses, and another was a director of a business associated with Mr Jameel. In the words of Lord Phillips, '[t]hey are members of the claimant's camp'.[64] With only two subscribers having apparently read the defamatory document who were

---

[60] [2005] EWCA Civ 75.
[61] Ibid. [8].
[62] Ibid. [14].
[63] Ibid. [16].
[64] Ibid. [17].

not connected to the litigation, the questions for the court were whether a substantial tort had taken place and/or whether an abuse of process would occur should the claim be allowed to proceed. On the former issue Lord Philips concluded that '[i]f the claimant succeeds in this action and is awarded a small amount of damages, it can perhaps be said that he will have achieved vindication for the damage done to his reputation in this country, but both the damage and the vindication will be minimal. The cost of the exercise will have been out of all proportion to what has been achieved. The game will not merely not have been worth the candle, it will not have been worth the wick.'[65] On the latter he concluded: [66]

 Highlight Defamation and abuse of process

It would be an abuse of process to continue to commit the resources of the English court, including substantial judge and possibly jury time, to an action where so little is now seen to be at stake. Normally where a small claim is brought, it will be dealt with by a proportionate small claims procedure. Such a course is not available in an action for defamation where, although the claim is small, the issues are complex and subject to special procedure under the Civil Procedure Rules.

It can now clearly be seen that s. 9 and *Jameel* follow similar reasoning, although arguably s. 9 goes further than *Jameel* in that it allows the court to dismiss applications where there may be a sufficient connection with the jurisdiction of England and Wales, that is, the *Jameel* standard, but where there is an identifiable jurisdiction in which it would be 'more appropriate' to bring the action. It is only these few cases though where the court may be convinced that the English courts are inappropriate, though sufficiently connected with the case, that s. 9 will be of impact.

As we awaited the first cases to be decided under the Defamation Act 2013 we got one final major decision made under the old legal settlement, *Sloutsker v Romanova*.[67] Mr Sloutsker is a Russian citizen and businessman. He was from 2002 to 2010 a Senator of the Russian Senate. In 2011 he emigrated to Israel where he still lives. Ms Romanova is a journalist who writes for the *Novaya Gazeta* newspaper and other outlets. Her husband was an ex-employee of one of Mr Sloutsker's companies. He was prosecuted and imprisoned in Russia for stealing assets from Mr Sloutsker's company. During 2011 and 2012 it was alleged that Ms Romanova wrote a number of libellous stories about Mr Sloutsker. Four publications were complained of in the claim: '(1) A blog post written by the defendant on the website of the Moscow-based radio station Echo Moscow; (2) and (3) two articles quoting the defendant published on the Russian website gazeta.ru; and (4) a programme broadcast on Radio Liberty.'[68] These variously contained a number of

---

[65] Ibid. [69].

[66] Ibid. [70].

[67] Although the Defamation Act 2013 came into effect on 1 January 2014 given the time delay in complex defamation actions most cases currently still being heard commenced before that date and are governed by the previous law. See e.g. *Bewry v Reed Elsevier (UK) Ltd* [2014] EWCA Civ 1411 as well as *Sloutsker v Romanova* [2015] EWHC 2053 (QB).

[68] *Sloutsker*, ibid. [7].

defamatory claims including 'that the Claimant had put a contract out for the murder of Alexei Kozlov, which was to be carried out whilst Mr Kozlov was being transferred to prison' (in the blogpost) and 'that the Claimant had ordered the fabrication of evidence in the criminal prosecution of Alexei Kozlov and had put a contract out for the murder of Mr Kozlov, which was to be carried out whilst Mr Kozlov was being transferred to prison' (the second article).[69]

The key question was could Mr Sloutsker, an Israeli resident Russian citizen find sufficient connection to the jurisdiction of England and Wales to successfully raise a defamation claim against a Russian resident Russian citizen? The analysis of this is spread across two judgments, the March 2015 judgment[70] and the July 2015 judgment.[71] In the March judgment Warby J reviewed the legal position. He recognized that the law was subject to change once s. 9 of the Defamation Act 2013 came into effect but that this did not apply to the case before him.[72] Instead he applied the common law test from *Berezovsky* and *Jameel*, that there must be a 'real and substantial tort' within the jurisdiction of the court.[73] He gave considerable weight to Lord Woolf MR's words in *King v Lewis*:

> The more tenuous a claimant's connection with this jurisdiction and the more substantial any publication abroad, the weaker the presumption in favour of England and Wales being the natural forum for the claim . . . the same principles apply to internet publication as apply to hard copy publication, except that the court's discretion in an internet context 'will tend to be more open-textured than otherwise'. It is clear from the context in which Lord Woolf made that remark that he intended it to be taken as an indication that the court should not be shy of allowing foreigners who publish via the internet to be sued in this jurisdiction, given that such publishers will have chosen to disseminate their information via a global medium.[74]

He also noted that 'in *King* the Court of Appeal rejected "out of hand" a submission that the court should take into account whether or not the defendant had "targeted" this jurisdiction, concluding that this was too subjective and nebulous a criterion, liable to manipulation and "much more likely to diminish than enhance the interests of justice."'[75] On this basis Warby J found that significant publication had taken place in the UK: 'Even on the defendant's figures, however, and allowing for the qualifications she puts forward, the sting of the allegations made on each of the Blogpost, the Second Article and the Third Article could easily have reached as many as 60,000 readers in this jurisdiction.'[76] This, along with the fact that the claimant is 'very well known' among the Russian and Jewish communities in the UK and has business interests in the UK[77] was enough to convince Warby J that the High Court could take jurisdiction over the case.[78]

In the July 2015 judgment Warby J revisits and develops much of this. He records that the claimant has provided 'further evidence of his links with this jurisdiction, referring

---

[69] Ibid. [9].
[70] [2015] EWHC 545 (QB).
[71] [2015] EWHC 2053 (QB).
[72] [2015] EWHC 545 (QB) [39].
[73] Ibid. [41].
[74] Ibid. [42]–[43].
[75] Ibid. [44].
[76] Ibid. [69].
[77] Ibid. [59].
[78] Ibid. [79].

to several visits to London over the past few months. I established that these were not all in connection with this case, but included business visits relating to real estate investment. He also explained his intention to relocate to London with his family over the next 2 years. Family means his 16-year-old son and 11-year-old daughter and his parents, both in their 80s but in good health. These are matters of obvious relevance to the extent of any need for vindication.'[79] Finding in favour of the claimant Warby J concludes:

> These were serious libels. The allegation of conspiracy to murder is the most serious, but the addition of imputations of corruption makes the matter worse. The allegations were published to a relatively substantial audience in this jurisdiction, where the claimant has a substantial and valuable reputation. My assessment of him as a witness is that he is a robust character, and that whilst his evidence of distress is genuine he has not suffered lasting emotional injury. He is however entitled to a sum that will vindicate him in the eyes of interested third parties who are unlikely to read this judgment. Adopting the approach I have indicated above, and taking account of all the factual matters I have identified, I have reached the conclusion that the appropriate global award of damages to compensate for the injury to reputation, and to feelings, and to ensure adequate vindication in respect of these serious allegations is £110,000.[80]

There is much about this judgment that is surprising. It is surprising that Warby J placed more emphasis on the judgments in *King* and *Berezovsky* than he did on *Jameel* given that most cases post-*Jameel* have followed that more closely than certainly *Berezovsky*. It is also surprising that having acknowledged in his judgment s. 9 of the Defamation Act he applied more closely the apparently outdated jurisprudence of *Berezovsky* and *King* rather than the fresher approach found in *Jameel*. Admittedly s. 9 was of no relevance to the case with the claim having begun before s. 9 came into effect, however it is suggested *Jameel* could have been applied more robustly. While admittedly the finding that 'the Blogpost, the Second Article and the Third Article could easily have reached as many as 60,000 readers in this jurisdiction' lifts it far from *Jameel* territory and more towards *King* in terms of volume, we should bear in mind the words of Gray J, another case *Al Amoudi v Brisard*, 'I am unable to accept that under English law a claimant in a libel action on an Internet publication is entitled to rely on a presumption of law that there has been substantial publication.'[81] In *Sloutsker* Warby J seemed to make such an assumption. All the figures which lead him to conclude 'the Blogpost, the Second Article and the Third Article could easily have reached as many as 60,000 readers in this jurisdiction' are extrapolated from general visitor numbers. This signals a return to the jurisprudence of *Berezovsky* and *King*: it equates availability with consumption and assumes that harm follows. Beyond this there are issues surrounding the level of damages awarded. To award £110,000 on that basis that 'He [the claimant] is however entitled to a sum that will vindicate him in the eyes of interested third parties who are unlikely to read this judgment' is barely credible. Damages may only be awarded as compensation for harm, unless punitive or exemplary damages are awarded, which was not the case here.[82] To suggest compensatory damages be set at a level to send a message to those 'unlikely to read this judgment' is baffling. As the claim was essentially

---

[79] [2015] EWHC 2053 (QB) [90].
[80] Ibid. [92].
[81] [2007] 1 WLR 113, 123.
[82] [2015] EWHC 2053 (QB), [74].

unchallenged, the defendant having effectively broken off all communication with the court, there was no appeal. It appears that having vindicated his reputation by winning in the High Court the claimant has taken no further action.

It seems likely that *Sloutsker* will be little more than a footnote in the history of defamation actions. Anyone who has begun an action since 1 January 2014 has to meet the more stringent test of s. 9 of the Defamation Act 2013. This is not to say that *Sloutsker* could not have met this standard had it been applied, it is simply to record that Sloutsker is unlikely to reset the steady jurisprudence the High Court and Court of Appeal has developed post-*Jameel*.

7.3 **Intermediary liability**

Finding a court willing to take jurisdiction over your claim is only the first stage in establishing a successful libel claim. Next you have to correctly identify the author, publisher, or distributor of the defamatory statement and have them brought before the court. In traditional publishing this is usually quite simple. The author often attaches his or her name to the article, byline, or book in question. The publisher is always identifiable by the addition of publishers' details in nearly all commercially produced material and the distributor will usually include the person who sold you the material in the first place. As with almost everything in the information society the addition of the digital elements of distribution confuses the usual principle. When the author of a defamatory statement signs him or herself as *noxious2256*, and when the site itself is published by an offshore anonymous corporation apparently domiciled in Panama or Russia it can prove difficult, if not impossible, to identify those primarily liable for the defamatory statement.[83] If you have been defamed online it seems all too often that the only party which can be identified as being liable is the ISP or local host who has carried the defamatory statement, or who has allowed access to it. Thus it is not surprising that an extensive body of litigation has grown up around the liability of ISPs and local hosts for hosting and carrying defamatory content.

7.3.1 *Godfrey v Demon Internet*

The first examination of ISP liability in the UK is to be found in the case of *Godfrey v Demon Internet Service*.[84]

 Case study *Godfrey v Demon Internet Service*

Dr Laurence Godfrey was a lecturer in physics, mathematics, and computer science based in London. On 13 January 1997, a posting, apparently originating in the US, was made to an ➥

---

[83] One way around this is the so-called Blaney Blarney order. See D Cran and G Warren, 'Service by Twitter—The UK Courts Embrace Technology' (2010) 21 *Entertainment Law Review* 81.
[84] [1999] EWHC 244 (QB).

→

internet newsgroup *soc.culture.thai* which, although we are not told the exact nature of it, is referred to by Moreland J as 'squalid, obscene and defamatory of the Plaintiff'.

Demon Internet carried the *soc.culture.thai* forum and stored postings for about a fortnight during which time the posting was available to be read by its customers.

On 17 January 1997, Dr Godfrey sent a fax to Demon Internet informing them that the posting was a forgery and that he was not responsible for its posting and requesting them to remove the posting from their Usenet news server as it was defamatory of him.

The defamatory posting was not removed as requested but remained available on the Demon Usenet server until its expiry on 27 January 1997. As a result of this Dr Godfrey raised a defamation action against Demon Internet.

There were two primary questions at issue. The first was, in applying the multiple publication rule were Demon Internet the publishers of the statement on each of the occasions a Demon customer accessed it via the Demon Server? The second was, could Demon avail itself of the defences contained in s. 1 of the Defamation Act 1996? On the first issue Moreland J was clear: 'In my judgment the Defendants were clearly not the publisher of the posting defamatory of the Plaintiff within the meaning of Section 1(2) and 1(3) and incontrovertibly can avail themselves of Section 1(1)(a).'[85] He was, unfortunately for Demon Internet, equally as unequivocal on the second question: 'However the difficulty facing the Defendants is Section 1(1)(b) and 1(1)(c). After the 17th January 1997 after receipt of the Plaintiff's fax the Defendants knew of the defamatory posting but chose not to remove it from their Usenet news servers. In my judgment this places the Defendants in an insuperable difficulty so that they cannot avail themselves of the defence provided by Section 1.'[86]

In effect the decision of *Godfrey* is to treat information society service providers as akin to distributors, or republishers, that is, they are immune from suit, under s. 1 of the Defamation Act 1996, until such time as they are made aware of the nature of the defamatory material. At this point then under s. 1(1)(c), their immunity is stripped and by s. 1(1)(b) they are required to 'take reasonable care in relation to its publication': in practice they must decide whether the statement is likely to be defamatory and if they believe it may be they must take steps to prevent further distribution or republication of the statement or face liability. This provides a balanced approach where information society providers are not expected to actively monitor content they carry and/or host but where, unlike the position in the US following the promulgation of §230 of the Communication Decency Act, liability may arise from a failure to act once they have been made aware of the defamatory nature of the content in question.

7.3.2 **Intermediary defences: the E-Commerce Directive and Regulations**

Soon after the *Godfrey* decision a change was made to the UK law in this area. The European Commission had for some time been looking to harmonize European law

[85] Ibid. [19].
[86] Ibid. [20].

in this area and in the Electronic Commerce Directive[87] a number of provisions were brought forward to harmonize the liability of ISPs for (a) carrying, (b) caching, and (c) hosting material including obscene material and defamatory material.

 Highlight Electronic Commerce Directive, Arts. 12–14

Article 12: Where an information society service is provided that consists of the transmission in a communication network of information provided by a recipient of the service, or the provision of access to a communication network, Member States shall ensure that the service provider is not liable for the information transmitted.

    Article 13: Where an information society service is provided that consists of the transmission in a communication network of information provided by a recipient of the service, Member States shall ensure that the service provider is not liable for the automatic, intermediate and temporary storage of that information, performed for the sole purpose of making more efficient the information's onward transmission to other recipients of the service upon their request.

    Article 14: Where an information society service . . . consists of the storage of information provided by a recipient of the service, Member States shall ensure that the service provider is not liable for the information stored at the request of a recipient of the service, on condition that: (a) the provider does not have actual knowledge of illegal activity or information and, as regards claims for damages, is not aware of facts or circumstances from which the illegal activity or information is apparent; or (b) the provider, upon obtaining such knowledge or awareness, acts expeditiously to remove or to disable access to the information.

Article 12 creates a 'mere conduit' defence similar to that given to telecommunications companies and which protects them from slander claims 'published' by the telephone network. This defence will not apply if the ISP originated or modifies the content of the message. Article 13 extends a caching defence. Again there are requirements that the ISP does not originate or modify the content of the message, but with this defence comes a further requirement that 'the provider acts expeditiously to remove or to disable access to the information it has stored upon obtaining actual knowledge of the fact that the information at the initial source of the transmission has been removed from the network, or access to it has been disabled, or that a court or an administrative authority has ordered such removal or disablement'.[88] This requires ISPs who retain cache copies of web pages or other content to remove such copies from their system once they become aware that the original has been removed for whatever reason. Failure to do so may expose such ISPs to liability for the content they cache. Article 14 provides that ISPs who host material have a form of distributor defence not dissimilar to that seen in *Godfrey*. In harmonizing the rules for liability of information society service providers the E-Commerce Directive does remarkably little to change the previous UK law, with perhaps the only major change being the introduction of the take-down requirement for cache copies found in Art.13(1)(e).

---

[87] Directive 2000/31/EC.
[88] Art 13(1)(e).

The UK gave effect to the E-Commerce Directive in the E-Commerce (EC Directive) Regulations 2002.[89] Regulations 17, 18, and 19 repeat the wording of the Articles 12, 13, and 14 almost verbatim. A significant addition to the Directive's provisions is though to be found in reg. 22. Reflecting criticisms made of the Directive in an earlier DTI consultation, reg. 22 attempts to address the issue of what constitutes 'actual knowledge' for the purpose of regs. 18 and 19. This provides an illustrative list of factors which a court may consider in determining whether a service provider has received notice through any means of contact that the service provider has made available, as required by reg. 6(1)(c).[90] To date, the Regulations appear to have functioned extremely smoothly. Despite some initial concerns that the Regulations may be abused by individuals and organizations who sought to use the notification procedure to take down critical comment, this appears not to have been the case.

Several cases have examined the intermediary defences. The first was *Bunt v Tilley & Ors*.[91] Mr Bunt claimed that Mr Tilley and two other individuals had made defamatory statements about him using online services. He wished also to bring proceedings against three information service providers on the basis that the individual defendants published the offending words 'via the services provided' by their ISPs, although as Eady J pointed out he did not plead that any of the three corporate defendants had at any stage hosted any website relevant to the claims.[92] The foundation of Mr Bunt's claims against the ISPs seemed to be that they had enabled the individuals in question to publish the allegedly defamatory statements by providing them with a connection to the internet. This claim raised substantial points of significance as to the basis upon which a provider of such services could, if at all, be liable in respect of material which is simply communicated via the services which they provide. Should Eady J side with Mr Bunt's interpretation of the Regulations, ISPs could be liable for any material they carried across their network, even if they themselves did not host said material, should they become aware of the nature of the material their customer was publishing and fail to take steps to block their customer from continuing to use their service. Fortunately for the information service industry Eady J dismissed Mr Bunt's claims. He held that ISPs fell within the definition of 'information society service' provider by applying the definition of an information society service given in reg. 2(1) of the E-Commerce (EC Directive) Regulations.[93] They were therefore able to rely upon defences within regs. 17–19 and the claims against the ISPs were accordingly struck out. In a sense *Bunt* merely confirms what we thought we already knew; that the Regulations prevent the attribution of liability to telephone companies or other passive telecommunications providers (such as ISPs) for the distribution of defamatory material over their communication networks.

The later case of *Metropolitan International Schools Ltd v Designtechnica Corp*. looked specifically at the liability of internet search providers.[94] Here, the claimant claimed

---

[89] SI 2002/2013.

[90] Regulation 6(1) obliges an ISP to make certain information available to the end user 'in a form which is easily, directly and permanently accessible'. Regulation 6(1)(c) refers to the service provider's contact details, including email addresses, which facilitate rapid and direct communication with the ISP.

[91] [2006] EWHC 407 (QB).

[92] Ibid. [5].

[93] Ibid. [41].

[94] [2009] EWHC 1765 (QB).

that the first defendant hosted several web forums in which threads were hosted which accused the claimant (a distance learning operator) of a number of faults including providing poor value for money, exploiting students, and being 'little more than a scam'. The third defendant in the action was search engine giant Google. The claimant claimed they were jointly liable as they: 'published or caused to be published at https://www.google.co.uk and/or https://www.google.com a search return for the Train2Game thread which . . . set out the following words defamatory of the Claimant as the third and fourth highest search result: "Train2Game new SCAM for Scheidegger"'.[95] Mr Justice Eady was asked by Google to deny a request to serve the order out of jurisdiction on Google. The case therefore became the first UK case to examine the liability of search engine providers for defamation committed on a catalogued website.

At the heart of the claim were Google's previews. Each search return displays not only a link to the page but also one or two lines of text which preview the page. It was these previews which contained the defamatory material referred to above. Eady J began by distinguishing the decision in *Godfrey*. He found that Google was not the 'publisher' of the snippet, noting that:

> A search engine is a different kind of Internet intermediary. It is not possible to draw a complete analogy with a website host. One cannot merely press a button to ensure that the offending words will never reappear on a Google search snippet: there is no control over the search terms typed in by future users. If the words are thrown up in response to a future search, it would by no means follow that the Third Defendant has authorised or acquiesced in that process . . . [and on this basis] I believe it is unrealistic to attribute responsibility for publication to the Third Defendant, whether on the basis of authorship or acquiescence.[96]

Eady J went on to consider whether the search engine giant could be liable as an intermediary carrier, and vitally whether the provisions of the E-Commerce (EC Directive) Regulations would apply to them. In the instant case he found no liability for Google on the basis of his previous analysis but found that:

> the United Kingdom government has so far taken the view that it is unnecessary or inappropriate to extend protection expressly to search engines. It would not be appropriate, therefore, for me to proceed as though there were a comparable statute in effect in this jurisdiction. I think that, for the Third Defendant to be classified as or deemed a 'host', statutory intervention would be needed.[97]

As a first instance decision this case is of influential authority only, although a dearth of alternative authorities suggests that it will be highly influential should similar facts arise. On this basis it is somewhat of a mixed victory for Google, for although Eady J found they were not liable as publishers, and vitally were found to have no duty to "take down" material under the *Godfrey* principle as they were 'not hosting a website and do not have anything from which to "take down" the offending words',[98] they have been denied entry to the safe harbour provisions found in the Regulations. No doubt Google would argue that it is better to be found not liable in the first place than to have to seek shelter in the safe harbour, and that is undoubtedly true, but to draw a

---

[95] Ibid. [15] (Scheidegger was the former trading name of the claimant).
[96] Ibid. [55], [64].
[97] Ibid. [112].
[98] Ibid. [78].

distinction between ISPs and hosts on the one hand and search engine providers on the other may yet have unforeseen consequences.

The liability of search providers has been revisited more recently in the case of *Hegglin v Persons Unknown*.[99] Here the court was asked to consider whether Google Inc. (registered in Delaware and located in California) could be served proceedings to appear in a hearing relating to the defamation of Mr Hegglin by persons unknown. On a series of internet websites a number of malicious, harmful, and defamatory comments had been made about Mr Hegglin, including that he was a paedophile, a murderer, a sympathizer of the Ku Klux Klan, a corrupt businessman, and a money launderer for the mafia. Mr Hegglin had been unable to identify who was so defaming him but he sought to bring Google into the action by applying sections 10 and 14 of the Data Protection Act 1998 (the prevention of data processing likely to cause damage or distress and the rectification, erasure, or destruction of inaccurate data). Mr Justice Bean found at an interim hearing that Google Inc, although they had been cooperative with Mr Hegglin in seeking to block access to sites containing the defamatory material, could be served, on the basis that: 'there is at least a good arguable case that Google is under an obligation, enforceable in this jurisdiction, to comply with the requirements of the 1998 Act when processing the claimant's personal data, both when hosting a website on which such data appears or . . . when operating a search engine such as google.co.uk on which his data is processed.'[100] Following this decision the case was settled, the terms of the settlement were not revealed but it appears Google agreed to increase its efforts to block access to the defamatory materials in question.[101] This case may be seen as an extended application of the Right to be Forgotten set out in the case of *Google Spain SL and Google Inc. v AEPD*.[102] Indeed one commentator suggested that Google had settled to avoid the 'opening of a floodgate of [defamatory material] claims in much the same way as the so-called "right to be forgotten" ruling has done.'[103] The same commentator though goes on to note that Google would likely face further cases in the future raised under the same basis: 'Google has deferred [this claim] to another day.'[104]

More commonly of late there has been a focus on the role of intermediaries who host social network sites and blogs. In two recent cases it is the operation by Google of the popular blog hosting service Blogger that came under scrutiny. First, in *Davison v Habeeb*[105] Ms Davison claimed a number of bloggers had defamed her, including some hosted by the Blogger service. She claimed that Google were not only publishers of the comments but were also promoters of the comments also as 'a Google search against "Peter Eyre", which brings up "Peter Eyre's Space" (one of the blogs complained of) as the second snippet and a reference to his articles in the Palestine Telegraph as the fourth snippet'.[106] Although HH Judge Parkes QC gave short shrift to the Google search

---

[99] [2014] EWHC 2808 (QB).

[100] Ibid. [20].

[101] O Bowcott and S Gibbs, 'Google settles online abuse court case', *The Guardian*, 24 November 2014.

[102] ECLI:EU:C:2014:317. Discussed in depth at 23.2.

[103] David Cook cybercrime specialist at Slater & Gordon cited in K Hall, 'Google dodges "costly" legal precedent, settles Daniel Hegglin case', *The Register*, 24 November 2014.

[104] Ibid.

[105] [2011] EWHC 3031 (QB).

[106] Ibid. [40].

facility forming part of the claim, 'The answer to that submission, of course, is to be found in the analysis in *Metropolitan International Schools v Designtechnica*: the operation of the Google search engine is entirely automatic',[107] he finds the operation of Blogger to be entirely different: 'Mr White submits that although there is no precise analogy between a service like Blogger.com and a search engine, it is clear from Eady J's reasoning in Metropolitan International Schools that Blogger.com is not a publisher, but simply a facilitator. It is true that there can be no intervention by Google Inc. in the process of posting material on Blogger.com. But then it is unclear that there could have been any intervention by Demon Internet in the process of posting on the newsgroup which it hosted in *Godfrey*. I accept that it is unrealistic to suppose that, absent notification, Blogger.com adopts as its own any of the content which it facilitates. But this is a summary application. In my view it must be at least arguable that the fifth defendant should properly be seen as a publisher responding to requests for downloads like Demon Internet, rather than a mere facilitator, playing a passive instrumental role.'[108] Thus for HH Judge Parkes QC, Blogger clearly is a publisher at English Law. He then revisited *Godfrey* and asked when Google could be responsible for material hosted on the Blogger service at English Law: 'it is arguable that [Google] is a publisher at common law, following notification it would be unable (or at least arguably unable) to establish that it was ignorant of the existence of the defamatory material on Blogger.com, or to rely on the defence at s. 1, Defamation Act 1996, exactly as the defendant was unable to rely on that defence in *Godfrey v Demon Internet*'.[109] This leaves one final question: do reg. 19 of the E-Commerce (EC Directive) Regulations and Art. 14 of the E-Commerce Directive protect Google from the claim? HH Judge Parkes QC embarked on a lengthy analysis of reg. 19 and Google's level of actual knowledge of the defamatory content. He concluded that the 'Blogger.com service provides an information society service'[110] meaning it qualified for reg. 19 protection and then found that it was impossible for Google to know with any degree of certainty whether the information was defamatory as they were faced with conflicting claims as to the defamatory nature of the content between the claimant and the operator of the blog: on this basis Google 'was in no position to adjudicate'.[111] Ultimately therefore Google were held to be a publisher in English law, but protected by reg. 19.

This position was reviewed in the following case of *Tamiz v Google Inc.*[112] Mr Tamiz raised a claim in relation to eight comments that were posted on a blog bearing the name 'London Muslim' in late April 2011. The blog was moderated by an individual who was unaware of Mr Tamiz's complaints until Google, with Mr Tamiz's permission, passed his complaint on to the blog moderator. The offending comments were then immediately removed by the blog moderator. Despite this Mr Tamiz decided to take legal action. Instead of suing the individuals who made the comments or even the blog moderator, Mr Tamiz attempted to pursue a claim against Google Inc. and Google UK Ltd. Google claimed that they were not the authors of the comments under English law and in any event even if they were they were protected by reg. 19 of the

---

[107] Ibid.
[108] Ibid. [41].
[109] Ibid. [46].
[110] Ibid. [56].
[111] Ibid. [68].
[112] [2012] EWHC 449 (QB).

E-Commerce (EC Directive) Regulations and Art. 14 of the E-Commerce Directive. In the High Court Eady J examined the line of cases that began with *Godfrey* and extended through *Designtechnica* and *Davison*. He highlighted the need for judges to be consistent in dealing with new technologies and that there was a need to remain proportionate in their decisions, in terms of Art. 10 ECHR.

Highlight Eady J

It seems to me to be a significant factor in the evidence before me that Google Inc is not required to take any positive step, technically, in the process of continuing the accessibility of the offending material, whether it has been notified of a complainant's objection or not. In those circumstances, I would be prepared to hold that it should not be regarded as a publisher, or even as one who authorises publication, under the established principles of the common law . . . its role, as a platform provider, is a purely passive one.[113]

He was then asked whether s. 1 of the Defamation Act 1996 made any difference to his finding. The confusion had arisen in *Designtechnica*, another decision of Eady J where he seemed to suggest a publisher at common law and a commercial publisher under s. 1 may be different. He replied quite unequivocally:

> In this brief and passing comment, I was contemplating the somewhat counter-intuitive hypothesis that Google Inc should be considered as a 'publisher', contrary to my primary finding. I was obviously finding it difficult to envisage how it could on that hypothesis, in any meaningful sense, not be 'a person whose business is issuing material to the public, or a section of the public, who issues material containing the statement in the course of that business.' All I was suggesting, in the passage at [80], was that if Google Inc was to be regarded as a publisher of the search 'snippets', it was difficult to see how it would not fall within the definition of a commercial publisher.[114]

Although perhaps not the clearest clarification in the world, here Eady J was telling us he does not see a commercial publisher as a separate classification from publisher, he was in essence musing when a platform provider would not be a commercial publisher. For the avoidance of doubt he added that 'whereas Google Inc in the course of its business makes facilities available, including by way of a platform for bloggers who use Blogger. com, it cannot be said to fall within the definition of a "commercial publisher".'[115]

Although he had already found that Google was not a publisher of the content, he took the time to review the application of reg. 19. He noted that in guidance issued by the CJEU *in L'Oréal SA v eBay International AG*,[116] the intermediary must be 'aware of facts or circumstances from which the illegal activity or information is apparent'[117] before the protection of Art. 14/reg. 19 is lost. In addition the CJEU noted that notifications made to intermediaries cannot be 'insufficiently precise or inadequately substantiated'.[118]

---

[113] Ibid. [39].
[114] Ibid. [46].
[115] Ibid. [42].
[116] [2011] ETMR 52. This case will be discussed in greater detail at 15.3.
[117] *L'Oréal* at [120]; *Tamiz* at [58].
[118] *L'Oréal* at [122]; *Tamiz* at [58].

Applying this guidance he found that 'it may be thought by Mr Tamiz to be implicit in his complaints that he was denying, outright, any allegation of theft or drug dealing, but it cannot be right that any provider is required, in the light of the strict terms of Regulation 19, to take all such protestations at face value. Clearly more is required for a provider to acquire a sufficient state of knowledge to be deprived of the statutory protection.'[119]

Mr Tamiz appealed this decision and on Valentine's Day 2013 the Court of Appeal issued their judgment.[120] In general the court supported the findings of Eady J but with, for Google, one major distinction. Counsel for Mr Tamiz tried to argue that Google was a publisher, acting not just through its employees but also through the bloggers who user the Blogger platform. He argued:

> it has control over the blogger, who in turn has control over the comments posted on the blog. Google Inc is therefore to be regarded as a primary publisher, potentially liable for defamatory material on the blogs, irrespective of knowledge or fault and irrespective of whether it has been notified of any complaint, subject however to any statutory defences. Alternatively it is a secondary publisher, facilitating publication in a manner analogous to a distributor, subject to the common law defence of innocent dissemination as well as to statutory defences, though it will be difficult to establish the defence of innocent dissemination if it has the power to prevent continuing publication and chooses not to exercise that power.[121]

This was rejected by Richards LJ.

 Highlight Richards LJ

Google was not in a position comparable to that of the author or editor of a defamatory article. Nor is it in a position comparable to that of the corporate proprietor of a newspaper in which a defamatory article is printed. There is no relationship of employment or agency between Google Inc and the bloggers or those posting comments on the blogs: such people are plainly independent of Google Inc and do not act in any sense on its behalf or in its name.[122]

In one important manner though Richards LJ departed from Eady J's judgment. He found that after Google had been notified of the complaint 'if Google Inc allows defamatory material to remain on a Blogger blog after it has been notified of the presence of that material, it might be inferred to have associated itself with, or to have made itself responsible for, the continued presence of that material on the blog and thereby to have become a publisher of the material.'[123] He felt the Eady J had been generous to Google in finding a five-week delay between notification and removal to be merely 'dilatory'. He suggested instead that 'it is in my view open to argument that the time taken was sufficiently long to leave room for an inference adverse to Google Inc. The period during

---

[119] *Tamiz* at [60].
[120] *Tamiz v Google Inc* [2013] EWCA Civ 68.
[121] Ibid. [22].
[122] Ibid. [25]–[26].
[123] Ibid. [27], [34]–[36].

which Google Inc might fall to be treated on that basis as a publisher of the defamatory comments would be a very short one.'[124]

Thus a clear warning was sent from the Court of Appeal to platform providers such as Google, but also to Facebook, Twitter, and others. You are not a primary publisher for the purposes of the Defamation Act but like Demon Internet, you may find yourself responsible as a distributor of the material if you are made aware of it and you fail to act to remove it in a reasonable time. In the instant case the court found Google were not liable, but not because they were shielded from liability but because applying the *Jameel* principle:

> the earliest point at which Google Inc could have become liable in respect of the comments would be some time after notification of the complaint in respect of them. But it is highly improbable that any significant number of readers will have accessed the comments after that time and prior to removal of the entire blog. It follows, as the judge clearly had in mind, that any damage to the appellant's reputation arising out of continued publication of the comments during that period will have been trivial; and in those circumstances the judge was right to consider that 'the game would not be worth the candle'.[125]

This was a very nervous 'win' for Google and one which no doubt was of concern to their counsel as well as advisors to other platform providers. The court in finding Google not liable did not consider reg. 19 but it is hard to imagine it would have saved Google once it was aware of the offending content.

7.3.3 **The operators of websites' defence**

A specific, and narrow, intermediary defence may be found in s. 5 of the Defamation Act 2013. Although s. 5 does not affect the outcome of decisions such as *Tamiz* it bolsters the defences available to some internet intermediaries, in particular those who operate a website. In essence, s. 5 gives intermediary defences similar to those found in the E-Commerce Directive to ordinary operators of websites such as bloggers but it would also appear to extend to anyone who operates a website on which third-party comments may be hosted, including Google's Blogger platform and social media platforms such as Facebook and Twitter. Under s. 5(2) it is a defence for the operator to show that they did not post the statement complained of on the website. Thus in the *Tamiz* case it is possible that both the operator of the London Muslim blog, and indeed Google, would be able to rely on a s. 5(2) defence. However, like the safe harbour provisions found in the E-Commerce Directive, and indeed s. 1 of the Defamation Act 1996 as applied in *Godfrey v Demon*, the defence comes with limits. By s. 5(3) the defence is defeated if the complainant could not identify the originator of the putatively defamatory statement and if a notice of complaint has been served on the website operator and they have failed to act accordingly. What does it mean to 'act accordingly', well, unlike the previous provisions found in the 1996 Defamation Act, or even the safe harbour provisions of the E-Commerce Directive, there is no requirement that the content be taken down by the website operator. This is not just another notify and takedown provision (at least not initially). Instead when a complaint is made to a website operator under s. 5(3)(b)

---

[124] Ibid.
[125] Ibid. [50].

this triggers the application of the Schedule of The Defamation (Operators of Websites) Regulations 2013.[126] This sets out an extremely complex procedure for the website operator to follow which has led to many criticizing the provision as being unduly administratively onerous on website operators who wish to rely upon the defence.[127] The first stage is that except in cases where the website operator does not know how to contact the poster of the statement complained of, or the complainant has successfully complained to the website operator at least twice before about the same or a related statement from the same poster, the website operator will pass the complaint on to the poster of the statement within 48 hours along with a notification that the statement may be removed. If the poster of the statement fails to respond to this notification within the time set out in the notification (which is 5 days after notification), or if they respond in part but fail to provide all necessary information as is required by the Schedule, then the post or message must be removed within 48 hours for the defence to remain in effect. Similarly, if the poster of the statement indicates they do not object to the statement being removed, the operator of the website must remove it within 48 hours. If the poster of the original content replies in full stating that they do not wish to have the statement removed, then the operator of the site should reply to the complainant within 48 hours noting that the statement will not be removed and if permitted to do so by the poster of the statement giving their contact details; if not permitted they must inform the complainant that they are not permitted to pass over these details. Thus an operator of a website may continue to host a statement which has been claimed to be defamatory in nature without fear of being held liable for statements they did not make. The idea behind this is to ameliorate the chilling effects of the notice and takedown approach used previously. The complainant may of course if they feel they have been genuinely defamed then make a Norwich Pharmacal application to have the website operator compelled to give up the identification details of the poster of the message or content allowing them to pursue an action directly.

7.3.4 Intermediary liability and Article 10 ECHR

The European Court of Human Rights made an important intervention into the debate in *Delfi AS v Estonia*.[128] At first glance *Delfi* appears to make major changes to the liability of internet intermediaries for defamatory content but upon reflection, and by taking account of the later case of *Magyar Tartalomszolgaltatok Egyesulete (MTE)* (discussed below) its impact is less than it may initially seem. An individual identified as 'L' who was the sole or major shareholder and a member of the supervisory board of SLK (or AS Saaremaa Laevakompanii (Saaremaa Ṡhipping Company)) brought the claim. On 24 January 2006 Delfi, an internet news portal, published a story entitled 'SLK Destroyed Planned Ice Road'. This story suggested that SLK (who operated a ferry between islands) had intervened to prevent a winter 'ice road' from being constructed between some

---

[126] SI 2013/3028.

[127] A Hurst, 'Defamation Act 2013: Section 5, it's decision time for website operators', 6 January 2014 <http://inforrm.wordpress.com/2014/01/06/defamation-act-2013-section-5-its-decision-time-for-website-operators-ashley-hurst/> and C Russell UK 'Defamation Act 2013, Update: Website Operators' September 2013 <https://www.charlesrussell.co.uk/UserFiles/file/pdf/Reputation%20Management/Defamation_Act_Website.pdf>.

[128] [2015] EMLR 26.

Estonian islands and the mainland. After all, stories on the Delfi site was the standard comments box. Here readers could publish unmoderated comments and read comments left by others. According to the report of the case:

> the articles received about 10,000 readers' comments daily, the majority posted under pseudonyms. Nevertheless, there was a system of notice-and-take-down in place: any reader could mark a comment as leim (an Estonian word for an insulting or mocking message or a message inciting hatred on the Internet) and the comment was removed expeditiously. Furthermore, there was a system of automatic deletion of comments that included certain stems of obscene words. In addition, a victim of a defamatory comment could directly notify the applicant company, in which case the comment was removed immediately.[129]

The complainant complained about twenty comments which had been left below the news story including: 'If there was an iceroad, [one] could easily save 500 for a full car, fckng [L] pay for that economy, why does it take 3 [hours] for your ferries if they are such good icebreakers, go and break ice in Pärnu port . . . instead, fcking monkey, I will cross [the strait] anyway and if I drown, it's your fault', 'they bathe in money anyway thanks to that monopoly and State subsidies and have now started to fear that cars may drive to the islands for a couple of days without anything filling their purses. burn in your own ship, sick Jew!' and 'The people will chatter for a couple of days on the Internet, but the crooks (and also those who are backed and whom we ourselves have elected to represent us) pocket the money and pay no attention to this flaming—no one gives a shit about this.' It appears all the comments in question were published on 24/25 January 2006. L, through his lawyers, complained to Delfi about these comments on 9 March 2006 and Delfi took them down on the same day. In their claim L's lawyers had sought 500,000 Kroons (circa €32,000) in non-pecuniary compensation, this was rejected by Delfi on the basis that they had taken the comments down immediately upon their notification of them.

L raised a civil claim against Delfi for damages. At a District Court hearing in Estonia in May 2007 his claim was dismissed as the Estonian Information Society Services Act, which implemented the safe harbour principles found in Arts. 12–14 of the E-Commerce Directive, protected Delfi. In October 2007 however the Court of Appeal remitted the case back to the District Court finding that it had erred in finding Delfi were protected by the Act and a second hearing in the District Court in June 2008 found that Delfi had held themselves out in such a way as be seen to be a publisher rather than merely a host or distributor of content found in the comments section of the website. As a result it could not disclaim liability and merely following notice and takedown was not enough to remove liability. The District Court awarded though only 5,000 Kroons (€320) damages.

The Court of Appeal upheld this decision, emphasizing that 'Delfi had not been required to exercise prior control over comments. However, having chosen not to do so, it should have created some other effective system which would have ensured rapid removal of unlawful comments from the portal. The Court of Appeal considered that the measures taken by the applicant company were insufficient and that it was contrary to the principle of good faith to place the burden of monitoring the comments on their potential victims. The Court of Appeal also rejected Delfi's argument that its

---

[129] Ibid. [12]–[13].

liability was excluded under the Information Society Services Act. It noted that Delfi was not a technical intermediary in respect of the comments, and that its activity was not of a merely technical, automatic and passive nature; instead, it invited users to add comments. Thus, they were a provider of content services rather than of technical services.'[130]

The Estonian Supreme Court agreed with the Court of Appeal that Delfi did not qualify for the protection of the Information Society Services Act on the basis that:

> a user of the defendant's service cannot change or delete a comment he or she has posted. He or she can only report an inappropriate comment. Thus, the defendant can determine which of the comments added will be published and which will not be published. The fact that the defendant does not make use of this possibility does not prompt the conclusion that the publishing of comments is not under the defendant's control. The defendant, which governs the information stored in the comment environment, provides a content service, for which reason the circumstances precluding liability, as specified in section 10 of the ISSA, do not apply in the present case.[131]

In one respect though the Supreme Court vacated the decision of the Court of Appeal. They found, vitally, that the removal of content could interfere with the personality rights and the freedom of expression rights of the writers of comments. As a result of this, and as a result of the costly new moderating process which Delfi had to set up to comply with the decision of the Supreme Court, Delfi applied to the European Court of Human Rights claiming that this interfered with their right to free expression under Article 10 and was in breach of the 2003 Council of Europe Declaration on Freedom of Communication on the Internet.[132]

The ECtHR initially ruled on the case in October 2013 when it found that there had been no violation of Art. 10 on the basis that the interference by the state had been proportionate and was for the legitimate aim of protecting the reputation and rights of others.[133] The case was then remitted to the Grand Chamber. In June 2015 the much-delayed decision of the Grand Chamber was published. It is (for the ECtHR) a lengthy 88 pages and unusually contains two concurring and one dissenting opinion. It is a decision which has been much commented upon but which we can hopefully reduce to a few key facts and issues.

The Grand Chamber began by effectively bypassing the question of supremacy of EU Law in the case by going straight to the ECHR principles. Once there the court reiterated the standard three stages normally applied to claims of an interference with Art. 10(1): that the restriction be lawful, achieve a legitimate aim, and be necessary in a democratic society. The court found that the Estonian law was lawful in the sense that it was sufficiently clear and the impact of the law was foreseeable.[134] The court found that 'as a professional publisher, the applicant company should have been familiar with the legislation and case-law, and could also have sought legal advice.'[135] As a result the actions were lawful. As the parties had already agreed that the restriction had pursued

---

[130] Ibid. [28]–[29].
[131] Ibid. [31].
[132] <https://wcd.coe.int/ViewDoc.jsp?id=37031>.
[133] *Delfi* (n. 128) [63].
[134] Ibid. [121].
[135] Ibid. [129].

the legitimate aim of protecting the reputation and rights of others, the court then examined the question of whether the restrictions were necessary. The court reiterated that the internet could be harmful as well as beneficial[136] and emphasized that the comments could be seen as hate speech and incitements to violence which on their face value were unlawful.[137] On this basis the court had little difficulty in finding the actions of moderators did not amount to private censorship and noted that a large news organization was better placed to police content on its website than a private citizen.[138] Finally the court found that a notice and takedown approach was insufficient to deal with hate speech of the nature of the comments in question:

> in cases such as the present one, where third-party user comments are in the form of hate speech and direct threats to the physical integrity of individuals, as understood in the Court's case-law, the Court considers, that the rights and interests of others and of society as a whole may entitle Contracting States to impose liability on Internet news portals, without contravening Article 10 of the Convention, if they fail to take measures to remove clearly unlawful comments without delay, *even without notice from the alleged victim or from third parties.*[139]

On this basis the action was necessary. It should also be noted that the court seemed to be influenced also by the low level of damages awarded.[140]

In the previous edition of this book I wrote 'It is unlikely we could extend *Delfi* to more nuanced speech which requires a value judgement, in particular defamatory speech which turns on accusations unknowable to the hosting site. As a result *Delfi* may be understood to be a balanced decision: one which creates a positive obligation on news sites and other such content sites[141] to police violent or hate speech without being over-restrictive.' The subsequent decision of the ECtHR in *Magyar Tartalomszolgaltatok Egyesulete (MTE) v Hungary*[142] suggests this might be correct. On 5 February 2010, MTE published an opinion piece titled, *Another Unethical Commercial Conduct on the Net* about two real estate management websites. The opinion piece explained that the sites offered a 30-day free trial for their services, after which they automatically charged a subscription fee. The piece also stated that the only way to remove personal data from the website was by paying overdue subscription fees. The piece generated comments and the court highlighted two of them: 'They have talked about these two rubbish real estate websites a thousand times already' and 'Is this not that Benkő-Sándor-sort-of sly, rubbish, mug company again? I ran into it two years ago, since then they have kept sending me emails about my overdue debts and this and that. I am above 100,000 [Hungarian forints] now. I have not paid and I am not going to. That's it.'[143] The opinion piece was

---

[136] Ibid. [133].
[137] Ibid. [153].
[138] Ibid. [158]–[159].
[139] Ibid. [159] (emphasis added).
[140] Ibid. [160].
[141] Delfi does not apply to social media platforms. This is made clear in the judgment: 'the case does not concern other fora on the Internet where third-party comments can be disseminated, for example an Internet discussion forum or a bulletin board where users can freely set out their ideas on any topics without the discussion being channelled by any input from the forum's manager; or a social media platform where the platform provider does not offer any content and where the content provider may be a private person running the website or a blog as a hobby' *Delfi* (n. 128) [116].
[142] [2016] 2 WLUK 62.
[143] Ibid. [12].

then reproduced verbatim on a website operated by Zrt and here more comments were left including the more colourful 'People like this should go and shit a hedgehog and spend all their money on their mothers' tombs until they drop dead.'[144] The company criticized in the opinion piece brought a civil action against both MTE and Zrt. The action alleged that the piece was false and offensive, while the comments violated the right to good reputation and therefore violated Hungary's Civil Code. Upon receiving notice of the suit, MTE and Zrt removed the comments in question.

The Hungarian court of first instance ruled that the comments violated the claimants' right to good reputation because they were offensive, insulting, and humiliating, and went beyond the scope of freedom of expression. The court also held that the comments constituted edited content and equated them to readers' letters. The appellate court upheld the decision, but disagreed that the comments were edited content. Particularly, the court held that, 'as the comments were injurious for the plaintiff, the applicants bore objective liability for their publication, irrespectively of the subsequent removal, which was only relevant for the assessment of any compensation.'[145] Hungary's Supreme Court upheld the judgments of the lower courts: 'It stressed that the applicants, by enabling readers to make comments on their websites, had assumed objective liability for any injurious or unlawful comments made by those readers. It rejected the applicants' argument that they were only intermediary providers which allowed them to escape any liability for the contents of comments, other than removing them if injurious to a third party.'[146]

The ECtHR began by first assessing the issue of intermediary liability. It reiterated that 'persons carrying on a professional activity, who are used to having to proceed with a high degree of caution when pursuing their occupation, can on this account be expected to take special care in assessing the risks that such activity entails.'[147] The court then held that it was satisfied on the facts of the case that Hungary's Civil Code 'made it foreseeable for a media publisher running a large Internet news portal for an economic purpose and for a self-regulatory body of Internet content providers, that they could, in principle, be held liable under domestic law for unlawful comments of third-parties.'[148] To determine the applicable standards to the case, the court reviewed 'the nature of the applicants' rights of expression in view of their role in the process of communication and the specific interest protected by the interference, namely—as was implied by the domestic courts—the rights of others.'[149] The court cited *Delfi* to establish that internet news portals must assume duties and responsibilities for comments and third-party content published on their platforms. However, the court differentiated *MTE* from *Delfi* in that the latter dealt with clearly unlawful speech amounting to hate speech and incitement to violence, while the current case dealt with offensive and vulgar speech. Reviewing first the context and content of the comments the court held that as the opinion piece discussed large real estate websites, which allegedly misled users, and as the websites' practices already resulted in complaints to Hungary's consumer protection agencies, the comments pertained to an issue in the public interest. Reviewing the

[144] Ibid. [14].
[145] Ibid. [20].
[146] Ibid. [22].
[147] Ibid. [49].
[148] Ibid. [51].
[149] Ibid. [60].

content of the comments, the court found that they were value judgments about a commercial activity, some even influenced by personal issues with the real estate websites. Furthermore, the court agreed that some of the comments were offensive and vulgar, but reiterated that vulgarity itself is not unlawful and that 'style constitutes part of the communication as the form of expression and is as such protected together with the content of the expression' and further that vulgar and offensive speech is a common attribute of online comments and that such commonality reduces their impact. [150]

Reviewing the measures taken by MTE and Zrt, the court found that the decision of the domestic courts to impose objective liability for unlawful comments made by readers by finding that allowing even some unfiltered comments made it foreseeable that those comments could be unlawful, as seemed permissible under *Delfi*, placed 'excessive and impracticable forethought capable of undermining freedom of the right to impart information on the Internet.'[151] The court held 'the decisive question when assessing the consequence for the applicants is not the absence of damages payable, but the manner in which Internet portals such as theirs can be held liable for third-party comments', such liability had a direct and indirect chilling effect on the freedom of expression on the internet.[152] Considering all of the above, the court ruled that the Hungarian courts failed to adequately balance the right to reputation and the right to freedom of expression, and followed *Delfi* in finding that the notice-and-take-down system that MTE and Zrt used offered an effective protection mechanism for the reputation of others.

Taken as a pair, *Delfi* and *MTE* give a much better understanding of the position of the European Court of Human Rights than *Delfi* does on its own. The court, it seems, used *MTE* as an opportunity to clarify that *Delfi* was, in fact, limited in scope to 'clearly unlawful' comments consisting of hate speech and incitement to violence; it was never about more nuanced speech which requires a value judgement, such as defamatory speech. We can now position *Delfi* as narrowly a case on unlawful speech as opposed to merely harmful speech.

7.4 **Social media defamation**

In the contemporary internet, User-generated content (UGC) carried by SMPs is king. In everything from consumer reviews in sites such as TripAdvisor to user-generated videos on YouTube, the modern 'social media' internet is built on UGC. The problem with UGC though is its completely unfiltered nature which increases greatly the risks of defamation occurring.

The best advice to give to individuals is to be cautious in any statement they publish, republish, retweet, or otherwise distribute. The reason for recommending caution is clear from the UK case law dealing with individual liability for statements made in the online environment. The first reported case was *Keith-Smith v Williams*.[153] This involved a series of claims made on a Yahoo! discussion group called 'In the Hole' by Tracey

---

[150] Ibid. [76] and [77].
[151] Ibid. [82].
[152] Ibid. [86].
[153] [2006] EWHC 860 (QB).

Williams about Michael Keith-Smith, a UK Independence Party candidate in the 2005 general election. Among other claims Ms Williams suggested that Mr Keith-Smith was a racist, a Nazi, a sex offender, and a sexual deviant. Ms Williams may have thought she was safe from litigation as she did all this hiding behind a pseudonym. Mr Keith-Smith obtained a court order requiring Yahoo! to identify Ms Williams and in an undefended action in the High Court in March 2006 he secured a total award of £10,000 in damages, being £5,000 in compensatory damages and £5,000 in aggravated damages. Although the judge notes with some regret that 'the defendant possibly, or indeed probably, does not have the means to pay an award of damages or costs',[154] he felt it important to make the award to clear Mr Keith-Smith's reputation.

This case has been followed by a flurry of other cases examining personal liability for postings in internet discussion forums. In *Sheffield Wednesday Football Club & Ors v Hargreaves*,[155] the court was asked to make a so-called 'Norwich Pharmacal Order', that is an order that a person who assists another in committing a tort must reveal the identity of the wrongdoer to allow the party who has suffered harm to take action. Mr Hargreaves was the operator of a site called *owlstalk.co.uk* a specialist site for fans of Sheffield Wednesday football club to discuss matters relating to the club. Although Mr Hargreaves himself never posted any inflammatory or defamatory statements several of his users did, including some statements questioning the financial probity of several of the directors of the club. Mr Hargreaves refused to name the individuals without a court order. In discussing whether or not to make the order to identify eleven users of the *owlstalk* board, Judge Richard Parkes QC noted a balance had to be struck between the rights of those allegedly defamed and the rights of the posters to privacy. Applying this balance he ruled that the identity of seven of the eleven individuals should be protected, stating: 'I do not think it would be right to make an order for the disclosure of the identities of users who have posted messages which are barely defamatory or little more than abusive or likely to be understood as jokes. That, it seems to me, would be disproportionate and unjustifiably intrusive.'[156] The remaining four though had posted statements which Judge Parkes thought 'may reasonably be understood to allege greed, selfishness, untrustworthiness and dishonest behaviour on the part of the Claimants'. He concluded 'in the case of those postings, the Claimants' entitlement to take action to protect their right to reputation outweighs, in my judgment, the right of the authors to maintain their anonymity and their right to express themselves freely'.[157] Thus four users of the *owlstalk* board were identified, although reports in the media suggest no further action was taken.[158]

7.4.1 Facebook libel

As may be expected the courts have dealt with a number of cases looking specifically at libels committed on Facebook and Twitter. The first such case was *Applause Store Productions Ltd & Anor v Raphael*.[159] On 19 June 2007, a false Facebook profile for

---

[154] Ibid. [15].
[155] [2007] EWHC 2375 (QB).
[156] Ibid. [17].
[157] Ibid. [18].
[158] P Gray, 'UK Libel Law v Freedom of Expression' *Liverpool Daily Post* 14 October 2008.
[159] [2008] EWHC 1781 (QB).

Matthew Firsht was set up, containing private information including reference to his date of birth, relationship status, purported sexual preferences, and his political and religious views. The following day a Facebook group was set up, with a link to the profile, called 'Has Matthew Firsht lied to you?' This contained material which was defamatory of him and his company Applause Store, indicating he owed substantial sums which he avoided paying with lies and implausible excuses.[160]

Mr Firsht discovered the false profile and group page on 4 July 2007 and requested it be removed. It was removed on 6 July 2007 and on 1 August 2007 his solicitors obtained a 'Norwich Pharmacal Order' order against Facebook for disclosure of the registration data provided by the creator of the offending material. That evidence indicated that the defendant created both the profile and the group page. The defendant was known to Mr Firsht, being a former close friend. This suggested he had indeed set up the profile page as whoever created the profile knew that Mr Firsht had a twin brother, was from Brighton, practised a variety of Judaism, and was familiar with his company and work as well as the unusual spelling of his name.[161]

Mr Raphael denied setting up either the profile or the group page: he suggested he had an alibi but this was rejected by Judge Richard Parkes QC. With this established the judge looked at the harm caused by the placing of the false statements on Facebook. The first problem Mr Firsht faced was overcoming the *Jameel* principle as Facebook does not store data showing how many users view a profile or group. Therefore he could not produce evidence of publication which extended beyond a small group of six who actually saw the material, all of whom were connected to him in some way.[162] However, Judge Parkes accepted that Facebook was a medium in which users regularly searched for the names of others whom they know, and anyone who had done so against Mr Firsht's name in the time between the publication of the false entries and their removal would have found the offending material without difficulty. He judged that it was likely 'a not insubstantial number of people [would] have done so. By that I have in mind a substantial two-figure, rather than a three-figure, number'.[163]

With the *Jameel* hurdle cleared it was necessary to show harm had occurred to Mr Firsht and his company. Judge Parkes commented that although the libel was 'not at the top end of the scale, it is serious enough to say of a successful businessman that (as I have found the words to mean) he owes substantial sums of money which he has repeatedly avoided paying by lying and making implausible excuses, so that he is not to be trusted in the financial conduct of his business and represents a serious credit risk'.[164] On this basis he awarded libel damages of £15,000 to Mr Firsht, including aggravated damages to reflect the fact that Mr Raphael denied making the remarks and £5,000 to Applause Store Productions.

Subsequently in *Bryce v Barber*,[165] a university student was awarded £10,000 in damages for remarks made by another student on his Facebook account. The defendant, Jeremiah Barber, posted indecent images of children on Raymond Bryce's Facebook profile along with the comment 'Ray, you like kids and you are gay so I bet you love this

---

[160] Ibid. [3]–[4].
[161] Ibid. [48].
[162] Ibid. [70].
[163] Ibid. [78].
[164] Ibid. [79].
[165] Unreported July 26, 2010 (HC).

picture, Ha ha.' Mr Bryce claimed that the material would be seen by more than 800 people (his Facebook friends and others within the network), defame his character, and even subject him to violence. The defendant also attached the names of 11 other individuals to the images which meant that they may well have been seen by thousands. Tugendhart J agreed and awarded him damages for stress endured and any ensuring anxiety brought by knowing that those close to him would have seen the offensive image stating that 'This was not only defamatory but a defamation which goes to a central aspect of Mr Bryce's public reputation.'[166]

7.4.2 **Twitter libel**

Twitter has been the cause of several defamation actions. One high-profile early case was *Cairns v Modi*.[167] The case was brought by former New Zealand international cricketer Chris Cairns against the Commissioner of the Indian Premier League, Lalit Modi. On 5 January 2010 Modi had sent the tweet 'Chris Cairns removed from the IPL auction list due to his past record in match fixing. This was done by the Governing Council today.'[168] He then sent a further tweet in reply to an inquiry from a journalist 'we have removed him from the list for alleged allegations [sic] as we have zero tolerance of this kind of stuff. The Governing Council has decided against keeping him on the list.'[169] Modi removed the offending tweets within a few hours and as a result at an interim hearing Mr Modi argued that no real or substantial tort had occurred in the United Kingdom. He argued that he had at the time about 90 followers on Twitter and of these, a proportion would not read the tweet once it had been sent out. He suggested that in the jurisdiction in proceedings only about 35 people would have actually seen the remarks.[170] Tugendhat J took advice from two experts who both sided with the suggestion of the defendant on actual publication numbers but neither went further as to how many might have seen the remarks through other means such as searching for the defendant.[171] Tugendhat J decided that given the sensationalist nature of the remarks and the fact that the remarks could have been searched and republished, and not just by the defendant's followers, that the actual number of direct followers that Mr Modi had was irrelevant.[172] He continued that the court was entitled to infer that publication in the United Kingdom had been far greater than the estimated figures for those who had received direct tweets from the defendant and that even if the publication in the particular jurisdiction could only be described as insignificant, there remains the possibility and real risk of wider publication[173] and in this instance, despite the fact that the remarks had been removed quickly the claimant could bring proceedings. At a later full hearing on the facts Bean J found that Mr Cairns had been defamed and awarded him damages of £90,000.[174]

---

[166] See 'Law student wins £10,000 after being branded a paedophile on Facebook' *Daily Telegraph* 28 July 2010.
[167] [2010] EWHC 2859 (QB).
[168] [2012] EWHC 756 (QB), [6].
[169] Ibid. [7].
[170] [2010] EWHC 2859 [20].
[171] Ibid. [19]–[20].
[172] Ibid. [30].
[173] Ibid. [41].
[174] [2012] EWHC 756 (QB) [138].

Subsequent to this case came the extremely high-profile case of *McAlpine v Bercow*.[175] This was a case brought by former Conservative Party treasurer Lord Robert McAlpine. After retiring from politics Lord McAlpine had settled outside the public eye, but on 4 November 2012 he was incorrectly identified by a large number of Twitter users as being implicated in a child abuse scandal in Wales following a botched *Newsnight* investigation broadcast on the BBC leading the BBC to later pay damages of £185,000 plus costs. It is estimated that over 10,000 Twitter users in the UK tweeted or retweeted messages which were defamatory of the peer. Obviously he could not sue all of them so he took a rather pragmatic approach. He offered to settle with all users who had fewer than 500 followers in return for an apology and a donation to BBC Children in Need.[176] He then chose to pursue actions against a few high-profile individuals. Initially it was reported that twenty high-profile individuals would be sued, including comedian Alan Davies, journalist George Monbiot, and Sally Bercow, the then wife of the Speaker of the House of Commons. Monbiot and Davies apologized and made reparation. Davies agreed to pay £15,000 in damages[177] and Monbiot reaching an interesting settlement where he agreed to do work for three charities over three years to the value of £25,000.[178] Sally Bercow however refused to apologize or settle and was the recipient of a writ.

 Highlight Sally Bercow's Tweet

Why is Lord McAlpine trending? *innocent face*

Lord McAlpine alleged that her tweet was defamatory as 'in their natural and ordinary meaning, and/or in the alternative, by the way of innuendo the Tweet meant that he was a paedophile who was guilty of sexually abusing boys living in care.'[179] In her defence Bercow claimed that her tweet was simply a question—the enquiry as to why Lord McAlpine was trending was 'entirely neutral, and there is nothing else to be inferred from the question. [The] question does not suggest any reason why [Lord McAlpine] was, or might have been, trending. [The] question was as neutral as the statement on the Twitter screen itself which listed the Claimant under the heading "Trends".'[180] The problem Ms Bercow faced was not the question itself it was the addition of the statement *innocent face*, as Counsel for Lord McAlpine pointed out, 'it is not neutral, even to a reader who knew none of the events of the preceding two days. The question is followed by the words "innocent face".'[181] The trial turned on the

[175] [2013] EWHC 1342 (QB).
[176] R Greenslade, 'Twitter users should learn lessons from Sally Bercow's libellous tweet', *The Guardian*, 24 May 2013.
[177] Mark Sweney, 'Lord McAlpine settles libel action with Alan Davies over Twitter comment', *The Guardian*, 24 October 2013.
[178] George Monbiot, 'My Agreement with Lord McAlpine' <www.monbiot.com/2013/03/12/my-agreement-with-lord-mcalpine/>.
[179] McAlpine v Bercow [2013] EWHC 1342 (QB), [33].
[180] Ibid. [34].
[181] Ibid. [67].

interpretation of this short phrase. Counsel for Lord McAlpine argued that 'the words "innocent face" are to be read as irony, that is, as meaning the opposite of their literal meaning. People sometimes ask a question to which they already know the answer. They may do that as an indirect way of bringing out into the open something they already know, or believe to be, a fact. They sometimes seek to conceal what they are up to (or pretend to conceal what they are up to) by putting on an expression which suggests that they do not already know the answer to the question. Sir Edward submits that the reasonable explanation for the Defendant inserting the words "innocent face" in the Tweet is to negate a neutral interpretation, and to hint, or nudge readers into understanding that the Claimant has been doing wrong.'[182] Counsel for Ms Bercow though claimed the meaning was quite different:

> the words 'innocent face' are to be read literally: that the expression which the reader is being invited to imagine on the Defendant's face in asking the question is 'deadpan'. It is an expression to convey that she is asking it in a neutral and straightforward manner. She has noticed that the Claimant is trending and all she is asking is that someone should tell her why.[183]

In weighing up the evidence Tugendhat J was not convinced by Ms Bercow's version of events: 'in my judgment the reasonable reader would understand the words "innocent face" as being insincere and ironical. There is no sensible reason for including those words in the Tweet if they are to be taken as meaning that the Defendant simply wants to know the answer to a factual question.'[184] He went on to note:

> the Defendant is telling her followers that she does not know why he is trending, and there is no alternative explanation for why this particular peer was being named in the tweets which produce the Trend, then it is reasonable to infer that he is trending because he fits the description of the unnamed abuser. I find the reader would infer that. The reader would reasonably infer that the Defendant had provided the last piece in the jigsaw.[185]

With this finding Ms Bercow's defence was pierced and rather than continue to fight the case she agreed to pay damages of an undisclosed amount, reported in some newspapers as being £15,000 and to make an apology in open court. The apology was made on 21 October 2013 and on 22 October 2013 in compliance with the terms of the settlement Ms Bercow communicated this via Twitter. Although the level of damages paid to Lord McAlpine under the settlement was not large Ms Bercow was also liable for his costs as well as her own with many estimates of costs being in the region of £100,000. This case illustrates just how easily a simple throwaway tweet can end up being extremely expensive in the longer term.

That lesson has been painfully learned recently by media commentator Katie Hopkins, who found herself at the heart of the most recent high-profile Twitter defamation case.[186] The case has its roots in an anti-austerity rally held in Whitehall, London on 9 May 2015, one day after the new Conservative administration was formed, an administration which in its manifesto was committed to further austerity measures. The rally turned violent and at some point someone spray painted the words 'Fuck Tory Scum' on the Memorial to the Women of WWII. This act was photographed and widely reported

---

[182] Ibid. [68].
[183] Ibid. [75].
[184] Ibid. [84].
[185] Ibid. [85].
[186] *Monroe v Hopkins* [2017] EWHC 433 (QB).

in the press. The action led to a debate on Twitter between Guardian columnist Laurie Penny who wrote in support of the act and Katie Hopkins, a right-wing columnist and media personality who objected to it. These tweets, at times vitriolic, are not directly the cause of action. Instead on 18 May 2015 Ms Hopkins tweeted to Ms Munroe 'scrawled on any memorials recently? Vandalised the memory of those who fought for your freedom. Grandma got any more medals?' Ms Monroe responded asking for the tweet to be deleted, offering at one point an exit for Ms Hopkins if she deleted the tweet and paid a donation to charity. Ms Hopkins did delete the tweet but then sent a further tweet linking Ms Munroe to Ms Penny (and her earlier support for the act) 'Can someone explain to me—in 10 words or less—the difference between irritant @PennyRed and social anthrax @Jack Monroe.' A few days later Ms Munroe launched a defamation action.

Ms Monroe claimed the first tweet suggested she had either vandalized a war memorial herself or she condoned such action. The second tweet she suggested bore a direct innuendo that she approved or condoned specifically the criminal vandalization and desecration of the women's war memorial in Whitehall during the anti-austerity protest. Ms Hopkins argued that the first tweet did not suggest or imply that Ms Monroe had herself vandalized any memorial. Rather it suggested she was supportive, politically, of those who had painted the slogan onto the monument. The second tweet, she argued, 'would have been understood [by] the ordinary reader as no more than a petulant acknowledgment by [her] that she had mistakenly identified [Ms Monroe] instead of Ms Penny. Alternatively, the Second Tweet bore the same meaning as the First Tweet: that Ms Monroe "was supportive—politically—of those who had painted the slogan onto the monument".'[187]

Warby J first spent some time looking at how the principles of defamation applied on Twitter. He acknowledged the disruptive effect of Twitter, noting 'these well-established rules are perhaps easier to apply in the case of print publications of long standing such as books, newspapers, or magazines, or static online publications, than in the more dynamic and interactive world of Twitter, where short bursts of pithily expressed information are the norm, and a single tweet rarely exists in isolation from others.'[188] He found the limiting characteristic of Twitter meant context was important, finding that Twitter 'is a conversational medium; so it would be wrong to engage in elaborate analysis of a 140 character tweet; an impressionistic approach is much more fitting and appropriate to the medium; but this impressionistic approach must take account of the whole tweet and the context in which the ordinary reasonable reader would read that tweet. That context includes (a) matters of ordinary general knowledge; and (b) matters that were put before that reader via Twitter.'[189] Applying this he found that many, although not all, of the readers of Ms Hopkins' first tweet would have been aware of the earlier events on 9 May and would connect the tweet to those events. This suggested Ms Monroe's support at least for such an act (or even perhaps culpability) and this was enough ultimately to find the tweet to be defamatory and to find that serious harm occurred to Ms Monroe's reputation by the sending of this tweet.[190] Warby J also found that the second tweet, which on its natural meaning 'conveyed Ms Hopkins' contempt for Ms Monroe' would be understood by the reasonable reader to mean that Ms Monroe

[187] Ibid. [28].
[188] Ibid. [34].
[189] Ibid. [35].
[190] Ibid. [74].

'condoned and approved of the fact that in the course of an anti-government protest there had been vandalisation by obscene graffiti of the women's war memorial in Whitehall, a monument to those who fought for her freedom.' In other words, it bore the same innuendo meaning as the first tweet.[191]

Ms Hopkins lost and Warby J awarded Ms Monroe damages of £24,000. At first glance this seems not too disastrous for Ms Hopkins. However Warby J makes an observation which reveals the disastrous effect of this decision on Ms Hopkins.

 Highlight Warby J observes

The case could easily have been resolved at an early stage. There was an open offer to settle for £5,000. It was a reasonable offer. There could have been an offer of amends under the Defamation Act 1996. Such an offer attracts a substantial discount: up to half if the offer is prompt and unqualified. Such an offer would have meant the compensation would have been modest. The costs would have been a fraction of those which I am sure these parties have incurred in the event. Those costs have largely been incurred in contesting the issue of whether a statement which on its face had a defamatory tendency had actually caused serious harm.[192]

Ms Hopkins refused Ms Monroe's offer, and later was refused leave to appeal to the Court of Appeal.[193] It was reported later that she faced legal costs in excess of £107,000 in addition to the damages award. In September 2018 it was reported that Ms Hopkins had applied for an insolvency agreement in a bid to avoid bankruptcy and had been forced to sell her home to cover costs. Her case is a salutary tale for anyone. Two tweets sent without thought, a few seconds' action, cost her everything.[194] This could be any one of us.

7.5 **Conclusion**

As a communications media the internet is an obvious breeding ground for comment which is harmful. In addition, several unique characteristics of cyberspace make the publication of defamatory content more likely online than in any other mass media forums. The impression of anonymity that the internet gives affords people the sense of security that encourages the making of reckless statements, some of which may be defamatory. The cross-border nature of the network allows individuals to defame from overseas and to seek the protection of provisions such as the First Amendment to the US Constitution. The internet archives material for later access in a more efficient way than other mass media, allowing defamatory statements to be found easily and accessed long after they were originally made. And finally, the encouragement to participate and create found in the interactive web, and especially on SMPs, is turning everyone into a social networker or citizen journalist.

---

[191] Ibid. [48].
[192] Ibid. [83].
[193] <http://www.5rb.com/wp-content/uploads/2018/01/1196_001.pdf>.
[194] Although it must be acknowledged that it was less the tweets themselves than her choice to press the case rather than accepting the offer to settle that ultimately cost her everything.

While there is no doubt that overall the freedom of expression afforded to individuals via the internet is a force for good in society, we cannot allow individual reputations to be sullied because of the thoughtless actions of a few. This is the challenge of online defamation. As we have seen throughout this chapter, issues such as the multiple publication rule, international and cross-border publications, and the liability of intermediaries and carriers have all been to the fore. The application of the multiple publication rule in cases such as *Gutnick* and *Loutchansky* have challenged the usual rules on both the time and place of publication. Although later cases such as *Jameel* and *Al Amoudi* have taken steps to rebalance the rights of the competing parties and legislative amendments introduced by the Defamation Act 2013 have attempted to 'reset' the multiple publication rule for the internet society, it is clear that internet republication has forced a substantial rethink of what it means to publish a statement.

Further, as often online defamation occurs in anonymity, or may be caused by the actions of an individual domiciled overseas where enforcement may prove difficult, we are likely to see a continuation of the line of cases on intermediary liability which began in the UK with the *Godfrey* case and which most recently may be seen in the *Tamiz* and *Davison* cases. The UK/EU law arguably strikes a sensible balance here through the safe harbour provisions found in the European law. The ECtHR meanwhile have attempted to strike an Art. 10 balance between clearly illegal and immediately harmful speech and more nuanced perhaps harmful speech such as defamatory speech in the *Delfi* and *MTE* decisions.

Finally, we come to the very topical and growing issue of defamation on SMPs. The explosion of interest surrounding social networking sites such as Facebook and Twitter has changed the nature of social interaction. Individuals no longer communicate in small groups in pubs, restaurants, or clubs; they now socialize online in large groups. While offline statements tended to stay in the ether for a few seconds before disappearing they are now retained in a publicly accessible forum. The growth of social network defamation is likely to be one of the defining points of information technology law in the next ten years. The *McAlpine* and *Monroe* cases are unlikely to be the last word on this. This is not necessarily a bad thing. Anything which causes people to show respect and consideration for their fellow user can only be positive.

TEST QUESTIONS

Question 1

When preparing the Defamation Bill, the Ministry of Justice noted: 'We do not believe that the current position where each communication of defamatory matter is a separate publication giving rise to a separate cause of action is suitable for the modern internet age.'

Prepare a short response, outlining whether or not you agree with the Ministry and why (or why not).

Question 2

Can it really be defamatory to say on Twitter 'Why is Lord McAlpine trending? *innocent face*'
What about 'scrawled on any memorials recently? Vandalised the memory of those who fought for your freedom. Grandma got any more medals?'

Do defamation claims in cases such as these risk chilling the expressive space that has developed on Twitter?

Question 3

Ada Lovelace is a regular and successful online gambler due to her mental arithmetic skills. Ada frequently uses the online gambling site Bettr which combines online casino games with a social media function. Ada does not use Bettr's social media or chat functionality, preferring to keep to herself while gambling.

Ada is a resident of Seattle, Washington, but has a brother, Charles, who is an entrepreneur based in the UK. Following a very profitable round of blackjack, which attracted the attention of thousands of Bettr users, Ada's Bettr profile went viral and she is now something of a global online gambling star. After this event, another Bettr user operating under the pseudonym 'John Montagu', posted comments on the Bettr website alleging, among other things, that 'Ada Lovelace is a cheat' and 'Ada Lovelace is a fraud, who uses her insider knowledge of the Bettr algorithms to cheat the system'.

Ada's brother Charles sees the comments and tells Ada about them. Ada is very upset and contacts Bettr UK (based in London) and Bettr Inc. (based in Arizona) to ask them to remove the comments. Bettr Inc. replies that it is clearly stated in its terms of service that the website is governed by the law of the State of Arizona for defamation purposes. It therefore refuses Ada's request to remove the posts. One month has since passed and Ada has initiated legal proceedings against Bettr UK before the High Court of England and Wales. Bettr UK seeks your advice as to whether (a) the High Court can claim jurisdiction in this case, given that only 2,000 UK-based Bettr users saw the comments, and (b) whether it can be held responsible for the publication of the comments.
Advise Bettr UK.

FURTHER READING

Books

M Collins, *Collins on Defamation* (OUP 2014)

A Kenyon (ed.), *Comparative Defamation and Privacy Law* (CUP 2016)

J Riordan, *The Liability of Internet Intermediaries* (OUP 2016)

Chapters and Articles

D Mangan, 'Regulating for responsibility: reputation and social media' [2015] *International Review of Law, Computer and Technology* 16

P Polański, 'Rethinking the notion of hosting in the aftermath of Delfi: Shifting from liability to responsibility' [2018] *Computer Law & Security Review* 870

J Rowbottom, 'In the Shadow of Big Media: Freedom of Expression, Participation and the Production of Knowledge Online' [2014] *Public Law* 491

A Scott, 'An unwholesome layer cake: intermediary liability in English defamation and data protection law' in D Mangan and LE Gillies (eds.) *The Legal Challenges of Social Media* (Edward Elgar 2017)

PART III

Digital content and intellectual property rights

Intellectual property law as applied to digital goods and services. How laws designed for 'creations of the mind' have been adapted and applied in the digital environment. The challenge of free content vs reward.

Intellectual property rights and the information society

Intellectual property is a subject with a complex and varied history. It can trace its roots back to the late medieval period, but for a long time little interest was shown by the legal profession in this marginal and esoteric subject. It was never taught in the undergraduate LLB syllabus and was rarely seen even at LLM level. Textbooks on intellectual property law were scarce with William Cornish's 1980 text *Intellectual Property* probably the first such book published in the UK. All this was about to change though. With the move from the post-industrial society to the information society, interest in intellectual property and intellectual property rights (or IPRs) exploded. The information society, and more importantly the information economy, placed value in information rather than in physical goods, industrial processes, or even services. The only body of law which had a relationship with information in its pure form was the long-neglected intellectual property rights and so lawyers and law schools had to reacquaint themselves quickly with this marginalized subject.

It quickly became apparent that intellectual property and the information society shared a common root: both dealt with protecting the economic value of intangibles. Nothing in the digital environment can be touched, held, or physically possessed. In nature this makes virtual goods similar in form to intellectual property. The parallels with, in particular, the law of copyright are clear. Copyright is awarded to the expression of an idea, rather than to a thing. But the expression must be recorded in some form for the copyright to take effect. Thus when we think of copyright goods we think of physical items, most commonly books manufactured from paper and binding or music CDs or video DVDs. Of course the physical element of the copyright product is not the part of the product protected by copyright: the book, CD, or DVD is merely a physical carrier for the informational product.[1] The same is true of digital goods in the information society: digital goods have no weight or form, and to be possessed we need a carrier or storage medium for them, usually in the form of a hard drive or an internet server or else in the form of a flash memory card or an old-fashioned CD or DVD/Blu-Ray. There is therefore a natural synergy between traditional intellectual goods and modern information goods. The character traits they share mean that, as the information society was going through its formative phase, intellectual property

---

[1] See JP Barlow, 'The Economy of Ideas: A framework for patents and copyrights in the Digital Age', *Wired 2.03*, March 1994.

rights, or IPRs, became the natural interface between the traditional legal world and the developing informational society. This interface still plays an important role today with copyright forming the backbone of our system for the protection and exploitation of software as well as forming a focal point for the ongoing debate between the rights of artists and creators to be rewarded in the information society and for individuals to share and distribute content of all types while the law of trademarks still drives domain name disputes and search engine keyword disputes. This section will examine some of the key relationships between IPRs and the information society, beginning here with a short introduction to IPRs, including a short discussion of their role and history.

8.1 **An introduction to IPRs**

Intellectual Property Rights are the collective name given to a suite of legal protections, mostly statutory, but some at common law, which seek to protect the creator, author, or inventor of an intangible creation. There are many theories as to the development and role of IPRs in modern society[2] although the most common theme is the protection of the incentive-innovation-reward cycle.[3] This states that innovations or creations which benefit society as a whole should be encouraged and the creator should be rewarded for their creation. As intellectual property is intangible it would be easy for a free-rider to replicate the valuable creation of the original author or inventor without rewarding him or her for their creativity. Thus the author of a book could find unauthorized copies of their book being printed and circulated with no reward to them for their creativity,[4] or the inventor of a new industrial process could find competitors using their invention to compete against them in the marketplace. As intellectual property can be so easily misappropriated without some form of legal protection for these 'fruits of the mind' there would no incentive to create.

Intellectual property rights, by protecting the creator/inventor/author, build a cycle of incentive-innovation-reward which benefits society as a whole. The cycle begins by incentivizing creative individuals to spend time indulging their creativity, secure in the knowledge that should they produce something valuable they will eventually be rewarded for this. By allowing creative individuals the time to create, they produce something innovative, whether that be an innovation capable of industrial application (an invention) or an innovative cultural product (such as a book, film, or music). Knowing that they are protected by IPRs that person then publishes or otherwise exploits their innovative output at which point they are rewarded through means such as royalty payments. The financial security this offers allows them to begin the whole process anew at the incentive stage.

---

[2] See W Cornish, *Intellectual Property: Omnipresent, Distracting, Irrelevant?* (OUP 2004); W Landes and R Posner, *The Economic Structure of Intellectual Property Law* (Belknap 2003); R Blair and T Cotter, *Intellectual Property: Economic and Legal Dimensions of Rights and Remedies* (CUP 2005); R Spinello and H Tavani, *Intellectual Property Rights in a Networked World: Theory and Practice* (Information Science Publishing 2004).

[3] C Waelde et al., *Contemporary Intellectual Property: Law and Policy* (4th edn, OUP 2016) 9.

[4] This often occurred in nineteenth-century USA which failed to recognize the copyright of other states. This policy was attacked by Charles Dickens in his lecture tour of the US in 1842.

IPRs are an essential part of modern society: they underpin a great number of creative industries including the music and film industries, the computer software and games industries, publishing, dance, theatre and drama, pharmaceuticals, and the computer industry. There are a large variety of IPRs ranging from the three central IPRs (copyright for the original expression of ideas, patents for inventions capable of industrial application, and trademarks for badges or signs capable of distinguishing the operation or product of one business from another) to the newer or less common IPRs, including the database right for organized bodies of information, registered and unregistered design rights for industrial and architectural designs, semiconductor topography rights for designs of microchips, and plant variety rights for newly engineered plant varieties. In this text we will focus only on those which have the greatest interaction with informational goods and services: copyright, patents (only in relation to computer software), trademarks, and the database right. In order to provide the backdrop to the chapters which follow there will now follow a short introduction to these four rights.

8.1.1 Copyright

Copyright developed in the sixteenth and seventeenth centuries as a response to the rapid growth of movable type printing presses which facilitated the production and distribution of printed text. We can think of copyright as the first legal response to a challenge of new technology and the development of copyright may be seen to be analogous to the development of legal rules and principles for the information society. Prior to the development of movable type printing press technology by Johannes Gutenberg in what is now modern-day Germany in the 1440s, the concept of having rights in creative works had never been considered. Creative works were nonrivalrous, meaning that the fruits of the labour of the mind could be shared between many.[5]

The nature of creative works meant that when the concept of exclusive property in land and goods was developed, there was no parallel for works of the mind. Throughout the intellectual highs of the ancient Greek and Roman worlds and the intellectual dark ages which followed, there was no exclusive property in the written or spoken word. During this period creative works were often distributed by travelling storytellers, usually wandering minstrels, who would travel from town to town and engage in singing, acting, storytelling, and comedy. With most citizens unable to read, the minstrel was often the only way for individuals to learn the stories from the scriptures, or to hear news of recent events such as famous victories in battle. The concept of anyone 'owning' such knowledge would have been quite impossible for the average medieval European to imagine.

The printing press changed all this. It industrialized the process of distribution, replacing the scribe or the minstrel with the press and the bookseller. This meant an industry grew up around publishing, a profitable industry in which often the profits went to the publisher and the bookseller, not the author, poet, or playwright.[6] For around 100 years

---

[5] As famously recounted by Thomas Jefferson in his *Letter to Isaac McPherson*, 13 August 1813, where he notes: 'He who receives an idea from me, receives instruction himself without lessening mine; as he who lights his taper at mine, receives light without darkening me.' Full text at <http://www.let.rug.nl/usa/presidents/thomas-jefferson/letters-of-thomas-jefferson/jefl220.php>.

[6] It is often recorded that William Shakespeare made his fortune through lands he purchased in Stratford-upon-Avon and from performances of his plays. He made little if any money from production of folios of his plays.

the publishing industry and the authors who supplied it with its raw materials were in dispute over who had the right to issue copies of works to the general public.[7] This dispute was ended in 1710 when the world's first Copyright Act, the Statute of Anne, came into force. This gave to authors of books, including play texts and poems, a monopoly right to control the publication of copies of their work for a period of 21 years (if the work was already published when the Act came into force) or 14 years (for new works).

The Statute of Anne is the foundation of modern copyright law, which for the UK is to be found in Part I of the Copyright, Designs and Patents Act (CDPA) 1988. Today copyright protects a wide variety of expression. It still protects the written word but now also protects music, dance, theatrical performances, works of art, photographs, sound recordings, films (and video recordings), television and radio broadcasts, and cable programmes. Copyright reaches into almost every aspect of our lives. The most common interactions that people have with copyright on a day-to-day basis are in their use of modern entertainment products. Music is nearly always sold subject to copyright terms. If you buy a CD or download a track from iTunes, you do not own that music. Instead you are awarded a non-exclusive licence to make use of that music. This does not extend to making copies of the music, playing or performing it in public, or selling or distributing further copies. You are given a basic right to listen to the music for your own consumption and usually, in the modern digital distribution model, to make a limited number of copies on smartphones, tablets, or similar devices. The same is true of movies or television programmes. You are entitled to watch a television programme or to make a single recording for the purpose of 'time shifting' the broadcast;[8] however, you are not entitled to sell, rebroadcast, or distribute any copy you may make.[9] The other primary point of interaction between the general public and copyright law is in relation to computer software. You are unlikely to own any software on your computer. Again, as with music and movies, computer software is licensed to the end user. When you first install any new software on your computer you will be asked to agree to an 'end-user licence agreement'. This lists all the terms and conditions of your agreement with the software developer who owns the copyright. Most people never read these agreements, simply clicking on the 'I accept' button. This is not good practice as these contracts are legally enforceable and usually contain a number of clauses which limit the software developer's liability for damage or harm and require the customer to accept and install software updates.

Today copyright arises automatically and persists for an extensive period. For literary, dramatic, musical, and artistic works, including computer software, this period is the lifetime of the author and for 70 years after his or her death. It is clear this period, designed for traditional literary and artistic works, rather overprotects modern copyright works such as computer software and games, which are unlikely to have a commercial lifespan of more than five years, and with hardware upgrades being constantly developed very few digital devices will survive long enough for original software and games to enter the public domain in a meaningful fashion. Also, thanks to international

---

[7] This dispute which mostly gave the 'copy-right' to publishers during the seventeenth century is discussed in detail in A Murray, *The Regulation of Cyberspace: Control in the Online Environment* (Routledge 2007) 169–75. See also R Deazley, *On the Origin of the Right to Copy: Charting the Movement of Copyright Law in Eighteenth Century Britain (1695–1775)* (Hart 2004).

[8] CDPA s. 70(1).

[9] CDPA s. 70(2).

cooperation, a copyright valid in one Berne Convention state will be recognized and enforced in other Berne Convention states,[10] meaning that copyright protection is extensive, almost global. It allows the copyright holder a series of exclusive rights to: (1) copy the work; (2) issue copies of the work to the public; (3) rent or lend the work to the public; (4) perform, show, or play the work in public; (5) communicate the work to the public; and (6) make an adaptation of the work or do any of the above in relation to an adaptation.[11] Anyone who commits any of these acts without the copyright holder's permission infringes copyright allowing the copyright holder to enforce their copyright and to seek an award of damages. Copyright is therefore a diverse and long-lasting right. Although not seen as a particularly powerful form of protection, its wide range of protection and lack of a record of pre-existing copyrights and copyright holders causes a high degree of tension in the information society, which is a short-term society with emphasis on immediacy and which has a tendency to 'cut and paste' information.

8.1.2 **Patents**

Patents are quite different to copyright in terms of aim, scope, and history. Patents originated as Letters Patent, a letter from a monarch or similar overlord issued to a tradesman offering him a monopoly over a process for a period of time in return for services to the state.

 Highlight John of Utynam's patent

The first recorded Letter Patent in England was issued by King Henry VI to John of Utynam in 1449. John was a glazer with a new methodology for producing coloured glass. The King gave John an exclusive grant of use of his methodology in England for a period of 20 years. In payment the King required John to create stained-glass windows for the King's new educational institutions: Eton College and King's College, Cambridge. Under the terms of the letter John had to tutor his assistants in the skills of making coloured glass, ensuring that his techniques would become part of the public domain in England once his patent expired.

The idea of Letters Patent was widespread throughout Europe but it is probably Venice which invented the modern patent system when in 1474 it passed a decree that tradesmen who disclosed a new technology would be granted a ten-year monopoly over the use of that technology.[12]

The first formal recognition of a patents system in England, as opposed to individual Letters from the Crown, came in the form of the Statute of Monopolies in 1624. This provided that patents would only be available to 'the true and first inventor' of processes and for a period of not more than 14 years.[13] This is the foundation of the modern

---

[10] The Berne Convention is the Berne Convention for the Protection of Literary and Artistic Works of 1886.
[11] CDPA s 16(1).
[12] Waelde et al. (n. 3) 366.
[13] Statute of Monopolies 1624 s. 6.

patent system but it left the award of Letters Patent to the discretion of the Crown; it was only in the nineteenth century that the modern system of patent law and procedure developed when in 1852 the Patent Office was established and with it a process for the examination of patent applications and the issuing of a UK patent.

The history of patents is therefore longer and more chequered than the history of copyright. Although Letters Patent predate Copy Rights, the modern system of copyright became established in the eighteenth century, whereas modern patent law owes much to nineteenth-century developments. This probably owes much to the technological drivers behind the two systems. Copyright became industrialized with the development of the movable type printing press in the 1440s whereas patents had to await the industrial revolution driven by the invention of the Boulton and Watt steam engine in the 1770s to become industrialized. This emphasizes the close historical relationship between IPRs and technology.

Modern UK Patent Law is to be found mostly in the Patents Acts 1977 and 2004, with the 1977 Act containing the bulk of the rules on patentability and enforcement. Strangely, the Act does not define an invention, merely defining the scope of protection offered to an invention.[14] Instead, the Act characterizes how an invention may be recognized by setting out a test for patentability.[15]

 Highlight Test for patentability

An invention must:

(a) be new (usually referred to as novel)

(b) involve an inventive step

(c) be capable of industrial application

(d) not be found within the list of excluded matter.

The list of excluded matter is extremely important as within this list we find 'a scheme, rule or method for performing a mental act, playing a game or doing business, or a program for a computer'.[16] This represents a long-standing principle that one should not be able to gain a monopoly over an intellectual or business process. The addition of computer software to this category suggests that a computer program is viewed primarily as a method of conducting business or perhaps as a substitute for a mental process and as a result steps are taken to exclude software from patentability.[17] In addition, it should be noted that material which is capable of protection by copyright is generally excluded from patentability[18] and, as we have already seen, the Copyright, Designs and

---

[14] Patents Act 1977 s. 125(1).

[15] Patents Act 1977 s. 1(1). For further discussion on the nature of patentability see Waelde et al. (n. 3) 408–68.

[16] Patents Act 1977 s. 1(2)(c).

[17] It should be noted that the framers of the Patents Act 1977 were bound to implement this exclusion as there was a similar exclusion in the European Patent Convention of 1973 to which the UK was a signatory.

[18] Patents Act 1977 s. 1(2)(b).

Patents Act 1988 treats software as a literary work.[19] Thus on two principles, one a direct exclusionary principle, the other an indirect exclusionary principle, software is not to be treated as a patentable invention. As we shall see though at 9.6, the application of this principle is not as simple as one may expect.

Should your invention clear all these hurdles you will be granted a patent after a lengthy examination of your patent application, including publication of the application to allow for public scrutiny of it. A patent is awarded for a maximum period of 20 years, although you will need to pay a renewal fee annually after the first 5 years of the patent's life. Unlike copyright, patents do not arise automatically; they must be registered, and unlike copyright patents are not automatically of international effect. A patent application is only valid in the state in which it is made, and claims often seen on consumer items that a 'worldwide patent [is] applied for' are inaccurate. A multinational patent application may be made under the Patent Cooperation Treaty. This allows a single application to be made in a PCT signatory state, and to undergo a single local examination before being passed to other PCT patent offices for registration. Multinational patent applications are very lengthy, complex, and expensive and thus in many ways we can see patents as the antitheses of copyright: they are a strong and effective monopoly right, but are limited both temporally and geographically, with multinational patents usually only preferred for inventions of a high degree of economic potential.

8.1.3 **Trademarks**

Trademarks are a more contemporary creation. Like the modern patents system they may be seen to be the fruit of the industrial revolution. Trademarks have their roots in the common law of 'passing off', a claim in tort which first appeared in the early nineteenth century.[20] Passing off allowed, and indeed allows, a business enterprise to protect the goodwill it has established in its trading name or brand identity to raise an action in tort against anyone who damages that goodwill by causing the public to confuse their brand, product, or service with that of the claimant.[21] The three essential elements of a passing-off claim were, and remain: (1) the establishment that the claimant has goodwill in the name, brand, or identity in question; (2) that there has been a misrepresentation (by the defendant); and (3) that misrepresentation has caused damage to claimant's goodwill.[22]

The problem with relying on the tortious claim was that the claimant always had to first establish goodwill. It would be much easier if the claimant could instead rely upon some form of presumption. This, along with the growing internationalization of trade in the late nineteenth century,[23] led to the Trade Marks Registration Act 1875. This created a domestic register of trademarks allowing businesses to protect their brand or identity without the need to establish goodwill during a passing-off claim. Unlike

---

[19] CDPA s. 3(1)(b).

[20] See C Wadlow, *The Law of Passing Off* (5th edn, Sweet & Maxwell 2016); H Carty, *An Analysis of the Economic Torts* (2nd edn, OUP 2010).

[21] See *Perry v Truefitt* (1842) 6 Beav 66.

[22] See *Erven Warnink BV v J Townend & Sons* [1979] AC 731; *Reckitt & Coleman Products v Borden, Inc.* [1990] 1 All ER 873.

[23] Waelde et al. (n. 3) 553–60.

patents, or even copyright, trademarks are protected for a potentially unlimited term. Provided the mark remains in use and the trademark holder renews their registration periodically the mark may be retained in perpetuity.[24]

The modern law of trademarks is to be found in the Trade Marks Act 1994. This provides that 'any sign capable of being represented graphically which is capable of distinguishing goods or services of one undertaking from those of other undertakings' may be registered as a trademark.[25] Once registered, the mark must be renewed every ten years.[26] The Act protects the trademark holder against a variety of threats, including piracy (the use in the course of trade of a mark or sign which is *identical* to the trademark and is used in relation to goods or services similar to those for which the trademark is registered); unfair competition (the use of a sign which is similar to the trademark and used in relation to goods or services identical with or *similar* to those for which the trademark is registered and there is a likelihood of confusion); and misappropriation (the use of a 'famous mark', being a trademark which has a 'reputation' in the UK in a manner which without due cause takes unfair advantage of, or is detrimental to, the distinctive character or the repute of the trademark).[27]

Internationally, trademark protection functions similarly to patent protection. There is no global or even international trademark.[28] Trademarks, like patents, are awarded by domestic trademark registries and are limited in effectiveness to the jurisdictional reach of the office which registered the mark. Like patents, there is a procedure to seek a basket of international trademarks through a cooperation procedure. This procedure is the Madrid system, which was created under the Madrid Agreement Concerning the International Registration of Marks of 1891. Under the Madrid system a trademark owner can apply to have their trademark protected in several countries simultaneously by filing a single application with their domestic trademark office and electing to have this application forwarded to any number of Madrid protocol nations.[29] A trademark so registered is equivalent to an application or a registration of the same mark effected directly in each of the countries designated by the applicant. If the trademark office of a designated country does not refuse protection within one year, the protection of the mark is the same as if it had been originally registered with that office. The Madrid system and the PCT system are very similar and, as with the PCT system, Madrid applications are lengthier, more complex, and more expensive than a domestic application and tend to be preferred for trademarks with a high degree of economic potential.

---

[24] It should be noted that UK Trade Mark No. 1 registered on 1 January 1876 (the first day of operation of the new register) by Bass Breweries is still in operation and use.

[25] TMA 1994 ss. 1(1) and 40(1).

[26] TMA 1994 ss. 42 and 43.

[27] TMA 1994 s. 10.

[28] There is though a community trade mark which has effect throughout EU member states and is managed by the Office for Harmonization in the Internal Market (Trade Marks and Designs) (OHIM), which is located in Alicante, Spain. This is similar to the European Patent which is administered by the European Patent Office in Munich, the main distinction between the two being that the European Patent Office is not an EU body but a treaty body created by the European Patent Convention of 1973.

[29] On 11 October 2018 there were 102 Madrid protocol signatories, including the EU, the UK, and the US. A full list may be accessed at: <http://www.wipo.int/treaties/en/ShowResults.jsp?treaty_id=8>.

8.1.4 **The database right**

Compared to these three traditional IPRs, the database right is a modern development. The database right came into effect following the promulgation of the Database Directive of 1996.[30] The database right, more properly known as the *sui generis* database right to distinguish it from copyright protection of databases, was brought in to meet the challenge of protecting increasingly valuable databases of information which may not qualify for copyright protection.

The information economy places considerable value in databases: everything from customer contact databases to direct marketing databases, to databases of customer shopping habits. Although commercially valuable it was not clear that the contents of a database were protected. If a company were to obtain a copy of a competitor's database and were to make use of it for their own commercial gain it was not clear if there would be an action open to the original owner of the database. In some EU states, most notably the UK, there was a suggestion that the contents of a database would be protected by copyright law. This is because the UK has a famously low standard of originality requirement for copyright protection of compilations of data.[31] In other states, notably France and Germany, the law of copyright clearly would not protect databases. This divide started to affect the market for database industries with most EU-based database industries deciding to base themselves in the UK. To harmonize the law, and to allow for a free market in the database industry, the directive was passed.

The directive provides for two different forms of database protection. Copyright protection is available where in creating the database the designer of the database displays a high level of skill or originality. This standard is found in the Copyright, Designs and Patents Act which states that copyright protection for databases is available when 'by reason of the selection or arrangement of the contents of the database the database constitutes the author's own intellectual creation'.[32] A database which fails to meet this higher standard will be protected by the *sui generis* database right. This protects the contents of a database for a period of 15 years from the end of the calendar year in which the making of the database was completed.[33] The protection of the database right is afforded to the maker of the database: that is, the person 'who takes the initiative in obtaining, verifying or presenting the contents of a database and assumes the risk of investing in that obtaining, verification or presentation'.[34] One peculiarity of the database right is that by reg. 17(3):

> Any substantial change to the contents of a database, including a substantial change resulting from the accumulation of successive additions, deletions or alterations, which would result in the database being considered to be a substantial new investment shall qualify the database resulting from that investment for its own term of protection.[35]

This means that a continually updated database may qualify for permanent protection as at some point during the 15 years of its original protection the accumulation of

---

[30] Dir. 96/9/EC.

[31] See *Ladbroke (Football) Ltd v William Hill (Football) Ltd* [1964] 1 WLR 273 (HL); *Independent Television Publications Ltd v Time Out Ltd* [1984] FSR 64.

[32] CDPA s. 3A(2), giving effect to Art. 3(1) of the Database Directive.

[33] The Copyright and Rights in Databases Regulations 1997 (SI 1997/3032), Reg. 17(1).

[34] Reg. 14(1).

[35] Reg. 17(3).

changes and amendments made to the database will cause it to qualify for a new, and further, period of protection. The *sui generis* database right protects the maker of the database from unauthorized extraction or reutilization of all or a substantial part of the contents of the database.[36] This suggests a level of protection somewhat less than that available at copyright law meaning the *sui generis* database right is rather weak. One advantage offered by the database right is that, like copyright, it requires no registration or recording by a public office to be of effect. Like copyright law it arises automatically and will be recognized by all states which recognize the database right, in effect all EU member states and the UK.

8.2 **IPRs and digitization**

As with all other areas of the law the way we think about and deploy IPRs is being challenged by the information society and the process of digitization. However, the interaction between IPRs and the developing discipline of cyberlaw is rather different to most other areas of law. At this point in this book we have examined the difficulties that traditional (physical) property law as well as principles of free expression and defamation have had in adapting to the information society. Further on we will look at how criminal law and commercial law are similarly finding the information society to be a challenge but IPRs, founded in the fires of technological developments past, and characterized as the focal point between legal controls and intangible (informational) products and services, are flourishing in the information society. The story of this part of the book is less about the need for the traditional legal rules to develop and evolve to meet the challenges of the information society, but more questioning whether the widespread adoption of traditional intangible property principles, as found in IPRs, are beneficial to the development of the information society.

It has become common to think of information technology law, or cyberlaw, as applied intellectual property law. Courses in information technology law at both undergraduate and postgraduate level in UK universities tend to devote a large proportion of their time to dealing with the IP/IT interface, looking at copyright in software; patents for software and business methods; trademarks for domain names and search terms; and the database right and copyright in cyberspace, including hypertext linking, deep linking, framing, and misappropriation of copyright material. Governments and intergovernmental organizations have also spent a considerable amount of time looking at these issues and the rump of decided cases in cyberlaw subjects are concerned with the application of IPRs in the digital environment. To observe all these is not to criticize. It is to be expected that when something becomes economically valuable there will be a move to 'enclose' it using property rights. It was difficult to extend traditional property models to cyberspace and so all parties with an interest turned to the models at hand to protect intangible property which were IPRs. But as cyberlaw continues to evolve and develop as a cognate discipline, critics are now challenging what many perceive as an over-reliance on models developed for another age and for different challenges in dealing with the information economy and the information society.

---

[36] Reg. 16(1).

Chief among these critics is Professor Lawrence Lessig who has campaigned tirelessly against what he sees as the misapplication of copyright law to create what he calls a 'second enclosure movement' in cyberspace.[37] Professor Lessig believes so passionately in this cause that he, along with like-minded individuals, founded the Creative Commons movement in 2001 to allow individuals the option of permitting certain uses of their creative works, including music, video, and photographs, rather than the 'all rights reserved' approach found in copyright law. This system, which Lessig branded 'some rights reserved' has proven to be extremely successful with in excess of 400 million works making use of Creative Commons licences.[38] It is not only copyright law which has attracted criticism in the digital environment. All of our four key IPRs have been the subject of criticism for overprotecting content or systems in the information society. Many commentators have critiqued the US Patent and Trade Mark Office for awarding patents for software and for business methods which have overprotected the patentee and have chilled innovation,[39] while the heavy-handed approach taken by trademark owners when dealing with individuals who register domain names which are similar to their pre-existing trademark or which use their trademark in a domain name as a means of operating a legitimate complaint site (so called 'sucks' sites)[40] have also been critiqued.[41]

What is clear is that there is a tension between what citizens of the information society want and expect: liberty, free use of content, and unfettered free expression, and what the intellectual property industry is seeking: protection, control over use and abuse, and reward. This tension is not unlike that seen in chapter 5 between those individuals who argue speech should be free and those who argue that in the interests of society it is necessary to place limits on free expression. It is clear that, if the information society is to function, a balance must be struck between the interests of IPR holders and the interests of the rest of us to 'rip, mix, and burn' digital content.

TEST QUESTIONS

Question 1

Describe which forms of intellectual property right are applied in the information society and how and to what are they applied.

Question 2

Do intellectual property rights need to adapt to the information society?

---

[37] L Lessig, *Free Culture: How Big Media Uses Technology and the Law to Lock Down Culture and Control Creativity* (Penguin 2004).

[38] Creative Commons stopped updating their data in 2010 at which point there were 400 million works. Based on exponential growth this is likely to be in excess of 1 billion works today but we have no up-to-date data.

[39] K Blind, J Edler, and M Friedwald, *Software Patents: Economic Impacts and Policy Implications* (Edward Elgar 2005).

[40] e.g. http://www.bmwsucks.com.

[41] M Mueller, *Ruling the Root: Internet Governance and the Taming of Cyberspace* (MIT Press 2002).

FURTHER READING

Books

A Brown, S Kheria, J Cornwell, and M Iljadica, *Contemporary Intellectual Property: Law and Policy* (5th edn, OUP 2019)

W Cornish, *Intellectual Property: Omnipresent, Distracting, Irrelevant?* (OUP 2004)

P Goldstein, *Copyright's Highway: From the Printing Press to the Cloud* (2nd edn, Stanford University Press 2019)

S Stokes, *Digital Copyright: Law and Practice* (5th edn, Hart 2019)

Chapters and articles

LC Becker 'Deserving to Own Intellectual Property' (1993) 68 *Chicago–Kent Law Review* 609

EC Hettinger, 'Justifying Intellectual Property' (1989) 19 *Philosophy and Public Affairs* 31

Sir N MacCormick, 'On the Very Idea of Intellectual Property: An Essay According to the Institutionalist Theory of Law' (2002) 3 *Intellectual Property Quarterly* 1

J Waldron 'From Authors to Copiers: Individual Rights and Social Values in Intellectual Property Law' (1993) 68 *Chicago–Kent Law Review* 841

Software

9.1 **Protecting software: history**

The information society is founded upon the symbiotic relationship between hardware devices and the software which operates these devices. Digital hardware cannot function without software, while software, without hardware to implement its commands, is merely a series of ones and zeros recorded on a storage device. As hardware without software was valueless, computer hardware was originally supplied with software pre-installed and maintained by the hardware manufacturer. Thus if you bought or—more likely, given the prohibitive cost—leased an early IBM mainframe computer such as the IBM 1401, the machine would be supplied complete with software, much in the same way that an e-reader is sold today.[1] There was no competitive market for the supply of computer software and as a result no software industry or interest in the ownership of IPRs in software. This changed as the 1960s drew to a close. IBM's success in the computer markets of the 1960s led the US Department of Justice to inquire whether IBM was committing antitrust violations both by leasing rather than selling mainframe computers and by selling hardware and software as a 'bundled' single product. As a response to these investigations and in an attempt to head off an antitrust suit IBM announced on 23 June 1969, that it would unbundle much of its software and would price and licence that software separately from its hardware and support services. From this date on, separate markets for computer hardware and computer software existed. Software was now a stand-alone product which would require legal protection in the marketplace lest any unscrupulous individual attempt to free-ride on the investment of another.

Almost immediately the legal profession became interested in the newly developing market in computer software. There were early questions as to how software should be protected. Should it be by the application of patent law or by the law of copyright or should it be a *sui generis* form of protection? Again, as in many areas involving the interface of law and the information society, early jurisprudence on this subject is to be found in the US. In 1972 in the case of *Gottschalk v Benson*,[2] the US Supreme Court ruled that a process which converted binary-coded decimal numbers into true binary numbers (a process valuable in software development) was not patentable. Justice Douglas in giving the opinion of the court said that this decision should not be seen to deny

---

[1] A typical IBM 1401 system would have cost about $370,000 if purchased outright in 1961 (the year of its launch). This is the equivalent of around $3,123,827 at 2018 values. To lease an IBM 1401 cost $2,000 per month or $16,885 per month at 2018 values.

[2] *Gottschalk, Commissioner of Patents v Benson & Ors* 409 US 63 (1972).

patentability to all software, and noted that 'It may be that the patent laws should be extended to cover these programs' but that this was 'a policy matter to which we are not competent to speak'.[3] The court revisited this issue only six years later in the case of *Parker v Flook*.[4] Here the court found that the addition of a new software-based system to calculate safety limits in a catalytic conversion process was insufficient to qualify the process as a whole for patent protection, the only novelty being in the software design.

The failure of the fledgling software industry to convince the Supreme Court, or the prior President's Commission on the Patent System,[5] that patents should be extended to software, led the industry to seek protection elsewhere. Almost as soon as IBM had unbundled its software development arm, Elmer Galbi, a consultant with IBM, had suggested the need for a *sui generis* form of legal protection for computer software based on modification of the patent system.[6] This idea received limited support from the Supreme Court, and led to Congressman Hamilton Fish Jr introducing a Bill which would enshrine *sui generis* software protection in the US Code.[7] The Bill was unfortunately seriously flawed and opponents claimed it was too heavily influenced by proposals emanating from IBM, which risked extending IBM's near-monopoly of the software industry. The Bill was therefore allowed to lapse and while the anti-protectionist movement continued to find success in cases such as *Gottschalk* and *Flook* they saw there was little need to make changes to the law as it stood.

The economic reality though was that unless some formal system of protection for computer software could be found, the fledgling software industry was under threat. With software patents at this point being rejected by the judiciary and the executive, and with no realistic prospect of an agreed approach to *sui generis* protection, it appeared that copyright offered the only realistic alternative. Copyright expansion was the preferred route of the World Intellectual Property Organization and offered several apparent advantages. First, as copyright law does not require prior registration to be effective the expansion of copyright to software would not increase the administrative burden of patents offices. Second, as copyright is a 'soft' protection, with only a broad requirement of originality required to gain copyright protection and no need to establish inventiveness or a development on the prior art, there was no need to establish a database of prior art for software. Further, as software, when written as source code, looks like written text it seemed apt to extend copyright, as the natural form of protection for literary works, to software.

The US introduced a new Copyright Act in 1976 and in this it was made clear that Congress intended to extend copyright protection to software.[8] What was not clear

---

[3] Ibid. 66.

[4] 437 US 584 (1978).

[5] Report of the President's Commission on the Patent System, *To Promote the Progress of Useful Arts*, S. Doc No. 5, 90th Cong., 1st Sess. (1967).

[6] E Galbi, 'Proposal for New Legislation to Protect Computer Programming' (1970) 17 *Journal of the Copyright Society* 280; E Galbi, 'Software and Patents: A Status Report' (1971) 14 *Communications of the ACM* 274.

[7] R Stern, *Computer Law: Intellectual Property Rights in Computer-Related Subject Matter Cases and Materials* (George Washington Law School 1997) ch. 13.

[8] The definition of literary works found in §101 of the 1976 Act states that they are 'works, other than audiovisual works, expressed in words, numbers, or other verbal or numerical symbols or indicia, regardless of the nature of the material objects, such as books, periodicals, manuscripts, phonorecords, film, tapes, disks, or cards, in which they are embodied'.

though was how much protection computer programs should be given and whether there should be special exceptions to the exclusive rights of the copyright owners, as with some other types of literary works. Because Congress didn't want to delay the passage of the Act, it appointed the National Commission on New Technological Uses of Copyrighted Works to report back about computer programs and other new technologies and put a placeholder provision in the Act.[9] The Commission reported back in July 1978. Its main recommendation was that a new definition be added to §101 of the Copyright Act to the effect that: 'a computer program is a set of statements or instructions to be used directly or indirectly in a computer in order to bring about a certain result'. This would fully extend copyright protection to software by affording them the status of 'a literary work'. As this required a change in the law Congress had to pass an amendment to the Copyright Act, and so it came to pass on 12 December 1980 that the US became the first country to formally extend copyright law to computer programs.

Meanwhile the UK had also been considering how to protect computer software. There had been discussions similar to those seen across the Atlantic and the prevailing view was that the listing of the source code of a computer program in a printout would protect that code as a literary work.[10] This assumption was tested in a number of interim hearings such as *Sega Enterprises v Richards*.[11] This case involved the early computer game *Frogger*. Mr Richards was alleged to have copied elements of the *Frogger* source code to produce his own copy of the *Frogger* game system which he then sold in competition to Sega. Mr Richards admitted he copied elements of Sega's code; the only question was whether Sega had copyright protection in their source code. The court examined this question and found that:

> copyright under the provisions relating to literary works in the Copyright Act of 1956 subsists in the assembly code program . . . the machine code program derived from it by the operation of the part of the system of the computer called the assembler is to be regarded . . . as either a reproduction or an adaptation of the assembly code program, and accordingly, for the purposes of deciding this motion . . . copyright does subsist in the program.[12]

This decision, although the result of only an interim hearing, is exactly what commentators had predicted. The 1956 Copyright Act was sufficiently flexible to protect software without the need for expensive amendment as the US had done.

Despite the limited success of the now well-established software industry in cases such as *Richards*, the industry remained nervous. None of the early cases in the UK had gone to a full hearing. Usually when the industry won an interim decision the defendant would settle and would move on to a new project. This was the time when computer games and even business software could be written at home as a hobby and if one

---

[9] §117 was the placeholder provision. It stated: 'Notwithstanding the provisions of sections 106 through 116 and 118, this title does not afford the owner of copyright in a work any greater or lesser rights with respect to the use of the work in conjunction with automatic systems capable of storing, processing, retrieving, or transferring information, or in conjunction with any similar device, machine, or process, than those afforded to works under the law, whether title 17 or the common law or statutes of a State, in effect on December 31, 1977, as held applicable and construed by a court in an action brought under this title.'

[10] D Bainbridge, *Information Technology and Intellectual Property Law* (7th edn, Bloomsbury 2018) 71–5.

[11] [1983] FSR 73.

[12] Ibid. 75. Nowadays we would tend to refer to the 'assembly code' as the source code.

project fizzled out another was always just around the corner. Then a case in Australia changed things quite dramatically. The case was *Apple Computers, Inc. v Computer Edge Pty Ltd* and the decision of the Federal Court for New South Wales was exactly what the software industry had feared.[13]

 Case study *Apple Computers, Inc. v Computer Edge Pty Ltd*

The defendants were importing computers from Taiwan which copied the design of the Apple II minicomputer. They were selling the machines under the name 'Wombat' and claimed the machines had no Apple software installed.

This claim was found to be false when the claimants proved that programs installed on three silicon chips found within the Wombat's hardware contained within them the names of several Apple programmers. The defendants argued that the code contained on the chips was not protected by the Australian Copyright Act 1968.

It fell to Beaumont J to decide the case. He found that none of the programs are literary works within the meaning of the statute, stating: 'in my view, a literary work for this purpose is something which was intended to afford "either information or instruction or pleasure in the form of literary enjoyment" [whereas] the function of a computer programme is to control the sequence of operations carried out by a computer'. He went on to add that should copyright require to be extended to software this was a decision for the legislature not the judiciary.

Although the Appeal Court quickly overruled the decision of Beaumont J,[14] the damage was done. The first common law case on software copyright outside the US, to go to a full hearing had found that copyright law did not automatically cover computer software. In panic, legislatures across the globe moved to place their now economically significant copyright industries on a sound legal footing, as the US had done in 1980. The Federal Australian Government passed the Copyright Amendment Act 1984 and in the UK the Copyright (Computer Software) Amendment Act 1985 finally and formally brought computer software within the protection afforded to a literary work under the Copyright Act 1956.

9.2 **Copyright in computer software**

9.2.1 **Obtaining copyright protection**

The current position UK law holds in relation to copyright for computer software is to be found in the Copyright, Designs and Patents Act 1988 (CDPA), as amended. The key provision is s. 3(1)(b) which states that '"literary work" means any work, other than a dramatic or musical work, which is written, spoken or sung, and accordingly includes

---

[13] *Apple Computers Inc. v Computer Edge Pty Ltd* [1983] FCA 328.
[14] *Apple Computers Inc. v Computer Edge Pty Ltd* [1984] FSR 481.

a computer program'. This means that all the general principles of copyright law developed with respect to literary works over the centuries now apply equally to software: including the requirements for the subsistence of copyright protection and the protection afforded by copyright. To gain copyright protection software is required to fulfil the subsistence requirements of a literary work: namely, that it is original,[15] it has been 'recorded',[16] and that it qualifies for protection in the UK.[17]

Originality is in UK law quite a low threshold test which essentially requires that the author of the work has not copied (plagiarized) the work or elements of the work from others. The normal standard that would be applied to test for this is the so-called *Infopaq* standard. This was developed by the Court of Justice of the European Union (CJEU) in the case of *Infopaq International v Danske Dagblades Forening*[18] and requires that the work created is the 'author's own intellectual creation'. The court defines this quite loosely:

> **Highlight** Originality (*Infopaq* standard)
>
> Regarding the elements of such works covered by the protection, it should be observed that they consist of words which, considered in isolation, are not as such an intellectual creation of the author who employs them. *It is only through the choice, sequence and combination of those words that the author may express his creativity in an original manner* and achieve a result which is an intellectual creation.[19]

It has been suggested this is at variance with the traditional UK test known as 'sweat of the brow' which arguably focuses more on labour than creativity. That test is drawn from the case of *University of London Press Ltd v University Tutorial Press Ltd*.[20] This case involved exam papers written by academics for the University of London. The question was, were exam questions sufficiently original to allow copyright law to protect them as literary works? Peterson J considered that 'The originality which is required relates to the expression of the thought . . . the Act does not require that the expression must be in an original or novel form, but that the work must not be copied from another work—that it should originate from the author.'[21] Some English courts have suggested *Infopaq* does little to vary the UK standard. In *Newspaper Licensing Agency v Meltwater* the Court of Appeal took the view that *Infopaq* made little or no difference.[22] However a later decision of the Court of Appeal suggests otherwise.[23]

The question of whether or not *Infopaq* has varied the traditional UK standard of 'sweat of the brow' or 'skill labour and judgement' to a higher standard of 'intellectual

[15] CDPA 1988 s. 1(1).
[16] Ibid. s. 3(2).
[17] Ibid. s. 1(3).
[18] ECLI:EU:C:2009:465.
[19] Ibid. [45] (emphasis added).
[20] [1916] 2 Ch 601.
[21] Ibid. 608–9.
[22] [2011] EWCA Civ 890, [20] per The Chancellor of the High Court (Sir Andrew Morritt).
[23] *SAS v World Programming* [2013] EWCA Civ 1482.

creation' (and whether the UK may move back to the old standard post-Brexit) is not important here. The Software Directive has harmonized the originality standard for all software works at the 'intellectual creation' standard.[24] The originality threshold for works of computer software is clearly therefore the *Infopaq* standard. What does this mean? In implementing the Software Directive the UK government did not amend UK law to specifically implement Art. 3(1), taking the view that the sweat of the brow standard complied with the new standard.[25] The European Commission disagreed and in their report on implementation of the Software Directive criticized that the UK's failure to vary the legal standard.[26] The Commission need not have worried unduly though. In the later case of *Navitaire v EasyJet* Pumfrey J observed 'it is not sufficient to say that the purpose of the act is to protect original skill and labour' in finding that copyright in computer programs did not protect programming languages, interfaces, and the functionality of a computer program.[27] Later in *SAS v World Programming* the Court of Appeal explicitly accepted Infopaq as the root standard for the author's own intellectual creation when dealing with software works.[28] It seems the UK standard of originality, for software at least, is harmonized at the *Infopaq* standard, even if doubts might remain in other areas of copyright.

The second requirement for copyright protection to arise is that the software must be 'recorded, in writing or otherwise'.[29] To be distributable software must be recorded: the very act of making software will usually fulfil this requirement. However, the manner in which software is recorded is unusual. Software will usually be distributed as encoded binary data (a series of zeros and ones) either stored magnetically (on an HDD) or electrical charges held on surface-mounted chips on a circuit board (flash or solid-state storage) or even as a series of electrical or optical pulses carried across telecommunications networks (as a download). The obvious question is whether a series of binary representations encoded in this fashion qualifies as being 'recorded, in writing or otherwise'. Section 178 of the CDPA assists slightly by giving a broad definition of 'writing' as 'includ[ing] any form of notation or code, whether by hand or otherwise and regardless of the method by which, or medium in or on which, it is recorded'. Although not definitive, the broad definition of writing given in s. 178 suggests that the courts would have little difficulty in applying this definition to any of the forms of distribution discussed above. In fact, there seems little question that even temporary copies of a software file or instruction is sufficient to meet the recording threshold as under s. 17(6) copyright may be infringed by 'the making of copies which are transient'. To state an infringing copy may be transient, is at least strongly indicative that the original may be equally transient.[30]

---

[24] Dir. 91/250/EEC, Art. 1(3).

[25] E Rosati, *Originality in EU Copyright: Full Harmonization through Case Law* (Edward Elgar 2013) 65.

[26] COM (2000) 199 final, 10.

[27] *Navitaire v EasyJet* [2004] EWHC 1725 (Ch) [80].

[28] *SAS* (n. 23).

[29] CDPA 1988, s. 3(2).

[30] In truth the requirement of recording is as much a requirement of evidence as copyright law. We require fixing of copyright materials in a recorded form so that should an infringement claim arise the court has a fixed record of the original work with which it can compare the allegedly infringing copy. Thus something which was fixed transiently could establish copyright, provided some archive of the event was kept which could be presented to the court.

The final requirement for copyright protection is that the work in question must qualify for protection under the CDPA; this is a requirement of domicile. The copyright holder is required to demonstrate that UK copyright law, as opposed to the copyright law of another state should be applied. There are a number of ways a literary work, including software, can qualify for protection under the CDPA. By s. 153, if the author is a British citizen, a citizen of a British overseas territory, was a domiciled British resident at the time the software was made, or is a UK-registered company then any work they produce is eligible for UK copyright protection. Alternatively, if the author falls into none of these categories then, if the software was first published in the UK, it qualifies for UK protection.

It should be noted though that even software which does not meet these strict criteria can qualify for protection in the UK. By s. 155(3) first publication overseas shall not preclude the author from being able to claim 'simultaneous publication' in the UK where the work is published in the UK within 30 days of the original publication. Despite those extremely generous provisions many reading this may assume that the requirement of a UK connection for the work may rule many software products out of UK copyright protection. If we take a computer game for example, like the well-known *Call of Duty* series, these are 'authored' by a company called Infinity Ward located in Encino, California, and published by Activision, a company based in Santa Monica, California. Should Activision choose to release the next *Call of Duty* game in the US on a date more than 30 days prior to its UK publication date, it does not qualify for UK copyright protection as the author does not meet the residency requirement and the work does not meet the publication requirement. This would suggest the game was not protected in the UK and would be open to all manner of infringing acts including the making and distributing of illegal (pirate) copies. This, obviously, is not the case as such a rule would affect not only software but movies, music, and works of literature. The truth is that once the work qualifies for US copyright protection, under the terms of the Berne Convention,[31] the UK agrees to extend copyright protection to that work as if it were a UK copyright work.[32] The Convention provides a truly global copyright protection with 176 signatories each recognizing the copyright of all the others.[33] Thus once you obtain copyright in any one of the Berne signatory states you are automatically protected in all 176. It is therefore almost impossible to imagine that a software work would not be protected in the UK on grounds of qualification.

9.2.2 The scope of copyright protection

Once copyright protection has been obtained in an original piece of software, what rights does this confer on the copyright holder?[34] As a literary work software qualifies

---

[31] Berne Convention for the Protection of Literary and Artistic Works 1886.

[32] Ibid. Art. 5(1).

[33] A full list of the UK's bilateral obligations under the Convention may be found in the Schedule to the Copyright and Performances (Application to Other Countries) Order 2008, SI 2008/677.

[34] It should be noted that the copyright owner may be a different person from the author. This is particularly important when dealing with computer software which may be created by a collaborative effort of many hundred programmers. Under s. 11(2) where a literary, dramatic, musical, or artistic work is made by an employee in the course of his or her employment, his or her employer is the first owner of any copyright in the work subject to any agreement to the contrary. Thus although Microsoft may have had several hundred programmers all acting as co-authors on the Windows 10 project the copyright holder will be Microsoft Corp.

for the same protection as books, movies, or music. This affords the copyright owner six 'restricted acts', actions that only the copyright holder may legally carry out or may permit others to carry out.

 Highlight The six restricted acts

1. to make copies of the work[35]
2. to issue copies of the work to the public[36]
3. to rent or lend the work to the public[37]
4. to perform, show or play the work in public[38]
5. to communicate the work to the public[39]
6. to make an adaptation of the work or do any of the above in relation to an adaptation.[40]

These acts all have specific meaning both within the CDPA, and within the broader scope of copyright law. By s. 17(2), copying is defined as 'reproducing the work in any material form'. This extends beyond making complete (or literal) copies of the work and may include copying the structure or plot of a play or story or the use of characters created by another.[41] This is particularly common with computer software as the value of the software is in the structure of the software and what it does rather than in the source or object code which are never usually seen by the consumer. Thus, a software designer may study the structure of an original piece of software—say, an original computer game such as Epic's *Fortnite*—and then by copying the gaming engine and underlying protocols produce a competing game such as *Rules of Survival*, a variant on the 'battle royale' theme. As *Rules of Survival* will not share any of the original code with *Fortnite* there can be no question of literal copying. Instead in cases of 'non-literal copying' the question becomes whether the latter piece of software has copied these elements of the original which are afforded protection.[42] As a result much of the case law discussed in the following section will focus on non-literal infringement.[43]

---

[35] CDPA 1988, ss. 16(1)(a), 17.

[36] Ibid. ss. 16(1)(b), 18.

[37] Ibid. ss. 16(1)(ba), 18A.

[38] Ibid. ss. 16(1)(c), 19.

[39] Ibid. ss 16(1)(d), 20.

[40] Ibid. ss 16(1)(e), 21.

[41] The use of structure and concepts was discussed in depth in *Baigent & Anor v The Random House Group Ltd (The Da Vinci Code)* [2006] EWHC 719 (Ch), aff'd [2007] EWCA Civ 247.

[42] For the avoidance of doubt the author does not suggest the producers of *Rules of Survival* committed any form of copyright infringement. It is perfectly acceptable and indeed normal practice to be inspired by a successful game and to produce variants on the game idea. However legal action was launched against *Rules of Survival* publisher NetEase by another games publisher PUBG in 2018 claiming infringement of their game engine. The case is ongoing at the time of writing.

[43] This is not to deny the massive effect software piracy has on the software industry. The 2016 *Business Software Alliance Global Online Piracy Study*, calculated that global software piracy cost the industry $52.2bn in 2015 with 39 per cent of all software installed being illegal copies. Software piracy is a legally clear issue. The production, distribution, and installation of pirated software are all infringements of copyright, with those who produce and distribute pirated software committing a criminal offence under s. 107 of the CDPA. The issue with software piracy is one of enforcement, not one of legal certainty.

An adaptation is specifically defined in relation to software in s. 21(3)(ab) of the CDPA as 'an arrangement or altered version of the program or a translation of it'. Adaptations tend to occur when a piece of software written for one operating system, such as Apple's Mojave OS, is rewritten to operate on a different operating system such as Microsoft's Windows 10. Adaptations can also occur when an original piece of software is rewritten, usually by an agent employed by the end user of the software, to allow the end user to cancel a contractual arrangement with the software vendor and replace the vendor's software with his or her own. With commercial software often leased at substantial service costs, which include fees for maintenance and upgrades, it is tempting for end users to seek to replace supplied software with their own version. This is of course perfectly legal provided the software they develop is neither copied from nor is an adaptation of the original software. As with non-literal copying there have been several cases on this issue which will be examined below.

The remaining rights reserved to the copyright holder, the right to issue copies of the work to the public and the right to communicate the work to the public are less problematic. These rights allow copyright holders to control the distribution of their work, and ensure that the copyright holder is adequately rewarded for their efforts. There is though one unusual aspect of the right to issue copies of the work to the public which should be highlighted; exhaustion of the right. The right conferred on the copyright holder under s. 18 is only the right to first distribute copies of the work in the European Economic Area. Once that has been done the right, with respect to *that copy* of the work, is exhausted allowing the owner of that copy of the work to sell it on. This can be clearly seen with an example.

 Example Exhaustion of the first sale right

Ana buys a legitimate copy of a computer program in Portugal. She then imports it into the UK when she moves to London. She later decided to sell her copy of the software on eBay.co.uk. The principle of exhaustion means Ana may legally sell her copy of the software in the UK without the permission of the copyright owner (assuming she removes any installations of the software from her computer).

Bárbara bought her copy of the same software in Brazil. She also moves to London. If Bárbara tries to sell her copy of the software on eBay.co.uk she would technically be in breach of copyright. As Brazil is not an EEA state, she may not resell her copy legally within the EEA without the permission of the copyright holder.

Similarly the exhaustion of the copyright holder's right to first distribution only gives Ana the right to resell her copy of the software. It does not allow her to rent or lease her copy, nor does it allow her to make additional copies of the software.

9.3 **Copyright infringement and software: literal copying**

To carry out any restricted act without the permission of the copyright holder invites an action for copyright infringement. An action for copyright infringement is usually a civil action, although many people imagine it to be a criminal action due to the language used by the copyright industry in campaigns such as the 'copying is theft' campaign operated by the Federation Against Copyright Theft. In truth only a small number of activities involve the criminal law, most of which involve making literal copies available to the public.[44] In fact the divide between the civil enforcement of copyright infringement and the application of the criminal law follows quite closely the divide between literal, or pirated, copies and non-literal copies.

9.3.1 Offline and online piracy

Literal copies, usually known as pirated copies, are precise copies of a work and are usually produced with a view to selling or otherwise distributing them as a substitute for the original. As a complete copy of a work there is no doubt that literal copies infringe. There are a variety of offline ways in which software piracy may occur. The most simple and obvious being the production of illegal copies on DVD or flash memory stick/card in a back-street factory which are then sold on in markets, on the street, or in pubs. Although this type of activity is more common overseas it does still occur infrequently in the UK (online piracy has generally overtaken offline sales). If such a case were to arise either the police or trading standards officers, often with the support of the copyright holder or the Federation Against Software Theft, would deal it with.

It should not be assumed that all piracy has moved online; variants of software piracy still occur in the UK. One variant is the illegal pre-loading of software by hardware suppliers. Here the hardware supplier installs the software onto the hard drive of a PC, tablet, or smartphone and then sells the device with the software pre-installed. There are many reported cases on this practice, including *Microsoft v Electro-Wide Ltd*,[45] in which Laddie J found that 'an original equipment manufacturer who pre-loads software onto a computer for sale to the public needs a relevant licence from the copyright owner each time he loads the software'.[46] Another, more common variant of pre-loading is multiple installations, or end-user piracy. This usually occurs where a small-to-medium size business installs more copies of a piece of software than they are licensed to, that is. where there may be a few dozen or a few hundred PCs but not quite as many licences.[47] This type of infringement is notoriously difficult to track down as it is widespread and usually at a low level, too low in terms of monetary value to pay for a detailed investigation. To combat this problem, commercial software manufacturers have employed a variety of authentication measures. This is usually achieved through a 'product activation key', a unique identifier supplied with the software which the end user must enter when the software is first installed. Today these are registered online with the copyright owner so that they may ensure only the licensed number of copies of the software is currently in use. Unregistered software will not be updated or supported. These systems are, however, open to attack through the use of key generators, small programs which can mimic the operations of the registration system used by the copyright owner to defeat the activation process. To attempt to defeat the use of key generators some software

---

[44] The bulk of criminal copyright offences may be found in ss. 107–12 of the CDPA 1988.

[45] [1997] FSR 580.

[46] Ibid. 582.

[47] The Business Software Alliance periodically audits and fines companies. In 2016 they required UK SMEs to pay out £914,587 in 'legalisation costs', essentially the costs of making unlawful software legal and legal settlements.

companies have developed further anti-piracy systems such as Microsoft's Office 365 program which it uses to protect its Office products. This sees the concept of software as a product replaced with the concept of software as a service. Instead of paying a fee to own your copy of Microsoft Office the user pays an annual subscription fee which sees the licensed user receive updates to the software, technical support, cross-platform licensing, and cloud storage space. By building an ongoing service relationship with the customer Microsoft hope to eventually weed out end-user piracy.[48]

More commonly today software piracy in the UK is an online activity, with fast and stable internet connections two online piracy methods have increased in importance. The first is client-server piracy. This is similar in effect to pre-loading piracy but with the distinction that only a single copy of the software is installed on a server which may then be accessed and used by any user on the network. This type of software installation is usually legal if you have the right form of licence but in some cases the number of end users exceeds the number of licences the network operator has purchased. In these cases infringement occurs. More damaging though in terms of both volume and value is the worryingly commonplace occurrence of file-sharing services. In the UK the practice of swapping discs or buying illegal copies of software in markets or car boot sales has been replaced with trading illegal files on file-sharing technologies such as BitTorrent. The size of the illegal peer-to-peer (P2P) market should not be underestimated. Data supplied by Statista reveals that although the use of P2P services to illegally share content is in decline, 19 per cent of UK internet users over twelve years of age used an illegal P2P service to access or share digital content in the months March to May 2018. This is much reduced from a six-year high of 35 per cent in late 2012 but remains significant.[49]

9.3.2 Employee piracy

The final, less common, but potentially extremely harmful form of literal infringement is employee piracy. This occurs when an employee leaves their employer's employ and takes with them a complete copy, or a copy of a section, of their employer's product, usually with a view to producing a competing product of their own. An example of this type of infringement may be seen in the case of *IBCOS Computers Ltd v Barclays Mercantile Highland Finance Ltd*.[50] This case involved a software developer, Mr Poole, who wrote a suite of programs for his employer, IBCOS, which handled accounts and payrolls for agricultural machinery dealers. This software, called ADS, was owned by the plaintiff. Under the terms of Mr Poole's contract he could not develop any competing products within two years of his termination of his contract of employment. After leaving IBCOS Mr Poole wrote a new software suite similar to ADS called Unicorn which he supplied to Barclays Mercantile for marketing and sale. Mr Poole was careful to ensure that Unicorn was not marketed until after his two-year limitation period had expired.

---

[48] Modern network enabled software suites like Office 365 are proving to be successful in reducing piracy rates. However The Business Software Alliance still reports that despite a 1 per cent drop in illegal installations in 2017, 21 per cent of all installed software in the UK was unlicensed. BSA, 'Use of Unlicensed Software Drops to 21 per cent in UK as CIOs are Concerned with Data Hacks' 5 June 2018 <https://www.bsa.org/news-and-events/news/2018/june/gl06052018gss>.

[49] Statista, *Use of peer-to-peer services to consume or share digital content in the United Kingdom (UK) from 2012 to 2018, by legality group* <https://www.statista.com/statistics/291481/use-of-peer-to-peer-services-to-consume-or-share-digital-content-uk/>.

[50] [1994] FSR 275.

IBCOS claimed that Mr Poole had used elements of the ADS code in the Unicorn program and raised an infringement action. When the two programs were compared side by side it became clear that Mr Poole had copied elements of the ADS code. There were common errors of punctuation and spelling in the comment lines of the programs[51] and the same programming errors and redundant code were found in the same places.[52] Faced with this evidence Jacob J had little difficulty in finding that copying had occurred. The only remaining question was whether the copying had been sufficient to qualify as a 'substantial part' of the original.[53] A key question here was whether Jacob J should consider each work separately and individually or whether he could treat the entire ADS software suite—which comprised of 335 program files, 171 record layout files, and 46 screen layout files—as a single work.[54] Rejecting an earlier suggestion made in an interlocutory hearing in the case of *Total Information Processing Systems Ltd v Daman Ltd*[55] that the mere linking of several programs is not in itself an original literary or artistic work, Jacob J found that ADS was a compilation capable of independent copyright protection which existed in addition to and separately from the individual copyrights in each of the elements.[56] With this decided, Jacob J then considered whether the evidence indicated that substantial copying had occurred of both the individual elements of ADS and of ADS as a whole. He found substantial elements of the individual programs were repeated in Unicorn and, in comparing the overall structure of Unicorn to ADS, found that both programs shared: nine levels of security; a unique ability to create different invoice types; a common internal sales system within the ordinary sales ledger package; month-end sales audits combined with VAT; a 22-character parts description; use of three separate programs for the stock ordering facility; 12 labour rates; five levels of sub-totalling; and both had a redundant and unnecessary holiday stamp facility.[57] These common features were in Jacob J's view too many in number and too similar in design to be caused by Mr Poole's programming style and his reuse of common routines. He therefore found in favour of IBCOS, finding infringement of both the individual elements of ADS and of ADS as a whole.

The principles Jacob J set out in *IBCOS* were later to be applied in the similar case of *Cantor Fitzgerald International v Tradition (UK) Ltd*.[58] Cantor Fitzgerald (CF) are inter-dealer brokers in bonds, which means they act as the middle-men in a bond transaction. In September 1991 CF dismissed their Managing Director, Mr Howard, who then approached Tradition with a view to setting up an inter-dealer brokerage for them. To get the Tradition system up and running Mr Howard hired a number of members of staff from CF including Mr Harland, then the head of the Systems Department at CF, and almost his entire programming team. CF claimed that in setting up their inter-dealer brokerage Tradition infringed several of CF's copyrights in its brokerage software. They claimed that Tradition had directly infringed by installing copies of the CF brokerage system on their

---

[51] Ibid. 297–8.
[52] Ibid. 299.
[53] By s. 16(3)(a) of the CDPA 1988 infringement by copying only occurs where the alleged infringer has copied 'the work as a whole or any substantial part of it'.
[54] Figures from *IBCOS* (n. 50) 289.
[55] [1992] FSR 171.
[56] *IBCOS* (n. 50) 292–3.
[57] Ibid. 304–5.
[58] [2000] RPC 95.

system. This was admitted by Tradition and was easily disposed of. CF further claimed that elements of the CF software had been copied in the design of the new Tradition software. Tradition admitted that they had included some of the CF code in their program but that this accounted for less than 4 per cent of the complete CF code. They therefore argued this was not a 'substantial part' as required by s. 16(3)(a) of the CDPA.

It fell to Pumfrey J to determine whether the elements copied were in fact substantial, and how substantiality should be measured. He first noted that due to the way a computer program operates there is an argument that 'every part of a computer program is essential to its performance, and so every part, however small, is a "substantial part" of the program'.[59] This he rejected as over-broad. Instead he preferred to follow the lead of Jacob J in thinking of computer software as similar to a literary work with the focus of substantiality resting on the quality of what is taken rather than the quantity: 'Substantiality is to be judged in the light of the skill and labour in design and coding which went into the piece of code which is alleged to be copied. It is not determined by whether the system would work without the code; or by the amount of use the system makes of the code.'[60] On this basis Pumfrey J went on to examine the software suites as a whole, and each of their component parts, as Jacob J had done in *IBCOS*. He found that the direct copies of the CF software loaded onto the Tradition system were infringing, but found that, mostly, because the Tradition programmers had copied small elements of the CF system with a view to developing a better program suite, little of the new Tradition software infringed CF's copyright, although on a few key elements including one called LIFFE.BAS there had been infringement. The case therefore brought a mixed result for both parties with CF claiming a partial win.

The *IBCOS* principle was again applied in 2013 in *Coward v Phaestos Ltd*.[61] The case is not factually dissimilar to IBCOS. Dr Coward had been chairman and a director of IKOS CIF Ltd, a company now wholly owned by the first defendant. While working for IKOS Dr Coward had written trading software in the Gauss language for the purposes of a trading business specializing in currencies and Japanese warrants. In 2009 he left IKOS and set up a new venture in Monaco utilizing the IKOS software. Upon leaving IKOS Dr Coward claimed ownership of the software and claimed IKOS's continued use of the software was in breach of his copyright, IKOS counterclaimed, asserting his use of the software in his new venture was in breach of their copyright.

As can be seen, the instant issue was who owned the copyright, Dr Coward or IKOS? That was an issue determined by partnership agreements and not relevant to this analysis. Ultimately Asplin J found that the software was necessarily partnership property meaning the copyright focus fell on the counterclaim.[62] The question was, in utilizing the IKOS software had Dr Coward infringed their copyright? Asplin J applied IBCOS and found that 'to prove copying the claimant can normally do no more than point to parts of his work and the defendant's work which are the same and prove an opportunity of access to his work. If the resemblance is sufficiently great then the court will draw an inference of copying.'[63] Doing this she found that his use clearly infringed IKOS's copyright.

---

[59] Ibid. 130.
[60] Ibid. 135.
[61] [2013] EWHC 1292 (Ch).
[62] Ibid. [214].
[63] Ibid. [23].

9.4 **Copyright infringement and software: non-literal copying**

Much less common than literal copying, but much more legally complex is the idea of non-literal copying. Non-literal copying occurs when the structure, design, or characterization of a literary work is copied. Famously in 2006 the High Court had to decide whether Dan Brown's blockbuster novel *The Da Vinci Code* (DVC) had copied elements of a previous non-fiction book *The Holy Blood and the Holy Grail* (HBHG).[64] The claim made by the authors of HBHG was that Mr Brown had copied the central theme (in chronological order) of HBHG, and that without this central theme there is very little structure to be found in either HBHG or DVC. They claimed that this central theme therefore formed a bridge between the two works by which Brown substantially copied HBHG in his own work DVC. This was a complex claim which took up a considerable amount of court time. When Peter Smith J finally produced his lengthy judgment he found against the claimants, finding that the shared central theme could not be identified from the evidence and that 'even if there is a Central Theme as alleged by the Claimants in HBHG it . . . is merely an expression of a number of facts and ideas at a very general level. There is nothing in them in my view that goes beyond that proposition. It follows therefore that the Central Theme as expressed is not such as to justify being protected against copying.'[65]

The Da Vinci Code case is a typical literary non-literal infringement case. Debates in such cases usually centre on the dividing line between shared ideas (which are not copyrightable) and shared structures, themes, and concepts (which may be). In cases involving literary works there is never any doubt that the reader is able to distinguish between the two works and will experience both rather differently; this is because with books the reader consumes the actual written word. In *The Da Vinci Code* case the issue was not that the consumer may buy DVC in preference to HBHG as one was a non-fiction book and the other a thriller novel, but rather that the author and publisher of DVC had profited from the expressed ideas of the authors of HBHG. With software the issue is very different. The end user rarely sees the source code and will never usually see the object code. The way we consume and experience software is therefore very different to other literary works. We do not consume the protected element of the work as we do with books, films, music, or with artistic works; instead we experience software through the 'user interface', usually a 'graphical user interface' which uses graphical icons, and visual indicators (icons) to control software operations. Because of this unique way we interface with software it is possible for the consumer experience to be replicated without copying any of the underlying code: this is known as 'look and feel infringement'.

9.4.1 **Look and feel infringement**

Look and feel infringement first came to the attention of the legal establishment in the 1980s but it was not until the 1990s that the UK developed any case law in the field. Initially look and feel infringement was driven not as an attempt to avoid the impact of copyright law while free-riding on the work of others, but more prosaically because a software program, or suite, written from one operating system (such as Windows) would

[64] *Baigent* (n. 41).
[65] Ibid. [259].

not run on a different operating system (such as IBM's O/S2). Thus a successful piece of software written for one operating system would need to be translated to work on another operating system. In making the translation every effort would be made to ensure the translated program would work in the same way as the original: in other words, would have the same 'look and feel'. If such a translation was carried out by the copyright holder there would be no copyright issue, but if a third party decided to translate, or 'port-over', a program without the permission of the copyright holder litigation may follow.

After considerable discussion of look and feel infringement in US courts,[66] the first opportunity for a British judge to examine the application of look and feel principles was Ferris J in *John Richardson Computers Ltd v Flanders (No. 2)*.[67] Mr Richardson was a pharmacist who had written a program which would print labels for dispensed drugs and keep a stock count of prescription drugs in a small dispensing pharmacy. This program was written in BASIC and could be used on Tandy and Video Genie machines. Although his program was successful Mr Richardson realized he was not a professional programmer and his program had some shortfalls. He therefore set up a company, John Richardson Computers (JRC) and employed Mr Flanders, a professional programmer. Mr Flanders rewrote the original program for the new BBC microcomputer with great success.

After leaving JRC's employ in 1986, Mr Flanders began work on a new program called 'Pharm-Assist' for the IBM series of computers. It was this subsequent program which led JRC to take action against Mr Flanders. This was the first major non-literal software copyright case in the UK. The case was allocated to Ferris J who had to decide both the scope and limits of copyright protection under the CDPA, and how to develop a test for infringement applicable to the UK. Following an analysis of the facts Ferris J concluded that there were six issues which he needed to address:

 Highlight Ferris J's six issues

1. Does copyright subsist in a computer program?

2. If it does, is the copyright in the BBC program vested in the claimant?

3. Assuming the above, what ought to be the approach of the Court to the appraisal of an allegation of breach of copyright in a computer program where it is not claimed that the source code itself has been copied?

4. Are there objective similarities between the BBC program and the defendant's program which enable the defendant's program to be regarded in any respect as a copy of the BBC program?

5. Were any such similar features in fact copied from the BBC program?

6. Is any copying which may be found to have occurred the copying of a substantial part of the BBC program?[68]

---

[66] *Whelan Associates Inc. v Jaslow Dental Laboratory Inc.*, 797 F 2d 1222 (3d Cir. 1986); *Lotus Development Corp. v Paperback Software*, 740 F Supp 37 (D Mass 1990); *Computer Associates International Inc. v Altai*, 982 F 2d 693 (2nd Cir. 1992); and *Lotus Development Corp. v Borland International Inc.*, 49 F 3d 807 (1st Cir. 1995).

[67] [1993] FSR 497.

[68] Adapted from [1993] FSR 497, 515.

Having established the first two questions were to be answered in favour of the claimant, Ferris J turned his attention to the key question 'what ought to be the approach of the court to the appraisal of an allegation of breach of copyright in a computer program where it is not claimed that the source code itself has been copied?' He reviewed prior English authorities on non-literal copying of literary works, and the US case law on non-literal copyright infringement before establishing a new four-part UK test for non-literal infringement based in part on the US authority *Computer Associates International Inc. v Altai.*[69]

 Highlight The John Richardson four-part test

1. Was the plaintiff's work protected by copyright?

2. Were there similarities between the plaintiff's and the defendant's programs?

3. Were these similarities caused by copying or were other explanations possible?

4. In the event copying is established did the copied elements constitute a significant part of the original work?

The complication of the test developed by Ferris J was that at its fourth stage, he envisaged the use of a test from *Altai* known as the abstraction-filtration-comparison test. This was an extremely complex test, one which was quickly abandoned in the United States in the following case of *Lotus Development Corp. v Borland International Inc.*[70] Some critics believe Ferris J never fully understood the complexities of the abstraction-filtration-comparison test and in adapting it to fit English law he made a number of errors in its application.[71]

These criticisms crystallized in the later case of *IBCOS*.[72] This case, discussed previously under the literal infringement heading, found Jacob J highly critical of Ferris J's approach noting that: 'For myself I do not find the route of going via US case law particularly helpful.'[73] In particular, Jacob J was concerned that the abstraction-filtration-comparison approach may be too strict for UK copyright law, noting that:

> United States copyright law is not the same as ours, particularly in the area of copyright works concerned with functionality and of compilations . . . United States case law has, ever since *Baker v Selden*, been extremely careful to keep copyright out of the functional field, either by saying there is no copyright in, or that copyright cannot be infringed by taking, the functional . . . I doubt that would have happened here.[74]

---

[69] *Computer Associates* (n. 66).

[70] *Lotus* (n. 66).

[71] R Arnold, 'Infringement of Copyright in Computer Software by Non-Textual Copying: First Decision at Trial by an English Court *John Richardson Computers v Flanders*' (1993) EIPR 250; D Rowland, U Kohl, and A Charlesworth, *Information Technology Law* (5th edn, Routledge 2016) 454; S Lai, *The Copyright Protection of Computer Software in the United Kingdom* (Hart 2000) 33.

[72] *IBCOS* (n. 50).

[73] Ibid. 302.

[74] Ibid. 292.

With this in mind Jacob J suggests an alternate four-part test:

 Highlight The *IBCOS* four-part test

1. What are the work or works in which the claimant claims copyright?
2. Is each such work 'original'?
3. Was there copying from that work?
4. If there was copying, has a substantial part of that work been reproduced?

Unlike Ferris J, Jacob J did not propose the use of the *Altai* test at any point, instead trusting judges to apply their forensic skills in the same way a judge would be asked to in a non-literal literary infringement case. It has been argued that these two decisions are compatible with each other as *IBCOS* was a literal infringement case, while *Richardson* was a case on non-literal infringement.[75] This cannot escape the fact though that in *IBCOS* Jacob J clearly stated that 'going via the complication of the concept of a "core of protectable expression" merely complicates the matter so far as our law is concerned. It is likely to lead to overcitation of US authority based on a statute different from ours.'[76] Clearly, therefore, *Richardson* and *IBCOS* suggest two different tests for non-literal infringement in English law and, as both cases were decided before the High Court, neither had greater authority. For a period therefore there were two equally valid tests at English law. This remained unresolved until Pumfrey J in the later literal infringement case, *Cantor Fitzgerald International v Tradition (UK) Ltd*[77] elected to follow the approach of Jacob J in *IBCOS*. Although *Cantor Fitzgerald* was again a High Court decision and could not overrule or enshrine either of the tests, Pumfrey J made it clear that in his view the *IBCOS* standard was to be preferred. This case probably signalled the end of the brief flirtation the English courts had with the *Altai* test, but does not signal the end of the development of the law in relation to non-literal infringement of computer software.

9.4.2 **Look and feel: *Navitaire v easyJet***

The High Court had another opportunity to review the *IBCOS* standard soon after in the case of *Navitaire Inc. v easyJet Airline Co. & Anor.*[78] This involved an attempt by a customer to reverse-engineer and replicate a piece of proprietary software. The software in question, called 'OpenRes'; was supplied under licence by the claimant to the defendant for use on their website. It allowed them to take bookings online and operate flights without the need to issue a physical ticket. By 1999 it became clear that easyJet wanted to radically overhaul their booking software to offer further routes, greater language support, and easier operability. EasyJet negotiated with Navitaire about this

---

[75] D Bainbridge, *Introduction to Information Technology Law* (6th edn, Longman 2007) 50.
[76] [1994] FSR 275, 302.
[77] *Cantor Fitzgerald* (n. 58).
[78] [2004] EWHC 1725 (Ch).

upgrade but no agreement could be reached. Instead easyJet approached the second defendant, BulletProof Technologies, with the request that BulletProof should write a new booking system which would allow easyJet to install these much-needed upgrades but which would operate in all other respects exactly the same as OpenRes. This was important for easyJet for two reasons. First, they did not want to have to retrain all their ticketing agents on a new booking interface and, second, they wanted to migrate databases held on the OpenRes system to the new system.

BulletProof worked closely with easyJet's IT department over an extended period to create a new booking system 'eRes'. In designing eRes, BulletProof did not examine or make use of the OpenRes code; instead they worked from an operational copy of OpenRes, copying the structure of the software and emulating the functions of OpenRes. Because none of the code had been directly copied Navitaire raised a non-literal infringement claim focusing upon eRes's emulation of OpenRes command codes used by operators,[79] as well as emulations of the screen displays used particularly in the report screens and the underlying business logic of the OpenRes system.

Pumfrey J examined each of these claims in turn and in depth. He rejected Navitaire's claim that their command codes were protectable forms of expression. He found that the use of 'single [command] words in isolation are not to be considered as literary works' and that as a result 'the individual command words and letters do not qualify'.[80] This is based upon a decision in an earlier case *Exxon Corp. v Exxon Insurance Consultants International Ltd*,[81] which had ruled that single words are unlikely to be sufficiently original to qualify for copyright protection unless sufficient skill, labour, and judgement have been expended on the creation of the word. He then examined whether strings of command codes such as; 'A13JUNLTNAMS' could qualify for protection. Again the answer was in the negative. These were not 'recorded' in the program code, rather they were commands entered by the user. In any event, Pumfrey J noted that Recital 13 of the Software Directive[82] appeared to forbid protection of user interfaces meaning that the command codes could not be protected.[83] He then went on to consider whether Navitaire had copyright in the screen displays produced by the OpenRes software. He found that there were two types of screen display: one a simple text-based display which provided an interface for the input of data, and the second more dynamic graphical user-interface screens which made use of icons. The former he held were not protectable, but the latter were protectable and, to the extent that the defendants had substantially copied these, there was an infringement of copyright.

The key claim though was the final one: that in copying the look and feel of the OpenRes system the defendants had infringed the underlying business logic of the

---

[79] 'Command codes' are strings of characters which function as a type of shorthand in the booking system. They are explained by Pumfrey J at [26]: 'For example, in OpenRes, the command A13JUNLTNAMS (where the flight date is 13 June, the originating airport is Luton (LTN) and the destination airport Amsterdam (AMS)) should produce a screen displaying the available flights on that day.'

[80] *Navitaire* (n, 78) [80].

[81] [1982] RPC 69.

[82] Dir. 91/250/EEC.

[83] Recital 13 reads 'Whereas, for the avoidance of doubt, it has to be made clear that only the expression of a computer program is protected and that ideas and principles which underlie any element of a program, including those which underlie its interfaces, are not protected by copyright under this Directive.'

OpenRes system. This was the most important aspect of this case. To the end user OpenRes and eRes were substantively the same. They looked the same, they operated in the same way and they produced the same results. eRes was a direct emulation of OpenRes. Whether or not this was a breach of copyright was likely to have far-reaching consequences. Pumfrey J described this as a question of 'copying without access to the thing copied, directly or indirectly'.[84] He noted that this claim was moving away from the literary element of software to its functional element:

> The claim depends first upon the contention that the manner in which a machine behaves under the control of a program represents part of the skill and labour that went into the program. This is not an unreasonable observation. On the contrary, it is the whole object of the programmer to get the computer to behave in the required manner.[85]

Despite seeing the merit of the claim Pumfrey J was not willing to extend copyright protection in this manner:

> The questions in the present case are both a lack of substantiality and the nature of the skill and labour to be protected. Navitaire's computer program invites input in a manner excluded from copyright protection, outputs its results in a form excluded from copyright protection and creates a record of a reservation in the name of a particular passenger on a particular flight. What is left when the interface aspects of the case are disregarded is the business function of carrying out the transaction and creating the record, because none of the code was read or copied by the defendants. It is right that those responsible for devising OpenRes envisaged this as the end result for their program: but that is not relevant skill and labour. In my judgment, this claim for non-textual copying should fail. I do not come to this conclusion with any regret. If it is the policy of the Software Directive to exclude both computer languages and the underlying ideas of the interfaces from protection, then it should not be possible to circumvent these exclusions by seeking to identify some overall function or functions that it is the sole purpose of the interface to invoke and relying on those instead. As a matter of policy also, it seems to me that to permit the 'business logic' of a program to attract protection through the literary copyright afforded to the program itself is an unjustifiable extension of copyright protection into a field where I am far from satisfied that it is appropriate.[86]

Pumfrey J closes his analysis with an analogy which is extremely helpful in understanding his logic:

 Highlight Pumfrey J's pudding analogy

Take the example of a chef who invents a new pudding. After a lot of work he gets a satisfactory result, and thereafter his puddings are always made using his written recipe, undoubtedly a literary work. Along comes a competitor who likes the pudding and resolves to make it himself. Ultimately, after much culinary labour, he succeeds in emulating the earlier result, and he records his recipe. Is the later recipe an infringement of the earlier, as the end result, the plot, and purpose of both (the pudding) is the same? I believe the answer is no.[87]

---

84 *Navitaire* (n. 78) [113].
85 Ibid. [114].
86 Ibid. [129]–[130].
87 Ibid. [127].

9.4.3 **Look and feel:** *Nova Productions v Mazooma Games*

The outcome of *Navitaire* was widely predicted[88] and has been widely welcomed.[89] In the years that have followed the courts have taken the opportunity to reinforce the *Navitaire* test. *Nova Productions Ltd v Mazooma Games Ltd* was the subsequent case and reached the Court of Appeal. Nova Productions designed, manufactured, and sold arcade games. It brought two actions for infringement of copyright in one of its pool-based arcade games, Pocket Money. The first action was against Mazooma in relation to the creation and use of software for a game called Jackpot Pool. The second action was against a company called Bell Fruit in relation to a game called Trick Shot. Both claims alleged infringement in artistic works, being the graphics and the frames generated and displayed to the user of the game, and the computer program as a literary work.

At first instance, Kitchin J found for the defendants. He concluded there was no reproduction of any artistic copyright work, first because the features of similarity relied upon were either implemented quite differently or were different in appearance, and second, because those features represented ideas expressed at a very high level of generality or abstraction with no meaningful connection with the artistic nature of the graphic works relied on.[90] Applying the principles of *Navitaire*[91] he then rejected the software claim on the basis that any similarities derived were cast at such a level of abstraction and were so general that they could not amount to a substantial part of the computer program.[92]

On appeal it was agreed that the individual frames stored in the memory of a computer were 'graphic works' within the meaning found in the CDPA.[93] However, save for the fact that they were of a pool table with pockets, balls, and a cue, nothing of the defendants' screens amounted to a substantial reproduction of a corresponding screen in Nova's game.[94] However, Nova argued that there was a further artistic work in the screen graphics, that being:

> something beyond individual freeze-frame graphics . . . there is a series of graphics which show the 'in-time' movement of cue and [power] meter . . . what the defendants had done was to create 'a dynamic re-posing' of the [original]—one in which the detail of the subjects had changed, but an essential artistic element of the original was carried through to the Defendants.[95]

Jacob LJ in giving the leading judgment rejected both claims. He found there was no reproduction of a substantial part of the screen display,[96] and further there was also no

[88] M Simons, 'EasyJet Software Case "a Complete Nonsense"', *Computer Weekly* 19 May 2003; JC Perez, 'Developer Sues Accenture Subsidiary', *Infoworld* 6 May 2003.

[89] S Stokes, 'The Development of UK Software Copyright Law: From John Richardson Computers to Navitaire' (2005) 11 *Computer and Telecommunications Law Review* 129; M Heritage and P Jones, 'The End of "Look and Feel" and the Invasion of the Little Green Men? UK Copyright and Patent Protection for Software after 2005' (2006) 12 *Computer and Telecommunications Law Review* 67.

[90] *Nova Productions Ltd v Mazooma Games Ltd* [2006] EWHC 24 (Ch) [245].

[91] Ibid. [248].

[92] Ibid. [253].

[93] Section 4(1).

[94] *Nova Productions v Mazooma Games Ltd* [2007] EWCA Civ 219 [12].

[95] Ibid. [13].

[96] Ibid. [18].

foundation for Nova's 'in-time' argument.[97] With the artistic copyright claim quickly disposed of the court could turn its attention to the claim that the defendants' programs infringed Nova's copyright in the Pocket Money program itself. Nova tried to persuade the court that notwithstanding the decision in *Navitaire* someone who copies the function of a computer program to write his own program to achieve the same result is clearly appropriating part of the skill and labour expended in designing the program.[98] Jacob LJ rejected this submission. He also saw nothing in the Software Directive to suggest, as Nova contended, that the preparatory design work of a computer program should be protected as such, even if it consisted only of ideas as to what the program should do. It was clear to Jacob LJ from the directive that for computer programs as a whole, including the preparatory design work, ideas were not to be protected. What was protected by way of preparatory design work was that work as a literary work, the expression of a design which was to go into the ultimate program, not the ideas themselves.[99]

What is most important about the *Nova* decision is not the actual outcome, which could have been confidently predicted prior to the first-instance hearing in the High Court, but the very definite response of the Court of Appeal to a challenge to the principles of *Navitaire*. Nova made an early attempt to have the case referred to the Court of Justice of the European Union (CJEU) on the basis that there was a need to interpret the Software Directive's references to 'literary works' and 'preparatory design material for a computer program'. This was robustly rejected by the court.[100] The court then took an equally robust view of attempts to reinterpret *Navitaire* and in so doing they gave *Navitaire* a stamp of authority.

9.4.4 **Look and feel:** *SAS Institute v World Programming Ltd*

The final case in our trilogy of standard non-literal infringement cases is *SAS Institute v World Programming Ltd*[101] This is an extremely complicated case involving copyright in the design of a software platform and the programming language used to develop that platform. SAS are a well-known business software supplier. In the 1970s SAS developed an analytical software suite called 'The SAS System' which allowed users to carry out a number of data processing and analysis functions by writing their own in the SAS language used by the SAS system. These additional modules would then interface with pre-existing SAS modules allowing for complete interoperability of the system. The problem for the customer was that they were then locked in to the SAS system as they had to continue using the necessary components of the SAS system in order to be able to run their existing SAS language application programs, as well to create new ones.

---

[97] Ibid. At [16] Jacob LJ notes: 'Graphic work is defined as including all the types of thing specified in s. 4(2) which all have this in common, namely that they are static, non-moving. A series of drawings is a series of graphic works, not a single graphic work in itself. No-one would say that the copyright in a single drawing of Felix the Cat is infringed by a drawing of Donald Duck. A series of cartoon frames showing Felix running over a cliff edge into space, looking down and only then falling would not be infringed by a similar set of frames depicting Donald doing the same thing. That is in effect what is alleged here.'
[98] Ibid. [48].
[99] Ibid. [50].
[100] Ibid. [35].
[101] [2010] EWHC 1829 (Ch).

The alleged infringer, World Programming Ltd (WPL), identified a possible market for alternative software capable of executing application programs written in SAS language. WPL tried to emulate the functionality of the SAS software in their own program, the 'WPL Program' but crucially did so without access to the SAS source code. Instead they studied the SAS manual and two versions of the SAS software Learning Edition (which is used to train programmers and users of SAS software) and Full Edition. SAS brought proceedings against WPL for copyright infringement. They challenged the decisions in *Navitaire* and *Nova* claiming it was a breach of copyright to study how a computer program functions and then to write a similar program to reproduce the functionality. In addition, SAS alleged that WPL copied the SAS manual to create the WPL program and its accompanying manual, copied vital SAS program components, and breached the terms of a licence agreement. The case raised three interesting questions:

 Highlight The SAS questions

1. the extent to which copyright protected ideas, procedures, methods of operation, and mathematical concepts as distinct from expressions of those ideas etc.

2. the extent to which copyright protected the functionality and interfaces of computer programs and the programming languages in which they were expressed

3. the test to be applied to determine what amounted to reproduction of a substantial part in cases such as the instant case.

In the High Court, the case came before Arnold J who produced an extremely lengthy and detailed judgment running to 333 paragraphs before referring the case to the CJEU. He found that the UK courts should interpret the 1988 Act so as to protect 'expressions' and not 'ideas, procedures, methods of operation and mathematical concepts as such'. Accordingly, it was necessary to distinguish between 'expressions', on the one hand, and 'ideas, procedures, methods of operation and mathematical concepts as such', on the other. What was protected by copyright in a literary work was the form of expression of the literary work itself. In particular it was the skill, judgement, and labour in devising the form of expression that was protected by copyright, not the structural material behind it which may be equated to ideas.[102] Clearly here Arnold J is following the lead of *Navitaire* and *Nova*. He went on to state that when considering whether a substantial part of a literary work had been reproduced, it was necessary to focus upon what had been reproduced and to consider whether it expressed the author's own intellectual creation.[103] He then examined whether a programming language could be protected as a copyright work. He supported the views of Pumfrey J in *Navitaire* that a programming language was not a work:

> I do not agree that this demonstrates, as counsel for SAS Institute argued, that an exclusion of programming languages was deliberately not included in the Software Directive. To the contrary, I consider that it indicates that Article 1(2) is to be broadly interpreted. Furthermore, I think that

[102] Ibid. [206]–[207].
[103] Ibid. [243].

the distinction which Pumfrey J drew between a computer program and the language it is written in is, despite his hesitancy on the point, perfectly consistent with the distinction between expressions and ideas, procedures, methods of operation and mathematical formulae.[104]

Applying this decision he found that on the assumption that Pumfrey J had correctly interpreted Art. 1(2) of the Software Directive, the defendant had not infringed the claimant's copyrights in the SAS components by producing WPS.[105]

His decision was hesitant though, just as Pumfrey J's had been. The key phrase in this decision was 'on the assumption that Pumfrey J had correctly interpreted Art. 1(2) of the Software Directive'. As Arnold J acknowledged, 'I also agree with Pumfrey J, however, that the correct interpretation of Article 1(2) of the Software Directive on this point is not *acte clair* and that a reference is required in order to determine it.'[106] Arnold J therefore sent a number of questions to the CJEU but the key questions for our purpose were:

[Q.1] Where a computer program (the First Program) is protected by copyright as a literary work, is Article 1(2) of Directive 91/250 to be interpreted as meaning that it is not an infringement of the copyright in the First Program for a competitor of the rightholder without access to the source code of the First Program, either directly or via a process such as decompilation of the object code, to create another program (the Second Program) which replicates the functions of the First Program?

. . .

[Q.3] Where the First Program interprets and executes application programs written by users of the First Program in a programming language devised by the author of the First Program which comprises keywords devised or selected by the author of the First Program and a syntax devised by the author of the First Program, is Article 1(2) of Directive 91/250 to be interpreted as meaning that it is not an infringement of the copyright in the First Program for the Second Program to be written so as to interpret and execute such application programs using the same keywords and the same syntax?[107]

In May 2012 the CJEU gave its answers to these key questions. It found quite unequivocally that 'neither the functionality of a computer program nor the programming language and the format of data files used in a computer program in order to exploit certain of its functions constitute a form of expression of that program for the purposes of art. 1(2) of Directive 91/250'.[108] This is about as clear guidance as it was possible for the CJEU to give. As such it is difficult to think of an occasion where non-literal copying would be upheld now. Although earlier UK cases like *Richardson* and *IBCOS* had suggested a form of non-literal copyright protection *Navitaire*, *Nova*, and now *SAS* suggest this is no longer correct at English or EU law and that software copyright is mostly restricted to direct infringement. The decision of the CJEU was then given effect by Arnold J who, following the CJEU ruling, dismissed all of SAS's claims in relation to their software copyright.[109] In a final twist SAS then appealed Arnold J's decision but the Court of Appeal upheld his decision.[110]

---

[104] Ibid. [217].
[105] Ibid. [332].
[106] Ibid. [218].
[107] The full list is at *SAS Institute Inc v World Programming Ltd* [2012] 3 CMLR 4, [AG35].
[108] Ibid. [39].
[109] *SAS Institute Inc. v World Programming Limited* [2013] EWHC 69 (Ch).
[110] *SAS Institute Inc. v World Programming Limited* [2013] EWCA Civ 1482.

9.5 **Copyright infringement and software: permitted acts**

Not all activities involving the reproduction of elements of computer software infringe the rights of the copyright holder: some acts are permitted by the CDPA. First, there is a wide range of acts classified as 'fair dealing'. These are permitted activities, regulated by the Act, which apply to all literary works, software included.

The list of permitted acts is contained in chapter 3 of the Act and covers an extensive variety of activities. In terms of software the most commonly useful fair dealing defences are likely to include the right to make copies for the purpose of private study[111] and copying in the course of criticism, review, or news reporting.[112] The private study exception allows an individual to make a copy of a literary work 'for the purposes of research for a non-commercial purpose'. This allows individuals to study the work but, crucially, in relation to software does not allow the user to 'convert a computer program expressed in a low level language into a version expressed in a higher level language'[113] or to 'observe, study or test the functioning of a computer program in order to determine the ideas and principles which underlie any element of the program'.[114] The reason for these exceptions is that there are specific fair use provisions for software found elsewhere in the Act which deal with these activities, and which will be discussed below.

The other general fair dealing right which may be implemented in relation to software is the criticism or review right. This allows the reviewer to carry out restricted activities in relation to the work for the purpose of 'criticism or review, of that or another work or of a performance of a work provided that it is accompanied by a sufficient acknowledgement'.[115] This right may be useful in particular when reviewing features of a piece of software in an online review or similar. Fair dealing rights also extend to a number of specific situations such as the use of copyright material in education and examinations,[116] libraries and archives,[117] and in the administration of justice,[118] but by far the most interesting section of the Act for those who deal with software design and development are the provisions contained in ss. 50A–50C, entitled: 'computer programs: lawful users'.

Sections 50A–50C contain four permitted acts specifically designed to allow for fair use of and development of computer software. These are the backup right, the decompilation right, the study and testing right, and the adaptation right. The simplest of these rights, and the most useful for an end user rather than developer, is the backup right contained in s. 50A. This allows a lawful user of a copy of a computer program to 'make any back up copy of it which it is necessary for him to have for the purposes of his lawful use'. This allows a lawful user[119] to make a copy of their software to be stored in case

---

[111] CDPA 1988, s. 29.
[112] Ibid. s. 30.
[113] Ibid. s. 29(4)(a).
[114] Ibid. s. 29(4A).
[115] Ibid. s. 30(1).
[116] Ibid. ss. 32–36A.
[117] Ibid. ss. 37–44A.
[118] Ibid. ss. 45–50.
[119] Helpfully defined in the Act as a person who 'has a right to use the program (whether under a licence to do any acts restricted by the copyright in the program or otherwise)', s. 50A(2). In effect this means anyone who has bought or otherwise licensed a legal copy of the software.

the software requires to be reinstalled at some point in the future should the original installation become corrupt. When this right was first introduced by the Copyright (Computer Programs) Regulations 1992[120] it was envisaged that the backup copy would be on a removable media such as a floppy disk but today with software usually requiring to be installed on to the HDD of the user before it can be used the 'backup' copy is usually the original installation disc. This raises the interesting, and as yet unanswered question of whether an end user could use s. 50A to allow them to install software on their hard drive.[121]

The remaining three rights are of greater use to software developers than users. The decompilation right contained in s. 50B, allows a lawful user of a copy of a computer program expressed in a low-level language (i.e. in object code) to convert it into a version expressed in a higher-level language, (i.e. source code) or, incidentally in the course of so converting the program, to copy it.[122] This right is subject to quite strict restrictions. One may only decompile for the purposes of the permitted objective 'to obtain the information necessary to create an independent program which can be operated with the program decompiled or with another program'.[123] Decompilation may only therefore be carried out to allow for interoperability of programs. The reason for the introduction of s. 50(B) is to ensure that software developers with a dominant position in either the operating systems market or part of the applications software market cannot use their market dominance to prevent competition. The fear was that dominant market players such as Microsoft would be able to prevent new entrants into the market by not revealing vital information about the APIs[124] used by the dominant software or about digital rights management systems they use to recognize and allow access to content. Imagine, if you will, a company wishes to produce a new word-processing program. When they launch this program they want their customers to be able to access and edit files sent by friends and colleagues using the market-leading Microsoft Word program, also they want files produced on their word processor to be equally accessible to users of Microsoft Word. This is interoperability, the ability of one program to interface with another. Without the ability to access the APIs Microsoft uses such interoperability would be impossible, or at least substantially compromised. This is remedied by s. 50B, which allows developers, when the designer of the original software withholds such information, to dissect the code of the original program to allow interoperability to take place.

The third permitted right is the right to 'observe, study or test the functioning of the program in order to determine the ideas and principles which underlie any element of the program if he does so while performing any of the acts of loading, displaying, running, transmitting or storing the program which he is entitled to do'.[125] This section

---

[120] SI 1992/3233.

[121] Although as yet unanswered the author is of the view that it is unlikely a judge would view an installed copy of a piece of software as a 'backup' as it would be the primary use piece of software.

[122] CDPA 1988, s. 50B(1).

[123] Ibid. s. 50B(2)(a).

[124] Applications programming interfaces or APIs are an expression of a software component in terms of its operations, inputs, outputs, and underlying types. An API defines functionalities that are independent of their respective implementations, which allows definitions and implementations to vary without compromising the interface.

[125] CDPA 1988, s. 50BA(1).

may seem to be rather superfluous. It suggests a lawful user may study a copy of their own software, surely something that sensibly shouldn't worry the courts? However, the reason for s. 50BA is twofold. First, it reinforces and gives some guidance as to the application of the idea/expression dichotomy which courts have had some difficulty with in relation to software. It also allows developers to produce software designs which emulate installed software, as in the *Navitaire* case, provided they do not copy the code of the original.

The final permitted right is the right for the lawful user of a piece of software to copy or adapt that software, including for the purpose of error correction.[126] Often the end-user licence supplied with a piece of software precludes the end user from carrying out repairs or corrections to the software. This may be problematic, particularly if the copyright holder elects to end technical support for that piece of software or if the commercial relationship between the software supplier and the end user breaks down. There are some inherent ambiguities in s. 50C, in particular what is the exact meaning of 'necessary' found in s. 50C(1)(a),[127] and what qualifies as an 'error' for the purpose of s. 50C(2)? Some guidance on the latter point may be gleaned from Jacob J's decision in *Mars UK Ltd v Teknowledge Ltd*.[128]

This was a case involving the upgrade of software on vending machines. Mars provide software on a programmable memory chip that allows vending machine operators to ensure only legal coins are accepted by their machines. This is done via a complex set of measurements including weight, size, and electrical resistance of coins. When coinage changes, as with the introduction of new 5p, 10p, and 50p coins in the 1990s these coin-sorter units must be reprogrammed. When this occurs Mars produce a reprogramming unit and licence agents to carry out reprogramming on their behalf. Teknowledge were a private company who in the 1990s reverse-engineered Mars' Cashflow software which managed most modern coin-sorter units. Mars claimed this was a breach of their copyright. Teknowledge claimed that they were permitted to produce a 'spare part' for replacement or repair, a common law defence found in an earlier House of Lords case, *British Leyland v Armstrong*.[129] In evaluating this claim Jacob J had to consider whether this common law defence had survived the passing of ss. 50A–50C of the CDPA. In finding the common law defence no longer applied he also seemed to indicate that the error correction defence was different to a repair or update defence. Thus it seems that 'error correction' is limited to correcting errors in coding which directly interfere with the operability of the software: anything which is required to be carried out to update or repair software caused by environmental changes (as in *Mars*) is not error correction. Thus if you need to upgrade software because of the development of a new virus threat, the development of a new standard protocol, or simply to reflect changes in operating practice this appears not to be error correction and not permitted by the s. 50C exception.

---

[126] Ibid. ss. 50C(1), (2).
[127] Section 50C(1)(a) states: 'It is not an infringement of copyright for a lawful user of a copy of a computer program to copy or adapt it, provided that the copying or adapting is necessary for his lawful use.'
[128] [1999] EWHC 226 (Pat).
[129] [1986] AC 577.

9.6 **Patent protection for computer software**

Section 1(2)(c) of the Patents Act 1977 is quite clear: 'the following (among other things) are not inventions for the purposes of this Act, that is to say, anything which consists of a scheme, rule or method for performing a mental act, playing a game or doing business, *or a program for a computer*'. Equally clear is Article 52(2)(c) the European Patent Convention, 'the following in particular shall not be regarded as inventions . . . schemes, rules and methods for performing mental acts, playing games or doing business, *and programs for computers*'. With two such unarguably clear statements of the law at both European and UK level it may be assumed that this final section of this chapter would be necessarily short but unfortunately the law on patent protection for computer software is less clear than one might hope. Software developers have long sought patent protection for their output. As previously discussed as early as 1972 in the case of *Gottschalk v Benson*,[130] the US Supreme Court examined the patentability of computer software, a question they were to return to in 1978 in the case of *Parker v Flook*.[131]

The UK courts had begun looking at the patentability of software processes even earlier. In *Gevers' Application*[132] the court examined whether a data processing operation using punch cards was a 'manner of manufacture' under the Patents Act 1949. Mr Gevers had designed an index of word trademarks using punched cards and a processing system which allowed use of these cards to check for similarity between applications for trademarks and previously registered marks. Graham J allowed Mr Gevers' application finding that his punched cards shared a similarity to a cam control for a lathe and could be distinguished from a card which contained written or printed information intended to convey information to the human eye or mind.[133] In the later case of *Burrough's Corporation (Perkin's Application)*,[134] the court held that 'computer programmes which have the effect of controlling computers to operate in a particular way, where such programmes are embodied in physical form, are proper subject matter for letters patent'.[135] Although it may be assumed that the 1977 Patents Act statutorily overruled these early cases[136] software designers have continued to seek patent protection for their output. This is because the level of protection offered by patent law is much greater than that offered by copyright law, with the core idea of the software being protectable by patent and although patents are of a short lifespan, only 20 years as opposed to copyright's 70 years plus, this is more than sufficient when dealing with most software applications which tend to be of a short shelf life. Further, the recent retreat from expansive look and feel protection seen in both the US and the UK has increased demand for software patents.

There is a problem with the wording of the Patents Act. There is a deliberate ambiguity designed to allow a patent to be awarded to an invention which contains a

---

[130] *Gottschalk* (n. 2).
[131] *Parker* (n. 4).
[132] [1969] FSR 480.
[133] Ibid. 486–7.
[134] [1973] FSR 439.
[135] Ibid. 450.
[136] On which see *Gale's Application* [1991] RPC 305.

software element, but is not solely software-based. This ambiguity can be seen if you look at s. 1(2)(c).[137]

 Highlight Patents Act 1977, s. 1(2)(c)

It is hereby declared that the following (among other things) are not inventions for the purposes of this Act, that is to say, anything which consists of a scheme, rule or method for performing a mental act, playing a game or doing business, or a program for a computer; but the foregoing provision shall prevent anything from being treated as an invention for the purposes of this Act only to the extent that a patent or application for a patent relates to that thing as such.

This ambiguity requires patent examiners to walk a very fine line. It is designed to ensure that patents may be awarded for inventions which rely upon software as an element of their design, think of a computer-controlled engine management systems or even a humble washing machine, but to exclude pure software inventions such as hyperlinking or 'cut and paste'. The problem is that courts are required to develop tests which allow through the patentable 'software-related invention' but which prevent the patenting of software. With such high values at stake it is no surprise that this fine distinction has come again and again under attack. The first attempt to define where this line should be drawn was the case of *VICOM/computer-related invention.*[138]

9.6.1 **VICOM/computer-related invention**

This was an application to the European Patent Office (EPO) under the Convention. It related to a new processing system for digital images, the process itself being described as a series of mathematical algorithms.

The Appeal Board of the EPO decided that a claim for a technical process, carried out under the control of a programme cannot be regarded as related to a 'computer program as such'. They reached this decision in applying an approach which became known as the 'technical effect' approach. It asks judges or patent examiners to examine the application as if the excepted element (the software) were not present and then to ask 'does the application without the excepted element meet the standard of patentability?' If the only novel or original element is in the excepted element the answer will be no and the application should be refused. If the software element is merely part of the novelty of the invention the answer will be yes and a patent should be awarded.

In allowing VICOM's appeal the Board noted that: 'the computer program referred to . . . merely serves to calculate the element values of the small generating kernel and the weighting values. It does not form part of the image processing methods claimed, nor

---

[137] The wording of the European Patent Convention is again similar. It states, at Art. 52: 'The following in particular shall not be regarded as inventions . . . schemes, rules and methods for performing mental acts, playing games or doing business, and programs for computers . . . only to the extent to which a European patent application or European patent relates to such subject-matter or activities as such.'
[138] [1987] 2 EPOR 74.

is it embodied in the apparatus claims. Indeed such a program would not be patentable in view of the Board's foregoing considerations.'[139] The Board also gave some helpful pointers as to what would be patentable and what not:

 Highlight Technical Board of Appeal guidance

1. A computer of known type set up to operate according to a new program cannot be considered as forming part of the state of the art.

2. A claim directed to a technical process which process is carried out under the control of a program (whether by means of hardware or software), cannot be regarded as relating to a computer program as such.

3. A claim which can be considered as being directed to a computer set up to operate in accordance with a specified program (whether by means of hardware or software) for controlling or carrying out a technical process cannot be regarded as relating to a computer program as such.

The *VICOM* decision was highly influential both before the Board of Appeal of the EPO and before the UK courts. It was applied by the Court of Appeal in *Merrill Lynch's Application*,[140] in which the court rejected Merrill Lynch's application to patent a system for automating market trades. The court found that the inventive step of Merrill Lynch's system was contained in the software which tracked the market and executed trades: as such the 'invention' was not patentable. Repeatedly throughout the late 1980s and 1990s *VICOM* was followed by the UK courts in a series of cases including *Genentech Inc.'s Patent*,[141] *Gale's Application*,[142] *Wang Laboratories Inc.'s Application*,[143] and *Fujitsu Ltd's Application*.[144] It appeared a clear and simple test to determine the patentability of software-related inventions, as opposed to pure software had been achieved. Yet even as this stability had established itself, activities were taking place elsewhere which threatened to undermine it.

9.6.2 **The effect of State Street Bank**

In the US look and feel protection had been reduced considerably in scope; functional elements of software such as command systems or interfaces were unlikely to be protectable. This led to a new wave of patent applications for software elements.

In *State Street Bank & Trust Co. v Signature Financial Group*,[145] the US Court of Appeals for the Federal Circuit found that a patent application which was, to all intents and purposes, the amalgamation of two excluded subject matters (computer software and a method of doing business) was patentable. The application involved a claimed invention

---

[139] Ibid. [18].
[140] [1989] RPC 561.
[141] [1989] RPC 147.
[142] *Gale's Application* (n. 136).
[143] [1991] RPC 463.
[144] [1997] RPC 608.
[145] 149 F 3d 1368 (Fed Cir. 1998).

of a 'Data Processing System for Hub and Spoke Financial Services Configuration'. In layman's terms this was a computerized system for moving funds within a series of accounts managed by the applicants. The case therefore shares many similarities with the English case of *Merrill Lynch*. In a departure from the previous case law the court found that systems such as these were patentable if it produces 'a useful, concrete and tangible result'.[146] Almost immediately the US Patent and Trade Mark Office issued new guidelines to examiners indicating that software which produced such a result may be patentable.[147] With the US Patent and Trade Mark Office now entertaining patent applications for software inventions pressure grew on other jurisdictions to follow suit. The EPO was well placed to consider an expansion of patent policy.

In February 1999 the Board of Appeal considered the case of *IBM's Application*.[148] This involved an application to patent a data processing system for Windows-based computers such that any information displayed in one window which is obscured by a second window is automatically moved to allow the first window to be clearly displayed. In a paradigm-shifting ruling, perhaps influenced by the *State Street* ruling in the US, the Board ruled that a computer program was not excluded from patentability per se. It stated that:

> the exclusion from patentability of programs for computers as such (Article 52(2) and (3) of the EPC) may be construed to mean that such programs are considered to be mere abstract creations, lacking in technical character. The use of the expression 'shall not be regarded as inventions' seems to confirm this interpretation. Programs for computers must be considered as patentable inventions when they have a technical character.[149]

 Highlight Decision of the Board of Appeal in *IBM's Application*

A patent may be granted not only in the case of an invention where a piece of software manages, by means of a computer, an industrial process or the working of a piece of machinery, but in every case where a program for a computer is the only means, or one of the necessary means, of obtaining a technical effect, where, for instance, a technical effect of that kind is achieved by the internal functioning of a computer itself under the influence of said program.

In short, the Board found that if the effect of the software was to cause a computer to function in a novel and inventive manner that software may be patentable.

This was to be the first in a long line of cases in which the EPO and the Board of Appeal gave ever narrower interpretations of the meaning of Art. 52(2)(c) of the Convention. In *PBS Partnership/Controlling Pension Benefits Systems*,[150] the Board of Appeal held that a program which calculated pension benefits and life assurance benefits could be

---

[146] Ibid. 1374. It should be noted that in the case of *In re Bernard L. Bilski and Rand*, 88 USPQ 2d 1385 (2008), the US Court of Appeals for the Federal Circuit overruled parts of the *State Street* test noting that 'those portions of our opinions in State Street and AT&T relying solely on a "useful, concrete and tangible result" analysis should no longer be relied on'.

[147] H Rockman, *Intellectual Property Law for Engineers and Scientists* (2004) 229–30.

[148] [1999] RPC 861.

[149] Ibid. 870.

[150] [2002] EPOR 52.

patentable, despite the fact that the program itself would usually be excluded subject matter under Art. 52 as well as the operation it was performing. This is an extremely complex decision. The process that the program was performing was a method of doing business which is excluded from patentability by Art. 52(2)(c), and the system or apparatus that was to be protected was software which was similarly excluded. But by a tortuous process of interpretation the Board found that although business practices were not patentable under the Convention and that a non-technical process for carrying out that activity was similarly not protected, 'An apparatus[151] constituting a physical entity or concrete product suitable for performing or supporting an economic activity, is an invention within the meaning of Art. 52(1) EPC.'[152] This is extremely difficult to conceptualize. While both the operation itself and software in the abstract were excluded subject matters, the design of a software-based system to carry out the process could be patentable:[153] as David Bainbridge notes: 'it seemed to diminish the exclusion of computer programs as such from inventions almost to vanishing point'.[154]

9.6.3 *De facto* software patents under the European Patent Convention

From this position it was a simple step to allow de facto software patents while the Convention retained the fiction that they were excluded subject matter. In *HITACHI/ Auction Method*[155] the Board considered a patent for an online Dutch auction system. The auction would start with a preliminary data exchange between the bidder's computers and the server (auction) computer in order to collect bids from the participants. Each bid would comprise two values, a 'desired price' and a 'maximum price in competitive state'. Once this was complete the auction would run automatically and requires no further bidder interaction. An auction price is set and successively lowered until it reaches the level of the highest bid or bids as determined by the 'desired price'. In the case of several identical bids the price is increased until only the bidder having offered the highest 'maximum price' is left who is then declared successful.[156] The Board found that there are three requirements which must be fulfilled for a claim of this nature to be patented:

 Highlight Technical Board of Appeal requirements for patentability[157]

1. It should be an 'invention'. That is, it must be new, inventive and industrially applicable.

2. The term 'invention' is to be construed as 'subject-matter having technical character'.

3. Verification that the claimed subject matter is an invention within the meaning of Art. 52(1) EPC must be done before performing the three other tests, i.e. the novelty, the inventive step and the industrial applicability tests.

---

[151] Being an organizational structure, including a suitably programmed computer or system of computers.
[152] *PBS Partnership* (n. 150) [5].
[153] Although in this case it was not as it lacked the necessary inventive step.
[154] Bainbridge (n. 75) 155.
[155] [2004] EPOR 55.
[156] Ibid. [19].
[157] Ibid. [20].

The Board then confirmed the fact that a mixture of a technical and non-technical feature may be patentable, finding that 'contrary to the examining division's assessment, the apparatus of claim three is an invention within the meaning of Art. 52(1) EPC since it comprises clearly technical features such as a "server computer", "client computers" and a "network"'.[158] Although the application in the instant case was ultimately rejected as it lacked an inventive step, this is, like the *Pension Benefits Case* before, an incredible decision. It seems to suggest that the clothing of a business method, or perhaps even a mathematical formula, or a scheme for carrying out a mental act in a technical apparatus may be patentable.

The Board seems to accept that this approach is controversial, perhaps even counter to the original intent of the drafters of the Convention, in noting that:

> the Board is aware that its comparatively broad interpretation of the term 'invention' in Art. 52(1) EPC will include activities which are so familiar that their technical character tends to be overlooked, such as the act of writing using pen and paper. Needless to say, however, this does not imply that all methods involving the use of technical means are patentable. They still have to be new, represent a non-obvious technical solution to a technical problem, and be susceptible of industrial application.[159]

The high-water point in this expansive interpretation of Art. 52 is to be found in the connected cases of *MICROSOFT/Clipboard Formats I*[160] and *MICROSOFT/Clipboard Formats II*.[161] Both cases involved patent applications made by Microsoft to cover aspects of their Windows clipboard system, in particular allowing non-file data to be transferred from one application to another via the clipboard. The Board followed *Hitachi* and found that a method applying technical means was an invention and that a computer system was a technical means. The Board emphasized the difference between a computer system and a computer program.

 Highlight The difference between a computer system and a computer program[162]

A method implemented in a computer system represents a sequence of steps actually performed and achieving an effect, and not a sequence of computer-executable instructions (i.e. a computer program) which just have the potential of achieving such an effect when loaded into, and run on, a computer. Thus, the Board holds that the claim category of a computer-implemented method is distinguished from that of a computer program. Even though a method, in particular a method of operating a computer, may be put into practice with the help of a computer program, a claim relating to such a method does not claim a computer program in the category of a computer program.

[158] Ibid. [26].
[159] Ibid. [34].
[160] [2006] EPOR 39.
[161] Ibid. 40.
[162] Ibid. [42].

This is the clearest exposition to date of the distinction between computer programs, which are excluded from patentability, and a computer-implemented method, which is not. Although the computer-implemented method may just describe the operation of the software, it is seen as distinct from the software. Again, patent examiners are being asked to walk a very fine line.

9.6.4 *Aerotel Ltd v Telco and Macrossan's Application*

The UK courts have watched all these developments with interest. Although the Board of Appeal has no authority over UK patent law, the relationship between a UK patent and a European patent is such that decisions of the EPO, and its Board of Appeal, are highly influential on UK patent law and policy. This tension between the expansive European approach and the UK approach which was still heavily influenced by *VICOM* came to a head in *Aerotel Ltd v Telco and Macrossan's Application*.[163]

The case concerned two inventions; one a system allowing for prepaid calls to be made from any telephone (Aerotel), the other an automated method of acquiring the documents necessary to incorporate a company through the use of an online database (Macrossan). In giving the judgment of the court Jacob LJ spent a considerable amount of time examining the prior UK case law, including *Merrill Lynch*, *Gale*, and *Fujitsu* and the Board of Appeal decisions including *Pensions Benefits*, *Hitachi*, and *Microsoft*. It was clear from his examination that little common ground now lay between the two jurisdictions and Jacob LJ found it was incumbent upon the court to review and modernize the UK law. He first of all noted that for the Court of Appeal English authority should be preferred over the recent EPO line of authority. He was quite forthright in his view on this: 'The fact is that this court is bound by its own precedent: that decided in *Merrill Lynch*, *Gale*, and *Fujitsu*—the technical effect approach with the rider.'[164] From this he developed a clear and simple test which brought the *Merrill Lynch* test up to date.

> **→ Highlight** The *Macrossan* test
>
> 1. Construe the claim
> 2. Identify the contribution
> 3. Ask whether the contribution is solely of excluded matter
> 4. Check whether the contribution is technical.

Macrossan may be seen as either an attempt to entrench the *VICOM* 'technical effect' approach, something to be criticized,[165] or as an attempt to bridge the divide between the UK approach and the European approach by inviting the Board of Appeal to reconsider post-*VICOM* developments in light of the fact that *VICOM* had never been expressly

---

[163] [2006] EWCA Civ 1371.
[164] Ibid. [38].
[165] Bainbridge (n. 75) 157.

overruled.[166] It is clear the court in *Macrossan* intended the latter,[167] however attempts to bridge the divide between the EPO and the English courts by finding a meeting place in the middle, inspired by *Macrossan*, failed. A referral to the Enlarged Board of Appeals of the EPO in 2008 by the then President of the Board led the Board to note that the EPO's interpretation of Arts. 52(2) and (3) were based on sound and consistent logic, and as having 'created a practicable system for delimiting the innovations for which a patent may be granted'.[168] The divide between the English courts and the EPO it appeared remained as distinct as ever.

In the meantime though the Court of Appeal had the opportunity to consider the application of the *Macrossan* test in the subsequent case of *Symbian Ltd v Comptroller General of Patents*.[169] This involved a rather complex patent application for the management of computer library functions (so-called dynamic link libraries or DLL) which can be called on by multiple application programs running on the computer. The patent applied for provided a way of indexing these library functions to ensure the computer continues to operate reliably after changes are made to the library. The claims were directed to a method, a device implementing that method and software arranged to implement the method. Essentially it was, though, a computer program which operates within a computer to improve the internal functioning of the computer.

In giving the judgment of the court Lord Neuberger MR carried out the most careful of balancing exercises, convincing not only himself but also readers of his judgment that the divide between the EPO and the English courts is more illusory than real. He analysed the approach of the EPO and of the English courts, in particular *Macrossan*, finding that the EPO is inconsistent in its approach:

> in a number of more recent decisions, the Board appears to have adopted an analysis which appears substantially more restrictive of the art 52(2)(c) exclusion of computer programs . . . Having said this, it is only right to add that, following Aerotel, there have been a number subsequent decisions of the Board on this issue. For example, apart from Duns and Gameaccount, there are Sharp T1188/04 and File search method/Fujitsu T1351/04, which contained the bald statement, 'The claimed method requires the use of a computer. It is therefore technical in character and constitutes an invention within the meaning of art 52 . . .'.[170]

He notes that there have been no references to the Enlarged Board of Appeal (essentially the EPO's equivalent to the Court of Appeal) and relying on this inconsistency of approach and the fact there is no conclusive determination from an Enlarged EPO Board he boldly sets out that the English courts should continue to apply the *Macrossan* test for 'if this court is seen to depart too readily from its previous, carefully considered, approach, it would risk throwing the law into disarray',[171] while suggesting the divide is less pronounced, as the *Macrossan* decision may have suggested it to be. He does so by acknowledging that 'it is, of course, inevitable that there will be cases where the

---

[166] D Booton, 'The Patentability of Computer-Implemented Inventions in Europe' (2007) *Intellectual Property Quarterly* 92.

[167] *Macrossan* (n. 163) at [29].

[168] *President's Reference/Computer Program Exclusion* [2010] EPOR 36 at [10.8.2] and [10.13.2].

[169] [2008] EWCA Civ 1066. For a discussion of the *Symbian* case see C De Mauny, 'Court of Appeal Clarifies Patenting of Computer Programs' (2009) 31 *European Intellectual Property Review* 147.

[170] *Symbian* (n. 169) [43], [45].

[171] Ibid. [46].

EPO will grant patents in this field when UKIPO should not, at least so long as the view in Pension Benefit and Hitachi is applied by the Board and is not applied here. The fact that the two offices and their supervisory courts have their own responsibilities means that discrepancies, even in approach or principle, are occasionally inevitable'[172] but he feels that 'it seems to us that the approaches in the two cases *and indeed in the great majority of cases in this jurisdiction and in the EPO*, are, on a fair analysis, capable of reconciliation.'[173] Thus for Lord Neuberger he believes the distinction between the two approaches is less an ideological divide, as Jacob LJ seemed to suggest, and more a difference in approach.

The problem with the *Symbian/Macrossan* standard is that while it informs how to approach the test for exclusion it does not give guidance as to how to resolve the question; for that one must look to *AT&T Knowledge Ventures LP v Comptroller General of Patents Designs and Trade Marks*.[174] This case involved a patent application for a 'content broker hosting service system', essentially a software system which selected multimedia files for delivery to the customer, based upon compatibility with the customer's device connected to the multimedia supplier. The judge, Lewison J, set out five signposts for indicating whether or not the invention made a technical contribution to the art in terms of the *Symbian/Macrossan* test.

 Highlight The *AT&T* signposts

1. Whether the claimed technical effect has a technical effect on a process which is carried on outside the computer;

2. whether the claimed technical effect operates at the level of the architecture of the computer; that is to say whether the effect is produced irrespective of the data being processed or the applications being run;

3. whether the claimed technical effect results in the computer being made to operate in a new way;

4. whether there is an increase in the speed or reliability of the computer;

5. whether the perceived problem is overcome by the claimed invention as opposed to merely being circumvented.

The first signpost refers to those occasions where a computer is being used to control a real-world apparatus or process such as a manufacturing process or an engine management system. These are generally permissible as they bring about a useful technical effect in the physical world and so go beyond abstract computer programs. The second signpost is rather more complicated. As we have already seen when discussing *MICROSOFT/Clipboard Formats* and *Hitachi*, any program can be said to bring about a change in the operation of a computer. Under the *Symbian/Macrossan* test such programs

---

[172] Ibid. [61].
[173] Ibid. [11].
[174] [2009] EWHC 343 (Pat).

are not considered patentable as their contribution is solely within excluded matter: what is required is a further technical effect or contribution. In *Symbian* the invention was ultimately found to be patentable as it solved a problem within the computer. This can be distinguished from inventions that depend solely on the data being processed or the applications being run, such as the invention in *Fujitsu Ltd's Application*.[175] In that case, the invention was a program for modelling crystal lattice structures and displaying the results on screen and the computer itself was held to simply be performing the kind of computational activities for which computers are used.

The third and fourth signposts are intended to give general examples of what might constitute a further technical effect or contribution, such as new functionality for the computer or an increase in speed. The emphasis is on what the computer program has achieved in the computer itself, although the effect may also apply to computer networks. In *HTC Europe v Apple Inc*.[176] the Court of Appeal expanded the fourth signpost to 'whether a program makes a computer a better computer in the sense of running more efficiently and effectively as a computer.'[177] In that decision, Apple's innovation of a touch screen control method called 'The Multi Touch feature' was found to be patentable as it provided a new interface for application programmers to create programs, in which conflicting inputs from the touch screen no longer needed to be resolved at the application level.

The fifth and final signpost is intended to prevent the patenting of programs that only result in a technical effect indirectly, that is by virtue of programming that reflects an organizational or administrative fix external to the program itself, rather than by an improvement to the technology itself.

The application of these signposts demonstrates a distinct approach to that of the EPO which despite Lord Neuberger's 'smoothing' approach in *Symbian* remains more laissez-faire than the English courts in this field. As Lord Neuberger acknowledged, the divide will remain for as long as both regimes are fixed in their approaches. In fact, the issue becomes even more confused when one adds the new unitary patent into the mix. This is an EU harmonization initiative which borrows elements of EPC infrastructure. As we saw earlier the EPO was formed by the EPC and is thus not an EU body. However, under the Unitary Patent Protection Regulation[178] and the Unitary Patent Co-operation Regulation,[179] a scheme for unitary patent recognition in EU member states was formed. The scheme will see the awards of a single unitary patent granted under the EPC which will be recognized in all EU member states which will be awarded for payment of a single application/renewal fee, subject to control by a single court (the Unified Patent Court) and uniform protection, meaning that that revocation as well as infringement proceedings are to be decided for the unitary patent as a whole, rather than for each country individually. This process has been on hold until recently due to two challenges against the legitimacy of the programme by the Kingdom of Spain. However, in May 2015 the CJEU rejected both challenges and found the process to be in compliance with EU Law.[180]

---

[175] *Fujitsu* (n. 144).
[176] [2013] EWCA Civ 451.
[177] Ibid. [51].
[178] Reg. 1257/2012 OJ L361/1.
[179] Known as the Translation Arrangements Regulation: Reg. 1260/2012 OJ L361/89.
[180] *Spain v Parliament and Council of the EU* ECLI:EU:C:2015:298 and *Spain v Council of the EU* ECLI:EU:C:2015:299.

The unitary patent is now moving ahead with the first applications expected in 2019. Thus it is likely within the next year or two that three patent regimes may be recognized in the UK: the UK patent issued by the UK Intellectual Property Office, the European patent issued by the European Patent Office, and the unitary patent issued by the European Patent Office.[181] The whole issue becomes murkier rather than clearer.

9.7 **Conclusions**

Of all the areas where law and the digital society interface, the question of how the law should protect computer software is probably the most complex. This is due to many factors. First, there is the long history: the software industry was the first fully formed digital industry, emerging in the 1970s before digital entertainment media, digital criminal activity, or e-commerce. Second, the product of the software industry is both traditionally the most valuable of any digital industry and the most complex. The software industry emerged before the legal system could adapt, meaning that software has never had a planned legal response in the way that computer crime, electronic contracting, or databases have. Whereas it may be argued that software is a unique product, and would have been suited to a *sui generis* form of protection, it has instead fallen between two stools: copyright protection designed primarily for artistic expression not functional goods, and patents which seek to protect inventions, not systems of performing human acts. In the 1980s any hope of a software patent law was abandoned in favour of expansive look and feel copyright protection. The 1990s and the 2000s have seen a strong move away from copyright protection for all except literal infringement and a shift back towards software patents both explicitly (as in the US) and implicitly (in Europe).

Whatever method of protection is followed, copyright law or patent law, the value of the software industry to the GDP of developed nations ensures some form of protection will be afforded to software. It is essential, however, that whatever form the next generation of software protection takes we do not repeat the mistakes of the look and feel cases of the 1980s and 1990s in providing a form of protection that is either under- or over-inclusive. Competition within the industry requires that innovation is not stifled by the application of IPRs, while free-riders must be discouraged. Protecting software products has proven to be one of the most intractable problems of the information society, a problem we have yet to deal with fully.

TEST QUESTIONS

Question 1

A client, Saadia, comes to see you for advice. Advise her of any potential claims she may have in copyright law. She is based in London:

---

[181] The UK has signaled it intends to remain in the unitary patent regime post-Brexit—see HM Government, *The Future Relationship Between the United Kingdom and the European Union* (Cm 9593, July 2018), [151].

Saadia owns a company Spinaround Games that specializes in producing games for children with motor control difficulties. They are highly interactive games which make use of motion sensor technologies, bright sounds, and bright colours designed to stimulate attention and movement among children between four and eight. A considerable amount of time has gone into developing a Spinaround system which uses both a specially designed hardware platform and carefully designed software, such as the bestselling 'Xander's Dance World' and their new product 'Flying with Allen'. Spinaround Games were until recently the only developer in this niche but valuable market.

Two months ago a rival developer PlayDay Games launched their own software but not hardware. Their games are designed to be compatible with the Spinaround system although Spinaround have not licensed them to use the Spinaround system and have never discussed with PlayDay any of the design specifications of the Spinaround system. Spinaround suspect PlayDay may have reverse-engineered their games software to ensure that PlayDay's products would work on the Spinaround system.

PlayDay have initially released two games 'PlayDate with Wendy' and 'Dance with Julio'. 'Dance with Julio' looks and plays exactly like 'Xander's Dance World' with similar characters, colours, movements, and goals. Also, PlayDay have announced that coming soon will be four more games including 'In the Air with Flair' which according to prelaunch advertising looks just like 'Flying with Allen'.

Question 2

Following the decision of the CJEU in *SAS Institute Inc. v World Programming Ltd* [2012] 3 CMLR 4 that the functionality of a computer program is not protected by copyright as it falls on the wrong side of the ideas/expression divide, and that the programming language used is also not protected by copyright as it is a functional element which allows instructions to be given to a computer, discuss what future role you believe copyright law will play in protecting computer software.

Question 3

You are legal counsel for Kumquat Inc. the world's leading supplier of smartphones, tablets, and computers. Kumquat have been working for several years on a new music streaming service and have recently purchased a streaming company DeadBeats to help get their streaming service off the ground. Kumquat are about ready to launch Kumquat Music publicly but yesterday they received a warning letter from counsel acting for a key competitor Yangtze Inc. warning them that a key component of the Kumquat Music service is in breach of both UK and EPO patents owned by Yangtze. The component in question was part of the technology bought from DeadBeats that Kumquat compliance checked at the time of purchase with no concerns being raised.

The Yangze patent is GB2981577/EP55721816 and is described as follows:

Music Integration and Streaming with Personalization: This invention allows a remote server to receive the following data from a consumer device (smartphone, digital music player, tablet, or similar): location data, local time data, local weather data, locally stored music preferences, internet search data, game playing data (preferred gaming apps, time playing, and other relevant data), RSS data, and related data. The remote server then following processing of this data selects and delivers a unique personalized musical play list which reflects the user's current mood and preferences to the end user by streaming data delivery through the pressing of a single virtual button.

Yangze call this their YangzeYou service and this is bundled on all Yangze Ice smartphones and tablets. It is part of the Yangze Elite music streaming service that costs £6.99 per month. Kumquat intends to offer a similar service called Kumquat Moods as part of its Kumquat Music service. There are now concerns that should Kumquat launch Moods, it will infringe Yangze's patents. You have been asked to brief the board as to whether Kumquat can successfully challenge Yangze's patents.
Prepare your brief.

FURTHER READING

Books

D Bainbridge, *Software Copyright Law* (4th edn, Tottel 2007)

P Leith, *Software and Patents in Europe* (CUP 2011)

Chapters and articles

D Booton, 'The Patentability of Computer-Implemented Inventions in Europe' (2007) *Intellectual Property Quarterly* 92

M Lemley, Software Patents and the Return of Functional Claiming (2013) *Wisconsin Law Review* 905

R Onslow and I Jamal, 'Copyright infringement and software emulation—SAS Inc. v World Programming Limited' [2013] 35 *European Intellectual Property Review* 352

P Samuelson, 'The past, present and future of software copyright: interoperability rules in the European Union and United States' [2012] *European Intellectual Property Review* 229

P Samuelson, T Vinje, and W Cornish, 'Does Copyright Protection Under the EU Software Directive Extend to Computer Program Behaviour, Languages and Interfaces?' [2012] *European Intellectual Property Review* 158

Digital creatives and copyright law

10.1 Content, creativity, and creation

The internet has afforded a new wave of human creativity. We are no longer simply consumers of content, a situation which only really came about in the twentieth century, we are also all content creators. In 2010 Google CEO Eric Schmidt observed that through the power of digital content creation and distribution tools we now created more content in 48 hours than in the entirety of human history to 2003.[1] Today we probably create as much information as we did in 48 hours in 2010 in less than 24 hours with the explosion of smart and IoT devices. In any given day, around 100 million images and videos will be posted to Instagram and every minute around 400 hours of video are uploaded to YouTube. The vast majority of newly created content will be original content, personal pictures or videos, or personal comments, musings, or stories. However a large proportion of user-generated content is derivative of content produced by others.

A derivative work is a work that is based on (derived from) another work; for example a painting based on a photograph, a collage, a musical work based on an existing piece or samples, a screenplay based on a book. An obvious example from the online world is fanfiction which is the creation of new literary works which use established characters from mainstream literature, film, television, or computer games without permission. These works may use characters from a single author or universe, such as the Harry Potter characters, or they may cross over characters between authors such as Harry Potter/Dr Who. Fanfic may be in many forms from fluff (a happy story) to smut (sexually explicit or pornographic). Smut can be a particular problem for authors who create children-oriented universes such as Harry Potter or wholesome stories such as *Little House on the Prairie*.

Musicians face similar challenges in the actions of fans who remix or mashup their music. Remixing usually involves sampling elements of music and then mixing them over other pieces of music, while mashups involve overlaying usually the vocals of one song on top of the music track of another.[2] Film and TV producers are not immune from the creativity of their customers either. Popular memes will be ripped, parodies like the wonderful and famous Downfall parody, and fansubbing of foreign language

---

[1] MG Siegler, 'Eric Schmidt: Every 2 Days We Create As Much Information As We Did Up To 2003' *TechCrunch* 4 August 2010.

[2] YouTube contains a number of Mashups but the author particularly commends the Snoop Dogg vs Guns N' Roses mashup at https://www.youtube.com/watch?v=GHDJhuoW1vQ.

content are all common reuses of video content. Finally, services such as Twitch allow for livestreaming and live recording of content. These services are used extensively to record video game playthroughs which necessarily replicate the content of the game creator. These are all legally problematic acts for as we shall see only the copyright owner has the right to authorize adaptations and reproductions of their work—this includes the making of a derivative work.

10.2 Copyright law and remixing and reusing content

As we saw in chapter 9, the Copyright, Designs and Patents Act 1988 affords the copyright owner six 'restricted acts', actions that legally only the copyright holder may carry out or permit others to carry out.

➡ Highlight The six restricted acts

1. to make copies of the work[3]
2. to issue copies of the work to the public[4]
3. to rent or lend the work to the public[5]
4. to perform, show or play the work in public[6]
5. to communicate the work to the public[7]
6. to make an adaptation of the work or do any of the above in relation to an adaptation.[8]

As may immediately be seen most of the actions of online creative communities who produce works which are derivative works are done so in breach of copyright. The main provisions which legally prevent the production of fanfiction, mashups, remixes, and the creation of memes and parodies are s. 16(1)(a), 'the owner of the copyright in a work has . . . the exclusive right to copy the work in the United Kingdom' and s. 17 'Copying in relation to a literary, dramatic, musical or artistic work means reproducing the work in any material form. This includes storing the work in any medium by electronic means.' The careful reader may think that although it is clear that in cases such as mashups, remixes, or the creation of memes and parodies where the original work is reused in full or in part that s. 16(1)(a) is infringed, it might be thought this does not catch fanfiction where only characters are replicated, the remainder being the original work of the writer of the fanfiction. However, it must first be noted that infringement does not require the whole work to be copied as references to infringement in the CDPA apply to the whole *or substantial part* of the work.[9] The essential question therefore is

---

[3] CDPA 1988, ss. 16(1)(a), 17.
[4] Ibid. ss. 16(1)(b), 18.
[5] Ibid. ss. 16(1)(ba), 18A.
[6] Ibid. ss. 16(1)(c), 19.
[7] Ibid. ss. 16(1)(d), 20.
[8] Ibid. ss. 16(1)(e), 21.
[9] Ibid. s. 16(3)(a).

what is a substantial part, and could that include characters created by the copyright holder? In *Nova Productions Ltd v Mazooma Games Ltd*,[10] which we discussed for different reasons in chapter 9, Jacob LJ observed that just because some element of copying occurred this did not mean that this qualified as a 'substantial part'.

 Highlight Jacob LJ on Copying

[It has been argued that] whenever copying has been found it must follow that a substantial part has been taken. I cannot agree. In many cases a coincidence in the copyright work and the alleged infringement of small, unimportant, details is an indication of copying. But no-one would say that those details alone meant that a substantial part of the copyright work had been taken—they are the starting point for a finding of infringement, not the end point.[11]

What then does qualify as a 'substantial part'? UK case law has emphasized this is a question of quality rather than quantity.[12] Thus an extract of twenty bars of music lasting fifty seconds from a four-minute musical work was substantial, as it constituted the section of the work recognizable by the public.[13] However the emphasis is not solely on quality. Separate acts of copying which on their own are insubstantial may as a series lead to a substantial act of copying.[14] In *Baigent &Anor v The Random House Group Ltd*[15] Peter Smith J found that the work *The Da Vinci Code* did not infringe on the claimant's earlier work *Holy Blood and the Holy Grail*. He emphasized that 'the line to be drawn is to enable a fair balance to be struck between protecting the rights of the author and allowing literary development.'[16] He made the point that the question of substantiality applies to the original work, not the copy: 'The differences between the two copyright works are not relevant and while the copied features must be a substantial part of the copyright work relied upon there is no need for them to be a substantial part of the Defendant's work',[17] and cited, with apparent approval Lord Scott in *Designer Guild Ltd v Russell Williams (Textiles) Ltd*[18] that 'the court should consider whether the Defendant has incorporated [a] substantial part of the independent skill, labour, etc. contributed by the original author in creating the copyright work and that that test is based on the principle a copier is not at liberty to appropriate the benefit of anothers skill and labour'.[19]

Characters, like every other element of a story may or may not be classified as a substantial part. In *Hodgson v Isaac* HH Judge Birss found that the elements reproduced were 'the main characters, many of the settings and contexts in which the events take

---

[10] [2007] EWCA Civ 219.
[11] Ibid. [26].
[12] *Ladbroke (Football) Ltd v William Hill (Football) Ltd* [1964] 1 WLR 273, 276 (per Lord Reid).
[13] *Hawkes & Son Ltd v Paramount Film Service* [1934] Ch 593 (CA).
[14] *Cate v Devon and Exeter Constitutional Newspaper Co* (1889) 40 Ch D 500. See also the discussion of the *sui generis* database right at 13.2.
[15] [2006] EWHC 719 (Ch), aff'd [2007] EWCA Civ 247.
[16] Ibid. [153].
[17] Ibid. [151].
[18] [2000] UKHL 58.
[19] Ibid. [64], cited in *Baigent & Anor* (n. 15) [185].

place and a good number of the incidents themselves.'[20] Although these were quantitatively not a substantial part of the original work, Judge Birss found that they were not generic elements of the story but were a recognizable element of the original work, therefore they were qualitatively a substantial part. Similarly the Court of Appeal in *Baigent & Anor v The Random House Group Ltd* found that 'the "text" of a literary work may cover more than the particular words in which it is expressed and extend to its overall content, including the selection, arrangement and development of ideas, theories, information, facts, incidents, characters, narrative and so on.'[21] More has been written on character protection in the United States. In *Detective Comics v Bruns* the court held that Superman's qualities, such as being a hero archetype, wearing a cloak, and being benevolent, should be considered as ideas, and ideas are outside the scope of copyright.[22] As Kaelyn Christian explains the US places particular value on the importance of the character to the story in determining whether characters are protected:

> The primary case for determining whether or not literary characters can be copyrighted, and therefore afforded copyright protection, is commonly referred to as the 'Sam Spade' case. In *Warner Bros. Pictures v. Columbia Broadcasting System* (1954) the Ninth Circuit court decided that 'it is conceivable that the character really constitutes the story being told, but if the character is only the chessman in the game of telling the story he is not within the area afforded by copyright.' This decision led to the Sam Spade test. This means that character-driven works are more likely to be able to copyright their characters than more plot-driven works. For instance, according to Nolan 'characters like those on Friends would constitute the story being told because they drive the action of their shows, while characters like those on *E.R., Law and Order,* or *C.S.I.* may have less protection because the plots are driven by action rather than the characters themselves.' However, this test remains open to interpretation and cannot be regarded as necessarily definitive.[23]

Characters who transcend the work they are in may also qualify more easily for protection. As Christina Ranon observes 'while stock or stereotyped characters are not copyrightable expression . . . they recognize that literary characters can be sufficiently distinctive, and note that the factors that contribute to this distinctiveness of character include expressive content such as the character's name and speech. This kind of expressive content moves characters from the realm of abstract ideas into concrete expression.'[24] Thus it might be suggested that in the jurisprudence of the United States at least characters easily recognized outside their origin material (be that books, film, television, etc.) are likely to be afforded copyright protection. As Christian notes, 'Harry Potter of J.K. Rowling's Harry Potter series is distinguishable outside the Harry Potter books because of his name, the fact that he is a wizard, and the lightning shaped scar on his forehead. In the case of characters like Harry Potter, where a character is well known, courts typically enjoin others from using the character in new works of fiction.'[25] The court may consider many factors in deciding whether a character is sufficiently distinctive and copyrightable including: (1) the name of the character; (2) their visual

[20] [2010] EWPCC 37, [77].

[21] [2007] EWCA Civ 247, [141] per Mummery LJ.

[22] *Detective Comics v Bruns Publications* 111 F.2d 432 (2d Cir. 1940).

[23] K Christian, 'Fan Fiction and the Fair Use Doctrine' (2013) 65 *The Serials Librarian* 277, 281.

[24] CZ Ranon, 'Honor Among Thieves: Copyright Infringement in Internet Fandom' (2006) 8 *Vanderbilt Journal of Entertainment & Technology Law* 421, 437.

[25] Christian (n. 23) 281.

appearance; and (3) the personality and attributes of the character. These elements combine to determine whether a character is recognizable outside their source material. For writers of fanfiction this suggests that works which make use of famous characters such as Harry Potter, Dr Who, or Luke Skywalker may be infringing the copyright of their creators or owners even if all other elements of the fan work are original to the fan.

10.2.1 *Coming Through the Rye*; *The Wind Done Gone* and other works inspired by other works

Although the UK courts have not had a chance to fully get to grips with works inspired by the work of others there have been several cases in the United States which are quite instructive of how the courts here may approach such works. The first major case on the re-imagining of the characters of another was *Suntrust Bank v Houghton Mifflin*.[26] This case involved the book *The Wind Done Gone* by Alice Randall, a book inspired by, and according to its author critical of *Gone with the Wind* by Margaret Mitchell. It was admitted by Randall that her book appropriated the characters, plot, and major scenes from *Gone with the Wind* as well as copying and summarizing famous scenes and other elements of the plot from *Gone with the Wind*. The Mitchell estate sued for infringement, Houghton Mifflin, the publisher of *The Wind Done Gone* argued that there is no substantial similarity between the two works or, in the alternative, that *The Wind Done Gone* was a parody of *Gone with the Wind*.

The court was clear in distinguishing unprotectable from protectable elements, finding that 'scenes a faire—the stock scenes and hackneyed character-types that "naturally flow from a common theme"—are considered "ideas", and therefore are not copyrightable' but that in the instant case:

> *The Wind Done Gone* copied far more than unprotected scenes a faire from *Gone with the Wind*: it uses fifteen fictional characters from *Gone with the Wind*, incorporating their physical attributes, mannerisms, and the distinct features that Ms Mitchell used to describe them, as well as their complex relationships with each other. Moreover, the various [fictional] locales, . . . settings, characters, themes, and plot of *The Wind Done Gone* closely mirror those contained in *Gone with the Wind*.[27]

After comparing the two works, the court found that *The Wind Done Gone* was largely 'an encapsulation of *Gone with the Wind* [that] exploit[s] its copyrighted characters, story lines, and settings as the palette for the new story.'[28] The court went on to find that *The Wind Done Gone* could make use of the statutory fair use defence of parody and so was not actually in infringement but without the defence it was clear that *The Wind Done Gone* would have been in breach of copyright.

This issue was revisited later in *Salinger v Colting*.[29] This case involved an unauthorized sequel to JD Salinger's *The Catcher in the Rye*. Unlike *The Wind Done Gone*, *60 Years Later: Coming Through the Rye* was not a parody and therefore could not qualify for the parody defence. The book instead continued the story of Salinger's hero, Holden Caulfield, sixty years on from the end of *The Catcher in the Rye* with Caulfield an old man living in

---

[26] 268 F.3d 1257 (11th Cir. 2001).
[27] Ibid. [35]–[36].
[28] Ibid. [37].
[29] 641 F.Supp.2d 250 (2009).

a nursing home. The book claimed to be written by John David California but this was actually a pseudonym for a Swedish writer and publisher named Fredrik Colting. Many reviews and reports of the book actually referred to it as fanfiction. At a preliminary hearing the court ruled 'that the character of Holden Caulfield is sufficiently delineated so that a claim for infringement will lie.'[30] Looking at the substantiality of the copying Judge Deborah Batts found that the:

> Defendants have taken well more from Catcher, in both substance and style, than is necessary for the alleged transformative purpose of criticizing Salinger and his attitudes and behavior. Most notably, Defendants have utilized the character of Holden Caulfield, reanimated as the elderly Mr C, as the primary protagonist of 60 Years. Mr C has similar or identical thoughts, memories, and personality traits to Caulfield, often using precisely the same or only slightly modified language from that used by Caulfield in Catcher, and has the same friends and family as Caulfield.[31]

On this basis she found that the material used in *60 Years Later* was substantial. A number of defences including parody and criticism were rejected and as a result she issued an injunction preventing the import to or sale of copies of *60 Years Later* in the United States. The court noted this seemed like the right balance in terms of copyright law:

> This approach is also consistent with the purposes of copyright in 'promot[ing] the Progress of Science and useful Arts', because some artists may be further incentivized to create original works due to the availability of the right not to produce any sequels. This might be the case if, for instance, an author's artistic vision includes leaving certain portions or aspects of his character's story to the varied imaginations of his readers, or if he hopes that his readers will engage in discussion and speculation as to what happened subsequently. Just as licensing of derivatives is an important economic incentive to the creation of originals, so too will the right not to license derivatives sometimes act as an incentive to the creation of originals. Accordingly, because it is likely that the publishing of 60 Years would harm the potential market for sequels or other derivative works based upon Catcher.[32]

From the *Suntrust* and *Salinger* cases we get an idea of how a US court would treat works of fanfiction. The reutilization of characters, settings, scenes, or language of the original would all point towards a likelihood of infringement absent a defence such as parody or criticism. Famous characters in particular seem to qualify as a substantial part of the original work is replicated closely. This suggests fanfiction works are likely to be found to be infringing.

Returning to other forms of user-generated content we can consider the legality of musical remixes and mashups. In *Newton v Diamond*,[33] the Central District Court of California held that the Beastie Boys' sampling of a three-note sequence and one background note from James Newton's song *Choir* in their song *Pass the Mic*, was neither qualitatively or quantitatively substantial. The Beastie Boys had managed to get license for the sound recording through Newton's record label, however they had not been able to obtain license for his underlying composition. Newton therefore sued the Beastie Boys for having infringed his copyright by copying a 6-second section of *Choir*. The

[30] Ibid. 254.
[31] Ibid. 263–4.
[32] Ibid. 268.
[33] 388 F.3d 1189 (9th Cir. 2004).

court concluded that the underlying composition, C—D flat—C, sung over a background C note, was of no musical significance and could therefore not be protected.

However in the later case of *Bridgeport Music, Inc. v Dimension Films*,[34] the US Court of Appeals for the Sixth Circuit came to a starkly different conclusion. The case centered on N.W.A.'s song *100 Miles and Runnin* on which N.W.A. had sampled a two-second guitar chord from Funkadelic's *Get Off Your Ass and Jam*, lowered the pitch and looped it five times without Funkadelic's permission and with no license from Bridgeport Music, which owned the rights to Funkadelic's music. Initially the District Court ruled that the sample 'did not rise to the level of a legally cognizable appropriation',[35] however on appeal this was overturned. The US Court of Appeals for the Sixth Circuit found that any unlicensed sampling, or using part of an existing sound recording in a new recording, is an infringement of the copyright in the original sound recording where the defendant does not dispute having sampled. The Sixth Circuit found that the US Copyright Act gave the owner the exclusive right to prepare a derivative work and that as a result 'a sound recording owner has the exclusive right to "sample" his own recording.'[36] This leads them to conclude 'if you cannot pirate the whole sound recording, can you "lift" or "sample" something less than the whole. Our answer to that question is in the negative.'[37]

This finding was unsurprisingly controversial, and arguably would not be followed in the UK given the requirement of 'a substantial part'. In his critique of the case John Schietinger argued the line that the Sixth Circuit was flawed for three reasons: 'first, a de minimis analysis applies to copyright infringement cases in general. Second, neither sampling case law nor the Copyright Act eliminates the de minimis analysis for infringement cases involving the sound recording copyright, and third, failing to conduct the de minimis analysis runs counter to the purposes of copyright law.'[38] Matthew Brodin meanwhile charges the court with making a decision against the very policy of copyright law:

> the purpose of copyright protection, as stated in the Constitution, is to promote the progress of a useful art. As the Sixth Circuit Court of Appeals put it, '[t]he copyright laws attempt to strike a balance between protecting original works and stifling further creativity.' However, the decision announced by the court of appeals in Bridgeport did everything possible to protect original works while backhandedly dismissing all evidence that its new rule would significantly stifle creativity.[39]

There is currently no UK case law on sampling however given the requirement of s. 16(3)(a) that infringement must be 'in relation to the work as a whole or any substantial part of it' it seems more likely that an approach similar to *Newton* would be preferred over *Bridgeport Music*. However whichever approach is followed it is doubtless the case

---

[34] 410 F.3d 792 (2005).

[35] *Bridgeport Music, Inc. v Dimension Films* 230 F.Supp.2d 830 (2002), 841.

[36] *Bridgeport Music* (n. 34) 800.

[37] Ibid.

[38] J Schietinger, 'Bridgeport Music, Inc. v. Dimension Films: How the Sixth Circuit Missed a Beat on Digital Music Sampling' (2005) 55 *DePaul Law Review* 209.

[39] M Brodin, 'Bridgeport Music, Inc. v. Dimension Films: The Death of the Substantial Similarity Test in Digital Sampling Copyright Infringement Claims—The Sixth Circuit's Flawed Attempt at a Bright-Line Rule' (2005) 6 *Minnesota Journal of Law, Science & Technology* 825, 857–8.

that mashups which normally require the entire work (or a quantitatively substantial portion of it) to be overlaid would be in infringement of copyright, while most remixes, which normally employ a qualitatively substantial portion of the original work to be replicated, would also be an infringement of copyright.

Before moving on we can finish this section with a brief reference to an early case on another form of user-generated content. Fansubbing is the creation of a subtitled version of a foreign film, television programme, or sometimes video game which has been translated by fans. These are done without permission of the copyright holder and involve the work as a whole being replicated, with added subtitles. It seems clear that such an act is an infringement of copyright and recently the District Court of Amsterdam has upheld this position. In *Stichting Laat Subtitles Vrij v Brein*[40] the court held that copyright is awarded to the dialogue spoken in a film, and that in the production of subtitles, the dialogue is translated into another language (in this case Dutch). As a result, for the production and publication of subtitles, permission is required from the copyright holder of the original work, otherwise the placing of subtitles is an infringement.

10.2.2 *Paramount Pictures v Axanar Productions*

There has to date been one major case on copyright and fanfiction. It is not a case involving traditional fanfiction, that is, the written word stored in an online database; this case involved video works which were crowdsourced and allegedly cost in excess of $1.5 million dollars to produce. The story began when *Star Trek* fans Christian Gossett and Alec Peters crowdsourced $100,000 (after asking for $10,000) to produce a short film called *Prelude to Axanar*. The film was produced to professional production values and starred a number of well-known actors including Tony Todd (Candyman) and Richard Hatch (Battlestar Galactica). It was filmed in two days at a cost of $80,000 and shown at Comic Con in San Diego in 2014. The film is set in the *Star Trek* universe and is a documentary-style film recounting the events surrounding the Battle of Axanar, a major clash between the Federation and the Klingons.[41] They produced the video knowing Paramount Pictures, which owns the rights to the *Star Trek* film production franchise, allows fan-made projects just 'as long as they agree not to sell anything—including tickets, merchandise, or copies of the finished film or series.'[42] Of course in setting this rule Paramount had not considered high-budget fan productions to be affordable, but crowdfunding changed all of this. Buoyed by the success of *Prelude to Axanar*, Gossett and Peters announced their intention to make a full-length feature *Star Trek: Axanar*, with production to begin in October 2015, for an early 2016 release. The original plan was to raise financing in sections, with the initial Kickstarter to raise enough money to obtain a warehouse, convert it to a sound stage, and build sets. However with *Star Trek* star George Takei sharing his interest in the film the project raised $638,000 in its initial financing round on Kickstarter, more than six times the target of $100,000.

---

[40] ECLI: NL: RBAMS: 2017: 2353.

[41] The video may be seen at: https://www.youtube.com/watch?v=1W1_8IV8uhA.

[42] A Devenish, 'The quest to make a studio-quality star trek movie on a kickstarter budget', *Wired* 22 July 2014.

With such large sums involved, and with the project aiming to produce a feature-length film Paramount decided to take action. On 29 December 2015, Paramount Pictures and CBS (who own the copyright in the original TV series) filed a lawsuit seeking damages in the US District Court for the Central District of California, stating Axanar's works infringed their rights by making use of the Klingon language and 'innumerable copyrighted elements of *Star Trek*, including its settings, characters, species, and themes.'[43] Early in the prosecution of the case film director JJ Abrams, director of both the rebooted *Star Trek* film, and its sequel *Star Trek: Into Darkness* was reported as saying 'This is not the appropriate way to deal with the fans. We should be celebrating this thing. We went to the studio and pushed them to stop this lawsuit and now, within the next few weeks, it will be announced that this thing is going away and the fans will be able to work on the project.'[44] Soon thereafter however Paramount and CBS released new fan film guidelines that were much stricter than the old laissez-faire system and continued to press the case.[45]

On 3 January 2017 US District Judge Gary Klausner issued an interim judgment. He dismissed a claim by Axanar Productions that the claim was not yet ripe for 'the motion picture is not completed'. Axanar Productions argued that without the completed *Axanar* Motion Picture, the court cannot make the necessary comparisons to determine copyright infringement. The Judge though disagreed, noting that 'evidence of a final shooting script satisfies the judicial standard for summary judgment.'[46] He went on to determine whether there was likely to be a substantive similarity between the *Axanar* film and the copyright materials of the plaintiffs. Taking inspiration from the plaintiffs' copyright works he noted that Axanar had access to the copyright materials: 'there is no dispute that Plaintiffs have ownership of copyrights to the Star Trek Copyrighted Works, and that Defendants have access to these Works. Thus, the copyright infringement claim can live long and prosper if the Axanar Works are substantially similar to the Star Trek Copyrighted Works.'[47] He noted that the plaintiffs demonstrated through the evidence that there were clear uses of copyright works including 'several costumes from the Star Trek Copyrighted Works similar to those Defendants use in the Axanar Works', 'two fictional species from the Star Trek Copyrighted Works: Klingons and Vulcans', and 'military spaceships including Klingon battlecruisers, Vulcan ships with an engine ring, and Federation spaceships with their iconic saucer-shaped hull'. As a result he had little difficulty in finding the Defendants' use of copyright-protected elements in the Axanar Works.[48] By examining the elements of the screenplay, the sets and costumes and the evidence of the previous *Prelude to Axanar*, he established that the Defendants had achieved their goal of creating authentic *Star Trek* films and scripts. He found that 'the Axanar Works are substantially similar to the Star Trek Copyrighted Works, at least under the extrinsic test', while acknowledging that the final question of substantive similarity would be decided by the jury at a full hearing.[49] He concluded by finding that it was unlikely Axanar Productions could rely on any fair use defence.

---

[43] *Paramount Pictures Corp. v Axanar Prods., Inc.* No. 2:15-cv-09938-RGK-E (CD Cal. 3 January 2017).
[44] J Fuster, 'J.J. Abrams Says Paramount Will Drop Lawsuit Against "Star Trek" Fan Film', *The Wrap* 20 May 2016.
[45] The new guidelines are at http://www.startrek.com/fan-films.
[46] *Axanar* (n. 43) 3.
[47] Ibid. 4.
[48] Ibid. 6–7.
[49] Ibid. 9.

Following the publication of Judge Klausner's opinion the parties settled the case with Alec Peters and Axanar Productions promising to make substantial changes to *Axanar* and agreeing to abide by Paramount's and CBS' Guidelines for Fan Films. Under the terms of the settlement, the filmmakers are allowed to release a maximum of two 15-minute films, instead of their planned 90-minute feature and the films must be non-commercial meaning they cannot be shown with adverts.

The Axanar tale is informative. It shows the line between small-scale fan projects which publishers, record labels, and TV and film studios normally allow as part of a vibrant fan community which support and promote the primary commercial works which are professionally produced and generate income, and projects viewed as a direct competitor to the primary commercial works and which will not be allowed. Copyright holders are happy to promote their work through fan productions; it shows a vibrant community who will demand more commercial works in time. What they cannot allow are works which appear to target the same market as the primary commercial works and which make use of their intellectual property.

10.2.3 Fair dealing defences

The above analysis suggests that nearly all forms of user-generated content from fanfiction to mashups by way of fansubbing and memes only exist because the owners of the copyright in the original content have actively chosen not to enforce their copyright. Except in cases where the content copied is not substantive this is probably the case but it should be acknowledged that in certain situations content may be reused without the permission of the copyright holder: this occurs when the user may establish a fair dealing defence.

A number of fair dealing defences are found in Chapter III (ss. 28–76) of the Copyright Designs and Patents Act 1988. A number of fair dealing defences are restricted to certain classes of people such as ss. 37–44A which are restricted to librarians and archivists and ss. 45–50 for those who work in public administration. The general fair dealing defences are found in ss. 28A-31 and of these only really ss. 30, 30A, and 31 are of direct use for user-generated content.

The first of these, s. 30 is the right of criticism or review or the reporting of current events. This allows the user to extract sections from a work in writing a review or critique of the work or to use a work, other than a photograph, to report current news events. This fair dealing right may prove useful to someone who operates a current affairs blog or news service or for someone who operates an online review site. However, it is unlikely to prove useful to wider works of fanfiction. In *Salinger v Colting* an attempt to fit the work within the American Fair Use defence of criticism, which is similar to s. 30, failed. On appeal Mr Colting claimed that '*60 Years Later* was never intended to be a sequel to *The Catcher in the Rye*, rather it was a critical examination of the character Holden and the way he is portrayed in Catcher, in this respect *60 Years Later* is similar to a work of literary criticism.'[50] The court though rejected this finding that 'the amount that Colting took and substantiality of the portion used in relation to the copyrighted work as a whole, [was] well more, in both substance and style, than

---

[50] *Salinger v Colting*, 607 F.3d 68 (2d Cir. 2010) 72.

is necessary for the alleged transformative purpose of criticizing Salinger and his atti-tudes and behavior.'[51] It is therefore extremely unlikely that the courts would accept a claim that fanfiction, or even a meme, was a form of criticism under s. 30.

For producers of user-generated content the most useful defence found in the CDPA is probably s. 30A. This is the parody defence and was added relatively recently by The Copyright and Rights in Performances (Quotation and Parody) Regulations 2014.[52] This provides that 'Fair dealing with a work for the purposes of caricature, parody or pastiche does not infringe copyright in the work.' This defence would almost certainly apply to the myriad of Downfall parodies available on the internet but can extend further. The UK defence is quite new but the US defence is much older so again we can get an insight as to how this might apply from US case law. All three literary cases discussed previously, *Suntrust Bank v Houghton Mifflin*, *Salinger v Colting*, and *Paramount Pictures Corp. v Axanar Productions* discussed the parody defence with varying degrees of success for the defendants. In *Suntrust* it was argued successfully that *The Wind Done Gone* was a parody of *Gone with the Wind*. The court noted that parody by definition must borrow elements from an existing work; parody needs to mimic an original to make its point, and so has some claim to use the creation of its victim's . . . imagination, whereas satire can stand on its own two feet and so requires justification for the very act of borrow-ing.'[53] Identifying whether a work is a parody can be difficult but the court in *Suntrust* referred to the decision of the US Supreme Court in *Campbell v Acuff-Rose Music, Inc.*[54] in finding that to qualify for the defence:

> a parodic character [must] reasonably be perceived in the allegedly infringing work. [However] the Supreme Court's definition of parody in Campbell is somewhat vague. On the one hand, the Court suggests that the aim of parody is 'comic effect or ridicule,' but it then proceeds to discuss parody more expansively in terms of its 'commentary' on the original. In light of the admonition in Campbell that courts should not judge the quality of the work or the success of the attempted humor in discerning its parodic character, we choose to take the broader view. *For purposes of our fair-use analysis, we will treat a work as a parody if its aim is to comment upon or criticize a prior work by appropriating elements of the original in creating a new artistic, as opposed to scholarly or journalistic, work.*[55]

In examining the nature of *The Wind Done Gone*, the court found it to be clearly parodic:

> the parodic character of TWDG is clear. TWDG is not a general commentary upon the Civil-War-era American South, but a specific criticism of and rejoinder to the depiction of slavery and the relationships between blacks and whites in GWTW. The fact that Randall chose to convey her criticisms of GWTW through a work of fiction, which she contends is a more powerful vehicle for her message than a scholarly article, does not, in and of itself, deprive TWDG of fair-use protection.[56]

In *Salinger* the defendant attempted a parody defence also, however this time without success. The problem was that while Mr Colting argued he was parodying the writer, JD Salinger, this did not qualify him for the parody defence as '*Campbell* and its progeny

[51] Ibid. 73.
[52] SI 2014/2356.
[53] *Suntrust Bank* (n. 26) [46]–[47].
[54] 510 US 569 (1994).
[55] *Suntrust Bank* (n. 26) [48] (emphasis added).
[56] Ibid.

define the limits of parody to include only those elements which criticize or comment upon the source author's works, rather than the author himself.'[57] Thus a work which parodies the writer's style, language, or compositions (as arguably was the case with *60 Years Later*) does not qualify. The work must be parodied, not the author. It is unclear if courts in the UK would take the same line, however it is suggested the wording of s. 30A 'fair dealing with a work' would lead to the same conclusion in the UK. Finally, in *Axanar*, the defendants argued that the film, and other works, were intended to be a 'mockumentaries'—fictions presented in a documentary form—which are a form of parody. However, Judge Klausner did not accept this claim finding that 'the Court has difficulty discerning from the Axanar Works any criticism of the Star Trek Copyrighted Works. This is not surprising since Defendants set out to create films that stay faithful to the Star Trek canon and appeal to Star Trek fans.'[58]

Although there is no UK case law on the parody defence as yet there is a decision of the CJEU. In *Deckmyn v Vandersteen*[59] the court was asked to rule on a difficult case from Belgium. At the heart of the proceedings was a calendar prepared by Mr Deckmyn as a gift for his fellow members of the Belgian far-right political party Vlaams Belang. The calendar contained a drawing which was a clear reference to one of the covers of a popular Belgian comic book Suske en Wiske, but with some xenophobic and racist undertones. The heirs of Mr Vandersteen, the author of Suske en Wiske, sued Mr Deckmyn for infringement of copyright and initially won in the Court of First Instance for Brussels. Mr Deckmyn appealed, claiming that the drawing in the calendar was covered by the parody exception. The Vandersteen heirs however argued that the specific criteria for the parody exceptions were not met. The Brussels Court of Appeal referred the matter to the CJEU, asking it to clarify two main issues: whether parody is an autonomous concept of the EU law and, if so, what conditions must a work meet to be a parody? The answer to the first question is not important here, suffice to record the court said yes. The second question though informs us as to how a UK court may interpret the s. 30A defence, even after Brexit.

In a short judgment the court said that the definition and limits of parody must be determined by considering its usual meaning in everyday language, while also taking into account the context in which it occurs and the purposes of the rules of which it is part.[60] The essential characteristics of parody are, first, to evoke an existing work while being noticeably different from it, and, second, to constitute an expression of humour or mockery.[61] This is similar to the US test as set out in *Campbell*, suggesting a UK court would take a similar line. The CJEU gave some further advice on how the defence would be applied inferring that when applying the parody exception, a fair balance must be struck between the interests of the copyright holder and the freedom of expression of the user who makes the parody of the protected work. Such balancing exercise is to be applied on a case-by-case basis by the national courts.[62]

The final defence that may apply in some unique situations is the s. 31 defence which states that 'copyright in a work is not infringed by its incidental inclusion in an artistic

[57] *Salinger* (n. 29) 257.
[58] *Axanar* (n. 43) 11.
[59] ECLI:EU:C:2014:2132.
[60] Ibid. [19].
[61] Ibid. [20].
[62] Ibid. [27].

work, sound recording, film'. This would possibly apply where someone made a video work for uploading to a site such as YouTube which happened to include elements of a copyright work but which work was not the focus of the video, such as a radio playing in the background on which the copyright work may be heard. The Court of Appeal considered this specific defence in *The Football Association Premier League Limited and Others v Panini UK Limited.*[63] This case revolved around collectible photo stickers of football players which are collected and stuck into albums. The photographs of the players included their team badge or crest and in a number of pictures the premier league logo also; both of these are copyright-protected images. Panini claimed these images were incidental to the main image, the photograph of the players and they were protected therefore by s. 31. In dismissing Panini's appeal Chadwick LJ observed that that while 'what is incidental' will depend on all the circumstances of each case, it is plain that 'incidental' was not intended to mean 'unintentional'. Section 31 is not confined to unintentional, or non-deliberate, inclusion. Mummery LJ gives some further guidance as to when something is incidental as opposed to being integral, or part of the work.

> The question whether the inclusion of copyright material in an artistic work is incidental is not answered by rushing to dictionaries or by searching the internet for substitute words and expressions; or by inquiring into the subjective intentions, motives, views or states of mind of the makers, distributors or collectors of the stickers and albums; or by the use of a non-statutory check list of possible indicators; or by recourse to the Copyright Act 1956 or to Hansard reports of the Parliamentary debates preceding the enactment of the 1988 legislation . . . Incidental is an ordinary descriptive English word. Parliament chose not to give it any special meaning. There is no need for the courts to define it. The range of circumstances in which the word 'incidental' is commonly used to describe a state of affairs is sufficiently clear to enable the courts to apply it to the ascertainable objective context of the particular infringing act in question.[64]

This advice mirrors that of the CJEU in *Deckmyn*: to paraphrase, the definition and limits of the defence must be determined by considering its usual meaning in everyday language, while also taking into account the context in which it occurs and the purposes of the rules of which it is part. In the instant case Mummery LJ agreed with Chadwick LJ that the defence was not made out as:

> the objective, when creating the image of the player as it appears on the sticker or in the album, was to produce something which would be attractive to a collector . . . there [can] be [no] doubt that it was of importance, in order to achieve that objective, that the player should appear in the appropriate club strip; and that the club strip be authentic and to be authentic it must include the club badge and where appropriate the FAPL emblem.[65]

10.3 **Computer-generated works**

There is one category of digital creative absent from our discussion so far. Computers as authors or artists, in particular, complex machine learning algorithms which can mimic human creativity are becoming more commonplace and the term 'computer-generated work' is beginning to take on a new and more expansive meaning than the

---

[63] [2002] EWCA Civ 995.
[64] Ibid. [39].
[65] Ibid. [27].

old-fashioned rendering of images following carefully programmed parameters where the creative control was always clearly in the hands of the human programmer or designer. Examples abound of what sophisticated AI can achieve already. They include *The Next Rembrandt*, a project funded by a Dutch bank which used AI to create an original artistic work in the style of the Dutch master[66] and the work Portrait of Edmond Belamy which was sold by Christie's in New York in October 2018 for $432,000 and which was created by a generative adversarial network.[67] The law is struggling to keep up with these developments with very few legal systems allowing for computer-generated works.

In the UK first ownership of a copyright work is awarded to the author of the work, this is defined by s. 9(1) of the CDPA as 'the person who creates it'. What does this mean for non-human authors, including AI authors? Well, interestingly, the UK is one of the few jurisdictions which has passed a specific law relevant to computer-generated works; however, as a law passed over thirty years ago it is arguably out of date for the current environment. The provision is s. 9(3) which provides that 'in the case of a literary, dramatic, musical or artistic work which is computer-generated, the author shall be taken to be the person by whom the arrangements necessary for the creation of the work are undertaken'. The phrase computer-generated is defined at s. 178 as 'the work is generated by computer in circumstances such that there is no human author of the work'. This means that in cases where the work is produced algorithmically the 'author' of the work is the person who makes the arrangements for the work to be produced. This normally will be the major investor in the project or the programmer or designer.

The courts in England and Wales have looked at this issue both before and after the passing of s. 9(3). In *Express Newspapers v Liverpool Daily Post & Echo* the High Court was asked to rule on whether a computer-generated work qualified for copyright protection under the Copyright Act 1956.[68] Counsel for the defendants claimed that 'although he was prepared to accept that computer programmes might well be copyright works, the result produced as a consequence of running those programmes was not a work of which it could truly be said that [the programmer who programmed the software] was the author.'[69] This however was rejected by Whitford J who found that 'the computer was no more than the tool by which the varying grids of five-letter sequences were produced to the instructions, via the computer programmes, of [the programmer]. It is as unrealistic as it would be to suggest that, if you write your work with a pen, it is the pen which is the author of the work rather than the person who drives the pen.'[70] On this basis the court found the programmer to be the author of the work.

This position was formalized in s. 9(3) and in 2006 the High Court reviewed this provision in *Nova Productions Ltd v Mazooma Games Ltd*[71] in which Kitchin J found that the principle games designer, and one of the principle shareholders in Nova games, was the author of their works *Pocket Money* and *Trick Shot* under s. 9(3). This confirms that s.

[66] https://www.nextrembrandt.com/
[67] J Jones, 'A portrait created by AI just sold for $432,000. But is it really art?', *The Guardian*, 26 October 2018.
[68] [1985] 1 WLR 1089.
[69] Ibid. 1093.
[70] Ibid.
[71] [2006] EWHC 24 (Ch).

9(3) made no change to the law and that the approach taken in *Express Newspapers* still applies. The approach is arguably sensible with the current state of AI as algorithmically generated works are produced to instructions and parameters produced by programmers. However, in time it seems likely machine learning algorithms will go beyond their programming and will start to be truly creative beyond their instructions. What then for copyright law? US law professor Annemarie Bridy argues that works produced by AI are copyrightable as 'despite their non-human genesis, they have a sufficient nexus to human creativity'.[72] As to who should own the copyright of these 'authors' she agrees that the current settlement seems to be best. AI may be seen as part of the wider 'Author-in-Fact' vs 'Author-in-Law' debate wherein the work made for hire doctrine that 'the employer or other person for whom the work was prepared is considered the author' seems appropriate.[73] This would class AI as a form of employee, the employer being the person who made arrangements for the AI to produce the work: similar to s. 9(3). This does seem to be the most likely settlement for the foreseeable future, and as Bridy points out this settlement fits the established pattern of case law in the automatic writing cases *Cummings v Bond*[74] and *Penguin Books USA v New Christian Church of Full Endeavor*.[75] Finally, as AI has no need of authorship, or of the concept of reward for investment, it seems unlikely there will be a drive towards autonomous rights for creative AI in the near future. Indeed, as another US law professor James Grimmelmann observes:

> It is possible that some future computer programs could qualify as authors. We could well have artificial intelligences that are responsive to incentives, unpredictable enough that we can't simply tell them what to do, and that have attributes of personality that make us willing to regard them as copyright owners. But if that day ever comes, it will because we have already made a decision in other areas of life and law to treat them as persons, and copyright law will fall in line. But unless those mechanical minds also invent workable time travel, their future existence is of no bearing now. The copyright issues we would face on that far off day are fundamentally different in kind from those we face today.[76]

TEST QUESTIONS

Question 1

You are a legal intern for a new start-up company based in London Extra Time. Extra Time is a sports-based news and social media platform. A key part of the Extra Time offering is 'The Fanzone'. The Fanzone allows users to post content including videos, text, audio files, and photographs to Extra Time servers based in London to be shared among other fans of sporting clubs, films and TV shows, and music acts. The Fanzone has been a massive hit and has led to a flurry of activity among Extra Time users. In the last week however Extra Time has received two

---

[72] A Bridy, 'Coding Creativity: Copyright and the Artificially Intelligent Author' (2012) *Stanford Technology Law Review* 5, 20.

[73] Ibid. 26. Note s. 11(2) of the CDPA provides a statutory 'work for hire' rule in the UK.

[74] (1927) 1 Ch. 167.

[75] No. 96 Civ. 4126, 2000 US Dist. LEXIS 10394 (S.D.N.Y. July 21, 2000).

[76] J Grimmelmann, 'There's No Such Thing as a Computer-Authored Work—And It's a Good Thing, Too' (2016) 39 *Columbia Journal of Law & the Arts* 403, 414.

letters from furious copyright holders suggesting their work has been infringed by posts made to the Fanzone and demanding that Extra Time take action immediately to remove the infringing posts before court action is begun.

- The first is a remixed version of a famous scene from the film Downfall and mocks England's performance at the 2016 European Championships (It may be viewed at https://www.youtube.com/watch?v=dma0P658mMg)
- The second is a Harry Potter/James Bond crossover Harry Potter and the Casino Royale (available at: https://www.fanfiction.net/s/7253248/1/Harry-Potter-andthe-Casino-Royale)

Extra Time seeks your advice as to whether these posts are likely to infringe copyright law in England and Wales and if so what they should do about them.

Extra Time has also employed an artificial intelligence known as 'ExtraBot' to write original content for the Fanzone. The ExtraBot has become a cult hit, not only with Extra Time users but across the internet. The ExtraBot code was written in-house and Extra Time own all the rights to the ExtraBot code. Yesterday a major publisher, Indiscriminate House, issued a press release saying that they were publishing a book called The Wit and Wisdom of ExtraBot in time for Christmas. They expect it to be a bestseller. Extra Time has not given permission to Indiscriminate House to do this and want to prevent the publication of the book as they have their own book planned with rival publisher CarperHollins.

Advise Extra Time on all these issues.

Question 2

Grimmelmann argues that 'For all present practical purposes, new copyright doctrines for computer-generated works are a terrible idea'. Is he right? Why, or why not?

FURTHER READING

Books

B Klein, G Moss, and L Edwards, *Understanding Copyright: Intellectual Property in the Digital Age* (Sage 2015)

L Lessig, *Remix: Making art and commerce thrive in the hybrid economy* (Bloomsbury 2008)

K McLeod and P DiCola, *Creative License: The Law and Culture of Digital Sampling* (Duke UP 2011)

Chapters and Articles

A Bridy, 'Coding Creativity: Copyright and the Artificially Intelligent Author' (2012) *Stanford Technology Law Review* 5

J Cohen, 'Creativity and Culture in Copyright Theory' (2007) 40 *UC Davis Law Review* 1151

U Gasser and S Ernst, 'From Shakespeare to DJ Danger Mouse: A Quick Look at Copyright and User Creativity in the Digital Age' *Berkman Center Research Publication No. 2006-05* <https://ssrn.com/abstract=909223>

J Grimmelmann, 'There's No Such Thing as a Computer-authored Work' (2016) 39 *Columbia Journal of Law & Arts* 403

Copyright in the digital environment

The move from physical to digital distribution models and the development of the internet are two of the most disruptive events of the twentieth century. They have changed the way the developed world trades, communicates, and socializes. But as with all disruptive technologies the positive benefits they bring are tinged with negative effects. As well as allowing people to keep in touch over long distances and allowing new models of commerce to develop they have also allowed the internet to become the largest and most efficient copying machine built by man. This development is not accidental it is in the DNA of the internet that it copies and distributes digital information.

The difficulty that the designers of the ARPANET had to overcome was how to supply data from one computer to another in a remote location. This entailed copying the data, splitting it into packets, and delivering these packets to remote locations: in essence the building of a platform for the copying and distribution of digital content. While computers were expensive and network connections slow, this was not a problem. The very idea that someone would pay several thousand dollars for a computer to allow them to download and store copies of music, movies, or games across a network connection which operated at 9,600 bits per second,[1] was frankly laughable. But in the last twenty-five years the cost of computers, storage media, and high-speed downloads have tumbled as the information society has become part of our everyday lives. This, coupled with an explosion of digital consumer devices such as tablets and smartphones, has created a new marketplace for digital consumer entertainment products, products that are at extreme risk of piracy given the nature of the internet as a copying and distribution device.

This chapter focuses on the battle between producers of content and free riders; between the copyright industries and their own consumers; between taking profit from content and making it free. It is a battle fought on many levels; an economic level, an artistic level, a legal level, and an ideological level. Some people believe passionately that the copyright industries have been profiteering; with HD movies on download services costing up to £13.99. These involve no cost of physical production (no need for a DVD/Blu-Ray case, insert, or even a carrier disc), no distribution costs (no need for fleets of vans to deliver Blu-Rays to shops), and no overheads for

---

[1] To underline how much download speeds have accelerated in the last twenty-nine years a standard 9600 bps modem in use in 1990 would take about 85 minutes to download a 6mb MP3 music file, today a 76MB/s fibre connection would take less than 1 second.

the retailer (download sites have no shops for which they need to pay rent, rates, heating, or staff costs). Others believe equally passionately that failure to control peer-to-peer file-sharing has had long-term deleterious effects for all copyright industries. Some believe passionately that the internet allows an artistic freedom which was impossible in the old distribution model when artists needed to be signed to a music label before their music could reach the shops; others worry about an explosion of mediocre music, films, and video games. Some believe that the illegal file-sharing of copyright protected media is the single biggest threat the copyright industry has faced. They believe there is a need to review, rewrite, and extend copyright protection to afford additional protection to copyright holders in an attempt to rebalance the interests of copyright holders and users. They argue this is necessary because the level of protection copyright holders had before the advent of the information society has been eroded by the simple, free, and (mostly) anonymous practice of file-sharing. Others believe the copyright industry is seeking to extend copyright protection in a way which may prove harmful to society at large. Finally, some believe that in the digital environment with its limitless supply of ones and zeros information wants to be and should be free. Others disagree. This will be the story of this chapter but before we get to the heart of the modern debate about file-sharing and free-riding copyright content we must begin with an analysis of how the internet has challenged the application and development of copyright law.

11.1 **Linking, caching, and the temporary reproduction right**

When ARPANET was designed and built in the 1960s few considerations were given to copyright issues. As the network was designed only to connect research computers the copyright in the material accessible on ARPANET was usually owned by the university or research centre where the mainframe computer could be found. As all involved in the ARPANET project were entering the project with the express aim of sharing research materials and findings there was no conceptualization of copyright infringement being pursued for any ARPANET activity.

Copyright became more of an issue as the network deregulated; the advent of private internet service providers saw copyright issues came to the fore. In particular the World Wide Web posed a major challenge to established copyright orthodoxy. It is founded upon hyperlinking: the very nature of its DNA being the ability to join together original content, or to draw original content from one place and place it in another (as is done with embedded images). This, coupled with the widespread geographical reach of the web and its foundations as an easy-to-use and easy-to-access platform, meant that quickly copyright law and web-based applications came into direct competition with each other.

11.1.1 **Weblinking**

First among common web-copyright issues was the issue of linking. It may seem clear that when one places original material on a website that it is the intent of the copyright holder that, absent a password protection system to control access, the material may be accessed and read (including making a cache copy of the content in the end user's browser cache),[2] but this is only part of the issue. Web pages function by getting referrals from other pages (links), these links are what make the web dynamic, and so one may assume that, as well as implying that placing content on a public web page allows for reading and caching of that content, it also allows for linking to that content. This is not necessarily the case.

This issue first arose in 1996 in the case of *Shetland Times Ltd v Wills*.[3] The pursuer was an established newspaper publisher producing a local newspaper servicing the Shetland Isles. Some time prior to October 1996 they began publishing an online version of their newspaper on the expectation that once this became popular they would be able to sell advertising space on the front page of the site. Dr Wills operates a web-only news publication, *The Shetland News*. In October 1996 it became clear to the pursuers that *The Shetland News* was embarking upon a programme of so-called deep-linking: this is linking directly to pages in the body of a site bypassing the front page. Their activities are described by Lord Hamilton:

> Since about 14 October 1996 the defenders have included among the headlines on their front page a number of headlines appearing in recent issues of *The Shetland Times* as reproduced on the pursuers' web site. These headlines are verbatim reproductions of the pursuers' headlines as so reproduced. A caller accessing the defenders' web site may, by clicking on one of those headlines appearing on the defenders' front page, gain access to the relative text as published and reproduced by the pursuers. Access is so gained and subsequent access to other such headlines also gained without the caller requiring at any stage to access the pursuers' front page. Thus, access to the pursuers' items (as published in printed editions and reproduced by them on their web site) can be obtained by bypassing the pursuers' front page and accordingly missing any advertising material which may appear on it.[4]

The final sentence here demonstrates the crux of the case. By deep-linking to *Shetland Times* news stories *The Shetland News* was misappropriating the advertising revenue from these stories. *The Shetland Times* sought an interim interdict (the Scottish equivalent of an injunction) to prevent *The Shetland News* from using any of their headlines on its site or from linking directly to any of their content other than their home page. Lord Hamilton had two decisions to make, (1) did a newspaper headline qualify as a 'literary work' under s. 17 of the Copyright, Designs and Patents Act, and (2) whether a web page constituted a 'cable programme' under s. 20 of the Copyright, Designs and Patents Act as then worded.[5] He evaluated both claims in an interim hearing. Due to

---

[2] For those unfamiliar with the operations of web browsers a cache copy is a stored copy of a web page previously visited by the user. These are used to reduce the amount of information that needs to be transmitted across the network during a browsing session as information previously stored in the cache can often be reused by the browser. This reduces bandwidth and processing requirements of the web server, and helps to improve responsiveness for users of the web. Modern browsers employ a built-in cache, but some ISPs also use a caching proxy server, which is a cache that is shared between all users of that network. Thus if a customer of BT broadband visits http://www.bbc.co.uk/news, BT will cache a copy in its server, then when the next customer requires http://www.bbc.co.uk/news instead of calling upon the BBC server to deliver the page BT will supply the copy from its server. The server periodically checks with the BBC server to see if a page update is needed.

[3] 1997 SC 316.

[4] Ibid. 318.

[5] It should be noted s. 20 of the CDPA 1988 has been completely rewritten since this case was heard. With new text being introduced by *The Copyright and Related Rights Regulations* 2003 (SI 2003/2498).

the nature of the hearing no authority was laid before the court making the opinion of little authority, however he found that:

> While literary merit is not a necessary element of a literary work, there may be a question whether headlines, which are essentially brief indicators of the subject matter of the items to which they relate, are protected by copyright. However, in light of the concession that a headline could be a literary work and since the headlines at issue (or at least some of them) involve eight or so words designedly put together for the purpose of imparting information, it appeared to me to be arguable that there was an infringement, at least in some instances, of s. 17.[6]

This at the time was of passing interest. The question of replicating headlines or short descriptions of text was no doubt important especially when one is creating a link to content on another site; the real question though was whether Lord Hamilton felt a website was itself capable of copyright protection. Although the wording of s. 20 has changed since the case, the decision on this final issue was of widespread importance. This may only have been an interim hearing, and the jurisdiction of the court may have been limited, but this was the first time a judge anywhere in the world had been asked to rule on the copyright status of a website. Lord Hamilton found that a web page operated by sending information across a network which fitted with the definition of a cable service as then defined as 'a service which consists wholly or mainly in sending visual images, sounds or other information by means of a telecommunications system, otherwise than by wireless telegraphy'.[7] On this basis, and on the basis that at an interim hearing the pursuer only needs to demonstrate a 'balance of convenience' in their favour, he found that 'the pursuers have, in my opinion, a *prima facie* case that the incorporation by the defenders in their web site of the headlines provided at the pursuers' web site constitutes an infringement of s. 20 of the Act by the inclusion in a cable programme service of protected cable programmes'.[8]

The *Shetland Times* case was at once unimportant and yet of international influence. As an interim hearing it carried almost no precedence, yet as the first published judicial opinion on copyright protection for web content, this four-page decision which discussed no previous authority was discussed and analysed globally.[9] Lord Hamilton was often, and unfairly, given the nature of the hearing, criticized for extending the definition of a cable programme to cover a website. The critics pointed out that the definition of a cable programme as one which 'sends visual images, sounds or other information' suggested a push media system, a type of media platform where a broadcaster sends programmes or other content unbidden (such as TV or radio), whereas a website is a pull media system, the customer must select what to receive and ask for it. Whatever they thought, Lord Hamilton had decided both that the contents of web pages could be protected by copyright law and that deep-linking without the permission of the

---

[6] 1997 SC 316, 319.

[7] This was found in s. 7(1) of the CDPA 1988. This section was repealed in whole by *The Copyright and Related Rights Regulations* 2003.

[8] 1997 SC 316, 319.

[9] Just a few of these papers include: H MacQueen, 'Copyright in Cyberspace' (1998) *Journal of Business Law* 297; J Adams, 'Trespass in a digital environment' (2002) *Intellectual Property Quarterly* 1; and J Connolly and S Cameron, 'Fair Dealing in Webbed Links of Shetland Yarns' (1998) (2) *Journal of Information Law and Technology* <www2.warwick.ac.uk/fac/soc/law/elj/jilt/1998_2/connolly/>.

copyright holder could infringe copyright. In making this decision the door had been opened for further copyright challenges to web-based content and, as may be expected, a number of cases followed looking at how copyright law should deal with linking and in particular deep-linking.

Across Europe claims were raised against deep-linking. In *Havas Numerique et Cadre On Line v Keljob*[10] the Tribunal de Commerce de Paris found the defendant's deep links to be parasitical and an unlawful appropriation of the claimants' work. On appeal though this decision was reversed.[11] The Grande Instance de Paris found that the defendant merely operated a search engine which provided results to its users and openly redirected them to pages within the claimants' sites. Consequently, there was no copying and no distribution in any manner which was unfair. In Germany in *Stepstone v Ofir*[12] the Landgericht (District Court) of Cologne held that the defendant, in deep-linking to content within the claimant's site, had infringed the claimant's exclusive right of copying, distribution, and representation, in particular the distribution right.[13] In the Netherlands in the case of *PCM v Kranten.com* the court held that deep-linking was not a reproduction of the copyright work and as a result no copyright infringement occurred,[14] but a contrary position was taken in Denmark in the case of *Danish Newspaper Publishers Association v Newsbooster.com*.[15] These cases suggested a split approach was developing. In France and the Netherlands authorities were in place suggesting that deep-linking was not an infringement of copyright,[16] while in Germany and Denmark a contrary position had developed. Of course it is not this simple; each case must be measured on its merits.

In Germany the decision in *Stepstone* was rendered less influential by the decision of the Bundesgerichtshof (Federal Court of Germany, Germany's highest court) in *Paperboy*.[17] Paperboy offered a news aggregation service comprising elements of a mainstream aggregation page. The court in a very different decision to the previous German law found that 'Where a hyperlink is made to a page on a third party's website which constitutes a work protected by copyright, the making of that hyperlink does not infringe the right of reproduction of that work'[18] and further that:

> a copyright owner who makes available on the internet a work protected under copyright law, without technological protection measures, must be taken to have enabled any use which an on-demand user can make. In general, there is no infringement of copyright where access to a work is facilitated by the setting of hyperlinks, whether in the form of ordinary links or through the use of deep links.[19]

---

[10] Tribunal de Commerce de Paris, 26 December 2000.

[11] *Cadremploi v Keljob*, Tribunal de Grande Instance de Paris, (5 September 2001).

[12] Landgericht, Köln, February 28, 2001: 28 O 692/00. Discussed in G Smith, *Internet Law and Regulation* (4th edn, Sweet & Maxwell 2007) 70.

[13] Stepstone also pursued Ofir in France. On this occasion the Nanterre Tribunal of Commerce held that the actions of Ofir did not infringe Stepstone's copyright. See *SARL Stepstone France v SARL Ofir France* Tribunal de Commerce de Nanterre 8 November 2000.

[14] *Algemeen Dagblad BV v Eureka Internetdiensten* [2002] ECDR 1.

[15] [2003] ECDR 5.

[16] Similar authority had been seen in Austria. See *Meteodata v Bernegger Bau* (Unreported, 17 December 2002, Supreme Court of Austria), discussed in Hobinger, 'Austria: Deep Linking: Copyright Note Allows Display of Foreign Contents on Website' (2003) (4) *World Internet Law Report* 18.

[17] *Verlagsgruppe Handelsblatt GmbH v Paperboy* [2005] ECDR 7.

[18] Ibid. [H7].

[19] Ibid. [H8].

The Danish Courts also moved away from the hard-line position found in *Newsbooster* in the case of *Home A/S v Ofir*.[20] In contradistinction to the earlier *Newsbooster* case the court found that Ofir's deep-linking to Home's database did not infringe Danish Copyright Law. In particular the court noted that deep-linking was a generally desirable function of the internet as a medium for searching and exchanging an incredibly extensive and steadily increasing quantity of information, stating that: 'it should be an ordinary practice that search engines make available deep links which allow the user to access the required information in an effective manner. Parties, including providers in the Internet, should thus expect that search services will establish links to these pages which are published.'[21]

11.1.2 *Google Inc. v Copiepresse SCRL*

By 2006 it appeared that a consensus had developed: deep-linking would be allowed, and should be expected except in those occasions where one party has acted in a manner which may be deemed to unfairly compete with the activities of another. Then the whole debate on linking was reopened by the Belgian case of *Google Inc. v Copiepresse SCRL*.[22]

The case surrounds two aspects of the Google search engine/portal. The first is the Google cache facility which Google offers on all its catalogued entries. The cache copy is a locally stored facsimile of the original site as it was catalogued by Google. The cache facility was described in some detail to the court in *Copiepresse*; the claimants argued that in making and then offering to their users access to the Google cache Google were reproducing and/or communicating to the public works (or parts of works) protected by copyright without having the authorization of the copyright holder.

 Highlight The Google cache facility

When Google crawls the Web it creates a copy of each page examined and stores it in a cache memory, which enables it to consult that copy at any time, and in particular when the original (or internet) page becomes unavailable. When you click on the link 'cached copy' of a web page, Google displays that page in the form that it was found the last time that it was indexed. Furthermore, the cached material forms the basis for a determination by Google as to whether a page is relevant to your search. When a cached page is displayed, it is preceded by a framed heading which reminds you that this is a cached copy of the page and not the original page and citing the search terms which led to its inclusion in the research results.

Copiepresse at [68]

---

[20] Unreported, 24 February 2006, Danish Maritime and Commercial Court, discussed in S Mercado-Kierkegaard, 'Clearing the legal barriers—Danish Court upholds "deep linking" in Home v. Ofir' (2006) 22 *Computer Law and Security Report* 326.

[21] Ibid. 332.

[22] [2007] ECDR 5.

The second issue was the operation of the 'Google News' service or on the Google.be site 'Google.Actualités'. Google News is available as an option at the top of the Google Search page. Today it operates just as a specific search targeted at news sites and blogs bringing up topical search returns so that users can search for current news stories. This is in part as a result of the *Copiepresse* case. Historically, if you clicked on the Google News link without entering a search term you were given a newspaper style offering of topical news stories, with acknowledgement of the source of each story and in traditional Google style a clear hyperlink taking you to the original version of the story. Like a traditional internet news site there were a variety of subheadings a user may select such as 'World News', 'Technology', and 'Sport'. For this reason the claimants argued that Google News was more than a search facility, it was an information portal, not unlike https://www.bbc.co.uk. The expert appointed by the court agreed. He felt that as 'the user finds articles without any action being necessary on his part and is not obliged to undertake a specific search . . . the Google News site is thus a portal for information drawn from the press'.[23] On this basis the claimants also contended that the Google News site was also in breach of Belgian copyright law as again, through this facility, Google were reproducing and/or communicating to the public works (or parts of works) protected by copyright without having the authorization of the copyright holder.

First the court examined the operation of the Google cache facility. They found that as the cache function operated by allowing a user access to a version of the original website held on the Google server rather than directing the user to the original site (as a hyperlink would do) the cache was 'a physical reproduction of the work and a communication of it to the public within the meaning of Art. 1 of the Law on copyright'.[24] The next question was whether or not Google had made the copy. In their defence Google claimed that as it only copied the HTML code for the page (a code which only contains the text and no image), they never created a copy of the page. Rather, the internet user creates a copy of the work when he or she accesses the cache. As such the user is the author of any reproduction or communication to the public, the only act undertaken by Google being the provision of a facility allowing or enabling a communication to be made to the public by internet users.[25] The court quickly dismissed this tortuous interpretation of the manner in which the copy was made, finding that 'Google stores in its memory a copy of webpages. The fact that that copy preserves the HTML code of those pages—i.e. that it is converted into computer language—does not seem particularly relevant.'[26] In summary the court held that Google's cache operation was both an act of reproduction and a communication to the public.

The court next turned to the Google News site. Google argued that Google News was not an information portal, rather it was:

[a] search engine . . . specialised in news material, which allows internet users easily to identify the news articles which may be of interest to them among the headlines published on the internet in the last 30 days and to consult them, at source, by going to the sites of the publishers making those articles available with just one mouse click.[27]

[23] Ibid. [92].
[24] Ibid. [71].
[25] Ibid. [72].
[26] Ibid. [74].
[27] Ibid. [86].

The court felt the distinction between an information portal and a search engine was unimportant as the same questions were raised however the Google News site was characterized.[28] The true question was about the nature of the Google News operation. The claimants argued that in producing the Google News service Google had specifically infringed their copyright by reproducing headlines and extracts drawn from their copyright work. This then raised the question of whether headlines could be protected at copyright law; one of the same questions Lord Hamilton had wrestled with over ten years previously. Google argued that headlines used in press articles are not original at all, claiming them to be merely turns of phrase in current use in language, citing by way of example 'The King visits Sweden' or 'Tom Boonen, world champion'. The court rejected this claim finding that: 'while not all the news article headlines can be considered as original—some of them in fact appear to be purely descriptive and do not therefore show the distinctive stamp of their author—nevertheless one cannot assume that a press article headline would never be sufficiently original to benefit from the protection of the Law on Copyright'[29] and went on to note that the short extract, usually the first two lines of the story, which was displayed alongside the link was equally susceptible to copyright protection.[30] The court therefore found that Google News did reproduce and distribute copyright protected works.

With the *Copiepresse* case established Google needed to bring forward a defence which would allow them to continue their activities. They laid two main defences: (1) Freedom of Expression under the ECHR, and (2) Fair Dealing. Google first argued that the Google News service was protected by Article 10 of the European Convention on Human Rights, arguing that freedom of expression protects the various aspects of the communication process, those being the freedom to receive and to communicate information.[31] Google recognized that the freedom to receive and to communicate information can be limited in order to protect the rights of others, including copyright, but argued nevertheless the restriction of the right of freedom of expression sought by the claimants was disproportionate as Google News was a free tool for access to information and did nothing more than perform a sign-posting function to facilitate research for information on the internet.[32] The court rejected this claim. It noted that copyright is based on a balance between, on the one hand, recognition of the legitimate interests of authors and, on the other hand, of the interests, which are also legitimate, of the public and of society in general and that copyright law had already been designed to take account of this balance by allowing fair dealing exceptions. Thus, Google could not claim a blanket Article 10 exception; they would need to establish that they fell within a fair dealing exception.[33]

---

[28] 'In relation to the argument that "Google Actualités" or "Google News" service is not a "mere search engine service" but is an "information portal", the Court noted that it is settled law that a hyperlink referring to a work protected by copyright is not a reproduction and that if there is a reproduction, it is the work of the internet user. However, this is not the case here as Google News reproduces and communicates to the public, on the homepage of its website, the headlines of press articles and an extract from those articles.' Ibid. [H12].

[29] Ibid. [105].

[30] '[I]n order to infringe the author's exclusive right, a reproduction does not need to be complete and may be merely partial, provided that there is some "borrowing", whether complete or partial, of that which makes the work "original".' Ibid. [109].

[31] Ibid. [53].

[32] Ibid. [54].

[33] Ibid. [56]–[62].

This left only one line of defence for Google to run. They offered two alternate Belgian fair dealing defences which mirror UK provisions: (1) quotation for the purpose of critique, argument, review, or teaching,[34] and (2) fair dealing in reporting the news.[35] The court rejected both defences. In response to the critique, argument, or review defence it noted that 'the Google News service is based on the automated indexing of news articles made available to the public on the internet by a robot. The classification of the articles by theme is done automatically, without any human intervention.'[36] Therefore 'Google News does not undertake any analysis, comparison or critique of those articles, which are not the subject of any commentary at all.'[37] In regard to the news defence the court noted that 'This argument by Google seems to contradict the argument presented previously when describing the Google News service, when Google presented its activity as a specialised search engine service and not as an information portal.'[38]

Google therefore was found to be in breach of copyright in the operations of both its cache operation and its Google News operation. Google appealed the decision but in May 2011 the Court of Appeal of Brussels upheld the decision of the Court of First Instance, reiterated the order, and imposed a fine for each day Google failed to comply with the order after ten days from publication.[39] Google then brought to bear its commercial might in the hope of forcing a settlement on the issue. Google removed the offending material from the Google News site and their cache, as required by the judgment, but also the company removed the newspapers represented by Copiepresse from the main Google index meaning they were no longer visible to users of Google worldwide.[40] This had an obviously deleterious effect on the online business model of the newspapers in question forcing them to seek a settlement with Google.

The question remained how would a UK court receive the continental line of authority? The authority of the *Shetland Times* case had been statutorily overruled: cable programmes have had no separate copyright protection since the Copyright and Related Rights Regulations 2003 came into effect. The question now would be whether the defendant had infringed copyright by communicating the infringing article to the public or (in relation to headlines and cache copies) had reproduced the original works. We now have an answer in the UK's very own news aggregation and scraping case *Public Relations Consultants Association (PRCA) v The Newspaper Licensing Agency (NLA).*[41]

11.1.3 The temporary reproduction right: *Public Relations Consultants Association v The Newspaper Licensing Agency*

The issues in the case are remarkably complex but also hide a central issue which is deceptively simple. The Newspaper Licensing Agency (NLA) acts as a clearance and collecting society for its members who are publishers of newspapers and current affairs

---

[34] For a similar UK provision see s. 30(1) of the CDPA.
[35] For a similar UK provision see s. 30(2) of the CDPA.
[36] *Copiepresse* (n. 22) [130].
[37] Ibid. [138].
[38] Ibid. [143].
[39] The full order is at <http://cdn.arstechnica.net/CopiepresserulingappealGoogle_5May2011.pdf>.
[40] M Lasar, 'Google v. Belgium "link war" ends after years of conflict', *Ars Technica*, 19 July 2011 <http://arstechnica.com/tech-policy/2011/07/google-versus-belgium-who-is-winning-nobody/>.
[41] [2010] EWHC 3099 (Ch) (High Ct.); [2011] EWCA Civ 890 (Court of Appeal); [2013] UKSC 18 (Sup. Ct.); ECLI:EU:C:2014:1195 (CJEU).

magazines. It operates its services in relation to both print and online publications. Meltwater BV is a multifaceted software as a service company which, among its portfolio, offers Meltwater News, a media monitoring service used extensively by public relations companies to monitor news reports in relation to their clients and their services. Part of the service offered by Meltwater News is an interactive analytical service. Meltwater monitors websites, including those operated by NLA members, and uses a spider program to scrape content from their servers. Its software then creates an index which records the position of every word in every article on every indexed website: in essence it is creating a searchable database at this point in the same way Google does. The client can then select any search terms they wish in order to search interactively through a search portal similar to Google search, but in addition they can set keyword alerts: this leads to the creation of a daily or weekly news monitoring report which is emailed to the client.

The Meltwater News report contains three things: (1) a hyperlink to each relevant article, the link consisting of the headline from the article (clicking on the link would take the customer through to the article as it appears on the original publisher's website); (2) the opening words of the article after the headline; and (3) an extract from the article showing the context in which the keyword appears.[42] Meltwater agreed to pay an annual licence to the NLA to hold a web developer licence (WDL). This allowed the licensee to carry out monitoring services such as those operated by Meltwater News, but according to the licence Meltwater may only supply its services to other licence holders, that is to say to end users also licensed by the NLA, by obtaining a separate web end-user licence (WEUL).[43] In short, according to NLA, both Meltwater and their clients required separate licences: Meltwater in carrying out their practice of scraping news content, indexing it, and then preparing the Meltwater News report required a WDL, while each of their clients required a WEUL to access the news story in full by following the link contained in the Meltwater News report. Thus the NLA not only required Meltwater to have a licence to extract the data, which is usual, but also that the end user have a separate licence to access the content on the website of the original publisher with intent to read the content found there.

This seems at odds with the usual position that it has always been assumed that a copyright holder cannot prevent passive enjoyment of copyright protected material. The general principle has always been that copyright law prevents illegal copies from being made, not the passive enjoyment of them. To analogize with the analogue world for a moment, if I buy (or am given) a 'pirated' book then I commit no copyright infringement if I read the book. Many infringements will have been committed upstream including the production and distribution of the book but so long as I make no copy or attempt to distribute the book, I commit no infringement. I need no licence or permission of the author to simply read content as it does not involve the making of a copy. Technology changes all of this. When we consume a digital file, by necessity a copy is made as part of the process of consumption. This is true of all digital content from movies to web-page content; when we access it we make a local copy in the RAM memory of the computer, and another copy as the screen display. It has always been

---

[42] The description of the service draws heavily from that of Proudman J at [2010] EWHC 3099 (Ch) [25]–[27].
[43] Ibid. [18].

recognized that there is the potential to use this technological development as a means to leverage end-user control in the way seen in *PRCA* where licences may be used as a method to control access to content in the same way that fences are used to delineate controlled access to physical property. Because this risk existed, steps were taken to ensure that digital content is not treated differently from analogue content. Article 5 of the InfoSoc Directive[44] was designed to ensure that the temporary acts of reproduction which are automatically carried out by digital systems did not lead to the consumption of digital content being treated differently to analogue content.

 Highlight Article 5(1) of the InfoSoc Directive

Temporary acts of reproduction, which are transient or incidental [and] an integral and essential part of a technological process and whose sole purpose is to enable:

(a) a transmission in a network between third parties by an intermediary, or

(b) a lawful use of a work or other subject-matter to be made, and which have no independent economic significance, shall be exempted from the reproduction right provided for in Article 2.

The intent of Art. 5 was to ensure that digital consumption and analogue consumption were treated equally. No matter in which format you consumed, you did not need a licence or permission from the copyright holder. The fact that your computer automatically made copies of content as part of the process of consumption was not legally relevant. Copyright infringement (if at all) occurred upstream of the consumer in the same way as had always been the case in the analogue environment.

The problem with Art. 5 has always been in the phrasing. What exactly is meant by 'essential' and what is meant by 'no independent economic significance'? These problems were magnified when the CJEU considered the case of *Infopaq International v Danske Dagblades Forening (Infopaq I)*.[45] This was a case not dissimilar to *PRCA* in factual origin. Infopaq also supply a media monitoring service similar to Meltwater News but with a different set of operating parameters. Rather than using a spider to scrape and gather news stories from websites, Infopaq would scan in material from hard-copy newspapers to produce a final report similar to Meltwater's which would then be sent to the client. There are many differences also between Infopaq and Meltwater. Infopaq did not have a licence, something Meltwater had conceded they would need, but more importantly the process Infopaq used was manual rather than automated. Their process involved five stages and in at least two of these stages a manual intervention was required to delete temporary copies made in the scanning and indexing process. The question was asked whether digital copies of the scanned material made then deleted during the scanning process fell within the temporary copies exception. Perhaps not surprisingly, the court found that the actions of Infopaq were not covered by Art. 5 as

---

[44] Dir. 2001/29/EC of the European Parliament and of the Council of 22 May 2001 on the harmonization of certain aspects of copyright and related rights in the information society.

[45] ECLI:EU:C:2009:465.

their actions, which required manual intervention, were not acts of temporary reproduction as these were, according to Recital 33, 'acts enabling "browsing" and "caching", [acts] which have the purpose of facilitating the use of a work or making that use more efficient. Thus, an inherent feature of those acts is to enable the achievement of efficiency gains in the context of such use and, consequently, to lead to increased profits or a reduction in production costs.'[46] The action of Infopaq in making a temporary copy that required manual intervention to delete was clearly not covered by Art. 5. This decision is undoubtedly correct. It is not, and never was, the intent of Art. 5 to licence manual acts of reproduction which, although temporary in themselves, create a new economic work. The problem of the necessarily narrow interpretation of Art. 5(1) which had been applied in *Infopaq I* became apparent when *PRCA* (then known as *Meltwater*) came before the High Court.[47] There Proudman J applied the narrow interpretation of *Infopaq I* and found that for s. 28A of the Copyright, Designs and Patents Act 1988 (which implements Art. 5 of the *Infosoc* Directive) to apply, *Infopaq*'s five conditions had to be met:

 Highlight *Infopaq*'s five conditions

1. The act must be temporary.
2. It must be transient or incidental.
3. It must be an integral and essential part of the technological process.
4. The sole purpose of the process must be to enable a transmission network between third parties by an intermediary or the lawful use of the work or protected subject matter.
5. The act must have no independent economic significance.

This is the position in *Infopaq I* but Proudman J added a twist to her interpretation. She was being asked a subtly different question to the court in *Infopaq I*: whereas they were looking at acts of reproduction designed ultimately to be consumed by third parties, she was being asked whether the end users required a separate licence, that is, for the act of consumption. To answer the question of whether consumption, in the form of a local computer-generated copy read and then automatically deleted, was covered by Art. 5 she referred to an early report from the European Economic and Social Committee, a report which had previously been cited with approval by Kitchen J in the case of *Football Association Premier League Ltd v QC Leisure*.[48] Unfortunately Kitchen J was looking at a different aspect of the report from Proudman J. While he was looking at the meaning of independent economic significance, Proudman J used the report to examine whether

---

[46] Ibid. at [49].
[47] The case commenced as *The Newspaper Licensing Agency and others v Meltwater Holding BV* as was so known in both the High Court and the Court of Appeal. It was renamed *Public Relations Consultants Association v The Newspaper Licensing Agency* upon appeal to the Supreme Court when PRCA took over as the lead appellant.
[48] [2008] EWHC 1411(Ch).

the temporary copying exception covered any copy in which end-user intervention was required. Applying the report, she found that it did, as the:

> exception cannot have been intended to legitimise all copies made in the course of browsing or users would be permitted to watch pirated films and listen to pirated music. The kind of circumstance where the defence may be available is where the purpose of the copying is to enable efficient transmission in a network between third parties by an intermediary, typically an internet service provider.[49]

This appears to be an incorrect interpretation. As already noted, it was in fact the intent of the temporary copying exemption to ensure that an act which had previously been permitted (consumption) remained so permitted. The wording of the directive seemed to ensure that: at Recital 33 it states that the temporary copying 'exception should include acts which enable browsing as well as acts of caching to take place, including those which enable transmission systems to function efficiently'. Proudman J by contrast seems to suggest that browsing is only permitted where it is an 'essential part of a technological process and carried out for the sole purpose of enabling either efficient transmission in a network between third parties by an intermediary, or a lawful use of a work'.[50] This position was then upheld on appeal.[51]

In the period following the decisions of both Proudman J and the Court of Appeal, the CJEU looked twice more at Art. 5. In a reference from the UK in *Football Association Premier League Ltd v QC Leisure*,[52] they essentially reviewed Proudman J's opinion that Art. 5 did not permit an unauthorized act of consumption as it remained in essence unlawful. The court found this was not the case noting that 'a use should be considered lawful where it is authorised by the right holder or where it is not restricted by the applicable legislation'.[53] For the avoidance of doubt the court went on to say that 'mere reception as such of those broadcasts—that is to say, the picking up of the broadcasts and their visual display—in private circles does not reveal an act restricted by European Union legislation or by that of the United Kingdom'.[54] Applying the *FA Premier League* decision, the same would be true of browsing a web page without a licence. In addition the CJEU revisited the original *Infopaq I* decision in *Infopaq International v Danske Dagblades Forening (Infopaq II)*.[55] The court was asked to clarify some of its earlier findings, in particular in relation to lawful use. It found that:

> in respect of the lawful or unlawful character of the use, it is not disputed that the drafting of a summary of newspaper articles is not, in the present case, authorised by the holders of the copyright over these articles. However, it should be noted that such an activity is not restricted by European Union legislation. Furthermore, it is apparent from the statements of both Infopaq and the DDF that the drafting of that summary is not an activity which is restricted by Danish legislation. In those circumstances, that use cannot be considered to be unlawful. In view of the foregoing, Article 5(1) of Directive 2001/29 must be interpreted as meaning that the acts of temporary reproduction carried out during a data capture process, such as those in issue in the

---

[49] *Meltwater* (n. 42) [110].
[50] InfoSoc Directive, Recital 33.
[51] [2011] EWCA Civ 890.
[52] ECLI:EU:C:2011:631.
[53] Ibid. [168].
[54] Ibid. [171].
[55] ECLI:EU:C:2012:16.

main proceedings, fulfil the condition that those acts must pursue a sole purpose, namely the lawful use of a protected work or a protected subject-matter.[56]

As a result of these decisions when *PRCA* came before the Supreme Court the decision of Proudman J, which had found favour in the Court of Appeal, was reversed. Lord Sumption gave the judgment of the court. He examined the case law which had taken place between the original decision of Proudman J (and the Court of Appeal) and suggested an alternative to *Infopaq*'s five conditions for the application of Article 5.

 Highlight *Lord Sumption's* six conditions

1. The exception in Article 5(1) applies to copies made as an integral and necessary part of a 'technological process', in particular the digital processing of data. For this purpose, the making of copies is a 'necessary' part of the process if it enables it to function 'correctly and efficiently': *Infopaq II*, at [30], [37].

2. These copies must be temporary. This requirement is explained and defined by the words which follow, namely that the making of the copies must be 'transient or incidental and an integral and essential part of a technological process'. It means (i) that the storage and deletion of the copyright material must be the automatic consequence of the user's decision to initiate or terminate the relevant technological process, as opposed to being dependent on some further discretionary human intervention, and (ii) that the duration of the copy should be limited to what is necessary for the completion of the relevant technological process: *Infopaq I*, at [62], [64].

3. The exception is not limited to copies made in order to enable the transmission of material through intermediaries in a network. It also applies to copies made for the sole purpose of enabling other uses, provided that these uses are lawful. These other uses include internet browsing: *Infopaq I*, at [63] and *Infopaq II*, at [49(4)]. The sole purpose of the process must be to enable a transmission network between third parties by an intermediary or the lawful use of the work or protected subject matter.

4. For the purpose of Article 5(1), a use of the material is lawful, whether or not the copyright owner has authorised it, if it is consistent with EU legislation governing the reproduction right, including Article 5(1) itself: *Premier League*, at [168-173], *Infopaq II*, at [42]. The use of the material is not unlawful by reason only of the fact that it lacks the authorisation of the copyright owner.

5. The making of the temporary copy must have no 'independent economic significance'. This does not mean that it must have no commercial value. It may well have. What it means is that it must have no independent commercial value, i.e. no value additional to that which is derived from the mere act of digitally transmitting or viewing the material: *Premier League*, at [175], *Infopaq II*, at [50].

6. If these conditions are satisfied no additional restrictions can be derived from Article 5(5).[57]

---

[56] Ibid. [44]–[46].
[57] [2013] UKSC 18 [26].

This is a comprehensive and helpful test. Not only has Lord Sumption analysed all the EU case law for us he has given the source of each part of his test and explained it. The key is that Lord Sumption agrees with, and applies, the key findings of *Infopaq II* and *FA Premier League* that (1) Article 5(1) is not limited to intermediary transmission but extends also to other lawful uses, including internet browsing; (2) that the authorization of the copyright owner is not relevant to Article 5(1); and (3) that temporary copies may have commercial value, as long as this does not amount to value added over that afforded by viewing or transmitting the material. This may be read as being in direct contradistinction to Proudman J's original position (pre-*Infopaq II* and *FA Premier League*) that 'the defence may be available where the purpose of the copying is to enable efficient transmission in a network between third parties by an intermediary, typically an internet service provider'.[58] Lord Sumption is clear throughout not to be critical of Proudman J's decision, nor the Court of Appeal's upholding of it, for they did not have the benefit of the later cases that he had. Having the benefit of these cases though it is clear that the Proudman analysis no longer stands. From here it seemed an obvious decision for Lord Sumption to find in favour of PRCA and dispose of the case. However, perhaps surprisingly, he chose not to do this. Having very clearly and carefully dissected both the meaning and application of Article 5, and the decisions of the lower Courts in Meltwater and the CJEU in both *Infopaq* cases and *FA Premier League* he then refers the case to the CJEU. With the law seemingly clear this may seem unusual but Lord Sumption, as always, has his reason:

> I recognise the issue has a transnational dimension and that the application of copyright law to internet use has important implications for many millions of people across the EU making use of what has become a basic technical facility. These considerations make it desirable that any decision on the point should be referred to the Court of Justice for a preliminary ruling, so that the critical point may be resolved in a manner which will apply uniformly across the European Union.[59]

This could be read as either an invitation or a challenge to the CJEU. Either 'having done all the hard work for you, I invite you to extend my reasoning across the EU providing Art. 5 protection to internet users in all 28 jurisdictions' or 'I challenge you to disagree with my reasoning'. It seems clear that Lord Sumption meant this as an invitation not a challenge: he was keen to see a harmonized application of Art. 5 in such an important matter.

The CJEU ruled in the *PRCA* case in June 2014.[60] The court agreed with all of Lord Sumption's analysis. They started by addressing the question of temporary copies, which had been a difficulty ever since *Infopaq I*. Were screen displays and cache copies made while browsing temporary? The answer on both counts was yes:

> it is apparent from the documents before the Court, first, that the on-screen copies are deleted when the Internet user moves away from the website viewed. Secondly, the cached copies are normally automatically replaced by other content after a certain time, which depends on the capacity of the cache and on the extent and frequency of Internet usage by the Internet user concerned. It follows that those copies are temporary in nature.[61]

---

[58] Text accompanying (n. 49).
[59] *PRCA* (n. 57) [38].
[60] ECLI:EU:C:2014:1195.
[61] Ibid. [26].

Next the Court revisited the two *Infopaq* decisions to address the question of essentiality, in essence could the internet function without these processes? First, the Court rejected the Proudman assertion that the copies were created by an act of the user: 'It is irrelevant, in this regard, that the process in question is activated by the Internet user'.[62] It then went on to find that 'on-screen copies and the cached copies must be regarded as being an integral [and essential] part of the technological process.'[63] On the basis of this analysis they rejected the claim made by the NLA that applying *Infopaq I* the actions of the user in initiating and ending screen displays meant the process was not a an incidental and technical process. Finally, to dispose of the case the court found that under Art. 5(5) 'although the copies make it possible, in principle, for Internet users to access works displayed on websites without the authorisation of the copyright holders, the copies do not unreasonably prejudice the legitimate interests of those rights holders.'[64] Their final ruling was clear and unambiguous and draws a line under all the confusion caused by the special circumstances of *Infopaq I*.

 Highlight The *PRCA Ruling*

Article 5 of Parliament and Council Directive 2001/29/EC of 22 May 2001 on the harmonisation of certain aspects of copyright and related rights in the information society must be interpreted as meaning that the copies on the user's computer screen and the copies in the Internet 'cache' of that computer's hard disk, made by an end-user in the course of viewing a website, satisfy the conditions that those copies must be temporary, that they must be transient or incidental in nature and that they must constitute an integral and essential part of a technological process, as well as the conditions laid down in article 5(5) of that directive, and that they may therefore be made without the authorisation of the copyright holders.[65]

This ruling has variously been called the ruling that saved the internet,[66] or potentially a Pirate's Charter.[67] In truth it is neither; it is the simple application of Art. 5 as was intended by the drafters. One thing which has been missed in the hyperbole which surrounded this case was that internet browsing was never under threat, this was a case about the *commercial* exploitation of copyright content not the simple act of browsing. It should be acknowledged, however, that had NLA won and established the principle that Art. 5 did not cover the transient copies made on-screen displays and in caches, it would have been possible at a later date for another claimant to seek to drive such a wedge home, so it is gratifying that the Supreme Court and the CJEU closed off such a possibility.

---

[62] Ibid. [30].
[63] Ibid. [33], [37].
[64] Ibid. [56].
[65] Ibid. [64].
[66] P Sherrell and W Smith, 'CJEU decision in Meltwater—the internet is saved, browsing does not require a licence', *Bird & Bird*, (2014) 5 June 2014. <www.twobirds.com/en/news/articles/2014/global/cjeu-decision-in-meltwater-the-internet-is-saved-browsing-does-not-require-a-licence>.
[67] M Hart, 'The legality of internet browsing in the digital age' [2014] 36 *European Intellectual Property Review* 630 (arguing the contrary).

11.1.4 **The temporary reproduction right after *PRCA***

The CJEU has added to the decision in *PRCA* in the case of *Stichting Brein v Jack Frederik Wullems (Filmspeler)*.[68] *Wullems* is one of many cases brought by Stichting Brein, a Dutch foundation that protects the interests of copyright holders. Mr Wullems sold multimedia players which came prefigured with installed open source software, making it possible to play copyright protected files through a user-friendly interface via structured menus which would take the user via hyperlinks to streaming websites (a so-called fully-loaded box). Stichting Brein brought an action against Mr Wullems, submitting that by selling the Filmspeler device he was making a 'communication to the public' in breach of the Dutch law on copyright. In reply Mr Wullems submitted that streaming of copyright works from an illegal source, as performed by the users of the Filmspeler device, was permitted on the part of the end user by Art. 5(1) as had been outlined in *PRCA*. The court begin its analysis by restating the five *Infopaq* conditions. They emphasized that as established in *Infopaq* those conditions are cumulative in the sense that non-compliance with any one of them will lead to the act of reproduction not being exempted.[69] In addition, they note that as established in *FA Premier League* and *PRCA* the *Infopaq* conditions must be interpreted strictly because Article 5(1) is a derogation from the general rule established by that directive that the copyright holder must authorize any reproduction of his protected work. Applying this, the court noted that the exception in Art. 5(1) must be interpreted in light of Art. 5(5), which requires that the exception is only to be applied in certain special cases which do not conflict with normal exploitation of the work and do not unreasonably prejudice the legitimate interests of the right holder.[70] The court decided that the applicability of the temporary reproduction exception in this case turned on the fourth *Infopaq* condition (the sole purpose of the process must be to enable a transmission network between third parties by an intermediary or the lawful use of the work or protected subject matter).[71] The streaming in this case was not a transmission by an intermediary, so it was necessary to examine whether the relevant streaming activity constituted a lawful use of the protected works. Unsurprisingly, the court held that the streaming activity made possible by the Filmspeler device did not constitute a lawful use of the relevant copyright works. In particular, the court noted that the main attraction of the player was the pre-installation of the software add-ons. In those circumstances, the court found that purchasers of the player used it to access unauthorized streams of protected works deliberately and in full knowledge of the unlawful nature of those streams. Considering the impact of Art. 5(5), the court considered that the relevant acts of temporary reproduction would also adversely affect the normal exploitation of the relevant works and cause unreasonable prejudice to the legitimate interests of the rightsholder, as there would be a diminution of lawful transactions relating to the protected works. In view of the above, the court held that acts of temporary reproduction on a multimedia player, of copyright protected works obtained by streaming from a third-party website without the consent of the right holder do not satisfy the conditions set out in Art. 5.[72]

---

[68] ECLI:EU:C:2017:300.
[69] Ibid. [61].
[70] Ibid. [62]–[63].
[71] Ibid. [64].
[72] Ibid. [70]–[71].

This decision answers Proudman J's concern that the Art.5 exception would 'legitimise all copies made in the course of browsing or users would be permitted to watch pirated films and listen to pirated music.'[73] Having found that the temporary reproduction exception cannot apply in the case of the Filmspeler player, it seems that the Court's reasoning may apply to any end user's enjoyment of an unlawful online streaming site. The temporary reproduction right does not 'cure' something illegal, it merely prevents a previously legal act from being deemed illegal due to the nature of digital distribution systems.

11.2 **The communication to the public right**

While our analysis to date has looked at the specific temporary reproduction exception found in Art. 5 of the InfoSoc Directive we must now turn our attention to the specific new right afforded to right holders in Art. 3. This creates a right, designed to assist copyright holders in enforcing their rights in an information society where the ability to distribute (communicate) copyright protected works by unauthorized third parties is facilitated by network communications and hyperlinking.

The WIPO Copyright Treaty of 1996 first promulgated the 'communication to the public right'.[74] Article 8 provided that 'authors of literary and artistic works shall enjoy the exclusive right of authorizing any communication to the public of their works, by wire or wireless means, including the making available to the public of their works in such a way that members of the public may access these works from a place and at a time individually chosen by them.' Importantly the Treaty footnotes that 'the mere provision of physical facilities for enabling or making a communication does not in itself amount to communication within the meaning of this Treaty'. This affords producers of end-terminal equipment such as computers, tablets, and smartphones and the producers of internet routing and other telecommunications equipment an exemption. As a contracting party to the Treaty the European Union had to give effect to Art. 8 and this was achieved by Art. 3 of the InfoSoc Directive.

 Highlight Article 3

1. Member States shall provide authors with the exclusive right to authorise or prohibit any communication to the public of their works, by wire or wireless means, including the making available to the public of their works in such a way that members of the public may access them from a place and at a time individually chosen by them.

2. Member States shall provide for the exclusive right to authorise or prohibit the making available to the public, by wire or wireless means, in such a way that members of the public may access them from a place and at a time individually chosen by them:

   (a) for performers, of fixations of their performances;

   (b) for phonogram producers, of their phonograms;

→

---

[73] Text accompanying (n. 49).
[74] WIPO Copyright Treaty 1996, TRT/WCT/001.

➡

(c) for the producers of the first fixations of films, of the original and copies of their films;

(d) for broadcasting organisations, of fixations of their broadcasts, whether these broadcasts are transmitted by wire or over the air, including by cable or satellite.

3. The rights referred to in paragraphs 1 and 2 shall not be exhausted by any act of communication to the public or making available to the public as set out in this Article.

This apparently simple provision has proven to be extremely challenging for national courts and very time-consuming for the CJEU with almost twenty references for a preliminary ruling, with a large number of these references referring to online distribution methods.

11.2.1 A communication: SGAE and TVCatchup

One of the earliest references under Art. 3 was *SGAE v. Rafael Hoteles*.[75] This reference came from Spain and concerned the playing of ambient music from hotel television sets. SGAE, which is the Spanish musicians collecting society argued this was a communication to the public without authorization. The court defined the public as 'an indeterminate number of potential viewers'.[76] On this basis the court found that the large number of successive viewers in hotel rooms, as well as of those who are present in the common areas of the hotel, constitute a 'public' within the meaning of Art. 3.[77] The court then noted that the distribution of a signal through TV sets in hotel rooms constitutes a communication 'made by a broadcasting organization other than the original one', which the author has the exclusive right to authorize or prohibit.[78] Regarding the viewers, such transmission is made to a public different from the one at which the original act of communication of the work is directed, that is, to a new public.[79] It is thus the right of the authors to grant authorization in respect of such further communication, which may well be provided for profit: in this case, as the court incidentally observed, Hotel Rafael distributed TV signals to its customers as an additional service, which had a direct bearing on the price of rooms. Furthermore, the ECJ clarified that for there to be communication to the public, no actual enjoyment on the part of customers is required; it is sufficient that the work be made available to them in such a way that they have access to it.[80] Finally, the court turned to the issue as to whether the private nature of hotel rooms is a bar to considering the communication of audiovisual works taking place in such rooms as communication to the public. In this respect, the court took the view that the public or private nature of the place where communication is carried out is immaterial, the relevant factor being whether a certain work is made available to the public, which is plainly a separate issue.[81]

---

[75] ECLI:EU:C:2006:764.
[76] Ibid. [37].
[77] Ibid. [38]–[39].
[78] Ibid. [40].
[79] Ibid. [42].
[80] Ibid. [43].
[81] Ibid. [50].

Careful readers will have observed that *SGAE* is not an internet case. It is though important for the online distribution cases that were to follow. In 2011 the UK referred the case of *ITV Broadcasting Ltd v TVCatchup Ltd*[82] This was to be the foundational case on whether streaming online constitutes a communication to the public. TVCatchup operated an online platform that retransmitted terrestrial and satellite TV channels enabling its subscribers to watch near-live UK television on their computers, tablets, mobile phones, and other devices. Several UK commercial broadcasters brought proceedings before the High Court contending that the streaming of their broadcasts (and works comprised therein) was an unauthorized communication to the public of their copyright works. The High Court took the view that it was not clear from previous CJEU case law that there was a communication to the public under circumstances such as this where works are streamed to subscribers who are already entitled to access the original broadcast signals via TVs in their own homes, and referred this question to the CJEU.[83]

In its reply the CJEU first found that as 'the principal objective of the Directive is to establish a high level of protection of authors, allowing them to obtain an appropriate reward for the use of their works, including on the occasion of communication to the public. It follows that "communication to the public" must be interpreted broadly.'[84] The court acknowledged that the directive does not define 'communication' and suggested that a contextual definition should be applied. In the instant case they noted that:

> from recital 23, the author's right of communication to the public covers any transmission or retransmission of a work to the public not present at the place where the communication originates, by wire or wireless means, including broadcasting. In addition, it is apparent from Article 3(3) that authorising the inclusion of protected works in a communication to the public does not exhaust the right to authorise or prohibit other communications of those works to the public.[85]

From this the court determined that 'the retransmission of a terrestrial television broadcast over the internet uses a specific technical means different from that of the original communication, that retransmission must be considered to be a 'communication' within the meaning of Article 3(1).'[86] The actions of TVCatchup were therefore a communication, separate to the original act of the broadcasters. Further, as Art. 3(3) makes clear the fact that the work had been previously transmitted by the broadcasters did not effect the need for TVCatchup to seek explicit permission for their act of communication.

The next question was whether this was a 'communication to a public'. Referring back to *SGAE* the court found that 'the term "public" in Article 3(1) refers to an indeterminate number of potential recipients and implies, moreover, a fairly large number of persons.'[87] As *SGAE* had established, the cumulative effect of access to the works in succession, as well as simultaneously, had to be taken into account. In this instance

[82] ECLI:EU:C:2013:147.
[83] [2011] EWHC 2977 (Pat), [23]–[24].
[84] *TVCatchup* (n. 82) [20].
[85] Ibid. [23].
[86] Ibid. [26].
[87] Ibid. [32].

TVCatchup's streaming of the protected works was aimed at all persons resident in the UK who had an internet connection and who claimed to hold a television licence. On this basis the court held that TVCatchup's retransmission of the protected works via the internet, fulfilled the *SGAE* criteria.[88]

This left one final question, had TVCatchup communicated to a *new* public? In *SGAE* the court had established that due to Art. 11*bis* of the Berne Convention 'a transmission [must be] made to a public different from the public at which the original act of communication of the work is directed, that is, to a new public.'[89] The court in *SGAE* had not given much guidance on the identification of this 'new public', merely noting that the clientele of the hotel had formed a 'new public'. In the later case of *FA Premier League v QC Leisure* the CJEU fleshed this out slightly by noting that a new public was 'a public which was not taken into account by the authors of the protected works when they authorised their use by the communication to the original public.'[90] In *TVCatchup* the court stated that it did not need to answer this question. In previous cases, such as *SGAE* and *FA Premier League*, the deliberate intervention of the operator made the original broadcasts containing the protected works available to a different public. In *TVCatchup* the case dealt with a new transmission, which required an individual and separate authorization from the copyright owners.[91] The question was however about to arise again.

11.2.2 A new public: Retriever Sverige; GS Media and Stichting Brein

The question of whether an online communication was indeed a communication to a *new* public arose again almost immediately in the Swedish case of *Nils Svensson & Ors v Retriever Sverige AB*.[92] In this case the court was asked whether a hyperlink to a story found elsewhere on the web was a 'communication to the public' under Art. 3. At issue were links to news stories on the Göteborgs-Posten website. The claimants, Nils Svensson and other Swedish journalists, had written articles for the Göteborgs-Posten, which published them in print as well as making them available on its website. Retriever Sverige AB operates a subscription-based service whereby customers can access newspaper articles through the provision of a hyperlink which links to the original website where the requested content is freely accessible. Svensson sued Retriever for equitable remuneration, arguing that Retriever had made his article available through the search-and-alert functions on its website. This, he maintained, falls within the copyright relevant acts of either communication to the public or the public performance of a work, neither for which he had given consent. Retriever denied any liability to pay equitable remuneration. They argued that the linking mechanisms did not constitute copyright relevant acts, and therefore no infringement of copyright law occurred. The Swedish District Court rejected the claimants' application. An appeal against the judgment of the District Court was then brought before the Swedish Court of Appeal, which referred the case for a preliminary ruling to the CJEU asking for a clarification on the

[88]   Ibid. [36].
[89]   *SGAE* (n. 75) [40].
[90]   *FA Premier League* (n. 52) [197].
[91]   *TVCatchup* (n. 82) [39].
[92]   ECLI:EU:C:2014:76.

interpretation of Article 3 of the Information Society Directive. The court had little difficulty in dismissing the claim:

> In the circumstances of this case, it must be observed that making available the works concerned
> by means of a clickable link, such as that in the main proceedings, does not lead to the works in
> question being communicated to a new public. The public targeted by the initial communica-
> tion consisted of all potential visitors to the site concerned, since, given that access to the works
> on that site was not subject to any restrictive measures, all Internet users could therefore have
> free access to them. In those circumstances, it must be held that, where all the users of another
> site to whom the works at issue have been communicated by means of a clickable link could
> access those works directly on the site on which they were initially communicated, without the
> involvement of the manager of that other site, the users of the site managed by the latter must
> be deemed to be potential recipients of the initial communication and, therefore, as being part
> of the public taken into account by the copyright holders when they authorised the initial com-
> munication. Therefore, since there is no new public, the authorisation of the copyright holders
> is not required for a communication to the public such as that in the main proceedings.[93]

The court on this basis quickly concluded that 'Article 3(1) must be interpreted as
meaning that the provision on a website of clickable links to works freely available
on another website does not constitute an "act of communication to the public", as
referred to in that provision.'[94]

The court has had cause to revisit this issue frequently since. In *BestWater International
GmbH v Mebes & Potsch*,[95] the court extended the *Svennson* analysis to find that embedding a video containing copyrighted material does not constitute copyright infringement. The respondents acted on behalf of a competitor of the complainant and both
operated websites where they promoted the products marketed by their client. They
each embedded a video produced by BestWater into their sites. BestWater argued that
by so embedding the video into their sites they had communicated it to the public
without permission. The court applied *Svennson* and found that the conclusion (from
Svennson) 'is not called into question by the fact that when users click on the link in
question, the copyrighted work appears giving the impression that it is shown from the
site where the link is found, when it actually comes from another site'.[96] This can be distinguished from earlier domestic cases such as *Shetland Times*, and the court acknowledged a risk in this approach:

> this technique can be used to make available to the public a work in avoiding the need to
> copy and so fall into the scope of the provisions relating to the reproduction right, but the fact
> remains that its use does not lead to what the work in question is communicated to a new public.
> Indeed, whenever and as long as this work is freely available on the site pointed to the Internet
> link, it must be considered that when the copyright holders have authorized this communica-
> tion, they have taken into account all Internet users as public.[97]

In *GS Media v Sanoma Media Netherlands*,[98] the question concerned images obtained
illicitly and then placed online. The case concerned photographs of the Dutch TV

---

[93] Ibid. [24]–[28].
[94] Ibid. [42].
[95] ECLI:EU:C:2014:2315.
[96] Ibid. [17].
[97] Ibid. [18].
[98] ECLI:EU:C:2016:644.

personality Britt Dekker taken for *Playboy* magazine. The images were leaked to GeenStijl a gossip blog site via a file locker site. GeenStijl placed a part of one of the photos on its website and linked to the file locker location where eleven photographs could be downloaded. The claimants argued that making available a hyperlink to a website on which a work has been posted without the consent of the copyright holder constitutes a communication to the public. GS Media argued the photographs were already on the web, they just linked to them and following *Svennson* and *BestWater* the images had already been communicated to all internet users when they published the link on their website. The court considered what it called the essence of the Dutch reference 'whether, and in what possible circumstances, the fact of posting, on a website, a hyperlink to protected works, freely available on another website without the consent of the copyright holder, constitutes a "communication to the public" within the meaning of Article 3(1).'[99] The court applied what has become known as the three-step test: (1) has there been an act of communication; (2) to the public; and (3) does it reach a 'new' public? The court stated in making this determination 'an individual assessment was needed in each case'.[100] Applying such an individual assessment the court reached the following conclusions. (1) Where a person acting not for profit publishes a link to a work available online without the consent of the rights holder, it is necessary to take account of the fact of whether the person knows, or cannot reasonably know, that the work has been published without consent.[101] (2) In contrast, where the person knew or ought to have known that the link provided access to a work published illegally online (for example, if they have been put on notice), or provides a link to circumvent restrictions which limit access to a work, the provision of that link would constitute a communication to the public.[102] (3) Finally, where links are posted for profit the person posting the links should carry out the necessary checks to ensure that the work linked to is not illegally published. There is therefore a presumption that the posting of the link has been done with full knowledge of the protected nature of the work and the possible lack of consent to its publication online. In these circumstances, unless the presumption is rebutted, the posting of the link would be a communication to the public.[103]

GS Media confirms that *Svensson* applies only to the situation where the works linked to were made freely available with the consent of the rights holder. The court also attempted to separate the sheep from the goats, or rather the ordinary internet user from the commercial user, something seen to some degree in *PRCA*. The court sought pragmatically to distinguish between the posting of links by ordinary internet users (who cannot be expected to perform a detailed assessment of the works to which they are linking and whether or not they are published with consent) and those users of the internet who seek to profit by sharing works of other people or who knowingly and deliberately infringe copyright. Importantly they stopped short of finding that hyperlinks are not a communication to the public at all; this was to be important for cases which followed.

[99] Ibid. [25].
[100] Ibid. [33].
[101] Ibid. [47].
[102] Ibid. [48]–[49].
[103] Ibid. [51].

The first of these cases was *Stichting Brein v Jack Frederik Wullems (Filmspeler)* discussed above at 11.1.4.[104] There discussion focused on Art. 5, used as part of Mr Wullem's defence. The case though also looked closely at Art. 3 and the question of whether the hyperlinks provided on the Filmspeler box were a communication to the public. Mr Wullems referred to Recital 27 which states 'the mere provision of physical facilities for enabling or making a communication does not in itself amount to communication within the meaning of this Directive' to claim that the boxes were not covered by Art. 3. The court disagreed, finding that:

> the present case does not concern a situation of the 'mere' provision of physical facilities for enabling or making a communication, Mr Wullems, with full knowledge of the consequences of his conduct, pre-installs onto the Filmspeler multimedia player add-ons that specifically enable purchasers to have access to protected works published without the consent of the copyright holders of those works. That intervention enabling a direct link to be established between websites broadcasting counterfeit works and purchasers of the multimedia player, without which the purchasers would find it difficult to benefit from those protected works, is quite different from the mere provision of physical facilities, referred to in recital 27.[105]

The court noted that the websites to which the player links are not readily identifiable by the public and that they change frequently. Consequently, the provision of a multimedia player with preinstalled add-ons which provide direct access to protected works without the rightsholder's consent is an act of communication within the meaning of Article 3(1).[106]

Turning to the question of whether the works had been communicated to a 'public,' the court noted that *TVCatchup* defined the public as an indeterminate number of potential viewers and implies a fairly large number of people.[107] The court observed that the multimedia player had been bought by a 'fairly large number of people'[108] and that the communication at issue covered all people who could potentially purchase the player and have an internet connection. This meant that there was a large but indeterminate number of potential recipients, which the court considered enough for the communication in question to be to a 'public' within the meaning of Art. 3(1).[109] Finally, the court noted that to complete the three-step test in order for there to be a 'communication to the public' there must be either: (a) a communication using technical means different to those used previously; or (b) a communication to a 'new public,' that being a public that was not taken into account by the right holder when they authorized the initial communication of their work.[110] The court held, following *GS Media's* third test: 'where links are posted for profit the person posting the links should carry out the necessary checks to ensure that the work linked to is not illegally published' that the sale of the Filmspeler device was made in full knowledge that the add-ons contained hyperlinks to websites which made protected materials available without the right holder's consent. Consquently, Mr Wullem's actions constituted a communication to the public within the meaning of Art. 3(1).[111]

---

[104] *Filmspeler* (n. 68) and accompanying text.
[105] Ibid. [41].
[106] Ibid. [42].
[107] Ibid. [32].
[108] Ibid. [45].
[109] Ibid. [46].
[110] Ibid. [33].
[111] Ibid. [49]–[52].

Finally, in this section we have the recent case of *Stichting Brein v Ziggo*.[112] This is another Dutch case brought by the same foundation that protects the interests of copyright holders. The factual background to this case is a little complex. Stichting applied to the Dutch courts seeking an injunction against internet service providers Ziggo and XS4ALL requiring them to block access to *The Pirate Bay* website. The Dutch law in this area is analogous to a s. 97A order in the UK which will be discussed below at 12.3 and in fact the Dutch and UK law on this subject share the same root, Art. 8(3) of the InfoSoc Directive. The key issue is that before an injunction can be awarded, the site to be injuncted must be infringing copyright or a related right. Stichting therefore had to establish the *The Pirate Bay* was an infringing site yet all it does is link to content held elsewhere. In essence there was little to distinguish *The Pirate Bay* from *Svennson* or *BestWater*.

The court found that *The Pirate Bay* was rather different to both *Svennson* and *BestWater*. Taking *Wullems* as its starting point the court found that a 'user makes an act of communication when he intervenes, in full knowledge of the consequences of his action, to give his customers access to a protected work, particularly where, in the absence of that intervention, those customers would not be able to enjoy the broadcast work, or would be able to do so only with difficulty.'[113] Applying this principle to the case, the court noted that there was no doubt that works were, by means of *The Pirate Bay*'s website, being made available to the public. The pertinent issue was instead who was responsible for this making available. The court acknowledged that the work was placed on the platform not by *The Pirate Bay* itself, but by its users.[114] Nevertheless, the court concluded that by making that platform available and managing it, '[*The Pirate Bay*] provides users with access to the works concerned. They can therefore be regarded as playing an essential role in making the works in question available.' As a result, the operation of the website 'must be considered to be an act of communication for the purposes of Art. 3(1).'[115]

The question was whether this communication was to a (new) public. Applying *GS Media* and *Wullems* quite easily disposed of this. The court found that *The Pirate Bay* had knowledge of the fact that its platform was being used by its users to infringe copyright. This was substantiated by the facts that: (1) the operators of the *The Pirate Bay* were informed that their platform provides access to works published without the authorization of the right holders; (2) *The Pirate Bay* made clear, on blogs and online forums, their intention that their platform be used to infringe and encouraged users to engage in such infringement; (3) a large number of torrent files on *The Pirate Bay* relate to works published without the consent of the right holders, meaning that its operators 'could not be unaware' that their platform provides access to works published without the consent of the right holders; and (4) the making available and management of *The Pirate Bay* is carried out for the purpose of obtaining profit, in the form of advertising revenues.[116] As a result of these findings the court concluded that *The Pirate Bay* does indeed communicate works to the public in breach of Art. 3(1).

---

[112] ECLI:EU:C:2017:456.
[113] Ibid. [26].
[114] Ibid. [32], [36].
[115] Ibid. [37]–[39].
[116] Ibid. [45]–[46].

11.3 **The EU copyright in the digital single market programme**

Before leaving this chapter we have to take some time to examine current develop-ments in the EU. In May 2015 the Commission adopted *A Digital Single Market Strategy for Europe.*[117] As the Strategy explains:

> a Digital Single Market is one in which the free movement of goods, persons, services and capital is ensured and where individuals and businesses can seamlessly access and exercise online activi-ties under conditions of fair competition, and a high level of consumer and personal data pro-tection, irrespective of their nationality or place of residence. Achieving a Digital Single Market will ensure that Europe maintains its position as a world leader in the digital economy, helping European companies to grow globally.[118]

The Commission has been driving this strategy since then and in December 2015 they published the communication *Towards a Modern, More European Copyright Framework.*[119] Here the Commission set out their aim that the EU should strive for a broad availability of online content services 'without frontiers' to deliver more choice and diversity to people. They noted though this was not the experience of EU citizens though as 'when it comes to copyright protected content crossing borders, the digital single market is not yet a reality. When people travel to another Member State, they frequently cannot access content they have subscribed to or acquired at home.'[120] They find a number of reasons why this is so, but find many are caused by the territorial nature of copyright licenses and the difficulty in achieving genuine cross-border licenses. As they note 'The financing of new European productions in the audiovisual sector is, to a large extent, based on territorial licensing combined with territorial exclusivity granted to individual distributors or service providers.'[121] The Commission states its aim is to bring about a functional single market in digital services and as part of this copyright reform is neces-sary to ensure 'an increase of legal certainty, transparency and balance in the system that governs the remuneration of authors and performers in the EU, taking national competences into account.'[122]

In September 2016 the Commission published its *Proposal for a Directive of the European Parliament and of the Council on copyright in the Digital Single Market.*[123] The proposal has proven to be massively controversial. Julia Reda a Pirate Party MEP from Germany has organized a campaign against the proposal, while academic experts have submitted written concerns about some of the contents of the proposal.[124] While much of the proposal is fairly neutral, and some provisions such as Art. 5 which allows member states to 'permit cultural heritage institutions, to make copies of any works or other

---

[117] COM(2015) 192 final.
[118] Ibid. 1.
[119] COM(2015) 626 final.
[120] Ibid. 3.
[121] Ibid. 4.
[122] Ibid. 10.
[123] 2016/0280 (COD).
[124] See letters at <https://medium.com/eu-copyright-reform/open-letter-to-the-european-com-mission-6560c7b5cac0> and <https://www.ivir.nl/publicaties/download/Academics_Against_Press_Publishers_Right.pdf>.

subject-matter that are permanently in their collections, in any format or medium, for the sole purpose of the preservation of such works or other subject-matter and to the extent necessary for such preservation' are broadly positive, the proposal has been attacked both for what is not there and what is. In particular, the proposal has been attacked for failing to provide any specific rights or exemptions to allow the reuse of copyright material in user-generated works, as specifically noted in the Opinion of the Committee on Culture and Education:[125]

 Highlight Opinion of the Committee on Culture and Education

The proposal does not acknowledge the position consumers, as service users, now occupy in the digital environment. No longer playing a mere passive role, they have become active contributors and are now both a source and recipient of content in the digital ecosystem. Indeed, information society services base the entire design, business model and optimisation of their services around the dual role of their users.

The Committee recommended the need for 'a new exception governing the digital non-commercial, proportionate use of quotations and extracts of copyright protected works or other subject-matter by individual users. Member States may provide for an exception for content uploaded by users where the content is used for criticism, review, illustration, caricature, parody or pastiche.'[126] Also missing is a harmonized 'freedom of panorama' right. While not an issue in the UK, taking and freely sharing pictures of public space is not allowed in all EU member states. In some countries, this infringes upon rights of architects and other creators of artworks located in public space, provided the buildings or artworks are still under copyright protection. Julia Reda organized a petition to ensure freedom of panorama throughout the EU which attracted over 550,000 signatures but which was ignored by the Commission.

Worse from many people's perspective is what may be found in the proposal, in particular Articles 11 and 13. Article 11, the so-called 'press publishers right' creates the first new copyright-related right since the right of communication to the public in 2001. It has been colloquially labelled the 'link tax' proposal by critics and is seen as a pushback against the *Infopaq II/Meltwater* line of cases as well as the *Svensson* decision. In its original formulation the right was a twenty-year right awarded to 'publishers of press publications' that would require anyone making use of snippets of journalistic online content to obtain a license from the publisher. It was envisaged that this would cover automatic link previews displayed on social media platforms such as Facebook and Twitter, which are generated when users share links, as well as anyone analysing news content on the web, like news aggregators such as Meltwater or Infopaq. As noted, this was in part a pushback against the *Infopaq II/Meltwater* line of cases and in part a response to the worsening financial position of mainstream media publishing. In September 2018 the European Parliament adopted Article 11 but with some

---

[125] 2016/0280(COD).
[126] Ibid. 5.

amendments. An amendment to Art. 11(1) introduced new qualifications to the right. It added a requirement that the right was limited to ensuring right holders 'may obtain *fair and proportionate remuneration* for the digital use of their press publications by information society service providers' and added a private use defence 'The rights . . . shall not prevent legitimate private and non-commercial use of press publications by individual users.'[127] A further 'hyperlink' defence was added that 'The rights referred to in paragraph 1 shall not extend to mere hyperlinks which are accompanied by individual words.' While these seem to be improvements on the original text there are a number of questions which are unanswered. What is 'fair and proportionate'? In light of cases like *Ziggo* and *Wullems* where, if the commercial/non-commercial divide? And 55how many words are 'individually' allowed? The right, if passed in its current form would seem to roll back much of the legal development of *Infopaq II/Meltwater* and will create considerable confusion around the entire line of Art. 3 cases from *Svennson* onwards.

Equally, if not more, controversial is Article 13, labelled 'censorship machines' or 'upload filters' by critics. It requires that internet platforms hosting large amounts of user-uploaded content must monitor user behaviour and filter their contributions to identify and prevent copyright infringement. Under this proposal once a right holder of any copyright work asks a platform provider to 'look out' for their work, the platform must start monitoring and scanning all future uploads to make sure that the content is never uploaded to their service. At least that is what the first version of Art. 13 said. In debate in the European Parliament this was subject to heavy amendment.

 Highlight Article 13(1) original text

Information society service providers that store and provide to the public access to large amounts of works or other subject-matter uploaded by their users shall, in cooperation with rightholders, take measures to ensure the functioning of agreements concluded with rightholders for the use of their works or other subject-matter or to prevent the availability on their services of works or other subject-matter identified by rightholders through the cooperation with the service providers. Those measures, such as the use of effective content recognition technologies, shall be appropriate and proportionate. The service providers shall provide rightholders with adequate information on the functioning and the deployment of the measures, as well as, when relevant, adequate reporting on the recognition and use of the works and other subject-matter.

 Highlight Article 13(1) amended text

Without prejudice to Article 3(1) and (2) of Directive 2001/29/EC, online content sharing service providers perform an act of communication to the public. They shall therefore conclude fair and appropriate licensing agreements with right holders.

[127] European Parliament, *Text Adopted on the proposal for a directive of the European Parliament and of the Council on copyright in the Digital Single Market* <http://www.europarl.europa.eu/sides/getDoc. do?pubRef=-//EP//NONSGML+TA+P8-TA-2018-0337+0+DOC+PDF+V0//EN>.

Eagle-eyed readers will note that the reference to 'effective content recognition technologies' has been removed. The provision has clearly been watered down considerably by the Parliament but the heart of the proposal remains platforms that rely on user-generated content, such as YouTube, Facebook, and Twitter, would be responsible for making sure that users don't share copyrighted material. This will make them potentially fiscally accountable for violations which is a change on the current position. If you are YouTube CEO Susan Wojcicki you will see this as a threat to your company and will suggest that:

> Article 13 as written threatens to shut down the ability of millions of people—from creators like you to everyday users—to upload content to platforms like YouTube. And it threatens to block users in the EU from viewing content that is already live on the channels of creators everywhere. This includes YouTube's incredible video library of educational content, such as language classes, physics tutorials and other how-to's.[128]

However those who work in the creative industries see this as a necessary pushback against platforms that free-ride on their creativity.[129]

The next stage for the proposal is trialogue discussions which are expected to conclude in early 2019. What is not clear at the time of writing (but which will be clear when you read this) is whether the proposal will be concluded in time to be adopted by the UK on Brexit day and thereby whether it will form part of the UK legal landscape post-Brexit.

11.4 **Conclusions**

This chapter has covered substantial ground. At the heart of the information society is a conflict between a culture of free use and access, of 'rip, mix, and burn' and of remixing and mashing and the culture of creative reward, publication, and commercial exploitation. This conflict is driven by the very nature of the information society in general and the internet in particular. The information society is built upon the sharing and exploitation of information, while copyright law is about the protection and control of information. One is about exploitation, the other reward. The internet is, when one thinks about it in simple terms, just a massive device for the copying and distribution of information: in a very real sense it is designed to infringe copyright massively. For the past twenty years (and no doubt for at the very least the next twenty) lawyers, judges, and lawmakers have been trying to establish where the legal balance in interests between these two extremes are to be struck. Some companies have become famously successful by trading in information; prime among these is Google. Some people see the activities of Google in not only cataloguing websites but also caching data, digitizing books, and appropriating newspaper headlines as being in breach of copyright and its values,[130] while others see it as the greatest success story

---

[128] YouTube Creator Blog, 22 October 2018 <https://youtube-creators.googleblog.com/2018/10/a-final-update-on-our-priorities-for.html>.

[129] <http://www.musicweek.com/opinion/read/we-have-badly-strayed-from-a-world-where-artists-control-their-work-rosanne-cash-on-today-s-copyright-directive-vote/073793>.

[130] See, e.g. H Porter, 'Google is just an amoral menace' *The Observer* 5 April 2009.

of the information society thus far.[131] This frames the predicament faced by judges, lawyers, and lawmakers: when is the exploitation of other people's data lawful and when, at copyright law, is it unlawful? In essence, what makes Google different from *The Pirate Bay*?[132]

The interface between copyright law and the information society is therefore one of the most complex and problematic in the contemporary legal landscape. This chapter has drawn together some of the challenges, including when and how one may link between content held on other websites and in particular the challenges of deep-linking, scraping, and caching content. These are all challenges almost as old as the World Wide Web itself and as we have seen over the years the courts have developed quite sophisticated approaches from the early cases, such as *Shetland Times*, through to *Google v Copiepresse*. The big change in the approach to online linking and consumption came with the InfoSoc Directive in 2001 which gave effect to the WIPO Copyright Treaty. This introduced two key measures, the 'Communication to the Public Right' in Article 3 which was balanced by the Temporary Reproduction Exception' in Article 5. Through a series of cases the CJEU has allowed us to develop a thorough understanding of both these provisions and we now have quite a mature understanding of both. However, the settled balance we have between commercial and non-commercial use and use with and without permission developed across these cases is arguably at risk due to the intention of the Commission to develop new, and further, rights and responsibilities in Articles 11 and 13 of the proposed Directive on copyright in the Digital Single Market. These have the potential to upset the delicate balance the CJEU has developed in recent years and by appearing to favour rightholders over end users and, in particular, failing to recognize the rights and interests of creators of UGC it has the potential to rebalance copyright law too far in favour of rightholders. This is a risk and challenge for the Commission, Parliament, and Council as the proposal goes through trialogue.

TEST QUESTIONS

Question 1

As the CJEU notes in GS Media, 'it may be difficult, in particular for individuals who wish to post such links, to ascertain whether website to which those links are expected to lead, provides access to works which are protected and, if necessary, whether the copyright holders of those works have consented to their posting on the internet. Such ascertaining is all the more difficult where those rights have been the subject of sub-licenses. Moreover, the content of a website to which a hyperlink enables access may be changed after the creation of that link, including the protected works, without the person who created that link necessarily being aware of it.'

In light of this, do you believe the current approach taken by the CJEU in applying Art. 3 strikes the right balance?

---

[131] See, e.g. D Vise and M Malseed, *The Google Story: Inside the Hottest Business, Media and Technology Success of Our Time* (Delta 2008).

[132] This question was raised by C Lundström at the conclusion of *The Pirate Bay* trial (discussed in chapter 12).

Question 2

Were the CJEU right to hold (in Ziggo) that 'the operators of the online sharing platform, by making that platform available and managing it, provide their users with access to the works concerned. They can therefore be regarded as playing an essential role in making the works in question available'?

Question 3

Critically analyse the outcome of the *PRCA v NLA* litigation? In particular, what do you make of the observation that 'the Supreme Court and the CJEU only had a nut to crack in this case. The lure of making a policy decision caused them to take a wrecking ball to it.'

FURTHER READING

Books

S Stokes, *Digital Copyright: Law and Practice* (5th edn, Hart 2019)

J Koo, *The Right of Communication to the Public in EU Copyright Law* (Hart 2019)

J Quintais, *Copyright in the Age of Online Access: Alternative Compensation Systems in EU Law* (Kluwer 2017)

Chapters and Articles

E Arezzo, 'Hyperlinks and making available right in the European Union—what future for the Internet after Svensson?' (2014) 39(6) *International Review of Intellectual Property and Competition Law* 524

E Rosati, 'GS Media and Its Implications for the Construction of the Right of Communication to the Public within EU Copyright Architecture' (2017) 54 *Common Market Law Review* 1221

E Papadaki, 'Hyperlinking, making available and copyright infringement: lessons from European national courts' (2017) 8 *European Journal of Law and Technology* 1

G Campus, 'Legal aspects of the video buffering process: the uncertain line between acts of reproduction and acts accessory to a communication to the public' [2017] *European Intellectual Property Review* 366

Copyright infringement in the digital environment

Linking, caching, the temporary reproduction right and the right to communicate to the public are not usually the first thing people think about when they are asked for their views on copyright in the digital environment. Although these issues are vital to the operation, development, and functionality of the internet, most media coverage of online copyright issues focuses on copyright infringement and the harm it causes to copyright industries. This perhaps is not surprising; as most early high-profile litigation in the United States in particular focused on this issue.

The problem is that, as noted in Chapter 11, the internet is to date the largest and most efficient copying machine built by man. In addition, most users access the internet from home in what they imagine is anonymity. Although in practice they can be traced, for the average user the idea that law enforcement agencies or copyright holders will track their activities while they are safely in their own bedrooms seems remote. It is not surprising therefore that the internet has been used extensively to share music, movies, and games without the permission of the copyright holder. The technology behind online file-sharing, and the ways file-sharing systems have attempted to get around copyright law have both grown in sophistication as the years have gone by. To date there have been at least four generations of file-sharing technologies, as well as a raft of accompanying litigation.

12.1 Early cases: Napster and Grokster

Although there had been earlier cases on digitally enabled copyright infringement such as *Recording Industry Association of America v Diamond Multimedia Systems Inc.*[1] and *UMG Recordings v MP3.Com,*[2] the case which most people associate with the rise of internet piracy is the first file-sharing case *A&M Records, Inc. v Napster, Inc.*[3]

Shawn Fanning created Napster as a 17-year-old freshman (first-year student) at Northeastern University in 1999. The idea that Fanning had was to create a music community site where fans of bands or singers could go, chat, and share music with each other.[4] The file-sharing aspect of Napster did not seem to hold primacy in Fanning's

---

[1] 180 F 3d 1072 (9th Cir. 1999).
[2] 92 F Supp 2d 349 (SDNY 2000).
[3] 239 F 3d 1004 (9th Cir. 2001).
[4] R Ambrosek, *Shawn Fanning: The Founder of Napster* (Rosen Publishing 2006) 30.

original design, rather his focus was on creating a music community, but as part of his design he included the ability for users to directly swap MP3 files with each other. In so doing, without perhaps realizing the groundbreaking nature of this development he created the first fully functional peer-to-peer (P2P) protocol, the Napster protocol. To explain the contribution of the Napster protocol we need to examine the distinction between P2P and traditional server-client file systems.

Prior to Fanning's development of the Napster protocol, online file transfers had always followed a server-delivery model where the file was stored on a web server which could be accessed by anyone with the requisite permission and then downloaded from that server. MP3.com had used a model such as this with their fêted (and fated) My.Mp3.com service. This model remains familiar to us today and is used by services as diverse as Apple's iTunes Store, BBC's iPlayer, YouTube, and streamed music systems such as Soundcloud or Spotify. Fanning though introduced the concept of P2P file-sharing to the masses. This operates very differently from traditional server-client file transfers. Instead of operating a central server containing all the files available for download a P2P system stores the files on the hard drives of the network subscribers. Subscribers choose which files they will share and these are placed in a 'shared' folder. The P2P software can access this folder and may transfer data out of this folder to another user by creating a network connection between the users or 'peers'.

 Example Shawn Fanning's party analogy

Fanning described the difference between client server networks and the Napster network by using an analogy of attending a party.

In the client server party each guest turns up empty-handed to the party and all the food and drink is supplied by the host. To get a drink you must ask the host to supply it and you can only have what the host has supplied. Your host may be efficient but he has to serve everybody and you may have to wait in a queue.

At a Napster party all the guests bring their own food and drink. There is still a host, but all he does is greet you at the door and take a note of what you have brought. Then anytime anyone wants a drink they can ask the host who has brought a particular product. The host can check his list and put them in touch with the right person and they can then exchange drinks directly with each other.

The Napster party works as long as people are not too greedy and are willing to share.

As the end user copies the files, not the service provider, this seemed to offer Napster a degree of protection against copyright infringement claims. The first line of defence was that they did not commit primary infringement; any sharing (and therefore copying) of files was done by their customers. Second, their customers would, it was imagined, be deemed to be acting in a noncommercial capacity allowing them to claim fair use defences should the copyright holders decide to pursue a claim.

There were though two problems with the Napster concept and design. The first was one that Shawn Fanning could not have imagined in the spring of 1999: Napster became a global phenomenon. Jupiter Media, the respected media research agency reported that by February 2001 Napster had 26.4 million users,[5] a remarkable reach for a program only released in June 1999. Although this may at first seem a positive outcome for Fanning and his internet start-up Napster, Inc., it meant that the music publishing industry and the Recording Industry Association of America quickly focused their attention on this fledgling company. The second was a design problem which was ultimately to prove to be Napster's downfall. If you recount the party host analogy given by Shawn Fanning, he explains that at the Napster party there is a host who keeps track of what each person has brought and who introduces guests to each other. In the Napster environment this function was fulfilled by 'the Napster server'. When a new user first downloaded and installed the Napster software, the software would catalogue the MP3 files he or she held on their computer and would place copies of these (with the user's permission) into a shared music folder. Then when the user first logged on to the Napster exchange site the Napster server would log their IP address (to allow sharing of files later) and the files which were in their shared music folder. The Napster server would then add this information to its searchable database allowing other users to discover what files the user had available for sharing. A keyword search of that database would return a list of users with file names which matched that keyword as well as details of how fast a connection they could offer. Thus a user searching for 'Backstreet Boys' (this was 2000 remember) would have returned a list of available files and users. They would then select one user, or peer, before the Napster server would instigate a digital handshake allowing the transfer to take place between users or peers. The Napster server meant that Napster always knew what files their subscribers were sharing and technically, as the Napster server had to make that digital handshake, could prevent the sharing of files between users of the service.

These two factors led a number of music publishers to file a complaint with the District Court for the Northern District of California. The plaintiffs contended that Napster's activities constituted 'contributory and vicarious federal copyright infringement'.[6] On 26 July 2000, the District Court granted the plaintiffs' motion for a preliminary injunction. The injunction was slightly modified by written opinion on 10 August 2000. The District Court preliminarily enjoined Napster 'from engaging in, or facilitating others in copying, downloading, uploading, transmitting, or distributing plaintiffs' copyrighted musical compositions and sound recordings, protected by either federal or state law, without express permission of the rights owner'.[7] Napster appealed to the Federal Court of Appeals for the Ninth Circuit. The case was heard on 2 October 2000 by Chief Judge Schroeder and Circuit Judges Beezer and Paez. On 12 February 2001 Judge Beezer issued the opinion of the court.

The court examined each of the plaintiffs' claims as well as three affirmative defences put forward by Napster. First, Judge Beezer examined the claim that 'Napster users are engaged in the wholesale reproduction and distribution of copyrighted works, all constituting direct infringement.'[8] Although the plaintiffs accepted that Napster never

---

[5] 'Global Napster Usage Plummets, But New File-Sharing Alternatives Gaining Ground, Reports Jupiter Media Metrix', *The Free Library*, 20 July 2001.

[6] Contributory and vicarious copyright infringement are two different forms of secondary infringement actionable under the Federal Copyright Act 1976. Although we have no direct equivalents in the UK ss. 22–26 of the CDPA 1988 cover much of the same ground and many similar concepts are discussed in *CBS Songs Ltd v Amstrad Consumer Electronics Plc* [1988] AC 1013.

[7] *A&M Records, Inc. v Napster, Inc.* 114 F. Supp. 2d 896 (N.D. Cal. 2000) 927.

[8] 239 F 3d 1004 [17].

actually copied any of the files in issue, the plaintiffs had to establish primary infringement on the part of Napster's users as without a primary infringement there could be no secondary infringement by Napster. Factually it was clear that the activities of Napster users were clearly in breach of the exclusive rights of the copyright holders; users were copying copyright protected music files and they were distributing them. It seemed all the copyright holders had to establish was that they were the rights-holders to the music in question to establish primary infringement had occurred, but Napster felt their customers could have an affirmative fair use defence and presented to the court three such defences: (1) sampling, (2) space shifting, and (3) use with permission.

Napster firstly claimed that its users 'download MP3 files to "sample" the music in order to decide whether to purchase the recording'.[9] Napster further argued that the District Court had erred in refusing a sampling defence as it '(1) erred in concluding that sampling is a commercial use because it conflated a noncommercial use with a personal use; (2) erred in determining that sampling adversely affects the market for plaintiffs' copyrighted music, a requirement if the use is noncommercial; and (3) erroneously concluded that sampling is not a fair use because it determined that samplers may also engage in other infringing activity'.[10] Judge Beezer rejected this claim noting that:

> [e]vidence relied on by the District Court demonstrates that the free downloads provided by the record companies consist of thirty-to-sixty second samples or are full songs programmed to "time out," that is, exist only for a short time on the downloader's computer. In comparison, Napster users download a full, free and permanent copy of the recording. The determination by the District Court as to the commercial purpose and character of sampling is not clearly erroneous.[11]

Napster then argued that 'Space-shifting occurs when a Napster user downloads MP3 music files in order to listen to music he already owns on audio CD.'[12] Again the court was not impressed, with Judge Beezer noting that 'it is obvious that once a user lists a copy of music he already owns on the Napster system in order to access the music from another location, the song becomes available to millions of other individuals, not just the original CD owner.'[13] This only left the defence of use with permission but as Judge Beezer pointed out the 'plaintiffs did not seek to enjoin this and any other noninfringing use of the Napster system',[14] thus this defence was also ruled out. The court therefore established that Napster users did not have a fair use defence and that the plaintiffs would likely succeed on a claim for copyright infringement against Napster users. On this basis the court moved on to examine the plaintiffs' claims for secondary infringement against Napster.

The court first examined whether Napster had committed contributory copyright infringement. Contributory infringement is established by the application of a two-part test. The defendant must (1) know, or have reason to know of the direct infringement; and (2) materially contribute to the infringing activity. This is where the Napster server proved to be Napster's downfall. As the Napster server recorded all files available for distribution in real time, and as many of these files contained material that was

---

⁹ Ibid. [39].
¹⁰ Ibid.
¹¹ Ibid. [40].
¹² Ibid. [44].
¹³ Ibid. [45].
¹⁴ Ibid. [46].

clearly being offered in breach of copyright Napster clearly had '*actual* knowledge that *specific* infringing material is available using its system, that it could block access to the system by suppliers of the infringing material, and that it failed to remove the material.'[15] As the Napster software and server hardware was essential to the swapping of copyright protected files the court therefore had little difficulty in finding the second arm of the test also proven: Napster were found liable for contributory infringement.

The court then turned to the question of vicarious infringement. Vicarious infringement requires the application of a three-part test: (1) there has been a direct infringement; (2) the vicarious infringer is in a position to control the actions of the direct infringer; and (3) the vicarious infringer benefits financially from the infringement. The first element of the test had already been established so the court focused on the remaining questions. Napster argued they did not benefit financially; they did not charge subscribers for either the software or access to the service. The court disagreed. It felt that without the availability of infringing files Napster would not have grown at the phenomenal rate at which it grew. This, the court felt, was a direct financial benefit to Napster by providing future revenue by increasing its user base.[16] This left only one final question, had Napster been in a position to control its users? Again the Napster server was the Achilles heel of the Napster operation; the court found that through it Napster had 'the ability to locate infringing material listed on its search indices, and the right to terminate users' access to the system'.[17]

There remained one crumb of solace for Napster. The court recognized that merely indexing file names did not mean that Napster had to have knowledge of what these files contained.[18] However this was not enough to save Napster. The Appeals Court did vary the terms of the injunction as they felt that the injunction of the District Court that 'Napster ensures that no "copying, downloading, uploading, transmitting, or distributing" of plaintiffs' works occur on the system' was overbroad. Instead the Appeals Court placed the burden of establishing infringement on the plaintiffs who were required to 'provide notice to Napster of copyrighted works and files containing such works available on the Napster system before Napster has the duty to disable access to the offending content.'[19] As this order seemed to offer Napster the opportunity to continue to operate, Napster remained in operation. A cat-and-mouse game developed between copyright holders and Napster users. The copyright holders gave Napster details of tens of thousands of infringing files which it was required by the injunction to block. Users would then change file names allowing the injunction to be circumvented and the whole process would begin anew. It proved impossible though for Napster to continue to meet the demands of the injunction and in July 2001 the Napster service was closed down.[20] Following protracted discussions to try and save Napster, including

---

[15] Ibid. [57].
[16] Ibid. [61].
[17] Ibid. [67].
[18] Ibid.
[19] Ibid. [86].
[20] On the last day of service the ten most downloaded tracks were reported to be: (1) Everly Brothers—Bye Bye Love; (2) The Clash—I fought the law (and the law won); (3) Jerky Boys—Fanning my balls (a play on Shawn Fanning's name); (4) Judge Jules—Gatecrasher; (5) Warren Zevon—Send Lawyers, Guns and Money; (6) Jimmy Buffet—A pirate looks at 40; (7) Metallica—Seek and Destroy; (8) Dr Dre—Bang Bang; (9) Red Hot Chili Peppers—Give it away; and (10) Doobie Brothers—Listen to the music.

a reported deal to sell the company to German music publisher Bertelsmann for $85 million, Napster eventually went into liquidation. Its trademarks and brand name were bought at a bankruptcy auction by Roxio Inc. and they rebranded their pressplay music service 'Napster 2.0'. Today Napster is owned by Rhapsody and operates as streaming music provider.

The music industry had claimed a victory, but at what cost? It seemed the Court of Appeals had suggested the P2P technology Napster had used was not in of itself illegal, but rather the problem was the Napster server which allowed Napster a high degree of oversight and control. If a P2P system could be designed which did not use a central index server it seemed its implementation would not infringe US copyright law.

Two such systems were quickly developed. One was to design a decentralized P2P network which operates more like the internet. This does away with the need to have a central server. Instead when one logs in to the network a connection is made to the nearest active user, or node, on the network. As this node already has onward connections any requests may be forwarded throughout the network without the need for a central server. Such decentralized P2P systems have some advantages but also strong disadvantages. As they are completely decentralized there can be no claim of a controlling mind and they are (in theory at least) difficult to disrupt. But they can be extremely slow and they carry a large amount of network traffic as requests are sent and replies received.

A better system, technically, is the semi-structured system allowed by the use of so-called 'supernodes'. A semi-structured system combines the advantages of the centralized and decentralized systems. Instead of having a central server, semi-structured P2P systems use a number of users as temporary information hosts, or supernodes. These hosts, or supernodes, act as local search servers and provide the backbone of the network. Cleverly though a supernode can leave at any time and be immediately replaced by another. The semi-structured network in effect decentralizes the server function as well as the file transfer and search functions.

Several P2P providers began offering either decentralized or semi-structured P2P services. Famous brand names to use one or other of these technologies included Kazaa, eMule, EDonkey, Gnutella, Grokster, and Morpheus. Users quickly migrated to these new P2P systems: it seemed that the music industry had won the battle but lost the war. Even worse for copyright holders, while Napster had only allowed the sharing of MP3 audio files, these new services allowed sharing of any type of file, meaning Hollywood movie studios, television networks, and software developers were now all affected. In spring 2003 a number of entertainment industry plaintiffs[21] raised an action against Groskter and Streamcast, suppliers of leading P2P technologies Grokster and Morpheus.[22]

Initially the legal omens looked good for the P2P service providers. At a preliminary hearing before Judge Steven Wilson of the US District Court for the Central District of California a motion by the defendants for summary judgment in their favour was granted.[23] Although Judge Wilson recognized that customers of Grokster and

---

[21] The plaintiffs fell into two camps: (1) the motion picture industry plaintiffs; and (2) the music industry plaintiffs.

[22] *MGM Studios, Inc. v Grokster, Ltd* 259 F. Supp. 2d 1029 (CD Cal. 2003); *MGM Studios, Inc. v Grokster, Ltd* 380 F.3d 1154 (9th Cir. 2004); *MGM Studios, Inc. v. Grokster, Ltd* 545 US 913 (2005).

[23] *MGM Studios, Inc. v Grokster, Ltd* 259 F. Supp. 2d 1029 (CD Cal. 2003).

StreamCast were engaging in unlawful activities he could see nothing to suggest either of the defendants had knowledge of their customers' activities or had the ability to control them.[24] He went on to note that although he shared some sympathy with the plight of the plaintiffs 'to justify a judicial remedy, however, [the] Plaintiffs invite this Court to expand existing copyright law beyond its well-drawn boundaries'.[25]

By removing the element of control and knowledge that the Napster central server offered, the second-generation P2P providers had escaped potential contributory or vicarious liability. The copyright holders appealed to the Court of Appeals for the Ninth Circuit. The court affirmed Judge Wilson's decision finding that 'the defendants are not liable for contributory and vicarious copyright infringement'.[26] The court was sympathetic to the plight of the copyright holders but noted that the defendants could not be held liable for either contributory or vicarious copyright infringement without the court expanding the scope of either or both forms of infringement.[27] At appeal the plaintiffs attempted to have the court extend the scope of vicarious liability by arguing that the defendants had 'turned a blind eye to detectable acts of infringement for the sake of profit'.[28] The court though rejected this claim: it was clear that any expansion of the law of copyright should come from Congress, not through judicial activism:

 Highlight Judge Thomas in *MGM v Grokster*

The introduction of new technology is always disruptive to old markets, and particularly to those copyright owners whose works are sold through well-established distribution mechanisms. Yet, history has shown that time and market forces often provide equilibrium in balancing interests, whether the new technology be a player piano, a copier, a tape recorder, a video recorder, a personal computer, a karaoke machine, or an MP3 player. Thus, it is prudent for courts to exercise caution before restructuring liability theories for the purpose of addressing specific market abuses, despite their apparent present magnitude.

Indeed, the Supreme Court has admonished us to leave such matters to Congress. In Sony the Court spoke quite clearly about the role of Congress in applying copyright law to new technologies. As the Supreme Court stated in that case, the direction of Article I is that Congress shall have the power to promote the progress of science and the useful arts. When, as here, the Constitution is permissive, the sign of how far Congress has chosen to go can come only from Congress.

[380 F.3d 1154, 1167]

The decision of the Court of Appeals for the Ninth Circuit is interesting on several levels. The court was sending a message to both the plaintiffs and to Congress. At the time of the *Grokster* case Congress was considering a revision to US copyright law, Judge Thomas was suggesting both that the plaintiffs would make better use of their time in

---

[24] Ibid. 1046.
[25] Ibid.
[26] *MGM Studios, Inc. v Grokster, Ltd* 380 F.3d 1154 (9th Cir. 2004).
[27] Ibid. 1160–2.
[28] This was a development of part of the *Napster* decision. See *Napster* (n. 8) 1023.

lobbying Congress, and that Congress was the proper forum to review, and if necessary amend the Copyright Act. Also he was expressing the need for copyright law to balance the interests of traditional copyright industries and the need to ensure new technology is allowed space to develop, given the monopolistic nature of copyright law. Finally, he was making a thinly veiled comment that the Supreme Court should not intervene given the current interest of Congress in the matter. Despite this, the plaintiffs appealed to the Supreme Court who agreed to hear the case.

The case was argued before the Supreme Court on 29 March 2005, with the decision of the court issued on 27 June 2005. The Justices of the Supreme Court were unanimous that the decision of the Court of Appeals should be overturned. Between the Ninth Circuit hearing and the Supreme Court hearing the plaintiffs had developed their 'turning a blind eye' argument. They presented the Justices with the argument that Grokster and StreamCast had 'clearly voiced the objective that recipients use it to download copyrighted works, and each took active steps to encourage infringement'.[29] By making this claim the plaintiffs were inviting the Justices to extend a principle from patent law, known as the 'active inducement' principle to copyright law.[30] The court was willing to hear this argument. Justice Souter, who gave the opinion of the court, noted that 'The rule on inducement of infringement as developed in the early [patent] cases is no different today. Evidence of active steps . . . taken to encourage direct infringement.'[31] Justice Souter was encouraged that there was a tradition of borrowing from patent law in cases such as this. He noted that '*Sony* took the staple-article doctrine of patent law as a model for its copyright safe harbour rule, the inducement rule, too, is a sensible one for copyright.'[32]

 Highlight The active inducement principle

We adopt it here, holding that one who distributes a device with the object of promoting its use to infringe copyright, as shown by clear expression or other affirmative steps taken to foster infringement, is liable for the resulting acts of infringement by third parties.

[Justice Souter, *MGM v Grokster* at 932]

In making this decision the Supreme Court had ignored its previous direction from *Sony v Universal Studios* that courts should not intervene to extend the scope of copyright protection,[33] and the plea from Judge Thomas that new technologies should be allowed to develop. The court did not clearly define when active inducement would be found, instead the court gave guidance as to what may or may not constitute 'active inducement'. Justice Souter noted that 'mere knowledge of infringing potential or of

[29] 545 US 913, 919.
[30] For a discussion of this see P Samuelson, 'Legally Speaking: Did MGM Really Win the Grokster Case?' (2005) 48 *Communications of the ACM* 19.
[31] *Grokster* (n. 29) 931.
[32] Ibid. 932.
[33] 464 US 417 (1984).

actual infringing uses would not be enough here to subject a distributor to liability. Nor would ordinary acts incident to product distribution, such as offering customers technical support or product updates, support liability in themselves. The inducement rule, instead, premises liability on purposeful, culpable expression and conduct, and thus does nothing to compromise legitimate commerce or discourage innovation having a lawful promise.'[34] What is clear therefore is that there must be some form of clear campaign or inducement which incites infringement to occur. Had the defendants been involved in such a campaign?

Justice Souter examined the evidence: of Streamcast he noted that they 'beamed onto the computer screens of users of Napster-compatible programs ads urging the adoption of its OpenNap program, which was designed, as its name implied, to invite the custom of patrons of Napster, then under attack in the courts for facilitating massive infringement'.[35] Meanwhile Grokster were 'distribut[ing] an electronic newsletter containing links to articles promoting its software's ability to access popular copyrighted music'.[36] In particular he found three things on the record to be damning of both defendants: (1) 'each company showed itself to be aiming to satisfy a known source of demand for copyright infringement, the market comprising former Napster users';[37] (2) 'neither company attempted to develop filtering tools or other mechanisms to diminish the infringing activity using their software';[38] and (3) 'StreamCast and Grokster make money by selling advertising space, by directing ads to the screens of computers employing their software. As the record shows, the more the software is used, the more ads are sent out and the greater the advertising revenue becomes. Since the extent of the software's use determines the gain to the distributors, the commercial sense of their enterprise turns on high-volume use, which the record shows is infringing.'[39]

12.2 *Sweden v Neij et al. (The Pirate Bay* case)

The decision in *Grokster* was arguably moot at the point the Supreme Court handed it down. The 'old fashioned' P2P technologies litigated in the US cases had been supplanted by the more efficient BitTorrent technology. BitTorrent works in a completely different manner to both centralized and decentralized P2P technologies. BitTorrent is an internet protocol, similar in function to File Transfer Protocol. To use the BitTorrent protocol you need a BitTorrent client, a specialized program which allows the transfer of files using the BitTorrent system. These BitTorrent clients are well known and include 'Vuze', 'μTorrent', and 'Deluge'. These have a similar relationship to the BitTorrent protocol as web browsers such as Internet Explorer and Chrome have to HTTP. Once installed a BitTorrent client allows for the uploading and downloading of BitTorrent files. To obtain a file via BitTorrent the user first has to obtain a small file called a Torrent file. This contains metadata used by the BitTorrent client to obtain the location

---

[34] *Grokster* (n 29) 932–3.
[35] Ibid. 933.
[36] Ibid.
[37] Ibid. 934.
[38] Ibid. 935.
[39] Ibid.

of the file. What makes BitTorrent both efficient and attractive is its method of sharing files. Instead of the file transfer taking place between two users (a P2P transfer) it
allows for an interaction between several users simultaneously (a multi-peer transfer) by
breaking large files down into smaller chunks and having different users transmit each
chunk independently. In truth BitTorrent is much more complex than this as people
are simultaneously uploading (seeding) and downloading (leeching) file chunks. For
the purposes of our analysis though the key part of the technology are torrent tracker
files; small files which are essential to finding all the parts of your larger music, video, or
software file. These tend to be made available through BitTorrent indexes, sites which
specialize in tracking and listing available Torrent files. The largest and historically best-
known index was the Swedish site The Pirate Bay, which due both to its high profile
and popularity as a Torrent index has had several confrontations with law enforcement
authorities and copyright holders.

On 31 May 2006 The Pirate Bay was raided by Swedish Police officers who removed all
of The Pirate Bay's servers and questioned three of The Pirate Bay's 'stewards', Gottfrid
Svartholm, Mikael Viborg, and Fredrik Neij, on suspicion of operating a business
infringing copyright. This, in Sweden, as in the UK, may be a criminal offence.[40] The site
was offline for three days and the Motion Picture Association of America claimed victory with MPAA chairman Dan Glickman announcing that 'The actions today taken in
Sweden serve as a reminder to pirates all over the world that there are no safe harbors for
internet copyright thieves.'[41] Despite this, reports of The Pirate Bay's death were premature. The site was up and running again on 2 June 2006, their logo amended to depict
their traditional pirate ship firing cannonballs at the Hollywood sign. The investigation
continued throughout 2006 and 2007 and eventually on 31 January 2008 The Pirate
Bay's operators Gottfrid Svartholm, Fredrik Neij, Peter Sunde, and Carl Lundström were
charged with 'promoting other people's infringements of copyright laws'.[42]

Two specific charges were levied: (1) 'complicity in the production of copyrighted
material', and (2) 'complicity to make copyrighted material available'.[43] The first related
to making copies available via The Pirate Bay site, the second to making and indexing
Torrent files via the site. The trial began on 16 February 2009 and on day two of the trial
the state prosecutor dropped the charge of 'complicity in the production of copyrighted
material'; this was reported to be in response to evidence given on day one about the
technical operations of The Pirate Bay.[44] The second, lesser charge remained.

The defendants argued that the actions of The Pirate Bay were no different to those of
other indexing and search websites such as Google, Yahoo!, or Bing. Those sites provide
a search facility for HTML-based content which may or may not be made available in
breach of copyright. There is no doubt that a proportion of content available on the
web is there without the permission or license of the copyright holder, but Google and
others do not take steps to positively identify which content is in breach of copyright

---

[40] The UK equivalent provision may be found in CDPA, s. 107.

[41] This quote, and all other factual data about The Pirate Bay raid is drawn from: Q Norton,
'Secrets of the Pirate Bay' *Wired* 16 August 2006.

[42] L Larsson, 'Charges filed against the Pirate Bay four' *Computer Sweden* 31 January 2008.

[43] K Fiveash, 'Pirate Bay prosecutor tosses infringement charges overboard' *The Register* 17
February 2009.

[44] Ibid.

and which is not. This, the defendants argued, also reflected how The Pirate Bay functioned. Torrents may contain material made available with the permission or license of the copyright holder, or they may contain content made available in breach of copyright, all The Pirate Bay does is index torrents; it does not question their content. The prosecution responded that unlike Google, The Pirate Bay actively use their technology to assist in the commission of copyright infringement and they directly profit from this. The prosecutor said he was not asking the court to rule on the legality of BitTorrent itself, but rather what the defendants did with the technology. He said that the Swedish Supreme Court had previously ruled that someone running a Bulletin Board which shared copyright material had been found guilty of assisting copyright infringement and that The Pirate Bay should be viewed in this light. He went on to estimate that the site had made between 5 million and 10 million kroner (£400,000–£800,000), turnover directly attributable to illegal file-sharing.[45] In making his case the prosecutor was clearly drawing on the same principles which had led the US Supreme Court to find that Grokster/Streamcast had actively induced copyright infringement.

On 17 April 2009 the District Court of Stockholm announced its decision.[46] All four accused were found guilty of complicity to make copyright material available, the court having rejected the defendant's 'Google defence'. They were each sentenced to one year in prison and collectively found liable for damages totalling 30m Swedish krona (around £2.4m). The defendants immediately appealed and their appeal was heard by the Svea Court of Appeal. Unfortunately for the four accused it did not reverse the judgment of the District Court.[47] Instead it found that:

> a search by its nature is such that it is primarily a valuable tool in lawful activity and generally socially, this legitimate use dominates, the diffusion or transfer of illegal materials which despite precautions cannot be excluded. The operation of such a service in objective terms may be regarded as permissible under the aforementioned theory. Regarding The Pirate Bay we can conclude that the Court of Appeals investigation shows that the service to the vast majority is used for file sharing of music, movies and games etc. How large proportion of the works entered in TPB's database of rightholders consent has not been clarified in the case.[48]

The Court of Appeal therefore upheld the District Court decision but varied the terms of the order. Their prison sentences were reduced, Neij to ten months; Sunde to eight months, and Lundström to four months. Gottfrid Svartholm was too ill to attend court and so a sentencing decision on him was postponed. The fine though was increased to 46m Swedish krona (around £4.1m). Three of the accused, Neij, Sunde, and Lundström then applied for leave to appeal to the Swedish Supreme Court while Svartholm left the country, fleeing to Cambodia. In February 2012 the Swedish Supreme Court ruled it would not hear the case,[49] Peter Sunde and Fredrik Neij applied to the ECtHR to have

---

[45] Information and data drawn from *The Pirate Bay Trial Day 10: Calls for Jail Time* <http://torrentfreak.com/the-pirate-bay-trial-day-10-calls-for-jail-time-090302/>.

[46] Stockholms Tingsrätt, No. B 13301–06, 17 April 2009 <http://www.ifpi.org/content/library/Pirate-Bay-verdict-English-translation.pdf>.

[47] Svea Hovrätt, No. B 4041–09, 26 November 2011 <http://www.scribd.com/doc/44068712/Pirate-Bay-appeal-ruling-Svea-Appeals-Court-Swedish>.

[48] Ibid. 24–5.

[49] Matt Peckham, 'Pirate Bay Founders Lose Supreme Court Appeal, Going to Jail' *Time* 1 February 2012.

their sentences overturned but their application was refused while Peter Sunde also applied for a pardon (which was rejected). Sunde then stood for election in the 2014 European elections as a candidate for the Pirate Party of Finland. He was eventually arrested in May 2014 near Malmo and transferred to Västervik Norra prison where he served his sentence. Carl Lundström served his time in prison, partly by electronic tag, and partly in prison in Gothenburg. Gottfrid Svartholm was arrested in Cambodia and was deported to Sweden where he was imprisoned for the full one-year term originally imposed. Fredrik Neij was arrested in Thailand in November 2014 and served two-thirds of his 10-month sentence in Skänninge prison in central Sweden. He was released on June 1 2015, bringing to an end the formal criminal process in *The Pirate Bay* case.

Despite the successes of copyright holders in cases such as *Napster, Grokster*, and *The Pirate Bay* the popularity of illegal file-sharing, both P2P and through so-called locker sites remains strong, with sites like *Putlockers Plus* and *123Movie* remaining popular. Even if Swedish prosecutors had been able to close down The Pirate Bay permanently, which seems unlikely given the number of global mirror sites on offer, other Torrent indexes would quickly have filled the void. Indeed most modern Torrent clients merge the index and client functions into a single package meaning the experience for the end user is no different to popular commercial sites such as Netflix or Amazon Instant Video. The days of closing down a few P2P site operators being an effective method to control the illegal trade in copyright protected music, video, and software files appear long gone in the completely decentralized world of BitTorrent. New techniques have therefore been developed in an attempt to stem the tide of illegal files.

12.3 **s.97A and site blocking**

One technique is to seek to block access to sites which offer file-sharing technology or indexes. Many websites which offer access to unlawful and illegal materials are blocked by intermediaries and ISPs. The technology is not new; the UK has been blocking access to sites that are known to contain child abuse images since 2004 through the application of the 'Cleanfeed' content-blocking tool. It is quite a simple operation to block access to a website, the difficulty, as we shall see is in making that block effective. Permission for site-blocking applications had been given by Art. 8(3) of the InfoSoc Directive which required member states to 'ensure that rightholders are in a position to apply for an injunction against intermediaries whose services are used by a third party to infringe a copyright or related right.'[50] The UK Government had implemented Art. 8(3) via the Copyright and Related Rights Regulations 2003[51] which by Reg. 27(1) had inserted a new s. 97A into the Copyright, Designs and Patents Act 1988. This new provision stated that 'The High Court (in Scotland, the Court of Session) shall have power to grant an injunction against a service provider, where that service provider has actual knowledge of another person using their service to infringe copyright.'

The case to test the limits of the effectiveness of this new provision was *Twentieth Century Fox & Ors. v Newzbin Limited*.[52] This case involved a service domiciled within

---

[50] Directive 2001/29/EC.
[51] SI 2003/2498.
[52] [2010] EWHC 608 (Ch).

the United Kingdom and therefore easily made subject to the jurisdiction of the High Court. Newzbin was an indexing service for Usenet files. It was a subscription-only service netting a substantial annual profit.[53] It was also clear that a substantial percentage of indexed content was there in breach of copyright. There was a fig leaf of a copyright enforcement system using a reporting and 'delisting' tool but Kitchin J did not believe it was offered as a genuine service to copyright holders: 'I have no doubt that this is another superficial attempt to conceal the purpose and intention of the defendant to make available binary content of interest to its users, including infringing copies of films. As will be seen, the defendant has done nothing to enforce this restriction.'[54] The claimants sought a wide injunction to prevent Newzbin from supplying links to *any* material in breach of copyright. Kitchin J felt he could not award such a widely drafted injunction, noting that he had only been briefed on the rights of the parties before him and that an injunction could only in his view be awarded to rights-holders (many of which were not represented before him). He did though grant a narrower injunction under s. 97A to the claimants. Almost immediately Newzbin Ltd was sold to a third party who resurrected the site with a Seychelles hosting agreement and operating from the same web address under the name Newzbin II. This prevented the claimants from recovering costs and allowed the site to continue to operate outside the jurisdiction of the High Court. The claimants then returned to the court with a new strategy. If Newzbin was now outside the jurisdiction of the court could they block access to it? The claimants returned to the High Court to seek a new and innovative injunction.[55] They were aware of the Cleanfeed system and now sought an order under s. 97A not against the host, which as it was located in the Seychelles was outside the jurisdiction of the Court, but against BT requiring it to add Newzbin to its list of blocked Cleanfeed sites. As most major UK ISPs share the Cleanfeed list for their content-blocking system, this would be effective beyond just BT customers and would in effect for most of the population block access to the Newzbin site in the same way as child abuse images are blocked from access.

There was though a problem that Arnold J had to overcome before he could grant the injunction. A Belgian case on ISP filtering had been referred to the CJEU for judgment. The final decision of the court was still outstanding at the time of the *Newzbin II* case but the opinion of the Advocate General had been issued and it was very negative in relation to applying the Belgian equivalent of s. 97A in a manner similar to that sought in *Newzbin II*. The case was *Scarlet Extended SA v SABAM*,[56] and it involved an application by SABAM, the Belgian authors collecting society to require Belgian ISPs to install a system for filtering file-sharing content with a view to preventing illegal file-sharing. Scarlet, one of Belgium's larger ISPs, refused to comply with the request. They argued this was 'contrary to Art. 15 of the E-Commerce Directive because it would impose on Scarlet, de facto, a general obligation to monitor communications on its network, inasmuch as any system for blocking or filtering peer-to-peer traffic would necessarily require general surveillance of all the communications passing through its network'.[57]

[53] Ibid. [15].
[54] Ibid. [45].
[55] *Twentieth Century Fox & Ors v British Telecommunications plc* [2011] EWHC 1981 (Ch).
[56] ECLI:EU:C:2011:771.
[57] Ibid. [25].

Highlight Article 15(1) of the E-Commerce Directive

Member States shall not impose a general obligation on providers, when providing the services covered by Articles 12, 13 and 14, to monitor the information which they transmit or store, nor a general obligation actively to seek facts or circumstances indicating illegal activity.

The Advocate General (AG) had recommended that the court find that Art. 15(1) prevented Belgian authorities from making and enforcing the order sought. He was strongly of the opinion that the injunction sought, which was for all communications on the ISP's network and for an unlimited time at the ISP's cost, was unreasonable. He noted that the solution was doubtless intended to be applied on a widespread basis, across all ISPs and to other major players involved in the internet, not merely in Belgium but beyond.[58] When the court decided the case in November 2011 they upheld the AG in full and found that:

> the injunction imposed on the ISP concerned requiring it to install the contested filtering system would oblige it to actively monitor all the data relating to each of its customers in order to prevent any future infringement of intellectual-property rights. It follows that that injunction would require the ISP to carry out general monitoring, something which is prohibited by Art. 15(1).[59]

Of course at this point Arnold J did not know this, but surely given the report of the AG he knew it was unlikely the court would depart from the opinion. He therefore had to anticipate whether the application before him would also offend Art. 15(1). Arnold J was extremely bullish in finding this would not be the case:

> I consider that the present case is clearly distinguishable from that case (*SABAM*). Quite simply, the Studios are not seeking an order that 'BT introduce, for all its customers, *in abstracto* and as a preventive measure, exclusively at the cost of that ISP and for an unlimited period, a system for filtering all electronic communications, both incoming and outgoing, passing via its services, in particular those involving the use of peer-to-peer software, in order to identify on its network the sharing of electronic files containing a musical, cinematographic or audio-visual work in respect of which the applicant claims to hold rights, and subsequently to block the transfer of such files, either at the point at which they are requested or at which they are sent.' On the contrary, the order sought by the Studios is clear and precise; it merely requires BT to implement an existing technical solution which BT already employs for a different purpose; implementing that solution is accepted by BT to be technically feasible; the cost is not suggested by BT to be excessive; and provision has been made to enable the order to be varied or discharged in the event of a future change in circumstances. In my view, the order falls well within the range of orders which was foreseeable by ISPs on the basis of section 97A, and still more Article 8(3) of the Information Society Directive. I therefore conclude that the order is one 'prescribed by law' within Article 10(2) ECHR, and hence is not contrary to Article 10 ECHR.

And with this thorny issue disposed of Arnold J went on to make the order applied for. This was a key victory for the copyright industry. Prior to this case it was not clear

---

[58] ECLI:EU:C:2011:255 [61].
[59] Scarlet Extended (n. 56) [40].

that s. 97A could be applied to an ISP in this form as they were unlikely to have 'actual knowledge' of infringement, and in any event it was assumed they would benefit from the defences of Arts.12 and 15(1) of the E-Commerce Directive. Indeed, the issue was so thorny that the government had introduced specific blocking legislation in the form of s. 17 of the Digital Economy Act 2010 which would allow the Secretary of State to pass Regulations permitting a court to make 'a blocking injunction in respect of a location on the internet which the Court is satisfied has been, is being or is likely to be used for or in connection with an activity that infringes copyright.'[60] But despite efforts of BT to argue they lacked actual knowledge and benefited from these defences, Arnold J stated that they had been put on notice by the applicants of the infringing nature of the Newzbin II site,[61] and he was equally dismissive of the applicability of Arts. 12[62] and 15.[63]

With the legal principle established, the copyright industry moved to reinforce their position. They quickly brought applications against a number of other ISPs requiring them to block *Newzbin II* and then moved to bring an action to block access to that significant thorn in their side, The Pirate Bay.[64] The Pirate Bay action began when a number of copyright holders made a joint s. 97A application against all of the UK's leading ISPs. It again came before Arnold J and he had little difficulty in following the path he had set out in *Twentieth Century Fox* and again the order sought was awarded. In the aftermath of The Pirate Bay block some people reported that it would be ineffective but data from Neilsen Media reported that in the twelve months following the blocking order traffic to The Pirate Bay from the UK dropped 75 per cent.[65]

Following this success, s. 97A orders have become the default method to block access to illegal file-sharing and streaming sites in the UK. In 2013 they were used to block access to file-sharing sites, Fenopy, H33t, and Kickass Torrents,[66] SolarMovie, and TubePlus[67] and the sports streaming website FirstRow Sports.[68] In 2014 file-sharing sites, including BTdigg, BTloft, ViTorrent, and LimeTorrents among others, were blocked,[69] alongside Viooz, Megashare, zMovie, and Watch32.[70] In 2015 in *Twentieth Century Fox Film Corp & Ors v Sky UK Ltd & Ors*,[71] an injunction was awarded against nine websites including popcorntime.io. In 2017 a further development occurred in *FA Premier League v BT & Ors.* when Arnold J awarded the first s. 97A blocking order against live broadcasts.[72] The FA specifically sought to block access to servers offering streams of live

---

[60] As an aside the government decided not to implement s. 17 of the Digital Economy Act 2010 following the successful application of s. 97A CDPA to obtain blocking injunctions.

[61] [2011] EWHC 1981 (Ch) [157]–[158].

[62] Ibid. [113].

[63] Ibid. [162].

[64] *Dramatico Entertainment Ltd & Ors. v British Sky Broadcasting Ltd & Ors.* [2012] EWHC 268 (Ch).

[65] Dave Lee, 'More piracy sites faced with blocking as BPI contacts UK ISPs' *BBC News* 23 October 2012.

[66] *EMI Records Ltd & Ors v British Sky Broadcasting Ltd & Ors* [2013] EWHC 379 (Ch).

[67] *Paramount Home Entertainment & Ors v British Sky Broadcasting Ltd & Ors* [2013] EWHC 3479 (Ch).

[68] *Football Association Premier League & Ors v British Sky Broadcasting & Ors* [2013] EWHC 2058 (Ch).

[69] *1967 Ltd & Ors v British Sky Broadcasting & Ors* [2014] EWHC 3444 (Ch).

[70] *Paramount Home Entertainment International & Ors v British Sky Broadcasting & Ors* [2014] EWHC 937 (Ch).

[71] [2015] EWHC 1082 (Ch).

[72] [2017] EWHC 480 (Ch).

football matches to viewers in the UK. To prevent the order falling foul of Art. 15 of the E-Commerce Directive (general obligation to monitor), the FA provided by confidential Schedule a list of the offending servers by IP address. In addition, by a further Schedule the claimant identified a subset of streaming servers to be blocked. The nature of how these were identified being confidential since if they were made public it would make it easier for the order to be circumvented. However, Arnold J did feel some of the process for targeting should be made public and revealed that 'first, FAPL and its contractor must reasonably believe that the server has the sole or predominant purpose of enabling or facilitating access to infringing streams of Premier League match footage. Secondly, FAPL and its contractor must not know or have reason to believe that the server is being used for any other substantial purpose.'[73] Arnold J explained what was unique about these orders. First, the order is a 'live' blocking order which only has effect at the times when live Premier League match footage is being broadcast. This is possible because of two technological advances: (1) The video monitoring technologies used by FAPL permit the identification of infringing streams with a very high level of accuracy in close to real-time during matches. The servers from which such streams emanate can be notified to the Defendants nearly instantaneously. (2) Advances in certain of the Defendants' blocking systems will allow them to block and unblock IP addresses during the course of Premier League matches, in some cases automatically. This means that blocking can be responsive to changes in the IP addresses being utilized by the operators of streaming services at the times when blocking is most needed to protect the rights in question. Second, the order provides for the list of Target Servers to be reset each match week during the Premier League season. This allows for new servers to be identified by FAPL and notified to the Defendants for blocking each week, and ensures that old servers are not blocked after the end of a week unless they continue to be observed as sources of infringing footage.[74] These new dynamic s. 97A orders are now a useful tool in the fight against live streaming services which can switch servers mid-stream.

In all of this though one case was more controversial than the others. In 2014 Arnold J had allowed an application from Cartier International to block access to a number of sites which traded goods in breach of trademark law. This cannot be achieved under s. 97A for it specifically only applies to copyright infringement. Instead Cartier argued, and Arnold J agreed, that s. 37(1) of the Senior Courts Act 1981 could substitute for the specific power found in relation to copyright infringements in s. 97A.[75] This case was to become the first UK site-blocking case to reach the Supreme Court.

12.3.1 *Cartier International AG v British Sky Broadcasting*

As noted, *Cartier* is not a copyright infringement case so strictly does not fit into this chapter but it is an extremely important decision for s. 97A cases and merits analysis here. The case began when Cartier sought blocking injunctions against a number of now-defunct sites that sold counterfeit Cartier and Mont Blanc items. The case first came before Arnold J in the High Court. He considered that, while there was no specific

---

[73] Ibid. [21].
[74] Ibid. [24]–[25].
[75] *Cartier International AG & Ors v British Sky Broadcasting & Ors* [2014] EWHC 3354 (Ch).

authority in English law for him to award a blocking injunction outside s. 97A which only applied to copyright holders, the UK government's failure to implement the third sentence of Article 11 of the EU Enforcement Directive[76] which states 'Member States shall also ensure that rightholders are in a position to apply for an injunction against intermediaries whose services are used by a third party to infringe an intellectual property right, without prejudice to Article 8(3) of Directive 2001/29/EC' meant that he had to look closely at extant English law for an equivalent position. In particular Arnold J noted that:

> When consulting on its implementation proposals in the *Consultation Paper: The UK Implementa-tion of the Directive on the Enforcement of Intellectual Property Rights* . . . the Patent Office stated in relation to Article 11: 'No action is required. The jurisdiction of the High Court to grant injunc-tions is derived from section 37(1) of the Supreme Court Act 1981. It may do so on such terms and conditions as it thinks fit (Section 37(2)).'[77]

This suggested the court already had the power to issue blocking injunctions under its equitable powers (as now found in the Senior Courts Act). The relevant section of the Act states 'the High Court may by order (whether interlocutory or final) grant an injunction . . . in all cases in which it appears to the court to be just and convenient to do so.' Arnold J noted that in the earlier case of *L'Oreal v Ebay*[78] the CJEU had stated 'that [as] the United Kingdom has not adopted specific rules to implement the third sentence of Article 11 of Directive 2004/48, the referring court will, when applying national law, be required to do so, as far as possible, in the light of the wording and the purpose the third sentence of Article 11.'[79] He took this to mean that he should apply the so-called *Marleasing* principle that that the courts of European Union member states have a duty to interpret national legislation in light of unimplemented European Union directives to find that:

> even if the Court would not have power to grant a website blocking injunction in a trade mark case upon a purely domestic interpretation of section 37(1), section 37(1) can and should be interpreted in compliance with the third sentence of Article 11 by virtue of the Marleasing principle. If it were otherwise, the UK would be in breach of its obligations under the Directive.[80]

This in itself was a controversial position to take but then he added to the controversy when considering who should pay the costs of installing and monitoring the system for enforcement of the blocking order. He suggested that 'the ISPs should generally bear the costs of implementation as part of the costs of carrying on business in this sector.'[81]

The ISPs appealed both the finding that under the *Marleasing* principle there was a general power to make blocking orders and the allocation of the implementation costs. The Court of Appeal issued their judgment in June 2016. They found that Arnold J was 'entirely correct' in finding that injunctions could be issued against intermediaries in cases other than copyright cases.[82] Giving the judgment of the court Kitchin LJ

---

[76] Directive 2004/48/EC.

[77] *Cartier* (n. 75) [116]. Note the Supreme Court Act 1981 may now be referred to as the Senior Courts Act 1981 by virtue of the Constitutional Reform Act 2005 (to prevent confusion with the powers of the UK Supreme Court).

[78] ECLI:EU:C:2011:474.

[79] Ibid. [137].

[80] *Cartier* (n. 75) [132].

[81] Ibid. [240].

[82] [2016] EWCA Civ 658 [35].

arguably went further than Arnold J did. He found that there was no need to rely upon the *Marleasing* principle and that the High Court could impose the injunction under its equitable power. He noted that while 'the ISPs are not guilty of any wrongdoing nor have they engaged in a common design with the operators of the websites offering counterfeit goods for sale' and have no specific duty of care to the trademark holders,[83] the operators of the infringing websites need the services of the ISPs in order to offer for sale and sell their counterfeit goods to UK consumers. Therefore, 'the ISPs are inevitable and essential actors in those infringing activities.'[84] Interpreting s. 37(1) in light of Art. 11 of the Enforcement Directive he finds that:

> Article 11 does indeed provide a principled basis for extending the practice of the court in relation to the grant of injunctions to encompass, where appropriate, the services of an intermediary, such as one of the ISPs, which have been used by a third party to infringe a registered trade mark. There is no dispute that the ISPs are intermediaries within the meaning of Article 11 and accordingly, subject to the threshold conditions to which I shall shortly come, I believe that this court must now recognise *pursuant to general equitable principles* that this is one of those new categories of case in which the court may grant an injunction when it is satisfied that it is just and convenient to do so.[85]

This is possibly an important finding as Kitchin LJ finds the court has the power to grant the injunction under equitable principles, not the *Marleasing* principle. This suggests that the UK government's failure to implement Art. 11 is unaffected by Brexit as the power to award the injunction is not a function of EU law.

The court divided on one issue. While Kitchin LJ and Jackson LJ agreed that Arnold J:

> was entitled to require the ISPs to bear the costs of the implementation of the orders in issue. He took proper account of the Enforcement Directive and the other parts of the EU legislative scheme, the guidance given by the Court of Justice, the nature of the orders sought and the circumstances of the case. He has made no error of principle and in my judgment there is no basis upon which this court can interfere with the conclusion to which he came.[86]

Briggs LJ felt that the specific cost incurred by the respondent ISP in complying with the order should be borne by the trademark holder, though not the cost of designing and installing any software required to comply.[87] This split gave the ISPs grounds to appeal to the Supreme Court on the issue of costs.

The Supreme Court hearing took place in January 2018 and the decision of the court was issued in June. The Supreme Court upheld the position of Briggs LJ and found that 'in principle the rights-holders should indemnify the ISPs against their compliance costs.'[88] The court noted that the compliance costs fell into five classifications:

   i   the cost of acquiring and upgrading the hardware and software required to block the target sites;

   ii the cost of managing the blocking system, including customer service, and network and systems management;

---

[83] Ibid. [54].
[84] Ibid. [56].
[85] Ibid. [65] (emphasis added).
[86] Ibid. [150].
[87] Ibid. [207], [211].
[88] [2018] UKSC 28 [36].

iii the marginal cost of the initial implementation of the order, which involves processing the application and configuring the ISP's blocking systems;

iv the cost of updating the block over the lifetime of the orders in response to notifications from the rights-holders, which involves reconfiguring the blocking system to accommodate the migration of websites from blocked internet locations; and

v the costs and liabilities that may be incurred if blocking malfunctions through no fault of the ISP, for example as a result of over-blocking because of errors in notifications or malicious attacks provoked by the blocking.[89]

The ISPs did not object to heads (i) and (ii); these being costs which would be 'incurred in any event for other reasons, for example to block access to child abuse images or to provide facilities for parental controls',[90] however they challenged heads (iii)–(v). The Supreme Court found that 'none of the Directives deal in terms with the position on costs as between the rights-holder and an information society service provider'[91] and as a result 'the incidence of compliance costs is a matter for English law, within the broad limits set by the EU principles of effectiveness and equivalence, and the requirement that any remedy should be fair, proportionate and not unnecessarily costly.'[92] The court attached importance to the fact that a 'mere conduit' ISP could not be liable for trademark infringement under English law, even in the absence of the liability protection provided by the E-Commerce Directive.[93] That meant that as an innocent intermediary its only duty was to comply with an order of the court. There was no legal basis for requiring a party to shoulder the burden of remedying an injustice if it has no legal responsibility for the infringement and is not a volunteer but is acting under the compulsion of an order of the court.[94] The court rejected the view that because ISPs benefit financially from the volume and appeal of the content available on the internet, including content which infringes intellectual property rights, it is fair to make them contribute to the cost of enforcement. This assumed a degree of responsibility on the part of the intermediary which did not correspond to any legal standard. Lord Sumption observed that the suggestion appeared to be that there was a moral or commercial responsibility in the absence of a legal one. But the law was not generally concerned with moral or commercial responsibilities except as an arguable basis for legal ones. Even if moral or commercial responsibility were relevant, Lord Sumption considered it would be hard to discern one in a case like this. Website blocking injunctions are sought by rights-holders in their own commercial interest. They are wholly directed to the protection of the claimant's legal rights, and the entire benefit of compliance with the order inures to the rights-holder. He considered that the protection of intellectual property rights is ordinarily and naturally a cost of the business which owns those rights and has the relevant interest in asserting them, rather than a cost of the business of an ISP which has nothing to do with the rights in question but is merely providing a network which

[89] Ibid. [5].
[90] Ibid.
[91] Ibid. [27].
[92] Ibid. [31].
[93] Ibid. [30].
[94] Ibid. [33].

has been abused by others. There was therefore no reason why the rights-holder should be entitled to look for contribution to the cost of defending its rights to anyone other than the infringers.[95]

What is the impact of *Cartier* on s. 97A orders? First, the Supreme Court has confirmed that there is a basis for granting site-blocking injunctions in domestic English law apart from under the EU Directives. This means copyright holders have an option of s. 97A or the general authority of the court under s. 37(1). More importantly, although not a case on s. 97A directly the decision of the Supreme Court seems to overrule the previous approach to costs allocation in s. 97A cases. The Court noted that in *Newzbin II* Arnold J had been of the view that because ISPs 'benefit financially from the volume and appeal of the content available on the internet, including content which infringes intellectual property rights, it is fair to make them contribute to the cost of enforcement.'[96] The Supreme Court explicitly rejected that position in *Cartier*, suggesting that in any future s. 97A cases any award of costs against ISPs for heads (iii)–(v) in the costs table are likely to be challenged. In future the substantive costs of complying with a blocking order are likely to have to be borne by right holders not ISPs.

12.4 **Speculative invoicing**

Speculative invoicing is a highly controversial enforcement system first introduced into the UK by law firm Davenport Lyons (DL), and then taken on for a period by niche firm ACS Law. It is now more widely practiced but due to the public perception of the practice as being little more than a 'legalized shakedown' it remains very much a niche practice.[97]

The practice first came to light in March 2007 when DL sent letters to five hundred individuals who, they claimed, had shared a computer game called Pinball Dreams 3D. The letters offered to settle the claim in return for a payment of in the region of £600; failure to settle would lead to DL taking further action.[98] This practice may be seen as a twist on the class action lawsuit where a collection of individuals bands together to pursue a corporation: here the corporation is ameliorating the costs of pursuing hundreds of actions by packaging them together and 'invoicing' each for part of the costs and damages.

The practice was initially attractive to copyright holders. As well as Topware Interactive, DL were retained by Codemasters, Reality Pump, Techland, and Atari to pursue claims relating to games titles such as *The Lord of the Rings,* the *Colin McRae Rally* series, and *Operation Flashpoint.*[99] Then a stream of bad publicity dogged the practice. First, it became clear that claims were being made based on IP address data alone.

---

[95] Ibid. [34]–[35].

[96] Ibid. [34].

[97] M Masnick, 'Court Lets Malibu Media Move Forward With Discovery In Copyright Case, But Blocks "Speculative Invoicing"', *TechDirt*, 19 August 2015.

[98] M Ballard, 'Games firm pursues 500 pinball "pirates" through UK courts', *The Register*, 28 March 2007.

[99] A Mostrous and J Richards, 'Computer games industry threat to downloaders: "pay up or we'll sue"', *The Times*, 20 August 2008.

This meant individuals who may not have adequately secured their wireless servers could find themselves receiving demands for the actions of individuals who had illegally piggy-backed on their server.[100] The bad publicity surrounding what many saw as strong-arm tactics reached a head in late 2008 with two separate episodes.

 Case study *Ken and Gill Murdoch*

In October 2008 Davenport Lyons sent a letter on behalf of Atari to Ken and Gill Murdoch of Inverness accusing them of sharing Atari's *Race 07* game. Ken (66) and Gill (54) said that they had never played a computer game before and contacted *Which?* The story quickly became a minor cause célèbre with Davenport Lyons dropping the claim but not before their tale was reported by *The Daily Express*, the *BBC*, and *The Daily Mail*.

 Case study *Davenport Lyons and Smut*

Davenport Lyons decided to represent the copyright holders of several hardcore pornographic titles. A substantial number of claim letters were issued in late 2008 relating to a number of film titles, all of which appear to be material which it would be illegal to trade in, or potentially even possess, in the UK. Quite apart from the question as to whether a Court of Equity would entertain an application from a copyright holder who is seeking to enforce their copyright in obscene material, Davenport Lyons had unfortunately sent several of their claims letters to respectable elderly citizens leading to a further round of bad publicity. This bad publicity led to Atari severing relations with the firm, while the tactics caused *Which?* to report the firm to the Solicitors' Regulatory Authority.

Immediately thereafter DL suspended their practice in speculative invoicing: the bad publicity surrounding these two events having caused a number of major clients including Atari to abandon the strategy and discourage the firm from continuing the practice. With the withdrawal of DL from the practice it was taken up by a number of others but in particular ACS:Law. For a period between 2008 and 2011 ACS:Law became a beacon for consumer anger as it developed a business model based on speculative invoicing. In essence ACS:Law acted for a small number of clients such as Media Cat Ltd. These are businesses which were given contractual permission of copyright holders to 'inquire claim demand and prosecute through the civil courts where necessary any person or persons identified as having made available for download a film for which [an agreement] has expressly licensed'.[101] These copyright monitoring companies then

---

[100] It is illegal under s. 125 of the Communications Act 2003 to 'dishonestly obtain an electronic communications service', this includes making use of another's wireless internet connection without permission. Despite thi,s the practice of 'war driving' is not uncommon. See J Leyden, 'UK war driver fined £500', *The Register,* 25 July 2005.

[101] *Media Cat Ltd v Adams* [2011] EWPCC 006 [5].

capture IP addresses from file-sharing sites in large numbers and pass them on to their legal representatives to allow for a Norwich Pharmacal application to be made. These applications would be made in huge volumes: *Media Cat Ltd v Adams* mentions 10,000 letters being sent out after a Norwich Pharmacal application. Following the Norwich Pharmacal award, it would then be served by the lawyers on the ISPs where subscriber identity was obtained. Then the 'invoice' letters before action would be sent out, threatening litigation if the subscriber did not pay up. It took nearly three years to get one of these cases to a full hearing and when it did in *Media Cat Ltd v Adams* HH Judge Birss QC was damning of the process. He found the claims far exceeded any damages likely to have accrued. He noted that the 'sum of £495 is demanded as compensation. This sum is said to include damages as well as "ISP administration costs (and its legal costs where applicable), a contribution to our clients legal costs incurred to date and all additional costs". However no breakdown of the figure is given.'[102] He was critical also of the distribution of money generated:

> I was provided with a copy of the agreement between Sheptonhurst (the copyright holder) and Media CAT which purports to give Media CAT the right to bring proceedings. Mr Tritton pointed out that the agreement shows (or appears to show) that a 65 per cent share of all revenues generated from this whole exercise will go to Media CAT's lawyers—ACS:Law. Media CAT receives 15 per cent and Sheptonhurst receive 20 per cent of the revenue. Mr Tritton submitted that the agreement was 'champertous' in that it was an assignment of a bare right to litigate and contrary to public policy.[103]

In the end HH Judge Birss threw the case out.[104]

A short period after the *Media CAT* decision a Solicitor's Disciplinary Tribunal suspended Andrew Crossley of ACS:Law for a period of two years and ordered him to pay costs in excess of £76,000.[105] In their report they were extremely critical of the speculative invoicing model, finding that it diminished the trust which the public placed in solicitors and encouraged solicitors' independence to be compromised because of the financial interest they had in the process.

At this point we may all have assumed that the process was dead in the water but recently it has resurfaced. In March 2012 a variation of the speculative invoicing process arrived at the door of the High Court. Instead of using a copyright monitoring company this time the actions are brought by the copyright holders themselves, both directly for their own work and as agents for other copyright holders. The case, *Golden Eye (International) Ltd v Telefónica UK Ltd*,[106] has a number of similarities to *Media CAT*. The applicants were seeking 9,124 personal details under a Norwich Pharmacal order to be served on Telefónica, operator of the O2 broadband network. They intended to send letters similar to those in *Media CAT* demanding a payment of £700. They were doing so in regard of their own work and under agreement for twelve other claimants who had contractually agreed for Golden Eye to represent them in the case in return for a proportion of any damages received. The claims are in relation to a number of

---

[102] Ibid. [19].
[103] Ibid. [41].
[104] Ibid. [98]–[102].
[105] *Solicitors Regulation Authority v Andrew John Crossley*, Case No. 10726–2011, 16 January 2012.
[106] [2012] EWHC 723 (Ch).

pornographic films produced by Golden Eye and Ben Dover Productions and a number of other porn producers and relate to their sharing by BitTorrent technology. At an initial hearing Arnold J examined closely the relationship between Golden Eye, their legal representatives, and the other claimants. He determined the case was distinguishable from *Media CAT* and awarded the Norwich Pharmacal order to Media CAT and Ben Dover Productions. However, with regard to the other twelve claimants, he was concerned the activity was close to champertous and refused to grant the order in relation to them.[107]

Golden Eye appealed this decision and in December 2012 the Court of Appeal reversed this decision.[108] Patten LJ gave the judgment of the court:

> The judge's refusal to grant relief to the Other Claimants was based on his disapproval of the recovery sharing arrangements with Golden Eye which is confirmed by his statement that to make the order would be tantamount to the court sanctioning the sale of the intended defendants' rights to the highest bidder. I have to say that I find those reasons difficult to follow. The court is not sanctioning the sale of anything. Indeed its ability to control the process (as the judge has done in this case) and ultimately to refuse relief was the primary reason why Arnold J rejected the submission that the litigation arrangements made with Golden Eye in this case do not jeopardise or undermine the proper administration of justice. If the arrangements are not therefore unlawful and are not simply a money-making exercise designed to take advantage of the vulnerability of the subscribers rather than a genuine attempt to protect the rights of the Other Claimants, I can see no justification for refusing relief based on a disapproval of those arrangements. Indeed it is difficult to articulate what that disapproval can be based on.[109]

This decision reopened the door of speculative invoicing. While the Court of Appeal trust their ability to manage the process and that of the Chancery Division and the Patents County Court, the problem is that the end effect is still individuals receiving letters through their doors demanding large sums of money for a copyright infringement they may or may not have committed, for as we know an IP address leads to a router not a person. Speculative invoicing letters continue to drop onto people's doorsteps. In July 2015 letters were sent by a US firm TCYK LLC, apparently set up to exploit the copyright in the 2012 Robert Redford film *The Company You Keep*, demanding payment of an 'appropriate fee' from alleged copyright infringers of their copyright to customers of Sky Broadband. It was reported in at least one reputable media outlet 'the piracy is alleged to have taken place in 2013, but the company making the claims is relying on subscriber data from 2015'.[110] Also Golden Eye (and other porn producers) began a second round of speculative invoicing claims against 1,400 Virgin Media customers in autumn 2014 (although only 800 names were disclosed under the Norwich Pharmacal Order).[111] Interestingly, there appear to have been no new cases in the UK since 2015 when Golden Eye took action against Sky broadband customers. It may be that with Golden Eye having pursued every avenue it could, the process is once more moribund in the UK.

---

[107] Ibid. [146].

[108] *Golden Eye (International) Ltd v Telefónica UK Ltd* [2012] EWCA Civ 1740.

[109] Ibid. [28].

[110] D Pegg, 'Sky Broadband customers targeted for allegedly pirating Robert Redford film', *The Guardian*, 15 July 2015.

[111] M Jackson, '800 Virgin Media Customers Pursued by Internet Porn Piracy Lawyers', *ISP Review*, 24 October 2014.

12.5 **Conclusions**

The development of digital distribution technologies and in particular peer-to-peer technologies has been one of the greatest rebalancing of user vs provider rights in history. From the minute Shawn Fanning built the Napster architecture, copyright holders lost control of their product in scale previously unimaginable. The old technique of going after the central distributor, or distributing technology, as seen in cases such as *Sony v Universal*[112] in the United States and *CBS v Amstrad*[113] in the UK, was gone. After copyright holders were observed to be following the frankly ridiculous pattern of suing their own customers while playing a game of 'virtual whack-a-mole' in an attempt to closedown the ever-burgeoning number of file-sharing services and sites the InfoSoc directive offered a way out. Article 8(3) has become perhaps the saviour of the European copyright industry. By replacing the old-fashioned intermediaries of broadcasters and publishers with the new intermediary internet information service provider (or ISPs) Art. 8(3) and its domestic equivalent s. 97A of the Copyright, Designs and Patents Act seems to be providing a relatively stable approach to the enforcement of copyright and related rights in the information society. The recent developments in *Cartier International AG v British Sky Broadcasting* have even extended s. 97A type protection beyond copyright and into trademarks (with other rights ready to follow, no doubt). The Supreme Court meanwhile used the opportunity to rebalance the costs of compliance in a way which seems, to the author at least, to be much more equitable with the bulk of costs being absorbed by the right holder who is the major beneficiary of any order. For the first time in many years we seem to have a functional enforcement system. This should hopefully spell the end of the terrible spectre of customers receiving letters demanding payment of significant sums of money which have done little to enhance the public reputation of the legal profession.

▌ TEST QUESTIONS

Question 1

Joanna is 12 and lives in London. One day she receives an email from her mobile phone company telling her that her details have been passed on to Urbane Music (a large music publisher) following the production of a court order. Joanna doesn't understand this, so she ignores it. Three months later a letter arrives addressed to her mother, Lewina. The letter alleges that Lewina, who is the account holder for Joanna's mobile phone account, illegally downloaded ten copyrighted music files from a file-sharing service. It goes on to say that the copyright holders will take action against Lewina and will seek damages for each song. The letter states that to avoid formal action the plaintiff record companies offer to settle for £2,500 (plus costs). Joanna admits downloaded the songs, but she didn't know she was doing anything illegal. She found the files on a site that was free to access, but there were no warning signs that the bands didn't authorize the site. She's a huge fan of these bands—she owns all of their CDs and just wanted to hear the new songs.

Lewina doesn't believe that she should be sued. She can't afford to pay the settlement fee, and she can't afford to hire a lawyer to fight the case in court. (The lawyer she spoke with asked for

---

[112] *Sony* (n. 33).
[113] *Amstrad* (n. 6).

a £5,000 fee retainer just to get started.) The plaintiff record companies claim that this is theft from their hardworking artists and that making Lewina pay the settlement fee will deter others from illegally downloading copyright protected music from the internet.

Jay-T, whose music Joanna copied, says that he should be paid for his creative works; fans should buy his CDs or download from reputable sites. Making music is his job, and musicians need to be compensated; they're losing money when fans illegally download their music. Coolplay, whose music Joanna also downloaded, has a different perspective and supports music file-sharing technology, even encouraging fans to download its latest album of MP3s for free or for whatever they want to pay. Coolplay believe file-sharing helps promote its music and encourages an even wider spectrum of music to be heard. Coolplay also allows its fans to remix its songs as long as the use is noncommercial.

Advise Lewina.

Question 2

In *Cartier v BSkyB* [2016] EWCA Civ 658, when presented with the two competing arguments for the establishment of blocking injunctions (EU law or domestic law) Kitchin LJ took the domestic route and therefore changed the direction of legal thinking. This is especially important post the Brexit vote, as it is now clear that this remedy does not derive from any European law but from the powers of the High Court. Further it explains the position of the court that the intermediary should bear the costs of implementation of such an order, a position which appears to conflict Art. 12(1) of Directive 2000/31/EC.

Discuss critically these aspects of the decision of Kitchin LJ in *Cartier v BSkyB*.

FURTHER READING

Books

C Doctorow, *Information Doesn't Want to Be Free* (McSweeney's 2014)

A Johns, *Piracy: The Intellectual Property Wars From Gutenberg To Gates* (Chicago University Press 2011)

N Netanel, *Copyright's Paradox* (OUP 2010)

W Patry *How to Fix Copyright* (OUP 2012)

Chapters and Articles

A Blythe, 'Website blocking orders post-Cartier v BSkyB: an analysis of the legal basis for these injunctions and the potential scope of this remedy against other tortious acts' [2017] 39 *European Intellectual Property Review* 770

B Danaher, M Smith, and R Telang, 'The Effect of Piracy Website Blocking on Consumer Behavior' available at <https://ssrn.com/abstract=2612063>

P Davies, 'Costs of blocking injunctions' (2017) *Intellectual Property Quarterly* 330

A Marsoof, 'The blocking injunction—a critical review of its implementation in the United Kingdom in the context of the European Union' (2015) *International Review of Intellectual Property and Competition Law* 632

Databases

One clearly identifiable effect the information society has had on the law is the introduction of a new, *sui generis* form of intellectual property protection in the form of the database right. Databases are structured collections of records or data stored in an indexed filing system usually, although not necessarily, held on a computer system. The structure is achieved by organizing the data according to a database model which allows data to be accessed, cross-referenced, recompiled, and extracted according to data labels. Databases are diverse in design and scope. At the most basic level a telephone directory may be classified as a database: it is ordered using an alphabetical structuring and data may be retrieved by users accessing at the correct page. At the other end of the scale are massive digital databases such as the Lexis/Nexis database which catalogues and cross-references case law, commentaries, newspaper reports, and statutory material from a number of jurisdictions. The Lexis/Nexis database also requires a much more sophisticated approach from the user as instead of merely following an alphabetical listing the user will use keywords and search phrases to find and extract the data they need. Technically the internet itself, or at very least the web, is a database with search engines such as Google, Yahoo!, and Bing providing the means to locate and extract data: few would think to classify the web as such though.

The database right is designed to protect the investment made in the gathering and indexing of data or files within a database model. It shares some similarities with copyright but is distinctively its own form of protection and has different boundaries to copyright protection. The database right was introduced throughout European Union Member States following the promulgation of Directive 96/9/EC of the European Parliament and of the Council of 11 March 1996 on the legal protection of databases.[1] In the UK the directive was implemented by the Copyright and Rights in Databases Regulations 1997,[2] which made some amendments to the Copyright, Designs and Patents Act (CDPA) 1988 to more clearly define the boundaries between copyright and *sui generis* database protection, and separately introduced the database right into the UK effective from 1 January 1998.

13.1 Copyright and the database right

The roots of the *sui generis* database right are to be found in copyright law. As we have seen throughout chapters 9 to 12 the relationship between informational products and

[1] OJ L 077, 27/03/1996.
[2] SI 1997/3032.

copyright law is a fraught one. Although copyright protection has the required flex-ibility to allow it to be moulded to new types of creative output it also often conflicts with the values or practices seen in the start-up industries which surround such new products. Thus many of the early software cases such as *John Richardson Computers v Flanders*,[3] reflected the conflict between the expansive protection copyright offered and the practice of translating software between operating systems common at the time, while the *Google v Copiepresse* decision suggests a conflict between the 'information wants to be free' ethos of the internet and the values protected by copyright.[4]

A similar conflict of values arose with regard to the protection of databases in the early 1990s. A database as a collection of (usually written) material seemed to fall naturally under copyright protection: a parallel could be drawn with anthologies of poetry or essays for which the publisher obtains copyright protection.[5] Databases became com-mon, and valuable, from the early 1980s as the cost of personal computers fell and major organizations saw the benefits of moving from old-fashioned paper-based records to the modern computer records. With database contents being of potentially great value, both internally as a business asset and on the open market as a commodity, businesses sought legal protection of their databases through the application of copyright law.

Within the UK this seemed perfectly possible, for a database could be categorized as a compilation under s.3(1)(a) of the CDPA, which meant that if it fulfilled the require-ments of originality and connection to the UK it would be protected as a copyright work. In the UK these requirements are not particularly onerous. The connection requirement may simply be achieved as under s.154(1)(c) of the CDPA: 'A work quali-fies for copyright protection if the author was at the material time a qualifying person, that is a body incorporated under the law of a part of the United Kingdom.' Thus any UK incorporated corporation would have the protection of the CDPA extended to their databases in the event they were deemed to be original. This meant the application of the skill, labour, and judgement test discussed previously in chapter 9, and drawn from *University of London Press Ltd v University Tutorial Press Ltd*[6] in which Peterson J stated that 'the Act does not require that the expression must be in an original or novel form, but that the work must not be copied from another work–that it should originate from the author'.[7] This means any original database, that is one in which the creator of the database has expended skill, labour, and judgement in its creation rather than simply copying it from another source, would be protected by copyright law in the UK.

It is important to be clear what is actually protected by this copyright. It is the design and structure of the database itself, not the individual contents of the database which may be separately protected by their own copyright as literary, artistic, or musical works. Thus if an individual were to create a database of photographs of cityscapes (a so-called photo-library), they could obtain copyright protection of the database as a whole (its structure, its selection of contents, and its 'model') while the copyright in

---

[3] [1993] FSR 497. Discussed fully at 9.4.1.

[4] [2007] ECDR 5. Discussed fully at 11.1.2.

[5] Anthologies will usually be classified as 'compilations' under CDPA, s. 3(1)(a). The editor or publisher will be awarded copyright protection for the original elements of the compilation (the selection and ordering of the works for instance), although copyright in the works themselves will remain with their original authors.

[6] [1916] 2 Ch 601. Discussed at 9.2.1.

[7] Ibid. 608–9.

each image in that database would remain with the original photographer. This means that a competing, and almost identical database may be built by a competitor provided they put in the work of gathering and cataloguing the images.

13.1.1 The listings cases

The application of the CDPA to listings of information in the form of a simple database was confirmed by two cases involving the publisher of a directory of solicitors and barristers in the late 1980s. The first was the case of *Waterlow Publishers Ltd v Rose*.[8] The plaintiff, under contract to the Law Society of England and Wales, compiled and arranged for publication *The Solicitors' and Barristers' Directory and Diary* which contained a geographical listing of solicitors and barristers by region. To enable them to produce this publication the Law Society gave to the plaintiffs a list of all solicitors. The publishers then supplemented and verified this data by sending questionnaires to all firms asking for further data, including areas of practice specialism. Prior to 1984 the defendant owned a printing company which printed copies of the directory; this work was then transferred to another firm. Following this, the defendant resolved to publish his own competing directory entitled *The Lawyers' Diary*. To launch his diary the defendant began by using a copy of the *Solicitors' Diary* to obtain the information he needed, which in his defence he said was necessary as 'it would have been impossible to do otherwise because the 1984 *Solicitors' Diary* was the only list of solicitors available'.[9] The defendant sent to solicitors copies of their entries in the current edition of the *Solicitors' Diary* and asked them to confirm whether the data was accurate and to make any necessary changes. The plaintiff argued that this action was in breach of their copyright in the *Solicitors' Diary*.

The Court of Appeal had to decide three factors: (1) was the *Solicitors' Diary* protected as a copyright work, (2) was the plaintiff the author of that work, and (3) did the defendant's actions breach copyright in the work? Slade LJ made short work of the first question, finding that 'Section 48(1) of the Copyright Act 1956 defines "literary work" as including "any written table or compilation". The "literary work" in which Waterlow claims copyright by its pleading is thus the "compilation" consisting of section 5 of the Solicitors' Diary 1984.'[10] Was the plaintiff the author of the work though? Here Slade LJ was less sure. He believed that the plaintiff was either the author or co-author of the work, 'I think it clear that if one accepts Laddie's definition of the author of a "compilation", Waterlow, if not the sole author, was at least a co-author of that compilation.'[11] In either event it did not matter as the plaintiff 'had a good cause of action for infringement of the copyright either as author or as co-author or by virtue of the presumption contained in section 20(4)'.[12]

Slade LJ then turned his attention to the final question. Had the defendant infringed the plaintiff's copyright? He noted that the defendant claimed that '[he was] designing

---

[8] [1995] FSR 207. NB: the case was actually decided on 27 October 1989 and was reported at the time in *The Independent* and *The Times* newspapers. It was not formally reported in the Law Reports though for some time.

[9] Ibid. 212.

[10] Ibid. 214.

[11] Ibid. 217–18.

[12] Ibid. 218.

his own directory on different lines and with a different layout from that of Waterlow's production, and [in] exercising his own independent skill and judgment in arranging the material, he would not be infringing'.[13] However this was rejected as:

> these submissions afford no valid defence to the claim of infringement: Mr Rose's suggestion that the database which he was in the process of constructing for his own directory was based solely on the material supplied to him by the solicitors with whom he had communicated is unsustainable. In 20 per cent of the cases where he sent out forms to individuals or firms, the recipients ignored them. The judge rejected his evidence that in such cases he proposed simply to omit them from the directory, and Mr Rose has not sought to challenge this rejection before this court. Furthermore, it has been common ground before this court that in 60 per cent of the cases the forms would be returned unaltered so that the material contained in them would be unchanged.[14]

The court therefore found in favour of the plaintiff and in so doing clearly established the principle that databases were protected as compilations under English law, and that the correct standard of originality was therefore the literary standard of skill, labour, and judgement.

A similar decision was reached in the following case of *Waterlow Directories Ltd v Reed Information Services Ltd*[15] This High Court case arose from the same publication, the *Solicitors' Diary*. The defendants on this occasion published another competing directory, the *Butterworths Law Directory*. In 1990 in order to update its directory, the defendant compared the *Solicitors' Diary* with their directory and highlighted those names and addresses which appeared in the *Solicitors' Diary* but not *Butterworths Law Directory*. The highlighted names and addresses were copied onto a word processor which was then used to produce letters inviting those solicitors and barristers to appear in the new edition of *Butterworths Law Directory*. Out of 12,620 firms of solicitors in the *Solicitors' Diary* about 1,600 were highlighted in this way.

The plaintiff argued this infringed their copyright in the *Solicitors' Diary*. Aldous J agreed, finding that:

> it is accepted that copyright subsists in the plaintiff's directory and that the plaintiff owns that copyright. Further, it is accepted that the defendant, using the plaintiff's directory, copied onto a word processor about 1,600 out of 12,600, names and addresses of solicitors and the names and addresses of organisations onto a computer. Thus it appears to me there has been reproduction and infringement if the amount reproduced constitutes a substantial part of the work. What is a substantial part of a work is a question of degree, depending on the circumstances, and it is settled law that the quality of that which is taken is usually more important than quantity. In the present case, it is a reasonable inference that the parts reproduced by the defendant were important in that they enabled the defendant to carry out a comprehensive mailing . . . That benefit was perceived to be substantial and at this stage of the action I hold that there is a strong case that the part taken by the defendant was a substantial part.[16]

On this basis Aldous J held that 'it was clear that a person could not copy entries from a directory and use such copies to compile his own directory. Even if it was correct that a person could use the information in a directory to compile another directory provided

13 Ibid. 222.
14 Ibid. 222.
15 [1992] FSR 409.
16 Ibid. 414.

that reproduction did not take place, that was not the case before the court. The defendant had reproduced the names and addresses from the plaintiff's directory onto a word processor and a computer.'[17] The second *Waterlow* case confirmed that extraction of data for a different application (in this case to turn directory entries into a mailing list) was an infringement of copyright. By the time of this second judgment, October 1990, it was clear that the CDPA provided considerable, perhaps even comprehensive, protection to original databases.

13.1.2 The Database Directive

The UK standard was causing difficulties at a European level. As we saw in chapter 9, the UK was unusual in applying the skill, labour, and judgement standard. Most states applied a more stringent standard which requires an intellectual contribution from the author. This distinction between the UK standard and the higher Continental *droit d'auteur* standard was leading to a fragmentation of the European database industry: with greater protection being found in the UK than in Continental Europe.[18] This was in turn affecting the internal market, with companies who deal in databases and their contents being more likely to setup operations in the UK than in Continental Europe.[19] To remedy this situation, and to harmonize legal protection of databases throughout the EU, the Commission issued a formal proposal for a directive on the legal protection of databases.[20] Following some amendment the proposal was passed in March 1996 as Directive 96/9/EC, usually known simply as 'the Database Directive'.

The Directive creates a two-tier approach to database protection by first creating a pan-European copyright in some databases, and then supplementing this with the *sui generis* database right where copyright does not apply. Article 1 defines a database (for the purposes of the directive) as 'a collection of independent works, data or other materials arranged in a systematic or methodical way and individually accessible by electronic or other means'.[21] Article 1 also clarifies that a program used to build, access, or update the contents of the database is to be distinct from the database itself, stating that '[p]rotection under this Directive shall not apply to computer programs used in the making or operation of databases accessible by electronic means'.[22] Thus if a software developer is asked to design a bespoke database management tool that is not part of the database: the database consists only of the data stored in the database. The software will though qualify separately for copyright protection, or perhaps even patent protection, as discussed in chapter 9.

The distinction between copyrightable databases and other databases is to be found in Art. 3(1): 'databases which, by reason of the selection or arrangement of their

---

[17] Ibid. 410.

[18] This is acknowledged in the text of the Database Directive where at Recital 1 it states 'Whereas databases are at present not sufficiently protected in all Member States by existing legislation; whereas such protection, where it exists, has different attributes.'

[19] This is also acknowledged in the Directive: 'Whereas such differences in the legal protection of databases offered by the legislation of the Member States have direct negative effects on the functioning of the internal market as regards databases and in particular on the freedom of natural and legal persons to provide on-line database goods and services on the basis of harmonized legal arrangements throughout the Community', at Recital 2.

[20] Proposal for a Council Directive on the Legal Protection of Databases, 35 OJ C 156/4 (1992).

[21] Art. 1(2).

[22] Art. 1(3).

contents, constitute the author's own intellectual creation shall be protected as such by copyright. No other criteria shall be applied to determine their eligibility for that protection.' The essential characteristic of copyright protected databases therefore is they must be 'the author's own intellectual creation'. This suggests a standard higher than the traditional UK standard of 'sweat of the brow', but unfortunately the Directive does not develop this further.

The UK government implemented Art. 3(1) by way of the new s. 3A of the CDPA, introduced by reg. 6 of the Copyright and Rights in Databases Regulations 1997.[23] Section 3A(2) implements Art. 3(1) almost word for word stating that: 'For the purposes of [copyright law] a literary work consisting of a database is original if, and only if, by reason of the selection or arrangement of the contents of the database the database constitutes the author's own intellectual creation.' What does this mean? The UK courts have had some interaction with s. 3A. In *Navitaire Inc. v easyJet Airline Co. & Anor*[24] Pumfrey J touched upon s. 3A in dealing with the extraction of data from an airline booking system. He seemed quite perplexed as to how to interpret s. 3A(2) within the spirit of the directive finding that:

> I cannot help but feel that section 3A is directed to the contents of the database. The one pointer against this conclusion is to be found in the Directive which section 3A is intended to implement. Recital 15 says 'Whereas the criteria whether a database should be protected by copyright should be defined to the fact (sic: the French text is "devront se limiter au fait que", which is clearer) that the selection or the arrangement of the contents of the database is the author's own intellectual creation; whereas such protection should cover the structure of the database.' In an electronic database, there is no compelling need to view the programs or scripts creating the database as part of the database, even though they define its 'arrangement' and 'structure'. Anyway, they acquire copyright even if no database is ever generated from them, and my inclination would be to say that they do so by virtue of the fact that they are computer programs.[25]

In the later case of *Pennwell Publishing (UK) Ltd v Ornstien and Ors*[26] Deputy Judge Fenwick QC, disappointingly did not engage fully with s. 3A(2) when invited to do so, but did comment that:

> it is not necessary, in the light of my other findings, for me to reach a conclusion as to whether the database either in its form on the Outlook system or in the form of the JuniorContacts.xls spreadsheet was an original work within the meaning of the Copyright Designs and Patents Act 1988, but it is right to indicate that I was far from persuaded that the exercise of assembling a list of contacts addresses would be sufficient to qualify.[27]

A much fuller picture emerged in *Football Dataco Ltd v Yahoo! UK Ltd*,[28] a Court of Justice of the European Union (CJEU) decision which originated in the UK courts as *Football Dataco Ltd v Brittens Pools Ltd*.[29]

---

[23] SI 1997/3032.
[24] [2004] EWHC 1725 (Ch) (2004).
[25] Ibid. [274].
[26] 2007 EWHC 1570 (QB).
[27] Ibid. [107(f)].
[28] ECLI:EU:C:2012:115.
[29] [2010] EWHC 841 (Ch); [2010] EWCA Civ 1380.

Case study *Football Dataco*

Football Dataco is a company owned by the FA Premier League, the Football League, the Scottish Premier League, and the Scottish Football League. It organizes and administers all football fixtures in the English and Scottish Leagues. Each season, through a complicated computer process accounting for a large number of variables, it produces the football fixture lists of that season for each league club. It then builds a database of all fixtures and licences others to extract data from that database such as football pools companies, betting sites, and news organizations. Football Dataco handle all requests to reprint or extract any part of the database within the UK. Internationally a subsidiary called Fixtures Marketing (whom we will discuss later at 13.2.1) handles overseas requests. It is reported that they charge £266 plus VAT to reprint the fixtures of one English club and that to reprint the fixtures of all clubs for one season costs around £3,931 plus VAT for a date-ordered listing. They attracted controversy for charging fanzines and non-profit organizations £1 plus VAT to reprint a single fixture.[30]

In 2004 Football Dataco's international subsidiary Fixtures Marketing lost a number of cases at the CJEU. These cases are discussed in depth below, but the key finding of these cases was that the database of football fixtures created by Football Dataco did not qualify for *sui generis* database protection because the makers of the database had not 'substantially invested qualitatively and/or quantitatively in either the obtaining, verification or presentation of the contents'.[31] Despite this reversal both Football Dataco and its international subsidiary Fixtures Marketing continued to pursue a number of actions in both the UK and overseas claiming that in spite of this finding they remained protected by traditional copyright protection under Art. 3(1) of the directive and s. 3A(2) of the CDPA. They based this upon the classic decision of *Ladbroke (Football) Ltd v William Hill (Football) Ltd*[32] In the High Court Floyd J agreed with this line of argument and found that the fixture lists were protected by database copyright, but not by the *sui generis* database right or any other copyright. This was appealed and at the Court of Appeal Jacob LJ ruled that while the application of Art. 7 was *acte clair* following the decision of the Court of Justice (CJEU) in the *Fixtures Marketing* cases the same was not true of Art. 3. He therefore, with the support of Hooper LJ and Rimer LJ, referred to the CJEU the questions:

(1) In Article 3(1) of Directive 96/9/EC on the legal protection of databases what is meant by 'databases which, by reason of the selection or arrangement of their contents, constitute the author's own intellectual creation' and in particular: (a) should the intellectual effort and skill of creating data be excluded? (b) does 'selection or arrangement' include adding important significance to a pre-existing item of data (as in fixing the date of a football match); (c) does 'author's own intellectual creation' require more than significant labour and skill from the author? If so what?

(2) Does the Directive preclude national rights in the nature of copyright in databases other than those provided for by the Directive?[33]

---

[30] D Conn, 'Fanzine Fight for the Right to Print Fixtures', *The Guardian*, 21 December 2005.
[31] Discussed fully at 13.2.1.
[32] [1964] 1 WLR 273.
[33] [2010] EWCA Civ 1380, [22].

The CJEU ruled on 1 March 2012. They rejected all of Football Dataco's claims. In a completely unambiguous judgment they ruled that Art. 3(1) of the directive must be interpreted as meaning that a database is protected by copyright only when the selection or arrangement of the data which it contains amounts to an original expression of the creative freedom of its author. As a consequence, the intellectual effort and skill of creating that data are not relevant in order to assess the eligibility of that database for protection by that right; it is irrelevant, for that purpose, whether or not the selection or arrangement of that data includes the addition of important significance to that data; and the significant labour and skill required for setting up that database cannot as such justify such a protection if they do not express any originality in the selection or arrangement of the data which that database contains. Further, the directive must be interpreted as meaning that it precludes national legislation which grants databases copyright protection under conditions which are different to those set out in Art. 3(1).[34]

The law now seems completely unambiguous in this area. It is indeed a higher standard of creativity than the UK standard of skill, labour, and judgement which is required for Art. 3(1) and s. 3A(2). Just as the CJEU had previously ruled in the *Fixtures Marketing* cases in relation to Art. 7, you cannot gain copyright protection for simply ordering something which is created or pre-existing for a different purpose. Article 3 protection is for creative collections, anthologies, and suchlike, not a way to supplement *sui generis* protection where an investment has been made in developing the database. We are now clear. Article 3 protection is a higher-level protection which exists where the author through their selection or arrangement has created something original. Article 7 covers the design and building of databases where there has been significant investment in the design and collection of the data for the database: unfortunately for Football Dataco and Fixtures Marketing, as shall be seen at 13.2.1 'The Fixtures Marketing cases', neither of these protections apply to the creation of 'spin-off' databases where the content of the database is created for another purpose and the database is only a subsidiary of that purpose.

13.2 **The database right**

The *sui generis* database right was introduced in Chapter III (Arts. 7–11) of the Database Directive. The right is awarded on creation of the database to the 'maker' of the database; in the directive this is defined simply as the person who 'takes the initiative and the risk of investing'.[35] The UK regulations give a far greater definition of a maker in reg. 14. The maker of a database is defined there as 'the person who takes the initiative in obtaining, verifying or presenting the contents of a database and assumes the risk of investing in that obtaining, verification or presentation'.[36] This is subject to several exceptions and limitations:

(1) where a database is made by an employee in the course of his employment, his employer shall be regarded as the maker of the database, subject to any agreement to the contrary;[37]

---

[34] *Football Dataco* (n. 28) [53].
[35] Dir. 96/9/EC, Recital 41.
[36] SI 1997/3032, Reg. 14(1).
[37] Ibid. Reg. 14(2).

(2) where a database is made by Her Majesty or by an officer or servant of the Crown in the course of his duties, Her Majesty shall be regarded as the maker of the database;[38]

(3) where a database is made by or under the direction or control of the House of Commons or the House of Lords the House by whom, or under whose direction or control, the database is made shall be regarded as the maker of the database, and if the database is made by or under the direction or control of both Houses, the two Houses shall be regarded as the joint makers of the database;[39] and finally,

(4) a database is made jointly if two or more persons acting together in collaboration take the initiative in obtaining, verifying or presenting the contents of the database and assume the risk of investing in that obtaining, verification or presentation.[40]

The UK regulations make clear that the maker of the database will be the first owner of the database right.[41]

Once the maker of the database has been identified, and for simplicity's sake we may assume that this is usually the person who pays for the database to be constructed, what rights does database right afford to the maker? The protection afforded by the *sui generis* right may be found in Arts. 7(1) and 7(5) of the Directive.

 Highlight Database Directive: Article 7(1)

Member States shall provide for a right for the maker of a database which shows that there has been qualitatively and/or quantitatively a substantial investment in either the obtaining, verification or presentation of the contents to prevent extraction and/or re-utilization of the whole or of a substantial part, evaluated qualitatively and/or quantitatively, of the contents of that database.

Some of these key terms are further defined: 'extraction' means 'the permanent or temporary transfer of all or a substantial part of the contents of a database to another medium by any means or in any form', while 're-utilization' means 'any form of making available to the public all or a substantial part of the contents of a database by the distribution of copies, by renting, by on-line or other forms of transmission. The first sale of a copy of a database within the Community by the rightholder or with his consent shall exhaust the right to control resale of that copy within the Community.'[42] Article 7(5) supplements the protection found in Art. 7(1).

---

[38] Ibid. Reg. 14(3).
[39] Ibid. Reg. 14(4).
[40] Ibid. Reg. 14(5).
[41] Ibid. Reg. 15.
[42] Dir. 96/9/EC, Art. 7(2).

Highlight Database Directive: Article 7(5)

The repeated and systematic extraction and/or re-utilization of insubstantial parts of the contents of the database implying acts which conflict with a normal exploitation of that database or which unreasonably prejudice the legitimate interests of the maker of the database shall not be permitted.

Collectively the effect of Arts. 7(1) and 7(5) are to ring-fence the contents of a database: their aim is to prevent competitors from either substantially recreating a protected database by the extraction of a substantial part of the original, or a series of insubstantial extractions, or from making use of a substantial part of a database without the permission of the database maker or owner.

The UK has implemented these provisions by reg. 16. The implementation of Art. 7(1) is found in reg. 16(1) which states: 'Subject to the provisions of this Part, a person infringes database right in a database if, without the consent of the owner of the right, he extracts or re-utilises all or a substantial part of the contents of the database.' Regulation 16(2) implements Art. 7(5): 'for the purposes of this Part, the repeated and systematic extraction or re-utilisation of insubstantial parts of the contents of a database may amount to the extraction or re-utilisation of a substantial part of those contents'. The final part of the implementation jigsaw is found in reg. 12(1) where 'substantial' is defined as 'substantial in terms of quantity or quality or a combination of both'.

The *sui generis* right is therefore rather different to a copyright. It has a different standard of originality, and protects in quite a different way. It is not copying per se which is restricted but rather *substantial* or *repeated* extraction or reutilization of the database contents. Also there are many restrictions contained within the directive and given effect in the regulations which limit the scope of the *sui generis* right. Article 8(1) provides that: '[t]he maker of a database which is made available to the public in whatever manner may not prevent a lawful user of the database from extracting and/or re-utilizing insubstantial parts of its contents, evaluated qualitatively and/or quantitatively, for any purposes whatsoever',[43] while Art. 9 provides three 'fair dealing' exceptions:

> Member States may stipulate that lawful users of a database which is made available to the public in whatever manner may, without the authorization of its maker, extract or re-utilize a substantial part of its contents:
>
> (a) in the case of extraction for private purposes of the contents of a non-electronic database;
>
> (b) in the case of extraction for the purposes of illustration for teaching or scientific research, as long as the source is indicated and to the extent justified by the non-commercial purpose to be achieved;
>
> (c) in the case of extraction and/or re-utilization for the purposes of public security or an administrative or judicial procedure.[44]

The term of protection is also less than with copyright law. By Art. 10(1) the right 'shall expire fifteen years from the first of January of the year following the date of

---

[43] Given effect by Reg. 19(1).
[44] Given effect variously by SI 1997/3032, Sch. 1 and Reg. 20(1).

completion', unless the database is subsequently made available to the public during this period in which case 'the term of protection by that right shall expire fifteen years from the first of January of the year following the date when the database was first made available to the public'.[45] However, there is one substantial qualification to these terms. By Art. 10(3), 'Any substantial change, evaluated qualitatively or quantitatively, to the contents of a database, including any substantial change resulting from the accumulation of successive additions, deletions or alterations, which would result in the database being considered to be a substantial new investment, evaluated qualitatively or quantitatively, shall qualify the database resulting from that investment for its own term of protection.' Neither the directive nor the UK regulations have a full and satisfactory definition of when a change is 'substantial'. One assumes though this is to be the same definition found as applied in reg. 7(1) for which there is some degree of case law discussed at 13.2.1 'The *Fixtures Marketing* cases' and 13.2.2 *British Horseracing Board v William Hill*, below. In any event, given that a database has to be continually updated to remain useful, it seems likely that most databases will undergo 'substantial' amendment in the 15 years that protection runs. For example, if you were to update as little as 0.01 per cent of the database on a daily basis you would cumulatively update over 54 per cent of the database over a 15-year period. Thus it seems that for any managed database perpetual protection will be available.

13.2.1 The *Fixtures Marketing* cases

With a completely new form of IP protection it is not surprising that the courts have been busy trying to set the limits of what is permissible and what is not. A series of questions arose in several national courts, almost all of which were eventually referred to the CJEU for interpretation. These questions included: (1) What amounts to a substantial investment for qualification of the right? (2) Does the right accrue where the database is a 'spin-off' from investment in another field—e.g. where broadcasters schedule television programmes the 'spin-off' is a database of scheduled television programmes? (3) What amounts to repeated and systematic extraction? (4) Does the right cover instances where information is generated/created and cannot be obtained from alternative sources? Many of these questions arose initially in a series of cases arising from the rights to football fixtures lists. These cases, known collectively as the *Fixtures Marketing* cases included *Fixtures Marketing Ltd v Organismos Prognostikon Agonon Podosfairou (OPAP)*,[46] *Fixtures Marketing Ltd v Oy Veikkaus AB*,[47] and *Fixtures Marketing Ltd v Svenska Spel AB*.[48]

All three involved material extracted from a database of football fixtures created by combining the individual fixtures lists of the English Premier League, the English Football League, the Scottish Premier League, and the Scottish Football League. This database was then managed by Fixtures Marketing on behalf of the leagues with a view to commercially exploiting the contents of the database. All three of the respondents had in various ways made use of details from the relevant fixtures lists without the

---

[45]   Dir. 96/9/EC, Art. 10(2).
[46]   ECLI:EU:C:2004:697. Case originated in The Athens Court of First Instance, Greece.
[47]   ECLI:EU:C:2004:694. Case originated in The Vantaa District Court, Finland.
[48]   ECLI:EU:C:2004:696. Case originated in The District Court, Gotland, Sweden.

permission of the claimant. OPAP were using fixtures drawn from the database on fixed-odds betting coupons; an online betting site in Greece, Oy Veikkaus, were using fixtures from the database for their football pools coupon in Finland; and Svenska Spel were doing likewise in Sweden. All three cases were heard together before the CJEU.

The questions referred varied from case to case but the key questions were contained in the OPAP reference which simply asked:

> (1) What is the definition of database and what is the scope of Directive 96/9 and in particular Art. 7 thereof which concerns the sui generis right? (2) In the light of the definition of the scope of the directive, do lists of football fixtures enjoy protection as databases over which there is a sui generis right in favour of the maker and under what conditions? and (3) How exactly is the database right infringed and is it protected in the event of rearrangement of the contents of the database?

Although wide in scope these are key questions. The judge of the Athens Court of First Instance was inviting the CJEU to clarify the scope of the directive and to determine what may amount to 'a substantial investment' under reg. 7(1), whether or not a 'spin-off' database may qualify for protection at all and finally what amounts to 'extraction and/or re-utilization a substantial part'.

The court gave full consideration to all these issues with a very full opinion given by Advocate General Stix-Hackl. As to the initial question, that of what qualifies as a 'database' under Art. 1(2), the court first noted that 'nothing in the directive points to the conclusion that a database must be its maker's own intellectual creation to be classified as such . . . the criterion of originality is only relevant to the assessment whether a database qualifies for the copyright protection'.[49] This confirmed the widely held view that the *droit d'auteur* standard of an *œuvre de l'ésprit* (in English usually referred to as a 'spark of originality') was not applicable to the *sui generis* database right. From here the court went on to answer the question finding that 'classification of a collection as a database requires that the independent materials making up that collection be systematically or methodically arranged and individually accessible in one way or another'.[50]

 Highlight Definition of a database (from *Fixtures Marketing*)

Any collection of works, data, or other materials, separable from one another without the value of their contents being affected, including a method or system of some sort for the retrieval of each of its constituent materials.

This makes clear that the definition of a database is to be interpreted broadly, certainly broadly enough to cover everyday directories such as telephone directories or legal directories such as seen in the *Waterlow* cases. This led on to the second element of the first question: what amounts to 'a substantial investment' under Art. 7(1)?

---

[49] *Fixtures Marketing Ltd v OPAP* (n. 46) [26].
[50] Ibid. [30].

Highlight Definition of a substantial investment (from *Fixtures Marketing*)

The expression 'investment in . . . the . . . verification . . . of the contents' of a database must be understood to refer to the resources used, with a view to ensuring the reliability of the information contained in that database, to monitor the accuracy of the materials collected when the database was created and during its operation. The expression 'investment in . . . the . . . presentation of the contents' of the database concerns, for its part, the resources used for the purpose of giving the database its function of processing information, that is to say those used for the systematic or methodical arrangement of the materials contained in that database and the organisation of their individual accessibility. Investment in the creation of a database may consist in the deployment of human, financial. or technical resources but it must be substantial in quantitative or qualitative terms. The quantitative assessment refers to quantifiable resources and the qualitative assessment to efforts which cannot be quantified, such as intellectual effort or energy.

Thus to qualify for protection under Art. 7(1) the maker of the database must have invested substantially, either in financial terms, or in terms of effort, skill, and manpower, and that investment *must* be made to ensure the database is accurate and/or functional. The investment cannot be for any other purpose, such as commercializing or marketing the database or for some other reason unrelated to the creation of the database itself.

The court then answered the second question. It noted that, given the wide interpretation of Art. 1(2), it had indicated that:

> the date and the time of and the identity of the two teams playing in both home and away matches are covered by the concept of independent materials within the meaning of Art. 1(2) of the directive in that they have autonomous informative value . . . [as such] it follows that a fixture list for a football league such as that at issue in the case in the main proceedings constitutes a database within the meaning of Art. 1(2) of the directive'.[51]

It also answered the question of whether a 'spin-off' database could ever be protected.

 Highlight Protecting 'spin-off' databases (from *Fixtures Marketing*)

The fact that the creation of a database is linked to the exercise of a principal activity in which the person creating the database is also the creator of the materials contained in the database does not, as such, preclude that person from claiming the protection of the sui generis right, provided that he establishes that the obtaining of those materials, their verification or their presentation, in the sense described at above, required substantial investment in quantitative or qualitative terms, which was independent of the resources used to create those materials.

[51] Ibid. [33], [36].

This ultimately proved to be Fixtures Marketing's downfall. The makers of the database were the professional football leagues of England and Scotland. The database was created as part of their primary function, namely the setting of league fixtures for the football season. Further, as they were the originators of the contents of the database, they did not need to verify the accuracy of the database. As the court recorded:

> Finding and collecting the data which make up a football fixture list do not require any particular effort on the part of the professional leagues. Those activities are indivisibly linked to the creation of those data, in which the leagues participate directly as those responsible for the organisation of football league fixtures. Obtaining the contents of a football fixture list thus does not require any investment independent of that required for the creation of the data contained in that list. The professional football leagues do not need to put any particular effort into monitoring the accuracy of the data on league matches when the list is made up because those leagues are directly involved in the creation of those data. The verification of the accuracy of the contents of fixture lists during the season simply involves, according to the observations made by Fixtures, adapting certain data in those lists to take account of any postponement of a match or fixture date decided on by or in collaboration with the leagues. Such verification cannot be regarded as requiring substantial investment. The presentation of a football fixture list is closely linked to the creation as such of the data which make up the list. It cannot therefore be considered to require investment independent of the investment in the creation of its constituent data.[52]

Ultimately, therefore, the database of football fixtures created by the football leagues and distributed under licence to Fixtures Marketing did not qualify for Art. 7 protection because the makers of the database had not 'substantially invested qualitatively and/or quantitatively in either the obtaining, verification or presentation of the contents'. With this decision made the court, unfortunately, declined to answer the third question.[53]

13.2.2 *British Horseracing Board Ltd v William Hill*

The *Fixtures Marketing* cases are an extremely important series of cases which usually would have been met with a fanfare at their outcome. The court had examined the scope of the Database Directive and had given guidance on the application of Art. 7(1), but they were little commented upon by the profession, academics, or the media for the same day the CJEU had given its opinion on an almost identical case, which had been bundled together with the *Fixtures Marketing* cases and which answered the third question that the court had declined to answer in the *OPAP* case: this was the case of *British Horseracing Board Ltd v William Hill Organisation Ltd*.[54]

The facts of this case are extremely similar to the *Fixtures Marketing* cases, and it is for this reason that *William Hill* was disposed with jointly with the *Fixtures Marketing* cases. William Hill operate a chain of high-street betting shops which among other things allow for betting on horse racing, an operation known as 'off-course bookmaking'. For many years William Hill had been operating their high-street bookmaking shops using information supplied from Weatherbys, a private company who compiled the Jockey

---

[52] Ibid. [49]–[51].
[53] Ibid. [54].
[54] ECLI:EU:C:2004:695.

Club database which contained advance information about race meetings, runners, and riders. In 1999 the Jockey Club database was merged with the British Horseracing Board (BHB) database, although Weatherbys continued to supply data to William Hill's high-street operation under a licence. The issue though was William Hill's website. They had no licence or permission to use data from the BHB database for online gambling. William Hill began to operate an internet gambling site in May 1999. It offered a variety of daily bets using information that had originated in the BHB database. William Hill argued they did not need a separate licence for this operation as the information they used was not subject to database protection; in particular William Hill argued that the information had been made publicly available via newspapers, teletext, and the specialist betting information service Satellite Information Services Limited ('SIS') which provides a raw data feed of all races taking place that day to all its subscribers, which includes William Hill. BHB argued that the database was a major part of their operation. It was estimated to contain some 800,000 entries and cost some £4m per annum to maintain, over 25 per cent of BHB's entire annual expenditure.[55] BHB argued that by extracting the daily data for races to be run that day William Hill extracted and reutilized a 'substantial part' of the database. Their argument was based on the principle that Art. 7(1) states 'substantial' is to be evaluated 'qualitatively and/or quantitatively'. Although the data extracted each day may be so small in proportion to the overall size of the database so as to be quantitatively insubstantial, it was, argued BHB, qualitatively substantial as the data extracted each day was the only data of commercial value for that day: by extracting that data William Hill effectively were avoiding payment to use the only commercially valuable part of the database for that day. In the alternative, BHB argued that by making daily extractions from the BHB database William Hill were actively involved in systematic extraction and/or reutilization of insubstantial parts of the contents of the database in breach of Art. 7(5).

BHB launched their case in the summer of 2000 and the initial hearings were before Laddie J who issued his judgment in February 2001.[56] He found that:

> Article 7(1) provides that substantiality is to be assessed by looking at the quantity and quality of what is taken but it does not require them to be looked at separately. It contemplates looking at the combination of both . . . Here what the defendant is doing is making use of the most recent and core information in the BHB Database relating to racing. William Hill is relying on and taking advantage of the completeness and accuracy of the information taken from the [Raw Data Feed], in other words the product of BHB's investment in obtaining and verifying that data. *This is a substantial part of the contents.*[57]

With regard to the subsequent claim under Art. 7(5), Laddie J found that 'William Hill's borrowing from [the database] from day to day comes within Article 7(5) as repeated and systematic extractions and re-utilizations of parts of its contents.'[58]

Unsurprisingly William Hill appealed this decision. The appeal was heard by the Court of Appeal (Peter Gibson, Clarke, and Kay LLJ) who stayed proceedings in July 2001 to refer the case to the CJEU.[59] The Court of Appeal referred 11 questions to the

---

[55] Ibid. [32].
[56] *British Horseracing Board Ltd & Ors v William Hill Organisation Ltd* [2001] EWHC 517 (Patents).
[57] Ibid. [53].
[58] Ibid. [73].
[59] *British Horseracing Board Ltd and Ors v William Hill Organisation Ltd* [2001] EWCA Civ 1268.

CJEU, some similar to those raised elsewhere in the *Fixtures Marketing* cases but many were important and were either unique to this reference or had not been answered elsewhere.[60] In a groundbreaking judgment the court substantially disregarded the opinion of Advocate General Stix-Hackl, the same Advocate General who had advised them on the *Fixtures Marketing* cases. The court went through the reference in great detail answering all the questions closely. It began by answering the prior questions:

> (2) What is meant by 'obtaining' in Article 7(1) of the Directive? In particular, are the facts and matters in [issue in the case] capable of amounting to such obtaining? and (3) Is 'verification' in Article 7(1) of the Directive limited to ensuring from time to time that information contained in a database is or remains correct?

The court applied the reasoning seen in the *Fixtures Marketing* cases in answering these questions. It ruled that:

> investment in the selection, for the purpose of organising horse racing, of the horses admitted to run in the race concerned relates to the creation of the data which make up the lists for those races which appear in the BHB database. It does not constitute investment in obtaining the contents of the database. It cannot, therefore, be taken into account in assessing whether the investment in the creation of the database was substantial.[61]

This is an application of the 'spin-off' principle discussed above. While BHB were creating data for another purpose the database was merely a spin-off from that purpose. Therefore the investment made in creating the data could not count towards a 'substantial investment' in the database: that would require to come from further investment in gathering or generating external data (i.e. data not required for the purpose of running BHB operations) or verifying the data.

This led to question 3: how high is the verification standard? The court unfortunately did not answer this directly, but they did indicate what did not qualify as verification:

> the process of entering a horse on a list for a race requires a number of prior checks as to the identity of the person making the entry, the characteristics of the horse and the classification of the horse, its owner and the jockey . . . However, such prior checks are made at the stage of creating the list for the race in question. They thus constitute investment in the creation of data and not in the verification of the contents of the database.[62]

At this point the court could have concluded its analysis by finding in a similar fashion to the *Fixtures Marketing* cases that the BHB database was merely a 'spin-off database' and as such did not qualify for protection because the makers of the database had not 'substantially invested qualitatively and/or quantitatively in either the obtaining, verification or presentation of the contents'. Fortunately though the court, perhaps influenced by the number of references which had been made under the directive, went on to analyse the remaining questions.

The court next addressed the seventh, eighth, and ninth questions together. These were:

> (7) Is 'extraction' in Article 7 of the directive limited to the transfer of the contents of the database directly from the database to another medium, or does it also include the transfer of works, data or other materials, which are derived indirectly from the database, without having

---

[60] The 11 questions may be found at ECLI:EU:C:2004:333 [AG27].
[61] *British Horseracing Board* (n. 54) [38].
[62] Ibid. [39], [40].

direct access to the database? (8) Is 're-utilisation' in Article 7 of the directive limited to the making available to the public of the contents of the database directly from the database, or does it also include the making available to the public of works, data or other materials which are derived indirectly from the database, without having direct access to the database? and (9) Is 're-utilisation' in Article 7 of the directive limited to the first making available to the public of the contents of the database?

These questions all came about because of William Hill's practice of drawing the information it needed for its online betting sites not from the BHB database directly, but from third party sources such as the SIS Raw Data Feed and newspaper listings such as *The Racing Post*. The court began with a general observation that:

> [t]he use of expressions such as 'by any means or in any form' and 'any form of making available to the public' indicates that the Community legislature intended to give the concepts of extraction and re-utilisation a wide definition . . . those terms must therefore be interpreted as referring to any act of appropriating and making available to the public, without the consent of the maker of the database, the results of his investment, thus depriving him of revenue which should have enabled him to redeem the cost of the investment.[63]

Following this, the court went on to find that:

> [s]ince acts of unauthorised extraction and/or re-utilisation by a third party from a source other than the database concerned are liable, just as much as such acts carried out directly from that database are, to prejudice the investment of the maker of the database, it must be held that the concepts of extraction and re-utilisation do not imply direct access to the database concerned.[64]

The court therefore found that:

> The terms 'extraction' and 're-utilisation' in Art. 7 of the Directive must be interpreted as referring to any unauthorised act of appropriation and distribution to the public of the whole or a part of the contents of a database. Those terms do not imply direct access to the database concerned. The fact that the contents of a database were made accessible to the public by its maker or with his consent does not affect the right of the maker to prevent acts of extraction and/or re-utilisation of the whole or a substantial part of the contents of a database.[65]

Finally, the court turned to the key questions:

> (1) May either of the expressions: 'substantial part of the contents of the database'; or 'insubstantial parts of the contents of the database' in Article 7 of the Directive include works, data or other materials derived from the database but which do not have the same systematic or methodical arrangement of and individual accessibility as those to be found in the database? (4) What is meant in Article 7(1) of the directive, by the expressions: 'a substantial part, evaluated qualitatively . . . of the contents of that database'? and 'a substantial part, evaluated quantitatively . . . of the contents of that database'? (5) What is meant in Article 7(5) of the directive, by the expression 'insubstantial parts of the database'? (6) In particular, in each case: does 'substantial' mean something more than 'insignificant' and, if so, what? does 'insubstantial' part simply mean that it is not 'substantial'? and (10) In Article 7(5) of the directive what is meant by 'acts which conflict with a normal exploitation of that database or unreasonably prejudice the legitimate interests of the maker of the database'? In particular, are the facts [of this case] capable of amounting to such acts?

---

[63] Ibid. [51].
[64] Ibid. [53].
[65] Ibid. [67].

While the preliminary issues were valuable, in particular the answer to questions 7, 8, and 9, what the court was about to do in answering these five questions was interpret the key provisions of Arts. 7(1) and 7(5), in particular what amounted to a 'substantial part' for Art. 7(1) and when would repeated extractions under Art. 7(5) infringe the maker's database right?

The court first turned to Art. 7(1) and sought first to clarify what constituted a 'substantial part' of a database.

 Highlight A 'substantial part' (from *BHB*)

The expression 'substantial part, evaluated quantitatively', of the contents of a database within the meaning of Art. 7(1) of the Directive refers to the volume of data extracted from the database and/or re-utilised, and must be assessed in relation to the volume of the contents of the whole of that database. If a user extracts and/or re-utilises a quantitatively significant part of the contents of a database whose creation required the deployment of substantial resources, the investment in the extracted or re-utilised part is, proportionately, equally substantial.

The expression 'substantial part, evaluated qualitatively', of the contents of a database refers to the scale of the investment in the obtaining, verification or presentation of the contents of the subject of the act of extraction and/or re-utilisation, regardless of whether that subject represents a quantitatively substantial part of the general contents of the protected database. A quantitatively negligible part of the contents of a database may in fact represent, in terms of obtaining, verification or presentation, significant human, technical or financial investment.

[at [70]–[71]]

This was a surprising outcome. While the definition of a 'substantial part, evaluated quantitatively' was in line with predictions, the definition of a 'substantial part, evaluated qualitatively' was not what had been expected. It had always been imagined that a 'substantial part, evaluated qualitatively' would refer to the commercial value of that part of the database as against the database as a whole. So, for example, in the current case the data for that day's race meetings would qualify as a substantial part of the database as a whole evaluated qualitatively. What the CJEU said though was it was not the value of the data at extraction which was to be measured; it was the value of the data at its addition to the database. Thus data which was difficult or costly to obtain or verify would be 'qualitatively substantial' whether or not this was subsequently of any greater value commercially than the rest of the database. As BHB had expended no greater effort or money in obtaining the data for the current day's races than for any other data in the database the court held that 'those materials do not represent a substantial part, in [quantitative or] qualitative terms, of the BHB database'.[66]

Finally the question of whether William Hill had infringed Art. 7(5) was addressed.

---

[66] Ibid. [74], [80].

Highlight Purpose of Art. 7(5) (from *BHB*)

The purpose of Article 7(5) is to prevent circumvention of the prohibition in Article 7(1) of the Directive. Its objective is to prevent repeated and systematic extractions and/or re-utilisations of insubstantial parts of the contents of a database, the cumulative effect of which would be to seriously prejudice the investment made by the maker of the database just as the extractions and/or re-utilisations referred to in Article 7(1) of the Directive would.

[at [86]]

In other words, the purpose of Art. 7(5) is not to prevent users from repeatedly accessing a database to extract or reutilize insubstantial parts of the database, as William Hill was doing; it was to prevent the cumulative construction of a competing database, or the accumulation of data from a database over a period of time which would lead to a cumulative 'substantial part'. Again this was somewhat surprising and had not been widely predicted. It made the application of Art. 7(5) extremely narrow, so narrow as perhaps to be of little practical application.

The end result of the immediate case was that BHB lost. On nearly every point the CJEU ruled against them. Their database was not sufficiently original to qualify for database protection as there had been no independent significant investment in the obtaining or verification of the data. Even if the database were protected, the actions of William Hill were not infringing: they neither extracted or reutilized a substantial part of the database, nor did they make repeated extractions or reutilizations which 'conflict with a normal exploitation of that database or which unreasonably prejudice the legitimate interests of the maker of the database' under Art. 7(5). The case was remanded back to the Court of Appeal for disposal and on 13 July 2005 the Court of Appeal gave judgment in favour of William Hill but not without reservation.[67] Clark LJ observed that 'I am conscious that in doing so I have agreed to allowing an appeal against a decision which I was inclined to think was correct when the case was last before the Court of Appeal in July 2001. The reason for my change of view is of course the decision and reasoning of the ECJ.'[68]

13.2.3 **After *BHB***

The immediate fall-out of the decisions of the CJEU of 9 November 2004, and in particular the *BHB* decision, was a concern that by interpreting Arts. 7(1) and 7(5) so narrowly the court had effectively undermined the protection offered by the *sui generis* database right. In the aftermath of the decision, news reports and professional journals reported that the effect of the decision was to effectively narrow the protection afforded to makers of databases.[69] This in time led to a number of similar academic articles.[70]

---

[67] *British Horseracing Board Ltd & Ors v William Hill Organisation Ltd* [2005] EWCA Civ 863.
[68] Ibid. [37].
[69] R Kemp, D Meredith, and C Gibbons, 'Database Right and the CJEU Judgment in *BHB v William Hill*: Dark Horse or Non-Starter?' (2005) 21 *Computer Law and Security Review* 108.
[70] S Kon and T Heide, 'BHB/William Hill—Europe's Feist' (2006) 28(1) *European Intellectual Property Review* 60; Tanya Aplin, 'The CJEU elucidates the database right' (2005) *Intellectual Property Quarterly* 204.

The common view of many of these comments is that the court had been forced to narrow the scope of the directive for there was a danger that 'this new property right would arise virtually everywhere there was a website'.[71] In time though a clearer view of the decisions of 9 November developed, at least in part formed by the Commission Evaluation of the Database Directive which was carried out immediately after these decisions.[72]

The report set out to evaluate three particular criticisms of the *sui generis* database right: (1) its scope is unclear and it is poorly targeted; (2) the database right 'locks up' data to the detriment of research and the academic community; and (3) the database right is too narrow in scope and fails to protect investors.[73] In evaluating these claims the Commission examined (1) the impact of the 9 November 2004 judgments; (2) whether there was an indication that the academic community and the research community at large were paying unnecessary costs to access data; and (3) the measure of the size of the EU database community.[74]

The outcome was rather surprising, in particular for critics of the *Fixtures Marketing/ BHB* decisions. In response to the question 'Has the CJEU's interpretation of the scope of the "sui generis" right devalued the uniform levels of protection achieved for "non-original" databases?', the findings of an online survey found that '43 per cent of the respondents believe that the legal protection of their databases will be the same as before the CJEU rulings (or even reinforced); only 36 per cent believe that the scope of protection will be either weakened or removed'.[75] Although this is not a statistically significant result it was not what may have been expected in the immediate aftermath of the 9 November decisions. Further it appeared that a majority of respondents actually welcomed the effect of the decisions:

> most respondents to the Commission services' on-line survey believe that the protection of databases is stronger than before adoption of the Directive. However, a majority of respondents feel that, after the CJEU's rulings, fewer databases will be protected by the 'sui generis' right. This allays fears of monopoly abuses which were usually expressed with respect to 'single-source' databases (databases where the database maker and the proprietor of the underlying information are the same person or entity).[76]

This suggests that many even within the industry were unhappy with the idea of a broad database right which would have protected spin-off—or in the Commission's terms, 'single-source'—databases. There was an obvious concern about market abuse with such databases, a concern allayed by the decisions of 9 November 2004.

In response to the other questions the Commission found the database right to be functioning well. They found that the research and academic communities were still able to access data and that the 9 November decisions had assisted in this[77] and that the database industry in Europe was healthy both before and after the 9 November

---

[71] Taken from Kemp, Meredith, and Gibbons (n. 69) 118.
[72] Commission of the European Communities, *First Evaluation of Directive 96/9/EC on the Legal Protection of Databases*, 12 December 2005.
[73] Ibid. [1.2].
[74] Ibid. [4.1.4].
[75] Ibid. [1.2].
[76] Ibid. [1.2].
[77] Ibid. [4.3].

decisions.[78] Thus the Commission Evaluation suggested that the decisions of the CJEU had actually proved positive for both our understanding and the health of the database right. By narrowing the scope of the right, the CJEU had actually restored confidence in the right, and had prevented overprotection of spin-off, or single-source, databases which may have harmed the competitiveness of European data industries as end users would have had to pay for access to single-source data which would have led to potential market abuse from companies in a dominant position. Following the publication of the Evaluation the views of commentators softened with the 9 November decisions now seen as broadly positive and reinforcing of the *sui generis* right, with most noting that the narrow interpretation promulgated has assisted all sides in the database industry, with the obvious exception of single-source database makers.[79]

13.2.4 **The *Football Dataco* decisions**

Much of this chapter appears to be taken up with the activities of Football Dataco and their subsidiary Fixtures Marketing. After losing the *Fixtures Marketing* cases and perhaps working on the assumption that eventually they would lose the *Football Dataco* fixtures listing decision, Football Dataco invested heavily in a new product called 'Football Live'. To create Football Live, Football Dataco sends reporters to football matches across the country to record details of the match on a minute-by minute-basis. The reporters, usually ex-professional footballers, record things like goals scored and when they were scored, goalscorers, yellow and red cards and who and when they got them, penalties and when they were awarded, and substitutions (who was substituted, when and by whom). In addition, they also are invited to make value judgements like 'man of the match' and most aggressive player in the last ten minutes. The contents of this database are then licensed to news organizations who can supply minute-by-minute match reports via websites and apps and to betting organizations that use them to allow betting in play on any number of options such as next player to score, next corner kick, or next player to receive a yellow card.

Although most people pay to extract data from the Football Live database a number of organizations, following the principles of the *Fixtures Marketing* cases were extracting data without a licence. Football Dataco brought a joint action against UK-based bookmaker Stan James and a German aggregation service, Sportrader, which operates a database of sports statistics called Betradar. Within Betradar is a section called Live Scores which reports information drawn from a number of live streams including internet streams. Much of what was reported in Betrader came from sources extracting data from the Football Live stream. Like much Football Dataco litigation this has been extensive and time-consuming. The case has seen three reported hearings from the High Court,[80]

---

[78] Ibid. [4.2].

[79] M Prinsley, 'An Opportunity to Improve Protection for Databases in Europe?' (2006) 6(3) *World Data Protection Report* 3; C Waelde, 'Databases and Lawful Users: The Chink in the Armour' (2006) *Intellectual Property Quarterly* 256; A Masson, 'Creation of Database or Creation of Data: Crucial Choices in the Matter of Database Protection' (2006) 28(5) *European Intellectual Property Review* 261.

[80] *Football Dataco Ltd v Sportradar GmbH* [2010] EWHC 2911 (Ch); *Football Dataco Ltd v Stan James (Abingdon) Ltd* [2012] EWHC 747 (Ch); and *Football Dataco Ltd v Sportradar GmbH* [2012] EWHC 1185 (Ch).

two of the Court of Appeal,[81] and one from the CJEU.[82] The key rulings are to be found in the CJEU and final Court of Appeal decisions.

The Court of Appeal drew a clear line between the fixtures database and the Football Live database. Sir Robin Jacob (formerly Jacob LJ before retirement) gave the lead judgment. The key question was: did the Football Live database exhibit the qualities required to gain protection under Art. 7? Sir Robin noted that 'this test has been considered by the court in the quartet of horseracing/football fixture cases'.[83] He noted that the common approach in all four: 'investment in creating data was not the right kind of investment. So that if only that kind of investment is involved in the creation of a database, there is no *sui generis* right in it.'[84] This was the contention of Stan James and Sportradar: the investment was all spent on the reporter who recorded the data and then entered it into the database. The database itself was merely an effect of the reports: 'Mr Silverleaf contended firstly that there can be no Art.7 right unless there is investment in collecting together materials which have already been recorded. The process of actually recording data is to be regarded as creative in the same way as the process of creating a football fixture list or list of finally approved runners and riders.'[85] Sir Robin felt differently that data is often pre-existing and that databases often reflect an investment in the gathering and verifying of this data. To Sir Robin there was a difference between the sporting fixtures cases where the data could only be created by the organization seeking to exert ownership over it, and who therefore invested in its creation and subsequently sought to profit from this by claiming database protection, and the instant case where the data was independent of the person recording it and the investment was made in the recording of the data:

> The factual data provided by the football analyst to the sports information processor and then recorded by the sports information processor (sometimes after some conversation to verify its accuracy) in Football Dataco's database is pre-existing data. Only a metaphysicist would say a goal is not scored until the football analyst tells the sports information processor that it has been scored. The same metaphysicist might also deny that a temperature exists unless and until it is recorded. But he would feel hot in a Turkish bath even without a thermometer . . . I am entirely confident that a scientist who takes a measurement would be astonished to be told that she was creating data. She would say she is creating a record of pre-existing fact, recording data, not creating it . . . the policy of the Directive is that databases which cost a lot of investment and can readily be copied should be protected. The right is created to protect the investment which goes into the creation of a database. If a database produced by collecting data ascertained (not created) by the database creator is not protected, there will be no incentive to create databases of that sort.[86]

On this basis Sir Robin had little difficulty in finding the Football Live database to be protectable under Art. 7. The clear distinction between this case and the sports listing cases was that the investment being made by Football Dataco was in the gathering of data for the purpose of creating the Football Live database; this was different from the

[81] *Football Dataco Ltd v Sportradar GmbH* [2011] EWCA Civ 330 and *Football Dataco Ltd v Sportradar GmbH* [2013] EWCA Civ 27.
[82] *Football Dataco Ltd v Sportradar GmbH* ECLI:EU:C:2012:642.
[83] *Football Dataco Ltd v Sportradar GmbH* [2013] EWCA Civ 27 [31].
[84] Ibid. [32].
[85] Ibid. [35].
[86] Ibid. [39], [44].

creation of data for other purposes and then incidentally entering it into a database.[87] With the question of protectability disposed of, he then went on to find both Stan James and Sportradar infringed Football Dataco's *sui generis* database right by allowing customers to extract data from the Football Live database without a licence.

13.3 **Databases and the information society**

Before leaving databases we must look at one final issue unique to online databases. With more databases publicly accessible via a web portal there is an increased risk of unauthorized linking to the contents of these databases. This raises issues similar to those discussed in the 'Linking, caching, and the temporary reproduction right' section of chapter 11.[88] Many of the cases discussed in that section including *Stepstone v Ofir*,[89] *Havas Numerique et Cadre On Line v Keljob*,[90] and *Google Inc. v Copiepresse SCRL*[91] involved claims not only of copyright infringement but also claims of unauthorized extraction and/or reutilization in breach of the Database Directive. Most of these cases though, with the exception of *Google v Copiepresse* and *NVM Estate Agents v ZAH*,[92] were decided prior to the decisions of 9 November 2004. However, the last part of the *Football Dataco* action was on this point. While the Court of Appeal felt capable of answering questions of protectability and unauthorized extraction, the one question which was referred to the CJEU was in this area. The CJEU was essentially asked one question in the reference from the Court of Appeal:

> where a party uploads data from a database protected by [the] *sui generis* right onto that party's webserver located in member state A and in response to requests from a user in another member state B the webserver sends such data to the user's computer so that the data is stored in the memory of that computer and displayed on its screen (a) is the act of sending the data an act of 'extraction' or 're-utilisation' by that party? and (b) does any act of extraction and/or re-utilisation by that party occur: (i) in A only; (ii) in B only; or (iii) in both A and B?[93]

The complication in the case was that Football Dataco was uploading data to a server in the UK. Sportrader though were a German/Swiss company who operated via servers in Austria and supplied data to a number of customers in a number of countries including Gibraltar. Sportrader therefore argued that their activities were not subject to the jurisdiction of the English courts and sought from the Landgericht Gera (Regional Court, Gera, Germany) a formal declaration that its activities did not infringe any intellectual property right held by Football Dataco. The High Court declared that it had jurisdiction to hear the claim insofar as it sought to establish joint liability on the part of Sportradar and those of its customers which use its website in the United Kingdom, but that it did not have jurisdiction to hear the claim insofar as it sought to establish primary liability on the part of Sportradar. Both parties appealed against the High Court's decision to the Court of Appeal, which made for the reference to the CJEU.[94]

---

[87] Ibid. [45]–[69].
[88] See 11.1.
[89] Landgericht, Köln, February 28, 2001: 28 O 692/00. Discussed in full at 11.1.1.
[90] Tribunal de Commerce de Paris, 26 December 2000. Discussed in full at 11.1.1.
[91] [2007] ECDR 5. Discussed in full at 11.1.2.
[92] 136002/KG ZA 06-25, LJN AV5236, 16 March 2006.
[93] *Football Dataco Ltd v Sportradar GmbH* ECLI:EU:C:2012:377 [AG13].
[94] Ibid. [AG11], [AG12].

The court first examined whether communication of the contacts of a database via a web server constituted extraction or reutilization of that data. They found that:

> the concept of 're-utilisation', must, in the general context of Art. 7, be understood broadly, as extending to any act, not authorised by the maker of the database protected by the *sui generis* right, of distribution to the public of the whole or a part of the contents of the database. The nature and form of the process used are of no relevance in this respect. That concept covers an act, such as those at issue in the main proceedings, in which a person sends, by means of his web server, to another person's computer, at that person's request, data previously extracted from the content of a database protected by the *sui generis* right. By such a sending, that data is made available to a member of the public.[95]

Therefore the court clearly determines that the process of scraping data from the database of another party and delivering it to customers via a web server is capable of infringing the *sui generis* right. The question then became whether the English courts had jurisdiction over Sportrader and for which parts of their operation. The court acknowledged that the directive does not aim to introduce a uniform law at EU level; rather it aims to remove the differences which existed between national laws in relation to the legal protection of databases, and which adversely affected the functioning of the internal market.[96] Sportrader argued that in that context, 'an act of re-utilisation within the meaning of Art. 7 must in all circumstances be regarded as located exclusively in the territory of the Member State in which the web server from which the data in question is sent is situated'.[97] The court rejected this and found that 'the protection by the *sui generis* right provided for in the legislation of a Member State is limited in principle to the territory of that Member State, so that the person enjoying that protection can rely on it only against unauthorised acts of re-utilisation which take place *in that territory*'.[98] 'The referring court will be entitled to consider that an act of re-utilisation such as those at issue in the main proceedings is located in the territory of the Member State of location of the user to whose computer the data in question is transmitted, at his request, for purposes of storage and display on screen.'[99]

What the court has decided therefore is that Sportrader (or anyone else who scrapes content) is subject not only to the jurisdiction of the court where their servers are based or from where the company operates but also any country where they target customers in relation to any data made available to those customers there. Whether or not a company targets users within the jurisdiction is a question for the national court to decide. In the instant case Sportrader admitted targeting English customers and therefore was liable for infringement in England.[100]

In the following Dutch referral *Innoweb BV v Wegener ICT Media* the CJEU returned to this issue.[101] This case involved a website, https://www.autotrack.nl, operated by Wegener on which a user may browse up to 200,000 second-hand cars for sale. Innoweb operated a meta search engine called, https://www.gaspedaal.nl which would index a number of automotive classified sites allowing the user to search multiple sites

---

[95] ECLI:EU:C:2012:642 [20]–[21].
[96] Ibid. [24]–[25].
[97] Ibid. [44].
[98] Ibid. [27] (emphasis added).
[99] Ibid. [43].
[100] *Football Dataco Ltd v Sportradar GmbH* [2013] EWCA Civ 27, [89].
[101] ECLI:EU:C:2013:850.

simultaneously. To allow GasPedaal to index AutoTrack when a GasPedaal customer input a search term it would be 'translated' into the format required by AutoTrack, then results displayed on the GasPedaal site. The court was told that:

> GasPedaal carries out approximately 100,000 searches on the AutoTrack website in response to queries. Thus, approximately 80 per cent of the various combinations of makes or models listed in the AutoTrack collection are the object of a search daily. In response to each query, however, GasPedaal displays only a very small part of the contents of that collection. In every case, the contents of those data are determined by the user on the basis of criteria which he keys into GasPedaal.[102]

Nine questions were referred to the CJEU from the Dutch court, the key one being:

> Is Article 7(1) of Parliament and Council Directive [96/9] to be interpreted as meaning that the whole or a qualitatively or quantitatively substantial part of the contents of a database offered on a website (online) is re-utilised (made available) by a third party if that third party makes it possible for the public to search the whole contents of the database or a substantial part thereof in real time with the aid of a dedicated meta search engine provided by that third party, by means of a query entered by a user in 'translated' form into the search engine of the website on which the database is offered?[103]

The court responded robustly to this question:

 Highlight Is meta-indexing a breach of Art. 7(1)?

The act on the part of the operator of making available on the internet a dedicated meta search engine such as that at issue in the main proceedings, into which it is intended that end users will key in queries for 'translation' into the search engine of a protected database, constitutes 'making available' the contents of that database for the purposes of Art. 7(2)(b) of Parliament and Council Directive 96/9.

That 'making available' is for 'the public', since anyone at all can use a dedicated meta search engine and the number of persons thus targeted is indeterminate, the question of how many persons actually use the dedicated meta engine being a separate issue.

Consequently, the operator of a dedicated meta search engine such as that at issue in the main proceedings re-utilizes part of the contents of a database for the purposes of Art. 7(2)(b) of Parliament and Council Directive 96/9.

That re-utilization involves a substantial part of the contents of the database concerned, if not the entire contents, since a dedicated meta search engine such as that at issue in the main proceedings makes it possible to search the entire contents of that database, like a query entered directly in that database's search engine. Accordingly, the number of results actually found and displayed for every query keyed into the dedicated search engine is irrelevant. As the Commission of the European Union observed, the fact that, on the basis of the search criteria specified by the end user, only part of the database is actually consulted and displayed in no way detracts from the fact that the entire database is made available to that end user.

[at [50]–[53]]

<hr />

102 Ibid. [13].
103 Ibid. [18]. Note the court only answered the first three questions.

This is an important decision for any meta-indexing site including price comparison sites. It does leave hanging of course the interesting question of what is the position of content not of sufficient originality to qualify for protection under Art. 7, the kind of content at the heart of the *BHB* and *Football Dataco* cases? This was exactly the scenario in the case of *Ryanair Ltd v PR Aviation BV*.[104]

This is a very interesting case and should be considered alongside the *PRCA v NLA* decision discussed at 11.1.3.[105] It started out as a standard meta-indexing/scraping case in the Netherlands but became something else along the way. PR Aviation operates a comparison website on which consumers can search through the flight data of low-cost airlines, compare prices and, on payment of commission, book a flight. Like GasPedaal (above) it obtains this information directly from the websites in question including Ryanair. At a first hearing before the Rechtbank (Local Court) in Utrecht Ryanair's database claim was thrown out, the court finding the data did not qualify for *sui generis* protection, although a copyright claim was successfully made out. An appeal to the Gerechtshof te Amsterdam (Court of Appeal, Amsterdam) found that PR Aviation had a defence against the copyright claim, and again found the database claim failed as Ryanair had not established the existence of 'substantial investment' in the creation of its data set. An appeal to the Hoge Raad der Nederlanden (Netherlands Supreme Court) saw the case take an unusual turn. The Hoge Raad referred a single question to the CJEU on the database right:

> does the operation of Directive 96/9 also extend to online databases which are not protected by copyright on the basis of Chapter II of that Directive, and also not by a sui generis right on the basis of Chapter III, in the sense that the freedom to use such databases through the (whether or not analogous) application of Arts. 6(1) and 8 in conjunction with Art. 15 of Directive 96/9, may not be limited contractually?[106]

What is this question about? It starts to become clear when you examine Ryanair's general terms and conditions, which PR Aviation agreed to in accessing their site. They say:

> this website and the Ryanair call centre are the exclusive distributors of Ryanair services. Ryanair.com is the only website authorised to sell Ryanair flights. Ryanair does not authorise other websites to sell its flights, whether on their own or as part of a package. You are not permitted to use this website other than for the following, private, non-commercial purposes: (i) viewing this website; (ii) making bookings; (iii) reviewing/changing bookings; (iv) checking arrival/departure information; (v) performing online check-in; (vi) transferring to other websites through links provided on this website; and (vii) making use of other facilities that may be provided on the website. The use of automated systems or software to extract data from this website or www.bookryanair.com for commercial purposes, ('screen scraping') is prohibited unless the third party has directly concluded a written licence agreement with Ryanair in which permits it access to Ryanair's price, flight and timetable information for the sole purpose of price comparison.[107]

Ryanair were claiming that, in the alterative to a database or copyright infringement, PR Aviation were in breach of these terms and conditions. PR Aviation were relying upon a number of statutory rights found, among other places, in the Database Directive, in particular Art. 6(1), 'the performance by the lawful user of a database or of a copy

---

[104] ECLI:EU:C:2015:10.
[105] ECLI:EU:C:2014:1195.
[106] ECLI:EU:C:2015:10 [28].
[107] Ibid. [16].

thereof of any of the acts listed in Article 5 which is necessary for the purposes of access to the contents of the databases and normal use of the contents by the lawful user shall not require the authorization of the author of the database. Where the lawful user is authorized to use only part of the database, this provision shall apply only to that part' and Art. 8(1) and (2):

> the maker of a database which is made available to the public in whatever manner may not prevent a lawful user of the database from extracting and/or re-utilizing insubstantial parts of its contents, evaluated qualitatively and/or quantitatively, for any purposes whatsoever. Where the lawful user is authorized to extract and/or re-utilize only part of the database, this paragraph shall apply only to that part. (2) A lawful user of a database which is made available to the public in whatever manner may not perform acts which conflict with normal exploitation of the database or unreasonably prejudice the legitimate interests of the maker of the database.

Importantly by Art. 15 of the Directive any contractual terms which attempts to interfere with the rights of end users as set out in Arts. 6(1) and 8 are null and void. In this way PR Aviation sought to have Ryanair's contractual terms rendered null. The problem for the Hoge Raad was though that although Ryanair had begun the case relying, in part, on having a *sui generis* database right, which had been found inapplicable by the courts. This is why they had referred that complex question to the CJEU. Essentially they wanted to know, if a claim to either a copyright right under Chapter II of the Directive or a *sui generis* right under Chapter III, failed what did this mean for Arts. 6(1) and 8, and vitally for Art. 15? The Court was clear:

> the answer to the question referred is that Directive 96/9 must be interpreted as meaning that it is not applicable to a database which is not protected either by copyright or by the *sui generis* right under that Directive, so that Arts. 6(1), 8 and 15 of that Directive do not preclude the author of such a database from laying down contractual limitations on its use by third parties, without prejudice to the applicable national law.[108]

These recent cases give us a strong impression of the future of database rights in the online environment. Those who operate meta indexes and scraping sites will have to ensure they comply contractually with the owner of the data or will have to ensure they meet the defences available under the Database Directive as implemented. The operation of unlawful price comparison or meta-indexing sites are controllable, by database rights, where the content qualifies, or by contractual law where it dos not. In the case of the latter though readers are reminded of Art. 5 of the InfoSoc Directive,[109] and the application of that in *PRCA v NLA*.[110] This may allow the narrowest window for a few services to escape through, but only for a few.

13.4 **Conclusions**

Anyone interested in the operation of the Database Directive has much to thank Football Dataco/Fixtures Marketing for. Their series of cases before the CJEU have settled the boundaries of both *sui generis* and copyright protection for databases. We know from

---

[108] Ibid. [45].
[109] Directive 2001/29/EC.
[110] *PRCA* (n. 105).

the *Fixtures Marketing* cases that *sui generis* protection extends only to cases where there has been significant investment in the gathering and verifying of data and the design of the database itself, not in the creation of the data. We also know from the *Football Dataco v Yahoo!* case that a higher level of creative investment, beyond skill, labour, and judgement, is required to qualify for Art. 3 copyright protection. Just as the CJEU had previously ruled in the *Fixtures Marketing* cases, you cannot gain copyright protection for simply ordering something which is created or pre-existing for a different purpose. Finally, the *Football Dataco v Sportrader* cases complete the jigsaw with two vital pieces of information. First, the excellent analysis of Sir Robin Jacob in the Court of Appeal clearly draws bright lines between the unprotectable at Art. 7 creation of data which leads to spin-off databases and, as seen in the *Fixtures Marketing* cases, the protectable gathering of data by observation. This is an extremely lucid analysis and also has the benefit of providing good policy: we will not protect by Art. 7 that which can only be created by one person or a defined group of persons as that creates a monopoly over not just the database but also the information in it, but we will protect those who invest in gathering data which others may gather equally by a similar investment. Finally, the CJEU dealt with the one outstanding issue of jurisdiction, again in a most lucid and sensible way. To decide otherwise than they did would have risked reintroducing a fractured Europe where informational intermediaries such as Sportrader gravitated towards countries with the weakest database protections as a safe harbour for the activities.

TEST QUESTIONS

Question 1

The *sui generis* database right is an unnecessary addition to the legal landscape. Copyright law was perfectly positioned to regulate the developing database industry. It has taken a number of cases involving sporting fixtures lists to even define what the scope of the right is, and in the end it is just about trying to harmonize the UK 'sweat of the brow' standard with European *droit d'auteur*. In the end though we still have two standards—Arts. 3 and 7: nothing has changed and the directive should therefore be repealed.

Discuss.

Question 2

Did the decision of the European Court of Justice in the case of *British Horseracing Board v William Hill* [2005] 1 CMLR 15 undermine the effectiveness and value of the *sui generis* database right?

FURTHER READING

Books

E Derclaye, *The Legal Protection of Databases: A Comparative Analysis* (Edward Elgar 2008)

T Hoeren and B Kolany-Raiser (eds.), *Big Data in Context: Legal, Social and Technological Insights* (Springer 2017)

M Davison, *The Legal Protection of Databases* (CUP 2008)

Chapters and articles

N Eziefula, 'Database Rights Back on the Sport Radar', 23(8) *Entertainment Law Review* 242 (2012)

M Koščík and M Myška, 'Database authorship and ownership of sui generis database rights in data-driven research' [2017] 31 *International Review of Law, Computers & Technology* 43

M Schellekens, 'A database right in search results?—an intellectual property right reconsidered in respect of computer generated databases' 27(6) *Computer Law and Security Review* 620 (2011)

C Waelde, 'Databases and Lawful Users: The Chink in the Armour', (2006) *Intellectual Property Quarterly* 256

Branding, trademarks, and domain names

The issue of 'branding' is one which lawyers have traditionally remained apart from, instead choosing to focus on the narrow legal question of protection of trade marks. However, one lawyer who does examine branding is Professor Cornish in his 2002 Clarendon Lectures.[1] His view is that branding and trademarks share a common foundation: 'branding is the watchword of marketers; lawyers talk of trademarks and associated get-up. By these terms the two groups mean broadly the same phenomenon; but each inclines to a contemptuous view of what the other contributes to business functioning and general welfare.'[2] A general definition of branding given by Colin Bates of BuildingBrands, a UK brand consultancy, is that it is 'a collection of perceptions in the mind of the consumer', which he goes on to develop saying: 'a brand is very different from a product or service: a brand is intangible and exists in the mind of the consumer'.

If this is the definition of branding as found in the marketing and branding industry what is a trademark as defined by the legal services industry? The answer is to be found in s. 1 of the Trade Marks Act (TMA) 1994 which defines a trademark as: 'any sign capable of being represented graphically which is capable of distinguishing goods or services of one undertaking from those of other undertakings'. It appears from this that Professor Cornish is correct: there is little substantive difference between the marketing concept of branding and the legal concept of a trademark. Both are intangible, both are distinctive and both are capable of definition and recording. Yet, despite these superficial similarities, the two live in very different environments, and an understanding of the conflict between the role of brands and trademarks is essential for the discussion that follows in this chapter, for it is this conflict which has been at the heart of a significant amount of litigation and arbitration.

In the modern consumer-driven society, brands have developed a purpose much greater than that intended for trademarks. To understand this purpose, take a second, look up from this book and look around (and at) yourself. Chances are, you and the surrounding environment are emblazoned with brand identities. Sony, Apple, Samsung, and Acer proclaim you buy their electronics while Ralph Lauren, Hugo Boss, Abercrombie & Fitch. and others proudly proclaim that you choose their clothes. You proudly wear these brands to identify yourself with a brand image: Prada, Louis Vuitton, and Versace (aspirational); Hugo Boss, Zara, and Paul Smith (professional); Marks and Spencer, Next,

---

[1] *Intellectual Property: Omnipresent, Distracting, Irrelevant?* (OUP 2004).
[2] Ibid. 73.

and Principles (practical); Topshop, French Connection, and H&M (fashionable). You may prefer an Apple laptop to an Acer as Apple portray themselves as creative and 'outside the box'; you probably choose which car you drive as much for its badge as for the practicalities of what it does.

The development of this 'brand society' and its interaction with the legal process was examined by Neil MacCormick in his paper 'On the Very Idea of Intellectual Property: An Essay According to the Institutionalist Theory of Law',[3] where he notes that intellectual property rights (IPRs) when viewed as a legal concept display three properties:[4]

 Highlight MacCormick's three legal properties of IPRs

1. They prescribe the circumstances in which the IPR comes into being and vests in a particular person.
2. The law provides what privileges and other rights belong to the holder of the IPR.
3. The law must specify how an IPR is extinguished and how it can be transferred from one person to another.

This is what MacCormick describes as the 'institutional facts' of IPRs. What is abundantly clear, though, is that this is a lawyer seeking to rationalize what intellectual property rights are from a legal perspective. He fails to capture, and indeed does not seek to, the complexity of trademarks as cultural icons. This is a weakness of the legal analysis. The lawyer talks of 'badges of identity', 'trademark registries', and 'infringement and enforcement', whereas the brand consultant talks of 'aspiration values', 'target audiences', and 'lifestyle choices'. The current value of trademarks is not measured in terms of brand recognition, as was the case in the past, but by brand identity. This means we no longer value brands by their ability to distinguish goods and services as being provided by a particular company or individual but by the lifestyle offered by that brand. This has allowed brands to develop quite astonishing dollar values. In the 2018 annual survey by Millward Brown, the *Brandz Top 100 Most Valuable Global Brands*, each of the top 25 global brands are valued as being worth in excess of $40bn each, with the global number one brand, *Google*, being valued at a staggering $302bn.[5] With such vast sums of money involved, and with more business being conducted in the online environment, it is only to be expected that both brand owners and their legal advisors would soon turn their attention to brand protection and development in the online environment. This has clear potential for a clash of cultures and it is this which forms

---

[3] [2002] *Intellectual Property Quarterly* 227.

[4] Ibid. 236.

[5] <http://www.millwardbrown.com/brandz/rankings-and-reports/top-global-brands/2018>. It should be acknowledged that other valuations are lower. Interbrand values Google at $155.5bn (its no. 1 is Apple worth $214bn) while Brand Finance is valued at only $120bn (its no. 1 is Amazon worth $150.8bn). Each valuation is though indicative of the huge value of brands.

the core of this chapter. The following discussion is split into three sections. First, we will analyse the UK law on trademark protection. From here we move on to a discussion of brand identity in the online environment, before we conclude with an analysis of the legal conflicts which have arisen from these culture clashes and the proposed legal solutions to these conflicts.

14.1 **Trademarks in the global business environment**

The legal system takes a narrow view of the role of trademarks, viewing a trademark as a tool of brand recognition rather than brand identity. There are two varieties of trademark, the registered trademark (or true trademark) and the common law of passing off (sometimes referred to as unregistered trademarks).[6] The more familiar of these to most people is the registered trademark which is sometimes referred to in literature by the addition of a commonly recognizable symbol ® or ™. The addition of such symbols is not though a prerequisite to a registered trademark and therefore one should never assume that an unadorned name or mark is not a registered trademark.

14.1.1 **Registered and unregistered trademarks**

In the UK registered trademarks are regulated by the Trade Marks Act 1994, which implemented the First Trade Marks Directive.[7] By s. 63 the Registrar of Trade Marks is required to maintain a register which contains a record of all registered trademarks. To gain registration in the register an applicant must make an application under s. 32. The procedure is governed by a set of rules which require the registrar to examine each application to see whether it complies with the Act and rules. If it does, he publishes it whereupon anyone objecting to the application may oppose it or make observations as to whether or not it should be granted. If no notice of opposition is given or all opposition proceedings are withdrawn or decided in the applicant's favour, the Registrar registers the mark unless it appears to him, having regard to matters coming to his notice since accepting the application, that it was accepted in error. If accepted onto the register the mark is registered for a period of ten years from the date of registration in the first instance,[8] which may be renewed for further periods of ten years.[9] Once registered, the proprietor of a registered trademark has exclusive rights in the trademark that are infringed by its use in the UK without his consent.[10] Those rights have effect from the date of filing of the application for registration.[11] However, no action may be taken before the date on which a trademark is registered and no offence is committed by anything done before publication of the registration.

---

[6] For more detail on both of these see L Bently, B Sherman, D Gangjee, and P Johnson *Intellectual Property Law* (5th edn, OUP 2018) ch. 31.

[7] Dir. 89/104/EEC.

[8] TMA, s. 42(1).

[9] Ibid. s. 42(2). The oldest trademark in the Registry is Trade Mark No. 1 of 1876 (the year the register was created). It is the red triangle logo of the Bass brewery.

[10] Ibid. s. 9(1).

[11] Ibid. s. 9(3).

Infringement of a registered trademark is regulated by s. 10 of the Act. This states that a trade mark may be infringed by using in the course of trade a sign:

(a) which is identical to the registered trademark in relation to goods or services which are identical with those for which the mark is registered;[12]

(b) where, because the sign is identical with the registered trademark and is used in relation to goods or services similar to those for which the mark is registered, or, because the sign is similar to the registered mark and is used in relation to goods or services that are identical with or similar to those for which that mark is registered, there exists a likelihood of confusion on the part of the public, which includes the likelihood of association with the registered mark;[13] or

(c) which is identical with or similar to the registered trademark and is used in relation to goods or services which are not necessarily similar to those for which the trademark is registered, where the trademark has a reputation in the UK and the use of the sign, being without due cause, takes unfair advantage of, or is detrimental to, the distinctive character or repute of the trademark.[14]

Use for these purposes includes affixing a sign to goods or their packaging, offering or exposing goods for sale, putting them on the market, stocking them for those purposes under such a sign, offering or supplying services under the sign, importing or exporting under the sign, or using it on business papers or in advertising.[15] Sections 11 and 12 of the Act provide that a trademark is not infringed, inter alia, by the use:

(a) of a person making use of his own name or address;[16]

(b) of indications concerning the kind, quality, quantity, intended purpose, value, geographical origin, time of production of goods, or rendering of services or other characteristics of goods or services;[17] or

(c) of the trademark where it is necessary to indicate the intended purpose of a product or service.[18]

Unregistered trademarks function similarly (without the registration process of course). The correct legal term for the protection of an unregistered trademark is 'the tort of passing off'. Unlike registered trademarks, which are a creature of statute, passing off is a common law invention. The modern law is to be found in a handful of cases of which the most recent are the decisions of the House of Lords in *Reckitt & Colman Products Ltd v Borden Inc.*[19] and *Erven Warnink BV v J Townend & Sons.*[20] In the first of those cases, Lord Oliver set out what is known as the 'Classic Trinity' which

---

[12] Ibid. s. 10(1).
[13] Ibid. s. 10(2).
[14] Ibid. s. 10(3).
[15] Ibid. s. 10(4).
[16] Ibid. s .11(2)(a).
[17] Ibid. s. 11(2)(b). This includes terms such as 'Scotch' Whisky or 'Lion Quality' Eggs.
[18] Ibid. s. 11(2)(c). This includes terms such as 'Ford' exhausts or games controllers for 'Sony Playstation4'.
[19] [1990] RPC 341.
[20] [1979] AC 731.

lies at the root of the modern English law of passing off. He said that a claim may be brought where:

(a) the claimant's goods or services have acquired a goodwill or reputation in the market and are known by some distinguishing feature; *and*

(b) there is a misrepresentation by the defendant (whether or not intentional) leading or likely to lead the public to believe that goods or services offered by the defendant are goods or services of the claimant; *and*

(c) the claimant has suffered, or is likely to suffer, damage as a result of the errone-ous belief engendered by the defendant's misrepresentation.[21]

14.1.2 **Trademark characteristics**

Both registered trademarks and the law of passing off share common characteristics of domesticity and specificity. Domesticity is the provision that a trademark will only be protected within the jurisdiction in which it is registered or used. For registered trademarks domesticity can be established by reference to s. 9(1) of the TMA: 'The proprietor of a registered trademark has exclusive rights in the trademark which are infringed by use of the trademark *in the United Kingdom* without his consent.' There is no cross-border protection of UK registered trademarks. The concept of domesticity in trademarks is reflected throughout the globe. There is no such thing as an 'international trademark'. Although two international agreements create provisions for the interna-tional protection of trademarks—the Paris Convention for the Protection of Industrial Property and the Madrid Agreement/Protocol—neither creates a truly international trademark as both require recognition by national governments and/or the domestic registrar of trademarks.

Unregistered trademarks also display domesticity. The clearest example of such a pro-vision in the UK is the case of *Anheuser-Busch v Budejovicky Budvar*.[22] In this case the Court of Appeal followed the so called 'hard-line' school of passing off in determining that goodwill, a necessary prerequisite for an action of passing off, has a territorial component. There is a separate 'soft-line' school of thought which is recognized in Australia.[23] This school claims to protect the unregistered trademarks of commercial organizations that do not trade within the jurisdiction in question.[24] Does this mean that unregistered trademarks, at least in some corners of the globe, do not demonstrate domesticity? The answer is no. In those cases where the soft-line approach is followed the court will look for evidence of reputation in the trademark within the jurisdiction in question.[25] The soft-line/hard-line dichotomy is not about domesticity, it is rather a question of whether the court is to look for goodwill on the part of the trademark holder or merely reputation. Whichever approach is correct, in both schools of thought unregistered trademarks benefit from domesticity.

[21] *Reckitt & Colman* (n. 19) 406.

[22] [1984] FSR 413.

[23] See H Carty, 'Passing Off and the Concept of Goodwill', (1995) *Journal of Business Law* 139; F Martin, 'The Dividing Line Between Goodwill and International Reputation', (1995) *Journal of Business Law* 70.

[24] See e.g. the case of *Conagra Inc. v McCain Frozen Foods (Aust) Pty* (1991) 23 IPR 193.

[25] Ibid. 237.

The second characteristic of trademarks is specificity. Put simply, you only gain protection if there is a likelihood of confusion on the part of the consumer. As the consumer is unlikely to be confused by similar trademarks on entirely dissimilar products, such as Penguin chocolate biscuits and Penguin books, protection is limited to those products which share characteristics with the trademark owner's product. In the UK, for registered trademarks, this is assured by categorizing all applications into one of 45 classes of goods/services.[26] The classification of the register in this manner ensures adequate protection for the trademark owner—no one else can use that mark for similar goods/services—while allowing others the right to make use of popular trade names/marks in different sectors of the economy where the public are unlikely to be confused.

Specificity of trademarks has a basis in equity, something which can clearly be seen when one looks at the common law protection offered to unregistered trademarks. Passing off as a common law delict/tort has a basis in equity. The concept of specificity has developed here also under a different title, 'the common field of activity'.[27] The common field of activity ensures that you cannot claim goodwill in your trade name/mark outside the class of goods or services in which you trade. It is designed to ensure one person does not gain a complete monopoly over a name or mark which would unfairly restrict others gaining access to a (different) market. Domesticity and specificity help create the 'one mark many owners' ethos. It has proved to be an extremely efficient method for regulating trademarks, allowing adequate protection but also free access. The internet domain name system, or DNS, though, uses a 'one mark one owner' ethos which is alien to experienced trademark practitioners. This clash of cultures has led many domain name/trademark disputes.

14.2 **Domain names as badges of identity**

DNS is the system of global navigation used on the internet. Each page of information, each image, and each file is given an address called a uniform resource locator (URL) which, like the address of every home, office, or shop, must be unique if the user is to locate it. This address is made up of several sections illustrated below.

 Highlight Properties of a uniform resource locator (URL)

http://www.lse.ac.uk/law

The above is the homepage of the Law Department at the London School of Economics.

The URL may be broken down as follows:

http://—This page uses hypertext transfer protocol.

www.—This page is found on the World Wide Web.

➡

---

[26] Full classificatory list at <https://www.gov.uk/guidance/how-to-classify-trade-marks>.
[27] *Rolls Razor Ltd v Rolls (Lighters) Ltd* (1949) 66 RPC 137; *Fortnum & Mason plc v Fortnum Ltd* [1994] FSR 438.

> →
>
> **lse.ac.uk**—The unique address of the London School of Economics. This is made up of two domain names: a top-level domain and a second-level domain. Internet addresses are read right to left. The top-level domain is the .ac.uk section of the domain. This tells the user the address is used by a UK registered academic organization. The second-level domain comes to the left of the first period, i.e. lse. This is the identifier of the site operator. As a whole the domain name must be unique. There can be only one lse.ac.uk address, although variations such as lse.com, or lse.co.uk are possible. Before they can be used, second-level domains require to be registered, of which more below.
>
> **/law**—This is a tertiary or file location domain. Any text which follows the top-level domain is used to identify individual pages of information within the site managed by the owner of the domain name. Such tertiary domains do not require registration and will not be discussed further.

The key aspect of a domain name is the second-level domain. Second-level domains are available on a first-come, first-served basis, and may be obtained through any one of a number of domain name registries. Registries are private companies who have been accredited by the relevant registrar[28] and may usually offer registration in any one of a number of top-level domains.[29] Registration of a second-level domain is extremely cheap and simple with .co.uk and .com registrations costing as little as £6.99 per year. To get a second-level domain all you need to do is fill out an online form and give the registry your credit card details.

Although functionally domain names, once registered, are addresses of pages of information in the online environment, there is an important distinction between these domain names and traditional addresses in that the make-up of a domain name, in particular the exact nature of the second-level domain, is chosen by the registrant. This is quite unlike a traditional address and more like a trademark registration in that the registrant has control over the allocation of the identifier. Thus, while McDonald's may have a restaurant in your town or city, when searching for that restaurant you will navigate in part by an assigned address (such as 36 South Street) and in part by the familiar, and protected, brand identifiers of McDonald's such as the Golden Arches. You would not expect your local McDonald's to have a specific address such as 1 McDonald Road, but due to the way domain names are allocated you do expect McDonalds online presence to be at specific domains including mcdonalds.com and mcdonalds.co.uk.

Due to this dual nature of domain names as both address tools and brand identifiers, some domain names have attracted high values, and many domain names have

---

[28] A registrar, as distinct from a registry, is the regulatory authority tasked with the role of overseeing a particular TLD. The key registrar is the Internet Corporation of Assigned Names and Numbers (ICANN) which manages the generic top-level domains including the new generic top-level domains or New gTLDs. Country code TLDs such as .uk, .jp, and .fr are managed at a national level. The .uk registrar is Nominet UK. We will examine the roles, and rules, of ICANN and Nominet UK below.

[29] Any individual may register in any ICANN-regulated generic TLD. Some country code TLDs are restricted to citizens of that country such as the Greek country code TLD (.gr). Others, such as the UK's .uk, are open to registration by anyone in a similar manner to the generic TLDs.

been litigated over. The most valuable domain names are varied, but tend to show two characteristics: (1) they are located in the .com top-level domain, which is the prime real-estate of the domain name world,[30] and (2) the second-level domain is usually a short, generic, English-language term. It is exceedingly difficult to get accurate data on domain name sales but according to one report the most expensive internet domain name sold to date, is carinsurance.com which was sold in 2010 for $49.7m,[31] with other high-value transactions including the domain names insurance.com which sold for $35.6m also in 2010, vacationrentals.com which sold for $35m in 2007, and privatejet. com sold in 2012 for $30.1m.

The commercial value of some domain names suggests that it is possible for domain names to have brand value far exceeding their role as mere internet addresses. This reflects their selection rather than allocation. Domain names have much more in common with trademarks than with addresses. They are selected and registered much like a trademark. In addition they are developed to reflect brand identities in a similar way to trademarks. Some of the most famous brand identities of our age are based upon domain names. The 'old-world' identities of Coca-Cola, Mercedes, and Tesco have been joined by Amazon.com, eBay.com, and Google.com. Second, domain names can be treated as traditional property. In *Kremen v Cohen*,[32] the court considered the question of whether a domain name was intangible property. The Court of Appeal for the Ninth Circuit stated that a domain name is a form of intangible property because

(i)   it represents an interest of precise definition,

(ii) it is subject to exclusive possession or control, and

(iii) a registrant has a legitimate claim to exclusivity.[33]

Thus more and more domain names start to look like trademarks. They have value, they are registrable, and they are (legally) intangible property rights. The key difference with domain names is that they are awarded purely on a first-come, first-served basis with no examination of the application as found with trademarks. This vastly increases the risks of names being registered which are in breach of a trademark of another business or individual or even, given the low cost and simple process of registration, the risk that individuals or companies will deliberately register marks similar to those of famous or well-known brands (such as coca-coladrinks.net, or barclaysbank-online.co.uk), a process known as cybersquatting, or based on misspellings of well-known marks (such as macdonalds.com or eboy.com), a process known as typosquatting. Thus risks surround trademarks in the online environment at every turn.

---

[30] In an earlier paper the author referred to the .com top-level domain as 'the electronic equivalent of Rodeo Drive or Bond Street'. See A Murray, 'Internet Domain Names: The Trade Mark Challenge' (1998) *International Journal of Law and Information Technology* 285, 301.

[31] J Styler, 'The top 25 most expensive domain names', *GoDaddy* 29 October 2018 <https://www.godaddy.com/garage/the-top-20-most-expensive-domain-names/>.

[32] *Kremen v Cohen*, 337 F 3d 1024 (9th Cir. 2003).

[33] It should be noted this was not the first decision to set out this position. Domain names had previously been found to be a form of intangible property in the cases of *Caesars World Inc. v Caesars-Palace.com*, 112 F Supp 2d 502 (ED Va 2000) and *Online Partners.com Inc. v Atlanticnet Media Corp.*, 2000 US Dist LEXIS 783, 101242 (ND Cal 2000).

14.3 **Early trademark/domain name disputes**

This conflict of values quickly led to disputes over rightful ownership of domain names. These issues were first brought to the attention of the wider public by a journalist for *Wired* magazine named Joshua Quittner. Mr Quittner, while preparing a story for *Wired* on the potential value of commercially recognizable domain names,[34] registered the domain name 'mcdonalds.com' in an attempt to illustrate the risks faced by the owners of famous or well-known names. After a short flurry of communications between Mr Quittner and McDonalds (and their lawyers) Mr Quittner assigned the name to the McDonalds Corporation in return for a donation towards computer equipment for a primary school. While the actions of Mr Quittner may be seen to be harmless, the courts were suddenly abuzz with trademark lawyers seeking to reclaim valuable cyber-property that their clients had failed to secure.

The UK courts first wrestled with this matter in the case of *Pitman Training Ltd v Nominet UK*.[35] The dispute in this case centred around the right to use the domain name pitman.co.uk, and the competing interests of two parties, Pitman Training Ltd and Pearson Professional Ltd.[36] Both the training company and the publishing company had at one time been owned by a single company, but in 1985 they had demerged and Pearson Professional had bought the publishing business. As part of the demerger, Pitman Training Ltd agreed not to use the name Pitman, except in relation to their core business. The problem arose when the two companies, who had coexisted peacefully in the actual world for 11 years, tried to register their presence on the internet.

On 15 February 1996, Pearson registered the domain name pitman.co.uk, but took no action to develop their web presence. Then, on 15 March 1996, Pitman Training Ltd also registered the domain name with Nominet UK.[37] They went on to establish a web presence in July 1996. Pearson had no knowledge of the Pitman Training website until December 1996, but immediately upon discovering it they contacted both Pitman Training and Nominet UK, demanding that the right to use the domain name be reassigned to them. On 4 April 1997 Nominet, following threats of legal action from Pearson's lawyers, agreed to reassign the domain name to Pearson, a transfer affected on 7 April. On 9 April, Pitman issued a writ against Pearson and Nominet requiring the immediate reinstatement of their rights to the domain name.

The problem for the judge was each party was entitled to make use of the Pitman trade name in their respective fields. Trademarks, registered or unregistered, benefit from specificity. In virtual reality though there is no specificity of domain names: there can be only one pitman.co.uk and there is no method of differentiating between Pitman Training and Pitman Publishing. It was this lack of specificity which led to the dispute before the court. The decision of the court was that the plaintiffs had no viable or reasonably arguable cause of action against the second defendant (Pearson) and the interim

---

[34] J Quittner, 'Billions Registered', *Wired*, October 1994.

[35] [1997] EWHC Ch 367.

[36] Pearson Professional own Pitman Publishing Ltd who produce academic/student texts.

[37] Nominet is the .uk registrar meaning they oversee the allocation of all .uk top-level domain registrations. Such a duplication of registration should not have occurred. In the event of parties who have equal claim to second-level domain names Nominet runs a first-come, first-served policy, see: Nominet UK: Rules for the .uk domain and sub-domains.

injunction was lifted, allowing Nominet to ratify the transfer of registration to Pearson. The impact of this case in UK law is that the High Court was willing to uphold the policy of Nominet that registration of second-level domain names should be allowed on a first-come, first-served basis.

14.3.1 Cybersquatting before the UK courts

The *Pitman* case was rather unusual. That was two parties with competing rights, a bit like the equal claims to the name 'Budweiser' in *Anheuser-Busch*.[38] More common among the early cases were cybersquatting claims. Probably the first such case was that of *Harrods Ltd v UK Network Services Ltd*[39] This case involved a well-known UK cybersquatter, Mr Michael Lawrie. Mr Lawrie registered the domain name harrods.com which he then warehoused. The court determined that Mr Lawrie's possession of the domain name, and the potential use he may make of it, constituted trademark infringement and passing off. Unfortunately as Mr Lawrie did not turn up in court the arguments to support this contention were not outlined or discussed in full. This though was quickly remedied by what is still the key decision on cybersquatting in the UK, *British Telecommunications plc & Ors v One in a Million Ltd & Ors*.[40]

This was an appeal to the Court of Appeal by the defendants against summary judgment given to a number of leading British companies in a series of actions against them. The defendants dealt in domain names. They specialized in registering well-known names and trademarks without the consent of the person or company owning the goodwill in the name or mark and offering those names for sale to the owners of such goodwill. They registered burgerking.co.uk which they offered to Burger King for £25,000 and bt.org which they offered to British Telecommunications for £4,700. The plaintiffs objected to the defendants' registration of, among others marksandspencer. com, britishtelecom.co.uk, ladbrokes.com, virgin.org, cellnet.net, and sainsburys.com. At trial the judge, Jonathan Sumption QC,[41] had granted injunctions to restrain the defendants from such registration and dealings, explaining that:

    (a) it was enough for a plaintiff to show that a defendant intended to infringe the plaintiff's rights in future even though the mere registration of a deceptive company name or a domain name did not amount to passing off; and

    (b) the use of a trade mark in the course of the business of a professional dealer for the purpose of making domain names more valuable and extracting money from the trade mark owner amounted to 'use in the course of trade'.

The appellants appealed on the basis that the action was premature. They submitted that if a name could be used for a legitimate purpose, it was not an instrument of fraud and relief should not be granted unless it was established that the defendant either threatened to pass off or was, with another, part of a common design to pass off. They said that in their case they registered domain names with a view to making a profit either by selling them to the owners of the goodwill, using the blocking effect of the

---

[38] *Anheuser-Busch* (n. 22).
[39] Unreported, High Court, Ch. D, 9 December 1996.
[40] [1999] 1 WLR 903.
[41] Later Lord Sumption, Supreme Court Justice.

registration to obtain a reasonable price, or, in some cases, selling them to collectors or to other persons who could have a legitimate reason for using them. They submitted that that could amount neither to passing off nor a threat to pass off.

In dismissing the appeal, Aldous LJ analysed several strands of authority which had held that in the law of passing off injunctive relief may be granted before the harm occurs.[42] He discerned from those cases that the court has jurisdiction to grant injunctive relief where a defendant is equipped with or is intending to equip another with an instrument of fraud. He added that the question as to whether a name is an instrument of fraud must depend upon all the circumstances: for instance, a name which by reason of its similarity to another name will inherently lead to passing off is such an instrument but not if it would not inherently lead to passing off. The court should consider the similarity of the names, the intention of the defendant, the type of trade, and all the surrounding circumstances. If, after taking all the circumstances into account, the court should conclude that a name was produced to enable passing off, was adapted to be used for passing-off, and, if so used, was likely to be fraudulently used, an injunction would be appropriate.

He identified three categories of cases in which a court would grant an injunction: 'First, where there is passing-off established or it is threatened; second, where the defendant is a joint tortfeasor with another in passing-off either actual or threatened, and third, where the defendant has equipped himself with or intends to equip another with an instrument of fraud.'[43] After reviewing the party-to-party correspondence and other dealings between the parties, Aldous LJ concluded that 'there was clear evidence of systematic registration by the appellants of well-known trade names as blocking registrations and a threat to sell them to others.'[44] He was also satisfied that threats to infringe the trademarks of the claimants had been established. The defendants sought to sell domain names that were confusingly similar to registered trademarks. Those domain names indicated origin, which was the purpose for which they were registered, and they were to be used in relation to the services provided by the registrant who trades in domain names. The Court of Appeal concluded that the deputy judge's analysis in respect of passing off and trademark infringement had been correct.

BT v One in a Million is still the leading UK case law on both passing off and trademark infringement in the case of cybersquatting and domain name warehousing, but we must analyse a few further decisions before we move on to look at the extrajudicial procedures which have extensively replaced court actions in such circumstances.

The first case is *Phones4u Ltd v Phone4u.co.uk*.[45] Phones4u Ltd was a UK chain of mobile phone retailers. It adopted the name Phones4u for some of its stores and its

---

[42] In *Farina v Silverlock* (1855) 1 K&J 509 the defendant sold materials for an infringing product. An injunction was granted, inter alia, to prevent the defendant from enabling passing off; in *John Walker & Sons Ltd v Henry Ost & Co Ltd* [1970] RPC 489 an injunction was granted to prevent the supply of bottles and labels to facilitate passing off abroad, and in *Glaxo plc v Glaxowellcome Ltd* [1996] FSR 388 where the defendant had incorporated a company combining the name of two well-known public companies just prior to their merger. These cases collectively are sometimes known as 'instruments of fraud cases'.

[43] *One in a Million* (n. 40) 927.

[44] Ibid. 934.

[45] [2006] EWCA Civ 244.

mail order business in 1995, and changed its corporate name and other shop names in 1997. By 1999 the company enjoyed an annual turnover of nearly £44m and the red, white, and blue Phones4u logo appeared on most of Phones4u's 63 shops countrywide. By 2004 the number of such shops exceeded 350. Phones4u registered the domain name phones4u.co.uk in 1999, and launched its website in October 2000. The second defendant was an individual, Abdul Heykali, who had worked for a small mobile phone retailer in London. Towards the end of 1999, Mr Heykali set up a mobile phone retail business called Mobile Communication Centre. In August 1999, he registered the domain name phone4u.co.uk. In November 1999, the site read, 'this site will be going mobile soon . . . Up and running by 1st of January 2000.' By September 2000, however, the site's content was merely an image of a phone followed by '4U.co.uk'. The site finally went live in July 2001. At that time, a disclaimer appeared: 'Phone4U.co.uk are solely an Internet based company and do not have the costs associated with running high street shops . . . Phone 4U.co.uk is NOT connected with the high street mobile phone retailer Phones 4U.'

Although some key facts were disputed, the judge accepted that Mr Heykali had chosen phone4u.co.uk at the recommendation of a friend and in ignorance of the claimants' business for use in connection with an internet-based mobile phone company. The court was persuaded that Mr Heykali thought it common practice on the internet to combine descriptive words with the phrase '4U'. However, by February or March 2000 Mr Heykali had become aware of the claimants while searching for a Vodafone dealership which he obtained from the claimants themselves in March 2000. The claimants by then knew of Mr Heykali's domain name and expressed concern that emails intended for them were being misdirected to Mr Heykali. In response to a cease-and-desist letter from the claimants, Mr Heykali incorporated a company under the name Phone4U Ltd (later changed to Phone4u.co.uk Internet Ltd) and denied any wrongdoing. He also recognized that his domain name was potentially very valuable. The court found that he deliberately exaggerated the number of misdirected emails he had received, and falsely suggested to the claimants that he had already been offered £100,000 for the domain name.

For reasons that were never adequately explained, the claimants took no further steps to stop Mr Heykali's activities until proceedings were issued in February 2004. Following a decision of the High Court in March 2005, in which the court found that the claimants had no goodwill in the mark 'Phones4U' in August 1999 when the domain name was registered and that there had been no deception in the use of the domain name across the five-year period it had been in use, the claimants appealed to the Court of Appeal. The lead judgment was that of Lord Justice Jacob. He found that the test for passing off was that of the *Jif Lemon* decision: '(a) reputation, i.e. goodwill; (b) misrepresentation; and (c) damage or its likelihood'. The court went on to state that there did not have to be evidence of direct diversion of sales caused by misrepresentation in order to prove damage. Jacob LJ adopted the 'more modern' definition of damage: '(a) by diverting trade from the plaintiffs to the defendants; (b) by injuring the trade reputation of the plaintiffs whose [goods are] admittedly superior in quality to that of the defendants; and (c) by the injury which is inherently likely to be suffered by any business when on frequent occasions it is confused by customers or potential customers with a business owned by another proprietor or is wrongly connected with that business'.[46]

The court agreed with the appellants on the four arguments raised in support of their appeal, namely that:

1. The judge applied the wrong test in deciding whether or not the appellants had protectable goodwill. Jacob LJ was convinced that the appellants had sufficient goodwill by the relevant date to found a claim in passing off. Looking at the evidence he stated that 'To infer from all that, that hardly anyone knew the name, that the name was not "an attractive force which brings in custom" by August 1999 is simply untenable.'[47] The court held that the judge had incorrectly applied the test for distinctiveness required to obtain a trade mark registration in holding that the phrase 'Phones4u' was not inherently distinctive and had muddled the test for registration with the test for goodwill sufficient for passing off.

2. At the date of registration of 'phone4u.co.uk' an instrument of fraud had been created.

3. The judge wrongly characterized a large number of instances of deception as 'mere confusion'. The defendants' email evidence showed that customers of the appellant thought they were communicating with those who owned and ran the Phones4u shops. Examining the evidence, Jacob LJ could see 'clear and convincing evidence of damage to goodwill . . . the emails collectively tell a clear story of people trying to contact and deal with or complain to or make inquiries of, Phones4u—the chain of shops they already knew'.[48]

4. The judge erred in placing significance on the parties' coexistence for five years without deception without first considering the extent of the defendants' use of the mark during that time which had been almost non-existent. Turning finally to the trade mark infringement claim, the court considered the effect of the colour limitations on the registration. Jacob LJ sought the view of the Registry before formally delivering the judgment. The Registry replied that the registrar has always regarded colour limitations on the face of the register to be a limitation of rights. On this advice, the court held that, despite the original certificate of registration and the original entry being in monochrome, the colour limitation stated on the register was effective to limit the registrations to the colours claimed. Had there not been such a limitation, Jacob LJ stated that the defendants' use of the words 'Phones4u' or a trivial variant would have infringed the appellant's trademark.[49]

Thus the appellants were ultimately victorious in their passing off claim but Jacob LJ criticized the long delay of four years between the original complaint and the

---

[46] Per Slade LJ in *Chelsea Man v Chelsea Girl* [1987] RPC 189, 202.
[47] [2006] EWCA Civ 244, [31].
[48] *Phones4u* (n 45) [37]–[38].
[49] Ibid. [49]–[50].

commencement of proceedings. He quoted the words of James LJ in 1879: 'the very life of a trademark depends on the promptitude with which it is vindicated'.[50]

More recently two decisions of the CJEU have thrown the applicability of *One in a Million* into doubt. In *Céline Sarl v Céline SA*[51] the ECJ held:

> the purpose of a company, trade or shop name is not, of itself, to distinguish goods or services but to identify a company, and the purpose of a trade name or a shop name is to designate a business which is being carried on. Accordingly, where the use of a company name, trade name or shop name is limited to identifying a company or designating a business which is being carried on, such use cannot be considered as being 'in relation to goods or services' within the meaning of Art. 5 (1) of the (First Trade Marks) Directive.

Although the court tempered this slightly by finding that 'where the sign is not affixed to goods, there is still use "in relation to goods or services" where a third party uses that sign in such a way that a link is established between the sign which constitutes the company, trade or shop name of the third party and the goods marketed or the services provided by the third party' this does not seem to apply in the case where a domain name is simply registered and warehoused, as in the *One in a Million* scenario. In the later case of *Belgian Electronic Sorting Technology NV v Peelaers*,[52] in a discussion of the Misleading and Comparative Advertising Directive, the court held that:

> registration of a domain name was not a form of representation which was made in order to promote the supply of goods or services. It was nothing other than a formal act by which the body designated to manage domain names was asked to enter it into its database and link internet users who type in that domain name only to the IP address specified by the domain-name holder. That purely formal act did not necessarily imply that potential consumers could become aware of the domain name and was therefore not capable of influencing the choice of those potential consumers. In contrast, the use of the domain name to host a website was clearly intended to promote the supply of the goods or services of the domain-name holder.

The Intellectual Property and Enterprise Court has considered the impact of the first of these cases, *Céline*, on *One in a Million* in the case of *Vertical Leisure v Poleplus Ltd & Bowley*.[53] This was a case similar to *One in a Million*; an individual, Mr Bowley, registered a number of domain names around the word 'silkii' including silkii.co.uk. The name referred to a particular product of the claimant, a tool allowing the connection of a length of silk to a pole dancing pole allowing for the material to be incorporated into a pole dancing routine. The product had been showcased in the UK in early 2013 but not launched until April 2013. Based upon knowledge of the product at the early showcase events it was claimed the second defendant had registered the domain names. The Judge, HH Judge Hacon, was unsure as to whether *Céline* had changed the authority of *One in a Million* in relation to a trademark claim:

> so far as infringement of the trade mark was concerned, the Court of Appeal held that the defendants had no realistic prospect of success against the allegation of infringement under section 10(3) of the 1994 Trademarks Act 1994, in other words, the equivalent to article 5(2) of the trademark directive. I would be wary of concluding, at least beyond any doubt, that the law as set

---

[50] *Johnston v Orr-Ewing* (1879) 13 Ch D 434, 464.
[51] ECLI:EU:C:2007:497.
[52] ECLI:EU:C:2013:516.
[53] [2014] EWHC 2077 (IPEC).

out in BT remains unaltered, bearing in mind in particular Case C-17/06 *Céline SARL v Céline SA* and Case C-407/07 *L'Oréal SA v Bellure NV*; at least I would be wary of reaching that conclusion without further argument on the law for which there was no time today.[54]

The question was moot though for Judge Hacon could dispose of the case under the secondary passing off claim, finding that:

> by registering the domain names Mr Bowley did trade in circumstances by which a misrepre-sentation would be made to the relevant public who consulted the register, and, secondly, he created an instrument of fraud. Mr Bowley offered, as I have mentioned, the domain names for sale to the claimant because, by implication, he realised the message that they would convey, which was the only reason they had any value for the claimant. He has no realistic prospect of defending the action. Therefore, essentially for the reasons given by Aldous LJ, I conclude the claimant is entitled to summary judgment against Mr Bowley.[55]

The cases mentioned, *Céline* and *L'Oréal* suggest that registration of an identity is not 'use' in terms of Art. 5(2) of the Trade Mark Directive (and thus s. 10(3) of the Trade Marks Act). This suggests that on trademark grounds *One in a Million* is no longer clearly good law. As HH Judge Hacon makes clear though *One in a Million* remains good law for the tort of passing off, and as most claims of cybersquatting may be brought under either head, assuming goodwill is present, it is unlikely to affect the course of most claims before UK courts.

The High Court was given the opportunity to review this position in *Yoyo.Email Limited v Royal Bank of Scotland Group Plc*.[56] The case concerned a number of new generic domain names registered by Yoyo including *rbsbank.email*, *rbs.email*, *natwest.email*, and *coutts.email*. These registrations were challenged by RBS and heard under the ICANN UDRP. The UDRP panel found them to be infringing and ordered their transfer. Yoyo challenged this decision in the High Court claiming to be guilty of no wrongdo-ing. In deciding the application for declaratory relief HH Judge Dight examined the passing off position. As might be expected, given that this was not a trademark case, he did not refer to *Céline* and *L'Oréal* and simply disposed of the case under *One in a Million* principles. RBS set out that they did not seek summary judgment on the basis of use by the claimant of the Domain Names, merely on the basis of registration,[57] while YoYo argued that 'the way in which it intends to use the Domain Names in the course of its business means that there is no risk of confusion with the defendants' business and therefore no misrepresentation.'[58] In his examination, however, Judge Dight found that *One in a Million* was still good law, noting that Judge Hacon in *Vertical Leisure* had concluded that 'the decision of the Court of Appeal in One in a Million was "undoubtedly good law by which I am bound"', a position that he agreed in finding '*One in a Million* establishes a principle of law by which I am bound and leads me to the conclusion that the registration of the Domain Names by the claimant amounted to passing off.'[59]

---

[54] Ibid. [16].
[55] Ibid. [21].
[56] [2015] EWHC 3509 (Ch).
[57] Ibid. [11].
[58] Ibid. [12].
[59] Ibid. [16].

A further opportunity for review came the following year when the Intellectual Property Enterprise Court heard the case of *Michael Ross v Playboy Enterprises International, Inc.*[60] The case is very similar to the *Yoyo* case in that it involved a new generic Top Level Domain (see 14.5) in this case *playboy.london*. Again like *Yoyo* the claimant had suffered a loss in the UDRP process and was seeking to challenge this finding. The Judge Amanda Michaels (sitting as a Deputy Enterprise Judge) looked briefly at both trademark and passing off claims, again without reference to *Céline* and *L'Oréal*. She dismissed the trademark claims on the basis that 'PEI has not put forward any explanation of how such use of the Domain Name would infringe any of its registered UK trademarks.'[61] In concluding a slightly more detailed passing off analysis the judge found that *One in a Million* should be applied and that as the 'use of the word Playboy as the distinctive part of the Domain Name would be liable to be seen by a substantial proportion of members of the public in the UK as indicating some sort of connection to PEI and its extremely well-known goods and services, . . . the mere registration of the Domain Name would lead to passing off'.[62]

These cases have reiterated that neither *Céline* nor *Belgian Electronic Sorting Technology* are likely to have an impact on the English courts' approach to domain name disputes. As disputes tend to be dealt with under passing off not trademark law *Céline* is not applicable. Further, as instruments of fraud require no communication to the public *Belgian Electronic* is also not applicable. The courts have confirmed at every turn that *One in a Million* is still good law in relation to passing off claims. Following *Céline* though it is less clearly still authoritative in trademark claims.

14.4 **The ICANN UDRP**

The increasing numbers of domain name/trademark disputes that were being taken to the courts internationally led to calls for a cheaper, more efficient and more streamlined system of dispute resolution to be put in place. The opportunity to review the dispute resolution procedure applicable to the generic top-level domains (including essentially the .com domain) arose in the late 1990s during a wide-ranging review of the management of generic top-level domains.

From 1991, the registrar for generic top-level domains had been a small private contractor called Network Solutions Inc. who had a complete monopoly over registrations in the .com, .net, and .org domain name space. By the mid-1990s, this monopoly was being challenged by campaigners who believed it was unsuitable given the developing commercial value of, in particular, .com domains. The campaigners proposed that Network Solutions' monopoly be broken up, and that a not-for-profit organization known as the Internet Society take over regulation of the domain name registration process.[63] To give effect to these proposals the Internet Society created a working group to take them forward. The group known as the International Ad-Hoc Committee

---

[60] [2016] EWHC 1379 (IPEC).
[61] Ibid. [45].
[62] Ibid. [50]–[51].
[63] J Postel, *New Registries and the Delegation of International Top Level Domains* (1996) <http://ww.watersprings.org/pub/id/draft-postel-iana-itld-admin-01.txt>.

announced they would create seven new top-level domain names which would compete with .com and Network Solutions' monopoly.[64] The US federal government then entered the debate by directing that the domain name system should be privatized and that competition within the domain name system should be increased.[65] The campaigners for reform started working alongside the US National Telecommunications and Information Administration; the body was given management of the federal domain name project, and between them they drew up the by-laws for a new regulatory authority and set out that the body should have responsibility for, among other things, internet protocol addresses and domain names. On 1 October 1998, the new regulatory and management body for internet addressing was named: it would be known as the Internet Corporation for Assigned Names and Numbers (ICANN). The new regulator would be an American not-for-profit corporation managed by a representative board of directors drawn from around the world. By the terms of its articles of association it was authorized to take responsibility for several key areas of internet stability and governance.

 Highlight ICANN's responsibilities

ICANN are to oversee the operational stability of the internet by:

I.   Coordinating the assignment of Internet technical parameters as needed to maintain universal connectivity on the Internet;

II. Performing and overseeing functions related to the coordination of the Internet Protocol (IP) address space;

III. Performing and overseeing functions related to the coordination of the Internet domain name system (DNS), including the development of policies for determining the circumstances under which new top-level domains are added to the DNS root system;

IV. Overseeing operation of the authoritative Internet DNS root server system; and

V.   Engaging in any other related lawful activity in furtherance of items (I) through (IV).

One of ICANN's first challenges was the development of policies regulating the management and allocation of domain names to allow for competition in the registry market for the generic top-level domains .net, .org, and .com. To this end, ICANN set to work on its first active project: creating a register accreditation system that would allow new registries to enter the market. Trademark holders were understandably apprehensive about any changes to be introduced into the market for domain names. They were concerned that, by creating competition in the market for the generic top-level domains, alternative routes for cybersquatting would open up. In an attempt to meet these concerns the US Department of Commerce placed the trademark holders' concerns at the

---

[64] Final Report of the International Ad Hoc Committee: Recommendations for Administration and Management of gTLDs, 4 February 1997 <http://mailman.apnic.net/mailing-lists/apple/archive/1997/02/msg00008.html>.

[65] The White House, *A Framework for Global Electronic Commerce*, 1 July 1997.

centre of its proposed reforms, and made trademark dispute resolution a key part of ICANN's mandate. The result was the creation of a new alternate dispute resolution (ADR) system applicable to those cases where the intellectual property right holder can establish that the domain name registration of the current holder is 'abusive'.[66]

 Highlight Abusive registration (ICANN Rules)

An abusive registration occurs when the domain name is identical or misleadingly similar to a trade or service mark in which the complainant has rights; and:

(i) the holder of the domain name has no rights or legitimate interests in respect of the domain name; and

(ii) the domain name has been registered and is used in bad faith.

The new policy, known as the ICANN Uniform Domain Name Dispute Resolution Policy (UDRP) was formally adopted on 24 October 1999. Although called the ICANN UDRP, the dispute resolution component of the policy is not to be supplied by ICANN itself; rather it uses 'approved dispute-resolution service providers' who supply panellists to hear claims and who manage the administration of complaints.[67] The first UDRP claim was raised on 9 December 1999, the domain name in dispute being worldwrestlingfederation.com; this led to success for the claimant on 14 January 2000.[68]

The UDRP is a 'mandatory administrative procedure' meaning that all registrants who have registered in the generic top-level domains administered by ICANN are required to submit to the UDRP if a challenge is raised to their registration.

 Highlight Prerequisites for a UDRP claim

You are required to submit to a mandatory administrative proceeding in the event that a third party (a 'complainant') asserts to the applicable Provider, in compliance with the Rules of Procedure, that:

(i) your domain name is identical or confusingly similar to a trademark or service mark in which the complainant has rights; and

(ii) you have no rights or legitimate interests in respect of the domain name; and

(iii) your domain name has been registered and is being used in bad faith.

[UDRP Policy para. 4(a)]

---

[66] WIPO, 'The Management of Internet Names and Addresses: Intellectual Property Issue, Final Report of the WIPO Internet Domain Name Process' 30 April 1999 [152]–[228] <https://www.wipo.int/amc/en/processes/process1/report/finalreport.html>.
[67] See <https://www.icann.org/en/help/dndr/udrp/providers>.
[68] *World Wrestling Federation Entertainment Inc. v Michael Bosman*, Case No. D99–0001.

The key aspect of this requirement is part (iii), the question of whether the registrant is *mala fides*. This is explained further in para. 4(b) of the UDRP Policy where it is stated that a panellist may use as evidence that the registration and use of a domain name is in bad faith:

(i) circumstances indicating that you have registered or you have acquired the domain name primarily for the purpose of selling, renting, or otherwise transferring the domain name registration to the complainant who is the owner of the trademark or service mark or to a competitor of that complainant, for valuable consideration in excess of your documented out-of-pocket costs directly related to the domain name; or

(ii) you have registered the domain name in order to prevent the owner of the trademark or service mark from reflecting the mark in a corresponding domain name, provided that you have engaged in a pattern of such conduct; or

(iii) you have registered the domain name primarily for the purpose of disrupting the business of a competitor; or

(iv) by using the domain name, you have intentionally attempted to attract, for commercial gain, Internet users to your web site or other on-line location, by creating a likelihood of confusion with the complainant's mark as to the source, sponsorship, affiliation, or endorsement of your web site or location or of a product or service on your web site or location.

When faced with a complaint the registrant (or formally, under the UDRP Policy, the Respondent) has a variety of defences set out in para. 4(c) of the policy. These are:

(i) before any notice to you of the dispute, your use of, or demonstrable preparations to use, the domain name or a name corresponding to the domain name in connection with a bona fide offering of goods or services; or

(ii) you (as an individual, business, or other organization) have been commonly known by the domain name, even if you have acquired no trademark or service mark rights; or

(iii) you are making a legitimate noncommercial or fair use of the domain name, without intent for commercial gain to misleadingly divert consumers or to tarnish the trademark or service mark at issue.

The process itself is quick and simple. The complainant opens the dispute by filing a complaint with the provider of his choice and sending a copy to the respondent at the address shown on the Whois database.[69] At this point, the provider reviews the complaint for compliance with the UDRP rules. If the complaint is in compliance, the proceeding continues; if the complaint is non-compliant, the complainant has 5 days to remedy the deficiencies or the complaint will be deemed withdrawn. Within 20 calendar days of the complaint, the respondent must respond specifically to the allegations in the complaint and offer any defences which allow for the retention of the domain name (see para. 4(c) above). The respondent will be deemed to have defaulted if no response is filed within this 20-day window. Assuming the respondent responds, after the receipt of the response, the provider has 5 days to appoint a panel to hear the dispute. The panel is usually made up of one independent panellist, but under certain conditions may consist of a panel of three panellists. The make-up of panels is detailed in para. 6 of the ICANN Rules for Uniform Domain Name Dispute Resolution Policy.[70]

---

[69] See <https://www.whois.net/>.
[70] At <https://www.icann.org/resources/pages/rules-be-2012-02-25-en>.

Basically, this sets out that if neither party seeks the appointment of a three-member panel then a single panellist will be appointed by the dispute resolution provider.[71] However, under para. 6(c) if either the complainant or the respondent elects to have the dispute decided by a three-member panel, then the dispute resolution provider is required to convene a three-member panel consisting of one member selected from a list compiled by the complainant, one selected from a list compiled by the respondent, and the third being appointed by the dispute resolution provider.[72] Once appointed, the panel decides the complaint by electronic communications and is normally required to make a decision within 14 days of appointment, this decision to be notified to the parties within 3 days of being made. There is no right of appeal under the ICANN UDRP, although recourse may of course be made to the courts.[73]

Since the first ICANN UDRP decision was issued in January 2000, the UDRP has handled more than 65,000 disputes.[74] This makes the UDRP by far the most success-ful and far-reaching aspect of ICANN's functions. However, despite its popularity, the UDRP has been heavily criticized. The most vociferous critic of the UDRP has probably been Professor Milton Mueller of Syracuse University. In his book, *Ruling the Root*, he describes the UDRP as: 'heavily biased in favor of complainants. It allows the trademark holder to select the dispute provider, thereby encouraging dispute resolution provid-ers to complete for the allegiance of trademark holders. The resultant forum shopping ensures that no defendant-friendly service provider can survive.'[75] This may explain the pre-eminence of the WIPO UDRP service, which is seen to be sympathetic towards trademark holders' interests. Another critic, Professor Michael Froomkin, focuses on the procedure's failure to comply with some of the basic principles of natural justice. He notes that the UDRP:

> would have little chance of surviving ordinary 'arbitrary and capricious' review, because it denies respondents minimal levels of fair procedure that participants would be entitled to expect . . . three aspects of the UDRP are particularly troubling: (1) the incentive for provid-ers to compete to be 'complainant friendly'; (2) its failure to require actual notice combined with the short time period permitted for responses; and (3) the asymmetric consequences of a decision.[76]

Elsewhere, the current author has focused upon the lack of training or experience of UDRP panellists, noting that 'almost half of all panellists employed by the two major

---

[71] Rules [6(b)]. Note: further the cost of appointing the panellist will be met by the complainant. There is no cost to the respondent under this scenario.

[72] The regulations on the selection and appointment of panellists in such cases are contained in Rules [6(e)]. The fees for a three-member panel shall be paid in their entirety by the complainant, except where the election for a three-member panel was made by the respondent, in which case the fees shall be shared equally between the parties [6(c)].

[73] On which see *Yoyo.Email Limited* (n. 56) and *Michael Ross* (n. 60).

[74] Accurate data is hard to come by, but data supplied by the two largest dispute resolution service providers, WIPO and the National Arbitration Forum, show that to October 2018 WIPO had taken 42,070 cases while to end 2014 the ADRForum had taken over 23,000. While smaller providers had also taken thousands of claims. Sources: <https://www.wipo.int/amc/en/domains/statistics/cases.jsp> and <http://www.adrforum.com/news#Item2574>.

[75] Milton Mueller, *Ruling the Root: Internet Governance and the Taming of Cyberspace* (MIT Press 2002) 193.

[76] Michael Froomkin, 'Wrong Turn in Cyberspace: Using ICANN to Route around the APA and the Constitution' (2000) 50 *Duke Law Journal* 17, 136.

UDRP providers[77] are untrained and inexperienced in adjudication',[78] and the potential bias of panellists noting that:

> the WIPO UDRP panel contains a high proportion of intellectual property practitioners. Of the 193 WIPO panellists currently practicing within the legal profession 110 (57%) list a specialism in intellectual property. In addition, of the 41 academic lawyers listed, 22 (53.7%) are listed as intellectual property professors or lecturers. Although it is to be expected that a high proportion of UDRP panellists would be experienced in intellectual property law given the nature of the disputes in question, and although there is no claim here made of individual bias by panellists in favour of intellectual property rights holders, for those panellists involved in the practice of IP law it may be difficult to maintain neutrality as the major aspect of their full-time vocation is the protection of IP rights from erosion and this might be expected to mean that certain 'habits of thought' are prevalent.[79]

The UDRP may therefore be classified as a policy which has been successful and popular with the community at large, but one which is controversial. But with much of ICANN's public image tied to the UDRP, ICANN has had to do everything possible to support the UDRP and its service providers.

14.5 **The new gTLD process and dispute resolution**

More recently ICANN have had an opportunity to review their dispute resolution procedures with the introduction of the new generic Top Level Domains (gTLDs). The scarcity of available domain name space has meant a push for a greater number of gTLDs to alleviate pressure on the ever-expanding use of the DNS. The creation of 'New gTLDs' formally began in 2008. It reached fruition in 2011 when the ICANN Board agreed to allow applications for new gTLDs from any interested party upon payment of a substantial management fee.[80] By October 2018 1232 New gTLDs had been approved,[81] falling mostly into four categories: trademarks such as .cartier, .toshiba, and .barclays; geographical such as .vegas, .london, and .sydney; vocational such as .pharmacy, .realtor, and .attorney, and speculative such as .beer, .porn, and .poker.[82]

With such an expansion of available domain names there were obviously concerns raised by trademark holders. ICANN has met their concerns in a two-part process, a pre-screening process for the gTLDs themselves,s then an expedited form of the UDRP for registrations made within the new gTLD space.

The first stage was pre-screening and allowing for challenges to applications to register the new gTLD itself. Once all applications were received by the deadline of 29 March 2012 a period of objection opened up where objections against grant could

---

[77] The two major UDRP providers being WIPO and the National Arbitration Forum.

[78] Andrew Murray, 'Regulation and Rights in Networked Space' (2003) 30 *Journal of Law and Society* 187, 203.

[79] Ibid. 216.

[80] ICANN, *Approved Board Resolutions—Singapore*, 20 June 2011 <https://www.icann.org/resources/board-material/resolutions-2011-06-20-en>.

[81] Up to date data is at <https://newgtlds.icann.org/en/program-status/statistics>.

[82] The full list is at <http://newgtlds.icann.org/en/program-status/delegated-strings>.

be lodged on one of four grounds: string confusion (where the applied for name is confusingly similar to an already in use or applied for string, such as .bom or .cam); legal rights objections (where the name is confusingly similar to a legal trademark or right in a name, such as .coach or .merck); community objections (where a challenge may be brought by representatives of a community to whom the name is impliedly or implicitly addressed, such as .amazon or .patagonia); and finally a limited public interest challenge which may be brought where the gTLD string is contrary to generally accepted legal norms of morality and public order that are recognized under principles of international law. Each objection gives rise to an arbitration process with the WIPO Arbitration and Mediation Centre dealing with legal rights objections; the International Center for Dispute Resolution dealing with string confusion objections; and the International Center of Expertise of the International Chamber of Commerce dealing with both community and public interest challenges. Any concerned trademark holder could therefore lodge an objection with the WIPO Arbitration and Mediation Centre under the legal rights head. This led to 71 claims being lodged with WIPO including objections to .delmonte, .coach, and .moto. Once the objection was lodged the procedure followed was very similar to the UDRP procedure. The only addition was a case manager who had the power to consolidate claims relating to the same domain space for simpler disposal,[83] thereafter a single expert or three-expert panel would dispose of the objection.[84]

WIPO have published data on the process which reveals that of the 71 claims, two were dismissed for non-compliance, six were terminated, in three cases due to the withdrawal of gTLD applications. Expert panels upheld four legal rights objections, with dissenting opinions in three of these cases and rejected 59 legal rights objections. The only successful challenges were .delmonte, .direct, .weibo, and .微博. This process is now complete but with future rounds of new gTLDs planned by ICANN it will be dusted off once round two begins, which is unlikely to be before 2022.

A second protection for trademark holders throughout the gTLD process was the operation of the Trademark Clearinghouse (TMCH). This is an ICANN-mandated centralized repository of data on trademarks that are registered, court-validated, or protected by statute or treaty. It provides authenticated information about trademarks to registries and registrars. Brand owners were invited to submit their trademark data into the database prior to the launch of the new gTLD process (it could also be added afterwards). After the data was verified, trademark owners received a unique authentication key which gave them first priority in the registration of gTLDs which related to their trademarks (the sunrise period). Additionally, if an application was made to register a gTLD that matched a trademark on record, the applicant would be alerted to the registered trademark and would have to acknowledge the trademark before completing registration. Finally, upon completion of registration, TMCH would notify the owner on record that the domain had been registered, allowing them to raise an objection with the WIPO Arbitration and Mediation Centre.

Now that the first new gTLDs are operating we move on to the second phase of the dispute resolution process. This is dealing with registrations within new gTLDs such

---

[83] WIPO, Rules for New gTLD Dispute Resolution for Existing Legal Rights Objections 20 June 2011 <www.wipo.int/export/sites/www/amc/en/docs/wipolrorules.pdf> [7].

[84] Ibid. [8].

as sony.london or microsoft.coding. There are two procedures for dealing with these; the first is the Uniform Rapid Suspension system (URS). Like the UDRP, which also applies to New gTLDs, this is offered by providers, in this case the National Arbitration Forum and the Asian Domain Name Dispute Resolution Centre. It is a fast-track procedure for the clearest trademark infringement cases. It is not intended for use in proceedings with open questions of fact or more involved legal scenarios. While the substantive criteria of the URS are similar to the UDRP criteria, the URS is supposed to carry a higher burden of proof for complainants. The URS also includes a range of additional registrant defences over an extended time period. The only remedy a URS panel may grant a successful complainant is the temporary suspension of a domain name for the remainder of the registration period. The URS Rules and Procedure are very similar to the UDRP except that it is only available to registered trademark or service mark holders,[85] it is only available against registrations in New gTLDs,[86] and has a higher standard of proof than the UDRP (being essentially an administrative rather than judicial process) of 'clear and convincing evidence'[87] as against a 'preponderance of evidence' (balance of probabilities) for the UDRP. In return for the higher standard of proof a simpler, cheaper, and more streamlined process is available for the claimant. Whereas the UDRP costs on average $1500, can take up to 60 days, and allows for unlimited annexes as well as amendments and supplemental filings, the URS costs $375, allows only three annexes and no amendments or supplemental filings, and vitally decides claims in under 21 days. Unlike the UDRP, and perhaps learning from the Nominet DRS (discussed in 14.6), the URS has an appeals process. By para. 12 of the Procedure:

> Either party shall have a right to seek a *de novo* appeal of the Determination based on the existing record within the URS proceeding for a reasonable fee to cover the costs of the appeal. An appellant must identify the specific grounds on which the party is appealing, including why the appellant claims the Examiner's Determination was incorrect.

The Procedure or Rules give little detail as to how appeals are to be run but make it clear that a panel must hear the appeal. The first URS decision was facebok.pw, decided in October 2013. The URS has however proven to be quite unpopular. WIPO does not offer URS while ADR Forum, who is far and away the major URS provider has dealt with only 930 cases from its launch to October 2018.[88]

In addition to the URS there is the Trademark Post-Delegation Dispute Resolution Procedure (Trademark PDDRP). This is a much more complex and judicial procedure intended to be used where a New gTLD Registry is accused of supporting trademark infringement at the top level or second level (i.e. where a trade ark owner believes a registry is facilitating trademark infringement *mala fides*). This like the Nominet DRS is a multi-part process. First a complaint must be filed with the relevant service provider, in this case the WIPO Arbitration and Mediation Centre. A complaint is limited to 5,000 words or 20 pages, excluding attachments, unless the WIPO Center determines

---

[85] URS Procedure [1.2.5].
[86] URS Rules [3(f)].
[87] URS Procedure [8.2].
[88] Data from <http://www.adrforum.com/SearchDecisions>. By comparison WIPO dealt with 3,074 UDRP cases in 2017 alone.

that additional material is necessary. Assuming the complaint is valid, within five days the complaint will be sent for a threshold review. This is a review by a single panellist to determine whether the complaint satisfies the criteria set out in Section 9 of the Trademark PDDRP.[89] Assuming the threshold review is successful, only then will the Registry be invited to file a response. This should be done within 45 days of the threshold review.[90] Thereafter the service provider has 21 days to form either a single-person or three-person review panel along lines similar to the UDRP,[91] and the panel must 'make reasonable efforts to ensure that the Expert Determination is issued within 45 days of the appointment of the Expert Panel and absent good cause, in no event later than 60 days after the appointment of the Expert Panel.'[92] The Panel have a number of remedies available to them. They may:

(1) order 'remedial measures for the registry to employ to ensure against allowing future infringing registrations, which may be in addition to what is required under the registry agreement, except that the remedial measures shall not:

   (a) Require the Registry Operator to monitor registrations not related to the names at issue in the PDDRP proceeding; or

   (b) Direct actions by the registry operator that are contrary to those required under the Registry Agreement';

(2) 'Suspend the accepting new domain name registrations in the gTLD until such time as the violation identified in the Determination is cured or a set period of time'; or

(3) 'In extraordinary circumstances where the registry operator acted with malice, providing for the termination of a Registry Agreement.'.[93] As with the URS there is an appeal *de novo* permitted under s. 20 and by s. 21 ICANN will suspend all remedies for 20 days to allow for an appeal. This procedure is unlikely to be used frequently and at the date of writing there are no PDDRP decisions or cases pending.

14.6 **The Nominet DRS**

Nominet UK set up their dispute resolution procedure in autumn 2001, with the first published 'Expert' decision coming on 15 November 2001.[94] Although based in part on the ICANN UDRP, there are essential differences between the Nominet DRS and the UDRP, most obviously the opportunity to obtain summary decision where the complaint is undefended, the addition of a mediation procedure in defended complaints, and the opportunity for an appeal against the decision of a Nominet expert.

---

[89] Available via <http://newgtlds.icann.org/en/program-status/pddrp>.
[90] Trademark PDDRP, s. 10.
[91] Ibid. s. 13.
[92] Ibid. s. 19.1.
[93] Ibid. ss. 18.3.1–18.3.3.
[94] *Eli Lilly & Company v Clayton* [2001] DRS 1.

To raise a complaint the complainant must file a complaint with Nominet, either physically, or via the Nominet website.[95] The rules governing the complaint (and the response if one is forthcoming) are then to be found in the 'Dispute Resolution Service Policy' (the Policy).[96] Paragraph 4(3) of the Policy sets out in full the requirements of the complaint document. There is a strict word limit of 5,000 words (not including annexes and appendices);[97] it must specify how and where the complainant may be contacted;[98] specify (where known) the respondent's contact details;[99] set out the domain name which is the subject of the dispute and the name or mark which is identical or similar to the domain name and in which the complainant asserts it has rights;[100] and describe in accordance with the Policy the grounds on which the complaint is made including, in particular, what rights the complainant asserts in the name or mark; why the domain name should be considered to be an abusive registration in the hands of the respondent; and discuss any applicable aspects of paragraph 5 of the policy, as well as any other grounds which support the complainant's assertion.[101] This complaint if found to be valid is then sent by Nominet's DRS team to the respondent who has 15 days to respond.[102] If no response is forthcoming the complainant can seek a summary decision.[103] If a response is received the complainant is then given a final five days to submit to them a reply to the respondent's response.[104] At the end of submission of the documents of pleading Nominet will (if both sides are engaged) refer the dispute to informal mediation under paragraph 10 of the Policy. The mediation procedure is done by telephone and email and may last for up to 10 days.[105] If mediation is unsuccessful, or if there is no reply to the complaint making mediation impossible, then the dispute may be referred to an independent 'Expert', who acts as an arbiter and decides the dispute.

To succeed under the DRS Policy a complainant must establish two things: (1) that they have rights in respect of a name or mark which is identical or similar to the domain name;[106] and (2) that the domain name, in the hands of the respondent, is an abusive registration.[107] The first limb of this test is relatively easy to establish with the Appeal Panel in *Seiko UK Ltd v Designer Time/Wanderweb* noting that '[t]he requirement to demonstrate

---

[95] Although it should be noted a physical (signed) copy of the complaint still requires to be lodged with Nominet.

[96] <https://s3-eu-west-1.amazonaws.com/nominet-prod/wp-content/uploads/2017/10/17150434/final-proposed-DRS-policy.pdf>.

[97] DRS Policy 4.3.1.

[98] Ibid. 4.3.3.

[99] Ibid. 4.3.4.

[100] Ibid. 4.3.5.

[101] Ibid. 4.3.6.

[102] Ibid. 7.1

[103] Ibid. 12.1.

[104] Ibid. 9.1.

[105] Ibid. 10.5.

[106] Ibid. 2.1.1. Note 'Rights' are defined as: 'rights enforceable under English law. However, a Complainant will be unable to rely on rights in a name or term which is wholly descriptive of the Complainant's business' in [1] of the Policy.

[107] Ibid. 2.1.2. Note an 'Abusive Registration' is defined as: 'a Domain Name which either: (i) was registered or otherwise acquired in a manner which, at the time when the registration or acquisition took place, took unfair advantage of or was unfairly detrimental to the Complainant's Rights; OR (ii) has been used in a manner which took unfair advantage of or was unfairly detrimental to the Complainant's Rights' in [1] of the Policy.

"rights" is not a particularly high threshold test'[108] with, among others, personal names,[109] and registered company names[110] being sufficient to establish this limb of the test.

The second limb is more testing. To establish an abusive registration the complainant is referred to paragraph 5 of the Policy, which sets out a number of situations in which abusive registration will be deemed to have occurred.

 Highlight Abusive registration (selected Nominet rules)

A non-exhaustive list of factors which may be evidence that the Domain Name is an Abusive Registration is as follows:

(A) Circumstances indicating that the Respondent has registered or otherwise acquired the Domain Name primarily:

   (i) for the purposes of selling, renting or otherwise transferring the Domain Name to the Complainant or to a competitor of the Complainant, for valuable consideration in excess of the Respondent's documented out-of-pocket costs directly associated with acquiring or using the Domain Name;

   (ii) as a blocking registration against a name or mark in which the Complainant has Rights; or

   (iii) for the purpose of unfairly disrupting the business of the Complainant;

(B) Circumstances indicating that the Respondent is using or threatening to use the Domain Name in a way which has confused or is likely to confuse people or businesses into believing that the Domain Name is registered to, operated or authorised by, or otherwise connected with the Complainant;

(C) The Complainant can demonstrate that the Respondent is engaged in a pattern of registrations where the Respondent is the registrant of domain names which correspond to well known names or trade marks in which the Respondent has no apparent rights, and the Domain Name is part of that pattern.

(D) The Domain Name is an exact match (within the limitations of the character set permissible in domain names) for the name or mark in which the Complainant has Rights, the Complainant's mark has a reputation and the Respondent has no reasonable justification for having registered the Domain Name.

In addition, under paragraph 5.3, Cybersquatters who are engaged in the process of warehousing domain names are caught by a specific provision that 'there shall be a presumption of Abusive Registration if the Complainant proves that Respondent has been found to have made an Abusive Registration in three or more Dispute Resolution Service cases in the two years before the Complaint was filed'.

Once the complainant has established a prima facie case the burden of proof switches to the respondent. Paragraph 8 of the Policy contains a non-exhaustive list of factors which may be evidence that the domain name is not an abusive registration.

---

[108] [2002] DRS 248, [9].

[109] *Stoneygate 48 Ltd v Rooney* [2006] DRS 3844.

[110] *JF Home Improvements Ltd v Giddy* [2005] DRS 3051.

Highlight Defences to Abusive registration (selected Nominet rules)

A non-exhaustive list of factors which may be evidence that the Domain Name is not an Abusive Registration is as follows:

(A) Before being aware of the Complainant's cause for complaint (not necessarily the 'complaint' under the DRS), the Respondent has:

   (i) used or made demonstrable preparations to use the Domain Name or a domain name which is similar to the Domain Name in connection with a genuine offering of goods or services;

   (ii) been commonly known by the name or legitimately connected with a mark which is identical or similar to the Domain Name; or

   (iii) made legitimate non-commercial or fair use of the Domain Name.

(B) The Domain Name is generic or descriptive and the Respondent is making fair use of it.

Perhaps unsurprisingly these defences have been the subject of a great degree of criticism and discourse. Possibly the most controversial decision was that of *Ryanair Ltd v Coulston*.[111] The respondent in that dispute was an individual called Michael Coulston. He once had a bad experience when travelling with Ryanair in which his luggage was temporarily lost and his holiday ruined, since when he devoted some considerable time and energy to publicizing what he perceived as deficiencies in the way in which Ryanair dealt with problems and complaints by its customers. He did this under the campaign name the 'Ryanair Refund Campaign'. As part of his activities he registered the domain name ryanair.org.uk on 20 September 2003 and used it as the address for his campaign by hosting a site critical of Ryanair.

Mr Coulston claimed he made a non-commercial fair use of the name as permitted under of the Policy. Ryanair claimed that the actions of Mr Coulston were designed to confuse Ryanair customers (and potential customers) and as such were for the purpose of unfairly disrupting the business of the complainant. In deciding the dispute. the expert, Anna Carboni, found that:

> Although I do not have full details of the chronology of statements and information posted to the Respondent's website, it is probable—as he asserts—that his initial purpose in registering the Domain Name was to tell his own story of the lost baggage and to comment on the Complainant's customer complaints policies. Nevertheless, my findings in relation to the inherent likelihood of confusion in adopting an essentially identical Domain Name to the mark Ryanair, lead me to conclude that the Domain Name was from the start registered in a manner which took unfair advantage of and was unfairly detrimental to the Complainant's Rights and, as such, was an Abusive Registration.

Unsurprisingly there has been a great deal of criticism of that decision with many commentators suggesting that somehow it is a restriction on the right to free speech. But

[111] [2006] DRS 3655.

if one examines the decision closely it is clear that it turned on some very narrow facts. Mr Coulston lost because the domain name ryanair.org.uk was simply too close in character to the complainant's ryanair.co.uk and customers were being confused. Mr Coulston admitted in his evidence that the emails he received at ryanair.org.uk were predominantly (in descending order of frequency): (1) spam; (2) messages from people who urgently need to change or correct booking details; (3) messages from people who have not received a confirmation of a booking; (4) messages from people with general Ryanair questions (e.g. about baggage allowances); (5) messages from people wanting to criticize Ryanair; and (6) messages from people wanting to praise Ryanair. Thus it is clear people were confusing his site with the official Ryanair site when it came to open-ing communications with the airline.[112] The decision of the expert was really that Mr Coulston's name selection for his site was deliberately chosen to mirror the name of the 'official' website which directly caused confusion. Mr Coulston was free to choose a more fitting domain name for his site such as ryanaircampaign.org, which he did and which following a further complaint by the airline to the ICANN UDRP was ruled not to be in bad faith.[113]

Once an expert decision is made either party then has 15 days to lodge an appeal.[114] If an appeal is made an appeal panel of three experts is convened. The appeal panel con-siders all the evidence laid before the expert at the original hearing and may addition-ally consider two further documents: an appeals notice and an appeal notice response, both of which are limited to 1,000 words. The panel has complete discretion to review all evidence from the original hearing and may make decisions by majority. Once the appeal decision is made the DRS is closed and the only route of further recourse open to the parties is to refer their dispute to the courts.

14.6.1 Reviewing the Nominet DRS

The DRS has proven to be extremely robust. It has dealt with in excess of 12,000 disputes, yet very few cases have left the DRS for the courts. The first was an attempt to by-pass the DRS procedure by seeking a judicial review of the initial DRS decision rather than following the appeal procedure set out in the policy. The case involved the domain name itunes.co.uk which had been registered by a company called Cyberbritain Group Ltd A DRS claim was raised by Apple Computer Inc., owners of the iTunes brand. The itunes.co.uk registration had been made before the UK trade-mark application was published. However, Apple Computer Inc.'s complaint related only to the later use of the name. In her decision the independent expert, Claire Milne, found that following the launch of Apple's iTunes music download service this use included:

(1) direction of traffic on the domain to a website owned by an associate company of Cyberbritain Group Ltd;

(2) an offer to sell the domain name to Napster;

---

[112] Admittedly this may have been out of frustration as Ryanair offer limited means of commu-nication except by premium rate telephone number.

[113] *Ryanair Ltd v Michael Coulston*, WIPO Case No. D2006–1194.

[114] DRS Policy 20.1.

(3) direction of traffic to Napster under an affiliate scheme (from which profit would be generated); and

(4) an offer to sell the domain name for £50,000. On the basis of these findings, the expert found that the registration was abusive and ordered transfer.

Mr Cohen (the owner of Cyberbritain Group Ltd) stated, following the decision, that he would not use the DRS appeals procedure but instead he intended to apply for judicial review. Cyberbritain Group Ltd duly started judicial review proceedings. Apple Computer, Inc. joined as an interested party and Nominet argued that (a) they were not subject to judicial review, and (b) failure to use the appeal stage of the DRS barred Cyberbritain from seeking judicial review. Apple Computer, Inc. also argued that Cyberbritain had waited too long to apply. At an initial hearing the judge rejected the application to judicially review Nominet, citing the failure to use the appeal process and the delay. He avoided the question of whether they were judicially reviewable, as he did not need to decide it. The domain name has since been transferred to Apple Computers, Inc. as decided by the expert.

A second, more recent, case asked whether the courts could review cases of abuse registration independently of the Nominet DRS.[115] Mr Toth is a well-known 'domainer', the accepted name for someone who speculates in the value of domain names (and who may or may not be a cybersquatter). He had registered the domain name emirates.co.uk and had then been subjected to the full application of the Nominet DRS following a complaint from Emirates Airline. At the initial hearing the expert found for Mr Toth and ejected the Emirates complaint, but on appeal the panel upheld the complaint and decided that the domain name should be transferred. Mr Toth then applied to the court for a declaration that the domain name was not an abusive registration within the meaning of the policy. Emirates argued that the parties had agreed to the Nominet DRS and that Mr Toth's contract with Nominet did not provide for a cause of action independent of that procedure. Mr Toth argued that the policy did not prevent a *de novo* challenge in the courts. Initially, before the Patents County Court, Mr Toth succeeded but on appeal to the Chancery Division Mann J overturned this and found that the court had no jurisdiction to review the decision of the DRS. He examined the contract that Mr Toth had agreed to when he registered the domain name and found 'the court can have no role to play in any determination about abusive registration. The contract creates and completely regulates the dispute in such a way as to leave nothing for the court to bite on.'[116] In reply to a query from Mr Toth as to what therefore was meant by para. 20 of the Procedure which requires Nominet to stay the DRS Procedure if court proceedings are brought, Mann J suggested this would be in relation to cases within the normal jurisdiction of the court such as a trademark disputes.

These cases have given considerable steel to the Nominet DRS. The independence the courts have granted it mean that it provides a strong regime for the resolution of disputes in the .uk domain name space.

---

[115] *Toth v Emirates* [2012] EWHC 517 (Ch).
[116] Ibid. [48].

14.7 **Conclusions**

To suggest that domain names and brand identifiers such as trademarks fulfil the same function is wrong, but to say they have similar functions (and often values) is right. The protection of brand identity, and brand values, online has been at the forefront of much litigation in recent years. The incredible growth of the domain name system caught out those who seek to protect traditional IP portfolios and those who regulated the domain name system were caught out by the huge potential values of what they had on offer. The early cases of cybersquatting, domain name warehousing, and concurrent use demonstrated a 'clash of cultures' between the two. The arrival of the extrajudicial dispute resolution procedures at the turn of the millennium has done much to solve this problem. Although neither the ICANN UDRP nor the Nominet DRS are perfect, they are bridging the divide between the two cultures and may be put down as one of the few successes of 'internet law'.

▌ TEST QUESTIONS

Question 1

Flutter Inc. (an online gambling site) has always operated from the domains Flutter.com and Flutter.co.uk but they have just become aware of two new websites Flutterbetting.com and Flutterwager.co.uk. The global board is concerned that the owners of these sites may harm their business by damaging their goodwill with existing and potential customers and want advice on what to do next. An investigation has revealed that Flutterbetting.com has been registered with registry GoMammy.com by an Italian gambling service Giochi Sportivi SpA. An under-construction page reveals that they intend to use it to run an online casino gambling service similar to Flutter's. An individual named Peter Flutterwager has registered Flutterwager.co.uk with the UK registry, 2&2.co.uk. The site currently resolves only to a 2&2 holding page saying the site is awaiting development. There is no other information available on Mr Flutterwager's intentions for Flutterwager.co.uk.

The board have asked for your advice on what actions, if any, they should institute against either or both these domain name registrations. The board is also considering registering the domain .flutter under the new gTLD process so they could offer sites such as slots .flutter, poker. flutter, blackjack.flutter, and roulette.flutter. They want to know how much this would cost and what procedure they need to follow.

Write your advice to the board on all of these issues.

Question 2

Do you believe the ICANN/Nominet UDRP procedures provide an equitable system for resolving domain name disputes? How could they be improved?

Question 3

Some have suggested the new gTLDs lead to excessive costs as defensive or precautionary measures are taken by brand identities. Are the new gTLDs a positive or retrograde step in your view?

FURTHER READING

Books

T Bettinger and A Waddell (eds.), *Domain Name Law and Practice: An International Handbook* (2nd edn, OUP 2015)

Ge Levine, *Domain Name Arbitration: A Practical Guide to Asserting and Defending Claims of Cybersquatting Under the Uniform Domain Name Dispute Resolution Policy* (Legal Corner 2015)

M Mueller, *Ruling the Root: Internet Governance and the Taming of Cyberspace* (MIT Press 2002)

J Wolfe and A Chasser, *Domain Names Rewired: Strategies for Brand Protection in the Next Generation of the Internet* (Wiley 2013)

Chapters and articles

L Helfer and G Dinwoodie, 'Designing Non-National Systems: The Case of the Uniform Domain Name Dispute Resolution Policy' 43 *William & Mary Law Review* 141 (2001)

J Lipton: 'Beyond Cybersquatting: Taking Domain Name Disputes Past Trademark Policy' 40 *Wake Forest Law Review* 1361 (2005)

A Murray: 'Internet Domain Names: The Trade Mark Challenge', *International Journal of Law and Information Technology* 285 (1998)

E Null and D Prahl, 'The New Generic Top-Level Domain Program: A New Era of Risk for Trademark Owners and the Internet', (2011) 101 *Trademark Reporter* 1757

Brand identities, search engines, and secondary markets

While the ADR procedures offered by among others ICANN and Nominet, discussed in chapter 14, remain the most commonly employed procedures with respect to online trademark disputes, with on average 289 cases per month raised with WIPO alone in 2018, much recent focus has been on the wider interaction between trademarks and the digital environment. Two key areas of dispute have arisen, the employment of marks by search engines and the use of marks in advertising on webpages and secondary marketplaces such as Ebay and Amazon. The first is due to a diminution of the role of domain names with the creation of so called omniboxes as replacements for the old-fashioned address bar in web browsers. Users rely on domain names much less following this development. Now a user is much less likely to type 'macdonalds.com' looking for the fast-food restaurant only to find that that is an advertising redirect portal; instead, they will type 'macdonalds' into the omnibox and be taken to the Google search page which opens with 'showing results for mcdonalds' and a link to the official McDonald's page. The second is the result of the increased value and importance of online advertising and online markets. To trade in the modern world means to be found online, and to be able to trade online. With the predominance of the ADR procedures in domain name disputes, recent case law has focused less on domain names and more on search, online advertising, and secondary markets such as eBay.

15.1 Jurisdiction and online trademark disputes

While the modern ADR systems for domain name disputes discussed in the previous chapter can avoid jurisdictional challenges through contractual agreements the question of jurisdiction, as so often seems to be the case, raises its head again in relation to online trademark abuses. Thus the question of whether my UK trademark is capable of being applied in a dispute I may have with Google about the placement of an advertisement which is carried on the google.com search page but not on the google.co.uk page is significant. Is that page somehow located in the United States or given that it may be accessed in the UK is there vitally 'use' of the mark by Google in the UK? Recently both the CJEU and the Court of Appeal have addressed this issue giving us clear guidance.

The CJEU addressed this question in *Wintersteiger AG v Products 4U Sondermaschinenbau GmbH*.[1]

 Case study *Wintersteiger AG v Products 4U Sondermaschinenbau*

Wintersteiger are an Austrian company who make and sell ski and snowboard servicing tools, replacement parts, and accessories which they sell internationally. It owns the Austrian trademark 'Wintersteiger'. Products 4U, is a German company. It also develops and sells ski and snowboard servicing tools. It also sells accessories for tools made by other manufacturers, in particular Wintersteiger. The sale of those accessories, which Products 4U described as 'Wintersteiger-Zubehör' (Wintersteiger accessories) was not authorized by Wintersteiger. Products 4U sells its goods internationally, including in Austria. In December 2008 Products 4U started to use the keyword 'Wintersteiger' in relation to adverts placed using the Google Adwords programme (which among other things placed ads next to Google natural search returns for that term). Vitally that use made by Products 4U of the term was limited to Google's German top-level domain, that is, the website google.de. The court noted that 'the advertisement on "google.de" gave no indication that there was any economic link between Wintersteiger and Products 4U. On the other hand, Products 4U had not entered any advertisement linked to the search term "Wintersteiger" in Google's Austrian top-level domain, this being the website "google.at".'

[at [12]]

Wintersteiger raised an action in the Austrian courts claiming that the Austrian courts had jurisdiction under Art. 5(3) of Brussels Regulation,[2] basing their argument on the fact that google.de could be accessed in Austria, and that the site was configured in German, the language that was also spoken in Austria. Products 4U argued that since google.de was directed exclusively at German users, the advertisement at issue was therefore also intended only for German customers and the Austrian courts had no jurisdiction.

The court took a narrow approach, probably to limit the option of forum shopping where local search pages such as google.de or google.at are accessible throughout the EU. The court began by observing that:

> the rule of special jurisdiction laid down, by way of derogation from the principle of jurisdiction of the courts of the place of domicile of the defendant, in Art. 5(3) of the regulation is based on the existence of a particularly close connecting factor between the dispute and the courts of the place where the harmful event occurred, which justifies the attribution of jurisdiction to those courts for reasons relating to the sound administration of justice and the efficacious conduct of proceedings.[3]

This meant that the mere accessibility of a web page from within a member state did not give that member state jurisdiction to hear claims regarding the alleged infringement of national trade mark rights.

---

[1] ECLI:EU:C:2012:220.
[2] Council Regulation (EC) No 44/2001. NB! The original Brussels Regulation has now been repealed and replaced by the 'recast' Regulation No 1215/2012.
[3] *Wintersteiger* (n. 1) [18].

The court confirmed that the last phrase of Art. 5(3) means both the place where the damage occurred (i.e., where the event which may give rise to liability resulted in damage); and the place of the event giving rise to the damage.[4] The place where the damage occurred is determined by identifying the 'centre of interests'[5] of the person whose rights have been infringed. In an action 'relating to infringement of a trademark registered in a Member State through the use, by an advertiser, of a keyword identical to that trade mark on a search engine website operating under a country-specific top-level domain of another Member State may be brought before the courts of the Member State in which the trademark is registered.'[6] The event giving rise to the damage in a case such as this would be 'the activation by the advertiser of the technical process' aimed at displaying the advertisement. On that basis, the 'place of the event' would be the place of establishment of the advertiser and not of the provider of the referencing service.[7] In the instant case therefore the relevant jurisdiction would be either Austria (as the place of registration of the trademark) or Germany (as the place of establishment of the advertiser), the location of the service provider or its servers was not relevant.[8]

The Court of Appeal has recently added to this analysis in the *Argos Ltd v Argos Systems Inc.* appeal.[9]

 Case study *Argos Ltd v Argos Systems Inc.*

Argos Systems Inc (ASI) provides computer-assisted design systems for the construction of buildings. It has been trading under the name Argos since 1991. In January 1992 it purchased the domain name *argos.com*. ASI has never traded in the European Union and apparently has no intention of doing so. In 1996 Argos Ltd obtained the domain name *argos.co.uk*. There is evidence customers who intended to visit Argos UK's website would mistakenly visit *argos.com*. From January 2012 Google Analytics revealed 89 per cent of traffic to ASI's website was from the UK and 85 per cent of these users navigated away from the website almost immediately. Given the level of UK traffic to its website, ASI signed up to Google's AdSense programme and used geo-targeting code so that the adverts were not displayed to internet users based in the US but they were displayed to those coming from the UK. Over the course of almost seven years ASI managed to make around $100,000 of revenue from adverts. Many of the adverts were for Argos Ltd. As a result, ASI received some of the money Argos Ltd paid to Google. Argos Ltd's case was that, in addition to its legitimate US operations, ASI was also operating a separate advertising business for the UK market. This meant it was 'targeting' the UK and was committing acts of infringement which came within the territorial scope of the English courts. In the circumstances, Argos Ltd claimed the use of the domain name *argos.com* as the front page for this UK-targeted advertising business constituted trademark infringement.

---

[4] Ibid. [19].
[5] Ibid. [21].
[6] Ibid. [29].
[7] Ibid. [37].
[8] Ibid. [36].
[9] [2018] EWCA Civ 2211.

The case initially came before Richard Spearman QC (sitting as a Deputy Judge of the Chancery Division). He found that ASI was not targeting UK consumers.[10] His reasoning was that the question is not one of the subjective intention of the advertiser, but rather one of the objective effect of its conduct viewed from the perspective of the average consumer.[11] The average consumer was split into sub-classifications, (i) enquiring and (ii) unenquiring. The first would assume some connection with their browsing history if they saw a third party advert on a website. The second would not worry about the reason for the advert being there.[12] The judge felt that although the ASI website was getting a lot of visitors from the UK, they quickly established the site was not a UK-facing website and left. If they saw adverts while there the 'enquiring' consumer would assume the adverts had been placed there by advertisers (including Argos Ltd), and not by ASI, based on their internet browsing history and cookies,[13] while the 'unenquiring' consumer would not regard the advert as being aimed or directed at him or her, even if the advert was viewed in isolation.[14] As a result the judge concluded that 'having regard to the perceptions and expectations of the average consumer, I am unable to hold that the proportion of UK visitors to ASI's website who would have regarded the site or any part of it as aimed or directed at them was such as to warrant the conclusion that it was targeted at them.'[15]

Argos Ltd appealed to the Court of Appeal and, while many of Deputy Judge Spearman's findings were upheld, the court overruled his findings on targeting. Floyd LJ set out the issue succinctly in his opening remark: 'Can a US corporation selling construction software only in the Americas under the name Argos be sued for infringement of a registered trade mark by a UK-based consumer goods retailer who trades mainly in the UK and Ireland under the same name?'[16] Floyd LJ, unlike Deputy Judge Spearman felt they could. He defined targeting as 'the criterion which the law has adopted for determining whether a foreign website which is accessible from the state in which the trademark is protected should be treated as using a sign in the course of trade in relation to goods or services in that state.'[17] This he noted was a jurisdictional requirement: 'Because trademarks are territorial in effect, those who are doing business exclusively outside the United Kingdom should not have their dealings subjected to the trademark law of the United Kingdom', in regard to online transactions he noted that 'the fact that a website is accessible from anywhere in the world, and therefore may attract occasional interest from consumers there when this is not intended, should not give rise to any form of liability. Thus, in order to make good its claim of trademark infringement, it was necessary for Argos Ltd to establish that ASI was using the sign Argos in the course of trade in relation to goods or services *in the United Kingdom*.'[18] The court notes that in the earlier case of *Merck v Merck Sharpe & Dohme*,[19] the Court of Appeal had indicated that a subjective intention to target could be a relevant factor that the court would take

[10] [2017] EWHC 231 (Ch).
[11] Ibid. [184].
[12] Ibid. [198]–[200].
[13] Ibid. [219].
[14] Ibid. [218].
[15] Ibid. [223].
[16] *Argos* (n. 9) [1].
[17] Ibid. [14].
[18] Ibid. [48] (emphasis added).
[19] [2017] EWCA Civ 1834.

into account in a finely balanced case, however 'subjective intention cannot . . . make a website or page (or part of a page) which is plainly, when objectively considered, not intended for the UK, into a page which is so intended.'[20] The question was, as Deputy Judge Spearman had also decided, 'whether the average consumer would regard the service of the provision of advertising space on ASI's website as targeted at UK consumers?' This is the point though at which the Court of Appeal diverged from the High Court for as Floyd LJ noted:

> the judge appears, at some points in his judgment, to have gone further and used the construct of the average consumer to determine the identity of the person who is targeting the activity at the UK. I do not think that is an appropriate use of the average consumer. If the relevant acts would be taken to be targeted at the UK consumer, the identity of the person who is seeking to target the UK is a question of fact to be determined from an evaluation of all the evidence.[21]

In determining this factual question Floyd LJ found that the adverts posted on the ASI website were a form of 'electronic billboard'. If when visiting websites the UK customer were to see adverts aimed at US citizens they would assume they were not the intended recipient of the advert, if however they see adverts relevant to them they are likely to assume the advert is aimed at them. As Floyd LJ concludes, 'the question for the UK average consumer is along the lines "is this website operator offering goods or services under the sign, in the course of trade, which are intended for me in the UK?"'[22] He was quite clear that on the facts 'it is difficult to escape the conclusion that the average consumers who looked at the contents of the billboard when they include ads of interest to them would conclude that someone was targeting the billboard service at them.'[23] On this basis ASI were found to be targeting UK customers.

Ultimately Argos Ltd lost their appeal on the separate issue that they could not establish that ASI's use of the name Argos in their advertising took unfair advantage of the distinctive character or repute of the Argos Ltd trademark. However this is not important here, what is important here is that this case provides further detail on when targeting will be established and jurisdiction taken by local courts. Additionally, as a case between a UK company and a US company (and website), this case is not one decided narrowly on the principles of the Brussels Convention. This is particularly valuable, as many cases in future will no doubt, like *Argos*, involve UK courts looking West more than East.

15.2 Search engines

In the modern internet, in a very real sense, if you are not listed in the first page of Google search returns you do not exist in the online world. Google dominates the online experience with in excess of 4 billion searches per day on Google, which represents about 86 per cent of all internet searches. Google determines in a very real sense how we experience the web. In addition as people switch from entering URLs

---

[20] *Argos* (n. 9) [51].
[21] Ibid. [55].
[22] Ibid. [57].
[23] Ibid. [60].

to search terms, Google controls more of our web experience.[24] Google obviously is a profit-making enterprise and a large part of Google's profits come from selling advertising on its search pages. This is through the delivery of ads placed at the head and right-hand side of a search return surrounding the natural search results. Obviously the Google algorithm determines the Google natural search returns and although they may be manipulated slightly it is now difficult to manipulate them extensively. If you want to be seen online, and you are not already a well-known name, it can be very difficult because, until you build up enough links and hits, you will languish in the lower reaches of a Google return.

 Example Getting seen on Google

Maria wants to open a new online business selling legal textbooks. She discovers quickly that her business is struggling to register in Google search returns as whenever anyone searches for a textbook like 'Andrew Murray Information Technology Law' the first page is taken up with major suppliers such as Amazon, Waterstones, and WH Smith.

She discovers an easy way around this is to buy an advertisement to be placed on the first page of search returns in the sponsored links section. She simply gives Google details of which search keywords she would like to have her advert displayed against, how much she would like to spend for each 'click through' she receives, and an overall budget for the day, week, or month. Then whenever someone types in a search term—say 'Information Technology Law' her advert will be displayed.

This is okay as long as someone is using a generic term like 'Information Technology Law' or a personal name like Andrew Murray. The problem is what to do when someone like Maria purchases a sponsored link using a trademark like 'Louis Vuitton', 'Chanel', or 'Gucci'.

This example illustrates the trigger point for the first in a series of cases referred to the CJEU between 2008 and 2012 in relation to the Google sponsored listing function.[25] The first began in France as a series of cases involving a number of trademarks including those owned by Louis Vuitton Malletier (LVM).[26] In early 2003 LVM became aware that when its trademarks were being used as Google search terms some of the adverts delivered provided links to sites offering imitation versions of its products. They discovered this was because Google offered advertisers the possibility of selecting not only keywords which correspond to LVM's trademarks, but also those keywords in combination with expressions indicating imitation, such as imitation and copy. Upon this discovery LVM brought proceedings against Google. The case was first heard in the Tribunal de

---

[24] The use of search in place of URLs is demonstrated by the list of most searched keywords for 2018. They were: (1) Facebook; (2) YouTube; (3) Google; (4) Gmail; and (5) Hotmail.

[25] There were five references in all but we will only discuss three. The five were *Google France, Google Inc. v Louis Vuitton Malletier* ECLI:EU:C:2010:159 (France); *Die BergSpechte Outdoor Reisen v Günter Guni* ECLI:EU:C:2010:163 (Austria); *Portakabin v Primakabin* ECLI:EU:C:2010:416 (Netherlands); *Eis.de GmbH v BBY Vertriebsgesellschaft mbH* ECLI:EU:C:2010:174 (Germany); and *Interflora Inc. v Marks & Spencer plc* ECLI:EU:C:2011:604 (UK).

[26] *Google France* (n. 25).

Grande Instance de Paris which held Google liable for trademark infringement. An appeal to Cour d'appel de Paris upheld this decision and Google appealed to the Cour de Cassation who referred the case to the CJEU for a preliminary ruling.[27] There were three key questions for the court:

(1) is the application of trade marks to the selection of advertisements to be displayed a use in the course of trade;

(2) is the use made by Google in placing sponsored listings likely to dilute the value of the trade mark; and

(3) can Google seek refuge in the safe harbour as an information society service provider by Art. 14 of the Electronic Commerce Directive?

The first question related to Google's use of the trademarks in selling advertising. Was this the kind of use of a trademark that could be prevented by a trademark holder? In essence was it use in the course of trade? The court began by looking at the activity of the advertiser rather than Google: 'use of a sign identical with a trade mark constitutes use in the course of trade where it occurs in the context of commercial activity with a view to economic advantage and not as a private matter'.[28] With regard to the advertiser purchasing the referencing service and choosing as a keyword a sign identical with another's trademark, it must be held that that advertiser is using that sign within the meaning of that case law.[29] What about Google though? The court ultimately decided that Google was not using the signs in the course of trade:

> The referencing service provider operates 'in the course of trade' when it permits advertisers to select, as keywords, signs identical with trade marks, stores those signs and displays its clients' ads on the basis thereof, it does not follow, however, from those factors that that service provider itself 'uses' those signs [in the course of trade] . . . A referencing service provider allows its clients to use signs which are identical with, or similar to, trade marks, without itself using those signs. That conclusion is not called into question by the fact that that service provider is paid by its clients for the use of those signs. The fact of creating the technical conditions necessary for the use of a sign and being paid for that service does not mean that the party offering the service itself uses the sign . . . a referencing service provider is not involved in use in the course of trade.[30]

Therefore, while the advertisers themselves are using the trademark in the course of trade, Google is not. This was a blow to LVM as most of the advertisers in question were not based within the EU and they would need to begin litigation elsewhere. The second question then was whether the use of the trademarks in paid-for advertising was likely to dilute the mark or cause loss to the trademark holder. The court saw a connection between the use of the trademarks on Google and elsewhere, 'With regard to the use by internet advertisers of a sign identical with another person's trade mark as a keyword for the purposes of displaying advertising messages, it is clear that that use is liable to have certain repercussions on the advertising use of that mark by its proprietor and on

---

[27] The case history is reported at [28]–[32].
[28] Per *Arsenal Football Club plc v Reed* ECLI:EU:C:2002:651 at [40].
[29] *Google France* (n. 25) [50]–[51].
[30] Ibid. [55]–[58].

the latter's commercial strategy.'[31] Again as with the first question the court found that the actions of the advertisers was likely to infringe:

> in the case of offers of imitations for sale where a third party attempts, through the use of a sign which is identical with, or similar to, a reputable mark, to ride on the coat-tails of that mark in order to benefit from its power of attraction, its reputation and its prestige, and to exploit, without paying any financial compensation and without being required to make efforts of its own in that regard, the marketing effort expended by the proprietor of that mark in order to create and maintain the image of that mark, the advantage resulting from such use must be considered to be an advantage that has been unfairly taken of the distinctive character or the repute of that mark.[32]

But, once again, when the court looked at Google it found it not liable for the actions of its customers, for as it had already ruled Google did not 'use' the trademarks.[33]

This left the remaining question somewhat moot but the court answered it anyway. The court here seemed to suggest that although Art. 14 protection was available to Google it was not clear Google would qualify for safe harbour protection:

> In order to establish whether the liability of a referencing service provider may be limited under Art. 14, it is necessary to examine whether the role played by that service provider is neutral, in the sense that its conduct is merely technical, automatic and passive, pointing to a lack of knowledge or control of the data which it stores . . . the role played by Google in the drafting of the commercial message which accompanies the advertising link or in the establishment or selection of keywords is relevant.[34]

This though was a question for the referring court to determine.[35] In the event, the referring court did not need to determine this as changes to Google's Adwords policy mean they comply with the decision of the court.[36]

Quickly on the heels of the *Louis Vuitton* decision the CJEU had another reference from the Netherlands.[37] The case essentially asked the same questions in regard to potential liability for search engines as *Louis Vuitton* and in essence the same answers were given. The one fresh issue dealt with in this case was a question of exhaustion. That is, once the trademark holder has put their goods into the market they are said to have exhausted their interest and they cannot then oppose the use of that trademark to commercialize the goods in a second-hand market—essentially this gives you the right to resell your old designer clothes on eBay with a full description including the name of the designer. Primakabin sells and leases new and second-hand mobile buildings. Among the second-hand units it leases are those manufactured by Portakabin. Primakabin was using Portakabin's trademark to buy Google advertising. Portakabin objected to this as they believed Primakabin were using their brand to advertise new Primakabin products at a loss to them. Primakabin argued they were advertising the second-hand Portakabin units they leased.

In a very confusing decision the court found that 'A trade mark proprietor is not entitled to prohibit an advertiser from advertising, on the basis of a keyword identical

---

[31] Ibid. [93].
[32] Ibid. [103].
[33] Ibid. [104]–[105].
[34] Ibid. [114], [118].
[35] Ibid. [119].
[36] See <http://support.google.com/adwordspolicy/bin/answer.py?hl=en&answer=6118>.
[37] *Portakabin* (n. 25).

with, or similar to, that trade mark, which the advertiser has chosen for an internet referencing service without the consent of the proprietor, the resale of second-hand goods originally placed on the market in the EEA under that trade mark by the proprietor or with his consent.'[38] But equally it found that:

> a trade mark proprietor is entitled to prohibit an advertiser from advertising, on the basis of a keyword identical with, or similar to, that mark, which that advertiser has selected for an internet referencing service without the consent of the proprietor, in relation to goods or services identical to those in respect of which the mark is registered, where that advertising does not enable average internet users, or enables them only with difficulty, to ascertain whether the goods or services referred to by the ad originate from the proprietor of the trade mark or from an undertaking economically linked to it or, on the contrary, originate from a third party.[39]

How then to connect the two? Well, the answer is again that the referring court must do a little work to determine whether or not the use made of the mark was in fact infringing. There is some guidance on how to achieve this. The court says the trademark holder may only oppose advertising in relation to 'exhausted' items when 'there is a legitimate reason which justifies him opposing that advertising, such as use of that sign which gives the impression that the reseller and the trade mark proprietor are economically linked or use which is seriously detrimental to the reputation of the mark'.[40] The court then gives some guidance to the referring court on how to determine this.[41]

This was a case more about the roles of advertisers and their competitors than the search intermediary but it does add one more piece to the jigsaw, one that is finally completed with reference to our final CJEU case in this section, *Interflora Inc. v Marks & Spencer plc*.[42]

 Case study *Interflora Inc. v Marks & Spencer plc*

This case originated in the UK and began when Marks & Spencer (M&S), the well-known high-street retailer began to advertise their M&S flower delivery service with a Google advertisement that could be triggered by the search terms 'Interflora'. Interflora is a trademark of Interflora Inc., a network of florists which allows customers to place orders for the flower deliveries in person, by telephone, or through their website. Once placed, the order is fulfilled by the network member closest to the address to which the flowers are to be delivered. It is a very old and efficient system which allows independent florists to operate a national flower delivery service. Once they became aware of the use of their trademark by M&S in this fashion, Interflora raised a trademark infringement action.

The case began before Arnold J in the High Court.[43] He quickly realized the complexity of the case and the need for a reference to the CJEU. He therefore stayed proceedings and referred ten questions to the CJEU for a preliminary ruling. However, following the

---

[38] Ibid. [78].
[39] Ibid. [54].
[40] Ibid. [89].
[41] Ibid. [93].
[42] *Interflora* (n. 25).
[43] [2009] EWHC 1095 (Ch).

decision of the court in *Louis Vuitton*, he withdrew six of these questions leaving four fresh questions for the court to consider.[44] The essence of the four remaining questions could be reduced to two key questions:

(1) whether the proprietor of a trade mark is entitled to prevent a competitor from displaying—on the basis of a keyword which is identical to that trade mark and which has been selected in an internet referencing service by the competitor without the proprietor's consent—an advertisement for goods or services identical to those for which that mark is registered; and

(2) in those circumstances, is it relevant

(i) that the advertisement concerned is liable to lead some members of the relevant public to believe, incorrectly, that the advertiser is a member of the trade mark proprietor's commercial network; and

(ii) that the provider of the internet referencing service does not permit trade mark proprietors to prevent signs identical to their trade marks being selected as keywords?[45]

The court answered the first question by reference to the decision in the *Portakabin* case:

a trade mark's function of indicating origin is adversely affected when internet users are shown, on the basis of a keyword identical with the mark, a third party's advertisement, such as that of a competitor of the trade mark proprietor, depends in particular on the manner in which that advertisement is presented. That function is adversely affected if the advertisement does not enable reasonably well-informed and reasonably observant internet users, or enables them only with difficulty, to ascertain whether the goods or services referred to by the advertisement originate from the proprietor of the trade mark or an undertaking economically connected to it or, on the contrary, originate from a third party.[46]

As had been indicated in the *Portakabin* decision, this was for the referring court to decide. As with *Portakabin*, the court gave guidance on how this may be achieved:

In carrying out its examination of the facts, the referring court may choose to assess, first, whether the reasonably well-informed and reasonably observant internet user is deemed to be aware, on the basis of general knowledge of the market, that M&S's flower delivery service is not part of the Interflora network but is, on the contrary, in competition with it and, second, should it become apparent that that is not generally known, whether M&S's advertisement enabled that internet user to tell that the service concerned does not belong to the Interflora network. In particular, the referring court may take into account that, in the present case, the commercial network of the trade mark proprietor is composed of a large number of retailers which vary greatly in terms of size and commercial profile. The Court considers that, in such circumstances, it may be particularly difficult for the reasonably well-informed and reasonably observant internet user to determine, in the absence of any indication from the advertiser, whether or not the advertiser—whose advertisement is displayed in response to a search using that trade mark as a search term—is part of that network.[47]

The second question was more complicated and the court separated off the two subquestions into questions of trademark dilution and unfair advantage. In relation to dilution the court directed that:

[44] [2010] EWHC 925 (Ch).
[45] *Interflora* (n. 25) [27]–[28].
[46] Ibid. [44].
[47] Ibid. [51]–[52].

When the use, as a keyword, of a sign corresponding to a trade mark with a reputation triggers the display of an advertisement which enables the reasonably well-informed and reasonably observant internet user to tell that the goods or services offered originate not from the proprietor of the trade mark but, on the contrary, from a competitor of that proprietor, the conclusion will have to be that the trade mark's distinctiveness has not been reduced by that use, the latter having merely served to draw the internet user's attention to the existence of an alternative product or service to that of the proprietor of the trade mark. If, on the other hand, the referring court were to conclude that the advertising triggered by the use of the sign identical to the Interflora trade mark did not enable the reasonably well-informed and reasonably observant internet user to tell that the service promoted by M&S is independent from that of Interflora and if Interflora were to seek moreover from the referring court, in addition to a finding that the mark's function of indicating origin has been adversely affected, a finding that M&S has also caused detriment to the distinctive character of the Interflora trade mark by contributing to turning it into a generic term, it would fall to the referring court to determine, on the basis of all the evidence submitted to it, whether the selection of signs corresponding to the trade mark Interflora as keywords on the internet has had such an impact on the market for flower delivery services that the word 'Interflora' has come to designate, in the consumer's mind, any flower delivery service.[48]

The final part of the second question was whether M&S had gained an unfair advantage through the availability of the Interflora trademark as an advertising keyword. The court found:

Where a competitor of the proprietor of a trade mark with a reputation selects that trade mark as a keyword in an internet referencing service, the purpose of that use is to take advantage of the distinctive character and repute of the trade mark. In fact, that selection is liable to create a situation in which the probably large number of consumers using that keyword to carry out an internet search for goods or services covered by the trade mark with a reputation will see that competitor's advertisement displayed on their screens. It is clear from those particular aspects of the selection as internet keywords of signs corresponding to trade marks with a reputation which belong to other persons that such a selection can, in the absence of any 'due cause', be construed as a use whereby the advertiser rides on the coat-tails of a trade mark with a reputation in order to benefit from its power of attraction. If that is the case, the advantage thus obtained by the third party must be considered to be unfair.[49]

This is a very strong finding in favour of the trademark holder. In essence, the question for the domestic court is to determine whether or not a 'reasonably well-informed and reasonably observant internet user' can tell that (or can only tell with difficulty) whether the advertiser and the trademark holder are economically connected.

With the fallout of the *Interflora* case still being felt in the courts of England and Wales two recent cases have demonstrated the lasting impact of the *Google France* decision in England and Wales. The first of these is *Cosmetic Warriors Limited, Lush Limited v Amazon.co.uk Limited, Amazon Eu Sarl*.[50] The issue in dispute in this case was the use by Amazon of the 'Lush' trademark to direct consumers to alternative products. Lush, a well-known ethical cosmetic company had taken the deliberate decision not to allow its goods to be sold on Amazon because it took issue with some of Amazon's business practices and did not wish to be associated with Amazon. As a result, no Lush cosmetics were on sale through Amazon. To direct consumers to alternative products, which

---

[48] Ibid. [81]–[82].
[49] Ibid. [86], [89].
[50] [2014] EWHC 181 (Ch).

Amazon did sell, they bid on the keyword 'Lush' as a Google AdWord. When a user searched for Lush on Google, the following sponsored advert would appear headlined 'Lush Soap at Amazon.co.uk' offering 'Low prices on Lush Soap' and 'Free UK Delivery on Amazon Orders'. The court noted that 'if a consumer clicks on the relevant link he is taken to the amazon.co.uk website and presented with the opportunity to browse or purchase equivalent products to Lush Soap. There is no overt message either within the advertisement or on the Amazon site that Lush Soap is not available for purchase from Amazon.'[51] Amazon also used another form of advertisement on Google, subtly different. This one was headlined 'Bomb Bath at Amazon.co.uk' and offered 'Low prices on Bath Bombs' and 'Free UK Delivery on Amazon Orders'. This advert did not mention Lush anywhere.

The court applied both *Google France* and *Interflora* and found that 'It is clear, following Google France, that if the ad appeared as a result of Amazon having bid on Lush as a keyword, Amazon has used the mark in the course of trade in relation to the relevant goods.'[52] However, there was a subtle difference in the two adverts. The first clearly mentioned the name 'Lush', whereas the second did not, did this make a difference? The judge, John Baldwin QC, thought it did. In relation to the first advert, which mentioned 'Lush' explicitly he found that:

> the average consumer seeing [the advert] would expect to find Lush soap available on the Amazon site and would expect to find it at a competitive price. Moreover, I consider that it is likely that if he were looking for Lush soap and did not find it immediately on the Amazon site, then he would persevere somewhat before giving up. My reason is that the consumer is likely to think that Amazon is a reliable supplier of a very wide range of goods and he would not expect Amazon to be advertising Lush soap for purchase if it were not in fact available for purchase.[53]

However, the second advert was different:

> In Interflora Arnold J held there to be infringement although the offending ad made reference only to 'M&S Flowers Online' and not to 'Interflora'. But that was, in part, because Interflora represents a network of flower shops and the court was not satisfied that the average consumer would appreciate that Marks & Spencer were not members of that network. So I think that case is different on the facts from the one before me. [In relation to the advert delivered], there was [also] an ad for a third party as well as one for Amazon. In my judgment the presence of such other ads makes the position even clearer. The average consumer could not reasonably fail to appreciate that the Amazon ad was just another ad from a supplier offering similar products to those requested by the internet searcher. My conclusion on this part of the case does not, however, depend on the presence of this other ad.[54]

On this basis the court found that the use of the Lush mark in the first advert was infringing, because the advert did not pass the test of enabling normally informed and reasonably attentive internet users to ascertain whether the goods or services referred to in the advertisement originated from Lush or from an unconnected third party, whereas in the second advert there was no infringement as the advert did not make use of the Lush mark and the average consumer would realize it was an advert for a competing product The judge took the view that consumers would expect an advert for Lush

---

[51] Ibid. [8].
[52] Ibid. [38].
[53] Ibid. [42].
[54] Ibid. [47]–[48].

products to include at least some reference to the Lush mark or some indication to distinguish it as a Lush advert from other adverts thrown up by a Google search. Although Marks & Spencer's flower delivery advert had been held to infringe Interflora's registered trademark, even though the advert did not mention Interflora, that case could be distinguished.

More recently the High Court has revisited the issue in *Victoria Plum v Victorian Plumbing*.[55] Victoria Plum Ltd and Victorian Plumbing Ltd are both bathroom retailers who retail primarily online. Both companies have been trading and co-existing on the marketplace, despite their very similar names, since 2001. Victoria Plum used the name 'Victoria Plumb' until July 2015, when it altered its name to 'Victoria Plum'. Victoria Plum owns a UK trademark registration for the mark *Victoria Plumb*, as well as other UK and EU trademark registrations for similar marks. Victorian Plumbing started bidding on the 'Victoria Plum' and 'Victoria Plumb' Google ad keywords in 2008, but its activity increased very substantially from 2012 onwards. Victoria Plum brought proceedings for trademark infringement, claiming that consumers would mistakenly assume that the adverts originate from Victoria Plum, or an economically linked undertaking.

The advertisements displayed in response to the keywords purchased by Victorian Plumbing fell into two categories: (1) Adverts that include the 'Victoria Plumb' trademark as a result of Google's dynamic keyword insertion service—this service automatically includes the internet user's search term in the resulting ad text if the search term matches one of the keywords purchased by the advertiser; and (2) Adverts that include the terms 'Victoria Plumbing' and/or 'VictorianPlumb' and/or 'Victorian Plumbing'. (NB! The claimant did not seek to restrain the use of the name 'Victorian Plumbing'). In relation to the first category, the defendant accepted that this was an infringement of trademark and submitted to judgment, and an injunction against further infringement, on that part of the claim.[56] In relation to the second category they claimed honest concurrent use in that the parties have traded for many years in a wide range of directly competing goods and while it is self-evident that the parties' names are so similar that there is a likelihood of confusion on the part of the public between them, in spite of actual confusion, the parties have co-existed peaceably for many years, each trading, without complaint, on an increasing scale.[57] They based this in part on the decisions of the CJEU in *Budejovicky Budvar NP v Anheuser-Busch Inc*.[58] and the Court of Appeal in *IPC Media Ltd v Media 10 Ltd*,[59] both of which recognized that honest concurrent use can constitute a defence to infringement.

Henry Carr J considered the honest concurrent use defence but ruled it did not apply in the current case as 'the use complained of is use by the First Defendant of the Claimant's Victoria Plum(b) marks (or trivial variations thereof) by bidding on them as keywords [and] a defence of honest concurrent use can entitle a defendant to continue to use its own name or mark. It cannot, in cases where the marks used by the claimant and defendant are different, entitle the defendant to use the claimant's mark.'[60] The question then was whether the use by Victorian Plumbing of the Victoria Plum(b)

---

[55] [2016] EWHC 2911.
[56] Ibid. [7]–[10].
[57] Ibid. [13].
[58] ECLI:EU:C:2011:605.
[59] [2014] EWCA Civ 1403.
[60] Ibid. [81]–[82].

marks was in infringement. This meant, applying both *Google France* and *Interflora*, whether the adverts enabled normally informed and reasonably attentive internet users to ascertain without difficulty whether the goods or services referenced in them originated from Victoria Plum or an undertaking economically connected to it, or from a third party. It was quite an easy decision for Henry Carr J to find that infringement had occurred as:

> the Claimant's trade marks have an enhanced distinctive character as a result of the use which has been made of them. The services in question, namely the bringing together of bathroom items enabling customers to conveniently view and purchase those goods via a website, are identical, as are the types of goods offered on the websites [and] the internet user who has searched for the Claimant's trade mark is likely to be expecting to find links to the Claimant's website.[61]

This did not dispose of the case though. The defendant counterclaimed that the Claimant had made use of the term 'Victorian Plumbing' in buying Google ads which resulted in the display of ads containing the term 'Victoria Plum(b)' (a practice they discontinued in 2016) must constitute passing off. Henry Carr J found that when Victoria Plumb began bidding on the 'Victorian Plumbing' keywords in 2011 the defendant had sufficient goodwill in the name to enable it to bring a passing off action against use of that name by the Claimant.[62] He found that:

> internet users who enter 'Victorian Plumbing' are likely to be looking for the First Defendant's website. When presented with Victoria Plumb advertisements for a business unconnected with that of the First Defendant, it seems to me that there is a propensity for confusion. There is nothing in those advertisements to indicate the absence of a connection between the parties. Some users are likely to have clicked through to the Claimant's website, and their confusion is likely to have continued. I consider that a substantial proportion of the relevant public are likely to have been misled into believing that the Claimant is, or is connected with, the First Defendant, and that this constituted a misrepresentation by the Claimant.[63]

As a result, he allowed the counterclaim.

15.3 **Secondary markets**

It is not only search engines that have been subject to this form of trademark litigation. eBay has found itself at the heart of litigation in both the United States and the EU. Litigation began in France, home of many luxury goods brands. In June 2008 a series of early cases established that eBay was liable under French law for allowing the abuse of trademarks in on their eBay France site. On 4 June the Tribunal de Grande Instance de Troyes, in *Hermes v eBay*,[64] found eBay to have 'committed acts of counterfeit' and 'prejudice' by failing to monitor the authenticity of goods being sold on its website by a user identified as 'Mrs Cindy F'. As a result, they were ordered to pay Hermes damages of €20,000 and to block the user from the eBay site. However, this case was a mere appetizer for the later joined cases of *Louis Vuitton Malletier v eBay, Christian Dior Couture*

---

[61] Ibid. [57].
[62] Ibid. [139].
[63] Ibid. [142].
[64] Decision available in French from <www.legalis.net/spip.php?page=jurisprudence-decision&id_article=2320>.

v eBay, and *SA Parfums Christian Dior v eBay*.[65] In all three cases eBay were found to have operated a site which supported both the trade in counterfeit goods and the illegal sale of genuine goods without a licence of the trademark holder. The cases related to a number of luxury goods brands and items including Dior and Louis Vuitton handbags and clothes, as well as Guerlain, Givenchy, and Kenzo perfumes and cosmetics. In total damages amounting to €38.6m were awarded to the claimants and eBay were banned from selling four perfumes—Christian Dior, Kenzo, Givenchy, and Guerlain in France. eBay appealed to the Cour de Cassation arguing that the French courts did not have jurisdiction to hear the case as eBay is a US/Swiss Corporation. The court rejected this in late 2010.[66] eBay then defended on the basis that they were an information society service host provider under Art. 14 of the Electronic Commerce Directive and as such were entitled to safe harbour protection. In May 2012 the court ruled that eBay were not simply hosts but played an active role that gave them the knowledge of or control over the data that they stock, which means they do not benefit from the safe harbour provisions of Art. 14.[67] They added that they considered that eBay plays an active role in its online marketplace, as it uses optimization services to assist sellers, sends unsolicited messages to the buyers to invite them to buy, and sends invitations to the unsuccessful bidders for them to participate in other offers. This decision left eBay liable in France for the actions of its sellers because of its active role which gives it the knowledge of and control over the unlawful items that it lists.

A later landmark decision of the CJEU suggests the reasoning of the Cour de Cassation has been proven right. The case was a reference from the High Court of England and Wales. It was brought by L'Oréal and a number of other beauty product companies in relation to a number of activities on eBay. L'Oréal and the other claimants had brought a number of items to eBay's attention and were dissatisfied with how eBay dealt with their complaints. The items were a mixture of counterfeit goods (in a few cases), unlawful imports from outside the European Economic Area, items not intended for sale (such as testers), and items sold without the packaging in which they were originally marketed. The case was referred to the CJEU by Arnold J who asked ten questions,[68] we will look at the three key questions: (1) was the use of the trademarks a use in the course of trade; (2) could the trademark owner prevent the sale of genuine but unboxed items; and (3) were eBay liable for the actions of the users of the site?

The first question was whether the sale of items on an auction site such as eBay was used in the course of trade. The court first determined that where an individual sells an item through an online marketplace this is not a sale in the course of trade. However, where 'the sales made on such a marketplace go beyond the realms of a private activity, the seller will be acting "in the course of trade"'.[69] In addition the court confirmed their earlier finding from *Louis Vuitton* that when eBay bought advertisements on Google they acted in the course of trade.[70] The next question then was: could the trademark

---

[65] Tribunal de Commerce de Paris, 30 June 2008. Decision available in French from <www.lega-lis.net/spip.php?page=jurisprudence-decision&id_article=2353>.

[66] *Louis Vuitton Malletier (Société) v eBay Inc. and eBay International AG* [2011] ILPr 16.

[67] Decision available in French from <www.legalis.net/spip.php?page=jurisprudence-decision&id_article=3398>.

[68] *L'Oréal SA and Ors v eBay International AG & Ors* ECLI:EU:C:2011:474 [50].

[69] Ibid. [55].

[70] Ibid. [87].

holders prevent the sale of unboxed goods which may be genuine? The court said yes and on two separate potential grounds, namely:

(1) where the consequence of that removal is that essential information, such as information relating to the identity of the manufacturer or the person responsible for marketing the cosmetic product, is missing, or

(2) where the trade mark owner has established that the removal of the packaging has damaged the image of the product and, hence, the reputation of the trade mark.[71]

The final and, for our purposes, key question was: were eBay liable for these actions? The court determined that eBay could be infringing the rights of trademark holders in two ways. First by advertising online using services such as Google sponsored links to advertise the claimants' products,[72] and second, by actively promoting sales on the eBay site via adverts and other promotional services such as mailings and re-offers, eBay could be liable for the infringements committed by their customers.[73] Could then eBay benefit from the Art. 14 safe harbour? Following the line of authority that began with *Louis Vuitton* the court concluded that 'the fact that the service provided by the operator of an online marketplace includes the storage of information transmitted to it by its customer-sellers is not in itself a sufficient ground for concluding that that service falls, in all situations, within the scope of Art. 14(1).'[74] An example of a situation when Art. 14 will not apply is when 'the service provider, instead of confining itself to providing that service neutrally by a merely technical and automatic processing of the data provided by its customers, plays an active role of such a kind as to give it knowledge of, or control over, those data'.[75] The final determination of this question is of course one for the referring court but the CJEU left clear guidance:

Article 14(1) must be interpreted as applying to the operator of an online marketplace where that operator has not played an active role allowing it to have knowledge or control of the data stored. The operator plays such a role when it provides assistance which entails, in particular, optimising the presentation of the offers for sale in question or promoting them. Where the operator of the online marketplace has not played an active role within the meaning of the preceding paragraph and the service provided falls, as a consequence, within the scope of Article 14(1), the operator none the less cannot, in a case which may result in an order to pay damages, rely on the exemption from liability provided for in that provision if it was aware of facts or circumstances on the basis of which a diligent economic operator should have realised that the offers for sale in question were unlawful and, in the event of it being so aware, failed to act expeditiously in accordance with Article 14(1)(b).[76]

Following the decision of the CJEU, the parties agreed a settlement in January 2014. This was unsurprising as eBay, not waiting for the outcome of the case, had made several changes to their business plan to ensure they would comply with a negative judgment.[77] The guidance from the CJEU is though clear.

---

[71] Ibid. [83].

[72] Ibid. [84]–[90].

[73] Ibid. [91]–[97].

[74] Ibid. [111].

[75] Ibid. [113].

[76] Ibid. [123]–[124].

[77] S Krawczyk, eBay's European government relations director stated afterwards 'A lot of cases will still have to be assessed by the national courts. We've moved on—we fulfill most of these conditions now anyways.' (2011) Source: *New York Times*, 12 July 2011 <https://www.nytimes.com/2011/07/13/business/global/ebay-suffers-setback-on-trademark-infringement.html>.

The High Court returned to this issue, and applied the *L'Oréal* guidance, in the previously discussed case of *Cosmetic Warriors Limited, Lush Limited v Amazon.co.uk Limited, Amazon Eu Sarl*.[78] In addition to the challenge to the two adverts placed on Google AdWords by Amazon, Lush also challenged the internal processes of Amazon's site, as explained by John Baldwin QC (sitting as a Deputy Judge of the Chancery Division):

> If a consumer searches for the word 'Lush' in the relevant 'department' of Amazon's UK site (e.g. 'Beauty' or 'Health and Personal Care'), the first thing to happen after the letters "lu" are typed, is that a drop down menu appears and various options are offered such as 'lush bath bombs' or 'lush cosmetics' or 'lush hair extensions', the consumer being offered the opportunity to click on one of these options whereupon a new page will appear. In the case of a consumer clicking on 'lush bath bombs' or 'lush cosmetics' the new page will offer similar products to those available from Lush without any overt reference to the Lush item not being available. In the case of a consumer clicking on Lush hair extensions, the consumer is presented with a page containing hair extensions from a third party manufacturer called Lush as well as other third party products. Slightly different results may be obtained if the consumer enters the term 'Lush' as a search into 'All Departments' (i.e. all departments of Amazon) but the general picture is the same. There will be a drop down menu identifying various Lush goods and a display of products which are similar to or equivalent to those sold by Lush, there will be no display of any Lush products of the Claimants and there will be no overt message to the effect that the Claimants' Lush products are not available from the amazon.co.uk website.[79]

This is not too dissimilar to the activities of eBay advertising L'Oréal products on their site. The court found that Amazon not only operated a marketplace but were the designers of the search facility: 'Amazon is both the designer and operator of the search engine and the operations on its site. Although it may be wearing different hats when it designs its search engines and sells its goods, I have no doubt that the design of the search engine is carried out in order to maximize the sale of goods from the site.'[80] From this it was a very short step to find Amazon used the Lush mark in the course of trade through its application to the drop-down menu.

 Highlight Trademarks in drop-down menus

The average consumer is unlikely to know how the drop-down menu has the content which it displays, but is likely to believe that it is intended to be helpful to him and is some consequence of other searches that have been carried out. In my judgment it would inform the average consumer that if he were looking for Lush Bath Bombs on Amazon, he would find them by clicking on that menu item. I reject the contention that the average consumer who was typing Lush into the search box would think that the drop-down menu reference to Lush Bath Bombs was a reference merely to products which were similar to or competitive with the Lush product . . . On the facts of this case, I do not think Amazon can escape from the conclusion that it has used the Lush sign in the course of trade in relation to the relevant goods based on the principles to be found in Google France and *L'Oréal v eBay*. It has used the sign as part of a commercial communication that it is selling the goods on its website.

[at [60–61]]

---

[78] See (n. 50).
[79] Ibid. [11], [13].
[80] Ibid. [57].

Finally, the question was whether this use had damaged the Lush trademark and again Baldwin QC had little difficulty: 'the use complained of by Lush clearly damages the original function and the advertisement and investment function of the Lush trade mark'.[81]

Ultimately, the use of the Lush trademark in the drop-down menu function was found to be infringing in relation to the menu options 'lush bath bombs' and 'lush cosmetics', but not in relation to 'lush hair extensions', that being the brand of a separate company in relation to the supply of clip-in hair extensions.

15.4 **Conclusions**

The nature of branding online has changed of late. Domain names have lost their focus as branding tools and the few brands which still rely on their domain name identity, such as Amazon.com, are mostly hangovers from that time in the development of the network where domain names were valuable pieces of real estate. With the replacement of the address bar by the multifunctional omnibox, much greater value has been attached to listing on search engines. Recently the focus of trademark holders has therefore turned to the invisible use of the brands and marks in search engine listings, particularly advertisements, and to the regulation of secondary markets which arguably support a trade in counterfeit goods. It was only a matter of time until the quasi deregulated environment of online commerce would come into conflict with brands and trademark values and thus we have had a series of cases at domestic and European level in the last six years. These cases have now established a strong legal framework for the legal regulation of trademarks and brand identities in relation to keyword advertising and use in secondary markets. With the law now more settled in this area we can expect a steady stream of cases in the next few years as trademark holders enforce their rights in this arena.

▌ TEST QUESTIONS

Question 1

A client, Jada, who is based in London, comes to see you for advice on the following scenario. Advise her of any potential claims she may have in trademark law.

Her company 'Streetbags' specializes in handbags and travel bags with designs supplied by famous urban artists including Blek Le Rat, D*face, and KAWS. Since their launch in 2014 they have quickly become a highly desirable fashion accessory featured in *Vogue*, *Elle*, and *Glamour*. Limited edition Streetbags can sell for up to £12,000. Collection bags range in price from £750 to £2,500.

Recently your client has noted that a search on Google using the term 'Streetbags' returns not only her company page but also 'Ads' for a number of unrelated sites. One ad links to the webpage of a UK-based dealer 'Cheap Designer Bags UK'. Their site offers Streetbags for sale

---

[81] Ibid. [75].

for between £80 and £150. An investigation by Streetbags reveals these are cheap fake bags produced in the Far East, not the genuine Streetbags product only ever produced in the EU. A second link takes the user to the home page of Streetbags competitor 'Urban Style', a start-up company which has recently begun to commission its own bags designed by less-well-known artists such as Isaac Cordaal and Lake. Yet to launch, Urban Style have indicated their bags will be priced in the £150 to £350 price range.

It has also come to the attention of Streetbags that auction site eBay hosts a number of Streetbags sales. Some appear to be genuine resales of genuine Streetbags by customers, but a number of listings seem to be suspect, offering new Streetbags for suspiciously low prices. Streetbags believe fake bags imported from the Far East are fulfilling these sales.

Question 2

To be an infringement of a trademark someone must mistakenly believe that good, service, or product is associated with the trademark holder in some way (confusion) unless the mark is an identical mark used for identical goods or services. Where goods are sold as being 'inspired by' or 'related to' or similar on eBay or Amazon Marketplace, is this trademark infringement?

Question 3

How would you have decided the *Interflora v Marks and Spencer* and *L'Oréal v eBay* cases?

FURTHER READING

Books

I Calboli and M Senftleben (eds.), *The Protection of Non-traditional Trademarks: Critical Perspectives* (OUP 2018)

Chapters and articles

A Blythe, 'Trade marks as adwords: an aid to competition or a potential infringement? An evaluation of the law in the light of recent decisions' [2015] 37(4) *European Intellectual Property Review* 225

J Davis, 'Revisiting the average consumer: an uncertain presence in European trade mark law' (2015) *Intellectual Property Quarterly* 15

J-S Dupont, 'Uncharted territories of trade mark use' (2013) 2 *Intellectual Property Quarterly* 139

C Morcom, 'Trade Marks and the Internet: Where Are We Now?' [2012] 34 (1) *European Intellectual Property Review* 40

E Moro, 'Protection of reputed trademarks and keywords: looking for Ariadne's thread among flowers, perfumes and bags' (2013) 2 *UCL Journal of Law and Jurisprudence* 64

PART IV

E-commerce

We all want to do business online but how can we be sure we are protected? How do we contract online? How do we make payments and how do we sign an agreement?

Electronic contracts

The ability to trade and to make payment is the foundation of all modern societies and the information society is no different in this respect. The information society has provided a number of commercial opportunities for entrepreneurs. Most famously software designers Bill Gates, Steve Ballmer, and Paul Allen became multibillionaires from their Microsoft software packages while competitors Steve Jobs and Stephen Wozniak made billions from both hardware and software development for Apple. Others, such as Michael Dell, focused on producing hardware while the next generation of internet entrepreneurs made money from either selling goods or services in the information society—as demonstrated by Amazon founder Jeff Bezos, eBay founder Pierre Omidyar, or Craigslist founder Craig Newmark—or have simply packaged and sold information as a stand-alone product, as done by Facebook founder Mark Zuckerberg; YouTube creators Jawed Karim, Chad Hurley, and Steve Chen; or most famously the Google guys Larry Page and Sergey Brin.

The cornerstone of the ability to extract revenue from all these products and services depends upon the binding legal agreement, or contract. Without the legal certainty offered by a contract all forms of commerce lack the necessary foundation of certainty and enforceability: this is why from earliest times the rules on pacts, or contracts, have been at the heart of all trading cultures and communities. This remains true of today's information society. Whatever form business takes, be it the trading of data, entertainment products, news and information, or systems for the management and development of software or hardware, certainty remains underpinned by the law of contract.

16.1 Contracting informally

Contracting is one of the most commonplace and simple applications of legal principles. Every day people enter into dozens of legally binding contracts without thinking about it. They enter into contracts of carriage with public transport operators, contracts of sale with shops, garages, and supermarkets, and contracts for the supply of services with hairdressers or dentists. These informal contracts are often entered into without a single word being exchanged, yet a contract is formed all the same.

Example Informal contracts

Kiera is travelling from home to university for class. She decides to take the bus. She gets on the bus and pays her fare (or shows a pass) and then takes a seat on the bus. She doesn't say anything to the driver; the driver doesn't say anything to her yet a contract has been formed where the customer agrees to pay the fare for the journey undertaken and to comply with the bus company's general conditions of carriage and the driver (as agent for the bus company) agrees to carry the customer in accordance with the same general conditions of carriage.

An equivalent type of transaction takes place daily in supermarkets where the customer offers to buy goods from the supermarket by taking them to the checkout and the checkout operator, as agent for the supermarket, accepts this offer. The customer agrees to pay the advertised price and in return the supermarket agrees to transfer title in the goods to the customer. The reason these contracts may be formed without the exchange of written, or even oral, terms is because these are informal contracts: contracts that have no legally defined form and which may be formed simply by a *consensus ad idem* or a meeting of the minds.

16.1.1 **Contract formation**

The rules for the formation of informal contracts seem extremely simple; to form a contract all parties to the contract must agree on the terms of the contract, and to be bound by these terms. In English law this is usually assumed to take place when an offer is accepted with consideration,[1] in Scots law the element of consideration is unnecessary.[2] This apparent simplicity though belies the complexity of contract law and in particular the rules of contract formation. Many of these rules affect the time and even place of formation of the contract, and even in informal contracts they prescribe certain conditions for the formation of a concluded contract which are of particular import in dealing with electronic and online contracts.

The basics of any form of contract are that a set of offered terms and conditions must be accepted. The question is how can one recognize an offer and an acceptance? Although this may seem a simple question, the intent of parties plays a significant role in determining when, or if, *consensus ad idem* has occurred.

This came to light in a series of shop display cases in the 1950s and 1960s. This series began with *Pharmaceutical Society of Great Britain v Boots Cash Chemists (Southern) Ltd*.[3] Boots, the well-known high-street pharmacy, had begun a trial of self-service shopping in some of its stores. This allowed customers to buy some pharmacy products by putting them in a basket and taking them to a cashier for payment. The Pharmaceutical Society argued this was in breach of the Pharmacy and Poisons Act 1933 which made it illegal to

---

[1] M Chen-Wishart, *Contract Law* (6th edn, OUP 2018) chs. 2 and 3.
[2] H MacQueen and J Thompson, *Contract Law in Scotland* (4th edn, Bloomsbury Professional 2016).
[3] [1953] 1 QB 401.

sell a listed poison without supervision of a registered pharmacist. The question before the Court of Appeal was whether the display of goods on the shelf was a standing offer to sell which was accepted by the customer upon placing the drugs in the basket or whether it was merely an 'invitation to treat' with the offer being made by the customer at the till and the acceptance being affected by the cashier. The court found the latter position was preferred with Birkett LJ noting that 'it would be wrong to say that the shopkeeper is making an offer to sell every article in the shop to any person who might come in and that that person can insist on buying any article by saying "I accept your offer."'[4]

This decision was later affirmed and developed in *Fisher v Bell*,[5] in which a shop window display was described as an invitation to treat, and *Partridge v Crittenden*,[6] in which a classified advert in a periodical was also similarly defined. These cases are very important in discussing electronic contracting, and in particular online contracts. We can draw on these cases to establish that a display on an e-commerce site such as Amazon should clearly be an invitation to treat and not a standing offer to sell.[7] The offer should come from the customer with the acceptance following at a later stage in the sales process. But one question remains, how should the contract formation process be structured when one of the parties is a computer? Traditionally, a contract is formed by a meeting of the minds, meaning both parties must agree to the terms and as a computer cannot form the necessary intent to form the agreement, this suggests that a human agent is required.

Computers are not the first non-human actor to be involved in contract formation. We have used vending machines for decades and ticket machines in stations and in car parks have stood in for human operators for some time. The role of automated ticket machines was reviewed by the Court of Appeal in the famous case of *Thornton v Shoe Lane Parking Ltd*.[8] The case, which is no doubt familiar to any student of English contract law, established the principle that a contractual term displayed or communicated to a contractual counterparty after *consensus ad idem* is reached is not incorporated into the contractual terms. What, though, is less often analysed in the many discussions of *Thornton* is the approach the court developed for dealing with contract formation and non-human actors. It is perfectly explained in the words of Lord Denning MR.[9]

 Highlight Lord Denning in *Thornton v Shoe Lane Parking Ltd*

The customer pays his money and gets a ticket. He cannot refuse it. He cannot get his money back. He may protest to the machine, even swear at it. But it will remain unmoved. He is committed beyond recall. He was committed at the very moment when he put his money into the machine.

The contract was concluded at that time. It can be translated into offer and acceptance in this way: the offer is made when the proprietor of the machine holds it out as being ready to receive the money. The acceptance takes place when the customer puts his money into the slot.

---

[4] Ibid. 407.
[5] [1961] 1 QB 394.
[6] [1968] 2 All ER 421.
[7] But see *Carlill v Carbolic Smokeball Company* [1893] 1 QB 256.
[8] [1971] 2 QB 163.
[9] Ibid. 169.

This is an important principle. Because a machine lacks the ability to form the necessary intent to conclude a contract, the court has rationalized the display constructed by the machine's operator as a standing offer similar to that found in the much earlier case of *Carlill v Carbolic Smokeball*.[10]

This standing offer reflects the intent of the machine operator and this is then capable of acceptance by the customer who indicates his or her acceptance of the terms by putting his or her money in the slot. This principle is assumed to extend to a number of self-service operations including vending machines and self-service petrol pumps.[11] This would suggest that an online e-commerce site such as Amazon would have to operate under this standing offer principle as they use non-human agents to conclude their contracts. This is at odds with our understanding from cases such as *Boots Cash Chemists*, *Fisher v Bell*, and *Partridge v Crittenden*, that shop displays, both interactive displays and passive displays, are merely invitations to treat. So the question is, is an e-commerce website like a shop display or like a vending machine?

16.2 **Regulating offer and acceptance**

With no case law to clarify the issue, commentators were left to speculate as to the nature of e-commerce sites. Most agreed that despite the lack of a human actor the interactive nature of websites rendered them more akin to self-service shop displays than to vending machines or ticket machines which issued a restricted choice of products.[12] The lack of clarity though raised the spectre of different approaches developing throughout Europe, with some countries taking the 'standing offer' principle while others followed the 'invitation to treat' principle. Such a lack of harmonization could adversely affect the development of e-commerce in Europe as a significant proportion of both business-to-business (B2B) and business-to-consumer (B2C) transactions were likely to take place across borders.

16.2.1 **Arts. 9–11 of the Electronic Commerce Directive**

To alleviate this risk, and to harmonize some rules on contract formalities, the Commission placed e-commerce, and electronic contracting at the heart of its fifth framework programme on the information society. The result was the Electronic Commerce Directive,[13] which is a wide-ranging document dealing not only with electronic contracting but also with SPAM emails and, as we have seen, protection for ISPs and other third-party intermediaries. The key provisions of interest to contract lawyers are to be found in Arts. 9–11.

Upon reading these, the first thing which becomes clear is that the Electronic Commerce Directive does not harmonize what is known as the contractual trigger—that

---

[10] *Carlill* (n. 7).
[11] Chen-Wishart (n. 1) 60–1.
[12] A Murray, 'Entering into Contracts Electronically: The Real W.W.W.' in L Edwards and C Waelde (eds.), *Law and the Internet: A Framework for Electronic Commerce* (Hart 2000); D Bainbridge, *Introduction to Information Technology Law* (6th edn, Longman 2007) 363.
[13] Dir. 2000/31/EC.

is, the moment at which *consensus ad idem* is legally deemed to have occurred. In earlier drafts of the directive it was proposed that this should be done with an original draft version of the directive suggesting that 'electronic contracts be concluded when the recipient of the service has received from the service provider, electronically, an acknowledgement of receipt of the recipient's acceptance, and has confirmed receipt of the acknowledgement of receipt'.[14]

This approach was criticized during the legislative passage of the directive with critics believing that in effect the directive was seeking to harmonize rules of contractual formation which lie outside the general competence of the Commission, and certainly well outside the competence of the information society programme. These critiques of the draft led to attempts to define a common contractual trigger being dropped. In their place we have a set of common principles with the key principles being found in Arts. 10 and 11.

Article 10 requires transparency in the contract-making process. While there is no common rule of contractual formation, there are a set of common principles which all e-commerce sites have to follow, including, essentially, by Art. 10(1)(a) the provision that the customer be informed of the technical steps he or she must follow to conclude the contract. Article 10 has been given effect in the UK by reg. 9 of the Electronic Commerce (EC Directive) Regulations 2002,[15] which enacts Art. 10 in full and without amendment. The combined effect of Art. 10/reg. 9 may be seen on any UK e-commerce website. If one were to visit Amazon UK and were to examine their conditions of sale, one would find that condition 1 states:

 Case study *Amazon's Conditions of sale*

Your order is an offer to Amazon to buy the product(s) in your order. When you place an order to purchase a product from Amazon, we will send you an e-mail confirming receipt of your order and containing the details of your order (the 'Order Confirmation E-mail'). The Order Confirmation E-mail is acknowledgement that we have received your order, and does not confirm acceptance of your offer to buy the product(s) ordered. We only accept your offer, and conclude the contract of sale for a product ordered by you, when we dispatch the product to you and send e-mail confirmation to you that we've dispatched the product to you (the 'Dispatch Confirmation E-mail'). If your order is dispatched in more than one package, you may receive a separate Dispatch Confirmation E-mail for each package, and each Dispatch Confirmation E-mail and corresponding dispatch will conclude a separate contract of sale between us for the product(s) specified in that Dispatch Confirmation E-mail. Your contract is with Amazon EU Sarl. Without affecting your right of cancellation set out in section 2 below, you can cancel your order for a product at no cost any time before we send the Dispatch Confirmation E-mail relating to that product.

Thus clearly the customer is informed, in accordance with reg. 9(1)(a) of the UK Regulations, that the web page operated by this retailer is to be treated as an invitation to treat in accordance with the principles of *Boots Cash Chemist*. The order placed by

---

[14] Draft E-Commerce Directive COM (1998) 586 final 18/11/98, Art. 11(1)(a).
[15] SI 2002/2013.

the customer is then to be treated as an offer to buy. An immediate acknowledgement of this order sent out by this retailer is just that—an acknowledgement of the offer, not an acceptance. Either party remains in a position to withdraw from the contract until such time as the retailer sends their dispatch confirmation email. This forms acceptance and concludes the contract.

At first glance this may seem to favour the retailer as they can withdraw from the contract at any time up to dispatch of the goods, but looking closely it is clear that the customer is also protected as they may withdraw their offer (cancel their order) at any point up to dispatch. This is the common position taken by almost all e-commerce sites. It allows for a human check to be made in the order process before the offer is accepted and the contract finalized. This prevents contracts from being formed by non-human actors on erroneous terms, as demonstrated in the Argos TV case of 2005 when a processing error led to a £350 television set being advertised at only 49p for 31 hours leading to 10,000 orders being placed, including one order for 80 TVs. Even though customers had completed the checkout procedure and had given their credit or debit card details to pay for the televisions ordered, Argos simply referred to their terms and conditions and cancelled all orders, refunding all monies paid.[16]

16.2.2 **Communicating acceptance**

This leaves one final question of contract formation. When, precisely, is acceptance effectively communicated to the offeror? To put it another way, does the delivery rule or the postal rule apply to acceptances which come in the form of a confirmation email? If we return to the example terms and conditions above we see they say that 'acceptance will be complete at the time we send the Dispatch Confirmation E-mail to you'. This though is not the complete picture because for an acceptance to be effective it has to be communicated to the offeror and there are two general principles which are used to determine when this is fulfilled. The first is the more commonplace principle that to be effective an acceptance must be delivered to the offeror. This principle applies in face-to-face oral negotiations but also to a number of 'at distance' communications. Most famously, in the case of *Entores Ltd v Miles Far East Corporation*,[17] Lord Denning (as Denning LJ) carried out an extensive examination of the principle of delivery in relation to an acceptance sent by Telex, concluding that 'the rule about instantaneous communications between the parties is different from the rule about the post. The contract is only complete when the acceptance is received by the offeror: and the contract is

---

[16] These errors are common. In January 2012 Argos also offered a £450 camera for £120. They also cancelled these orders. In March 2012 Tesco refused to honour purchases of a 64GB third generation iPad offered online for £49.99 instead of £659, while in January 2014 tools and hardware retailer Screwfix had an error which caused all items including sit-on lawnmowers worth £1600 to be priced at £34.99. It cancelled all orders except those already delivered or collected. Sometimes they are honoured. In 2002 Kodak fulfilled orders for a digital camera sold for £100 instead of its intended price of £329. This was because Kodak's terms and conditions at the time stated the contract would be concluded when they sent the order confirmation email, not the later dispatch confirmation stage. Kodak have since amended their terms and conditions. Also in January 2012 Marks & Spencer honoured sales of a £599 television wrongly priced at £199, following a petition. However, it is believed few orders were made as the error was in the early hours of Sunday morning.

[17] [1955] 2 QB 327.

made at the place where the acceptance is received.'[18] This conclusion brings about several consequences for electronic contracting. First, it suggests that communications by Royal Mail are a *sui generis* form of communication for the purposes of contract formation rules, and that it is only they which are regulated by the postal rule in place of the delivery rule. This principle was later affirmed in the House of Lords case of *Brinkibon Ltd v Stahag Stahl und Stahlwarenhandels-Gesellschaft*.[19] More recently two Scottish cases, *McIntosh v Alam*[20] and *Carmarthen Developments Ltd v Pennington*,[21] have extended the *Entores/Brinkibon* principle to facsimile communications.

Elsewhere, and before the implementation of the Electronic Commerce Directive, I had suggested that email communications may be treated differently to those other forms of telecommunications on the basis that one of the key arguments in support of the postal rule is that the offeror in accepting a posted letter of acceptance accepts the risk of delay or misdirection of a non-instantaneous means of communication.[22] The Electronic Commerce Directive, though, suggests this is unlikely. Article 11(1), as given effect by reg. 11(2)(a) of the Electronic Commerce (EC Directive) Regulations, states that 'the order and the acknowledgement of receipt will be deemed to be received when the parties to whom they are addressed are able to access them'. Regulation 11(2)(a) strictly only applies to the offer (termed here the order) and the acknowledgement of receipt of that offer, not to the acceptance, which will usually occur much later when the goods are dispatched. Despite this, it is hard to imagine a court accepting an argument that the delivery rule applies to offers and acknowledgements but not to acceptances. Therefore, it seems likely, that should the question arise, a UK court would find that the delivery rule applies to acceptances sent by email which conclude an online commercial transaction, such as a dispatch confirmation email.

Before leaving this issue it is important to note that Art. 11(1) first indent and Art. 11(2), and reg. 11(1) of the UK Regulations 'shall not apply to contracts concluded exclusively by exchange of electronic mail or by equivalent individual communications'.[23] This does not affect the preceding analysis on contract formation as the sections excepted are to do with delays and input errors in the contracting process not the provision found (in the UK Regulations in reg. 11(2)(a)) that 'the order and the acknowledgement of receipt will be deemed to be received when the parties to whom they are addressed are able to access them.'

16.3 **Contractual terms**

Having established when a contract is formed, the next question is what are the terms of the contract? The terms of any contract, whether it is an electronic contract or a traditional contract, will be those agreed upon by the parties at the time the contract

---

[18] Ibid. 334.

[19] [1983] 2 AC 34.

[20] 1997 SCLR (Notes) 1171.

[21] [2008] CSOH 139.

[22] Murray (n. 12) 24–5. See further P Lambert, *Gringras: The Laws of the Internet* (5th edn, Bloomsbury 2018) 38–40; J Dickie, 'When and Where are Electronic Contracts Concluded?' (1998) 49 *Northern Ireland Legal Quarterly* 332.

[23] The Electronic Commerce (EC Directive) Regulations 2002, reg. 11(3).

is concluded. This can clearly be seen in the series of cases known as the ticket cases concluding in *Thornton v Shoe Lane Parking Ltd*[24] Here Lord Denning led the Court of Appeal in finding that the issue of the ticket by an automated ticket machine was the point at which the contract was concluded, meaning that the terms of issue printed on the reverse of the ticket did not form part of the contract. This is the latest of a long line of ticket cases where terms printed on tickets or receipts have been held only to be validly incorporated into the contract if the terms have been brought to the other party's attention before the contract is concluded.[25] Thus terms not brought to the attention of the counterparty to the contract before the delivery of the final acceptance will not form part of the contract. How does one incorporate terms into the contract? As any student of contract law knows, contractual terms usually fall into one of three categories: express terms, terms incorporated by reference, and implied terms.[26]

16.3.1 **Express terms**

The incorporation of express terms into electronic contracts poses little difficulty. Such terms will be clearly set out in the transmission of information between parties and as such should be easily identified. There are, though, two problem issues regarding express terms which parties should always bear in mind when negotiating an electronic contract. The first is that parties must take care to identify the document or documents which are intended to constitute the contract. This will be more common with contracts concluded by email, which have to be individually drafted and which have the potential for prolonged exchanges between the parties at the negotiation stage, than with online contracts. The second potential problem of express terms is their interpretation by the courts in the event of a dispute. Contracting parties should attempt to limit as far as possible any inconsistencies or ambiguities in their contractual terms. In the event of any disagreement between the parties on the terms of the contract the court will apply the established rules of contractual interpretation.[27]

16.3.2 **Terms incorporated by reference**

The structure of the web, with its use of interconnected, hyperlinked pages, lends itself to incorporation by reference.[28] Consequently, terms incorporated by reference are common in relation to electronic contracts. The terms that the contracting party wishes to incorporate are set out in a separate document and are incorporated into the final contract by a reference to this separate document somewhere in the contractual documentation. Commonly, this document is a separate web page hosted on the same server as the online shop or marketplace. This is usually known as the terms and conditions page and is accessible via a hypertext link embedded at several points in the order system usually being expressly referred to during the checkout process.

---

[24] *Thornton* (n. 8).
[25] See in particular *Parker v South Eastern Railway Co.* (1877) 2 CPD 416.
[26] For detail on these categories see Chen-Wishart (n. 1) ch. 10.
[27] Ibid.
[28] As do email systems which support HTML and allow for embedded hypertext links.

To be effectively incorporated, the terms must not only be clear and unambiguous, they must also clearly have been intended to form part of the contract. This means that the party relying upon these incorporated terms must take all steps to bring them to the attention of the other party before the contract is concluded and in such a manner as to make it clear these terms are intended to be contractual terms.[29] These terms and conditions must therefore be clearly signposted. A passive link to terms and conditions contained on another page will not necessarily be sufficient to incorporate these terms into the contract. To effectively incorporate any external terms and conditions, the site operator must offer a clearly marked and prominent link to the specific terms and conditions they wish to incorporate into the contract before the customer makes their offer.

Fortunately, the site operator can easily ensure the terms and conditions have been incorporated into the contract by requiring the customer to indicate they have knowledge of, and have accepted, these terms and conditions before processing their order. This is done by requiring the customer to check a box during the checkout process acknowledging they have read and accept the terms and conditions or by expressly stating at the submission of the order that the customer agrees to these terms and conditions as a condition of the order being placed. If the customer has acknowledged they are aware of the terms, then the terms and conditions will be incorporated into the contract even if the customer has not actually read them.[30]

16.3.3 **Implied terms**

Finally, as with traditional contracts, there may be occasions where terms will be implied into electronic contracts. As implied terms usually come about apart from the contract formation process, the fact that a contract has been concluded in cyberspace will be of no impact to the rules on formation of contract. Implied terms may be implied by fact, such as terms required to give a contract business efficacy,[31] and terms implied on the basis of custom or usage.[32] Additionally, terms may be implied by the common law such as the implied term of seaworthiness implied into contracts for the carriage of goods by sea,[33] and the implied rule of non-derogation from grant.[34] As the introduction of these terms is uniform, no matter how the contract was negotiated and concluded, the use of electronic means to conclude the contract will not affect the established rules, and reference should be made to traditional contract texts for further guidance on implied terms.[35]

---

[29] Thus courts have continually held that where 'contractual' terms are found in places where the customer would not expect to find them they do not form part of the contract. See *Chapelton v Barry UDC* [1940] 1 KB 532; *Taylor v Glasgow Corporation*, 1952 SC 440 (both involving tickets/ receipts); and *Lightbody's Trustees v Hutchison* (1886) 14 R 4 (advertising leaflet).

[30] Some terms will require a greater degree of highlighting than others. Exclusionary terms for instance will require a significantly greater degree of explicitness. See Denning LJ in *Spurling v Bradshaw* [1956] 2 All ER 121, 125F: 'Some clauses which I have seen would need to be printed in red ink on the face of the document with a red hand pointing to it before the notice could be held to be sufficient.'

[31] *The Moorcock* (1889) 14 PD 64.

[32] *London Founders Association Ltd and Palmer v Clarke* (1888) LR 20 QBD 576.

[33] *Steel v State Line Steamship Co.* (1877) LR 3 App Cas 72.

[34] *Lyme Valley Squash Club Ltd v Newcastle under Lyme BC* [1985] 2 All ER 405.

[35] Chen-Wishart (n. 1) 10.6.

16.4 **Formal contracts**

Not all contracts are as simply accommodated into the framework of the information society. While the vast majority of everyday contracts are informal in nature, there are a small number of core contractual agreements which require to be formally concluded, usually in writing and sometimes with the requirement of a signature. These contracts tend to be for higher-value items or of a nature so as to create an ongoing contractual undertaking: they include contracts for the sale or transfer of an interest in land, guarantees, or an assignment of intellectual property rights.

The initial problem with many formal contracts was that for many there was a statutory requirement that they be 'in writing'. Although one could define an electronic document such as one created on a web page or via email as a written document in the colloquial sense there was a degree of debate as to whether it met the statutory definition of writing found in the Interpretation Act 1978 as 'includ[ing] typing, printing, lithography, photography and other modes of representing or reproducing words in a visible form'.[36] This rather dated definition of writing as being something in a tangible form suggested that should the rule of *ejusdem generis* be applied it was unlikely that a series of binary digits would qualify.

Some form of updating of the law was required and this became urgent when in 1996 the United Nations Commission on International Trade Law (UNCITRAL) adopted its Model Law on Electronic Commerce.[37] The model law requires all UNCITRAL states (including the UK) to formally recognize electronic contracts. Article 5 requires that 'Information shall not be denied legal effect, validity or enforceability solely on the grounds that it is in the form of a data message.' Building upon this principle, the model law goes on to ensure that all supporting principles required to provide for recognition of electronic contracts are in place. First, Art. 6 endows equivalence for electronic documentation by requiring that, 'where the law requires information to be in writing, that requirement is met by a data message if the information contained therein is accessible so as to be usable for subsequent reference'; then, through Art. 7, it requires that states give legal recognition to electronic signatures; finally and perhaps most importantly, Art. 11 formally provides for the legal recognition of electronic contracts.

As we have seen UK law could comply with Arts. 5 and 11, at least in relation to informal contracts, but with the Interpretation Act suggesting 'contracts in writing' had to be in a tangible form and with signatures often required to be 'in writing' there was an inability to comply with Arts. 6 and 7. This led the Department of Trade and Industry to undertake a review of the UK legal position, a review which concluded that: 'the position on the requirement for information to be "written" or "in writing" . . . cannot at present be met using electronic means'.[38] The DTI recognized that 'these uncertainties and limitations . . . are important barriers to the development of

---

[36] Interpretation Act 1978, Sch. 1.

[37] The UNCITRAL Model Law on Electronic Commerce (1996) with additional Art. 5 bis as adopted in 1998.

[38] DTI, 'Building Confidence in E-Commerce: A Consultation Document' 5 March 1999 URN 99/642 at [16].

electronic commerce',[39] and opened consultation on the best approach to removing these barriers.[40]

This led to the Electronic Communications Act 2000. The Act was designed to ensure the UK complied fully with the UNCITRAL model law, and to position the UK to allow for smooth implementation of the Electronic Commerce Directive,[41] which was also under construction at this time as a means to ensure the EU, which is a separate UNCITRAL member, also complied with the model law. The main provision of the Electronic Communications Act was s. 8. It allows for electronic documentation to be used in the formation of a contract where some sort of formality is required. It states that ministers may make subordinate legislation allowing for electronic communications to be used where appropriate to do anything which is 'required to be or may be done or evidenced in writing or otherwise using a document, notice or instrument' or which 'is required to be or may be done by post or other specified means of delivery'.[42]

Immediately it is clear that s. 8 does not give complete equivalence to all 'data messages' in accordance with Art. 6. Instead s. 8 enabled ministers to take a case-by-case approach to equivalence, designing specific rules to allow the integration of electronic data messages into existing statutory schemes with the least disruption. In a process that took many years to complete over sixty regulations and orders were passed. The UK approach was originally criticized for being slow, costly, and cumbersome to design and implement, but now parties, and the courts, have a clear framework to apply in the event of a challenge to the legality or enforceability of any formal contract concluded electronically.

16.5 **Electronic signatures**

Allowing electronic forms and delivery to be used for formal contracts is only half of the solution to online formal electronic contracting. Most formal contracts not only have requirements of form, they also usually require adoption of the terms of the contract, usually through the addition of a signature, stamp, or seal. This, obviously, proves extremely difficult for an electronic document which has no physical structure upon which a signature may be added. We have had to be extremely inventive in designing structures to replace traditional signatures as there is no way to simply replicate a manuscript signature, which is by far the most common form of signature, when dealing with intangible, digital documents. To this end a number of techniques were tried in the 1990s, including digitally encoding a signature made with an 'electronic pen and paper system',[43] or using biometric data such as fingerprints

---

[39] Ibid. [17].

[40] Ibid. at [18] the DTI set out two broad approaches and asked for views to be expressed by members of the public. The approaches considered were (1) to allow for individual Acts and Statutory Instruments on a case-by-case basis or (2) allow, through enabling legislation, a power for government ministers to adopt changes through statutory instruments where necessary. This is the approach taken and may be found in s. 8 of the Electronic Communications Act.

[41] Dir. 2000/31/EC.

[42] Electronic Communications Act 2000, s. 8(2) lists a number of 'purposes' for which a minister may make a s. 8 order.

[43] B Wright, 'Alternatives for Signing Electronic Documents' (1995) 11 *Computer Law and Security Report* 136.

or iris scans.[44] However, it soon became clear that systems such as these attempted to replicate physical signatures instead of seeking to fulfil the function of a signature: in other words, systems like these promoted form over function.

This was made clear in an excellent article by Professor Chris Reed called 'What Is a Signature?' In this, Reed distinguishes between the form of a signature—being usually facsimiles of the traditional manuscript signature such as 'the use of initials, marks, seals (for some but not all types of document), the adoption of a printed name and the use of rubber stamps'[45]—and the function of a signature. Reed notes that:

> the approach adopted by the courts . . . was to determine whether the particular form of signature adopted had already been recognised as valid in previous decisions, and if not, to decide whether it was acceptable in the particular circumstances. Often no reasons were given to explain why the signature method in question was legally acceptable; it appears that the judges in each case simply satisfied themselves that the method adopted achieved the same authentication effects as a manuscript signature.[46]

This, as noted by Reed, is not necessarily the best way to approach the adoption of a system to formalize electronic documents given the radically different nature of the intangible, nonrivalrous, and easily replicable digital document when compared with the tangible, rivalrous, and difficult to reproduce nature of an original manuscript signature, or its facsimiles. Reed suggests we focus on the function of a signature. He identifies three functions of a signature; one primary and two subsidiary.

 Highlight The primary function of a signature

The primary function is authentication. This reflects that a signature is an evidentiary tool used to reduce reliance on post-agreement oral evidence which attempts to deny the apparent accuracy of a document or explain its true meaning.

This primary function consists of three 'sub-functions'. These are that a signature provides evidence of:

1. the identity of the signatory;

2. that the signatory intended the 'signature' to be his signature; and

3. that the signatory approves of and adopts the contents of the document.

In addition to this primary function there are two subsidiary functions of a signature: (1) to validate official action (such as a judge signing an order of court), and (2) for consumer protection reasons.[47] Quite rightly Reed suggests that the function of a signature

---

[44] C Reed, 'What is a Signature?' (2000) 3 *JILT* <http://www2.warwick.ac.uk/fac/soc/law/elj/jilt/2000_3/reed/>.

[45] Ibid.

[46] Ibid.

[47] Reed is not strongly in favour of recognizing this as a separate function. He notes that 'The consumer's signature merely supplements this method of protection by providing evidence (a) that the other party has supplied the required information, and (b) that the consumer has agreed to the terms. Thus, although signatures have a secondary effect in respect of consumer protection, this effect is achieved through their primary functions as evidence of identity and agreement.'

should take priority over its form. There is no need for the traditions of physical signatures being carried over into the information society. Reed argues that the (at that time) newly adopted Electronic Communications Act 2000 and Electronic Signatures Directive[48] show that the primary method for promulgating electronic signatures is to be through the use of encryption technology.

16.5.1 Identity and electronic signatures

Article 7 of the UNCITRAL Model Law on Electronic Commerce required signatory states to adopt a provision that:

> Where the law requires a signature of a person, that requirement is met in relation to a data message if: (a) a method is used to identify that person and to indicate that person's approval of the information contained in the data message; and (b) that method is as reliable as was appropriate for the purpose for which the data message was generated or communicated, in the light of all the circumstances, including any relevant agreement.

This may be seen as enunciating Reed's primary function of authentication. As with Reed, there is no discussion of form, merely function.

To implement Art. 7 the EU originally enacted the Electronic Signatures Directive 1999. This has since been repealed and replaced (from 1 July 2016) by Section 4 of the Regulation on electronic identification and trust services for electronic transactions in the internal market (commonly referred to as 'eIDAS' Regulation) 2014.[49] This is the culmination of a lengthy review programme. Despite the legal framework for electronic contracts and electronic signatures dating from the late 1990s, the uptake of electronic signatures has been somewhat disappointing and the number of digital contracts formalized by electronic signatures remains low, due to the complexity and cost of the procedure and the fact that the different member states had different interpretations of the Electronic Signatures Directive. In 2006 the Commission issued a report on the uptake of electronic signatures in the EU and proposals as part of the Commissions i2010 project. Viviane Reding, then Commissioner for Information Society and Media, noted that although the framework provided by the directive provided 'A reliable system of electronic signatures that work across intra-EU borders the Commission was not fully satisfied with the take-up of e-signatures.'[50] This failure eventually led the Commission to propose a new draft directive on electronic identification and trust services for electronic transactions in the internal market.[51] This eventually was replaced with the eIDAS Regulation, adopted because a Regulation allows for both repairing the weaknesses of the current legal framework and the creation of a new single market in digital services. As the Commission notes, the Regulation:

> (1) ensures that people and businesses can use their own national electronic identification schemes (eIDs) to access public services in other EU countries where eIDs are available, and

---

[48] Dir. 1999/93/EC (since repealed).

[49] Reg. (EU) No 910/2014.

[50] See Europa, 'Electronic Signatures: Legally Recognised but Cross-Border Take-up too Slow' <http://europa.eu/rapid/press-release_IP-06-325_en.htm?locale=no>.

[51] COM(2012) 238/2.

(2) creates an European internal market for electronic Trust Services—namely electronic signatures, electronic seals, time stamp, electronic delivery service and website authentication—by ensuring that they will work across borders and have the same legal status as traditional paper based processes. Only by providing certainty on the legal validity of all these services, businesses and citizens will use the digital interactions as their natural way of interaction.[52]

The Regulation is wide-ranging and covers a number of eID and Trust services. Articles 6–12, cover electronic identification. These provide that where member states issues electronic identification to citizens or businesses of that state that these identifiers shall receive mutual recognition in other member states if it meets the qualification requirements.[53] Essentially mutual recognition is available when the eID is issued by the notifying member state; under a mandate from the notifying member state; or independently of the notifying member state but recognized by that member state;[54] and that identification can be used to access at least one service which is provided by a public sector body and which requires electronic identification in the notifying member state.[55] eIDs are classified in one of three levels of assurance: low, substantial, and high.[56]

 Highlight Low, substantial, and high assurance

Assurance level low shall refer to an electronic identification means in the context of an electronic identification scheme, which provides a limited degree of confidence in the claimed or asserted identity of a person, and is characterised with reference to technical specifications, standards and procedures related thereto, including technical controls, the purpose of which is to decrease the risk of misuse or alteration of the identity;

   Assurance level substantial shall refer to an electronic identification means in the context of an electronic identification scheme, which provides a substantial degree of confidence in the claimed or asserted identity of a person, and is characterised with reference to technical specifications, standards and procedures related thereto, including technical controls, the purpose of which is to decrease substantially the risk of misuse or alteration of the identity;

   Assurance level high shall refer to an electronic identification means in the context of an electronic identification scheme, which provides a higher degree of confidence in the claimed or asserted identity of a person than electronic identification means with the assurance level substantial, and is characterised with reference to technical specifications, standards and procedures related thereto, including technical controls, the purpose of which is to prevent misuse or alteration of the identity.

When giving recognition to eIDs from other member states there is only a requirement that recognition is given to those which meet or exceed the assurance level required by the recognizing state for the activity in question.

The Regulation does not require member states to create an eID scheme where one is not already in use but it does require them to notify the Commission of any schemes in

[52] <http://ec.europa.eu/digital-agenda/en/trust-services-and-eid>.
[53] Reg. (EU) No 910/2014, Art. 6.
[54] Art. 7(a).
[55] Art. 7(b).
[56] Art. 8(1).

use and any changes made to those schemes,[57] and to notify both the Commission and other member states who offer mutual recognition, should there be a security breach.[58] In the UK the eID scheme is GOV.UK Verify which was recently pre-notified to the Commission.[59] When a citizen goes online to carry out a number of services on a gov.uk website they are directed to Verify to prove their identity. One of five certified identity providers, Barclays, Digidentity, Experian, Post Office, and SecureIdentity, carry out the identification procedure.[60] Like the eID standards of the Regulation there are four levels of assurance. Level 1 is used when a relying party needs to know that it is the same user returning to the service but does not need to know who that user is. This equates to 'low' on the eID scale. Level 2 is used when a relying party needs to know on the balance of probabilities who the user is and that that they are a real person. This equates to 'substantial' on the eID scale. Level 3 is used when a relying party needs to know beyond reasonable doubt who the user is and that that they are a real person. This equates to 'high' on the eID scale. Level 4, which is currently only planned, is as level of assurance 3, but with a biometric profile captured at the point of registration. This would clearly be 'high' on the eID scale and indeed would go beyond the scale somewhat.[61]

Chapter III of the Regulation goes on to create a legal framework for the recognition and regulation of trust service providers; these are certification companies who carry out the process of identification and who issue eID certificates. These already have a role in EU law in anti-money laundering provisions but the Regulation creates a new regime for a single framework for recognition and regulation, not dissimilar to the data protection regime that we will see in future chapters. Article 17 requires member states to designate a supervisory authority for trust service providers; this can either be a domestic regulator or one shared with another or other member state or states.[62] This body, among other powers and duties, confers, and can withdraw, qualified status on trust service providers.[63] This is important for the purpose of recognizing qualified electronic signatures, which will be discussed further. The Regulation also provides that member states 'lay down the rules on penalties applicable to infringements of this Regulation [and that] the penalties provided for shall be effective, proportionate and dissuasive',[64] and that trust service providers will be liable 'for damage caused intentionally or negligently to any natural or legal person due to a failure to comply with the obligations under this Regulation.'[65]

For our purposes though the key part of the Regulation is Section 4 of Chapter III, Arts. 25–34. This is the new law on electronic signatures and whereas the old law described two types of electronic signature a [standard] electronic signature and an advanced electronic signature, we now find three varieties: (1) electronic signature; (2) advanced electronic signature; and (3) qualified electronic signature.

---

[57] Art. 9.

[58] Art. 10.

[59] European Commission, *GOV.UK Verify eID scheme pre-notified under eIDAS* 28 August 2018 <https://ec.europa.eu/cefdigital/wiki/display/CEFDIGITAL/2018/09/11/GOV.UK+Verify+eID+scheme+pre-notified+under+eIDAS>.

[60] In addition, Royal Mail and CitizenSafe can provide identity services as part of GOV.UK Verify, but cannot create a new account.

[61] Cabinet Office/CESG, *Good Practice Guide No. 45 Identity Proofing and Verification of an Individual*, October 2015, Ch. 4.

[62] In the UK the Information Commissioner's Office is the designated supervisory body for UK trust service providers.

[63] Art. 17(4)(g).

[64] Art. 16.

[65] Art. 13(1).

Highlight Forms of electronic signatures

1. An 'electronic signature' is data in electronic form which is attached to or logically associated with other data in electronic form and which is used by the signatory to sign; 'standard' electronic signature is one in which 'data in electronic form are attached to or logically associated with other electronic data and which serve as a method of authentication'.

2. An advanced electronic signature shall meet the following requirements:

   (a) it is uniquely linked to the signatory;

   (b) it is capable of identifying the signatory;

   (c) it is created using electronic signature creation data that the signatory can, with a high level of confidence, use under his sole control; and

   (d) it is linked to the data signed therewith in such a way that any subsequent change in the data is detectable.

3. A qualified electronic signature [is] based on a qualified certificate issued in one Member State [and] shall be recognised as a qualified electronic signature in all other Member States. Qualified certificates for electronic signatures shall contain:

   (a) an indication, at least in a form suitable for automated processing, that the certificate has been issued as a qualified certificate for electronic signature;

   (b) a set of data unambiguously representing the qualified trust service provider issuing the qualified certificates including at least, the Member State in which that provider is established and:

   – for a legal person: the name and, where applicable, registration number as stated in the official records,

   – for a natural person: the person's name;

   (c) at least the name of the signatory, or a pseudonym; if a pseudonym is used, it shall be clearly indicated;

   (d) electronic signature validation data that corresponds to the electronic signature creation data;

   (e) details of the beginning and end of the certificate's period of validity;

   (f) the certificate identity code, which must be unique for the qualified trust service provider;

   (g) the advanced electronic signature or advanced electronic seal of the issuing qualified trust service provider;

   (h) the location where the certificate supporting the advanced electronic signature or advanced electronic seal referred to in point (g) is available free of charge;

   (i) the location of the services that can be used to enquire about the validity status of the qualified certificate;

   (j) where the electronic signature creation data related to the electronic signature validation data is located in a qualified electronic signature creation device, an appropriate indication of this, at least in a form suitable for automated processing.

What is immediately clear looking at the distinction between an advanced electronic signature and a qualified electronic signature is that the EU is using qualified here to, in the common language definition, 'possesses a certain quality or qualities' rather than in the usual legal definition 'limited or modified' (as in qualified acceptance). To be qualified a signature is required to meet much stricter standards than those required to be 'advanced'.

What is the difference between the three? An electronic signature is of little legal value whatsoever, only being subject to a non-discrimination provision: 'An electronic signature shall not be denied legal effect and admissibility as evidence in legal proceedings solely on the grounds that it is in an electronic form or that it does not meet the requirements for qualified electronic signatures.'[66] In essence, the evidentiary value of an electronic signature is no greater than any other documentary materials. An advanced electronic signature is afforded a different but no greater evidentiary value. In essence their role is within public services. By Art. 27(1), 'if a Member State requires an advanced electronic signature to use an online service offered by, or on behalf of, a public sector body, that Member State shall recognise advanced electronic signatures, advanced electronic signatures based on a qualified certificate for electronic signatures, and qualified electronic signatures.' Thus the role of an advanced electronic signature is directed towards the provision of public services. It is the qualified electronic signature which in law is the equivalent of a traditional manuscript signature: in fact, Art. 25(2) says as much: 'a qualified electronic signature shall have the equivalent legal effect of a handwritten signature'. The attachment of a qualified electronic signature is therefore probative of the document. This is why qualified status on trust service providers is so important for, to be a qualified electronic signature, all certification of the signature must be from a qualified trust service provider. What then in practice is a qualified electronic signature?

16.5.2 **Qualified electronic signatures**

A qualified electronic signature is a form of electronic signature based in encryption technology with a matching certificate issued by a qualified trust service provider. While there are many ways to demonstrate one has accepted the terms of a document and intend to be bound by them, all are at risk of forgery or fraud, except for one system known as public key encryption or PKE signatures. The attachment of an unencrypted form of identification risks interception and/or reproduction without authorization, even a biometric signature could be replicated or added at a later date by a forger. Further digital documents, unlike physical documents, may be changed with no apparent trace of the change: words could be deleted or altered, a value of $1 per unit could be changed easily to $2 per unit without any obvious change on the face of the document. And as a digital document may be signed at a distance there is no way for a counterparty to prove identity without there being some form of third-party witness to prove the identity of a signatory.[67]

---

[66] Art. 25(1).

[67] This point may be demonstrated by a short experiment. Should a disgruntled employee of a firm want to take revenge on his employer he may pose as a member of senior management of that firm and enter into an online transaction on unfavourable terms. Assuming the counterparty never meets this person, then when he 'signs' the document acting on behalf of the company the counterparty has no reason to suspect anything is amiss. It is only when the contract comes to be fulfilled that the issue will come to light. When dealing at a distance, therefore, you want some system of independent identification of counterparties.

The system, which fulfils all these requirements, is an authenticated digital signature; this is the system adopted by the EU in describing both advanced and qualified signatures. Digital signatures use a particular functionality of encryption technology. Encryption is a well-known and tried system for protecting the content of messages, but previously it has not been of much use as a methodology of identifying the originator of the message, or demonstrating their intent to be bound to the message. This was because of the nature of traditional or symmetric key encryption.

When using symmetric keys the originator of the message and the recipient of the message would use the same key to encrypt and decrypt the message.

 Example Symmetric encryption

Romeo has a message that he must transmit securely to Juliet. To secure the message he uses the Caesar cipher. Caesar cipher is one of the simplest and most widely known encryption techniques. It is a type of substitution cipher in which each letter in the plaintext is replaced by a letter some fixed number of positions down the alphabet. For example, with a shift of +3, A would be replaced by D, B would become E, and so on. Using a +3 shift the message 'attack' becomes 'dwwdfn'. The method is named after Julius Caesar, who used it to communicate with his generals. Romeo chooses his cipher and sends the key to Juliet. He then separately encodes his message and sends that to Juliet as 'ciphertext'.

Note: Romeo and Juliet use the same key to encode and decode the messages.

Thus a basic cipher such as Caesar cipher relied on both the originator and recipient of the message having the same cipher key. This is good for sending secure messages (assuming the key is kept secure) but no good for proving identity as at least two people have copies of the key. Thus a message sent in encrypted form could be sent by any one of two people (or more depending on how many copies of the key there are).

Asymmetric or public key encryption (PKE) works differently. Here two keys are created: one known as the private key, the other the public key. The keys are mathematically linked but vitally you cannot discover one key by examining the other, and the keys only work in pairs—that is, if you encrypt a message with one key it can only be decrypted by the other. This technology was first suggested in the nineteenth century but was not developed until more powerful computers could be used to create the pairs of keys.

PKE is extremely powerful as an encryption tool as one never has to send the decryption key to the message recipient. One weakness of symmetric encryption is that you must at some point communicate to the recipient of your message the key you are using; this is liable to intercept, allowing your enemies to decrypt all your messages.[68] With PKE keys need never be traded in this fashion.

---

[68] There are two very famous examples of intercepted keys from the history books. It is believed that Sir Francis Walsingham, spy master of Queen Elizabeth I of England, obtained a secret code used by Queen Mary I of Scotland to communicate with a Catholic nobleman named Anthony Babington from Chartley Hall, Staffordshire, where Mary was being held. This allegedly unearthed a plot to overthrow Elizabeth leading to the execution of Mary. In another example, in World War II the German 'Enigma' code was broken by scientists at Bletchley Park with the help of a captured Enigma machine recovered from a German U-boat in 1941.

Example Asymmetric PKE encryption

Romeo has another message that he must transmit securely to Juliet. To secure the message he uses PKE. He takes his message and encrypts it using Juliet's public key. As this message can only be decrypted by the paired key (the private key) the public key may be made publicly available anywhere including on the internet at no risk to the security of the message.

Romeo then sends the encoded (ciphertext) message to Juliet, who then decrypts it using her private key. The private key never leaves Juliet's possession making the entire transaction secure.

Note: This time Romeo and Juliet use different keys to encode and decode the messages.

This was the reason for the design of PKE. It allowed British agents in Moscow to send messages back to London with no risk of the key being compromised. In addition, PKE encryption is resistant to so-called 'brute force' attacks, making it the preferred choice of encryption today for all secure services and internet sites.[69]

One interesting side effect of PKE, though, is that it may be used in reverse. An individual who wishes to prove their identity may encrypt a message (or even part of that message) using their private key. They can then send this to someone else and, providing the public key they have previously published can decrypt the encrypted part of the message, there is overwhelming proof that the message must have been encrypted using the private key, and as the private key is within the possession of one person we therefore have a way of proving identity, and the desire to adopt the contents of a digital document: in other words, a signature.

Example Asymmetric PKE signatures

Romeo now wants to 'sign' a contract with Juliet. To achieve this he encrypts all (or more likely part of) the document using his private key. He then sends the document to Juliet. She then uses Romeo's public key to decrypt the encrypted part of the document. If she is successful, she knows the document part could only have been encrypted using Romeo's private key, and as only Romeo has access to that key it is as unique, in evidentiary terms, as a manuscript signature.

The problem with a PKE signature is that by itself it does not prove identity: only possession of a key pair. To explain, there is nothing to stop me from setting up a fake website passing myself off as the UK operation of an international company who does not yet trade in the UK, someone like China Telecom. I then create a matching key pair and place the public key on my website. Then if I induce someone to trade with me I sign all contractual documents using my private key. When my victim checks my signature using my public key it will, of course, demonstrate that the signature is valid, but

---

[69] Secure Socket Layer (SSL), the standard encryption used for secure websites (such as financial transactions and online banking) is a form of PKE.

of course I am not who I say I am. This returns us to the common problem of proving identity when people are in remote locations.

The solution for electronic signatures is to issue a certificate of authenticity; a virtual ID card for key pairs. To create an authenticated signature (in particular a qualified, and therefore probative, signature) the user either creates his or her own key pair and sends them to a certification agency such as Barclays, Digidentity, or Experian along with proof of identity, or more usually and commonly he or she approaches the certification agency and asks them to create a key pair and simultaneously issue a certificate. The certification agency must carry out necessary checks to establish the identity of the individual or business before issuing the certificate, and may be held liable for damages should someone rely upon that certificate to their loss through any fault of the certification agency.[70]

Now when the signatory signs his or her message by attaching their private encryption to a portion of the message they also include a copy of the certificate. This shows who issued the certificate, when it was issued, and whether or not it is still valid. If the contractual counterparty is at all suspicious, they can contact the certification agency and ask for the identity of the signatory to be confirmed. Through the joint use of a secret, and in theory incorruptible, private key and the certificate of identity all of Reed's functions of a signature may be fulfilled, including the two subsidiary functions. In fact, in some ways, a digitally signed document is preferable to a physical document. A digital signature can be used not only to authenticate a document but also to guarantee the document has not been altered. In the real world we use forensics to determine whether a document has been altered post-signature but the risk remains that a page may be removed and replaced by a different page or gaps filled with additional words or numbers. With an electronically signed document we can reduce the risk of such fraud. All electronic documents have an in-built integrity check known as a 'checksum' or a 'hash sum'. This is a numerical value of all the data held in the file and is used by computers to check for accidental damage (corruption) or transmission errors in the file. In any complex file that number is uniquely created by the value of the contents of the file and will record any change, no matter how minor in the document, even the addition or removal of a single space. To protect the integrity of a signed document it is commonplace to encrypt the hash value of the document when signing. This both creates the electronic signature and protects the integrity of the document.

16.6 **Smart contracts**

We can't leave a chapter on electronic contracts without looking at least briefly at smart contracts. The term has become almost ubiquitous in the last three years yet the subject can be hard to define. Perhaps this is because there is no single accepted definition of a 'smart contract'. Computer scientist Nick Szabo first coined the term in 1994 and defined it as 'a computerized transaction protocol that executes the terms of a contract'. Building on this he explained that a smart contract is designed to 'satisfy common contractual conditions (such as payment terms, liens, confidentiality, and even enforcement), minimize exceptions both malicious and accidental, and minimize the need for trusted

---

[70] Art. 13(1).

intermediaries.'[71] A good starting point for anyone seeking a more contemporary legal definition is Surden's definition of a 'data-oriented contract'.[72] Surden starts by explaining what is different about a smart or data-oriented contract from a traditional contract: 'in a conventional contract, parties express their contracts using words—written (or spoken) descriptive language . . . by contrast, in a data-oriented contract, parties express some part of their contract—for example, key terms or conditions—as computer data and rules.'[73] Surden then points out that, vitally, smart contracts are very much still legal instruments not just lines of code, 'the data-oriented label simply suggests that the parties have decided that *some* subset of key terms or conditions would benefit from being represented as computer processable data.'[74] Another definition is that of Max Raskin: 'A smart contract is an agreement whose execution is automated. This automatic execution is often effected through a computer running code that has translated legal prose into an executable program.'[75] By drawing together Surden and Raskin's definitions we get a workable definition of a smart contract; it is a contract in which elements of the agreement have been recorded in computer code and which may execute those elements by code.

So far this analysis has been highly theoretical so what does a smart contract look like in reality?

 Example Simple smart contract

Arvin agrees to sell 10,000 shares in his company XSmart to Bryony if the share price reaches £10 before 31 December 2019. Bryony is happy to accept these terms and the two agree a contract. Instead of using a normal contract they agree to code elements of the agreement. Bryony's bank allows the software managing the contract access to her bank account and permission to transfer £100,000 at any point up to close of the market on 30 December 2019 to Arvin's bank account. At the same time the share register for Arvin's company allows the transfer of 10,000 shares from Arvin's holding to Bryony's holding.

Once the share price hits exactly £10 both protocols trigger and £100,000 is automatically transferred to Arvin's account while 10,000 shares are automatically transferred to Bryony. If the share price fails to reach £10 by the close of the market on 30 December 2019 the transfers do not execute and the protocols time out.

This is an extremely simple automated execution of contractual terms. It means that neither party has to monitor the markets to check the current share price and it means that if the contract terms are met there is no chance of either party defaulting on the terms. This type of very simple automated contract is nothing new. This is how a vending machine operates—you put in coins to a certain value and the machine, once it checks their value, vends the required item. There are a number of examples of automated execution as

---

[71] Nick Szabo, *Smart Contracts* <http://www.fon.hum.uva.nl/rob/Courses/InformationInSpeech/CDROM/Literature/LOTwinterschool2006/szabo.best.vwh.net/smart.contracts.html>.

[72] H Surden, 'Computable Contracts' (2012) 46 *University of California, Davis Law Review* 629.

[73] Ibid. 640.

[74] Ibid. (emphasis in the original).

[75] M Raskin, 'The Law and Legality of Smart Contracts', (2017) 1 *Georgetown Technology Review* 304.

forms of simple 'smart contracts'. Raskin for instance tells the reader of how a technology called a starter interrupter can be paired with a smart, self-enforcing contract:

> A starter interrupter is a device that is installed in an automobile that allows for a remote party to prevent the engine from starting. It allows a user who controls the starter interrupter to remotely shut off an automobile. These devices often also include global position systems, so that the collateral can be located. *The New York Times* reported on an Arizona company, C.A.G. Acceptance Corporation, which offers its automobile loans on a condition that if the debtor is in default, the company reserves the right use the device to prevent the car from starting.[76]

Raskin explains how these devices can be paired with a 'smart' contract to automatically disable vehicles and transmit their location for collection upon a scheduled payment being missed. This though is only the start of the smart contract story.

The point of smart contracts is to take enforcement out of the hands of the courts: parties use them to keep themselves out of the public court system. As Raskin observes 'Automated execution of a contract is a preemptive form of self-help because no recourse to a court is needed for the machine to execute the agreement.'[77] There is a theory that a smart contract lowers the cost of contracting as the risks of enforcement action are minimized, even removed if the contract is well-designed. This means legal costs of enforcement (and the time invested in enforcement actions) are removed from the cost of contracting. It may be argued however that costs are simply reallocated as the upfront costs of designing the contractware to execute the contract adequately reflect a different but no less burdensome cost.[78] The real problem of smart contracts though is trust. If the point of a smart contract is to avoid going to the public courts to solve disputes you need to have a trustworthy alternative which all parties can sign up to. So far, I have kept the examples simple; two counterparties and automated execution and enforcement. However, let's complicate things in a way that takes the agreement outside the framework of a simple execution of terms.

 Example Complex smart contract

Arvin agrees to sell Bryony his copy of Edvard Munch's *The Scream* for £120m. The item is to be delivered to Bryony's office in London and upon authentication Bryony undertakes to pay the agreed price. In accordance with the contract Arvin ships his copy of *The Scream* while Bryony places $120m in an escrow account under the management of the contractware. The $120m will be released upon authentication of the item.

When *The Scream* arrives Bryony's expert authenticates that it is a genuine Munch but it is not the version agreed to be sold by the parties. Bryony's expert is insistent that this is the 1895 version not the 1893 one. Arvin sends his expert who confirms it is indeed the 1893 version as agreed and Arvin demands the funds be released.

---

[76] Ibid. 330.

[77] Ibid. 333.

[78] There are very high costs of failure if you design your contractware incorrectly. For example, in 2016 a loophole in the DAO smart contract allowed a hacker to withdraw the equivalent of $70m from a total investment fund of $250m. Although the funds were recovered the hack showed the weakness of smart contracts. There have been several subsequent hacks and bug exploits.

In a normal contractual situation the parties would take their case to court and ulti-mately a judge would issue a judgment in favour of one party or the other. A not dissim-ilar case is the famous 1864 case of *Raffles v Wichelhaus*, in which controversy arose over a cotton shipment contract when two ships named *Peerless* could both fulfil the terms; one party claimed he intended one ship, the other party, the other.[79] If the contract is unclear as to whether the version intended for sale was the 1895 version or the 1893 version it would be up to a judge to decide by interpreting the terms of the contract as to whether Arvin had indeed fulfilled his part of the bargain. However, the point of a smart contract is to avoid judges and with Arvin and Bryony in dispute we cannot allow either side to set the terms if trust is to remain. How then do we adjudicate disputes or clear up confusion in smart contracts?

Now the engaged reader will have already come to the conclusion that the contract-ware will have thought of this and will determine which version was the one contracted for. However, when the parties are negotiating the contract each has their interpreta-tion of the terms. To allow one party to then fix these terms in the code of the con-tractware means the counterparty is bound, perhaps unlawfully, to the interpretation of the contracting party who designs the code. As Raskin observes 'a machine owned by one of the parties of a contract does not solve the problem of interpreting or writ-ing the contract. The problem, briefly stated, is that an independent third party must interpret the contract in accord with the intentions of the parties.'[80] If the public courts are not the forum to solve this dispute ,we need a different trusted third party. This is where distributed ledger technology, more commonly known as blockchain, comes in. While blockchain has taken on almost mythical status of late, it is in fact a rather simple technology to do a rather simple task.[81] Generally our 'trust systems' are central-ized. We trust the courts to interpret and enforce the law, we trust banks to maintain our financial records and protect our investments, and we trust public records like the Land Register to maintain records of ownership. A blockchain is a way to replace these centralized trust and authority systems with a decentralized collection of data that is verified by members of a peer-to-peer network. Essentially it is just a ledger of transac-tions that is held on thousands or even millions of computers rather than with a central server. It is the ledger equivalent of replacing servers with peer-to-peer systems. Rather than writing your terms directly into your smart contract you write them onto the blockchain. You start with a block which records basic data such as Arvin's ownership of *The Scream* or Bryony's credit balance of £120m. You then encode your transaction onto the blockchain: On delivery of Arvin's copy of *The Scream*, Bryony will transfer £120m to Arvin (obviously your contract can be much more complicated than this). Now going back to our original dispute, it is the blockchain which records whether Arvin has fulfilled the contract terms or not; the views of Arvin and Bryony are not relevant. How does the blockchain do this?

Well we've got part of the story of the blockchain so far; we have the block but not the chain. Arvin's ownership of *The Scream* will be recorded in the blockchain database not as a single block but as a series, or chain, of blocks. Thus if we imagine *The Scream* was originally owned by Xander and his ownership was recorded as a genesis block

---

[79] 2 H. & C. 906 (1864).
[80] Raskin (n. 75) 316–17.
[81] DLT and Blockchain are discussed further at 17.3.2.

(this is the original block hardcoded into the blockchain) and he then sold *The Scream* to Yvie, this would be recorded as a new block linked to Xander's original block, chaining them together. Yvie then sells *The Scream* to Zayn and another block connected to the first two is written to the ledger. Finally, Zayn sold to Arvin, writing another block to the ledger. The blockchain thus records Arvin's ownership as an immutable record from Xander to Arvin. If we imagine Bryony is paying in cryptocurrency (on which see 17.2) then her ownership of the relevant coins or tokens is also recorded in the ledger. Now when the contract is written it is written not as whether or not Arvin will transfer the 1893 or 1895 version of the painting, it is written as Arvin will transfer his ownership as recorded on the blockchain in return for payment by transfer of Bryony's cryptocurrency. When Arvin and Bryony dispute which version of the painting is to be transferred, this will be decided by the blockchain which determines whether or not Arvin has transferred the copy of *The Scream* recorded in the ledger. A process of authentication does this.

 Highlight Authenticating the transaction

1. Arvin sends a crypto token which records his ownership of *The Scream* to Bryony.
2. The transaction is broadcast and is now waiting to be picked up by a miner on the according blockchain.
3. Miners on the network select the transaction (and the corresponding counter transaction representing Bryony's payment) and form them into a 'block'.
4. To add this block of transactions to the blockchain, the block needs a signature. Solving a very complex mathematical problem that is unique to each block of transactions creates this signature. Each block has a different mathematical problem, meaning each miner will work on a different problem that is unique to the block they built, but all of these problems are equally hard to solve. In order to solve this mathematical problem, a lot of computational power is needed (and thus a lot of electricity). This is the process referred to as mining.
5. The miner that finds an eligible signature (solution) for its block first, broadcasts this signature to all the other miners.
6. Other miners now verify if that solution corresponds with the problem of the senders' block (the hash input actually results in that signature). If it is valid, the other miners will confirm the solution and agree that the block can be added to the blockchain.
7. If the majority of the miners reaches consensus, the block gets added to the blockchain.

Thus, if the majority of miners agree that the transaction is correct; that is, Arvin has transferred the correct version of *The Scream* according to the record of ownership on the ledger, then the transaction will execute. It does not matter what Bryony's interpretation of the contract is, or Arvin's come to that, all that matters is what the miners confirm. Of course Bryony still feel aggrieved and this is where the Achilles heel of smart contracts comes in.

While smart contracts are designed to remove human fallibility and the costs of traditional enforcement models built around human judges, they have clear failings. First, by trying to reduce a contract to algorithmic data there is an attempt to remove the human elements of contextualization and perhaps even compassion or the concept of 'justice' as opposed to simply interpretation and enforcement from the process. This is likely to concern a lot of people simply because machines cannot exercise these human qualities. Second, and more importantly for the widespread adoption of smart contracts, the technology finds ambiguity very difficult to deal with. The example given of a painting with many versions is actually one that smart contracts would find very difficult to solve as, while humans are very good at working with ambiguity, machines are not. For example, as Ruskin observes, 'a potential problem comes with imperfect performance. Courts in the United States do not demand perfect performance for a contract to be recognized and enforced. The common law doctrine of substantial performance permits a contract to be recognized even if the performance does not fully comport with the express terms laid out. This is the kind of leeway that a computer program cannot recognize because it involves an outcome that was not contemplated and specified by the parties. Imagine, for instance, a contract for a painting that is contingent on the reasonable personal satisfaction of the buyer.'[82] For this reason, so far, smart contracts have mostly been focused on transactions involving financial instruments and investment instruments as these tend to be more easily reducible to code.[83]

One final note before leaving smart contracts; occasionally you will come across claims that smart contracts somehow sit outside the legal system. One such recent suggestion to this end came rather surprisingly from Supreme Court Justice Lord Hodge who in a speech delivered in October 2018 claimed 'No-one, including a court, can stop the performance of a smart contract. The courts will not be able to cancel the performance of the contract.'[84] This is not legally true. Whether it is technically true depends upon how the contract is set up. However, these contracts are not extra-legal. They are still governed by contract law and by law we can determine the limits of what they may or may not do. The idea that somehow smart contracts are outside the legal system is a fiction created by a few people who imagine that somehow blockchain is fairer or more democratic, due to its decentralized nature, and who also believe that regulation by code is preferable to regulation by law. They are a minority even within the blockchain/smart contract community.

16.7 **Conclusions**

Contract formation is probably the most commonplace legally regulated activity in the online environment. It is at once also the simplest and yet most complex online activity from a legal perspective. As we have seen, informal contracts are easily concluded, yet raise a number of issues. Where is the contract domiciled, what are the terms of the contract, and when is the contract concluded? These three W's are the WWW of contract lawyers. Traditional rules on contract formation, as seen in cases like *Thornton v Shoe*

---

[82] Raskin (n. 75) 326.
[83] P Paech, 'The Governance of Blockchain Financial Networks' (2017) 80 MLR 1073.
[84] Lord Hodge, *Financial Technology: Opportunities and Challenges to Law and Regulation. Speech delivered to East China University of Political Science and Law, Shanghai, China* on 26 October 2018 < https://www.supremecourt.uk/docs/speech-181026.pdf>.

Lane Parking and *Entores Ltd v Miles Far East Corporation*, assist greatly in the domestic interpretation of these issues. But in the online environment a consumer is just as likely to conclude a contract with an American or French trader as a UK-based trader. Here provisions such as the UNCITRAL model law and the Electronic Commerce Directive assist. Additionally, consumer protection laws assist a consumer should they find themselves disputing the position with their counterparty.

This is only part of the story though. Formal contracts have rules as to form and often require a signature; something impossible in the traditional sense when dealing with a digital document. Complex rules have been developed as to the form of both documents and signatures, with heavy reliance being placed on highly technical solutions such as PKE encryption technology. Finally, we examined the relatively new technologies of distributed ledger technology and so-called 'smart' contracts which seek to use blockchain technology to automate transactions and to reduce the role of the courts. Yet, despite all these challenges, we find in reviewing this chapter an almost complete absence of case law dealing with these subjects. Why is this? It is because, on the whole, we make it work without the need for legal interventions. Online retailers have extremely detailed terms and conditions and generally those who do not act reasonably and fairly do not last long in the cut-throat online business environment. Although an essential body of law, the rules on electronic contract formation and interpretation will, in all likelihood, continue to be little relied upon in court.

TEST QUESTIONS

Question 1

How (legally) do electronic contracts differ from traditional contracts? In your opinion have the E-Commerce Directive and Regulations solved the unique problems of e-contracts?

Question 2

What are 'smart contracts'? What legal implications arise in smart contracts?

Question 3

The requirements needed to obtain a qualified electronic signature are far too onerous and mean there is no comparison between a simple manuscript signature and the qualified electronic signature which is designed to replace it. Until a simpler method of replicating the manuscript signature is found for the digital environment the use of electronic signatures will remain uncommon.

Discuss

FURTHER READING

Books

H Halilovic, *Harmonisation of Electronic Contracting Law in Europe* (Independent 2018)

S Mason, *Electronic Signatures in Law* (4th edn, IALS 2017)

F Wang, *Law of Electronic Commercial Transactions: Contemporary Issues in the EU, US and China* (Routledge 2014)

Chapters and articles

J Dumortier, 'Regulation (EU) 910/2014 on electronic identification and trust services for electronic transactions in the internal market (eIDAS Regulation) in A Lodder and A Murray (eds.) *EU Regulation of E-Commerce: A Commentary* (Edward Elgar 2017)

A Lodder, 'Directive 2000/31/EC on certain legal aspects of information society services, in particular electronic commerce, in the internal market' in A Lodder and A Murray (eds.) *EU Regulation of E-Commerce: A Commentary* (Edward Elgar 2017)

M Raskin, 'The Law and Legality of Smart Contracts', 1 *Georgetown Technology Review* 304 (2017)

C Reed, What Is a Signature? 3 *JILT* (2000)

Electronic payments and cryptocurrency

17.1 **Payments**

Like contracting, payment is one of these complex legal relationships we tend not to think of on a day-to-day basis. When we buy something we hand over some banknotes, or place our credit or debit card into a chip and PIN device, or, more likely today, simply wave our smartphone over a contactless payment reader. Behind this though is a complex banking system which allows all this to function: the ability to make payment allows services to be supplied immediately and orders for products to be processed without delay. Online, the issue of secure payment at a distance (i.e. without both parties being present at the same place at the same time), sometimes over borders, is a more complex problem and, as we shall see, the solution used to date has been relatively inelegant, while alternatives have proven difficult to develop and establish.

17.1.1 **Token payments**

The most familiar payment system is the token system. Tokens are the method used in physical currency where a token (a banknote or coin) is exchanged for the supply of goods and services. The token system has a number of benefits which led to it becoming the dominant form of real-world currency for over 3,000 years.

First, tokens have, over the years, become easily portable and easily stored with banknotes replacing old-fashioned coin-based currency from the eighteenth century onwards. Second, tokens such as banknotes and coins are both fungible and divisible. This means that they are interchangeable (one £10 note is as good as the next) and are capable of subdivision into smaller units (a £10 note can be divided into two £5 notes or ten £1 coins). These functions are essential to liquidity; the function of money that allows it to be traded at a fixed value, including for other currency. This allows for change to be given allowing goods of a lesser value to be traded for a banknote of a higher value with change (tokens of a lower value) being used as the makeweight in the transaction. Third, tokens are a physical store of value. This is vital to retain confidence in a currency and leads to most tokens being secured or guaranteed by the central bank or treasury.[1] Collectively tokens are an extremely efficient way of fulfilling the three key functions of money:

Highlight The key functions of money

The three key functions of money are to act as:

1. a means of exchange
2. a unit of measurement
3. a comparator of the value of goods and service.

Tokens also fulfil the secondary function of liquidity:

Highlight The qualities that assist liquidity

The three key qualities of money that assist liquidity are:

1. portability and storability
2. fungibility
3. divisibility.

If any new form of monitory exchange is to replace cash tokens it must at least fulfil these functions.

17.1.2 **Alternative payment systems**

Several alternatives have developed over the years, mostly based upon substitution of a debt, novation, and funds transfer. The most common alternative to the token system of currency until recent years was debt substitution. This is where a debt owed to one party is 'paid off' by substituting a debt owed by another. This is the design of the cheque payment system wherein a debt owed by the bank to its customer is used to make payment to a third party. Thus a customer has money on deposit with her bank; the bank is her debtor to the value of the money she has on deposit. The customer then buys goods and pays by cheque. In doing so she pays her debt for the goods she has bought by transferring part of the debt the bank owes her. The bank pays her debt and reduces its indebtedness to her by the same amount.

Debt substitution is a way of reducing the risks associated with carrying money, but it has few of the benefits of cash tokens. It cannot be used as a unit of measurement or as a comparator of the value of goods or services. It is not fungible, is not divisible,

[1] In the UK Bank of England notes are issued by the central bank while coins are issued by the Royal Mint, an executive agency of the Treasury.

and vitally is not as easily transferrable as cash tokens. In other words, forms of debt substitution are strictly not money but are a money substitute. The cheque was initially popular for higher-value transactions where the allied risks of carrying large amounts of money could be negated. Recently a new phenomenon has seen debt substitution become the dominant form of debt settlement in the UK, due to the replacement of the cheque with the chip and PIN (and contactless) debit card. The general and wide-spread use of the debit card even for low-value transactions, thanks to the convenience it offers, has seen debt substitution become increasingly popular and now the value and number of debit card transactions eclipses cash token transactions in the UK high street.[2] Many people refer to chip and PIN or contactless debit card transactions as electronic payments, although as we shall see, this is not strictly true; rather, they are electronically enabled payments, meaning that the payment technology uses digital tools to make the system more reliable and secure, but they are in form debt substitution payments, not true electronic payments.

Another popular payment system, which has proven in particular to be extremely popular with internet transactions, is payment by credit card. Although to the user a credit card transaction may appear to be functionally the same as a debit card transaction—a piece of plastic is handed over and a PIN is used to authorize the transaction—they are in fact very different in function. Whereas a debit card relies upon money the customer has placed with the bank (or perhaps an agreed overdraft), a credit card works by having the credit card company assume the customer's debt for them and then providing the customer with credit to the same value. This uses a principle known as novation: the replacing of one contract or obligation with another. When a customer pays by credit card, the credit card company agrees to take on the debt the customer owes to the supplier and makes payment as if it were the customer. It simultaneously issues credit to the customer to the same value as the debt incurred, creating or extending contractual relationships between the credit card company and the supplier, and the credit card company and the customer. In function a credit card payment, like a debit card payment, is a money substitute not a form of money. Like a debit card it offers none of the functions of money. Also in common with a debit card payment, although people often think of credit card payments as electronic payments they are not—they are electronically enabled payments only.

Finally there is payment by fund transfer. This is not an option for traditional high-street transactions as it involves a direct transfer from one bank account to another. It tends to be used for commercial transactions and for property transactions, as well as for regular payments such as bills and subscriptions, and for payments using internet banking services. There are a number of names for different types of fund transfer: a standing order is an order to pay a predetermined amount at the instigation of the account holder on a certain date or at a certain frequency; a direct debit allows the payee to debit varying amounts from the payer's account at the payee's request, while a CHAPS transfer is a same-day inter-account transfer. These types of transfers are often collectively known as 'electronic fund transfers' (EFTs), along with internet account transfers and direct credits. This terminology has also extended to cover credit and debit card

---

[2] R Jones, 'Cash no longer king as contactless payments soar in UK stores', *The Guardian*, 12 July 2017; PA, 'UK in-store contactless payments overtake chip and pin—Worldpay', *The Guardian*, 16 October 2018.

purchases with these often being referred to as 'electronic funds transfers at the point of sale' (EFTPoS). Again the common message is that none of these alternative payment systems are money in the true sense of the word. Money remains, with the possible exception of cryptocurrencies discussed further at 17.3, the only form of payment that possesses the functions of money. This raises the obvious question: if more and more trade occurs in a purely digital environment where cash tokens cannot be exchanged and over distances where it is impractical to send cash tokens by traditional means, how do we develop functional methods of payment for the information society?

17.2 **Online payments, e-money, and e-payments**

In the early days of e-commerce a number of innovative e-money systems were developed. These included the Mondex smart payment card system introduced in 1994. One would 'charge up' the card by visiting specially enabled ATM machines and then one could spend amounts from the card by visiting retailers who accepted Mondex. Mondex was a version of electronic cash. It had many of the features of cash tokens: it was easily portable, fungible, and divisible and, like cash tokens, the Mondex user was anonymous. Mondex-style technology is now being used in current near field communication (NFC) smartcard systems including the London Transport Oyster Card and Apple Pay/Android Pay. The problem with Mondex was that it was inconvenient. Only Mondex registered businesses which had installed Mondex readers would accept it for payment. In addition, if your Mondex card was lost or stolen, then, like real cash, you lost whatever was charged on to it. Consumers continued to prefer debit cards over Mondex and soon it was removed from the market. Other systems vied to be the new cash for the online world. Digicash was a software-based solution which installed an 'electronic wallet' on your hard drive: a protected space which, using encryption technology, was secure. The customer could buy Digicash tokens which were simple encrypted files containing some tracking data to prevent forgery (a digital serial number) which was stored in the wallet. When the customer wanted to pay a retailer he or she could transfer tokens to the value of the goods bought, just like real cash. It functioned like Mondex for online transactions. It fulfilled most of the functions of cash. It was fungible, divisible, and anonymous. However, it was not easily portable (it was tied to the wallet, which was tied to the hard drive) but as it was designed as an online currency this did not matter. For the first time it offered the opportunity to develop a true digital cash system which fulfilled the three key functions of money. It was possible to use Digicash as a means of exchange, a unit of measurement, and as a comparator of the value of goods and service. Digicash spawned a number of imitators including Cyphermint and later Peppercoin, a system designed to make so-called micropayments. Today the nearest modern equivalent are cryptocurrencies which will be discussed in 17.3.

These systems all failed to capture the public imagine though, but why? There are a number of reasons First, consumers are extremely conservative with cash and payment methods. Given the perceived risks of financial loss, consumers tend to trust established names with their money: high-street banks such as Barclays, Lloyds, and NatWest are trusted, even after the recent financial crisis. Companies with no track record such as Digicash do not have the same position of trust. Second, consumers were happy to use their credit and debit cards both online and offline. The perceived advantage of anonymity offered by e-cash systems was outweighed by the advantage that the card issuer would assume most of the risks of fraud associated with online transactions.[3] Third, the technology was unreliable and untested. Who provided the best system? Which was most secure? There was no way for consumers to know. Fourth, and most importantly, all these electronic cash providers were private companies. Nearly all of them were recent start-ups with no record of financial stability. Consumers tend only to have confidence in cash tokens issued by, and/or guaranteed by, either the central bank or government of the issuing state. This was the problem with cyberspace. There was no government, no central bank, and no pre-existing financial framework, only private organizations and competing technologies.

As a result of this, true electronic money never took off. Instead, alternative payment systems dominate online and offline. The most popular payment method remains by some distance the credit or debit card. A number of more innovative payment systems are though emerging. Led by market leader PayPal who has been offering an alternative online payment method since 1998, new systems such as Amazon Pay, Venmo, and Due are slowly establishing market share. The reason that systems have begun to emerge in the last few years is a refresh in the legal framework which makes it easier to process e-payments and to issue e-money.

17.2.1 **PSD II and EMD II**

The original legal framework for Europe was found in the e-Money Directive 2000[4] and the Payment Services Directive 2007.[5] The e-Money Directive regulated the issue and redemption of e-money, defined in the directive as 'monetary value as represented by a claim on the issuer which is: (i) stored on an electronic device; (ii) issued on receipt of funds of an amount not less in value than the monetary value issued; and (iii) accepted as means of payment by undertakings other than the issuer'.[6] The Payment Services Directive regulated who could process payments throughout the EU. Neither proved to be particularly happy or effective ultimately. To instill consumer confidence the e-Money Directive introduced extremely restrictive capital and business restriction requirements on electronic money issuers (EMIs) which made it almost impossible for them to operate profitably. Even PayPal, which at one time was a UK-registered EMI, made the decision to instead take a banking license in Luxembourg to allow it to escape the restrictive regime of the e-Money Directive. The Payment Services Directive was initially more successful. Better designed than the e-Money Directive it did allow a number of new payment institutions to begin to offer services in competition to the banks and major card issuers Visa, Mastercard, and Amex. However, a failure to ensure equal access to the interbank clearing system and to end-user account details hamstrung these new payment institutions. As a result, both have been overhauled through two new directives the e-Money Directive 2009 (or EMD II)[7] and the Payment Services Directive 2015 (or PSD II).[8]

---

[3] I Grigg, 'How DigiCash Blew Everything' <http://cryptome.org/jya/digicrash.htm>.
[4] Dir. 2000/46/EC.
[5] Dir. 2007/64/EC.
[6] Dir. 2000/46/EC, Art. 1(3)(b).
[7] Directive 2009/110/EC.
[8] Directive (EU) 2015/2366.

Two of the main reasons the original e-Money Directive ultimately failed were the capital requirements for e-money issuers and the business restrictions imposed upon them. Under the original e-money regime an EMI was required to hold initial capital of €1m and to retain that level of capital for as long as they remained an electronic money institution. In addition, they were required to retain operating funds at least equal to the higher of the value of all electronic money they had in current circulation or the average value of their money in circulation in the preceding six months, these funds to be held in approved low-risk, high-liquidity form of investment vehicles.[9] EMIs were also prohibited from carrying on any business beyond that of issuing and managing e-money.[10]

To end these restrictions EMD II brings major changes. The initial capital requirement is reduced and the rules on liquidity are changed. EMD II has a complex set of calculations regulating capital and liquidity but essentially the core requirement now is that an EMI must have an initial capital of at least €350,000[11] and must hold a fund of at least 2 per cent of the average outstanding electronic money.[12] This brings EMIs in line with the less restrictive requirements of payment institutions, as set out in the first Payment Services Directive. Vitally, EMD II also sweeps away the rule restricting electronic money issuers to carry on business as solely an electronic money issuer by Art. 6(1).

 Highlight Article 6(1)

Institutions shall be entitled to engage in any of the following activities:

(a) the provision of payment services listed in the Annex to Directive 2007/64/EC;

(b) the granting of credit related to payment services referred to in points 4, 5 or 7 of the Annex to Directive 2007/64/EC, where the conditions laid down in Article 16(3) and (5) of that Directive are met;

(c) the provision of operational services and closely related ancillary services in respect of the issuing of electronic money or to the provision of payment services referred to in point (a);

(d) the operation of payment systems as defined in point 6 of Article 4 of Directive 2007/64/EC and without prejudice to Article 28 of that Directive;

(e) business activities other than issuance of electronic money, having regard to the applicable Community and national law.

This finally allowed mobile network operators like Vodafone and technology companies such as Apple or Google to be licensed as electronic money institutions without fear of this affecting their ability to carry on their core business.

There is little doubt that this was a long-overdue development: by relaxing the key provisions on liquidity and allowing EMIs to carry on unrelated business, the

---

[9] Dir. 2000/46/EC, Arts. 4–5.
[10] Ibid. Art. 1(5).
[11] Directive 2009/110/EC, Art. 4.
[12] Ibid. Art. 5(3).

millstones of the old directive were swept away. What is interesting is what electronic money became in the nine years between the original directive and the new one. In 2000 it was envisaged that the problem was with online payments. Customers were relying on credit and debit cards to make payment; this was extremely inefficient with high transaction costs and with no means for consumer-to-consumer payments. It seemed that what was missing was an internet currency—money rather than payments methods. The Commission believed there was a demand for electronic money to facilitate online electronic commerce and believed that the Electronic Money Directive would provide the framework for this to grow. We now know there is little demand for electronic money in the online environment.[13] Customers like the security and convenience offered by card payments or payment institutions such as PayPal or Amazon Pay. Payment institutions have also recently been given a boost by the provisions of PSD II. This provides a revised framework for payment institutions designed to offer consumers greater protection online by requiring that, in cases of payment fraud 'where the payment instrument is not present at the point of sale, such as in the case of online payments, it is appropriate that the payment service provider be required to provide evidence of alleged negligence since the payer's means to do so are very limited in such cases'[14] and by requiring the 'payment service provider applies strong customer authentication where the payer: (a) accesses its payment account online; (b) initiates an electronic payment transaction; or (c) carries out any action through a remote channel which may imply a risk of payment fraud or other abuses.'[15]

More important than all this though are the 'open banking' provisions of PSD II. While the increased protections for customers no doubt helps to instill consumer confidence, there needed to be a regime which gave payment institutions fair access to the full range of banking services controlled by traditional banks. This is achieved through Title II, Chapter 2 (Arts. 35–7). This requires that:

> rules on access of authorised or registered payment service providers that are legal persons to payment systems are objective, non-discriminatory and proportionate and that they do not inhibit access more than is necessary to safeguard against specific risks such as settlement risk, operational risk and business risk and to protect the financial and operational stability of the payment system.[16]

In the UK this has been given effect by reg. 103 of The Payment Services Regulations 2017[17] but also by the adoption of the Open Banking API. The Open Banking API is a shared application programming interface that allows banks, payment institutions, and e-money issuers to share date in a secure yet open format allowing more innovative products, such as Monzo the challenger bank that operates uniquely as a smartphone app.

---

[13] Even the truly virtual currency bitcoin has arguably gone from being a currency to an investment vehicle. Perhaps the only place where online virtual currencies have thrived are in game cash for online gaming such as 'Gold' in World of Warcraft, 'Platinum Pieces' in Everquest, and 'Points' in Xbox Live.

[14] Directive (EU) 2015/2366, Recital 72.

[15] Ibid. Art. 97(1).

[16] Ibid. Art. 35(1).

[17] SI 2017/752.

As a result of EMD II and especially PSD II, electronic money has begun, surprisingly, to flourish in the real world rather than the online world. People carry less cash than they used to as they rely more on payment methods. This means it is more likely that people will not have change for small-value transactions such as paying for parking, for transport, or for low-value items such as coffee or a newspaper. Additionally, for banks and for vendors coins are very inefficient. They cost a lot to transport and need constant security. Conversely, at low values, payment methods are also inefficient due to the transaction costs involved. Electronic money, although it does still come with transactions costs, is a cheaper simpler method of real-world payment and, with the widespread adoption of near field communication technology (used for contactless payments including Apple Pay and Google Pay), it is now clear that the high street, not the internet, is the natural home for the next stage of electronic money development. And with the relaxation of the strict rules found in the first Electronic Money Directive the EU is finally in the right place to reap the rewards of such technologies, as we are seeing in a variety of exciting applications such as Apple Pay (which can be installed on your phone or your Apple Watch), Google Pay, Pingit, and Circle. Also in the next few years we can expect a national travel card system, like Oyster, known as ITSO to be effective across England and Wales.

17.3 **Bitcoin and cryptocurrencies**

One area which has developed quite independently of the European legal framework, is cryptocurrency, of which the best-known example is bitcoin. Cryptocurrencies work on similar principles to smart contracts which were discussed in chapter 16. Just as a smart contract is a peer-to-peer contract, cryptocurrencies are peer-to-peer currency. They do away with the idea of a central trusted party who verifies the monetary value of the currency (such as a central bank or financial institution). Instead it is, in the words of its creator, Satoshi Nakamoto,[18] 'an electronic payment system based on cryptographic proof instead of trust, allowing any two willing parties to transact directly with each other without the need for a trusted third party.'[19] The system works through two vital underpinnings. The first is a chain of electronic signatures, the second a distributed ledger of transactions known as the blockchain.

17.3.1 **Crypto**

The first part of any cryptocurrency is the crypto part. Before we embark on an explanation of how the crypto element of cryptocurrency works, take a banknote out of your purse or wallet and look at it.[20] Look at the reverse of the banknote (the side that doesn't have the Queen on it). You will see a serial number repeated twice. Once printed vertically on the left hand side and once printed horizontally in the bottom right corner. It

---

[18] Satoshi Nakamoto is a pseudonym of either an individual or a group. Several attempts have been made to 'unmask' Nakamoto but none have to date been convincing.

[19] S Nakamoto, *Bitcoin: A Peer-to-Peer Electronic Cash System* <https://bitcoin.org/bitcoin.pdf>.

[20] I acknowledge that, as already discussed, modern payment systems such as contactless payment mean fewer people are carrying banknotes on them today. So if you don't have a banknote to hand, borrow one from someone nearby (just don't forget to return it afterwards).

will be in a format like: DB45 153603. This essentially is all a banknote is today. It is a carrier for a serial number. The Bank of England has a record of all serial numbers in issue which allows it to keep track of the complete value of banknotes in circulation. The reason the serial number is replicated is to allow the bank to replace damaged notes. If your banknote is partially eaten by your dog, or destroyed by an overactive toddler, the Bank of England will replace the money for you if you can supply over 50 per cent of the note including one serial number. As a banknote is merely a carrier medium for a serial number there is no legal reason why we need the physical banknote at all. As we have seen throughout this book, the process of digitization has divorced information from physical carriers and the same is true for serial numbers. The first thing you need for a cryptocurrency therefore is a way of tracking value—that is, a serial number for your currency.

This is achieved using public key encryption.[21] The first stage to owning (and spending) cryptocurrencies is to install a wallet onto your device. A wallet is a software program that stores private and public keys and interacts with the blockchain to enable users to send and receive digital currency and monitor their balance. Into this wallet you must load your currency which you get in one of three ways: you can buy them from an exchange, receive them as payment for goods or services, or you can mine for them (more on this at 17.3.2). For most initial users this means buying tokens from an exchange or dealer, of which there are many. When you buy the currency you don't actually receive anything. Instead, value is loaded into your wallet (much like a prepay mobile phone) and this is recorded in the blockchain as a transaction (see 17.3.2). How is all of this kept secure? That is, how does anyone know that you are the rightful possessor of that value, or that it has gone to the right recipient? This is where the public key encryption comes in. Much like serial numbers on banknotes each wallet has unique identifiers, which makes sure the value is going to the right place and from the right place. In your wallet is your private key this is your unique identifier for sending value. There is also your public key which acts both as your address to receive value and allows others use to receive value from you. Let's look at a crypto transaction.

 Example Buying bitcoin

Mischa decides to buy some bitcoin. She installs a wallet onto her phone then visits an exchange to buy ฿5. She pays the exchange by debit card and in return the exchange transfers value equivalent to ฿5 to her. It does this by creating a transaction message which it encrypts using its private key. It sends this message to Mischa at her wallet address which is a shortened version of her public key. The message is then authenticated using a technique called mining, discussed in 17.3.2, and once authenticated the value is deducted from the wallet of the exchange and added to Mischa's wallet. The use of the private key to encrypt the transaction message ensures the value originated from the exchange. As Mischa's public key is embedded in the message in the form of her wallet address, the value can be tracked as having passed from the exchange to Mischa.

[21] Public Key Encryption was discussed in 16.5.2.

The transfer of value is similar to the transfer of value in traditional fiat currency (cash). Instead of transferring value in the form of serial numbers contained in banknotes (or physical coins) the transfer of value is recorded in a publicly recorded (and immutable) record on the ledger, recording the transfer (this is the blockchain which will be discussed shortly). Now that Mischa has the bitcoins in her wallet she can spend them as token payments. While exchanges quote the market price for one bitcoin (on 2 November 2018 this was £4,891.25) you are rarely going to spend a whole bitcoin (except when 'cashing in' an investment). In fact, bitcoin does not really work with whole bitcoin, but with a smaller unit, called a satoshi (after Satoshi Nakamoto). 1 bitcoin equals 100,000,000 satoshi so the smallest amount you can spend is 1 satoshi or around 0.0049p on 2 November 2018. Thus to buy a coffee at £2.40 you would spend 48,275 sat.

Example Spending bitcoin

Mischa decides to invest in some artwork. She sees Lucian is selling an original watercolour £1500, or 30,456,195 sat. She creates a transaction message (the software in her wallet will do this automatically) which she encrypts using her private key. She transmits this message to Lucian at his wallet address. Once the message is authenticated 30,456,195 sat. are deducted from her wallet and added to Lucian's.

Eagle-eyed readers may spot a potential risk in all of this. When I spend fiat money (cash) I physically hand over the banknote or coin. Replicating (counterfeiting) banknotes in particular is difficult due to security measures placed into the notes. However a recurrent theme of this book is that data may be easily copied. What is to stop Mischa from spending the value, then simply topping up her wallet and spending it again? This is known as the double spending problem and is solved by blockchain.

17.3.2 **Blockchain (distributed ledger) technology**

The solution to the double spending problem is a technology which has multiple applications, much wider than just cryptocurrency. We already touched on blockchain in chapter 16 while discussing smart contracts. As was noted there, while blockchain has taken on almost mythical status of late it is in fact a rather simple technology to do a rather simple task. The task is to decentralize the trust and authentication of transactions. We trust fiat currency because the issuer, usually the central bank, authenticates it, whether that is money in physical form as banknotes or in an electronic form as a balance held in a bank account or loan account. The bank centrally authorizes the currency by issuing blocks of currency (serial numbers) and has systems to check for fraud and for counterfeits, and guarantees the currency as a store of value. A distributed ledger (or blockchain) is a way to replace these centralized trust and authority systems with a decentralized collection of data that is verified by members of a peer-to-peer network.

When a cryptocurrency is first offered, usually following an Initial Coin Offering, new tokens are created and for each token issued a genesis block (an original block hardcoded into the blockchain) is created.[22] This records who the initial owner of this token is by recording his or her public wallet address. When they want to transfer the value represented by this token they follow the pattern already discussed, they create a transaction message with the value to be transferred, and the address of the recipient, and encrypt that message using their private key. The part of the process that was passed over before was the process of authentication and how that worked. This is the process of mining blocks on the blockchain. When the transaction message is sent it is not sent directly to the recipient. Instead it is broadcast by the wallet application and can be picked up by a miner for authentication. As long as it is not picked up, it hovers in a 'pool of unconfirmed transactions'. This pool is a collection of transactions on the network that are waiting to be processed. Miners on the network select transactions from these pools and form them into a 'block'. A block is basically a collection of transactions (at this moment in time, still unconfirmed transactions). Every miner constructs their own block, but multiple miners can select the same individual transaction to be included in their block.[23] To add this block to the blockchain (to register the transactions), the block needs a signature. Solving a very complex mathematical problem that is unique to each block of transactions creates the signature.[24] Each block has a different mathematical problem, meaning each miner will work on a different problem that is unique to the block they built, but all of these problems are equally hard to solve.[25] Once a miner finds an eligible signature (solution) for their block they broadcast this to all the other miners. The other miners will now verify if that solution corresponds with the problem of the senders' block. If it is valid, the miners will confirm the solution and agree that the block can be added to the blockchain. Every time another block gets added on top of this block it references the previous block in its record and thereby it counts as another confirmation for the block beneath it.

From this we can see that the blockchain becomes a chain of blocks. The ledger records all transactions of value in a chain of transactions. When you transfer bitcoin (or satoshi) you digitally sign a hash of the previous transaction and the public key of the next owner and add these to the end of the coin. This creates a chain of ownership (which is anonymous as no one is certifying identity of any of the owners of the key pairs) showing each transaction and the identity of the new owner. Also as the whole process is cryptographically secure it cannot be altered once written (is immutable). The recipient of the payment can verify the signatures to verify the chain of ownership, thus preventing theft and embezzlement, and double spending. Why do miners give over valuable time (and electricity) to authenticating transactions? The first transaction in any block, the 'minting' of the coin creates a new coin owned by that person. There is though no central mint to create the coins so Nakamoto drew an analogy to gold mining: 'the steady addition of

---

[22] The other way of first acquiring transactions is through a coinbase transaction (rewarding a miner). See <http://learnmeabitcoin.com/glossary/coinbase-transaction>.

[23] e.g. imagine two miners, A and B. Both miners can decide to include transaction Y into their block. Before adding the transaction to their block, the miner checks if the transaction is eligible to be executed according to the blockchain history. If the senders' wallet balance has sufficient funds according to the existing blockchain history, the transaction is considered valid and can be added to the block. If not, it is invalid and rejected.

[24] See further M Nielsen, 'How the Bitcoin protocol actually works' <http://www.michael-nielsen.org/ddi/how-the-bitcoin-protocol-actually-works/>.

[25] For more detail on mining/hashing see <https://blockgeeks.com/guides/what-is-hashing/> Note: in order to solve this mathematical problem, a lot of computational power is needed (and thus a lot of electricity). This consumption of resources is often held up as the Achilles heel of blockchain.

a constant of amount of new coins is analogous to gold miners expending resources to add gold to circulation. In our case, it is CPU time and electricity that is expended. The incentive can also be funded with transaction fees.'[26] Thus if you mine blocks you get rewarded in coins. The problem is the more miners there are the longer it takes to mine coins. As bitcoin attracts a lot of speculation, recent estimates suggest it costs between $4,000–$6,000 to mine a single coin. This is approaching break-even point with a bitcoin worth $6375 on 2 November 2018. Soon it may not be economic to mine bitcoin and the whole process may stop until enough miners leave to make it profitable again.

17.3.3 Cryptocurrency and the law

What is the legal position of cryptocurrency in the UK? It is not issued by an EMI and therefore is not legal under the Electronic Money Directive 2009. Equally it is not issued by a central bank, and in England and Wales it does not qualify as legal tender under s. 1 of the Currency and Bank Notes Act 1954 or s. 2 of the Coinage Act 1971. It doesn't even qualify for the same status as Scottish or Northern Irish banknotes as authorized and approved currency under Part 6 of the Banking Act 2009. Essentially, the crypto-currency has no legal status in the UK, but despite this many UK-based websites and even shops and cafés accept bitcoin, or at least they did until the market value of one bitcoin skyrocketed in 2017 from $930 in January to at one point $19,783 in December. What had happened was that bitcoin effectively withdrew from being a currency (no one wanted to buy a coffee with something that was appreciating at 2,027 per cent per annum) and became an investment vehicle. At the time of writing it is not clear whether cryptocurrencies will ever operate as true currencies or payment methods. For a while between 2011 and 2016 it appeared that bitcoin was operating as a currency and could be a real alternative to fiat currencies. However, the 2017 bull run on bitcoin suggests it is now seen as a commodity not a currency. This has had a halo effect on other major cryptocurrencies such as Ethereum, suggesting these are now viewed as investment vehicles by speculators not transactional tokens. However, should these currencies ever wish to be accepted as payment methods as a viable alternative to fiat currency, they will need to be legally recognized.

The widespread acceptance of bitcoin into the mainstream prior to 2017 caused government and regulators to slowly interact with and acknowledge bitcoin. On 3 March 2014 HMRC published its policy paper *Bitcoin and other cryptocurrencies*.[27] In this HMRC reviewed the tax implications of payment in cryptocurrency, in particular whether or not Value Added Tax (VAT) was due on cryptocurrency operations and payments. The advice was that income received from bitcoin mining was not subject to VAT, and that when bitcoin is exchanged for sterling or other currencies, no VAT is due on the value of the bitcoins themselves. However, 'VAT is due in the normal way from suppliers of any goods or services sold in exchange for Bitcoin or other similar cryptocurrency. The value of the supply of goods or services on which VAT is due will be the sterling value of the cryptocurrency at the point the transaction takes place.' This essentially treats cryptocurrency like cash payments. In 2017 when bitcoin surged in value, HMRC reminded

---

[26] Nakamoto (n. 19).
[27] <www.gov.uk/government/publications/revenue-and-customs-brief-9-2014-bitcoin-and-other-cryptocurrencies>.

traders that 'Where an asset (including Bitcoin) is held as an investment—as opposed to being working capital in a trading activity—the presumption is that any profit or gain on its disposal will be charged to Capital Gains Tax.'[28] Again this treats cryptocurrency as a foreign currency for as the *HMRC Capital Gains Manual* explains 'Currency other than sterling is a chargeable asset and its disposal can give rise to a chargeable gain or an allowable loss.'[29] The Bank of England meanwhile issued several bulletins on cryptocurrency and, among other things, focus on the potential uses of the blockchain ledger for traditional currencies.[30] Andrew Haldane, the Chief Economist of the Bank even suggested the Bank could issue its own cryptocurrency, maybe even to replace paper currency.[31] While it seems unlikely the Bank will be issuing cryptocurrency any time soon the Financial Policy Committee announced in March 2018 that the Bank 'recognises the potential benefits of the technologies underlying crypto-assets and of their potential to create a more distributed and diverse payments system', and welcomed 'the work of the Bank and other authorities to explore ways of achieving these benefits in a robust and efficient manner'.[32] The Bank was keen to 'distinguish the crypto-assets themselves from the distributed ledger and cryptographic technologies upon which many of them rely', noting that 'these underlying technologies have significant potential and, over time, could have material benefits, including for the efficiency and resilience of the financial system.'[33] The Bank concluded that cryptocurrencies 'do not currently pose a material risk to UK financial stability.'[34] The UK's financial markets regulator, the Financial Conduct Authority, does not currently regulate cryptocurrency markets but has notified that cryptocurrency futures and derivatives are financial instruments under the Markets in Financial Instruments Directive II (MIFID II).[35] They have noted that 'although we do not consider cryptocurrencies to be currencies or commodities for regulatory purposes under MiFID II. Firms conducting regulated activities in cryptocurrency derivatives must, therefore, comply with all applicable rules in the FCA's Handbook and any relevant provisions in directly applicable European Union regulations.'[36]

Cryptocurrency has also begun to be acknowledged in legislative measures. The explanatory note to s. 44 (5) of the Consumer Rights Act 2015 (right to a refund for digital content) records that:

> subsection (5) does not mean that a trader can refund the consumer by giving them back the virtual currency. Rather, to satisfy this requirement a trader must give the consumer back the money originally paid for the in-game currency, using the means of payment that the consumer

---

[28] T McMullan, 'If you've made cash from Bitcoin in the UK, you could face a hefty tax bill' *Alphr* 20 March 2018 <http://www.alphr.com/cryptocurrency/1008865/bitcoin-tax-cryptocurrency-hmrc-capital-gains-ethereum>.

[29] HMRC, *Capital Gains Manual*, CG78300.

[30] R Ali, 'Innovations in payment technologies and the emergence of digital currencies' *Bank of England Quarterly Bulletin* Q3 2014 <https://www.bankofengland.co.uk/quarterly-bulletin/2014/q3/innovations-in-payment-technologies-and-the-emergence-of-digital-currencies>; Robleh Ali, 'The economics of digital currencies' *Bank of England Quarterly Bulletin* Q3 2014 <www.bankofengland.co.uk/publications/Documents/quarterlybulletin/2014/qb14q3digitalcurrenciesbitcoin2.pdf>.

[31] A Haldane, *How low can you go?* 18 September 2015
<https://www.bankofengland.co.uk/quarterly-bulletin/2014/q3/the-economics-of-digital-currencies>.

[32] Bank of England, *Financial Policy Committee Statement from its policy meeting*, 12 March 2018, 2.

[33] Ibid. 7.

[34] Ibid.

[35] Dir. 2014/65/EU.

[36] FCA, *Cryptocurrency Derivatives* 6 April 2018.

used to buy that in-game currency (unless the consumer expressly agrees otherwise). However, digital currencies (or cryptocurrencies) that can be used in a variety of transactions with a number of traders, and exchanged for real money, are much more akin to real money (e.g. bitcoins). Where the consumer uses these types of digital currency to pay for digital content, the trader can (and must, unless the consumer agrees) repay the consumer in the digital currency.

Also the explanatory note to s. 14 (3) of the Serious Crime Act 2015 (seized money etc.) records that:

> subsection (3) inserts new subsections (7A) and (7B) into section 67 which confer a power on the Secretary of State to amend, by order, section 67 [of the Proceeds of Crime Act 2002] so as to apply the money seizure power to money held by other financial institutions or other realisable cash or cash-like instruments or products, for example share accounts, pension accounts or 'bitcoins'.

Thus although not yet of any specific legal standing in the UK, cryptocurrencies, and in particular bitcoin, have attracted the attention of the central bank, the tax authorities, the financial markets regulator, and the legislature.

17.4 **Conclusions**

According to the song, 'money makes the world go round'. While, hopefully, we are not as avaricious a society as to be dominated by our desire for money, there is no doubt that e-commerce needs to be able to service the basic financial requirements of any commercial sector if it is to continue to grow. Initially there were concerns that the development of e-commerce would be negatively affected by an inability to pay for goods and services online by any means except card payment systems. Card payments lacked many of the functions of money—in particular, they lacked anonymity and they were expensive to operate. It was feared that the lack of anonymity meant that users would worry about identity fraud and they would not buy goods or services online which may cause embarrassment. For suppliers there was a concern that the transaction fees meant that they could not be used economically for small-value transactions as the fees payable would outweigh the payment received.

All these predictions have proven to be false. Customers have embraced payment by card. They do fear identity fraud, but know their card issuer will reimburse them for any losses they incur. They have no embarrassment about using their cards to make payment because the feeling of anonymity a computer screen gives means they would rather buy Viagra online than in a pharmacy, and in any event goods bought online have to be shipped to their home anyway so why worry about giving your credit card details. Industry, realizing that cards were to become the dominant online payment system, developed alternatives to cash payments for low-value transactions—using a mixture of subscription services and advertising supported services.

Some things initially not predicted have also come to pass. Electronic money has found a new lease of life in the real world—the convenience of payment by mobile phone being the driving force behind one arm of the technology while the familiarity of smart card systems as a means of payment for public transport is driving another. For all involved in the money supply chain the benefits offered by electronic money are clear. The risks of forgery are reduced, the costs of production are removed, and, most importantly, there are no cash deposits in banks, stores, or in armoured cars to steal. It seems that the rise of cryptocurrencies could herald the next movement in money as a form of token. Token-based payment systems (cash money in old language), may, like music, film, and photographs become a series of ones and zeros. However, movements in the last three years suggest that currently crypto is viewed more as a commodity than a currency, an investment vehicle not a payment token. To reinvigorate cryptocurrencies as an actual currency it may ironically involve a central bank who is willing to experiment with crypto as an alternative to cash. The idea of centralized crypto may just be ironic enough to the crypto community to cause the elusive Satoshi Nakamoto to reveal him- or herself.[37]

TEST QUESTIONS

Question 1

Is it too late to develop an effective online e-money sector in Europe? Did the first Electronic Money Directive kill off any chance of such a business sector developing due to its draconian rules on liquidity?

Question 2

Is it now time to formally bring cryptocurrency systems within the framework of the Electronic Money Directive? Advise the European Commission on what you see as being the key provisions of a model Cryptocurrency Directive.

FURTHER READING

Books

J Brito and A Castillo, *Bitcoin: A Primer for Policymakers* (Mercatus 2016)

S Hoegner (ed.), *The Law of Bitcoin* (iUniverse 2015)

P Vigna and M Casey, *Cryptocurrency: How Bitcoin and Digital Money are Challenging the Global Economic Order* (Vintage 2015)

Chapters and articles

T Cutts, 'Modern Money Had and Received' (2018) 38 *Oxford Journal of Legal Studies* 1

M Kohlbach, 'Making Sense of Electronic Money', 1 JILT (2004)

VD Roman, 'Virtual Currencies: Can Regulators Keep Pace?' *Jusletter IT*, September 2015

N Vandezande, 'Between Bitcoins and mobile payments: Will the European Commission's new proposal provide more legal certainty?' (2014) 22 *International Journal of Law and Information Technology* 295

---

[37] After publishing the paper *Bitcoin: A Peer-to-Peer Electronic Cash System* and helping to set up the original bitcoin architecture, Nakamoto disappeared from public view. No one knows his or her identity.

Consumer protection

One of the complexities of e-commerce is that the consumer is put in a quite unique position of never meeting the retailer, never inspecting their place of business, and, most importantly, they cannot inspect or sample the goods they are buying before they make a purchase. In addition, the consumer has added complications and costs including paying to receive the goods and, in the event that the goods are not satisfactory or fail to meet their requirements, they have to arrange shipping and absorb the shipping costs of returning the goods. All of these issues exacerbate the pre-existing imbalance of power between suppliers and consumers of products or services. Although it may be argued that the availability of information, review, and comparison sites may offer to rebalance this natural imbalance somewhat,[1] that does not affect the need for strong consumer protection laws, especially when the consumer may be dealing with a trillion-dollar corporation domiciled in a state different from his or her own.

18.1 Distance and online selling

Consumer contracts concluded online, whether that is by web page or by email or other form of distance communication, are all dealt with similarly. The European framework document is the Consumer Rights Directive[2] which classifies contracts into three categories: (1) standard or 'on-premises'; (2) 'off-premises'; and (3) distance. On-premises contracts (which are not labelled as such in the directive; they are merely labelled as 'other than distance or off-premises contracts') are contracts concluded in the presence of the parties on the business premises of the trader. This is the standard where you buy goods in a shop for instance. Off-premises contracts are contracts which are 'concluded in the simultaneous physical presence of the trader and the consumer, in a place which is not the business premises of the trader'[3] or 'concluded on the business premises of the trader or through any means of distance communication immediately after the consumer was personally and individually addressed in a place which is not the business premises of the trader in the simultaneous physical presence of the trader and the consumer'.[4] In essence these are contracts concluded after an agent or salesman visits your home or speaks to you in a neutral location such as in a hotel room or

---

[1] L Labrecque et al., 'Consumer Power: Evolution in the Digital Age' (2013) 27 *Journal of Interactive Marketing* 257.

[2] Dir. 2011/83/EU.

[3] Art. 2(8)(a).

[4] Art. 2(8)(c).

conference hall. Distance contracts are 'any contract concluded between the trader and the consumer under an organized distance sales or service-provision scheme without the simultaneous physical presence of the trader and the consumer, with the exclusive use of one or more means of distance communication up to and including the time at which the contract is concluded'.[5] These are contracts concluded where the parties never meet. As a result, normally all e-commerce contracts will be classified as 'distance' agreements whatever form of communication: web page, email, instant messenger, or text message, is used.[6]

18.1.1 Jurisdiction, choice of law, and consumer disputes

The first problem many consumers will encounter is that the contractual counterparty may be located outside their jurisdiction and as a result they may find that the contract is governed by law (and courts) outside their home state.

 Case study *Amazon.co.uk* Conditions of use and sale

14. APPLICABLE LAW

These conditions are governed by and construed in accordance with the laws of the Grand Duchy of Luxembourg, and the application of the United Nations Convention of Contracts for the International Sale of Goods is expressly excluded. If you are a consumer and have your habitual residence in the EU, you additionally enjoy the protection afforded to you by mandatory provisions of the law of your country of residence. We both agree to submit to the non-exclusive jurisdiction of the courts of the district of Luxembourg City, which means that you may bring a claim to enforce your consumer protection rights in connection with these Conditions of Use in Luxembourg or in the EU country in which you live.

Two things are immediately apparent from this. The first is that the company a UK consumer deals with when they buy from Amazon.co.uk is not as they might expect a UK company. Instead, you buy from Amazon EU SARL, a Luxembourg registered corporation. It is important to note that a .co.uk web address does not mean a UK trader. Second, while Amazon excludes other forms of international instrument which may undermine their applicable law clause, they are required within the EU to allow the consumer to elect to raise a claim in their country of residence, as this is a 'mandatory provision of law'.[7] What is this mandatory framework that protects the consumer from having to make a costly trip to Luxembourg to enforce their rights?

---

[5] Art. 2(7).

[6] For UK implementation see Reg. 5 of The Consumer Contracts (Information, Cancellation and Additional Charges) Regulations 2013, SI 2013/3134.

[7] The analysis which follows is an analysis rooted in EU law and mutual recognition by courts in EU member states. By the time you read this book the UK will no longer be a member state. At the time of writing the final Brexit settlement is still unknown, however as the European Union (Withdrawal) Act 2018 provides that EU law in effect in the UK on Brexit day remains in effect after Brexit, and in the hope that a similar recognition will be extended in the EU27 this section assumes the law discussed here will remain unaffected by Brexit.

There are in fact two Regulations which ensure the consumer can:

(i)   raise an action in their domestic courts rather than having to travel to the place where the business is domiciled or has stated as having exclusive forum in an applicable law clause; and

(ii) rely upon their domestic law as opposed to the law of another member state as a result of domicile or an applicable law clause.

The first is the Brussels (Recast) Regulation.[8] This requires, by Art. 18, that 'a consumer may bring proceedings against the other party to a contract either in the courts of the member state in which that party is domiciled or, regardless of the domicile of the other party, in the courts for the place where the consumer is domiciled.' In addition, by Art. 17(1)(c) this includes traders who 'direct such activities to that Member State or to several States including that Member State.' Thus if a UK consumer buys goods from a US-based website, and that website is happy to trade with EU-based customers and perhaps signals this by pricing items in Euros or Pounds or by offering shipping to the UK, then under this targeting principle they may be brought under the provisions of the Brussels Regulation. It should be noted though that the consumer provisions of the Regulation only applied in business-to-consumer contracts, not in consumer-to-consumer transactions.[9] This means so-called peer-to-peer trading such as on eBay does not automatically qualify for protection. In addition, it should be noted that the protection of the consumer is reciprocal. By Art. 18(2) proceedings may be brought against a consumer by the other party to the contract only in the courts of the member state in which the consumer is domiciled. This prevents a UK consumer from having to defend a claim in a foreign jurisdiction (often in a foreign language) and having to engage local representation.

The Brussels (Recast) Regulation is only half of the framework however. Theoretically the consumer could end up raising their claim in an English Court only to have Luxembourg law applied by the applicable law clause they accepted when buying from a website or other online supplier. To prevent this we can apply the Rome I Regulation.[10] Whereas the Brussels Regulation deals with jurisdiction, that is, which court or courts have legal standing to hear a claim, the Rome I Regulation deals with choice of law, that is, which law applies to the dispute. Consumers are protected by Art. 6 which states:

> a contract concluded by a natural person for a purpose which can be regarded as being outside his trade or profession (the consumer) with another person acting in the exercise of his trade or profession (the professional) shall be governed by the law of the country where the consumer has his habitual residence, provided that the professional (a) pursues his commercial or professional activities in the country where the consumer has his habitual residence, or (b) by any means, directs such activities to that country or to several countries including that country, and the contract falls within the scope of such activities.

This is an almost exact mirror of the Brussels provision. The consumer when engaged in a business-to-consumer agreement is entitled to rely upon the law of the state of

---

[8] Reg. (EU) No. 1215/2012.

[9] By Art. 17(1)(c), the counterparty to the transaction must be a 'person who pursues commercial or professional activities'.

[10] Reg. (EC) No 593/2008.

their habitual residence. As with the Brussels Regulation there is a targeting principle so that if the business 'directs such activities to that country or to several countries including that country' they are caught by the provision. Art. 6(2) does allow
the parties to derogate from Art. 6(1) but such agreed derogation cannot 'deprive
the consumer of the protection afforded to him by provisions that cannot be dero-
gated from by agreement by virtue of the law which, in the absence of choice, would
have been applicable on the basis of paragraph 1'. In other words, such derogation
must comply with the law of the place from which derogation is sought. As UK consumer protection law would deem such a clause to be a term 'which may or must
be regarded as unfair' under s. 63 of the Consumer Rights Act 2015[11] with the result
that it would be 'not binding on the consumer' under s. 62(1) it would not be effective in UK law.

18.1.2 Consumer rights in distance contracts

As consumers are at a particular detriment when dealing at a distance, there are
particular protections for consumers who enter into distance contracts. The legal
framework may be found in the Consumer Rights Directive[12] as implemented by
the Consumer Contracts (Information, Cancellation and Additional Charges)
Regulations 2013.[13]

The Regulations seek to ensure that consumers are fully informed of all their contractual obligations, as well as their consumer rights and cancellation rights before they
enter into a distance contract. By regs. 13 and 14 and Schs. 2 and 3, a supplier of goods
or services must supply a considerable amount of information before a distance contract concluded by electronic means is concluded, including the price of the goods or
service including all taxes, any delivery costs, arrangements for payment and delivery, the main characteristics of the goods, services or digital content, the geographical
address at which the trader is established, and, where available, the trader's telephone
number, fax number, and email address, to enable the consumer to contact the trader
quickly and communicate efficiently, and information about any after-sales services
and guarantees. Should a trader fail to supply the material required then by regs. 13(1)
and 14(5) the consumer may not be bound by the contract and the trader may not be
able to enforce (any of) the terms of the contract against the consumer. This is a considerable disadvantage to the trader and therefore ensures compliance, but with some
provisions the penalty is greater.

Where a trader fails to inform a consumer of their right to cancel, or when the consumer may have to bear reasonable costs of cancellation or returning items, they may
commit an offence under reg. 19 which could see them fined at a level up to point 5
on the standard scale (currently £5000). Finally, with reference particularly to contracts
concluded on websites or via apps, the Regulations require clear labelling as to when
payment is required, this may be seen as a response in particular to apps which are
unclear on in-app purchases. Regulation 14(3) provides that 'the trader must ensure

---

[11] See Sch. 2, Part 1, para. 20: 'A term which has the object or effect of excluding or hindering
the consumer's right to take legal action or exercise any other legal remedy.'
[12] Consumer Rights Directive (n. 2).
[13] SI 2013/3134.

that the consumer, when placing the order, explicitly acknowledges that the order implies an obligation to pay' while reg. 14(4) provides that:

> if placing an order entails activating a button or a similar function, the trader must ensure that the button or similar function is labelled in an easily legible manner only with the words 'order with obligation to pay' or a corresponding unambiguous formulation indicating that placing the order entails an obligation to pay the trader.

A failure to comply with either of these provisions releases the consumer from any obligations under the contract or order under reg. 14(5).

Moreover, as the consumer cannot inspect the goods prior to purchase or evaluate the supplier in the same way they can with an on-site purchase, consumers who enter into off-site or distance contracts (including electronic contracts) are given a cooling-off period, during which time they may reject and return the goods in question. By reg. 29 the consumer is given a right to cancel a distance or off-premises contract at any time in the cancellation period without giving any reason. The normal cancellation period is found in reg. 30. For contracts for the supply of services or for the delivery of digital content supplied without a carrier medium it is 14 days after the day on which the contract is entered into. For the supply of goods it is 14 days after the day on which the goods (or if multiple items are ordered the day upon which the final item) come(s) into the physical possession of the consumer or their agent. There is also an extended cancellation period under reg. 31. This applies when the trader does not provide the consumer with the information on the right to cancel, which as we have seen is also an offence under reg. 19. In such cases the cancellation period does not begin until the trader gives the consumer the requisite information, or if they fail to do so within 12 months the period will be 12 months and 14 days.[14] It should also be noted that by regs. 27 and 28 some contracts cannot be cancelled. By reg. 27(2) there is no right to cancel contracts for the supply of prescription medicines, for products supplied by the NHS or other healthcare provider, or contracts for passenger transport services. By reg. 28 the right to cancellation does not apply to, among others, price-sensitive goods such as gold or shares, personalized goods, perishable goods, the supply of a newspaper, periodical, or magazine, sales concluded at public auction, and the supply of accommodation, transport of goods, vehicle rental services, catering, or services related to leisure activities, if the contract provides for a specific date or period of performance. In addition, by reg. 28(3) the consumer may lose their right to reject under certain circumstances. The right to reject will cease to be available when

(a) in the case of a contract for the supply of sealed goods which are not suitable for return due to health protection or hygiene reasons, if they become unsealed after delivery;

(b) in the case of a contract for the supply of sealed audio or sealed video recordings or sealed computer software, if the goods become unsealed after delivery; or

(c) in the case of any sales contract, if the goods become mixed inseparably (according to their nature) with other items after delivery (such as mixing sand with cement to create mortar).

---

[14] Reg. 31(3).

Special rules apply to the supply of services and digital content within the cooling-off period. Both have similar provisions under regs. 36 and 37 but for our purposes the more interesting and important is reg. 37 which applies to digital content. By reg. 37(1) where there is a contract for the supply of digital content not on a tangible medium, the trader must not begin supply of the digital content before the end of the cancellation period. This obviously is quite unworkable, when you ordered an app on an app store or a piece of music on iTunes or Google Play you would have to wait 14 days for it to be delivered to you. Thus there are exceptions: reg. 37(1) will not apply if the consumer has given express consent, and the consumer has acknowledged that the right to cancel the contract under reg. 29(1) will be lost. This is achieved via terms and conditions for the app store or content store agreed to whenever the store software is installed or updated.[15]

The Regulations also make some special provisions with regard to returning items and shipping costs. The consumer must send back the goods or hand them over to the trader without undue delay and in any event not later than 14 days after the day on which the consumer informs the trader that they wished to cancel and return the goods.[16] In addition, by reg. 35(5) the consumer must bear the direct cost of returning goods unless either the trader has agreed to bear those costs, or the trader failed to provide the consumer with the information about the consumer bearing those costs, but by reg. 34(2) and (3) the trader must reimburse the consumer for delivery costs incurred unless the consumer expressly chose a kind of delivery costing more than the least expensive common and generally acceptable kind of delivery offered by the trader, in which case the trader must reimburse any payment for delivery received from the consumer up to the amount the consumer would have paid if the consumer had chosen the least expensive common and generally acceptable kind of delivery offered by the trader. This is for the practical reason that sellers could inflict disproportionately high shipping costs on the buyer which they could then not recover following a rejection of the goods. Thus if a T-shirt was advertised at £4.99 plus £15 postage and packaging, then without this protection upon a rejection of the item the consumer would only be in line for a refund of £4.99, but with this protection is eligible for a refund of the whole amount of £19.99. The buyer is in turn, though, normally responsible for return shipping costs. This is because the buyer may control the costs of shipping by choosing the most competitive service; there is therefore less risk of abuse of process.

This particular issue was reviewed by the European Court of Justice when discussing similar provisions found in the now repealed Distance Selling Directive[17] in *Handelsgesellschaft Heinrich Heine GmbH v Verbraucherzentrale Nordrhein-Westfalen*,[18] where the claimant, a mail order company, stated in its general terms and conditions that the consumer was to pay a flat-rate charge for delivery, which the claimant would not refund in the event of withdrawal from the contract. The court determined that the Distance Selling Directive imposed on the supplier, in the event of the consumer's withdrawal, a general obligation to reimburse which covered all of the sums paid by the consumer under the contract, regardless of the reason for their payment.[19]

---

[15] Interestingly, while the Google Play store gives a seven-day cancellation period in replacement of the statutory period, Apple give a fourteen-day cancellation period in iTunes and the App Store.
[16] Reg. 35(4).
[17] Dir. 97/7/EC.
[18] ECLI:EU:C:2010:189.
[19] Ibid. [43].

18.2 **The Consumer Rights Act 2015**

Further protections, not specific to distance contracts, may be found in the Consumer Rights Act 2015. The Act focuses upon attempts by suppliers of goods and/or services to restrict liability for negligence or harm, or to avoid statutory duties. In addition, it provides some basic quality standards provisions for goods or services supplied. By s. 65 a party to a contract cannot exclude liability for death or personal injury caused by negligence,[20] while by ss. 31, 47, and 57 suppliers cannot contract out of liability for legal minimum provisions of quality in relation to order contracts for the sale and supply of goods, contracts for the sale and supply of digital goods, and contracts for the supply of services. These minimum provisions in part replace provisions found previously in the Sale of Goods Act 1979 and the Supply of Goods and Services Act 1982 and in part are new.

Statutory provisions as to the quality of goods are found in ss. 9–18 of the Act. These include that the goods are of satisfactory quality; they are fit for purpose, and are as described. An important new provision is that by s. 16 if the goods supplied contain a digital component which does not meet the standard contracted (or the statutory minimal standards including 'satisfactory quality') the goods may be rejected for the failure in the digital component. Similar provisions relating to the quality of services supplied are to be found in ss. 49–53 and require that services be performed with 'reasonable care and skill' and within a reasonable time.

Completely new provisions are to be found in Part 1, Chapter 3, 'Digital Content'. By ss. 34–41 a set of minimum quality provisions, similar to those found in ss. 9–18 are applied to digital content. Digital content is defined in s. 2 as 'data which are produced and supplied in digital form.' This would include software, digital music and video, and e-books and applies however that content is delivered—that is, there is no difference between a music or movie download or stream than music or movies delivered on CD or DVD. By s. 34 digital content must be of satisfactory quality, while by ss. 35–36 it must be fit for purpose and as described. Section 39(5) is a useful new addition to the consumer's armoury. It provides that the processing facility for digitally supplied contact must be available for a reasonable time. Thus if you pay £15 to access and download an online article and due to network failures you can't download it right away, the supplier must give you a reasonable time to make the download. It should be noted that where the consumer agrees to an express term limiting access (such as 24 hours access), then that term would apply, assuming it is reasonable.

In the event that goods, including digital goods, or services fail to meet the statutory minimum quality threshold then under ss. 19–24, 42–45, and 54–56, consumers are given a variety of enforcement rights, including (for goods), a right to reject the goods under s. 20 and a right to repair or replacement under s. 23, (for digital goods), a right to a refund under s. 45 and a right to a price reduction under s. 44, and (for services) a right to a repeat performance under s. 55. In general the rights across all three classifications boil down to repudiation (rejection and refund) or repair, reperformance, or reduction in price.

In addition to these specific statutory terms there is also a general prohibition on unfair terms.

---

[20] Note a similar provision applying to B2B contracts may be found in s. 2 of the Unfair Contract Terms Act 1977.

Highlight The Consumer Rights Act, s. 62

(1) An unfair term of a consumer contract is not binding on the consumer . . .

(4) A term is unfair if, contrary to the requirement of good faith, it causes a significant imbalance in the parties' rights and obligations under the contract to the detriment of the consumer.

(5) Whether a term is fair is to be determined—

(a) taking into account the nature of the subject matter of the contract, and

(b) by reference to all the circumstances existing when the term was agreed and to all of the other terms of the contract or of any other contract on which it depends.

This means that in any B2C contract if the court finds that term to be biased in favour of the supplier of the goods or services it may be struck out. The Consumer Rights Act is so new that we have as yet no case law on its terms (it only came into effect on 1 October 2015). The House of Lords though did discuss the meaning of an unfair term under the previous law, the Unfair Terms in Consumer Contracts Regulations 1994, in *Director General of Fair Trading v First National Bank Plc* where Lord Bingham described it as:

> causing a significant imbalance in the parties' rights and obligations under the contract to the detriment of the consumer in a manner or to an extent which is contrary to the require-ment of good faith. The requirement of significant imbalance is met if a term is so weighted in favour of the supplier as to tilt the parties' rights and obligations under the contract sig-nificantly in his favour. This may be by the granting to the supplier of a beneficial option or discretion or power, or by the imposing on the consumer of a disadvantageous burden or risk or duty.[21]

Schedule 2, Part 1 provides an excellent illustrative list of the types of terms which may be found to be unfair. These include terms which 'inappropriately exclude or limit the legal rights of the consumer in relation to the trader or another party in the event of total or partial non-performance or inadequate performance by the trader of any of the contractual obligations' and which 'irrevocably bind the consumer to terms with which he had no real opportunity of becoming acquainted before the conclusion of the contract'.

18.3 **Regulation of spam**

In addition to protecting consumers once they have entered into agreements with traders, consumer protection law has a vital role to play in ensuring that consum-ers have access to fair and unbiased information before they enter into an agree-ment and that they are not unduly pressured into making bad agreements. A vital part of the consumer protection framework is therefore laws that regulate direct marketing.

---

[21] [2002] 1 AC 481, 494.

Our experience teaches us that the digital environment is awash with unsolicited commercial communications, or spam.[22] Is that true? The answer appears to be yes.

 Highlight Spam data

Reports from Symantec and Cisco suggest the high-water mark of spam was in July 2010 when approximately 230 billion spam messages were in circulation each day, accounting for in excess of 90 per cent of all email traffic. Since then the number of spam messages has reduced but tends to stay over 50 per cent of all messages sent. Statistics for September 2018 record that spam messages accounted for 55.1 per cent of all email traffic. With estimates suggesting 281 billion messages were sent daily in 2018, this suggests there are still in the region of 155 billion spam messages sent daily.[23]

Somewhat surprisingly there have been few surveys of consumer responses to spam, but in 2002 a Harris Poll revealed that 80 per cent of those surveyed said that they found spamming very annoying and 74 per cent favoured making spam illegal.[24] Why then do spammers continue? There are two predominant reasons for this. The first is that unlike traditional unsolicited commercial communications (such as junk mail or cold-calls), digital commercial communications are infinitely replicable, easy to store and, the key for spammers, almost costless to send. As any internet user knows you only pay for your access cost. Once you are connected to the network the costs of carrying data across the network are borne by the telecommunications providers, not the customer. Excepting issues of bandwidth availability, it costs no more to send 1 million emails than to send one. The same is not true of traditional media: 1 million telephone calls will cost around 1 million times the cost of a single telephone call and 1 million letters will cost (bulk discounts aside) 1 million times the cost of a single letter. Thus it seems email is almost designed for spam messages. For the spammer there are almost no overheads and massive reach. But if everyone just filters and deletes their spam why do spammers keep doing it? Well surprisingly spam brings about substantial revenue despite all the filters and other technologies used to prevent spam. A 2012 paper by Justin Rao and David Reiley showed that not only was spam very cost-efficient[25] but

---

[22] Unsolicited Commercial Communications are colloquially known as spam because of the Monty Python sketch in which a couple go into a restaurant and the wife tries to get something other than spam. In the background are a bunch of Vikings who sing the praises of spam. Pretty soon the only thing you can hear in the sketch is the word 'spam'. That same idea would happen to the internet if large-scale inappropriate postings were allowed. You couldn't pick the real postings out from the spam.

[23] Symantec Intelligence Report for September 2018 <https://www.symantec.com/security-center/publications/monthlythreatreport>.

[24] Harris Interactive, 'Large Majority of Those Online Wants Spamming Banned', 3 January 2003.

[25] 'Direct mail is the most expensive form of advertising, due to printing and postage costs; this medium thus requires high breakeven conversion rates of at least 2 percent. For the case of $50 profit per sales, standard online display advertising can be profitable down to a conversion frequency of 2 per 100,000 ads, while "premium display" would require 10 per 100,000 ads. Retail spam is profitable down to 0.2 conversions per 100,000. Bulk spam through wholesale botnet rental is sustainable with a mere 0.06 conversions per 100,000 ads, or about 1 in 2,000,000. Clearly, spam can be orders of magnitude less effective than traditional forms of advertising and still remain profitable.' J Rao and D Reiley, 'The Economics of Spam' (2012) 26 *Journal of Economic Perspectives* 87, 102.

also very profitable: 'Overall, we feel comfortable with an estimate of total industry revenue for spam-advertised goods on the order of $300 million per year.'[26] Revenues of this magnitude encourage spammers to continue operations, as Rao and Reiley acknowledge, their own study showed the profits can be high—'The authors estimate that the Cutwail botnet earned $1.7–4.2 million in profit during the 14-month period of study.'[27] As a result, regulation of spam is essential.

18.3.1 Regulating spam: the Directive on Privacy and Electronic Communications

Despite the obvious appeal of spam to a number of people, the question of how to regulate spam is clearly a major issue. Steps have been taken in both the European Union and the US to control spam. The EU regulatory framework is currently being reviewed and so in this section we will look briefly at the law prior to 2019 and then at the proposed future framework.

The EU began consultation on spam regulation in the summer of 2000 when they began to consider the Commission proposal for a directive on privacy and electronic communications. In their explanatory memorandum the Commission noted that:

> Four Member States already have bans on unsolicited commercial e-mail and another is about to adopt one. In most of the other Member States opt-out systems exist. From an internal market perspective, this is not satisfactory. Direct marketers in opt-in countries may not target e-mail addresses within their own country but they can still continue to send unsolicited commercial e-mail to countries with an opt-out system. Moreover, since e-mail addresses very often give no indication of the country of residence of the recipients, a system of divergent regimes within the internal market is unworkable in practice. A harmonised opt-in approach solves this problem.

On the basis of this, the Commission proposed that the draft privacy in Electronic Communications Directive use an opt-in approach where only those persons who had given prior consent to the receipt of unsolicited messages could lawfully receive them. This approach is highly controversial, not least with the business community and during the parliamentary hearings on the draft directive this was replaced with an opt-out approach instead. However at the last stage of the co-decision procedure the Council reinstated the opt-in proposal and the final wording as passed in the *Directive on Privacy and Electronic Communications*[28] stated:

 Highlight Article 13(1) of the *Directive on Privacy and Electronic Communications*

Electronic mail for the purposes of direct marketing may only be allowed in respect of subscribers who have given their prior consent.

---

[26] Ibid. 103.
[27] Ibid. 101.
[28] Dir. 2002/58/EC.

Recital 40 makes clear that 'prior *explicit* consent of the recipients is obtained before such communications are addressed to them', the use of the term explicit making clear that an opt-out system is incompatible with the directive. There remains though one important exception to Art. 13(1). Under Art. 13(2) if there has been a prior commercial relationship between the sender of the communication and the recipient thereof the communication may be sent without prior explicit consent 'provided that customers clearly and distinctly are given the opportunity to object, free of charge, and in an easy manner, to such use of electronic contact details when they are collected and on the occasion of each message in case the customer has not initially refused such use'. In effect what Art. 13(2) says is that if you have a prior commercial relationship the opt-in requirement is reversed and it becomes an opt-out requirement.

The directive was given effect in the UK in December 2003 when The Privacy and Electronic Communications (EC Directive) Regulations 2003 came into force. By reg. 22(2) it became a harm to: 'transmit, or instigate the transmission of, unsolicited communications for the purposes of direct marketing by means of electronic mail unless the recipient of the electronic mail has previously notified the sender that he consents for the time being to such communications being sent by, or at the instigation of, the sender'. The Art. 13(2) exception is given effect in reg. 22(3).

Rather disappointingly for many anti-spam campaigners it is not an offence to send spam; rather reg. 30(1) states that: 'a person who suffers damage by reason of any contravention of any of the requirements of these Regulations by any other person shall be entitled to bring proceedings for compensation from that other person for that damage'. The trouble with this is that it effectively makes it a tort claim and in most cases where individuals receive spam messages the harm or damage suffered is either unquantifiable or of such low value as to be *de minimis*. That is not to say the Regulations are unenforceable.

18.3.2 *Mansfield v John Lewis*

There had been few cases enforcing the Regulations. In December 2005 Nigel Roberts, a businessman from Alderney, lodged a claim under the Regulations in Colchester County Court against Logistics UK, a Stirlingshire-based company. Logistics UK did not defend the action and agreed to pay Mr Roberts £270 in damages and £30 in costs. Then in March 2007 it was reported that Gordon Dick, an electronic marketing specialist from Edinburgh, won £750 in damages and costs of £616.66 when he pursued Henley-on-Thames-based Transcom under the Regulations. In June 2013 Steve Higgins, a businessman form Northampton, won £750 in damages and £60 costs against Jean Patrique cookware.

In 2014 though the County Court in the unreported case of *Mansfield v John Lewis Partnership* may have made a key contribution to the effectiveness of the Regulations. The value and importance of this decision should not be overstated; it is merely a County Court Small Claims decision and therefore is of no binding authority yet it is probably the fullest discussion of the Regulations to date. According to reports, Mr Mansfield had been browsing the website of Waitrose supermarket, which is owned by John Lewis, to check the price of a home delivery. The Waitrose website requires all potential customers to supply an email address before it allows access to the home delivery finder, this he did but he then left the Waitrose website without buying anything. Mr Mansfield subsequently began receiving marketing emails from the John Lewis Partnership. After writing an objection to the receipt of these emails using a standard form available online,[29] he raised a small claims action. John Lewis argued that because he had not opted out of receiving their emails, he had opted in; this is called soft opt-in and is used on many websites. However Mr Mansfield argued that an opportunity to opt out that is not taken is simply that, it does not convert to automatic consent under the law. In the alternative, John Lewis's lawyers argued that because he had browsed the website he had negotiated with them for a sale and a business relationship existed between them; this would have permitted John Lewis to email Mr Mansfield under reg. 22(3)(a).

Mr Mansfield relied sensibly on the Information Commissioner's Office guidance on direct marketing.[30] At paragraph 68 this states that 'Best practice is to provide an unticked opt-in box, and invite the person to confirm their agreement by ticking. This is the safest way of demonstrating consent, as it requires a positive choice by the individual to give clear and explicit consent.' Further in para.71 which deals with soft opt-in (or opt-out if one prefers): it states:

> An opt-out box is a box that the user must tick to object or opt out of receiving marketing messages. However, the fact that someone has failed to object or opt out only means that they have not objected. It does not automatically mean that they have consented. For example, they may not even have seen the box if they were using a smartphone or other small screen device. For this reason, we would always advise the use of opt-in boxes instead.

Mr Mansfield laid all of this before the judge who agreed with him that he had not consented to the receipt of marketing emails from John Lewis in terms permissible by reg. 22. As a result, Mr Mansfield was paid undisclosed damages. This was an important case as it was the first time that a soft opt-in (or opt-out) was explicitly rejected by a UK judge. Of course this case has no authority, there is not even a written judgment so it is impossible to read too much into it. In any event the Regulations were about to be superseded by a new legal framework for spam regulation.

18.3.3 Regulating spam: the GDPR and ePrivacy Regulation

In January 2011 the European Data Protection Supervisor published an opinion *A comprehensive approach on personal data protection in EU*.[31] This called for a wholesale revision of EU data protection law including a new legislative framework which would harmonize data protection laws across the EU, strengthening the rights of individuals. This led the Commission to propose in January 2012 a comprehensive reform of data protection rules.[32] It took time to give effect to these extensive changes but eventually the General Data Protection Regulation (GDPR) came into effect on 25 May 2018.[33] At

---

[29] This form used to be available from <http://www.scotchspam.org.uk/resources.html>. However, the service appears to have been discontinued, along with this site, and therefore the form is no longer available.

[30] <https://ico.org.uk/media/for-organisations/documents/1555/direct-marketing-guidance.pdf>.

[31] <https://edps.europa.eu/sites/edp/files/publication/11-01-14_personal_data_protection_en.pdf>.

[32] <http://europa.eu/rapid/press-release_IP-12-46_en.htm>.

[33] Regulation (EU) 2016/679.

the time of writing we still await the second pillar of the new framework, the proposed ePrivacy Regulation.[34]

The GDPR will be discussed in depth in chapters 22–24 but for our purposes here it is important to note some important changes the GDPR makes to the regulation of spam. First, and most importantly, the GDPR confirms the approach of the court in *Mansfield*. Soft opt-ins (or opt-outs) are no longer permissible. Consent must now be by way of 'clear affirmative action'[35] and cannot be regarded as freely given if the individual has no genuine or free choice or is unable to refuse or withdraw consent without detriment.[36] In addition, there are fresh requirements for the gaining of consent. The consent to processing, including consent to send commercial messages must be separate to other terms and conditions,[37] meaning that combined consent of the nature seen in *Mansfield* is no longer permissible. The GDPR also strengthens the right of the individual to withdraw consent at any time and for any reason,[38] and individuals have the right to object to their data being processed automatically for the purpose of profiling them.[39] Also, and this is very important given that most spam originates outside the EU,[40] the GDPR extends beyond the boundaries of the EU to regulate the activities of any individual or organization who processes or controls the personal data of data subjects who are in the Union where the processing activities are related to, either (a) offering of goods or services to individuals within the EU, or (b) the monitoring of their behaviour as far as their behaviour takes place within the Union.[41] This means that legally anyone sending a commercial communication to recipients within the EU must comply with GDPR. The weakness of this of course is enforcement. As we have already seen interstate enforcement is complex and the costs of identifying and locating a spammer makes interstate enforcement unlikely.

The GDPR was supposed to be supplemented by the new ePrivacy Regulation when it came into force. However, there have been extensive delays in the drafting and promulgation of the Regulation, which means it is now likely to be introduced in 2019 or 2020. The draft Regulation builds upon the GDPR by adding additional layers of protection for individuals. In particular, if a customer gives their email address to a business for the purpose of facilitating the sale of a product or a service, the business may only contact the customer for direct marketing of its own similar products or services only if customers are 'clearly and distinctly given the opportunity to object, free of charge and in an easy manner, to such use.'[42] Additionally, anyone who uses electronic communications to send marketing

---

[34] Proposal for a Regulation of the European Parliament and of the Council concerning the respect for private life and the protection of personal data in electronic communications and repealing Directive 2002/58/EC, COM (2017) 10 final.

[35] GDPR (n. 33) Recital 32 and Art. 4(11).

[36] Recital 42.

[37] Recital 43.

[38] Art. 7(3).

[39] Art. 22.

[40] Spamhaus retains a list of 'worst spam enabling countries'. As of 8 November 2018 the world's worst Spam Haven countries for enabling spamming were: (1) United States; (2) China; (3) Russia; (4) Ukraine; (5) Japan; (6) UK; (7) Hong Kong; (8) India; (9) Brazil; (10) Nigeria: https://www.spamhaus.org/statistics/countries/.

[41] GDPR (n. 33) Art. 3(2).

[42] Proposed ePrivacy Directive (n. 34) Art. 16(2).

communications is required to 'inform end-users of the marketing nature of the communication and the identity of the legal or natural person on behalf of whom the communication is transmitted and shall provide the necessary information for recipients to exercise their right to withdraw their consent, in an easy manner, to receiving further marketing communications.'[43]

18.4 **The proposed online sales and digital content Directives**

Before leaving this chapter we should note that the European Commission has proposed two additional directives for the digital consumer sphere. The first is the draft Online Sales Directive. The draft of the Directive was published in 2015 and amended in 2017.[44] The other is the draft Digital Content Directive.[45] Both are yet to be adopted. At the time of writing it is unclear whether or not they become part of the UK consumer acquis will depend upon the nature of the UK's exit from the EU and its ongoing relationship with the EU27.

The purpose of the proposed directives is to the respective differences in contract law regulation between member states. According to the Commission, differences in contract law between member states generate additional transaction costs when concluding cross-border transactions that deter both consumers and businesses from engaging in such transactions. The Commission believes the existence of different domestic provisions governing the contractual rights of consumers generates uncertainty among them as to the extent of their rights when purchasing from another EU jurisdiction. This lack of legal certainty deters consumers from making cross-border purchases, in particular online. Consequently, consumers do not exploit the potential of having access to a wider choice of goods and digital content at more competitive prices. The proposed directives will harmonize consumer rights, creating a single set of rules providing the same level of consumer protection across the European Union.

The draft Online Sales Directive applies to sales contracts for tangible movable goods that are concluded online or through any other means of distance communication, such as telephone or mail.[46] By Art. 3 it requires member states to ensure they 'shall not maintain or introduce provisions diverging from those laid down in this Directive including more or less stringent provisions to ensure a different level of consumer protection'. This is important. If adopted in this form the directive will fully harmonize consumer contract protection rather than just setting minimum standards. The body

---

[43] Ibid. Art. 16(6).

[44] The amended proposal COM/2017/0637 final—2015/0288 (COD) may be found at <https://eur-lex.europa.eu/legal-content/EN/TXT/?uri=COM:2017:0637:FIN>.

[45] COM/2015/0634 final—2015/0287 (COD)<https://eur-lex.europa.eu/legal-content/EN/TXT/?uri=COM%3A2015%3A635%3AFIN>.

[46] Arts. 1 and 2(e).

of the directive covers much of the same ground as the UK Consumer Rights Act 2015. The key provision is Art. 5 which provides that goods shall be:

(1) fit for all the purposes for which goods of the same description would ordinarily be used;

(2) be delivered along with such accessories including packaging, installation instructions or other instructions as the consumer may expect to receive; and

(3) possess qualities and performance capabilities which are normal in goods of the same type and which the consumer may expect given the nature of the goods.

In cases where goods fail to meet these standards 'the consumer shall be entitled to have the goods brought into conformity by the seller, free of charge, by repair or replacement'.[47] In addition, the consumer is given a number of related rights including a choice between repair and replacement under Art. 11, a right to receive a price reduction under Art. 12 and a right to cancel is given to the consumer by Art. 13. This ultimately allows the consumer to terminate the contract where goods fail to comply with Art. 5.

The draft digital content directive covers contracts for the supply of digital content in exchange for a price or for personal data or any other data actively provided by the consumer.[48] Unlike the Online Sales Directive, the Digital Content Directive does not limit its scope of application to distance contracts. Its purpose, as set forth in the recitals, is to avoid legal fragmentation between different distribution channels.[49] The directive introduces a broad definition of digital content that is wider in scope than the one employed under the Consumer Rights Directive. The purpose is to make the regulation technologically neutral and resistant to the passage of time, and ensure it effectively covers the rapid technological developments of the sector.[50]

The directive will apply (if adopted) to contracts in which the supplier agrees to provide the consumer with 'data which is produced and supplied in digital form, for example video, audio, applications, digital games and any other software'[51] This is regardless of the medium used for its transmission, whether in durable form, for example DVD or other carrier medium, or by any other means, such as downloading or streaming, and irrespective of the way the content has been developed, including digital content developed by the supplier according to the consumer's specifications.[52]

It will also apply when the supplier supplies digital services to the consumer. In particular, it includes services such as cloud computing that allow consumers 'the creation, processing or storage of data in digital form, where such data is provided by the consumer', and access to the use of social media platforms that allow consumers to 'share of and any other interaction with data in digital form provided by other users of the service.'[53] The directive is highly innovative in that by Art. 3(1) it applies to 'any contract where the supplier supplies digital content to the consumer or undertakes to do so and, in exchange, a price is to be paid *or the consumer actively provides counterperformance other than money in the form of personal data or any other data.*' In so doing,

[47] Art. 9(1).
[48] Art. 3.
[49] Recital 12.
[50] Recital 11.
[51] Art. 2(1)(a).
[52] Art. 3(2).
[53] Arts. 2(1)(b) and (c).

the directive takes into account that in the contemporary market, information about individuals has a monetary equivalent value. However, this does not happen if the data collected is 'strictly necessary for the performance of the contract or for meeting legal requirements and the supplier does not further process them in a way incompatible with this purpose.'[54] Importantly, Art. 3(1) does not apply where the supplier collects information about the consumer without him or her actively supplying it, for example by means of cookies.[55]

In a similar fashion to the Online Sales Directive the Digital Content Directive attempts to set standard quality requirements for digital goods and services. By Art. 6 digtial content must be:

(1) of the quantity, quality, duration, and version and shall possess functionality, interoperability, and other performance features such as accessibility, continuity, and security, as required by the contract;

(2) fit for any particular purpose for which the consumer requires it and which the consumer made known to the supplier;

(3) be supplied along with any instructions and customer assistance as stipulated by the contract; and

(4) be updated as stipulated by the contract. Similarly to the Online Sales Directive the consumer has a variety rights including repair/replacement or price reduction, all under Art. 12, and ultimately a right of termination under Art. 13. Again from a UK perspective the Consumer Rights Act 2015 has already implemented most of this in UK Law.

With the directives still in draft it is hard to say how they might develop and when, or if, they will become part of the European Consumer Acquis. If they do it is unlikely the UK will need to make changes to the law as the Consumer Rights Act 2015 suggests we are already compliant so no changes to UK law may be expected in the medium term.

18.5 **Conclusions**

Consumer protection is an important area of Information Technology Law. Data from Eurostat shows that in 2017 82 per cent of UK consumers bought at least one product online,[56] while 51 per cent of UK consumers say they prefer to shop online instead of at physical stores.[57] Against this backdrop consumer protection is vital. Consumers must have confidence that when they buy online they have effective means of enforcement. Given the global nature of e-commerce and the local nature of consumer protection laws, this means that the first line of defence for the consumer is the ability to raise actions in his or her local courts, and applying their local laws. To this end the Brussels (Recast) Regulation and the Rome I Regulation provide essential safeguards. It is vital

---

[54] Art. 3(4).
[55] Recital 14.
[56] See <https://ec.europa.eu/eurostat/statistics-explained/index.php/E-commerce_statistics_for_individuals>.
[57] See <https://ecommercenews.eu/51-uk-consumers-prefer-to-shop-online-than-in-store/>.

these safeguards, and their recognition by courts, survive the Brexit process if cross-border e-commerce is to thrive in the UK.

Even when e-commerce transactions do not cross borders the form of an e-commerce transaction, as a distance contract, marks it for particular consumer protections beyond those one would expect in a high street transaction. Here the framework of the Consumer Rights Directive and its implementation by the Consumer Contracts (Information, Cancellation and Additional Charges) Regulations is vital in ensuring consumers are fully aware of who they are dealing with and what their rights, including inspection and rejection rights, are. These rights are then combined with the rights in the Consumer Rights Act 2015 which include requirements as to quality, fitness for purpose, and the requirement that goods and/or services are as described to create a comprehensive consumer protection framework.

Finally, this chapter looked at the long-established framework for the regulation of commercial speech and unsolicited commercial communications (spam). We find that despite a long history of EU regulation in this field it has only been partially successful in regulating spam communications. This is mostly because spam originates as a form of speech outside the EU, and also that most spammers have little inclination to comply with regulations as they operate in the shadows anyway. The regulatory regime has though been successful in regulating legitimate businesses and operations and European commercial operators now have a strong framework for privacy and communications which most work within. We could at best call Europe's spam regime a qualified success.

TEST QUESTIONS

Question 1

Liam is a student in London. He has recently bought a new laptop computer from 'computadoras para la venta' (CPV), an online retailer in Spain. The laptop was sold under CPVs standard terms and conditions which state that the contract is concluded when the goods are shipped and that goods may only be returned for a refund if they are faulty under Spanish law. They also state that the contract will be governed by Spanish law and is subject only to the jurisdiction of the Spanish courts. They further state that refunds will only be given if goods are returned in their original packaging within seven days of receipt and that the buyer must bear the cost of both the return and original shipping costs. The CPV website makes no reference to any right to cancel under distance selling regulations and indeed gives few details about CPV. There is no business address, company registration, or tax details. The returns address is simply a PO Box. Liam has had the laptop for six weeks and has found in the last two weeks that there are problems with the power supply, which means that at times the laptop is rendered unusable. This could be remedied by simply having a new power supply module supplied but CPV say they do not do this and in any event this does not make the laptop faulty under Spanish law and more than seven days has passed. They refuse to talk to Liam any further.

Liam wants to know what he can do about this. He is unsure what rights he has and is concerned that he could not afford the costs of raising a case in Spain but he is sure he could raise a small claims action in England if that were possible. He seeks your advice.

Question 2

The European Commission have claimed that 'The level of consumer confidence in cross-border shopping is low. One of the causes of this phenomenon is the fragmentation of the Consumer Acquis. The fragmentation and the related uneven level of consumer protection make it difficult to conduct pan-European education campaigns on consumer rights and to carry out alternative dispute resolution mechanisms.' Is this true?

Question 3

Do you agree with the following statement? 'Consumer protection measures for online purchases are actually of little value as the individual consumer is not likely to pursue an action for the small amounts of money involved. It would be much better to allow freedom for online retailers and consumers to contract as they see fit. Retailers would then pass on cost savings to the consumer and this would be a real and tangible, benefit.'

FURTHER READING

Books

C Riefa, *Consumer Protection and Online Auction Platforms: Towards a Safer Legal Framework* (Routledge 2015)

G Woodroffe, C Willett, and C Twigg-Flesner, *Woodroffe & Lowe's Consumer Law and Practice* (10th edn, Sweet & Maxwell 2016)

Chapters and articles

Z Akhtar, 'Distant selling, e commerce and company liability' (2012) 33 *European Competition Law Review* 497

P Cachia, 'Consumer contracts in European private international law: the sphere of operation of the consumer contract rules in the Brussels I and Rome I Regulations' (2009) 34 *European Law Review* 476

J Krebs, 'Twixt cup and lip: liability of traders under consumer contracts for digital content damaged in transit' [2017] *Journal of Business Law* 378

C Markou, 'Directive 2011/83/EU on Consumer Rights' in Arno Lodder and Andrew Murray (eds.) *EU Regulation of E-Commerce: A Commentary* (Edward Elgar 2017)

J Smits, 'New European Union Proposals for Distance Sales and Digital Contents Contracts: Fit for Purpose?' (2016) *Zeitschrift für Europäisches Privatrecht* 319

Z Vernadaki, 'Consumer protection and the reform of the European consumer acquis' [2010] 21 *International Company and Commercial Law Review* 316

PART V

Criminal activity in the information society

The information society offers opportunities for criminals as well as law-abiding citizens. How does the law reduce the risks of criminal activity in the information society?

Computer misuse

Computer misuse is the collective term for a number of criminal offences committed by means of a computer and regulated by the Computer Misuse Act (CMA) 1990 (as amended). These include computer hacking (unauthorized access); the creation and distribution of computer viruses and other malware; and denial-of-service attacks. The need for specific legislation in this area became clear in the winter of 1984 when two computer hackers, Stephen Gold and Robert Schifreen, gained unauthorized access to the BT Prestel computer network and successfully accessed several secure areas of the service.[1]

Their story began in spring 1984 when they obtained a Prestel username and password. There are a variety of tales as to how they did this, and neither has ever confirmed the truth. What does appear to be the case is that they did not obtain these details by watching a Prestel engineer enter his username and password at a trade show as is widely reported on some internet sites.[2] It would appear the password and username were either obtained through the acquisition of a private phone book belonging to a BT engineer[3] or by the actions of Robert Schifreen attempting a variety of passwords and usernames until one was accepted, a so-called 'brute force attack'.[4] Whatever approach was used it appears Prestel did not take security seriously. The Prestel network required that a username was always a ten-character string of letters and/or numbers, and that a password was a four-character string. The username/password combination discovered by Gold and Schifreen was 2222222222/1234. Using this new-found information Gold and Schifreen spent a considerable amount of time on the Prestel network. They identified several weaknesses in Prestel's security and gained system-manager-level access when, in October 1984, in another security breach, a BT engineer left his log-in details on his log-in page.[5] They soon learned how

---

[1] Prestel was an early commercial computer network service in the UK. It was a 'Videotex' system which carried text and simple graphics across telephone lines for display on a domestic TV via a terminal. It allowed access to a wide range of content as well as allowing emailing between Prestel customers. Prestel was for a while an important commercial service used by banks, financial institutions, travel agents, and media organizations to supply and trade data and to carry out transactions.

[2] See Wikipedia, *Entry for Computer Misuse Act* http://en.wikipedia.org/wiki/Computer_Misuse_Act; 'What is the Computer Misuse Act of 1990?', *Wisegeek*, http://www.wisegeek.org/what-is-the-computer-misuse-act-of-1990.htm.

[3] H Cornwall, *The Hacker's Handbook* (Century 1985) 209.

[4] P Mungo and B Clough, *Approaching Zero: The Extraordinary Underworld of Hackers, Phreakers, Virus Writers and Keyboard Criminals* (Random House 1992) 34.

[5] Cornwall (n. 3) 209.

to enter subscription-only areas of Prestel,[6] though their most infamous act was about to begin their downfall. They managed to gain access to subscribers' personal email accounts, including the email account of the Duke of Edinburgh. One hacker (it is not clear which) sent an email, allegedly from the Duke to the Prestel System Manager, saying 'I do so enjoy puzzles and games. Ta ta. Pip! Pip! HRH Hacker.'[7] This act, along with a further act which could only have been carried out by a Prestel engineer with the highest network clearance (or a hacker with similar clearance),[8] caused BT to reset all system manager passwords and then set a trap for the hackers. They were soon identified and were arrested on 10 April 1985.

The problem for the authorities was what were they to be charged with? It was not clear that they had committed a criminal act. There was no theft or damage to property and although there was deception it was not clear they had committed fraud. The authorities could not simply let them go for that would send the signal that hacking was okay. Eventually they were charged under s. 1 of the Forgery and Counterfeiting Act 1981: 'A person is guilty of forgery if he makes a false instrument, with the intention that he or another shall use it to induce somebody to accept it as genuine, and by reason of so accepting it to do or not to do some act to his own or any other person's prejudice.' The argument of the Crown was that the defendants had infringed this provision since, when asked to log in to the Prestel network, they had given false details. In the words of counsel for the Crown '[t]he relevant instrument was the control area of the user segment of the relevant Prestel computer whilst it had recorded and/or stored within it the electronic impulses purporting to be a customer identification number and customer password'.[9] The problem for the Crown was the definition of 'instrument' found in s. 8 of the Act: an 'instrument' is 'any document, whether of a formal or informal character . . . [including] any disc, tape, sound track, or other device on or in which information is recorded or stored by mechanical, electronic, or other means'.[10] This suggests a degree of permanence is required, but in the Prestel system the username and password were only held for a fraction of a second while the system authenticated them.

At trial the defendants were found guilty and fined.[11] Both immediately appealed and before the Court of Appeal argued, among other things that 'in the context of section 8(l)(d), storage does not include temporary storage in the input buffer because it is immediately passed elsewhere; and (b) the instrument is not *ejusdem generis* with

---

[6] Ibid. 210–11.

[7] Ibid. 211. In another 'prank' they managed to issue a FT newsflash claiming that the pound was worth fifty dollars on international currency exchanges.

[8] The act itself was a minor one. It was the nature of the way it was carried out which forced Prestel to act. It is reported by Mungo and Clough (n. 4) in some detail: 'When subscribers dial into Prestel, they immediately see page one, which indexes all other services. Only the system manager can alter or update listings on this page, but [Schifreen], exploiting his [system manager] status, made a modest change and altered the word Index to read Idnex. Though it was perfectly harmless, the change was enough to signal to Prestel that its security had been breached. The other pranks had been worrisome, but altering the first page was tantamount to telling Prestel that its entire system was insecure', at 36.

[9] *R v Gold and Schifreen* [1988] 1 AC 1063, 1064.

[10] Forgery and Counterfeiting Act 1981, s. 8(1)(a) and (d).

[11] *R v Gold and Schifreen* [1987] QB 1116, 1117.

disc, tape and sound track since there was no evidence that the device was in any way physically altered. The impulses always remained separate from the device itself.'[12] The Court of Appeal upheld their claim. In giving the judgment of the court Lord Lane CJ found that:

> the user segment in the instant case does not carry the necessary two types of message to bring it within the ambit of forgery at all. Moreover, neither the report nor the Act, so it seems to us, seeks to deal with information that is held for a moment whilst automatic checking takes place and is then expunged. That process is not one to which the words 'recorded or stored' can properly be applied, suggesting as they do a degree of continuance.[13]

On this basis the court found that 'the language of the Act was not intended to apply to the situation which was shown to exist in this case . . . It is a conclusion which we reach without regret. The Procrustean attempt to force these facts into the language of an Act not designed to fit them produced grave difficulties for both judge and jury which we would not wish to see repeated.'[14]

The Crown appealed to the House of Lords, but were unsuccessful in their attempts to have the decision of the Court of Appeal overturned with Lord Brandon of Oakbrook going out of his way to criticize the Crown for prosecuting the case in this manner.

 Highlight Lord Brandon's rebuke

I share the view of the Court of Appeal (Criminal Division), as expressed by Lord Lane CJ, that there is no reason to regret the failure of what he aptly described as the Procrustean attempt to force the facts of the present case into the language of an Act not designed to fit them.

The Crown had lost the first case on computer hacking in the UK and had done so in a blaze of publicity and with a stinging rebuke from both the Court of Appeal and the House of Lords. There was a great deal of concern both that the UK was unable to deal with the growing threat of computer hacking and that the outcome of this case may encourage others to take up hacking as a hobby.[15] Against this background moves were made to introduce a new Act which would close this loophole in the criminal law. The Law Commission and the Scottish Law Commission produced a joint report recommending that a new offence of unauthorized access to computer data be created,[16] and in the next parliamentary sitting Conservative MP Michael Colvin sponsored a private member's Bill which would give effect to the Law Commissions' recommendations: the Bill, supported by the government, became the CMA 1990.

---

[12] Ibid. 1118–19.
[13] Ibid. 1124.
[14] Ibid. 1124.
[15] It is suggested by Mungo and Clough (n. 4) that the outcome of this case encouraged another young hacker, Nick Whitely, to begin a campaign which included wiping data from university networks as well as computer firm ICL, a practice which led to him being dubbed 'the Mad Hacker', at 39–41.
[16] Law Commission, Report No. 186: Computer Misuse (Cm.819 1989).

19.1 **Hacking**

The Act in its original form was remarkably concise comprising only 18 sections with no schedules. This may be due to the origins of the Act as a private member's Bill rather than as a government Bill. The meat of the Act was in part I (ss. 1–3) entitled 'Computer Misuse Offences'. Here were to be found three new criminal offences: the unauthorized access offence, the aggravated unauthorized access offence, and the unauthorized modification offence. The first two of these were designed to deal with computer hacking.

Section 1, the main hacking provision, is a well-designed criminal law provision. It does not use colloquial terms such as 'hacking',[17] 'phreaking',[18] or 'cracking'[19] and instead simply defines the illegal activity. It states:

 Highlight Computer Misuse Act, s. 1(1)

A person is guilty of an offence if:

(a) he causes a computer to perform any function with intent to secure access to any program or data held in any computer, or to enable any such access to be secured;

(b) the access he intends to secure, or to enable to be secured, is unauthorised; and

(c) he knows at the time when he causes the computer to perform the function that that is the case.

Despite its clarity and brevity several questions remained. The first was what was meant by unauthorized access: was this an offence designed to prevent hacking as portrayed in the media—that is, using one computer to gain access to another, or could the unauthorized access be simply the obtaining of access to a single computer by accessing it directly without permission? In other words, to commit the s. 1 offence did one need to hack into a computer or network from an external source? Guidance could be found in s. 17(5) which states that:

Access of any kind by any person to any program or data held in a computer is unauthorised if—

(a) he is not himself entitled to control access of the kind in question to the program or data; and

(b) he does not have consent to access by him of the kind in question to the program or data from any person who is so entitled.

This seemed to clearly suggest the latter approach was correct, i.e. that access could include direct access to a single computer. This, though, was thrown into doubt when

---

[17] Strictly speaking, a hacker is anyone who displays skilled software development. They are not always malicious and the term is often applied to skilled programmers working in all aspects of software development.

[18] Phreaking is using a computer or other device for tricking telephone systems to obtain free calls. Phreaking used to be common when internet access was obtained on a cost-per-minute dial-up account. It is less common now.

[19] A cracker, rather than a hacker, is someone who breaks into someone else's computer system, by-passes passwords or licences in computer programs, or in other ways intentionally breaches computer security.

the case of *R v Cropp* was heard before Snaresbrook Crown Court.[20] Mr Cropp was charged with unauthorized access to a computer with intent to commit a further offence under s. 2 of the CMA 1990. He had returned to the premises of an ex-employer to purchase goods on behalf of his current employer. When left alone by the salesperson for a few minutes Mr Cropp entered a discount code onto the Point of Sale computer effecting a 70 per cent discount on the goods sold, meaning that his new employer was invoiced for only £204.60 (plus VAT) instead of £710.96 (plus VAT). His activity was traced and he was charged but when he came to trial the defence counsel entered a plea of no case to answer. The grounds for this claim were that in order to contravene s. 1(1) (and therefore s. 2(1)) of the Act the prosecution had to establish that the accused had used one computer to gain access to another computer. Somewhat surprisingly the judge upheld the submission, finding that:

> It seems to me, doing the best that I can in elucidating the meaning of s. 1(1)(a), that a second computer must be involved. It seems to me to be straining language to say that only one computer is necessary when one looks at the actual wording of the subsection: 'Causing a computer to perform any function with intent to secure access to any program or data held in any computer.'

This outcome caused consternation for the Crown. It had been assumed that unauthorized access meant any access: this decision threatened to limit the scope of the Act extensively. As a result the Attorney General sought clarification of this issue from the Court of Appeal by way of an Attorney General's reference.[21] The Court of Appeal ruled that the judge in *Cropp* had erred. Lord Taylor CJ gave the opinion of the court:

> The ordinary cannons of construction require this court to look at the words of the section and to give them their plain and natural meaning. Doing that, we look again at the relevant words. They are, 'he causes a computer to perform any function with intent to secure access to any program or data held in any computer'. . . . It is a trite observation, when considering the construction of statutes, that one does not imply or introduce words that are not there when the plain and natural meaning is clear. In our judgment there are no grounds whatsoever for implying or importing the word 'other' between 'any' and 'computer' or excepting the computer which is actually used by the offender from the phrase 'any computer' at the end of subsection 1(a).[22]

This was a relief for the law enforcement bodies. If the Court of Appeal had confirmed the original outcome of the case the CMA could have been undermined by its first application.[23] As it was, by confirming that the unauthorized access offences could be committed on a single computer, they opened up a further role for ss. 1 and 2. They had confirmed it could be used not only to prosecute the traditional computer hacker as imagined and portrayed in the media; it could also be applied to employees who accessed data held on their employer's computers without permission.

---

[20] *R v Cropp*, Snaresbrook Crown Court, 5 July 1991, unreported, but see case note at (1991) 7 CLSR 168.

[21] AG's Reference No. 1 of 1991 [1992] 3 WLR 432.

[22] Ibid. 437.

[23] E Dumbill, 'Computer Misuse Act 1990—Recent Developments' (1992) 8 *Computer Law and Practice* 105.

19.1.1 **Employee hackers**

In the few years following promulgation of the CMA there were a number of cases involving employee misuse of their employer's resources: many centred on abuse of the Police National Computer system (PNC) by serving police officers and civilian support staff.

The first was *R v Bennett*.[24] Superintendent Bennett used the police national computer (PNC) to identify his ex-wife's new partner by using details he had gathered on him by observation. Superintendent Bennett pleaded guilty to a breach of s. 1 and was fined £150. Several subsequent cases followed, including *R v Bonnett* in which a special constable was convicted under s. 1 for unlawfully accessing the PNC without authority to find out who owned the car registration number BON1T, because he wanted to buy it,[25] and *R v Begley*, in which a WPC used the PNC to access records in an attempt to track down a woman who had had a relationship with her boyfriend.[26] These cases, and many similar cases from the private sector,[27] were easily dealt with by the courts. They were simple criminal prosecutions where the only question was whether or not the accused had committed the infringing act. The first major challenge to the application of ss. 1 and 2 to these 'insider hackers' was to come in the case of *DPP v Bignell*.[28]

Bignell was another in the series of cases involving misuse of the PNC. The respondents were two married police officers Paul and Victoria Bignell. They accessed the PNC to extract details of motor vehicles owned by a Mr Howells, the new partner of PC Bignell's ex-wife for purposes not entirely clear from the case report. At trial at Bow Street Magistrates' Court both defendants were found guilty of breaching s. 1 of the CMA and were fined. However, as a conviction would mean that they were both likely to lose their jobs as police officers, they appealed this decision. On appeal they challenged the decision of the stipendiary magistrate on the basis that 'their use of the computer, even if it was found to be for private purposes, was not within the definition of "unauthorised access" provided by s. 17(5) of the Act because the access had been with authority even though that authority was used for an unauthorised purpose'.[29]

This extremely complex and convoluted defence became known as the defence of 'authorized access for unauthorized purpose'. Basically the respondents were arguing that, despite the fact they were using the PNC for purposes for which they were not authorized to use it, they did have authority to use the computer system, meaning that broadly their access was authorized and it was only their purpose which was not. As the Act states that the s. 1 offence is committed when 'the access he intends to secure is unauthorised'[30] no offence was committed.

---

[24] Unreported, Bow Street Magistrates' Court, 10 October 1991.

[25] Unreported, Newcastle-under-Lyme Magistrates' Court, 3 November 1995.

[26] Unreported, Coventry Magistrates' Court. This case and the others discussed in this section are discussed in M Wasik, 'Computer Misuse and Misconduct in Public Office' (2008) 22 *International Review of Law, Computers & Technology* 135.

[27] Private sector cases included *R v Borg* in which a computer officer at a financial services firm was cleared of unlawfully accessing her employer's system with a view to defrauding £1m, and *R v Speilmann* in which an ex-employee of a financial news service was found guilty of a breach of s. 1 in accessing his ex-employer's system to modify and delete emails. Details of these unreported cases, and many others may be found at <www.computerevidence.co.uk/Cases/CMA.htm>.

[28] [1997] EWHC Admin 476.

[29] Ibid. [4].

[30] Computer Misuse Act 1990, s. 1(1)(b).

This appeal was upheld at Southwark Crown Court in September 1996 but the Crown appealed to the Divisional Court. Astill J and Pill LJ heard the appeal and on 16 May 1997 they issued their judgment: they would reject the appeal and uphold the decision of the Crown Court. Astill J gave the decision of the court. He examined both the original Law Commission Report and the wording of s. 17 before concluding that the respondents were entitled to access data contained on the PNC as part of their normal duties as police officers; therefore they were entitled to access the data, although their purpose for accessing it may have been unauthorized. Astill J attempted to quell concerns that this left employers with little control over how employees used their computer systems by pointing out that 'The authority of the Commissioner is not undermined because the respondents remain subject to internal disciplines. The use of the computer for an unauthorised purpose involves the use of a false Reason Code and that is a matter subject to disciplinary procedures. In addition the respondents could have been prosecuted under the Data Protection Act 1984.'[31]

There has been a considerable amount of analysis of the *Bignell* decision.[32] While some acknowledge that the Crown may have erred in not raising a prosecution under the Data Protection Act,[33] most commentators were highly critical of the outcome. The problem was the way Astill J had interpreted s. 17(2) and (5). Section 17(2) states that:

A person secures access to any program or data held in a computer if by causing a computer to perform any function he—

(a) alters or erases the program or data;

(b) copies or moves it to any storage medium other than that in which it is held or to a different location in the storage medium in which it is held;

(c) uses it; or

(d) has it output from the computer in which it is held (whether by having it displayed or in any other manner).

While s. 17(5) states:

Access of any kind by any person to any program or data held in a computer is unauthorised if:

(a) he is not himself entitled to control access of the kind in question to the program or data; and

(b) he does not have consent to access by him of the kind in question to the program or data from any person who is so entitled.

Astill J concluded that:

s. 17(2)(a) to (d) sets out four ways in which a person secures access. S.17(5)(a) and (b) define unauthorised access by reference to access 'of the kind in question'. That refers to the four kinds of access set out in s. 17(2)(a) to (d) and the respondents did have authority to secure access by reference to s. 17(2)(c) and (d) at least. It therefore follows that 'control access of the kind in

---

[31] *Bignall* (n 28) [17].

[32] C Gringras, 'To Be Great Is to Be Misunderstood: The Computer Misuse Act 1990' (1997) 3 *Computer and Telecommunications Law Review* 213; Z Hamin, 'Insider Cyber-threats: Problems and Perspectives' (2000) 14 *International Review of Law, Computers and Technology* 105; Wasik (n. 26).

[33] To be fair to the Crown, an earlier attempt to prosecute a serving police officer under the Data Protection Act 1984 for extracting data from the PNC with a view to passing it on to a friend who worked for a debt collection agency had failed. See *R v Brown* [1996] 1 AC 543.

question' in s. 17(5)(a) must apply to the respondents because they were authorised to secure access by s. 17(2)(c) and (d).[34]

Thus, for Astill J, s. 17(5) is tied to s. 17(2), but as has been pointed out by several commentators this should not be the case. Clive Gringras notes that:

> The Bignells instructed that a false 'reason code' be typed into the police national computer. Why? They wanted the computer to perform this function to allow them to gain access to data which were 'not necessary for the efficient discharge of genuine police duties'. In other words, they were not authorised to secure access to the data. The offence should have been made out. The reason that the court did not come to this conclusion was because they did not restrict their analysis of the facts with the precise wording of the statute. The Act is drafted in terms of 'causing a computer to perform a function' together with the intention to 'secure unauthorised access to any program or data'. It is therefore an error in law for the court to have provided a judgment littered with references to 'accessing a computer'. The Act does not sanction those who access computers; it sanctions those who use computers to secure access to data and programs. This difference is fundamental and because it was not appreciated by the Divisional Court we, those who rely on the safety of the material stored by computers, are left again waiting for an appeal to set straight the Act.[35]

David Bainbridge was equally forthright, 'As part of their normal duties, the police officers were entitled to access such computer information. *But being entitled to access computer material is not the same as being entitled to control access to such material.* This is an important and crucial distinction which the court failed to make.'[36] What Astill J had failed to do was distinguish between 'access to data', as defined under s. 17(2) which forms the *actus reus* of the offence under s. 1(1)(a) and '*unauthorised* access' as defined by s. 17(5) and which forms the *mens rea* of the offence under s. 1(1)(b). In effect the Divisional Court had fused the two elements together leaving what David Bainbridge called 'an unsatisfactory gap in the Computer Misuse Act 1990'.[37]

The opportunity for the courts to revisit *Bignell* came quickly. Sometime between January 1996 and March 1997 Joan Ojomo, an employee of American Express working in the credit section of the company's office in Florida, gained access to customer accounts and extracted confidential information which she passed on to others, including a Mr Adeniyi Allison who was resident in London. The information she gave to him was then used to encode blank credit cards which could then be used fraudulently to buy goods and to obtain money from ATMs. Miss Ojomo was arrested, and as a result of the subsequent investigation Mr Allison was arrested and held in London on suspicion of conspiracy to: (1) secure unauthorized access to the American Express computer system with intent to commit theft; (2) secure unauthorized access to the American Express computer system with intent to commit forgery; and (3) cause unauthorized modification to the contents of the American Express computer system. At committal the magistrate declined to commit Mr Allison on the first two charges but did commit him on the third. The US government then sought extradition of Mr Allison, while Mr Allison brought a *habeas corpus* claim on the basis that none of the offences were

---

[34] *Bignall* (n. 28) [17].
[35] Gringras (n. 32) 215.
[36] D Bainbridge, *Introduction to Information Technology Law* (6th edn, Longman 2007) 443 (emphasis added).
[37] Ibid. 443.

extradition offences. A series of cross-appeals from both the US government and Mr Allison emerged before, on 13 May 1998, the Divisional Court certified a question of law of general public importance:

> Whether, on a true construction of s. 1 (and thereafter s. 2) of the Computer Misuse Act 1990, a person who has authority to access data of the kind in question none the less has unauthorised access if:
>
> (a) the access to the particular data in question was intentional,
>
> (b) the access in question was unauthorised by a person entitled to authorise access to that particular data,
>
> (c) knowing that the access to that particular data was unauthorised.

The case, *R v Bow Street Magistrates Court and Allison, ex parte Government of the United States of America*,[38] was heard on 13 July 1999 with the full judgment issued on 5 August 1999. This was remarkable timing. It had been just over two years since the *Bignell* decision and now the House of Lords had been referred a case on exactly the same point of law. Lord Hobhouse gave the decision of the Court. He found first of all that offences committed under ss. 2 or 3 were clearly extraditable as s. 15 of the Act clearly stated that they were to be so.[39] The question then remained, had there been an offence under either of these sections? It was clear that in her daily work it was possible for Miss Ojomo to access all customer accounts held on the American Express database but she was only authorized to access those accounts that were assigned to her. However she had accessed various other accounts and files which had not been assigned to her and which she had not been given specific authority to work on. This meant the court had to revisit the *Bignell* decision and determine whether these activities of Miss Ojomo were in breach of s. 2.

Lord Hobhouse was extremely critical of the approach taken in *Bignell*.[40] He found that the actual interpretation of 'control' and 'access' was much simpler:

> Section 17 is an interpretation section. Subsection (2) defines what is meant by access and securing access to any programme or data. It lists four ways in which this may occur or be achieved. Its purpose is clearly to give a specific meaning to the phrase 'to secure access'. Subsection (5) is to be read with subsection (2). It deals with the relationship between the widened definition of securing access and the scope of the authority which the relevant person may hold. That is why the subsection refers to 'access of any kind' and 'access of the kind in question'. Authority to view data may not extend to authority to copy or alter that data. The refinement of the concept of access requires a refinement of the concept of authorisation. The authorisation must be authority to secure access of the kind in question. As part of this refinement, the subsection lays down two cumulative requirements of lack of authority. The first is the requirement that the relevant person be not the person entitled to control the relevant kind of access. The word 'control' in this context clearly means authorise and forbid. If the relevant person is so entitled, then it would be unrealistic to treat his access as being unauthorised. The second is that the relevant person does not have the consent to secure the relevant kind of access from a person entitled to control, i.e. authorise, that access.
>
> Subsection (5) therefore has a plain meaning subsidiary to the other provisions of the Act. It simply identifies the two ways in which authority may be acquired—by being oneself the person

---

[38] [2000] 2 AC 216.
[39] Ibid. 222–3.
[40] Ibid. 225.

entitled to authorise and by being a person who has been authorised by a person entitled to authorise. It also makes clear that the authority must relate not simply to the data or programme but also to the actual kind of access secured. Similarly, it is plain that it is not using the word 'control' in a physical sense of the ability to operate or manipulate the computer and that it is not derogating from the requirement that for access to be authorised it must be authorised to the relevant data or relevant programme or part of a programme. It does not introduce any concept that authority to access one piece of data should be treated as authority to access other pieces of data 'of the same kind' notwithstanding that the relevant person did not in fact have authority to access that piece of data. Section 1 refers to the intent to secure unauthorised access to any programme or data. These plain words leave no room for any suggestion that the relevant person may say: 'Yes, I know that I was not authorised to access that data but I was authorised to access other data of the same kind.'[41]

Bignell was distinguished and a commonsense approach prevailed. Lord Hobhouse clearly set out the different roles of s. 17(2) and (5). Authority to access data was to the specific data, or for a specific purpose; there was to be no aggregation of data as 'data of a specific kind' as set out in *Bignell*. Because Miss Ojomo had no permission to access the specific data in question her access was unauthorized and therefore in breach of s. 1. Further, because this access was secured with the intent to go on and commit fraud, this was an extraditable offence under s. 2.

Allison remains the leading case on unauthorized employee, or insider, hacking. Employees who access data without authority risk prosecution under the CMA, even if they are authorized to access other data of that type. The *Allison* principle has been applied in several subsequent but unreported cases including *R v Culbert*,[42] in which an ex-employee of Associated Newspapers pleaded guilty to two counts of making an unauthorized modification to a computer system and one of gaining unauthorized access after he offered to damage his employer's computerized print centre in return for £600,000; *R v Carey* in which a computer engineer deleted a number of design drawings over a dispute about payment;[43] and *R v Curzon* in which an employee at Royal Wootton Bassett Academy accessed the school's email system using the login and password of another school employee to read private emails from the Head.[44] The risk of insider hacking remains high, as was recorded in reports by the Audit Commission,[45] the Information Commissioner,[46] and PWC,[47] but prosecution for more serious breaches continues to discourage this type of attack.

19.1.2 **External hackers**

Of course when the CMA was passed it was external hackers in the mould of Stephen Gold and Robert Schifreen who most people had in mind. Following the *Cropp* decision a number of cases followed, including *R v Goulden*,[48] in which a software contractor in dispute with a client over unpaid fees 'locked' the client's computer system by

---

[41] Ibid. 223–4.
[42] Unreported, Southwark Crown Court, 13 October 2000.
[43] Unreported, Hove Crown Court, 19 September 2002.
[44] Unreported, Swindon Magistrates Court, 17 August 2012.
[45] The Audit Commission, *ICT Fraud and Abuse*, June 2005.
[46] Office of the Information Commissioner, *Annual Report 2004* (July 2004) 34–6.
[47] PWC, *Managing Insider Threats*, February 2015.
[48] Southwark Crown Court, *The Times*, 10 June 1992.

installing a security program and refused to hand over the password until his fees were paid, was fined £1,650; and *R v Pryce*,[49] in which teenage hacker Richard Pryce—aka the 'Datastream Cowboy'—pleaded guilty to 12 charges of unlawful access after accessing websites operated by among others, Lockheed Martin and the US Air Force.

The most famous early case was probably the 'addicted hacker' case *R v Bedworth*.[50] Paul Bedworth, along with co-accused Karl Strickland and Neil Woods, was charged under ss. 1 and 3 of the CMA. Together they formed a group called Eight Legged Groove Machine (8LGM). They gained access to a number of high-profile networks including JANET (the Joint Academic Network), the National Assessment Agency, BT, the *Financial Times*, and the European Commission. Once in they often left messages signed 8LGM or 'eight little green men'. They did not meet, or even know each other or their real names until they were introduced by the arresting officers; all contact was by bulletin boards. Strickland and Woods entered guilty pleas and both were sentenced to six months in prison.[51] Bedworth however pleaded not guilty. For some reason the prosecution had charged him with conspiracy to commit offences under ss. 1 and 3 of the CMA, rather than the direct offences. Why this was done is not clear as he appeared to be equally culpable with his co-accused. In any event, Bedworth claimed he was addicted to computer use and by virtue of that addiction was unable to form the necessary intent. The defence called expert witnesses to impress upon the jury that Bedworth had an addiction described as 'computer tendency syndrome' and the jury duly acquitted, despite the fact that the judge had made it clear to the jury that obsession and dependence were no defence to criminal charges. This outcome was surprising, and was heavily criticized.[52] It appears though to be a unique case. At the time there was a considerable amount of concern that the case would establish a precedent which would be followed by other defendants, but this has not turned out to be the case. Instead it seems that the jury was influenced by the defendant's background: at the time he was 18 and about to start university. If so, he can count himself most fortunate.

Cases of external attacks prosecuted under ss. 1 and 2 continue to be seen with some regularity. Few are reported but the evidence suggests that although incidences of external hacking attacks remain high the law is quite effective in dealing with offenders. In *Ellis v DPP (No. 1)* the appellant appealed against three convictions under s. 1.[53] Mr Ellis was an ex-student and alumnus of the University of Newcastle upon Tyne. On three occasions he had used non-open access computers on campus to browse the internet. Mr Ellis did this knowing he was not permitted to use these computers for this purpose, having been previously advised by an administrative officer at the university that as an alumnus he could only make use of public access computers in the library. On each occasion Mr Ellis did not enter a false password or make any other false declaration to gain access to the computers as they had been left logged in by authorized users who had failed to log out after using them.[54] The question for the court was whether using

---

[49] Unreported, Bow Street Magistrates' Court, 21 March 1997.

[50] Unreported, Southwark Crown Court 21 May 1993.

[51] *R v Strickland, R v Woods*, Unreported, Southwark Crown Court 21 May 1993.

[52] See among others 'The Case of the Artful Dodger' *Computer Weekly* (25 March 1993); C Christian, 'Down and Out in Cyberspace' (1993) 90 *Law Society Gazette* 2; A Charlesworth, 'Addiction and Hacking' (1993) *New Law Journal* 540.

[53] *Ellis v DPP (No. 1)* [2001] EWHC Admin 362.

[54] Mr Ellis in interview drew an analogy between what he did with the computers and picking up someone else's discarded newspaper to read. *Ellis v DPP (No. 1)*, ibid. [8].

a logged-in terminal without permission was unauthorized access under s. 1. Judgment was given by Lord Woolf, CJ. He found that s. 1 was 'sufficiently wide to cover the use which was made of the computers by the appellant',[55] and that the 'evidence of Mr Hulme, the administrative officer, was perfectly satisfactory evidence on which the magistrates could decide that the appellant was aware that he was unauthorised to use the computers in the way which he did'.[56] As a result the Divisional Court upheld Mr Ellis's convictions.

A further ambiguity was clarified in the later case of *R v Cuthbert*.[57] Mr Cuthbert made a donation through the Disasters Emergency Committee (DEC) website to support the Asian Tsunami Appeal in the aftermath of the natural disaster on 26 December 2004 but became suspicious as to the veracity of the site when he did not receive an immediate acknowledgement of his donation. As he was a freelance information security consultant, he decided to test the security of the website by increasing his privileges to see if he could find anything amiss. In so doing he was caught by the site's security measures and reported to the authorities. Given that Mr Cuthbert's actions were in good faith, surprisingly he was prosecuted and at trial he was fined £400 plus costs.[58] In sentencing, District Judge Purdy said that it was 'with some considerable regret' that he passed down a guilty verdict, but the Act made it quite clear that Cuthbert had knowingly performed unauthorized actions against DEC's systems.[59] This case makes clear that intent does not affect the applicability of s. 1. Although Mr Cuthbert was of good intention, he was still strictly guilty of the unauthorized access offence. This has led some commentators to suggest that professionals involved in testing security systems could find themselves liable to prosecution under the CMA, but as Richard Walton points out:

> penetration testing for security purposes is a legitimate and legal activity. The starting point for all such testing is the cooperation and authorisation of the owners of the system under test. No unauthorised activity is involved and so no breach of the CMA can occur. Uninvited security testing is a form of vigilanteism that is not legitimate and clearly breaches the CMA. Professionals avoid this sort of behaviour.[60]

19.1.3 **Extradition cases**

Recently there has been considerable focus on the ability to extradite so-called hackers for breaches of ss. 1 and 2 (and ss. 3, 3A, and 3ZA) of the CMA. The Police and Justice Act 2006 has made several amendments to ss. 1–3 of the CMA.[61] One of the key changes made by the amendments was that penalties for the s. 1 offence were increased with considerable extensions to penalties available for cases prosecuted on indictment. When the CMA was introduced s. 1 was a summary offence only with the maximum penalty being 'imprisonment for a term not exceeding six months or to a fine not

---

[55] Ibid. [16].

[56] Ibid. [17].

[57] Unreported, Horseferry Road Magistrates' Court 6 October 2005.

[58] He also lost his job as a freelance information security consultant at ABN Amro Bank.

[59] Reported in Richard Walton, 'The Computer Misuse Act' (2006) 11 *Information Security Technical Report* 39, 43.

[60] Ibid. 43–4.

[61] The bulk of the amendments are to s. 3 and the introduction of a new s. 3A. These will be discussed at 19.3 'Denial of service and supply of devices, and 19.3.2 'Section 3A'.

exceeding level 5 on the standard scale or to both'.[62] This was quite different to the s. 2 offence which carried much heavier penalties on indictment 'on conviction on indictment, to imprisonment for a term not exceeding five years or to a fine or to both'.[63] With the enactment of s. 35 of the Police and Justice Act 2006, the s. 1 offence became indictable with a maximum penalty much closer to the s. 2 offence of 'imprisonment for a term not exceeding two years or to a fine or to both'.[64] The reason for this extension is to be found in the All Party Internet Group Report, 'Revision of the Computer Misuse Act'.[65] There they outline that 'Raising the tariff to one year would make the offence extraditable. Making s. 1 indictable would make it possible to prosecute for a criminal attempt at the offence, viz: it would not have to actually succeed.'[66] By making s. 1 an indictable offence with a maximum penalty of two years' imprisonment it achieves this double aim. This has not been uncontroversial, particularly against the highly charged political debate surrounding the CMA and extradition centred on the Gary McKinnon and Laurie Love cases.

Gary McKinnon became the focus of much debate on the scope and application of anti-hacker legislation. McKinnon was a UK hacker who gained access to a number of US military sites including the Department of Defense, the US Army, Navy, and NASA. He appears to have been originally motivated by a desire to discover evidence of extraterrestrial visits and technologies which he, in common with other UFOlogists, believes are held in US military files. Whatever his original motivation McKinnon gained entry to a number of sensitive systems including 53 Army computers, 26 Navy computers, 16 NASA computers, and one at the Department of Defense. It is alleged he gained access to administrative accounts and installed unauthorized remote access and administrative software called 'remotely anywhere' that enabled him to access and alter data upon these computers at any time and without detection by virtue of the program masquerading as a Windows operating system. He appears to have become more political in his intentions as time went by, posting a message on one computer 'US foreign policy is akin to Government-sponsored terrorism these days . . . It was not a mistake that there was a huge security stand down on September 11 last year . . . I am SOLO. I will continue to disrupt at the highest levels.'[67]

McKinnon was tracked down by the UK National Hi-Tech Crime Unit and was arrested in March 2002 for breaches of the CMA.[68] He was bailed to appear before the courts on 9 October 2002 but was informed in September 2002 that he would not need to appear as the US authorities had decided not to proceed with an

---

[62] See s. 1(3).

[63] See s. 2(5)(c). Section 2 could also be charged as a summary offence in which case the maximum penalty is 'imprisonment for a term not exceeding twelve months or to a fine not exceeding the statutory maximum or to both', s. 2(5)(a).

[64] See s. 1(3)(c). It should also be noted that the maximum sentence on summary procedure is now 'imprisonment for a term not exceeding 12 months or to a fine not exceeding the statutory maximum or to both' (s. 1(3)(a)).

[65] All Party Internet Group, *Revision of the Computer Misuse Act*, June 2004. <https://www.cl.cam. ac.uk/~rnc1/APIG-report-cma.pdf>.

[66] Ibid. [93].

[67] *McKinnon v Government of the USA and Secretary of State for the Home Department* [2007] EWHC 762 (Admin), [8].

[68] I Grant, 'US Took 39 Months to Demand McKinnon's Extradition' *Computer Weekly*, 19 January 2009.

extradition request.[69] Then in June 2005 he was arrested pursuant to an extradition request from the US government. By then the controversial Extradition Act 2003 had been brought into force making it easier for the US authorities to extradite McKinnon. Between June 2005 and summer 2010 McKinnon and his supporters repeatedly challenged the right of the US authorities to extradite him, which if successful could have seen him charged under USA-PATRIOT Act of 2001 which could lead to a maximum prison sentence of 70 years. He unsuccessfully challenged the Home Secretary's decision to issue an extradition certificate before the Divisional Court[70] and the House of Lords.[71]

Following his defeat in the House of Lords McKinnon signed a statement admitting offences under the CMA, including under ss. 2 and 3. He hoped that this might convince the Crown Prosecution Service to prosecute him in the UK. Following this, his case was referred to the Director of Public Prosecutions, but on 26 February 2009 the CPS issued a statement: 'Having reached our conclusions on these matters, as is our wider duty in accordance with the Attorney General's guidance for handling criminal cases in the USA, we also reconsidered in which jurisdiction the case is best prosecuted—and that remains the US.'[72] McKinnon's legal team raised a judicial review action, arguing that due to his recently diagnosed Asperger's Syndrome, the decision to certify his extradition was illegal as the Secretary of State failed to account for this supervening event which affects McKinnon's human rights as he was required to do under s. 6 of the Human Rights Act 1998.[73] This application was lost in July 2009 and it appeared certain McKinnon would be extradited.[74] Then amazingly, following a change of government, the new Home Secretary Theresa May announced she would reconsider McKinnon's case afresh.[75] Another lengthy delay followed until 16 October 2012. Home Secretary Theresa May then announced to the House of Commons that the extradition had been blocked, saying that 'Mr McKinnon's extradition would give rise to such a high risk of him ending his life that a decision to extradite would be incompatible with Mr McKinnon's human rights'. She stated that the Director of Public Prosecutions would determine whether McKinnon should face trial before a British court.[76] On 14 December, the Director of Public Prosecutions announced that McKinnon would not be prosecuted in the United Kingdom because of the difficulties involved in bringing a case against him when the evidence was in the United States.[77]

---

[69] Ibid.

[70] *McKinnon* (n. 67).

[71] *McKinnon v Government of the US of America & Anor* [2008] UKHL 59.

[72] Steve Ragan, 'UK Refuses to Charge McKinnon—NASA Hacker One Step Closer to Extradition' *The Tech Herald*, 26 February 2009 <www.thetechherald.com/articles/UK-refuses-to-charge-McKinnon-NASA-hacker-one-step-closer-to-extradition/4550/>.

[73] *McKinnon v Secretary of State for the Home Department* [2009] EWHC 170 (Admin).

[74] *R (on the Application of Gary McKinnon) v Secretary of State for Home Affairs* [2009] EWHC 2021 (Admin).

[75] Home Office, *Latest on Gary McKinnon Case*, 4 November 2010 <www.homeoffice.gov.uk/media-centre/news/mckinnon-case>.

[76] 'Gary McKinnon's Mother "Overwhelmed" as Extradition Blocked', *BBC News*, 17 October 2012. <www.bbc.co.uk/news/uk-19968973>.

[77] M Kennedy, 'Gary McKinnon Will Face No Charges in UK', *The Guardian*, 14 December 2012.

This case has been highly controversial for many reasons, not least the extended time Mr McKinnon spent under threat of extradition. Most commentaries focus on the long delay between McKinnon's first arrest in 2002 and his subsequent arrest in 2005. This also meant that the 2003 Extradition Act applied to the eventual extradition request, an Act which itself has been the subject of controversy for the procedure it put in place wherein, at the extradition hearing stage, requests from the USA, Canada, Australia, and New Zealand are no longer required to be supported with evidence of a *prima facie* case against the accused. The key controversy, though, is why McKinnon was never charged under the CMA. There is no doubt the UK authorities could have charged McKinnon in 2002 or subsequently. For the Act to apply, the act must have a connection with the UK. This is defined under s. 5(2) as being *either*:

(a) that the accused was in the home country concerned at the time when he did the act which caused the computer to perform the function;

(b) or that any computer containing any program or data to which the accused secured or intended to secure unauthorised access by doing that act was in the home country concerned at that time.

As McKinnon was in London at the relevant time he is clearly liable to the regulation of the CMA 1990 under s. 5(2)(a), even though the computers he hacked into were in the US. Further, as he purportedly admitted offences under ss. 1–3 there was no need for a long and costly trial. Although the harm may have occurred in the US there is no barrier to simply disposing of the McKinnon case at very little further cost to the public purse by having him tried in the UK where he would admit the charges. It is certainly not unusual for UK hackers to be prosecuted here for harm which they have caused overseas. In *R v Caffrey*,[78] a UK teenager, was charged—and later cleared—of an offence under s. 3 of the CMA for a distributed denial-of-service attack (DDoS) carried out on the Port of Houston Authority, while in *R v McElroy*[79] another UK teenager who hacked into a US Department of Energy Research Lab was given 200 hours' community service under the CMA. Why the UK authorities refused to charge McKinnon in the UK is a mystery, especially as hundreds of thousands of pounds of costs accumulated as he fought extradition. The final decision of the DPP not to prosecute him in the UK seemed, at last, a sensible application of his discretion.

Since the McKinnon case there have been two further high-profile extradition cases. The first involved Pakistani student Usman Ahzaz.[80] He had been operating a botnet of over 100,000 computers, at least 800 of which were in the United States. He was caught in an FBI sting operation. He appealed on the basis that he had committed no offence under s. 1 or s. 3 of the CMA. He had been asked by an FBI agent to install software he thought was malware onto the botnet but it was in fact benign. Counsel for Mr Ahzaz argued at worst he committed an attempt to commit the offences detailed. Gross LJ rejected this. He found that 'by his knowingly unauthorised action in installing the

---

[78] Unreported, Southwark Crown Court, 17 October 2003. See R Allison, 'Youth Cleared of Crashing American Port's Computer', *The Guardian*, 18 October 2003.

[79] Unreported, Southwark Crown Court, 3 February 2004. See J Leyden, 'Victory for Commonsense in Nuke Lab Hacking Case', *The Register*, 4 February 2004.

[80] *Ahzaz v United States* [2013] EWHC 216 (Admin).

software believed to be malicious onto the computers in question, the conclusion is inescapable that the Appellant was altering the data on those computers, so constituting an offence under s. 1, read with s. 17(2)(a) of the 1990 Act.'[81] For good measure Gross LJ also found he had committed an offence under s. 3:

> it is plain that the Appellant's conduct would, if proved, constitute an offence under s. 3. In the present case, the Appellant (on the facts as alleged) had control of the computers in question without the knowledge or authorisation of their owners. The Appellant, for reward, agreed to install, surreptitiously, and did install, software he believed to be malicious on those computers. There is no dispute that his action in doing so was, to his knowledge, unauthorised. The obvious reason for the Appellant acting as he did was to impair the operation of the computer or the program or data in question, within the meaning of s. 3(2)(a) and/or (c) of the 1990 Act.[82]

On this basis he, along with Gloster J, upheld the extradition order.

The second case is that of Lauri Love. Love was indicted in the districts of Virginia, New Jersey, and New York between various dates in 2012 and 2014 for a number of computer misuse offences. For example, in 2013 in Federal Court in New Jersey it was alleged that he hacked into US Army computers and placed hidden backdoors within the networks, which allowed them to return to the compromised computer systems at a later date and steal confidential data,[83] while in 2014 in Federal Court in Virginia he was charged with illegal access to a computer operated by the Department of Energy, the Department of Health and Human Services, and the FBI's Regional Computer Forensics Laboratory, among others.[84] The United States sought to extradite Love to stand trial. The parallels between this case and the McKinnon case are striking. Like McKinnon, Love was charged with hacking into US military and federal computer systems. Like McKinnon, Love committed these acts from the UK and like McKinnon, Love was diagnosed with Asperger's Syndrome.

The extradition hearing was heard at Westminster Magistrates' Court in June 2016. The Presiding Magistrate, Judge Tempia found that she was 'satisfied the conduct alleged would amount to extradition offences, namely offences under sections 1 and 2 of the Computer Misuse Act 1990 (carrying maximum sentences of 2 years and 5 years imprisonment respectively).'[85] Unlike the McKinnon case, she did not believe that extradition to the United States would lead to an appreciable suicide risk over and above that which Mr Love would experience in UK prisons and she ordered his extradition. Love immediately appealed and in February 2018 he was successful in that appeal. The appeal centred on s. 83A of the Extradition Act 2003. This new provision,

---

[81] Ibid. [22].

[82] Ibid. [21].

[83] US Attorney's Office, *Alleged Hacker Indicted In New Jersey For Data Breach Conspiracy Targeting Government Agency Networks*, 28 October 2013 <https://www.justice.gov/usao-nj/pr/alleged-hacker-indicted-new-jersey-data-breach-conspiracy-targeting-government-agency>.

[84] FBI, *Hacker Charged with Breaching Multiple Government Computers and Stealing Thousands of Employee and Financial Records*, 24 July 2014 <https://www.fbi.gov/contact-us/field-offices/washingtondc/news/press-releases/hacker-charged-with-breaching-multiple-government-computers-and-stealing-thousands-of-employee-and-financial-records>.

[85] *The Government of the United States of America v Lauri Love*, Westminster Magistrates' Court, 16 September 2016, [15] <https://www.judiciary.uk/wp-content/uploads/2016/09/usa-v-love-judgment-1.pdf>.

known as the Forum Bar, had been specifically introduced following the McKinnon case.[86] The forum bar requires the judge or magistrate at an extradition hearing to consider whether the relevant activity was performed in the UK and whether the extradition is in the interests of justice. At the extradition hearing Judge Tempia had felt the forum bar was not met as the harm had occurred in the United States and 'there are over twenty witnesses, all of whom are in the United States. The digital evidence could be given in the United Kingdom but the witnesses reside in the United States and as a matter of desirability and practicality it is easier for them to give evidence in the United States.'[87] She also took account of the fact that the Crown Prosecution Service seemed unwilling to take action in the UK (England and Wales) but eventually decided that their silence was 'neutral'.[88]

On appeal the Divisional Court disagreed. Lord Burnett CJ and Ouseley J found that although the United States was the place where the harm occurred no specific interests of the victims had been identified which pointed to trial in the United States. In fact, the court quite pointedly stated that 'it is likely that their interests included Mr Love being tried, and tried at the least inconvenience to themselves.'[89] They also disagreed with Judge Tempia's view that the silence of the CPS was 'neutral'. The court felt that 'in view of the fact that the CPS did not express any view adverse to the prosecution of Mr Love in the United Kingdom on any of the grounds potentially available to it, this silence is a factor which tells in favour of the forum bar', for 'it can certify under section 83B that it has decided formally that [Love] should not be prosecuted in the United Kingdom, for certain specific reasons; if it does so certify, the forum bar cannot apply.'[90] As a result the court discharged the extradition warrant against Love. The US government did not appeal the decision, closing the extradition case. However, this is not technically the end of the Lauri Love case. In their judgment Lord Burnett CJ and Ouseley J were very clear:

> we emphasise that it would not be oppressive to prosecute Mr Love in England for the offences alleged against him. Far from it. If the forum bar is to operate as intended, where it prevents extradition, the other side of the coin is that prosecution in this country rather than impunity should then follow, as Mr Fitzgerald fully accepted. Much of Mr Love's argument was based on the contention that this is indeed where he should be prosecuted.[91]

At the date of writing no charges have been brought. This seems to end the Lauri Love case in a similar fashion to the Gary McKinnon one. No charges successfully pressed on either side of the Atlantic. Again, though, this case seems to suggest a failure of prosecutors in both the UK and the US. It must be assumed the extradition cases were brought so that sensitive information would not form part of a trial in England and when this failed English prosecutors decided they did not have enough evidence to proceed. However, as noted above, the fact McKinnon seemed to admit his offences would seem to obviate this problem.

---

[86] *Lauri Love v The Government of the United States of America* [2018] EWHC 172 (Admin), [12].
[87] *USA v Love* (n. 85) [90F].
[88] Ibid. [90C].
[89] *Love v USA* (n. 86) [29].
[90] Ibid. [34].
[91] Ibid. [125].

19.2 **Viruses, criminal damage, and mail-bombing**

Section 3 is deliberately vague and has been the subject of a great deal of speculation and rewriting over the years. As originally passed in 1990 s. 3 stated:

 Highlight Computer Misuse Act, s. 3 (original 1990 wording)

(1) A person is guilty of an offence if:

    (a) he does any act which causes an unauthorised modification of the contents of any computer; and

    (b) at the time when he does the act he has the requisite intent and the requisite knowledge.

(2) For the purposes of subsection (1)(b) above the requisite intent is an intent to cause a modification of the contents of any computer and by so doing—

    (a) to impair the operation of any computer;

    (b) to prevent or hinder access to any program or data held in any computer; or

    (c) to impair the operation of any such program or the reliability of any such data.

This offence, known rather unimaginatively as the 'unauthorized modification' offence was to fulfil three separate roles:

(1) to regulate and control the production and distribution of computer viruses and other malware by making it an offence to distribute software which impaired the performance of any computer;

(2) to formalize the law on 'digital criminal damage'; and

(3) to criminalize the installation of software devices such as Trojans which allow hackers backdoor access to computers and computer networks almost at will.

One of the first challenges for s. 3 was to clarify the law with relation to 'digital criminal damage'; this is when someone directly amends or erases data held on a computer without permission. While the pre-CMA case of *Gold and Schifreen* had clearly demonstrated that the pre-existing law could not adequately deal with computer hacking, the pre-existing law on criminal damage was unclear. The Criminal Damage Act 1971 states that 'a person who without lawful excuse destroys or damages any property belonging to another intending to destroy or damage any such property or being reckless as to whether any such property would be destroyed or damaged shall be guilty of an offence'.[92] The definition of property may be found in s. 10 which states it is to be 'property of a tangible nature, whether real or personal, including money'.[93] This would seem to suggest that it would not cover information which by nature is intangible but this was rejected in the case of *Cox v Riley*.[94] Here the accused erased programs from a printed circuit card used to control his employer's computer-controlled saw. He was charged

---

[92] Criminal Damage Act 1971, s. 1(1).
[93] Ibid. s. 10(1).
[94] (1986) 83 Cr App R 54.

under the Criminal Damage Act 1971 but argued that the programs were not tangible property within the meaning of the Act. Nevertheless, he was found guilty on the basis that the printed circuit card had been damaged and was now useless. This approach was confirmed in the later case of *R v Whitely*.[95]

Case study *The Mad Hacker*

Nicholas Whitely was a 21-year-old hacker known as the 'Mad Hacker'. He was charged with ten offences of intending or recklessly damaging property by hacking into various university computer networks via the Joint Academic Network (JANET) between March and July 1988. He deleted and added files, made sets of his own users, and then deleted any files which would have recorded his activity. He managed to attain the status of a system operator which enabled him to act at will without identification or authority. As a result of his actions, computers failed, were unable to operate properly, or had to be shut down for periods of time.

He was found guilty at Southwark Crown Court on 24 May 1990 and appealed to the Court of Appeal. By the time his appeal was heard the CMA was in force but, as his charges predated the Act, the question remained: had Mr Whitely breached s. 1 of the Criminal Damage Act? Lord Lane CJ gave the judgment of the court. He dismissed the appeal, stating that 'the Act required that tangible property had been damaged, not that the damage itself should be tangible'.[96] He added that 'there could be no doubt that the magnetic particles upon the metal discs were a part of the discs and if the defendant was proved to have altered the particles in such a way as to cause an impairment of the value and usefulness of the disc to the owner, there would be damage within the meaning of section 1',[97] before citing with approval the judgment of Auld J in *Cox v Riley* that 'the term "damage" for the purpose of this provision, should be widely interpreted so as to include not only permanent or temporary physical harm, but also permanent or temporary impairment of value or usefulness'.[98] Thus despite the Criminal Damage Act appearing to be restricted to tangible property, the courts had interpreted it widely as applying to data stored on disks and servers.

It was the intent of the Law Commission that s. 3 should replace the Criminal Damage Act when dealing with damage to computer data. In its report 'Computer Misuse',[99] the Law Commission came to the conclusion that clarification of the pre-existing law was required. They looked at the definition of property in the 1971 Act and concluded that 'for the commission of a criminal offence to depend on whether it can be proved that data was damaged or destroyed while it was held on identifiable tangible property not only is unduly technical, but also creates an undesirable degree of uncertainty in the operation of the law'.[100] The promulgation of s. 3 had the desired effect for, although the Criminal Damage Act remained a possible alternative method to prosecute acts of

[95] *R v Whitely* (1991) 93 Cr App R 25.
[96] Ibid. 28.
[97] Ibid.
[98] Ibid. 29.
[99] Law Commission (n. 16).
[100] Ibid. [2.29].

digital criminal damage, subsequent cases have all been decided under the CMA, and an amendment introduced by the Police and Justice Act 2006 seeks to remove any confusion by introducing s. 10(5) into the Criminal Damage Act which reads: 'For the purposes of this Act a modification of the contents of a computer shall not be regarded as damaging any computer or computer storage medium unless its effect on that computer or computer storage medium impairs its physical condition.'

A number of cases have been successfully prosecuted under s. 3 dealing with both criminal damage and the creation and sending of viruses. One of the first was *R v Goulden* which has been previously discussed.[101] As well as being found to have infringed s. 1 Mr Goulden was found to have infringed s. 3 by installing the security program which he used to lock his client's computer. Also found to have infringed s. 3 were Gareth Hardy, a computer engineer who 'time locked' his employer's computers so that one month after his employment was ended all data became encrypted;[102] Jeremy Feltis, a computer operator who worked for Thorn UK, who 'sabotaged' his employer's computers by disconnecting vital connections;[103] and Alfred Whittaker who installed bespoke software on a client's machine with a hidden time lock, which locked the client's computers when he was not paid on time.[104]

Without doubt though the first cause célèbre of s. 3 was the case of the 'Black Baron'.[105]

 Case study *The Black Baron*

Christopher Pile was a self-taught computer programmer who became fascinated with the design of computer viruses. He designed several viruses including the infamous SMEG.Pathogen and SMEG.Queeg viruses, named after expressions from the BBC television series 'Red Dwarf'. The reason Pathogen and Queeg were seen to be so dangerous was that they were early examples of polymorphic viruses, viruses which can mutate to take on different forms in an attempt to defeat antivirus software. The SMEG part of the virus referred to an encryption code system which could change the shape and nature of the virus at each infection: this was made available by Pile to other virus writers as part of a toolkit.

Pile was traced and arrested by officers from the Computer Crime Unit (the forerunner of the National Cyber Crime Unit). He pleaded guilty to five charges under s. 2 and five of unauthorized modification of data under s. 3 and was sentenced to 18 months' imprisonment. Pile was the first virus writer to be successfully prosecuted under s. 3 and prosecutions for the writing and distribution of viruses remain rare, with the most recent cases being of an individual found guilty of mass-mailing viruses who infected thousands of computers,[106] and an individual who used malware attached to spam to spy on victims using their webcams and steal personal information.[107]

[101] *Goulden* (n. 48).
[102] *R v Hardy*, Unreported, Old Bailey, 1992.
[103] *R v Feltis* [1996] EWCA Crim 776.
[104] *R v Whittaker*, Unreported, Scunthorpe Magistrates Court, 1993.
[105] *R v Pile*, Unreported, Plymouth Crown Court, 15 November 1995.
[106] *R v Vallor*, Unreported, Southwark Crown Court, 21 January 2003.
[107] *R v Anderson*, Unreported, Southwark Crown Court, 22 October 2010.

The value of s. 3's wide definition came to be recognized as new harms developed. In 1997 the first successful prosecution for web defacement took place. Two defendants, Ian Morris and Richard Airlie, hacked into the website of an estate agency and replaced pictures of homes for sale with pornographic images. They were convicted under ss. 2 and 3 and were fined £1,250 and sentenced to 100 hours' community service.[108] In 2006 another individual was sentenced to eight months' imprisonment, suspended for two years, and given a two-year supervision order for defacing members' profiles on love-andfriends.com dating website,[109] while in 2015 an individual was jailed for 18 months for hacking into 900 phones and defacing the Twitter account of his ex-employer.[110]

Section 3 has also been applied to 'mail-bombing' attacks. These occur when the attacker sends huge volumes of email to an address in an attempt to overflow the mail-box or overwhelm the server where the email address is hosted. To mail-bomb, one merely sends tens, or even hundreds of thousands, of emails simultaneously to the same email server causing the server to fail and thereby denying the lawful user of the server the ability to use it, thus denial-of-service.

The first mail-bombing prosecution in the UK took place in 2005 when David Lennon, a 16-year-old from London, was charged under s. 3 for mail-bombing the network of Domestic and General Group plc. Lennon had been employed by D&G for three months but then had been dismissed. He decided to take revenge by mail-bombing the D&G network by using an automated mail sender to send email messages purporting to come from D&G's HR manager to random recipients within the company. By using this methodology, he managed to generate in excess of 5 million emails which caused network failures in the D&G network. He was arrested and charged.

Following his arrest he admitted sending the emails but said that his intention was to cause a 'bit of a mess up' in the company; that he did not consider what he was doing was criminal; and it was not his intention to cause the damage to D&G.[111] On 2 November 2005, District Judge Kenneth Grant, sitting as a Youth Court in Wimbledon, ruled that there was no case to answer on the basis that s. 3 was intended to deal with the sending of malicious material such as viruses, worms, and Trojan horses which corrupt or change data, but not the sending of emails.[112] The Director of Public Prosecutions appealed to the Divisional Court which held that:

> The critical issue is that of 'consent' as that word is used in s. 17(8) of the Act. [There is] a clear distinction between the receipt of emails which the recipient merely does not want but which do not overwhelm or otherwise harm the server, and the receipt of bulk emails which do over-whelm it. It may be that the recipient is to be taken to have consented to the receipt of the former if he does not configure the server so as to exclude them. But in my judgment he does not consent to receiving emails sent in a quantity and at a speed which are likely to overwhelm the server. Such consent is not to be implied from the fact that the server has an open as opposed to a restricted configuration.[113]

With the ruling of the Divisional Court clear, the case was remitted back to Wimbledon Youth Court, and on 23 August 2006 Lennon was sentenced to a two-month curfew

---

[108] *R v Morris and Airlie*, Unreported, Cardiff Crown Court, 1997.
[109] *R v Byrne*, Unreported, Southwark Crown Court, 7 November 2006.
[110] *R v Neale*, Unreported, Guildford Crown Court, 24 August 2015.
[111] *DPP v Lennon* [2006] EWHC 1201 (Admin).
[112] Ibid. [7].
[113] Ibid. [14].

with electronic tagging.[114] More recently a man who bombarded Sussex Police's contact centre with 3,000 emails in six hours, pleaded guilty under s. 3 and was sentenced to ten months' jail, suspended for 18 months.[115]

19.3 **Denial-of-service and supply of devices**

Mail-bombing is only one type of denial-of-service (DoS) attack. More sophisticated attacks can take down complete networks and/or web servers rendering websites unavailable. There are a variety of DoS techniques which all take the form of asking the recipient server to deal with more requests for information than it can deal with, causing it to overload.[116] There are two basic varieties of DoS attack, the standard DoS attack where one individual with considerable resources, or more likely a number of individuals acting in a coordinated fashion, attacks a single server or web server, and DDoS where malicious code such as a Trojan is used to create a network of 'slave' computers under the control of one operator which can all be triggered at one time to carry out the attack.

Under the CMA as passed in 1990 DoS attacks were probably not illegal, while those engaged in DDoS attacks would probably only be liable for the installation of the Trojan software not the actual attack itself, meaning the authorities would need to track down at least one infected 'zombie' computer to introduce as evidence. This is because s. 3 as originally enacted required the accused to carry out an act of 'unauthorised modification of the contents of any computer' but a DoS, or even a DDoS attack, does not modify the contents of any computer; it merely stops it from functioning while the attack is ongoing and once an attack concludes the server is released and returns to service.[117]

This raised several problems both legal and practical. Practically it meant that it would prove to be extremely difficult to prosecute for a DoS, or even a DDoS, in the UK unless either some further offence was committed (such as blackmail or fraud) or unless the prosecuting authorities could establish either a s. 1 or s. 2 offence, or they could find evidence of unauthorized modification of contents. Legally this meant the UK was failing in its duties under the Council of Europe Convention on Cybercrime.[118] Articles 4 and 5 of the Convention, on data interference and system interference, were much more widely drawn than s. 3 of the CMA. In particular, Art. 5 required signatory states to 'adopt such legislative and other measures as may be necessary to establish as criminal offences under its domestic law, when committed intentionally, the serious hindering without right of the functioning of a computer system by inputting, transmitting, damaging, deleting, deteriorating, altering or suppressing computer data'. This is clearly aimed at DoS attacks in any form.

---

[114] J Oates, 'Kid Who Crashed e-Mail Server Gets Tagged', *The Register*, 23 August 2006.

[115] *R v Mochizuki*, Unreported Lewes Crown Court 19 August 2016.

[116] For a quick primer on denial of service attacks see US Computer Emergency Readiness Team, 'Cyber Security Tip ST04–015: Understanding Denial-of-Service Attacks' <https://www.us-cert.gov/cas/tips/ST04-015.html>. For greater detail see Richard Overill, 'Computer Crime: Denial of Service Attacks: Threats and Methodologies' (1999) 6 *Journal of Financial Crime* 351.

[117] There is a difference with a mail-bombing attack (as Mr Lennon found to his cost) as the emails themselves are stored in the mail server and as such may be an 'unauthorised modification of the contents of any computer'.

[118] CETS No. 185, Budapest, 23.XI.2001.

Faced with both a clear failure in the current law, and the demands of the international community, the UK All Party Internet Group (APIG) reviewed the scope of s. 3 as part of their 2004 revision of the CMA.[119] They reported a split in opinion as to whether s. 3 was adequate as it stood to deal with DoS attacks noting that 'almost every respondent from industry told us that the CMA is not adequate for dealing with DoS and DDoS attacks . . . We understand that this widespread opinion is based on some 2002 advice by the Crown Prosecution Service that s. 3 might not stretch to including all DoS activity',[120] while also reporting 'the Government, many academic lawyers and also, we understand, the NHTCU, believe that s. 3 is sufficiently broad to cover DoS attacks.'[121]

This inherent uncertainty was enough to convince APIG to recommend that:

> the Home Office rapidly bring forward proposals to add to the Computer Misuse Act an explicit 'denial-of-service' offence of impairing access to data. The tariff should be set the same as the s. 1 'hacking' offence. There should be a further 'aggravated' offence along the lines of the current s. 2 where the denial-of-service is merely one part of a more extensive criminal activity.[122]

These proposals eventually formed part of the review of the CMA found in ss. 35–8 of the Police and Justice Act 2006. Section 3 was substantially rewritten to ensure it criminalizes all forms of DoS/DDoS attacks. The current wording states:

 Highlight Computer Misuse Act, s. 3 (current wording)

(1) A person is guilty of an offence if–

    (a) he does any unauthorised act in relation to a computer;

    (b) at the time when he does the act he knows that it is unauthorised; and

    (c) either subsection (2) or subsection (3) below applies.

(2) This subsection applies if the person intends by doing the act–

    (a) to impair the operation of any computer;

    (b) to prevent or hinder access to any program or data held in any computer;

    (c) to impair the operation of any such program or the reliability of any such data; or

    (d) to enable any of the things mentioned in paragraphs (a) to (c) above to be done.

(3) This subsection applies if the person is reckless as to whether the act will do any of the things mentioned in paragraphs (a) to (d) of subsection (2) above.

The 'unauthorized amendment' offence of the original s. 3 has been replaced with an 'unauthorized impairment' offence which clearly covers all forms of DoS/DDoS attack and which came into force on 1 October 2008.[123] It has been highly controversial both in

---

[119] All Party Internet Group (n. 65).

[120] Ibid. [60].

[121] Ibid. [61].

[122] Ibid. [75].

[123] Like the changes to s. 1 discussed above this was brought into force by The Police and Justice Act 2006 (Commencement No. 9) Order 2008, SI 2008/2503.

the planning and the execution. In particular a number of critics argue that DoS/DDoS attacks can take the form of a legitimate protest. The Swedish academic Mathias Klang in his essay 'Virtual Sit Ins, Civil Disobedience and Cyberterrorism'[124] wrote that, 'the present legislative trend which criminalises DoS attacks . . . are much too far reaching and seriously hamper the enjoyment of individuals' civil rights'.[125] Klang's argument is that a DoS attack can, and should be allowed to, function as a form of virtual sit-in. When protestors wish to be heard on a variety of issues from equality and civil rights to enfranchisement or to protest the actions of government, one well-known approach is to occupy a public place to make themselves heard and to reach the media.[126] This argument found itself in the mainstream as people drew comparisons between the activities of groups such as Anonymous and mainstream civil rights movements such as Occupy.

In his book *The Net Delusion*, Evegny Morozov writes:

> Many cyber-attacks—especially those of the DDoS variety—may simply be construed as acts of civil disobedience, equivalent to demonstrations in the streets. It's not obvious that a campaign to limit the public's ability to practice those would abet the cause of democratization. If society tolerates organizing sit-ins in university offices and temporarily halting their work, there is nothing wrong—at least, in principle—with allowing students to organize DDoS attacks on university websites.[127]

Yochai Benkler meanwhile highlights that DDoS is a nonviolent action, 'it causes disruption, not destruction, and the main technique that Anonymous has used requires participants to join self-consciously and publicly, leaving their internet addresses traceable. By design, these are sit-ins: Participants illegally occupy the space of their target. And they take personal responsibility for the consequences.'[128] It is arguments such as these which led Anonymous to launch a White House petition in January 2013 to ask the US government to recognize the validity of DDoS attacks as a form of civil disobedience.[129] The petition unfortunately only received 6,048 signatures, far short of the 25,000 signatures needed for a response at that time, and as a result has been archived.

Despite these arguments, these activities are clearly illegal in the UK. The question is should we be worried about this development? If Klang, Morozov, and Benkler are right, a serious restriction on civil liberties has occurred: as well as criminalizing DDoS attacks

---

[124] M Klang, 'Virtual Sit Ins, Civil Disobedience and Cyberterrorism' in M Klang and A Murray (eds.), *Human Rights in the Digital Age* (Routledge Cavendish 2005).

[125] Ibid. 145.

[126] Klang notes that: 'While the origins of the sit-in are difficult to locate, a popular point of origin stems from 1960 when four African-American college students in Greensboro, North Carolina protested against the whites-only lunch counter by sitting there every day. After the publication of an article in the *New York Times* they were joined by more students and their actions inspired similar protests elsewhere.' Ibid. 138.

[127] E Morozov, *The Net Delusion: The Dark Side of Internet Freedom* (Public Affairs 2011) 228.

[128] Y Benkler, 'Hacks of Valor: Why Anonymous Is Not a Threat to National Security' *Foreign Affairs*, 4 April 2012. <www.foreignaffairs.com/articles/2012-04-04/hacks-valor?page=show> (subscription required).

[129] The petition was entitled: *Make, distributed denial-of-service (DDoS), a legal form of protesting*. It stated: 'With the advance in internet technology, comes new grounds for protesting. Distributed denial-of-service (DDoS), is not any form of hacking in any way. It is the equivalent of repeatedly hitting the refresh button on a webpage. It is, in that way, no different than any "occupy" protest. Instead of a group of people standing outside a building to occupy the area, they are having their computer occupy a website to slow (or deny) service of that particular website for a short time.'

which are carried out for criminal purposes such as fraud or blackmail, s. 3 also prevents the use of DoS or DDoS as a peaceful tool of protest. While clearly Klang, Morozov, and Benkler are right to draw our attention to this, it may be argued that the outcome of s. 3 is not as dark as they suggest. Sit-ins are not absolutely protected speech in UK law and a sit-in which occupies private property, or which blocks a public highway, may be broken up and protestors arrested. Further, a virtual sit-in is not akin to a real-world sit-in. A real-world sit-in has a highly visible presence where the protestors may be seen and heard: in fact, this it may be argued is the prime import of the sit-in: it is less about appropriation of place and more about communication of a message. A virtual sit-in affected through a DoS attack is very different. There is no visible presence, rather the opposite: the web page or server in question merely lists an error message when sought, without explanation of why the error occurs.[130] In a real-world equivalent it is like protestors building some form of barrier around a property which screens it from public view without explanation as to why they have done it. Further, the internet as a whole is a communications media; there are much more effective means for protestors to be heard online than through a DoS/DDoS attack. They may set up a protest site, buy advertising through Google or similar, or make themselves heard through social network sites such as Facebook, Twitter, or YouTube. A DoS/DDoS attack is an extremely damaging form of attack, especially for e-commerce sites; it does not seem unreasonable to criminalize those involved in such an assault.

The actions of Anonymous provide an opportunity to review this. The media has extensively covered a number of Anonymous campaigns such as Operation Avenge Assange. Their actions often take the form of DDoS attacks and, as we have seen, they draw an analogy to the actions of the Occupy movement in real space. A number of individuals have been arrested and charged with Anonymous activity in the US and UK. One of the first members of the collective to come to trial in the UK was James Jeffery. He was charged under ss. 1 and 3 of the CMA after he illegally gained access to the British Pregnancy Advisory Service and downloaded details of 10,000 users of the site which he considered publishing. He also defaced the website with the Anonymous logo and a statement. He attacked the site because he disagreed with termination advice given by the service.[131] A larger-scale case involving a number of Anonymous members saw the first successful prosecutions for DDoS attacks in the UK. Four men were charged with being part of the DDoS attack on a number of attacks on payment sites such as PayPal, Visa, and Mastercard in December 2010 as part of Operation Payback. All four were convicted with two, Christopher Weatherhead and Ashley Rhodes, being given prison sentences for their actions. It is reported that in his sentencing remarks, Judge Testar said: 'The defendants were actually rather arrogant. They thought they were far too clever to be caught and used various methods to try to cloak and preserve their anonymity. It seems to me that the police were a little bit more clever than the conspirators.'[132]

---

[130] Although it must be acknowledged that groups such as Anonymous promote a great deal of publicity around their DDos attacks, the counterargument then is that the DDoS is not itself necessary as a means of communication.

[131] *R v Jeffery*, Unreported, Southwark Crown Court, 13 April 2012. S Malik, 'BPAS hacker jailed for 32 month', *The Guardian*, 13 April 2012.

[132] *R v Weatherhead, Rhodes, Gibson & Burchall*, Unreported, Southwark Crown Court, 24 January 2013. See J Halliday, 'Anonymous Hackers Jailed for Cyber Attacks', *The Guardian*, 24 January 2013.

19.3.1 **Section 3ZA**

Section 3ZA is the recently added provision of the Act, added by s. 41 of the Serious Crime Act 2015. It came into effect on May 3, 2015 and is in effect an aggravated form of the s. 3 offence.

 Highlight Computer Misuse Act, s. 3ZA

Unauthorised acts causing, or creating risk of, serious damage:

(1) A person is guilty of an offence if—

    (a) the person does any unauthorised act in relation to a computer;

    (b) at the time of doing the act the person knows that it is unauthorised;

    (c) the act causes, or creates a significant risk of, serious damage of a material kind; and

    (d) the person intends by doing the act to cause serious damage of a material kind or is reckless as to whether such damage is caused.

(2) Damage is of a 'material kind' for the purposes of this section if it is—

    (a) damage to human welfare in any place;

    (b) damage to the environment of any place;

    (c) damage to the economy of any country; or

    (d) damage to the national security of any country.

(3) For the purposes of subsection (2)(a) an act causes damage to human welfare only if it causes—

    (a) loss to human life;

    (b) human illness or injury;

    (c) disruption of a supply of money, food, water, energy or fuel;

    (d) disruption of a system of communication;

    (e) disruption of facilities for transport; or

    (f) disruption of services relating to health.

(4) It is immaterial for the purposes of subsection (2) whether or not an act causing damage—

    (a) does so directly;

    (b) is the only or main cause of the damage.

There is little explanation from government as to why this was felt necessary given that a prosecution on indictment raised under s. 3 carries a maximum tariff of ten years' imprisonment, the same as the tariff for the aggravated offence under s. 2. It seems this may have been driven by fears over cyberattacks by terrorist groups driven by fears over Islamic terrorism and groups like the Islamic State. Such risks are, though, blown quite out of proportion and in any event there are already a number of legal redresses available for dealing with such an attack including s. 3 of the CMA, the Terrorism Acts

2000 and 2006, and common law offences such as murder, criminal damage, or actual or grievous bodily harm. The few indicators given by government give little away. In their fact sheet on the Act, the Home Office state simply that 'hitherto the most serious offence under the Act was the section 3 offence of unauthorised access to impair the operation of a computer. The maximum sentence of 10 years' imprisonment which this offence carried did not sufficiently reflect the level of personal and economic harm that a major cyber attack on critical systems could cause.'[133] The explanatory notes to the Serious Crime Bill are equally unclear 'The Government's UK Cyber Security Strategy included a commitment to "review existing legislation, for example the 1990 Act, to ensure that it remains relevant and effective". Following that review, this Part introduces a new offence in respect of unauthorized acts in relation to computers causing serious damage.'[134]

It seems unlikely s. 3ZA will be used often, if at all. In fact in their impact assessment the Home Office acknowledge that 'we assume there will be one case every other year (high estimate); one case every two or three years (best estimate); or no cases in a ten year period (low estimate)'.[135] What we can say is that the *actus reus* requirement is that the accused undertakes an unauthorized act in relation to a computer and that act causes, or creates a significant risk of causing, serious damage of a material kind. The *mens rea* requirement is that the accused, at the time of committing the act, knows that it is unauthorized and intends the act to cause serious damage of a material kind or is reckless as to whether such damage is caused. The term 'material kind' is as defined in s. 3ZA(2). The new offence is triable by indictment only and the maximum penalty, as set out in s. 3ZA(6) is fourteen years imprisonment, however should the defendant's act cause loss of life, injury or illness or cause serious damage to national security the maximum penalty under s. 3ZA(7) is life imprisonment.

19.3.2 Section 3A

Section 3A was introduced by s. 38 of the Police and Justice Act 2006, and amended by the Serious Crime Act 2015.

 Highlight Computer Misuse Act, s. 3A

(1) A person is guilty of an offence if he makes, adapts, supplies or offers to supply any article intending it to be used to commit, or to assist in the commission of, an offence under section 1, 3 or 3ZA.

---

[133] Home Office, *Serious Crime Act 2015 Fact sheet: Part 2: Computer Misuse*, March 2015 <https://www.gov.uk/government/uploads/system/uploads/attachment_data/file/415953/Factsheet_-_Computer_Misuse_-_Act.pdf>.

[134] Serious Crime Bill, Explanatory Notes: <https://www.publications.parliament.uk/pa/bills/cbill/2014-2015/0116/en/15116en.htm>.

[135] <www.parliament.uk/documents/impact-assessments/IA14-21B.pdf>. At the time of writing no cases have been brought in the three and a half years that s. 3ZA has been in effect.

➔

(2) A person is guilty of an offence if he supplies or offers to supply any article believing that it is likely to be used to commit, or to assist in the commission of, an offence under section 1, 3 or 3ZA.

(3) A person is guilty of an offence if he obtains any article

(a) intending to use it to commit, or to assist in the commission of, an offence under section 1, 3 or 3ZA, or

(b) with a view to its being supplied for use to commit, or to assist in the commission of, an offence under section 1, 3 or 3ZA.

(4) In this section 'article' includes any program or data held in electronic form.

Section 3A, like the changes to s. 3, was introduced to meet the UK's international commitments under the Cybercrime Convention. Article 6 requires signatory states to criminalize the production and distribution of devices designed to circumvent security protection or to facilitate in attacks on computers and computer systems. The aim of Art.6, and therefore s. 3A, is to criminalize so-called 'hacking tools'. These are software tools which make it easier to infiltrate computer networks or to design and build viruses, Trojans, and other malware. This seems like a pretty straightforward issue but it has in fact proven to be extremely controversial.

When APIG reviewed the CMA in 2004 they recommended that the UK use an opt-out in Art. 6 to not implement it in full.[136] The reason for this recommendation was that 'such offences would result in significant difficulties because almost all these tools are "dual use" and are widely employed by security professionals and system administrators'.[137] These concerns led the House of Lords Committee on Science and Technology to note that s. 3A left 'security researchers . . . at risk of being criminalised because of the recent amendment to the Computer Misuse Act'.[138] The government replied that this was not the case as 'those in the legitimate IT security sector, who make, adapt and supply tools as part of their daily work should have confidence that the new offence will be used appropriately and be assured that their practices and procedures fall within the law'.[139] The government stated that the security industry would be protected in CPS guidelines to be issued when the new law came into force. This guidance was duly published on the CPS website.[140] It states that the following factors, among others, should be taken into account by prosecutors when considering a prosecution under s. 3A CMA:

> Section 3A(2) CMA covers the supplying or offering to supply an article 'likely' to be used to commit, or assist in the commission of an offence contrary to section 1 or 3 CMA. 'Likely' is not

---

[136] All Party Internet Group (n. 65) [82].

[137] Ibid. [80].

[138] The Government Reply to the Fifth Report from the House of Lords Science and Technology Committee, Session 2006–07 HL Paper 165, 3.

[139] Ibid. 3.

[140] At <https://www.cps.gov.uk/legal-guidance/computer-misuse-act-1990>.

defined in CMA but, in construing what is 'likely', prosecutors should look at the functionality of the article and at what, if any, thought the suspect gave to who would use it; whether for example the article was circulated to a closed and vetted list of IT security professionals or was posted openly.

In determining the likelihood of an article being used (or misused) to commit a criminal offence, prosecutors should consider the following:

- Has the article been developed primarily, deliberately and for the sole purpose of committing a CMA offence (i.e. unauthorised access to computer material)?
- Is the article available on a wide scale commercial basis and sold through legitimate channels?
- Is the article widely used for legitimate purposes?
- Does it have a substantial installation base?
- What was the context in which the article was used to commit the offence compared with its original intended purpose?

This guidance appears to do little to protect IT security professionals. One specialist website for such professionals notes that 'sadly the CPS guidance, far from clarifying the matter, at first sight seems likely to increase the confusion. It offers examples where there is little or no ambiguity. But it apparently fails to address the hugely important grey area of security testing tools that by definition can also be exploited maliciously.'[141]

As many experts predicted at the time s. 3A has been little relied upon. It seems there have only been five convictions achieved in the eleven years s. 3A has been in effect. These are *R. v Paul McLoughlin* (Southwark Crown Court, 13 May 2011); *R. v Glenn Mangham* (Southwark Crown Court, 17 February 2012); *R v Lewys Stephen Martin*;[142] *R v Tyrone Ellis* (Central Criminal Court, 14 November 2013); and *R v Shaun Turner* (Peterborough Crown Court 30 January 2017). None of the five could be mistaken for computer security professionals; all were involved in extended computer misuse activities. It seems that s. 3A will be of limited use and will only be used alongside charges under ss. 1–3.

19.4 **Conclusions**

There is little doubt of the value and need for the Computer Misuse Act 1990. It is a vital tool in the armoury of the police and the CPS. Without the CMA there would be no simple way of prosecuting those who illegally gain access to computer networks and systems, perhaps with a view to committing further offences or doing harm. However, the utility of the Act has been somewhat undermined by amendments and alterations over the years. While the Act as passed in 1990 has been robust enough to withstand the challenge of dealing with insider (employee) attacks and the *Bignall*

---

[141] The H-Security, *UK Crown Prosecution Service Publishes Computer Misuse Act Guidance* <www.h-online.com/security/news/item/UK-Crown-Prosecution-Service-publishes-Computer-Misuse-Act-guidance-735749.html>.

[142] [2013] EWCA Crim 1420.

defence, malicious attackers such as the *Mad Hacker* and even the challenge of extradition and the long running *McKinnon* case. The need for s. 3A is understandable, and provides compliance with the Convention on Cybercrime. However, the rather vague wording of the section and the CPS guidelines mean that it is rarely prosecuted and is arguably unnecessary given that in three of the five successful prosecutions so far under s. 3A the defendant was also charged with offences under s. 1 or s. 3. Its direct utility it seems has been restricted to two cases in eleven years. It is equally difficult to imagine a raft of cases under s. 3ZA which seems to be beyond all else a grandstanding move by the government. There have to date been no cases in the over three years it has been in effect and even the impact assessment notes a possibility of no cases in ten years being brought under s. 3ZA. If and when cases are brought, it seems beyond doubt that s. 3ZA will be part of a portfolio of charges brought against anyone accused. The need to add a new criminal offence onto the statute books to deal with what would appear to be covered elsewhere in the criminal law seems questionable at best.

TEST QUESTIONS

Question 1

The actions of so-called 'ethical hacking' groups such as Anonymous are illegal and clearly in breach of s. 3 of the Computer Misuse Act 1990 (and Art. 5 of the Convention on Cybercrime). There is no defence or justification for their actions. They should be arrested and prosecuted as a matter of urgency.

Discuss.

Question 2

Should Gary McKinnon and/or Lauri Love have been tried in the UK under the Computer Misuse Act?

Question 3

'Insider Hacking' is a contradictory concept.

Discuss.

FURTHER READING

Books

O von Busch and K Palmås, *Abstract Hacktivism* (OpenMute 2006)

H Cornwall, *The Hacker's Handbook* (Century 1985)

J Erickson, *Hacking: The Art of Exploitation* (2nd edn, No Starch 2008)

S Fafinski, *Computer Misuse: Response Regulation and the Law* (Willan 2009)

Chapters and articles

A Karanasiou, 'The Changing Face of Protests in the Digital Age: On Occupying Cyberspace and Distributed-Denial-Of-Service (DDoS) Attacks' (2014) 28 *International Review of Law, Computers and Technology* 98

M Klang, 'Civil Disobedience Online' (2008) 2 *Journal of Information, Communication & Ethics in Society* 2

N MacEwan, 'The Computer Misuse Act 1990: lessons from its past and predictions for its future' (2008) *Criminal Law Review* 955

A Nehaluddin, 'Hackers' Criminal Behaviour and Laws Related to Hacking', 15 (7) *Computer and Telecommunications Law Review* 159 (2009)

M Wasik, 'Computer Misuse and Misconduct in Public Office', 22 *International Review of Law, Computers and Technology* 135 (2008)

Obscenity in the information society

The human obsession with pornography and obscenity is as old as society itself.[1] Erotic imagery is common in all cultures and societies including ancient Rome[2] and Greece,[3] to the India,[4] China, and Japan[5] of the Middle Ages, and the early modern period up to the present day. In common with this cultural obsession one of the first roles played by any new technology has been to improve and streamline the distribution and production of erotica and pornography. As soon as humans divined how to make cave paintings they produced erotic images. With the process of industrialization, more efficient methods of producing images and text were developed and at every development erotica and pornography seemed to lead the way. Early photography produced the first nude and erotic images[6] leading to the development and sale of the infamous 'French Postcards' of the latter part of the nineteenth century. Then the moving image began to take over from the still image. Again, erotica and pornography were at the forefront of developments with the introduction of 'stag' films such as *Red Headed Riot* and burlesque films such as *Peeping Tom's Paradise*.

Through the first half of the twentieth century the main outlets for pornography remained these film rolls and still photographs. Then in the 1940s photo magazines began to be produced culminating in the launch of *Playboy* in 1953. Basically, the technology behind pornography remained unchanged until the development of home video cassettes. This allowed people to watch pornographic films in the comfort of their own home for the first time without needing specialist equipment. In the 1970s it was the porn industry in America that is widely credited with the eventual success of the VHS video format over rival Betamax,[7] although it should be noted that other

---

[1] Erotic cave paintings found across Europe which are estimated to be up to 40,000 years old depict highly realistic drawings of sexual activity including recreational (i.e. non-reproductive) sexual activity.

[2] A number of erotic frescoes have been discovered preserved in Herculaneum and Pompeii.

[3] Erotic images are often found on Greek vases, and Greek plays and texts often contain erotic themes.

[4] Most famously recorded in the *Kama Sutra*.

[5] China and Japan shared an erotic art tradition known as Shunga. It can be traced back to fourteenth century China but has its peak in Japan in the seventeenth to nineteenth centuries.

[6] In *Nude Photography, 1840–1920*, Peter Marshall notes: 'In the prevailing moral climate at the time of the invention of photography, the only officially sanctioned photography of the body was for the production of artist's studies. Many of the surviving examples of daguerreotypes are clearly not in this genre but have a sensuality that clearly implies they were designed as erotic or pornographic images' <http://web.archive.org/web/20070218141330/http://photography.about.com/library/weekly/aa013100a.htm>.

[7] P Johnson, 'Pornography Drives Technology: Why *Not* to Censor the Internet' (1996) 49 *Federal Communications Law Journal* 217.

factors contributed to VHS's eventual success. The home VCR began a 'golden age of porn' where the industry grew to a massive size.[8] It is no surprise therefore that the internet with its unique ability to host and distribute text, video, audio, and image has proven to be an attractive home for modern producers and distributors of pornography. When the accessibility and reach of the internet is paired with the economic benefits of convergence for the producers of pornographic content (4KHD video cameras are now available on mobile phones available for free if the user signs a carrier contract while ultra-high quality 4KHD-Camcorders are on sale for less than £100) it is no surprise that there has been an explosion of the availability of pornographic and obscene images: the question is how does the law deal with this?

20.1 **Obscenity**

As erotica started to give way to pornography and obscenity the law became involved in the control of pornographic goods. The law intervenes in several ways. First, it draws a line between types of erotica: erotic content (such as erotic art or literature—this is material produced around a sexual theme but not produced wholly or principally for the purpose of sexual arousal); pornographic content (this is material produced solely or principally for the purpose of sexual arousal);[9] obscene material (this is material likely to deprave and corrupt persons);[10] and extreme content (this includes child abuse images and violent or extremely obscene content). The law then intervenes to determine how each class of erotic, pornographic, or obscene content is to be controlled.

Erotic material may, in general, be sold and distributed freely and usually with few controls.[11] Bookshops often have an erotic literature section and there is no law which prevents a bookseller selling a 15-year-old a copy of *Fanny Hill* or *Tropic of Cancer* (although many booksellers may voluntarily refuse to sell such titles to minors). By comparison, pornographic content is more closely regulated. It is content which it is legal to sell and distribute but usually within closely restricted channels. For example, material rated as R18 (or restricted 18) by the British Board of Film Classification may only be shown to adults in specially licensed cinemas, and DVDs may only be supplied to adults in licensed sex shops and not by mail order.[12] By comparison, obscene content may not legally be imported, published, or supplied in the UK[13] although it may be legally possessed, provided there is no intent to publish, whereas extreme content may not be imported, supplied, published, or possessed.[14]

---

[8] L Glass 'Second wave: feminism and porn's golden age', *Radical Society*, October 2002.

[9] This definition is taken from s. 63(3) of the Criminal Justice and Immigration Act 2008.

[10] This definition is taken from s. 1(1) of the Obscene Publications Act 1959. It should be noted this is not restricted to sexually obscene material. This definition would also include violent material such as snuff movies and other such content.

[11] Although, as we shall see, this was not always the case.

[12] Video Recordings Act 1984, s. 12.

[13] Obscene Publications Act 1959, s. 2; Customs Consolidation Act 1876, s. 42.

[14] Currently in the UK it is illegal to view or possess images of child abuse under s. 160(1) of the Criminal Justice Act 1988, while by s. 45 of the Sexual Offences Act 2003 a child is defined as anyone under 18 years of age. It is further illegal to possess 'extreme pornography' under s. 63 of the Criminal Justice and Immigration Act 2008 (as amended) and 'non-photographic pornographic images of children' under s. 62 of the Coroners and Justice Act 2009.

20.1.1 **The Hicklin principle**

The way the law has traditionally dealt with pornography and obscenity is illuminating. The UK common law standard is known as the 'Hicklin principle' after the case of *R. v Hicklin*.[15] Here Lord Cockburn CJ famously stated that the test was whether there is a tendency 'to deprave and corrupt those whose minds are open to . . . immoral influences, and into whose hands a publication of this sort may fall'.[16] According to *Hicklin* the essence of corruption is the suggestion of impure thoughts. Moreover, publications likely to have this effect on young or other vulnerable people are to be ruled obscene, regardless of the literary or artistic merits of the work.

The *Hicklin* principle was voraciously applied and led to works such as *Lady Chatterley's Lover*, *The Well of Loneliness*, and *Tropic of Cancer* being banned from publication in the UK. This did not prevent publication of these books in English elsewhere (both *Lady Chatterley* and *Tropic of Cancer* were published in Paris) but to import such editions was in itself an offence under s. 42 of the Customs Consolidation Act 1876. The dual effect of banning the publication of obscene material in the UK and banning the importation of obscene material from outside the UK allowed the state to control quite strictly the availability of obscene content. Prior to 1959 little distinction was drawn between erotic, pornographic, and obscene content with almost all sexually explicit content likely to be classified as obscene under the *Hicklin* standard. But that year the obscenity laws were relaxed slightly. Following recommendations from a House of Commons Select Committee, the Obscene Publications Act was passed.

 Highlight Obscenity: Obscene Publications Act 1959

For the purposes of this Act an article shall be deemed to be obscene if its effect or (where the article comprises two or more distinct items) the effect of any one of its items is, if taken as a whole, such as to tend to deprave and corrupt persons who are likely, having regard to all relevant circumstances, to read, see or hear the matter contained or embodied in it.

Although it retained the spirit of the *Hicklin* principle it changed it in one key aspect; the new test is that it asks the jury to consider the effect of the content on persons who are likely to see the content in question (i.e. adults) rather than 'those whose minds are open to immoral influences' (i.e. children or other vulnerable groups). Following the entering into force of the 1959 Act, a number of important cases clarified that the new obscenity standard was indeed distinct from indecency (the usual standard of pornographic material) including most famously *R. v Penguin Books Ltd*.[17]

20.1.2 **The Obscene Publications Acts**

The law on obscenity has remained mostly unchanged since 1959, the only amendments being the addition of a number of extreme obscenity offences which criminalize

---

[15] (1868) LR 3 QB 360.
[16] Ibid. 371.
[17] [1961] Crim LR 176.

possession, rather than the importation, sale, or possession with intent to supply materials, and the new offence of publishing so-called 'revenge porn'.[18] To control the supply of pornography, and to restrict the supply of obscene content the UK law enforcement authorities continued to rely on a mixture of border controls and supply controls. By restricting the availability of pornographic content to licensed sex shops the authorities could oversee the type of content that was being made available to ensure it did not breach the Obscene Publications Act; additionally it meant that pornography produced in the UK, for the most part met community standards. Further, by strictly enforcing border controls the authorities could restrict the supply of unclassified (and often obscene) materials.[19]

The arrival of the internet changed the nature of the distribution model for all forms of content including pornographic content. Like other entertainment products, including music, film, and video games, much so-called 'adult entertainment' is now produced and distributed in a disintermediated digital format. The demand for purely digital distribution of adult content has, like music and mainstream film and TV, increased exponentially in the last ten years and has particularly increased with the availability of high-speed ADSL, LTE (4G) and fibre connections and the development of video streaming technology. This has left our border authority quite impotent for, as predicted by David Johnson and David Post in 1996, the borderless nature of the internet undermines effective border controls.[20]

This loss of ability to adequately police our borders has by turn rendered the Obscene Publications Act ineffective. For while the Obscene Publications Act remains enforceable, its focus on the supply or possession with intent to supply obscene material within the UK is undermined by the fact that the vast majority of indecent and obscene material to be found online is hosted overseas. This is why it is not surprising to find that, despite surveys which show that 56 per cent of UK adults watch online pornography occasionally or regularly while 34 per cent of children are believed by their parents to have so done,[21] there have been no prosecutions in England and Wales under either the Customs Consolidation Act or the Obscene Publications Act 1959 for privately viewing obscene material using an internet connection. The authorities have instead focused their meagre resources on extremely obscene material and UK distributors of obscene material with, to date, nearly all prosecutions for internet obscenity centring on the storing and distribution of child abuse images[22] or extremely pornographic images,[23] the prosecution of those who disclose private sexual photographs (the legal definition

---

[18] These will be discussed in full later. Further, it should be noted that as obscenity is tested on the so-called community standard, the classification of obscene materials has weakened over the years. In 2004 for the first time a movie which portrays actual sex between actors was given an '18' certificate. The movie *9 Songs* attracted little public outcry; a considerable change from the controversy surrounding *Women in Love* which in 1969 portrayed male full-frontal nudity for the first time or *Last Tango in Paris* which in 1972 had portrayed anal sex on screen.

[19] The courts would tend to strictly apply the provisions of the Obscene Publications Act when dealing with material seized at the border. See *R. v Uxbridge Justices, ex parte David Webb* [1994] 2 CMLR 288.

[20] D Johnson and D Post, 'Law and Borders—The Rise of Law in Cyberspace' (1996) 48 *Stanford Law Review* 1367.

[21] J Mann, 'British Sex Survey 2014' *The Observer*, 28 September 2014.

[22] *R v Barry Philip Halloren* [2004] 2 Cr App R (S) 57; *R v Snellman* [2001] EWCA Crim 1530; *R v James* [2000] 2 Cr App R (S) 258.

[23] *R v Burns (Robert)* [2012] EWCA Crim 192; *R v PW* [2012] EWCA Crim 1653.

of revenge porn),[24] or the prosecution of those who run pornographic websites from overseas servers but who are resident in the UK and profit from this activity.[25]

20.2 **Pornography**

The dividing line between indecent content and obscene content is a vital one. Although pornographic content may be either indecent or obscene, it is only obscene content which may not be published, supplied, or imported: in other words one may legally trade in indecent content, provided all necessary regulations are complied with, but one cannot legally trade in obscene content.

20.2.1 **The UK standard**

As discussed, the dividing line between indecency and obscenity is defined by a community standard. Since 1959 that standard has been to determine whether the content in question will tend to deprave and corrupt persons who are likely to read, see, or hear the content. This line is not fixed and will vary with changes in society. In 1961 the focus of the test was on literary works such as *Lady Chatterley's Lover*. The jury on that occasion found Penguin Books not guilty of a breach of s. 1 of the Obscene Publications Act 1959, but today the very concept that a publisher may be tried for obscenity for publishing a book of the nature of *Lady Chatterley's Lover* seems nonsensical: society has moved on. Even the publication of Bret Easton Ellis's 1991 novel *American Psycho* with its graphic descriptions of sexual abuse, torture, and murder did not cause the UK authorities to consider a prosecution under the Obscene Publications Act; although the novel was subject to restrictions in other parts of the world.[26]

Similarly standards in mainstream films have moved on considerably. In 1969 a film adaptation of DH Lawrence's *Women in Love* sparked a great deal of controversy when the British Board of Film Censors (later to become the British Board of Film Classification) passed it for cinema display. The film contained the first full-frontal male nude scene as Oliver Reed and Alan Bates wrestled naked. A few years later a great deal of controversy (although no prosecutions for obscenity) dogged films like *A Clockwork Orange*, *Straw Dogs*, and *Last Tango in Paris*. Today mainstream movies frequently portray sex, and often sex and violence are mixed in so-called 'torture porn' movies such as *Hostel*. Despite some controversy there is little call for these movies to be banned. Also, the way sex is portrayed in mainstream movies shows how community values have changed. It had always been assumed that the portrayal of the erect male member would automatically rule a film unclassifiable as certificate 18 but that changed in 1999 when Catherine Breillat's movie *Romance* became the first movie to display an erect penis to be passed

---

[24] Crown Prosecution Service, *Prosecutors continue to tackle revenge porn across the country*, 13 August 2015 <http://www.womensgrid.org.uk/news/?p=4585>.

[25] *R v Ross Andrew McKinnon* [2004] 2 Cr App R (S) 46; *R v Stephane Laurent Perrin* [2002] EWCA Crim 747.

[26] In Germany, the book was deemed harmful to minors, and its sales and marketing were severely restricted from 1995 to 2000. In Australia, the book is sold shrink-wrapped and is classified R18. The book may not be sold or loaned to those under 18. In New Zealand, the Government's Office of Film and Literature Classification has rated the book as R18. The book may not be sold or lent in libraries to those under 18.

for cinema display. Since then several movies which portray actual sexual intercourse between actors have been passed for display including Mike Winterbottom's *9 Songs* which in 2004 became the first film certified 18 to show full sexual intercourse including ejaculation.

This change in community values led to the creation of the R18 certificate in 1982 for adult movies which may be supplied through licensed sex shops and displayed in licensed 'adult only' cinemas. The number of R18 titles has increased dramatically since 2000 when Mr Justice Hooper upheld a decision of the Video Appeals Committee of the British Board of Film Classification that R18 certificates should not be withheld to adult entertainment products on the basis that they had the potential to cause harm to children.[27] Hooper J (in a finding not dissimilar in effect to the move from the *Hicklin* standard to the new Obscene Publications Act standard in 1959) held that 'the risk of [the videos in question] being viewed by and causing harm to children or young persons is, on present evidence, insignificant'.[28]

The most dramatic case to date though on developing community attitudes is *R v Peacock*.[29] Michael Peacock is a distributer of hardcore gay pornography. Some of the DVDs he distributed contained films which featured extreme sexual acts between men, such as BDSM (including whipping, staged kidnapping, and rape play), fisting, and urolagnia. The jury found Peacock not guilty of an offence under the Obscene Publications Act, deciding that the scenes depicted in the DVDs were unable to deprave or corrupt any viewer watching them. Defence solicitor Nigel Richardson later told the press that the jury had recognized that the pornography found in the DVDs would only be seen by 'gay men specifically asking for this type of material' and not by the general public.[30]

It is clear that the UK has become a considerably more permissive society in relation to indecency and obscenity in the sixty years that the Obscene Publications Act has been in force. The problem with internet pornography is that the UK legal definition of the community standard is in danger of being overtaken by external community values. This is arguably what happened in *Peacock*. While UK community standards have moved on considerably, the law in the UK is still strict in its application of both indecency regulations (such as the R18 standard) and obscenity laws. Despite the *Peacock* decision, which as a jury decision does not set a precedent;[31] so-called 'hardcore' pornography may only legally be supplied by licensed sex shops and only strictly to those over the age of eighteen and never by mail order. 'Soft' pornography is more widely available with newsagents permitted to sell so-called 'top-shelf' magazines, again though only legally to those over eighteen. The internet is, however, at least in relation to pornography, a case study in cyberlibertarianism.[32]

As we saw in chapter 4, the cyberlibertarian ethos that traditional lawmakers could not enforce their laws against citizens of cyberspace due to the nature of cyberspace as

---

[27] *R v Video Appeals Committee of British Board of Film Classification, ex parte British Board of Film Classification* [2000] EWHC Admin 341.

[28] Ibid. [47].

[29] Unreported, Southwark Crown Court, 6 January 2012.

[30] 'Not guilty verdict in DVD obscenity trial' *BBC News*, 6 January 2012 <https://www.bbc.co.uk/news/uk-16443697>.

[31] Despite it having no binding legal effect it arguably does show how internet content has dramatically moved community values.

[32] See 4.1 'Cyberlibertarianism'.

a unique and separate jurisdiction has been widely debunked by the cyberpaternalist school which demonstrated that control of content and the actions of persons could be effected in cyberspace through code (or design-based) controls. But to effect such controls requires a degree of cooperation among lawmakers. In some areas cooperation has been forthcoming, as with regulation of the domain name system discussed in chapter 14 or in relation to hacking and other computer misuse offences discussed in chapter 19, but with pornography and, in particular, the dividing line between indecency and obscenity there is a problem.

As we have seen, the line between indecency and obscenity is a community standard and the internet plays host to individuals from many social backgrounds in one place. Lawmakers across the globe cannot agree a common standard: what is considered sexually explicit but not obscene in England may well be considered to be obscene in the Republic of Ireland, and almost certainly material considered obscene in the Islamic Republic of Iran or in the Kingdom of Saudi Arabia would not be felt to be noteworthy in England. Similarly, material which would be considered to be obscene in England would probably not be censored in Germany, Spain, or Sweden where a more tolerant approach to erotica and pornographic material is taken. What we are seeing in these differences is a spectrum of obscenity which ranges from extremely conservative to extremely liberal, and upon which individual states position themselves. In general, this system has functioned quite effectively in the real world due to the existence of physical borders and border controls. These traditional measures are predicated though upon the assumption that the items in question will be fixed in a physical medium, and that they will require physical carriage to enter the state. With the advent of the digital age both of these assumptions have been rendered null. The development of a global informational network has dismantled traditional borders: a point which was so eloquently made by David Johnson and David Post in their seminal paper *Law And Borders—The Rise of Law in Cyberspace*.[33]

> Cyberspace has no territorially-based boundaries, because the cost and speed of message transmission on the Net is almost entirely independent of physical location: Messages can be transmitted from any physical location to any other location without degradation, decay, or substantial delay, and without any physical cues or barriers that might otherwise keep certain geographically remote places and people separate from one another. The Net enables transactions between people who do not know, and in many cases cannot know, the physical location of the other party. Location remains vitally important, but only location within a *virtual* space consisting of the 'addresses' of the machines between which messages and information are routed.[34]
>
> The Net thus radically subverts a system of rule-making based on borders between physical spaces, at least with respect to the claim that Cyberspace should naturally be governed by territorially defined rules.[35]

Thus the traditional concept of border controls is undermined in the digital environment, making it very difficult for individual states to enforce and protect their community standard in the face of competing community standards found elsewhere. This can be demonstrated with an example.

---

[33] Johnson and Post (n. 20).
[34] Ibid. 1370–1.
[35] Ibid. 1370.

Example Access

Richard is a UK resident who accesses and downloads pornographic images held on a server based in Germany. The image is in compliance with the German community standard but arguably is in breach of the UK community standard.

To consider a prosecution against Richard the UK prosecuting authorities would first have to identify that the item is obscene by applying the UK community standard, a task now further complicated by *Peacock*.[36] If the image was found to be 'obscene' under the UK community standard, they would next have to prove that either Richard imported the item in breach of s. 42 of the Customs Consolidation Act 1876, or that he possessed the item with intent to publish in breach of s. 2 of the Obscene Publications Act 1959. Neither of these claims would necessarily succeed. The second claim would only succeed in relation to members of communities which trade or share images or files: for individuals who merely access and view pornographic websites there would be no intent to further publish or distribute, and therefore no offence under the Obscene Publications Act. The former claim is one mired in extreme complexity. Whereas identification of an importer was relatively straightforward when dealing with physical goods, it becomes much more complex in relation to digital information. The question is: does the consumer import the image into the UK, or is the image imported into the UK by the supplier, or even their internet service provider (ISP), who then makes it available to the consumer? The answer may at first seem straightforward: if Richard downloads an obscene image from a German website then he should be deemed to be the importer. But what if the website appears to be from the UK? Perhaps the supplier is using a UK-based domain name like www.ukporn.co.uk,[37] and seems to be implying they are based in the UK. In such circumstances does Richard exhibit sufficient intent and knowledge to be classed as an importer? As UK border controls are nullified, the consumption of pornography is de facto deregulated, meaning that the point of control over pornographic content is at its point of supply: as very little online pornographic content is hosted in the UK, this means that we are reliant upon the community standards found elsewhere.

20.2.2 **A global standard?**

Pornography is hosted on web servers sited across the globe; there is no one community standard that prevails, but one community has greater impact than any other. Although there are no completely reliable statistics detailing where most pornographic websites are hosted, it is clear that the US hosts substantially more sexually explicit web

---

[36] If they could not establish the item to be in breach of s. 1 of the Obscene Publications Act, then he would be entitled to view the item under Art. 28 of the Treaty on the Functioning of the European Union. See *Conegate Ltd v HM Customs & Excise* [1987] QB 254 (ECJ); *R v Forbes* [2002] 2 AC 512 (HL).

[37] At the time of writing no site or registration existed in relation to this address.

pages than any other state, with one survey suggesting it hosts around 60 per cent of all adult web pages. The same survey reveals that only around 7 per cent of global adult content is hosted in the UK.[38] Together these two statistics suggest that in effect much of the pornography available in the UK has met the US community standard rather than the UK standard.[39]

The US is in many ways a unique marketplace for the production and distribution of pornography due to the effects of the First Amendment. Whereas UK citizens are willing to accept that free expression does not mean limitless freedom to say or do whatever one wishes, US citizens strongly support their First Amendment right to enjoy freedom of speech, even where that right strays into the potentially destructive areas of pornography and hate speech. The question of whether it is appropriate to apply the First Amendment to pornographic content has long vexed US scholars and judges. Some scholars have argued that there can never be a true marketplace of speech in relation to pornographic imagery because there is no real freedom of speech for women in a country in which women are relegated to the particular gender roles that society gives them,[40] others, though, argue that pornographic magazines 'consciously attempt to express a view of social and sexual life'.[41] Whatever position one holds on the validity of First Amendment protection for pornographic imagery the law is quite clear: material of a sexual nature will be protected by the First Amendment unless that material is determined by the court to be obscene.[42] The current US standard of obscenity was set out in the landmark case of *Miller v California*,[43] wherein the Supreme Court established a three-part test for obscenity.

 Highlight The *Miller* standard

To be obscene, a judge and/or a jury must determine:

(1) That the average person, applying contemporary community standards, would find that the work, taken as a whole, appeals to the prurient interest; AND

(2) That the work depicts or describes in a patently offensive way, as measured by contemporary community standards, sexual conduct specifically defined by the applicable law; AND

(3) That a reasonable person would find that the work, taken as a whole, lacks serious literary, artistic, political and scientific value.

[38] D Holmes, 'Infographic: What countries host the most porn?' *Pando*, 13 August 2013 <https://pando.com/2013/08/05/infographic-what-countries-host-the-most-porn/>.

[39] In fact, it's the California community standard as the same survey reveals that 66 per cent of US-hosted adult content is hosted in the State of California.

[40] This is known as the MacKinnon/Dworkin debate and is found most clearly in the work of Catherine MacKinnon and Andrea Dworkin. See C MacKinnon, *Feminism Unmodified: Discourses on Life and Law* (Harvard University Press 1987) 127–213; A Dworkin, 'Against the Male Flood: Censorship, Pornography, and Equality' (1985) 8 *Harvard Women's Law Journal* 1.

[41] W Brigman, 'Pornography as Political Expression' (1983) 17 *Journal of Popular Culture* 129. See also A Dershowitz, 'Op-Ed' *New York Times*, 9 February 1979.

[42] *Roth v US*, 354 US 476 (1957).

[43] 413 US 15 (1973).

Chief Justice Burger went on to make clear that 'Under the holdings announced today, no one will be subject to prosecution for the sale or exposure of obscene materials unless these materials depict or describe patently offensive "hard core" sexual conduct specifically defined by the regulating state law, as written or construed.'[44] Although at the time it was felt that such a widely drawn standard would lead to wide local differences in obscenity laws this did not turn out to be the case. The scope of community standards was narrowed the next year in *Jenkins v Georgia*,[45] when the court found that the film *Carnal Knowledge* could not be found to be patently offensive to the local community. Later, further guidance would come in the case of *Pope v Illinois*,[46] which found that the test for literary, artistic, political, or scientific value, had to be based upon national, not local, standards.

Cyberspace not only removed the barriers between states, it also broke down barriers between communities. The US's approach to policing obscenity, much like the UK's, was predicated on the existence of a product fixed in a physical medium and sold or displayed through a physical outlet. The digitization of pornography rendered the *Miller* concept of 'contemporary community standards' redundant. In cases where pornographic material was posted onto a publicly accessible Bulletin Board System (BBS) or website it was more difficult to prosecute using local community standards, as in these cases it was not possible to show knowledge or intent to trade within a particular community. This was demonstrated in cases such as *American Libraries Association* et al. *v Pataki*[47] and *PSINet v Chapman*,[48] where attempts to apply local community standards had to be carefully handled lest they be found to be in violation of the implicit confines on state power imposed under the US Constitution's Commerce Clause.[49] During the 1990s, the quantity of online publicly available pornographic content grew rapidly through the development of BBS trading communities, free access websites, and fledgling file-sharing systems.[50] With more pornography becoming freely available, US lawmakers were faced with a new problem: children were able to access all content, including adult content, as quickly and easily as adults, for as noted by Lawrence Lessig 'a kid in Cyberspace need not disclose that he is a kid'.[51]

20.2.3 **US statutory interventions**

Faced with a growing problem of children being exposed to online adult content, state and federal lawmakers attempted to take legal control of the online environment. In 1996 two such attempts came to public prominence, and provoked controversy. In the State of New York, Governor George Pataki oversaw the introduction of §235.21(3) to the New York State Penal Code (NYSPC). This made it a crime to disseminate information 'harmful to minors' via a computer system. At the same time the Federal

[44] Ibid. 27.
[45] 418 US 153 (1974).
[46] 481 US 497 (1987).
[47] 969 F Supp 160 (SDNY 1997).
[48] 63 F 3d 227 (4th Cir. 2004).
[49] Article I, Section 8, Clause 3 of the US Constitution.
[50] D Thornburgh and H Lin *Youth, Pornography, and the Internet* (National Academy Press 2002) Ch. 3: <https://www.nap.edu/openbook.php?record_id=10261&page=71>.
[51] L Lessig, *Code and Other Laws of Cyberspace Ver2.0* (Basic Books 2006) 248.

Government introduced the Communications Decency Act 1996 (CDA) as Title V of the Telecommunications Act of 1996. Both measures were felt to be in breach of the First Amendment by free speech advocates and were immediately challenged. §235.21(3) of the NYSPC was challenged by an extensive coalition of groups including the American Library Association, Peacefire, and the American Civil Liberties Union.[52] They contended that the change in the NYSPC was unconstitutional as it unduly burdened free speech in violation of the First Amendment and it unduly burdened interstate commerce in violation of the Commerce Clause. At a summary hearing on 20 June 1997, the plaintiffs succeeded in their claim and were awarded summary judgment. District Judge Loretta Presky noted that 'individuals who wish to communicate images that might fall within the Act's proscriptions must thus self-censor or risk prosecution, a Hobson's choice that imposes an unreasonable restriction on interstate commerce.'[53]

Pataki establishes that although State Legislatures retain the power to control the supply of obscene material, a power which the Supreme Court recognized in *Miller v California*,[54] attempts to control the supply of sexually explicit, though not obscene, material are unlikely to be effective. The problem faced by State Legislatures was that they could not sufficiently precisely define the terms of the content they were seeking to control, a problem exacerbated by the lack of a common national standard. What may be deemed to be acceptable in California, may be felt to be unacceptable in Tennessee, and with State Laws requiring individuals to self-censor it is almost impossible to imagine how such regulations could not offend against the Commerce Clause. What was clearly needed was a federal response.

Senators James Exon, a Democrat from Nebraska, and Slade Gorton, a Republican from Washington, introduced The Communications Decency Act to the Senate on 1 February 1995, in response to the previously discussed fears that internet pornography was on the rise. In March 1995, the Senate Commerce Committee unanimously adopted the Exon/Gorton proposal as an amendment to the in-progress Telecommunications Reform Bill. In June 1995, the Senate attached the Exon/Gorton amendment to the Bill by 84 votes to 16. On 1 February 1996, the Bill was passed by both Houses, becoming law on 8 February 1996.

The introduction of the CDA explicitly outlawed, intentionally, communicating 'by computer in or affecting interstate or foreign commerce, to any person the communicator believes has not attained the age of 18 years, any material that, in context, depicts or describes, in terms patently offensive as measured by contemporary community standards, sexual or excretory activities or organs'.[55] Opponents of the Act argued that 'just as a librarian cannot be expected to determine the age and identity of all patrons accessing a particular book in the library's collection, the provider of online information cannot be expected to police the usage of his or her online offerings. To impose

---

[52] *Pataki* (n. 47).

[53] Ibid. [91].

[54] *Miller* (n. 43). Chief Justice Burger made this clear by stating: 'This Court has recognized that the States have a legitimate interest in prohibiting dissemination or exhibition of obscene material when the mode of dissemination carries with it a significant danger of offending the sensibilities of unwilling recipients or of exposure to juveniles' (at 16).

[55] §502(2).

such a requirement would result in reducing the content of online material to only that which is suitable for children.'[56]

A campaign against the Bill began on its introduction and by 1 February 1996 over 115,000 signatures had been collected on a petition against the Act. On 2 February 1996, in response to the adoption of the Act by Congress, thousands of websites turned black for forty-eight hours as part of the Electronic Frontier Foundation's, 'Turn the Web Black' protest. On 8 February 1996 the EFF launched its blue ribbon 'Free Speech Campaign.' This asked those who ran web pages to display a distinctive blue ribbon logo in support of their campaign against the CDA and almost overnight the blue ribbon logo populated the web. Publicity campaigns such as these were, though, merely a sideshow to the main event. As soon as President Clinton signed the CDA on 8 February, the American Civil Liberties Union and 23 other co-plaintiffs, including the Electronic Privacy Information Center, the Electronic Frontier Foundation, and the Planned Parenthood Federation of America, raised a complaint before the Federal District Court in Philadelphia seeking a temporary restraining order against the implementation of the indecency provisions of the CDA on the grounds that 'the Act is unconstitutional on its face and as applied because it criminalizes expression that is protected by the First Amendment; it is also impermissibly overbroad and vague; and it is not the least restrictive means of accomplishing any compelling governmental purpose'.[57] The complaint was heard by District Judge Ronald Buckwalter, who, on 15 February, granted the plaintiffs an order insofar as the CDA referred to indecent, but not obscene content.[58] With the order in place the plaintiffs then extracted from the Federal Government a stipulation that they would not 'initiate any investigations or prosecutions for violations of 47 USC Sec.223(d) for conduct occurring after enactment of this provision until the three-judge Court hears Plaintiffs' Motion for Preliminary Injunction'.[59] With this safeguard in place to ensure that the CDA would not be enforced while a question mark remained over its constitutionality the plaintiffs prepared a case to be heard before the District Court.

Hearings were quickly arranged and held over six days from 21 March to 10 May.[60] The decision was given on 11 June and all three judges agreed that on the face of it the CDA was unconstitutional. Chief Justice Sloviter reflected the views of the Court in noting: 'I have no hesitancy in concluding that it is likely that plaintiffs will prevail on the merits of their argument that the challenged provisions of the CDA are facially invalid under both the First and Fifth Amendments.'[61] The Federal Government, as expected immediately sought to appeal the decision to the US Supreme Court, and on 6 December 1996 the Supreme Court noted probable jurisdiction and agreed to hear the case on 19 March 1997. The government filed its brief on 21 January; the plaintiffs' briefs were filed on 20 February. Oral argument was heard, as scheduled, on 19 March,

---

[56] D Sobel, 'The Constitutionality of the Communications Decency Act: Censorship on the Internet' (1996) 1 *Journal of Technology Law & Policy* 2.

[57] Complaint filed before the US District Court, Eastern District of Pennsylvania, 8 February 1996, Civ. No. 96–963: <www.epic.org/free_speech/censorship/lawsuit/complaint.html>.

[58] *ACLU v Reno* 929 F Supp 24 (1996).

[59] Stipulation of 23 February 1996. <https://www.epic.org/free_speech/censorship/lawsuit/stipulation.html>.

[60] The plaintiffs' case was heard on 21 and 22 March and 1 April while the government's case was put on 12 and 15 April. Closing arguments were heard on 10 May.

[61] *ACLU v Reno* 929 F Supp 824 (1996) 856.

following which everyone waited for the court's ruling. The court finally issued its decision on 26 June, and by a 7:2 majority it found in favour of the plaintiffs. The first decision the court had to come to was whether the First Amendment applied in cyberspace. Here Justice Stevens, who gave the majority opinion, was clear:

 Highlight The First Amendment of cyberspace

The Internet provides relatively unlimited, low-cost capacity for communication of all kinds. The Government estimates that 'as many as 40 million people use the Internet today, and that figure is expected to grow to 200 million by 1999'. This dynamic, multifaceted category of communication includes not only traditional print and news services, but also audio, video, and still images, as well as interactive, real-time dialogue. Through the use of chat rooms, any person with a phone line can become a town crier with a voice that resonates farther than it could from any soapbox. Through the use of Web pages, mail exploders, and newsgroups, the same individual can become a pamphleteer. As the District Court found, 'the content on the Internet is as diverse as human thought'. We agree with its conclusion that our cases provide no basis for qualifying the level of First Amendment scrutiny that should be applied to this medium.

[*Reno v ACLU* 521 US 844 (1997) 862.]

Thus with the prior question of whether First Amendment protection could be applied within Cyberspace clearly answered in the affirmative the Court could go on to assess the constitutionality of the CDA. Again, Justice Stevens was clear:

> In order to deny minors access to potentially harmful speech, the CDA effectively suppresses a large amount of speech that adults have a constitutional right to receive and to address to one another. That burden on adult speech is unacceptable if less restrictive alternatives would be at least as effective in achieving the legitimate purpose that the statute was enacted to serve.[62]

The plaintiffs' success was complete. They had won every round and the Supreme Court had, as they hoped, extended First Amendment protection into Cyberspace. The effect of this decision cannot be overstated. Not only had the narrow victory ensured that the *Miller/Pope* obscenity standard was to be applied in cyberspace, a much more important victory had been won: the Supreme Court had confirmed that the US Constitution, including the First Amendment protection for indecent but not obscene content, applied to that part of cyberspace over which the US government and courts could exert authority. This meant that two years later when the Clinton administration attempted to resurrect parts of the Communication Decency Act in the Child Online Protection Act 1998 the US Supreme Court again ruled such legislation was unconstitutional.[63]

---

[62] Ibid. 880.

[63] The Child Online Protection Act 1998 attempted a slightly different wording to the CDA by putting more emphasis on knowledge and intent: 'Whoever knowingly and with knowledge of the character of the material, in interstate or foreign commerce by means of the World Wide Web, makes any communication for commercial purposes that is available to any minor and that includes any material that is harmful to minors shall be fined not more than $50,000, imprisoned not more than 6 months, or both.' It was ruled unconstitutional by a 5:4 Supreme Court majority in the case of *Ashcroft v ACLU* 542 US 656 (2004).

20.2.4 **The decision heard 'round the world'**

The *Reno* decision had impact not only in the US. As previously established, the inability of UK border authorities to prevent the massive influx of digital pornographic content hosted outside the UK means we are reliant on regulation at the point of supply and/or production of pornographic content. As a considerable proportion of that content is produced in and hosted in the US, the *Reno* decision had massive impact in the UK. Further the impact of *Reno* is more far-reaching than may have been initially recognized. On the surface it meant that any producer of pornographic content could use the US as a 'safe haven' for their content as any content hosted on a US-based server would effectively gain First Amendment protection, provided their material was not obscene, applying the *Miller/Pope* standard; a standard which is far more permissive than the UK standard. This suggested, if online pornographic content were to be effectively regulated, international cooperation would be required since any form of regulation would require the cooperation of enforcement authorities in the US. This, though, would prove extremely difficult to achieve in the post-*Reno* environment for, as explained by Douglas Vick, 'The *Reno* decision will constrain the international community's efforts to establish a comprehensive body of common rules for regulating Internet content. Under American law, treaties and other international accords are hierarchically inferior to the provisions of the US Constitution. A treaty provision, just like a congressional statute, is unenforceable if it fails to conform with First Amendment law.'[64]

This handicap could clearly be seen in negotiations to draft the Council of Europe, Convention on Cybercrime.[65] The Convention deals with only one 'content-related offence', that being the production or distribution of child abuse images using a computer system.[66] We know several of the states that took part in the drafting process were keen to include further content-related offences, but that these never made the final text. The reason for this is to be found in the Explanatory Report:[67]

> The committee drafting the Convention discussed the possibility of including other content-related offences, such as the distribution of racist propaganda through computer systems. However, the committee was not in a position to reach consensus on the criminalisation of such conduct. While there was significant support in favour of including this as a criminal offence, some delegations expressed strong concern about including such a provision on freedom of expression grounds.[68]

Although the identity of the delegations in question are not revealed, it is clear that at least one of these would be the US delegation: the US delegation could not, as Douglas Vick had predicted, sign the US government up to any treaty provisions which would conflict with First Amendment protection. With child abuse images being clearly classed as obscene in US law,[69] Art. 9 could be left in place, but any attempts to extend the Convention into more general content regulation could not be countenanced by the US delegation because of the principle of the First Amendment.

---

[64] D Vick, 'The Internet and the First Amendment' (1998) 61 MLR 414, 419.

[65] Council of Europe, ETS No. 185, *Convention on Cybercrime*, Budapest, 23 November 2001 <http://conventions.coe.int/Treaty/en/Treaties/Html/185.htm>.

[66] Art. 9.

[67] Council of Europe, ETS No. 185, *Explanatory Report on the Convention on Cybercrime* <http://conventions.coe.int/Treaty/EN/Reports/Html/185.htm>.

[68] Ibid. [35].

[69] *New York v Ferber* 458 US 747 (1982).

In the twenty-plus years since the *Reno* decision, sexually explicit content on the internet has been effectively deregulated. This has not led; as some predicted, to the internet becoming mired in obscene content and sexually explicit content remains a small proportion of internet content.[70] There remains though the problem of more vulnerable members of society, especially children. One of the reasons R18 videos may only be sold through licensed sex shops is to prevent children from gaining access to them; but with the internet hardcore pornographic content may be streamed directly to the laptop, or smartphone of teenagers or even pre-teens. The focus switches from regulating the supply of pornographic content to the adult population to the protection of minors.

20.2.5 **Age-verification**

A variety of techniques have been employed to protect children from exposure to indecent content. These include parental control settings on mobile phones, software tools such as FamilyShield and KidLogger, and the use of server side controls such as Sky Broadband Shield and BT Cleanfeed, but the legal system was until recently little involved in these self-regulatory regimes. This all changed with the Digital Economy Act 2017. By s. 14(1) 'A person contravenes this subsection if the person makes pornographic material available on the internet to persons in the United Kingdom on a commercial basis other than in a way that secures that, at any given time, the material is not normally accessible by persons under the age of 18.'[71] This provision, known as age-verification is designed to ensure that children are not exposed to pornographic content. This is achieved by a new age-verification mechanism set out in the Act. By s. 16 the Secretary of State may designate an age-verification regulator. The designated age-verification regulator is the British Board of Film Classification, on the basis that their experience of classifying R18 content will give them the experience they need to fulfill this role.[72]

The age-verification regulator has considerable responsibility and power. By s. 25 the regulator:

> must publish, and revise from time to time
>
> (a) guidance about the types of arrangements for making pornographic material available that the regulator will treat as complying with section 14(1); and
>
> (b) guidance for the purposes of section 21(1) and (5) about the circumstances in which it will treat services provided in the course of a business as enabling or facilitating the making available of pornographic material or extreme pornographic material.

The first set of guidance was recently published by the BBFC.[73] This provides that:

> The BBFC recognises that age-verification is an evolving and fast changing technology. It expects that advances will improve the capability and variety of systems that will become available. Consequently, the BBFC will adopt a principle-based approach when assessing new age-verification arrangements and shall maintain a dialogue with stakeholders in order to take any developments into consideration and will from time to time update this guidance accordingly.[74]

[70] See discussion in M Castelman, 'Dueling Statistics: How Much of the Internet Is Porn?' *Psychology Today*, 3 November 2016.
[71] Pornographic material is defined at s. 15.
[72] <https://www.bbfc.co.uk/about-bbfc/age-verification>.
[73] BBFC, Guidance on Age-verification Arrangements (October 2018) <https://www.ageverificationregulator.com/assets/bbfc-guidance-on-age-verification-arrangements-october-2018-v2.pdf>.
[74] Ibid. 9.

Although the guidance notes that it does 'not provide an exhaustive list of approved age-verification solutions, but sets out the criteria by which the BBFC will assess that a person has met the requirements of section 14(1) of the Act' it gives advice as to what types of system will be required:[75]

Highlight Age-verification requirements

The criteria for affective age-verification are:

a. an effective control mechanism at the point of registration or access to pornographic content by the end-user which verifies that the user is aged 18 or over at the point of registration or access;

b. use of age-verification data that cannot be reasonably known by another person, without theft or fraudulent use of data or identification documents nor readily obtained or predicted by another person;

c. a requirement that either a user age-verify each visit or access is restricted by controls, manual or electronic, such as, but not limited to, password or personal identification numbers. A consumer must be logged out by default unless they positively opt-in for their log in information to be remembered;

d. the inclusion of measures which authenticate age-verification data and measures which are effective at preventing use by non-human operators including algorithms.

The BBFC also list a number of tools which do not meet their requirements:

Highlight Not effective for age-verification

The criteria for affective age-verification are:

a. relying solely on the user to confirm their age with no cross-checking of information, for example by using a 'tick box' system or requiring the user to only input their date of birth;

b. using a general disclaimer such as 'anyone using this website will be deemed to be over 18';

c. accepting age-verification through the use of online payment methods which may not require a user to be over 18. (For example, the BBFC will not regard confirmation of ownership of a Debit, Solo or Electron card or any other card where the card holder is not required to be 18 or over to be verification that a user of a service is aged 18 or over);

d. checking against publicly available or otherwise easily known information such as name, address and date of birth.

---

[75] Ibid. 9–10.

Some guidance as to what may form effective means of age-verification are given, 'a range of solutions to age-verify online is currently available on UK-hosted pornography services. These solutions draw from numerous datasets including credit card, passport, driving licence and mobile phone age-verification.' When the Act was initially passed in May 2017 it was the intention that mandatory age-verification under s. 14 would come into effect in April 2018. However, delays and confusion as to which systems would be compliant (and subsequent delays in the issuing of the initial guidance by the BBFC) held up implementation. The government plan to have the system go live in 2019 and in October 2018 eventually published the long-overdue enabling legislation, the Online Pornography (Commercial Basis) Regulations 2018 which define who is defined as a commercial supplier of pornography under s. 14(1). They provide that pornography is provided on a commercial basis if either (a) it is supplied for payment, or (b) it is made available free of charge and the person who makes it available receives (or reasonably expects to receive) a payment, reward or other benefit in connection with making it available on the internet. Vitally, the Regulations provide that they do not apply 'in a case where it is reasonable for the age-verification regulator to assume that pornographic material makes up less than one-third of the content of the material made available.' This means social media platforms such as Imgur, Tumblr, Twitter, and Reddit are not caught by the regulations.

Once s. 14(1) is in force, which should be by the time you read this book, the age-verification regulator is given extensive enforcement powers. By s. 18 the regulator may issue an information notice on any person to whom it believes s. 14 applies requiring them to provide any relevant information sought by the regulator. A failure to comply with the notice, or to comply with s. 14 itself, may lead to an enforcement notice or a fine being issued under s. 19. The fining power is rather extensive and modelled on the General Data Protection Regulation being a fine of up to £250,000 or 5 per cent of qualifying turnover.[76]

Of course all of this is worth naught if the supplier of pornographic content is based overseas and has no assets or employees in the UK. We run up once more against the enforcement problem that we discussed so extensively at 5.3.5–5.3.7. the answer is a variation of the s. 97A order discussed at 12.4. By s. 23 the regulator may issue a blocking notice. These will be issued on UK-based ISPs and will require them to 'take steps specified in the notice, or if no such steps are specified to put in place arrangements that appear to the provider to be appropriate, so as to prevent persons in the United Kingdom from being able to access the offending material using the service it provides.' To ensure over-blocking does not occur s. 23 notices may only be issued once the regulator has informed the Secretary of State of its decision and notified the party in breach of its intent to issue the notice. In addition by s. 21 the regulator may notify payment service providers and ancillary service providers (which could include Google) of sites which fail to comply with s. 14.

If, as proposed, age-verification goes live in 2019 the UK will be the first country in the world to implement such a regime and many other countries are watching with interest. However the scheme is extremely controversial with campaigners arguing that

---

[76] See s. 20(2).

there are real risks to privacy and sensitive data,[77] freedom of expression,[78] and over-regulation and censorship. There are also concerns that the system will not achieve its primary objective of preventing children from accessing adult content[79] and that the technological challenges are likely to lead to ongoing problems.[80] We await its implementation with interest.

20.3 **Child abuse images and pseudo-images**

Child abuse images are the most extreme form of pornographic image and are always obscene no matter which community values apply.[81] There are a number of reasons why child abuse images are treated differently to adult pornography but prime among them are that to produce a child abuse image a child must be abused: thus the image is a record (and evidence) of a crime in a way pornographic images are not. This is known as the 'direct harm rationale'. To produce images of child abuse a child must be harmed: as a result the law must take steps to protect children and to prevent such harm and to do so the production, distribution, and even possession of child abuse images are criminalized.[82]

Although nearly all countries agree the need for the criminalization of child abuse images on the direct harm rationale the enforcement of this agreement is though not as simple as it sounds. First, there is the relatively simple question of how old is a child? This is not an issue when one is dealing with young children; all governments and lawmakers agree that a 5-year-old is a child. What, though, about a 17-year-old? Or even perhaps a 15-year-old? A strict application of the direct harm rationale assumes that in the production of a child abuse image a child has been abused: this means the 'child' cannot have legally consented to the production of the image in the way adult performers do. This is true only if the 'child' has not reached the age of consent within their state: once they reach majority they can legally have sex, and equally they can consent to it being recorded without direct harm having occurred to them.

---

[77] Open Rights Group, *The government is acting negligently on privacy and porn AV* 8 May 2018 <https://www.openrightsgroup.org/blog/2018/the-government-is-acting-negligently-on-privacy-and-porn-av>.

[78] L Hughes, 'Age checks to stop children accessing online pornography is a breach of human rights, UN warns', *The Telegraph*, 12 January 2017.

[79] D Gayle, 'Millions of porn videos will not be blocked by UK online age checks', *The Guardian*, 18 October 2018.

[80] V Warrington, 'Porn Age Verification Rules—Expensive, Ineffective and a Hacker's Delight' *Computer Business Review* 11 April 2018.

[81] There is a debate over terminology for images such as these. The Internet Watch Foundation note on their website that: '"child pornography", "child porn" and "kiddie porn" are not acceptable terms. The use of such language acts to legitimise images which are not pornography, rather, they are permanent records of children being sexually abused and as such should be referred to as child sexual abuse images.' I will refer to these images as 'child abuse images' but may refer to them being of a pornographic nature.

[82] Under s. 1 of the Protection of Children Act 1978 it is an offence to 'take, or permit to be taken, any indecent photograph of a child' and to 'to distribute or show such indecent photographs'. While by s. 160 of the Criminal Justice Act 1988 it is an offence for a person to have any indecent photograph of a child in his possession.

The first problem is that different states have different ages of majority. Until relatively recently the age of consent in Canada was 14,[83] while in the UK it is 16. Throughout the US it varies from 16 to 18 while in some states it is as high as 20 (Tunisia) while in others as low as 12 (Angola).[84] With child abuse images streaming across borders as easily as other forms of pornographic imagery some form of agreement is needed on this basic issue.

This has been achieved in part though the Convention on Cybercrime.[85] Article 9 seeks to form international agreement and cooperation on 'Offences related to child pornography.' Article 9(3) states: 'For the purpose of [this provision], the term "minor" shall include all persons under 18 years of age. A Party may, however, require a lower age-limit, which shall be not less than 16 years.' Thus although there may be no common agreement on the age of sexual majority between member states there is agreement that when dealing with child abuse images they will adopt a common age of 18 in most circumstances.[86] As the majority of child abuse images are consumed in Western Europe, Japan, and North America, the Convention provides a useful point of commonality among law enforcement authorities who can then organize international operations to attempt to break so-called 'child pornography rings'.

A second problem is that it is not always clear how old a 'child' in an image actually is. Again with young children this is not an issue, but a 14-year-old can look 18 and vice versa. Should the law ban the production, distribution, and possession of images of young adults who appear to be younger than they actually are? Equally, should an individual who possesses a pornographic image of a person who appears to be over 18 face prosecution if it is subsequently established that the person in question is in fact a minor? These are questions that have been faced in courts overseas. In Sweden a child is defined as 'a person whose puberty development is incomplete, or when it can be discerned from the image or from the circumstances around it, is less than 18 years old'.[87] In a challenging test case the defendant paid two 16-year-old girls to take part in pornographic films. The girls informed him of their age before filming took place but the films were produced anyway. The Stockholm District Court and the Court of Appeal both interpreted the law to mean that if the age of the girls could not be discerned by the images the man could not be guilty of producing or distributing child pornography despite the fact that he was aware of their age. The courts found that as the girls had passed through puberty and therefore it was not possible to understand from the images that they were under age these were not images of child pornography as defined in the Criminal Code.[88]

---

[83] The Tackling Violent Crime Act 2008 raised the legal age of sexual consent in Canada from 14 to 16, the first time it had been raised since 1892.

[84] R Morgan and N Baker, 'What are the ages of sexual consent around the world?' *SBS News* 12 March 2018 <https://www.sbs.com.au/news/what-are-the-ages-of-sexual-consent-around-the-world>.

[85] Council of Europe (n. 65).

[86] The UK has taken steps to ensure UK law complies with Article 9. In England and Wales s. 45(2) of the Sexual Offences Act 2003 amends s. 7(6) of the Protection of Children Act 1978 to read '"Child" . . . means a person under the age of 18.' In Scotland the relevant provisions are to be found in the Protection of Children and Prevention of Sexual Offences (Scotland) Act 2005.

[87] Swedish Criminal Code Chapter 16, para. 10a.

[88] Stockholm District Court Case nr B 7047–01. Discussed in full in M Eneman, 'The New Face of Child Pornography' in M Klang and A Murray (eds.), *Human Rights in the Digital Age* (Routledge-Cavendish 2005).

To prevent these issues arising in the US, the Child Protection and Obscenity Enforcement Act 1988 requires that producers of pornographic material keep records of all performers engaged by them with proof that they were over 18 at the time the material was produced.[89] The UK strikes a middle ground between these approaches. There is no requirement of record-keeping but we are less laissez-faire than the Swedish position. By s. 160 it is an offence to possess an image of a person under 18, whether or not they look older than they actually are.[90] Therefore in the UK it is not technically illegal to possess an indecent image of a person 18 or over who looks younger than they are, but it is illegal to possess a computer-manipulated or computer-generated image which is specifically designed to create the impression that a minor is portrayed: these are so-called pseudo-images.

20.3.1 Policing pseudo-images in the UK

Pseudo-images are mostly a product of the digital society. The creation of pseudo-images involves powerful computer software such as Photoshop or Paint Shop Pro to either create photorealistic images which portray children being abused or to manipulate pre-existing pornographic images to make adult actors appear prepubescent by digitally removing pubic hair (and other post-pubescent hair such as chest hair or underarm hair) and the resizing of genitals and breasts. These images raise a number of issues. First among them is the simple question of whether we should criminalize such images at all. As discussed, child abuse images are criminalized under the direct harm principle. Pseudo-images are quite different: in the same way that actors are not actually killed in violent action movies or horror movies, no children are harmed in the production of pseudo-images. But, there are compelling arguments which suggest we cannot consider pseudo-images so lightly.

There is strong evidence which points to a connection between viewing child abuse images and the act of abuse itself.[91] In current research there are four main hypotheses on the paedophile's use of child abuse images: (1) to develop their sexual motivation, (2) to lower their level of sexual impulse control, (3) as a substitute for sexual contact with a child, and (4) to break down the child's resistance while attempting to seduce the child. A study presented in 2003 showed that two-thirds of perpetrators arrested for internet sex crimes against children also possessed stills pictures and film sequences containing child abuse images.[92] Therefore there is a clear psychological link between the consumption of child abuse images and the act of child abuse; further as most pae-dophiles do not differentiate between pseudo-images and genuine images and as genu-ine images are easier to produce than pseudo-images producers will tend to continue to produce genuine images. All of these factors suggest that although children may not

---

[89] US Code, Title 18 §2257.

[90] If the 'child' in an image or video cannot be identified, not uncommon where images may have come from overseas, the question of whether a person in an image is under 18 becomes a question of fact for the jury to decide. See *R v Land* [1998] 1 Cr App R 301 and *R v Charles William Owen* (1988) 86 Cr App R 291.

[91] C Bagley and K King, *Child Sexual Abuse* (Routledge 1989) 219; C Itzen (ed.), *Home Truths About Child Sexual Abuse* (Routledge 2000) Ch. 7.

[92] J Wolak, K Mitchell, and D Finkelhor, *Internet Sex Crimes Against Minors: The Response of Law Enforcement*, Crimes against Children Research Center November 2003, University of New Hampshire <www.unh.edu/ccrc/pdf/CV70.pdf>.

be directly harmed in the production of pseudo-images such images do cause indirect harm on several levels.

This 'indirect harm rationale' is applied in Art. 9(2)(c) of the Convention on Cybercrime which states that 'the term "child pornography" shall include pornographic material that visually depicts realistic images representing a minor engaged in sexually explicit conduct'. The UK was an early adopter of legislation to criminalize pseudo-images with the Criminal Justice and Public Order Act 1994 extending the ambit of both the Criminal Justice Act 1988 and the Protection of Children Act 1978 to cover such images.[93]

The newly extended scope of s. 160 was examined by the Court of Appeal in *R v Fellows and Arnold*.[94] Mr Fellows was a computer officer at Birmingham University. Without the knowledge of the university he constructed a large database of child abuse images on the university network and made it available via the internet. Mr Arnold was a 'customer' of Mr Fellows who was granted access to Mr Fellows's database in return for supplying him with further images. Both were prosecuted under the Protection of Children Act and both claimed that the Act did not extend to their activities as 'computer data was not a "photograph" for the purposes of section 1'.[95]

This argument was rejected by Evans LJ. He began by examining the dictionary definition of a photograph as 'a picture or other image obtained by the chemical action of light or other radiation on specially sensitised material such as film or glass': this he said could not apply to an indecent image held on a computer hard drive as 'There is no "picture or other image" on or in the disc; nothing which can be seen.'[96] But, he went on to note that under s. 7(2) a photograph was defined as including 'a copy of an indecent photograph', could the images on the hard drive be such a copy? Evans LJ believed so: 'There is nothing in the Act which makes it necessary that the copy should itself be a photograph within the dictionary or the statutory definition, and if there was, it would make the inclusion of the reference to a copy unnecessary. So we conclude that there is no restriction on the nature of a copy, and that the data represents the original photograph, in another form.'[97]

He then gave an *obiter* opinion on the scope of the new pseudo-photographs provisions. As the appellants had been charged prior to s. 84 of the Criminal Justice and Public Order Act 1994 coming into effect they could not be charged with possession or distribution of pseudo-photographs but Evans LJ believed he should examine the scope of the new provision in any event. He noted that it was the view of the Court that '[these new provisions] seem to us to be concerned with images created by computer processes rather than the storage and transmission by computers of images created originally by photography'.[98] Thus the collective view of the *Fellows* court was that digitized images

---

[93] Section 84 of the Criminal Justice and Public Order Act 1994 made the necessary amendments to s. 160 of the Criminal Justice Act 1988 and ss. 1, 4, 5, and 7 of the Protection of Children Act 1978.

[94] [1997] 2 All ER 548; [1997] 1 Cr App R 244.

[95] [1997] 1 Cr App R 244, 245–6.

[96] Ibid. 253.

[97] Ibid. 254.

[98] Ibid. 255.

held on hard drives were not photographs but were copies of photographs originally taken in the traditional manner and that pseudo-images were only images created by computer and could not be images stored on computer.

If the law had been left in this form it could have caused substantial difficulties for the prosecuting authorities. A completely digital picture (taken with a digital camera and then downloaded onto a hard drive) would appear to fall between these two definitions: being not a photograph nor a copy of a photograph nor a pseudo-image. In one of those strange twists that often occurs though when new legislation is introduced, there remain outstanding appeals on the old legislation. Even as Evans LJ gave the judgment of the court in *Fellows* he knew that it had already been replaced by statutory developments, for his judgment was given on 27 September 1996 while the wording of s. 7(4) of the Protection of Children Act had been changed on 3 February 1995 to read 'references to a photograph include (a) the negative as well as the positive version; and (b) data stored on a computer disc or by other electronic means which is capable of conversion into a photograph'. Therefore, while Evans LJ had to follow a complicated line of reasoning to find that data held on a hard drive could be a copy of a photograph, the new wording of s. 7(4), if it had applied in the case before him, would have allowed him to simply find the appellants guilty of distribution of 'indecent photographs'. The UK continues to take a hard line with the possession of both actual and pseudo-images being aggressively prosecuted.

 Highlight Prosecuting possession of child abuse images

Akdeniz reports that between 1988 (when the possession offence was introduced) and 2004 there were 1,831 prosecutions under s. 160 (with 1,267 convictions) and 624 police cautions. Meanwhile between 1980 and 2004 there were 4,771 prosecutions under s. 1 of the Protection of Children Act with 3,789 convictions and 732 police cautions. Subsequent research by McManus and Almond shows that between 2005 and 2013 there were 1,834 convictions under s. 160 and 8,043 convictions under s. 1. Further, McManus and Almond show that the trend for convictions is upward with the greatest number of convictions under s. 160 being 278 in 2011/12 and under s. 1 being 1247 in 2012/13.

[Y Akdeniz, *Internet Child Pornography and the Law* (Ashgate 2008), 25; and MA McManus and L. Almond, 'Trends of indecent images of children and child sexual offences between 2005/2006 and 2012/2013 within the United Kingdom' (2014) 20 *Journal of Sexual Aggression* 142]

It may be that the law enforcement authorities prosecute aggressively because the courts have indicated they take a hard-line stance in enforcing the provisions of both s. 160 and s. 1. Many cases of what would usually be thought of as possession of child abuse images are being prosecuted under s. 1 of the Protection of Children Act for the more serious offence of making indecent images.

This follows the decision of the Court of Appeal in *R. v Bowden.*[99]

 Highlight *R v Bowden*

A person who either downloads images on to disc or who prints them off is making them.

The Act is not only concerned with the original creation of images, but also their proliferation. Photographs or pseudo-photographs found on the Internet may have originated from outside the United Kingdom; to download or print within the jurisdiction is to create new material which hitherto may not have existed therein.

The impact of this decision is that anyone who 'saves' an indecent image (even if the copy is merely in their browser's cache) is deemed to have 'made' an image under s. 1: this does seem to stretch the framer's original intent in framing both s. 1 and s. 160 and given that the s. 1 offence carries a maximum term of imprisonment of ten years, as compared to five years under s. 160, seems to suggest this was intended to prevent the more serious offence of *original* creation of indecent images. But *Bowden* demonstrates the hard-line approach taken in the UK. We can see this at work again when dealing with pseudo-images. In *Goodland v DPP*, the Divisional Court suggested that the creation of a crude pseudo-photograph by Sellotaping two images together and then photocopying the resultant gestalt image, could trigger the Protection of Children Act.[100]

20.3.2 **Non-photographic pornographic images of children**

Recently the law has moved on from *Goodland.* Although in that case the image crudely produced was found ultimately not to be a pseudo-photograph, the introduction of s. 62 of the Coroners and Justice Act 2009 may have changed that position. *Goodland* was interesting as it examined the potential line between pseudo-images and other forms of content. Simon Brown LJ noted that 'there being several features of this combination of images which give the lie to [the fact that this appears to be a genuine photograph] . . . in my judgment, an image made by an exhibit which obviously consists, as this one does, of parts of two different photographs Sellotaped together cannot be said to "appear to be a photograph."'[101] In the same case counsel for the prosecution tried to define the line between pseudo-images and legal-to-possess artistic content: 'The exhibit must appear to be a product of photography rather than, for example, a cartoon, sketch, painting, or other indecent representation of a child.'[102] This distinction is now rendered practically moot as s. 62 of the Coroners and Justice Act puts non-photographic pornographic images of a child (NPPICs) on the same footing as a pseudo-image. The image in question must be pornographic and grossly offensive,

---

[99] [2001] QB 88.
[100] [2000] 1 WLR 1427, 1442, per Simon Brown LJ.
[101] Ibid.
[102] Ibid. 1441.

disgusting, or otherwise of an obscene character. To be pornographic it must be of such a nature that it must reasonably be assumed to have been produced solely or principally for the purpose of sexual arousal. Finally, the image must fall within s. 62(6) and (7). This requires that it is an image which focuses solely or principally on a child's genitals or anal region and that it portrays a prohibited act.[103]

The definition of a child is given in s.65. It is that the impression conveyed by the image is that the person shown is a child, or the predominant impression conveyed is that the person shown is a child despite the fact that some of the physical characteristics shown are not those of a child. This is less than precise and has been criticized by Julia Hörnle for requiring juries to make subjective evaluations of the impression conveyed by a purely imagined image.[104] This is a serious offence with a maximum penalty of three years in prison and a fine.[105] It does have a number of defences under s.64 which are in common with those found under extreme pornography provisions. Interestingly the Act does not criminalize publication of NPPICs although Julia Hörnle points out that this would be an offence under the Obscene Publications Acts 1959 and 1964.[106] This is perhaps less certain following *Peacock* but is still likely to be true.

At the date of writing s.62 has been discussed in sixteen reported cases but little has yet been learned about its scope. Probably the most important case to date is *R v Richard Palmer*.[107] The defendant pleaded guilty to three offences of possessing prohibited images of children contrary to s. 62. He had been contacting a 12-year-old girl via the internet and her parents reported him to the police. When the police investigated they found the images in question. Despite Palmer suffering from Asperger's Syndrome, HH Judge Curran sentenced Palmer to two years in prison. This seemed extremely severe for such a low level of offending and on appeal it became apparent that 'the judge had in mind the need to protect the public from the potential risk which he thought the appellant posed to young girls, arising out of his internet contact. A Sexual Offences Prevention Order could only be made if there were a sentence of at least two years' imprisonment.'[108] On appeal the sentence was reduced to a 24-month community order with a 12-month supervision order. In giving the judgment of the court Langstaff J noted 'we prefer to approach the appeal on [the] basis that this statute does not merit sentences of the same length or of the same gravity as do offences charged under the Sexual Offences Act in respect of indecent images.'[109] The other reported cases are mostly appeals against sentence and contain little discussion of the scope and application of s. 62. Thus although there clearly remains much to be determined about the

---

[103] The prohibited acts are: (a) the performance by a person of an act of intercourse or oral sex with or in the presence of a child; (b) an act of masturbation by, of, involving or in the presence of a child; (c) an act which involves penetration of the vagina or anus of a child with a part of a person's body or with anything else; (d) an act of penetration, in the presence of a child, of the vagina or anus of a person with a part of a person's body or with anything else; (e) the performance by a child of an act of intercourse or oral sex with an animal (whether dead or alive or imaginary); or (f) the performance by a person of an act of intercourse or oral sex with an animal (whether dead or alive or imaginary) in the presence of a child.

[104] J Hörnle, 'Countering the dangers of online pornography—shrewd regulation of lewd content?' (2011) 2 *European Journal of Law and Technology* 1.

[105] Coroners and Justice Act 2009, s. 66(2)(b).

[106] Hörnle (n. 104).

[107] [2011] EWCA Crim 1286.

[108] Ibid. [24].

[109] Ibid. [25].

scope and application of s. 62, what is clear though is that prosecutions are successfully being obtained under the Act.

20.4 **Extreme pornography**

Extreme pornography is a relatively new term in UK law. It arrived in summer 2005 when the Home Office and the Scottish Executive launched their joint consultation paper: 'Consultation: on the possession of extreme pornographic material.'[110] The consultation was launched after a campaign from Liz Longhurst to ban possession of violent pornography; images portraying sexual asphyxia, necrophilia, and rape, following the rape and murder of her daughter, Jane, in March 2003 by Graham Coutts, a man seemingly obsessed with violent sexual imagery.[111] The consultation process led eventually to the promulgation of s. 63 of the Criminal Justice and Immigration Act 2008 which came into force on 26 January 2009.[112] Section 63 outlaws the possession of extreme pornographic images: these are pornographic images (defined in s. 63(3) as an image of such a nature that it must reasonably be assumed to have been produced solely or principally for the purpose of sexual arousal) which portray 'in an explicit and realistic way' one of five categories of act or activity.

 Highlight Extreme pornography: the categories

(a) an act which threatens a person's life,

(b) an act which results, or is likely to result, in serious injury to a person's anus, breasts or genitals,

(c) an act which involves sexual interference with a human corpse,

(d) a person performing an act of intercourse or oral sex with an animal (whether dead or alive), or

(e) an act which involves the non-consensual penetration of a person's vagina, anus or mouth by another with the other person's penis, or an act which involves the non-consensual sexual penetration of a person's vagina or anus by another with a part of the other person's body or anything else, and a reasonable person looking at the image would think that the persons were real.

This is a far-reaching addition to the list of banned items. Before January 2009 only child abuse images (and pseudo-images) were proscribed in this manner. Why has the government extended the law in this fashion? The answer is given in the original consultation paper.[113]

---

[110] Home Office/Scottish Executive, *Consultation: on the possession of extreme pornographic material*, August 2005 <http://news.bbc.co.uk/1/shared/bsp/hi/pdfs/30_08_05_porn_doc.pdf>.

[111] For discussion of the Longhurst campaign and the events surrounding it see A Murray, 'The Reclassification of Extreme Pornographic Material' (2009) 72 MLR 73.

[112] By The Criminal Justice and Immigration Act 2008 (Commencement No. 4 and Saving Provision) Order 2008, SI 2008/2993.

[113] Home Office/Scottish Executive (n. 110) [1].

Highlight Banning possession of extreme pornography

The issue arises due to the wide range of extreme pornography available via the internet which cannot, in practice, be controlled by our existing laws. Extreme pornography featuring violent rape, sexual torture, and other abusive non-consensual acts existed in various forms before the internet but the publication and supply could be controlled by the Obscene Publications Acts 1959 and 1964, the Civic Government (Scotland) Act 1982, and by Customs legislation (the Customs Consolidation Act 1876 and Customs and Excise Management Act 1979). Closing down sources of supply and distribution obviated the need for a possession offence. However, the global nature of the internet makes this approach much more difficult.

This demonstrates the problem highlighted originally by Johnson and Post in 1996,[114] that although the community standards applied in obscenity regulations are local, the internet both fails to respect traditional borders, and is largely given the benefit of the US First Amendment following the *Reno* decision.[115] Faced with the inability to control this most extreme of pornographic content the government felt compelled to act in light of Mrs Longhurst's high-profile campaign. The only effective method of control which they could apply was to pass a possession offence: basically bracketing extreme pornography with child abuse images. The difficulty with this approach is that while we may justify the criminalization of the possession of child abuse images on the direct harm rationale (and pseudo-images and even NPPICs on the indirect harm rationale) it is more difficult to justify a blanket ban on the possession of extreme images.

An examination of the proscribed content found in s. 63 reveals that it covers five broad headings: (1) snuff and similarly highly violent content; (2) sado-masochism and 'torture porn'; (3) necrophilia; (4) bestiality; (5) rape porn. Although all of these acts may themselves be criminal offences if carried out against an unwilling victim, in most cases pornographic content of this nature is produced in much the same way as action movies produce scenes of violence and murder: using actors and careful stage direction. The direct harm approach cannot be therefore justified in all cases. Although there are no doubt cases where actual criminal activity may be recorded in the making of extreme pornography, the definition given in s. 63(7) and (7A) that the image must 'portray, in an explicit and realistic way' the act in question is too wide to justify the application of the direct harm principle when in most cases these images will be staged by paid actors.[116]

During consultation the government attempted to make an indirect harm argument, suggesting that 'it is possible that such material may encourage or reinforce interest in violent and aberrant sexual activity to the detriment of society as a whole'.[117] The

---

[114] Johnson and Post (n. 20).

[115] In fact it is reported that the UK Government approached the US Government asking them to take steps to close down a number of necrophilia websites at the heart of the Graham Coutts case, including 'Necrobabes' which was frequently visited by Coutts ahead of the murder, but were told the sites were protected by the Constitution. C Brown, 'Blunkett presses for curb on US porn', *The Telegraph*, 7 March 2004.

[116] The obvious exception is the bestiality provision since animals, like children, cannot consent.

[117] Home Office/Scottish Executive (n. 110) [27].

difficulty with this argument is though that while there is extensive statistical data to prove a link between the consumption of pseudo-child abuse images and further offending by paedophiles there is little evidence of a link between consumption of extreme pornography and further offending,[118] a fact admitted by the government.[119]

The government therefore took the decision to outlaw the possession of such images on public policy grounds rather than on the harm principle. The policy justification was that 'there is a small category of pornographic material which is so repugnant that, in common with child abuse images, its possession should not be tolerated'.[120] The danger with a public policy argument though is that you must judge the mood of the public correctly: with s. 63 it is arguable that the government failed to meet the public mood fully. By outlawing possession of BDSM images an extensive backlash occurred, led by members of the BDSM community who were concerned that the provision would be used to strike at their community. A strong campaign from the BDSM community assisted by anti-censorship groups and human rights organizations forced the government to make a number of concessions while s. 63 was being debated in Parliamentary Committee.[121]

Section 63 has been extensively prosecuted. The Crown Prosecution Service gives up-to-date statistics on numbers of prosecutions in their annual *Violence Against Women and Girls Report*.[122] The 2018 report shows that from the years 2011/12 to 2017/18 an average of 1,550 prosecutions have been brought *per annum* under s. 63; a considerable increase on the 30 or so cases *per annum* that the Ministry of Justice estimated would be prosecuted when the law was first introduced.[123]

It seems though, despite the high level of prosecutions being brought, it is unlikely that it has much effect on the large amount of extreme pornographic content available on the internet. As has already been discussed most of this content is hosted in the US where much of it can gain the protection of the First Amendment: therefore s. 63 is unlikely to close down many pornographic websites.

As a result, steps have been taken in the Digital Economy Act 2017 to block access to sites which host such content. In the same way as we saw at 20.2.5 the age-verification regulator (the BBFC) can issue a blocking notice under s. 23 where they consider that a person is 'making extreme pornographic material available on the internet to persons in the United Kingdom.' Such notices will require UK-based ISPs to 'take steps specified in the notice, or if no such steps are specified to put in place arrangements that appear to the provider to be appropriate, so as to prevent persons in the United Kingdom from being able to access the offending material using the service it provides'. In addition, by s. 21 the regulator may notify payment service providers and ancillary service providers (which could include Google) of sites which fail to comply. Thus the compliance mechanisms designed for age-verification will also apply to sites which make extreme

---

[118] Murray (n. 111). See also See M Popovich, 'Establishing New Breeds of (Sex) Offenders: Science or Political Control?' (2007) 22 *Sexual and Relationship Therapy* 255; A D'Amato, 'Porn Up, Rape Down' *Northwestern Public Law Research Paper* No. 913013: <www.ssrn.com/abstract=913013>.

[119] Home Office/Scottish Executive (n. 110) [31].

[120] Ibid. [33].

[121] A full discussion of the progress of s. 63 through Committee may be found in Murray, (n. 111).

[122] The 2018 report may be found at <https://www.cps.gov.uk/sites/default/files/documents/publications/cps-vawg-report-2018.pdf>.

[123] Erika Rackley and Clare McGlynn, 'Prosecuting the Possession of Extreme Pornography: A Misunderstood and Mis-used Law' [2013] *Criminal Law Review* 400, 404.

pornography available to the UK. As this content is illegal to possess there is no equivalent to s. 14 to allow them to become compliant. To avoid being blocked they will need to remove the offending content from their site.

In terms of UK enforcement to date, it appears that the police do not devote substantial resources to a crime that they see to be of relatively low priority when compared to more serious offences, such as possession of images of child abuse, and the large number of prosecutions have mostly come as a result of investigations into other matters or via reports made by members of the public. The first person charged with possession of extreme pornographic images was investigated after an engineer found the images on his computer while carrying out a repair,[124] while the first person to receive a custodial sentence under s.,63 was arrested on drugs offences with the images in question coming to light in the course of the drugs investigation.[125] In the over five years it has been in effect s. 63 has been at the centre of a number of successful prosecutions but in most cases it is one of a volume of charges usually alongside other charges,[126] with the images often coming to light either during a supervision meeting made under a sexual offences supervision order or during a license review for ex-prisoners released on license.

An important consideration is when one is deemed to be 'in possession' of the images in question. This was the subject of one of the first appeals against conviction in the case of *R v Ping Chen Cheung*.[127] The police had stopped the appellant in the street and had asked to search his laptop bag which appeared swollen, bulked out by content. Inside the bag the officers found a large amount of counterfeit DVDs. Although most were mainstream movies a small bundle of eight DVDs was found that formed the charge under s. 63. The appellant claimed he was unaware these DVDs were in the bag which had been given to him by a third party. The question was whether or not the appellant was said to be in possession of the DVDs absent his knowledge of the nature of the DVDs. The court found possession was a simple statutory question like drugs possession: 'The offence created under the 2008 Act is a new offence. However, we have no doubt that the concept of possession in section 63 does carry with it both a physical and a mental element in the same way as possession has been interpreted in offences under the Misuse of Drugs Act 1971.'[128] This position has been upheld and even reinforced in a number of cases since. In *R v Oliver (Philip)*, the Court of Appeal upheld a conviction under s. 63 for an ex-prison governor who had downloaded extreme images before their criminalization in January 2009 and who despite not accessing them following criminalization allowed others to access them through software which allowed for the contents of his hard drive to be shared. The court did not accept his assertion that he had no recollection of the images or how they got on his computer.

More recently the court reviewed the position of images sent by messaging systems and stored on a phone application in *R v Okoro (Cyprian)*.[129] The applicant had been convicted of possession of extreme pornographic images contrary to s. 63(1). Three videos

---

[124] 'Man had "grossly offensive and disgusting" porn images on computer', *St Helens Star*,18 June 2009.

[125] J Fae, 'First prison sentence for extreme porn' *The Register*, 29 September 2009.

[126] See *R v Smith* (Robert) [2013] EWCA Crim 167; *R v Horn (Stephen)* [2014] EWCA Crim 653; *R v Labonn (Jacque Cecil)* [2014] EWCA Crim 1652.

[127] [2009] EWCA Crim 2965.

[128] Ibid. [14].

[129] [2018] EWCA Crim 1929.

had been found on his phone, two of which were stored in a vault application and one in the memory of his phone. The applicant averred that the videos had been sent to him using WhatsApp and that he had not requested or sourced any of the images and did not know what they contained until he downloaded or opened the videos. He believed that he had deleted the images and he had only accessed them once, as he found them disgusting. He maintained that he had never sent or forwarded any of these images and had not accessed such material via any other computers or mobile device.[130] He relied upon the statutory defences of s. 65(2)(b) and (c): 'that the person had not seen the image concerned and did not know, nor had any cause to suspect, it to be an extreme pornographic image' or 'that the person was sent the image concerned without any prior request having been made by or on behalf of the person, and did not keep it for an unreasonable time'.

Giving the judgment of the court Irwin LJ noted that the Act fails to define possession.[131] In the absence of a statutory definition he turned to the case law decided under s. 160 of the Criminal Justice Act 1988 (possession of child abuse images). He found that in *Atkins v DPP*,[132] the Divisional Court held that where a defendant had viewed indecent images on his computer but, unknown to him, the images were automatically saved to the cache, it had to be shown that the defendant knew of the existence of the 'cache' of images as knowledge was an essential element of the offence.[133] He also noted though that in *R v Porter* the court, held that in order for a person to have possession of an image it required the particular individual to be capable of retrieving the image.[134] Finally, he examined the previously discussed case of *Ping Chen Cheung* and noted that 'Thomas LJ, giving the judgment of the court, held that the prosecution had to establish to the criminal standard that the appellant had knowledge of the existence of the "things" that were in his custody or control, but did not have to prove the defendant's knowledge of the quality, or contents, of the thing.'[135] On the basis of the prior cases he found that:

> the statute requires proof by the Crown of possession of the pornography or images of child abuse, as a preliminary step before the burden of proof shifts to the accused, to establish the statutory defences. An accused cannot be convicted in relation to material of which he was genuinely totally unaware. Nor could a defendant be said to be in possession of a digital file if it was in practical terms impossible for him to access that file. However, for these statutory purposes we are clear that possession is established if the accused can be shown to have been aware of a relevant digital file or package of files which he has the capacity to access, even if he cannot be shown to have opened or scrutinised the material. That appears to us to be consistent with the criminal law of possession in other fields, such as unlawful possession of drugs.[136]

In the current case where messages are delivered by a messaging service such as WhatsApp, Irwin LJ held that 'two elements had to be made out in order for an individual to have possession: (1) the images must have been within the appellant's custody or control; and (2) he must have known that he possessed an image or a group of images'.

---

130 Ibid. [8].
131 Ibid. [37].
132 [2000] 2 Cr App R 248.
133 *Okoro* (n. 129) [37].
134 [2006] EWCA Crim 560.
135 *Okoro* (n. 129) [40].
136 Ibid. [45].

He went on to explain that 'where unsolicited images are sent on WhatsApp, and automatically downloaded to the phone's memory, it is highly likely that the first element will be fulfilled. The second element will depend on whether the defendant knew that he received an image or images.'[137]

20.5 **Non-consensual disclosure of private sexual images**

The prevalence of digital photographic devices and the use of images as a form of communication rather than as a repository of memory have caused an explosion in the number and circulation of sexualized images. Most often these take the form of so-called 'sexting' images; the sending of sexually explicit, or sexualized, images from one person to another, usually that person's partner or someone they are sexually interested in. There are a number of social problems linked to the practice of sexting. Prime among these is the prevalence of sexting among children and youths for whom it has become socially normative. In their paper 'Cyber safety for adolescent girls: bullying, harassment, sexting, pornography, and solicitation',[138] Smith, Thompson, and Davidson record that in Europe 15 per cent of 11–16-year-olds had received peer-to-peer sexual messages or images while 3 per cent said they had sent or posted such images, while the UK levels were 12 per cent and 4 per cent.[139] They also report much higher levels of sexting in the United States, noting that 'the prevalence of adolescent sexting varies widely, from 9.6 per cent to 28 per cent', while also noting the prevalence of sexting in the UK seemed to be rising' noting that The Child Exploitation and Online Protection Command (CEOP) identified a marked increase in self-generated indecent images (SGIIs) being uploaded to the internet.[140] Even if we were to assume that the number of children receiving sexually explicit peer messages in the UK were around 12 per cent and those sending messages were around 4 per cent with around 3.7million children in the 11–16 age bracket in the UK, that would equate to 444,000 children receiving such images and, more worryingly, 148,000 children generating such images. Predominantly the issue of children sharing such images is not a legal problem, the issue is societal not legal. The law already has a regime to deal with the making and distribution of images of children under the age of 18 through the Protection of Children Act and the Criminal Justice Act.[141] The problem with sexting is often the sender and recipient will both be under 18 and it is often not appropriate to apply the full force of the law.[142]

The rise in the prevalence of sexting has though had another unintended side effect. With sexual partners often using sexting to supplement their relationship a large number of young adults now possess images of their partners in sexualized poses. When a

---

[137] Ibid. [46].
[138] P Smith, F Thompson, and J Davidson, 'Cyber safety for adolescent girls: bullying, harassment, sexting, pornography, and solicitation' (2014) 26 *Current Opinion in Obstetrics and Gynecology* 360.
[139] Ibid. 362.
[140] Ibid.
[141] See 20.3.
[142] The Crown Prosecution Service guidance 'Child Sexual Abuse: Guidelines on Prosecuting Cases of Child Sexual Abuse' advises that it would not usually be in the public interest to prosecute the consensual sharing of sexual images between children and this would suggest most of these incidents be dealt with informally, at [80].

break-up occurs it seems a not insignificant number of jilted ex-lovers take to the internet and share these images against the wishes of their ex-partner. This practice is so commonplace that is has been given a specific name: revenge porn. The posting of revenge porn can take a number of variations. There are websites, not hosted in the UK, where one can send images to be hosted and shared. One of the most infamous of these sites was IsAnyoneUp.com. The website operated as a revenge porn site between 2010 and 2012. During that time nude and semi-nude images of thousands of women were posted with links to their Twitter accounts and Facebook pages. However, an investigation revealed that a large number of images had been hacked rather than posted by ex-partners and eventually the site operator Hunter Moore was charged with computer misuse and identity theft charges. In February 2015 Moore pleaded guilty and was sentenced to two years in prison. Despite this, a large number of revenge porn sites continue to operate.

An alternate approach used is more direct, less permanent, but often more damaging. That is, to directly post images or video to popular social networking sites, such as Twitter or Facebook, identifying the victim (often images are posted directly to the victim's Facebook page). Clearly this is very harmful to the victim both psychologically and socially, yet until recently there was little the law could do. When the victim in *AMP v Persons Unknown*[143] had intimate photographs removed from her mobile phone in 2008 she had to resort to a mixture of copyright law and a rather inventive application of the Protection from Harassment Act to attempt to gain control over illegally obtained, and circulated, images. At the time no one who distributed the images committed an offence, at least not until they were formally notified that such distribution was in breach of the order of the court.

Today *AMP* would find a drastically different legal landscape. Recognizing the harm that revenge pornography causes to victims, a number of jurisdictions have passed specific revenge porn laws including all the jurisdictions of the UK. The law for England and Wales is found in ss. 33–35 of the Criminal Justice and Courts Act 2015.[144] This makes it an offence to 'disclose a private sexual photograph or film if the disclosure is made (a) without the consent of an individual who appears in the photograph or film, and (b) with the intention of causing that individual distress.' The offence has a number of defences for law enforcement purposes, journalism, and the public interest or where the image was previously made available for reward. Consent, according to s. 33(7) could be general consent or specific consent. The key phrase for the offence is 'private sexual' and these components of the offence are defined in s. 35. A photograph or film is 'private' if it shows something that is not of a kind ordinarily seen in public,[145] while it is sexual if '(a) it shows all or part of an individual's exposed genitals or pubic area, (b) it shows something that a reasonable person would consider to be sexual because of its nature, or (c) its content, taken as a whole, is such that a reasonable person would consider it to be sexual.'[146] The new offence came into effect on 13 April 2015 and in its first three years of operation the CPS brought 1,135 prosecutions.[147] To date though

---

[143] [2011] EWHC 3454 (TCC).

[144] In Scotland the equivalent provisions are ss. 2–4 of the Abusive Behaviour and Sexual Harm (Scotland) Act 2016, while in Northern Ireland they are ss. 51–3 of the Justice Act (Northern Ireland) 2016.

[145] See s. 35(2).

[146] See s. 35(3).

[147] Crown Prosecution Service (n. 122).

there has only been one reported case, that of *R v Bostan (Amar)*.[148] This was simply an appeal against sentence so contains no examination of the law. What we can learn from this case was that the Court of Appeal felt that a sentence of 2 months' detention was appropriate where a single topless image of an ex-girlfriend was texted to her mother by the appellant with a warning that he would expose the image more widely.

Recourse to the criminal law is not the only option open to victims of revenge porn. There have recently been successful civil claims brought in Northern Ireland and in England and Wales. The case in Northern Ireland involved a then 14-year-old girl who from November 2014 to January 2016 saw her nude picture posted several times on Facebook as 'an act of revenge', without her consent. Lawyers for the girl raised an action against Facebook alleging misuse of private information, negligence, and breaches of the Data Protection Act. Unfortunately, there is no judgment as it was reported in January 2018 that a confidential settlement had been reached between the claimant and Facebook.[149] In a similar action in England and Wales, YouTube star Chrissy Chambers settled an action in breach of confidence and misuse of private information for 'substantial damages' arising out of the non-consensual uploading of sexual videos without her consent to a pornographic website. The ex-boyfriend responsible accepted liability and also agreed to pay Chambers' legal costs, as well as assigning her the copyright in the videos allowing her to have them removed from the site.[150]

20.6 **Private regulation of pornographic imagery**

As the discussion throughout this chapter has demonstrated, the development of web hosting and delivery of pornographic content has undermined the effectiveness of state regulators to control their borders and to police the production, distribution, and consumption of pornographic content in all forms, be it indecent, obscene, or extremely obscene. Pornography and obscenity are the areas where there is arguably the greatest need for alternative regulatory measures, such as those predicted by Lawrence Lessig in *Code and Other Laws of Cyberspace*,[151] which make use of the design features of the internet to allow for effective regulation. Some such measures have been implemented by ISPs, mostly designed to restrict the supply of child abuse images and pseudo-images. In the UK a hybrid hierarchical/design control system known as Cleanfeed is used.[152] Cleanfeed is a two-part hybrid system: first, suspect images need to be identified and blacklisted; this is carried out by a private regulatory authority known as the Internet Watch Foundation, then the suspect images, pages, or sites are blocked though the Cleanfeed technical protocol.

Central to the functioning of Cleanfeed is the Internet Watch Foundation (IWF). The IWF was formed in 1996 following agreement between the government, police forces, and the ISP industry that something had to be done to tackle the problem of child abuse

---

[148] [2018] EWCA Crim 494.

[149] H McDonald, 'Facebook warned it faces legal action from "revenge porn" victims', *The Guardian*, 12 January 2018.

[150] J Kleeman, 'YouTube star wins damages in landmark UK "revenge porn" case', *The Guardian*, 17 January 2018.

[151] L Lessig, *Code and Other Laws of Cyberspace* (Basic Books 1999); *Code Ver. 2.0* (Basic Books 2006) discussed in depth in Ch. 4.

images on the Usenet system. The ISPs suggested a self-regulatory body which would operate a 'hotline' to allow members of the public to report potentially illegal images; the experts at the IWF would then establish whether the report had identified an illegal image of child abuse and if they adjudged the image to be illegal they would add it to their blacklist of banned images or sites which ISPs would then block access to, thus protecting them from the risk of being prosecuted for possession of an indecent image of a child under s. 160 of the Criminal Justice Act. Over time, the focus of the IWF's work has moved from Usenet to content hosted on websites and that now forms the bulk of the IWF's day-to-day work. As well as informing ISPs of material that should be blocked, the IWF also passes relevant information to the law enforcement authorities allowing them to take steps to trace the source of the illegal material: material hosted in the UK is reported directly to the relevant local UK police service or the National Crime Agency's CEOP Command, whereas material hosted offshore is reported to the Virtual Global Taskforce for investigation.[153]

Once a site is blacklisted by the IWF it is passed on to its industry partners for blocking. This is usually achieved through the Cleanfeed content blocking system. The system uses the blacklist and a number of proxy servers to block access to the content in question. For example, if there is blacklisted content on the website *yourpiccshere.com/ nastynasty/porn*, then when a user requests access to any content on the yourpiccshere. com server that request will be sent to a Cleanfeed server where the blacklist is held. If the content requested is not on the blacklist (say *yourpiccshere.com/holiday/spain*), then the proxy will allow access to the content, though if the customer is seeking to obtain access to the blacklisted content they will be blocked from accessing the site.

A problem with Cleanfeed was that the end user did not know that Cleanfeed had blocked his access. There was no 'blocked by Cleanfeed' message; instead the user simply received a 'not found' error, meaning there was no way the average user could tell if content had been blocked by Cleanfeed or was just unavailable, and as the IWF does not publish its blacklist we had no way of knowing how many sites had been blocked in error, or had been blocked in full when only one page or image held on that site was illegal. This has now changed and the IWF Blocking: Good Practice note[154] 'strongly recommends that all relevant members serve a splash page with an agreed standard text' which states that 'access has been denied by your internet access provider because this page may contain indecent images of children as identified by the Internet Watch Foundation'. This should mean that if sites are blacklisted by the IWF in error, or if over-blocking were to occur, end users should be aware of it and should be able to take steps under the Content Assessment Appeal Process to have the block removed.[155]

[152] Cleanfeed is actually the internal BT project name for the system; its actual name is the BT Anti-Child-Abuse Initiative. Over time though Cleanfeed has become the common label of the system.

[153] To learn more about the NCA's CEOP Command and the Virtual Global Taskforce visit their websites at <https://www.ceop.police.uk/safety-centre/> and <www.virtualglobaltaskforce.com/> respectively.

[154] <https://www.iwf.org.uk/become-a-member/services-for-members/url-list/url-blocking-good-practice>.

[155] <https://www.iwf.org.uk/content-assessment-appeal-process>.

20.7 **Conclusions**

The regulation of pornographic and obscene content is one of the greatest challenges for the information society. As an 'informational product' pornography benefits from the same economies of production and distribution seen in music and video production but with the potential for far greater negative social impact. There are several challenges which will continue to test communities and lawmakers in the next ten to twenty years. First among them is how to prevent children from coming into greater contact with pornography than they already do. Since children routinely have their own computer, tablet, or smartphone from an early age, this is becoming a major problem. Second is the question of how we wrest back local community values in a place where there is no local community. This may prove impossible, but it is certainly worth exploring. Third is to determine where obscene content becomes unacceptably obscene: this to date has led to the banning of the possession of images of child abuse, pseudo-images, NPPICs, and 'extreme pornographic images'. Should we add to this list? Or would it be an infringement of our freedom of thought and expression if we continually grow a list of banned items? Finally, we may wish to consider how technology is changing the nature of sexual encounters and question how we wish to deal with online advertising of brothels, and how to deal with new phenomena, including sexting (in addition to the regulation of revenge porn), and online grooming. Some of these will be discussed in the next chapter.

TEST QUESTIONS

Question 1

On the morning of Tuesday 1 August 2019, the Metropolitan Police raided the offices of a major corporate client of your firm. The raid revealed a series of potentially unlawful images on the client's cloud server, based in San Francisco. These images belonged to one of the client's employees who had originally stored them on his desktop but had transferred them to the cloud server before deleting them from his PC. The employee in question admitted in an interview that he likes to look at pornographic materials during his lunch hour. He claims the images are perfectly legal and 'not unlike those you will find in any top-shelf magazine'. The client's representatives have looked at some of the sites he is visiting and are extremely concerned that some of the models look to be under 18. The employee says that all the models are over 18, but that the images are morphed a little using photo-manipulation software to make them look a little younger and that the site carries a disclaimer saying all models are over 18. The same employee also has several images on his computer of him engaging in what the client describes as 'dangerous, and potentially even fatal, sexual acts'. During his interview with the client the employee dismissed that the acts were dangerous, stating that it was just 'a bit of fun between consenting adults'.

You have been asked to determine whether the actions of the employee are potentially illegal in English law and whether the client is doing anything illegal, or whether it could be liable for its employee's actions.

Question 2

Can we treat 'extremely pornographic images' in the same way as images of child abuse images? Is s. 63 of the Criminal Justice and Immigration Act proportionate to the harm?

Question 3

Will age-verification (as set out in the Digital Economy Act 2017) be effective at all? Is the age-verification process proportionate to the risk or harm?

FURTHER READING

Books

A Gillespie, *Child Pornography: Law and Policy* (Routledge 2011).

M Hall and J Hearn, *Revenge Pornography* (Routledge 2017)

A Nair, *The Regulation of Internet Pornography: Issues and Challenges* (Routledge 2018)

Chapters and articles

A Gillespie, '"Trust me, it's only for me": Revenge porn and the criminal law' (2015) *Criminal Law Review* 866

J Hörnle, 'Countering the dangers of online pornography—shrewd regulation of lewd content?' (2011) 2 *European Journal of Law and Technology* < http://ejlt.org//article/view/55/121 >

A Murray, 'The Reclassification of Extreme Pornographic Images' (2009) 72 Modern Law Review 73

E Rackley and C McGlynn, 'Prosecuting the Possession of Extreme Pornography: A Misunderstood and Mis-used Law' [2013] *Criminal Law Review* 400

J Rowbottom: Obscenity laws and the internet: targeting the supply and demand (2006) *Criminal Law Review* 97

Crime and law enforcement in the information society

As most online transactions take place with the identity and location of participants hidden behind the computer screen, opportunities arise for those with criminal intent to reach out globally to commit fraud, theft, and harassment; to offer illegal gambling and pornography, and to commit direct cyberattacks.[1] Although by far the most common form of illegal activity online is simple copyright infringement,[2] there are a growing number of criminal activities being operated through the internet including the unregulated production and distribution of pornography, revenge porn images and child abuse images,[3] direct cyberattacks such as denial-of-service attacks and privacy attacks including hacking, phishing, and the installation of Trojans,[4] computer fraud, online harassment, grooming, and bandwidth theft. Such activities often take place overseas but target UK citizens. The most infamous form of computer fraud is the advance fee fraud (discussed below), which was for a period so prevalent in Nigeria that it became known internationally simply as the '419 Fraud': 419 referring to the Article of the Nigerian Criminal Code dealing with such fraud.[5] A variation of the 419 Fraud, the 'Russian Scam', targets users of online dating sites and is often perpetrated by criminals based in Russia and Eastern Europe, while 'cheque overpayment fraud' or 'criminal cashback' schemes are common on internet auction sites. This chapter will look at advance fee fraud as well as a number of other criminal activities common in the information society, including the illegal appropriation of personal data, commonly known as phishing, and offences against the person committed through information and communication technologies including harassment, cyberstalking, and grooming.

---

[1] Of course IP addresses offer a route to track criminals, but the average computer user does not know how to trace an IP address and even when law enforcement authorities become involved they often find that the address is either 'spoofed' through a re-router or leads to an internet cafe.

[2] Discussed in Ch. 12.

[3] Discussed in Ch. 20.

[4] Discussed in Ch. 19.

[5] Article 419 forms part of Chapter 38, 'Obtaining Property by false pretences: Cheating.' It (along with the rest of the Nigerian Criminal Code) may be found at: <www.nigeria-law.org/Criminal%20Code%20Act-Tables.htm>.

21.1 **Fraud and identity theft**

21.1.1 **Fraud**

The risk of online fraud is extensive. In June 2017 the UK National Audit Office issued their report 'Online fraud'.[6] In this they recorded that 'fraud is now the most commonly experienced crime in England and Wales, and most takes place online. In the year to 30 September 2016, the ONS reported an estimated 11.8 million incidents of crime in England and Wales. For the first time, the official figures revealed an estimated 3.6 million fraud incidents, of which 1.9 million incidents (53 per cent) were cyber-related.'[7] They revealed that there were approximately 1.4 million cases of card-not-present fraud, an increase of 103 per cent since 2011, and that losses associated with card-not-present fraud through the internet were £308.8 million in 2016.[8] The 2017 Annual Fraud Indicator suggests the overall annual loss to the UK economy in all forms of fraud, offline and online, was estimated to be £190 billion with £6.8 billion of that falling directly on individuals,[9] The £6.8 billion figure represents an average loss per UK adult of £135.

Many aspects of fraud are, of course, criminalized with much of the current law of England and Wales to be found in the Fraud Act 2006. The Act was introduced to replace the old deception offences found in the Theft Acts.[10] The problem with the deception offences was that to commit deception it was widely accepted that a human mind had to be deceived. Deception of a computer system which would process an instruction automatically without human intervention was apparently not covered by the Theft Acts.[11]

The Fraud Act 2006 was enacted in response to the growing threat of computer and online fraud, much of which could be operated directly on a computer system. The Act came into force in January 2007: it creates three new forms of fraud and a further offence of obtaining services dishonestly. Section 1 states that a person is guilty of fraud if he commits any of the offences listed in ss. 2–4: these are (1) fraud by making a false representation;[12] (2) fraud by failing to disclose information;[13] and (3) fraud by abuse of position.[14] These new offences, although all still offences of deception, have been extended to clearly cover fraud committed on an automated system. For instance, s. 2(5) clearly states that 'a representation may be regarded as made if it (or anything implying it) is submitted in any form to any system or device designed to receive, convey or respond to communications (with or without human intervention)'. Thus it will clearly cover all types of electronic communication including email, SMS, and IRC, as well as instructions sent to an automated system like an online bank or credit card clearing system. If a UK-based fraudster were therefore to make a false representation, in

---

[6] <https://www.nao.org.uk/wp-content/uploads/2017/06/Online-Fraud.pdf>.

[7] Ibid. [6].

[8] Ibid. [1.10]–[1.11].

[9] Experian, *Annual Fraud Indicator 2017* <https://www.experian.co.uk/assets/identity-and-fraud/annual-fraud-indicator-report-2017.pdf>.

[10] These were obtaining property by deception (1968 Act, s.15); obtaining an money transfer by deception (1968 Act, s.15A); obtaining services by deception (1978 Act, s.1); and evasion of liability by deception (1978 Act, s.2).

[11] In *DPP v Ray* [1974] AC 370, Lord Morris stated: 'For a deception to take place there must be some person or persons who will have been deceived.'

[12] Fraud Act 2006, s.2.

[13] Fraud Act 2006, s.3.

[14] Fraud Act 2006, s. 4.

breach of s. 2, such as to give false credit card details to an online bank or e-commerce site with a view to making a gain,[15] he would commit an offence. This would cover most forms of online fraud, including card-not-present fraud where the fraudster improperly gains credit card details and uses them to buy goods and services online; asset transfer fraud where a fraudster gains access to online banking services, or similar, and transfers assets to himself; and most forms of advance fee fraud where the fraudster tricks the victim into advancing them funds in the hope of making a future gain.

The problem is that in the online environment fraud, like pornography, usually originates overseas but has its effects in the UK. As discussed in the introduction to this chapter the best known is probably the 'Nigerian Advance Fee Fraud', known colloquially as the '419 Fraud'. There are many variations of the 419 Fraud but they all follow a similar pattern.

 Case study The 419 Advance Fee Fraud

The victim receives an email from someone claiming to represent a company or individual with a large sum of money or similar assets which they require to transfer. They claim to have no ability to transfer the funds or assets directly themselves, usually due to banking regulations or some other legal impediment. They ask the victim for their assistance in making the transfer and in return offer them from 10–40 per cent of the value of the asset or funds (usually worth millions of pounds).

When the victim offers to help, the fraudster begins to ask for funds to be paid to effect the transfer. These may include small amounts to bribe officials or larger amounts required to show the victim is in good financial standing. Once the funds are transferred the fraudster disappears with the funds.

A variant of the 419 Fraud, popular in Eastern Europe, is the 'Russian Scam'.

 Case study The 'Russian Scam'

The victim is usually selected from a dating site, or singles site. They are contacted by a young woman who claims to be looking to marry a UK citizen. She will often send pictures of herself and will spend some time communicating with the victim by email, social media, or perhaps even by telephone (although this is unusual as the fraudster is usually a man; when this occurs women are hired by the fraudsters to make such calls).

The fraudster will then make requests for funds. These may involve payments for medical expenses for the young woman's mother, or for assistance with housing costs. She will then indicate that she is willing to travel to the UK to meet the victim and will ask for expenses for visas, travel tickets, and hotel rooms. The fraudster then disappears with the funds.

---

[15] Gain is defined in s. 5(2) as '(a) gain in money or other property; (b) include any such gain or loss whether temporary or permanent; and "property" means any property whether real or personal (including things in action and other intangible property).'

Although these frauds have names which reflect where they developed, advance fee frauds can originate anywhere. Many 419 frauds are now affected from China and former Soviet Bloc countries, as well as Nigeria and other sub-Saharan African countries, while Russian scams often originate in Africa and China, as well as in former Soviet Bloc countries. Advance fee fraud is, though, only one form of internet-based fraud.

Whereas advance fee fraud tends to be practiced in developing nations, other more sophisticated forms of fraud are practiced in Europe and other developed nations. Here the most common form of dishonest representation is 'card-not-present' fraud. Like the 419 fraud, there are a variety of ways this is practiced but the end result is usually the same.

Case study 'Card-not-present' fraud

The fraudster gets hold of personal credit card details including the name of the account holder, the card number, expiry date, and the card verification code (CVC). This may be acquired in a number of ways: either simply by using discarded credit card receipts, or by 'skimming' a card in a restaurant, bar, or shop, or by 'phishing' for such details online (discussed in greater depth at 21.1.2).

Once these details are known the fraudster may purchase goods or services online. The fraudster may also choose to sell the information on to third parties, this, although not a breach of s. 2 of the Fraud Act, may amount to the common law offence of conspiracy to defraud.

Thus common frauds committed though the application of Information and Communication Technology (ICT) would in most cases be either a breach of s. 2 of the Fraud Act 2006 or one of the subsequent sections, depending upon the nature of the fraud, or may, if involving two or more people amount to conspiracy to defraud at common law. But, with so many frauds originating overseas, can the international community effectively police this activity?

Some basic standards for international cooperation are found in the Council of Europe Convention on Cybercrime.[16] Article 8 requires that:

> Each Party shall adopt such legislative and other measures as may be necessary to establish as criminal offences under its domestic law, when committed intentionally and without right, the causing of a loss of property to another person by:
>
> > (a) any input, alteration, deletion or suppression of computer data, [or]
> >
> > (b) any interference with the functioning of a computer system, with fraudulent or dishonest intent of procuring, without right, an economic benefit for oneself or for another person.

It is clear though that Art, 8 only covers certain forms of fraud. Card-not-present fraud is covered by Art, 8 as it requires the inputting of computer data with fraudulent intent.

---

[16] CETS No. 185, Budapest, 23.XI.2001.

However, advance fee fraud appears not to be covered unless one takes an extremely expansive view of the term 'input of computer data' to cover the contents of emails or instant messages sent by the fraudsters to their victims.

The reason for the narrow scope of Art. 8 may be because the Convention is focused on 'cybercrime' or as the preamble to the Convention puts it 'the present Convention is necessary to deter action directed against the confidentiality, integrity and availability of computer systems, networks and computer data as well as the misuse of such systems, networks and data by providing for the criminalisation of such conduct'. It is less focused on traditional criminal activity which makes use of ICT as a communications media, and more focused on new forms of criminal activity which makes use of the unique nature of ICT communications.

The recent growth in advance fee frauds is as a result of the 'globalization effect' of the information society. Fraudsters, often based in the poorest parts of the world, can use ICT to contact potential victims in the richest nations at a relatively low cost: there is nothing uniquely technology-driven about this form of fraud: instead it is an old form of fraud being reborn through the global reach that the information society offers.[17] By contrast, internet-enabled card-not-present fraud is a new form of an old fraud. Card-not-present fraud, as it name suggests, is based on giving false credit or debit card details to a vendor or supplier of services when the card is not available for inspection. As such, it tended historically to be carried out by mail or by telephone. Internet-based card-not-present fraud is a new way of carrying out card-not-present fraud not previously available: as such, it is unlike advance fee fraud as it has created a new way of committing this fraud rather than merely a new way of communicating with victims.

Alongside these common online frauds a number of new frauds has developed, mostly around online auction sites. These include overpayment fraud and escrow fraud.

 Case study Overpayment fraud

This begins when a buyer pays for goods (usually bought via an internet auction site) with a cheque drawn for a higher amount than the agreed price.

The buyer/fraudster will then ask the seller/victim to refund the overpayment by wire transfer. The seller/victim pays the cheque into his bank account and after three or four days assumes the cheque has cleared. He will then usually send the goods and refund the difference as requested.

After about 16–20 days the seller/victim's bank will bounce the cheque for being a forgery leaving the seller/victim with no payment but having both shipped the goods and paid an amount of cash to the buyer/fraudster. The goods plus cash element of this fraud lead to it being dubbed in some quarters 'criminal cashback'.

---

[17] The Advance Fee fraud was originally known as the 'Spanish Prisoner Fraud' and can be dated back to the early 1900s.

Case study Escrow fraud

This occurs when a buyer offers to buy a high-value item such as a car, boat, or designer watch. The seller will not wish to send the item without knowing the money for payment is secured; the buyer will not want to release the funds until they receive the item in case the seller is fraudulent. The answer is to escrow the funds: putting them in the hands of a reputable third party to hold until such time as the goods are received and the buyer is satisfied they are as described.

This is commonplace and there are a number of reputable escrow agencies but in the case of escrow fraud a fraudulent agency has been set up. The seller then sends the item believing the funds to be safely escrowed, but both the buyer and the escrow agency then disappear.

These are only a few of the number of current online frauds but by far the commonest form of online fraud currently is identity fraud.

21.1.2 **Identity theft and identity fraud**

Online identity fraud is now a massive industry. We are particularly susceptible to identity fraud in the information society for a number of reasons, but prime among these are: (1) the way information is gathered and stored in the information society, and (2) the increased use of identity proxies to prove our identity.

The information society is, as we have seen, both a social and economic market built around the ownership, storage, manipulation, and transfer of data. Much of this data may be used to identify the individual, including IP addresses, dates of birth, name, address, telephone number, credit card details, and banking details, among others. There are therefore large amounts of personal data held by companies and organizations with whom we do business. There is always a risk of loss of this data either by the data controller, or in transit between the data subject and the data controller.[18] A loss of data can lead to identity fraud. There is no easy way to prove the identity of an individual when they deal with a website for there are no biometric indicators which we use in real life to establish identity: as Lawrence Lessig says 'In cyberspace . . . you enter without an identity and you identify only what you want—and even that can't be authenticated with any real confidence.'[19] Thus we use customer IDs, passwords, and passkeys to identify ourselves. Often these passwords and passkeys give access to financial data and resources; in particular, online bank accounts or credit card accounts or other payment accounts like PayPal, or they allow others to fraudulently use our accounts to buy or sell goods such as our internet auction accounts.

These proxies for identity are highly prized by the criminal fraternity and have led to the rise of a new form of identity fraud known as 'phishing'.

---

[18] This will be discussed further in chs. 22–3.
[19] L Lessig, *Code and Other Laws of Cyberspace Ver2.0* (Basic Books 2006) 248.

Case study Phishing

Phishing[20] is usually carried out by email. An email is sent to many tens of thousands of email accounts at random and says something like the user's account has been suspended due to unusual activity, or that security measures are being upgraded and they need to confirm their details. The email will contain a link which will take the user to a 'shell' website made to look like the genuine site but when they enter their details they are retained by the fraudster who then uses them to gain access to their accounts.

Like advance fee fraud and card-not-present fraud, phishing represents a real harm to the UK economy with UK banks absorbing losses of £134m in online banking fraud in 2017.[21] The tactic for dealing with phishing has largely been the same as with other forms of online fraud: suppression in the UK and cooperation on an international level.

On a domestic level the Court of Appeal has reviewed phishing in a number of appeals against sentence, including the case of *R v Jabeth & Babatunde*.[22] In giving judgment Holroyde J noted that 'these applicants admitted involvement in a substantial international conspiracy which involved the obtaining of bank account details and other confidential data by the use of disguised emails in the criminal activity known as phishing.'[23] The case was a complex international conspiracy involving the applicants and a hacker in Egypt who obtained personal details. The court found that on one occasion, Christmas Eve 2011:

> Miss Jabeth succeeded in passing herself off as Miss Budow and managed to change the contact number to which the one-time password would be sent. Armed with that information and using a computer at her home, the conspirators were able to transfer funds out of Miss Budow's accounts. They made in all 376 transfers in the space of about 24 hours, until they reached the point at which both accounts had been emptied of funds. In all, £1,051,967 was obtained.[24]

The court in part allowed the appeal which saw Miss Jabeth's sentence reduced from four years' imprisonment to three years and six months' imprisonment. Mr Babatunde's sentence of five years and six months' imprisonment was confirmed.

Sentences such as these demonstrate how seriously the UK courts are taking the risk of phishing, a risk recognized internationally and which has led, like advance fee fraud, to a high level of international cooperation. In 2004 the United Nations organized an expert group on fraud and the criminal misuse and falsification of identity. The group met twice (in March 2005 and January 2007) and recommended that states take steps to update their laws to reflect recent technological developments, that states should ratify or accede to, the United Nations Crime Conventions and Council of Europe Cybercrime Convention, and that states should review rules on territorial jurisdiction to keep pace

---

[20] This is a false representation and is illegal under s. 2 of the Fraud Act 2006.
[21] Experian (n. 9).
[22] [2014] EWCA Crim 476.
[23] Ibid. [1].
[24] Ibid. [11].

with ongoing evolution of fraud and identity-related offences and consider establishing extraterritorial jurisdiction in lieu of extradition.[25]

The expert group recommendations were passed on to the United Nations Office on Drugs and Crime, a body that fosters cooperation in the international fight against drug trafficking and organized crime. They created a further Expert Group on Identity-Related Crime to examine the issue. The group discussed 'legal approaches to criminalize identity theft',[26] and reported that they had doubts 'as to whether a single unified offence would be viable in most legal systems, but noted that it should be possible to address the problem through a combination of adjustments to existing crimes and the development of a series of new offences to address the novel forms of crime'.[27] They went on to recommend that 'in developing materials with respect to criminalisation and other legislative responses to identity related crime, it was important to adopt a flexible approach'.[28]

The final outcome of the Group's work was the *United Nations Office on Drugs and Crime Handbook on Identity Related Crime*, published in April 2011.[29] The *Handbook* has taken on board the recommendations of the Expert Group by setting out a range of options to be taken into account when addressing domestic law in relation to identity-related crimes. For lawmakers the most useful part of the guide is probably Part V, the practical guide to international cooperation. It lists all the international instruments that allow for international cooperation, extradition, and extraterritorial actionability of orders. It also sets out a series of case studies in areas such as phishing, card cloning, and auction fraud and suggests strategies that lawmakers and law enforcement bodies may take to regulate the activity. In addition to the *Handbook*, the Economic and Social Council (ECOSOC) have passed a series of resolutions culminating in resolution 2009/22 on 'International cooperation in the prevention, investigation, prosecution and punishment of economic fraud and identity-related crime'.[30] This encourages member states to undertake a number of activities to reduce the risk and prevalence of identity-related crime, including:

(a) to combat economic fraud and identity-related crime by ensuring adequate investigative powers and, where appropriate, by reviewing and updating the relevant laws;

(b) to develop and maintain adequate law enforcement and investigative capacity to keep abreast of and deal with new developments in the exploitation of information, communications and commercial technologies in economic fraud and identity-related crime, including websites and other online forums used to

---

[25] Taken from <http://www.itu.int/osg/spuold/cybersecurity/pgc/2007/events/presentations/session5-chryssikos-C5-meeting-14-may-2007.pdf>.

[26] Commission on Crime Prevention and Criminal Justice, *Papers for the Eighteenth Session, Vienna, 16–24 April 2009: Thematic discussion: Economic fraud and identity-related crime*: <https://www.unodc.org/documents/treaties/organized_crime/ECN152009_CRP12.pdf>.

[27] Ibid. [6].

[28] Ibid. [9].

[29] <www.unodc.org/documents/treaties/UNCAC/Publications/Handbook_on_ID_Crime/10-57802_ebooke.pdf>.

[30] <https://www.unodc.org/documents/treaties/organized_crime/ECOSOC_resolution_2009_22.pdf>.

facilitate trafficking in identity information or documents, such as passports, driving licences or national identity cards;

(c) to consider, where appropriate, the establishment of new offences and the updating of existing offences in response to the evolution of economic fraud and identity-related crime, bearing in mind the advantages of common approaches to criminalization, where feasible, in facilitating efficient and effective international cooperation;

(d) to strengthen international cooperation to prevent and combat economic fraud and identity-related crime, in particular by making full use of the relevant international legal instruments;

(e) to develop an approach for the collection of comparable data on the nature and extent of identity-related crime, including, where feasible, from the victim's perspective, that would allow the sharing of data among appropriate law enforcement entities and provide a central source of data at the national level on the nature and extent of identity-related crime, taking due account of national law.

In 2013 ECOSOC, concerned about levels of identity theft rising, passed a further resolution inviting member states to provide extra-budgetary resources for the purpose of fighting identity theft and to extend the budget of the United Nations Office on Drugs and Crime.[31] Despite these efforts, the data suggests the problem continues to grow.[32]

21.2 Grooming, harassment, and cyberstalking

As well as offering an opportunity for fraud, the anonymous and intrusive nature of the information society allows users to stalk, harass, and groom others from a distance. We may classify these as offences against the person, enabled and supported by ICT. Each of these offences is slightly different and has produced a slightly different legal response. All are illegal in the UK and in many cases the law has recently been amended or updated to account for changes in technology.

21.2.1 Grooming

Grooming is the act of befriending or establishing an emotional connection with a child, in order to lower the child's inhibitions in preparation for sexual abuse. Grooming is not new; it existed before the advent of the information society and would be carried out through personal interaction with a child, perhaps at a public place such as a park or by a person with a position of trust such as a teacher, religious leader, or group leader (such as a scoutmaster). The information society makes it easier for strangers to groom children due to the nature of the communications media. First, children are comfortable: they are usually sitting at home and using websites familiar to them such as Habbo, Playkids, or Club Penguin, or if older PopJam, Facebook, WhatsApp, or Instagram; this causes them to lower their guard. Second, internet social networking sites such as the ones mentioned cause children not to recognize 'stranger danger' as easily since they

---

[31] ECOSOC resolution 2013/39 of 25 July 2013.
[32] See (n. 21) and related text.

are accustomed to meeting new people in this environment and so do not equate new people to 'strangers'. Third, the anonymity offered by social networking sites allows adults to pose as children so the victim believes they are talking to someone of the same age as them; this again causes them to lower their defences.

Grooming was only formally criminalized in 2003. Prior to the passage of the Sexual Offences Act 2003 law enforcement authorities had to use a hotchpotch of legislation to prosecute many of the acts which the offender may have committed in grooming a child, including the Obscene Publications Act 1959 or the Protection of Children Act 1978 (as offenders would often use pornography to convince a child it was okay to engage in sexual conduct); the Malicious Communications Act 1988 (which outlaws the sending of offensive or threatening communications); and the Protection from Harassment Act 1997 (which outlaws activity which the offender knows amounts to harassment).

These were felt to be inadequate to deal with the increased risk of grooming following the development of ICT communications such as email, IRC, and social networking sites. In their famous 2001 report, *Chat Wise, Street Wise*,[33] the Internet Crime Forum reported that a US survey had found that 'just under one in five of 10–17 year olds surveyed claimed to have received some kind of sexual solicitation on the Internet within the previous twelve months',[34] and that the UK law as it stood did not adequately deal with the issue of 'online enticement of a child'.[35]

The solution was s. 15 of the Sexual Offences Act 2003. This introduces the complicated offence of 'Meeting a child following sexual grooming', a provision which as its name suggests doesn't criminalize the act of grooming itself, but rather the further act of intending to meet a child following grooming. To commit the offence the offender (who must be aged 18 or over) must either have met or communicated with the child (being a person under 16) on at least one previous occasion;[36] the offender must then either meet the child or travel with the intention of meeting the child; and at that time, the offender has the intention of committing a relevant sexual offence (including sexual activity with a child, causing a child to engage in sexual activity, engaging in sexual activity in the presence of a child, or causing a child to watch a sexual act). The reason why the offence is framed in this way is to prevent the risk of criminalizing innocent communications with children, by including the final element that the offender must either meet or travel with intent to meet the minor for the purpose of some form of sexual encounter; it removes any element of uncertainty.[37] The offence has been prosecuted extensively, with among others a serving police child protection officer and a priest facing charges.[38]

---

[33] Internet Crime Forum, *Chat Wise, Street Wise* March 2001 <www.internetcrimeforum.org.uk/chatwise_streetwise.pdf>.

[34] Ibid. [56].

[35] Ibid. Executive Summary.

[36] The law used to require at least two previous communications but this was amended by s. 36 of the Criminal Justice and Courts Act 2015.

[37] House of Commons Select Committee on Home Affairs, *Fifth Report*, 24 June 2003, Ch. 5: <www.publications.parliament.uk/pa/cm200203/cmselect/cmhaff/639/63908.htm>.

[38] BBC News, 'Priest "paid for girl's grooming"' *BBC News*, 15 May 2007 <http://news.bbc.co.uk/1/hi/england/merseyside/6657715.stm>; 'Child Protection Officer On Grooming Charge' *Police Oracle*, 29 April 2009 <https://www.policeoracle.com/news/Child-Protection-Officer-On-Grooming-Charge_19061.html>.

In 2010 the Court of Appeal had an opportunity to review grooming, albeit in relation to offline communications in *R v G*.[39]

Case study *R v G*

The case involved a man known to the family of the victim. He appeared to be a close family friend and had known the victim and her family for some time. It is reported the victim's family and his family intended to holiday together.

He was accused of assaulting the victim on five occasions and was convicted under s. 15. The appellant appealed this conviction arguing that the previous communication he had had with the child was of a non-sexual nature; all he had done was arrange to meet her, as a family friend, after school. In essence his appeal was based on the claim that the prior communication must have been undertaken with a view to instigate a sexual relationship for the s. 15 offence to be made out and in his case this was not true.

The decision of the court was given by Leveson LJ:

On the face of it, the fact that the description of the offence in the heading is 'meeting a child following sexual grooming etc' might be taken to suggest that the behaviour antecedent to any arranged meeting must itself be sexual in nature. The phrase 'sexual grooming', however, does not appear in the section and although the origin of the offence might have been a concern that paedophiles could use the internet to contact and groom children, the language of the provision is far wider than 'virtual' sexual contact. Thus, the only requirement prior to the intentional meeting during which A (over 18) intends to do anything to B (under 16) which, if carried out, would involve the commission by A of a relevant offence is meeting or communication 'on at least two occasions'. There is absolutely no requirement that either communication be sexual in nature . . . The aim of the statute is to penalise those who use a relationship which they have developed (whether innocently or otherwise) as a platform from which to launch sexual offending.[40]

He also took the opportunity to clarify the *mens rea* element:

The statute visualises the commission of an offence whether or not that meeting takes place; it is sufficient if, with the intention of meeting, A travels to B or B travels to A. In each case, however, A must intend to commit a relevant (sexual) offence. Thus, either when A travels to B, waits for B to arrive or at the moment of meeting, A's sexual intention must be proved. It is not enough that, during the course of a meeting, started without any such intention, A then decides to take advantage of the situation and commit an offence: the crime then will be the commission of or the attempt to commit that offence. The offence contained within s. 15 is not engaged.[41]

In the instant case he found that the offence had been made out and that the judge's direction to the jury had been correct, and he dismissed the appeal.

R v G tells us quite a lot about the scope of the offence. It is now clear that in essence it is about two things: (1) has the accused been in contact with the victim prior to the

[39] [2010] EWCA Crim 1693.
[40] Ibid. [16].
[41] Ibid. [17].

meeting in question? The nature of that contact is not important, and (2) what was the intent of the accused at the time they travelled to meet the victim?

21.2.2 **Sexual communication with a child**

As technology has advanced, the grooming offence has been less effective in dealing with online abuse of children. In particular, the advent of HD webcams and instant messaging services now means paedophiles can abuse children virtually and at a distance. In their 2013 report *Threat Assessment of Child Sexual Exploitation and Abuse* the Child Exploitation and Online Protection Centre identified online child sexual exploitation as one of four 'key threats' to children's safety online.[42] Children are becoming sexualized at an earlier age and can easily be fooled into thinking they are trading intimate images with someone close to their age. Paedophiles pose as children and once they receive a sexual image from a child will use this to blackmail the child into sending more, often more explicit, images. As the paedophile never travels, nor intends to travel, to meet the child they do not commit the offence of grooming. As a result, the NSPCC ran a campaign suggesting a new offence was needed to target paedophiles who communicate sexually with a child. The government considered the proposal and, at the WePROTECT summit in December 2014, the Prime Minister announced the intention to create a new offence in response to the campaign.[43]

The new law is to be found in s. 15A of the Sexual Offences Act 2003, as introduced by s. 67 of the Serious Crime Act 2015. This makes it an offence when an adult (being a person over 18) communicates with a child (being under 16) 'for the purpose of obtaining sexual gratification'. To commit the offence the communication must be sexual or is intended to encourage the child to make a communication that is sexual. That is, the communication must be of a sexual nature or it is trying to elicit a sexual communication (such as an indecent image) from the child. The maximum sentence under s. 15A is two years' imprisonment.[44] The provision is intended to criminalize the act of communicating with a child either directly in a sexual manner or with the intent to elicit sexual communications from the child. This was felt to be a necessary addition to the law for, although a paedophile who received a sexual image of a child would have committed an offence under the laws which regulate child abuse images (see 20.3), the act of soliciting such an image was not previously an offence. The new law came into effect in April 2017. The first reported case under the new offence was *R v Price (Wayne)*.[45] This involved a 35-year-old appellant who was convicted of two counts under s.15A of communicating with girls aged 13 and 14 via WhatsApp. The appeal was an appeal against sentence involving a number of more serious offences so unfortunately little about the operation of s.15A may be learned from this.

---

[42] CEOP, June 2013 <https://www.norfolklscb.org/wp-content/uploads/2015/03/CEOP_Threat-Assessment_CSE_JUN2013.pdf>.
[43] S Swinford, M Holehouse, and V Ward, 'New law will prevent paedophiles soliciting pictures from children', *The Telegraph*, 10 December 2014.
[44] Sexual Offences Act 2003, s. 15A(3)(b).
[45] [2018] EWCA Crim 1528.

21.2.3 **Harassment and stalking**

Harassment and stalking are rather different to grooming. Harassment is behaviour intended to disturb or upset, and, which is usually found threatening or disturbing, stalking is an aggravated form of harassment where victims finds themselves followed and continually contacted by the offender.[46] In harassment and stalking cases the victim is usually an adult, although in law it is possible to harass or stalk a minor. In a legal sense there is little distinction between the two and both are regulated by the Protection from Harassment Act 1997. This provides that a person 'must not pursue a course of conduct (a) which amounts to harassment of another, and (b) which he knows or ought to know amounts to harassment of the other'.[47] This raises the question of how one ought to know that their course of action amounts to harassment, given that many harassers/stalkers suffer from mental impairment? This is covered though by s. 1(2) which provides that 'the person whose course of conduct is in question ought to know that it amounts to harassment of another if a reasonable person in possession of the same information would think the course of conduct amounted to harassment of the other'.

If found guilty of harassment the offender may both be charged under s. 2, which can lead to a maximum six months' imprisonment, and may be issued with a restraining order under s. 5, which if breached, may lead to up to five years' imprisonment.[48] If the harassment is of such a nature as to put the victim in fear of violence on at least two occasions, then under s. 4 of the Act the offender may be charged with the aggravated offence of 'Putting People in Fear of Violence', this, like breaching a restraining order under s. 5, can lead to imprisonment of up to five years.

In addition to the provisions of the Protection from Harassment Act, online harassment (or cyberstalking as it is usually known) may also lead to prosecutions under the Malicious Communications Act 1988 or the Communications Act 2003. By s. 1 of the Malicious Communications Act 1988 it is an offence to send an indecent, offensive, or threatening letter, electronic communication, or other article to another person. This is a summary offence and as such may only lead to a maximum sentence of imprisonment of six months, as is the offence of improper use of the public electronic communications system under s. 127 of the Communications Act 2003, which makes it an offence to send, by means of a public electronic communication system, a message or other matter that is grossly offensive or of an indecent, obscene, or menacing character; or which is sent for the purpose of causing annoyance, inconvenience, or needless anxiety to another and which is known to be false. As both of these offences are summary in nature, and as the court cannot issue a restraining order unless the prosecution is brought under the Protection from Harassment Act, the authorities will tend to prosecute under the Protection from Harassment Act rather than the Malicious Communications Act or the Communications Act.[49]

---

[46] Stalking is an aggravated form of the harassment offence found in s.2A of the Protection from Harassment Act 1997.

[47] Protection from Harassment Act 1997, s. 1(1).

[48] Protection from Harassment Act 1997, s. 5(6).

[49] An extensive discussion of harassment and bullying on social network platforms can be found at 6.4.

21.3 **Cyberterrorism**

Cyberterrorism is now seen as part of the front line of the 'war on terror'. The concept of 'informational warfare', that is, states fighting campaigns using informational tools and weapons in addition to traditional ordinance, is well established and dates from at least the early 1990s.[50] The concept of cyberterrorism, that is, individuals or groups using the network capabilities of the information society to launch unlawful attacks and threats of attack against computers, networks, and the information stored therein to intimidate or coerce a government or its people in furtherance of political or social objectives, is newer, dating from around the turn of the millennium.[51] Although terrorist acts are clearly criminal, it was not clear initially that the types of activities carried out by cyberterrorists would be illegal. Cyberterrorists may carry out denial-of-service attacks, which as we saw at 19.3, were not clearly criminalized until 1 October 2008 when ss. 35–38 of the Police and Justice Act 2006 were brought into force; otherwise they may commit offences of unlawful access to data or unlawful modification of data under ss. 1–3 of the Computer Misuse Act 1990, but often they would simply publish materials in support of terrorist organizations or aims, or incite hatred. Prior to the passage of a series of anti-terror measures from 2000 onward this was not illegal unless the materials were in support of an organization proscribed by Sch.1 of the Prevention of Terrorism (Temporary Provisions) Act 1989, a list which predominantly listed Irish dissident groups in a time when the rising risk was from extremist Islamic organizations.

The law since, though, has changed substantially. The Terrorism Act 2000 introduced several new offences which could take place online. Prime among these were: possession of items for a terrorist purpose; possession of information or documents of a kind likely to be useful to a person committing or preparing an act of terrorism; and inciting terrorism overseas.

Section 57 provides that it is an offence to possess an article in circumstances which give rise to a reasonable suspicion that possession is for a purpose connected with the commission, preparation, or instigation of an act of terrorism. On conviction or indictment, this may lead to a maximum sentence of imprisonment of fifteen years.[52] The wording of the section, and the fact that there was a separate offence of possession of information or documents of a kind likely to be useful to a person committing or preparing an act of terrorism under s. 58, punishable by up to ten years in prison,[53] may lead one to suspect that by 'article' the framers of s. 57 had in mind items such as weapons, bomb-making equipment, training videos, or similar articles. Unfortunately, the definition of 'article' found in s. 121 is extremely vague, defining it simply as 'includes substance and any other thing'. This has led the authorities to attempt to prosecute possession of information or data under s. 57.

---

[50] Information Warfare was first introduced in a formal sense in 1992 in the US Department of Defense Directive TS3600.1. See P Kaomea, S Hearold, and W Page, 'Beyond Security: A Data Quality Perspective on Defensive Information Warfare' *MIT Total Data Quality Management Program Working Papers* 1994 <http://web.mit.edu/tdqm/papers/other/kaomea.html>.

[51] This definition is taken from one of the early discussions of cyberterrorism before the Special Oversight Panel on Terrorism of the US House of Representatives Committee on Armed Services which took place on 23 May 2000. It is taken from the testimony of Dorothy Denning, then Professor of Computer Science at Georgetown University.

[52] Terrorism Act 2000, s. 57(4)(a).

[53] Terrorism Act 2000, s. 58(4)(a).

In the first case of this type, *R v M*,[54] the prosecution claimed that possession of data stored electronically on computer hard drives or CDs was capable of being an 'article' under s. 57. The prosecution's case was that the s. 57 articles were electronic storage devices such as hard drives, CDs, and DVDs, a USB storage device, and a video recording, as well as two documents. At the preliminary hearing, the defendants submitted that 'data' was not an article arguing that the prosecution's interpretation of s. 57 made s. 58(1)(b) completely redundant and made nearly all of s. 58(1)(a) redundant. The defendants argued that the only conduct which would be caught by s. 58 if the prosecution's interpretation was allowed would be collecting information but not writing it down. The Court of Appeal allowed the appeal, finding that the issue was whether the items listed were 'articles'. They found that CDs and computer hard drives holding electronic data were capable of being articles within the meaning of s. 57, but that it was clear that Parliament had laid down a different regime for documents and records under s. 58 and 'articles' under s. 57.

This decision which seemed to sensibly delineate the difference between 'articles' and 'data' or 'information', was though unfortunately not followed in the later case of *R v Rowe* in which a five-judge bench found *R v M* to be *per incuriam*.[55] Mr Rowe had been arrested in possession of a notebook which contained mortar instructions and a substitution code which listed components of explosives and places of a type susceptible to terrorist bombing. The prosecution case was that the appellant was shortly to embark on a terrorist venture and that the notebook and the code were held for terrorist purposes. Mr Rowe was charged and found guilty of possession of a terrorist article under s. 57. Following the decision in *R v M* he appealed against conviction. On this occasion the Court of Appeal refused his appeal. The judgment of the Court was given by Lord Phillips CJ:

> There is undoubtedly an overlap between section 57 and 58, but it is not correct to suggest that if documents and records constitute articles for the purpose of section 57, section 58 is almost superfluous. Collecting information, which falls within section 58 alone, may well not involve making a record of the information. Equally a person who possesses information likely to be useful to a person committing or preparing an act of terrorism may well not be in possession of it for a purpose connected with the commission, preparation or instigation of an act of terrorism. Sections 57 and 58 are indeed dealing with different aspects of activities relating to terrorism. Section 57 is dealing with possessing articles for the purpose of terrorist acts. Section 58 is dealing with collecting or holding information that is of a kind likely to be useful to those involved in acts of terrorism. Section 57 includes a specific intention, section 58 does not. These differences between the two sections are rational features of a statute whose aims include the prohibition of different types of support for and involvement, both direct and indirect, in terrorism. There is no basis for the conclusion that Parliament intended to have a completely separate regime for documents and records from that which applies to other articles. For these reasons we have concluded that the decision in *R v M* was based on false assumptions and false analysis and that it was wrong.[56]

This suggests that possession of data for publication on a website or some other forum may amount to a s.57 offence if that data or information is of a nature as to be directly associated with a specific terrorist purpose. The nature of s. 57, and s. 58, has though arguably been changed by new provisions introduced by Part I of the Terrorism Act 2006 and we shall return to this analysis.

[54] [2007] EWCA Crim 298.
[55] [2007] QB 975.
[56] Ibid. 985–6.

The other major provision of the Terrorism Act 2000 which may apply to online activities is the s. 59 offence of inciting terrorism overseas. This formed the focus of one of the most high-profile cyberterrorism cases in the UK to date. The case involved a group of young men who operated a network of at least thirty-two websites and a number of chat forums dedicated to fighting a Jihadist cause, in particular in Iraq. According to evidence:

> the sites included assertions that it was the duty of Moslems to fight armed Jihad against Jews, crusaders, apostates and their supporters in all Muslim countries and that it was the duty of every Muslim to fight and kill them wherever they are, civilian or military. There were also films, much of it emanating from Al-Qaeda in Iraq, posted to the websites showing very explicit acts of terrorist murder, including the beheading of civilian hostages, attacks on the police, government officials and on coalition forces in Iraq. In the internet chat forums individuals disposed to join the insurgency were provided with routes by which to travel into Iraq and manuals of weapons and explosives were requested.[57]

Those involved included Younes Tsouli, a Moroccan-born UK resident who called himself Irhabi_007; 'Irhabi' being the Arabic word for terrorist, and '007' a reference to the fictional secret agent James Bond. Tsouli had been among the most-wanted supporters of terrorist activity of UK and US law enforcement agents. All involved were charged under s. 59 for inciting terrorists to commit murder overseas. On 4 July 2007, after two months at trial, Tsouli and his co-defendants Waseem Mughal and Tariq Al-Daour pleaded guilty to 'inciting another person to commit an act of terrorism wholly or partly outside the UK which would, if committed in England and Wales, constitute murder' and admitted to conspiring together and with others to defraud banks, credit card companies, and charge card companies to pay for the hosting of the websites and chat rooms. Tsouli was sentenced to ten years' imprisonment, Mughal to seven and a half years, and Al-Daour to six and half years.[58]

The Attorney General referred these sentences to the Court of Appeal for being unduly lenient, and on 18 December 2007 the sentences of all three men were increased: Tsouli's sentence was increased to sixteen years, Mughal to twelve years, and Al-Daour twelve years.[59] In giving the judgment of the court Gage LJ noted that:

> The offenders' conduct involved the preplanning of a sophisticated and intricate misuse of computers. Its execution was funded by the proceeds of fraud and was carried out with no little technological skills . . . their purpose was to facilitate publication of material on the website and in the chat room forums, exhorting in strong terms others to participate in acts of extreme violence on a very large scale. The material which was published leaves no doubt about what was intended. It was also published in the context of the armed conflict in Iraq involving, as it did, British and American soldiers. Their conduct covered a comparatively short period. However, we infer that but for their arrest their conduct would have covered a much longer period.[60]

The use of the Terrorism Act 2000 to prosecute those operating terrorist websites and chat forums has now arguably been superseded by Part I of the Terrorism Act 2006. By s. 1(2) it is an offence to publish a statement or to cause another to publish a statement

---

[57] Attorney General's References (Nos. 85, 86, and 87 of 2007) [2007] EWCA Crim 3300.
[58] Ibid. [4].
[59] Ibid. [41].
[60] Ibid. [40].

which is likely to be understood, by some or all of the members of the public to whom it is published, as a direct or indirect encouragement or other inducement to them to the commission, preparation, or instigation of acts of terrorism or Convention offences, if at the time it is published it is intended to encourage members of the public to be directly or indirectly encouraged or induced to commit, prepare, or instigate acts of terrorism. This offence is punishable on indictment with a prison sentence of up to seven years. In addition, there is a separate offence under s. 2 of dissemination of terrorist publications. This makes it an offence to distribute, sell, circulate, offer for sale, or *transmit electronically* material intended to encourage members of the public to be directly or indirectly encouraged or induced to commit, prepare, or instigate acts of terrorism. Like s. 1, the penalty for such an offence may be seven years' imprisonment if charged on indictment. Section 3 lays out specific provisions to regulate the publication of terrorist materials via the internet.

Due to the risk of a website being hijacked or defaced without the knowledge of the operator of that site, or of comments made in an unmoderated forum being published without the forum operator's knowledge, there is a notification procedure. The procedure requires that a constable gives notice, either in person or by sending it by recorded delivery to the last recorded address of the 'relevant person' (usually the operator of the site),[61] which declares that in the opinion of the constable giving it, the statement or the article or record is unlawfully terrorism-related.[62] The notice requires the relevant person to secure that the statement or the article or record, so far as it is so related, is not available to the public or is modified so as no longer to be so related;[63] warns the relevant person that a failure to comply with the notice within 2 working days will result in the statement, or the article or record, being regarded as having his endorsement;[64] and explains how he may become liable by virtue of the notice if the statement, or the article or record, becomes available to the public after he has complied with the notice by republication elsewhere.[65] If the recipient of the notice fails to take steps to remove the material or render it inaccessible to the public within two working days, then under s. 3(2) the statement is deemed to be 'endorsed by the relevant person',[66] this allows for criminal prosecution under either or both of ss.1 and 2. Part I came into force on 13 April 2006[67] and has, perhaps unsurprisingly, been the subject of a number of reviews by the appellate courts.

The case of *R v Zafar* allowed the Court of Appeal to consider the interplay between s. 57 of the 2000 Act and Part I of the 2006 Act.[68] *Zafar* is the conclusion of the *R v M/Rowe* line of analysis discussed earlier. The defendants here were the same ones in *R v M* (that being an earlier interlocutory appeal). All had been charged with the possession of articles for a purpose connected with the commission, preparation, or instigation of an

---

[61] Terrorism Act 2006, s. 4.
[62] Terrorism Act 2006, s. 3(3)(a).
[63] Terrorism Act 2006, s. 3(3)(b).
[64] Terrorism Act 2006, s. 3(3)(c).
[65] Terrorism Act 2006, s. 3(3)(d).
[66] There are defences under s. 3(5) and (6) when a statement is republished without the knowledge or assistance of the original publisher.
[67] Terrorism Act 2006 (Commencement No. 1) Order 2006, SI 2006/1013.
[68] *R v Zafar* [2008] QB 810. It should be noted that *Zafar* has been subject to a mildly disapproving review from the House of Lords in *R v G* [2009] UKHL 13. The decision was not however overruled and the principles discussed in this text are still unmoved by the *R v G* decision.

act of terrorism under s. 57, the articles in question being 'documents, compact discs or computer hard drives on which material had been electronically stored. The material included ideological propaganda as well as communications between the defendants and others which the prosecution alleged showed a settled plan under which the defendants would travel to Pakistan to receive training and thereafter commit a terrorist act or acts in Afghanistan.'[69] Following the decision in *Rowe*, the Recorder of London gave a further ruling that he would be bound by that decision. That ruling was upheld in a second interlocutory appeal,[70] and at a subsequent trial the accused were found guilty on almost all charges.[71] All appealed against conviction. Their appeal was upheld with Lord Phillips CJ again giving the judgment of the court. A crucial part of the court's deliberation was how Part I of the 2006 Act could be read alongside s. 57 of the 2000 Act. Applying the extremely expansive interpretation of s. 57 found in *Rowe* seemed to suggest Part I of the 2006 Act was unnecessary. Here Lord Phillips noted that 'Parliament, did not envisage that [s. 57] would extend to possessing propaganda for the purpose of incitement to terrorist acts. That belief is strengthened by the fact that Parliament considered it desirable to legislate in relation to possessing propaganda with the intention of inducing acts of terrorism by section 2(2)(f) of the Terrorism Act 2006.'[72]

Where does this leave the interplay between s. 57 of the 2000 Act and Part I of the 2006 Act? It appears that if one possesses documents, including digital data, with the intent to use them to instigate a *specific* terrorist attack (i.e. what may be defined as preparatory materials). this will cause a prosecution to be brought under s. 57. If though the materials are rather in the form of propaganda materials, then it falls within the scope of Part I of the 2006 Act. However. against this is the further confusion that the authority of Attorney General's References (Nos. 85, 86, and 87 of 2007) still applies also. This means that if one operates a website which promotes or supports terrorist activity in the widest sense, one would probably be charged under Part I of the 2006 Act. If one offers support or advice, including instruction or maps, via a website or other forum to individuals planning a particular terrorist attack, one would probably be charged under s. 57. If, though, as Younes Tsouli and his co-defendants did, one operates a website or forum which provides advice and encouragement to terrorists overseas to commit a terrorist act, such as murder or endangerment to life, one may be charged under s. 59 which allows for sentences up to a mandatory life sentence.

The more recent case of *R v Brown* dealt with the question of whether the Terrorism Acts 2000 and 2006 were an unreasonable restriction on the fundamental right to free expression.[73] Mr Brown sought leave to appeal his conviction under both s. 58 of the Terrorism Act 2000 and s. 2 of the Terrorism Act 2006. He had for some time been selling via his website the famous 1971 publication *The Anarchists Cookbook*, a publication which details bomb-making recipes as well as recipes for toxins. He accepted that the publication could be useful to terrorists but argued that his motivation for selling it was commercial rather than ideological, pointing out that the terms and conditions of his website bound buyers to only use it for lawful purposes. After being arrested and

---

[69]   Ibid. 816–17.
[70]   *R v M (No. 2)* [2007] 3 All ER 53.
[71]   [2008] QB 810, 818.
[72]   Ibid. 822.
[73]   [2011] EWCA Crim 2751.

sentenced to three years' imprisonment Mr Brown sought to appeal against his conviction and sentence. He argued that s. 2 and s. 58 breached his fundamental right to free expression. The decision of the court was given by the Lord Chief Justice who found that neither provision infringed on Mr Brown's right to free expression. In relation to s. 58 he noted that:

> In relation to the offence created by section 58 of the 2000 Act, a statutory defence is provided: that there was a reasonable excuse for the applicant's action or possession of information likely to be useful to an individual committing or preparing an act of terrorism. In other words, the prohibition in section 58 is not itself absolute, once the offence created by section 58 is not an offence of strict liability. The actions which would otherwise constitute the offence may be excusable. The question whether the excuse is reasonable on the basis of the exercise of the right to freedom of speech or freedom of expression may be left to the jury to be decided as a question of fact in the individual case.[74]

In relation to s. 2, the answer was similar:

> it is difficult to see how a criminal act of distribution or circulation of a terrorist publication with the specific intent, or in the frame of mind expressly required as an essential ingredient of this offence to encourage or assist acts of terrorism, can be saved by reference to the principle of freedom of speech, unless that principle is absolute, which, as we have indicated, it is not.[75]

The Court of Appeal recently revisited this issue in *R v Ali (Humza)*.[76] The appellant had been convicted under s. 2 of disseminating, via a chat group, ISIS propaganda videos showing prisoners confessing sins against IS prior to being executed, as well as an ISIS recruitment video. Mr Ali denied that the videos were terrorist publications and he denied having the necessary state of mind when sending them. He asserted that he was ignorant of the content of the execution videos and said that he had only watched the opening 2 minutes of the 11-minute propaganda video. He had thought that the video simply concerned Islam and the situation in Syria, and he had sent it in order to raise awareness.[77] He argued that the judge in summing up had not protected his Art. 10 right sufficiently. The court disagreed, finding that:

> in relation to Counts 2 and 3 (the execution videos), where the appellant claimed ignorance of the contents of the videos, it is hard to see how his Article 10 rights were engaged in respect of those videos. As to Count 4 (the propaganda video) where the appellant's case was that he had only viewed the opening part of the video and thought that it concerned Islam and the situation in Syria, and that he had sent it in order to raise awareness, his Article 10 rights were potentially engaged. However, his factual defence in this respect was left to the jury and was rejected. For these reasons, we are unpersuaded that there was, as asserted, a failure adequately to take account of the appellant's Article 10 rights.[78]

These outcomes are hardly surprising outcomes given Art. 10(2) of the European Convention on Human Rights:

> The exercise of these freedoms, since it carries with it duties and responsibilities, may be subject to such formalities, conditions, restrictions or penalties as are prescribed by law and are

---

[74] Ibid. [22].
[75] Ibid. [23].
[76] [2018] EWCA Crim 547.
[77] Ibid. [12].
[78] Ibid. [21]–[22].

necessary in a democratic society, in the interests of national security, territorial integrity or public safety, for the prevention of disorder or crime, for the protection of health or morals, for the protection of the reputation or rights of others, for preventing the disclosure of information received in confidence, or for maintaining the authority and impartiality of the judiciary.

Finally we have the Supreme Court case of *R v Gul*.[79] This is a case at the very heart of the Terrorism Acts; the definition of terrorism itself. Mr Gul had uploaded videos to a number of websites, including YouTube, showing attacks by al-Qaeda, the Taliban, and other proscribed groups on military targets in Chechnya, and on the coalition forces in Iraq and in Afghanistan, the use of improvised explosive devices against coalition forces, excerpts from martyrdom videos, and clips of attacks on civilians, including the 9/11 attack on New York. According to the report of the case 'these videos were accompanied by commentaries praising the bravery, and martyrdom, of those carrying out the attacks, and encouraging others to emulate them.'[80] Mr Gul was charged under s. 2 of the 2006 Act. He argued that the provision did not apply to these videos as they showed a justified use of force by freedom fighters resisting occupation of their country. He particularly argued three claims:

(1) The first is that the 2000 Act, like the 2006 Act, was intended, at least in part, to give effect to the UK's international treaty obligations, and the concept of terrorism in international law does not extend to military attacks by a non-state armed group against state, or inter-governmental organization, armed forces in the context of a non-international armed conflict, and that this limitation should be implied into the definition in section 1 of the 2000 Act;

(2) it would be wrong to read the 2000 or 2006 Acts as criminalizing in this country an act abroad, unless that act would be regarded as criminal by international law norms; and

(3) as a matter of domestic law and quite apart from international law considerations, some qualifications must be read into the very wide words of section 1 of the 2000 Act.[81]

The court, in the joint judgment of Lords Neuberger and Judge, found against Mr Gul. In response to his first claim the court noted that 'there is no accepted norm in international law as to what constitutes terrorism'[82] and that while it is true that some other provisions of the 2000 and 2006 Acts give effect to treaties that do not extend to insurgent attacks on military forces in non-international armed conflicts, there was no reason why the United Kingdom could not go further in the 2000 Act than the treaties had. And even if those treaties had intended to limit the definition of terrorism that they applied, that would only affect the particular provisions of the 2000 Act that implemented those treaties.[83] This claim was thus refused. In response to the second claim, the court found that this claim was irrelevant as 'the present case does not involve a defendant who has committed acts, which are said to be offences, abroad: the

---

[79] [2013] UKSC 64.
[80] Ibid. [2].
[81] Ibid. [24].
[82] Ibid. [44].
[83] Ibid. [54].

activities said to be offences were committed in the UK—and by a UK citizen'.[84] This only left the final, domestic, claim. Here the court found that:

> unless it is established that the natural meaning of the legislation conflicts with the European Convention on Human Rights (which is not suggested) or any other international obligation of the United Kingdom (which were considered and rejected), our function is to interpret the meaning of the definition in its statutory, legal and practical context. We agree with the wide interpretation favoured by the prosecution: it accords with the natural meaning of the words used in section 1(1)(b) of the 2000 Act, and, while it gives the words a concerningly wide meaning, there are good reasons for it.[85]

In all, this is not a terribly surprising outcome. One man's terrorist is another man's freedom fighter and in terms of the rule of law we cannot allow individuals to interpret definitions to suit their own ends. The seriousness of Mr Gul's challenge, particularly the international law aspects of it, may be seen in the fact that the case made it to the Supreme Court. This was an extremely important issue and the very wide definition of terrorism given in the Acts may be rightly criticized, but, given the high level of sophistication of modern terrorist groups such as the Islamic State, which uses social media and online video to great effect, it is perhaps no surprise that the Supreme Court upheld the wide definition. This issue will continue to press lawmakers and judges in the coming years as recruitment videos for groups like Islamic State continue to be posted online. The problem is that there can sometimes be a very fine line between protected religious speech and unprotected speech which promotes or supports terrorist activity, and the courts have to ensure that while restricting and controlling the latter they do not inadvertently and illegally restrict the former.

21.4 **The Convention on Cybercrime**

A common theme across several of the examples of online criminal activity we have examined in this section (hacking and viruses; indecency, pornography, and obscenity; fraud and identity fraud; and also cyberterrorism) is that with a truly global network criminals in any part of the world can impact on any other part of the world. Criminal law is the one area where the warnings of the cyberlibertarian school have been proven substantively correct. There are of course solutions to some of these problems, including the installation of filters, such as the IWF/Cleanfeed filter and localizing the offence as the UK has done by outlawing the possession of extreme pornography and NPPICs. But to deal with the underlying problem of child abuse images being produced in such diverse places as the Ukraine, the US, and Vietnam, or fraud being perpetrated in Nigeria, China, and Russia, we need to harmonize law enforcement provisions and seek measures to reduce jurisdictional disputes. To date though international cooperation has been limited, with only one substantial international convention being agreed, despite some twenty-five years of discussion.

Only the Council of Europe Convention on Cybercrime[86] attempts to harmonize international cybercrime laws. As of 10 November 2018 the treaty had been signed

---

[84] Ibid. [56].
[85] Ibid. [38].
[86] Council of Europe (n. 16).

by forty-six Council of Europe states, including the UK, and four non-European states.[87] It has been ratified by and has entered into force in sixty-one states, including the US and the UK.[88] The substantive provisions are all found in Chapter II, Section 1 and fall into five subsections: offences against data and systems;[89] computer-related offences;[90] content-related offences;[91] offences related to infringement of copyright;[92] and ancillary offences.[93] In addition, the Convention provides for procedural systems to support the enforcement of the substantive provisions. Mutual assistance and cooperation provisions found in Arts. 23 and 25 require states parties to cooperate in the investigation and evidence gathering of convention crimes reported to them by other states partners: or to put it another way, as favoured by critics of the convention:

> The treaty requires that [domestic] governments help enforce other countries' 'cybercrime' laws—even if the act being prosecuted is not illegal [domestically] . . . That means that countries that have laws limiting free speech on the Net could oblige [local law enforcement] to uncover the identities of anonymous [domestic] critics, or monitor their communications on behalf of foreign governments. [Domestic] ISPs would be obliged to obey other jurisdiction's requests to log their users' behaviour without due process, or compensation.[94]

Although there is some element of truth in these criticisms of the Convention, critics have blown the risk out of proportion. Article 25(4) states that 'except as otherwise specifically provided in articles in this chapter, mutual assistance shall be subject to the conditions provided for by the law of the requested Party or by applicable mutual assistance treaties, including the grounds on which the requested Party may refuse cooperation'. This means that the requested state can refuse a mutual assistance request where it exceeds the agreed parameters of the requested state except in specific cases set out, mostly in Art. 27, which itself provides safeguards.[95]

From a UK perspective the Convention changes little, except in the area of cooperation. Even before implementation, the UK fulfilled all the substantive

---

[87] These are: Canada, Japan, South Africa, and the US.

[88] Beyond the signatories the Convention has entered into force in Argentina, Australia, Cape Verde, Chile, Costa Rica, the Dominican Republic, Israel, Mauritius, Morocco, Panama, Paraguay, Philippines, Senegal, Sri Lanka. and Togo by accession.

[89] These are: Art. 2: illegal access (hacking); Art. 3 illegal interception of data; Art. 4: data interference (criminal damage and viruses); Art. 5 system interference (denial of service); and Art. 6 production or use of a device for any of the aforementioned purposes.

[90] These are: Art. 7: computer-related forgery and Art. 8 computer-related fraud.

[91] This is a single offence under Art. 9 of production, distribution, or possession of child pornography.

[92] This is a single Article, Art. 10 which requires signatories to cooperate in the detection and prosecution of criminal copyright infringement under the Paris Act of 1971, the Rome Convention, and the WIPO Copyright and Phonograms and Performances Treaties.

[93] These are: Art. 11 attempts and aiding and abetting; Art. 12 corporate liability; and Art. 13 sanctions and measures.

[94] D O'Brien, 'The World's Worst Internet Laws Sneaking Through the Senate', *Electronic Frontier Foundation* 3 August 2006 <https://www.eff.org/deeplinks/2006/08/worlds-worst-internet-laws-sneaking-through-senate>.

[95] By Art. 27(4) 'The requested Party may, in addition to the grounds for refusal established in Art. 25(4), refuse assistance if: (a) the request concerns an offence which the requested Party considers a political offence or an offence connected with a political offence, or (b) it considers that execution of the request is likely to prejudice its sovereignty, security, *ordre public* or other essential interests.'

requirements of the Convention through domestic provisions that was partly the catalyst for the reforms to the Computer Misuse Act found in the Police and Justice Act 2006. Even the procedural elements of Art. 25 change little in the UK as previously (and indeed currently) that was/is met by the mutual assistance provisions of the Crime (International Cooperation) Act 2003. As we have seen repeatedly in this section, greater cooperation in these fields can only be positive despite the concerns of the EFF.

21.5 **Conclusion**

As with all aspects of life the information society offers opportunities for criminal activity to those attracted to that lifestyle. It also offers challenges to law enforcement authorities, courts, and legislators. The challenges are on several levels. The first was that the information society both afforded opportunities for new and unique harms, such as hacking, denial-of-service, and the writing and distribution of viruses and Trojans. Second, it afforded new ways of committing old harms such as the production and distribution of obscene, harmful, violent, or abusive content, fraud and theft, and harassment and stalking. These were issues which called for the law to be updated and the UK government has been extremely busy over the last twenty years in implementing the necessary changes to the law found in the Computer Misuse Act 1990, the Protection of Children Act 1978, the Police and Justice Act 2006, the Terrorism Acts 2000 and 2006, the Protection from Harassment Act 1997, and the Criminal Justice and Immigration Act 2008, among others. Our laws are among the most well-developed for dealing with the threats of e-crimes of all varieties: computer misuse crimes, content-related crimes, and computer-enabled crimes. The next challenge was designing effective law enforcement structures to deal with the challenges of cybercrime. Here too the UK was an early adapter, setting up the National Hi-Tech Crime Unit in 2001 to investigate computer fraud, hacking, data theft, and network attacks, as well as supporting the work of the Internet Watch Foundation in dealing with content-related crime, in particular images of child abuse. Many of these operations have now been assumed under the umbrella of the National Crime Agency with the National Hi-Tech Crime Unit becoming the NCA's National Cyber Crime Unit, while the Child Exploitation and Online Protection Centre, created in 2006 to work with the IWF and Scotland Yard's Child Abuse Investigation Command, also comes within the NCA framework as CEOP Command. We therefore have a highly integrated investigation and evidence-gathering organization in the NCA. We also give leadership on international cooperation. The UK leads the way in forging international partnerships in dealing with child abuse images, and the NCA's forerunner SOCA has provided vital leadership in the international campaign to deal with Nigerian e-fraud. We have also finally ratified the Cybercrime Convention, meaning that we are now in full partnership with those other countries that have ratified and enacted the Convention.

TEST QUESTIONS

Question 1

According to the House of Commons e-crime report, 'the majority of cybercrimes could be prevented by better awareness by the user'. Do you agree? Provide examples from the crimes we have discussed in this chapter.

Question 2

Is the UK law on grooming sufficiently robust to adequately protect children online? Does the law of harassment adequately protect adults?

Question 3

Discuss critically the decision of the Court of Appeal in Attorney General's References (Nos. 85, 86, and 87 of 2007). Were the sentences out of proportion to the harm? In particular, are there any grounds for mitigation on principles of freedom of expression?

FURTHER READING

Books

J Clough, *Principles of Cybercrime* (2nd edn, CUP 2015)

A Gillespie, *Cybercrime: Key Issues and Debates* (Routledge 2015)

D Wall, *Policing Cybercrime: Networked and Social Media Technologies and the Challenges for Policing* (Routledge 2014)

M Yar and K Steinmetz, *Cybercrime and Society* (3rd edn, Sage 2019)

Chapters and articles

A Gillespie, 'Cyber-bullying and Harassment of Teenagers: The Legal Response' [2006] *Journal of Social Welfare and Family Law* 213

A Gillespie, 'Cyberstalking and the law: A response to Neil MacEwan' (2013) *Criminal Law Review* 38

B Mann, 'Social networking websites—a concatenation of impersonation, denigration, sexual aggressive solicitation, cyber-bullying or happy slapping videos' [2009] *International Journal of Law and Information Technology* 252

H Harrison Dinniss, 'The Threat of Cyber Terrorism and What International Law Should (Try To) Do about It' (2018) 19 *Georgetown Journal of International Affairs* 43

A Gillespie, 'Cyber-bullying and Harassment of Teenagers: The Legal Response' [2006] *Journal of Social Welfare and Family Law* 213

PART VI

Data privacy

The financial value of data is such that individual privacy is often set aside in the pursuit of commercial advantage. The information society makes it easy for individuals to be monitored and tracked: how much data are we willing to trade for convenience? How does the law strike a balance between data privacy and data brokering? How is the law in this area developing?

22

Data protection: the legal framework

As has been the theme throughout this book, the information society divorces identity from the physical person, and as more of our everyday lives are ordered digitally (from electronic mail, to social media activity, to online shopping and banking) we increasingly use proxy data to identify us. In addition to our proxy identity, sometimes labelled as your 'data self', we generate vast amounts of personal information as we 'surf' or trail through this digital environment. By our actions we reveal our location, including where we live and where we work; we reveal our preferences for food, clothing, entertainment, and travel; we even reveal our sexuality, our family connections, our loves, and our religious beliefs. We can reveal our innermost secrets: do we support or object to a right to choose an abortion? Are we a remainer or a leaver? Do we support or object to open borders and free movement of persons?

The risks of misapplication, mishandling, or misprocessing of data in this 'data-driven' environment cannot be understated. Risks extend from something as simple as failing to secure data, a charge laid before the UK government at several points during 2007 as they in quick succession lost data relating to 25 million child benefit recipients,[1] 3 million candidates for the driving theory test,[2] 168,000 NHS patient records,[3] and 40,000 housing benefit claimants;[4] to bias and errors caused by data that is inaccurate, incomplete, or out of date, leading to an unfair outcome in computerized (or even human) decision-making processes.[5] Or more simply with money to be made from data mining, our data may be packaged and sold, or otherwise transferred against our wishes, to third parties for purposes such as profiling and marketing.[6] These (and more) risks will form the focus of this chapter and the next.

---

[1] For a full discussion of the affair see K Poynter, *Review of information security at HM Revenue and Customs: Final Report* (HMSO 2008) <https://ntouk.files.wordpress.com/2015/06/poynter_review250608.pdf>.

[2] H Mulholland, 'Details of 3m learner drivers lost, government admits', *The Guardian*, 17 December 2007.

[3] D Rose, 'More personal data lost as nine NHS trusts admit security breaches', *The Times*, 24 December 2007.

[4] J Ungoed-Thomas, 'More financial data discs lost', *The Times*, 2 December 2007.

[5] Famously lampooned in the 'Little Britain' sketch 'computer says no'. For those on the receiving end of a computerized decision-making process though there is little to laugh about. See J Bing, 'Code, Access and Control' in M Klang and A Murray (eds.), *Human Rights in the Digital Age* (Routledge-Cavendish 2005).

[6] A Daly, *Private Power, Online Information Flows and EU Law: Mind The Gap* (Hart 2016); P Bernal, *Internet Privacy Rights: Rights to Protect Autonomy* (CUP 2014).

22.1 **Digitization, data, and the regulation of data industries**

Today digital information is commercially more valuable than analogue information as it may be manipulated and processed in conjunction with other data to reveal hidden patterns and truths, a process known as data analytics. As a result, a multibillion-pound industry had grown up around this new product.

A number of data analytics companies gather data to act as an adviser to others. An example of such a company would be Experian. Experian are the world's largest credit reference and scoring agency. They ingather data from a variety of sources such as records held by lenders, the electoral roll, and the list of County Court judgments. They then use this data to give a numerical score to the risk of lending to an individual. All credit agencies from mortgage lenders and credit card issuers to local shops which offer credit, use their services, or the services of one of their competitors, to determine whether to extend credit to individuals.

Other companies gather data to improve their service to their customers. Examples of such schemes include customer loyalty cards such as the Tesco Clubcard and the Nectar Card. They gather data on customer buying habits and allow the retailer to tailor their stock and staffing levels accordingly, as well as offering customers rewards such as discount vouchers and promoting to customers related goods and services.

A third type of company carries out market research using gathered data with a view to selling their insights, or tailored advertising products, to clients. These include traditional market research companies like Brand Institute and Neilsen, but more likely today will be the global internet giants; Google being a leading provider in this area. Google gathers vast amounts of search and passive tracking data and then sells specialist online advertising (Google Ads) which are much more focused on the target market than traditional media advertising. By offering this service Google has become the largest media advertising company globally, the only other company even coming close to Google's ad pull being Facebook.[7]

Fourth, there are companies who act as information brokers for others. These companies gather information and sell it on as packaged data for the purposes of product development, advertising, and promotion, or other purposes. This may include social networking sites such as Facebook, mobile network operators like Vodafone, or hardware suppliers like Apple or Samsung. Or it may be specialist information gatherers such as so-called tracking companies, like Datalogix or Acxiom, who gather data on internet habits and then sell that information on to third parties.

Finally, there are the organizations on the fringes of what is legal. These are groups that gather data to create massive databases of customer details including mailing lists, email lists, and phone lists. These are then used for direct mailing or cold calling to try to sell goods and services. Some organizations involved in this industry are responsible and act legally, such as Marketing File, Electric Marketing, or even BT. Others though are less responsible and exist at the fringes of what is required under the General Data Protection Regulation and the Data Protection Act.

---

[7] J Kollewe, 'Google and Facebook bring in one-fifth of global ad revenue', *The Guardian*, 2 May 2017.

All these companies want personal data. It is the lifeblood of their operations but it is costly to gather and process. As a result, a number of digital processes have been developed to make it easier and cheaper to ingather and store such data, but such automation of data gathering risks our data privacy since computers lack the ability to evaluate the nature of data or its sensitivity. Thus, a strict legal regime is required to regulate the industry as a whole. This regime ensures that when data is gathered individuals are aware of what data is being gathered, why it is being gathered, and how it will be stored. It ensures that there are standards within the industry to ensure data is accurate, up to date, secure, and fairly processed. Further, it ensures that if sold or transferred, data remains protected and cannot be sold or transferred for reasons unconnected with its original gathering. Finally, there is an enforcement procedure to ensure all these things are done and that there is oversight of the industry as a whole.

22.1.1 The changing face of data protection laws in Europe: the GDPR

There is a long history of data protection legislation in Europe dating back to the *Hessisches Datenschutzgesetz*, the original data protection law passed in the German state of Hesse in 1970, and the Swedish *Datalagen*, the first national data protection law, passed in 1973. In more recent history European data protection law was first fully harmonized as a result of the Data Protection Directive 1995[8] which was given effect in the UK through the Data Protection Act 1998.

Recently however European data protection law has been comprehensively reviewed and modernized. When the Charter of Fundamental Rights of the European Union[9] was agreed in 2000 EU citizens gained a new fundamental right: the right to the protection of personal data concerning him or her.[10] When the EU Charter formally became part of the EU's legal settlement in December 2009,[11] the view from the European Commission was that the state of data protection law at that time did not meet the fundamental right standard. As a result in 2012 they issued a citizen factsheet explaining why reform of data protection law was necessary:

> the current rules need to be modernised—they were introduced when the Internet was still in its infancy. Rapid technological developments and globalisation have brought new challenges for data protection. With social networking sites, cloud computing, location-based services and smart cards, we leave digital traces with every move we make. In this 'brave new data world' we need a robust set of rules. The EU's data protection reform will make sure our rules are future-proof and fit for the digital age.[12]

To implement the changes necessary EU Commission Vice-President Viviane Reding published specific proposals to reform European data protection rules, including a draft for a new Data Protection Regulation.[13]

---

[8] Directive 95/46/EC.
[9] 2000/C 364/01.
[10] Art. 8(1).
[11] Although agreed in 2000 the Charter did not become legally binding until the entry into force of the Treaty of Lisbon, in December 2009. See 2012/C 326/02.
[12] <http://ec.europa.eu/justice/data-protection/document/review2012/factsheets/1_en.pdf>.
[13] COM(2012) 11 final (Brussels, 25 January 2012).

The need for a new framework was apparent: the Data Protection Directive, passed in 1995, had been drafted and negotiated in the period 1992–1995. This was a time before the modern internet, smartphones, social media platforms, and major data corporations such as Google and Facebook. The CJEU had been forced to sometimes take expansive and creative interpretations of the law to make it fit for the modern world.[14] In addition, as a Directive the law had been subject to divergent interpretation, both in implementing legislation and by domestic courts, meaning that it was no longer the unified regime it was intended to be. The General Data Protection Regulation (GDPR) was to correct this but was subject to extensive delay and renegotiation. An almost complete version of the text was agreed in December 2015, following the successful conclusion of six months of trialogue negotiations between the European Commission, the European Parliament, and the Council of the European Union.[15] The text was finally agreed and adopted in May 2016 and came into force two years later on 25 May 2018 as the General Data Protection Regulation (GDPR).[16]

The regulation harmonizes and extends our data protection rights. The real strength of the new law though is the way it was enacted. As a regulation rather than a directive it creates a binding legal regime for all EU member states, sweeping away the fragmented approach of the old Data Protection Directive. The problem was that in the twenty-one years since the directive had been promulgated the business of data gathering and processing had changed beyond recognition. The arrival of e-commerce and social network platforms, along with online tracking and data gathering technologies meant that an online business, or indeed any business with an online presence was likely to be found to be gathering data in all EU member states simultaneously, and thereby likely to be subject to the controls of twenty-eight different national data protection regimes and authorities. The driving force behind the Regulation was twofold:

(1) to ensure non-EU companies, such as Tumblr, were subject to EU data protection regulation when they target or process the data of EU citizens; and

(2) to ensure companies established in the EU such as Google (whose European Headquarters are in Dublin) and Facebook (also Dublin) could submit themselves to the supervision of one local supervisory authority and know they are in compliance with EU data protection law across the Union.

When the new law came into effect in May 2018 you probably noticed its effect, even if you didn't know why, as websites and other digital service providers asked you to reconfirm your permissions or to check and reconfirm your cookie settings. A number of services specifically not compliant with the new law, such as Klout, closed on that date.

22.1.2 The geographical scope of the GDPR

The first substantial change in the GDPR is the scope of the Regulation. The 1995 Directive had a relatively narrow scope in its original form. Taking its lead from the 1981 Convention for the Protection of Individuals with regard to Automatic Processing of Personal Data,[17]

---

[14] As, for example, in *Google Spain SL and Google Inc. v AEPD* ECLI:EU:C:2014:317.
[15] COM(2012) 11.
[16] (EU) 2016/679.
[17] Council of Europe, CETS 108.

the directive applied only where the data controller or processor was established within the territory of an EU member state.[18] In essence, this meant that they were either established in a member state or had localized equipment or personnel for the processing of data in that member state. This made sense in the 1990s as processing normally was a localized practice with established data centres or customer call centres. However, as technology advanced and as services became more generalized, offered over cloud servers, or simply were a result of online activity, this concept of localization became ever more dated. As a result, the CJEU has repeatedly been asked to explain the scope of European data protection law and over time they became ever more inventive as to what qualified for establishment under the 1995 Directive.

In *Weltimmo* the court used Recital 19 to create a 'flexible' approach to establishment.[19] The Recital explains that 'establishment on the territory of a Member State implies the effective and real exercise of activity through stable arrangements and that the legal form of such an establishment, whether simply branch or a subsidiary with a legal personality, is not the determining factor in this respect.' The court suggested this meant that this:

> results in a flexible definition of the concept of 'establishment', which departs from a formalistic approach whereby undertakings are established solely in the place where they are registered. Accordingly, in order to establish whether a company, the data controller, has an establishment, both the degree of stability of the arrangements and the effective exercise of activities must be interpreted in the light of the specific nature of the economic activities and the provision of services concerned. This is particularly true for undertakings offering services exclusively over the Internet.[20]

As a result, the court held that a Slovakian-registered company which operated a property-dealing website advertising Hungarian properties in Hungarian was established in Hungary and was therefore subject to supervision by the Hungarian data protection authority.

To determine whether or not a business operating an online presence would be established in a state, the court set out a three-stage test:

1. Is there an exercise of real and effective activity—even a minimal one?
2. Is the activity sufficient to constitute a stable arrangement?
3. Is personal data processed in the context of the activity?

A similar expansive approach was taken in the *Google Spain* case.[21] This case, which will be discussed in much greater detail at 23.2, dealt with an application by a Spanish citizen to have data about him removed from Google search returns (the so-called 'right to be forgotten'). It was clear that Google's Spanish subsidiary, Google Spain, was established in Spain and was subject to supervision by the Spanish data protection agency (Agencia Española de Protección de Datos). The issue was whether the authority of the agency could extend to Google Inc. which had no direct establishment in Spain, but which operated search facilities there. In this regard the case is very similar to the *Yahoo! France* and *Google v Equustek* cases discussed in chapter 5.

---

[18] Data Protection Directive, Art. 4(1).
[19] *Weltimmo s.r.o. v Nemzeti Adatvédelmi és Információszabadság Hatóság* ECLI:EU:C:2015:639.
[20] Ibid. [29].
[21] *Google Spain* (n. 14).

The court found that the activities of Google Inc., as a search engine operator, and those of its establishment, were 'inextricably linked' as Google's search engine service is closely related to the activity of selling advertising space via its Spanish subsidiary.[22] The court noted that 'the Spanish Government and the Commission have pointed out, Article 4(1)(a) of Directive 95/46 does not require the processing of personal data in question to be carried out "by" the establishment concerned itself, but only that it be carried out "in the context of the activities" of the establishment.'[23] Applying the principle that 'the objective of [the Data Protection] Directive of ensuring effective and complete protection of the fundamental rights and freedoms of natural persons, and in particular their right to privacy, with respect to the processing of personal data, those words cannot be interpreted restrictively',[24] they found that:

> the processing of personal data for the purposes of the service of a search engine such as Google Search, which is operated by an undertaking that has its seat in a third State but has an establishment in a Member State, is carried out 'in the context of the activities' of that establishment if the latter is intended to promote and sell, in that Member State, advertising space offered by the search engine which serves to make the service offered by that engine profitable.[25]

The *Weltimmo* and *Google Spain* decisions clearly illustrated how the world had changed since 1995. Data controllers and processors were now more likely to be established outside the state seeking to regulate them; indeed they are in many cases likely to be established outside the EU entirely. As a result, the GDPR has started from the flexible approach outlined in *Weltimmo* and *Google Spain* and has widened the geographical scope of EU data protection law substantially.

 Highlight GDPR Article 3

1. This Regulation applies to the processing of personal data in the context of the activities of an establishment of a controller or a processor in the Union, regardless of whether the processing takes place in the Union or not.

2. This Regulation applies to the processing of personal data of data subjects who are in the Union by a controller or processor not established in the Union, where the processing activities are related to: the offering of goods or services, irrespective of whether a payment of the data subject is required, to such data subjects in the Union; or the monitoring of their behaviour as far as their behaviour takes place within the Union.

3. This Regulation applies to the processing of personal data by a controller not established in the Union, but in a place where Member State law applies by virtue of public international law.

This is an extremely wide scope and we await guidance from both courts and the newly formed European Data Protection Board on the application of the new law.[26] However,

---

[22] Ibid. [56].
[23] Ibid. [52].
[24] Ibid. [53].
[25] Ibid. [55].
[26] The European Data Protection Board (EDPB) is the replacement organization for the Article 29 Working Party. It is formed under Art. 68 GDPR.

we can say that in addition to EU established data controllers/processors who are regulated by Art. 3(1), and who will continue to be held to the *Weltimmo/Google Spain* standard,[27] by Art. 3(2) organizations that may previously not have been caught by the 1995 Directive will now clearly fall under the territorial scope of the GDPR. These essentially fall into two classifications:

(1) Non-EU established organisations who process personal data about EU data subjects in connection with the offering of goods or services (payment is not required); and

(2) Non-EU established organisations who process personal data about EU data subjects in connection with monitoring their behaviour within the EU.

Recital 23 helps us understand this first group. They are 'a controller or processor offering goods or services to data subjects who are in the Union'. The recital gives guidance as to when this is likely to be established:

> The mere accessibility of the controller's, processor's or an intermediary's website in the Union, of an email address or of other contact details, or the use of a language generally used in the third country where the controller is established, is insufficient to ascertain such intention, factors such as the use of a language or a currency generally used in one or more Member States with the possibility of ordering goods and services in that other language, or the mentioning of customers or users who are in the Union, may make it apparent that the controller envisages offering goods or services to data subjects in the Union.

The simple operation of a web page accessible from within the EU, or the operation of a simple service such as the facility to receive emails from within the EU, is insufficient to bring the service provider within the scope of the Regulation. However, targeting indicators such as using the local language of an EU member state, where that is not the local language of the service provider, (for example a Brazilian site offering the option to browse a site in Italian), pricing goods and services in euros, or specifically offering shipping rates to EU states may bring them within the scope of the Regulation. The CJEU has examined when an activity (such as offering goods and services) will be considered 'directed to' EU member states in the joined cases of *Pammer* and *Hotel Alpenhof*.[28] There the court noted that an intention to target EU customers may be illustrated by:

(1) 'patent' evidence, such as the payment of money to a search engine to facilitate access by those within a Member State or where targeted Member States are designated by name; or

(2) other factors—possibly in combination with each other—including the 'international nature' of the relevant activity (e.g. certain tourist activities), mentions of telephone numbers with an international code, use of a top-level domain name other than that of the state in which the trader is established (such as.de or.eu), the description of 'itineraries . . . from Member States to the place where the service is provided' and mentions of an 'international clientele composed of customers domiciled in various Member States.'[29]

This list is not exhaustive and the question is to be determined on a case-by-case basis.

The second group of processors is unsurprisingly defined in Recital 24. This informs us that 'in order to determine whether a processing activity can be considered to monitor

---

[27] GDPR, Recital 22.
[28] ECLI:EU:C:2010:740.
[29] Ibid. [83].

the behaviour of data subjects, it should be ascertained whether natural persons are tracked on the internet including potential subsequent use of personal data processing techniques which consist of profiling a natural person, particularly in order to take decisions concerning her or him or for analysing or predicting her or his personal preferences, behaviours and attitudes.' This means any site which gathers identifying data through tracking cookies or other forms of profiling data. It suggests passive sites are not within the scope of the Regulation but sites that seek to profile their customers are. There is a little guidance from the Art. 29 Working Party who described 'regular monitoring' (under the 1995 Directive) as: ongoing or occurring at particular intervals for a particular period; recurring or repeated at fixed times; or constantly or periodically taking place. Meanwhile 'systemic' monitoring was occurring according to a system; pre-arranged, organized, or methodical; taking place as part of a general plan for data collection; or carried out as part of a strategy.[30] Examples given of monitoring were:

> operating a telecommunications network; providing telecommunications services; email retargeting; profiling and scoring for purposes of risk assessment (e.g. for purposes of credit scoring, establishment of insurance premiums, fraud prevention, detection of money-laundering); location tracking, for example, by mobile apps; loyalty programs; behavioural advertising; monitoring of wellness, fitness and health data via wearable devices; closed circuit television; connected devices e.g. smart meters, smart cars, home automation, etc.[31]

Before leaving this section it is important to record that a final decision on the geographical scope of the 1995 Directive is due to be issued by the CJEU (and should have been issued by the time you read this) in the case of *Google Inc. v Commission nationale de l'informatique et des libertés (CNIL)*.[32] This case is discussed in detail at 5.3.7. Although it is of limited assistance in understanding specifically the scope of Art. 3 of the GDPR it affords a valuable insight generally into the extraterritorial effect of data protection law and the reader is directed to read it to complete their understanding of this section.

22.2 **Data and data processing**

Although the GDPR is directly effective the UK government has implemented it domestically through the Data Protection Act 2018. As the Act essentially recognizes the authority of the GDPR and supplements it by filling in those sections of the Regulation that are left to individual member states to interpret and implement, references throughout this and the following chapter will be mostly to the GDPR itself rather than to the Act.

The Regulation begins by defining its scope. We are told by Art. 1(1) that it applies to 'natural persons with regard to the processing of personal data and rules relating to the free movement of personal data'. The Regulation does not therefore apply to legal personalities such as corporations, clubs, or societies.[33] Nor does it apply once the natural person dies. This is expanded upon by Art. 2, which sets out the material scope of the Regulation.

---

[30] Article 29 Working Party, *WP243 Guidelines on Data Protection Officers (DPOs)* December 2016, 8.
[31] Ibid. 9.
[32] Case C-507/17.
[33] See further, Recital 14.

Highlight Material scope (Art. 2)

1. This Regulation applies to the processing of personal data wholly or partly by automated means and to the processing other than by automated means of personal data which form part of a filing system or are intended to form part of a filing system.

2. This Regulation does not apply to the processing of personal data:

(a) in the course of an activity which falls outside the scope of Union law;

(b) by the Member States when carrying out activities which fall within the scope of [the EU common foreign and security policy];

(c) by a natural person in the course of a purely personal or household activity;

(d) by competent authorities for the purposes of the prevention, investigation, detection or prosecution of criminal offences or the execution of criminal penalties, including the safeguarding against and the prevention of threats to public security.

There are a few things to be taken away from this. First, the Regulation only applies to personal data. This is defined by Art. 4(1) as:

> any information relating to an identified or identifiable natural person (data subject); an identifiable natural person is one who can be identified, directly or indirectly, in particular by reference to an identifier such as a name, an identification number, location data, an online identifier or to one or more factors specific to the physical, physiological, genetic, mental, economic, cultural or social identity of that natural person.

However, what at first glance may appear to be straightforward is actually more complicated. While it is clear that personal data can include personal names and addresses, as well as online identifiers such as IP addresses and mobile device IDs (including telephone numbers) and even pseudonymous data,[34] it is not true that under every circumstance these forms of data will *always* be personal data. The Information Commissioner's Office explains this by reference to a common name:

> A name is the most common means of identifying someone. However, whether any potential identifier actually identifies an individual depends on the context. By itself the name John Smith may not always be personal data because there are many individuals with that name. However, where the name is combined with other information (such as an address, a place of work, or a telephone number) this will usually be sufficient to clearly identify one individual.[35]

They go on to explain that a name is though only one possible identifying characteristic 'Simply because you do not know the name of an individual does not mean you cannot identify that individual. Many of us do not know the names of all our neighbours,

---

[34] Art. 4(5) defines 'pseudonymisation' as 'the processing of personal data in such a manner that the personal data can no longer be attributed to a specific data subject without the use of additional information, provided that such additional information is kept separately and is subject to technical and organisational measures to ensure that the personal data are not attributed to an identified or identifiable natural person'.

[35] Information Commissioner's Office, *Determining what is personal data* (ICO 2012), 7.

but we are still able to identify them.'[36] Essentially, to be personal data you must be able to identify *a* living individual from that information, either on its own or in combination with other information you possess or which you may be able to possess. The information may be information which is true or false. Thus if you were to hold personal data about me which allowed you to identify me (perhaps by reference to my current employer and job title) but which was inaccurate (such as you have recorded my address incorrectly) this is still personal data. This actually is an important point for, as we shall go on to see, the data subject has a right to correct errors in any data held or processed on them.

A key provision of the definition of personal data is that it is 'any information *relating to* an identified or identifiable natural person.' That is a key phrase—when is data 'relating to' an individual? This is a question that has been returned to over the years by the courts. In the controversial case of *Durant v Financial Services Authority*[37] the Court of Appeal examined the question of when data 'related to' the applicant. The case is discussed in greater detail at 23.1.1 but for now it is important to note that when asked whether files held by the FSA relating to Mr Durant's complaint against Barclays Bank were personal data, Buxton LJ recorded that 'on the ordinary meaning of the expression, relating to him, Mr Durant's letters of complaint to the FSA, and the FSA's investigation of that complaint, did not relate to Mr Durant, but to his complaint'. He explained that 'the [Data Protection] Act would only be engaged if, in the course of investigating the complaint, the FSA expressed an opinion about Mr Durant personally, as opposed to an opinion about his complaint'.[38] This decision was criticized at the time,[39] and now is no longer considered good law.

In 2007 the Article 29 Working Party clarified that 'in general terms, information can be considered to "relate" to an individual when it is about that individual'.[40] They go on to give useful examples of when data 'relates to' an individual. First, they demonstrate the direct link: 'in many situations, this relationship can be easily established. For instance the data registered in one's individual file in the personnel office are clearly "related to" the person's situation as an employee. So are the data on the results of a patient's medical test contained in his medical records, or the image of a person filmed on a video interview of that person.' Then there is the possibility of an indirect link; this is where for example information relates to an object which can be tied to an individual. The example they give is of a house price valuation. This seems not to be personal data but as the Working Party explain 'under certain circumstances such information should also be considered as personal data. Indeed, the house is the asset of an owner, which will hence be used to determine the extent of this person's obligation to pay some taxes, for instance. In this context, it will be indisputable that such information should be considered as personal data.'[41]

---

[36] Ibid.

[37] [2004] FSR 28.

[38] Ibid. [80].

[39] L Edwards, 'Taking the "Personal" Out of Personal Data: *Durant v FSA* and its Impact on the Legal Regulation of CCTV' (2004) 1 *SCRIPT-ed* 342; S Chalton, 'The Court of Appeal's interpretation of "personal data" in *Durant v FSA*—a welcome clarification, or a cat amongst the data protection pigeons?' (2004) 20 *Computer Law & Security Review* 175.

[40] Article 29 Working Party, *Opinion 4/2007 on the concept of personal data*, 9.

[41] Ibid.

They go on to identify three further ways in which data may indirectly relate to the individual. The first is where the *content* of the information relates to the individual. This is where information is clearly 'about' a person. As the Working Party explain:

> information 'relates' to a person when it is 'about' that person, and this has to be assessed in the light of all circumstances surrounding the case. For example, the results of medical analysis clearly relate to the patient, or the information contained in a company's folder under the name of a certain client clearly relates to him. Or the information contained in a RFID tag or a bar code incorporated in an identity document of a certain individual relates to that person, as in passports with a RFID chip.[42]

Second, there is data which *purpose* it is to 'to evaluate, treat in a certain way or influence the status or behaviour of an individual.' An example would be a call log for a telephone. Although the log may not directly contain personal data, the log would allow a company to monitor the employee who uses that phone and, in addition, can provide information on who called, or was called, and can be used to determine when the employee is in or out of the office. Finally, there is data which when processed produces a *result* 'likely to have an impact on a certain person's rights and interests, taking into account all the circumstances surrounding the precise case'. The Working Party give an example of location data held by a taxi company for the purpose of optimizing the service. As the they point out, while the location of cars may not immediately be personal data, 'the system does allow monitoring the performance of taxi drivers and checking whether they respect speed limits, seek appropriate itineraries, are at the steering wheel or are resting outside, etc. It can therefore have a considerable impact on these individuals, and as such the data may be considered to also relate to natural persons.'[43]

These clarifications suggested that *Durant* was wrong in finding that the files regarding Mr Durant's claim were information about his complaint (not personal data) rather than information about him (personal data). This position was revisited domestically in *Edem v IC & Financial Services Authority*.[44] Here the Court of Appeal considered the application of the test set forth in *Durant* and concluded that the meaning of personal data should be interpreted in accordance with the Information Commissioner's technical guidance note,[45] rather than the more restrictive interpretation of *Durant*. In particular, the court confirmed that the more restrictive test in Durant should apply only in limited circumstances, namely where the information in question is not obviously about an individual, or clearly linked to them.[46]

The leading case on this is currently is not a domestic case. It is *Nowak v Data Protection Commissioner*, a CJEU decision following a reference from Ireland.[47] The case arose as a result of the Institute of Chartered Accountants of Ireland (CAI) refusing a request by an accountancy student, Peter Nowak, for a copy of his failed exam script. The CAI concluded that the exam script did not contain personal data and therefore did not fall within the scope of data protection law. Nowak submitted a formal complaint to the Irish Data Protection Commissioner, who also determined that the exam script

---

[42] Ibid. 10.
[43] Ibid. 11.
[44] [2014] EWCA Civ 92.
[45] Information Commissioner's Office (n. 35).
[46] *Edem* (n. 44) [21].
[47] ECLI:EU:C:2017:994.

was not personal data. Nowak appealed eventually to the Supreme Court of Ireland. At the Supreme Court, the Data Protection Commissioner relied on the opinion of the Advocate General in the case of *YS and Others* that: 'only information relating to facts about an individual can be personal data. Except for the fact that it exists, a legal analysis is not such a fact. Thus, for example, a person's address is personal data but an analysis of his domicile for legal purposes is not.'[48] The Supreme Court referred a question to the CJEU as to whether the written answers provided by a candidate at an exam, and any examiner's comments with respect to those answers, constitute personal data.

The CJEU held that written answers provided by a candidate and any comments made by the examiner with respect to those answers constitute information relating to that candidate, and are therefore personal data. It found that 'the content of those answers reflects the extent of the candidate's knowledge and competence in a given field and, in some cases, his intellect, thought processes, and judgment. In the case of a handwritten script, the answers contain, in addition, information as to his handwriting.'[49] Further 'the purpose of collecting those answers is to evaluate the candidate's professional abilities and his suitability to practice the profession concerned',[50] and 'the use of that information, one consequence of that use being the candidate's success or failure at the examination concerned, is liable to have an effect on his or her rights and interests, in that it may determine or influence, for example, the chance of entering the profession aspired to or of obtaining the post sought.'[51] As a result the court held that both the exam answer, as well as the examiner's comments were 'by reason of content, purpose or effect, linked to that candidate [and this] is not called into question by the fact that those comments also constitute information relating to the examiner'.[52]

There is one interesting wrinkle of the *Nowak* decision. The exam was anonymously marked. This meant that the exam paper was in terms of data protection law pseudonymous. The examiner never knew Mr Nowak's identity (and indeed could not know), only the CAI had both his candidate number and his name. This brings us finally to the identifiability criterion. You should remember that according to Art. 3(1) 'an identifiable natural person is one who can be identified, directly or indirectly.' Again the Recitals offer assistance. By Recital 26 we are told that:

> to determine whether a natural person is identifiable, account should be taken of *all the means reasonably likely to be used*, such as singling out, either by the controller or by another person to identify the natural person directly or indirectly. To ascertain whether means are reasonably likely to be used to identify the natural person, account should be taken of all objective factors, such as the costs of and the amount of time required for identification, taking into consideration the available technology at the time of the processing and technological developments.

The fact that the CAI had possession of both the exam paper, with comments, and a means to identify Mr Nowak suggested he was identifiable. Fortunately for the court it could refer to an earlier case, *Breyer*, which is actually very important for all Information Technology Law students.[53]

---

[48] ECLI:EU:C:2013:838, [56]

[49] *Nowak* (n. 47) [37].

[50] Ibid. [38].

[51] Ibid. [39].

[52] Ibid. [44].

[53] *Patrick Breyer v Bundesrepublik Deutschland* ECLI:EU:C:2016:779.

Breyer concerned the question of whether an IP address could qualify as personal data. Mr Breyer's IP address was dynamically allocated (i.e., each time he connected to the network, his device is issued with a new IP address). Ordinarily, a dynamic IP address does not provide a website operator with sufficient information to directly identify an individual user, unless additional information is also available (e.g., the user logs into the website and provides information that enables the website operator to identify that user). The parties agreed that the IP address in question did not directly identify Mr Breyer. The question was whether Mr Breyer was indirectly identifiable, from his dynamic IP address in combination with other available information. The parties agreed that Mr Breyer could be indirectly identified by the combination of his IP address plus account data held by his ISP. The court had to determine whether the test for determining identifiability is:

a. objective (i.e., the IP address is personal data in everybody's hands because the ISP can link it to Mr Breyer's real world identity, even if nobody else can legally do so); or

b. relative (i.e., the IP address is personal data in the ISP's hands, but would not be personal data in the hands of another party who had no lawful means of accessing the information held by the ISP).

The court determined it was a question of relative indentifiability:

> a dynamic IP address registered by an online media services provider when a person accesses a website that the provider makes accessible to the public constitutes personal data within the meaning of that provision, in relation to that provider, where *the latter has the legal means which enable it to identify the data subject* with additional data which the internet service provider has about that person.[54]

Applying *Breyer* the court in *Nowak* found that 'there is no requirement that all the information enabling the identification of the data subject must be in the hands of one person'.[55] The fact that Mr Nowak could be identified rather easily meant the identifiability criterion was met.

22.2.1 Data subjects, data controllers, and processors

The Regulation defines the personnel of the data protection environment, identifying four key actors. The first are data subjects, which are defined as 'an identified or identifiable natural person'.[56] The Regulation does not therefore apply to legal personalities such as corporations, clubs or societies—as Recital 14 puts it: 'this Regulation does not cover the processing of personal data which concerns legal persons and in particular undertakings established as legal persons, including the name and the form of the legal person and the contact details of the legal person.' Of course, the divide between natural and legal persons is not always as clear as the Regulation suggests. Often micro-undertakings will share a name with their owner (imagine Sam Smith Legal Services Ltd) and operate from the private address of their owner which then doubles as the

---

[54] Ibid. [49].
[55] *Nowak* (n. 47) [31].
[56] In this section all definitions are taken from Art. 4.

address of the undertaking. It is quite easy to combine personal data and identifiers of people in their capacity as natural persons with data of legal persons. This requires courts to carefully unpack the legal personality from the natural one—when is the data about the company and when is it data about the person? Only the latter is protected by the GDPR. Where the data is shared: such as address data or phone numbers, it will be treated as personal data as it relates to a natural person.

Second, data controllers are 'the natural or legal person, public authority, agency or other body which, alone or jointly with others, determines the purposes and means of the processing of personal data'. The data controller is the party primarily responsible for compliance with the Regulation. By Art. 24(1) the controller is required to 'implement appropriate technical and organisational measures to ensure and to be able to demonstrate that processing is performed in accordance with this Regulation' and to ensure 'those measures shall be reviewed and updated where necessary'. There may be joint controllers, defined in Art. 26(1) as 'two or more controllers [who] jointly determine the purposes and means of processing'. The controller (or controllers) have significant responsibilities to the data subject including that they will comply with Chapter 3 of the Regulation where considerable rights to the data subject are awarded, including subject access rights, the rights to rectification and erasure of data, and the notification obligation.

The role of data processor has recently been given consideration in the CJEU in the *Facebook fan page* case.[57] The case involved a private educational company who offered services by means of a fan page hosted on Facebook. Administrators of fan pages can obtain anonymous statistical information on visitors to the fan pages via a function called 'Facebook Insights' which Facebook makes available to them free of charge under non-negotiable conditions of use. The information is collected by means of cookies, each containing a unique user code, which are active for two years and are stored by Facebook on the hard disk of the computer or on other media of visitors to fan pages. The user code, which can be matched with the connection data of users registered on Facebook, is collected and processed when the fan pages are opened. The data protection supervisor for Schleswig-Holstein (a federal state in Germany) ordered the operator of the fan page to deactivate the page or face a fine as neither it nor Facebook, had the permission of the visitors to the page to have the tracking cookie installed on their machine and to process their data connected to it. The operator of the page challenged this finding, arguing that the processing of personal data by Facebook could not be attributed to it and that it had not commissioned Facebook to process data that it controlled or was able to influence. They argued that the data protection supervisor should have acted directly against Facebook instead of it.

The case was referred to the CJEU and there the court noted that the 'aim [of] Article 2(d) of the directive defines the concept of "controller" broadly as the natural or legal person, public authority, agency or any other body which alone or jointly with others determines the purposes and means of the processing of personal data'.[58] This, the court

---

[57] *Unabhängiges Landeszentrum für Datenschutz Schleswig-Holstein v Wirtschaftsakademie Schleswig-Holstein GmbH* ECLI:EU:C:2018:388.

[58] At [27]. Note this is the same definition found at Art. 4(7) of GDPR.

noted 'is to ensure, through a broad definition of the concept of "controller", effective and complete protection of the persons concerned'.[59] Who were the controller, or controllers, in the instant case? As the court observed, Facebook were clearly a controller for they 'primarily determine the purposes and means of processing the personal data of users of Facebook and persons visiting the fan pages hosted on Facebook'.[60] In addition, the operator of the fan page was also a controller for while 'the mere fact of making use of a social network such as Facebook does not make a Facebook user a controller jointly responsible for the processing of personal data by that network, it must be stated, on the other hand, that the administrator of a fan page hosted on Facebook, by creating such a page, gives Facebook the opportunity to place cookies on the computer or other device of a person visiting its fan page, whether or not that person has a Facebook account'[61] and 'the creation of a fan page on Facebook involves the definition of parameters by the administrator, depending inter alia on the target audience and the objectives of managing and promoting its activities, which has an influence on the processing of personal data for the purpose of producing statistics based on visits to the fan page . . . Consequently, the administrator of a fan page hosted on Facebook contributes to the processing of the personal data of visitors to its page.'[62]

Operators of fan pages are therefore data controllers; however, the court was at pains to point out that different data controllers may have different levels of responsibility, noting that:

> the existence of joint responsibility does not necessarily imply equal responsibility of the various operators involved in the processing of personal data. On the contrary, those operators may be involved at different stages of that processing of personal data and to different degrees, so that the level of responsibility of each of them must be assessed with regard to all the relevant circumstances of the particular case.[63]

Our third actor is data processors. These are 'a natural or legal person, public authority, agency or other body which processes personal data on behalf of the controller'. These are the agents of the data controller who actually carry out the day-to-day storage and processing of the data. An example would be the Tesco Clubcard scheme. Although the data controller would be Tesco plc, the operation of the scheme is not managed by Tesco but by a private company Dunnhumby Ltd. In this scenario Dunnhumby is the data processor to Tesco's data controller. Processors, like controllers, have specific responsibilities under GDPR including that they 'provide sufficient guarantees to implement appropriate technical and organisational measures in such a manner that processing will meet the requirements of this Regulation and ensure the protection of the rights of the data subject'[64] and that they shall not subcontract any processing without specific authorization.[65] Since data processing is often outsourced to specialist companies, the data controller/data processor distinction allows the GDPR to control both aspects of data management and processing.

---

[59] Ibid. [28].
[60] Ibid. [30].
[61] Ibid. [35].
[62] Ibid. [36].
[63] Ibid. [43].
[64] Art. 28(1).
[65] Art. 28(2).

22.2.2 **Data processing and the data protection principles**

At the heart of the Regulation is the data controller/data processor relationship and their responsibilities to the data subject. These responsibilities are captured in the Data Protection Principles. By Art. 5(2) 'the controller shall be responsible for, and be able to demonstrate compliance with, paragraph 1 ('accountability')'. The Principles are found in Art. 5(1):

 Highlight The Data Protection principles

Personal data shall be:

(a) processed lawfully, fairly and in a transparent manner in relation to the data subject ('lawfulness, fairness and transparency');

(b) collected for specified, explicit and legitimate purposes and not further processed in a manner that is incompatible with those purposes; further processing for archiving purposes in the public interest, scientific or historical research purposes or statistical purposes shall, in accordance with Article 89(1), not be considered to be incompatible with the initial purposes ('purpose limitation');

(c) adequate, relevant and limited to what is necessary in relation to the purposes for which they are processed ('data minimisation');

(d) accurate and, where necessary, kept up to date; every reasonable step must be taken to ensure that personal data that are inaccurate, having regard to the purposes for which they are processed, are erased or rectified without delay ('accuracy');

(e) kept in a form which permits identification of data subjects for no longer than is necessary for the purposes for which the personal data are processed; personal data may be stored for longer periods insofar as the personal data will be processed solely for archiving purposes in the public interest, scientific or historical research purposes or statistical purposes in accordance with Article 89(1) subject to implementation of the appropriate technical and organisational measures required by this Regulation in order to safeguard the rights and freedoms of the data subject ('storage limitation');

(f) processed in a manner that ensures appropriate security of the personal data, including protection against unauthorised or unlawful processing and against accidental loss, destruction or damage, using appropriate technical or organisational measures ('integrity and confidentiality').

Although all the principles are of equal weight in many ways the key principle is the First Principle. This is the general principle that data processing shall be carried out in a lawful, fair, and transparent manner. This is an extremely vague term, which although supported by conditions for the fair processing of data has caused problems for courts in the UK and further afield.

The first issue is the rather vague term 'processing'. This is defined broadly by Art. 4(2) of the GDPR (while the Data Protection Act essentially gives the same definition but in a slightly different order).

Highlight Processing data (Art. 4(2))

Processing means any operation or set of operations which is performed on personal data or on sets of personal data, whether or not by automated means, such as collection, recording, organisation, structuring, storage, adaptation or alteration, retrieval, consultation, use, disclosure by transmission, dissemination or otherwise making available, alignment or combination, restriction, erasure or destruction.

This definition makes it clear that mere consultation of data is a data process as is the act of collecting and recording data. Thus creation of data, as well as its destruction, is a data process in of itself. Further, some data attracts additional protection: this is data known as 'special data' and it is defined in Art. 9.

 Highlight Special Data

Processing of personal data revealing racial or ethnic origin, political opinions, religious or philosophical beliefs, or trade union membership, and the processing of genetic data, biometric data for the purpose of uniquely identifying a natural person, data concerning health or data concerning a natural person's sex life or sexual orientation shall be prohibited.

The common theme of special data is that it is data which may be used to discriminate against an individual. As such, there is a special regime for such data both in the Regulation and the Data Protection Act.[66] In particular, the Act applies special conditions to the processing of data of this nature in Schs. 8 and 10.

Not every action with personal data is processing in terms of the Regulation and Act. If we return to Art. 2(1) we see that processing must be 'wholly or partly by automated means' or manual processing of data 'forming part of a filing system or intended to form part of a filing system.' This means the data must be stored or processed electronically or it should be stored or processed as part of a filing system which is 'any structured set of personal data which are accessible according to specific criteria, whether centralised, decentralised or dispersed on a functional or geographical basis'.[67] This means that a simple act of recording or processing personal data not as part of an organized record, such as noting down the registration number of a vehicle parked outside your house or asking your friend if she knows the name of another person at a party, is not covered by the Regulation and Act. More structured processing will though bring the data within the scope of both the Regulation and Act, such as searching the DVLA database to find out who owns the car in question or adding the name to your list of contacts on your smartphone. However, even allowing for this qualification, in the

---

[66] See ss. 35(8) and 42, and Schs. 8 and 10.
[67] Art. 4(6).

modern digital environment the definition of processing is potentially a very expansive set which could cover anything from hardcore data mining of gathered personal data by commercial organizations to individuals mentioning friends and family on personal web pages without permission or otherwise in accordance with the Regulation and Act. Is this really the intent of EU data protection law?

The leading case to date on the question of 'processing' is the Swedish case of *Bodil Lindqvist*.[68] Mrs Lindqvist, in addition to her day job as a maintenance worker, worked as a catechist in the parish of Alseda in Sweden. She took a data processing course to allow her to develop an online presence for her church. At the end of 1998, Mrs Lindqvist set up internet pages using her personal computer in order to allow parishioners preparing for their confirmation to obtain information they might need. At her request, the administrator of the Swedish Church's website set up a link between those pages and that site.

The pages in question contained information about Mrs Lindqvist and eighteen colleagues in the parish, sometimes including their full names and in other cases only their first names. Mrs Lindqvist also described, in a mildly humorous manner, the jobs held by her colleagues and their hobbies. In many cases family circumstances and telephone numbers and other matters were mentioned. She also stated that one colleague had injured her foot and was on half-time on medical grounds. It was established that Mrs Lindqvist had not informed her colleagues of the existence of those pages or obtained their consent, nor did she notify the Datainspektionen (Swedish supervisory authority for the protection of electronically transmitted data) of her activity. She removed the pages in question as soon as she became aware that they were not appreciated by some of her colleagues.

Mrs Lindqvist was charged by Swedish authorities with breach of the Swedish Data Protection Act on the grounds that she had: (a) processed personal data by automatic means without giving prior written notification to the Datainspektionen; (b) processed sensitive personal data (injured foot and half-time on medical grounds) without authorization; and (c) transferred processed personal data to a third country without authorization. Mrs Lindqvist accepted the facts of the case but challenged that her activities (placing material on a website) did not qualify as 'processing' data under the Data Protection Directive 1995 and thereby the relevant Swedish law. The Swedish Court of Appeal referred the case to the European Court of Justice for their interpretation of the Directive.

In a wide-ranging opinion the ECJ found that:

 Highlight The decision of the ECJ in *Bodil Lindqvist*

(1) The act of referring, on an internet page, to various persons and identifying them by name or other means constituted the processing of personal data.

(2) The processing of personal data such as that described in answer to the first question was not covered by any of the exceptions given in the Directive.

➡

---

[68]   ECLI:EU:C:2003:596.

➞

(3) Reference to the fact that a colleague had injured her foot and was on half time on medical grounds constituted personal data concerning health within the meaning of [sensitive personal data].

(4) The provisions of the Directive did not, in themselves, bring about restrictions which conflicted with the right to freedom of expression. It was for the national courts responsible for applying implementing legislation to ensure a fair balance between the rights and interests in question.

This clearly gives an extremely expansive interpretation of 'processing'. Even the simplest act of placing information on a personal we site qualifies.

22.2.3 The domestic purposes exception

Of course to suggest that every act of every individual in which data is processed in a manner covered by the *Lindqvist* decision would make data protection law oppressive and almost impossible to apply. It would suggest the keeping of an address book on a mobile phone or writing a list of gifts for friends could only be done in accordance with the data protection principles. This would be somewhat overbearing and overreaching so the Regulation carves out an exemption for purely domestic processing.[69]

The domestic purposes exemption is carried over from the Directive and the 1998 Act so we have some case law to clarify when the exemption applies and when it does not. In fact, the first case to look at this was *Lindqvist* itself. Mrs Lindqvist argued that her activities were carried out in a private capacity and that the web page onto which she loaded data was a private one. The court disagreed, finding that:

> as regards the exception provided for in the second indent of Article 3(2) of Directive 95/46, the 12th recital in the preamble to that directive, which concerns that exception, cites, as examples of the processing of data carried out by a natural person in the exercise of activities which are exclusively personal or domestic, correspondence and the holding of records of addresses. That exception must therefore be interpreted as relating only to activities which are carried out in the course of private or family life of individuals, which is clearly not the case with the processing of personal data consisting in publication on the internet so that those data are made accessible to an indefinite number of people.[70]

More recently the CJEU has returned to this issue in the case of *Ryneš v Úřad pro ochranu osobních údajů*.[71] Mr Ryneš had installed a CCTV camera on the exterior of his house, which recorded movements not only on his private property, but also the public footpath outside. He said he installed the camera to protect his family and his property, as there had been previous vandalism to his property. After the installation of the CCTV, his house windows were broken once more. The CCTV footage was used to identify two individuals, one of whom questioned whether the use of the CCTV system was

---

[69] GDPR Article 2(2)(c); Data Protection Act 2018, s. 21(3).
[70] *Lindqvist* (n. 68) [46]–[47].
[71] ECLI:EU:C:2014:2428.

permissible under the Czech data protection law. Mr Ryneš argued that the 'domestic processing exception' found in Art. 3(2) of the Directive applied.[72]

The Czech court referred this question to the CJEU, asking:

> Can the operation of a camera system installed on a family home for the purposes of the protec-
> tion of the property, health and life of the owners of the home be classified as the processing
> of personal data 'by a natural person in the course of a purely personal or household activity'
> within the meaning of Article 3(2) of Directive 95/46/EC, even though such a system monitors
> also a public space?[73]

The court first clarified that the capture of an identifiable image of a person on a CCTV system is personal data within the definition of the directive.[74] It then clarified that 'surveillance in the form of a video recording of persons, as in the case before the referring court, which is stored on a continuous recording device—the hard disk drive—constitutes, pursuant to Article 3(1) of Directive 95/46, the automatic processing of personal data.'[75] This just left the question of whether Mr Ryneš was covered by the domestic processing exception. The court noted that the decision in *Google Spain SL and Google Inc. v AEPD*[76] provided that 'the protection of the fundamental right to private life guaranteed under Article 7 of the Charter of Fundamental Rights of the European Union (the Charter) requires that derogations and limitations in relation to the protection of personal data must apply only in so far as is strictly necessary'.[77] As a result, the court found:

> The processing of personal data comes within the exception provided for in the second indent
> of Article 3(2) of Directive 95/46 only where it is carried out in the purely personal or household
> setting of the person processing the data. Accordingly, so far as natural persons are concerned,
> correspondence and the keeping of address books constitute, in the light of recital 12 to Direc
> tive 95/46, a "purely personal or household activity" even if they incidentally concern or may
> concern the private life of other persons. To the extent that video surveillance such as that at
> issue in the main proceedings covers, even partially, a public space and is accordingly directed
> outwards from the private setting of the person processing the data in that manner, it cannot be
> regarded as an activity which is a purely "personal or household" activity for the purposes of the
> second indent of Article 3(2) of Directive 95/46.[78]

The court, as in Lindqvist, ultimately applied an extremely strict interpretation of the domestic processing exemption. This is possibly because Art. 3(2) said it only applied to 'a *purely* personal or household activity'. One other thing to note is that the court did find that the domestic court was correct not to fine Mr Ryneš as 'the application of Directive 95/46 makes it possible, where appropriate, to take into account—in accordance, in particular, with Articles 7(f), 11(2), and 13(1)(d) and (g) of that directive— legitimate interests pursued by the controller, such as the protection of the property, health and life of his family and himself, as in the case in the main proceedings.'[79]

---

[72] Art. 2(2)(c) of the GDPR extends the domestic processing exemption into the modern framework.

[73] Ibid. [18].

[74] Ibid. [22].

[75] Ibid. [25].

[76] *Google Spain* (n. 14).

[77] *Ryneš*, (n. 71) [28].

[78] Ibid. [31]–[33].

[79] Ibid. [34].

It may be argued that *Lindqvist* and *Ryneš* are now less authoritative than they were. This is due to Recital 18 of the GDPR (emphasis added):

> This Regulation does not apply to the processing of personal data by a natural person in the course of a purely personal or household activity and thus with no connection to a professional or commercial activity. Personal or household activities could include correspondence and the holding of addresses, *or social networking and online activity undertaken within the context of such activities*. However, this Regulation applies to controllers or processors which provide the means for processing personal data for such personal or household activities.

It is clear that GDPR in moving with the times has recognized that people spend large amounts of their lives online now. It is therefore unlikely that if a modern Mrs Lindqvist were to post to Facebook her sympathies for a friend who had broken a leg that the courts would find that today to be in breach of the domestic purposes exemption. However, as Art. 2(2)(c) retains the vital term 'a *purely* personal or household activity' it means that both *Lindqvist* and *Ryneš* retain their authoritative status, despite this slight variation in scope given in Recital 18. This means that, if she were to repeat her actions of placing the information (unnecessarily) on a web page, the outcome would likely be the same as in her original case. This makes the interpretation of 'fairness' of paramount importance, as only when data is processed 'fairly and lawfully' is the first data protection principle met.

22.2.4 **Fairness and lawfulness**

The leading UK case on fairness is *Johnson v Medical Defence Union Ltd*.[80] The claimant, Mr Johnson, was a consultant orthopaedic surgeon with over 20 years' clinical experience. He was, from 1980, a member of the Medical Defence Union (MDU), a mutual society which provides advice and professional liability insurance cover to its members. He was reported as having 'never been the subject of a claim for alleged professional negligence'.[81] However, it was reported that 'over the years he [had] sought advice and assistance from the MDU in relation to professional questions and problems that concerned him, including complaints made against him. His contact with the MDU, and that from others about him, gave rise to the opening at least since 1991 of 17 MDU files.'[82]

As a result of a review of their files the MDU wrote to Mr Johnson in January 2002 informing him they would not renew his membership at the end of his current subscription. The letter gave no reasons. Mr Johnson sought the reasons, but none were provided. As a result of the MDU's actions, Mr Johnson claims he suffered damage to his professional reputation and financial loss. He made a claim under s. 13 of the Data Protection Act 1998 seeking compensation for unfair processing of his personal data.

At an initial hearing before Rimer J in 2006 all of Mr Johnson's claims were dismissed.[83] In particular, he found that:

> [The MDU's risk policy] was formulated against the background of a contractual relationship between the MDU and its members under which the MDU had and has an absolute discretion to terminate a member's membership and in which it was in the interests of all members that it

---

[80] [2007] EWCA Civ 262.
[81] Ibid. [2].
[82] Ibid.
[83] *Johnson v The Medical Defence Union Ltd* [2006] EWHC 321 (Ch).

should have a sound risk assessment policy. There might be legitimate scope for disagreement between those competent to judge these things as to whether the MDU risk assessment policy was sound or otherwise, or as to whether it could be improved. But I have no reason to believe that it was arrived at other than after proper consideration and that it was regarded as other than the most appropriate policy for the needs of the MDU . . . The MDU could process his data in the circumstances in which it did perfectly fairly without his [Mr Johnson's] input, and the evidence from the MDU witnesses satisfied me that his input would be unlikely to have made any difference to the assessment of his case: because, put shortly, the policy regards a member's input as essentially irrelevant.[84]

Therefore, according to Rimer J, Mr Johnson's suggestion that he 'was entitled to have his data processed and case considered by reference to his own inexpert assertions as to the risk assessment policy that the MDU should apply' should be rejected.[85]

Mr Johnson appealed. His appeal was based on the foundation that the MDU's policy was flawed. In particular, he believed two flaws led to his personal data held by the MDU being processed unfairly. The first was that the MDU's policy of assessing members according to the number of incidents or complaints rather than according to their outcome meant he was penalized, and second, because of that policy, the Risk Assessment Review process used by the MDU did not allow any explanation by the member of the various incidents reported to it.

On 28 March 2007 the Court of Appeal dismissed Mr Johnson's claim. They held that the MDU's processing of Mr Johnson's personal data for the purpose of conducting a risk assessment review was, in relation to all but two of the files in question, fair and lawful under the Act, and dismissed Mr Johnson's claim for compensation. Arden LJ noted that 'Mr Johnson gave his consent to the processing of personal data for a number of purposes, including risk management. The directive requires consent to be unambiguous. However, in my judgment, Mr Johnson did not have to know the nature of the MDU's risk assessment policy to give a valid consent for this purpose.'[86] She went on to note:

the judge [Rimer J] did not accept Mr Johnson's submission, either in relation to the lead files or the non-lead files, that the MDU had an obligation to consult Mr Johnson about the processing exercise or to invite his representations upon it. In my judgment the judge was right to hold that the fairness principle did not require this. As a general proposition a party to a contract cannot in my judgment use the fairness principle as a means of upsetting any contractually permitted use of information where, as here, processing was foreseeable. I see no basis for displacing this general proposition in this case.[87]

The unfair processing of the remaining two files was held not to have caused damage to Mr Johnson. The court paid particular regard to the fact that Mr Johnson had signed up to the MDU's risk assessment policy and agreed to the processing of his personal data for this purpose, and the court held that the review was carried out within the terms of this policy. In terms of compensation, the court held that even if Mr Johnson had shown there to be a breach of the Data Protection Act, there is nothing within the Act that would give him the right to compensation for a general loss of reputation. The

[84] Ibid. [110].
[85] Ibid. [202].
[86] *Johnson* (n. 80) [145].
[87] Ibid. [148]–[149].

court noted that a defamation claim would be a more appropriate course of action for this; however, the court did note that had the MDU breached the Data Protection Act in processing Mr Johnson's personal data, he would have been able to claim for losses and distress 'by reason of a data controller's contravention of the Data Protection Act'.[88]

What is apparent from the cases we have discussed is the complexity of processing in accordance with the regulatory provisions. Mrs Lindqvist appeared to be engaged in an innocent activity, which she no doubt felt was a private matter; likewise Mr Ryneš believed he was processing for a private purpose and for the protection of his property. Both, however, fell foul of the law as their actions went further than their domestic purposes and had potential to impact on the data privacy of others. By comparison, The Medical Defence Union was involved in high-level data processing with the potential to adversely affect the professional career of Mr Johnson and others that were subject to its risk assessment review. Ultimately, though, we know that Mrs Lindqvist's actions were in breach of the Swedish data protection law (and the Directive) while Mr Ryneš' actions were similarly in breach of Czech data protection law (and the Directive), while the actions of the Medical Defence Union were ultimately fair and lawful. How can a data controller process data with confidence given the complexity of the first data protection principle?

22.3 **Conditions for the processing of personal data**

To assist data controllers in fulfilling the First Principle, Art. 6(1) lists conditions in which the principle is met.

 Highlight Lawfulness of processing

Processing shall be lawful only if and to the extent that at least one of the following applies:

a. the data subject has given consent to the processing of his or her personal data for one or more specific purposes;

b. processing is necessary for the performance of a contract to which the data subject is party or in order to take steps at the request of the data subject prior to entering into a contract;

c. processing is necessary for compliance with a legal obligation to which the controller is subject;

d. processing is necessary in order to protect the vital interests of the data subject or of another natural person;

e. processing is necessary for the performance of a task carried out in the public interest or in the exercise of official authority vested in the controller;

f. processing is necessary for the purposes of the legitimate interests pursued by the controller or by a third party, except where such interests are overridden by the interests or fundamental rights and freedoms of the data subject which require protection of personal data, in particular where the data subject is a child.

---

[88] Ibid. [72].

In cases of special data Art. 9(2) is applied instead. This states that the processing of such data should only take place on one or more of the following occasions.

 Highlight Processing of special categories of personal data

a. the data subject has given explicit consent to the processing of those personal data for one or more specified purposes, except where Union or Member State law provide that the prohibition referred to in paragraph 1 may not be lifted by the data subject;

b. processing is necessary for the purposes of carrying out the obligations and exercising specific rights of the controller or of the data subject in the field of employment and social security and social protection law in so far as it is authorised by Union or Member State law or a collective agreement pursuant to Member State law providing for appropriate safeguards for the fundamental rights and the interests of the data subject;

c. processing is necessary to protect the vital interests of the data subject or of another natural person where the data subject is physically or legally incapable of giving consent;

d. processing is carried out in the course of its legitimate activities with appropriate safeguards by a foundation, association or any other not-for-profit body with a political, philosophical, religious or trade union aim and on condition that the processing relates solely to the members or to former members of the body or to persons who have regular contact with it in connection with its purposes and that the personal data are not disclosed outside that body without the consent of the data subjects;

e. processing relates to personal data which are manifestly made public by the data subject;

f. processing is necessary for the establishment, exercise or defence of legal claims or whenever courts are acting in their judicial capacity;

g. processing is necessary for reasons of substantial public interest, on the basis of Union or Member State law which shall be proportionate to the aim pursued, respect the essence of the right to data protection and provide for suitable and specific measures to safeguard the fundamental rights and the interests of the data subject;

h. processing is necessary for the purposes of preventive or occupational medicine, for the assessment of the working capacity of the employee, medical diagnosis, the provision of health or social care or treatment or the management of health or social care systems and services on the basis of Union or Member State law or pursuant to contract with a health professional;

i. processing is necessary for reasons of public interest in the area of public health, such as protecting against serious cross-border threats to health or ensuring high standards of quality and safety of health care and of medicinal products or medical devices, on the basis of Union or Member State law which provides for suitable and specific measures to safeguard the rights and freedoms of the data subject, in particular professional secrecy;

j. processing is necessary for archiving purposes in the public interest, scientific or historical research purposes or statistical purposes in accordance with Article 89(1) based on Union or Member State law which shall be proportionate to the aim pursued, respect the essence of the right to data protection and provide for suitable and specific measures to safeguard the fundamental rights and the interests of the data subject.

22.3.1 **Consent**

Most commonly data is processed according to the first condition of processing data. That is 'the data subject has given consent to the processing of his or her personal data for one or more specific purposes', or for special data, 'the data subject has given *explicit* consent to the processing of those personal data for one or more specified purposes'. What in practice does this mean?

Assistance is found in Art. 7 'conditions for consent'. This tells us that 'where processing is based on consent, the controller shall be able to demonstrate that the data subject has consented to processing of his or her personal data.' Thus the burden of proof for consent-based processing rests with the data controller. This, in part is why on or around 25 May 2018, when the GDPR came into force you were faced with a flurry of requests to reaffirm your agreement (consent) to be on any number of mailing lists and to allow web pages to install cookies and similar. Any organization that did not have a clear record of your consent to have your data gathered and processed was not compliant with GDPR if that processing was based upon consent. What form must that consent take? Recital 32 tells us 'consent should be given by a clear affirmative act establishing a freely given, specific, informed and unambiguous indication of the data subject's agreement to the processing of personal data relating to him or her, such as by a written statement, including by electronic means, or an oral statement'. This form of consent may be 'ticking a box when visiting an internet website, choosing technical settings for information society services or another statement or conduct which clearly indicates in this context the data subject's acceptance of the proposed processing of his or her personal data.' As consent must be an affirmative act, 'silence, pre-ticked boxes or inactivity should not constitute consent'. Article 7(2) makes it clear that where consent is sought in the framework of a wider set of declarations or documents (such as the terms and conditions of use of a web page or social media platform) 'the request for consent shall be presented in a manner which is clearly distinguishable from the other matters, in an intelligible and easily accessible form, using clear and plain language'.

The consent must be specific to the processing purpose.[89] Thus consent should cover all processing activities carried out for the same purpose or purposes, and when the processing has multiple purposes, consent should be given for all of them. This prevents data gathered for one purpose being processed for a different unrelated purpose. The data subject has the right to withdraw his or her consent at any time. Vitally, by Art. 7(3) it is a requirement that 'it shall be as easy to withdraw as to give consent.' This prevents data controllers from making withdrawal complex, or hiding links to systems which allow deregistration or unsubscribing options. Finally, in determining whether consent has been freely given, the GDPR allows regulators and courts to take account of whether the performance of a contract, including the provision of a service, is conditional on consent to the processing of personal data that is not necessary for the performance of that contract.[90]

The GDPR treats children as a special case. By Art. 8(1) where an information society service (including any social media or communications service) is offered to a child,

---

[89] Art. 7(2).
[90] Art. 7(4).

being a person under the age of 16, processing of the personal data of that child shall only be lawful if the consent is given not by the child but by 'the holder of parental responsibility over the child'. Member states are allowed to lower this age to 13 should they wish and the UK has chosen to do so, electing to set the age limit at 13 by s. 9 of the 2018 Act. Importantly, by Art. 8(2) the data controller is required to 'make reasonable efforts to verify in such cases that consent is given or authorised by the holder of parental responsibility over the child, taking into consideration available technology'. This means the data controller has to take steps to attempt to identify when young people are under 16 (or 13 in the UK) and to ensure that the right consents have been given. Recital 38 explains the reason for this:

> Children merit specific protection with regard to their personal data, as they may be less aware of the risks, consequences and safeguards concerned and their rights in relation to the processing of personal data. Such specific protection should, in particular, apply to the use of personal data of children for the purposes of marketing or creating personality or user profiles and the collection of personal data with regard to children when using services offered directly to a child.

22.3.2 Other conditions for the processing of data

Although many talk of the GDPR as being a consent-based model,[91] consent is not the only condition under which processing will be fair and lawful. Article 6 has a number of additional conditions, most of which allow for the usual functioning of pre-existing legal obligations such as the right to process to conclude or perform a contract,[92] or the right to process to comply with a legal obligation,[93] or in the public interest or in the exercise of official authority.[94]

Two interesting conditions are Art. 6(1)(d): processing in the vital interests of the data subject and Art. 6(1)(f): processing necessary for the purposes of legitimate interests pursued by the data controller. Recital 46 gives more detail as to what are meant by 'vital interests'. We are told 'the processing of personal data should also be regarded to be lawful where it is necessary to protect an interest which is essential for the life of the data subject or that of another natural person'. The Information Commissioner's Office in their GDPR guidance explain 'it is likely to be particularly relevant for emergency medical care, when you need to process personal data for medical purposes but the individual is incapable of giving consent to the processing'.[95] Recital 46 notes that 'some types of processing may serve both important grounds of public interest and

---

[91] See E Carolan, 'The continuing problems with online consent under the EU's emerging data protection principles' (2016) 32 *Computer Law & Security Review* 462; T Zarsky, 'Incompatible: The GDPR in the Age of Big Data' [2017] 47 *Seton Hall Law Review* 995.

[92] This may be relied upon if the data controller needs to process the data subject's personal data to fulfil a contractual obligation to them; or because they have been asked to do something before entering into a contract (e.g. provide a quote).

[93] This applies when the data controller is obliged to process the personal data to comply with the law. An example would be where an employer needs to process personal data to comply with its legal obligation to disclose employee salary details to HMRC.

[94] This applies when it is necessary to process personal data 'in the exercise of official authority' or to perform a specific task in the public interest that is set out in law. Examples include HMRC's calculations of tax due to be paid or the operation of the DVLA driver database.

[95] <https://ico.org.uk/for-organisations/guide-to-the-general-data-protection-regulation-gdpr/lawful-basis-for-processing/vital-interests/>.

the vital interests of the data subject as for instance when processing is necessary for humanitarian purposes, including for monitoring epidemics and their spread or in situations of humanitarian emergencies, in particular in situations of natural and man-made disasters'.

Legitimate interests are probably the most interesting ground excepting consent. This allows the data controller to process data without specific consent where processing is 'necessary for the purposes of the legitimate interests pursued by the controller or by a third party'. This is the only point in the conditions for processing where specifically the interests of a third party, or of the data controller, are acknowledged. Again, the recitals give some guidance; this time Recital 47 is relevant. It states 'such legitimate interest could exist for example where there is a relevant and appropriate relationship between the data subject and the controller in situations such as where the data subject is a client or in the service of the controller'. It is noticeable that this guidance is less precise than that given in relation to the other conditions, and indeed Recital 47 states 'the existence of a legitimate interest would need careful assessment including whether a data subject can reasonably expect at the time and in the context of the collection of the personal data that processing for that purpose may take place'. The Information Commissioner's Office (ICO) gives further guidance noting 'legitimate interests are the most flexible lawful basis for processing, but you cannot assume it will always be the most appropriate. It is likely to be most appropriate where you use people's data in ways they would reasonably expect and which have a minimal privacy impact, or where there is a compelling justification for the processing.'[96]

The legitimate interest test is three-fold. The data controller must: (1) identify a legitimate interest; (2) show that the processing is necessary to achieve it; and (3) balance it against the individual's interests, rights, and freedoms. This is known as the purpose, necessity, and balancing test. We have not yet received guidance from the European Data Protection Board on the application of legitimate interests under the GDPR but the Article 29 Working Party did issue an opinion on legitimate interests under the directive.[97] They first make is clear that an interest is distinct from a purpose, so 'a company may have an interest in ensuring the health and safety of its staff working at its nuclear power-plant. Related to this, the company may have as a purpose the implementation of specific access control procedures which justifies the processing of certain specified personal data in order to help ensure the health and safety of staff.' The justification for processing relates to the interest, not the purpose, and the interest 'must be sufficiently clearly articulated to allow the balancing test to be carried out against the interests and fundamental rights of the data subject.'[98] The interest must of course be 'legitimate'. In the view of the Article 29 Working Party this means that it passes a balancing test between the rights and interest of the controller and the rights and interest of the subject. They note that the interest may even be trivial, such as conventional direct marketing,[99] but this may be legitimate if 'the controller can pursue this interest

---

[96] <https://ico.org.uk/for-organisations/guide-to-the-general-data-protection-regulation-gdpr/lawful-basis-for-processing/legitimate-interests/>.

[97] Article 29 Working Party, *Opinion 06/2014 on the notion of legitimate interests of the data controller under Article 7 of Directive 95/46/EC*, 844/14/EN WP 217.

[98] Ibid. 24.

[99] Recital 47 of the GDPR acknowledges this, stating 'the processing of personal data for direct marketing purposes may be regarded as carried out for a legitimate interest'.

in a way that is in accordance with data protection and other laws: in other words [it is] "acceptable under the law"'.¹⁰⁰ The key therefore is balancing the rights of the data subject with the rights of others including the data controller. The Article 29 Working Party imagines this as two spectrums of rights and interests: one belonging to the data subject, the other to the third party or parties.¹⁰¹

Highlight The balancing test

It is useful to imagine both the legitimate interests of the controller and the impact on the interests and rights of the data subject on a spectrum. Legitimate interests can range from insignificant through somewhat important to compelling. Similarly, the impact on the interests and rights of the data subjects may be more or may be less significant and may range from trivial to very serious.

Legitimate interests of the controller, when minor and not very compelling may, in general, only override the interests and rights of data subjects in cases where the impact on these rights and interests are even more trivial. On the other hand, important and compelling legitimate interests may in some cases, and subject to safeguards and measures, justify even significant intrusion into privacy or other significant impact on the interests or rights of the data subjects.

Relatively minor invasions into personal data privacy may therefore be more easily justified under the legitimate interest principle than more serious invasions or abuses. The Article 29 Working Party gives examples to illustrate the balancing principle.

Example Permissible legitimate interests

Claudia orders a pizza via a mobile app on her smartphone, but does not opt out of marketing on the website. Her address and credit card details are stored for the delivery. A few days later Claudia receives discount coupons for similar products from the pizza chain in her letterbox at home.

This is likely permissible. The pizza restaurant has a legitimate, but not particularly compelling, interest in attempting to sell more of its products to its customers. On the other hand, there does not appear to be any significant intrusion into Claudia's privacy, or any other undue impact on her interests and rights. The data and the context are relatively innocent (consumption of pizza). Other factors that may be considered include whether the restaurant provided an easy-to-use opportunity to opt out of marketing on the website or app.

---

¹⁰⁰ Article 29 Working Party (n. 97) 25.
¹⁰¹ Ibid. 30.

> **Example** Impermissible legitimate interests
>
> The pizza restaurant stores not only Claudia's address and credit card details but also her recent order history. In addition, her purchase history is combined with data from the supermarket where Claudia does her online shopping (which is linked to the restaurant). Claudia is provided with special offers and targeted advertisements based on her order history for both the restaurant and the supermarket. She receives the adverts and special offers both online and offline, by regular mail, email, and placement on the website of the companies, as well as on the website of a number of selected partners. Her browsing history (click-stream) is tracked as well. Her location data is also tracked via her mobile phone. An analytics software is run through the data and predicts her preferences and the times and locations when she will be most likely to make a larger purchase, willing to pay a higher price, susceptible to being influenced by a particular rate of discount, or when she craves most strongly for her favourite pizza or ready-meals.

In this case the processing goes far beyond what Claudia may have expected when ordering pizza or groceries. The scale of data collected and the techniques used to analyse it are far beyond minimal intervention. In this case, it is highly unlikely this type of processing could rely upon the legitimate interests condition.

22.4 **Conclusions**

Despite all the guidance, it is difficult to explain with any certainty when any of these conditions is fulfilled given the rather generic nature of them. It is hard to imagine what form of processing may be *necessary* for the purposes of legitimate interests pursued by the data controller rather than merely convenient or expedient. As Professor Lloyd observes '[a]lthough many situations may be identified in which it will be useful for the data controller to hold information, the restrictions associated with the adjective "necessary" must constantly be borne in mind'.[102] What is clear is that the protections afforded by the data protection principles are limited. Processing may take place for any number of conditions without the consent of the data subject. Although the data protection principles provide a framework that says processing is fair and reasonable, and although they require data to be kept secure and up to date, the true means of scrutiny and supervision of data controllers are to be found elsewhere in the GDPR.

TEST QUESTIONS

Question 1

Marie is a keen, if unsuccessful, blogger (with a very limited following) who writes mostly about online gambling. Marie's most recent blogs want to dispel the myth that online gamblers are

---

[102] I Lloyd, *Information Technology Law* (8th edn, OUP 2017) 109.

addicts. She describes a number of her friends—a reputable dentist living in the Kensington area, a journalist who has recently been nominated for a prestigious award, and a teacher in a primary school close to Marie's home, and outlines how they use online gambling sites for multiple purposes, including socializing with other gamblers. Although Marie does not name these individuals, she is contacted by one of them and asked to edit her blog post to remove some of this information. She refuses and her friend complains to the Information Commissioner's Office (ICO). When investigating, the ICO also realizes that Marie is an avid 'Go-Pro' user and posts her 'Go-Pro' footage, filmed all over London, on her blog.

Marie seeks your advice as to whether she is in fact processing personal data within the meaning of data protection law and, if so, whether there are any exemptions that she could invoke to avoid data protection regulation.

Question 2

In the current setting, the broad definitions of personal data, processing of personal data, and controller are likely to cover an unprecedented wide range of new factual situations due to technological development. The scope of EU data protection law is therefore too broad and should have been limited in the data protection reform process.

Discuss.

FURTHER READING

Books

C Kuner, L Bygrave, and C Docksey, *Commentary on the EU General Data Protection Regulation* (OUP 2019)

O Lynskey, *The Foundations of EU Data Protection Law* (CUP 2015)

P Voigt and A von dem Bussche, *The EU General Data Protection Regulation (GDPR): A Practical Guide* (Routledge 2017)

Chapters and articles

F Borgesius et al., 'Tracking Walls, Take-It-Or-Leave-It Choices, the GDPR, and the ePrivacy Regulation' (2017) 3 *European Data Protection Law* 353

F Ferretti, 'Data protection and the legitimate interest of data controllers: Much ado about nothing or the winter of rights?' (2014) 51(3) *Common Market Law Review* 843

B-J Koops, 'The Trouble with European Data Protection Law' (2014) 4 *International Data Privacy Law* 250

N Purtova, 'The law of everything. Broad concept of personal data and future of EU data protection law' (2018) 10 *Law, Innovation and Technology* 40

23

Data protection: rights and obligations

Data controllers are supervised using a variety of means including public scrutiny, oversight by the Information Commissioner, and where necessary the application of the criminal law. However, the primary control mechanism for day-to-day enforcement of data protection principles is through the actions of data subjects. This chapter will focus on the data subject and how he or she can self-police their own data under the GDPR and the DPA 2018 before concluding by looking at the role of the Information Commissioners Office in enforcing data protection rights when the actions of the data subject prove to be inadequate.

23.1 **Data subject rights**

Self-policing of personal data is a key aspect of the Act and to assist with this data subjects are given an assortment of low-level enforcement powers. The foundation for this are basic transparency rights. Articles 12–14 of the GDPR and s. 44 of the Data Protection Act 2018 ensure that the data subject should always be fully informed of when and why their data is collected, who controls it and what use is being made of it. It begins with the general principle under Art. 12 that the data controller 'shall take appropriate measures to provide any information referred to in Articles 13 and 14 . . . in a concise, transparent, intelligible and easily accessible form, using clear and plain language, in particular for any information addressed specifically to a child'. The information to be provided under Arts. 13–14 varies depending upon whether the information is provided when the data is gathered from the individual (Art. 13) or from a third party (Art. 14).

 Highlight Information to be provided where personal data is collected from the data subject (Art. 13)

a. the identity and the contact details of the controller and, where applicable, of the controller's representative;

b. the contact details of the data protection officer, where applicable;

c. the purposes of the processing for which the personal data are intended as well as the legal basis for the processing;

➡

➡

d. where the processing is based on [legitimate interests], the legitimate interests pursued by the controller or by a third party;

e. the recipients or categories of recipients of the personal data, if any;

f. where applicable, the fact that the controller intends to transfer personal data to a third country or international organisation and the existence or absence of an adequacy decision by the Commission.

In addition, the controller shall, at the time when personal data is obtained, provide the data subject with the following further information necessary to ensure fair and transparent processing:

a. the period for which the personal data will be stored, or if that is not possible, the criteria used to determine that period;

b. the existence of the right to request from the controller access to and rectification or erasure of personal data or restriction of processing concerning the data subject or to object to processing as well as the right to data portability;

c. where the processing is based on [consent], the existence of the right to withdraw consent at any time, without affecting the lawfulness of processing based on consent before its withdrawal;

d. the right to lodge a complaint with a supervisory authority;

e. whether the provision of personal data is a statutory or contractual requirement, or a requirement necessary to enter into a contract, as well as whether the data subject is obliged to provide the personal data and of the possible consequences of failure to provide such data;

f. the existence of automated decision-making, including profiling, and at least in those cases, meaningful information about the logic involved, as well as the significance and the envisaged consequences of such processing for the data subject.

The list under Article 14 is similar but slightly different.

 Highlight Information to be provided where personal data has not been obtained from the data subject (Art. 14)

a. the identity and the contact details of the controller and, where applicable, of the controller's representative;

b. the contact details of the data protection officer, where applicable;

c. the purposes of the processing for which the personal data are intended as well as the legal basis for the processing;

d. the categories of personal data concerned;

e. the recipients or categories of recipients of the personal data, if any;

f. where applicable, the fact that the controller intends to transfer personal data to a third country or international organisation and the existence or absence of an adequacy decision by the Commission.

➡

→

In addition, the controller shall provide the data subject with the following information necessary to ensure fair and transparent processing in respect of the data subject:

a. the period for which the personal data will be stored, or if that is not possible, the criteria used to determine that period;

b. where the processing is based on [legitimate interests], the legitimate interests pursued by the controller or by a third party;

c. the existence of the right to request from the controller access to and rectification or erasure of personal data or restriction of processing concerning the data subject or to object to processing as well as the right to data portability;

d. where the processing is based on [consent], the existence of the right to withdraw consent at any time, without affecting the lawfulness of processing based on consent before its withdrawal;

e. the right to lodge a complaint with a supervisory authority;

f. from which source the personal data originate, and if applicable, whether it came from publicly accessible sources;

g. the existence of automated decision-making, including profiling, and at least in those cases, meaningful information about the logic involved, as well as the significance and the envisaged consequences of such processing for the data subject.

The idea behind these combined provisions is that the data subject should always be aware of who is gathering his data and for what purpose(s). As Recital 60 says 'the principles of fair and transparent processing require that the data subject be informed of the existence of the processing operation and its purposes.' However, such transparency is not without risk. Given the everyday nature of data gathering and processing today, the large number of notices generated under Arts13–14 are likely to lead the data subject to suffer informational overload, leading to data protection fatigue. How often do you immediately dismiss cookie notices on websites? Do you ever read the full details of what is being gathered and for what purpose? How often do you read the full privacy terms on Facebook? Because there is a risk that transparency does not achieve the full level of supervision by data subjects and compliance by data controllers, the transparency provisions are supplemented with a number of more powerful tools for the data subject.

The first of these is that data subjects may under s. 45 of the Data Protection Act make a subject access request.[1] This requires data controllers to reveal to the data subject if they hold data on them and what use they make of that data. This includes detailing what data the data controller holds, who, if anyone, they disclose that data to, and any information, if available, as to the source of the data. This information should be given to the data subject 'without undue delay', and in any event within one month of the application being received by the data controller.[2] The information provided must be

---

[1] Giving effect to Art. 15 GDPR.
[2] See s. 45(3) and s. 54(2) DPA 2018.

provided to the data subject in a concise, intelligible, and easily accessible form, using clear and plain language.[3] The aim of s. 45 is to allow data subjects to check what data is held on them and how that data is being processed and/or transmitted onwards. This investigatory right then arms data subjects with the necessary information to allow them to take further action, such as applying for data to be deleted or corrected, or if necessary to report the actions of the data controller to the Information Commissioner for investigation.

That is not to say this procedure is without risk. It would obviously be a breach of the data protection principles if data were revealed under a s. 45 application to the wrong person.[4] To prevent this, there are a number of measures designed to protect the data subject. By s. 52(4) the data controller may require the data subject to provide further information to prove his identity and may refuse to comply with a subject access request (SAR) until this information is supplied. This information may take the form of personal identifiers, such as passwords or identification numbers, or it may take the form of physical identifiers, such as a passport or driving license. Further to this, there is the risk of conjoined or commixed data. These are forms of data in which the information held on the data subject is linked to data held on other persons. Conjoined data is data which is held in a single file or folder about two or more data subjects, but which as far as possible treats data subjects separately. An example may be a personnel review file on a sales and marketing team which evaluates each member of the team in comparison with each other, rating their relative strengths and weaknesses and evaluating their teamwork. Commixed data is data relating to two or more persons which has come together to form a single file or entry. An example may be a joint mortgage application of two persons which forms a single mortgage file with the lender.

To ensure the rights of one person, do not interfere with or infringe the rights of another; both the GDPR and the Data Protection Act take steps to protect parties whose data may be conjoined or commixed. By Art. 23 of the GDPR, rights awarded to data subjects may be restricted, inter alia, to protect the rights and freedoms of others. The UK government has adopted specifically in Sch. 2 of the Data Protection Act 2018 that:

> Article 15(1) to (3) of the GDPR, and Article 5 of the GDPR so far as its provisions correspond to the rights and obligations provided for in Article 15(1) to (3), do not oblige a controller to disclose information to the data subject to the extent that doing so would involve disclosing information relating to another individual who can be identified from the information.[5]

In such a situation the information may be handed over where (a) the other individual has consented to the disclosure of the information to the data subject, or (b) it is reasonable to disclose the information to the data subject without the consent of the other individual.[6] If the balancing principle is not met, the data controller should not hand over commixed or conjoined data. The questions of what qualifies as 'information relating to another individual who can be identified' and when it is reasonable to comply

---

[3] See s. 52(1), giving effect to Art. 12(1) GDPR.

[4] Imagine if you will an investigative journalist obtaining medical details of a well-known political or business figure by means of a false application under s. 45.

[5] Sch. 2, para. 16(1).

[6] Sch. 2, para. 16(2).

with a request absent the other data subject's permission, was first considered by the Court of Appeal in *Durant v Financial Services Authority*.[7]

23.1.1 Subject access: *Durant v the Financial Services Authority*

The appellant was an erstwhile customer of Barclays Bank, against whom he had brought proceedings which ended unsuccessfully for the appellant in 1993. Since then he had sought, without success, disclosure of various records in connection with the dispute giving rise to the litigation because he believed that the records might assist him to reopen his claims or to secure an investigation into the conduct of the bank. In September and October 2001 he made two requests to the FSA in its role as the regulator for the financial services sector, seeking disclosure of personal data held by it, both electronically and in manual files. The FSA in response provided Mr Durant with copies of documents it held in computerized form, some of which had been redacted so as not to disclose the names of others. It refused his request for access to the unredacted documents. It also refused the whole of his request for information held on manual files on the ground that the information sought was not 'personal' within the definition of 'personal data' in s. 1 of the Data Protection Act 1998 and that, even if it was, it did not constitute 'data' within the separate definition of that word in s. 1(1)(c) in the sense of forming part of a 'relevant filing system'.

The court was faced with several questions: (1) What is a 'relevant filing system'? (2) Which data is 'personal' data under that Act? (3) Does a data subject have an entitlement to have access to unredacted data under s. 7? and (4) What limits may be placed on access to conjoined and commixed data?

In answering the first two questions the court first divided all the files Mr Durant sought access to into four categories. These were:

(i) a file relating to the systems and controls Barclays Bank was required to maintain and which was subject to control by the FSA. This file was in date order and also contained a few documents relating to part of the appellant's complaint against the bank, which concerned such systems and controls;

(ii) a file relating to complaints by customers of Barclays Bank to the FSA. The file was subdivided alphabetically by reference to the complainant's name and contained, behind a divider marked 'Mr Durant', a number of documents relating to his complaint filed in date order;

(iii) a Bank Investigations Group file, relating and organized by reference to issues or cases concerning Barclays Bank, but not necessarily identified by reference to an individual complainant. It contained a sub-file marked 'Mr Durant', which contained documents relating to his complaint. Neither the file nor the sub-file was indexed in any way save by reference to the name of the appellant on the sub-file itself; and

(iv) Company Secretariat papers comprising a sheaf of papers in an unmarked transparent plastic folder held by the FSA's Company Secretariat, relating to the Mr Durant's complaint about the FSA's refusal to disclose to him details and the outcome of its investigation of his complaints against Barclays Bank. This file was not organized by date or any other criterion.

---

[7] [2004] FSR 28.

The court found:[8]

> **Highlight** Relevant filing systems (from *Durant v FSA*)
>
> A relevant filing system for the purpose of the Act, is limited to a system:
>
> (1) in which the files forming part of it are structured or referenced in such a way as clearly to indicate at the outset of the search whether specific information capable of amounting to personal data of an individual requesting it under s. 7 is held within the system and, if so, in which file or files it is held; and
>
> (2) which has, as part of its own structure or referencing mechanism, a sufficiently sophisticated and detailed means of readily indicating whether and where in an individual file or files specific criteria or information about the applicant can be readily located.

On this basis it was found that none of the further types of files were 'relevant filing systems' as 'none of the files in question is so structured or indexed as to provide ready access to it . . . an ability of staff readily to identify and locate whole files, even those organized chronologically and/or by reference to his and others' names, is not enough'.[9]

This was a rather surprising outcome as it had been thought data held in organized files were covered and as in particular file (ii), the Barclay's complaints file, was organized by reference to the complainants' names this seemed to fit the definition of 'relevant filing system' in s. 1 of the Act. What Auld LJ pointed out though was that the Act requires the information to be structured in such a way that 'specific information relating to a particular individual is readily accessible'. In the FSA file Mr Durant's complaint recorded in file (ii) was not so structured. The data was indexed firstly by reference to Barclays Bank, then by complainant: in effect this was a file about Barclays Bank which mentioned Mr Durant, rather than a file about Mr Durant. Thus, with respect to Mr Durant, it was not 'relevant' to him. This though did not dispense with the question of how to deal with conjoined and commixed data. Although it may be that the files were not 'relevant', they may still contain personal data.

To this end Auld LJ began his analysis of what constitutes personal data with a warning.[10]

> **Highlight** Auld LJ's warning
>
> [The subject access right] is not an automatic key to any information, readily accessible or not, of matters in which he may be named or involved. Nor is to assist him, for example, to obtain discovery of documents that may assist him in litigation or complaints against third parties. As a matter of practicality and given the focus of the Act on ready accessibility of the information—whether from a computerised or comparably sophisticated non-computerised system—it is likely in most cases that only information that names or directly refers to him will qualify.

---

[8] Per Auld LJ at [50].
[9] Ibid. [51].
[10] Ibid. [27].

With this said Auld LJ then went on to analyse what qualifies as 'personal data':[11]

 Highlight Personal data (from *Durant v FSA*)

Mere mention of the data subject in a document held by a data controller does not necessarily amount to his personal data . . . It seems to me that there are two notions that may be of assistance. The first is whether the information is biographical in a significant sense, that is, going beyond the recording of the putative data subject's involvement in a matter or an event that has no personal connotations, a life event in respect of which his privacy could not be said to be compromised. The second is one of focus. The information should have the putative data subject as its focus rather than some other person with whom he may have been involved or some transaction or event in which he may have figured or have had an interest, for example, as in this case, an investigation into some other person's or body's conduct that he may have instigated. In short, it is information that affects his privacy, whether in his personal or family life, business or professional capacity.

This is a vital distinction that may be best thought of in terms of a stage play. There are characters who are central to a stage play, for instance, Hamlet in the eponymous Shakespeare tragedy. Then there are characters which support the telling of the story: for instance, Ophelia and Laertes. No one would claim the play is about Ophelia or Laertes, but they are essential for the story of Hamlet. So is the case of personal data. Personal data is, in Auld LJ's words, information which has 'the putative data subject as its focus': it is about the lead character not the supporting cast. In the instant case none of the data Mr Durant requested access to was 'personal data'. In each case, although he was mentioned and details about him and his complaints were recorded, he was not the central character of the files in question.

How then does one know if they are a central character or merely supporting cast in any given file? According to Auld LJ it is a question of 'a continuum of relevance or proximity to the data subject as distinct, say, from transactions or matters in which he may have been involved to a greater or lesser degree'.[12] This means data controllers and perhaps later the Information Commissioner or judges will have to evaluate the degree to which the data subject is the focus of the data in question, based upon the biographical focus of the data. Data which is clearly focused on the data subject will be personal data, even if others are mentioned; data which is clearly focused on a third party is not, even if it mentions the data subject. Data in between remains somewhat in a grey area to be decided on the facts in a case-by-case analysis.

The answers to these questions led to the dismissal of Mr Durant's claim to access the further information which had been withheld from him, but what about his claim to have unredacted versions of data already supplied to him? Auld LJ suggested a two-stage approach be taken when considering redaction of data. The first is to ask whether the data redacted 'is necessarily part of the personal data that the data subject has requested'.[13]

---

[11] Ibid. [28].
[12] Ibid.
[13] Ibid. [65].

He defines 'necessarily' as 'Where a data controller cannot comply with the request without disclosing information about another individual who can be identified from the information.' If such information about another is not 'necessarily' part of personal data sought, then 'the data controller, whose primary obligation is to provide information, not documents, can, if he chooses to provide that information in the form of a copy document, simply redact such third-party information because it is not a necessary part of the data subject's personal data'.[14] If the data is 'necessarily' part of the data subject's personal data then the second stage is applied. This requires the data controller to balance the interests of the data subjects in question. Should the revealing of personal data about other data subjects appear to be a greater intrusion of privacy, or carry greater risk of harm, than the process of redacting does to the original data subject's access request, then the data may be redacted. Should there be little risk to other data subjects, then the interests of the data subject who made the access request should be protected and unredacted data should be supplied. In Auld LJ's words:

> In short, it all depends on the circumstances whether it would be reasonable to disclose to a data subject the name of another person figuring in his personal data, whether that person is a source, or a recipient or likely recipient of that information, or has a part in the matter the subject of the personal data. Beyond the basic presumption or starting point, I believe that the courts should be wary of attempting to devise any principles of general application one way or the other.[15]

This left one final question for the court: what discretion do the courts and data controllers have when dealing with subject access requests which may involve conjoined or commixed data? Mr Durant had asked the court to compel the FSA to release to him the data they had retained and redacted under s. 7(9). Although this became a moot point during the analysis applied in answering the prior questions, Auld LJ did question when it may be appropriate for a court to so do. His answer was not terribly clear but he did make two points strongly. The first was that the court's discretion under s. 7(9) is general and untrammelled, the second that, when dealing with the disclosure of data relating to a third party, it may be difficult for a court to order the data be retained if it found it to be reasonable for the data subject to have access to the data. This seems to be a weak support for the view that if the data relating to a third party forms a necessary part of the data relating to the data subject's access request, the court should order the data to be released to the data subject, notwithstanding the effect this may have on the third party.

In sum, *Durant* is a simple case dealing with complex issues. The case is simple because as noted by another of the judges in the case, Buxton LJ, 'the information sought by Mr Durant was by no stretch of the imagination a borderline case'.[16] Mr Durant was seeking to use the subject access right (SAR) found in the Data Protection Act to effect pre-trial discovery in the hope of finding evidence to allow him to raise a further claim against either Barclays Bank or the FSA. This was a clear abuse of the s. 7 procedure. The complexity of the case was in the type of data in question: most data is not 'clean' data about a single

---

[14] Ibid.

[15] Ibid. [66]. In the instant case the court found Mr Durant had no right to unredacted copies of the data supplied to him as in most cases it was not 'necessarily part of the personal data that he had requested'. On the two occasions the data redacted did pass the first hurdle of the test it fell down at the second hurdle as 'they were of the name of an FSA employee which, in itself, can have been of little or no legitimate value to Mr Durant and who had understandably withheld his or her consent because Mr Durant had abused him or her over the telephone' (at [67]).

[16] Ibid. [80].

data subject. Data is processed and reordered regularly. It is commixed and conjoined to create new data and identifying 'a' data subject or 'the' data subject is increasingly difficult. It is less often about Hamlet: a central character surrounded by supporting cast. More often we are dealing with a complex ensemble piece with no clear central role.

23.1.2 Revising subject access

From as soon as the *Durant* decision was handed down it was felt to be flawed. How could the court find that files ordered by Mr Durant's name not be data about him, even if they were sub-files of a larger file about Barclays Bank? Mr Durant may not have been Hamlet in the larger Barclays file but he clearly was in the sub-file ordered by his name— it might be said that in that file he, like Hamlet, was the eponymous hero.

It was therefore not surprising that in reviews of the *Durant* decision it has been distinguished and can no longer be said to be good law. The Court of Appeal reviewed the decision in *Durant* in the case of *Edem v IC & Financial Services Authority*.[17] Mr Edem had made an earlier complaint to the FSA about a UK Bank. He clearly felt that that complaint had been mishandled as he requested 'a copy of all information that the Authority held about him and "my complaint that the FSA had failed to correctly regulate Egg PLC"' under the Freedom of Information Act 2000. The FSA refused to release certain information which they believed could identify three employees, on the basis that there was an exemption under s. 40(2) of the Data Protection Act 1998 for data which falls within the definition of personal data under the Data Protection Act. Mr Edem challenged this on the basis that it defeated his Freedom of Information Act request, which had been made for legitimate reasons, and on the basis that individuals could not be identified just by their names as attached to emails. By the time the case arrived at the Court of Appeal a single issue remained live; whether information amounting to the names of these three individuals who had worked on the complaints constituted 'personal data' under s. 1(1) of the Data Protection Act. The individuals in question were all junior employees who did not have public-facing roles. In giving the decision of the court Moses LJ began by reviewing the guidance of Auld LJ in *Durant*. In that case, of course, Auld LJ had famously stated 'mere mention of the data subject in a document held by a data controller does not necessarily amount to his personal data'[18] suggesting the data in this case may not qualify as personal data under s. 1(1). To determine whether it did, one would usually apply the *Durant* test (as we have just seen) to determine whether or not data is personal data which is: (1) biographical, or (2) focused on the data subject. This is exactly what the first-tier tribunal had done in *Edem*,[19] but Moses LJ believed this was incorrect:

> The First-Tier Tribunal were wrong to apply Auld LJ's 'notions' in this case. There is no reason to do so. The information in this case was plainly concerned with those three individuals. Neither of Auld LJ's notions had any application and to seek to apply them runs contrary to the Statute, the Directive, and the jurisprudence of the Court of Justice, to which I have already referred. It is important not to misunderstand the context in which Auld LJ referred to those 'notions'.[20]

---

[17] [2014] EWCA Civ 92.
[18] *Durant* (n. 7) [28].
[19] *Edem* (n. 17) [16].
[20] Ibid. [17].

What did Moses LJ mean by this? After a short discussion of the circumstances which led Mr Durant to bring his claim, Moses LJ concludes that the 'notions' were Auld LJ's way of 'explaining why information and documents in which Mr Durant's name appeared were not personal data relating to him'.[21] In the current case the question was whether disclosure of a person's name is disclosure of personal data. As Moses LJ notes: 'a name is personal data unless it is so common that without further information, such as its use in a work context, a person would remain unidentifiable despite its disclosure'.[22]

This position has been revisited in two recent cases, both of which support the *Edem* position over the *Durant* one. The first is *Dawson-Damer v Taylor Wessing LLP*.[23] This is a complex case with quite a simple data protection angle. The claimants were the beneficiaries of a trust held in the Bahamas. They made a subject access request under the Data Protection Act 1998 to the respondents, the legal representatives of the trust in the UK. The respondents refused to comply with the requests, contending that much of the personal data was exempt from the data subject access provisions in the Act as it consisted of information in respect of which a claim to legal professional privilege could be maintained in legal proceedings, for the purposes Sch. 7 to the 1998 Act.[24] The claimants subsequently brought a claim for declarations that the respondents had failed to comply with their requests and orders under s. 7 of the 1998 Act requiring them to do so. Before the Court of Appeal Arden LJ examined the scope of the legal professional privilege defence. She found that the exemption for legal professional privilege applies only to a claim which would be recognized in legal proceedings in the UK. It does not extend to privilege under any other system of law,[25] and, further, the privilege does not extend to documents which are not the subject of legal professional privilege but which are the subject of rules of non-disclosure (such as a trustee's right of non-disclosure).[26] On this basis she found that Taylor Wessing was a data controller, regardless of whether it was acting as an agent of the trustee. It must claim privilege in support of its client but is otherwise in no special position, and therefore the privilege did not apply.[27]

She then went on to determine whether it would be disproportionate for the data to be supplied. She noted that:

> there are substantial public policy reasons for giving people control over data maintained about them through the system of rights and remedies contained in the Directive, which must mean that where and so far as possible, SARs should be enforced. Moreover, most data controllers can be expected to know of their obligations to comply with SARs and to have designed their systems accordingly to enable them to make most searches for SAR purposes.[28]

---

[21] Ibid. [20].
[22] Ibid.
[23] [2017] EWCA Civ 74.
[24] The same protection may be found in Sch. 2, para. 19 of the Data Protection Act 2018.
[25] *Dawson-Damer* (n. 23) [44].
[26] Ibid. [51]–[54].
[27] Ibid. [56].
[28] Ibid. [79].

On this basis she found that Taylor Wessing should have complied with the request. Finally, she examined whether there were any grounds under which Taylor Wessing may have legitimately not complied with the request. She began by noting that:

> the rights given by the Directive are to protect fundamental rights conferred by EU law. We have been shown nothing in the DPA or the Directive which limits the purpose for which a data subject may request his data, or provides data controllers with the option of not providing data based solely on the requester's purpose. The data controller has property rights as well, but they do not override the proper exercise by the data subject of his rights.[29]

This led directly on to a discussion of *Durant*. Taylor Wessing had, in part, refused to hand over the data on the basis that it would be used for a legal challenge. The advice was that following *Durant* SARs could not be used as a proxy for discovery. Finding in favour of the claimants, Arden LJ pointed out though that this case was quite different to *Durant*. In *Durant* Auld LJ held that a person could not claim that something was personal data because it would assist him in obtaining discovery or in litigation or complaints against third parties (in other words data which was not strictly personal could not be made into personal data because it would assist him in his claims). In the present case, the issue was whether the claimants were entitled to data which was personal data even though it had the collateral purpose of assisting in litigation. Arden LJ was convinced this was quite different and ordered the data to be transferred to the claimants.[30]

The other case is the joint appeal in *Ittihadieh v 5–11 Cheyne Gardens and Deer v The University of Oxford*.[31] This involved two separate refusals to provide data following subject access requests (SARs). Mr Ittihadieh became concerned that other residents of Cheyne Gardens had been keeping a file containing his personal data, during the course of various disputes he had with them. He submitted a SAR to the company that manages Cheyne Gardens and, in response, the company disclosed more than 400 documents. Mr Ittihadieh was not satisfied and brought a claim under the Data Protection Act claiming information had been held back. Similarly, Dr Deer had submitted two SARs to Oxford University, stemming from an ongoing employment dispute. The University rejected several of Dr Deer's requests, but did disclose some information in response to the requests.

In the Court of Appeal Lewison LJ gave the judgment of the court. In a wide-ranging judgment looking at everything from the form a SAR should take to the purpose of a SAR and what forms a response should take, he gave a clear insight into the current approach of the Court of Appeal. He took some time to examine what qualified as personal data, reviewing *Durant* and *Edem* as well as *Dawson-Damer*. He found that the definition of personal data was actually quite simple: 'the definition of "personal data" consists of two limbs: (i) Whether the data in question "relate to" a living individual; and (ii) Whether the individual is identifiable from those data.'[32] He discusses at length what types of data qualify, noting that from *Lindqvist* it 'undoubtedly covers the name of a person in conjunction with his telephone details or information about his working

---

[29] Ibid. [107].
[30] Ibid. [110]–[114].
[31] [2017] EWCA Civ 121.
[32] Ibid. [61].

conditions or hobbies as well as information that a person has been injured and is on half time'; their name and address;[33] name, date of birth, nationality, gender, ethnicity, religion and language, relating to a natural person, who is identified by name, although it does not apply to legal analysis;[34] a person's salary;[35] and an image of a person recorded by a camera.[36] He went on to examine *Durant* and *Edem*, finding that there was no conflict between the two cases, noting that:

> what Mr Edem wanted was a specific piece of information, namely the names of the officials who dealt with his case. The question was whether the three officials were identifiable from these data. Plainly they were. What Mr Durant wanted was any document in which he was mentioned. His error was the submission that the contents of any document in which he was mentioned were, without more, his personal data . . . the fact that in *Durant* Mr Durant was asking for information about himself, and that in *Edem* Mr Edem was asking for information about third parties is irrelevant to the definition of 'personal data'.[37]

On this basis the *Durant* interpretation was distinguished and Lewison LJ followed the line developed in *Edem* and *Dawson-Damer*.

He went on to look at the question of proportionality which had recently been reviewed in *Dawson-Damer*. He noted that 'there are indications in the Directive that the EU legislature did not intend to impose excessive burdens on data controllers'[38] and that in a number of CJEU cases the court had applied the proportionality principle.[39] On this basis he agreed that a proportional response from data controllers was reasonable for 'in the case of a wide-ranging SAR, a simple search of a computerised system (for instance a server, or a personal e-mail account) by reference to the surname or forename of the data subject is highly likely to reveal a mass of material, particularly if the search terms are used disjunctively.' He went on to explain:

> If the data subject has a common name, say 'Smith' or 'Patel', the search may retrieve data which have nothing to do with the data subject at all. It may then be necessary to refine the search, or it may be necessary for a human being to review the material to decide whether the named individual is indeed the data subject. Even where the retrieved data do mention the data subject, much of that material is likely to contain personal data of individuals other than the data subject. Under section 7(4) of the DPA the data controller is not entitled to disclose those data without the consent of that other individual, unless it is reasonable in all the circumstance to disclose it without that consent. It follows that the mere retrieval of the personal data of the data subject is only the first stage in compliance with the SAR. Moreover, whether it is reasonable to disclose information about another individual is an evaluative judgment which must, as it seems to me in the current state of technology, be carried out by a human being rather than by a computer.[40]

The recent *Dawson-Damer* and *Ittihadieh* cases have added considerable richness to our understanding of the earlier *Durant* and *Edem* cases. Prior to these cases, too often data controllers would refer to *Durant* as an unbendable authority on the question. To many

---

[33] From *Rotterdam v Rijkeboer* ECLI:EU:C:2009:293.
[34] From *YS v Minister voor Immigratie* ECLI:EU:C:2014:2081.
[35] From *Rechnungshof v Österreichischer Rundfunk* ECLI:EU:C:2003:294.
[36] From *Ryneš v Úřad pro ochranu osobních údajů* ECLI:EU:C:2014:2428. Overall analysis taken from *Ittihadieh* (n. 31) [62].
[37] *Ittihadieh* (n. 31) [66].
[38] Ibid. [96].
[39] Ibid. [97]–[98].
[40] Ibid. [101].

observers this seemed rather inflexible and the new interpretation found post-*Edem* deals with these concerns and also gives greater guidance to data controllers. *Durant* may now be seen as a narrow internal test. It applies when data subjects are seeking specific information about themselves in records and files; it is about defining the character or role of the data subject—are they Hamlet or Laertes? The *Edem* interpretation is an external test. It applies when individuals are seeking to obtain contextual data about themselves. In such a situation the data controller must be careful since ,when data is conjoined or commixed, they must be aware of potential infringement of the rights of others as found in Art. 8 of the EU Charter of Fundamental Rights.[41] As a result, the test is different; it is simply to apply Art. 4(1) of the GDPR: personal data means information relating to an identified or identifiable natural person.

23.1.3 Correcting and managing data

Following a subject access request (or even without one) the data subject may make a number of applications to have the data corrected or, if necessary, destroyed. Article 16 GDPR, as given domestic effect by s. 46 of the DPA 2018, gives the data subject the right to obtain from the controller without undue delay and at the latest within one month of receipt of the request, the rectification of inaccurate personal data concerning him or her. This includes the requirement that the data controller complete incomplete information, where this makes the information inaccurate, by way of adding information provided by the data subject.[42] This right may be seen as the mirror of the controller's obligation under the accuracy principle found in Art. (5)(1)(d) GDPR. While this sounds straightforward, as with all things data protection, there are some complications. First, the data controller may legally not comply with the application for rectification where the request is manifestly unfounded and excessive.[43] It is not yet clear what that means but the advice is that this will be a high threshold. More complex is the position where the parties dispute the accuracy of the data.

Where the data subject believes the data to be inaccurate but the data controller believes it to be accurate, there is clearly a subjective dispute as to the accuracy of the data. In such cases the Information Commissioner's Office (ICO) advises data controllers to 'let the individual know you are satisfied that the personal data is accurate, and tell them that you will not be amending the data. You should explain your decision, and inform them of their right to make a complaint to the ICO or another supervisory authority; and their ability to seek to enforce their rights through a judicial remedy.'[44] In such a case the data subject may request under Art. 18(1) GDPR and s. 47(3) DPA 2018 restriction of processing. By Art. 18(1)(a) where the accuracy of the personal data is contested by the data subject, the data subject shall have the right to obtain from the controller restriction of processing for a period enabling the controller to verify the accuracy of the personal data. Where processing has been restricted, then by Art. 18(2) GDPR,

---

[41] 2000/C 364/01.

[42] Data Protection Act 2018, s. 46(2).

[43] See s. 53(1) and Art. 57(4). Note this also applies to subject access requests under s. 45 and the right to erasure under s. 47.

[44] <https://ico.org.uk/for-organisations/guide-to-the-general-data-protection-regulation-gdpr/individual-rights/right-to-rectification/>.

the personal data may only be stored and 'can only be processed with the data subject's consent or for the establishment, exercise or defence of legal claims or for the protection of the rights of another natural or legal person or for reasons of important public interest of the Union or of a Member State'. In addition, the data subject may make a request under s. 51 to the Information Commissioner to check that the refusal of their request was lawful. The commissioner can then carry out an informal assessment or may choose to use their enforcement powers under the Act to prosecute that enquiry.[45] There is a further right under s. 100 to apply to a court to have the data rectified.

Should the data subject prefer not to correct data but instead to withdraw their data and take their custom elsewhere, the GDPR can help. By Art. 20 GDPR where the processing of data is based upon either consent or for the performance of a contract and is carried out by automated means 'the data subject shall have the right to receive the personal data concerning him or her, which he or she has provided to a controller, in a structured, commonly used and machine-readable format and have the right to transmit those data to another controller without hindrance from the controller to which the personal data have been provided'. This is the data portability provision. Essentially, it allows data subjects to move data from one data controller to another. The theory behind this is that it will encourage competition in data markets and break up dominant providers. One of the problems of Facebook, for example, is that it is very hard to set up a competing service. Due to network effects (the number of your friends on Facebook) and switching costs (the time spent rebuilding your Facebook presence somewhere else) people will not switch to start-up competitors. Article 20 is designed to make switching easier. The Regulation imagines that providers will work together on interoperable data formats.[46] However, the evidence suggests Art. 20 may not work as simply as envisaged. Early indications from researchers are that while large data companies are happy to provide your personal data in a portable format, as required by Art. 20, they do not provide any value added to that data by their processing of that data, so none of the algorithmic processes linking data to other data. In addition, the Electronic Frontier Foundation report that while Facebook, for example, do now allow the user to download their list of friends (vital if you were to migrate to another provider) it is provided 'in the form of plain-text names without unique identifiers. This makes it impossible for a user to take their list of friends to a competing service.'[47]

Faced with such a weight of difficulty in migrating their data, the data subject may choose the nuclear option of data erasure (the so-called right to be forgotten) but before we get to that option there is one further right which the data subject may want to consider. These are the rights to object to data processing under Arts. 21–22. By Art. 21 the data subject may object at any time to the processing of their data carried out either in the public interest or for a legitimate interest. When an objection is made, the controller must no longer process the personal data unless the controller can demonstrate 'compelling legitimate grounds for the processing which override the interests, rights

---

[45] See s. 142 Information Notices and s. 146 Assessment Notices.

[46] Recital 68.

[47] B Cyphers and D O'Brien, 'Facing Facebook: Data Portability and Interoperability Are Anti-Monopoly Medicine', *Electronic Frontier Foundation* 24 July 2018 <https://www.eff.org/deeplinks/2018/07/facing-facebook-data-portability-and-interoperability-are-anti-monopoly-medicine>.

and freedoms of the data subject or for the establishment, exercise or defence of legal claims'. Further, by Art. 21(2) and (3):

> where personal data are processed for direct marketing purposes, the data subject shall have the right to object at any time to processing of personal data concerning him or her for such marketing, which includes profiling to the extent that it is related to such direct marketing. Where the data subject objects to processing for direct marketing purposes, the personal data shall no longer be processed for such purposes.

These rights are added to and expanded upon by Art. 22. This gives the data subject the right to object to automatic processing of their data. Many people have concerns about algorithmic risks and biases and may prefer to have their data reviewed by a human; Art. 22 supports this interest. Article 22 applies to processing on all grounds, including implicit consent. It states: 'the data subject shall have the right not to be subject to a decision based solely on automated processing, including profiling, which produces legal effects concerning him or her or similarly significantly affects him or her'. This right cannot be exercised if the data subject has given their explicit consent to such processing, the processing is necessary for entering into, or performance of, a contract between the data subject and a data controller; or if the processing is legally authorized and such legal authorization 'lays down suitable measures to safeguard the data subject's rights and freedoms and legitimate interests'.[48]

If all of these safeguards fail to satisfy the data subject that their data is secure, accurate, up to date, and fairly processed, they may choose instead to request their data be completely erased. This is usually known as an exercise of the right to be forgotten.

23.2 **The right to be forgotten**

If at any time the data subject wishes to have their data permanently deleted, they may make an application under Art. 17 GDPR/s. 47 DPA 2018. The right to data erasure as set out in full in Art. 17:

 Highlight Right to erasure

The data subject shall have the right to obtain from the controller the erasure of personal data concerning him or her without undue delay and the controller shall have the obligation to erase personal data without undue delay where one of the following grounds applies:

a. the personal data are no longer necessary in relation to the purposes for which they were collected or otherwise processed;

b. the data subject withdraws consent on which the processing is based, and where there is no other legal ground for the processing;

c. the data subject objects to the processing pursuant to Article 21(1) and there are no over-riding legitimate grounds for the processing, or the data subject objects to the processing pursuant to Article 21(2);

➡

---

[48] See also ss. 14, 49, and 50 DPA 2018.

d. the personal data have been unlawfully processed;

e. the personal data have to be erased for compliance with a legal obligation in Union or Member State law to which the controller is subject;

f. the personal data have been collected in relation to the offer of information society services referred to [an offer of information society services directly to a child].

As is explained in Recital 65: 'A data subject should have a "right to be forgotten" where the retention of such data infringes this Regulation or Union or Member State law to which the controller is subject. In particular, a data subject should have the right to have his or her personal data erased and no longer processed where the personal data are no longer necessary in relation to the purposes for which they are collected or otherwise processed, where a data subject has withdrawn his or her consent or objects to the processing of personal data concerning him or her, or where the processing of his or her personal data does not otherwise comply with this Regulation.' The right to be forgotten (RTBF) was originally designed to be a new right introduced by the GDPR. However, the courts fashioned an equivalent right under the 1995 Directive in the groundbreaking case of *Google Spain SL and Google Inc. v AEPD*.[49]

 Case study *Google Spain*

In the late 1990s a Spanish citizen by the name of Mario Costeja González was the subject of a debt recovery action by the Spanish state. It appears that he owed the Ministry of Labour and Social Affairs debts by way of social security payments. At the time it is certain neither he nor the Spanish state could imagine the impact his debt and the recovery of it would have. As part of the process of recovering the debt the Ministry ordered a public auction of items of real estate by way of a public auction and to maximize the return at auction they placed an announcement of the auction in the newspaper *La Vanguardia*. The auction proceeded and in the normal run of affairs that would have been the end of the matter.

Unfortunately, *La Vanguardia* later digitized that copy of the newspaper and now it can be accessed online.[50] This of itself would not be a problem for Sr González except this data (like much internet data) was then indexed by Google which meant that when you searched for his name the most prominent data returned was this information relating to a long-extinguished debt. Obviously, Sr González felt this affected his standing in business and generally reflected data which should be deleted under the principles of Art. 6(1)(c) of the 1995 Data Protection Directive, that data must be 'adequate, *relevant* and not excessive' and Art. 8 of the Charter of Fundamental Rights of the European Union that one has a right to data privacy. Therefore, in March 2010 Sr González lodged a complaint with the Agencia Española de Protección de Datos (AEPD), the Spanish data protection agency claiming that *La Vanguardia* must delete or amend the irrelevant data in a way to prevent his identification and that Google must stop linking to it in search returns.

---

[49] ECLI:EU:C:2014:317.
[50] <http://hemeroteca.lavanguardia.com/preview/1998/01/19/pagina-23/33842001/pdf.html>.

In July 2010 AEPD issued their findings. They found that *La Vanguardia* needed to take no action as they simply recorded information which had legally been published and which was correct.[51] However, they found that Google in producing search returns were processing data and were subject to data protection provisions. This suggested Google's actions were in breach of Spanish data protection law.[52] Google challenged this decision before the Spanish High Court and they referred it to the CJEU. The long-awaited decision of the CJEU was published in May 2014 and it has had wide-reaching implications for operators of websites and search engines. The court found that search engine operators were data controllers for the purpose of Art. 2(d) of the Data Protection Directive as they 'determine the purposes and means of that activity (search) and thus of the processing of personal data that it itself carries out within the framework of that activity'[53] and that they processed data in accordance with Art. 2(b).[54] This meant the directive covered the activities of search engine operators such as Google and the defence that Google had argued that they merely indexed data held by others was not made out.

The next question was whether the provisions of the directive only applied to Google Spain (as established in the EU) or whether they also applied to Google Inc. when dealing with an EU citizen. The court found that the operations carried out by Google Inc. outside the EU but for the purpose of providing a service through their establishment in the EU, and through which profit was generated by advertising and promotion, were within the geographical scope of the directive.[55] On this basis the court found that:

> it follows that Article 4(1)(a) is to be interpreted as meaning that processing of personal data is carried out in the context of the activities of an establishment of the controller on the territory of a Member State, within the meaning of that provision, when the operator of a search engine sets up in a Member State a branch or subsidiary which is intended to promote and sell advertising space offered by that engine and which orientates its activity towards the inhabitants of that Member State.[56]

This merely left the question of whether Google had a duty to remove links to out-of-date information upon request of the data subject. The court began by noting that under Art. 12(b) data subjects have the right to request erasure or rectification of data which does not comply with the provisions of the directive,[57] while under Art. 14(a) data subjects have the right to object to processing of personal data where they have not given permission for its processing and the processing is not in compliance with a legal or contractual obligation.[58] Starting from this base the court noted that processing was likely to significantly impact the data subject's right to both privacy and data protection and that, as a result, 'it is clear that it cannot be justified by merely the economic interest which the operator of such an engine has in that processing'. The court did however note that others may have a legitimate interest in being able to access this information

---

[51] *Google Spain* (n. 49) [16].
[52] Ibid. [17].
[53] Ibid. [33].
[54] Ibid. [25]–[32].
[55] Ibid. [55].
[56] Ibid. [60].
[57] Ibid. [70].
[58] Ibid. [76].

for it is not the intent of data protection law to allow private censorship of data. To counterbalance this risk the court noted that:

> a fair balance should be sought in particular between that interest and the data subject's fundamental rights under Articles 7 and 8 of the Charter [with those of others interested in the data]. Whilst it is true that the data subject's rights protected by those articles also override, as a general rule, that interest of internet users, that balance may however depend, in specific cases, on the nature of the information in question and its sensitivity for the data subject's private life and on the interest of the public in having that information, an interest which may vary, in particular, according to the role played by the data subject in public life.[59]

Having done this balancing exercise the court found that Sr González was justified in his application:

> in order to comply with the rights laid down in those provisions (Arts. 12(b) and 14(a)) the operator of a search engine is obliged to remove from the list of results displayed following a search made on the basis of a person's name links to web pages, published by third parties and containing information relating to that person, also in a case where that name or information is not erased beforehand or simultaneously from those web pages, and even, as the case may be, when its publication in itself on those pages is lawful.[60]

The immediate fallout from this decision was extensive and wide-reaching. The European Commission published a fact sheet for citizens and for operators of web pages and other intermediary services.[61] Newspapers and journals attacked the judgment as being a form of private censorship (despite the balancing provision set out in the judgment);[62] Google was criticized for the way they were handling RTBF requests;[63] while Google sought clarification of the ruling.[64] Meanwhile the UK House of Lords produced a highly critical report on the judgment finding that 'neither the 1995 Directive, nor the Court's interpretation of the Directive, reflects the current state of communications service provision, where global access to detailed personal information has become part of the way of life' and 'it is no longer reasonable or even possible for the right to privacy to allow data subjects a right to remove links to data which are accurate and lawfully available'.[65] Despite these initial teething problems, the RTBF has been an unqualified success, at least from the point of view of data protection law. Google details, through its transparency reports, how many requests it has received under RTBF and how many URLs it has delisted as a result of these requests.[66] At 27 November 2018 this reveals that

---

[59] Ibid. [81].
[60] Ibid. [88].
[61] <https://www.inforights.im/media/1186/cl_eu_commission_factsheet_right_to_be_forgotten.pdf>.
[62] A Hern, 'Wikipedia swears to fight "censorship" of "right to be forgotten" ruling', *The Guardian*, 6 August 2014; J Ball, 'EU's right to be forgotten: Guardian articles have been hidden by Google', *The Guardian*, 2 July 2014; R Williams, 'Telegraph stories affected by EU "right to be forgotten"', *Daily Telegraph*, 3 September 2015.
[63] S Gibbs, 'Google hauled in by Europe over "right to be forgotten" reaction', *The Guardian*, 24 July 2014.
[64] A White, 'Google Seeks Feedback on EU Right to Be Forgotten', *Bloomberg News*, 28 August 2014.
[65] House of Lords, European Union Committee: *EU Data Protection law: a 'right to be forgotten'?* (HL Paper 40 TSO 2014), 22 <http://www.publications.parliament.uk/pa/ld201415/ldselect/ldeucom/40/40.pdf>.
[66] <https://transparencyreport.google.com/eu-privacy/overview?hl=en>.

Google has received 748,482 requests to delist, covering 2,866,801 distinct URLs. Of these 91,595 requests have originated in the UK, covering 386,889 URLs.[67] The report reveals that in 44 per cent of cases URLs were delisted; in 56 per cent they were not.

It is too early yet to say whether Art. 17 will bring about any material changes to the way the RTBF will operate. Further cases have, however, assisted, and will assist, in our understanding of the operation of the right. The first is the decision of the High Court in *NT1 and NT2 v Google LLC*.[68] This was a decision in two joined cases. In the first (NT1) a businessman was convicted of conspiracy to false account, having transferred monies to offshore companies to cheat the revenue. He received a four-year custodial sentence, and was released in the early 2000s. His sentence, at the time, was of such a length that it would not have been deemed 'spent' for the purposes of the Rehabilitation of Offenders Act 1974. However, it became spent following a change in the law in March 2014 due to the passing of the Legal Aid, Sentencing and Punishment of Offenders Act 2012 (which had retrospective effect).[69] NT1 sought the delisting of three URLs from the search results returned upon entry of his name into Google's search engine. Two of the URLs related to contemporaneous media reports of NT1's conviction; the other was a book extract which referred to the conviction. NT2 is also a businessman. He was involved in a business which had attracted public controversy for environmental reasons. Individuals seeking to disrupt it targeted the business and NT2 took steps to identify those individuals; this included sanctioning the use of unlawful phone and computer hacking. NT2 was convicted for his part in this and received a six-month custodial sentence, of which he served six weeks. His conviction also became spent in March 2014 (but it would have become spent in July 2014, even if the law had not changed). NT2 complained of eleven URLs, some being contemporaneous reports of his prosecution and conviction, and some more recent. Warby J summarized the case in his judgment:

> The main issues in each case, stated broadly, are (1) whether the claimant is entitled to have the links in question excluded from Google Search results either (a) because one or more of them contain personal data relating to him which are inaccurate, or (b) because for that and/or other reasons the continued listing of those links by Google involves an unjustified interference with the claimant's data protection and/or privacy rights; and (2) if so, whether the claimant is also entitled to compensation for continued listing between the time of the delisting request and judgment. Put another way, the first question is whether the record needs correcting; the second question is whether the data protection or privacy rights of these claimants extend to having shameful episodes in their personal history eliminated from Google Search; thirdly, there is the question of whether damages should be paid.

Google sought to argue that the claims were an abuse of process as they 'amount in substance to claims for damage to reputation which are intended to outflank the limits on reputation claims in the law of defamation and section 8 of the 1974 Act'.[70] Warby J had little difficulty in setting this aside: 'As a general rule, it is legitimate for a claimant to rely on any cause of action that arises or may arise from a given set of facts. This

---

[67] The largest volume of requests comes from France with 164,209 requests relating to 573,309 URLs.

[68] [2018] EWHC 799 (QB).

[69] It might be noted that had his sentence been one day longer, the position would not have changed and it would have remained permanently unspent.

[70] *NT1 and NT2* (n. 68) [58].

is not ordinarily considered to be an abuse just because one or more other causes of action might arise or be pursued instead of, or in addition to, the claim that is relied on.'[71] Google then claimed it could rely on the journalistic exemption found at s. 32 of the Data Protection Act 1998 (and restated at Art. 85(2) GDPR and para. 26 of Part 5 of Sch. 2 of the 2018 Act). This was also set aside by Warby J. who noted that Google's search function was indiscriminate, and that the exemption 'is not so elastic that it can be stretched to embrace every activity that has to do with conveying information or opinions. To label all such activity as "journalism" would be to elide the concept of journalism with that of communication.'[72]

With the preliminaries settled he looked at the issues at hand. Following a lengthy discussion of the data protection principles, Warby J found the right approach was a balancing principle: balancing the rights of the data subjects in having the data delisted against the interests of the public at large to have access to this data. The test to be applied, on this principle, was 'with appropriate adaptation, the *In re S* approach must be followed: neither privacy nor freedom of expression "has as such precedence over the other"; the conflict is to be resolved by an "intense focus on the comparative importance of the specific rights being claimed in the individual case"'.[73] He was content that this approach was consistent with the *Google Spain* decision:

> What the CJEU was saying, in the passages at [81] and [97] on which Mr Tomlinson relies, is that in the majority of cases of this kind the facts will be such that the factors in favour of delisting will outweigh those in favour of the continued availability of the data, via an Internet search engine. The 'general rule' to which the court was referring was a descriptive, not a prescriptive one.[74]

He then went on to apply this test to the cases before him. He noted that the idea that results which contain references to spent convictions should immediately become delisted as soon as the conviction is spent was a 'blunt instrument' incompatible with the balancing interest of freedom of expression. Thus, although a spent conviction was a 'weighty factor' in considering delisting, it could not of itself be determinative.[75] Applying the balancing principle to the cases before him, he found that NT1 had been convicted of a serious dishonesty offence, and received a relatively lengthy sentence of four years. When it was imposed he could have had no expectation that the conviction would ever become spent and NT1 continued to refuse to accept, or fully accept, culpability for his crime. Further, he found NT1's case on harm not especially compelling, it being largely to do with harm to reputation.[76] Finding against NT1 he found that:

> his business career since leaving prison made the information relevant in the past to the assessment of his honesty by members of the public. The information retains sufficient relevance today. He has not accepted his guilt, has misled the public and this Court, and shows no remorse over any of these matters. He remains in business, and the information serves the purpose of minimising the risk that he will continue to mislead, as he has in the past. Delisting would not erase the information from the record altogether, but it would make it much harder to find.[77]

---

[71] Ibid. [61].
[72] Ibid. [98].
[73] Ibid. [132].
[74] Ibid. [133].
[75] Ibid. [166].
[76] Ibid. [167].
[77] Ibid. [170].

The NT2 case was quite different. Warby J found that his crime was much less serious and had not been committed for financial gain. He had pleaded guilty at an early opportunity and expressed considerable remorse for a one-off mistake. He had received only a six-month sentence, which would always have become spent in the fullness of time. On this basis, and vitally as 'his past offending is of little if any relevance to anybody's assessment of his suitability to engage in relevant business activity now, or in the future. There is no real need for anybody to be warned about that activity' he upheld NT2's application.[78]

This seems like a good framework for future RTBF cases. It balances the competing rights of the data subject and the interests of the data controllers and wider public. Central to the opposing decisions were whether or not the processing of the data remained relevant. In NT1's case it was as 'his business career since leaving prison made the information relevant in the past to the assessment of his honesty by members of the public'. In NT2's case it was not as 'his past offending is of little if any relevance to anybody's assessment of his suitability to engage in relevant business activity'. Nothing in Art. 17 of the GDPR should effect this approach for Art. 17(3)(a) allows for a balancing principle to be applied. Before leaving the RTBF we should acknowledge the ongoing case of *Google Inc. v Commission nationale de l'informatique et des libertés (CNIL)*. This case was discussed at length at 5.3.7 and will in time set the geographical scope of the RTBF. As was noted there the opinion of the Advocate-General is that RTBF should be restricted to the geographical confines of the EU with the addition that operators of services such as Google should take such reasonable steps to geo-block access to content on global sites to prevent searches from within the EU producing the delisted materials.[79] As was noted at 5.3.7 this seems to be a sensible settlement ensuring that global listings are not directly effected by EU law outside its normal jurisdictional reach but also giving real effect to orders of EU and member state institutions within the globally linked environment.

23.3 **Supervising data controllers**

Both the GDPR and the DPA 2018 have a number of mechanisms to ensure compliance with the data protection framework. By Art. 51 GDPR each member state must have a supervisory authority, described as 'one or more independent public authorities to be responsible for monitoring the application of this Regulation'. In the United Kingdom this function falls upon the Information Commissioner's Office (ICO). By Part 5 of the DPA 2018 the ICO is given considerable regulatory and enforcement powers. The lower level regulatory functions of the ICO include the issuance of codes of practice. These are non-binding guidelines designed to form a template for good practice within an industry sector. Under the DPA 1998 the ICO issued a number of such codes in industry sectors such as CCTV, health, education, and marketing. In addition, a number of general codes cover subjects such as data security, information sharing, and dealing with enquiries. The DPA 2018 requires the ICO to maintain a number of specific codes, including by s. 121 a data sharing code which is to give 'practical guidance in relation

---

[78] Ibid. [223].
[79] *Google v CNIL* ECLI:EU:C:2019:15.

to the sharing of personal data in accordance with the requirements of the data protection legislation'; a direct marketing code under s. 122 which gives 'practical guidance in relation to the carrying out of direct marketing in accordance with the requirements of the data protection legislation'; and for the first time by s. 123 an age-appropriate design code 'which contains such guidance as the Commissioner considers appropriate on standards of age-appropriate design of relevant information society services which are likely to be accessed by children'.

In addition to extending the regulatory role of the ICO, the DPA 2018 extends the ICO's investigative and enforcement remit. By s. 129 the ICO may carry out a consensual audit of data controllers or processors. This allows the ICO, with the consent of a controller or processor, to carry out an assessment of whether the controller or processor is complying with good practice in the processing of personal data. This allows businesses who believe there is a risk of non-compliance to work with the ICO to improve their compliance model. For more serious cases, the primary investigative weapon of the ICO is the Information Notice which may be served under s. 142. This requires the data controller to furnish the ICO with the information set out in the Information Notice within a time specified in the notice. It is an offence to give false information in response to an Information Notice under s. 144 and failure to comply with the notice allows the ICO to obtain an Information Order under s. 145. Failure to comply with such an order would be contempt of court. Under s. 146 the ICO may issue an Assessment Notice. These require the controller or processor to permit the commissioner to carry out an assessment of whether the controller or processor has complied or is complying with the data protection legislation.

If at any point the ICO is unhappy with compliance with its notices, or if it finds through the application of Information and Assessment Notices that a breach of data protection principles is occurring, it has a number of measures at its disposal. The first is an Enforcement Notice under s. 149. This permits the ICO to 'give the person a written notice which requires the person (a) to take steps specified in the notice, or (b) to refrain from taking steps specified in the notice, or both. If this is insufficient to deal with the problem the ICO has the ultimate sanction; under s. 155 they may issue a penalty notice. You have probably read about penalty notices in the media as much of the focus of the introduction of the GDPR focused on this issue. Whereas under the DPA 1998, as amended, the maximum penalty that the ICO could issue was £500,000, the new penalty powers are far beyond this. By s. 157(5) and (6) standard and higher penalty maximum amounts are set out. Whether or not data controllers or processors are open to standard or higher penalties depends upon the type of breach. The standard maximum penalty is set out in s. 157(6) and is 'in the case of an undertaking, 10 million Euros or 2 per cent of the undertaking's total annual worldwide turnover in the preceding financial year, whichever is higher, or (b) in any other case, 10 million Euros'. The higher maximum penalty is found in s. 157(5) and is 'in the case of an undertaking, 20 million Euros or 4 per cent of the undertaking's total annual worldwide turnover in the preceding financial year, whichever is higher; or (b) in any other case, 20 million Euros'. As some newspapers have reported, for a company like Facebook with a turnover of $40.7bn in 2017, this allows for a maximum penalty of $1.6bn; for Google which reported $110bn in 2017, it could allow penalties as high as $4.4bn. At the time of writing the ICO has not issued a penalty notice under these new limits. Widely reported penalties such as the $500,000 penalty issued to Facebook for failure to protect customer data from abuse by Global Science Research Ltd[80] and the £350,000 penalty issued to Uber for failing to protect customers' personal information during a cyberattack[81] were taken under the DPA 1998 framework. It is possible that the first monetary penalty notice under the DPA 2018 regime may be issued against the data analytics firm AggregateIQ who were issued an Enforcement Notice in October 2018[82] for its use of personal data to target online adverts at voters during public polls. It has been reported that they were paid nearly £2.7m by Vote Leave to target adverts at prospective voters during the Brexit referendum campaign.[83]

Finally, the ICO has an additional role as part of the GDPRs transparency requirements. As the supervisory authority data controllers are obliged to notify the ICO of any data breaches without undue delay, and where feasible, not later than 72 hours after becoming aware of it.[84] This notice must contain:

(a) a description of the nature of the personal data breach including, where possible, the categories and approximate number of data subjects concerned and the categories and approximate number of personal data records concerned;

(b) the name and contact details of the data protection officer or other contact point from whom more information can be obtained;

(c) a description of the likely consequences of the personal data breach; and

(d) a description of the measures taken or proposed to be taken by the controller to address the personal data breach, including, where appropriate, measures to mitigate its possible adverse effects.

In addition to this duty to notify the ICO, the data controller must also inform the data subjects concerned, without undue delay, where 'the data breach is likely to result in a high risk to the rights and freedoms of individuals'.[85]

23.4 **Conclusions**

Data management and data processing are ubiquitous activities in the information society. The unique properties of digital data make it more valuable and therefore more commercialized than analogue data ever was. But with so many decisions automated and so much personal information now held in the form of proxy data the risk of harm to the individual is great. The GDPR and the Data Protection Act 2018 are our first line of defence against invasions of data privacy and against unfair and unreasonable data processing.

---

[80] See <https://ico.org.uk/media/action-weve-taken/mpns/2260051/r-facebook-mpn-20181024.pdf>.

[81] See <https://ico.org.uk/media/action-weve-taken/mpns/2553890/uber-monetary-penalty-notice-26-november-2018.pdf>.

[82] See <https://ico.org.uk/media/action-weve-taken/enforcement-notices/2260123/aggregate-iq-en-20181024.pdf>.

[83] C Baraniuk, 'Vote Leave data firm hit with first ever GDPR notice', *BBC News*, 20 September 2018.

[84] DPA 2018, s. 67(1).

[85] DPA 2018, s. 68(1).

The framework is, as we have seen in this chapter and the preceding one, less directive and more a series of guidelines for data controllers and data processors. The heart of the framework is in the data protection principles found in Art. 5 and in the conditions for processing seen in Arts. 6 and 7. The application of the data protection law, due to its framework approach can sometimes seem counter-intuitive. To find Mrs Lindqvist responsible for processing data in an unfair fashion for placing some humorous anecdotes on a web page, or Mr Ryneš for operating a camera for the protection of his private dwelling, while holding that the Medical Defence Union acted within the terms of the Act in processing Mr Johnson's data to determine whether to continue to offer cover to a client who had never made a claim on his insurance seems perverse; yet when one thinks of the GDPR and Act as frameworks or guides for fair processing these decisions make sense. The MDU had a clear policy which was fair and reasonable; Mrs Lindqvist and Mr Ryneš acted without thought, policy, or permission.

There remains though the concern that this framework approach does little to protect the data privacy of individuals. The framework it may be argued focuses on data integrity and data security more than strictly data privacy. The concern is that data protection laws, originally designed in the 1990s for an environment where most data was gathered in a traditional form and was merely stored and processed on computer are out of date in an environment where data is gathered from a multiplicity of sources and is processed and transferred automatically and instantly. This is the complex data environment we find ourselves in now, which arguably the revisions in the GDPR fail to fully account for.

TEST QUESTIONS

Question 1

Marie has a friend Louis who has been experiencing serious migraines recently and is thinking of visiting a famous physician in Kensington, Jean d'Oubli. Marie publicly states on her Facebook page that Jean d'Oubli was investigated for clinical malpractice in France 15 years ago, before moving to London as his reputation was in tatters. She therefore recommended that Louis and other friends avoid his practice in Kensington. Dr d'Oubli has contacted Marie directly and asked her to remove the content but she has refused, saying that her comments are made for 'purely personal purposes' and therefore data protection rules don't apply to her. She adds that even if they did, she has a right to freedom of expression and it is true that Dr d'Oubli was investigated for malpractice. Dr d'Oubli has therefore contacted Facebook and asked it to remove the comments. Facebook wants to know whether it is a data controller for the purposes of data protection law, and, if so, what obligations it has under data protection law vis-à-vis Dr d'Oubli.

Question 2

You are an adviser to Bettr an online gambling service. Bettr recently fired Todd who was spending all his free time brushing up on his rights under the EU General Data Protection Regulation. Before his dismissal Todd had been the subject of a disciplinary procedure. He has contacted Bettr seeking access under the GDPR to (a) all email correspondence in which he is mentioned by name or by his Bettr handle @BettrthanU, and (b) the names of the attendees of the meeting where his dismissal was first discussed. Todd, who worked in an open-plan office, is also arguing that the use by Bettr of CCTV cameras in this space is incompatible with GDPR and therefore that images of him breaching company policy are unlawful and cannot be used against him. Bettr suggests that the presence of CCTV cameras in the office is well documented and that their CCTV policy allows data storage for one year.

Advise Bettr as to its responsibilities to Todd under EU data protection law.

FURTHER READING

Books

G Brock, *The Right to be Forgotten: Privacy and the Media in the Digital Age* (Tauris 2016)

B Custers et al., *EU Personal Data Protection in Policy and Practice* (Springer 2019)

G González Fuster, *The Emergence of Personal Data Protection as a Fundamental Right of the EU* (Springer 2014)

V Mayer-Schönberger, *Delete: The Virtue of Forgetting in the Digital Age* (Princeton 2009)

Chapters and articles

D Erdos, 'From the Scylla of Restriction to the Charybdis of License? Exploring the Scope of the "Special Purposes" Freedom of Expression Shield in European Data Protection Law' (2015) *Common Market Law Review* 119

J Kokott and C Sobotta, 'The distinction between privacy and data protection in the jurisprudence of the CJEU and the ECtHR' (2013) 3 *International Data Privacy Law* 222

I Lloyd: 'From ugly duckling to swan: the rise of data protection and its limits' (2018) 34 (4) *Computer Law & Security Review* 779

K O'Hara and N Shadbolt, 'The Right to be Forgotten: Its Potential Role in a Coherent Privacy Framework' (2015) 1 *European Data Protection Law Review* 178

J Powles, 'The Case that Won't be Forgotten' (2015) 47 *Loyola University Chicago Law Journal* 583

24

The international trade in personal data

It is a widely reported aphorism that 'data is the new oil'. No one is quite sure who first said this but it may have been the man behind the Tesco Clubcard scheme, Clive Humby, who in 2006 said 'Data is just like crude. It's valuable, but if unrefined it cannot really be used. It has to be changed into gas, plastic, chemicals, etc to create a valuable entity that drives profitable activity; so must data be broken down, analyzed for it to have value.'[1] Whoever first said it, it is clear that in the modern economy data driven transactions are essential. The OECD estimated that in 2015, the global volume of data stood at 8 zettabytes (8 trillion gigabytes), an eight-fold increase on 2010. By 2020, that volume is forecast to increase up to 40 times over, as technologies including the Internet of Things create vast new data sets.[2] According to the McKinsey Global Institute, cross-border flows of data grew 45 times from 2005 to 2014, and accounted for $2.8 trillion (approx. 3.3 per cent) of global GDP in 2014; again this is a figure rapidly rising.[3] To get an idea of the future value of data the Boston Consulting Group has estimated that across Europe, the quantifiable benefit from personal data applications could reach €1 trillion annually by 2020—with two-thirds of that benefit accruing to consumers, and one-third to businesses.[4] All of these reports and predictions point to the same conclusion: a modern economy must trade data. This is potentially a problem for data protection laws. As data is today mostly a purely digital item it is, as John Perry Barlow explained in 1994, and discussed in chapter 1, merely a 'highly liquid pattern of ones and zeros'.[5] The flow of personal data across borders unchecked is the common theme throughout this book. It is this unchecked flow that makes the policing of illegal content, including obscene content and content in support of terrorism, difficult to police. It is the flow that effects copyright and trademark enforcement and it is the same flow that undermines local enforcement of data protection and data privacy provisions.

This is a major challenge for the European data protection regime. If all a data controller had to do was to transfer personal data from a controller in Germany, who is subject to the European data protection regime, to one in Chile, who is not, then European data protection law would not be worth a candle. We have already touched

[1] M Palmer, 'Data is the New Oil', *ANA Blogs* 3 November 2006 <https://ana.blogs.com/maestros/2006/11/data_is_the_new.html>.

[2] OECD, *Data-driven Innovation: Big Data for Growth and Well-being* (OECD Publishing, 2015) 20.

[3] McKinsey Global Institute, *Digital Globalization: The New Era of Global Flows*, March 2016, 10.

[4] Boston Consulting Group, 'The Value of our Digital Identity' *Liberty Global*, November 2012, 55.

[5] JP Barlow, 'The Economy of Ideas: Selling Wine without Bottles on the Global Net', *Wired 2.03*, March 1994.

upon the tension between a local legal framework and a global trade in personal data at 22.1.2 where we saw that reg. 3 of the GDPR provides that its geographical scope reaches far beyond the borders of the EU to both non-EU established organizations who process personal data about EU data subjects in connection with the offering of goods or services; and to non-EU established organizations who process personal data about EU data subjects in connection with monitoring their behaviour within the EU. That though is about the territorial scope of the GDPR when the data controller may be beyond the geographical borders of the EU. What about the more direct issue of data exportation (data transfers) from within the EU to ouside it? This is a practice that goes on all the time. Think how much of your personal data is likely to end up in servers operated from 1 Infinite Loop; Cupertino, California (Apple), 410 Terry Avenue North, Seattle, Washington (Amazon), or 129 Samsung-ro, Yeongtong-gu, Suwon-si, Gyeonggi-do, Korea (Samsung). To deal with this the European data protection framework has developed complex provisions to regulate the transfer of data outside the European Economic Area (EEA).

24.1 **Transfers of personal data to third countries**

The transfer of personal data to states outside the EEA was regulated by the 1995 Data Protection Directive and the 1998 Act and continues to be regulated by the GDPR and the 2018 Act. To fully understand the legal framework requires a working knowledge of both the old framework and the new framework. This is because vital case law under the old framework remains authoritative and informs our understanding of the GDPR framework.

Article 25 of the Data Protection Directive provided that 'Member States shall provide that the transfer to a third country of personal data which are undergoing processing or are intended for processing after transfer may take place only if, without prejudice to compliance with the national provisions adopted pursuant to the other provisions of this Directive, the third country in question ensures an adequate level of protection'. This was reinforced by the eight data protection principle: 'Personal data shall not be transferred to a country or territory outside the European Economic Area unless that country or territory ensures an adequate level of protection for the rights and freedoms of data subjects in relation to the processing of personal data.' The reasoning behind the Article and Principle were that, as already noted, without some form of transfer limitation unscrupulous data controllers could simply export data to a state which offers a lower level of protection to data subjects for processing, then transfer the results back into the EU for action.

The first question was what qualified as a 'transfer to a third country of personal data'? For example could the placing of data on an internationally accessible web page qualify as a transfer of data? This was examined in the case of *Bodil Lindqvist*[6] which was discussed in depth in chapter 22. As was discussed there, one of the issues which attracted the attention of the Swedish data protection authority was that Mrs Lindqvist, in placing the data on a publicly accessible web page which was accessible from any

---

[6] ECLI:EU:C:2003:596.

part of the world had transferred processed personal data to a third country without authorization. The court received a number of competing observations on this point. The European Commission and the Swedish Government considered that:

> the loading, using a computer, of personal data onto an internet page, so that they become accessible to nationals of third countries, constitutes a transfer of data to third countries, and that the answer would be the same if no one from the third country had in fact accessed the data or if the server where it was stored was physically in a third country.[7]

A different view was put forward by the government of the Netherlands who argued that 'the term, [transfer], must be understood to refer to the act of *intentionally* transferring personal data from the territory of a Member State to a third country and, [accordingly] loading personal data onto an internet page using a computer cannot be considered to be a transfer of personal data to a third country'.[8] The UK government took a similar but slightly different approach to the Dutch approach arguing that the Directive 'concerns the transfer of data to third countries and not their accessibility from third countries. The term transfer connotes the transmission of personal data from one place and person to another place and person.'[9]

The court considered these alternatives before coming down in favour of the UK interpretation, finding that 'personal data which appear on the computer of a person in a third country, coming from a person who has loaded them onto an internet site, were not *directly transferred* between those two people but through the computer infrastructure of the hosting provider where the page is stored'.[10] On this basis the court concluded that 'there is no transfer [of data] to a third country within the meaning of [the] Directive where an individual in a Member State loads personal data onto an internet page which is stored with his hosting provider which is established in that State or in another Member State, thereby making those data accessible to anyone who connects to the internet, including people in a third country'.[11] The placing of data on a web page therefore is not a transfer of data. Before leaving *Lindqvist* we should note that the court observed that:

> given the state of development of the internet at the time [the] Directive was drawn up and the absence of criteria applicable to use of the internet, one cannot presume that the Community legislature intended the expression transfer [of data] to a third country to cover the loading, by an individual in Mrs Lindqvist's position, of data onto an internet page, even if those data are thereby made accessible to persons in third countries with the technical means to access them.[12]

The lawmaking institutions of the EU have, of course, now had a second opportunity to review the application of the data protection framework to the internet and the placing of content on web pages in the drafting of the GDPR. In terms of data transfers, the GDPR makes no significant changes on the previous law as found in the directive, suggesting that the EU institutions are satisfied with the settlement found in *Lindqvist*.

---

[7] Ibid. [53].
[8] Ibid. [54] (emphasis added).
[9] Ibid. [55].
[10] Ibid. [61].
[11] Ibid. [71].
[12] Ibid. [68].

Data transfers are covered by Chapter 5 (Articles 44–50) but for the purposes of the immediate analysis we need to look to Art. 44. This provides that:

> any transfer of personal data which are undergoing processing or are intended for processing after transfer to a third country or to an international organisation shall take place only if, subject to the other provisions of this Regulation, the conditions laid down in this Chapter are complied with by the controller and processor, including for onward transfers of personal data from the third country or an international organisation to another third country or to another international organisation.

This is not dissimilar to the old wording of Art. 25(1) of the 1995 Directive 'Member States shall provide that the transfer to a third country of personal data which are undergoing processing or are intended for processing after transfer may take place only if, without prejudice to compliance with the national provisions adopted pursuant to the other provisions of this Directive, the third country in question ensures an adequate level of protection.' The main distinction between the 1995 wording and the 2018 wording is not around the definition of the transfer itself but rather the addition of 'international organisations' defined in Art. 4(26) as 'an organisation and its subordinate bodies governed by public international law' to the classification of 'third country'. The GDPR specifically does not seek to define transfer, suggesting that *Lindqvist* remains the applicable law in this area.

24.1.1 **The data exportation framework**

It is clear from the wording of Art. 44 that there is a framework for the legal exportation of data outside the EEA. This is necessary as data transfers occur continually; data is after all the oil that lubricates our modern economies. Article 44 says 'any transfer of personal data . . . shall take place only if *the conditions laid down in this Chapter* are complied with'. The framework for effective legal transfers of data is therefore fully contained within Chapter 5 (Articles 44–50) of the GDPR.

An examination of Chapter 5 reveals three frameworks for the exportation of data from the EEA to a non-EEA state. These are particularly important for us in the UK post-Brexit when the UK ceases to be an EEA state. It means that as you are reading this all transfers from the EEA to the UK are regulated in accordance with Chapter 5. At the time of writing it is unclear what form of settlement has been reached to allow transfers of data to the UK from the EEA. If the UK has managed to negotiate a withdrawal agreement based on the Prime Minister's Chequers plan, as agreed by the European Council on 25 November 2018, the UK government and the EU will be negotiating a deal based on so-called 'adequacy plus', a formal recognition that UK data protection law meets EU standards.[13] However, I have written elsewhere that the current UK law may not meet formal adequacy requirements.[14] Whatever the final legal position, the two sides (the UK and the EU) are given until 31 December 2020 to negotiate an agreement by Art. 71 of the agreed text of the withdrawal agreement, which states that during the transition

---

[13] HM Government, *The Future Relationship Between the United Kingdom and the European Union*, CM9593 July 2018, 3.2.
[14] A Murray, 'Data transfers between the EU and UK post Brexit?' (2017) 7 *International Data Privacy Law* 149.

period EU law will apply in the UK 'in respect of the processing of personal data of data subjects outside the United Kingdom'.[15]

If the UK has 'crashed out' without a deal being in place, emergency measures will have had to be implemented. This will be based on the guidance note prepared by the Department for Digital, Culture, Media and Sport in September 2018.[16] This notes that there is no change in domestic law (no doubt a relief to all of you who have read chapters 22 and 23) as 'the Data Protection Act 2018 would remain in place and the EU Withdrawal Act would incorporate the GDPR into UK law to sit alongside it'. The note observes, however, that 'the legal framework governing transfers of personal data from organisations (or subsidiaries) established in the EU to organisations established in the UK would change on exit'. The advice from DDCMS is the UK government would hope to get an adequacy decision, but as these take time to agree at the point of Brexit organizations should have standard contractual clauses (discussed at 24.4) in place to allow them to continue to transfer data from the EEA to the UK. Although this might seem odd to you reading this text in late 2019, or later, at the time of writing (30 November 2018) it is not clear at all if the UK will leave the EU in an orderly fashion or will simply crash out.

Already you have read the word 'adequacy' several times. This is the 'Rolls-Royce' system for data transfers from within the EEA to outside it. The framework for adequacy is found in Art. 45 GDPR. This states that 'a transfer of personal data to a third country or an international organisation may take place where the Commission has decided that the third country, a territory or one or more specified sectors within that third country, or the international organisation in question ensures an adequate level of protection. Such a transfer shall not require any specific authorisation.' Thus if your country or organization is deemed to be 'adequate' by the Commission you may transfer data into and out of the EU as if your country or organization was an EEA member state, this is the settlement the UK government hopes to achieve post-Brexit. How do you receive adequacy recognition? Article 45(2) gives a framework checklist for the Commission to follow. To find adequacy they must find:

a. rule of law, respect for human rights and fundamental freedoms, relevant legislation, both general and sectoral, including concerning public security, defence, national security and criminal law and the access of public authorities to personal data, as well as the implementation of such legislation, data protection rules, professional rules and security measures, including rules for the onward transfer of personal data to another third country or international organisation which are complied with in that country or international organisation, case-law, as well as effective and enforceable data subject rights and effective administrative and judicial redress for the data subjects whose personal data are being transferred;

b. the existence and effective functioning of one or more independent supervisory authorities in the third country or to which an international organisation

---

[15] Agreement on the withdrawal of the United Kingdom of Great Britain and Northern Ireland from the European Union and the European Atomic Energy Community, as endorsed by leaders at a special meeting of the European Council on 25 November 2018.

[16] Department for Digital, Culture, Media and Sport, *Guidance: Data protection if there's no Brexit deal*, 13 September 2018 <https://www.gov.uk/government/publications/data-protection-if-theres-no-brexit-deal/data-protection-if-theres-no-brexit-deal>.

is subject, with responsibility for ensuring and enforcing compliance with the data protection rules, including adequate enforcement powers, for assisting and advising the data subjects in exercising their rights and for cooperation with the supervisory authorities of the Member States; and

c. international commitments the third country or international organisation concerned has entered into, or other obligations arising from legally binding conventions or instruments as well as from its participation in multilateral or regional systems, in particular in relation to the protection of personal data.

In practice this means an extensive period of negotiation between the Commission and the country seeking adequacy, followed by the publication in the Official Journal of the text of the adequacy decision. Currently there are full adequacy decisions in place for eleven countries[17] and limited adequacy decisions for two: Canada which has an adequacy decision only in relation to data held or processed by commercial organizations, not public bodies or non-commercial organizations, and the United States Privacy Shield (which will be discussed at 24.3). In addition, negotiations are ongoing with South Korea for recognition.

Adequacy decisions are open-ended but the Commission is required by Art. 45(3) to review the country (or organization) at least every four years to ensure that they continue to meet the standards required for adequacy. In addition, by Art. 45(4) the Commission is tasked to continually monitor developments in the country or organization. If at any time the Commission finds the country or organization no longer meets the adequacy standard, they may repeal, amend, or suspend the original decision by Art. 45(5). If they do so they are required by Art. 45(6) to re-enter negotiations with the country or organization in question 'with a view to remedying the situation'.

Probably the most controversial adequacy decision is the one between the EU and the United States. When the 1995 Directive was passed, it required adequate levels of data protection from third countries before data could be exported to them.[18] This was a problem for EU–US data flows which are the backbone of data transfers globally. To remedy this, the Commission and the US State Department and Department of Commerce negotiated an agreement, called the 'safe harbour agreement' which would allow the Commission to issue an adequacy decision in favour of the United States. The EU eventually formally recognized the agreement in July 2000 and it took effect.[19] However, the agreement was unlike any adequacy decision which was to follow. Essentially, it allowed US organizations to voluntarily agree to abide by seven principles and to register with the US Department of Commerce.[20] As a self-certification scheme, it was clear

---

[17] Andorra, Argentina, Faroe Islands, Guernsey, Israel, Isle of Man, Japan, Jersey, New Zealand, Switzerland, Uruguay.

[18] The equivalent to Art. 44 GDPR was Art. 25 DPD which stated that 'the Member States shall provide that the transfer to a third country of personal data which are undergoing processing or are intended for processing after transfer may take place only if, without prejudice to compliance with the national provisions adopted pursuant to the other provisions of this Directive, the third country in question ensures an adequate level of protection'.

[19] Commission Decision of 26 July 2000 pursuant to Directive 95/46/EC of the European Parliament and of the Council on the adequacy of the protection provided by the safe harbour privacy principles and related frequently asked questions issued by the US Department of Commerce 2000/520/EC.

[20] The seven principles were: Notice; Choice; Onward transfer; Security; Data integrity; Access; and Enforcement.

to observers that it did not strictly meet the standards of Art. 25 DPD and it was extensively criticized.[21] Eventually the safe harbour settlement was legally challenged by privacy activist Max Schrems (in a case discussed in detail at 24.2) and was struck out. It has been replaced with a new agreement, the so-called 'privacy shield' agreement.[22] In essence, this is a beefed-up version of the safe harbour agreement. As with safe harbour, US-based corporations can self-certify to the Department of Commerce that it complies with the Privacy Shield Principles.[23] What is different about privacy shield is that enforcement and data subject rights are strengthened with, inter alia, requirement that US organizations respond to data subject complaints within 45 days. They must have a data protection policy which includes statements regarding the enforcement body, arbitration rights, disclosures to public authorities, and the company's liability for onward transfers; limitations on access rights to data by US public authorities; and a stronger enforcement and oversight procedure operated by the Federal Trade Commission. The privacy shield agreement has since also been challenged, and these challenges will be discussed at 24.3.

If a country or organization does not hold an adequacy decision then data transfers must be legitimized in some other way: this means appropriate safeguards under Art. 46 GDPR. Article 46(2) lists a menu of safeguards which may be 'appropriate'. These include 'a legally binding and enforceable instrument between public authorities or bodies'; transfers subject to binding corporate rules; standard contractual clauses; and an approved code of conduct together with binding and enforceable commitments of the receiver outside the EEA. These appropriate safeguards ensure that both the EEA-based data controller and the receiver of the transfer are legally required to protect individuals' rights and freedoms for their personal data.

The most common form of appropriate safeguard is binding corporate rules (BCRs) under Art. 47. These are internal codes of conduct operating within a multinational group, which applies to restricted transfers of personal data from the group's EEA entities to non-EEA group entities. They can be rules for a single corporate group or rules for a group of undertakings or enterprises engaged in a joint economic activity, such as franchises or joint ventures. According to Art. 47 these rules must:

(a) be legally binding and apply to and are enforced by every member concerned of the group of undertakings, or group of enterprises engaged in a joint economic activity, including their employees; and

(b) expressly confer enforceable rights on data subjects with regard to the processing of their personal data. In addition, they must meet the extensive requirements of Art. 47(2).

---

[21] W Long and M Quek, 'Personal data privacy protection in an age of globalization: the US-EU safe harbor compromise' (2002) 9 *Journal of European Public Policy* 325; M Zimmer, 'Internet Privacy across Borders: "Trading Up" or a "Race to the Bottom"?' in RJ Beck (ed.), *Law and Disciplinarity: Thinking Beyond Borders* (Palgrave 2013); N Purtova, 'Who decides on the future of data protection? Role of law firms in shaping European data protection regime' (2014) 28 *International Review of Law, Computers & Technology* 204.

[22] Commission Implementing Decision (EU) 2016/1250 of 12 July 2016 pursuant to Directive 95/46/EC of the European Parliament and of the Council on the adequacy of the protection provided by the EU–U.S. Privacy Shield, C/2016/4176.

[23] The principles are the same seven as originally agreed under safe harbour.

Before taking effect BCRs must be submitted for approval to an EEA supervisory authority in an EEA country where one of the companies is based. An alternative for an organization that does not want to seek formal BCRs, or who cannot use them as they are transferring data not within their corporation or group but to third parties, is to use standard contractual clauses under Art. 46(2)(c) and (d).

Standard contractual clauses (SCCs) are four sets of model contractual clauses adopted by the Commission under the 1995 Directive (no new clauses for the GDPR have been issued yet but they are planned).[24] The clauses contain contractual obligations on the data exporter and the data importer, and rights for the individuals whose personal data is transferred. Individuals can directly enforce those rights against the data importer and the data exporter. There are two sets of standard contractual clauses for restricted transfers between one controller and another controller, and two sets between a controller and processor. SCCs must be adopted in the contractual agreement between the data exporter and the data importer in their entirety and without amendment. The parties are allowed to include additional clauses on business-related issues, provided that they do not contradict the SCCs. SCCs may offer a tantalizing alternative to BCRs as they do not need to be approved by a supervisory authority and they can be used to export data to unconnected third parties. However, they are subject to a current challenge from privacy advocate Max Schrems which makes the current adoption of SCCs risky as they may be ruled invalid by the CJEU in 2019.

24.2 **Challenging the data exportation framework:** *Schrems v Data Protection Commissioner*

As already noted, to comply with EU data exportation rules, originally in Art. 25 DPD and now in Art. 44 GDPR a number of countries have adopted data protection laws and principles which have been found to be 'adequate' by the Commission. One particular sticking point over the years though has been data exportation to the United States. The United States takes a philosophically different view to the EU on how data protection should be effected. Whereas the EU supports a holistic, rights-based approach which protects all data of the data subject, the United States favours a sectoral and self-regulatory approach.[25] To allow for the free flow of data from the EU to the United States a legal fiction was created: the safe harbour agreement. I call it a legal fiction for as we have seen it was a self-certification scheme which did not appear to strictly meet the standards of Art. 25 DPD. However, it was an effective fiction that allowed for the massive volumes of international transfers of data between the EU and the US, transfers

---

[24] Commission Decision of 15 June 2001 on standard contractual clauses for the transfer of personal data to third countries, under Directive 95/46/EC; Commission Decision of 27 December 2004 amending Decision 2001/497/EC as regards the introduction of an alternative set of standard contractual clauses for the transfer of personal data to third countries; and Commission Decision of 5 February 2010 on standard contractual clauses for the transfer of personal data to processors established in third countries under Directive 95/46/EC of the European Parliament and of the Council.

[25] G Steinke, 'Data privacy approaches from US and EU perspectives' (2002) 19 *Telematics and Informatics* 193; L Movius and N Krup, 'US and EU Privacy Policy: Comparison of Regulatory Approaches' (2009) 3 *International Journal of Communication* 169.

which are the lifeblood of technology companies such as Apple, Facebook, Google, and Microsoft.

In summer 2013, though, the Edward Snowden revelations threatened to undermine the safe harbour agreement. Among the many revelations in the Snowden documents, discussed in full in chapter 25, was the exposure of a program known as Prism. Prism is a large-scale state data-gathering program in which the US National Security Agency gathers and stores large volumes of internet communications data from technology and telecommunications companies based in the United States, such as Google, Microsoft, Facebook, and Apple. The data is requested under a warrant obtained under the FISA Amendments Act of 2008.[26] The disclosure of the Prism program suggested the safe harbour agreement was unable to provide the level of protection needed to meet the requirements of Art. 25 for although other EU states, including the UK, have parallel data-gathering programs at state level, the EU member states are bound by the principles of the EU Charter, whereas the United States Federal Government is not.

One man who took this view was Maximilian Schrems, an Austrian privacy activist and founder of civil society group Europe v Facebook.[27] He had been campaigning against Facebook's data-gathering program before the Snowden revelations. He first became interested in Facebook's data privacy program when studying law during a semester abroad at Santa Clara University in Silicon Valley. It is reported that Schrems decided to write a paper on Facebook's lack of awareness of European privacy law, after being surprised by what the company's privacy lawyer, Ed Palmieri, said to his class on the subject.[28] He later made a request under Art. 12 to receive what information Facebook held on him and received a CD containing over 1,200 pages of data, which he published at Europe v Facebook with personal information redacted. In summer 2013 he filed a complaint with the Irish Data Protection Commissioner alleging that Facebook's policy of exporting data to the United States was unlawful under Art. 25 due to its role in and compliance with the Prism program.[29] When the Data Protection Commissioner ruled that Facebook had no case to answer, Schrems filed an application for judicial review in the Irish High Court. When the case was heard in June 2014 the court immediately referred the case to the CJEU.

The High Court sent two questions to the CJEU:

(1) Whether in the course of determining a complaint which has been made to an independent office holder who has been vested by statute with the functions of administering and enforcing data protection legislation that personal data is being transferred to another third country (in this case, the United States of America) the laws and practices of which, it is claimed, do not contain adequate protections for the data subject, that office holder is absolutely bound by the Community finding to the contrary contained in [Decision 2000/520] having regard to Article 7, Article 8 and Article 47 of [the Charter], the provisions of Article 25(6) of Directive [95/46] notwithstanding?

(2) Or, alternatively, may and/or must the office holder conduct his or her own investigation of the matter in the light of factual developments in the meantime since that Commission decision was first published?

---

[26] See 25.1.4.
[27] <http://europe-v-facebook.org/EN/en.html>.
[28] K Hill, 'Max Schrems: The Austrian Thorn In Facebook's Side', *Forbes* 7 February 2012.
[29] Facebook's European Headquarters are in Ireland, hence the complaint to the Irish DPC.

The first question essentially asks whether the Irish Data Protection Commissioner is bound by the safe harbour agreement and must find data transfers which comply with it to be lawful, notwithstanding the rights to privacy, data privacy, and an effective remedy found in the EU Charter. The second asks whether the Commissioner may by his own investigation find that the export does not comply with the Directive, notwithstanding the safe harbour agreement.

The court gave its decision on 6 October 2015 and in so doing perhaps went further than the High Court had envisaged when it referred the case.[30] The court first answered the questions referred. It noted that the very act of transferring data was a data process in and of itself[31] and that by Art. 8(3) of the Charter and Art. 28 of the Directive

> national supervisory authorities are responsible for monitoring compliance with the EU rules concerning the protection of individuals with regard to the processing of personal data, each of them is therefore vested with the power to check whether a transfer of personal data from its own Member State to a third country complies with the requirements laid down by Directive 95/46.[32]

This means that national supervisory authorities such as the Irish Data Protection Commissioner have a general supervisory authority which they can use to block data transfers. However, as Art. 25(6) allows the Commission to adopt a decision finding that a third country ensures an adequate level of protection, as is the case with the safe harbour, in these cases:

> until such time as the Commission decision is declared invalid by the Court, the Member States and their organs, which include their independent supervisory authorities, . . . cannot adopt measures contrary to that decision, such as acts intended to determine with binding effect that the third country covered by it does not ensure an adequate level of protection. Measures of the EU institutions are in principle presumed to be lawful and accordingly produce legal effects until such time as they are withdrawn, annulled in an action for annulment or declared invalid following a reference for a preliminary ruling or a plea of illegality.[33]

As such the answer to the first question is that the Irish Data Protection Commissioner is bound by Decision 2000/520 (the safe harbour decision) until it is declared invalid. What happened next though was a powerful message from the court. It found that it would be:

> contrary to the system set up by the Directive and to the objective of Articles 25 and 28 for a Commission decision adopted pursuant to Article 25(6) to have the effect of preventing a national supervisory authority from examining a person's claim concerning the protection of his rights and freedoms in regard to the processing of his personal data which has been or could be transferred from a Member State to the third country covered by that decision.[34]

As a result, the court found that state supervisory bodies such as the Irish Data Protection Commissioner do have the right to review the transfer of data under a decision such as the safe harbour decision, notwithstanding the normal principle.[35]

---

[30] *Maximillian Schrems v Data Protection Commissioner* ECLI:EU:C:2015:650.
[31] Ibid. [45].
[32] Ibid. [47].
[33] Ibid. [52].
[34] Ibid. [56].
[35] Ibid. [66].

This was only the appetizer though; the main course was to come. The court noted that:

> as is apparent from the referring court's explanations relating to the questions submitted, Mr Schrems contends in the main proceedings that United States law and practice do not ensure an adequate level of protection within the meaning of Article 25 of the Directive. As the Advocate General has observed in points 123 and 124 of his Opinion, Mr Schrems expresses doubts, which the referring court indeed seems essentially to share, concerning the validity of Decision 2000/520.

As a result, the court declared that 'in such circumstances, having regard to what has been held in paragraphs 60 to 63 of the present judgment and in order to give the referring court a full answer, it should be examined whether that decision complies with the requirements stemming from Directive 95/46 read in the light of the Charter.'[36]

This was what Mr Schrems had hoped for but was strictly beyond what the referring court had asked. The court now was going to examine the legality of the safe harbour agreement itself. Remember, at this point, that the safe harbour agreement was the only thing which permitted the safe transfer of personal data from the EU to the US under Art. 25. Should the court find the agreement to be unlawful, it had a direct impact upon a multibillion-dollar industry.

 Highlight The decision of the CJEU in *Schrems*

(1) Decision 2000/520 does not contain any finding regarding the existence, in the United States, of rules adopted by the State intended to limit any interference with the fundamental rights of the persons whose data is transferred from the European Union to the United States, interference which the State entities of that country would be authorised to engage in when they pursue legitimate objectives, such as national security.

(2) Nor does Decision 2000/520 refer to the existence of effective legal protection against interference of that kind.

(3) The Commission's own analysis of Decision 2000/520 shows that the United States authorities were able to access the personal data transferred from the Member States to the United States and process it in a way incompatible, in particular, with the purposes for which it was transferred, beyond what was strictly necessary and proportionate to the protection of national security.

(4) Data subjects had no administrative or judicial means of redress enabling, in particular, the data relating to them to be accessed and, as the case may be, rectified or erased.

(5) Legislation permitting the public authorities to have access on a generalised basis to the content of electronic communications must be regarded as compromising the essence of the fundamental right to respect for private life, as guaranteed by Article 7 of the Charter

➡

---

[36] Ibid. [67].

→

(6) Legislation not providing for any possibility for an individual to pursue legal remedies in order to have access to personal data relating to him, or to obtain the rectification or erasure of such data, does not respect the essence of the fundamental right to effective judicial protection, as enshrined in Article 47 of the Charter.

(7) Consequently, without there being any need to examine the content of the safe harbour principles, it is to be concluded that Article 1 of Decision 2000/520 fails to comply with the requirements laid down in Article 25(6) of Directive 95/46, read in the light of the Charter, and that it is accordingly invalid.

As may be expected, the fallout from the *Schrems* decision was great. On the European side of the Atlantic the decision was greeted as a strong vindication of the fundamental right of privacy. The European Commission[37] and the Article 29 working party[38] made bullish statements about how this protected fundamental rights. Meanwhile, US regulators were understandably less enthusiastic. Federal Trade Commissioner Julie Brill admitted that 'although I and other close observers of the European privacy scene have been discussing the potential implications of the Schrems case for some time, the decision clearly came as a shock to many policy makers and companies in the United States', and that:

> during a discussion held just last week in the heart of Silicon Valley, a Member of the US House of Representatives who hails from that area of California stated that the Schrems decision measured 7.8 on the Richter scale. For those of you not as familiar with earthquakes as they are in California, that is an enormous shock that would seriously test most bridges. It also makes the need for building stronger and more durable bridges that much clearer.[39]

Unsurprisingly, both sides were quick to mobilize to try and find a replacement for the safe harbour agreement. A communication from the Commission committed it to developing a 'renewed and sound framework for transfers of personal data to the United States'.[40]

---

[37] European Commission Statement: First Vice-President Timmermans and Commissioner Jourová's press conference on Safe Harbour following the Court ruling in case C-362/14 (Schrems) (6 October 2015) <http://europa.eu/rapid/press-release_STATEMENT-15-5782_en.htm>.

[38] Article 29 Data Protection Working Party, Statement on the Implementation of the Judgment of the Court of Justice of the European Union in *Schrems v Data Protection Commissioner* (16 October 2015) <http://ec.europa.eu/justice/data-protection/article-29/press-material/pressrelease/art29_press_material/2015/20151016_wp29_statement_on_schrems_judgement.pdf>.

[39] J Brill, 'Transatlantic Privacy After Schrems: Time for An Honest Conversation' Keynote Address at the Amsterdam Privacy Conference, 23 October 2015 <https://www.ftc.gov/system/files/documents/public_statements/836443/151023amsterdamprivacy1.pdf>.

[40] Communication from the Commission to the European Parliament and the Council on the Transfer of Personal Data from the EU to the United States of America under Directive 95/46/EC following the Judgment by the Court of Justice in Case C-362/14 (Schrems) COM(2015) 566 final.

24.3 **Challenging privacy shield**

The negotiations led in time to the adoption of the privacy shield agreement.[41] As already noted, privacy shield replicates much of the framework of the safe harbour but with added protection for EU data subjects. The key issue in *Schrems* was the ability of US law enforcement and security bodies to access locally held data using FISA warrants or similar without any form of redress for EU data subjects under US Federal or State Law. Privacy shield attempts to plug these problems. Part III of the agreement covers access and use of personal data transferred under the privacy shield by US public authorities. This requires written assurance from the US Federal Government that any access of public authorities to personal data will be subject to clear limitations, safeguards, and oversight mechanisms. US Federal authorities, as part of the agreement, had to affirm the absence of indiscriminate or mass surveillance,[42] and companies who hold data on EU data subjects in the US will be able to report approximate number of access requests; a move from the previous position where they were not allowed to reveal if requests had been made.

Most importantly, though, a new system of redress is created through the EU–US Privacy Shield Ombudsperson.[43] The ombudsperson is an office created by the US government but who by the terms of the agreement must be 'independent from, and thus free from instructions by, the US Intelligence Community.'[44] The ombudsperson is tasked with ensuring 'that individual complaints are properly investigated and addressed, and that individuals receive independent confirmation that US laws have been complied with or, in case of a violation of such laws, the non-compliance has been remedied'.[45] The current ombudsperson is Acting Under Secretary of State for Economic Growth, Energy, and the Environment, Manisha Singh, who was appointed to the role in on 28 September 2018. Her appointment was only confirmed after a number of delays and following a letter from a number of US technology and business groups to US Secretary of State Pompeo calling for the urgent appointment of the ombudsperson.[46]

There is currently considerable concern in Europe that the US Federal Government is not meeting its side of the agreement. In addition to a protracted period with no ombudsperson in place, now resolved, the European Parliament resolved in June 2018 for privacy shield to be suspended if the US Federal Government had not fully complied with it by 1 September 2018, although no such suspension has yet been announced.[47] This followed a Commission review in October 2017 which concluded that although:

> overall Privacy Shield continues to ensure an adequate level of protection for the personal data transferred from the EU to participating companies in the US, at the same time, the Commission considers that the practical implementation of the Privacy Shield framework can be further improved in order to ensure that the guarantees and safeguards provided therein continue to function as intended.[48]

---

[41] Privacy Shield (n. 22).

[42] At [82].

[43] See [116]–[121] and Annex III.

[44] Ibid. [121].

[45] Ibid. [117].

[46] <https://www.bsa.org/~/media/Files/letters/082018LettertoSOSPompeo.pdf>.

[47] European Parliament, *Motion for a resolution on the adequacy of the protection afforded by the EU-US Privacy Shield* (2018/2645(RSP)) <http://www.europarl.europa.eu/sides/getDoc.do?type=MOTION&reference=B8–2018–0305&language=EN>.

[48] European Commission, *Report from the Commission to the European Parliament and the Council on the first annual review of the functioning of the EU–U.S. Privacy Shield* COM(2017) 611 final, 4.

It was further reported that in July 2018 Věra Jourová, the EU Commissioner for Justice, wrote to US Commerce Secretary Wilbur Ross, warning that the US had three months to comply with the EU's demands that they meet privacy shield requirements.[49] The report suggests the protectionist approach to trade prevalent in Washington along with the passing of the Clarifying Lawful Overseas Use of Data Act or CLOUD Act of 2018[50] had caused concerns in Brussels.

In addition to these political concerns, the privacy shield agreement has been the subject of two separate legal challenges. The first brought by the privacy group Digital Rights Ireland (DRI).[51] They brought an action before the General Court of the CJEU arguing that under Art. 263 of the Treaty on the Functioning of the European Union (TFEU) '[a]ny natural or legal person may, under the conditions laid down in the first and second paragraphs, institute proceedings against an act addressed to that person or which is of direct and individual concern to them, and against a regulatory act which is of direct concern to them and does not entail implementing measures'.[52] They argued both that DRI had standing to bring an action in its own name, or, as an alternative, in the name of its members, its supporters, and the general public.

The claim in DRI's own name rested on three claims:

(1) that, given that it possesses a mobile phone and a computer, its own personal data are liable to be transferred to the United States pursuant to the contested decision;[53]

(2) that privacy shield decision affects its situation as controller of the personal data of its supporters;[54] and

(3) that there is a risk that the use of electronic communication services to process the data of which it is controller will result in their transfer to the United States by a provider of those services.[55]

Unfortunately the court struck out all three claims. The first was summarily dismissed as 'the applicant is a legal person and its official title does not identify any natural person, it cannot avail of the protection of personal data'.[56] The second was dismissed as 'recital 14 of the contested decision specifies that the Privacy Shield applies to American organisations, whether they act as controller or as processor. It is also apparent from recital 15 of that decision that the principles of the Privacy Shield apply to the processing of personal data by an American organisation only if that processing does not fall within the scope of EU legislation, and that the Privacy Shield does not affect the application of EU legislation governing the processing of personal data in the Member States.'[57] The third because 'the applicant could not be criticised for having breached

---

[49] Michael Baxter, 'Jourová puts Trump administration on notice with letter to America' *GDPR:Report* 31 July 2018 <https://gdpr.report/news/2018/07/31/jourova-puts-trump-administration-on-notice-with-letter-to-america/>.

[50] PL 115–41.

[51] *Digital Rights Ireland Ltd v. European Commission* ECLI:EU:T:2017:838.

[52] Ibid. [18].

[53] Ibid. [23].

[54] Ibid. [29].

[55] Ibid. [38].

[56] Ibid. [26].

[57] Ibid. [34].

its obligation of lawful processing by having carried out a transfer of personal data in accordance with the applicable rules'.[58] As a result DRI did not have personal standing.

The court then examined whether DRI could stand in for 'its members, its supporters and the general public'. The court found, and DRI did not dispute, that DRI was a company not a member association,[59] that Art. 263 TFEU does not, in principle, allow for the possibility of an applicant to bring an *actio popularis* in the public interest,[60] and that an attempt to find standing under Art. 80(2) of GDPR which allows a not-for-profit body, organization, or association to make a representative complaint was impossible because GDPR was not in force at the time the complaint was made.[61] As a result the court found DRI had no standing and dismissed the complaint.

Moreover, the DRI complaint was not the only challenge to privacy shield. Max Schrems, flush from his success in the safe harbour litigation had started a second round of litigation against Facebook Ireland. The focus of that litigation was initially standard contractual clauses and the case will be discussed in more detail at 24.4, with specific reference to SCCs. However, when the Irish High Court referred eleven questions to the CJEU in April 2018 a number of them were specifically on the operation of privacy shield. The first question is quite procedural. It asks whether for the purposes of Art. 25(6) of the DPD (and presumably by extension for Art. 46(2) GDPR) the privacy shield decision constitutes a finding of general application binding on data protection authorities and the courts of the member states to the effect that the US ensures an adequate level of protection. If it does not, what relevance, if any, does the privacy shield decision have in the assessment conducted into the adequacy of the safeguards provided to data transferred to the United States which is transferred pursuant to the SCC Decision? This, in essence, determines the limits of the authority of the Irish Data Protection Commission. If privacy shield is the equivalent of a full adequacy decision it means it would not be possible for the Irish Data Protection Commission to intervene. If, however, it is less than a full adequacy decision, it gives them leeway to intervene in individual cases.

More interesting, however, is the following question. This is:

> given the findings of the High Court in relation to US law, does the provision of the Privacy Shield ombudsperson under Annex A to Annex III of the Privacy Shield Decision when taken in conjunction with the existing regime in the United States ensure that the US provides a remedy to data subjects whose personal data is transferred to the US under the SCC Decision that is compatible with Article 47 of the Charter?'[62]

This question is extremely provocative. In her earlier determination of the case Costello J was quite forthright, stating:

> it seems to me that there is a well-founded argument that the Ombudsperson mechanism does not respect the essence of that fundamental right. It does not afford EU citizens judicial protection. The Ombudsperson is not a judge and she is not on the face of it independent of the executive. The office arguably does not meet the indicia of a tribunal established the ECJ in Denuit [2005] ECR I-923 at para 12 that the body is established by law, is permanent, whether its

---

[58] Ibid. [41].
[59] Ibid. [47].
[60] Ibid. [50].
[61] Ibid. [52].
[62] Art. 47 is the right to an effective remedy and fair trial.

jurisdiction is compulsory, whether its procedure is inter partes, whether it applies rules of law and whether it is independent. Critically, her decisions are not subject to judicial review. It is also arguable that the remedy is not an effective remedy as required by Article 47.[63]

If the CJEU agrees with her assessment, this would render the privacy shield agreement deficient of a procedure for an individual to pursue legal remedies in order to have effective judicial protection, as enshrined in Art. 47 of the Charter, which as we know from *Schrems*, was one of the major reasons safe harbour was ruled illegal. It is not impossible that some time in 2019 the CJEU could strike out privacy shield completely on this basis.

24.4 Challenging standard contractual clauses

The Schrems II challenge was not originated as a direct challenge to privacy shield, although, as we have just seen, it may ultimately provide a killer blow to the operation of the agreement. It originated as a challenge to the use of SCCs. This is because, in the immediate aftermath to the *Schrems* decision and the striking down of safe harbour, Facebook (and others) continued to export personal data from the EU to the US under SCCs. Max Schrems believed, not unreasonably, that if the United States was not felt to be a safe enough trading partner for personal data under the safe harbour, then data transfers on SCCs should equally be stopped for the reasons given in the *Schrems* decision, in particular, data-gathering programs such as Prism continue to be operated by the NSA and under a FISA warrant Facebook and others would still be compelled to hand over personal data of EU data subjects, whether that data were transferred to them under the safe harbour agreement (now defunct) or SCCs. Additionally, as SCCs do not allow the data subject administrative or judicial means of redress, enabling the data relating to them to be accessed, rectified, or erased, SCCs demonstrate identical flaws to the safe harbour agreement.

Schrems raised his claim with the Irish Data Protection Commission as a result of the outcome of the *Schrems* case at the CJEU. He claimed that the fact that data held in the US remains subject to surveillance under a number of legal provisions, many of which afford no judicial remedy that would allow the data subject to take appropriate action, means that transfers under SCCs were in breach of Art. 8 of the EU Charter. The Data Protection Commissioner then made an application to the Irish High Court to refer a number of questions to the CJEU to assist it in making its decision, or, in the alternative, to issue a judgment answering these questions if they were *acte claire*. The court issued its judgment in October 2017 referring eleven questions to the CJEU. In her judgment, Costello J outlined that in her view 'SCCs alone cannot ensure an adequate level of protection in the third country for data protection rights and freedoms. Despite the provisions of the SCCs, nonetheless data transferred pursuant to the SCCs to third countries may not enjoy the adequate level of protection mandated by reason of the laws of the individual third country.'[64] She went on 'it follows therefore that the provisions of the law of that third country may provide the basis for concluding that data transfers

---

[63] *The Data Protection Commissioner v. Facebook Ireland Ltd and Maximillian Schrems* [2016] No. 4809 P.3 October 2017 [301] <http://www.europe-v-facebook.org/sh2/HCJ.pdf>.

[64] Ibid. [150].

effected pursuant to SCCs under Article 26 (2) do not provide adequate safeguards for the personal data of data subjects.'[65] This led her to conclude:

> if there are inadequacies in the laws of the United States within the meaning of Union law, the SCCs cannot and do not remedy or compensate for these inadequacies. The private contractual clauses cannot bind the sovereign authority of the United States and its agencies. This conclusion means that the terms of the SCCs themselves does not provide an answer to the concerns raised by the DPC in relation to the existence of effective remedies for individual EU citizens in respect of possible infringement of their data privacy protection rights if their data are subject to unlawful interference.[66]

Eleven questions were referred to the CJEU in May 2018. As we have already seen, some refer to the privacy shield agreement. In relation to SCCs, the key questions are probably questions 3, 4, and 8. Question 3 asks:

> when assessing whether a third country ensures the level of protection required by EU law to personal data transferred to that country for the purposes of Article 26 of the Directive, ought the level of protection in the third country be assessed by reference to:
>
> (a) the applicable rules in the third country resulting from its domestic law or international commitments, and the practice designed to ensure compliance with those rules, to include the professional rules and security measures which are complied with in the third country; or
>
> (b) the rules referred to in (a) together with such administrative, regulatory and compliance practices and policy safeguards, procedures, protocols, oversight mechanisms and non judicial remedies as are in place in the third country?

This invites the CJEU to state whether rules for the protection of personal data are enough to allow data transfers or whether effective enforcement procedures are also required. Question 4 asks quite bluntly, 'Given the facts found by the High Court in relation to US law, if personal data is transferred from the EU to the US under the SCC Decision does this violate the rights of individuals under Articles 7 and/or 8 of the Charter?' This is self-explanatory. Finally, question 8 asks:

> if a third country data importer is subject to surveillance laws that in the view of a data protection authority conflict with the clauses of the Annex to the SCC Decision or Article 25 and 26 of the Directive and/or the Charter, is a data protection authority required to use its enforcement powers under Article 28(3) of the Directive to suspend data flows or is the exercise of those powers limited to exceptional cases only, in light of Recital 11 of the Directive, or can a data protection authority use its discretion not to suspend data flows?

This is inviting the CJEU to rule in a similar fashion to *Schrems* that the EU Charter is superior to the remainder of the legal acquis and that subject to this, supervisory authorities are required to step in to protect the rights of data subjects where they are aware of risks of harm.

As can be seen, the possible impact of this case is as great as that of the original *Schrems* case. However, there is a rub; well, two actually. The first is that many people believe the case to be moot. The law upon which the case is being argued, the 1995 DPD, has now been repealed and replaced by GDPR. The Commission will soon issue

---

[65] Ibid. [151].
[66] Ibid. [154].

new standard contractual clauses under Art. 46 so is there any mileage in this claim? Well, possibly. Facebook made a request in April 2018 to have the reference to the CJEU delayed as there was a risk of unquantifiable potential loss, which they argued was incapable of being remedied if the court ultimately found against them. In that reference they argued, in the words of Costello J 'obliquely' that the Directive having been replaced by GDPR means 'the legal basis for the SCCs will be fundamentally altered, and the question in respect of the Directive will be moot'.[67] In dismissing this request, Costello J noted that she felt Facebook was deliberately 'running out the clock' so as to make the application of the Data Protection Commission moot, noting 'the existing delays have already potentially gravely prejudiced the DPC and Mr Schrems. I do not propose to exacerbate this potential prejudice any further.'[68] In a further twist, after initially refusing leave to appeal, the Irish Supreme Court allowed Facebook leave to appeal on 31 July 2018 against both the findings of fact and law at the High Court.[69] A hearing in that case has now been fixed for 21 January 2019. With no hearing yet fixed for the CJEU case, it is the intention of Facebook to ask the Supreme Court to halt the referral to the CJEU. However, it is not clear if legally it is possible for a superior court to withdraw a referral once it has been made by an inferior court.

The outcome of this case is as difficult to predict as the Brexit settlement. At one end of the spectrum it could rule both the privacy shield agreement and the use of SCCs incompatible with Art. 8 of the EU Charter and have both struck out. At the other end the Irish Supreme Court could withdraw the reference (if possible) or the CJEU could find most of the questions to be moot given that GDPR has replaced DPD 1995. It is another example of the current lack of certainty in data protection law.

24.5 **Conclusions**

This chapter opened with a modern aphorism 'data is the new oil'. We might conclude with reference to a reportedly ancient curse 'may you live in interesting times'.[70] With data flows and data exportation now essential to just about every commercial transaction globally (even if you buy a piece of commercial real estate there will be the name of company officers, email addresses, and telephone numbers exchanged to service the transaction), it is vital we keep data flowing. EU data protection law in this area is, however, necessarily complex and while some, possibly the Trump White House in Washington, may view the laws on data transference as economically protectionist, from this side of the Atlantic the need for strong data protection and data transference rules are clear, from the fundamental rights principle enshrined in Art. 8 of the EU Charter. The actions of, in particular, Max Schrems but also other data activists have arguably complicated the political and economic position but have helped the CJEU to set out the legal position. It might be argued that to be a member state of the EU (or the

---

[67] *The Data Protection Commissioner v. Facebook Ireland Ltd and Maximillian Schrems* [2016] No. 4809 P, 2 May 2018 [27] <http://www.europe-v-facebook.org/sh2/HCJ_stay.PDF>.

[68] Ibid. [33].

[69] <https://noyb.eu/wp-content/uploads/2018/08/sc_leave_cjeu.pdf>.

[70] Although purportedly an ancient Chinese curse, no authentic Chinese saying to this effect has ever been found according to FR Shapiro, *The Yale Book of Quotations* (Yale UP 2006) 669.

EEA) in these 'interesting times' is valuable for you are protected from the buffeting of the winds of the data exportation framework, and there is no doubt that for many years the UK has benefited from this protection. However, at 11pm on 29 March 2019 we will suddenly find ourselves outside the protective harbour of EU membership, either in the relatively calm waters of having secured a withdrawal agreement or perhaps in the stormy and unwelcoming waters of a no-deal Brexit. Should we find ourselves there, it may prove to be most uncomfortable.

TEST QUESTIONS

Question 1

Transnational data flows require consensus between States, brokered through negotiation and compromise. The *Schrems* judgment of the European Court of Justice is illegitimate and impractical and will do nothing to facilitate such transnational convergence.

Discuss.

Question 2

Although a number of countries around the world have data protection laws, there is insufficient international protection for data privacy in the digital age. We therefore need an international treaty on data protection. Such a treaty could be based on existing legal instruments (including GDPR) and administered by the UN. This would finally give us the effective international protection we need for data processing on a global level.

Discuss.

FURTHER READING

Books

L Bygrave, *Data Privacy Law: An International Perspective* (OUP 2014)

C Kuner, *Transborder Data Flows and Data Privacy Law* (OUP 2013)

Chapters and articles

D Bender, 'Having mishandled Safe Harbor, will the CJEU do better with Privacy Shield? A US perspective' (2016) 6(2) *International Data Privacy Law* 117–38

E Fraser, 'Data Localisation and the Balkanisation of the Internet' (2016) 13 *Script-ed* 360

C Kuner, 'Reality and Illusion in EU data transfer Regulation Post Schrems' [2017] 18 *German Law Journal* 881

A Murray, 'Data transfers between the EU and UK post Brexit?' (2017) 7 *International Data Privacy Law* 149

25

State surveillance and data retention

The digitization of data affects not only digital information held on a computer or in a relevant filing system. It also affects how information is gathered, processed, and interpreted in the real world by states. Digital surveillance is now the cornerstone of signals intelligence (SIGINT) and computer network exploitation (CNE) in all states, with vast sums being expended on SIGINT and CNE programmes.[1] These can take a number of forms from basic digital interception, storage, and transmission facilities, to device tracking, biometric tracking, and threat assessment. It can also use a variety of tools from remote video surveillance tools such as CCTV and drone surveillance, to tracking tools such as GSM and GPS tracking, and data and identity authentication tools such as biometrics. By choosing a selection of tools it is possible for governments, or private citizens, to track an individual, to monitor his or her behaviour, and to monitor his or her communications network, which data may be used for a variety of purposes.[2] This chapter will examine some of the technologies involved, discuss the challenge they pose to the current legal settlement and ask what, if anything, needs to be done to protect the rights of the individual against the forever-developing technologies for digital surveillance.

25.1 State surveillance

We have always understood that governments have had the ability to intercept communications, to monitor and track movements, and to obtain data from third parties under warrants, but until the revelations of NSA contractor Edward Snowden in 2013 we were unaware of the truly massive scale of state surveillance programmes. New terms entered the lexicon based upon Snowden's considerable data release. We learned of Prism (a clandestine surveillance program under which the United States National Security Agency (NSA) collects internet communications from at least nine

---

[1] Computer Network Exploitation is essentially the hacking by state intelligence services of computer networks. It already accounts for 30 per cent of the raw intelligence that Government Communications Headquarters (GCHQ) collects, and will no doubt continue to increase.

[2] NSA General Counsel Stewart Baker has said, 'metadata absolutely tells you everything about somebody's life. If you have enough metadata, you don't really need content.' While General Michael Hayden, former director of the NSA and the CIA, upped the stakes saying 'We kill people based on metadata.' See D Cole 'We Kill People Based on Metadata', *The New York Review of Books* May 2014.

major US internet companies), Upstream (interception and collection by the NSA of telephone and internet traffic from the internet backbone), Tempora (the UK equivalent of Upstream, a data gathering system that is used by Government Communications Headquarters (GCHQ) to buffer internet communications extracted from fibre-optic cables, so that these can be processed and searched at a later time), XKeyscore (a computer system first used by the NSA for searching and analysing global internet data), and Bullrun/Edgehill (a highly classified project aimed at defeating, or undermining or influencing, encryption standards and implementations operated by the NSA/GCHQ) in day-to-day communications. Prior to late 2013 though we were unaware of the existence of all of these programmes (and many more).[3] Some have called Edward Snowden a hero,[4] others a traitor.[5] Whatever your view is of Edward Snowden, it is clear that the so-called 'Snowden files' have realigned the privacy/surveillance discourse in the UK and further afield as changes to surveillance laws have been seen in the United States, the European Union, the United Kingdom, France, Germany, the Netherlands, Switzerland, and many more places as governments seek to place their state surveillance policies on a sound legal footing.

25.1.1 The current UK legal framework for interception

We, as citizens, understand that part of our contract with the state allows the state to carry out surveillance programmes for the purposes listed in Art. 8(2) ECHR: 'in the interests of national security, public safety or the economic wellbeing of the country, for the prevention of disorder or crime, for the protection of health or morals, or for the protection of the rights and freedoms of others'. As a result, we accept that law enforcement agencies and the security and intelligence services will carry out surveillance operations in our collective interests. We rely on the principle of proportionality to ensure that these operations do not become a form of state control over the populous, as happened in former East Germany. As their powers of surveillance and data gathering are so extensive, legislative controls are necessary to prevent abuse or unwarranted intrusion. This is why we have a strict legal framework to control the powers and ability of the state to monitor its own citizens and those external to the state.

The first control is the ECHR itself and Art. 8. As already noted, state surveillance is only compliant with Art. 8 where it fits within the Art. 8(2) exceptions, which require that the interference with privacy be necessary in a democratic society, in accordance with law, and proportionate. The ECtHR has given guidance in all three of these. In *Klass & Ors v Germany*,[6] the court started from the premise that democratic societies were under threat from highly sophisticated forms of espionage and terrorism with the result that the state had to be able, in order effectively to counter such threats,

---

[3] An overview of the Snowden Files can be obtained via <www.theguardian.com/us-news/the-nsa-files>.

[4] S Chakrabarti, 'Let me be clear—Edward Snowden is a hero', *The Guardian*, 14 June 2015; T Huddleston Jr, 'Steve Wozniak: Edward Snowden is "a hero to me"', *Fortune Magazine*, 26 May 2015.

[5] M Hastings, 'Snowden's clearly an anarchist and traitor. Those who endorse him are just as dangerous', *Daily Mail*, 8 April 2015; C Moore, 'Edward Snowden is a traitor, just as surely as George Blake was', *Daily Telegraph*, 5 July 2013.

[6] (1978) 2 EHRR 214.

to undertake the secret surveillance of subversive elements operating within its jurisdiction. The court therefore accepted that the existence of some legislation granting
powers of secret surveillance over the mail, post, and telecommunications was, under
exceptional conditions, necessary in a democratic society in the interests of national
security and/or for the prevention of disorder or crime. In fixing the conditions under
which the system of surveillance is to be operated, the court noted that the domestic
legislature enjoys a certain discretion, and that it is certainly not for the court to substitute for the assessment of the national authorities what might be the best policy in this
field. However, although domestic legislatures have a wide discretion, this is not unlimited. Because of the danger that such a law poses to democracy, the court emphasized
that states do not have unlimited discretion to subject persons within their jurisdiction
to secret surveillance measures in the name of the struggle against espionage and terrorism. As powers of secret surveillance of citizens characterize a police state, they are
tolerable only insofar as the means provided for by the legislation to achieve such aims
remain within the bounds of what is necessary in a democratic society. The interest of
the respondent state in protecting its national security must be balanced against the
seriousness of the interference with the applicant's right to respect for his private life.[7]

This raises the question of whether the activity of the state is in accordance with law.
In a line of case law, the court has established that this requirement will only be met
when three conditions are satisfied.

 Highlight In accordance with law according to ECtHR[8]

(1) the impugned measure must have some basis in domestic law and, with regard to the quality
of the law at issue,

(2) it must be accessible to the person concerned and

(3) it must have foreseeable consequences.

This was reviewed in *Malone v UK*.[9] Mr Malone had been charged with an offence based
in part upon information received through a telephone tap placed on his phone line
under a warrant from the Secretary of State. Mr Malone argued there was no law permitting this, the only relevant provision being s. 80 of the Post Office Act 1969 which said:

> A requirement to do what is necessary to inform designated persons holding office under the
> Crown concerning matters and things transmitted or in course of transmission by means of postal
> or telecommunication services provided by the Post Office may be laid on the Post Office for the
> like purposes and in the like manner as, at the passing of this Act, a requirement may be laid on the
> Postmaster General to do what is necessary to inform such persons concerning matters and things
> transmitted or in course of transmission by means of such services provided by him.

---

[7] Ibid. See also *Leander v Sweden* (1987) 9 EHRR 433.

[8] *Kennedy v United Kingdom* [2011] 52 EHRR 4; *Rotaru v Romania* [2000] ECHR 192; *Kruslin v
France* (1990) 12 EHRR; 547; *Huvig v France* (1990) 12 EHRR 528; *Amann v Switzerland* (2000) 30
EHRR 843.

[9] 7 EHRR 14.

The court accepted that the requirements of the Convention, notably in regard to fore-seeability, could not be exactly the same in the special context of interception of com-munications for the purposes of police investigations. In particular, the requirement of foreseeability could not mean that an individual should be enabled to foresee if and when the authorities were likely to intercept his communications so that he could adapt his conduct accordingly. Nevertheless, the law should be sufficiently clear in its terms to give citizens an adequate indication as to the circumstances in which and the conditions on which public authorities were empowered to resort to this secret and potentially dangerous interference with the right to respect for private life and corre-spondence. Since the implementation, in practice, of measures of secret surveillance of communications was not open to scrutiny by the individuals concerned or the public at large, it would be contrary to the rule of law for the legal discretion granted to the exec-utive to be expressed in terms of an unfettered power. Consequently, the law should indicate the scope of any such discretion conferred on the competent authorities and the manner of its exercise with sufficient clarity, having regard to the legitimate aim of the measure in question, to give the individual adequate protection against arbitrary interference.[10]

In the joined cases of *Kruslin v France* and *Huvig v France*, the court reflected that tap-ping and other forms of interception of telephone conversations represented a serious interference with private life and correspondence and had accordingly to be based on a law that was particularly precise. It was essential to have clear, detailed rules on the subject, especially as the technology available for use was continually becoming more sophisticated.[11]

Finally, the interference with liberty must be proportionate. This was considered in *S & Marper v UK*.[12] The case concerned two individuals who had fingerprint and DNA evi-dence taken from them during criminal investigations. In one case the individual was acquitted at trial, in the other charges were not pressed. The individuals then applied to have their collected information destroyed but the police refused. In the House of Lords Lord Steyn referred specifically to the value of the fingerprint and DNA databases built up by the police under s. 64(1A) of the Police and Criminal Evidence Act 1984:

> almost 6,000 DNA profiles had been linked with crime-scene stain profiles which would have been destroyed under the former provisions. The offences involved included 53 murders, 33 attempted murders, 94 rapes, 38 sexual offences, 63 aggravated burglaries, and 56 cases involv-ing the supply of controlled drugs. On the basis of the existing records, the Home Office statistics estimated that there was a 40 per cent chance that a crime-scene sample would be matched immediately with an individual's profile on the database. This showed that the fingerprints and samples which could now be retained had in the previous three years played a major role in the detection and prosecution of serious crime.[13]

On this basis, he found the law to be proportionate:

> Lord Steyn saw five factors which led to the conclusion that the interference was proportionate to the aim: (i) the fingerprints and samples were kept only for the limited purpose of the detec-tion, investigation and prosecution of crime; (ii) the fingerprints and samples were not of any

---

[10] This judgment led directly to the passing of the Interception of Communications Act 1985.
[11] *Kruslin v France; Huvig v France* (n. 8).
[12] (2009) 48 EHRR 50.
[13] Ibid. [17].

use without a comparator fingerprint or sample from the crime scene; (iii) the fingerprints would not be made public; (iv) a person was not identifiable from the retained material to the untutored eye; and (v) the resultant expansion of the database by the retention conferred enormous advantages in the fight against serious crime.[14]

The ECtHR, however, felt otherwise: it found the actions of the UK authorities to be disproportionate on four grounds.

 Highlight Marper's grounds of disproportionality

(1) The gathering of blanket biometric data from all those suspected of offences whatever their age or the seriousness of the offence, and without a time limit for storage was disproportionate.

(2) There was no independent review of decisions as to whether data should be retained.

(3) Some data is particularly sensitive, the retention of cellular samples is particularly intrusive given the wealth of genetic and health information contained therein.

(4) The mere retention of data could impact an individual through stigmatization or disturbance of the presumption of innocence.

Any UK law which allows for the interception, storage, and examination of digital data must therefore comply with these principles. The current primary provisions are to be found in the Investigatory Powers Act (IPA) 2016. It begins by repeating the *Malone* principle that interception must be carried out in accordance with law. By s. 3 it is an offence for any person (either a person involved in an investigation of a law enforcement body or a private person) to intercept any communication in the course of its transmission by means of a public or private telecommunication system. This covers not only telephone calls but also emails, SMS/MMS messages, IM messages (including SnapChat, WhatsApp, and similar), and all other forms of communication (such as Facebook updates, Tweets, or search terms). It was the predecessor to s. 3 (s. 1 of the Regulation of Investigatory Powers Act 2000) which brought the *News of the World* royal affairs editor to justice after he was found guilty of hacking the voicemail messages of members of the Prince of Wales' staff in 2006 and which led eventually to Operation Weeting, the police operation that led to the arrests of, among others, Neville Thurlbeck, *News of the World* chief reporter; Ian Edmondson, former *News of the World* news editor; and James Weatherup, *News of the World* assistant news editor, for breaches of the Act; and ultimately Rebekah Brooks, News International chief executive and former *News of the World* editor who was arrested (although cleared at trial) on suspicion of conspiring to intercept communications, contrary to s. 1(1) of the Criminal Law Act 1977. An exception is given in s. 44 where all persons have agreed to the interception of the communication; otherwise a warrant will normally be required. Legal interception of communications can only be carried out with a warrant authorizing such interception. There are a variety of warrants that may be issued under the IPA but here we will focus on two: targeted interception warrants and bulk interception warrants.

[14] Ibid. [21].

25.1.2 **Targeted interception warrants**

Targeted interception warrants are issued under Part 2, Chapter 1 of the IPA (ss. 15–43). There are three types of targeted warrant:

(1) a targeted interception warrant (a warrant which authorizes the interception of a communication or the obtaining of communications data, or the disclosure of such data);[15]

(2) a targeted examination warrant (a warrant which authorizes the examination of intercepted material obtained under a bulk interception warrant);[16] and

(3) a mutual assistance warrant (which allows communications to be intercepted or communications data to be examined as part of a mutual assistance request under EU or other Treaty requirements).[17]

All warrants are issued by the Secretary of State under s. 19(1), in practice normally the Home Secretary, or by an appropriate member of the Scottish Executive under s. 21(1) where devolved powers are involved. There is currently no role for judicial warrants in the IPA as are frequently found elsewhere in the world (as we shall see at 25.1.4 when we discuss §702 of the US Foreign Intelligence Surveillance Act 1978). The process is an executive process and IPA warrants are more like executive orders than warrants in the normal legal sense. There is a safeguard process to prevent abuse of executive power. By s. 23(1) a judicial commissioner must review the warrant to ensure it is 'necessary on relevant grounds'[18] and that the conduct that would be authorized by the warrant is proportionate to what is sought to be achieved by that conduct. This review should be carried out before the warrant is issued, although in urgent cases the warrant may be issued without the review being carried out. In such cases under s. 24 the warrant must be reviewed by a judicial commissioner within three working days and if not approved the warrant ceases to be of effect. This process was introduced following a series of reviews held from 2014–2015 which collectively recommended a 'double-lock' system where warrants issued by an executive officer would be reviewed by a judicial officer either before taking effect or, in urgent cases, as soon as possible thereafter.[19]

By s. 23(2) judicial commissioners are told they must apply the same principles as would be applied by a court on an application for judicial review, and consider the matters with a sufficient degree of care so as to ensure that the judicial commissioner complies with the duties imposed by s. 2, which are to have specific regard to the privacy interests of the public. Where the judicial commissioner refuses to approve

---

[15] See s. 15(2).

[16] See s. 15(3).

[17] See s. 15(4).

[18] The relevant grounds are found in s. 20(2), they are: (a) in the interests of national security, (b) for the purpose of preventing or detecting serious crime, or (c) in the interests of the economic well-being of the United Kingdom so far as those interests are also relevant to the interests of national security. (Note: A warrant on this ground can only be issued if the information which it is considered necessary to obtain is information relating to the acts or intentions of persons outside the British Islands.)

[19] Parliamentary Intelligence and Security Committee, *Privacy and Security: A modern and transparent legal framework* HC 1075 (HMSO 2015); Independent Reviewer of Terrorism Legislation, *A Question of Trust: Report of the Investigatory Powers Review* (HMSO 2015); Royal United Services Institute, *A Democratic Licence to Operate* (RUSI London 2015).

a decision to issue a warrant, they must give the Secretary of State written reasons for the refusal and there is a limited form of appeal under s. 23(6) in that where the judicial commissioner who considered the warrant was not the Investigatory Powers Commissioner, the Secretary of State may ask the Investigatory Powers Commissioner to decide whether to approve the decision to issue the warrant. Who are these judicial commissioners? They are all appointed in accordance with s. 227 and must be persons who hold or have held a high judicial office (within the meaning of Part 3 of the Constitutional Reform Act 2005). The chief judicial commissioner (for want of a better term) is the Investigatory Powers Commissioner. They are appointed on the joint recommendation of the Lord Chancellor, the Lord Chief Justice, the Lord President of the Court of Session, and the Lord Chief Justice of Northern Ireland. Lower Judicial Commissioners also need the approval of this powerful quartet but in addition the approval of the Investigatory Powers Commissioner. The current Investigatory Powers Commissioner is Lord Justice Fulford and, although the Act doesn't specifically allow for this, he is assisted by a Deputy Commissioner, Sir John Goldring formerly the Intelligence Services Commissioner and Senior Presiding Judge for England and Wales. There are currently twelve judicial commissioners, all of whom have sat in High Court, the Court of Session, or the Court of Appeal for Northern Ireland. There are as yet no published reports of the Investigatory Powers Commissioner's Office so we have no idea how many warrants are approved and how many refused. In time that information will become known for under s. 234 the Investigatory Powers Commissioner is required to prepare an annual report to the Prime Minister detailing, among other things, statistics on the use of the investigatory powers, including the number of warrants or authorizations issued, given, considered, or approved during the year, information about the results of such use, and information about the operation of the safeguards conferred by this Act in relation to items subject to legal privilege, confidential journalistic material, and sources of journalistic information. The Prime Minister is required by s. 234(6)(a) to publish the report, meaning in time we will get access to this data.

Targeted interception warrants, once issued, are valid for six months, following which they require to be renewed,[20] and are addressed to an intercepting authority. These are the only authorities permitted to carry out interception in terms of the IPA. The list of intercepting authorities is found at s. 18(1), they are: (a) a person who is the head of an intelligence service (Director General of the Security Service, Chief of the Secret Intelligence Service, and Director of GCHQ); (b) Director General of the National Crime Agency; (c) Commissioner of the Metropolitan Police; (d) Chief Constable of the Police Service of Northern Ireland; (e) Chief constable of the Police Service of Scotland; (f) HMRC Commissioners; (g) Chief of Defence Intelligence; or (h) a person who is the competent authority of a country or territory outside the United Kingdom for the purposes of an EU mutual assistance instrument or an international mutual assistance agreement.

As its name suggests, a targeted interception warrant must be specifically targeted. This means that the warrant must comply with s. 15(2) which targets the form of communication and s. 17 which targets the focus of the warrant.

[20] See s. 32(1).

Highlight Targeting form—s. 15(2)

A targeted interception warrant is a warrant which authorizes or requires the person to whom it is addressed to secure, by any conduct described in the warrant, any one or more of the following:

(a) the interception, in the course of their transmission by means of a postal service or telecommunication system, of communications described in the warrant;

(b) the obtaining of secondary data from communications transmitted by means of a postal service or telecommunication system and described in the warrant;

(c) the disclosure, in any manner described in the warrant, of anything obtained under the warrant to the person to whom the warrant is addressed or to any person acting on that person's behalf.

In effect, this allows the security services and law enforcement bodies to intercept any form of communication carried by a postal service or a telecommunications service. It does not allow them though to carry out a general trawl of data (a so-called fishing expedition) it only allows them to gather data on the specified target and any secondary data the primary data generates. Secondary data is defined in s. 16 and is essentially metadata that is attached to the primary data. This is important as metadata can tell security and law enforcement bodies more about the person than primary content data such as their location, their contacts, what device(s) they use, what services they use, even potentially passwords and authorizations if sent insecurely.

 Highlight Targeting scope—s. 17

(1) A warrant under this Chapter may relate to:

  (a) a particular person or organisation, or

  (b) a single set of premises.

(2) In addition a warrant may relate to:

  (a) a group of persons who share a common purpose or who carry on, or may carry on, a particular activity;

  (b) more than one person or organisation, or more than one set of premises, where the conduct authorised or required by the warrant is for the purposes of a single investigation or operation;

  (c) testing or training activities.

(3) Testing or training activities means in relation to a targeted interception warrant:

  (a) the testing, maintenance or development of apparatus, systems or other capabilities relating to the interception of communications in the course of their transmission by means of a telecommunication system or to the obtaining of secondary data from communications transmitted by means of such a system, or

  (b) the training of persons who carry out, or are likely to carry out, such interception or the obtaining of such data.

The scope of a targeted warrant is therefore restricted to a person, organisation or place. Thus a warrant may be issued for Mr Eric Allan of 29 Acacia Road, London, or for the premises at 221B Baker Street, London. In the former the warrant would be able to cover Mr Allan wherever he went such as his place of work and would be able to intercept his email, status updates on social media, and mobile communications wherever he sent them. In the latter the warrant would only cover the place named but would apply to anyone at that location. So any telephone calls made to the occupants or letters sent to the occupants at that address but not to any other address. Similarly any email sent or received, status updates sent, or any web visits made from that address would be covered by the warrant whoever made or received them. However once the occupants leave the named place the warrant would not cover the persons when they are in a different location.

However, s. 17(2) does expand a little the scope of targeted warrants. By s. 17(2)(a) 'a person' can in fact be 'a group of persons who share a common purpose or who carry on, or may carry on, a particular activity' or 'more than one person or organization'; while a 'single set of premises' can include 'more than one set of premises'. These are called thematic warrants and they have to be connected by being part of 'a single investigation or operation'. These warrants have specific conditions laid down by s. 31. By s. 31(4) a warrant that relates to a group of persons who share a common purpose or who carry on, or may carry on, a particular activity must: (a) describe that purpose or activity, and (b) name or describe as many of those persons as it is reasonably practicable to name or describe. By s. 31(5) a warrant that relates to more than one person or organisation, or more than one set of premises, where the conduct authorized or required by the warrant is for the purposes of a single investigation or operation, must: (a) describe the investigation or operation, and (b) name or describe as many of those persons or organisations, or as many of those sets of premises, as it is reasonably practicable to name or describe. In the Interception of Communications Draft Code of Practice, the Home Office notes 'a thematic warrant may be appropriate where the relevant statutory tests are met and where a series of individual warrants is not practicable or where the proposed activity for which the authorisation to be sought is most suitably dealt with by a thematic subject-matter in light of, for example, the operational circumstances'.[21] They give detail on what is expected in relation to such warrants through the use of two examples.

Example A Identifiable parties

Where it is reasonably practicable to individually name those falling within the subject matter of the warrant.

An intercepting authority wishes to intercept the communications of three people for the purposes of an investigation in to human trafficking. The agency applies for a warrant in relation to 'more than one person for the purpose of operation "X" and those persons are known to be "Mr A", "Mr B" and "Mrs C".' As it is reasonably practicable to do so their names must be included in the warrant at the point of issuing. Once issued the warrant authorizes the interception of the communications of 'Mr A', 'Mr B', and 'Mrs C' which are identified by factors specified in the warrant.

---

[21] Home Office, *Interception of Communications Draft Code of Practice*, December 2017, 23 <https://www.gov.uk/government/consultations/investigatory-powers-act-2016-codes-of-practice>.

Example B Non-identifiable parties

Where it is not reasonably practicable to individually name those falling within the subject matter of the warrant.

An intercepting authority wishes to identify persons accessing terrorist material online. The authority seeks a thematic warrant in relation to more than one person for the purpose of a single investigation, with the subject matter of the warrant being 'persons accessing the terrorist website "X".' In such a case, it may not be reasonably practicable to name or describe those persons any further than by a description which is based on their use of website 'X'. Once issued the subject matter of this warrant is any person known to be accessing the terrorist website 'X' and the interception of the communications of any person falling within that description is lawful. There is no requirement to modify the warrant in accordance with s. 34 to add names or descriptions of persons accessing the website.

As can be seen, especially from example B, these thematic warrants can have a large target area. As has been pointed out by Paul Scott, 'though the terms of these provisions are such that they do not permit the granting of "bulk" warrants this is obviously far broader than a genuinely targeted warrant and will permit the interception of communications sent or received by persons who are not named nor otherwise personally identified, within the warrant'.[22] Thematic warrants are somewhat of a middle ground therefore between a true targeted warrant and bulk warrants and for that reason are somewhat controversial.[23] If the security services or law enforcement agencies want to carry out generalized surveillance they should use bulk powers rather than targeted ones but, as we shall see, the scope for bulk interception of communications is restricted and cannot be used for communications which take place completely within the British Isles. This makes thematic warrants all the more controversial.

25.1.3 **Bulk interception warrants**

Where a larger volume of communications data is to be intercepted, a bulk interception warrant is required. Bulk interception warrants allow the security services to intercept large volumes of information without reference to an individual (or group of individuals) or place. A bulk interception warrant could, for instance, cover all communications going into or out of the Twitter servers. Because of the highly intrusive nature of such warrants there are provisions to prevent their abuse. First, and most importantly given our previous analysis of thematic warrants, bulk interception warrants do not apply to purely domestic communications (for example letters sent from London to Edinburgh).

---

[22] PF Scott, *The National Security Constitution* (Hart 2018) 80.

[23] PF Scott, 'General warrants, thematic warrants, bulk warrants: property interference for national security purposes' (2017) 68 *Northern Ireland Legal Quarterly* 99; *Privacy International*, Destroying Democracy Under the Cloak of Defending It, *Medium* 7 March 2016 <https://medium.com/privacy-international/destroying-democracy-under-the-cloak-of-defending-it-4a46727ea272>; Liberty, *Briefing on Part 2 of the Investigatory Powers Bill for Committee Stage in the House of Commons*, April 2016.

By s. 136(2) a bulk interception warrant must have as its main purpose either (or both) the interception of overseas-related communications and/or the obtaining of secondary data from such communications. What is an overseas-related communication? This is defined by s. 136(3) as communications sent by individuals who are outside the British Islands, or communications received by individuals who are outside the British Islands.[24] However, as we shall see at 25.1.5 in our analysis of the *Liberty and Privacy International v GCHQ* case, this has some surprising outcomes.[25] For if someone living in London writes a message on the Facebook page of a friend living in Manchester, this qualifies since the Facebook servers are outside the British Islands, meaning the communication is received by individuals who are outside the British Islands. Perhaps even more surprisingly, the government considers a Google search to be covered because the search is in fact two communications: one from the user to Google servers overseas and another a reply from the servers to the user. Second, given the nature of these warrants they may only be issued on national security grounds. By s. 138(1)(b) the Secretary of State may only issue such a warrant if they are satisfied that either the warrant is necessary in the interests of national security, or *on that ground and* on any other grounds falling within subsection (2).[26] For this reason the list of people who may receive and operate such a warrant is also very limited, being only 'the head of an intelligence service' thereby restricting these warrants to the Security Service, the Secret Intelligence Service, and GCHQ. This means, as no devolved powers are involved, Scottish Ministers cannot issue bulk warrants, only the Secretary of State (normally the Home Secretary for the Security Service, and the Foreign Secretary for the Secret Intelligence Service, and GCHQ).

The same principles on obtaining secondary data and approval by judicial commissioners as apply to targeted warrants also apply to bulk warrants by ss. 137 and 140, although in this case there is no power for the Secretary of State to issue an urgent warrant and to have it retrospectively reviewed by a judicial commissioner. However, bulk warrants may be modified by the Secretary of State to 'add, vary or remove any operational purpose specified in the warrant as a purpose for which any intercepted content or secondary data obtained under the warrant may be selected for examination'.[27] In such a case the variation may be done 'urgently', in which case under s. 147 the modified warrant takes effect subject to a review by judicial commissioner within three working days. Finally, as with targeted warrants, the warrant needs to be renewed every six months or it will cease to be of effect.[28]

The bulk interception warrant (and its predecessor the s. 8(4) RIPA warrant) are the backbone of the UK's SIGINT capability. A small number of bulk interception warrants held by GCHQ allow them to operate vast programmes of communications data collection, such as Tempora. These programmes allow GCHQ to gather an immense volume of data with the intention that most of it will never be selected for examination and will be deleted after a pre-set period. A small amount of this data will, though, be selected for examination

---

[24] The British Islands are the UK, Channel Islands, and Isle of Man as per the Interpretation Act 1978, Sch. 1.

[25] *Liberty & Ors v GCHQ & Ors* [2014] UKIPTrib 13_77-H. Discussed in depth at 25.1.5.

[26] These are for the purpose of preventing or detecting serious crime, or in the interests of the economic well-being of the United Kingdom, so far as those interests are also relevant to the interests of national security.

[27] See s. 145(2)(a).

[28] See s. 143(1).

(in essence, in much the same way as Google selects data from the internet following a search request). The argument from the security services, and in particular GCHQ, is that bulk data collection is not a wide-scale infringement of privacy as only a tiny subset of that data is ever examined. The security services view the dataset as a vital tool in the event of an attack or other form of breach of national security, such as the Manchester Arena bombing or the London Bridge attacks. After the event they can comb through that intercepted and retained data to see who the attackers were communicating with. An opposing view is that the mere act of collecting data is a surveillance act which alters people's behaviour and that therefore the mass interception of data does affect the privacy of all the people in the database of intercepted communications since the mere act of being observed, rather than the act of that data being consulted, is a surveillance act.[29]

25.1.4 State surveillance: Five Eyes, Upstream, and Tempora

The focus of this text is on the laws of the UK's jurisdictions but, as we have seen, the bulk interception powers are focused not on the UK but on communications outside the British Islands. As noted these powers are extremely important to GCHQ in particular, which is the lead agency in the UK's SIGINT capability. This means it is incumbent upon us to take a little time out to discuss some of the capabilities of states by looking at some of the most invasive digital surveillance programmes in place.

I have already mentioned in outline some of the better-known programmes operated mostly through the NSA and GCHQ. The first thing to be aware of is the data sharing agreements in place between friendly states. Both the US and the UK are members of a group known as 'Five Eyes'. This is an intelligence alliance between the US, the UK, Canada, Australia, and New Zealand. It is based on a series of multilateral agreements known collectively as the UKUSA Signals Intelligence Agreement which began in 1940 and which co-opted the last Five Eyes members (Australia and New Zealand) in 1956.[30] The network grew in importance and scope throughout the cold war and several foreign security services were co-opted to share data within the Five Eyes network. This has led to speculation about the existence of shadow intelligence sharing networks such as Nine Eyes, which adds Denmark, France, the Netherlands, and Norway; Signal Seniors Europe (sometimes called Fourteen Eyes) which includes Germany, Belgium, Italy, Spain, and Sweden; and even Forty-one Eyes adding in all others in the allied coalition in Afghanistan.[31] In fact in 2013 *The Guardian* reported that:

> the exclusivity of the various coalitions grates with some, such as Germany, which is using the present controversy to seek an upgrade. Germany has long protested at its exclusion, not just from the elite 5-Eyes but even from 9-Eyes. Minutes from the UK intelligence agency GCHQ note: 'The NSA's relationship with the French was not as advanced as GCHQ's . . . the Germans were a little grumpy at not being invited to join the 9-Eyes group.'[32]

---

[29] This fits with Bentham's concept of the Panaopticon and Foucault's Panopticism. See M Foucault, *Discipline and Punish* (Penguin 1991).

[30] Agreements from 1940 to 1956 were declassified in 2010 and may be found at the National Archive site <http://discovery.nationalarchives.gov.uk/results/r/?_q=ukusa>.

[31] E MacAskill and J Ball, 'Portrait of the NSA: no detail too small in quest for total surveillance', *The Guardian*, 2 November 2013.

[32] Ibid.

It is clear therefore that considerable intelligence sharing goes on between states, with the UK at the heart of the highest-level intelligence sharing networks. In fact it is likely the case that the relationship between the NSA and GCHQ is the heart of all intelligence sharing activities across the North Atlantic.[33] Against this backdrop Edward Snowden has revealed details of some of the key programmes operated by Five Eyes partners. Primary programmes include Upstream a programme operated by the NSA. This is a large-scale data gathering programme in which the NSA gathers the content and meta-data of communications as they pass through fibre-optic cables. The data is gathered under Executive Order 12333[34] which grants wide authority to the agencies within the US Intelligence Community 'to collect, retain or disseminate information concerning United States persons only in accordance with procedures established by the head of the agency concerned and approved by the Attorney General'.[35] Where there are gaps in the Upstream data, such as where that data is encrypted, this can be filled in by the Prism programme, another NSA programme.[36] This is a large-scale data gathering programme in which the NSA gathers stored internet communications data from technology and telecommunications companies based in the United States such as Google, Microsoft, Facebook, and Apple. The data is requested under a §702 warrant obtained under the FISA Amendments Act of 2008. This allows the Foreign Intelligence Surveillance Court, which meets in secret, to authorize the NSA (or other national security or law enforce-ment body) to carry out surveillance 'for a period of up to 1 year from the effective date of the authorization, the targeting of persons reasonably believed to be located outside the United States to acquire foreign intelligence information'.[37] These warrants are then served on the relevant technology or telecommunications company and may require the handing over of metadata, call records, details of contents of calls, emails or web searches, or any number of other types of data. It is reported that much of the data is handed over in unencrypted format or with a backdoor through any encryption.[38] This means the NSA can use Prism requests to target communications that were encrypted when they travelled across the internet backbone.

There are limitations to the Prism programme. As warrants are awarded under §702 it cannot legally target those resident in the United States. Often this is misreported as US citizens but it is clear that §702 is a residence qualification not one of naturalization and US citizens may often be surveilled using the Prism system when outside the US. Also, as we shall see at 25.1.4, again with Tempora there is a problem with restrictions based upon geographical location when it comes to using internet data. While in the days of analogue communications it was easy to identify if a telephone was based in the US or in Vietnam, it can be very difficult to determine the difference between domestic and external communications using internet technology. As we saw in chapter 2, the

---

[33] N Hopkins and J Borger, 'Exclusive: NSA pays £100m in secret funding for GCHQ', *The Guardian*, 1 August 2013.

[34] <http://www.archives.gov/federal-register/codification/executive-order/12333.html>.

[35] Ibid. [2.3].

[36] An overview of the NSA programmes and how they fit together may be found at B Kaufman, 'A Guide to What We Now Know About the NSA's Dragnet Searches of Your Communications', *ACLU Blog*, 9 August 2013 <https://www.aclu.org/blog/guide-what-we-now-know-about-nsas-dragnet-searches-your-communications>.

[37] HR 6304.

[38] G Greenwald et al., 'Microsoft handed the NSA access to encrypted messages', *The Guardian*, 12 July 2013.

network uses packet-switching technology and will send packets by the most efficient route in terms of network capacity, not in terms of network geography. Thus there is no reason to assume that if files are transmitted from a computer in New York to one in Chicago, they will follow the most direct route. If the network between New York and Chicago is extremely congested one packet may go via Toronto, another via Tijuana, and another possibly even via Tel Aviv. As a result, it has been reported by the *Washington Post* that when intelligence analysts search collected and stored data, 'analysts key in "selectors", or search terms, that are designed to produce at least 51 percent confidence in a target's "foreignness".'[39] The authors of the report note that this 'is not a very stringent test'. Additionally, there are few protections for UK citizens or residents[40] and none at all for non-UK EU citizens or residents. This was the foundation of the legal challenge against the legality in EU law of the process of data exportation from the EU to the US under the so-called safe harbour agreement in the case of *Schrems v Data Protection Commissioner*,[41] discussed in chapter 24.[42]

In the UK, GCHQ operates an equally invasive data gathering and retention programme. The main component of this is a programme known as Tempora, which operates with arguably less legal oversight than Upstream/Prism. Tempora is in essence a locally stored buffered version of internet communications carried via the undersea fibre-optic cables that form the backbone of the internet. In June 2013 *The Guardian* newspaper reported documents discovered in the Snowden files which showed that GCHQ had installed taps on 'more than 200 fibre-optic cables and was able to process data from at least 46 of them at a time. Each of the cables carries data at a rate of 10 gigabits per second, so the tapped cables had the capacity, in theory, to deliver more than 21 petabytes a day—equivalent to sending all the information in all the books in the British Library 192 times every 24 hours. And the scale of the programme is constantly increasing as more cables are tapped and GCHQ data storage facilities in the UK and abroad are expanded with the aim of processing terabits (thousands of gigabits) of data at a time.'[43] As the authors noted, 'For the 2 billion users of the world wide web, Tempora represents a window on to their everyday lives, sucking up every form of communication from the fibre-optic cables that ring the world'.[44] As the documents went on to explain the buffer could store these massive amounts of data for a considerable period, 'Tempora allowed the agency to set up internet buffers so it could not simply watch the data live but also store it—for three days in the case of content and 30 days for metadata.'[45] In essence GCHQ had the capacity to buffer 21 petabytes of data per day, both content and metadata, and to store all that data for three days and the metadata for thirty days in 2013. That data being, like Upstream data, drawn directly from

---

[39] Ibid.

[40] There is an informal protection for UK citizens between the Five Eyes partners. A pact between partners agrees that Five Eyes partners, including the United States, must treat UK citizens as if they were their own. See GCHQ and Second Parties in GCHQ, 'Operational Legalities', *The Intercept*, 22 June 2015 <https://theintercept.com/document/2015/06/22/operational-legalities-gchq-powerpoint-presentation/>.

[41] ECLI:EU:C:2015:650

[42] At 24.2.

[43] E MacAskill et al., 'GCHQ taps fibre-optic cables for secret access to world's communications', *The Guardian*, 21 June 2013.

[44] Ibid.

[45] Ibid.

the fibre-optic cables that make up the internet backbone.[46] How was all this legal? Well, according to GCHQ it is because they hold relevant bulk interception warrants.

The role played by bulk interception warrants is therefore similar to that of §702 FISA warrants in the US. They are intended to allow for mass surveillance of external communications (that is communications external to the state) while protecting the communications of those resident within the state from mass state surveillance. The idea behind both §702 and bulk interception warrants is that the state must be free to spy on external threats through programmes of mass surveillance and data gathering but that it must not turn those same powers onto its own citizens. Two things are, though, immediately apparent when one compares the §702 legal authorization scheme used in Prism with the bulk interception scheme. The first is that §702 warrants are issued by a judge, albeit one in a secret court which approves 99.97 per cent of all applications,[47] whereas s. 136 warrants are issued by the Secretary of State, albeit with approval by judicial commissioners under s. 140. This means there is no clear separation of the Executive and the Judiciary in the s. 136 process, and remember that under s. 140 the judicial commissioner 'must apply the same principles as would be applied by a court on an application for judicial review'. This means that they can only overturn the Secretary of State's decision if they believe it to be illegal, irrational, procedurally improper, is disproportionate, or is a breach of a legitimate expectation.

The second is that §702 warrants are targeted on persons whereas s. 136 warrants are targeted on communications. This is an important but subtle distinction. It means that to comply with §702 an analyst carrying out a Prism inquiry has to be able to demonstrate (even if it is only to 51 per cent as reported) that the inquiry does not 'intentionally target any person known at the time of acquisition to be located in the United States' and does not 'intentionally target a person reasonably believed to be located outside the United States if the purpose of such acquisition is to target a particular, known person reasonably believed to be in the United States'. In addition, the inquiry must be carried out in a manner consistent with the Fourth Amendment to the Constitution of the United States. This means that if an NSA analyst knows a communication has been sent between someone in Syria and someone in Syracuse, New York, and the intent of the inquiry is to carry out an investigation into the individual living in Syracuse, then a §702 warrant does not cover this. However, as s. 136 is concerned with communications rather than persons, an equivalent GCHQ analyst examining a communication buffered by Tempora that originated in Iran and terminated in Irby, Merseyside, it would be legal under the terms of a bulk intercept warrant issued by the Secretary of State for that message to be read as part of an inquiry into the UK resident recipient of the message. Because of this there are specific safeguards in ss. 150–152 of the IPA which seek to provide UK residents with a similar form of protection to that seen in §702. The key provision, or second 'narrow section', is s. 152(4) which prohibits the selection of the

---

[46] We must assume the intercept and storage capacities have both increased since then. In evidence to the Joint Parliamentary Committee on the Draft Investigatory Powers Bill, Eric King, Director of Don't Spy on Us, suggested that GCHQ could have the capacity to actively intercept up to 25 per cent of global internet traffic <http://data.parliament.uk/writtenevidence/committeeevidence.svc/evidencedocument/draft-investigatory-powers-bill-committee/draft-investigatory-powers-bill/written/26357.html>.

[47] Conor Clarke, 'Is the Foreign Intelligence Surveillance Court Really a Rubber Stamp? *Ex Parte* Proceedings and the FISC Win Rate' (2014) 66 *Stanford Law Review Online* 125.

intercepted content for examination if 'any criteria used for the selection of the intercepted content for examination are referable to an individual known to be in the British Islands at that time' and 'the purpose of using those criteria is to identify the content of communications sent by, or intended for, that individual'. This seems to provide similar safeguards as §702.

25.1.5 *Liberty and Privacy International v GCHQ*

The question of safeguards was at the heart of a legal challenge to GCHQ's role in the Prism programme, and to the operation of the Tempora programme.[48] Challenges against operations carried out by GCHQ cannot be taken to the normal courts. Challenges to the operations of any of the intelligence services must be taken to a secret court, the Investigatory Powers Tribunal.[49] Such a challenge was brought by a group of civil liberties groups led by Liberty and Privacy International. The groups essentially brought two challenges. The first was on the alleged factual basis[50] that:

> the US Government's 'Prism' system collects foreign intelligence information from electronic communication service providers under US court supervision . . . the Claimants' communications and/or communications data might in principle have been obtained by the US Government via Prism and might in principle have thereafter been obtained by the Intelligence Services from the US Government. Thereafter, the Claimants' communications and/or communications data might in principle have been retained, used or disclosed by the (British) Intelligence Services (a) pursuant to a specific request from the intelligence services and/or (b) not pursuant to a specific request from the intelligence services.

In such a case, the question for the tribunal was, 'does this satisfy the Art. 8(2) [of the ECHR] "in accordance with the law requirement"?'[51] The second challenge was based on the alleged facts that:

(a) the Intelligence Services operate a programme, described as Tempora, under which fibre-optic cables are intercepted. This involves making available the contents of all the communications and communications data being transmitted through the fibre optic cables;

(b) the intercepted communications and communications data may be retained for an indefinite period and automatically searched through the use of a large number of search terms, including search terms supplied by the United States National Security Agency; and

(c) the intercepted communications and communications data may then be further retained, analysed and shared with other public authorities.'

On this basis the question was 'does the alleged Tempora programme and/or the s. 8(4) regime give rise to unlawful discrimination contrary to (i) Art. 14 of the ECHR (as read with Art. 8 and/or Art. 10)?'[52]

---

[48] *Liberty & Ors v GCHQ & Ors* [2014] UKIPTrib 13_77-H.

[49] Regulation of Investigatory Powers Act 2000, s. 65.

[50] The tribunal will not examine the factual basis of any claim as to do so would require an inquiry into operational matters. Instead inquiries before the tribunal proceed on the basis of assumed or alleged facts. A form of moot analysis if you will.

[51] *Liberty* (n. 48) [14].

[52] Ibid. [78]–[79]. Note s. 8(4) of the Regulation of Investigatory Powers Act 2000 was the predecessor to s. 136 and authorized bulk interception warrants.

In some ways the challenge was most interesting for what it unearthed in terms of operational parameters in use at GCHQ. In a witness statement provided by Charles Farr, then Director General of the Office for Security and Counter Terrorism,[53] the nature of an external communication for the purposes of bulk interception was discussed.[54]

 Highlight Charles Farr explains 'external communications'

The distinction in paragraph 5.1 of the Code between (i) the routing of a communication and (ii) the location from which it is sent/where it is received is intended to address these different factual scenarios, and to indicate that the route that a message takes is immaterial. A 'communication' for these purposes, both in RIPA and the Code, has both a particular sender and a particular recipient. Under Paragraph 5.1 of the Code, the relevant question to ask is not via whom (or what) a message has been transmitted, but for whom (or what), objectively speaking, the message is intended. Thus, an email from a person in London to a person in Birmingham will be an internal, not external communication for the purposes of RIPA and the Code whether or not it is routed via IP addresses outside the British Islands, because the intended recipient is within the British Islands.

A person conducting a Google search for a particular search term in effect sends a message to Google asking Google to search its index of web pages. The message is a communication between the searcher's computer and a Google web server (as the intended recipient). The Google web server will search Google's index of pages for search results and in turn send a second communication—containing those results—back to the searcher's computer (as intended recipient). Google's data centres, containing its servers, are located around the world; but its largest centres are in the United States, and its largest European centres are outside the British Islands . . . In such a case, the search would correspondingly involve two 'external communications' for the purposes of section 20 of RIPA and paragraph 5.1 of the Code.

Mr Farr goes on to confirm that a YouTube search and video delivery, the sending of a tweet, or the posting of a status update, message, or any other file on Facebook would all involve external communications.[55] This is factually correct in terms of recording the form of communication in place. The servers are outside the British Isles and as a result the communication is an external communication if one takes what Orin Kerr calls an 'external perspective', that is, 'the viewpoint of an outsider concerned with the functioning of the network in the physical world rather than the perceptions of a user'.[56] However, the issue is confused by Mr Farr following what Kerr calls

---

[53] Now Chairman of the Joint Intelligence Committee and Head of the Joint Intelligence Organisation at the Cabinet Office.

[54] Witness statement of Charles Farr in *Liberty & Ors v GCHQ & Ors* Case No. IPT/13/92/CH, [129]–[134] <https://www.liberty-human-rights.org.uk/sites/default/files/Witness%20statement%20of%20Charles%20Farr%20on%20behalf%20of%20the%20Intelligence%20Services%2016th%20May%202014.pdf>. The Code referred to is the *Code of practice for the interception of communications* <www.gov.uk/government/uploads/system/uploads/attachment_data/file/97956/interception-comms-code-practice.pdf>.

[55] Ibid. [135]–[138].

[56] O Kerr, 'The Problem of Perspective in Internet Law' (2003) 91 *Georgetown Law Journal* 357, 360.

an internal perspective when dealing with emails between London and Birmingham routed outside the British Islands. The internal perspective is 'the point of view of a user who is logged on to the Internet and chooses to accept the virtual world of cyberspace as a legitimate construct'.[57] What we see, therefore, is what often occurs with law enforcement bodies and security services; an inconsistent approach applying both the internal perspective 'cyberspace is a place' and the external perspective 'cyberspace is a communications medium' simultaneously. Why should a UK resident or citizen assume that an email sent from London to Birmingham was legally different to an internet search conducted in (in their view) the privacy of their own home, or a tweet or Facebook message intended to be read by friends in Manchester? This is a major problem with the interpretation of the law in bulk interceptions. Although there is a logical explanation for the difference in approaches, the inconsistency in applying the internal and external perspectives makes it very difficult for the average individual to understand.

In his review of the distinction between internal and external communications the Independent Reviewer of Terrorism Legislation noted that 'This was not clear prior to the publication of Mr Farr's statement. Some have considered those distinctions counter-intuitive: for example, many people might not consider a Google search to be a communication at all, let alone an external communication.'[58] He goes on to note that 'Further potential confusion follows from the fact that internal communications are collected under external warrants . . . As explained in the Charles Farr Statement, it is inevitable that there is "by-catch" of internal communications because s. 8(4) bulk interception takes place at the level of communications cables. It is generally accepted that the collection of such material cannot be avoided.'[59] This is the same side effect we noted with respect to *Prism* and §702 warrants: there is no way to extract purely internal communications from the data feed at the point of collection, they can only be identified when examined. Thus, as technically a bulk interception warrant (either under the old law of s. 8(4) or the new law of s. 136) can only be targeted at 'overseas-related communications', all internal (UK) communications ingathered under the warrant are technically illegally intercepted. This is remedied by s. 136(5)(a) which allows for collateral data to be collected if it is 'necessary to undertake in order to do what is expressly authorised or required by the warrant'. However, once again we are left with the feeling that although the letter of the law is being met the spirit of it is not.

The eventual outcome of the *Liberty v GCHQ* case was an unusual yet ultimately pyrrhic victory for the claimants. The tribunal found that the activities of GCHQ were lawful and in compliance with the ECHR on the basis that the disclosures made to the tribunal in the course of its hearings (and which were published in the judgment at paragraphs 47–48 and 126) revealed 'the existence of a safeguard rendering it less, rather than more, likely that there will be objectionable interference with privacy or arbitrary conduct by the Respondents'.[60] However, in a later order published in February 2015 the tribunal found that: '"prior to the disclosures made and referred to in the Tribunal's Judgment of 5 December 2014 and this judgment" the Prism and/

---

[57] Ibid. 359.
[58] Independent Reviewer of Terrorism Legislation (n. 19) [6.52].
[59] Ibid. [6.53].
[60] *Liberty* (n. 48) [154].

or Upstream arrangements contravened Articles 8 or 10 ECHR, but now comply'.[61] In other words, in a rare victory for the claimants the tribunal found that GCHQ had been acting illegally in processing Prism/Upstream data before 5 December 2014 when the safeguards were publicized in the tribunal's own judgment, however the very act of the judgment being published corrected that illegality, rendering the programme compliant with the ECHR.

25.1.6 The European Court of Human Rights and bulk interception

The ECtHR received, not unsurprisingly, a number of applications around and following the Snowden revelations and has now built up a considerable jurisprudence in this area. In December 2015 the ECtHR in *Roman Zakharov v Russia*[62] found that although interception of communications could be pursued for the legitimate aims of protection of national security and public safety, and prevention of crime and protection of the economic well-being of the country, systems of mass, secret, surveillance 'may undermine or even destroy democracy under the cloak of defending it'; for that reason 'the Court must be satisfied that there are adequate and effective guarantees against abuse'.[63] In looking at the specifics of the Russian scheme for surveillance the court concluded that there were insufficient safeguards against mismanagements in the use of the system, such as arbitrariness or abuse. They noted that this risk is particularly high in a system, such as the one in Russia, where the secret services and the police had direct access, by technical means, to all mobile telephone communications.

Following this case, in *Szabó and Vissy v Hungary*[64] the ECtHR noted that:

it is a natural consequence of the forms taken by present-day terrorism that governments resort to cutting-edge technologies in pre-empting such attacks, including the massive monitoring of communications susceptible to containing indications of impending incidents. The techniques applied in such monitoring operations have demonstrated a remarkable progress in recent years and reached a level of sophistication which is hardly conceivable for the average citizen, especially when automated and systemic data collection is technically possible and becomes widespread. In the face of this progress the Court must scrutinise the question as to whether the development of surveillance methods resulting in masses of data collected has been accompanied by a simultaneous development of legal safeguards securing respect for citizens' Convention rights.[65]

In examining the Hungarian provisions the court found that:

given that the scope of the measures could include virtually anyone, that the ordering is taking place entirely within the realm of the executive and without an assessment of strict necessity, that new technologies enable the Government to intercept masses of data easily concerning even persons outside the original range of operation, and given the absence of any effective remedial measures, let alone judicial ones, the Court concludes that there has been a violation of Article 8 of the Convention.[66]

---

[61] *Liberty & Ors v GCHQ & Ors* [2015] UKIPTrib 13_77-H, [32].
[62] (2016) 63 EHRR 17.
[63] Ibid. [232].
[64] [2016] ECHR 579.
[65] Ibid. [68].
[66] Ibid. [89].

In early 2018 the court built on this emerging jurisprudence in *Centrum För Rättvisa v Sweden*.[67] The case was brought by a Swedish civil rights organization after the Swedish parliament extended the powers of the Försvarets Radioanstalt (FRA), Sweden's equivalent of GCHQ, to allow the bulk interception of communications and communications data running through cables. The Signals Intelligence Act established that 'all cable-based cross-border communications' would be transferred to points of collection so that the FRA may conduct foreign signals intelligence based on detailed tasking directives which were to be routinely issued by governmental offices, the armed forces, the security police, and the national operative department of the police authority.[68] This case therefore closely matches the operation of Tempora and the contribution to Prism by GCHQ.

In its examination the court recognized that there were eight possible justifications for foreign SIGINT collection under the Swedish law:

(1) external military threats to the country;

(2) conditions for Swedish participation in international peacekeeping or humanitarian missions or threats to the safety of Swedish interests in the performance of such operations;

(3) strategic circumstances concerning international terrorism or other serious cross-border crimes that may threaten essential national interests;

(4) the development and proliferation of weapons of mass destruction, military equipment and other similar specified products;

(5) serious external threats to society's infrastructure;

(6) foreign conflicts with consequences for international security;

(7) foreign intelligence operations against Swedish interests; and

(8) the actions or intentions of a foreign power that are of substantial importance for Swedish foreign, security or defence policy.[69]

Prior to launching any operation or accessing and querying information collected, the FRA must secure a permit from the Foreign Intelligence Court, except in the case of exigent circumstances where delay might make the operation futile. The Foreign Intelligence Court applies a proportionality test in considering the reasoning for the request, the search terms or categories of search terms to be used, and the proposed duration of surveillance (up to six months, with possible routine extensions).[70] In this the operation looks very similar to the IPA with one notable exception; warrants are issued judicially rather than by executive order with a judicial review process. Similar to the IPA there are protections for domestic communications, but as the Independent Reviewer of Terrorism Legislation had noted in relation to the law in the UK, the ECtHR noted that although 'concerns of personal integrity were taken seriously by the FRA and formed an integral part of the development of its procedures . . . there were practical difficulties in separating domestic cable-based communications from those crossing the Swedish border. Any domestic communications that were not separated at the automated stage were instead separated manually at the processing or analysing stage.'[71]

---

[67] No. 35252/08, Judgment 19 June 2018.
[68] Ibid. [8]–[9].
[69] Ibid. [12].
[70] Ibid. [18]–[22].
[71] Ibid. [62].

The court explicitly found that 'the decision to operate a bulk interception regime in order to identify hitherto unknown threats to national security is one which falls within States' margin of appreciation'.[72] From this starting point the court then determines that its list of minimum safeguards, must be adapted 'where necessary to reflect the operation of a bulk interception regime'.[73] On this basis the court found that 'mindful of the potentially harmful effects that the operation of a signals intelligence scheme may have on the protection of privacy' there was a need to acknowledge 'the importance for national security operations of a system such as the one examined in the present case'.[74] Examining the Swedish law they found that 'while [there were] some areas where there is scope for improvement—notably the regulation of the communication of personal data to other states and international organisations and the practice of not giving public reasons following a review of individual complaints—the Court is of the opinion that the system reveals no significant shortcomings in its structure and operation'.[75] Accordingly, the court found 'the structure and operation of the system are proportionate to the aim sought to be achieved, [and] accordingly no violation of Article 8 of the Convention'.[76]

Given the line of authority from *Zakharov* to *Szabó and Vissy* it is maybe a little surprising to find the court coming to such a conclusion. However, what we may perceive here is the court giving guidance to states that they accept that mass surveillance has become an essential part of the armoury of state security agencies in the modern world and if a system is well-designed and proportionate in terms of protecting individual rights, especially Art. 8, then they will consider this within the margin of appreciation of states. What they are signalling is there is 'good' mass surveillance as well as 'bad' mass surveillance. This is a departure from the previous position where it seemed all mass surveillance was bad.

Finally, we come to the recent case of *Big Brother Watch & Ors v The United Kingdom*.[77] This is the combined challenge by a group of UK-based human rights groups to the operation of Tempora and the GCHQ contribution to Prism. The claims were essentially the same claims as the *Liberty v GCHQ*. The case was adjourned in April 2014 to await the outcome of *Liberty v GCHQ*. The adjournment was lifted in November 2015 allowing the case to proceed, with the judgment finally coming in late 2018. The case has been described in some circles as a blockbuster and at 212 pages and 525 paragraphs, and with two partly concurring, partly dissenting, opinions adding another 56 paragraphs, it is worthy of the label. Fairly obviously such a rich, complex and detailed case cannot be given full attention here so the analysis will focus on the 'headlines'. The first headline is that the UK government lost the case but maybe not the war for while the court finds that the UK's surveillance programme under the now-repealed Regulation of Investigatory Powers Act was deficient in important respects, and in violation of Arts. 8 and 10 of the Convention,[78] it at the same time normalizes mass surveillance

---

[72] Ibid. [112].
[73] Ibid. [114].
[74] Ibid. [179].
[75] Ibid. [180].
[76] Ibid. [181].
[77] Nos. 58170/13, 62322/14 & 24960/15, Judgment 13 September 2018.
[78] Ibid. The court held by 5 votes to 2, that there had been a violation of Art. 8 of the Convention in respect of the s. 8(4) regime; by 6 votes to 1, that there had been a violation of Art. 8 of the Convention in respect of the Chapter II regime; by 6 votes to 1, that there was a violation of Art. 10 of the Convention in respect of the s. 8(4) regime and the Chapter II regime; but by 5 votes to 2, that there had been no violation of Art. 8 in respect of the intelligence sharing regime.

programmes. In particular, the court decided that bulk interception programmes are not categorically disproportionate, as privacy activists have argued.[79] Second, in a similar vein, the court finds that prior judicial authorization is not indispensable for the legality of bulk interception even if prior judicial authorization could be seen as best practice.[80]

Given the massive overhaul in the operation of UK mass surveillance laws in the IPA 2016, much of what the court found to be illegal has already been repealed and replaced and that which has not can quickly be updated to ensure compliance going forward. While the applicants undoubtedly carried the day, a considerable victory after four years of campaigning, it may, like the IPT case before it, prove to be a pyrrhic victory. For while GCHQ operations under the RIPA regime were found to be a breach of both Arts. 8 and 10 and the court emphasized that access to metadata could be just as intrusive as access to content data and should be dealt with in the same way as content data, if we look more closely at the judgment, we see that what the court condemns are mainly techniques used by the GCHQ. These include the fact that, in some respects, the United Kingdom did not match its monitoring system with sufficient safeguards and adequate oversight mechanisms. The 'killer blow' that the applicants sought, a ruling that mass surveillance of the type carried out by GCHQ was per se a breach of Art. 8, did not materialize. Worse, reinforcing the earlier decision of *Centrum För Rättvisa* the court found that 'it is clear that bulk interception is *a valuable means* to achieve the legitimate aims pursued, particularly given the current threat level from both global terrorism and serious crime'.[81] This pushes the jurisprudence on from *Centrum För Rättvisa's* statement that 'the decision to operate a bulk interception regime falls within States' margin of appreciation' and suggests what Asaf Lubin has called 'the new normal', namely the proliferation of intelligence laws with a mass surveillance dimension.[82] In return, the ECtHR expects states to ensure such surveillance is limited with conditions and safeguards. *Big Brother Watch* is arguably the case that determines once and for all that it is no longer a question of the legality of mass surveillance policies, but rather a question of how to operate them.

25.2 **Data retention**

There is enough content in the Investigatory Powers Act to write a book, or indeed several books, and indeed these books are now appearing.[83] Books will be written on equipment interference (state-sanctioned computer hacking), bulk personal datasets, communications data, and internet connection records (in more depth than will be done so here), but this is not the place for all these discussions. This is a book on information technology law, not surveillance law and powers. There is, though, one area we must discuss before we can treat this chapter as complete and that is data retention powers.

---

[79] Ibid. [314].
[80] Ibid. [318]–[320].
[81] Ibid. [386] (emphasis added).
[82] A Lubin, 'Legitimizing Foreign Mass Surveillance in the European Court of Human Rights', *Just Security* 2 August 2018 <https://www.justsecurity.org/59923/legitimizing-foreign-mass-surveillance-european-court-human-rights/>.
[83] S McKay, *Blackstone's Guide to the Investigatory Powers Act 2016* (OUP 2018); Scott (n. 22).

As the war on terror continues, security forces find themselves constantly stretched. The risk is that at some point their stretched resources mean vital information is being lost. This was illustrated in the immediate aftermath of the 7 July 2005 attacks in London. The attacks were committed by a small group of UK nationals who had obviously been in contact with supporters of terrorism but who had not been under surveillance. What security forces feared was that there were other cells ready to commit further attacks, a fear raised further after the abortive attacks of 21 July 2005. The security forces' attempts to piece together the events preceding 7 July were hampered by their lack of available data. They wanted to know to whom the bombers were talking, whom they were emailing, and what information they were accessing online. To assist with future investigations the UK government, as chair of the Council of Europe, suggested new measures be taken to retain private communications data in case it were needed in future by security services or law enforcement bodies. The end result was the Data Retention Directive (now repealed).[84]

This provided that member states could require telecommunications and internet service providers to retain certain forms of data for a period of not less than six months and not more than two years.[85] The types of data affected were all set out in Art. 5 and are usually known as communications data or metadata. They were:

(1) data necessary to trace and identify the source of a communication;

(2) data necessary to identify the destination of a communication;

(3) data necessary to identify the date, time, and duration of a communication;

(4) data necessary to identify the type of communication;[86] and

(5) data necessary to identify users' communication equipment or what purports to be their equipment.[87]

This data was required to be retained by the telecommunications or internet service provider for the prescribed time and had to be made available to the relevant authorities upon a formal request. The UK implemented the Data Retention Directive in two stages: first, the Data Retention (EC Directive) Regulations 2007,[88] and then subsequently the Data Retention (EC Directive) Regulations 2009.[89] The 2007 regulations covered only telecommunications data—that is, data relating to telephone calls made from fixed-line and mobile telephones. They required that telecommunications providers retain session data for voice calls (that is, the telephone numbers of the caller and recipient of the call, the date and duration of the call, the telephone service used, the IMSI and the IMEI of both of the telephones and, for cell phones, the cell location in which the call was made and received) for a period of 12 months.[90] The 2009 regulations extended and

---

[84] Dir. 2006/24/EC (Repealed).

[85] Art. 6.

[86] Such data as the telephone or internet service used.

[87] This is data such as the calling and called telephone numbers; the international mobile subscriber identity (IMSI) or the international mobile equipment identity (IMEI) of the called or calling party, or the digital subscriber line (DSL), or other end point of the originator of an internet communication.

[88] SI 2007/2199.

[89] SI 2009/859.

[90] SI 2007/2199, regs. 4 and 5. In addition, reg. 5 requires that where a call is made from an anonymous prepaid phone, the service provider must retain a record of the date and time of the initial activation of the service and the cell ID from which the service was activated.

revoked the 2007 regulations to cover internet communications as well. After repeating the requirements of the 2007 regulations with respect to fixed-line and mobile tele-communications, they then went on to require internet service providers and internet access providers to retain:

(1) the name and address of the subscriber or registered user to whom an internet protocol (IP) address, user ID or telephone number was allocated at the time of the communication;

(2) the DSL or dial-up number of the subscriber;

(3) the date and time the subscriber logged on and off from the service;

(4) email user ID details; and

(5) the internet service used.

Again, this was required to be retained for 12 months.[91] These provisions are discussed in the past tense as they have all been ruled illegal and have been repealed by the decision of the CJEU in *Digital Rights Ireland and Seitlinger & Ors.*[92]

25.2.1 *Digital Rights Ireland and Seitlinger & Ors*

As may be deduced from the first claimant this is a challenge to the Data Retention Directive that originated in Ireland, and then was joined by a similar challenge from Austria. Both sets of claimants raised similar objections to the legality of the directive. The High Court of Ireland sent a series of questions to the CJEU asking, among other things, whether the directive was compatible with the right to privacy laid down in Art. 7 of the Charter of Fundamental Rights of the European Union (the Charter) and Art. 8 ECHR, whether it was compatible with the right to the protection of personal data as laid down in Art. 8 of the Charter, and whether it was compatible with the right to freedom of expression as laid down in Art. 11 of the Charter and Art. 10 ECHR.[93] The Austrian court asked rather more succinctly 'Are Articles 3 to 9 of Directive 2006/24 compatible with Articles 7, 8 and 11 of the Charter?'[94] In a concise judgment of 73 paragraphs the court answered emphatically, no. In first addressing the question of Arts. 7 and 8, the court made a few strong points that 'the obligation imposed by Articles 3 and 6 of Directive 2006/24 on providers of publicly available electronic communications services or of public communications networks to retain, for a certain period, data relating to a person's private life and to his communications, such as those referred to in Article 5 of the directive, constitutes in itself an interference with the rights guaranteed by Article 7 of the Charter', and that 'the access of the competent national authorities to the data constitutes a further interference with that fundamental right.[95] Accordingly, Articles 4 and 8 of Directive 2006/24 laying down rules relating to the access of the competent national authorities to the data also constitute an interference with the rights guaranteed by Article 7 of the Charter.'[96]

---

[91] SI 2009/859, reg.5, Sch. Part III.

[92] ECLI:EU:C:2014:238.

[93] Ibid. [18.2].

[94] Ibid. [21.1].

[95] Citing *Leander v Sweden*, (n. 7), *Rotaru v Romania*, (n. 8) and *Weber and Saravia v Germany* [2006] ECHR 1173.

[96] *Digital Rights Ireland* (n. 92) [34]–[35].

With interference established, the question was whether it was proportionate. The court acknowledged that the directive satisfies an objective of general interest (the prevention of offences and the fight against crime, in particular organized crime and international terrorism),[97] but in examining whether the data retention principles of the directive were proportionate found that the 'Directive covers, in a generalised manner, all persons and all means of electronic communication as well as all traffic data without any differentiation, limitation or exception being made in the light of the objective of fighting against serious crime'[98] and that it:

> does not require any relationship between the data whose retention is provided for and a threat to public security and, in particular, it is not restricted to a retention in relation
>
> (i)   to data pertaining to a particular time period and/or a particular geographical zone and/or to a circle of particular persons likely to be involved, in one way or another, in a serious crime, or
>
> (ii) to persons who could, for other reasons, contribute, by the retention of their data, to the prevention, detection or prosecution of serious offences.[99]

As a result, the directive was found not to proportionately comply with Arts. 7 and 8 of the Charter.[100] Having made this finding the court first declined to deal with the Art. 11 question, it now being moot, and then vitally struck down the directive.

25.2.2 The Data Retention and Investigatory Powers Act 2014 (DRIPA) (now repealed)

The impact of the *Digital Rights Ireland* decision was that all domestic legislation passed to give local effect to the directive was now rendered illegal under EU law, including the Data Retention (EC Directive) Regulations 2009. For a short period after the judgment, given on 8 April 2014, the UK government was silent as to the impact of this. Then suddenly it seemed as if a panic button had been pressed in Downing Street. On the morning of 10 July 2014 the Prime Minister and Deputy Prime Minister together announced the need for 'emergency legislation' to replace the now defunct regulations. A Bill, The Data Retention and Investigatory Powers (DRIP) Bill was published the same morning with the support of the Leader of the Opposition. The Bill cleared the Commons at 10pm on 15 July 2014 and was passed into law, having had a single day of debate in the Lords, on 17 July.

At the time a large number of Parliamentarians expressed barely disguised fury about the way Parliament had been sidelined. Prominent Conservative back bencher (at the time and now again) David Davis MP stated:

> My understanding is there was an argument inside government between the two halves of the coalition and that argument has gone on for three months. So what the coalition cannot decide in three months this House has to decide in one day. This seems to me entirely improper because of the role of Parliament—we have three roles. One is to scrutinise legislation, one is to prevent unintended consequences, and one is to defend the freedom and liberty of our constituents. This undermines all three and we should oppose this motion.[101]

---

[97] Ibid. [41]–[44].
[98] Ibid. [57].
[99] Ibid. [59].
[100] Ibid. [69].
[101] HC Deb vol. 584 (15 July 2014) col. 690.

Prominent Labour backbencher (at the time) Tom Watson MP made the highly unparliamentary statement that the Bill was 'democratic banditry, resonant of a rogue state. The people who put this shady deal together should be ashamed',[102] while another Labour backbencher David Winnick MP stated baldly 'I consider this to be an outright abuse of parliamentary procedure. I will certainly vote against the motion, and I hope that a number of hon. Members will do so as well.'[103] The Bill did pass and became the Data Retention and Investigatory Powers Act 2015 (DRIPA). The Act was a very short eight sections and sought essentially to replace the data retention powers lost in the *Digital Rights Ireland* outcome.

DRIPA was designed as a stopgap measure until the major project of the comprehensive review of surveillance legislation ahead of the IPA 2016. As a result ,DRIPA contained a sunset clause that ensured the Act be repealed by automatic operation on 31 December 2016. To ensure that DRIPA would not fall foul of the decision in *Digital Rights Ireland* s. 1 replicated the data retention provisions of reg. 4 of the repealed regulations with one essential difference. Whereas reg. 4 stated it was 'the duty of a public communications provider to retain the communications data specified', s. 1 stated that 'The Secretary of State may by notice require a public telecommunications operator to retain relevant communications data if the Secretary of State considers that the requirement is necessary and proportionate for one or more of the purposes falling within paragraphs (a) to (h) of section 22(2) of the Regulation of Investigatory Powers Act 2000.'

This was the government's attempt to ensure that DRIPA was proportionate where the directive was not. Whereas the directive was a blanket order to retain all data for the specified period, or as noted by the court in *Digital Rights Ireland* covered 'in a generalised manner, all persons and all means of electronic communication as well as all traffic data without any differentiation',[104] s. 1 required the issuance of a notice which must comply with s. 22 of RIPA. The government believed, this distinguished DRIPA from the directive and ensured DRIPA was proportionate where the directive was not.

Despite the amendment to the retention procedure in s. 1 (and its limited life span) many believed DRIPA was also incompatible with Arts. 7 and 8 of the EU Charter as the directive had been, and a legal challenge was brought by two of the MPs who spoke out against DRIPA, supported by Liberty. David Davis and Tom Watson brought a judicial review of the decision of the Parliament they were members of. Bean LJ and Collins J heard the case and with incredible symmetry they gave their judgment on 17 July 2015, exactly one year after the DRIPA came into force. The Divisional Court found that s. 1 of DRIPA was unlawful.[105]

 Highlight DRIPA s. 1 unlawful

The Claimants are entitled to a declaration that section 1 of the Data Retention and Investigatory Powers Act 2014 is inconsistent with European Union law in so far as:

(a) it does not lay down clear and precise rules providing for access to and use of communications data retained pursuant to a retention notice to be strictly restricted to the purpose of

---

[102] Ibid. col. 691.
[103] Ibid. col. 689.
[104] (n. 98).
[105] *Davis & Ors v Secretary of State for the Home Department* [2015] EWHC 2092 (Admin) [114].

→

preventing and detecting precisely defined serious offences or of conducting criminal prosecutions relating to such offences; and

(b) access to the data is not made dependent on a prior review by a court or an independent
administrative body whose decision limits access to and use of the data to what is strictly
necessary for the purpose of attaining the objective pursued.

The government immediately appealed this decision and on 20 November 2015 the
Court of Appeal gave its judgment in *Secretary of State for the Home Department v David
Davis MP & Ors.*[106]

The Court of Appeal took a different interpretation of the *Digital Rights Ireland* decision. The court did not believe it was the intent of the CJEU to lay down a mandatory
requirement automatically applicable to national legislation. In fact, the court thought
this was highly unlikely: 'we consider that it would be surprising if the CJEU were here
seeking to lay down a mandatory minimum standard of universal application without
referring to any of the relevant case law and without any consideration of the competing considerations.'[107] Finding it impossible to say with certainty what the intent of the
CJEU was the court took the only sensible decision it could; it referred two questions to
the CJEU. They were:

(1) Did the CJEU in *Digital Rights Ireland* intend to lay down mandatory requirements of EU
law with which the national legislation of Member States must comply? And

(2) Did the CJEU in Digital Rights Ireland intend to expand the effect of Articles 7 and/or
8, EU Charter beyond the effect of Article 8 as established in the jurisprudence of the
ECtHR?[108]

The reference from the Court of Appeal became joined to a related reference from
Sweden and in December 2016 the CJEU issued its judgment in *Tele2 Sverige AB v Post-
och telestyrelsen and Secretary of State for the Home Department v Tom Watson and Others*
(Tele2).[109] After taking some time to consider the preliminary point of whether domestic legislation on retention and access to data fell within the scope of the e-Privacy
Directive,[110] ultimately deciding that it did,[111] the court moved on to the main question. Was 'general and indiscriminate' data retention compliant with EU law? Starting
from the point that the e-Privacy Directive was applicable, the court recalled that the
directive 'contained specific provisions designed . . . to offer to the users of electronic
communications services protection against risks to their personal data and privacy
that arise from new technology and the increasing capacity for automated storage and

---

[106] [2015] EWCA Civ 1185.

[107] Ibid. [87].

[108] Ibid. [118].

[109] ECLI:EU:C:2016:970. Note by this point David Davis had been appointed Brexit Secretary
and as a member of government could no longer remain a claimant in the case, as to do so would
mean he was pursuing an action against himself.

[110] Directive 2002/58/EC.

[111] *Tele2* (n. 109) [81].

processing of data'[112] and noted that by Art. 6 of the directive 'the processing and storage of traffic data are permitted only to the extent necessary and for the time necessary for the billing and marketing of services and the provision of value added services'.[113] More important was the general principle of confidentiality in Art. 5(1):

> the principle of confidentiality of communications established, as a general rule, any person other than the user is prohibited from storing, without the consent of the user concerned, the traffic data related to electronic communications. The only exceptions relate to persons lawfully authorised in accordance with Article 15(1) of that directive and to the technical storage necessary for conveyance of a communication.[114]

The Art. 15(1) exception, the court noted, was that Art. 15(1) cannot permit the exception to the directive's confidentiality obligation to become the rule, as this would render the confidentiality obligation meaningless.[115]

The court turned next to the heart of the debate; the application of the EU Charter of Fundamental Rights. After observing that Art. 15 must be interpreted by reference to Charter Rights, the court noted that while 'the first sentence of Article 15(1) provides that Member States may adopt a measure that derogates from the principle of confidentiality of communications and related traffic data where it is a "necessary, appropriate and proportionate measure within a democratic society"', Recital 11 'states that a measure of that kind must be "strictly" proportionate to the intended purpose' and 'in relation to, in particular, the retention of data, [this means] that data should be retained "for a limited period" and be "justified" by reference to one of the objectives stated in the first sentence of Article 15(1).'[116] In considering whether the national legislation complied with these requirements of strict necessity, the court observed that 'the legislation provides for a general and indiscriminate retention of all traffic and location data of all subscribers and registered users relating to all means of electronic communication' and that the retention obligation on providers is 'to retain the data systematically and continuously, with no exceptions'.[117]

Applying these findings, and the decision in *Digital Rights Ireland* the court held that general and indiscriminate data retention legislation entailed a 'very far-reaching and particularly serious' interference with the rights to privacy and data protection, and that the user concerned is likely 'to feel that their private lives are the subject of constant surveillance'.[118] On this basis, 'given the seriousness of the interference in the fundamental rights concerned represented by national legislation which, for the purpose of fighting crime, provides for the retention of traffic and location data, *only the objective of fighting serious crime is capable of justifying such a measure.*'[119]

DRIPA however went much further than this with retention being justified, inter alia, for 'for the purpose of preventing or detecting crime or of preventing disorder', note not serious crime, just crime, and 'for the purpose of assessing or collecting any tax, duty, levy or other imposition, contribution or charge payable to a government department'.

---

[112]   Ibid. [83].
[113]   Ibid. [86].
[114]   Ibid. [85].
[115]   Ibid. [89].
[116]   Ibid. [95].
[117]   Ibid. [97].
[118]   Ibid. [100].
[119]   Ibid. [102] emphasis added.

As a result, it was no surprise that the court found DRIPA not to be compliant with EU law, noting that, while the fight against serious crime may depend on modern investigative techniques for its effectiveness, this objective cannot in itself justify the finding that general and indiscriminate data retention legislation is necessary for this fight against crime,[120] and that the domestic legislation applies to persons for whom 'there is no evidence capable of suggesting that their conduct might have a link, even an indirect or remote one, with serious criminal offences'.[121] As a result, the court held that DRIPA exceeded the limits of what is strictly necessary and cannot be considered justified under Art. 15(1), read in light of the Charter.[122]

DRIPA, like the Data Retention Directive before it was therefore incompatible with EU law. However, as with the analysis of the ECtHR jurisprudence on bulk interception which moved from a strict approach in *Zakharov* and *Szabó and Vissy* to a more permissive one in *Centrum För Rättvisa* and *Big Brother Watch*, we also find a movement away from substantive impermissibility towards procedural impropriety in this case. Moving on from the detail of the legislation in question, the court highlighted that Art. 15(1) 'does not prevent a Member State from adopting legislation permitting, as a preventive measure, the targeted retention of traffic and location data, for the purpose of fighting serious crime, provided that the retention of data is limited, with respect to the categories of data to be retained, the means of communication affected, the persons concerned and the retention period adopted, to what is strictly necessary'.[123] To be compliant with EU law the court suggested that 'the national legislation must be based on objective evidence which makes it possible to identify a public whose data is likely to reveal a link, at least an indirect one, with serious criminal offences, and to contribute in one way or another to fighting serious crime or to preventing a serious risk to public security'.[124]

Finally the court addressed the procedural questions:

(1) does EU law preclude national data retention legislation if that legislation does not restrict access solely to the objective of fighting serious crime, and

(2) does EU law preclude national data retention legislation if that legislation does not require access to be subject to prior review by a court or independent body?

In relation to the first question the court noted that 'the list of objectives set out in the first sentence of Article 15(1) of Directive 2002/58 is exhaustive, access to the retained data must correspond, genuinely and strictly, to one of those objectives' and that 'access can, as a general rule, be granted, in relation to the objective of fighting crime, only to the data of individuals suspected of planning, committing or having committed a serious crime or of being implicated in one way or another in such a crime'.[125] However, the court conceded that 'in particular situations, where for example vital national security, defence or public security interests are threatened by terrorist activities, access to the data of other persons might also be granted where there is objective evidence from which it can be deduced that that data might, in a specific case, make an

---

[120] Ibid. [103].
[121] Ibid. [105].
[122] Ibid. [107].
[123] Ibid. [108].
[124] Ibid. [111].
[125] Ibid. [115], [119].

effective contribution to combating such activities'.[126] In relation to the second question, the court noted that 'in order to ensure, in practice, that those conditions are fully respected, it is essential that access of the competent national authorities to retained data should, as a general rule, except in cases of validly established urgency, be subject to a prior review carried out either by a court or by an independent administrative body'.[127] In light of both of these findings the court answered that domestic legislation which did not comply with these conditions would be precluded pursuant to Art. 15(1) as read in light of the Charter. However, it was for the relevant national courts to examine whether such conditions were satisfied in the present case.[128]

In January 2018, long after DRIPA ceased to be law, the Court of Appeal published its final judgment. In giving the judgment of the court, Lord Lloyd-Jones agreed 'that DRIPA was inconsistent with EU law to the extent that it permitted access to retained data, where the objective pursued by that access was not restricted solely to fighting serious crime, or where access was not subject to prior review by a court or an independent administrative authority'.[129] Of course this disposition of the case was moot and in the interim the Home Office had issued a consultation on how it would meet the challenge of the CJEU decision by amendment to the Investigatory Powers Act 2016.[130]

25.2.3 Data Retention under the Investigatory Powers Act 2016

The Investigatory Powers Act is, as has already been acknowledged, wide in its scope. It brings together in one place the body of the UK's interception, data retention, and equipment interference laws. We have already looked in some depth at the interception provisions of the Act and here we look at the data retention provisions. The Act essentially restates the provisions of DRIPA with a few extensions and additions. This is why the outcome of the reference to the CJEU in *Secretary of State for the Home Department v David Davis MP & Ors* was vital to the government. By s. 87 'The Secretary of State may, by notice and subject as follows, require a telecommunications operator to retain relevant communications data if the Secretary of State considers that the requirement is necessary and proportionate for one or more of the following purposes' and the decision to give the notice has been approved by a judicial commissioner:

 Highlight Data retention purposes

(i) in the interests of national security,

(ii) for the applicable crime purpose. (In this section, the applicable crime purpose means—(a) to the extent that a retention notice relates to events data, the purpose of preventing or

➜

---

126 Ibid. [119].
127 Ibid. [120].
128 Ibid. [124].
129 *Secretary of State for the Home Department v Tom Watson MP* [2018] EWCA Civ 70 [13].
130 Home Office, *Consultation on the Government's proposed response to the ruling of the Court of Justice of the European Union on 21 December 2016 regarding the retention of communications data*, November 2017 <https://assets.publishing.service.gov.uk/government/uploads/system/uploads/attachment_data/file/663668/November_2017_IPA_Consultation_-_consultation_document.pdf>.

➡

detecting serious crime; (b) to the extent that a retention notice relates to entity data, the purpose of preventing or detecting crime or of preventing disorder),

(iii) in the interests of the economic well-being of the United Kingdom so far as those interests are also relevant to the interests of national security,

(iv) in the interests of public safety,

(v) for the purpose of preventing death or injury or any damage to a person's physical or mental health, or of mitigating any injury or damage to a person's physical or mental health,

(vi) to assist investigations into alleged miscarriages of justice.

The Act also adds a checklist for the Secretary of State which should provide transparency to his decision-making process and so head off the issue set out in paragraph 61 of *Digital Rights Ireland* that 'Directive 2006/24 does not contain substantive and procedural conditions relating to the access of the competent national authorities to the data and to their subsequent use.' The checklist is given at s. 88.

 Highlight Matters to be taken into account before giving retention notices

(1) Before giving a retention notice, the Secretary of State must, among other matters, take into account—

(a) the likely benefits of the notice,

(b) the likely number of users (if known) of any telecommunications service to which the notice relates,

(c) the technical feasibility of complying with the notice,

(d) the likely cost of complying with the notice, and

(e) any other effect of the notice on the telecommunications operator (or description of operators) to whom it relates.

(2) Before giving such a notice, the Secretary of State must take reasonable steps to consult any operator to whom it relates.

In addition to this check, s. 90 allows telecommunication operators to refer notices back to the Secretary of State for review.

There is, however, one final sting in the tail of the Investigatory Powers Act. By s. 87(11) the definition of relevant communications data is extended to cover 'in particular, internet connection records'. These are defined at s. 62(7):

Highlight Internet connection records

Internet connection record means communications data which:

(a) may be used to identify, or assist in identifying, a telecommunications service to which a communication is transmitted by means of a telecommunication system for the purpose of obtaining access to, or running, a computer file or computer program, and

(b) comprises data generated or processed by a telecommunications operator in the process of supplying the telecommunications service to the sender of the communication (whether or not a person).

These were a highly controversial addition to the data retention powers of the state. In her oral statement to Parliament when the Investigatory Powers Bill (as was) was being considered, the Home Secretary played down the impact of these.

 Highlight The Home Secretary on internet connection records[131]

It cannot be right that today the police could find an abducted child if the suspects were using mobile phones to coordinate their crime, but if they were using social media or communications apps then they would be out of reach. Such an approach defies all logic and ignores the realities of today's digital age. So this Bill will also allow the police to identify which communications services a person or device has connected to—so called Internet Connection Records.

Mr Speaker, some have characterised this power as law enforcement having access to people's full web browsing histories. Let me be clear—this is simply wrong. An Internet Connection Record is a record of the communications service that a person has used, not a record of every web page they have accessed. So, if someone has visited a social media website, an Internet Connection Record will only show that they accessed that site, not the particular pages they looked at, who they communicated with, or what they said. *It is simply the modern equivalent of an itemised phone bill.* (Emphasis added)

Many however saw this as much more invasive than that.

 Highlight Paul Bernal on internet connection records[132]

This means, essentially, that a rolling record of a year of everyone's browsing history will be stored. Not, it seems, beyond the top level of website (so that you've visited 'www.bbc.co.uk' but not each individual page within that website, nor what you have 'done' on that website).

---

[131] Home Secretary: Oral Statement to the House of Commons on the Publication of draft Investigatory Powers Bill HC Deb vol. 601, col. 970 (4 November 2015).

[132] P Bernal, 'A Few Words on Internet Connection Records' (5 November 2015) <https://paul-bernal.wordpress.com/2015/11/05/a-few-words-on-internet-connection-records/>.

→

The significance of this data is very much underplayed, suggesting it is just a way of checking that so-and-so accessed Facebook at a particular time, in a similar way to saying 'so-and-so called the following number' on the phone, and thus the supposed 'restoring of capabilities' referred to. That, however, both misunderstands the significance of the data and of the way that we use the technology.

Our 'online life' isn't just about what is traditionally called 'communications', and isn't the equivalent of what we used to do with our old, landline phones. For most people, it is almost impossible to find an aspect of their life that does not have an online element. We don't just talk to our friends online, or just do our professional work online, we do almost everything online. We bank online. We shop online. We research online. We find relationships online. We listen to music and watch TV and movies online. We plan our holidays online. Monitoring the websites we visit isn't like having an itemised telephone bill (an analogy that more than one person used yesterday) it's like following a person around as they visit the shops (both window shopping and the real thing), go the pub, go to the cinema, turn on their radio, go to the park, visit the travel agent, look at books in the library and so forth.

As a result of the highly contentious nature of internet connection records an amendment was introduced into the Bill as it passed through the House of Lords. This amendment became s. 67 of the Act. This states that officers of a local authority cannot access internet connection records, and other designated officers under the Act can only access them if one of three relatively strict conditions is met.

At this point the final analysis gets very confused and confusing. With numerous challenges to data retention laws passing through the courts the government have chosen to bring into force some parts of the Investigatory Powers Act but not others. For example, the data retention provisions contained in Part 4 including ss. 87 and 88 are currently in force and have been since 30 December 2016 (although, as we shall see, they have been recently amended). However, almost all of Part 3 of the Act has not yet been brought into force. These provisions provide vital authorization for designated senior officers to gain access to retained data. This means that currently access to retained data remains governed by s. 22 of the Regulation of Investigatory Powers Act 2000. More confusingly, while s. 87 is in effect meaning that for data retention purposes, relevant communications data includes 'in particular, internet connection records' s. 62 is not yet in effect meaning that in law there is no definition of internet connection records, which as we saw are defined at s. 62(7). How did we end up in this situation? It is all due to the continued confusion surrounding the legality of data retention provisions. The government is trying to ensure that the IPA 2016 provisions are not struck down in the same way as the directive and the DRIPA 2014 provisions. For this reason, after the CJEU decision in *Tele2* came out the Home Office immediately issued a consultation on how it would meet the challenge of the CJEU decision by amendment to the IPA 2016.[133] The consultation ran from 30 November 2017 to 18 January 2018,

---

[133] Home Office (n. 130).

after which the government published its response.[134] While all of this was ongoing the High Court heard the case of *R (Liberty) v Secretary of State for the Home Department*.[135] This was a challenge by civil rights group Liberty to the data retention provisions of the IPA. Liberty sought to have those parts of the Act which were not compliant with the *Tele2* judgment ruled unlawful and in effect be struck out by the court. The court refused to go that far but did find that:

> part 4 of the Investigatory Powers Act 2016 is incompatible with fundamental rights in EU law in that in the area of criminal justice:
>
> (1) access to retained data is not limited to the purpose of combating 'serious crime'; and
>
> (2) access to retained data is not subject to prior review by a court or an independent administrative body.[136]

At the same time, however, the court recognized the lawfulness of the data retention regime as a whole, noting:

> objectives concerned with, for example, the interests of national security and public safety and the investigation of miscarriages of justice have sufficient intrinsic importance to be capable of justifying an interference with Articles 7, 8 and 11, without the need to superimpose any 'seriousness' threshold. The degree of seriousness involved in any situation falling within any of these cases is adequately dealt with through the application of the necessity and proportionality tests in section 87(1) and other parts of the 2016 Act. The addition of a 'seriousness' threshold would add nothing of substance to the legislative scheme.[137]

In light of these findings, (1) that data retention was generally legal, and (2) that the current formulation of the IPA did not meet the requirements of EU law, the court ordered that 'the legislation must be amended within a reasonable time and that a reasonable time would be 1 November 2018, which is just over 6 months from the date of this judgment.'[138]

This judgment was given in the knowledge that the Home Office consultation was ongoing and that in the fullness of time amendments would be made to the IPA. In essence, the court was giving the Home Office a deadline to make these amendments. The amendments were finally made by the Data Retention and Acquisition Regulations 2018 which came into force on 1 November 2018, thereby meeting the court's deadline.[139] These regulations made a number of amendments to the Act, including the insertion of s. 60A, which grants the Investigatory Powers Commissioner oversight powers. Now before retained data can be consulted the relevant public authority (this is any body who has authorization to access data under the Act including the Security Service, Secret Intelligence Service and GCHQ) must make an application to the Investigatory Powers Commissioner before data may be accessed. Before such a request

---

[134] Home Office, *Investigatory Powers Act 2016: Response to Home Office Consultation on the Government's proposed response to the ruling of the Court of Justice of the European Union on 21 December 2016 regarding the retention of communications data*, June 2018 <https://assets.publishing.service.gov.uk/government/uploads/system/uploads/attachment_data/file/724142/June_2018_IPA_regulations_-_Government_Response_to_consultation_on_response_to_ECJ_judgment.pdf>.

[135] [2018] EWHC 975 (Admin).

[136] Ibid. [186].

[137] Ibid. [161].

[138] Ibid. [187].

[139] SI 2018/1123.

may be authorized it must meet a three-part test. It must be relevant data, meaning it must be within the data retention purposes discussed above; it must be necessary for the purposes of a specific investigation or a specific operation, or for the purposes of testing, maintaining or developing equipment, systems or other capabilities relating to the availability or obtaining of communications data; and it must be proportionate. This does seem to meet the first arm of the *Tele2* and *Liberty* requirements that access to data is 'subject to prior review by a court or an independent administrative authority'.[140]

The second requirement to be *Tele2* compliant is that 'access can, as a general rule, be granted, in relation to the objective of fighting crime, only to the data of individuals suspected of planning, committing or having committed a serious crime or of being implicated in one way or another in such a crime'. The regulations have made amendments to the Act to also meet this requirement. By a very confusing and complicated amendment in ss. 60A, 61, and 61A (authorization to access data) and s. 87 (power to require retention of data) we are introduced to the concept of an 'applicable crime purpose'. This is defined in s. 87(10A): 'In this section, "the applicable crime purpose" means: (a) to the extent that a retention notice relates to events data, the purpose of preventing or detecting serious crime; (b) to the extent that a retention notice relates to entity data, the purpose of preventing or detecting crime or of preventing disorder.' Similar definitions are given in ss. 60A, 61, and 61A.[141] To understand what this means you have to search out the meanings of 'events data' and 'entity data'. Both of these are defined in s. 261. 'Events data means any data which identifies or describes an event (whether or not by reference to its location) on, in or by means of a telecommunication system where the event consists of one or more entities engaging in a specific activity at a specific time.' 'Entity data means any data which (a) is about an entity, an association between a telecommunications service and an entity, or an association between any part of a telecommunication system and an entity, (b) consists of, or includes, data which identifies or describes the entity (whether or not by reference to the entity's location), and (c) is not events data.'

Given that the court in *Tele2* had said quite clearly that 'access can, as a general rule, be granted only to the data of individuals suspected of planning, committing or having committed a serious crime or of being implicated in one way or another in such a crime', why make this distinction? The answer is that the government is trying to make a distinction between retained communications data which would be 'events' data as it would record an event, being a telecommunications message sent across a network, and retained subscriber data (such as billing data) which police routinely ask mobile network operators for in the investigation of a crime. The theory the government is applying here is that at EU law it is acceptable to limit only access to events data while allowing entity data (i.e. data which does not record specific data about the data subject at a specific time) to be accessed for all forms of law enforcement. Given that police have routinely sought entity data from telecommunications companies for decades across Europe without issue, they might be right in this. However, it does leave scope for further challenges from privacy groups, so watch this space.

---

[140] It should be noted that in urgent cases s. 61A allows 'senior officers' to authorize access to data. This is also Tele2 compliant as the court ruled that 'it is essential that access of the competent national authorities to retained data should, as a general rule, *except in cases of validly established urgency*, be subject to a prior review carried out either by a court or by an independent administrative body'.

[141] In ss. 60A(8), 61(7A), and 61A(8).

25.3 **Conclusions**

The power of the information society is that it sets us free. We no longer need to travel to the local shops to buy goods or obtain services. We can have a tailored, personalized service based upon our previous actions and decisions and we can communicate more freely and more easily than ever before. There is, though, a price to be paid for this freedom. The warning of Wendell Phillips that 'eternal vigilance is the price of liberty' is probably of greater truth today than at any point in the last 200 years. The very digital technology which sets us free also allows for perfect control and observation. Everywhere we travel online our movements are tracked and recorded. These movements may be stored for extended periods, intercepted, and interrogated by highly sophisticated computer programs. Data from one person's movements online may be combined with movements of another to create new datasets, our conversations may be remotely monitored, tagged, and then traced.

The problem is that digital technology may not in fact be making us freer. As is made clear throughout this chapter and by the efforts of Edward Snowden, the technology affords the state the opportunity to perfectly monitor and control us much more tightly than even George Orwell imagined in his dystopian classic, *1984.*

TEST QUESTIONS

Question 1

YourSpace is an online social media and messaging platform. It is expanding its operations across the EU and wants particularly to provide its services in the UK. The YourSpace board have been advised they may need to comply with s. 87 (including s. 87(11) 'internet connection records') of the Investigatory Powers Act 2016. YourSpace is concerned about the costs that such a retention requirement will entail for it and seeks your legal advice on the potential viability of a successful legal challenge against any retention notice issued on it under s. 87.

Advise YourSpace.

Question 2

Systematic mass and indiscriminate data retention can never be compatible with the right to private life and to data protection. Such data retention contradicts the very essence of the right to private life.

Discuss.

FURTHER READING

Books

P Bernal, *Internet Privacy Rights: Rights to Protect Autonomy* (CUP 2014)

C Farivar, *Habeas Data Privacy vs the Rise of Surveillance Tech* (Melville 2018)

G Greenwald, *No Place to Hide: Edward Snowden, the NSA and the Surveillance State* (Metropolitan 2014)

H Nissenbaum, *Privacy in Context: Technology, Policy, and the Integrity of Social Life* (Stanford 2009)

D Solove, *Nothing to Hide* (Yale UP 2011)

Chapters and articles

D Anderson, 'The investigatory powers review: a question of trust' (2015) 4 *European Human Rights Law Review* 331

I Brown, 'Government Access to Private-Sector Data in the United Kingdom' [2012] 2(4) *International Data Privacy Law* 230

I Cameron, 'Balancing data protection and law enforcement needs: Tele2 Sverige and Watson' (2017) 54(5) *Common Market Law Review* 1467

N Richards, 'The Dangers of Surveillance' (2013) 126 *Harvard Law Review* 1934

C Walker, 'Data Retention in the UK: Pragmatic and Proportionate, or a Step Too Far?' (2009) 25 *Computer Law & Security Review* 325

INDEX